An Exposition of the Prophecy of Hosea

by
Jeremiah Burroughs

completed by
Thomas Hall and Edward Reynolds

revised and corrected by
James Sherman

biographical preface by
Joel R. Beeke

REFORMATION HERITAGE BOOKS
Grand Rapids, Michigan
2006

REFORMATION HERITAGE BOOKS
2965 Leonard St., NE
Grand Rapids, MI 49525
616-977-0599 / Fax 616-285-3246
e-mail: orders@heritagebooks.org
website: www.heritagebooks.org

10 digit ISBN #1-892777-94-0
13 digit ISBN #978-1-892777-94-2

Previously published
Edinburgh: James Nichol, 1863

BIOGRAPHICAL PREFACE

Jeremiah Burroughs (c. 1600 -1646)

Jeremiah Burroughs (or Burroughes) was baptized in 1601 and admitted as a pensioner at Emmanuel College, Cambridge, in 1617. He graduated with a Bachelor of Arts degree in 1621 and a Master of Arts degree in 1624. His tutor was Thomas Hooker.

Burroughs's ministry falls into four periods, all of which reveal him as a zealous and faithful pastor. First, from about 1627 until 1631, he was assistant to Edmund Calamy at Bury St. Edmunds, Suffolk. Both men became members of the Westminster Assembly. Both men strongly opposed King James's Book of Sports. Both refused to read the king's proclamation in church that dancing, archery, vaulting, and other games were lawful recreations on the Lord's Day.

Second, from 1631 to 1636, Burroughs was rector of Tivetshall, Norfolk, a church that still stands today. Despite the best efforts of his patron, Burroughs was suspended in 1636 and deprived in 1637 for refusing to obey the injunctions of Bishop Matthew Wren, especially regarding the reading of the Book of Sports, and the requirements to bow at the name of Jesus and to read prayers rather than speak them extemporaneously.

Third, from 1638 to 1640, Burroughs lived in the Netherlands, where he was teacher of a congregation of English Independents at Rotterdam, formerly ministered by William Ames. William Bridge was the pastor and Sidrach Simpson had established a second like-minded church in the city. Thus, three future dissenting brethren were brought together, all of whom would serve as propagandists for congregationalism later in the 1640s.

In the final period from 1640 to his death in 1646, Burroughs achieved great recognition as a popular preacher and a leading Puritan in London. He returned to England during the Commonwealth period and became pastor of two of the largest congregations in London: Stepney and St. Giles, Cripplegate. At Stepney, he preached early in the morning and became known as "the morning star of Stepney." He was invited to preach before the House of Commons and the House of Lords several times. Thomas Brooks called him "a prince of preachers."

As a member of the Westminster Assembly, Burroughs sided with the Independents, but he remained moderate in tone, acting in accord with the motto on his study door: *Opinionum varietas et opinantium unitas non sunt hasustata* ("variety of opinion and unity of opinion are not incompatible"). Richard Baxter said, "If all the Episcopalians had been like Archbishop Ussher, all the Presbyterians like Stephen Marshall, and all the Independents like Jeremiah Burroughs, the breaches of the church would soon have been healed."

In 1644, Burroughs and several colleagues presented to Parliament their *Apologetical Narration,* which defended Independency. It attempted to steer a middle course between Presbyterianism, which they regarded as too authoritarian, and Brownism, which they regarded as too democratic. This led to division between the Presbyterians and Independents. Burroughs served on the committee of accommodation, which tried to reconcile the differences, but on March 9, 1646, he declared on behalf of the Independents that presbyteries were "coercive institutions." Burroughs said he would rather suffer or emigrate than submit to presbyteries. Ultimately, the division between Presbyterians and Independents helped promote the cause of prelacy after the death of Oliver Cromwell.

Burroughs pursued peace to the end. He died in 1646, two weeks after a fall from his horse. The last subject on which he preached became his *Irenicum to the Lovers of Truth and Peace,* an attempt to heal divisions between believers. Many of his friends believed that church troubles hastened his death.

Burroughs was a prolific writer, highly esteemed by Puritan leaders of his day, some of whom published his writings after his death. Nearly all of his books are compilations of sermons and are eminently readable. *An Exposition of the Prophecy of Hosea,* a mammoth and fine 700-page exposition reprinted by Soli Deo Gloria as recently as 1990, has been one of Burroughs's most urgently sought titles. The present printing by Reformation Heritage Books is a facsimile reprint of the 1863 James Sherman edition. Burroughs died before finishing the work, but two of his closest friends, Thomas Hall and Edward Reynolds, finished the commentary. Spurgeon called this work "masterly," noting that it is "a vast treasure-house of experimental exposition." No work on Hosea has since superseded this commentary. We pray that God will use this reprint as a valuable tool especially for ministers and Bible teachers as they prepare messages on this graphic prophet.

In addition to his commentary on Hosea, we would encourage you to read more of Burroughs. Banner of Truth Trust has kept in print for a few decades now, Burroughs's classic, *The Rare Jewel of Christian Contentment.* You might want to begin here with your reading of Burroughs. In this book on contentment (Philippians 4:1, "I have learned in whatsoever state I am, therewith to be content"), Burroughs presents two major themes: (1) peace among believers of various persuasions, and (2) peace and contentment in the hearts of believers during "sad and sinking times." Burroughs expounds what Christian contentment is (chap. 1), unveils its mystery (chaps. 2–4), shows how Christ teaches it (chaps. 5–6), and describes ten of its fruits (chap. 7). He then addresses the evils and aggravations of discontentment (chaps. 8–11). He concludes by showing how to attain contentment (chaps. 12–13). Throughout, Burroughs provides numerous practical remedies for the spiritual disease of discontent.

To whet your appetite further, Soli Deo Gloria has performed a mammoth service over the last twenty years in bringing the following titles by Burroughs back from oblivion in a newly typeset, edited format:

> *The Evil of Evils, or The Exceeding Sinfulness of Sin,* first printed in 1654, consists of sixty-seven short chapters that expose sin and urge believers to choose affliction over sin. Burroughs organizes his material around seven major thoughts: (1) there is more evil in the least sin than in the greatest affliction; (2) sin and God are contrary to each other; (3) sin is directly against our good; (4) sin opposes all that is good; (5) sin is the evil of all other evils; (6) sin has infinite dimension and character; and (7) sin makes us comfortable with the devil. *Evil of Evils* is invaluable for sensitizing our consciences to the "exceeding sinfulness of sin" (cf. Rom. 7:13).
>
> Based on Numbers 14:24 ("Caleb was of another spirit; he followed God fully"), *The Excellency of a Gracious Spirit* is divided into two parts: (1) what this gracious spirit is, and (2) what it means to follow God fully. Burroughs says we must strive to live in the fear of the Lord to depart from evil and draw closer to Him. Living out of godly fear is the sum and substance of a gracious spirit.
>
> *Gospel Conversation* is a masterful treatise that deals with the right living of believers. It includes seven sermons on Philippians 1:27 ("Let your conversation be as becometh the gospel of Christ"), three on John 18:36 ("My kingdom is not of this world"), and a sermon on Exodus 14:13, titled "The Saints' Duty in Times of Extremity."
>
> Burroughs moves the reader to mourn his alienated state and yearn for the spring of holiness, union, and communion with Christ. He stresses there can be no works of sanctification before union with Christ. But once in Christ, the Christian must give evidence of that union by fervently pursuing the pious life to which God calls him. Good works are dangerous if they are made the foundation of justification, but are necessary and useful in sanctification. The conversation and conduct of believers must be on a higher plane than that of unbelievers.
>
> *Gospel Fear: Developing a Tender Heart that Trembles at the Word of God* focuses on the need for reverence, a concept nearly forgotten in our day, even by many who regard themselves as Christians. We are irreverent because we are ignorant of God and His holiness. As Burroughs writes, "The reason men worship God in a slight way is because they do not see God in His glory." These sermons (on Isaiah 66:2, "he that trembleth at my Word" and on 2 Kings 22:19, "because thine heart was tender") are a

corrective to prevailing ignorance. The entire volume shows our need for reverence and awe towards God and His Word.

There is no more important issue for any one than how to be right with God. In *Gospel Reconciliation*, a treatise of eighty-one chapters on 2 Corinthians 5:19, 20 ("God was in Christ reconciling the world unto Himself"), Burroughs answers questions about reconciliation. Christ's atoning work is the only way for fallen sinners to be reconciled with God, for a finite creature can never satisfy the justice of an infinite God. Burroughs explains the consequences of our reconciliation in Christ, showing that this reconciliation is a deep mystery, that it is free, sure, full, honorable, firm, and eternal, but also a difficult work, for we are only saved by divine accomplishment, not by human achievement.

Gospel Remission: True Blessedness Consists in Pardon of Sin consists of a series of sermons on Psalm 32:1, which Burroughs preached after finishing his masterpiece on sin, *The Evil of Evils.* As a tender pastor, Burroughs knew that after hearing about the deadly nature of sin, his congregation would need to hear about the remission of sins offered in the gospel. Burroughs covers five areas of forgiveness: (1) the many gospel mysteries in remission; (2) the glorious effects proceeding from remission; (3) the great mistakes made about remission; (4) the true signs and symptoms of remission; and (5) the ways and means to obtain remission. Burroughs stresses the dishonor done to God by not resting on the mercy of His remission.

In *Gospel Revelation: Finding Worth in Knowing Christ*, Burroughs treats God's revelation regarding Himself and His Son, Jesus Christ. He also gives precious insight into the worth of the human soul, as it is created to joyously serve and glorify God. Whereas sin debases a man, a right relationship to God elevates him to the position of worth and dignity with which God created Adam. Burroughs shows how true Christians can find great joy in so good a revelation.

Gospel Worship, subtitled *The Right Manner of Sanctifying the Name of God in General* is a call to propriety and sobriety in the worship of God, based on Leviticus 10:1–3. It deals with the believer's sanctification through "three great ordinances": (1) hearing the Word; (2) receiving the Lord's Supper, and (3) prayer. In a day that promotes man-made forms of worship, *Gospel Worship* is a call to biblical worship of the Triune God through the means that He has instituted. Burroughs shows how important worship is to God and teaches us how to "give unto the Lord the glory due unto his name" (Ps. 29:2). He makes plain that we do not need new forms of worship to be relevant, but to renew old forms of worship.

Hope, a treatise based on 1 John 3:3, ("And every man that hath this hope in him purifieth himself"), first establishes that every believer is a hopeful person; second, that where true hope resides, it will purge the heart; and third, provides ten ways in which believers can purify themselves by hope. Burroughs also shows the origin, object, and ground of hope. The book concludes with an exhortation to put away sin. This is a timely, succinct masterpiece for an impure world lost in sin and full of despair.

Appendixed to *Hope* is a 63-page sermon by Burroughs on the misery of those who have hope only in this life, based on Psalm 17:14b ("From men of the world, which have their portion in this life").

Irenicum to the Lovers of Truth and Peace, subtitled, *Heart-divisions opened in the causes and evils of them, with cautions that we may not be hurt by them, and endeavors to heal them,* contains the last sermons Burroughs preached before his death. Burroughs pleads for unity among his brethren, addresses the issues that seriously divided believers in his day, and offers practical ways to promote unity. He explains when one should plead his conscience, provides rules to know in what areas we are to bear with our brethren, and shows that "every difference in religion is not a differing religion." He discusses the role of pride, self-love, envy, anger, rigidity, rashness, willfulness, inconsistency, jealousy, contentiousness, covetousness, and gossip in division. He concludes that the answer for division does not lie in blanket tolerance of all religions nor in a compromising attitude towards sin, but in a biblical striving for peace. Given the divisiveness of Christians in all generations, this treatise is extremely applicable.

The Saints' Happiness offers a detailed exposition of the Beatitudes. In forty-one sermons, the author covers our Lord's Sermon on the Mount in compelling detail. Though Burroughs does not match Thomas Watson in popular appeal or Robert Harris in exegetical skill on the Beatitudes, his work is a significant contribution for proper understanding of the most famous sermon in history.

The Saints' Treasury is a compilation of five sermons on the holiness of God, Christ as all in all, faith's enjoyment of heavenly things, the natural man's bondage to the law and the believer's liberty by the Gospel, and preparation for judgment.

A Treatise of Earthly-Mindedness is a timely reprint for our earthly-minded age, containing two treatises: a serious warning against the evils of being earthly minded and an explanation on how to "get our hearts free from earthly-mindedness"; and a discussion on what it means to be heavenly-minded, with an accent on living godly in Christ Jesus. Several chapters deal with how to foster heavenly conversation and a heavenly walk.

Reading Burroughs is always a treat for the spiritually-minded. His writings are expositionally sound and reliable, sane and usable, warm and devotional. Let this commentary on Hosea move you to read more by this great Puritan divine.

Joel R. Beeke
Puritan Reformed Theological Seminary
Grand Rapids, Michigan

BRIEF NOTICE

OF

THE REV. JEREMIAH BURROUGHS, A. M.

It is deeply to be lamented that no life was given to the church of this excellent minister of Christ; concerning whom Mr. Baxter says, "If all the Episcopalians had been like Archbishop Usher, all the Presbyterians like Mr. Stephen Marshall, and all the Independents like Mr. Jeremiah Burroughs, the breaches of the church would soon have been healed." From the few scattered notices of him in different authors, and chiefly from those of his enemies, we learn that he was born in 1599. He studied and took his degree at Emmanuel College, Cambridge; after which he became colleague with the Rev. Edmund Calamy, at Bury St. Edmund's. In the year 1631 he became rector of Tivetshall, in the county of Norfolk; but upon the publication of Bishop Wren's Articles and Injunctions, in 1636, he was suspended and deprived of his living.

The Earl of Warwick, who was the friend and patron of the persecuted ministers, and one of their constant hearers, gave him an asylum in his house, till the fire of persecution, which raged so strongly against him, obliged him to fly to Holland. He was chosen assistant minister to the church at Rotterdam, of which the Rev. William Bridge was pastor. The violence of party strife at that period raised against him many accusations for leaving his country, but his vindication of himself and his conduct in retiring to Rotterdam is so ample and circumstantial, and withal written in so meek and humble a spirit, as to raise in the reader a high estimation of his veracity and piety.

The church at Rotterdam gave him a most hearty welcome, and he laboured among them, in conjunction with Mr. Bridge, with great acceptance and usefulness for several years. After the commencement of the civil war he returned to England: "Not," says Granger, "to preach sedition, but peace; for which he earnestly prayed and laboured." The renown which he had acquired at Rotterdam accompanied him to his native land. His popular talents as a preacher, his peaceable spirit, and his exemplary character, soon excited great attention; and as a proof of it, he was chosen lecturer to the congregations of Stepney and Cripplegate, then accounted the largest and wealthiest in England. At Stepney he preached at seven o'clock in the morning, and Mr. Greenhill at three in the afternoon: one was called *the morning star,* and the other *the evening star, of Stepney.* He was chosen one of the Assembly of Divines, and united with his brethren, the Revds. Thomas Goodwin, Philip Nye, William Bridge, and Sydrach Simpson, in publishing their "Apologetic Narration" in defence of their own distinguishing sentiments, which contain the general principles by which congregational churches are governed in the present day. In the year 1645 he was elected one of the committee of accommodation, and was of great service in all their important deliberations.

Though, after his exile, he never accepted a parochial benefice, or became pastor of a separate church, he laboured extensively in preaching at various and distant places, and in rendering other important services to the church of Christ. But his incessant labours, and grief for the distractions of the times, brought on consumption, of which he died in the forty-seventh year of his age.

In the spirit of union among all Christians, which he so powerfully advocated, he was far before the opinions of his day. The following sentiment, in reply to one of his bitterest enemies, does equal credit to his piety and discernment: "I profess, as in the presence of God, that upon the most serious examination of my heart, I find in it, that were my judgment presbyterial, yet I should plead and preach as much for the forbearance of brethren differing from me, not only in their judgment, but in their practice, as I have ever done. Therefore, if I should turn Presbyterian, I fear I should trouble Mr. Edwards, and some others, more than I do now; perhaps my preaching and pleading for forbearance of dissenting brethren would be of more force than it is now." The last subject on which he preached, and the last treatise he published, was his "Irenicum," or an attempt to heal the divisions among Christians. Oh that we had more of his spirit among all who take the lead in the Christian church! The estimation in which he was held by unprejudiced persons who were capable of forming a judgment of his spirit and character, was very high. Granger says, "he was a man of learning, candour, and modesty, and of an exemplary and irreproachable life." And Fuller has classed him among the learned writers of Emmanuel College, Cambridge.

The following Exposition was delivered in lectures to the wealthy citizens of London, at St. Michael's, Cornhill, where crowds constantly attended to hear his luminous exhibitions of truth, and forcible appeals to the conscience. The first volume only was published during his life, in the preface to which he remarks, the expositions "were taken from me in preaching. I perused the notes, but I could not bring the style to the succinctness that I desired, except I had written all over again, for which I had no time." Both this volume, and those published after his death, were most imperfectly printed; unimportant sentences were reprinted over and over again; and the supervisors had literally, as they say, done little more than usher the books into the world with the sanction of their names. Mr. Burroughs lived to carry on the Exposition as far only as chap. xiii. ver. 11. The remaining verses of that chapter were expounded by the Rev. Thomas Hall, who published his Exposition as a supplement to that of Mr. Burroughs, and will be found exceedingly valuable. The fourteenth chapter had been previously treated in a very able manner by Bishop Reynolds, who must ever rank high as an expositor of God's word. The whole are united in this volume, and form a most useful comment on this difficult book of Scripture, to aid the minister of Christ and the private Christian in rightly interpreting the sacred text. Dr. Williams, in his "Christian Preacher," observes, that the Exposition of Mr. Burroughs on Hosea, is a pleasing specimen, to show how the popular preachers of his time applied the Scriptures in their expository discourses to the various cases of their hearers.

The editor has only to remark, that the present volume is produced at great labour and expense; that the most scrupulous regard has been paid to accuracy, and in no single instance has a sentiment of the writer undergone any change to adapt it to the editor's mind. He commits it to the blessing of the great Head of the church with much prayer and hope that it may prove equally useful with the other Expositions which he has ventured to publish.

Surrey Parsonage,
Jan. 14, 1843.

THE ORIGINAL PREFACES.

TO THE EXPOSITION

ON

THE FIRST THREE CHAPTERS.

TO THE READER.

You have these lectures as they were taken from me in preaching. I perused the notes, but I could not bring the style to the succinctness that I desired, except I had written all over again, for which I had no time; my perusal was but cursory, therefore many things have slipt me: you have them as I preached them, without any considerable alteration. I had thought to have been far briefer, but meeting with so many things almost in every lecture so nearly concerning present times, caused me to go something beyond an expository way. In the remaining part of the prophecy, if God gives life to go through it, I shall keep myself more closely to exposition. What here you have, take it as you find it; what good you meet with, receive it in. This will be the encouragement of

Thy friend in Christ,

J. B.

TO THE EXPOSITION

ON THE

FOURTH, FIFTH, SIXTH, AND SEVENTH CHAPTERS.

TO THE READER.

Reader,

We here present thee with a continuation of Expositions and Observations upon other four chapters of the prophet Hosea, delivered by that worthy man, now with God. Himself in his life-time published the three first chapters: these, now made public, were compiled out of the manuscripts which himself under his own hand left, which, being short, have been filled up and enlarged out of the best copies of sermon notes taken from his own mouth. We must not undertake for all imperfections or mistakes that haply may be found, though a diligent and a skilful hand had the collecting of them. We only give letters of credence to them, that they are genuinely the author's, and that they are singularly worthy of all acceptation, especially by such readers as have their thoughts exercised in observing the ways of God's proceedings in and towards the nations of the world where his name is called. One great piece of his dispensations under the Old Testament, was that towards the ten tribes, who remain in captivity to this day, and who were set up (as their predecessors in the wilderness) as types of God's dealing in like cases with us under the New Testament, 1 Cor. x.; Rev. vii.; as we may see in the instance of the Eastern and Grecian churches that have groaned under the Mahometan tyrannies and oppressions, of whom the ten tribes may seem to be the liveliest pattern, as the condition of the saints in the Western European churches under the pope was exemplified in the captivity of Babylon, which befell the other two tribes. Yet so as, both in sins and punishment, the one and the other are general examples unto us, "upon whom the ends of the world are come," in which God acts over with a quick and swift motion, as being the last act, what was done more slowly under the Old. The worthy author was one of the most accurate spectators in his time, that with a curious and searching eye beheld what God was a doing in the world. He was as one of those "wise men that knew the times," (as it is said of Ahasuerus's seven counsellors, Esth. i. 13,) and skilled therein not, as they, in a human or political way, but as the transactions in the world do relate unto God, who governs this world by the rules and precedents in his word. He was one of those who, as the psalmist speaks, Psal. cxi., had pleasure to seek out the great works of the Lord, and to parallel those in these times with those of old under the Old Testament; and unto that end, in the entrance to these alterations in our times, he pitched upon the explication of this prophecy, which the studious reader will with much delight read over, when he shall observe how he made application all along to the dispensations of that time in which he preached them. The Lord bless them to them of this nation, for which they were principally intended.

THOMAS GOODWIN, WILLIAM BRIDGE,
SYDRACH SIMPSON, JOHN YATES,
WILLIAM GREENHILL, WILLIAM ADDERLY.

TO THE EXPOSITION
ON THE
EIGHTH, NINTH, AND TENTH CHAPTERS.

TO THE READER.

WHAT we have by way of preface set before the edition of the fourth, fifth, sixth, and seventh chapters, may sufficiently serve for a premise to these eighth, ninth, and tenth chapters, as holding forth the use and scope of the whole prophecy, and the author's intentions in his comment thereon: so as we shall only need now to give letters of credence before the world, to the passing of these, as the best and most authentic notes that could any way be obtained, both as the extracts of the best notes of sermons taken from his mouth, and chiefly his own writings, which were more brief. Expect shortly the eleventh, twelfth, and thirteenth chapters from the same hand. We commit them, and the reader, to the blessing of God.

THOMAS GOODWIN, WILLIAM BRIDGE,
SYDRACH SIMPSON, JOHN YATES,
WILLIAM GREENHILL, WILLIAM ADDERLY.

TO THE EXPOSITION
ON THE
ELEVENTH, TWELFTH, AND THIRTEENTH CHAPTERS.

TO THE READER.

GOD, who alone is perfect in himself, has retained this prerogative to himself, that his work should be perfect (as Moses speaks); and, as another holy one hath it, doth all his pleasure. Paul, though in whatever he was to commit to writing (in matters sacred) had infallibility of assistance, yet perfected not all he intended: "These things we will do, if God permit," said he to the Hebrews, Heb. vi. But we no where find extant any evidence, that he accomplished what he there intended, namely, a full, methodical discourse upon those first principles and foundations of religion, which that speech had reference unto. It is no wonder then, that if such a kind of imperfection accompanied the works of so great a master-builder, it attend those who build on this foundation, and are not privileged (as yet he was) from building hay and stubble.

This sort of incompleteness hath befallen the works of this worthy author, in respect to the finishing of this prophecy, which he intended, and had performed; wherein yet to the church of God there shall be no loss, there being no thoughts nor notions suggested to any man, which, though for the present they die with him, but the same Spirit who is the inspirer of all, doth bring to light in some one or other servant of God, in his own time.

What a treasury of thoughts seemed to be lost and to die with the Saviour of the world, which he had not, could not then utter! which yet the Spirit, that filled him without measure, distributed amongst the apostles that came after him, according to the measure of the gift of Christ in each. There is no beam of Divine light has shone into any man's heart, that shall finally and for ever be put under a bushel, but in the end shall be set up, to give light to the whole house.

The purpose of this preface is, to consign the passport through the world of these last notes of the author upon this prophecy, namely, the eleventh, twelfth, and thirteenth chapters; and to assure the reader, that they are the best and most genuine that can be expected, being collected out of those under his hand, all along, and the best copies of those that took them from his mouth; and to subjoin this hearty prayer, for a blessing from Heaven on these, and the rest of these our brother's labours that are published, that his works may follow him, and he receive (at the latter day) a full reward, even according to the fruit of his doings.

THOMAS GOODWIN,
WILLIAM GREENHILL,
SYDRACH SIMPSON,
WILLIAM BRIDGE,
JOHN YATES,
WILLIAM ADDERLY.

POSTSCRIPT BY THE SUPERVISOR

OF

THE LAST SERMON BY BURROUGHS.

THE author was prevented by several providences from preaching the foregoing sermon for some months together, insomuch as himself wondered what purpose God had in it; till at last God visited him by sickness, whereof he fell asleep in the Lord: his disease was thought to be infection, but without any sore, yea, and (as the gentlewoman his wife has related) without any spots or tokens of the plague; there was only a black settling of blood on one side of his back, which she supposed might have arisen from a fall from a horse, which he had met with not long before. This is mentioned by occasion of some contrary reports concerning his death. About the time of his immediate dissolution, he lifted up his eyes, and was heard to speak these words, "I come, I come, I come:" and so gave up the ghost.

It had been much to be wished that the author had been more concise and brief in some amplifications, which, though all exceedingly useful, yet have deprived us of his preaching and completing both the former sermon, and the rest of the prophecy. But God was pleased (for our sin no doubt) to deprive us of that mediator-like instrument between the divided godly parties of this nation, and of the further mind of the Holy Ghost which he had revealed to this his servant, touching the scope and use of this prophecy in these days.

God took him away in the strength of his parts and graces, that he might not lose in the reputation of his ministry or piety, as some have before their death.

Also, though we cannot affirm, as one of Josiah, that he was taken away lest the evil of the time should have wrought upon his temper; yet we may say, as another doth, he was "taken away from the evil to come," Isa. lvii. 1.

Moreover, it is not an unuseful note, that the Preface to the Tigurine Bible hath, whereof the inference is, That whilst in some weighty point we labour for great exactness and preparation, we are either disabled by our diligence, or prevented by our tardiness and delay; whereas moderate preparation seasonably applied might be more useful to the church, than such exactness so deferred. Which is not spoken to reflect any thing on our reverend author, but to admonish others.

Now among other arguments (good reader) to commend this excellent piece, this is one, That it has been brought to thy hand through several elements, having been in danger, part of it to be rotted in the earth where it was buried; part of it to be consumed in the fire wherewith much of the town where it was flamed;* part of it to be lost in by-holes where it was hidden in the midst of enemies. Make special use therefore of what is come (as it were) through fire unto thee for that end. And if thou find that fruit the supervisor did in preparing it for thee, thou wilt not repent thy pains or penny. Farewell.

* The original was with the supervisor in Colchester when besieged, and much of the town burnt.

THE ORIGINAL PREFACES.

TO THE EXPOSITION BY BISHOP REYNOLDS,

ON

THE FOURTEENTH CHAPTER.

TO THE READER.

CHRISTIAN reader, understanding that my sermon, which was preached three years since before the Honourable House of Commons, on the day of their solemn humiliation, was to be reprinted, I thought fit to peruse, transcribe, and enlarge six other sermons, in which I had, at mine own charge in the country, on the ensuing fast days, briefly explained and applied that whole chapter, (a portion only whereof was in the first handled,) and to send them forth together with it to the public: which I was the rather induced to do for these two reasons: 1. Because it has pleased God in his righteous and holy providence to make me, by a long infirmity, unserviceable to his church in the principal work of the ministry, the preaching of the gospel (which is no small grief unto me). So that there remained no other means whereby my life might, in regard of my function, be useful to the church, and comfortable to myself, than by inverting the words of the psalmist, and as he made his "tongue the pen of a ready writer," Psal. xlv. 1, so to make my pen the tongue of an unready speaker. 2. I considered the seasonableness and suitableness of these meditations to the condition of the sad and disconsolate times wherein we live, very like those which our prophet threatened the ten tribes withal throughout this whole prophecy, unto which this last chapter is a kind of use, and a most solemn exhortation, pressing upon all wise and prudent men such duties of humiliation and repentance, as might turn threats into promises, and recover again the mercies which by their sins they had forfeited and forsaken: which being restored to them according to their petition, they are here likewise further instructed in what manner to return unto God the praises due to his great name. And these two duties of humiliation and thanksgiving, are the most solemn duties to which in these times of judgments and mercies, so variously interwoven together, the Lord so frequently calls us.

Places of Scripture I have, for brevity sake, for the most part, only quoted and referred thee to, without transcribing all the words, and have usually put many parallel places together, because by that means they do not only strengthen the doctrine whereto they belong, but mutually give light one to another.

The Lord make us all in this our day so wise and prudent, as to understand the righteous ways of our God towards us; that we may not stumble at them, but walk in them, and be taught by them to wait upon him in the way of his judgments, and to fix the desires of our soul upon his name as our great refuge, and upon his righteousness as our great business, Isa. xxvi. 8, 9: till he shall be pleased, by the dew of his grace, to revive us as the corn, to make us grow as the vine, and to let the scent of all his ordinances be over all our land, as the smell and as the wine of Lebanon.

It will be an abundant return to my poor and weak endeavours, if I may have that room in thy prayers which the apostle Paul desired to have in the prayers of the Ephesians, "That utterance may be given unto me, that I may open my mouth boldly, to make known the mystery of the gospel," Eph. vi. 19.

The Lord sanctify all the ways of his providence towards us, that when we are chastened we may be taught, and may be greater gainers by the voice of his rod than we are sufferers by the stripes.

AN EXPOSITION

OF

THE PROPHECY OF HOSEA.

CHAPTER I.

Verse 1.

The word of the Lord that came unto Hosea, the son of Beeri, in the days of Uzziah, Jotham, Ahaz, and Hezekiah, kings of Judah, and in the days of Jeroboam the son of Joash, king of Israel.

This day we begin a Scripture exposition, an exercise which has lost much of its honour by its disuse. The best apology for it is to begin it immediately. It is an ancient practice in the church of God, old enough to speak for itself. In Neh. viii. 8, we read that Ezra, Jeshua, Bani, and the rest read in the book of the law, and gave the sense, and caused the people to understand the reading.

I have determined to expound first the books of the minor prophets, of which Jerome remarks, * I know not which to wonder at most, the brevity of speech, or the greatness and abundance of sense. And the prophet Hosea in this respect is most excellent, of whom the same author says he is † exceedingly concise, and speaks by sentences. Why I chose rather to begin with Hosea than with Isaiah, I shall afterward inform you. If God continue life and this exercise, we may go through all the prophetical books, both small and great. In these prophets we have most admirable truths revealed to us; and it is a pity that the mind of God contained in them should be so little known, even unto his children; that such treasures of heavenly truths should lie hid from so many for so long a time.

We might preface our work by labouring to raise your hearts to the consideration of the excellency of the Scriptures in general. Luther uses a high expression about them; he calls them ‡ the highest genus, that contains in it all good whatever. Take away the Scripture, and you even take away the sun from the world. What is the world without the Scriptures, but hell itself? We have had indeed the word of God as the sun in the world, but oh how many mists have been before this sun! Seldom the sun shines clearly to us. Seeing there is such a glorious sun risen, it is distressing that there should be a misty day. Now the work to which we are called is, to dispel the mists and fogs from before this sun, that it may shine more brightly before your eyes, and into your hearts.

Chrysostom§ in his twenty-ninth sermon upon Genesis, exhorting his auditors to get the Scriptures into their houses, and diligently to exercise themselves in them, tells them that by them the soul is raised, elevated, and brightened, as with the beam of the Sun of righteousness, and delivered from the snares of unclean thoughts. In the Scripture the great God of heaven has sent his mind to the children of men; he has made known the counsel of his will, and opened his very heart unto mankind. The Bible is the epistle that God has sent into the world. Did we but hear of a book dictated immediately by God himself, to show the children of men what the eternal counsels of his will were for conducting them to eternal happiness, and his thoughts and intentions concerning their everlasting condition; did we, I say, but hear that there was such a book in the farthest part of the Indies, should we not rejoice that the world was blest with such a mercy? What strong and vehement desires should we have to enjoy but one sight of it before we died! We should be willing to venture upon any hazard, to pass through any difficulty, to be at any expense, that we might have but a glance at such a book as this. My brethren, you need not say, Who shall go to the farthest part of the Indies to fetch us this book? who shall descend into the depth, or go to the uttermost part of the earth, to gain us a sight of this book of Scripture? for, behold, the word is nigh unto you, it is in your houses, and we hope in your hearts, and in this exercise it is to be in our mouths, not only to tell you what it saith, but to explain to you the mind of God in it.

Quid est Scriptura sacra, nisi quædam epistola omnipotentis Dei ad creaturam suam? Greg. l. 4. Ep. 40. ad Gregorium Theodorum Medicum. Sacræ Scripturæ expositio est omnium, quæ ad cultu Dei fiunt, opus maximum, et utilitates humano generi maximas afferens. Wolfius in loc.

To exercise ourselves in this book is sweet indeed.

* Nescio utrum brevitatem sermonum, an magnitudinem sensuum admirari debeas.

† Commaticum et quasi per sententias loquentem.

‡ Genus generalissimum omnium bonorum. Si hoc auferas, solem e mundo sustulisti: quid mundus, sublato verbo, quam infernus?

§ 'Αλλὰ καὶ οἴκαδε μετὰ χεῖρας λαμϐάνειν τὰ ϑεῖα βίβλία· ἡ ψυχὴ πτερȣται καὶ μετάρσιος γίνεται, τῷ φωτὶ τȣ̃ τῆς δικαιοσύνης ἡλίȣ καταυγαζομένη, &c.

Ego odi libros meos, et sæpe opto eos interire, quod metuo, ne morentur lectores et abducant a lectione ipsius Scripturæ, quæ sola omnis sapientiæ fons est, &c. Luther in Gen. c. 19.

Luther professes himself out of love with his own books, and wished them burnt, lest men, spending time in them, should be hindered from reading the Scriptures, which are the only fountain of all wisdom: I tremble, said he, at the former age, which was so much busied in reading Aristotle and Averroes. We read in Neh. viii. 5, 6, when Ezra opened the book of the law to expound it to the people, he "blessed the Lord, the great God: and all the people answered, Amen, Amen." And now blessed be the Lord, the great and gracious God, for stirring your hearts up to such a work as this, and blessed be his name for those liberties we have thus freely to exercise ourselves in this service. Oh praised be the name of the great God for this day's entrance into so good a work as this. Yea, they not only blessed God, but "they lifted up their hands, and bowed their heads, and worshipped the Lord with their faces to the ground." Why? Because the book of the law was read to them and expounded. How came it to pass that their hearts were so ready to hear the book of the law expounded to them? Surely it was because they were newly returned out of captivity. When they came into their own land, and heard the law of God opened to them, they blessed his great name, and bowed their faces to the ground, worshipping him. This day, my brethren, witnesses our great deliverance and return from bondage. Not long since we could not have either ordinances, truths, or religious exercises, but according to the humours of vile men. But now, through God's mercy, a great deliverance is granted to us, that we may come and have free liberty to exercise ourselves in the law of our God. O bless the Lord, and bow your faces to the ground, worshipping him!

In the 12th verse of that chapter we read, that after they had heard the law read and expounded to them, they "went their way to eat, and to drink, and to send portions, and to make great mirth." Why? "Because they had understood the words that were declared unto them." I hope, if God shall please to give assistance in this work, many of you shall go away from this assembly rejoicing, because you know more of God's mind revealed in his word than formerly; and this will be the comfort of your meat and drink, and of your trading, and the very spirit of all the joys of your lives. As the sweetness of the fruit comes from the graft, rather than from the stock; so your comforts and the blessing of grace must come from the word ingrafted in your souls, rather than from any thing you have in yourselves.

In the 1st verse, Nehemiah saith, "All the people gathered themselves together as one man into the street that was before the water gate," to desire Ezra to bring the book of the law, and to read it and to open it unto them. Behold, it is thus this day in this place; here is a great company met together, some to know what the business will be, some for novelty, and some for other ends; but we hope many have come that they may have the book of the law read and opened unto them. Now we expect that from you which is said of them, ver. 3, "And the ears of all the people were attentive unto the book of the law," when it was read and expounded. And truly that attention which now you show promises that we shall have an attentive auditory. But yet that is not all; let us have further a reverential demeanour and carriage in the hearing of the law, as it becomes those who are to deal with God. It is said, ver. 5, that when Ezra opened the book of the law, "all the people stood up." We do not expect the same gesture from you, but by way of analogy we expect a reverential demeanour in your carriage during the whole work, as knowing we are to sanctify God's name in it. Those people after the first day's exercise were so encouraged, that they came again the second day: ver. 13, "On the second day were gathered together the chief of the fathers of all the people, the priests, and the Levites, unto Ezra, to understand the words of the law." And I hope God will so carry on this work, that you shall find encouragement too to come again and again, that you may know more of the mind of God; and that this work shall be profitable not only to the younger and weaker class, but to the fathers, to the priests and Levites also.

Let it be with you as it was with them; according as you have any truth made known unto you, submit to it, yield to it, obey it immediately, and then you shall know more of God's mind: "If any man will do his will, he shall know of the doctrine whether it be of God," John vii. 17. Thus did they; for, ver. 14, when they found it written in the book of the law, that the children of Israel should dwell in booths in the feast of the seventh month, (this was one passage of the law which was expounded, how they should keep the feast of tabernacles, and what booths they should make,) the people immediately went forth to the mount, and fetched olive branches, and palm branches, and branches of thick trees, and made themselves booths, every one upon the roof of his house. In this prophecy of Hosea you will find many truths suitable to the times wherein we live; the Lord grant you obedient hearts to what shall be delivered.

I must not retard the work, nor your expectations, any longer with a larger preface, only somewhat might have been said about the rules for the interpretation of Scripture; I will only observe that, to the interpretation of Scripture, a Scripture frame of heart is necessary, a heart holy and heavenly, suitable to the holiness and heavenliness which are in the word. As it was said of Tully's eloquence, that nothing but the eloquence of Tully could describe its excellency; so it may be said of the spirituality of Scripture, nothing but a heart filled with Scripture spiritualness can set forth its excellencies. And because the authority of Scripture is supreme, we desire the prayers of you all to God for us that his fear may fall upon our hearts, that seeing we are men full of error and evil, yet we may not bring any scripture to maintain any erroneous conceit of our own heads, nor any evil of our own hearts: this we know to be a dreadful evil. It was a fearful evil for Lucifer to say, "I will ascend into heaven, I will exalt my throne above the stars of God: I will sit also upon the mount of the congregation, in the sides of the north: I will ascend above the heights of the clouds; I will be like the most High," Isa. xiv. 13, 14. It is as great an evil for any to seek to make the Highest appear like Lucifer; for they who make the Scripture justify any erroneous opinion, or any way of evil, go about to make the blessed God and the Holy Ghost to be the fathers of lies. It is counted a great evil in a commonwealth to put the king's stamp upon false coin; and to put the stamp of the Spirit of God upon an error, upon a conceit of a man's own, is certainly a great evil before the Lord. God made the priests vile and contemptible before the people, because they were partial in the law, Mal. ii. 9. And for you, my brethren, our prayer shall be, that the fear of God may fall upon you likewise, that you may come to these exercises with Scripture frames of heart.

What frame of heart is a Scripture frame? The Holy Ghost tells you, Isa. lxvi. 2, God looks at him that trembleth at his word: come with hearts trembling at the word of God; come not to be judges of the law, but doers of it. You may judge of your profiting in grace by the delight you find in Scripture; as Quintilian was wont to say of profiting in eloquence, a man may know that by the delight he finds in reading Cicero. It is a true sign of profiting in religion, when

Eum debere scire se aliquid profecisse, cui Ciceronis lectio est valde jucunda.

the Scriptures are sweeter to us than the honey and the honeycomb.

And now the work we have to do is, to open the difficulties and to show you the Divine truths contained in this portion of Scripture. May they spring up from the fountain of life itself, and be presented to your minds with freshness and power.

These five things are to be inquired concerning the prophet whose prophecy I am now to open, which are contained either in the 1st verse or in the chapter:

I. Who he was.
II. To whom he was sent.
III. What his errand was.
IV. His commission.
V. The time of his prophecy.

I. Who this prophet was.

I will explain only what you have of him in the 1st verse, "Hosea the son of Beeri." His name signifies a saviour, one that brings salvation; it is the same root from which Joshua is derived; and many saving and savoury truths we shall find this prophet bringing to us. He was the son of Beeri. We do not find who this Beeri was in Scripture, only that he is here named as the father of the prophet. Surely it is *honoris gratia* to the prophet, and hence

ישע in Hiphil הושיע Salvavit.

Obs. That parents should so live and walk, that it may be an honour to their children to be called by their names, that their children may neither be afraid nor ashamed to be named with them.

The Jews have a tradition which is generally received among them, that whenever a prophet's father is named, that father was a prophet as well as the son. If that were so, then surely it is no dishonour for any man to be the son of a prophet. Let the children of godly, gracious ministers be no dishonour to their parents, their parents are an honour unto them. But we find by experience that many of their children are far from being an honour to their godly parents. How many sons of ancient godly ministers, who heretofore hated superstitious vanities, have of late been the greatest zealots for such things. It reminds me of what the Scripture says concerning Jehoiakim, the son of Josiah, and of the difference between his father and him. When Josiah heard the law read, his heart melted, and he humbled himself before the Lord, 2 Kings xxii. 19. But when Jehoiakim his son heard the law of God read, he took a pen-knife, and cut the roll in which it was written in pieces, and threw "it into the fire that was on the hearth, until all the roll was consumed," Jer. xxxvi. 23. There was much difference between the son and the father: and thus it is between the sons of many ancient godly ministers and them; their fathers indeed might be an honour unto them, but they are a dishonour to their fathers.

"The son of Beeri." The word Beeri is derived from באר *puteus*, a well that has springing water in it, freely and clearly running. So ministers should be the children of Beeri; that which they have should be springing water, and not the mud, and dirt, and filth of their own conceits mingled with the word. This only by way of allusion.

II. To whom was this prophet Hosea sent?

He was sent especially to the ten tribes. I suppose you all know the division of the people of Israel which took place in Rehoboam's time; ten of the tribes went from the house of David, only Judah and Benjamin remained with it. Now these ten tribes, rending themselves from the house of David, separated themselves also from the true worship of God, and horrible wickedness and all manner of abominations grew up amongst them. To these ten tribes God sent this prophet. He sent Isaiah and Micah to Judah, Amos and Hosea to Israel; all these were contemporary. If you would know the state of Israel in Hosea's time, read but 2 Kings xv. 24, "Jeroboam did that which was evil in the sight of the Lord, he departed not from all the sins of Jeroboam the son of Nebat, who made Israel to sin." But notwithstanding Israel was thus notoriously wicked, and given up to all idolatry, yet the Lord sent his prophets Hosea and Amos to prophesy to them even at this time. Oh the goodness of the Lord, to follow an apostatizing people, an apostatizing soul! Mercy yet pleaded while God was speaking in anger; but woe to that people, to that soul, concerning whom the Lord shall give in charge to his prophets, Prophesy no more to them!

III. What was Hosea's errand to Israel?

His errand was to convince them clearly of their abominable idolatry, and those other wickednesses in which they lived, and to denounce severe threatenings, yea, most fearful destruction. This was not done before by the other prophets, as we shall afterward make appear; but it was Hosea's errand specially to threaten an utter desolation to Israel more than ever was before, and yet withal to promise mercy to a remnant to draw them to repentance; and to prophesy of the great things that God intended to do for his church and children in the latter days.

IV. What was his commission?

The words tell us plainly, "The word of the Lord came to Hosea." It was the word of Jehovah. It is a great argument to obedience to know that it is the word of the Lord which is spoken. When men set reason against reason, and judgment against judgment, and opinion against opinion, it prevails not; but when they see the authority of God in the word, then the heart and conscience yield. Therefore however you may look upon the instruments that bring it or open it to you, as your equals or inferiors, yet know there is an authority in the word that is above you all; it is "the word of the Lord."

And this word of the Lord "came to Hosea." Mark the phrase: Hosea did not go for the word of the Lord, but the word of the Lord came to him; he sought it not, but it came to him, אשר היה אל-הושע that is, the word of the Lord came or was made into him, was put into him. Such a kind of phrase you have in the New Testament, John x. 35, "If he called them gods, unto whom the word of God came," πρὸς οὓς ὁ λόγος τοῦ Θεοῦ ἐγένετο, that is, to whom the commission came to place them where they were. So the word of the Lord came to Hosea. The knowledge of a call to a work will help a man through the difficulties of the work. One of the most notable texts of Scripture to encourage a man to the work to which he sees he is clearly called, is that which is spoken of Christ himself, Isa. xlii. 6, "I the Lord have called thee in righteousness." What follows then? "I will hold thy hand, and will keep thee, and give thee for a covenant to the people, for a light to the Gentiles." If we know God's call to a work, (as for the present this of ours is exceeding clear unto us,) though the work be difficult and liable to much censure, yet the Lord will hold our hands, and will be with our minds, and our tongues, and our hearts, and make us instruments to give some light to others.

Magna semper fecerunt, qui, Deo vocante, docuerunt. Luther.

V. What was the time when Hosea prophesied?

You have it in the text, "In the days of Uzziah, Jotham, Ahaz, and Hezekiah, kings of Judah, and in the days of Jeroboam the son of Joash, king of Israel." It is computed by chronologers that Hosea lived about 814 years before Christ. In his time the city of Rome was built. It was the beginning of the Olympiads. Eusebius tells us that there was no Grecian history, and if no Greek learning, then not any that was of any author-

Ab hoc tempore Græca de temporibus historia vera creditur. Euseb. de

Præpar. Evan. l. 20. c. ult.

ity, extant before the time of Hosea.

He prophesied in the reigns of Uzziah, Jotham, Ahaz, and Hezekiah. We have much more of God's mind revealed in this than at first view we apprehend. Hosea prophesied a very long time, probably fourscore years; but it is certain he was in the work of his ministry above seventy years. I make that clear thus: He prophesied in the days of Jeroboam, who though he is here named last, yet was the first of these kings that took up some of his time. But suppose you reckon from the end of Jeroboam's reign, from that to the beginning of Hezekiah were seventy years, and yet the text declares he prophesied both in Jeroboam's time and in Hezekiah's time. After the death of Jeroboam, Uzziah lived thirty-eight years. He reigned fifty-two in all. He began his reign in the twenty-seventh year of Jeroboam, 2 Kings xv. 1. Now Jeroboam lived after that fourteen years, for he reigned forty-one in all. Take fourteen out of fifty-two, and there remains thirty-eight. After him Jotham reigned sixteen years, and then Ahaz succeeded him, and reigned sixteen years more. So that between these two kings, Jeroboam and Hezekiah, were seventy years, in which Hosea prophesied, besides the forty-one years of Jeroboam, and twenty-nine years of Hezekiah, in both whose reigns too you see he lived; and therefore it is probable that Hosea continued in the work of his prophecy at least fourscore years. See what of God's mind will spring from this.

Obs. 1. It pleases God sometimes that some men's labours shall abide more full to posterity than others, though the labours of those others are greater and as excellent as theirs. Hosea continued so long, and yet there is not much of his prophecy extant, only fourteen short chapters. This is according to the diversity of God's administrations. Let the ministers of God learn to be faithful in their work, and let God alone to make them eminent by having their labours extant.

Obs. 2. It appears from hence that Hosea must needs begin to prophesy very young. If he were a prophet fourscore years, certainly he was very young when he began to prophesy; and yet he was called to as great an employment as any of the prophets. It pleases God sometimes to stir up the hearts of young ones to do him great service. He sends such sometimes about great works and employments; so he did Samuel, and Jeremiah, and Timothy. Therefore let no man despise their youth.

Obs. 3. Hosea prophesying thus long, it appears he lived to be old in his work. When God has any work for men to do, he lengthens out their days. So he did the days of John the disciple, who lived a hundred years, if not more; for the time of writing his Gospel was in the ninety-ninth year of Christ, sixty-six after the ascension. Let us not be too solicitously careful about our lives, to maintain our health and strength; let us be careful to do our work, for according as the Lord hath work for us to do, so he will continue to us our health, and strength, and life. When you come to die, you may die comfortably, having this thought in you: Well, the work that the Lord appointed me to do is done, and why should I seek to live longer in the world? God has others enough to do his work. It was a sweet expression of Jacob, "Behold, I die: but God shall be with you, and bring you again unto the land of your fathers," Gen. xlviii. 21. So may a prophet of God say, who has been faithful in his work, Behold, I die, but the Lord shall be with you; my work is finished, but God has others who are young to carry on his work.

Obs. 4. You may see by Hosea's continuance in so many several kings' reigns, that he went through a variety of conditions. Sometimes he lived under wicked kings, sometimes under moderate kings, sometimes he had encouragement from godly and gracious kings, though they were kings of Judah. Not only the people of God, but especially God's ministers, must expect a variety of conditions in the world; they must not promise to themselves always the same state.

Yet further, Hosea prophesied in all these kings' reigns. Here appears the constancy of his spirit, notwithstanding the many difficulties he met with in his work; for, prophesying in the time of Jeroboam, Jotham, and Ahaz, who were wicked princes, he must surely have met with many discouragements: and though he continued fourscore years, yet he saw but little success of his labour; for the truth is, the people were not converted to God by his ministry. Nay, it is apparent they grew worse and worse; for it is said of that Jeroboam in whose time Hosea began his prophecy, that he did evil in the sight of the Lord, and continued in the ways of Jeroboam the son of Nebat, 2 Kings xv. 24; but after we read most horrible things of which Israel was guilty In 2 Kings xvii. 17, it is said, "They caused their sons and their daughters to pass through the fire, and used divination and enchantments, and sold themselves to do evil in the sight of the Lord, to provoke him to anger;" besides many other dreadful things you may read in that chapter. This was in king Hoshea's time, which was towards the end of Hosea's prophecy.

Obs. 5. God may continue a prophet a long time amongst a people, and yet they may never be converted. It is a distemper in ministers' hearts to incline to abandon their work because they see not desired success. Latimer, in one of his sermons, speaks of a minister who was asked why he left off preaching, who replied, because he saw he did no good: this, says Latimer, is a very naughty answer. What we have here may be a great stay to those who have laboured many years in the work of the ministry, and yet think they have done little or no good; Hosea was fourscore years a prophet to Israel, and yet did not convert them. But notwithstanding all these discouragements, he continued constant, and that with abundance of freshness and liveliness, even to the end of his prophesying.

Obs. 6. It is an honour to the ministers of God, who meet with many difficulties and discouragements in their way, yet continue fresh and lively to the very end. Many young ministers are fresh and lively when they begin first: oh how full of zeal and activity are they then! but after they have been a while in their work, or when they have gained what they aimed at, they grow cold, and that former vigour, freshness, and zeal which appeared to be in them become much flatter. Like soldiers, who at the first are forward and active in service, but afterward come to live upon their pay, and can do no service at all; or rather, as vessels when they are first tapped, the wine is very quick and nimble, but at last grows exceeding flat. As we commend that vessel of wine that draws quick to the very last, so it is an excellent thing for a minister of God to continue fresh, and quick, and lively to the last end. It is true, nature and natural abilities may decay, but a spiritual freshness may appear when natural abilities are decayed. To see an old prophet of God, who has gone through many difficulties and sufferings, and yet continues fresh and lively in the work of the ministry, and has spiritual excellencies sparkling in him then, this is a most honourable sight, and calls for abundance of reverence.

Obs. 7. It pleases God many times to let his prophets see the fulfilling of their threatenings upon the people against whom they have denounced them. Hosea prophesied so long, that he most probably saw the fulfilling of his prophecy; for he continued prophesying till Hezekiah's time, and in the sixth year of Hezekiah's reign came the destruction of Israel. Hosea had threatened an utter taking of them away, but it was not done till then. Perhaps the people go away, and scorn and contemn the prophets, and their words are but wind with them; but God often lets his ministers live to see their words fulfilled upon them. For it is common with individuals, when upon their beds of sickness or death, to say, Ah, the word of the Lord is true that I heard at such a time, it is now come upon me! So God dealt with the people in Jeremiah's time; they laughed and contemned him, but Jeremiah lived to see the fulfilling of those threatenings. And if they live not to see the fulfilling of their words, yet soon after their death they are fulfilled, as it was at Hippo, where Austin threatened judgments against the people; they were not executed in his time, but soon after he was taken away they came.

Hosea not only prophesied in these kings' days, but in the days of Jeroboam king of Israel. Here are three questions:

1. What is the reason that Jeroboam, who in truth was the first of these kings, is named last?

2. Why only one king of Israel is named, and three kings of Judah? for in the time of Hosea's prophecy there were six other kings of Israel, Zachariah, Shallum, Menahem, Pekahiah, Pekah, Hoshea.

3. Why Jeroboam is named at all?

One answer will be sufficient for the first two questions, why Jeroboam is named last, and why there is but one king of Israel named. The answer is this, God took no great delight in the kings of Israel, for they had forsaken the true worship of God. Though there was much corruption in Judah, yet because they kept to the true worship of God, God took more delight in Judah than in Israel. Therefore he names Jeroboam in the last place, though he was first, and only him.

But why was Jeroboam named at all?

It was that you might understand the state of the people of Israel at the time of Hosea's prophecy. Much is to be learned from hence. The state of the people of Israel in the time of Jeroboam's reign was very prosperous, though their wickedness was very great. 2 Kings xiv. shows you, that a little before this they had been in very great distress, and under sore afflictions; but in Jeroboam's time they had the greatest prosperity they had ever known. For this Jeroboam was not the first Jeroboam, the son of Nebat, that caused Israel to sin, and occasioned the rent of the ten tribes from the house of David; that occurred above a hundred and forty years before this; but the Jeroboam in whose time God sent Hosea to prophesy this great wrath against the house of Israel, was the son of Joash. Now in all this time the kingdom was never in a more prosperous condition than in the days of this Jeroboam.

Two things are to be observed concerning the condition of the people at this time.

First, That they were a little before this in great adversity, and then afterwards they grew up to great prosperity. That 14th chapter of the Second of the Kings informs you that they were under sore affliction, ver. 26, "There was not any shut up, nor any left, nor any helper for Israel." It is a comparison taken from shepherds, that shut up their flocks when they would keep them safe from danger; but now here was such a general desolation and woeful affliction upon Israel, that there was none shut up, nor any helper left. But then comes this Jeroboam, and it is said, ver. 25, that "he restored the coast of Israel from the entering of Hamath unto the sea of the plain." And, ver. 28, "He recovered Damascus and Hamath, which belonged to Judah, for Israel." This Hamath of which he speaks was of great use, it was the inlet of the Assyrians; and for Jeroboam to conquer that place, to recover Damascus, and to add that to the crown of Israel which belonged to Judah, shows that after their bitter affliction God granted a great mercy by Jeroboam's means, and that now Israel flourished greatly, and grew exceedingly prosperous. There is much of God's mind held out to us in this: as, in that the people of Israel had been under sore affliction, and delivered, yet God sent Hosea to them to show them their horrible wickedness, and to threaten destruction.

Obs. 1. Hence see the perverseness of the children of men, that after great deliverances granted them from bitter and sore afflictions, yet they will continue in their wickedness and rebellion. The Lord grant this may not be true concerning us. God has delivered us in great measure from those sore and bitter afflictions and heavy oppressions under which we lately groaned, and has restored to us many gracious liberties; now have we not need of an Hosea to be sent unto us to rebuke us, and to threaten judgment for the evil of our ways? This is a sad thing.

Obs. 2. God may let a sinner continue a long time in the way of his sin; and when he has flourished many years, and thinks surely the bitterness of death is past, God may threaten judgment. Jeroboam reigned one and forty years, and Hosea must have prophesied in the latter end of Jeroboam's time. Jeroboam might think, Why does he come to contest with me, and to tell me of my sin and wickedness, and to threaten judgment? have not I continued these forty years king, and have prospered? and surely God hath been with me. Well, a sinner may hold out long, and yet afterward judgment may come.

Obs. 3. A people in a flourishing condition, when they prosper most, and overcome their enemies, and have all according to their hearts' desire, even that may be the time for God to appear in his wrath against them. So it was here; therefore we must not judge our enemies to be happy, nor fear them, because of their present flourishing state, nor be secure ourselves because of the mercies we enjoy. God does not always act thus, but sometimes he is pleased, as here, to stay till sinners are at the height of their prosperity, and then to come upon them. Sometimes God is more sudden. Zachariah the son of this Jeroboam thought he might venture as well as his father: My father prospered in such ways forty-one years, and why may not I? No, God came upon him in six months, 2 Kings xv. 8.

Secondly, When Hosea came to prophesy against Israel, he saw them in their prosperity, and yet continued to threaten judgment against them. It was a further argument of the Spirit of God that taught him, and of the special insight which he had into the mind of God, that he should thus prophesy destruction to them, when they were in the height of their prosperity. It is true, if Hosea had prophesied in Zachariah's days, when the kingdom was declining, or in Shallum's time, and others after him, then he might have seen by the working of second causes that the kingdom was going down. But he comes in Jeroboam's time, when there was no appearance from second causes of their destruction, and then prophesied destruction unto them.

Obs. 1. It is a sign of the special insight the soul has in the ways of God, that can see misery under the greatest prosperity. The prophet did not think Israel in a better condition because of their outward prosperity; a sign his prophecy was from God. Yet further, this being in the reign of Jeroboam, when they were in great prosperity, their hearts were exceedingly hardened against the prophet; and it cannot be imagined but that they entertained his prophecy with scorn and contempt; for it is a usual thing, when men are in the height of their pride, like the wild ass's colt, to scorn and contemn all that comes against them.

Obs. 2. It is easy for a minister of God to deal plainly with people in the time of adversity, but when men are in their pride and jollity, to deal faithfully with them then is very difficult. That their great prosperity raised up and hardened their hearts with pride against the prophet appears plainly, if you will read Amos vii. 10; (for we must find God's mind by comparing one place with another;) there you see the fruit of Jeroboam's prosperity, for Amos and Hosea were contemporary. When Amos was prophesying, "Amaziah the priest of Beth-el sent to Jeroboam king of Israel, saying, Amos hath conspired against thee in the midst of the house of Israel: the land is not able to bear his words." This was said of Amos, and it is likely that Hosea did not meet with better treatment. Amaziah the priest of Beth-el did this. If there be any enemies against faithful ministers, they are the priests of Beth-el, idolatrous and superstitious ministers. And what course do they take? They send to the king, to the governors; O they have conspired against the king, they are seditious persons, factious men, who stir up the kingdom, and break the peace of the church, the land cannot bear their words. Such a message as this you see Amaziah sent to the king concerning Amos; he turns off all from himself to the king, and all the punishment that must be inflicted upon Amos must be in the name of the king. And mark the 12th verse of that chapter, "Also Amaziah said unto Amos, O thou seer, go, flee away into the land of Judea, and prophesy there." We are not holy enough for you, forsooth we are idolaters, we do not worship God aright, we are no true church; get you to Judah among your brethren, and prophesy not any more here at Beth-el. Why? Because "it is the king's chapel, and it is the king's court." It seems then in those times that the king's chapel and the king's court could not bear with a faithful prophet. And what was the ground of it, but because at this time Jeroboam prospered in his way, and the kingdom was in a more flourishing condition than it ever was before. Here then was the trial of the faithfulness of Hosea's spirit yet to go on in the work of his prophecy.

Yet further; in that Hosea prophesied in the time of Jeroboam, it will appear that he was the first prophet that ever brought these hard tidings to them of the utter destruction of Israel. "The Lord said not that he would blot out the name of Israel from under heaven: but he saved them by the hand of Jeroboam the son of Joash," 2 Kings xiv. 27. Mark, there is given the reason why the Lord saved them by the hand of Jeroboam, because he had not yet said he would blot out the name of Israel from under heaven; that is, the Lord never before sent any of his prophets thus plainly and fully to declare his intention to them, to blot out the name of Israel, upon their going on in their sins. So that it is clear that Hosea was the first that was sent about this message. And certainly it was so much the harder, he being the first of all. For they might have said, Why do you come with these new things, and in so great severity? who ever did so before you? We know if a minister come with any thing that seems to be new, if he presents any truth to you that has but a show of novelty, though it be never so good and comfortable, he finds little encouragement. Nay, if he but comes in a new way, as this very exercise, because it is likely to be pursued in a way that has been disused, it will meet with many discouragements. What then will the threatenings of hard things, of judgments and destruction, do when they come with novelty? Surely Hosea had a hard task of this, and yet he went on faithfully with it. Thus much for the time wherein Hosea prophesied.

Ver. 2. *The beginning of the word of the Lord by Hosea. And the Lord said to Hosea, Go, take unto thee a wife of whoredoms and children of whoredoms: for the land hath committed great whoredom, departing from the Lord.*

Some from these words gather, that Hosea was the first of the prophets whose writings have come down to us. Though it is true we cannot gather it directly from hence, yet it is apparent that notwithstanding Isaiah is set first, yet Hosea was before him; for if you look into Isa. i., you find that his beginning was in the days of Uzziah. Now Hosea was in the days of Jeroboam, and Jeroboam was before Uzziah. And this may be one reason why, though I intend the whole prophetical books, yet I rather begin with Hosea, because indeed he was the first prophet: it is clear you see from the Scripture, though we cannot gather it from these words in this 2nd verse.

But yet thus much we may gather from these words, "The beginning of the word of the Lord by Hosea," that this was the beginning of his prophecy. And what was this beginning? what did God set him about first? Mark the next words, "And the Lord said to Hosea, Go, take unto thee a wife of whoredoms and children of whoredoms;" and so declare to the people of Israel that they had "committed great whoredom, departing from the Lord:" the most grievous charge and most severe and terrible expression of God's wrath against that people that you meet with in all the book of God. This is Hosea's work, and he was very young when first he went about it. Now, as I told you before, God sometimes calls young ones to great services; but to call a young man to go to this people with such a message, in the midst of all their pride and flourish to contest with them thus, and to tell them that they are children of whoredoms, and no longer the people of God, for a young man to do this! Why, men grown old and sodden in their sins might reason, If this indeed came from the mouth of some old prophet, reverend for his years and experience, it had been somewhat; but to come from a green-head, for an upstart to upbraid us with such vile things! But let us know, my brethren, if God send any message unto us, though by young persons, he expects our entertainment of it. When God would destroy Eli's house, he sends the message by young Samuel; but Eli did not reason thus, What, this young boy to come and speak thus malapertly to me! No, he stoops to it, and saith, "Good is the word of the Lord."

Again, Hosea must tell them that they are children of whoredoms, and not the people of God. What, for a minister when he comes first among a people to begin so harshly and severely! is it not better to comply with the people, to come with gentle and fair means, to seek to win them with love? if you begin with harsh truths, surely you will make them fly off immediately. Thus many reason. Now I beseech you take heed to your own hearts in reasoning thus. Many have done so, and have sought to comply with the people so long, till they have complied away all their faithfulness, and conscience, and vigour. When they come to great men, rich men, men in place and eminence, they will comply with such; but let them have any of God's people in their parish who are of a mean rank and poor, they comply little enough with them, but are harsh and bitter to them, and regard not the tenderness of their consciences at all.

It is true, if ministers have the testimony of their own consciences that they would take no other way but what shall be for the greatest profit of their people, maintaining such a disposition as to be willing to undergo any sufferings to which God shall call them, they may say first when they come to a house, Peace be to this house, especially when they come to a place that has not had the means before. But if it be to a people who act directly against the light of their consciences, a superstitious people, that cannot but be convinced, and have had many evidences, that their conduct is against the mind of God, and yet for their own base ends will go on and not amend; in such a case we may come with harshness at the very first. So Paul gives a charge to Titus in dealing with the Cretians, who were evil beasts and slow bellies, that he should "rebuke them sharply" (so we translate it); the word is, ἀποτόμως, cuttingly, Tit. i. 13.

"The beginning of the word of the Lord by Hosea." The particle which is translated *by* signifies *in* as well as *by;* it is not *El*, but *Beth*, and so it is read by some, The word of the Lord came in Hosea. This expression notes the inward and intimate converse that the Lord had with the spirit of Hosea in the work of his ministry. The Lord spake first *in* Hosea, and then Hosea speaks *out* unto the people. Some such expression we have concerning Paul, Gal. i. 16, That Christ may be revealed in me; not only to me, but in me. The more inwardly God speaks and converses with the hearts of his ministers, the more inwardly and efficaciously they are able to speak to the people. This is deep preaching, when it is from the heart to the heart. And so Augustine says of Hosea, because that which he spake was so deep, it wrought more strongly. Hosea's prophecy must needs be deep, for God spake in him before he spake out to the people. We say that which comes from the heart will go to the heart; surely that which comes from the voice of God in the heart, will go beyond the ears to the hearts of people. And blessed are the people that have such ministers who will speak nothing *to them*, but what has first been spoken by God *in them*.

Quanto profundius quidem loquitur, tanto operosius penetratur. August. de Hosea, l. 18. de Civ. c. 28.

Again in this 2nd verse he twice uses the same expression: "The beginning of the word of the Lord by Hosea;" and again, "The Lord said to Hosea;" and yet in the beginning of the 1st verse, "The word of the Lord came to Hosea." Why all this three times? With good reason; for Hosea was to come with a terrible message to the people, and to reprehend them with much sharpness, to tell them that they were the children of whoredoms, and that they had departed from the Lord, and he would have no more mercy upon them, but would utterly take them away. He had need therefore have an express command for what he did, and to have much evidence of the Spirit, that what he said was from God, and not any thing of his own spirit. When a minister of God shall come and reprehend a people severely for their sins, and threaten God's judgment, let him then, if ever, look to it that he has a good warrant for what he saith, that what he shall deliver may be nothing but the word of God in him, the sheer word of God, without any mixture of his own. It is an ordinary thing for ministers in reprehending sin, and denouncing threatenings, to mingle much of their own spirit and wrath. But if at any time ministers should take heed of mixing their own wrath, then especially when they denounce God's wrath, then they should bring nothing but the word of the Lord; for it being a hard message, the spirits of men will rise up against it. If they once see the spirit of the minister in it, they will be ready to say as the devil in the possessed man, "Jesus I know, and Paul I know; but who are ye?" So they, The word of the Lord I know, but what are you? here is your own passion, your own humour. O let not any think to oppose sin with sin; "the wrath of man worketh not the righteousness of God," James i. 20. You that are ministers, would you have a sentence? I will give you one: When you are called to reveal God's wrath, conceal your own.

The scope of the prophecy is the very same as the scope of this chapter, to declare, first, The evil condition in which the ten tribes were, both in regard of their sins, and the punishment that was to be executed for their sins. Secondly, Gracious promises of mercy to a remnant; to Judah, in the 7th verse; and to Judah and Israel both, from the 10th verse to the end of the chapter.

First, God begins with conviction, to show them their sin, and the dreadfulness of it. Conviction should go before correction. You must not presently fly in the faces of those who are under you when they cross you; first instruct them, and then correct them. God would first convince them of the greatness of their sins, not by verbal, but by real expressions. Things that assail the ear slowly stir and work upon the heart, but things that are presented before the eye are more operative; and therefore Hosea must not tell them only that they had committed whoredom, but must tell them in this way; he must go and take a wife of whoredoms, and beget children of whoredoms.

Segnius irritant animos demissa per aurem, Quam quæ sunt oculis subjecta fidelibus, et quæ Ipse sibi tradit spectator. Horat. de Arte Poet.

In the entrance of the prophecy you see we meet with a great difficulty. First, a command from God, from the holy God, to a prophet, a holy prophet, to go and take "a wife of whoredoms;" not an ordinary harlot, but a most prostitute woman, "a wife of whoredoms:" as, in the Scripture phrase, a man of bloods, is a man who has shed much blood; and a man of sorrows, is a man who has been exercised with many sorrows; so "a wife of whoredoms," is one who has committed vile, notorious lewdness. Yet such a wife must the prophet take to himself, and his children must be children of whoredoms too. How can this be?

St. Austin, who had been a Manichee, having to deal much with Manichees, met with this objection against the Old Testament from one Faustus, a Manichee: That Old Testament of yours, Moses and the prophets, said Faustus, is that of God? do you not find there a command to take a wife of whoredoms, and can this be from God?

Austin answers it thus: Though she had been a prostitute before, yet she might be reclaimed; and so she might be called a wife of whoredoms, from that whoredom of which she was heretofore guilty. And so he thinks that it was a reality that Hosea did take to himself a wife of whoredoms.

Quid adversum clementiæ veritatis, quid fidei Christianæ si meretrix, relicta fornicatione, in castum conjugium commutetur? &c. Aug. cont. Faust. l. 22. c. 80.

Theodoret is somewhat angry with those who think it was not really done, but only in a way of vision. I find many of our later men are of the same mind: so Arias Montanus, Piscator, Pareus, Tarnovius, and others think, and they explain it thus; that it is a command of God, and therefore though it had not been lawful for Hosea to have done it, yet, God commanding it, he might do it. As they instance in other cases that seem to be somewhat of the like nature, as the children of Israel's borrowing of the Egyptians, Abraham's killing his son, and the like.

Eorum audaciam mirari satis nequeo, qui non verentur dicere verba hæc esse rebus destituta. Theod. in Hos. enar. c. 1.

If this should be so, (and as many interpreters so explain it, it appears a thing not impossible,) we might learn thus much from it.

Obs. 1. That God's command takes away all matter of offence. It would be a notorious, offensive thing for a prophet, a minister of God, to marry a wicked harlot; yet so far as the offence is, God's command is enough to take it away. For the subject of offence is not duty, but indifference: any thing that is a duty to be done, we must perform it, though it be never so offensive to others; but if it be a thing of indifference, then we may stop. God's command takes away all plea of offence. I speak not thus of man's command, for men, even magistrates themselves, are bound not to offend their brethren, as well as others.

But then it may be said they should command nothing at all, for some or other would be offended. And shall not they command because some weak ones may be offended? It is true, that which they believe in their consciences to be their duty, they are bound to command, and they would sin against God if they did not command it, and require obedience to it; they must do it, though never so many be offended. But in matters which they themselves acknowledge to be neither for God's service or for the good of a commonwealth, the rule binds them as well as others in regard of offences to forbear.

Obs. 2. That the prophet must suffer much in his credit before men, only to be serviceable to God for a further expression of his mind. Our credit, our names, and all we are or have, must lie down at God's feet to be serviceable to him in the least thing, if but in a way of expression of his mind, much more in bearing witness to his truth.

Obs. 3. We see the wisdom of God in putting the prophet in the very first service upon a very difficult work. It could not but be a thing exceedingly irksome to his spirit to marry such a one, yet God commands him to do it. It is the usual way of God, when he calls any to great services, at the beginning to put them to such difficult works as shall try them, that if they go through them, then they may be confided in, that they will go through more afterward.

But we shall rather understand this in a way of vision, as others do; not that Hosea did really marry such a wife, but it appeared to him in a vision, as if such a thing were really done, only to declare what the condition of the people of Israel was at this time in respect of God: as if God should say, Hosea, this people of Israel is to me no other than as if thou shouldst have a wife that were the most notorious harlot in the world, and all their children are to me as if thy children were the children of whoredom and fornication. And this I conceive to be more directly the mind of God. I will not give you my mere conception of it, but reasons why it must be so.

First, Because we find in Scripture that which is historically related was sometimes done in a way of vision. It is a usual way of Scripture to express that which is done in vision as if it were a history, as if it were really done. I will show you two examples for this: one of Jeremiah, when he was at Jerusalem, yet the Scripture speaks as if he had been at Babylon; and the other of Ezekiel, when he was at Babylon, it speaks as if he had been at Jerusalem. It is as fully related as this is here, and both must therefore needs be understood as in a way of vision. First, for Jeremiah, you have it chap. xiii. 4. God requires there that he should "go to Euphrates, and hide his girdle there in a hole of the rock:" but this river was a river in Babylon, and Jeremiah was not in Babylon at that time, nor in all the time of the siege, nor in the time of the captivity; neither could he go to Babylon, for the city was now besieged, and when he did but essay to go a little way to Anathoth, his own town, he was seized as if he had been a traitor to his country. Therefore that which is declared as a history was only done in a vision. So Ezekiel was at Babylon (for he was the prophet that prophesied to the people who were carried captive to Babylon; God sent a prophet to them to help them there in their captivity); yet, chap. viii. of his prophecy, Ezekiel seems to be brought to Jeremiah and he is bidden there to dig a hole in the wall to see the wicked abominations that the ancients of Israel did there. Now Ezekiel was not there, he was at Babylon; but it is declared as if the thing had been done really. So we are to understand Isaiah's going naked twenty days, and Ezekiel's lying three hundred and ninety days on the one side, and forty-three on the other, Ezek. iv.

Secondly, That it was a vision, and not really done. We observe, it was God's command, Lev. xxi. 7, that the priest must not marry with a whore. Of all men's wives, God is most careful of the wives of those who are in the work of the ministry, and who are church officers; therefore when, in 1 Tim. iii. 11, but a deacon is described, his wife is described also, that she should be "grave, no slanderer, sober, and faithful in all things." You never read that when God appoints what a magistrate's office should be in a commonwealth, that he takes such care to set down what his wife should be; but when he appoints the lowest officer in a church, a deacon, he appoints what his wife should be too. Therefore the wives of ministers should go away with a lesson from hence, and know that God has a more special eye to them than to the wives of all the men in the world besides. God is tender of the credit of the officers of his church, and so should man be, for their discredit is a hinderance to their work.

Yea further, we read, Amos vii. 16, that it was threatened as a curse to Amaziah the priest of Beth-el, that his wife should be a harlot, for resisting the prophet: shall then the wife of Hosea be a whore? for Amos and Hosea prophesied both at the same time. And the Scripture saith, 1 Cor. xi. 7, that "the woman is the glory of the man." What a glory would Hosea have had in such a match as this! The woman is the glory of the man; how? In two respects she is so. 1. Because it is a glory to a man that he has such an image, for she is from the man; and as the man, being the image of God, shows the glory of God, because he is the image of God and from him; so the woman, being from the man, and as it were his image, she is the glory of the man. 2. Because man has such an excellent creature brought under subjection to him. Man is not only made glorious by God, in that God has put all other creatures under him; but especially in this, that God has put such an excellent creature under him as the woman, for the woman is the glory of the man. This could not be here in such a match as this.

Thirdly, It could not be that it was a real thing, but a vision, from the prophecy itself. If real, Hosea must have stayed almost a whole year before he could have gone on in his prophecy. For, first, he must take to him a wife of whoredoms, and beget a child of whoredoms; then he must have stayed till the child had been born, before he could have come to the people and said, My child is born, and his name is Jezreel, and it is upon this ground that I have named him thus; and then he must have stayed almost a year more before he could have had Lo-ruhamah; and then after that he must stay almost another year longer before Lo-ammi could be born.

Fourthly, The expression used here is, that God spake *in* Hosea; speaking and appearing to him by an inward vision, as it were in an ecstasy, saith Polanus; therefore we must understand that this wife of whoredoms whom Hosea was to marry was in a way of vision. It was to signify that Israel was to God as a wife of whoredoms, and as children of whoredoms should have been to the prophet if he had been married to her.

From all these reasons there is this result, that the people of Israel were gone a whoring from God. Idolatry is as the sin of whoredom; and I cannot open this scripture, except I show you wherein idolatry is like the sin of whoredom. The idolatry of the church, not the idolatry of heathens, is whoredom. One that commits adultery gives herself to another. The heathens, because they were never married to God, their idolatry is not adultery; but the people of God, being married to the Lord, their idolatry is adultery.

1. Adultery breaks the marriage bond. There is nothing breaks the marriage bond between God and his people but the sin of idolatry. Though a wife may be guilty of many failings, and be a grievous trouble and burden to her husband, yet these do not break the marriage knot except she defile the marriage bed. So though a people may be guilty of notorious and vile sins, yet if they keep the worship of God pure, they are

not guilty of whoredom, but still God is married to them.

2. Whoredom is a loathsome thing. Though delightsome to men, yet loathsome to God. Idolatry is the same; therefore the Scripture describes the idols that men set up by a גלולים a word which signifies the very excrement that comes from creatures, Ezek. xxii. 3. Idolaters think their way of idol worship to be very delightsome, but that which they call delectable God calls detestable, if you compare these two scriptures: Isa. xliv. 9, they call their idols "delectable things;" but in Ezek. v. 11, God calls them "detestable things." Idolatry is a detestable, loathsome thing.

3. There is nothing causes so irreconcilable a breach between a man and his wife as defiling the marriage bed by adultery: Jealousy is the rage of a man, and he will take no ransom. There is nothing wherein God is so irreconcilable to a people as in the point of false worship.

4. Adultery is a besotting sin. "Whoredom and new wine take away the heart," saith the prophet, chap. iv. 11; and in Isa. xliv. 19, saith God, He hath no understanding to say, "I have burned part of it in the fire; yea, also I have baked bread upon the coals thereof; I have roasted flesh, and eaten it: and shall I make the residue thereof an abomination? shall I fall down to the stock of a tree?" He hath no understanding to consider this. Idolatry is a besotting sin, as well as adultery. And therefore we need not marvel, though men of great parts and abilities continue in their superstitious way of worship, for nothing besots men's hearts so much as that.

5. Whoredom is a most dangerous sin. "The mouth of strange women is as a deep pit: he that is abhorred of the Lord shall fall therein," Prov. xxii. 14. Oh most dreadful place to an adulterer! If there be any adulterer in this place this day, when thou goest home turn to that scripture, and let it be as a dart to thy heart, "The mouth of strange women is as a deep pit: he that is abhorred of the Lord shall fall therein:" a sign of a man abhorred of God. And so is idolatry; for in 2 Thess. ii. 11, 12, God gave them over to believe a lie, that they might be damned. Those that follow the idolatries of antichrist are given over by God to believe a lie. That lie of popery altogether is one lie. Hence it is that the popish party invent so many such strange lies, all to uphold that great lie. Why is this? That they might be damned. Idolatry is a dreadful, dangerous sin. Though idolaters think they please God in and by such ways of worship, yet they are given over by God that they may be damned. If this prove to be a place that concerns those who follow antichrist, and if Rome proves to be as that scripture describes her, it is a dreadful text to all papists.

6. Harlots are accustomed to deck themselves in pompous attire and gaudy raiment. So idolaters deck up their idols in bravery, and lavish gold (as the Scripture speaks) upon their idols; whereas "the King's daughter is all glorious within," and the simplicity of the gospel will not permit such things.

7. Though women go a whoring from their husbands, yet still they retain (before the divorce) the name of wives, and their children (though bastards) retain the name of children, and bear the father's name. So idolaters retain the name of the church, and those that they beget must still be called the only sons of the church.

But how are his children said to be children of whoredoms? for suppose his wife were a wife of whoredoms, yet, being married to her, wherefore should the children be called children of whoredoms?

To that is answered, 1. Some think upon this ground, because the children when they grow up would follow the way of the mother, as is usual for children to do. Therefore you need take heed how you enter into the estate of marriage for your children's sake, for they will follow the way of the mother. Or rather, 2. Because, though they were begotten after marriage, yet they will lie under suspicion as those that are illegitimate. The children of one that has been a harlot are always suspected, and so in repute they are the children of fornication: so says God, These people are to me as if their children were accounted children of fornication.

"For the land hath committed great whoredom." Or, as Arius Montanus reads it, In going a whoring it will go a whoring. They not only have, but will; they are set upon it, they are stout-hearted in the way of idolatry. It is the land that has done it, the people of the land.

Fornicando fornicatur: or, as Arius Montanus. Fornicando fornicabitur.

But why the land? It is a secret check to them, and an upbraiding them for their unthankfulness, that when God gave them so good a land, the land of Canaan, that flowed with milk and honey, the land of promise, and gave it to them to nourish up the true worship of God, yet they made this land of God, this land of promise, to be a land to nourish up most vile idolaters.

"Departing from the Lord," from Jehovah. The more worthy the husband is, the more vile and odious the adultery of the wife. What! to go a whoring from God, the blessed God, in whom is all beauty and excellency, and turn to blind idols? What! change the glory of the invisible God into the similitude of an ox that eateth grass? With what indignation doth God speak it! O you that go a whoring after your sinful lusts, this will lie most dreadfully upon your consciences one day, that it was from the Lord that you departed, from that infinite, glorious, eternal Deity, the fountain of all good, to cleave to base, sinful, and unclean lusts.

Who is this whore? and what are the children that are begotten to Hosea by her?

Ver. 3. *So he went and took Gomer the daughter of Diblaim; which conceived, and bare him a son.*

We must obey God in things that seem to be never so much against our reason and sense.

"He took Gomer the daughter of Diblaim." The word Gomer, גמר comes from a word which signifies both perfection and defection; and so it may be applied both ways. Some apply it to perfection; that is, a harlot that was perfect and complete, both in her beauty and in her fornication. The word likewise signifies rottenness, corruption, and consumption: so indeed are all things in the world; as soon as they grow to any perfection, they begin to decline quickly to corruption. All but spiritual things do so; they indeed grow still higher and higher.

This Gomer we will take rather in the second acceptation of it, as it signifies rottenness and consumption. Who was this Gomer? She was בת־דבלים "the daughter of Diblaim." The signification is, according to some, "one that dwells in the desert," in reference to that famous desert Diblath, of which we read Ezek. vi. 14, noting the way of idolaters, that they were wont to go into woods and deserts, and there to sacrifice to their idols. But rather, according to most, Diblaim signifies bunches of dried figs, which were the delicacies of those times; so Œcolampadius, from which he observes, that rottenness and corruption proceed from voluptuous pleasures and delicacies. Though the pleasures of the flesh are very contentful to you, yet destruction is the fruit of them; destruction is the daughter of sensual pleasures and delights; so saith the Scripture: "If ye live after the flesh, ye shall die," Rom. viii. 13. "Whose end is destruction, whose God is their belly, whose glory is in their shame," Phil. iii. 19.

But to apply it to Israel. Israel was as "Gomer the daughter of Diblaim;" that is, the people of Israel were now near to destruction, and were the daughters of sensual delights, they gave themselves over to sensual pleasures.

It is the usual way of those idolaters who forsake the true worship of God, to give themselves up to the pleasures of the flesh. Sensuality and idolatry usually go together. When the people of Israel sacrificed to the calves, what did they? They ate and drank, and rose up to play; that was all their work, and good enough for the worshipping of such a god, a calf. You know the more we began to decline in the worship of God, we began to be more sensual; there must be proclamation to people to take their sports and delights upon the Lord's day; and indeed it usually accompanies defection in the way of God's worship. False worship lays not such bonds upon men's consciences for the mortifying the lusts of the flesh as the worship of God does. Therefore those men who love to give liberty to the flesh are soonest enticed to ways of superstitious worship. Jeremiah, in chap. xxiv. 9, sets forth the state of those naughty Jews that were in captivity by the similitude of a basket of rotten figs; which is agreeable to this, and the more confirms this interpretation, that Israel was as Gomer the daughter of Diblaim, that is, rottenness, the daughter of sensuality.

Thus for the mother. But now the son that is begotten of this mother is Jezreel.

Ver. 4. *And the Lord said unto him, Call his name Jezreel; for yet a little while, and I will avenge the blood of Jezreel upon the house of Jehu, and will cause to cease the kingdom of the house of Israel.*

"Call his name Jezreel." The prophet must give a name to his son. It belongs to parents to give names to their children. Godfathers and godmothers (as they call them) are of no use for this, or for any thing else that I know; and, in such holy things as sacraments are, we must take heed of bringing in any unuseful, any idle things.

But here we are to inquire, First, The signification of this name; Jezreel signifies the scattered of the Lord. Secondly, The reasons why the son of Hosea must be called by this name, יזרעאל Jezreel. Five reasons may be given.

First, That hereby God might show that he intended to avenge that blood which was shed in Jezreel.

Secondly, To show that Israel had lost the honour of his name, and was no more Israel, but Jezreel. There seems to be much similarity between the name Israel and Jezreel, but there is a great deal of difference in the signification; for Israel is one that prevails with God, "the strength of the Lord;" Jezreel is one that is "scattered by the Lord." Many outlive the honour of their name and reputation. These ten tribes are no more worthy to be called by the name of Israel, their famous progenitor; but now Jezreel, the scattered of the Lord.

Thirdly, Jezreel, to show the way that God intended to bring judgment upon these ten tribes. And what was it? God would scatter them.

God brings judgment specially upon a kingdom when he scatters the people. We read, 1 Kings xxii. 17, that when Micaiah saw the destruction of Ahab and his people he had this vision; "I saw all Israel scattered upon the hills, as sheep that have not a shepherd." There is a twofold scattering; a scattering among ourselves by divisions, and a scattering by the enemy one from another to flee for our lives. The one part of this judgment (the Lord be merciful to us) is upon us already, and in this sense we may be called Jezreel. Oh how is our kingdom divided! how is it scattered! The Lord keep us from the other scattering, that we be not scattered one from another by being forced to flee for our lives before the enemy. It is just with God, that if we scatter ourselves sinfully by way of division, that God should scatter us in his wrath to our destruction by giving us up to our enemies. If we love scattering, if we delight in division, we may soon have scattering enough, there may soon be divisions enough one from another.

Fourthly, Call his name Jezreel, to note that the Lord would scatter them even in that very place wherein they most gloried, as they did in the valley and city of Jezreel. But God would scatter them even in that place in which they so much boasted.

Fifthly, Jezreel, because the Lord would hereby show that he would turn these conceits and apprehensions that they might have of themselves quite the contrary way. As thus: Jezreel signifies indeed scattered of the Lord, but it signifies also the seed of the Lord, or sown of the Lord; and so the Jews were ready to take the name Jezreel, and would be content to own it, because it signified the seed of God: and hence it comes to signify scattered too, because that seed is to be scattered when it is sown; and hence it was that they might glory so much in that name. O, they were the seed of the Lord, in an abiding condition, as being sown by the hand of God himself. No, saith God, you are mistaken, I do not call you Jezreel upon any such terms, because you are sown of me; but quite the other way, because you shall be scattered and eventually destroyed by me. It is usual with God to turn those things which men take as arguments for their comfort to their confusion. Haman made a false interpretation of the action of Esther's inviting him to the banquet alone with the king, the right interpretation of it had been that it was to his destruction. And so here; whereas they might make such interpretation of Jezreel, as that they were the seed, the sown of the Lord, the true interpretation is that they are the scattered of the Lord.

All these five reasons you have either in the nearness of the name Israel with Jezreel, or otherwise in the words that follow after.

"For yet a little while, and I will avenge the blood of Jezreel upon the house of Jehu." Here now we come to that which is the main part of this scripture; and these four questions are of great use, and will tend much to edification.

I. What is this "blood of Jezreel" that God will avenge?

II. Why God "will avenge the blood of Jezreel upon the house of Jehu?"

III. Why is it called "the house of Jehu," and Jehu alone, without the addition of the name king, as it is usual in others, as Hezekiah king of Judah, and such a one king of Israel; but here only the house of Jehu?

IV. What is this "little while" God speaks of? "yet a little while."

The words are read and passed over ordinarily, as if there was little in them; but you will find that they contain much of the mind of God.

I. What was the "blood of Jezreel" that here God threatens to avenge? You may read the history of it in 2 Kings ix. 10, 11. It was the blood of the house of Ahab, the blood of Jezebel, the blood of the seventy sons of Ahab, whose heads the elders of Jezreel sent to Jehu in baskets. This was the blood that was shed in this place, which God saith he will avenge. God will certainly avenge blood; and if God will avenge the blood of Ahab, he will surely avenge the blood of Abel; if the blood of Jezebel, then surely the blood of Sarah; if the blood of idolaters, then the blood of his saints. What vengeance then hangs over antichrist for all the blood of the saints that has been spilt by him! The scarlet whore has dyed herself with this blood; yea, and vengeance will come for that blood of our brethren which hath been shed in Ireland, upon those who have been instrumental in it, great or small: certainly the righteous God will not suffer that wicked and horrid work to go unavenged, even here upon the earth. Let us wait a while, and we may live to see that time wherein it shall not only be said by the voice of faith, but by the voice of sense itself, "Verily there is a God that judgeth the earth."

II. Why will God "avenge the blood of Jezreel upon the house of Jehu?"

Indeed this at first sight is one of the strangest things we have in all the book of God. Compare it with other scriptures, and nothing appears more singular than that it should be said that the Lord would avenge the blood of Jezreel upon the house of Jehu. For in 2 Kings ix. 7 you find that Jehu was anointed by the Lord on purpose to shed that blood. He had a command from God, he was bidden to go and shed it, and the holy oil was poured upon him for that end, that he might shed that blood; yet now it must be avenged, and avenged upon the house of Jehu. Yea, chap. x. 30, God said, because he had shed the blood of the house of Ahab in Jezreel, he would reward him for it, and that his children to the fourth generation should sit upon the throne of Israel and govern that kingdom. But that which Jehu was anointed and commanded to do, that for which God afterward rewarded him for doing, now God says he will avenge, and avenge it upon his house. What are the reasons of this? There are three reasons why God would avenge this blood upon the house of Jehu.

1. Because though Jehu did it, yet he looked at himself and his own ends rather than at God in it; his aim was to get the kingdom to himself, but he never aimed at God in the work, therefore God says he will avenge it upon his house.

2. Because though he did that which God set him about, yet he did it but by halves. Indeed he destroyed Ahab's house, but he should have destroyed Ahab's idolatry too; but he omitted that, and therefore now God comes upon him.

3. Yea, though he was made Ahab's executioner for his idolatry, yet he proved Ahab's successor in his idolatry. He was God's rod in punishing Ahab, but he continued in the sins that Ahab committed; therefore now God saith he "will avenge the blood of Jezreel upon the house of Jehu."

From hence we have most excellent observations that spring naturally, as a fountain bubbles up fresh and springing water. I will only show them to you, and so pass them over.

Obs. 1. That a man may do that which God commands, and yet not obey God. He may do that which God would have done, and yet not please God. He may do what God requires, and yet serve himself therein, and not God.

Obs. 2. A carnal heart is contented to go so far in God's commands as will serve his own turn, but there he stops. So far as might serve the elevation of Jehu to the crown of Israel, to setting him on the throne, so far he goes in the way of God's command, but no farther. Such a heart is like the hand of a rusty dial: suppose the hand of a rusty dial stand (as now) at ten o'clock; look upon it, and it seems to go right, but it is not from any inward right state of the clock it does so, but by accident; for stay till after ten, and come again at eleven or twelve, and it stands still as before at ten. So let God command any thing that may hit with a man's own ends, and be suitable to him, and he seems to be very obedient to God; but let God go on further, and require something that will not serve his turn, that will not agree with his own ends; and here God may seek for a servant; as for him, he will go no farther.

Obs. 3. God knows how to make use of men's parts and abilities, and yet to punish them for their wickedness notwithstanding. Jehu was a man of a brave and valiant spirit, full of activity and courage, and God would make use of this for the destruction of the house of Ahab; yet Jehu must not escape. Many men have excellent parts of learning and state policy, which God may use for pulling down his proud adversaries; yet God may punish them afterward notwithstanding. Many that have but weak parts, and can do but little, shall be accepted of God; and others that have strong parts, and can do much, shall be punished by God. We read, Rev. xii. 16, "the earth helped the woman;" yet, chap. xvi. 1, the vials of God's wrath were poured forth upon the earth: men may be useful for the public, and yet not freed from the wrath of God.

Obs. 4. The Lord knows how to make use of the sins of wicked men to further his own counsels; yet no excuse to them, but his curse will come upon them at last for those sins. God knows how to make use of the proud heart and ambitious spirit of Jehu to fulfil his purpose against the house of Ahab; and yet afterward, when God has done with him, he comes against Jehu with a judgment. There are many whose strong lusts God overrules for himself, and overpowers for the furtherance of his own ends. Many a scholar who, through the mere pride of his heart, will study hard and preach very often and well, God makes use of for the good of others, and yet the minister may be damned himself.

Obs. 5. God may sometimes reward a work in this world, yet may curse a man for the work afterward. Many there are who perform some outward service for God, and perhaps rejoice in it, and think that God must needs accept them: they have been excellent men in the commonwealth, they have stood for ministers, they have been forward in a good cause. Well, thou hast done these: has not God rewarded thee? Hast thou not health and strength of body. Look upon thy estate; art not thou blessed there? look upon thy table, thy wife and children; art not thou blessed there? Thou hast thy penny for what thou hast done. But yet, after thou hast had thy pay here in this world for what thou hast done, God may curse thee hereafter even for the sinfulness of thy heart in that work which for the matter of it was good. God may reward thee for the matter, but curse thee for the manner of thy work.

Obs. 6. It is a most dangerous thing for men to subject the works of God, especially the public works of God, to their own base ends; God will be sure to be even with them for that. The more excellent any work is, the more dangerous it is to subject it to a lust. It is an evil thing to make meat, and drink, and clothes serviceable to our lusts; but to make public services to God stoop and be serviceable to your base lusts must needs be grievous indeed. It is accounted burden enough for the basest servant to be serviceable to some base lust of his master; but if the master should make his wife serviceable to his filthy uncleanness, oh what a villany were that! So I say, the greater the thing is any man makes serviceable to his lust, the more vile and the more dangerous is the sin. Hearken to this, you that are professors of religion. The drunkard makes beer serviceable to his lust, and he shall be damned for that: but you make the worship of God, prayer, and hearing, and fasting, serviceable to your lusts; oh what shall become of you! A base wretch, that sits tippling in an alehouse, you account vile, but it is a poor creature that he subjects to his base lust. A minister or a magistrate subjects things of a higher nature to their lusts: oh this is exceeding vile. We had need, my brethren, all pray earnestly for those whom God employs in public works, that they may not only have strength to assist them, and success in them, but that they may have hearts to give God all the glory of them; for though they may do never so worthily for God in the church or in the commonwealth, yet if they be not careful to give God all the glory, God will curse them at last notwithstanding.

Obs. 7. When but half the work is done, God curses the whole for our neglect of the other half. Jehu does somewhat which God commanded him, but not all. I remember Calvin upon this place likens Jehu to king Henry the Eighth: Henry, saith he, cast off some degree of popery so far as would serve his own turn, but there were the five articles in force still, for which many suffered at that time; and so he was like Jehu in that. God will be served with the whole heart; for all our good is in God, and therefore all our hearts must make out after God. God must have perfect obedience in the desire and endeavour, or else he will have none. Certainly that which must make any man acceptable, is not so much that there is somewhat done, but that that which God commands is done, or done in regard of the endeavour; for that indeed will be acceptable: though we cannot do all at once, if we bring somewhat to God as a part, and acknowledging the whole debt, work for the remainder, it will be accepted. As suppose a man owes you one hundred pounds, and brings you but fifty in part of payment, yet if he acknowledge the rest, and promise the payment of it, if you know he will be faithful in the payment of the other, you will accept it; but if a man bring you fourscore pounds in lieu of all, you will not accept it. So it is here; hypocrites say they cannot be perfect in this world, and so think to put off God with a little. It is true, if thou hadst an upright heart, and didst bring God but part and labour after the whole, he would accept it; but if thou bringest him ten times more than a sincere heart can bring him, it will not be acceptable, no, not ninety-nine pounds will be accepted, if brought instead of the whole. God must have a man according to his own heart, such a one as David: you know what was said of David, "I have found a man after my own heart, that shall fulfil all my wills;" for the word is plural in the original, not all my will, but all my wills.

Obs. 8. Jehu did but half, and the worst half too, and therefore God comes upon him. For the great care of Jehu was only to reform things in the state and kingdom, and therefore that indeed he did thoroughly; he transferred the government from the house of Ahab, and set up another government. But for the matter of the worship of God, he cared not what became of that. Still the calves continued in Dan and Bethel. He took no care that the people of Israel should go up to Jerusalem, the place that God had appointed to worship him in a right way. This is that for which God thus cursed him and his house. It is a very evil thing in reformers, who have power in their hands, to be more careful of the state than of the church; to be more solicitous about affairs in civil policy than in religion; to be so afraid to meddle with religion, because of hinderances and disturbances in civil policy, that they sacrifice religion for it: this is an evil thing and a bitter. Or if they reform the church, yet to reform only that which is notoriously evil and vile: so far Jehu went; he destroyed the priests of Baal, but not the priests of Dan and Bethel; the idols of Baal were destroyed, but the idols of Dan and Bethel were retained.

πρῶτον περι θείων ἐπιμέλει. Arist. Pol. l. 7. c. 8.

It is the speech of the philosopher in his politics, when he gives a rule of policy, The care of divine things must be first; and that is the best policy. Politicians must trust God in the way of policy, and take care of divine things first. Yea, and go to a thorough reformation too; for Jehu did something in religion, but left other things, therefore God cursed him. Men must take heed of betraying the cause of God for the maintenance of state policy; let them be never so excellent in their way, yet if they do thus, God will blast them.

Obs. 9. Men can see the evil of sin in others, rather than in themselves. Jehu saw the danger of that wicked and abominable sin of idolatry in others, but he could not see it in himself. "What peace," said he to Joram, "so long as the whoredoms of thy mother Jezebel" continue? What peace? Then what peace, Jehu, so long as the whoredoms of Israel continue afterwards? This is common, my brethren, for men to see evil and danger in the sins of others; but when they come to themselves, to be blind there: to inveigh against the sins of other men, when they seem to be far off from them, or that they cannot make use of them; but when they can make use of them, then to embrace them. Thus it was with Saul; he was exceedingly severe against witchcraft, all the witches in Israel must be put to death; but in his hour of need Saul himself goes to the witch of Endor.

Obs. 10. Those ways of sinful policy, by which many think to raise their houses or themselves, are the means to ruin them. Jehu thought, by retaining the calves in Dan and Bethel, to preserve the kingdom to his posterity, and this proved the ruin of his posterity. He that walks uprightly walks surely.

Obs. 11. Let them who punish the sins of others take heed what they do, lest they be found guilty themselves; for if they be found guilty, God will plague them, as if they did the greatest act of injustice. God punishes Jehu because he continues in the same sin that Ahab was punished for. This is of excellent use, especially to magistrates; and indeed it is a dreadful place to magistrates, if considered. As for instance, suppose a magistrate should take away the life of a man lawfully for that for which God would have him take it away; yet if this magistrate should be guilty of the same sin, or that which amounts to the same sin, God will avenge himself upon this magistrate as upon a murderer: as here, God avenges himself upon the house of Jehu as for murder, yet Jehu was a magistrate, and this was commanded Jehu by God himself. So suppose a magistrate fine a man for any evil, and that justly; yet if he be guilty of the same himself, God will deal with this magistrate as if he robbed by the highway-side, and took away a man's money by violence. It is apparent out of the text. Certainly, my brethren, great wrath and vengeance hangs over the head of wicked magistrates. All this you learn from what is here said, that God "will avenge the blood of Jezreel upon the house of Jehu."

III. Why is it called "the house of Jehu?"

The house of Jehu is his posterity, or family who were to succeed. Though it was to the fourth generation till God came against them, yet the posterity of the ungodly, especially idolaters, shall suffer for their fathers' sin. It is very observable, that God in no other commandment but the second threatens the sin of the fathers upon the children. The reason is this:

That commandment forbids images, and superstitious worshippers, above all men, are strengthened by the tradition of their fathers. Our fathers did thus and thus, and what shall we be wiser then our forefathers? We have now a company of upstart men, and they will be wiser than their ancestors. Because superstitious worshippers harden themselves so much from the example of their fathers, therefore in that very commandment against making and worshipping of images God threatens to visit the sin of the fathers upon the children, and in no other.

What, the *house* of Jehu, after *Jehu* was dead! how can that be? Yes, as a prince that has to punish two traitors, both of whom have deserved death, but the prince is inclined to show mercy. Against the one there comes this accusation, This man's father was a traitor, and his grandfather and his great grandfather were traitors. Then let him die, saith the prince. But of the other, that is guilty of as much as this man was, it is told the king, Sir, this man's father performed excellent service for the commonwealth, not one of his house but was a loyal person. This man is spared, though he deserveth death equally with the other for the same treason; and the king is just in this. The first man may be said to die for his fathers' sin; that is, he would not have been executed if his forefathers had not been in the fault. Take heed what you do in the course of your lives; if you regard not yourselves, yet, for your children's sake, leave not a curse behind you upon your offspring; look upon them, pity them. Though you yourselves may escape in this world, yet you may leave the inheritance of your sins unto your children. Pity your children, that they may not have cause to curse the time that they were born of such parents, and wish that they had rather been the offspring of dragons, and a generation of vipers, than to be born of such parents that have left them a curse for an inheritance. It had been better if you had not left them a penny, than to leave them to inherit the curse of your wickedness.

"Upon the house of Jehu." The house of Jehu fares the worse for Jehu. Those who desire to raise and continue the honour of their houses, let them take heed of ways of wickedness; for wickedness will bring down any family whatsoever. But why is it "the house of Jehu," without any addition of Jehu the king, as in other cases it is usual? Hereby God would give a check to Jehu, and bid him look back to the meanness of his birth, for Jehu was not of the kingly race: yet how unthankful was he, who was raised from the dunghill, thus unworthily to depart from the Lord! You whom God has raised up on high to great honours and estates, look back to the meanness of your beginning, from which God has raised you, and labour to give him an answerable return of obedience. Those who will not give God the glory of their honours and estates, it is just that their honours and estates should be taken from them.

IV. What is this "little while" God speaks of?

"Yet a little while." This is to be understood either in reference to Jehu, or in reference to the house of Israel. "Yet a little while, and I will avenge the blood of Jezreel upon the house of Jehu, and will cause to cease the kingdom of the house of Israel." It was a long while before God came upon the house of Jehu, still he saith, yet but a little while, I will stay but a little longer ere I avenge the blood of Jezreel upon the house of Jehu. It was now the third generation since Jehu committed those sins, nay, it will appear that it was above a hundred years from the sins of Jehu to God's avenging the blood of Jezreel upon his house: for Jehu reigned twenty-eight years, his son Jehoahaz seventeen years, and Jehoash his son sixteen years, and Jeroboam his son forty-one years, and then in the days of Zachariah, the son of this Jeroboam, God came to avenge this blood, which was above a hundred years, 2 Kings x. 36; xiii. 1, 23. Oh the patience of the Lord towards sinners! But though he stayed long, he saith, "yet a little while."

Obs. 1. That God sometimes comes upon sinners for their old sins. Sins a long time ago committed, and perhaps forgotten by you, yet remain, are filed and recorded in heaven above a hundred years after the commission. It is likely that these sins of Jehu were forgotten, yet God comes now at last to avenge the sins of Jehu upon his house. So he did for the sins of Manasses, and for the sins of Joseph's brethren. It was twenty-two years before they had their consciences troubled, and then say they, "We are verily guilty concerning our brother; therefore is this distress come upon us;" and now (saith Reuben) "behold also his blood is required," Gen. xlii. 21, 22.

Look to yourselves, you that are young, take heed of youthful sins. Youthful sins may prove to be the terrors of age. Perhaps you think it was a great while ago, when you were a young man, that you were in such a tavern or in such a journey, and committed such and such sins. Have you repented for them? have you made your peace with God for them? Though you were then young, and did not fear the wrath of God to come upon you; yet now you are old the wrath of God may come upon you for sins committed in your apprenticeship. "A sinner being a hundred years old shall be accursed," Isa. lxv. 20.

Obs. 2. A long time after the flourishing of a nation God may reckon with it in ways of judgment. "Yet a little while, and I will cause to cease the kingdom of the house of Israel." This nation had continued a pompous, successful nation, though idolatrous, for about two hundred and sixty years before that wrath of God came upon it which was here threatened. This may make us look back to the sins committed in the days of Henry the Eighth, and of Queen Mary. Let us not plead from our forefathers for the maintenance of superstitious worship, but let us look to the sins of our forefathers, and bewail them before the Lord, for God may come upon a nation for former sins after it hath flourished a long time. You ask me, Was it really but a little while from the beginning of this prophecy till the ceasing of the kingdom of the house of Israel? No, my brethren, it was many years. And it is very observable, that from the beginning of this prophecy, which was in the end of the reign of Jeroboam, to the fulfilling of what was here threatened, viz. to the ceasing of the kingdom of the house of Israel, it was seventy-six years. For, from the end of this Jeroboam, spoken of ver. 1, unto the time of Hezekiah, was seventy years, and in the sixth year of Hezekiah Israel was destroyed by the king of Assyria; and yet God saith here by Hosea, "yet a little while."

Obs. 3. Seventy-six years are but a little while in God's account. Sinners think, either in ways of judgment or mercy, a little while to be a great while. If God defer mercy seven years, it is a great while in our account. We think our parliament has sat a long time: how long? Almost two years. A great while! We think every day a great while, but seventy-six years, yea, a hundred, a thousand years, are but as one day unto God. So for judgment: a sinner, if he has committed a sin seven years ago, he thinks it is a great while, and he has not heard of it, therefore surely it is forgotten. But what if it be seventy years ago? You that are sinners of seventy years old, all is but a little while in regard of God.

Obs. 4. The apprehension of a judgment just at hand is that which will stir the heart and work upon it most. "Yet a little while," and God will cause the kingdom to cease; therefore if ever you repent, repent now, for it is but a little while ere God will cause the kingdom to cease. The apprehension of a sinner to be upon the brink of judgment, beholding his poor soul ready to launch into the infinite ocean of eternal destruction, and to lie under the scalding drops of the wrath of the Almighty; this works upon the heart indeed. It is the way of the flesh and the devil to put far from us the evil day, to make us believe the day of death is a great way off. But it is the way of God to exhibit things present and real; and in this consist the efficacy and power of faith to make things future as if present. We say in nature there must be a contiguity and nearness between things that must work. So we must apprehend a nearness between the evil that is to come upon us and ourselves, that so it may work upon our hearts.

An excellent scripture you have to this purpose in 1 Kings xiv. 14; where the Lord threatens to "raise him up a king over Israel who should cut off the house of Jeroboam that day: but what?" (he immediately recalls his word;) "even now:" you may think the day a great way off, but it is "even now;" and therefore now come in, return and repent. O sinners, consider that your danger is now; not only in that day of Christ: but what? even now, it may be at hand.

Obs. 5. God suffers some sinners to continue long, others he cuts off speedily. Jeroboam had continued above forty years in his sin, but now Zachariah his son, upon whom this threatening was fulfilled, continued but six months. Perhaps he thought to escape as long as his father. No; though the father continue old in his sins, if the son presume to follow his steps he may be cut off presently.

"And I will cause to cease the kingdom of the house of Israel." Kingdoms and monarchies are subject to change. What is become of all the glorious monarchies in the world? how hath the Lord tossed them up and down as a man would toss a ball! Idolatry is enough to destroy the greatest monarchy in the world.

But there is some instruction in the elegance of the word והשבתי "and I will cause to cease." It is a metaphor (according to some) taken from instruments, that a man uses for a while, and when he has done with them, either hangs them up against a wall and regards them no more, or else brings them to the fire to be burned. So saith God, "yet a little while, and I will cause to cease," &c. As if he should say, Indeed there was a time wherein I made some use of the rent between Judah and Israel, and of this kingdom; but I have done with that use, there is an end of it, and now I will cause to cease the kingdom, I will take them away, they shall be to me as an instrument not to be used any more, or for the fire. When the Lord has any use of a people, or of any particular men to do him service, he will preserve them, though they are wicked; and when he has done with them, he either lays them aside, or else brings them to the fire. A husbandman, so long as he can use thorns to stop a gap, he destroys them not, but when there is no further use for them, he brings them to the fire: so God here, "I will cause to cease the kingdom of the house of Israel."

But how and where will God cause to cease the kingdom of Israel?

Ver. 5. *And it shall come to pass at that day, that I will break the bow of Israel in the valley of Jezreel.*

By "breaking the bow," is here meant the blasting and bringing to nothing all the strength of their warlike power, all their arms and ammunition; for the bow was a great warlike instrument in those days; therefore, in Psal. xlvi. 9, "He maketh wars to cease; he breaketh the bow, and cutteth the spear in sunder."

But here, by "breaking the bow," something more is meant. There is this particular reason why the bow is instanced here, because, whereas Jehu did many memorable things in his warlike affairs, yet none more than that he did by his bow. Mark that place, 2 Kings ix. 24, "And Jehu drew a bow with his full strength, and smote Jehoram between his arms, and the arrow went out at his heart." So that the victory that Jehu obtained over the two kings of Israel and Judah was by the bow especially. What observe we from hence?

Obs. 1. That even in those things wherein wicked men have been most prosperous and successful, God will curse them, and let out his wrath upon them.

Obs. 2. Carnal hearts trust much in their warlike weapons, but they are nothing when God breaks a people's strength. "Break the bow," blast all the power of their ammunition. God has the power of all ammunition. The Lord is called the Lord of hosts, and he delights much in this title, first, because God has not only the power over ammunition and all warlike weapons, so that they cannot be used but by him; but secondly, because when they are used, they can have no success at all but by him: and so the Lord is the Lord of hosts in a peculiar sense. He is the great General of all armies, more than all other generals, for the success of all depends upon him. My brethren, why then need the church of God fear the strength of weapons, the bow, the cannon, or all the ammunition of the enemies of the church, seeing our Lord is the Lord of hosts? No weapon can be used or have success but by this Lord of hosts: he can break the bow, though of steel, when he pleases, and can give his people strength to do so too. For this you have an admirable promise, Isa. liv. 16, 17; "Behold," (saith God,) "I have created the smith that bloweth the coals in the fire, and bringeth forth an instrument for his work; and I have created the water to destroy. No weapon that is formed against thee shall prosper." What need the church fear then? God breaks the bow when he pleases; for as God has a providence over all the things in the world, so he has a specialty of providence to order battles, to give the victory not to the strong or to the multitude, but sometimes to the weak and few, even as he pleases. And therefore he is the Lord of hosts, because though his providence is general over all creatures, yet there is a specialty of providence exercised by God in warlike affairs.

But what was this valley of Jezreel?

It is worthy our time to inquire after this valley, in which God will break the bow of Israel. There were two places called Jezreel, the one belonging to Judah, Josh. xv. 56, the other belonging to Israel, Josh. xvii. 16; xix. 18. Jezreel was a fruitful valley, ten miles long, and by it there was a famous city built, which, in Ahab's time, was the metropolis of the kingdom, in which was a glorious tower, from whence they might see over Galilee and Jordan. Now there were two great cities that belonged to the ten tribes, Samaria and Jezreel; as we in England have two principal cities, London and York. But this Jezreel was the most fortified, in which they put much confidence, yet God saith here, "He will break the bow of Israel in the valley of Jezreel;" that is, in that very city which they accounted the great strength of their kingdom, there he would break the bow of Israel.

Obs. 3. Fortified cities cannot help when God comes out against a people. If we can fortify our cities against sin, we may soon fortify them against an enemy. If sin once get in, the enemy will quickly follow. "All thy strong holds shall be like fig trees with the first-ripe figs: if they be shaken, they shall even fall into the mouth of the eater," Nah. iii. 12. With the least wind, like the first-ripe figs, all your strong holds shall fall; yea, "thy people in the midst of thee are women: the gates of thy land shall be set wide open unto thine enemies: the fire shall devour thy bars," ver. 13. You see what the valley of Jezreel is, and the meaning of it.

But why will God "break the bow of Israel in the valley of Jezreel?" There are these two reasons for it: 1. Because God would deal with this people of Israel as judges deal with malefactors; hang them up where their fact was committed, as we see some hanged up in chains near to the city, at or about the place where their villany was done. So in Jezreel was shed the blood of Jezebel, and the blood of the seventy sons of Ahab, and the blood of Jehoram, and there will God break the bow. Hence guilty consciences are often afraid to go near the places where they have committed wickedness, because they fly in their faces, for fear God should come upon them where the crimes were perpetrated.

But, 2. He "will break the bow of Israel in the valley of Jezreel," that is, in that fortified place in which they so much gloried.

Obs. 4. Even in the place in which a kingdom most glories, and seems to trust most in, God many times comes and breaks the kingdom in that very place. "Art thou better than populous No, that was situate among the rivers, that had the waters round about it, whose rampart was the sea, and her wall was from the sea?" Nah. iii. 8. Mark, a people just like England in this case. What! we overcome by the enemy? we that have the seas for our wall, and such a multitude of people amongst us? These have been and still are the two pleas which England uses for herself, because our people are many, and we have the seas for a wall: but "art thou better than populous No? Yet was she carried away, she went into captivity," ver. 10. Thus the prophet pleads with them.

But further; These trusted in Jezreel, they seemed to scorn the prophet. What! the kingdom of Israel cease! what think you of Jezreel, such a strong place as that? Just as we should say, What! an enemy come to us! what say you to London, a brave city, a strong city? What say you to the ammunition, to the militia, to the strength that is there? Are they not able to resist all that can come against it? Have we cause to fear danger? It is true, the kingdom has cause to bless God for London, and London has not yet been "the valley of Jezreel," but Israel, the strength of the Lord, and has prevailed with God, as an instrument: and therefore we bless God for the protection we have had. But yet let us not trust in it, for even in London, in the valley of Jezreel, the bow may be broken; and God knows how to bring things about, so as to make the ammunition of London to be broken in pieces, and turned against its people: O, therefore, do not trust here. Only let it be your care, ye people of this city of London, that you prove not the valley of Jezreel, and then we shall do well enough, our bow shall not be broken. What attempts have there been to make London by this time the valley of Jezreel, that is, a scattered valley, and to bring divisions into this city, that it might be a scattered people! And woe to the kingdom if this had been effected! better these men had never been born, than that they should have had success in that horrid enterprise. O London, now the blessing of God is over you, the means of grace abundantly among you, the eyes of the kingdom are upon you; take heed you be not the valley of Jezreel; your divisions will cause great thoughts of heart: continue you united one to another, and then you are as one Israel of God, the instrument of God for our strength.

Thus we have done with the mother and with the first son.

Ver. 6. *And she conceived again, and bare a daughter. And God said unto him, Call her name Lo-ruhamah: for I will no more have mercy upon the house of Israel; but I will utterly take them away.*

"She conceived again." This conception sets out also the estate of Israel in regard of her sin and misery: sin is fruitful, and what does it bring forth? Parents bring forth a likeness to themselves, and so does sin; and what is that? nothing but ruin and misery.

This second child is a daughter, denoting the weakness of the ten tribes at this time. They were grown effeminate in regard of their lust, and the baseness of their spirits; and in regard of their strength also they were weak like the female sex.

There are three estates of the people signified by the three children of Hosea; first, their scattered estate, and that was signified by Jezreel, the first son; and the story of that you have 2 Kings xv. 9—19, where you may read their woeful seditions; for Zachariah reigned but six months, and then Shallum slew him, and reigned in his stead, and he reigned but one month, for Menahem came and smote Shallum and slew him, and reigned in his stead: so here were nothing but murders and seditions amongst them. A scattered people.

The second state of the people of Israel was their weak condition, signified by this daughter; and the history of that you have from ver. 16 of that chapter onwards, where, when Pul the king of Assyria came against Israel, Menahem yielded to him his demand, gave him a thousand talents of silver to go from him, and laid a tax upon the people for it. Here they were brought into a very low and weak condition. And afterwards this king of Assyria came to them again, and carried part of them into captivity.

The third child was Lo-ammi; and the history of the state of the people signified by that you have in 2 Kings xvii. 6, where they were fully carried away, and wholly rejected for ever. And because they were a little before that time grown up to some strength more than formerly, therefore this last was a son. We are now to speak of the second.

"She conceived again, and bare a daughter."

From the interpretation I have given, this denotes the weakness and effeminacy of the people at this time, a little before their ruin.

When the manliness, and courage, and vigour of the spirits of people are taken away, they are under a fearful judgment and near to ruin. Even when their men shall be as women, as Nah. iii. 13; when there shall be such baseness of spirit in people, that for the enjoyments of their present ease and quiet they yield to any thing. So it was with these, and their effeminateness was showed,

1. When the king of Assyria came to them, they yielded to any terms he would appoint; and when the taxes were laid upon the people, they inquired not whether they were just or no, but merely for their peace and safety paid them. We must take heed of bringing ourselves into trouble, we had better pay this than venture the loss of all; we must not displease those that are above us, we know not what hard things may follow; it is our wisdom, though things are hard, and we complain the taxations are heavy, to suffer something. They had rather have a little, though with baseness, than venture any thing for further peace and liberty for themselves and their posterity.

2. The effeminateness of their spirits was shown in this, that they were willing to submit to the government of most vile murderers, without any inquiring after them, or taking any course to find out their murders and wickedness. Zachariah was slain by Shallum; then came Menahem, and he killed Shallum; after Menahem reigned Pekahiah, and against him conspired Pekah, the son of Remaliah, and smote him in Samaria, and with him killed fifty men, and reigned in his room; then came Hoshea the son of Elah, and made a conspiracy against Pekah, and slew him, and reigned in his stead. Here were murderers upon murderers, and yet the people all this while bow down their necks, and look not after these things: They have gotten power in their hands, and we must take heed of inquiring after those things that are above us, it will displease them, we had better be quiet and hold our peace: and so they bowed their necks to the yoke. Such horrible guilt of murders must not be questioned, because the murderers had got power in their hands. Their cowardly, timorous spirits were much like the temper of Issachar: "Issachar is a strong ass couching down between two burdens: and he saw that rest was good, and the land that it was pleasant; and bowed his shoulder to bear, and became a servant unto tribute," Gen. xlix. 14, 15.

And when men's spirits are effeminate with respect to the civil state, they quickly grow so in regard of their consciences, and religion too. Purity of religion in the church cannot stand long with slavery admitted in the state. We read, Rev. iv. 7, of four ages of the church set out by four living creatures: the third living creature had the face of a man, and that was to note the state of the church in the time of reformation; they began then to be of manly spirits, and to cast off that yoke of bondage which was upon them, to inquire after what liberty God had granted to them. Not like those we read of, Isa. li. 23, that would obey such as would say to their souls, "Bow down, that we may go over."

This, my brethren, was the condition of many of us; there has been that effeminateness of spirit in us that we have bowed down our necks, yea, our souls, to those that would go over us; yea, as it is in Isa. li. 23, they made themselves the very street to them that went over them, their very consciences were trampled upon by the foot of pride, and all for the enjoyment of a little outward accommodation in their estates, in their shops, and in their trading; O, they dare not venture these, rather yield to any thing in the world. And truly we were afraid, not long since, that God was calling us by the name of this daughter Lo-ruhamah, for our effeminateness of spirit; that the Lord was departing from our nation. But blessed be God, that now there is a rising of spirit among us, especially among our worthies in parliament; and their warmth, and vigour, and life have put warmth, vigour, and spirit into the whole kingdom. Now our kingdom will never bow down and submit their consciences, nor estates, nor liberties, to the former bondage and oppression. No, they had rather die honourably than live basely. But why do I make such a disjunction? Die honourably, or live basely! Had we spirits we might free ourselves and posterity from living basely, and we need not die at all; for the malignant party has neither spirit to act nor power to prevail: if we keep up our spirits and are strong in the Lord, we are safe enough, we shall not have our name Lo-ruhamah, but Ruhamah; the Lord will have mercy upon us.

In 1 Kings xiv. 15, God threatens to smite Israel, that they shall be "as a reed shaken in the water;" and mark what follows, and then "he shall root up Israel out of this good land, which he gave to their fathers." If this judgment be upon England, that our spirits be shaken as a reed with the wind, that we bow and yield to any thing in a base way, the next may justly follow, that the Lord may root us out of this good land. As Israel grew effeminate before their destruction, so do Judah also before theirs: Isa. iii. 2, 3, when God intended judgment against them, you may observe that he took away "the mighty man, and the man of war, the judge, and the prophet, and the prudent, and the ancient, the captain of fifty, and the honourable man, and the counsellor;" men of truly noble spirits were removed, their nobles became vile and sordid, and yielded to any humours and lusts, then they were near ruin; and ver. 12 saith, "women rule over them:" for women that have manly spirits to rule is no judgment at all, but for women of revengeful spirits to rule over a nation is a most fearful judgment. But so much of the first, that it is a daughter born to Hosea.

What is this daughter's name? Call her name "Lo-ruhamah," either not beloved, or one that has not obtained mercy, for God's mercy proceeds from his love.

"I will no more have mercy," or, I will add no more mercy; noting that God had showed abundance of mercy to Israel before, but now he declares, I will not add any more, I will show no further mercy to them.

"But I will utterly take them away;" so turned by some, in taking them away I will take them away; others, I will lift them up, that I may cast them down so much the more dreadfully. The old Latin thus reads, *obliviscendo obliviscar*, forgetting I will forget. And this was upon a mistake of the Hebrew word, because there is little difference in the Hebrew between נשה signifying to forget, and נשא which signifies to take away. The Septuagint, ἀντιτασσόμενος ἀντιτάξομαι, setting myself against them I will set myself against them. Well, the name of the child must bear this upon it, that God will have no more mercy upon them. Hence,

Obs. 1. Sometimes the very children of families, and in a kingdom, bear this impression upon them, that God will have no mercy upon this family. My brethren, one may read such an impression upon the children of many great families in this kingdom, when we look upon the horrible wickedness of the young that are growing up. How different from their former religious ancestors! We may see, with trembling hearts, such an impression of wrath, as if God had said, I have done with this family, I intend no further mercy to it. As sometimes, when we see in a family gracious children, gracious young gentlemen, noblemen, we may see the impression of God's mercy to that family; Ruhamah, I intend mercy to it.

It was not long since that we might, and we thought indeed we did, see such an impression upon the young people of this kingdom, in the city, and in the chief families in the country, that we were afraid Lo-ruhamah to England was written upon them; for, oh the rudeness and wickedness of the young! But blessed be God that we see it otherwise now. Because of that graciousness and forwardness of so many young people amongst us, we think we see written upon them Ruhamah to England, mercy to England; God has taken away his Lo, and writes only Ruhamah, mercy to you. The great ground of the hope we have for mercy to England, is the impression of God upon the young: when God has tender plants growing up in his orchard, certainly he will not break down the hedge or dig it up.

Obs. 2. There is a time when God will not have mercy upon a kingdom, or upon a particular people. "Gather yourselves together, yea, gather together, O nation not desired; before the decree come forth," Zeph. ii. 1, 2. There is a time for the decree to come forth against a kingdom; a time when, though Noah, Job, and Daniel should stand before him, yet he will not be entreated; though they cry, cry early, cry aloud, cry with tears, cry with fasting, yet God will not be entreated. God's mercy is precious, and he will not let it run out to waste, he will not be prodigal of it; a time wherein God will say, Now I have done, I have done with this people, mercy has had her turn. It is true, except we had that immediate revelation which the prophets had we cannot now determine the particular time. Those who laboured most to search God's mind in his word, were afraid that this decree had gone out upon us in England. It is true, God seems for the present to tell us that he has a prerogative, and he will have mercy upon whom he will have mercy. But they are not altogether to be blamed who, even in their own hearts, determined that mercy was gone, except they wholly limited God, and left nothing of prerogative to him. It was God's ordinary way, and except God had wrought with us in a way of sovereignty otherwise than ever he did with any nation before, they concluded that the decree was gone forth: and so it might be true; and what God may do with us yet we do not know. But this we can say, if the decree be not gone forth, if there be mercy for us, God shows his prerogative, that he will now go on in a way different from his former paths in the world; and if God *will* do so, who can say against it?

A time there is likewise for God to say against particular persons, he will not have mercy upon them; a time when God will say, Those men that were bidden shall not taste of my supper, Luke xiv. 24; he that *will* be filthy, let him be filthy still, Rev. xxii. 11; my Spirit shall no longer strive with them, Gen. vi. 3. He has no need, my brethren, that we should receive or entertain his mercy; we have need that God should grant it. God many times is quick in the offer of his mercy; "Go and preach the gospel; he that believeth shall be saved, he that believeth not shall be damned." A quick work God makes many times in the effect of mercy.

Obs. 3. "I will not have mercy:" this is pronounced as the most dreadful judgment. What! not have mercy upon them? then indeed is a state or kingdom in a dreadful condition, when God shall say of them, that he will not have mercy. "Woe to you," saith the Lord, "when I depart from you!" woe then to you, when my mercy is for ever gone! then all judgments and miseries must needs flow in upon a nation, or a particular soul. When the sea-bank is broken up, then the waves will all flow in. "All ye beasts of the field, come to devour, yea, all ye beasts in the forest." Why, what is the matter? "His watchmen are blind," Isa. lvi. 9, 10. I argue from thence, if the prudence of the watchman is taken away, which should stop misery, then all evils come flowing in upon a nation. What then, if the mercy of God, that should stop misery, be taken away? whither should the poor creature go if mercy be gone? to what creature should it look for help? if it cries to any creature, the creature saith, I can afford no comfort, because God affords no mercy. What shall uphold the heart when it has no hope at all? It must needs sink.

Obs. 4. Men best know what the worth of mercy is, when mercy is taken away from them. I will not add mercy; showing that what good they had received before, it was from his mercy, though they would take no notice of it. Well, saith God, you shall have no more; you have taken no notice that it was my mercy that helped you before, but when my mercy is gone, then you will know it; but then I will not add more.

Obs. 5. God usually takes not away his mercy fully from a people, or from a soul, until after much mercy has been received and abused. You have a parallel place to this, Judg. x. 13: "I will deliver you no more," saith God; I have delivered you many times, my mercy has been abused, I will deliver you no more. It is just with God, when mercy is abused, that we should never know further what mercy means. Mercy, as it is a precious thing, so it is a tender thing, and a dangerous thing to abuse. There is nothing that more quickly works the ruin of a people, or of a soul, than abused mercy.

Obs. 6. God's second strokes usually are more dreadful than the first. "I will utterly take them away." Before it was only that they should be scattered, the name of the first child before was but Jezreel, that they should be the scattered of the Lord; but the second is Lo-ruhamah, that they shall have no more mercy from the Lord. God begins first with the house of correction before he brings to the gallows. There is branding first, before hanging: there are warning pieces before murdering pieces. God makes way for his wrath by lesser afflictions before he comes with destroying judgments.

I remember Knox, in his History of Scotland, relates that Sir James Hamilton, having been murdered by the king's means, he appeared to him in a vision with a naked sword drawn, and struck off both his arms, with these words, Take this before thou receive a final payment for all thy impieties; and within twenty-four hours two of the king's sons died. God comes to nations and particular persons with a sword, cuts off arms before he takes their lives. As when the Lord comes in a way of abundance of mercy, lesser mercies make way for greater mercies. When manna was rained down, the dew ever came before it: so, lesser judgments to the wicked are forerunners of, and make way for, greater judgments; first they are parboiled, before they come to be roasted in the fire.

Obs. 7. With God a multitude of sinners is no argument for their escape of judgment. I will not add mercy to the house of Israel. He does not say, I will not add mercy to this or that particular man of Israel, but to the house of Israel. It is a rule, indeed, with man, *Multitudo peccantium tollit peccatum*, Multitude of offenders take away their offences: men know not how to execute the offenders when they are in multitudes; here and there some of the ringleaders may be taken, for example' sake. But it is no rule with God; though it be the whole house of Israel, God has no mercy for the whole house of all the people of Israel. Let no man presume to sin against the Lord because there are multitudes that offend, and think that he shall escape with the multitude. No; all the nations of the world with the Lord are but as the drop of a bucket, and as the small dust of the balance; nothing, even less than nothing.

Obs. 8. The nearness of any to God exempts them not from the wrath of God. "No more have mercy upon the house of Israel;" though it be the house of Israel, yet no mercy upon her. If it were the house of Pharaoh it were not so much; but what! no mercy upon the house of Israel! God hates sin, and hates sin most in those nearest to him: "You only have I known of all the families of the earth; therefore I will punish you for all your iniquities," saith the Lord, Amos iii. 2. As we hate a toad in our bosoms more than when it is at a farther distance, so God hates sin in those that are nearest to him more than in those that are farther off; for "God will be sanctified in all those that draw nigh unto him."

But why will God have no more mercy upon the house of Israel? What hath the house of Israel done that God should be so angry with it? It is worth our searching and inquiring after, it concerns ourselves nearly.

1. The first and a main reason is, because of their continuance in their false worship, notwithstanding all the means that God had used to bring them off; not only by his prophets, sending them again and again to show them its evil in those two calves that were set up in Dan and Bethel, but by most remarkable works of his providence against them. As for example; the work of God against Jeroboam, when he was stretching out his hand against the prophet that came to denounce judgment against the altar upon which he was offering sacrifice; his hand dried up, so that he could not pull it in again to him, and upon the prayer of the prophet it was restored, and became as it was before, 1 Kings xiii. 4, 6. Again, the remarkable work of God in anointing Jehu to destroy the house of Ahab and his seed for their idolatry. Yet, notwithstanding these prophets, and these works of God, with many others, they still persisted in their way of idolatry; and this caused the Lord now not to have mercy upon the house of Israel.

Let us take heed of this: God has used and still uses means to bring us off fully from all ways of false worship; not only by sending his ministers from time to time to declaim against such things, but by wonderful and remarkable works of his providence towards England, especially at this day. Never had any nation, never had England heretofore, more remarkable works of God to draw them off from all ways of false worship, to bring them to worship God in the right way according to his will. Now let us tremble at this sentence; I will not add mercy, I will have no more mercy. God has added mercy to us again and again, from time to time. And now, methinks, in this work of God's mercy, that he is about concerning us, he speaks to us as he did to the people, "Come and put off thy ornaments from thee, that I may know what to do unto thee," Exod. xxxiii. 5; come now and humble yourselves that I may know what to do; as if God should say, Come and give in your last answer. Now I am showing mercy once more, take heed of rejecting it, lest you have a Lo-ruhamah upon you, I will add no more mercy. Consider not only what we have done, but what we do; how we have abused mercy, and how we now abuse present mercy; how opposed the spirits of most are to the work of reformation now commencing, who even say to the Lord Christ, Depart from us, we desire not the knowledge of thy ways. When the people of Israel were offered Canaan, and God bade them go in and possess it, they were then near unto it; but as they then refused Canaan, God sware in his wrath that they should not enter into his rest. If ever a people were offered Canaan, were offered the ordinances of God in his own way, certainly we are at this time. Let us tremble lest God, if we reject this mercy, should swear in his wrath, I will have no more mercy upon you, and so we prove to be a Lo-ruhamah indeed.

2. But a second reason why this people could have no mercy, might be because of their forsaking God even in the civil state: for the people of Israel had not only left God in their church state, and defiled themselves with false worship, but they had in their civil government wickedly departed from those whom God had appointed over them; they had departed from the house of David, and rent themselves from it. It is true, this was of God's permission, but yet it was the wickedness of their hearts, and no excuse at all for them. Hence, Hos. viii. 4, God charges them that they had set up kings, but not by him. From whence we observe,

Obs. 9. It is a most dangerous thing for a people to forsake, or to rebel against, the civil government which God sets over them. When the people, in 1 Sam. viii. 7, required a king, and would not be ruled by judges any more, the Lord saith to Samuel, "They have not rejected thee, but they have rejected me, that I should not reign over them." A most fearful declaration: and I confess freely to you, this one text of Scripture was the first that made impression upon my thoughts and heart, about fearing to adopt a way of church government that God had not appointed. For thus I reasoned: What! is God so provoked against a people that will reject but a civil government that he has appointed, which concerns but the outward man? Then if God has appointed any government in a church, which is a Divine institution, which concerns the good of the soul, and is immediately to work upon that, surely God will be much more provoked for rejecting it. And though we have not a civil government appointed by God, as the Jews had, yet for the church state we have one appointed even by God himself. And reason there must be for it; for whatever has a spiritual efficacy upon the heart, must have a spiritual rule for its warrant and direction. Indeed prudence and reason are enough for ordering things that concern the outward man, except God will come in with his own institution: but when it comes to the ordering of the heart, and there is a spiritual efficacy expected, as in all church ordinances there must be, and that authority by which they are executed gives a great influence into them, nothing can go beyond its principle, therefore it must have a Divine institution to give it its efficacy.

It may here be demanded, whether God has not appointed over us a particular civil government, as he did over the Jews? That our government, and all lawful government of other nations, is appointed by God, we must conclude is a certain truth. But not so appointed by God as the government of the Jews was. And the reason is this, because the church and commonwealth of the Jews were involved in one, and therefore the apostle, speaking of the Gentiles, saith they were "aliens from the commonwealth of Israel;" it was meant of the church state. There was such a kind of pedagogy under the law, that the church and state were involved in one, for Christ would be the Head of the church and commonwealth too, and appoint them laws; and so their government was immediately from heaven. Now for us: that we should have a government according to the rules of wisdom and justice, that indeed is appointed by God. God would have us have a just and wise government; but he leaves the ordering of that government to general rules of prudence and justice. So that now it is lawful for any kingdom or country to agree together, and, according to the rules of wisdom and justice, to appoint what kind of government they will, as whether it shall be a monarchy, or an aristocracy, or a democracy; and to limit it according to covenants of agreement, as whether the fundamental power shall be wholly put out, or any part reserved, how far this or that man or society of men shall have the managing of it, and the like; then so far as it is agreed upon, we are bound in conscience to obey either actively or passively, but no further are we bound to obey any man; conscience is not tied. Though such men be in authority, yet not to do what they would have, is no resisting of authority. Yea, though the thing be lawful which they command, if it be not according to the law of the kingdom, to the first agreement, I may be bound by the rules of prudence to save myself; but it is not authority that binds me to obey out of conscience: for we must of necessity distinguish between men in authority, and the authority of those men. Wherefore so long as we seek to keep authority in the right channel, that it flows not over the banks, we cannot be charged with resisting the government God hath set over us, though we do not obey the will of those who are set over us; and therefore there is no cause that we should fear, that God should say to England, upon this ground, Lo-ruhamah, he will have no mercy.

Ver. 7. *But I will have mercy upon the house of Judah, and will save them by the Lord their God, and will not save them by bow, nor by sword, nor by battle, by horses, nor by horsemen.*

The people of Israel might say, Hosea, thou art a severe preacher; what! preach nothing but judgment, nothing but wrath, to be utterly taken away? Is there no mercy at all? Is not God a merciful God? Yes, saith the prophet, though you be taken away, God knows how to glorify his mercy; he has others that he can make objects of his mercy, though you be destroyed.

Obs. 1. Though God utterly reject some, yet in the mean time he has others to whom he can show mercy. Therefore it is no plea for any sinner to say, Well, I have sinned indeed, but God is merciful. What if God be merciful? so he may be, though thou perish everlastingly. Yea, whole kingdoms and nations may perish, yet God may be merciful, God has still infinite ways to glorify his mercy. Many people, in desperate moods, lay violent hands upon themselves, and certainly there is a kind of spirit of revenge in it, as if they thought there would be some trouble about it, and so God should lose some honour. But if you will have your will in this, or in any thing else, though you be dead, and your souls perhaps in chains of darkness, God will have ways to be glorious in his mercy, whatever become of you.

Obs. 2. God will always have a church. He will never destroy his church at once. The Lord loves public worship in the world. Though he will utterly take away the house of Israel, yet he "will have mercy upon the house of Judah." Israel might say to the prophet, What! will not God be merciful to us? What does Judah get by worshipping God in that which you say is the only right way? Judah indeed keeps herself to Jerusalem, and to worship in the temple, but what does she gain by it? for aught we see, Judah is in as hard an estate, and as low a condition, as we? Well, saith God, let Judah be what she will, I will have mercy upon her.

Obs. 3. Though carnal hearts, when they look upon the low condition of the true worshippers of God, think that there is no difference between those who are in a good way, and themselves who walk in the ways of sin, yet God will make a difference; I will have mercy upon Judah, but not upon Israel. Many carnal men please themselves with arguing thus: I see others who are strict, who pray in their families, who run to sermons, and will not act as others, yet they are as poor, in as mean a condition, as others; what do they get by their forwardness in religion? Are not we in as good a condition as they? Well, friend, though thy carnal heart think there is no difference "between him that serveth God and him that serveth him not," God has a time to manifest a difference: "Then shall ye return, and discern between the righteous and the wicked, between him that serveth God and him that serveth him not," Mal. iii. 18. I will not have mercy upon Israel, "but I will have mercy upon Judah."

Obs. 4. If a people keep the worship of God pure, God will favour them, though there be many weaknesses, yea, many wickednesses, amongst them. Judah indulged at this time in many gross and fearful evils. It would require much time to show you the horrible wickedness of Judah; yet God saith, "I will have mercy upon the house of Judah." What is the reason of this? Because though Judah had many gross evils, yet Judah kept to the right way of worshipping God, kept to Jerusalem and to the temple; and so far kept the worship of God pure. It is true, many spirits are most bitter against those who seek to worship God in the right way; if they observe them tripping in any small thing, they charge it against them with all bitterness. This is not like God, who favours those that worship him in a right way, though in other respects he may have many charges against them.

But, you will say, this seems to contradict what you said before, that the nearer any are to God, the more he hates their sins; and the sins of those that make a show of worshipping God in a pure manner are worse than the sins of others. It is true, but as their relation to God in the nearness of his worship is an aggravation of their sins, so their relation to God is a foundation of their hope of mercy from God. How is this? It makes their sin indeed worse, so as to provoke God to punish them sooner, and perhaps more bitterly; yet their relation to God keeps this ground of faith, that God is their God still, and will have mercy upon them at last. But the wicked, though God spare them longer than his own people, yet when he comes against them he rejects them utterly; so he did Israel. Judah indeed was punished, but yet Judah had mercy at last; but, saith God, "I will have no more mercy upon the house of Israel; but I will utterly take them away."

Obs. 5. God sometimes shows mercy to poor afflicted ones, and yet rejects those who are greater and enjoy more prosperity in the world. Israel had prevailed a little before against Judah, for in 2 Kings xiv. 12—14, you find that "Judah was put to the worse before Israel; and they fled every man to their tents. And Jehoash king of Israel took Amaziah king of Judah, the son of Jehoash, the son of Ahaziah, at Beth-shemesh, and came to Jerusalem, and brake down the wall of Jerusalem from the gate of Ephraim unto the corner gate, four hundred cubits: and he took all the gold and silver, and all the vessels that were found in the house of the Lord, and in the treasures of the king's house, and hostages, and returned to Samaria." And this was but a little before this time, Israel had thus prevailed against Judah, and brought Judah under; yet now, saith God, I will have mercy upon Judah, but not upon Israel. Many who are in a low, afflicted condition, God looks upon and shows mercy unto them, when brave ones that carry it out, and thrive and live gallantly in the world, are often rejected of God. Mark what God saith, Zeph. iii. 12, "I will also leave in the midst of thee an afflicted and poor people, and they shall trust in the name of the Lord." God looks not at the brave and gallant ones of the world, but at the poor and afflicted ones, and they shall trust in the name of the Lord. We must not then judge of the happiness of men from their success in the world; for you may now be delivered, and others kept under affliction, yet afterwards you may be rejected, and they received to mercy.

Obs. 6. How impartial the ministers of God ought to be in their work. Hosea was the prophet of Israel, he was sent to the ten tribes, yet Hosea tells *them*, whose prophet especially he was, that God would have no more mercy upon them. And he speaks to Judah, (to whom he was not sent,) and tells them that God would have mercy upon them. Ministers must not go according to their private engagements with any people, though bound to them in many respects: if they be wicked, they must deal faithfully and plainly, and denounce the judgments of God. And if others, though strangers to them, be godly, they are to give them that comfort which belongs unto them. My brethren, partiality in those in public places, especially of the ministry, is a great evil: it was for this that God said he had made the priest and the Levite "contemptible and base before all the people:" why? because they were "partial in the law," Mal. ii. 9.

Obs. 7. It is a great aggravation of the misery of some, that God shows mercy to others. For it is here set down as a part of the threatening against Israel, "I will have no more mercy upon the house of Israel, but I will show mercy to Judah." To aggravate the misery of Israel, God manifests his mercy to Judah. Mark how God, in Isa. lxv. 13, makes it a part of his threatening against the wicked, that he will show mercy to his servants: "Behold, my servants shall eat, but ye shall be hungry: behold, my servants shall drink, but ye shall be thirsty: behold, my servants shall rejoice, but ye shall be ashamed: behold, my servants shall sing for joy of heart, but ye shall cry for sorrow of heart, and shall howl for vexation of spirit." These "buts" are cutting ones to the heart of the wicked. And observe, the word "behold" is four times used in setting out the difference that God will make between his servants and the wicked; and how God will aggravate the misery of the wicked by showing mercy to his people, because it is a thing much to be considered. A similar passage you have in Matt. viii. 11, "Many shall come from the east and west, and shall sit down with Abraham, and Isaac, and Jacob, in the kingdom of heaven; but the children of the kingdom shall be cast out into outer darkness: there shall be weeping and gnashing of teeth." Mark, they shall gnash their teeth when they shall see how they are rejected and others received, gnash their teeth for envy and vexation of spirit, for it is a great aggravation of men's misery. And is it not fulfilled this day? How do many gnash their very teeth to see the mercy that God shows to his people in these days; giving them liberty to meet together, and encouragement in his service, while he casts shame and contempt upon their faces, and brings them forth to answer for their wickedness, and to suffer condign punishment!

It is observable, that, in Acts xxii. 21, 22, Paul was speaking a great while to the Jews, and they heard him quietly till he came to that sentence, "Depart: for I will send thee far hence unto the Gentiles. They gave him audience unto this word, and then lifted up their voices, and said, Away with such a fellow from the earth! for it is not fit that he should live." What! to disgrace us thus, and to think that the Gentiles should come to have more mercy than we! Away with such a fellow from the earth! We have such an expression likewise in Luke iv. 25—29; our Saviour, Christ, told the Jews of the widow of Sarepta, that Elias the prophet was sent only to her, and that Naaman the Syrian, of all the lepers in Israel, was cleansed. They of the synagogue, when they heard these things, "were filled with wrath, and rose up and thrust him out of the city, and led him unto the brow of the hill whereon their city was built, that they might cast him down headlong." They were so vexed at Christ's sermon that they would have broke his neck as soon as he had done preaching. It was at this statement, "many widows were in Israel in the days of Elias, but unto none of them was Elias sent, save unto Sarepta, a city of Sidon, unto a woman that was a widow. And many lepers were in Israel in the time of Eliseus the prophet; and none of them was cleansed, saving Naaman the Syrian." Christ intimated, that though there were many of the people of Israel, yet the Lord would have mercy but upon a few of them; yea, that God would choose to show mercy to other people rather than to them: at this they were enraged. And certainly this will be the aggravation of the misery of the lost, to know the mercy of God to others. It may be wicked parents shall see their children at the right hand of Jesus Christ in glory, and themselves cast down into eternal torment; this will be a stinging aggravation of misery, no mercy unto thee, but mercy unto thy gracious child; the child that thou rebukedst for being forward is now at the right hand of Christ, and thou cast into everlasting misery. So a poor servant, or a poor boy in a family, may stand at the right hand of Jesus Christ hereafter, and ascend with him in glory; while his rich master, that murmured at him, and would not suffer him to have the least time for God's service, but checked and mocked him in every thing with, O, this is your preciseness, finds himself cast down into eternal misery.

Dives magis uritur gloria Lazari, quam suo incendio. Chrysologus.

But yet further; God declares, "I will have mercy upon the house of Judah." Here is another remark very observable, and which much concerns our present condition. God promises to Judah mercy, after Israel's rejection; yet if we search the Scriptures we shall find that both before and after the rejection of Israel was executed, Judah was under very sore afflictions. In 2 Chron. xxviii. 6, you find that "Pekah the son of Remaliah slew in Judah an hundred and twenty thousand in one day." We never heard of such a slaughter; we wonder when we hear of five or ten thousand slain in the field; here we have one hundred and twenty thousand slain, and this slaughter was made after this promise: yea, further, ver. 8, there were besides "carried away captive two hundred thousand, women, sons, and daughters;" yea, further, ver. 17, "again the Edomites had come and smitten Judah, and carried away captives." And, ver. 18, "The Philistines also had invaded the cities of the low country, and of the south of Judah; and they dwelt there:" and, ver. 19, it is said, "the Lord brought Judah low:" and, ver. 20, it is said, "Tilgath-pilneser, king of Assyria," (whom Ahaz had sent to help him,) "came unto him and distressed him, but strengthened him not." Pekah, the son of Remaliah, slays one hundred and twenty thousand, and carries away captive two hundred thousand: then come the Philistines and invade the country; and then the Edomites carry away captives, and God brings them low; and then comes Tilgath-pilneser, and he, instead of helping, distresses them. What a case were they in now! Yet this was after the promise, for this promise was made to Judah in the beginning of Hosea's prophecy; so it is, ver. 2, "The beginning of the word of the Lord by Hosea," which was before the rejection of Israel. It was in the reign of Ahaz that Judah was brought into this low condition, about twenty-two years before the execution of the sentence against Israel, for that was fulfilled in the sixth year of the reign of Hezekiah, which, if you take it from the beginning of the reign of Ahaz, who reigned sixteen years, makes twenty-two years. Now this promise to Judah was made in the days of Uzziah, king of Judah, and of Jeroboam, king of Israel, which was at least seventy-six years before the rejection of Israel; and yet, after the making of this promise, Judah is reduced to this sad condition.

Yea, and we shall find, besides, that though God had said he would reject Israel, and be merciful to Judah; so that when Israel was rejected a man would think that Judah should come into a better condition than ever; yet see how Judah was dealt with. 2 Kings xviii. 13 saith, that "in the fourteenth year of Hezekiah, Sennacherib king of Assyria came up against Judah;" and this was after the casting off of the ten tribes, for that was in the sixth year of Hezekiah, as ver. 10: and seven years after came Sennacherib against Judah, thinking to prevail against them as they had done before against Israel; and then Hezekiah was disposed to give him all the silver that was found in the house of the Lord, and in the treasures of the king's house; yea, ver. 16 saith, that "Hezekiah cut off the gold from the doors of the temple of the Lord, and from the pillars, and gave it to the king of Assyria." Now the Lord keep our kingdom and our parliament from giving the gold of the temple doors in any way of compliance with any malignant party, who regard with an evil eye the beauty of our Zion.

Yea, and after Sennacherib had gotten this, not content with it, he sends Rabshakeh from Lachish, with a great host against Jerusalem. The adversaries of the church are never satisfied, yield to them, gratify them in what you will: this is the first temptation. What! will you be so strict and rugged, and yield to them in nothing? say some: but if they prevail with you to begin to yield, they will encroach upon you. Hezekiah yielded to Sennacherib, even to take away the gold of the temple doors, yet a little while after he comes again with a great host, so that Hezekiah said, it was "a day of trouble and rebuke," chap. xix. 3. Nothing will quiet them but the ruin of the church, they must needs have that; "Down with it, down with it, even to the ground!" nothing else will satisfy them.

To this low estate and sad condition was Judah brought, though God promises mercy to them.

Obs. 8. God may intend much mercy, yea, God may be in a way of mercy to a people, yet may bring that people into very great straits and difficulties. The promises of God's mercies are always to be understood with the condition of the cross. If we think that upon the promise of mercy we shall be delivered from all trouble and affliction, we lay more upon the promise than the promise will or can bear. It is a great evil, which proceeds from much weakness of spirit and distemper of heart, in people for whom God has done great things, if there come any difficulty or trouble, to say, Now we are all lost, now God has left us; we hoped that there would have come mercy, we looked for light, and behold darkness; now the heart sinks, and all hope is abandoned. Know, my brethren, this is an evil, unthankful, and unbelieving heart. God has indeed done great things for us; yet how ready are we, though God be in such a glorious way of mercy, if we hear of any difficulty, any combining of the adversaries together, to expect nothing but blood, and to bid adieu to all our peace: we thought to have had happy days, but now the Lord is coming out against us, and all that is done must be undone again. Why are you so full of unbelief? Surely this is unworthy of Christians that profess an interest in God, and unworthy of all the good that God has done for us. Though Peter had walked upon the sea through the power of Christ, when the waves came, he cried, "Master, save, or else I perish." Has not God made us walk upon the waves of the sea all this while? wrought as great a miracle for us in England as he did for Peter? Yet when a wave does but rise a little higher than before, we are so distressed in our spirits that we can scarcely cry, O Master, save us; but we look one upon another, and instead of crying unto God, we cry out one to another in a discouraging way, and so pine away in our iniquities. Certainly God is exceedingly angry at such a demeanour as this, and yet this is common, both with nations and particular persons.

With nations: it was so with Judah. Though God had made this promise to Judah, yet if we look into Isa. vii. 2, (Isaiah was contemporary with Hosea, and it was not much after the making of this promise,) we shall see how they were troubled with fear: "It was told the house of David, saying, Syria is confederate with Ephraim. And the heart of the king of Judah was moved, and the heart of his people, as the trees of the wood are moved with the wind;" they were afraid, and shook as the very leaves of the trees shake. Well, but God speaks to the prophet, in chap. viii. 11—13, "with a strong hand, and instructed him that he should not walk in the way of this people, saying, Say ye not, A confederacy:"—Oh, the king of Israel and the king of Syria are confederate together; what shall we do? we are undone, we are lost for ever! "Say ye not, A confederacy, to all to whom this people shall say, A confederacy; neither fear ye their fear, nor be afraid. Sanctify the Lord of hosts himself; let him be your fear, and let him be your dread." Thus God would have his saints act now. When you hear of confederate enemies, or any ill tidings abroad, exclaim not, Oh, the papists are linked together, a confederacy, a confederacy! Do not say, A confederacy, fear not their fear, but "sanctify the Lord of hosts himself, and let him be your fear, and let him be your dread; and he shall be for a sanctuary" to you. And mark the resolution of the prophet afterward, ver. 17, "I will wait upon the Lord, that hideth his face from the house of Jacob, and I will look for him." Oh that this were the disposition of our hearts! Take that note away with you, amongst many, though you cannot remember all: when you hear so many rumours of fears and troubles, as if all were gone, and there were now no more hope, let this be your answer, "I will wait upon the Lord, that hideth his face from the house of Jacob;" for God is in a way of mercy, and mercy certainly we shall have, let us look for it then.

With particular persons: though God be in a wonderful way of mercy towards them, yet if they do but feel their corruptions stirring never so little, how common is it for them to say, All is lost! I was indeed in a good way, but God is gone, Christ is gone, mercy is gone, and all is gone, surely God intends no thoughts of good to me. O, be not faithless, but believing: for this is the way of God, though he promises great mercy, yet in the mean time he may bring into great afflictions.

"I will no more have mercy upon the house of Israel, but I will utterly take them away; but I will have mercy upon the house of Judah, and will save them." For a people to be saved when others near them are destroyed, is a great display of God's goodness to them: as to stand upon the shore safely, and see others suffer shipwreck before us, is a great augmentation of God's mercy towards us. When the people of Israel stood upon the banks, and saw the Egyptians tumbling in the Red Sea, and their dead bodies cast upon the shore, then "sang Moses and the children of Israel unto the Lord," Exod. xv. 1. And this kind of mercy the Lord has granted to us in England, for while neighbouring nations have been in a combustion, and many of them spoiled, we have sat under our own vines and fig trees, and our greatest afflictions have been only the hearing of what our brethren have suffered, and yet do suffer. All about us is as the fiery furnace, and we walk in the midst of it like the three children, and our garments are not touched, nor the smell of the fire passed on them. We see all countries as Gideon's fleece, wetted with the tempest of God's wrath, yea, with their own blood; but, behold, we are dry, and the sunshine of God's mercy is upon us; the blackness of the misery of our brethren is the brightness of our mercy.

"I will save them." It is the Lord that will save them. This is an upbraiding of Israel. O Israel, you think to be saved by your own policy, you have gone beyond God; you are afraid that the people should go up to Jerusalem to worship, therefore you have set up the two calves to save yourselves. But Judah shall be saved, and saved after another way: Judah need not go to such carnal policies to save themselves, for the Lord shall save them. Though carnal hearts think and endeavour to save themselves only by their own policy and carnal ways, yet let God's people know that they have a stronger means to save them than all the policy in the world. So long as the wisdom, the power, the mercy, the faithfulness of God is for them, they need no other string to their bow.

"I will save them by the Lord." This, by interpreters, is expounded concerning Christ: that God the Father promises to save by Christ. In Dan. ix. 17, we have such an expression in prayer, "Now therefore, O our God, hear the prayer of thy servant—for the Lord's sake;" that is, for Christ's sake: so here, God will save by the Lord; that is, by Christ.

Obs. 9. The administration of God's grace to his people is given into the hands of Jesus Christ. It is Christ that saves the people of God, and has saved them in all former times: "As for thee also, by the blood of thy covenant I have sent forth thy prisoners out of the pit wherein is no water," Zech. ix. 11. All the prisoners of God's people, ever since the world began, have been sent out of the pit by the blood of the covenant, by the merits of Christ: and not only so, but Christ, in the administration of God's grace, has been the chief; he has been the Angel of God's presence, who has stood up for his people in all their necessities; he has been the great Captain and Deliverer, the Saviour of them all. Let Christ then have the honour of a sovereign to us with respect to our salvation in outward deliverances. Let us look up to him for salvation in all our straits. And if Christ was the Saviour of his people in all ages, and still will be, then surely those ages and places where Christ is most known and honoured may expect the greatest salvation. And this is our comfort, for above all the ages since the world began, Christ is most known and honoured in this age; and of all places in the world, here in England, and amongst our countrymen; and if Christ will be a Saviour of those places where he is known and honoured, surely England may expect a salvation. England has had it; and as England is peculiar in the knowledge of Christ, so England shall be peculiar in God's grace to her.

Obs. 10. It is a great upbraiding of a people when it

can be said of them, that they have forsaken the Lord. "I will save them by the Lord their God." Not *your* God, O Israel, but their God. Thus he upbraids the people of Israel that they had forsaken their God; that Judah had kept their God, but Israel had not. It is a woeful thing not to have God to be our God at all; when conscience can charge upon a man what Daniel did upon Belshazzar, "That God in whose hand thy breath is, and whose are all thy ways, hast thou not glorified," Dan. v. 23: but it is dreadful when conscience can charge this, That God, whom thou hast chosen, and with whom thou hast entered into covenant, O thou apostatized soul, thou apostatized nation, thou hast forsaken, he is not now thy God. This is a sore and heavy charge indeed.

Obs. 3. Those, then, who do not worship God in a right way, God will not acknowledge himself to be worshipped by them at all. It seems he is the God of Judah, though Judah had many evils, but not the God of Israel. The people in the wilderness proclaimed a fast to Jehovah, and yet the apostle, 1 Cor. x. 7, calls them idolaters; and it is said they sacrificed to idols, because they worshipped God by a calf, and not in God's way. Though we may think we worship God, yet if we do not worship him in his own way, he does not own himself worshipped by us at all.

Obs. 4. Carnal hearts cannot endure that any one should think they have more interest in God than themselves. This could not but sting Israel, that Judah should be thought to have more interest in God than Israel had. Thus they scorned at Christ: O, he trusted in God, he thinks he has more interest in God than others, now let his God come and save him. We read in the Book of Martyrs, that the papists were much vexed with the protestants, because they used to say, our God, and our Lord, by which they seemed to claim more interest in God than others. And, indeed, what is the cause of the quarrel against God's people, but because the world think they claim more peculiarity and interest in God than others? And this is the reason that soul-searching preaching cannot be endured, because it makes a difference between the one and the other, and shows that some have an interest in God more than others. Hence it is that in no places in the world men's spirits so fret against preaching as in England. Why? Because there is not such soul-examining, such soul-distinguishing preaching in the world as in England. Yea, that is the reason of the bitterness of one professor against another, because one is a protestant at large, and the other manifests more power of godliness, is more strict in his course, and seems to claim a greater share in God than the former. Profession in England is a more distinguishing profession than in other places.

Obs. 5. So long as God is our God we need not fear our adversaries. God is the God of Judah still, therefore God will save them. You have heard of the Palladium of the heathens in Troy. They imagined that so long as that idol was kept safe, they were unconquerable, all the strength in Greece was not able to prevail against it. Wherefore the Grecians sought by all the means they could to get it from them. I have read that the men of Tyrus were afraid their god Apollo should forsake them: they therefore chained and nailed that idol to a post, that they might be sure of it, because they thought their safety was in it. Let us fasten ourselves to God in an everlasting covenant, and certainly God will be fast to us, and then we are safe enough.

Ejus simulachrum catenis constrinxerunt clavisque basi affixerunt.

"I will save them:" but how? What shall Judah be saved by, and not Israel? Judah, a poor, contemptible people! How saved?

"And will not save them by bow, nor by sword, nor by battle, by horses, nor by horsemen." It shall not be by any outward means, but by the immediate hand of God. This promise, that God would save them not "by bow nor by sword," was performed two several times, and there is a third time for the fulfilling of it, which is yet to come. It was done first when "the angel of the Lord went out, and smote in the camp of the Assyrians an hundred fourscore and five thousand," 2 Kings xix. 35: and God tells them that the king of Assyria should "not shoot an arrow there, nor come before the city with a shield:" so God saved them without bow, for they had no need to use the bow then, because the angel of the Lord destroyed them. The second time was when he saved Judah in their return from captivity, then, as it is Zech. iv. 6, he saved them "not by might, nor by power, but by my Spirit, saith the Lord of hosts." Mark the phrase; as if God should say, I have strength, for I am the Lord of hosts; I can command armies, if I would, to save you; no, though I be the Lord of hosts, yet I will not save you "by might, nor by power, but by my Spirit." Therefore, Isa. xxx. 7, "their strength" is said to be "to sit still;" and ver. 15, "in quietness, and in confidence, shall be your strength." Thus they were saved, "not by bow, nor by sword." Then the third time, which is yet to come; that is, in the wonderful work of God in calling the Jews, when God shall raise up out of them a glorious people to himself, and save Judah once again, and it shall not be by sword, nor by bow, but by the Lord their God; for, as it is said, Dan. ii. 34, the stone that smote the image "was cut out without hands;" so there shall be a power not visible from whence it comes, but Jesus Christ shall come from heaven to do his great works. "As the lightning cometh out of the east, and shineth even unto the west; so shall also the coming of the Son of man be."

Obs. 1. God ties not himself to the use of outward means in procuring good to his people. Though all outward means fail, yet there may be ways of salvation for the saints. Wicked men's hearts presently sink, if outward means fail. And if our hearts faint when outward means fail, it is a sign that we before rested upon the means, and if we had had the means we should have robbed God of his honour. We must use means, but not rely upon the means. I might show you excellent texts of Scripture for this, as Psal. xxxiii. 16, "There is no king saved by the multitude of an host: a mighty man is not delivered by much strength." And Psal. xliv. 5, 6, "Through thee will we push down our enemies: through thy name will we tread them under that rise up against us. For I will not trust in my bow, neither shall my sword save me."

Obs. 2. Deliverance of a people without bow and without sword is a great mercy. For such are the woeful miseries that a people suffer when war comes, that usually the victory will scarce pay the charges of the battle. Though we are sure to be saved at last, yet if we must be saved by bow and by sword, the misery that we may suffer in our salvation may be more than the salvation. It was the height of that mercy promised, Isa. ix. 5, that it should be without "confused noise, and garments rolled in blood." Such a mercy we have had; and had Christ come to have reigned amongst us, though he had come riding upon his "red horse," with his garments rolled in blood, we should willingly have entertained him; but behold, he comes riding upon his "white horse," in peace and mercy. The mercies we have had have been very cheap, they have not been by bow, nor by sword. And if God should come at length by the sword, and bring perfect salvation to us by blood, which God forbid, we have had already more mercy without blood than our blood is worth. Should we now have our blood shed, God has paid us beforehand. Who almost in this congregation, but two or three years ago would have lost his blood to procure so much mercy to England, as England has had already?

Obs. 3. Such is the love of God to his people, that he is pleased to work for them beyond means. The other point was, that he can save his people without means; this, that he will do it beyond means: for the grace and love of God to his people is so high and glorious, that it is beyond that which can be conveyed by means, therefore it must be done more immediately. "Thy right hand, O Lord, is become glorious in power; in the greatness of thine excellency thou hast overthrown them that rose up against thee," Exod. xv. 6, 7. First, it is the "hand of God." Secondly, it is "the right hand of God." Thirdly, it is "the right hand of God in power." Fourthly, this is "glorious in power." Fifthly, there is "excellency." And sixthly, there is "the greatness of excellency." It is a high expression, ברב גאונך in the greatness of thy lifting up; for the same word signifies pride, which is here translated excellency; and if God be lifted up in any thing it is when he shows himself for his people. Now take all these six expressions, God's hand, God's right hand, his right hand in power, a right hand that is become glorious in power, his excellency, the greatness of his excellency, and all this for his saints; surely this is more than can be conveyed by means; God must come immediately and save them by himself.

Obs. 4. The more immediate the hand of God appears in his mercy to his people, the more sweet and precious ought that mercy then to be. "Be thou exalted, O Lord, in thine own strength: so will we sing and praise thy power," Psal. xxi. 13. When God comes in his own strength, and not in the strength of the creature, then the saints sing and praise the power of God. We are accustomed to say, *Dulcius ex ipso fonte*, that which comes immediately comes exceeding sweetly. Then the saints may boast in God, when he comes immediately with his salvation: "Thou hast saved us from our enemies, and hast put them to shame that hated us." What follows? "In God we boast all the day long, and praise thy name for ever," Psal. xliv. 7, 8. So that the saints of God then praise God; nay, they may lawfully give up themselves to boast, when God works immediately. When God works by means, then they must take heed of ascribing to the means; but when God comes immediately, then they see his hand, and may well boast.

It is the blessedness of heaven, that God's mercy comes immediately. Created mercies are the most perfect mercies. Suppose God had been with them by bow and by sword when Sennacherib came against them, could the salvation have been so precious? God's hook that he put in his nose, and the bridle that he put in his lips, (for so God said he would do with him, that is, use him as a beast,) were better than their sword or bow. Surely, if ever any nation knew what it was to have immediate mercies come down from heaven, England does; if ever nation saw God exalting himself in his own power, England has; we have lived, blessed be God, to see the Lord exalting himself in his own power. O, let us cry out with the psalmist, "Be thou exalted, O Lord, in thine own strength," amongst us; "so will we," still, and still, and still, "sing and praise thy power."

Ver. 8. *Now when she had weaned Lo-ruhamah, she conceived, and bare a son.*

We finished the signification of the name of the second child of Hosea, Lo-ruhamah. We now come to its weaning, and the begetting of the third child, Lo-ammi.

"When she had weaned Lo-ruhamah." We do not read that the first child, Jezreel, was weaned; but that the second child, Lo-ruhamah, was weaned, before the third child, Lo-ammi, was conceived. What is the meaning of this?

This second child, Lo-ruhamah, was to typify the people of Israel being carried out of their own country in captivity to Assyria: it was to signify to them that they should be weaned from the comforts and delights which were in their own land; that they should be taken away from their milk and honey, and be fed in Assyria with hard meat, even with the water of affliction and the bread of adversity. The first child only signified their scattering, especially in regard of their seditions amongst themselves; but the second child signified the carrying them away wholly into captivity from their own land; therefore the second child is weaned. *Cibis sustentabitur immundis*, so Jerome interprets it. They should be carried amongst the Gentiles, and be fed with unclean meat, they should be deprived of prophecy, of the milk of the word, and of the ordinances that they enjoyed: so Vatablus.

Vaticinantur hic dura, ut destituantur verbo Dei, prophetiis et gratiis. Vatab. in loc.

Ordinances are as the breasts of consolation, out of which the people of God suck soul-satisfying comforts. "That ye may suck, and be satisfied with the breasts of her consolations; that ye may milk out, and be delighted with the abundance of her glory," Isa. lxvi. 11. And, "We will remember thy love more than wine," Cant. i. 4. The Vulgate reads it, We will remember thy breasts above wine; and so the words will bear. These people should be deprived of those breasts out of which they had sucked much sweetness before; even deprived of all comfort in God. God's people hang upon God, and draw comfort from him, even as the infant upon the mother's breast, which sucks sweetness, and comfort, and nourishment from thence.

Memores uberum tuorum super vinum.

This expression, then, of weaning the child, implies these two things:

1. That the enjoyment of the comforts of a sweet native land, specially where Divine ordinances abound, is a very great blessing of God; and to be deprived of it is a great affliction, yea, to some it comes as a curse. The very sucking of our native air is certainly a great blessing from the Lord. Those who have been banished and deprived of it, have been more sensible of it than many of you who always have enjoyed it. Many have lain so long sucking the sweetness of our English air, and the comforts which flow from their accommodations, till they have sucked in that which, if God's mercy had not prevented, would have proved poison to their souls. But I speak not of all, I make no question but there have been many of God's dear servants that have tarried in their native soil, and kept the uprightness of their hearts and consciences as clear as others that went away. It is true, the comforts of a native soil are sweet, but except we may enjoy them with the breasts of these consolations, the ordinances of the church, they are not able to satisfy the soul; yea, except we may suck out of these breasts sincere milk, not soiled nor soured by the inventions of men, better a great deal that we were weaned from all the sweetness and accommodation we have in our native soil, by the mortifying of our affections to it, than that God should wean us from it, by sending us into captivity, or by giving the adversary power over us, or by making the land too hot for us.

2. That it is an evil thing for a child to be taken from the mother's breast too soon, and sent away to be nursed by others. The expression fully implies this, for it is to tell us the evil condition of the people, that they should be taken from their own and sent to another country. The affliction is set out by a child's being taken from its mother's breast. It could not express what it intended, except it were to intimate

thus much unto us; that it is an evil thing for a child to be taken from its own mother's breast. It is unnatural then for mothers, out of daintiness and pride, to deny the fruit of their wombs the comfort of their breasts. It is true, in time of weakness and danger, when it may be dangerous to themselves and the child, God permits it. But when it is merely out of pride and affectation, certainly it is an evil against nature itself. Hannah's care of her son Samuel is recorded, and it is mentioned by the Holy Ghost in her commendation, that she gave him suck; "The woman abode, and gave her son suck until she weaned him," 1 Sam. i. 23. It is said of the ostrich, Job xxxix. 16, "She is hardened against her young ones, as though they were not hers:" the ostrich is reckoned among the fowls that are unclean: and Lam. iv. 3, "Even the sea monsters draw out the breast, they give suck to their young ones: the daughter of my people is become cruel, like the ostriches in the wilderness;" more cruel than the very sea monsters themselves, that draw out their breasts and give suck to their young ones. The instruction of the son belongs to the father, the nursing of the son belongs to the mother. The mother's milk is the most profitable and wholesome for every one, (saith Pliny,) except it be in some extraordinary case. We read, in 2 Tim. iii. 3, that in the latter day, when evil times should come, some should be ἀστοργὸι, "without natural affection:" that στοργὴ, which is there spoken of, is the affection of the parents to the children, as well as of the children to the parents.

Lac utilissimum cuique maternum. Plin. l. 28. c. 9.

But enough of this; if not too much, to such as with their pride and daintiness, the children of their own fancies, neglect nature's duty to the children of their bodies.

But further observe here, That the Lord stays for the weaning of the child; he stays till Lo-ruhamah was weaned, before Lo-ammi was conceived. And there is much to be known in this. Why does God stay? This is to show the great patience of God toward his people; for God was now about to reject them utterly from being his people; God was coming in the height of his wrath, to declare that they were no more his people; and here God makes a stop, stays till Lo-ruhamah was weaned. I have read that it was the custom of the Jews to be a long time, three years sometimes, before they weaned their children. God then it seems stayed long here, till the third child, Lo-ammi, was born, before he would come with that dreadful sentence, "Ye are not my people, and I will not be your God." First, when Jezreel was born, they are scattered up and down, but they are not all carried away captive. Then Lo-ruhamah is born, and then they are carried away captive, never to return again. But for all this, God may yet own them in their captivity. This is not so bad as for God to say, I will have no more to do with you as my people. Lord, though we be under affliction, under the power of our enemies, own us still, acknowledge us to be thine; though we be in the fiery furnace, yet let us have thee to be our God. No, (saith God,) you shall not only be scattered, but you shall be all carried away captive, and I will not own you, I will cast you off, you shall not be my people, neither will I be your God. Now before this God makes a stop. Hence,

Obs. 1. That God stops in his anger for a while, as long as he pleases. God is called, Nah. i. 2, The Lord of anger; so the words בעל חמה signify, though translated otherwise. We may apply it at least thus, God is the Lord of his own anger, he can let it out as far as he will, he can stop it when he will, he can command it to come in when he pleases. It is not so with us; our passions are lords over us; if we once let our anger arise, we cannot get it down again when we would, we cannot still our passions when we please; if we let our affections run, we cannot rein them in in a moment. That is the frame of spirit which we should all labour for, to be like God, though angry, yet sin not, so that we can stop when we will, and command our anger as we please. God says to the proud waves, "Hitherto shalt thou go, and no further." Oh that we were able to say to those proud waves of our passions, Hitherto are you gone, but you shall go no further!

Obs. 2. Those who have been once the people of God must not be suddenly rejected from being God's people. Mark here, God stops in his anger for a while. When this dreadful judgment was about to be executed, God is even ready to say, as he said afterward in this prophecy, "How shall I give thee up, Ephraim? How shall I deliver thee, O Israel?" Hos. xi. 8. When we are about either to reject any particular person, who has made profession of religion, from being God's, or to reject a church from being God's, we had need pause, and examine the matter well; yea, and when we have examined it, to stop again, and bethink ourselves what we do. We must not be too sudden in rejecting those who have been once the people of God, from being the people of God now. Many men are too hasty, in rejecting both particular servants of God, and particular churches from belonging to God, as soon as they see some few things amiss in them; especially if there be any thing gross, immediately they are no churches at all, they are altogether antichristian, they belong to the beast; and so, while they strike at the beast, they wound the Lamb. Certainly there is to be acknowledged much of Christ, not only in particular saints, but with respect to the church ordinances of many particular congregations in England: we must take heed therefore of too sudden rejection of them from belonging to God, or refusing them, as his people, church fellowship.

"She conceived, and bare a son." We come now to the conception of the third child; it was a son, and his name was Lo-ammi. The second child a daughter, but the third a son; what is the meaning of this? I told you, that by the second child was noted the state of the people at that time, that it grew weaker and more effeminate; weaker in regard of their outward strength, and more effeminate in regard of their spirits: and that statement I made good to you out of the history of those times in the Book of the Kings. Well, but now it is a son; what! do they grow stronger now they are nearer to destruction than before? Yes, though nearer to ruin, and more heavy wrath, than they were before, yet they get up a little strength before that time; therefore the third child is a son. Concerning the strength this people had a little before their utter rejection, upon which their spirits were raised, you shall find the history in 2 Kings xvii. 4, where you have a declaration of the state of the ten tribes when Lo-ammi was born; for the text tells us, that they began to join in confederacy with the king of Egypt; and whereas formerly they had done homage, by presents, to the king of Assyria, now being confederate with the king of Egypt, they refused to bring any more presents to him; they begin now to be a jolly people, and hoped to cast off that Assyrian yoke of bondage under which they had groaned.

Obs. God sometimes permits men, and nations, and churches, to rise a little out of their affliction before their utter ruin; he gives them a little reviving before their death. Many men think themselves in a very good condition, if, having been in affliction, their afflictions begin to abate, and they begin to rise a little; now they think they are safe, and they are ready to say, with Agag, "Surely the bitterness of death is past," surely the worst is gone, 1 Sam. xv. 32. But you may sometimes be recovered, when God intends you should be suddenly rejected. Many may be preserved from some judgments, because they are reserved to greater judgments. The Lord has begun, indeed, to give to us in England a little reviving, a little strength to enable us to rise against the cruel oppressions of our adversaries: but let us not be secure, notwithstanding this; for though we have some little reviving, if we follow not God in the way of humiliation and reformation, this our little reviving may be but a lightning before our death.

And yet further, it is very observable what the condition of Israel was at this time, when God was about to say, "Lo-ammi, they are not my people;" what it was not only in regard of their strength, but of their very sins. For if you examine the history, you find that the people of Israel not only had gotten somewhat more strength, but they were somewhat better in regard of their sins than they had been; I mean, they had less sins than they had before: yet now God is saying to them, "Lo-ammi, ye are not my people." And if you read 2 Kings xvii. 2, you will observe that the very time of the utter rejection of Israel was in the days of Hoshea, a king who did "evil in the sight of the Lord, but not as the kings of Israel that were before him." He was not so bad as the former kings of Israel, and yet in his days there comes utter destruction upon Israel. Yea, and as the king was not so bad as others before him, so it seems the people were not so bad as in former time, for ver. 9 saith, that "the children of Israel did secretly those things that were not right against the Lord their God." They were sinful, but their sinfulness was secret, they did not sin with such an open, impudent face as heretofore. Yet in this king's time, and when these people were thus improved, comes their utter ruin.

Hence we learn, that sometimes when there are greater sins patience stays judgment; and yet afterward, when a people seem to be in a better condition, not only in regard of their outward strength, but in regard of their sins too, then God comes with his wrath upon that people. Let us not flatter ourselves, although we can say that some things amongst us are not so bad as they were heretofore. Suppose there be some partial reformation, this is not ground enough to secure us. We cannot reason thus, Why heretofore the land was more sinful than now, and the governors were more oppressing than now. This is not enough, we may be nearer the sorest misery at this time, if our reformation be not a thorough reformation, than we were before. And the reason is this, because God, when he comes against a nation, does not only come against it for the present sins of which they are actually guilty, but to reckon with them for their sins committed before, though the judgment is inflicted just at that time. A concourse of events in God's providence might so meet as to suit with God's ends, that the destruction of this nation should be now, rather than some time ago, yet the nation not more sinful than before, but in order to fulfil other events of providence that God intends; and then he comes to reckon with them for sins that were long ago committed and for their present sins all together. As he does sometimes with particular persons: perhaps they have been drunkards, unclean, wicked, twenty years ago; God has spared them; afterward, upon some lesser sins, God may take advantage to come against them for all their other sins together. We commonly say, It is not the last blow of the axe that fells the oak: perhaps the last may be a weaker blow than any of the former, but the other blows made way for the felling of it, and at length a little blow comes and completes it. So our former sins may be the things that make way for our ruin, and then at length some lesser sins may accomplish it.

Ultimus ictus non sternit quercum.

You that have been guilty of gross sins, take heed of small sins; for though God has spared you when you were guilty of great sins, do not say that he will spare you now you commit lesser sins; at this very time of committing lesser sins, you may be called to an account for grosser. Did you never know a house stand out against many strong and blustering winds, yet afterward some little puff of wind has thrown it down? So it is with nations and people that sometimes stand out through God's patience, when their sins are gross and vile, and afterwards upon some lesser sins are utterly undone.

Ver. 9. *Then said God, Call his name Lo-ammi: for ye are not my people, and I will not be your God.*

The name of this son is Lo-ammi, and the word signifies, as it is interpreted here by God himself, "ye are not my people, and I will not be your God." The people to whom Hosea prophesied might have objected against him thus: What! Hosea, do you say that God will not have any more mercy upon us? What! will not God have mercy upon his own people? Is not God our God? Why do you threaten such things as these? The prophet answers, It is true, God has been your God, and you have been his people, but there is an end of those days; God now degrades you from those glorious privileges that you formerly possessed, he will own you no more to be his, and you shall have no further right to own him to be yours. From whence,

Obs. 1. A people that have been once a people dear to God, may be so rejected as never to become a people of God more. For so these did not, though afterwards we shall hear of the promise for others in other ages. God has no need of men. God is able to raise up a people what ways he pleases, even from the very stones in the street "to raise up children unto Abraham." Rome may boast that she has been a glorious church. True, there has been heretofore a glorious church in Rome. What then? Those who were his people are now no more his people. We shall meet further with this in the next chapter.

Only here observe but this thing, the great difference between the estate of a Christian in communion with Christ by grace, and a church estate. Men and women may lose their church estate, and that for ever; but their estate in communion with Jesus Christ by grace they can never lose. This is a great difference, and affords abundance of comfort. True, our church state, I mean in regard of an instituted church in congregations, is a great privilege and mercy; but our communion with Jesus Christ is a higher privilege, and that privilege can never be lost: we may be cut off from the one, but never cut off from the other.

Obs. 2. It is a most heavy judgment for any to have been heretofore the people of God, now to be unpeopled, for God to be no more theirs, and for them to be no more the Lord's. A heavy judgment for the Lord to say, Well, I will be no more a God to you, whatsoever I am to others, no more yours in my goodness, in my mercy, in my power, or whatsoever I am in myself.

The being cast off from God, 1. Takes us off from that high honour that was before upon a people. "Since thou wast precious in my sight, thou hast been honourable," Isa. xliii. 4. The people of God gathered together in church communion, certainly are in an honourable condition; when they are dispeopled, they are cast off from this their privilege, from their honour. 2. They have not the presence of God with them, nor the care of God towards them, nor the protection of God over them, nor the delight of God in them, nor the communication of God to them as before. But, among other privileges, they want this, namely, that great privilege of pleading with God for mercy upon this relation, which was the usual way of the prophets to plead with God, because they were the people of God: so Isa. lxiv. 9, "Be not wroth very sore, O

Lord, neither remember iniquity for ever." Upon what ground? "Behold, see, we beseech thee, we are all thy people." This is a good argument. Again, Jer. xiv. 9, "Why shouldest thou be as a man astonished, as a mighty man that cannot save? yet thou, O Lord, art in the midst of us, and we are called by thy name; leave us not." This text is ours this day, and well may we say, "O Lord, why shouldest thou be as a man astonished?" Yet if we can but take up the second part, and say, "We are called by thy name," we may make more comfortable use of the former, "Why shouldest thou be as a man astonished?" How doth a man astonished stand? He stands still in a place, as if he knew not which way to go; he is in a kind of distraction, first he goes one way, and by and by he returns again. The Lord knows his purpose from eternity, but the Scriptures are pleased to express God's ways towards us in this similitude. Has not God stood amongst us "as a man astonished?" God has been in a way of mercy, and then stood still, and then gone forward a little, and afterward gone back again, and yet back and back still; and we have prayed and cried, and God has again stood as a man astonished, as if he were not yet resolved which way to go. Let us pray earnestly to God that he would not stand as a man astonished, but that the way of the Lord's mercy may be made clear before him, and clear before us. But this I bring in to show that the relation which a people have to God, is the ground of their encouragement to pray to God, and when a people is rejected they lose this privilege. Our relations to God are very sweet and glorious things, though ordinarily they are exceedingly abused. As it is said of other relations, Relations are of the least entity, but of the greatest efficacy; so it is here, our relations to God are of very great efficacy, whatever the entity be; and therefore to lose our relations to God, especially this relation of God's being ours, and we being his, is a sore and heavy curse.

Obs. 3. We first begin with God in our apostacy, before God begins with us in his rejection. Mark here; the first is, "you are not my people," before the second comes, "I will not be your God." I would not have withdrawn myself from being your God if you had not first rejected me, and would not be my people. When God loves, he begins first; we love not him, but he loves us first: but when it comes to departing, it begins on our side, we first depart before the Lord does: and this will be a dreadful aggravation to wicked men another day, to think with themselves, This evil is come upon us, God is gone, mercy is gone; but who began this first? where is the root and principle? Thy perdition is of thyself. I began first, and therefore all the loss of that grace and mercy that is in God, I may thank this proud, this distempered, this base, passionate, wretched heart of mine own for it.

Obs. 4. It is a greater misery to lose God himself, than to be deprived of whatsoever comes from God. "I will not be your God." He does not say, You shall not have the fruit of my patience to be yours, you shall not have my creatures to be yours, you shall not have those fruits of my bounty to be yours: no, but I will not be yours, I myself will not be yours. This is the sorest threatening that can possibly be to a gracious heart. And this indeed is one special difference between a hypocrite and a truly gracious heart; a hypocrite is satisfied with what comes from God, but a truly gracious heart is satisfied with nothing but God himself. Though God lets out never so many fruits of his bounty and goodness to him, yet he must have union with God himself, or else he is unsatisfied. It is a notable speech of Bernard, "Lord, as the good things that come from me please not thee without myself, so the good things that come from thee please not me without thyself." This is the expression of a gracious heart. Let us tender up to God never such duties, with never so great strength, except we tender up to God ourselves, they never please him. So let God bestow never so many favours upon us, except God give us himself, they should never please us; I mean, please us so as to satisfy us, so as to quiet us, if for our portion.

You know what God said to Abraham, "Fear not, I am thy shield, and thy exceeding great reward. But Abram said, Lord God, what wilt thou give me, seeing I go childless?" Gen. xv. 1, 2. What is all this to me, so long as I have not the promise fulfilled, that so I may come in Christ to enjoy thyself? And Moses would not be contented though God told him his Angel should go before thm; no, saith he, "If thy presence go not with me carry us not up hence," Exod. xxiii. 20; xxxiii. 15. The harlot cares not so much for the person of her lover, as for his gifts; but the true lover cannot be satisfied with love-tokens, but she must have the person himself. So it is with a gracious heart. It is very observable that David, in Psal. li. 9, prays, "Hide thy face from my sins;" it seems God's face was angry; and yet presently, ver. 11, "Cast me not away from thy face, or presence." God's face was an angry face, yet David would not be cast away from this face of God: O no, rather let God be present with a gracious heart, though he be angry; though his anger continue, yet let me have his countenance. In that God says not, I will not give you these and these favours, but "I will not be your God;" this is the sorest threatening that possibly can be to a gracious heart.

Cujus faciem timet, ipsius faciem invocat. Aug.

Obs. 5. This is the judgment for sin, God not being their God. It hence appears that sin carries along with it in itself its own punishment. How is that? Thus: by sin we refuse to have God to be our God; by it we depart from God, we do not trust God, nor love him, nor fear him. The very nature of sin causes a sinner to depart from God, yea, to reject God from being a God to him; and this is the punishment, "I will not be your God." And this is the sorest punishment to a sinner, that he shall not have God for ever for his God.

Obs. 6. When any forsake God, and disavow him to be their God, we should do as God does, reject them from being ours. If they will not be God's, neither should they be ours. Will not such a man have acquaintance with God, will he forsake him and his ways, then he shall not have our acquaintance, we will forsake him. How far we may withdraw from a church that it shall not be ours, we shall fully meet with in the second chapter. Only now thus much: though it be true, when a people forsake God, we are to forsake them, yet let them grow never so wicked, our natural and civil relations cannot be broken because of their wickedness; but the relations of husband and wife, father and child, master and servant, must be acknowledged; servants must be dutiful to their masters though never so wicked; and the wife must be loving and dutiful to her husband, though he be never so wicked a man. But any intimate familiarity with those, not thus joined in such relations, ought not to exist; if they reject God, if they will not be God's, they should not be ours. It is said, Job viii. 20, that God will not help the evildoers; it should be true of us all, that we should not take the ungodly by the hand, to help them in evil. Thus much for the name of this third child, "Lo-ammi: ye are not my people, and I will not be your God."

That which remains in the chapter, is a promise of mercy both to Israel, ver. 10, and afterwards to Israel and Judah together, ver. 11. To Israel first, and that is,

Ver. 10. *Yet the number of the children of Israel shall be as the sand of the sea, which cannot be measured nor numbered; and it shall come to pass, that in the place where it was said unto them, Ye are not my people, there it shall be said unto them, Ye are the sons of the living God.*

And so he goes on with wonderfully gracious promises of mercy to Israel in future generations, though for the present God had determined what to do with Israel. Here then we have, first, a promise of mercy to Israel. Secondly, this mercy to be in future generations. And thirdly, to consist in the multitudes that should be gathered to Israel.

I. Here is a promise of mercy to Israel.

Obs. 1. That the Lord in judgment remembers mercy. It is a sore thing when God in mercy remembers judgment, but it is as comfortable when God in judgment remembers mercy. When God threatens most dreadfully, yet he promises most graciously. We should therefore, when we most fear the threats of God, look up to the promises of God, look up to see, when wrath is denounced in the most hideous and dreadful way, whether we can spy a promise, whether there be not yet a little cloud, though but as big as a man's hand, whether there be not yet a little crevice, through which we may see whether God doth not break forth with a little light in a way of promise.

Obs. 2. It is usual, when we are in prosperity to forget all threatenings, and when we are in adversity to forget all promises. When we hear of mercy to God's people, we never think of God's wrath; and on the other side, when we hear of his wrath, our unbelieving hearts never think of his grace and mercy. We ought to sanctify the name of God in both; when God is in a way of justice, look up to his grace; and when he is in a way of grace, look up to his justice. For that end I shall give you two notable texts of Scripture, as famous as any I know in the book of God: the one declares to you that when God expresses the greatest mercy, yet then he declares the greatest wrath; and the other, when God expresses the greatest wrath, he then declares the greatest mercy: and I shall show you how the name of God ought to be sanctified in both.

The first is in Exod. xxxiv. 6, 7; when the Lord passed by before Moses he "proclaimed, The Lord, the Lord God, merciful and gracious, longsuffering, and abundant in goodness and truth, keeping mercy for thousands, forgiving iniquity and transgression and sin." What abundance of mercy is here expressed! Now it follows, "and that will by no means clear the guilty; visiting the iniquity of the fathers upon the children, and upon the children's children, unto the third and to the fourth generation." Here is an expression of great wrath. And then for our sanctifying of God's name in this, it follows, ver. 8, And when Moses heard this, he "made haste, and bowed his head toward the earth, and worshipped." Thus we must bow and worship before God, sanctifying his name in both his mercy and justice.

On the other side, Nah. i. 2, "God is jealous, and the Lord revengeth; the Lord revengeth, and is furious; the Lord will take vengeance on his adversaries, and he reserveth wrath for his enemies." Dreadful expressions! Yet, ver. 3, "The Lord is slow to anger;" there is a mitigation at first: then he advances in expressions of wrath, but he is "great in power, and will not at all acquit the wicked:" and ver. 5, "The mountains quake at him, and the hills melt, and the earth is burned at his presence, yea, the world, and all that dwell therein: who can stand before his indignation, and who can abide in the fierceness of his anger? His fury is poured out like fire, and the rocks are thrown down by him." What more terrible expressions of wrath than these? Now mark, ver. 7, "The Lord is good, and a strong hold in the day of trouble; and he knoweth them that trust in him." What a strong expression of grace is here! observe it, my brethren, that in the midst of God's anger, yet God is good still. A gracious heart must acknowledge, though God be provoked to anger, yet he is a good God still; and it is a good sign for the soul to fall down before God when he is in the way of his wrath, and to say, "The Lord is good." As that good old man Eli did, after the denunciation of that dreadful sentence against him and his house by Samuel, "It is the Lord, let him do what seemeth him good."

Obs. 3. God, in the midst of his anger, knows those that trust in him. All of you will say, when God bestows favours upon you, The Lord is good, O blessed be God, he is a good God: but when God reveals his greatest wrath, truly then the Lord is good. Luther declared he would acknowledge God to be a good God, though he should destroy all men in the world.

Deus bonus est, etiamsi omnes homines perderet. Luther.

Much more then is he to be acknowledged in a day of trouble, when he appears most graciously to his saints. "The Lord is good, and a strong hold in the day of trouble." God is a strong hold now, when such wrath is revealed, to his saints in the day of trouble; and he knoweth those that trust in him; though his wrath is abroad in the world, he knoweth those that trust in him. When men are angry they scarce know the difference between their foes and their friends. If any displease them, they come home and are angry with their wives, with their servants, with their children, with their friends, with every one about them. While they are in their passion, their wives, and children, and servants wonder what the matter is with them: Surely some one has displeased my master to-day, he is so touchy, and angry at every little thing. My brethren, it is a dishonour to you in the eyes of your servants, and it lays low your authority in your families, for them to see you come home in such a pet that you know not how to be pleased, though they have done nothing to displease you. God does not act so; though he be never so angry, yet he knows those that trust in him. Let God's anger be never so public and general in the world, if there be but a gracious soul that lies in a poor cottage, or in a hole, the Lord knows it, and takes notice of it, and that soul shall understand too that God knows it. It is true, when the wrath of God is revealed abroad in the world, it seems as if it would swallow up all the saints; and those whose spirits are weak and fearful are afraid that they shall be swallowed up in the common calamity. But be of good comfort, God knows those that trust in him, even when his wrath is never so dreadful and general. In this case it is with God's children as it is with a child in the mother's arms; if the father violently lays hold upon his servant, and thrusts him out of doors for his demerits, there is such a terrible reflection of the father's anger against the servant upon the child, that the poor child begins to cry. So when the children of God see God laying hold upon wicked men, to execute wrath upon them, they cry out, they are afraid lest some evil should befall them too. O no, be of good comfort, "The Lord is good, and a strong hold in the day of trouble; and he knoweth them that trust in him," when his anger is never so great and general. So though this Israel be "not my people," yet "the number of the children of Israel shall be as the sand of the sea." So in Nah. i. 15, "Behold upon the mountains the feet of him that bringeth good tidings, that publisheth peace!" What! at this time, though God's way be in the whirlwind, and so terrible, yet now, "behold the feet of him that bringeth good tidings, that publisheth peace." God abroad publishes war, yet he has a messenger to publish peace and life to some.

Is it not so this day? It is true, the wrath of the Lord is kindled, and burns as an oven against the ungodly, but peace shall be upon Israel. And let us sanctify the name of God in this too, for so it follows,

Nah. i. 15, "O Judah, keep thy solemn feasts, perform thy vows: for the wicked shall no more pass through thee; he is utterly cut off." And because God reveals such rich grace in the midst of judgment, let this engage your hearts to the Lord for ever.

Obs. 4. Not only when God threatens judgments, but when judgments are actually upon us, let us sanctify God's name in looking up to promises. Suppose we should live to feel most fearful judgments of God, yet even then we must look up to promises, and exercise faith, and have an eye to God in the way of his grace at that time; this is more difficult than in threatenings. You have a notable passage in Isa. xxvi. 8, "In the way of thy judgments, O Lord, have we waited for thee; the desire of our soul is to thy name." Blessed be God, my brethren, the Lord calls us to wait upon him in the ways of mercy for the present. Not long since the Lord was in a way of judgment toward England; and some of God's people would wait upon God and keep his ways; but there were many, when they saw that they were likely to suffer, departed from God and declined his ways. Much cause of bitterness of spirit, and of dread of humiliation, have they that did so. But others may have comfort to their souls, that in the very way of God's judgments they waited for him, and they can now with more comfort wait upon God, when he is in the way of his mercy. But if God should ever come unto us in the way of his judgments, let us learn even then to wait upon God and keep his way.

Jer. xxxiii. 24 may seem more pertinent to illustrate this truth: "Considerest thou not what this people have spoken, saying, The two families which the Lord hath chosen, he hath even cast them off? thus they have despised my people, that they should be no more a nation before them." Mark the low condition of the people at this time; God has cast them off, they are despised and contemptible, not worthy to be accounted a nation: but though they were brought low, and in a condition contemptible, yet now God confirms his covenant with them: for observe, ver. 25, 26, "Thus saith the Lord; If my covenant be not with day and night, and if I have not appointed the ordinances of heaven and earth; then will I cast away the seed of Jacob, and David my servant." As if God had said, Let them know that whatever their condition is now, yet my love, my mercy, my faithfulness, is toward them as sure as my covenant with day and night, and as the ordinances of heaven and earth. An admirable text to help not only nations, but individuals, when they are under the contempt of ungodly men. Yet at that time the Lord is most ready to confirm his covenant with them, to be as sure as his covenant with day and night, and heaven and earth. It brings honour to God when at such times we can look up to him and exercise faith. And indeed this is the glory, and dignity, and beauty of faith, to exercise it when God's judgments are actually upon us.

II. To whom did this promise refer? It was not a promise to any who then lived, but to be fulfilled in future ages, yet introduced by the prophet as a comfort to the people of God then living. Hence

Obs. Gracious hearts are comforted with the promises of God made to the church, though not to be fulfilled in their days. If the church may prosper and receive mercies from God, though I be dead and mouldering in the grave, yet blessed be God! When Jacob was dying he said to Joseph, "Behold, I die; but God shall be with you, and bring you again unto the land of your fathers," Gen. xlviii. 21; he will fulfil his promises to you though I am dead. Our forefathers, that generation of the saints who lived a while since, how comfortably would they have died, if God, before their death, had revealed to them, that within three, or four, or seven years, so much mercy should come to England as we now see! Yea, how comfortably would any of us have died (I appeal to any gracious heart here) if God had said thus to thee, Go and be gathered to thy fathers in peace, within these two years such things shall be done for England as we now live to see! would not we willingly have died? would it not have been comfort enough against the fear of death, to have had revealed to us what should have been done to our posterity? What mercy then is it now, that it is not only revealed to us, but enjoyed by us!

III. What was this promise? "That Israel should be a multitude, that the number of them should be as the sand of the sea shore." We shall examine the excellency of the mercy of God in this promise by and by. Only for the present, inquire we a little why God should manifest his grace "to multiply them as the sand of the sea shore?"

If we compare Scripture with Scripture, we shall find that God promises this, because he would thereby show, that he remembered his old promise to Abraham, that God would multiply his seed "as the stars of heaven, and as the sand which is upon the sea shore;" and now God a long time after renews this promise. Hence

Obs. That the Lord remembers his promises, though made a long time since. "God is ever mindful of his covenant," Psal. cxi. 5. When we have some new and fresh manifestations of God's mercy, our hearts rejoice in it, but the impression of it is soon gone. When some of you have been seeking God, have had many manifestations of his love, and God has entered into covenant with you, for a while you have been comforted, but you lose all your comfort again within a short time. O remember, "God is ever mindful of his covenant," though made twenty or forty years ago; he remains the same still; be you the same still; be you ever mindful of your covenants. When men are brought into the bond of the covenant, their consciences are awed with it, at first they walk very strictly, and dare not in the least thing go from the covenant; but after a few months or weeks are over their heads, they forget the covenant they made with God. There is not such a strong bond upon their spirits as there was before. O my brethren, know that this is a great and sore evil in you; "God is ever mindful of his covenant," so you should be.

And as of his covenant, so of his threats too, by way of proportion. God remembers his threats that were made many years ago: we are affected with God's threats for the present, but within a while the impression is gone; but let us know, time alters not God as it does us.

We must, however, inquire more fully into this promise, because it is often declared in Scripture, that the children of Israel should be like the stars of the heaven, and as the sand upon the sea shore. Why did God express himself thus in his covenant to Abraham?

First, Abraham left his father's house and all his kindred at God's command, and upon that God made this covenant with him, that he would make his seed "as the stars of the heaven, and as the sand which is upon the sea shore." As if God had said, Abraham, be willing to leave your father's house, I will make a great house of you, a great family of yours.

Secondly, Observe that afterwards God confirmed this covenant to Abraham, and that with an oath. When he came first out of his country, and left his father's house, God made this promise of increasing his seed, but not with an oath; but afterwards, in Gen. xxii. 16, 17, God renews this promise of multiplying his seed, and that by an oath: "By myself have I sworn, saith the Lord, for because thou hast done this thing, and hast not withheld thy son, thine only son: that in blessing I will bless thee, and in multiplying I will multiply thy seed as the stars of the heaven, and as the sand which is upon the sea shore." Mark here, it was upon Abraham's being willing to offer up his son Isaac, his only son Isaac. Abraham was willing at God's command to offer up his own son, and upon that God promises to multiply his seed as the stars of heaven, and as the sand of the sea. Yea, with an oath, By myself I swear, saith the Lord, that I will do it, because thou hast done this.

Obs. 1. There is nothing lost in being willing to lose for God. Abraham was willing to lose his father's house, the comfort of his family, for God: I will make thee a glorious family as the stars of heaven, saith God. Again, Abraham was willing to lose one son, his only son, for God. Art thou willing to lose one son for me, saith God, thou shalt have ten thousand sons for this one thou losest, yea, though it be lost but in thy intention. Thou shalt have thy own son, and yet have ten thousand sons besides. O, let us not be afraid to part with any thing for God. God's people know how to make up in God whatever they lose for God. But God will not only make it up in himself, but will make it up even in the very creature itself thou losest for God. Art thou willing to lose a little of thy estate? Thou mayst with comfort expect, as far as, if thou knewest all, thou thyself wouldst desire, to have it made up in abundance, even in that very way. You know the promise, "And every one that hath forsaken houses, or brethren, or sisters, or father, or mother, or wife, or children, or lands, for my name's sake, shall receive an hundredfold, and shall inherit everlasting life," Matt. xix. 29. How hath God fulfilled this promise this day in many of our eyes, and to many of our experiences! How many have you known who were willing to part with what they had, and to put it out, as it were, to the wide world! But God has made it up to them, not only in himself, but in the very thing itself; and thereby taught them, and all the world, to be willing to venture to part with any thing for God and his cause.

Obs. 2. When we are willing to lose for God, then is the time when God will renew and confirm his covenant with us. God confirmed his covenant with Abraham when he was willing to part with his son, to be deprived of all his seed. The way to make sure of what we have is to be willing to part with it. You all desire to be sure of your estates; Oh that we could in these times, wherein we see nothing sure, make our estates sure! Would you make sure of your estates? Be willing to employ your estates for God and for a good cause. This is the way to have God renew his covenant to you for an assurance that way. This is the best assurance office in the world.

But how comes this promise in at this time, and to this people, in Hosea's prophecy? Because the Lord, by the prophet, would answer an objection of the people. They might have said, Hosea, do you thus threaten the destruction of Israel? You promise mercy to Judah, and Judah is but a handful to us; we are the ten tribes, and with us is the greatest part, almost all the seed of Abraham, and yet you threaten our destruction; it can never possibly be. What will become of God's promise to Abraham, that his seed should be as the stars of heaven, and as the sand on the sea shore? You seem to speak contrary to God; God said that he would multiply that seed, and you take a course to make men believe that the seed of Abraham shall be brought to nothing.

The prophet answers thus: Do you say, What will become of Abraham's seed? Know that God can tell how to provide for his church and fulfil his promise made to Abraham, whatever becomes of you. You are mistaken in thinking that you alone are the seed of Abraham. Abraham has not only a carnal, but a spiritual seed; all those that shall join in the faith of Abraham, and subject themselves to the God of Abraham, shall be the seed of Abraham, and so they shall be the children of Israel as well as you. Thus God will make good his word. To expound this truth the apostle quotes this promise, "As he saith also in Hosea, I will call them my people which were not my people," Rom. ix. 25; and applies it to the Gentiles. The Holy Ghost, who is the best interpreter of Scripture, there shows that it is at least in part fulfilled in so many of the Gentiles coming in, and being converted to the faith of the true Messiah.

This and many other excellent prophecies concerning the glory of Israel, were made good in part in the first times of the gospel. They were, however, but the first-fruits of the fulfilling of those promises and prophecies; the accomplishment of them is yet certainly to come, when the fulness of the Gentiles shall come in, and the Jews be converted. Then not only the spiritual seed, but the very carnal seed of Abraham shall have this promise made good, and be multiplied, and come into the faith too, Rom. xi. 26. The apostle speaks there of a general salvation of Israel that was to come after the fulness of the Gentiles. So it appears plainly, that those prophecies concerning the glory of Israel, though they were in part made good in the first times of the gospel, yet there was a further accomplishment of them, when there should be a fulness of the Gentiles come in, and then all Israel should be saved. From hence

Obs. 1. All believers, though of the Gentiles, are of the seed of Abraham, they are of Israel, and therefore have the same privileges with Israel, the same in effect, yea, better. They are all the heirs of Abraham, who, Rom. iv. 13, is said to be "the heir of the world;" they have the dignity of Israel, to be the peculiar people of the Lord, to be God's treasure and portion. Whatever you read of excellent titles and appellations about Israel, they belong now to all believers, though they are Gentiles. A comfortable and most sweet point to us Gentiles.

Obs. 2. God has a time to bring in abundance of people to the profession of the faith; multitudes, even as the sand of the sea shore. He will do it, and he has ways enough to accomplish it. Though for the present men cast this reproach upon the people of God, that they are but few, a company of poor mean people, a handful, that are nothing in comparison of the rest. But this reproach will be wiped away, and we may yet expect, that before the world come to an end, the greatest part of its inhabitants shall embrace the faith of Christ, and become godly too. Isa. xlix. 19—21, "Thy waste and desolate places, and the land of thy destruction, shall even now be too narrow by reason of the inhabitants." This yet has not been fulfilled. Thy children shall say, "The place is too strait for me, give place to me that I may dwell. Then shalt thou say in thine heart, who hath begotten me these?" When was this fulfilled? "The stone," in Dan. ii. 35, "that smote the image became a great mountain, and filled the whole earth." God's people shall fill the whole earth. Now take all Christians to be God's people that only acknowledge Christ to be the Son of God, they are computed to be not above the sixth part of the world; and yet this must be fulfilled, that the church shall be as the stone that smote the image, become a great mountain and fill the whole earth. "John saw," in the Revelation, "the holy city, new Jerusalem, coming down from God out of heaven, prepared as a bride adorned for her husband," Rev. xxi. 2, 10: and when God comes to dwell with men by his Spirit, all people shall come and flock to the church, as the prophet saith, like "the doves to their windows," Isa. lx. 8; and they, you know, fly together in flocks. In Christ's time the people of God were a little flock; "Fear not, little

τὸ μικρὸν ποίμνιον.

flock." The Greek has two diminutives, little, little flock, and so it may be translated, "Fear not, little, little flock; for it is your Father's good pleasure to give you the kingdom," Luke xii. 32. It was a little flock then, but it shall be a great flock when the Father shall come to give them the kingdom. Christ is promised to have the "heathen for his inheritance, and the uttermost parts of the earth for his possession," Psal. ii. 8; he shall possess them. A king does not possess a kingdom who only possesses some town, or one shire of it: Christ shall possess the uttermost parts of the earth. Yea, it shall be said, "The kingdoms of this world are become the kingdoms of our Lord, and his Christ," Rev. xi. 15. They are the Lord's indeed in some sense always; but he speaks in a special sense, wherein it shall be said not only a few congregations are the Lord's, and his Christ's, but the whole kingdoms of the earth, which, with their great kings, shall come and bring their glory into the church.

Obs. 3. Is it so? let every one then come in, and help on this work. Has God promised this, that there shall be multitudes come into the church? Come thou in then, and thou! What! shall so many embrace the faith of Jesus Christ, and shalt thou stand out, and be shut out at last amongst the dogs? Do you come in and add to the number, to make good this word of the Lord. Yea, let us seek to draw in all others as much as we can: therefore it is that we have such excellent promises in the Scripture to encourage us to draw in others to the faith. "He that turneth many to righteousness shall shine as the stars for ever and ever," Dan. xii. 3.

Obs. 4. Although God defers fulfilling his promise for a time, yet at last he does it gloriously. The paucity of the number of the saints of God now shall not discourage always; let us be above this stumblingblock. There are but few yet; what then? there shall be many, "The number of the children of Israel shall be as the sand of the sea." What though we do not see ways how this promise shall be fulfilled for the present, yet let us believe it. For, observe, when God first made this promise to Abraham, that his seed should be as the stars of heaven, and as the sand of the sea shore, it required much exercise of faith in Abraham to believe it. It was twenty years after this promise before Abraham had a child. At last he had a child, and a child by promise; then he must go and kill that child; but he was spared. Well, Isaac grows up, and he was forty years old before he married; all this while there was but one of the promised seed. When Isaac married, Rebekah his wife continued twenty years barren; what became of the promise all this while, that the seed of Abraham should be as the sand of the sea? Here are twenty years gone, and forty years gone, and twenty years more gone, and yet there are no other children of the seed by promise but Isaac. Nay, it appears that upon their going into Egypt, which was two hundred and fifteen years after the promise, there were but threescore and ten of them all. Where is the promise then, that Abraham's seed should be as the stars of heaven for multitude? But now mark, God afterwards comes on apace, for in Numb. i. 46, you find that at the end of the next two hundred and fifteen years they were reckoned when they came out of Egypt, and "they were six hundred thousand and three thousand and five hundred and fifty" fighting men of twenty years old and upwards, besides all the women and children, and all the tribe of Levi, which made two and twenty thousand more, Numb. iii. 39. In the first two hundred and fifteen years they were but threescore and ten, and the next two hundred and fifteen years, while they were in bondage, they increased to six hundred thousand and three thousand and five hundred and fifty, besides women and children, and the tribe of Levi. Thus, though it was long, yet when God's time came he fulfilled the promise to Abraham. So though we do not for the present see God making good the promise, yet let us believe, for God has ways to fulfil all, and he will do it, and when he comes he will come gloriously above our faith.

We can hardly believe there should be such great things done in England as we desire and expect, but there is nothing yet to accomplish which is more difficult than that which has been already done, therefore we may believe: and when God once comes in the way of mercy, he triumphs gloriously; therefore let us be willing to wait his time. Let us not proportion out God's ways, nor draw an argument from what has been done in one time, that therefore no more shall be done in another. You see what he did in the fulfilling of the promise to Abraham; and you may observe in your reading of the New Testament, what low beginnings there were of the church at the first: therefore saith Christ, "Where two or three are gathered together;" as noting that there would be but a very few at the first. When Paul was called by a wonderful vision, in which he saw a man of Macedonia appearing to him, and praying him to come over to Macedonia and help them, Acts xvi. 9; one would have thought that when he preached there, all would have come flocking to hear, and there would have been a glorious work done, that he would have brought in a great number to the faith. But when he came to Macedonia he was fain to go into the fields by a river's side to preach, and only a few women came there to hear him. That was all the auditory he had, and amongst them there was but one poor woman wrought upon, "God opened the heart of Lydia." This was the present result only of such a mighty call; and yet we know how gloriously God wrought by Paul. This I note to confirm you in this, that though the beginnings be very small, yet we may expect a glorious increase afterward. As it was with the church at the beginning, so it will be here: that which Bildad said of Job, chap. viii. 7, may well be applied to the church, "Though thy beginning was small, yet thy latter end shall greatly increase."

Obs. 5. As God has a time to multiply his church, so it is a great blessing to the church of God when it is multiplied. It is a fruit of God's great grace and mercy to make the church a numerous people: as "in the multitude of people is the king's honour," Prov. xiv. 28; so it is the glory of Jesus Christ, and therefore it was prophesied of him, that converts should come into the church as the "dew of the morning," Psal. cx. 3. Thus it began in the primitive times, and soon after multitudes united with the church. I remember that Jerome, writing to Cromatius, affirms, that there might be computed for every day in the year (except the first of January) five thousand martyrs; therefore the church was grown to a numerous multitude. And Tertullian, in his Apology to the Heathens, states, they were become so numerous in his day, that they had filled their cities; and that if they would they had strength enough to make their party good against them, but they were patient and submitted themselves to their tyranny.

I know many make this statement of Tertullian an argument that men ought to lay down their necks, if those who rule over them will it; and that if they cannot obey actively, they must obey passively, any thing that is according to the will of their rulers. Why, say they, did not the Christians resist in the primitive times? Yes, though they were under idolaters, and were commanded to deny Christ, which was utterly unlawful, if they could not obey actively, they obeyed passively, they submitted themselves to their rage; and though they had strength yet they would not resist. Why should not Christians do so now?

You are exceedingly deceived with this argument. True, we are bound to obey authority, actively or passively, and yet this argument does not serve the turn. There is much difference between authority abused, and men that are in authority commanding; here the difference lies not in authority abused, but in that which is no authority at all. For there is no authority that we are subject to now, but according to the laws and constitutions of the country in which we live. Not to the commands and mere will of men are we bound in conscience to submit, either actively or passively. Though it be a good thing that is commanded, conscience does not bind to it, *ea ratione*, to yield to it because it is commanded, till it be brought to a law, and is according to the agreements and covenants of the country wherein we live. And suppose this authority is abused, and there is an ill law made, then I confess, if that law be of force, we must either leave the country, or submit, or suffer, for then the power of God is in it, though it be abused, and we are to be subject to all powers. When then it comes to be a power, to be a law, it is authority, though abused, and we must yield obedience to it, either actively or passively. But we must inquire whether it be a power; it is not because the man that is in authority commands it, except he command it by virtue of that authority which is according to the nature and condition of the fundamental constitutions of the country where he lives.

Now in the primitive times they submitted themselves to suffer when they could not do the things that were commanded, as to deny Christ, because by the constitutions of that country they had a legal power to proceed against them. Therefore the Christians were willing rather to suffer any thing than to resist; and were ours the same case we should do so too. If once it come to pass, that mischief be established by a law, though it be mischief, yet if we cannot obey it actively, we are bound to suffer, or else to quit the country, if it be urged upon us. We may seek what we can to get it alleviated, but we must either do or suffer, if once it be framed into a law; otherwise we are not bound in conscience; bound we may be in regard of prudence, and for preventing other disturbances, but conscience does not bind to the will of men, but to laws. Thus much for the satisfaction of conscience in this case.

Obs. 6. We should rejoice in multitudes joining the church. The Christians were wonderfully increased at this time. Now we know we are to rejoice when the church is increased, and to esteem it as the great blessing of God when its members are made as the sand upon the sea shore. In Psal. lxxii. 8, there is a large prophecy made of the kingdom of Christ, and of his glory in this particular: " He shall have dominion from sea to sea, and from the river unto the ends of the earth:" then ver. 11, " All kings shall fall down before him: all nations shall serve him:" and ver. 17, " His name shall endure for ever: his name shall be continued as long as the sun: and men shall be blessed in him: all nations shall call him blessed." Mark how the saints rejoice and bless God; what! shall all nations come in and serve Christ? shall there come multitudes in and join the church? " Blessed be the Lord God, the God of Israel, who only doeth wondrous things, and blessed be his glorious name for ever: and let the whole earth be filled with his glory; Amen, and Amen," saith the church of God then. Let all the saints send forth their echo, Amen; yea, and Amen too to this, that all the earth shall be filled with the glory of Christ; this is that with which they are affected, this is that they desire, as if they should say, This is a blessed thing indeed!

My brethren, it is a good and comely sight in a gracious eye to see multitudes flock to Christ and to his ordinances. It is true that the spirit of antichrist, which is in many, cannot look upon this but with a malevolent eye, and their hearts rage and fret. They love to scatter Christ's church up and down, but to see people flocking to ordinances, to see multitudes come and join themselves to Christ, this they cannot endure. The same malicious spirit that was against Christ, of which we read in the Acts of the Apostles, yea, and in the Gospels too, we find still in such kinds of men. Mark that text, Acts xiii. 44, 45: " Almost the whole city came together to hear the word of God;" to hear a sermon. Now when the Jews " saw the multitude, they were filled with envy:" why, what harm was there done? They saw no harm done, but merely saw the multitude, and they speak against those things that were spoken by Paul, contradicting and blaspheming. Mark again the vile spirits of the Pharisees, who envied at the multitude that followed Christ himself: not only did they envy the apostles, for they might be factious and singular men in their esteem; but what say you to Christ himself? John xii. 19, " The Pharisees said, Perceive ye how ye prevail nothing? behold, the whole world is gone after him." Certainly the same Pharisaical spirit has prevailed in our days. We know that many a godly, painful, conscientious minister, has been ousted of all he had in an instant, and his mouth stopped, though his persecutors had nothing against him, no, not for their own laws, but because he was a popular man, and multitudes followed him. What a dangerous thing has it been of late times for men to be popular, that is, to be such as multitudes would flock to the word preached by them. Certainly it is an evil spirit, for the promise of God to his church is, that there shall come multitudes and join with the people of God in his ordinances.

I know some reply to this, they do not object that multitudes should follow that which is good, but it is the humour and pride of such men to have multitudes to follow after them, and that they oppose. Take heed of putting this accusation off with such a plea. Consider whether it will hold at that great day. The devil himself never pleaded against Christ or any of his ways, but with some colour. Surely these men judge thus by looking into their own hearts; they know that if multitudes should come to them their hearts would be lifted up, and so they judge accordingly of others. But suppose it be so, for men are but men, that they, through corruption, should have any such workings of pride, yet do they say any thing that is not justifiable? do they preach any thing that is not according to Christ? If they do not, then thou shouldst encourage that which is good; and as for that which is evil, leave it to the coming of Christ, except thou canst by prayer and instruction help to remove it. It is worse to envy at multitudes coming to hear the gospel now, than it was for the Jews to envy Paul for multitudes following him, for they thought they could contradict the false doctrine which they supposed Paul preached, and therefore they had some colour for their conduct. But here it is nothing but merely because multitudes come to hear the word. If men preach first in corners privately, where they have but a few auditors, they object: well, if they preach publicly, and multitudes come to hear them, then they cry out of that too. Nothing can please envious and malicious spirits. If we keep ourselves retired, that has exceptions enough, and if we come in a public way, they have exceptions to that too. Here the gross malice and cunning of Satan appear, because when the thing itself cannot be excepted against, he runs to the intention of the heart, and to men's inward aims, and bringeth an argument against that which he knows no man can confute. For who can say that that is either true or false, that men have inward aims of pride, and vain-glory, and self-seeking, in multitudes flocking after them? Nay, suppose we profess before the Lord and Christ, as we desire to stand before him, and answer it at that day, what our aims are, this will not serve the turn. Why, then, my brethren, if men will choose such an argument as cannot possibly be answered before the coming of Christ, and so make a stumblingblock, there is no help, but men must stumble and fall; and many do stumble and fall. However, let "wisdom be justified of her children;" let the saints rejoice in this, that multitudes come to the ministry of the word and to the ordinances of Christ. Be careful and wise in your coming, and give no just occasion for reproach, but all due respect to those to whom you have the most relation.

This you see is the promise, that there shall come in such multitudes to the church. But mark how the promise runs:

"As the sand of the sea." Rabbin Ezra makes an allusion from hence: "As the sand," saith he, "keeps the waves of the sea from breaking in, and drowning the world; so Israel, so the saints, keep the world from being drowned by the waves of God's wrath." I do not say that this is the intention, but the intention of God is mainly to signify the multitudes that should come into the church. Only this idea we may use, as being a comfortable and pretty allusion, and it is a truth that Israel is as the sand of the sea, not only in respect of multitudes, but as the sand to keep in the waves of God's wrath from drowning the world. Were it not for the church of God, the waves of God's wrath would overflow all the world, and the world would quickly be confounded. So saith he, "When the waves of God's anger seem as if they would overflow all the world, they do but see Israel and immediately return back; they retire, and are not able to overflow the world as they desire."

Quando fluctus maris volunt obruere, et submergere mundum, vident Israelem et redeunt et franguntur in seipsis, et non possunt dominari mundo.

Luther, in his comment upon this prophet, makes the second chapter to begin at the tenth verse; from which to the end we have the promise of future mercy to Israel, both to Israel and Judah together. Some part of God's promise of mercy to Israel we have expounded. Now we proceed:

"And it shall come to pass, that in the place." This, according to some, has reference to the land of Canaan, that God will have a very glorious church there, especially in Jerusalem, before the end of the world come; and many prophecies seem to incline that way, as Zech. xii. 6, "Jerusalem shall be inhabited again in her own place, even in Jerusalem." This cannot be meant only of their return out of captivity, that was in the time of Cyrus. The prophet saith, in the day that Jerusalem shall be inhabited, "the feeble among them shall be as David; and the house of David shall be as the angel of God;" and also that God will "pour upon them the spirit of grace and supplication; and they shall look upon him whom they have pierced," ver. 8, 10. The return of their captivity at first was not glorious; if you read the story of it, you find that even all that while they were in a contemptible condition before the surrounding nations. But God speaks here, and in other places, of a glorious return of their captivity, and coming into their own land.

The Jews have a tradition, that there is a time that all the Jews, wherever they die, shall come through *meatus terræ*, and rise again at Jerusalem; and therefore when some of them think they have not long to live, they sell all their possessions, and go and live near Jerusalem, to prevent the trouble of coming through those *meatus terræ*, of which they speak. Thus they are deluded in their conceits.

Buxtorfii Synagoga Judaica.

But yet more generally, "In that place."

Whereas the place of my people was confined to a little and narrow room, hereafter it shall be enlarged. Where I was not known, amongst the heathen, even there shall I be known, and there I shall have a people; and not only a people, but sons, the sons of the living God; and that so apparently, that it shall be said unto them, "Ye are the sons of the living God."

Thus St. Peter seems to interpret this place: 1 Pet. ii. 10, speaking of the Gentiles, that God would have a people among them, the apostle saith, "Which in times past were not a people, but are now the people of God." Interpreters generally conclude that the apostle had reference to this very place in Hosea. We may build then upon this interpretation, that it is the intention of the Spirit of God, that God would call home the Gentiles to himself, and so they that were no people should become his people, his sons. It should be said in that place where before it was said that they knew him not, that now they are his sons. Yea, the heathen shall be brought in, they shall be convinced of the vanity of their idolatry. We worshipped dead stocks; our gods were dead stones. We were vassals to them: but now we see a people come in to the profession of this Christian religion, they worship the living God, their God is the true God: certainly here are the sons of the living God. This is the scope of the Holy Ghost.

Obs. 1. It is a comfortable thing to consider that where God has not been known and worshipped, that afterward in those places God shall be known and worshipped.

That such nations, countries, and towns, which have been in darkness and idolatry, should now have the knowledge of the true God, that the true God should be worshipped amongst them, is a blessed thing. England was once one of the most barbarous nations in the world, and in that place, where it was said, "Ye are not my people," where there was nothing but a company of savage barbarians that worshipped the devil; how in this place, in England, is it said, even by the nations round about us, Surely "they are the sons of the living God!" And so many times in dark corners in the country, where they never had the knowledge of Jesus Christ, but were nursed in popery, and in all kinds of superstitious vanity, God is pleased to send some faithful minister to carry the light of the knowledge of Christ unto them, and efficaciously to work faith in their hearts, and then, oh what an alteration is there in that town! It may be said of many a house and family, in which nothing but blasphemy, atheism, scorn of religion, uncleanness, and all manner of wickedness have been, now it is a family filled with the servants and sons of the living God. As it is a grievous thing to think that in a place where God has been truly worshipped, the devil should be served there; so it is a comfortable thing to think of other places wherein the devil has been served, that God is now truly worshipped there. The Turks have possession of the temple at Jerusalem; there where the ark, and the cherubim, and the seraphim dwelt, now are tigers, and bears, and savage creatures: but on the other side, consider that in places where there have been none but tigers, and bears, and savage creatures, they are now filled with cherubim and seraphim; this is a comfortable thing.

Obs. 2. God has a time to convince the world of the excellency of his saints. It shall be said they "are the sons of the living God." They shall not only be the sons of the living God, but it shall come to pass that it shall be said they are the sons of the living God: all about them shall see such a lustre of the glory of God upon them, that they shall say, Verily, whatever other people have said heretofore, whatever the thoughts of men have been, these are not only the servants, but the sons of the living God. We have an excellent prophecy of this in Zech. xii. 5, "The governors of Judah shall say in their heart, The inhabitants of Jerusalem shall be my strength in the Lord of hosts their God." Not only the people shall be convinced of this, but the governors of Judah shall say in their hearts, Our strength is in the inhabitants of Jerusalem, in the Lord of hosts their God. However they were heretofore scandalized as seditious and factious, and as enemies of the state, yet now the governors of Judah shall acknowledge that their strength is in them, and in the Lord their God, that this Lord of hosts is their God. That time will be a blessed time when the governors of Judah shall come to be convinced of this; when God shall so manifest the excellencies of his saints, as that both great and small shall confess them to be "the sons of the living God." It is promised to the church of Philadelphia, Rev. iii. 9, that the Lord would make them that said they were Jews and were not, and said they were the church and were not, but were "of the synagogue of Satan, to come and worship before their feet, and to know that I have loved thee." There is a time that ungodly men shall be forced to know that God loves his people.

And one thing, amongst the rest, that will much convince the men of the world of the excellency of the saints, will be the beauty of God's ordinances that shall be set up amongst them, that shall even dazzle the eyes of the beholders. For this you have an excellent promise, Ezek. xxxvii. 28, "The heathen shall know that I the Lord do sanctify Israel." How shall they know it? "When my sanctuary shall be in the midst of them for evermore:" they shall know that I the Lord do sanctify Israel, when the beauty of my ordinances shall appear in them.

And if God be not only satisfied in doing good to his people, but he will have the world know it, and be convinced of it; let the people of God then not be satisfied only in having their hearts upon God, but let the world know that they love God too. You must do that which will make it appear to all the world that you are the children of the living God. "Let your light so shine before men, that they, seeing your good works, may glorify your Father which is in heaven." It is one thing to do a thing that *may* be seen, and another thing to do a thing that *it* may be seen: and yet God's people may do both; not do good only that may be seen, but if they keep the glory of God in their eye, as the highest aim, they may desire, and be willing too, that it may be seen to the praise of God. But this, I confess, requires some strength of grace, so to act, and yet to keep the heart upright. The excellency of grace consists not in casting off the outward comforts of the world, but to know how to enjoy them, and to overrule them for God: so the strength of grace consists not in forbearing such actions as are taken notice of by men, or not daring to aim to publish those things that have excellency in them, but in having the heart enabled to do this, and yet to keep it under, and to keep God above in his right place.

Obs. 3. It is a great blessing to God's children that they shall be accounted so before others. It shall be said they are sons.

Not only that they shall be so, but that they shall be accounted so. "Blessed are the peacemakers: for they shall be called the children of God," Matt. v. 9. This is a blessing, not only to be God's children, but to be called God's children; we must account it so, and therefore we must walk so as may convince all with whom we converse that we are the children of God. Let us not think this sufficient; Well, let me approve my heart to God, and then what need I care what all the world thinks of me. God promises it as a blessing to have his people called the children of God; then this must not be slighted. You find in the gospel that Christ often made it his great business to make it manifest to the world that he was sent of God; he would have them know that his Father sent him, and that he came from him: so the people of God should count it a blessing, and walk so as they may obtain such a blessing, that the world may know that they are of God.

Obs. 4. The grace of God under the gospel, is more full and glorious than the grace of God under the law. "In the place where it was said unto them, Ye are not my people, there it shall be said unto them, Ye are the sons of the living God."

Mark, it is not in the place where it was said they "are not my people," it shall be said to them, they are my people. No; but further, it shall be said they are sons, and "sons of the living God:" this goes beyond being his people.

For this is spoken of the state of the church under the gospel: they were God's people indeed under the law; but the appellation, "the sons of the living God," is reserved for the times under the gospel. Sometimes under the law they are called by the name of sons; but it appeareth by this text, that in comparison of that glorious sonship which they shall have under the times of the gospel, that in former times they were rather servants than sons. There is very little of our adoption in Christ revealed in the Old Testament. No, that was reserved for the Son of God, for him that came out of the bosom of the Father, and brought the treasures of his Father's counsel to the world to reveal. Both adoption and eternal life were very little made known in the time of the law, therefore St. Paul saith, that "life and immortality were brought to light through the gospel," 2 Tim. i. 10.

(2.) Sons, because, in the time of the gospel, the spirits of the saints are of son-like dispositions, they are ingenuous, not mercenary. In the time of the law, God induced his people to obey by offering rewards, especially prosperity in outward things; but in the time of the gospel we have no such rewards in temporals. In the time of the law afflictions are not much spoken of, but much outward prosperity; but in the time of the gospel more affliction, because the dispositions of the hearts of people should not be so mercenary as they were before, they should be an ingenuous, willing people in the day of Christ's power.

(3.) Sons, because of the son-like affection toward God their Father, out of a natural στοργὴ, that they should have more than in the times of the law. I suppose some of you have heard of the story of the son of Crœsus; though he was dumb all his days, when he perceived a soldier striking his father his affection broke the bars of his speech, and he cried out to the soldier to spare his father. This is the affection of a son, and these affections God looks for from his children, especially in the time of the gospel, that they should hear no wrong done to him; but though they could never speak in their own cause, yet they should be sure to speak in their Father's cause.

(4.) Sons, because they have not such a spirit of servility upon them as they had in the time of the law. Christ is come to redeem us, that we might "serve the Lord in holiness and righteousness before him, without fear, all the days of our life;" to take away the spirit of fear. Hence the apostle saith, 2 Tim. i. 7, We have not received "the spirit of fear; but of power, and of love, and of a sound mind:" and Heb. ii. 15, Christ is come "to deliver them who through fear of death were all their lifetime subject to bondage." The spirit of a son is not the spirit of fear: "Ye have not received the spirit of bondage again to fear; but ye have received the Spirit of adoption, whereby we cry, Abba, Father," Rom. viii. 15. It is unseemly in the children of God, especially in the time of the gospel, to be of such servile spirits as to fear every little danger; to be distracted and amazed. Has not God revealed himself to us as a Father to his children, that we should not fear? He would not have us fear himself with a servile fear, as men do, and therefore surely not to fear men, be they what they will. We are sons.

(5.) Sons. Not *only* sons, for we might find in Scripture where the people of God, under the law, perhaps are sometimes called so, but elder sons, sons come to years; (it is true, they were before us, and so in that respect we are not elder;) not children under tutorage, not under schoolmasters and governors, as they were under the law. You know what comparison the Scripture makes of the difference between the church in the time of the gospel, and that in the time of the law. In the time of the law it is true indeed they were children; but how? they were children under tutors and governors, they were not as yet come to years, they were but as young children that were put out to school. But now, as the apostle saith, Gal. iv. 5, Christ hath redeemed us from being under the law, "that we might receive the adoption of sons:" mark, that we *might* receive it; so that now the state of the church is like a child that is of age, and by that is freed from his tutors and governors, and comes to his inheritance, *sui juris*, as it were.

Therefore the saints now are not to be dealt with as if still they were in their childish condition. How were the Jews dealt with in their childish condition? Thus, they had external things to gain them to serve God, they worshipped God much in external things. As we deal with children, we give them apples and fine things to induce them to obey, so God dealt with them. And as children, when they begin to learn, must have a great many pictures in their book; so God taught the Jews with outward ceremonies, which afterward the Scripture calls but beggarly rudiments. Children, you know, are pleased much with gay things; and they that would bring Jewish ceremonies, or ceremonies of their own invention, into the church, treat the church as if in her childish condition still, as if gay things would please her. Therefore they must have pictures, and images, and such things to gratify the people, which make the people of God beneath themselves, as if they were yet children. No, in the state of the gospel they are come to the adoption of sons. And so children you know are pleased with hearing music, and pipes, and such things, which men would bring still into the church in the time of the gospel. I remember Justin Martyr, in answer to that about musical instruments, saith that they are fit for children and fools, as organs and the like, and therefore they were not in use in the church. And indeed, for the childish state of the church those things are fit, but now when they are come to the adoption of sons, other services that are more spiritual are more suitable and honourable. As a man, that is grown to be a man, would think himself wronged much to be taught as a child, to be put off with gay things; so should the people of God under the gospel think it a great wrong that has been done them, when men have sought to teach them with pictures and images, instead of spiritual instruction.

Τὸ μετὰ τῶν ἀψύχων ὀργάνων ᾆσαι τοῖς νηπίοις ἁρμόδιον, διὸ ἐν ταῖς ἐκκλησίαις προαίρεται ἡ χρῆσις ὀργάνων καὶ τῶν ἄλλων νηπίοις ὄντων ἁρμοδιῶν. 107. Quest. ad Orthodoxos.

Obs. 5. When God is pleased to be reconciled to a people, he is as fully theirs as ever, yea, sometimes more fully. "It shall be said, Ye are the sons of the living God." Israel, that was cast off from God, now shall be brought in more fully than before. He comes rather with more full grace than formerly he did.

People before, but sons now. Oh what an encouragement is this to all apostatizing souls that have fallen off from God! Come in, come in, and be reconciled to God, and thou shalt not only find God as good as ever thou didst, but thou shalt find him much better and much sweeter than ever thou didst in all thy life. Seldom we act so. When men fall out one with another, though possibly they may be reconciled, yet it is seldom that they are so fully reconciled, so fully one as they were before; they are but as a broken vessel soldered together, that is very weak in the soldering place; or as garments that have been rent, and are mended, soon torn, and quickly ready to fall in pieces in the place where they were mended: it is not so between God and a penitent soul.

Again, "sons," not only of God, but "of the living God." There is much in this, that the people of God under the gospel should be called the "sons of the living God." The life of God is the glory of God: he swears by his life: by this he is distinguished from the heathen gods, that he is the living God. Life is the most excellent thing in the world: Austin therefore saith, that the life of a fly is more excellent than the sun in the firmament: and certainly it is the glory of God, that he is the living God. God, as the living God, is the object of our faith, and so he is the happiness of his people: "Trust in the living God," 1 Tim. vi. 17. "My soul thirsteth for God, for the living God: O when shall I come and appear before God?" Psal. xlii. 2.

But why is God called "the living God" in reference to his church here? This is a treasure of comfort to his people, that he is called the living God in reference to his church. God would hereby declare to them that all that is in him shall be active for the good of his church for ever. He will show himself not only to be a God, but a living God. He will show all his attributes to be living attributes, for the good of his people. Did God show himself active for his people in former times? much more may his church in the time of the gospel, expect the Lord to manifest himself to be active amongst them. Therefore we may make use of what we read of God's activeness for the good of his church in former times, to plead with God to show himself as active now. See how the church pleads it: "Awake, awake, put on strength, O arm of the Lord; awake, as in the ancient days, in the generations of old. Art not thou it that hath cut Rahab, and wounded the dragon? Art thou not it which hath dried the sea, the waters of the great deep?" Isa. li. 9, 10. O Lord, hast thou not shown thyself glorious in defence of thy people, in helping thy servants in their great straits, and in destroying thine enemies? wilt not thou be so still? In the times of the gospel we may expect more activeness of God than ever he manifested since the world began. Therefore, when God would set out the state of the church under the gospel, mark how he takes that title to himself. Rev. iv. 9, the four living creatures (mentioned in the verses before, by which is meant the state of the church under the gospel) "give glory and honour and thanks to him that sat on the throne, who liveth for ever and ever;" and ver. 10, "the four and twenty elders fell down before Him that sat on the throne, and worshipped him that liveth for ever and ever;" and chap. v. 14, both join together: "The four living creatures said, Amen. And the four and twenty elders fell down and worshipped him that liveth for ever;" and chap. x. 5, 6, "The angel which I saw stand upon the sea and upon the earth lifted up his hand to heaven, and sware by him that liveth for ever and ever." Thus life, the attribute of God, is made use of for the state of the church in the gospel, to show how active God will be for them. Hence, Heb. xii. 22, the church is called "the city of the living God." Now to apply this to ourselves.

Obs. 1. If we expect that God should be a living God to us, it becomes not us to have dead hearts in his service. If God be active for our good, let us be active for his honour. A living, and a lively Christian, is beautiful in the eyes of God and man. Let us labour not only to be living, but to be lively, for God and his cause. Abundance of service and good may living and lively Christians do in the places where they live, especially in these times. But oh how few are there, who are active and stirring, and are carried on by the spirit of wisdom and zeal for God and his cause! Away now with our cold and dead wishes and desires, let us up and be doing, and the Lord will be with us. The adversaries are lively; so saith the psalmist, "Mine enemies are lively, and they are strong," Psal. xxxviii. 19. We may well make use of that expression too; our enemies are lively and strong; shall they be more lively and active for Satan, and for their lusts, than we for the living God? As God is the object of our happiness as he is the living God, so we are the object of God's delight as we are living too. "God is not the God of the dead, but of the living."

Obs. 2. We should be lively and active, for we live upon the bread of life, and drink the water of life, we have lively oracles, lively ordinances, therefore life and activity are required of us: "fervent in spirit, serving the Lord," Rom. xii. 11; be burning, boiling up in your spirits, for you are serving the Lord, the living God: dead spirits become not the services of the living God. Grace is called "the Divine nature," 2 Pet. i. 4. It is also called the very "life of God," Eph. iv. 18. It is impossible, then, but a Christian must needs be active, seeing his grace is the very life of God in him.

Τῷ πνεύματι ζέοντες.

Obs. 3. By being lively and active, we shall prevent abundance of temptations that otherwise will befall us. A dead, lazy spirit is liable to a thousand temptations: as when the honey is boiling, the flies will not come to it; when it is set in the window and grows cold, then they come to it: so when the spirits of men are boiling hot for God, Beelzebub, the god of flies, with his temptations, comes not upon them; but when their spirits begin to cool, and grow dull and heavy, then comes Beelzebub, and all manner of temptation, upon their souls. The breath that comes from the body of a man is warm, but the breath that comes from a pair of bellows is cold, because it is artificial; so when men are cold in the services of God, it is to be feared that their breath in praying, and other duties, is but artificial; it is not the breath of life; if it were living it would be warm. That was the reason why God would not have an ass offered him in the law in sacrifice, but his neck must be broken, because the ass is a dull creature: God loves not dull creatures in his service.

I have read of a people who worshipped the sun for their god, to which they sacrificed a flying horse; the reason was this, because they would offer to the sun somewhat suitable to it. They honoured the sun for the swiftness of his motion, and a horse you know is a swift creature, and therefore somewhat suitable, especially having the emblem of wings upon him. They that would honour the sun as a god for swiftness, would not offer a snail, but a flying horse; so if we honour God for a living God, an active God, let us not offer snails to him, dull, heavy, sluggish services, but quick and lively hearts.

That which the courtiers of Nebuchadnezzar flatteringly said unto him, in the name of God say I to you, "Live for ever." Saith Christ, "As the living Father hath sent me, and I live by the Father; so he that eateth me, even he shall live by me," John vi. 57. Christ was active, exceedingly active, in the work he was sent about; why? because "the living Father sent him:" so let us consider that in all our services and employments it is a living God that sets us about them, and we should be active as Christ was.

I am willing a little to enlarge on this, because of its importance to our present times, and give me leave to do it by telling you what this Christian activeness is.

1. Stay not for company in any good cause. An active spirit will not stay till he see others to accompany him, but if he must go, rather than the cause should fall he will go alone. Mark that saying, Isa. li. 2, "I called Abraham alone, and blessed him." Be not discouraged, if God give thee a zealous spirit, and others will not appear; God calls thee alone, and he will bless thee.

2. When you have company do not lag behind, but be willing to be foremost, rather than any cause of God should suffer by your indolence. Do not wait till others go before you. Hence in Prov. xxx. 31, amongst the goings of many things, the going of the he-goat is said to be very comely; why? because he is accustomed to go before the flock. Those who, out of love to the cause of God, are willing, if they are called to it, to go before the flock, go comely in the eyes of God.

3. Do not forbear the work till all difficulties about it are over. That is a sluggish spirit that will not begin the work, till they can see how all the difficulties about the work are, or may be, removed. You must up and be doing, be doing presently, and fall to work wisely, to prevent and avoid the difficulties that come in it. As those active spirits did, of whom we read in Neh. iv. 17; when they were at work, with one of their hands they wrought, and with the other hand they held a weapon; they did not stay the building of the wall of Jerusalem till all their adversaries were quashed, but immediately began it. This is an active spirit.

4. We must not be active in a sudden mood, and upon a mere flash, and then give over, but in a constant, solid way. Active, yet solid. Many indeed are stirring and active for the present, but are like the flame of a wisp of straw, which makes a noise and a great stir for the present, but soon after there remains nothing but black, dead ashes. But we must be considerately active. Therefore observe, the Scripture saith (speaking of the saints, specially in the time of the gospel) that they are "lively stones," 1 Pet. ii. 5. What! a stone, and yet lively? A stone, of all things, is most dead, and so it is used to describe a dead spirit in the story of Nabal; when Abigail came to tell him of the business of David, "his heart died within him, and he became as a stone." What is this but to show, that though we must be lively and active, yet we must be solid, firm, and substantial in our activeness; and again, that when we are solid, firm, and substantial, yet we must be lively. There are many that know not how to be active solidly, and therefore grow slight and vain in their activity; and many others, striving to be solid and substantial, quickly grow dull; many, through a kind of affected gravity, would forsooth be accounted solid and wise, and so become at last dull, and heavy, and of very little use in the church of God. Take heed of either, and labour to unite both together: that is acceptable to God, to be living stones before him.

Ver. 11. *Then shall the children of Judah and the children of Israel be gathered together, and appoint themselves one head, and they shall come up out of the land: for great shall be the day of Jezreel.*

Here you have a promise both to Israel and Judah together. Great was the enmity between Judah and Israel heretofore. They worshipped the same God, but in divers manners. Judah worshipped God according to his own institution; and Israel worshipped the same God, but according to their own inventions, as might best suit with their political ends. Bitterness and vexation abounded between these two people, though worshipping the same God; and God here makes it a great matter to bring these two together, that they should be gathered together in one. Here we have the promise: First, that there shall be a union. Secondly, that there shall be a union under one head. Hence

Obs. 1. The enmity of such as seem not to differ much in matters of religion, and yet do differ, is sometimes exceedingly great and bitter. There shall be a union between Judah and Israel, saith God. Here is a mercy, a wonderful work of the Lord. It requires a mighty work of God to reconcile those who differ even but little. It appears it was so between Judah and Israel. 2 Chron. xxviii. 9, the prophet Oded tells the children of Israel, when he came to reprove them after the slaughter committed by them of the children of Judah, "Ye have slain them in a rage that reacheth up unto heaven." What a rage was this! and yet thus the people of Israel were enraged against the people of Judah; yea, they were often more bitter against each other, than they were against the heathen, the Philistines, Assyrians, and Egyptians, who were round about them.

Thus it has been, and until that blessed time come here spoken of, thus it will be. Though the Calvinists and Lutherans agree together against papists in fundamental articles, yet, oh the bitterness of their spirits one against another! A Lutheran is scarce so bitter against a papist as he is against a Calvinist. Luther himself complains,* Not only openly wicked men are our enemies, but even our friends, and those who at first received the doctrine of the gospel from us, persecute us most bitterly. And he complains particularly of Zuinglius;† Zuinglius accuses me of every wickedness and cruelty, so that the papists do not tear me so much as these my friends. Again, speaking of Carolostadius,‡ He is more deadly against me, more set against me, than any of mine enemies ever were. Even he, whom God used for the furtherance of the gospel, has bitterness to another, with whom he agrees in doctrine.

And has it not been so amongst us? Those who are protestants, and such as are nick-named puritans, though they agree in all the fundamental points against popery, yet for some difference in matter of discipline and ceremonies, oh what bitterness of spirit is there! It is so much the more sinful in those who say that discipline and ceremonies are but indifferent things; they are specially to be blamed for bitterness on their side, because the conscience of the other is bound up, and cannot yield. Yea, not only such as contend against popish discipline, but such as go a degree further in reformation of discipline, yet because they differ in some few particulars, oh the bitterness of spirit that exists even among them! These are times that call all the people of God to see in what they can agree, and in that to join against the common adversary, and not to tear one another by dissensions. God may justly give us over to our adversaries, if we agree not among ourselves, and they may chain us together. Perhaps a prison may make us agree, as it was said of Ridley and Hooper. Ridley opposed Hooper in point of ceremonies, and they could not agree, yet when they came to prison they agreed well enough there. The Lord deliver us from that medicine of our dissensions, that we be not made so to agree; yea, that we be not soldered together by our own blood.

Obs. 2. God has a time to gather Judah and Israel together, that is, to bring peace to his church. God has a time to gather all his churches together, that there shall be a universal peace amongst his churches.

For though it be meant here of Judah and Israel literally, yet Israel and Judah set out to us all the churches of God that shall exist among the Gentiles: and as God will fulfil this scripture literally, so he will fulfil it spiritually, to bring Judah and Israel, that is, all the churches of God, under one head. "Ephraim shall not envy Judah, and Judah shall not vex Ephraim," Isa. xi. 13. Ephraim envied Judah, because Judah challenged to himself the true worship of God; and Judah on the other side envied Ephraim, because he was the greatest; they were vexing spirits one against another. This shall not always be, saith God, but "the envy of Ephraim shall depart," I will take away this envious, vexatious spirit. Those two staves of which the Holy Ghost speaks in Zech. xi. 10, 11, 14, the staff of "Beauty," and the staff of "Bands," were both broken, but God has a time to unite them together again, and for that, mark that excellent prophecy in Ezek. xxxvii. 16, 17, 22, 24. There you find declared, God brings Judah and Israel, and joins those sticks together again. "Son of man, take thee one stick, and write upon it, For Judah, and for the children of Israel his companions: then take another stick, and write upon it, For Joseph, the stick of Ephraim, and for all the house of Israel his companions: and join them one to another into one stick; and they shall become one in thine hand." And then, ver. 19, this is interpreted of the union of them, "Behold, I will take the stick of Joseph, which is in the hand of Ephraim, and the tribes of Israel his fellows, and will put them with him, even with the stick of Judah, and make them one stick, and they shall be one in mine hand:" and ver. 22, "I will make them one nation in the land upon the mountains of Israel; and one king shall be king to them all." And in the 24th verse that king is said to be David, which we shall afterward show more fully, when we describe the head which they shall be under. Now this God has never yet fulfilled, that the ten tribes, and Judah and Benjamin, should come together and be set in one stick; he has never set together the staff of Bands that was broken, and yet this must be done; it is the great blessing of God upon his churches, the bringing about of this union. Mark that text, Jer. xxxiii. 11; God having promised that in the latter days he would bring Judah and Israel together, and build them as at first: in the 14th verse, "Behold, the days come, saith the Lord, that I will perform that good thing which I have promised unto the house of Israel, and to the house of Judah." What is that good thing that God had promised to the houses of Israel and Judah? That good thing, my brethren, is the building them up together as they were at first. "Behold, how good and how pleasant it is for brethren to dwell together in unity! It is like the precious ointment upon the head, that ran down upon the beard, even Aaron's beard: that went down to the skirts of his garments; as the dew of Hermon, and as the dew that descended upon the mountains of Zion: for there the Lord commanded the blessing, even life for evermore," Psal. cxxxiii. In the churches of God, where this peace and union dwell, there is blessing, there is God commanding blessing, that is, blessing comes powerfully and efficaciously, the blessing of life, and life for evermore. Oh, who would not then love union and peace in the churches! "The Lord shall be king over all the earth: in that day shall there be one Lord, and his name one," Zech. xiv. 9. The churches now have one Lord, they all acknowledge God and Christ to be their Lord; yea, but this Lord has not one name: though they all pretend to honour Christ, and set up Christ, yet this one Lord has many names. But here it is prophesied that there shall be but one Lord, and his name

* Non solum hostes palam impii persequuntur nos, sed etiam hi qui fuerunt dulces amici nostri, qui a nobis acceperunt doctrinam Evangelii, fiunt insensissimi hostes nostri, persequentes nos acerrime.

† Nihil est scelerum aut crudelitatis, cujus me non reum agat, adeo ut nec papistæ me sic lacerent hostes mei, ut illi amici nostri. Ep. ad Mich. Stifelinum.

‡ Infensior mihi est quam ulli hactenus fuerint inimici. Luther ep. ad Spalatinum.

shall be but one. And Zeph. iii. 9, "Then will I turn to the people a pure language, that they may all call upon the name of the Lord, to serve him with one consent." The words in the original are, שכם אחד one shoulder; all the people of God shall have but one shoulder, that they shall set to the service of God. O blessed time, when they shall be so united as to have but one shoulder! And the greater this blessing of Judah's and Israel's gathering together will be, if you consider these two things; I beseech you observe them.

First, That they shall have this perfect union together, even then, when "Israel shall be as the sand of the sea." When there shall be such multitudes flocking to the church, yet then they shall be united in one, and then there shall be peace in the churches. It is not a hard matter, when there are but very few of a church, perhaps half a dozen or half a score, for them to be of one mind, and to agree lovingly together, and to have no divisions nor dissensions among themselves; but when a church grows to be a multitude, then lies the difficulty. When did ever any church, though never so well constituted at first, but increase in divisions and dissensions, as they increased in number and multitude? You find it very hard in a meeting in any society, when any business concerns a great many, so to agree as to be of one and the same mind. An instrument, as a watch, or any thing that has many wheels, is sooner out of frame than that which has but a wheel or two. So when numbers come together about any business, it is mighty hard to bring them to be united in one. There are few families that consist of many persons, but quickly dissensions grow among them: perhaps, where there are two or three in a family they keep well enough together; but where there are seven in a family they cannot so well agree, nor so long a time together, as the seven devils did in Mary Magdalene. But God has made this promise to the church, that though it shall increase as the sand on the sea shore, and that multitudes shall come flocking to it, yet they shall be all gathered together into one, under one head, and they shall have peace.

Secondly, They shall agree in one, not only when they are a multitude, but when they enjoy the full privileges and liberty that Christ has purchased for them, even then there shall be a blessed agreement. For it is spoken here of those times, when they shall come under one head, and Christ alone shall rule them, and not men's inventions. Christ will grant his church those privileges that he has purchased for them, and rule them according to those, and then there shall be a blessed agreement among them all. Men now think it impossible for those liberties to be enjoyed without dissensions; O, say they, let them have but such liberty as they speak of, and we shall have nothing but babbling and divisions. What! shall every man be left to do what he list? why then we shall have nothing but breaches in the church, and heart-burnings one against another. No; Christ has never purchased so much liberty, for every man to do what he lists in things apparently unlawful, against the common principles of religion; in those there may be compulsion. But the liberty which Christ has purchased, is the lawful use of things indifferent, and the lawful use of his ordinances. And though now many think that, in things indifferent, if men be left at their liberty, there will be heart-burning and dissensions, and no peace at all in the church, they are much mistaken in this; for the only way to have true peace in the church, is to leave things as Christ has left them, and to force nothing upon men's consciences that Christ would not have forced; this is the way of peace. And the special way of dissension (we have had experience of it) has been, and ever will be, the urging upon men's consciences those things Christ would not have urged; this makes the greatest rent and division in the church. The urging of uniformity in all indifferent things as necessary to unity, is a most false principle. It is a principle that many have been led by, but it is a false and corrupt principle, and is, and will be found to be, the cause of the greatest distractions.

When the time comes here prophesied of, there shall not be such need of any antichristian chain to unite the servants of God together, but they shall be one without any such doings. It is true, papists and prelatical men cry out against others; they say, there are such divisions among them, none of them can agree, there is more uniformity and unity with us than with them. Mark these two answers to that.

1. They have little cause to boast of their unity, if we consider all; for though many thousands of Christians, and hundreds of faithful, painful, and conscientious ministers of God, (that did more service to God and his church than ever they will do,) be banished out of their country, and put upon miserable extremities, and endure sore afflictions for their conscience' sake, this is no breach of unity with them.

2. But suppose by their power they could have brought all to a uniformity in their own inventions and innovations, as they desired. What then? they have little cause to boast of that unity. Certainly, there the remedy would have been worse than the disease, and work a greater mischief. Their boasting of unity would have been, as if a couple of prisoners chained to a block, and kept close all day, should see others go abroad in the streets at a distance, and should cry out to them, Why do you not take example by us? you keep at a distance one from another; see, we keep close together from morning to night: pray take example by us, and do not go so distant one from another. Would not such an argument be most ridiculous? What is the reason of their union, but their chain? Certainly, there is the same argument in pleading for that uniformity which they force upon men by such a kind of antichristian chain. What breach of unity is it if, in a broad street, one goes a little distant from another? and so what breach is it if, in matters of indifference, one take one way and another another? It is the corrupt and perverse spirits of men that think they cannot have unity, and yet have things as Christ has left them. Christ needs no such things to cause unity in his church, the spirit of his people, which loves truth and peace, is enough to cause the unity he would have. And oh that this gathering together were come, of all churches to be made one, and to be under one head! for abundance of mischief is done now among the churches, and in the world, by the spirit of division and dissension. The devil delights (especially that devil that is the spirit of division) to live in the region of the church. There are some devils especially that are spirits of pride, as the dumb devil, and some of dissension, and some of one kind, and some of another. Cajetan remarks upon Mark v. 8, 9, where our Saviour Christ cast the devils out of the possessed man, they besought him that he would let them enter into the swine, and that he would not send them out of that region; because, saith he, they have several regions where they most haunt, and they that are in such a region are loth to be put out of it, but would fain keep their place. Whether that be so or no we will not say, but this we say, that if there be any region in the world which the unclean spirit of division loves, and is loth to be cast out, it is the region of the church, for there he does the greatest mischief. But Christ has a time to cast this unclean spirit out of the region of the church so effectually, that he never shall return again.

This point, as we meet with it so fitly, and is so fully agreeable to the necessity of our times, I cannot tell, though I go a little beyond the ordinary way of expositions, how to get away from it.

This union of the church is that which will be the stability of it. You have an admirable place for this, Isa. xxxiii. 20, "Thine eyes shall see Jerusalem a quiet habitation." Oh that our eyes might be blessed to behold Jerusalem a quiet habitation! then we should be willing with old Simeon to say, "Lord, now lettest thou thy servant depart in peace, for mine eyes have seen thy salvation." Mark then what follows: "a quiet habitation, a tabernacle that shall not be taken down; not one of the stakes thereof shall ever be removed, neither shall any of the cords thereof be broken. But there the glorious Lord will be unto us a place of broad rivers and streams, wherein shall go no galley with oars, neither shall gallant ship pass thereby." The kingdoms of the world, though they seem to be built upon mountains, yet God will toss them up and down, and they shall come to nothing; but the church, when it is made a quiet habitation, though it be but a tabernacle and set upon stakes, yet this tabernacle shall not be taken down, nor one of the stakes thereof ever removed; though it be tied by lines, yet not a cord thereof shall be broken. Yea, in this the glory of the church consists, for when it is a quiet habitation, the glory of God shall be there, God shall dwell among them as a glorious God. No church was more honourable than the church of Philadelphia, for that is the church the adversaries must come and bow before, Rev. iii. 9, and that church carries brotherly love in its very name, for so it signifies. Cant. vi. 9, "My dove, my undefiled is but one, the only one of her mother." What follows? "The daughters saw her and blessed her; yea, the queens and the concubines, and they praised her." When Christ's dove and undefiled comes once to be but one, the daughters shall see her and bless her. In Isa. xi. 13, you have a promise of Judah and Ephraim's joining together. Mark what follows, chap. xii. 1, "And in that day thou shalt say, O Lord, I will praise thee." Observe, "in that day." And again, ver. 4, "And in that day shall ye say, Praise the Lord, call upon his name, declare his doings among the people, make mention that his name is exalted. Sing unto the Lord; for he hath done excellent things: this is known in all the earth. Cry out and shout, thou inhabitant of Zion." God indeed does excellent things, when he makes Ephraim and Judah to be one. Therefore saith the apostle, 1 Cor. xii. 31, "Yet show I unto you a more excellent way." What is that way? In the chapter following, he writes his commendation of love, the highest commendation of any grace found in the book of God; that is the more excellent way. In Cant. iii. 9, the church is compared to the chariot of Solomon: "The pillars thereof of silver, the bottom thereof of gold, the covering of it of purple, and the midst thereof being paved with love." Then the church rides in triumph in her chariot, when there is much love and peace in the midst of it.

It is true, my brethren, considering the weakness and peevishness of the spirits, yea, of good men as well as evil, we may wonder however this shall come to pass: Is it possible that this shall ever be so? Indeed it must be a mighty work of God to do it. We must not think to effect it by struggling one with another, and to say, We will make them be at peace and unity, or they shall smart for it, and we will pull them together by law. This will not do it; but we must look up to God for the accomplishing of this great thing. Jer. xxxiii. 3, "Thus saith the Lord, Call unto me and I will answer thee, and show thee great and mighty things which thou knowest not." What are those great and mighty things that we must call upon God for? Amongst others, this is a principal one, ver. 7, "And I will cause the captivity of Judah and the captivity of Israel to return, and will build them as at the first," and so make them both one. And then, ver. 9, "It shall be to me a name of joy, a praise and an honour before all the nations of the earth, when they shall hear all the good that I do unto them." Mark, joy, praise, honour, yea, a name of joy, praise, honour, follows upon this blessed union, and that before all the nations of the earth. For the accomplishing of this, "come, Lord Jesus, come quickly!"

Yet let us further observe the difference between the scattering of the wicked, and the scattering of the saints. Judah and Israel were scattered, but now they shall be gathered together.

Obs. 1. There is a great deal of difference between the scattering of the saints, and the scattering of the wicked. When God scatters the saints, he scatters them that they may be gathered; when he scatters the wicked, he scatters them that he may destroy them. Psal. lxviii. 1, "Let God arise, let his enemies be scattered." How scattered? "As smoke is driven away, so drive them away." Smoke, you know, is so driven away and scattered, that it comes to nothing. Psal. cxliv. 6, "Cast forth lightning and scatter them, shoot out thine arrows and destroy them." This is the scattering of the wicked. But as for the saints, they may be scattered, but it is to spread abroad the gospel by them in the world. Acts viii. 4, "They that were scattered abroad" (by reason of the persecution of Saul) "went every where preaching the word." But within awhile our God shall come, and all his saints with him, and he will gather together the outcasts of Israel with abundance of mercy. Micah iv. 6, "In that day, saith the Lord, will I assemble her that halteth, and I will gather her that is driven out, and her that I have afflicted." Isa. liv. 7, "For a small moment have I forsaken thee, but with great mercies will I gather thee." God will gather his people with great mercies. God has fulfilled this in a great part in our eyes even this day. Many of those who were driven out of their places and country, those that were afflicted, and those the land could not bear, God has gathered together these outcasts of Israel. Let every one take heed how he hinders this work of the Lord, and how he adds affliction to those that have been afflicted.

Obs. 2. The more the gospel prevails, the more peace there shall be. They shall "be gathered together;" that is, in the time of the gospel, when that shall prevail, then Judah and Israel shall be gathered together.

The gospel is not the cause of divisions, of seditions, of factions. No; it is a gospel of peace, the Prince of it is a Prince of peace, the embassage of it is an embassage of peace. It is next to blasphemy, if not blasphemy itself, to say that since the preaching and profession of the gospel we have had no peace, but it causes factions and divisions among the people. People who are in the dark sit still and quiet together, as it is said of the Egyptians, when they were in the dark for those three days together, they stirred not from their seats, there was no noise among them; shall the light be blamed, because afterward, when it came, every one stirred and went, one one way, and another another? So when we were in gross darkness, we saw nothing, we knew nothing; now light begins to break forth, and one searches after one truth, and another after another, and yet we cannot attain to perfection; shall we accuse the light for this? Yea, but we see too apparently that those who seem the strictest of all, that would worship God (as they say) in the purest manner in his ordinances; yet there are woeful divisions and distractions even amongst them. How then is the gospel a gospel of peace?

Consider this one reason in answer to this, to satisfy your consciences, that the gospel may not be blamed, for indeed where the gospel comes there is promised peace. Because so long as we are here we are partly flesh and partly spirit. Those who have the gospel prevail with their consciences, cannot move any further than they can see light for, and their consciences will give them leave. But other men have more liberty, they quarrel not one with another; why? because they have wide, elastic consciences: having ends of their own, they will yield to any thing to attain those ends; so that here they have this advantage, that if they see contention will bring them more trouble than they conceive the thing is worth, they will condescend, though it be against the light of conscience; whilst others upon whom the light of the gospel has prevailed, have that bond upon conscience, that though all the world should differ from them, they must be content to lie down and suffer; they cannot yield; though you would give them all the world, they cannot go against that light. They may search, and it may trouble them that their apprehensions of things should be different from the apprehensions of their brethren, and that they cannot yield to that to which their brethren yield. It is true they should be humbled, and suspect their hearts, and look to themselves, and fall down before God and pray, and use all means for advice and counsel, and consider of things again and again. But suppose they have done all this, and yet the Lord does not reveal to them any further light, though it be a sad affliction to them, yet they must lie down under it, for they cannot yield; one known truth is more to them than all the world; therefore, unless others will bear with them in their infirmity, they will suffer whatever men will lay upon them.

The world calls this obstinacy, and stiffness, and being wedded to their own opinion; but they know it is otherwise, and can appeal to God and say, Lord, thou knowest what a sad affliction it is unto me, that I cannot see what my brother sees, and that I cannot yield to what my brother yields: thou hast hid it from me: I will wait upon thee till thou shalt reveal it; and in the mean time I will be quiet, and not make disturbance in the places where I come, but pray, pray, pray for light, and that thou wouldst incline the heart of my brethren unto me, that they may not have hard thoughts of me. Do but thus, thou shalt have peace with God, and in thine own heart.

If we would have light let into us, we must so prize it, as to be willing that in the discussion of truths there should be some hazard of differences in lesser things. If a man have a house closed on every side with a thick brick wall, and he is so desirous to keep his house safe and strong, that he will rather all his days sit in the dark, than be at the trouble to have a hole digged or a few bricks broken to let in any light, we should accuse that man of folly. It is true, we must not be so desirous of light, as to break so much of the wall as to endanger the house, we must keep that safe; but yet it is difficult to let in light without taking away some bricks, and occasioning some trouble. A child, when he sees the workman with his tools breaking the wall, and making a deal of rubbish, thinks he is pulling down the house; but a wise man knows it is but a little trouble for the present, to let in light that shall be for the beauty of the house afterward.

Agreement in error is far worse than division for the sake of truth. Better to be divided from men that are erroneous, than to agree with them in the ways of their error. A company gathered without the covenant of peace, without the observance of God's law, is a headless multitude, says Bernard, it has much of Babylon, but little of Jerusalem.

Ubi sive fœdere pacis, sive observantia legis, sive disciplina et regimine, Acephala multitudo congregata fuerit, non est civitas sed confusio, Babylonem exhibet, Hierosolymaticum nihil habet. Bern. Ser. 5. de dedic. Eccles.

Obs. 3. As soon as any are converted to the faith, they are of a gathering disposition. They desire to gather to the saints immediately. Every child of God is a gatherer; as Solomon is called Ecclesiastes, in the Greek, but the Hebrew word is interpreted by some, a soul gathered, because it is in the feminine gender. None in the world love good fellowship so much as the saints of God. They fly as doves to their windows, and doves you know fly in great flocks, thousands together. The more spiritual any one is, of the more joining and uniting nature he is. Thousands of beams of the sun will meet together in one, better than the beams of a candle. In the apostles' times, when men were converted, it is said, they "were added to the church," they gathered presently. So, in Isa. lxvi. 20, it is observable: "They shall bring all your brethren for an offering unto the Lord out of all nations upon horses, and in chariots, and in litters." How comes this? Those who dwell a great way off shall not make that their excuse for not joining the people of God, It is a great journey; no, but there are horses to be got. But it may be some cannot ride? Then get chariots. But some, perhaps, are so weak that they can neither ride on horses nor in chariots. Then they will get litters; and litters you know are to carry weak and sick persons. This shows the intention of spirit in the people of God to be gathered to the church, either to be carried on horses, or in chariots, or in litters, one way or other they will come and join themselves to the people of God. For there is the presence of Christ, and the protection of Christ, and the communication of Christ in their union and communion, and "Wheresoever the body is, thither will the eagles be gathered together." Oh they love a life to be going towards Zion, gathering one to another, as in Psal. lxxxiv. 7, "They go from strength to strength, every one of them in Zion appeareth before God." "From strength to strength," that is, thus: from one place of the country perhaps there come half a score, or twenty, to go toward Zion, and perhaps before they come to such a town or turning they meet with half a score more, and so they grow stronger; when they are a mile or two farther perhaps they meet with another town coming, and they join presently and are stronger; and so they go from strength to strength comfortably together till they come before God in Zion.

קהלת

"They shall appoint themselves one head." Although they are multitudes, and are as the sand of the sea, yet this is no great matter, unless they come under one head, and a right head too. Multitudes are not a sufficient argument of truth. A multitude coming under one Head, under Christ as one Head, they are the true church. The papists give universality as the mark of the church, that there are so many papists in the world.

But, 1. We must not regard how many the people are, but under what head they are: they shall be gathered under one head: look to the head they follow; for St. Paul tells us, that there shall be an apostacy before the revelation of that man of sin, 2 Thess. ii. 3. And Rev. xiii. 3, "All the world wondered after the beast:" and ver. 2, "The dragon gave him his power, and his seat, and great authority:" and Rev. xvii. 1, "The great whore that sitteth upon many waters;" and, ver. 15, these "many waters" are interpreted to be "peoples, and multitudes, and nations, and tongues." The whore sits upon them, that is, uses them vilely and basely; sits upon the very consciences of them in a base manner. And who does she sit upon? Upon peoples and multitudes. It is not an argument then of a true church, though they are multitudes, though they are as the sand of the sea, though they are gathered together, for they must be gathered under one head, under Christ.

2. Neither is unity a sufficient argument of the verity of the church. They shall be gathered together, they shall be joined together in one way, with one consent; but if it be not under one head, they are like Simeon and Levi, brethren in iniquity. It is not enough that we are one, unless we are one in Christ; and that is a blessed union: for there shall be much unity under an-

tichrist. "These have one mind, and they shall give their power and strength unto the beast," Rev. xvii. 13. And chap. xviii. 5, "her sins have reached unto heaven." Their sins cleave together, and so get up to heaven. Here is a union of persons, and a union of sins amongst them. The Turks have as little dissension in their religion as any; they are all united in one. But well may that garment have no seam, that has no shape. Look at Psal. lxxxiii. 5, "They have consulted together with one consent, they are confederate against thee." There are two or three things exceedingly observable in this psalm about the union of the wicked: First you have ten countries join together against the church; ver. 6—8, "The tabernacles of Edom, and the Ishmaelites; of Moab, and the Hagarenes; Gebal, and Ammon, and Amalek; the Philistines with the inhabitants of Tyre; Assur also is joined with them: they have holpen the children of Lot." And it was not by accident that they joined, but in a deliberate way, "they consulted together," and not only consulted together, but consulted together "with one consent," or heartily, for לב יחדו which is translated there, with one consent, signifies, with heart together, their very heart was in the consultation; but mark, it was "against thy hidden ones," so ver. 3. Let them consult together, let ten of them consult together, and consult with their hearts, yet the saints are God's hidden ones. "They shall surely gather together, but not by me: whosoever shall gather together against thee shall fall for thy sake," Isa. liv. 15. My brethren, peace, though we should all desire it, yet not at too costly a price; peace is too chargeable when it costs us the loss of any truth. Take heed of any such costly peace: "Though hand join in hand" together in wickedness, yet they "shall not be unpunished," Prov. xvi. 5. And Nahum i. 10, "While they are folded together as thorns, they shall be devoured as stubble fully dry." Wicked men are as thorns to prick the people of God, yea, they are thorns folded together, there is a peace amongst them: yet, though they be folded together, they shall be devoured, they shall be devoured even in their folding. The division that comes by truth is better than the union that comes by error. It is a notable speech of Luther, Rather than any thing should fall of the kingdom of Christ and his glory, let not only peace go, but let heaven and earth go too: we should love peace, yet peace and truth better.

Potius quam aliquid regno Christi, et gloriæ ejus decedat, ruat non solum pax, sed cœlum et terra. Luther.

What is this "head?"

I find both the Jews and divers of the ancients, Theodoret, Cyril, and others, would make this head to be Zerubbabel, and only to have reference to the return of the people from their Babylonish captivity. But this certainly cannot be, for these two reasons, to name no more.

First, Because both Israel and Judah are here to join together and to return out of the land: there it was Judah, and not the ten tribes, that were delivered from their captivity.

Secondly, Compare this scripture with others, and we shall find that Zerubbabel cannot be meant. In Ezek xxxiv. and xxxvii., we have expressions such as plainly appear that they are but comments upon this text of Hosea (for Ezekiel prophesied after Hosea): and especially in the 37th chapter we have a prophecy of the union of all the tribes together, Judah and Israel; and ver. 24, "David my servant shall be king over them;" and ver. 25, "My servant David shall be their prince for ever." The one head which they shall have when they come together shall be David. And so in chap. xxxiv. 23, "I will set one shepherd over them, and he shall feed them, even my servant David;" and ver. 24, "I the Lord will be their God, and my servant David a prince among them." That head then that they shall have shall be David, not Zerubbabel. Now by David we are to understand Christ clearly, for in other places, as in Isa. lv. 3, "I will make an everlasting covenant with you, even the sure mercies of David," they can only be meant of the sure mercies of Christ; and so it is interpreted by St. Paul, Acts xiii. 34. Therefore, then, we conclude certainly this is meant of Christ; they shall appoint Christ to be their Head.

This is then the first great point in this text, a head-point of divinity indeed, that Jesus Christ is the Head of the church. And, secondly, he shall be so appointed.

Obs. Jesus Christ is the Head of the church, and shall appear so hereafter, further than now he doth.

The church is not a headless multitude, it is a community of saints who have a glorious Head. That body cannot be contemptible that has a Head so honourable. It is he that is the brightness of his Father's glory, in whom "all fulness dwells," yea, "the fulness of the Godhead bodily." It is he by whom all things consist, that is the beginning of all things. It is he that is the Head of angels themselves: "Ye are complete in him, which is the Head of all principality and power," Col. ii. 10.

1. He is the Head of angels; how?

(1.) Because the angels are joined together with the church, and are part of the church triumphant, and so Christ is their Head.

(2.) Yea, the angels have influence from him. That grace which they have from God, which is beyond naturals, is from Christ, for Christ is *canalis gratiæ*, the channel of grace from God. Their establishment in their condition is from Christ, for it is not due to them in a natural way; yea, the glory they shall have in joining with the church is above that which is due to their natural state, and all that is from Christ.

2. He is the Head of all men; "the Head of every man is Christ," 1 Cor. xi. 3. "The Head of every man;" how? What! are all men in the world the body of Christ? if he be the Head, then it seems they are all the members. No, though Christ be the Head of angels, yet angels are not said to be members of him; yea, in the same place of the Corinthians, God is said to be the head of Christ, and yet Christ is not a member of God. So that he may be the Head of every man, and yet every man not a member of Christ. He is the Head of every man in regard of that superiority that Christ has over every man, and some kind of influence even from Christ comes to every man; he enlighteneth every man that cometh into the world.

3. Yea, he that is the Head of his church, is the Head of all things; "God hath given him to be the Head over all things to the church," Eph. i. 22. Mark it, it is a most admirable place, that Christ is "the Head of all things." But how? "To the church," for the sake of the church, as aiming at the good of the church especially.

(1.) It is the honour of the church to have such a Head, who is the brightness of his Father's glory, the Head of angels, the Head of every man, the Head of all things for the good of his church.

(2.) He is their Head because he is their strength. Christ is the Head of the church in regard of the strength that the church has by him. An oppressed multitude cannot help itself if they have no head, but if God shall please to give them strength and a head, and that in a legal way, if they have hearts they may deliver themselves from oppression, this God has done for us; if therefore God does not vote us to misery and slavery, if we be not a people given up of God to ruin, we may have help. The church is a communion of saints oppressed here in the world; their strength is in heaven, in their Head, who has received all power to exercise it for them; to him they cleave, for him they bless God, even the Father, because he is their strength.

(3.) He is their Head, because the saints hold all upon Christ; all that they have they hold *in Capite*, as the best tenure of all. The tenure upon which the saints hold all their comfort, all their good in this world, is in another way than other men hold it: other men have what they have through the bounty and patience of God; but the saints hold all *in Capite*, in their Head, in Christ, in the right they have in him.

(4.) He is their Head, because their safety is in him: though all the members of the church be under water, yet all is safe when the head is above water; our Head is in heaven. Luther said he was even as a devil to some, they so violently accused him; but let Christ live and reign. Christ is above, the head is above water.

Lutherus apud illos Satan est, sed Christus regnat et vivit.

(5.) He is their Head in regard of his compassion to his church and people. The meanest member here, if wronged, Christ is sensible of it. When but the toe is trodden upon, the head cries, Why do you hurt me? Christ the Head cries, "Saul, Saul, why persecutest thou me?" And observe, the meaner and the poorer the members of Christ are here in the church, the more is Christ sensible of their sorrows and afflictions, and the more will he appear for them, when he shall appear a Head yet more gloriously than ever he has done. Ezek. xxxiv. 16—26, is very notable. You find there, Christ is said to be "one shepherd" to his people, and "a prince" to them; but mark what is promised, That he will "bring again that which was driven away, and will bind up that which was broken, and will strengthen that which was sick: but he will destroy the fat and the strong, and feed them with judgment.—And he will judge between cattle and cattle, between the rams and the he-goats.—He will judge between the fat cattle and the lean cattle; because ye have thrust with side and with shoulder, and pushed all the diseased with your horns, till ye have scattered them abroad." When Christ shall appear, he will not show such respect to the brave, stout, jolly spirits of those that were in the church, who thought to carry all before them with force. No; he will look to the poor of the flock; and those that thrust with the side, and pushed with the horns, and scattered the poor and the lean, they shall be judged.

My brethren, have you not known times when stout-hearted and cruel men have thrust with the side, and pushed with the horn, and scattered up and down in divers countries, thousands of weak and tender-conscienced Christians? Well, but here is a promise, that Christ our Head will come, and he shall be one Shepherd, and he shall show his tender affection toward the poor afflicted of the flock, he shall take away from the land the evil beasts, as you have it there in the 25th verse. He is the Head in regard of his compassion.

(6.) Christ is their Head in regard of guidance and direction. The body is to be moved and guided by the head; so all truths, all doctrines of religion, must hold on Christ. Col. ii. 19, the apostle, rebuking worshipping of angels and other false opinions, saith, that they did not hold the head. All doctrines in the church therefore must hold the Head, and must not be obtruded upon the church, but as they come from the Head, and hold there.

(7.) And that principally, and upon which we must stay a while, which is most of all intended in the text, Christ is their Head in regard of his rule and government; and therefore he that is called "one head" here, is called "a prince" in those two forenamed chapters, Ezek. xxxiv. and xxxvii. It would spend time needlessly, to show you in Scripture how governors are called heads, that I suppose you are all acquainted with. This, therefore, is the main thing that we are now to open, how Christ is the Head of the church in regard of his rule and government. There are many things of importance in this point. I shall desire to decline, what possibly I may, all things that are controversial, especially with our brethren, and only speak of what I think for the present you are fit to bear.

There are four things, especially of the government of Christ in his church, for which he is to be accounted the Head.

1. All offices and officers in the church hold upon Christ, and are from him as from the Head. As in a civil body, the offices of a civil state hold of the king, hold upon him in a legal way; the power of the king being regular, it regulates all power in all other officers; that which is done, is done in the name of the king. So all the officers and offices in the church are in the name of Christ, they all hold on him. There can be no officer nor offices in the church, but such as Christ himself has appointed, for they must be by institution. I beseech you observe the difference between officers in a civil state, and officers in a church.

(1.) A civil state, because it reaches only to the outward man, has liberty to appoint what officers it please, according to the rules of prudence and justice; and more or less, according to the necessity of the country and place. But it is not so in the church, there we have no liberty to go according to the rules of prudence, merely to erect any office because we think it may make for the good and peace of the church. I say, therefore, to erect any new office not established before in the word, we have no liberty, we cannot do it, we are too bold if we attempt it, for such an office will not hold of the Head. In the state, none can erect new offices, new courts, but by the supreme legislative power; so in the church, none can erect new offices, but only from the Head. In the civil state, God leaves a great deal of liberty; there may be change of officers, those that are good now, perhaps, may seem not so fit afterwards, and those in one country may not be so fit for another. But for the officers of the church, they must be all the same in all places, where they can be had, and no more than those appointed by Christ.

(2.) The civil state may limit their officers as they think fit. They may choose one into an office, he shall have power but in so many things; this shall be the object of his power, when he is come hither there he shall stop; though he that was before him had more power, yet he that comes after him may not have that power, the civil state may limit that, if it see fit. But in the church state it cannot be so; and upon this ground, because they hold upon the Head. Indeed the men that bear any office in the church, are designed to it by the church, but they do not hold of the church, they hold of Christ the Head; therefore it is not in the power of the church to limit them being in it, but they must go to the word, for their office once taken upon them, whether it be the office of teachers or of pastors, they cannot then be limited by any power, but what the word saith is the office of a teacher or of a pastor: they cannot have the rule so propounded to them, as, You shall go but thus far, and you shall do so much of the office of a teacher and no more; but when they are once in, they are in without any limitation of the power of their office; it is only from Christ the Head.

(3.) In a civil state there may be alteration, raising the dignity of the office, and making it lower than before; but in the church no such thing, the officers of the church are always the same, no raising, no depressing; why? because they hold upon the Head. Others depend upon man's prudence, but these are institutions by Christ, and hold of the Head.

2. Christ is the Head in regard of rule, because all ordinances, laws, and institutions hold upon him. It is not in the liberty of man to erect any new spiritual

ordinance in the church, no nor to make spiritual laws in the church, for the government of the spirits of men. No new ordinance, no new institution, can be in the church. In the civil state there may be thousands of new institutions.

I call that an institution that has an efficacy in it for attaining such an end by virtue of the institution, not by virtue of any naturalness in the thing. As for example, to instance in Divine institutions: The sacrament is an institution, and therefore there is a virtue, a spiritual efficacy, to be expected from that and by that, through the strength of the institution, more than it has in it in any natural way. So in preaching the word, and ecclesiastical censures, there is more to be expected, more efficacy to work upon the soul, for the spiritual man, by virtue of the institution, than there is in the natural things that are done there. So for laws: Christ makes a law in the church, it being an institution, there is to be expected a spiritual efficacy and virtue to go with that thing which Christ commands, beyond what it had before it was commanded. Now then, in this way, no man in the world can make any church institution, no, nor law for the church, so as to appoint any thing, to have any spiritual efficacy by virtue of that institution, beyond what it has in a natural way. We must take heed of being so bold, that when Christ has made an institution, an ordinance, and revealed it to us, for us to think we may imitate Christ, and make another ordinance, or another institution, like that; because Christ has done so, because we find such a thing in the word, therefore we may do so too. No, this is too bold, this is to set our post by God's post, for which the Lord charged the people, Ezek. xliii. 8. In Isa. xxxiii. 22, it is said, "The Lord is our judge, the Lord is our lawgiver, the Lord is our king" in this thing.

We are to consider that there are some things belonging to the church (I beseech you observe) common with all other societies; and therefore they have that which belongs to them, natural and civil, concerning which laws may be made: there the power of man may come in, there the rule of prudence may order things. Those things, I say, that belong to the church, that yet are not so peculiarly the church's, but belong to other societies, there man's reason may come in. As for instance: First, a church is a spiritual society and community, they must meet together, and if they do meet, they must meet in some place: this is common to all societies in the world, if they will meet, they must meet in a place. Yea, Secondly, if they meet in a place, this place must be determined where it shall be. This also is common to all societies. Thirdly, this likewise is common to them with all other societies, that what they do in that place, must be done decently and in order. As if many things are to be done, one thing must be before another, one thing must not exclude another; if they come together, they must come together as befitting men in a decent way. Therefore that rule of the apostle, "Let all things be done decently and in order," is not properly an institution, it is nothing but the dictate of right reason; so that if we had never found such a maxim in Scripture, it had been a truth that we were bound in conscience to observe. Again, if men will come and meet together, it is natural and common to all societies, that they should be decent in their garments and otherwise.

But then you will say, When is it an institution proper only to Christ, with which none must meddle?

Thus, when any man shall by virtue of any law, or imposition, put more efficacy in an institution for the worship of God, than God or nature has done, this we call sinful.

As for instance, (1.) Suppose we instance only garments. That all who meet together in Christian assemblies, ministers and others, should meet in decent garments, the light of nature tells us; and there may be law, if men will be refractory, to compel them so to meet. But now, if we say, such a garment shall be decent for God's worship because it is appointed, whereas if it were not appointed, it would not be decent at all; then I say all the decency does not depend upon what God has put into it, or what is natural to it, but merely upon the institution of man. For some kind of garments, if men were left to their freedom, and there were no institution, would not be decent to wear; if it would not be decent, then it seems it is the institution that puts all honour upon them, and more than nature, or the God of nature, has put upon them.

2. There is more put upon a thing, than nature hath put into it, when there shall be expected, by virtue of an institution, some kind of spiritual efficacy to work upon the soul; then it is sinful. As thus, when that creature, by virtue of the institution and appointment, shall be made, esteemed, or accounted more effectual to stir up my mind, or to signify such a thing, to purity or holiness, than another creature that has as much in it naturally to signify the same thing, and to stir up my mind; this is to imitate God's institution, which is too much boldness in any man.

As, when God appoints a thing in his church, a ceremony or the like, he will take something that has a resemblance, to put men in mind of such a holy thing, that has some kind of metaphor or likeness in it. But when God has taken this creature and separated it from others, this creature must be expected to have more efficacy to signify the thing to my soul, and to stir up my soul to think of this holiness, than any creature in the world, not so appointed, though other creatures have as much in them naturally to do it. This is God's institution. Now man's institution, that comes near to God's, where there is a setting our post by his post, is when man shall take one creature from thousands of others, and all those thousands have as much in them naturally, and put into them by God, to remind me of holiness, and to stir up my heart; but this creature shall be separated from the rest, and by virtue of an institution put upon it, there shall be expected more efficacy in this to stir up my mind, and to draw my heart nearer to God, than other creatures, that only do it in a natural way. This, I say, is intrenching upon that which belongs to the government of Christ.

Therefore I beseech you, my brethren, be not mistaken in this, because I know you are ordinarily led by that speech of the apostle, "Let all things be done decently and in order." Understand it aright: it is true we must do so, and it is a sin not to do things decently and in order, in the worship of God; but this does not at all countenance any institution of man, to draw the heart nearer to God, or God nearer to the heart, by virtue of man's separation of it from common use.

I might instance other things, such as places: that there should be a convenient place for God's worship, the light of nature will tell us; but when any man shall set one place aside separated from another, and shall make the worship of God to be better, and have more efficacy to draw men nearer to God, or God nearer to men, than another place that has as much natural decency and fitness in it as that place has; then it has evil in it.

By these few instances you may judge of all things, when they come to be institutions in God's worship, and beyond the rule of the apostle, "Let all things be done decently and in order." This is the second thing of Christ's government, that all ordinances, all laws in the church, must hold on him the Head.

3. Those laws which Christ makes for the ordering and government of his church, not only hold on him as

the Head, but have such a virtue and efficacy in them as coming from the Head, that they bind the consciences of men. Because they come from him who is the Head of the church, they lay bonds upon consciences, and that primarily, and more efficaciously than any law of any man in the world can. Yea, they lay such a bond upon conscience, that though a thing be commanded that has no other reason for the command but merely the will of Christ, and that we cannot see to what good the thing tends, but merely because Christ will have it, yet we are bound to obey, yea, and that in secret; yea, so far as the rule goes, we are bound to do what is required by it, though we should suffer never so much prejudice to ourselves. Here is the binding power of Christ in binding conscience. But no law of man can in this way bind conscience.

But what will you say then to that text of Scripture, which I suppose is in every one of your thoughts, and would be ready in every one of your mouths if you were from the assembly, "Let every soul be subject unto the higher powers; for there is no power but of God, the powers that be are ordained of God. Whosoever therefore resisteth the power, resisteth the ordinance of God; and they that resist shall receive to themselves damnation," Rom. xiii. 1, 2. Yea, "ye must needs be subject, not only for wrath, but also for conscience sake," ver. 5. This text seems to imply that the laws of men do bind the conscience; and we find how this is urged by many, so that there is no institution of man whatever, (except we can apparently show it is contrary to the word of God,) but they think by virtue of this text the consciences of men are bound; they do not submit to authority, they sin against their consciences. Many men will jeer at those who are so conscientious in God's commands about those which seem to be but little things (and in themselves are little things); O, they dare not disobey because they are bound in conscience; they will jeer at the scrupulosity of their consciences. But when it comes to man's commands, then they must obey in the least thing, whatever it be; though in its own nature it be never so indifferent, yet they must obey for conscience sake.

I shall desire, as fully and as clearly as I am able, to satisfy conscience in this very thing. To open therefore that scripture unto you:

First, You must observe, that every one is bound to be subject to the higher powers. Mark, it is not to the man first, but it is to the power, "Let every soul be subject unto the higher powers," wherever this power lies. It is not to the will of a man that has power, but it is to the power of that man. Now the power, the authority, is that which man has in a legal way. That first must be understood.

Secondly, We must consider in what they must be subject. The laws of men are of three sorts.

Some perhaps command that which is simply unlawful, to which we all yield the Scripture does not bind us to be subject; there "we must obey God rather than man." Others command things that are lawful; and they are of two sorts.

Either such things as tend, by the rules of justice and prudence, to the good of the community of which we are members; and there we are bound to obey for conscience sake. But still this is not according to that obedience we owe to Christ our Head, it is secondary, not primary, because commanded by man: and then, because there exists a law of Christ to us, to walk and live according to the rules of justice and prudence; so we are bound for conscience in those things, but not primarily, and so they cannot be said to bind conscience, as Christ's laws do.

There are other things which are commanded by man, (and that especially concerns our question,) and these are such things as indeed are neither here nor there for the public good. The good of the community does not at all depend upon them, and there is nothing in them but merely the satisfaction of the will of those who are in authority. Now here is the question, how far those laws bind men, and bind conscience? Indeed many poor Christians who are conscientious have been extremely snared in these things.

To that I answer, that though such things should be commanded to be done, yet if they be not done, (so that they are not omitted out of contempt, nor so as to bring scandal upon the authority that enjoins them, and those that omit them patiently and willingly submit to what punishment the law of the land shall require,) in such things a man's conscience shall not, nor need not, bind him over to answer before God, that he has sinned against that rule.

You will say, How do you prove that? How doth it appear? I will make it appear from the nature of subjection required in the text, and from reason.

First, this text, Rom. xiii. 4, gives this as the ground why we are to be subject, "For he is the minister of God to thee for good." So that that which is the special ground of our subjection is, because they that are in place are ministers for our good. But here is then an abuse of their power, if they command what does not tend to the good of the public, but merely the satisfaction of their own minds.

But suppose it to be an abuse, the text saith we must be subject.

Mark, therefore, the text saith not, you must do the thing for conscience sake; (I beseech you observe it;) it saith, ἀνάγκη ὑποτάσσεσθαι, you must be subject, we must not resist, but be subject; the meaning is, we must be subordinate for conscience sake. Here is all that is required, that I must be subordinate and not resist, that is, if there be a thing commanded by authority, though this authority should be abused, yet I may not resist, I must be subject. If then out of that reverent respect I have to authority, though I do not the thing, yet I do not forbear out of contempt: it is a thing exceedingly prejudicial unto me, and it is not for the common good, but yet I am so careful that authority shall not be despised that I will keep it secret, I will not refuse to do it so as shall be a scandal unto authority. And yet further, if authority shall so far urge upon me as to inflict punishment because I do it not, I will patiently bear it. Now when these three things are done, here is that subordination to authority which the apostle in that scripture requires.

And the reason why this of necessity must be granted, is, because otherwise all that Christian liberty of which the Scripture so much speaks, may be utterly taken away in the practice, and be in the power of man wholly to deprive us of it. This scripture cannot be so understood, that all the liberty we have in things in their own nature indifferent, should be so under the power of men, as that we for the practice, and for our consciences too, must be tied, that we cannot have liberty, no, not in secret. Certainly, that is against the judgment of all orthodox divines of the Reformed churches.

But it may be said, Who shall be judge whether things tend to the public good or not? will you take upon you to judge yourself? To that the answer is plain, that indeed those who are appointed by law have the power to judge legally and authoritatively, to judge so as to bind others. But every man has liberty so far as concerns his own act to judge at his peril. And that a twofold peril. First at his peril, lest he, judging himself, should sin against God in this, that he should judge that not good for the public which indeed is good; that he should perhaps judge that to be of an indifferent nature that justice and prudence require of him. Here he misjudges at his peril, he sins against the

Lord, against the rules of justice and prudence, and endangers his own soul if he go amiss. Secondly, if he misjudge, it is at his peril by the laws of men, as he is in danger then to suffer what the laws of men shall inflict upon him. And so submitting this way, his conscience may have some ease; and yet no gap open at all to liberty, or any disturbance to any lawful authority. This is necessary for men to know, that they may understand aright how to answer that question about laws binding of conscience. You hear it is the prerogative of Christ our Head, so to be our lawgiver, as to lay bonds upon conscience in such a manner as no man can do the like. That is the third.

4. Christ is the Head of the church, say some, even personally, so as to come and rule in the world in a glorious manner, personally. They think this may be interpreted, that Christ shall be a Head, that he shall come personally, and rule and govern things even in this world. As Christ in his own person exercised his priestly and prophetical offices, so they think in his own person he shall exercise his kingly power and office. Which opinion, because the further discussion of it I suppose generally you are not able to bear yet, therefore in modesty I will forbear; and though out of modesty I shall for the present forbear, yet out of conscience I dare not altogether deny it, but so we will leave it, to see what truth may be in it. We must expect to have light let in by degrees.

In these four things then we have the rule of Christ, three determined of, the fourth only propounded, about which Christ in time will show further light. Christ is then the Head.

Now from all this there follows three consequences that are very useful,—That seeking after the right government of Christ in his church is not a light matter, it concerns the headship of Christ.—By what has been said, we may learn to know what is properly antichristian, and what not;—and we shall come to have light how far the king may be said to be head of the church. In these things you will find it needful for conscience to be informed, and I shall carry them on too, I hope, with modesty, fulness, and safety.

1. I say it follows from hence, that it is not a light matter to seek after the right government of Christ in his church, it concerns the headship of Christ in a special manner. There are some other things in which the headship of Christ consists, which perhaps may be spoken of hereafter, but in this place especially that. In the primitive times, the greatest contention was about the doctrines of religion, what doctrines should hold upon Christ and what not, and the people of God suffered most for contending about them. They would not receive a doctrine but what held on Christ; and what was obtruded upon them, not holding upon Christ the Head, they rejected. And Luther upon this place saith how much the church in after-time suffered for this very thing; What kind of dangers environed the church, and do environ it for acknowledging Christ to be the Head, these our times sufficiently testify. And further, because we preach Christ to be the whole Head, therefore we are subject to anathemas, and to all kinds of punishment. In these latter times, it is likely that the great contention will be, rather about the headship of Christ in the point of his government, than in the other, the other being so clear unto us; and the sufferings of the people of God will be so much the more grievous, because this is accounted such a little thing, such a poor business. And rather, because this does not seem to be altogether so clearly revealed in the Scripture, as other doctrinal points that hold upon Christ the Head. Christ has so disposed of things, that this should not be so clearly revealed, because he intended to suffer antichrist to rise to his height: and it cannot be imagined, if the doctrine of Christ's government in his church had been clearly and demonstratively laid down, so as there could have been no gainsaying it, how it is possible for antichrist to have risen to the height he has attained. But the nearer the time comes for antichrist to fall, the more clearly this shall be revealed.

2. By this we may learn, what to account antichristianism, and what not. For there are many amongst us, who cry out against every thing that displeases them, that it is antichristianism, and yet understand but very little what antichristianism is. But by what has been said, you must know that antichristianism is not every error. It is true, in a large sense antichrist is as much as against Christ, and so every sin, every error, is against Christ, and is antichristianism, if you take it so. But you are to know the Scripture speaks of antichrist, and of antichristianism, in a special acceptation. What is that?

Antichristianism is that which shall oppose Christ as a Head, and set up another headship; this is the peculiarity of antichrist and antichristianism.

First, Whoever shall obtrude any doctrine upon the church, to be believed by his own authority, he is guilty of antichristianism; not whoever shall preach or hold an error in the church. But when any shall presume to obtrude upon the church any doctrine that holds upon human authority, to be urged by the authority of those that impose it, this, I say, is properly antichristianism, for it opposes Christ in his headship. Secondly, The intrusion of such offices and officers in the church, as merely belong to the spiritual man, such as are properly church offices, that do not hold upon Christ the Head, but only hold upon men, this is antichristianism. Thirdly, The imposing of any ordinance, any new institutions, upon the church, belongs to antichristianism. Fourthly, The imposing of laws so to bind conscience as the laws of Christ do, here is antichristianism.

Not only because these things are directly against the headship of Christ, but because these things set up another head; and so the word antichrist may signify as well for one to be instead of Christ (for so ἀντὶ, the Greek, signifies, sometimes as well for, as against; as, of his fulness we receive grace for grace, it is χάριν ἀντὶ χάριτος, grace for grace). So antichrist is one that shall claim to himself that headship which is proper unto Jesus Christ, and not to be communicated to any from Jesus Christ.

Now the apostle saith that there were many antichrists in his time, and this mystery of iniquity did work then; but now it grows to a great height in that great antichrist of Rome, for (you know) in these four special things he is the antichrist: Because he obtrudes doctrines, articles of faith, upon the church by his own authority. He makes all offices of the church to hold on him; and appoints laws, ordinances, and institutions likewise to hold on him. He claims the binding of consciences, which is proper only to Jesus Christ. All those who hold thus on antichrist, and are his abettors in these things, are guilty of this great sin of antichristianism.

3. The third consequence. You say Christ is the Head, but you know the king is called the head of the church; in what sense are we to understand that? or how may we come to understand aright the oath of supremacy?

These things (my brethren) are necessary for information of conscience, and the burden lies upon us to make them out as clearly unto you as we can, that you may go along with the more freedom of spirit and conscience in your way, and yet give every one their right too. You are to know, therefore, that the oath of supremacy came into England thus: In the time of popery, the pope claimed to himself the headship of the church: he being excluded, then came in that oath to acknowledge the king or queen the head of the church. But now you must know, first, that this title, The head of the church, as it has been attributed to the king, has been much abused, and has given some advantage to our adversaries; for the king is not the head of the church, neither as Christ is, nor as the pope claimed it.

Not as Christ is. Christ is the Head to govern unlimitedly. No limits or bounds are set to the government of Christ, but only his own will. No prince in the world is so the head to govern. But all governors nave a twofold limit; they are limited by the laws of God, and by the laws of man.

Neither is he the head as the pope challenges to himself. How is that? you will say. In the forenamed four things, the pope challenges holding of doctrines, and holding of offices, and the like, upon him. Offices do not so hold upon any governors, upon the king or others, as the pope challenges to hold upon him. How does he challenge them to hold upon him? Thus, that all are in him virtually, and so to be derived from him to others. And in great part many of our prelates say that they are the head of the church, thus; that is, that all the offices hold on them, that they are all in them virtually, and so go from them to others. Hence they account none others ministers but their curates, and they must not pray but as they will, and do nothing but what they will. Why? because they are but their substitutes, as if all offices were virtually in them, and so came from them to others; whereas every officer in the church, even the meanest, holds upon Christ the Head.

Now, in the civil state in some sense it may be said, that the officers of the commonwealth are virtually in the king, he being the supreme; but you must not think that all are thus virtually in him in church affairs, for if they were virtually in him, then he could himself dispense those things that others dispense by virtue of their offices, but that he cannot, as to give the sacrament and the like.

But how is he the head, then, or in what sense may we quiet our consciences in acknowledging the king to be the head of the church? Only thus; he is said to be the head because he is the supreme to govern in a civil way, not only the civil state, but even affairs that belong to the church. We do not deny the power of princes even in affairs that belong to the church. And because the king is the supreme in that civil power, to govern by civil laws, to see Christ not dishonoured, to keep out idolatry, to protect the church, to punish enormities that exist, to defend it from enemies, in that sense he is said to be the head; but the title of supreme governor, being understood in a civil way only, is more proper.

To make it a little plain that the king has some supremacy, not only in the civil state but in church affairs. For we must not exclude the king quite out of all church affairs, as some would do; but though we would inform your consciences aright, yet we would not by any means take away any lawful power God has put into him. Now that he has power even in church affairs, there are many reasons that fully move me to be persuaded in it.

The first that I shall name I think will least prevail (though it be the most ordinary) with them that make most doubt of it, therefore I will not stand upon it, only name it. We know that among the Jews in the time of the Old Testament, the governors, and kings, and princes had power in affairs that belong to the church, as well as to the state. But this I say I do not think to be the greatest strength in this point, especially to persuade them that make any scruple of it; they will tell us that the power there was but typical and the like, and so binds not now.

There are therefore other reasons that persuade the same thing.

The first is this, because I find that in the prophets, where we have a prophecy of the state of the church in the times of the gospel, God promises that he will make kings to be their nursing fathers, and queens their nursing mothers. Now if they are to be nursing fathers of the church, surely they must have some influence by their power in it.

Secondly, Rom. xiii. 4, speaks indifferently, and saith, "he is the minister for thy good." It does not say for this good, or that good, for this civil good, or ecclesiastical good, but "he is the minister of God to thee for good," for all good unto thee so far as his power can reach. It is a hard thing, you know, (if men will put us unto it,) to show in the New Testament the power that kings had, because there was then no king but heathens, yet saith he, they are ministers for thy good, and he speaks to Christians.

But thirdly, and that which yet may seem to have more in it, I find in the New Testament that St. Paul, when he was accused by his brethren in matters of religion, appealed unto Cæsar, Acts xxv. 19, who was a heathen magistrate, his accusation was in matters of religion, in questions about their law, and about "one Jesus that was dead, whom Paul affirmed to be alive." Yet in his answer to those things he appealed to Cæsar, therefore there is somewhat that Cæsar has to do in overlooking the affairs of the church.

But you will say, How can he be a competent judge? Can Cæsar, a heathen, be a competent judge in matters of religion? is that possible? Or suppose that a governor be wicked, can he be a competent judge in matters of religion?

I answer, a governor, though he be a heathen, yet loses not his power, he has still a true and lawful power; yea, he has some oversight in things that concern church affairs. How can that be? I answer, Christianity gives not the authority, but enables to execute the authority; a heathen magistrate has authority, it is his duty to see that Christians be not wronged, and if he does not, it is his sin; but if he becomes a Christian, he is the better able to do what he ought, but this puts not the power into him.

But if a man be wicked, and understand not the things of the church, how can he be a judge? Thus; though the king be not a competent judge of the principles upon which the church acts, whether right or no, yet he may have ability to judge between man and man, whether one wrongs the other in matters of religion. As thus; though he does not think the principles upon which they act to be right, yet he can judge whether according to those principles they do right one to another, or whether according to their principles they do not wrong one the other. And this is a great matter, to be able to judge and to punish with civil punishment when any of the church wrongs his brother against the principles which he himself professes.

As for example, a man who is not a physician does not understand the difference between poison and a wholesome medicine, yet when things are brought before him, he may be a competent judge, by evidence, to condemn a physician who has poisoned a man instead of giving him wholesome physic. And that objection against his competency in judging in the affairs of the church, has no more power than if it should have been objected that he must not judge a physician, whether he has poisoned a man or no, because he himself is not a physician.

Thus we have done with these three consequents that follow upon the opening of the headship of Christ in point of his government. And now we see more clearly how Christ is Head, and none but Christ, and what glory we are to give to Christ as the Head of the church.

There is one thing more belongs to the headship of Christ, which must not be passed by, though it is not so fully aimed at in the text as that which has already been expounded, and that is, the influence of spiritual life which comes to the church by Christ the Head, as the animal spirits come from the head to the members. And this is the very reason, first, why grace in the saints is of such a beautiful and glorious nature as it is, because it comes from Christ the Head. Secondly, this is the reason of the power and efficacy of grace in the saints, because it comes from Christ the Head. Thirdly, this is also the reason why grace in the saints is of such an everlasting nature. It has more beauty, it has more power and efficacy, and it is of a more everlasting nature, than the grace Adam possessed, because the grace of the saints holds upon Christ the Head, and has an influence from Christ, God-man, in a special and peculiar way, such an influence as Adam had not. This is the excellency of grace in the saints.

And to conclude this point of the headship of Christ. God the Father thus advanced Christ to be the Head, because he was willing to stoop so low, to be as a worm under foot, for so he saith of himself, "I am a worm, and no man," Psal. xxii. 6. Christ was low in his own eyes, and submitted himself to such a condition; and now, behold, the Father has advanced him, God has made him "Head over all things," Eph. i. 22; has made him Head over principalities, and powers, and dominions, over angels, and over all men and all things in the church; has advanced him to this high and glorious dignity. We see somewhat of it now, and we shall see more gloriously the headship of Christ hereafter.

In this God the Father shows, that as he has dealt with his Son, so he is willing to deal with the members of his Son. His Son, who was willing to be so low and under foot, is now advanced to such high glory that all must stoop, and yield, and submit to him. Let us be willing to lie low, though it be under foot, to be trodden upon by the wicked and ungodly in the world; though we cannot expect to be advanced to be head, yet we may expect to be advanced to glory and dignity. You know what God said to Saul, "When thou wert little in thine own eyes, then I made thee king," 1 Sam. xv. 17. The less any of us are in our own eyes, the more are we likely to be advanced by God; for God will observe a proportion between his dealings with Christ the Head, and his dealings with all his members.

"And appoint themselves one head." In Eph. i. 22, it is said, God gave Christ "to be the Head over all things to the church." How then is it said here that they shall "appoint to themselves one head?"

It is true, God the Father has advanced his Son, and extolled him above all things, and given him to be Head over all; but yet when the church chooses Christ to be their Head, when they shall willingly submit themselves unto him, lifting him up above all, honouring his ordinances, laws, and institutions, and depending upon him for light, then they are said to appoint Christ to be their Head. Though God's eternal decree has made himself to be the God of his saints, yet when the saints choose God to be their God, God accounts himself to be made their God by them; they make God to be their God in choosing him. So though Christ by the Father is appointed to be Head over all, yet the act of the church in choosing Christ, and coming to him freely, and submitting to him as to the Head, is accounted an appointing of Christ to be Head.

This is that happy work which the saints have been doing, and which we are to do now, and which they will do to the end of the world. Though there be some special time to which this text refers, yet in all ages of the church, when the saints choose Christ to be their Head, they are said to appoint him.

Let us join in this blessed work, an honourable work for creatures, to appoint the Lord Jesus to be Head over them. Let us say, as Hushai did in another case, 2 Sam. xvi. 18, "Whom the Lord, and this people, and all the men of Israel, choose, his will I be, and with him will I abide." So, he whom God the Father shall give to be Head over all things, he whom the saints have in all times chosen for their Head, he shall be our Head and our King; his will we be, and with him will we abide. Let us give Christ the pre-eminence, prizing his government, his ordinances, above all the comforts we have in this world. "If I prefer not Jerusalem above my chief joy," Psal. cxxxvii. 6. The words are על ראש שמחתי if I make not Jerusalem to ascend above the head of my joy; whatever is high in our thoughts, as a head, let Christ be above it. Christ in his ordinances must be above the head of our joy, for otherwise he is not a Head unto us. If you invite a man of quality to your table, though you provide excellent cheer for him, yet if you set any people of mean quality above him, he would not regard all your courtesies. When you tender up any thing unto Christ, when you seem to entertain him with the greatest respect, yet if there be any thing you set above him, especially if a vile lust be set above him, he cares not for all your entertainment. We read in Col. ii. 19, that there were some blamed for not "holding the Head:" what is that? because they gave more honour to angels than was due to them; though never such glorious creatures, yet by overprizing them they come not to hold the Head. What! is the giving undue honour to angels enough to take us off from Christ the Head? Certainly, then, prostrating ourselves before our vile and base lusts, much more takes us off from holding Christ to be the Head. Let us look at all the offices and ordinances of Christ, as holding upon him the Head, that so we may have a more reverent esteem of them. Let us depend upon him for influence of life, and not depend upon means. Let us manifest in our conversation the spirit and life that we have received from such a Head as Christ is, that we may not be a dishonour to this our Head. Chrysostom, in his comment upon the first chapter of the Ephesians, says, in this respect we must be better than angels, yea, greater than archangels. He has three most excellent remarks, to prove that Christians should take heed of dishonouring Christ their Head.

Τῶν ἀγγέλων βελτίους εἰναί χρὴ καὶ τῶν ἀρχαγγέλων μείζους, &c.

First, saith he, Suppose a man had a precious diadem upon his head, or a crown of gold, that would be some argument to him to make him take heed of doing things unworthy of that ornament: but we have not a diadem, not a crown of gold upon our heads, we have Christ himself to be our Head, therefore let us do nothing unworthy of this our Head. Secondly, he remarks, Oh the honour that God affords to us in this! the thought of this were enough to terrify us from sin, more than the setting of hell itself before our eyes. And indeed so it is. The right understanding of Christ to be our Head, and having so near a union with him, is of power to terrify us from sin more than the sight of hell, if it were before us. Thirdly, he observes, What! is Christ your Head? Do you know next to whom this your Head sits in heaven? Is he not placed at the right hand of the Father, above all principalities and powers? And shall the members of this Head be trampled upon by the devil? God forbid.

And yet so honour the Head, as to give due honour likewise to those he has placed under him for the administration of any of his ordinances to us. We must not, under pretence of giving Christ all the honour, dishonour those that are set over us by Christ. St. Paul, in 1 Cor. i. 12, when reproving the dissensions of the church of Corinth, remarks, "Every one of you saith, I am of Paul, and I of Apollos, and I of Cephas, and I of

Christ." Why, are these all blamed? how could those who said that they held Christ be blamed? Thus: amongst the Corinthians there were some that made divisions, some were for one officer, others for another: We are for Paul, said some; We for Apollos, said others; and, We for Cephas; And for our parts, said others, we are neither for Paul, nor for Apollos, nor for Cephas, but for Christ. What are men? what are officers? what are ordinances? what are all those to us? Christ is all in all to us, he is our Head, and we are complete in him, and we hold upon him. These are blamed as well as the other, because we must so hold upon Christ, as to give all due honour to the ordinances, institutions, officers, and offices of Christ.

Yet I confess, if any that are in Christ's stead, to dispense his ordinances to us, prove to be wicked, of all people in the world they are the most contemptible, and a just judgment of God is upon them. Isa. ix. 15, "The ancient and honourable, he is the head, and the prophet that teacheth lies, he is the tail." Mark, the prophet speaks against those who were in place and power, though they were naught, yet still they retained the name of ancient and honourable; but the prophet that teacheth lies, a contemptible name is put upon him, he is the tail; no generation in the world more contemptible than those, when once they degenerate.

But you will say, though they are vile in their lives, yet their wickedness does not hinder the virtue and efficacy of the ordinances, they depend not upon the officers. True, the efficacy of no ordinance depends upon men, and it is not either because the minister is vile, or communicants are wicked, that the virtue of an ordinance is lost, if the church contract no guilt upon themselves by retaining such in place, and by not casting out such as come into communion with them. Take for granted that there is no guilt contracted, and then it is not the wickedness of the minister, or of the people, that hinders the efficacy of any ordinance. But if it prove that there be guilt contracted upon the church through their negligence of duty, then the case is the same with those of Corinth, 1 Cor. v. 6, "A little leaven leaveneth the whole lump;" what is that whole lump but their communion?

They shall "appoint themselves one Head?" But was not Christ the Head before. It is spoken of a glorious time, when the Jews shall be called again, and Israel and Judah shall join together. Now they shall appoint themselves one Head, Christ to be their Head. Christ was the Head to the fathers under the law, how now is he appointed their Head? I answer,

Christ indeed was a Head to the forefathers, but now in the times of the gospel, especially at the calling of the Jews, the time spoken of here, Christ will appear a Head in another manner, to govern in another way, far more gloriously than he now does, and far more influence of grace and light will come from him to his members. Though Christ has always been a Head to his church, yet there is a time coming when the seventh trumpet shall be sounded, spoken of Rev. xi. 15; when that voice shall be heard that yet was never heard, "The kingdoms of this world are become the kingdoms of our Lord, and of his Christ, and he shall reign for ever and ever."—A time coming, wherein Christ shall say to his people, "To him that overcometh will I grant to sit with me in my throne, even as I also overcame, and am set down with my Father in his throne," Rev. iii. 21. The throne that Christ sits upon now, is his Father's throne; he does not call it his; and at the day of judgment, the Scripture tells us that he shall give up the kingdom unto his Father. There is a time therefore for the throne of Christ to be exalted more than it has been, which Christ has promised to those that overcome.—A time coming, when there shall be heard the noise, not only of "many waters," but as of "mighty thunderings, saying, Alleluia; for the Lord God omnipotent reigneth," Rev. xix. 6. He shall be a Head another way.

Now if it be true, that Christ himself is appointed by the church to be Head, then the officers and ministers of the church should not think much to be appointed in their places by the church too. It is true, their offices hold on Christ the Head, but the designation of the persons must be from the church. We do not now list to enter into the controversy, who of the church should do it, but there must be more than a civil act to make any man a pastor or teacher of a church; somewhat to make conscience yield and submit to him as an officer that Jesus Christ has placed over them. Christ himself would be appointed a Head by his people, that they might submit to him the more cheerfully, and give glory to him with the more freedom of spirit. And as for all such as thrust themselves upon a people, no marvel if they complain of want of respect from them, or of their going away from them. They never did any thing towards appointing them as officers over them.

They shall "appoint themselves one Head;" not force Christ upon others by fire and sword. Heretics are to be burnt with fire, saith Luther; but with what fire? the fire of charity.

Igne charitatis comburendi sunt hæretici. Luther.

They shall appoint to themselves. Let others choose what head they please, yet the saints will appoint to themselves the Lord Christ to be their Head; they will bless themselves in Christ, he shall be a Head unto them, whatever he is to others. Others, it may be, will choose to themselves other heads, but the saints say as they in Micah iv. 5, "All people will walk every one in the name of his god, and we will walk in the name of the Lord our God for ever and ever." Other people will walk in their ways, and choose to themselves such as give them most liberty; they perhaps think the government of Christ too strict for them: but for us, we will bless ourselves in our Christ, we will never prostitute our consciences to men, or to lusts and humours, as we have done; Christ shall be our Head, and we will submit to him. *Secreta mea mecum*, (is a Hebrew proverb,) My secret is with myself; what good we find in Christ it is to ourselves: let Christ be a stumbling-block and a rock of offence to others, to us he is precious, he is one of ten thousand, "he is altogether lovely," Cant. v. 16.

They shall "appoint themselves one head." But one; the church is not a monster of divers heads, it has but one head. There cannot be a ministerial head of the church, Christ is always present, and has left his laws with his people. If we consider the difference between ecclesiastical power and civil power, we shall see clearly that there cannot be a ministerial head of the church. A ministerial head is absurd. In the civil power, it is not against any institution of Christ, nor against any law, that there should be one head over all the world. But to have one head over the church, yea, to have any general officers over all the churches, cannot be. The reason is, because there can be no delegation of power that belongs to the church. There may be a delegation of a civil power, one man may be king over many countries, and he may appoint substitutes under him, and delegate them to officiate for him. But in the church there is no delegation of power from one to another. Grant but once delegation of the teaching power, and you establish non-residency; grant but delegation of the ruling power, and you immediately establish a papacy. There is no such thing therefore.

Again, the civil power is by way of coaction; a magistrate is not always bound to give a reason of his injunctions, he may by way of compulsion require obedience. But church power is to deal with conscience;

and therefore every one that has any power must officiate himself, and deal with the consciences of men to persuade and to instruct.

These two things being granted, it is impossible that there can be a head over all the churches, yea, or over many. We must join nothing with Jesus Christ, in the way of his headship. As Alexander said to Darius, when he sent to him that he would be willing to divide the kingdom; No, said Alexander, there is but one sun in the firmament, and there can be but one king in a kingdom. So saith Christ, But one Head: he must be Head alone, or no Head at all; nothing must be joined with him as head. Indeed, the heathen gods were contented to divide their honours: and hence the senate of Rome rejected Christ from taking him in to be a God, after they consulted about it; For, said they, if Christ is acknowledged as a God, he will not share with the rest, he will have all himself; and so upon this reason they refused him. Thus many reject Christ as God, and as a Head, because Christ will not share with others, he must be but one.

And a special help is here given to our faith, in looking up to Christ for help and protection when all means fail; I beseech you, observe it. Does Christ require of us that we should make him Head alone, and join nothing with him? Then we may well expect from him protection in all our wants, and that he alone will help us. Or, otherwise, the condition of a Christian were worse than the condition of a heathen; for the gods of a heathen would be content to have but part of the honour of the heart and life, because they could help but in part. If a heathen god should require the whole soul to be lifted up to him above all, and he alone to be honoured and worshipped as a god, yet, when help and protection are required, he could do nothing without another joined with him, a heathen might well reason the case against him, as doing him wrong. Certainly Christ will never wrong his people, so as to require them to lift up him alone, and join no other with him, and yet when they require help and succour, that there should be need to call in others besides himself to their help. Therefore, as Christ challenges us to make him our Head alone, so we may challenge Christ to help us alone, when there is no other help for us.

Thus we have finished both the headship of Christ, and the church's appointing him to be that Head.

Now follows the next blessing, and that but in a word, and then we come to the conclusion of this chapter.

"They shall come up out of the land." Jerome interprets it, *a terrenis affectibus*, a coming up from their earthly affections; Luther, *a vita miserabili*, a coming up from their miserable life and condition. But rather thus, "come up out of the land," that is, out of their captivity. Judah and Israel shall join together in coming to Jerusalem, and so unite in the same kind of worship. As they were wont to come out of all parts of the country to worship at Jerusalem, and there were united in one kind of worship, so they shall now come from all parts of the world where they are scattered, and join in the same way of worship, yea, and it is very probable in their own land.

There was a time when the people of God sang songs of praise in the wilderness, Exod. xv.; but the time shall come when they shall do it in their own land; and this shall be a blessing of God upon them. "In that day shall this song be sung in the land of Judah; We have a strong city; salvation will God appoint for walls and bulwarks," Isa. xxvi. 1. It shall be sung in the land of Judah. "In the mountain of the height of Israel, saith the Lord God, there shall all the house of Israel, all of them in the land, serve me: there will I accept them, and there will I require your offerings, and the first-fruits of your oblations, with all your holy things," Ezek. xx. 40. "I will take the children of Israel from among the heathen, whither they be gone, and will gather them on every side, and bring them into their own land," Ezek. xxxvii. 21.

This blessing has God granted to many of his servants this day, who never thought to have seen their own good land: but God has been pleased to gather them up, not only to come into their own land, but they find the arms and hearts of the saints open to embrace them, and call them to public employments. Not long since the land could not bear them; we hope that the time will come ere long, that the Lord Christ may so rule in our land, that it will as hardly bear wicked and ungodly men as it has borne the saints; though it were difficult to say that so much violence should be used, even to keep them from sin, as was used against the saints to keep them from their God. Yet, time may come ere long, that wicked men may be glad to flee, though not forced into another land, because they cannot have the enjoyment of their lusts so freely here; as the saints have been forced to flee out of their land that they might serve the Lord, and keep their consciences clear.

But we let this pass, and come now to the close of the chapter, to the epiphonema of it all.

"For great shall be the day of Jezreel." They shall "appoint themselves one head, and come up out of the land; for great," &c. Tremellius renders it, although the day of Jezreel be great: and the Hebrew particle כי signifies *quamvis*, as well as *quia*, it may be translated "although," as well as "for." And translating it, although the day of Jezreel be great, takes it in this sense, that is, although the people of Israel shall be brought into great affliction, yet God will be so merciful when his time comes, that they shall be gathered together again, and appoint themselves one head, and come up out of the land. And from such an interpretation of the words there might be an excellent meditation raised, and it is this.

Obs. That the greatness of the misery of the church is no hinderance to the course of the freeness and abundance of God's mercy towards it. Although the day of Jezreel be never so calamitous, never so afflictive, never so grievous, yet they shall come up out of the land, and appoint themselves one head. The greatness of the church's misery is no hinderance to the church's deliverance. Why? because their deliverance depends upon a God who delights not only to manifest some power, but the excellency and the glory of his power, in their deliverance. Isaiah (lxii. 8) speaking of these very times of God's being merciful to his people, saith, "The Lord hath sworn by his right hand;" and we have not only mention there of God's right hand, and swearing by it, but his arm too; mark that, "and by the arm of his strength:" there is God's hand, God's arm, the arm of his strength, and God swearing by it. Surely when God delights to put forth such power for the deliverance of his church, it is no great matter whether its afflicted state be great or small. It makes no greater hinderance to the church's delivery than if you should see two bubbles of water rise up, one having a little thicker skin than the other. Now there is as much difference in the difficulty of bursting that thick-skin bubble above the thinner, when a mighty piece of ordnance is shot off with a weighty ball against them, as the greatest and sorest affliction that the people of God were ever under in this world makes a difference in the difficulty of their deliverance from the least affliction that ever the church endured, when they have to deal with an infinite God. If a child should see the thicker-skin bubble, he might think it is harder to be broken than the thinner; but if a cannon be shot off, nay, if it be but a gust of wind, it makes no difference. Now the afflictions of God's people are to this right hand of God's power, and the arm of his strength, but as a bubble of water before a mighty cannon. Yea, if there be no help at all to deliver God's people in time of affliction, God can create help, "He will create Jerusalem a rejoicing, and their people a joy." Yea, suppose their condition be such as never was the like since the beginning of the world, yet, "since the beginning of the world men have not heard, nor perceived by the ear, neither hath the eye seen, O God, beside thee, what he hath prepared for him that waiteth for him," Isa. lxiv. 4.

And as the greatness of the church's deliverance is no hinderance to God's power in delivering them, so it should be no hinderance to the work of our faith. Common prudence and reason will go a great way to uphold us under some afflictions, but when the affliction becomes grievous and long, prudence and reason sink under the burden; but then should faith lift up itself, and cast an eye upon this right hand of God's power, this arm of his strength by which he has sworn, and exercise itself in the glorious acts it has wrought. For certainly faith is appointed for such a time as this, when the church is under grievous extremities. The ordinary afflictions of the church do not call for such a work of faith, but when they come to extraordinary calamities, these require such a power of God for their deliverance, and call for a work of faith proportionable. As Alexander, when he was in great danger, said, Now there is a danger fit for the spirit of Alexander to encounter; so when the church is in any great danger, all the members of it should say, Here is a danger, here is a trouble, fit for the spirit of Christians, fit for the spirits of those that are able to exercise the most noble and glorious acts of faith.

Jam periculum par animo Alexandri.

We are scarcely for the present put to this glorious exercise of faith, for reason and sense see much help. They see that the cause of God at this day has the better of the adversary. Let us not look upon every difficulty as a thing that calls for such a mighty, glorious work of faith, when men, by reason and prudence, may carry themselves under such difficulties much better than most of us do. However, we do not know but the Lord may call us to such difficulties and dangers as will require such an exercise of faith as I have spoken of. Let us therefore lay up this instruction for the time to come.

"For great shall be the day of Jezreel." If the words be read as they are in your Bibles, and yet have reference to the calamitous time and grievous extremities of the day of Jezreel, then

Obs. 1. That God's bowels of compassion work toward his church because of the greatness of their affliction. When their afflictions are very great, and the greater they are, the more God's bowels of compassion work toward them. We know the misery of God's people was a marvellous quickening argument to the compassion of God; "I have surely seen the affliction of my people, and their sorrows, and therefore am come down to deliver them," Exod. iii. 7, 8. If the greatness of the affliction of the church move the bowels of God's compassion, then let not the greatness of affliction hinder our faith. Let not the greatness of trouble reason down our faith, but let it rather reason up our faith, for so indeed it should; and so the saints of God heretofore have done. It is time for thee, O Lord, to work, for men have almost destroyed thy law; yea, the high time is come for thee to have mercy upon Zion, for thy people begin to favour the dust thereof. Was this a good argument, "For thy name's sake, O Lord, pardon mine iniquity, for it is great," Psal. xxv. 11, to move God withal? Surely then this is a good argument, Deliver us in afflictions, for they are very great. For sin makes more distance between God and us than afflictions: yet if the greatness of sin can be put as an argument for God's mercy and compassion to work, much more the greatness of afflictions. Yet this is the grace of God in the second covenant, that even the sins which before made the creature an object of hatred, now make it an object of compassion. So afflictions, that before were part of the curse, are turned to arguments for moving the bowels of God's tender compassion toward his people.

Obs. 2. The promise is the only support of the soul, and that which carries it through the greatest affliction. Afflictions are as lead to the net; the promise is as the cork, which keeps above water when the lead pulls down. But I leave these meditations, though I find many interpreters run this way; and I rather take it as a further expression of God's wonderful mercy to his church.

"For great shall be the day of Jezreel;" that is, God has a great day of mercy for Jezreel. They shall appoint themselves one head, they shall be gathered together and be made one, they shall come up out of the land; why? for God has a great day of mercy to his people, a "great day of Jezreel." And herein, therefore, God makes use of the name of Jezreel in a good sense. They who interpret Jezreel the other way would have the name signify, great is the day of scattering, or of the scattered people. But Jezreel signifies likewise the seed of God. Before God used their name in the worst sense, that he would scatter them according to their name; now he uses their name in the best sense, they are the seed of God, and there is great mercy from God for them.

Obs. When God is reconciled to a people he takes all in the best sense, and makes the best acceptation of every thing, as he does here of the name Jezreel. We have only these two things to consider in this expression: That the saints of God are God's Jezreel; that is, they are the seed of God. And that there is for this seed of God a great day.

1. They are the seed of God; the seed of the blessed, and there is a blessing in them. They are the precious seed which God preserves in the world, and has done ever since the beginning of the world. They are that seed that preserves the glory of God in the world. Were it not for a few gracious, holy people in the world, where would the glory of God be? what would become of it? The godly, however contemptible in the world, are the precious seed, that God reserves for great and glorious ends. They are the seed to preserve the continuation of the doctrine of the gospel; as Isa. vi. 13, "The holy seed shall be the substance thereof." Though they are under great afflictions, yet there shall be a holy seed that shall be the substance thereof, and there shall be his blessing. Psal. lxxii. 17, "His name shall endure for ever;" the words are read by Montanus, *Filiabitur nomen ejus*, His name shall be childed; that is, so continued as families are continued, one generation after another, one begetting another. Thus shall the name of Christ continue in the world, as it has done.

Though seed be but a handful in comparison of the harvest, so the saints of God then were, and yet are but as a handful in comparison of the glorious harvest that shall arise, yet they are very precious before God, and God will make the world hereafter know that they are the precious ones of God. Isa. lxi. 9, "All that see them shall acknowledge them that they are the seed which the Lord hath blessed." A man will be careful of his seed, whatever becomes of his other corn. In time of dearth, the husbandman will rather pinch his stomach, than have his seed-corn spent. So in times of common calamity or dearth, God's care is over his seed. The saints are (as I may say) God's seed-corn, to preserve his name in the world to succeeding generations, he will not therefore have them destroyed.

Seed is the most precious of the corn, which is most

winnowed and cleansed; so are the saints the clean and the most precious ones. God winnows them more than others by the fans and winnows of afflictions; why? because they are his seed. Other corn which has chaff in it, the husbandman will give to the fowls and the cattle, he bestows not much winnowing upon it; but the corn that is for seed he carefully winnows, he would not willingly have a darnel amongst it. It may be thou complainest thou art more winnowed than other men; perhaps thou art more precious in God's eyes, and thou art reserved as seed, as the seed of the blessed.

The wicked indeed are seed too, but a corrupt seed, "a seed of evil-doers," Isa. i. 4; the grandfather was an enemy unto God, yea, the great-grandfather; and the father, and the children after him, continue enemies to God. And God, in mercy unto his church, many times cuts down the wicked before they seed too much. You who have gardens, if you see the weeds come up and grow towards seed, you think then that it is time to pull them up, you will not suffer them to seed. God looks upon many families, and sees wretched and sinful men as "a seed of evil-doers" ready to seed, and if they be not cut down suddenly, there will be a wretched brood of wicked ones in such a family. This is the reason of God's sudden cutting down many wicked families.

But to come to the point chiefly intended, that is, that this seed of the Lord shall have a great day.

"Great shall be the day of Jezreel." The men of the world have their day in which they ruffle it out. St. Paul seems to speak of this in 1 Cor. iv. 3, that he did not regard "man's judgment," the words are, ἀνθρωπίνης ἡμέρας, man's day. Now men have the day, they have all the bravery of the world; well, observes St. Paul, I do not regard man's day, I expect another day. I know not how it is otherwise translated; you translate it judgment in your books, but in the original it is day, man has a day. As men have a day, so shall God's saints have a day too. We used often to say, when we saw our enemies jocund and merry, Surely they hope to have a day. My brethren, be joyful in the Lord, God has a day for you, and a great day too, "Great shall be the day of Jezreel." The beginning of God's mercy to his people, is called "a day of small things," Zech. iv. 10; and that must not be despised, "Who hath despised the day of small things?" It was the beginning of the reformation, and deliverance of the people of Judah from their captivity. But God has a day of great things, and certainly that day shall be honourable.

1. It shall be a great day, in which the glory of God shall exceedingly appear, wherein God shall be (as I may so speak with holy reverence) as it were in his robes. As we know princes upon great days put on their robes, so the King of glory shall have a day for his people, wherein even he himself will put on his robes: Psal. cii. 16, "When the Lord shall build up Zion, he shall appear in his glory." It seems, while the church is in affliction, and the witnesses prophesy in sackcloth, that God is as it were clothed in sackcloth, "in all their afflictions he was afflicted;" but because God has a day, a great day to his churches, he will reserve his robes till then, and when that day comes he will put them on. A great day it shall be for Jezreel, for the seed of the Lord.

2. It shall be a great day, for this day shall be the riches of the world. Mark, Paul, speaking of the Jews, saith, "If the fall of them be the riches of the world, and the diminishing of them the riches of the Gentiles; how much more their fulness?" Rom. xi. 12. It was a rich mercy to the Gentiles when they were brought out of darkness, and called to the knowledge of Jesus Christ. But God has a greater day than that, for it is spoken of here as a day that is to come; that is, their fall was the riches of the Gentiles, much more their calling in again. So then, there is such a day of calling home the people of God, as shall be the riches of the Gentiles, the riches of all the world.

3. Great shall be this day, for it shall be as a day of resurrection from death to life: so Dan. xii. 2, "Many of them that sleep in the dust shall awake, some to everlasting life, and some to shame and everlasting contempt." This is not spoken of the great resurrection at the last day of judgment; for, first, it is spoken but of some that shall arise. Secondly, the greatest glory that is here put upon the just, is but to shine as the stars in the firmament; but at the last day, the saints shall shine as the sun in the firmament, more and above the stars. Yea, thirdly, that which is here revealed to Daniel, must be sealed up as a great secret till the appointed time come; but the resurrection at the last day is no great secret, that they knew well enough. But this resurrection is to be sealed up as a great secret that was not known in the world, nor should be much known till the appointed time should come. And then, lastly, it was promised to Daniel in the 13th verse, that he should "stand up in his lot," as a peculiar and special favour that God would bestow upon him. Now it is not such a peculiar and special favour for a saint to stand up at the last day, but this was a favour to Daniel as an eminent saint, that he should stand up in his lot. Therefore this resurrection is the same with this great day of Jezreel, wherein there shall be such a glorious work of God in calling Israel and Judah together, and the fulness of the Gentiles, that it shall be as the resurrection from death to life; so the apostle calls it in Rom. xi. 15, "What shall the receiving of them be, but life from the dead?"

4. "Great shall be the day of Jezreel;" for this day shall bring refreshing to all the saints, this is "the time of refreshing," Acts iii. 19. There shall be such things then as will refresh and revive the spirits of all the saints.

5. A great day, for it shall be the day of restitution of all things. Acts iii. 21, "Until the times of restitution of all things, which God hath spoken by the mouth of all his holy prophets since the world began." I know this text is ordinarily interpreted concerning the last day; but that it cannot be so appears, because that then there shall not be the restitution of all things, but the annihilation of many things. Further, this speaks of a restitution of all things, that was spoken of by the mouth of all the holy prophets. Now the holy prophets spake but very little concerning the day of judgment, or the life to come; and therefore the apostle, in 2 Tim. i. 10, saith, that "life and immortality are brought to light through the gospel." Not but that it was known somewhat before, but it was very darkly known, there was very little spoken of life and immortality in the prophets: but this speaks of a time of which all the holy prophets spake, as an argument that was the general theme of them all. And, indeed, there is no argument whatever that is more general among the prophets, than this great argument of this great day of Jezreel.

6. A great day, for it shall be the day of a new creation; a new heaven and a new earth shall be made, when this great day of Jezreel shall come. "Behold, I create new heavens and a new earth," Isa. lxv. 17. In ver. 18, you see what this new heaven and new earth is: "But be ye glad and rejoice for ever in that which I create: for, behold, I create Jerusalem a rejoicing, and her people a joy." Those are the new heavens and the new earth which are to be created, and plainly mean the church, for ver. 21 speaks of "building houses," and "inhabiting them," and of "planting vineyards," and "eating the fruit" of them, upon these new heavens and this new earth's creation. And, 2 Pet. iii. 13, "Nevertheless we, according to his pro-

mise, look for new heavens and a new earth, wherein dwelleth righteousness." This is usually taken for the kingdom of heaven hereafter. But where is this promise? We do not find it any where, but in Isa. lxv. 17. Now it is apparent that promise speaks of a state of the church in this world; it speaks of a new earth, as well as of a new heaven; if it only spoke of new heavens, it had been another matter, but it speaks of a new earth likewise, therefore meant of a state in this world, that is, there shall be such glorious things done by God, as shall manifest a creating power, as if God now made "new heavens and a new earth."

7. "Great shall be the day of Jezreel," for it shall be as another world, when this day comes. "Unto the angels hath he not put in subjection the world to come, whereof we speak. But one in a certain place (Psal. viii. 4) testified, saying, What is man, that thou art mindful of him? or the son of man, that thou visitest him? Thou madest him a little lower than the angels; thou crownedst him with glory and honour, and didst set him over the works of thy hands: thou hast put all things in subjection under his feet," Heb. ii. 5—8. This the apostle interprets of Christ, as ver. 6, that all things must be subjected to him as man, "What is man, that thou shouldst regard him?" that is, that thou shouldst advance the nature of man so far as to unite it to thy Son, and "put all things in subjection under his feet." But, saith he, "we see not yet all things put under him," that time is yet to come, for, saith he, "he hath not put in subjection the world to come, whereof we speak." Therefore, mark, my brethren, there must be such a time wherein all things, all creatures, must be put under subjection to Christ, and this is in the world to come. It cannot be meant of that world to come, where the saints shall reign gloriously in heaven, for the heavens must depart as a scroll, and many things shall then rather be annihilated, and the kingdom must then be given up by Christ to God the Father, 1 Cor. xv. 24. But this place speaks of a time when all creatures must come under subjection to Christ, and it is called "the world to come;" why? because of the great change there shall be of things, it shall be, as it were, a new world. As we call this world from Noah's time, a new world, and when we speak of the other world, we call it the old world; so the Scripture calls it, 2 Pet. ii. 5, God "spared not the old world;" and, chap. iii. 6, "The world that then was, being overflowed with water, perished." So, this world in which we live shall be as the old world; this day of Jezreel shall make such a glorious change, all things being put in subjection to Christ, that it shall be as it were a new world. God has made an excellent world, in which there is much beauty and glory, and yet his enemies have the rule here; what then will that world be that God intends for his saints?

8. "Great shall be the day of Jezreel," for it shall be such a great day that all former things shall be even forgotten because of the lustre and glory of that great day. As Isa. lxv. 17, the former heavens and the former earth "shall not be remembered, nor come into mind." And so Jer. iii. 16, 17, "In those days, saith the Lord, they shall no more say, The ark of the covenant of the Lord: neither shall it come to mind: neither shall they remember it; neither shall they visit it; neither shall that be done any more. At that time they shall call Jerusalem the throne of the Lord; and all the nations shall be gathered unto it, to the name of the Lord, to Jerusalem: neither shall they walk any more after the imagination of their evil heart." Mark, my brethren, "In those days the house of Judah shall walk with the house of Israel, and they shall come together out of the land of the north to the land that I have given for an inheritance unto your fathers," ver. 18. It is apparent that it is spoken of this great day of Jezreel; for now God declares he will gather Judah and Israel together, and they shall walk together, and that then former things shall be forgotten. "They shall call Jerusalem the throne of the Lord." Heretofore, even the temple itself, the glory of Jerusalem, was but as the place of God's feet, and the ark of God was but his footstool. 1 Chron. xxviii. 2, "As for me, I had in mine heart, saith David, to build a house of rest for the ark of the covenant of the Lord, and for the footstool of our God:" and Isa. lx. 13, "I will make (Zion) the place of my feet glorious." But now in this great day, Jerusalem, that was but God's footstool, shall be God's throne. A great day certainly this shall be, when all things are thus forgotten.

9. "Great shall be the day of Jezreel," because it shall be a day after which there shall be no night. And that you will say will be a great day indeed, in which the saints shall be raised to such a state of prosperity and happiness, that it shall never be darkened any more. The churches here have often had some little release, they have had their days of peace for a while, but it has soon grown to be night, and a dismal night of darkness. But when this great day shall come, it shall be a day that shall never be succeeded by night, for so God promises here to his Jezreel, to make it an eternal excellency, and to make Jerusalem an everlasting joy; and, Dan. ii. 44, God shall in the days of those kings "set up a kingdom which shall never be destroyed," that is, the great day of Jezreel.

This will more clearly appear, if we consider more fully what shall be done for the church and the world on this day. (1.) There shall be the deliverance of the churches from woeful affliction, in which they shall be found a little before. For so the Scripture tells us, Dan. xii. 1, that before this day "there shall be a time of trouble, such as never was since there was a nation even to that same time: and at that time thy people shall be delivered." I might tell you how much some of the ancients have spoken of this; though it be a point that seems to be somewhat strange to us, yet it was one of the most ordinary things known in the primitive times. It was then so generally acknowledged, that Justin Martyr, who was but thirty years after St. John, observes, There is no man who is of the orthodox faith in all things, but acknowledges this. Lactantius shows the glory of this great day of Jezreel, but withal declares that a little before there shall be most grievous times, such times as that all right shall be confounded, the law shall perish, nobody shall know what is his own, the wicked shall have the pre-eminence, and the saints shall be persecuted; so that though in this our time wickedness is grown to such a height, that a man would think it could increase no higher, yet in comparison of the time a little before that great day, these times may be called golden ages. So that great times of affliction will be before that great day; and it is therefore called a great day, because of God's appearing so gloriously in the deliverance of his church. The Scripture speaks of wonderful things which God will do, and show himself marvellous, as he did when Israel came out of Egypt. Who knows but that God is now sending abroad so much of the light of his gospel, and so working in the hearts of men, and giving us such a time of reviving, and calling so many youths as he does, because this great day is at hand, and because before this day we may have a day of dismal darkness, and by this he will prepare people for those times? God will have a numerous seed in the world, therefore so many young people are converted and are so forward, because, I say, God means to prepare them, by this light that we now have, for this great day. And you that are young may expect to go through some difficulties and hardship before this great day

Ego autem et qui sunt per omnia orthodoxæ sententiæ Christiani, &c.

L. 7. c. 15. 24. 28.

comes, but be of good comfort, you may hope to live to see all the glory of this great day: God gives you now time that you may lay up, and be fit seed for such a glorious day as this, that, when sufferings come, you may not be found among the number of the fearful ones, spoken of in Rev. xxi. 8, who "shall have their portion in the lake which burneth with fire and brimstone." Those who through base cowardice and compliance shall yield to vile superstitious vanities, shall be cast out among dogs when that great day comes. God now gives you a day that you may see the evil of superstitious vanities, that you may have truths revealed to you with more freedom than formerly; and who knows but this may be to prepare you for that darkness which may come a little before this great day of Jezreel?

(2.) There shall be the subduing of the adversaries of the church. Though they shall have great power a little before; yet when that great day of Jezreel comes, they shall certainly be all subdued and brought under. Christ, when he shall come in this great day, shall have his "vesture dipped in blood," in destroying the wicked and ungodly, Rev. xix. 13; and when the saints see the wicked destroyed as the Egyptians were in the sea, they shall again "sing the song of Moses," Rev. xv. 3. What was this song of Moses, but the praising of God for the destruction of their adversaries in the sea? God has another sea to destroy the wicked, and another day for his saints to sing over the song of Moses again, especially for the destruction of popery. My brethren, be not troubled to see papists flock together, for when this day shall come, God will so order things that his adversaries shall flock together, but it shall be that they may be destroyed, for God has a great feast and a great sacrifice, and he will sacrifice them especially. And therefore Lactantius, who lived one thousand three hundred years since, speaking of this day, saith, I have a thing to say, but I even tremble to utter it, but I must speak it; and what was it? *Romanum nomen de terra tolletur*; the Roman name shall be taken off from the earth. In those primitive times he prophesied of the destruction of Rome. Perhaps, though he did not see it so clearly, God might intend it for these times. God will destroy the enemies of his churches then. Yea, Ezek. xxviii. 24, there is a promise to the saints that there shall be no more "a pricking brier, nor any grieving thorn," of any that are round about them that despise them; and in another place God saith, that he will "take away the Canaanite out of the land."

Romanum nomen, horret animus dicere, sed, dicam quia futurum est, tolletur de terra. L. 7. c. 15.

(3.) The glorious presence of Christ among the saints shall be displayed. Let it be personal, or what it will, we determine not, but thus far we may confidently affirm, that there shall be a more glorious presence of Jesus Christ among his people, than ever yet was since the beginning of the world. Rev. xxi. 22, "The Lord God Almighty and the Lamb are the temple of it:" and chap. xxii. 3, 4, "The throne of God and of the Lamb shall be in it; and his servants shall serve him: and they shall see his face." And the very last words of Ezek. xlviii. are, "the name of the city from that day shall be" Jehovah-shammah, that is, "The Lord is there."

(4.) Glory shall there be put upon the saints. Glory shall be put upon them, first in regard of their admirable gifts and graces, which shall be heightened and enlarged; the weak shall be as David, and they that are as David shall be as the angel of God at that day. Their adversaries shall bow down before them. They shall have high esteem, even in the thoughts and judgments of many great ones of the world; they shall be called up to heaven, that is, those that are in highest place and dignity shall advance and honour them in that day; yea, the kings of the earth in that day shall come in, and bring their glory to the church. Therefore it is apparent that Rev. xxi. 24 cannot be understood of heaven; for it is said, "the kings of the earth do bring their glory into it;" they shall not bring their glory to the church, when the church shall be in heaven.

(5.) There shall be a wonderful change of all creatures, and glorious, fruitful times. Lactantius says, that the rocks themselves should issue forth honey and precious things; but that we cannot affirm; yet that there shall be a wonderful change of all things, and all creatures brought to a further happiness, even the sensitive creatures, as well as others, than they had before, the Scriptures are clear enough. And we are to understand many scriptures literally that tend this way, concerning the fruitfulness of the earth, and the external glory that there shall be in the creatures. As upon a great marriage feast, or coronation day, all the servants of the prince are in their best array; so when Christ, this Bridegroom, shall come and meet his spouse, all creatures shall be put into a new dress, shall have further glory.

Terra aperiet fœcunditatem suam, et uberrimas fruges sua sponte generabit, rupes montium melle sudabunt, &c. Lactant. l. 7. c. 4.

(6.) A multitude of all nations and people shall flock to the church, that they shall be as "the sand of the sea." But this I have spoken of before at large. Now put all these things together, and "great shall be the day of Jezreel."

Tunc qui erunt in corporibus vivi, non morientur, sed per mille annos infinitam multitudinem generabunt, et erit soboles eorum sancta, et Deo chara. Lactant. ibid.

Yea, but shall these things be so? Though flesh and blood may reason against these things, yet I may apply that place, Zech. ii. 13, "Be silent, O all flesh, before the Lord, for he is raised up out of his holy habitation." God has made known in his word the great things he intends to bring to pass. And Zech. viii. 6, "Thus saith the Lord of hosts; If it be marvellous in the eyes of the remnant of this people in these days, should it also be marvellous in mine eyes? saith the Lord of hosts." These things may seem marvellous to your eyes, especially because we have been but little acquainted with them, but they are not marvellous in the eyes of God. Yea, we find it, that these things were to be kept hidden till the appointed time should come, till we draw near to that great day. God tells us that they were to be sealed up even to the time appointed, Dan. xii. 4; and God tells John that he "must prophesy again before many people, and nations, and tongues, and kings," Rev. x. 11; that is, before the time of the fulfilling of all things, that book of the Revelation shall be made out as clear as if John were come to prophesy again before men. And we hope it is coming, because God begins to let in light, and the morning star seems to arise.

In Zech. xiv. 6, 7, you have mention of a day, that we may apply to the present day: "And it shall come to pass in that day, that the light shall not be clear, nor dark; but it shall be one day which shall be known to the Lord, not day nor night: but it shall come to pass, that at evening time it shall be light." Mark what shall be in that day, ver. 8, "And it shall be in that day, that living waters shall go out from Jerusalem;" and ver. 9, "In that day shall there be one Lord, and his name shall be one;" and then ver. 20, "In that day shall there be upon the bells of the horses, Holiness unto the Lord;" and ver. 21, "In that day there shall be no more the Canaanite in the house of the Lord of hosts." Certainly, my brethren, these scriptures speak of a glorious day that is approaching, but yet, in the beginning of it, it is just such a day as we have at present, wherein the light is neither clear nor dark. It is true, not long since it was dark, now this darkness begins to be a little dispelled, but it is not clear yet, many things for the present darken the light. Opposition and many damps are upon the hearts of God's people, and things go not on as we desire; but blessed be God, it is not night with us; though it be not so dark as it was, or as clear as we desire, it is as it were twilight. Well, but "it shall be one day," that is, a special day; and indeed it is our day now, it is the greatest day that ever yet England had. "It shall be one day which shall be known to the Lord," a day in which the Lord has great purposes to do great things; and, certainly, this our day is known to the Lord, great things God is about to do for his churches, and lay a foundation of glorious things for the good of his people. And then mark, though it be "neither day nor night," yet "at the evening time it shall be light." What a strange expression is here! It shall be a dusky, cloudy day, and then a man would think that at evening it should be quite dark. To be cloudy at noon, and darkish at three or four of the clock in the afternoon, surely then it must needs be more dark in the evening. No, though it be not clear now, though it be a cloudy day, yet at the evening time it shall be light. When light is least expected, and when we most fear darkness, when we are ready to conclude, Our day is gone: once God did bring a day to England, a comfortable day; though it was a little dark, yet there was a glorious light in comparison of what we had before; but now the evening begins to shut upon us, "we looked for light, but behold darkness." If we see things go on with difficulty and opposition, we shall be ready to have our hearts sink within us, and to cry, Now our day is gone, and the evening is coming. But, my brethren, be of good comfort, for "at evening time it shall be light;" when we expect evening, when it is most unlikely to be light, then shall the light of the Lord break forth most gloriously. For whenever this day of Jezreel comes, there must be such a glorious work of God, as may magnify his name before the eyes of all men, and therefore at the evening it shall be light. "And it shall be in that day, that living waters shall go out from Jerusalem:" we have had some drops of living waters in this our day, but there is a day coming wherein living waters shall even flow out of Jerusalem.

Now, to wind up all, there is a day for the saints, a rest for the people of God, a day wherein God will deliver them from all afflictions. I have met with one, who, observing that the Jews might kindle no fire upon their sabbath, because that rest was to signify the rest of the saints, remarks, That was a type that there is such a time of rest for the saints, that they shall be delivered from all fiery trials, all their afflictions shall be taken away. "Great shall be the day of Jezreel."

Obs. 1. Let the consideration of this be a strong argument to draw all people to the ways and love of godliness, to come and join with the churches in appointing Christ Head over them. All you wicked ones who have forsaken the Lord hitherto, come in and join now, and submit unto Jesus Christ as your Head, "for great shall be the day of Jezreel." There is a great day for the church of God, a day of glory, a day of abundance of wonderful mercy from God to the churches. They shall have their day; come you in and embrace religion, that you may partake of their glory. Certainly, the saints of God shall have the best of it, shall have the day of all the world, let the world strive against them as they can. Every man desires to follow the stronger party, and to cleave to that. Would you cleave to the stronger part? Cleave to the saints of God, for certainly they are the stronger part. The church is rising, and will rise more and more till it be risen unto the height. Though there be some opposition, yet it is such as shall make the glory of the day so much the more.

Those men who now stand up to plead for antichrist, and to oppose this work of God, are men born out of time, born in an ill hour. Papists and superstitious people heretofore prospered in their way, because the day of God was not so near, but that was the day of his patience in permitting antichrist to continue. But dost thou resist now? what! superstitious now? what! opposing the work of God now, when God is coming out to fight against popery and superstition, when God is about to do such great things for his churches? Thou fightest against God, and God will fight against thee, and thou shalt be thrown. Thou art born in the worst time that possibly could be, worse than all the adversaries of the truth in former times.

Obs. 2. If there be such a day, let us be willing to suffer a little for a while, and to mourn for the churches a while in that way of mourning to which God calls us, for there is a recompence coming, glory enough coming even in this world. There is a time of triumphing, let us be content with our warfare here for a while.

Obs. 3. Let us study these things. It is useful for people in these times to search into these truths of God, that they may be the better prepared to meet Christ their Bridegroom when he comes. Ezek. xl. 4, speaks of the glorious times of the gospel, especially of these times which I am describing; where God saith to the prophet, "Behold with thine eyes, and hear with thine ears, and set thine heart upon all that I shall show thee." And what did God show him? The measure of the temple, and all the glorious things that should be in the church in future times. So I say to you, my brethren, concerning all I have spoken of the great day of Jezreel; behold with your eyes, look into God's book and see what is said there, and hear with your ears, and set your hearts upon what has been set before you. In Isa. xli. 20, you have a passage somewhat like this: speaking of the mercies of God to his church in latter times, the prophet saith, "That they may see, and know, and consider, and understand together, that the hand of the Lord hath done this, and the Holy One of Israel hath created it." Mark how one word is heaped upon another, that they may "see, and know, and consider, and understand" what God would do for his people. And when God revealed the glorious things he intended for his church in future times in the book of the Revelation, mark how he begins. It is said, God gave this first to Christ; secondly, Christ to the angel; thirdly, the angel to John; and then there is pronounced a blessing to him that reads and hears the words of this prophecy, and understands it. What a solemn way of blessing is here! There is no instance in the Bible of a blessing so solemnly proclaimed to the reading and hearing of any of the books of God, as to that book. Therefore, though they are things that seem to be above us, yet, certainly, God would have us to inquire into these things. It is the fruit of the purchase of the blood of Christ to open these seals, Rev. v. 9. There was no man in heaven nor in earth that was able to open the book, and to loose the seals thereof; only the Lamb that was slain, and that hath redeemed us unto God by his blood, he was only worthy to open the seals. It is a fruit, I say, of the slaughter of Christ and of his blood, and therefore cry to him to open these things to thee. And though thou art very weak in regard of parts, and thinkest, How can I understand such things as these? know that Christ through his blood comes to open these seals, and seeing it is a fruit of his blood, it is no matter whether thou art weak or strong if he open them to thee. God saith to the prophet, Jer. xxxiii. 2, "Call unto me, and I will show thee great and mighty things which thou knowest not;" so I say to you, be a praying people, call upon God, and he will cause you to understand great and excellent things that you have not known.

Obs. 4. Seeing these things shall be thus, what manner of persons ought we to be! how heavenly our conversation! Our hearts should rise up from the earth, seeing

God intends to do such great things for his people. "Arise, shine; for thy light is come, and the glory of the Lord is risen upon thee," Isa. lx. 1. So I say to the churches now, Arise, arise, shake off the dust of your earthly affections, for the light of God is now ready to arise upon you. Now *sursum corda*, now lift up your hearts above the things of the world. We read in Rev. iv. of the four living creatures that appeared unto John; the first was like a lion, and the second like an ox, and the third had a face as a man, and the fourth was like a flying eagle. They are, according to the interpretation of Brightman, to describe to us the four states and conditions of the church. The primitive times were lion-like for their valour; the second age like an ox, to bear the burden of antichrist; the third had a face as a man, that stood for their liberties, and would not be under slavery, and they are our times; and then the fourth as an eagle that soared aloft. In the state of the church hereafter, they shall be like an eagle, have heavenly hearts, no such drossy, base, earthly hearts as we have now. Labour we even now to be so that we may be fit for that day.

Obs. 5. Let us all prepare for the Bridegroom against his coming. How shall we prepare? The clothing then shall be "white linen, which is the righteousness of the saints." That great doctrine of our justification by the righteousness of Christ shall be the great business of that day, in which the glory of the saints shall much consist; they shall be clothed with that; it shall be clearly understood of all men; they shall be ashamed to rest upon duties and ordinances as now they do. Let us study the doctrine of the righteousness of Christ aforehand, for that is to be our clothing at that day, that is the white linen of the saints which shall be their glory. Let us prepare our lamps, and keep them all burning and shining; the oil not only of justification, but of sanctification, active, stirring in our hearts; that so we may be fit to entertain the Bridegroom whenever he comes.

Obs. 6. All of you labour now to instruct your children in the knowledge of God and of Christ, bring them up in the fear of the Lord, that they may be seed for that day. Acquaint them with these things, for though perhaps you may be dead and gone before this great day, yet they may live to see it; therefore catechise them, and instruct them, and drop into them those principles that may fit them for meeting Jesus Christ their Bridegroom.

Obs. 7. To conclude all, Let us be all praying Christians. It is that which is charged upon us in Isa. lxii. 6, 7, "Ye that make mention of the Lord, keep not silence, and give him no rest, till he establish, and till he make Jerusalem a praise in the earth." God has a day to set up Jerusalem as the praise of the whole earth; O be praying, praying Christians every one of you, and give God no rest till he effect this. Remind God of all his promises, search the prophets, search the book of God, and urge God with these promises to the church. And you that are the weakest, be not discouraged in your prayers, you may be a means to further and hasten this great day of Jezreel. Psal. cii. 17, the psalmist had spoken before of God's building up Zion, (and certainly that psalm is a prophecy of the future, glorious times of the church,) mark what he now saith, "He will regard the prayer of the destitute, and not despise their prayer." Speaking of those who shall live a little before this day of Jezreel, the Lord shall regard the prayer of the destitute. The word הערער translated destitute, signifies a poor shrub in the wilderness, that the foot of every beast is ready to tread down; and that poor shrub, that perhaps is despicable in the eyes of the world, and despicable in his own eyes, yet saith the text, the Lord shall regard the prayer of that poor shrub. Is there ever a poor shrub present, though never so destitute or despicable in the eyes of the world, or in thine own eyes? yet be thou a praying Christian, praying for those glorious things for the church, and God will regard thy prayer, he will not despise thy prayer. Perhaps thou art ready to despise thy prayers thyself, but God will not despise them. Let all our hearts be lifted up, and let us all cry with the church, Come, Lord Jesus, come quickly. O let this day come, "for great shall be the day of Jezreel."

CHAPTER II.

Ver. 1. *Say ye unto your brethren, Ammi; and to your sisters, Ruhamah.*

SOME join the first verse of this chapter to the end of the former; and (according to a sense that may be given of the words, agreeable to the scope of the latter part of the former chapter) it may seem more fit to be made the end of that, than the beginning of this. There God was promising mercy to his people, that those who were not his people should be his people, and those that had not received mercy should receive mercy. Now he calls upon all whose hearts were with God, to speak to one another of this great favour of God to his people, for their mutual encouragement, and for the praise of his name. As if he should say, Well, you have been under dreadful threats of God, your sins have called for severe punishment, but my grace is free, it is rich and powerful, therefore you that were not my people shall become my people; you that had not obtained mercy shall obtain mercy: "Say unto your brethren, Ammi; and to your sisters, Ruhamah;" that is, O you that are godly, speak one to another, and tell one another, for the quickening of one another's hearts, of this great favour of God, his free grace! O say, Ammi, Ammi, the people of God; Ruhamah, God's mercy: we were not his people, but now Ammi again, God has promised to make us his people, we were rejected from mercy, but mercy is come again, now Ruhamah. Oh the mercy of God! oh that free grace of our God! that we who have been so vile, we who have so provoked the eyes of his glory, we who have so sinned against mercy itself, that mercy should thus follow us, to make us his people, and to save us from his wrath! Ammi! Ruhamah!

Obs. 1. It is a good thing to speak of the loving-kindness of our God. "It is a good thing to give thanks unto the Lord, and to sing praises unto thy name, O Most High; to show forth thy loving-kindness in the morning, and thy faithfulness every night," Psal. xcii. 1, 2. That psalm is appointed for the sabbath. It is a work of the sabbath to be speaking one to another of the goodness of God; especially in this case, when a people were afraid that they should have been for ever rejected, and yet God calls them again, Ammi, my people, and says now that he will have mercy upon them. "One generation shall praise thy works to another, and shall declare thy mighty acts: I will speak of the glorious honour of thy majesty, and of thy wondrous works," Psal. cxlv. 4, 5. Mark what the works of God are toward his church, when he comes in the ways of mercy; they are wondrous works of God, they are the mighty acts of God, they are such wherein the honour of God appears, yea, they are the honour of his majesty, yea, they are the glorious honour of his majesty. He displays majesty, honour of majesty, glorious honour of majesty, the mighty works of God, the wonderful works of God. When these appear, these are fit to be declared indeed. And for them to be able to say to one another, Ammi, and Ruhamah, it was to declare the wonderful works of God, and the glorious honour of his majesty. Yea, it follows further in that psalm, ver. 6, "men shall speak of the might of thy terrible acts: and I will declare thy greatness." And ver. 7, "They shall abundantly utter the memory of thy great goodness." Montanus renders it, ***eructabunt***, they shall not be able to keep it in, but break forth in the memory of thy goodness.

Happy are those people to whom God grants such subjects of discourse, that they may say to their brethren and sisters, Ammi, and Ruhamah. It was not long since, that, when we met with our brethren, we could not have such a subject of discourse as this, but usually when Christians met together, after their salutations, their first question was; Oh! what shall we do? what course shall we take? All the news almost in the kingdom, and the subject of discourses, specially among the saints, was this; Such a minister silenced in such a place, such a one banished in another place, such a one imprisoned in another place, such a one high-commissioned in another place, such signs of the wrath of God upon us, we are afraid that God is going, if he be not quite gone already; we are afraid that he will not only reject us from being his people, but reject us from being a people upon the face of the earth.

But, blessed be God, he has changed the subject of our discourses. Now, God's ways have begun to be towards us as if he intended to make us again his people. Now, when we meet together, we have plentiful subjects of discourse about God's grace and mercy; we say, Ammi, Ruhamah, O the Lord manifests goodness to an unworthy nation, we have hope that yet he will own us to be his people, that yet he will show mercy to us, though never so unworthy. Who would have thought to have seen and heard such things as we have seen and heard! who would have thought to have seen the hearts of the adversaries so daunted, their power so curbed, their rage so quelled, the wicked in their own works so insnared, and their hopes so disappointed! Who would have thought to have seen the saints so rejoicing, their liberties so enlarged, their hearts and expectations so raised! This is the free grace of God: Ammi, Ruhamah, we have obtained mercy, God has dealt with us in abundance of grace. But we must not discourse of this when we meet as matter of news only, we must speak of it to the praise of God, for the sanctifying of our hearts.

Our brethren in Ireland have another subject of discourse at this day. When a brother and a sister meet, they say, Oh my father, my mother, taken such a day by the rebels and cruelly massacred; such a kinsman, such a kinswoman, taken such a day and fearfully murdered; such houses were fired, such cities and towns were taken! and with what sorrowful faces do they look one upon another, when they are thus relating these sad things? The word of God came out against England, but it has lighted upon Ireland. O unworthy are we of these mercies which we enjoy, if, when we meet together, our discourses be frothy and light, about vain and trivial things, when God has given us such a subject of discourse as he has done by such gracious, wonderful, and glorious ways of his mercy towards us in this latter age.

Obs. 2. As the mercies of God are to be inculcated upon our spirits, we should not only tell them one to another, but again and again impress them upon our hearts. "Say to your brethren, Ammi; and to your sisters, Ruhamah." Indeed God's mercies at first seem to take impression upon our spirits, but the impression is soon vanished.

Obs. 3. A gracious heart should rejoice in God's mercies towards others. "Say to your brethren;" that is, according to some, Let Judah, to whom God showed special mercy, say to Israel, to the ten tribes, which were more threatened to be cast off from being the people of God, than Judah was. Let Judah rejoice in this, that their brethren are received again to mercy. God's mercies are an infinite ocean, there needs no envying there, no grieving for that which others have. When one man is richer than another, another is ready rather to envy him than to rejoice. A courtier envies the favour another has at court; why? because these are narrow things. But when we come to God's mercy, there is room enough there; that soul which has been made partaker of mercy, counts it a great happiness when in any way the mercy of God is magnified.

Obs. 4. Those whom God has received unto mercy, we should receive into brotherly affection. "Say to your brethren and sisters:" has God showed mercy to such and such, well may we account them our brethren and sisters then. If God takes them to mercy, we must be ready willingly to take them into brotherly society.

But if we take these words as the beginning of the second chapter, we shall see them interpreted in a different way. And taking them so, as most do, I shall first show you the scope of the chapter in the parts of it, and then in what sense the words may be expounded, as the beginning of this chapter.

The scope of this second chapter is much according to that of the first, viz. to show to Israel their sin and danger; and, secondly, to promise God's abundant grace and mercy again. The first is especially from the beginning to the 14th verse; and the second from the 14th verse to the end of the chapter.

Yet this is not an exact division, neither can we give one, more than we could give of the other chapter, because things are so intermixed. They are the pathetical expressions of a loving, and yet a provoked, husband. He is convincing his spouse who has dealt falsely with him, and showing her her sin and danger; but whilst he is manifesting his displeasure, the bowels of his compassion begin to yearn, and he must use some expressions of love in the midst of all; then, when he has had some expressions of love, he again rebukes her and shows her her sin, and then his bowels yearn, and he returns to expressions of love again. We have found it so in the former chapter, and shall find it so in this: for though the beginning of this chapter, to the 14th verse, is specially spent in convincing of sin and threatening of judgment, yet in the 6th and 7th verses there are promises of mercy and favour, and expressions of love; and then in the 8th verse he threatens again, and in the 14th verse begins to express mercy again.

As God acts in this case, so should we. When we rebuke others we should manifest love to them; and when we manifest love, to do it so as to take notice of what is amiss, and to reprove them. Many parents know not how to rebuke their children, they do it with nothing but bitterness; and they know not how to manifest their love, they do it with nothing but fondling and immoderate indulgence. God unites both together.

What then must be the sense and the scope of the words, "Say to your brethren, Ammi," &c. Something must be supplied for making up the full sense. As if God had said, O Ammi, you whom I have reserved to be my people, you to whom I have showed mercy, there yet is remaining a handful of you; while you remain to be my people, and others cast off, and you obtaining mercy, and others rejected, let it be your care to exhort, persuade, convince, and to use all the means you can to bring your brethren and sisters to that grace of God which you have received. "Say to your brethren:" say; it is not expressed what they should say, but by that which follows we may understand what the meaning of God is. When he saith, "Plead with your mother," &c., that is, You, the remnant, that have received mercy, and are my people, do not think that, so long as you escape, and are well enough yourselves, it is no great matter what becomes of others; O no, but let your hearts be much toward your brethren and sisters, let your bowels yearn toward them. O seek, if it be possible, to draw them unto God, that they may receive mercy too; labour to convince them; say, and speak to them, that they may not yet stand out against God and be obstinate: "Say to your brethren, Ammi, and to your sisters, Ruhamah."

Obs. 1. That in the most corrupt times God usually reserves a people, to deliver some from the guilt of the general corruptions of the place where they live. This Ammi and Ruhamah were a remainder, whom God delivered through his grace from the general corruptions of the place where they lived; for otherwise they had not been fit to have said to their brethren, or to have spoken to their sisters, in this sense.

Obs. 2. Those whom God delivers from the guilt of general corruptions, are to be acknowledged the people of God. Such as have received mercy from God in a special manner. It is free grace that has made this difference between you and others. Augustine remarks on 1 Kings xix. 18, "I have left me seven thousand in Israel," God says not, there are left seven thousand, or they have left themselves, but I have left. It is the special work of God to preserve any for himself in evil times.

Reliqui mihi septem millia, non ait relicta sunt vel reliquerunt se, sed reliqui; reliquiæ per electionem gratiæ. August. de Bon. Persev. l. 2. c. 18.

Obs. 3. The Lord takes special notice of those who are thus by his grace preserved in evil times. Ammi, Ruhamah. There are a people among these that are Ammi, my people, that have obtained mercy from me, mine eyes are upon them, my heart is toward them; there is a number who have kept their garments undefiled even in Sardis, and I will remember this for ever for their good. "Noah was a just man and perfect in his generations," Gen. vi. 9; and what then? chap. vii. 1, "Come thou and all thy house into the ark; for thee have I seen righteous before me in this generation."

Obs. 4. Such as keep themselves from the corruptions of the times wherein they live, they, and only they, are fit to exhort and reprove others. Those that are not guilty themselves as others are, are fit to speak to others, to say to their brethren and to their sisters. They are fit to exhort, who perform the duties themselves that they exhort unto. We say it is a shameful thing for one to be teaching, if he be guilty himself; he cannot with freedom of spirit say to his brethren and sisters, Ammi.

Turpe est doctori, cum culpa redarguit ipsum.

Obs. 5. It is the duty of those whom God has delivered from the corruption of the times, to seek to draw all others to God; to seek to convince others of their evil ways, and so bring them in to the truth. We read, Lev. xix. 17, "Thou shalt not hate thy brother in thine heart: thou shalt in any wise rebuke thy neighbour, and not suffer sin upon him." Surely those who have obtained mercy, and have the impression of God's mercy upon their spirits, are far from having hateful hearts; now it is hatred for any to suffer sin to lie upon his brother, and not to do what in him lies to help him. It is desperate pride for men to triumph over others in their falls, and it is wicked cruelty to suffer others to lie down when they are fallen, if they can raise them. Seafaring men, who are delivered themselves from shipwreck, and all is safe with them, if they see another ship ready to sink in the sea, and those on ship-board cry out to them to come to help to save them, though they be never so far remote, yet if it should be known that they decline to go out to help them, all the seamen would cry out shame on such, and be ready to stone them for letting a ship sink when they might have helped. Certainly it is the same case with those to whom God has showed mercy, if others lie in their sins, and they do not what they can for their help.

Obs. 6. The nearer the relation of any persons is to us, the more should our compassion be towards them, in seeking to deliver them from their sins. "Say to your brethren, and to your sisters." There is more likelihood of prevailing with your brethren and sisters. Has God converted you, and have you a brother or a sister not converted, or any of your kindred? go, and tell them of the danger of their evil ways, tell them of the excellency of the ways of God, exhort them to come in, and to make trial of the blessed ways of God. When a brother speaks to a brother, or a sister to a sister, it is the bringing a hammer of gold to work upon gold, and of silver to work upon silver.

Obs. 7. Exhortations to and reprehensions of others, should be given with much love and meekness. "Say to your brethren and sisters." Look upon them as brethren and sisters, though they have not yet obtained the like mercy that you have. St. Paul, 2 Thess. iii. 15, speaking of one that walks inordinately, from whom we are to withdraw in familiar society, yet, saith he, "admonish him as a brother." Those who reprove and admonish others with bitterness of spirit and evil speaking, are like a foolish fowler, who seeks to get the fowl, but goes boisterously, and makes a noise: the way, if he would get it, is to go on quietly, softly, and gently; so the way to gain a brother, is not by boisterousness and violence, but softness, and gentleness. It is observed by some of the Jews concerning Exod. xxv. 3, where the matter of the tabernacle is said to be gold, and silver, and brass, still you do not hear of iron required for the building of it; no, iron, rigid, severe, hard dispositions, are not fit either to be matter of the tabernacle themselves, or to draw others to be the matter of it.

Yea, but if saying will not be enough to do the deed, then follows pleading. That is the second. Say to them, admonish them, exhort them, but what if that will not do? do not leave them immediately, but "plead," yea, and "plead with your mother" too, not only with your brethren and with your sisters, but with your mother.

• Ver. 2. *Plead with your mother, plead: for she is not my wife, neither am I her husband: let her therefore put away her whoredoms out of her sight, and her adulteries from between her breasts;*

ריבו Plead, Litigate, so some, *Contendite*, Strive; the Vulgate reads *Judicate*, Judge your mother. It may seem to be a harsh phrase at first, but we shall labour to acquaint you with the mind of God in it. Here is an exhortation to the private members of the church, to all, one or other, to plead with their mother, to plead even with the church of which they are members, and so to plead as to deal plainly, and to tell her that she is not the wife of God.

Obs. 1. Here we see God's condescension, that he will have us plead the case betwixt others and himself, as Isa. v. 3, "Judge, I pray you, betwixt me and my vineyard." This shows the equity of God's dealing. Plead the case; perhaps some of you might think I deal hardly with your mother in so rejecting her, and in bringing such judgments upon her. No, not so, but plead you the case, plead rather with her, than complain of me for my dealing with her.

Obs. 2. When exhortations and admonitions will not do, we must strengthen ourselves by pleading. If there be any way more powerful than exhortation and admonition, we should take that way, and not presently give over; for though it is not said here, Plead with your brothers and sisters, yet they are included in this, when he saith "Plead with your mother."

Obs. 3. It is a hard thing to convince idolaters of their sin, and of the justice of God coming against them for their sin. "Plead with your mother, plead;" she will not acknowledge it, she will stand it out, and say she has not done so ill, she is not worthy to be cast off; you had need plead, and plead hard with her. Idolaters have so many distinctions, evasions, and pretences, that it is a thousand to one if you prevail with them. When you deal with papists about worshipping of images, they will have such distinctions of worship *per se*, and worship *per accidens*, of honouring the creature *propter se, et propter aliud, proprie, improprie*, and a hundred of such distinctions and evasions, till they distinguish away the truth, and scarce understand themselves what they mean by their distinctions. Hence, idolaters scorn at judgments threatened, they think only a company of foolish and timorous people fear such things; they cry out, Say they that we are idolaters, and that grievous judgments of God are coming upon us? a company of foolish, melancholy people, they fear their own fancies! Was it not so heretofore, when we were going on in the ways of idolatry apace? Was it not the jeer and scorn of all such spirits? If any seem but to question about idolatry, they would never be convinced of such a sin, nor ever fear any judgment hanging over our heads. Though God has prevented it through his grace, and has showed his prerogative in the ways of his mercy, yet certainly there was sign enough of dreadful wrath hanging over us, and what yet may be we know not.

Obs. 4. God loves to have people dealt with in a convincing way. "Plead with your mother, plead." It is a forensic word, and carries with it such a kind of pleading as must be convincing and powerful. The Lord does not declare to the prophet, or to those other good people who were free from idolatry, that the people of Israel were generally corrupted; he does not bid them go and terrify them, and speak bitterly to them; but go and plead the cause with them, seek to convince them, not rail upon them, but convince them. God loves to have people dealt with in a convincing way. Let not therefore any one think it enough, either minister or layman, that he can speak terribly to people, and cry out against their sins; but let him labour to convince them, to deal with them as rational creatures, and to take away their secret objections and shifts, and to make their sins plain before their consciences. A convincing preacher, and a convincing Christian, is such a one as may be very useful, and do abundance of good to the church of God.

Obs. 5. It is very fit that God should have some to plead for him, to plead his cause, as well as Satan has to plead his. The devil never wants pleaders. When did there ever such a bad cause come to a bench, or to any society, but found some that would plead for it? A shame that the worst cause in the world should have pleaders for it, and many times the cause of God suffers by men being mute. God will take this very ill at their hands. It is true, God saith he will plead his own cause, and we are bound to pray, according to the psalmist, that God would "arise and plead his own cause." And indeed, if God had not risen and pleaded his own cause better than we did, his cause would have been in the dirt before this. God is raising up his own cause, no thanks to us; we have cause to lay our hands upon our mouths as guilty, in that we so basely and cowardly let the cause of God suffer; and God appearing so immediately and gloriously, is the rebuking of us because we did not, we would not, before stand up to plead his cause.

Obs. 6. When any have found mercy from God, the sweetness of that mercy so warms their hearts, that they cannot endure to see that blessed God dishonoured. Plead you, Ammi, Ruhamah: What, my people, those to whom I have showed mercy, what though it be your mother, what though it be any dear to you, what though they be great ones, what though they be a multitude, yet plead, plead for me against them. God's mercy is so sweet, it so inflames them, that they must plead for God against any in the world.

"Plead with your mother." That is, with the church, called a mother, because, as the mother is as it were the root from whence children come, and divides herself into branches; so the community of a commonwealth or a church is called in Scripture a mother, and the particular members are as several branches that grow from that root, they are as children. Therefore you have such expressions in Scripture, as "the daughters of Jerusalem;" and there is no great difference between calling Jerusalem which is the state, mother, or Jerusalem which is the church, mother; for indeed the church and state were mixed both together. Learn hence,

Obs. 7. It is lawful for children to plead with their parents. Though it is true, this aims at something higher than what is between natural children and their parents, yet from the expression this is intimated and implied, That it is lawful for children to plead with their parents. If children see their parents in an ungodly way, they may lawfully plead with them, and their parents are bound to hearken to their pleading God's cause. It is a speech of Tertullian's, The begetter is to be beloved, and we may add, he is to be honoured, but our Creator is to be preferred. Children must give due respect to their parents, yet so, as preferring the Lord before them; and if the parents go against God, even their children must plead against them. As it is a great sin for parents to prefer their children before God, so it is a great sin for children to prefer their parents before God.

Amandus generator, sed præponendus Creator.

Do not think I aim to set children against their parents, be but content to hear to the end, and you will be convinced that it is fit for children to plead with their parents when they go from God. Thus we see it was with Jonathan, 1 Sam. xix. 4; he pleaded with his father, when he saw him in such a passionate mood and cruel spirit toward poor David, "Let not the king sin against his servant, against David." "Let not the king," he gives him very respectful words, and shows his due honour to his father: "Let not the king sin against his servant," and then goes on and tells his father of the good service David had done, and that David did not deserve such ill usage from him. Thus, when children see their fathers or mothers in a passion, it is fit enough for them in a humble, submissive manner to say, I beseech you, father, or mother, consider that by these distempered passions, instead of helping yourself, you sin against God; you know by experience, that often in such passion many sins have broken from you, and you have grieved for it afterwards, oh do not again that which your conscience has so often checked you for. If children thus plead with their parents, they do no more than their duty, and their parents are bound to hearken to them. I confess, they should be very careful to preserve due respect to their parents, and not speak pertly, but with all reverence and submission; and privately too, if possible, not to divulge their parents' weaknesses. You know Ham was cursed for discovering his father's nakedness, though he was drunk, he did not show due respect at that time to him; but if he had sought to cover his father's nakedness, and after had come and pleaded the case with him, certainly he had not been cursed, but received a blessing.

Yea, and there is a great deal of reason that children should plead with their parents, and that you should give them leave so to do, because, you know, children are the worse for your sins, God threatens to "visit the sins of the parents upon the children, to the third and fourth generation;" there are many threatenings against children for the sins of their parents, therefore it concerns your children that they should plead with you, and that you should suffer them. For if you say, Sirrah, what have you to do with me? what does it concern you? Yes, the child, if he does it in modesty and humility, may say, O father, it does concern me, I may fare the worse for your sins; God may come upon me for them; therefore give me leave, I beseech you, to plead the cause of God with you. And if you will not give your children leave in this, they may rise up as witnesses against you another day.

It is a very suitable and powerful pleading, that when children cannot prevail by humble and submissive address, then to plead with tears. We read that when Cranmer and Ridley came to King Edward the Sixth, and were so earnest that he should give way to his sister, the Lady Mary, to have mass, he stood out and pleaded the case with them, and told them it was a sin against God. They used many carnal arguments to persuade the king, but he withstood them a great while. At length, when King Edward, who was but about fifteen years of age, saw he could not prevail by pleading with words against those grave men, he burst into tears, and that so prevailed with them, that they went away, and concluded that the king had more divinity in his little finger than they had in all their bodies, and so yielded to him. Certainly, in such pleadings, the heart of a parent must needs be much hardened if he will not break and yield to his child.

You that are parents, look upon your children's pleading with you, and consider with yourselves, What! does God send one of my children to come and plead the cause of God with me, to draw me from the ways of sin, and to do good to my soul for ever? surely it is a mercy to have one out of my own bowels to stand for the cause of God; surely God is in it; I see this child in other things walks humbly and obediently unto me. As indeed you children, that plead with your parents, need be careful so much the rather to be obedient to them, and not use an unseemly manner to check and reprove them; and then it cannot but convince the heart of a parent. What a blessing will it be to you children, if you, who have received your natural life from your parents, should be a means of their spiritual and eternal life!

Obs. 9. The members of a state and church should behave towards it as children to a mother. They should have the affection of children to it, they should take much to heart those things that concern it, the sufferings of state or church should be the sufferings of all its members. There are children of Belial risen up among us, a viperous generation, who are even tearing the bowels of our mother; let our hearts break for this, as Psal. xxxv. 14, "I bowed down heavily, as one that mourneth for his mother." Let us not lift up our heads and be merry now, but for the present bow down heavily, as those that are called, though in some respects to rejoice, yet, in many others, to mourn this day for our mother. Yea, let our hearts rise against those vile monsters that join with a party to bring such woeful confusion and trouble to our mother. We may say to them justly, as Saul said to Jonathan passionately, "You children of the rebellious and perverse, why have you chosen to join with them to your own confusion, and to the confusion of your mother's nakedness?" Let us do what we can to help. Shall we see her bowels torn, and not stir at all? She calls now to us to come and help her, and lets us know that if it go ill with her it cannot go well with us. If the mother's breast, through some incurable disease, must be cut off, the tender father takes away the children, and will not suffer them to behold the torture of their mother. Who knows but that this has been God's end in taking away his dear children in former times, because he would not have their tender hearts see so much sorrow and evil as should befall their mother? And what God has reserved for us to see in the sufferings of our mother, we do not know. However, let her not suffer by us, let her not suffer for want of our help, let her not suffer without us, let us not be so unnatural as every one to be shifting for himself, neglecting our mother, that should be as dear to us as the bowels out of which we came.

Obs. 10. Those that are godly should not only devote themselves to do good to themselves or friends in private, but they are to labour to do good to the public also. Not only say to your sisters and your brethren, but "plead with your mother." There are many narrow-spirited men, who, if they can discharge, as they think, their consciences with their families, and can plead with their servants and children, or some of their own near acquaintance, they have done enough, though for the public they take no care at all.

Obs. 11. It is apparently implied, that all those who are members of any church ought to be men of knowledge. Why? because they are such as are called upon to plead with their mother. It is not for an ignorant sot to plead with a church of God. The members of every church, therefore, should be enlightened, as in some cases they must plead with their mother.

Obs. 12. God gives liberty to some private members of churches, yea, it is their duty in some cases to plead with the whole church. This we must speak of a little more. God's ways and his cause are so equal, that private Christians, though they are very weak, yet they may be able to plead with a church. It is true, a poor, weak, private Christian has a great disadvantage when he is to deal with a whole church, where there are many godly and learned: but if there is a disadvantage one way, the advantage is as much the other way, as the cause of God is on the one side, and not on the other. The goodness of the cause is as great an advantage, as the abilities and number on the other side is a disadvantage. And sometimes particular members of a church have no other way to free themselves from the guilt of the sins of the church, but by pleading with them.

Yea, and sometimes God has blessed the pleading of some few, and of weak ones too, with a multitude. Perhaps you may have heard of that notable story we have in ecclesiastical history of Paphnutius, who being in the council of Nice, where there were three hundred and eighteen bishops, and the business was about the marriage of ministers; generally they decided, that those who were single should not marry. Paphnutius alone pleads against them all in that case, and God so wrought, that he carried the cause, and he, one man, convinced all these three hundred and eighteen bishops. Therefore it is no discouragement for one man to stand up and plead against a great many. So Petrus Waldensis, in the story of the Waldenses, though he was but one at first, yet he stood against many thousands, and God blessed that which he did for the conversion of thousands. And Luther, you know, stood against almost all the world.

Yea, and though this one man may be but a private man, a weak man, God may bless that which he saith sometimes more than that which more learned men shall say. I have read in the Centuries this story: A company of bishops being met together, there was a philosopher that stood out against the Christian religion, and so reasoned against them all, that he seemed to have the better of it. Amongst them there was one very godly and holy man, but a very weak man; he, seeing the cause of God likely to suffer, desired leave to speak and encounter this philosopher. All the rest were troubled at it, thinking that God's cause would suffer more by him, knowing that he was a very weak man; but yet, knowing withal that he was a very holy man, none would oppose, but let him speak. So he began with the philosopher, reciting many articles of the faith; Tell me, said he, with majesty and authority, do you believe that these things are so? do not so reason the case about these articles of our faith, but do you believe? Presently the philosopher acknowledged himself overcome. Hitherto, said he, I have heard words, and returned words, but now I feel the Divine power, and I cannot further answer; and so yielded to be a Christian upon the pleading of this poor weak man, yet a very holy and godly man. God has blessed the pleading of weak ones, though against those that are very strong, therefore they must not be contemned.

Hactenus verba audivi et verba reddidi, sed cum divina virtus accessit, ultra respondere non potui.

Œcolampadius saith,* Christ would be contemned and dishonoured, if we would not hear, were it but a child speaking with his Spirit, though all the world should be against it. And in Isa. xi. 6, there is a promise, that in the times of the gospel the spirits of men should be so brought down, that they should not stand upon their greatness and learning, but "a little child should lead them;" that is the humble temper that God would have under the gospel.

But it may be said, Will not this argue self-conceit? What! for one man, a private man, to plead with so many, with a church? It is a sign that such a one is very opinionated, that should think that what he apprehends is sufficient to stand against the apprehension of so many learned and godly men as are in the church. How can this be freed from arrogance and proud conceitedness? I answer, not so, it may be conscience, and not self-conceit, for the rule of conscience is not the abilities, nor the holiness, nor the multitude of others, but it is that light that God lets in to convince according to his word. Nay, further, I suppose I may convince you that this pleading for God may proceed from much self-denial, and the not pleading may proceed from vile, sinful self-respect. How will that appear? Thus: for a private man when he sees the truth of God suffer, if he be of a humble and an ingenuous spirit, it cannot but be exceeding grievous to him to think, that he must contest with such a multitude of able and godly men. He would rather a hundred times, if he looked at his own quiet and ease, sit down: For, thinks he, if I speak, by this I shall be endangered to be accounted self-conceited, I shall have the accusation of pride, I shall displease many of my friends, I shall make a great disturbance in myself; I am sure of my own peace, whatever I do to others, and how much better were it for me to sit still and be quiet. A humble spirit would reason thus, but conscience puts him upon it: I shall contract guilt to myself if I be not, at least, a witness for God's truth; therefore though I shall suffer so much in it, yet, rather than the truth shall suffer, rather than conscience shall plead against me, I will plead, though never so much to my disadvantage. Now, if such a one carry it humbly and quietly, certainly he is rather to be accounted a self-denying man; for it is a very hard task. Whereas, on the other side, self-love is more likely to think thus: It is true, these things are not right, I see they are not according to the truth of God. Conscience indeed would have me speak, but I shall trouble myself, and what will they think of me on the other side, where there are so many able and godly men? surely I shall be thought a conceited fool, and therefore I were as good hold my peace, and sleep in a whole skin, and be quiet. Thus because they have so much self-respect, and love their own quiet, and cannot endure to suffer any trouble, they will leave the truth to suffer, and their consciences to be pleading against themselves, rather than thus plead for the cause of God.

Certainly they that are charitable would rather take things in the better part, than in the evil. It is possible that a man may through pride of spirit plead with others, but yet you may perceive it in the general course of his conduct. Now if, in the general course of a man, he carries himself humbly and submissively, so that you see him yielding as much as he can in all lawful things, and when he pleads against an evil he is not sudden, nor rash, nor pleads against every light evil, but approaches it with trouble in his spirit, and carries it with all quietness and humility; it is your rigidness, and that spirit which does not beseem a Christian, which is not the spirit of Christ in this thing, to judge this to be pride. For certainly under this false judgment the cause of God has suffered much.

You will say, How can it be imagined, that one man should see more than many, more than others equally able? To that I answer, In a community, where there are many, though they should be godly, yet many of them may have their spirits biassed with prejudice and self-ends, and so not come to see the truth, though they are more able. Again; perhaps, though they may be more able in most things, yet in some one thing God may leave them; yea, though they may be more able at other times, yet for some one time God may leave a man in a thing that he is very able in at another time. And perhaps a great many of them for the present may have so much distemper of spirit, as they may not speak according to what they think themselves. Therefore it may be useful for some one man to be pleading with many others.

I beseech you consider this, it is very useful. Men must not think that God dispenses the knowledge of his truth always according to natural abilities. For want of this consideration many are led into much evil. For they think with themselves, if a man have more ability to understand natural things than others have, therefore he must needs have more ability to understand spiritual things than others have. This is a mistake. A learned man may have great abilities, and understand the rules of nature, yet a poor weak man may have the mind of Christ more than he has. For the promise is to them that fear God: "The secret of the Lord is with them that fear him," Psal. xxv. 14. It may be another man has more abilities, but his spirit may be more distempered than the poor weak man's. "I thank thee, O Father, Lord of heaven and earth, because thou hast hid these things from the wise and prudent, and hast revealed them unto babes. Even so, Father: for so it seemed good in thy sight," Matt. xi. 25, 26.

If multitudes had been an argument against the truth, then in the primitive times, when the Christian religion began, certainly very few would have followed Jesus Christ. Yea, and there is not more disadvantage and disproportion between one or two private members of a church and the whole church, than there was at that time between the whole church and the world. St. John saith, "We know that we are of God, and the whole world lieth in wickedness," 1 John v. 19. "We know:" what a singular spirit was here! here was singularity indeed, if you talk of singularity; you are afraid you should be counted self-conceited and singular in differing from others. "We know that we are of God, and *the whole world* lieth in wickedness."

Thus we see the thing a little cleared, as this point had need be, but we have not yet done with it. There must be some rules given, or otherwise we should wrong the point in naming it.

* Contemneretur ecclesia Christi, si vel unum puellum ejus Divino Spiritu loquentem non audiremus, etiamsi omnes reclament. Œcolampadius.

Christians may plead with their mother, yet they must observe these rules.

First, They must not plead with her for every light thing; for the Scripture gives us this rule, " Love covereth a multitude of sins." We must not stand pleading for every infirmity with our brother, but rather pass by many and cover them; much less then with the church. But if there be that which is notorious, so that I cannot have communion with them, and I shall be wrapped up in the guilt except I testify the truth, certainly then I am bound to plead.

Secondly, It must be orderly done; that is, if possible, you must make the officers of the church to be your mouth in pleading. I say, if it can be. If it come to declaring the evil to the church, it should rather be by him whom God has appointed to be his mouth to the church; for you do it in God's name, therefore the most orderly way to do it, if it may be done, is by him that is God's mouth.

Thirdly, It must be so as you must manifest all due respect to the church; showing in your carriage, that you are apprehensive and sensible, even at this time, of that distance that is between you and that whole society whereof you are a member.

Fourthly, You must do it in a very peaceable way, so as to manifest that you desire peace, and not to be the least disturbance to the peace of the church, but that the peace of it is dear and precious to you. Therefore, when you have witnessed the truth, and discharged your conscience, you must be then content to sit down quiet, for so the rule is in that case; that the spirits of the prophets must be subject to the prophets. But if it should prove that the church continues the evil, after all means used and all patience exercised in such a case, you may desire to be dismissed from it, and depart; but in as peaceable a way as possible, continuing due respect to the church, though you should depart, only leaving your witness behind you.

The papists cry out against us for pleading against them, and say it is an ill bird that will defile its own nest, and they tell us the curse of Ham is upon us for discovering our parent's nakedness. They are to know this, that there is more liberty for a member of a church to plead with a church, than for a child to plead with his parent. Though there be liberty for a child, yet there is more liberty for the member of a church. For a parent, though he should be never so evil, yet he does not lose his right over his child. Though your parents should be very wicked, yet know, that their wickedness does not discharge you of your duty; that all children should take notice of. But a church may so fall off from God, as that the members of it may be free from their duty to it, and therefore may have more liberty to plead, than a child with his parent. And certainly, so far have they fallen from God, when they discharge those that plead against them.

Well, but if a member may plead with a church, with their mother; certainly, then, there is no one member of a church so high, but he may be pleaded with by another; yea, any that is an officer of a church may be pleaded with, even by private people in that church. Col. iv. 17, " Say to Archippus, Take heed to thy ministry." It is an exhortation to all the church, to say to Archippus, and admonish him to look to his ministry. For though the officer of a church be nearer to Christ the Head than other members are, as the arm is nearer the head than the hand; yet if the arm shall send forth any thing to the hand that it has not from the head, (as in a flux of putrid humours that rest in the arm,) then it would be the strength of the hand to resist those ill humours which the arm sends forth. So if any officer of the church shall send forth that which he did not receive from the Head, to any member, but some putrid humour of his own, it is the virtue of that member to resist the receiving of any such humour.

It is the pride of many that scorn any private person's pleading. Pride in men, which, through want of that right order which should be in all churches, is grown to such a height, that those who take to themselves, as proper, the name of clergy, think it a dishonour to them for any one who is not a clergyman to speak to them or admonish them, or to reason with them about any thing; or when they have preached, to come to them for further satisfaction in somewhat that they have delivered; or if they be negligent in their duty, to tell them of it, though never so submissively and meekly; their pride makes them rise so high. And observe, that they do so upon the ground that they are the clergy, which signifies God's inheritance and God's lot, and so contemn others as inferior. You shall find in Scripture, that the people are called clergy in distinction from the ministers, and never the ministers in the New Testament in distinction from the people, the word κληρος is not attributed to them to my remembrance, but I am sure it is attributed to the congregation, to the private members, by way of distinction from them. That you see in 1 Pet. v. 3, " Neither as being lords over God's heritage." Μηδ' ὡς κατακυριεύοντες τῶν κλήρων, not lording it over God's clergy, over God's lot. Certainly, that exhortation is addressed to the officers of the church, that they must not lord it over God's inheritance, that is, over God's clergy. The word κληρὸς, therefore, from whence clergy comes, is, you see, attributed to the people. We find in Acts xviii. 24, that Apollos, " an eloquent man and mighty in the Scriptures," and a man of a fervent spirit, permitted Aquila and Priscilla, who were private people, to take him unto them, and expound to him the way of God more perfectly." Where have you an Apollos now, an eloquent man, a scholar, a great clergyman, but would scorn and contemn a poor man and his wife, who should attempt to take him home and instruct him in the way of God more perfectly? Yet Apollos, an eloquent man and mighty in the Scriptures, took it well, and was willing to receive further instruction from these people. And we find, Cant. v., that in the time of the reformation of the church, the church went to the watchmen, and the watchmen beat her, she had more relief from the daughters of Jerusalem than from them.

There may, however, be a notorious abuse of both these, and it is exceedingly difficult for a people to understand their liberty without abusing of it, either against the church, or against the officers of a church. This power may be abused by persons, who in pride, arrogancy, and a spirit of contention, take delight in contradiction. There are many people of such a humour, that it is their very delight to contradict, and they think they are nobody except they have somewhat to say against their officers, or against what is delivered; and upon that very ground will quarrel not out of mere conscience, but that it may appear to others that they see farther than other men. And if they be in a community, they conceive that every one would think them nobody if they say nothing, therefore, that they may appear to be somebody, they will find fault, though they scarce understand what they say, or whereof they affirm, showing their disapprobation in a virulent spirit, and insulting those whom God has set over them. Certainly, this is a gross and abominable thing, whereas the rule of Christ is, "Rebuke not an elder, but entreat him as a father," 1 Tim. v. 1; do not think that because you may plead with them, and God's cause may suffer by your silence, that therefore you may rebuke them in an undecent and unseemly manner. You may indeed go in a humble manner, acknowledging the distance betwixt you and him, he being an officer, and so "entreat him as a father." Do many of you so when you go and reason the case with a minister, whom you yourselves will acknowledge to be an officer of Christ? It may be that sometimes, through bitterness of spirit, you cast them off from being officers of Christ before you have sufficient warrant for it; and therefore the apostle saith in the same chapter, ver. 19, "Against an elder receive not an accusation but before two or three witnesses:" mark, you must not "receive an accusation," much less a condemnation, for the credit and honour of the ministers of Christ are very dear and precious unto him; therefore take heed how, through a violent and turbulent spirit, you cast any dishonour upon those whom Christ has set over you.

Thus I have endeavoured to discover the truth to you, and so limited as I hope it may be for edification, and not for injury to any.

"She is not my wife, neither am I her husband." This pleading has much bitterness in it, yet it is in as fair terms as can be set out. "She is not my wife." He does not bid them say to their mother, she is a harlot, but, "she is not my wife." You will say, Why? what difference is there between her not being his wife, and her being a harlot? May we not call things as they are? True, the thing is the same, but hence the Spirit of God teaches us, that those who plead against others must not give ill terms, especially when they plead against superiors; you may declare your minds fully, but in as fair, modest, comely, and the least provoking terms possible. It is a foul evil in many, if they see ministers or churches act improperly, to give reviling speeches; they cry out, There is one of Baal's priests; every thing they dislike they call antichristian; whereas they should study if there be any term more mollifying than another, and use that: although the fault you plead against might bear a harsher term if rebuked by one in authority, yet they who are but private Christians should be very careful, in the fairest, gentlest terms to reprove what they dislike.

"She is not my wife." That a people who have been God's people, may prove not to be God's people, we have already met with in the former chapter. We shall not speak of it as then we did. Only now we have it more fully, that a church may come to be unchurched. This is a difficult case. When I began this prophecy of Hosea, though I had spent some time in it before, I little thought to have met with so many things so fully presented to me as I have found, that, by God's providence, so nearly concern us and the times. I would not violently introduce any thing but what is so presented to us, but I should injure the Scripture, and you, not to notice it. We have already met with difficult points, and this also is exceeding difficult. I desire in this to interpret as I have done, your own consciences witnessing with me as in the other, without the least spirit of contention and division, or meddling with controversies, but laying the truth in the principles of it plainly before you.

When may a church, that had God before to be her Husband, come not to have God to be her Husband?

I confess that I cannot find any thing to pitch upon certainly, when the Jewish church ceased to be a church, but this; either when God sent them a bill of divorce by some extraordinary men, (as they always had some prophets amongst them,) or when they wholly left off the schoolmaster which God put them under; for I find that their idolatry was not enough actually to cut them off from being a church. It is true their idolatry deserved it; they broke the marriage bond by their idolatry, but God did not always take advantage of that, and always send them a bill of divorce when they committed idolatry. These ten tribes had been idolaters a long time before God said to them they were not his wife. Therefore, idolatry merely did not cut off the Jews. Neither do I think that all idolatry (if it be through ignorance) cuts off a church now in the time of the Christians. The Lutherans are certainly guilty of idolatry by consequence, and so other churches may be through ignorance, and yet they do not cease to be churches. Therefore, in the time of the Jews, I say I do not find any particular sin that actually cut them off, so long as they kept under the pedagogy of the law; unless God by some extraordinary messenger sent them a bill of divorce, they yet remained the people of God. "Where is the bill of your mother's divorcement?" saith God, Isa. l. i. It is true you have deserved it; but where is it? I have not given you a bill of divorce; therefore they were a church.

But for the time of the gospel, this I think may very safely be asserted, that so long as there is a communion of saints embodied, holding forth the profession of all fundamental truths, and joining in all ordinances as far as they are convinced, this multitude, though it should have abundance of corruptions, though many wicked be mingled amongst them, yet they are a church of God. Though they should not set up all ordinances, though perhaps, through ignorance, they are not convinced that such an ordinance is an ordinance of God; yea, though they be convinced that it is an ordinance, and yet perhaps they are not convinced that it is God's mind they should set it up, though this should be their error, yet this communion of saints embodied remains a true church of Christ. Yet, though it be a true church of Christ, it may be such a church, that perhaps you, or I, or another, cannot have communion with.

You will say, How is that possible for any church to be a true church of Christ, and yet we may not have communion with it? I answer, communion we may have, so far as to acknowledge it to be a church, and to have communion in some duties; but it may be a true church of Christ, and I may acknowledge it so, and yet not have communion in all ordinances. In what cases may that be? First, if this church shall so mingle any ordinance, any work of their public communion, as I for the present cannot join without contracting guilt upon me, as not seeing God's will in it, I cannot have communion with them in such ordinances. Yea, secondly, if a church shall require me to yield in my judgment, and subscribe to such things as I cannot satisfy my conscience in, they put me off communion with them. It is not my fault, but they violently keep me off. Thirdly, when they shall not suffer me to do the duty that God requires of me, I cannot have communion with them; because if I should join with them, not doing my duty which my conscience tells me I am bound to do, I thereby contract guilt. Nay, further, a man may be of a church, and perhaps they may not be so ill, but it may be lawful to have communion with them in many ordinances, and yet, for those who are free, and are not by any special call of God tied to such a place, they are bound in conscience in some cases not to join with them, as members, in a constant way. As thus:

(1.) When I cannot enjoy all ordinances with them, but God opens a door to another place where I may have communion in all ordinances, I may receive sacraments with them occasionally, and yet not be constantly with them as a member of that church. If God did shut the door that I could not enjoy all ordinances any where, then it were better to join with a church that has not all, though I do but enjoy some.

(2.) When God offers me elsewhere that I may enjoy the ordinances with more power, purity, and freedom of spirit, and I am not tied; then, if there be nothing but outward accommodations that shall cast the balance on the one hand, and the purity and power of the ordinances on the other, if I shall rather choose the one than the other, it will be apparent that I love my body better than my soul. In this case conscience bids me to show more respect to my soul than my body. This can be no controversy, for it is generally acknowledged by all, that if one will but remove his residence from one parish to another, he may go and join with that parish. But that which I affirm is not so far as that; I only suppose that a man is free, and not yet actually joined; then he should regard more the purity and power of the ordinances than outward accommodations.

Obs. 1. The end of all pleading and exhortation, is reformation, and not contention.

Plead with her; to what end? "let her put away her whoredoms." Plead with her that she may reform, do not plead for contention's sake. There are many men who will rebuke others, and plead with others, but what for? merely in a spirit of contention, merely that they may triumph over them, and shame them; not out of love, to reform them, they care not whether they reform or not; if they have vented their gall and malice, they have what they wish.

But how will you know that? How can you know a man's heart?

First, You shall know that men plead not for reformation, but for contention, if they rather make it appear that they are glad of the sins of their brethren, and do not grieve for them. Many a man comes in a fury to rebuke those against whom he has advantage, but not with a spirit of sorrow and mourning; if he came to plead and rebuke them for reformation, he should have come with a mourning spirit. Ye should have mourned, that such a one "might be taken away from among you," saith the apostle to the Corinthians, 1 Cor. v. 2. You should mourn at your very hearts, that the church, or the member of it, has offended.

Secondly, When men are partial in their pleading, when they will sharply rebuke others who are distant, but are careless of such as are near.

Turn ye, turn ye, that ye may not die, Ezek. xviii. 32, "turn yourselves, and live." Now the word is השיבו do you make to return, for so the Hiphil form may well be translated. Arias Montanus renders it *reverti facite*, make others to return. You must plead so as to desire reformation, not that you may get the victory and have the better of it by your pleading, but with bowels of compassion seek reformation; you must not cut as an enemy to conquer, but as a surgeon to heal. Therefore before you go to rebuke and to plead, you must go to prayer, that God would bless your rebuking and your exhortation to your brethren; and when you have done, pray again to God for a blessing upon it. And look after your reprehensions, and see what becomes of them; and if they do not prosper to reformation, then mourn, and cry to God for your brethren; and if they prosper, then bless God that you have converted a soul. Thus when the tribes on this side Jordan pleaded with the tribes on the other side Jordan, you find that the answer of their brethren "pleased the children of Israel; and the children of Israel blessed God, and did not intend to go up against them in battle," Josh. xxii. 33. So you should go and plead with your brethren; perhaps your brethren may plead best, and convince you that that which you apprehend to be a sin is not a sin. Now many men perhaps are angry, and will not be convinced that it is a sin; Shall I go away with the shame? shall I rebuke him of a sin, and is it no sin? Many a man holds on in an argument which he has begun, and is loth to yield that it is not a sin, whereas he should be glad to yield it. If a minister plead or preach that men commit that which he conceives is a sin, and another come and convince him that it was no sin, it is a vile spirit in any minister not to bless God that he is mistaken: why? because the guilt of his brother is removed from his heart. If I had not been mistaken, my credit had been greater; but I am mistaken, the sin is removed from my brother; oh blessed be God that my brother is not guilty, though I am mistaken. If we plead against others with such a spirit as this, God will bless it.

"Let her therefore put away her whoredoms out of her sight, and her adulteries from between her breasts." "Plead with your mother," and plead so as to tell her plainly that she is no more my wife, she has her bill of divorce, she is now none of mine. Well, it seems then there is no hope, no help, God has forsaken us, he has said we are no more his wife, we have our bill of divorce, and must be gone. Not so either, but now it follows, "let her put away her whoredoms out of her sight, and her adulteries from between her breasts." Hereby insinuating at least, that her condition, notwithstanding the greatness of her sin, and the fearfulness of the threat, is not altogether hopeless, but he would have those that plead with her, exhort her and bid her even then to put away her whoredoms. It is true, when a man puts away his wife for whoredom, and gives a bill of divorce, he will never take her again upon any terms. Jer. iii. 1, Will a man, when he putteth away his wife, return unto her again? As if he should say, No, certainly, no man will do it. "But thou hast played the harlot with many lovers; yet return again to me, saith the Lord."

Obs. 1. God mercies are beyond man's. There is no dreadful threatening against any sinner in the word of God for any sins, (if we except the sin against the Holy Ghost,) but there is a door of hope left. Here seems to be the greatest sin, idolatry and forsaking of God; and the most dreadful threatening, "she is not my wife," she is divorced from me. Yet here is insinuated a hope of mercy. See that notable text, Judg. x. 13, 14, compared with ver. 16. In the 13th and 14th verses, saith God, "Ye have forsaken me, and served other gods;" what then? "I will deliver you no more." I am resolved against you now; I have delivered you often, but now "I will deliver you no more. Go and cry unto the gods which ye have chosen; let them deliver you in the time of your tribulation." One would think this people to be in an ill case, to whom God thus spake; for observe these four things: First, God charges them with the greatest sin, they had forsaken God and turned themselves to idols. Secondly, This great sin is aggravated with the most aggravating circumstance, they had done it notwithstanding God was wonderfully merciful to them, and had often delivered them. Thirdly, Here is one of the most peremptory resolutions against showing mercy that we can imagine, "I will deliver you no more," now I have delivered you so oft. Fourthly, Here is a most bitter sarcasm, a biting, upbraiding, taunting speech for their serving other gods. As if he should say, What! do you come now? do you cry and howl to me now you are in your trouble? In your prosperity I was no God for you, you left me then for other gods, and now I will be no God to you; to other gods I leave you; go now and cry to those other gods, and see whether they will help you. Put these together, and one would think this people were in a hopeless condition. Is there any help for this people yet? are they not a lost people? Is not repentance too late for them? No, for all this, repentance is not too late; for mark the 15th verse, "And the children of Israel said unto the Lord, We have sinned; do thou unto us whatsoever seemeth good unto thee; deliver us only this day:" and ver. 16, "They put away the strange gods from among them, and served the Lord." They do not lie down sullenly in their sins, and say, There is no help, therefore we may as well go on in our sinful ways; but they venture to put away their strange gods, and cry unto the Lord, and tell him that they had sinned. What then? The "soul" of the Lord "was grieved for the misery of Israel." Though he had thus pronounced against them, yet his soul was grieved for them. It is true he said, "I will deliver you no more," you impenitent ones; but God did not say he would not give them repentance; but when they had put away their strange gods, though they had grieved God's Spirit with their sins, God was grieved for their affliction; though God had thus threatened them, yet his bowels now yearn towards them; he comes again with mercy, subdues their enemies under them, he conquers the children of Ammon, and gives them twenty of their cities, Judg. xi. 33.

God never threatens any people, but the condition of mercy upon repentance is either expressed or implied. It is therefore the frowardness and sullenness of the hearts of sinners to give up hope, upon the thought of the greatness of their sins, or the severity of God's threatening against them. Oh no, you great sinners, who have been guilty of many horrible sins, come in and repent. I may say to you, as Shecaniah did to the people in another case, of a grievous sin, " There is hope in Israel concerning this thing," Ezra x. 2.

Many carnal hearts cavil against many faithful and zealous ministers, that they do nothing but preach judgment and threaten damnation, and say people shall be damned, and go to hell, and the like. This they speak against them, not mentioning the conditions upon which damnation and hell is threatened. Certainly, there can scarce a minister in the world be found that threatens damnation or hell absolutely, but upon the terms of impenitence. I will give you one scripture, to show how the perverse spirits of men will take a piece of the words of the prophets, and separate the threatening from the condition, on purpose that they may cavil at the word. In Jer. xxvi. 4, 5, saith God to the prophet, " Thou shalt say unto them, Thus saith the Lord; If ye will not hearken to me, to walk in my law, which I have set before you, to hearken to the words of my servants the prophets, whom I sent unto you; then will I make this house like Shiloh, and will make this city a curse to all the nations of the earth." See how fairly the words of the prophet go, " If ye will not hearken to me, to walk in my law, which I have set before you, to hearken to the words of my servants the prophets, whom I sent unto you," then I will do so and so. The prophet delivers his message fairly. But see now their perverseness in the 8th verse, " It came to pass, that when Jeremiah had made an end of speaking all that the Lord had commanded him to speak unto all the people, that the priests and the prophets and all the people took him, saying, Thou shalt surely die." What is the matter? " Why hast thou prophesied in the name of the Lord, saying, This house shall be like Shiloh?" They leave out " if," whereas he said, " If you will not return and hear the words of the Lord, this house shall be as Shiloh." They lay hold upon him with violence, " Why hast thou said, This house shall be like Shiloh?" and leave out the other. This is the perverseness of the hearts of men. Well then, the conclusion of this observation is this, that the best pleading against any for their sins, is not to sink them in despair, but to turn their hearts towards God that they may receive mercy. " Let her put away her whoredoms."

Obs. 2. While God is pleased to speak to a people, and exhort them to turn to him, the condition of that people is not desperate. After such pleading, that included in it a most dreadful threatening, " She is not my wife," yet God exhorts, " Let her put away her whoredoms." Exhortations from God argue that the condition of a people may be hopeful. So long as the king is but speaking to a traitor, especially giving him good counsel, there may be hope. If he turn his back upon him, and will speak no more, then he looks upon himself as a lost man. Many people are troubled, that God continues exhorting so constantly by his ministers and others, and they cannot be at rest. If thou hadst such a quiet, as that God should leave exhorting and drawing thee from thy sins, woe to thee, thou wert a lost creature! Make much of exhortations and threatenings.

Come we now to the exhortation itself, " Let her therefore put away her whoredoms out of her sight, and her adulteries from between her breasts." " Her whoredoms," and " her adulteries," in the plural number, they were many, she must put them all away. If a wife who has been naught, shall be contented to forsake divers of her lovers, and retain but one, there is no reconciliation, all her adulteries must be put away.

Let her put them away out of her sight. The eye is the receiver of much uncleanness into the heart, and by it the uncleanness of the heart is much expressed. The Scripture speaks of eyes full of adultery. " Let her put her whoredoms out of her sight," let them be abominable now in her eyes; those things that before were delectable, let them now be detestable. Let them cast away their idols, and with indignation say, Get ye hence.

Or, from before her face, so it is in the Hebrew, noting her impudence in her idolatry, that it appeared in her very face. Though men at first may be a little wary, yet at length they grow to manifest outwardly their idolatry in their very face.

And because Israel did not, according to the exhortation of those who pleaded with her, put her whoredoms out of her sight, God put Israel out of his sight, for so we have it, 2 Kings xvii. 22, 23. " The children of Israel walked in all the sins of Jeroboam which he did; they departed not from them;" promises could not draw them, threatenings could not deter them; " until the Lord removed Israel out of his sight." They might have prevented this; if they had put their whoredoms out of their sight, God would never have put them out of his sight.

" From between her breasts." Harlots used to discover their filthiness, either in the nakedness of their breasts, or in those ornaments which they hung about them, as they were wont to do in those countries, to entice their lovers.

The nakedness of the breasts has been condemned, not only in the churches of God, but amongst the heathen. Tertullian, in his book de Habitu Muliebri, has this expression: Women adorning themselves immoderately with gold, and silver, and precious apparel, is *crimen ambitionis*, the sin of ambition; but for them to seek to adorn themselves solicitously about their hair and their skin, and those parts that draw the eyes, this is *crimen prostitutionis*, the sin of prostitution.

Tertul. de Hab. Mul. c. 4.

Yea, besides, Tertullian, in his De velandis Virginibus, introduces the heathen rebuking Christian women in those times. The very women of Arabia, saith he, shall judge you, for they not only cover their faces, but even their heads; rather than immodestly expose their whole face, they will let the light but into one eye. Now if the heathen did so, if they would not have their nakedness in any thing appear, much more should Christians cover those parts that are incitements to lust. That which is the maniac's madness, and the beggar's misery, namely, nakedness, that is the harlot's pride and glory.

Judicabunt vos Arabiæ fœminæ Ethnicæ, quæ non caput sed faciem quoque ita totam tegunt ut, uno oculo liberato, contentæ sint luce frui dimidia potius quam totam faciem prostituere. Tertul. de vel. Virgin. c. 17.

" Let her therefore put away her whoredoms out of her sight, and her adulteries from between her breasts." That which is intended especially here, is, that they should not be content merely with a change of their hearts, to say, Well, we will acknowledge the Lord to be the true God, and our hearts shall wholly trust in him, but for these external things, what great sin is there in them? Oh no, they must abstain from all appearance of evil, from the badges of idolatry, there must not be so much as the garb and dress of a harlot upon them, they must take away their adulteries from between their breasts."

The breasts of the church are her ordinances, for out of them the saints suck sweetness and spiritual nourishment; so they are called in Isa. lxvi. 11, "That ye may suck and be satisfied with the breasts of her consolations." Now certainly it is an evil thing, for any thing that is adulterous to be in the ordinances of the church. No, the breasts are so near the heart, that it is a pity any thing should be upon them but Christ himself; it is most fit that he should lie there. Cant. i. 13, "A bundle of myrrh is my well-beloved unto me, he shall lie all night between my breasts." Myrrh we know is a bitter thing, but though Christ were as a bundle of myrrh, and brought many afflictions which add bitterness to the flesh, yet the church would have Christ lie between her breasts, and she would rejoice in Christ; Christ was sweet to the church, though with afflictions, As "a bundle of myrrh is my well-beloved." So, many faithful ministers of God have been contented, yea, joyful, to keep Christ between their breasts, and in the ordinances, though as a bundle of myrrh: he has brought some afflictions to them; yet, rather than they would endure any expression of that which is adulterous upon the ordinances, the word and sacraments, Christ Jesus, a bundle of myrrh between their breasts, has been delightful to them.

I find another reading of the words in the Septuagint translation. Whereas we render it, "Let her put away her whoredoms out of her sight;" they regard it as a speech of God, and translate it, ἐξαρῶ τὴν πορνειαν αὐτῆς ἐκ προσώπου μου, I will take away her whoredoms from my face. And Cyril, reading the words thus, has an excellent remark: God, saith he, threatens that he will take away her whoredoms from his face; as when a member of a body is so putrified that it cannot be cured by medicine, it is cut off, and the disease removed: so God labours to cure the people of Israel by admonitions, by exhortations, by threatenings, by promises of mercy, and when all would not do, he threatens to cure them another way, that is, by cutting them off by the Assyrians; I will send an enemy against them, and he shall take them out of their own land, and carry them into a strange land, and then they shall be far enough from their calves, far enough from Dan and Bethel; so I will take their whoredoms from before my face. Thus, many times God takes away the sins of a people, or of a particular person, from before his face. As for instance, thou drunkard, thou unclean person, hast had exhortations, threatenings, and many merciful expressions from God to draw thee from thy sins; they will not do; God comes with some noisome disease upon thy body, that thou shalt not be able to act thy sin any more, and God takes away the act of thy sin in such a violent manner by his judgments. Sometimes men and women who have estates will be proud, and vain, and make their estates the fuel of their lusts; when the word cannot take away their sins and the expressions of their wickedness, God by some violent judgment takes away their estates, that they shall not be able to commit those sins they did before, though they would never so fain. This is a dreadful taking away of sin. Yea, God shall so take away the sin of men and women, as to take away their souls together with their sin: for so it is threatened, Job xxvii. 8, "What is the hope of the hypocrite, though he hath gained, when God taketh away his soul?" Thou that wouldst not suffer the word to take away thy sin, must expect that God will take it away another way, even by taking away thy soul. It may be said of some sinners, as in Ezek. xxi. 29 God threatens, their "day is come, when their iniquity shall have an end." God will suffer them to live no longer to sin against him: he will take away their sins, but so as to take away their souls, they shall not sin any more against God in this world.

"Ονπερ γὰρ τρόπον τῶν ἐν τοις σώμασι τραυματων τὰ δυσχερῆ ἢ σιδήρῳ τέμνεται ἤγουν νικᾶται πυρί. &c. Cyril. in Hos. c. 2.

Ver. 3. *Lest I strip her naked, and set her as in the day that she was born, and make her as a wilderness, and set her like a dry land, and slay her with thirst.*

There is much in these words, and because they are so exceeding suitable unto us, you must give me liberty to insist a little upon them.

"Lest I strip her naked." It seems by this that Israel, when she was born, had been in a very low condition, in a very pitiful estate; but God had put many ornaments upon her; and now he threatens to bring her again into the same condition, and to strip her naked.

"In the day that she was born." This, I find, interpreters refer to divers conditions of Israel, but most to the time of their deliverance out of Egypt, called here by God, "the day that she was born." We must inquire, first, What was the condition of Israel "in the day that she was born." Secondly, What ornaments God had put upon her afterwards: and then we shall come to see the strength of the threat, that God would "strip her naked, and set her as in the day that she was born."

For the first two we shall not need to go far, we have them fully and most elegantly set out unto us in Ezek. xvi. That chapter may be a comment upon this, what Israel was in the day wherein she was born, and what ornaments God had put upon her. In the third verse, "Thus saith the Lord God unto Jerusalem; Thy birth and thy nativity is of the land of Canaan; thy father was an Amorite, and thy mother an Hittite."

When thou wert born, thou wert in this condition. What! their father an Amorite, and their mother an Hittite? Abraham was their father, and Sarah their mother; why here an Amorite and an Hittite? Because there were other nations besides Amorites and Hittites, there were the Jebusites and the Perizzites; why rather an Amorite and Hittite, than a Jebusite and Perizzite? These two questions must be answered.

First, Though Abraham was their father, yet, because they were in such a disposition, so like the Amorites and Hittites, so vile and so wicked, they deserve not to have the honour of Abraham's being their father, but to be called the children of the Amorite and the Hittite. As John Baptist calls the Pharisees the viperous, the serpentine brood, so those that are like the devil, are called the children of the devil.

Secondly, Why the Amorite and Hittite rather than others? For the first, the Amorite; because the Amorites were the chiefest of those nations in Canaan which were driven out. All the five were called by the name of Amorite: "The sins of the Amorites are not yet full." Secondly, the Hittite, because they seemed to be the vilest of the five, and there is a text of Scripture that seems to infer so much. Gen. xxvii. 46, "I am weary of my life" (saith Rebekah) "because of the daughters of Heth." She only mentions the daughters of Heth, and those that were now called Hittites were of the daughters of Heth: and saith she, "What good will my life do me, if Jacob take a wife of the daughters of Heth?" Why, there were other daughters besides them, but those were the vilest, therefore she only mentions them. Yea, but what was Israel at this time, when they were delivered out of Egypt? for that is the time wherein she was born that is spoken of here. Were they in so ill a condition, as that their father was an Amorite and their mother an Hittite at that time? There are two most useful observations that flow from hence, before we proceed any further in the explication of the words.

Obs. 1. Israel, though they had been four hundred

years in Egypt under grievous afflictions, yet they continued exceeding abominable and wicked. The fire of their afflictions seemed to harden their hearts, as much as the fire of the furnace hardened the bricks. Their hearts were clay, foul, dirty hearts, and were hardened by their afflictions.

Obs. 2. When God came to deliver Israel out of Egypt, God found them in a very wicked condition. Then their father was an Amorite, and their mother an Hittite. They were thus vile when God came to deliver them, in the day wherein they were born. Oh the freeness of God's grace! God often told them that his grace was free, and so indeed it was. Read the story of the people of Israel, and you find, when God sent Moses unto them, they were a very wicked and stubborn people, even at that very time when God came with his deliverance.

Let us then raise up our hearts, and look up to the free grace of God even toward us. We are vile, we are wicked; mercies and chastisements have hardened us; and yet all this hinders not the free grace of God for the deliverance of a people. God has begun to deliver us; and when did he begin? Certainly England, never since it was born, since it was delivered out of spiritual Egypt, out of the bondage of popery, was in a worse condition than when God came in lately with his mercies to us. Then, if ever, it might be said, that our father was an Amorite, and our mother an Hittite. We were in the very highway towards Egypt again, when God came with his free grace to deliver us. As he dealt with his own people, so he has dealt with us. Magnified be the free grace of God towards us, an unworthy people!

Further, Ezek. xvi. 4, "Thy navel was not cut." The loathsomeness of their condition is set out by that. Naturalists observe, that the nourishment which the child hath from the mother is by the navel: as afterward, the child sucks the breasts, and so is fattened; but all the while it is in the womb, by a string in the navel it draws nourishment from the mother. Now when God delivered Israel from Egypt, they had not their navel cut, that is, they drew their nourishment from Egypt; they fattened themselves, and sucked out the Egyptian manners, and customs, and superstitions; and in their growth up, they seemed rather to have their nourishment from Egypt than from God; so God himself charges them, Ezek. xxiii. 8, "Neither left she her whoredoms brought from Egypt."

Is it not thus in part with us? Let me a little speak of this, by way of allusion at least. Is our navel cut to this very day? It is true, God has delivered us from popery, from Egypt, as he did Israel, but still do not we continue sucking, drawing nourishment from our old superstitious ways of popery? We seem to live still upon them, and to have our hearts delighting in them. Oh how just were it with God, to come in a violent way and cut our navel, even by the sword! It is mercy he comes not thus to cut it, and so take from us all those secret hankerings that we have after the old Egyptian customs.

Yet again, seeing it is such a full allusion, we may apply it to those that seem to be born again; those that seem now to make very fair profession of religion, and to forsake many evil ways in which formerly they have delighted: but yet their navel is not cut; they secretly suck sweetness from their former lusts; the curse of the serpent is upon them, upon their bellies they go, and dust they eat; their souls even cleave to the dust.

"Neither wast thou washed in water." This also sets forth the woeful condition of Israel when he was born, he was not washed. When the infant comes into the world, it emerges from blood and pollution in which it was wrapped, so that (as Plutarch saith) it is rather like a child killed, than a child born; and were it not for a natural affection stirring in parents, they would even loathe the fruit of their bodies. It is true, parents may see that with their bodily eyes, but there is more pollution in their souls; they are wrapped up in original sin and filth, more than their bodies were wrapped up in blood and pollution in the womb. Therefore infants are washed; but thou wast not washed, thou wast let go in thy filth. The barbarous Lacedemonians, when their children were born, used to throw them into the river, to consolidate their members and to make them strong.

Αἵματι πεφυρμενος καὶ λελυθρωμενος, καὶ φονευομενῳ μᾶλλον ἢ γεννώμενῳ ἐοικώς, οὐδενος ἐστιν ἅψασθαι ἢ τοῦ φύσει φιλοῦντος. Plut. de Amore Prolis.

"Thou wast cast out in the open field." What is the meaning of this? We cannot understand it fully, without examining the custom of the people in those times. We find in histories, that the custom of divers of the heathen was, when their children were born, to observe by their countenance, or by the structure of their members, whether they were likely to be useful to the commonwealth or not; if not, they threw them away, and if they were likely to be useful they nourished them up. They nourished up no other children but those that they judged by their countenance or shape would do good to the commonwealth. Strabo tells us that the Indians and Brahmins had certain judges appointed for that very end; their office was, that when any child was born, to judge by the countenance and parts of the body of the child, whether it was likely to do any good in the commonwealth, and so either to save it or cast it out. So likewise Ælian tells us, that the Thebans made an express law among them in these words, That none of them should cast out their children; noting thereby that it was wont to be the custom amongst them. So Clemens Romanus tells us, as a thing peculiar to them, that amongst the Jews their children are not cast out.

Strab. l. 15.

Ne cui Thebano liceat infantem exponere. Ælian variar. Hist. li. 11.

Nunquam apud eos infans natus exponitur.

So that the Holy Ghost alludes to the way of the Gentiles and barbarous people, and tells Israel that they were as a child cast out, such a one as the countenance promised no good. "Thou wast cast out in the open field," because they never hoped to have any good of thee; and indeed (as if God should say) if I had regarded what I saw in you, I might have passed this judgment upon you too, there was little hope of good from you.

But what though the child be cast out in the field, yet some may pass by accidentally, as Pharaoh's daughter did, who may pity the child, and have compassion on it. No, saith God, thou wast not only cast out, but worse than this, thou wast so cast out as "none eye pitied thee." You have sometimes poor children laid at your doors, and left there, some in baskets, or other ways, yet, when you open them and see a child, and a child weeping, there is some pity in you, and you will take care some way or other that it may be fed and brought up. But, saith God to Israel, "thou wast cast out in the open field," and "none eye pitied thee;" that is, all the heathen were against you, and others in the land rose against you; the Egyptians came out to destroy you, you had the sea before you, and them behind you, none had pity upon you. This was the condition wherein you were born.

Now see what ornaments God had put upon them. They were in a sorry condition, you see, when they were born. But mark, I took thee, "and entered into covenant with thee, saith the Lord God, and thou becamest mine," Ezek. xvi. 8. That is the way a people become God's, his entering into covenant with them. The Lord has begun to enter into covenant with us, and we with him in former protestations, and if any further covenant binding us more strictly to God be tendered to us, know that God in this deals with us as he did with his own people. We are as children cast out in the open field, and no eye pities us; but many plot against us and seek our ruin. If God will be pleased now to enter into covenant with us, and give all the people of the land hearts to come closer to the covenant, to renew their covenant with him, and that to more purpose than in former covenants, the Lord yet will own us. The covenant of God was the foundation of all the mercy the people of Israel had from God, and we are to look upon it as the foundation of our mercy; and therefore, as in the presence of God, willingly and cheerfully to renew it with him.

After God's taking this people to himself as his own, it follows, ver. 11—14, "I decked thee also with ornaments, and I put bracelets upon thy hands, and a chain on thy neck. And I put a jewel on thy forehead, and earrings in thine ears, and a beautiful crown upon thine head. Thus wast thou decked with gold and silver; and thy raiment was of fine linen, and silk, and broidered work; thou didst eat fine flour, and honey, and oil: and thou wast exceeding beautiful, and thou didst prosper into a kingdom. And thy renown went forth among the heathen for thy beauty." Thus God did with the people of Israel; he added to what they had when they were born. Miserable they were then; but the mercies of God toward them are thus set out. And now he threatens that he will strip them naked, and set them as in the day wherein they were born.

Yet further, for the opening of this, we must know that it was the custom among the Jews, when any married, that what dowry they brought their husbands was written down in a table; and if afterward he should divorce his wife, except there could be proved some gross and vile thing against the woman, though she should go away, yet she was to go away with her table, with her dowry, she must not go away naked. But if there could be proved some notorious villany that she had committed, then she was sent away *sine tabulis*, naked, without those tables wherein her dowry and other things were written, and destitute of all things, as being unworthy of them, because she had played the harlot. Thus God threatens this people. "She is not my wife," but unless she put away her whoredoms from before her face, and her adulteries from between her breasts, I will strip her naked as in the day wherein she was born. She shall be sent away without any tables, naked and wholly destitute. Thus you have the opening of the words.

Obs. 1. The beginnings of great excellencies are sometimes very low and mean. This plainly rises from the opposition of her condition when she was born, and what she had gotten from God afterward; "lest I strip her naked, and set her as in the day that she was born." Therefore it is clear she was born in a very mean condition, and gotten up to a very excellent condition; though now high and glorious, yet once very low and mean. God many times raises up golden pillars upon leaden bases, and the most glorious works of God have had the lowest beginnings. This beautiful frame of heaven and earth was raised out of a chaos of confusion and darkness. This is true, both personally and nationally, and that in regard of outward conditions, or spiritual. How poor, and low, and mean have many of your beginnings been in the world! Who could ever have thought that such low beginnings could have been raised to such high things, as some of you have been raised to in the world? It was not long since when you came hither to this city, (which may be said to be the day wherein you were born for your civil estate, though not for your natural,) you were low enough, mean enough; you had but little to begin withal; you came hither "with your staff," and "now behold two bands."

It is sometimes so, likewise, in regard of the spiritual estate. You may remember, not long since, what darkness and confusion abounded in your minds and hearts; what poor, low, and mean thoughts had you of God, and the things of his kingdom; what unsavoury spirits, when at first God was pleased to work upon you! Oh what a poor condition were you in then! Though you had some light put into you, yet you were as a child new born, wrapped up in filth and blood, many noisome distempers there were in your hearts, as it is usual with new converts; like a fire newly kindled, where there is a great deal of smother and smoke, that afterward wears away. But now, behold the shining of God's face upon your souls. Oh the abilities that God has given you to know his mind and do his will! Oh the blessed communion that you have with God, and the sparkling of that Divine nature! The glory and beauty of the Divine nature is put upon you.

So for nations, we will not go farther than our own. How low and mean were we at the first! We were as rude, barbarous, and savage a people, almost, as lived upon the earth. Britons had their name from hence; in the old Britain language, Brith signifies blue-coloured, because those who lived here, instead of good clothes, as you have, with woad besmeared their bodies blue. *Tania* was added, as it is usual in other languages, for the signification of such a region, or country, as Mauritania, Lusitania, Aquitania, &c. So that Britannia is as much as to say, The region of the blue-coloured people; so called because they were thus painted. The best food they were wont to eat (historians tell us) was bark of trees and roots. Hollinshed in his Chronicle says, There were old men that he knew who told of times in England, that if the good man in the house had a mattress or flock-bed, and a sack of chaff to rest his head on, he thought himself as well lodged as the lord of the town, for ordinarily they lay upon straw pallets covered with canvass, and a round log under their heads instead of a bolster. They said pillows were fit only for women in child-bed; and in a good farmer's house it was rare to find four pieces of pewter, and it was accounted a great matter that a farmer could show five shillings or a noble in silver together.

Camden, in his Britannia, tells of Aylesbury, a town in Buckinghamshire, where there was a king's manor, and the condition of holding certain lands there was, that the possessor or holder of them should find straw for litter for the king's bed, when he came there. Latimer, in a sermon before King Edward, relates, that his father, who, he says, kept good hospitality for his poor neighbours, and found a horse for the king's service, brought him (Latimer) up at learning, and married his sisters with five pounds, or twenty nobles, apiece for their portions. This was the poor and mean condition of those times. And Jerome, contra Jovinianum, and Diodorus Siculus, tell us concerning the people in Ireland, our neighbours, that the best delicacies they used to eat in former times, was the flesh of young children; that the ships they used, were sallows wreathed together, and boughs twisted, and covered with the hides of beasts; and the wives they had, were common to all their brethren and parents. As for their religion, they offered to the devil man's flesh, they worshipped Apollo, and Jupiter, and Diana. And Gildas, one of the most ancient historians, who relates the condition of these British people, says the idols they had were horrible, devilish, monstrous things, and that they even surpassed the Egyptian idols in number. No people had so many idol-gods, and so monstrous, as the Egyptians, and yet these went beyond them.

Portenta diabolica, pene numero Ægyptiaca vincentia.

Afterward, no people in the world were more rent and torn with civil wars than England has been. And in the times when popery was here professed and established, oh the outward and spiritual bondage we were under then! Our bodies, our souls, our estates, our consciences, were in miserable thraldom.

It is the most sordid and miserable slavery possible for a rational creature to be under, not only to be bound to practise, but to believe for truth, the dictates and determinations of men, yea, and that upon pain of eternal damnation. To believe what they say, as the articles of faith upon which salvation or damnation depends, and conscience must not question, or scruple any thing; if any man that is a rational creature should think there is any such distance between man and man, he debases himself beneath a man, and advances the other above a man. Better it is to be in slavery to another, to scrape kennels, than to be in this slavery. And to have the Scriptures kept from us, the epistle that God has sent from heaven to us, that which enlightens the world, revealing the great counsels of God concerning eternal life, is worse bondage than to be chained up in dark holes all the days of our lives. To have no ordinances but according to the lusts and humours of vile men, how great a slavery is this! The manifestation of the least suspicion of the falseness of the vilest errors, dislike of the basest practices, was enough to confiscate estate, to imprison, yea, to take away life. Was not this a low condition, a base slavery, in which England was? could any bear it, but such as were slaves to their own lusts? But now, what ornaments has God put upon us! No nation under heaven more renowned than we have been, our renown has gone through the earth. England; its people, Angli, *quasi Angeli;* and itself, Albion, from the whiteness of its cliffs. From our happiness we see now, that glorious excellences have many times low beginnings.

Obs. 2. God's mercy is a people's beauty and glory. When we have any excellency, any beauty upon us, it is God's mercy that is all our beauty. "I will strip you naked, and set you as in the day wherein you were born." If you have any excellency, it is my mercy. We have nothing belonging to us but shame, confusion, and misery; if we have any ornaments, it is mercy, free mercy: therefore, in Ezek. xvi. 14, Thou wert perfect in beauty; how? "through my comeliness, which I had put upon thee, saith the Lord." Let God take away his mercy, we are quickly left naked, and poor, and miserable; like the rugged walls in the court, when the king goes away, and all the rich hangings are taken down, what a difference is there in their appearance! the beauty of the walls were the hangings, when the king was there. So, if we have any thing that makes us beautiful, they are the hangings that God has put upon us; his mercies are those hangings of gold, and silver, and needle-work; and when they are gone, we are poor, and ragged, and miserable.

Obs. 3. Though sinners deserve great evils, to be stripped of all comforts, yet God, in patience and clemency, continues them a long time. "Lest I strip her naked." God had said before, that she was not his wife, she was guilty of whoredoms, yet it seems she was not yet stripped naked; she was yet left with God's ornaments upon her, notwithstanding her sin. Sinners may be under fearful threatenings, and yet retain many comforts; yea, the truth is, it is possible for a people to be cast off from God, and yet to continue for a while in outward prosperity. The tree that is cut up by the roots, may have the leaves green for a while. Saul was rejected of God, 1 Sam. xiii. 14, yet, after that, God suffered Saul to prosper exceedingly in overcoming the Philistines and the Amalekites.

Obs. 4. The mercies that God bestows upon a nation, are but common favours, not spiritual graces, they are such ornaments as a people may be stripped of. The great mercies a people have, they may wholly lose. Here is the difference between true spiritual graces, in which Jesus Christ adorns his spouse. When Christ not only takes in an outward way a people to himself, but marries them to himself in a spiritual way, he decks the soul with such ornaments, bestows such mercies upon them, as shall never be taken away. Such a soul has no cause to fear that ever it can be stripped, as in the day wherein it was born, you need not fear that you shall ever lose the jewels given you at that marriage day. You may be stripped of common graces and gifts, as many professors are, who have not truth at heart. When they prove naught, God takes away their gifts from them; they have not that gift of prayer they were wont to have; though they have excellent words, yet a man may perceive such an unsavouriness mixed with their gifts, that it breeds loathing in others to join with them. As, when the king goeth away from his palace, the hangings are taken down; so, when God departeth from a soul, (as from such he may,) then their hangings, those excellent gifts, are taken from them. But of spiritual gifts they are never stripped. We read in Ezek. xlvi. 17, when a king gave gifts to his servants, they were to return to him again at the year of jubilee; but when he gave them to his sons, they were to be their inheritance. There are many who are outwardly in the church as God's servants, they have many gifts, but God will take his gifts away, and strip them naked; but then there are his children, they shall have their gifts as an inheritance for ever. It is true, God may stay a while: as, when the king is gone from court, if there be any thought of his return the hangings continue, but if the message come, The king will not be here these twelve months, or a long time, or, it may be, never any more, then the hangings are taken down; so, though these gifts of the hypocrite may stay a while, yet they will vanish at last.

Obs. 5. Continuance in sin, and especially the sin of spiritual whoredom, is that which will strip a nation from all their excellences, from all their ornaments and beauty. The continuance in that sin especially; for so the words imply, "Let her put away her adulteries from between her breasts, lest I strip her naked." If she continue thus, certainly naked she shall be. This always brings nakedness meritoriously, but if continued in, effectually, it makes them naked. In Exod. xxxii. 25, you may see what made the people naked at that time: the text saith, that "Aaron had made them naked," that is, Aaron, by consenting to the people to make the calf, had made the people naked; that is, destitute now of God's gracious protection, deprived of those favours from God, which formerly they had. And as the priest had made them naked, so you may find, in 2 Chron. xxviii. 19, that the king made them naked too: "The Lord brought Judah low because of Ahaz king of Israel; for he made Judah naked, and transgressed sore against the Lord." "He made Judah naked," that is, by countenancing idolatry, by siding with those who were idolaters, he made Judah naked at that time.

Here we may see who they are that are likely to strip us, if ever God should come to strip us. We have many amongst us that see false burdens of all the miseries and troubles that come upon the nation; they blame the puritans, and others that they say are factious, seditious, and turbulent spirits, and all must be laid upon them. Certainly, whoever has eyes in his head, may easily see who makes us as naked as we are, and, if we be made more naked, who will be the cause of all. Those who stand against the way of reformation, those that will keep their whoredoms in their sight, and their adulteries between their breasts, those that will not be willing that the church should be purged from that filth and whorish attire it uses; these are they that make us naked. We read in Lam. ii. 14, "Thy prophets have seen vain and foolish things for thee: and they have not discovered thine iniquity to turn away thy captivity; but have seen for thee false burdens, and causes of banishment." Mark it, "Thy prophets have seen vain and foolish things, and they have not discovered thine iniquity;" they have not dealt plainly with thy people, neither have they told them the reason of their captivity; "but have seen for thee false burdens and causes of banishment." The prophets say, It is a company of these precise and strict ones, that will not be obedient to authority, and will not do what is commanded in such and such things, and (when there were corruptions in God's worship) they would not submit to such and such orders. The prophets lay the blame upon them; but they see false burdens, saith the text, and false causes of banishment. We have many such prophets amongst us, who see false burdens and causes of banishment, and they blame those who certainly are the causes of our peace, and of the good of the kingdom. Tertullian tells us, that in the primitive times, if they had any ill weather, or trouble, they would blame the Christians as the cause of it, and presently the voice was, *Ad leones*, Let the Christians be dragged to the lions, and devoured by the lions. It has been so amongst us. But may we not answer, as Elijah answered Ahab, when Ahab told him that he was the man that troubled Israel, "I have not troubled Israel, but thou and thy father's house." May we not well say to them, as Jehu to Jehoram, when he asked him whether there was peace, "What peace, so long as the whoredoms of thy mother Jezebel and her witchcrafts are so many?" Those that have been popish, certainly they have endangered us of being stripped of all. Who were the causers of the first disturbances amongst us, even of all the persecution here of God's saints, and of all the discontent among the people? who were they that persuaded the bringing in of an arbitrary government? who were the cause of laying such things upon the people, that they could not bear? who were the causers of the troubles in Scotland, and sending of books thither full of superstitious vanities? was it not that prelatical faction, who are those that hinder the reformation at this day? Certainly, if it were as apparent that they who are called puritans, had been the cause of such charge to the kingdom, and disturbance to the state, as the prelatical faction has been; it had been impossible for them to go in the streets, but they would have been stoned to death. I speak not this as though we should do the like, but to show what the virulence of their spirits would have been to them, if it had been apparent that they had been such charge to the kingdom, and such disturbers of the state. The truth is, we may charge our papists, and others that are of that way, (and we know who are next to them,) as the cause of stripping us so naked as we have been. It is clear enough, those that put not away their whoredoms from them, but continue still superstitious and idolaters, they are they who endanger a people to be stripped naked.

Obs. 6. That it is time for people to plead, when there is danger of desolation. "Plead with your mother, plead." Why so? why should we not be quiet? "Lest I strip her naked, and set her as in the day that she was born." What! you are in such a condition as you are in danger to be stripped naked, and to be left desolate as a wilderness? Is it not time then to plead? O plead with God, and plead with those that are in authority, and plead one with another, and plead with all; stir up yourselves, and do what you can; let there be no sluggish spirit, no neutralizing spirit. It is no time for any to be neuters now. It is time now for all to come and plead, not so much now to dispute of things, but for every one to stand, and appear, and plead, not only verbally, but otherwise, as God calls them to it. When John saith, "The axe is laid unto the root of the trees," Luke iii. 9; what then? Then every one cometh and saith, "What shall we do?" "He," saith he to some, "that hath two coats, let him impart to him that hath none;" and to the soldiers, when they say, "What shall we do?" "Do violence to no man, neither accuse any falsely; and be content with your wages." Mark, "when the axe is laid to the root of the trees," every one then comes in, and saith, "What shall we do?" You that are women and inferior, do you pray, and cry, and further your husbands in all good. Be not you backward, do not draw them away, through your extravagance and folly, when they would be liberal and forward, and adventure themselves. And you that are men of estates, if you ask what you should do, it is apparent; "He that hath two coats, let him impart to him that hath none," be willing to part with much of your estates in such a cause as this. And so, soldiers, if you ask what you should do; behave yourselves so as you may convince others; "Do violence to no man," but act according to an orderly way: and "be content with your wages;" perhaps it may not come in so fully afterwards, yet let it appear that it is the cause that strengthens you, rather than your wages. Thus, every one should be of an inquiring spirit when "the axe is laid to the root of the trees." When we are in danger to be stripped of all, it is not time then to stand about curiosities and niceties.

Obs. 7. Those who will not be convinced by the word, God has other means to convince them besides the word. If pleading and convincing arguments will not do it, well then, stripping naked shall do it. The expression is usual in the Scripture, "Then ye shall know that I am the Lord," when I do thus and thus. As you do with those who are of a sleepy disposition; if you call up a servant that is sluggish and sleepy, he answers, Anon, and then falls down and sleeps again; you call him again, and he answers, and sleeps again; at length you come up and pull the clothes off him, and leave him naked, and that will awake him. So God calls upon them to leave their whoredoms and idolatries, and to repent; he threatens, and offers mercy, and they seem a little to awake, but to it again. Well, saith God, I will come another way, and strip you naked, and that will do it.

Obs. 8. Whatever are the means of stripping a nation naked, it is God that doth it. "Lest I strip her naked, and set her as in the day wherein she was born." Lest *I* do it. It is God that gives, and it is God that takes away. But let that pass.

Obs. 9. It is a grievous judgment, for one that is advanced from a low to a high degree, to be brought down again. "Lest I strip her naked, and set her as in the day wherein she was born." Thus Job (chap. xxix. and xxx.) aggravates his misery: "The candle of God shined upon my head; I washed my steps with butter, and the rock poured me out rivers of oil; my glory was fresh in me, and my bow was renewed in my hand," &c. "But now, they that are younger than I have me in derision, whose fathers I would have disdained to have set with the dogs of my flock." Thus he aggravates his judgment, because he was brought into a low condition, having once been in a high one. The like aggravation of misery have we, Lam. iv. 2, "The precious sons of Zion, comparable to fine gold, how are they esteemed as earthen pitchers, the work of men's hands!" and ver. 5, "They that did feed delicately are desolate in the streets: they that were brought up in scarlet embrace dunghills." Thus the Scripture is clear, and your experience is enough to confirm it. For a man who has been a bond-slave in the galleys, and afterward ransomed by the liberality of his friends in

England, if he should be taken and brought back again to the galleys, oh how tedious and grievous would it be! but if he had lived long here, and flourished, and gotten preferment, and had grown a great merchant, and after this to be brought again to the galleys, how much more terrible would this be to him! If some of you that have been beggars heretofore, if God by some way or other should bring you to your former poverty, oh how tedious would it be! We see that many men, who have been raised from a low estate to a high one, are so afraid of returning to a low estate again, that they will venture soul, and conscience, and God and all, rather than they will endanger themselves in the least degree in their estates.

Hence it is very observable, that the chief curse that God threatens the people of Israel, is that they should return to Egypt again, that the Lord would bring them back to the condition wherein once they were. That whole chapter, Deut. xxviii., is spent in denouncing most dreadful curses upon the people; now the conclusion of all is the chief curse of all the rest, ver. 68, "The Lord shall bring thee into Egypt again with ships, by the way whereof I spake unto thee, Thou shalt see it no more again, and there ye shall be sold unto your enemies for bondmen and bondwomen, and no man shall buy you."

Were it not a sad thing for us who have been acquainted with the glorious light of the gospel, and with the blessed privileges that come in thereby, for us to be brought into popish bondage and thraldom again? We may reason with Ezra, "Now for a little space grace hath been showed from the Lord our God, to leave us a remnant to escape, and to give us a nail in his holy place, that our God may lighten our eyes, and give us a little reviving in our bondage. Should we again break thy commandments, and join in affinity with the people of these abominations?" Ezra ix. 8, 14. As for ourselves, who have had of late a little taste of the sweetness of our outward privileges and liberties, who could endure to be under that bondage in which we were three or four years ago, under every apparitor, promoter, pursuivant, commissary, chancellor, and tyrannical prelate, as formerly? We could not have met together, and enjoyed the liberty of such exercises as these; no, you could not have met in your families to pray, but one or other would have been upon you and endangered your estates. The bondage was intolerable; we may well complain, it was a yoke that neither we nor our fathers could bear.

Obs. 9. When God has delivered a people out of misery, and bestowed upon them great mercies, it is their duty often to think of the poor condition in which they were, and to use all the means they can that they may not be brought thither again. God loves this, that we should remember and seriously take to heart what once we were. "Lest I strip her naked, and set her as in the day that she was born;" as if he should say, I would have you consider what a low condition you were in when you were born, and consider the danger you are in to be brought thither again, look then about you, and seek to prevent it, if you have the hearts of men in you. This we shall find in Deut. xxvi. 1, 2, 5, 6, When thou art come into the land which the Lord giveth thee for an inheritance, and dwellest therein, "thou shalt take of the first of all the fruit of the earth, which thou shalt bring of thy land that the Lord thy God giveth thee, and shalt put it in a basket, and shalt go unto the place which the Lord thy God shall choose, to place his name there. And thou shalt speak, and say before the Lord thy God, A Syrian ready to perish was my father, and he went down into Egypt, and sojourned there with a few, and became there a nation, great, mighty, and populous: and the Egyptians evil entreated us, and afflicted us, and laid upon us hard bondage." And Isa. li. 1, "Look unto the rock whence ye are hewn, and to the hole of the pit whence ye are digged." It is very useful for us to consider our former low condition. Mr. Deering, in a sermon preached before Queen Elizabeth, uses this bold expression to her, If there were a time that you thought yourself *tanquam ovis*, as a sheep ready to be slain, take heed that the words of the prophet be not now true, that you be not *tanquam indomita juvencula*, as an untamed heifer. You may note the difference between the spirits of men in former times, in their plainness and boldness; and if there were an excess that way, how far the other way are our court sermons now! Queen Elizabeth was once in a very low condition, and she thought herself to be as a sheep appointed for the slaughter. It is usual for men raised up from a low condition to forget God and themselves, and to grow proud and scornful. Nothing is more sharp than a low thing when it gets up high; so there is none that have more proud and scornful spirits than those who are raised from the dunghill, they know not then where they are: as the proverb is, Set a beggar on horseback, and he knows not how nor whither to ride.

Asperius nihil est humili cum surgit in altum.

Thus it was with Saul: the way to humble Saul, was for him to consider what he once was; and that is the way to humble us all who are subject to be proud of our prosperity, to which God has raised us. When thou wast little in thine own sight, then thou wert made the head of the tribes of Israel. There was a time that he was little in his own eyes, and I beseech you observe the difference between the spirit of Saul when he was in a low condition, and his spirit when he was raised. When Saul was in a low condition, his spirit was low, therefore, in 1 Sam. x. 27, you find that though there were some children of Belial that would not have Saul to reign over them; What! say they, "how shall this man save us? And they despised him, and brought him no presents. But he held his peace." But, chap. xi. 12, when Saul had gotten some credit and honour by his victories, some of the people said, "Who is he that said, Shall Saul reign over us? bring the men that we may put them to death." No, saith Saul, "There shall not a man be put to death this day." Oh how meek was Saul! what a quiet spirit had he before he got up high! But afterward, when he had had many victories, what a furious and outrageous spirit had Saul! You know the story of the fourscore and five priests that must be slain in the city of Nob, and the whole city, men, women, and children, sucklings, oxen, asses, and sheep, must be put to the sword. Why? because one of them only gave a little refreshment to David. What a different spirit is here in Saul to that which he had when he was low!

Is it not so with many of you? When God has brought you low, you seem to be humble, meek, and quiet; then you are content with every thing, and prize every little mercy. Oh a hundred times more mercy will not serve your turn now, as you would have been glad of then, and blessed God if you had had it. But now you know not yourselves, your hearts are raised up as your estates are. Well, it is good for you to look to the condition you were in when you were low; as we read of Agathocles, that king, who was a potter's son, and after advanced to a kingdom, would always be served at his table in earthen vessels, to put him in mind of the condition he was in before. Certainly, if in any place in England it be seasonable to speak of this, it is in London, where many that have been potters' children, and in a low degree, have been raised up high, and acquired great estates. Let them remember in what condition they were, that they may be humbled, and so may prevent the danger of being brought thither again. Many put others in mind of it in a taunting way,—I know what you were not long ago,

I know what your father was! but do you put your own souls in mind of this in a humbling way? this is the way to continue mercies.

But now apply we it a little to ourselves generally, and then we shall conclude all. Let us work this upon our hearts. Look we back to what we were lately, and let us check our hearts for any discontent in our present estate. Not long since would not many of us have been willing to have laid down our lives, to have purchased that mercy we have had this year or two? God has granted to us our former mercies, and raised us from our low condition, of free cost hitherto. God has been beforehand with us; and what if those mercies that are to come, are at somewhat dearer rate than those we have had already? Those mercies we have had already have been very precious and sweet; but surely they that are to come are more precious and sweet, and therefore we may be content though they cost us dear. Yet how vile are the spirits of men in forgetting the sad condition they were in, the taxes, and monopolies, and uncertainty of enjoying any thing that was your own! and now, if there be but a little charge, you immediately murmur and repine: Oh these heavy burdens! the parliament burdens the kingdom and the country, and as good have ship-money and other taxes as these burdens. O, unworthy, unworthy are you to live to see the goodness of the Lord in these days! unworthy to have your eyes open to see what God has done, and thus to murmur! Thou shouldst magnify God's mercies, and not murmur at his proceedings. We have a notable parallel to this (Numb. xvi.) in the story of Korah, Dathan, and Abiram; those murmurers, when they were but in a little strait, came to Moses, and said, "Is it a small thing that thou hast brought us up out of a land that floweth with milk and honey?" ver. 13. What land was that, that Moses brought them up out of, that they said flowed with milk and honey? It was the land of Egypt, the land of their bondage. Indeed they were promised a land of Canaan, that should flow with milk and honey, and they put that upon the land of Egypt; though they had been in bondage and slavery in Egypt, and were now going to Canaan, yet when they endured some trouble in the way, and had but some opposition, and were put to some straits, then Egypt was the land that flowed with milk and honey, and who would come out of Egypt? So though God be bringing us to Canaan, to a blessed land that flows with milk and honey, yet because there are some straits in the way, some difficulties, some oppositions that may cost us something, how do men cry out, We were better before! you talked of reformation, but, for our part, would we might have but what we had before, and be as quiet as we were then! why will you bring us out of a land that flows with milk and honey? O base, murmuring, and discontented spirits, that forget what once they were, and rather prize the bondage they were in before, than are thankful for God's present mercies.

For us not to look back to God's former mercies, goes to the very heart of God. God has an expression in Ezek. xvi. 43, that it frets him to the very heart; "Because thou hast not remembered the days of thy youth, but hast fretted me in all these things." It is a thing that frets God to see a people so unworthy of mercy, when God comes in such ways of mercy to them. My brethren, God has done great things for us, whatever others say and think. Let them murmur, and repine, and say what they will; let us say God has done great things for us. Let us lay to heart our late condition, that so we may be stirred up now to seek after God, that we may never be brought into that condition again. If they would have it again, much good may it do them; but for us, let it be our care to seek God, and to use all lawful means to prevent our bringing back to it again.

For even our present straits are an aggravation of our former misery and present mercy, it should not therefore make our former misery, or present mercy, seem less, but greater. How is that? you will say. Thus; if now we have so much help and power to hinder a party that seek our ruin, yet they have so much strength and resolution, what would have become of us if this had been before, when we had no way nor means to help us? If men complain now, what would they have done then? Therefore, whereas some make use of our straits to lessen our former misery, and think we are now in a worse condition than before, rather let us make it an aggravation of God's mercy towards us; and if we be in such straits now, when God has raised up such means beyond all our thought to resist the flowing in of misery upon us, Lord, whither were we going? what would have become of us if the stream, which had been so long swelling, had broken in upon us when there was no means to have resisted it? We may well see now, that if their intentions and resolutions are so strong for mischief as will not be hindered, notwithstanding the present strength God has granted us to oppose them, surely they had most vile intentions, and dreadful things were determined against us, which would have brought us low indeed, and have made us the most miserable people upon the earth, if God had not come in so miraculously for our help, as he has done at this day.

Therefore, as we read in Jer. xxxvii. 20, "Let my supplication," saith he to the king, "I pray thee, be acceptable before thee, that thou cause me not to return to the house of Jonathan the scribe, lest I die there." So let us present our supplications to the King of heaven, that we may not be sent back to that condition we were once in, that God may not strip us and leave us naked. We have many blessings; Lord, do not strip us, do not strip us of all the ornaments thou hast put upon us.

And would you not have God strip you of your ornaments? be you willing to strip yourselves of your ornaments. Exod. xxxiii. 5, God calls upon the people there, "Put off thy ornaments from thee, that I may know what to do unto thee." This is true and seasonable at this time, in the literal sense, you are called now to strip you of your ornaments. Strip from your fingers your gold rings now when there is need of them; perhaps one of your gold rings would serve to maintain a soldier a month or five weeks, or more; and yet you may have the benefit of it again afterward. Strip your cupboards from your pompous show of plate. It is much if you should not be willing to have your fingers stripped naked, when we are in danger to have the state stripped naked of all our comforts and ornaments. Is it such a great matter to have your cupboard naked of plate now? what if a white cloth were upon it, and all that glittering show taken away, were that such a great sacrifice now, when God is about to strip us naked, and set us as in the day wherein we were born? Certainly all of you, who shall keep your plate now for the pompous adorning of cupboards, cannot but be ashamed of it. Surely you must rather keep it up in your trunks. It cannot but be both a sin and a shame to see such glittering pomp and glory in such times as these.

Strip yourselves of your ornaments, that God strip you not; and not only outwardly, but strip yourselves of your ornaments by your humiliation, for that is the meaning of that place in Exodus. O come and humble yourselves, and come now with naked hearts before the Lord; open your hearts before God, bring them naked and sincere before him, lest he strip you and the kingdom naked. Cry unto God for mercy: O Lord, thou knowest what a vile heart I have had, a base, time-serving heart; yet, Lord, I desire to take away all these cloaks now, and to rend and bring this heart naked before thee; though it be a filthy heart, yet open it. Lord, thou knowest those vile things, those innovations, those superstitions, those horrible wickednesses that were in danger to be let into the church and commonwealth, yet they were things that went down very well with me, and I had distinctions to colour them; but, Lord, it was my base heart that I could not trust thee, but now here I open it naked before thee. O Lord, these ordinances of thine, of the purity and power of which others spake so much, they have been things unsavoury to me, I had no skill in such things. Thou knowest I had a neutralizing spirit, I looked which way the wind blew; how just were it for thee to give me up to be of a desperate malignant spirit! Now, Lord, I come as a naked, wretched creature before thee, in the shame and guilt of my sin, and here I acknowledge thou mayst justly strip me naked of all the comforts of my estate, and leave me in the most miserable condition in which ever poor creature was left. My heart is open before thee, show me what I shall do; and if thou dost reserve any of my estate and comforts which I have forfeited, in testimony of my humiliation for my former sins, I bring it before thee, and am willing to give it up for the public good, and to prevent that evil and mischief that I am sure my sins call for, for my sins cry for wrath against the land, that thou shouldst strip it naked. If all had been such base spirits as I have been, what would have become of the land by this time? In testimony therefore of my humiliation for my sins, here I bring in this of my estate; though indeed, if I had not been guilty of such sins, yet, out of common prudence, and respect to my own security, I might bring in some part; but here is so much the more of my estate, because my conscience tells me of my former guilt. And, Lord, for the time to come, I am resolved to do the uttermost I can for thee and thy cause. And those worthies that carry their lives in their hands for me, God forbid that I should have the least hand in betraying them, in withdrawing my hand and assistance from them. Lord, here I give up myself to thee, and my estate, I surrender it to thee in an everlasting covenant. This is to come with a naked heart indeed before the Lord.

Were it not better that we should be willing to strip ourselves naked, than that God should do it by violence, that God should send soldiers into our houses to strip us naked, as they have dealt with our brethren in Ireland? they took not away their estates only, but all their clothes, and sent them in droves as naked as they were born. We know we have deserved the like. If you will not strip yourselves of your superfluities, God may justly by them strip you naked; and not only bring you into the same condition you were in, but into a far worse; for so he threatens in Deut. xxviii., You shall not only be carried back again into Egypt, but "there you shall be sold unto your enemies for bondmen and bondwomen, and no man shall buy you;" they should be in a worse condition than when they were first in Egypt. So, if there be any of you willing to sell your consciences in hope of preferment, the other side may get power and prevail, and so, instead of being preferred, you may be disappointed, not only be brought into as ill, but into a far worse condition. And perhaps, though you would have sold yourselves, yet nobody will buy you; if the papists come to have the power of your bodies and estates, you may miss that preferment you think of. So saith Ezra, chap. ix. 14, after he had spoken of God's mercy in giving them liberty, and remitting their captivity, "Should we again break thy commandments, and join in affinity with the people of these abominations? wouldst thou not be angry with us till thou hadst consumed us, so that there should be no remnant nor escaping?" And, certainly, if God do not awaken the hearts of people now, if God do not give the people throughout the kingdom a heart to stick to the cause of truth, and to those whom they have intrusted with their estates, liberties, and lives, in every good way, it would be the heaviest judgment of God that ever was upon a nation since the beginning of the earth, it would never be paralleled; that a people should have such an opportunity put into their hands to help, and to vindicate themselves from slavery and bondage, yet, out of I know not what respects, to betray all those that have ventured their lives for them, I say it would be such an example as were not to be paralleled since the beginning of the world. Therefore I beseech you, my brethren, let us lay this to heart, and the Lord make known to us all what is to be done in such a time as this, that we may not be "stripped naked, and set as in the day wherein we were born."

"And make her as a wilderness, and set her like a dry land." God would bring this people, who dwelt in the land of Canaan, flowing with milk and honey, and were, for the beauty which God had put upon them, "excellent for beauty," now to be "as a wilderness." In the former chapter, the state of the ten tribes was set out by Hosea's wife, whose name was "Gomer," and this Gomer was the "daughter of Diblaim." Gomer signifies perfection, and what Diblaim signifies I told you then. But there is another signification of this Diblaim, which we are to refer to this expression of the Lord in this place, that he will "make her as a wilderness;" for you find, Ezek. vi. 14, that mention is made of a desolate country, and a "wilderness towards Diblath," to which this that the prophet speaks of Gomer seems to have reference.

Diblath then, it appears, was a place where there was a very desolate wilderness, and Gomer was the daughter of this Diblath, from whence Diblaim; that is, though the ten tribes were as Gomer, in regard of their beauty, perfect, for so they were; yet she was the daughter of Diblath, or Diblaim, that is, she came forth out of a low and mean condition, and was even brought out of a wilderness; now she shall be brought again into the same estate wherein she was, for I will set her "as a wilderness."

"As a wilderness." The church of God is in itself God's garden, Cant. iv. 12, "A garden enclosed is my sister, my spouse." It is the place of God's delight, not a place for beasts to invade, but enclosed, they are to be kept out of it; a place where very precious fruits grow, which are very pleasing to God; a place that has the dew, the showers of God's blessing, "the dew of Hermon," the dew "that descended upon the mountains of Zion; there God commanded his blessing, even life for evermore," Psal. cxxxiii. 3. But now she must come to be "a wilderness."

For, first, the hedge, the pale, the wall of God's protection shall be taken away from her, and she shall be laid open, liable for all wild beasts to come in and devour her. They loved liberty, and were loth to be enclosed, though it were in God's garden, though it was with the pale and wall of God's protection; well, seeing you will have liberty, you shall have liberty, and this pale and wall of my garden shall be taken away, and your condition shall be like the condition of the beasts in the wilderness.

Again, you shall be "as a wilderness." There shall no good grow among you. No good thing grew amongst you, that was your sin; and there shall no good grow among you, that shall be your plague and punishment. The blessing of God shall be taken away from you, you shall not have those showers of blessing as formerly you were wont to have, but you shall be "as a wilderness." "Cursed be the man that trusteth in man, and maketh flesh his arm, and whose heart departeth from the Lord." Why? "For he shall be like the heath in the desert, and shall not see when good cometh; but shall inhabit the parched places in the wilderness, in a salt land, and not inhabited," Jer. xvii. 5, 6. Vatablus interprets this judgment upon the hearts of idolaters; they are dry, unsavoury; they are destitute of all spiritual good.

Anima idololatriæ dedita, nullos profert fructus, estque inutilis prorsus ut desertum in quo nihil nascitur. Vatab.

"And I will set her like a dry land." The Septuagint read it, I will order her as a dry land. Your sins bring you out of order; but God's plagues order that which sin disorders. "As a dry land." This is contrary to the blessing of the godly man, for he is said to be as the "tree planted by the rivers of waters," Psal. i. 3. The graces and comforts of God's Spirit are compared to waters in the Scripture: "All my springs are in thee," Psal. lxxxvii. 7; all my comforts, all my gifts, all the graces that I have, are in thee. But now God will set them as a dry land, he will take away his gifts and their comforts from them, and so leave them waste and desolate.

Καὶ τάξω αὐτὴν ὡς γῆν ἄνυδρον.

Obs. That sin is of a wasting nature: sin lays waste countries and places in which people live. We have a most remarkable place of Scripture for that, Zech. vii. 14, "They laid the pleasant land desolate." They; who are they? you shall find it, ver. 12, those that "made their hearts as an adamant stone, lest they should hear the law, and the words which the Lord of hosts hath sent in his spirit by the former prophets;" they made the pleasant land desolate. We not only blame those that strip and waste, but commence actions against them. O let us not lay waste this pleasant land, this good land of ours, this garden of the Lord. It is indeed as an Eden, as a paradise; our forefathers have left us this our land, as God's garden; let not us, through our sins, leave it to our posterities as a wilderness, and a dry land. In Psal. cvii. 34, there is a threatening that God will turn "a fruitful land into barrenness, for the wickedness of them that dwell therein." Sin has heretofore laid waste as pleasant and fruitful countries as ours. Those who travel in Germany, their hearts bleed within them to see the spots where famous towns have stood, now overgrown with nettles, and laid waste as a wilderness. And in this God acts after the manner of great kings, who, when their subjects obey them not, threaten to lay their countries waste, and to destroy their cities. Ecclesiastical stories tell us of Theodosius, who laid great taxes upon the city of Antioch, at which the inhabitants were much grieved, and imagining, it seems, that the queen had a special hand in it, they pulled down the brazen statue of the queen, that was in the city, in anger. Upon this, Theodosius threatened to lay the city and country waste, as a fruit of his displeasure. It is a fruit of the anger of kings, according to their power, to manifest it, not only upon particular men, but to lay whole countries waste. God is the great King, and he threatens this against his people for their sins, that he will lay them waste as a wilderness. God had rather that the wild beasts should eat up the good of the land, than that wicked, stubborn sinners should enjoy it: God had rather have a land under his curse, to have nothing but thorns and briers brought forth of it, than that wicked wretches should partake of the sweetness and fruit of it; for sin not only pollutes the sinner, but the land, and puts both the sinner and the land under a curse.

"And slay them with thirst." In Psal. xxxvi. 8, we have a full expression of the plentiful provision of God's people that dwell in the house of the Lord; "They shall be abundantly satisfied with the fatness of thy house; and thou shalt make them drink of the river of thy pleasures." Oh what a sweet promise to those that dwell in God's house, and walk with God as beseems those that are in his house! they shall have fatness, and drink of the river of his pleasures; but here is threatened, that God will not only take away those rivers, but even drops of water; they shall not have a drop to cool their tongues, but shall be slain with thirst. There was a time when God had such pity upon his people that he would cause water to gush out of the rock, rather than their thirst should not be satisfied: but now God threatens that he will make "the heavens as brass, and the earth as iron;" and though a little water might save their lives, they should not have it, he will slay them with thirst. Oh what an alteration does sin make in God's administration of his ways towards us!

It is a great judgment thus to be slain with thirst. I knew a man once, lying in a burning fever, profess, that if he had all the world at his disposal he would give it all for one draught of beer: at so low a rate is the world at such a time as that. If the want of a little beer or water to satisfy thirst for a little while, be so great a judgment, what is it for all good to be eternally withdrawn from all the faculties! I have read that when Darius fled from his enemies, and being in great thirst, (though those kings had a delicate drink that was peculiar to them, which they called *coaspis*, and others, ὕδωρ βασιλικὸν,) he met with a dirty puddle of water, with carrion lying in it, but he drank very heartily of it, and professed, that it was the sweetest draught that ever he drank. If a little dirty water can afford so much comfort when the faculties are in such a disposition as fits them to draw comfort out of it, oh, then, what comfort and goodness are there in an infinite God, when he shall communicate to his creature all that good which is communicable! and when all the faculties of soul and body shall be in a full disposition to receive all the good that is communicated; and not put into a disposition by reason of want, but by reason of the excellency of the faculty raised to such a height, and enlarged to receive what good God himself has to communicate to his creature.

Cum in fuga aquam turbidam et cadaveribus inquinatam bibisset, negavit unquam se bibisse jucundius, nunquam scilicet (ut Cicero lib. 1. Tusc. ait) sitiens bibisset.

But further, it is observable, though God brought them into a wilderness, and set them in a dry land; yet if they might have some drink, though but water, to refresh them in the wilderness, and in this dry land, it were not so much. Though they were in a scorching country, in the wilderness, parched with heat, might they have but some refreshment there, the judgment were not so great; but they shall be in a wilderness, in a dry land, and there they shall be scorched with heat, and then God shall deny them all succour. He will slay them with thirst.

Obs. God brings wicked men into extremity, and there leaves them destitute of all succour. We have an excellent scripture for this, in Ezek. xxii. 20, "I will gather you in mine anger and in my fury;" and what then? "I will leave you there, and melt you," saith God. This may be a comment upon this text, I will bring into the wilderness, and set them in a dry land, and slay them with thirst. The saints may be brought into great extremity, but God leaves them not there. God makes their extremity his opportunity for mercy, he brings refreshing to them then. They never have more sweet refreshings from God than when they are in the greatest extremities in regard of trouble and affliction. God promises that he will be "a shadow for them in the day time from the heat, and for a place of refuge, and for a covert from storm and from rain," Isa. iv. 6. This is God's peculiar mercy to the saints; perhaps they have no shelter now, but when the storm comes they have a shelter then; and they have a shadow when the heat comes; in their extremity they have comfort. But it is otherwise with the wicked; the wicked perhaps may have many shelters before the storm comes, but when it arrives they are destitute;

they may have many shady places before the heat comes, but when it is felt they are left succourless, then they are slain with thirst. When wicked men are in prosperity, there may come one blessing after another (I mean that which is in itself a blessing) heaped upon them, but when they come into adversity, when they have most need of comfort, they are left destitute.

This slaying "with thirst" is applied by some spiritually; I will bring a spiritual famine upon them. When they shall be in a wilderness, in a dry land, when they shall have most need of comfort for their souls, they shall be deprived of it. Many men, in the time of their health and prosperity, have sweet promises of the gospel revealed to them, many blessed manifestations of God's free grace and goodness in his Christ made known to them, but they slight and disregard them. But when God brings them into the wilderness, and causes them to be under the torment of a scorching conscience, then perhaps they may long, Oh that I had one drop of water, one promise out of the word to comfort me! Oh that I might have but never so little refreshing! Oh that I might hear again those things I have heretofore heard and neglected! But then God may deny one drop of water to cool their scorching consciences, and slay their souls with thirst at that time: and thus many poor creatures are slain with thirst, who so little regarded those rivers of consolation, which in the time of their prosperity they might have had.

Ver. 4. *And I will not have mercy upon her children, for they be the children of whoredoms.*

I confess, at the first view, looking upon this verse, I thought I might quickly pass it over; the rather, because we had some such expressions in the former chapter, where God threatened that he would have no mercy upon them: but the Scripture is a vast depth, and there are many excellent treasures in it, there is always *aliquid revisentibus*, something for those that come and look again, and this something will appear to be much more than before had been observed.

"And I will not have mercy." This particle *and* has much in it, it is a most terrible *and*. This conjunction many times in Scripture is as a pleonasm, and does not serve for much use; but in this place it is of great use, and is filled with terror, as full as it is possible for such a little particle to hold.

I know there may be many curious observations of particles and conjunctions; but we shall not meddle with any curiosity, but speak of that which is plain, and the intention of the Holy Ghost here. I say this *and* is most dreadful; mark the conjunction, you had four *ands* before: saith God, I will "strip her naked, *and* set her as in the day wherein she was born, *and* make her as a wilderness, *and* set her as a dry land, *and* slay her with thirst." Is not here enough? O no, there comes a fifth, and that is more terrible than all the former four; "*And* I will have no mercy upon her children." This adds terror to all the rest. Suppose that all the other four had been executed, "I will strip her naked, and set her as in the day that she was born, and I will make her as a wilderness, and set her as a dry land, and slay her with thirst," yet if there might be mercy in all this, their condition had not been so miserable; but (saith God) I will do all these, "and I will not have mercy upon them." O this has terror in it, impossible for the heart of a man that apprehends it to stand under.

And for the opening of this, I shall show you that all the former four, not only may stand with God's mercy, but that they have stood with God's mercy; that God had heretofore showed mercy to them when they were in the low condition in which they were born, when they were in the wilderness, when they were in a dry land, yea, when he did slay them, he showed mercy unto them. But now he saith, he will do thus and thus, and show no mercy unto them. So that then, though this *and* be conjunctive in grammar, yet in divinity it is a disjunctive, and a most dreadful disjunctive, to part them and mercy asunder, yea, to part many of them and mercy eternally asunder. To show you, therefore, that in the four former God showed them mercy; and that this is a more dreadful condition in which God will show them no mercy,—observe,

First, "In the day wherein they were born," they were "cast out in the open field," and they were "in their blood," and "not washed," and the like: but mark, "I passed by thee, and looked upon thee; behold, thy time was the time of love; and I spread my skirt over thee, and covered thy nakedness: yea, I sware unto thee, and entered into a covenant with thee, and thou becamest mine," Ezek. xvi. 8. Here are the highest and fullest expressions of God's grace; first, "I looked upon thee," and then, "the time was a time of love," and then, "I spread my skirt over thee, and I entered into covenant with thee, and thou becamest mine:" here are all these expressions of mercy, at that time when they were cast out as forlorn in the open field, and no eye pitied them; but now they are threatened to be cast out into the field again, and no eye to pity them in heaven or in earth; no, nor the eye of God to pity them: now God threatens to cast them off for ever, so that he will see them in their blood, but it shall be no more a time of love, but a time of wrath, and he will no more enter into covenant with them, neither shall they be his.

Secondly, When God brought them into the wilderness, he there showed them mercy: see Deut. xxxii. 10, "He found him in a desert land, and in the waste howling wilderness;" but mark, "he led him about, he instructed him, he kept him as the apple of his eye." Though they were in a waste howling wilderness, yet they were as dear to God "as the apple of his eye." Yea further, ver. 11, "As an eagle stirreth up her nest, fluttereth over her young, spreadeth abroad her wings, taketh them, beareth them on her wings, so the Lord alone did lead him." Paulus Fagius, citing Rabbi Solomon upon this verse, observes, The eagle carries her young ones not as other birds, for other birds carry their young ones in their claws, the eagle bears hers upon her wings; and this is the reason, because the eagle is more tender of her young ones than other birds are; why? for the other birds carrying their young ones in their claws, if any shoot at them, they hit the young ones and kill them first, and may miss the old one, but the eagle carries hers upon her wings, that whoever shoots her young ones, they must shoot through her first. So saith God, I carried you in the wilderness, as the eagle carries her young ones upon her wings, that if any shoot at you to hurt you, they must shoot through me before they can come at you. This was God's mercy to them when they were in the waste howling wilderness; here is not such an *and*.

Thirdly, God brought them into a dry land. In this wilderness they wanted water, yet (though they were ready to murmur) "he made them suck honey out of the rock, and oil out of the flinty rock," Deut. xxxii. 13. You will say, When did God make them suck honey out of the rock? we read indeed, that water gushed out of the rock in a dry land, but here the Scripture speaks, that "he made them suck honey out of the rock, and oil out of the flinty rock." Chrysostom, speaking upon God's making them suck honey and oil out of the rock, remarks: Not, saith he, that indeed honey or oil came out of the rock, but because they being in the wilderness, and in such great want, the water that came out of the rock was to them as sweet and delightful, as if it had been honey or oil. Thence he gathers, that want and necessity will make every thing very sweet and comfortable, water will be as honey and oil to them that want. When you are at your full tables, this wine pleases you not, and that beer gratifies you not; but if you were in necessity, water would be as wine, it would be as honey and oil to you.

Yea, but what say you to the fourth *and*, "He will slay them with thirst?" Can you show us any place wherein God slew his people, yet showed mercy to them? Yes, I can. There is a place where it is said, God slew his people, yet at that very time he showed abundance of mercy to them; God came with his sword in his hand, yet with abundance of compassion in his heart. The scripture is Psal. lxxviii. 34, 35, "When he slew them, then they sought him: and they returned and inquired early after God, and they remembered that God was their rock, and the high God their redeemer." Well, "they sought him;" and "they remembered" this, that "the high God was their redeemer;" but did God redeem them at that time? Yes; ver. 38, "He, being full of compassion, forgave their iniquity, and destroyed them not: yea, many a time turned he his anger away, and did not stir up all his wrath;" or, as the old translation has it, He called back his anger, which here he will not do. He was "full of compassion," and "forgave their iniquity," and called back his anger, though he slew them at that time. He denies to do so here, he lets out his anger to the full, and will not call it back; "I will have no mercy upon them." And it is observable, that the psalm declares before that, they did but flatter God with their mouth: though they did but flatter God with their mouth, yet such was God's mercy toward them, that he called back his anger. My brethren, God has a high esteem of his worship in a nation; though it should be but external, (but we must not rest in that,) yet external humiliation and worshipping of God in a nation, has been effectual to deliver them from external judgments. Therefore we have much cause to be encouraged, in that God stirs up our nation at this day, and those particularly who are going in that expedition and service for the kingdom, to worship him. Our adversaries come against them with oaths and curses, and they go against them with fasting and prayer, not externally only, but we hope many of them internally, and thousands that join with them in our nation. And if God will show so much mercy to them when they did but flatter him with their mouth, surely, when there are so many true worshippers of him, yea, those that are the instruments of the work, we have much cause to think that God will show mercy to us, and that if anger were come out against us, yet God will call it back.

Thus then we see, that so long as God's people be God's people, though they may be brought to great troubles, yet still there is mercy for them; so long as the knot is between God and them, and they are in covenant, there is mercy for them. But now when they are cast off, there comes an *and*, I will do thus and thus, bring them into these extremities, and I will show no mercy to them, there shall be judgment without mercy.

Obs. The observation then from hence is, When God comes upon the wicked with wrath, he comes with pure wrath, wrath without mixture of mercy; and this is intolerable. We have a remarkable passage in Ezek. vii. 5, "An evil, an only evil, behold, is come." Mark, there may come an evil to the people of God, that which materially is evil, but it can never be said of God's people, that an evil, an only evil, is coming; if an evil come, there comes a great good with that evil: but upon the wicked an evil, and an only evil, is coming. God threatens, Psal. lxxv. 8, that he has "a cup" in his hand, "full of mixture;" the mixture is an aggravation of the wrath in it: but here there is a cup in God's hand without mixture, and the want of mixture is the aggravation of the evil of this cup.

1. When wrath is pure, then it is grown beyond anger, and grown to hatred. So long as it is but mere anger, it admits of mixture of love, but when once it is (as we may speak) grown to that height of sourness, that all the mixture of love is gone, then it is turned to hatred. There was a time when Israel spake in a murmuring way, that God brought them into the wilderness because he hated them, Deut. i. 27. But now God threatens to bring them into the wilderness, and to hate them indeed, according to Hosea ix. 15, "All their wickedness is in Gilgal, for there I hated them." David prays, Psal. vi. 1, that God would not "rebuke him in his anger, neither chasten him in his hot displeasure;" but what then? "Have mercy upon me, O Lord." So long as God shows mercy, he does not chasten in his sore displeasure; but when God comes with afflictions, and denies mercy, then he comes in sore displeasure indeed, it is hatred.

2. When God comes without mercy, he comes upon the wicked in the most unseasonable time for them. That is the difference betwixt the evils that come upon the godly and the wicked. There may be evils (that materially are so) upon the godly, yet they shall come upon them when it shall be seasonable for them; but when they come upon the wicked, it shall be when they are most unseasonable for them. As a husbandman, if he would cut his tree so as only to lop it that it may grow and flourish again, he will be sure to do it in due time, as in January or February, but if he would cut it that it may die, he will lop it when it flourisheth most, at midsummer. God indeed lets wicked men grow up and flourish to the height of their prosperity, and then he lops them, because then he knows they must die and perish. It were better to be lopped in January, in winter time before you flourish, then you may live for your good; but if you stay till the summer, you die for it. You have an excellent scripture, Zeph. ii. 4, "They shall drive out Ashdod at the noon day." In those countries where the sun was exceedingly hot and scorching, shepherds, and others who had their business abroad, used to keep within their houses at noon day, or get into some shady places and sleep. Now when God threatens a judgment in wrath, and denies mercy, he saith, "They shall drive out Ashdod at noon day," in the worst time that Ashdod can be driven out, in the midst of scorching. Because God intended to destroy them, he drives them out at noon day.

3. When God comes upon the wicked and denies mercy, he regards not the proportion of any affliction or any evil; whether it be enough or not enough for them, what is that to him? When he comes upon his own people he weighs out his wrath. Never did any skilful apothecary more carefully weigh every dram of the potion which is to be given to a child, than God weighs out every affliction which he sends upon his children. The difference is, just as if you should go to the apothecary's to take ratsbane to poison vermin; you do not weigh out how much you should take, but give them it at an adventure, and let them take as much as they will, and die: but if you take any thing for your child, if it have any strong virtue in it, or without composition may poison, you will take heed not to take a dram or a grain too much, but will be sure to weigh it out exactly. Thus, though when God comes to his children, he weighs out their afflictions, yet when he comes with judgments upon the wicked, he cares not how much, how many or great they be, whether suitable to their conditions or no, whether they can bear them or no, whether their backs break or no; he comes with judgments upon them to destroy them.

4. When affliction comes without mercy upon the

wicked, God stops his ears at their cries. If they cry when God comes with judgments against them, he calls their crying howling; he tells them, though they cry aloud, yea, cry with tears, he will not hear them, Hos. vii. 14; Ezek. viii. 18.

5. God commands all creatures that they shall deny help to them. They may stand and be amazed, but help them they cannot. They all say, How can we help, seeing God helps not?

6. There is the curse of God mixed with every judgment to drive them further from God, and to harden them more in their sins.

7. One judgment is but the making way for another; yea, all judgments in this world are but the forerunners of eternal judgments. This is the portion of the cup of the wicked, when God saith he will show them no mercy. The afflictions of the saints may seem to be more grievous outwardly, but thus God never afflicts them, there is mercy always for them. Wherefore, all ye saints of God who are under any affliction at any time, be patient and contented under it, for though your afflictions are sore and grievous, yet God delivers you from such afflictions as these, wherein he saith he will show no mercy.

"I will not have mercy upon her children." "Her children." The judgment of God in punishing the sin of the fathers upon the children, we spoke somewhat of in the chapter before; we will wholly let that pass now, and only consider children politically, for certainly that is the meaning of the text; "I will not have mercy upon her children," that is, I will not have mercy upon the particular people that belong to Jezreel. Private persons are called the daughters of Jerusalem, the daughters of such a country. So that the whole community together, with the officers and governors, are as the mother, and private persons are as the children. So that when God saith he will have no mercy upon her children, he not only threatens the state and the church, the governors and the whole community thus, but he threatens every particular person of them. Though you that are in the multitude perhaps think you may escape in the crowd; No, saith God, I will look to every one of the private and particular persons of Israel, and my wrath shall not only come out against those that are in higher place, but it shall come out against you also, I will slay her children. It is true, indeed, the heads and governors of places are usually most involved in the guilt of the sins of nations, and their judgments are usually most dreadful when God comes with national judgments; as Numb. xxv. 3, 4, "Israel joined herself to Baal-Peor, and the anger of the Lord was kindled against Israel, and the Lord said unto Moses, Take all the heads of the people, and hang them up before the Lord, against the sun." The Lord's anger was kindled against the people, but he bade Moses especially look to the heads, and take them and hang them up before the Lord, that the fierce anger of the Lord might be turned away from Israel. Certainly execution of wrath upon such as have been heads in evil, is a sacrifice exceedingly well pleasing to God. But though God aim at them especially in national judgments, yet private persons must not think to escape; and that upon these grounds.

First, Because for their sins God often suffers their governors to do so much evil as they do. As Israel had sinned, and God was wroth with Israel, therefore David did what he did in numbering the people. When you see your governors do that which is naught, lament for your own sins; do not spend your time only in crying out against them, but look to yourselves, it is for your sins that God has left them to do as they have done.

Secondly, The reason why governors do not reform, may be the perverseness of people, that they are not in a preparation to receive that good which, otherwise, our governors had in their hands and hearts to accomplish. As 2 Chron. xx. 33, "Howbeit the high places were not taken away:" why? "for as yet the people had not prepared their hearts unto the God of their fathers." Should they have pulled down the high places? No; but they should have been in a preparation for the pulling of them down. Certainly this is the great cause why our high places are not pulled down, why reformation has gone on no better than it has, and why we have so much evil remaining amongst us, because the people have not prepared their hearts, are not in a disposition to receive the mercy that our governors have hearts to bring to us. They have hearts to work for us, but when we speak to them of what is fit to be done, their answer is, But is England in a fit disposition to receive such a thing? So that the truth is, although you are ready to blame your governors, and to say, They have power in their hands, why do they not reform things? yet the guilt, in great part, devolves upon the people, they are not in a fit disposition to receive such reformation; therefore God threatens the children, the people, here.

Again, further, It may be that the governors who are evil, are so much encouraged and abetted in that which is evil by you; though you do it not, yet you so much encourage them that the guilt redounds upon you.

Yea, lastly, If you obey them in any thing that is evil, the guilt devolves upon you, for you should not do it, but rather obey God than man. Many think to make this their plea, they are commanded to do thus, and governors would have them do it, and it is a law, and the like; and they think upon this plea they may do any thing in the world. This will not secure you, God may come with judgment without mercy upon the children, as well as upon the mother. And if God's wrath should come in national judgments against England, let the people know that they are likely to smart most dreadfully, for never was there a time in our days, nor in our forefathers' days, that so much depended upon the people as at this day; never were they called to afford such help as they are now. So that the people now may have reformation and blessings, if it be not through their own fault. As in Cant. vii. 1, the church is described in her beauty, and it begins at her feet, "How beautiful are thy feet!" And in Cant. v. 11, Christ is described in his beauty, and it begins at the head, "His head is as the most fine gold." God sometimes makes use of the people to be great means, and perhaps the beginning of means, to bring beauty to the church, though they cannot perfect it. Heretofore private persons could do little; alas, they were under grievous oppressions, they knew not how to help themselves. Many men that had purses, and strength, and heads, and hearts, and all, knew not what to do, but make their moan one to another, and to Heaven; but now it is otherwise, you may do somewhat besides making your moan one to another, yea, besides making your moan to Heaven: you that have purses may see ways to employ them for the public good, for religion, for liberty; you that have strength of body may know what to do; you that have parts, you are called to help, you may join together for good, and the good of your country, you may do much more than heretofore could be done. Wherefore now, if you should desert the cause of God, and those you have trusted, you must expect the most dreadful wrath of God upon the people, and that without mercy, that ever was upon any nation since the beginning of the world; for never any nation had more depending upon the people, than there is at this day upon the people of England. Consider it, and oh that all the people of the land did but know what God would have them to do in such a time as this!

"I will not have mercy upon her children;" upon

particular private persons in the society. One note more upon that, It is a dangerous thing for men in any society to do as the most do. If they be in a civil society, or in a church, to give their votes, and to act as the greater part act, without any examination, is dangerous. For though the community may do that which is evil, you shall not be excused by saying, Why, what could I help it, when the most did the same? God comes upon private and particular men, upon the children, even every one of them: and why?

"For they are the children of whoredoms;" that is, either passively or actively: passively, because they were begotten of whoredoms, and brought up, their education had been in whoredom, they had it from their parents: or else they are "the children of whoredoms" actively, they live in the same whoredoms their mother did. From hence,

Obs. 1. There is little hope of children who are educated wickedly. If the dye have been in the wool, it is hard to get it out of the cloth. If evil principles have been dropped into children, there is little hope of them for good, especially of those children who have been brought up in ways of superstition and idolatry, their hearts being so defiled and hardened in superstitious and idolatrous ways, that they seldom come to any good. Therefore that which has been proposed is very good, namely, to take the children of papists, and to bring them up in the education and knowledge of the truth.

Obs. 2. This shall not excuse children, though they be "children of whoredoms." It is no excuse for them to say, they had it from their parents, and they did as their parents have done, and as they commanded them, and according as they brought them up, for the wrath of God cometh upon "the children of disobedience." Then what a mercy is it for us to be brought up in the truth; to have parents that profess the truth, and for our education to be in the way of truth! It is a mercy of which we do not consider to give God the glory. How dangerous is it to have superstitious, idolatrous parents, and to have such kind of education! If they have Turks, or Jews, or papists to their parents, and such education, it is not one of ten thousand that alters his religion. Therefore it is likely our condition would have been the same, if God had not ordered it, that our parents should be such as profess the truth, and our education be according to the truth. Bless God for this. And you that are parents, look to your children, and bring them up in the truth. Children who have gracious principles dropped into them, and watered by prayers and tears, there is hope of them; and not of them alone, but of the nation where they live.

Obs. 3. When God's judgments are abroad in the world, let "the children of whoredoms" look to it, God threatens "he will have no mercy upon them, for they are the children of whoredoms." They are the butt of God's wrath when his judgments come. God saith in Isa. xxvii. 4, "Fury is not in me," that is, it is not in me toward my saints; though I come out in fury, yet it is not in me towards them. What then? "Who would set the briers and thorns against me in battle? I would go through them, I would burn them together." When my wrath comes against the briers and thorns, I will go through them and burn them together; but toward my children, "fury is not in me." When God's wrath is abroad in the world, let not the children of the bride-chamber fear, but let the children of whoredoms tremble. Let briers and thorns fear, but not the fruitful trees in God's garden. God's judgments know how to make a difference between men, they are distinguishing things when they come abroad: God sends not his judgments hand over head, but puts into them a distinguishing quality. God has a chamber of rest and safety for his people, wherein he will hide them till his indignation be overpast; but for the children of whoredoms, superstitious, idolatrous, wicked, and ungodly people, they are the people of God's indignation, they are like Idumea, the people of God's curse, as you have it in Isa. xxxiv. 5.

There are a people this day amongst us who are certainly the people of God's curse, and let them look to it well. Rev. xiv. 8, "Babylon is fallen, is fallen," saith an angel; and mark what follows, ver. 9, 10, "And the third angel followed them, saying, with a loud voice, If any man worship the beast and his image, and receive his mark in his forehead or in his hand, the same shall drink of the wine of the wrath of God, which is poured out without mixture into the cup of his indignation." According to this text, God will have no mercy, they shall drink of the wine of the wrath of God, without mixture of any mercy at all. And further, "He shall be tormented with fire and brimstone in the presence of the holy angels, and in the presence of the Lamb; and the smoke of their torment ascendeth up for ever and ever; and they have no rest day nor night, who worship the beast and his image, and whosoever receiveth the mark of his name." Here is a dreadful threat against such as follow the ways of that great whore of Babylon. Blessed are they that in these times have testimony in their own consciences, that it has been their care above all things to draw themselves out from the guilt of all superstitious and idolatrous vanities, and to keep themselves, according to the light that God has discovered to them, pure from the pollutions of that man of sin. Blessed, I say, are these, they need not fear this day; but for those who have involved themselves in the guilt of those pollutions, they have need to humble their souls before God, and to cry mightily, for wrath is going out against the children of whoredoms. It is not meant only of hell hereafter, but of judgment even in this world. And above all times that have been since antichrist began, it is a most desperate thing to be a papist in these days, because now is the time for God to make these children of whoredoms the very butt of his wrath and indignation.

We hear of wars, and rumours of wars: my brethren, keep your hearts chaste to God, and fear not, for God has another manner of people to deal with than you; you shall be sealed first, before the wrath come out. Though I cannot excuse you altogether from suffering some afflictions, these children of whoredoms may bring some trouble upon the saints for the present, yea, perhaps some of you may have your blood spilt, but God has mercy to bestow upon you: but for them there is wrath, and wrath without mixture, God saith he will have no mercy upon the children of whoredoms.

Let such as are going forth then in the service of religion and liberty, go forth with courage and undauntedness of spirit; why? for they fight against none but those whom God fights against. Who are they, but those who have showed themselves fighters against God, most abominable swearers and blasphemers, such as make no other use of the light of the gospel, but to scorn and contemn it; such as are open despisers of God and his truth, and of his people? Certainly, if there be a cursed generation upon the face of the earth, these are the people, whose mouths are full of curses; and God's curse is upon them, who are so full of cursings themselves. If there be any of you here that are now going, or hereafter may go forth in this service, your spirits should rise with indignation against such monsters upon earth, and go against them as David against Goliath, What! shall this uncircumcised Philistine defy the host of the living God? Thus your hearts should rise if you have any love to God and his truth; Shall a company of cursed monsters, that do nothing but blaspheme, and curse, and swear, and defy God, and his servants, and his tabernacle, and worship; shall these uncircumcised Philistines go on thus, defying God and his truth? If you have the hearts of men within you, especially of Christians, methinks you should not be able to bear it, but go forth against them with fulness of spirit and resolution. Certainly, God will make them a prey to you; they are such as not only have put off Christianity, and are become atheists, but they have put off all kind of humanity, and are rather turned monstrous beasts, or devils. Fear them not, though their hearts be full of pride and rage, and though they boast never so much what they are, or what they have done, or what they will do; I say, fear them not, for this is part of the curse of God upon them, that though God fights against them, they will not see it, they shall not see it because God intends to destroy them; though judgments are out against them, yet they will not repent. You find divers times in the book of the Revelation, that those who followed antichrist, though they were tormented, and all the judgments of God were against them, yet they repented not, Rev. ix. 21; xvi. 9, 11. This, I say, is the curse of God upon such, God will not give them repentance unto life, for they are the children of whoredoms, upon whom God intends to have no mercy: therefore the higher their rage rises, the higher your hearts should rise against them.

Ver. 5. *For their mother hath played the harlot: she that conceived them hath done shamefully: for she said, I will go after my lovers, that give me my bread and my water, my wool and my flax, mine oil and my drink.*

"Their mother," that is, the state and the church, for they were both involved in one, "hath played the harlot." This "for" has reference two ways; either it may have reference to those words, "I will not have mercy upon them," for not only they are defiled with whoredoms, but their mother also, she has played the harlot: or secondly, it has reference only to the latter part, "they are the children of whoredoms, for their mother hath played the harlot:" either it refers to the reason why God will not have mercy upon them, because their mother hath played the harlot; or to the reason why they are the children of whoredoms, for their mother hath played the harlot. And from both these references we have very useful observations.

Obs. 1. God cannot endure a succession in wickedness. I will not have mercy upon them, "their mother hath played the harlot," and they are children of whoredoms themselves, there is a succession of wickedness among them, and that I cannot bear. The ground is, because those that keep up a succession of wickedness from the mother to the children downward, are guilty of all the wickednesses that went before them in that line: else, how can that be understood, where Christ saith he will require all the blood from Abel to Zacharias upon that generation, but because they, continuing in that way of sin, kept up the succession of that sin; and so that generation was guilty of all the sins of that kind that went before, even unto Abel. The father is a whoremonger, and the child proves to be one too, and so it descends; the child is not only guilty of his own sin, but of his father's, and of his grandfather's, and of all that kind of sin committed before, even up to the beginning of the world; why? because he keeps up the succession of that sin in the world. This is a most terrible thing to consider, enough to wound the strongest heart in the world, especially of those that know they have had wicked parents.

Obs. 2. Children usually follow the example of their parents. "For their mother hath played the harlot," is assigned as the reason why they are children of whoredoms. It is a usual thing where there are profane parents, to have profane children; if the parents swear, to have swearing children; if parents be superstitious, to have superstitious children; if parents be scorners at religion, to have children scorners too. That new nick-name brought against the godly in room of the former, is as frequent in the mouths of children as in others, because children follow their fathers. 2 Kings ii. 23, when Elisha the prophet was going up to Bethel, "there came forth little children out of the city, and said unto him, Go up, thou bald-head; go up, thou bald-head." The thing that I note it for is this, that not only the children did it, and so were destroyed, (for two she-bears came out of the wilderness, and tare forty-two of them,) but what children were they? If you observe the text, you find that they were the children of Bethel; and what place was that? one of the places where the calves were set up, a place of much superstition, and the children were as superstitious as their parents. A place that had the name, The house of God; but no place degenerated more from the name than it, it was a Beth-aven, a house of vanity and wickedness. The place was most superstitious, and its children were those who scorned at the prophet. Again, the prophet saith, Jer. vii. 18, "The children gather wood, and the fathers kindle the fire, and the women knead their dough:" the children joined, you see. Pelagius thought that there was no sin came into the world, but by children imitating their parents. Certainly, imitation is of great power and force to prevail with the hearts of children. You that are wicked parents, had need look to what you do before your children. He that sins before a child, especially a parent, sins doubly, for a child will be ready to imitate it. What! will you not only sin against God, and be enemies unto him, but will you leave a succession, part of yourselves, to blaspheme God after you are dead? Suppose, parents, you had a plague-sore upon you, would you go amongst your children and breathe upon them? This cruelty is much worse: will you go into your families, and breathe infection into your children, and so make them like you, and guilty of your sins, and of the plagues of God together with you? O cruel parents!

Qui peccat coram puero bis peccat.

On the other hand, as they were children of whoredoms, because "their mother hath played the harlot," why then should not children be gracious and godly, who have gracious and godly parents? Why should it not be said, This child is a godly child, for his mother was a gracious woman, his father was a godly man? Children, let this be your encomium, You are godly and gracious children, because you had godly and gracious parents; this will be your honour before the saints. But how vile is it, when it may be said, Here is a wicked wretch, yet he had a godly father and mother; here is an unclean and filthy liver, yet he had gracious parents! It is no wonder to say, This man is filthy, for his father was unclean, and his mother was a harlot; but to look upon one and say, Here is an adulterer, yet his father was a godly, gracious man; here is a harlot, yet her mother was a holy woman: oh how vile is this! The reverend Mr. Bolton, upon his death-bed, called his children to come to him, and thus addressed them, "I do believe not one of you will dare to meet me at the tribunal of Christ in an unregenerate condition." You that are evil children of godly parents, let me, in their names, speak to you: With what face do you think you shall dare to meet your godly father and gracious mother before the judgment-seat of Christ Jesus? at that day, if your godly father stand at the right hand of Christ, how can you appear before that face in the guilt of those horrible wickednesses in which you now live? Certainly, the thought of this has power to daunt your hearts.

"She hath done shamefully." The word הוֹבִישָׁה is in Hiphil, and may be translated transitively, she hath made ashamed, as well as done shamefully; and by some it is thus interpreted, she has made ashamed her husband, she has made ashamed her children, she has made ashamed herself: and all these three may be meant; yea, I conceive the intent of the Holy Ghost is to express them all.

Her husband first. The church is the spouse of Jesus Christ; Christ is the husband of the church; and you know the Scripture saith that "the woman is the glory of the man:" so the church, being the spouse of Christ, should be the glory of Christ. The woman should be the glory of the man, but yet, being wicked, she makes her husband ashamed. The evil of the wife is a shame to the husband; so the evil of the church is a shame to Jesus Christ. The church in Scripture is called the glory of Christ: If "our brethren be inquired of, they are the messengers of the churches, and the glory of Christ," 2 Cor. viii. 23. "Upon all the glory shall be a defence," Isa. iv. 5. It should be so; but when it is defiled it shames Christ, its wickedness reflects upon Christ. Christ is said to "walk in the midst of the seven golden candlesticks," Rev. ii. 1. Every church is a candlestick, and it should be a golden candlestick; but if it be a filthy and rusty candlestick, it is a dishonour to Christ who walks amongst them. Wicked men do not shame Christ, but the godly do. My brethren, let us take heed of that; it is an evil thing to bring shame to ourselves and one another, but to bring a shame upon Jesus Christ is the greatest evil. Many of you perhaps are ashamed *of* Christ, take heed that you be not a shame *to* Christ. They are ashamed of Christ that are ashamed to appear in the cause of Christ; but as for you that are so, Christ has more cause to be ashamed of you, for you are a shame to him. I cannot deny, but many churches of God of late have brought shame to Jesus Christ by their dissensions and fractions. They have taken shame to themselves, and have acknowledged it to the glory of Christ, and thus, in some measure, have washed off that shame which they have brought to Christ.

Again, wicked parents are a shame to their children. When a child appears in a place, and is known to be very hopeful, some who knew his family say, I wonder to see him so forward, for his father is a drunkard, and his mother of a vile and malignant spirit: how the child is ashamed to hear of the evil of his father, and of the evil of his mother! As foolish children are a shame to their parents, so wicked parents are a shame to their children. You that have gracious children, take heed you be not a shame to them, and so a shame to yourselves.

And then a shame to herself. "She hath played the harlot: she hath done shamefully." Wherein had she done shamefully? I will only mention one particular. Her shame was especially in subjecting religion to carnal policy. For what was the great sin of the ten tribes? It was this, they were afraid, if they went up to Jerusalem to worship, the people would then depart from the house of Jeroboam to the house of David, therefore out of political regards they would have worship set up at Dan and Bethel; there they would have calves, and they would not go up to Jerusalem, the place which God had appointed for worship. This was a mere politic fetch, for they could not but acknowledge that God required them to worship at Jerusalem where the temple was. Here then they did shamefully.

Obs. 1. For governors, or any other persons, to subject religion to policy is a shameful thing. (1.) It is shameful to make religion an underling, and to make policy the head. Perhaps they call this wisdom, prudent conduct. We must, say they, be careful and wise to foresee inconveniences that may follow. But what if God give it another name? God may give it a name of base temporizing, a name of folly and wickedness. To subject religion to policy is shameful, because it abases that which is the great honour of any country, and makes it an underling. What is the excellency of man but religion? what is the excellency of a country but religion? and what has England been glorious for more than for religion? Now to put an excellent thing under an inferior, is to put the crown, which is for the head, under one's foot: although a thing has in itself but little excellency, if it be brought beneath itself under other things which have not so great an excellency in them, it makes it vile.

(2.) Shameful, because it holds forth this, that we dare not trust God for our civil estate, and for our peace, therefore religion must come under.

(3.) Shameful, because it is gross folly; for there is no such way to breed disturbance, or to undo a state, as to make religion an underling to policy. Was it not so here? That very way which they took to uphold their policy, was the way to destroy their state; and did destroy it at last. What cause had they then to be ashamed, when God took that by which they thought to help themselves, and made that the very thing that caused their ruin! And certainly it will be so; they that use the most deep and politic artifices, if they think to secure themselves, and preserve their peace, by the principle, that religion must come under, God will make them ashamed one way or other, it will be the only way to undo themselves and us. In matters of religion some commands are affirmative precepts; these, though they *ligare semper*, yet not *ad semper*, there is not a necessity that at every time and instant they should be urged; so that a people may be in such a frame that men cannot but by degrees bring in a reformation, and then it is not carnal policy to bring in such ways of God gradually, as are commanded by affirmative precepts: but negative precepts bind *semper* and *ad semper;* and the state must see, that they do nothing against Christ out of policy, that they do not hinder the gospel of Christ by any positive law; for though Christ may be willing to forbear some ordinances for a time, and out of mercy to a people, and will have mercy and not sacrifice, yet he will never allow any thing done against him in that time. If, out of any state policy to preserve peace, or to gratify an evil party, they sacrifice any part of religion, or any godly person, Christ accounts this a shameful thing; and whoever does so will be ashamed of it at the last. Now, my brethren, why should not God be trusted? Let us look at religion in the first place, and pray that those who are reformers, who have power in their hands, may never prove guilty of putting religion under policy. When Joshua had brought the people of Israel over Jordan, which you know was the beginning of their entrance into Canaan, they were to encounter all their enemies. You may imagine, that when Joshua had passed the river, Israel might suppose that all the country would be about their ears. One would think, that policy would have taught them to lay aside all thoughts of religion then, and to look to their enemies who were at hand; If ever they are outrageous it will be now, therefore now let us mind nothing but arming ourselves against them. But mark, God goes another way to work; as soon as they were gone over Jordan, and were upon the borders of the land of Canaan, they must circumcise themselves, and when they were circumcised they could not fight. Simeon and Levi destroyed a whole city when they were circumcised, because they were not then able to fight or defend themselves, but lay at the mercy of their enemies. But this was God's wisdom. Nay further, they must keep the passover too, they must mind and attend to religion: and mark the latter end of the chapter, that after they had been circumcised and kept the passover, then appeareth one to Joshua with a drawn sword, and saith, "I am the Captain of the host of the Lord." The Captain of the Lord's host appeared to fight for them when they had obeyed; whereas, had they neglected circumcision and the passover, and thought of fighting only, they might have missed the Captain of the Lord's host to have fought for them, and what would have become of them then? So you see, God would have us mind religion in the most dangerous times; and though we think we must mind our peace and safety, and lay our hands upon our swords for our defence, yet let us be careful of our religion, and then we shall have a Captain of the Lord's host come and fight for us.

In Mark viii. 15, we are charged to take heed of two sorts of leaven, "the leaven of the Pharisees, and the leaven of Herod." The leaven of the scribes and Pharisees is corruption in church affairs; the leaven of Herod is corruption in religion, in bringing the things of God under the affairs of the state: for in this Herod was like Jeroboam, he was afraid of his kingdom, as Jeroboam was; he had many ways and plots to keep himself in that kingdom, as Jeroboam had; and many cleaved to Herod in his plots, as Israel clave to Jeroboam in his; therefore says Christ, Take heed not only of the leaven of the scribes and Pharisees, but of the leaven of Herod. And it may be, the Lord saw us too prone to ways of sinful compliances, even ready to have sacrificed much of his worship and many of his saints, for obtaining peace in the state, and so to have fallen off from that reformation that both God and his people expected; hence he has taken the work into his own hands; he will bring about his own work, though it may cost us dear, who knows how much blood?

Obs. 2. That sin, but especially whoredom, is a shameful thing. Prov. xiii. 5, "A wicked man is loathsome, and cometh to shame." Prov. xiv. 34, "Sin is a reproach to any people." Sin, of its own nature, let it be what it will, is shameful. All sin brings a man beneath the excellency of a man, it is contrary to the image of God in man, to that wherein true honour, beauty, glory, consist. It makes men vile: Dan. xi. 21, "And in his estate shall stand up a vile person." Who was that? It was, according to interpreters, Antiochus Epiphanes, the great king of Assyria, and yet a vile person. Josephus tells us, when the Samaritans were in danger of suffering from him, because he thought them to be Jews, they wrote to him in this manner, To Antiochus the mighty god; and his very epithet, Epiphanes, is in English as much as illustrious, Antiochus the illustrious, the famous, bright in his glory. He that was so illustrious and great a prince, as to be addressed as the mighty god, yet in Scripture language, being wicked, is "a vile person." It is a special mark of one that is fit to dwell in God's mountain, Psal. xv. 4, that he is able to see the vileness of sin through all the glory of the world; "in whose eyes a vile person is contemned." Sin is a shame, because it deceives a man: "The way of the wicked shall deceive him." "What fruit had ye then of those things, whereof ye are now ashamed?" It is a good sign of grace, to be able to see into the deceits of sin, so as to be ashamed of it. But, though all sin be shameful, yet whoredom especially, and that either bodily or spiritual.

First, bodily. The expression of shamefulness, though it especially aims at their idolatry, yet has its rise from bodily whoredom; if that were not shameful, the expression could not be appropriate, that she had played the harlot, and done shamefully. Prov. vi. 32, 33, "Whoso committeth adultery with a woman, lacketh understanding, he that doeth it destroyeth his own soul. A wound and dishonour shall he get; and his reproach shall not be wiped away." It makes one to be as one of the fools in Israel: "And I," (saith Tamar, when Amnon defiled her,) "whither shall I cause my shame to go? and as for thee, thou shalt be as one of the fools in Israel," 2 Sam. xiii. 13. Amnon, though a king's son, yet by his uncleanness makes himself as one of the fools in Israel. Deut. xxiii. 18, "Thou shalt not bring the hire of a whore, or the price of a dog, into the house of the Lord;" they are joined together, for Scripture makes those to be dogs who are unclean and filthy. When Ishbosheth charged Abner with the sin of uncleanness, 2 Sam. iii. 8, "Am I a dog's head," saith he, "that thou chargest me to-day with a fault concerning this woman?" Many adulterers go very fine and spruce, many young wantons are bravely dressed, but in God's esteem they are as dogs for their uncleanness. It is not a harsher title than the Spirit of God gives them. I have read of a people amongst the heathen, who condemned this sin with a shameful death, according to its nature. The adulterer's or adulteress's head was put into the paunch of a beast, and stifled to death; a punishment fit for so filthy a sin. This sin is ever shameful, but especially the more lovely any yoke-fellow is who is forsaken, and the more vile and foul the harlot is, so much the more shameful is the sin. Athenæus introduces Plato, bewailing himself and his own condition, that he was taken so much with a filthy harlot. It is more shameful for Christians than for heathens, because they know that the covenant of marriage is the "covenant of God," Prov. ii. 17.

But further, corruption in God's worship is most shameful, for that is aimed at especially here. The shamefulness of corrupting the worship of God is expressed in Exod. xxxii. 25. Aaron made the people naked unto their shame; how was that, but by false worship, though it was of the true God? In false worship there is shame, because in that a man subjects his conscience to vile things. Conscience, which is not to be subject to any creature, only to God himself, is here made subject to low and vile things. It is not shameful to subject our consciences to God in the use of creatures, though never so mean, if appointed by himself; but those that subject them to creatures in ways of false worship not appointed by God, subject not their consciences to God but to those creatures, and that is shameful. In false worship, though there may seem to be a great deal of humility, yet there is notorious pride and presumption, and therefore much shame. For a creature to take upon him, by his own fancy and conceit, to raise up creatures higher than God has raised them, to put higher respects upon creatures than God has done, is boldness and presumption. Yea, he presumes, by his own conceit, to raise up the creature so high, that God himself must come nearer to men, and be more present with these creatures than otherwise he would. Thus men presume to bring God under their fancies; and is not this shameful?

Further, it is extreme folly, for we contradict ourselves when we think to honour God, and yet go against him, when we put high esteem upon such things as are abominable and detestable. "I sent unto you all my servants the prophets, rising early and sending them, saying, Oh, do not this abominable thing that I hate," Jer. xliv. 4. Mark, God cries out with energy, All my servants the prophets I sent, saying, "Oh, do not this abominable thing;" it is a delightful thing in your eyes, but abominable in God's. And, Ezek. xxii. 3, they are denominated גלולים a word that signifies the very excrements of a man; they glory in them, but he saith, they defile themselves by them. When God opens their eyes they will see false worship a shameful thing; and when they do so God will show them the excellency of his own. "Son of man, show the house to the house of Israel, that they may be ashamed of their iniquities: and let them measure the pattern.

And if they be ashamed of all that they have done," that is, of all their false worship; what then? "show them the form of the house, and the fashion thereof, and the goings out thereof, and the comings in thereof, and all the forms thereof, and all the ordinances thereof, and all the forms thereof, and all the laws thereof: and write it in their sight, that they may keep the whole form thereof, and all the ordinances thereof, and do them," Ezek. xliii. 10, 11. Mark, my brethren, you see how God stands upon forms, "all the forms thereof," and "all the forms thereof," and "the whole form thereof." Let us not slightly account any thing in God's worship, for God stands much upon his own form in his own worship. Many who have no religion but a form, yet neglect God's form. Men love to stand much upon their own forms; let them know God stands much upon his forms, and it is no hinderance, but a furtherance, to the power in religion, to keep close to God's form. If we would know what are God's ordinances, for many cry out, Oh that we could but know what is the right way, this is one way for you to know: First, be ashamed of what you have done, be ashamed of your former false worship, and then God will show you the ordinances of his house, and the true beauty of his worship: till then there are so many distinctions, and evasions, and objections, that you never come to understand it. When God humbles the heart, and makes it ashamed of what has been naught before, all the distinctions, and evasions, and objections, vanish away as the mist before the sun.

And the more excellent the Lord is, and those ordinances are, from which we depart, the more shameful is that false worship to which our hearts decline. "She hath done shamefully:" why? she has forsaken such a Husband, the Lord Jesus Christ, who is so lovely; she has forsaken the blessed ordinances that God has appointed, and turned herself to vanities of her own. Christ is said, Cant. v. 16, to be altogether lovely, there is loveliness enough in Christ to satisfy the soul for ever. Ezekiel says, chap. vii. 20, "As for the beauty of his ornament," (speaking of God's ordinances in his temple,) "he set it in majesty: but they made the images of their abominations and of their detestable things therein." Oh how shameful was this! This shows the shamefulness of it, because God set the beauty of his ornament in majesty. The ordinances of God which he appointed himself, are God's "ornament," they are "the beauty of his ornament," they are "the beauty of his ornament set in majesty;" and shall these beautiful and glorious things be forsaken for vanities of our own inventions? This is shameful.

Obs. 3. Sin, especially whoredom, either bodily or spiritual, if suffered to grow, will make those who commit it not only shameful, but shameless in their doings. "She hath done shamefully, for she hath said." Here it is implied, that the thing done was not only shameful, but that she was shameless. "Were they ashamed when they had committed abomination? Nay, they were not at all ashamed, neither could they blush," Jer. vi. 15. At first, sin may seem to be a little shame-faced, but afterward it grows brazen-faced; modest a little at first, but bold, impudent, and daring afterward. If men were told beforehand what they would do afterward, they would be ready to say, as Hazael to the prophet, "But what! is thy servant a dog, that he should do this great thing?" their hearts would even shake at the thought of it: yet, when sin has hardened their hearts, they will do it, and that with open face too. Whoredom, you know, at first, is that at which every man blushes; but, within a while, unclean ones can boast of their filthiness. But especially spiritual whoredom, the corruption of God's worship, at first may be a little modest, but see to what a height it grows if in time it be not prevented. I will give you a notable example of this. At first we find Solomon very modest in the matter of idolatry. 2 Chron. viii. 11, saith, that he "brought up the daughter of Pharaoh out of the city of David, to the house he had built for her, for he said, My wife shall not dwell in the house of David king of Israel;" why? "because the places are holy, whereunto the ark of the Lord hath come." Mark, how careful Solomon was not to pollute any thing that had any seeming holiness in it. I have so much respect to the ark of God, to the worship of God, and to those places that are holy, that my wife shall not so much as dwell there. But oh what did Solomon grow to afterward! he suffered idolatry most shamefully, he "went after Ashtaroth the goddess of the Zidonians, and after Milcom the abomination of the Ammonites,—and built a high place for Chemosh, the abomination of Moab, in the hill that is before Jerusalem," 1 Kings xi. 5, 7; just there he built it too, as if it had been in defiance to the temple of God and his true worship; and that "for Molech the abomination of the children of Ammon; and likewise did he," saith ver. 8, "for all his strange wives, which burnt incense and sacrificed unto their gods." Thus shameless was he grown! And thus we see it in experience. How fair are men in their ways of superstition at first! decency is all they plead for. Well, afterward it rises from decency to significancy, that is a little higher, to put men in mind. Thirdly, from significancy it rises to efficacy, to stir up the dull mind of man. Fourthly, from efficacy it rises to necessity, that now it must be done, and the worship of God cannot be without it, and there shall be no ordinance, no administration at all without it. Decency, significancy, efficacy, and necessity; thus it rises to be shameful at last. So, amongst the papists in their traditions, at first they came with this argument, What! will you not regard them as you would other books and histories? they are the traditions of our forefathers; but at length they came to this, in the fourth session of the council of Trent, the synod "doth take and honour the books of the Old and New Testament, and the traditions of the fathers, with equal affection of piety and reverence." To this shamefulness they grew at last. And so for worshippping of images, why, it is for the decency of churches to have them, and they are but to put you in mind, at the most; but at length these are the very words, "the same honour is due to the image and to the exemplar."

Omnes libros tam Veteris tam Novi Testamenti necnon traditiones ipsas pari pietatis affectu ac reverentia suscipit ac veneratur.

Idem honor debetur imagini et exemplari.

Obs. 4. When men grow shameless in evil, there is little hope of them. "I will have no mercy upon them;" why? for they have done thus, they are grown thus impudent. It is a good thing to keep the bridle of shame as long as we can upon our children, servants, and any of our inferiors: therefore take this one instruction, be not too ready to rebuke and chastise your servants, or your children, in a reproachful manner before others, lest you bring them to see that they have no honour to lose, and then there is little hope of them: evermore keep such a hand over your children and servants that they may see they have some respect to lose; that they may not be so shamed by you, as for them to think they cannot be worse, or more disgraced; there is no such way to make them desperate as that. It is very great wisdom in governors to keep the bridle of shame. Your bridewell or jail-birds seldom or never come to good; why? because they have no bridle to keep them in, they have lost all their honour, and they can lose no more; and there is no rational creature but would have honour. Not the meanest servant you have but has a respect to honour, and that will do more than blows, except they are become very beasts.

But how does he prove that it is shameful? Thus:

"For she said, I will go after my lovers, that give me my bread and my water, my wool and my flax, mine oil and my drink."

Obs. 1. Deliberate sins are most shameful sins. She hath said. This is a proof of her shamefulness, because that which she has done, she has done upon deliberation; she said she would do thus and thus, she considered before what she would do, and yet she did it. Wickedness committed *de industria, ex consilio,* of purpose resolved upon, is very shameful. Godly men may be overtaken with a fault: "If a man be overtaken with a fault," Gal. vi. 1. It is one thing to be overtaken with a sin, and another thing to overtake a sin; a gracious heart may have sin overtake it, but it is a shameless heart that overtakes sin.

'Εὰν καὶ προληφθῇ ἄνθρωπος.

Obs. 2. Those who are guilty of whoredom usually grow extremely wilful. "She said, I *will* go." As if she had said, Let all the prophets say what they can, let them talk out their very hearts, I will have my mind, I will follow my lovers still. Of those who commit this sin bodily, it is said, Prov. ii. 19, "None that go unto her return again, neither take they hold of the paths of life." It is a most dreadful scripture against all adulterers and unclean persons: make it out how you will, there is "none that go unto her return again, neither take they hold of the paths of life." These are the words of the Holy Ghost: I leave the words with you. So Prov. xxiii. 27, "A whore is a deep ditch, and a strange woman is a narrow pit;" they cannot easily get out, nor will they easily get out, they are so plunged in. "Having eyes full of adultery, and that cannot cease from sin," 2 Pet. ii. 14. Why cannot they cease to sin? it is not because they have a heart but no power, but their wills are brought into that bondage and subjection that they cannot will otherwise; therefore in Ezek. xlvii. 11, we find that though the waters of the sanctuary were very healing, yet the miry places and the marshes were not healed: miry, filthy, unclean hearts are very seldom healed by the waters of the sanctuary. Ælian reports, that there was a harlot who boasted she could easily get scholars away from Socrates, but Socrates could get no scholars from her, none of her followers. It is true that a harlot is prevalent, and when she has once overcome, it is almost impossible to get away from her. Therefore Heb. vi. 6, which speaks of that sin from which it is impossible to be renewed again to repentance, is interpreted by Tertullian to be no other than the sin of uncleanness. The author of this Epistle (saith he) knew no promise of second repentance to the adulterer and fornicator; showing how ordinarily those that are guilty of that sin, and are given up to it, grow wilful in it. And therefore in Eph. iv. 19, these two are put together, "being past feeling," and "having given themselves over unto lasciviousness." Wantons usually grow past feeling.

Ælianus variar. Histor.

And for spiritual adultery, that usually is very wilful too, for those who are left by God to superstition and idolatry, seldom return again, but grow exceeding wilful in that wickedness. You have a notable text for that, Jer. xliv. 16, 17; the people say there, "As for the word thou hast spoken to us in the name of the Lord, we will not hearken unto thee; but we will do whatsoever cometh out of our own mouth, to burn incense to the queen of heaven." We will go on to burn incense to the queen of heaven, talk as long as you will. And so Jer. ii. 10—12, "Pass over," saith God, "the isles of Chittim, and see; and send unto Kedar, and consider diligently, and see if there be such a thing. Hath a nation changed their gods, which are yet no gods?" Men are settled in the ways of idolatry, and will never give over worshipping their gods: "but my people have changed their glory for that which doth not profit:" therefore "be astonished, O ye heavens, at this, and be horribly afraid, be ye very desolate, saith the Lord." So Micah iv. 5, "All people will walk every one in the name of his god." Their hearts are set upon it, they *will* do it. Spiritual whoredom mightily besots the heart. Isa. xliv. 19, 20, "None considereth in his heart, neither is there knowledge and understanding to say, I have burned part of it in the fire; yea, also I have baked bread upon the coals thereof; I have roasted flesh, and eaten it; and shall I make the residue thereof an abomination? shall I fall down to the stock of a tree? He feedeth on ashes: a deceived heart hath turned him aside, that he cannot deliver his soul, nor say, Is there not a lie in my right hand?" And so Rev. xvi. 11, where those who were given up to antichrist, though they were tormented they "blasphemed the God of heaven, because of their pains and their sores, and they repented not of their deeds."

Obs. 3. Wilfulness in any sin, but especially in this sin, is a very great aggravation of it. "I will have no mercy upon them," I will give them up; why? they have done shamefully, and they have said, "I will go after my lovers." There are many who, in their passion, think it a brave spirit to say, I will, and I will, and I care not, say what you can, or whatever becomes of it, I will do, or I will have this. Especially men in place, and of estates, are not able to endure the controlling of their will in any thing; and therefore when their wills are but crossed, they burst out into outrageous speeches, and fall blaspheming, and swearing, and saying they will have their will, though it cost them their lives. Thus we find it in the people of Israel, 1 Sam. viii. 19, when Samuel came from God and told them in a long narration what hardship they should endure in having a king, for that was not then according to God's mind; they heard him all that he said, and they do not stand to answer any of Samuel's arguments, but presently they break out into this resolution, "Nay, but we will have a king." Those whom God leaves to hardness of heart, and intends to ruin, he usually gives them up to this wilfulness in their evil ways. The Scripture records Pharaoh as a famous example of one hardened and prepared for ruin. He was of a most wilful spirit. Exod. xv. 9, you shall find his wilfulness expressed four times in that one verse: "I will pursue," saith he; and then again, "I will overtake;" and, thirdly, "I will divide the spoil;" and then, fourthly, "I will draw my sword." There are two other expressions to the same effect, which are equivalent to the former, even in the same verse, "My lust shall be satisfied, my hand shall destroy them." Put all these six expressions, which you have in that one verse, together, and where have you such an exhibition of a wilful creature as Pharaoh was? and what became of him you all know. Only one more example I find in Scripture parallel to this, and that is the king of Babylon: Egypt and Babylon were two countries most eminent for idolatry, and the persecution of the church, and these are the two most famous examples for wilfulness. In Isa. xiv. 13, 14, you have in those two verses five times *I will:* 1. "I will ascend into heaven." 2. "I will exalt my throne above the stars of God." 3. "I will sit also upon the mount of the congregation." 4. "I will ascend above the height of the clouds." 5. "I will be like the Most High." And what became of him you likewise know; yea, the next words tell you, "Yet thou shalt be brought down to hell."

These two little words, *I* and *will*, do a great deal of mischief in the world. Luther, upon Psal. cxxvii., saith, I am of that opinion, and verily persuaded, monarchies would far longer endure, if those who are high monarchs would but omit this one pronoun, *I*. It is true, in public ways they

Ego in ea opinione sum, monarchias longe diutius duraturas, si monarchæ hoc unum pronomen *ego* omisissent. Luther in Psal. cxxvii.

express themselves in the plural number, *we*, but private resolutions are in the singular number, *I*. The second is *will*, "I will," that is a little word too; but I may say of this *will*, as James saith concerning the tongue, It is indeed "a little member" in the body, but "it setteth on fire the course of nature, and it is set on fire of hell." So it is true that this little *will* is but a little word, but it sets whole kingdoms on fire, towns and cities on fire, and is itself set on fire of hell. Bernard remarks, Take away *will* once, and there will be no hell. Oh the mischief that it does in the world! I will only say these two things to those that keep such ado with these two little words, *I*, *will*.

Tolle voluntatem et non erit infernus. Bern.

First, That which thou usest with so much pride, and thinkest thyself such a man that canst say, I will, know, it may be as heavy a judgment of God as can befall thee in this world, for God to give thee up to thy will. There is nothing wherein God pours out his wrath upon the children of men in this world, more than in giving them up to their will. Therefore, tremble when thou usest so many expressions, I will, and I will do this. Observe what the Scripture saith of those who had their will in ways of false worship; "Go ye, serve ye every one his idols, and hereafter also, if you will not hearken unto me," Ezek. xx. 39. Go, saith God, you will not hearken to me; you hear out of the word what should be the way of my worship in its purity, but you say, I love novelty, and you will not have it thus; you answer not God's arguments, but you cast off his worship, and say you will not have it: Well, saith God, if you will not hear me, if you are set upon your will, go and serve your idols, and take your fill of your own ways. And Psal. lxxxi. 11, "My people would not hearken to my voice, and Israel would none of me;" they were all upon their will, they would not and they would not. Mark what follows; "so I gave them up unto their own hearts' lusts, and they walked in their own counsels." You will have your own counsels, and your own will, and so God gives you up to them; and then woe to you, you are undone!

Secondly, You that are set upon your will in that which is evil, know, God is and will be as wilful toward you as you can be toward him. Mark that notable text, Jer. xliv. 25, which sets out the notorious height of wickedness that was in the people of those times: "Ye and your wives have both spoken with your mouths, and fulfilled with your hand," that which is evil; you will not only say you will do it, but will do it indeed. Well, saith God, you have done so, "ye and your wives have both spoken with your mouths, and fulfilled with your hand, saying, We will surely perform our vows that we have vowed, to burn incense to the queen of heaven, and to pour out drink offerings unto her: ye will surely accomplish your vows, and surely perform your vows." You will go on in your false ways of worship. Mark what follows in ver. 26, "Therefore hear ye the word of the Lord, all Judah that dwell in the land of Egypt; Behold, I have sworn," you have vowed, and I have sworn, "I have sworn by my great name, saith the Lord, that my name shall no more be named in the mouth of any man of Judah in all the land of Egypt:" and ver. 27, "Behold, I will watch over them for evil, and not for good: and all the men of Judah that are in the land of Egypt shall be consumed by the sword and by the famine, until there be an end of them." God will be as resolute as the stoutest sinner: you will, and God will; who shall have their will, think you? Answer to this, you stout-hearted that are away from God; answer to this, you stout-hearted children, and servants, and wives. A wilful man never wants woe. If you will be resolute in any thing, my brethren, be resolute in that which is good; be resolute in the work of repentance, with David, Psal. xxxii. 5, "I will confess my transgressions:" indeed I had many thoughts to come and shame myself, and open all unto God, but I could not get it off; at length I grew resolute and said, I will, and I have sworn to keep thy righteous precepts: and as they, Micah iv. 5, "We will walk in the name of the Lord our God:" and as Joshua, I and my house will serve the Lord; do you what you will, we are resolute that we will serve the Lord. This is a blessed wilfulness indeed. Oh that the stoutness and wilfulness of many people might be turned to this resolution for God and for his truth! Especially, carry this note home with you, you that give such often expressions of your will, and turn it to the willing of that which is good. I will follow my lovers, says the apostate from God: I will follow my beloved, who is altogether lovely, let every gracious soul say.

Obs. 4. Professed sins are shameful sins. "She said," she professed what she would do. It is an evil for sin to lie lurking in any one's heart, but for sin to break out into open profession, is a greater evil. This is to prove that she had done shamefully, because she said she would do it. There is a great deceit in the hearts of many men, they are ready to say, I may as well say so as think so; I say so, and perhaps others think so, it were as well for me to speak it as to keep it in my heart. My brethren, there are two deceits in this kind of speaking.

First, You suppose that when you speak so, it is not in your heart, and you make the comparison of what is in other men's hearts and in your mouths; as if the evil were in your mouths only, and in their hearts only; as if the comparison lay thus, they think and do not speak, and you speak and do not think. Here is the deceit, for if you speak you have it in your hearts too, you both speak and think, for so the Scripture assures us, that "out of the abundance of the heart the mouth speaketh:" if you speak maliciously, you have a malicious heart; if you speak uncleanly, you have an unclean heart; if oaths be in your mouths, you have a profane heart.

Secondly, Here likewise lies the deceit, as if you should have less in your heart because you vent it; as passionate people will say, I may as well vent my mind, and then I shall be quiet. Thou deceivest thyself; the venting of corruption that lies in thy heart will never lessen it, but increase it. It is not with the corruption of our hearts as it is with liquor in a vessel, that the more it is let out the less is within; but as it is with a fire in a house, that when it is kindled within, and bursts out, there is not less within because it bursts out; no, the more it flames out, the more it burns within: and as it is with water in a fountain, when it flows out of the fountain, there is not the less water in the fountain; it may rather have the less by stopping, and fire may be lessened by smothering. Know, therefore, that professed wickedness is aggravated wickedness. Secret sins may be more dangerous in regard of the cure, but these are more abominable to God in regard of the open dishonour that is done to him by them. The aggravation of the blood that was shed by the people is described, The blood that was shed, "she poured it not upon the ground, to cover it with dust; that it might cause fury to come up to take vengeance," Ezek. xxiv. 7, 8; you did not conceal the blood, you did not cover it, but set it "upon the top of a rock." What then? Not being covered, but being professed and laid open, this caused fury to come up with vengeance against them. God's anger would have been against them if they had shed blood, though they had covered it; but to shed blood and not to cover it, causes the fury of the Lord to come with vengeance. So you know he saith in Isa. iii. 9, "They declare their sin as Sodom, they hide it not. Woe unto their soul!" woe unto them when they shall presume to declare their sin as Sodom. And as I said before, God will be as wilful in punishing a sinner, as a sinner is wilful in sinning; so here, God will be as professed in plaguing, as thou shalt be professed in sinning. In that forenamed place of Ezekiel, they did not cover the blood; well, mark it: saith God, "I have set her blood upon the top of a rock, that it should not be covered. Therefore thus saith the Lord God; Woe to the bloody city! I will even make the pile for fire great." I will be as professed in my plagues and punishments as you are professed in your sins.

My brethren, if we will profess any thing, let us profess that which is good, let us do that as openly as we can. 2 Cor. ix. 13, saith, that God is glorified for their professed subjection to the gospel; for their subjection of profession, so the words are. It is not enough to be subject to the gospel, but there must be a professed subjection to it: therefore, in Rom. x. 10, confession with the mouth is made as necessary to salvation as believing with the heart, they are put together. There may be times that confession may be called for, as well as believing, and as necessary to salvation. When the friends of Gordius, a martyr, came to him, and would have him keep his heart to himself, and only with his mouth deny what in his heart he believed was true; O no, saith he, it is fit that my mouth, which was made for God, should speak for God. And Zuinglius is of the opinion, that we may as well worship the altar of Jupiter, or Venus, as hide our faith and profession when we live under antichrist. The way to honour religion and bring it into credit, is for those who are godly to profess what they know. I knew one that was noble both in birth and grace, and who had to act often with those of his rank, who scorned at religion under the name of puritanism: he would usually take this course,—when he entered into such company, he would begin and own himself to be one of those whom they called puritans, and by that means prevented much sin in them, and much scorn of religion, by thus avowing it. It is certain, that the best way to honour religion is for every one to own it, though ignominious terms are put upon it. If ever we were called to profess what we believe, we are now called to it in these days. Certainly, God professes for us; God not only respects us, but he does it professedly, in the eyes and before the faces of our adversaries. Let us not only have God in our hearts, but profess his name openly before the faces of our adversaries. It is time now to do it. It had been well, if you had professed heretofore when God's truth called for it. It may be, many of you are found guilty of betraying the truth of God, for professing no sooner than you did; but, however, betray it not now for want of profession; be willing now to profess of what party you are, that, as we read of Jonah, chap. i. 9, when he was in the storm, and the mariners awoke him, he said unto them, "I am an Hebrew, and I fear the Lord, the God of heaven, which hath made the sea and the dry land," making an open profession of himself. My brethren, if we be not in a present storm, yet the clouds grow black; therefore, awake, you sluggards, you that are secure, awake out of your security, and now profess what you are. I am a Hebrew that fears God; however they give such men ignominious terms and titles, I am one of them, and I am willing to appear so. Like Nicodemus, many of you come to Jesus by night, you are afraid to be seen. You would give money to the parliament, and help forward that work which God has in hand, but you are afraid to be seen. I know there may be possibly some reason why some men should not appear, but not many, the cases are very rare; ordinarily, it is not enough to do it, but to do it professedly, let it be declared who you are, and what side you take.

'Επὶ τῇ ὑποταγῇ τῆς ὁμολογίας.

Ad aras Jovis aut Veneris adorare ac sub antichristo fidem occultare. Zuin. ep. 3.

If you say, We live in evil and wicked times, it is dangerous to appear; I may not only keep my heart right, but I will do as much as another, but why should I appear? 1. The worse the times are, the more thou shouldst appear. Mark viii. 38, "Whosoever therefore shall be ashamed of me and of my words in this adulterous and sinful generation; of him also shall the Son of man be ashamed, when he cometh in the glory of his Father with the holy angels." If the generation were holy, it were nothing to appear, not to be ashamed or afraid; but we must not be either ashamed or afraid in the midst of an adulterous generation. 2. Why should wickedness have this advantage, that it dares appear, but godliness dares not? 3. If all should reason as you do, what would become of the cause? Why should others venture themselves more than you? What is your flesh, your estate, your liberty, more than theirs? 4. You must appear for example sake, to provoke others. This is a duty as well as any. 5. If the adversaries prevail, they will find you out, except you mean to give up your consciences to them, and then you will escape no more than others; to be sure, you will not have so much peace as others who have most appeared.

Obs. 5. It is a very dangerous and sinful thing for the people of God to join in association with foreigners who are of an idolatrous religion, and to expect help from them. "I will go after my lovers;"—who are they? either the Egyptians or Assyrians with whom they associated, or their idols. Let us suppose the former: the people of God, Jer. xlii., were determined to have association with Egypt, and they could not be brought from it: if you read that story, their conduct will appear very vile and dangerous; they seemed to yield to God, that they would do what he would have them, and they would not go into Egypt if he forbade it; but in chap. xliii., when Jeremiah told them the mind of God, that they should continue in the land of Judah, and not go down into Egypt, "Then spake Azariah the son of Hoshaiah, and Johanan the son of Kareah, and all the proud men, saying unto Jeremiah, Thou speakest falsely: the Lord our God hath not sent thee to say, Go not into Egypt to sojourn there." They are loth to break off their association with Egypt. Gualter, in his comment upon Hosea, though not upon this text, states that the Grecian churches, who in the year 1438 were afraid of the Turks breaking in upon them, sent to the bishop of Rome, and offered to be under his subjection, merely that they might have the help of the Latin churches to keep them from the rage and tyranny of their adversaries; but within a few years they were destroyed, Constantinople and the empire were subdued, so that heathenism and atheism prevailed; and this is the fruit, saith he, of seeking the association of others in a sinful way. But because this is not the chief thing that is aimed at, we pass it by. She said she would go after her lovers, that is, her idols. Hence,

Obs. 6. Idolaters usually keep good thoughts of their idols. They call them their lovers, they look upon their idols as those that love them; and hence they used to call them Baalim, from Baal, a husband. So it should be the care of the saints evermore to keep good thoughts of God, to look upon God as their lover, as one that attends to their good. My brethren, let us not be ready to entertain hard thoughts of God, it is a dangerous thing. God's great care is to manifest to us and to all the world that he loves us. He has done much to manifest to us in England, and to our brethren of Scotland, that he loves us and them. In Rev. iii. 9, Christ saith of the church of Philadelphia, that God loved them. Forty years ago, Mr. Brightman interpreted that text of the church of Scotland. Philadelphia signifies brotherly love. You know how they are joined in covenant one with another, and we see that those who said they were Jews, that they were the church, but proved themselves to be of the synagogue of Satan, are forced to bow before them; and if they were not mad with malice, they must needs acknowledge that God has loved that church. And since God has done great things for us, to manifest that he is the lover of England, let us keep good thoughts of God.

Obs. 7. Idolaters highly prize the love of their idols. They do not only maintain good thoughts of their idols, or think that their idols are their lovers, but they set a price upon them. She said, I will follow my lovers; I make account of their love, they will do me good, for aught I know, more than any thing you speak of. It is true both of bodily and spiritual whoredom. I will only make use of one scripture, to daunt the heart of unclean persons, who so much prize the love of their harlots. You prize their love, but what get you by it? you get God's hatred by it. You rejoice that you have their love; and for that God hates and abhors you. Make that good, you will say. I will: "The mouth of a strange woman is a deep pit: he that is abhorred of the Lord shall fall therein," Prov. xxii. 14. What get you by this? your harlots embrace you, and God abhors you. If there be any unclean wretch in this congregation, either thou art an atheist, or this text must strike thee at thy heart. Art thou in that way, and yet not repenting, thou art the man whom this day God tells thee to thy face, that he abhors thee.

But how then should we prize the love of Jesus Christ our Husband! "We will remember thy love more than wine," Cant. i. 4. The church prizes the love of Jesus Christ, more than men in the world prize their delight in wine. And, my brethren, do you prize Christ's love; then Christ will prize yours: and it is observable, that according to the degree and way of your prizing Christ's love, so Christ will prize your love. In Cant. iv. 10, you have the same expression of Christ's love to his church, answerable to hers before: "Thy love is better than wine," saith the church to Christ; "How much better is thy love than wine!" saith Christ to the church.

Obs. 8. The hearts of whoremongers and idolaters follow hard after their uncleanness in bodily and spiritual filthiness. "I will follow them;" not only say they are lovers, but I will express it by following them. For bodily filthiness, observe how unclean men follow their lovers. Josephus, in his Antiquities, states, that Decius Mundus offered to give many hundred thousand drachms, which amounted to six thousand pounds sterling, to satisfy his lust one night with a harlot, yet could not obtain his desire. Will not ye be content now who have been guilty of spending a great part of your estate in uncleanness, now to do as much for religion, for God, and Christ, and his kingdom, as ever you have done for that sin? If there be any in this place who have been profuse for their uncleanness, and yet now are strait-handed in these public affairs, such are fitter to be taken out of Christian congregations, and to be shut up in prisons.

For spiritual whoredom, I shall show you how superstitious and idolatrous people, as they prize their idols, so they follow hard after them. When the calf was to be set up, upon proclamation all the men and women took off their earrings and their jewels, and brought them to Aaron to make the calf. What a shame will it be to us if we should keep our earrings, and our jewels, and things perhaps that have not seen the sun a great while, now when God calls for them! Let women do that for God and his truth, for their own liberties and posterities, that they did for their idol. Though you have earrings, and jewels, and rings, that you prize much, yet let them be given up to this public cause. And it were a shame that gold rings should be kept merely to adorn the fingers, when the church and state are in such necessity as they are. Away with your niceties, your fineness, and bravery, now, and look to necessities, to the preservation of the lives and liberties both of yourselves and your children. If you should see a malignant party come with their spears and pikes, and your children writhing upon the tops of them, and their blood gushing out, what good would your gold rings and all your ornaments do you?

The Scripture strikingly describes the eagerness and earnestness of spirit which idolaters manifest in following after their idols. Isa. lvii. 5, exhibits them "inflaming themselves with idols." In Jer. l. 38, God says, "they are mad upon their idols." In Isa. xlvi. 6, it is said, "they lavish gold out of the bag." They not only gave their gold rings which were of no use, and parted with that which they could well spare, but they lavished gold that was in the bag; they would not only bring some of it, but they lavished it; and they lavished not their silver, but their gold; and that not a piece or two out of a paper, but out of the bag, they brought their bags of gold, and lavished gold out of them. This they did for their idols: oh what a shame is it then that any should be penurious, and not act generously, in the public cause of the church and commonwealth!

In Jer. viii. 2, we have five expressions in one verse, describing the pursuance of the heart of idolaters after their idols; the like we have not in all the book of God. First, he saith, "whom they have loved." Secondly, "whom they have served." Thirdly, "after whom they have walked." Fourthly, "whom they have sought." And, fifthly, "whom they have worshipped." Oh how are the hearts of people set upon the ways of idolatry! Camden reports that Canute, king of England, spent as much upon one cross, as the revenues of the crown came to in a whole year, he was so profusely liberal about his superstitious vanities. Calvin, in a sermon upon that text, "Seek ye my face," remarks: Foolish idolaters! they endure much in their pilgrimages, spend their money, waste their bodies, and are abused in their journey; yet they go on, and think all sufficiently recompensed, if they may see and worship some image of a saint, or holy relic. Shall the beholding some dead carrion, or apish idol, have more power to strengthen them, than the face of God in his ordinances shall have to strengthen us?

"My lovers, that give me my bread and my water, my wool and my flax, mine oil and my drink." What were these idols? The idol that gave their bread was Ceres, she was the goddess whom the heathens worshipped for corn. Luna, the moon, was the idol they worshipped for their drink, and all moist things. For their wool and flax, Ashtaroth was their god; and for their oil, Priapus. The Seventy translate that "clothes" which we call here "wool;" and that which we term "flax" they translate "linen."

Obs. 1. Idolaters have a great many idols to supply their several wants. "My lovers," in the plural number. The idols of the heathen do not supply all good, but one one thing, and another another thing. And that is the difference between the true God and idols. The excellency of the true God is, that he is a universal good; we have all good, flax, oil, bread, and wine, and all in one, in our God, in our lover. And that is the reason why God challenges the whole heart. Idols are content with a partial obedience, because they are but partial in bestowing good things; but God justly requires the whole heart of his worshippers, because he is a universal good to them.

Obs. 2. The end at which idolaters aim in their worship is very low. They follow their lovers, and are very earnest; for what, I pray? for their wool and their flax, and their bread and their water, their oil and their drink. They desire no more, they look no higher; satisfy their flesh, give them but liberty to sport on the Lord's day, to have their feasts, their wakes, and merry meetings, and they care for no more. Their spirits are vile, and so accordingly is their worship. Therefore their worship is external, it is bodily, because their aims are at external and bodily things. As a man's end is, either base or honourable, so is he. There are some men who seem as if they aimed at God and religion in many things they do, they make a noise about religion, and God, and Christ, and his ordinances, and the public good; but the truth is, their aims are at gain and credit, at their wool and their flax; and herein they show the baseness of their spirits; like lapwings, that scream aloud as if they were come near their nests, when their nests are some where else. Whatever their cry be, for God or the public good, if you mark them, their nest is in their wool, in their flax, in their profit, in their honour and preferment, in these outward things. But the end of the true worshippers of God is higher, they soar aloft, there is a spiritual height of soul whereby they are raised upwards by the grace of God. A godly man's feet are where a wicked man's head is; that which he accounts his chief good, a godly man can trample under his feet. He looks at God himself, and his service. He worships the high God: he is a child of Abraham; not Abram, but Abraham; what is the signification of that? *Pater excelsus*, A high father, for he is the father of children of high spirits, not only of children that are believers, but of those that have high and raised spirits. Cleopatra told Marcus Antonius, that he was not to angle for gudgeons and trout, but for castles, and forts, and towns; so I may say of a Christian, he does not angle, especially in matters of religion, for wool, and flax, and oil, he has no such low and base ends, but at God, and Christ, and heaven, and glory, and immortality. He desires these things only that by them he may be fitted more to serve God. One who has been acquainted with the free grace of God in Christ, will serve God for himself without bargaining with him, he will be willing to go into God's vineyard, and not indent for a penny a day. You that will indent with God in his service, and have your penny, you who have such low and mean spirits, God may give you your penny, and there's an end of you.

Obs. 3. That way of religion by which we can get most bread, and wool, and flax, and oil, is the religion that most people will follow, because the hearts of most people are low and base, and aim at no higher things. That religion which brings the largest estate, and can please the sense, is the religion that pleases most people. Pamchtius, a heathen, once said, Make me a bishop, and though I be now a heathen yet I will be a Christian as well as any other. He saw in what pomp the bishops lived, and by that he thought it was a fine thing to be a Christian. By outward pomp and glory antichrist draws many followers; they go where they can have most wool and flax; they can get most preferment that way. Æneas Silvius observed, the reason why the pope prevailed against the council, though it was a general council, which was above the pope, was this, that the pope had a great many places of preferment and honour to give, the general council had none: the general council can inquire after truth, and present its decision, and can tell what is God's mind, but it has no honour, no promotion, no preferment to give; therefore, alas, the general council prevails little, the pope gets all, and all because he has bishoprics, and cardinals' places, and livings, and great honours, to bestow. Luther, in his comment upon this text, relates that one whom he knew, who lived like a nobleman by his many ecclesiastical preferments, when excellent bread and wine were brought to the table, pointing to them, said, These are the things that make me that I cannot leave this kind of life. These are the arguments that prevail most in the world; arguments taken from bread, and flax, and wool, and oil, are stronger arguments than any taken from the Scripture, than any thing taken from the honour of the Father, Son, and Holy Ghost. When men come with Saul's arguments, 1 Sam. xxii. 7, "Will the son of Jesse give every one of you fields and vineyards, and make you all captains of thousands, and captains of hundreds?" will you follow him? can he prefer you? O no, he can do little for you. And when men argue, I pray what will this way bring you in? what preferment will you get by this? you may get preferment in the other way; this draws, this prevails. In a speech delivered by the vice-chancellor, not many years ago, in a public commencement at Cambridge, speaking to the young scholars, and wishing them to take heed of being puritans, he said, What can you get in that way? you shall live poorly, perhaps you may have some three-halfpenny benefice in following them; but come to be children of the church, and then you may be sure of good benefices, you may come to be prebends, to be deans, to be bishops. Thus he persuaded the young scholars to take heed of puritanism. There is mighty strength in this argument upon the hearts of most.

Fac me pontificem et Christianus ero.

Novi hominem non ex uno canonicatu nobilem commonstrantem digito delicatiorem panem, et vinum quod præstantissimum erat appositum, Hæc, inquit, sunt quæ faciunt ut hoc vitæ genus deserere non libeat. Triobulare Beneficium.

Magis soliciti de mero quam de vero, φιλήστονοι μᾶλλον ἢ φιλόθεοι, magis amant mundi delicias quam, Christi divitias.

Hence the poverty of Christ is a great scandal and offence to most people. When they see that religion will not bring them flax, and wool, and oil, but that they must live poorly, they are offended at this exceedingly. Charles the Great, having war with Aygolandus, king of Africa, who, being anxious to make peace with Charles, made some profession to become a Christian; Charles was very glad of this, and brought him to his court to parley with him. There he saw thirty poor persons whom Charles fed, who were halt, and maimed, and blind, and in a very poor garb. Charles the Great did this, because he would have poverty before his eyes continually, that he might not be too high in and proud of his prosperity. When Aygolandus saw them, he said, Who are these? These, saith Charles, are the servants of God. Nay then, replied he, if your God keep his servants no better, I will be none of his; I thought to be a Christian, and to serve your God, but seeing those that serve him have no better food or raiment than these, I will be none of those servants. Thus it is with many, though their consciences are convinced which is the best way, yet, because of the want of flax, and wool, and oil, they will not decide for Christ.

Obs. 4. It is a shameful thing for men to put religion in subjection to their wool, and corn, and oil. Before I showed, that it is shameful to subject religion to the political affairs of a kingdom, but to subject religion to our own base sensualities, for profit and preferment, this is very shameful. Gain gotten this way, is filthy lucre, as the Scripture calls it, yet *hujusmodi lucri dulcis odor*, the smell of this gain is very sweet to many. Is thy religion serviceable only to gain a trade, to gratify sensual lusts? what is this, but to stop the hole of a mud wall with diamonds and precious pearls? That were a folly, you will say, to make such precious things serviceable to such base ends: thou dost as much, thou wouldst make religion subject to that which only satisfies the flesh. Religion, my brethren, is the glory of a man, and the glory of a nation; and shall we turn this glory into shame? It is a base thing in magistrates, to subject the acts of justice to their base ends, for gain and profit; for a judge, or a justice of peace, or a prelate, to show most favour where there is most flax, and wool, and oil, where butts of beer or rundlets of sack are to be gained, this is baseness in them. But to subject religion to such ends as these, this is the villany of all baseness. A generous spirit is far from this. It is observed of the generous spirit of Luther, that when a papist was vexed at him for his preaching and writing, one bishop remarked to another, There is such a stir with this Luther, why do you not stop his mouth with preferment? He presently answered, That German beast cares not for money, he is above money. He called him beast in his anger, whereas he might have called him an angel, because his spirit was above these things, his mouth would not be stopped with them. A bishop in this land, hearing that a kinsman of his was a zealous preacher; Well, saith he, let me alone, I will silence him; and indeed he did; how? he gave him two livings, and they silenced him presently. Some men's lust of malice goes beyond their lust of covetousness, like those cockatrices, Jer. viii. 17, that "will not be charmed." It is a shameful thing then, that our zeal for God should not go beyond our lust for gain. To subject your religion to flax, and wool, and oil, springs from a base diffidence in God, as if he would not provide for us such outward things; therefore Luther saith in his comment upon Hosea, They followed their idols for bread, and wool, and flax, and oil, as if God would not give bread to his church, or as if it were more safe to go to Satan for it. O let us trust God for all, for our clothes, for our meat and drink, for our estates, for our children; God certainly will feed his church. And yet the men who have hearts so base themselves, think it impossible for any man not to be taken with such arguments; They may talk of religion and conscience, say they, but I will warrant you they may be bought with money, and preferment, and places of profit and honour. They think it impossible for men to stand against these arguments. It reminds me of that speech that Balak used to Balaam, "Did not I earnestly send unto thee to call thee, wherefore camest thou not unto me? Am I not able to promote thee to honour?" As if he had said, Thou art a strange man indeed; did not I send thee word that I would promote thee to great honour, and give thee silver and gold, or whatever thou wouldst have? What! will not preferment and money tempt you? I thought this would have tempted any man in the world. And thus many men think: but let all such know that there is a generation of men in the world of true generous spirits, who are above these things, and take as much delight, and have as much sweetness, in denying these places of honour, and preferment, and gain, as those that offer them have in enjoying them. It was a notable speech that Pliny made concerning Cato, in his Epistle Dedicatory to his Natural History, Cato took as much glory in those dignities and honours which he refused, as he did in those which he enjoyed. Certainly it is so with the saints, the true generous spirit of Christians take as much content in those places of preferment they deny for Christ, as in any gain they enjoy. There is no tempting such men.

Germana illa bestia non curat aurum.

Quasi vero Deus nolit dare lanem ecclesiæ suæ, aut satius sit a Sathana petere.

Let us pray therefore for those who are intrusted by us, not only for civil things, but for matters of religion, that bread, and corn, and wool, and flax, and wine, and oil may never tempt them; that preferment and gain may never bias their spirits. Such ways have not been left untried by some, and have prevailed; but through God's mercy he has preserved others, and made the world know that Christ has a people to whom religion and the public good are more dear than all the flax, and wool, and wine, and oil in the world; than all the estates, and high places, and great preferments that can be offered them. And now, the Lord our God keep this in their and in our hearts for ever.

Obs. 5. Prosperity and success in an evil way, harden the hearts of men in sin. I will follow after my lovers, for they give me bread, and water, and wool, and flax. Eusebius reports that Maximilian the emperor, in an edict against the Christians, vilifying the Christian religion as an execrable vanity, and seeking to confirm the heathens in the worship of their idols, remarks, Behold, how the earth brings forth fruit for the husbandman in abundance, how our meadows are adorned with flowers and herbs, and moistened with the dews of heaven, what health we have, and what quiet and peaceable lives. Thus, by their prosperity, he seeks to confirm the hearts of idolaters in their wicked ways. Prosperity in a wicked way is exceedingly hardening. Dionysius, having committed sacrilege against the idols, by robbing their temples, yet his voyage being prosperous, boasted that though he did not worship the gods as others did, he prospered as much as they. In that year when those innovations in God's worship were principally brought in amongst us, especially in the diocess of Norwich, it proved to be a very fruitful year; and one commissary, among the rest in his court, after the harvest was taken in, addressed the countrymen in this way, Do you not see how God prospers us? What a plentiful harvest have we had this year! This is since you began to worship God with more decency than you were wont to do. Thus attributing all the goodness of God to that way. Let it be all our prayer, that God would never prosper us in a sinful way.

Obs. 6. Carnal hearts look upon what they enjoy as their own, and think they may use it as their own; and especially such as are idolaters. It is very observable, how often this word "my" is iterated: give me my bread, and my water, and my flax, and my oil, and my wool; nothing but *my*. Though they will acknowledge that what they have comes from the idols, as here they did, for they said their lovers gave it them, yet when they had these things, they thought they might do with them what they would; they were theirs, Mine, mine, all is mine. Thus it is usual for carnal spirits to acknowledge in general, that what they have comes from God; but when they have it, they think it is their own, not that God reserves the propriety of what they have after he has given it them. You mistake, if you think that that is all the acknowledgment you owe to God for what you enjoy, that you had it from God; but you must acknowledge likewise, that God reserves his propriety after he has given it you. God never gives any thing in the way that one friend gives to another. A friend may give you a gift, yet, when you have it, it is your own, and you may use it as you please, your friend parts with his own propriety. God never gives any thing so as to part with his own propriety; though he has given it you, yet you cannot say, It is mine; in respect of God, it is still his.

There is no such bond upon conscience to use all the comforts we have for God as this, to look up to God, and see that all comes from him in the way of the covenant of grace. I say, that will lay a bond upon conscience, to make use of your estates, and of all you enjoy, for God, and not think to employ them for your own ends. It is not the slight acknowledgment idolaters make, that all comes from God, will do it. Carnal men look upon what they have coming from God through second causes, and no further; but a Christian looks upon that which he has as coming from God in a covenant of grace, and this engages the heart strongly to use all for God, from whom all is received in such a way.

Ver. 6. *Therefore, behold, I will hedge up thy way with thorns, and make a wall, that she shall not find her paths.*

This verse and the following are the workings of God's bowels of mercy, a parenthesis of grace to the elect, though mingled with some severity. They are indeed the epitome of the whole chapter, declaring Israel's sin, with threatening judgment, and yet promising mercy unto the elect, the penitent amongst them.

"Therefore." This has reference to somewhat before, and answers to wherefore: Because I have dealt with you by the way of my prophets, in convincing, in admonishing, in threatening, and all this will not do, "therefore" I will deal with you in another way.

"Therefore, behold." That way of mine of which I now speak, is a singular way; you shall find much of my grace in it, the way in which I will deal with you is full of wonders, "Behold."

"I will hedge up thy way." There is a two-fold hedge that God makes about his people. There is the hedge of protection to keep evil from them, and there is the hedge of affliction to keep them from evil. The hedge of protection you have, Isa. v. 5, where God threatens that he "will take away the hedge" from his vineyard, that is, he will take away his protection; and it is said of Job, that "God had hedged him about." But the hedge here meant, is the hedge of affliction. "I will hedge up thy way," that is, I will bring sore and heavy afflictions upon you, but yet in a way of mercy; these afflictions shall be but as a hedge to keep you from evil, they shall not do evil to you, or bring evil upon you.

"I will hedge up thy way with thorns." That is, I see you will go on in these ways of idolatry and false worship, I will make them difficult to you, you shall go through thorns; if you will get to your idols, you shall be pricked. It is a metaphor taken from a husbandman, who, when the cattle will break over pastures, makes thick and prickly hedges to prevent them, and to distress them if they attempt it: so I will deal with you, saith God. Or, when a husbandman observes passengers make a path in his ground where they ought not, and spoil the grass or the corn, he lays thorns in the way that they cannot go into his corn; or if they do, they shall go with some pain and trouble: so saith God, "I will hedge up thy way with thorns."

"And make a wall." I will wall a wall, so the words are. It may be they will get through the thorns, but if they do, I have another way to deal with them, I will come with stronger afflictions, and they shall be of more power to keep them from their sin, they shall be as a wall; and though they get through the thorns, they shall not get over the wall.

"That she shall not find her paths." Mark the change of the person, "I will hedge up thy way," first; and then I will "make a wall, and she shall not find her paths." It often occurs in Scripture, and signifies some perturbation of spirit. That manner of speech is usual amongst men when their spirits are troubled, they speak sometimes in one person, sometimes in another; and, indeed, the Lord here speaks after the manner of men, as if his spirit were troubled with the perverseness of his people. Besides, the change of the person is to express some indignation of God against their perverseness, therefore he speaks as if he would turn from them, and rather speak to somebody else; as if he should say, I speak to these, yet they are stubborn; well, I will speak to all the beholders, Take notice of their stubbornness and perverseness, and judge between them and me.

Obs. 1. Though such as are in covenant with God, may for their sins be involved in the same judgment with others, yet God will make a difference between them and others that are not in covenant with him. God will have other ends in his afflictions towards his people, than he has towards the wicked; though the difference be not in the *things* they suffer, yet it is very broad in the *ends* for which they suffer. When the briers and thorns, Isa. xxvii. 4, are set before God, the fire of God's anger passes through them to destroy them; but when God comes to his people, though some anger be stirred up for a while, yet all the fruit thereof is to take away their sin, ver. 9. See what difference God makes between persons even under the same affliction. In Jer. xxiv. 5, God saith, "Like these good figs, so will I acknowledge them that are carried away captive of Judah, whom I have sent out of this place into the land of the Chaldeans for their good." Though they be carried into the land of the Chaldeans, I will acknowledge them there to be my people, and it shall be for their good. Well, now there was likewise a basket that had "very naughty figs," and they were carried away captive too, both went into captivity; what does he say of them? ver. 9, "I will deliver them to be removed into all the kingdoms of the earth for their hurt;" I will aim at their hurt when I deliver them into captivity.

This should be a mighty support to the saints under all their afflictions, though the affliction be the same to sense and view with that of the wicked, yet you see the difference is broad. It is true, may the troubled heart say, there may be different ends of God's afflicting some and others; he may afflict some for trial, and others for their sins; but what will you say if an affliction come upon us for our sins? Is there a difference here? Yes, my brethren, though your afflictions come upon you for your sins, if you be in covenant with God, the difference still may hold: so it is here; those afflictions which God calls the hedge and the wall, were sore afflictions, and they were for their sins, yet God intended good and mercy to them in those afflictions. This is the virtue of the covenant of grace, that it takes out the sting and curse even of afflictions, which are not only for trial, but for sin. If God bring some misery upon you, yet being in covenant with him, his blessing causes those troubles to keep you from greater misery that else would befall you.

Obs. 2. There is even in the saints such a slavish disposition remaining, that they will stand out against God a long time, even against the admonitions, exhortations, convictions, and threatenings of his word. Not only the reprobate, but such is the perverseness of the hearts of men, that even the elect of God will many times do so; this is a sore and a grievous evil, that it should be said so of them. If there be ingenuousness in the spirits of men, the very intimation of the mind of God is enough to cause the heart to yield; and surely grace makes the heart of a man ingenuous. God expects that there should be melting of spirit at the very notice given of his displeasure; yet, behold, even in the hearts of the godly there remains so much slavishness, that they will not return but upon God's dealing very hardly with them. They must have many afflictions, they must be whipped home before they will return home; God must send the dog many times to worry his sheep before they will come into the fold. This God complains of: Jer. ii. 14, "Is Israel a servant? is he a home-born slave? why is he spoiled?" ver. 17, "Hast thou not procured this unto thyself?" So it may be said of many of the saints, when we see the dealings of God towards them; yea, even God himself speaks thus, What! is such a one a servant? is he a slave? is not such a one my child? how is it then that he must be dealt with like a slave, like a servant?

Obs. 3. When one means will not keep ourselves or others from sin, we must not rest there, but look after other means to prevent it. What! will not this do it? Is there any thing else that possibly may do it? That means then shall be used. Thus God (we speak with reverence) studies his administrations towards his people, when he is frustrated in one, if that will not do, he bethinks with himself, Is there any thing else will do it? if there be any thing in the world can do it, it shall not be left unattempted. God does not presently cast off his people, because they stand out against him in the use of one means. It is true, for others that are not in covenant with him, God is quick with them, and if they come not in presently, he cuts them off, and will have no more to do with them; but for his own people, though they stand out long, yet God tries one means after another. This is the grace of God towards his own.

It should be our care to imitate God in this. When you are to deal with others who are under you, with your children or servants, do not satisfy yourselves with, I have admonished them, and threatened them, and persuaded them, yet they will not come in; what, then, will you have no more to do with them? will you cast them off presently? You should study what further course may be taken, study their dispositions; What do I think will work upon them, if this do not? will fair means? will foul means? will any thing do it? If any thing will, you should labour to deal with them that way. So for your own hearts, when you are convinced of the evil of your sin, your consciences will not be quiet unless you use some means against it. Well, but I have used means, I have laid the threatenings, the promises, to my heart, and I have followed God's ordinances. Will they not do? will not thy heart come off? is there no other means to be used? What do you say to the afflicting of your soul? Try that: you have laid the word to your heart, and you find it does not work; try the afflicting of your souls in humiliation, fasting, and prayer, for the overcoming of your sins. "This kind goeth not out but by prayer and fasting." Thus, when admonitions and exhortations of the prophet will not do, God saith, I will try another way, I will bethink me of some other course; "I will hedge up their way with thorns," and I will see whether I can bring them in that way.

Obs. 4. For God to make the way of sin difficult to sinners, is a most singular mercy. "Behold!" It is better for the way of sin to be hedged with thorns, and to be made difficult to us, than to have the smoothest path for its commission. As it is one of the greatest judgments of God upon wicked men to lay stumbling-blocks before them in the way of righteousness; so it is one of the greatest mercies of God to his children to lay stumblingblocks and difficulties before them in the way of sin. It is usual with God in dealing with reprobates, to make their sins, and his providences, stumblingblocks to them in the way of life. They hate godliness, and therefore the hedge of thorns compasses about the way of righteousness to the wicked. In Prov. xv. 19, it is said that "the way of the slothful man is an hedge of thorns;" that is, a slothful man looks upon any duty that he should perform, as compassed about with a hedge of thorns. God, in his just judgment, suffers such difficulties at least to appear to the wicked in the way of his duties as make him have no mind to them. Now this is a grievous judgment of God, to cause the way of his fear to appear so difficult, and to scare them from it: What should I do meddling with such ways? I see I must suffer much; there are these stumblingblocks that I must go over, these troubles that I must meet; I had better sit still and be quiet, I shall never be able to go through them. Such stumblingblocks God lays in the way of godliness before the wicked, and they stumble at them, and fall, and ruin their souls. On the other hand, God, in abundance of mercy, casts stumblingblocks in the way of sin before his people, which they cannot get over; if they stumble, it is but to break their shins, and to save their souls. But when the wicked stumble, they break their necks, and damn their souls. But the ways of God "are all plain to him that understandeth, and right to them that find knowledge," Prov. viii. 9. God's ways are very plain to the godly, and sin's ways are very difficult; but on the other side, to the wicked God's ways are very difficult, and the ways of sin are very plain. O unhappy men, says Luther, when God leaves them to themselves, and does not resist them in their lusts! but woe to them, at whose sins God winks! When God lets the way to hell be a smooth and pleasant way, it is a heavy judgment, and a sign of God's indignation against men, a token of his rejection of them, that he does not intend good unto them. You bless yourselves many times, that in the way of sin you find no difficulty; if a lewd or a malicious man, who would accomplish his own ends, find all things go on as he desires, so that he has not in his way so much as a thorn, he blesses himself. Bless thyself! if thou knewest all, thou hast cause to howl, and wring thy hands, for the curse of God is upon thee, a dreadful curse to make the way of sin pleasant. On the other side, perhaps many of God's saints, when they find the ways of sin somewhat difficult to them, are troubled that they cannot have their will. Troubled! thou hast cause to bless God who has thus crossed thee, for it is an argument of much love to thee. There is a "Behold" put to this, that God should be so merciful to make their ways of idolatry and superstition difficult to them.

O infelices et miseros quando relinquit Deus homines sibi ipsis, nec resistit eorum furori et cupiditatibus: sed væ illis ad quorum peccata connivet Deus. Luther.

Obs. 5. There is much brutishness in the hearts of backsliders. "I will hedge up her way with thorns." Not only slavishness, but brutishness. That is, they must not only be dealt hardly with, as slaves, and so be brought home, but, as brute beasts, they must have some present evil put upon them. They will not return from their evil way, except their sin be grievous and troublesome to them. It is not enough, you know, to threaten beasts, but if we would keep them from the place to which we would not have them go, we must use something that will give them pain when they attempt to enter it. A man who has some understanding, though he has a slavish spirit, may be kept from sin by fear of future evils; but when nothing but present evils will keep him off, he is worse than a slave; he cannot be kept from sin by the exercise of his reason, God must deal with him then as a brute beast, God must make some hedge prick him, or else he will go on in an evil way. This is brutishness, even in the hearts of the saints.

Obs 6. See the proneness of men's natures to idolatry. The way must be hedged up to keep them from it. It is not enough to forewarn men of it, for all means that can be used are little enough to deter them. How wicked then is the way of many amongst us, who seek to make the way to idolatry as smooth, plain, and open as they can! Yea, instead of stopping such as have inclinations to it, they lay before them the inciting and enticing occasions, which add to their own propensity such delectation as puts them forward with a swift facility.

Obs. 7. Afflictions to the people of God, are God's hedges to keep them from sin. The command of God is one hedge, and affliction is another. Therefore sin is called by the name of transgression; that is, going beyond our bounds, going over the hedge; a man that sins goes over the hedge. We find, Eccl. x. 8, "Whoso breaketh an hedge, a serpent shall bite him:" it is true in regard of the hedge of God's command, he that will venture to break that hedge, must expect the biting of conscience, its anguish and horror. But when that hedge is broke, God comes with another hedge to keep his people from sin; so you have it expressed in Job xxxiii. 17, 18: speaking of afflictions, By them "he withdraweth man from his purpose," and "he keepeth back his soul from the pit." Suppose a beast running in a pasture, bounded by a hedge at the brink of a precipice, perhaps he does not see the hedge; if he should run a little further, he would fall over and be destroyed; but the husbandman sets a hedge there, that when the beast comes to the thorns, they may withdraw him from his purpose, and so preserve his life: so it may be with a man that is running to such a sin, when he meets with something that hinders him, he is withdrawn from his purpose, and his soul is kept back from death. If you live in the country near ditches and pits of water, you will hedge them about, for fear your children should fall into them; and so the hedge keeps the children alive. As afflictions keep the saints from sin, as a hedge to them, so the difficulties in God's ways keep the wicked from God. When difficulties therefore happen, it should teach us to consider what way we are in: why? for God uses to compass about sinful ways with difficulties, on purpose to keep his people from them. Well, I am going on in this course, I am sure I am compassed about with difficulties, it may be these difficulties are but God's hedges to keep me from sin; how shall I know that? Sometimes difficulties are but trials of our graces, and they lie in the most blessed ways of God's people; then the work of the saints should be to stir up their graces, and to break through this hedge, though they be pricked and torn thereby. It is the excellency of their faith that will carry them through all difficulties in God's ways. Therefore here is the trial; when I meet with difficulties, I must not forbear because there are difficulties, but I must examine, Is it the way of God or not? If it be the way of God, then lay aside the thought of difficulties; if I have authority for it, let the difficulties be never so many, and the hedge never so thick, I must break through, and God is so much the more honoured by it: but on the other side, if, upon examination, I find the way I am in is not warranted by God, then I must know that God's end in laying difficulties in the way, is to stop my going on in it, and it is desperateness in me to seek to break through; in seeking to break through I may break my peace: therefore I must examine whether I have warrant from God for those ways in which I walk.

Oh that men would think of this when they meet with difficulties in their ways! How many of the saints have met with difficulties in their paths, and yet have gone on with strength! That of Jacob is one of the most famous examples we have in the book of God. The difficulties he met with were all in the way that God himself bade him take. God commanded him to return to his father Isaac, and yet he met with six or seven most prodigious difficulties, enough, one would have thought, to make him doubt whether he was in God's way or not, and to cause him to return back again. First, Laban pursued him, and intended mischief against him; then Esau comes to meet him with a purpose to destroy him; then his wife's nurse died; then Rachel herself died; then he had his daughter Dinah defloured; and then his two sons committed that horrible wickedness in murdering the Shechemites! All these things fell out in Jacob's journey; he might have said, Am I in the way that God would have me? Yes, Jacob was in his way, he had an express warrant from God to go that journey. Difficulties therefore must not discourage us, but we must break through them, especially in these times. It were a low and poor spirit, to be kept from a good way because of a few thorns that it meets in the way. If we know it be God's way, go through it in the name of God, let the difficulties be what they will. But if the way be not warranted by God, let the difficulties we meet with stop us, for God intends them to be a hedge to keep us from sin.

Again, it should make us content when any affliction befalls us, because it is more than we know but that God intends abundance of good to us. It may be, if this affliction had not befallen thee, thou hadst undone thyself: if this affliction, that thou dost so wriggle to get out of, and thinkest thyself so miserable under, had not befallen thee, thou mightest have fallen into the pit and been lost; therefore be not troubled so much at the affliction, but examine whether it be not a hedge that God has set, to keep thee from a further misery.

Obs. 8. The perverseness of a man's heart is such, that he will break through many difficulties to sin. It seems that a hedge will not serve, there must be a wall, as well as a hedge.

We read of idolaters, who would cause their children to pass through the fire to their idols; that was more than a hedge of thorns. We see often, that men's hearts are so strongly bent upon their sins, that though they were to pass through much trouble, though they prick and tear themselves, yet they will have their sin. Ambrose tells us, that Philotimus, who brought his body to grievous diseases by uncleanness and drunkenness, when the physicians told him, that if he did not abstain he would certainly lose his eyes; as soon as he heard that, he answered, *Valeat lumen amicum*, Farewell, O pleasant light; rather than I will deny myself in this, I will never see light more: he would venture the loss of his eyes, rather than lose the satisfaction of his lusts. Thus it is with many. Oh what do they venture for their lusts! What an argument should that be to us to venture much for God, to endure hard things for the blessed God! though there be some hardship between us and our duty, break through all to get to that duty; wicked men will break through great difficulties to get to their sins. There need be a wall as well as a hedge.

Obs. 9. God, when he pleases, will keep men from their sins in spite of their hearts, that they shall not have their desire. Well, if there be need of a wall I will have a wall, saith God; though she may break down the hedge, she shall not break down the wall, it is too strong and too high. When God sees men set upon their wicked desires, if they be those that belong not to him, perhaps God may condemn them for their wicked desires, and yet they shall not have them; they shall go to hell for them, and never accomplish them. How desperately set was Saul to mischief David? but God made a wall that he could not get to have his desire, do what he would. Many, especially great men, how strongly are they set upon their desire! they must have it, and they will have it, nothing comes from them but must and will: well, they may be deceived, God knows how to cross the most stubborn and stout hearts that live upon the earth, that they shall not have what they would have in this world. "I will make a wall." God thus makes a wall about men's sins, by sending sore and heavy afflictions. When God brings some grievous disease upon the drunkard's body, perhaps he is so stopped that he cannot drink, that is a wall about his sin, that he cannot follow it according to his desire: so the unclean person, God brings such a disease upon him, that he cannot have the pleasure of his lust though he earnestly desires it: so God brings poverty upon others, that they cannot follow their ambition and pride, do what they can: these are as walls to them. But God does not always send this in a way of mercy.

Obs. 10. When lesser afflictions will not serve to keep men from their sins, God usually comes with greater and sorer. First a hedge, and then a wall. I see some of them will break through the hedge, "I will make a wall" therefore, that is, I will come with stronger and greater afflictions, and so keep them off. Lev. xxvi. 18, 19, "If you will not yet for all this," saith God, "hearken unto me, then I will punish you seven times more for your sins. And I will break the pride of your power." You think there is a power in your hand, and there is pride in your power, for power raises the heart up to pride; I will break it, I will never leave till

I have broken your hearts in spite of you: and you will find in that chapter four or five times mention of "seven times more." This is after the hedge, then there comes a wall.

Obs. 11. God is able to strike men with blindness, that they shall not see their way. "And they shall not find their paths." Though there be an evil way of mischief before them, though there be nothing to hinder them in it, God can strike men with blindness one way or other, that they shall not be able to see their way before them. We have it this day exceedingly fulfilled in our eyes; how does God blind and besot our adversaries, that they cannot see their way! The truth of Job v. 13, is this day before our eyes, "He taketh the wise in their own craftiness; and the counsel of the froward is carried headlong." How has God taken wise men in their own craftiness! their spirits are froward, because they are crossed and vexed, and their counsel is carried headlong; God takes away their understanding, and baffles them in their own counsels. "The stout-hearted are spoiled, they have slept their sleep; and none of the men of might have found their hands," Psal. lxxvi. 5; they are cast into a slumber, and know not how to make use of that power which they have in their hands. It follows, ver. 6, "At thy rebuke, O God of Jacob, both the chariot and horse are cast into a dead sleep:" a strange expression, that a chariot should be "cast into a dead sleep;" the meaning is, they can no more tell how to make use of them, than if they all lay dead, or asleep. Let us not be afraid of the power of adversaries; suppose they had power in their hand, God can strike them with blindness, they shall grope to find the door, they shall be baffled in their own ways, they shall not tell how to make use of their power. Isa. xxix. 14, "Behold," (saith God,) "I will proceed to do a marvellous work among this people, even a marvellous work and a wonder." What is it? "The wisdom of their wise men shall perish, and the understanding of their prudent men shall be hid." This is a wonderful thing that God will do; yea, and he will "mingle a perverse spirit in the midst of them." Thus, Isa. xix. 11, "Surely the princes of Zoan are fools, the counsel of the wise counsellors of Pharaoh is become brutish:" and ver. 12, "Where are they? where are thy wise men?" And again, ver. 13, "The princes of Zoan are become fools, the princes of Noph are deceived;" and ver. 14, "The Lord hath mingled a perverse spirit in the midst thereof; and they have caused Egypt to err in every work thereof, as a drunken man staggereth in his vomit." Here is the judgment of God upon men; when he list, he can blind them in their way that they shall err in their work, and stagger in their counsels and designs, as a drunken man in his vomit; they shall not find their paths, nor know what to do.

Well, thus God deals with wicked men: but now let us consider this in reference to the saints, to God's own people, "they shall not find their paths;" then,

Obs. 12. It is a good blindness for men not to see the way of sin. It is promised here in a way of mercy, that "they shall not find their paths." This darkness is not "the shadow of death;" but "the way of life." It is rich mercy. Maris, bishop of Chalcedon, a blind man, whom Julian the apostate called a blind fool, because he had rebuked Julian for his apostacy, answered him thus, I bless God that I have not my sight to see such an ungracious face as thine. So, many may bless God for their bodily blindness, because it has prevented abundance of sin that might have been let in at the casements of their eyes. But especially for blindness, not to see the way of sin, if we may call that blindness. It is a mercy that God does not grant to all, it is a singular mercy to the saints: for you find abundance of people exceedingly quick-sighted in the way of sin, that can find the path there, and yet are exceedingly blind in the way of God, and cannot find the path there. On the other side, the saints are blinded in the way of sin, but are quick-sighted in the ways of God. How many men are wise to do evil, as the Scripture saith, able to see into the depths of Satan, and are profound to damn themselves; they can find out so many objections against the ways of God, they can answer such arguments against their own ways, and have such cunning devices to accomplish them; but when they come to the ways of God, they are as blind as moles; they cannot see the necessity for such strictness; they cannot understand, though men of great parts and of great understanding otherwise, yet they have no skill in the ways of God. "I thank thee, O Father, Lord of heaven and earth," saith Christ, "that thou hast hid these things from the wise and prudent, and hast revealed them unto babes." Hence the saints, though babes, are able to see far into the excellency and glory of God's ways, they have understanding there, though but weak otherwise; the beauty of the great mysteries of God, dazzles all the glory of the world in their eyes. They are not so easily caught with temptations, but can see into the subtleties of the devil that would draw them out of God's ways; but when they come to the ways of sin, there they want understanding, and it is God's mercy to them that they do; there they are but bunglers, they grope as blind men, they are not cunning artists in those ways. As the apostle saith, 1 Cor. ii. 12, "We have received not the spirit of the world," we cannot shift for ourselves as the men of the world can, we are not so cunning to contrive plots, and tricks, and devices for our own ends as the men of the world; but "we have received the Spirit of God," we can understand things (through God's mercy) to eternal life. There are many men cunning for their own destruction, they can find every secret path of sin; though sin be a labyrinth, they trace it, and find out every by-path in that way. When the ways of God are propounded to wicked men, there is a mist before their eyes, they cannot see; and when the ways of sin are propounded to the saints, God in mercy casts a mist before their eyes that they cannot see. Eccl. x. 15, The fool "knoweth not how to go to the city;" wicked men know not the path to the church of God, to the ordinances of God; they talk much about such and such ordinances, and setting up of Christ in the way of his ordinances, but they know not what the true worship of God means. No, a fool does not understand the way to the city of God, he cannot find out that path. But the saints, though they know not the ways of sin, yet they can find out the paths of God, they know the way to the city. Possidonius tells us, that when wait was laid for Austin's life, through God's providence he missed his way, and so his life was preserved, and his enemies were disappointed. So many times when you are going on in such a way of sin, perhaps you little think what danger there is in it; God in mercy therefore casts a mist before your eyes, and you miss that way and save your lives.

Ver. 7. *And she shall follow after her lovers, but she shall not overtake them; and she shall seek them, but shall not find them: then shall she say, I will go and return to my first husband; for then was it better with me than now.*

In the 5th verse it was but אלכה *vadam*, "I will go after my lovers;" but here it is, רדפה "she shall follow," from a root which signifies *persequor*, to follow with eagerness; not only *sectari*, but *insectari;* the word is the same that is used for persecutors, who eagerly pursue those they persecute. Psal. vii. 5, David speaks of his enemies following him, and uses the same word, "Let the enemy persecute my soul." The form of the word being in Piel, signifies to do any thing anxiously, diligently, carefully, whereas in Kal it signifies barely doing a thing. Thus it is interpreted by Polanus, *anxie prosecuta est*, she has prosecuted or followed with a great deal of care. So that this is more than the other, for it seems that after she had some affliction she grew worse for a while, and was more eager upon her idols than she was before.

καταδιώξαι, Sept.

"But she shall not overtake them." Though she be never so much set upon that way of evil, yet I will take a course to keep her from it, she shall not overtake them. Yea,

"She shall seek them, but shall not find them." The word בקשתם signifies, to seek with much endeavour, not only to seek in one's thought and mind, but to walk up and down, that we may find. The Seventy use divers words, which signify a seeking more than ordinary.

ἀναζητέω, ἐκζητέω, ἐπιζητέω.

"But shall not find them." Let her be never so set upon her ways of idolatry, yet I will keep her from them.

"Then shall she say, I will go," &c. This shall be the effect of it. One would think all this were nothing but threatening; O no, it is mercy, for it is for this end, that she might at length say, "I will go and return to my first husband," &c.

You may take then the scope of this and the preceding verse in this short paraphrase: as if God should say, O Israelites, you have grievously sinned against me, in forsaking me and following your lovers. Sore and heavy evils are ready to befall you, even you, my elect ones, upon whom my heart is set for good. You have involved yourselves in the common guilt of this wickedness, therefore even you must expect to be involved in the common calamity that shall come upon the nation. When you are under those calamities, know that I understand how to make a difference between sinner and sinner, though guilty of the same sin, and under the same affliction. What shall be for the destruction of some, shall be in mercy to you, it shall hedge up your ways, keep you from further sinning, and make your ways of sin difficult, that so your souls may be saved; and although your hearts will be a long time perverse, and will not submit to me, yet I will so order things, in the way of my providence, that at length I will so work upon your hearts, that you shall return unto me. You shall bethink yourselves, and remember what sweetness once you had in my ways; and you shall take shame to yourselves, and acknowledge that it was then far better with you than it is now; and so I will remain to be your God, and you shall give up yourselves to worship and serve me for ever. This is the meaning and scope of the words.

Obs. 1. Until God subdues the heart to himself, men will grow worse and worse in their sins. Even God's elect, to whom he intends mercy at last, till God comes with his grace to subdue their hearts, they may grow worse and worse. They would before "go after their lovers," and now here afflictions come upon them; yet still they will follow their lovers, and that with more eagerness of affection, and with more violence, than before. Afflictions in themselves are part of the curse of God, and there is no healing virtue in them, but an enraging quality to stir up sin, till God sanctify them by his grace; and God may suspend for a time the sanctifying work of his grace to those to whom he intends good at last. Isa. li. 20, speaks of some whose afflictions were not sanctified, that "they lie at the head of all the streets, as a wild bull in a net: they are full of the fury of the Lord." They were full of the fury of the Lord, yet lay like a wild bull in a net, in a raging manner. This distemper of heart proceeds from two grounds. 1. When outward comforts are taken away by affliction, the sinner, having no comfort in God, knows not where to have comfort but in his sin; and if conscience be not strong enough to keep from it, he runs madly upon it. 2. Because he thinks others look upon him as one opposed by God for his sin; therefore, that he may declare to all the world that he is not daunted, and that he has no misgiving thoughts, (though perhaps he has nipping gripes within,) he will put a good face upon it, and follow his ways more eagerly than formerly.

Obs. 2. A man may follow after the devices of his own heart, and yet may not overtake them. "She shall follow, but she shall not overtake." There is a great deal of difference betwixt following God's ways, and our own ways: there was never any in the world that was disappointed, if he knew all, in following God's ways, he obtained either the very thing he would have, or something that was as good, if not better, for him; but in the ways of sin, in our own ways, we may and do meet with disappointment. Why should we not then rather follow God than our own desires? The desires after sin, as they are *desideria futilia*, so they are *desideria inutilia*, as one speaks; as they are foolish, so they are fruitless desires, they do not attain what they would have. How has God disappointed men in our days! they have not overtaken what they greedily sought after. Our adversaries blessed themselves in their designs, they thought to have their day, they propounded such an end and thought to have it; but how has God disappointed them! But whether God has done this in mercy to them, as it is here, we know not; we hope God has crossed some of them in a way of mercy, though perhaps he may deal in another way with others.

Obs. 3. Disappointment in the way of sin is a great mercy. As satisfaction in sin is a judgment of God, and a fearful judgment; so disappointment in sin is a mercy, and a great mercy. God says in Prov. xiv. 14, "The backslider in heart shall be filled with his own ways." A dreadful threatening to backsliders and apostates! When God has no intention of love and mercy for backsliders, he will give them their own devices, they shall have their fill of their own ways; you would have such a lust, you shall have it, you shall be satisfied to the full, and bless yourselves in your own ways. This is the judgment of God upon backsliders. But for the saints, when tempted to such a way of sin, God will disappoint them, they shall not have it. We account it ordinarily very grievous to be disappointed of any thing, and many times I have had this meditation upon it; What! does it so trouble the heart of men to be disappointed almost in any thing? oh what a dreadful vexation and horror will it be for a man to see himself disappointed of his last hopes! Remember this, when you are troubled at any disappointment; what will be the terror and anguish of spirit then, if it should prove that any of you are disappointed of your hopes for eternity! But those whom God disappoints in the way of sin, may have hope that God will deliver them from that great disappointment.

Obs. 4. Governors should take such a course as to remove idols and superstitious vanities from those that will worship them, and sin against God by them. She would have her idols, but God will take them away; though she follow after them, and have a great mind to them, yet "she shall not overtake them." The meaning is, God will remove them from their idols, or their idols from them; they should not come to their Dan or Bethel, they should either be removed far enough from their calves, or the calves from them. Hence governors must either take people away from those vanities, or their vanities from them; they should not so much as suffer those things to be enticements and snares for the hearts of people; though they are very grand, and abundance of gold and excellent artificial work are about them, yet, "Thou shalt not desire the silver or gold that is on them, nor take it unto thee, lest thou be snared therein: but thou shalt utterly detest it, and thou shalt utterly abhor it; for it is a cursed thing," Deut. vii. 25, 26. You shall not look upon the ingenious work of their idols, and upon the great cost bestowed upon them, and therefore spare them because of that; O no, but take them away, that men may not be insnared by them.

Obs. 5. Idolaters' hearts are after their idols when they cannot get them. "She shall follow after her lovers, but she shall not overtake them." Though they cannot get them, yet they will be following them. Their conduct is of excellent use for us: so should we do in pursuing after God's ordinances; though perhaps, for the present, we cannot enjoy the ordinances of God, yet be sure to keep our hearts working after them. Many deceive themselves in this; they say, We would have all the ordinances of God, but we see we cannot; and so upon that sit still, and do not labour to keep their hearts in a burning desire after them; and hence, many times they let slip the opportunities of enjoying them. But now if thou canst not have the beauty of an ordinance, if thou keepest thy heart in a burning desire after it in the use of all means for attaining it, know then, that the want of an ordinance is an ordinance to thee. You shall find in the English Chronicle of Edward the First, that he had a mighty desire to go to the Holy Land; and because he could not go, he gave charge to his son upon his death-bed that he should take his heart thither, and appointed £32,000 to defray the charges of carrying his heart to the Holy Land, out of a superstitious respect he had to that place: though he could not attain it, his heart should. Thus should our hearts work after ordinances.

And now we come to the blessed fruit of all this. "She shall follow after her lovers, but she shall not overtake them; and she shall seek them, but shall not find them." What follows after all this? Now mercy appears; they shall return, at length they shall bethink themselves. "Then shall she say, I will go and return to my first husband; for then was it better with me than now."

Obs. 1. In times of affliction, the only rest of the soul is to return to God. They kept wriggling, and shifting up and down, to provide for themselves, but they could find no rest. As a poor prisoner that is shackled keeps a stir with his chains, but instead of getting any freedom he galls his legs. But when the poor soul, after all shiftings, and turnings, and vexings, comes to think of returning to the Lord, and of humbling and repenting itself before him, then it finds rest. "Return to thy rest, O my soul." Remember, after all your afflictions, here is your rest, in returning to the Lord.

Obs. 2. So long as men can have any thing in their sinful way to satisfy themselves with, they will not return to God. Then they shall say, that is, when they are so stopped in their way, when they are hedged, and walled, and cannot overtake their lovers, then they shall return to the Lord. There is that perverseness of spirit in men. Only when men are stopped in the way of sin, that they can have no satisfaction nor hope, then they begin to think of returning to God. As the prodigal; what shift did he make! he goes to the farmer, to the swine, to the husks to fill his belly, and it is likely if he had had his bellyful of them he would never have thought of going to his father; but when he came to the husks, and could not tell how to fill his belly there, when he was in a desperate state, then he begins to think of returning to his father. So you have it, Isa. lvii. 10, "Yet saidst thou not, There is no hope: thou hast found the life of thine hand; therefore thou wast not grieved;" thou wast not brought to such a desperate stand as to say, There is no hope: that intimates that till men are brought to such a stand that they can say, Certainly, there is no hope or help this way, they will seldom think of returning to God. Thus is God infinitely dishonoured by us. It is very strange how the hearts of men will hanker after their sin this way and that way, and till God take them quite off from hope of comfort by it, they will never have a thought to return to God. God is fain to be the last refuge. We account ourselves much dishonoured when we are the last refuge; when nobody will, I must. It seems God is fain to yield to this; when no one will give satisfaction to the soul, then men come to God, and God must.

Cum nemini obtrudi potest, itur ad me.

Obs. 3. Returning to God, if it be in truth, though it be after we have sought out all other helps, yet God is willing to accept. This is an observation full of comfort, the Lord grant it may not be abused; but it is the word of the Lord, and a certain truth, that returning after men have sought other means, and can find no help, though they are driven to it by afflictions, yet it may be accepted by God. Man will not accept upon these terms, but the thoughts of God are as far above the thoughts of men, as the heaven is above the earth. It is true, sometimes God will not, nay, God threatens, Prov. i. 28, Though "they call upon me, I will not answer;" though "they seek me early," yet "they shall not find me." God is not thus gracious to all at all times; therefore you must not presume upon it. God sometimes at the very first affliction hardens his heart against men, that he will never regard them more, for his mercy is his own; but those that are in covenant with him, though they come to him upon such terms, yet they may be accepted of him; therefore, take this truth for helping you against this sore temptation, which, when you are in affliction, will be apt to intrude: Oh! I cry to God now in my affliction; I should have done it before, surely God will not hear me now. I confess I cannot speak in this point without a trembling heart, lest it be abused; but the text presents it fairly to you, and you must have the mind of God made known to you, though others abuse it. "Mine eye mourneth by reason of affliction: Lord, I have called daily upon thee," Psal. lxxxviii. 9. This is spoken by Heman, and God did accept him, as it is apparent in the psalm, yet he cried by reason of affliction. And Psal. cxx. 1, "In my distress I cried unto the Lord, and he heard me;" though it were in my distress, yet the Lord heard me. Only take this one note about it: Though our being stopped in all other ways may make us cry to God, and God may hear us, yet, when God does hear us, he works more than crying out by reason of that affliction; at first our affliction carries us to God, yet, before God has done with us, and manifests any acceptance of us, he works our hearts to higher aims than deliverance from our affliction.

Obs. 4. A heart effectually wrought upon by God is a resolute heart to return to God. "I will go and return." As they were resolute in their way of idolatry, "I will go after my lovers;" so their hearts, when converted, shall be as resolute in God's ways; "she shall say, I will go and return to my first husband." When God works upon the heart to purpose, he causes strong arguments to fasten upon the spirit, and nothing shall hinder, no, not father, nor mother, nor the dearest friend. Perhaps the Lord begins to work upon the child, and the father scorns him, and the mother says, What shall we have of you now? a puritan? This grieves the spirit of the child; yet there are such strong arguments fastened by God upon his heart, that it carries him through, he is resolute in his way, he will return.

Obs. 5. Those who have ever found the sweetness of Christ in their hearts, though they should be backsliders, have something remaining that will at length draw them to him. Christ has such hold upon their hearts, as at one time or other he will get them in again; there will be some sparks under those embers, that will inflame and draw the soul to return again to Christ. Therefore, if any of you have friends in whom you were verily persuaded there was a true work of grace, though they have exceedingly departed from Christ, do not abandon your hope, for if ever there were any true taste of the sweetness that is in Christ, Christ has such a hold upon their hearts, that he will bring them in again one time or other.

Obs. 6. There is nothing gotten by departing from Christ. "I will go and return to my first husband, for then was it better with me." You go from the better to the worse, whenever you depart from him: "What fruit had ye in those things whereof ye are now ashamed?" Rom. vi. 21. "I am the Lord thy God which teacheth thee to profit," Isa. xlviii. 17: sin does not teach you to profit, you can never get good by that, but the Lord teaches to profit. You may think to gain something by departing from Christ, but when you have cast up all the gain, you may put it into your eye, and it will do you no hurt. "What is the hope of the hypocrite, though he hath gained, when God taketh away his soul?" Job xxvii. 8. Perhaps a hypocrite, or a backslider who has departed from God, once forward in the way of godliness, but who now, like Demas, has forsaken those ways and cleaves to the world, thinks he has gained, and perhaps is grown richer, and lives braver than before; yet what hope has this backslider, this hypocrite, when God taketh away his soul? then he will see that he has gotten nothing. As it is said of the idolater, Isa. xliv. 20, "He feedeth upon ashes: a deceived heart hath turned him aside, that he cannot deliver his soul, nor say, Is there not a lie in my right hand?" What! shall there be more in a lust than in the blessed God? than in Jesus Christ, who is the glory of heaven, the delight of angels, the satisfaction of the Father himself? Can a lust put thee into a better condition than Christ, who has all fulness to satisfy God himself? Certainly it cannot be.

Obs. 7. There must be a sight and an acknowledgment of our shameful folly, or else there can be no true returning to God. "I will go and return to my first husband, for then was it better with me than now." As if the church should say, I confess I have played the fool, I have done shamefully, I have lost by departing from Christ, it was better far than it is now. Jer. iii. 25, "We lie down in our shame, and our confusion covereth us, for we have sinned against the Lord our God," saith the church; so it should be with all that return to Christ, they must lie down in their shame. This is very seasonable in these times: we have many now, who not long since were vile apostates; they have gone with the times, they saw preferment went such a way, and their hearts went that way; now they see they cannot have preferment in that way, and God of his mercy has changed the times, they will be converts. We have in England many parliamentary converts, but such we are not to confide in. Do you ask, Why should we not confide in them? If they repent and return, God accepts them, and why should not we? It is true, such a one was before an enemy, and followed superstitious vanities, but now he is grown better and preaches against them, and why should not we receive him? I answer, it is true, if deep humiliation has gone before that reformation; if, together with their being better, they have been willing to shame themselves before God and his people, to acknowledge their folly in departing from God, and be willing to profess before all that knew them, and have been scandalized by them. It is true, God began with me and showed me his ways when I was young; I began to love them, and to walk in them; but when I saw how the times went, and preferment went, the Lord knows I had a base, time-serving heart, I went away from God. No arguments satisfied my conscience, but merely livings and preferment, and now I desire to take shame and confusion of face to myself. Woe unto me for the folly and falseness of my heart! it is infinite mercy of God ever to regard such a wretch as I. If they did thus take shame to themselves, and acknowledge their folly, this were something. We read in the primitive times of Ecebolius, who, when he had revolted from the truth, came to the congregation, and, falling down upon the threshold, cried out, *Calcate, calcate insipidum salem;* Tread upon me, unsavoury salt; I confess I have made myself unsavoury salt by departing from the truth, let all tread upon me. It was a sign of true returning, when this went before, and reformation followed. We have done foolishly, it was better with us than now.

Obs. 8. Though acknowledgment must go before, yet returning must follow. "I will return." It is not enough to see and acknowledge, but there must be a returning; for as reformation without humiliation is not enough, so humiliation without reformation suffices not. And I speak this the rather, because these are times wherein there is a great deal of seeming humiliation, and we hope true humiliation: but many in the days of their fasting will acknowledge how sinful, how vile, how passionate they have been in their families, how worldly, what base self-ends they have had; and they will make such catalogues of their sins in those days of their humiliation, as cause admiration: the thing itself is good; but I speak to this end, to show the horrible wickedness of men's hearts, that after they have ripped up all their sins, and with all aggravations acknowledged the folly of their evil ways against God, yet they often manifest no returning; after all this, they are as passionate in their families, as froward, as peevish, as perverse, as earthly, as light and vain in their carriage as ever. They will acknowledge what they have done, but they will not return. Remember, humiliation must go before reformation, but reformation must follow after humiliation.

Obs. 9. How much better it was when the heart cleaved to Christ, above what it is since its departure from Christ, is an effectual means to cause the heart to return to him. This is the way that Christ himself prescribed, Rev. ii. 5, "Remember therefore from whence thou art fallen, and repent." Thou wert in a better condition once than now thou art: O return; and that thou mayst return, "remember from whence thou art fallen." I will give a little glimpse of what might be said in this point more largely. The reasonings of the heart in the sight of this may briefly be hinted thus: Heretofore I was able through God's mercy to look upon the face of God with joy. When my heart cleaved to him, when I walked close with God, then the glory of God shined upon me, and caused my heart to spring within me every time I thought of him; but now, now, God knows, though the world takes little notice of it, the very thoughts of God are a terror to me, the most terrible object in the world is to behold the face of God. Oh, it was better with me than it is now.

Before my backsliding I had free access to the throne of God's free grace, I could come with humble and holy boldness to God, and pour out my soul before him; such a chamber, such a closet, can witness it: but now I have no heart to pray, I must be haled to it by conscience; yea, every time I go by that very closet where I was wont to have that access to the throne of grace, it strikes a terror to my heart; I can never come into God's presence, but it is out of slavish fear. Oh, it was better with me then than it is now."

Before, oh the sweet communion my soul enjoyed with Jesus Christ! one day's communion with him, how much better was it than the enjoyment of all the world! But now Jesus Christ is a stranger to me, and I a stranger to him. Before, oh the sweet enlargements that my soul had in the ordinances of God! when I came to the word, my soul was refreshed, was warmed, was enlightened; when I came to the sacrament, oh the sweetness that was there! and to prayer with the people of God, it was even a heaven upon earth to me: but it is otherwise now, the ordinances of God are dead and empty things to me. Oh, it was better with me then than it is now.

Before, oh the gracious visitations of God's Spirit that I was wont to have! Yea, when I awaked in the night season, oh the glimpses of God's face that were upon my soul! what quickenings, and enlivenings, and refreshings did I find in them! I would give a world for one night's comfort I then had by the visitations of God's Spirit, but now they are gone. Oh, it was better with me then than it is now.

Before, oh what peace of conscience had I within! however the world railed and accused, yet my conscience spake peace to me, and was a thousand witnesses for me: but now I have a grating conscience within me; oh the black bosom that is in me, it flies in my face every day! I could come before from the society of the saints, and my conscience smiled upon me; now I go to wicked company, and when I come home, and in the night, oh the gnawings of that worm! It was better with me then than it is now.

Before, the graces of God's Spirit were sparkling in me, active and lively! I could exercise faith, humility, patience, and the like; now, I am as one bereft of all, unfit for any thing, even as a dead log. Before, God made use of me, and employed me in honourable services; now I am unfit for any service at all. Oh, it was better with me then than it is now.

Before, I could take hold upon promises, I could claim them as mine own, I could look up to all those blessed, sweet promises that God had made in his word, as mine inheritance; but now, alas, the promises of God are very little to me. Before, I could look upon the face of all troubles, and the face of death, with joy; but now the thoughts of affliction and of death, God knows how terrible they are to me. Oh, it was better with me then than it is now.

Before, in all creatures I could enjoy God, I tasted the sweetness and love of God even in my meat and drink; I could sit with my wife and children, and see God in them, and look upon the mercies of God through them, as a fruit of the covenant of grace; oh how sweet was it with me then! But now the creature is as an empty thing unto me; whether it come in love or hatred I do not know. Oh, it was better with me before than now.

Before, I was under the protection of God wherever I went, but now I do not know what danger and miseries I am subject to daily, what may befall me before night, God only knows. Before, the saints rejoiced with me in my company and communion; now every one is shy of me. Before, I was going on in the ways of life; now these ways I am in, God knows, and my conscience tells me, are ways of death. Oh, it was better with me then than it is now.

Now then, put all these together, as I make no question these thoughts are the thoughts of many backsliders, if we knew all that were in their hearts. As the prodigal, when he was feeding upon the husks, began to bethink himself; What! is not there food enough in my father's house? every servant there has food enough, and here I am ready to starve. So may many backsliders say, Alas! before, I had sweetness enough, and was satisfied with those abundance of pleasures that were in the house of God, and in his word and ordinances; now I feed upon husks, and amongst swine: oh that it were with me as it was before! As Job speaks in another case concerning his afflictions, "Oh that I were as in months past, as in the days when God preserved me; when his candle shined upon my head, and when by his light I walked through darkness!" Job xxix. 2, 3. Before, I had some afflictions, but I could walk through all afflictions by the light which I had from God. Oh that it were with me now as it was then; "as in the days of my youth, when the secret of God was upon my tabernacle, when the Almighty was yet with me!" It may be said of many backsliders, as Lam. iv. 7, 8, they were once as polished sapphires, but now they are become "blacker than a coal."

But oh that you had hearts to say, Let me return, let me return, because it was otherwise with me heretofore than it is now! Oh that this day there might an angel meet thee, as he met with Hagar when she fled from Sarah! the angel said to her, "Hagar, Sarah's maid, whence comest thou, and whither wilt thou go?" So I say to thee, O backslider, whence comest thou, and whither wilt thou go? Mark, "Hagar, Sarah's maid, whence comest thou?" Dost thou come from Sarah? from Abraham's family, where God is worshipped, where the church of God is? and whither goest thou? canst thou be any where so well as there? So I say to thee, thou who wert a forward professor before, whence comest thou? Dost thou come from such ordinances, from such communion with the saints? What hast thou gotten by those base ways? Thou canst eat, and drink, and laugh a little, and have some esteem with such as are carnal; oh, whither wilt thou go? Oh that God would show you this day whither you go!

Obs. 10. Seeing there is so much grief and shame in complaining of our backsliding, whenever God awakens us it should teach all that are not yet apostates, to take heed what they do, that they may never bring themselves into such a condition. It is a note of caution to you who are, through God's mercy, in his way; you are now well, know when you are well, and keep well. And you young ones who are beginning to give up your names to God, take heed that you do not decline from what you now do, that you do not apostatize from God afterward, lest this be your condition at best; for this is at best, thus to lament the change of your condition. Perhaps you will go on, and God will never cause you to see your shame and folly, till you be eternally undone; but at best you must be brought to this shame and confusion of face, to acknowledge how much better it was with you before than now. How much better was it when I lived in such a family, under such a master, in such a town! oh it was better then with me than it is now! Oh the precious days that once I had when I was young! those days are gone, and whether ever they will come again, God knows.

Yet, further, when the judgment passes on God's side, that it was better before than now, then the soul is in a hopeful way. So long as the judgment holds for God and his ways, though thou art a backslider, though perhaps thy heart be drawn aside from God, and thy affections be unruly, thou art not in a desperate condition, there is hope of thee. There are two sorts of apostates. There are some apostates, who though they are so through the unruliness of their affections, and the strength of temptation, yet they keep their judgment for God's ways, and acknowledge God's people to be best, and his ordinances to be best, and themselves in the danger; these are properly backsliders. But there are some apostates who so fall off from God and his ways, that they begin in their very judgments to think that those ways which they professed before were but fancies, and that the people of God are but a company of humorous people, and bless themselves in their own ways, and think that they are better now than they were before. Oh, this is a hideous thing. If thy judgment be once taken, that thou thinkest the ways of sin to be better than those ways of God, that thou professedst before, then the Lord have mercy upon thee, thou art even a ruined man. We do not know what God will do with thee, but in the judgment of man thou art undone.

Latimer, in a sermon before King Edward, has this passage: I have known many apostates, but I never knew more than one that proved a scorner, and yet returned again. Take heed therefore, saith he, of apostacy. Though a man may fall from God, and possibly return; yet, if he fall off, so that his judgment is taken that he is become a scorner, that is a woeful condition, such a one scarce ever returns. Many such apostates you have in England, and I would challenge you all to give me one example of any one that ever returned again that so fell. I know many scorners are converted, but they that have been forward in professing, and then fall off, and prove scorners, where have you any of them come in? In Lev. xiii. 44, you find when the priest shall come and see a man that has the leprosy in his head, he shall pronounce him utterly unclean; for the plague is in his head. Observe, when the priest found uncleanness in any other part, he was to pronounce it unclean, but if the leprosy be in the head, he shall pronounce the part utterly unclean; there is not that utter uncleanness any where as when the plague is in the head. So I may say here, when a man falls off from the ways of God by some strong temptation or unruly affection, this man is unclean, verily, he is unclean; but when it comes to the head, that his judgment is against the ways of God, and so contemns them and those that follow them, and thinks his own ways better, this man is utterly unclean, for the plague is in his head. The Lord deliver you from that plague.

Obs. 11. Backsliders may have hope of attaining their former condition, to be as well as ever they were: "I will return to my first husband; for then was it better with me than now."

In this, God's goodness goes beyond man's abundantly. "They say, If a man put away his wife, and she go from him, and become another man's, shall he return unto her again? shall not that land be greatly polluted? but thou hast played the harlot with many lovers; yet return again to me, saith the Lord," Jer. iii. 1. Hence, ver. 22, the Holy Ghost exhorts to return upon this very ground, "Return, ye backsliding children, and I will heal your backslidings." Is there any backsliding soul before the Lord? God now offers to heal thy backslidings, thou knowest that it is not with thee now as heretofore; lo, God tenders his grace to thee that thou mayst be in as good a condition as ever. Oh that thou wouldst give the answer of the church there, "Behold, we come unto thee; for thou art the Lord our God. Truly in vain is salvation hoped for from the hills, and from the multitude of mountains: truly in the Lord our God is the salvation of Israel." It is true, God might justly satisfy thee in thy present ways of backsliding, as sometimes he does. "The backslider in heart shall be filled with his own ways," Prov. xiv. 14; he shall have enough of them; and Prov. i. 31, "They shall eat the fruit of their own way, and be filled with their own devices." But, behold, wisdom itself calls thee now to return again, and makes this fair promise, Prov. i. 23, "Turn you at my reproof: behold, I will pour out my spirit unto you." There is not only a possibility of being received into thy former condition, but Christ woos thee, and calls after thee, he promises to pour out his Spirit unto you, yea, and there would be triumph in heaven upon thy returning.

But let me say thus much to thee, though there be a possibility of coming again into as good a condition as thou wast in before, yet, 1. There had need be a mighty work of God's Spirit to raise thy heart to believe this. It is not an easy thing for one who has been left of God to that fearful sin of backsliding, to believe that ever God should receive him, and that he should return to the ways of mercy and comfort as before. Yea, 2. Though there be a possibility to be recovered to mercy, yet you must be contented to be in a meaner condition if God shall please. You must come to God with such a disposition as to be content with the lowest condition, only that thou mayst have mercy at the last; as the prodigal, "Make me as one of thy hired servants." And know, lastly, that if you do not return upon his gracious offer, God may give thee up for ever, take thy fill and there is an end of thee. "He which is filthy, let him be filthy still."

Yet, further, this expression strongly presents occasion to digress a little in comparing our present times with former, to examine whether we can say, it was better with us heretofore than it is now? In these days there is much comparing our present times with times past, and divers judgments about present times; some complaining of the hazards and dangers we are in, in these present times, Much better was it heretofore, say they, than it is now.

To such let me say, first, as the Holy Ghost saith, Eccl. vii. 10, "Say not thou, What is the cause that the former days were better than these? for thou dost not inquire wisely concerning this." Certainly, those people who make such grievous complaints of present times, comparing them with times past, do not wisely inquire concerning this thing. There are many sad things for the present amongst us, things that our hearts have cause to bleed for, such misunderstanding between king and parliament, some blood shed already, and danger of shedding much more; yet, perhaps, if we inquire wisely concerning this thing, we shall find that, notwithstanding all this, we have little cause to complain that it is worse with us now in comparison of what was before.

Consider, first, that which men most complain of, which makes the times hardest now, is but the breaking out of those mischievous designs that lay hid long before, and would have done us a great deal more mischief if they had been kept in. Now they break forth, and break forth as the desperateness of the hopes of those who had such designs; because they could now go no longer underhand, but being brought into a desperate pass, they are fain to see what they can do in ways of violence; and this certainly is better than that mischief should work secretly under-board. Secondly, by this we have a discovery of men, which way they stand, what was and is in their hearts; and this is a great mercy. Thirdly, with the breaking forth of these things, God grants that help now to England, that it never yet had so fully in the like way, and puts such a fair price into the hands of the people of England, that never yet was put into their hands. Yea, and consider, fourthly, that the more violent men are now, the more does it tell us what a lamentable time was before; for if now, when there is such means of resistance, and yet the adversaries prevail so much, what would they have been by this time, if this means of resistance had not been? What a case were we in then, when they might do what they would, and we had no means to help ourselves? Certainly things then lay at more hazard than now. Fifthly, though there be many sad things amongst us, yet God hath been beforehand with us, we have had already, even of free cost, as much mercy as all these troubles come to. Sixthly, these troubles are making way for glorious mercies to come; though there be some pangs, yet they are not the pangs of death, they are but the pangs of a travailing woman that is bringing forth a man-child. Any prince would think, that though his queen should be put to some pain in travail, yet her condition is better than when she had no pain and was barren, or than that she should lie upon her sick bed, and bereft of her senses, and ready to die. The pains of a travailing woman are better than a senseless dying. Yet further, if you think that you had better times heretofore than now, to what times will you refer in making the comparison? I suppose you will instance the times of the first reformation; then things were in a good way when those worthy lights of the church and blessed martyrs had such a hand in the reformation. Many magnify the times of the beginning of reformation for their own ends, that they may thereby hinder reformation now. This, you know, is the great argument that prevails with most: What! were not those prayers composed by learned, godly men, as Cranmer, Latimer, and Ridley, and others? and can we be wiser than they? did not they seal their profession with their blood?

My brethren, we need go no further to show the weakness of this argument, but only to show how it was in the church in those times, and you will find that you have cause to bless God that it is not so with you now as it was then; and if that will appear, then the argument you will see can no further prevail with rational men. Certainly, those first reformers were worthy lights and blessed instruments for God: I would not darken their excellency, but weaken the argument that is abusively raised from their worth. It is reported of Mr. Greenham, that famous practical divine, that in a letter to the bishop of Ely, in giving his reasons for refusing subscription and answers to that prelate's objection against him, that Luther thought such ceremonies might be retained in the church; he thus replied, I reverence more the revealed wisdom of God, in teaching Luther so many necessary things to salvation, than I search his secret judgments, in keeping back from his knowledge other things of less importance. The same I say of those worthy instruments of God's glory in the first reformation; and that it may be clear to you that God kept back his mind from them in some things, consider, whether you would be willing that should be done now that was then: as in the administration of baptism, we find that in the book of liturgy in King Edward's time, which was composed by those worthy men; first, the child was to be crossed in the forehead, and then on the breast; after a prayer used; then the priest was to say over the child at the font, "I command thee, thou unclean spirit, in the name of the Father, and of the Son, and of the Holy Ghost, that thou comest out of this infant; thou cursed spirit, remember thy sentence, remember thy judgment, remember the day is at hand wherein thou shalt be burnt with everlasting fire prepared for thee and thy angels, and presume not hereafter to exercise any tyranny over this infant whom Christ hath bought with his precious blood." Then they dipped the child thrice in the water, the godfathers and the godmothers laid their hands upon the child, and the priest put a white vestment over it, called a chrysome, saying, "Take this white vesture for a token of thine innocency, which by God's grace in this holy sacrament of baptism is given to thee, and for a sign whereby thou art admonished as long as thou livest to give thyself to innocency." Then the priest must anoint the infant upon the head, saying, "Almighty God," &c., "who hath regenerated thee by water and the Holy Ghost, who hath given thee remission of all thy sins, vouchsafe to anoint thee with the unction of his Holy Spirit." Would you now have your children baptized after this order? yet these learned, holy men thought that to be a good way. So at the burial of the dead, the priest casting earth upon the corpse shall say, "I commend thy soul to God the Father Almighty, and thy body to the ground;" and in another prayer, "Grant to this thy servant, that the sins he committed in this world be not imputed to him, but that he, escaping the gates of hell and pains of eternal darkness, may ever dwell in the region of light."

You will say, things are otherwise now. True; therefore I say, there is no strength in that argument, that those men who composed the liturgy were worthy lights in the church; for they were but newly come out of popery, and had the scent of popery upon them, therefore it is too unreasonable to make that which they did the rule of our reformation now, as if we were to go no further than they did. The like may be said of the primitive times, which many plead for the justification of their superstitious vanities, for the Christians then came but newly out of heathenism, and lived among heathens, and therefore could not so soon be delivered from their heathenish customs. I could relate to you sad things there were in Queen Elizabeth's and in King James's days; but I must not take too much liberty in this digression; only let us hereby learn not so to cry out of evil times in which we live, as to be unthankful for present mercies; let us bless God for what we have had, and look to him and his word for further reformation.

Ver. 8. *For she did not know that I gave her corn, and wine, and oil, and multiplied her silver and gold, which they prepared for Baal.*

The Spirit of God returns here again to convincing, upbraiding, accusing, threatening of Israel. The sin of Israel went very near to the heart of God, and God speaks here as a man troubled in spirit for the unkindness, unfaithfulness, unreasonableness of the dealings of his spouse with him. It runs in his thoughts, his heart is grieved at it, and he must vent himself, and when he has told his grief and aggravated his wrong, he is upon it again and again, still convincing, upbraiding, charging Israel for dealing so unfaithfully and treacherously with him, all showing the trouble of his spirit. These words depend upon the 5th verse, for the 6th and 7th are as a parenthesis: "She that conceived them hath done shamefully: for she said, I will go after my lovers, that give me my bread and my water, my wool and my flax," &c. She did thus and thus, "for she did not know that I gave her corn, and wine," &c.

What! was Israel worse than the ox or the ass, that knows his owner, and his master's crib? It is impossible but Israel, who were the only people of God in those times, where God was most, nay, we may say, only known in the world, should know that God was the cause of all the good they had; certainly, they could not be ignorant of that, for in their creed (as Buxtorf and others mention) they had thirteen articles, and this was the first article, I believe with a true and perfect faith, that God is the Creator, the Governor, the Sustainer of all creatures, that he wrought all things, still works all things, and shall for ever work all things. And at their feasts they had these expressions, Blessed be thou, O Lord our God, King of the world, that dost create the fruit of the vine. The master of the feast himself came in publicly to bless God for the fruit of the vine; and yet the text saith that they did not know that God gave them wine. When they came to take bread they had this speech, Blessed be thou, O God, that art the King of the world, that bringest forth bread out of the earth. And at the end of the feast this, Let us bless him who hath sent us of his own, of whose goodness we live. The question answered, And blessed be he of whose goodness we live. Yea, to bless God solemnly

Buxtorf. Synag. Judaic. c. 1. 7.

for the sweet and fragrant smell of spices and herbs, was their constant way: and yet here God charges them that they did not know that he gave them bread, and wine, and oil; they did not lay it to heart.

We shall see afterward of what great use this is to us, to show what profession they made of acknowledging that God gave them all, and yet God charges them that they did not know that he gave them; what? "corn, wine, and oil, and multiplied her silver and her gold." Here God expresses himself more largely than they did before, in what they received from their idols: they talked in the 5th verse of receiving from their idols "bread, and water, and wool, and flax," &c.; but here is "wine, and oil, and silver, and gold," more than they had from their idols. God sets out his mercy to them, to upbraid them.

"Which they prepared for Baal."

We must inquire here, first, what this Baal was. The word בעל signifies primarily, a lord (and then a husband): because they attributed dominion, acknowledging their idols to be lords, therefore they called them by this name; and because they chose them as their husband, therefore also they gave them this name: so with Bel too, for Baal and Bel are the same, the letter ע being omitted, and the points being altered in the Chaldee.

Now this Baal either was some special idol, or else a general name given to all idols: sometimes it is a name given generally to all, in the plural number, Baalim; Jer. ix. 14, They "have walked after the imagination of their own heart, and after Baalim." But it likewise notes a special idol, an idol that was the same with that of the Zidonians, which they called Jupiter Thalassius, or their sea Jupiter; that idol was called Baal in a special manner. In 1 Kings xvi. 31, you may see how the worship of Baal came into Israel at that time. It is true it had been introduced in Israel a long time before, for in Judg. ii. 11, you find that they "served Baalim;" yet the idolatry of Baal was often cast out by the people of God: but see how it came in a fresh; "Ahab took to wife Jezebel the daughter of Eth-baal, king of the Zidonians, and went and served Baal, and worshipped him;" that was the occasion, Ahab marrying a Zidonian; to the end that he might ingratiate himself with his wife's kindred, he would worship his wife's god.

And this Baal has divers additional names. Sometimes in Scripture he is called Baal-zebub, or Beelzebub, and that signifies the god of flies; the reason why Baal had that name was, because in those countries they were extremely perplexed with flies, and they attributed the power of driving them away, and of helping them against their molestation, to their god Baal; hence they called him Baal-zebub. We have other manner of deliverances by the goodness of our God than this, yet for this Baal-zebub was one of their principal gods, therefore it is said of Christ, that "he cast out devils by Beelzebub, the prince of devils," which is, "by the god of flies;" and in Matt. x. 25, he is called Βεελζεβοὺλ, Beelzebul, which is as much as, the dung god, Zebel in the Syriac signifying dung. Then there was Baal-perazim, that addition was only from the place, the mountain where he was worshipped. There was also Baal-berith, that signified only the covenant they entered into with that god. So that it seems the very idolaters bound themselves to worship their god by solemn covenant, to teach us to be willing to bind ourselves in worshipping the true God by all the legal bonds we can, to make God to be the God of our covenant, as their god was. It is needless to name more who had this name. I shall afterward show how God himself had once the name of Baal, for the word signifying the name of husband, or lord, was as due to God as to any other, and God himself took that name. But here we are to understand it of their idols.

They prepared them for Baal, עשו לבעל they made them for Baal. It imports these two things:

First, that they sacrificed these things to their Baal, for so *facere*, to make, is often as much as *sacrificare*, to sacrifice. And Bellarmine, taking advantage of this word, when Christ saith, "Do this," draws an argument that the Lord's supper is a sacrifice, for the word to do is used sometimes to sacrifice.

But, secondly, they prepared them, that is, of their gold and silver they made images of this their idol god Baal; they would not spare their gold and silver, but laid aside and prepared it to make images of Baal, and they thought that gold and silver thus laid out as good as any in their purses.

Obs. 1. It is God that supplies all the outward good of his people. "They did not know that I gave them," &c. I gave not only mine ordinances, but I gave them corn, and wine, and oil, and gold, and silver. It is the Lord himself that supplies all outward good to his people; he does not only prize the souls of his people, but he takes care of their bodies too, and outward estates. "He keepeth all his bones," Psal. xxxiv. 20. Yea, he takes care of the very hair of their heads. The bodies of the saints are precious in the eyes of God, the most precious of all corporeal things in the world: the sun, and moon, and stars are not so precious as the bodies of the saints; how much more precious are their souls!

Austin, upon Psal. lxiii. 1, "My soul thirsteth for thee, my flesh longeth for thee," has this note: If the flesh has any need of bread, of wine, of money, or cattle, seek this of God, for God gives this too; for mark, "My flesh longeth for thee." Those who thirst for God must thirst for him every way; not only their souls thirst for him, but their flesh must thirst for him; for, saith he, did God make the soul, and did the devils, or any idols, make the flesh? No, he that made both soul and flesh feeds them both; therefore all Christians must say, "My soul thirsteth for thee, my flesh longeth for thee." If then we can trust God for our souls, and our eternal states, that he will provide for them, we must trust him for our bodies also, for our flesh, for our temporal estates, that he will provide for them also.

Nunquid animam tuam Deus fecit, et carnem dæmonia fecerunt? qui fecit ambas res ipse pascet ambas. Aug. in Ps. lxiii.

Obs. 2. All our supply that we enjoy in this world, is the free gift of God. "They did not know that I gave them corn, and wine," &c. All of us live upon the mere alms of God; the greatest man in the world is bound to go to God's gate and beg his bread every day; though he were an emperor over all the world he must do it, to show his dependence upon him, that he lives wholly upon alms. Men think it hard to live upon alms, and because they have so much coming in by the year, such an estate in land, they think they are well provided for many years. But whatever estate thou hast, though by thy trading thou hast gotten much, yet God requires this of thee, to go to his gate, and beg thy bread of him every day; so Christ teaches, "Give us this day our daily bread:" and certainly, if we did but understand our dependence upon God for all outward comforts, we could not but fear him, and seek to make peace with him, and keep peace with him. It would be a means that our hearts should be enlarged to give to others who need our alms, seeing every man and woman of us is an alms-man and an alms-woman.

Obs. 3. It is a duty that we owe to God, to know and take notice of God as the author of all our good. They know not, that implies they ought to have known. This is a special duty of that worship we owe to God: it is the end of God's communication of all good to us, that he may have active as well as passive glory from his rational creature; and there is no creature else in the world that God has made capable of knowing any thing of the first cause but the rational creature; therefore it is the excellency of such, that they not only enjoy the good which they have, but that they are able to rise up to the highest and first cause of all their good. It is observed of doves, that at every grain of corn they take in their bill they cast their eyes upward; and in the Canticles you find the eyes of the church are called "doves' eyes," because they look so much up to heaven upon every good they receive. They have not dogs' eyes; the men of the world have dogs' eyes: dogs, you know, look up to their masters for meat, and when they have it they presently look down to the ground; so the men of the world will pray to God when they want, but when they enjoy what they have, they look no more upward, but downward.

This taking notice of God to be the author of all our good, and to give him praise, is all the rent we pay to God for what we enjoy, therefore it is fit we should do that. If we do any thing for God, God takes notice of that to the uttermost; yea, though he enables us to do it, yea, though it be but a little good mingled with a great deal of evil, God takes notice of it, and will reward it; surely then we should take notice of the good that he gives out to us. This sweetens our comforts, to see that they all come from God. Observe the difference between the expression of Jacob's blessing and Esau's blessing; when Isaac came to bless Jacob, he expresses himself thus, Gen. xxvii. 28, "God give thee of the dew of heaven, and the fatness of the earth, and plenty of corn and wine." Now when he comes to bless Esau, mark his expression then, ver. 39, "Thy dwelling shall be the fatness of the earth, and of the dew of heaven from above;" but he never mentions God in that. It is not Esau's blessing, "God give thee of the dew of heaven, and of the fatness of the earth," though it is true Isaac meant so; but yet he does not mention the name of God in Esau's, as in Jacob's blessing. Certainly, my brethren, the seed of Jacob count their blessing to be a double, a treble blessing, that they can see God in it. Carnal hearts do not much regard God, if they can have their flesh satisfied in what they desire, from what hand it comes they do not much care; but a gracious heart, a child of Jacob, rejoices more in the hand from whence it comes, than in any good he can possibly enjoy.

Obs. 4. God does a great deal of good in the world that is little taken notice of, or laid to heart. Many of God's dispensations are invisible, the angels, Ezek. i. 8, are described with their hands under their wings. God does great things sometimes so invisibly that he cannot be seen; and when he does great things that we might see, yet, through the neglect, stupidity, and drossiness of our hearts, we do not see them. The most observing eye in the world, that takes the exactest notice of God's mercy, and has the greatest skill to set forth the riches of God's goodness to himself and others, yet, alas, notices very little. It is with the quickest-sighted Christians as with a skilful geographer, who takes notice of and understands many parts of the world, and is able to set out the several parts distinctly to you in such a climate, in such a country, but yet leaves a great space for a *terra incognita*, for an unknown world, and that unknown world, for aught we know, may be five times bigger than the known world. So they who have the most observant eye of God's mercies, and take the most notice of them, who can best set out the mercies he bestows, spiritual mercies, temporal mercies, preventing mercies, past mercies, present mercies, delivering mercies, &c.; yet when they have done all, they must leave a great space for the *terra incognita*, for the unknown mercies of God.

The truth is, those mercies of God which are obvious to our knowledge every day, one would think were enough to melt our hearts: but besides the mercies we notice, there are thousands and thousands of mercies that we know not of. As we daily commit many sins that we know not, so daily we receive many mercies that we know not likewise. And as, in our confession of sins, we should pray to God first to pardon the sins we know, and so to name them in particular; and when we have done, then, Lord, forgive us our unknown, our secret sins. So in our thanksgiving, first bless God for the mercies before us, and when we have done, Lord, blessed be thy name for all thy unknown mercies, of which I have taken little notice.

Scire tuum nihil est, nisi te scire hoc sciat alter.

We soon grow cold and dead if we do good, and men take no notice of us. Neither what we know, nor what we do, is any thing to us, except others know it too; but this is the vanity and pride of men's hearts. It is God's prerogative above his creatures, to do all for himself, for his own glory, and yet he doth much good in the world that none see. We are bound to deny ourselves in what we do, not to seek our own glory. The most excellent piece in the most excellent of our works, is our self-denial in it; why should we not then do all the good we can cheerfully, though it be not known? We should do good out of love to goodness itself; and if we would do so, we should be encouraged in doing good secretly.

Obs. 5. In God's account, men know no more than they lay to heart and make good use of. The schools distinguish between *nescientia*, and *ignoratia:* nescience is of such things as we are not bound to know, it is not our sin not to know them; but ignorance is of such things as we are bound to know, and that ignorance is twofold. There is an invincible ignorance, let us take what pains we can, we can never know all that we are bound to know; and there is an affected ignorance, when through carelessness we do not mind what is before us; and when we have minded it so far as to conceive it, yet if we lay it not to heart as we ought, in God's account we know it not; if we digest not what we know into practice, God accepts it not. As God is said not to know when he does not approve, "I know you not;" so when any man has a truth in notion, and it is not embraced by the heart, God accounts that that man knows it not. Therefore, in Scripture it is said, The seer is blind; it is a strange expression, and seems to be a contradiction; but it is not so, because God accounts those that have never so much knowledge, if it do not sanctify the heart so as to give him the glory, blind. The knowledge of the saints is another kind of knowledge than other men have. We have, saith Cyprian, no such notions as many of your philosophers, but we are philosophers in our deeds, we do not speak great things, but we do great things in our lives. In 1 Thess. iv. 9, 10, you have an excellent example of this: "Ye yourselves are taught of God to love one another." What follows? "And indeed ye do it." That is an evidence that you are taught of God when it prevails with your hearts; when it may be said, indeed so you do. Who is there in the world, but knows that we should love one another? but men are not taught of God to love one another, until it may be said of them, that indeed so they do.

Philosophi sumus factis, non verbis, nec magna loquimur, sed vivimus. Cypr. de Patientia.

There is nothing more obvious to the understanding of a man than the notion of a Deity, that there is a God: we may, as it were, grope after him, as the Holy Ghost speaks; but yet, 1 John ii. 4, "He that saith, I know him, and keepeth not his commandments, is a liar, and the truth is not in him." Any man, whoever he be, though the greatest scholar in the world, if he say he knows God, and yet keeps not his commandments, he has the lie told him to his teeth, he does not know God at all. Though this be the most obvious thing to the understanding, yet Christ saith, "No man knoweth the Father, save the Son, and he to whomsoever the Son will reveal him," Matt. xi. 27. Hence, when a soul is converted, you shall hear these expressions; I never knew God before, I never knew what an infinite Deity meant, I never understood the infinite sovereignty and majesty of the great God, I never knew what sin meant before: yet if you had asked him before, he would say, I know God is a Spirit, that he is infinite and eternal; I know that sin is the transgression of the law. I never knew what Christ was before; yet before he would have told you, that Christ was the Son of Mary, and came into the world to die for sinners. A German divine, when upon his sick bed, said, In this disease I have learned what sin is, and how great the majesty of God is: this man, though a preacher, and doubtless he could preach of sin and of the majesty of God, yet he professed he knew not these things until God came powerfully upon his heart to teach him what they were. The Hebrews say, words of sense carry with them the affections, or else they are to no purpose: when men have notional knowledge, that comes not down into the heart, they are like men who have weak stomachs and heads, when they drink wine its fumes fly up to the head and make them giddy; but if the wine went to the heart, it would cheer and warm it: so all this man's knowledge flies up to his head and makes him giddy, whereas, if it were digested and got to the heart, it would warm and refresh, yea, it would sanctify it. Eli's sons, 1 Sam. ii. 12, "knew not the Lord;" they were priests of God, yet they were "sons of Belial," and "knew not the Lord." Be not offended at great scholars, who have skill in languages, arts, and sciences. Do not say, Would such great and knowing men do thus, if things were as you say? They are not *knowing* men; God saith that Eli's sons did not know the Lord: the things of God are hid from them; "I thank thee, O Father, Lord of heaven and earth, that thou hast hid these things from the wise and prudent, and hast revealed them unto babes."

Hoc morbo didici quid sit peccatum, et quanta majestas Dei. Gaspar Olevianus.

Obs. 6. Affected ignorance coming through distemper of heart, is no excuse, but rather an aggravation. "They did not know." It is a high degree of ingratitude not to prize God's mercy, but not to take notice of God's mercies, what a high ingratitude is this! That which shall be part of God's charge against sinners, can be no excuse of their sin. God threatens to cut people off, to have no mercy upon them, for want of knowing, as well as for not doing: "It is a people of no understanding; therefore he that made them will not have mercy on them, and he that formed them will show them no favour," Isa. xxvii. 11. Ambrose saith, Thou dost sin greatly, if thou dost contemn the riches of God's longsuffering, but thou sinnest most of all if thou dost not know it.

Graviter, O homo, peccas, si divitias Dei longanimitatis contemnis, gravissime si ignoras. Ambro.

Obs. 7. The not taking notice of and considering God's mercies, and laying them to heart, is the cause of vile and shameful evils in men's lives. Therefore they "did shamefully," therefore they "went after their lovers," because they "did not know:" the cause of almost all the evil in the world is from hence. "They that know thy name will trust in thee;" those who know the Lord will fear him and his goodness. Isa. i. 4, "Ah sinful nation," saith God: God fetches a sigh under the burden of it, his spirit is laden and troubled with it. What was the matter? "The ox knoweth his owner, and the ass his master's crib, but Israel doth not know, my people doth not consider," they were more stupid than the brute creatures. O sinful soul, this is the cause of all thy inordinate walking, of all thy profaneness, of all the ungodliness in thy ways, because thou dost not know, thou dost not consider, thou dost not lay to heart the ways of God towards thee. In Jer. ii. 5, God charges his people that they were "gone far from him;" and, verse 7, that they had "made his heritage an abomination." What is the reason given for both these? It is in the 6th verse, "Neither said they, Where is the Lord that brought us up out of the land of Egypt?" They did not take notice of what the Lord had done for them, therefore they were gone far from him. If thou hadst but a heart to consider what God has done for thee, it is impossible thou shouldst go so far off from God as thou dost. For these deductions are easy and obvious to any from such a principle.

1. Justice, common equity, requires living to God, seeing we live by and upon God.

2. Common ingenuousness calls for requiting good with good; the publicans and heathens will do good to those that do good to them.

3. If all be from God, then all still depends upon God.

4. How much good is there in God from whence all this good and mercy comes! When God shall show another day to men and angels, how he was the Fountain of all good, it will confound those who have not laid it to heart.

Obs. 8. God is more bountiful to his people than the idols can be.

The idols, by their own confession, gave them but their bread, and water, and flax, and oil, &c.; but God gave them wine, and silver, and gold. God gives better pay a great deal than the devil, yet the devil usually has more servants to follow him than God has, though his wages be less and worse. It is usual for men to get soldiers from adversaries, by giving them more pay: this is the way God takes, he offers a great deal better pay to those that will follow him, than they have that follow Satan, yet God can get few to follow him. This shows the vileness of man's heart against God.

Obs. 9. When men get abundance, they soon grow wanton.

When I gave them corn, and wine, and oil, and multiplied their silver and their gold, then they followed Baal. This is the reason of so many solemn charges of God. Take heed when thou art full, that thou dost not then forget the Lord. As they that are nearest the sun are the blackest, so those to whom God is nearest in regard of outward mercies, are many times blacker than others. It is observed, that the fatter men's bodies are, the less blood and the fewer spirits they have; so, often, the fatter men's estates are, the less spirit they have to any thing that is good; God has less spirit from them; sin has much more. We read of the sun melting the manna that fell down, but the same manna was able to bear the fire; so many a man's heart is able to bear affliction, and the affliction does him good, and prepares him for much good, as manna was prepared to be eaten by fire; but prosperity melts him, makes him useless. Many men, when they were poor and in a low condition, were very useful; but when they grow high and rich, they are of very little use in the places where they dwell. Trajan, the emperor, was wont to liken a man who had become rich, to the spleen in the body; for as the spleen grows big, the body grows less: so when men's estates grow bigger, they grow less useful. Evagrius notes it as a special commendation of Mauritius the emperor, that, notwithstanding his prosperity, he retained his ancient piety: it is a very rare thing to see men advanced to high places, who preserve their former devotedness.

Obs. 10. Even those creatures that wicked men abuse to their lusts, God gives them. "Which they prepared for Baal." Though he does not give them for that end, yet those creatures which they use for such an end are given of God. If thou art a drunkard, that wine or drink which thou dost sacrifice to thy lust, who giveth it thee? does not God? Thou hast a good estate more than other men, and all the use thou makest of thy estate, is merely that it might be but as fuel for thy lusts. Who gave thee this thy estate? did not God? God gives thee clothes, and thou sacrificest them to thy pride; thou hast more money than others, and so canst vent thy malice more than others; from whence hast thou this? Thou hast more strength of body than others, and thou ventest it in uncleanness; where hadst thou this? Consider this, and let this meditation prevail with thy heart to stop thee in thy sinful way; let it be seconded with the next; namely,

Obs. 11. That it is most horrible wickedness and abominable ingratitude, for any men to take God's creatures, and abuse them against God. What! "I gave them corn and wine, and multiplied their silver and their gold," and have they prepared these for Baal? God speaks of this as of a monstrous sin, as if God should say, Let all my people lament my condition, that I should do so much for them, and they do nothing for me, but all against me, sacrifice all to Baal. Some of you have been kind to your friends, and have raised them, and made them, as we say; if these men should turn your enemies, and that estate which they have obtained by you, they should use to do you a mischief, would you not call in your neighbours and friends, to join with you in lamenting your condition? What! did you ever hear of such an example, that I should do so much for them, and they turn all against me? God does so here; he makes this his grievous complaint. This is as if a bird should be shot with an arrow whose feathers came out of her own body. We should even pity a bird in that case. Many men make no other use of their estates, but to turn them against God; they are not as the slothful servant who hid his talent in the napkin, that were not such guilt; but they take their talents and employ them against God. Would it not go to your heart if one should sue you in law, and bear the charges of the suit out of your own estate? We complain, Such a man sues me, and it is my own money with which he goes to law. So thou goest against God, and he is made as it were to bear all the charges. Is it not against the light of nature? The very heathens, publicans, and sinners will do good to those that do good to them. Thou art worse than a publican and sinner: wilt thou do hurt to God who does thee good? When Julius Cæsar saw Brutus come to give him a stab in the senate house, he cried out, What thou, my son, wilt thou do it? But suppose that Julius Cæsar had given him the dagger with which he stabbed him, then, O thou, my son, what stab me with that dagger I gave thee! If, when Jonathan gave David his sword and bow, David had turned against Jonathan and killed him with his own sword and bow, would not the unkindness, or rather the abominable wickedness, have pierced deeper into his heart, than any swords or arrows possibly could? If you can find any creature that is not God's, with which to fight against him, you may do it; but if all you have is from him, it is horrible wickedness to take that, and to sacrifice it to Baal. Certainly, God gives it for other ends. To cross God's ends is an evil thing: when God aims at such a thing, for us not to join with God in the same end at which he aims, is an evil; but for us to aim at a quite contrary end, is horrible wickedness.

Καὶ σὺ τέκνον.

Obs. 12. When once superstition and idolatry have entered a place, though there be much done to oppose it, it is not easy to drive it out. Hence, God so often complains of Baal. In Judg. ii. 11, (I think that is the first place in which it is mentioned that they served Baal,) it appears that they fell off from Baal, yet they returned to him again; for in Judg. viii. 33, after Gideon's death it came to pass "that the children of Israel turned again, and went a whoring after Baalim, and made Baal-berith their god." It speaks as if it were a new thing now, that they should worship Baal after they had left worshipping him; after his death. And, 1 Sam. vii. 4, "The children of Israel did put away Baalim;" yet, if you read chap. xii. 10, they confess that they had sinned, because they had "forsaken the Lord and served Baalim;" though they had put him away before, yet he had got up again. So in 1 Kings xvi., Ahab would serve Baal; it is introduced as a novelty, because Baal had been so much suppressed. 2 Kings x., Jehu sought to destroy Baal and all his priests; but yet Baal was not so driven out, but he got in again, for 2 Kings xxiii. 4, saith, that Josiah, who was long after that time, caused the vessels that were made for Baal to be taken away and burnt.

This is seasonable for our times. If superstition be opposed, though it be cast out, as we think, in a great degree, yet, if there be not a thorough reformation, it will wind in one way or other again. If we think it enough to cut things short, and to take away their strength, and their enormities, we deceive ourselves; they will grow up again; it is but cutting the weeds a little; if branch and root be not taken away, Baal will rear up his head one way or other.

Cluverus, a late historian, yet much approved, saith, that one gave this counsel concerning Rome, when it was much annoyed with wolves; "There is no way to save Rome from wolves, but to cut down the woods wherein these wolves breed and live, for otherwise you may kill, but they will breed again." So certainly, this is the way to destroy superstition from amongst us, to take away the places and revenues of those men that have been maintainers and upholders of superstitious ways of worship. Let us, by cutting down the woods, destroy these wolves.

Ver. 9. *Therefore will I return, and take away my corn in the time thereof, and my wine in the season thereof, and will recover my wool and my flax given to cover her nakedness.*

In the former verse, Israel is accused for abusing her silver and gold in the service of Baal; now it follows, "Therefore I will take away my corn in the time thereof:" if there be a "therefore," we must inquire wherefore it was; "because they did prepare their corn," &c. for Baal.

Let us inquire, 1. What is the meaning of returning. 2. What the meaning of the time and season thereof, "and take away my corn in the time thereof, and my wine in the season thereof." 3. What that phrase imports, "I will recover my wool," &c.

1. For the first, "Therefore will I return," that is, I will change the way of my administrations toward them; I will go out of my way of mercy, and turn into my way of judgment, I will go back again. I was in a way of judgment toward them, and they cried to me, and I turned into a way of mercy; but I will go back again into a way of judgment, "I will return." Montanus remarks, Whereas God has heretofore bid them not to be afraid of all the tokens of the soothsayers; that is, when they saw by astrology some signs of death which might follow, they were afraid; Be not afraid, saith the Lord, but know your corn, and wine, and oil depend on me, not on second causes; though second causes make against you, yet fear not, for I will give you corn, and wine, and oil: but now it is quite contrary, though second causes promise all kind of plenty, so that there shall be abundance of corn, and wine, and oil, yet I will take away your plenty, there shall be a dearth of all things amongst you.

2. "I will take away my corn in the time thereof;" that is, first, in the time of harvest, just when their corn is to be gathered; and in the time of their vintage, I

will then take it away; whereas I might take it away in the seed, I will let it grow till the harvest, and then take it away. 2. In the time when they have most need of it, when they are in the greatest straits, and know not what to do without these creatures. 3. *In tempore suo*, so some, in the time I have appointed, though I have let them go on and enjoy the creatures in abundance, yet my time is come that I will take away all.

3. "And will recover;" the word הצלתי signifies, I will snatch it away, I will spoil you of it; and it has reference to two things.

First, I will recover it as out of the hands of usurpers; you have my corn, and wool, and flax, as usurpers, but I will recover them out of your hands: as a man that has his goods usurped by others, by some means recovers them; so, saith God, you have my corn and wine, and, as you have carried the matter, you are but usurpers, I will sue you for them, you shall not enjoy them long.

Secondly, "I will recover:" it has a reference to prisoners and bond-slaves; when the enemy gets any of our soldiers into their power, and makes them bond-slaves, a greater power goes against the enemy, and recovers them out of his hands; as Abraham recovered Lot and his goods, Gen. xiv. Or, as if mariners should recover those galley-slaves the Turks have taken. And as if God should say, These creatures of corn, and wine, &c., are in bondage, and I will recover them out of your hands. You know the creatures groan under their bondage while they are in the possession of wicked men. My creatures are in bondage to you, and they cry to me, and I will recover them out of your hands, Rom. viii. 22. There are many precious truths to be presented to you out of the words.

Obs. 1. Though God gives mercy out of free grace without cause in ourselves, yet he takes not away mercy without cause; there is a "therefore" for taking away mercy, but we have many mercies given without a "therefore." When God takes away mercy we have cause to look into ourselves to find out a "therefore;" but for thousands of mercies which God gives to us, you shall find never a "therefore" for them. It is not so great a wonder that thousands are in misery, as that any one enjoys mercy, for misery has a "therefore" in ourselves, for mercy there is reason only in the breast of God.

Obs. 2. Sin causes God to change the way of his administrations towards his people. Though God walk in the ways of mercy, yet sin may put him out of those ways, and make him return to a way of judgment again. How much better were it for sinners to return, than that sin should cause God to return! O sinner, return out of thy evil ways; if God return, it will be a sad return. Not long since God was in ways of judgment against us, and lately he has come into ways of mercy, and now he seems to return again to his former ways of judgment. Jer. xiv. 9 asks, "Why shouldest thou be as a man astonied?" A man astonished stands still; or if he moves, it is up and down, as if he knew not which way to go. Though we have suffered hard things, we cannot yet say, God is returned, but he seems as a man astonished, that knows not which way to go. Thus God is pleased to speak of himself after the manner of men. Let us cry to him that he may not turn out of his way of mercy into those sad ways of wrath to which he seems looking.

Obs. 3. Abuse of mercy causes the removing of mercy. "Woe to the idol shepherd that leaveth the flock! the sword shall be upon his arm, and upon his right eye: his arm shall be clean dried up, and his right eye shall be utterly darkened," Zech. xi. 17. Has God given a right hand any abilities? take heed God does not strike that right hand: or right eye, any quickness of parts? take heed that, through abuse, it be not put out. How many shepherds, when they were young, had many excellent parts, great abilities, but, having abused them to their lusts, God has taken them away! So in children, there is no such way to lose your children as to abuse them; if your hearts be inordinately set upon them, God takes them away. I will relate a remarkable providence concerning this; and the rather, because I was an eye and ear witness of it, living not far from the place. A godly man desired his friends to meet and bless God for a plentiful harvest. After dinner was over a very lovely little child came in; Ah, said the father, I am afraid I shall make a god of this child. By and by the child was missing, and when they went to look for him, he was found drowned in a pond. Consider this, ye parents, who have your hearts inordinately set on your children.

Obs. 4. God keeps the propriety of all that we have. "I will take away my corn, and my wine, and my wool, and my flax." Mark, in the former verse, they said they were their own; now, God challenges them for his. Here we have "my," "my," "my," repeated on God's side, as often as before it was on theirs. Though God gives all, yet he keeps the propriety of all in his own hand. God has a greater propriety in our estates than any prince in the world has. Subjects have propriety in their estates, and enjoy them with as true a right as their sovereigns; but no creature has any propriety in what it has, compared to God. Not only what we have, but what we do, and what we are, is all God's: yea, says Luther, Even our thanksgiving to God for gifts is a gift of God; it is therefore a very vile thing to attribute to ourselves what is his. When God has enriched us, we add this odious phrase, I have done it, I have done it. By this you may see they are not your goods which you abuse. It is a great argument to be bountiful and liberal for good uses, because what we have is God's. "For all things come of thee, and of thine own have we given thee," 1 Chron. xxix. 14. David thought not much of his bounty towards the temple, because all was God's.

Gratiarum actio, ipsa confessio donum est acceptum, quanto magis ipsa dona. Luther. Postquam locupletati sumus hanc odiosam particulam addimus, ego feci. Id.

Obs. 5. The taking away the good things which we enjoy, is a means of making us return to God. "Therefore I will take away." "Therefore" has not only reference to the abuse of them, but to the 7th verse, "And she shall follow after her lovers, but shall not overtake them," &c.: "then shall she say, I will go and return to my first husband; for then was it better with me than now." God makes this a means of working that frame of spirit in them of returning to their first husband. It is a special means to convince us of sin, when God comes with some special providence against us. Some real expression of God's displeasure works more upon us than when we merely hear the threat. You that are tradesmen, and run into debt, and your creditors tell you they will come upon you, yet you go on, till the bailiff comes into your house, and takes away your bed from under you, and all your goods. When you see all go, then you think of your negligence, and then the husband and wife wring their hands. So, though God threaten you for the abuse of the creature, that he will take it away, yet you are not sensible of it till God indeed takes away all, and then conscience begins to awake and fly in your face. When David saw God taking away his people, then his heart smote him for numbering them; he was told of the evil of his way before by Joab, but he went on in it. When Samuel prayed for rain in wheat harvest, and there came thundering and lightning, then "the people feared exceedingly," and acknowledged their sin in asking a king. Those who have abused their estates in these times, when the enemy comes, what gratings of conscience will they have! Then these thoughts will arise, Have I used my estate for God? have I done what I might have done? have I not satisfied my lusts with those things which God has now taken from me? There is usually a grating of conscience for the abuse of any thing when God takes it away. When God takes away a wife, if the husband has any tenderness of conscience, his first thoughts are, Have I performed the duties of my relation to my wife as I ought? have I not neglected my duty towards her? When he takes away a child, Have I done my duty to this child? have I prayed for it, and instructed it, as I ought? This causes sad thoughts.

Obs. 6. There is an uncertainty in all things in the world; though they promise fair, yet they are ready to fail us when they promise most. "I will take away my corn in the time thereof, and my wine in the season thereof." A husbandman who has a good seed-time, promises much to himself; it comes up and thrives, and yet at harvest it is all blasted. Hab. iii. 17, "Though the labour of the olive shall fail," the phrase is, Though the labour of the olive כחש "shall lie;" that is, the olive promised fair, it grew up, and looked very fair, and ripened; but it did lie, that is, it did not perform what it seemed to promise, for in the time thereof it vanished and came to nought. I had certain information from a reverend minister, of a singular work of God this way. In his own town there was a worldling who had a great crop of corn; a good honest neighbour walking by his corn, said, Neighbour, you have a very fine crop of corn, if God bless it. Yea, saith he, speaking contemptuously, I will have a good crop; and before he could get it into the barn, it was blasted, so that the whole crop was not worth sixpence. Here we see the uncertainty of the creature in the time thereof, when it seems to promise never so fair, when we are ready to take it into the barn, it depends on God, as well as when it is under the clods. Oh the blessedness of God's servants, who are sure of their good for time to come! We may promise ourselves certainty, even for the future, in the things of Christ; but temporal things are never sure, no, not when men have them in their hands. Many things fall out between the cup and lip, as we have it in the proverb.

Obs. 7. God often shows his displeasure to those who provoke him, when they are at the greatest height of prosperity. When affliction seems to be farthest off from them, then it comes heaviest upon them; when they think least of it, when they think all sure, then God visits them with his displeasure, when it is most bitter to them; for that is the strength of the point, he will not only take them away in the time thereof, but when the affliction shall be most grievous to them. Job saith, chap. xx. 22, "In the fulness of his sufficiency he shall be in straits." A man may seem to have sufficiency of the creature, and may have his fulness of sufficiency, yet God saith, he shall be in straits in the fulness of his sufficiency. I give you another admirable work of providence to illustrate this very thing; it came from that worthy divine, Doctor Preston, and happened in the town where he was born. There was a man who of a long time had no child, but when God gave him one, at the weaning of it he called his friends and neighbours to rejoice with him for this great mercy; and while the nurse was dandling the child, the point of a knife which she had placed in her bosom ran into its bowels, when all his friends were about him to rejoice with him. When men think the bitterness of death to be past, (as Agag did,) the curse of God comes on them. "While the meat was yet in their mouths, the wrath of God came upon them," Psal. lxxviii. 30, 31.

Pope John XXII. said, he knew by the position of the stars that he should live a long time, and boasted that he could cast his nativity; and the same night, by the fall of a chamber which he had newly built for his solace, he was slain. I have heard credibly reported, that a drunken fellow in an inn was swearing most dreadfully, and one came in and said, Sir, what if you should die now? He replied, I shall never die; and going down-stairs from his chamber, he fell down and broke his neck.

When Bibulus, a Roman, was riding in triumph in all his glory, a tile fell from a house in the street, and killed him. As, on the contrary, God's ways and dealings with the saints are such, that when their condition is most dark and gloomy, he comes with mercy to them; so, when the wicked are in the height of their prosperity, God smites them. When "the iron entered into" Joseph's "soul," God delivered him. When the apostle "had the sentence of death" in himself, God comforted him, 2 Cor. i. 9. When Abraham was lifting up his hand to slay Isaac, the angel of the Lord stayed his hand. As it is observed in nature, that a little before day-break it is darkest, so a little before the happiness of God's people, there are some great afflictions. "At evening-time it shall be light," Zech. xiv. 7.

Obs. 8. When men abuse mercies, they forfeit their right in those mercies, they are then only usurpers. "I will recover my wool," &c. They are not usurpers merely for the use of mercies, but for their abuse; they are not charged for their right to use them, but for their not using them aright: there is great difference between these two.

It has been taught by many, that all wicked men have no right at all to use any creature, but are to answer as usurpers before God. But certainly there is a mistake. It is certain, man has forfeited all, but God has given a right by donation to all that they enjoy in a lawful way. They have not such a right as the saints have, a right in Christ; once in Christ, we may challenge of God all things that are good for us. Another man has right; but how? When a malefactor is condemned to die for his offence, he has forfeited all his estate, and all the benefit of a subject. But if the king be pleased out of his bounty to allow him provision for a day or two, till the time of execution, he cannot be challenged as a usurper, for that which he has, he has it by donation: such a right all wicked men have; they are under the sentence of condemnation, and have forfeited their right, and all the good of the creature, only the Lord is pleased, out of his bounty, to give them such and such enjoyments, they shall have such houses and such lands for a time, till the day of execution comes.

This might daunt the hearts of wicked men: You look upon yourselves as great men, you have your shops full, you have large estates; you are like some malefactors, who have a better supper before execution than others. But, still, your not using them aright may make you usurpers before God. You command your servant to buy certain commodities; suppose your servant run away with your money, do you not follow him as a thief? you trust him with a stock, to keep such markets, he has right to use your estate for you, but if he run away with your estate, and use it against you, if you meet with him again you will say, What a thief are you to run away with your master's estate, and abuse it against him! "I will recover my wool," &c.

Obs. 9. All the time the creature serves wicked men, it is in bondage, and God looks upon it with pity. God has made all things for his own praise. He gives the children of men many mercies, but for his own glory; when therefore these creatures which were given for the glory of God, are abused to thy lust, the creature groans under thee. Thou drinkest wine, but the creature groans under thy abuse; never any galley slave groaned more under the bondage of the Turks, than thy wine and thy dishes on thy table groaned under thy abuse, Rom. viii. 22. As God hears the cry of the widow and fatherless, so he hears the groans of the creature.

Cornelius à Lapide states, that a famous preacher, showing this bondage of the creature, brings in the creatures complaining thus: Oh that we could serve such as are godly! Oh that our substance and our flesh might be incorporated into godly people, that so we might rise into glory! but if our flesh be incorporated into the flesh of sinners, we shall go to hell; and would any creature go to hell? The very creatures shall be in hell eternally which wicked men consume on their lusts, being incorporated into their bodies. The creature one day will have a kind of revenge upon ungodly men, and divers think that hell will be a turning all creatures into a chaos, into a confusion again, as at the first, and the wicked put into that, and so tormented there; there shall not be an annihilation, but God shall take away all the beauty, comfort, and glory of the creature, and whatever shall be for the torment of ungodly men shall abide; and so they shall be tormented eternally by the very creatures which they abuse.

As in such a building as this, there are stones and mortar, and the art of man puts a beauty upon them; but suppose all the art of man were taken away from this building in an instant, what would become of us then? it would bury us in its rubbish; now it is useful and delightful, but if the art were taken away, it would be our destruction. So the creatures of God, which God suffers wicked men to enjoy, have much of God's wisdom, power, and goodness in them; but God will take away all his wisdom, beauty, and goodness, so that nothing but the confusion and rubbish of the creature shall be upon the wicked to all eternity.

Obs. 10. God gives his blessings to us, not for luxury, but for necessity. "I will recover my wool and my flax given to cover her nakedness." Therefore when our Saviour teaches us to pray, it is for daily bread, or bread which is for our substance; so much bread as serves for our substance, and that but for a day. Most are abusive in their desires after and use of the creature, they look at luxury rather than necessity. As Cyprian observes, It is not the heat of their clothes, *non calor*, but *color*, the colour, is rather regarded by many. God expects now, especially, that we should cut off our superfluities, when our brethren want necessaries.

Ἄρτον ἐπιούσιον.

"To cover her nakedness." Our nakedness needs a covering. Sin has made nakedness shameful. Hence, our bodies are called vile bodies; those bodies that we study so much to pamper and adorn, are bodies of vileness, as the apostle speaks, Phil. iii. 21; yea, of that vileness, with an article, or of the vileness: to be proud of our clothes that cover our nakedness is an unreasonable thing. Would you have your bodies adorned? labour for godliness, and then you shall have bodies like the glorious body of Jesus Christ; you will then have bodies that shall not finally need a covering.

Τὸ σῶμα τῆς ταπεινώσεως.

Obs. 11. When abundance is abused, it is just with God that we should want necessaries. "I will take away my corn," &c. How many are there who have lavished out their estates, upon whom you may see God's judgment so grievous that they want a piece of bread! You often tell your wasting servants, they will be glad of a crust before they die; it proves true often of masters and mistresses also, who, out of pride and delicacy of spirit, will be so fine and live above their rank, that God blasts them that they have not to cover their nakedness. Those who had gorgeous and splendid attire, are threatened with "baldness," and "a girding with sackcloth," Isa. iii. 24; and such as come to misery by their wasting superfluity have none to pity them.

Alfonsus, king of Spain, when a knight, fell into want, and being arrested for debt, a petition was sent to the king to succour him: Yes, replied the king, if he had spent his estate in my service, or in that of the commonwealth, it were reasonable he should be provided for by me, or by the commonwealth, but seeing he has spent all in riotousness, let him suffer.

Consider this, you who are so loth to part with your estates for the public good; you murmur at every thing required of you for that, but you are profuse in expenses for your lust; God has ways to bring you low enough in your estates.

Ver. 10. *And now will I discover her lewdness in the sight of her lovers, and none shall deliver her out of mine hand.*

"And now," that is, when I recover my wool and flax, "I will discover her lewdness;" I will take their coverings from their own eyes, and from the eyes of others. Wicked men, and especially idolaters, have divers coverings for their lewdness. These people had three.

The first was their outward prosperity: Do you speak so bitterly against us, as if we were idolaters, as if we had forsaken God? are we not in as good a condition as Judah, who you say has not forsaken God?

Secondly, their external worship, in that they yet retained something according to God's mind, they yet kept the sabbath and some solemn days according to the law, in this covering they rested; as if they should say, Why do you accuse us as if we did not worship the true God? have not we God's service with us, and our solemn assemblies?

Thirdly, they had other services which were not God's, yet they covered them with pompous days of solemnity, pretended for God; but being of their own invention, they were hateful. Well, saith God, I will take away your prosperity, and I will take away those things in which you think to put me off, I will take away your solemnities, and all the pomp in your services.

"I will discover their lewdness." The word נבלתה lewdness, comes from נבל which signifies to fall; it intimates the falling of the spirit to low, poor, vile, and unworthy things. Hence the Hebrews use it for a fool; one that has a vile spirit, set upon base, contemptible things, is Nabal, a fool. Hence that speech of Abigail concerning her husband, As is his name, so is he; he is Nabal, and folly is with him. The Seventy translate this by another word, which signifies uncleanness, the mixture of their spirits with vile things that make them unclean. The English word lewd, comes from *loed*, an old Saxon word, which signifies one that is of a servile disposition. Some are of servile spirits naturally, they are born to a kind of servility; they are inclined to baseness and vileness by their natural genius: others are of more sublime spirits naturally, as if they were born for great things: these people are lewd, they have vile spirits, forsaking the blessed God and his glorious ways, turning to vanities that can do no good. So we say of many, they are lewd, base fellows, that is, they are of such sordid dispositions, that they seek only after such things as have no worth in them, and satisfy themselves with things beneath the excellency of a man, unseemly in a rational creature to take content. The Greek word in Acts xviii. 10, translated lewdness, elegantly sets forth the disposition of a lewd man, namely, one easily drawn to any wicked way.

ἀκαθαρσίαν.

Ῥᾳδιούργημα, ἁ ῥᾴδιον, καὶ ἐργάζομαι.

"I will discover her lewdness in the sight of her lovers." "In the sight;" this is a great aggravation of their shame. God will discover them, not before those who are strangers, but those before whom they would be honoured. Calvin's remark seems to reach the meaning of the Holy Ghost, alluding to harlots who have favourites with princes at the court for their lovers; they rest on their power, and confide on their greatness, and care not what their husbands can do against them.

I will take away their confidence, though their lovers, the Assyrians and Egyptians, be never so great, they shall have no power to help you, but I will discover your lewdness before their face. From hence take these observations.

Obs. 1. All wickedness, and especially idolatry, has many covers. Except we look very narrowly to those who are superstitious and idolatrous, we shall not see the evil of that sin. Some covers are subtilly woven, but it may be said of them all, as Isa. xxviii. 20, "The bed is shorter than that a man can stretch himself on it, and the covering narrower than that he can wrap himself in it."

First, Prosperity in a sinful way is a great cover. This glitters in so many men's eyes, that the filth of sin is hid; many a foul hand is under a fair, perfumed glove; an ill complexion may have a painted face, and prosperity is no other to wicked men than a painted face to a foul woman. As a painted face is no argument of a fair complexion, so neither is prosperity, of a good condition. Crooked and diseased bodies may have fine clothes. Green leaves on a tree may hide the rifts, the mosses, and blackness of the body which appears in winter. Many men are abominably false in their ways, cruel and bloody in their hearts against God and good men, their spirits are envenomed, they have given up themselves to most horrible sins; yet so long as they have power about them, all is covered: were all their prosperity taken from them, and all their glory and greatness, and nothing but their falsehood and hatred of the ways of God appeared, what dreadful creatures they would be!

Secondly, Retaining some truths in worship is a great cover to much falseness. When some wicked persons have to pay a great sum, they shuffle in a counterfeit sixpence or shilling, or a light piece of gold: so some, though they retain many errors, yet because they keep some truths, think to cover much superstition. False wares will be holpen off amongst good, and a man accustomed to falsehood will sometimes tell some truths to put off a lie. A man that is a base self-seeker will often deny himself; the proudest spirits are as crouching and subject to their superiors as any, and so by seeming humility cover a great deal of pride. So the evil of ceremonies, and false discipline, pass without much contradiction: You must not trouble yourself about these things; have not we as wholesome, soul-saving doctrine as any church in the world? Because of this the corruption of the other is covered. Much hypocrisy is covered under excellent gifts; the gifts are gifts of God's Spirit, but they often cover much vileness.

Thirdly, Outward, pompous devotion in God's worship is a great colour of notorious idolatry. Gilded crosses, painted churches, pompous ceremonies, have covered the most desperate hatred to the power of godliness.

Obs. 2. God has a time to discover wickedness. "I will discover thy lewdness," it shall appear one day in its colours! Vile and abominable wickedness shall not always go uncovered. God will not discover her infirmities, neither should we; we should do as God does, discover the lewdness of men, but not their infirmities. Love covers a multitude of faults, if they be but infirmities. And when you discover the lewdness of others, take heed you do not discover your own lewdness at the same time. Many who discover the lewdness of other men, manifest such bitterness of spirit, and such rejoicing that they have obtained an advantage against those who are religious, that, whether true or false they care not, they relate it confidently. This is for men to discover their own lewdness, when they cry out against the lewdness of others. Those who are wise and discerning are able easily to see it; but if we would not have God discover our lewdness, let us get such a cover as shall never be uncovered. You may have many expedients to cover your sins that are not large enough, but I will tell you of a cover amply sufficient to cover all. What is that? The righteousness of Jesus Christ. "Blessed is he whose transgression is forgiven, whose sin is covered," Psal. xxxii. 1. That is a cover which hides from the eyes of God and man for ever.

Obs. 3. When God discovers men's lewdness, they shall do little hurt. "I will discover her lewdness in the sight of her lovers." I will take such a way to manifest her vile lewdness before her lovers, that she shall neither prevail with them, nor be upheld by them. "But they shall proceed no further: for their folly shall be manifest unto all men," 2 Tim. iii. 9. There are many men who have secretly gained on the spirits of others by fair pretences, that they seek nothing but the public good, and desire only the furtherance of the gospel; but when opportunity serves, their intentions are discovered to go another way than their words seem to import, and then they shall proceed no further, for they shall be vile and contemptible in the eyes of those with whom they prevailed before.

Obs. 4. When God sets himself against his enemies, he will go through his work in the face of all those that seek the contrary. "In the sight of her lovers." God needs no tricks or devices to carry on his work, but he can carry it on in the sight of his adversaries, and shame them in the sight of their lovers, and bring them down. God can make use of the wisdom and policy of men, nor less of their indiscretion. The great works of God amongst us of late have been carried on with a high hand, in the sight of those who have been our adversaries: what discoveries have there been of the filth of men! how has their nakedness been made naked! what changes in their conditions! what contempt has God cast in the face of those who were the great champions for lewdness, and that in the very face of their lovers! Their lovers looked on them, there was little or no change in their hearts, which were as eager for them as ever, yet their shame has been discovered.

Obs. 5. Dishonour before those from whom we expect honour, is a sad and great evil. "In the sight of her lovers." Oh, said Saul, honour me before the people, 1 Sam. xv. 30. Saul cared not much if he were dishonoured before strangers, but he would be honoured before his own people. It is such a disgraceful thing to be dishonoured before those by whom we would be honoured, that the stronger a man's spirit is, the more intolerable is the burden: one of a mean and low spirit cares not much for dishonour any where, but a man of elevated spirit counts it the worst thing that can happen, to be dishonoured before those that love him. Many tradesmen who are modest at home are lewd among strangers. Those who love God and the saints, are most afraid to have their evil discovered before God and the saints, for a gracious heart desires honour from them most. A godly man can bear any contemptuous abuse from the profane, rather than from one that is godly. Wicked men care not for dishonour among the saints, because they care not for their love. If dishonour before lovers be such a shame, what will dishonour before God at the great day be, and before the saints, and wicked men too who were your lovers!

Obs. 6. Carnal friends esteem men when they are in prosperity, but when they are in adversity they contemn them. "I will discover her lewdness in the sight of her lovers." When I take away their corn, and wine, and flax, and these things, their lovers will be ashamed of them. When huntsmen would single out a deer, they shoot her first, and as soon as the blood appears, all the rest go out of her company, and push her from them. It is so with carnal friends, if a man is in affliction, if they see their friend shot, they look aloof from him. We have had woeful experience of this formerly; when many godly ministers were persecuted, those who before seemed to be their lovers, grew strange unto them. When the sun shines, men that pass by look on a dial; but in a dark, stormy day, a hundred may ride by it and never look at it. When we are in a sun-shine day of prosperity, men will look towards us; but if the gloomy day of adversity come, then they pass by without regard to us. If a man of fashion come to a house, the dogs will be quiet; but when a beggar comes in rags, they fly upon him. It is apparent, that men in their prosperity are not regarded for any thing in themselves, but for their prosperity's sake, for their money's sake, for their clothes' sake. Suppose when you go to a friend's house, and your servant accompany you, if all the respect and kindness shown to you were only for your servant's sake, you would take it ill. This is all the respect that men have from false lovers, it is not for any good in them, it is for their prosperity, for their servant's sake. Oh how vain is respect from the world! If you be gracious, God will not deal with you thus; if you have your estates taken from you, God will not despise you as carnal friends do. "For he hath not despised nor abhorred the affliction of the afflicted," Psal. xxii. 24. When the saints are afflicted, God does not hide his face from them, but when they cry to him he hears them.

Obs. 7. Carnal hearts have much confidence in many things in which they trust; in time of danger they will not believe but they shall escape. "None shall deliver her out of my hand." Let us not be troubled at the confidence of our enemies; they expect to prevail; this is from the curse of God upon them; their case is never so desperate, but they have something to shelter themselves in their own thoughts. Oh what a shame is it that any thing is rather trusted in than God! The husbandman casts seed-corn, that costs dearer than other corn, into the ground. The merchant trusts all his estate to the winds and waves of the sea, and if they fail, all is gone. You trust servants with matters of weight. If you go to Westminster, you trust your lives in a boat half an inch thick. God is not trusted so much; that blessed God, who is the only true object of soul-confidence.

Obs. 8. Lastly, when God sets himself against a generation of men, or any individual, all the means in the world shall not help. The prophet Ezekiel (chap. ix.) had a vision of six men with weapons of war in their hands; there were six principal gates in Jerusalem, and God would set these six men with weapons in their hands at each gate, that if they run to this, or the other, or any gate, the man with the weapon in his hand should be sure to take them, they should not escape. "Seek him that maketh the seven stars and Orion," Amos v. 8; why are these named, "the seven stars and Orion?" the one is the extreme of cold, and the other of heat. The Lord has the power of both: if they escape the heat, the cold shall take them; if the cold, the heat shall destroy them; and I, likewise, saith the Lord, can make both these helpful to you as I please. Hence there is such blasting of means, for the cursing of those whom God opposes; let us not be afraid, though our adversaries have great assistance, they are in God's hand, and none can deliver out of his hand; all their great strength is but as tow or flax before the flame of fire. "There is none that can deliver out of my hand: I will work, and who shall let it?" Isa. xliii. 13. Wherefore it is a fearful thing to fall into the hand of God when he is in a way of wrath, and it is a blessed thing to be in his hand when he is in a way of mercy. Christ holds the stars, not only ministers, but all his elect, in his hand, and none can take them out. In the time of the massacre at Paris, a poor man for his deliverance crept into a hole, and when he was there a spider wove a cobweb before the hole. When the officers came to search for him, one observed, Certainly he is got into that hole. No, said another, he cannot be there, for there is a cobweb over the place; and by this means the poor man was preserved. The hope of the wicked, Job saith, chap. viii. 14, is as the spider's web; yet, if God please, he can make a cobweb to deliver his people. The least things shall deliver when he will, and the greatest means of deliverance shall not deliver when he pleases.

Ver. 11. *I will also cause all her mirth to cease, her feast days, her new moons, and her sabbaths, and all her solemn feasts.*

In this verse we have a sore threat against Israel, for it is in part spiritual.

"Her mirth," משושה εὐφροσύνας, Sept. The word signifies the right temper and posture of the mind; when the mind is in a right frame, then it may be merry; Whosoever is merry, let him sing, James v. 13; the word, though not the same, signifies the same thing; whoever has his mind in a right frame, let him sing. εὐθυμεῖ.

"I will cause *all* her mirth." God many times takes away from his saints much of the matter of their mirth, but never takes away all. This is a dreadful threat, to cause all their mirth to cease.

"I will cause it to cease." I will turn it away, Ἀποστρέψω, Sept. I can soon have all their mirth down, they shall never be able to rejoice more if I please; it is gone with the turn of a hand. It appears that Israel, though an apostatizing people, designed to dreadful judgments, yet were a merry, jocund people, they went on still in their mirth and joviality.

That which is here implied, is more fully expressed in Amos, chap. vi. 4—6, who was contemporary with Hosea, and, like Hosea, he was the prophet of the ten tribes: see there how Amos sets forth the mirth of this people; "That lie upon beds of ivory, and stretch themselves upon their couches, and eat the lambs out of the flock, and the calves out of the midst of the stall; that chant to the sound of the viol, and invent to themselves instruments of music, like David; that drink wine in bowls, and anoint themselves with the chief ointments." This was their condition when they were under such fearful guilt, and in such dreadful danger. Sensual men, while they prosper, look upon themselves as above the word, and bless themselves in satisfying their own carnal desires, as if it were but a poor, low, and mean thing for them to fear sin and threatenings. Come, say they, let us sing away all care, let us live merrily, let us take our pleasure for the present, and crown ourselves with rose-buds. This is the disposition of carnal hearts under all their guilt and danger. They swim delightfully in that river of Jordan, and suddenly fall into the Dead Sea; they spend their days in pleasure, and in a moment go down into hell. This is all the portion of their cup which they receive from the Lord. They have a little joy here, this is all they are like to have, and therefore they will take their fill of what they have. But this will not hold, I will cause this mirth to cease.

Obs. 1. Sin and mirth can never hold long together; there must be a separation between them. The union between sin and mirth at any time is a forced union; God never joins them together; and if you will join those things that God never joined, your joining cannot hold: sin is of such a canker-fretting nature, that it will soon fret out all the varnish of mirth and joy upon it. If you will not take away sin from your mirth, God will take away mirth from your sin. It is the happiness of the saints that they shall have everlasting joy; the "pleasures at God's right hand" are "for evermore," but the pleasures of sin must cease.

Obs. 2. When afflictions come upon the wicked they are all dejected, their joy and mirth are gone. We say of fire, it congregates things of the same kind, and separates things that are of diverse kinds. So the fire of affliction congregates things of the same nature, as sin, horror, trouble, anguish, sorrow, vexation, accusation of conscience, condemnation; these are of the same kind; sin and these are homogeneal: now, when affliction comes, it congregates all these: you sin, but sorrow, anguish, and horror of conscience seem now not to unite with your sin; but when the fire of affliction comes, it joins all these together. On the other side, sin, and joy, prosperity, and peace, these are heterogeneous things of another kind; now when the fire of affliction comes, it separates these heterogeneous things; then the hearts of the wicked sink as lead, they lie down in sorrow, the candle of the wicked is blown out, all their mirth and joy are but the light of a candle, affliction makes all to be but as a snuff. When affliction comes, ungodly men have the poorest spirits of any men, they quickly die, they succumb, they fall down under the least weight of affliction; they seem to outbrave the word of God, but they have mean and low spirits when they bear God's hand upon them; affliction takes away all that they conceive and understand good. There is nothing within them to support them, but darkness and blackness; nothing but guilt and the gnawings of the worm: they look upon every suffering they endure but as the beginning of eternal suffering; and the venom and curse of God go with their affliction, which drinks up their spirits.

Oh the happy advantage which the saints have in their afflictions above the wicked! They have spirits that may well be called brave spirits, which can stand under the greatest weight of affliction, and with joy in the midst of them. Paul can rejoice in tribulation, yea, and glory in it too. They have comfort in the creature, but they are not beholden to the creature for comfort; they depend not upon the creature, their joy is a great deal higher: that is precious light indeed, that no storm can blow out. See an example of a brave spirit, that in the midst of affliction can have the light of joy, Hab. iii. 17, 18: "Although the fig tree shall not blossom, neither shall fruit be in the vines; the labour of the olive shall fail, and the fields shall yield no meat; the flock shall be cut off from the fold, and there shall be no herd in the stalls:" what then? "yet I will rejoice in the Lord, I will joy in the God of my salvation." Perhaps in times of affliction they may abate somewhat of their outward joy, but all their mirth shall not cease, there shall be joy within, though none without.

Obs. 3. All our mirth depends upon God, he can take it away when he pleases. "I will cause all their mirth to cease." God is called in Scripture, "The God of all consolation." Joy is God's propriety, he gives it when he will, and takes it away when he will. "Give them sorrow of heart, thy curse unto them," Lam. iii. 65. Mark, the word מגנת translated sorrow, comes from one which signifies a helmet, or a shield to fence off any thing, or to cover a thing, as a thing is covered by a shield and helmet; and it notes to us that disease which physicians call *cardiaca passio*, a disease whereby the heart is so oppressed, and there is such a stopping, that it is, as it were, covered *sicut scuto*, as with a shield, to keep out all things that should comfort the spirits: let the most precious cordials in the world be given to those who have that disease, they cannot be refreshed by any of them; and so the heart is at last suffocated with sorrow. This is the meaning of the word here, Lord, "give them sorrow of heart;" put them in such a condition, that their hearts may be so stopped and stifled with sorrow, that whatever means shall be used to bring any comfort to them, no creature in the world may be able to afford the least refreshment. They were wont to shield and fence off thy word, which contains the treasures of thy mercies, and they heard the sweet promises of the gospel opened, yet they fenced off thy word as with a shield; now, when they are in affliction, let there be such a fence put upon their hearts, that though there be never so many promises brought to them, they may be fenced off by thy secret curse. We find many wretches who have lived under the gospel, and resisted the treasures of mercies when opened to them, who in affliction have been in horrible desperation, and whenever any comforts of the gospel have been presented to them, they have ingeniously fenced them off. Those who read the story of Spira, will wonder what cunning he possessed to fence off all comfort that was brought to him. This was from the Lord. Lord, "give them sorrow of heart," that is, Lord, put such a shield upon their hearts, as all comfort may be fenced off from them.

We see, my brethren, how we depend upon God for comfort; we all cry for comfort, let us know our dependence upon God for it; God can fence our hearts from comfort when he pleases, let us take heed we do not fence off his word from our hearts.

"I will cause all her mirth to cease, her feast days." These two are put together; for the hearts of men, when they enjoy a more liberal use of the creature than ordinary, and are amongst cheerful company, are warmed, raised, and inflamed. If the heart of a man be gracious, and he feasts in a gracious way, his heart is warmed and cheered, and enlarged in things that are good; so the hearts of the wicked, when they are at their feasts, their lusts are warmed, and their spirits are raised and strengthened in things that are evil. You have a notable example of cheering and raising the hearts of men in good things, in the time of the feast that Hezekiah made for the people of Jerusalem in that great passover, they "kept the feast of unleavened bread seven days with great gladness: the whole assembly took counsel to keep other seven days: and they kept other seven days with gladness," 2 Chron. xxx. 21, 23. Now mark how their hearts were raised mightily by this; chap. xxxi. 1, "Now when all this was finished, all Israel that were present went out to the cities of Judah, and brake the images in pieces, and cut down the groves, and threw down the high places and the altars out of all Judah and Benjamin, in Ephraim also and Manasseh, until they had utterly destroyed them all." Their feasts being in a gracious way, their hearts were so inflamed that now they took upon them a mighty courage in doing great things for God.

It were well if it were always so with us when God calls us to feasting, that our hearts were always warmed and enlarged to do much good. That has been the honour of this city, that in their companies feasting yearly, they were wont when their hearts were up, to consult together what good to do for the countries in which they were born, and then to resolve to send the preaching of the word to one great town, and to another town. This was a gracious feasting, and for this they were much envied. And though these feasts were prohibited upon other pretences, yet the hindering this good done at those times, lay at the bottom of that prohibition.

Feasting also warms the lusts and desperately inflames the wicked resolutions of ungodly men. When a company of ungodly men get together in a tavern, and there have drunk and eat liberally, how desperately are they set against the ways of godliness! then they scorn and jeer godly ministers, and parliament, and Christians: when their lusts are heated by wine and good cheer, they are then as if they were above God, their tongues are their own, and who shall control them? Mark that Scripture, Psal. xxxv. 16, "With hypocritical mockers in feasts, they gnashed upon me with their teeth." Here is scorning and violence, gnashing upon the psalmist with their teeth, and this at their feasts. Hos. vii. 5, "In the day of our king the princes have made him sick with bottles of wine: he stretched out his hand with scorners." They brought bottles of wine, and when his lusts were heated with the wine and good cheer, he joined with them in scorning the ways and worship of God; they scorned at all those that would go up to Jerusalem to worship according to the institution, These must be so precise that they will not join with us, as if we had not the worship of God among us; they tell tales to Jeroboam, and the other princes, of the godly who would not yield to their idolatrous ways of worship: now, saith the text, the king "stretched out his hand with scorners;" takes them by the hand, and encourages them, and tells them he will take a course with them, not one of them shall be suffered to live in his dominions.

But God has a time to take away feasting times from a people, a time when those who have delighted themselves so in the use of the creatures, shall have all those merry meetings cease, never feast more, never meet with such merry company more. As Pope Adrian said, when he was dying, O my soul, whither art thou going? thou shalt never be merry any more.

Animula mea vagula, blandula, quo vadis? non amplius jocos dabis, &c.

For kingdoms also, though there be times for feasting, yet there is a time of mourning; and God seems this day to be coming to us to take away our feasts, to call upon us to spend our time in another way. It were good for us to do what we can to prevent God by voluntarily humbling ourselves, to take away our own feasts, and to change our festivities into humiliations. The times call for fasting now, rather than feasting; and it is a most dreadful sin for men to give liberty to themselves for feasting, when God calls for mourning and fasting. You are not at liberty to feast when you will. Isa. xxii. 12—14, might make the hearts of those who are guilty of this tremble: "And in that day did the Lord God of hosts call to weeping, and to mourning, and to baldness, and to girding with sackcloth: and behold joy and gladness, slaying oxen, and killing sheep, eating flesh, and drinking wine: let us eat and drink; for to-morrow we shall die. Surely this iniquity shall not be purged from you till ye die, saith the Lord God of hosts." While the bread is taken away from our brethren, and the land is miserably spoiled, and when such a black cloud hangs over our heads, there is no time for festivities. Whatever your customs have been, at the time now approaching, (I mean that which you call your Christmas festivity,) you are certainly bound to turn it into a time of mourning. For if we should grant it lawful for men to appoint holy days for feasting, yet certainly it cannot but be sinful, so to set those days apart, that whatever providence of God happens they must be observed. You will all grant this, that if it be lawful to keep this time of festivity, yet that God has not set it apart and enjoined it. We never have it required by Christ or by his apostles, that at the beginning of the year we should have days of festivity. Well then, at the most, if we suppose it lawful, it is but the institution of man; if it be man's institution, then it must give way to God's work, to providence. For man to put so much upon his institution, because he has appointed such a day at the commencement of the year for rejoicing, that whatever providence happens that calls for humiliation and fasting, yet he will hold to his own institution; what is this, my brethren, but to make the commandments of God to be of none effect through man's traditions? It is the commandment of God now, that you should mourn and fast; if then, because of man's institution, you put by the command of God, and spend time in feasting and rejoicing, which ought to be only when God shines upon a kingdom in ways of mercy, know this is sin unto you. If you can say that God shines upon us now in present extraordinary mercies, then we may feast. I confess they are extraordinary mercies in regard of what we may hope to be the event and effect of them; but for the present administrations of God towards us, they are such as, if ever they called for fasting, they call for it at this day. Therefore, by God's works amongst us, we know we have God's will revealed to us, namely, to fast; the other, at most, is but man's institution and tradition. Now the traditions of men must yield to the commandments of God.

With what conscience now can you take such a plentiful use of the creature, and suffer your brethren to want clothes and bread? If God have granted you such a comfortable estate that you have so much to spare as to feast, know you are bound in conscience to lay that out in relieving your brethren who have been so cruelly used; therefore God brings them to you to be objects of your compassion. It would be very acceptable to God, if so much as any of you have usually spent in feastings, or intended to spend in these twelve days, you would set it apart for the relief of those who want bread, and set the time apart also for mourning in your families, that God would pardon the sin of these times. And now, not only feasts in private families should cease, but the feasts of companies in your public halls likewise.

What abundance of poor plundered people might be relieved, if all that were spent in one year in the feasts of your companies were laid aside for their use! These are times for mercy, not for festivity; if we will not cease our feastings, let us know, God has thousands of ways to take away feasts from a kingdom, and to bring "cleanness of teeth" among us: I will take away their feasts, saith the Lord.

The main thing in this verse to be opened to you is, what these feasts of the Jews were.

The words here are חגה feasts, and מועדה, solemn feasts; they are both in your English translated feasts, but the words in the Hebrew differ much, the first comes from a word that signifies to rejoice and leap, the second from a word that signifies a stated, a settled time; our English word feast is derived from the Greek *ἑστία*, the goddess which the Latins call Vesta, the goddess both of the earth and of fire.

The Jews had their civil feasts, and their holy feasts. Amongst their holy feasts, some were of God's appointment, and some of their own. Of God's appointment, some were more solemn, some less.

Their civil feasts were times wherein they took a more liberal use of the creature, in rejoicing one with another upon some special occasion, this they called a good day, not a holy day; Esth. viii. 17, "The Jews had joy and gladness, a feast and a good day." It will appear by examining that text, that though the day was appointed to be kept every year, yet it was but as a good day to them, and could not be said to be a holy-day; we do not read of any religious solemn exercise that they had for the day. Such a day I take to be our fifth of November, a good day, not a holy-day, wherein we have a more liberal use of the creature than at other times, and remember the mercies of God with thanksgiving. But we know the day is not set apart for this end, so that it is unlawful to be exercised in any other thing.

Their religious feasts, which they presumed themselves to make holy, were *their* feasts, rather than God's; for that, you have the example of Jeroboam, he appointed a feast of his own head, which the prophet speaks of, 1 Kings xii. 32, 33, "And Jeroboam ordained a feast in the eighth month, on the fifteenth day of the month, like unto the feast that is in Judah. So he offered upon the altar which he had made in Beth-el the fifteenth day of the eighth month, even in the month which he had devised of his own heart; and ordained a feast unto the children of Israel." Mark here, Jeroboam is rebuked for appointing a feast of his own heart, like the feast God had appointed; this is no excuse, that he would be an imitator of God. This reason, many think, will justify their superstitious way, they do but imitate what God did; as thus, God had an ephod for the priests, therefore they will have a holy garment; God had a temple consecrated, they will have one so too; God had his feast days and holy-days, they will have theirs too in imitation of God. This very thing that Jeroboam did, he is rebuked for, that he would set up something as God did.

Where God has set his stamp upon any thing, we must take heed we presume not to set our own stamp. Suppose any one should take a piece of silver, and stamp it as near as he can like the king's coin. The silver is his own; well, but if he be examined, Why did you thus? What hurt, saith he, is there in it? I have done no more than the king did; why, may we not follow his example? Will this answer, think you, serve his turn? It is as much as his life is worth. Just such a plea is this, they will do such and such things in God's worship; why? God has done so before, and they do but imitate God; there is as much strength in the one as in the other. Therefore that word "devised" in the Hebrew comes from a word that signifies to lie, Jeroboam did lie. So in Isa. xliv. 25, "That frustrateth the tokens of the liars." Jeroboam, in setting this day apart, did it under a pretence to honour and worship God; but though it might seem to make God's honour and worship better than before, yet the Scripture puts the lie upon it. I think this was the reason he set it apart in the eighth month; the feast of tabernacles was the fifteenth day of the seventh month; now he would not alter the day, but have it the same day that God appointed, but in the eighth month. The feast of tabernacles was appointed to praise God for the in-gathering of the fruits of the earth. It was as upon our September; now, upon the fifteenth of September, perhaps, all the produce was not gathered in, therefore Jeroboam might have this device, he would stay till every thing was gathered into their barns and their vessels, and was fit to eat and to drink; then saith Jeroboam, Now is the time to praise God; you praised God before when you were taking in the fruits, you could not use them, but now having them all in, and being able to make use of them, now is the time to praise God. This was Jeroboam's wisdom, by which he thought to make a feast to please the people, rather than God's feast. There are no superstitious men but will have some plea to induce the hearts of people to embrace their ways, rather than God's simple, plain, and pure ordinances. But though Jeroboam did it under this pretence, yet he lied; so, those men who will take upon them to sanctify days, or places, or garments, or any vesture, that God never did, though they say they do it for God's honour, to make God's worship more glorious and decent, yet it is a lie. Just as those who will make images, brave, golden images of God, O, say they, it is for the honour of God; but mark what is said, Hab. ii. 18, "What profiteth the graven image that the maker thereof hath graven it; the molten image and a teacher of lies?" If images be laymen's books, they are books that have abundance of errata in them, they are full of lies.

בדא
בדים
Mendaces.

Now arises the question, whether there may be holy feasts (taken so in a proper sense) by man's appointment? Jeroboam is accused of it plainly: and in Gal. iv. 10, 11, there is a very severe charge upon the Galatians, "Ye observe days, and months, and times, and years. I am afraid of you, lest I have bestowed upon you labour in vain." It appears by this, that people's hearts were mightily set upon their feasts, their days, and months, and years, they were loth to be taken off from them; so that the apostle speaks with bitterness of spirit, "I am afraid of you, lest I have bestowed upon you labour in vain." And indeed when godly ministers take pains amongst people whose hearts are set upon such things as these, for the most part they lose their labour, little good is done.

Yes, some will say, to observe the Jewish days after they were abolished by God, was sinful and dangerous. but we do not keep Jewish days. But mark what these men say, God abolishes his own, and yet they think he gives liberty to man to set up others. If upon God's abolishing his own, men have liberty to set up theirs, then Christians are under a more heavy bondage, and grievous pedagogy, than ever the Jews were, for it is better to have a hundred days of God's appointing, than one of man's, and more honourable. Further, if God appoint, there needs no scruple, as if man appoint: yea, if God appoint, we may expect a special blessing, and efficacy, and presence of God; we cannot expect such things in man's appointment. Now, if when God has taken away Jewish ceremonies and days, man might lawfully appoint others as he pleases, we may pray to God with good reason to bring us under the bondage of the law again, rather than to be thus under man's power.

Thus far we grant, that upon any special work of God, the revolution of the year naturally reminds of it; and so far as it is natural, it is good, I may make use of it. Therefore, I dare not say that it is altogether unlawful at such times to have some outward rejoicing, when God does not call for mourning some other way (except the argument from the extraordinary abuse there has been of it may be of force). Nay, that there may be advantage taken of the people's leisure, to preach the word and to hear sermons upon such days, we deny not. We know that Christ was in the porch of the temple at the feast of dedication, which was one of the days of their own appointing, not that he was there to countenance or honour the feast, but because he had been there before, at another feast of God's appointment. Now there being a multitude of people at that time also gathered together, he took advantage of the concourse, to come to the outer porch to preach to them. So much therefore as we may grant, we will not deny.

For the right understanding of setting apart days, I suppose these two things will be questioned.

First, Why may not governors of the church set apart days, as well as appoint times for preaching; or as well as others who appoint such times, as once a week so much time set apart for a lecture?

Secondly, We may appoint fast days, and days of thanksgiving, these are set apart by man: how happens it that a man may appoint a time for preaching constantly once a week, and he may appoint times of fasting, and days of thanksgiving, and yet not have this liberty, to make a day that may properly be called a holy-day?

We must clear that point from this objection, or else we do nothing; and for the clearing this we must know there is a great deal of difference in these three things, the right understanding of which will clear all the matter:

Between the deputation, and the dedication, or sanctification of a thing.

I may depute a creature to be used to help me in holy things, and yet this creature is not sanctified by its deputation: and so for a lecture, such an hour in such a day is deputed, but the time is not made holy by it; the place is deputed, but is not made holy by it. Yea, I will appoint such a garment when I am in such a service such a day to wear, but yet the garment is not made holy by it. A creature is not made holy merely by being used at a holy exercise, or in a holy thing. As thus, suppose I read the holy Scripture, I make use of a candle to read it by, I do not make the candle holy by this. If the using of a creature in a holy duty did make the creature holy, then it would be the same in all creatures. I use the very light of the air when I am reading and speaking holy things in public assemblies, but I do not make the light and air holy because I use them in holy things; so I use this hour to preach in, though I use it in a holy duty, I make it no further holy than a man does his spectacles that he reads the Scripture by. A deputation is this, when such a creature as I shall think most commodious for such a service, shall be set apart for such a service; or when such a creature as I use for such a service, will be a natural and useful help to me, to appoint it for that service upon that ground.

The second is dedication, that is, when I give a thing out of my own power for a pious use, so that I cannot use it for any thing again. As when a man has given so much of his estate to build a school or an hospital, it may be said to be a kind of dedication; he has devoted, given away, so much of his estate to that end, so that he cannot make use of it for another purpose. Now we do not so set apart the time of preaching, as that we cannot use this time for any other end, we may, as we see cause, alter it, where it is from nine to eleven we make it from two to four; whereas, if it were a thing that we had dedicated, that is, given out of our own power, then it cannot be changed by us. That is a second degree.

Now sanctification is beyond dedication, that is, when any creature or time is so set apart for holy things, as it must not be used in any thing but that which is holy; and though the same holy actions be done at another time, and with the use of another creature, they shall not be accounted so holy as at this time, and when this creature was used. Sanctification is the setting apart of any day which God gives me to use for my ordinary avocations, and so to devote it for such a business that it may not, without sin to me, whatever happens, be used for any other occasion. And, secondly, when I have set it apart, if I so exalt it, as if the same holy actions performed at another time, shall not be accounted as holy as at this time, although that time has as much natural fitness in it, then I sanctify a time to myself; but this I cannot do without sin. There are two things in all holy feasts, and, indeed, in all things which are accounted holy. First, it was a sin for them to use that time for any other thing, or in any other way, than God had appointed. Secondly, the actions they did at that time were such as were more acceptable to God than if they had done the same things at another time. Yea, it was so in their very days of humiliation. The day of expiation must not be used for any thing else; if they humbled themselves or fasted upon another day, that would not have been so acceptable to God as upon this day. So in all superstitions of men, when they set apart either days, or places, or things, they put these two upon them. As for places, they say we may appoint a place for people to meet in a religious way. Yes, but it becomes superstitious, first, when it is so set apart, as I shall make conscience of using it for no other purpose. Secondly, when I am persuaded in my conscience, that God accepts the service in this place better than in any other, though as decent as this. So for superstitious garments. You say, May not ministers be decent? I have heard a great doctor give this argument for a surplice: Sometimes I ride abroad to preach, and my cloak is dirty, is it fit for me to come into a pulpit with a dirty garment? and therefore there is always appointed somewhat to cover it; it is decent. Suppose it be so, but if this garment must be used only for such a holy exercise; and, secondly, if I think the wearing of it honours the service, and that God accepts the service performed in such a garment rather than in another; this is superstition: as in one place in Suffolk, when that garment was lost, there was a strict injunction to the poor countrymen that there might not be any service or sermon till they had got another; for which they were appointed ten days, and this being upon a Friday, there were two sabbaths without any service; therefore it is apparent they put the acceptance of the duty upon it. So for days, if any man set apart a day, so that his conscience condemn him before God as sinning against him if he do any thing upon that day but such holy duties; secondly, that though the same holy duties be done upon another day, they shall not be accounted so acceptable to God as done upon that day; this is superstitious. Yet, certainly, of this nature have many of our days been, for if you opened your shops what disturbance was there in the city! it was profaning the day, every proctor had power given him to molest you. Did not they also account it a greater honour to God to have service read that day than to have it read upon an ordinary Tuesday or Thursday? yea, preaching upon a lecture day that was not one of their holy-days, they accounted not so acceptable to God as upon one of them. Here comes their institution, which puts more upon it than God does, and thus it becomes sinful. So if you set apart the time you call Christmas, so as to make conscience of not doing any other service or work on that day, and think that to remember Christ, and to bless God for Christ, upon another day, is not so acceptable to God as to do it upon this day, here is the evil of man's instituting days.

Well, but this is not cleared except we answer another objection: Do not the king and parliament command days of fasting and of thanksgiving, and are not they of the same nature? Will not you say it is sin for us to open shops upon these days? I answer, our days for fasting and thanksgiving have not those two ingredients in them, for, first, if God by his providence call any individual to special business in his family, then he need not have his conscience condemn him though he spend all that day in that business. They may set apart a day to be spent publicly, yet with this limitation, not to enjoin every individual, that to whatever God's providence specially calls him, he must leave off all, and make as much conscience of doing this as upon the Lord's day.

You will say, Upon the Lord's day, if any thing extraordinary happen, we may go a journey, or transact business, as a physician may ride up and down, works of mercy may be done, therefore this makes no difference between God's day and these of man's appointment. I answer, though a physician do a work of mercy upon the sabbath day, yet he is bound to do it with a sabbath day's heart; whatever calls him from those services that are God's immediate worship, he sins against God if he follow it as the business of his calling, as upon another day; but if he do it with a sabbath day's frame of heart, as a work of mercy, he keeps the sabbath in that. But if there were a necessity to ride upon a fast day, a man's conscience need not to condemn him before God, if he went about that work as the work of his calling. It is not therefore so dedicated, but God's providence may oblige us to do other civil actions, and that as the works of our calling. Secondly, neither is it so sanctified, as if the same works done on another day were not so acceptable to God as when done upon this day. Our fast days are fixed for the last Wednesday of the month, but to think that the work done upon another day were not so acceptable to God as done upon that day, is to sanctify the day, and such a sanctification is sin. The same answer may be given for days of thanksgiving.

Besides, there is another thing to be considered, that is, in stating the time. Though men may thus depute and appoint days to worship God, yet they cannot state any such days, but as God's providence permits, according to the present occasion. Therefore it would be a sin for a state to appoint nominally a day for religious fasting: God did so, but men have no power to do so, because they do not know but God may call them to rejoicing upon that day, they have not knowledge of the times. All that we can do is this, when God calls us to fasting, we must appoint days of fasting; when God calls us to rejoicing, we must appoint days of rejoicing. Therefore to appoint the time of Lent as a religious fast is sinful, and the statute itself threatens a mulct upon that man who shall call it a religious fast: stated fasts, which are not limited by Providence, are certainly evil. The monthly fasts now enjoined, if we should say we will have them once a month till this day twelvemonths, or two years, I persuade myself the state should sin; but to have it as long as God's hand is upon us, as long as the occasion lasts, and God's providence calls us to it, is justifiable.

Our brethren in Scotland wholly deny the appointment, both of stated fasts and feasts: nay, they will scarce agree to the monthly fasting we have, because they are so loth to yield to any *stata jejunia.* King James once made a speech in Scotland, in which he blessed God that he was born in such a time, and was a member of such a church; the reason he gave was this: The church of Scotland exceeds in this all other churches. England, though it has pure doctrine, has not pure discipline; other reformed churches have pure doctrine and discipline, but they retain the observation of many holy-days; but the church of Scotland has pure doctrine and discipline, and keeps no holy-days, and therefore it is a purer church than any in the world.

Thus I have endeavoured to show you how far things may be set apart, and how far not, when it becomes a sin for any one to sanctify a day. By this we may see what a mercy it is to be delivered from those men who have robbed the kingdom of many days, and put many superstitious respects upon them, and so have involved us in much guilt; bless God for delivering us from them, and for those days in which God gives us liberty to exercise ourselves in his worship. Thus much for those feasts called their feasts, that were of their own appointment.

"Her new moons." The ordinance of God in the new moons, is in Numb. xxviii. 11, "And in the beginning of your" new moons, or "months, ye shall offer a burnt offering unto the Lord," &c. It was God's ordinance, that the Jews at the beginning of every month, when they had a new moon, should keep that day holy to God. That which the Latins call the calends, were their new moons.

The holy solemnity of these days consisted in three things.

First, The offerings that were there appointed by God particularly for that time, were many and chargeable; two young bullocks and one ram, seven lambs of the first year without spot; besides their flour and oil for their drink-offerings, and one kid of the goats for a sin-offering.

Secondly, At these times they were wont to repair to the prophets for instruction, to know the mind of God. The husband of the Shunammite said to his wife, "Wherefore wilt thou go to him to-day? it is neither new moon, nor sabbath," 2 Kings iv. 23: if it were new moon or sabbath, you might go, but since it is neither, why will you go? That implies, that to repair to the prophets for instruction, and to hear God's word from them, upon those days was common among the Jews.

Thirdly, It was unlawful to buy and sell upon those days. Amos viii. 5, "When will the new moon be gone that we may sell corn?" they were weary of it, it seems, because they might not buy and sell in it.

Buxtorf, who describes the Jewish customs, relates three other things they were wont to do in their new moons.

1. Those who were most devout among them, set the day apart for fasting and prayer, to entreat God to bless the new moon to them.

2. As soon as there was an appearance of the new moon, one steps up, and cries, O thou Creator of the moon, be ever blessed,* and so he goes on in blessing God for this creature.

3. They used to leap and to reach toward the moon as soon as they saw it, speaking after this manner: We, stretching to the moon, cannot reach it; so all our enemies that aim at us, are as unable to reach us to our hurt, as we that.†

But why did God appoint this feast of the new moon? It was appointed for these four ends.

(1.) Because God would be acknowledged to have the government of all inferior things in the world, and especially of all the changes of times. As the sabbath was to put us in mind of God's creating the world, so the new moons were appointed for them to bless God for the government of the world. Many nations have attributed much of the government of the world to the moon; the tides, you know, ebb and flow according to the moon, the great works of God in the seas seem to be governed by God in the use of that creature; yea, things seem to be governed more sensibly by this creature than by others: that they might not rest therefore in the creature, but give God the glory, he appointed the feasts of the new moon; if they had any changes of times and seasons, God caused it, rather than this creature. As the heathens called the moon "the queen of heaven," so did Israel; and would not be hindered from offering cakes to her, because they attributed all their prosperity to her, Jer. xliv. 17—19. Now from this God would take them off, therefore he appointed this solemn feast of the new moon.

(2.) God would hereby teach, that the bringing of any light unto us after darkness is merely from himself, and he must be acknowledged in it. The moon is a glorious creature, and causes much light; but soon after there is darkness, and after this darkness light springs up again: this is the work of God. We are taught a moral lesson from this feast; that is, has God at any time brought darkness upon a kingdom, or upon a family, or an individual? does he begin to bring light? he must be acknowledged and praised for it.

(3.) God would teach them, also, that the beginnings of all mercies are to be dedicated to him. When God renews a mercy, at the very first, before it comes to perfection, it is to be given up unto God; they were to celebrate this feast upon the beginning of the light of the moon.

* Benedictus esto Conditor tuus, O luna, benedictus esto Dominus tuus.

† Ter subsiliunt cœlum versus quod, quanto sublimius possunt, tanto melius est, lunamque alloquentes, quemadmodum, inquiunt, nos te versus subsilientes attingere te non possumus, sic hostes nostri omnes nos ad malum attingere nobisque nocere non poterunt. Buxtorf. Synag. Judaic. c. 17.

(4.) This aimed at Christ, as all other ceremonies of the law did. It pointed out our condition in our depending upon Christ; for our light must be renewed by our conjunction with Jesus Christ, who is the Sun of righteousness; as the light of the moon is renewed by her conjunction with the sun, that gives the great light to the world. And as the light of the moon increases as it takes it from the sun, so our light increases as we take it from the Sun of righteousness. Thus this feast was typical, and thus we see these feasts were of special use.

But when they abused these feasts, God said, I will take them away, you shall have no more; and therefore God professes a loathing of their feasts, and, amongst others, of their new moons, Isa. i. 14. Not but that they were holy in themselves, but when they abused them, by adding their own superstitious vanities, or by not observing the due end for which God appointed them, then God is offended. Now, saith God, you acknowledge darkness and light to be from me, and change of time to be from me, but what use do you make of your time? You seem to give up the mercies you receive to me, but you do not honour me with them, nor for them.

You seem to think of the Messias in these things, but your hearts are not with him, all your ways are after your lusts. I loathe your feasts. Just as when a man comes to God, and prays devoutly, Lord, lead me not into temptation; and as soon as he has done, immediately goes into wicked company. God loathes you for going quite cross to your prayers. You pray, Lord, give us this day our daily bread; as if you said, Lord, I depend upon thee every day for my bread, and for a blessing upon all my outward estate; and as soon as you have done, you overreach, and cheat, and go to Satan for your bread: God loathes these prayers of yours, as God loathed their new moons, because when he appointed such worship for those ends, yet they went quite contrary.

Yet there are two things very observable about these new moons. We often read these things, but pass them over and but little mind them.

1. God will have the glory of his creature, of the new moon, and that solemnly, yet it must be at that time when the moon is very little. God does not ask to be glorified in that creature when it is fullest of glory; but when it is, as we may say, in the meanest condition, when it exhibits but little light, scarce any at all, then God will be glorified. This is the instruction and moral lesson from hence, which is no strained one, but I think intended by God himself, in appointing this feast; in that God will have the glory due to him from this creature in the beginning of its light, rather than at any other time. We are taught in this,

Obs. That there is much danger when we are giving God the glory of the creature, of resting in the creature, and not passing through the creature speedily to God. God is very jealous of his glory this way. God has made many glorious creatures, and he would have us give due esteem to them all; but when we esteem them for any excellency, God is jealous lest any of his glory should rest in the creature, therefore he calls for it at the time when the creature is most mean. That is the reason why God's ordinances are so plain, we have but plain bread, and plain wine, and a plain table, and no pompous attire, because God saw that when we are to deal with him spiritually, if we had pompous things we should rest in them. We see men so attracted with pompous things, that they give not God that glory which is due to him, but honour the creature rather than God. It seems that the heathens who made the moon to be their goddess, looked at it when it was most light, as appears, Job xxxi.; therefore Job, to clear himself from that idolatry, saith, ver. 26, "If I beheld the sun when it shined, or the moon walking in brightness." They used to worship the moon when they saw it "walking in brightness;" because they could not reach the moon, they kissed their hand, and bowed to it in acknowledgment of a deity; therefore, Job would free himself from worshipping this creature. When the creature is most glorious, there is danger of giving God the less. It is thus with us; God has often more glory from us when our estates are small, than when they are very great: many a man, when he has been in full light of prosperity, never minded God, but when God brought him into darkness, he gave God glory; and then it has been most acceptable, because then he sees God's hand helping him without the creature. God had most glory from the moon when it had the least light, so God may have glory from us though our light be extinguished.

2. There is yet another remarkable thing concerning this feast. You observe what difference there is between the feasts of the new moons by God's appointment under the law, and the feasts of the new moons as they are set forth to us in Ezekiel. Those chapters in Ezekiel from the fortieth and so on, though they seem to speak of the Jews' ceremonies, and temple and feasts; yet their scope is to describe the glorious condition of the church of God in the time of the gospel; as in Isa. lxvi. 23, "And it shall come to pass, that from one new moon to another, and from one sabbath to another, shall all flesh come to worship me, saith the Lord;" that is, their constant worship shall be in comparison as a sabbath, and they shall not only worship me at the beginning of the moon, but at all times, it shall be full and constant: therefore, though Ezekiel there speaks of new moons and other feasts, yet it is to set out the condition and blessed state of the times of the gospel under those shadows and types, according to the phraseology of the Jews. This being granted, let us compare the institution of the feast of the new moon, in Numb. xxviii., with what is said in Ezek. xlvi. In Numb. xxviii. they were to offer for a burnt-offering, two bullocks, one ram, and seven lambs; but in Ezek. xlvi. 6, in the days of the new moon, there should be but one bullock and six lambs. God himself had said, that in their new moons they should offer two bullocks and seven lambs; yet when the prophet sets out a more glorious condition of the church, they must not offer so much as they did before, but one bullock and six lambs. What are we taught from this? Two excellent lessons, which are the reason of the difference.

First, that there is a blessed state of the gospel coming, which shall not be subject to such changes as heretofore, but a more settled condition of peace and rest; so that they shall not have the same occasion to bless God for his providence in the changes of times as before they had. Their solemnity of the new moon, was to do that spiritual thing in a ceremonial way, that is, to give God the glory for the change of times: but in the times of the gospel, they shall not have so many sacrifices, to make it such a solemn business. Why? Because the church shall be in a condition of more rest and safety, and more constancy in their ways, not hurried up and down by men's humours, and lusts, and will, as before.

Secondly, as the state of the gospel shall not be so subject to danger as it was before, there shall not be that occasion to bless God for bringing light immediately after darkness. After it had been dark a long time, and they could not see the moon, as if that creature had been lost out of heaven, when they saw it again they were to bless God for it: but in the time of the gospel that is coming, there shall be no such darkness; this time, however, is not yet come, we have need of our seven lambs and two bullocks, for we have much darkness.

"And her sabbaths." Plutarch thought that the sabbath of the Jews was from Sabbos, a name of Bacchus, that signifies, to live jovially and merrily. Indeed, the sabbaths which many keep may have such a derivation; their sabbaths are sabbaths of Bacchus, to be merry, and to eat, and drink, and play, is the end of them all.

σαβάζειν, jovialiter vivere.

But the word has a better root. God would have us upon the sabbath rest from all other works, that we may be free to converse with him; therefore it is so much the more inexcusable if, when we have nothing else to do, we shall refuse to converse with God as he requires of us. If a friend came to your house to converse with you, and he should know you have no business to take up your time, yet you will scarce see him, or spend a little time with him, will he not take it ill? If, indeed, you had an excuse that your business was extraordinary, it would not be so ill taken; but when he knows you have nothing to do, and yet you refuse time to converse with him, will not this be taken for slighting him? Thus you deal with God: had you indeed great business to transact upon that day, though you did not converse with God in holy duties, God might accept of mercy rather than sacrifice. But when he appoints you a day to rest, wherein you have nothing to do but to converse with him, yet then to deny it, is a slighting the majesty of God.

Now the Jews had divers sabbaths; amongst others, these were principal ones, the sabbaths of days, and the sabbaths of years.

The sabbaths of days. Every seventh day they had a sabbath, and it was kept unto the Lord. Now this feast of theirs had somewhat in it memorative, somewhat significative, and somewhat figurative. It was a memorial, a sign, and a figure.

First, it was memorative; a memorial of two things:

1. Of the work of God's creation. After God had finished his works of creation, then he rested, and sanctified the seventh day. Psal. xcii. is appointed for the sabbath, the argument of it is, the celebrating the memorial of God's great works.

2. Of their deliverance out of Egypt, in remembrance of the rest that God gave them from their bondage. "Remember that thou wast a servant in the land of Egypt, and that the Lord thy God brought thee out thence through a mighty hand and by a stretched out arm: therefore the Lord thy God commanded thee to keep the sabbath day," Deut. v. 15.

Secondly, it was significative, a sign. Exod. xxxi. 17, "It is a sign between me and the children of Israel for ever:" and ver. 13, "It is a sign between me and you, that I am the Lord that doth sanctify you." God made it a sign, that as this day was by his command to be sanctified, set apart from other days, so God had set apart this nation of the Jews from other nations.

Thirdly, it was figurative, it prefigured or typified the rest that remained for the people of God. Heb. iv. 9, "There remaineth therefore a rest to the people of God," both here, in the time of the gospel, and in heaven eternally.

Now there was some specialty in this day of rest, in this sabbath of the Jews, more than in any other sabbath. As,

(1.) In the antiquity of it. It was the most ancient of all the days set apart for any holy use, being from the time of the creation.

(2.) It was written with God's own finger in the tables.

(3.) God rained no manna upon this day, and that even before the law was given in Mount Sinai for the honour of this day.

(4.) The whole week takes denomination from the sabbath. Luke xviii. 12, "I fast twice in the week," δὶς τοῦ σαββάτου, twice a sabbath. So Mark xvi. 2, "The first day of the week," the first of sabbaths, τῆς μιᾶς σαββάτων.

(5.) This sabbath is called an everlasting covenant by way of eminency, as if nothing of God's covenant were kept if this were not. Exod. xxxi. 16, "Ye shall keep the sabbath for a perpetual covenant."

(6.) Yea, God puts a remembrance upon this day, and not upon any other sabbath. If a friend who would fain converse with you, send to you a week beforehand, saying, I pray think of that day, I will come to you then and converse with you, we will enjoy communion together; now, if when he comes he find you employed in unnecessary businesses, will he take it well? God does so with you: I desire to converse with your souls, and I appoint you a day, think of it, remember that day, that you and I may be together, and converse sweetly one with another: if God find you then occupied in unnecessary businesses, he will not take it well.

This sabbath the Jews rejoiced much in, and blessed God for it, Neh. ix. 14, as a great mercy. Philo Judæus, speaking of the fourth commandment, saith, It is a famous precept, and profitable to excite all kind of virtue and piety. The Hebrews say we must sanctify the sabbath at its coming in and going out, and bless God who gave it to us. Yea, it is called by some of the Hebrews, the very desire of days. Drusius tells of a Jew, who, when the sabbath day approached, was wont to put on his best clothes, saying, Come, my spouse, &c., as being glad of that day, as a bridegroom of his spouse. It is not my work to handle the point of the sabbath day, or Lord's day now, but to open it as we have it here in the text, to show what kind of sabbath the Jews had. Only observe this one thing about this sabbath; if you compare Numb. xxviii. 9, with Ezek. xlvi. 4, you find that the offerings in the time of the gospel, were more than those in the time of the law. In Numbers, you find but two lambs; but in Ezekiel, six lambs and a ram, for the sabbath. This by way of type shows, that in the settled times of the gospel, God's worship upon the Christian sabbath should be solemnized more fully than it was in the time of the law.

Quartum præceptum egregium præceptum, et ad omnem virtutem excitandam utile, pietatem vero præcipue.

The next is, *the sabbaths of years*, and they were of two sorts. There was one to be kept every seven years, and another every seven times seven, every fiftieth year. Every seventh year there was a rest of the land; as every seventh day there was a rest of the labour of their bodies: Exod. xxiii. 10, 11, "Six years thou shalt sow thy land, and shalt gather in the fruits thereof: but the seventh year thou shalt let it rest and lie still;" they must not prune their vines, nor gather their vintage. The sabbath of days signified that they themselves were the Lord's, therefore they ceased from their own labours. But the sabbath of years, the resting of the land signified that the land was the Lord's, at his disposal, and that they were to depend upon the providence of God for their food in the land. When they ploughed, and when they sowed, and gathered in the fruits, God would dispose the land as he pleased.

And we must acknowledge, for that is the moral of it to ourselves, that all lands are the Lord's, and the fruit that we enjoy from the land is at his disposing. If any man ask, What should we eat that seventh year? seeing they might not plough, nor sow, nor reap, neither have vintage, nor harvest; the Lord answers them, Lev. xxv. 21, "I will command my blessing upon you in the sixth year, and it shall bring forth fruit for three years." God, you see, will not have any to be losers by his service. Let us trust God then, though perhaps you have now one year in which you have no trading. People cry out, Oh this twelvemonth we have had no trading in the city! we can get no rent out of the country! Do not murmur, trust God; it may be God has been before-hand with many of you, you have had full trading formerly which may preserve you comfortably now. If not before, trust God for the next: the Jews were to trust God every seventh year, they had nothing coming in for one year in seven. If once in all your lifetime God takes away your trading upon an extraordinary occasion, do not murmur, do not give less to the poor: I speak to those whom God has blessed in former years, so as that they are not only able to subsist, but to give too: "Beware that there be not a thought in thy wicked heart, saying, The seventh year, the year of release, is at hand; and thine eye be evil against thy poor brother, and thou givest him nought; and he cry unto the Lord against thee, and it be sin unto thee," Deut. xv. 9. If a poor company of distressed and plundered people come to you and desire your help, because you have not such a full income as you were wont to have in your trading, you refuse to relieve them, if they cry unto God against you, it will be sin unto you.

This rest of the land was also to put them in mind that there was a time coming when God will free them from labour. Now they were fain to eat their bread in the sweat of their brows, but God would supply them once in seven years, without the sweat of their brows in tilling the land, showing, that there was a time wherein God would bring his people to such a rest, that they should have full supply of all things without labour.

The second thing in this seventh year was, all debts that their brethren owed to them were to be released. Deut. xv. 2, it is called there, "the Lord's release;" the Lord is merciful to those that are in debt. God knows what a grievous burden it is for his people to be in debt; rich men, who are full-handed, do not understand what a burden it is to be in debt to every man they deal with; they cannot sleep quietly, they can have but little joy and comfort in their lives, the burden is so grievous. Now God, in mercy to his people, that they might not all their days go under such a burden, and so have little joy of their lives, granted this favour to them, that once in seven years their debts were to be released. But it was the debt of a Hebrew, Deut. xv. 12; foreigners' debts they were not bound to release. By that we are to learn, that there should be more pity and commiseration shown to those who are our brethren in the flesh, or in the Lord, with respect to their debts, than others. There is a complaint that many of the godly have little care and conscience in paying their debts; the justness of that complaint I know not, but there may be slothfulness, if not unfaithfulness, and if there be carelessness and unfaithfulness in some, it is enough to cast an aspersion upon all. Though those who are godly should be more careful to pay their debts than others, yet if you see them godly and laborious in their calling, and the providence of God only prevent, and not any negligence of theirs, it must be a vile and wicked heart that would take advantage of their being godly, to oppress them; no, you are bound to show them much commiseration. Beware there be not an evil heart in thee, to be less merciful to thy poor brother because of the seventh year's rest of the ground, or because the debt was to be released that seventh year: but "thou shalt surely give him, and thy heart shall not be grieved when thou givest unto him; because for this thing the Lord thy God shall bless thee in all thy works, and in all that thou puttest thy hand unto," Deut. xv. 10. Notwithstanding there must be a cessation of ploughing, and sowing, and vintage, in the seventh year, yea, notwithstanding they were bound to release their debt in the seventh year, yet they must do this, and not do it grudgingly; they must not murmur and say, Does God require of us that we must neither plough nor sow, and that we must release our debts, and give too, nay, and give, and not have our hearts grieved too, that we must not complain of this? O my brethren, God loves exceedingly cheerful givers, and hearts enlarged with bowels of compassion, not hearts grumbling and objecting against giving. Many men have no quickness of understanding in any thing else but against works of mercy; how quick are they in their objections, and find such subtle ways to save their purses, that we are astonished! Against this there is a solemn charge, Deut. xv. 11, "Thou shalt open thine hand wide unto thy brother, to thy poor, and to the needy, in thy land."

The third thing to be done once in seven years was the release of servants, they too must go free, and they must not be sent away empty neither: "It shall not seem hard unto thee, when thou sendest him away free from thee," Deut. xv. 18; you must give them liberty, as ver. 14. It is true, we are not bound to the letter, every seven years to do thus, but there is a moral equity in it; when servants have done you faithful service, you must not think that it is enough that you give them meat, and drink, and clothes, but you must be careful of your servants how they should live after they are gone from you. This was the first sabbath of years.

But the second was the most famous, and that was the rest that was every seven times seven years, the fiftieth year, which was called the year of jubilee, from the trumpet by which they were wont to proclaim that year, which, as the Jews tell us, was of a ram's horn. In this year divers of the same things were done as in the seventh year, as the release of debts, the release of servants. But there are some things observable that were done at this time beyond what was done every seventh year.

As for servants, the release of them was not only of such as had then served seven years, yea, if they had served any time, they were then to be released; but there were some that would not be released, and there was a command given by God respecting it, Exod. xxi. 6, if there were a servant that loved his master and would not go free, then his master should bring him to the post of the door, and with a nail bore his ear, and then the text saith, "he shall serve him for ever." Now, that "for ever" is by interpreters interpreted but for the time of jubilee, and then he should have rest. Here it is to be understood of the fiftieth year, the year of jubilee.

There are some kind of spirits so slavish, that when they may have liberty they will not; they deserve to have their ears bored, to be slaves to the fiftieth year, if not for ever. Many amongst us at this day have such spirits. God offers us a release from bondage; how many of us love servitude still! It is just with God that we should have our ears bored, and that we should be slaves even for ever; but we hope there will be a jubilee come at length for our deliverance. God would have a jubilee even to deliver those that were of the most servile spirits. When God began with us at the commencement of our parliament, like the seventh year he offered to us a release, and we refused it then, and we deserve that our ears should be bored; but God is infinitely merciful, though we be of servile spirits, and know not how to pity ourselves, we hope the Lord will pity us, and grant us, out of free and rich grace, a jubilee, even to deliver those who have a mind to be bond-slaves. I am sure God does so spiritually; if God did not deliver those who are willing to be slaves, he would deliver none.

It was a great mercy so to provide for servants, that they might thus be delivered. The greater, because servants endured a great deal of hardship then, more than now; they were bought and sold, not only other nations, but the Hebrews were bought for servants also, as you find it, Exod. xxi. 2. Besides, servants were in such bondage then, that if the masters beat them with a rod until they had killed them, yet they must only be punished, they must not have blood shed for their blood; yea, though the servant died under his master's hand, yet the master was only to be punished; and if the servant lived but two or three days after, the master was not to be punished at all: "And if a man smite his servant, or his maid, with a rod, and he die under his hand; he shall be surely punished. Notwithstanding, if he continue a day or two, he shall not be punished: for he is his money," Exod. xxi. 20, 21.

Oh that servants would consider this, and bless God for the liberty they have now, more than servants had in former times! It was so likewise with the Romans, the word "servant" comes from *servando*, because the Romans used to have such for servants as were preserved in time of war, who would otherwise have been put to death; whether they were those or others, yet the condition of all was very servile both amongst Jews and Romans. This may justly rebuke the pride of servants now; if they be but crossed in the least thing, they make such a complaint as if they were exceedingly wronged. Let servants rather bless God for their condition, than murmur at a little hardship; the hardship of servants in former times was more severe than any you can endure now, who have the hardest masters. Hence, in the time of jubilee the servants so rejoiced. Jewish antiquities tell us, that nine days before their release, the servants feasted and made merry, and wore garlands, because of their freedom approaching.

Godwin, Jewish Antiq. lib. 3. c. 10.

The second thing extraordinary in the day of jubilee was, that not only debts, but lands were released: Lev. xxv. 23, "The land shall not be sold for ever." And there were divers reasons, why the land must not be sold for ever, but must return to the first possessors in the year of jubilee.

1. One reason is in Lev. xxv. 23, "For the land is mine," saith God, "for ye are strangers and sojourners with me." God would hereby teach them that they must not account themselves absolute lords of the land; "the land is mine," and you that are the greatest landlords of all, are but as strangers and sojourners with God, the land is still God's. Ver. 28, "But if he be not able to restore it to him," nor his kinsman for him, it shall remain unto the year of jubilee, and in the jubilee it shall go out, and he shall return unto his possession. If he could redeem his land himself, or a kinsman for him, he was to redeem it before; but if a man was so poor that he could not give any thing to redeem it, yet in the year of jubilee it should return to him.

2. God would not have his people too greedy to bring the possession of the country in to themselves, to have a perpetual inheritance to themselves and their posterity. This is the greediness of many covetous and ambitious men, they lay land to land, and house to house, to get a perpetual inheritance for themselves and posterity. God would not have his people be of so greedy dispositions, for a few of them to get the whole country into their own possession; therefore no man gained a possession for ever, but once in fifty years that possession must return to the original owner again.

3. The land was to return to the first owner, that the distinction of tribes might be continued, which was known much by continuance of the possessions that belonged to every tribe and family. God had great care before Christ's time to keep the distinction of tribes, that it might be clear out of which tribe Christ came.

But further, this year of jubilee aimed at something higher, it was a type of Christ, to set out the blessed redemption we have by him. The trumpet of the gospel which ministers blow is a trumpet of jubilee. Isa. lxi. 1, 2, seems to have reference to a jubilee. Christ was appointed to proclaim liberty to the captives, and the opening of the prison to them that are bound, to proclaim the acceptable year of the Lord; now that acceptable year was the year of jubilee, there was the opening of the prison, and the releasing of them that were bound. "Blessed is the people that know the joyful sound," Psal. lxxxix. 15; that hear and know the jubilee. Oh blessed are our ears who live at such times, to hear the trumpet of jubilee blowing in one congregation or other almost every day! Now, first, we have a release of our debts and bondage, this is the joyful sound. We are all by nature in debt, (sins, you know, are called debts in the Lord's prayer,) every soul is bound over to God's eternal justice to answer to the law, for not obeying it; now comes this jubilee and releases all debts. And, secondly, we are all bond-slaves, in bondage to sin, to the law, and to the devil; now comes the gospel, this jubilee, and releases our bondage, sets us at liberty. And, thirdly, we have forfeited our right to the creature, yea, to heaven itself; the gospel comes and restores all, we have right now to the comforts of this world, and to heaven. Canaan was a type of heaven, and the loss of their inheritance was a type of the loss of heaven, and the bringing of them again to the possession of it, a type of the restoring of right to heaven. Oh happy are they who hear this joyful sound, not only with the ears of their body, but who have it sounding in their hearts, by the work of the Spirit of God in them!

In this year of jubilee, there is one thing further very remarkable, and that is, the time when this trumpet was to blow that proclaimed this year. Lev. xxv. 9, the trumpet was "to sound on the tenth day of the seventh month." What remarkable thing is there in this that the trumpet must be blown the tenth day of the seventh month? The tenth day of the seventh month was their day of expiation, (the day of atonement, their public fast,) this day was appointed every year for all Israel to afflict their souls before God, to humble themselves for their sins, and so to seek mercy from God. It is a strange thing, that upon the day in which they were to afflict their souls before God, and to mourn for their sins, the trumpet of jubilee was to sound, that was to proclaim joy and mirth, things of a contrary nature to humbling and mourning. Yea, but this affords us divers excellent instructions. As,

1. God would have his people so to mourn, as to know there is joy coming. In the darkest day they had, wherein they were bound to afflict their souls most, yet they were so to mourn, as to know there was a jubilee at hand. We are not to mourn as those without hope; in our most grievous mournings, we must not have our hearts sink in desperation, we must so mourn as to expect a jubilee.

2. The saints' mourning is a preparation for a jubilee. Joy then is near at hand, when the saints most mourn in a godly manner. Did not the Lord deal graciously with us the last fast day, when we were mourning before him? There was, amongst our brethren in other parts, a kind of trumpet of jubilee blown; the Lord was then working for us; what great deliverance did God grant that very day at Chichester! God shows that the mournings of his people make way for joy.

3. The sound of the trumpet of jubilee is sweetest, when we are most afflicted for our sins. When we are most apprehensive and sensible of the evil of sin, then the joy of God, the comforts of the gospel, are sweetest to the soul. When the trumpet of jubilee is blown in congregations, if it meets not with hearts sensible of sin, they are not delighted with its sweet sound, it is not melody in their ears, it rejoices not their hearts: but let a poor soul be brought down, and made sensible of the evil of sin and God's wrath, then let but one

promise of the gospel be sounded forth, how sweet, how joyful is it!

4. Pardon of sin is the only foundation of every jubilee. For this tenth day of the seventh month, wherein the trumpet of jubilee was to be sounded, was a day of atonement. What is that? A day of covering, (as the word means,) of pardon of sin to the people of God. Many men keep a continual jubilee, live merrily, do nothing but eat, and drink, and play, and dance, and laugh, and cannot endure these sad melancholy people. What is the foundation of this thy jubilee? Art thou sure there is an atonement made between God and thy soul? Art thou sure thy sin is pardoned? Is this the foundation of thy rejoicing? Know it will not last, it is not God's, but the devil's jubilee, except there be an atonement made between God and thee, as the foundation of it.

5. When God has pardoned us, then our hearts are in a fit frame to pardon others. Now, now comes the jubilee; and now you must release your debts, and your lands, and forgive those that owe you any thing. This is the day wherein God testifies his mercy in pardoning your sins. They might well say, Now, Lord, command us what thou wilt, in showing mercy to our brethren; we are ready to pardon, to release them, to extend the bowels of our compassion towards them, for thou hast pardoned our sins. The reason of the rigidness, cruelty, and hardness of the hearts of men, and straitness of their spirits to their brethren, is, because God has not witnessed to their souls the pardon of their own sins; an atonement between God and them.

Their "solemn feasts." Among their feasts, they had three that were especially more solemn than others: and they were the feast of passover, pentecost, and tabernacles.

These three were united in one thing; that is, upon these three feasts all the males were to ascend up to Jerusalem to worship in the place which God chose. "Three times in a year shall all thy males appear before the Lord thy God in the place which he shall choose; in the feast of unleavened bread, (that was the passover,) and in the feast of weeks, (that was pentecost,) and in the feast of tabernacles," Deut. xvi. 16.

But how could the ten tribes then keep these feasts, for they went not to the temple? You may as well say, How had they an ephod? Jeroboam was wise enough to keep the feasts, though not in the way God appointed; he could tell them that going to the temple was but a circumstance of place.

See chap. iii.

From the connexion of these three together in their solemn feasts, there are divers things to be noted.

First, We may see a reason why there were sometimes so many believers at Jerusalem. An argument is brought by some from Acts xxi. 20, to prove that there may be in one church more than can possibly assemble together in one congregation; "Thou seest, brother, how many thousands of Jews there are which believe," πόσαι μυριάδες, how many myriads. Now, say they, so many could not join in one congregation. The answer to this is clear, that the time of which the passage speaks, was when the people of the Jews were all assembled together at Jerusalem to keep the feast of pentecost; for chap. xx. 16, states, that the apostle "hasted, if it were possible for him, to be at Jerusalem the day of pentecost." Now, reading the story on, it plainly appears that, by hastening his journey, he arrived at Jerusalem at the day of pentecost, and being there at that time, no marvel they said unto him, "Thou seest, brother, how many thousands of Jews there are which believe;" for all the males of the people of the Jews were together at Jerusalem, according to that law to which as yet they submitted. They were not in a church state at Jerusalem, therefore there is no strength in that objection against congregational churches.

Secondly, Where there is a national church there must be a uniting of the nation in some way of national worship. The Jews, by institution from God, were united in national worship three times in a year at the temple. And there should be some kind of individual worship not in the same species; that is, as others are praying, so are we, and as others are hearing, so are we; for so all the churches in the world may be joined; but to join in one act of worship together, as that was of going up to the temple, that made the Jews a national church. But we have no such institution now; no nation in the world can, in a proper sense, be said to be a national church as theirs was; in some figurative sense we may so call it, but not in that proper sense as it was among the Jews.

Thirdly, There are some ordinances that cannot be enjoyed but in the way of church fellowship. The Jews could not enjoy these feasts as they ought, unless they went together to Jerusalem in the way that God appointed. As among the Jews there were some ordinances they might enjoy in their synagogues and private houses, but some which they could not enjoy but in the temple; so there are some ordinances we may enjoy in our families, but others that we cannot enjoy but in church communion, of which Jerusalem is a type.

Fourthly, These three times, wherein they were to go up together to Jerusalem, were all in summer. The first, which was the feast of the passover, was in the latter end of our March, and the beginning of April; the feast of pentecost was fifty days after; the feast of tabernacles was about the middle of our September. It was very laborious for them to go up to Jerusalem to worship; but God so commiserated them, that they were not to go in winter time. That is the reason of that phrase in Acts xxvii. 9, "Sailing was now dangerous, because the feast was now already past;" that is, the feast of tabernacles was past, which was about the fifteenth of September, and so it began to be winter. It would be an affliction to go up to Jerusalem in the winter, and therefore God would be so indulgent to his people, that they should go in summer time. Oh what an affliction is it, then, to fly from Jerusalem before our enemies in the winter time! We had need pray the more hard now for those that are in danger of the enemy, that God would be merciful to them in this.

Fifthly, When they went up to these three feasts they must not go empty, but full-handed: "They shall not appear before the Lord empty," Deut. xvi. 15; noting thus much, that whenever we come to acknowledge God's mercy for any thing, we must come with full hands and liberal hearts, with hearts ready to distribute, or otherwise we only take God's name in vain.

Sixthly, The wonderful providence of God toward them, that though all the males in the whole country were to come up to Jerusalem three times in the year, yet their country should not be in danger of the enemies. The Jews had not such walls of seas about their country as we have, but they lived in the very midst of their enemies, who surrounded them; on the east, the Ammonites and Moabites; the west, the Philistines; the south, the Egyptians, Idumeans; the north, the Assyrians, to whom the prophet seems to have reference, Zech. i. 18. Now they might say, If all our males go up to Jerusalem three times a year, then our enemies that lie close in our borders, (for they lay as near them as York is to us,) may come upon us and destroy us: therefore God made provision for their encouragement; "Neither shall any man desire thy land, when thou shalt go up to appear before the Lord thy God thrice in the year," Exod. xxxiv. 24. God took care that none should desire their land. Let us go on in God's service, and he will take care to deliver us from our enemies. Often out of slavish fear of enemies, and the disturbance they are able to make among us, we are ready to betray the cause of God, and neglect his worship. Let us learn from hence to go on in God's ways, and not fear any injury which our enemies can do us. God saith he will take care, when they are all at Jerusalem in the exercise of his worship, that none should desire their land.

Now, by opening these several feasts, you may be helped to read the Old Testament profitably, for much of it is spent in things that concern some of these.

The first was *the passover*. You have the history of it Numb. xxviii. 16, 17, and in divers other scriptures. That feast was in the beginning of the year. It is true, our September was the beginning of their civil year, but the month Abib, which was the middle of March and part of April, was the ecclesiastical year; and upon their deliverance out of Egypt, when God commanded them to celebrate their passover, he apppointed that that month should be unto them the beginning of months, the first month of the year. Deliverance from great evils are mercies that we are highly to prize; the Jews were to begin their year in memorial of the mercy they received in that month.

The name "passover" arose from God's sending forth a destroying angel that "passed over" the houses of the Israelites that night; he went through the land and destroyed all the firstborn of the Egyptians, but saved the Israelites. This feast was also called "the feast of unleavened bread," Luke xxii. 1, because they were to go out of Egypt in haste, and could not have time to leaven their bread. Josephus tells us that they took only a little flour mingled with water, that might serve them with great economy for thirty days. God taught them thus to depend upon him. We are ready to murmur if we see not enough to serve us for many years, if our armies have not enough for so long a time; but many hundreds of thousands had but a little meal and water to serve them for thirty days, and they knew not where to have more when that was spent: no marvel that it is said of Moses, Heb. xi. 27, "by faith he forsook Egypt." This bread is called "the bread of affliction," Deut. xvi. 3; and it was unleavened bread, not only to typify that we must not have our hearts leavened with malice, but to put them in mind of the sore affliction they endured both when they were in Egypt, and when they went out of Egypt.

Now this passover was partly memorative, and partly figurative.

Memorative. First, To remember the deliverance of their first-born.

Secondly, To remember their deliverance from the bondage of Egypt.

Obs. 1. When others are smitten and we are "passed over," it is a great mercy.

Obs. 2. Deliverance from the bondage of the outward man, and from bondage in respect of religion and conscience, is a mercy for ever to be celebrated. God is pleased now to offer us this mercy of deliverance from both these kinds of bondage; certainly we are a people devoted to misery if we take not God's offer of mercy. We have been in bondage in our estates and liberties, God offers us freedom, and freedom also from antichristian bondage, which is worse than Egyptian bondage. The text saith, when they were delivered from the bondage of Egypt, "Moses sang;" and in the Revelation, when they were delivered from antichristian bondage, "they sing the song of Moses," Rev. xv. 3. We were long since delivered from a great part of this bondage, now the Lord offers to deliver us altogether.

Obs. 3. When God offers us mercy of deliverance we should not go forth slowly. They were to eat this passover with their staves in their hands, this was to note their hasty going out of Egypt. Our misery at this day is, that the Lord offers deliverance, and we lie slugging on our beds, and are like that foolish child the prophet speaks of, that sticks in the birth: we have stuck these two years in the birth, whereas we might have been delivered long before this. It concerns us all to consider what the cause is, and to lament it before the Lord, that we may make our peace with him.

Obs. 4. In thanksgiving for a mercy, we are ever to remember what we were before that mercy. They must eat unleavened bread at this feast, the bread of affliction, to remind them of the afflictions they were in before they had this mercy. When we bless God for a deliverance, we must really present before our souls the sad condition we were in before we were delivered.

But the special thing aimed at in the passover was, that it should be a type of Christ, who was the paschal Lamb that was to take away the sins of the world; he that was roasted in the fire of God's wrath for our sins, as that lamb that was to be eaten in the passover was roasted in the fire. And if ever the angel of God's vengeance pass over us, it is through the blood of that Lamb sprinkled upon our hearts, which was signified by sprinkling the blood of the lamb upon the posts of their houses. In the Lord's supper we celebrate, in effect, the same feast of the passover they did; and by this we may learn,

Obs. 5. There is little comfort in the remembrance of our outward deliverances, except we can see them all in Christ. They were in this feast to remember their deliverance out of Egypt, but they were in it to have a figure and type of Christ. That sweetened their remembrance, that made the feast a joyful feast, when they could see it as a fruit of Christ's sufferings; when this lamb that put them in mind of it, put them in mind likewise of Christ the paschal Lamb. If you would have the remembrance of deliverances from any kind of affliction sweet unto you, you must look upon them all in the blood of Christ, and then your hearts will be enlarged to bless God.

This was the ordinance of God in the passover; but besides God's ordinance, the Jews added divers other things.

The first thing they added, was earnest prayer to God for the building of the temple, which many of them observe to this day. Buxtorf tells us, that because the temple is destroyed where they were to go up thrice in the year to solemnize these feasts, therefore they pray earnestly and mightily for the temple in this manner: they cry all together to God,* Lord, build thy temple shortly, very quickly, very quickly, most quickly in our days. And then they go over it again, Merciful God, great God, kind God, high God, sweet God, with divers other epithets, now build thy temple quickly, very quickly, &c. Now, now, now, five times together. They teach us how much the temple concerns us. Their mistake was, they rested in the material temple, and did not consider that this temple was a type of Christ; therefore as earnestly as they prayed for the building of their material temple, let us pray for the building up of the mystical body of Christ; Now, Lord, build quickly, do not defer it, even in our days do it!

A second thing they added was the manner of casting out unleavened bread. In this they observed three things, their inquisition, their extermination, their execration. First, with a candle they would narrowly search every corner of the house to see if they had the

* Templum tuum brevi, valde cito, valde cito, in diebus nostris, citissime, nunc ædifica templum tuum brevi. Misericors Deus, magne Deus. benigne Deus, pulcher Deus, dulcis Deus, virtuose Deus, Judaice Deus, nunc ædifica templum tuum brevi, valde cito, in diebus nostris, valde cito, valde cito, nunc ædifica, nunc ædifica, nunc ædifica, nunc ædifica, nunc ædifica templum tuum cito, robuste Deus, fortis, potens Deus, &c. Buxtorf. de Synag. Jud. c. 13.

least crumb of leaven; if any were found they cast it out with solemnity; and then they used to wish a curse upon themselves if there were any left in their houses that was not cast out.

This moral observation may be taught from it; it should be our care when we are to receive the sacrament, to make narrow inquisition, to get the candle of the word, and to search every corner of our hearts, every faculty of the soul, to see if there be no leaven in it. 2. Whatever we see, to cast it out of doors. And, 3. To be so much set against sin, as to be willing to take a curse upon ourselves, if we should willingly let any known sin be in our hearts, and to acknowledge that God might justly curse us in his ordinance if we be false in this.

Thirdly, they used to display all their treasures; if they had any splendid clothes, or furniture, or curiosity, they would show all at this feast. By their superstition we may learn, that in the time of our coming before God, it is fit for us to exercise and manifest all those beautiful graces with which the Lord has endowed us by the work of his Spirit; for in them the riches of a Christian, his splendid clothing, his jewels, and all his excellences, consist.

Fourthly, after the passover was at an end, they fasted three days, to humble themselves for their failings in keeping that feast. This was not God's institution, but it was their custom; and we may learn from it, (though we do not bind ourselves to do as they did,) to look back to our receiving the sacrament, and to bewail all our miscarriages: I believe, if things were examined to the quick, in our receiving the sacrament, we should find matter enough to fast and pray, and to humble our souls for our miscarriages.

Lastly, in the passover they used to read the book of the Canticles, because that book treats especially of the conjunction of the soul with the Messiah, which is sealed up specially in the passover. And that, indeed, is a special meditation for us when we come to the Lord's supper, to meditate upon our conjunction with Christ.

The next is the feast of *pentecost*. This feast is called also the feast of weeks, because there were seven weeks to be reckoned, and at the end of them it was solemnly to be kept, Lev. xxiii. 15. In the feast of the passover, the first day of seven, and the last day of seven, were solemnly kept; now they were to count from the morrow after the first sabbath, seven sabbaths, that is, seven weeks complete; the first sabbath of the passover was the fifteenth day of the month Abib, and the next day from that they were to count seven weeks, and at the end of seven weeks the feast of pentecost was to be kept. Now in this first day, wherein they began to count their weeks, you find the first-fruits were to be offered up to God; it was a kind of distinct feast, called the feast of the first-fruits, in which they were to bring a sheaf of the first-fruits of their harvest to the priest, to be offered to God; and the reason was, because now their harvest began: as soon as the passover was killed, and they had kept the first sabbath of the passover, (for they were to keep it seven days,) they began their harvest; they must not put a sickle into the corn, nor reap any thing of their ground, until they had kept the passover.

Now their harvest began in the month Abib, that is, part of our March and part of April, and thence it has its name, for Abib signifies, an ear of corn. Harvest began so soon in the land of Canaan, not only because it was a hot country, for it is observed that Africa was a hotter country than theirs, and yet their harvest began later, but because of the blessing of God upon that land; therefore, Jer. iii. 19, it is called, "a goodly heritage," because of the timely bringing forth the fruit; the words translated "goodly heritage," signify an heritage of comeliness; the same word translated "goodly," signifies "a roebuck," to which this land was compared, and so it may be said to be a land of a roebuck, because of the speedy and swift ripening of the corn.

נחלת צבי Hereditatem elegantiæ.

Obs. 1. It is the blessing of the church to have their fruit ripe betimes, for Canaan was a type of the church. You young ones, consider this, the Lord loves to have the fruits of Canaan ripe betimes: if you grew in the wilderness, though you did not bring forth fruit in your youthful days, God would not so much regard it; but if you live in his church, in Canaan, the Lord expects you should begin betimes, in the very spring of your years, to bring forth fruit unto God. Men rejoice much in early fruits, they are lovely; yea, and God rejoices in them too, Micah vii. 1, "My soul desired the first-ripe fruit;" this is true of God himself. Your parents and godly friends may say, Our soul desires that grace may spring up betimes in these young ones: so it may be said of God, his very soul desires to see the first-fruits; fruit in young ones is that which is pleasing to God's soul.

Obs. 2. We cannot enjoy any sweetness or blessing from any fruits of the earth, but through the blood of Jesus Christ. After they had solemnized the memorial of the blood of Christ, then they might put a sickle in the corn and reap it, not before; and as soon as they had solemnized the remembrance of Christ in the passover, they might go with comfort and take the fruits of the earth and rejoice in them, but not before.

Obs. 3. When we have had communion with God in holy things, then we may have a holy and more comfortable use of the creatures. As when we have solemnized the blood of Christ, then we may enjoy sweetness from the comforts of the earth; so when we have enjoyed communion with God in his ordinances, it is a fit time to have a holy use of the creatures, yea, then you must be careful to have a holy use of the creatures; as soon as ever they came from the passover, the first day they were to celebrate the first-fruits unto God.

Obs. 4. After the blood of Christ is sprinkled upon the conscience, men will be ready to dedicate things unto God. Then, as Zaccheus said, "Half of my goods I give to the poor," Luke xix. 8; here are my goods, here is my estate: does the church, do my brethren, stand in need of help? lo, we are ready to offer them up to God.

Obs. 5. The first of blessings are to be offered up to God. God gives them charge, that the first of the first of all the fruits of their land should be offered to him, all that come afterward should be the more blessed. Learn this, you young ones, dedicate the first of your years unto God, the very first of your first, the dawning of your years, Exod. xxiii. 19.

Obs. 6. If you dedicate your young days to God, when the consummation of your years comes, how may you keep a feast of pentecost! The Jews dedicated the first-fruits fifty days before, and at the fifty days' end kept their joyful feast of pentecost: so might you if you dedicated your young years unto God. On the other side, what a sad thing will it be for old men that but now begin to think of God and Christ! it is well you do so, but you cannot do it so comfortably as you might have done, if you had begun in your younger years. If the Jews, when their harvest was done, had brought two loaves to God, might God say, Why did you not bring the first-fruits unto me? God might so upbraid you; but, however, come in to God, and he will not upbraid you, he upbraids no man; but the comfort will not be so much, because your consciences will upbraid you.

Obs. 7. Happy is that man, who, when he comes to reap the fruit of his actions, shall have a feast of joy. Thus it was with the Jews, the very beginning of their harvest was with a feast, and the conclusion with a feast too. All the actions of our lives are a sowing of seed, if you sow sparingly, you shall reap sparingly; and happy those men when they come to reap, who find both the beginning and conclusion of their reaping a joyful feasting. Many sow merrily, but they reap horror and anguish; but when the saints come to reap, they shall have a feast of joy. " At thy right hand are pleasures for evermore."

Obs. 8. Much praise is due to God for the fruits of the earth, for outward comforts. On the fiftieth day they were to solemnize the mercy of God in giving them the fruits of the earth for their harvest. How much praise then is due for Jesus Christ, and all spiritual mercies in him! Though we ought to bless God for the things of the earth, yet we should be so swallowed up in blessing God for his word and ordinances, and spiritual mercies, that in comparison our hearts should be above the fruits of the earth. Therefore, observe that when Ezekiel prophesies of the blessed state of the church, by the Jewish feasts, though he mentions the passover, and new moons, and sabbaths, and the feast of tabernacles, yet not the feast of pentecost; there is no mention of keeping a feast for blessing God for these things. Not but that they should do so, but that their hearts should be so carried up with abundance of spiritual mercies, that then they should be all for Christ, and for heaven, and for eternity.

Obs. 9. It was a great engagement to them rightly to use the creatures, when they had first dedicated them to God, and in the conclusion of harvest had solemnized his mercy in giving them. For God thereby taught them that they might be further engaged to use all creatures for his service. If God give a heart to dedicate the beginning of a mercy to himself, and when the mercy is fulfilled, in a solemn manner to bless God for it, it is a mighty engagement to make use of this mercy for God's honour. The reason why many are so loose in their conversations, and do not employ the creatures of God to his glory, is, because they do not in a solemn manner bless God for that they enjoy. As in your trading, if you have comfortable incomes, and you take these comforts, and thank God in a slight manner for them, how do you use them afterwards? only for yourselves and for the flesh. But when you hear of riches flowing in upon you, if you can immediately take the first-fruits and give some part to God's service as a testimony of thankfulness, and in your families and closets in a solemn manner give God the glory for the good success you have had in your estate, this will be a mighty engagement to you to use your estates for his service.

Mark that at the first, in their preparation, they were to bring but a sheaf, but afterward, Lev. xxiii. 17, they were to bring " two wave loaves;" in the first they were to offer " one he lamb without blemish," but afterward " seven lambs, and one young bullock, and two rams," &c., both burnt-offerings, and sin-offerings, and peace-offerings, when they had received the full harvest.

Obs. 10. Though you are forward to give God glory when you are young, the first-fruit of your years, yet when you come to be old, you should still flourish in the courts of God's house. First they offered but a little unto God, afterward abundance. Do you so? I appeal to all old men who are here this day, if God gave you heart to give up your young years to him, bless him for it; but now when you are old, are you as forward as ever you were? You ought to be not only so, but much more abundant in the work of the Lord. Nay, cannot others witness against you, that there was a time wherein you were more forward, and that now you begin rather to temporize? The Lord forbid this should be spoken of any old men. God expects more afterward than at the first-fruits; and though nature may decay, yet there is a promise that in their old age they shall flourish in the courts of God's house, and shall manifest the graces of his Spirit much more. We are ready at the first-fruits to offer unto God somewhat, when his mercy comes first; but when mercy comes afterward more fully, we should be more full in our offerings.

You will say, What is the meaning of this, that there is a burnt-offering, a sin-offering, and a peace-offering in the feast of pentecost? what is the difference of these three offerings?

The difference is this; the burnt-offering was in testimony of their high respect to God, that is, they tendered up something to God as a testimony of the high and honourable esteem they had of his majesty, it was wholly to be given up to him. Now in the other they had respect to themselves, the sin-offering was not to offer a sacrifice merely to testify respect to God, but to be a typical signification of Christ's sacrifice for sins; they were to look through their sacrifice to Christ, and their sin-offering was to be an atonement for their sin. The peace-offering was in thanksgiving for a mercy, or when they would petition to God for a further mercy. All this must be done in the day of pentecost.

But, beside solemnizing the mercies of God in their harvest, there is another object that is constantly affirmed by the Jews, and I find many divines making no question of it; but it is not so clearly laid down in the word. They say, God in this feast solemnized the giving of the law, and this is their ground; because fifty days after their coming out of Egypt, God gave the law, and so they say pentecost was appointed to bless God for giving the law. The Jews say that God dealt with them as a king might deal with a poor man in prison, first he releases him of his bondage, and then tells him, that after such a time he will marry him to his daughter; now, say they, will not this man count every day till this time come? so, when God delivered us out of Egypt, he told us, that after such a time he would give us his law, and marry us to his daughter, which is the law; and this is the reason why we count so diligently the very weeks, nay, the days, as longing for that time when we are to be married to the law.

Obs. From whence we may note, that we are not only to keep God's law, but to rejoice in it; not only to look at what is commanded as a duty, but as a high privilege, and so bless God for the law. It is a higher thing to love God's law and rejoice in it, than to obey it: Great peace shall they have that love thy law. David professed that he loved the law of God more than silver and gold, that it was sweeter to him than the honey, and the honeycomb. The Jews at this day rejoice when the law of God is read, and in their synagogues, when the law of God is brought out, they lift up their bodies in a kind of exultation, rejoicing that God gave this law to them.

Further, the time of their pentecost was the time of the descending of the Holy Ghost upon the apostles: as God at that time gave the law by Moses, so the Spirit at that time came by Christ, to show that we are in the gospel to receive the Spirit of God, to enable us to fulfil the law. They had the letter of the law, but, in comparison of what we have, they had not the Spirit, but now the Holy Ghost is come in a full measure; as he then came upon the disciples, so he comes now in the time of the gospel in a fuller way than formerly, there is a continual pentecost.

But the works of God do not of themselves sanctify any time: hence observe, that we may run into a thousand absurdities if we argue, because the Jews had such a time, we may have such a time, or because there were such blessings at that time, therefore we may sanctify that day. No, the works of God do not sanctify any time, of themselves; it must be either the word written, or some immediate dictate of the Spirit, that must sanctify any day. Certainly, the work of our redemption itself is not enough to change the sabbath, if we had not some footing for a new institution. We usually give this ground for the change of the day, because of the greatness of the work; but though the works of God be never so great, we sin in sanctifying any set and stated time for such work; except there come an institution, it will be but will-worship in us, and God will not be put off with this. What! is not this as great a work as the Jews had, and may not we celebrate the memory of it as they did? But God will say, "Who required these things at your hands?" Thus far you may do, that is, bless God for those works all the days of your lives; but to sanctify any particular day for them, certainly that cannot be done without sin: we have our warrant for the Lord's day, as well as the greatness of the work, because of the practice of the apostles, who were inspired by the Holy Ghost.

The next is the feast of trumpets: only one particular about it at this time, because Providence makes it so seasonable. In the seventh month (which was the first month of their *annus civilis*) there were three feasts; of trumpets, of expiation, and of tabernacles.

The first was THE FEAST OF TRUMPETS. There was a threefold use of trumpets among the Jews: 1. For the calling of the congregation together, as we do with bells. 2. The calling of them to war. 3. For the solemnizing of their feasts.

There are four ends given by divines for the feast of trumpets; some I confess are very improbable, but there are two very probable. The one is, this feast was to celebrate the new year with them; as every new month they had the feast of the new moon, to celebrate the beginning of the month, so in the beginning of the year they had a feast to celebrate its commencement; that was this feast, for it was on the first day of their civil year: so that it is very probable this feast was appointed to bless God for the new year, as well as one to celebrate the new month. Yet this can be no ground for us now to consecrate the beginning of every new year to God: that was Jewish, and it ceased: if we will have any consecration of a new year, it must be by virtue of some institution or other; let who can, show the institution: we must not think because it has a show of wisdom, and seems reasonable, therefore it may be; this is not enough in matter of worship, you must strictly tie yourselves to an institution. As it is Jewish, so it is heathenish; the heathens consecrated their new year to the honour of their god Janus; and we read in Concilium Antisiodorense, in France, in the year six hundred and fourteen, it was the judgment of that council, that it is not lawful to observe the festivities of the Gentiles, to keep their worship and observe their calends, (that is, the beginning of their months,) to adorn houses with laurels and green bays, for all these practices (saith the council) savour of paganism. And likewise an ancient writer saith, that the calends of January are rather to be taken heed of, than to be accounted calends, and so to be sanctified. And further, he saith, the church has appointed a solemn feast to be upon that very day, because of the notorious abuses there were wont to be upon that day. And Polydore Virgil saith, that these solemnities of laurel, and bays, and masks, and mummings, and such vanities, come from the heathens' Bacchanalia and Saturnalia, that were wont to be at that time of the year. However, therefore, we think we honour Christ, and call it the circumcision day of Christ, yet by those customs we dishonour him, for they are rather heathenish than Christian.

Non licet iniquas observationes agere calendarum et otiis vacare Gentilibus, neque lauro aut viriditate arborum cingere domos. Omnis enim hæc observatio paganismi est. Canon. 74.

Statuit universalis ecclesia jejunium publicum in isto die fieri. Alcuinus de Divinis Offic. c. 4.

Though there may be some natural reason of rejoicing, yet no ground for consecration.

Let no man object and say, These solemnities have been a long time in the church. It is true these are ancient, but from whence comes the antiquity? From hence, because Christians, being newly converted from paganism, kept as much as possible of the pagan customs, only they gave them a turn to Christian solemnities; therefore all the argument of antiquity, either for these days, or ceremonies, or prelatical government, comes from their pagan customs. They lived among pagans, and having been lately pagans, they savoured and smelt of heathenism still. So now, many plead that such things were in the first reformation: no marvel they retained them, for they were newly come out of popery, and they savoured and smelt of popery. Indeed to plead the antiquity of these things, which men must show when they are put to it, is one of the greatest arguments against them. Thus the feast of All-saints was turned from the heathens' feast Pantheon; and on the feast of the purification of the virgin Mary, which they call Candlemas, the heathens had the festivity of their goddess Februa, (who was the mother of Mars,) from whence comes the name of our month February, and they celebrated that time with candles, and such things as papists do now.

The like may be said for the argument of antiquity for the prelates. O, say some, such government has been ever since the Christian religion has been in England. Grant that there has been some kind of bishops ever since, but from whence came they? We find in histories, that when the pagans were in England they had their flamins, and their archflamins, London was one, and York was another; and when they were converted to the Christian religion, still keeping some of their heathenish customs, instead of their archflamins they made archbishops, and of their flamins, bishops, and that in their very places, as London and York, and some say Chester. This is the very ground of the antiquity of them; therefore, my brethren, let not us be put off with such arguments as these; men delude you, and baffle you by these arguments.

The second reason of that feast, the Hebrews think, was a remembrance of Isaac's deliverance, when he should have been sacrificed, and the ram was caught by the horns to be sacrificed in his stead; they draw it from this argument, because that feast is called a memorial, (say they,) to remember the deliverance of Isaac, and it must be by the trumpets of rams' horns, to call this to remembrance; but it seems to be far from the meaning of the Holy Ghost. A third reason of the feast of trumpets, some say, (Cajetan among others,) was instituted for a memorial of God's giving the law by sound of the trumpet. But that is not likely, because this feast was not kept at the time of God's giving the law; if there were any time for the celebration of giving the law, it must be at the feast of pentecost. A fourth, it was for a celebration of a memorial of all the mercies of God to them in their wars, which was declared by the blowing of the trumpets. But I rather take another reason, to be a main and principal reason of God's institution of this feast; to be a preparation to the feast of atonement and expiation. It is called "a memorial," saith Calvin, Lev. xxiii. 24, for this reason, to put them in mind to humble themselves before God, "to afflict their souls" in the day of atonement; and, secondly, "a memorial" before God, that God may remember them for mercy; so the Jews observe, that from the first day of the seventh month to the tenth day, there were more than ordinary exercises in giving of alms, in praying, in going to their synagogues; they were very devout for those ten days in preparation for the day of atonement. From whence

Obs. Ministers should blow their trumpets to the

people to prepare them for the day of fasting. God has accepted those poor fasts that we have kept, abundance of mercies we have received on them; scarcely one, but we hear good news after it; if we had kept fast days as we ought, if we had been prepared as we should, oh what might we have obtained of God by this time! If God accepts such poor things as we do, (as God knows they are poor and mean,) if we had every time a trumpet blown before us to prepare us for the day of atonement, what atonements might England have made with God before this time!

The next feast was, THE FEAST OF EXPIATION, in the tenth day. I thought not to have spoken of that, because the feast of expiation is a fast rather than a feast; but that is meant here as well as any of the other, for this reason, though it were a fast, yet the Hebrew word translated solemn feasts, signifies only a settled, stated, solemn time. And, secondly, it was a great mercy to them to have such a fast day; though the day of atonement was a day for afflicting themselves, yet it is the cause of rejoicing to a nation that God grants them such a day of atonement; it is a special means to make way to the joy of a nation, and therefore is included amongst the other: now the history of that you have in those two famous scriptures, Lev. xvi. and xxiii. In this day of atonement, there are divers things very observable and useful.

1. The solemn charge that God gave for afflicting men's souls upon that day. In a few verses, three several times God charges them to afflict their souls, to humble their souls, Lev. xxiii. 27, 29, 32. God appointed one day in the year for all the Jews to afflict their souls, to make an atonement between God and them in a day of fast, and they were charged to afflict their souls; and that soul that did not, God threatened to cut it off.

2. The priest was to go into the holy of holies, where he went but once a year; Lev. xvi., the beginning and the latter end compared together, you shall find it. This may teach us, that if ever we are to look upon Jesus Christ in the presence of God, in the holy of holies, making intercession for us, it is in the day of atonement. In the day of a public fast of the kingdom, we are to exercise our faith upon Christ, as entering before God into the holy of holies for us. After we have charged upon our souls our sins, and afflicted them, we must likewise cast up an eye of faith, beholding Jesus Christ our High Priest at that day before the Father, making intercession for us.

3. On that day the priest was to make an atonement for all the holy things; in Lev. xvi. 20, "When he hath made an end of reconciling the holy place, and the tabernacle of the congregation, and the altar," &c., the priest was not only to seek to make reconciliation between God and the people, but to reconcile the holy places; even the holy of holies, and the tabernacle, and the altar had a kind of pollution in them, and must be reconciled: so infectious is the sin of man. This teaches us, that in a day of atonement, of fasting, we are to have a special care to seek mercy from God, to be reconciled to us, in respect of all our holy duties and offerings; we are to seek then to get the best services that ever we performed in all our lives cleansed, that God may be pacified in regard of the filth and uncleanness that cleaved even to them. In the day of a fast, you are not only to confess your notorious sins to God, those which in their own nature are sinful; but you are to examine all your holy duties, and seek to make peace with God in regard of the uncleanness that has been in them. This few think of; in the day of a fast, they confess such sins as are vile in themselves; but to be sensible of the uncleanness of holy duties is as necessary.

4. In their day of atonement the priest was to lay the sins of the congregation upon the scape-goat. The story of the scape-goat was this, the priest must come and confess the sins of the congregation, laying his hand upon the head of the goat, and then he must send this goat into the wilderness. The meaning is of great use to us; Jesus Christ is the scape-goat, and in the days of our humiliations we are to come and lay our hands upon Jesus Christ, and confess all our sins over him, and look upon all our sins as laid upon him. Now the scape-goat was to be sent into the wilderness. What is that? That is, sent into a land of forgetfulness, so as the Jews should never see that goat again upon which their sins were laid; it signified to them, that their sins were now so forgiven, that they should never hear of them again. Thus are our sins upon Christ, as we shall never see nor hear more of them. In the day of our fasts we should thus exercise our faith upon Christ.

5. A fifth thing that was to be done, was to sprinkle the blood of the slain goat upon the mercy-seat, and before it. It is the blood of Christ that is upon and before God's mercy-seat, that procures mercy from thence for us.

6. The priest must "take a censer full of burning coals of fire from off the altar before the Lord, and his hands full of sweet incense beaten small," Lev. xvi. 12; to teach us, that in the day of our solemn fasts we must be sure to get our hearts full of burning coals from the altar, full of affection and zeal, full of mighty workings of spirit to God. Although you that are godly, and so are priests to God, at other times come with few coals from the altar, your affections scarce heated; but in a day of atonement you must come with your hearts full of coals, and be sure it be fire from the altar, do not satisfy yourselves in natural affections then, but be sure you be full of spiritual affections. And then, "full of sweet incense." What was that? It typically represented our prayer; you must be sure to have your hearts full of prayer, to send up abundance of incense before God. The incense must be of spices "beaten small." What is that? The prayers that we are to send up to God in the day of atonement, must come from much contrition of spirit, our hearts must as it were be beaten small to powder, then they are able to send forth such incense as is a sweet savour to God. Many of you in the day of a fast seem to be full of prayer, but is this prayer a sweet incense to God or no? How shall I know that? By this; God has appointed the incense upon the day of atonement to be such as must come from spices beaten; if thy heart be beaten to powder, and thy prayers be the savour and odour of thy graces, which are as spices, and heated by the fire of God's Spirit, then there will be incense that pleases God: first, graces, which are the spices; secondly, the contrition, that is the beating small; then the fire of God's Spirit, to cause the incense to rise up before God as a sweet savour.

7. In the day of atonement, the cloud of the incense must cover the mercy-seat, ver. 13; and then the blood both of the bullock and the goat must be "sprinkled upon the mercy-seat," and that "seven times;" and, ver. 15, the blood of the goat must be sprinkled, not only "upon the mercy-seat," but "before the mercy-seat." What is the meaning of this? must our mercy-seat be clouded in the day of atonement? we had need have it appear to us, and not be clouded. Yes, in the day of atonement it must be clouded, but with incense; the incense that was sent up was a type of the sweet perfume of the merit of Jesus Christ. Now, in days of atonement, we must look up to the mercy-seat, and see the merit of Jesus Christ round about it as a cloud covering it; to teach us, that no man must dare to look upon the mercy-seat of God as it is in itself, but must have the incense of the merit of Christ round about it. The reason was given why the Lord must have the in-

cense as a cloud, "lest he die;" if he had entered into the holy place and there looked upon the mercy-seat, not clouded by incense, he must have died for it. Those who think to come into God's presence, and to receive mercy from God out of Christ, they die for it. This is the damnation of men's souls. Mercy is an attribute of God, but if we, who are sinful creatures, dare to look upon this attribute of mercy, and not have the incense of Christ's merit, it is the way to destroy our souls. Oh how many thousands are in hell for this! Many who are afflicted for their sins, and cry to God to forgive them, and think to exercise their faith upon God as merciful, yet not looking upon the mercy-seat as clouded with the merit of Christ, it proves the destruction of their souls. In a fast, you must not look upon God as the Creator of heaven and earth, or as merciful in himself barely, but upon God's mercy in his Son, and so exercise your faith; or else you can never make an atonement, but rather will procure God's wrath. It is not only dangerous, but horrible, once to think of God without Christ, says Luther.

Non solum periculosum, sed horribile est de Deo extra Christum cogitare. Luther in Psal. cxxviii.

Again, the blood of the bullock and the goat must be sprinkled "seven times" upon the mercy-seat. When we come to make our atonement with God, we must exercise faith in the blood of Christ, and sprinkle it seven times, that is, again and again, upon the mercy-seat. We look upon God, when we pray to him, as a God of mercy, and we present ourselves in humiliation before the mercy-seat; but know this, that the mercy-seat will do us no good without the blood of Christ; faith must take this blood of Christ, and sprinkle it, tender it up to God the Father for the atonement of our souls, and procuring our mercy. Not only so, the blood of the bullock and the goat must be sprinkled *upon* the mercy-seat, and *before* the mercy-seat; we must not only think there can be no mercy obtained from God but by the blood of Christ, but we cannot so much as have access to God's mercy-seat. We must know, that all sinners are banished from the presence of God, and cannot have access to God's presence as they are in themselves.

8. Lastly, this day divers times is called "a sabbath of rest," that is, a sabbath of sabbaths; so it is in the original, as one of the principal sabbaths they had. I did not handle it amongst the sabbaths, because it comes in now more fully amongst these solemn feasts. There must be more rest in the day of atonement, than in their other solemn days. That was permitted in others that was not permitted in this, to teach us, that in the day of fasting, above any day, we must get our souls separated from the world, there must be a rest in our hearts, a rest from sin, a rest from the world; it must be a sabbath of sabbaths unto us.

Now, notwithstanding God had given this solemn charge for this day of atonement, yet, Theodoret tells us, that in his time they had so degenerated, that they spent it in sports, and made it a day of mirth. God grant, that from the ordinariness of our days of atonement this abuse may not spring, as in some places it does; by the wickedness of men's natures, the most solemn things that ever God gave us in charge in time degenerate.

One note more from this feast of expiation. We find in Grecian history, that yearly the Greeians were wont to have a kind of expiation for their cities, in imitation of the custom of the Jews. Certain condemned persons were brought forth, with garlands in manner of sacrifices, and were cast down from some steep place into the midst of the sea, and offered to Neptune the god of the sea, with these words, Be thou a περίψημα for us. In times of public infection in their cities, to make an atonement between them and their gods, certain men were brought to be sacrificed to their gods, for an expiation for the whole city; and they were called καθάρματα: this word was used to signify, that that man who was to expiate for all the sins of their cities to their gods, having all their sins upon him, was accounted as filth and offscouring. The apostle, in 1 Cor. iv. 13, uses the same expression, by which we may understand the meaning of those two words he employs; "We are (saith he) made as the filth of the world, and are the offscouring of all things;" περίψημα, καὶ περικαθάρματα, alluding to the custom of the Grecians. We, for our parts, (saith he,) are made as despicable and odious in the sight of the people, and are as much loaded with curses, as those condemned persons who had all the sins and curses of the people laid upon them, and were offered to their gods for expiation.

Suidas.

THE FEAST OF TABERNACLES. The history of this feast is in Lev. xxiii. 34. The Jews were to take boughs off the trees, and make booths of them; and those that write the history of their manners tell us, because they could not make booths and tabernacles for all the people, some of them thought it sufficient to carry boughs in their hands, and those boughs they used to call hosanna; Do thou fold, or prepare, the hosanna. Therefore, when Christ came to Jerusalem, they cried, "Hosanna to the Son of David;" the meaning was not a prayer, Save us, O thou Son of David, as some would have it; but, Hosanna to the Son of David; that is, We hold forth these boughs to the honour of the Messiah, the Son of David. Now for those boughs, ver. 40, there was a command of God, that they should be of goodly trees, palm trees, or willows of the brook; but why so? It denoted, that whereas they had lived forty years in the wilderness, in a dry place, they were now brought to a fruitful land, that had much water, which was a great advantage in those hot countries; and therefore they were to bring boughs of the willows of the brook, and of goodly trees, that might most testify the goodness of God in delivering them from the wilderness, and in bringing them to a land filled with sweet and pleasant brooks. Observe the reasons why God would have this feast kept. He aims at these three things chiefly.

Necte hosannam.

I. God would have them bless his name for his mercies to them in the wilderness, when they dwelt in booths. He appointed, that once a year they should call to mind the great mercies of God in his dispensation towards them, who for forty years were in the wilderness, and had not a house all that time, but dwelt in tabernacles. This was a mighty work of God! That so many hundred thousands should live forty years without a certain dwelling, manifested his exceeding protection over them, and his providence every way to supply necessaries for them, even as well as if they had had the strongest houses. God would declare thereby, that the church in this world is not to expect any settled condition, but to be as men that dwell in tents, removing up and down, and so seek after a city that hath foundations, as is said of Abraham. At this feast, the Jews were wont to read the Book of Ecclesiastes, principally because it speaks so much of the works of God's providence. All the while God's people dwelt in booths and tabernacles, God himself would dwell in a tabernacle. God would not have a house built unto him, till he had brought his own people to be settled in houses of their own; and therefore when David began to think that he had a house of cedar, and surely God must have one too, God tells him, Did I ever speak, saying, "Why build ye not me an house of cedar?" as if he had said, As long as my people went up and down in booths and tabernacles, I was content to have a tabernacle for my dwelling. Thus God is willing to suit himself to the condition of his people: saith God,

If your conditions be afflicted and unsettled, I will be so too. In all their afflictions, God was afflicted; in all their unsettledness, God seemed to be so too. Afterwards, when God's people were settled in Jerusalem, then God would have a house built him. God would hereby teach us, that if he be content to be in a condition like us, then we must be content to be in a condition like him; as thus, when we are afflicted, will God be afflicted with us? when we are unsettled, will God be (as it were) unsettled with us? then let us not think it much, if God's truth and gospel suffer, to suffer with God. When God is magnified and praised, our hearts should be enlarged too, and rejoice in his praise. We should consider the condition that God is in in the world, and suit ourselves with that.

Obs. 1. It is good to have a real remembrance of our former low and mean condition. Does God now bring us into a more settled condition than heretofore? Let us not forget our former afflicted and unsettled condition, how ready we were to fleet up and down. If God should grant his people to think themselves settled in their own kingdoms, yet let them never forget the time when they were unsettled in this and other countries. Many of the people of God have thought, what shall become of them, and whither shall they go, unless there be some special mercies of God to prevent their scattering; and yet that may be the condition of thousands in the land, before a year has closed. If God should prevent you, ever remember your fleeting condition. It was God's great care of the people of Israel, that they should never forget their dwelling in tabernacles.

Obs. 2. After our humiliations for our sins, and making up our peace with God, it is good to keep our hearts low with meditation of the uncertainty of all things in the world. Note, the time of their feast of tabernacles, they were to dwell in booths upon the fifteenth day of their month, which was but five days after their day of atonement; as if God had said, You have been humbling yourselves, and making your peace with God, yet, when your hearts are comforted with the hope of atonement made, keep them low, take heed of pride; the feast of tabernacles must be kept. And one special means to keep our hearts low, is to remember the uncertainties of the comforts of this world. If your hearts are lifted up, and conceive some excellences in things here, go into your booths, and work your hearts down, keep your feast of tabernacles.

Obs. 3. To keep those humbled who are raised from a low condition to a high one, it is good actually to go into the houses of the poor, and look into their cupboards, and see what provision they have. This will be a means to humble your hearts, when you consider, This was once, or might be now, my condition. God would have Israel's hearts kept low by actually going into booths and tabernacles. Though they had fair and sumptuous houses in the city, yet they were to go out, and live in their booths a while. You might think, Was it not enough for the priest to bid them remember their dwelling in tabernacles, but they must go forth from their houses, and abide in booths?

II. A second end of this feast was, to bless God for all the fruits of the earth they had received, when they had gathered in their vintage. The feast of pentecost was to bless God for their first-fruits, and their harvest; but now they were to join all together, and to bless God for all the fruits of the earth. That this is God's end, is clear in Deut. xvi. 13—15, "Thou shalt observe the feast of tabernacles seven days, after that thou hast gathered in thy corn and thy wine: and thou shalt rejoice," &c.; "because the Lord thy God shall bless thee in all thine increase, and in all the works of thy hands, therefore thou shalt surely rejoice."

From hence there is this lesson.

It is useful to remember what a poor condition we were once in, and the uncertainty of all things we have, even when we have got our riches into our houses. We think them uncertain when they are growing in the field, but after the vintage was gotten in, then they were to keep the feast of tabernacles, to remember the uncertain condition of all things in the world: this we are very loth to do, it is unsuitable to our natures, and therefore this feast of tabernacles was much neglected among the Jews. When God carried them into Babylon, and brought them back again into their own country, they kept the feast of tabernacles more solemnly than ever they had done; Neh. viii. 17, "Since the days of Joshua the son of Nun unto that day had not the children of Israel done so;" they never kept the feast of tabernacles so solemnly from their first coming into Canaan, as then they did. Now, having come out of prison, they could remember the uncertainty of things in the world; men forget this, but if they be driven from house and home, and lose all, then they remember what they have heard and confessed of the uncertainty of all worldly things. Some of our brethren who are plundered and driven from their habitations, if God should ever restore them to their habitations again, their hearts would be enlarged in blessing God, they would be more sensible of the uncertainty of the comforts of the creature than before.

III. The feast of tabernacles had an aim at Christ and the state of a Christian. It was to typify Jesus Christ coming into the world, and pitching his tent amongst us; as John i. 14, he "dwelt amongst us;" he came and pitched his tabernacle amongst us, ἐσκήνωσεν ἐν ἡμῖν. The state of a Christian, likewise, is a tabernacle; 2 Cor. v. 1, "If our earthly house of this tabernacle be dissolved:" till we go where Jesus Christ is gone before us, to prepare mansions for us, our dwelling is in tabernacles.

In the offerings that God appointed to offer in this feast, Numb. xxix. 12, there are some things very observable, but it is difficult to understand their precise meaning. The feast was to be kept seven days; the first day was a great day, and the last day a great day; the first day thirteen bullocks were to be offered, and fourteen lambs; the second day but twelve bullocks, the third day but eleven, the fourth day but ten, every day one decreased, and the last day there was but one offered. Now, divers expositors have sought to find out the meaning of this. Calvin confesses that he does not understand its meaning, and rather than guess, I will, saith he, be silent in it; and yet he ventures upon a very unlikely conjecture, therefore I shall not name it. That which is most likely seems to be in two things: the first is, they must offer every day less and less, that is, (saith another interpreter,) to show their increase in sanctification, that they should grow to more and more perfection every day of their feast, and so have less need of sacrifices than they had before. Thus, it will afford a good note to us, that when we keep days to God, every day we should grow more and more in sanctification, and have less and less sin to answer for, than we had before.

Another interpretation is, that it was to show the cessation of the sacrifices of the Jews, that they were to decrease day by day; and this I take rather to be the meaning, because the last day but one bullock was offered, and yet that was the great day of the feast. "In the last day, that great day of the feast, Jesus stood and cried, saying, If any man thirst, let him come unto me, and drink," John vii. 37. There is somewhat to be noted about Christ there: though it is true it was the feast of dedication, which was their own feast, from whence many would prove the lawfulness of holy-days, yet the truth is, upon examination you shall find there is scarce strength enough from that place to prove it, though it be lawful to take the advantage of such times; but it will appear there, that it was the feast of tabernacles, as in 2 Chron. viii. 9. Their feast of the dedication of the temple was at the same time as the feast of tabernacles. One thing is to be observed from Christ's being at the feast. Why did Christ upon the great day of the feast cry out thus, "If any man thirst, let him come unto me, and drink?" One reason may be, because when men are most strongly possessed with the uncertainties of all outward things in the world, they are fit to entertain the gospel, fit to hear of Jesus Christ. When their hearts are taken off from the world, and they look upon all things here as unsettled, the conclusion of that feast is a special preparation to the gospel. Isa. xl. 6, 7, &c., the preparation to the good tidings of the gospel, is the proclamation that "All flesh is grass, and all the goodliness thereof is as the flower of the field;" yea, the withering of the grass and the fading of the flower must be proclaimed again and again. And then seasonably and acceptably it follows, ver. 9, "O Zion, that bringest good tidings," &c., "say unto the cities of Judah, Behold your God!"

Tremelius thinks, that the expression of Christ at this time had reference to the custom of the Jews at this feast. At the feast of tabernacles the Jews were wont with great joy to bring water out of the river of Shiloh to the temple, where, being delivered to the priest, he poured it out upon the altar, together with wine, and all the people sung that song of Isaiah, "With joy shall ye draw water out of the wells of salvation," Isa. xii. 3. Though it was their own invention, Christ improves it, as if he said, What do you expect from this ceremony of yours? your custom will die and perish in the use of it, but come to me, and there you shall have water; I am the well of salvation; a spring of grace shall be continually in the heart of that man that believeth in me.

One note more is observable in this feast. We have a prophecy, that the feast of tabernacles should be kept in the times of the gospel, that is, in the truth of it, not in the ceremony. In Zech. xiv. 16, there is a prophecy, that when Christ comes, then all people shall "worship the King, the Lord of hosts, and keep the feast of tabernacles." Why is it there prophesied that all people shall come and keep that feast? The reason this feast is named may be this; because in the times of the gospel, men shall acknowledge their outward comforts to be from God, and the uncertainty of all things here, and that they are strangers and pilgrims on earth. In the times of the gospel this shall be made more evident to the hearts of people than ever before. The more Jesus Christ is known in the world, the more shall the hearts of men be taken up with this knowledge, and of the uncertainty of every creature, and have them taken off from the comforts of the world, and never expect any settled condition here, but account themselves pilgrims and strangers. It is a sign that the gospel has prevailed with your spirits, if you have your hearts taken off from the creature, and you look upon yourselves as strangers in the world, and expect an abiding city; then do you keep, in an evangelical sense, this feast of tabernacles.

Thus you have had a view of the chief of the Jewish feasts, which God threatens here shall cease.

There are only these three observations to be drawn from all together.

Obs. 1. Even those things which are appointed by God himself, if once abused, God will not own them, they are then accounted ours rather than God's. "Her sabbaths;" why not my sabbaths? why not God's sabbaths? God appointed them, but because they were abused, God would not own them: "her sabbaths, and her solemn feasts." The ordinances of God, though never so good in themselves, if you pollute them, God rejects them, they are your ordinances then, and not God's. See then that all ordinances are as God would have them.

Obs. 2. It is a grievous and lamentable affliction upon any people, for God to deprive them of his sabbaths and ordinances. His ordinances are included in their solemn feasts. Nay, (saith God,) you will go on in your wickedness, and would put me off with your sabbaths and solemn meetings, which were once my ordinances, and attempt to satisfy me with them, though you continue in your wickedness; no, you shall be deprived of them, you shall have no more sabbaths, no more solemn feast days. It is a sad affliction for a people to have no more sabbaths. How many of you neglect solemn meetings of God's people! Time may come, when God will rend these privileges from you, and then your consciences will grate upon you: Oh the sabbaths that once we had! oh the solemn meetings that once we enjoyed! but our hearts were vain and light; we did not make use of them, and now they are gone. Perhaps thou mayst be cast into a jail, or a dungeon, and there thou shalt keep thy sabbaths, and think upon thy solemn meetings. Oh how unworthy is this land of sabbaths! how did many persecute those that kept sabbaths! never any such thing occurred in any Christian nation: other places, though they are somewhat loose upon their sabbaths, yet they never persecute them that will keep sabbaths. How justly might God have taken away our sabbaths! let us acknowledge God's free grace. What reproach has it been in England to assemble to hear sermons! how justly might God have taken away these solemn assemblies from us long before this! Let us pray, that whatever judgment God sends upon us, he will not take away our sabbaths, nor our solemn assemblies; but that we may still enjoy those we have, and enjoy them to better purpose than ever we have done.

Obs. 3. God has no need of our services. If God call upon us to worship him, it is for our good, not for any need he has of what we do. What do I care, saith God, whether I have any sabbath kept or no? I can provide for my glory, whatever becomes of your duties; I need them not, I can be glorious without you.

But these threats are but to take away spiritual things; carnal hearts think, if they may live and prosper in the world, what care they for sabbaths, and for solemn meetings? Tell them of taking away ordinances, or removing the truth of God's worship, what is that to them? Let us have our peace, our trading, and our outward blessings, and truth will follow. O no, a gracious heart will rather reason thus; O Lord, let us have thy ordinances, let us have thy gospel, and then for our vines and fig trees, our tradings and our outward blessings, we will leave them to thy disposal; if thou wilt give us thy sabbaths and thy ordinances, we will trust thee for our vines and for our fig trees. But if the Lord be so angry as to deny us his ordinances, how can we think that he will be so merciful to us, as to continue our peace, or our civil liberties? No, be sure, if truth be gone, vines and fig trees will not stay long: the next words therefore are, "I will destroy her vines and her fig trees." The Lord may suffer those places that never had sabbaths and ordinances to prosper in their civil peace a long time; but where they had these, and the wrath of God is so incensed as to take them away, it cannot be expected that outward peace and plenty can hold long there. "Seek ye first the kingdom of God and his righteousness," saith Christ, "and all these things shall be added unto you." No, (say they,) let us first seek the kingdom of earth, and the things of heaven will be added to us; which shows the slightness of their account of heavenly things. As the paper and the thread in a shop is given in with the commodity, if a man bargain for the paper and thread, and think the commodity will be given in, what a folly were it? Many men have their thoughts altogether upon the things of this life, and they think the gospel will be given into the bargain; as, if they have peace, they shall, no question, have truth; as if the gospel were the paper and the thread, and the things of the world were the commodities. It is your wisdom, if you would enjoy outward peace, to fix your hearts on ordinances, to cry to God for ordinances, and then God will take care you shall sit under your vines and under your fig trees in peace.

Ver. 12, 13. *And I will destroy her vines and her fig trees, whereof she hath said, These are my rewards that my lovers have given me: and I will make them a forest, and the beasts of the field shall eat them. And I will visit upon her the days of Baalim, wherein she burned incense to them, and she decked herself with her earrings and her jewels, and she went after her lovers, and forgat me, saith the Lord.*

In the former verse God threatens Israel to take away spiritual mercies, their sabbaths, and ordinances, and solemn feasts; but because such a judgment would not be so grievous to many as the destroying of the fruit of the ground, the spoiling of their land, and the loss of those things wherein their riches and outward comforts lay, therefore God joins this threat with the former, "And I will destroy her vines and her fig trees." In vines and fig trees there is a synecdoche, by these are meant all her outward prosperity; I will not lop their vines, I will not cut down some branches of their fig trees only, but destroy them.

Obs. If God stays long before a judgment comes, he comes fearfully indeed, he comes with destroying judgments; then he strikes at the very root of a people's prosperity, and leaves them hopeless of ever recovering themselves. It concerns us to humble ourselves under God's hand, when he only cuts off some branches of our vines and fig trees, of our outward comforts, lest ere long there follows a destroying judgment, cutting to the very root. Does God come into your families, and cut off a branch or two, a child or two? Humble your souls before him, he may cut down the tree, stub up the root ere long, come to the mother or the father, and so root out the family. So in a nation: that is a very remarkable passage in Ezek. xxi. 27, "I will overturn, overturn, overturn." This was spoken to Israel, and to Israel when they were in captivity, and yet God threatens them thus even there, "I will overturn, overturn, overturn."

"Whereof she hath said, These are my rewards that my lovers have given me:" the word תנה translated "rewards," signifies *merces meretricia.* It comes from תנה which signifies to hire with wages, but such wages as are given to harlots; and yet idolatry makes her so impudent, that she uses that very word, "These are my rewards."

Obs. 1. Whoredom is a costly sin to many a man. Many men secretly waste and consume their estates, and their neighbours wonder how they come to be so low. Uncleanness is as a gangrene, as it will consume the body, so the purse; it beggars many men, when the world little thinks the cause.

Obs. 2. God may suffer men in wickedness to prosper, to gain their hearts' desires. "These are my rewards;" these, that you call idols, give me liberal rewards, I have what I served them for.

Obs. 3. It is a dangerous thing for sinners to look back to the sins which they have committed, and then to bless themselves, as if they had gained by them. Before a sin is committed, the sinner by temptation may be persuaded there is much gain to be had; and in the very act of commission, he may find some flash of false contentment and delight; but usually after the act is over, when he looks back, he sees nothing but shame, guilt, and horror. Sinners dare scarcely look back to their sins, after they are committed, except such as are most desperately hardened; but here you see, they look at what they have done, and bless themselves, as if they had obtained a goodly reward by it. As the sight of the evil consequences of sin is a means to humble, so the apprehending of gain by sin is a special means to harden in sin. Judas thought it a brave thing to get the thirty pieces of silver, yet when he saw the evil fruit his sin had produced, he looked with horror upon his sin, and his soul sunk under the burden of it. If Judas, looking back upon his sin, has his spirit filled with horror, what hope is there then of any one, who, looking back upon it, blesseth himself as a gainer by it? If a man prospers, either at the time he sins, or more a little after he has committed it than he did before, or so prospers as that he conceives his sin to be some way instrumental to bring in the gain that he obtained; this hardens exceedingly.

Obs. 4. It is a provoking sin to attribute the blessings of God to our own wicked, sinful ways, and thereby to harden our hearts in those ways. "These are my rewards that my lovers have given me." It is too much to attribute any of God's blessings to second causes, even to our lawful endeavours, to our industry, to our care, to any instruments; but to attribute them to our wickedness is abominable. God expects glory in the acknowledgment of every mercy, and improvement of it to him: where then there is not only a denial of this to him, but a giving it to his enemy, to wickedness, to the devil, whom he hates; this goes exceeding near to the heart of God. It is a great part of our sanctifying of God's name in the use of all the creatures, to acknowledge him in all, that all depends upon him, and thereby to be quickened in his service: but to think all depends upon that which is contrary to God, and therefore, if we want what we would have, to begin to think we have not served our lusts enough, and to be urged to serve them more; this exceedingly provokes him. I will give you a notable example of this wretchedness of man's heart. There was a consultation of many of the Lutheran ministers of Germany, in Hamburgh, to find out the cause why the hand of God was so heavy in those parts of Germany where they lived, that so they might reform what was amiss, and make their peace with God. The issue of their consultations came to this, that the reason of all their calamities and troubles was, because the images of their churches were not adorned enough; and therefore, for preventing the continuance of those calamities, they unanimously consented to improve all the strength they had, to beautify and adorn the images in their churches more. It was a sad thing for ministers who profess against popery, as the Lutherans do, to keep images in churches. But could it be thought that they should be thus vain, yea wicked, as to attribute the unfruitfulness of their vines and fig trees to the want of their superstitious vanities, and to bring their consultations to this conclusion, that if they were more zealous in the one, they should be more prosperous in the other? was not this a sore and a grievous evil, going near the heart of God?

Many attribute the increase of their estates to their lying, their overreaching, and their swearing, and rejoice, This I have gained by these ways. Zeph. i. 9, God threatens to "punish all those that leap on the threshold, which fill their masters' houses with violence and deceit;" that is, the servants of great men, who by oppression and fraud bring in gain to their masters' houses, and then they leap upon the threshold for joy, applauding themselves in the success they have had in their wicked ways. It is usual if men meet with prosperous success, to bless themselves, as if this success came because of their ways, let them be never so wicked. Of late, have not some made the world believe they have had great success, and have argued that their ways were good, and that God had blessed them on account of them, though we know their ways are such as bring most fearful guilt upon themselves and their families; we have all cause to tremble for them, and to pray, "O Lord, forgive them, for they know not what they do:" and as for the success of which they boast, who would not, if he might, wish such success to his enemy?

Obs. 5. Idolaters encourage themselves in their ways from the good they suppose they derive by them; how much more should the saints encourage themselves in the rewards they have from their lover, from the Lord Christ! Psal. cxix. 56, "This I had," (saith David,) "because I kept thy precepts;" this is the reward I have had from my lover; I bless God, I have in some measure got my heart to break before the Lord, and to melt after him, and the Lord has come mercifully to me. Though there is no worthiness in what I have done, yet the Lord has been gracious, he has encouraged his poor servant in his way: these and these mercies the Lord has given me as a fruit of seeking him; he has not said to the seed of Jacob, Seek ye me in vain; I have sought for comfort, for peace, and at last it is come: I will call upon the name of the Lord as long as I live. We should consider what mercies from God we have, and rejoice in them; these are the rewards, these are the love-tokens, that come from our dearly beloved. Hereafter, when the saints come to heaven, how will they bless God, and bless themselves in their God, for those glorious things, those blessed rewards, that they shall then receive from their beloved, and enjoy for ever with him! Then they shall triumphantly say, The world said heretofore, What profit is there in serving of the Lord? But blessed be God that I went on, notwithstanding, in the ways of God, and now I see there is profit to purpose: O these joys! O this glory! O this crown! O this happiness! these are the rewards that I have from my beloved.

Obs. 6. Whatever any man gets by sin, or looks upon as gotten by sin, or uses as a means to harden himself in sin, the curse of God is in it, and it will rend him from it, or he shall never enjoy it. "I will destroy her vines and her fig trees, whereof she hath said, These are my rewards that my lovers have given me." Ahab blessed himself in getting Naboth's vineyard by the device of Jezebel; 1 Kings xxi. 16, he "rose up to go down to take the vineyard of Naboth the Jezreelite, to take possession of it;" but, ver. 19, "Thus saith the Lord, Hast thou killed, and also taken possession? In the place where dogs licked the blood of Naboth, shall dogs lick thy blood, even thine." What! you have got the vineyard, you have obtained possession; how? by wickedness. Though you bless yourselves in it now, as a reward of your vile ways, certainly the Lord will either force you, in the anguish and terror of your souls, to vomit up those sweet morsels again, or some fearful judgment of God upon you will rend them from you. That which many have obtained by unjust and sinful ways, they have rejoiced in for a while; but after a while that estate has been in their consciences, as drops of scalding lead in the very apple of a man's eye; so terrible has it been unto them. I will give you a late example, that came to my own hands, in restoring that that was wrongfully obtained many years ago, from one near myself. I name it because the party desired that the thing might be made known to the glory of God. He sent that which he had wrongfully obtained, many years after, with a letter, with these expressions; "Many a throb of conscience had I about it, many an aching heart, and many promises have I made of restitution, and thousands of times have I wished unto you your silver again. What shall I do? to keep it, it is to continue in sin; to give it to the poor, alas, it is not mine own, or at least the evil purchase of gain hoarded up in the stuff of my iniquity; to send it home, the owner is dead: I would to God I had sent it before, that it might not have lain so hard upon me; but seeing that is past, and cannot be recalled, here I send it you; I ask God forgiveness, and I ask you forgiveness, and pray you fail not to pray for me. Sweet Jesus, forgive me." It was kept divers years, but was biting all the while in the conscience of the poor man, and at length it must break forth in such expressions as these. Consider this, every one who has obtained any thing dishonestly, and has blest himself in it; This is the reward I have got by such a cunning device, by such an unjust and deceitful way: you got it cleverly, and have enjoyed it, and been merry with it; well, one day it may thus lie grating in your consciences. Oh then how terrible will it be to you! The best way to be rid of the rewards of sin, when they begin to cause aching in your consciences, is to cast them out yourselves; all your praying to God for forgiveness will never ease you without, if you be able to restore; but if you will not do so, God may come by some hideous judgment, and force them from you in spite of your hearts; and then how terrible will it be to you when you look upon them as being rent by God from you! Oh, now I must part with all that gain and sweetness, that such ways of sin have brought me! the gain, the sweet is gone; but the guilt, the curse, the dregs, the filth remain upon my spirit, and, for aught I know, must stick by me to all eternity. God's judgments will come upon you one day, as strainers, to let out whatever is sweet and delightful to you, and to keep in the filth and dregs. Remember this, you that have got rewards by sinful ways, your rewards of sin may now delight you, but there is a time you shall have rewards for your sins that will not please you.

"I will make them as a forest." God threatens his people to make them as a forest; the Seventy read, θήσομαι αὐτὰ εἰς μαρτύριον, that is, μισθώματα, I will put those things (the rewards) as a witness. You will say, Here is a great difference; "I will make them as a forest," and, I will put those things as a witness: those things, that is, those rewards; they rejoice in the rewards of their iniquity, but I will make them as a witness against them. Certainly there is a truth in this; those things in which you rejoice, as obtained by sin, the Lord will make rise up and witness against you. Be sure now you cast them out, they will else be witnesses against you another day. A guilty man would be glad, when he knows one that would witness against him was dead, or out of the way: have you gained any thing by a sinful course? put it out of the way, for otherwise it will be a witness against you, either upon your sick bed, or at the great day of judgment. But how can these two readings be reconciled, I will make them as a witness against you, and "I will make them as a forest." It is true the English words seem to be very wide from the Septuagint, but there is an easy mistake that might cause the Seventy to render them thus, I will put them as a witness, for יער signifies a forest in the Hebrew, and יעד to witness, so it is used Zech. iii. 6. Montanus reads those words, *contestabatur angelus;* now those that are skilful in the Hebrew know that, there being no more difference in the words than in those letters ר and ד which are so like one another, there might easily be a mistake. But we take it as it is here, "I will make them as a forest." The church is God's garden, hedged in with God's protection, but God threatens to take away the hedge, and let in the wild beasts. The wild beasts are one of God's sore judgments often threatened; those who will not be subject to the blessed holy God, shall be subject unto the ravening and rage of beasts; and it is probable the

Seventy understood it literally of the judgment of noisome beasts to be let in upon them; for I find that they add to the words, "the beasts of the field shall eat them," *καὶ τὰ πετεινὰ τοῦ οὐρανοῦ καὶ τὰ ἑρπετὰ τῆς γῆς*, and the fowls of the heaven and the creeping things of the earth shall devour; but they are not in the Hebrew text, and therefore we must let them pass, and only speak of what we have here, of the beasts' eating. Now, according to most interpreters, I am persuaded that it is the intention of the Holy Ghost, to express a judgment beyond the interpretation, of letting in noisome beasts, namely, the Assyrians, the adversaries of Israel, who should come upon them as ravening beasts to devour them.

Obs. 1. Sin makes men like beasts, the beasts of the earth. He means the Assyrians, great ones, and yet he calls them the beasts of the earth. To be like a beast is worse than to be a beast; for to be a beast is but to be as God made the creature, it is no dishonour to it; but to be like a beast is the corruption of a creature, and the deformity of it, the worst deformity that possibly can be. Chrysostom shows it thus, Beasts (saith he) have but some particular evil, take the worst of all, as the swine, sensuality; the tiger and the bear, cruelty; the fox, subtlety, &c.; but wicked men have all evils that all beasts of the world have in them. One wicked man has the sensuality of a swine, and cruelty of a tiger, of a bear, the subtlety of a fox; and whatever is set out emblematically by any beast, a wicked man has it all in his heart; yea, and further, wicked men are worse than beasts in this, that they corrupt themselves in those things which they have in common with beasts, more than beasts do. As the drunkard corrupts himself in his drink, which a beast will not do; a glutton corrupts himself in his meat, more than ordinarily a beast will do: and that I think is the meaning of that text in the Epistle of Jude, ver. 10, "These speak evil of those things which they know not: but what they know naturally, as brute beasts, in those things they corrupt themselves." As for their intellectual parts, they will take upon them as if they knew much; but the truth is, they understand little, and yet will speak evil of that they know not. It is a dreadful text against such, as cry out against men and their ways, when in truth they know not what they are. But, further, "what they know naturally, as brute beasts, in those things they corrupt themselves;" that is, in things they know merely by sense, as they know by tasting, and by smelling, as brute beasts do, in those very things they corrupt themselves more than brute beasts, that is, by excess in meats and drinks.

Would not any account it to be one of the greatest judgments that could befall him, if God should turn him into the fashion of a beast while he lives in this world, though he should still retain the mind of a man? Suppose God should inflict this judgment upon a drunkard, he would still have his intellectual parts as he now has, but his body should be turned into the form of a swine, or a railer into the form of a dog, as they say Hecuba the wife of Priam was, for her railing: would not this be a fearful judgment? Lactantius, from Cicero, observes, If it would be such a judgment as a man would be willing to endure any misery in the world, rather than to have his body turned into the fashion of a beast; is it not as great a misery to keep the fashion of the body, and to have the mind become like a beast, to keep a human shape with the soul of a beast? surely it is worse than to have the shape of a beast with the soul of man.

Si nemo est quin emori malit quam converti in aliquam figuram bestiæ, quamvis hominis sit mentem habiturus, quanto est miserius, in hominis figura animo esse efferato. Lactant. l. 5. c. 1.

Obs. 2. God looks upon wicked men, who do great things in the world, with a contemptible eye. "The beasts shall devour;" that is, the great king of Assyria, and all his courtiers above him, and cavaliers with him, shall come to devour them; they are but beasts. God speaks in a contemptible manner, as he does against Sennacherib king of Assyria; in Isa. xxxvii. 29, God threatens to "put a hook in his nose, and a bridle in his lips," because of his rage and of his tumult; that is, he would use him as a beast, to hook his nose, and to put a bridle into his jaws. Mark, likewise, how contemptibly God speaks of the great king of Babylon, and his whole army, Joel ii. 20, "His stink shall come up, and his ill savour shall come up, because he hath done great things." And so in Psal. lix. 7, "They belch out with their mouth," (saith David,) "they make a noise like a dog, and go round about the city." David means his adversaries that were about Saul in his court. And in Ezek. xxxviii. 3, 4, God says to "the chief prince of Meshech and Tubal, I will put hooks in thy jaws." In Dan. vii. the four great monarchies, Babylonian, Persian, Grecian, Roman, are described by four beasts, and the fourth monarchy, which is by most interpreted the Roman empire, Dan. vii. 7, is described to be "dreadful and terrible, and strong exceedingly; and it had great iron teeth: it devoured and brake in pieces, and stamped the residue with the feet of it: and it was diverse from all the beasts that were before it." Now, this beast raged first in the heathen empire, and after it gave its power to the beast antichrist, as you may read in Rev. xiii., and that beast was like a leopard, spotted, full of uncleanness and filth; or, as some translate it, a panther, who by his scent draws other beasts to him, but devours them; and his feet like a bear, and his head like a lion. Thus, you see how God describes the great ones of the world as beasts, and looks with contempt upon them.

Obs. 3. It is a sore and heavy judgment for a people to be delivered up to the rage of cruel adversaries. "The beasts shall devour them." I will give you up to cruel, wicked men, who will bring you under; you will not be obedient to me, but to them you shall. Hence David prayed, "Let me not fall into the hand of man;" when God put him to choose what judgment he would have, he was quickly resolved to refuse to be given up to the hands of men; that he knew was dreadful: and, Psal. lv. 6, 7, he prays, "Oh that I had wings like a dove! for then would I flee away and be at rest. Lo, then would I wander far off, and remain in the wilderness." In the wilderness! why he would be among the wild beasts in the wilderness, and yet he cries, Oh that I had the wings of a dove! What is the reason? It was because of the cruelty of Saul and his courtiers: David apprehended that he had better fall into the hands of tigers and wild beasts in the wilderness, than into theirs. When Scipio came against Numantia in Spain, and the inhabitants were afraid it would be taken, all the young men first took all the old people in the city, and killed them with as easy a death as they could; then they brought all the riches and treasure of the city to the market-place, and set all on fire; and after that they all took poison; and thus, in one day, old and young, and all in the city, were quite destroyed, rather than they would fall into the hands of their enemies. "Deliver my soul," saith David, "from the sword; my darling from the power of the dog," Psal. xxii. 20. The power of the dog, and the sword, is but one the interpretation of the other. Paul declares, 1 Cor. xv. 32, "If after the manner of men I have fought with beasts at Ephesus:" some interpret this literally, that he did indeed really fight with beasts, as being one way of torment to which they subjected the Christians; but most interpreters think that the meaning is, with men that were beastly, with cruel men; and Estius thinks the men to be those who are mentioned in Acts xix. 9, "Divers were hardened, and spake evil of that way before the multitude." Paul then "departed from them, and separated the disciples." Paul saw that it was a most devilish design, to get the multitude together, and there to speak against him and his doctrine, and against Christ; upon which the spirit of Paul was so provoked, that "he departed from them, and separated the disciples." Thus with many, the more sedition is raised, the better are their designs furthered. Christ tells his disciples, Mark xvi. 17, 18, that serpents shall do them no hurt, poison shall not injure them, and they shall have power over devils; but in Matt. x. 17, "Beware of men:" they might say, Why, blessed Master, serpents shall do us no hurt, we shall have power over devils, what need we be afraid of men? But Christ bids them take heed of men; as if there were more danger from wicked men, than from devils, or from serpents. Therefore St. Paul, in 2 Thess. iii. 2, prays that they may be delivered from ἀτόπων, absurd men; those that had lost the very principle of reason, and were even as beasts. There is a generation risen up amongst us, who have sucked the poison of the old serpent, who are set on fire of hell, and the poison of asps is under their lips. As Romulus and Remus, the founders of Rome, were, as reported, suckled by wolves; so these, who desire to build up Rome again, are like the first founders of that Rome, they seem to be men suckled by wolves; or as the poets feign of Lycaon, turned into wolves for their cruelty; or as it is said of their St. Dominic, who was the father of the Dominicans, that before he was born, his mother dreamed that she brought forth a wolf, with a firebrand in his mouth; and according to that representation in her dream, so he proved afterwards. If we look at the cruelty and rage of these men, we may think, that their mothers have indeed brought forth wolves with firebrands in their mouths: Satan rages in them, and we hope therefore his time is but very short. Had they prevailed, to bring every thing under their power, no chronicle of any nation under heaven, would afford similar stories of horrid cruelties, as the chronicles of these times. Where they have prevailed, in Ireland, such barbarisms have commenced, as here would have risen to the perfection of cruelty. The Lord deliver us from being scourged with these scorpions. Let us humble our souls before God, that God may not humble us before such beasts; that he may not say that England shall be as a forest, and these beasts shall devour them. In the mean time, let us not be offended at their prevailing in some places, for then we should be as beasts ourselves. "So foolish was I and ignorant, I was as a beast before thee," saith David. God saith, He will require of the beasts the blood of his people, Gen. ix. 5. Certainly, God will require of these beasts the precious blood they have drunk: had it been corrupt blood, God would not so much have cared for it, but it is the blood of his saints. Let us believe that God will turn the rage of man, the rage of beasts, to his praise, Psal. lxxvi. 10. Surely the Lord cannot possibly behold without indignation his lambs, who are so precious in his eyes, torn and worried by such beasts as these. We may well say with the prophet, Hab. i. 2—4, "O Lord, how long shall I cry, and thou wilt not hear! even cry out unto thee of violence, and thou wilt not save! Why dost thou show me iniquity, and cause me to behold grievance? for spoiling and violence are before me: and there are that raise up strife and contention. Therefore the law is slacked, and judgment doth never go forth: for the wicked doth compass about the righteous; therefore wrong judgment proceedeth." When the Jews made use of Philo to apologize for them to Caius the emperor, Caius used him very ruggedly; when he came out of his presence, to encourage the Jews he said, Surely Caius will arm God against himself for us.

But, some may say, surely these men are not beasts, for they are skilful warriors: mark that text of Ezek. xxi. 31, "I will deliver thee into the hand of brutish men, and skilful to destroy;" they are skilful to destroy, and yet brutish men. We have a promise from God, and our prayers should hasten its fulfilment; "I will cause the evil beasts to cease out of the land;—the beast of the land shall no more devour them," Ezek. xxxiv. 25, 28. Oh that that time were come! Oh that the Lord would so work for us as to cause our beasts to cease out of our land, that they might no more devour! Such a time is coming; "No lion shall be there, nor ravenous beast shall be found there; but the redeemed shall walk there," Isa. xxxv. 9. In the mean time, though our brethren endure hard things by these cruel beasts, and though God may perhaps bring some of us under the rage of them, let us be patient, and comfort ourselves in these promises.

Ver. 13. *And I will visit upon her the days of Baalim, wherein she burned incense to them, and she decked herself with her earrings and her jewels, and she went after her lovers, and forgat me, saith the Lord.*

This is the conclusion of the threatenings in this chapter; now God will punish them for all their sins together. If a generation succeed in wickedness, God may justly come upon that generation, for all the sins of former generations; all the blood from Abel to Zachariah shall be required of this generation. "I will visit upon her all the days of Baalim;" ever since they served Baal. Let men take heed of continuing in the ways of sin: who can tell what sin may put a period to God's patience with a nation, a family, or an individual? Though God has spared heretofore, upon the next sin committed he may put such a period to forbearance as to come upon the family, not only for that sin, but for all the sins it has committed since it was a family; and so for all the sins of a nation, since it was a nation; and for all thy sins, ever since thou wast a sinner! Men go on awhile in the ways of sin prosperously, but when God visits, what will become of them? "What will ye do in the day of visitation, and in the desolation which shall come from far? to whom will ye flee for help? and where will ye leave your glory?" Isa. x. 3. Now you are merry, now you fear nothing, but "what will ye do in the day of visitation?" what will become of you then? whither will you flee then? "and where will you leave your glory?"

"I will visit upon her the days of Baalim;" in the plural number, Baalim; by which some think, and not improbably, that their inferior gods are meant, which they called Baalim; for the heathen had their chief gods, and their *Dii minores*, their lesser gods, who were as mediators to their chief gods; and so our papists have their *Dii minores*, lesser gods, who are tutelar gods, either over nations, or over families, or over particular diseases, &c. As they say, for England, St. George; for France, St. Dennis; for Ireland, St. Patrick; for Wales, St. David; for Scotland, St. Andrew, &c. These saints are in imitation of the heathens. Baal, or, in the Chaldee dialect, Bel, was the first king of Babylon after Nimrod, the first that was deified, and reputed as a god after death; whence those men who were deified after their death, and worshipped as gods, as the papists worship their saints, they called Baalim; as from Julius Cæsar, those kings who followed after were called Cæsars. This interpretation throws light upon 1 Cor. viii. 5, 6, "Though there be that are called gods, whether in heaven or in earth, (as there be gods many, and lords many,) but to us there is but one God, the Father, of whom are all things, and we in him; and one Lord Jesus Christ." If the apostle had spoken in Hebrew, it would have been, "Though there be many Baalim, there is to us but one God, and one Baal;" for in Hebrew, Baal is Lord; there are many gods, (say they,) i. e. divers greater gods, and many lords, i. e. many Baalim, which are mediators to their chief gods; but to us (saith he) there is but one God, and but one Lord, but one Baal; we have not Baalim, not many mediators between us and God; but as we have but one God, so we have but one Lord, but one Mediator, who in regard of his human nature is inferior to the Father, but yet such a Lord, "by whom are all things, and we by him:" the papists acknowledge but one God, but they have many lords, many mediators, many that must stand between God and them. This is a heathenish opinion.

Again, Baalim, in the plural number. Another reason not improbable, given by some, is, that it intimates the several images they had of their Baal, in various places, even in their private houses; for idolaters did not satisfy themselves with worshipping their gods in public, but worshipped them in their private houses also. Now, though the Jews had only two idols set up, one in Dan, and another in Bethel; yet they had some representations of those images in their private houses, which may be grounded upon Hos. x. 5, "Because of the calves of Beth-aven," that is, of Bethel, calves of Bethel. Why, how many calves were there there? there was but one calf set up there, and yet here it is plural: now the reason of that is given, that though there was but one calf set up for public worship, yet they had in their private families the picture of that calf, and so brought the worship of Baal into their families. A good lesson for Christians, not to satisfy themselves with public worship, but to bring as much of the worship of God as they can into their families.

"Wherein she burned incense to them." Incense was a typical signification of prayer, in two respects. First, in the sweet savour of it. And secondly, in its ascending by fire: so all our prayers should be as incense, sweet before the Lord, and ascend up with the fervency of zeal and faith: it is proper to God alone to have such incense burnt to him: the heathens burnt incense to their idols, imitating the worship of God.

"She decked herself with her earrings and her jewels." They worshipped their idols in a sumptuous manner, adorning themselves with costly apparel, especially in front: the word נזמה translated jewels, signifies the nose jewel; and in Isa. iii. 21, is translated "nose jewels:" they hanged upon their faces jewels to make themselves beautiful before their idols. Harlots adorn themselves more pompously than grave matrons. By this many simple people are drawn to the love of idolatry, which is spiritual whoredom. They thought that God would accept of their service the rather, because of the costly jewels, that hung about their ears and nostrils. From whence

Obs. To think that God will accept our service the rather because of any apparel, or any thing of our own devising, is to deal with God as the heathens with their idols. We must take heed of that. The heathens instituted garments that they might be accepted. A council in the year of Christ 333, by one of its canons, anathematizes all those who shall judge one vesture more holy than another. We are to learn from idolaters to beautify and adorn our souls when we come into the presence of God; did they deck their bodies and hang jewels about ears and noses, when they came before their idols for acceptance? let us beautify our souls every time we come before the living God. And would you know what fine clothes you should wear when you come into God's presence? I will tell you, and especially those women who delight so much in fine clothes, 1 Pet. v. 5, "Be clothed with humility:" the word ἐγκομβώσασθε, means, to clothe with a dress that gentlewomen used to wear in those times, of ribands about their heads: Well, (saith the apostle,) would you have a fine dress, ye women? "be clothed with humility," the finest dress you can possibly have. I will tell you of another garment, 1 Pet. iii. 4, adorned with "a meek and quiet spirit, which is in the sight of God of great price," πολυτελὲς, much set by of God, so translated in some of your books. If you come into God's presence with quiet and meek spirits, and clothed with humility, you will be beautiful in the very eyes of God; but withal remember, both men and women, except you come clothed and decked with the robe of Christ's righteousness, you can never find acceptance.

Concilium Gangrense anathematizat eos qui aliam vestem alia sanctiorem, aut plus facere ad pietatem, judicant.

"She went after her lovers, and forgat me, saith the Lord." Their lovers were remembered, but I was forgotten, saith God. God here speaks as a man bemoaning his sad condition; as if he had said, How am I slighted by my people! the idols can be followed, they can be remembered; but I am neglected, I am forgotten; they have activity for their idols, but none for me; memory for them, but none for me!

Obs. God takes it very ill, when men can find memory, strength, and activity enough for their sinful ways, but none for him. Many complain of weakness, but who was ever so weak, but had strength enough to sin? though memories are weak, yet sinful ways can be recollected.

"Forgat me;" that is, first, they have forgotten what a God I am; secondly, what I have done for them, the great works I have done before them; thirdly, all their engagements to me. Many follow wicked ways, yet sometimes they have checks of conscience, some remembrances of God, and so long there is hope; but when a sinner has so far departed from God, and followed his ungodly ways, as that God is quite worn out of his thoughts, then he is in a sad case indeed. I appeal to you, is it not the case of some here? There was a time when you had mighty impressions of God upon your spirits, and then you could never transact your business, or go into the streets and fields, or awake in the night season, but the thought of God was in your hearts; but there was some haunt of wickedness which you hankered after, temptation came, and you have given way to it, and now, friend, you can go one day after another, and scarce think of God at all. Why have you no thoughts of God now, as you were wont to have? Now and then there come darting in some thoughts of him, but your guilty conscience knows they are very terrible to you; now you can never have a thought of God, but it is as a dagger at your heart. Well, take heed what thou doest, O sinner, go not on in thy sinful ways, till thou wearest out all thoughts of God. Some have done so, though they had checks of conscience. When they have been in wicked company, God has come into their thoughts, and troubled them; but they have gone to wicked company again, and some thoughts of God have followed them; but they have gone again and again, and now they have forgotten God as much if there were no God in heaven; as if God had nothing to do with them, and they nothing to do with God. Oh this is a sad condition indeed! If any of you are declining into such a condition as this, the Lord stop you this day; the Lord awaken your consciences! Ordinarily, the more prosperity men have, the more forgetful they are of the Lord. They "forgat me." As, Gen. xlviii. 20, Jacob set Ephraim before Manasseh, first Ephraim, then Manasseh; Ephraim signifies fruitfulness, and Manasseh signifies forgetfulness: thus it is with men; Ephraim comes first, fruitfulness, God is fruitful to you, and blesses your estates; and then comes Manasseh, forgetfulness. My brethren, if always we had such impressions of God as we have sometimes, oh how happy were it! When God shall again present himself to you, and cause you to remember what impressions of his Divine majesty once you had, it will terrify you. I will give you this rule for your lives: Live such lives, as by them you may hold forth to your brethren such remembrances of God, that they may conclude by what they see in your conversation, Certainly there are deep impressions of the Divine majesty upon the heart of this man; there was a time when he walked lightly, vainly, and foolishly; but now he is serious, considerate, heavenly, and walks with fear. If we act so, how joyful will it be to us hereafter, when God shall appear in his glory! Then to have our consciences tell us, I now see the glory of the great God shining, and, blessed be his name, even this God that appears so gloriously, has appeared often to my soul before; I have kept the impressions of his glory upon my heart, and he was continually in my thoughts. It is a wonder that God should ever think of us, who are so forgetful of him. Psal. viii. 4, "What is man, that thou art mindful of him?" What is man? The word אנוש translated man, some would derive from נשה which signifies forgetfulness. I find Eusebius taking it thus: "What is man, that thou shouldst remember him?" that is, what is forgetful man, that thou shouldst remember him? Yet I think it comes rather from אנש which signifies weakness, sickness: what is weak man, what is sick man? yet if this word come not from the root that signifies to forget, I am sure there is a word derived from such a root, used for women, because of their forgetfulness. We would be glad to have God remember us in the day of our adversity; let us remember God now. All you young ones, remember your Creator in the days of your youth: you old people, whatever you forget, forget not the Lord: let us all remember the Lord, who has remembered us all; who has remembered England in her low estate, for his mercy endureth for ever.

לנשים "As women." Jer. li. 30.

Ver. 14. *Therefore, behold, I will allure her, and bring her into the wilderness, and speak comfortably unto her.*

The former part of this chapter was spent in conviction, threatening, and pronouncing of judgment; but from ver. 14 to the end, contains the opening up of the free and rich grace of God to Israel. It may be said of this chapter, "Mercy and truth are met together; righteousness and peace have kissed each other," Psal. lxxxv. 10. There is a blessed connexion between threatening of judgment and proffering of mercy; but where is the copula of this conjunction? what is it that knits these two together? Here is a bond of union, but it is a very wonderful one, it is in the first word, "therefore;" "*Therefore* I will allure her:" wherefore? This "therefore" has a very strange and wonderful wherefore, if we dwell on what precedes: "She went after her lovers, and forgat me, saith the Lord. Therefore, behold, I will allure her:" there needs indeed a behold to be put to this therefore. "Therefore, behold, I will allure her." Lyra could not see how these things could be joined together, therefore he thinks that this verse has not reference to the one immediately preceding, but to the words in the beginning of the chapter; "Say ye unto your brethren, Ammi," my people, "and to your sisters, Ruhamah," she that hath obtained mercy; "therefore, behold, I will allure her." And Cornelius à Lapide, not understanding the cause of such a connexion, would refer the beginning of this verse to the end of the seventh; "She shall say, I will go and return to my first husband; for then was it better with me than now: therefore, behold, I will allure her." Both of these, though learned men, are papists, and therefore understand but little of the free, rich grace of God, and hence are so much at a loss to connect what goes before with this "therefore;" but the right knowledge of the fulness and the riches of the grace of the covenant, will help us out of this difficulty, and tell us how these two, the greatness of man's sin and the riches of God's grace, may have a connexion one with another, and that by an illative "therefore." I confess, the Hebrew word is sometimes *conjunctio ordinis*, rather than *causalis;* a conjunction intimating the order, rather than at all implying the cause of a thing; but the reading here by way of inference, I conceive to be according to the scope of the Spirit of God, and it gives us this excellent note.

לכן

Obs. Such is the grace of God to those who are in covenant with him, that it takes occasion from the greatness of their sins, to show the greatness of his mercy; from the vileness of their transgressions, to declare the riches of his grace. And the Scripture often adopts this form of expression; as in Gen. viii. 21, "The Lord said in his heart, I will not again curse the ground any more for man's sake;" why? "for the imagination of man's heart is evil from his youth." Strange reasoning: "I will not curse the ground any more for man's sake, *for* the imagination of man's heart is evil from his youth." One would have thought it should have been rather, I will therefore curse the ground for man's sake, because the imagination of man's heart is evil from his youth; but the grace of God knows how to make another manner of inference than we could have imagined. So likewise, Isa. lvii. 17, 18, "For the iniquity of his covetousness was I wroth, and smote him: I hid me, and was wroth, and he went on frowardly in the way of his heart. I have seen his ways," saith God: now one would have thought that the next word should have been, I will therefore plague him, I will destroy him, I will curse him; but mark the words that follow, "and will heal him: I will lead him also, and restore comforts unto him and to his mourners." This is a consequent at least, if not an inference. David understood this reasoning to be agreeable to the covenant of grace, and therefore pleads thus with God, Psal. xxv. 11, "Pardon mine iniquity, for it is great:" Lord, my iniquity is great, therefore pardon it. Hearken, ye saints, hearken, I say, this is the great blessing of God to you, this is the glorious fruit of the covenant of grace; whereas otherwise your sins should have made you objects of God's hatred, they now render you objects of his pity and compassion.

I would saints alone heard me in this thing; but why do I say so? I will recall my word; let all sinners hear me, let the vilest, the worst sinners in the world, hear of the riches of the grace of God in this his covenant, that, if they belong to God's election, they may, seeing the fulness and the glory of God's grace, be enamoured and have their hearts ravished with it, and never be at rest till they get evidence to their souls, that God indeed has actually received them into this his covenant. If, then, God be pleased in the riches of free grace to make such an inference, let us take heed that we cross not the mind of the Spirit, by dwelling on the greatness of our sins, instead of the infiniteness of God's grace. God reasons thus: You have followed your lovers, you have forgotten me, therefore will I allure you. An unbelieving heart would make this inference: I have followed my lovers, I have followed after vanity and folly, and therefore God has rejected me, God will have no mercy upon me, I am undone, the gates of mercy are shut against me. O unbelieving heart, do not sin against the grace of God: he saith, You have forgotten me, therefore will I allure and speak comfortably to you; do not you say, I have forgotten the Lord, and therefore the Lord will for ever reject me: these discouraging, despairing therefores are very grievous to the Spirit of God, which would have us all entertain good thoughts of God, and not to regard him

Tota Scriptura hoc agit ne dubitemus, sed speremus, confidamus, credamus, Deum misericordem esse benignum, patientem. Luther.

as a hard master. It is an excellent saying of Luther, That the whole Scripture principally aims at this; that we should not doubt, but that we should hope, and trust, and believe, that God is a merciful, bountiful, gracious, and patient God to his people. Master Bradford, in one of his epistles, thus expresses himself: O Lord! sometimes, methinks, I feel as if there were no difference between my heart and the wicked, a blind mind as they have, a stout, stubborn, rebellious spirit, a hard heart as they have; shall I therefore conclude thou art not my Father? nay, I will rather reason otherwise; because I do believe thou art my Father, I will come to thee that thou mightest enlighten this blind mind, that thou mightest soften this hard heart, and sanctify this unclean spirit. This is good reasoning indeed, and worthy of one who professes the gospel of Jesus Christ. Again, as the inference of the unbelieving heart is grievous to God's Spirit, as it draws its therefore from the greatness of sin against God's mercy; so the profane heart taking its therefore from the greatness of God's mercy, to the hardening of itself in sin, "treasures up for itself wrath against the day of wrath." What! shall God make his therefore from our sin to his mercy, and shall we make our therefore from his mercy back again to our sins? Where sin abounds, grace abounds; but where grace abounds, sin must not abound. Because God takes occasion from the greatness of our sins to display the greatness of his mercy, let not us take occasion from the greatness of his mercy to be imboldened in the greatness of our sins.

"Behold." Here is a wonder in this inference to occupy the thoughts of men and angels to all eternity; behold, notwithstanding all this, yet you, men and angels, behold the fulness, the riches of God's grace. "I will allure her." What! will not God cast us away notwithstanding the greatness of our sins? let not us then reject God's ways, notwithstanding the greatness of any sufferings we meet with in them: this surely is most reasonable: you should bear with sufferings in God's ways, and yet embrace them, as God bears with sins in your hearts, and yet embraces you. But there follows, "I will allure." The Hebrew word translated "allure," signifies to entice, and is often used in a bad acceptation, *blandiendo decipere*, to deceive by subtle enticing: the Seventy, in their translation, render it by πλανῶ, "I will deceive them;" the Vulgate, by *lactabo;* and others, by *seducam*, "I will seduce them:" God made use of the word to express the sweet and gracious ways in which he intends to deal with them from his gracious affection towards them.

פתה

What God means by alluring his people, when once he is reconciled to them, may be expressed in these three things.

First, I will unfold the beauty and excellency of the infiniteness of my goodness and loving-kindness, and set in array before their souls the exceeding glory of the riches of my grace.

Secondly, Whereas before they went a whoring from me, because their hearts were allured by their lovers, proffering unto them various contentments, and so subtlely beguiling their minds; I will now deal with them in a more powerful manner than their lovers possibly could, and outbid them all. Did their lovers proffer to them comfort? I will bid more than they. Did their lovers proffer gain? I will bid more gain. Did they proffer more honour and respect? I will outbid them in this too: so that I will persuade their hearts that they shall enjoy more in me, than they possibly could in all that their lovers could do for them. And indeed, then the gospel has the true, full, and gracious work upon the heart of a sinner, when it yields to its proffers, as finding that all that the world can bid is now outbidden, and that there is more gain in Christ than in all else besides. You know, when one comes to offer so much for a commodity, and another outbids him, he carries it away: so when the world and sin proffer to the soul such and such contents, if God come and outbid all, the bargain is made up, and God carries away the heart.

Thirdly, I will come upon them even unawares, and, as it were, steal away their hearts by a holy guile; as St. Paul tells us, that he caught the Corinthians with guile, 2 Cor. xii. 16. I will secretly insinuate myself, and draw their hearts in such a sweet and hidden way, that I will take them before they are aware. God deals thus with many a soul, taking it before it is aware, and the soul afterward comes to understand some of the dealings of his grace. Indeed the sinner himself sees he is not where he was before: Surely there has been something working on my heart; I find it is otherwise with me now than it has been; but how this comes to pass I understand not at present, but shall understand hereafter. "Or ever I was aware, my soul made me like the chariots of Ammi-nadib," Cant. vi. 12; that is, the chariots of "a willing people," so the word Ammi-nadib signifies. My heart was caught, and run amain to God, before ever I was aware; God's grace came in such a manner into my heart, and so ravished my soul, that it ran freely and swiftly after the Lord. And this is a blessed deceit when the heart is so deceived and so allured. Thus Christ sometimes sends such a glance of his eye into the heart of a sinner, as surprises the soul, and brings it involuntarily into love with the ways and with the truths of God. His grace has a subtlety in it, as well as the serpent, Prov. i. 4. It is a blessed thing to be thus outwitted, as I may so speak, for the grace of God to be too subtle for our sins. As I remember, Luther, when he was charged with apostacy, acknowledged it, saying, "I confess I am an apostate; but how? an apostate from the devil, falling off from the devil, and returning unto God; such an apostate I am." And happy that man who can say, Blessed be God, I am deceived indeed; but so deceived that my sin is beguiled: I am seduced, but it is out of the ways of sin, into the paths of God and of peace.

"And bring her into the wilderness."

There is some difficulty here; how comes this in between alluring, and speaking comfortably? I told you, that this second part of the chapter was altogether mercy; what can be meant then by bringing into the wilderness? Some, in order to show that it is yet a way of grace that God intends by this phrase, "and bring her into the wilderness," translate the words, after I have brought her into the wilderness, *postquam perduxero eam.* So Tremelius, who was a Jew, and therefore could well understand the Hebrew, renders them; telling us that ו which we translate *and*, is equivalent to אחר *postquam, after*, and then the meaning would be, after I have humbled them thoroughly, as I did their forefathers in the wilderness, then will I speak comfortably unto them. God humbled their forefathers in Egypt, yet that did not suffice; he humbled them afterwards in the wilderness, and then brought them into Canaan. Many times God sends successive afflictions upon his own people, to break their hearts, to humble them thoroughly, and at last "speaks comfortably unto them." It has been so with us; the Lord, not many years since, brought us into bondage, it might have humbled us and broken our hearts before him; but when we began to be delivered, the Lord brought us into the wilderness, and follows us with afflictions to this day, that he may thoroughly subdue us; and yet our trust is, that these trials are working together for our good, making straight the paths, and preparing the way for us into Canaan.

והלכתיה

But, secondly, if you take it as it is here translated,

"I will allure her, and bring her into the wilderness;" then the scope of it may be not the afflicting part of the wilderness, but only a declaration to Israel, that he would show to them the great and wonderful works of his power, and wisdom, and goodness, as he did to their forefathers in the wilderness. Whatever the condition may be into which you shall be brought, yet you shall have me working in as a glorious way for your good and comfort, as ever I did for your forefathers when they were in the wilderness; and this exposition is rather strengthened by that which we have *ex Thargum Jonathæ*, "I will work miracles, great, wonderful, and famous things for them, such as I wrought in the desert."

Operabor miracula, et grandia facinora, qualia edidi in deserto. Thargum Jonathæ.

Has God wrought gloriously for his people hitherto in the ways of his mercy? if reconciled to him, they may expect the same wonderful manifestations for their good, even to the end of the world. We may read the stories of God's wonderful power displayed in delivering his people out of their straits in the wilderness, and make them our own; and plead with God, that he would show forth that old, that ancient power, and wisdom, and goodness of his, as he did unto his people formerly. This is the ground of that excellent prayer, Isa. li. 9, 10, "Awake, awake, put on strength, O arm of the Lord, awake, as in the ancient days, in the generations of old. Art thou not it that hath cut Rahab, and wounded the dragon? Art thou not it that hath dried up the sea, the waters of the great deep?" Awake, awake, thou art he who hast done such great things formerly. It is a great help to our faith to consider what God has done for the church of old.

But, thirdly, Pareus saith, this expression is taken from the condition of a poor man drawn aside out of his way by a thief, who, having allured him from his path, carries him into some desolate place. Then the man begins to bethink himself where he is, and seeing himself in a sad condition, knows not what to do; and yet at that very time there may come in supply, comfort, and help. So, saith God, I will bring you into the wilderness, that is, I will allure you, as the thief allures, and put you into a condition similar to that in which such a poor man is placed. I will, by specious proffers of abundance of good, draw you into situations wherein you shall meet with very great straits for a while, and be confounded, and sore amazed, as not knowing what to do; and then, in the midst of all your distresses, will I come with the fulness of my grace, and "speak comfortably" to your hearts. Thus, though God speaks of bringing into the wilderness, yet still it is with an intention of showing mercy there. And does not this just agree with our condition? have not the ways of God towards England for these two or three years been ways of allurement? God has proffered to us a great deal of mercy, and raised the hopes of his people; and the ministers of God have spoken encouraging words, that surely the Lord intends great goodness towards us, and God knows that we have endeavoured to follow the leadings of his providence, and to render instant obedience to its commands; and yet we are now brought even into the wilderness, into a kind of desolate condition, that for the present we are at a stand, and see afflictions round about us, and the very beasts ready to come and tear us, and pull us in pieces: and yet we can say, to the comfort of our hearts, Lord, if we be deceived, thou hast deceived us; for, Lord, thou knowest that whatsoever we have done, it was our duty to do; and although we are brought into great straits for the present, yet we repent not of having thus followed thee, and the gracious intimations of thy mercy towards us in the beginning of the parliament. We will not therefore say, What is now become of all our hopes? but we expect God, even in this wilderness, to "speak comfortably" unto us. Let not men then upbraid us for what we have done: we repent not, for God has brought us into this situation; and if we are in no other wilderness than that into which he has allured us, we may fully expect deliverance. In this lies the difference between men bringing themselves into trouble, or being brought into it by the allurements of the devil or the world, or by the dealings of God's providence. In the one we cannot, but in the other we may confidently, expect that God will speak comfortably unto us.

Further, there is yet another interpretation, which I think the fullest and most genuine. That you may understand what I shall advance, you must know, that from the beginning of this part of the chapter to the end, God is expressing himself to his people conjugally; that is, whereas his people had gone a whoring from him, yet he would receive them again into conjugal affection and communion. By this expression, then, of God's "bringing into the wilderness," the prophet appears to me to allude to a custom observed by the Jews in their marriages. The bridegroom used to conduct his bride out of the city into the fields, and there they sang their nuptial songs, and delighted themselves one with another; and afterwards he brought her back again, leaning upon him, into the city, to his father's house, where they rejoiced together, and solemnized the nuptials. Now, these fields are called the wilderness, either because they might be some champaign, dry fields surrounding the city; or, because he would allude to the mercy of God in bringing his people up out of Egypt into Canaan, and by giving these fields this title, would remind them of it. Allusion seems to be made to this custom of the Jews in Cant. viii. 5, "Who is this that cometh up from the wilderness, leaning upon her beloved?" Such was the ceremony of marriage, they came out of the fields, leaning upon their beloved, and so were brought into the house of the bridegroom's father. So Christ brings his spouse through this world, which is as the wilderness, and here has his nuptial songs, and takes "his delights among the children of men;" and the church, leaning upon her Beloved, is carried onward to his Father's house, where, ere long, she shall be with him for ever, solemnizing her marriage with the Lamb in a more glorious manner. Thus then we may see the meaning of this expression, "I will allure her, and bring her into the wilderness." As "the bridegroom rejoiceth over his bride," so, God saith, I will deal with you in the fulness of my grace, I will perform all the nuptial rites with you, and be married again to you; and look, whatsoever solemnities are publicly regarded as most sacred and most glorious in your city of Jerusalem, or in any other of your cities, with these will I betroth thee unto me for ever. Let all backsliders, then, amongst us learn from hence, that if they return and repent, God is willing to manifest all expressions of love and goodness to them. "Turn, O backsliding children, saith the Lord; for I am married unto you: and I will take you one of a city, and two of a family, and I will bring you to Zion," Jer. iii. 14.

"And speak comfortably unto her."

The words translated, "And I will speak comfortably," mean, And I will speak to her heart; I will speak to her, either so as to prevail with her heart, or speak to her so as to do her good at the very heart. Many scriptures may be brought to show, that speaking kindly, friendly, or comfortably, the Hebrews express by "speaking to the heart:" thus, Gen. xxxiv. 3, "Shechem spake kindly unto the damsel," the Hebrew is, Shechem spake to the heart of the damsel: so, Ruth ii. 13, "Thou hast spoken friendly unto thine handmaid;" that is, Thou hast spoken to the very heart of thy handmaid: and in Isa. xl. 2, "Speak ye comfortably to Jerusalem;" that

ודברתי על־לבה

is, Speak ye to the heart of Jerusalem. What should be spoken to the heart of Jerusalem? "Cry unto her, that her warfare is accomplished, that her iniquity is pardoned." These are the comfortable words which God required should be spoken to the heart of Jerusalem. Oh that God would speak thus to England! it would do her good at the very heart, if God would cry from heaven, Thine iniquity is pardoned, and thy warfare is accomplished. But a place still more in accordance with the expression in the text, is Judg. xix. 3; there you have the story of a Levite, who was willing to be reconciled to his wife after she had played the harlot, and the text saith, that he "went after her, to speak friendly unto her;" now the words are in the Hebrew, he went after her to speak to her heart; and indeed it is a word that must reach the heart of an adulterous spouse, if that heart be humbled, when she knows that her husband will be willing, notwithstanding all her transgressions against him, to be reconciled to her. This was the condition of Israel, they had gone a whoring from God, and when God promises a renewal of the marriage rites, he saith he will speak to her heart; from whence we might

Obs. 1. That an apostatizing people, or an apostate soul, require words of comfort spoken to their hearts, or else their terrified consciences can find little ease. We read that Spira, that famous apostate, had words of comfort enough spoken to his ear; but God did not come in and speak to his heart, therefore his conscience could not be quieted, the tumult of it could not be allayed. How many lie under the troubles of an accusing conscience, and have to endure the corrodings of a guilty spirit, because they have been backsliders from the truth; and though they come to sermons one after another, and hear the covenant of grace opened to them in all its fulness, and the riches of God's goodness set before them in all its beauty, yet go away without comfort, because the words come to the ear first, God all this time speaks not to the heart! Sometimes, however, it pleases God, when the time of his love is come, to take but the hint of a truth, and dart it upon the heart of a troubled sinner, to work effectually in him, so that he is constrained to say, Well, this day God has spoken to my heart; and he then goes away rejoicing, eased, comforted, and pacified. God shows hereby that it is not in the word of man to comfort an afflicted conscience.

Hence an expression Luther has in his comment upon Genesis, It is far harder to comfort an afflicted conscience than to raise the dead. You think it is nothing to apostatize from the Lord, you think it is easy to receive comfort; you will find it no such light matter. But you told us before, how, in the riches of his grace, God takes advantage from the greatness of our sins, to show the greatness of his mercy. Grant it, let the grace of God be never so rich, but till this grace be applied, till God be pleased to speak himself to the heart of a sinner, it will avail nothing. One who had made profession of religion, afterwards apostatized and scoffed at it. His acquaintance told him that he now did what he would smart for one day; but he thought that he understood something of the gospel, and that it was merely to believe in Jesus Christ, that he came to pardon sinners. On his sick-bed, however, being in great horror of conscience, and bitterly lamenting his apostacy, there came some of his acquaintance to him, and spake words of comfort, and told him that Christ came to save sinners, and that he must trust in God's mercy, &c. At length he began to close with this, and to get a little ease by applying it to himself; upon which his companions began to be hardened in their ways, because they saw, after a life so ill spent, it was so easy a matter to gain comfort; but not long before he died, in a most miserable anguish he exclaimed, Oh! I have prepared a plaster, but it will not stick, it will not stick. We shall find, though the grace of God be rich, and the salve a sovereign one, unless God be pleased to apply it by speaking to our hearts, human efforts are unavailing.

Multo difficilius est conscientiam afflictam consolari quam mortuos excitare. Luther.

Obs. 2. That as, when God speaks comfortably to his people, he speaks to their hearts; so God's ministers, when they come to speak in his name, should labour to speak to the hearts of his people. It is true, indeed, it is impossible for man of himself to reach the heart, but God both assists and blesses the earnest endeavours of his servants; and though I know God can take that which comes but from the lips, and render it effectual, yet, ordinarily, that which comes from the heart goes to the heart. Ministers, therefore, when they come to declare the great things of the gospel, should not seek so much for eloquent terms and enticing words of man's wisdom; but try to get their own hearts warmed with the grace of the gospel, and then they are most likely to speak to the hearts of their hearers. Ribera saith,* Let ministers remit somewhat of their care for fine, curious words, brave, neat phrases, and cadences in their sentences; but let them bend their studies to manifest humility and mortification, and to show love to the souls of people; otherwise, though they speak with the tongues of men and angels, they shall become but "as sounding brass, or a tinkling cymbal." A Jesuit thus expresses himself, and it were surely then a great shame for God's ministers not to labour to speak so, that they may speak to the hearts of the people. You must be desirous of such kind of preaching as you find speaks to your hearts, not that which comes merely to your ears. Many men love to sit, like Israel of old, listening to the words of the preacher as to "a pleasant song;" but when you find a ministry which speaks to your hearts, close with it, bless God for it, and count it a sad day when you go from a sermon unaffected.

But because many godly and learned men understand by "the wilderness" a continued series of afflictions, wherein God would comfort his people, I dare not wholly reject that interpretation: and we may on this

Obs. 1. That there are many obstructions in the hearts of men whilst in prosperity; but when afflictions come, though they cannot of themselves convert the heart, yet by them God often opens a way for his word to reach their hearts. Many of you have heard thousands of sermons, and scarce know of one that has come to your hearts; but when God casts you upon your sick-beds, and you apprehend death, then you feel the same truths that you were not sensible of before; the threatening word of God that went but to the ear before, now reaches the heart, now it terrifies, now you lament your sins, and relish the sweet promises of the gospel that afflictions make way for. To his brother, who was a riotous and profane soldier, Bernard gave many good instructions, wholesome admonitions and counsels; but his brother seemed to slight them. Bernard came to him, and putting his hand on his side, said, God will one day make way to this heart of yours by some spear or lance; meaning God would wound him in battle, and so open a way to his heart, and then his admonitions would get to his heart: and as he said, so it happened, for going into war, he was wounded, and then he remembered his brother's admonitions, they lay upon his heart to purpose. If God should let the enemy in upon us, their swords or bullets may make way to our hearts, that God's word may come to have entrance

* Remittant aliquid de cura nitoris cultusque verborum venustatis et numerositatis sententiarum, et veræ humilitati et mortificationi, impendant ut charitatem habeant, sine qua si linguis hominum loquantur et angelorum, facti sunt sicut æs sonans vel cymbalum tinniens. Ribera.

there: the Lord rather pierce our hearts by his Spirit, than gain that way to our hearts.

Obs. 2. Great afflictions are the time for God's mercies. This should make us not be so much afraid of afflictions. How alarmed are we! how do we shrink back when we see them coming! Why art thou so cast down, O Christian? the time of affliction is the time for God to speak to the heart of a sinner: many a one may say that their condition has been like Jacob's, who never had a more sweet vision of God than when he lay abroad in the fields, with no other pillow under his head than a stone. It may be God will take away all your outward comforts, and when they are all gone, then may be God's time to speak comfortably to your heart.

Obs. 3. The words of mercy, oh how sweet are they when they come to the heart after an affliction! "When their judges are overthrown in stony places, they shall hear my words; for they are sweet," Psal. cxli. 6.

Again, There is yet one more interpretation put on this expression, of bringing into the wilderness, and speaking to the heart; but as it is not very probable, I will only briefly mention it for the sake of the improvement to be drawn from it; it is this: that, by bringing into the wilderness, God means that he would take them off from their engagements, from their houses, lands, shops, estates, friends, and acquaintance, from all the pomp and glory of the world which they enjoyed, and were snared by in their own country; and so carry them aside into desolate places, and there, when he has got them, as it were, alone, instruct them. God often works thus toward those upon whom he has set his love. There is an illustration of it in Mark viii. 23, where it is said of the poor blind man, whose eyes Christ intended to open, that Christ took him by the hand, and carried him out of the city, and there, apart from the tumult of the people, wrought the miracle upon him: so many of God's people have found by experience, that, whereas there were many truths of his word which they had read and heard much of here, and in some slight measure understood, yet would not be persuaded of them, and still their consciences bore them witness that they were not walking against its light; but when God took them aside from their engagements, and from the pomp and glory of their own land, and carried them into remote places, where the glory of their own country did not so glitter before their eyes, they then could clearly discern truths which they saw but imperfectly before, and their hearts were opened to receive them in the "full assurance of faith." When God had taken them aside, then God opened their eyes.

Ver. 15. *And I will give her her vineyards from thence, and the valley of Achor for a door of hope: and she shall sing there, as in the days of her youth, and as in the day when she came up out of the land of Egypt.*

Some translate the word כרמיה her vine-dressers, and indeed the Hebrew words for vine-dressers, vines, and vineyards, differ only in the vowel points; but we will read it as it is here. "From thence;" either from the time they are in the wilderness, or from that condition of their affliction in it, wherein I will speak comfortably to her, thence I will give her her vineyards: God threatened to destroy her vineyards, now God saith, he will give vineyards.

Obs. God can as easily restore, as he can destroy. It is an easy thing for men to make havoc, and do mischief, but not so easy for them to restore; it is easy to ravage a country, but not so easy to heal the breaches thereof. Psal. lii. 1, "Why boastest thou thyself in mischief, O mighty man?" There is no reason for this vain-glorying. Plutarch tells us of one commending the power and valour of Philip, for having utterly destroyed Olynthus, a city of Thrace: a Lacedemonian standing by, answered, But he cannot build such a city. And some amongst us make it their boast, that they can roam about the country, plundering, spoiling, and making havoc; but it is not in their power, nor in the power of thousands such as they, when peace comes, to remedy the unhappy consequences of their actions. This is God's property alone, who, when reconciled to a nation, can restore her her vineyards, and "bless her latter end more than the beginning."

Plut. l. de Trac.

But, moreover, on this passage Calvin remarks, that God saith not, I will give them their corn, that is, supply their necessities, but, I will give them their vineyards, that is, minister to their delights. When God is reconciled to a people, he will not only give them subsistence, but abundance; even for delight, as well as for necessity.

Obs. 1. When God is reconciled to a people, although he reserves an abundance of mercy for the future, yet he always comes immediately with some real evidences and demonstrations of love. He saith not only, I will speak comfortably to Israel, and they may expect mercies hereafter; no, but "I will speak comfortably to her, and I will give her her vineyards" again; I will give them present manifestations of my love: so it should be with us, when we come in to be reconciled to God, we should approach him with real expressions of unfeigned repentance. Many, when they lie upon their sick-beds, will promise what they will do for God, if he restore them; but they cannot resolve on an immediate surrender of themselves to his service, and so the opportunity passes away unimproved. When, therefore, you find your hearts wrought upon, broken, and melting, do not content yourselves with fair promises, but set upon the work presently, and so engage your hearts to God; and if once you be engaged by doing something, the work will go on. This is of the greatest consequence, for a man has even a natural reluctance to turn back, after having put his hand to the plough.

Obs. 2. When God restores vineyards, after speaking to the heart, then they are blessings sweet indeed, for they are the fruits of reconciliation with him. Many a poor afflicted soul knows the comfort I allude to: I thought my sinfulness had forfeited all my mercies, and God indeed took away many comforts from me; but it pleased him to come in graciously upon my heart, and in some measure to break and humble it before him; so that I hope peace is made. Notwithstanding those great offences of mine, he has now restored mercies; he took away a child, but he has given another, a better; he has taken away one mercy, and he has given a greater; and this I do confidently, yet humbly regard as a fruit of my reconciliation with God. Oh how sweetly may such a one enjoy that mercy from God! If after the meltings of thy heart after God, he then comes in with mercies to thee, thou mayst take them as tokens of love; now thy house is a comfortable blessing to thee, and thy yoke-fellow, and thy children about thee; yea, the meat on thy table is sweet with a double sweetness, when thou canst look upon all as the fruit of God's reconciliation with thee: as the Christians, when they once believed on Christ, "did eat their meat with gladness and singleness of heart, praising God," Acts ii. 46, 47. We may enjoy all our common mercies, in another manner than other men, they will be blessings doubled, yea, a hundred-fold increased: I will speak to her heart, and then, "I will give her her vineyards." Perhaps God has given thee an estate in the world, more than thy neighbours, or brother; but has God spoken to thy heart? Are God's blessings upon thee as a fruit of God's speaking to thy heart, through reconciliation? Otherwise it is but a flat comfort, to have an estate, and not to feel God speaking to our hearts.

I will restore unto you your vineyards *from thence.* From whence? From the wilderness.

Obs. 1. God can bring vineyards out of wildernesses. Let us not be afraid, only let us make up our peace with God, and then, though we be in a wilderness, God can from thence bring us vineyards. Our brethren have found vineyards in the wilderness, and many of God's people in the midst of their straits have found abundance of mercy.

Obs. 2. "From the wilderness:" they shall have more love, mercy working more strongly for them now, it seems, than it did before. They had vineyards before, but they had none in the wilderness. God will draw now mercies out of those things that were unlikely; he will bring forth good to them, from what seemed to be for evil: the Lord has done so for us, out of those things which seemed against us; God has brought much good, as if he had made vineyards to spring out of a wilderness. But the close of all is,

Obs. 3. Those mercies that come to us out of great difficulties, and seem to be raised out of contraries, are sweet mercies indeed, and what we are to rejoice in; and therefore it follows, "and she shall sing." Deut. xxxii. 13, "He made him to suck honey out of the rock, and oil out of the flinty rock." When did God so? when did God cause his people to "suck honey out of the rock," or, "oil out of the flinty rock?" we read, indeed, that the rock was smitten, and water gushed out; but where is it said that oil or honey came out of the rock? No where; and the meaning therefore is, that God brought forth water out of the rock by a mighty hand, and it was as oil and honey to them, being given in an hour of greatest need. So all the mercies which God gives his people when he brings them out of difficulties and straits, are sweet and glorious mercies. Let us be patient awhile; though we seem to be in the wilderness, and see nothing to fetch out water from, but only rocks, stones, and difficulties, God at length will bring mercies out of those difficulties; and they will be honey mercies unto us, mercies for which we shall sing and praise the name of our God with joyful hearts.

"And the valley of Achor for a door of hope." The words are an excellent expression of mercy to Israel. To open which, these three things are to be inquired into.

I. What this "valley of Achor" was.

II. The reason of the name.

III. Why said to be "a door of hope."

I. Achor was a very pleasant and fruitful valley, near Jericho; the first place that Israel came to when entering upon and taking possession of the land of Canaan. "And Sharon shall be a fold of flocks, and the valley of Achor a place for the herds to lie down in, for my people that have sought me," Isa. lxv. 10. First, It is joined with Sharon, Cant. iii. 1, "I am the rose of Sharon," which was a sweet, pleasant place. Secondly, It is said to be "a place for the herds to lie down in;" a fat pasture that they shall even tumble in. And, thirdly, It is promised as a blessing to them that "have sought the Lord."

II. The reason of the name Achor. Josh. vii. shows that Achan, who, in 1 Chron. ii. 7, is also called Achar, having taken the accursed thing; God left the camp, and Israel fell before the men of Ai, which was the first battle they fought for the possession of Canaan. Upon this their minds were exceedingly troubled: notwithstanding all the experiences of God's mighty power going along with them, so lately bringing them over Jordan in such a wonderful manner, and so miraculously giving them Jericho; yet at the loss of thirty-six men their hearts begin to fail, and Joshua falls with his face upon the earth. Josephus, in his Jewish Antiquities, gives us his prayer at large, and in it occur these expressions: "Beyond all expectation, having received an overthrow, being terrified by this accident, and suspicious of thy promises to Moses, we both abstain from war, and after so many enterprises, we cannot hope for any successful proceedings; by thy mercy relieve our present sorrow, and take from us the thought of despair, wherein we are too far plunged."

God then asks him why he lay upon his face, and bade him get him up, for Israel had sinned in the accursed thing. Upon search being made, Achan is detected; whereupon Joshua tells him, that he had troubled the host of Israel, and God would trouble him; upon which they stoned him, and from hence the valley was called עמק עכור the valley of Achor, that is, the valley of trouble.

עכר
Turbavit.

III. Why this valley is called "a door of hope." And here we shall inquire, first, How it was "a door of hope" to Israel then, when they first came into Canaan: secondly, How it is promised to be "a door of hope" to repenting Israel in after-times.

1. It was "a door of hope" for them in two respects.

First, Because it was the first place of which they took possession in Canaan, and began to have outward means of subsistence, and to eat of the corn of the land. While they were in the wilderness, although God provided wonderfully for them, by sending them manna from heaven; yet because they had no way of subsistence by ordinary means, they always feared lest they should want upon any strait into which they were brought. Now in this valley God gave them outward means, and this raised their hopes that their danger was over, and that they should do well enough. This is our nature, when ordinary means fail, our hearts fail; yea, though, in regard of God's extraordinary workings, we have never so many gracious encouragements; and when God grants means again, then we hope.

Secondly, God made their great trouble there a means of much good to them, for by that they were brought to purge their camp; they learned to fear the Lord, and were prepared, more than before, for so great a mercy as the further possession of the promised land. The Septuagint, instead of "a door of hope," render the clause, διάνοιξαι σύνεσιν αὐτῆς, "to open their understanding;" for there indeed they learned the dreadfulness of God, who, for one man's sin, was so sorely displeased, and began clearly to see that the God that was amongst them was a holy God, and that he would have them to be a holy people.

2. How this "valley of Achor" was to be "a door of hope" to Israel in after-times.

First, The Jews think that Israel shall return into their own country again by the same way to Canaan, by that valley, which shall thus be a door of hope to them.

Secondly, As God turned this valley of trouble to much good to them; so he would turn all the sore afflictions of Israel in after-days to their great advantage, grievous afflictions should make way for glorious mercies.

Thirdly, and chiefly, In this expression God follows the allegory of marriage: now it was the custom amongst the Jews for the husband to give his spouse, as a dowry, some piece of ground, more or less, according to his means; and this, as a pledge of love, to assure her that whatever was his, she should have the benefit of: so saith the Lord, Although you have gone a whoring from me, and may justly expect that I should for ever reject you, yet I will betroth you to myself, and fully perform all marriage rites, to show my love towards you to the uttermost; and that you may know that you are married to a wealthy husband, I will give you a rich and plentiful dowry, that valley of Achor; and this but as a token and pledge of further love, mercy, and riches, that you shall receive at my hand as the first-fruits of all those glorious things that I have treasured up for you.

From this "valley of Achor," as it concerned Israel of old, we may

Obs. 1. Sometimes when God gives men their hearts' desires, and they think themselves happy, as if all trouble were past, then he visits them with great and sore afflictions.

Obs. 2. Although God has been humbling men's hearts with long and sore afflictions, yet, just before he bestows great mercies, he afflicts again, to humble and break their hearts still more.

Obs. 3. Sin will make the pleasantest place in the world a place of trouble.

Obs. 4. The afflictions of the saints are not only harbingers of mercies, but doors of hope to let in mercies, means to advance their progress. God commands light to shine, not only after darkness, but out of darkness. Joseph's prison, David's persecution, Daniel's den, made way for the glorious mercies God had in store for them. That which once Themistocles said to his children and friends, the saints have much more reason to say to theirs; I had been undone, if I had not been undone; had it not been for such a grievous affliction, I had never come to the enjoyment of such a mercy. Hence we must learn not only to be patient in tribulation, but joyful.

But the especial thing intended in this expression is this. When God is reconciled to his people, then present mercies are doors of hope to let in future mercies. Every mercy a door to another mercy, and all mercies here put together, are a door to eternal mercy. When Rachel had a son she called his name Joseph, saying, "The Lord shall add to me another son," Gen. xxx. 24. Every mercy the saints have may well be called Joseph, it brings assurance of mercy to be added; such is the high privilege of the saints: every mercy that a wicked man has, he may look upon as his utmost, his all, he may write a *ne plus ultra* upon it. One misery, one judgment upon a wicked man makes way to another, but not one mercy: however God in the riches of his forbearance may extend mercies to him, yet it is more than he should expect, and he has rather cause to wonder that he has received so much, than reason to look for more. But God ever draws out his loving-kindness to his saints. "Continue thy loving-kindness unto them that know thee; and thy righteousness to the upright in heart," Psal. xxxvi. 10. First, The good which others receive from God is bounty, patience; but that which the saints have is loving-kindness. Secondly, That which others have is in no way tied to them by promise, but that which the saints have they have by promise, it is righteousness. Psal. xxiii., Thou makest me lie down in green pastures, thou anointest my head with fresh oil, my cup runneth over. Here is much; but is this all? no, ver. 6, "Surely mercy and goodness shall follow me all the days of my life." What we read of David in 2 Sam. v. 12, is very observable; from God's prospering him in his present way, he draws an argument to assure himself for the future, that his kingdom was established to him: why? did not Saul prosper at the beginning of his reign, as well as David? and yet it was no evidence of his establishment: but David could see God's mercy coming to him after another manner than Saul could. All mercies the saints have, come from the covenant in which there is a most rich treasure of mercies, a blessed connexion of mercies. The covenant between David and Jonathan was, 1 Sam. xx. 15, That loving-kindness must not be cut off from the house of Jonathan. The covenant between God and the saints is, That loving-kindness shall never be cut off from them, but the links of mercies shall be fastened one to another, so as to be coeval with eternity.

Mercies to the saints proceed from love, and *amor nescit nimium*, love knows no such thing as excess. The saints, understanding this mystery in the dealings of God's grace toward them, follow on to seeking his face then, especially, when he is most in the way of mercy; whereas the men of the world, who know not this, seldom seek after mercy, but in times of affliction, when God is in a way of justice and wrath: this is their folly.

Infinite reason there is, O ye saints of the Lord, that one duty should be but an inlet to another, seeing mercy ever succeeds mercy. Here lies the great difference between performing duties from the strength of common grace, and from the power of sanctifying grace; in the one, the spirit after a few efforts is wearied, and thinks it may now rest; but in the other, the very doing still increases strength, and incites the heart to greater activity. But may not security promise continuance of mercy? Yes, but if so, then when affliction comes, the heart will sink from an apprehension of continuance in misery, as before it hoped for continuance of mercy.

When then may we assure ourselves that our mercies are doors of hope to further mercies?

First, When they are created mercies, wrought by the more immediate hand of God. Generation may be imperfect, but creation never: *omne creatum est perfectum.* "Lord, thou wilt ordain peace for us;" what is the argument? "for thou also hast wrought all our works in us," Isa. xxvi. 12.

Secondly, When they are spiritual mercies. Ezek. xxxix. 29, "Neither will I hide my face any more from them;" what is the argument? "for I have poured out my spirit upon the house of Israel." But is not this your private opinion that this argument will hold? No, the words following are, "Thus saith the Lord God."

Thirdly, when mercies carry us to the God of mercy, and are turned into duties. As if we can turn our duties into mercies, that is, account every duty a mercy, it is a good argument that we shall persevere in duty; so when we can turn mercies into duties, that is, make every mercy an engagement to duty, it is a good argument that mercy will continue to abound.

But are there not interruptions many times in the course of God's mercy to his own people?

It must be granted, that an interruption may sometimes occur, as after Israel's return from captivity and beginning to build the temple, from various hinderances seventy years elapsed before it was finished; but though there may be a temporary interruption, yet the work ceases not entirely; there is still strength in the grace of the covenant sufficient to carry it on, and perfect it at last. By ceasing in one way of mercy, God prepares for another; the very ceasing in such a way may be a mercy. We ourselves at this day are a sad spectacle of the interruption of the course of God's mercies towards a nation. Mercy, that formerly shone in her beauty upon us, now seems in a great measure to have withdrawn the beams of her glory; our door of hope, which we thought so wide open, appears almost shut against us. I dare not say that it is shut, lest I should wrong the present grace of God yet continued to us. But,

1. Sin, yea, our many and fearful sins, lie at this our door, Gen. iv. 7.

2. A crowd of difficulties seem even to stop up the door, they come thronging still to it, as if they would certainly shut it against us.

3. As the prophet, Ezek. xi. 1, 2, saw "at the door of the gate five and twenty men;" among whom there were some "princes of the people who devised mischief, and gave wicked counsel in the city:" so may we at this day see many, even of the chief ones, devising mischief, and giving wicked counsel, by which they

labour to shut, yea, to lock and bolt up this our door of hope.

4. We hoped that this our door of hope would have been like the doors that entered into the oracle, of which we read, 1 Kings vi. 31, 32, made of the olive tree, yea, the side posts and lintels of olive tree, and carvings of palm trees and cherubims, all overlaid with gold; but now our door seems to be of iron, and the way to our help and mercy must be through the iron gate, we must get to it by suffering hard things.

5. Our door that was wide, at which mercy began to flow in freely, now seems to be straitened, and we must be content to strip ourselves of a great part of our estates, of many of our outward comforts; yea, we must venture them all, and judge ourselves happy "if by any means at length" we may crowd in.

6. Yea, our door-posts are like the Israelites' in Egypt, besprinkled with blood; the keeping up our means of mercy has cost us much blood, and may cost more.

7. Now when we knock, and would step in, the dogs bark at us, and are ready to fly upon us; yea, the servants, yea, some of our brethren, are discontented with us, frown upon us, and speak against us.

8. Alas, we have rejected the right key that should have opened this our door; no marvel, then, though we stand blundering before it and it open not to us. What is that right key which would have opened it before this time, had we made use of it? That "key of David" that we read of, Rev. iii. 7, which "openeth and no man shutteth." This key the church of Philadelphia had, therefore it follows, ver. 8, "I have set before thee an open door, and no man can shut it."

But what is this key of David?

It is the ruling power of Jesus Christ in his church. David in his government was a special type of Christ, the first godly king over the people. Government is emblematically set forth by a key: thus, Isa. xxii. 22, God promises to commit the government to Eliakim by this expression, "The key of the house of David will I lay upon his shoulder." And in Isa. ix. 6, 7, the government is said to be upon Christ's shoulder, and he sits upon the throne of David. It is worthy of remark, that to Eliakim there was promised only the key of the house of David; but to Christ, the key of David himself: the one was to govern but as a steward, the government of the other was to be princely. If we had been like the church of Philadelphia, united in brotherly love, and had this key of David amongst us, we might before this time have had set before us an open door that no man could have shut; but woe unto us! how many amongst us say of Christ, "We will not have this man to rule over us!" Mr. Brightman, more than thirty years ago, compared this church of Philadelphia with the church of Scotland, applying it typically to set forth the dealings of God toward that church in after-times; and, indeed, in many things they have been similar. 1. They are both Philadelphians, united in a brotherly covenant, no churches in any kingdom more. 2. It was said of Philadelphia, it had but a little strength, and yet it kept God's word. What churches in any nation have been more contemptible than those in Scotland? They have been accounted a poor, beggarly people, despised of all, and yet God has enabled them to do great things. 3. God has caused their enemies to come and bow before them, and to know that he has loved them; even those who said "they were Jews and were not," that they were the only church, when indeed they were "the synagogue of Satan;" and they have rejected false government, and received much of the government of Christ; the key of David is more amongst them than in any kingdom in the world: no wonder, then, that their door be so opened through God's mercy, that none can shut it. Our houses of parliament have cast away the false key, the Lord deliver them and us from ever meddling with it any more, whatever befall us. They have, moreover, professed their desire to inquire after the true key. This door of hope, we trust, will open to us in due time, so that none shall prevail to shut it.

9. We have lost many fair opportunities for the opening this door, and we cannot look back upon them without trembling hearts; we may see cause to lament their loss with tears of blood. Even already it has cost us much, and is likely to cost much more blood.

10. Yea, woe unto us! our Father comes forth and seems to be angry with us, and commands the door to be shut against us, yea, he shuts us out himself. Is not that complaint of the church's truly ours, "O Lord God of hosts, how long wilt thou be angry with the prayer of thy people?" Psal. lxxx. 4. If God be angry with our knocking, what shall we do?

11. And well may God command the door to be shut upon us, for we have shut it upon ourselves. This our door of hope has a spring lock, and is easily closed, but cannot so easily be opened again: we have stood wrangling and struggling one with another, and shut the door upon ourselves before we were aware. Hos. vii. 1, belongs as truly to us, as ever it did to Israel; "When I would have healed Israel, then the iniquity of Ephraim was discovered, and the wickedness of Samaria." When the Lord would have healed England, then its iniquity has been more fully developed. The vilest spirit of malignity against godliness, against the saints, against the way of Christ in his ordinances, now rages. Men care not though they ruin themselves, bring themselves and posterity to be bond-slaves, so they may but gratify themselves in the suppression of the godly. The controversy now is almost grown to such a height, that the kingdom divides itself into those who have some show of religion, and the haters of it. The times complained of in Micah vii. 5, are even ours; "Trust ye not in a friend, put ye not confidence in a guide: keep the door of thy mouth from her that lieth in thy bosom:" yea, we are almost come to the pass spoken of in the 4th verse, "The best of them is a brier: the most upright is sharper than a thorn hedge." There is much frowardness and perverseness even in the best, many contentions and grievous breaches amongst them; they cannot endure you should be jealous of them, and they give you cause of jealousy daily. The greater part of this generation show themselves to have spirits so defiled with superstitious vanities, and so imbittered by a spirit of malignity, that we may fear God has no pleasure in the generality of it: yea, Moses and Aaron have sinned, the best have so sullied themselves with antichristian pollutions, that it were just with God that this whole generation should be first taken away, and that the young, who have not so defiled themselves, should have this door into Canaan opened to them, that they only might go into and possess that good land, but our carcasses fall in the wilderness.

Ye godly youths, whose hearts began betimes to yearn after Christ, know that his heart yearns after you: and although some of you may fall fighting for your brethren, and so be received into heaven; yet you are of that generation to which God will open this door of mercy, you shall go in and possess Canaan, all this valley of Achor is but a door of hope to you. Continue then in your sincerity, and God will reveal himself more fully to you than he has done to us. If we be cut off before those treasures of mercy that God has ready for his people be opened, we must accept of the punishment of our iniquity, and even bear this indignation of the Lord, because we have sinned against him.

12. Yea, the Lord has struck us with blindness at the door, we grope up and down and cannot find it, Gen. xix. 11. Never were a people at a greater loss, or in

greater confusion, than we now are; every man runs his own way, and we know not what to do, nay, the truth is, we know not what we do.

13. Many, because they have found some difficulties at the right door, have gone away from it, and sought back doors to help themselves by, even base, false, shifting, treacherous ways, seeking to comply for their own private ends, as if themselves must needs be saved, whatsoever becomes of the public.

14. This enhances our misery, that we are groping up and down at the door, and night is coming upon us, storms and tempests are rising, dangers are approaching, and yet God opens not to us.

15. Above all our misery, this is yet the greatest, that even our hearts are shut up too: were they open, our condition had still comfort in it; but there lies a stone rolled at their door, and such a stone, as is beyond the power of an angel to remove.

What then shall we do?

1. Let us yet resolve to wait at this door, wait upon God in those ways of help which in mercy he still affords us: certainly we are at the right door; let us then say with Shecaniah, "We have trespassed against our God: yet now there is hope in Israel concerning this thing," Ezra x. 2. Let us resolve, whatever becomes of us, not to go from our Father's door; if we perish, let us perish at his gates.

2. It is said, Ezek. xlvi. 2, 3, "The prince shall worship at the threshold of the gate," and "the people of the land shall worship at the door:" so let us worship the Lord at this our door, though we be not entered in; let our hearts bow before our God in acknowledgment of his greatness, power, dominion over us, to do with us what he pleases.

3. Let us look in at the key-hole, or at any crevice that we can, to see something of the riches of mercy into which this door opens. We may discern within, liberty of conscience, enjoyment of ordinances, the blessing of God's true worship, and the ways of God and his saints made honourable in this kingdom, in a higher degree than any where upon the face of the whole earth; we may see too many sweet outward liberties, the free enjoyment of our estates, peace, plenty, and prosperity in abundance: all these, and more than we can think of, would appear, if this door were but once opened to us: however, it is good to look in, to quicken our hearts meanwhile, and to excite more strongly our desires and endeavours. Oh how happy were we if we possessed these mercies!

4. Let us knock louder still, and cry still louder at our Father's door. But did not you tell us our Father seemed to be angry at our knocking? Yes, but mark what we have in that very scripture, where the church complains that God is angry with her prayer; Psal. lxxx. 4, "How long wilt thou be angry against the prayer of thy people?" Yet, ver. 14, "Return, we beseech thee, O God of hosts: look down from heaven, and behold, and visit this vine: and, ver. 19, "Turn us again, O Lord God of hosts, cause thy face to shine; and we shall be saved."

5. Let every one sweep his own door, and take away the sins that contribute to stop up this avenue of hope. "Again have I thought in these days to do well unto Jerusalem and to the house of Judah: fear ye not." But mark what follows; "These are the things that ye shall do; Speak ye every man the truth to his neighbour; execute the judgment of truth and peace in your gates: and let none of you imagine evil in your hearts against his neighbour," Zech. viii. 15—17. Both private men and men in public place must reform. How far are we from this! Never more plottings, more heart-burnings one against another, and those in public station neglect the execution of judgment; they would stretch their policy beyond God's wisdom. God joins these two together, the execution of judgment and peace, and commends one as a means to the other; but they aim at something more, they will not execute judgment for fear of the breach of peace. It is just with God that we should never have peace till we can trust God for it in his own way.

6. Let us seek to God again, and call to him for the right key. Lord, reveal the way of thy worship and thy government to us, and we will yield ourselves unto it.

7. Let us stir up ourselves against all difficulties. Things are not yet so bad, but we may help ourselves if we took courage. Our Father hears us, he can command many angels to come to help to roll away the stone; yea, he has opened divers doors to us already. We are indeed come to the iron gate, yet the Lord can make that at length fly open of its own accord; as, in Acts xii. 10, the church was praying, and after the prison doors were opened to Peter, and he had passed the first and second ward, he came to the iron gate that led unto the city, and there he found as easy passage as any where else. "In the mount will the Lord be seen."

8. Let faith act as well as prayer; let us exercise faith in the blood of Christ; let us, as it were, besprinkle this our door with the blood of the Lamb; yea, look up to Christ as the true door to all mercy.

9. Let us now especially watch all opportunities of mercy, and take heed we no more neglect, as we have many times most inexcusably, lest hereafter we knock and cry, "Lord, open to us," and it proves too late.

10. Let us open to God who knocks at our doors, if we would have him open to us. God knocks at the door of every one of our hearts, let us set all wide open for him. "Lift up your heads, O ye gates; and be ye lift up, ye everlasting doors, and the King of glory shall come in," Psal. xxiv. 6, 7. Those who do thus are the true generation that seek the Lord. Let England open, for God yet stands at the door and knocks, and if we will yet open to him, he will yet come in and sup with us, and we shall sup with him. It is true, God rebukes and chastens us severely; so he did Laodicea at the time when he stood at her door and knocked, Rev. iii. 19, 20. If any church was like to that of Laodicea, it is ours; we have been lukewarm as she was; a mixture in God's worship has been amongst us, more than in any other reformed church; we have been a proud people, thought ourselves rich, and wanting nothing, whereas we knew not that we were indeed wretched, and miserable, and poor, and blind, and naked; and those who *would* be the angels of this church, how has God spued them out of his mouth, and cast them forth as an abominable thing! With all that belonged to their courts, they have made themselves loathsome. He is now at our door and knocks, calling to us to let him in, that he may come and rule us, and bring peace and salvation unto us; but, however, whether Christ be admitted by the state or no, yet let the saints who are willing that Christ should rule over them, hold on to the end; the promise is, even to those in Laodicea, "To him that overcometh will I grant to sit with me in my throne, even as I also overcame, and am set down with my Father in his throne."

11. Let us encourage, as far as we are able, all our faithful door-keepers, those who are the public instruments of God for our good, and upon whom, under God, so much of the great affairs of the kingdom depends.

And for the quickening of our hearts that we may do all we can, that this our door of hope be not shut against us, consider further,

First, This door was opened to us when we began to think, yea, almost to conclude, that all doors of hope had been shut against England, and were ready to give up all for lost.

Secondly, It was opened to us after much knocking by prayer. If ever there was a parliament of prayer since the world began, this was, and is. How dreadful then would it be to have this door shut against us!

Thirdly, It was opened by a mighty hand of God. Josephus tells us of a door of the temple that used to have thirty men to open it, and yet, as a prognostication of some great occurrence, it opened of its own accord. This our door was more hard to be opened; thousands of men could not have prevailed, it was work for the mighty hand of God to effect.

Fourthly, It is a door which opens to the greatest mercies that ever England had: how happy would England be in the happy success of this parliament!

Fifthly, It is a door which our adversaries have laboured all they can to shut, by policy and by force; but hitherto, through God's mercy, they have laboured in vain.

Sixthly, How sweet have the manifestations of God been to us, in the beginnings of his goodness, and in the infancy of our endeavours! "My beloved put in his hand by the hole of the door, and my bowels were moved for him. I rose up to open to my beloved; and my hands dropped with myrrh, and my fingers with sweet smelling myrrh, upon the handles of the lock," Cant. v. 4, 5. The hand upon the door is sweet; what then would the work completed be!

Seventhly, If this door should be wholly shut against us, what a miserable people would we be! If these men have their wills, then never expect parliaments more, nor any good from parliaments; they will be the most contemptible and servile things imaginable, doors to let in all misery, agents to legalize mischief. Then what would we and our posterity be, but slaves? The popish party must, yea, would, be gratified, and their designs effected: what contempt of the saints and of religion would ensue! what hatred! what persecution! what horrid blasphemies! how will they be hardened in all manner of wickedness! our estates, our liberties, our religion sacrificed; yea, perhaps our very lives, and if not, so miserable would our existence be, that it were better to have the grave open her mouth upon us and shut us in, than to live to see, and hear, and feel such things as we and our friends are like to hear, and see, and feel.

It would be the most horrid judgment that ever befell a nation, a thing to be told to all the kingdoms of the world: God gave England a fair opportunity to help itself, to be a most happy nation, but they had no hearts, they were besotted, blinded, their hearts taken from them; the worthies whom they chose, and who ventured themselves for them, they basely deserted and betrayed: moreover, they vilely betrayed themselves, their liberties, their religion, their posterity, and are now become the most miserable nation, the most fearful spectacle of God's wrath, upon the face of the whole earth. Wherefore, beloved in the Lord, let us at all risks make sure of Christ, who is our hope, and who saith of himself that he is "the door;" as indeed he is, to let in upon us all the mercies of God, that however our hopes here be frustrated, yet we may not be disappointed of our last hopes; and that though it should prove that here, looking for light, behold darkness, yet when looking for the light of God's face eternally, we may not be driven out into the blackness of darkness for ever. But shall I end thus? nay, the close of all shall rather be the close of the 31st Psalm, "Be of good courage, and he shall strengthen your heart, all ye that hope in the Lord;" hope yet that God will make our valley of Achor a door of hope unto us. The next words in the prophecy before us are words of joy, "She shall sing as in the days of her youth." Was there ever a time wherein England had cause to sing praise unto God? there are times coming that shall be as joyful as ever yet times have been; God hath mercy in store for his people, he hath singing times for them.

"And she shall sing there, as in the days of her youth, and as in the day when she came up out of the land of Egypt."

You heard of the valley of Achor, which God gave to his people to be a door of hope. This day you shall hear of God's people standing singing at this door of hope. Though it be but a door of hope, yet at that day she "shall sing there, as in the days of her youth, and as in the day when she came up out of the land of Egypt."

There are six things needful to be opened, for the meaning of God's mind here, in their singing at the door of hope.

First, The reading of the words are to be cleared.

Secondly, The scope is to be showed.

Thirdly, What the days of youth here spoken of are.

Fourthly, What was the song of the days of their youth.

Fifthly, What cause they had to sing in this, the day of their youth.

Lastly, How this is applicable to repenting Israel, and what time this prophecy aims at, are likewise to be manifested.

I. The reading of the words. There are only two words that require explanation.

First, the word translated singing. Secondly, that which is translated, coming out of the land of Egypt.

The word for singing the Sept. translate, She shall be humbled; a sense very different from what is in our books; but I find several translate the words so; amongst others, Cyril and Theodoret, who explain it, that she shall be humbled by the Assyrians as she was before humbled by the Egyptians. But certainly this is not the meaning of the words, for it is spoken of ascending or coming up out of the land of Egypt. But they might easily mistake in rendering the words, because the Hebrew signifies both to be humble, and to sing; as it is usual with that language, by the same word to express contrary things; thus ברך signifies both to bless and to curse, and many similar might be named.

ταπεινωθήσεται.

עָנָה, in Kal. humiliavit, in Niphal. humiliatus, afflictus fuit, in Piel. cecinit, cantabit.

The word translated singing, signifies also "she shall answer," and it is so rendered by some, as Cyril and others observe on this. "She shall answer as in the days of her youth." What answer did she make? Thus, God in the days of her youth, when she came out of Egypt, declared to her his covenant; "Now therefore," saith God, "if you will obey my voice indeed, and keep my covenant, then ye shall be a peculiar treasure unto me above all people:" a sweet promise to all in covenant with God, that they "shall be a peculiar treasure unto me above all people," Exod. xix. 5. Now, ver. 8, "All the people answered together, and said, All that the Lord hath spoken we will do." And some would explain the passage before us by referring to this; as if the meaning were, Whereas God in the days of their youth told them, that "if they would keep his covenant," they should be "a peculiar treasure unto him above all people," and they all with one consent answered, "All that the Lord hath spoken we will do;" so, saith God, when I shall again convert them to myself, I will renew my covenant with them, and upon my setting it before them they shall freely and willingly answer, Lord, we accept of this thy covenant. Thus some interpret the passage; and the exposition is very sweet.

But we shall join both these significations of the original together, which I take indeed to be the meaning of the Spirit of God: they shall sing by way of answering; thus, they were wont to sing *alternis choris*, in their joyful songs to answer one another, *his præci-*

nentibus, aliis succinentibus, some singing before, and some answering, a *canticum dramaticum,* or a kind of song admitting of alternate responses. And thus, saith God, shall be the melody of my people, when I am again reconciled to them upon their repentance, there shall be mutual singing; one singing to another, and the others answering in a joyful way.

The other word requiring explanation is, עלותה "when she came," that is, ascended "up out of the land of Egypt." They may be said to have *ascended* out of the land of Egypt, partly because Egypt was a country that lay very low; but chiefly because they were in a low condition, their lives being made "bitter with hard bondage."

II. The second thing to be showed, is the intent of the Spirit of God: they shall sing as in the days of their youth, when they ascended out of the land of Egypt. Read it so, and

It is a further expression of the nuptial solemnity that there should take place between God and his people, in the time of their reconciliation, as if he should say, Marriage is an ordinance I have appointed for the mutual joy and delight of the man and his wife; so I will bring you and betroth you to myself, and there shall be the singing of the Epithalamium, the nuptial song, between us, and I will rejoice over you. Think with yourselves the greatest joy that ever you experienced in your lives, and I will realize it all to you. Whatever mercies you received when you came out of the land of Egypt, and rejoiced in, you shall hereafter enjoy again. Did I then appear in a miraculous way to you? I will do so again. Were mercies long promised fulfilled, blessings long prayed for bestowed? you shall receive the like again. Did Moses and Miriam go before you singing, and you follow after, making melody in your hearts unto the Lord? the like time shall come again, when both governors and people shall join together in singing and praising the name of the Lord.

III. What is meant by "the days of her youth?" This is the same that is afterward expressed by "the day when she came up out of the land of Egypt," that is, the time when they were delivered out of bondage, after they had passed through the Red Sea, and seen the great works of God in their deliverance. "I remember thee, the kindness of thy youth, the love of thine espousals, when thou wentest after me in the wilderness, in a land that was not sown," Jer. ii. 2. When this people were delivered from Pharaoh, and saw the great works of God in the wilderness, that is the season of their youth. In the time of their bondage they did not outwardly appear to be the Lord's; but when God manifested himself so gloriously in their deliverance, then he took them, as it were, again to be his people, and they seemed to be born again, and the years they passed in the wilderness were God's training time. For a people under bondage can scarce be said to be born, they are at least in that prison but as the embryo in the womb, they cannot be said to be a people, a living people. Hence, chap. xiii. of this prophecy, when they were in bondage under Jeroboam's wicked commands, it is said, ver. 1, that they died; "When Ephraim spake trembling, he exalted himself in Israel; but when he offended in Baal, he died."

But here a question arises: How can God refer to this time, and tell them they shall sing as then, whereas in the beginning of the chapter we find, that when God threatens them, he tells them he will set them as in the day wherein they were born? so that there to be brought again into the same condition, would appear to imply a threatening; how can it here be a promise?

We may answer, It is very true, when they came up out of Egypt was indeed a time of much mercy, but still they were in great straits with regard to outward means, a succourless and helpless people. When therefore God threatens to set them as in the day wherein they were born, he only refers to their former destitute condition with regard to creature-helps; but when he promises mercy, and tells them he will bring them into the state they were in in their youth, he rather looks at all the loving-kindness shown them in their deliverance out of Egypt. As it is a great affliction for a people to be brought into the same condition they once were in, that is, to have all the sour and bitter without any of the sweet; so it is a great privilege for a people to be brought into a former condition, when they shall have all the blessings without the cursings; when God shall take away all the bran, and give them only the pure grain, strain out all that is evil, and give them all that is good. Such mercy the promise before us holds forth.

IV. What the song was that they then sang in the days of their youth, when they came out of the land of Egypt. That song you find, Exod. xv. 1, "Then sang Moses and the children of Israel this song unto the Lord," &c.; and afterwards you read that "Miriam and all the women" sang likewise. In this song of theirs there are these five things observable.

First, This song of Moses, Exod. xv., was the most ancient that we know of. Orpheus, Musæus, and Linus, the earliest of the poets, were five hundred years after this time.

Secondly, It was a song of triumph; "Then sang Moses and the children of Israel, The Lord hath triumphed gloriously," &c. When they saw God's judgments upon the adversaries, then they sang in a triumphant manner. But you will say, How could they sing thus when they saw such a dreadful spectacle before their eyes, the Egyptians so miserably destroyed; when they heard their shrieks and doleful cries, and beheld their bodies cast upon the sea shore? shall Moses and the people of Israel sing then, and triumph over their adversaries thus fearfully perishing? To that we answer, We must not be more pitiful than God is; "The righteous shall rejoice when he seeth the vengeance: he shall wash his feet in the blood of the wicked," Psal. lviii. 10.

But you will say, This is austerity, they are cruelhearted people who could do so.

Not so. Moses was the meekest man that ever lived upon the face of the earth, the most full of tender compassion; yet Moses sang thus when he saw the Egyptians destroyed: so that to rejoice in God's judgments against the ungodly, may consist with meekness and quietness of spirit, with a loving and sweet disposition as Moses had. It is true, we ought not to insult over wicked men in way of revenge on our own account; but when we consider the righteous judgments of God on his adversaries, we may be swallowed up in the consideration of his justice, and rejoice in it; but so, as not altogether to be without some pity and commiseration of the persons perishing; as Titus Vespasian is said to have wept when he saw the destruction of Jerusalem, though a hostile city. But there is a time coming, when all the saints shall be so swallowed up with God, that they shall rejoice in the destruction, yea, in the eternal damnation, of the wicked, without the least mixture of pity or commiseration; they shall wholly have a regard to God and his glory without consideration of them; yea, though they were the fruit of their own bodies, and came out of their own loins. But for the present, though we are to rejoice and triumph in the works of God and his judgments upon the wicked, yet our joy is not to be unmixed with feelings of pity and compassion towards the persons of the sufferers.

And mark by the way, the difference with which God regards his own people and the wicked. When God's people come to be in a distressed condition, if there be any that dare to rejoice over them, God will avenge himself on them; yea, if they do but look upon his afflicted servants with any kind of satisfaction, the Lord will be avenged on them for it. But when the wicked are destroyed, God not only gives us leave to look at them, but to rejoice and sing praises to God for their destruction. Thus, Obad. 12, "Thou shouldest not have looked on the day of thy brother in the day that he became a stranger; neither shouldest thou have rejoiced over the children of Judah in the day of their destruction." Mark, God has a quarrel against them who only looked upon the day of their brother's distress and rejoiced. But when destruction comes upon the enemies of God, then the people of God may look, and rejoice, and triumph.

Thirdly, It is a song most excellent, in regard of the elegance of the expressions, and variety of the matter. There is great force and beauty in the expression, ver. 1, "He hath triumphed gloriously," or, He is become gloriously glorious, or, In magnifying himself he hath magnified himself; or, as some render it, He is magnified above the magnificent. All God's works are glorious, but some are gloriously glorious; and so is the work of God toward his people. Rivet observes on this, The greatest glory of God, in which he is most glorious, is in doing good to his own people: so, adds he, great men should account their true glory to consist, not in spoiling others, especially those that are their own, but in doing good. In Isa. xiv. 20, a dishonourable burial to the king of Babylon is threatened, "because," saith the scripture, "thou hast destroyed thy land, and slain thy people:" yea, the threatening is continued to his seed, "the seed of evil-doers shall never be renowned."

Again, the abstract terms employed are very elegant, thus, "The Lord is my strength and song, and he is become my salvation."

So, beside many other instances, that elegant epiphonema, with which he breaks forth in the midst of the song, though it would more properly have been introduced at the close as a summary of all the rest; "Who is like unto thee, O Lord, among the gods? who is like thee, glorious in holiness, fearful in praises, doing wonders?"

Fourthly, A prophetical song, not only narrating the past, but prophesying of what is to come: "The dukes of Edom shall be amazed; the mighty men of Moab, trembling, shall take hold upon them," &c., ver. 15.

Fifthly, A typical song, that is, a song pre-signifying the rejoicing of God's people in after-times, when the saints shall overcome antichrist, and the song of Moses shall be sung over again. Of those that overcome the beast, Rev. xv. 2, 3, saith they sung "the song of Moses," that is, they sung that song of which this of Moses was but a type.

Sixthly, A miraculous song, according to some; so Augustine, De Mirabilibus Scripturæ, calls it, a miracle worthy of unlimited admiration.

Enormi admiratione dignum miraculum. August.

Wherein did he think the miracle of this song to consist?

In this; he imagined that both Moses and all the people were at once inspired by God to sing this song: which idea has been received by some; but as we have no authority for this from Scripture, we rather think that God inspired Moses only, and the rest of the people followed him as he sung.

I note it the rather, because hereby we may see that singing is an ordinance in the church of God, not only in the time of the law, but in the time of the gospel; for this place, "she shall sing as in the days of her youth," refers to gospel times. Therefore, not only when one man has an extraordinary gift (as the Scripture speaks, if any one hath a psalm, an extraordinary gift in the congregation of making a psalm) he should sing; but others are enjoined to unite with those who have the gift of making a psalm; so were the people to do here.

V. The reason of their singing thus in the days of their youth. It was briefly this, they sang on account of the great deliverance they had experienced out of Egypt. Observe,

First, They then sang because of their freedom from outward bondage. Bondage implies three things.

1. That a man is under the power of another, under some law, without his consent given, either explicitly or implicitly.

Here you may see the difference between a free subject and a slave; the former, as in England, is not bound to any laws of men, as men's laws, but such as some way or other he gives his own consent to; whereas the latter, like the Turks, are subject to the mere will of their rulers.

2. That a man serves another, aiming to satisfy his will alone, without any reference to his own benefit. A slave is forced to obey thus, although there is naturally no such distance between man, that one should serve another, without respect to his own good. Such a distance indeed exists between God and us, and the more we are swallowed up in aiming at God, and the less at ourselves, it is the better and more reasonable service; but as regards our fellow creatures, it is far otherwise. In England, therefore, when any thing is granted to the king, it is usual to send up some other bill for the good of the subject, thus giving the ruler somewhat, but withal expecting some benefit from him in return. Indeed in our very service to men we are to aim at God, and in the condition God has put us, to seek to glorify him, more than to provide for ourselves; but as regards man only, we are not bound to serve him, further than with respect to ourselves, and the good of others. Wherefore subjects may know that they are not made merely for the will of those above them; they indeed render them obedience, but do it for the good they expect from them.

3. That a slave is forced to serve with rigour; his service is not one of love.

Now the people of Israel were under bondage in all these three respects. First, they were forced to serve without any consent at all. Secondly, they who governed them, did not at all aim at their good; it concerned not them; Let them perish as dogs, we will have our work done, and well done too. When men govern so as to care not what becomes of thousands of others, provided they may have their own wills satisfied, this is to make free subjects bond-slaves. And thirdly, all was done with rigour; the Egyptians "made their lives bitter with hard bondage," but cared not for Israel's love. Wherefore when freed from these three things, they sang, and they had cause to do so.

Secondly, They sang when they came out of the land of Egypt, because they were not only in bondage in Egypt, but in bondage under such a king. For, consider this, and surely to be delivered from such a one afforded abundant matter for rejoicing.

1. They were bond-slaves to a king of another nation. Sometimes regard for country and kindred moves compassion; but of Israel, being strangers, he desired merely to get his own turn served, and cared little what eventually became of them.

2. They were bond-slaves to a king whose rule was arbitrary, and his will the law, who imposed what tasks he pleased, the number of bricks they should make, and when he pleased took away their straw, and yet tied them to making the number. He governed them not by law, but by will.

3. They were in bondage under a cruel king, who in the Scripture is called a dragon, on account of his cruelty; "I am against thee, Pharaoh king of Egypt, the great dragon," Ezek. xxix. 3.

4. They were in bondage to an unnatural king. A progenitor of the Israelites had saved Egypt from perishing, and the king and his family from destruction; yet now, without any regard to former services, the new king who "arose up over Egypt" "made their lives bitter with hard bondage."

5. They were in bondage under a king, in whose eyes they were impure and unclean. "The Egyptians might not eat bread with the Hebrews; for that is an abomination unto the Egyptians," Gen. xliii. 32.

6. They were in bondage under a wilful king. We scarcely read of any one so set upon his will as this king was. Judgments were denounced and executed in vain, his language still was, "I will pursue, I will overtake, I will divide the spoil; my lust shall be satisfied upon them; I will draw the sword, my hand shall destroy them," Exod. xv. 9. Something similar has been remarked of the king of Babylon, but of none else; and the text refers partly to their deliverance from under the king of Babylon also; as if he should say, You sang joyfully when you came up out of Egypt, because you were delivered from such a cruel, wilful king; you shall sing so once more, for you shall hereafter be delivered from a like bondage: for though all the ten tribes came not back, yet it was in part fulfilled to many of them.

7. They were in bondage under a king suspicious and jealous, lest they should "multiply" and rise up against him, Exod. i. 10. It is a sad thing when there are such suspicions betwixt a king and his people, that they cannot confide in and trust each other. Well might they sing therefore in the days of their youth, when they came up out of the land of Egypt.

Thirdly, They sang when they came up out of the land of Egypt, because they were then freed from hinderances in the exercise of religion; as Moses told Pharaoh that they could not sacrifice in Egypt, but must go three days' journey into the wilderness to sacrifice unto the Lord their God, Exod. viii. 25—27.

Fourthly, They sang, because their deliverance out of Egypt was wrought with a mighty hand: "The Lord hath triumphed gloriously," hath been gloriously glorious, Exod. xv. 1; and, ver. 6, "Thy right hand, O Lord, is become glorious in power." The "hand of God" is God's strength, the "hand of God in power" implies something more, and still more "God's right hand in power;" but, "the right hand of God is glorious in power," is a most forcible expression, denoting the greatness of the work wrought by God in their deliverance: and to enhance it still more, it is said, ver. 16, "by the greatness of thine arm;" not only God's hand, but his arm, and "the greatness of his arm," were engaged on their behalf. In ver. 7, there is a phrase more expressive still, "in the greatness of thine excellency," in the multitude of thine elation, or proud lifting up of thyself (for the word translated excellency there signifies pride also); and God indeed in this wrought for his people in the multitude of his excellency, that is, in a manner which combined in it a multitude of glorious works, which if you could analyze, you would find each replete with a multitude of glorious excellences. Well might they sing, when God did manifest himself thus.

Fifthly, They sang when they came up out of the land of Egypt, because this mercy was the fulfilling of a promise made long before. "At the end of four hundred and thirty years, even the self-same day, the hosts of the Lord went out of the land of Egypt;" which refers to a promise, and shows us that God kept his word to a very day. Hence, Exod. xv. 2, "He is my God, I will prepare him an habitation; my father's God, and I will exalt him." As if he would say, O Lord, thou didst make promises to our forefathers, and now thou hast fulfilled them to us, thou art our God and our fathers' God.

Sixthly, It was a mercy got by much prayer. They cried unto God by reason of their afflictions, Exod. iii. 7; and their prayers being now answered, their hearts rejoiced.

Seventhly, It was a mercy succeeding a sore and long bondage.

Eighthly, It was a mercy precursive to an entrance into Canaan; therefore this they mention as the especial cause of the joy of their hearts, in ver. 13, "Thou hast guided thy people in thy strength to thy holy habitation;" and, ver. 17, "Thou shalt bring them in, and plant them in the mountain of thine inheritance." The Holy Ghost speaks here as if the thing were done already; O Lord, thou hast indeed granted unto us a great mercy in delivering us out of Egypt, but herein we especially prize it, as bringing us to thy holy habitation, and planting us at length in the mountain of thine inheritance.

Now, saith the Lord, you shall sing as you did then; look, whatever causes you had then for rejoicing, you shall have the same when I am reconciled to you.

VI. The time referred to when this was fulfilled, is the last thing requiring explanation; and this prophecy seems to relate to four periods.

First, It began in some degree to be fulfilled at their return out of captivity from Babylon. Though it is true, few of the ten tribes returned; yet it is clear from Scripture, that many of them did then rejoice in the first-fruits of this mercy. The whole of Isa. xii. is a song, blessing God for their return; "Jehovah is my strength and my song, he also is become my salvation."

Secondly, In reference to spiritual Israel, it is applied, as in Rom. ix., to the calling of the Jews and Gentiles together, when the gospel was first preached. Jews and Gentiles being then called home, became the spiritual Israel of God, and there was singing: "And again he saith, Rejoice, ye Gentiles, with his people," Rom. xv. 10.

The third period referred to, is the delivery of God's people from under the tyranny of antichrist, typified by that of the Egyptians: "And I saw as it were a sea of glass mingled with fire: and them that had gotten the victory over the beast, and over his image, and over his mark, and over the number of his name, stand on the sea of glass, having the harps of God. And they sing the song of Moses the servant of God, and the song of the Lamb, saying, Great and marvellous are thy works, Lord God Almighty; just and true are thy ways, thou King of saints. Who shall not fear thee, O Lord, and glorify thy name? for thou only art holy: for all nations shall come and worship before thee; for thy judgments are made manifest," Rev. xv. 2—4. In this song, which I make no question but the scripture before us refers to, there are divers things observable.

First, The singers were those "that had gotten the victory over the beast, and over his image, and over his mark;" that is, a full victory, not only abominating antichrist himself, but the very image or character of him, any thing whereby they might seem to allow of him, to be owned by him.

Secondly, They stood upon "a sea of glass mingled with fire." The sea of glass I find interpreted, Christian doctrine; so called for its clearness; though not so clear as afterward it should be, for there is some darkness even in glass, but clear in comparison of what it was before, for, 2 Kings xxv. 13, the sea was of brass, which is far thicker and more opaque. But there was fire mingled with this sea of glass; that is, though they had a clearer doctrine than before, yet there were many contentions in the church through diversity of opinions, and much division even amongst the godly. It is a sad condition indeed, yet not unusual, especially when doctrines are first cleared, to have great contentions arise in the church among godly men. It is no wonder that they should differ in opinion, yea, and contend with some heat of spirit, when the light first breaks forth. When men are in the dark they sit together, and walk not at such a distance from each other; but when light comes, it cannot be expected but there will be differences. But yet, mark, the godly then did not reject the doctrine, because there was fire, heat of contention, mingled with it; but, "stood on the sea with their harps in their hands," professing the doctrine, and rejoicing that ever they lived to have the gospel so clearly revealed to them.

"And they sing the song of Moses," and not only of Moses, but "the song of the Lamb" too. What was that? First, "Great and marvellous are thy works;" in that we see we are delivered from antichristian bondage, as the people of Israel from Egyptian, with a mighty hand of thine: oh it is a marvellous work of God that we are thus freed. Therefore know this, that whensoever the church shall be delivered from antichristian bondage, it shall be by an extraordinary manifestation of God's power; and let us not be discouraged, because we meet with some trials by the way, for our deliverance would appear as nothing marvellous, except our difficulties were many and great.

Further, "Just and true are thy ways." God, in that deliverance, will show the fulfilling of all his promises, and will fully satisfy the hearts of his people who have been a long time seeking him, and suffering for him. Whereas the adversaries, who, because of the forbearance and long-suffering manifested towards them, thought there was no God in heaven that regarded them, but scoffed at the fastings, and prayers, and faith of the saints, will find that God avengeth his own elect; and the hearts of the saints, ready to fail, at last shall say, "Just and true are thy ways;" Lord, we now see all thy good word fulfilled, all thy promises performed; now we see it is not in vain to seek thee, and to wait upon thee, for "just and true are thy ways."

"Thou King of saints." God is indeed the King of the world now, and the King of his saints; but the glory of Christ's kingdom, being now obscured by the surrounding shades of this world's sin and guilt, its manifestations do not shine forth so brightly as they will then appear. We have somewhat indeed of his priestly and prophetical office discovered to us, but very little of his kingly; but when God shall fully deliver his people, then shall they magnify Jesus Christ as in very deed the King of saints.

Lastly, Who will not fear thee, thou King of nations, "for thy judgments are made manifest:" as if they should say, We see now it is good to fear God, he has now made a difference "between him that feareth God, and him that feareth him not." The angel, John saw flying "in the midst of heaven, having the everlasting gospel to preach," cries, "with a loud voice, Fear God, and give glory to him," Rev. xiv. 6, 7. The fear of God will powerfully constrain the hearts of the saints in those times. This is the song of Moses to which this scripture refers; and they shall thus sing, as Israel did in the days of her youth, when she came up out of the land of Egypt; yea, and their song shall be much the more glorious one.

The last period this prophecy refers to, is the great calling in of the Jews. Then the Scripture saith, "Everlasting joy shall be upon their heads: they shall obtain gladness and joy; and sorrow and mourning shall flee away," Isa. li. 11. They shall sing as those who will mourn no more in this world, on account of the malice and rage of adversaries. This was not fulfilled at their return from the Babylonish captivity, but the Scripture is explicit about its accomplishment even in this world: Rev. xxi. 4, is almost a repetition of the words of the prophet; "God shall wipe away all tears from their eyes; and there shall be no more death, neither sorrow, nor crying, neither shall there be any more pain." The former things shall be passed away for ever, and they shall sing, as they did in the days of their youth, when they came up out of the land of Egypt.

From these remarks many important observations will flow.

Obs. 1. It is a great mercy for people to be delivered from outward bondage. It will be found a great mercy, when the world shall be delivered from their outward bondage, and men shall see that they were born freemen, and not slaves; and that the world was not made for twenty or thirty to do what they pleased in, and to account all the rest as beasts, yea, dogs; as if the lives of thousands might be recklessly squandered for the gratification of their humours and lusts. When men shall become sensible that they are subjects and not slaves, men and not beasts, and so shall not suffer themselves, like beasts, to be driven at the will of others, this will be a great mercy.

But to be delivered from antichristian bondage, is a greater mercy than it was for the children of Israel to be delivered from their Egyptian bondage. For,

First, We read not of any attempt in Egypt to bring their consciences under the thraldom of any false worship. Pharaoh did not this, but antichrist forces to idolatry.

Secondly, Though Pharaoh imposed heavy tasks and burdens, yet he did not kill them; at length indeed he commanded their first-born to be slain; but the people of Israel themselves continue to exist, though with their lives made bitter by hard bondage. But antichrist thirsts for blood; papists are men of blood.

Thirdly, It was the affliction of God's people to be in bondage in Egypt, but not their sin; but to be in bondage under antichrist, is not only an affliction, but it is sin, and that of a high nature.

Fourthly, Though under Egyptian bondage, yet they were delivered from Egyptian plagues; but those who are under antichristian bondage, shall come under antichristian plagues. "Come out of her, my people, that ye receive not of her plagues," Rev. xviii. 4. You must not think to escape as they did out of Egypt; if you stay in that bondage, you will be involved in their plagues. How, therefore, should we regard those who would bring us into this bondage again, when God has begun to revive us a little! "O my lord the king," (saith Jeremiah,) "let my supplication, I pray thee, be accepted before thee; that thou cause me not to return to the house of Jonathan the scribe, lest I die there," chap. xxxvii. 20. So let us cry to the King of heaven and earth, O Lord, our King, let our supplication be accepted before thee; since we are begun to be delivered from that bondage, cause us not to return to that house again.

Obs. 2. A reconciled condition is a singing condition. When there is a harmony between heaven and the soul, between God and a sinner, there is sweet melody indeed, there may well be singing. "The ransomed of the Lord shall return, and come to Zion with songs and everlasting joy upon their heads," Isa. xxxv. 10. And chap. xliv. 23, "Sing, O ye heavens; for the Lord hath done it: shout, ye lower parts of the earth: break forth into singing, ye mountains." "We being justified by faith have peace with God," saith the apostle, and not only rejoice in hope of the glory, but we even "glory in tribulation also." Having peace with God, though war with all the world, we rejoice.

Obs. 3. It is a great mercy when magistrates and people join together in praising God; when Moses begins, and Miriam and the leaders of Israel follow, and then all the people join in, and answer one another in their singing. When that day shall come that God shall stir up the hearts of the magistrates and the great ones amongst us, to sing hallelujahs to him that sitteth upon the throne, and to the Lamb for evermore; and when he shall so move the hearts of the people, that they shall answer one another in their singing, and join, with one accord, in this sweet melody; this will be a blessed time indeed. Now, perhaps, in one place there is singing and blessing of God for what is done; in another, cursing and blaspheming against those engaged in praise. Some men's hearts are rejoicing, whilst others fret and rage when they hear of the great things God is doing; and this discourse has rent asunder, not only the political, but the social relations of life. Such is our condition at this day, but there are better times coming, when our Moseses, our Aarons, and Miriams, and all our people, shall join together in singing praises to our God.

Obs. 4. Thankfulness to God for mercy implies joyfulness. A sad, grumbling, discontented spirit consists not with true thankfulness of heart. God will not accept, in this sense, of the bread of mourners. It is grievous to his Spirit, that we should hang up our harps and be sad in the midst of abundance of mercies.

Obs. 5. When God brings into straits, yet if he sanctify them and make them means of good to us, we have cause to rejoice. "She shall sing there." Where? At the "door of hope" in "the valley of Achor;" that is, that God would make the greatest troubles and afflictions of his church to be a door of hope, an inlet to mercy. "In the wilderness shall waters break out, and streams in the desert; and the parched ground shall become a pool, and the thirsty land springs of water." What seemed most contrary to you, I will make to work for your good, saith God; and "*then* shall the lame man leap as an hart, and the tongue of the dumb sing," Isa. xxxv. 6, 7. Though our tongues be dumb, yet it should make us sing when we see God bringing good out of evil; and things that of themselves tend to our ruin, and would reduce us to misery, that are as the valley of Achor, yet rendered by his mercy a door of blessed hope. If men, we ought; if Christians, though dumb before, we must sing and tell of all his loving-kindness.

Yea, this overruling providence is introduced as an argument to strengthen the weak hands and the feeble knees, and as a reason why those who are faint-hearted should not fear; but stay themselves upon God, who brings sweet out of bitter, good out of evil. "Say to them that are of a fearful heart, Be strong, fear not, behold your God will come with vengeance, even God with a recompence: he will come and save you."

Are we in "the valley of Achor," a place of trouble and straits? we have cause to sing even there, for we have not yet been brought into any difficulties which God has not overruled for our good; he has turned "the parched ground into a pool, and the thirsty land into springs of water." And it is our great sin, that when God calls us to singing, we are dejected and cast down, and ready to conclude that "all these things are against us." Oh no, God calls you to singing, notwithstanding all your difficulties. "Sing, O heavens; be joyful, O earth; and break forth into singing, O mountains: for the Lord hath comforted his people, and will have mercy upon his afflicted." But mark now what follows: "But Zion said, the Lord hath forsaken me, and my Lord hath forgotten me." At the very time when the Lord was calling them to singing, even then they were concluding of rejecting. Let us take heed that this be not our condition.

Obs. 6. When the Lord is beginning with his saints in the ways of his mercy, though they have not all they desire, yet is theirs a singing condition. That is, that valley of Achor was some special mercy, which God gave at first as a door of hope to further mercies which he had in store, and there they should sing. Though you be but brought into the valley of Achor, and only at the door of hope, and not yet entered in, nor gotten possession of all the mercy God intends for you, yet he expects you should sing. You must not stand complaining and murmuring because you have not all that you desire; though God makes you wait at the door, you must wait there singing. It may be said of his mercy as of his word; "The entrance of thy word giveth light," Psal. cxix. 130; so the entrance of God's works of mercy gives light. And Psal. cxxxviii. 5, "Yea, they shall sing in the ways of the Lord: for great is the glory of the Lord." In the ways of the Lord they shall sing, though their day be but still the day of small things.

Because we stand at the door murmuring and quarrelling one with another, whereas God expects that we should wait there singing and praising his name, is certainly one great reason why our door of hope is not yet fully opened, or, at least, that we have not that abundant entrance into it which we desire. Yet, though the mercy we look for should be reserved for the generation that shall follow, we have cause to bless God that ever we lived to this day, to see so much of God as we have done. Let us then stand singing at our Father's door; and if we must sing at the foot of Zion, what song shall we sing when we come to the height! "They shall come and sing in the height of Zion, and shall flow together to the goodness of the Lord," Jer. xxxi. 12.

If God is dealing with any of you in a way of mercy, though you can see but a little light through the keyhole, yet you should sing there. There are many poor souls, with whom God is beginning in very gracious ways, yet because they have not their minds enlightened, their hearts humbled, as they desire, complete power over corruptions, and ability to perform duties; are presently ready to conclude against themselves, Surely the Lord will not have mercy, we are rejected. They think they have nothing, because they have not all they desire. O unthankful heart! this is the very thing which keeps thee under bondage; because, when the Lord is setting open a door of hope to thee, thou wilt not take notice of it, but art presently murmuring and repining, because all thy desires are not fulfilled. Wouldst thou enter in at this door, and have God perfect the mercy he has begun? be observant of the beginnings, and bless God for what thou hast. This would be of marvellous use to many a drooping soul, if it taught them, by this day's coming hither, to sing hereafter at the door of hope.

Obs. 7. It is often the condition of God's own people, when first made free, to be in a singing condition, but afterwards to lose their joy. "She shall sing there, as in the days of her youth." When God's mercies were new to them, in the days of their youth, oh how their hearts were affected! how then with joy and gladness sang Moses and all the people! but in process of time it appears they kept not up this singing, this making melody in their hearts; therefore God promises they should sing as in the days of their youth.

We find it so when people first come out of a state of bondage to enjoy church liberties. How they rejoice in them! how they bless God for them! how sweet are these mercies to their very hearts! they rejoice that ever they lived to this time; but soon the flower of their youth is gone, and the "teats of their virginity bruised." At first, indeed, oh the sweetness, the blessed condition that God has brought us to, to have these liberties and ordinances according to his own way! But stay a while, and you shall find contention or scandal arising among them, or deadness of heart befalling them; and we may say, as the apostle to the Galatians, "Where is then the blessedness you spake of?" Gal. iv. 15. They "would have plucked out their eyes" for Paul. What is become of all now? All their beauty and glory is quite faded. Let us take heed that, when our hearts seem raised and strongly affected by mercies, we do not soon lose the vigour and warmth of our zeal.

When the city of Berne was first delivered from antichrist, they wrote the day of their deliverance upon pillars, with letters of gold. Was it not so with us in England? When mercies were fresh we rejoiced in them exceedingly. I will only instance that deliverance upon the fifth of November; how mightily were both king and parliament affected with it! their hearts elated, and blessing God for having saved them from papists. Then there were prayers and thanksgivings set forth, and in them this expression against popery, "Whose faith is faction, whose religion is rebellion, whose practice is murdering of souls and bodies." When the mercy was new, how did their spirits work! then they protested against all kinds of popery. From the proclamation about the solemnity of that time, and the expressions in the prayers then set forth, one would verily think that popery could never more have prevailed in England; who would have deemed it possible for a popish army ever to be countenanced in England again? Certainly, if it had been raised then, when men's feelings were so excited, all the people of the land would have risen and beaten them to pieces, if it had been but with clubs.

It is so with many young persons, when God first begins to work upon their hearts; oh how zealous are they for the Lord! then their spirits are mightily up for Christ. "O satisfy us early with thy mercy; that we may rejoice and be glad all the days of our lives," Psal. xc. 14. It is a sweet thing when the latter part of that prayer follows, when God satisfies young people with his mercy, and that satisfaction abides, so that they rejoice all the after-days of their lives in him. The Lord many times satisfies young ones with his mercy, but they quickly grow dead and cold; their hearts soon become hardened and polluted, and they cease to rejoice.

Obs. 8. Restored and recovered mercies are very sweet and precious. "She shall sing as in the days of her youth." They were once in a sweet singing condition, but had lost it; and now God promises to recover them. "Oh that I were as in months past, as in the days when God preserved me; when his candle shined upon my head, and when by his light I walked through darkness; as I was in the days of my youth, when the secret of God was upon my tabernacle!" Job xxix. 2—4. The patriarch desired this earnestly, that he might have restored, recovered mercies. What a happy condition should I be in, saith he, if it were now with me as in the days of my youth! May not many in this place say so? God has been gracious to them in former days, given them many sweet manifestations of his love, many soul-ravishing communications of himself; but oh, how have they lost them! They may well say, Oh that it were with us as in the days of our youth! Oh that God would restore to us the mercy we once had! how blessed then would be our condition!

But God here gives a gracious promise that he will restore them, that he will grant them the petition of David, "Restore to me the joy of thy salvation," Psal. li. 12: Lord, I have lost it; oh that I might have it again! how happy should I be! So Psal. cxxxvii. 1, 2, "By the rivers of Babylon, there we sat down, yea, we wept, when we remembered Zion. We hanged our harps upon the willows." If one had come to them and said, What will you say if you be restored and go to Zion again, and have songs there, as many and as delightful as before? Their hearts could not but have leaped for joy. This mercy would be like the wine mentioned Cant. vii. 9, so sweet that it "causes the lips of those that are asleep to speak:" if there be any life left, such a mercy would raise and animate it. "When the Lord turned again the captivity of Zion, we were like them that dream. Then was our mouth filled with laughter, and our tongue with singing," Psal. cxxvi. 1, 2. As a poor prodigal, who, having left his father's house and become reduced to want, misery, and bondage, sits down beneath a hedge, wringing his hands, lamenting the loss of his father's house, and, considering what comfort he had in that father's presence, exclaims at his own folly and madness: if one should then come and say to him, Your father is reconciled to you, and sends for you home, and promises to put you into as comfortable a condition as ever; what heart-music would this cause! Thus God promises to his people, that he will restore them to their former singing condition.

Obs. 9. Promised mercies are sweet mercies. "Blessed be the Lord God of Israel; for he hath visited and redeemed his people, and hath raised up an horn of salvation for us in the house of his servant David; as he spake by the mouth of his holy prophets," Luke i. 68—70: and ver. 72, "To perform the mercy promised;" there is the cause of singing. Blessed be the Lord God of Israel, that hath performed the mercy promised.

The declaration of a promise is sweet to a gracious heart, it can sing then; much more sweet is the promise fulfilled. 2 Chron. xx. 17, "Stand ye still, and see the salvation of the Lord;" there is the promise. Mark now how Jehoshaphat and the people were affected with it: ver. 18, 19, "And Jehoshaphat bowed his head with his face to the ground: and all Judah and the inhabitants of Jerusalem fell before the Lord, worshipping the Lord. And the Levites, of the children of the Kohathites, and of the children of the Korhites, stood up to praise the Lord God of Israel with a loud voice on high." And ver. 21, "He appointed singers unto the Lord, that should praise the beauty of holiness, and say, Praise the Lord; for his mercy endureth for ever." Jehoshaphat had not the promise fulfilled, it was only made; they had not obtained the victory over their enemies; but only a promise that God would be with them, and presently Jehoshaphat and all the people began singing. A gracious heart sees cause enough to sing if it receive but a promise, but much more when it is enjoying the fulfilment. If the promise of a mercy has such sweetness in it, what sweetness then has the mercy of the promise!

Obs. 10. When God appears remarkably, with a high hand in delivering his people, then the mercy is to be accounted precious indeed, and all the people of the Lord should sing and praise him; as in Isaiah, when God had told of an extraordinary manifestation of mercy, I will plant them in the wilderness, and so on: then, saith he, shall this be, that they may "see, and know, and understand, and consider, that the hand of the Lord hath done this, and the Holy One of Israel hath created it." When a thing is effected by God's hand immediately, which helps a people much, he expects that they should see, and know, and consider, and understand together: all these expressions are heaped one upon another. And if any people be called to this, we are at this day; God has appeared extraordinarily to us. Oh that we had eyes to see! oh that we had hearts to consider and understand, that we might give God the glory due to him!

Obs. 11. Mercies which have been much sought for, and to obtain which many cries have been sent up to God, when once granted, should cause us to sing his praises. The people of Israel cried much before God granted them deliverance from Egypt. "I have heard their cry," saith God, Exod. iii. 7. And here, They shall sing as in the day when they came up out of the land of Egypt. "*They* shall praise the Lord that seek him," Psal. xxii. 26. The more we seek to God for any mercy, the more we shall praise him when we have obtained it. "Blessed be the Lord, because he hath heard the voice of my supplications; my heart trusted in him, and I am helped." What follows? "Therefore my heart greatly rejoiceth, and with my song will I praise him," Psal. xxviii. 6, 7. Because God had heard the voice of his supplication, therefore with his song he would praise him. The mercies we get by crying unto God are singing mercies indeed; such as come to us only through a general providence, without seeking to God, are not so sweet: as Hannah said to Eli concerning her son, whom she obtained by prayer, (and therefore named Samuel, that is, "Asked of God,") "As thy soul liveth—for this child I prayed; and the Lord hath given me my petition which I asked of him." This she spake, triumphing in God's goodness. Mercies gotten by prayer may be triumphed in. When you want a mercy, pray much for it; the more you pray for it, the more you will sing when you receive it; and the less prayer that went before, the less praise will follow after.

Obs. 12. Mercies which make way for the enjoyment of ordinances are truly sweet, singing mercies. They shall sing as they did when they came up out of the land of Egypt. Why did they sing then? Because the deliverance from Egypt made way for that richer mercy, the enjoyment of God's worship in his ordinances, as appears from Exod. xv. 2: "I will prepare him an habitation," saith Moses, rejoicing that Israel was now going on in the way to build God a habitation; and ver. 13, "Thou hast guided them in thy strength unto thy holy habitation:" as if he should say, It is indeed a great thing to be delivered out of bondage, but it is only a foretaste of a higher mercy that we look for, that is, the guiding of thy people "in thy strength unto thy holy habitation:" we look upon this present mercy of our deliverance, for which we now sing, and give thee praise, in this light; and although, Lord, there are many difficulties between this and our coming to enjoy thy habitation, thou wilt guide us in thy strength, and carry thy people all the way through to the house of thy holiness: this made them sing so cheerfully. And again, ver. 17, "Thou shalt bring them in, and plant them in the mountain of thine inheritance, in the place, O Lord, which thou hast made for thee to dwell in, in the sanctuary, O Lord, which thy hands have established." So David, Psal. xxvii. 4, "One thing have I desired of the Lord, that will I seek after; that I may dwell in the house of the Lord all the days of my life, to behold the beauty of the Lord, and to inquire in his temple." This is a choice mercy, therefore all mercies that make way for it are indeed sweet. So we should look upon all our deliverances from outward troubles, and whatsoever peace God gives us, as sweet and comfortable preludes to this mercy of enjoying God's mountain, of living in God's habitation, that we may dwell there all the days of our life.

Obs. 13. New mercies should recall the memory of old. They shall sing as in the day when they came up out of the land of Egypt; that is, I will grant to them yet further mercies, and these shall renew the memory of all the former ones they have enjoyed from me. As new guilt summons up the recollection of former transgressions, so new mercies recall the memory of former ones. Has God rescued you from any danger now? were you never delivered before? if even when a child, the present deliverances should remind you of what you then received. So in a nation; does God grant it any new mercy? this should bring to their remembrance all the mercies they ever have received. "Bless ye God in the congregations, even the Lord from the fountain of Israel," Psal. lxviii. 26. You who are true Israelites, bless God now; but in your praises, let present mercies be to you as streams to lead you to the fountain. Consider in order the whole series of them till you come to the source, even that covenant which God has made with Israel.

Obs. 14. All former mercies to God's people should strengthen our faith in future ones. Why does the prophet remind them of coming out of the land of Egypt? that he might help and strengthen their faith in believing the mercy which was to come. As if he should say, That God who has wrought so wonderfully for you, in delivering you out of the land of Egypt, is able and willing to make good his word in granting you deliverance hereafter. Many scriptures confirm this, as Psal. lxvi. 6, "He turned the sea into dry land, they went through the flood on foot: there did we rejoice in him." Mark, "they went through the flood," and "there did we rejoice in him." How did we rejoice in him? it was many hundred years after, that we rejoiced. But by the manifestation of God's great goodness to his people in former days, our faith is strengthened in his mercies for our times; and "there did we rejoice in" his leading of Israel through the Red Sea upon dry land, as an argument to us of the power, goodness, and faithfulness of God. Again, Hos. xii. 4, "He had power over the angel: he found him in Bethel, and there he spake with us." Mark, "He had power over the angel: he found him in Bethel." Who "found him?" Jacob, who lived many years before. But "there he spake with us;" not with Jacob only, but with us, that is, whatsoever goodness the Lord showed to Jacob in Bethel, it concerned us for the strengthening of our faith. So, Matt. xx. 31, 32, "Have ye not read that which was spoken unto you by God, saying, I am the God of Abraham, and the God of Isaac, and the God of Jacob?" This was spoken to Moses many hundred years before; but that expression of God's grace then, was a strengthening of the faith of the godly when Christ spake, and now confirms ours.

Obs. 15. Mercies ought to be met with proportionate thankfulness. They shall sing as they did in the days when they came out of Egypt. I will grant you as great mercies as they had, and I expect as much gratitude: as they sung to my praise, so must you sing also. God shows as much mercy to you now, as heretofore, and I appeal to you, nay, God appeals to your consciences, Is there proportionate thankfulness? There has been a time when your hearts have been enlarged to ascribe praise to God, why should it not be so now?

Obs. 16. Deliverance out of Egypt is an ascending condition, as in the original, "They shall ascend out of the land of Egypt:" as then God would never rest till he brought them up to Mount Zion; so when he begins to deliver his people from antichristian bondage, they should never rest in their minds until they reach the height of their deliverance, that is, come to enjoy God's ordinances in his own ways, in the purity and power of them. Our misery and baseness lead us upon some little deliverance presently to rest, whereas we should aim yet higher and higher, and expect that God would go on still with us, and exalt us in the ways of mercy, until he has brought us even to the top of Mount Zion.

Obs. 17. When God raises the spirits of people to rejoice in his mercy, and their hearts are warmed, inflamed, and enlarged with his goodness; then is the time, if ever, to set upon a thorough reformation, to cast out all the remainders of superstition, and every species of false worship. This observation is derived from the connexion of these words with what follows, "And it shall be at that day, saith the Lord, that thou shalt call me Ishi; and shalt call me no more Baali; for I will take away the names of Baalim out of her mouth, and they shall no more be remembered;" that is, there shall be a most glorious reformation, and so complete, that they shall be delivered from all the remainders of their idol worship, and not so much as remember the very names of their false gods. "Thou shalt weep no more: he will be very gracious unto thee at the voice of thy cry," Isa. xxx. 19: the Lord promises abundance of mercy, tells them that they shall weep no more, and that he will be very gracious; now, mark what follows in ver. 22, " Ye shall defile also the covering of thy graven images of silver, and the ornament of thy molten images of gold: thou shalt cast them away as a menstruous cloth; thou shalt say unto it, Get thee hence." And 2 Chron. xxx. 26, you find " there was great joy in Jerusalem" on the celebration of their passover, such joy as was not " since the time of Solomon." Mark then the beginning of the next chapter; " Now when all this was finished," that is, when they had celebrated a passover so full, and had such abundance of joy as had not been in Jerusalem since the time of Solomon, " all Israel that were present went out to the cities of Judah, and brake the images in pieces, and cut down the groves, and threw down the high places and the altars out of all Judah and Benjamin." Their hearts were inflamed with the joy, and they went with full purpose of mind, and brake down the images, &c. And mark, it was Israel that did this; " Israel went out to the cities of Judah, and brake the images in pieces, and threw down the high places, and the altars out of all Judah." What had Israel to do with Judah? Judah and Israel were divided; but now their hearts were so inflamed for God, that they were not able to suffer any false worship among their brethren. Though it belonged to Judah, yet they would help their brethren to cast down all their images, and to cut down their groves and altars, when their hearts were warmed with joy in blessing the name of God. In such a case, men will do much for God; they will not stand examining every point, but commence work directly; the joy of the Lord will be the strength of their hearts. As when wicked men get together drinking, at feasts and in taverns, and their lusts become inflamed, what desperate resolutions to do evil are they filled with! so when God's saints are exercised in his ordinances, and refreshed with the sweetness of his love, when *that* lies glowing at their hearts, how resolved are they for God! they can then do any thing for him. Now the very names of Baalim must be taken away.

Ver. 16, 17. *And it shall be at that day, saith the Lord, that thou shalt call me Ishi; and shalt call me no more Baali. For I will take away the names of Baalim out of her mouth, and they shall no more be remembered by their name.*

Here we have a prophecy and promise of a thorough reformation of the church, as full as any I know of in Scripture. God has a time to reform his church thoroughly, the very names of their idols and the remembrance of them shall be taken away. This reformation is God's work, I will do it, saith God, " I will take away the names of Baalim."

" Thou shalt call me Ishi, and shalt call me no more Baali."

Why? what great difference is there between these two names, Ishi and Baali, that God will have one, but not the other?

Both of them signify almost the same thing; names very fit for a wife to apply to her husband. But Ishi comes from a word signifying strength, and the woman being the weaker vessel, therefore calls her husband Ishi, my strength; for the husband should be strength to the wife, he should live with her as a man of knowledge, be a protection to her, and help her in all her weaknesses and afflictions. Baali signifies my lord, as well as my husband; it is a word denoting rule and authority, and marking the inferiority of the wife; but Ishi has more love and familiarity in it: now God saith he will be called Ishi, but not Baali. Why? the word Baali is a very good word, and has a good signification, and is as proper to God as any name that can be given to him by the church (except that God forbade it here): for when the church calls God Baali, it only means, O God, that art my Lord, my Husband, who art to rule and govern me: yea, and we find that God applies to himself this name, Isa. liv. 5, " Thy Maker is thine husband;" in the Hebrew, Thy Maker is thy Baal; so that husband and Baal are the very same. But now, because they had abused this word Baal, and given it to their idols, therefore God would have it no more. As the word *tyrannus* was a name once for a king, kings were called tyrants, without any such bad meaning as now; but because when kings had gotten the sole power into their own hands, they so often abused it to oppression, therefore oppressors were called tyrants. So *fur*, a thief, was once the ordinary term for a servant, *fures* and *servi* implying the same; but because many servants were false and dishonest, therefore *fures* began to be altogether understood in the worst sense, and at length applied only to thieves. So *sophista*, a sophist, was one who studied wisdom; but because they so much degenerated, and many, under pretence of the study of wisdom, deceived others, therefore the name sophist became equivalent to deceiver. I might instance many others.

But further, God saith that he would " take away the names of Baalim out of her mouth." May not we use then this word Baali?

Yes, it is not unlawful for us to use it, notwithstanding this, for the Holy Ghost long afterwards saith, " I have reserved to myself seven thousand men, who have not bowed the knee to the image of Baal," Rom. xi. 4. Thus it is mentioned and remembered even by the Spirit of God, therefore it is not a sin. Nay, not only the word Baal, but it is not unlawful to mention the names of any idols of the heathen; for the Holy Ghost, Acts xxviii. 11, speaking of the ship Paul sailed in, saith, " whose sign was Castor and Pollux," the names of two heathen idols. And you may observe, that in our text the remembering is as much forbidden as the mentioning. Now if it were a sin merely to mention the names of the heathen gods, it were a sin to remember them; therefore God means the mentioning of them *honoris gratia*, by way of honour, or without marked detestation of them.

From the words thus opened, there arise many observations very useful and seasonable for our times.

Obs. 1. There is much danger in words and names. You shall call me Ishi, I will not have you call me Baali, I will not have that word used. The devil has obtained much by words and names, formerly by the word puritan, though men knew not what it meant, and now by this new name that he has lately invented; the devil has always some words, some names, in which he sees advantage to distinguish men. Speaking of the ways of religion in the language of superstition does much injury. Concerning this, we have a notable observation from the papists themselves in the Rhemist Testament, in their notes on 1 Tim. vi. 20, " Keep that which is committed to thy trust, avoiding profane and vain babblings;" so we translate it: they render it, profane novelties, and observe on it, " Let us keep our forefathers' words, and we shall easily keep our old faith. The heretics call repentance amendment, but let us" (say they) " keep the old word penance; they call it the Lord's supper, but we will keep the old word mass; they say communion table, but let us retain the word altar; they use the terms elders and ministers, let us say priests; they say superintendents, but let us retain the word bishop;" (it is a Scripture word indeed, but not in the sense they use it, for in the Scripture sense every presbyter is a bishop;) " they say sacrament, let us keep the words sacrifice and host; they say congregation, let us keep the word church; they, morning and evening prayer, let us keep the words matins and evening song; and so oblation, and Lent, and Palm Sunday, and Christmas day," &c. This was the policy of papists, and it has been the means many of us have used to bring in popery. Let us take heed of this, for the devil is subtle in it, and though these words have some kind of good sense in the original, yet there is danger in the use of them. Augustine, in the preface to his Commentary on the Psalms, has this expression, "It is a better thing for Christians to speak according to the manner of the church." So we may well say, It had been better, that in the mouths of protestants there had been the ordinary language of protestants, and not the language of papists. Certainly, if God had not been very merciful to us, the very language of papists that began to be used amongst us would have done abundance of mischief; and you should avoid it, and take heed, whatever pretence they may have for their words. In that place of the Rhemist Testament quoted, they say, "Let us take heed of the words of heretics;" they there confess that heretics (as they call us) use many words which have no great danger in them; but because they are the words of heretics, let us not (say they) use them: they are wise in their generation, they will not use our words; though they confess the words themselves contain no harm, yet because they consider them as our proper language, distinct from themselves, therefore no catholics should use them. Why should not we be as wise as they?

Melior in ore Christiano ritus loquendi ecclesiasticus. August. in Præf. Enar. in Ps. xciii.

Obs. 2. Idolatry is a most loathsome and abominable thing. Why? Surely that is most loathsome that we may not so much as mention, nor even remember. We must seek to abolish the very name, the very remembrance, of idolatry as much as possible. We do not love the presence of one whom we hate; if we hate him very much we do not love so much as to see him; and if, perhaps, we see him afar off, our hearts rise against him; but if we cannot endure to name him, that is a greater degree of hatred; and if not even to remember him, it evidences still more our hatred. Yet thus should it be in our manifestation of our hatred to idolatry; we should not admit it into our company, much less then into the ordinances of God. We should not admit the sight, the name, no, not even the memory of it, without much indignation. "Oh, do not this abominable thing that I hate," saith the Lord, Jer. xliv. 4; exclaiming emphatically, as, if any of you should see one ready to murder your child or your father, you would shriek out, Oh, what mean you to do! do not such a horrible villany as this. So God as it were cries out, "Do not this abominable thing." It is observable in the second commandment, that God saith, He will visit the sin upon the third generation of them that hate him: none seem to love God more than will-worshippers; they not only worship God as he has appointed, but devise ways of their own; and yet God charges the breakers of no other commandment with hatred of him but these. As if God should say, You pretend love to me, in finding out new ways to worship me by you pretend decency and reverence, but I account it hating me, you can in nothing provoke me more. Tertullian remarks, Idolatry is the most heinous crime of mankind, it is the chief guilt of the world, and the only cause of judgment in the world.

Principale crimen generis humani, summus seculi reatus, tota causa judicii, idololatria. Tertul. lib. de Idololat.

It were good therefore, seeing God hates and loathes it so much, that we should hate and loathe it also, and therefore cast out even the name and memory of it; it were a happy thing if the names of popish, as well as heathenish, idols could be banished from the church; but I know not how it happens that we Christians still retain the use of them; the very days of the week among us are called by the names of planets, or heathen gods: not that I think it a sin, when it is the ordinary language of the world, to speak so as may be understood, for the apostle mentions the name of Castor and Pollux; but if there could be an alteration by general consent, (as our brethren in New England have,) it were desirable; and still more so, that our children might not be educated in the use of heathen poems, whereby the names of heathen idols are kept up fresh amongst us: the papists themselves acknowledge so much in the Rhemist Testament, in their notes on Rev. i. 10: "The name Sunday is heathenish, as all other of the week-days, some imposed by the Romans after the name of planets, some from certain idols which the Saxons worshipped, and to which they dedicated their days before they were Christians. These names the church rejecting, has appointed to call the first day *Dominic*, (the Lord's,) the others by the name of *Feries*, successively to the last day of the week, which she calls by the old name sabbath, because that was of God, and not by imposition of the heathen." And in their Annotations upon Luke xxiv. 1, "The first day of the sabbath; that is, the first after the sabbath, which is our Lord's day. And from the apostle, 1 Cor. xvi. 2, commanding a collection to be made on the first day of the sabbath, we learn," (say they,) "both the keeping that day as the sabbath, and the church's naming the days of the week the 2nd, 3rd, and 4th of the sabbath, and so on, to be apostolical, which St. Sylvester afterward named the 2nd, 3rd, and 4th *Feriam*." Thus you have the papists acknowledging the Lord's day to be apostolical, and the calling of the days of the week the second, the third, the fourth, &c., to be likewise apostolical. The heathenish Roman names of the days were taken from the seven planets: 1. *Sol*, thence *Dies solis*, Sunday, dedicated to the sun. 2. *Luna*, Monday, dedicated to the moon. 3. *Mars*, Tuesday, dedicated to Mars. Our Tuesday is a Saxon name, from Tuisco, who they say was, since the tower of Babel, chief leader and ruler of the German nation, who, in honour of him, called this day Tuesday, Tuisco's day. 4. *Mercurius*, to whom Wednesday is dedicated, and we call it so, is from the Saxons' Woden, who was a great prince among them, and whose image they adored after his death. 5. *Jupiter*, to whom Thursday is dedicated; so called by us from the Saxon Thor, the name of an idol which they anciently worshipped. 6. *Venus*, to whom our Friday, which name is given it from Friga, an idol of the Germans. This idol was an hermaphrodite, and reputed to be the giver of plenty, and the causer of amity; the same perhaps which the Romans called Venus. 7. *Saturnus*, dedicated to Saturn, whence our Saturday; or, as others think, from Seater, an idol of the Germans. Exod. xxiii. 13, we have this charge, "In all things that I have said unto you, be circumspect: and make no mention of the names of other gods, neither let it be heard out of thy mouth." And Psal. xvi. 4, David professes he will not take the names of idols into his lips.

Obs. 3. In God's worship, even trivial things, any way tending to idolatry, are to be avoided. The mere mention of the word Baali one would think to be one of the smallest things imaginable; but yet we see God would have his people avoid even that.

There is no commandment in which God speaks of himself as a jealous God, but in the second. Now jealousy, you know, not only causes one to be offended at some gross action, but with any thing tending to it; as a husband, if jealous, watches suspiciously the very looks of his wife. So saith God in this commandment, "I am a jealous God;" to note, that though we should not agree to gross idolatry, yet if we do any thing that even tends that way, that faintly approaches superstition, the Lord is jealous of that, and displeased even by such a thing. In his worship little things are not to be contemned, when we come to deal with him we should conscientiously perform even the smallest. The Pharisees, doubtless, when they washed their hands, and Christ would not wash his, would be ready to accuse him of being too scrupulous; What! is there any harm in the washing of a man's hands? yet Christ would not wash his. Though this might appear a little matter before others, yet because it tended in some measure to show some respect to their superstitious observances, Christ would not consent.

That noble servant of God and minister of the church, Marcus, bishop of Arethusa, in the time of Constantine, caused the overthrow of an idol's temple. When Julian came to be emperor, and forced the people of that place to rebuild it, they were ready to do it, but he refused; whereupon the people over whom he had been bishop, took him and stripped him of all his clothes, abused his body, and gave it up to the children to lance with their pen-knives, and then caused him to be put in a basket, and having anointed his naked body with honey, set him in the sun to be stung with wasps. All this cruelty they showed because he would not do any thing toward the building up of this idol temple; nay, they were content to spare him, if he would do even the least thing towards it, or give the merest trifle: but though the aiding in the smallest degree the re-edification of that idol temple might have saved his life, he would not do it; for a little thing in that which concerns the worship of God in religion, is of more concernment than your life or mine.

Theodoret recounts that Valentinian, who was afterwards emperor, going before Julian into the temple of the goddess Fortune, the priest had his holy water, (just as the papists, who imitate the heathen,) and as he sprinkled it upon Julian, there came by accident a drop on Valentinian, who presently struck the priest, and taking his garment, cut that part of it in pieces upon which the water had fallen. Some would say, Alas, why that? It was but a little water that dropped on him, and that by accident; yet, in detestation of idolatry, he cut in pieces that part of his garment. We cannot show our hatred against idolatry fully, except we show it in little, as well as in things very gross and vile.

Theodoret, lib. 4. cap. 15, tells of the zeal of children of Samosaten, who because a tennis ball with which they played had but touched the foot of the ass whereon Lucius, their heretical bishop, rode, they cried out it was defiled, and burnt it in the market-place. Hatred is much shown in little things.

Obs. 4. It is the duty of all God's people, to keep themselves as free as possible from all appearance of idolatry and superstition. Here they are forbidden so much as to mention the names of their idols, certainly therefore they must scrupulously avoid idolatry. We must not think it enough to say, Can any man convince us that this is idolatry? Though it be not, yet if it borders on it, it is our duty to abstain. "There shall be no strange god in you," or "by" you, Psal. lxxxi. 9. It is not only forbidden you to worship a false god, but you shall not even have a false god by you: as Deut. xxv. 13, when God would forbid the sin of injustice, of selling wares by false weights, mark the expression, "Thou shalt not have in thy bag divers weights, a great and a small;" it was a sin to have a great and a small weight in a man's bag. Why? Because, on detection, a man might say, But can you prove that ever I sold wares by the small, or took wares in by this great weight? Yea, but, saith God, that you may be far off from the sin of injustice, I require of you that you shall not have them in your bag: God would have us keep from the very verge of that sin, much more from idolatry, which is the worst of all sins. Isa. lxv. 4, God charges upon them, not only that gross sin of "eating swine's flesh," but having the "broth of abominable things in their vessels." They might say, We use not the flesh but the broth. No, you must not have the broth of abominable things in your vessels; you must keep far off from that defilement: as the Lord speaks concerning "the strange woman," "Remove thy way far from her, and come not nigh the door of her house," Prov. v. 8. If one should say, We will not commit uncleanness; But, saith God, you must remove your way far from her, and not come nigh her, no, not nigh the door of her house. We must not come nigh popery, but abstain from the appearance of that evil. Certainly, it has been a great distemper in many of your hearts, that you went so nigh to popery, especially when the tide was coming in upon you. To stand at the edge of the water when the sea is coming in, especially in some places, as in the Washes in Lincolnshire, is dangerous; but when the tide is going away, is less dangerous. Many of you, when the tide of popery and superstition was flowing, stood upon the very edge of the water: this is a sin of which you ought to repent.

Obs. 5. The church of God must not worship God after the manner of idolaters. They must not even make mention of the names they did; certainly, then, not worship God in a manner conformably to their customs. Deut. xii. 30, 31, "Take heed to thyself, that thou be not snared by following them, after that they be destroyed from before thee; and that thou inquire not after their gods, saying, How did these nations serve their gods? even so will I do likewise. Thou shalt not do so unto the Lord thy God:" and ver. 32, "What thing soever I command you, observe to do it: thou shalt not add thereto, nor diminish from it." Thou shalt not so much as inquire how others serve their gods, what their rites and ordinances and manner of serving their gods are, thou shalt not worship me so. As if he should say, "Whatsoever thing I command you, observe to do it, thou shalt not add thereto, nor diminish from it;" you must keep to that, and not think to worship me as others worship their idols. The Lord insists much on this, though the thing in itself be lawful, yet because adopted by idolaters, it must therefore be rejected. In Ezek. xliv. 20, there is a commandment to the priests of the Lord, that they shall not "shave their heads," nor suffer their "locks to grow long;" but "they shall only poll their heads." Arias Montanus translates the words, "They shall clip equally their hair all of a length;" and the old translation, "They shall round their heads," both which are agreeable to the Hebrew, and refer to the practices of the idolatrous priests, and their several ways of worshipping their idols; some of them shaving their heads, others wearing long hair as women, and both carrying it to an extreme. Now, saith God to his priests, you shall do neither, but "only poll" or "round your heads." Certainly, the devil forgot this scripture, when he raised up such a name as Round-heads, to reproach men by; seeing the word of God is thus express on the point. And on the other side, when the Scripture would describe the enemies of God, it notices, on the contrary, their "hairy scalp," Psal. lxviii. 21.

Tondendo æque attondebunt.

When the Lacedemonians wished to reform excess in apparel, which prevailed amongst them, they at length resolved, that there should be a law forbidding any but harlots to wear rich and showy clothes; thinking by this means to induce all women who regarded their reputation, to adopt mean or plain clothing, and they succeeded. If by the light of nature, when a thing became fashionable with harlots, grave and sober matrons disused it; then what idolaters adopt in worship, the church should abstain from: if there must not be a conformity between matrons and harlots, there must not surely be a conformity between the church of God and idolaters.

—Tredecim mensas lapideas in Atriis exterioribus fuisse, quibus adstantes homines orarent; fuere vero illæ partim ad meridiem, ad occasum, ad septem trionem sitæ, ad orientem nulla. Montan. de fabrica Templi, l. 96.

Arias Montanus saith, that the Jews report of thirteen tables of stone that were in the outward court of the temple, at which men were wont to pray, all of them were made, so that some looked to the north, some to the south, and some to the west, but not one toward the east. And God built his temple so that the holy of holies should not look toward the east, but toward the west. Hence, Ezek. viii. 16, it is said that those who worshipped the sun with "their faces toward the east," had "their backs toward the temple;" so that it appears plainly that the temple stood westward. As there were so many among whom the Jews lived that were worshippers of the sun, and in their adorations would ever look eastward, for that very reason the Lord would not have the holy of holies built eastward. Now all your chancels in England are built eastward; and it used to be the custom of your superstitious worshippers, when they came into such a place, to look eastward, and bow solemnly themselves not only to the altar, but toward the east. I have myself seen a bishop, when the communion table was set in another place, neglect that, and go to the east end of the chancel and bow himself, though his back was toward the table. And you may observe, that in all your burials the corpses are laid east and west, in order (say some) that when Christ comes to judgment they may be ready to look him in the face; it being a tradition that he shall come from the east. You must not think that those who do not follow the old customs of superstition are influenced by perverseness of disposition; God thus enjoined his people, when they saw idolaters worship one way, that they should worship another. We must refrain from borrowing of the Egyptians, lest with the imaginary riches we contract their botches and boils. We have sufficient in the word of God, and need not to imitate idolaters and papists in their forms of worship.

Obs. 6. Things that, in themselves considered, are harmless, yet, if abused to the service of idolatry, must be cast away. On this the text is most explicit: "I will take away the names of Baalim out of her mouth." The name was good, but being abused, was to be taken away; yea, not only such things as originate with idolaters, but even such as at first were of God's own institution; if they cease to be so, if he require not the continuance of them, they must be not only reformed, but wholly rejected from God's worship. Many will easily grant that the inventions of idolaters should be rejected by us; but they say that the present ceremonies originated with the ancient fathers in the primitive times, before popery appeared. For a full answer to this objection you have an express command, Exod. xxxiv. 13, "Ye shall destroy their altars, break their images, and cut down their groves." Here the groves were to be cut down, and they originated not with idolaters, for Gen. xxi. 33 saith, that "Abraham planted a grove, and called there on the name of the Lord, the everlasting God:" groves had a good original in Abraham, but afterwards being abused by idolaters, God requires them to be cut down. And 2 Kings xviii. 4, the "brazen serpent" spoken of originated with God himself, as a temporary ordinance, and they might think and plead that it was kept as a religious monument; but Hezekiah, according to the command of God, beat down the brazen serpent, and called it, by way of contempt, Nehushtan, a piece of brass. It had once been a notable instrument of good to the people of Israel, but now it was but Nehushtan, a piece of brass. And further, to the abolishing things that have been abused to idolatry, there is added a gracious promise, Isa. xxvii. 9, "By this therefore shall the iniquity of Jacob be purged; and this is all the fruit to take away his sin; when he maketh all the stones of the altar as chalk-stones that are beaten in sunder." Then indeed has Jacob's correction produced the desired effect on him to purge away his sin, "when he maketh all the stones of the altar as chalk-stones." And Josiah is commended, 2 Kings xxiii., for destroying the high places, the groves and altars, and the chariots for the sun. And repenting Manasseh, 2 Chron. xxxiii. 15, is commended for taking away the strange gods, and the idol out of the house of the Lord, and all the altars. And Daniel, chap. i., would not eat of the king's meat, because it had been abused and consecrated to his idols.

But to explain this matter fully it will be necessary to meet an objection. You will say, Do not those prohibitions particularly concern the Jews, and not so fully apply to us? they sometimes are forbidden to take off the gold and silver off the idols; do such prohibitions concern us in every thing abused to idolatry?

For answer, I confess, I think we are not bound in every particular to follow the commandments that God gave them; neither do I think that if they had not been prohibited by some express commandment, their using the silver or gold of an image for some civil purpose, had been no sin in them; these things being required of them by a positive law, and not contained in the second commandment, further than by moral implication.

But how far do these commands bind us?

In a three-fold manner.

First, We must retain nothing that conduces to honour any false worship. If Mordecai would not bow to a living monument of that nation whose name God had ordained to be blotted out from under heaven, much less should we reverence dumb monuments of those idols which God has devoted to destruction. We must not show respect to any thing that idolaters have abused, when our reserving or respecting them may in any way maintain their honour. Therefore, certainly, this is true, that to take a ceremony from papists, and introduce it into the most solemn ordinance of Christ, yea, to incorporate it with it, that it may add to the honour of that ordinance, can never be justified. There never was any ceremony more abominably abused than that of the cross: now though it be not a sin to make a cross, yet to bring it into one of the most solemn ordinances of Christ's church, and to make it there conduce to the honour of that ordinance, is plainly a great evil, if men will but open their eyes to the extent of it. So for vestments; suppose there might be some use in them, yet to bring them to add decency to the worship of God, to think that those vestments that have been so notoriously abused should do honour to Divine worship, must needs be sinful: surely all those scriptures that required the Jews to abolish things abused by idolaters, if they carry any moral obligation in them, prohibit these.

Secondly, When any thing once abused to idolatry, implies in the use of it any communion with idolaters, then it must be rejected. This is clear from Rev. ii. 20, where the church of Thyatira is charged that they did "eat things sacrificed unto idols." Why? the meat sacrificed to idols was good meat, a good creature of God, for we know that "every creature of God is good, if it be sanctified by the word and prayer," yet they are charged as sinning against Christ in the use of it. You will say, What is it to them if it were offered to idols? they might eat it as God's creature. But it was a sin, because the eating argued communion with the idolaters: this is plain in 1 Cor. x. 18—21, where you have the argument of the apostle against eating things offered to idols, and he reasons thus; When you eat the same bread in the sacrament, it is a mark of your communion one with another; so your eating of the things sacrificed to idols, is an acknowledgment of your communion with them. Such is the argument of the apostle in that place, and upon that ground it is made a sin; "You cannot" (saith he) "be partakers of the Lord's table, and of the table of devils;" in eating of their meat you communicate with them, and so sin.

Thirdly, It is a sin against God to make use of any thing abused by idolaters when it becomes a scandal to our brethren, a snare to the weak, 1 Cor. x. 28. Eating meat offered to idols is forbidden in the place before referred to, on the ground of communicating; but in this place it is forbidden upon the ground of scandal. Calvin, in his Epistle to the Lord Protector in King Edward's days, saith, What were the ceremonies maintained in England, but so many pleasing allurements, that insnare poor miserable souls, and bring them into evil? Certainly, what we have retained have brought in abundance of evil, and been the means of insnaring many souls. In these three things the rules that concern the Jews have a bearing on us.

Quid enim illæ ceremoniæ aliud fuerint quam totidem lenocinia, quæ miseras animas ad malum perducerent?

But yet they must be observed with some cautions, and understood to regard,

First, Things that are not ordinances continued by God; for certainly if it be an ordinance that God has appointed, though idolaters abuse it never so much, we must maintain it. It is true, the brazen serpent was an ordinance of God, but only to serve a temporary occasion, and therefore, being abused to idolatry, was to be destroyed; but when a thing is an ordinance appointed by God to be continued in the church, we must persevere in the use of it, though it be abused. As in baptism, the ordinance is water; though they abuse water we must continue its use: in the Lord's supper, the elements are bread and wine; and though they are abused we must continue them. Why? Because no abuse is an argument to refuse that which is a duty: the subject causing scandal may in itself be a thing indifferent; but if it be an ordinance, we must continue our obedience, whether men be offended or not.

Secondly, Neither do any of these rules affect any thing indispensably necessary for the worship of God. Suppose idolaters have abused a place of meeting for God's worship; when we have no other place to assemble, this is, for the present at least, necessary for God's worship; a place is required, and if no other can at the time be had, we are bound to worship in that place: the abuse of men must not hinder the service of God. God has never put his worship under the power of wicked men, that they should deprive his people of it at their pleasure.

Thirdly, Any ceremony that naturally, and not merely by virtue of man's appointment, has such decency in it, that its absence would be improper, then, though never so much abused, we are to preserve; for it is the duty of God's people to worship him in a decent way; it is the rule of the apostle, "Let all things be done decently," that is, conformably to what the light of nature teaches, though not expressly revealed in the Scriptures. Such a decency as a thing derives from the institution of man is not here referred to; but such as God in the nature of the thing puts upon it, so that if it were wanting there would be a deficiency. But if the things be merely man's inventions and institutions, having their supposed decency, not from what is indeed in the things themselves, but from that which man's institution puts on them, then they come not under that rule of the apostle; but the abuse of them is a sufficient argument for their rejection.

But it may be objected, If we can instruct people what the abuse is, and what right use they may make of such things, will not that excuse the retaining of them?

No, certainly; it was not allowed the Jews to use the name Baali, though their prophets might teach them in what the abuse of it consisted. Things that have had poison in them, none will be so unwise as to keep by them, under pretence of washing them clean; if they be broken vessels of which there is no use, they are cast upon the dunghill with less trouble and more safety.

All things that are of man's invention, yea, those things that have been God's ordinances, but now are out of date, the Scripture calls "beggarly elements:" you cannot compare men's inventions to clothes, or any thing worth the airing or keeping; but the truth is, all such things as have been abused to idolatry, are but as dirty rags and plasters laid upon plague-sores.

But, further, you will say, If the use we retain them for be not the same they were employed in, why may we not do so?

The text answers that, though the Jews should call God Baali in a right sense, it was not enough, they must wholly reject the very mentioning of the name. The church is the wife of Christ, he is jealous, and has cause to be so, for he knows, while we are in the flesh, that we are prone to spiritual adultery; and if we take any ceremony from popish idolatry, and join it with his ordinances, and think to plead that we intend to make no ill use of it, this will not satisfy Christ.

If any say, Why should we not retain our liberty if the things be good?

But why shouldst thou not manifest thy hatred to all idolatry? And why shouldst thou not tender thy brethren so, as to prevent all scandal that may come by the use of such things?

But, you will say, the idolatry of papists and the idolatry of heathens is not the same, there is a great deal of difference between the heathens in their worship of their idols, and the papists worshipping of God, though in a false way.

Indeed the difference seems great, but yet the idolatry is the same in both; for you are mistaken, if you think that many of the heathens worshipped a false god, otherwise than the papists do; though they made stocks and stones their idols, yet they worshipped the God that was *Primum Ens*, the First Being, in and through those idols. Therefore, Austin upon Psal. xcvi. introduces one answering thus, We do not worship a stone, but the virtues, the strength, and the powers of the great God. And one Maximus Madaurensis, whom Austin speaks of in his 43rd Epistle, saith, Who is so mad, or so void of sense, as to doubt whether there be more gods than one? we invocate the virtues of this one God, under many names, diffused through the frame of the whole world. What more fair answer can papists give for their idolatry? Therefore the thing continues still clear, that (with the rules and cautions before-mentioned) such things as have been abused to idolatry must be wholly cast away; we must not retain them and think to excuse ourselves to God with such distinctions. To what end do we retain them? Is there not sufficient in the worship of God itself to make it acceptable to him?

Non lapidem colimus, sed virtutes Dei magni.

To add a word or two more upon this subject; it has always been the care of the churches of God, to distinguish their worship from that of idolaters. The Manichees were wont to keep their fasts on the Lord's day, on account of which the churches utterly prohibited the keeping of fasts on that day, because they would not do as the Manichees. Tertullian saith, it is *nefas*, a detestable wickedness, to fast on the Lord's day. And Ignatius saith, to fast on the Lord's day is to kill Christ. Tertullian states, that a Christian soldier in the army of the heathen, who, when they, in honour of their idol gods, wore on their heads coronets of bays, instead of wearing his on his head, held it in his hand; upon which there arose a great mutiny in the army, his fellows being indignant that one soldier should be in a different garb

Tert. de Coron. Milit. Ignat. ep. 3. ad Philip.

from all the rest: Surely this is some nice-conscienced soldier, that, forsooth, cannot do as others, he must hold the coronet of bays in his hand, whereas others wear it on their heads. The murmurs of the soldiers reached at length the officers of the army, and the Christian being asked why he differed from his fellows, gave this answer, I am a Christian, and therefore it does not beseem me to do as these do, who wear the bays on their heads in honour of their idol gods: at this they were all greatly incensed, and not only he himself, but all the Christians near at hand, were in danger of great persecution. Nay, there was much murmuring amongst other Christians, that this one man, by such over-scrupulousness, should endanger not only himself, but others. Tertullian therefore, in his defence of this soldier, saith, that he was holier than his brethren, who thought and presumed they might serve two lords, that, in order to avoid persecution, they might comply with the heathens in their superstitious observances; and exclaims, in commendation of this action, O most glorious soldier, who would thus venture himself, and refuse to comply with idolaters! And whereas some, even Christians, who would rather comply than endanger themselves, would plead against him, and say, Where is it written in all the word of God, that we should not wear bays upon our heads? Tertullian replies, Where is it written that we may do it? We must look into the Scriptures to see what we may do, and not think it enough that the Scripture does not directly forbid this or that particular act. By this we see, that some, to avoid trouble and persecution, will, as far as possible, comply with the ways of idolatry; yet those who are truly of a Christian spirit, will courageously refuse, and rather hazard the sorest persecution.

Sanctior cæteris fratribus qui duobus dominis servire se posse præsumunt. Tertul. de Corona Militis.

O militem in Deo gloriosum! Ubi scriptum est ne coronemur? at ubi scriptum est ut coronemur? Tertul. ibid.

Thus it should be with us, we must not retain, with the view of doing it honour, any thing that has been abused to idolatry; we must not so comply with idolaters, and especially in regard of that great idol, the cross, as to retain it, and bring it into the ordinances of God, into the very sacrament, which is surely doing it a great honour; yea, and too great an honour is put upon it, by placing it in the highest part of the city, and thinking it is an ornament to it, whereas it is indeed a great disgrace and dishonour, and retains the memory of your forefathers' superstition and shame. Augustine saith, It is better to die with hunger than to eat things offered to idols: so far were these ancients from conforming with idolaters. Gabriel Biel saith, The church of Rome thought fit to use leavened bread, lest in unleavened they should seem to resemble Ebion the heretic; and Bellarmine would not have Paul called *divus Paulus*, but *beatus*, because *divus* and *diva* were terms applied by the heathen to their gods and goddesses.

Melius mori fame quam idolothytis vesci. August. de Bono Conjug. c. 18.

Obs. 7. When God is reconciled to his people, there will be a thorough reformation both outward and inward. This promise to take away the names of Baalim, is introduced upon God's reconciliation to this people. Idolatry is cast out not only from the heart, but from the mouth; the taking away the names from their mouths is a synecdoche, and denotes the utter abolishing of all ways of idolatry in the outward practice, as well as in the inward affection. The more perfect the reconciliation with God is, the more enmity against idols and superstitious worship. A fearful proof then it is, that we in England were never thoroughly reconciled to God, because we never yet have cast off our idols. As some remnants of superstition, still abiding amongst us, not long since broke forth in the most horrid and vile forms of false worship; so some remainders of God's wrath amongst us this day break forth into a most dreadful flame. When the Jews shall be called again, and God shall be perfectly reconciled to his churches, then idolatry shall be wholly rejected, and their idols shall not even be mentioned any more; and to these times this text refers, and shall then be perfectly fulfilled.

Obs. 8. When a people is reconciled to God, then they call God theirs. My husband, "Ishi." Psal. xvi. 3, 4, David professes that he would not so much as take up the names of idols into his lips; and mark what follows, ver. 5, The Lord is my portion; when the prophet is so taken off from idols, as not to mention their names, then "the Lord is the portion of his inheritance:" so here, now, "Ishi," the Lord is my husband; now can we claim a peculiar interest in God. This is the evil of sin, it hinders a nation, it prevents a soul, from claiming this interest in God. God is a blessed and glorious God; yea, but what is that to this apostatizing people? what is that to this apostatizing soul? but when the soul comes to God, and begins thoroughly the work of reformation, then, This God is my God, Ishi, my husband. Can any comfort, any profit, that you have in ways of sin counterbalance this great loss? you gain some contentment to the flesh, some profit in your estate; but you lose the comforts of your interest in God, and "what profiteth" it you? Think of this when temptation comes; I may by yielding to it gratify so far the flesh, but I shall lose the blessed privilege of claiming an interest in my God, I shall not be able to say, Ishi, my husband.

Obs. 9. God delights to have his people look upon him with love and delight. It is his care and good pleasure that his people should not look upon him so much as one that has dominion over them, but regard him with joy and love, and call him Ishi, and not Baali. But the more reconciled we are to God, the more may we use loving appellations. For a soul to be always under the spirit of bondage, to look unto God merely as the Lord of all, is not so pleasing to him; but when you come to have the spirit of adoption, the spirit of grace, an evangelical spirit, so that you can regard him with affection, and use that title of love and goodness, Ishi, my husband, this is well-pleasing to God. It is reported of Augustus, that he refused the title of lord, and would rather have his people look upon him under the notion of love as a father, than fear him as a lord. It were happy if all princes were of this mind, to desire that their people should rather love than fear them! It is a most wicked and cursed principle, that which some infuse into the mind of princes, Let your people fear you, no great matter whether they love you or no. Suetonius relates of Augustus, that when a poor man came to present him a petition, with hands shaking and trembling from fear, the emperor was much displeased, and said, It is not fit that any should come with a petition to a king, as if a man were giving meat to an elephant, fearing every moment to be destroyed by him. God loves not the bread of mourners to be offered up in sacrifice; but to have his people come before him with a holy boldness, with a filial, not with a servile and slavish spirit. Christ laid down his life to redeem us, that we might serve the Lord without fear.

Obs. 10. The church should look upon Christ as the strength of it. "They shall call me Ishi," that is, My strength. "Thy Maker is thine husband;" and who is he? "The Lord of hosts is his name: thy Redeemer; The God of the whole earth shall he be called." When the people of God can look upon Christ their husband as the Lord of hosts, and their Redeemer as the God of the whole earth, then they find quiet and satisfaction in their minds. Psal. lxxxix. 17, God is said to be the glory of the strength of his people: though we be weak in regard of outward aid, let us look up to Christ our strength, he has been our strength, and is "the glory of it."

Obs. 11. Repentance must be proportionable to men's sins. How do we infer that? Ver. 13, God charged them that they had forgotten him, "She went after her lovers and forgat me, saith the Lord." Now, saith God, your idols shall be forgotten: your hearts were so set upon your idols that you forgat me; now in your repentance your hearts shall be so fixed on me, that you shall forget your idols. Men who have been heretofore so wicked and ungodly that they have forgotten God, God has not been "in all their thoughts," he now expects from them that their lusts should be "no more remembered." It is not enough that you forbear the act, but you must not roll the sweets of them in your thoughts; you must not so much as remember them, except with detestation. If there be not a proportion between your repentance and your former sins, you may expect there will be a proportion between God's wrath and your former sins.

Obs. 12. "And they shall no more be remembered by their name." All superstitious vanities, though they may seem for the present very glorious, yet in time will vanish and come to nothing; God has a time to make them vanish, so that they shall not even be thought of. In Col. ii. 22, it is said of the rudiments of the world which are according to the doctrine of men, that they "all are to perish with the using;" that is, they effect nothing that they seem to be appointed for, no present good arises from them, but in the very use they come to nothing; and God in his time will cause them all to perish utterly, and the very remembrance of them shall be taken away. It is true, that for the present, while men's hearts are set upon their superstitions, they are glorious in their eyes; but these glorious things will come to nothing; whereas those ordinances of God which seem to be but mean, and in which only the simplicity of the gospel appears, shall be manifested to be full of beauty; and though at present they be obscured, yet shall they be glorious in the eyes of the saints to the end of the world. Not long since, what a stir was there about the more than decent, nay, even superstitious, embellishing of temples, and building of altars, and splendid canopies! what sumptuous and fine trappings had they, and all to adorn a pompous, superstitious mode of worship, which altogether prevailed! As for the purity and simplicity of God's ways and worship, how were they trampled under feet as unworthy and contemptible! But those things which for a while seemed so glorious, begin to vanish, and we hope ere long will come to nothing; the very memory of them shall perish. The purity of God's worship, and the simplicity of the gospel in God's ordinances, shall recover their pristine beauty and glory, when those braveries shall be no more.

Obs. 13. A true penitent cannot remember former sins without indignation, for so the phrase "they shall not remember" signifies. Some of us may remember how we have been entangled in ways of false worship, and how we have defiled our consciences therein. We said we would yield as far as we could, but we yielded farther than we could, for *id possumus quod jure possumus*, &c., and have cause to remember it with shame and confusion of face. Ye old men may remember the sins of your youth; but how can you remember them and speak of them with joy and merriment? That is a desperate sign, that you are in a high degree left of God, and given up to hardness, when you so remember the sins of your youth, as to tell tales of the pranks of your younger days with joy? You should remember them with shame and indignation, the sweet morsels of former sins coming up into remembrance should be bitter and sour unto you.

Obs. 14. The taking off men's hearts from idolatrous ways, is a special work of God. "I will," saith God, "take away the names of Baalim out of their mouths." The people in these times cleaved to their false ways of worship, and had many arguments to uphold them; but there shall come a day, saith the Lord, when I will take away the names out of their mouths; I will stop your mouths, I will take off your hearts from all those reasonings by which you maintain those ways, I will silence all; and then you shall see convincingly to your shame, that you have been gulled by such vain and false distinctions. What numerous means God uses to take off men's hearts from ways of false worship! What a number of distinctions and objections have men, their hearts cling to them, unwilling to be loosed from them! Now and then their consciences are wrung, yet they hold fast; and then conscience has another wring, and then they have another objection, and another distinction; and yet perhaps true grace exists notwithstanding this.

But God having love to them, by some way or other takes off their hearts, either by settling truths upon their souls by his Spirit, or by some notable works of providence. As long as men cannot enjoy their estates, liberties, and comforts, without yielding to the ways of superstition, they will not be taken off from them; they please themselves (and perhaps speak what they think) that they do nothing against the light of their consciences; for why? their engagements keep off the strength of truth, that it comes not with a full conviction to the conscience. But when God by any work of his providence takes off their hearts from engagements, and sets before them the same truths as formerly, they see now a convincing evidence in those truths, and wonder that they discerned it not before. They read books before that had the same arguments against their ways, and for the truth, but they could not see their full strength; now they see it apparently, and are ashamed of themselves every time they go into the presence of God. Now they see them with such clearness, that they think they could lay down their lives for them; whatever they suffer for time to come, they can never yield to what they have yielded before. Why? God has come with power! God has taken off their hearts! When God thus comes, the thing will easily be done.

Let us take heed we do not stand out too long, lest God take off our hearts by some dreadful judgment. It were better our mouths were stopped, our objections silenced, and all the relics and remainders of false worship taken from us through the word and Spirit of God. If that will not do, God will come in some other way, and take the name of Baalim out of our mouths. If we will keep the memory of superstitious ways, God may extirpate the memory of them by such ways as may prove fearful to us, and make our hearts ache, and our ears tingle. "In all your dwelling-places," saith God, "the cities shall be laid waste, and the high places shall be desolate that your altars may be laid waste and made desolate, and your idols may be broken and cease, and your images may be cut down, and your works may be abolished," Ezek. vi. 6. Observe, "In all your dwelling-places the cities shall be laid waste;" to what end? "that your altars may be laid waste." So that God will lay waste their cities for this very end, that he may lay waste their altars; if they will not lay waste their altars, if they will not abolish their superstitions, God will abolish their cities. God has begun to put it into the heart of our governors to abolish many superstitious pictures and crosses in divers places; there is yet one great one remaining, and we hope God, upon the same grounds, may put into their hearts to abolish that. It would be a dreadful thing if we should not obey God, now calling upon us to cast out the remainders of idolatry and superstition, to lay waste all idolatrous pictures, images, and crosses; and he should lay waste your cities, to lay waste your altars, crosses, and relics of idolatry. You see, God threatens this here, as if God did not really desire to lay waste their cities, he would preserve them; but because he could not (we speak according to the manner of men) abolish their altars, but by laying waste their cities, saith God, Rather than your altars shall stand, your cities shall fall. God has ways, and most terrible ways too, to take away the memory of superstitious vanities. Oh that we had hearts to join with God before he comes in so dreadful a manner, to abolish the memory of such things! Were our prelates in their power, such a speech as this could not be borne. When Master Udal, a godly preacher in Queen Elizabeth's days, was charged with this expression, "If it come in (that is, the true government of Christ, as he means) by that means which will make all your hearts ache, blame yourselves;" for these words especially was he then condemned to be hanged: such was the rage and potency of the prelates in those days. What I have said may be against the spirits of such as cleave to superstitious vanities; but we have no cause to fear exasperating such, for surely they cannot be more angry than they are, and it would be a foolish thing to provoke God, for fear of further exasperating those who are already exasperated so much against us. What is the exasperation of vile men, to the abiding of the wrath of God upon us!

Ver. 18. *And in that day will I make a covenant for them with the beasts of the field, and with the fowls of heaven, and with the creeping things of the ground: and I will break the bow and the sword and the battle out of the earth, and will make them to lie down safely.*

In this verse God promises peace and security; peace, in regard of their deliverance from the beasts of the field, and fowls of the heaven, and creeping things of the ground; peace from the hostility of their adversaries, he "will break the bow and the sword and the battle out of the earth:" and security, "I will make them lie down safely."

I. The first part of the promise is peace with the creatures: "And in that day will I make a covenant for them with the beasts of the field, and with the fowls of heaven, and with the creeping things of the ground."

Some allegorize these words, "the beasts of the field," and say they mean cruel men; the fowls of the air, ambitious, who are lofty in their thoughts and counsels; "the creeping things of the ground," subtle adversaries: God here promises, they say, to deliver them from all these. But I desire not to allegorize, unless there is a necessity, and therefore understand the words literally. But how may God be said to "make a covenant for" his people "with the beasts of the field, and with the fowls of heaven, and with the creeping things of the ground?" for, to speak properly, none but rational creatures are capable of a covenant with God.

The meaning is, there shall be such an establishment of God's work on the beasts, and fowls, and creeping things for the good of his church, as if God had bound them to serve it by way of covenant; that dealing of God is called "making a covenant with them," here and elsewhere; as in Jer. xxxiii. 20, "If ye can break my covenant of the day, and my covenant of the night, that there should not be day and night in their season." How does God covenant with the day, and with the night? Thus, there is an establishment of God's decree on the day, and on the night, that it should be in such a way from the creation to the end of the world; and that establishment is called God's covenant: so Œcolampadius renders my text, I will order inviolably and unalterably, there shall be an establishing decree upon these creatures, that they shall do you no hurt, but good.

Ita ordinabo inviolabiliter.

Obs. 1. Sin has caused enmity between man and the creatures; this is implied here, I will, saith God, upon your reconciliation with me, and your reformation, make a covenant with the creatures, now they shall be at peace with you; denoting, that by our sin there is grown enmity between us and God's creatures. We have lost by sin a great part of the dominion which God gave us over his creatures, and which resulted from the image of God wherein man was created. Therefore when you see any creature rebel against you, call to mind your rebellion against God. It is true, God maintains, in some measure, man's dominion over the creatures still, that the world, and human society, may be preserved. Sometimes you may see a little child driving before him a hundred oxen, this way or that, as he pleases, showing that God has continued somewhat of man's dominion over them. But a great part is lost by our sin. If we, who are the servants of God, rebel against him, it is just with God that the creatures, which were subjected to us, should rebel against us. And you who are superiors, when any of your inferiors are stubborn against you, your servants or your children rebellious, raise your hearts up to this meditation, My servant is rebellious against me, how have I been rebellious against the Lord! my child stubborn against me, how has my heart been stubborn against the Lord my Father!

Obs. 2. Peace with God brings peace with the creatures. "I will make a covenant with the beasts of the field," with the fowls of the air, &c. In Job v. 23, you have a strange promise, "Thou shalt be in league with the stones of the field: and the beasts of the field shall be at peace with thee." This goes somewhat deeper than that which is here promised; There shall be a league, not only with the beasts, but with the stones of the field. How in league with the stones of the field? It is more easy to be understood to be in league with the beasts of the field, for they are many times hurtful unto us; but how with the stones of the field? It was customary (and so it is still in many places) in fixing the bounds of their fields, to set up stones for landmarks, and engrave them, to denote to whom this or the other parcel of ground belonged. Now the Lord promises that he would be so gracious to his people, that they should enjoy the bounds of their own habitations securely, they should not be wronged, nor their landmarks taken away. "Thou shalt be in league with the stones of the field;" that is, the stones of the field that stand for your landmarks shall abide, and none shall take them away; I will preserve your bounds, as if you were in league with the stones that are your landmarks, as if they had agreed with you, and covenanted that they would stand, and set out the bounds of your fields for ever.

But you will say, Sometimes the beasts of the field do injure the saints, how then does God make a covenant with them?

Many answers might be given. In ver. 17, of the chapter of Job referred to, he speaks of a time when "God correcteth," and men "despise not the chastening of the Almighty:" now the expression in ver. 23, relates to that time; that is, when any make use of God's correction, do not despise it, but reverently submit to his hand, then God will make this "league with the stones of the field," and "with the beasts of the earth." If God has corrected you with any sickness, and you do not profit by it, it is just with God that some or other of his creatures should meet you, and be more terrible to you than ever your sickness was. And the promise here in Hosea is to those who are reconciled to God, and have cast off their superstitious vanities; and because we are not perfectly reconciled, therefore this promise is not perfectly fulfilled. But I make no question but the Holy Ghost here refers to the time of the calling of the Jews; and then I verily believe that this promise, and those in Isaiah and other places, where God says he will make "the lion to eat straw with the ox, and that "no venomous creature shall do them hurt," shall be literally fulfilled. When the calling of the Jews shall take place, the creatures shall be restored to a state of excellence, resembling their condition with Adam in Paradise. The lion was not at its creation made to live upon prey, nor the creatures formed to devour one another, therefore the promise is, that the lion shall return to its state previous to the fall. And at the calling of the Jews it is very probable there will be such "a restitution of all things," Acts iii. 21, that the creature will be restored to its original excellency. And though this may be partly fulfilled to God's people, that the beasts of the field shall do them no hurt, that is, if they prevail against them it shall be for some gracious ends which God has in view; yet the literal accomplishment of the promise is reserved for that day.

Obs. 3. When God is reconciled to his people, shall the beasts of the field, and the fowls of the air, and the creeping things of the earth be at peace with the saints? what a wicked and ungodly thing is it then in men, that the more any are reconciled to God, the greater enemies are they to them! God promises, when his people are reconciled to him, the creatures shall be reconciled to them; yet, thou vile wretch, when thou seest one grow up in the ways of reconciliation with God, thy enmity increases towards him: what horrible wickedness is this! it is far more than brutish, it is desperate wickedness. As with those five kings of Canaan, spoken of Josh. x. 5, who, as soon as the Gibeonites had made peace and a league with Joshua, conspired against them. They lived quietly enough before with them, but when they heard that they had made a covenant with Joshua, they immediately made war upon them. Thus it is with many at this day, when your companions would drink, swear, and break the sabbath, and be unclean, and scorn with you, they were good fellows, then you embraced them, and delighted in them; but as soon as God wrought upon their hearts, and they were brought from enmity into a state of reconciliation, your minds rise against them, and you regard them with hatred and abhorrence. Oh horrible and desperate wickedness! the Lord rebuke you this day, the Lord strike upon such hearts. Before Saul's conversion he was in much repute, but as soon as he became a Christian, he was a "pestilent and seditious fellow:" "Away with such a man from the earth, he is not worthy to live;" and forty of them conspired together and bound themselves with an oath, that they would neither eat nor drink till they had killed him.

Obs. 4. Covenant mercy is excellent mercy indeed. "I will make a covenant," saith God, you shall have this mercy, and have it by covenant. The same mercy coming in the course of general providence is nothing so sweet, nothing so firm, as that which arises from the covenant. When the saints receive a mercy, though it be in external circumstances, they rejoice not in it, merely because they have some comfort and contentment to the outward man by it; but because they see that even this outward mercy comes to them by virtue of God's covenant, which sweetens and confirms every gift; when they go up and down the field, and the beasts come not upon them to destroy them, they can look upon their present safety as enjoying it in the covenant.

You will say, the wicked can walk up and down in the fields, and the beasts not destroy them. Though they can, yet a godly man has more enjoyment as he can see that this his safety arises from the covenant: when he goes on a journey, his beast is not made an instrument of God's wrath to dash out his brains; perhaps it is so with his wicked neighbour who accompanies him; but the preservation of the godly man is a mercy from the covenant which God has made with him, "to preserve him in all his ways," whereas to the other it is but general providence. Wicked men may have the same mercies for the matter of them that the godly have, yet there is a kernel in the mercy which only the saints enjoy.

There are two things observable in mercies coming by covenant. First, They are more sweet. "All the paths of the Lord are mercy and truth unto such as keep his covenant," Psal. xxv. 10. This is a sweet promise, a soul-satisfying promise, more worth than all the riches of your city: all the dealings of God's ordinary providence "are mercy and truth unto such as keep his covenant." Mark, perhaps they are mercies to you, there is a general bounty in your ordinary preservation, but they are not "mercy and truth" to you; there lies the emphasis; they are "mercy and truth" to the godly, that is, they are such mercies as are bound to them by covenant; therein David rejoices, and therefore saith in the beginning of the Psalm, "Unto thee, O Lord, do I lift up my soul," as amongst other reasons, so for this, that all the paths of God are not only mercy, but "mercy and truth." You have been preserved, and have had many mercies from God; well, they are God's mercies to you, but are they mercies and truth to you? that is, do they come to you in a way of promise? Look to that, the sweetness of a mercy consists in it, and it is a good sign of a gracious heart to look more to the source whence mercy comes, than to the outward advantage it conveys.

Secondly, They are more firm. Isa. liv. 10, "The mountains shall depart, and the hills be removed; but my kindness shall not depart from thee;" why? for "the covenant of my peace shall not be removed." The mercy which you have, I give in a way of covenant, and the hills and mountains shall be removed rather than that kindness of mine shall depart from thee.

Obs. 5. Is it such a blessed thing for God to make a covenant with the beasts for us? what a mercy is it then for God to make a covenant with our souls! The covenant which God makes with his people is a covenant in Christ, and abounds in mercy. In Gen. xvii. you find that, in ten verses, God repeats his covenant which he made with Abraham thirteen times, to impress this, that that was the mercy indeed which must satisfy Abraham in all his troubles, sorrows, and afflictions: as if God should say, Be satisfied with this, Abraham, that I have entered into covenant with thee and thy seed, that I am your covenant God. And 2 Sam. xxiii. 5, David saith, "Although my house be not so with God, (as I desire, as I expect,) yet he hath made with me an everlasting covenant, ordered in all things, and sure: for this is all my salvation, and all my desire, although he make it not to grow." Take this scripture, Christians, take it, I say, and make use of it in these times of trouble; though things do not go as you desire, yet say as David did, "yet the Lord hath made a covenant with us, ordered in all things and sure, and this is all our salvation and all our desire."

Obs. 6. Is it a mercy for God to make a covenant with the beasts for his people? what a mercy is it then for him to make a covenant with his Son for his people! If we are to bless God, that he will make a covenant with brute beasts for our good, how should we extol and magnify his name, in that he has made a covenant with his own Son for our eternal good, and brought the second person in Trinity, to be the head of this covenant for us. The apostle speaks, Tit. i. 2, of "eternal life, which God, that cannot lie, promised before the world began." Why, what promise was there ever made before the world began? to whom was it given? who was there before the world began for God to make any promise unto? The Son of God alone, the second person in the Trinity; and there was a most blessed transaction between God the Father and God the Son, for our everlasting good, before the world began, and upon that depends all our salvation and all our hope. When we read the promises of the gospel which the Lord has given to us as branches of the covenant of grace, we are ready to think we are poor, weak creatures; we cannot keep covenant with God, we cannot perform its conditions: but, Christian, know this, thy peace, the salvation of thy soul, does not depend so much upon a covenant God has made with thee, as upon the covenant he has made with his Son; there is the firmness, the original, the foundation of all thy good, and all thy salvation; and though thou art a poor, weak creature, not keeping covenant with the Lord, yet the Son of God has perfectly performed all the conditions the Father required of him; by him the work has been perfected, and herein is our comfort. Raise up then your drooping hearts by this meditation.

II. The second part of this peace, is a promise of deliverance from the hostility of their adversaries: "I will break the bow and the sword and the battle out of the earth."

Obs. 1. Peace is a great blessing, it is a great mercy to have the bow and the sword broken. It is a part of the covenant that God makes with his people, to take away the instruments of hostility. Isa. ii. 4, God promises the beating of swords "into ploughshares, and spears into pruning-hooks." You find, on the contrary, when God denounces judgments on a people, Joel iii. 10, that he threatens to beat their ploughshares into swords, and their pruning-hooks into spears. It is a great deal better that the swords should be beaten into ploughshares, than that the ploughshares should be beaten into swords; that the spears should be made pruning-hooks, than that the pruning-hooks should be made spears.

Obs. 2. Peace is a most amiable thing, and lovely in all our eyes, every man desires it, and God promises it to his people in many places as a most special fruit of his love. Isa. xxxiii. 20, "Jerusalem shall be a quiet habitation, a tabernacle that shall not be taken down." And Numb. vi. 25, 26, "The Lord make his face shine upon thee, and be gracious unto thee: the Lord lift up his countenance upon thee, and give thee peace." The shining of God's face appears in the giving of peace to a nation: therefore, Jer. xvi. 5, where God threatens to take away peace, mark the expression, "I have taken away my peace from this people, saith the Lord, even loving-kindness and mercies." He does not say, I have taken away peace, but I have taken away "my peace;" and then, when "my peace" is taken away, I will take away "even loving-kindness and mercies." How easy were it to discourse largely in commendations of peace! God teaches us in these days to set a high price upon it. We have had peace a long time, and the Lord knows we have not prized the mercy; now we know what a sad thing it is to have war in our gates. And if peace be a fruit of God's covenant, we have cause to bewail the breach of it with us. Surely there is great displeasure of God out against us; this cup of blood which is prepared, poured forth, and in a great measure drunk, is a most dreadful one. Our brethren have drunk deep of it, and we have long feared it, having heard of rumours of wars; and when the cup was abroad, we prayed that, if it were possible, it might pass from us, and it did pass to our brethren in Ireland; but now is it come to us; the sword has had its circuit and is now in our midst, and that which aggravates the evil is, that our wars are not with foreign enemies, but civil. I have read in the Roman chronicles, that in a battle between Sylla and Marius, a soldier by accident killed one, not knowing who it was; but after he was slain, seeing it was his brother, presently, in anguish of spirit, he ran his sword into his own bowels. This we find occurring ordinarily among us, even brother to be against brother, yea, son against father. Certainly, therefore, it is time for us to fall on our knees, and to be humbled before the Lord for the breach of our peace.

Obs. 3. Peace is a sweet mercy, therefore it is a pity that it should be abused and not improved. Oh how have we abused our former peace! God gave us peace before; to what end? That we might be edified, and so built up in the fear of God and comfort of the Holy Ghost; as, Acts ix. 31, it is said, "The churches had rest, and were edified; walking in the fear of the Lord God, and in the comfort of the Holy Ghost." We have not made this use of the rest which God has been pleased to afford us, but have grown wanton with that precious jewel peace, and just it is with God to take it from us. And now we desire peace; but to what end? to have more freedom to satisfy our lusts and make provision for the flesh, is the very ground of most men's desire of peace; whereas if we understood the true worth of peace, we would think it were a very low end to desire it only for the attainment of this. Mark the promise in Ezek. xxxvii. 26, "I will make a covenant of peace with them; it shall be an everlasting covenant with them: and I will place them and multiply them, and will set my sanctuary in the midst of them for evermore." Yea, that is a comfortable peace, desirable indeed, when God by peace shall make way to set his sanctuary in our midst. If we truly desired peace upon these terms, we might soon expect an answer from the God of all peace.

Obs. 4. Peace is sweet, therefore not to be falsified. Psal. xxviii. 3, there are some that "speak peace to their neighbours, but mischief is in their hearts." It is pity that such a precious thing as peace should be made serviceable to men's lusts, that it should be pretended only to compass mischievous designs; peace is too good to serve men's base ends.

Obs. 5. Peace is a great blessing, therefore it is a pity not to endeavour by every means to attain it. Yea, cursed be that war which has not peace for its end. *Sic quærimus pacem*, Even thus do we seek peace, ought to be as the emblem written on the sword of every soldier. It is a great deal better to have a war that aims at and effects peace, than to have a peace which aims at and creates war. It is true, war produces very dreadful effects; but war that shall bring forth peace, is better than peace that produces war; and the more we commend peace, the more do we still commend the war that tends to bring forth true peace, rather than to seek for a false peace, which will produce afterwards most dreadful war.

Obs. 6. Peace is a great blessing from God, but we must take heed we buy it not too dear: we may say of this as we are wont to say of gold, We may buy gold too dear.

You will say, How is it possible to buy peace at too dear a rate? If you give these three things for it.

First, If you sell truth for it; selling any truth for peace, is buying peace too dear, for the least truth of God is better than all the kingdoms of the earth. It first cost the blood of Christ, and since has been watered by the blood of thousands of martyrs.

Secondly, If you betray those who have been most active for the public good, only that, by way of compliance, you may provide for your own particular peace.

Thirdly, If, through desire of peace, you subject

yourselves to tyranny or slavery. This is peace at too dear a rate, and the posterity that comes after, may curse that baseness of spirit and cowardice of their forefathers, who purchased peace at so dear a rate as to bring not only themselves, but their posterity, under the bondage of miserable tyranny and woeful slavery. It is true, it is a great deal easier for a man who is striving and fighting with his enemy, to lie down, than to spend his strength in the combat: why will he weary himself? is it not better to lie down upon the soft grass, than to tire oneself in the conflict? but if by lying down he has his throat cut by his enemy, has he, think you, done wisely for himself? to spare exertion he has lost his life. If we should be so weary of present troubles as to lie down and be destroyed by our adversaries, shall the generation to come commend either our wisdom or valour? When a stream runs strong you cannot expect to stop it without some trouble; and the war now on foot amongst us, though it has much trouble in it, and many of our brethren suffer grievously, yet, let us consider it is a means to stop a stream of misery which was coming upon us, and that it is better to undergo some difficulties in damming it up, than tamely suffer it to flow in till all be past recovery. Our adversaries exclaim that we are enemies to peace, and they are all for peace, that is, they would have us to be so quiet as to let them do their pleasure; they would fain have us so to love peace as to give up our strength to them, and to be irrecoverably under their power. Therefore let this generation be wise, for great things depend upon the present affairs of the kingdom, which concern not only their own outward comfort, but the glory of God, and the good of their posterity, to many succeeding generations.

Obs. 7. Peace is God's peculiar work. We may treat about peace, but until God is pleased to permit it, it will not ensue. If God comes in with exceptions, our treaties and our plots will never succeed. "I will break the bow,"saith God. Jer. xlvii. 6, 7, "O thou sword of the Lord, how long will it be ere thou be quiet? put up thyself into thy scabbard, rest, and be still." The answer is, "How can it be quiet, seeing the Lord hath given it a charge against Ashkelon?" Till God give a commission to the sword, it cannot "rest, and be still." Job xxxiv. 29, "When he giveth quietness, who then can make trouble? and when he hideth his face, who then can behold him? whether it be done against a nation, or against a man only." If he cause trouble, who can make quietness? O no, none can! It is God that is to be regarded in the breaking of treaties, it is he who hardens the hearts of men that they shall not make peace till his time come. In Josh. xi. 19, 20, it is said, "There was not a city that made peace with the children of Israel, save the Hivites the inhabitants of Gibeon: all other they took in battle. For it was of the Lord to harden their hearts, that they should come against Israel in battle, that he might destroy them utterly." Of all the cities in Canaan which God's people "came against," though his hand was very remarkable in going along with them, working many miracles for them, yet the text observes that there was none that would make peace with them, save Gibeon only. Why? "For it was of the Lord to harden their hearts, to come against Israel in battle, that he might destroy them utterly." God intended to destroy them, and therefore hardened them that they should not make peace with his people. God is the Prince of peace, and therefore disposes of it as he will: many devices may be in the hearts of men, many plots and contrivances, but the counsel of the Lord shall stand. "The Lord sitteth upon the flood; yea, the Lord sitteth King for ever. The Lord will give strength unto his people; the Lord will bless his people with peace," Psal. xxix. 10, 11. That is not the peace for God to bless his people with, for which they must expose themselves to every danger, and betray his cause, God need give no strength for that; but his way is to "give strength unto his people," and then "to bless them with peace." We love peace, but let us take care to gain it through the strength of God: join these promises together, and plead them; and though we seem weak, yet "the Lord will give strength unto his people," and so "bless his people with peace." We must procure our peace by working in God's strength, and not think to obtain it by a sluggish compliance, and base, unworthy yielding to our adversaries. Jer. xiv. 19, "We looked for peace," it seems they were forming some treaties, "and there is no good; and for the time of healing, and behold trouble!" all their treaties came to nothing: but mark what follows, ver. 20, "We acknowledge, O Lord, our wickedness, and the iniquity of our fathers." O Lord, we dwell amongst people that are set on fire, and when we speak of peace, yea, when they speak of peace, they have mischief in their hearts: "O Lord, our wickedness, and the iniquity of our fathers," is great. O Lord, pardon our iniquity. To make our peace with God is the way to obtain peace.

Obs. 8. Thorough reformation is the way to procure peace. Mark the gradation, "They shall call me no more Baali," then "will I break the bow;" when they shall break off thoroughly from their idolatry, then will I break the bow and the sword: so long as they worship false gods, war shall be in their gates; but when they shall thoroughly reform, and set up my worship in the way that I choose, then will I break the bow. So should we act if we had sufficient reliance on God. Our baseness is, that we will not trust God in this way of peace; but are ready to think that reformation will introduce disturbance, whereas reformation is the way to a thorough peace. Let our wisdom be pure, and then certainly it will be peaceable. In Isa. xxxiii. 20, Jerusalem is promised to be "a quiet habitation." What follows? ver. 22, "For the Lord is our judge, the Lord is our lawgiver:" the more we regard him as our judge and lawgiver, the more peace we shall have. Isa. ix. 7, "Of the increase of his government and peace there shall be no end." When the government of Christ is felt, then comes peace. Zech. vi. 13, "He shall sit and rule upon his throne; and be a priest upon his throne: and the counsel of peace shall be between them both;" that is, when Christ shall be advanced in his kingly as well as in his priestly office, then there shall be a counsel of peace. What is the reason that the counsel of peace has not prevailed to this day? We have cause to fear it has not been set between the kingly and priestly office of Christ to advance them. Isa. xxxii. 17, 18, "The work of righteousness shall be peace; and the effect of righteousness quietness and assurance for ever. And my people shall dwell in a peaceable habitation, and in sure dwellings, and in quiet resting-places." See how the Holy Ghost adds one word to another to show that true peace is in the ways of righteousness. When men strive for peace by unfair means, and seek to serve their own ends, disregarding the honour of God, it is just with him to dash all their counsels. "The way of peace they know not," saith God, "and there is no judgment in their goings: they have made them crooked paths: whosoever goeth therein shall not know peace," Isa. lix. 8. We know the path of the serpent is crooked, it winds up and down: so many of our counsellors of peace have gone, like the serpent, winding up and down in their carnal policies; have not studied reformation, but pursued crooked paths, and therefore have not effected true peace. But further, in Jer. xxxi. 22, 23, when the Lord was about to deliver his people from captivity, he asks, "How long wilt thou go about?" that is, you do not go steadily on, but compass about, and hope, by time-serving compliances, to escape the difficulties in your path, and by various means to avoid troubles. What follows? "The Lord bless thee, O habitation of justice, and mountain of holiness." Endeavour to make your way to be the "habitation of justice, and the mountain of holiness," and the work is done; execute justice upon delinquents, and set up the ordinances of God in the right way of worship, and this will lead to assured peace. Oh that the Lord would deliver our great counsellors from unworthy compliances.

III. The effects of this peace. "I will make them to lie down safely."

Obs. 1. God's peace alone brings safety. If we patch up a false peace on base and unworthy terms, we must not think "to lie down safely;" but when God promises peace as a fruit of the covenant, then follows, "I will make them to lie down safely." And I suppose none of you would like any other peace, but such as would enable you to lie down safely; and how is it possible, do you think, to do so, except the Lord destroy the evil beasts out of the land? "I will give peace in the land, and you shall lie down, and none shall make you afraid: and I will rid evil beasts out of the land," Lev. xxvi. 6. What is the end of our present war, but to "rid the evil beasts out of the land," that so we may "lie down safely?" Can you think to dwell safely among them, exasperated, as their fury is, to the highest degree? Certainly, if a false and patched-up peace were made, we should be in a condition full of hazard. Could those amongst us who have openly espoused the cause of God, and showed themselves most faithful, lie down safely, confiding in such a peace? If you have the hearts of true Englishmen, you would never desire any peace, but such as would enable you and your brethren, your ministers, and those worthies in parliament, and all that have stood forth in your behalf, "to lie down safely." Acts xxvii. 13, 14, we read of a "south wind that blew softly;" but the text adds, that not long after there arose "a tempestuous wind called Euroclydon." So if we have a false peace, it may blow as that south wind, "softly;" but certainly Euroclydon, that most terrible east wind, will succeed. 2 Chron. xx. 30, "The realm of Jehoshaphat was quiet: for his God gave him rest round about." Suppose we should be quiet, and our own base counsels and compliances should procure us rest, our peace would never be certain, but dismal things would follow; for a people dwell safely only when they have the peace of God together with the God of peace. "The peace of God which passeth all understanding, shall keep your hearts," Phil. iv. 7. Then follows, ver. 9, "The God of peace shall be with you." We would be loth to be without the God of peace, let us then refuse to have any but the peace of God. You all desire peace, and so the adversary pretends: take heed you be not deluded with vain words; that which your thoughts regard as the end, is with them a means to further their designs; and what good will such a peace do you? you will be no more secure than you are now, nay, your danger will be far greater.

Tranquillitas ista tempestas erit. Hieron.

Obs. 2. "To lie down safely," is God's own gift to his people. It is an additional blessing to having the sword and bow broken. We may be delivered from our enemies, but the Lord may affright our consciences with visions in the night, he may terrify us a thousand ways and take away our security; therefore, when he saith, "I will break the bow and the sword," he adds, "I will make thee to lie down safely." This is a precious mercy, it is *recumbere faciam, in fiducia dormire faciam fiducialiter*, I will make them to lie down in trust and confidence, that is, without any fear of evil befalling them before morning. We little think what a mercy it is, to have many nights lain down safely, and slept quietly, and risen up comfortably; and little do we think of praising God on this account. Many of our brethren in various countries would prize such a mercy now, they are afraid of every stir, and can scarce obtain a night's sleep unbroken by alarms. What would some of them give for one night's calm repose, that when they go to bed they might say, Well, I hope this night I shall enjoy quiet rest, tranquil and uninterrupted sleep! In many places they sleep in the day, and watch during the night. Here in the city, indeed, you can go to bed and sleep quietly, and rise quietly; but oh, think of those who are deprived of this mercy, and while you enjoy it, give God the glory. It is a great blessing for the Lord to calm our minds in these dangerous times, in these days of trembling, when every man's hands are upon his loins. Many who are free from their adversaries, yet, through the timorousness of their spirits, cannot enjoy one night's quiet, but agitate themselves with their own thoughts, Oh, what will become of us hereafter! It may be the enemies will come, and we shall lose our lives, and all will be torn from us; and this makes them that they cannot lie down safely, though danger be not yet near them: but when God is pleased so to stay the heart on him, that in the most troublesome times you can lie down securely, this is a choice mercy, a fruit of the covenant.

This mercy the Lord promises, Prov. iii. 23, "Then shalt thou walk in thy way safely, and thy foot shall not stumble." And mark the 24th verse, "When thou liest down thou shalt not be afraid: yea, thou shalt lie down, and thy sleep shall be sweet. Be not afraid of sudden fear: for the Lord shall be thy confidence, and shall keep thy foot from being taken." This made good to one in these days were a text worth gold indeed. So Psal. cvii. 3, "He giveth his beloved sleep;" others labour and toil, and "eat the bread of sorrow," and are mightily perplexed, but "He giveth his beloved sleep;" that is, takes away care and thought from his beloved, and gives them rest, so that they can repose quietly as in his bosom.

There is a false rest and security of the wicked when they make a covenant with death and with hell, as Isa. xxviii. 15, "Ye have said, We have made a covenant with death, and with hell are we at agreement; when the overflowing scourge shall pass through, it shall not come unto us: for we have made lies our refuge, and under falsehood have we hid ourselves." This text is as applicable to our adversaries as any one I know of in the Scriptures; they all promise to themselves security and safety, they make a covenant with hell and death; but how? they make lies their refuge, and under falsehood have they hidden themselves. Here is a security, and that by a covenant with hell and death; but this text points to "a lying down safely" by virtue of another covenant, even the covenant of God; therefore there follows, ver. 16, "Behold, I lay in Zion for a foundation a stone, a tried stone, a precious corner-stone, a sure foundation: he that believeth shall not make haste." This text wonderfully suits our times; we have a security on that ground, that though the overflowing scourge break down all, yet, saith God, "I lay in Zion for a foundation a stone," &c.; you may rest secure, though your enemies vaunt themselves, and boast in their own ways, that they "have made a covenant with death, and with hell are at agreement;" but, for you "I lay in Zion a corner-stone, a sure foundation: he that believeth shall not make haste." Although God come not with present deliverance, yet, believers, quiet yourselves, and "lie down safely," and do "not make haste." "A horse," saith the Scripture, Psal. xxxiii. 17, "is a vain thing for safety," vain is all creature-dependence; but, "behold, the eye of the Lord is upon them that fear him," ver. 18; they are more secure than if troops of horses lay round about to defend them. So ver. 20, "Our soul waiteth for the Lord; he is our help and our shield:" and Prov. xxi. 31, "The horse is prepared against the day of battle: but safety is of the Lord." Let us therefore cry with the psalmist, "Lord, lift thou up the light of thy countenance upon us; then we will lie down in peace, and sleep, for thou only makest us dwell in safety." Would you have quiet sleep in these troublesome times? make your peace with God. If there be peace within, then you may lie down safely notwithstanding all the rumours and tumults of war abroad; but if your heart be unreconciled, though you should live to see outward peace, your sins would pursue you, the terrors of the Almighty would be upon you.

But, Lord, what is all this except we may have communion with thyself, except we may have communion with Jesus Christ? is the voice of a gracious heart: therefore follows that blessed promise, as a further fruit of the covenant which God would make with his people, I will betroth thee unto myself; I will be yours, and there shall be a most blessed union and conjugal communion between us; you shall enjoy me in all the sweetness and love in which the wife enjoys the husband, though you have most wretchedly departed from me.

Ver. 19, 20. *And I will betroth thee unto me for ever; yea, I will betroth thee unto me in righteousness, and in judgment, and in lovingkindness, and in mercies. I will even betroth thee unto me in faithfulness: and thou shalt know the Lord.*

But how betroth? This phrase seems to be very strange; she had been the wife of God before, and departed from him; though God were reconciled to her, one would have thought it should rather have been, I will receive you again: no, but "I will betroth thee;" to note, that God would receive her with the same love as if she had been a pure virgin, and never upbraid her with her former departure from him: You have been an adulteress, bear your shame; but for my own name's sake I will be content to receive you again: nay, "I will betroth thee unto me," you shall be as a bride, and your sins shall be no more remembered, but passed over as if they had never been committed.

Obs. When God pardons sin he will remember it no more, the Lord will never charge upon sinners their former transgression. And if God will not remember the sins of his repenting people, to charge them upon them, we should not remember them, to upbraid them for them; whatever they have been before, if now converted, it is too much boldness in any of us to upbraid them for any of their former sins. I remember that Beza relates, that the papists reproached him much with the sins of his youth, the lascivious poems he made before his conversion; but he answered them thus, *Hi homines invident mihi gratiam divinam*, These men envy me the grace of God.

The repenting church might say, 1. How is it possible that so vile an adulteress, one who has so shamelessly forsaken the blessed God, her glorious Husband, and continued so long in filthy whoredoms, should yet expect to receive mercy? What! such a mercy as to be betrothed to God, to be taken by him as if she were a chaste spouse? Yes, saith God, I will do it; and therefore, to assure the humbled, repenting church that he will fulfil his promise, there is repeated three times emphatically, "I will betroth," "yea, I will betroth," "even I will betroth;" to show how much the heart of God is set upon it. As if God should have said, Though you may think such a thing can never be, and see nothing but cause for doubt and discouragement in yourselves, yet I will do it, yea, I will do it. This repetition marks also the excellency of the mercy; an excellent one indeed, that the Lord should take a people into so near a communion with himself; and from it flow other most glorious mercies.

But will this mercy hold? is it sure? I have already apostatized from the Lord, and have still an apostatizing heart, and am like to fall off from God again, and so my condition to be worse than ever. No, saith God, "I will betroth you unto myself for ever," my heart shall be for ever towards you, and your heart shall be for ever towards me, there shall never more be any breach of conjugal love and communion between us.

2. But the Lord is a righteous God, a God of infinite justice, and I have most fearfully transgressed against him: oh the hideous sins that I stand guilty of before him! how shall that infinite justice of God be satisfied? This is the care of a repenting heart, not only to obtain mercy for pardon, but satisfaction for the justice of God. Yes, saith God, I will have a way for that too; though you have been very sinful, yet when I receive you to mercy, I will do it so that I shall be righteous, as well as gracious, I will do it "in righteousness;" my taking you again to myself shall cast no stain on my righteousness. And I will put such a righteous frame into your hearts, that the nations shall not blaspheme my name, that I have betrothed such a one as you to myself.

3. But what reason can there possibly be that God should act thus? God has ten thousand ways to honour himself, though we perish for ever, and no people have ever provoked him as we have done, saith this repenting Israel. Well, saith God, though you know no reason why it should be done, yea, indeed, though there exist none at all in yourselves, yet what I shall do I will do in judgment. What I now promise you, I have exercised my wisdom about from all eternity; it is not only a work of my grace and mercy toward you, but of my wisdom also, which shall one day appear and be justified gloriously in this my work of taking you unto myself again. I know what I do in it, yea, and on your part, though hitherto you have seen no such excellency in my ways to cleave to them, but have departed from them and followed other lovers; yet when I come with mercy to you, I shall so convince you of the vanity of all other objects of desire, and of the fulness of good which there is in me to satisfy your souls for ever, that you shall see infinite reason to join yourselves unto me in an everlasting covenant. You thought the ways of false worship wore a more specious appearance, but when you shall be reconciled, you shall see there is infinite reason in the service your souls have heretofore rejected; you shall not only have your affections a little roused and warmed for the present, but the change which shall take place in you shall be in judgment, "I will betroth thee unto me in judgment;" in judgment on my part, I will have reason for what I do; and in judgment on your part, you shall see reason for what you do; so much reason for coming to me, that you shall wonder at the former folly of your hearts, when you departed from me, and sought your comforts elsewhere. The workings of my heart shall be in judgment toward you, and the workings of your hearts shall be in judgment toward me.

4. But suppose that my heart does indeed come in to God, yet I shall remain a poor, sinful, weak creature, there will hang upon me many infirmities that will be grievous to the Spirit of the holy and just God. Well, saith God, "I will betroth thee unto me in loving-kindness:" I will deal gently and favourably with you; I will not take advantage of your failings and infirmities; I will remember you are but flesh, and have a tender regard to you.

5. But, perhaps, there will not only be some ordinary infirmities which may grieve, but I may even fall into offences that will provoke the Spirit of God bitterly against me, and so my condition become worse than before. No, saith God, "I will betroth thee unto me in mercies" as well as "in loving-kindness;" my bowels

of mercy shall yearn towards you, not only to pass over the lesser infirmities, but to swallow up the greater transgressions. And accordingly, I will work in you gracious dispositions of loving-kindness toward me, and create a most sweet and ingenuous spirit, and cause your services to flow from principles of love; that perverse, distrustful spirit of yours toward me shall be changed into a sweet, gentle, dependent frame. And when I am once reconciled to you, you shall be reconciled one to another; and the hearts that were so rugged, so harsh, and unkind towards one another before, shall be joined together in the bonds of love. And as my bowels yearn towards you, so your bowels shall yearn towards me; as it shall pity my soul to see you in misery, so it shall pity your souls to see me dishonoured; and you shall likewise be compassionate one toward another, pitying, helping, and relieving one another in the greatest straits.

6. But there are many glorious promises which we find God made to his people, and great things to be done for them; shall ever those promises be made good to us? If we may have mercy, though in never so low a condition; if God's loving-kindness be manifested to us in a way of reconciliation, though we be but as hired servants; if we may be spouses, though kept hardly, it will be well with us. But, saith God, there are glorious promises made to the church, and I will fulfil them all to you; though you have departed from me and provoked me against you, yet, upon your returning, you shall become interested in them. I will fulfil them all to you, for "I will betroth you unto me in faithfulness," as well as "in mercy." Look, whatever I have said concerning my church, is yours to be made good to the uttermost; and there is nothing that concerns me as a loving husband to do, but you shall assuredly receive: and as for you, however your hearts have been hitherto unfaithful toward me in departing from me, yet now you shall have put into you a faithful spirit; your hearts shall confide in me, that I will deal faithfully with you, and my heart shall confide in you, that you will deal faithfully with me; so that whatever befalls you, you shall still be faithful to me, and to each other. "I will betroth you unto me in faithfulness."

7. And whereas it is but little that you yet have known of me, and this ignorance has been the cause of all your unworthy wanderings; therefore "you shall know the Lord;" know him in a manner far different to your former experience; I will show my glory to you, I will open my very heart to you, the secret of the Lord shall be with you, though your conceptions be but weak and mean, yet you shall all be taught of God; perhaps you may be ignorant of other things, but "you shall know the Lord."

8. And as for outward blessings, you shall receive them also in abundance; all the creatures shall be moved towards you to comfort and to succour you: "And it shall come to pass in that day, I will hear, saith the Lord, I will hear the heavens, and they shall hear the earth; and the earth shall hear the corn, and the wine, and the oil; and they shall hear Jezreel." There shall be in them a readiness to help, an eagerness to relieve you; yea a combination of them all, established by me for the good of Jezreel.

9. But yet we are a people scattered about the world, and most of us consumed: But, "I will sow her unto me in the earth:" you were scattered in judgment, but now it is turned to a mercy; your scattering is as seed, whereby you shall fructify and increase abundantly, and so be a blessing to the whole earth.

10. But we have been under the curse of God a great while, and have seemed to be rejected: But, saith God, "I will have mercy upon her that had not obtained mercy."

11. Lastly, we are a proverb in all the world, a byword, a scorn, and a reproach amongst all people; God, say they, has rejected us, and so they trample upon us. No, saith God, I will not only betroth you to myself, but make it manifest to all the world that you are my people; "I will say to them which were not my people, Thou art my people;" though you be a people scorned and vilified in the world, yet I will acknowledge you openly; your low and miserable condition shall not hinder me from saying, "Thou art my people:" and as for you, whatever you shall meet with in my ways, whatever you suffer for my worship, though it be scorned and despised of men, yet you shall confess it before the world, and say, "Thou art my God."

Thus you have a short paraphrase upon this and the succeeding gracious expressions of God to his reconciled people, a slight view of the mercy of the Lord to his saints.

But when was all this fulfilled? you will say; or to what times does this prophecy refer?

This prophecy is partly fulfilled when a soul is brought to embrace the gospel; but the full accomplishment shall be at the calling in of the Jews; then not only the spiritual estate of particular converted souls shall be thus happy, but the whole visible church shall be betrothed unto the Lord for ever. We cannot say so of any visible church at present, none of them but may fall off; but when God shall bring in the Jews, they shall never lose the visibility of their church communion. Rev. xxi. 2, 3, seems to have reference to this prophecy: "And I John saw the holy city, new Jerusalem, coming down from God out of heaven, prepared as a bride adorned for her husband. And I heard a great voice out of heaven, saying, Behold, the tabernacle of God is with men, and he will dwell with them, and they shall be his people, and God himself shall be with them, and be their God." This contains almost the same words which we have here in this prophecy to be fulfilled in that glorious church estate, when God calls home to himself his own people. Mark there, "God himself shall be with them:" God is always with his people; but "God himself," that is, a more especial, and immediate, and full presence of God, shall be with them.

But the words must yet be more fully examined.

"I will betroth thee." The Scripture often mentions espousals and marriage, to express the great mystery of the grace of God to his people. The Holy Ghost seems to delight much in this allegory: there is none more frequent in Scripture, and it sheds very great honour on the marriage state; and the lives of those united in marriage ought to resemble the blessedness, as far as possible, of the condition of a people reconciled to God, for in all comparisons a similitude should exist. Married people should so live, that all who behold the sweetness, the happiness of their lives, may be reminded thereby of the sweetness and happiness which is in the church's communion with Jesus Christ. I appeal to you, are your lives thus?

Now in a married condition there are these four things most remarkable.

First, There is the nearest possible union. "They two shall be one flesh." Consider this power of God in an ordinance; two that perhaps not a month before were mutually strangers, never saw each other's faces, and knew not that there were such in the world, when they enter into this, though but a civil ordinance, these two shall be nearer one to another than the child that came out of the mother's womb. Whence arises this, but merely from the power of an ordinance? One would think that the affection of a mother to the fruit of her own body should be more than it were possible for her to have to a stranger she had never seen before in her life; but it is not so; when a woman comes under the obligation of this ordinance, she should entertain more affection to one who was ere while a stranger, than to her own child. Such is the power of God's ordinance, though but a civil one. Now then, what efficacy must Divine ordinances have! Certainly, most powerful on the soul, when they are administered in the way of God's appointment. So here, "I will betroth thee:" as if God should say, Thou wast not long since as a stranger to me, as one cast off, yea, as an enemy; but now all the creatures in heaven and in earth, the very angels themselves, shall not be more dear to me, nor in closer communion, than you. This is true of a wretched, sinful creature, who has not only been as a stranger, but as an enemy to God; on conversion and union with Christ he is admitted into a nearer connexion and more intimate communion with God, in some respects, than the very angels in heaven, for they are never said to be the spouse of the Son of God, as the saints are. Such is the mighty power and love of God in uniting his saints to his Son.

Secondly, In nothing in the world is there so full a communication of one creature to another as in marriage: so in our spiritual marriage with Christ there is a most intimate communion. God has two ways of communicating himself: one is infinite, that is, to his Son in that inconceivable mystery of Divine generation; the other modes are of a finite kind, and of these, the greatest is his communication of himself to his saints in Christ. God does not so communicate himself to the creatures generally indeed: in comparison he communicates little or nothing of himself to the whole frame of heaven and earth. As far as communion is wanting in marriage, so far is the blessing of it from being complete. The communion of God to his church is a full communion; his wisdom, power, riches, are made over to the saints; the merits, the righteousness of Christ, are all theirs.

This communication is mutual: one converted to God, lets out his heart into God in a fuller manner than any creature can do to another. Suppose all the beauty and excellency in the world were combined together and presented to thee, to be an object of thy delight, yet it were not possible that thou shouldst communicate thyself so fully to it, as thy soul will to God upon thy conversion. The soul yields itself to God, as into an infinite ocean of goodness, so that it would retain nothing of its own; but, as a drop of water in a vessel of wine, assume the flavour and colour of that with which it is united. And hereby you may know whether your conversion be real or not, if as that which is Christ's comes to be thine, so that which is thine comes again to be Christ's. "My Beloved is mine, and I am his," saith the church. Hence it is that the honour which Christ the husband has, is reflected on the saints; they shine with the brightness of his beams. "Since thou wast precious in my sight, thou hast been honourable," Isa. xliii. 4. Among the Romans, when the newly married wife was brought home, she was wont to say, Where you are Caius, I am Caia. How mean soever the woman may be before, yet, when married, she partakes of the honour of her husband. So the saints, whatever they were before, are now looked upon as honourable in the eyes of the triune God; and in those of the angels and of the rest of the saints, who are able to discern their excellency. And on the other side, (for it is ever mutual,) as the church derives honour from the lustre of the beams of Christ's glory, so also is the church a glory unto Christ. As the Scripture saith, "The wife is the glory of the man;" so, in truth, the church is the glory of Christ.

How is that? you will say. True, Christ is the glory of the church; but that the church, which is a company of poor creatures, should be the glory of Christ, how can that be?

Yes, it is so, Christ accounts himself glorified before the Father in having such a spouse. Thus, 2 Cor. viii. 23, "Whether any do inquire of Titus, he is my partner and fellow helper: or our brethren be inquired of, they are the messengers of the churches, and the glory of Christ." Titus and the brethren are there called "the glory of Christ." And Eph. i. 23, the church is said to be "the fulness of him that filleth all in all." However low we should be in our own eyes, yet this is certain, that it is the glory of Christ before the Father and the blessed angels that he has such a spouse. Hence, Rev. xxi. 9, one of them saith, "Come hither, and I will show thee the bride, the Lamb's wife:" the very angels rejoice in this; Come, behold the bride, the Lamb's wife! Certainly they would not, in such triumph, have called all to behold the bride, had it not been for the glory of Christ in her. Psal. xlv. 14, the church is described as brought in to the King all glorious and beautiful, "in raiment of needlework." Christ rejoices, and his very heart even springs forth, to present his church to his Father; Father, he saith, here behold my spouse that I have married unto myself. It is true, a child may sometimes marry against his father's consent, one whom he may be ashamed to bring to his father's house, because she will disgrace it; but how mean and sinful soever we are in ourselves, when once we are betrothed to Christ, he will not think it any dishonour to acknowledge us even before his Father, but account it his glory, before him and the blessed angels, that he has such a spouse.

But further, this communion makes the afflictions between Christ and his church mutual. There is a communion in things evil as well as good. The very sins of the church are to be charged on Christ. As a woman who had contracted debts before marriage, and so was liable to arrest, when married is no more troubled with the officers of justice, but all claims are to be made on the husband: so, though we be in debt, owing a debt of punishment because we have not paid the debt of obedience, and whilst out of Christ may fear every moment to have some sergeant of the Lord to arrest us, and to hale us to prison, there to lie until we have paid the uttermost farthing; but when the soul is married to Christ, all debts, all sins, are all transferred upon and charged to him; and if the law now require satisfaction, if justice pleads against you, you may send it to your husband Christ, and he will joyfully answer all demands. An earthly husband perhaps may take it ill, and think he has brought himself to misery, when arrested for his wife's debts, and his heart may be alienated from her; but Christ will never love you the worse for all the debts charged against him on your account, but will willingly discharge them, and rejoice in it before his Father. And if any affliction befall you, Christ sympathizes with you: "In all their affliction he was afflicted," Isa. lxiii. 9. So, on the other side, all the afflictions of Christ are the afflictions of the church. Doth Christ suffer? you are affected as if you suffered yourselves. Christ feels for your sufferings as if they were his own, and you sympathize in those of Christ in return.

Thirdly, In a married condition there is a mutual, entire love. That is,

1. Loving the person more than the benefits received from him. True conjugal love is fixed on the persons, rather than on the estates, or any thing they enjoy by them. So, on Christ's part, his love is fixed on the persons of the saints, more than on their actions. It is true, all the gracious actions you do are lovely before Christ, for they are the fruits of his Spirit; but Christ's greatest love is toward your persons. So your chiefest love, if it be a true conjugal affection, settles on the person of Christ rather than on any thing derived from him. Notwithstanding those riches of pardon of sin and precious promises which thou enjoyest through him, his person is that which ravishes thy soul.

2. True love can be satisfied with nothing else but love. Love vilifies every thing tendered, except it comes

as a fruit of love; and where love exists, even a little cup of cold water is more highly prized than a kingdom without it: the giving the body to be burned, without love, is nothing. I will give you two scriptures, one wherein the saints prize God's love, the other wherein God prizes the love of the saints. Psal. xxxvi. 7, "How excellent is thy loving-kindness, O God!" Psal. xci. 14, "Because he hath set his love upon me, therefore I will deliver him: I will set him on high, because he hath known my name."

3. This entire love is a love in all conditions. Christ loves his church in their afflictions as entirely as after their deliverances. "He found him in a desert land, and in the waste howling wilderness; he led him about, he instructed him, he kept him as the apple of his eye," Deut. xxxii. 10. Mark, they were in the wilderness, "in the waste howling wilderness," yet even there they were dear to Christ, and were "kept as the apple of his eye." The church in return regards Christ in his afflictions as lovely still as ever: "A bundle of myrrh is my well-beloved unto me, he shall lie all night betwixt my breasts," Cant. i. 13. Myrrh is a bitter thing, yet the church professes that Christ, though bitter in his afflictions, should still be most dear to her. Herodotus and Pliny report of Artemesia, queen of Halicarnassus, that after her husband's death, she took his ashes and drank them in wine, from excess of love to him though dead. The church loves a crucified Christ, as well as a glorified Christ. A most remarkable example of the love of a spouse to her husband we have in our English History. King Edward the First, having been wounded by a poisoned dagger, his wife Eleanor, to show the entire love she bare him, and because she thought if the venom was suffered to remain there would be no possibility of a cure, herself sucked the poisoned wound, and so ventured the loss of her own life to preserve her husband's. Here was love in a spouse to her husband. The church bears a like love to Christ. If he be wounded with the poisonous tongues of ungodly men in reproaches and blasphemies, and persecuted in the world, the truly gracious are willing to suck in that very poison to themselves, so they may take it from him. Let the reproaches of Christ fall upon me; oh let me suffer rather than Christ. It was Ambrose's wish, Oh that God would turn all the adversaries of the church upon me, that they might direct against me all their weapons, and satisfy their thirst with my blood: and such is the disposition of a true spouse of Christ.

Utinam Dominus avertat adversarios ab ecclesia, et in me omnia sua tela convertant, meo sanguine sitim suam expleant. Ambr.

4. In it there is unspeakable delight. Communion has delight; the greatest communion, the greatest delight: the greatest delight that God has is to communicate himself, first to his Son, and then to his saints. If God delights in communicating out of his fulness to the saints, one would think the saints must needs delight in flowing out into God. God delights in imparting mercy to his saints, because he was well pleased with the death of his own Son as a means conducing thereto. One would think that the death of Christ should be most abhorrent to the heart of God, yet the Scripture saith God was well pleased with it, Isa. liii. 10. Why so? Because he saw this opened the way for him to communicate himself in the fulness of his grace to his church, and, therefore, though it cost him so dear as the death of his own Son, yet was he well pleased. And as for Christ, he takes delight in communicating himself to his people; after his suffering, he was satisfied, saith the prophet, when he saw of the travail of his soul. As if Christ had said, Oh let me have a church to communicate myself to, and though I see it has cost me my blood, and all these fearful sufferings, yet am I satisfied, and think all well bestowed, so I may have a people to partake of my love and mercy for ever. "Thou hast ravished my heart, my sister, my spouse, thou hast ravished my heart with one of thine eyes," Cant. iv. 9. Then for the saints, the delight they have in intimate communion with Christ is unutterable. "Stay me with flagons, comfort me with apples, for I am sick of love," saith the church, Cant. ii. 5. "My soul shall be satisfied as with marrow and fatness; and my mouth shall praise thee with joyful lips: when I remember thee upon my bed, and meditate on thee in the night watches," Psal. lxiii. 5, 6.

Observe, The more fully you lay out yourselves for Christ, the more comfort you shall have in your lives. Here is the great difference between the hypocrites and the sincere. It is impossible that a hypocrite can have the same comfort in his life as a gracious heart has, and for this reason, because a hypocrite makes reservations, and gives not himself wholly to Christ, but always keeps somewhat back, and thereby loses his comfort; but a gracious heart, fully giving itself up to Christ, derives comfort and sweetness in the service of its Master, far above all the joy of the hypocrite. Perhaps you think that the only comfort you can have is by receiving some benefit, some mercy from God: you are much mistaken; the letting your hearts out to God is a greater comfort than any you can derive from his gifts.

And now, how happy are they to whom Christ is thus espoused! How comfortably may you live, being affianced to Christ! and how comfortably may you die! It is our work to seek to draw souls to Christ, to allure them to be in love with him. In Gen. xxiv. 35, you see the course which Abraham's servant took to excite the love of Rebekah and her friends to his master's son; he begins with telling them, that he is the servant of Abraham, and that the Lord had blessed his master greatly, so that he was become great; and that the Lord had given him flocks, and herds, and silver, and gold; and that he had an only son who was to inherit all. This is the work of ministers, to tell people what riches of mercy there are in God, and that all the treasures of those infinite riches of the infinite God are in Jesus Christ, and to be communicated through him. Yea, it is not only the work of ministers, but it should be the work of every gracious heart, thus to seek to draw souls to Christ; as Rev. xxii. 17, not only the angels say, Come, but "the bride saith, Come. And let him that heareth say, Come. And let him that is athirst come. And whosoever will, let him take the water of life freely."

Were I not thus expounding, we surely could not leave such a point as this; but for the present I shall only add, Know that it is not want of any worth in you than can hinder communion with Jesus Christ; and do not reason thus, I am a poor, wretched, sinful creature, will ever Christ be married to me? It is not thy sinfulness, nor thy base condition, that can hinder it: Christ never joins himself to any because they *are* worthy, but that they *may be* worthy; and he makes them so by the very act of union. The woman is not married to the king because she is a queen, but the king marries her to make her a queen.

And further, remember, if your hearts be not taken with Christ, to join with him in this holy marriage, if he be not your husband to enjoy conjugal communion with you, he will be your judge to condemn you.

But besides this betrothing between Christ and a soul, there is a betrothing between Christ and a visible church, especially the church of the Jews when called in.

God shall appear in his glory when this marriage shall take place between Christ and the Jewish church. If a wealthy man has a son to marry, and intend to solemnize the nuptials according to his means, he arrays himself in his best attire: so, at the calling of the Jews, the King of heaven will put on the robes of his majesty, and appear in a more glorious manner to the world than he ever did since the creation. Yea, and as the bridegroom on the marriage day decks himself sumptuously, so Jesus Christ will then appear; whether personally or otherwise, we say not, but certainly he will then appear resplendent with glory. So Tit. ii. 13, We look "for the glorious appearance of the great God, and our Saviour Jesus Christ." And 2 Thess. i. 10, Christ shall come so as "to be admired in all them that believe:" the church likewise shall then be clothed with beauty, "arrayed in fine linen, clean and white: for the fine linen is the righteousness of saints," Rev. xix. 8; and in that day the great doctrine of justification by Christ shall be made out full and clear. Yea, and as in a great marriage the servants in the house receive new clothes; so at that day the creatures, her servants, shall put on new raiment, and the face of the world shall be changed. Then will follow the marriage supper, and happy shall those be that shall then be found worthy to enter the bridal chamber. Let us now love Christ, cleave to him, and suffer for him; we may, perhaps, be of those, who, beside their eternal enjoyment of Christ in heaven, may enjoy him in this marriage upon the earth. But we must pass on, as we spake something of this in the end of the first chapter.

"And I will betroth thee unto me for ever." "For ever;" this addition to the mercy makes it glorious, this "for ever" renders a misery, though never so slight, an infinite misery; and a mercy, an infinite mercy. This betrothing for ever shall be fulfilled in a visible church communion to the Jews, and in the spiritual communion of Christ with the soul at present. Of the visible form first.

"I will make thee an eternal excellency, a joy of many generations," Isa. lx. 15. I think this not only regards the spiritual happiness of the saints, but that God has a time to make his visible church to be "an eternal excellency, and a joy of many generations;" an excellency that shall never have an end. And this their perpetual condition, their enduring happiness, shall arise from these three grounds.

First, from the precious foundation that shall be laid of that church when it shall appear: Isa. liv. 8, "With everlasting kindness will I have mercy on thee, saith the Lord;" but mark the ground, ver. 11, "Behold, I will lay thy stones with fair colours, and lay thy foundations with sapphires;" all the rubbish shall be removed, it shall not be raised on such a foundation. God will lay "the foundations of that church with sapphires;" and then with everlasting mercy he will embrace it.

Secondly, That church shall be in a peaceable condition, no rent, no division there, therefore in a perpetual condition: "A tabernacle that shall not be taken down; not one of the stakes thereof shall ever be removed," Isa. xxxiii. 20. Why? The very words before show the reason; "Jerusalem shall be a quiet habitation."

Thirdly, This church shall look wholly at Christ as their Judge, their Lawgiver, and their King: "The Lord is our Judge, the Lord is our Lawgiver, the Lord is our King," Isa. xxxiii. 22. Churches are ready to change while they mix other things with the worship of Christ, and the laws of men with his laws; but when they can look to him, I mean in that which is spiritual, as their Lawgiver, as their Judge, and as their King; then their happiness shall be perpetual even in this world, the Lord Christ will betroth them unto him for ever.

Though I verily think the Holy Ghost refers chiefly to this, yet we are further to understand this "betrothing for ever," of the spiritual communion the soul has with Christ. When Christ betroths himself to a soul, it is "for ever:" the conjugal love of Christ with a gracious soul shall never be broken. At first, man's condition was such, that man laid hold upon God, and let go his hold; but now God lays hold upon man, and he will never let go his. The bond of union in a believer runs through Jesus Christ, is fastened upon God, and his Spirit holds the other end of it, so that it can never be broken. This union is in the Father, who has laid "a sure foundation," 2 Tim. ii. 19; Rom. ix. 11. In the Son, who loves his to the end, John xiii. 1. In the Spirit, who abides in the elect for ever, John xiv. 16, 17. "The mountains shall depart, and the hills be removed; but my kindness shall not depart from thee, neither shall the covenant of my peace be removed, saith the Lord that hath mercy on thee," Isa. liv. 10. My loving-kindness shall be more stable with thee, and endure longer, than the mountains themselves. It is as sure as the ordinances of heaven. "Thus saith the Lord, which giveth the sun for a light by day, and the ordinances of the moon and of the stars for a light by night: If those ordinances depart from before me, saith the Lord, then the seed of Israel also shall cease from being a nation before me for ever," Jer. xxxi. 35, 36. And chap. xxxiii. 20, 21, "Thus saith the Lord; If ye can break my covenant of the day, and my covenant of the night, and that there should not be day and night in their season; then may also my covenant be broken with David my servant." You have these three expressions of the abiding of God's love with his people: 1. The continuance of the mountains. 2. The continuance of the ordinances of heaven and earth. 3. God's covenant with night and day. Here is the ground of consolation to the saints, they shall be "kept by the power of God," 1 Pet. i. 5. As if God should say, The special power I mean to exert in this world, shall be to uphold the spirits of my saints, and to bring them to salvation; and certainly, the special work in which God has in this world to exercise his power, is to keep Christ and the saints together. Though it be through God's power that the heavens and the earth are sustained, yet if God must withdraw his power from one, he would rather withdraw it from upholding heaven and earth, than from sustaining one gracious soul that has union with his Son.

The union between Christ and his people is too near a union ever to be broken. Luther has a remarkable expression about this:* As it is impossible for the leaven in the dough to be separated from it, after it is once mixed, for it turns the nature of the dough into its own: so it is impossible, saith he, for the saints ever to be separated from Christ, for Christ is in the saints as the leaven in the dough, so incorporated, that Christ and they are, as it were, one lump. Christ, who came to save that which was lost, will never lose that which he has saved. Heb. vii. 16, it is said that Christ was made a priest "not after the law of a carnal commandment;" that is, he was not made a priest as the priests in the law, after a ceremonial way, "but after the power of an indissoluble life;" *cœlesti virtute*, by a celestial energy, as Calvin on the place saith. The argument why Christ's life is indissoluble, rather than the priests in the law, is because they were made "after the law of a carnal commandment," not by a celestial power. So those who profess godliness, in a ceremonial way, "according to a carnal commandment," may fail, vanish, and come to nothing in their way of worship, as many have done; but such as are professors of religion by the virtue of God's Spirit in them, have the power of a life indissoluble.

Κατὰ δύναμιν ζωῆς ἀκαταλύτου.

There are two soul-staying and soul-satisfying grounds to assure of Christ's betrothing himself for ever.

First, when a soul is taken in to Christ, it receives not only pardon for all the sins previously committed, but there is forgiveness in store for all future transgres-

* Sicut impossibile est fermentum mixtum a pasta separari, quia immutaverit pastæ naturam, ita impossibile Christianos rapi a Christo, quia est in eis Christus fermentum, ita incorporatus, ut unum sit corpus, una massa. Luth.

sions. "There is forgiveness with thee," Psal. cxxx. 4. There lie pardons with God beforehand for all that is to come, as well as for that which is past. "There is therefore now no condemnation to them which are in Christ Jesus," Rom. viii. 1; that is, there is no instant of time after they are once in Christ Jesus, wherein it can be said that they are under the sentence of condemnation. Now, were it not that there was a pardon laid in beforehand for all future sins, they might upon commission of some new transgression be brought under condemnation; for if the least sin remain unpardoned, there is condemnation; but this cannot be. I do not say the sin is pardoned before it is committed, for it were harsh and improper to say so; for when we speak of pardoning sin, we speak of a work applied to the creature, not of that which is in God: a pardon is laid up to be applied by God whenever the sin is committed, so that there shall no time elapse wherein the sinner is unpardoned, and so under condemnation. Then surely he can never fall from Christ; for what endangers his safety, but the commission of sin? Christ has as well merited at the hand of God pardon for any future sin, as he has pardon for sin past. Do not say that this opens a gap to licentiousness, and that then we need not care; no, the grace of Christ has no such malignity in it; in saying thus, thou speakest against thine own life.

The second soul-staying argument for perseverance is, that it is a spiritual mercy purchased by Christ, as well as any other grace. "Blessed be the God and Father of our Lord Jesus Christ, who hath blessed us with all spiritual blessings in heavenly places in Christ," Eph. i. 3. Now you will say, faith, and humility, and joy, are all blessings, and we have them in Christ; is not perseverance then a blessing, a spiritual blessing also? Christ has as truly and as really laid down his life to purchase thy perseverance, as to purchase thy pardon, or any other thing he has procured for thee. That which Christ has shed his blood to purchase, surely must be obtained, he cannot have died in vain. Have you any thing by virtue of that purchase? Thou mayst be as sure of perseverance, for Christ has laid down his life to purchase that also.

Christian, then, satisfy thy soul, God gives thee comforts in this world, but he gives them not for ever; but when he betroths thee unto his Son, he betroths thee for ever. Perhaps the Lord, in mercy, has made thy life here in this thy pilgrimage very comfortable, by giving thee a meet yoke-fellow; in this thy betrothing thou art happy, but this happiness continues not; thou canst look on thy companion as a mercy of God, making thy pilgrimage sweet, yet there must be a dissolution between thee and her; but thy union with thy husband Christ is for ever, it shall never be dissolved. Perhaps some of you have lost comfortable yoke-fellows, death has come and snapped asunder the union between you, and you complain, Never woman lost such a husband, never husband such a wife; if you be godly, you have a Husband that you shall never lose, one who will fill up all relations, who saith, "Thy Maker is thine husband," Isa. liv. 5.

And further, this is mutual; "I will betroth thee unto me for ever," and give thee a heart that thou shalt cleave unto me for ever. This will afford us another useful meditation, viz. When the Lord chooses any soul to himself, as he sets his own heart for ever on that soul, so he imparts to it a principle of grace to cleave unto him; and to yield itself to him in an everlasting covenant. Psal. cxix. 112, "I have inclined mine heart to perform thy statutes alway;" is not that enough? no, he must have another word to express the "alway," "even unto the end." David's heart was much taken with the statutes of God; O Lord, through thy mercy my heart is inclined to keep thy statutes, yea, and it is so always, and it shall be "even unto the end." This is a kind of pleonasm, or rather the expression of the fulness of his heart, in his resolutions never to depart from God.

But what are those riches which Christ bestows on his people whom he betroths to himself? The bracelets and ornaments he puts on their necks and on their hands are these:

"I will betroth thee unto me in righteousness, and in judgment, and in loving-kindness, and in mercies. I will even betroth thee unto me in faithfulness: and thou shalt know the Lord."

There is much of the gospel in this.

"In righteousness." This, according to some, is understood as opposed to dissimulation, and that by this he assures his people that they shall find his dealings with them altogether just and equal; and so I expect from you, and will effect it in you, that in your dealings towards me, you shall be the same, there shall be nothing feigned betwixt us, all shall be plain, right, and just. There is often much dissimulation in marriages, great promises, and overtures of what one should enjoy in the other, and when they meet not with what they expect, it causes great dissension between the parties, and makes their lives very uncomfortable. But now, saith God, there shall be no dissimulation between us, I will deal with you in the plainness of my heart, and you shall do so likewise. So the word "righteousness" is taken in Scripture. Isa. xlviii. 1, "They make mention of the God of Israel, but not in truth, nor in righteousness;" the one explains the other: Though you have departed from me, I will receive you again in the very integrity of my soul; do not fear, do not suspect me, do not think though I make a show of love and of great favour to you, yet that I intend to cast you off at last: these are the jealous thoughts of many troubled consciences. Indeed, I hear of mercy, and God is working as if he intended mercy to me; but I am afraid he will finally reject me. No, saith God, do not fear; this mercy I offer in the very sincerity of my heart, therefore let not such suspicious thoughts arise between us; you may be sure that what is fit and right for you to have from such a husband as I am, you shall certainly receive. This I conceive a part, though not all, of the meaning of the Holy Ghost here, "I will betroth thee unto me in righteousness;" that love I profess to you, I do it not to mock you, saith God, but I do it in truth. From whence very useful observations may be drawn.

Obs. 1. Guilty hearts are full of suspicions of God's real meaning in all his expressions of love and mercy. They judge God by themselves. As they first slight sin, and see not such a dreadful evil in it, they think God sees it not: so after they have sinned, they measure God's mercy by their own, and think thus, If any had offended us as we have offended God, though we might say we would be reconciled to him, yet we could not bring our hearts wholly to it, some grudge would remain: they therefore think the like of God, and suspect that he is not really sincere in his expressions of love and mercy to them. But beware of this, do not judge of God by yourselves; though you have a base and cruel heart, and cannot be reconciled to those who provoke you, it is not *therefore* so with God. There are these two evils in sin: first, in the nature of it, there is a departing from God; secondly, it causes jealousies and suspicions of God, and so hinders the soul from returning to him again.

Obs. 2. God is very careful to prevent all these suspicions in the hearts of his people. He desires you to entertain good thoughts of him, and we plead with you, and so often open the riches of God's grace, for this very end, and to remove your jealousies and suspicions of him, as if there were no real intention in all the proffers of mercy he makes you; do not think that all those riches of God's grace are mere words, they are certain intentions of God's heart towards you. "I will betroth thee unto me in righteousness."

And for your part I will give you a heart, and you shall return to me in sincerity and truth. There was a time, indeed, when God complained of his people, that they sought him and returned unto him, "nevertheless they did flatter him with their mouth, and they lied unto him with their tongues," Psal. lxxviii. 34—36; there was no reality in their returning to him, nor in their professions of obedience: But, saith God, there shall come a time that you shall have righteous hearts, and that which you promise to me you shall truly perform; you shall no longer make a show of love, but shall return to me with all your hearts "in righteousness."

God has much difficulty at first to make us believe that he is sincere in his proffers of mercy; and long is it before our hearts can be prevailed on to turn to him in good earnest.

Obs. 3. One reason why God betroths "for ever," is, because he does it in the sincerity of his heart; and this is also a good reason why the saints continue for ever, because what they do to God is in the sincerity of their hearts. Those who return to God hypocritically will fall off, but they that return in uprightness will continue constant. Prov. viii. 18, it is said of wisdom, that with her "are durable riches and righteousness;" they are conjoined: where there is true righteousness in the heart, *there* are durable riches.

But there is yet another thing in this betrothing in righteousness, and that I think of even more importance than the former. God will be reconciled to his church so as yet to manifest himself to be a righteous God. In the works of the riches of his grace he will manifest the glory of his justice too: I will do it "in righteousness:" though indeed the Lord intends to glorify rich grace, yet so as to declare his righteousness to men and angels, that in this very work of his he may be acknowledged by them, to all eternity, to be a righteous God. That place, Rom. iii. 25, 26, confirms this; "Whom God hath set forth to be a propitiation through faith in his blood." How? "To declare his righteousness for the remission of sins." Mark it! it is not that he had set forth Christ to be a propitiation, to declare his mercy in the forgiveness of sins; you will say, What is there in the forgiveness of sins, but only the mercy of God? Yes, there is somewhat else, there is righteousness too; and the Lord declares his righteousness in the forgiveness of sins, and therefore it is that he has set forth Christ to be a propitiation. If the Lord had said but thus, Well, you are great and grievous sinners, I will be content freely to forgive you all your transgressions; this would have declared God's mercy, but not his righteousness: but now, when the Lord has set forth Christ as a propitiation, and forgives sins through the blood of his Son, in this God declares as much righteousness as grace. This text Luther had great difficulty in understanding, and prayed much before he could discern the right meaning of it. Yea, it is repeated again, "To declare, I say, at this time his righteousness: that he might be just, and the justifier of him which believeth in Jesus;" not that he might be merciful in justifying him that believeth in Jesus, but that he might be just.

And this is the great mystery of the gospel, this it is which the angels desire to look into; and the saints and angels shall admire and bless God to all eternity, for reconciling the riches of mercy and infinite justice; this it was that engaged the infinite wisdom of God from all eternity how to find a way to save sinners, and to be infinitely righteous notwithstanding. If all the angels in heaven, and all the men in the world, had been asked this question, How shall sin be pardoned, the sinner reconciled unto God, and yet God glorify his justice? they could never have answered it; but God in his infinite wisdom has found out a way. This cost God dear, even the life of his own Son, and that was a sign that God's heart was much in it; and indeed we are not Christians until in some measure we see, and have our souls taken with, the glory of God in this mystery. We must look at righteousness in our reconciliation, as well as at loving-kindness and mercy.

When God is reconciled to a sinner, not only his mercy is glorified, but, in the plan for a sinner's salvation, the glory of his justice is magnified as much, yea, more than if the sinner were eternally damned in hell.

How is that? you will say.

I prove this three ways.

First, When God appointed his Son as a surety, and charged the debt of his justice upon him, in that God would not spare this Son of his the least degree of punishment, would not remit any thing, he hereby showed a stronger and more intense love to justice, than if he had damned ten thousand thousand creatures. Suppose a malefactor comes before a judge, and the judge refuses to spare him without satisfaction to the law, this shows that the judge loves justice; but if the judge's own son be a delinquent, and it is made manifest before all that the judge will not spare him, unless the penalty of the law is paid to the uttermost, you will say the judge honours justice more in this than in condemning many other malefactors. So when the Lord shall cast many thousands into hell, there to be tormented for ever, this will show that God loves justice; but when his own Son takes our sins upon him, but by imputation, and God will not spare him, (for such are the very words of Scripture, "He that spared not his own Son," Rom. viii. 32,) this declares God's love to righteousness more than if all the world had been damned.

Secondly, Suppose the reconciled sinner had been damned, then the justice of God had been but in satisfying, and never had been fully satisfied; but in the way that God has found out to save a sinner, his justice is not only satisfying, but it is fully satisfied at once and for ever. Now it is a greater honour to justice to be fully satisfied than to be in satisfying. As for instance, suppose a creditor has one who owes him five thousand pounds, and the man is poor, and the utmost he can pay is but sixpence or twelvepence a week; suppose the creditor should put him in jail until he had paid all, this man would be receiving something, but would never be paid as long as the debtor lived; but if another rich man should come and lay down five thousand pounds at once, the man is satisfied forthwith. Such is the difference between God's satisfying his justice on sinners and upon Jesus Christ: God comes on the sinner and requires the debt of punishment, because he did not pay the debt of obedience; casts him into prison; the uttermost he can pay is but little, and therefore he must be still paying and paying eternally, which is the very ground of their eternal punishment in hell, because they cannot pay enough in any finite time: now Christ interposes and fully pays the debt, so that justice saith it has enough, it is satisfied, and the greater glory accrues to the justice of God.

Thirdly, If the sinner had been sent down to hell, God had had the glory of his justice passively upon him, he should be for ever under its power and stroke; but in the mean time the sinner would have hated God for his justice, and abhorred justice itself: but when justice is honoured actively, the sinner falls down and acknowledges himself guilty, puts himself under the stroke, and accepts of the punishment of his iniquity: now God is delighted more abundantly in this active way of glorifying his justice than if the sinner had been satisfying it eternally in hell.

And now devils and all wicked men must needs have

their mouths stopped for ever, they cannot cry out against God because he will marry himself to such sinners; This is mercy, but where is his righteousness? where is the glory of his justice? Here is an answer to them all, Though the Lord sets his love upon vile sinners, yet he does it in righteousness. And this is a great encouragement to come in and believe, for if the sinner be terrified with the apprehension of his sins, and sees that by them the wrath of God is incensed, and that infinite justice demands satisfaction; this bids the sinner know likewise that God has a way to satisfy infinite justice, and yet to save his soul; he will marry him unto himself, and yet he will do it in righteousness.

And this is a great help to a sinner against all failings afterwards, a mighty establishment against a thousand objections the sinner may make against himself. Thus we must seek to God when we seek to be received again when we have departed from him; whatever God does for us, he must do it in the way of righteousness as well as in the way of mercy. Take this with you, sinners, if ever you have a pardon sealed to you, it must be sealed in the court of justice as well as in the court of mercy; therefore, ye need not appeal from the court of justice to the mercy-seat, for in the mystery of God's reconciling himself to a sinner, there may be as much comfort in standing before the bar of justice as at the mercy-seat; that is, by standing there, in and through Christ, for he has made justice propitious to us, and now it pleads to mercy for us.

And indeed this is the very work of faith, thus to go to God, when by faith the sinner shall present to God the Father the righteousness of Jesus Christ for an atonement and satisfaction for sins: this brings the comfort of justification. When you come to God in any other way than this, it is but in a natural, and not in a true evangelical way; a man by nature may know thus much, that when he has sinned he must seek unto God for mercy, to pardon his sin, or else become miserable; but to seek to God for pardon with a price in our hand, to tender the merits of Christ as a satisfaction to Divine justice, here is the mystery of faith; faith is not only to rely upon God's mercy for pardon, but speaks thus, I see riches of grace in Christ, that he, as my surety, has made an atonement, has laid down a price, and now I tender up this to God the Father, and I thus believe my soul shall be accepted through him.

What a mighty engagement is this for us to be righteous before God! the Lord betroths us unto himself in righteousness, and we should give up ourselves to him in righteousness also. O my brethren, take this away with you, whatever you forget: if the Lord has thus engaged himself to us in a way of righteousness, and if it has cost him so dear to show himself righteous unto us; what an infinite engagement lies upon us to be righteous before him, to glorify God's righteousness in our conversation! I will do it in righteousness, and you shall have such a righteous heart, as you shall never be a dishonour to me before the people; neither devils nor wicked men shall ever be able to upbraid me, that I set my love upon such creatures as you, because, whatever you were, you shall be now righteous. When we profess ourselves to be the spouse of Christ, and be unrighteous in our conversation, we upbraid Jesus Christ, and are a dishonour to him before men and angels; What you, the spouse of Christ! where is this ornament, this bracelet of righteousness, then? Whomsoever Christ marries, he puts on them this jewel of righteousness. He blasphemes religion which he seems to honour, says Cyprian, who makes not good in his life what he professes.

Blasphemiam ingerit religioni quam colit, qui quod confitetur, non ante omnes impleverit. Cypr. de sing. Cler.

"And in judgment." Some interpreters understand this and righteousness to be the same, according to Psal. xxxiii. 6, "He loveth righteousness and judgment," and so pass it over; but we must not do so, for we shall find much of God's mind in this.

Others take judgment, as frequently it is understood in Scripture, for sanctification; so they would make this promise correspond with that of Christ, John xvi. 7, 8, I will send the Comforter, and he shall "convince the world of sin, of righteousness, and of judgment." Righteousness there is of the same sense as here: judgment there, by many interpreters, is understood of sanctification; because the prince of this world is judged, the power of Satan is already broken, he is already cast out of your hearts. And they think to strengthen that by Matt. xii. 20, He will not quench the smoking flax, nor break the bruised reed, "till he send forth judgment unto victory;" that is, until he perfect the work of sanctification, that it shall overcome corruption. The text in Matthew is quoted from Isa. xlii. 3, but there we have the words somewhat different, "He shall bring forth judgment unto truth." Now, if that should be the meaning, that by judgment is meant sanctification, then we may learn an excellent note from the comparing these two texts together; that it is all one to bring judgment, sanctification, unto truth, and to bring it unto victory, when it is in truth it will certainly be in victory. But we shall a little more examine this interpretation of judgment presently; for my part, I do not think that that is meant either in this text, or in any of the texts named.

I find others understand "in judgment," to be God's judgment against the adversaries of the church. "I will betroth thee unto me in righteousness;" I will deal with you in a way of righteousness; and I will deal with your adversaries in a way of judgment, you shall have judgment against them. So Luther interprets it, and he says, that judgment here is the second pearl of the husband's ring* which he gives to his spouse, God promises to exercise judgment and vengeance against the adversaries of the church, and so applies it to his times in Germany: "For these many years, wicked magistrates have oppressed the church, and profane doctors have corrupted its doctrine, but Germany has seen God judging his adversaries."† If we understand it in this sense, Isa. liv. 5 confirms it, where God tells his church, that he that is her Maker is her husband, even the Lord of hosts, and her Redeemer, the God of the whole earth; the word there is *Vindex*, the Avenger; he that will avenge thee of thine enemies, is the God of the whole earth, is thy husband. This might afford a sweet meditation, that the Lord will defend his church from the rage of adversaries, as the husband will defend his spouse because he is betrothed to her. The Lord certainly will take a valuable consideration at the hands of the adversaries who wrong his church. But this I think not to be the scope of the phrase.

"In judgment;" that is, say others, though things be now out of order, and seem to be in confusion, yet the time is coming when all things shall be ordered in the church according to equity and right.

The two preceding interpretations are applicable to the former texts: "He will convince the world of judgment," that is, the world shall be convinced that Christ has all judgment committed to him, and he shows it in this, that the prince of this world is judged: so that passage, "I will cause judgment to return unto victory;" that is, though the adversaries of the church be many, yet he will cause them all to be vanquished, judgment shall conquer them all; though there be much opposition and confusion in the church, yet I will order

* Secunda gemma maritalis annuli. Luther.

† Jam multos annos hoc agit Sathan ut per impios magistratus ecclesia opprimatur et doctrina per prophanos doctores depravetur, sed videt Germania Deum judicantem. Luther in loc.

and compose all things in the church according to equity.

In Isa. iv. 4, the Lord saith, he will purge his church "by the spirit of judgment, and by the spirit of burning." I know some interpret it as if it were meant of the spirit of sanctification, that is as fire to consume lusts; but rather as there were those who oppressed the church by false judgment, the Lord would cleanse her from wrong and oppression, by giving a spirit of judgment to its officers, and by consuming its adversaries.

But I think we have not yet the full scope of this place, and would rather settle on this, as principally intended, though the other may be in some degree included: viz. "I will betroth thee unto me in judgment;" that is, there shall be good reason for what I do; that which I will now do in betrothing thee to myself, shall not be done rashly, nor unadvisedly, but with understanding and good deliberation; I know what I do in it, and I know what glory I shall have by it; I will do it "in judgment." So I find the word judgment taken in Scripture, Jer. iv. 2, "Thou shalt swear, The Lord liveth, in truth, in judgment, and in righteousness." "In judgment," that is, when you swear, know it is worshipping God, and you must do it in judgment: you must not only swear "in truth," that is, swear to that which is true; and "in righteousness," that is, not to the wrong or prejudice of your neighbour, for you may sin in swearing, (though you swear in truth,) if you have an intent to wrong any; but, thirdly, you must swear "in judgment" too; you must understand what you do, that is, when you take an oath, you must know that it is not as the oath *ex officio* was, to swear to answer to every thing that shall be asked you; but you must understand before-hand what you are to swear to, and so swear "in judgment." So saith God, "I will betroth thee unto me in judgment," that is, I have considered what I am to do in this thing, and I do it from judgment. And for your parts, when you shall close with me, in this blessed conjugal union and communion, you shall do it from judgment also. "I will betroth you in judgment," so as to make it appear before the world that I had good reason so to do; and you shall likewise so close with me, that you shall be able to justify it before men and angels, that you had good reason for what you did, that it was done "in judgment."

In nothing is there more need of judgment than in marriages and contracts; therefore the heathens were wont to set Mercury, their god of wisdom, by Venus, their goddess of marriage, to note that there was need of judgment there; yet there is nothing, usually, in the world undertaken with more rashness and inconsiderateness, which is the reason of so much subsequent unhappiness. But though there be many contracts between men and women that are not out of judgment, yet, saith God, "I will betroth you in judgment." Christ's union with his church is an union out of judgment. Christ considers of our meanness before he marries us; knows fully what we are, our sinfulness, our wretchedness; knows we are in debt, and whatever else we can think might be a hinderance, he knows as perfectly as ever he shall know it, and yet he goes on. Yea, the marriage between Christ and his church is that which has been planning in heaven from all eternity; it is not a sudden, rash engagement, but arranged in the "counsel of peace," between the Father and the Son, from everlasting. God the Father gives consent to this union; God the Holy Ghost is sent to draw the hearts of his people to come in and consent to it likewise, as a union out of the deepest judgment.

Though it be true that God can see no reason in us why we should be thus united to his Son, yet he can see abundance of reason in himself; therefore the conversion and salvation of a soul is not only out of God's mercy, but it is also from God's wisdom. Hence the Scripture attributes our predestination and our calling to his wisdom, as well as to the freeness of his grace; as Eph. i. 11, "Being predestinated according to the purpose of him who worketh all things after the counsel of his will." Mark, it is not only because God will, "I will have mercy because I will have mercy;" I will choose such, and I will refuse such; I will do it: no, but it is "after the counsel of his will." Our wills are often bent on doing a thing when there is no reason for it, *there* is no counsel of our will; but God, even in this thing that we can see no reason for at all, works according to "the counsel of his will:" and, Eph. iii. 10, the apostle, having said before, ver. 8, that he was "to preach the unsearchable riches of Christ," adds, he was to preach to the intent that now might be "known by the church the manifold wisdom of God." In all things in the gospel there is much wisdom. Vocation is one of the mysteries of the gospel; and, 1 Cor. i. 24, the gospel is said to be "the power of God, and the wisdom of God:" the apostle there instances what one would think has as little reason in it as any thing in the gospel, that is, the leaving of the rich, wise, and noble, the great ones of the world, and calling the poor; but herein is not only the power, but the wisdom of God; God does even this in judgment. And although we can now understand little or nothing of any reason that there can be of God's choosing us to himself; yet this will be made known at the great day of judgment. It will be a great part of the glory of that day for the Lord to make known "the counsel of his will:" we now know his will, but we shall then know "the counsel" of it, and praise him to all eternity for it: this shall be the glory of the saints, that they shall see into the counsel of God's will in choosing and calling them, and suffering others to perish.

God's betrothing himself thus to his people in judgment, is an especial reason of the perpetuity of this betrothing. "I will betroth thee unto me for ever." Why? First, It is "in righteousness," therefore it will continue. Secondly, It is "in judgment," therefore also it will continue. Things done rashly seldom hold, and though eager for them at present, we quickly undo them afterwards; but that which is done in judgment abides: the calling of a sinner, and uniting him to Christ, is done in judgment, therefore it will hold; that is the ground of his perseverance. If a man, before marriage, understands thoroughly all the faults his wife has, or ever shall have, and knows perfectly her estate, and all the encumbrances he shall have with her, yet loves her out of judgment, surely this love will continue. It is so between Christ and his church; Christ, before he betroths his church, perfectly knows all the faults the church has, or shall have, all the sins that she shall ever commit, and all the encumbrances and dishonour he shall have; yet out of judgment he betroths her to himself, and therefore surely this will remain stedfast. Comfort yourselves with this, Christians, though there may be many failings after your coming to Christ, Christ knew them all before you were united to him, yet out of judgment he betrothed you to himself.

There must also be judgment on our parts: I will put into you a judicious heart, to choose me out of judgment. The saints who choose Christ know what they do. "They shall be all taught of God; every one therefore that hath heard, and learned of the Father, cometh unto me." None cometh unto me, but such as are taught of God; they who hear and learn of the Father, come to me out of judgment. "I know whom I have believed," saith Paul; and so may every Christian say. They do not embrace Christ and his ways because they are new things, as many do, and so vanish to nothing; though it is true there is always some new excellency in Christ, something revealed more than we knew

Christus est novitas semper renovanda.

before, and delightful he is in that respect, if we love novelty. It is not a sufficient plea against any truth, that it is only now revealed, and was not known before. 2 Pet. i. 12, "Be established in the present truth." Though truths be from the beginning, yet they are present truths in regard of manifestation; but the saints must not therefore receive them, merely because they are new to them, neither must any reject them, because they are now revealed, whereas before they lay hid; but all must proceed with judgment, and when any truth is presented, reject it not because you have not heard of it before, neither adopt it for that reason; but try it, and when you are convinced, then from judgment embrace it. Neither must the saints follow God, or any way of truth, merely from the example of others, but from their own judgments. Perhaps you see some of whom you have a reverent esteem, and that justly, doing thus and thus; I confess, that is enough to put you on examining, to make you bethink yourselves, Surely there is something in it, or else it is not probable they would do it; but that must not be the only reason; but if on examination you find it to be good, then embrace it out of judgment; never rest till you come to that which the men of Samaria said to the woman, "Now we believe" that this is the Messiah, "not because of thy saying," not because you told us so, "for we have heard him ourselves, and know that this is indeed the Christ, the Saviour of the world." At first, they came to Christ upon her relation, but they did not believe in Christ until they had seen and heard him for themselves. You may come to examine the ways, the truths of God upon the relation and example of others, but you must not engage your hearts in them till you see the reality of them yourselves.

You must embrace Christ and his ways out of judgment, not out of sudden flashes of affection, which pass away as quickly as they come. You have a remarkable example of this, Luke xiv. 15: "Blessed is he that shall eat bread in the kingdom of God," they exclaim; this is blessed doctrine indeed. But by that which follows, we may infer that they were such as presently went to their farms and to their oxen, and prized them before Christ, and refused to come to the supper. Sudden flashes there were in those that shouted Hosanna, Hosanna, but presently their cry was, "Crucify him, crucify him." In Josh. xxiv. 19, the people seemed to be moved with sudden affections, they *would* "serve the Lord," yea, that they would; but they considered not what they said; "Ye cannot serve the Lord," said Joshua to them. So Deut. v. 27, "All that the Lord our God shall speak unto thee, we will hear it, and do it;" but presently saith God, Oh that there were such a heart in this people to do it! The truth is, they know not what they say, they have sudden affections, but they will quickly vanish. We must choose Christ out of judgment.

You must not choose him from mistake; we must understand who he is, we must sit down and count with ourselves beforehand what we are like to suffer in his ways. Compare Cant. v. 9, with the beginning of chap. vi.: "What is thy beloved," say they, "more than another beloved?" Let us know what thy beloved is. Then the church begins commending her beloved; and in the beginning of chap. vi., "Whither is thy beloved gone? whither is thy beloved turned aside? that we may seek him with thee;" that he may be our beloved too.

Nor out of by-ends, but from a right knowledge of the excellences of Christ, having our judgments overcome by them. We must not choose any truth or ways of God, because the times favour them: we have now a number of parliament converts, who were formerly prelatical and ceremonial, they see how the times sway; but this is not from judgment. Every Christian should be a judicious Christian: such adorn religion, and are an honour to Christ. As the more deliberation and judgment there are in sin, the worse it is; so the more deliberation and judgment there are in godliness, the better it is. When a soul chooses Christ and his ways on this ground, I see a beauty in the Lord Jesus that I never saw before, I see him to be the character and the engraved form of the image of the Father; in him dwell all treasures, the very Godhead dwells in him bodily; he is the most precious among ten thousand, and the ways of God are holy and righteous! here is the rule of eternal life, here lies the happiness of the rational creature, these are the ways that my soul closes with, and shall cleave to for ever, whatever I suffer in them, for I see the excellency, the beauty, the equity, and the glory of them, and that the Lord is worthy of all honour from all his creatures: this is a choice which will hold. The world thinks the saints are fools; why? because they cannot see any reason for what they do; they cannot see ground enough in reason for such activity, strictness, and zeal; they think they do *incalescere in re frigida*, that they are very hot about a very poor, sorry, cold business, and therefore they count their ways folly: so any man, when he sees another do a thing that he understands not the reason of, will either suspect his own judgment, or think the man foolish; now wicked men are too proud to suspect their own judgments, to think their own reason folly, therefore they count the ways of God foolishness. They look on his ways from a distance, and therefore think there is no reason for them.

It is reported of the famous Marcus Galeasius, that he was converted by a sermon of Peter Martyr's, in which he expressed the excellencies of God's ways, and the mistakes of the world, by this similitude; The men of the world (said he) mistake God's ways: as, if a man were to see a company of musicians playing and dancing according to the exactest rules of art; regarding them from a distance, he sees them skipping and leaping up and down as a company of mad men, and wonders what they mean; but when he comes nearer, and hears the melodious sound, and observes how all their motions are directed agreeably to rules of art, then he begins to change his thoughts: so the men of the world look on the ways of God and on the saints from a distance, and think their motions and ways are madness; but when they come nearer, and observe the exactness of the rule they walk by, and the wisdom of God that appears in them, they change their judgments, and begin to think, surely there is something in them more than they conceived. This similitude God blessed, so that it was the means of converting that nobleman, and made him leave all his possessions in Italy, and come to Geneva, where he became a pattern of self-denial, such as scarce any age has ever produced. When you come near God's ways, and see them indeed, you will discern infinite reason in them, and charge yourselves with infinite folly that you should have had such low thoughts of them heretofore.

This is the reason why the saints hold on in their ways. This judgment is as the ballast of the ship. Many hurry on in a profession of religion, and the truth is, they know not what they do nor what they profess; if there be any new opinion, I mean, not only in regard of new manifestation, but in regard of the thing itself, presently they follow it, that they may be counted something, and seem to go beyond other men: they are as a ship that moves at a mighty rate, all the sails are up, and winds blow fairly, but there is no ballast; so it is tossed up and down, but never comes to the end of the voyage. When the seed was sown in the stony ground, it sprung up presently; but because there wanted moisture at the root, it "withered away," Luke viii. 6. This judgment is as moisture at the root. We read, that notwithstanding the stony ground "received the word with joy," yet when "persecution arose because of the word, by and by they were offended:" they were mightily taken with the ways of God, with the great things of the gospel, at first; but not having judgment, as soon as suffering came, "by and by they were offended." If times should change again, and the adversary should prevail, (which God forbid,) we shall soon have experience enough of abundance of professors, who, having chosen the ways of God not out of judgment, will by and by be offended.

"I will betroth thee unto me in loving-kindness." Though Christ takes us to himself, and will not cast us off, yet he may see such failings and frailties in us as may render us so grievous and burdensome to his spirit, that we shall enjoy but little sweetness in our communion together, through the wretchedness of our hearts. No, saith Christ, "I will betroth you unto me in loving-kindness;" my heart and ways toward you shall be full of gentleness and sweetness, and I will put such a frame likewise into your hearts, both toward me and toward one another, that you shall have hearts full of sweetness and gentleness.

בחסד

The Scripture speaks much of the loving-kindness of God to his people in Christ. Eph. ii. 7, "The exceeding riches of his grace in his kindness toward us through Christ Jesus." Tit. iii. 4, "After that the kindness and love of God our Saviour toward man appeared." You have these epithets given unto God's kindness: "Great kindness," Neh. ix. 17. "Marvellous kindness," Psal. xxxi. 21. "Merciful kindness," Psal. cxix. 76. "Everlasting kindness," Isa. liv. 8. "Excellent loving-kindness," Psal. xxxvi. 7. "Multitude of loving-kindnesses," Isa. lxiii. 7. Thus full is the Scripture of the loving-kindness of God towards us in Christ.

To open it a little. The kindness of God to us in Christ consists,

First, In the freeness of God's goodness. Kindness in a friend is seen much in this, when he does a thing freely, with good nature; when he does a kindness so as not to burden it, nor upbraid his friend with what he has done; nor in a mercenary spirit, as if he expected great matters in lieu and recompence, but leaves it to his friend to answer him in a way of kindness again as he thinks fit. Thus, in all God's dealings with us, he looks not for much at our hands before, but what he does is out of his free grace, and not burdened with conditions; he "giveth liberally and upbraideth not," James i. 5. But does not God burden his kindness, requiring that we should give up ourselves to him, and serve him, and suffer for him in return? I answer, God requires nothing in lieu of all his kindness to us; but it is an additional kindness in God to enable us to do, and a further kindness in him to accept at our hands when we have done it, and *therefore* is his kindness free. The heathens were wont to paint their *Gratiæ*, their goddesses of kindness, naked; for this reason, because all actions of kindness should be free, unclogged and unburdened. "The blessing of the Lord, it maketh rich, and he addeth no sorrow with it," Prov. x. 22. The kindnesses of this world are ordinarily clogged, scarce worth the having; the kindness of God not so, it is free.

Secondly, Kindness consists much in our tenderness over those to whom we show kindness. The kindness of God in Christ is much in compassionating our weakness, and dealing with us in all his ways accordingly. Isa. lvii. 16, "I will not contend for ever, neither will I be always wroth;" why? "for the spirit should fail before me, and the souls which I have made." He considers our weakness: Psal. ciii. 14, "For he knoweth our frame; he remembereth that we are dust." Isa. xl. 11, Christ "shall gather the lambs with his arm, and carry them in his bosom, and gently lead those that are with young." Isa. lxiii. 9, "In his clemency" (so the word is) "he redeemed them; and he bare them, and carried them all the days of old." Kindness makes one long-suffering, he bare them always and continually. It is kindness for the man to consider all the weaknesses of the wife, and to deal with her in a loving way accordingly, intending her good: this is the kindness of Christ to his church.

Thirdly, Kindness in passing by all infirmities, not taking advantages of his people because of them. Christ notices all the good that is in his people, though it be never so little; but that which is a weakness he will pass by. The Lord is not "strict to mark iniquity," but the Lord is strict to mark what we do well; if there be never so little good in an action that has a hundred weaknesses in it, Christ will mark the good and pass by all the weaknesses. Sarah is commended by Peter for calling her husband lord: in that speech of hers there was nothing but sin, saving that expression, and yet the Holy Ghost takes notice of that one word and passes over all the rest. If thou aimest at serving Christ, and canst appeal to him that thy heart is toward him to honour him as he requires, I say, though there be a hundred weaknesses in an action, if there be but one thing good, all thy weaknesses are passed by, and that one good thing is taken notice of.

Fourthly, Kindness is in a loving, sweet, amiable carriage toward one another in our converse one with another. Oh the sweet, amiable carriage that Christ exhibits toward his people! and that Christ expects likewise from them to him again. In the Canticles you find what sweet, amiable expressions there are between Christ and his church; what rebounding, as it were, there is of love and kindness one to another; "Thy love is better than wine," saith the church to Christ; and, "Thy love is better than wine," saith Christ to his church. In 1 Cor. xiii. 4, love is said to be "kind," no moroseness, but all sweetness in it, and such should exist between husband and wife.

χρηστεύεται.

Fifthly, Kindness consists in easiness to be entreated; "peaceable, gentle, and easy to be entreated," Jam. iii. 17. Thus, in Christ, he is easy to be entreated by his church, and the church should easily be entreated, and indeed is: when the hearts of the saints are right, there is an ingenuousness in them, and they are soon moved to any service Christ requires.

Lastly, Kindness is compassionate, sensible of all sufferings; so Christ and his saints mutually are.

Such loving-kindness as this should be in all marriage communion; where this does exist there is a sweet conjugal communion indeed, and so far as this is wanting, so far the blessing of a marriage estate is from being complete. One reason, amongst others, why God makes so much use of this allegory of marriage, to express so great a mystery of godliness as the union between Christ and his church, is, to teach those who are married, to live so together as to show forth all that excellency of communion which exists between Christ and his saints. Now I put it to you who are married, is there such loving-kindness in you as may shadow forth the loving-kindness which exists between Christ and his spouse? So far as you come short of this, so far there is an evil. When you go home take this lesson with you, labour to show such mutual loving-kindness as may express the loving-kindness of Christ to your souls. There are many frailties in each, but not so many as there are in you in reference to Christ; he bears with more infirmities in you than you can bear with in your wife, and yet is not morose, nor a bitter husband to you. I have read of Monicha, Austin's mother, that she had a husband of a very cross and perverse disposition; and that a heathen, who lived near her, came to her once, and asked, How is it that you and your husband live so well together? We know your husband is of a very cross and perverse disposition, yet we see nothing but a great deal of sweetness and love between you; it is not so with us, we cannot do so for our lives. Monicha gave her this answer, It may be, when your husband is untoward and perverse, you are perverse and answer unkindly in return; but the Christian religion teaches me, when my husband comes home and is in a passion, to be as loving, and dutiful, and amiable to him as I can, and so I have won his heart. It were a happy thing if all women would take this home with them, and learn of Monicha, Austin's mother. And likewise, on the other hand, the man should so act in reference to his wife: this loving-kindness exists between Christ and his spouse, let it then appear between husband and wife, who profess an interest in Christ.

And this loving-kindness of Christ, oh how should it draw our hearts to him! What more powerful means to attract than loving-kindness? Mark that passage in proof of its power, 2 Chron. x. 7, "If thou be kind to this people, they will be thy servants for ever," say those ancient counsellors of Rehoboam, who counselled him wisely. If this be the way to draw the heart, surely Christ must needs have ours; he is not "a bloody husband," but a kind one to us; let us then be his "servants for ever." It were a good thing for all governors to consider that it is kindness that wins the hearts of people; and as they rule not over beasts, but men, if they would rule with comfort and safety to themselves, they should temper their authority with kindness. Hence, Cant. iii. 10, it is said that the chariot of Solomon was "paved with love for the daughters of Jerusalem;" thus expressing Solomon's gentleness toward its people. When the mother and wife of Alexander Severus would incite him to severity, and objected to him his mildness and readiness to yield to his subjects, saying, You have made your power more contemptible by your kindness and compliant spirit; his answer was, *At securiorem*, But more secure and lasting. Certainly, if magistrates would follow the advice of the ancient counsellors, to be kind to the people, they would be their servants for ever, and their own peace and safety be better secured.

Christ expects loving-kindness from you to himself, and loving-kindness likewise one to another.

First, Christ expects you should be full of loving-kindness to him. O blessed Redeemer, what is it that we should do, that we should be kind to thee? The very phrase seems to be too low for Christ, that he should look for our kindness. Yes, Christ looks for it, and prizes it dearly, nothing in the world is valued by him more than it; as a fond husband prizes nothing more than kindness in his wife. But how kind to Christ?

1. When you cleave to him when he stands most in need of you. 2 Sam. xvi. 17, Absalom saith to Hushai, "Is this thy kindness to thy friend?" that is, Is thy friend in danger, and requiring thy present aid, and dost thou now forsake him? thou shouldst now be with him in the time of his need, and thus prove thy kindness. So, I say, there are times in which Christ stands in more need of us than at other, in suffering times, in times wherein his cause has many enemies, and our help is called for; if we should forsake him then, may not Christ, nay, may not the holy angels and saints say, "Is this your kindness to your friend?" To come to Christ when you have need of him is not so much kindness, but to come to him when he has need of you, this is kindness.

2. It is kindness when we serve Christ in the midst of difficulties. You have this strongly marked in Jer. ii. 2, "I remember the kindness of thy youth, the love of thine espousals, when thou wentest after me in the wilderness." To be willing to follow Christ in the wilderness, that is kindness. Christ does not account it kindness for us to serve him when we may prosper in his service; when it may suit our own ends, when we may keep our shops, our lands and possessions, when no difficulty at all presents itself, what great kindness is this? But when, from love to the ordinances and the truths of Christ, you are willing to follow him even in the wilderness, this is kindness, and Christ will account it such: however, some have thought that they have shown great kindness to Christ, because they have staid and borne the brunt; but how have they borne it? by yielding to superstitious vanities, and being ceremonial and prelatical. It will be found that those who have been willing to follow Christ in the wilderness, from love to him, his truth and ordinances, that Christ will remember such service as kindness.

3. It is a kindness for young people to dedicate their prime to Christ. By way of allusion, at least, we may make use of that Scripture, "I remember the kindness of thy youth:" when thy bones are full of marrow, and the world seeks to draw thy heart after its vanities, when thou mayst have thy delights and pleasures in the flesh to the full; if then thou art willing to deny all, and to give up thyself to Christ, this is loving-kindness. One that is old may possibly reach heaven on repentance; but what kindness is it for him, who has nigh worn out all his days and strength in the ways of sin, and the delights of the flesh, when he is leaving the world, and can have no more pleasure in his sins, to come to Christ for mercy; what kindness is here? here is self-love indeed, but little kindness.

Secondly, Loving-kindness one to another. "I will betroth you unto me in loving-kindness:" I will put such a spirit into you of loving-kindness unto your brethren, as I have towards you. The word חסד here rendered loving-kindness, often in Scripture is used for saints. Those who are called godly, and saints, in the English Bible, in the Hebrew are called kind ones: thus, Psal. iv. 3, "Know ye that the Lord hath set apart חסיד לו him that is godly," or, the kind one, "for himself;" the Lord hath set apart for himself those that are kind, those who are of sweet, gentle dispositions. And Psal. xvi. 10, Not "suffer thine Holy One to see corruption," the Hebrew is, חסידיך thy kind one. So Psal. cxlix. 1, "Sing his praise in the congregation of the saints," חסידים of the kind ones; and the same word again, ver. 5, "Let the saints be joyful in glory;" that is, the kind ones. All come from the same root with that which here is translated "loving-kindness," denoting what an ingredient loving-kindness is to saintship and to godliness; therefore it is not enough for Christians to be godly, but they must be kind one to another also. 2 Pet. i. 3, "And to godliness add brotherly kindness." You think you are godly; but are you of a rugged, rough-hewn disposition, surly, severe, and perverse? here is the exhortation to you this day from God, if you will approve yourselves to be godly, "Add to your godliness brotherly kindness;" except you add that, you can have little comfort in your godliness. It is impossible indeed for one who has the power of godliness, and its true comfort and sweetness, to be of a harsh and unkindly disposition; such a heart has in God such infinite satisfaction, that there is nothing that can come from without that can make it bitter; there is so much sweetness in the satisfaction it enjoys in God, that not all the bitterness from without can sour such a heart; as the scripture saith, "A good man is satisfied from himself."

If you have a vessel of honey, a little gall will make it all bitter, yet a little honey will not make sweet a vessel of gall. But in grace, though there be much bitterness in men or women, though they be naturally harsh, yet a drop of true saving grace will sweeten all that gall; and if they be once gracious, a great deal of gall and bitterness from without will not imbitter that sweetness. I beseech you to

Obs. 1. When God has left men they grow more passionate and froward than they were before. And I verily believe one ground of the frowardness and passionateness in professors is, that they have made breaches between God and their souls, and their peace being broken, nothing then can give them content. As when a man has been abroad and others have angered him, and his inward comfort and joy are gone, then every thing annoys him, he is pleased with nothing, his countenance is louring, and he is unkind to all; and why? because he has lost the sweetness of his own spirit, and now all seems bitter, nothing from without can content him: but let this man go abroad and things succeed with him, let him make a good bargain, hear excellent news, that his goods are come home safely, he can now bear a hundred times more than before, and you can scarce anger him; why? because his heart is filled with sweetness. So, let a Christian walk close with God, maintain his peace with him, and he will have so much sweetness in his heart that it will not be easy to incense him. Why? He has enough within. Perhaps his friend, his wife, his neighbour is unkind, but his Christ is loving: Though there be little comfort in my marriage with one who is so peevish and perverse, yet in my marriage with Christ there is satisfaction enough. But when the heart has made breaches between Christ and itself, when it has lost the sweetness of that marriage communion, no marvel if there be no sweetness in the other.

A remarkable example of this is Saul, who, before his breach with God, was of a sweet, mild, and loving disposition, but afterwards perverse, cruel, and froward. When first chosen king, how humble was he! he acknowledges himself to be of "the least of the tribes of Israel," and "the least in his father's house;" and when some contemptuously exclaimed, "Shall this man reign over us?" the text saith, "he held his peace;" and when others would have had them killed, No, by no means, they must not be slain, because God had shown him mercy in a late victory. But after Saul had fallen from God, how rugged, perverse, and cruel his disposition then! even to Jonathan his son, a gracious, loving youth, he saith, "Thou son of the perverse, rebellious woman," and casts a javelin at him to kill him; then the fourscore and five priests in the city of Nob must be all slain in his anger. What was the reason of all this? The breach between God and his own soul. Oh take heed of those breaches, for what does a man get by the want of this kindness and loving disposition! he troubles himself; Prov. xi. 17, "He that is cruel," of a harsh disposition, "troubleth his own flesh." I appeal to you who are married, do you not lose much of the sweetness of your lives? what comfort have you in them when there is nothing but snarling at and crossing one another? you trouble your own house, and your own flesh; whereas, if there were loving-kindness between you, it would sweeten all your comforts, yea, all your crosses.

Obs. 2. The loving-kindness of a man or a woman is their beauty. "The desire of a man is his kindness," Prov. xix. 22; and of a "virtuous woman" who had "done excellently," among other high commendations, this is one, "In her tongue is the law of kindness," Prov. xxxi. 26; kindness gives a law to her mouth: many women are under no restraint, and their tongues are lawless when they are provoked; but of a woman commended by God, the text saith, "The law of kindness is in her tongue," the kindness of her heart guides her lips, and that is the honour of a woman.

To be of a sweet, kind disposition, is an exceeding beauty, adding a glorious lustre to any man. Isa. xl. 6, "All flesh is as grass, and all the goodliness thereof is as the flower of the field;" the word for goodliness is חסד the same word that is used here, and translated "kindness," denoting that kindness is "the goodliness" of the spirit of a man or woman; as the flower imparts beauty to the field. Justin Martyr, in his Apology for the Christians, saith, That their adversaries hated only the name of a Christian, but had nothing against the Christians; and what is there, saith he, in the name? Nothing but that which is good and lovely enough: now, it is not just to hate what is profitable and gentle, yet so the word may signify, if you call them *Christiani*, from χρηστὸς, mild, profitable; and so they are indeed, profitable, gentle, and kind people, and why should you hate such? 2 Cor. vi. 6, "By kindness, by the Holy Ghost," are put together, and there is much of the Holy Ghost where there is much kindness. The spirit of Christ is a spirit of kindness and gentleness, and though you may think that your harshness and severity argue courage of mind, (for it is usual for froward and passionate people to think they have more courageous spirits than others,) know that they only prove you more base and degraded. I will cite, in proof only, Psal. xlv. 4, where it is said of Christ, "In thy majesty ride prosperously because of truth and meekness;" now the word for meekness is, in 2 Sam. xxii. 26, translated "gentleness;" "thy gentleness hath made me great:" mark, gentleness and majesty may consist together, yea, Christ is magnificent and full of majesty in the gentleness and quietness of his spirit; Ride on in thy majesty prosperously, because of thy meekness, because of thy gentleness. Would you have a brave spirit, like to the spirit of Christ in his glory? let your spirits be gentle, sweet, and loving.

Τὸ δὲ χρηστὸν μισεῖσθαι οὐ δίκαιον. Just. Mar.

"I will betroth thee unto me in mercies."

Loving-kindness and mercies may seem, at first view, synonymous, but there is much difference in them.

"And in mercies;" *viscera*, so the word is; "I will betroth thee unto myself in bowels." Not the fruit only, but the root; not the water only, but the fountain; thou shalt have the fountain of all good, my very bowels, from whence flow all mercies. Wherefore, Christians, you need not fear the want of the supply of mercies; why? because you have the Fountain from whence mercies spring. God may grant to wicked men many fruits of his bounty and goodness; but they have not his bowels, they have not the fountain, the root from whence all mercies issue.

Here is the happiness of a Christian, not only to have much good from God, but to have those very bowels from whence that good comes. Herein lies the dignity, the glory of a Christian, the vastness of his riches.

Christians, you need not therefore fear to resign any mercy God requires at your hands, for the bowels of mercy are yours; the spring-head of all mercy, whence you may fetch all seasonable and all suitable supplies at pleasure, is yours. Here is the reason why many carnal persons, when they have received a mercy from God, cling to it so closely, and are so unwilling to part with it, though God requires it again: why? because they are not acquainted with the true privilege of a Christian, know not what it is to possess the bowels of God, nor where to go for more, and therefore are loth to part with what they have. Now the saints can part with any thing for God; Let him take what he will, let him strip me as naked as he pleases, I have the bowels of God, the spring-head, to resort to for new mercies. If there were a scarcity of water, and you had only some in a cistern, and your neighbour came to borrow of you, you would be unwilling to lend any; but if you have a well-spring, a fountain, that never was and never will be drawn dry, is it a great matter for you to lend water then? So, the men of the world are needy creatures, they have something indeed, but it is as water in a cistern, when that is gone they think that all is gone; therefore they will not lend it, no, not unto God himself when he requires it of them. But the saints have the bowels of mercy, the spring-head of all grace, therefore whatever God calls for, they presently say, Lord, here take all, I know where to have it again, and much more than that. This makes godly men so ingenuous for God, and so free-hearted to him, and to his servants.

But let us search a little into these mercies: it is an argument that has much depth in it.

1. They are a depth swallowing up the greatest evils of sin or affliction. If you pour a pail of water on the boards of your chamber, it seems like a little sea; but take the same and pour it into the deep ocean, it is there swallowed up, and appears nothing. Our afflictions and our sins in themselves seem great, but when they are swallowed up in these bowels, in these depths of God's mercies in which he betroths himself to us, they are as nothing in comparison. Therefore the Scripture uses such strong expressions for the wonderfulness of God's mercies to his people in Christ.

There are three chiefly remarkable words to express the fulness of God's mercies in Christ. The first in Eph. ii. 7, "The exceeding riches of his grace," the riches that are cast in over and above.

Τὸν ὑπερβάλλοντα πλοῦτον τῆς χάριτος.

The second in Rom. v. 20, "The grace of God did much more abound;" there is a second ὑπερ.

Ὑπερεπερίσσευσεν ἡ χάρις.

And the third in 1 Tim. i. 14, "The grace of our Lord was exceeding abundant." There was a pleonasm before, but here is a super-pleonasm. Here ὑπερ is three times repeated, to mark the riches of the glory, and the depth of the mercy, of God in Christ.

Ὑπερεπλεόνασεν ἡ χάρις.

2. Consider these mercies in the effects. They set on work all the fulness of God for the good of his people. If there be any thing that God's wisdom, or power, or all that blessedness which is in God, can effect, they will engage all to work for thy good, for the bowels of mercy yearn towards thee, if thou art in Christ.

3. It is the great design, yea, the greatest design, that ever God had from all eternity, to honour his mercy, and to set out the infinite glory and riches of it in Christ. Certainly God had great designs in doing such mighty things as he has done, but, above all the designs that ever God had in all his works, to glorify the riches of his mercy in Christ is the chiefest. They are indeed bowels of mercy when they are such, as that in the glory of them God attains his great design in making the world, for he would never have created it had it not been for that.

4. They are the heart-blood mercies of Jesus Christ, such mercies as cost the blood of Christ; and his was certainly most precious blood. When Christ sees any converted and brought home to him, to be made a subject of God's mercy, he thinks his blood well bestowed. The Scripture saith, "He shall see of the travail of his soul, and shall be satisfied." I have enough for all the blood I shed. I came indeed from my Father, and was made a servant, a curse; yea, I suffered the wrath of my Father, and my blood was shed; but if this be the fruit of it, that such a soul shall obtain this mercy, I have recompence sufficient.

5. Yea, God the Father is well pleased with it, he thinks the blood of Christ but a valuable price to purchase such mercies as these. As for all the glory of the world, God can give it to men whom he hates, to reprobates: as Luther saith of the whole Turkish empire, It is but a crumb of bread that the master of the house throws to his dogs: but when his mercies in Christ are concerned, they are such as are worth the blood of his Son, which alone could purchase them.

Turcicum imperium, quantum quantum est, mica est quam paterfamilias canibus projicit. Luth.

6. They are such mercies as God designedly bestows, that he may declare to all eternity, before angels and all his saints, to what a height of excellency and glory these infinite mercies are able to raise a poor creature. These must needs be great.

7. Yea, they must be an object for angels and saints to wonder at, and adore and magnify the name of God everlastingly.

What shall I say more in naming the fruits of these mercies? Such mercies as, whereas before sin made thee the object of God's hatred, it now makes thee an object of his pity; God takes occasion from thy sin to display his mercy. Take heed of abusing it, it is children's bread; let us not sin that grace may abound, but rather, seeing thy sin cannot overcome God's goodness, let God's goodness overcome thy sin. Let us learn also to wonder at these riches of mercy in Christ, and to exercise much faith about them. Certainly we would thrive in godliness much more if we exercised faith in the bowels of God in Christ. Those fruits, like your apricots and May cherries, that grow up by a wall and enjoy the warm beams of the sun, are sooner ripe, and have more sweetness, than those which grow in shady places; your grass that is shaded by the trees in orchards, is sour: so the fruit which Christians bring forth under discouragements and despairing thoughts, is very sour; some things they do, for conscience compels them to duties, but, alas, it is sour fruit; though it be better to do what conscience requires than not, yet to do it merely because conscience compels, is but as sour grass. But when a Christian can by faith set himself before the sunshine of these mercies of God in Christ, and continually live in the midst of the beams of that grace, he grows ripe sooner, and his fruit is sweeter.

You may easily know whether the Sun of righteousness shines on you. Does your fruit grow ripe? and is it sweet? Those who talk of mercy, and of Christ, and have his name in their mouths, but bring forth sour and crabbed fruit, are not in the Sun; they are blind, and cannot discern it; and are but in a light of their own fancy, and in a heat of their own making.

In Eph. iii. 18, 19, the apostle prays that the Ephesians "may be able to comprehend with all saints, what is the breadth, and length, and depth, and height" of the riches of God in Christ. Mark, the philosophers tell us of only three dimensions, but here are four; and what is the fruit of this? "To know the love of Christ, which passeth knowledge, that ye might be filled with all the fulness of God." Here is the effect of it; when we know the breadth, and length, and depth, and height of God's love, and have that knowledge by the Spirit of God, that passeth all natural knowledge, then we are filled with all the fulness of God. Here now is a glorious Christian; a Christian filled with all the fulness of God. Would you be so? Learn then to exercise faith much about the infinite riches of the mercy of God in Christ, this will fill you with all the fulness of God. You complain of barrenness and emptiness in your hearts and lives, it is because you give such little heed to this.

God betroths his church to himself in mercies, in bowels. Let us learn, when we are in any strait, to plead with God for bowels of mercy. Isa. lxiii. 15, "Look down from heaven, and behold from the habitation of thy holiness and of thy glory: where is thy zeal and thy strength, the sounding of thy bowels, and of thy mercies toward me? are they restrained?" Lord, hast thou not said that thou wilt betroth thy church unto thyself in bowels? Where is "the sounding of thy bowels?" Lord, let us have these bowels of thine in which thou hast betrothed us through Christ.

Oh what confusion will there be one day to those who

shall miss these mercies of God, in which the Lord has betrothed himself unto his church! What! will you content yourselves now with crumbs which God casts to dogs, with the fruits of his general bounty and patience, when you hear of such glorious mercies in Jesus Christ? These things should raise our hearts, so that we should protest as Luther did: I protest, saith he, God shall not put me off with these things of the world, with my portion here. O no, the Lord has showed me greater riches, and though I be unworthy of any, yet, as I know his mercy is free, why then should not I have my portion in these glorious things?

Valde protestatus sum me nolle sic satiari ab eo. Luth.

Come in, then, come in, O sinful soul, be in love with Jesus Christ and the ways of godliness; know that all these mercies are tendered to thy soul this day, to break thy heart, even that hard heart of thine; and they are as free for thee as for any. There is nothing more pleasing to God, than for thee to be taken with the glory of the riches of his mercy. Thou canst perform no duty so acceptable to God as this, to have thy heart broken on the consideration of his bowels, to have thy bowels yearn again, and to come in and close with this infinitely rich and glorious grace. Which if thou dost, know that, the first moment thou art united to Christ, thou dost launch into the infinite ocean of mercy, dost breathe in the element of mercy, and live on nothing but mercy.

Is it so? Then know God expects a merciful disposition from thee too. God betroths thee in righteousness, and puts righteousness into thee; in judgment, and gives thee judgment too; in loving-kindness, and makes thee loving and kind likewise; and in mercies, and puts mercies into thee.

First, toward himself. Can we be merciful to God? What good can we do to God? God expects you should have bowels toward him. How? Thus. Dost thou see the name of this blessed God thy husband dishonoured in the world? Oh, thy bowels should yearn. What! does God look upon thee in thy blood, in thy misery, and do his bowels yearn toward thee? Canst thou look on God in his dishonour, and his cause trampled under foot, and do not thy bowels yearn toward him? It should move thy soul to see this blessed God so much dishonoured in the world as he is, to see that there are so few that love and fear him, who is thy God and has done thee so much good. Is there any good cause in which the name of God may be honoured? Thy bowels should forthwith work toward it. "My beloved put his hand by the hole of the door, and my bowels were moved for him," Cant. v. 4. When Christ but began to open the door, but put in his hand, my bowels were moved, saith the church, and I could never be at rest till I had inquired after, yea, and found my beloved. Is there any beginning amongst us to let Christ in his government into the kingdom? Do we feel him putting his hand in at the door? certainly, if skilled in his way, we may feel him. Oh that our bowels then would yearn, and cause our hearts to flow out to the bountifulness of the Lord, and join with Christ in this blessed work which he is commencing.

Our bowels must be toward the saints also. It is extremely against the Spirit of Christ, for a Christian to be hard-hearted toward his brethren. Christ expects bowels; and as you would account it a grievous misery to have your bowels diseased, know it is a greater evil to have your hearts unmerciful, than to have a disease in your bowels: as the Scripture phrase is, Amos i. 11, "He cast off all pity, and his anger did tear perpetually," so it is in your English Bibles; but the words in the original are, "and corrupted his bowels;" their bowels were corrupted when they were not pitiful toward their brethren in misery. The condition of Jehoram was grievous, when his bowels came forth by reason of his disease, 2 Chron. xxi. 15. An unmerciful heart is a worse disease.

What are we, and who are we, that God's mercies should be shown to us? and why not our mercies toward our brethren? The Scripture expressly requires mercy in the saints towards one another. "Put on, as the elect of God, bowels of mercy, and kindness," Col. iii. 12. Would you have an argument to yourselves that you are God's elect? put on bowels then. Never was there a period in your own life, or that of your forefathers, in which God called for bowels of mercy, more than now. Do you hear of the miseries of your brethren, their goods spoiled, houses burnt, wives and children ravished, themselves imprisoned, their bodies wounded, and yet have no bowels all this while? what! do you remain hard-hearted? Are you the elect of God? Why, I pray you, what is your flesh more than the flesh of others? What are your comforts more than the comforts of others? Why should you lie soft and safe more than others? Is there any such difference between you and your brethren, that they should be in misery, and you pampered, and scarce feel the very wind blow on you? You will say, It is God that has made the difference. I grant it, and it would not grieve God to make such a difference between you and them, if he saw your bowels yearn towards them. But if God lay such afflictions on your brethren who are better than you, and have done more for him than ever you have, and yet you continue hard-hearted, this will grieve God at the heart. "Whoso hath this world's good, and seeth his brother have need, and shutteth up his bowels of compassion from him, how dwelleth the love of God in him?" 1 John iii. 17. If thou hast bowels and shuttest them up from thy brother, surely thou never knewest what the love of God meant.

Mark what encouraging expressions we have to bounty and liberality towards our brethren, in 2 Cor. ix. 8, "God is able to make all grace abound toward you; that ye, always having all sufficiency in all things, may abound to every good work." There is no such text in all the book of God to encourage the opening our bowels to the administering to the necessities of the saints, for that scripture expressly bears on the point; and if you believe any thing in the word of God, if you have any experience of God's bowels towards you, read over this, and see if it will not open your bowels. "God is able to make all grace abound:" "grace abound," that is something; "all grace," something more; but all kind of grace, that is still more, and that from God's almighty power too; but even that is not enough, mark, "that ye, always having all sufficiency in all things." It were enough, one would think, for God to say, You shall have things needful, nay, you shall have sufficiency in that you have; but no, he saith, You shall have "all things," and "sufficiency in all things," and "all sufficiency in all things." Yea, but I may want before I die? No, you shall have "always all sufficiency in all things." Well, this may make us do something, and you may think, If I do this or that good work, it were enough: no, but you must abound, you must do every good work, and abound in every good work. But I shall exhaust myself if I be so abundant in every good work: no, God is able to make all grace in you to abound towards you, "that you, always having all sufficiency in all things, may abound." You shall never be drawn dry, for you have the bowels of God's mercy. Some asked Alexander, when giving large gifts, What will you keep for yourself? *Spes*, replied he; I will keep hope for myself; I believe that there are still greater things in store for me: what he had he gave away, because he had a spirit that looked after and hoped for great things to come. Certainly, Christians have hope left always; why? because they can have recourse to the bowels of God's mercies.

One thing more, to knit all together; all righteousness, all judgment, all loving-kindness, all mercies, come from God through our union with Christ.

Though God be an infinite ocean of goodness, yet we can expect nothing from God, but through our union with Christ. Man has forfeited the title he had to all the goodness of God, and now the title upon which he is to hold all his good, is the union he has with this husband, with Jesus Christ, by virtue of this marriage. Whenever faith goes to heaven for any good from God, it goes by virtue of this right, and obtains all the blessings it gets from God, by virtue of that conjugal union which the soul has with Jesus Christ.

How blessed then was the time when Christ was first revealed to the church! "Behold king Solomon with the crown wherewith his mother crowned him in the day of his espousals, and in the day of the gladness of his heart," Cant. iii. 11. The things explained regarding our espousals with Christ, must needs make that day the day of the gladness of our hearts: oh how dear should this Christ thy husband be to thee! how happy, when thou shalt have full communion with him! When Isaac met Rebekah, he carried her into his mother's tent: when the Lord Christ shall meet his spouse, he will carry her into his Father's palace. Behold the riches, the glory of my Father whom I told you of, these are all yours in my right eternally.

"I will even betroth thee unto me in faithfulness."

Here is a third betrothing, "I will betroth, I will betroth, I will betroth." Jerome remarks that it is thrice repeated, to note the three several times of God's betrothing himself to his people: 1. When he called Abraham. 2. After they went out of Egypt and were in the wilderness at Mount Sinai. 3. In the time of the gospel. And of this exposition, Calvin saith, it may be accounted witty, but frivolous; and gives himself a better reason for the repetition, which I think agreeable to the mind of the Holy Ghost; Because apostatizing Israel could hardly believe that God would do such a thing as this. What! after the Lord had cast her away, yea, cast her to the beasts, (for so he threatens in the former part of the chapter,) yet now betroth her to himself? this was unlikely.

"I will *even* betroth thee;" so it is in your Bibles: the particle here rendered "even" is the same that is before translated "and;" but because it is repeated the third time the translators thought there was an emphasis in it, and therefore, to express that, employed the word "even."

"In faithfulness," or steadiness: I will betroth thee unto me in a steady way; my goodness toward thee shall be stable and firm: so the word is often used in Scripture: "His hands were steady," Exod. xvii. 12; and Deut. xxviii. 59, I "will make thy plagues of long continuance;" thy plagues stable and constant: in both which places the same word is used that is here translated "faithfulness." Thus 1 Sam. ii. 35, "I will raise me up a faithful priest; and I will build him a sure house:" there the word is of the same root; "a sure house," a firm, steady house. Faithfulness here imports God's stability and steadiness in his covenant with his people. It denotes not so much the perpetuity, for that was before, "I will betroth thee unto me for ever;" but firmness and constancy, as opposed to fickleness and uncertainty.

There is much inconstancy and fickleness in our love one to another; but the love of God to his people is a stable, settled, firm, and constant love. That is the meaning in the first place, though not all. "As the bridegroom rejoiceth over the bride, so shall thy God rejoice over thee," Isa. lxii. 5; that is, the love of Christ, after thousands of years, is still but as the love of a bridegroom on the wedding day; then, ordinarily, love is ardent, and shows itself much. There is no moment of time in which Christ does not rejoice, not only as a husband, but as a bridegroom, over every faithful soul.

Christ's love is steady, because it is pure, without mixture; it is a holy love. Compare Isa. lv. 3, where "the sure mercies of David" are promised, with Acts xiii. 34, where that scripture is quoted, and there it is, the holy things of David. Τὰ ὅσια Δαβίδ. Thus noting, because the love of God is holy, therefore it is sure and stedfast.

Christ's love to his people is from the sweetness of his nature, and therefore it is steady and firm: "with him there is no shadow of change." It is grounded on a sure covenant, and therefore firm. Though indeed the love of Christ may be to us as the sun, not always in the fruits of it, shining out with equal glory; yet still like the sun, steadily pursuing its course, though sometimes obscured by clouds.

The saints should fasten on the love of Christ in the covenant; and though other things be very uncertain, yet they should quiet their hearts in this, that their happiness in the covenant of grace is sure. Perhaps the love of our friends is very fickle and inconstant; they may speak smooth things, and seem as if their hearts were with us; but what sullen moods and fits, at times, come over them! and when you have most need of them, you know not where they are to be found: but the love of Christ is certain and stable. Mark how David comforted himself in the stability of God's covenant love: Though he causes not my house to grow, "yet he hath made with me an everlasting covenant, ordered in all things, and sure: for this is all my salvation, and all my desire," 2 Sam. xxiii. 5; that is, that the covenant is sure and stedfast.

And this faithfulness must be mutual. "I will betroth thee in faithfulness," and make thee faithful too; that is, thou shalt have a firm and stable spirit in thy love to me: though not to be compared with Christ's love to them, yet there is a reciprocal stability in the hearts of the saints, they are not carried up and down, as other men, with every wind of doctrine, with every breath of temptation. "The righteous is an everlasting foundation," Prov. x. 25. "The righteous shall hold on his way," Job xvii. 9. It must needs be so, because the affections of the saints to Christ are holy affections also; and though they have some mixture, and therefore some instability; yet they are holy, and therefore stable.

And they choose Christ in righteousness and in judgment. They have the Divine nature in them; and as that has no shadow of change, they attain to some shadow of its immutability. Isa. xxvi. 3, a godly man is described as one "whose mind is stayed upon God:" he has a stable, not a wandering, fickle spirit, and has fixed himself on God, and can say, "My heart is fixed." The men of the world, because they have not that which can satisfy, run up and down, first after one contentment, then after another, and can settle no where; but the saints find an all-sufficiency in God; there their hearts are satisfied, and there they fix: as a bee, lighting on a flower, and finding but little honey, tries many in succession; but when it comes to one laden with sweets, it settles there. The hearts of the saints find a fulness of good in God, and there stay themselves.

A fickle, wavering, unstable spirit, is exceedingly unbecoming a Christian. As in the body, some, who have flushings of heat, have a very good colour for a while; but when we know that this is but a flush, it is rather a proof of disease, than of a good complexion. A candle burning down in the socket gives some flashes of light now and then; but a candle set up upon a table yields a steady and constant light. Mad people, you know, have their lucid intervals; but you may perceive they are insane, because there is not constancy and evenness in their actions. This stableness, this evenness in a Christian way, is its beauty and glory. Though you be forward sometimes in that which is good; yet, if at other times your hearts be off, there is no beauty in your conversation. Give me a Christian whose ways are even, in whom you find a constancy.

Those who have such fickle, uncertain, inconstant hearts, are never likely to excel; if they have any truth in them, yet they will never be eminent Christians. Gen. xlix. 4, it is said of Reuben, " Unstable as water, thou shalt not excel :" so it may be said of an unstable Christian, He is one of good affections ; at some times very zealous, but being unstable as water he shall not excel.

Constancy in love is exceedingly comely and beautiful between married persons, it adds much to the lustre and comfort of their lives; and to this allusion is here made. For men to seem sometimes very fond, and at other times to be bitter and unkind, like Nabals; or the wife to show much love occasionally, and to be grievous at other times; this takes away the beauty, the comfort of their lives.

But there is more in this faithfulness than stability and firmness: " I will betroth thee in faithfulness ;" I will certainly perform all the good which is befitting a husband, yea, such a husband as I am, to do to my spouse; you may confide in me, I will be faithful to you; not only my love, but my faithfulness, shall bind me to you. My loving-kindness, my merciful disposition, is a great bond, but my faithfulness shall bind me also; I will be content to engage myself to you, to engage all that I am and all that I have to you, that you may certainly confide in me; so as not only to expect it from my love, but to challenge it from my faithfulness. We deny not God's providence to other creatures; but the spouse has a claim on God's care, saith Bernard, which is beyond his providence, grounded on his faithfulness as well as his love. Christ here condescends to his spouse, as a man is willing to give satisfaction to his wife and her friends; and though indeed he would do any thing in the world from love to his wife, yet in regard of her weakness, and to satisfy some friends, he is content to enter into bond, to do whatsoever is fitting. It is good to make all things sure beforehand, say her friends: he presently yields, in order to satisfy their minds, for it is only what he is willing to do without bonds. Thus it is between Christ and his spouse: the love of Christ is enough, sufficient to insure a supply for all wants; but we are weak, and would fain have things made sure; therefore, saith Christ, in condescension to our infirmity, I will even enter into bond, and you may then rest assured I will be faithful: I will bind my faithfulness to you for all the good you desire.

Providentiam creaturis non negamus, curam sponsa sibi vindicat. Bern.

And this faithfulness of Christ respects either the great marriage covenant, there he will be sure to be faithful to his spouse, or all particular promises contained in it. There is the great marriage covenant, about reconciling God, and paying all debts, and satisfying God's justice, and bringing to eternal life; but there are many under-promises, and Christ will be faithful in them all. In Psal. xxv. 10, you have a promise worth a kingdom, " All the paths of the Lord are mercy and truth ;" not only mercy, but mercy and truth, mercy engaged. Wicked men may have mercy from God, from the general bounty and goodness and merciful disposition of God; but what the saints have is from truth, as well as from mercy, it is theirs by covenant.

God urges much that the hearts of his saints should confide in him. He accounts not himself honoured without it: therefore mark how Christ suits himself to our weakness, that we may confide in his faithfulness. What is it (saith he) that you poor creatures do one to another, when you would make things sure between you? We answer thus, Lord, we engage ourselves by promise. I will do so, saith Christ, you shall have my faithful promise. Acts ii. 39, Peter invites to baptism on this ground, because " the promise is unto you, and to your children, and to all that are afar off, even as many as the Lord our God shall call." In the first clause he addresses the Jews, in the other the Gentiles. As if he should say, Come in and receive baptism, for to you and to your children the promise is made; to you that are Jews and to your children, and to the Gentiles and their children likewise, they have the same promise as you, and come under the same covenant for the main. And this promise in which Christ has engaged himself, is no other than a draught of that which was from all eternity, and therefore is so much the more sure. Tit. i. 2, the gospel is called a promise before the world began. All promises in Scripture are but a draught of that grand promise which God the Father made before time to his Son. As if Christ should say, Will you have an engagement by promise? This is past long ago, my Father has engaged himself to me from all eternity, and if you have any promise now, it is but a draught of the first copy of that great promise which my Father has made me from all eternity.

What do you more when you would make things sure one to another? We answer, We not only make a verbal, but a written promise. God has therefore given us his Scripture, and the chief thing in it is the promise, God has set to it his hand. Hence, Luther saith, The whole Scripture especially aims at this, that we should not doubt, but believe, confide, and hope that God is merciful, kind, and patient.

Here you have my promise and my hand, is there any thing else you are wont to do, to make things sure? We answer, Lord, we take witnesses. I will do so too, saith God. When we would make things sure indeed, we sometimes take not only two, but three, or four, or more witnesses. You shall have witnesses, saith God, as many as you will, witnesses of all kinds, witnesses in heaven, and witnesses in earth. In heaven, " the Father, the Word, and the Holy Ghost," witnesses authentical, of credit sufficient, the three persons in the Trinity. On earth, " the spirit, the water, and the blood," 1 John v. 7, 8.

What do you more? Lord, we set to our seals likewise. You shall have that too, saith God, you shall have seals of all kinds; you shall have the broad seal of heaven, the sacraments, the seals of the covenant; and you shall have my privy seal, I will take my ring off my finger, I will give you even the seal the Spirit; show but this seal, it will carry with it sufficient authority.

Is there any thing remaining? Yes, we answer, there is one thing more, we take an oath. I will do that too, saith God, that you may confide in my faithfulness: " God, willing more abundantly to show unto the heirs of promise the immutability of his counsel, confirmed it by an oath," Heb. vi. 17. As if he should say, There is no need of an oath, but I will abound toward you, because I would have you trust me, and confide in me thoroughly. And mark, this is for the sake of the heirs of promise, God would never have done this for other men; it is for your sakes only, because of your weakness he confirms all with an oath. And if we would have things sure, we will not have the oath of such as are of no great credit. Mark, therefore it is God that swears, and that by the greatest oath; " because he could swear by no greater, he sware by himself," Heb. vi. 13.

Is there any thing more, saith God, that you are wont to do amongst yourselves, to make things sure? Yes, Lord, we are accustomed to take a pledge. You shall have that too, saith he, I will give you a pledge, and such a one that if you never had any thing more you would be happy. What is that? 2 Cor. i. 22, "Who hath also sealed us, and given the earnest of the Spirit in our hearts." I will send my Spirit to be an earnest in your hearts of all the good that I intend to do for you everlastingly.

Is there any thing else you would require of me to confide in me? Yes, if God would do some great and notable work, as a beginning and engagement of that which is to come after, this is yet more than an earnest. When some special thing is done as an opening to our expectations, then we have not merely a promise under hand and seal, an oath and a pledge; but the matter is actually begun, and so begun, that the difficulty is over. Those who live under the gospel see the greatest part of our salvation already accomplished. God made a promise of sending his Son into the world; now the performing of that promise, that God-man should come into the world to be made a curse for sin, is the greatest work of all eternity, and if God could have failed in any thing, it would have been in that. It is not so much for God to deliver us in this world, nor to bring us to heaven, as it is to send his Son into the world to be made a curse for us. Now when God has done so great a work, and been faithful in that great promise, he has taught us for ever to trust in him, to believe his faithfulness in accomplishing the rest. If a man who owes five thousand pounds, pays you four thousand nine hundred of it, you think surely he will never break for one hundred, I may trust him for the rest, seeing he has dealt so faithfully with me in the great sum. God has paid the four thousand nine hundred, and much more; in comparison of what God has done for us, take all the glory of heaven, and we have not one hundred of the five thousand left behind, therefore surely we may well confide in him for the payment of the rest.

It is true, God is faithful; but is God able? This is seldom an objection, at least an explicit objection in the *mouths* of people, but surely an implicit one in the *hearts* of many; that appears by the cautions God gives to remove it. "Commit the keeping of your souls to him in well-doing, as unto a faithful Creator," 1 Pet. iv. 19: as if he had not said enough in declaring he is faithful, he adds, "faithful Creator;" as if he should say, If there be no means to help you, I will create means, I will put forth my almighty power to aid you, and you shall have help. "He shall confirm the covenant," Dan. ix. 27; the word translated "confirm," הגביר is of the same root with that for "mighty one," in Gen. x. 8. God will come forth as a giant, as a mighty man, to perform the covenant he has made with his people; if there be any thing in the world wherein God will stir up his infinite power, the excellency of his might, and the glory of his right hand, it will be in confirming his covenant to his saints. "Trust ye in the Lord for ever: for in the Lord Jehovah is everlasting strength." "Thy Maker is thine husband; the Lord of hosts is his name; The God of the whole earth shall he be called," Isa. xxvi. 4; liv. 5.

Seeing God is so faithful, let not us be faithless. But things go very cross, and how shall we believe, our faith wavers? The true, genuine love of the saints is such as will love God for himself alone, without gifts; so genuine faith is to believe in God without experiences, yea, though things seem against us. That is but a poor love that loves God only for that which we receive from him for the present; and that but a weak faith which trusts God only for things that are seen. Do things go cross? they are corrections, and may come from faithfulness, as well as any thing the church enjoys: Psal. cxix. 75, "I know, O Lord, that thy judgments are right, and that thou in faithfulness hast afflicted me." As God comes down and suits himself to you as his poor creatures; so you should labour to raise your hearts to him, and to believe in him as a great God. God deals with you as with weak creatures, you should deal with him as with an infinite God. You must give God leave to do his work in his own way. The object of our confidence in God is, that the thing *will* be done; not *how*, or *when*, but that God will eventually complete his work. Shall our weakness be so much regarded as that things must not work so as to evince God's power? Certainly, it is too much for us to expect such consideration for our weakness. One would think it enough for God to express himself so to you that you *may* believe; would you have God condescend to reveal himself, so that he should not have the glory of his work, nor you the glory of your faith? this were too much. Though we be bound to deny ourselves much because of the weakness of our brethren, must God deny his glory because of our weakness? We burden God too much with our infirmities. It is for God's glory things happen as they do: Lazarus was dead, and dead so long, that the work of God might appear.

But I find not things turn out as I had hoped; I think I have believed, and sometimes in prayer I have thought my heart closed with the promises of God, but yet things have not answered my expectations.

It may be God calls for new acts of thy believing, and a renewing of thy faith in his faithfulness. You must know, the continual actings of faith draw out the continual actings of the power of God. I will give you, in proof, one remarkable text; perhaps you may have read and heard it often, but not perceived its force; "Oh how great is thy goodness, which thou hast laid up for them that fear thee!" but mark what follows, "which thou hast wrought for them that trust in thee," Psal. xxxi. 19. "Great is thy goodness, which thou hast laid up." God's goodness is wonderfully great for them that fear him; but how? it is "laid up" for them; but now mark, "for them that trust in thee."

All the goodness that is in God, is for them that fear him; but it is not fearing God that will bring it to work. Do you fear God? God has laid up abundance of goodness in a treasury for you, but you must not expect this will work for you, unless you trust in him; your faith must bring it forth into action, and that "before the sons of men. Thou shalt hide them in the secret of thy presence from the pride of man." Would you be hid in the secret of God's presence from the pride of men? you must not only fear God, but trust in his faithfulness. Matt. xiii. 58, Christ "did not many mighty works there because of their unbelief." And Mark vi. 5, "He could there do no mighty work." One says he did not, and the other says he could not. When we have a promise, let us put forth faith, to get the goodness of God to work. A remarkable example of a believing heart laying hold on a promise for God's faithfulness to work out, occurs in 1 Chron. xvii. In the former part of the chapter God promised David to establish his house, to build him a sure house. Well, as soon as David had received this, mark how he works on God's word; as if he had said, Seeing I have got his word, I will hold him to it, he shall not go from it. "Therefore now, Lord, let the thing thou hast spoken concerning thy servant and concerning his house be established for ever, and do as thou hast said," ver. 23: thou hast spoken it, do as thou hast said. And ver. 24, "Let it be even established;" I expect and rely on it, seeing thou hast been pleased in such a gracious way to promise it to me; "let it even be established, that thy name may be magnified for ever." I will plead thy name in it, if there be one thing more than another to be pleaded, I will plead it before thee. But is not this enough? Ver. 25, "For thou, O my God, hast told thy servant that thou wilt build him an house: therefore thy servant hath found in his heart to pray before thee."

He had said before that God had spoken it; here he goes over it again, as magnifying God's word; Thou hast told me, and I pray for nothing but what thou hast told me. Nay, David encroaches yet still more upon God: ver. 26, "Now, Lord, thou art God, and hast promised this goodness unto thy servant." I have not to deal with a man that will be fickle and inconstant, wavering and unfaithful; but thou art God, and I will trust in thee as God; thou art God, and thou hast promised this goodness; it is thine own goodness, now therefore do it. See how he urges God's promise; and mark what admirable effects followed, chap. xviii. After this he prospered: when Hadarezer came against him, he took "a thousand chariots, and seven thousand horsemen, and twenty thousand footmen. And when the Syrians came to help Hadarezer, he slew of them two and twenty thousand men." "After this:" mark the connexion of the chapters; "Now after this," after David had improved the promise, he might have what he would; thus the loving-kindness of God was laid up in a promise, but wrought out by David's faith. It is our misfortune that we do not plead this faithfulness of God; we lose abundance by it, and prove that we have base spirits. It is a great evil between husband and wife, when they cannot confide one in another, but are jealous; how can such live comfortably together? So we are jealous of God, and lose our comfort in him. Jealousy comes often from meanness of spirit and self-guiltiness; because we are of such base hearts ourselves, we are jealous of God. Where much love exists between husband and wife, there cannot be much jealousy; and if there were entire love in the spouse of Christ, there would not be jealousy. You have a suitable passage in John v. 40, "Ye will not come to me that ye might have life;" you will not believe in me, that is the meaning: then ver. 42, "I know you, that ye have not the love of God in you." Is there any thing in the world more grievous to a husband than that the wife should be jealous of him? think of it; the same grief it is to the Spirit of Jesus Christ, that thou shouldst be jealous of him, and not confide in his faithfulness.

Surely, if we did trust in God's faithfulness we should not compound with him as we do, but improve his promise to the uttermost. As long as you merchants confide in your debtors, you will not compound with them for less than your debt; if you should go to one that owes you money, and say, I pray, sir, pay your debt to me, and I shall be content to take ten or fifteen in the hundred, the party would think himself disgraced: What! do you distrust me? do you think I will break? No, I will pay you every penny. The truth is, we, poor wretches, because we have not God's promises immediately fulfilled, would fain compound with God; that is, if he would give us any little present comfort we would be satisfied, rather than wait for that which is to come, though it be infinitely more: this is a great dishonour to God, and an argument of our unfaithfulness. It were an argument of little faith if thou couldst be satisfied, should God give thee ten thousand worlds for the present. Were he to say, What will you have? Would you have your enemies destroyed? Would you have your peace, and your trading in the world, your ease and quietness, assured? Is this all? This is to compound with God for twelvepence in the pound, as it were. No, saith a gracious heart; Lord, thou hast promised me mercy, and I expect it to the full, I will not abate the least farthing. God loves we should stand with him for his promise to the uttermost. No, but I hope God will give me heaven at last, yet I doubt he will forsake me here. This is to compound with God in another way. There are some who, perhaps, will pay eighteen or fifteen shillings in the pound; but it is dishonouring God to abate one shilling: therefore we must not only believe in God for heaven, but for earth, and for safety and comfort, and that in times of greatest trouble. God is well pleased with such kind of holy impudence, as we may say; that is, with our following him for the uttermost, and urging him on his word again and again, to pay what he is engaged for.

Again, had we faith in God we should attempt great things, though we see but little means. Many of you who have but small stocks, yet, if you have rich friends that have given you encouragement, and that you know will be faithful to you, you will trade for great things with your little, because you know you have friends who will stand by you: so, though we have but little strength, if God call us, we should be willing to undertake great things, because God has stock enough, and has engaged himself to stand by us.

"I will betroth thee unto me in faithfulness." As I will be faithful to you, and you shall confide in my faithfulness, so you shall be faithful to me, that I may confide in your faithfulness; as I fulfil all my promises and covenant with you, so you shall make good all your promises and covenant with me. The spouse of Christ is one that the Spirit of Christ can confide in. It is said of the virtuous woman, Prov. xxxi. 11, "The heart of her husband doth safely trust in her." Let him be abroad or at home, in what company soever, yet his heart trusts in her, he can leave all his business, his writing, or any thing that concerns him with such a wife. Where this trust is wanted in the heart of the husband toward the wife, there is want of comfort in their lives: thus God saith of his people, Isa. lxiii. 8, "They are children that will not lie;" I can confide in them, I can employ them on any business that I will, for "they are children that will not lie."

They are faithful to God first in the great covenant, in surrendering themselves to God, as they do at their first closing with Christ. Then every gracious soul enters into solemn covenant with God, and it will be faithful in that covenant. And they will be faithful likewise in all their inferior promises and vows which they make to God, in days of fasting, and thanksgiving, and at other times. As God's promises are God's gifts to us, so should our promises be as gifts to God. "According to his own purpose and grace, which was given us in Christ Jesus, before the world began," 2 Tim. i. 9; not only promised, but given unto us in Christ Jesus.

So in thy conversation thou must be faithful to Christ, not prostitute thyself unto another, but keep thyself for Christ. Indeed, the spouse of Christ may be ravished by open violence, but she will not prostitute herself to any other, she keeps herself only for Christ. Thus the saints are described, Eph. i. 1, "Faithful in Christ Jesus." There is a kind of natural faithfulness, as I may so speak; as in Isa. viii. 2, "I took unto me faithful witnesses:" Calvin saith it is meant of Urijah, that base, temporizing man, who made the altar according to the pattern that Ahaz sent from Damascus; he is said to be faithful, that is, he was a fair, honest dealing man, his word was as good as his bond: so, many civil men will be faithful to their word. But mark here, it is "faithful in Christ Jesus;" not only faithfulness between man and man, for many heathens were so, they would rather die than cheat one another; but this is a higher degree of faithfulness. The saints must be faithful, faithful *to* Christ Jesus, and faithful *in* Christ Jesus. They who are thus faithful, are fit for the service of Christ; Christ has much work to do, they only are fit for it. Rev. xvii. 14, "The Lamb shall overcome;" why? "for he is Lord of lords, and King of kings: and they that are with him, are called, and chosen, and faithful;" not called faithful, but called and faithful; and therefore the Lamb shall overcome. If all who are in the public service of the kingdom, and profess to be with Christ in his cause, were called and faithful, the work would soon be at an end. It is for faithfulness we shall be hereafter rewarded: "Well done, good and faithful servant;" not, Well done, good and rich servant, or servant who had great employment in public works, but, "Well done, good and faithful servant." Every one of us cannot be eminent, every one cannot be employed in public services, but you may every one be faithful: you that are poor servants may be faithful, as well as a magistrate or as a minister: you that are poor labouring men, porters and watermen, the meanest of you may be faithful, as well as the nobles of a kingdom. God regards faithfulness rather than service; he has no need of the services of men, great or small, but he looks upon the faithfulness of their hearts.

And as you must be faithful to God and his cause, so you must be faithful one to another. You who are godly servants, be sure you be faithful to your masters, that there may be no occasion of such scandal as is often used concerning professors; Such a servant must go to sermons, and he is set against ceremonies, &c.; I never had any so faithful, that, if mine eye were off him, he did not cease to work presently. God forbid there should be such scandals given of you. Wives who profess godliness, be sure you be faithful to your husbands; and tradesmen who profess more than ordinary strictness in religion, be you faithful in your dealings. Has Christ married himself unto thee in faithfulness? he expects that his faithfulness to thee should have that reflection upon thy heart as to make thee faithful to others.

I add one note, taken from all together. As if God should say, O Israel, you have dealt unrighteously with me, you have broken your covenant, but I will betroth you to me in righteousness. You have done foolishly in departing from me, but I will betroth you unto me in judgment. You have been unkind to me, but I will betroth you unto me in loving-kindness. It has not pitied your souls to see me dishonoured, but I will betroth myself in bowels of mercy to you. You have been unfaithful to me, but I will even betroth you unto me in faithfulness. The note from thence is this,

Obs. God deals not with those in covenant with him as they deal with him. This remark is of admirable use and comfort. Mark the difference between God's dealing with others and those that are in covenant with him. Let others deal with God in a perverse way, God will deal with them so too. Psal. xviii. 26, "With the froward thou wilt show thyself froward." Will you be froward with God? God will show himself froward with you. Will you be proud with God? In the thing you are proud God will be above you. Will you be subtle, and contriving mischief against God and his truth? God will meet with the wicked, and insnare them in the work of their own hands. Are you resolute in wickedness? God will be as resolute as you, Jer. xliv. 25, 26. But when God deals with his saints in covenant, though they deal frowardly with him, he will deal gently with them: though they deal proudly with him, he deals in a way of condescension with them; though they be unfaithful to him, yet he will be faithful to them. O my brethren, this point has abundance of sweetness in it, take heed of abusing it. Thy sins cannot overcome God's goodness, let God's goodness then overcome thy wickedness.

"And thou shalt know the Lord."

But why does this follow, "In faithfulness; and thou shalt know the Lord."

Thus, upon these two reasons:

First, The church shall know Christ to be the Lord, and this shall be the means to keep his spouse in faithfulness for ever. As if Christ should say, The reason of all your vile departings from me is, you do not know me, you do not see my bounty and glory, or discern the excellency of my worship. Hence you are gone from me, and have been unfaithful to me; but when I betroth you to myself again, you shall know me, you shall see so much beauty and excellency in me and my ordinances that you shall never depart from me.

Obs. Low thoughts of God are the cause of superstitious vanities. Had men high and honourable thoughts of God, they would never think to put him off with such poor bauble-worship as they do. Acts vii. 2, it is said, "The God of glory appeared to Abraham;" that is given as a ground why Abraham forsook his country, his father's house, and his kindred. If we once knew the Lord, and that the God of glory had appeared to us, we should be ready to forsake all for him, and give up ourselves unto him in an everlasting covenant.

Secondly, This is as a fruit of my betrothing myself unto them, a fruit of the covenant. "They shall teach no more every man his neighbour, and every man his brother, saying, Know the Lord: for they shall know me, from the least of them unto the greatest of them, saith the Lord: for I will forgive their iniquity," &c., Jer. xxxi. 34. It is a fruit of the conjugal union betwixt Christ and the soul. When a man and his wife are but suitors, or well-willers, they do not communicate their secrets one to another; but when they are married, they open all their hearts, there is no secret but they will disclose one to another. So saith God, When I am once married to you, I will even open my whole heart to you: "The secret of the Lord is with them that fear him." Those who have but natural knowledge, understand something of the ways of religion. A man in the dark may know where he is; by feeling, he may discover the length and thickness of many things in the house; but when the light of the day comes, he knows what there is in the room after another manner than he did in the dark: this is the difference between knowledge of God in a natural man, and the knowledge of one espoused to Christ. By his natural knowledge he may understand the history of the gospel, and have some general notions of God and of Christ; but when the Sun of righteousness arises, he sees the excellency and glory of God shining in all his attributes, he sees that in Christ which draws his heart unto him in an everlasting covenant. As we read, Cant. vii. 5, Christ "is held in the galleries;" that is, Christ, as soon as he is married to the soul, takes her, as it were, by the hand, and walks in the galleries, and there opens his heart unto her. There is many a sweet turn that a gracious heart has with Christ in his ordinances, wherein Christ opens his whole soul unto it. "All things," saith Christ, "that I have heard of my Father, I have made known unto you," John xv. 15. An admirable text; surely you cannot but know the Lord then. Here is the fruit of our union with Christ. Oh that our hearts were inflamed with desire after further conjugal communion with him! According to the capacity of the soul, so Christ makes known to it what he has heard of the Father. Certainly Christ has heard great things of the Father; he is the wisdom of the Father; he has been with the Father from all eternity; and the Father loves him, he will tell him all the glorious things he has in his heart, and Christ will hide none of those things from his saints! This is the privilege of a saint. Who would not be godly, by which he shall come to know the mind of the Father, according to what Christ knows of it?

Yea, and Christ makes God known to the saints in another way than others know him. גליתה את־און 2 Sam. vii. 27, "Thou, O Lord of hosts, God of Israel, hast revealed to thy servant:" the Hebrew reads, Lord, thou hast revealed this to the ear of thy servant. I wonder how the words "to the ear" come to be left out in your books, in which the emphasis lies. When God makes known himself to his people he reveals things to their ear, as we to a friend who is intimate with us. Many a secret Jesus Christ speaks in the ears of his saints, with which others are never made acquainted. 2 Cor. iv. 6, "God, who commanded the light to shine out of darkness, hath shined in our hearts, to give the light of the knowledge of the glory of God in the face of Jesus Christ." It would require time for fully opening the gradations of this scripture; here is "knowledge," and "the knowledge of the glory of God," and "the light of the knowledge of the glory of God; and "shining," and "shining into our hearts," and "into our hearts in the face of Jesus Christ." Surely, then, they shall know the Lord, and they shall know him in a very spiritual way. The light of the saints is a light three stories high. First, They have the light of reason, which other men have. Secondly, They have the light of common gifts, which other men have too, and that is a story higher than the other. Thirdly, They have the light of a sanctifying Spirit, that is a third loft; and they shall come to a fourth story, and that is the light of glory. The light that other men have, is but as the light which you have in a lower room, in warehouses, which in some is so little that you use a candle at noon-day; others have somewhat more light, they have common gifts, which is like the light in the next story, somewhat more clear; but the light of the saints is higher than all these, they know God as their God. Great is the excellency of this knowledge; the soul has blessed satisfaction in it: "Show us the Father, and it sufficeth us." The sanctification of the heart by the presence of the beams of the glory of God, transforming it into the same image, is the very beginning of eternal life. What superior means have we to know God than the heathens had! The Roman histories describe the poor and mean ways those wise men took to know God; as thus, they would look into the entrails of beasts, thereby to find out the minds of their gods; they would observe how the beasts came to the slaughter, whether willingly or unwillingly; they would observe the fire of their sacrifices, whether the flame ascended right or not: thus they attempted to ascertain the mind of their gods. What poor ways are these! We have Jesus Christ, God blessed for ever, the eternal Son of the Father, who is come from the bosom of the Father, to make known to us the mind of God, his and our Father. We know the truth as it is in Jesus, Eph. iv. 21, not only as it is in the works of nature. Some know much of God in the works of creation and providence, and we may learn much of God in those great things which the Lord has lately done amongst us; but to know the truth as it is in Jesus, to know God in Christ, is another kind of knowledge than to know God in the way of his works. Here we see the truth really, when we see it in Christ Jesus. Certainly, then, no one united to Christ in a conjugal union can be an ignorant sot, for Christ engages himself in his faithfulness, upon this marriage of a soul with himself, to reveal himself and the Father unto it. John viii. 54, "Of whom ye say he is your God;" but mark the next words, "yet ye have not known him." A likely matter, that he should be your God, and you not know him! a likely matter, that Christ should be your Saviour, and you not know him, seeing he has engaged himself in his faithfulness, that if you be married to him you shall know him and his Father!

Ver. 21—23. *And it shall come to pass in that day, I will hear, saith the Lord, I will hear the heavens, and they shall hear the earth; and the earth shall hear the corn, and the wine, and the oil; and they shall hear Jezreel. And I will sow her unto me in the earth; and I will have mercy upon her that had not obtained mercy; and I will say to them which were not my people, Thou art my people; and they shall say, Thou art my God.*

Now, after the assurance of mercy in the covenant, come temporal promises, promises of corn, and wine, and oil: God would hereby teach us this lesson, that all our outward things (at least the sweetness and comfort of them) depend on the covenant in Christ.

"I will hear:" the word may be rendered, I will answer; God will so hear that he will answer. אענה Many times a poor man cries to the rich, and he hears him, but he will not answer; but, saith God, I will hear so that I will answer. This is a most elegant expression: "I will hear the heavens, and they shall hear the earth; and the earth shall hear the corn, and the wine, and the oil; and they shall hear Jezreel." *Mira orationis sublimitas*, A wonderful sublimity of speech, saith one expositor; *Hyperbolica metaphora*, A hyperbolical metaphor, saith another; *Pulcherrima prosopopœia*, A most beautiful and delightful prosopopœia, saith another; these creatures being addressed as if they understood what they did. As if the Lord should say thus, My people, you have indeed, through your sins, been brought into great straits, you have wanted corn, and wine, and oil, and have been scattered in your banishment; but when I shall betroth myself to you, and enter into a covenant with you, then, when you cry, Oh that we might have these outward comforts! immediately the corn, and the wine, and the oil, as if they heard your complaints, shall say, O Lord, we would help Jezreel, and satisfy these thy servants: the corn shall cry to the earth, O earth, let me come into your bowels, I will rot there that so I may bring forth fruit for this people: the vines and the olive shall desire the earth to receive them, to impart juice and nourishment to them, that they may refresh these reconciled ones to God: the earth shall say, Oh that I might receive the corn, and wine, and oil, that I may be fruitful in my kind; but, ye heavens, I can do nothing except I have your influences and the warm beams of the sun to make me fructify; come, therefore, and assist me, that I may bear fruit for Jezreel: and the heavens shall cry, Lord, we would fain help the earth, that the earth may help the corn, and wine, and oil, that they may supply Jezreel; but we can do nothing without thy hand; therefore, hear us, and suffer us to rain upon the earth, that it may become fruitful. Thus the creatures are introduced, pleading that they might help Jezreel. Hence

Obs. 1. Our condition in this world is such, that although reconciled to God, yet, while here, we must be beholden to the corn and wine, to the earth and heavens, and cannot do without them.

Obs. 2. When we are reconciled to God, then the creatures will be serviceable to us, yea, they will be desirous to do us good, they will cry for it. Let us take heed of provoking God, the creatures then will be against us. Gordius, a martyr, gave this answer to those who urged him to deny the truth. If I deny it, the sun, and moon, and stars will deny me light. If we serve God, the creatures will account it their happiness to serve us.

Obs. 3. God is wont to work good for his people by second causes. He sends not things immediately from heaven, but the heavens hear the earth, and the earth hears the corn and the wine. We must look to second causes, but take heed of resting on them. It has been God's work amongst us of late, by detecting plots and giving successes, to manifest himself very strangely, when the means have been very weak; nay, indeed, God has made as much use of men's weakness, as of their strength; but let not us therefore be slack in the use of means, but do the best we can. Though God sometimes works beyond means, and even contrary to them, yet, ordinarily, he uses second causes, not only to work *ad præsentiam*, as Biel the schoolman, and others say, that is, conjointly with the creature; for they assert that there is no efficacy at all in them to produce results; but the truth is, God does make use of second causes, so that they are efficient to accomplish that which he purposes.

Obs. 4. There is a concatenation in second causes, and not merely a use; every one in their order ministers to the other; the heavens hear the earth, and the earth hears the corn. If we could discern the comely order of the creatures, we should see them all linked together by a golden chain: as in the joints of the body, one bone supplies another, one part is hollow to receive another; so in nature, one thing supplies and aids another. As in our salvation there is a golden chain, Rom. viii., so in the creatures there is a golden chain of beauteous order and mutual suppliance.

Obs. 5. Nothing can be done by any link of the chain of second causes, but by God's being at the uppermost link. Jezreel must cry to the corn, and wine, and oil, and they must cry to the earth, and the earth must cry to the heavens, he must be the highest cause.

Obs. 6. It is most comely, and a great blessing, when the right order and chain of second causes hold; as in nature, so in any society, when all preserve their due subordination; as when the tradesman works in his way, the magistrate in his, the minister in his, every one in his place. But when they are out of order, it is a great misery to a city or kingdom. As once among the Athenians, Themistocles said of his son, a bold youth, This boy can do more than any man in all Greece. Why? Because, the Athenians command the Grecians, I command the Athenians, my wife commands me, and my son commands my wife: here was the concatenation of that government. God deliver all societies from such a concatenation, that the beginning of any public work, I mean the lower link of the chain, should be in an ungodly man, and he should command one, and that one another, and so on in succession. Wheresoever this occurs, it is a fearful judgment.

Obs. 7. God, the giver of all plenty, accounts it his glory to give rain. In Jer. v. 24, God wonders that men will not fear him because of that; "Neither say they in their heart, Let us now fear the Lord our God, that giveth rain." As if he should say, It is strange in men; what! will not they say in their hearts, Let us fear God, seeing he gives us rain? Thus God glories in this great work of hearing the heavens, and the heavens the earth. The heavens will be as brass over us, and the earth as iron, unless God hear them, and send rain. Therefore let God be acknowledged in that rain which we have had of late: the creatures wanted grass, and the grass cried to the heavens, and the heavens cried unto God, and God has heard the heavens, and sent down rain; and so we see the earth has been refreshed, and abundance of good has come to us by these showers. Give God the glory of this.

Obs. 8. All plenty is given for the sake of the saints. How? God hears the heavens, and the heavens hear the earth, and the earth hears the corn, and the wine, and the oil, and they hear Jezreel. It is all for Jezreel's sake. Were it not for the saints, the earth would soon come to confusion; they are "a blessing in the midst of the land," Isa. xix. 24.

Obs. 9. If the creatures work so graciously for us, how should we then work for God, and for one another! What! shall the creatures cry one to another, and hear one another for our good, and shall God cry to us, and we not hear God? The senseless corn cries to the earth, O earth, help me, that I may help Jezreel; and the earth cries to the heavens, O heavens, send down your influences; and the heavens say, We will hear, and the earth saith, I will hear: shall the earth hear, and the heavens hear for our good, and shall not we hear when God cries for help? God often cries to you to help in his cause, and wilt not thou hear, to work for him? O vile creature, how unreasonable are thy ways before the Lord!

Obs. 10. How should we hear the cries of the poor! When we are in want, the corn cries to the earth, and the earth cries to the heavens, and the heavens cry to God for us. When the poor, I mean God's poor, whom God's hand has made poor, cry, will you not hear? Will you be more hard-hearted than the earth and the heavens are? seeing they hear you, do you hear the cry of your poor brethren.

Obs. 11. If God will hear the creatures when they cry for us, how much more will he hear Jesus Christ when he cries for us! It is a part of our happiness, that we have all the creatures crying to God for our good; but the summit of our bliss is this, that we have Jesus Christ, the Mediator of the new covenant, making intercession at the right hand of God continually for us.

Obs. 12. God's mercies go on to perfection, when they work for the saints; the corn begins to cry to the earth, that stays not there, but the earth goes on and cries to the heavens, and the heavens to God. God's mercies to his saints never cease till the thing is perfected.

"And I will sow her unto me in the earth."

What great mercy is this for God to grant plenty, if he destroy his people? Our country is plentiful, but if God should consume us out of the land, what good would our plenty do us? Therefore saith God, "I will sow her unto me in the earth." Indeed, she is now a poor, contemptible people, and there are but few of them remaining on the earth; but I will make them a seed, and a seed that the Lord has blessed.

"I will sow her." Here the Lord alludes to the name Jezreel, which signifies the seed of the Lord. It was used in the first chapter as a reproach; and in the latter end of the same in a way of mercy. I spoke of it there, therefore I shall now say only this, God uses the word here, to remind her of what she deserved; as if he should say, Though thou art a Jezreel, and deservest to be scattered, yet, out of free grace, I will be merciful to thee, I will sow thee; there shall come a blessing upon thee, and though scattered in the earth, yet in all places thou shalt be as seed from whence my church shall spring. Hence we may

Obs. 1. God's people are the seed of the earth. But of that I have spoken before, in the latter end of the first chapter, and shall now only add an observation of Ribera. The seed, saith he, lies under the clods, and at length fructifies: so should the saints be content to lie under the clods, and though, because of their afflicted condition, they may seem as dead, yea, rotten, yet shall they afterwards fructify and be glorious. Before the time of the church's glory, times of great calamity and distress came, which this rotting of the seed before fructification shadows forth.

Obs. 2. Every godly man should so live, as, either in life or death, to be as a seed from whence many may spring; he should be a means that many should be begotten to God. In the history of the church, it is recorded of Cecilia, a poor virgin, that by her gracious behaviour in her martyrdom, she was the means of converting four hundred to Christ. As in the Indies, one grain yields many hundreds; so we should labour to convert as many as we can, that some that live after may continue to bear up the name of Christ, and the profession of his truth. Especially be careful of your children, leave them as seed to hold up the name of God in your family when you are dead and gone.

Obs. 3. The saints are sown unto Christ, they are seed for Christ, therefore all their fruit must be consecrated to Christ. "I will sow her unto me." Christ must have all the fruit we bear: who should have the fruit, but he that sows it? Therefore it is said, Cant.

vii. 13, "At our gates are all manner of pleasant fruits, new and old, which I have laid up for thee, O my beloved." Are we able to bear any fruit? We must not sow to ourselves, not to the flesh, for then we shall reap corruption; but lay it all up for Christ Jesus, for it is he that soweth us unto himself.

"And I will show mercy upon her that had not obtained mercy."

Many things about God's showing mercy after rejection have been spoken of in the first chapter; and I shall at present only

Obs. 1. There are none so rejected that they can conclude that they shall never have mercy, those that have committed the sin against the Holy Ghost excepted. Though Israel "had not obtained mercy," though they were cast out, yea, cast out to the beasts to be devoured, yet, saith God, I will show mercy upon her.

Obs. 2. Children of wicked parents may at length obtain mercy from God. Though Israel be cast off, yet her children shall have mercy: a comfort to us in regard of the idolatry of our forefathers, yea, a comfort in regard of the children to come. Our forefathers have broken the covenant, why may not we obtain mercy? But suppose we should be the generation of God's wrath, and not obtain mercy, yet we may hope that our posterity shall.

Obs. 3. Mercy after it is thought to be past, if then it come, oh it is sweet mercy indeed! when she seemed to be utterly rejected, then to have mercy shown, this was sweet.

Obs. 4. Mercy is the cause of all the good the saints receive. Psal. lvii. 3, "He shall send from heaven," saith David. David was in the cave, in a poor condition, hunted for his life, persecuted by Saul; I see little help from earth, therefore, saith he, "He shall send from heaven." What! shall God send angels from heaven to deliver thee, David? No, but mark what follows, "God shall send forth his mercy and his truth:" as if he should say, Lord, though I have no help in earth, though I see no angels from heaven to aid me, yet let me have thy mercy and truth, and that suffices. It satisfies a gracious heart if he may have God's mercy and his truth, that is, God's mercy revealed in a promise.

Obs. 5. God has a special day of mercy for his people, for his churches. "I will have mercy upon her that had not obtained mercy." Let us cry to God to hasten this day; let us open before him the miseries of our own kingdom, and of Ireland: Oh when shall this day come, that thou wilt show to thy people the mercy of which thou hast told us! Oh that that day may hasten! Come, Lord Jesus, come quickly.

"And I will say to them which were not my people, Thou art my people."

This is what we had in the first chapter, with only some slight difference; there it is, "In the place where it was said, Ye are not my people." And when I explained that place, I showed you, both out of the Romans and out of Peter, how the apostles make use, both of the expression in the first chapter and this in the second, and shall here only

Obs. 1. God takes a special interest in his people; they are his people, they are called his "peculiar people," Tit. ii. 14. The word has this emphasis in it, God looks upon all other things as accidents in comparison, and his substance is his people; they are his very portion, as Deut. xxxiii. 29; Exod. xix. 5; they are his peculiar treasure above all people in the world; and Isa. xix. 25, "Assyria the work of my hands, and Israel mine inheritance:" I have made all people, but Israel is mine inheritance. This is the happiness of the saints, therefore they are not as other people are; Numb. xxiii. 9, "This people shall dwell alone, and shall not be reckoned among the nations." This is a great ground of prayer, Lord, leave us not, we are thy people, called by thy name, we have an interest in thee.

λαον περιούσιον.

Obs. 2. Our being God's people is an argument so to walk that he may not be dishonoured by us. If those in a man's family walk disorderly, it is a dishonour to the master. It is no dishonour to him for a stranger, or one who has but little connexion with him, to do so; and it is not so much dishonour to God for the wicked to walk disorderly, as for the saints, because of their nearness to him: and, besides, their light is (as I told you) three stories high, and if they sin, they sin against a greater light than others, their sin is greater than the sin of the wicked in that respect.

Obs. 3. It is a great mercy for God to make it known to the world, that his people *are* his people. "I will say to them which were not my people, Thou art my people." The world will not believe it, they think they are a poor, contemptible people; but there shall come a day in which I will make it known that they are mine: and amongst other things by which God will make all the world to know that his people are his, this is one, by setting up the beauty of his ordinances amongst them. Ezek. xxxvii. 27, "My tabernacle also shall be with them: yea, I will be their God, and they shall be my people; and the heathen shall know that I the Lord do sanctify Israel, when my sanctuary shall be in the midst of them for evermore." Thus they shall know, saith God, that they are my people, and that I am their God, when I have set my sanctuary in the midst of them for ever. Were the ordinances of God set up in their purity amongst us in England, were reformation perfected, and did the saints walk humbly and peaceably as they should, the whole world would be convinced that these are indeed the people of the Lord, and that God is amongst them.

"And they shall say, Thou art my God."

Obs. 1. God must begin with us; we cannot begin and say, "Lord, thou art my God;" but God must first say, "You are my people." There are a great many who say God is their God; but God never said they were his people. John i. 12, it is said of those who believed in Christ, that God "gave them" ἐξουσίαν, "*power* to become the sons of God;" the word signifies authority, that they might with authority acknowledge themselves to be the sons of God, and call God Father; they had the broad seal for it. Will you call God, Father? where is your ἐξουσία, your authority? If God call you children, if he say, You are my people; you may give the echo to God's mercy, and say, Thou art our Father, thou art our God.

Obs. 2. When God speaks mercy to us, we must answer accordingly. Does God say, You are my people? we must answer, Lord, thou art our God. This is a great fault amongst Christians; God manifests himself to many a gracious heart in abundance of love and mercy, and they return an answer to God of despondency and discouragement. God's ways toward thee speak thus, "Thou art one of my people;" but thy heart works as if God were none of thy God. Has not God done much for thee? thou thinkest all that thou dost is hypocritical, whereas the truth is, it is the fruit of his love and kindness to thee. He speaks aloud in what he has done for thee, that thou art one of his people; and yet thy heart thinks that he is thine enemy, that he hates thee, and will cast thee off at last. The ways of God are full of mercy to thee, and he has set his stamp on thee, and, by his dealings of love, tells thee that thou belongest unto him. O unbelieving soul, answer, Lord, thou art my God! and lay aside these discouraging and despairing thoughts of thine! Oh that thou wouldst go away with such an answer in thy mouth! Do not answer God's loving-kindness, and his gracious dealings toward thee, with a distrustful heart; it is dishonourable to him, and grievous to his Spirit.

Obs. 3. God works an answerable disposition in the hearts of his people to him. This is thy duty, but God will work it in time if thou belongest to him. As thus: does God choose us to be his people? then the hearts of the saints choose him to be their God. Does God say, You are my people? the saints say, Lord, thou art our God. Does God say, I will dwell with them? they answer, Lord, thou art our habitation. Does God say, I delight in them? they say, Lord, our delight is in thee. Does God say, I will rest in them for ever? the church saith, O my soul, return unto thy rest. Here is a sweet answer, a rebound of all God's loving-kindness.

Obs. 4. The saints must profess God to be theirs. It is not enough to believe with the heart, but thou must confess with the mouth.

Obs. 5. It is the highest happiness of the saints, that God is their God; then they can say, they have enough. If we could say, This house is mine, this street, this lordship, this city, kingdom, or world is mine; what is all this? A Christian can say, The God that made all is mine. As it is reported of the French and Spanish ambassadors meeting together: My master is king of Spain, said the former. My master (replied the French) is king of France. My master, said the Spaniard again, is king of Naples. And my master, returned the other, is king of France. My master is king of Portugal. And, My master is king of France: still he answered with, My master is king of France, as being equivalent to all the different kingdoms of the Spaniard. So one saith, I have this house, this stock, this estate, this trade; Yea, but, saith a Christian, I have God, God is mine. Surely, having him, thou hast enough. And if God be thy God, he will be a God to thee. 1 Chron. xvii. 24, "The Lord of hosts is God of Israel, even a God to Israel." So it must be with thee, if thou art a saint *of* God, be a saint *to* God: are we a people of God? then we must be a people to God. Blessed are the people, that are in such a case; yea, happy are the people, whose God is the Lord.

Thus have we opened the gracious manifestations of God to his church, in part realized spiritually, to spiritual Israel here; but to be more sensibly fulfilled at the great day of Jezreel, that is, when the Jews shall be called, then the spouse of Christ shall visibly be thus married to him, and the Lord will be their God. Jerome saith on the text, All the things here promised to the church, the Jews expect at the end of the world, after the time of antichrist: and I question not, that though in a spiritual sense this scripture is fulfilled now to the saints, yet in a more visible and sensible manner it will be all made good to the people of the Jews; and the Gentiles then joining with them even literally, the glory of the church shall be visible and apparent.

Quæ omnia Judei post antichristum in fine mundi præstolantur. Hieronym. in locum.

CHAPTER III.

Ver. 1. *Then said the Lord unto me, Go yet, love a woman beloved of her friend, yet an adulteress, according to the love of the Lord toward the children of Israel, who look to other gods, and love flagons of wine.*

The close of the former chapter had in it much mercy, and this contains the expression of much love also to Israel; but yet God tells them of the mean and low estate they are likely to be in, before the time comes for the fulfilling of all the good which he intends for them. God purposes great mercy, but they must, for a long time, bear their iniquity, and be brought into a vile and desolate condition in their captivity; even until a second appearing of Christ. But in all this time the heart of God would be toward them; his intentions would be strong for good to that people, above all the people on the face of the earth, as a people that he intended yet to marry unto himself; and in time, mercy should break forth gloriously upon them, and his name be magnified in their so returning to him, that their hearts should melt toward his goodness, and not abuse it any more as formerly they had done; but they should "return, and seek the Lord their God, and David their king; and shall fear the Lord and his goodness in the latter days." This is the scope of the chapter:

In which you have three things.

1. God's love continued to "an adulteress," Israel.
2. The low and mean condition of this "adulteress" for a long time.
3. The return of God in infinite mercy toward them at the latter day, together with their return to him.

"Then said the Lord unto me, Go yet, love a woman beloved of her friend, yet an adulteress."

We have here a new injunction to the prophet, and that more difficult than the former. In the first chapter God commanded him to go and "take a wife of whoredoms," but here, to "love an adulteress," which is somewhat more than to take her unto himself. What was meant by taking "a wife of whoredoms," has been explained in the former chapter, and may save us some labour in this. Here there is a vision, as there; as if God should say, Hosea, it is just with me as it would be with thee, if thou hadst a wife an adulteress; notwithstanding all the love she has found, yet still an adulteress; and thine affections were fixed on her, so that thou couldst not withdraw them, but must needs continue to love her: so this people, whom I have loved, and to whom I have done so much good, have gone a whoring from me, and are an adulteress; yet, for all that, my heart cannot be estranged, but is still toward them; I yet love them.

Obs. It is through the strength of the covenant that God's love is so permanent. Others, who are not in covenant with him, God casts off for lesser sins, for any sins; but as for his covenant people, not even their adulteries, their idolatries, alienate the heart of God wholly from them. Surely then, if thou canst appeal to God; O Lord, thou that knowest all things, knowest that there is nothing of thy mind revealed to me but my heart is ready to do, and if I fail in any thing, thou knowest it is the greatest burden to my soul; oh that I knew more of thy mind! and that I had power to do more! surely God will love thee. You hear he loves his people, though an adulteress: so, now take this lesson, as thy sins cannot overcome God's goodness, let God's goodness overcome thy sinfulness.

"A woman beloved of her friend, yet an adulteress."

That is, (as Calvin, Vatablus, and many others interpret it,) beloved of her husband; as if God should say, Had they any such excuse for departing from me, that I have been a bitter husband to them, that I have used them hardly, and with rigour, then indeed they might have some plea; but I have loved them dearly, done much for them, and ever treated them in the kindest manner; yet are they gone a whoring from me. The wife that follows other lovers, thinks, if she can but say, her husband is hard to her, cares not for her, and loves her not, it palliates her adulteries; and so if the adulterous husband can say, What will you have me to do? I never come home but my wife is ill-tempered; and she loves other men: he thinks this is plea enough for him. But Israel could not have this excuse for herself, for she was an adulteress, yet beloved of the Lord. If we understand the passage thus, we may briefly

Obs. 1. The husband should be a friend to his wife.

There should be nothing inconsistent with a friendly demeanour between them. Yea, the love of the husband to the wife should far surmount the love of any friend in the world; he should be, at least, a friend to comfort and cherish her in time of sorrows, to bear the burden of affliction with her: and so the wife in return should act toward the husband.

Obs. 2. A base heart will prove base against all bonds of love. "Beloved of her friend, yet an adulteress." If you should ask, Who is he, or where is he, that is so base? Lay thy hand on thine own heart, and consider what the love of God has been toward thee all the days of thy life, and what return thou hast made to him. Thou hast had from God love that might break the heart of a devil; yet when any temptation comes to draw thee from God, thy base heart listens to it.

Obs. 3. It is a great aggravation of sin to sin against much love. We ought to fulfil our relative duties, though others do not so towards us. If a wife has an unkind, churlish, ungodly husband, yet she is bound to love and to obey him, to be observant of him in whatever may give him all lawful content. So, if servants have froward, churlish, cruel masters or mistresses, yet are they bound to be obedient to them: "Servants, be subject to your masters with all fear; not only to the good and gentle, but also to the froward," 1 Pet. ii. 18. It is no sufficient excuse for the wife to say, My husband is froward and unkind, and therefore what shall I do? nor for the servant to say, My master, or mistress, is unreasonable and cruel, what can I do? You must do your duty to them, though they do not theirs to you. But if you have a loving husband, tender over you, then love is required much more. Love, above all things, should draw the heart; the knowledge that it is our duty may force obedience, but it is love that draws the heart most kindly. So, if a servant have a godly master and mistress, who respect and tender his good; if he should sin against them, this aggravates the sin exceedingly. To wrong love is a very great sin. *Delicata res est amor*, Love is a most delicate thing, and must not be rudely handled. A man who is of an ingenuous spirit had much rather be wronged in his estate than in his love; he cannot bear the injury done to it; when his love is abused it goes to his very heart: so it affects God when his people sin against his love; therefore it is said of the saints, when they sin, that they grieve the Spirit of God: he never says so of the wicked; they anger God, but the saints grieve him, because they sin so much against God's love. Charge this aggravation of your sin on your souls, and be humbled; collect together all the expressions of God's love to you, and let them lie glowing at your hearts, and melt them.

But inasmuch as God bids him take "a woman beloved of her friend," and calls not this friend husband, I think those express the intention of the Holy Ghost in this more fully, who interpret it thus: this friend is not meant of one who is fully married, but rather one in a way of marriage. Among the Jews it was usual for women to be under the protection of men: "And in that day seven women shall take hold of one man, saying, We will eat our own bread, and wear our own apparel: only let us be called by thy name," let us be under your protection, Isa. iv. 1. Even "the strange women," Prov. vii. 5, were wont, though they had many lovers, yet to have some in particular, under whose protection and care they might be; who was to see that they were not wronged, and to make provision for them; and such a one they were wont to call their friend; and often these friends would so provide for them, as to give them good hopes of marrying them at length, if they would be reclaimed, and forsake all their other lovers. Arias Montanus refers us to the second Elegy of Propertius, respecting the charge and care of such a friend. The Grecians had a similar custom; they called him under whose protection they put themselves, *ἑταῖρος*, and the woman, *ἑταῖρα*. It is said of Plato, that he had one Archenassa, who was called Plato's *ἑταῖρα*. Here the Lord would have the prophet take an adulteress beloved of her friend, that is, one that was a common adulteress, and yet under the protection of some special friend; so that if he could supplant that friend, and in time reclaim the love and affection of this adulteress, he might marry her to himself. This is according to the love of God to his people, that is, as if God should say, This people is going a whoring, but I will be content to take them unto myself, I will be as their friend, and so protect them, and care for them, until there be some proof of their being reclaimed, and then I will marry this adulteress fully unto myself. For God is not now fully married to the Jews, neither will that marriage take place until the glorious time of their calling comes; but yet God is as a friend to them to this day, that is, God takes this people yet under his protection, though they seem to be in a rejected condition, and so gives hope, yea, makes many promises, that upon their return to him he will marry them unto himself; yea, there shall be a more glorious marriage between the Jews and the Lord Christ, than ever yet there was between him and any people on the face of the earth. This I think to be the very scope and meaning of the words, "beloved of her friend."

Somewhat suitable we have Deut. xxi. 12, 13: when one of the Jews took captive a woman, he might not forthwith marry her; but if he loved her, she was to continue a certain time, and undergo certain purifications, and then he might take her. The Jews are for the present as that captive woman, in bondage, yet God has a love for them unto this day; but so, that they must abide a while until God be married to them; they are beloved of God, but as yet with the love of a friend.

The Seventy read the words "beloved of her friend," "one that loveth evil things," a mistake easily arising from the Hebrew words, for friend, and רע evil, differ only in the points.

"Who look to other gods."

Their eyes are upon other gods. Where the heart is, there is the eye. *Timor figit oculum*, so *amor*; Fear fastens the eyes, and so does love. The workings of the soul appear as much in the eye as in any member; it well conveys emotions of love, of trust, and of confidence. They "look to other gods," that is, they have confidence in other gods. Looking up to a thing, in Scripture phrase, is to have some confidence in it. Psal. cxxi. 1, "I will lift up mine eyes unto the hills from whence cometh my help;" that is, I look for help, and confidently expect it. But how from the hills? What! does David's help come from them? Some think this to be the place where afterward the temple was built, and the same as was then the place of the sanctuary; but because that is usually in Scripture in the singular number, the hill of God, not the hills; therefore I find Calvin, Mollerus, and others, think that David here speaks of confidence in the creature, because he presently retracts in the second verse, "My help cometh from the Lord." As if he should say, I lift up mine eyes unto the creature for help, this is the frailty of my nature and of the nature of man, to look for auxiliary forces from Jerusalem (which was a hilly place); I look for forces to come from thence, but they come not; well, I will not trust any longer in them, Jehovah is my help. So they interpret it. But now I would rather free the prophet from vain confidence in the creature, and so the words may, if you read them thus, Do I lift up mine eyes unto the hills? do I expect help from the creature? God forbid I should, for "my help cometh from the Lord."

Further, sometimes the Hebrew אל is used for על and so might be translated "above the hills;" other men look to the hills, I look above the hills. But rather thus, "I lift up mine eyes to the hills," that is, I look to God; why? because the place where the temple was to be built was hilly; and so this expression refers to those two hills, or rather, two ridges of the same hill, on which it was built, Moriah and Zion: as 2 Chron. iii. 1, "Then Solomon began to build the house of the Lord at Jerusalem in mount Moriah;" and Psal. ii. 6, "Yet have I set my king upon my holy hill of Zion." I look, saith David, unto God, my faith has reference to the place which God has chosen for himself: that this is the meaning will appear if we compare this with Psal. lxxxvii. 1, "His foundation is in the holy mountains;" not mountain, but mountains. The respect idolaters had for their idols, being manifested by lifting up their eyes to them, therefore God commanded them not so much as to lift up their eyes to their idols, Ezek. xxiii. 27: and indeed, we had need take heed of so much as lifting up our eyes to look on the enticements of the flesh; many will not commit their former sins, but they love to be looking that way. I have read of a loving wife, who, being at the marriage of Cyrus, was asked how she liked the bridegroom? How? saith she; I know not, I saw no one but my husband. Love and respect draw the eye either to God or to the creature. According as our hearts are, so our eyes will be.

אשישי

"And love flagons of wine." The word comes from one which signifies *fundavit*, he has established. The Vulgate renders it, *vivacia uvarum*, the leaves, skins, and stones of the grape that remain after pressing, and sink down into the bottom of the vessel; noting thereby, how sapless, tasteless, and degrading idolatrous worship is in comparison of the true worship of God. The true worship of God is sweet, and lovely, and excellent; but man's institutions, how unprofitable are they! The spirits of such as plead for and delight in superstitious vanities, the devices of men, how dead and vapid do they soon become! though heretofore they have had some life and energy, yet, if once they delight themselves in the inventions of men in God's worship, their spirits grow very unsavoury to those with whom they converse.

But take the translation as it is in your Bibles, "flagons of wine," called by this name in the Hebrew, because the flagon, broad at the bottom, stands securely; that is, (as some interpret it,) they are as drunkards that call for one flagon after another. Superstitious and idolatrous people, when they have one mode of superstition, call for another; and when they have got that, they will have another, and are still desirous of more, never satisfied, but, as drunkards, they still thirst after their flagons.

Or rather, to denote the sensuality of the forms of their idolatrous worship, their flagons of wine are joined to their gods. The Seventy translate the word πέμματα, *bellaria*, delicacies made of wine and grapes by every art they could devise in order to please the appetite. From thence this observation evidently arises:

Obs. Spiritual adultery and carnal sensuality go together. They used flagons of wine in their idolatrous solemnities, and that made them love their idols so much the more. In the true worship of God, there is abundance of sweetness to satisfy the hearts of the saints, they need not sensual pleasures to complete their happiness; but in superstitious worship there is none such, therefore they are fain to call for flagons of wine, and other sensual things, to make up a full delight to themselves. Superstitious and idolatrous rites bring with them pleasure to the flesh, and hence are they loved and followed; people can hardly ever be taken off from them. In their idolatrous solemnities, they were wont to have feasts to pamper the flesh. Judg. ix. 27, "They went out into the fields, and gathered their vineyards, and trod the grapes, and made merry, and went into the house of their god, and did eat and drink, and cursed Abimelech." So Amos ii. 8, "They drink the wine of the condemned in the house of their god." What is that? By oppression and violence they would rend the estates of men from them, and then make merry, yea, come into the house of their gods, and drink bowls of wine which they had gotten from the possessions of those whom they had wrongfully condemned. Let idolaters have their lusts satisfied, and they care not what god they serve. 1 Cor. viii. 10, "If any see thee which hast knowledge sit at meat in the idol's temple;" "at meat," they had their flesh satisfied in the idol's temple. Thus God complains of his people here. As if he had said, Let all bemoan my condition, for though I have loved Israel dearly, she has gone a whoring from me, and loves flagons of wine; and because she has more pleasure to the flesh in serving idols, she *will* serve them. What an abominable thing is it to forsake the blessed God merely for the love of wine! How many are there in the world who forsake all that good which is in God, in Christ, in heaven, in eternity, merely for flagons of wine!

Calvin renders it flagons of grapes, so the words are in the Hebrew, not flagons of wine; and observes, of grapes rather than wine, because there were artificial means used by them to make their superstitions more grateful to them: as when drunkards have drunk even *ad nauseam*, and begin to loathe what they delighted in, then they will use some artificial mixture of grapes or something else with the wine, to give it a new flavour, that they may still delight themselves in drinking: so, (saith he,) because their old superstitions have nothing in them to satisfy the heart, therefore they invent new kinds to please themselves with; and although they boast of their antiquity, yet the truth is, they are devising new ceremonies every day, to give a fresh lustre and pomp to their worship, or else it would grow loathsome even to themselves. We have seen in our own experience, that the wantonness of men's hearts in superstitious ways is very great, they are ever inventing new devices to uphold their old moth-eaten vanities.

Ver. 2. *So I bought her to me for fifteen pieces of silver, and for an homer of barley, and an half homer of barley:*

The prophet obeys God in this other hard command. God many times sends his prophets on very irksome duties, yet they must be willing to serve the Lord in the hardest work. "So I bought her."

The word here translated "bought," signifies also to dig, and is taken (as some think) from the piercing of the servant's ear, who was to be a slave until the year of jubilee, to denote the slavish condition this people should be in for a long time.

אכרה

It signifies also to cut, *excidit*, "he has cut asunder." These different significations may be reconciled by reference to the customs of the Jews, who in their bargainings were wont to cut a beast in sunder, and so to go between the two pieces; or because they joined their right hands together, and then another came and put his hand between theirs, (as a spade is put into the earth,) and so did, as it were, cut them asunder: thence arose the various acceptations in which the word was used.

cognatum cum כרה Pagn.

Contrahentes dextras invicem datas ut rem ratam esse significarent, percutiendo discindebant, sicut et in fœderibus bestiæ dissecabantur. Pagn.

"To me." This buying was in order to marrying, that she might be under his care for a while, and then come to be his wife. It was the custom of men in those days to buy their wives. Jacob served twice seven years for Rachel, and so bought her. David bought his wife for a hundred foreskins of the Philistines; and Christ purchased his church to himself at a dear rate, even by his own blood: but "I bought her" (saith he) "for fifteen pieces of silver."

There is a necessity for fully explaining these words, that you may not only see the meaning of this, but likewise better understand some other passages of Scripture.

"Fifteen pieces of silver." How much is that? Fifteen shekels; for it is a rule among the Hebrews, when a piece of silver, and not the sum, is named, always to understand a shekel; and when a shekel is set down, and the metal not expressed, there silver is understood. Now the common shekel was, according to some, of the weight of one hundred and sixty grains of barley; according to Jerome on Ezek. iv. it weighed half an ounce. Josephus saith its value was about four drachms; that is, about eighteen or twenty pence of our money; and so I find most consider it, though much difference exists among interpreters.

This was to signify the vile and base condition into which Israel had brought herself, for thirty shekels of silver was to be given for the price of a maid-servant. Exod. xxi. 32, "If the ox shall push a man-servant or a maid-servant, he shall give unto their master thirty shekels of silver." Thirty shekels must be given as a recompence for the loss of a slave; yet the prophet must buy this adulteress for half as much, fifteen shekels. Israel, all the ten tribes, yea, the whole people of the Jews, are signified by this adulteress, beloved of her friend. So that now Israel, who were heretofore the dearly beloved of God's soul, his only people on the face of the earth, the peculiar treasure of God, his portion, his inheritance; had now by their sin brought themselves into a meaner condition, and were worth but half as much as any poor bond-woman in Israel. This thirty pieces of silver was the goodly price Christ was valued at by the Jews, Zech. xi. 12; Matt. xxvii. 9. This showed how Christ was humbled, that he must be sold for no more than was the price of a slave. But the price of Israel is but fifteen pieces, half as much. Israel was proud in the day of her prosperity, but now she has brought herself by her sin into a meaner condition than a slave.

"And for an homer of barley, and an half homer of barley." What that homer of barley was, and what the Holy Ghost intends by mentioning it, must be inquired into. First, an homer contained ten ephahs, and an ephah is nearly as much as our bushel, so that this homer contained about ten of our bushels. In Ruth ii. 17, it is said, that when Ruth gleaned in the field after the reapers, she beat out that she had gleaned, and it was an ephah of barley. And by this you may know the meaning of Isa. v. 10, "The seed of an homer shall yield an ephah:" why an homer was ten bushels, how then should the seed of nearly ten bushels yield but one bushel? It was a threatening of a famine, that though they sowed much they should reap but little, they should sow ten bushels, and reap but one.

Some, however, interpret an homer to be about the burden that an ass was able to bear; for חמיר in the Hebrew signifies an ass, and so the burden of that creature was called an homer; but Ezek. xlv. 11, tells us plainly that an ephah is the tenth part of an homer.

There is great difficulty in understanding this, if we compare it with Exod. xvi. 16, where it is said they were to gather of the manna "every man according to his eating, an homer for every man;" and ver. 36, "an homer is the tenth part of an ephah." This seems contradictory, here an ephah is the tenth part of an homer, and there an homer is the tenth part of an ephah. But those who understand Hebrew know that these words are written with different letters, though in our English the pronunciation is the same; that in Exodus with ע and the other with ח in English the former is Gnomer, the latter Chomer, and so they should be read. Now this homer of manna which God gave for each man daily, was almost the tenth part of a bushel, four or five times as much as the Roman *dimensum* or *chœnix*, the allowance given by them to their servants; noting thereby that God is exceedingly liberal to his people.

But why "an homer of barley?" Because it was a mean food, and in those times rather the food of beasts than of men; God promised to feed his people with the finest of the flour of wheat: therefore, Rev. vi. 6, "A measure of wheat for a penny, and three measures of barley for a penny." But what means this, that there must be an homer of barley, and a half homer of barley, given for this adulteress, whom the prophet was to take unto himself? The scope of all is, to signify the mean condition in which the ten tribes, and afterward all the Jews, should be, till Christ came to marry them to himself. First, they should be in a contemptible condition, they should be valued but at half the price of a slave. Secondly, they should be fed but meanly and basely, even as slaves, or rather as beasts; this homer and half of barley should be for their sustenance.

This not only referred to the time of their captivity before Christ, but to all their captivity ever since, and that which they shall endure until their calling. Their mean condition, in the time of their first captivity, you may see, Lam. iv. 5, "They that were brought up in scarlet, embraced the dunghills;" they either lay in filthy places, like beasts, or else they were employed in carrying dung up and down. And to this day, we know that, in the esteem of others, the Jews are the vilest people on the face of the earth. An historian tells us of an emperor travelling into Egypt, and there meeting with some Jews, by whose appearance he was so disgusted, that he cried out, O Marcomani, O Quadi, &c., at length I have met with men viler than such or such, reckoning up divers of the basest people on the face of the earth. And to this day the Turks will suffer no Jew to turn Mahometan, unless he first become a Christian: so much more they esteem the Christians, acknowledging that Jesus Christ, though not God, yet was a great prophet; but as for the Jews, they think them a dishonour to the Turkish religion. And we read that the Romans, when they conquered other nations, would permit the vanquished to call themselves Romans, except in the case of the Jews, though never so willing to conform themselves to their customs, and to be their servants; lest the glory of the Romans should be tarnished by that odious people. Thus we see what shame God has cast on that people even unto this day, that they are counted as the very off-scouring of all nations. Suetonius tells us, that in the exactions that the Romans require of people, they imposed on the Jews more than on any other people. Thus, history and our own experience prove the fulfilling of this scripture, which I am now opening to you: She shall be bought for fifteen pieces of silver, and fed with barley; she shall be in a very low, base, and mean condition, until Christ shall come and marry her to himself.

O Marcomani, O Quadi, O Sarmatæ, tandem alios vobis deteriores inveni. Ammian. lib. 2.

Alios Romanos appellari permitterent, non Judæos, ne quid labis adhæresceril nomini ab odioso ac sordido genere. August. in. Psal. lviii.

Suetonius in Domitiano, c. 12.

Hence we may

Obs. 1. A people who have been high in outward glory, when they depart from God, make themselves vile and contemptible. God casts contempt on wicked men, especially on the wicked who corrupt his worship. Do we not see it at this day? In Mal. ii. 9, it is threatened that the priests, who departed from the law, and corrupted their ways, should be base and contemptible before the people. Has not the Lord done thus at this day? Even those who, not long since, gave themselves the title of the triumphant clergy, and the triumphant church, and boasted as if they would outface heaven itself, and scare all men with their high-commission court. But what shame has God cast on this generation! the people loathe them, and we hope in time the Lord will sweep away the proud and haughty of them as the refuse of the earth. Yea, our whole nation has been a proud nation; what vaunting has there been of what a glorious church we had! Never such a one on the earth! We sat as a queen amongst the nations, and have behaved ourselves haughtily, and God may justly cast contempt upon us. The Jews called themselves "The temple of the Lord," "The temple of the Lord;" but God has now made them the basest nation on the earth. And indeed God has now begun to cast much shame upon us. The time was when the kingdom of England was a terror to other people, but of late they have been the scorn and contempt of nations. "When Ephraim spake trembling, he exalted himself in Israel; but when he offended in Baal, he died:" he became as a dead, poor, vile, contemptible people, Hos. xiii. 1. The Lord loves to stain the pride of men. How many have you known who have been proud and lofty, and the Lord has cast shame and contempt in their faces! even before those whom they looked upon heretofore with contempt, have they now been humbled.

Obs. 2. Though a people be under contempt, yet God's heart may be towards them to do them good at the latter end. The love of God's election still is on this people; God remembers them, and yet intends good to them. Who knows what contempt God may cast upon us? Perhaps he may let our proud adversaries trample us under their feet; but we hope he will not, because he sees their hearts so proud. But if he should, we should not despair; we must not conclude that God has quite cast off England, though he should bring all his people under contempt, so as to be trampled under the foot of pride. And if there be any of you whom God has so depressed as to render you contemptible, humble yourselves before God, but do not despair, the Lord may yet have a love for you; though you are now under shame and contempt, who knows but that this was the only way that God had to bow your hearts? God puts his own people under contempt, and yet it is all from love to them, and with an intent to do them good at last.

Obs. 3. After many promises of God's mercy and of a glorious condition, which he intends for his people, he may yet hold a very hard hand over them for a great while; and this we should especially remember. God having promised so much mercy in the former chapter, Israel might quickly grow wanton, and say, Though we be vile and wicked, yet God will marry us to himself, and we shall be a glorious people; and why need we take care? Nay, saith God, stay, though my heart be toward you, yet this generation shall suffer, and the next generation, and the succeeding one, shall suffer hard things, you shall be brought into the very vilest condition; yet my promise shall be fulfilled at the last. Here we see what care God takes that people should not grow wanton with his mercy, and think, O we are in covenant with God, and God has pardoned our sins, what need we care? Take heed of growing wanton, thou mayst suffer fearful things in this world. Though God may save your souls, yet you may be brought into as woeful a condition in your own apprehensions as ever any creature was on the earth. And for England, though it is true we have as many proofs of the love of God to us as any nation ever had, yet who knows what this generation may suffer, that has so sullied itself with superstitious vanities? We may be brought into woeful slavery, and then God may raise up unto himself another generation, upon whom he will bestow the mercy intended.

Obs. 4. Those who will delight their flesh to the full in a sensual use of the creature, it is just with God they should be cut short, and made to live meanly and basely, made to feed on coarse fare. The Jews had their delicacies before, and fared deliciously; now they must be fed with barley, worse than their servants, and eat that which was meat for beasts. How many has God thus dealt with, who not long since had their tables furnished with the choicest fare, and are now, perhaps, glad of a barley loaf for themselves and their children!

Obs. 5. If God will not utterly destroy a people as he might, but reserve mercy for them at last, yet they have cause to bless God, though their subsistence for the present be most mean. Though there be a threatening here, yet it contains a promise. The people of Israel, had they known all, had no cause to murmur at God's dealing, but to wonder at his mercy, though they had but a little barley to sustain them. And suppose God should bring us, in England, into such a low condition as to be glad of a barley loaf; and we know famine commonly follows war, and God may bring that upon us in a manner far beyond what we or our forefathers ever knew; but yet if the Lord do not cast us off utterly from being his people, though he feed us with brown bread, though we have never so mean a subsistence for the present, we shall have cause to bless his name. It was wont to be a phrase, Brown bread and the gospel are good fare.

Obs. 6. It is the way of God to humble those to whom he intends good, to prepare them for mercy, by cutting them short of outward comforts. If any of you have lived full-handed, your wives, perhaps, brought you good portions, and now all is lost; you had good friends in the country, and many of them now are plundered in their estates; and you fare meanly, and if you have bread for your children think it well; but, consider this, Is not God now humbling me, and thereby preparing my heart for himself? Oh blessed be God for this my condition; this bread is sweeter to me than all the provisions of my former life. When you sit in your house with your wife and children, and have nothing but barley bread to feed on, have these thoughts; I hope God does this in love and mercy, he is making this my condition the best I was ever in, and the greatest blessing to me.

Ver. 3. *And I said unto her, Thou shalt abide for me many days; thou shalt not play the harlot, and thou shalt not be for another man: so will I also be for thee.*

You shall not only be in such a low condition as a slave, and worse than a maid-servant, and be fed with barley; but you shall abide thus, and that for "many days." Thus they have abode these sixteen hundred years since Christ's time, besides their former captivity. The Lord would fully prove Israel, that their hearts were thoroughly humbled, before he would take them to mercy again. Never did any people deal more falsely with God in their humiliations, than they formerly. How often when they were in misery did they come with their seeming repentance and cry for mercy, and God showed them mercy; and as soon as they were delivered, they fell off again and went after their idols; and then, being in misery again, they cried to God and he delivered them, and then presently they returned to their idols again! Well, saith God, I will not deal so with you hereafter, I will not trust you as I have done; you have been in misery, and I have delivered you when you have cried to me, and then you have returned to your sins; but now you shall be thoroughly humbled, you shall be many years in this low and mean condition, and then your hearts will be completely broken, so that, when you return to me again, you shall never backslide. God has dealt so with many of you; you have been in affliction, and he has delivered you, and you have returned to your sins; you have been in affliction again, and he has delivered you once more, and you have backslidden again; and thus you have trifled with the great God: God may bring a sore and long affliction on you, that you shall be so thoroughly humbled, that you shall never return to your sins again as you have done. This is the meaning of "abide many days." When we would thoroughly cleanse a filthy garment, we do not only wash it, but we lay it soaking a great while, and let the frosts of many a night fall upon it: the Jews have so lain many hundred years. The hardness of man's heart is such, that afflictions will not work immediately. Though many wedges be inserted, and many blows struck on knotty wood, it stirs not: some metals are long in melting, yea, though the fire be very fierce.

Obs. 1. When God promises mercy, it is his ordinary method to seem to go quite contrary to a people, to seem as if he would quite destroy them. I will marry myself unto them in loving-kindness and in mercies: but yet I will let this people be above sixteen hundred years in this forlorn condition. And so it has been in all God's administrations since the beginning of the world.

Obs. 2. When God comes to humble sinners, they must be content to be humbled God's own time; they must not impatiently exclaim, "Lord, how long?" I have been thus long in a sad condition; I have prayed thus long. Is your sadness and affliction eternal? O no, a year or two perhaps; yet you have deserved an eternity of misery.

"Thou shalt abide for me many days; thou shalt not play the harlot, and thou shalt not be for another man: so will I also be for thee." That is, All this time you must take care that you do not seek after other lovers; let me have experience that you will now worship the only true God, and I will promise to stay for you as you abide for me.

"Thou shalt not be for another man." The Hebrew phrase, "to be" to or "for another man" means, thou shalt not marry another. Ezek. xvi. 8, "I entered into a covenant with thee, saith the Lord God, and thou becamest mine." *Fuisti mihi*, thou wert to me, that is, thou wert married to me. Lev. xxi. 3, "A virgin which hath no husband:" *quæ non fuit viro*, a virgin that was not to another man. Hence we may profitably

Obs. 1. That husbands must be to their wives, and wives to their husbands; that is, live to them: whatever thou hast, any knowledge, any parts, any grace, it must be to thy wife, for the benefit of thy wife; and what the wife has must be to the husband.

Obs. 2. In the time of the sorest affliction and trouble we must take heed we forsake not God. "You shall abide for me many days." Though I use you hardly for a long time, yet you must not think to go and shift for yourselves any other way. In time of affliction, though trouble continue long, we must not seek to help ourselves by false comforts. We have an excellent text, Psal. xliv., which describes a most afflicted state of God's people. Ver. 11, "Thou hast scattered us amongst the heathen." Ver. 12, "Thou sellest thy people for nought." Ver. 13, "Thou makest us a reproach to our neighbours, a scorn and a derision to them that are round about us." Ver. 17, "All this is come upon us; yet have we not forgotten thee, neither have we dealt falsely in thy covenant." And, ver. 19, 20, "Though thou hast sore broken us in the place of dragons, and covered us with the shadow of death. If we have forgotten the name of our God, or stretched out our hands to a strange god." As if he should say, God forbid such a thing as this; though we be in the place of dragons, under reproach, and in great affliction, yet we have not lifted up our hands to another god. We must not say as king Jehoram, 2 Kings vi. 33, "What should I wait for the Lord any longer?" He seemed to be humbled, and put on sackcloth; but would not be contented to wait longer for the Lord. Men's spirits under affliction are prone to think, Why should I wait for God any longer? I will now seek to help myself in mine own way, to shift for myself. The Lord forbid that such thoughts should be in any of our hearts. *Sedebis mihi*, Thou shalt be quiet, though thou dost abide in this sad condition a long while. Isa. xxx. 7, "Their strength is to sit still." And, ver. 15, "In returning and rest shall ye be saved; in quietness and in confidence shall be your strength." Alas! thou art now afflicted; where wilt thou find help, poor soul? Wilt thou go to false gods, to thy former sinful lusts? that is not the way to help thee; thou must abide until God's time come to show mercy to thee. The heart of man is strongly set upon good, and cannot be content to stay God's time; but if God subdue thy heart so far as to render it content to abide, though never so long, for God, and that it will not try to relieve itself by any unlawful means, this is a good sign that there is much love in reserve for thee. It is a proof of a strong affection in a woman, when there occur things that hinder the match between her lover and herself; Well, saith she, though there be some obstacles, and you make many objections, I will never marry as long as I live, except I may have him: this argues fervour and strength of affection. So here, I will marry you unto myself, saith God, and many things are to be done before that day, but then, after you have stayed my time, I will come to you in a glorious manner. As God deals with the Jews, so often in his marrying himself to a particular soul.

Obs. 3. God not only commands them to do it, but it is a promise and a prophecy that they shall do it. "Thou shalt abide," &c. But you will say, How have the people of the Jews abode for God? Thus; they have never to this day chosen any other god, and though they have not received the Messiah, yet ever since the captivity they have hated idolatry, and that was the thing God specially meant in this; Thou shalt not have any more idols, thou shalt choose no other god, no other husband; though thou hast been very wicked and sinful in this way, and formerly chose all manner of gods, the gods of the Amorites, and Moabites, and of all the heathens round about you, yet now thou shalt choose no other gods but me. Thus to this day the Jews have acknowledged Jehovah to be the only true God, and cannot endure images. There is a remarkable passage relating to this in Eusebius's Antiquities, cap. 18. When Caius Caligula sent one Petronius to set up an image in the temple of Jerusalem, many of the Jews pleaded with Petronius, saying, Sir, what is it that you do? we beseech you do it not, deprive us of our lives first; for it is impossible, while we live, to submit to this, we will all die first. But, replied he, it is the command of the emperor; opposition is vain, it must be done. They answered, Seeing you will not transgress Cæsar's command, neither will we violate the command of our God; we are not so faint-hearted, nor have we such a vain desire for the continuance of our lives, as to enjoy them at the risk of that eternal life, which is proposed for the keeping of God's commands. Such was their spirit then, and to this day they will not endure idols; and their being scattered here and there among papists, and seeing so much idolatry among them, they are thereby stumbled at Christianity, and their conversion greatly prevented; but if God would once pull down popery, certainly the Jews would quickly come in. God now seems about to do it, therefore all of us should assist as far as we can to demolish all monuments of idolatry, to make the worship of God more pure, and this will be a means to bring about the conversion of the Jews, and in this respect they have abode for God all this while: such I conceive to be the meaning of the text.

"So will I also be for thee." What is the meaning of that? First, though you shall be long in captivity, saith God, and in a low condition, be content, do not take any other god as your husband; I will be content, I will stay, I will have no other people upon the earth but you, all the time you are in captivity.

But how does God abide for Israel now? God has chosen the Gentiles, how then does he stay for them?

First, All the Gentiles who are called come in to God, as being joined to the people of the Jews; God honoured the Jews so far, as that all the Gentiles who come in are to be made the Israel of God.

But rather thus, God abides for the people of the Jews to this day, in this sense, God never has taken, nor ever will take, to himself any nation upon the earth to be a national church, as the Jews were, and as it is probable the Jews shall be at their conversion: though God takes the converted Gentiles by their several congregations to be churches, yet to marry himself to a whole nation, as he did to the Jews, that is, if a man be born of that nation it shall be sufficient to make him a member of the church, this God never did since the Jews' rejection, and never will till the Jews be called again. God chooses kingdoms now, and so, in some figurative sense, a nation perhaps may be called a church; but to speak properly and strictly, there is no such national church as the Jews were. But then God will be married to that nation in a more glorious manner than ever; and God abides to this day for the glory which he intends for Jesus Christ, until they come in. And this I take to be a great reason why God, for the present, suffers his churches to be persecuted as they are. The church, ever since Christ's time, has been in a low and persecuted condition; the wicked have prevailed. What is the reason? God abides for this people of the Jews, and he is pleased himself to undergo many sufferings; and seems to say, In the mean time do you abide for me. I will be content to suffer much dishonour myself: many shall come in to Christ; but yet they shall be a poor, contemptible people, the wicked of the world shall prevail against them, shall scorn them, shall contemn them, so that I shall not appear to the world to be their husband, until you be called again: but when you shall return to me, then I will manifest myself indeed; you shall be a most glorious church, and there shall be such a full marriage between us, that all the world shall acknowledge it, and shall say, Come, behold the bride, the Lamb's wife. This is the scope of this scripture.

Obs. 1. Husbands should not require of their wives any thing but what they will answerably do for them. God doth so here; "Abide for me," saith he, "and I will abide for you;" there shall be *par pari*, like for like. Many husbands will require hard things from their wives, but will do little themselves; and, on the other side, wives expect great things from their husbands, but do little themselves. There must be a proportion between what they expect from each other, and what they do to or for each other.

Obs. 2. In our sad condition God suffers as well as we. This may help us in our sufferings, to think, though we suffer much, God suffers as much as we. The people of the Jews, if they had hearts, might see now that God stays for his honour till they come in. So in all the persecutions of the church, does not Christ suffer, because the great work of reformation does not advance? If we are grieved, the Spirit of God is grieved as well as we, and suffers as much as we; God, as it were, abides for us, and stays for his glory. We desire that God would come and manifest himself, then we might be happy and rejoice; but so long as God stays our happiness, he stays his own glory. What abundance of glory does God lose in those praises he would have if the reformation were immediately perfected! but God has other ends, and is content to stay for his praises. Let us be content to stay for what we desire to have; it concerns God to hasten the work as much, yea, far more than it concerns us to desire it; we suffer something for want of it, but God suffers more.

Obs. 3. That soul which endures hardship a long time for God, and resolves to reserve itself for him, so that if it cannot have comfort in God it will have none elsewhere, may assure itself that God reserves himself for it. Certainly, nothing shall take off the heart of God from that soul, but there will be a blessed marriage between it and him. Is there ever a poor creature here with whom God seems to deal hardly, yet finds in himself this frame of spirit, Well, though God seem to leave me, and I am thus desolate, yet if I can have no comfort here, I will have none elsewhere; I will be content to wait; no creature shall have my heart. It is true, I am not able to guide myself, but I am resolved Satan shall never guide me; I am not able to do the will of God, but I will never do the will of the devil: and if God should leave me never so long, nay, leave me eternally, I will never have any other husband, I will rather die a widow; if he do not marry himself to me, I will be without comfort as long as I live. Is thy heart in this frame? Peace be unto thee; certainly God intends thoughts of mercy to thy soul; there will certainly be a marriage between God and it. And wheresoever this frame of heart is, oh how will it help against temptation! When a soul is in distress, and God seems to go off farther and farther, it exclaims, I have prayed long, and yet God seems not to hear, and afflictions prevail. We may ask, Why do you pray any more? why do you come and hear any more? if God will never come, you might as well take your pleasure for a while, you can but perish at the last. But when the heart answers, It is true, the Lord indeed seems to be gone, and I have cause to fear lest he should reject me; but, become of me what will, yet I will never have any other husband but God, never any other comfort but God's comfort, no other peace but the peace of God, and I am resolved that, if I perish, I will perish crying for it. In this frame thou art waiting for God, and God is waiting for thee in ways of mercy; and at length the bowels of God's mercy will yearn towards thee, as the bowels of Joseph yearned towards his brethren. For a long time Joseph used his brethren roughly, but they behaved themselves humbly and submissively towards him, and at length he could not refrain: so God may be using thee somewhat hardly for a while, yet keep thou in a humble and submissive frame of spirit towards him, do that which beseems a creature to do, whatever God does to thee; say, It is fit God should exercise his absolute power over me, and that I should do my duty to him: do this, and be sure thou art a soul that God will marry to himself in the end.

Obs. 4. So far as we are willing to be for God, God is willing to be for us. God requires that you should seek him with your whole heart, Jer. xxix. 13. Mark how God answers, "I will rejoice over them to do them good, and I will plant them in this land assuredly with my whole heart and with my whole soul," Jer. xxxii. 41. Will you seek God with your whole heart? I will do you good, saith God, with my whole heart. If all the faculties of your souls work toward God, all the attributes in God shall work for your good. If thy estate be wholly given up for God, God's riches shall be wholly for thee. Wouldst thou know how God's heart works towards thee? lay thy hand upon thine own heart; according to the beatings of thy heart towards God, so are the workings of the heart of God towards thee: thou mayst determine it thus; thou canst not go up to heaven to know it, but go into thine own heart, and there thou mayst know: as a man may discover by the working of an engine within, what its operations are abroad. That is the reason why the saints, when they have had their hearts enlarged in prayer, have resolved what God will do for them, or for his church: as it is said of Luther, when he had been one time more than ordinarily earnest with God in prayer, he came to his friends and said, Well, it shall go well with Germany all my days; look ye to it afterward. He knew what was decreed in heaven, by what took place in his own heart. We may know in a great measure what God means to do with his church, according to the inward beatings of our own hearts.

Obs. 5. See the happy advantage of the saints, beyond the men of the world, thus: Be you for me, saith God, and I will be for you. The men of the world can say, I am for the world, and the world is for me; I am for my honour, and my honour is for me; this is all their happiness: but now a saint can say, I am for God, and God is for me.

Oh the goodness of God towards us, that he is willing to be for us as we are for him! For him! alas, what can we be for him? we are poor worms, vile creatures in ourselves, what can we do? he has no need of us, we are bound to do all that we do. It is as if a king should come to a poor beggar, and say, Poor man, thou hast but little, yet do what you can for me, I will do what I can for you. This were a mighty disproportion. Alas, what can the beggar do for the king? If you will but use your staff or what you have for me, I will use my riches, and glory, and all for your good, saith the king to the beggar. So saith God to a poor creature, Be you for me, and I will be for you; stand for me, and I will stand for you; use any thing you have for me, and I will use what I have for you. Oh the blessed condition of the saints! Who would not be for God? Do not now say, Alas! I am a poor, vile, and unworthy creature; so were the Jews: do not say, I have gone a whoring from God, and dealt falsely with him; the Jews did so: Yet, saith God, whenever you will be for me, I will be for you. It is now the great question amongst us, Who are you for? I will put the question to you all, Who are you for? Are your hearts wholly given up to God, or are you for your lusts, for the creature? Certainly the creature will deceive you ere long, and bring you no good: if you be not for God now, he will send you to the creature in the time of your distress. There is a time coming that every one of us shall see the need we have that God be for us; let us be for God now, that God may be for us then. When we cry to him, and say, O Lord, let thy mercy and goodness be for us; he will say, Who were you for? You were for your lusts, now go to your lusts; you would have none of me before, I will have none of you now. "You would none of my reproof: I also will laugh at your calamity; I will mock when your fear cometh," Prov. i. 25, 26. Mark, they would have none of God's reproof: he does not say, They would have none of my mercy, they would have none of my grace, therefore I will laugh at their destruction; but they would have none of my reproof. Why? The reproofs of God are the bitterest and harshest things; yet, because they would have none of God's reproofs, he laughs at their destruction. What shall become of them then, who will now have none of the riches of God's grace offered to them in Christ?

Ver. 4, 5. *For the children of Israel shall abide many days without a king, and without a prince, and without a sacrifice, and without an image, and without an ephod, and without teraphim: afterward shall the children of Israel return, and seek the Lord their God.*

Here is much privation, six "withouts:" 1. "Without a king;" 2. "Without a prince;" 3. "Without a sacrifice;" 4. "Without an image;" 5. "Without an ephod;" 6. "Without a teraphim:" but the last verse makes up for all; "They shall return, and seek the Lord their God, and David their king." These "withouts" show the woefully confused estate that Israel was to be in for "many days," many years, both in regard of their civil and of their church estate. The civil state, "without a king, without a prince." Their church, without the four things which succeed. Though once they were the happiest people on the face of the earth in both respects, yet now they shall be most miserable. This they had brought on themselves, by setting up their idols in Dan and Bethel; Dan, the place of judgment; Bethel, the house of God; there was abundance of corruption both in places of judgment, and in the house of God; and now there comes on them abundance of confusion both in their civil and in their church estate. They received their laws, as well for civil as for church government, from God himself out of heaven, which no other people ever did; but they leave God's institutions, and so are brought into all confusion.

They shall be "without a king."

How "without a king?" When they were in captivity, they yet were under a king, the kings of Babylon and Assyria; and they are still, in their dispersion, under the government of kings and princes. I answer, they have kings over them, but not of their own nation; and that is the judgment: neither are they governed by their own, or rather by God's, laws: and for them to be in slavery under kings, is to them as bad, yea, worse, than to have no king at all. How sad a condition, for a people to be without a king to protect them, and to maintain their laws, privileges, and liberties!

When men reject God from ruling over them, it is just with God to put them under the rule of tyrants, of oppressors, of destroyers, and public enemies to their state. The blessing of government is very great, if just; and therefore the Persians were wont, on the death of their king, to let all the people be for five days without any government at all, that, seeing the inconvenience and mischief resulting, they might the more willingly submit to government, and be more obedient when under it.

It is a question among politicians, whether tyranny or anarchy, tyrannical government or no government at all, be preferable. Though tyranny (unless carried to a great extreme) may be better than anarchy, yet certainly it is not better than to reduce power under good regulations, though that be attended with some trouble. The Power which first raises power, designs such persons and families to hold it, and puts limit to it, surely cannot be unable to regulate it that it should not prove its own destruction.

But here they were not only to be "without a king," but "without a prince" also. The word שר translated "prince," signifies a ruler, judge, or governor, and so I find it often used in Scripture. "All these were the rulers," the princes, "of the substance," 1 Chron. xxvii. 31. And Neh. iii. 9, "The ruler," the prince, "of the half part of Jerusalem." So that by "prince" here is meant judges, or any kind of rulers; they shall be "without a prince," that is, without any judges or rulers. Though they had no kings, yet if the government had been in the hands of eminent men, judges over them, their condition had not been so sad. No long time had elapsed since their happiness consisted not in being governed by kings; they were in a flourishing condition before they had any, and when first they came under their government it was from their own choice. God professed they had rejected him, and sent them their first king in his wrath. Therefore their misery certainly did not depend wholly on being without a king. If God restrain not kings, they often desire to encroach on those liberties which the laws of the land, the light of nature, and God himself, give to subjects. Plutarch tells us, that, on Pyrrhus' coming to Athens, the Athenians, to show their respect and do him honour, admitted him, contrary to their custom with strangers, into their citadel, to sacrifice there to Minerva. When he came out, he told them that he was much indebted to them for that great favour, and in requital would give them this advice: Take heed that you never let a king again enter this place; intimating how easily they may be persuaded to intrench on the liberties of those who come under their power.

Plutarch in Vit. Pyrrhi.

And this should "abide for many days." It did abide for 700 years and upward before Christ. From the sixth of Hezekiah to Christ, the ten tribes never were under any governor of their own in all that time; and since Christ's time neither Judah nor Israel have had either king or prince of their own. Oh what a blindness is there upon this people! how dreadful is that darkness in which they now are; that, notwithstanding the prophecy was so clear, that "the sceptre should not depart from Judah until Shiloh came," and they have now been without a prince these 1600 years, yet they will not believe that Shiloh is come! Thus, when God gives men over to blindness and hardness, the clearest declarations will not be believed.

But their confusion in their church estate is more grievous than their civil; they shall "be without a sacrifice, and without an image, and without an ephod, and without teraphim." Two of these four express their being deprived of God's own ordinances, and the other two, of their being deprived of their false worship. They made a mixture in worship, and would have their sacrifice and their ephod, but, together with them, their image and their teraphim.

Obs. 1. Man's perverseness leads him to introduce mixtures into God's worship, he will retain something of that which is God's, but will also bring in something of his own, and that spoils all. An emperor of Rome, in one temple would have Christ and Orpheus worshipped both together. And of those who were sent into Samaria by the king of Babylon, we read, 2 Kings xvii. 33, "They feared the Lord, and served their own gods;" but, ver. 34, it is said, "they fear not the Lord;" that is, though they acknowledged the true God, yet they would mix the worship of idols with his worship, and so God rejected all; "they did not fear the Lord" at all. It is no fear of God except we fear him only; it is no acceptable worship of God unless we worship him only. The heathens are content with mixture in their worship; you may worship one god, and join with it the worship of another, because there is not one of them who challenges to himself to be the universal good; but our God being the universal good, must be worshipped alone, without mixture.

There are two things in which we must take heed of mixture: the one is in Divine worship; the other is in that great point of justification. It is as much as our lives are worth to introduce foreign matter into either of these, we must in them both adhere to the rule laid down closely and strictly. These people had both, and God threatens they should be without both; seeing they would not confine themselves wholly to his institutions, they should have none at all; neither God's institutions nor their own.

We this day much resemble Israel. With respect to our civil state, much confusion is in that, though not altogether so much as was in theirs. And our church estate is very similar: we have neither the right way of worship, nor the false, in respect to the government of the church; the false is cast away and professed against, and yet we have not the true; only here is the mercy of God, that we are inquiring after the true, and "seeking the Lord, and David our king." The Lord gives us hearts to inquire to purpose.

The Septuagint translate these four words, זבח מצבה אפור ותרפים by terms expressing true worship only; and therefore they render מצבה by θυσιαστήριον, an altar; תרפים by ἱερατειας, priesthood; and אפור by δήλωσεως, or δήλων, manifestations, a word used for the Urim and Thummim. But the Hebrew means, "Sacrifice, image, ephod, and teraphim," as expressed in your books.

First, then, to inquire into that which was the right and true worship, "sacrifice and ephod," and in what it consisted; and then into the other, "image and teraphim."

"Sacrifice." They should have no sacrifice at all, for since their temple was destroyed it was impossible they could. Hence it is that they pray with that mighty fervency of spirit, that God would build the temple again, "Lord, build, build, build thy temple in our days, in our days, in our days," &c.; because they knew they could have no sacrifice so long as their temple was in ruins. This was their sad condition, and to this day they have not the legal sacrifices, nor that which was typified by them. There were these three things in their sacrifices:

1. Their dedicating of themselves to God, showing their respect to him in the way he required, in their burnt-offering.

2. Seeking the expiation of sin, in their sin-offering.

3. Seeking for mercy, and rendering thanks, in their peace-offering.

Now to have no sacrifice in any of these three kinds, that is, to have nothing to offer up to the high and blessed God to show our respect to him; to have no means to expiate our sins when we have offended him; to have no way to seek to God for mercy in our necessities, nor to return praise; this must needs be a sad condition: this is the present state of the Jews. We have Christ, who is to us all these. Presenting him to God, is showing the greatest possible respect to God; presenting him is the expiation for our sins, the seeking of whatever blessing we desire, and our eucharistical sacrifice too for all our mercies. But those who are without Christ, are to this day without sacrifice, they have nothing to present to God. If thou wilt offer up thine estate, thy body, thy liberty, or thy name, this is no sacrifice acceptable to God; except thou hast Christ to present it to him, and canst offer all in him and through him, then indeed God graciously accepts. When thou hast sinned, what sacrifice wilt thou offer to God to expiate thy sin? all thy prayers, thy tears are nothing, unless accompanied with this sacrifice, Jesus Christ; in him, indeed, a contrite heart is an offering very acceptable to God. But so long as thou art without Christ, the judgment of the Jews is upon thee, thou art without a sacrifice.

"And without an ephod."

By this he means, first, that they should be without the priesthood. They should not have any church officers. And, secondly, they should have no means to know the mind of God. That this is the scope, appears thus:

First, That by the "ephod" is meant the priests, is evident from that expression, 1 Sam. xxii. 18, where it is said that Doeg "slew on that day fourscore and five persons that did wear a linen ephod;" that is, fourscore and five priests.

Secondly, Without the means of knowing God's mind, for the Urim and the Thummim were on the breastplate that was fastened upon the ephod; so that when they were without the ephod, they must needs be without their breastplate, for it was attached to the ephod, and could not be used for discovering the will of God, but only by applying it to the ephod. 1 Sam. xxx. 7, 8, "David said to Abiathar the priest, Ahimelech's son, I pray thee, bring me hither the ephod. And David inquired at the Lord, saying, Shall I pursue after this troop?" It was by the presence of the ephod that he inquired what God wished him to do in the matter, whether he should follow the troop, or not. And the 6th verse is very observable: you may see when it was that David was so anxious to make use of the ephod, to know of God what he should do. He was in an exceedingly distressed condition, for Ziklag, his own city, of which he had the charge, was burnt; and the men were all "grieved in soul," and talked of stoning him, because the Amalekites had come in his absence and taken away their goods, their wives and children, and burnt the town. If the acts of men in public places turn out unsuccessfully, the people are ready to fall in a rage upon them; this renders their condition very dangerous and troublesome, and should lead us to pray much for them. We are ready to envy those above us, who are employed in public services; but considering their danger, and how far the blame of every thing that falls out otherwise than we desire, is forthwith laid upon them, their condition is not so happy as we imagine. In this state was David, nay, in a worse, for the text saith that he and the men that were with him "lifted up their voice and wept, until they had no more power to weep," their hearts were so broken; yet in this sad and grievous condition "David encouraged himself in the Lord his God," and called for the ephod, to inquire of God what he should do. You observe, that this is the first time we read that David in his battles called for the ephod: when he went to Achish, he did not inquire; when he invaded the Geshurites and Amalekites before, he did not inquire; but now, when he was brought into straits, when his heart was broken, when he was in a weeping condition, he called for the ephod. When God brings men into straits and humbles them, then they will inquire of God with purpose of heart. We are now about to inquire of God, to know his mind; but we are not humbled enough, our straits have not broken our hearts, and perhaps we shall not so readily know God's mind; God may yet humble us more; and then we will come to inquire God's mind more effectually.

אפד Accinxit.

But to open this garment a little. The word "ephod," signifies, to close in, or gird about, because of the fitting of the garment to the priests, and the girding of it about them. There were various sorts of ephods: one peculiar to the high priest, which you have Exod. xxviii. 6. Others which the ordinary priests wore, and that you have in the place before referred to, about the fourscore and five priests slain by Doeg. A third was common to the Levites; thus Samuel, 1 Sam. ii. 18, "ministered before the Lord, being a child, girded with a linen ephod." A fourth, worn by others in their holy actions, especially by kings; "David danced before the Lord with all his might; and David was girded with a linen ephod," 2 Sam. vi. 14. And to this day the Jews have a kind of linen garment, but not like our ephod, yet with some resemblance to it, which they wear upon their heads, and suffer to hang down. When Alexander came to Jerusalem, Jaddus the high priest, arrayed in all his priestly garments, met him; which caused him, out of reverence, to fall down and prostrate himself before him. Josephus tells us, that the people likewise came with white garments, garments that had some kind of resemblance to this ephod; and adds, that the ephod was a garment a cubit in length, covering only the shoulders and the breast, open above and on either side, and girt around the chest. Others make it a long robe reaching down to the very feet. But the ephod was worn also over another robe: so Christ appeared to John, Rev. i. 13, "clothed with a garment down to the foot, and girt about the paps with a golden girdle," like the priests, for so they were wont to be arrayed; and Rev. xv. 6, the ministers of the churches, called by the name of "angels," are described as "clothed in pure and white linen, having their breasts girded with golden girdles;" not girt about their loins, but about their breasts, near their hearts. That which makes ministers of the gospel ready prepared for their work, is the girdle of truth, and this must be about their hearts; if their own devices and selfish aims gird them, that is, incite them to do what may advance their own interest, this is not the golden girdle, but like that rotten girdle of Jeremiah's, that "was profitable for nothing," chap. xiii. 7.

This ephod then was a holy garment, and others must beware of meddling with such, or of seeking to imitate them. When God had given Gideon a great victory over the Midianites, he imitated this ephod; and of the spoil he took from the Midianites, he made a rich and a glorious ephod; but the text observes, that thing proved to be "the destruction of Gideon's house," for "the people went a whoring after it:" he made it with a good intention, to testify his thankfulness to God for his victory, not thinking that it would be ever worshipped. It is dangerous for governors to imitate God's ordinances in garments or the like, and to preserve them amongst people; though with never so good an intention, that will not excuse them. Gideon's presumption in making an ephod, in imitation of the ephod appointed by God, proved to be the destruction of his house; yet this was that Gideon who a little before had destroyed the altar of Baal, and though then so much against idolatry, yet now he does that which promotes it. So may governors, if they take not heed, pull down one kind of false worship and set up another.

The Jews have many mysteries about this garment, it would weary you to hear them. I shall only observe, as most useful for you, that we must not read the books of the Old Testament as if they concerned us not. First, upon the shoulders of the ephod were set ranks of precious stones, with the names of the twelve tribes, according to their generations, engraven on them. And in the middle of the ephod, upon the breastplate, which was to be four-square, there were four rows of precious stones, and upon them likewise were engraven all the names of the tribes of Israel; and he bore them upon his heart. There is much to be observed in this.

Obs. 1. Let the tribes be never so mean in themselves, yet, upon the ephod, they were precious stones. The priest wearing the ephod was a type of Christ: let the godly be never so mean in themselves, yet, in Christ, God looks upon them as precious stones.

Obs. 2. These precious stones, that were upon the shoulders of the ephod, are called "a memorial," Exod. xxviii. 12. First, to signify Christ bearing the names of all the saints before his Father for a memorial, those twelve tribes representing all the churches that should be unto the end of the world. When God remembers his church, it is through Christ. God never remembers his church, but by Christ's carrying it before him: and that is the comfort of the saints; he therefore can never remember them to revenge himself upon them, for he never thinks of them but only as Christ presents them unto him.

Secondly, a memorial, (say the Jews,) not only because the priests were to bear the names of the twelve tribes, engraven in those stones, for a memorial before the Lord, but to signify that the priests themselves were to remember to pray for the tribes.

And thirdly, a memorial, to signify that both the priests and all the people were to remember their godly ancestors and predecessors, and to follow their virtues, and not in any wise to dishonour them.

But the first is the chief. These precious stones with the names of the tribes, were first upon the shoulder, and then upon the heart: upon the shoulder; this notes that Christ carries his church upon his shoulder, bears its burden, all their weight, all their afflictions. The shoulder of Christ stands under the churches, certainly therefore they shall never sink.

But may they not be so burdensome to Christ as to induce him to shake them off? No, Christ carries the memorial of his churches at his heart as well as upon his shoulders, and that makes Christ labour strenuously for the good of the churches. There is an infinite comfort in the spiritual meaning of this ephod, that belongs to all the godly; Christ night and day has thee upon his shoulder, and upon his heart, as a precious stone before God the Father. One thing further is observable about it. In Exod. xxviii. 12, the names of the twelve tribes were to be engraven on these stones in order, according to their birth: now in Rev. xxi. the twelve apostles, who in regard of their doctrine are made the twelve precious stones of the foundation of the new Jerusalem, are all the very same precious stones by name, excepting four, and these four I find interpreters think to be the same as the others, only under different names; for precious stones, either in regard of the places where they are found, or their quality or colour, bear various names; so that it is very probable that the stones in the Revelation were the same with those in Exodus: but there we do not find that they are set according to any dignity in one apostle above another, as there was in the setting of the names of the tribes; for the first precious stone to be laid of the foundation of the new Jerusalem, of the glorious church that should be, is the stone of Benjamin, who was the youngest; and if there might be any mystery in it, we may think it signifies thus much, at least we may thus adapt it by way of allusion, that the Lord will make use of the young ones of this generation, to open the way for the new Jerusalem, before any of the other tribes; God will cull out them to be the first stone of the foundation of that glorious church. In that we find there was not such order observed among the apostles as among the tribes, we are taught that Christ would not have us regard the apostles as superior one to another, and therefore you find they are never named in one unvarying order; in one evangelist they are set down in one order, and in another in another, as Matt. x.; Mark iii.; Luke ix.; so Acts i.; noting thereby, that there is no superiority nor inferiority in the ministers of the gospel.

Upon the ephod there were likewise the Urim and Thummim. It is very hard to tell the true signification of these; men have differed so much about it, that it would be tiresome even to enumerate their various opinions. Augustine, in his 117th question upon Exod., saith, it is hard to discover what this Urim and Thummim was; and Cajetan declares, that none yet have ever explained it; and they add, that even the Rabbins themselves say, the Jews were very ignorant on this point. But most probably one of these two, especially the latter. Some think that they were stones set in the breastplate, which by their brightness or darkness gave an answer to what they demanded of God; that is, when the high priest went to inquire of God what was to be done in any great and public affairs, he presented this breastplate with these stones before the Lord, and if God would give an affirmative answer, the stones gave a more than ordinary brightness and lustre; but if a negative, then the stones were darker than before. But we are not certain of this, and may rather conclude, on the other hand, that the Urim and Thummim (though we know not what matter they were made of, no more than we know what manna was made of) were somewhat that God gave Moses to put into the breastplate, which by him was appointed as an ordinance, and to be presented before the Lord by the priest when they would know the mind of God; and when this was presented, God usually gave an answer to the priest, either by an audible voice, or by secret inspiration; yet not always obliging himself to answer thus, for we find that sometimes God did not reply when sought to by Urim and Thummim, as when Saul thus inquired of God no answer was returned. And it seems likely Josiah would not have sent only to Huldah the prophetess, if he might have had an answer by Urim and Thummim; but the answer depended on the pleasure of the Lord.

Fatentur Rabbini summam esse apud Hebræos harum rerum ignorantiam.

The words Urim and Thummim signify "lights and perfections:" some would make them to signify the knowledge and integrity of life that should be in ministers; but I rather think the meaning is, that they were bright, precious stones, perfected and fitted to do that for which God appointed them. The Septuagint calls them λόγιον, the oracle. Hence, 1 Pet. iv. 11, "If any man speak, let him speak ὡς λόγια, as the oracles of God."

Now this must be on the breastplate of the priest, which the priest using, the people thereby came to know the mind of God. This was to signify that we must look for the mind of God by Christ. It is Christ who is come from the Father to reveal his counsels to us, and if we expect a revelation of the will of God in any other way than through him, we are mistaken. And further, this Urim and Thummim, this breastplate of judgment, was to be on the heart of the high priest, and that when he went in before the Lord, Exod. xxviii. 30.

Obs. 1. The answer that any minister of God in the name of Christ should give his people, should be an answer from his very heart, he must speak nothing but what it dictates; when he would answer any case of conscience, or make known any thing of the mind of God, his answer must proceed from his heart.

Obs. 2. It must be as in the presence of the Lord, as before God; he must consider in whose place he stands, to answer as from God through the great Prophet of the church.

To be threatened with the deprivation of the Urim and Thummim, seeing it was of so much use to them, is a great judgment. And this should be for "many days." Josephus saith, that they were without this two hundred years before he wrote his Antiquities, that was a hundred and five years before Christ; but it appears that they had no Urim and Thummim long before that time, for at their return from captivity, Ezra ii. 63, "the Tirshatha," that is, the ruler, "said unto them, that they should not eat of the most holy things till there stood up a priest with Urim and with Thummim;" therefore they had not then a priest with Urim and Thummim, but expected to have one; whether that hope was realized afterwards is not known. This was the reason of that grievous complaint of Asaph, Psal. lxxiv. 9, "We see not our signs, there is no more any prophet, neither is there any among us that knoweth how long." Now it is probable that Psalm was made about the very time of their return from captivity, for in Ezra ii. 41, Asaph is named among those that came to Jerusalem from the captivity: "The singers, the children of Asaph, an hundred twenty and eight." But let it be then or afterwards, by this Psalm we may find that it was very lamentable to be without Urim and Thummim.

Obs. 3. The result of all is, that it is a grievous thing to the saints, when in the time of their straits they know not God's mind. When God at any time brings his people into straits, yet if they can discover the mind of their God, they are refreshed and encouraged; but when they shall seek to know God's mind, and the

Lord refuses to declare it to them, this is a sad condition indeed.

About their being without an ephod—Jerome observes, That the hardness of the hearts of the Jews is very remarkable: that they should be so many hundred years without sacrifice and without ephod, without the true worship of God among them, or means to know his mind; and yet not guilty of any greater sin than the sin of idolatry, except it be the killing of Jesus Christ; is it not surprising that they do not reason thus, What sin is it that thus provokes God against us more than ever? Surely there is some greater sin than we have ever yet committed.* But, saith he, they can never find any offence, except the killing of Christ, to be a greater offence than idolatry, and yet they have a heavier judgment on them than ever they had, though they are not guilty of that sin as formerly. Surely, were they not extremely hardened, they would be convinced that all this is because of their rejecting and crucifying Christ the Son of God.

As they had the ordinances of God, so they had ways of false worship of their own, images and teraphim. I must show you what those were, and then how it is a threatening that they should be without them.

"Without an image," seems to refer to the two calves they had set up in Dan and Bethel, in which they so much gloried; they should be taken away.

"Teraphim;" that likewise should be taken away. Now if you ask what this teraphim was? in the general, *Taraph* is a divining image: as the ephod was God's ordinance by which to know the mind of God; so the teraphim was an invention of Satan to foretell things that were to come.† The teraphim was the image of the head of a man wrung off his body, perfumed by precious spices. Upon this head was a plate of gold with the name of that spirit by whom they would divine, or, (as some,) put under the tongue of this head; and this being set up upon a wall, burning candles and incense were offered to it, under some constellation: ‡ thus they inquired concerning something that was to come. It was an oracle of the devil, that told them what success they should have in this or the other business; and sometimes it hit right. See the superstition of the Jews; they desired much to know the mind of God, but because they were afraid they should not know all by the ephod, which was the ordinance of God, they would join with the ephod the teraphim.

Obs. It is a very great and fearful evil, when men, in searching to know any thing of God's mind, do not keep themselves to God's ways of knowledge, to God's own ordinances. It concerns us much now at this day. We are about inquiring the mind of God, that we may know it in matters which regard the commonwealth, but more especially concerning religion. I suppose there is none of us but will acknowledge, that the medium which God has appointed for the revealing of his will, is the Scriptures; that we must look into them, and seek to know God's mind there. So far is good, but let us not join teraphim with them. Then do we join teraphim, when we rest not upon Scripture alone, but search after rules of man's devising, and what may consist with our own carnal ends. The Lord may justly meet with us in wrath, if we presume to join our teraphim with his ephod. Pray that at this day, where there is so much searching after God's mind, that those who are employed in it may confine themselves to the ephod, to the Scriptures, to that which is God's ordinance for the revealing of his mind, that they may not join the teraphim, their own fancies and inventions of men, with them. So long as we keep to that rule, we may hope to do well enough; but if the teraphim be joined with the ephod, if any thing be joined with the Scriptures, though apparently never so rational, we have cause to fear God will leave us.

We find this word teraphim used sometimes in Scripture for the image of a man: as 1 Sam. xix. 13, when Michal took an image and laid it in the bed instead of David, the word in the Hebrew is teraphim: so when Rachel stole away her father's images, the word is, she stole away her father's teraphim; and some think they were her father's divining images, and that she rather stole those than any others, because she would not have her father divine which way they were gone. Zech. x. 2, it is said, "The idols have spoken vanity;" the word is, the teraphim: by which we may see they were wont to consult their idols about their successes. And sometimes we find in Scripture that idolatry is called by this name, as 1 Sam. xv. 23, "stubbornness is as iniquity and idolatry;" the word is, is as teraphim.

But here occurs the question; God threatens to take away the sacrifice and the ephod, and that plainly is a threatening, but how is it so to take away the image and the teraphim?

You may understand it as a threatening thus: It is as if God would threaten to bring Israel into as desolate condition as a strumpet is brought into, when not only all her kindred and true friends leave her, but when all her lovers forsake her too, even those who pretended the most love to her, in whom she took abundance of comfort, and from whom she expected protection; yet now she is brought into such a condition, that she sitteth desolate, forlorn, and helpless: so shall ye be, saith God, your sacrifice and your ephod, yea, and teraphim, shall leave you.

Or rather thus: Howsoever it is a mercy for God to take away false worship from a people, images and teraphim, yet here it is a threatening, because it would much disquiet them to be deprived of these images and teraphim, and would be in their apprehension a judgment: as for instance, what trouble have we when the people conceive that any false worship is about to be taken away from them! they think they are undone; nay, when the inventions of men in God's worship are but questioned, what excitement is there! men think their gods are taken away; as Judg. xviii., when the children of Dan came to the house of Micah and took away his ephod and his teraphim, he cried out after them, "Ye have taken away the gods that I have made, and what have I more?" what worse thing could you have done more? I had rather you had taken away all I had; and yet you say unto me, "What aileth thee?" Is it not so at this day? What is it that now breeds such disturbance in England, but that people think their teraphim shall be taken from them? whereas they have heretofore worshipped God in a false way, after the inventions of men, and now he is pleased to shed some light, and there is an inquiring after a right form of church government, and the true manner of worshipping God, they are even mad at this, and would rather lose their lives and their estates, than that their teraphim should be taken away: let that be taken away, and how shall they be able to pray? what! will you take away their religion? This is the language of

* Quæ sit causa tam grandis offensæ ut tanto tempore relicti sunt? maxime cum idola non colant, præter interfectionem Salvatoris aliam non valent invenire. Hieron. in loc.

† Quemadmodum per ephod Deo consecratum quid agendum esset consulentibus significabatur, ita per teraphim idolorum prædictiones declarabantur. Procop. in Sam. xv. 23.

‡ Mactabant hominem, cujus caput torquendo præscindebant, quod postea sale et aromatibus condiebant, scribebantque super laminam auream nomen spiritus immundi, qua supposita capiti ejus, ponebant illud in pariete incendentes coram eo candelas, et adorantes coram eo, supponebant nomen spiritus immundi sub lingua ipsius, et ille alloquebatur eos. Sic R. Eliez.

men in many ignorant places in this kingdom, yea, the very language of many even amongst us here; they are verily persuaded that the parliament intend to abolish all religion in the kingdom; and the adversaries go about to infuse into men, that the parliament are a company of Brownists, merely because they anxiously inquire after the true way of worshipping God, and would have the land purged of all superstitious vanities: thus people cry out for their teraphim: "Great is Diana of the Ephesians." When King Edward the Sixth had but banished the mass, an army rose in Devonshire, and sent several articles to the king about their grievances, as causes of their rising. First, they said that their children were denied baptism: and as they now cry out that none but a company of Anabaptists do all this; so then the popish priests infused into the people of those remote counties, that they were to have no more children baptized, thinking this would exasperate them then against king and parliament. And secondly, they complained that their service, meaning the mass, was taken from them. King Edward was fain to write, to tell them that they were exceedingly abused, that they should still enjoy what was according to the word of God, that their children should be baptized; and as for the mass, that the Common Prayer Book was just the same, only whereas it was in Latin before, it was now turned into English: and so he quieted and satisfied the people. Thus it comes to be a threatening, that God will take away their image and teraphim, because the hearts of people are so vexed when their forms of superstition are abolished.

Now upon this confusion, when they are without king, prince, sacrifice, ephod, image, and teraphim, what shall be the result?

Ver. 5. *Afterward shall the children of Israel return, and seek the Lord their God, and David their king; and shall fear the Lord and his goodness in the latter days.*

A little before God's time is come to raise the most glorious church that ever existed in the world, the greatest confusion is likely to arise. Lactantius tells us, that just before the glorious church, all right shall be confounded, laws shall perish, men shall possess all things by force, good men shall be scorned and contemned; and though, in the times in which we live, one would think that wickedness had reached its highest, yet, in comparison of those evil days that shall happen just before this glorious time, these may be called the golden age. God will reduce all to a chaos first, as he did in the first creation, and then bring out of it a glorious building. We know the raising of that glorious church of which so much is prophesied, is called a creation, "a creating a new heaven and a new earth;" and it is probable enough, that as the heavens and the earth were first made out of a chaos, so those "new heavens and new earth" will be raised out of a chaos, out of that which seems to us to be but confusion. Of what do people complain at this day but of confusion? All things, they say, are brought into confusion. It is true, confusion is an evil thing, and we are to grieve for it, and to seek to prevent it; yet let us not be too much troubled, for you see, when the greatest confusion comes on the people of the Jews, then follows the greatest mercy, then they shall "return, and seek the Lord their God;" never return before that time. Indeed, till men be taken off from all others they will not return to God. When Saul had but a witch to whom he could go, he would rather have recourse to her than seek the face of God in repentance. Because God seems to leave us for the present, and suffers us to be in confusion, and we know not what to do, let not our hearts be disquieted, let us not recur to unlawful means; for mark, it

Lib. 7. cap. 15. 24, and 28.

was just a little before Saul was to be destroyed that he had attained that height in evil. There was a time that Saul inquired after God's mind, and God refused to answer him, but yet he would not then adopt such an unlawful course, but searched to see what sin was amongst the people that caused God to refuse him an answer. When Jonathan took the honey, "Saul asked counsel of God, but he answered him not that day. And Saul said, Draw ye near hither, and see wherein this sin hath been this day," 1 Sam. xiv. 37, 38: but afterward he became so evil, that when he was in a strait, and God answered him not, he forthwith went to the witch; but this was when he was near destruction.

Obs. 1. Wicked men near destruction, (as Saul was,) finding things in confusion, and God not showing them what is to be done, are soon in a rage against God, and seek after unlawful means to deliver themselves. The Lord forbid that this should be our condition. Let not us say, Things are now in such disorder that we cannot discover the mind of God; we consult ministers, and they know not what to say; they have cast out one government, and they know not what to bring in; and therefore it were better we were as before. If this be our reasoning, it is a sign that we are, like Saul, nigh to destruction. Let us be content to wait; they shall be "many days without a king," &c., and "then they shall return;" the fruit of their being without king, and prince, and ephod, and sacrifice, shall not be vexation and disquiet, but a returning to God and repentance. If things be worse, and we be brought into greater straits than ever we supposed, let us not murmur, but let us repent. Every one is complaining, but who is repenting? if there were as much repenting as there is murmuring, then we should soon know the mind of God.

Obs. 2. The use of sanctified affliction is to cause returning to God: "Then they shall return." Jerome expresses the life of an impenitent sinner by a line stretched out, he goes from the centre in a right line, and so goes *in infinitum* from it; but a penitent sinner is like a line bent, and turning back to the centre, though by sin he goes from it, yet by repentance he turns to it again: They are gone from me a great way, saith God, but I will turn them, they shall bend back again and return to me.

Obs. 3. Repentance is described by the word "return," to denote the folly of sin. In sin thou goest out of the way, and the truth is, though you think you choose a good path for yourself, yet you must either return or perish. It is just like a traveller, who sees a dirty lane before him, and is told that is the way he must go; but on the other side of the hedge there is a green and pleasant path, and he gets over into it, and so rides on a mile or two, till at length he is compassed about with ditches and rivers, so that he must either turn back or else lie there and perish; he returns with shame, and if any one that before told him of the other way see him, he now reproaches him with his folly. So it is with sinners; there are ways of God that lead directly to heaven, but because these ways are rugged, and they meet with trouble and persecution in them, and they see by-paths, though leading to hell, yet more plain and smooth, they will transgress, (for that is the word for sin,) will pass over, and for a while, in this their way, enjoy pleasure: but, friend, you must come back again, and if ever you mean to be saved, you must go in the way that you have refused.

Obs. 4. Here is an encouragement for old sinners. "They shall return, and seek the Lord their God." The Jews have been above sixteen hundred years in this woeful condition, forsaking God; but in their latter days they shall return, and seek the Lord, and God shall be merciful to them. Hast thou been forty, fifty, sixty years going from God? there is hope for thy soul: O return, return, ye old sinners.

But further, they shall return to "Jehovah," and seek him. Jer. iv. 1, "If thou wilt return, O Israel, saith the Lord, return unto me." They shall not turn from one false way of worship to another, but from the false way to the true, they shall return to God. It is that we now should look to. We must not think it enough to cast one false mode of government out of the church, and turn to another, though not so bad, yet not God's mode; if from any carnal policy we reject the way of God, it will prove a sore evil to us: it is one thing not to be able to bring in the way of Christ, another to reject it.

They shall seek Jehovah. The word "seek" signifies, *conatu ac studio quærere*, to seek with endeavouring and study, rather than merely to ask and inquire; they shall be studious in seeking after God. They "shall seek the Lord," that is,

First, They shall seek his face and favour for the pardon of all their evil ways; they shall come and acknowledge their false ways and doings, and seek mercy to pardon.

Secondly, They shall seek the true worship of the Lord. Calvin, in a sermon on "Seek ye my face," interprets it to be a seeking of the ordinances and the true worship of God. So Psal. cv. 4, "Seek the Lord, and his strength:" what is meant by the strength of God there? It is the ark, for that Psalm was made at the bringing of the ark into the place which David had prepared, as you may see by comparing with 1 Chron. xvi. where the ark of God is called the strength of God, and Psal. lxxviii. 61, He gave "his strength into captivity." Surely, if the true worship of God be the strength of God, it is our strength too: a people are then strong when they entertain the ark of God, the true worship of God; and then indeed we seek God aright, when we seek to know the way of his worship.

Lastly, They shall seek to know his will in all their ways, and to do it.

Obs. It is not enough for them to be content to do just that which he has commanded, but they shall seek to know his mind, and what his worship requires. Some yield thus far to God, if any convince them that this should be done, then they will do it, they dare not then but comply; but when the heart is in a true repenting frame, it is in a seeking frame, it is laborious and industrious to know the mind of God. Whereas the heart of a sinner heretofore lay dead and dull, never stirred after God, now it is in a stirring, in an inquiring way; which is a sign of much good. Though thou hast not what thou seekest for, yet be comforted in this, that thou art seeking; "Their hearts shall rejoice that seek the Lord." Though thou complainest, I have been seeking a long time, but I know not the mind of God, I cannot apprehend the love of God, and the pardon of my sins: True, but the hearts of those "shall rejoice that seek the Lord;" if thou art in a seeking way, thou art in a saving way, there is cause thou shouldst rejoice in this, that God has led thee thus far.

They "shall seek the Lord," and that not faintly, but anxiously and effectually. Jer. l. 4, 5, They, "the children of Israel, and the children of Judah," when they shall be together, "shall go weeping, and seek the Lord their God; and they shall ask the way to Zion with their faces thitherward." Many of you ask questions, but your hearts are not right, your faces and the strength of your spirits are not set to yield to the will of God when it is revealed to you. And mark how it appears that their faces are thitherward, "Come," (say they,) "and let us join ourselves to the Lord in a perpetual covenant that shall not be forgotten." To seek God, is not merely to go to a minister and ask him a question, but to go with the strength of our spirits set to know the mind of God above all things, and so to resolve to obey, as to be willing to enter into a perpetual covenant, to bind ourselves to yield to whatever God shall reveal. When you come to a sermon, come not to get a little notional knowledge, but with your faces toward Christ and his truth previously; if you be a true seeker, enter into covenant with God, that to whatever God reveals to be his mind you will yield; and though you have heretofore opposed many revealed truths, say, Lord, here I am, ready and willing to enter into an everlasting covenant to be under the command of every truth. This is seeking God aright.

They "shall seek the Lord their God." This "their God" has two references, either to what is past, or to what is to come. To what is past; "their God," that is, the God who was once the God of the Jews, the God of their forefathers, the God of Abraham, of Isaac, and of Jacob. And secondly, "their God," that is, that God who is yet ready and willing to be reconciled to them, notwithstanding all their sins. Thus they "shall seek the Lord their God."

Obs. 1. It prevails much with the heart of a backslider, to think what God was once to him before he apostatized, and what he was to his godly parents and progenitors. There was a time that I enjoyed God sweetly, when I went to prayer I had blessed communion with him; it is otherwise with me now, I have apostatized. Let this consideration catch hold on thy heart and turn it this day: O turn, turn, thou apostate soul; God, who was once thy God in a gracious manner, is the same that thou hast vilely forsaken, yea, thy father's God also. Thou hadst a godly father, a godly grandfather; remember what a blessed God he was unto them, and return.

Obs. 2. The apprehension of a possibility to obtain mercy from the Lord, is a strong means to draw the heart to return to him. "Their God," the God whom they may yet hope to enjoy, notwithstanding all their departings from him. When they look on God as a God in covenant with them still, there is nothing to prevent his yet becoming their God. Let this argument arrest the spirits of all sinners who have departed from God. Backslider, thou hast departed from God in a foul and vile manner, but men and angels know nothing to the contrary but that he may be thy God for all this. Let me speak to the vilest sinner in this place before the Lord this day. Thou hast indeed most desperately and wickedly sinned against God; the Jews have done so. Hast thou crucified Christ? they have done so. Hast thou denied the truth and followed false ways? they have done so. Notwithstanding all thy wicked and evil ways, seeing thou art yet alive, I do this day yet once more pronounce to thee in the name of the great God, that there is nothing to the contrary, that either angels or men can possibly know, but that God may be thy God, and that this day God may enter into covenant with thee, and thou with him; this night he may come in and sup with thee, and thou with him; there may be a blessed reconciliation between God and thee; return, return, thou sinful soul.

"And David their king." That the Jews shall return and believe in Christ, is most ordinarily spoken and believed by the faithful, saith Augustine. In this their return and seeking God, they "shall seek David their king."

Judæos in Christum nostrum credituros, celeberrimum est in sermonibus cordibusque fidelium. August.

For the explanation of this, there are five things to be inquired into.

1. Who this David was.
2. Why David is named rather than any other.
3. Why he is mentioned in this place.
4. Why joined with seeking of Jehovah.
5. Why this epithet is added to David here, "David their king."

First, By "David" is evidently meant Jesus Christ. Nothing is more manifest than that Christ is meant by the name of David, saith

Nihil est in ista prophetia manifestius quam David regis

nomine significatus intelligitur Christus. Aug. de Civit. lib. 18. c. 28.

Augustine. The Scripture is explicit on this, in the New Testament calling Christ by the name of David. Compare Isa. lv. 3, with Acts xiii. 34. Isaiah saith, "I will give you the sure mercies of David." What are they? In Acts xiii., where that place of Isaiah is quoted, the words are *τὰ ὅσια Δαβὶδ*, the holy things of David; the Holy Ghost there adopting the translation of the Septuagint, as is usual in the New Testament. And Psal. xvi. 10, where David seems to speak in his own person, "Thou wilt not leave my soul in hell; neither wilt thou suffer thine Holy One to see corruption;" is applied to Christ, Acts xiii. 36, 37. And Acts xv. 16, in the assembly of the church of Jerusalem, James, in his speech to the assembly, tells them of a prophecy that God would "return and build again the tabernacle of David," that is, convert the Gentiles to the profession of Christ. But you will say, Is this quoted right? for it was James's intention in the assembly (and it concerns all in such a grave assembly) to speak to the point; but how does James so here? The question at issue was, the calling of the Gentiles, and he proves it by that scripture where it is said, that God would "build again the tabernacle of David;" but how does that prove that God would call the Gentiles? You may see, if you examine the prophecy whence this was quoted, that this text was most appropriate; it is in Amos ix. 11, 12, where, after he had said that he would "build again the tabernacle of David," there follows, "that they may possess the remnant of Edom, and of all the heathen, which are called by my name." So that the tabernacle of David is indeed the tabernacle of Christ, and it shall be raised to this end, that he may possess the remnant of Edom, and of all the Gentiles that were to be called by the name of God. David is Christ because he was his type, and Christ was the seed of David.

Secondly, Why David is named rather than any other, rather than Abraham, Isaac, or Jacob; others were types of Christ as well as he, and Christ was their seed as well as David's. The reason is, because David typified Christ, especially in his kingly power over his own people, David was the first godly king over God's own people. Melchisedec was a king, king of Salem; but over the people of God David was the first type of Christ.

Thirdly, Why he is mentioned in this place, why the Holy Ghost adds to seeking the Lord, that they shall "seek David?" Was it not enough if the Holy Ghost had said, When the ten tribes of Israel (for he speaks of them especially) shall return they shall "seek the Lord" and the Messiah, but that they shall "seek the Lord and David." The reason is, the expression is introduced to remind these tribes of their great sin in revolting from the house of David; when they shall repent, this will lie near their hearts, they will mourn for this their transgression, and when they choose Christ to be their King, shall do it under the name of David; as if they should say, We indeed have cast off the house of David sinfully, but we now come and choose the Son of David to be our King. Thereby reminding us that,

Obs. True penitents, in mourning for their sin and returning to God, will go as far as possible to the foot of their transgressions, to their first defection, and mourn for that, and labour with all diligence to reform in that very thing wherein originated their sin.

Fourthly, Why joined with seeking the Lord; "they shall seek Jehovah, and David their king." It is added to show us, that none can seek God rightly but through Christ, they must seek God in Christ. "This is life eternal, to know thee, and Jesus Christ whom thou hast sent:" to know God alone is not eternal life, but to know God and his Son; so to seek God alone is not eternal life, nor will it ever bring to eternal life, except there be a seeking of God in Christ, seeking Jehovah and David conjointly. Grace from God the Father and from the Lord Jesus Christ must go together: no grace from God the Father, but from him through Christ; so no seeking of God the Father, Jehovah, but it must be with seeking of David likewise. It is not only dangerous, but terrible, to think of God without Christ; the very thought of him out of Christ is most dreadful to the hearts of those who know God. There are some indeed who have bold, presumptuous hearts, who will go into God's presence though reeking in the very guilt of their lately-committed sins, and seek to God for mercy, and never think of Christ the Mediator; they understand not the necessity of seeking God in Christ, because indeed they know not with what a God they have to deal; but the soul that knows what God is, dares not think of God, much less come into his presence and seek him, but only through Christ. Plutarch, in the Life of Themistocles, relates, That when the Molossians would seek the favour of the prince, they were wont to take the king's son in their arms, and so go and kneel before his altar in his chapel; and that Themistocles did so when he sought the favour of King Admetus. So Christians, in seeking the face of God the great King, should take up his Son in the arms of faith. Luther, on Psal. cxxx., observes, Often and willingly do I inculcate this, that you should shut your eyes and your ears, and say you know no God out of Christ, none but he that was in the lap of Mary, and sucked her breasts; he means, none out of him. We must not, we should not, dare to look upon God but through Christ, and seek him together with David.

Non solum periculosum, sed horribile est de Deo extra Christum cogitare. Luth.

Ego sæpe et libenter hoc inculco, ut extra Christum oculos et aures claudatis et dicatis nullum vos scire Deum, nisi qui fuit, in græmio Mariæ et suxit ubera ejus. Luther.

This is the evangelical way of seeking God; when we have sinned, if there be any way of help, it must be by seeking a merciful God; thus far nature goes, and most people go no farther; yea, most Christians, though they have the name of Christ in their mouths, yet their hearts go no farther than natural principles carry them. But the seeking God in Christ, is the true spiritual and evangelical way, "the mystery of godliness," to present a Mediator to God every time we come into his presence. I fear that many of our prayers are lost for want of this. There is much fasting and prayer, through God's mercy, amongst us, and I would to God there were no abatement; but though we ask, Will God leave his people when there is such a spirit of prayer? let us know, if it be not a seeking God in his Son, it is our own spirits rather than the Spirit of God. We may be earnest in prayer and cry mightily to God, yet if we take not up his Son in the arms of faith, and present him to the Father, thousands of prayers and fasting days may be all lost for want of this. The truth is, we must not depend so much on our prayers, though we are to rejoice and to bless God that there is so much prayer; but God's dealings towards us seem as if he would take us off, not from the practice of prayer, but from relying on it, to rely upon free grace in Christ alone. As this is the supernatural seeking of God, so it is the most powerful. It is not enough to seek God by virtue of a promise, except we seek him by virtue of Christ, who is the foundation of all the promises. We seek him because he is merciful, that is one way; yea, we seek him because he has promised mercy, this is a step higher; but we must go higher yet, we must look to his Son, in whom all the promises are Yea and Amen; otherwise, though we seek him never so earnestly, though we challenge his promises, and cry to him to remember them, yet if we do not act our faith on his Son, we may altogether fail.

And herein we sanctify that great name of God in that which is his great work, his master-piece, as we may say, or the great design he has to honour himself by in the world here, and everlastingly hereafter. Certainly, though God has made the creature for his own glory, and expects we should honour his image in it; yet the great design God has to honour himself in and by is, that the children of men may behold this his glory as manifested in his Son, and reflect it on his own face; except you glorify God in this, he cares not much for whatever other glory you can give him.

When you seek God, you must not, therefore, expect good things from him merely because he is merciful, you must not think that the mercy of God serves to eke out our righteousness. Perhaps some will say, It is true, we are poor sinful creatures, and what can we expect from God, being sinful? but we hope that the mercy of God will pardon our sin, and so accept of our poor services. This is the way with most, they, as it were, employ God's mercy in a work that God never intended it for, that is, they would make the mercy of God to eke out their own righteousness, that so both joined together might serve as a means of atonement. No, you mistake God's mercy; the work of God's mercy is not this, but it is to show us our unrighteousness, our misery, our uncleanness, to show us Jesus Christ, to draw our hearts to him, to empty us of ourselves that we may wholly rely upon that righteousness that is by faith in him, and present that to the Father for sanctification and atonement: this is the work of God's mercy, and when it thus works, then it has its true, genuine effect.

Fifthly, Why this epithet is added to David, "David their king." True, we must seek the Lord and Christ, but why Christ the King? Because Christ in the latter days shall be fully honoured in his kingly power; they shall look upon him not only as Prophet and Priest, but as King. Hitherto Christ has been much honoured in his prophetical and priestly office, but not so much in his kingly; but in the latter days, when God shall call home his people, (the Jews,) then Christ shall be fully honoured in his kingly office. The tabernacle of Christ was raised in the primitive times, according to that speech of St. James, Acts xv. 16, "God shall build up again the tabernacle of David," he speaks of its accomplishment then; but there is a time when God shall not only raise the tabernacle of David, but the throne of David; Christ the King shall appear in glory. Ezek. xxxvii. 24, 25, "And David my servant shall be king over them;" it was spoken on the union that should take place between Judah and Israel, then "David my servant shall be king over them." David was long dead, but there is a time when David must again be king, that is, Christ shall reign on the union of all the tribes together. And again, the text adds, "David shall be their prince for ever;" when they are brought back into their own land: surely this prophecy is yet to be fulfilled. And Luke i. 32, 33, "The Lord God shall give unto him the throne of his father David: and he shall reign over the house of Jacob for ever; and of his kingdom there shall be no end." I know we usually think that this is meant only of his spiritual reign, but certainly there is to be a fulfilling of this prophecy in a reign that shall appear outwardly before the children of men. This opinion gathers strength by comparing this with other passages. Rev. xi. 15, "The kingdoms of this world are become the kingdoms of our Lord, and of his Christ; and he shall reign for ever and ever." In a spiritual sense the kingdoms of this world are always the kingdoms of the Lord and of his Christ, but a time is here spoken of, when the kingdoms of this world shall manifestly appear to be the Lord's and his Christ's, and then "he shall reign for ever and ever." Rev. iii. 21, "To him that overcometh will I grant to sit with me in my throne, even as I also overcame, and am set down with my Father in his throne." Mark this text, as one of the most remarkable we have. That kingly rule which Christ has for the present, is on his Father's throne; he is not yet on his own, but reigns conjointly with the Father; but there is a time in which Christ will have a throne himself.

Now you will perhaps think that that throne of Christ is in heaven at the day of judgment; but we find, 1 Cor. xv. 24, that at that day he comes to resign the kingdom; the words do not seem to import that he came to take it, but to give up the kingdom unto God the Father; therefore there is a time for Christ himself to have a throne, and with him the saints shall reign. Matt. xxi. 9, the children cried out, "Hosanna to the Son of David," because they looked upon the Son of David as one who was to reign.

In these "latter days" Christ shall break the kings of the earth who stand against him, as, indeed, many, yea, most of the kings of the earth have ever stood out to hinder this his kingdom. There will be a mighty shaking of the kingdoms of the earth when this shall be: "Whose voice then shook the earth: but now he hath promised, saying, Yet once more I shake not the earth only, but also heaven;" quoted in Heb. xii. 26, out of Hag. ii. 6, 7. God, in giving the law, shook the earth, but then he will shake the earth and the heavens, which some interpreters expound thus: not only the power of the meaner people, but that of the highest kings and emperors, and whatever is lofty in the world, shall be shaken when Christ comes to take the kingdom to himself; the Father will set him King upon his holy hill. Though "the kings of the earth set themselves, and the rulers take counsel together, against the Lord, and against his Anointed, saying, Let us break their bands asunder, and cast away their cords from us; he that sitteth in the heavens shall laugh: the Lord shall have them in derision. Then shall he speak unto them in his wrath, and vex them in his sore displeasure. Yet have I set my King upon my holy hill of Zion:" "yet" have I done it, though the kings of the earth and great ones of the world fret, and vex, and rage, and collect their might; though they blaspheme, and say he shall not reign, the Lord sitteth in heaven and laughs at them; let them do what they can, and gather what strength they can, and oppose it to the uttermost, "yet have I set my King upon my holy hill of Zion."

This is acceptable news, it is the joyful voice of the gospel, to tell you of Christ's coming to reign in the world. Isa. lii. 7, "How beautiful upon the mountains are the feet of him that bringeth good tidings!" What are those "good tidings?" those that say unto Zion, "Thy God reigneth." This, indeed, is the triumph of the church. Isa. xxxiii. 22, "The Lord is our judge, the Lord is our lawgiver, the Lord is our king;" for then shall the churches be delivered from the oppression of all tyrants in the world.

And this kingdom of Christ shall indeed be like David's kingdom; Christ shall be "David their king." I might show you many parallels, but I will only instance these two:

First, David was one of the most gentle of princes, and exceedingly loving and kind to his subjects: 1 Chron. xxviii. 2, "Then David the king stood up upon his feet, and said, Hear me, my brethren, and my people." Mark how he, a king, speaking to his people, addresses them; he stood upon his feet, and said, "Hear me, my brethren, and my people." Thus the kingdom of Christ is declared to us, Psal. xlv. 4, "In thy majesty ride prosperously, because of truth and meekness." Christ shall be a most meek king; not a king of blood, ruling with violence and harshness, so as not to care for the love of his people, making his finger heavier than the loins of others; but he shall rule his people with all gentleness. Therefore the government of Christ is expressed by "a shepherd gently leading those that are with young;" and in this David and Christ are alike: Psal. lxxviii. 70, 71, "He chose David also his servant, and took him from the sheepfolds: from following the ewes great with young, he brought him to feed Jacob his people, and Israel his inheritance." So Isa. xl., having spoken of the glad tidings of Christ's kingdom, adds, "He shall feed his flock like a shepherd; he shall gather the lambs with his arm, and carry them in his bosom, and shall gently lead those that are with young." When Christ shall reign, he shall have great respect to the good and comfort of his people, he shall not disregard their liberties, but their benefit and his own glory shall be blended in one.

Secondly, "David their king," in regard of faithfulness. David was very faithful to his people, and therefore the mercies of God in Christ are called "the sure mercies of David," because "David was found faithful before the Lord." In Psal. xlv. 4, a prophecy of Christ's kingdom, the text saith, "In thy majesty ride prosperously, because of truth, and meekness, and righteousness:" there shall be righteousness in the kingdom of Christ. It is a blessed thing when we may confide and fully venture our estates, our liberties, and our lives on the promises of those who are above us. We know how many there are about great personages to draw them from things that they have promised with the utmost seriousness, and most solemn protestations to perform. I will give you one or two remarkable instances of this. King Edward the Sixth sends letters to London in the behalf of the duke of Somerset, the then protector; many of the lords had risen up against him, thinking he oppressed the people, and they sent at the same time to London for aid and assistance. On this there was a common council called in the city, and amongst them a wise and an honest man, one George Stadlowe, addressed the council thus: I remember a story in Fabian's Chronicle, of the wars between Henry the Third and his barons; the barons then demanded aid of the city of London, as our lords do now, and that in a rightful cause, for the good of the commonwealth, for the execution of divers good laws which the king would not suffer to be enforced; and the city did aid them, and an open battle ensued, and the lords prevailing, took the king and his son prisoners. The lords afterwards restored the king and his son to their freedom, on certain conditions, amongst which this was one, that the king should not only grant his pardon to the lords, but also to the citizens of London; and the conditions of this accommodation of peace were ratified by act of parliament; but what followed? was it forgotten? no, surely, nor forgiven neither, during the king's life: the liberties of the city were taken away, strangers appointed to be our head and governors, the persons and goods of the citizens endangered, and one persecution succeeded another. Again, in the history of Queen Mary's time we find, that because there was some dispute about her coming to the crown, she went to Suffolk, to the place where the duke that then rose up for another was most hated; and being at Framlingham castle, the Suffolk men came to her and promised their aid, on condition that she would not attempt the alteration of religion, which her brother King Edward had just established: she promised them there should be no innovation in religion, no, God forbid, yea, she promised it so solemnly that no one would or could doubt the performance; but afterward, when she got the power into her hand, the Suffolk men came to make supplication to her, that she would be pleased to perform the promise she made them, and she replied thus: Forasmuch as you, being but members, desire to rule your head, you shall one day be made sensible that members must obey their head, and not expect to bear rule over the same. And not only so, but to cause the more terror, one Master Dobs, a gentleman that lived near Windsor, who presumed in a humble address merely to remind her of her promise made to the Suffolk men, was three times set in the pillory, and others for the same cause sent to prison. We may see what hold heretofore promises have had on those who had the power to break them, and what temptations they have to withdraw their hearts from the fulfilment of their engagements. But when this our Prince comes, David our King, we shall find "the sure mercies of David," we shall find nothing but faithfulness in all his dealings.

"And shall fear the Lord and his goodness in the latter days."

"Shall fear the Lord." The words are, shall fear *to* the Lord, *pavebunt ad Dominum.* The fear of God is much upon the heart of a sinner in his return to God. Such a sinner has high and honourable thoughts of God. They shall return, and fear the Lord. The unthinking vanity of his spirit, the boldness of his heart, are gone, and the fear of God rules in it. The majesty, the power, the authority of the great God are strongly impressed on him; when he comes to worship, the fear of God makes him worship God as God, it abides with him even all the day long, you may see written on his life the fear of the great God. And this not a servile, slavish fear, but a holy, reverential, filial fear. Isaac had such a fear of God, that from it God is called "the fear of Isaac." This is a most precious fear: others fear poverty, imprisonment, disgrace, their fellow men; but, saith a true repenting heart, "I fear the Lord:" this fear is the well-spring of life to him, it is the very treasure of his soul, Isa. xxxiii. 6.

I shall speak of the fear of God here only as it concerns this place. It is introduced here, to show that when this glorious church shall be formed, when God shall call home his own people the Jews, and bring in the fulness of the Gentiles, then shall the fear of God mightily prevail upon the hearts of people; and the greater God's goodness shall be, the more shall the fear of God be on their hearts. It is remarkable, that almost all the prophecies which speak of the glorious condition of the church, ever make mention of the fear of God that should rest then on the hearts of the people. One would rather think there should be a reference to the joy they would have, and that there should be nothing but mirth and triumph in those times; but the Scripture speaks much of fear that shall be then, and more then than at any other time. Thus in Rev. xi. 18, a most remarkable prophecy of Christ's coming, and taking the kingdoms of the earth, and bringing his reward with him, it is said, he shall come and give a reward to those that fear him. And Rev. xiv. 6, 7, "I saw another angel fly in the midst of heaven, having the everlasting gospel to preach unto them that dwell on the earth, saying with a loud voice, Fear God, and give glory to him." Mark an angel when he comes to preach the everlasting gospel, how does he preach it? what, Cast now away fear and rejoice in this everlasting gospel? No, preaching this everlasting gospel, he saith with a loud voice, "Fear God and give glory to him." So Rev. xv. 3, 4, contains the song of the saints when they are delivered from the power of antichrist, and what saith it, Rejoice and be glad? No; "Great and marvellous are thy works, Lord God Almighty; just and true are thy ways, thou King of saints. Who shall not fear thee, O Lord, and glorify thy name? for thou only art holy: for all nations shall come and worship before thee; for thy judgments are made manifest." And again, Rev. xix. 5, "And a voice came out of the throne, saying, Praise our God, all ye his servants, and ye that fear him, both small and great."

But why fear the Lord in these times?

For these four reasons.

First, Because of the glory of Christ their King. They shall behold their King in glory that shall cause fear. Rev. xix. 12, 13, 15, 16, Christ is described with his "eyes as a flame of fire, and on his head many crowns; and he was clothed with a vesture dipped in blood; and out of his mouth goeth a sharp sword, and he hath on his vesture and on his thigh a name written, King of kings, and Lord of lords." Thus they shall behold Christ, and therefore they shall fear.

Secondly, Because of the great works of God that shall then take place; "the heavens shall depart like a scroll, and the elements melt with fervent heat." This is meant of the time when there shall be "new heavens and a new earth," and refers to the prophecy of Isaiah, and apparently, and so interpreters generally explain it, regards the state of the church. Heb. xii. 26, quoted out of Hag. ii. 6, "Whose voice then shook the earth, but now he hath promised, saying, Yet once more, I shake not the earth only, but also heaven." There shall be wonderful works of God in the earth when those days come, therefore there shall be much of the fear of God.

Thirdly, Because the holiness and purity of the worship of God, and of his ordinances, shall cause fear. Did we see the ordinances in their true and native purity and holiness, it would inspire us with much awe. Some have but seen the execution of that one ordinance of excommunication solemnly performed, and it has daunted their spirits, and struck awe into the most proud, profane, stubborn, and wicked hearts; the beholding, then, of all the ordinances, and all duties of worship, in their native purity, holiness, and glory, cannot but cause much fear. Psal. lxviii. 35, "O God, thou art terrible out of thy holy places:" God will be terrible out of his holy places and out of all his holy ordinances.

Fourthly, Because the holiness of the saints, appearing brightly in their very faces and conversations, shall strike great fear. "Holy and reverend is thy name," is said of God, and so it shall be said of the saints in that day; their graces shall be much exalted, they shall sparkle with abundance of the graces of God's Spirit resting on them; their wisdom and holiness shall make their faces shine, "holy and reverend shall be their names." Psal. lxxxix. 7, "God is greatly to be feared in the assembly of the saints;" saints who walk close with him have a majesty in their appearance which appals guilty consciences. I appeal to apostates, to professors who frequent secret haunts of wickedness; when you come but into the presence of one who is a truly gracious and godly person, whom your conscience tells you walks close with God, does not even the very sight of such a one awe you? the very lustre of the holiness you see in such a one strikes on your conscience; then you think, he walks close with God indeed, but I have basely forsaken the Lord, and have frequented haunts of wickedness, and have brought dreadful guilt on my soul since I saw him last. Ecclesiastical history tells us, when the officers came to apprehend Basil, being then engaged in holy duties, such a majesty and lustre came forth from his countenance, that the officers fell down backward (as they did who came to apprehend Christ) and were not able to lay hold of him. Surely, when the saints shall be exalted in their holiness, when every one of them shall have their souls filled with God, it will cause abundance of fear in the hearts of all those who shall even converse with them.

But the wicked shall fear too, as well as the saints. Luke xxi. 26, "Men's hearts shall fail them for fear," shall be verified in these days, as it was in the destruction of Jerusalem.

The saints shall "fear the Lord and his goodness;" the words in the original are, they shall fear אל־יהוה to the Lord, and אל־טובו to his goodness. It is in effect the same; the goodness which God shall manifest shall excite this fear in their hearts.

You will say, What goodness? what shall that goodness of God be that shall move the hearts of this people with so much fear?

I will tell you briefly, for I have spoken of it at large on the last words of the first chapter of this prophecy, "great shall be the day of Jezreel;" and shall now only add, The goodness of God which in that day they shall fear, shall be this:

First, That ever he should regard such a wretched people as they, and pardon all their sins. What! Israel, the ten tribes, who had most wretchedly forsaken God, who had crucified Jesus Christ, crucified David their King, yet that that blood which they shed should be applied to them for the pardon of their sin! Oh the goodness of God! They shall fear this goodness in showing mercy to such a hard-hearted, stubborn, stiff-necked people as they have been; this goodness of God will break their hearts.

Secondly, Because God shall then make the difference between him that feareth God and him that feareth him not. Then shall God take away all the reproach of his saints. What bitter reproach has there been on the saints since the beginning of the world, especially since the times of the gospel! Reproach, first, because they are a mean people. Secondly, because they suffer so much, and God lets his adversaries prevail over them. Thirdly, because they wait upon God, and God seems not to come, the adversaries say, Where is your God? no marvel you pray and fast, what is become of all? Here will be manifested the goodness of God at that day in wiping off all this reproach. They shall have so much mercy, so much honour from God, that it shall appear before all the world that it was good to wait upon him; so much as shall compensate abundantly all their sufferings; they shall bless God that ever it was put into their hearts to suffer for him, and to wait upon him. And because God foresees what goodness he has laid up for his people, which they shall enjoy ere long, (and we know a thousand years with him are as one day,) is the reason why he suffers them to be so oppressed for the present; he knows he has such goodness for them hereafter, yea, in this world, that all the world shall say that God has dealt well with them, that he was not a hard master to them, to make them wait so long, and to let them suffer so much as they do. I will give you for this one excellent scripture, perhaps you have not considered the emphasis of its argument, it is Heb. xi. 16, "But now they desire a better country, that is, an heavenly: wherefore God is not ashamed to be called their God: for he hath prepared for them a city." The poor persecuted saints wandered up and down, were content to leave their own country, their estates here, and sought another country, a heavenly, but they had it not, their enemies prevailed over them, as if God had forsaken them; but "God is not ashamed to be called their God;" why? "for he hath prepared for them a city." Mark the force of the argument, "for he hath prepared for them a city." This city is the one referred to in the text I am now speaking of: sometimes it is described as a tabernacle, "The tabernacle of God shall come down from heaven;" sometimes as a city, sometimes as a country, as a kingdom, sometimes as an inheritance; here, "God hath prepared for them a city," that is, there is a glorious time for God's people, when they shall have the new Jerusalem come down from heaven unto them. Now then, saith God, though my people be in a suffering condition, "I am not ashamed to be called their God," I am not ashamed to own them, for I have glory enough for them: as if God would be ashamed that he should ever profess such an interest in this people, and they such an interest in him, if there were nothing in store for them, if there were not a time to recompense all their sufferings. As if a master should have a servant, or a prince a subject, and they suffer extremely, and have no help; but still when they expected aid, none should arrive, and when they think, Surely now it will come, still it should fail them; yet if you know that at such a day you shall be able to recompense them for all this, and to advance them and bring them to such honour that they will bless God that ever they were in your service, you will not be ashamed to own them. But if these servants shall suffer in your cause, and you have no time nor ability to recompense them, but they must suffer, and suffer for ever, you would be ashamed to own them. So God is pleased to speak here; Because I have prepared for them such a city, though they be in present persecution, I am not ashamed to own them for my people, and do not account it any dishonour to me, for there is a time coming that will answer all objections. This is the goodness of God.

They shall fear this goodness. Fear it; how?

In these several respects.

First, They shall admire "his goodness," and in their admirations stand even amazed at it; the fear of amazement shall possess them. 2 Thess. i. 10, when Christ shall come, "he shall come to be admired in all them that believe." In Luke v. 26, it is said, "They were all amazed, and glorified God, and were filled with fear, saying, We have seen strange things to-day." When this "goodness" of God shall come, all the saints shall stand admiring it with amazement, and say one unto another, We did heretofore hear of prophecies and promises, and we thought when they were opened to us, our hearts did burn within us; oh, they were blessed things! but now here is goodness we never thought of, this is higher and more glorious than we ever imagined. Thus they "shall fear the Lord and his goodness." You have a similar place in Jer. xxxiii. 9, "It shall be to me a name of joy, a praise and an honour before all the nations of the earth, which shall hear all the good that I do unto them: and they shall fear and tremble for all the goodness and for all the prosperity that I procure unto it."

Secondly, They shall upon this fall down and worship this God with fear. Oh how shall their hearts adore this God, because of this his goodness! As we read Exod. xxxiv., when God had told Moses that he would "make all his goodness pass before him;" when God came and "passed by before him, and proclaimed, The Lord, the Lord God, merciful and gracious, long-suffering, and abundant in goodness and truth, keeping mercy for thousands, forgiving iniquity and transgression and sin;" the text adds, When Moses heard this, he "made haste, and bowed his head and worshipped" before the Lord. Indeed nothing will cause a gracious heart to make more haste to worship God, than the beholding the glory and lustre of God's grace and goodness; then the heart will not stand dallying and trifling any longer, but will make haste to worship before the Lord. God often shows his greatness to you, and that convinces your consciences a little, and you think you must abandon your sinful courses; then temptation prevails over you again; but when God comes and makes known his goodness, then the heart stands out against the Lord no longer, but gives up itself to him in an everlasting covenant.

Thirdly, They shall fear to offend this goodness of God. It shall be a mighty engagement on their hearts to walk close with God. It is a sweet disposition indeed when the heart has been both humbled before God and his justice, and fears God and his goodness.

Obs. Whereas many will say, Oh the goodness of God will break our hearts, if ministers did preach only it; but when they preach the law, when we hear of terror, that hardens our hearts: take heed of this, there is more evil in it than you are aware. A truly gracious heart will fall down before any exhibition of the Lord, and it is not a good sign to be wrought upon only by the goodness of God, but may arise from much stubbornness of heart. Have you never known a perverse servant, or child, that as long as you are displeased with them, would resist you; but, perhaps, if you would yield a little, they would yield to you? Is this a good disposition? does it not arise from obstinacy in a child, or in a servant, or in a neighbour, that they will never yield to you till you yield to them? This is precisely the disposition of many; as long as they hear of God's greatness, and the terrors of the law, and God's justice, they are hardened; and why? because they stand out stoutly against God, notwithstanding his wrath is revealed from heaven. But, say they, when God's goodness is preached, then we yield; that is, except God will yield to them they will not yield to God. But when I can yield both ways, fear his goodness and his justice, then it is a sign of a gracious disposition indeed.

Fourthly, They "shall fear his goodness," so that they shall no longer slight nor abuse the goodness of God; they shall not do evil because God is good, but shall fear his goodness. We have a generation of men who, at this day, extremely abuse the goodness of God, even God's goodness in the gospel, in those blessed things revealed to us in Jesus Christ. As thus: we find this revealed in the gospel, that it is God that must work the will and the deed; the covenant of grace to be such, as that God does not only require, but work all for us: how is this goodness misinterpreted and abused! Therefore, say they, what need we do any thing? why do ministers urge people to duties? Your principle is good; the truth is good, that it is God that works all in the covenant of grace, but it is very absurd and vile, and an abuse of God's goodness, to infer that therefore you must not work together with the Lord as rational beings. Again, the gospel reveals to us "the righteousness of God in Christ," that we must not stand before God in our own, but in the righteousness of Christ; this principle is good, but how is it abused! false deductions and absurd consequences drawn from it: therefore say they, To make conscience of duties, what is it but legal? and they who do it, what are they but duty-mongers? Oh! wanton, wanton spirits, who do not fear God and his goodness, but abuse them both! Again, the Scripture tells us in the gospel, that all sins are pardoned to believers in Christ, all sins both great and small; "there is, therefore, now no condemnation to them that are in Christ Jesus," no, not one moment after they are once justified: this is God's goodness, and thou shouldst fear it: the principle is right, but it is vile to deduce as a consequence, that to preach that we must be humbled for sins is legal preaching; neither will these men ever confess their sins because of this goodness of God. This is to be wanton indeed, not to fear this goodness of God. Moreover the goodness of God in the gospel tells us, that the grace of God is strong, that the saints shall persevere, that those that are once in Christ shall never fall away; therefore say they, Let us indulge ourselves; why need we be careful of our ways, seeing the grace of God will carry us through? Oh! thus to abuse this goodness of God is wicked; the heavens may blush to behold it, and the earth tremble under it. But we have not so learned Christ; the more of the goodness of God in Christ that is made known to us, the more should we fear him.

The goodness of God in the gospel is so rich, that, the truth is, because the hearts of men are so vile, and so ready to abuse it, we are almost afraid to preach it. Oh! is this the fruit of the preaching of the gospel? Never was the gospel so clear as in England, and in no age as in this; and is this the fruit of all, that men should draw such absurd consequences from it, and go away harder from that which is the softening word? When we come to preach the goodness of the gospel, we come, I say, with fear, yea, trembling, lest it should cost the damnation of some soul. The preaching the goodness of God in the gospel certainly causes, *ex accidente,* the damnation of many a soul. Therefore, meanwhile, you who are God's saints, know how dearly God tendereth you, when he will have the goodness of the gospel preached to you though at the risk of the damnation of many a soul. You had need prize it therefore, and make a good use of it. Let this meditation cause you to improve to the uttermost what you hear of all the goodness of the Lord: That which I hear is costly to some, it costs the perishing of many a soul that I may have it; and though God see that many souls will be hardened by it, Yet, saith God, let them be hardened, these my servants shall not want it, though they perish for ever. When a man hath a thing in his house, and he hears that it cost dear, even the lives of many men, he has other thoughts of it than before. David had a reverent respect to the water of the well of Bethlehem, because procured at the hazard of men's lives. Learn then to fear God and his goodness.

Fifthly, In all rejoicing in and praising God for his goodness, there shall be a mixture of fear. They shall be well skilled in this mystery of godliness, when they enjoy so much of God's goodness, and are called upon to sing and rejoice, yet sing with a mixture of fear. Their hearts shall be very serious and spiritual in all their joy. It is very hard for us to rejoice in God's goodness, and not to have our hearts grow light and vain, to keep a day of thanksgiving with a serious spirit; for joy commonly causes vanity in the hearts of men. But now the goodness of God shall be so strong in their hearts, that though they shall seek and rejoice abundantly in God's goodness; yet with such an abundant mixture of fear, that their hearts shall be kept serious, holy, and spiritual in his service: thus, in Exod. xv. 11, when Moses was blessing God for his goodness in delivering the people out of Egypt, (which was a typical song, as appears in the Revelation, that bondage typifying antichristian bondage,) mark the expression, " Who is like unto thee, O Lord, among the gods? who is like thee, glorious in holiness, fearful in praises?" God is to be praised, but so praised, that his name must be "fearful in praises." Consider this in all your joyful celebration of the memorial of God's goodness; you must so rejoice and bless God, as to manifest this before all you converse with, that the name of God is fearful in the praises you offer to him: this a slight, trifling spirit cannot do. So Psal. lii. 6, "The righteous also shall see, and fear, and shall laugh at him." Mark what a mixture is here, " The righteous shall see, and fear, and laugh," he "shall rejoice," but "with trembling," Psal. ii. 11.

God much delights to have the glory of his goodness appear thus. We have much goodness of God at this day, and he calls us to fear him and his goodness: if we give him not his glory in this, he may soon call us to fear him and his greatness; to fear him and his justice; to fear him and his wrath. This is the argument now, " There is forgiveness with thee, that thou mayest be feared." But how soon may God justly turn this, and oblige us to say, There is wrath, vengeance, sword, fire, blood, storm, an horrible tempest, with thee, therefore thou shalt be feared! Our consciences are ready to misgive us when we have any evil tidings, for we have much guilt on our spirits; we have had much goodness indeed from God, (who ever thought to have lived to see the goodness that you have seen?) but because you have not feared God and his goodness, this is the reason of your hearts misgiving at evil tidings, and saying, Oh, now God is coming against us with his wrath that he may be feared.

Something might be said to explain a little the difference between fearing God and his goodness, and fearing God and his wrath and justice in a legal way; but I shall only briefly observe,

1. Such a fear as enlarges the heart, is the fearing God and his goodness; other fear contracts it. We have an excellent text for this in Isa. lx. 1, compared with ver. 5: " Arise, shine; for thy light is come, the glory of the Lord is risen upon thee:" and so he goes on describing God's goodness, in reference to the times that we are speaking of; then adds, "Thou shalt see, and flow together, and thine heart shall fear, and be enlarged:" when the heart so fears that it is enlarged unto God, this is the fearing God and his goodness aright.

2. It is a fear that leads the heart to cling to God for ever; it drives not from God, but makes the heart cleave closer to him; such is the force of the Hebrew here, they shall fear *to* God and *to* his goodness: "I will put my fear in their hearts, that they shall not depart from me." This binds the heart to God.

3. This fearing God and his goodness works the heart to a high degree of sanctification. 2 Cor. vii. 1, "Having therefore these promises, let us cleanse ourselves from all filthiness of the flesh and spirit, perfecting holiness in the fear of God:" and Heb. xii. 28, " Wherefore we receiving a kingdom which cannot be moved, let us have grace whereby we may serve God acceptably with reverence and godly fear."

Lastly, It is a fear joined with love, whereas the other fear leads the heart to have hard thoughts of God. Beware of that fear of God that makes you to think hardly of him. In times of danger many begin to fear, and presently they wish they had never engaged themselves so much in ways that succeed so ill; and cry out of others, You would needs do thus, and you see the result. But the fear of God and his goodness, is joined with blessing God that ever you knew his ways and were engaged in them.

" In the latter days."

God is content to stay for that which is indeed his chief glory until the latter days, for though in these former days God has had glory, yet he has had but very little. Let this be an argument for our patience; though we have sufferings now, let us wait as God waiteth.

But " the latter days," when are they? The times of the gospel are generally called "the latter days;" but this, though it refers indeed to the whole time of the gospel, yet especially to the latter times of those latter days. If you would know what these latter days are, though I will not take upon me to give you the day, or week, or month, or year, yet I will show you that probably these " latter days" are at hand.

For understanding this, we are much assisted by what we have in Daniel concerning the four kingdoms, and the prophetical chronology; it comprises the time from the captivity of the Jews to that in which the counsel of God shall be fulfilled. You have there a description of four several monarchies, the Babylonian, Assyrian, Grecian, and Roman; now in the last of these, Daniel saith, chap. ii. 44, "shall the God of heaven set up a kingdom, which shall never be destroyed: and the kingdom shall not be left to other people, but it shall break in pieces and consume all these kingdoms, and it shall stand for ever." In this last (namely, the Roman) has the kingdom of Christ begun to appear already; but God tells Daniel, chap. xii. 13, "Thou shalt stand in thy lot at the end of the days." Now observe, the chief prophecy we have respecting the time of these latter days is contained in that expression of "time and times and half a time;" and compare with this Dan. vii. 25, " And they shall be given into his hand until a time and times and dividing of time," and Rev. xi. 2, " The holy city shall they tread under foot forty and two months," and ver. 3, The "witnesses shall prophesy a thousand two hundred and sixty days;" now a thousand two hundred and sixty days, are the days of a "time and times and half a time," or of three years and a half, and so are the days of forty-two months. Then the woman in the wilderness, Rev. xii. 6, shall be fed there a thousand two hundred and sixty days, still the same number; the witnesses shall prophesy a thousand two hundred and sixty days; the holy city shall be trodden under foot forty-two months; and the woman in the wilderness shall be there a thousand two hundred and sixty days. And again, Dan. xii. 11, "From the time the abomination that maketh desolate is set up, there shall be a thousand two hundred and ninety days;" a few days more, not many. You see then the Scripture prophesies of some great thing to be done at this time, at the end of which are these "latter days."

But all the difficulty consists in understanding when the three years and a half, or forty-two months, or one thousand two hundred and sixty days, begun; having discovered it, we may know when these latter days shall be. Brightman makes the one thousand two hundred and ninety days begin at Julian's time, when he would have set up the abomination, that is, the Jewish worship again, by rebuilding the temple; and reckoning one thousand two hundred and ninety days for one thousand two hundred and ninety years, his time by computation will fall about the year 1650. The other passage in the Revelation (and that in Daniel refers to the same) denotes the time that the churches shall be under the persecution of antichrist; for a thousand two hundred and sixty years the beast shall prevail, and the witnesses prophesy in sackcloth, and the woman abide in the wilderness.

But when did antichrist begin to reign?

For that observe, It must be at the time when the Roman empire was broken up, and the dragon resigned his power to the beast; when the power of the dragon that persecuted the Christians under the Roman empire was given to antichrist, so that they became subject to persecution under him: here the one thousand two hundred and sixty days begin.

That the Roman empire must be given up first, appears, 2 Thess. ii. 7, "For the mystery of iniquity doth already work: only he who now letteth will let, until he be taken out of the way;" that is, as expositors generally interpret it, when the power of the Roman empire is "taken out of the way," then shall that wicked one be revealed; there were many antichrists before, but then that wicked one that shall "exalt himself above all that is called God," shall have power to persecute the church. Hence it is observable, that the custom of the church was to pray for the continuance of the Roman empire, because they knew when that was broken antichrist would come. Now the dissolution of the Roman empire was at the raising up of those ten distinct governments, called in the Revelation, ten kings; and the raising up of those kings was about four hundred years after Christ; it is hard to fix on the precise year, so much difference exists in chronologers' computations; and after that period there must be one thousand two hundred and sixty days, that is, one thousand two hundred and sixty years. Make this computation, and compare all these passages together, and it would seem that the time cannot be distant, but that in the present century these latter days shall come, when the people of God and the Jews shall "return to Jehovah and David their king, and fear the Lord and his goodness." The nearer the time comes the more will these things be cleared: Dan. xii. 9, "Go thy way, Daniel: for the words are closed up and sealed till the time of the end:" none of the wicked shall understand, but the wise shall lay it to heart.

But one point remains, why the Scripture expresses this rather by so many days, than years? The reason is, because God would have his people think the time until his goodness should be revealed but short; if he had said they should be one thousand two hundred and sixty years under antichrist's persecution, it would have sounded harsher: No, saith he, it shall be but so many days (though flesh and blood may think even this time long); yet look upon it as days; it is but a short time to me, and it will be a short time to you; within one thousand two hundred and sixty days you shall be delivered from his tyranny, and then you shall have this voice from heaven, "The kingdoms of the earth are become the kingdoms of the Lord and of his Christ, and he shall reign for ever;" and then shall ye, together with the Jews, seek the Lord and David your king, and fear the Lord and his goodness.

Now, by God's goodness, we have gone through these three chapters. Tertullian saith, *Adoro plenitudinem Scripturarum*, I adore the fulness of the Scriptures. By searching thus into the Scriptures, we may come to see rich treasures in them, and so, like him, adore their fulness. How do we read over texts, as if they contained nothing! but certainly God has revealed much more of his mind in them than we are aware of: let us all then be in love with the study of the Scriptures.

CHAPTER IV.

Ver. 1. *Hear the word of the Lord, ye children of Israel: for the Lord hath a controversy with the inhabitants of the land, because there is no truth, nor mercy, nor knowledge of God in the land.*

IN this chapter we have,

I. A suit commenced.

II. The pleading of God.

III. Judgment pronounced.

IV. Exhortation to Judah to beware that she come not into the same condition.

V. Execution, God in his wrath giving up Ephraim to himself.

I. A suit commenced. Israel is cited: "Hear the word of the Lord, ye children of Israel."

Obs. 1. The knowledge that any truth is the word of the Lord, is a special means to prepare the heart to receive it with reverence and all due respect, even though it be hard and grievous to flesh and blood. It was a hard message that Hosea had to bring, to tell them of God's controversy; he therefore makes this preface, "Hear the word of the Lord." Hard truths are hardly borne; but when the authority of the infinite God appears in them, be they either for us or against us, our hearts must bow to them; they lay bonds upon the conscience, and bind over to eternal death those who reject them. 2 Chron. xxvi. 12, Zedekiah, a king, is charged with not humbling himself before the prophet Jeremiah. Though the prophet be never so poor and contemptible in himself, yet if he bring the word of the Lord, Zedekiah the king must humble himself before him.

Obs. 2. The nearness of a people to God, exempts them not from God's contending with them for sin. "Ye children of Israel." In this appellation God puts them in mind of the covenant he had made with them and they with him: You are not heathens, but the children of Israel, in covenant with me, a people near to me, yet I have a controversy with you. Neither should nearness to us exempt any from our contending with them. "If thy brother, the son of thy mother, or thy son, or thy daughter, or the wife of thy bosom, or thy friend, which is as thine own soul, entice thee secretly, saying, Let us go and serve other gods; thine eye shall not pity him, neither shalt thou spare, neither shalt thou conceal him: but thou shalt surely kill him; thine hand shall be first upon him to put him to death," Deut. xiii. 6, 8, 9.

Obs. 3. The nearer the relationship the more grievous is the controversy. "Hear the word of the Lord, ye children of Israel." It is a sad thing for one nation to have a controversy with another; much more for a people to be at controversy with itself; yet more sore and grievous is it when the controversy comes nearer, into the family, between husband and wife, between father and child, between dearest friends who were before to each other as their own souls: Prov. xviii. 19, "A brother offended is harder to be won than a strong city: and their contentions are like the bars of a castle."

Quid dicturus es, o propheta, qui tanta diligentia vocas ut audiatur verbum Domini. Œcolamp. in locum.

"Hear ye." O prophet, saith Œcolampadius, what is it thou hast to say, that with so much earnestness thou callest to have the word of the Lord heard? The solemn message of the prophet to this people is, "The Lord hath a controversy with the inhabitants of the land."

The word ריב translated "controversy," signifies a debate, or contention, and comes from ריב *contendere vel privatim vel coram judice*, to contend privately or before a judge. As in Exod. xxiii. 3, "Neither shalt thou countenance a poor man in his cause." The Septuagint render it κρίσις, *judicium*. The same word is translated by them also δίκη, Job xxix. 16, where the word for "cause," is the same as here translated a "controversy." The Lord hath a cause to plead with this people; the prophet stands up for God to plead against them in his name, he pleads for the King, the King of heaven: so should all faithful ministers take heed that they be on God's side, pleading his cause, for they are God's sergeants at law, his attorneys, his solicitors. The king's lawyers are sworn that they shall never plead against him, nor take fee on the other side; and yet how many, even in the exercise of their ministry, show that they have taken fee on the other side! How many plead against God, against his sabbaths, against his ordinances, yea, plead sometimes against the power of godliness, against those things wherein the chief dignity and glory of God consists! Truly, the devil has not more cordial solicitors and pleaders for him than those who would be accounted the prophets of the Lord.

"The Lord." As if the prophet should say, Though you think you can make your cause good with me, and with Amos, and the other prophets, know you have not to deal with us; God will no longer stand pleading with you by his ministers, he will take the cause into his own hands, and will plead by his judgments. So the Lord tells the people, Gen. vi. 3, that his Spirit should no longer strive with them. What is that? That is, in the way of Noah's ministry; but that he would come and strive himself after another manner, by bringing the flood upon them.

Obs. 1. For God to take the controversy into his own hand, and to contend with them in a way of judgment, is most dreadful for sinners; "It is a fearful thing to fall into the hands of the living God." You think ministers are harsh, and preach terrible things; but if you had to deal with God immediately, if he did not speak to you by man, but come himself and plead with you, you would find it much harder. When Job's friends were pleading with him, he could with them easily sustain his cause; but in chap. xxxviii. 2, God himself comes and speaks out of the whirlwind, "Who is this that darkeneth counsel by words without knowledge?" And Job answereth the Lord and saith, "Behold, I am vile," chap. xl. 4. And the Lord still pleading with him, he is constrained to exclaim, "I have heard of thee by the hearing of the ear; but now mine eye seeth thee: wherefore I abhor myself, and repent in dust and ashes," chap. xlii. 5, 6. In Psal. cxxx. 3, David uses similar language, "If thou, Lord, shouldest mark iniquities, O Lord, who shall stand?" The sense would have been complete thus, If thou, Lord, shouldst mark iniquities, who shall stand? there would have been a mighty emphasis in the word Jehovah; who shall stand, for it is thou, O Jehovah? but the word Lord is repeated, to show that the sight of having to deal with God in our sins, without a Mediator, is very terrible. If thou, Lord, shouldst mark, then, O Lord, who shall stand?

Obs. 2. Sin causes a most dreadful controversy between God and the soul, between God and a nation. For this, God comes to strive, to contend for his glory, and the sinner strives and contends against God: and here we may remark,

1. That God is infinitely above every sinful impenitent soul, and every sinful impenitent nation; vainly do they strive with their Maker. "Let the potsherd strive with the potsherds of the earth," Isa. xlv. 9. The Lord is far above them. And to intimate therefore the distance between God and us in this controversy, our text saith, "The Lord hath a controversy with the inhabitants of the land," poor earth-creeping creatures that have dwellings here below, whose houses are houses of clay, and God is the great God of heaven and earth.

2. The controversy that God has with a sinner is a just controversy, God has right on his side, and the injury done to him is great.

3. It is a controversy which we have begun; God did not begin it with us, but we began it with him, and must have the worst of it.

4. It is an old controversy, a controversy of our forefathers, a controversy which God has had with one generation after another, and we, as a wretched generation, stand forth to hold up the old controversy. As in England in the times of the barons there were wars for hundreds of years; and when one generation was gone, the generation after stood forth to hold up the controversy: so it has been between God and man; God has had a controversy with the children of men ever since the fall of Adam, and one generation after another has stood forth to hold up the controversy. And thou, wretched sinner, standest up in thy generation, in thy place, to sustain the controversy that mankind has had with God since his expulsion from Paradise.

5. It is a controversy which stirs up all the power and all the wrath of God against a sinner. A man who has a controversy with another, employs and exerts all the strength he has against his opponent; and if God have any power in him, it shall be put forth in making his cause good against a sinner: "If ye walk contrary unto me, I will walk contrary unto you;" my power, my wisdom, all mine attributes are against you, Lev. xxvi.

6. This controversy is a deadly controversy, one which strikes at our lives, at our souls, at our eternal state.

7. This is a controversy with God, who is determined to have satisfaction in some way or other for all the wrong we have done to him.

8. It is a controversy which only the Lord Christ, that great Mediator, that great Peace-maker, is able to make up. None can reconcile God and a sinner but Christ, God-man. He must stand before God to satisfy for the wrong the sin of man hath done unto him.

9. A controversy with him who has thee at infinite advantage, who has thee under his feet, and the point of the sword of his justice at thy heart.

10. A controversy which, if thou look not to it, is likely to prove an everlasting controversy. "I will not contend for ever, neither will I be always wroth: for the spirit should fail before me," Isa. lvii. 16. This

is spoken to those who are in covenant with God, in regard of the lesser controversies which after their reconciliation may exist between God and them: but with thee who art yet in the great controversy that God has with sinful man, it may prove an everlasting controversy, if thou dost not look to it, and become reconciled to God in Christ. The Lord has appointed a certain period for thy coming in to make up thy peace with him, to "lay hold of his covenant;" if thou neglectest that time thou art lost, undone for ever. God will certainly overcome thee, God will have the day of thee, the Lord will overcome when he judgeth. Julian strove a great while against the Lord, but at length he was forced to acknowledge with his blood cast up into the air, *Vicisti, Galilææ, vicisti*, Thou hast conquered, O Galilean, thou hast conquered.

It is a vain thing for thee to stand out striving with this great God. Job xl. 2, "Shall he that contendeth with the Almighty instruct him?" So it is translated in your Bibles, but the original is perhaps better rendered by Pagnine and others, "Is there any wisdom," or any learning, "in contending with God?" any knowledge showed in that? No, certainly, there is no knowledge, no wisdom, in contending with the Almighty: our greatest wisdom is to fall down and be humbled before the Lord.

My brethren, this is no time to have any controversy with God, to stand out against him in ways of enmity. When such blackness of darkness is upon us, even storms of blood hanging over our heads, it surely is time to be at peace with Heaven: "Because there is wrath, beware lest he take thee away with his stroke," Job xxxvi. 18. The Lord is come forth from his place, he is pleading his cause, and now in the ways of his administration he declares, that he will have glory from his creature; he "hath sworn by himself, the word hath gone out of his mouth in righteousness, and shall not return, That to him every knee shall bow, every tongue shall swear." It is no time, therefore, now for us to have controversies with God, to have controversies with God and man both, with heaven, and earth, and with our own consciences. What shall become of us? "Be not thou a terror, O Lord, unto me," saith Jeremiah, "for thou art my hope in the day of evil." If God be a terror, and the days be evil, what will become of us?

Consider this, you who are so often in controversies with your neighbours, that God has a great controversy with you; and satisfy not yourselves with this, that you are able to clear yourselves before men, for what avails that, so long as this controversy continues?

It is wisdom to make an end of it betimes: "The beginning of strife is as when one letteth out water; therefore leave off contention before it be meddled with," Prov. xvii. 14. The beginning of strife, especially with God, is most dreadful; if thou go on but a little while, thy heart may be most desperately set against God, and for ever left to strive against him, never to come in and be humbled before him. This is the reason (I verily believe) of the horrid wickedness of some amongst us; we wonder that they, one after another, should dare to venture on such horrid wickednesses. At first, it may be, there was some dreadful breach between God and their souls when they were young, and they fell (though the world perhaps knew it not) into some foul and abominable sin; and having departed so far from God then, they now go on and fight against the God of heaven in such a desperate manner as no age but this can afford us any examples of. God has a controversy with nations also for their sin. Those who are to sue for God may well charge us, that the Lord has a controversy with the inhabitants of the land at this day. If ever he had a controversy with a people he has it with us. The Lord has a fearful controversy with us, most fearful things to charge this land with. I might instance some that are more peculiar to this nation than to any other on the face of the earth.

1. The hatred, contempt, and persecution of the power of godliness. No nation on the face of the earth has ever had such guilt in this respect as England; persecuting faithful and godly ministers of the same religion, holding with them all fundamental truths, yea, all the articles of religion and every point of doctrine; I say, never any nation was guilty of such persecution as we; silencing many for mere trifles; persecuting others for keeping the sabbath. It is true, other countries are loose in their observation of the sabbath, but no country on the face of the earth has ever persecuted the keeping of it as England has done; and that by the countenance of those in authority. We are sinners, and others are sinners, but the Lord has a controversy with us for these things in a more special manner than with any people on the face of the earth this day.

2. This controversy which the Lord has against us, is an old controversy too. I may apply that which God speaks, Jer. xxxii. 31, concerning the city of Jerusalem, unto us, "This city hath been to me as a provocation of mine anger and of my fury, from the day that they built it, even unto this day." So, ever since the Reformation commenced have we been a provocation to the Lord.

3. A general controversy, even with all sorts; a controversy with our kings and princes, with our nobles, our gentry, our cities, countries, universities, common people; with wicked people, with godly people, with the saints, with all.

4. It is the most unkind controversy on our part that any nation was ever engaged in; for God had dealt with us in a way of love more than with any nation in the world besides, he made us even as "the dearly beloved of his soul," and yet, for all this, we have contended against him. This unkindness goes even to the very heart of God.

5. The Lord has sent many faithful ambassadors to plead his cause with us. He never to any nation on the earth sent more faithful ambassadors, that have pleaded his cause with more power and evidence of the Spirit, than to us in England; yet we have stood out.

6. We have had as many offers of mercy as ever people had. Many a time have we been upon the brink of judgment, and the bowels of God have been towards us, and he has said, "It shall not be."

7. The Lord has been as patient, and forborne as long as ever he did with any people before he came to execution. Where do we read of a people that has had, as we, nearly a hundred years' peace? no where that I know of in all the Scripture.

8. The Lord has had us at advantages as much as can be; we have broken as many treaties as ever people broke. When we seemed to yield to God, we have but flattered him with our lips and dealt dissemblingly with him.

9. God has broken the backs of others with whom he has had a controversy. He has had a controversy with Germany, and how has he dealt with it? It is reported that in Germany, when the war was but twenty or thirty miles off, they went on in their trading, and followed their businesses, buying and selling, and hoped that they should be safe; but God came in his judgments, and desolated Germany. Thus is he beginning to deal with us. Is not some part of England at this day as desolate as Germany itself?

10. Those that knew most of God's mind, have been so afraid of this controversy, that they have fled for fear of the wrath of God; and we have slighted, jeered them for it, ascribed it to their foolish timorousness and melancholy conceit: the Lord now seems to justify their fear

The Lord is now for the present out against us in as dreadful a way of wrath as ever he was against any people of the earth. I never read in Scripture nor in history of a more dreadful wrath of God against a people, all things considered, than is against us at this day. Amos vii. 4, "The Lord called to contend by fire:" surely the Lord does it at this day, he calls to contend with England by fire, in a most dreadful way; and who knows what the end shall be? That he has a most dreadful controversy against England, will appear if we further consider,

1. That a people complaining of bondage heretofore, yet, when God offered deliverance, should be so far left of him as to prefer making themselves and their posterity slaves. Surely God has a dreadful controversy against us, it were else impossible that such a thing should be in the hearts of men. Men love liberty, and groan under bondage: we did groan but a few years ago, and the Lord was coming to help us, and yet we are now so left of God that we even turn again to our former bondage, and would have our ears bored that we might be perpetual slaves, Exod. xxi. 6; Psal. xl. 6.

2. We not only turn again to bondage, but do so out of a spirit of enmity against the yoke of Jesus Christ. This is the very ground of it; in a great part of the kingdom, whatever yoke they have upon them, they are resolved they will not have the yoke of Christ, out of a spirit of enmity against the godly party, who desire and endeavour reformation.

At the beginning of this parliament, when we began to hope for some liberty and reformation, what joy was there generally in the kingdom! all men agreed together; but when the wicked and carnal began to see that their godly neighbours rejoiced and blessed God that their desires were being fulfilled, presently they turn, out of a spirit of malice against them; Rather than they shall rejoice, rather than they shall be gratified, we will turn back again to the former bondage, and we will stand and oppose that which heretofore we rejoiced in. They have therefore turned malignants against that cause which a man would wonder that ever rational men should oppose. But there is also a spirit of malice against Christ and his ordinances: men *would* enjoy their lusts; they think if reformation come they should not have them with their former liberty; hence arises the opposition of the gentry and others in the country. Surely God has a controversy with us.

3. That men should so vilely desert those whom they have chosen and trusted, and who have been faithful, those worthies in parliament, who have ventured their lives for them; basely and unworthily now to desert them, is one of the greatest judgments of God upon the hearts of men. If they complain of them now, they would have complained much more of them if they had complied. Suppose the parliament had made up a patched reformation and a crazy peace, liable to be broken on every occasion, would not the people of the land have cried out of their unfaithfulness? But now, when they venture themselves and labour so hard for a sound peace, to be deserted! An unworthy generation, a generation that we have cause to fear is become the generation of God's wrath and the people of his curse. People are affected according to success; we complain of those in parliament because of some difficulties in the work, yet if they had not done what they did they would have been complained of much more. So of ministers: sometimes ministers speak and stir up people because their consciences tell them they would be unfaithful to their country and to the cause of God if they did not; and forthwith men call them, as they did Luther, the trumpets of sedition and rebellion; whereas, on the other side, if they had said nothing, then the cry would have been, that they had betrayed their country, and that they were not so faithful in their places as they should, and therefore people were so bad as they were. Thus hard it is for God or man to please people.

But further, that not only the people, but that so many nobles, and some members even of the parliament, should desert their brethren, and join with papists, French, and Walloons. Not long since, a company of vile wretches were gathered together to fight against our brethren of Scotland; yet these people, vile as they were, could not by any means be induced to fight against them. But now, not the vile ones, but nobles, knights, and gentry, can be brought to fight against the parliament, their own brethren. Is not here a mighty hand of God against us? Could this ever be if God had not a dreadful controversy against England?

4. That men should be so blinded as to think the protestant religion should be maintained by an army of papists, the laws and liberty of the subject, by an army of delinquents and strangers; yea, that the king with papists, delinquents, French, and Walloons, should better maintain the liberty of the subject and the protestant religion, than with the parliament; is not the hand of God upon the people of this land when they believe this? Are they not infinitely besotted? can we think that men endued with reason should do this? Surely not, if the judgment of God rested not fearfully on their souls.

5. God surely contends fearfully with us when he suffers such an ill cause to prosper and attain to such a height. Both England and the countries around us stand amazed at this success. Surely the Lord is against us, or else it could not have been.

6. When there exists a design so desperate, so long maturing, carried on by such means, and now at such a time breaking forth with such violence, and yet men cannot see it. The track of the design is as apparent as the sun at noon-day, and by comparing one thing with another we may clearly see how it has proceeded step by step. Would you not think it a besotting thing, if there should be a train of gupowder laid along the streets from some place to the parliament house to blow it up, and yet that men should pass by and say, they see no such thing? Certainly the design against our religion and state, to bring us under tyranny and slavery, is as evident and plain in its progress, as ever was a train of gunpowder laid to a place that men desired to blow up; and yet men see it not. Surely God's hand is out against us.

7. That we should have so little fruit of our prayers as we have at this day, yea, that God should seem to be angry with the prayers of his people. This argues a fearful controversy. And in this one particular amongst others; what prayers in England have been sent up to God for the Palsgrave's children! and that now, instead of answering our prayers, God should send two arrows, as it were, out of those loins to do us mischief, that it should come from them for whom England has done so much, and sent up so many prayers to God; that they in return for all this should come hither to make havoc of the kingdom, surely proves that the hand of God is out against us.

8. That our brethren should be so spoiled, and ourselves in such danger of drinking the dregs of the cup, yet where are our hearts? The judgment of God is upon the hearts of men, that they stir not and act like men, but see their brethren spoiled before them; and in the mean time, all that keeps them quiet is only that they hope they shall be the last. God's hand is upon the hearts of men, else this could not be. Could one ever have thought that Englishmen could have borne this? If one had told them before that an army of papists should rise up with French, Walloons, and Irish, to spoil the kingdom, to destroy our brethren, would one have ever imagined that Englishmen should

have borne it, and stirred no more than they have done? You talk indeed of this and that, and of going forth every fourth man; but all such resolutions and such great words generally fall to the ground, as if men were willing and content to lay down their necks upon the block. Surely the guilt of the blood of our brethren may justly come upon us, and God may have a controversy with us for suffering it to be spilled.

9. That God should put so many opportunities of mercy into our hands, and we neglect all, manifests the hand of God to be against us, and is a fruit of his controversy with us.

10. That God himself should take away our opportunities, that when we are nigh to deliverance he should drive us back, is an argument of a heavy controversy indeed. Numb. xiii., when the people were come very near to Canaan, and were even ready to take possession, God resolved against them, that none but Caleb and Joshua should enter, and they were beaten back again: and in chap. xiv. 33, it is said, that the people, when they heard this, mourned greatly, for they saw the hand of God out against them. The truth is, we have been on the very borders of Canaan. O! what an opportunity God put into our hands in the west! I say not we lost it, but there God's own hand showed itself against us; Bristol then might have been saved, but God would not. And so when we were even near deliverance God seemed to drive us back, as if saying to us, I approve not, I have somewhat more to say to this generation; it may be I may show mercy afterward to their young ones, but against this my wrath shall be let out. Surely we may be afraid, from the ways of God's present administration, lest this should be in God's heart. However, let us consider it, and mourn greatly before the Lord. God "hath a controversy with the inhabitants of the land."

It is no time now to have controversies one with another, to be wrangling one with another about matters of opinion. It is time for us now to lay down all our private controversies, and fall to making up the controversy with our God. It is no time now for brethren to strive with brethren, but to strive and wrestle with God in prayer. If we have any strength with us, let it not be spent in contending one with another, but let all our strength be spent in seeking to make peace with our God. It is said of the Romans, that they had a temple of Concord, and none were to go to offer any further sacrifice, till they had first offered in that temple. The Lord expects the same of us; we should agree one with another, lay down all our own controversies, and then give up ourselves, as one man, to this great work of making up our controversy with him. If two chickens be fighting and the kite come near, they will leave pecking one another and run to the hen for shelter. We stand pecking and snarling one at another, and many, that say they will do thus and thus for the public cause, take exception against this man and that man, and at this thing and that thing, and so let their private grudges come in and draw them off. O, let us not be quarrelling now the kite is coming near, let us run and shelter ourselves under the protection of God, by making our peace with him.

As for the controversy that is this day between the king and us, we can in that appeal to God, that there is no just cause the king should contend with us, as we only desire to deliver ourselves from tyranny and slavery. Our privileges and liberties are dear to us, they are our right as truly as his honour is his. That which he inherits was his forefathers', and that which his forefathers, his predecessors, inherited, came at first from the people, who set up such a family to rule and govern them; and certainly they never set it up but for the public good, not for their misery and ruin. We can appeal to God, that we desired nothing else but to live peaceably and to serve God in our land, enjoying only what God, and nature, and the laws of our land had made our own. We know the relation between him and us, and the bond is mutual; and if there be any thing done now that perhaps cannot be justified by any positive, explicit law of the land, let men know that yet it may be justified by the very light of nature and by the law of arms. It cannot be imagined but if those that ought to be the protectors of the law, against law deal so hardly with us, that we must have recourse then to the law and light of nature; it is impossible this should be otherwise, and this God himself approves.

Whatever, therefore, becomes of this controversy between him and us, whether reconciliation or not, yet we have peace in this, that what we have done in resisting a deluge of misery that was coming upon us, if we had not done it, our consciences would have upbraided us, generations to come would have cursed us, the nations around us, yea, our very enemies, would have scorned us for our base cowardliness, for our sordid spirits; would have derided us as an unworthy generation, that could see itself and posterity sinking into misery and brought under slavery, and out of base fear and sluggish litherness, and effeminate softness of spirit, could suffer all to be brought into bondage to the humours and lusts of a few men. We can, therefore, with comfort and boldness stand at God's tribunal, and plead the uprightness of our hearts and justness of our cause in this controversy, whatever ensues. But in the controversy that God has against us, there we fall down at his feet, and acknowledge ourselves guilty before him; yea, we come with sackcloth upon our loins, and ashes on our heads, with ropes on our necks, and plead mercy only for our lives. And this is the work that we have to do in all the days of our humiliation, to seek to make an atonement between God and our souls and the land, in regard of that dreadful controversy he has against us. Now, blessed God, because thou tellest us in thy word, "Because I will do this, therefore prepare to meet thy God, O Israel;" thou threatenest hard, great and sore evils, and thou callest now to us, Because thou wilt do this, England, O England, prepare to meet thy God; we come, (oh that this might be our answer,) we come, Lord, and meet thee with our souls bowed towards thee, with our hearts bleeding that we have provoked thee to cause so much bloodshed of our brethren amongst us. O Lord, our hearts are open to thee, and with trembling spirits we cry to the Lord, What wilt thou have us do? If thou proceed against us in thy controversy, we are undone, we are undone. O Lord, forgive; O Lord, arise and be merciful, we beseech thee; for by whom shall Jacob rise, for he is small? by whom shall the people arise? by whom shall the power of godliness and thine ordinances be maintained?

How happy were we (think some) if the controversy between the king and us were at an end, that we might have peace! Oh if the people were happy that were in such a case, how happy the people that were at peace with the King of heaven! If the controversy between God and us were at an end we should be happy indeed. The Lord and the land is at a controversy, and this makes us cry out unto God; but yet woe unto us! here is the misery, we still keep our sins that cause the controversy. Jer. xxxv., "Will the Lord reserve his anger for ever? will he keep it unto the end?" mark what the answer is, "Behold, thou hast spoken and done evil things as thou couldest." Thus you have said; but what is the fruit of this? You have done evil as you could. We in the days of our fasts cry, Lord, wilt thou reserve thine anger for ever? wilt thou keep thine anger unto the end? Behold, thus we speak, but we continue to do evil as we can. "We wait for light," saith Isa. lix. 9, 10, "but behold obscurity; for brightness, but we walk in darkness. We grope for the wall like the blind." We indeed grope as if we had no eyes, and we stumble at noon-day as if it were night. Men to this day are ready to cry out and say, What shall we do? as if the way were not clear before us what we should do. The way is clear enough if we had hearts, but "we grope as if we had no eyes, and we stumble at noon-day as in the night." In many places of the kingdom they "roar all like bears," and they have cause to do so; for they are miserably spoiled, their wives ravished, their houses plundered, themselves imprisoned: and for the rest of us, "we mourn sore like doves," night and day; and "we look for judgment, but there is none; for salvation, but it is far off from us:" mark what follows, "For our transgressions are multiplied before thee," (there is the ground of that controversy between God and us,) "and our sins testify against us, for our transgressions are with us." Surely, my brethren, God is willing to be at peace with England again; the controversy is great and sore, yet we may confidently declare that the Lord is yet willing to be at peace with England, and the sufferings of England go as near the heart of God as ours. Oh that we knew then what it is that is the great makebate between God and us, that we might get rid of it! Would you know it? In 2 Sam. xx. 21, Joab saith, Deliver us Sheba the son of Bichri, and we will depart from the city and go every one unto his tent. If amongst us delinquents were punished as they ought, if the hearts of people were prepared to have the remainders of superstition and idolatry cast out, if they were willing to receive Jesus Christ as King among them, the sound of retreat would soon be heard, the controversy would soon be at an end; and except this be the foundation of our peace, either there will be no peace at all, or it will not hold long. In our raising of forces therefore to help ourselves and our brethren, (seeing we pretend we will do more than before, and it is time we should if we be not a people destinated to destruction and ruin,) be sure we begin here, let us do more than ever we did before to make up this controversy with God. It is reported of Achior, one of Holofernes' captains, that he counselled Holofernes to inquire first, whether the Jews had offended their God, before he attempted to make war against them; for if they had, he then assured him that that would be their ruin, and that he might go up and overcome them; but if he could not hear that they had sinned against their God, it was in vain for him to strive against them. Truly, it concerns us nearly to make up our peace with God, that when our adversaries come out against us they may not indeed be made use of to avenge God's quarrel upon us, for then they will thus easily improve all their advantages, and say, that they, indeed, are not come out against us without the Lord. Every victory they now get, they are ready to flatter themselves, and say, that God fights against us, and God approves them; and tell us, the reason they prevail is, because God is against us; and so we know Rabshakeh did, though a foul railer: "Are we come up without the Lord?" said he. And the enemies of David spake against him, "saying, God hath forsaken him; persecute and take him: for there is none to deliver him," Psal. lxxi. 10, 11. Thus they will be ready to say upon every occasion, The Lord has forsaken them, let us persecute and take them. And certainly, if the Lord should suffer them to prevail, many of them would think they did God good service by slaying and rooting out the generation of God's people that is here in England, and would be confident that it was the mind of God that they should be rooted out. Therefore we had need look to it to make up our peace with God, that the controversy between him and us may not prove to be their victory.

Obs. 5. Men should be willing that the cause that is between them and their inferiors should be pleaded. God having to deal with poor earthen creatures, might presently have let his wrath out against them and destroyed them. But mark, God is willing to have his cause pleaded with vile creatures, so that all the while he is pleading there is time and space for them to come in; as if a controversy be between husband and wife, though the one be superior and the other inferior, they think it right to debate it between themselves with meekness and love. Job, chap. xxxi. 13, professed he did not despise the cause of his man-servant, when he contended with him, but he would have that pleaded and made out. Jehovah, the mighty God, condescends to put his cause to a suit, he will not pass sentence upon poor creatures till it come to a trial. Be not then surly and scornful towards your inferiors.

Obs. 6. Whatsoever mercy you have from God, you are to look upon it as a fruit of God's faithfulness to you, (if you be God's,) and as a ground of your obedience to him, and his pleading with you if you walk not answerable to it. "The inhabitants of the land." The inhabitants of the land; what land? The inhabitants of the land of Canaan, a controversy with them! Mark, God fulfilled his promise in bringing them into the land of Canaan, and now he pleads with them for the forfeiture of their promise. Psal. cv. 44, 45, he tells them, that he had given them the lands of the heathen, "that they might observe his statutes and keep his laws;" that was their condition. God fulfilled his part by bringing them into the land, but when they were in the land they minded not their part. You know, God often charged them when they came into the land to do this and that, and they promised they would do it, but when they were once brought into the land they forgot it, and forsook God. God now comes and pleads with the inhabitants of this land; as if he should say, I have done my part in bringing you into the land, now I come to plead with you for breaking your promise and covenant.

"The inhabitants of the land." Jerome has another note upon it, but as it is farther off, I will only name it. "Rightly," saith he, "are they called to answer and to judgment who are the inhabitants of the land, and do not look upon themselves as sojourners and strangers in the land; but he that can truly say with the prophet, 'I am a pilgrim and a stranger here,' such a one can never do that which may cause God to have a controversy against him. The reason why men do that which causes God to have a controversy with them, is because they look upon themselves as possessors of the land, and not as pilgrims and strangers." But this is too far off.

II. The pleading of God. A suit first is entered against a man; when the court day comes, there is calling for a declaration, the lawyer declares: God does so, and the prophet is God's lawyer, and here are three articles put in this declaration, "Because there is no truth, no mercy, no knowledge of God in the land."

Obs. 1. God contends not with a people without a cause. How many are there that strive and contend one with another without any cause at all! they vex and rage, contend and sue, and great controversies exist, great dust is raised; but if we sift the matter, we can see just nothing, they themselves know no cause, they can give no rational account of all their pleading one against another. As David said to Eliab, his eldest brother, 1 Sam. xvii. 29, when he came and wrangled with him, "What have I now done? Is there not a cause?" Eliab's spirit was up through his envy; but, saith David, Have not I a cause for what I did? Thus many have their spirits up, chiding and wrangling, but examine the cause, and they can show none at all. How many bitter spirits go about like mad dogs, snarling at every one, even at those they know not, with whom they had never any thing to do, yet railing upon them every where! Ask them, Do you know the man? can you prove any thing against him? The truth is, they are not able to make good what they say, only there is a general report that such and such men do thus and thus, and they bite and snarl, and rage against them, but after all they know no cause. Such men, they say, disturb the kingdom and trouble the people. The foundations of the earth are out of order, but what have the righteous done? You would think, when you hear such railings against such men, that they were the most monstrous men upon earth; but examine what it is that they have done, and there is nothing. God does not so with you; God never contends with man but for a just cause.

Obs. 2. God contends not against a people for little things. When God saith he "hath a controversy with the inhabitants of the land," it is not for trifles, for ordinary infirmities, for daily transgressions, but for great, notorious sins. Not that little things do not deserve a controversy, but it is from the virtue and fruit of the covenant that this comes to pass; in others that are not in covenant, little things make a controversy, but between God's children and himself little things make not a controversy. But men are of froward spirits, every trifle is enough to make a controversy between them. Yea, usually the greatest controversies between nearest friends is some trifle or other. Do a man and his wife live lovingly and sweetly many years, and yet fall out afterwards? Is there a bitter controversy? Examine it, it is but about some toy. I could give you examples in histories of bitter controversies between nearest friends on small and trivial grounds. Camerarius tells a story of two brethren, who walking out in a star-light night, one of them said, Would I had a pasture as large as this element; and the other, Would I had as many oxen as there be stars. Says the other again, Where would you feed these oxen? In your pasture, replied he. What, whether I will or no? Yea, said he, whether you will or no. What, in spite of me? Yes, said he. And thus it went on from word to word, till at length each sheathed his sword in the other's bowels. This verifies that saying of James, chap. iii. 5, "Behold how great a matter a little fire kindleth!" So it is in many families: sometimes a look is the beginning of a great controversy: one thinks such a one does not look lovingly upon him, and then he begins to suspect that things boil within him; afterward some words come forth that seem to argue discontent, and then that word begets another, and so a miserable breach arises in a family. It is an argument that these people have gunpowder spirits, when a little spark of fire so quickly blows them up. Truly, in the controversy here in England, the ground of it at the first beginning was little enough on our parts; and had there not been a desperate design in our adversaries, it were impossible that such a little beginning should ever have attained to such a height. But God does not so, they are great things for which he "hath a controversy with the inhabitants of the land."

But what is the declaration? "No truth, nor mercy, nor knowledge of God in the land." These three, but especially the first, very nearly concern us.

First, "No truth." God is a God of truth, he is true in all his ways. He justly pleads with them that have dealt falsely with him. "No truth;" no reality in their religion; that is something, but that is not all. God comes upon them for the breaches first of the second table; for they are more convincing, and more likely to affect the conscience of a natural man, than matters of religion. If you speak to them concerning sins in matters of religion, they will say they acknowledge the true God, and they worship him. Well, therefore the prophet here begins first with the second table, concerning the want of truth between man and man; as if he should say, Talk what you will concerning your worshipping the true God, there is "no truth" between one another, you deal falsely and cruelly, and are merciless to your brethren; never therefore talk of religion and of acknowledging the true God.

Obs. 3. That it is in vain for any man to talk of his religion, if he make no conscience of the second table as well as the first. For a man to talk of praying and hearing sermons, if he be cruel and hard-hearted, and false in his dealings, the Lord rejects all such, let him talk what he will.

"No truth" in your dealings one with another. First, there is abundance of flattery amongst you. You flatter one another in your sin, you do not deal unfeignedly one with another. You flatter your princes, and your princes have little truth in their courts. It was once said, All things were plentiful in the court except truth. And this is the unhappiness of great men, that those about them usually deal falsely with them, telling them that their bloodshedding and ruining of kingdoms is but the maintaining of their just honour and prerogative. I have read of Dionysius's flatterers, that when he spat upon the ground they would lick it up, and then tell him, that that spittle was sweeter than any ambrosia and nectar they ever tasted, merely to please him: and so you have many near great men, who, though they see them do things never so abominable, things that make never so great breaches between God and them, between them and the people, yet tell them, that they do more bravely than ever any of their ancestors did. "There is no truth."

"Truth" here some take for justice; and so it is sometimes taken in Scripture. Zech. viii. 16, "Speak ye every man the truth to his neighbour; execute the judgment of truth and peace in your gates." As if he should say, You do not execute judgment upon malignants that are in your power; you speak of raising arms to fetch in delinquents, but you execute not judgment upon those that you have in their hands; you will have God in a solemn manner to be blessed because he has delivered you from them, but judgment is not executed in truth as it should be. Nor "no mercy," that is, you show no mercy to the innocent; you talk of indulgence, but your indulgence to delinquents is cruelty to innocents. Oh how many of our brethren, in Oxford and other places, suffer most dreadful things because these here enjoy so much liberty and favour! So there is neither mercy to the innocent nor justice to the guilty.

But the special thing here intended is, That you are not true in your dealings, nor in the trust committed to your charge. There is no equity in your dealings. Isa. lix. 14, "And judgment is turned away backward," (it is turned upon those that it should be executed upon,) "and justice standeth afar off." If one be greater than another, the meanest shall come under the stroke of justice and be executed, and the greater not. And "truth is fallen in the street." How comes that in? Thus, as if he should say, It is true, they that are in authority will not execute judgment and justice, but are not the common people faithful in their dealings one with another? No, "truth is fallen in the street." This seems to refer to the multitude. "And equity cannot enter." The word here translated "equity," comes from one which signifies a thing that is just before one: as if he should say, Those very things that one would think the plainest and most evident, that are just before us, that have so much equity and reason in them; yet these things cannot enter into their hearts, nor be entertained, there is such a general confusion and corruption among the people. And is not this in a great measure our condition at this time?

There is "no truth," they are false in the trust committed to their charge. Oh, here is a controversy indeed that God may have against us. Was there ever a time, that either England or any other country knew, when there was so much falseness in men in the trust committed to them? All things in Israel at this time were come into such confusion, that, through the falseness of men, things of the greatest consequence were betrayed. It is a sign of God's fearful wrath upon our nation, that there is no truth in men, when people are left to the treachery and perfidiousness of others; that persons of whose truth we thought ourselves confident, nay, would have ventured our lives on it, yea, such as a long time before were faithful to admiration, yet at last, when they think they may suffer, they will betray all the trust that is reposed in them, and venture even their own undoing rather than endure further hazard. Such cursed selfishness is there in men that have not the grace and true fear of God to balance their hearts; they will even betray God himself, and a whole kingdom, for their own private ends. But what an unworthy thing is this, when so much mischief may ensue! It is as if a man should set a house on fire to roast an egg: what are men's own particular ends in comparison of a kingdom? not so much as an egg in comparison of a house. This was the complaint in Micah's time of Judah, as well as of Israel here: (Micah was contemporary with Hosea:) "Trust ye not in a friend, put ye not confidence in a guide: keep the doors of thy mouth from her that lieth in thy bosom. A man's enemies are the men of his own house," Micah vii. 5, 6. But though many of them are thus corrupt, and there is no truth in them, are there not some of them better? Mark the 4th verse: "The best of them is as a brier: the most upright is sharper than a thorn hedge." In evil times you find those in whom you most confide, so perverse in some of their ways, that if you go to them for shelter, they will prick you; even those men that you most esteem, and from whom you expect to receive most. And this, indeed, is the day of the perplexity of a kingdom; what shall we do in this case? Mark the 7th verse: "Therefore I will look unto the Lord; I will wait for the God of my salvation; my God will hear me." As if he should say, If I look to man I have little help or comfort there, the best of them is a brier; if I trust in men, I see what they will do, verily, every man is altogether vanity; therefore our condition is very sad and miserable; Lord, what shall we do? "I will look unto the Lord; I will wait for the God of my salvation: my God will hear me." Men cannot save me; God will hear me, though they will not.

God's controversy with covenant-breakers, with those that betray their trust, is very dreadful. I will cite an example or two out of the Scripture and out of history.

First, when there was a famine in the days of David three years together, David would know why it was, and God gave him this answer, That it was "for Saul, and for his bloody house, because he slew the Gibeonites," 2 Sam. xxi. Because Saul would not keep to the Gibeonites the trust that was promised them, God therefore brings a famine upon the whole land for three years together. I beseech you, mark the aggravation of God's displeasure against any that break trust. First, this promise was not made by Saul, but by Saul's progenitors, above three hundred years before this time: and to whom was it made? unto a heathenish people, to the Gibeonites; and this promise was obtained by craft, they deceived Joshua. Secondly, it was a promise made them without asking counsel of God, Josh. ix. 14. A promise, too, that was against the mind of the congregation; ver. 18, "All the congregation murmured against the princes." Thirdly, when Saul slew the Gibeonites, he did it not from a perfidious spirit, but with a good intent, for so saith 2 Sam. xxi. 2, "He sought to slay them in his zeal to the children of Israel," because he thought that the Gibeonites remaining amongst them would, perhaps, prove some hinderance to the good of Israel. Fourthly, this work of God comes not upon Saul then when he broke the trust, but upon his posterity afterward, and that shows the wrath to be greater. Lastly, it comes so upon them as that it will not be appeased till it has their lives: you may see then how determined God is to punish promise-breakers.

Another example as remarkable is in Ezek. xvii. 15. When Zedekiah the king of Judah had made a covenant with the king of Babylon, he broke it, and "rebelled against him in sending his ambassadors into Egypt, that they might give him horses and much people. Shall he prosper?" saith the Lord, "shall he escape that doeth such things? or shall he break the covenant, and be delivered?" This covenant was made with a wicked man, with a tyrant, and yet God calls it his oath and his covenant, ver. 18; and with what an emphasis does God speak this! "He despised the oath by breaking the covenant, when, lo, he had given his hand:" yea, ver. 16, God professeth it shall cost him his life: "As I live, saith the Lord God, surely in the place where the king dwelleth that made him king, whose oath he despised, and whose covenant he brake, even with him, in the midst of Babylon, he shall die:" yea, further, God swears against him, and that by his own life, ver. 19: "Therefore thus saith the Lord God, As I live, surely mine oath that he hath despised, and my covenant that he hath broken, even it will I recompense upon his own head:" further, God tells him, all the strength that he had got, and all his policy and cunning devices, should not help him: ver. 20, "I will spread my net upon him, and he shall be taken in my snare, and I will bring him to Babylon, and will plead with him there for his trespass that he hath trespassed against me:" and lastly, the wrath of God shall not only be upon him, but upon all those that joined with him and abetted him in the breaking of this covenant: ver. 21, "All his fugitives with all his bands shall fall by the sword, and they that remain shall be scattered towards all winds." I know not two scriptures more full for God's being set to contend with men for breach of promise. Oh! take heed, all you that are intrusted with any public charge, that you break not covenant.

And as you have examples of this in the Scripture, so there is also an example or two in history exceedingly to the point. Rodolphus set his hand to a covenant with Henry IV., which he afterward broke; and when his right hand was obliged to be amputated, his conscience accused him: "Oh," saith he, "this is that right hand that subscribed the covenant, and now God revenges the breach of it upon this right hand." But above all, that part in the history of the Hungarians is the most remarkable, concerning Udislaus the king of Hungary, and Amurath the Great Turk. In it we are told that Udislaus making war with Amurath contrary to promise, when the Turks were about to be worsted; Amurath having with him the covenant made between the king of Hungary and him, and seeing himself put to the worse, plucked the covenant out of his bosom, and with his eyes fixed toward heaven, spake thus, "This, O Jesus Christ, is the covenant that thy Christians have struck with me; O holy Jesus, they have done it in thy name, and sworn by thy Majesty, and yet they have violated it; they have perfidiously denied their God. Now, O Jesus, if thou art a God, as they say, and as we guess thou art, revenge this wrong that is done unto me and unto thyself upon these that have violated their faith and promise, and show unto us that know not thy name, that thou art an avenger of such as betray their trust, and then we shall know thee to be a God." Now upon this, God ordered it that the Hungarians, having the better of the day, broke off the fight, and, through covetousness of the prey, fell upon the laden camels, whereupon the Turks totally routed the Hungarians, Udislaus their king was slain, and a famous victory left to Amurath.

Thus you see how God will be avenged for the breach of trust, and how certainly he will follow those that have been guilty of it. If we have to deal with papists, how is it possible that we can confide in any thing they promise or agree to? for we know it is their very opinion, that *fides non servanda hereticis*, faith is not to be kept with heretics; that for the Catholic cause they may break all their trust, promises, and covenants. Certainly, that people are besotted who shall so depend upon and be carried away by papists, as to lay their lives, liberties, and outward comforts at their feet and their mercy, for certainly there is no truth in them. What will be our state, if we lie at the mercy of those who have no truth in them, when afterwards we find they break asunder all their bonds of agreement, and we knew that this was their opinion before, that they would enter into league with us merely to serve their own turns, and when they obtained power, make our estates, lives, and liberties a prey to them?

Secondly, "No mercy." The merciful God sets himself against unmerciful men, and has a dreadful controversy against them; and when this controversy is pleaded, unmerciful men will be confounded before the Lord; for God will lay his plea thus: What! you that stood in so much need of mercy every moment to keep you out of hell; you that lived upon mercy continually as you breathed in the air; you who are begging at my gates every day; you who are undone for ever if you had not mercy supplied every hour; and yet you unmerciful to your brethren? This plea will stop the mouths of all unmerciful ones. It was the controversy that God had with Sodom itself, because they were unmerciful: much more then hath God a controversy with the inhabitants of the land of Israel if they be unmerciful. In Ezek. xvi. 49, God lays his charge against Sodom, That they did not "strengthen the hand of the poor and needy." Unmercifulness is a sin against the very light of nature. Josephus reports of Herod, that wicked and ungodly king of whom we read in the Gospel, That when there was a great famine in Judea, he melted all his movables of gold and silver that were in his palace, he spared nothing of his plate, either for the preciousness of the matter, or for the excellency of the fashion of it, no, not so much as those vessels wherein he was daily served at his table, but he melted them all and made money of them, and sent it into Egypt to buy corn, which he distributed to the poor. He appointed bakers to provide bread for the sick; he provided raiment for the naked, because the sheep were likewise dead and the poor had no work; yea, he sent to his neighbours the Syrians corn, that might be seed-corn for them to sow. This was that wicked Herod, who yet in time of public calamity was thus merciful to the poor. Surely, then, God must needs have a controversy with Israel, with Christians, that have received so much mercy from the Lord, if they shall be unmerciful in times of common calamity. And if ever unmercifulness were a vile sin and provoked God against a people, it must needs do now at such a time as this, when there are so many objects of pity and commiseration daily presented before us: if this should but prove to be our charge, that there is no mercy in the land at this day, God must needs have a fearful controversy against us. The whole land cannot be said to be charged now as once it might have been. Not long since many were crying out of violence and wrong, those which ruled over us ruled with rigour and cruelty, according to that complaint, Ezek. xxxiv. 4, "With force and cruelty have ye ruled" my people. They have turned "judgment to wormwood," Amos v. 7. The courts of judicature, which should have been for right judgment, have been turned into bitter wormwood and have been full of cruelty. What have many of them cared for the lives or the comforts of thousands, or for the extreme misery they created, provided their own humours and lusts might be satisfied? as if all other men were but as dogs except themselves. The Lord at this day charges this upon some of them, and will charge it more. I remember a speech of a reverend divine in this city, now with God, whom you all honoured when alive; being brought before the high commission court, when he came home one day, speaking of what he observed there, I heard, said he, much crying out of Grace, and please your Grace, and much crying out of Peace, peace, if there were any noise; but I saw no mercy there, nothing but cruelty.

Antiq. B. 5. c. 12.

In Jer. l. 17, you see what indignation God shows where men, though the greatest upon earth, are cruel to his people: "This Nebuchadrezzar king of Babylon hath broken his bones." Who was this Nebuchadrezzar? A mighty and great prince, yet God looks upon him with indignation when he sees him breaking the bones of his people. We have amongst us those who, as Psal. xxvii. 12, "breathe out cruelty," and indeed act nothing less; "cruel hatred" being in their hearts and ways, Psal. xxv. 19. No marvel therefore though heretofore our brethren left the kingdom, because they found such cruelty here, no mercy in the land; they did but according to that to which the church calls its members, Cant. iv. 8, "Come with me from Lebanon, from the lions' dens, from the mountains of the leopards." When they went from us, they went from the lions' dens, and from the mountains of leopards. No marvel now the Lord is so severe against our land, because there has been so little mercy in it. That is the second article against Israel, That there was "no mercy."

Thirdly, "Nor no knowledge of God." In the Hebrew it is, *and* no knowledge; but now *Vau*, rendered there and, signifies sometimes *quia*, as well as *et;* and so it may indeed be well rendered here, *Because* there is no knowledge of God in the land; the reason why there is no mercy, is because there is no knowledge of God. The knowledge of God will make wicked men merciful. Cruel men know not God. These two are joined together most elegantly, Psal. lxxiv. 20, "The dark places of the earth are full of the habitations of cruelty." The knowledge of God will make men civil and humane at least, but when there is no knowledge of him men grow cruel and savage. And do we not find this to be true at this very day? To what places are men that now rise up to plunder, to shed blood, to cruelly perpetrate the most desperate outrages, to what places are these men beholden for their assisters and abettors? Are they not beholden to places where they are in ignorance, where they have no knowledge of God, where there is no preaching? In the countries round about, observe those parishes, those towns, where there has been least or worst preaching, where they have had least knowledge of God, and there you see most malignants that are bloody and cruel. No marvel, then, that our adversaries are such enemies to the faithful preachers of the word of God; no marvel, then, they are made the butt of their malice; for indeed if they bring the knowledge of God into the land, they will bring humanity, civility, mercy, and love, and these will find few or none to aid them in their wickedness. Indeed they complain that the parliament sets ignorant men in places, but certainly this complaint is but a pretence, for it were better for their turns that all the congregations in England had but ignorant men, none to bring the knowledge of God amongst people; but they know well enough, notwithstanding what they say, that those that are sent are such as do bring the knowledge of God among people, and that nothing injures them more than this knowledge of God.

"No knowledge of God." This is a heavy charge indeed: "Pour out thy fury upon the heathen that know thee not," Jer. x. 25. Though they be heathens and yet know not God, the wrath of God is to be poured forth upon them; surely then God's wrath must be upon Israel that know not God. And Isa. xxvii. 11, They are "a people of no understanding: therefore he that made them will not have mercy upon them, and he that formed them will show them no favour." 2 Thess. i. 7, 8, "The Lord Christ shall be revealed from heaven with his mighty angels, in flaming fire, taking vengeance on them that know not God." What! no knowledge of God? what glory then can God have from such a people? God has done great things in the world, he has manifested himself an infinite and a glorious God, and his end in all his manifestations is, that angels and men might behold this, might adore, admire, worship, fear, and praise him; but where there is no knowledge of God, there all God's glory passes by and there is no notice taken of it. To what purpose is the world made? such a one can never sanctify the name of God in any duty, nor worship in the use of any creature. Where there is no knowledge of God, there all good is kept out, there the unclean spirit, a spirit of darkness, dwells. When the crow has picked out the eyes of the lamb, then it preys upon it. As in dark vaults there are toads and filthy creatures, so in dark souls there are crawling and filthy lusts: as in blind alehouses there is abundance of disorder, so in a blind heart there are distempers and disorders in abundance.

ואין־דעת οὐδὲ ἐπίγνωσις.

"No knowledge of God." The Septuagint render the word for knowledge, by a word which signifies *recognition* or *acknowledgment*, there is no acknowledgment of God in the land. People should walk so in all their ways as to hold forth the glory of the great God whom they profess to serve. If they know God to be such as he is revealed in all his attributes and works, they should in their lives so walk as to hold this forth before the children of men. I appeal to you in this: perhaps some of you can speak concerning God, and tell us what he is, and concerning his attributes; yet, are your lives in your families, in your conversations, such, that one, beholding them, may see inscribed the glorious attributes of God? are they such, that in all your ways you carry with you the glory of the great God, holding forth your fear of him, your love of him, and giving up yourselves to this all-sufficient God, who is worthy of all? There should be this acknowledgment of God, as well as knowledge; and he has a controversy with a land, with a family, with a particular soul, when there is not an acknowledgment of him in all their ways.

"In the land." *In the land*, here is the emphasis. Oh this is a sad thing: What! in the land of Israel no knowledge of God? Psal. lxxvi. 1, "In Judah is God known: his name is great in Israel." God was not known to any people in all the world but Judah and Israel; and here ten tribes are charged for not having the knowledge of God in their land. Surely they refused to know the Lord, they shut their eyes against the knowledge of God, they say to God, "Depart from us, we desire not the knowledge of thy ways." Men may live where there is the means of knowledge, and yet be ignorant all their days. How many men of excellent parts, in respect of all outward affairs, are there both in the country and city, to whom, if you speak about matters of state, they will speak intelligently, and discover much acquaintance with state affairs; confer with them about merchandise or their trades, they will speak understandingly; but speak to them about God, about Christ, about the things of eternal life, how poorly, how weakly, how childishly, how sottishly, shall you have them speak about these things! Men of parts, and living under much means, may yet be very ignorant in the knowledge of God. However the want of knowledge may seem to be a little matter, even in places where there are means, yet let men know, that it is a fearful brand of reprobation for people to live under the means, and not to have the knowledge of God: 2 Cor. iv. 3, "If our gospel is hid, it is hid to them that are lost." And it is pronounced as a great curse for a man to live without knowledge, Job xxxvi. 12, "They shall perish by the sword, and they shall die without knowledge." Oh how many at this day do perish by the sword, and die without knowledge! It concerns us now to get the knowledge of God, because the sword may be nearer than we are aware of; and what will become of us if it fall out to be our portion to perish by the sword, and to die without knowledge?

But though they had some means of knowledge, yet their means did grow very short. And there are two special reasons why at this time there was no knowledge of God in the land of Israel.

1. Because that Jeroboam had, in the defection of these ten tribes of Israel, set up the lowest of the people in the place of the priests' office. Any man that desired to be a priest, though never so base and vile, Jeroboam would set him up. In 1 Kings xii. 31, you find "he made an house of high places, and made priests of the lowest of the people, which were not of the sons of Levi;" no marvel then they had not the knowledge of God amongst them. Thus it has been in Ireland, and therefore no marvel there is so little knowledge of God there: any tradesman that scarce understood right reason, less divinity, was set up there to be a priest, and what horrible cruelty has ensued! So in England: however some of them complain of ignorant men at present in the ministry, the truth is, they have set up men of far less understanding in former times: for a little money to a bishop's clerk, might not any tradesman, any cast butler or serving-man, get into orders, read their prayers, and so become a priest? This has been the cause of much ignorance. How many cast serving-men have been placed to do what they can do, whereas learned and godly divines must be cast out of the kingdom, and denied to have any liberty to preach the knowledge of God unto his own people! Here is the reason of our ignorance, even that which was Jeroboam's sin, the setting of the lowest of the people in the ministry; and now that there is an examination of men, we find what abundance of vile men there are in places, and the people in those places are like to them, such prophet, such people, and the truth is, people love to have it so. In 2 Chron. xv. 3, a complaint is made that for a long season Israel had been "without the true God, and without a teaching priest." (This Israel includes both Judah and Israel, as elsewhere in Scripture.) "Israel hath been," (saith he,) "without the true God and without a teaching priest." This was a sad condition indeed, and mark how they are joined, "without the true God, and without a teaching priest, without law." A people are without God that are without a teaching priest and without the law. If they have not means to instruct them in the knowledge of God, they are a people without God. But now, observe what follows this, ver. 5, 6, "And in those times there was no peace to him that went out, nor to him that came in, but great vexations were upon all the inhabitants of the countries. And nation was destroyed of nation, and city of city: for God did vex them with all adversity." Truly, our condition is almost like the condition of Israel at that time. And here we may see what the fruit of this controversy was, they were without a teaching priest and without law, and in those times there was no peace to him that went out, nor to him that came in, but great vexations, city destroying city, and nation destroying nation, for "God did vex them with all adversity." Oh how doth the Lord

even vex us at this very day! and this as a fruit of God's controversy with us, because there is so little knowledge of God in the land.

2. Because the pure worship of God and his ordinances were shut out of doors, and men's inventions were introduced in their room. For after the ten tribes' defection from Judah, they left the right worship of God, ceased to worship in the temple at Jerusalem, and set up their calves in Dan and Bethel, and so brought in their own inventions instead of the true worship of God; and no marvel though there came dismal darkness upon the land when this took place. Be assured, my brethren, whenever the pure ordinances of God and the right way of his worship is shut out from a kingdom, there will come woeful darkness upon that kingdom. The right knowledge of God vanishes, when men's inventions in his ordinances come to be honoured. As painted glass in your windows hinders the light, so the more inventions of men there are in God's worship, the less light comes into the hearts of the people. As some, not contented with ordinary plain letters, make such flourishes about them that you can scarce tell what they are; and write their names so that you cannot tell what to make of them; so, many men that will not content themselves with plain ordinances, with the ordinances of Christ, but must have flourishes of their own inventions, at length darken the right understanding of the mind and truths of God, so that you know not what to make of them. "To the law and to the testimony," (saith the prophet,) "if they speak not according to this word, it is because there is no light in them." If they will leave the law and the testimony, and will go according to their own inventions in Divine worship, it is because there is no light in them, they are in darkness, and they will bring darkness upon the people. In Col. ii. 22, it is said of the rudiments of the world and the ordinances of men, that they "perish with the using;" that is, there is no efficacy at all in them to do any good unto the souls of men. Our adversaries call images and pictures, books to teach laymen; but the Scripture tells us they teach a lie. And if they be laymen's books, they are full of errata in every page, yea, there are more errata than true lines. The best that we can say of any ceremonies brought into the church by men (because people would endeavour to excuse the first Reformers) is, that they thought at that time they were required because of the dulness of men; for so they say in the preface to the Common Prayer Book, that it was to stir up the dull minds of men. But mark, if it could possibly be imagined that there could be any use of them in the first Reformation (which indeed there was not, but rather they did hurt and made men's minds more dull, as I dare appeal to you who have lived continually under such inventions of men in God's worship); but if possibly (I say) there could be imagined any use of them at the first, they were at best but as horn-books and fescues for the childhood and infancy of the church. They say themselves that they needed such things, but they could have needed them only as children need horn-books and fescues. And is it seemly always to learn upon them? what knowledge will be acquired, if, when you set your children to learn to read, they shall be kept ten, twenty, or thirty years to their horn-books? Now thus would our prelates have debased people, to keep them continually to learn the knowledge of God by these their beggarly elements.

Now take these two reasons together, unteaching priests, and man's inventions, they keep out the knowledge of God from a people; and they are brought on purpose to induce blindness, because that is most fit and suitable to the design that men have to bring people under slavery. So it was here; Jeroboam, at the time when Hosea prophesied, designed to bring the people under slavery, to keep them from the house of David to be his slaves; and what course does he take? He first sets up the basest and lowest of the people to be their priests; and secondly, he introduces false worship, and that is attended by blindness and ignorance, and so by this means he knew he should soon bring them under slavery. And nothing is more clear, than that it has been the design of many that would have been rulers of the church, and that they have laboured with all their might, (in subservience to others,) to bring blindness and ignorance into the land, that so they might reduce the land under slavery; and nothing has vexed them more, than that there is so much knowledge in the land. Therefore their spirits were so enraged at people's flocking unto sermons; it was even matter enough to silence any minister, to have people crowding to hear him preach: and they were enraged, too, at people's repeating of sermons in their own private families, because it also was a way to bring in knowledge. Any thing that tended to that, their hearts were enraged against it. Why? Because they knew knowledge would so mould men that they would never bear servitude. And truly it is a very strange thing, that though in some countries, (as in Wales and other places,) where men have not knowledge, they are contented to become slaves; but that in these parts, where there is, though not so much as should be, yet some degree of the knowledge of God, one would think it impossible that men should suffer themselves to be brought into slavery here; and that they fear most. We read that when the Philistines had taken Samson, they put out his eyes, and then made him to grind in the mill. So these men would fain make us to grind in the mill; as it is said, some have threatened to make the dames of London work for a penny a day in bridewell. They would fain make you all slaves, but first they would put out your eyes; they would take away knowledge, and then they know they shall soon succeed in their object. Well, the Lord hath promised, Isa. xxv. 7, that "he will destroy in this mountain the face of the covering cast over all people, and the veil that is spread over all nations." And mark, ver. 9, "It shall be said in that day, Lo, this is our God; we have waited for him, and he will save us." O come, Lord Jesus, come quickly and destroy the covering, the veil that is upon the eyes and hearts of a great part of the people of this land. The work would soon be done if the Lord would but destroy the veil of darkness that is upon the eyes and hearts of people, and we should triumph in our God and say, Lo, this is our God, we have waited for him, and he will save us, yea, he hath saved us.

Ver. 2. *By swearing, and lying, and killing, and stealing, and committing adultery, they break out, and blood toucheth blood.*

You see what a catalogue of gross sins are here mentioned. And indeed when idolatry prevails in any country, there will be all manner of wickedness. We found it so here in England, that the more superstition prevailed amongst us, the more abominable wickedness was generally spread over the country.

First, For "swearing." The word here translated swearing, is of אלה and signifies to curse, to swear, and to be perjured, and likewise also signifies to howl out: as in Joel i. 8, "Lament like a virgin girded with sackcloth:" so that the same word which signifies cursing, swearing, and forswearing, signifies also to howl and cry, for God has a time to make such to howl and cry out. An oath is a sacred thing, a part of God's worship, and therefore the abusing of this is a dreadful sin; especially if it be abused to swear to that which is false. Paulus Phagius, in his comment on Gen. xlii.,

In Egypto siquis juret per caput regis et non præstet, morte plectitur, nec permittitur ut auro vel aliâ re vitam redimat.

saith, It is reported of the Egyptians, that if any man did but swear by the life of the king, and did not perform his oath, that man was to die, and no gold or any thing in the world could redeem his life: so did heathens hate that sin of perjury. Yea, we have found others that have not had much religion in them, who yet have extremely hated the sin of ordinary swearing. Louis IX. of France, punished that sin by searing the lips of swearers with a hot iron: which law being executed upon a citizen of Paris, some said it was too cruel; which he hearing of, replied, I would to God, that by so searing mine own lips, I could banish out of my realm all abuse of oaths. He could be willing to sear his own lips with hot iron, that he might banish the abuse of swearing. Chrysostom, in some sixteen continued homilies, if not more, whatsoever his text was, always concluded against swearing, as being such a vile and notorious sin. And because some pleaded custom, he urges, If you would but punish it thus, that if there were an oath sworn in your house, the servant or child that swore the oath should not dine that day, that would in some measure put a stop to it; yet, saith he, the command of God is less efficacious. Divers other expressions I might name, but must hasten on. Jer. xxiii. 10, is remarkable and appropriate, "For because of swearing the land mourneth; the pleasant places of the wilderness are dried up. And their course is evil, and their force is not right."

Οὐδε γαρ πρόφασιν ἐχουσι ἀλλα κατα φρόνησιν μονὸν. Hom. 11. Ad pop. Antioch.

It is a sin that has more malignancy in it against God by how much the less is the temptation to it. I verily believe, that if God had never made the third commandment, there would never have been so many oaths in the world; but it springs from a mere malignancy of spirit in men against God because he has forbidden it; for no profit can arise from the practice.

If men be guilty of this sin merely through a vain custom, what high indignity is this against God! what slighting and neglect of God is there! as if sinning against God were an argument of so little weight that a habit, senseless and unprofitable, could weigh it down. Custom, indeed, may prevail in things of no moment, as postures of the body, gestures, and the like, because in their very nature they are unimportant: but that custom should suffice to be set against the high displeasure of the blessed God, or against his solemn profession that he will not hold that soul guiltless that taketh his name in vain, this argues a most insufferable vilifying of his sacred Majesty.

Secondly, To swear that thereby the words of men may be graced, is more horrid impiety: as if the polluting of the holy name of the most holy God were the best ornament of thy speech; as if the dishonour put upon God were the best grace to thy language.

Thirdly, To swear out of a conceit that this argues braveness of spirit, as if according to the fulness of mouthing of oaths, there were a spirit of valour and courage, is still more hideous wickedness; as if the courage and excellency of our spirits consisted in flying in the very face of God. Whence it is that many men, if angered, fall a cursing and swearing, that is, when others displease them they will fly in God's face; for this is your language, though you will not dare to say so; but this is the language of your practice, Others displease and anger me, and I to revenge myself will fly in the very face of God. A hideous wickedness there is in this, that you do not think of. When you passionate spirits come home, and your wives and children or servants anger you, and you fall to cursing and swearing, know you do no other than this; this is the language of your practice, They displease me, and to revenge myself I will fly in the very face of God. Many gentlemen and noblemen and those that belong to them are great swearers, because they imagine that it is an argument of some braveness of spirit, and that thereby they manifest courage of a higher strain than other men. Oh hideous and abominable wickedness! This is all the valour that many men have, that they dare sin against the glorious God and never be troubled at it: whereas a godly man is described in Scripture, Eccles. ix. 2, to be a man "that feareth an oath;" but for these, it is not for them to fear, it is for timorous, melancholy, poor spirits, but they are men of brave spirits, and they would have men know that they can swear and not be troubled at it, they have stronger minds than other men have. Thus is the blessed God dishonoured by this sin more than we are aware of.

Fourthly, There is a class more guilty than these, those who swear that they may not be accounted puritans, or of the number of such a faction; if they go into company where they think they may be suspected to be inclined to that party, what do they? to give evident demonstration to the contrary, they swear lustily, and rap out oaths one after another. Oh what horrible opposition to God and to the Spirit of Christ is this! Christ saith, "that our light must so shine before men, that they, seeing our good works, may glorify our heavenly Father." Now, they let their wickedness appear before men, that it may be known what they are; and hereby they give testimony that they can be brought to yield to any thing, for that is their intent; they do (I say) by that testify to the other party, that they can be brought to yield unto any thing and that they can serve their turns; and this is the reason why they would willingly entertain no other than such as these, for if they hear a man swear lustily, then they think, Such a man surely either has no conscience at all, and so is fittest for our turn, as he will not be a scrupulous fool, or if he had a conscience he has broken it, and now it cannot prevail over him; therefore let us put upon him what we will, if it suit with his own ends and with his own profit, this man will do it; but as for your puritans, that are so conscientious we cannot effect our objects by means of them, therefore we will have none of them. Hence the puritans are so much hated, and the others, that they might be entertained by them, and give full testimony that they are fit for their turns, therefore swear. Oh how black are men's mouths at this day by their cursed oaths, new execrations newly invented, that the world never before heard of! Wherefore then, though God might make these men as scorpions for a while to scourge us, yet if our spirits were up we need not fear them, for certainly they that are so full of curses in their mouths, are the people of God's curse.

"And lying." "By swearing and lying." These two go together: there is no man that makes not conscience of an oath, that will make conscience of a lie; though the world would think to part them, and say, Oh you will not swear, but you will lie; but God saith otherwise. Swearing and lying go together; those that will swear, certainly will lie. But for God's own people, God frees them from this sin of lying, though the world would cast it upon them, for no sin more offends against godliness. In Isa. lxiii. 8, God saith of his people, "Surely they are my people, children that will not lie." God engageth himself for his people, These are the people that will not lie. Are you in profession any of God's people? God doth engage himself for you in this, that certainly you will not lie. It is said of the devil, that he is a liar, and the father of lies. And women that carry false tales up and down and are slanderers, are in Scripture called devils, 1 Tim. iii. 11, "Even so must their wives be grave, not slanderers;" μὴ διαβόλους, not devils: a woman that is a slanderer, that carries false tales up and down to the prejudice of her neighbour, the Scripture there calls that woman by the name of a devil. And the word that signifies detractor, in Hebrew is רכיל and some think that from it comes our English word rakehell, one that makes no conscience to speak falsely.

This sin of lying is the breaking of all society, there can be no converse between man and man where it prevails. Augustine, writing to his friend that sent to him to have his judgment concerning an officious lie, (that is, a lie that tends not to the hurt of any but of him that tells it,) returns this answer: That a man must not tell a lie to save the whole world; if it were to save thy father or thy mother out of hell, if that were possible, thou must not tell a lie; if it were to save kingdoms from destruction, thou must not tell a lie. That is his opinion; and certainly it is correct, for God will never be beholden to the devil to do good through his means. Surely then thou must not tell a lie to gain a groat, or a shilling, or to procure a good bargain, or to prevent the displeasure of thy master or mistress; but rather willingly confess the truth than attempt to cover the fault by a lie. It is practical atheism that induces servants and children, when they have done amiss, to seek to cover it by a lie. God is exceedingly displeased with this sin, and has a controversy on account of it against nations, families, and against particular persons; and therefore, Prov. vi., you shall find if you read from ver. 16—19, that after the Lord has said, that six things he hateth, yea, seven are an abomination unto him, that amongst these seven he repeats lying twice, though under different terms; and that in Rev. xxi. 8, it is expressly said, that "all liars shall have their part in the lake which burneth with fire and brimstone." Take that home with you, you servants, and children, and tradesmen that will tell lies for gain: God ranks and chains up liars together with notorious sinners, that shall all have their portion in the lake of fire and brimstone, which is the second death.

There are none in the world that make such advantage of lying as the antichristian party, inventing all manner of lies, either to draw a party to themselves or to discourage those against them, inventing all manner of lies. And because the malignants invent so many themselves, if any thing is said against them, you presently hear them exclaim, That 's a lie: they think all men are liars because they are conscious that they themselves are continually so. And no marvel that the antichristian party are so full of lies, for the very doctrine of popery, as a whole, is altogether called a lie: 2 Thess. ii. 10, 11, God gave men over, that did not entertain the truth in the love of it, "to believe a lie," that they might be damned. Do you ask the question, why so many learned men and persons of understanding turn to the popish party? Mark the reason here, "because they received not the truth in the love of it, God gave them over to believe a lie." A lie; what is that? that is the doctrine of popery. So the very quintessence of it is a lie. That lie of popery being therefore the great lie in the world, it must have a company of lesser ones, if I may say so, to underprop and uphold it. Isa. xxviii. 15, "They make lies their refuge." It is a text as suitable to our times as any I know, showing the practice now, that when men cannot get any thing by fair means, then they invent lies and make them their refuge. The maxim of the Jesuits is, *Calumniare audacter, aliquid hærebit*, Slander and lie fearlessly, and something will adhere; for every one that may hear the report, may not hear of the answer that can be given to it. And their policy is to spread abroad lies as much as they can, and especially of those that are most eminent and active in public affairs; and hence those strange inventions raised of such as are most active in parliament, in the city, and in the ministry; things so hideous, that if they were true, would render men altogether unfit to be entertained in a commonwealth. But you will say, What can they get by it when it proves to be false? Yes, because their lies spread a great deal farther than the refutation. And those in Jer. xx. 10, do fully set out the condition of these men: "I heard the defaming of many," saith the prophet. How? "Report, say they, and we will report it." This was their plot; We must defame Jeremiah; we see that he has got a great deal of credit and prevails with the people, and we know not how to help ourselves; only if we can but defame him, if we can but raise up something that may take away his esteem with the people, we may then have our end; therefore devise somewhat, report, and we will report it, we will spread it abroad. As now, if a company of malignants get into a tavern, there they will talk against this minister and the other, against this parliamentarian and the other, against this citizen and that: What shall we do? say they; we see they prevail, let us devise somewhat that may defame them, report somewhat and we will spread it. To this day this has been the way of maintaining that antichristian party, that great lie. Jer. ix. 3, "They bend their tongues like their bow for lies;" and ver. 5, "They have taught their tongue to speak lies." They are now become practised in it, and they do it the rather because they know it will please some great ones. It was so in former times: Prov. xxix. 12, "If a ruler hearken to lies, all his servants are wicked." If any officer, or any about him, see that it will humour him to raise ill reports against God's servants, the servants of such a ruler will be wicked and invent lies enow. And amongst other places, Hos. vii. 3 is remarkable, where the text saith, "They make the king glad with their wickedness, and the princes with their lies." It is spoken of Jeroboam and the other kings that followed him, that set up false worship. Now there were a great many in Israel whose consciences would not give them leave to follow that way of false worship: whereupon the promoters, apparitors, bailiffs, and some courtiers, would invent lies against those that must needs go up to Jerusalem to worship, and would not content themselves with the calves that the king set up. Now these their inventions respecting some of the most zealous men amongst the people, they brought to the king, and said, Did your Majesty hear such a thing? There are such men in your Majesty's dominions dwelling in such towns, and they are forsooth so scrupulous that they will not be content with the law-established religion, but they must go up to Jerusalem to worship, yea, and there they privily commit such and such wickedness, and live in such and such vile practices: and thus they came and told the king tales of them, and the text says, "They made the king glad;" the king was pleased, and gave them encouragement. Certainly, amongst us there have not been wanting men that have endeavoured this, that would have accounted this their happiness, to get a tale, though never so false, to tell of a puritan, or of a godly minister.

"And killing." Murder is a provoking sin; God seldom suffers it to go unrevenged in this world. Whence are all those discoveries of murders; scarce any one but can tell strange stories of them. We have a vain distinction of murder and man-slaughter, as it is called, that, forsooth, if a man be angry, and in a passion kills another, this is man-slaughter, and no murder. God will not own that distinction; for if you shall by your passion make yourself a beast, and so kill a man, God will require this at your hand; for, Gen. ix. 5, God saith, that he will require the blood of man "at the hand of every beast;" much more at the hand of a man that by his passion makes himself a beast. The life of a man is precious to God, and God will not suffer any creature to have absolute power over it, but reserves dominion over men's lives to himself. Mr. Ainsworth on Gen. ix. 6, cites the Jewish doctors, affirming that a murderer, though it were possible for him to give all the riches of the world, yet must be put to death, because the life of the murdered is the possession of the most holy God; this is their argument. Certainly it is not in the power of any man upon earth, be he what he may, to save a murderer. The greatest man upon earth has no liberty, no prerogative, from God to save a murderer; "whoso sheddeth man's blood, by man shall his blood be shed." God avenges the blood that Manasseh shed a long while after his death; 2 Kings xxiv. 4, "And also for the innocent blood that he shed; which the Lord would not pardon." Though Manasseh did repent, (and so we have cause to hope well in regard of his soul and his eternal estate, though Calvin seems to be of the contrary opinion,) yet the Lord came upon the nation after his days, and would not pardon his shedding of innocent blood. How much do we find in the law concerning the killing of a man! Deut. xxi. 1—9, when a man was found dead in the fields nigh unto a city, the elders of that city must come to the dead body, wash their hands over the heifer to be slain, and take a solemn oath that they had no hand in the murder, and so clear the city. This shows how precious the life of man is in God's esteem, and that God hath a controversy with a land for shedding of blood.

And if this be so, what a controversy, think you, has God against many in this kingdom at this day! How fearful is God's controversy against some that must feel it for the blood that has been shed in Ireland! There is upon record one hundred and forty thousand that have been murdered there since the beginning of this rebellion, and everybody will say, it is plain murder. And they, whosoever they are, that have participated in and abetted this, and strengthened the hands of the murderers, what will they be able to answer unto God? Shall the blood of one righteous Abel cry aloud in the ears of God, and never leave crying until it has had vengeance, and shall not the blood of one hundred and forty thousand innocents? (I mean innocents in regard of the cause for which they were murdered.) We now in England begin to be somewhat sensible what it is to have the guilt of murder lie upon a nation. In the last declaration of the affairs of Ireland, the parliament intimates some fear they have, that possibly the guilt of the blood of King James may in some way lie upon us. God has a controversy for murder wheresoever it lies, if it be not punished accordingly. And for all that blood that has been shed here of late, wherever the cause lies, God will find it out one day. Oh the blood that will be upon the head of some! Jer. li. 35, "The violence done to me and to my flesh be upon Babylon, shall the inhabitants of Zion say; and my blood upon the inhabitants of Chaldea, shall Jerusalem say." So let all Christians, (they may do it, and they have warrant from God to do it,) let all godly people in this kingdom that have had their husbands, their children, their apprentices, their friends butchered in these unhappy wars, let them say, The violence done to my flesh be upon the Babylonish, the popish party; and the blood that has been shed of our husbands, of our children, of our servants, of our friends, be upon the inhabitants of Chaldea, the popish party dwelling amongst us, that have risen up and shed so much blood. Oh how vile and cursed are men's hearts, that are so set upon their designs, that to attain them they will go through streams of blood that lie in their way, and care not for the lives of thousands of men so their desires may be satisfied! How are men vilified in this, that their lives and bodies must go to gratify the lusts of a few others! Certainly God never made such a difference, never put such a distance between one and another.

But now, in the execution of justice we must not account the shedding of blood to be killing. God has not a controversy with a land for bloodshed in it; nay, on the contrary, the Lord has a controversy against a people when there is not shedding of blood that way: Jer. xlviii. 10, "Cursed be he that keepeth back his sword from blood:" such a case may be. And 1 Kings xx. 42, when Ahab let Benhadad go, the text saith, that a prophet came to him in the name of the Lord, saying, "Because thou hast let go out of thy hand a man whom I appointed to utter destruction, therefore thy life shall go for his life, and thy people for his people." So when we have men in our hands whom God has appointed to destruction, who are guilty of death, who have sought not the blood of some few, but the massacring of a city, if for private ends of our own we let them go, God may require our lives for theirs. And this perhaps is one of the reasons, that there is so much bloodshed amongst us at present, because there is no execution of justice upon offenders, and God requires the blood of many for many. It is true, papists are not to be put to death for their religion, that we acknowledge; but the Lord, because he intendeth the ruin of that party, will leave them to act so that they shall be guilty of death by the law of the land, and by the law of arms, and then the putting them to death is the execution of justice, and not the breach of the sixth commandment.

But some will say, Oh, killing is a grievous thing, we never were acquainted with it as we have been of late: were it not better we were all at peace, than that still so much blood should be shed?

God forbid any of us should be bloody men, or desire the shedding of blood. No, let us all labour to have peace that there may be no more bloodshed. This speech simply considered is good, and we are all I hope of the same mind. Cursed be that man, I say, that shall not yield to this. And certainly peace, though upon hard terms, were to be desired, if it would save blood; yea, though half our estates went to procure it: but what if it prove that that peace we talk of should be a means of more bloodshed? If you should let into your city such men as bloody papists, French, Walloons, and Irish rebels, and that merely upon their bare word that they would do you no hurt, do not you think if they were once admitted, that you would every night be in danger of being massacred? and would there not be much more bloodshed than has yet been? Therefore say not that those are bloody men that will not yield up their throats to men of blood, but will stand up to defend their brethren from being massacred; they take up arms, not to shed, but to prevent the shedding of blood: and certainly, if the city and country had in the beginning of these wars risen up as one man and gone forth, they might have saved much of the blood that has been shed. Many thousands that have now lost their lives might have been preserved, if you had resolutely taken up arms sooner than you did: but when every county looks to itself, and the enemy goes to one, and then to another, shedding blood, and you sit still and do nothing, God may require the blood of your brethren at your hands; and you cannot clear yourselves from being guilty of it, when you do not, to the uttermost you are able, strive to subdue the power of those that shed it. We cannot see any way to preserve the blood that is now in our veins, but by subduing the malignant and antichristian party that have already tasted so much of the blood of the saints.

And so with those rebels that in Ireland have tasted so much blood, and now are come over here to join with papists, you cannot possibly conceive any safety but by subduing that party. Is that a way to prevent the shedding of your blood, to lay your necks upon the block? for that peace proffered under a specious name, may be in truth no other but a laying your necks upon the block, and giving up your wives and children to be a sacrifice to their malice.

The Lord has a controversy for blood. We know, when we have to deal with papists, what they have been of old, and therefore we hope God has a controversy with that party, that as they have drunk the blood of the saints, so they shall at last swell and burst themselves in pieces. In the time of the massacre in France, when history tells us of more than ten thousand protestants that were murdered in one night in Paris, they were in as fair a way of peace as possible, and there was a marriage solemnized, and a great deal of rejoicing for the union of one party with another, and yet (I say) in that night so many were slain; and you may expect no other if the malignant party get power. You will say, They have not done so to other cities which they have taken. No, they have not got the day yet, their design is but progressing; but if once they get this city, then, having attained their chief object, you may expect all manner of cruelty from them. And this massacre in France went on to other cities, for within a few days after there were forty thousand more computed to be murdered. I remember that the history of France tells us of that King Charles IX., by whose commission this was done, that afterward God struck him with such a disease, that there issued out of his body at several places nothing but blood, so that in that sickness he would sometimes fall down and wallow himself in his own blood. Be men great or small, yet, being guilty of blood, at one time or other the Lord will manifest that he has a controversy against them.

"And stealing." God sets bounds, as to men's habitations, so to men's estates, and he will not have one to break in upon another; no, not so much as to covet that which is another's. Seeking therefore an increase of our estates in any sinful way, is, as it were, saying, God's care is not over me to provide needful things for me, and seeing I cannot have them from God, I will try if I can have them from the devil. This is the language of all kind of gain that we get by any unlawful way; you do not say so in words indeed, but this is the language of your actions. Saith a poor person, I am in want, I want bread for my family, and clothes, and many outward comforts, money to pay my rent, &c.; I see in God's providence he does not provide for me; well, I will go to the devil then, and will see whether he will do more for me than God: I cannot have it by God's allowance, for if so, I might get it by lawful means, therefore, saith he, I will have it whether God will or no. This is the language of all kind of stealing: and the curse of God is upon that which is gotten so unjustly, and all the repentance in the world is not sufficient for a man who has gotten his estate unjustly, unless he make restitution of it again to the uttermost of his power.

And this stealing refers not only to open robbery, but to all wrongful gain gotten by way of trade. If I were preaching of this argument at large, much might be said to those that live by trade. But for the present take that one scripture, Ezek. xxviii. 18, "Thou hast defiled thy sanctuaries by the multitude of thine iniquities, by the iniquity of thy traffic." Let merchants and tradesmen that have gotten any thing unlawfully, take this text home with them, "Thou hast defiled thy sanctuaries by the iniquity of thy traffic." It may be, by trafficking unjustly you have gotten an estate, and you come to God's sanctuaries as if you were very holy, and no one should suspect you for your false books and dealings; to you God saith in this text, that you defile all the ordinances by the iniquity of your traffic. Perhaps you think, out of your unrighteous gains, to give somewhat to adorn such a place as this: it is well enough, but you do defile them.

So for all kind of oppression, for that too is meant by stealing. Latimer, in one of his sermons before King Edward, saith, that the greatest man in the kingdom cannot so hurt an oppressor, as a poor widow may; and with what arms I pray? saith he; can he bring the judges to condemn? The arms are these, the tears of the poor, which run down their cheeks and go up to heaven, and there cry for vengeance. The text here speaks not of the meanest, but of the greatest thieves. Calvin, on the place, saith, those that had the most power by their honour and riches, and were oppressors of the people, are the thieves here spoken of. And Isa. i. 23, "Thy princes are rebellious, and companions of thieves." And Isa. xxxiii. 1, "When thou shalt cease to spoil, thou shalt be spoiled." This is a text for our spoilers at this day: it may be God will let them go on till they have done their work, and then come upon them; and when they have done spoiling, they shall be spoiled. O! that controversy seems to be upon England, which was threatened and was upon the people in that place we read of, Isa. xlii. 22, "This is a people robbed and spoiled; they are all of them snared in holes." If they had come into the field, perhaps it had been better with them; but they crept into holes, and they are snared and spoiled: "They are for a prey, and none delivereth; for a spoil, and none saith, Restore. Who among you will give ear to this?" Mark what the text saith, "Who will hearken and hear for the time to come? Who gave Jacob for a spoil, and Israel to the robbers? Did not the Lord, he against whom we have sinned? for they would not walk in his ways, neither were they obedient unto his law. Therefore he hath poured upon him the fury of his anger, and the strength of battle: and it hath set him on fire round about, yet he knew not; it burned him, yet he laid it not to heart." We are a people robbed and spoiled; because we have not walked in the ways of God, nor been obedient to his law, therefore the Lord hath poured his fury upon England at this day, and his fire burneth; and who hath laid it to heart?" Nobody stirs; because the fire is not kindled in the city, you lay it not to heart, and you suffer your brethren in one county after another to be spoiled. Take heed, if you stir not more than you have done, as many of you may answer for the blood of your brethren, so for the spoiling of their goods, because you do not lay to heart this heavy judgment that is at present upon the land, the execution of this controversy.

But yet you must know, that the taking away of men's goods is, in times of war, no stealing, nor no breach of the eighth commandment; for it is against common sense and reason, that in such times we should be wholly tied to those positive laws .f a state that are made for seasons of peace: but it accords with the law of nature, the law of God, and the law of arms, that our enemies should be deprived of what may strengthen them against us. Therefore let none cry out about stealing and robbing in these times; indeed, it is not fit that any should be suffered to rob, but yet it is just that those that will not be on one side should be taken as enemies to the other; and (I say) it is agreeable to the laws of nature, of God, and of arms, that in times of just war, (and regarding ours, I hope you cannot but be fully satisfied,) that what may strengthen the enemy may be taken away. Indeed, *they* plead for law who wholly break it themselves, because they would have all the privilege they can to strengthen themselves by our goods and the goods of others; but certainly God permits us, being in a lawful war, to strengthen ourselves by the estates and goods of those that appear our enemies, without breach of peace or of the positive law of the land, or of his own commandment. Thus much for the fourth charge.

"And committing adultery." The generation of a rational creature who must live to all eternity, is a work that God challenges a special hand in, to appoint it to all at his pleasure; therefore the breach of God's order in this, to satisfy the brutish lust of man or woman, is a most cursed evil, against which God carries on a most dreadful controversy. It is a breach of the blessed covenant of God, and a sin most opposite to his nature. And all you that are guilty of this; for perhaps many that are professors of religion, and live fairly amongst their neighbours, may yet be secretly guilty of it; all of you take this text home with you, "The mouth of strange women is a deep pit: he that is abhorred of the Lord shall fall therein," Prov. xxii. 14. Go thy ways, thou canst know no otherwise by thyself, but that thou art the man or the woman that art abhorred of God. Thou art beloved of thy whore, but the Lord abhors thee. And Tertullian, speaking on Eph. v. 6, "Let no man deceive you with vain words," uses an expression which I confess I would not dare to employ; He that preacheth of repentance to adultery, especially adultery in a forcible way, deceiveth men with vain words. You see his conception of the sin; we dare not justify what he saith, but it serves to show you how dreadful he apprehended the sin to be. And in Heb. vi., speaking of the sin that is unpardonable, he saith, We never read, nor ever knew, a second repentance promised to an adulterer or fornicator. He admitted but one repentance after baptism: see lib. de Penitentia, et de Pudicitia. These were his thoughts of adultery. The Athenians made a law, that if any man found his wife in the act of adultery, he might presently kill her. And I have read of a people among the heathen, that have punished this sin for its filthiness, by thrusting the adulterer's head into the paunch of a beast and keeping it there, and so stifling him. If heathens hated it so much, surely God must have a controversy, because of this sin, with those that profess themselves Christians; and the greater controversy because it is so little punished by men. And though many great ones can escape man's punishment, yet they cannot get beyond this controversy. I remember Mr. Cleaver reports of one that he knew, that had committed the act of uncleanness, and in the horror of conscience hung himself; that when he was about to hang himself, he wrote on a paper to this effect, I indeed acknowledge it to be utterly unlawful for a man to kill himself, but I am bound to act the magistrate's part, because the punishment of this sin is death. God would have that sin punished with death, but the magistrate did not punish it accordingly, therefore he, in horror of conscience, lays violent hands upon himself. We justify not his act, but it shows what a controversy God has with men that commit this sin. Thou committest that abominable sin, and thou hast some pleasure and delight in it; go thy way, thou art a dead man in God's eyes; look to thyself, one way or other God may bring death upon thee, and though man's law take not hold on thee, God's may, thou knowest not how soon. I have read of a king of Navarre, that by adultery had weakened his frame very much, and in consequence, his physicians caused his body to be wrapped about with a cerecloth dipped in aqua vitæ, and the party that sowed the cerecloth, having done, went to burn off the thread with a candle, which presently took hold of the cloth and consumed both it and the king.

Nunquam mæcho aut fornicatori secundam pænitentiam esse permissam.

And as God has a controversy for this sin, which is so little punished by man's law, but by God's law is death; so the rather has God a controversy for it, if it be committed by men of knowledge, by learned men, by men that are in public places, by men that carry a show of holiness, by men that are in the ministry; if they commit it, God has, in a special manner, a dreadful controversy with them. Jer. xxix. 22, 23, "The Lord make thee like Zedekiah and like Ahab, whom the king of Babylon roasted in the fire; because they committed villany in Israel, and have committed adultery with their neighbours' wives." It was a proverb, "The Lord make thee like Zedekiah and like Ahab, whom the king of Babylon roasted in the fire." This was not King Zedekiah and King Ahab, but two false prophets of the name, unclean wretches; and though it were the king of Babylon, a heathen, yet he so hated that sin of adultery, that he caused them to be roasted in the fire; for to burn or roast the offenders in the fire, was the punishment of that nation for capital offences. Therefore those that are ministers, that are learned men, that have any show of holiness more than others, if they be guilty of this sin God has a most dreadful controversy with them.

And see how we should have a controversy too against this sin of uncleanness, especially when forced. In Judg. xx. 17, you read there that there were four hundred thousand men, all men of war, that were raised up as one man, and they all said, ver. 8, "We will not any of us go to his tent, neither will we any of us turn into his house." And why did all these men rise? The cause was this: there was a Levite that had a concubine, which had played the harlot and gone from him, and he going to fetch her back, the men of Gibeah, a city of Benjamin, came in a violent way and abused her until she died; upon this the Levite took the dead body and divided it into twelve several pieces, and sent them into all the coasts of Israel. Upon this the hearts of all the men of Israel were raised as one man, and they covenanted among themselves, that they would none of them turn into their houses until they had brought the delinquents, that had committed that horrible offence, to condign punishment. Mark now, that the hearts of people should be so set upon it, and think it a sufficient reason to gather an army of four hundred thousand. Have we not heard of worse than this amongst us wheresoever the soldiers have come? what horrible villanies have been committed in this respect, taking not men's concubines and whores, but grave matrons, and purposely those whom they think to be most godly, and defiling them before the eyes of their husbands, and then murdering them! and yet we stir not for all this to fetch in these delinquents. Now we have rapes and ravishments of thousands amongst us, and yet our hearts stir not, though no question the same thing is intended against us here that is done to our brethren in other countries, for you can expect little else from such as these. In Judg. v. 20 the mother of Sisera saith, "Have they not divided the prey, to every man a damsel or two?" They aim as much to satisfy their lusts upon you as upon your goods; you must not think your lives will satisfy them, but their lusts must be first gratified. If you regard not your lives, and estates, and liberties, yet regard such horrible villany as this, which is committed in the face of heaven. These here resolved not to go to their tents nor to turn into their houses till this was done. Be content to shut up your shops for a while, and to leave your trades and to lie in the fields, until you have brought these delinquents to their just punishment. Be not discouraged with a little ill success; there were forty thousand of the better side slain here before Israel got the victory, until they had thoroughly humbled themselves, and then they succeeded. Though our adversaries meet with success in their ways, let us not be discouraged; they that stood to defend this horrible wickedness of the men of Gibeah, got the first and second days, yet they persevered till they had brought the offenders to condign punishment. We should resolve never to follow our business, nor regard our houses and private estates, until we have got this wickedness punished in this land, and wiped off its guilt from the kingdom.

"They break out." That is, like the eruption of waters: as waters break over the banks when it has been kept in a while, so they thus break out and overflow all bounds. When sin is not mortified, though it be restrained for a while, it will break out: as many young men that have lived in good families and had good governors, and so have had their sin restrained, afterward, when they come to manage themselves, then break out, sin grows to a strength that nothing can restrain; like that man that had an unclean spirit and lived among the graves; "no man could bind him, no, not with chains," Mark v.

Obs. Breaking out is a great aggravation of a man's sin. It argues strength, impudence, and desperateness in sin. And this breaking out of sin is not merely as the overflowing of water at some times or tides, but rather like the bursting out of fire, or, if you will, like water gushing forth from some fountain: now you know, if water break out of a fountain, not a diminution, but rather an increase ensues; and when a house is on fire, it will smoulder a long while, but when it bursts out at the roof or elsewhere, then it flames the more and increases with more violence. So it is no diminution to sin that it breaks out; as many foolish people that will speak horribly wickedly in their passion, I will let it go, as good out as in; foolishly concluding there is so much less corruption within, and that is a diminution of sin, whereas it is an aggravation, and denotes impudence in sin.

"And blood toucheth blood." That is, as some will have it, one gross and abominable sin, accounted a bloody sin, follows another. But some understand it thus, one murder follows another, one oppression succeeds to another: "Blood toucheth blood;" now thy wickedness is broken out there is no end of it, but one murder follows another. Pareus thinks it refers to the same times as 2 Kings xv., where you may read what murders there were, and how blood touched blood; as if the prophet here said, They being used to murder, there is now nothing else, you hear of murders every where. Thus, if the Lord raise not up means to control and subdue the rage of ungodly men, if it get head and overcome the opposition it meets, blood will then touch blood, one messenger shall not have done his relation of one horrid and cruel murder, before another messenger will be at his heels to tell you of another, still more horrid and more vile. So it is in some countries, there comes one and saith, In such a place such a man and all his family were murdered; and presently another comes and tells you, In such a town such a friend of yours was murdered; thus the messengers rapidly succeed one another, and relate of blood touching blood. So some interpret it.

But I rather thus, They defile themselves incestuously, (so that this is somewhat more than bare adultery,) not regarding the nearness of blood, but "blood toucheth blood;" they that were nearest in blood mingled themselves one with another in filthy and abominable lusts. So the Septuagint translate it, μισγουσι, they mingle: and Jerome, *sanguis sanguinem tetigit*, they mingle and touch blood with blood, those that are near of kin come near one another in filthy lusts. Now this was a sin for which God cast the very heathen out of Canaan, that good land, and therefore well may he have a controversy with the people of the land now; as you may find Lev. xviii. 6, "None of you shall approach to any that is near of kin to him, to uncover their nakedness: I am the Lord." And so afterward goes on to show what degrees of consanguinity we must observe; and then, ver. 24, 25, "Defile not ye yourselves in any of these things: for in all these the nations are defiled that I cast out before you: and the land is defiled: therefore I do visit the iniquity thereof upon it, and the land itself vomiteth out her inhabitants." The rather still has God a controversy with a people for this sin, because it is so little punished. I ask, what punishment is there at this day amongst us for incest, or for any uncleanness, except that the man must support the child; and as to the ancient punishment of coming into the court and being enjoined to wear a white sheet, they could dispense with it for a very little money. Hence we may fear that God's controversy is so much the more against us, and pray to him that speedily the land may deliver itself from this guilt by having severe laws for the punishment of this horrible wickedness, lest God come and punish it himself, and then woe unto us!

Ver. 3. *Therefore shall the land mourn, and every one that dwelleth therein shall languish, with the beasts of the field, and with the fowls of heaven; yea, the fishes of the sea also shall be taken away.*

You have heard that God in this chapter commences a suit against the ten tribes. He puts in his action, and he declares, and then judges. The articles of his declaration or charge against them we have discussed. Hereupon judgment is passed, "Therefore shall the land mourn."

"The land." How can the land be said to mourn? As when the land is fruitful it is said to laugh and sing, and meadows that are green to rejoice; Psal. lxv. 13, "The valleys also are covered over with corn; they shout for joy, they also sing:" so when a land is desolate and God brings famine, then it is said to mourn. Jer. xii. 4, "How long shall the land mourn, and the herbs of every field wither, for the wickedness of them that dwell therein? the beasts are consumed, and the birds; because they said, He shall not see our last end." And likewise a place, when left desolate of people that were before the beauty of it, is then said to mourn: Isa. iii. 26, "Her gates shall lament and mourn." Lam. i. 4, "The ways of Zion do mourn, because none come to her solemn feasts." As now in time of plague, the streets of your city may be said to mourn because they are deserted and look desolate, when the grass grows between the stones; "Her gates shall lament and mourn." The expression here is designed to upbraid the hardness of the hearts of the ten tribes. As if God should say, Notwithstanding all their dreadful sins, that should break their hearts and make them howl and cry out, yet they will not mourn; therefore their land shall mourn. When God will upbraid men for stopping their ears and refusing to hear, and to obey, he calls to the heavens, Isa. i. 2, "Hear, O heavens, and give ear, O earth;" to upbraid the the deafness of men that will not hear: and Jer. ii. 12, "Be astonished, O ye heavens:" because men will not fear, therefore, to upbraid them, God calls to the heavens to be astonished: so, because men's hearts are hard, therefore God calls to the land to mourn, yea, saith it "*shall* mourn." The deformity of your sin, that is the meaning, shall appear in the miserable desolation of your country. There is an ugly face of sin, and it were well if you saw it as it is in your own hearts, the guilt that you have brought upon your own spirits; but seeing you will not apprehend sin as in your own hearts, you shall see the sad effects of it in all things of the land. God will have sin appear vile to us one way or other. The Lord this day is making our land mourn because we have not mourned, because we do not mourn. Many countries know what this expression means, their country mourns, their land mourns. The very sight of the dreadful effects of sin upon many parts in England is sufficient to break any man's heart. As in Germany, persons that have travelled there, and seen towns and places, formerly of great riches and traffic, now overgrown with nettles, it breaks their hearts, they see the land to mourn; and it begins to be so amongst us in many places of England, in Yorkshire, and in the west. Oh that we all could mourn in the bitterness of our spirits, that our land and cities might no further mourn! But we must not give liberty to ourselves in pathetical or affectionate ways, but keep as near as we can to an explicatory course.

"And every one shall languish." The word translated languish here, signifies the withering of a flower, or the withering of herbs and trees: and so in Nah. i. 4, "The flower of Lebanon languisheth;" the same word occurs as here, "every one shall languish," and the signification of it suggests this useful note.

Obs. 1. All the glory and pomp of the men of the world, is but as a flower; and even as soon as a flower withereth, so soon do they pass away.

Obs. 2. Times of affliction take down the jollity and bravery of men's spirits, and make them fade, wither, and pine away.

ואמלל The word here is translated by some, and they shall be made weak. When wicked men are prosperous, their hearts are stout and strong to sin, they can stand out against God and against all threats; but when the hand of God is upon them, then their spirits are poor, they are weak and presently cast down. Oh the difference between the brave, stout spirits of wicked men in their prosperity against God, and their poor, weak, withered, and dejected spirits in the time of their adversity! Psal. xxxix. 11, "When thou with rebukes dost correct man for iniquity, thou makest his beauty to consume away like a moth: surely every man is vanity. Selah."

And a notable expression we have of the withering, the languishing, of the spirits of wicked men in the time of their adversity, that whereas now in their prosperity their tongues are their own, and they must and will ask, Who is the Lord? they are then loud in their oaths and blasphemies; but mark them now in their adversity; Isa. xxix. 4, "Thou shalt be brought down, and shalt speak out of the ground, and thy speech shall be low out of the dust, and thy speech shall whisper out of the dust." This is the fruit of the languishing of their spirits in the time of their trouble. As a riotous and boisterous gallant, that would so mouth it when he was in prosperity, yet let God but lay his hand upon him in sickness, and his conscience then accusing him, he whispers and speaks low out of the dust. Then follows,

"With the beasts of the field, and with the fowls of heaven; yea, the fishes of the sea also shall be taken away."

Jerome allegorizes this, and would take it to mean several sorts of men. But we must not stand to that, but rather take the words as they are literally. Only as to the reading of them a word or two first.

"With the beasts of the field, and with the fowls of heaven." In the Hebrew, ב which is translated *with*, is sometimes equivalent to *for*, "*for* the beasts of the field:" as in chap. v. 5, "Israel and Ephraim shall fall in their iniquity," or, for their iniquity. So if here we translate it, *for* the beasts of the field, and *for* the fowls of heaven, then we have this note.

Obs. 3. We may here see the poorness of our condition, that when but the beasts of the field and the fowls of the air are destroyed, our comforts are forthwith gone. The comforts of natural men depend upon poor things, on the beasts of the field, the fishes of the sea, the fowls of the air; if God's hand be but upon them, and the cups be taken from their mouths, and the full dishes from their tables, presently they languish. It is otherwise with a gracious heart: Hab. iii. 17, 18, "Although the fig tree shall not blossom, neither shall fruit be in the vines; the labour of the olive shall fail, and the fields shall yield no meat; the flock shall be cut off from the fold, and there shall be no herd in the stalls: yet will I rejoice in the Lord, I will joy in the God of my salvation." A gracious heart does not languish because the beasts of the field and the fowls of the air are taken away: let them be taken away, yet he can rejoice in God, his spirit will be sustained.

"Shall be taken away." The word in the Hebrew is יאספו they shall be gathered, for it is observable both in fowls and in fishes, that when they perceive any thing noxious unto them, or that they are in any danger, they gather themselves together: and that is the reason that fishes at some periods of the year are in such shoals; going from one place to another, and finding them noxious and hurtful, or perceiving some danger, they gather together. And so fowls migrate in the winter time. I have heard many in Holland say of the storks, that they gather themselves in the space of a week or thereabouts, and so take their flight together from that country. Thence I take the word here, they shall be gathered together, to mean, that there shall be such times of danger, and such infection in the air, and in the very waters of the sea, that the fishes and fowls shall perceive it, and so shall be gathered together (as they use to be gathered when they perceive any such thing) to go away; and being so gathered together, they shall be destroyed. It is good for men, like these creatures, in times of danger to gather together and to join one with another, and not be scattered one here and another there. This only for the reading of the words.

The scope of the Holy Ghost here, in threatening to take away the beasts and the fowls and the fishes, is this, To show the severity of God's wrath against the ten tribes; that as a king not only executes a traitor, but pulls down his house and burns all that is in it; so the great wrath of God shall so be upon these ten tribes, that he shall not only destroy them, but for their sakes bring destruction even upon the creatures. And this seems to be a threatening of greater wrath than God let out when he destroyed the world. In that destruction, we do not read of any hurt unto the fishes of the sea; but here the beasts of the field, the fowls of the air, and the fishes of the sea, shall be taken away. It refers to some fearful plague, wherein not only the air, but the waters are pestilential, and the cattle and the fish die. So it has been in other countries, and even in England, in the time of Edward the Third, such a pestilential quality was in the air and water, that birds and fishes were found with infectious blotches. And then in one church-yard, (I think about the Charter-house,) in one year's space, fifty thousand were buried of pestilential diseases. Such power has God over us, that he can let out his wrath by such ways as these, and such plagues are very fearful fruits of his wrath upon a country. What cause have we to bless God that he has delivered us from the infection of the air! If God had but brought a plague upon London last year, it would have been the heaviest calamity brought on any kingdom in the world; if we had had but such a plague as would have caused men to have fled and the parliament not have sat, its dissolution would have reduced the whole kingdom into a lamentable estate at this day. Let us bless God for that.

I remember upon this text a Jesuit that wrote but very lately, Cornelius a Lapide, has a most audacious lie. Since Scotland and Ireland, saith he, have departed from the catholic faith, (that is, from popery,) God's judgments are out against them; and whereas they were wont to be such plentiful countries for fish, God has cursed their very waters, and now their trade of fishing is nothing like to what it was formerly. He includes not England in this observation, for he was one that wrote lately, and had it seems some hope that England was coming to them again. But through God's mercy both Ireland, and Scotland, and England, have found it otherwise in this respect.

Hence,

Obs. 4. The good or evil of the creature depends on man; because it was made for man, man is punished or blessed even by the creature, and the creature comes to feel good or evil, according as man's behaviour is towards God. Let then mercy and pity toward the creature be an argument to keep us from sin. If you have not cruel hearts towards the creature, abstain from sin, for you do not only undo yourselves, but the creation, by your sin. And when at any time we see the hand of God out against any creature, let us reflect in our own hearts, My sin is the cause that this creature feels that evil which it does: and as Judah said unto Tamar, "She is more righteous than I;" so do you say of the creature, Indeed God's hand is out against it, but the creature is more righteous than I.

Obs. 5. God, when in a way of wrath, can cause his wrath to reach to those things that seem to be most remote. As the fishes in the sea seem to be most remote, therefore they are named here; "yea, the fishes in the sea also:" as if he had said, My wrath shall burn fiercely, and shall reach not only to yourselves and houses, your cities, and land, and cattle, but to the very fish in the sea. God can let out his wrath as far as he pleases.

Obs. 6. No creature can help man in the time of God's wrath; why? for every creature suffers as well as man. How vain then are the hearts of men, who solace themselves in hope of comfort from this or that creature, in the day of God's wrath! If you cry unto the mountains and hills, and say, Help us; they will echo back, Help us; for they need help as well as you; for the wrath of God is upon the creature in the day of his wrath, and therefore they are unable to aid.

Ver. 4. *Yet let no man strive, nor reprove another: for thy people are as they that strive with the priest.*

"Yet." The Hebrew word is, אך *Vere*, as if he should say, Truly it is in vain for any one to stand striving or reproving his neighbour, or seek to convince or admonish him, it is in vain for one friend to meddle with another; for they are so violent in their wicked ways, so far from hearkening to private admonition, that they will contend with the priest, even with him that is set by God, and designed by special office, to teach and reprove. Some interpret it thus, They are so vile, and their wickedness so general, that no man is fit to reprove his brother for his sin. But I incline to the former interpretation, which imports thus much to us in the general.

Obs. 1. Sin cannot be got from men without striving. Such is the perverseness of men's hearts, that they take fast hold of deceit, Jer. viii. 5, and you cannot get them away without striving; like men in a frenzy, you cannot get them off from that which will injure them without struggling with them. When you admonish and reprove men for sin, you must expect beforehand that they will contend against you, yet afterwards, perhaps, they will bless God for you: at first you may be hardly used; What! you come to judge us? as they said to Lot, "Who made you a ruler?" So you generally receive very ill language from men at first when they are reproved, yet be not discouraged, they may bless God for you afterwards, they may say as David unto Abigail, "Blessed be God, and blessed be thy advice, and blessed be thou for thy counsel."

Obs. 2. Even private men, (as implied in the former note,) so long as there is any hope, should strive with their brethren, by way of admonition and reprehension, to bring them from their sin. We must not say, Are we our brother's keepers? that is the language of a Cain. There is much striving and contending one with another for our own ends; oh that there were more striving and contending for God and his glory! It is a sign that the glory of God and the souls of our brethren are not precious in our eyes, when we can so strive and contend to have our own wills, and though God loses his glory, and our brother's soul is like to perish, we cannot strive and contend there, not even those of us that are full of strife otherwise.

Obs. 3. It is a great aggravation of sin, and a forerunner of destruction to a people, not to regard the strivings, admonitions, and reprehensions of others. "Let no man strive;" It is in vain to strive now (that is the meaning); indeed, so long as there was hope there might be striving, but now they are past striving. This was the height of wickedness that they were grown unto, and the forerunner of that wrath of God which was now ready to fall upon them, that they were now past all reprehension and admonition. I will cite two or three notable texts of Scripture to fasten this upon your hearts, that it is a most fearful thing for people to stand out against admonition and reprehension. In 1 Sam. ii. 25, the text saith of Eli's sons, that they hearkened not unto the voice of their father; why? "because the Lord would slay them." O you children, hearken to this scripture, turn to it, read it over, you that are stout and rebellious, whose parents are reproving you for your sins and admonishing you, but you will not hearken to them; and in the pride of your hearts and stoutness of your spirits you refuse admonition; but if you read that scripture, and believe that it is the word of God, O tremble at it; "They hearkened not unto the voice of their father, because the Lord would slay them." Another text you have in 2 Chron. xxv. 16, a speech of the Lord's prophet to Amaziah; when the prophet came to rebuke him for worshipping the gods of that people whom he had overcome in battle; (here is the infinite vanity and sottishness of idolaters, Amaziah falls to worship those very gods that could not deliver themselves nor their people out of his hands;) when the prophet (I say) came to reprove him for it, in what a rage was he! one would have thought that it was reasonable for his spirit to yield to the prophet's reproof, but saith the king, "Art thou made of the king's counsel? forbear;" it may be he has other plans and intentions, what have you to do to meddle? The prophet did forbear indeed, but mark what he said, "I know that God hath determined to destroy thee, because thou hast done this, and hast not hearkened unto my counsel." Here was his inference, because the king would not regard admonition and reproof, certainly God purposed to destroy him. And it is observable of this king that he should now stand out so; for in the chapter before, he seems to be of a yielding spirit, though a wicked man: when he had hired a hundred thousand out of Israel to join with him in battle, and had given them all pay; yet, when God did but command him by the prophet to send them back with the loss of the hundred talents which he had paid the soldiers, on the very word of the prophet he sends back a hundred thousand of his soldiers, and loses all their pay; and yet this Amaziah, so yielding then, how stubborn was he against the prophet at another time! and therefore when he did so yield to God, God prospered him in the battle, and he overcame his enemies gloriously; but when, after that victory, he fell a worshipping the idols he had overcome, and was stout against the prophet, soon after he was destroyed. The last scripture is that in Prov. xxix. 1,

"He that being often reproved hardeneth his neck, shall suddenly be destroyed, and that without remedy." It is a dangerous thing to stand out against reproof and admonition.

Obs. 4. Sin increases where it is let alone. Let no man strive, nor reprove another. You may see that this people were become worse than they were before, for in the second chapter of this prophecy, "Say to your brethren, Ammi; and to your sisters, Ru-hamah." The godly amongst them are there admonished to speak to their brethren and to their sisters; but now it is come to such a pass, that there must be no more striving, no more admonishing. Those that once were capable of admonition, going on in sin and hardening their hearts, grow quickly past all reproof.

Obs. 5. There is a time when men may, yea, men should give up striving with, admonishing, and reproving others, when they should let them alone. Especially in these two cases; when those they admonish scorn their admonition, when they trample their reproofs under their feet as swine, or turn again on them and rend them as dogs. There are two sorts not to be admonished or reproved, swine and dogs. When they become such, then you may leave, yea, you ought to leave admonishing them. For admonitions and reprehensions are precious things, pearls, that must not be cast to swine; Matt. vii. 6, "Give not that which is holy unto the dogs, neither cast ye your pearls before swine," they are holy and precious things: for I do not take that place to be meant of the sacrament only; it may, by an argument *a minori ad majus*, be applied to it, but it is primarily meant of admonition and reprehension. So that admonition is to be looked upon as a holy thing, as a pearl, you are to prize it, and therefore not to be angry when we come to admonish you; but you are to look upon the holiness of God in it, and so reverence it; and regard it as a mercy of God, and bless him for it. There are many in heaven now blessing God for the admonitions which they have received from others, as David blessed God for Abigail and her counsel. Many think it a great happiness to them that they can reject admonition and counsel; and when they are gone from such as have admonished them, and are among their companions, they can boast and say, Oh, such a one came and reprehended me, but I said thus and thus to him; and so they rejoice how they have rejected admonition. But if they knew all, they have cause to mourn; it is a great misery for them when it comes to that, that God shall bid those that have to deal with them to strive no more with them: when you have so rejected the admonitions of others, that you think you have succeeded in stopping their mouths, and that you have fairly rid yourselves of all their reproofs, oh, your misery is the greater. For,

1. You have deprived yourselves of a special ordinance of God. Admonition and reprehension, even brotherly admonition and reprehension, is an ordinance of God.

2. Those who strive thus, who admonish and reprove you, must give an account to God what is become of their admonition and reprehension. You must give an account to God one day, and so must they also; yea, they should do it at present, thus: after they have admonished, they must go to God and tell him how it has succeeded, for they have done it in his name if they have done it right; and if their admonition and reproof have prevailed with you, they are to return to God with blessing, to bless God that he has been pleased to bless their admonition. And on the other hand, if you reject their admonition, they are to tell that too, and to lament your condition, and to entreat of him to look upon you, and to say, Lord, I have been thus and thus admonishing such a one in thy name, but, Lord, he contemns and rejects it. When you are laughing that you have rejected such a friend's admonition, then he that has been faithful to you, he is telling God of it; and do you not think there will come somewhat of this one day?

3. You are left to God's striving and rebuking, and "it is a fearful thing to fall into the hands of the living God." It is better when God strives with you by men, than that he should come and strive with you himself. As now, if a father send his servant to go and fetch in a child, to receive a rebuke, and he return and tell the father, He cares not for what I say; then the father goes himself, and it is worse for the child: so God sends thy brother to rebuke thee, and to fetch thee in, and thou carest not for him, but regardest him as thy fellow creature; and so thy brother goes to God, Lord, he regards not what I say. Then, saith God, I will rebuke him myself: and God's rebukes in this case will be "furious rebukes;" Ezek. v. 15, "When I shall execute judgments in thee in anger, and in fury, and in furious rebukes." Mark it, "furious rebukes;" the rebukes of a brother are loving rebukes, but if thou reject them, God's rebukes may come, and they will prove furious rebukes. The rebukes of a brother are out of love, but, Amos vii. 4, "The Lord called to contend by fire." When Job's friends strove with him they could not prevail, but, chap. xxxviii. 1, 2, "The Lord answered Job out of the whirlwind, and said, Who is this that darkeneth words without counsel?" The Lord out of the whirlwind calls to contend with Job, and so overcomes him. If thou regardest not friends contending with thee, the Lord himself, out of the whirlwind, may come and contend with thee. Take heed how thou rejectest the strivings of a brother with thee, for God may not only say he shall strive no longer, but, My Spirit shall no longer strive with thy soul.

"For thy people are as they that strive with the priest." That is the reason why they must not strive one with another. Here, only these two things require explanation:

1. Why it is said "with the priest," rather than with the prophet?

2. Why it is said, "For thy people are *as* they that strive with the priest?" Did they not strive with the priest? why then is it not said, This people are a people that strive with the priest?

To answer these two briefly, observe,

1. It is said that they "strive with the priest," rather than with the prophet, though the prophet did rebuke and strive with them, for this reason; because the priest was a standing office in the church of God, whereas the prophet was an extraordinary office, and they could not be sure whether he were a true prophet or no, but according to the event of the prophecy; but the priest they acknowledged to be an officer of God, and hence he is here named rather than the prophet.

2. It may be, the priests, being Jeroboam's, scarce strove at all, but rather joined with them in their wickedness; therefore he could not say they actually strove with the priests, but yet so vile were their hearts, that God saw that if there were priests to strive with, they would strive with them. Or, it may be, because indeed those priests of Israel at this time were not such as were called of God, for in 1 Kings xii. 31, the text saith of Jeroboam, that "he made priests of the lowest of the people, which were not of the sons of Levi;" and chap. xiii. 33, "Whosoever would, he consecrated him, and he became one of the priests of the high places." But the people received them as priests still, for they thought that the king's authority was a sufficient reason for their reception, as if the king had absolute power to make all church officers. So it was then, and this may be the reason of the expression, "*as* they that strive with the priest."

Obs. 1. It is the work of the priest to contend against

men for their sin. That is the proper work of a priest, to strive with men against their sin. They are the salt of the earth, and so they should have some acrimony in them. In 1 Tim. iii. 3, it is said, indeed, of the minister of God, that he should be ἄμαχον, no striver. A minister of God should in office look to the souls of people, and be no striver; how will you say then that he should strive? It means, he should never strive with men for his own ends, or for his own ways; he should be no brawler, but one of a quiet and gentle spirit, willing to pass by wrongs done unto himself: but when he stands up for God he should be a striver. All faithful ministers should be strivers when they come in God's cause. Œcolampadius, writing to his fellow ministers, I remember, has a notable expression; "Let not our zeal and anger burn when we are scorned and reproached ourselves; but when the truth and the name of God are in danger, then let our heat arise, then let us strive." This, indeed, is the character of a true godly minister, that he is in his own cause gentle and yielding, but when it comes to the cause of God, zealous and fervent, ready to strive and contend with men in the ways of their sin.

Obs. 2. When ministers do reprehend and strive with people, they must expect to be striven withal by people. These are "as they that strive with the priest;" they have such vile hearts, that, had they never such faithful and godly officers set over them by God, they would strive with them. And indeed all faithful ministers must expect, that if they strive with men for their sins, men will strive with them. If there had ever any faithful ones been sent among them by God, they would have been ready to have cried out against them and told them, You are the cause of our misery, for you are so strict and precise that you will not yield to Jeroboam: you threaten us that judgments will come upon us, but you are the cause of our misery; were it not for you we should have all the people yield to what the king has set up, but you stir them up against it and so disquiet us. Thus no question but they would be ready to strive with the priest at that time. And thus they did with Amos, chap. vii. 12, "Go to Judah and prophesy there." They strove with Amos, who was contemporary with Hosea, prophesying at this time unto this people, and the land say they cannot bear Amos's words, let him go to Judah; he tells us we are a superstitious people, and that we do not worship God in the right manner and in the right place, let him go thither, we wish he were out of the country; he, and such as he is, raise a fire in the land. Thus when ministers discharge their consciences, showing people their sins and the mind of God, this is ordinarily their recompence. Thus it was with Jeremiah; chap. xv. 10, "Woe is me, my mother, that thou hast borne me a man of strife and a man of contention to the whole earth! every one curseth me." Jeremiah, a grave and holy prophet, yet a man of contention to the whole earth, and every man cursed him! A strange thing, that he should meet with such hard dealing; and yet he appealed to God in the matter of his sincerity, he desired not the evil day, and he prayed for the people until God bid him pray no more; when they were railing on him, he was praying for them. This was his unhappy situation; and so it was with other prophets besides him. I might name other texts in Jeremiah, as chap. xx. 7, 8, "I am in derision daily, every one mocketh me. For since I spake, I cried out, I cried violence and spoil; because the word of the Lord was made a reproach unto me, and a derision, daily." After I threatened that there should come some judgment upon the nation, I cried out of the violence and spoil that they for the present made in the nation, and then they mocked and scorned me. The like we have in Isaiah, he had the same dealings from the people: chap. xxviii. 13, "But the word of the Lord was to them precept upon precept, precept upon precept; line upon line, line upon line; here a little, and there a little; that they might go, and fall backward, and be broken, and snared, and taken." You will say, How do they strive against the prophet in this? I take it this scripture is often mistaken, and the intent of these words is, to show how the people jeered and mocked the prophet in his preaching. But the word of God was to them "precept upon precept," that is, they scorned at God's word; What! we have nothing but precept and precept, one precept after another, and commandment one after another, and one prophecy after another, a line upon line, and now you would have a little more: it is spoken contemptuously. I take this to be the meaning, because the threatening follows after, "that they might go, and fall backward, and be broken, and snared, and taken. Wherefore" (saith the text in the very next words) "hear the word of the Lord, ye scornful men." They manifested a scornful spirit in such kind of expressions, retorting upon the prophet in such a manner; and God's anger riseth, "Wherefore hear the word of the Lord, ye scornful men." It is usual with many scornful men, that if they can lay hold of any thing that ministers speak, by their manner of pronouncing it, or otherwise, to express their contempt: so did they with Isaiah, who was one of the most eloquent of the prophets, a man that spake in his time so as never man spake, for he spoke in a most high style, being himself of the kingly race, and a great man by birth; yet, when he came to prophesy to this people in the name of God, they thus jeered and scorned him. And Isa. xxx. 10, "Which say to the seers, and to the prophets, Prophesy not unto us right things, speak unto us smooth things;" tell not us of such and such things as these are: thus they contemned him. Yea, and in Christ's time we find, that when Christ himself preached, once, as soon as he had done his sermon, the people got him up to the brow of a hill that was upon the side of the city, and would have thrown him down and broken his neck; that was the reward he should have had. And of Paul, one of the best of preachers, whom Austin wished he could but see in the pulpit, when he came to preach, "What will this babbler say?" and, "He is a pestilent fellow," one that is of a furious spirit and an incendiary, and wherever he goes he turns the world upside down. Such kind of entertainment had the apostles. And Luther, I remember, has such an expression, *Quid est prædicare evangelium?* What is it to preach, unless it be this, to turn all the fury of people upon oneself, if one would preach conscientiously? And in Matt. v. 12, Christ tells his disciples what revilings and persecutions they were likely to meet with; "For so," saith he, "persecuted they the prophets which were before you." And Acts vii. 53, "Which of the prophets have not your fathers persecuted?" Thus those that by their office are sent to speak to the people, must expect, if they would be faithful in their administrations, to be striven withal.

But though wicked men do strive, yet, as Samson said to the men of Judah that came to bind him that they might deliver him into the hands of the Philistines, "Do not ye fall upon me yourselves," it were well if faithful ministers were not often striven with by those that are godly. It is not so much for a faithful minister to have wicked and ungodly men to strive with him. Though *they* bind them, O brethren, do not *you* bind them. After that, in conscience of their duty and love to your souls, they have hazarded all the hatred and malice of the adversary, even to stand in the forefront of the battle; yet, in requital for all this, even many that are godly, if they see them grow troublesome, are ready to strive with them; because wicked men are exasperated by the word of God preached, therefore even such as make profession of godliness could wish that such ministers had never come amongst them. Is here a requital of the hazard that faithful ministers undergo? I appeal to you, Are there any people in the kingdom that stand as a butt against the malice of the adversary so much as godly and faithful ministers? Do not think that, from precipitancy or rashness, we do not consider what danger we stand in, in doing what we do. Yes, we consider it beforehand; but from a conscientious regard for our duty, and in faithfulness to your souls, we hazard our lives, we hazard all the rage and malice of the enemy. Now, when we have done all this, we expect a far better requital from many people than we find. When Moses and Aaron came to the people of Israel, when they were in Egypt, to deliver them, (for that was their message,) because for the present their bondage was increased, and the wrath of Pharaoh more incensed, therefore they were weary of Moses and Aaron, and fell to striving with them, as if they were the cause of their misery: Why, it was better with us before than since you came; if you had never come amongst us it would have been better with us: so now, because those that are faithful, out of conscience, labour to declare to you the mind of God, and to draw you to those duties that God requires; you are ready to think they have brought us into this state, they have kindled the fire, telling us it is the cause of God, and exhorting us to come in with our estates; and now the king is exasperated against us, and our adversaries are enraged, and we are likely to be in some misery: and so all the strivings of even the better sort are ready to devolve upon the ministers, and they strive with them as the only incendiaries and troublers of the places where they come. Well, however ministers may meet with hard dealing from some, even professors, yet their way is with the Lord, and their judgment is with the Almighty. There is a most admirable promise to help those that have been most forward to rebuke sin, and zealous for God, though men are enraged against them, in Isa. xlix. 2, "He hath made my mouth like a sharp sword; in the shadow of his hand hath he hid me." This text is true of every faithful minister. Mark, "He hath made my mouth like a sharp sword:" why, if I did speak smooth things, I were not like to be in so much danger; but if I speak sharp things, do not I hazard myself much? I shall incur the rage and anger of all kinds of people. But mark, "He hath made my mouth as a sharp sword;" but "in the shadow of his hand hath he hid me." Ministers whose mouths are as sharp swords, are in a great deal of danger; yea, but let such be comforted, here comes a promise presently; "in the shadow of his hand hath he hid me." So that those ministers whose mouths are sharpest in the name of God, and who speak but the truth of God, are under his protection more than those who have held their peace, they are in more safety, hid in God's hand, "in the shadow of his hand." So God comforted Jeremiah, chap. xv. 11; after he had cried out, Woe is me, I am a man of strife! Well, saith God, "Verily it shall be well with thy remnant; I will cause the enemy to entreat thee well in the time of evil and in the time of affliction." It may be, many of you think it is a weakness in ministers to endanger themselves so much, and that they cannot be quiet as others are. Many of more moderate spirits, and who deal more wisely for themselves, keep in and say nothing, and so may escape, whatever side prevail; and may not they escape? No, they are in more danger than the other, for the former are under a promise, the latter not; they are so studious for themselves and for their own safety, that God will take no care of them. Our Saviour Christ takes care to encourage his disciples against the strivings of people with them: we have in Luke vi. many blessings pronounced; "Blessed are the poor; Blessed are they that hunger and thirst after righteousness; Blessed are they that mourn," &c. But they that understand the original shall find the word "ye" is not in, only blessed are the poor, and blessed are they that mourn, &c. But when he comes to his disciples, ver. 22, he addresses them more particularly: whereas people shall speak evil of them, and cast out their name as filth, then there is, "Blessed are ye," with an ἐστε, more than there was in all the other blessednesses; that shows God has a special care of his ministers when men speak evil of them and strive with them. But on the other side, "Woe to you when all men speak well of you!" is true indeed of all Christians; but I take it, that the scope of Christ in that place concerns ministers that were to go and preach, and woe to them when all men speak well of them! The word that is translated "well," is καλῶς, that speak of you so as to commend you as a curious, neat teacher; there are such and such fiery men, but here is a preacher, a quaint, refined man, a man that uses fine language, and such they will never persecute. The others are pronounced blessed when they are reviled and cast out as evil.

μακάριοί ἐστε.

Obs. 3. To strive with those who come in God's name to reprove, is a great aggravation of sin and a hastening of judgment. God expects when he sends his ministers, that you should obey them in the Lord, and not strive with them. In 2 Chron. xxxvi. 12, God took it ill that King Zedekiah did not humble himself before Jeremiah the prophet; and in ver. 16, of the same chapter, it is said, They mocked the prophets, and contemned them, until the wrath of God arose against his people, and there was no remedy: no remedy when once they strove with those that God sent amongst them. Those that are sent by God, they are the special witnesses of God. Rev. xi. it is said of those two witnesses, that if any do them hurt and contend with them, fire shall go out of their mouths and devour their enemies. Those that are sent by God, and come in God's name, have the power of Jesus Christ with them: Matt. xxviii., "All power is given to me," &c.; "Go and teach," &c. As if he should say, Know, as I have all power given to me, it shall go along with you, to do good to those that obey your doctrine, and to execute vengeance upon all those that strive with you. The apostles were to shake off the dust of their feet in contempt of those who contemned their doctrine.

But you will say, May we not in any case strive with the minister?

I confess, in popery they would so exalt their priestly office, that all people must be brought into a blind obedience to them, and the people must receive whatsoever doctrine they preach; the priest's lips only must preserve knowledge, the people must not so much as examine it, but implicitly obey. It is one of the pope's canons concerning himself, that though he should carry down with him by heaps souls to hell, yet no mortal man must presume so much as to rebuke him or find fault with him; for he, being spiritual, as they say, (for so they abuse the Scripture,) judgeth all men, and no man judgeth him: and in a proportion, all their priests would fain claim some measure of the same power. And this certainly has been the policy of our priests of late, to bring the people into ignorance, so that they might not be able to contend with them, let them do what they would. They cry out, There was never such a time, when every tailor and every shopkeeper had so much knowledge that they can contradict their minister as now, and try their doctrines. They rage at this, that poor men have so much knowledge as to be able to try the doctrines they preach; they would fain teach, that you must be led, like a company of sheep, what way they would lead, and believe whatever they preach. Certainly, so many

Nullus mortalium præsumat redarguere, quia cunctos ipse judicaturus a nemine est judicandus. Lex Canonic.

gross errors and doting conceits of popery could never have prevailed, but by the people rendering blind obedience. Therefore there may be some striving with ministers, and that according to God, though here striving is forbidden: as thus; Christ requires that his sheep should know the difference between his voice and the voice of a stranger: yea, we know that there is a charge, that if any preach any other doctrine he should be accursed; even people should regard those that come to them to preach any other doctrine as accursed; therefore they are required to know; and they are commanded to try every thing, and "not to believe every spirit," yea, not to bid them "good speed" who bring other doctrines. And they are to "say to Archippus, Take heed to thy ministry, which thou hast received, that thou fulfil it." So far the people are empowered: yet still it must be done with respect to them. If they look upon them as true officers, (whether they be or no, yet, if they regard them as such,) the rule will apply, "Against an elder receive not an accusation, but before two or three witnesses;" you must not be so ready to strive with those that you look upon as officers. And "rebuke not an elder, but entreat him as a father:" it must not be in a malapert way, but with respect and reverence. And when you have done that, contended by witnesses, and spoken to them with reverence as owning the place wherein they stand, you have liberty then, if they bring strange doctrine, or their life be bad, to strive and contest with them in the name of the Lord, and not to suffer yourselves to be under such bondage as to believe whatever they would have you, without calling them to any account at all. There was wont to be crying out against people if they went from their parish churches, (as they called them,) Oh, it could not be suffered; and yet they themselves would be away a whole year together; as if the relation were not mutual, and they bound as much to continue with their people as the people tied to keep unto them: if the minister may have leave to go away, certainly the people may enjoy the same freedom; whereas, indeed, neither ought to go away, so long as the one is looked upon as an officer, and the other as under that officer. But I speak of that bondage into which they would have brought you, whereby in time they would so wholly have freed themselves, that you should have had nothing to do with them in church power. And then they would be the clergy; whereas it is an absurd thing that they should be accounted the clergy; for the Scripture, speaking of the people in distinction from the ministers, calls the people the clergy, 1 Pet. v. 3: Let them not lord it over God's clergy, των κλήρων, which in the same verse is called the flock. But they would be accounted the church and the clergy, as if the people were no part of the church at all, and all church power should come into their hands. And then they endeavoured to free themselves, as the papists you know do, from all civil power too, and were going many steps to it; therefore they would send forth things in their own names, and in time they would have wrought themselves free from all civil power, and have had all church power in their hands, and so, indeed, you could not strive with them. Bless God for the deliverance he has now given you.

Obs. 4. If public means prevail not, there is little hope of private. Why should one man strive with another? these "are as they that strive with the priest." Though they had never so good public means, they resisted, surely then they will resist private. Therefore, public means are to be preferred before private; when a man can speak as an officer to another, that is more to be regarded, and will be more efficacious to those God has a love unto, than private means. If this be so, let parents take heed how they teach their children to deride public means: when you have been at a sermon, perhaps you will despise what you have heard: it is just with God they should despise your admonition and reproof, for you have taught them to despise public means.

Obs. 5. To reject those that we look upon in office, though their calling be not good, is yet a wickedness that God will revenge. I say, though their calling be not right, so long as you regard them as true officers, and yet despise what they do according to God's will, so long God will avenge it. If they come in God's name, you must not oppose them, so long as you have any apprehensions that they are true officers: though, perhaps, if they were examined, they have no true calling; yet, if you cannot see but they have a true calling, you are to have such a reverence and respect unto them, that you are to be subject to them.

Ver. 5. *Therefore shalt thou fall in the day, and the prophet also shall fall with thee in the night, and I will destroy thy mother.*

Mark, though private men are here bid not to strive one with another, or reprove one another, yet Hosea goes on in his striving and reproving. "Therefore shalt thou fall in the day, and the prophet also shall fall with thee in the night." Hence,

Obs. 1. Those in office must go on though they be striven against; as long as they remain in office they must still go on, though people strive against them. I remember, Latimer saith in one of his sermons, Many ministers will not preach; and if they be asked the reason, it is this, because they can do no good to people. Oh, this (saith he) is a bad answer. Certainly, as long as you continue in that place, whether you do good, or whether you do not, you must go on in your work.

Obs. 2. When a threatening comes to individuals, then it works. "Therefore shalt *thou* fall." He directs the judgment to the individual, *thou*, every one of you, in the singular number. Perhaps some might think, Well, though the generality suffer, I may escape. No, look to yourselves, every one of you.

וכשלת translated here, "thou shalt fall," is a word that signifies the falling of a man by stumbling in the dark; a punishment suitable to their sin; they had no knowledge, therefore they shall stumble in the dark.

"In the day." Thou shalt stumble as a man in the dark, but it shall be in the day to thee; and yet thou shalt stumble. "In the day;" that is, first, in thy prosperity, for in the latter times of the second Jeroboam, (which was a little before the destruction of the ten tribes,) they were in a better situation than they had been in before, yet from thence they began to fall. I say, not long before their ruin, they were in more prosperity than they had been in many years before, therefore it is here said, "thou shalt fall in the day," even when thou art in a prosperous condition. Or, secondly, "thou shalt fall in the day," that is, you shall see your misery before you, yet you shall fall, you shall not be able to prevent it; it shall be in the day time, at noon-day, and you shall see plainly where your misery lies, yet shall you, as if you were in the night, stumble and fall.

O my brethren, this is a scripture that nearly concerns us here in England. If England fall and perish now, it falls and perishes in the day. We see, apparently, our evil before us; we see means to prevent it. God does not bring night upon us in this sense, that is, he does not bring misery so upon us, that we do not know how it comes, or by what means, or how we should prevent it. No, we are not so in the night, but in the day; we have seen the misery that has come upon us by a continued design, we know almost the very source and origin of that design, how it has gone on by degrees, step by step; we see now the reason of its breaking out, because the stream is stopped it bursts forth violently: we know who are the causers of our evil, what their counsels, intentions, what their ways are, notwithstanding all their protestations; we see what we are like to be brought into, if we do but yield a little, and do not appear to quit ourselves like men; and we see clearly what God would have us to do; we see ways and means to help us if we will, we have power to help ourselves, and direction too; we all of us know, or may know, clearly what we should do, and what, in an ordinary course of providence, would relieve us. Yet, Lord, how do we fall! notwithstanding this, we fall even in apparent day-light. So that if this kingdom be brought into slavery, it will be the heaviest wrath that ever fell upon a nation. Never any nation fell in a clear, open sunshine, as we are like to do if we perish now, having such means for our help.

Again, "Thou shalt fall in the day," *hodie*, that is, soon, presently, your destruction shall not be long.

"And the prophet also shall fall with thee in the night." There seems to be some difficulty in this. How comes this in, "thou shall fall in the day, and the prophet also shall fall with thee in the night?"

Obs. 3. The falls of the prophets are falls of the night. "The prophet also shall fall with thee in the night." The blind lead the blind, and they both fall into the ditch. You gave yourselves up to false prophets to be guided by them, and here is all the good you shall have, both you and they shall perish together; the prophet also shall fall as well as ye.

Obs. 4. It is a most sad judgment for a people to be in affliction, and to have no prophet at all amongst them; no prophet to tell how long it shall continue, or to declare to them any part of God's mind. In the captivity of the ten tribes, they had no prophets, nor have had since. Judah was carried into captivity, yet in their misery they had prophets among them, Ezekiel, and Zechariah, and Haggai, to direct them. But Israel shall be carried into captivity and shall have no prophet to help them. Look to yourselves that you regard the prophets of God now; otherwise, when brought into misery, under the power of your adversaries, you shall have no minister among you, none to show you God's mind, or to open up to you his will. It was so with Israel, they never had any prophet since the captivity to tell them the mind of God.

Thus the prophets shall fall, but why "in the night?" Some, because they think hard of the different expression, read it thus; You shall fall in the day with the prophet, in the night your mother shall be destroyed: and it may fairly be so rendered. But I had rather read it as we have it, "thou shalt fall in the day, and the prophet also shall fall with thee in the night," for these two reasons:

1. Because God would inflict a greater darkness upon the false prophets in his just judgment, than upon the people. Those who abuse most light come into the grossest darkness, and therefore it is a usual expression in Scripture when prophets are threatened, to threaten that darkness shall be upon them: Micah iii. 6, "Therefore night shall be unto you, that ye shall not have a vision; and it shall be dark unto you, that ye shall not divine; and the sun shall go down over the prophets, and the day shall be dark over them:" over the prophets in a special manner. And Zech. xi. 17, "His right eye shall be utterly darkened;" the chief understanding that he has, his pregnancy of parts, shall be besotted. Do we not see it even at present, that the prophets fall in the night? There is more darkness now on wicked ministers amongst us, than upon ordinary people. Ordinary people understand more of the will of God than wicked ministers. God besots them in their very parts and abilities, and they do nothing but cry out still for that which will bring themselves and us into slavery. Were it not for them, people would see sufficiently well what to do, and the great darkness that is upon them comes from the prophets; they bring darkness on the people, therefore their own darkness is the greater. In divers towns are there not many people who know the mind of God, and see need of, and desire, a reformation in God's worship? and yet, notwithstanding, their ministers will see no need.

2. The distress that shall be on the prophets shall be greater than on other people, it shall be night to them indeed; not only shall there be more darkness on their understandings, but more darkness in regard of their afflictions; they shall be in greater horror of conscience and distress than any other people, for they shall see that they have brought you into all misery. And the truth is, that the great present misery on England is through false prophets, through wicked ministers, and their doctrines. We had never been in such a condition as we are, had not they flattered at court, and told there that all was at the king's power and pleasure, and there ought to be no resistance, and to refuse whatsoever he would have was rebellion. Had they not taught such things as these, we never had had such times. Now if this kingdom be destroyed, it may be God may bring horror on their consciences, and however they may desire to throw the blame on others, yet, those that have any light remaining in them, the Lord may cause horror and distress in their minds, as the cause of all that evil that shall be upon us. They shall fall in the night, a black, dismal night shall be upon them when judgments come. Therefore in times of public judgment, God's ministers are to look on his hand as especially against them, and more horror and distress of conscience shall be upon them than upon others.

"And I will destroy thy mother." They boasted of their mother, as the papists do of their mother the church; but "their mother," that is, their church state and civil state, shall be destroyed; and so there shall be no hope of this people, both children and mother being destroyed: it seems to have some allusion to that in the the law, where we are forbidden to take the dam with the young ones, because of the preservation of succession; but here, saith God, my wrath shall be so hot, that I will not only take the young ones, but the dam; they shall be destroyed together with their mother.

The word דמיתי here translated destroyed, signifies, shall be brought to be silent, for indeed this word signifies silence, as noting thus much, in times of God's judgments wicked men shall have nothing to say for themselves, but shall be forced to lay their hands on their mouths and be silent.

Ver. 6. *My people are destroyed for lack of knowledge: because thou hast rejected knowledge, I will also reject thee, that thou shalt be no priest to me: seeing thou hast forgotten the law of thy God, I will also forget thy children.*

"For lack of knowledge." As if he had said, If they had the knowledge of God they might have prevented all this, but they were ignorant and sottish people, and this was the forerunner of their misery and destruction. The heathens were wont to say, if their god Jupiter would destroy one, he would first besot him: so these people were first besotted and then destroyed. Ignorance is not the mother of devotion, but rather the father and mother too of destruction. How diametrically opposed is the language of the Scripture and the doctrine of papists! Ignorance is the mother of devotion, say they: Ignorance is the mother of destruction, saith God; they perish "for lack of knowledge." In the beginning of this chapter we have the sin of ignorance set forth, here we have its danger. There we had the charge, that they had "no knowledge of God in the land;" here we have the judgment, that they "are destroyed for want of knowledge."

Ignorance is not only the deformity of the soul as blindness is the deformity of the face; though a man or woman have never such a comely visage otherwise, yet, if they be blind, or have but one eye, it mars their beauty: so ignorance takes away the beauty of the soul; and not only so, but is dangerous and destructive, and that in these respects:

1. The rational creature is very active of itself, and will always be in motion, always working; and it is surrounded by pits and snares; if then it be blind, how dangerous will it be for it! as a mettled horse that is in the midst of deep snares and pits, and will be curvetting and dancing, and will not stand still, in what danger will he be, if blind! No creature is so full of activity as the rational creature is, he will be active in the world; and then, wanting knowledge, how dangerous is his situation!

2. Man's way is for eternity, and there is but one way that leads to an eternity of happiness, and that lies in the midst of a hundred cross-ways and by-paths. If he have not light, if he want knowledge, what shall become of him?

But you will say, Though he be dark himself, yet he may have some others to guide him, and so he may do well enough.

3. Therefore consider in the third place, That man is not only going onward through dangers and by-ways, but he must go on with his own light. All the light of all the angels in heaven, or of all the ministers in the world, cannot help a soul in his journey to eternity, except this light be conveyed into his own eyes. It is true, a man physically blind may have help, though it be but by a dog; but the soul that is ignorant, no angel in heaven can help, except as an instrument of God to bring sight into his eyes.

4. The work we are to do about our souls and eternal estates, is the most curious and most difficult piece of work, and we must do it by our own light. Surely, if a man were engaged in a work requiring ingenuity, as a curious watch or the like, he need have light: put such a one in the dark, and what can he do? The work of grace, God must enable us to do; but we must work together with God. God enables a man to make a watch, by giving him skill; but he must work with God: so it is with the work of grace, we must have light in our own souls; therefore ignorance is dangerous.

5. Blindness in this world makes men objects of pity and compassion, but this ignorance and blindness make men to be the objects of the hatred and curse of God. When you see a poor blind man here, is he loathsome in your eyes because he is blind, do you hate him? No, you pity him. But now the blindness of your souls makes you abominable in the sight of God, and God will be avenged on you for it. But you will say, How can we help it? We have put out our own eyes; God gave us light at first, and we brought ignorance upon ourselves.

If ignorance then be so dangerous that people perish for "lack of knowledge," how vile is it to deny the means of knowledge to men, merely to satisfy the humours of others! How many hundred congregations are there that have been deprived of their ministers, for a surplice, or a cross, or some such thing!

But you will say, Obedience to a church is an important matter.

The answer is, Therefore it is the fault of a church, or governors, to require such things as God never required; and after requiring them, it is a greater fault for them to insist so much on them, that many thousands must perish rather than their humours not be satisfied.

If this be the ground of perishing, then, though divers countries have felt the hand of God most fearfully, yet we hope that England shall not perish, for the knowledge of God is begun to shine among us, and never since the world began has it shone more brightly on a kingdom than upon us. We hope, therefore, though God intends to chastise us, we shall not perish.

"Because thou hast rejected knowledge." Only let us take heed that we do not reject knowledge, and despise it. The word מאסת signifies to reject with despite and contempt; it is *ignorantia non meræ negationis, sed pravæ dispositionis,* affected ignorance. "Thou hast rejected knowledge" two ways. First, when the means of knowledge are rejected, then knowledge is rejected. Secondly, when the directions of our knowledge are rejected, when we refuse to be guided by it, upon this our knowledge decays, and eventually is contemned.

Now this is a great sin in any, but especially in the priests. When others think that the knowledge of God and his truth is too slight, too mean a thing to engage their thoughts, this is vile. When merchants and tradesmen think they must busy their heads about some other matters, but as for this knowledge of the Scriptures, it is no great matter, they may be happy without that; let them have their tradings, and bargainings, and houses, and receipts; let them have their tables spread, and their dishes full; but for this Scripture, and these points of religion, these are things too mean for them. These men now despise knowledge, for so the word here signifies, reject it, as undervaluing its importance. But, I say, when the priests shall reject knowledge, the priests that should have laboured to have filled their souls with knowledge, if they shall seek to gratify the lusts of the flesh, and care not either to have the knowledge of God in their own souls, or to bring it to the people, but look upon it as nothing worth, this is in a more special manner a most grievous sin. How many are there amongst us at this day, that study to get preferment, &c., and then sell their books, and never after pursue knowledge! And others, if they have knowledge and learning, and prize it in some respects, yet in this they contemn it, they prize knowledge merely as serviceable to their lusts. It is not for the beauty and excellency of the knowledge of God, nor for the sweetness that they find in Christ, that they so laboriously study; but that they may be accounted scholars, men of understanding and learning. When we thus seek knowledge merely to subserve our lusts, we may be justly charged with despising knowledge.

But further, These priests, and such as were eminent in Israel, rejected knowledge, because they had their houses, and goods, and revenues amongst the ten tribes. (I beseech you observe it, for this concerns us.) I say, the priests that were amongst the ten tribes were settled there, and had their houses, incomes, and estates there; but now this was taught, that we must worship God at the temple in Jerusalem, and they rejected this knowledge especially, for they saw that if they embraced that truth of worshipping God in his own way, then, Farewell our incomes, farewell our livings, farewell our houses, we must leave our brave dwellings, and all our maintenance, and go from Samaria, and we must go to Judah; and how shall we live there? Upon this they shut their eyes against the knowledge of that very truth that should have brought them to the true worship of God; rather than they would lose their estates, they would reject that knowledge. And that I think to be the meaning of the Holy Ghost here; they despised, as other knowledge, so that knowledge of the true worship of God; so it is rendered by some, *scientiam illam,* that kind of knowledge they rejected. For they knew that those truths were suffering truths. Now suffering truths are truths that will hardly go down with either people or ministers, they had therefore rather be ignorant of them; as the Holy Ghost in Ezekiel speaks of men that shut their eyes against the sabbath, so they shut their eyes against those truths which should have brought them to the true worship of God. And in this case it is not enough for a man to say, God knows I go not against my conscience; if my conscience were convinced that such and such things must be in the worship of God agreeably to his word, I would obey it. But the reason they see not this to be the word of God is, because they have no mind to know it, they reject that knowledge, it is against their ease and preferment, and it is suffering truth, and therefore they shut their eyes against it. This is no excuse. Mark the judgment that follows.

"I will also reject thee." You despise knowledge, I will despise you; so the words may be read, as well as reject you. God scorns wicked men as much as they scorn him; "with the froward he will deal frowardly," and with the scornful he will deal scornfully, that is, he will laugh them to scorn. What! do you look on God's ways and worship as a vile thing? are the truths of God vile in your eyes? You are vile in God's eyes, he looks upon you and your spirits with as much contempt as you can regard his worship, his saints, and his ordinances. You despise knowledge, and I will despise you, saith God.

And "I will reject thee." The word ראמאסאך here translated reject, has a letter in it more than it has in any other place in all the Scripture; and Tremelius from thence observes, there is a letter in this word in the Hebrew that is redundant, and it denotes the extraordinary manner of God's rejecting them, he will cast them out of the hearts of his people, as he does apostate ministers, whom, above all others, God rejects with contempt, pouring shame and contempt upon them more than on any in the world. That is his note upon this; he will reject them with contempt; yea, for ever. You heard before, in Luke vi., that Christ pronounced his disciples, faithful preachers, blessed, when their names were cast out as evil, when they were vilified by men. But now mark, when a minister goes on faithfully in declaring the mind of God unto people, and there be shame cast upon him, that minister is blessed; but if the minister be wicked, and there be shame cast upon him, that shame is a part of the curse, for then he is cast out as unsavoury salt, and men tread upon it, saith Christ. Wicked men would cast out the godly, but God and God's saints embrace them, and bless God for them; but if you be wicked, and men cast you out as unsavoury salt, then men contemn you, then you are trodden upon; yea, so rejected, as never to be received again. In Ezek. xliv. 13, the priests that did forsake the Lord, when Israel forsook him, must never again come near unto God, no, not so much as near unto the priest's office: a notable text, which it concerns you to know for your direction about receiving in persons who have wickedly apostatized in evil times. Perhaps now they preach good sermons, but you are to inquire what they were when others were superstitious and evil; and although we are not utterly to reject them, yet, until there be further evidence of their repentance, they are not to be received. God threatens an utter rejection of those Levites that forsook him when Israel forsook him.

Now the observations that I would derive from hence, are,

Obs. 1. Unfaithfulness in service provokes God to cast us out of service. I cannot stop to set an edge on this.

Obs. 2. It is a great judgment to be rejected from the priest's office, from the office of a minister: "I will reject thee, that thou shalt be no priest to me." To be rejected from any employment is a great judgment: Neh. v. 13, "So God shake out every man from his house, and from his labour, that performeth not his promise." It is a judgment to be shaken out of our labour, but to be shaken out of such an office, whereby we draw so nigh unto God as to be the mouth of God to the people, and the mouth of the people unto God again, is a sore evil.

Again, whereas it may be said, Israel had no true priests, therefore it was no judgment for them to be rejected out of that office: but yet to be cast out of what we *seem* to have, is likewise a judgment of God, Luke viii. 18.

"Seeing thou hast forgotten the law of thy God, I will also forget thy children."

"Seeing thou hast forgotten the law of thy God." You live so as to show that you never think of the law, of its holiness, equity, and authority, and the threats annexed unto it, for if you remembered these you could not go on so quietly in a course of sin; but you have cast off all the remembrance of the law, it is even worn out of your memory. The book of the law of God was lost for a long time in Judah, surely in Israel much more.

"I will also forget." גם-אני *Etiam ego*, Even I. It is a sad thing to be forgotten by our friends when we are in misery, Oh that such a dear friend, such a father or such a mother, should forget me! but how sad a thing is it for God to forget you!

"Thy children." That is, there shall be no succession in the priestly office. This was threatened against Eli's house, 1 Sam. ii. 20. It is a blessing for the godly children of godly ministers to succeed them in the office, and the contrary is a judgment. Your children shall not succeed you in this office, but they shall be forgotten by me. The families of wicked ministers, through God's judgment, are many times forgotten. You have forgotten me, I will also forget you and your children. I will not here speak how the child may suffer for the father's offence, we often meet with it; only now, as it concerns the posterity of wicked ministers, they are, through God's judgments, often forgotten. But let not the families of godly ministers, especially if their children be godly too, oh let them not be forgotten. It is a judgment threatened upon these wicked priests, that God would forget their children, therefore it is not so evil though men forget them; but if there be any that have been faithful ministers, God forbid their children should be forgotten after they are dead. This city has been honoured for its respect to godly ministers; but have you never forgotten their children, their families that have been left behind? When they were with you, and preached among you, you seemed mightily to respect them; but are there not many that belong unto their families that live now with you, in a hard condition? yea, their children and families that are godly, their widows too, how are they forgotten! If the godly children of pious ministers should go unto God and complain thus, would it not be a sad thing? Lord, thou didst threaten idolatrous priests that forgot thee, that thou wouldst also forget their children; but, Lord, my father was in the city a faithful minister, he remembered thee, and was a faithful remembrancer for thy people, yet we are forgotten; is this according to thy word? shall the judgment threatened on the children of idolatrous priests be the judgment upon us that are the children of faithful ministers? are we to be thus forgotten though our fathers forgot not thee? Look, therefore, into the families of godly ministers, look after their children, and as their fathers did not forget God, do not you forget them; let not the judgment threatened on the children of wicked ministers be upon them, but let there be a distinction made between the children of faithful and godly ministers, and the children of idolatrous priests.

Ver. 7. *As they were increased, so they sinned against me: therefore will I change their glory into shame.*

The Lord is here further charging these ten tribes, but especially their priests, at them he aims most. They had before rejected the knowledge of the Lord, and the Lord threatened rejection of them. The knowledge, הדעת *that* knowledge, *scientiam illam*, that knowledge of the true worship of God, that he was to be worshipped at Jerusalem alone: that truth was a suffering truth, therefore that truth they did especially reject; and in this seventh verse there is some ground for their rejection of the knowledge of God, "As they were increased, so they sinned against me." God had increased them, they were become a great multitude, and as their number increased, so their sins increased. But that which I especially conceive to be the meaning of the Holy Ghost here, is, As their prosperous condition increased, so their sins increased; they were grown up to a height of prosperity, and that made them sin against and reject the knowledge of God.

The first is not to be rejected, viz. As they increased in multitude: so the Seventy, κατὰ τὸ πλῆθος, according to their fulness. And it may be understood both ways, fulness of number, or fulness of their prosperous estate.

Obs. Where there is an increase in number, there is usually an increase in sin. The more meat there is in the pot, the more scum arises. So in great cities, what a great deal of filth is there, filth of sin, moral filth! Where there is any confluence of people, as at fairs and markets in the country, or in any corporation, what abundance of defilement is there continually! In churches, at their first beginning, a few, called saints, can agree well together, and go on sweetly in their way; but, ordinarily, as they increase in number they begin to corrupt and increase in sin. They should increase so much the more in godliness; but this is the corruption of man's heart, every one bringing in some evil, therefore as the number, so the sins, increase.

But because the second appears the true interpretation, to speak to that a little: As they increased in their prosperous estate. At this time the ten tribes were in a very prosperous condition, grown rich and great, and so increased, especially the priests; for they had the favour of Jeroboam and of the princes; for their main design was to uphold their false worship, and the priests served for their turns best, therefore they countenanced those priests of Dan and Bethel, the priests of the calves, and they flourished at this time in the court and in the country, and were much increased in their prosperous estate; and "as they increased, so they sinned." This is man's vile disposition, that increase of mercies should be the increase of their sin. Thus was it with the church; when in a lower condition, then there was more holiness and more sincere love to the truth, but when it began to flourish in outward prosperity, it began to decay in true piety. And, therefore, ecclesiastical history tells us, that when the church received from Constantine great donations, then there was heard a voice in the air, *Hodie venenum infunditur, &c.*, To-day poison is poured forth into the church: when great livings and great estates were given to the ministers of the church, then poison was poured forth into it. And so when Boniface, the martyr, was asked whether it were lawful to receive the communion in wooden chalices, he well answered, Time was, when in the church there were wooden chalices and golden priests; but now, there are golden chalices, but wooden priests. And on Innocent the Third showing Aquinas a table of gold and silver, and saying, We have no need to say as Peter once did, "Silver and gold have we none:" Neither, replied Aquinas immediately, can ye say, "Arise and walk;" as you have more money than they had, so you have less gifts, and not so much of the Spirit of God. It was so in the increase of the prosperity of the church, and is generally the case. As with the spleen, the greater it grows, the less the body is; so, the more prosperity, the leaner and weaker are the spirits of men. Deut. xxxii. 15, "Thou art waxed fat, thou art grown thick, thou art covered with fatness: then he forsook God which made him, and lightly esteemed the Rock of his salvation." How many, when they were low and poor in their estates, were more holy and gracious, and more spiritual, than now! It is true in particular persons, in churches and countries, but most true in ministers. It was a complaint once made to a prelate here, that he had a kinsman, a very zealous preacher in the country: Well, said he, I will silence him: and his mode of silencing was this, he gave him two livings, and that stopped his mouth: when he came once to have fatted livings, then his zeal quickly abated. And Jerome, in the life of Malachus, saith, When the church came to Christian princes, and there had countenance, we may well say of it, that indeed it was fatted with riches, but diminished in virtue and godliness.

Quando ecclesia ad principes Christianos venit, factam fuisse opibus pleniorem, sed virtutibus minorem, ait Jerom.

God threatens here, that seeing they abused their prosperity, he therefore would turn their glory into shame. God loves to stain the pride and haughtiness of men. He would turn the glory of the people, and the glory of the priests, but especially the glory of the priests, (for so it is meant, but we must include all,) into shame: either, first, he would instead of glory bring shame; or, secondly, he would make that wherein they most gloried, to be their shame.

1. That he would bring shame instead of glory. So God is wont to do. Women that glory in their beauty and splendour, should mark well Isa. iii. 16—24, "Moreover, the Lord saith, Because the daughters of Zion are haughty, and walk with stretched-forth necks, and wanton eyes," &c.; therefore, "instead of well-set hair, there shall be baldness; and instead of a stomacher, a girding of sackcloth; and burning instead of beauty." If any will glory in parts, the Lord justly brings shame upon them, blasting their gifts. As is reported of Albertus Magnus, that great scholar, that for five years before his death he lost his faculties so completely that he could not read. God can soon blast men's parts when gloried in, and turn them to shame. If any glory in riches, God can soon turn that into shame also. History tells us of an earl of Exeter, that married the sister of King Edward the Fourth, of whom yet Philip de Commines reports, that he was seen barefoot, and begging his bread, in the Low Countries. God can soon take away the riches of men, and turn that, their glory, into their shame. And then, if any glory in honour, God can soon turn that into shame, as in the case of Herod, who gloried in the applause of the people when they cried out, "It is the voice of a god, and not of a man;" and presently was he consumed by worms.

And much shame comes to men that glory in these things. Mark, according to the glory of men in external things, so is their shame when God takes them away. Here is the difference between the saints and the wicked when they lose these outward things. When the saints lose them, much shame comes not to them, because they gloried not in them when they had them; but carnal hearts, because they know no higher things than these, when they are taken from them, much shame accrues to them, for they gloried in their possession.

2. God makes the very things they glory in to turn

to their shame. He not only takes away their parts, and brings ignorance and dotage instead of them, but makes their very gifts to be their undoing, and uses them to bring them to shame. He makes their very riches and honours, and their glorying in their success, to turn to their shame. As now, when men glory in this, that they had such success and such a victory at such a time; and thence infer, Surely God is with us, and blesses and owns us; in this they glory: well, God turns this into their shame, when he appears against them, and, blasting their success, makes it manifest to all, that though they have all outward means, yet they avail nothing: now, where is the argument of God's owning their cause, and their reason for glorying, if success be the test. Those that shall make that the only or principal argument that God is with them, how does God turn their glory into shame, when he apparently denies them success, and that when they have most outward means for its attainment! The saint's shame is turned into glory, but the wicked's glory is turned into shame. When the saints suffer any shame for God, they can glory: the apostles, Acts v. 41, rejoiced that they were accounted worthy to suffer; that they had the honour to endure dishonour, so the words properly signify; they gloried that they bore about them the marks of the Lord Jesus. Thus, what the world accounts their shame, is their glory; and that which the world judgeth to be their glory, is their shame.

Κατηξιώθησαν ἀτιμασθῆναι.

But it is especially meant of the priests, for the prophet is speaking of them. God will turn "their glory into shame." The priests, though they did reject the knowledge of God and their duty, and never regarded that wherein the true glory of their office consisted; that blessed knowledge of God, which might have made them glorious indeed, was despised by them, and the faithful administration of their office neglected: yet they would glory for all this, they would bear it out as if they were *the* men: why, they were countenanced at court, had good livings, and they could lord it over their brethren; and in that they gloried. It is usual with wicked priests, if they can have but countenance from them that are in public places, and can have but estates and livings, though they be never so negligent of their office, and never so ignorant, yet to glory. How has it been thus amongst us of late! How have they carried their heads on high, and accounted themselves the triumphant church, and all must be made to yield to them! The land was not able to bear the pride of prelates and prelatical men. Cyprian saith, Ambition and pride sweetly sleep in the bosom of priests. And there are none indeed so much puffed up with vain pride as they are, especially the more ignorant they are; and the more they neglect that in which the true glory of their office consists. On such God delights to pour shame and contempt, therefore, in Isa. ix. 15, saith, "The prophet that teacheth lies, he is the tail," the very meanest; and Mal. ii. 9, "Therefore have I also made you" (speaking of the priests that had been partial in the law and had not kept the ways of God) "contemptible and base before all the people;" and Rev. iii. 16, "I will spue thee out of my mouth," as loathsome; and Matt. v. 13, "If the salt have lost his savour, wherewith shall it be salted? it is thenceforth good for nothing, but to be cast out, and to be trodden under foot of men," as a contemptible and vile thing. Thus God casts shame upon wicked priests.

Ambitio et superbia suaviter dormiunt in sinu sacerdotum. Cypr. de Jejun. &c.

Ver. 8. *They eat up the sin of my people, and they set their heart on their iniquity.*

"They eat up the sin of my people." There is some difficulty in these words. To eat up sin, to eat up the sin of people, what is that? There is much in this to be learned.

The word חטאת here translated sin, has in Scripture three acceptations.

First, It is used for that which is properly sin, the transgression of God's law: for that I need not cite any scripture.

Secondly, It is used for the punishment of sin: "He shall bear his sin," his punishment of sin. Christ "was made sin." And,

Thirdly, It is used for the sacrifice that was offered for sin: Lev. x. 17, "Wherefore have ye not eaten the sin" (that is, the sin-offering) "in the holy place?"

The observation from hence (by way of allusion, at least) is,

Obs. 1. Ministers should eat the revenues they have by their office in a holy place; that is, their houses, in which they spend their income, should be holy places; for the offerings of the people were what the priests had in return for their services, and they were to eat them in a holy place: so ministers now should eat the means they have coming in, in holy places, their houses should be sanctuaries. Let those priests that spend their time in play, in pleasures of the flesh, in taverns, and make their houses very sinks of vice, let them hearken to this.

But where lies the charge here, "They eat up the sin of my people?"

First, in that they flattered them in their sin, and so got advantage thereby. So Gregory: Why or how are they said to eat up the sin of people, but because they nourish the sins of delinquents for their own advantage? So all your court flatterers and others, that flatter men in their sin for their own advantage, may be said to feed on the sins of the people.

Cur peccata populi comedere dicuntur, nisi quia peccata delinquentium, &c.

Secondly, Because they were negligent in their office, and took all the profits and advantages resulting, but neglected their charge, let people go on in their sin, and cared not what became of them in that respect, provided they received their tithes and revenues; such ministers may be said to live upon, or to eat, the sins of the people, and to wear their sins; their very backs may be said to be covered, and their tables spread, with the sins of the people. A writer on this place relates a story of a prelate in Charles the Fifth's time, that, inviting his friends to his house, and preparing good cheer, they did not eat of it: What, saith he, will you not eat of dainties that are bought at so dear a rate? this meat which I have prepared for you, and you will not eat, is like to cost me the pains of hell. He was convinced in his conscience of the neglect of his duty, and so regarded the very food on his table as the sins of his people, and that which was like to cost him eternal misery.

But further, to open it far more clearly, "They eat up the sin of my people;" that is, the sacrifices which were offered for sin.

But you will say then, How is this so deep a charge, that they should eat of the sacrifices that were offered for sin? for God allowed the priests to eat the sin-offering, as that place, Lev. x. 17, shows.

In this, therefore, consisted the evil, that they were greedy of the people's sacrifices, not that God might have honour, but that they themselves might gain advantage. It is true, God had honour by the people's offering of sacrifice, but they looked not to that so much as to their own profit. Hence, they urged people as much as they could to sacrifice, teaching them to rest in their sacrifices, and indeed making light of their sin; Though you sin, come, and I will offer for your sins, and they shall be pardoned. Just as the papists at this day teach the people, though they sin, yet by so many masses, and Pater-nosters, and indulgences, and dirges, they shall be delivered; and by this means they get the wealth of kingdoms, and eat up the sins of the people. The priests in those times were apt emblems of the papists now.

Again, They were glad when people did offend and sin against God, because then their sacrifices must be multiplied, and so their gains increased: and so it is a rebuke of the covetousness of priests. It is a most abominable thing for those that are to watch over souls, to regard their own profit and carnal gratification, more than the good of souls: just like your chancellors' and commissaries' courts of old, they cared not what offences there were, they rejoiced at long presentments, all brought grist to their mill. And, it seems, there were such priests in Bernard's time; in his 77th sermon on the Canticles, he quotes this place, and saith, They eat up the sin of my people; as if he should say, they exact the price of their sin, but take not due care for the sinners. And again, Give me any one of those that are governors in the church, that does not watch more to empty people's purses than to save their souls.

Populi mei peccata comedunt; quasi dicat, peccatorum pretium exigunt, et peccantibus debitam solicitudinem non impendunt. Et rursum, Quem dabis mihi de numero prepositorum qui non plus invigilet subditorum vacuandis marsupiis quam vitiis extirpandis. Bern.

Obs. 2. It is a most cursed thing to desire or rejoice in the sins of others because of our own advantage. How many are there that watch for the falls of their enemies, and rejoice in their sin! I appeal to you: had you an enemy and you heard of his fall, though it were a sin against God, yet, if it tended to his disgrace, would you not rejoice and be glad of it? because the more an enemy is disgraced, the more you think yourself justified and honoured. This is truly horrible! O, be humbled before the Lord for it, and seek unto God, that, if it be possible, he may pardon the thoughts of thy heart in this thing. What! to rejoice that the infinite, blessed God is dishonoured because thou thyself hast an advantage! it is most horrible and accursed. How many are there, that, looking on the professors of religion, whom they think to be their adversaries, rejoice when they see them fall! Why? because they think by their disgrace they themselves are justified. This is to feed upon the sins of people. You shall have vermin and swine rooting in filth and in dung; so there are many that feed upon the defilement of others, on the filth of their sins. It is a vile and cursed wickedness, to be glad, for our own advantage, of the afflictions of our neighbour, much more to rejoice at his sin. When thy neighbour falls into affliction, thou shouldest not rejoice at his affliction, though thou art advantaged by it; but when thy neighbour falls into sin, to be glad of it for thine own advantage, is a most cursed thing indeed. Were a surgeon to rejoice at another man's wounds, and to prolong the healing of them, because he thereby received some profit, would not every one cry out against him? and truly this were wicked. So for soldiers to love war, and willingly to lengthen it out, and care not what becomes of the lives of men, and the woeful miseries of a kingdom, that they may have continued pay, this you will all account a great wickedness; but this is not so bad as to be glad of the sins of people for our own advantage. Certainly, as surgeons may be said in such a case to feed upon the matter and stuff of the wound; and those soldiers may be said to drink of the blood of people; and those cups of wine that go down so merrily, and those dishes of meat that they are so jovial with, may be said to be the flesh and the blood of people; yet, all this is not so bad as to feed upon the sins of others. Thou that feedest upon the sin of thy brother, dost thou not know that this diet of thine must needs breed diseases? It is not wholesome food, but such as will one day breed the worm of conscience, and create such remorse as humiliation and repentance will hardly purge thee of. It was once wittily said of a prelate that was very fat, that he became so by so often eating his own words; and no marvel, though men grow to have fat hearts that feed upon the sins of people. As this is the ordinary diet of many, so especially of ministers: and for ministers to feed upon the sins of people, so as to keep them alive by their flatteries and connivance, is surely evil; but if by their faithful preaching they did first slay the sins of the people, and then receive maintenance for their work, this is allowed by God, and this they may do. When God bade Peter, Arise and eat, he first bid him slay, "Arise, Peter, slay and eat:" so ministers, if first they would arise and slay the sins of the people by their preaching, may eat, that is, may then comfortably receive maintenance and allowance for their work; but, if they keep their sins alive, then their diet is evil, for they feed upon their sins.

What! is there such wickedness in the hearts of men as to rejoice in the sins of others for their own advantage? Oh how much more then should the saints rejoice, for their Master's sake, in the graces of God as manifested in others! In Ezek. viii. 17, you have an expression which seems hard to be understood. God charges the people there, as with other notorious evils, so with this among the rest, that "they put the branch to their nose." I conceive the meaning to be this; The people are there charged with idolatrous service, rendered to either the sun, or Vesta, the goddess of the earth, because they believed that by them the sweet flowers and branches of trees came forth; and when they worshipped either of these, in acknowledgment of the honour due to them they took a branch and put it to their nose, thereby showing their respect and homage unto them, as rejoicing in that good and sweet fruit which was caused by this, their god or goddess: so that God charges them here for so rejoicing in these creatures, as to worship the sun or the earth as their cause. To apply this to our purpose; As idolaters, because they looked upon the sun or the earth as the cause of such flourishing plants, and sweetness of branches and flowers, put them to their nose and delighted in them, and thereby showed their reverence for their idols; so should we take the graces of the Spirit of God in our brethren, that are the fruits of the Sun of righteousness, and put them to our nose, smell at them, account them fragrant, and so do honour unto Jesus Christ as their sole author. Thus much for that phrase, "They eat up the sin of my people."

"And they set their heart on their iniquity." The words are ישאו נפשו they lift up every one his heart, not נפשים their hearts. It may be interpreted either of the heart of the priests, or the heart of the people, according to the scope of the Spirit of God.

Calvin.

First, The heart of the priests, they lift up their hearts to the iniquity of the people. This phrase, lifting up of the heart to a thing, intimates in Scripture, the earnest desire that there is in the heart to attain such a thing; as in Deut. xxiv. 15, speaking of poor men, it is said, "He is poor, and sets his heart upon his hire." A poor man that wants provision for his family, sets his heart upon his wages; and the word used in this text is, he lifteth up his heart to his hire, Oh my hire, that it might come! And Jer. xxii. 27, "To the land whereunto they desire to return, thither shall they not return;" that is, the land whereunto they lift their hearts, for which they have an earnest desire. And Ezek. xxiv. 25, "When I take from them their strength, the joy of their glory, the desire of their eyes, and that whereupon they set their minds, their sons and daughters:" it is applied to their love unto their children, they lift their minds, or their hearts, to their sons and their daughters: so that then it signifies the earnest desire the priests had unto the sins of the people, that they might have the greater advantage by them: as some who are of poor, servile spirits, and whose greatest means arise from burials, are said to be glad and rejoice when they hear the bell ring; and are ready to desire the death of men out of regard to their own fees, because the more and the richer that die, the more advantage accrues to them. So the priests at this time desired the multiplying of the sins of the people, that they might thereby have the more sacrifices.

But I rather think, according to other interpreters, the passage to refer chiefly to the lifting up of the hearts of the people; that is, that the priests might have the more advantage by their sacrifices; they encouraged the people in their sins, lightening and lifting up their hearts above their guilt, persuading them that if they offered up sacrifice all should be well, they should be fully cleared, and need not be further troubled; whereas, indeed, the priests ought to have convinced men's consciences of the evil of their sins, and when they came to sacrifice, showed them how they deserved death for them, and that the death of the animal, and their laying their hands upon the head of it, signified that their sins deserved the death eternal of their souls; and they should have instructed the people how the sacrifices typified the blood of Christ, and have told them, You come now to offer sacrifice, and to have the blood of beasts shed, this shadows forth the Messiah that is to come into the world, the Son of God, that is to be made man, and to shed his precious blood to pacify the wrath of God for your sins; and you are to exercise your faith upon this Messiah that is to come. They should have told them that no sin could be pardoned but by the blood of Christ; they should have burdened their consciences with their guilt, and made their sins heavy; but they lightened their minds by persuading them, that if they did but offer sacrifice all would be well, they might indulge themselves; and though they committed sin again, yet still a sacrifice could atone for it.

This was a most abominable sin of the priests. Calvin, on this place, introduces Plato inveighing against the absurdity and ridiculousness of people's offering sacrifice, thinking thereby to pacify their gods, and gain a liberty to sin again: thus even a heathen thought it an abuse of a heathen god, for people to think it enough to offer sacrifice. And yet, do not many amongst us commit sin, and take liberty to themselves to satisfy the lusts of the flesh, and then they will pray to God to forgive them? and some go so far that they will fast, and then sin, and then pray and fast, and return to their sins again, thinking to put off God with such kind of sacrifices as these are; and so making repentance, that should be the death of their sins, a means to nourish their sins. The priests here abused the type, the sacrifices, lightening the hearts of people by telling them that there remained a sacrifice to expiate their sin. And have you not at this day many that abuse the Antitype as much, that tell the people thus; Sin as fast as you can, there is a sufficient sacrifice for sin; it is but to believe in Christ, who has shed his blood for the greatest of all sins; you may then sin as fast as you can, the penalty is paid. There may indeed be truth in the words, that there is a sacrifice for the greatest sin, but there is a manner in declaring it that either encourages or deters people from sin. I appeal to you, whether you have not many that do so reveal Christ, and open the rich and glorious free grace of God in Christ, as an encouragement to people to sin. It is true, when examined they deny it: No, God forbid; they encourage not men to sin, they only tell them of God's free grace. Yea, but they tell them of it in such a manner, without such cautions as prudent, wise, conscientious ministers use: and therefore you find that all your lewd and looser sort of professors follow them. It appears that in Jerome's time there were such people, for he saith, When they saw any to live wickedly they would say thus to them, You sin and offend, but God requires of us nothing else but only to abide in the truth of the faith; to believe, and that is enough. And again, Which faith, if you do but keep, God regards not so much what your lives are, only looks that you do believe. And by this means (saith he) men repent not, neither are they humbled, but walk up and down with a stretched-out neck, in proud security, because they think they hold the true faith, and so take liberty to sin. The church has been continually troubled with this generation, and no marvel there be such men now amongst us; for the reformation being yet incomplete, some kind of liberty is for the present permitted to such, and therefore I say, no marvel that we have such among us; men who abuse the free grace of God, and lighten the hearts of sinners continuing in their sin, by telling them there is a sufficiency in Christ's sacrifice to atone for all transgression.

Ver. 9. *And there shall be, like people, like priest: and I will punish them for their ways, and reward them their doings.*

The Lord, threatening the ten tribes, especially directs his denunciations against the priests, as the great cause both of the sin and punishment of the people; evil ministers in a country being often a chief cause of its guilt and misery. Divers of God's threats against them we saw before, and still there follows,

"There shall be, like people, like priest." Here is a mixed threat both against priest and people. They have made themselves like one another in sin; God will make them resemble each other in punishment. They join themselves together in sin, and were alike there; God will join them in judgment, and they shall be alike there too. There is a likeness between people and priest on two grounds, I mean in evil especially.

First, They generally are like in sin one to another, from the just judgment of God. When people dislike the powerful ministry of the word, and their hearts cannot bear its spirituality and force, God, in just judgment, sends unto them ministers according to their very lusts, ministers that shall be suitable to harden them in that very disposition of their hearts. And this is a fearful judgment on a people. They may rejoice, and bless themselves in it, and think themselves now quiet and secure, and say they have got a very honest and peaceable man amongst them; but while they are rejoicing, the wrath of God is in a most dreadful manner let out against them, in sending them a minister according to their lusts. As God threatens in Ezek. xiv. 4, "If a man set up an idol in his heart, God will answer him according to his idol;" so, when people set up idols in their hearts, and are bent on such and such lusts and wicked ways, God, in his just judgment, will answer them according to their own hearts' lusts, and they shall have such ministers sent amongst them as will harden them in their wickedness.

Secondly, They come to resemble one another in evil from the great influence they mutually exercise over each other: sometimes from the people to the priests; if the people be malignants, superstitious, loose, and vain, the priests among them, being carnal, will seek to humour them; loving to be praised by them, they will preach things agreeable to them. But this is very vile, and an extreme dishonour to the ministry of the word, to subject it to the lusts of men. It is this that makes it so contemptible in the eyes of the wicked, though they be pleased with it. How is that? you will say. They are pleased with it, commend such men, and like them well, while they do so; yea, like what they say; yet they contemn the ministry, because they come to see that even it is subservient to and aims to please their humours: hence they look upon themselves and their lusts as above the ministry, and so despise its authority. They are pleased with the suiting of it to their lusts, but they despise it in regard of any authority, for they see apparently it is under their humours. In Rev. xix. 10, when John did but fall down to worship an angel, the angel came to him and said, "See thou do it not;" why? "I am thy fellow servant, and of thy brethren that have the testimony of Jesus." What! you a minister that have the testimony of Jesus, to fall down to an angel? An angel! what is an angel? their glory is to be fellow servants with you, and to have the same testimony of Jesus that you have. A minister must not in his ministry fall down under the lusts of any man living, because he has the testimony of Jesus with him. It is true, ministers, with regard to themselves, should be willing to be under all; servants unto all for Christ: they should, I say, be willing to put their persons under every man for Christ, but they should keep their ministry above every man. Their ministry, and its authority, are to be kept above the greatest, and that for Christ's sake.

Again, A great influence, as from people to the minister, so from the minister to the people. Look, how ministers are, so usually the people are: "Like priest, like people;" especially in evil, they have a great influence. You know that in almost all places where you have malignant, superstitious ministers, you have likewise such kind of people. Jer. xxiii. 10, "The land is full of adulterers," saith the text; then in the next verse, "For both prophet and priest are profane;" that is the reason. And again, ver. 14, "I have seen also," saith God, "in the prophets of Jerusalem, an horrible thing: they commit adultery, and walk in lies: they strengthen also the hands of evildoers, that none doth return from his wickedness." Here we see how they harden others in sin; they walk in lies, they tell people we need not be so strict, we may take more liberty, it is but the fancies and humours of such and such men; they walk in lies, and so they strengthen men's hands in wickedness, and none returns from his wicked ways. And then ver. 15, "From the prophets of Jerusalem profaneness is gone forth into all the land;" if they be profane and wicked, they have an influence quite through the land to make the whole country wicked and profane. And on the other side, there is often a great influence in the ministry of the word upon people for good. If ministers continue painful, faithful, conscientious, it is very rare but that they bring people to some kind of obedience or other. Very few such ministers have lived any time in any place, but have left some savour of their spirits discoverable afterwards in their people. It was wont to be said, *Da Ambrosios et habebimus Theodosios*, Let us have Ambroses, and we shall have Theodosiuses. Let us have godly ministers at court, and we shall have godly princes. The reason why the emperor Theodosius was so good, was because he had an Ambrose. So we find it in 2 Kings xii. 2, that Jehoash, so long as Jehoiada the priest lived, did that which was right in the sight of the Lord: so long as he had a godly minister with him that instructed him, he did that which was right in the eyes of God. No marvel, then, so much evil at court and other places, because we know what kind of ministers they ever have had. And because of the influence that a minister exerts on the people, the evil and malignant party ever desire to cherish such; and the force of their rage and malice is directed against godly ministers, for like minister, like people, they think: and, indeed, supposing their principles these, they act prudently to attain their ends, for godly ministers discover to people their evil and wicked ways, and cause those to whom they preach to cleave to the truth, and their spirits vex and rage when they see the ministry of the word to prevail thus with the people. With such policy Xerxes acted when he was in straits by reason of Agesilaus, who prevailed much in his country. He sent men with good store of money to gain over the towns in Greece, and they went and corrupted Athens and Thebes, and so caused such great disturbance in Greece, that Agesilaus was sent for home, to look to his own country. They went especially to the universities, Athens and Thebes, and there corrupted the orators. And it has been the policy of our men in these days to corrupt the seats of learning, thinking by scholars and others there to prevail most. It is fabled, that when the wolves would make a league with the sheep, they insisted chiefly on one article, which was that their shepherds should be delivered up to them, and then they would be at peace with the sheep, and do them no hurt. I make no question but if our adversaries should come to covenant with us, there is no one thing on which greater stress would be laid than the delivery up of faithful shepherds. "Like people, like priest."

They are like in evil, and they shall be like in punishment; they shall be involved in the same punishment. I will make the priests as contemptible and as miserable as the vilest of the people; their places exalted them above others, but their sin has abased them, and so they shall be dealt with accordingly. You will say, What great judgment is here threatened, that, "like people, like priest?" Certainly to them the judgment was very bitter and grievous, for the priests have at all times been puffed up with their callings, so that they looked upon themselves as far above the people, whom they regarded with scorn and contempt. Thus the Pharisees in John vii. 49, "This people who knoweth not the law are cursed;" this same vulgar sort are they that are accursed: so these priests here, though the truth is, they themselves were of the vilest of the people, (for Jeroboam's time is spoken of,) yet, being once raised into that place, they were puffed up as if they had been of another kind of mould than the people. It is usual for wicked ministers, though never so base and vile, either in birth or breeding, when they get up a little, and are come to preferment, to regard others with great contempt. It is a master-design in popery to raise the priesthood high above the people; and we know, that of late in this kingdom our gentry were nothing but slaves and vassals to the popish priests, especially the prelates. And if we did not look at the hand of God in his dreadful judgment besotting men, we could not conceive why the gentry should desire to have prelacy come in again, knowing how they were contemned and despised by them before. There was scarce a vicar in the country, but if he were *filius ecclesiæ*, (as they called him,) a child of the church, but vaunted himself as superior to the gentry; and it was an evident argument of the coming in of popery upon us, that whilst the priestly office was too much extolled, that wherein the true honour of the office consisted, the faithful preaching of the word, was not regarded. To give you an instance or two of their pride and their assumption of authority, as here of late, Riconius saith, The priest excelleth the king as much as a man a beast; yea, as much as God is above a priest, so is a priest above the king: these are his very words. And Pope Innocent II. would have Lotharius the emperor painted in his palace as a vassal lying down at his feet. And so Becanus calls the pope the chief priest, the shepherd; and emperors and kings are their dogs and curs, saith he; and if they will be faithful and ready to obey the call of the shepherd, they must be caressed, but if lazy and troublesome, they must be removed. Is it possible now that kings and great ones should ever love popery, and attempt to introduce it with a view to their own honour, when they thus advance their priesthood far above them? No; only for the present they would incite them to strive for an arbitrary government, with the hopes that that government should be under their own control. There is a spirit of fornication (as follows afterward) upon men, else were it impossible they should be so besotted as they are.

But though they thus lifted up themselves above the people, yet, saith God, I will make them in punishment like to the people. God is no respecter of persons, to spare any above another for their place; so neither should we: we should not say, Oh it would be a disgrace to the calling, therefore it must be passed over; but rather, Because he is a priest or magistrate, or in some exalted situation, yet, proving to be a delinquent and an enemy to the state, he must certainly be dealt with, and made an example in judgment. For the meaner sort to be punished, and the high to escape with impunity, God forbid ever such a thing should be. He is no accepter of persons, neither should men be.

Yea, but perhaps you will say, "Like people, like priest;" one would rather think that God should say, I will make their judgment greater than the judgment of the people, for the sin of the priests is far greater than the sin of the people.

To that I answer, first, It is true the sin of the priests is greater than the sin of any of the people, but it is not greater than the sin of the whole congregation. In Lev. iv., compare ver. 3 with ver. 13, and you shall find that the same sacrifice that was offered for the sin of the whole congregation, is offered for the sin of the priest; so that the sin of the priest is accounted equivalent to the sin of the whole congregation. So there is a parallel here, "like people, like priest," that is, I will deal with the priests as with the whole congregation.

Yet further, for a second answer, As the condition of the person aggravates the sin, so the condition of the person aggravates the judgment. It is a greater punishment for a man of a high condition to suffer the same thing that a man that is of a lower condition suffers.

"And I will punish them for their ways." ופקדתי may be rendered, I will visit them for their ways; and so it is, I think, translated in some of your books, *Super vias ejus;* I will visit them upon their ways, or visit their ways upon them. Hence we may

Obs. 1. God has his days of visitation, wherein he will narrowly inquire into the ways of men, and call them to an account for sins long before committed. Exod. xxxii. 34, "In the day when I visit, I will visit their sin upon them;" I will spare them for the present, but I have a day to visit, and then I will come upon them even for this sin. God spares sinners now; why? because the day of his visitation is not yet come; but when that is come, then look to your old sins: look that now your repentance be thorough, for otherwise you may be spared a while, but when the day of visitation comes, then all your old sins shall be called over. In some late visitations by men, the more conscientious and godly persons were, the more were they aimed at, and it always went worst with them; but it shall be otherwise in this visitation of God's; God will visit the visitors, and visit them for their visitations, and then, as Isa. x. 3, "What will ye do in the day of visitation?" You knew what to do in the day when you yourselves did visit, but what will you do in the day of God's visiting of you? As Micah vii. 4, "The day of thy watchmen and thy visitation cometh; now shall be their perplexity." Certainly those visitors did begin to be in perplexity, for their day was coming, and we hope their day yet cometh.

Obs. 2. In the day of God's visitation men's own ways will come upon them: "I will visit their ways upon them." Men may have shifts to put off God for a while, but when God shall visit, then they shall see that all the evil that is come upon them is from their own ways; and that will be the very torment of the damned in hell, that they shall clearly see that all the evil that is upon them, is but the fruit of their own ways. As birds are sometimes snared by materials which they themselves supply, so out of men's sins doth God make his lime-twigs to take them withal; that is, the judgment that comes upon them is no other than the fruit of their own ways, they have procured this unto themselves.

"And reward them for their deeds." ומעלליו here translated deeds, signifies *cogitationes*, *studia*, their studies, their thoughts, as well as *opera*, their works: from whence there may be these two observations.

Obs. 1. First, That God will call men to account for their thoughts; the uncleanness of your thoughts, their vanity, envy, and malice. You must look to your thoughts, they are not free before God.

Obs. 2. That studied wickedness, thoughtful wickedness, is the worst wickedness: when men shall plot evil in their thoughts God will especially come to visit it.

"And reward them." There is a great elegancy in these words, which in your English you pass over very lightly. "Reward them their doings:" we know that God will reward every one according to their doings; but I say the original אשיב לו signifies properly *Redire faciam*, I will make to return your doings, I will make your doings return back upon you. Whence

Obs. 1. Sin passes away in the act of it with much sweetness, but God will make it return back again in the guilt of it with much bitterness. As Gideon said, in Judges viii. 7, to the men of Succoth, "When I return I will tear your flesh with the thorns of the wilderness, and with briers." How many have passed over the act of their sin very pleasantly, but within a period of long, it may be, or short duration, God has made their sin return upon them; and it has returned as Gideon did upon the men of Succoth, and torn them with briers and thorns, that they have lain roaring in the anguish of spirit for the horror that hath been upon them for their sins. You sinners, that have not returned unto God in the way of repentance, remember that all those pleasant, delightful sins of yours will one day return upon you, and that in the way of terror.

Obs. 2. The good works of the saints shall return upon them with comfort and peace. I will "reward them their doings," that is, I will make to return their doings, I will make their doings return back upon them. It may be you have some troublesome afflictions in the flesh in some of your works and services, yet know they shall return with abundance of peace and joy. Do not think that what you do for God shall be altogether lost: never in your own, nor in the times of your forefathers, was there a more full opportunity to glorify him than at this day; I refer to the calling in of our brethren the Scots into the nation; it is such an opportunity of serving God as you never had, nor probably ever will have the like as long as you live; for it is not the bringing in of so many men into the kingdom, but the engaging of a kingdom for us; and not only so, but the greatest testimony of the goodness of our cause before all the surrounding nations: for though now the nations about us know not which part to take, there having been such protestations on both sides, yet when they shall hear that a kingdom that heretofore carried themselves so loyally, that the king himself by proclamation declared them to be his faithful and good subjects, when, I say, they shall hear that these, having an army in England for the king, yet went away in peace, and that they now espouse our side, certainly this will be a strong testimony to all the surrounding nations, and undoubtedly gain many amongst ourselves. Therefore I say, it is the highest and fullest opportunity for the service of God and good of your country, that you or your forefathers have ever had; and though you have done somewhat, nay, much already, yet you never had such an opportunity as this, which you may bless God that he has afforded you. And do not think now that what you do is quite gone and lost: O no, the Lord will make it return, you shall have a good return for it. You that are merchants, are you not willing to venture your stock at sea, upon the expectation of a good return? you will rely in this on winds, and waves, and seas, and servants that may prove unfaithful. You never ventured any thing in all your lives in which you could have such assurance of a good return, as what you venture in such a case as this. It is not adventured, for God will certainly make your good works to return, as he will make the doings of the wicked return upon them.

Ver. 10. *For they shall eat, and not have enough: they shall commit whoredom, and shall not increase: because they have left off to take heed to the Lord.*

"For they shall eat and not have enough." Some would interpret these words, They shall still grow worse and worse in eating the sin of my people; and so would refer to the eating of the sin of the people in that sense which you heard before, that is, they shall never think they have advantage enough from the sin of the people: they desire the sin of the people for their own advantage; well, they shall eat their sin in that respect, but they shall never have enough, they shall never be satisfied, but still desire that people may sin more and more, that they may gain more by their sacrifices.

But I rather take it, and evidently more according to the words, thus, Howsoever they think to provide for themselves by that which they get in such a base, sinful way, yet they shall find no satisfaction to themselves in it, they shall be deceived. The truth is, if they found satisfaction, it were of little consequence, seeing they must answer for it afterwards; but they shall not only be judged for it hereafter, but for the present they shall find no satisfaction in that in which they promised to themselves satisfaction; they will get an estate, perhaps, acquire money and riches this way, and prosper in the world, but I will curse that which they have gained. Even in goods lawfully gotten there is a vanity, a vanity in goods gotten even by fair means; though we have them, we cannot enjoy them except God give us the power. God is the God of all consolation, and it is his mercy and goodness conveyed through creatures that can alone bring comfort in the use of them. If a man should think to satisfy himself with wind, it were an idle expectation; but it were worse if he should open his mouth wide to fill himself with plague-infected air: when thou thinkest to satisfy thyself with goods never so well got, it is but opening thy mouth to the wind, but when thou thinkest to satisfy thyself with goods unlawfully acquired, it is opening thy mouth to draw in pestilential air, there is no satisfaction, but ruin in them: "He that loveth silver shall not be satisfied with silver," Eccles. v. 10. Howsoever men think with themselves, that if they had such an estate they would live happily, when they have it they find it otherwise. Those that hunger and thirst after righteousness shall be satisfied, but they that hunger and thirst after any thing in the world shall find it to be an empty thing unto them. It is true, there is a kind of satisfaction which God gives sometimes to wicked men, but it is accursed in its nature, a fearful judgment of God. "The backslider in heart shall be filled with his own ways," Prov. xiv. 14; that is, they shall have enough of them; as when a man will go on in his own ways, although he suffer much in consequence, we say, What! have you not enough of such a course? So the wicked shall be satisfied, he shall have enough of his own ways, that is, he shall find such attendant plagues and miseries that he shall be satisfied, he shall be filled with them. It is spoken of an apostate, a backslider in heart, one that will apostatize from God, and think to provide for himself better in the ways of his apostacy, he "shall be filled," but it shall be "with his own ways."

"They shall commit whoredom, and shall not increase."

If we understand this of bodily whoredom, then the sense is, that God will cross them even in that, "they shall commit whoredom, and shall not increase." You will say, What great judgment is that? whoremongers care not for increasing. It is true, they desire only to satisfy their lusts; and in this respect, as much as in any, resemble evil and wicked ministers, who desire only to please the fancies of their auditors, and never look after begetting children unto God. But when the prophet prophesied, increasing in a numerous offspring was a special thing that all gloried in; therefore they sought it, not only by marrying many wives, but by their concubines and strange women; but God threatens to send out a curse upon them, that they shall not increase. And hence we may in general

Obs. Whatsoever a man undertakes unlawfully, he can never expect to prosper in. This is remarkably exemplified in Solomon: you know he had seven hundred wives and three hundred concubines, a thousand in all; yet we read but of one son that he left behind him, Rehoboam, whom the Scripture calls a child when he was above forty years old, 2 Chron. xiii. 7. When Rehoboam was young and tender-hearted, he had a childish and foolish, though a rugged and churlish heart. Solomon was not blessed with a numerous progeny, notwithstanding he indulged himself in so much carnal liberty. But on the contrary, we read that Isaac, from whom came the promised seed, that were to be as the stars of heaven and as the sand of the sea-shore for number, had but one wife; he took not that course which many of the patriarchs did, to marry many wives, but contented himself with one, and yet from him came the promised seed, so many as the stars and the sand for number. From which we may infer, that it is the best way for us to keep to God's ordinances; we shall prosper more in what we would have, to keep to God's ways, than to go out into our own sinful courses.

"They shall not increase." The words are read otherwise by some: Jerome renders it, They have committed whoredom, and have not ceased; and his note upon it is this, They have committed fornication and whoredom, till they have spent all their strength, yet have they not ceased, their hearts are still that way: just as it is with many long habituated to carnal indulgence, they have committed uncleanness, and spent their strength in impurity, yet cease they not, their lusts still boil within them notwithstanding. And if you read the words so, and then take it for spiritual whoredom, They have committed whoredom, and have not ceased, that is, they still go on and on in the ways of idolatry, idolaters seldom come in and return.

Tarnovius reads it otherwise, They shall not break forth, for so יפרצו may well signify; they think to take liberty in their whoredom and idolatry, they break forth from God's laws and punishments, and think still to escape laws and punishments, to break forth from all bonds whatsoever. No, saith God, they shall not break forth; I will lay fetters upon them. This is good, but, however, I take the former to be the legitimate interpretation. and so we shall leave that expression, "they shall commit whoredom, and shall not increase." Here follows the reason.

"Because they have left off to take heed to the Lord."

There is a great deal of elegance in this expression; They have left the Lord to take heed, so you may translate לשמר *ad custodiendum*, to keep themselves within any bounds of the commandment of God; as if the prophet should say, They run wild, and have left off to take heed of God, or any of his ways. Perhaps they have not left the Lord wholly, for they will render God some external worship, but he cares not for that, they have left the Lord to take heed of him. Though we think to follow the Lord in any external duties, if we cease to take heed of God in all his ways, he notices it not: that may be one note.

But the thing specially meant is, though at first a temptation prevail against a professor of religion, yet he having an enlightened conscience, the truth of God will continue working in his conscience and in his heart; but now if he still give way to that lust, at length it will so far prevail that he will wholly leave minding and regarding the truth of God, which opposes his sin, and give himself fully up unto the ways of his own heart: and this man's condition is very dangerous. Oh take heed of this, take heed of this not taking heed! You that begin to decline, and find some secret lust prevailing in your heart; you yet have the truth of God working in your souls, and it will not let you go on quietly; but yet your lusts strive against this truth: well, if this lust be not mortified, if you give way to it, that it continue a while, you will come to be weary of that truth which opposes it, and you will turn your eyes from it, and leave off to take heed further to think of that which makes against your sin; and when you are come to this pass your condition is truly dangerous. Hence we may especially

Obs. 1. The way to keep the heart and life in order, in the paths of obedience, is "to take heed to the Lord;" to take heed to the infinite, glorious, blessed Majesty of the holy and great God; to mind God in his sovereignty, in his authority, in that infinite worthiness which is in him of all obedience from all his creatures; to look upon God the only Jehovah, the high and eternal God. This is the way to keep our hearts and lives in order, to "take heed to the Lord" thus, to have him in all our thoughts and hearts, and to observe diligently him and his ways.

Obs. 2. It is an evil thing for any, in matters that concern the worship of God, not to take heed to God's word. That they did leave off to take heed to God in point of worship, is the thing that God especially charged them with: that kind of worship which they thought most suitable to their own reason and politic ends, that worship they set up; but now to take heed to God, and to look up unto him, that whatsoever they had in his worship should be according to the rule he prescribes, that they left off to regard, and were altogether intent on their own ends. And it is an evil thing in any kingdom that men should leave off so to take heed, as is now almost come to pass with us. I make no question but that at first, for the government of the church, the primitive Christians had a special eye to the rule, to apostolical institution; but, I know not how, it is now almost a general conclusion amongst men, yea, amongst good men, and even good divines, that we can scarce have a rule of institution, they think we need not directions, and can find no such thing at all in the word, and so have altogether ceased even to examine it on this point. But though in civil things we are left to prudence and reason, when we come to matters of worship, in every particular properly ecclesiastical, properly church work, we must, I say, in every such thing take heed to the word of God. On this point Luther forcibly remarks, In religion we ought not to look so much at what is commanded, as who commands it: and he cites Seneca, who gives this rule, Observe not who commands, but what is commanded: so in the church, saith he, and in matters of religion, we should adopt this, and regard not so much *quid*, but *quis*, *qualis*, and *quantus*; but the devil changes this into *quid*, *quale*, *quantum*, that is, he changes this Who, and what manner of a person, and how great a one, commands, into, What, what manner, and how great a thing. Many thus despise some ordinances in the church, Why, what great matters are there in these things? they look to the thing, and not to the institution; whereas, did we look to Christ, the Institutor, as we should, we would have more regard to the institution than to the thing itself. Let the thing commanded be never so low and poor, never so mean in itself, yet the institution must be honoured. Let us take heed to God, especially in the point of worship.

Ver. 11. *Whoredom and wine and new wine take away the heart.*

The Holy Ghost still especially addresses the priests; for their whoredom, their wine and new wine, did take away their hearts. "Take away:" the words יקח-לב may be translated diversely; either, "take the heart," or, "take away the heart."

"Take the heart:" so some render it; meaning, these lusts do take possession of their hearts. It is one thing for a man to be overtaken with a lust, and another thing for a lust to take a man. It is said of the godly, that they are overtaken; but it is said of these, that their lusts take them: and now when it comes to this, that you not only yield to a temptation, but a temptation takes you captive, then whoredom and wine and new wine have taken your hearts.

But I rather understand it thus: these lusts "take away the heart." It is true, there is not one lust harboured in the heart of a man, but in time will take away his heart, will eat out all the juice, and strength, and vigour of any grace in him. That is the reason why many professors grow so sapless, so heavy, so dull, so dead in the way of religion; there is some secret lust or other that they have a desire after, and that takes away their hearts, and they become like vapid liquor, all their spirit and life quite gone, their lust has eaten them out: that man is indeed in a sad condition, whose vigour and strength are gone and eaten out by some heart-lust.

From the context we remark, that they left off to take heed to God in point of his worship, and now it seems they are left to the sins of whoredom and drunkenness. Hence,

Obs. 1. It is just with God, that they that will not seek to satisfy their souls in himself, shall be given over to base and filthy delights of the flesh, that they shall never have any other comforts but those. Let them have those comforts, saith God, that is all the comfort they shall ever find. So we read in Rom. i., that when they did not glorify God as God, he gave them up unto unnatural affections and sins of uncleanness.

But to speak of these two sins as they are here set forth to us, whoredom and drunkenness. I shall not discuss their nature, as I have somewhat enlarged on that in the beginning of the chapter, but I shall follow here the dictates of the Holy Ghost, and endeavour to show you briefly how these "take away the heart."

First, Both the sins, in general, are sins of sensuality. Hence,

Obs. 2. Sensuality is a besotting sin, sensuality either in whoredom, or intemperance in drinking. You know how it took away the heart of the wise Solomon, as his concubines turned him from God, to worship idols. And so with Samson, who was so strong, when Delilah had first taken his heart then she took it away; for you know, in the story, though she sought his destruction many times, and he saw plainly that she designed to give him up into the hands of the Philistines, yet for all that his heart could not be taken off from her. The Scripture speaks of the sin of lust most fully in this respect, Prov. ii. 19, "None that go unto her return again, neither take they hold of the paths of life." None that go unto "the strange woman" return; or, as some would read it, interrogatively, Do any return that go unto her? It is a rare thing for any one to return whose heart is thus insnared, or ever to enter into the paths of life. The Holy Ghost speaks this, make of it what you will. And again, 2 Pet. ii. 14, "Having eyes full of adultery, and that cannot cease from sin:" when eyes come to be full of adultery they cannot cease from sin, their hearts are so alienated from all good. And Prov. xxiii. 27, "A whore is a deep ditch; and a strange woman is a narrow pit:" it is hard to get out of a deep ditch, especially if the mouth be narrow too; those that are got in there, are like to Jeremiah who was put in the dungeon where there was no water, but filth and mire, so that he sank in the mire; and except the Lord send from heaven long cords of his mercy, it is improbable they should ever come out, but they must die and perish: and how many thousands do so die and perish! Nothing ever deadened David's heart more than that sin of adultery; Psal. li., he cries out, "Uphold me with thy free Spirit;" as if he should say, Lord, I was wont to have more power over temptation, but now I am weak and quickly overcome; Lord, "uphold me." And as the sin of uncleanness takes the heart away from God and from truth, therefore 1 Pet. ii. 18, speaks of professors who were allured "through the lusts of the flesh, through much wantonness," even such as had escaped, "clean escaped," the pollutions of the world, and separated "from them who live in error." So drunkenness, that likewise takes away the heart; wine takes away the heart exceedingly. When Solomon gave himself "unto wine," he "laid hold on folly," Eccles. ii. 3; though somewhat of his wisdom remained, yet wine in a great measure took away his heart. He gave himself liberty, as appears by that scripture, though we read not of drunkenness, yet he gave himself liberty to satisfy himself with wine, and then he laid hold on folly. Those that indulge themselves in drinking wine and strong drink are besotted in their very intellects, as you know by experience; they are as a snuff of a candle in a socket, drowned in the tallow; a while since it spread a good light over the room, but now there is nothing left but a little smoke and snuff, and little or no light: so many men, when young, were like a candle upon the table, diffusing light to all about them; but now, having given themselves up to that filthy and vile lust of drinking, all their parts are become extinct, drowned in the fumes of intoxication. Or rather, they are become as a quagmire: if the husbandman sow never such precious seed there, what fruit will it bring forth? Austin saith, Just as when the ground has too much rain it grows miry and dirty, and is not fit for seed, so are those that indulge themselves in drink. Therefore in Ezek. xlvii. 11, it is said, the waters of the sanctuary did not heal the miry places and the marshes: drunken hearts are seldom healed by the waters of the sanctuary. Basil, in a sermon on intemperance, compares drunkenness to the idols spoken of in the Psalms, that have ears and hear not, and eyes and see not, and feet and walk not; it takes away their standing and their understanding likewise, their very intellects are debased, and they are left at liberty to indulge in all kinds of wickedness. How many are there that were excellent when young, yet being taken with that lust, how are they grown like Esau, who sold his birthright for a mess of pottage! these will so sell heaven for a cup of wine; yea, they are more profane than Esau, for he was in a strait, he had come out of the field and was very hungry, and thought he should die if he had not the pottage; so he might plead that he sold his birthright for a mess of pottage out of a kind of necessity; but these will sell their souls, and heaven and all, merely to indulge that humour: for that lust, they will venture the health of their bodies, the waste of their estates, the loss of their friends, the shaming of themselves, the ruin of their names, and the damnation of their souls. Oh how does this besot men of otherwise excellent parts!

Well, but these two are applied here unto the priests, and so we must make special use of them: That whoredom and wine and new wine did take away their hearts, for these priests (as before we have heard) rejected the knowledge of God, and so left off the work they were appointed to do, the instruction of the people, therefore the people were brought up in ignorance; now they, leaving their office, their duty that they should perform in the place they were set in, gave themselves up to sensuality, to whoredom and to wine. From hence we may

Obs. 3. Ministers, when they are negligent in preaching, usually grow sensual. We find it so by experience, we need not go about to prove it. Have there not been many that in their younger time have been forward preachers, and when they have gotten livings and preferment, never minded their study and preaching any longer, but gave themselves to satisfy the flesh in uncleanness, filthy lusts, and drunkenness? Do we not know some such? People are but in an evil case when they have such ministers. Isa. lvi. 9, "All ye beasts of the field, come to devour, yea, all ye beasts in the forest." What is the matter? The 12th verse shows what kind of priests and prophets they had; "Come ye, say they, I will fetch wine, and we will fill ourselves with strong drink; and to-morrow shall be as this day, and much more abundant:" such kind of priests they had; and then, "All ye beasts of the field, come to devour," for they lie open to all kind of misery. Paul would have Timothy, when he was weak, drink a little wine for his stomach's sake and often infirmity; he, good man, though he were but weak, out of conscience it seems would drink only water, yea, for fear lest it might do hurt, he would drink but water till he had a commission from Paul; he was fain to exhort him to drink wine, and yet but a little, drink a *little* wine. Those in public places especially should take heed of intemperance. I have read of some heathens, who made it death for a king or a magistrate to be drunk.

Ver. 12. *My people ask counsel at their stocks, and their staff declareth unto them: for the spirit of whoredoms hath caused them to err, and they have gone a whoring from under their God.*

There is a little more difficulty in these words than in the former. First, however, the connexion affords this useful note.

Obs. 1. Bodily and spiritual whoredom are wont to go together. "Whoredom and wine and new wine take away the heart;" and then, they "ask counsel at their stocks, and their staff declareth unto them." First they are besotted with these lusts, and then they fall into the grossest idolatry, for the words in this verse seem to express idolatry of the grossest and most stupid kind. "They ask counsel of their stocks, and their staff declareth unto them;" when they had given up themselves to the lusts of their hearts, then they grew most sottish in their idolatries. Therefore we are not to marvel, though men, apparently of understanding, yet will worship stocks and stones, as your papists; why? they give themselves up to their lusts, and then the grossest idolatry in the world will meet with their sanction. I remember to have read of one, who, seeing a person go to mass, and presently after to a house of ill fame hard by, exclaimed, *A lupanari missam tantum esse passum;* that is, There is but one step from the mass to uncleanness. Spiritual whoredom and bodily go together; their hearts are taken away by their whoredom, and they "ask counsel at their stocks." Jewel, in his Apology, relates, on very credible report, that search being made, in the year 1565, for harlots belonging to the stews in Rome, there were found in that city alone twenty-eight thousand. Thus you see how bodily and spiritual whoredom go together; twenty-eight thousand such women found in one city, in that city which we know is called in regard of spiritual whoredom, idolatry, "the great whore," Rev. xix. 2.

Now to explain this, "My people ask counsel at their stocks, and their staff doth teach them."

"Their stocks;" that is, their images, God puts that contemptible name upon them; they ask counsel of them. And that is to be observed too, "*my* people," there is the emphasis; mine by profession, not wholly cast off yet, yet these "ask counsel at their stocks," their images, which, although perhaps beautified with silver and gold, yet God calls "stocks."

"And their staff teacheth them." Here is a peculiar form of idolatry, to be taught by their staff. Vatablus and others interpret it of the false prophet, upon which they leaned, as upon a staff; but I rather think it is to be understood literally. There was a kind of idolatry which the Jews had, a way to ask counsel by the staff, and with this the prophet here charges them. The Romans likewise, after this, practised the same, calling it *ῥαβδομαντεία*, or *βελομαντεία*, *divinatio ex virgis*, divination by rods, sticks, arrows, or staves; and there were four ways by which they did divine by these. The first was to put arrows or staves into a closed case, having the names written upon them of what they divined about; and then drawing out one or two, they determined their business according to what they found written; thus their staff declared to them either good or bad; and thus Nebuchadnezzar seems to have done, Ezek. xxi. 22. Interpreters there show, that Nebuchadnezzar, being in doubt whether he should war against Philadelphia or against Jerusalem, took two arrows, and wrote the name of Jerusalem on the one, and Philadelphia on the other, and so divined which way he should go. And this is the first mode of declaring by the staff. A second was by casting up staves or arrows into the air, and according as they fell, on the right hand or on the left, before or behind, so they divined their good or ill luck, as they called it. A third way was this, they used to peel off the bark of some part of a stick, and then cast it up, and divined according to which part of the pith, either black or white, appeared first. A fourth was, as we find in the Roman antiquities, that their augurs or soothsayers used to sit upon the top of a tower or castle in clear and fair weather, with a crooked staff in their hand, which the Latins call *Lituus*, and having quartered out the regions of heaven, so far as to answer their purpose, and offered sacrifices and prayers to their gods, they stretched it forth upon the head of the person or thing they would divine for, and so foreboded good or ill luck, according to what at that time they observed in the heavens, the birds flying, &c. This was the custom of the Romans, and perhaps derived from the Jews.

By all this we may see what poor ways idolaters have had to know the minds of their gods. When men forsake the right way of knowing God's will, what poor expedients have they recourse to! Oh how should our hearts be raised up to bless God, that we have such a way to know his mind, as the word; and that we have his Son, who came out of his bosom, to declare to us the eternal counsel of his Father!

Now follows the ground of this miserable condition of idolaters; "For the spirit of whoredoms hath caused them to err, and they have gone a whoring from under their God."

"For the spirit of whoredoms." Some would understand it thus, that as there are particular sins, so there are particular devils to attend upon them; one especially to attend upon idolatry, another on whoredom, another on drunkenness, another on envy, pride, and the various evil passions: and so "the spirit of whoredom" (say they) is the devil that especially attended upon this sin. But I think this not to be the scope, but rather, that impetus of "the spirit of whoredoms" that was in them; there is an impetus, a strong inclination, of their spirits to such a sinful course, which carried them on, and caused them to err. The Scripture often speaks of different sorts of spirits, as sometimes the spirit of perverseness, Isa. xix. 14; in your books it is translated, "a perverse spirit," but the words are רוח עועים a spirit of perversenesses; there is an impetus of spirit that has caused Egypt to err in every work thereof. So the spirit of uncleanness, Zech. xiii. 2, translated in your books, "the unclean spirit," but the words are ואת-רוח הטמאה the spirit of defilements, or uncleanness. So the spirit of lying, 1 Kings xxii. 22; "the spirit of error," 1 John iv. 6: "We are of God: he that knoweth God heareth us; he that is not of God heareth not us. Hereby know we the spirit of truth, and the spirit of error." That is, there is an impetus, a strength of spirit, which carries men on to such erroneous ways. And the consideration of that will be of marvellous use to us. Let us look to our spirits, my brethren, and consider what spirit we are of; especially when carried impetuously to any thing we desire, let us take heed to ourselves: when you find, I say, your spirits very eagerly and strongly set upon a thing, examine well that it be not a spirit of lust, of envy, of malice, such as sometimes exists in men's hearts, when they are carried to any object with more than ordinary strength. Many people find themselves hurried on with such a fervent impetus, that they cannot endure to be crossed, no, they must have it: as in Samuel, they that desired a king, when they heard all the reasons that could be urged to persuade them against it, would return none other answer than, "Nay; but we will have a king." So a man that has such a spirit will rush upon a thing without due examination, and even if there appear any truth against it, he presently slights it; why? because he has a spirit which impels him to it, and if the truth come even so strongly that he is convinced by it, yet his spirit carries him on, and though he meet with many difficulties in the way, he will break through them all. Oh, it is a dangerous thing when men have a spirit of error, or a spirit of bitterness. You will find some men that have much of antichristianism remaining in them; do but speak to them of any thing that concerns an ordinance of Christ, of Christ's institution, of the will of Christ in the word, as soon as it is but mentioned, you hear no answer to the argument, but may perceive immediately arising a spirit of bitterness and aversion. So you find men, and sometimes good men, with whom if you but discourse of some things which you know are in accordance with the mind of Christ, yet having been brought up otherwise, and imbibed other principles, they have a spirit of bitterness, anger, and vexation, which presently will appear in them to reject any truth suggested.

But let us labour, on the other side, rather to be actuated by the Spirit of God; the children of God are "led by the Spirit of God." And it is true, that as wicked men have a spirit of uncleanness in them, so God's children are carried on with a spirit of holiness; the love of Christ has taken hold of their hearts, and perhaps they are weak, and cannot reason out the case with some subtle sophists; yet they have "the Spirit of Christ," an impetus of his spirit which carries them on. But take heed, the Spirit of Christ is joined with much humility and holiness: do not say you are impelled by the Spirit of Christ, when bitterness and pride are mixed with it; but if there be humility and holiness, then perhaps, though you cannot answer every objection of every sophist, yet the Spirit of Christ dwelleth in you. As wicked men, then, have a bias on their hearts, influencing their judgments, so the godly have a bias on their hearts, the truth and love of God, which swaying, carries them on with strength in the ways of God: as the poor man, the martyr, who said, I cannot dispute for the truth, but I can die for it. There was a spirit of love in him to Jesus Christ, that impelled him onwards, and made him relish and love holy things, though he could not dispute for them.

We are to pray to God that he would satisfy us not only in body and in soul, but in spirit, that that impetus of spirit may be sanctified, for great things depend upon it; almost all things in the world are carried by the impetus of men's spirits. Hence it is that men, although very wicked, will, on their death-beds, hearken to your words, and listen to reason; why? because then their affliction abates the impetus of their spirits, the activity and keen fervour of their minds, and you may say any thing unto them.

"And they are gone a whoring from under their God." Drusius renders it, by a periphrasis, thus, They have cast off the yoke of God. In the Hebrew, if rendered word for word, it is, "from under their God;" and so the Septuagint translate it. And it denotes these two things.

מתחת אלהיהם Καὶ ἐξεπόρευσαν ἀπὸ τοῦ Θεου αὐτῶν.

First, They have gone from under the command of God. The pride of their hearts refused to be under the command of God, especially in his worship. O my brethren, we should look to this, to God above us, and be willing to lie under the command and authority of God, especially in his worship. Take heed of the rising of your thoughts in the matter of God's worship.

Secondly, They are gone from under the protection of their God. From under the command of their God, and consequently from under his protection. As wives, so long as they keep themselves under their husbands in due subjection, are under their protection also; but when they will forsake their husbands, and refuse to obey their commands, they at the same time put themselves from under their protection. So do my people, saith God, they will be from under my commands, and so are from under my protection. Hence two observations.

Obs. 1. All false worship puts a people from under the protection of God. No marvel that miseries befall a people who corrupt the worship of God. Oh, we were in a sad case not long since, even from under the protection of God, and things ran on at riot with us; and even now, because the people of this land have not yet hearts to entertain the true worship of God, we may fear lest we should not enjoy his wished-for protection. Would you have the protection of God? then keep close to the rule of his worship.

Obs. 2. So far as we are from being under God's command, so far are we from being under his protection. Obedience and protection are conjoined. In sin, you wander from under God's command, and from under his protection too. But he watches over us for good when we are in his ways. Keep close, then, to God's commands, and although troubles befall you, yet still you are under God's protection. The difference between a man that is under the command of God, and will closely observe it, and another that will have liberty, is as a deer in a park: so long as it is within the place, it is under the care of the keeper, who watches that no dogs or any thing else injure it, and in snowy weather, when there is no grass to be got, provides it with sustenance; but if the deer will wander forth, it may indeed enjoy more liberty, but then every dog pursues it, and it is subject to a thousand dangers more than when within the pale. So it is with a man that is willing to be within the pale of God's command, there he enjoys the watchful care of God; but if he will have more liberty, and transgress, let him not expect the protection of God in his wanderings. Oh that those that are gone astray from God would observe this! It may be, the consciences of some here tell them that they have wandered from under God's commands: there was a time that they trembled at his word, and their hearts fell down under the dreadful authority of those commands, then was it well with them; but now you have got from under this, you do not fear God's word as before, you will not tremble at his commands, you now go astray in your own ways. Poor wanderer, whither art thou gone? thou art gone from under the protection of the Lord.

Ver. 13. *They sacrifice upon the tops of the mountains, and burn incense upon the hills, under oaks and poplars and elms, because the shadow thereof is good: therefore your daughters shall commit whoredom, and your spouses shall commit adultery.*

In the former verse the prophet, in the name of God, had charged Israel with having the spirit of fornication, and accused them for going a whoring from under their God, and now he shows to them wherein they had so offended.

Obs. 1. General accusations, without particular specification, will not prevail with stubborn hearts. Above all, idolaters must be convinced wherein they have committed idolatry. They will stand it out stoutly if you charge them only with idolatry in general, of going a whoring from God, except you demonstrate wherein. It is so with many sinners. Ye have despised my name, and yet "ye say, Wherein have we despised thy name? Ye offer polluted bread upon mine altar; and ye say, Wherein have we polluted thee?" Mal. i. 6, 7. Stubborn hearts will stand it out with God a great while, until the evils they have committed be particularly specified, wherein they have done such and such evils. And it is wise, therefore, for all God's ministers not to deal in general accusations, if they would have their ministry a convincing ministry. Instancing preaching is the most convincing preaching.

Now the prophet instances that kind of idolatry which seems the most specious and fairest of any in the world, and in which one would have thought that as little evil as possible existed. Why, what great matter is it? they might say. You accuse us for going a whoring from under our God; we only offer sacrifice upon mountains, and burn incense under trees; is that so great a matter? It is sacrifice, and you cannot say but we sacrifice to the true God; we do not sacrifice to idols, how then do we go a whoring from God? This is very specious, that they should sacrifice thus upon mountains, and under trees, and in this they pretend to be more devout than Judah was: the people of Judah sacrificed only in one temple, and as it were confined and limited God to that place, and they sacrificed only upon one altar; Now, say they, we think God worthy of a great deal more than this; we think it is fit to sacrifice to him every where, in every place, and especially upon mountains, for it is to the high God that we sacrifice. Just as the papists at this day will have their images in every place, and their crosses in every highway as they travel, that by them they may be reminded of God continually. What a specious pretext is this! Yet the Lord, by the prophet, charges them with going "a whoring from under their God," and establishes the accusation by instances taken from services which they considered, if not meritorious, at least excusable.

Obs. 2. What seems most specious in our eyes, if it be not according to the rule, may prove most abominable in the eyes of God.

Obs. 3. Ministers should especially labour to present to the people the foulness of those things in which they think there exists the least evil. To exclaim against wickedness which they themselves cannot but acknowledge to be notorious, will never so convince as thoroughly to humble: but to close with them, and to open the evil of their ways in those things in which they most bless themselves, and to show how, even in these, they make themselves abominable unto God, that is the way to make our ministry a convincing and a humbling ministry indeed. Thus the prophet, You sacrifice upon the mountains and high places, and under the shadow of every tree. Jerome upon this place remarks, Israel loveth high places, for they have forsaken the high God; and they love the shadow, for they have left the substance. It is thus with men, when they have left the high God, then they have somewhat or other that they set up high in their hearts; they forsake the shadow of the wings of God, and then seek after vain shadows to be their protector.

But to open this scripture yet more clearly, to show wherein their sin lay here, that they sacrificed upon the mountains, and hills, and under trees. We are to know, that in former times, before the ark, and the tabernacle, and the temple were built, it was lawful to sacrifice in any place, and God approved of sacrificing in mountains, directing Abraham to go and sacrifice his son on mount Moriah, Gen. xxii. 2; and in Gen. xxi. 33, we read of Abraham's planting a grove when he called upon the name of God; so that their forefathers did sacrifice upon mountains, and planted groves and trees by the places where they sacrificed; there was no hurt then in such things. But afterward God prohibits this: "Take heed to thyself that thou offer not thy burnt-offerings in every place that thou seest: but in the place which the Lord shall choose in one of thy tribes, there thou shalt offer thy burnt-offerings," Deut. xii. 13, 14. God would limit them the place of his worship. When the ark and the tabernacle were made, they were bound to come and sacrifice there, and no where else; and so when the temple was built, that became the sole appointed place. Yea, then the Lord commanded them to pull down the high places, and to cut down the groves and trees: "Ye shall utterly destroy all the places wherein the nations which ye shall possess served their gods, upon the high mountains, and upon the hills, and under every green tree," Deut. xii. 2. When once God had appointed a place of worship, then they were to destroy the other places where the heathens were wont to serve their gods. Hence,

Obs. 4. When God chooses a place or thing, he stamps it with peculiar holiness. If God appoint a way of worship of his own, this forbids all other. If God consecrate a place, this forbids to make any place holy but that. So of things, and ceremonies, if once God sets upon them the impress of holiness, we must confine ourselves to them, and not think to imitate God, by dedicating any thing of the same kind. It was now a sin in them, and God, we see here, stands much upon circumstances in his worship. Many plead, Why should men be so strict and scrupulous about circumstances? what, must we have every circumstance commanded in the word of God? My brethren, that which is natural and moral, and but likely to subserve religion, may, indeed, be left to prudence; but where religion is directly involved, though it be but a circumstance, God insists much upon it, and we must have for it the sanction of a Divine rule. Here they are not accused for sacrificing things they ought not to sacrifice, doubtless they offered what was commanded, sheep, and beeves, and the like; but only with respect to the circumstance of place, they did not sacrifice where God appointed, therefore he charged them, that in this they went "a whoring from under their God." It is true, we read of some godly men's sacrificing elsewhere; Gideon under an oak, Judg. vi; and Samuel on a high place, 1 Sam. ii.; and David in the threshing-floor of Araunah, 2 Sam. xxiv. Now, to all these instances the answer generally given by divines is, that they could not lawfully have done so, but by some special dispensation of God himself; else it could not but have been sin. For the kings of Israel and Judah are also charged with their sacrificing in the high places; even of Solomon himself, when, in 1 Kings iii. 3, he is commended for loving the Lord, and walking in the statutes of David his father at first, yet the text saith, "Only he sacrificed and burnt incense in high places." And amongst other high places, we read in 2 Chron. i. 3, that Solomon went to Gibeon, which was a great high place. And though some excuse him, because it is said the tabernacle was there, and therefore he might go to sacrifice, yet Austin, in his Questions on Judges, thinks Solomon is to be blamed, though the tabernacle was there, for it seems he put a more than ordinary respect upon that high place; wherefore else is it called *the* great high place? and he went there, not only for the sake of the tabernacle, but because it was that great high place; and therefore is to be blamed. So that if we go to the ordinances of God where yet there are other mixtures, and we do the rather go and esteem them because there is some addition of man's inventions, this is a sin against God. And further, it is observable, though Solomon were blamable for going thus, yet we find that God revealed himself unto him, in a wonderfully gracious manner, even in that place, and bade him ask what he would. So certainly many of God's people have found, that though sometimes they have been in the use of ordinances where there have been such mixtures that they have been polluted to them in consequence, yet the Lord has been so gracious to them, that he has accepted of the uprightness of their hearts, and they have had, even in them, many sweet manifestations of his favour: they can remember when they have been at sacrament, and they have known that they have offended against God by reason of some pollutions, yet they have, notwithstanding, found God shedding abundance of mercy on them, and refreshing their souls with comfort and joy in the Holy Ghost. This was God's mercy. Do not think, therefore, that there was no evil in it, because God was so far gracious unto you. There was evil in Solomon's respecting this high place, yet there God favoured him abundantly. Other kings there were, who were exceedingly blamed that they did not take down their high places, which were the same as the mountains here spoken of.

Yet there were some of them that were very careful in this respect. Amongst others Hezekiah and Jehoshaphat. So, in 2 Kings xviii. 22, Hezekiah is charged by Rabshakeh with taking down the high places, "Is not that he, whose high places and whose altars Hezekiah hath taken away?" God approves of it, though Rabshakeh thinks he has done ill; O, saith he, do you trust in Hezekiah? he has taken down the high places. He thought that Hezekiah had therefore been an enemy to religion, and to the worship of God. Thus it is with ignorant people at this day, who understand not the way of God's worship; because some in the parliament seek to take away corruption in the worship of God, many cry out that they are enemies to all religion. Thus it is reported by your country people that dwell far off, as in Wales, and in other places, that the parliament are a company of vile men, that seek to take away all religion out of the kingdom. But this is so but in the understanding of a Rabshakeh, that confounds the taking away of high places with the abolition of religion.

Jehoshaphat, likewise, is commended for taking away the high places, and it is noted of him, that his heart was much lifted in the ways of God when he did it: for this sacrificing on the high places, the people were so attached to, and thought it a great thing that they should go up to a high place to offer unto the high God; therefore when Jehoshaphat took them away, the text saith, his heart was lifted up in a more than ordinary manner. So it should be with governors, when they see corruptions in God's worship, though the people stick close to them, yet they should have their hearts lifted up with courage and zeal to go on in the work. In 2 Chron. xvii. 6, "His heart was lifted up in the ways of the Lord: moreover he took away the high places and groves out of Judah." Here are two things that Israel is charged with, "the high places, and the groves;" Jehoshaphat took them away, and took them away out of Judah. He was of a lifted-up mind, and his heart took boldness for the ways of God, as the Vulgate renders it. But mark, what course did Jehoshaphat take to remove "the high places and the groves?" In the 7th verse you find this, "He sent to his princes, to teach in the cities of Judah." Mark here, princes are become preachers; "He sent to his princes to teach in the cities of Judah; and with them he sent Levites and priests. And they taught in Judah, and had the book of the law of the Lord with them, and went about throughout all the cities of Judah, and taught the people." This is the course to take them away; if he had only by an edict removed them, he could not have done so much, but he wisely sent faithful preachers throughout all the country, especially all the great cities. So that it appears it was because of the bad preachers they had before, or because they had none at all, that it was so difficult to remove the high places. How easy would it be in England at this day to make a reformation, to take away corruptions from the worship of God, if in all cities and towns there were faithful preachers! For we see evidently, that people brought up in ignorance adhere most to these things. Let a faithful minister come into a congregation, and so exert himself, that the people may see and be convinced that he is pains-taking, and let him expound the Scripture to them, and they will soon begin to confess, We get more by this than by all the mere reading of prayers; and this demands more to the minister. They would, I say, be convinced of this, if instructed. Jehoshaphat acted thus; and oh how happy were it if we took the same course! But there is something more observable; it is said in this 7th chapter, that Jehoshaphat took away the high places; but in chap. xx. 33, it is said he took them not away; but how is it? It is put upon the people; the text saith, "The high places were not taken away: for as yet the people had not prepared their hearts unto the God of their fathers." The people were the cause. Now to reconcile these two places: it seems in chap. xvii., Jehoshaphat did his utmost, therefore God accounts it as done with respect to him, but because the people were so stubborn, that they would not yield to the command of the king, therefore in this 20th chapter the blame is all laid upon them; as if God should say, They were not taken away, because the people had not prepared their hearts; but as for Jehoshaphat, his heart was right in my sight. God will accept the intention of governors; let them do what they can, and if it be not effected the fault will rest on the real cause. You may see by this, that people may hinder the work of reformation much: "their hearts were not prepared," that is, they were not fit to receive the instructions sent to them. And truly, in England many people are not yet prepared to receive the work of reformation. We never read, and that is observable, of any difficulty that any of the kings, either of Judah or Israel, met with, in introducing any false worship; but when good kings sought to bring in true worship, and to cast out false, it was too difficult a work for them. Thus men's hearts cleave more to false than they do to true worship.

But further, it is observable, with respect to the high places, that it is not only said here, that they sacrificed on the mountains, but "upon the tops of the mountains." There are two things very observable from hence.

Obs. 5. Idolatry is shameless, and loves publicity. They would not do it in a corner, but gat them up to the mountains, to the top of the mountains, and were not ashamed. Oh why should we not have the true worship of God as public! It is a lamentable case when it must get into holes and corners, and dare not appear in public; and even this necessary concealment draws down persecution. Well, my brethren, let us pray, and endeavour as far as we can, to bring in the true worship in the most public manner; and let us not be ashamed of it before the world. In Rev. xiv. 6, there is mention of an angel flying in the midst of heaven, having the everlasting gospel in his hand, to preach to them that dwell on the earth: now it is usual in the Revelation to signify the ministry of the gospel by an angel, and so it is a prophecy that the ministry of the gospel shall fly in heaven, aloft, publicly, and that all the world shall see it. And mark what follows upon this; ver. 8, "And there followed another angel, saying, Babylon is fallen, is fallen." So that we may note from thence, That when the ministry of the gospel and its ordinances come to be made openly public, then is the time for Babylon to fall; and so long as Babylon stands, and antichrist stands, so long is the gospel fain to be preached in corners; but when the time of Babylon's fall comes, then shall the ministry of the gospel be publicly manifested in the eyes of all the people.

Obs. 6. They sacrificed not only upon the mountains, but "upon the tops of the mountains." Idolaters seek to rise to the greatest height, to go the greatest lengths in false worship; they content not themselves with hills and mountains, but the very uppermost part of hills and mountains; if there were any higher than other, if they could ascend to heaven, they would do it. Idolaters do not content themselves with a lower degree of false worship. How much less should we in the way of God's worship! we should not content ourselves with low attainments, but get up to the top of godliness, and labour to gain the very height of the worship of God; not content ourselves in one ordinance, but get all ordinances, and get them as far as possible in full exercise. Thus, in Eph. v. 15, "Walk" accurately, "circumspectly, not as fools, but as wise;" the word is ἀκριβῶς, as if he said, Walk to the top of godliness, to the height; if there be any degree higher than another, labour to attain it; as idolaters will get up to the tops of mountains. Thus for their sacrificing upon the mountains.

"Under oaks and poplars and elms." These trees are such whose leaves are broad, and did abide longest upon them. But why did they and the heathen also seek to sacrifice under trees, and such trees as these? There seem five or six reasons for it.

1. The heathens consecrated many trees to their idols; the poplar to Hercules, the vine to Bacchus, the myrtle to Venus, the bay to Phœbus. They consecrated several trees to their several gods, and sacrificed under them.

Populus Alcidæ gratissima, vitis Iaccho, formosæ myrtus Veneri, sua laurea Phœbo. Virg. Ecl. 7. 61.

2. They sacrificed there in imitation of the patriarchs, as I showed before. Abraham built a grove by the altar he made, and so did many of the patriarchs; and in imitation of them these here, and the heathen generally, for the devil strove much to imitate the form of the true worship of God; but now, when the ancient practice of the patriarchs was abused, God removes it.

3. They thought that places dark, by the shadiness of these trees, might strike some fear and reverence into the hearts of the worshippers. There does exist in woods, where there are high trees and shady places, a kind of solemnity, they are calculated to inspire awe; for even the heathen themselves, when they worshipped their idols, sought to have the hearts of the worshippers filled with reverence.

4. They thought that the spirits of their heroes frequented the woods and groves. This was the current tradition of the heathen, and they were taught it by their priests. Virgil, in Æn. 6. 673, makes one of them say, *Nulli certa domus, lucis habitamus opacis*, We have no certain habitation, but dwell in dark and shady groves.

5. They were fit places for the commission of impurity. Many of the sacrifices of the heathen were mixed with filthy and abominable uncleanness, and those places were adapted for them, and therefore the devil liked them well. So Philo; and Sozomen, in his history, mentions this reason.

6. Many of the heathens thought that it was to the dishonour of God to be worshipped in any place covered above, or circumscribed within limits. Even some of the heathens looked upon God as infinite, and for him to be worshipped within any covered place they thought a dishonour, therefore would worship him in the open fields and under trees.

"Because the shadow thereof is good." The Holy Ghost instances only this one reason; "the shadow thereof is good," that is, they pleased themselves in their own ways, they thought there was more solemnity in this than in the temple service. The shadow was good, oh it was a fine thing to go to the open fields, and more solemn to worship there than in the city. The shadow was good; they applauded and blest themselves in this way.

Obs. 8. Usually superstition thinks it has a great deal of reason for what it does; therefore it is observable of the papists, that although their form of worship is most ridiculous and absurd, yet they write whole volumes to show reason for what they do, as if theirs were a reasonable service. In Col. ii. 23, it is said of "will-worship," that it has "a show of wisdom;" λόγον σοφίας, the reason of wisdom, for so it may be rendered; and thus in Rom. iv. 18, "reasonable service," is λογίκην λατρείαν. So idolaters think that it is not only wisdom, but that they have the very reason, the very quintessence of wisdom, in their way of false worship, and that "the shadow thereof is good;" especially they think their worship is more sumptuous and more solemn than the ordinances of God.

Obs. 9. It is the pride of men's spirits to think that God's ordinances are too plain. They think they can devise a way to embellish the worship of God, they will show additional reverence and respect. But certainly, if it be not God's own ordinance, whatsoever outward respect can be given unto God in it, he regards it with abhorrence. I have read, that when a lady in Paris saw the splendour of a procession to a saint, she cried out, Oh how fine is our religion compared with that of the Huguenots! (that is, such as we in England call Puritans;) they have a poor, mean, and beggarly, but we have a sumptuous religion. So your papists, with their embellished churches and altars, their prostrations and their bowings, have a fine and showy religion, their "shadow is good," there is splendour and solemnity in it. O, take heed of thinking that any addition of man's renders God's worship more solemn and more reverend. It is the worst argument you can use, to say, Can we do things in God's worship with too great reverence? Have you warrant out of God's word for it? does God enjoin it? have you not at least some rule or ensample for it? If you think to render it by your own addition more reverend, this very argument spoils it, though it were in other respects lawful. Suppose some gesture were indifferent, yet if you think that by it you put more reverence and respect upon God's worship than there is, you thereby spoil it; upon that ground it cannot be justified. Therefore the Lord forbade his people, when they were to make an altar to him, to lift up a tool upon it, for then, saith he, you pollute it. They might have said, Lord, we would fain have thine altar not so plain, we would fain bestow carving and some cost upon it, and so show some respect to it. No, saith God, if you lift up a tool upon it, you pollute it. So if you think to put more reverence and solemnity upon God's worship by any invention of your own, you certainly defile it. That was the sin of Israel at this time, they would sacrifice here; why? because "the shadow was good." So much for their high places, and their worshipping under trees. Now follows the judgment threatened:

"Therefore your daughters shall commit whoredom, and your spouses shall commit adultery."

You commit adultery in going a whoring from me, you shall be punished in the like kind, your daughters and your spouses shall go a whoring from you.

We may regard this in two points of view:

I. As a judgment of God upon them.

II. As that of which they themselves were the cause.

I. As a judgment of God upon them. Hence,

Obs. 1. God sometimes punishes sin with sin, he punishes spiritual adultery with corporal uncleanness. Corporal pollutions are the fruit of spiritual filthiness. So Rom. i., They worshipped not God as God, but in an idolatrous way, after the similitude of an ox that eateth grass, therefore God gave them up to uncleanness. If men be not careful to maintain purity in God's worship, God cares not for their bodily chastity. If you pollute my worship, be then unclean, saith God. Not that he doth permit it as lawful, but in just judgment he gives them over to it. What care I for all your carnal defilements, if you pollute my worship. Bodily and spiritual adultery are usually conjoined. The word *Roma*, with the letters reversed, forms *amor;* and there is much impurity in Rome, as I showed before. Where there is most idolatry there is most adultery.

Obs. 2. The sin of parents is often punished in the children and in the family. Your daughters and your spouses, I will leave them, saith God, and my hand shall be upon them. When a parent or a husband sees the hand of God against his child or against his wife, he should consider, How does God meet with me in this? is it not a sign of God's displeasure against me in this particular? It is observable of the woman of Canaan, Matt. xv. 22, that when her child was vexed with an unclean spirit, she saith, "Have mercy on me, O Lord, thou Son of David, my daughter is grievously vexed with a devil;" she did not say, Lord, have mercy on my child, but, Lord, have mercy on me, for my child is vexed with an unclean spirit; as if she should say, O Lord, this unclean spirit may be the punishment of my sin, therefore, Lord, have mercy upon me, and forgive me my sin, that hath caused such a thing as this; yea, Lord, it may be, I have had an unclean spirit, and this my child imitated me in somewhat that was evil, and so thy hand is come upon it; I am the original, therefore, Lord, have mercy upon me, for my child is vexed with an unclean spirit. So should you, when you see the hand of God upon your children, cry out, Lord, pardon my sin. And does God leave your children in wickedness? do you see unclean spirits in your children, the spirit of filthiness? cry out, Lord, have mercy upon me. Perhaps it was by imitating of you that they came to have such unclean spirits.

Obs. 3. It is a great reproach to any family to have uncleanness committed in it. Fornication and adultery is a great reproach to a family, especially when the daughter or the wife is unclean. It is a reproach to a family if a servant prove naught, especially to some families more than others, as those of ministers, magistrates, or men in public place and esteem: which, by the way, should teach governors to be more careful of their families than they are, for often, through their carelessness, God sends such a judgment, puts this disgrace upon them. Many of you, for your pleasure and delight, can go to your country houses, and while you are there your servants are committing evil; but you should have an especial eye over them, lest God, as a just judgment upon you for your neglect, bring this reproach upon your families. But especially your children, your daughters, and your spouses; and above all, the children of ministers. In Lev. xxi. 9, it is said, If the daughter of a priest "profane herself by playing the whore, she shall be burnt with fire." Now, though adultery was, yet fornication was not, punished with death, in any other instance.

Obs. 4. Our unfaithfulness with God is made more sensible when those that are near unto us are unfaithful to us. Well, saith God here, you go a whoring from me, your spouses shall go a whoring from you; you have been unfaithful to me, your children shall be unfaithful to you; they shall go a whoring too, and then by that anguish and trouble that you have when you see this in your wife, or in your child, you shall be made sensible how grievous it is to my spirit, that you go a whoring from me. Many parents, if they heard that their daughters had dishonoured themselves, oh how would they beat their hands upon their breasts, and tear their hair, and in agony cry out, I am undone, I am undone! and though they had never such great estates, they would think they had no comfort in any thing, but would even look upon themselves and their family as utterly ruined. And if you should hear that your wife had played the whore, how would it be as a dagger in your hearts! Are you so sensible of this? then, by the extremity of grief you would experience in such a case, know, that God so grieves when a child of his goes a whoring from him. If his people depart from him, in ways of superstition and idolatry, yea, even in things that otherwise seem to be but small, (here but a circumstance of place is spoken of,) yet the Spirit of God grieves at it, as a husband or father over the dishonour of a wife or daughter. Oh that you would consider that there is this grief in heaven when God sees his people forsaking his true worship! We think, indeed, that murder and blasphemy are displeasing to God, but we little reflect how the corruption of his worship provokes him. Let us know, that the great provocation of the most high God is the corruption of his worship, I mean, when his people shall corrupt his worship any way.

And further, Do your children prove stubborn and rebellious to you? oh how often does the father or mother retire into their chamber and bemoan themselves, Oh what a stubborn, rebellious child have we, nothing will reform him, admonitions are vain! Well, are you so sensible of the stubbornness of your children? O consider how sensible God is if you carry yourselves so toward him. If a husband have a wife froward and troublesome, that grieves his spirit and loves him not, he laments his condition, and thinks himself one of the most miserable men on the earth. Is this so grievous to you? oh how grievous is it to Jesus Christ to have his church so to him! And have you any friend that has dealt unfaithfully with you? Such a friend, you say, has dealt unfaithfully with me; was ever any served so? O consider how you have dealt unfaithfully with God; and as your hearts are affected by the falseness of a friend, so does your unfaithfulness go to the heart of God. And thus much for the words under the first consideration, of God's retributive justice. I will make you sensible, saith God, of your dealings with me; if nothing will do it, it shall be thus, "your daughters and your spouses shall commit adultery."

II. As that of which they themselves are the cause. Now the people of Israel were the causes of the uncleanness of their daughters and wives, by this their way of false worship, in two respects.

1. By going abroad from their families to hills and mountains to worship, they afforded them opportunity meanwhile of committing adultery. Calvin observes on the place, As it is in popery when they go a pilgrimage, it is the most opportune time for impure indulgences; so here, when they went unto the hills and mountains to worship, then the unclean places were most frequented. So when husbands and parents go up and down without any lawful call, then their wives and families do oft miscarry. Therefore it should teach them to abide at home until God calls them out: if they have a lawful call, they may trust God with their families; if not, some mischief may befall them before their return.

2. By carrying them into mountains, and groves, and under trees, because (as I said before) those places were chosen on purpose, as the fittest for lewdness. It is dangerous for young women to go into such places, and parents and husbands are exceedingly to blame, and it is to be charged as a great evil upon them, when they venture so to expose their daughters or wives to temptation.

Ver. 14. *I will not punish your daughters when they commit whoredom, nor your spouses when they commit adultery: for themselves are separated with whores, and they sacrifice with harlots: therefore the people that doth not understand shall fall.*

This is as severe an expression as any that we have in Scripture; They shall commit whoredom and adultery, yet I will not punish them. Strange! God has threatened whoredom and adultery with death, and threatened the priests' daughters that committed fornication, with fire; and this here refers to the priests especially; yet, saith he, I will punish none of them when they commit whoredom or adultery.

These words are read by some interrogatively, "Will I not punish them?" and then they carry another sense; but I think not according to the intention of the Spirit.

Others read these words comparatively, and, I confess, with some probability: I will not punish them, that is, I will not punish them in comparison with you, for your example makes them what they are, you should restrain them; and though their sin be great, yet, in comparison of you, they shall not be punished at all. Wicked parents look upon their children, when swearers, liars, unclean, as those with whom it will go very ill. Well, it shall go ill with them indeed; but if you be so too, it shall be worse with you. Many wicked parents are loth their children should be so too; I have known some who have put their children to be educated by puritans: they are wicked themselves, yet their consciences tell them it is not good for their children to be so. But the truth is, if you be wicked and your children also, though they may perish in their sins, yet you shall perish with a sevenfold destruction.

But thirdly, it is read plainly by most thus, I will not punish them when they commit adultery, that is, I will show my wrath against you in this, that I will even give up your children and your wives, let them do what they will, I will not restrain them by any punishment. And this is often the course of God's judgment against the wicked, that he will not restrain them in their evil ways. The especial note from these words is:

Obs. 1. It is one of the most fearful judgments of God in the world, not to restrain men from sinning. Jerome, upon those words in Ezek. vii. 4, "I will not spare," saith, God does not spare, that he might spare, he has not mercy, that he might have mercy upon people; that is, when God intends any good, then he will not spare; he will afflict and chastise those that he loves, but if you be bastards and not children, he cares not for chastising you. As long as a parent regards a child, and intends he should inherit, he corrects him; but when once he has cast him off, and is fully resolved he shall never inherit, he lets him go on and take his course. So a physician will give a patient potions, and bitter potions, while there is hope; but if the disease be grown too strong, and hope depart, he lets him alone: thus God often deals with sinners in this world. Origen, in one of his sermons on Exodus, quoting this scripture, hath this expression, Will you hear the terrible voice of a provoked God! "I will not punish your daughters when they commit whoredom, nor your spouses when they commit adultery;" this is the most terrible thing, the greatest imaginable wrath and judgment; here is a terrible voice of God indeed, I will not punish you. So Luther: Woe to those men at whose sins God winketh! It is a fearful judgment to fall into the hands of the living God, but it is a more fearful judgment to fall out of the hands of the living God, in this respect. Many men bless themselves that they can go on in the world, and, although continuing in sin, still prosper and thrive: they do not pray in their families as others do, are not so scrupulous in their consciences as others are, not so strict to walk exactly, yet they thrive in their trades, they are as rich, healthful, have as fine persons and as handsome children, as others; and thereby they are hardened in their sin. O but know, though thou mayst bless thyself in this thing, yet it is the heaviest curse of God that can be on thee, unless he should send thee quick unto hell. There is no such mark of reprobation as this, for God to suffer a wicked man to prosper in his sin.

Origen, Hom. 8. in 20. cap. Exod. Vis indignantis Dei terribilem vocem audire, &c. Luther, Væ illi ad quorum peccata connivet Deus.

Jerome observes on these words, When thou seest a sinner flow with wealth, when thou seest him boasting of his power, when thou seest him healthy, and delighting in his wife, a number of fine children around him, then say, the threatening of God by the prophet Hosea is fulfilled upon that man.

Quando videris peccatorem divitiis affluentem jactare se potentia et sanitate abundare, delectare conjuge, coronâ circumdare liberorum, dic in illum comminationem compleri.

Thy judgment is very great in this, that the less punishment thou hast now, the more thou art like to have hereafter. The less punishment, the more sin, and so the more misery. Know that justice will have somewhat, and much too, for the forbearance of her act, of her stroke; and certainly, it were better for thee who art a wicked and ungodly man, that thou shouldst beg thy bread from door to door. Perhaps now thou hast great revenues, thou liest soft and farest daintily, while others are put to miserable extremities, and yet thou art ungodly and wicked; know, that it were better for thee, and thou wilt one day say it, and wish it thyself, that thou hadst been as the poor beggar at thy door; and it is God's wrath upon thee, that thou art not now as miserable as they. Let us therefore stop the troubles of our thoughts with this, when we see the wicked, how they prosper in the world, and how vile men are exalted, though they undertake causes which we know are abominable in the eyes of God, and by their iniquities provoke the God of heaven. They are, indeed, ready to take this, their prosperity, as an argument that God approves of their ways, and loves them. O let us not (I say) be troubled at their prosperity, for it is so far from being an argument of God's approbation of their ways, that it is one of the greatest judgments that can possibly befall them in the world, when God shall say, Let them go on and fill up the measure of their sins; they shall have their heart's desire for a while, and so shall be fattened up to their destruction. This few but the spiritual will understand. Carnal hearts are ready to call the proud happy, and to think those to be in the best condition that are most prosperous in the world; but this text teaches us the contrary.

"For themselves are separated with whores." Here interpreters remark, that God charges the persons by way of indignation. As when one man is speaking to another and his anger rises, he turns from him and speaks to some one else; so God seems here to have his anger awakened so against his people, that he turns, as it were, from them, as if he spake to some one else, though indeed he means them; "themselves are separated," or divided themselves.

Junius reads it, they have separated; and, not improbably, interprets it, they have separated fat and plentiful things, the choicest and richest things that they had at home, and set them apart under pretence of consecration to a religious use, and then, when they went to sacrifice, they would eat them among their whores, and so deceive their spouses at home.

Others interpret it thus, they have separated themselves from their God; first in spiritual whoredom, and then from their wives in bodily uncleanness.

Or else thus: "separated;" that is, they withdraw themselves into secret, where they might not be known, as the filthiness of that sin causes men to desire concealment; and when they have got into a secret place, or separated themselves from all that know them, then they commit impurity; as many men, when they are gone abroad from their own houses, in their journeys, in their inns, that is a fit opportunity for their filthiness.

Thus God gives the reason why their daughters and their wives commit this uncleanness, because they themselves do so. Hence we may remark,

Obs. 2. When parents are filthy and unclean, what can be expected but that their children should be so too? Take it either with respect to bodily or spiritual uncleanness. In bodily, David commits adultery, and Amnon commits incest: and in spiritual, "The children gather wood, the fathers kindle the fire, and the women knead their dough, to make cakes to the queen of heaven," Jer. vii. 18. If fathers and mothers be idolaters, children will be so too: so it is at this day, the children of those who adhere to the old superstitions, are superstitious likewise; and if the parents be malignants, it is strange to hear how the children, though young, will speak. Which should be a strong caution to all parents to make them take heed what they do before their children: he that sins before a child, sins twice, for the child will do as his father does, he thinks it enough that his father said so, or his father did so. Take heed then how you sin before your children.

The word translated "whores," has a further signification than our English conveys. According to most interpreters, it presents to us those women that worshipped Baal-peor, or Priapus, that unclean god. In 1 Kings xv. 13, it is said of Asa, that he took away Maachah his mother from being queen: now it is interpreted by some, that he removed her that she might not be a special queen in the solemnity of that unclean god Baal-peor, which idol she had set up in a grove. So then these people separated themselves, not to ordinary whores, but to those that were consecrated to the service of that impure god, and in his worship committed with them uncleanness.

"Sacrifice with harlots." If we were to take this merely according to our translation, "harlots," then the observation is only this:

Obs. 3. The filthy and unclean will yet sometimes make some show of religion. Harlots, and yet sacrifice! how can these two consist? One would think harlots should cast off all sacrifice. No; often will the filthy and unclean make a show of religion, thinking to cover all their impurities with some religious action; as the "strange woman," in Proverbs, had peace-offerings, and made them but preparations for the commission of uncleanness. What horrible wickedness is this! yet this is not unusual, for many are very devout in some religious duties, and think that thereby they have served God well, given him his portion, and so conceive they may the more indulge the flesh afterward. It is true we are sinners, and cannot serve God always, but it is an abominable thing to unite impurity and sacrifice.

But the word translated "harlots" here, conveys much more than our English can well express; הקדשות "harlots," is meant of the adultery of the priests with the consecrated ones. This the rather justifies the interpretation of the other word "whores," for I told you by that was meant those women that worshipped Baal-peor, for there the word signifies the consecrated ones, the holy ones. You will say, How can it be translated harlots then? Yes, by antiphrasis, for so the Scripture expresses things and words, and so other languages too, as wood is called so by a name that comes from light. So there, "holy ones," that is, as devoted to filthiness as others are consecrated to God, and therefore called holy ones by antiphrasis. And that, I think, is the meaning of this place; by the priests of Baal-peor are here meant those for whom this people did separate themselves.

Jerome upon this place remarks, that the Romans, to disgrace the French, used to separate priests of their nation for that idol, and to make them eunuchs; from whence all such priests to that their idol, which resembled the Baal-peor of the Jews, they used to call Gallos, Frenchmen, by way of ignominy upon that nation, for some especial revenge they cherished against them.

Take it thus, then, and it will afford us very profitable instruction. These people were grown so corrupt that they had forsaken the true priests of God, and the prophets of the Lord, and separated themselves from the Lord to join in sacrificing with these filthy priests of Baal-peor, that unclean idol which is termed in Scripture "that shame."

But how can it be meant of priests, when the word in the Hebrew is in the feminine gender? We answer, because of the effeminateness of these priests, some of them eunuchs, and so sottish and filthy that they had forfeited the very name of men. Therefore Aquila renders it, with the changed, so he calls the effeminate; they were changed from men into women: and so the Scripture speaks of men that have lost their true character, calling them women, or men of womanish spirits, Isa. iii. 12. And so the heathen poet Virgil, in imitation of Homer, calls the Trojans women, not men, because in character they were rather of the feminine than the masculine gender. Therefore the priests here of that unclean idol are in like manner designated priestesses.

Μετὰ τῶν ἐναλλαγμένων.

Ὦ vere Phrygiæ, neque enim Phryges. Æn. 9. 617.
Ἀχαιΐδες οὐκ ἔτ' Ἀχαιοί. Hom. Il. 2. 235.

Cyril, Theophylact, and others, however, think that these priests seemed to be men, but were indeed women. So that by this text is meant persons vilely impure, that were consecrated to be as priests to the service of this unclean idol. Now then we may remark from hence, their degradation in forsaking the priests of the Lord, separating themselves from them and joining with such unclean priests as these of Baal-peor. Here were separatists indeed. Have we not many amongst us at this day as vile and wicked as these, whose hearts, being opposed to the faithful ministers of God, and the purity of God's ordinances, they separate themselves to any drunken, impure, malignant priest? It was so here, there were the true priests and ordinances of God in Judah, and yet these men, rather than join in his true service, will separate themselves to these filthy and unclean priests of Baal-peor, and think there is more to be gained by uniting with them, than with the true priests of the Most High. How has God of late discovered the filthiness and malignancy of our superstitious priests, who cared not what became of our liberty as men, or our religion as Christians, so they had their lusts gratified! yet how debased are men still, that though faithful and conscientious ministers are sent amongst them who would reveal the mind of Christ and the way of heaven, that they may now know more in one month than before they knew in many years, if they had hearts to hearken to them, yet they will separate themselves, and join rather with such as are not only malignants, but manifestly ungodly in their lives, and commend and love them. Heretofore, when they had but some Sir John, that could only read prayers, sent by the bishop, and godly ministers were thrust out, if men went from their parish church to hear a sermon, how did they immediately exclaim that they were sectaries and schismatics; but now, when men of vile and malignant spirits are by a better authority removed for their wicked lives, and godly and holy men inducted, yet these they will not hear, though it be in their own parish church; but if a malignant preacher be in the city, to him they will flock. Who is the separatist or schismatic now? They separate themselves now to such men, and think they may hear those by whom they can most profit, that is, those that preach things suitable to their own spirits and inclinations. When the case comes home, how partial are men in their judgments! I know nothing so expressive of the condition of these men as these words, though, as they are read in your books, no such thing appears, but the words, according to the original, signify, separating themselves to unclean priests.

"Therefore the people that do not understand shall fall." Well might he say, that they are a people that understand not, indeed.

Obs. 4. Idolaters are not an understanding people, they do not understand, they are ignorant people. You will say, Ignorant? many of them are scholars, and learned. But they are ignorant of the ways of God, even their priests, and for the most part the people; and their very design is to bring ignorance into places, that their idolatrous ways may be the sooner embraced.

"The people that do not understand shall fall." Understand what? what did not these people understand, that was the cause of their fall? They did not understand these things:

1. The design entertained by Jeroboam and those princes that followed him. Poor simple people, they were led by vain pretences. Jeroboam pleaded, that he was for the true religion, and the worship of the true God, only he would not have the people fatigued by going up thrice a year to Jerusalem, that was not so necessary. But in truth, Jeroboam, notwithstanding all his pretences of worshipping the true God, and being a friend to the true religion, designed to bring them under his own government, and to tyrannize over

them. Now this people did not understand this, they were carried away with fair words; if Jeroboam made but a show of religion, and professed that he acted merely out of respect and love, and in favour to them; it was sufficient to blind them, though he designed far otherwise. They did not understand the design of Jeroboam and his princes.

2. That the acceptableness of God's worship did not depend upon its outward pomp and splendour, but upon the observation of what God required. They understood not this. They were led away merely with the fair shows and pomp of religion, but understood not that all the acceptableness of divine worship depends on its being a divine ordinance. Most people at this day understand not this, and hence great evil ensues.

3. That their safety depended more upon the true worship of God, than upon all the politic wisdom that could be. They understood not that their protection depended on God's service and worship, but thought to go politicly on, to provide for their own safety, and relied on the wisdom of their wise men.

4. They did not understand, that whatsoever was commanded by their governors, or taught by their priests, yet, if it was against the mind of God, it would not excuse them from judgment and deliver them from the wrath of God, though their magistrates commanded, and their priests taught it.

They understood not these four things, and therefore they shall fall. This it was that brought down and ruined this people.

There are divers degrees of not understanding.

1. When people do not understand merely from want of the means of knowledge. This excuses not wholly, but they shall even fall though they have no means.

2. When men have means, yet, through their negligence in the use of them, they do not understand.

3. When they are not only guilty of negligence, but wickedly oppose and shut their eyes against the means of knowledge. Then they shall fall indeed.

4. When, having knowledge heretofore, they now lose it by their often resisting its injunctions, and so become dull in their understandings.

5. When they so provoke God, as that he gives them up to a sottish spirit, so that they shall not understand. now these fall deepest. Where all these five are conjoined, as they are in many places, surely that people must needs fall. My brethren, have we not cause to fear our not understanding at this day, that in these different points of view we understand not the vain pretences of our adversaries the Cavaliers, who say,

1. That they fight for religion, and intend nothing but the liberty of the subject. Many people are led away with these pretences, and understand not that their design is to bring them under slavery, and to take away their religion: and this blindness is like to cause us to fall.

2. People understand not that the worship of God and the government of the church must be according to the word. They think what most suits with the reasons of understanding men is best.

3. People at this day think there is too much to do about religion, and desire us rather to act with policy and provide for ourselves. As for religion, why should we injure or trouble ourselves so much about it? we have done so too much already. They think not their safety is in religion, therefore they shall fall.

4. People think the authority of their ministers sufficient sanction. Is it not so with us now? Therefore we have cause to fear that the Lord intends us a grievous fall.

Yea, as those four objects, so the four degrees of want of understanding.

In many places they have no means, many towns and countries have scarce a sermon in half a year.

In many places where there are most means, there they are negligent of them, rebel and shut their eyes against them.

And others that have had knowledge heretofore, have resisted their light, and are grown sottish; yea, it is to be feared that God, in his just judgment, has delivered many amongst us over to a sottish spirit, otherwise it is impossible they should remain so ignorant. Is it not a stupid insensibility in men, that after all the oppression and misery that they have suffered, yet they will not understand, but join with their oppressors, and lay all the blame upon those that venture their lives to deliver them? That when men come and spoil them of their goods, and ravish their wives and children, that they yet rather exclaim against those that venture their lives to do them good, as if they were the cause of their misery? Surely these people do not understand, and can it be expected but that they should fall, themselves and their posterity, into the depth of the misery of perpetual bondage.

Obs. 5. Idolatrous people shall fall: "They shall fall." An angel proclaims this, "Babylon is fallen, is fallen." It is fallen already, my brethren; however idolaters seem to lift up their heads high, yet they are falling, and fall they shall, God has pronounced it, and the time is at hand; they have fallen off from God, and fall they shall by the hand of God, and the prouder they grow the nearer is their fall; pride goes before a fall: while the gospel of Christ and his pure ordinances, that are now so opposed, shall stand, all superstitious ways, and persons, shall fall. It is observable in that place before named, Rev. xiv. 6, an angel flies in the midst of heaven, and preaches the everlasting gospel; and within another verse or two, another angel cries out, "Babylon is fallen, is fallen." When Babylon with all their idolatrous ways shall be fallen, then shall the everlasting gospel be preached: the gospel and the ordinances of Christ shall be everlasting, shall continue for ever; when all superstitious vanities shall have passed away. We find it so; however they thought to give perpetuity to their superstitions by all the means that the devil or wicked men could devise, yet have we not found that God has blasted them, and many of them are fallen? and though God brings his people into affliction, yet they shall rise, the ways of God shall rise, Zion shall rise, Babylon shall fall: the people that understand not, they shall fall.

A word or two about the meaning of ילבט here rendered "shall fall." It comes from לבט which does not occur often in Scripture, and I find divers translations of it. Some render it, shall be beaten; others, shall be brought into captivity; and others again, and not improperly, shall be perplexed. The word signifies, to be brought into perplexity and doubt with respect to the course one ought to pursue; such is the force of the word: I say, by their hesitancy, and being perplexed in their counsels, they come to stumble and fall. This people that do not understand shall thus fall. Indeed this translation is more proper and suitable to the words before; they do not understand, therefore they must needs be perplexed in their ways, and not know which way to go, and therefore must fall: as a man in the dark stumbles; so when men have left the true light and are in the dark, they shall fall, and when fallen they shall be perplexed in the misery that ensues. From whence,

Obs. 6. It is a fearful judgment of God, and a forerunner of a grievous fall, to leave men to perplexed counsels. When men are perplexed in their counsels, utterly uncertain what measures to adopt, it is a sure forerunner of falling into grievous misery. In Isa. xix. 14, the Lord threatens Egypt that he will send a perverse spirit in the midst thereof, and they shall err in every work, as a drunken man staggereth in his vomit; they shall err in their counsels, and this from a perverse spirit. The Lord often sends a spirit of perplexity and perverseness in judgment upon men; and what ensues? they reel and stagger up and down in their counsels, first have recourse to one expedient and then another, and so bring on themselves a great deal of sorrow and trouble. The Lord grant our enemies these perplexed counsels, and deliver us from them.

Obs. 7. When the wicked are fallen, they shall be so insnared and perplexed that they shall not know what to do. Idolatrous and superstitious men, and those whom God leaves to themselves, are in miserable perplexity when fallen, they are as those poor blinded men in 2 Kings vi., whom Elisha led to Samaria instead of Dothan. What miserable perplexity were they in when they found themselves in Samaria among their enemies! So when men are left to themselves, and God has brought them into difficulties, the fruit of their own perplexed counsels, how grievous will it be! On the contrary, when a man walks according to the rule of God's word, and in the uprightness of his heart desires to be directed agreeably thereto, though such a one should meet with trouble and fall into affliction, he need not be perplexed; quietness and peace shall possess his spirit in the midst of his trials, because he has followed God, and walked according to his rule. It may be, he knows not God's end, he understands not the depth of his ways, in bringing him into affliction; yet, having endeavoured in the sincerity of his heart to walk according to God's will, he understands this much, to stay his perplexed soul on God.

Ver. 15. *Though thou, Israel, play the harlot, yet let not Judah offend; and come not ye unto Gilgal, neither go ye up to Beth-aven, nor swear, The Lord liveth.*

The close of this chapter is a warning to Judah to take heed that she sin not as Israel sinned, in regard of the vileness of their transgressions, the fearfulness and suddenness of their judgment.

"Though thou, Israel." Thou wretched, wicked, stubborn, stout-hearted Israel, that no means will reclaim, though thou "play the harlot, yet let not Judah offend."

The word translated "offend," is from אשם and signifies also to desolate, because sin brings desolation. The Hebrews have divers words to express at once sin and punishment, because they are so near akin. Israel plays the harlot, and so is like to bring desolation on herself, but let not Judah likewise offend and bring the same on herself.

The prophet Hosea was sent especially to Israel, to the ten tribes, but here we see he turns his speech to Judah.

Obs. 1. Ministers should especially look to those whom they are bound unto by office, but yet so as to labour to benefit others when occasion offers. And not only ministers, but others likewise. We should all purpose good, especially to those that are under our charge, but yet neglect no opportunity to benefit all.

Obs. 2. When we see our labour lost on those we desire most to benefit, we should try what we can do to others. If these get not good by our ministry, by our admonitions, exhortations, and counsels, yet the Lord may bless our endeavours upon those; let us try what we can do there.

"Let not Judah offend." Let not Judah do as Israel did. There was a great deal of danger that Judah should be insnared and polluted with Israel's idolatry, which is the ground of this seasonable admonition of the prophet. Though Israel do thus and thus, yet let not Judah do so; as if he should say, Judah is indeed in great danger of being defiled by Israel, and that in many respects.

1. They lived near to them; and there is a great deal of danger in living near to idolaters or wicked persons. All sin, especially idolatry, is as leaven that will spread: and you may see the danger that there was in living so near them, in Ezek. xvi. 46, where, as one special reason of the iniquity of Jerusalem, it is said, "Thine elder sister is Samaria, she and her daughters that dwell at thy left hand: and thy younger sister, that dwelleth at thy right hand, is Sodom and her daughters:" that was an especial reason of the iniquity of Jerusalem, their elder sister, Samaria, that is, the ten tribes, were on the left, and their younger sister, Sodom, on the right hand. To be near idolaters and wicked ones is very dangerous; much more to be in the same town, in the same family, where superstitious and wicked persons are, there we had need to take heed to ourselves, for there is much danger.

2. They were brethren, and so the danger of being drawn aside by them was the greater. If you have a kinsman, if you have one that is near to you, not only in place, but in nature or affection, that is superstitious, take heed of being defiled by such. Oh how many have by this means suffered shipwreck of their faith, and been drawn aside from the ways of God! Hence arises the severity that God would have used against a brother or a friend that seeks to entice us to idolatry, because the Lord sees there is so much danger in it: Deut. xiii. 6, 8, 9, "If thy brother, the son of thy mother, or thy son, or thy daughter, or the wife of thy bosom, or thy friend, which is as thine own soul, entice thee secretly, saying, Let us go and serve other gods, which thou hast not known, thou, nor thy fathers; thou shalt not consent unto him, nor hearken unto him; neither shall thine eye pity him, neither shalt thou spare, neither shalt thou conceal him: but thou shalt surely kill him; thine hand shall be first upon him to put him to death." Though he be thy brother, or the wife of thy bosom, or thy friend that is as thine own soul, thou shalt not pity him, but thou shalt seek the very death even of such a one, if he seek to draw thee into ways of idolatry. Because God saw the danger, therefore the severity of this admonition.

3. Israel was the greater number. Israel was ten tribes, but Judah and Benjamin only two, little Benjamin together with Judah were but a few in comparison of Israel. To draw others to their ways, idolaters often plead their number. The whole world admire after the beast; the world and the nations do, and that is a mighty argument to draw: the greater part of people think that this mode of worship is the best, there are but a few, and they inconsiderable, that are opposed. No question but it was their argument here, as if they should say, What! do not ten tribes know the mind of God as well as those two? Is there any reason why we should think that the ten tribes, the greater part of the children of Abraham, should not know the mind of God? It is the argument at this day, with many that are superstitious and would go on in their old idolatry, They that are against such ways are but a few, an inconsiderable party, but the greatest in number and influence of all sorts, you see, favour us. We are to take heed of this. Oh let not Judah, though Israel be the greater number, follow a multitude to do evil.

4. Israel was rich and in a flourishing estate, therefore there was danger that Judah might be carried away by them. Israel carried things before them in outward pomp and glory, and we know that men are soon brought to close with these; and the way of Israel, when Hosea prophesied, did much thrive and prosper, Israel prevailed mightily in the world, When Ephraim spake there was trembling; therefore it was a wonder-

ful grace of God to keep Judah from following their example. We find by experience, let even a persecuted cause be but once countenanced in the world, and men will cry it up; do we not see at this day, that those things which before men would not profess, because of persecution, they now suddenly view in a different light and applaud? The very things before persecuted, if once countenanced by the great ones and by multitudes, how will men praise them! Things that their hearts opposed, and against which they argued and reasoned, yet now because they have more public countenance, their judgments are changed; and, agreeably to the deceit of men's hearts, the way that is most countenanced in the world, that way they will adopt, especially in the worship of God.

5. Israel had many colours and pretences for what they did. They did not profess themselves idolatrous and superstitious; no, they professed that they served the Lord, the true Jehovah, and the difference between them and Judah was but the circumstances of place; You must worship God at Jerusalem, and we would have you worship at Dan and Beth-el, and those images that are set up, are merely intended to remind you of the God whom you worship.

Obs. 3. The nearer a false worship approaches to a true one, the more dangerous it is. Israel came nearer to the true worship of God than the heathens: now the prophet saith not, Though the heathens be idolaters, yet let not Judah be so too; but, "Though Israel play the harlot, yet let not Judah offend." There was more danger that Judah should be drawn aside by Israel, than that they should be drawn aside by any of the heathen. And so there is more danger that we, at this day, should be drawn aside by those that join with us in many things that are right, than by papists, who are hateful to us, and whose ways we see to be abominable. There is not so much danger, especially for those that profess godliness, of being drawn aside by those who grossly violate the laws of God, as by brethren that join with us in many things that are right, and come very near to the true worship of God.

Well, Judah must not do so, though Israel did. As there were many things wherein Judah was in great danger to be drawn aside by Israel, so there were many arguments why Judah should not do as Israel did.

1. God had graciously distinguished Judah from Israel by abundance of mercy, and Judah must not now make himself like Israel in sin, seeing God had made them unlike in mercy. God had in mercy made a difference between Judah and Israel, let not then the wickedness of their hearts make them similar. God had kept Judah to the house of David and to his temple, to be his own people.

2. Judah had more means than Israel had, therefore Judah's sin would be more vile than Israel's was: for Judah had the true priests of God to teach them, had the temple and the right ordinances of his worship among them; therefore, for Judah to be drawn aside to the ways of Israel would be a greater sin in them. Whatsoever Israel does, that has in it none but superstitious, idolatrous priests, priests made of the lowest of the people, Israel, that has in it but the calves, and not the right ordinances of God, whatsoever they do, yet let not Judah, surrounded with privileges, offend. Those that enjoy God's ordinances in a true way, should take heed of doing as other people do.

3 Judah was not compelled by her governors to act as Israel, for Israel, you know, by Jeroboam and other of the princes, was compelled to adopt these measures, and they might pretend that it was for their own safety, for the preservation of their lives and their estates; but no such necessity lay on Judah, for God many times sent it godly and gracious princes, and there was not such compulsion used, they were not so necessitated (if we may speak of a necessity to embrace evil) to adopt false worship as Israel was. When God gives people liberty, that they need not (except they will) be idolaters, for them to close with ways of idolatry and superstition is more sinful. True, heretofore there might have been some excuse for us, we were forced to it, it was as much as our estates were worth, we must have been cast into prison and persecuted, and that made us do that we did. The Lord be merciful to us, for that we, rather than endure sufferings, would join in the prevalent superstitions. But now, through God's mercy, we are delivered from that bondage, and therefore our sin would be so much the greater, were our hearts to cleave still to those beggarly elements.

4. God had no other people upon the face of the earth but Judah and Israel to worship him. Well, Israel is gone from him; and will Judah go too? what will then become of the worship of God? A mighty argument to those that profess godliness, to keep them from the ways of false worship and wickedness in any kind. If you too depart from God as others do, what honour will he have in the world? what will become of his service? Is not God worthy of all honour and of all service from all his creatures? It is a pity there should be any creature in the world that do not honour and serve the blessed and infinite God; but we see the most do not, and there are but a few, a handful of people, that regard his worship; and shall this few, this handful, forsake God? Shall Judah go away too? then the Lord will have no church, no worship, no service in the world.

5. God had much mercy in store for Judah, more than for Israel, therefore "let not Judah offend;" for Christ was to come from that tribe, and the Lord promised, when he had said he would reject Israel, to show mercy unto Judah. Though Judah was carried into captivity as well as Israel, yet God was with Judah, and promised them a return; but he never promised a like return to Israel. Therefore, since God had the more mercy in store for Judah, "let not Judah offend."

Hence we should

Obs. 4. We must not do as others do, especially with respect to God's worship; we must not make the example, even of our brethren, nor of those that profess religion, nor of those that prosper in the world, precedent or rule in matters connected with God's worship. Indeed the consideration, how others sin against God, should be so far from being an argument to draw us to sin, that it ought to be the greatest to deter us. Every sin against God is a striking at God. It is true, if a common enemy come into a city or town, every one desires to have a blow at him; and when men make the example of others an argument for their sin, they deal with God as with a common enemy. When thou pleadest, that such and such sin, therefore I may sin, thou dost in reality say, Such and such strike at God, let me too have a blow at him. Oh take heed of pleading the example of others in ways of wickedness, and remember this one expression, that thou doest in effect as if thou shouldst say, Others about me strike at God, and I must have my blow at him too as well as they. In any sin we must take heed of example, but above all in matters of worship. Hence, Deut. xii. 30, "Take heed to thyself that thou be not snared by following the nations, after that they be destroyed from before thee; and that thou inquire not after their gods, saying, How did these nations serve their gods? even so will I do likewise." Take heed, saith God, thou dost not so much as inquire how these people serve their gods, and say, I will do so likewise. God would not have us use that argument. Take heed therefore of pleading thus, Other people and nations do so and so, why may not we? It is evil to plead example in matters of worship, I mean especially that worship which here Judah is forewarned of, that is, worship by institution. In any thing else there may be more plea for example than in instituted worship; and the reason is this, because that other things, as the moral law, are in some measure written in man's heart, by the law of nature; but institutions depend merely upon God's revealed will. Therefore, though we might have a plea to follow the example of others in point of morality, yet, with regard to institutions, we must be sure to keep to the rule of God's word; to look above all things to what is written, and never to plead example as a precedent.

Obs. 5. It goes nearer to the heart of God when his people offend, than when others offend. "Yet let not Judah offend." Judah was the only people of God, the only true church that remained in the world. When God's own people offend, oh that goes nearer to the heart of God than when others offend! As Christ said to his disciples, "Will ye also go away?" and as Julius Cæsar said to Brutus in the senate, when he came with a dagger to stab him, What! and thou, my son Brutus? so saith God, when those that are professors of religion, that are his own people, and near unto him, when they sin against the Lord, What! and you also? will you also come and strike me? There are many reasons for this.

1. There is more unkindness in their sins. Others provoke the Spirit of God, but God's saints grieve his Spirit; for grief proceeds from love, and the more God loves any, the more their offences grieve him. As the more you love any object, the more it goes to your heart if they do any thing to incur your just displeasure.

2. There is more unfaithfulness in their sins. They have dedicated themselves to God in a manner different from others, and the heart of God reposes more confidence in them. What! thou, my friend, that hast eat bread at my table, wilt thou lift up thy heel against me? And Isa. lxiii. 8, I said, "They are children that will not lie." God confideth in them, and for them to be unfaithful, for Judah to sin, this goes to the heart of God indeed.

3. God's name is more polluted by them. The wicked offend the will, but do not, so much as his own people, pollute the name, of God.

4. The excellency of their graces makes their sins worse. As spots of dirt on sackcloth is not so great an evil, as when on cambric or lawn, and some garments, as your safeguards, that you make of coarse materials, you care not so much though they be soiled and dirty: so the wicked are of a coarse thread, their spirits are little worth, therefore though they be sullied and defiled it matters little; but the spirits of the saints are renewed, they have the image of God impressed, therefore a spot on them is much worse. As a spot of dirt on an ordinary deal board is of little consequence, but if there be a curious image or picture drawn on a table, to have that besmeared is a great deal worse; so if thou art godly, thou hast the image of God drawn on thy soul, and a sin, a spot in thee, is worse than in others. Therefore, whatever others do, yet let God's people take heed to themselves that they do not offend.

Yea, the saints of God, they are the very salt of the earth, the very light of the world, they are those for whose sake God continues the world in that way he does, they are the supporters of all; and if they depart from God also, what will become of the world?

5. They go nearer to the heart of the saints than the sins of others. The sin of one saint affects the heart of another saint more than the sin of any other man doth. Offences of brethren amongst brethren are the greatest of all. As Samson said to those that came to bind him, Do not you bind me; I care not for the Philistines so much, only do not you bind me: so all the railings and persecutions of ungodly men are not so much as the unkindness of the saints. Unkindnesses from such as we look upon as godly, go nearer to the heart of the godly, than all the railing and persecutions of ungodly men. If some godly saints should suffer opposition, yea, even persecution, from such as they esteem godly, oh how would that cut their hearts! their complaints to their Father of this would be sore complaints indeed.

Now all this might be thus applied to us at this time: Though prelates, and such as were superstitious and corrupt, were bitter against and did persecute my servants, yet let not those who have professed godliness, let not those who have been painful and laborious ministers, let not those whose consciences have been heretofore in many respects tender, let not them offend by any bitterness, or any harshness against their brethren: this, beyond all, will grieve the Spirit of God, and distress the heart of the saints. All the persecutions of all the prelates and papists, and of all your popish priests, and such kind of men, would not be a thousandth part so much as any bitterness or harshness toward the saints from the spirits of those who are regarded as godly; especially such as heretofore have professed so much tenderness of conscience, and have thereby suffered so much, because they could not do what was enjoined; if they now, after having got liberty to their own consciences, should become harsh and bitter against others that are godly, oh how sad would this be to God and to his people! Oh, whatever Israel do, "let not Judah offend."

"And come not ye unto Gilgal, neither go ye up to Beth-aven."

There are two things to be inquired here.

I. What this Gilgal and Beth-aven were.

II. The reason of the prohibition, why they must not come to Gilgal, nor go up to Beth-aven.

The words are ordinarily read and passed over without any great observation, but they contain much of God's mind.

I. Gilgal was a place in the borders of Israel, famous heretofore for many things. I know no place, except Jerusalem, that there are more glorious things spoken of than of Gilgal. It was famous for these things.

1. That great circumcision after Israel came out of the wilderness, took place there, when God "rolled away" their reproach; whence the name Gilgal. For during the forty years that Israel was in the wilderness, none of their children were circumcised, God being so indulgent to his people for that time, because they were to remove up and down, they knew not how soon, according to his requirements, and if their children were circumcised they could not so readily have been carried with them. But yet it seems it was an affliction, for God saith, "I have rolled away the reproach of Egypt from off you;" and therefore commanded that they should be circumcised. Now, when they came over Jordan, as soon as they were about to set foot on the land of Canaan, then God required them to circumcise their children. And if we observe it, it was a strange command, for they were now come into the very mouth of their enemies, and all the people of Canaan, all the kings and princes of the country, were gathered together to fight against them; yet now they must circumcise all those under forty years, even their fighting men, who had been in the wilderness so long, though they were in the very mouth of their enemies; and by reason of the soreness attendant on circumcision, they would be unable to stir out against them to battle; notwithstanding all this, they must be circumcised. Thus we see God, when he pleases, will have his worship, rather than our own safety, regarded. And upon this the place was called Gilgal: "This day," saith God, "have I rolled away the reproach of Egypt from off you. Wherefore the name of the place is called Gilgal unto

this day," Josh. v. 9. The word is from גלל which signifies to roll; the Hebrew letter Gimel being doubled and interposed, it forms Gilgal. That is the first thing observable of this place, that there was the great circumcision.

2. The first passover kept in the land of Canaan was observed there, as appears from Josh. v. 10.

3. In Gilgal the manna ceased, and the people were fed with the bread of the wheat of the country of Canaan, Josh. v. 12; God there giving them that first possession of Canaan, to "eat of the fruit of the land," and intimating that they should not henceforth need such extraordinary providence of God to feed them by manna.

4. Joshua pitched there those twelve stones which they took out of Jordan, for a memorial and perpetual remembrance of that great deliverance given them by God, in drying up the waters of Jordan from before them until they were passed over, as appears, Josh. iv. 20.

5. Joshua himself, together with the camp, kept much in Gilgal, and that after even Jericho and Ai were taken and the five kings slain, Josh. x. 6. Yea, after the whole country was possessed, yet still he kept at Gilgal, together with the camp, as appears from Josh. xiv. 6.

6. At Gilgal the angel of God appeared to Joshua, Josh. v. 13, and told him he was captain of the host of the Lord, and bade him loose his shoes from off his feet, for the place whereon he stood was holy.

7. At Gilgal Saul was anointed king, and thither he and Samuel often repaired, 1 Sam. xi. 15.

8. Gilgal was the place for sacrificing, and the tabernacle was much there, as appears, 1 Sam. x. 8; xv. 21. And ver. 33 of the same chapter, when Samuel hewed Agag in pieces in Gilgal, the text saith, "It was before the Lord."

9. Elijah and Elisha came often to Gilgal and prophesied, as 2 Kings ii. 1; iv. 38. Thus you see how famous Gilgal was, and yet though in these nine particulars a place of such renown, God gives his people a charge, that of all places they must not come to Gilgal. I will give you the reason of the prohibition presently, but I must first tell you what Beth-aven was.

Beth-aven was no other than that town which so often in Scripture is called Beth-el, that is, "the house of God," a name given to it by Jacob, on God's appearing to him when he fled because of his brother Esau, Gen. xxviii. This place had before been called Luz, from the abundance of almond trees which were there, the word Luz signifying an almond tree; but on God's appearing to Jacob the name was changed, and it was called Beth-el, "the house of God:" and a very sweet note we may have from thence, and that is, that God's appearing to his people in any place puts more honour on it than all the pleasant fruits that can grow in it. A garden or orchard filled with almond trees, and the most pleasant fruits imaginable, yet are not, and should not be, so delightful to us, nor would they be if our hearts were right, as the house of God, where God appears. If God appear to us in any place, even a wilderness, it should be esteemed more than the most pleasant garden in the world, where we have not the like manifestation. God's appearing makes that place the house of God, and renders it far more delightful than all the beautiful and pleasant fruits in the world possibly can do. Thus you see what both places were; but now they are strictly charged not to go thither. The reason of the change of the name from Beth-el to Beth-aven I shall show you presently, in explaining why they must not come to Gilgal nor to Beth-aven.

Now the reason why they must not come thither was this, because though they were such famous places before for God's true worship, yet now they were become the chiefest places for idolatry in the whole land, therefore there is a charge here not to come to Gilgal nor to Beth-aven. So in Amos v. 5, you have the like charge almost in the same words, "Seek not Beth-el, nor enter into Gilgal;" there it is called Beth-el: Though (saith God) it takes the name from my house, and there was once a glorious manifestation of mine there, yet now do not seek to Beth-el, do not so much as enter into Gilgal.

That both these places were now very corrupt by idolatry, I will make apparent. As I have showed you how famous these places were before, so I will show you how corrupt they afterward became. As to Gilgal, it appears plainly in Hos. ix. 15, "All their iniquity is in Gilgal," above all places there is the greatest iniquity committed; and "there I hated them." It was the place where God loved his people and manifested himself to them, but now, "there I hated them," I saw so much wickedness therein. And this corruption was of early date, for in Ehud's time, the third judge from Joshua, idols were then begun to be set up in Gilgal: thus Judg. iii. 19 saith, that Ehud "turned again from the quarries that were by Gilgal;" now פסילים translated "quarries," some render idols, "from the idols;" it signifies also to engrave, he came from the engravings. There were idols at Gilgal then. And the reason of this corruption there was, that Gilgal had been an eminent place, and accounted very holy, because of the great things that had been done there; upon which they set up their images in it, and regarded the place with much superstitious respect and honour. Their respect to the place arose from God's often appearing there, and the great things that had been done in it, and now they began to think the place essentially holy, and so abused it. Hence,

Obs. 6. Men are prone to abuse places, esteeming them holy, because of some special things done in them. We see papists do so at this time, regarding the sepulchre of Christ; oh what a deal of stir was there about going to visit it! And the very cross whereon Christ was crucified, what a stir was there about that! as if it were more holy than any other piece of wood; one chip of it was counted worth I know not how much. And the sepulchres of the martyrs and cells of the monks, men have gone many a sore journey to visit. This is the same will-worship as existed amongst the people of the Jews. Whereas, the truth is, that it is not the place that can sanctify a work, except it be appointed thereunto by God's institution; but if there be any sanctity in a place, it is sanctified by the work, and not the work by the place; and if the work do sanctify it, it is but for the present, during the performance of the holy duties. We may say this is the house of God, where the congregation meet for performance of holy duties, but it is so only in regard of the work; when the work is done there remains no impression of holiness on the place, as if God's worship in any other place were not as acceptable. This was the vain opinion of the Jews, they therefore abused Gilgal because such great things had been done there, and God so much the more hated it; I charge you, saith he, come not to Gilgal, that superstitious place. They thought, because it was a place eminent for many manifestations of God, it was therefore the more holy; I do therefore abhor it, saith God.

The reason why they must not come to Beth-aven appears from the change of the name; it was once Beth-el, and now it is Beth-aven, and the difference betwixt these two names, Beth-el and Beth-aven, is wide and great; Beth-el is the house of God, and Beth-aven is the house of iniquity, the house of vanity, the house of labour, and the house of affliction, for it signifies all these. That which was my house, which I did once own, being corrupted, is no other but the house of iniquity and vanity, and the house that brings affliction. Beth-aven was one of the places where Jeroboam set up one of his calves, and in this he took advantage of the opinion that the people entertained of the holiness of that place, thinking thereby to prevail with the people so much the more: now God charges them that they should not come thither. There was indeed another town, as in Josh. vii., called Beth-aven, but generally that by interpreters is understood as different from Beth-el; but this town here is no other than that Beth-el of which we have such frequent mention in the Scripture. Some, as Aquila and Symmachus, render the word Beth-aven, *Domus inutilis*, an unprofitable place, for indeed sin and idolatry make places unprofitable. Whence,

Obs. 7. We must not approach places calculated to draw us into sin, especially to false worship. Places dangerous for bodily pollution we must shun. Prov. v. 8, "Remove thy way far from her, and come not nigh the door of her house." Do not come so much as nigh her door. Say not, Why may not I go such a way? may not I go by her house? No, you must not go by her house, nor by that way that leads to her house. This is a strange admonition, you will say. Mark the words that precede it, in the 7th verse, "Hear me now therefore, O ye children, and depart not from the words of my mouth." What are the words of his mouth? "Remove thy way far from her, and come not nigh the door of her house." Thus wisdom herself counsels us. Many, however, think they may allow themselves to come near a temptation, near to such a place, and many have come so near that they have fallen into the pit. As sometimes in your houses, when you light a candle, you see moths and flies that will flutter up and down the light, and at first they will keep at some distance, and then approach nearer, till at length they singe their wings and perish: so it is with many; at first they think they will not do such a thing, Oh! God forbid they should do so and so; but they will come nigh a temptation, and be tampering with it, till at length they are insnared by it and destroyed. It is dangerous to indulge our curiosity in visiting places of idolatry, and going to see mass, and the fashions of superstitious countries. Dinah went thus abroad, but she came home dishonoured: so there are many that *will* go abroad to see the fashions of countries out of mere curiosity, (I speak not of going when God calls us to it,) it is just in God that they should come home maimed and despoiled. In the Lord's prayer we pray that God would not lead us into temptation. How do men mock God when they pray to God daily, "Lead us not into temptation;" yet will venture on temptations, frequent haunts of impurity, and go to many places where they know there will be wicked company; yea, even thrust themselves into it needlessly, with this pretence alone, they will take heed to themselves, and they mean no hurt! When you are tempted to go to places of sin, to theatres, and scenes of vice, satisfy not yourselves with this plea, I mean no hurt: have you any call from God for this? can you approve it before God, and say, Lord, thou hast called me hither? I suppose you have heard of that story that Tertullian has of a Christian woman, who being at a play became possessed of a devil; and other Christians coming to cast him out, asked the evil spirit how he durst possess one that was a Christian? he answered, I found her in my own place: so if we would take heed of the devil, let us take heed of wicked places.

Obs. 8. Places corrupted lose their honour. Rome formerly was a famous church, as in Rom. i. we find that the faith of Rome was spread abroad throughout the world; and so they will yet plead for the glory of Rome, because once it was famous. But it is no matter what it has been, what is it now? suppose it has been the seat of Peter, what is it now? If once they are corrupt in themselves, they lose the honour of what once they had. Oh let us take heed to ourselves also in this. True, England has also been a place renowned for religion, and travellers that have come hither have blessed themselves, and blessed God for seeing what they have seen, they never saw so much of God as in England: but if we shall corrupt our ways and become idolatrous and superstitious, we may, by God's just judgment, be made as infamous and vile as any people on the face of the earth. And so of particular persons, that heretofore have had much honour among the saints, men of admirable parts and very useful to the church, it may be, temptation prevails so much with them, tells them, You have had such a name, you have done such and such things, and now may be quiet, you cannot but be esteemed for what you have done. But let a man in his younger days or afterward act never so worthily in the church of God, or commonwealth, if he decline afterward he loses all his honour, both with God and men, and may be as unsavoury salt, spurned out and trodden under foot of men; as Gilgal and Beth-aven, though honoured before, yet now the people are charged not to come to them. One would have blest himself to be in the company and families of some men; but now they are grown so sapless in their spirits, so carnal, so malignant, superstitious, and vain, that it is dangerous now to associate with them; we may even hear a voice from God calling to us, Go not into such a man's company, as here, Go not to Gilgal. Thus you have the mind of God in these words opened to you, "Come not ye unto Gilgal, neither go ye up to Beth-aven." There follows,

"Nor swear, The Lord liveth." Swearing in itself is lawful, yea, it is a part of the solemn worship of God, when God requires it; and it constitutes such a part of God's solemn worship, as that sometimes it is put in Scripture for the whole worship of God, Psal. lxiii. 12; Isa. xix. 18. Therefore oaths are to be esteemed so much the more sacred: for as God puts such an honour on prayer, that sometimes the whole worship of God is called prayer, "He that calleth on the name of the Lord shall be saved;" "My house shall be called the house of prayer." So God honours oaths, that all his worship has sometimes the name of an oath. Therefore the abuse of oaths is the more vile; and when swearing is requisite, it should only be by the name of the Lord; we should swear by the Lord when it is lawful to swear, and in no other way, for by this we acknowledge the Lord to be the searcher and judge of all hearts, the all-seeing God, fit to witness to all men's ways, and to be an avenger of all their unfaithfulness. And here is the reason that we must swear by none but by God, because in swearing (I say) we acknowledge him we swear by to be the searcher of our hearts, the witness of all our secrets, and the supreme judge if we be unfaithful: now this honour, whether secret or open, is only due to God. God esteems it highly, and will not give it to another. And when we do swear by his name, the life of God is the greatest title we can give him. It is the greatest oath of all; God himself doth often swear by his life; and the angel, by the living God. God loves that his creature should acknowledge him to be the living God for ever, that is, living to reward that which is good, and to revenge that which is evil. And therefore, Jer. iv. 2, there is an injunction, "Thou shalt swear, The Lord liveth," but it must be "in truth, in righteousness, and in judgment." And indeed it is God's mercy to us, that he will grant us the use of his name, that he is willing to be called to witness to our affairs.

But then you will say, Why doth God forbid it? In that place of Jeremiah you see it is, "Thou shalt swear, The Lord liveth;" and here, "nor swear, The Lord liveth." How shall we reconcile these? Thus; that God would not have his name and this his solemn worship abused by idolaters. When they were before their idols, yet still they would make use of God's name, and would seem to honour him; Oh, Jehovah liveth, we acknowledge him, and honour him as a living God. This was the vain show of those idolaters, who, though they forsook the true worship and commandments of God, yet would seem to revere him much; "The Lord liveth," and we desire to honour this living God. Now, saith God, why do you pursue such idolatry as this, and take my name into your mouths? what have you to do to take my name into your mouths, seeing you hate to be reformed? I will have none of this honour from you, saith God, you shall not swear any more, "The Lord liveth." Many superstitious persons will make much use of the titles of God, and employ many expressions that carry a great air of devotion; they will cry out, Our blessed Saviour, Our Lord and Saviour, and, The blessed God; but God cares for none of these, while they worship him according to the traditions of men, after their own inventions: God cares not for all the seeming honour they render him, for all their lip service; let them appear to men to be never so devout, God rejects those devotions, when they reject his pure and sincere worship. God loves not to have his worship mixed. In Zeph. i. 5, God charges them with swearing by the Lord and by Malcham; what is the meaning of that? Malcham there signifies a king, for such is the meaning of the Hebrew; and it seems, that though it is true they would sometimes call their idols by the name of king, *Honoris gratia*, by way of respect, yet that in this place more is intended, namely, that they would worship God and worship their king too, they would swear by God and by Malcham, they made the honour paid to their king come too near the honour rendered to God; this seems here to be specially intended. It is true, both are to be honoured, but one is to be honoured more than the other, and the true distance between them is duly to be observed; we must not swear by God and swear by Malcham, much less prefer the will of our Malcham, our king, before the will of our God. God cares not for any honour given to him in common with others. It is true indeed, God rejects not the worship of his saints because of some mixtures of evil, for there are none that worship him so as not to mix some sin with it; but such as choose to themselves some way of sin, that set it up in their hearts and lives, and then think it sufficient to yield God some outward service, and expect to put him off with that, while at other times they follow their own lusts, such worship God rejects: therefore saith the Lord here to these idolaters, "You shall not swear, The Lord liveth."

Ver. 16. *For Israel slideth back as a backsliding heifer: now the Lord will feed them as a lamb in a large place.*

Here, first, Israel, the ten tribes, is compared to a heifer, and to "a backsliding heifer." A heifer, that noted the wantonness of Israel. And here is one argument why Judah must not offend as Israel doth; Let not Judah offend as Israel doth, for Israel is a backsliding heifer: Israel, through his sin, has brought himself to be a vile, wanton heifer; but the emblem of Judah is to be a lion: Gen. xlix. 9, "Judah is a lion's whelp: from the prey, my son, thou art gone up: he stooped down, he couched as a lion, and as an old lion; who shall rouse him up?" Judah should not refuse the yoke through wantonness and perverseness, but through a magnanimous spirit, he should not be willing to be brought under the yoke of bondage. Israel is as a heifer, that through wantonness refuses to be brought under the yoke; but let not Judah do thus, for Judah is as a lion: and although Judah be a lion, yet he should come under God's command, and be subject to him; but when it comes to be in bondage to men, and that in matters of religion, Judah should have a magnanimous, lion-like spirit, and cast off the yoke: Let not Judah be like Israel; Judah is as a lion, Israel as a heifer.

And the word סררה which is translated backsliding, cometh of סרר signifying perverseness, as well as backsliding. It is translated in Scripture, stubbornness, rebellion, as in Deuteronomy, about the stubborn and rebellious child; and many other scriptures might be shown how this word is understood otherwise than here. Israel is a stubborn, a rebellious, a perverse people, therefore let not Judah be so. And I find the Seventy translate it thus, *δαμάλις παροιςρῶσα*, that is, Israel, the ten tribes, were a stung bullock, *Juvenca œstro percita*, as if by a kind of witchery, or by the bite of some venomous thing, they had been excited to fury or madness: such is the force of the word, according to their translation. There is a great deal of difference between the wantonness of a beast, and a beast that runs up and down in a fury and madness, as being bit with a mad dog. Thus this people was. Ephraim goes on madly: as many wicked men go on in ways apparently against light and conscience, and against the word, though they know it will prove to be their eternal ruin and destruction; conscience tells them so, yet they go violently on, in a madness and rage, even down to the pit. This was Ephraim's condition here.

And that which made Ephraim do so, was his prosperity. Ephraim was grown prosperous, and had plenty of food, was fed full and large, and that made them go on madly in the ways of wickedness and sin. That was now fulfilled of Ephraim which was prophesied of him, Deut. xxxii. 15, "Thou art waxen fat, thou art grown thick, thou art covered with fatness; then he forsook God which made him, and lightly esteemed the Rock of his salvation." Oh, when a people is waxen fat and grown prosperous, then they kick and spurn, and forsake God that made them, and lightly esteem the Rock of their salvation; God and his truth, his saints and his ordinances, are nothing to them, they lightly esteem them; why? because they are waxen fat, they are in their prosperity. Many men on their sick beds highly esteem the ministers of God, and his word and worship, and exclaim then, Oh send for such and such to come to us: but when they are in prosperity, all these are forgotten. This was the condition of Ephraim. Where have you a man almost, but grows wanton in prosperity, except God comes in with abundance of his grace? Judah was almost in the same state; though here the Lord would not have Judah to be like Ephraim, as a wanton heifer, spurning and kicking with the heel, yet it appears in Jer. ii. 24, that Judah was not much dissimilar: Judah is there compared to "a wild ass used to the wilderness, that snuffeth up the wind at her pleasure; in her occasion who can turn her away? all they that seek her will not weary themselves," to take her when she is full of spirit and strength, and there is no dealing with her; but, saith God, "in her month they shall find her," when she is more weakened, then "they shall find her:" so many men; take them when swollen with pride and prosperity, and there is no dealing with them; but when God has tamed them by affliction, then you may talk with them, and then they will hear you.

But further, the word translated "heifer" here, is in the feminine gender, though spoken of the ten tribes, because, being stubborn and raging mad in wickedness, though they seemed to themselves and others to be full of fiery courage, yet the Lord looks upon them as people base and effeminate, poor and weak. The stubborn and proud always think themselves to possess more than ordinary courage, they are the only brave spirits; but the Lord regards them as base and weak, and therefore speaks of them here in the feminine gender.

"Now the Lord will feed them as a lamb in a large place." Mercer and Vatablus would thus interpret this: *Lautè ut agnus pastus, mox mactatur*, As a lamb when it hath large food, it is soon slain; so God threatens Ephraim here, that he will soon make an end of them, only he will let them prosper for a while, and feed them largely, but it shall be for the slaughter. Many men that are fed largely, and are in prosperity, think themselves blessed, but God intends them only for the slaughter; I think, however, that is not the meaning of the place, "they shall be fed as a lamb." But thus,

"As a lamb." They are as a heifer, raging mad, but I will make them as a lamb, I will bring such affliction upon them, that I will tame the pride of their hearts. Have you not seen instances of this kind? did you never see a blasphemous, proud, stubborn spirit, when the hand of God was upon them, tamed?

Fed as a lamb. *Parce ac tenuiter*, not fed as a heifer, that denoted their prosperity; but fed as a lamb, that notes their adversity; for the food of a lamb differs from the food of a heifer, that which will feed a lamb will starve a heifer. They have been proud and wanton, saith God, by their prosperity, but now they shall have spare fare, I will bring them down, I will lay them low, they shall be but as a lamb that picks up the grass in the wilderness.

"As a lamb in a large place." That is, dispersed among the countries, amongst the Assyrians and Medes in their captivity, who occupied a very large country. They would not be satisfied with Canaan, and with that sheep-fold of mine that was there; they shall have more room, saith God, they shall go into a large place, but it shall be a place of captivity.

Or rather, which I conceive to be the full scope of the passage, "I will feed them as a lamb in a large place;" that is, as a lamb that shall be alone; one lamb, he speaks of them singly, because they shall be scattered. They had society, and might have made good use of it, but they cared not to avail themselves of it, to edify each other in the fear of God, therefore they shall be scatttered, one in one place, and another in another, and they shall be as a lamb alone in the wilderness, succourless, helpless, surrounded by dangers, and with no eye near to pity, no hand to help it. What will become, think you, of this lamb? what an unfriended condition is it in! So, saith God, they have been wanton heifers, but I will "feed them as a lamb in a large place;" they shall be carried into captivity, and there they shall be lamenting and mourning, and in danger of wolves, but there shall be none to regard, and none to succour them. It is a great deal safer for a lamb to be in the flock, though it be more confined, than to be thus alone in a large place. Hence,

Obs. 1. Liberty may prove to be one's misery. To keep within the compass of God's commands is the best liberty of all; as David professes, Psal. cxix., Then shall I have liberty, when I keep all thy commandments. As for all other liberty, it will certainly bring us into straitness; therefore, Rom. ii. 9, where "tribulation and anguish" is threatened to be upon the head of every one that worketh wickedness, the word translated "anguish" signifies straitness of place, they shall have straitness of place: You would be at large, and would fain get out of God's limits: though God may for a time let you have such liberty, yet the conclusion will be anguish of spirit. O my brethren, there is largeness, there is room enough in God, in him our souls may expatiate, we need go no further for liberty. If we would have liberty out of God, and out of his bounds, our liberty will prove our undoing. Let us then value highly the society of the saints while we are not yet, through God's mercy, scattered up and down in other countries, as some of our brethren have been, though, through his mercy, some even there have met with and been kept in his own fold; but others have wandered to and fro, and have had none to help them in any strait. Our condition is not yet such; but we may meet together, we may be in God's fold and have our hearts refreshed, we may go into our families and pray together, and sing together. Let us then bless God that this judgment denounced against Israel, that they should be "as a lamb in a large place," bleating up and down and none to regard them, has not befallen us; let us, I say, bless God for this his forbearance and long-suffering.

Ver. 17. *Ephraim is joined to idols: let him alone.*

You have heard before, that God warns Judah to take heed of the sins of the ten tribes of Israel; and many arguments are used; some you have heard, others remain.

This 17th verse contains two principal points.

I. Ephraim engaging himself in false worship, is now so inwrapped in that sin and guilt that he cannot tell how to extricate himself; "Ephraim is joined to idols:" as it is usual with idolaters, and the effect of the curse of God upon them, that when they are once engaged in that sin, it is very hard ever to recover them out of it; so, Judah, take heed that you come not into it.

II. The Lord has given him up to his idols. The curse of God rests on him, and saith, "Let him alone." O Judah, take heed then what you do. These words are thus introduced as a twofold argument to persuade Judah not to do as Israel has done, and indeed all the remainder of this chapter has the same tendency. To speak then of these:

I. "Ephraim is joined to idols." Why Ephraim? Ephraim was dead long ago. He was the child of a patriarch, and the grandchild of Jacob, from whom he received a great blessing; Gen. xlviii. 20, "In thee shall Israel bless, saying, God make thee as Ephraim;" intimating that such special blessings would rest on him that the tribes should say, "God make thee as Ephraim;" and yet now it is said, that "Ephraim is joined to idols." Why then Ephraim?

1. The chief of the ten tribes that were now joined to idols, were the children of Ephraim, for Ephraim and Manasseh had received Joseph's inheritance in Israel, and at this time were the chief of the ten tribes. Whence,

Obs. 1. Wicked children are a great dishonour to their parents. Ephraim, who was dead long before, suffers dishonour by his children that are now joined to idols. Let children, out of reverence and respect to their parents, take heed what they do.

2. Jeroboam and the princes were all of the tribe of Ephraim, and therefore all is attributed to them. He does not say the ten tribes are joined to idols, but Ephraim is; because indeed the idolatry of all the other nine tribes sprang from the idolatry of Jeroboam, and the princes that were of the tribe of Ephraim. Whence again,

Obs. 2. Governors are usually the causes of the evils of the people. If governors be superstitious and will favour idolatry, all the people, or the generality of them, will imitate, but they contract all the guilt. Ephraim, Jeroboam and the princes of that tribe, contract all the guilt of the idolatry of all the ten tribes, therefore it is said, Ephraim, as if Ephraim only was joined to idols. Governors therefore that are superstitious and idolatrous, incur woeful guilt, and we have exceeding cause to lament their condition. We read in the second of Matthew, that the wise men who came to inquire after the King of the Jews, came from a far country, and said they had seen his star, and desired to know the place in which he should be born. Herod, and all Jerusalem with him, were troubled what this strange thing should mean, that such wise men should come from so far a country, and tell of a star that had appeared, and of a King of the Jews that should be born; and they called a council of all the chief priests and the scribes, and such as were expert in the law, to know where Christ should be born, and this council pointed out Bethlehem as the place; and upon that, the wise men, according to their direction, or according to the star, proceeded thither: but mark, you do not read of any one of all the people of Jerusalem that went with the wise men; although they were stirred at it, and thought it wonderful that a star should thus appear, and that these wise men should come and inquire for the King of the Jews, and that their own teachers should tell them that he was to be born at Bethlehem, and that thereupon they should go thither to find him, yet (I say) we do not read that any of the people went with them; no, they durst not, because of Herod. He was the prince, and it met not with his approbation, and therefore not one of the people would accompany the wise men to search after Christ. So it usually happens, that when governors discountenance the ways of God, they are followed by the people. And especially governors inclined to superstition and idolatry, and who, together with these, will indulge people in their lusts, they will indeed, as Jeroboam and the rest of the princes did, find followers in abundance. As appeared partly before, and will further appear in this prophecy, this scope and liberty given to their lusts was one special way by which they gained the hearts of the people to them in their false worship. Let any princes and governors set up and countenance any false way of worship, and together with it give liberty to the people for the satisfying of their lusts, and they will gain enow unto them; there is no cause to wonder that such princes should have so many to cleave unto them, seeing the people know that by cleaving unto them they shall have liberty to enjoy their lusts. Whence,

Obs. 3. Idolaters' hearts are strongly attached to their idolatrous ways. "Ephraim is joined to idols." The word is חבור and signifies in the participle, *incantatus*, such a kind of joining as that whereby your enchanters in their conjurations join their unclean spirits to them: so Ephraim is joined to his idols, cleaveth to his idols, or (as some render it) is glued to his idols, and that unclean spirit which carries him on to the ways of idolatry is become incorporated with him. As it is said of believers, that they are joined to the Lord Christ, and so they are one spirit; so idolaters are joined to the devil, and are become as one spirit with him. So Jer. viii. 5, "They hold fast deceit;" they will not easily be taken off. And Jer. ii. 10, 11, "Pass over the isles of Chittim, and see; and send unto Kedar, and consider diligently, and see if there be such a thing. Hath a nation changed their gods, which are yet no gods?" Kedar was one of the vilest places: Woe is me, saith David, that I have my habitation in the tents of Kedar! yet, saith God, go thither, and see whether they have changed their gods. The most vile idolaters will not yet change their gods, their hearts are joined to them; let their hearts be never so base, and their gods never so vile: as the Egyptians would worship leaves, and garlick, and cats, and would listen to no admonitions against their idolatrous ways. I have read, too, of a people in India, in the isle Zolon, that worshipped an ape's tooth; and when it was taken from them, they offered an inconceivable sum of treasure to regain that their idol again: so attached are idolaters to "their gods, which are yet no gods." And especially if they have outward prosperity, to be as the glue and cement to join their hearts to their false worship, then they are joined indeed. If men that are superstitious prosper in their ways, this, their prosperity, is the glue and cement to join their hearts strongly to those ways, there is no alienating them from them. And long continuance in false worship makes them not like it a whit the worse. I beseech you, observe this, that antiquity will make false worship venerable, and they will plead for it on account of its antiquity, and say, it is thus and thus ancient, and was the religion of their forefathers. Of the true worship of God men are quickly weary, and because they have had it a great while they desire some change, some novelty. Many people are much affected with the truth when first revealed to them, and their hearts are much taken with sermons, but within a while they loathe and forsake this manna. Such is the wickedness of the hearts of men.

But will idolaters thus adhere to their idols? will their hearts be united to them? are they willing to be one spirit with them? oh how much more should we join to the Lord our God, join to Jesus Christ, to be as one spirit with him! That exhortation of Barnabas, Acts xi. 23, that with full "purpose of heart they should cleave unto the Lord," is seasonable even at all times. O let us cleave to God and his worship, so that whatever arguments are used, yet our hearts may never be taken off from the love of the truth; but let us say as once that martyr did, Though you may pluck my heart out of my bowels, yet you shall never pluck the truth out of my heart. And the less there is between God and our hearts, the more firmly shall we be joined to him. The godly and gracious need not the cement of outward prosperity to join their hearts to God, the very sweetness that they find in God alone is enough to unite their hearts to him, even in an everlasting covenant. Those who seem to be joined to God and his worship, yet if united merely by the cement of outward respects, they will quickly fall off; but those that are immediately joined to God will for ever keep to him, when there is nothing but God and their hearts together, nothing between God and them.

"Ephraim is joined to idols." The word עצבים translated idols, is by some rendered, and justly, *dolore afficere*, pains or troubles. For this latter signification there are two reasons.

1. Because that idolaters were willing to endure much pain and trouble in the worshipping of their idols; which should teach us not to account the worship of God tedious, though it be somewhat hard to the flesh.

2. Such worship will bring pain and trouble to them in the end.

This however is not the principal thing intended here, but the force of the argument is, "Ephraim is joined to idols," therefore meddle not with him, do not you do as they do. So that when we see people set up false ways of worship in any place, and they are resolute for them, we must take heed of communicating with them in these their idolatries; but to enter on this would occupy too much time.

II. The Lord has given him up to his idols.

"Let him alone;" *Demitte eum*, Let him go, saith God, he is joined to his idols, let him go. This admits of three expositions.

1. As addressed to Judah. Let Ephraim go, saith God to Judah. Ephraim, they indeed are the ten tribes, the greater part of the Jews, but yet seeing they set up false worship, let them go, have nothing to do with them, do not converse with them. Here,

Obs. 4. It is a heavy judgment of God upon a people when the saints withdraw from them. If God had any saints in the world they were in Judah, and saith God to these saints of his, Let Israel alone and withdraw from them, have nothing to do with them, though they be your brethren and countrymen, yet, let them alone. Many wicked men make nothing of this, and when the most strict, and holy, and gracious people of God withdraw from them, and, as heretofore, forsake the land because they see it so defiled with superstitious vanities, they say, Let them all go, we are well rid of them: and who knows but you may be thus spoken of before you die? that you may have many that will be willing to be rid of those that are most godly and gracious? Well, whatever men think and say, let them know it is a dreadful curse of God on a nation, for the saints of God to withdraw and go from them; for such is the import of God's command here, Judah, let them alone, have nothing to do with them: so when God commands his saints to withdraw from others of their brethren, it is one of his most dreadful judgments on a people, whatever they think of it. You know that expression, conveying the most fearful curse of God on the wicked, which you have, 1 Cor. xvi. 22, "If any man love not the Lord Jesus Christ, let him be Anathema Maran-atha." "Anathema," let him be accursed; but the meaning of "Maran-atha" is, the Lord cometh: *Maran* signifies the Lord, in the Chaldee and Syriac; and is so used by Daniel, who lived in Chaldea. Thus Dan. iv. 19; v. 23, "My lord, the dream be to them that hate thee," and, "Thou hast lifted up thyself against the Lord of heaven;" the word מרא whence *Maran* in the Syriac, is there translated Lord; and *atha* signifies to come; as in Deut. xxxiii. 2, The Lord *cometh* with thousands of his saints, the word in the original is אתה so that you have in Scripture these two words *Maran* and *atha*. What then is the meaning of that, "Let him be Anathema Maran-atha?" This simply; when men shall forsake Christ and the ways of his worship, after means have been used with them, then "Anathema Maran-atha," that is, let all the saints of God leave them to the coming of Jesus Christ; let them alone, do not meddle with them; when you have used all means you can, then withdraw yourselves from them, and leave them to the coming of Christ, and Christ will deal with them: let them not only be excommunicated, but so excommunicated that they be let alone to the coming of Christ. So when the godly shall first labour by admonition, and persuasion, and counsel, with the ungodly and sinners, and they shall be refractory, and stout, and stubborn, and be as swine to trample under feet those pearls, or as dogs to turn again and rend them, they are then to let them alone, that is, to let them alone to the coming of Jesus Christ; and even in their own hearts say, Well, we see no means can do them any good, "Maran-atha," the Lord cometh, and he shall deal with them himself when he cometh.

2. The Lord speaks here to the prophet, as if he should say, Hosea, you can do no good to them, it is in vain for you to meddle with Ephraim. Just as Christ directed his disciples when he sent them forth to preach the gospel, that if any place rejected them, they should go away and shake the dust off their feet, as a testimony against them; so saith God here to the prophet, Let them alone, spend not your strength any more upon them. The exhortations which come from the saints, but especially from sincere ministers of the gospel, be they what they may, are pearls and precious things, and God will not have them despised, he will not have them spent in vain; therefore there is a time even for the ministers of God to let people alone. In Exod. xxxiii. 7, we read, that when the people had notoriously sinned against God, Moses took the tabernacle of the congregation, and pitched it without the camp, and went away from the people, and would not come amongst them, till they repented: so there is a time even for the ministers of God to hold their peace and let people alone. Many think they are troubled with ministers, and they could wish they would let them alone; Why do they trouble us? we were quiet enough before they came; we would they would let us alone. And there are many guilty consciences, that cannot come to a powerful ministry but they find that the minister has in every sermon to do with them, and that he will not let them alone in their wickedness, and this troubles them, and they had rather be let alone. Had you so? It is one of the most dreadful judgments in the world for God to say, Let such a ministry let a man alone. It may be, some of you may be weary of the faithful ministers of God; you may get rid of them perhaps, God may take them away, and you may be let alone; but yet know, in this rests on you the brand of God's wrath.

3. It shows that God himself would let them alone too, it is an evidence of his rejection of this people. It is as if a father, that had used means to reclaim a rebellious child, would at length, when he disregarded all his admonitions, exclaim, Let him alone. What do you think would the father mean? it is as if he should say, I have done with him, I will own him no more, I will meddle no more with him. If a servant should be stubborn and rebellious, and all the many means used to reclaim him should fail; the master saith, Let him alone, let him take his own course, I will have no more to do with him. So here, when God saith, Let them alone, it is as if he should say, Let them take their own ways, let them have their lusts to the full, let them join themselves to their idols, and satisfy themselves with their own devices, let them alone. Hence arise two profitable observations.

Obs. 5. God has a time to give men over to themselves, to say that his Spirit shall no longer strive with them. Oh, many a man has felt the Spirit of God working, struggling, striving with him to draw him from such and such wickedness; he has felt (I say) God's Spirit mighty and strong, pleading, Will you still go on in this way of wickedness, uncleanness, drunkenness, oppression, injustice, profanation, hypocrisy, self-seeking, and the like? but he has been striving against, and his lusts have even gotten the victory over, the Spirit, so that God saith, "My Spirit shall no longer strive," I will not struggle in vain, but let him go on and be filled with his own devices. Oh, it is dreadful when the Lord saith of a drunkard, of an unclean person, of a hypocrite, I have been struggling so long with them, but yet their hearts have been opposed to me; let them alone, let them go on and satisfy themselves in their iniquities. Psal. lxxxi. 11, 12, They "would none of me," saith God, they would none of my ways, "so I gave them up to their own counsels." Oh, this is a dreadful gift! Many men will set their counsels against God's counsels, and will do it so long, that God at length gives them up to their own counsels: You will set your thoughts against my truth, your counsels against mine; well, take your own counsels, satisfy yourselves in your own ways. And you know that place in the latter end of the Revelation, "He which is filthy, let him be filthy still." Let him alone, saith God: will you be filthy? be filthy then. And that in Ezek. xxiv. 13, "Because I have purged thee, and thou wast not purged, thou shalt not be purged from thy filthiness any more." I will let them alone, saith the Lord, I will never seek, either by my word, or by my works, to do them any further good, they shall be purged no more. And the reasons are,

1. Because God has no need of men. God does this to show that he has no need of you. Indeed he seeks by his word to draw you to obedience to his service, and you stand off, and draw from him, and will not come in: at length God will manifest that he has no need of your service, he can honour himself without you, though you perish everlastingly.

2. He knows how to fetch out glory to his own name from their sins. You will continue in your wicked

ways, you will be stubborn and stout, saith God; do you think so to hinder me of my glory? well, take your fill of your lusts, I know how to glorify myself out of that sin whereby you offend so much against my glory, therefore be ye filled with your own devices.

Obs. 6. It is the most woeful judgment of God upon any people, or person, when he saith in his wrath, "Let him alone." The words are הנח־לו and is equivalent to, Let him be quiet: that quiet will prove a dreadful storm. You know what the wise man saith, "Woe to him that is alone!" Oh, woe to him, of whom God saith, "Let him alone," that is thus alone! Many men bless themselves when they are let alone, and desire it; Let us alone, say they. Oh, but when God shall say, Let them alone, this is a most dreadful thing indeed. It proved to be a fearful evil to Adam in Paradise, when God let him alone: when he left Adam to himself what became of him? As far as he could, he undid himself and all his posterity, when left to his natural abilities. Yea, and when God but leaves his own saints, that have grace in them, for a little while to themselves, oh what mischief ensues! As in 2 Chron. xxxii. 31, when God did but for a little leave Hezekiah to himself, to try what was in his heart, what a deal of misery did he bring on himself! What! do such evil consequences attend on Adam left alone in Paradise, and the saints left alone here? oh what a dreadful thing must it be, then, when God shall leave a sinner alone! I mean one that has nothing else but sin in him, one wholly destitute of grace. This is a most grievous judgment for many reasons.

1. It is a testimony of very great disregard in God for his creatures, in this, that he accounts them not worthy of any further meddling with, he loves them not so well as to interpose any further on their account; it is a sign, I say, of great disregard on the part of God for them; it is as if he should say, There are others indeed that are wicked, that are very great sinners; but I have mercy for them, I intend to draw them to myself, I intend to show them the evil of their ways, and to turn them to me that they may be saved; but as for these, I have nothing to do with them, saith God, I have no mercy for them, let them alone.

2. Because those let alone are going apace to misery. To let a man alone when he is at home in his house and all things convenient about him, matters not; but if you were to see one madly rushing to water, or into fire, to destroy himself, no one then would hesitate to interpose; to let him alone were a great judgment. But now the Lord sees sinners running headlong into misery, into the bottomless pit, and even then God saith, Let them alone.

3. They were in the midst of abundance of dangers. When a man is in safety among his friends, and you let him alone, it matters not; but suppose you knew of one environed with adversaries, or around whom were wild beasts ready to devour, and this message were brought to you, Oh there is such a friend of ours in great danger, and you should say, What if he be, let him alone, let him shift as well as he can; it would be a grievous judgment: yet all sinners that are going on in their evil ways are in woeful danger on every hand, and the Lord sees and takes notice that they are in the midst of dangers, yet saith God, Let them alone, they shall not have my protection and help. And this is a just punishment of God on sinners that will go on in their wickedness.

4. God intends by this to make way for some fearful wrath that is to come upon them. Let my mercy and goodness let them alone, but it is that they may fall into my wrath; and that will not let them alone, that will trouble them. They cannot endure to be troubled by my word, by my messengers, by my Spirit; but my wrath shall trouble them afterward, that shall not let them alone: as in that place of Ezekiel before quoted, "Thou shalt not be purged from thy filthiness any more, till I have caused my fury to rest upon thee," chap. xxiv. 13; they shall have no outward means to trouble them for a while, but at length my fury shall rest upon them. When the Lord seems to be quiet toward men and lets them alone, it is but to make way for fearful wrath that is coming upon them.

5. God will not, after the infliction of this judgment, vouchsafe to hear them speak unto him any more. If once the Lord shall say, They would not hear me, they shall never hear me more, let them alone; God will then likewise say, I will not hear them; let them cry in the anguish of their spirits, I will let them alone. It seems evident, that when God shall let sinners alone with respect to his mercy, when the greatest wrath shall be upon them he will let them alone also. As thus; when they shall come into the greatest afflictions, the most dreadful miseries and torments in this world and eternally in the world to come, when they shall then be crying out in the anguish of their spirits unto God, Oh that God would now have mercy upon us! God will let them even then alone: I will bring them into the fire, saith God, and then I will leave them there. Oh think of this, when you feel that there was a time when God was stirring and striving with your hearts, and implore of him to recover you out of the snares of the devil.

6. It is a dreadful sign of reprobation: and we shall briefly consider what reprobation is, and in what respect this is a sign of it.

1. What is reprobation? Reprobation certainly means not that God decrees to damn men, that is not the first act of God upon any man; but that God decrees, whereas there are some that he has set his heart upon, is resolved to do them good, there are others, whom he does not presently decree to damn, but he determines to leave to themselves, that what they *earn* they may have, and no more; he will deal with them according to their works; he will do them no wrong, will not be unjust to them, he will not condemn them but for their sin: he never decrees to damn any but for sin; but he decrees this, I will give them what is fit for them to have in creation, I will make such a covenant with them, and then I will leave them to themselves, and in course of justice, what they work for, that they shall have. For God to decree to leave a man to himself when he had no sin in him, as God did not make man with sin at first, were an act of reprobation: suppose you were now made according to the image of God, without sin, yet if God should decree to leave you fully and eternally to yourself, you were but a reprobate: but there is a second and more dreadful reprobation, when God sees a man in the gall of bitterness and in the bond of iniquity, and leaves him to himself.

2. Wherein the reprobation here consists. That God now doth manifest that he intends to fetch his glory from this sinner out of his ruin. Certainly God will have glory from every creature; however they may resist, God will have it, he will fetch it out from you. God would have his glory from his creature in the ways of obedience and service; but they deny him this, they will not give him this glory, they will have their own will, and set up themselves in God's throne. Well, saith God, I have used such and such means to draw their hearts from those ways to myself, but they stand out, let them be now: as if he should say, I have thought now of another way to fetch out my glory from them. As he in the Gospel reasoned, when he could not provide for himself one way, I know what I will do, saith he: so saith God, I am denied my glory one way, I will adopt other means, that is, I will glorify

my infinite justice and the power of my infinite wrath; they have refused to give me glory by obedience and submission to me, I will not have my glory that way, but now I will rather choose to have my glory from them in their everlasting misery; they shall be spectacles of my wrath and justice, and it shall be known to angels and men to all eternity, what my infinite justice and power is able to do; therefore let them alone, saith God.

7. It is greater than all earthly judgments. Too many of you are afraid of sickness, of being spoiled of your goods, afraid that God should let the enemy in upon you, and all should be taken from you; and this were a great judgment, but the judgment in the text is far greater. If you were stripped of all the comforts in the world, and brought into the most miserable condition with respect to outward circumstances, yet you were not under such a dreadful judgment as this, for God to say, Let them alone. Better any judgments than spiritual judgments. As the spiritual blessings of God bestowed on the saints are the greatest blessings, "Blessed be the God and Father of our Lord Jesus Christ, who hath blessed us with all spiritual blessings in heavenly places in Christ," Eph. i. 3: so the spiritual judgments of God are his most dreadful judgments on the children of men. Oh that we could have our hearts possessed with a fear of those spiritual judgments more than all the judgments in the world!

8. It is worse than to be given up to the devil. If God should give up any man to the devil, and say, Take him, possess him, (as once he possessed many in Christ's time,) it were not such a fearful judgment as this, to say, Let lusts take him and rule him, let him be given up to his own heart's lusts, let him alone to them. And this is apparent from that place where the apostle directs the incestuous person to be given over to Satan, for the destruction of the flesh, that his soul might be saved: when one is given up to the devil in excommunication, or any other way, it may prove the salvation of his soul; but this judgment of God, saying, Let a man alone, is for the destruction of his soul, not of the flesh; it tends directly to the destruction of the soul, though, it may be, in the mean while the flesh may be saved. It is so with many; there are many whom God lets alone, and that proves the destruction of the soul, but perhaps the saving of the flesh: as thus, perhaps many that went on in wickedness, God was chastising and afflicting, and this tended to the destruction of the flesh, though to the saving of their soul; but they would rather live in prosperity and ease, and indulge their sin; Well, saith God, you shall do so, you shall have ease and prosperity, and have your sin; that is, your flesh shall here be saved, but your soul shall eternally be destroyed. Therefore it is worse than to be given up to the devil.

9. It is worse than to be sent down to hell presently; for when one is left alone to himself, he will increase his sin most dreadfully throughout his life-time, and as his sin increases, so his torment: therefore it is a most dreadful thing to be let alone.

10. Though he be without grace, he must answer for it as though he had it; there lies the further evil of it. When God leaves a man alone, he must not think he is not to answer still for the motions of God's Spirit though he has them not, and for the means of grace though he enjoy them not, for he has deprived himself of them; for look, what means of grace we, through sin, have deprived ourselves of, we must answer for them. And there is none of you but may be convinced of this. I will give you a plain instance. Suppose you send your servant to market to buy a commodity, and give him money wherewith he may do it, but he goes into an alehouse or tavern and drinks it away; he cannot bring you what you sent him for, but you may justly require it, and punish him for not doing of it: he may say, Would you have me do that I cannot? I cannot bring it to you without money: yea, but you may reply, I gave you money, it is your fault you have embezzled it. So God may justly require of these men all that they might have done by all the means of grace they should have had: God gave you that means, you have embezzled it by your sin.

11. Now all the means of grace are made unprofitable to him, yea, cursed to him, and they have quite a contrary effect; for the word will work one way or other, either to be the savour of life unto life, or of death unto death; and so the sacrament, either to be the seal of salvation, or the seal of damnation. Now all those means that do other souls good, are to him unprofitable. It may, be the poor child of a wicked parent comes to the word, and there finds God revealing himself to him, and the Spirit of God drawing his heart to himself; but there is his parent, of whom God has said, Let him alone, he sits under the means and gets no good: so perhaps the master is one on whom this judgment is past, Let him alone; and he sits under the means without benefit, whilst his poor servant comes, and his soul is enlightened, his heart is enlarged.

O my brethren, upon this (because the point is of so great consequence I could not pass by it lightly) you may learn from hence,

1. What poor creatures we all are. God need not say, Let my power, and wrath, and justice come upon them, to make them miserable; if God but say, Let them alone, we are presently miserable, we are lost and undone. As in nature, if God should say to any of you as soon as born, Let this creature alone, and let none help him, how miserable were our condition! So with respect to our souls, take one that has the most excellent gifts in all this congregation, yea, take one that has the most excellent graces, if God should but say, Let him alone, he would quickly bring himself to misery. It is through the strength of that grace in the covenant that God will never say to those that are members of his Son, Let them alone for ever.

2. To fear and tremble at this judgment. Especially let them deeply consider this, who have felt the Spirit of God stirring in their hearts, and the word coming to their consciences, yet have gone on, directly against God's word and the motions of his Spirit. Oh that this day the fear of this great God may fall upon them, lest God should say, Let them alone! Perhaps God has not said so yet, but who knows but that upon the next wilful sin thou committest, God may say concerning thee, Let him alone? and then thou art undone for ever. Oh, fear and tremble.

Perhaps some of you may say, God has surely said this of me already, I should not else be so unprofitable under the means, I should not hear such powerful sermons and get so little good, I should not have such and such corruptions prevailing over me; I am afraid this is pronounced already against me.

I am loth when I speak of this dreadful judgment (which is indeed the most dreadful in all the book of God) to let any poor soul go that has need of comfort, without receiving what is due to him.

To answer thee, then:

1. It is a good sign that God has not let thee alone, when thou art troubled with such a fear. Commonly, those whom God has left alone go on and are quiet, and are never troubled about it, but please themselves in their own hearts' lusts.

2. It is a good means to keep thee from being let alone. Those that are afraid lest God should leave them alone, and upon that can say in the uprightness of their hearts, Oh I tremble under this judgment, I had rather God should give me up to all the Cavaliers, to all the devils in hell, than to my own heart's lusts,

it is a sign that this judgment is not upon thee, and it is a means to keep it from thee.

3. If thou hast not a heart to let God alone, God has not a heart to let thee alone. So long as thy heart keeps close to God that thou wilt not let him alone, (you know it is the Scripture phrase, used when Moses was so earnestly seeking God in prayer,) and though thou findest not him coming to thee as thou dost desire, yet thou attendest him in the word, in reading, in meditation, and in all the means thou knowest, and, notwithstanding thou dost not find God, thou art not weary of his service, but art resolved thou wilt not let him alone, and that if thou perish thy last breath will be crying to God; peace be to such a one, God has not let thee alone so long as this frame of heart abides in thee. Those of whom God saith, Let them alone, usually begin to be more sluggish in prayer than before, to discontinue it in their families, in their closets, and then perhaps to raise objections against it, Why, what is there to prove such things must be done? and so by degrees they will come to have no heart for any holy duty; but if thy heart be kept in quickness, and activity, and life, to seek God and to resolve not to let him alone, surely God will not let thee alone. Learn hence,

1. To bless God if thou dost find that he has not inflicted this judgment upon thee. Though perhaps thou hast many outward judgments in the world, it may be some of you are spoiled of all your goods, and have great afflictions on you, yet let this be a means to quiet your hearts, that though God has taken from you many comforts in this world, yet, blessed be his name, he has not left me alone; I yet find his Spirit within me, I find his grace within me, and his word working in my heart: there are many others who have outward comforts, fair houses, great possessions and lands, but the Lord has let them alone; though I have afflictions upon me, yet, blessed be God, he has not inflicted this judgment upon me, he has not let me alone.

2. To bless God that he has not inflicted this judgment on the kingdom. Surely the ways of God toward this land are such that we have reason to hope that God has not pronounced this judgment upon it. God might have said, England "is joined to idols, let him alone." One would have thought that a little more than three years ago we were in a condition fit to be let alone; but since, the Lord has so worked for England that it may appear evidently that God will not let us alone; and blessed be God that he will not, that he will scourge and afflict us sorely, rather than not purge out our idols. And that people, and that soul, which had rather have God purge them soundly than let them go on in any sin, surely God does not let that people and soul alone. It is true, indeed, great chastisements are upon us, but still they all hitherto tend to our purging, not our ruin, and originate in this, that the Lord will not let us alone. It may be, many think it would be better if it were with us now as it was four years since, then we had no such noise and rumours of war, no such spoiling and killing, as now. What, I ask, is their real meaning? It was well with us when we were going on in superstitious and idolatrous ways, going to Rome so fast, that God might have said then, Let England alone: if God had said, Let them go to Rome, let idolatry be set up there, this would have been a greater judgment than all the present bloodshed in England: but in that the Lord is yet striving with us, though we be struggling against him, let us bless his name.

Ver. 18. *Their drink is sour: they have committed whoredom continually: her rulers with shame do love, Give ye.*

"Their drink is sour." I find some interpret this word, as if it noted their excess in drunkenness and luxury, as if they poured down drink till it soured in them, and then vomited it up. Luther translates the words, *fœdè crapulantur*, and on the place observes, Idolaters love to pamper the flesh, they drink even to vomiting again, but for the true worshipping of God, that they curtail in outward things, it is hungry and cold. We find that the false prophets were pampered at Jezebel's table, when poor Micaiah was fain to be fed with the bread and water of affliction. Thus Luther and many others interpret the word. But I think there is more in it.

The word סבאם here translated "drink," refers to their festival meetings, and imports that their feasts and their meetings were as wine that is sour, and has lost its spirit and savour. By "drink," then, we understand their drinkings, that is, the comforts that they have in this world; as your superstitious, idolatrous people always seek to pamper their appetites, and to secure outward comforts: now, saith he, all this is sour. And indeed all the comfort of this world when God is forsaken, it is but as sour drink; the sweetness, and quickness, and life of all is taken away, when God and his worship are forsaken: so you may take their drink, by a synecdoche, for all the comforts of this world, even all those carnal things wherewith they seek to satisfy their flesh, it is all sour, for God is gone when his worship is gone. Perhaps if you had had superstition and idolatry set up amongst you in England, you might have had your drink and wine at your tables more plentifully; but if God and his worship had been gone, all, notwithstanding, had been sour and ungrateful. I appeal to those who have apostatized to enjoy comforts to the flesh, how sour and unsavoury have these proved! whereas let a people keep close to God and his worship, and then their drink, if it be but water, will be sweet to them: as in Acts ii., the saints that believed "did eat their meat with gladness and singleness of heart." We were wont to say, Brown bread and the gospel is good cheer: let us have but bread and water with the gospel and the ordinances and the worship of God, and it will be sweet to us; but let us have wine and all manner of drink at our tables, if we have not the ordinances and worship of God, all will prove sour to us. The ten tribes had as good drink as Judah, yet all the drink of the ten tribes was sour. But further, the meaning may be,

Their society is unsavoury and sour, for so their *convivia*, their meetings together for feasting and drinking, is taken often for closeness of communion, as they were a means to maintain their mutual converse and familiarity: so the meaning is, what relish can any gracious heart take in their converse one with another, when they meet together at one another's tables and drink together? You may observe how unsavoury the superstitious people that have heretofore lived amongst you, have been in their converse; perhaps, before they were forward in the ways of religion, and if then conversed with, there were some life and quickness in them, but when they have once yielded to superstitious vanity, all this is gone. It would have been so with you if these times had not come, you might perhaps have met and caroused together; but the truth is, all your merry meetings would have been sour and sapless, there would have been no sweetness in your converse, and those of your brethren that had been gone from you into the howling wilderness, would have found more savour in the water there, than you could have had in all the drinks your ingenuity could have devised.

"Their drink is sour." That is, all their worship and their sacrifices, for so "their drink" is taken by others, for all their drink-offerings: they were wont to have feasts in their sacrifices, but now, saith God, all their offerings are sour, the savour, and sap, and life of them is gone. These are the four interpretations offered, which may enable us to understand what is meant in these words, "Their drink is sour."

"They have committed whoredom continually." They are unwearied in their wickedness, continually they go on in their whoredom, both bodily, but now especially spiritual; that is, when they are worshipping of their idols they are never weary, "they commit whoredom continually." Oh what a shame it is that the godly should be weary of the service of God, when idolaters are not weary of the service of their idols! What rebuke is this to you who are weary under a sermon, if the glass be but run out a little; but if you were to sit up all night in company, in a tavern, you would not be weary at all! "They commit whoredom continually;" at the service of their idols and the satisfying of their lusts they are never weary, but they are soon weary of my service.

הזנה הזנו

But I think there is somewhat further meant: *fornicantur in fornicando*, in committing fornication they commit fornication, that is the force of the Hebrew; that which they do they do it intensively, in doing they do it. As the apostle saith of Elijah's prayer, James v., In praying he prayed, that is, he prayed intensively, he prayed powerfully, with his whole strength put forth: so the words are here, in committing fornication they committed fornication, that is, they give up their strength to their idols, they are mightily intent on their idols. And therefore have nothing to do with them, (still the argument goes on,) Have nothing to do with them, lest that fearful judgment befall you before spoken of: have nothing to do with them, because their society and converse are unsavoury: have nothing to do with them, because they give up themselves to their lusts. How should we give up ourselves to the service of God, pray in praying, hear in hearing, &c., seeing idolaters are devoted in their service!

"Their rulers." The word translated "rulers" is מגניה their shields, that is, their protectors, so the word in the Hebrew signifies. And there is a very special note to be learned from hence.

Obs. 1. Rulers should be shields to the people where they live; and so they are called, Psal. xlvii. 9, "The princes of the people are gathered together, even the people of the God of Abraham, for the shields of the earth belong unto God." That is, the governors and rulers of the earth, so I find interpreters understand it, belong unto God; they are in God's stead, and they govern in God's name. Rulers, governors, are to be the shields of the people, for they are to be willing to put themselves forward to ward off all the dangers about to come on the people. Have not our worthies in parliament shown themselves to be shields in this respect? Have not they put themselves between us and our dangers? And do you not think that if the adversary prevail they will first swallow up them, I mean those of them that are faithful? Whereas those that before regarded it as an honour to be parliament men, and when there was no danger made such brave speeches, but when they saw things approaching a crisis, and that there were darts shot against the people, and that they must be the shields to keep them off, forsook us; they were showy in appearance, like fine golden or enameled shields, but fit for no service. We are therefore to honour these that still stay, and though they are not perhaps so showy and gilded as those, yet they are proved to be shields of good metal, that will not break, but will keep off the darts shot against the people. And indeed rulers and governors should be men of good metal, willing to bear off much hardship from the people; and they should not think to be honoured only, but should take their honour as a burden also. We are not therefore to regard our rulers as too much honoured, when we consider the danger connected with it. So it is true the governors in armies have pay more than others, but if they be faithful they hazard their lives more, and are the shields of the people. It is an evil thing when a commonwealth have none but wicked magistrates; in such a case they are as if they had nothing to defend them but shields of rotten wood.

"With shame do love, Give ye;" so it is in your books: but I find it rendered אהבו הבו קלון by some, They love to bring shame, they love not to say, Bring ye, but they love to bring shame; and you can translate it thus by merely altering the points in the Hebrew; and the meaning is, they, being of vile spirits themselves, do not care what becomes of the people, let them perish as dogs, and let them do that which shall be a perpetual reproach to them to all posterity, so they may have their lusts satisfied.

Others translate the words thus; With shame they call, Bring ye; that is, with shame they call for pleasure to the flesh: so Arias Montanus, Let us have our pleasure, our tables furnished, our honours, and it matters little what becomes of the people. Such rulers and governors had the ten tribes when they were such idolaters; and it is just with God, when people forsake the true worship of God, that he should send them such governors.

But I rather understand the passage as a rebuke to them for their bribery, "They with shame do love, Give ye." They will not only indulge this propensity in private, but they are grown so impudent that they will sell all the good of a kingdom, and the liberty of the subject, for their own gain. They say "with shame, Give ye." It is a great judgment of God on a people when magistrates and governors are given to bribery, to regard gifts and the increase of their estates more than the public good. "A wicked man taketh a gift out of the bosom to pervert the ways of judgment," Prov. xvii. 23. It is a sign of a wicked man to take a gift, though it be but secretly, out of the bosom; but if he take it openly, it evinces more impudence. A wicked man takes a gift out of the bosom, is loth to be seen at first, and he does it to pervert judgment; these men, that should be as shields to the people, for base ends will betray them. What! to subject such a glorious thing as justice to base ends? justice, which is the glory of God, the glory of a kingdom, and the glory of a man, which he should be clothed with as a robe, as a diadem, to subject it to base ends, for gain to say, Give ye; this is abominable! For a justice of peace to be struck dumb at the appearance of angels, is surely an evil thing: for justices to be bound to the peace by a gift in a basket, is surely most abominable. Exod. xxiii. 8, "A gift blindeth the wise, and perverteth the words of the righteous." Though men are of excellent understanding, and eloquent, yea, though they seemed heretofore very honest and just in their ways, yet when they come to high places, a gift will blind, or, as some render it, pluck out their eyes, irradiate their eyes, that they cannot see. *Auro loquente, iners omnis oratio*, saith an ancient, Let gold but speak, and all other speeches are to little purpose. Therefore magistrates, of all men, should be without covetousness, fearing the Lord. So God himself characterizes them, as men "fearing God, and hating covetousness." In 2 Chron. xix. 6, 7, "Take heed what ye do: for ye judge not for man, but for the Lord, who is with you in the judgment. Wherefore now let the fear of the Lord be upon you; take heed and do it: for there is no iniquity with the Lord our God, nor respect of persons, nor taking of gifts." Justice must run down as a river, not be paled in as a pond for private advantages. Magistrates must shake their hands from bribery, and despise the gain of oppressors, Isa. xxxiii. 15. As we read of Paul, that when a viper came on his hand, he shook his hand and the viper fell into the fire; so should magistrates, when one brings them a gift to pervert

Gregor. Naz. in distichis.

justice, regard it as a viper, and shake their hands of it and let it fall even into the fire, and say as Peter to Simon Magus, "Thy money perish with thee:" They should look upon such as bring them gifts with indignation, and even say, Thy money perish with thee in this wicked enterprise. Even Cicero, a heathen, in an epistle to Quintus his brother, a magistrate in Asia, saith, That he should not only show himself an enemy to them that received gifts, but to them that gave them; he should account them his enemies. And Isa. v. 23, "Woe to them which justify the wicked for reward, and take away the righteousness of the righteous from him!" Many righteous men come before some of you, and their cause is true and good, but you will speak bitterly against them to gratify others from whom you expect a reward. Deut. xxvii. 25, saith, There shall be a curse pronounced against such as take gifts, "and all the people shall say, Amen." If any magistrate love to take gifts, the curse of the people is upon him, and God requires that all the people should say, Amen. And I have read, that among the Romans, if it could be proved against any magistrate that he had taken bribes, he was to be punished with death, without any deliverance. And Psalm xv., in answer to that question, "Who shall abide in thy tabernacle?" it is said, "He that taketh not a reward against the innocent." If you would ever dwell with God, either here in his church, or in heaven hereafter, you must not take bribes against the innocent. I have read in the life of that saint which you call St. Edmund, that he was wont to say, There is little difference between these two words, to take, and to hang, the words are almost alike in Latin, *prendere* and *pendere*, signifying thereby, that those that would take gifts showed what they deserved. Prov. v. 27, "He that is greedy of gain troubleth his own house; but he that hateth gifts shall live." It is not enough for a magistrate not to take gifts, but he must hate gifts, for "he that is greedy of gain," though he think it not, "troubleth his own house."

Ver. 19. *The wind hath bound her up in her wings, and they shall be ashamed because of their sacrifices.*

The word רוח here translated "wind," signifies also a spirit, and so I find Jerome takes the meaning of the words to be, that the evil spirit hurries them up and down, and carries them on violently in their wickedness. As in Deut. xxxii. 11, God is said to carry his people on his wings; so the devil here carries idolaters, who are set upon their wicked ways, as it were on his wings, with impetuous violence.

But we are rather inclined to understand the expression metaphorically, to signify the power, the suddenness, the violence, and swiftness of God's judgments, carrying them into captivity and into misery. "The wind hath bound" the people of Israel, the ten tribes, "up in her wings;" that is, the judgments of the Lord shall come upon them with sudden and overwhelming violence, and take them away from their own country, and carry them into captivity and misery. The power and violence of the judgments of God are often expressed in Scripture by the wind, by storms and tempest. There is a mighty power in the wind: 1 Kings xix. 11, "A great and strong wind rent the mountains, and brake in pieces the rocks." Job xxviii. 9, "That overturneth the mountains by the roots." The winds are the voice of the Lord, that breaks the cedars, even the cedars of Lebanon, and shakes the wilderness, Psal. xxix. Sabelicus tells us of Cambyses, that his soldiers being in a wilderness, in a sandy place, suddenly a violent wind came and drove the sand with such force that thousands of them were buried in it. And here, by the way, we may have hinted unto us a very profitable meditation. How great is the glory and power of the infinite God! For the wind, what is it but a vapour? and what more weak than a vapour? We are wont to say, As weak as water: but many drops together will make the waters terrible, and the seas are called the mighty waters; but vapour is weaker than water, and yet the winds are nothing but a number of vapours joined together, and then what a mighty power have they to rend the rocks and turn up the mountains by the roots! Oh, then, what is the power of the mighty God! for in him there is nothing but infinity, and to him nothing can be added. If a weak vapour being multiplied have such strength, what power then is there in the infinite God, to whom, as having all fulness dwelling in him, nothing can be added!

The wind is of great power, and so are the judgments of God. Hence observe, That the judgments of God upon wicked men who have been spared a long time, when they come, they come swiftly, violently, and suddenly: but of this before.

"And they shall be ashamed because of their sacrifices." As long as they prospered in their course of false worship they were not ashamed, but gloried in it; and the ten tribes, Israel, rather despised and sought to cast contempt upon Judah, who worshipped God aright, as appeareth plainly from Amos vii. 12; "Go," (saith Amaziah there to Amos scornfully,) "flee thee away unto the land of Judah, and there eat bread, and prophesy there." They scorned and contemned Judah, and gloried in their own false worship. Hence,

Obs. 1. The superstitious and idolatrous look upon God's ordinances as vile, and their own inventions as glorious; but God has a time to honour his ordinances and to cast shame upon their sacrifices. The true worship of God is often in such low esteem among men, that its servants are exceedingly vilified, and many are deterred from embracing it, because they cannot bear the attendant shame and ridicule: but God has a time to honour his ordinances, to manifest the beauty of them before all the world, and to cast shame and reproach on all ways of superstition and idolatry; "they shall be ashamed because of their sacrifices;" a time to make even those that gloried most in them, to be ashamed of them. Isa. ii. 20, 21, "In that day a man shall cast his idols of silver, and his idols of gold, which they made each one for himself to worship, to the moles and to the bats; to go into the clefts of the rocks, and into the tops of the ragged rocks." And Isa. xxx. 22, "Ye shall defile also the covering of thy graven images of silver, and the ornaments of thy molten images of gold: thou shalt cast them away as a menstruous cloth; thou shalt say unto it, Get thee hence." They thought them curious ornaments, but the time shall come when God shall make idolaters see their impurity, and cause them to cast them away with indignation, and say, "Get ye hence." That place in Isa. lxvi. 5, bears on this point, "Hear the word of the Lord, ye that tremble at his word; Your brethren that hated you, that cast you out for my name's sake, said, Let the Lord be glorified: but he shall appear to your joy, and they shall be ashamed." There are some of you that tremble at my word, and dare not do any thing in my worship but what my word requires; others have looser consciences, and can venture on things that they have no warrant for in my word: but you that tremble at it, and are scorned for your scruples, whom your brethren cast out because you will not be of the like judgment with them, and because your hearts and consciences are more tender than theirs; whom they would willingly be rid of, and think it would be better with the land when you are gone; and of whom they say, "Let the Lord be glorified," pretending that they desire nothing but the peace of the church and the glory of God; of whom they, even your brethren that cast you out, say, "Let the Lord be glorified;" God shall appear for your glory and for their shame; the Lord will honour you in that his worship which you adopt according to his word, though you suffer at present much ignominy and contempt for it; and though they may for a while seem to carry all before them, having that which is countenanced more publicly, the Lord will appear at length to their shame, the Lord will make them ashamed of their sacrifices.

Four things principally cause shame.

1. Disrespect from those from whom we desire honour. When one comes to a superior, and expects respect from him, and finds that he is cast out, this is a great shame. So they shall be ashamed of their sacrifices; they think that they shall have honour from me by reason of their sacrifices, but I will cast shame upon them, they shall have nothing from me but proofs of disrespect. In 1 Kings ii. 16, when Bathsheba came to Solomon to ask a petition of him, "Deny me not," she said; the old Latin has it, *Ne confundas faciem meam*, Do not confound my face, do not make me ashamed; and the Hebrew is, *Ne avertere faciem meam*, Do not cause my face to be turned, that is, do not make me ashamed by showing me disrespect, when from you I expect honour. When God casts off the sacrifices of men and shows disrespect to them, that causes shame, it confounds, or should confound, their faces.

2. When a man takes a great deal of pains and it all comes to nothing. So all superstitious ways will bring shame at last; as in Col. ii. it is said of all superstitious ceremonies, that they "perish with the using," there comes from them no good result. Idolaters take a great deal of pains in their false worship, but all will come to nothing; in their utmost need all their modes of superstition and idolatry will leave them destitute and helpless, and so cast shame upon them.

3. Disappointment of hope. "Let me not be ashamed of my hope," saith David, Psal. cxix. 116. If I hope for good and be disappointed, this will bring shame. Many passages confirm this. So when those that are superstitious and idolatrous shall raise up their hearts with great expectation of good from God in their ways of false worship, and shall be disappointed of all their hope, in this God will cast shame upon them.

4. When God discovers that to be vile which a man glorieth in. So idolaters, that glory in their superstitious forms, the Lord in time will discover them to be base, and vile, and worthless things, for indeed they are all but poor beggarly elements, fitter to please children than God. God will make this manifest.

If it be objected, that they seem not to be such poor and weak things, but more glorious and pompous a great deal than the rites observed by the true worshippers of God; yea, even true worship of God in itself seems to be a poor and mean thing;

The answer is, the institution stamps a glory on the observance: now they never having been instituted, must be regarded as mean and beggarly elements. Besides, the promise and engagement of God's presence in his own ordinances puts an honour on them, which attaches not to the ways of superstition.

It is good for those who have defiled themselves with superstitious worship, to prevent God by casting shame on themselves; for if they do not, God will cast shame upon them, he will make them to be ashamed. It is our best way, to come in and to prevent God, to take shame unto our own souls and to lie down therein. God knows how we have polluted ourselves, even all of us, in the ways of superstitious worship; and the truth is, God is casting shame upon them all at this day. Happy are those that before these times took shame to their own souls for all these their defilements. Howsoever, before God doth yet further force it upon us, it will be our wisdom to humble ourselves on this account. Ezek. xliii. is very apposite: first in the 10th verse, "Show the house to the house of Israel, that they may be ashamed;" show them the true form of my worship, that they may be ashamed. The truth is, if we did but understand the beauty and excellency of God's ordinances, in the purity and simplicity of the gospel, that were enough to make us ashamed, if there were nothing else; we would even be very vile in our own eyes, to think that, while our hearts have been taken up about such vain and vile superstitions, such glorious ordinances of God, and such beauty of holiness, have been neglected by us: Show them the way of my house, "that they may be ashamed." But further, in the 11th verse, "If they be ashamed of all that they have done, show them the form of the house, and the fashion thereof, and the goings out thereof, and the comings in thereof, and all the forms thereof, and all the ordinances thereof, and all the forms thereof," (again,) "and all the laws thereof: and write it in their sight, that they may keep the whole form thereof, and all the ordinances thereof, and do them." First, show them my house, let them have some kind of general knowledge of my ways and ordinances, perhaps that will make them ashamed: and at this day we know, though there be but a few rays shed upon us, to show us a little more of the ways of God's worship than we saw before, that we begin to be ashamed of what we have done: but now, if indeed we be thoroughly ashamed before God of all our false forms of worship, of all our sacrifices, then mark what a promise is here; then saith the text, "If they be ashamed of what they have done, then show them the form of the house, and the fashion of the house," &c. Thus here is one word heaped on another to show, that it is a mercy of God to people when they not only understand in general God's worship, but know "the form, the fashion, all the ordinances, all the laws," and circumstances in detail. For we must regard nothing in the worship of God as to be neglected, but must have respect to all the forms and ordinances of his house; and it is his great mercy to reveal them to us in all their fulness. True, man stands much on form, and God insists on it likewise. Many deny the power of godliness, but keep the form of it; they are much set on their forms, and God is much set on his. If you desire forms in God's worship, they are already prescribed by his own appointment. And mark, when we are ashamed of what we have done, then shall we understand the laws of the house, the right way of God's worship in his own temple; but first we must be ashamed and thoroughly humbled for our former superstitious sacrifices, we must not expect it before. Many people cry out, We are at a loss, we know not what to do; we have rejected indeed false worship, and in some measure see its vileness; but we know not the forms and fashions of God's house; and the hearts of people tremble to think of the result, fearing lest the acceptable forms be not discovered, and dissensions ensue. Would you understand the right worship and government of God's house? be ashamed of your sacrifices, be ashamed of what you have done, and they shall be shown unto you.

And those that are intrusted to find out the laws, and forms, and fashions, and ordinances of God's house, are, above all men, to be ashamed of what they have done, to be ashamed first of their sacrifices. And you should pray that God would humble them for all their former superstitious observances, that these things may be revealed to them; and being revealed to them, they may reveal it to you. There is a necessity for this previous repentance, let them be men of never such excellent parts and abilities, before they can expect to understand the ways of God's house in its forms, and fashions, and ordinances. In Ezek. xliv. 10—13, God threatens those priests that departed from him in Israel's defection to false worship, that they should bear their iniquity, that they should never come near to him; seeing they partook of the general departure, and did not keep close to the true worship of God, they must bear their iniquity, they must not come near unto God; only God would permit them to be employed in some meaner out-services: and therefore it may be that he will not use some men amongst us of choice parts, in any great work of his, to do him any great service; though they be employed in some meaner duties, yet, for their sinful compliances and conformity to superstition, they shall not come near him. Except there be extraordinary repentance and taking of shame to themselves, though they may be men of excellent parts, the Lord may remember what they did when our Israel departed from God, and what their compliances were; and though he may still make use of them in some ordinary service, yet he may lift up his hand against them, that they shall never be employed, never made a special blessing, in any choice work. God may justly leave them so that they shall cast themselves in a great measure out of the hearts of the saints, and their shame shall stick upon them while they live; and the more honour they seek, the more shame will God certainly cast upon them. In Jer. iii. 25, the church saith, "We lie down in our shame." There is cause indeed that such men should lie down in their shame; those that are of discerning spirits, and observe the ways of men and the ways of God, cannot but be sensible of this, for so long as yielding to superstitious vanities and submission to false power were useful to them to save their estates, their liberties and livings, they yielded, and submitted, and altered their judgments to suit the times, yea, and so altered it as presently to grow even bitter against their brethren who differed from them. Surely they, and we, and all of us, should take shame to ourselves, lie down in our shame a while, and act with all humility, and with all meekness, in suspicion of ourselves and of our own judgments, and in love to our brethren, remembering that we ourselves not long since held other views and other sentiments; therefore should our hearts, I say, be very low, gentle, and full of forbearance. But further,

Obs. 2. God has a time to make all idolaters ashamed of their sacrifices. We will raise our meditations somewhat higher on this, "They shall be ashamed of their sacrifices." All sacrifices, not only the superstitious and idolatrous, but all other sacrifices that come short of the rule, will at length cause shame. As carnal men that tender up many services to God, and lay such weight upon them as on their account to claim heaven and an interest in God, God has a time to make them ashamed of all these sacrifices. And now, as God shall discover the vanity of their services, if he would but show to us all here each other's hearts in time of prayer; when we have been offering up that sacrifice unto God, and have seemed very devout, yet, oh the vanity of our hearts, the vile, impure, foolish, and ungodly thoughts that have passed through them! If God should write our prayers before us, and interline them with all these, and then bid us read them, and bid others read our prayers thus interlined, would we not be ashamed of our sacrifices? The best sacrifice that ever we rendered up to God in all our life we would be ashamed of. God has a time (except all be pardoned in Christ and covered in him) to make men that lay such weight upon their prayers, discern such native deformity in them, as to make them lie down in their shame.

Obs. 3. Duties performed with a carnal heart are mixed with base ends. We seem to draw near to God, and would honour and worship him: oh, but the hypocrisy of our hearts! what vile and base ends are there, to give content to this and the other, to display our parts and abilities in services! These things have been manifest in God's sight, and except we be ashamed of them now, and repent, and get them pardoned in Christ, God will set all our base ends before angels and men; and shall we not then be ashamed of our sacrifices?

Obs. 4. Our sacrifices are defiled by the foulness of our hearts. Not only by actual sin mixed with them, by base thoughts and ends, but our services have come forth from unclean hearts, and it is impossible that out of the unclean there can come any thing that is clean. And when God shall show the infinite holiness of his majesty, and the extent of his justice and righteousness, and how infinitely worthy of sacrifices far other than ever we have tendered to him, oh then how shall we be ashamed!

How will our hearts be overwhelmed with confusion and shame, when, apprehending the infiniteness of the glory of the great God, we shall see how utterly unworthy all our duties were of that surpassing excellency and majesty! Men think highly of the sacrifices that they tender up unto God because of the ability they display in them, but they know not with what a God they have to do. When the Lord shall show unto us the lustre of his glory and the greatness of his majesty, (as it will be seen by us one day at the glorious appearing of the great God,) then we shall see how unworthy all our services were of such a God as he is, and that will make us ashamed if we have not been ashamed heretofore; nothing will be more grievous and more confound the hearts of men, than to be put to shame for their sacrifices.

You will say then, What are those sacrifices we should render God that we shall never be ashamed of? God will one day make all superstitious and carnal people ashamed of their sacrifices, this will be a dreadful thing when it comes to pass, what then are those sacrifices which the saints of God shall never be ashamed of? If you would offer such sacrifices,

1. Be sure they be his own, worship God in his own way. It is not what you think will please God, and will make an excellent appearance, but look to the word, be sure it his own.

2. Let them come from faith; let your hearts be actuated by divine principles in whatsoever you tender up unto God; rest not in the action, but consider the source from whence it flows.

3. Let your ends be high; O take heed of base and low ends in all your sacrifices. It is too much that men should have base and low ends in their outward affairs, when even in them they should have their hearts high upon the glory of the great God; but when they come to their sacrifices and holy duties, then *sursum corda*, then lift up your hearts indeed, be sure then your ends be high and holy.

4. Let your whole strength be engaged in them so as to sanctify the name of God; let the whole soul be carried out unto God, for God is worthy of the whole; if you had ten thousand times more strength than you have, God is worthy that it should be put forth in the services you tender unto him.

5. Offer up yourselves as a sacrifice to God. Be not satisfied to offer up a prayer as a sacrifice, or alms, or such duties only, but be sure, together with these, to offer up yourselves as a living sacrifice to God; as the apostle saith, Rom. xii. 1, "I beseech you therefore, brethren, by the mercies of God, that ye present your bodies a living sacrifice, holy, acceptable unto God." God cares for none of your sacrifices except you offer yourselves. That is a very observable place in the latter end of 1 Kings viii., where you find that Solomon offered "two and twenty thousand oxen, and one hundred and twenty thousand sheep;" a great sacrifice indeed to be offered at once unto God! but mark what,

notwithstanding, God saith to him in chap. ix. 4, presently after the sacrifice was done, "If thou wilt walk before me, as David thy father walked, in integrity of heart, and in uprightness, to do according to all that I have commanded thee, and wilt keep my statutes and my judgments," &c. God puts it to an *if;* Notwithstanding all these sacrifices, if thou thyself, in the constant obedience of thy life, wilt be a constant sacrifice, then will I do thus and thus. But ver. 6, "If ye shall at all turn from following me," if, notwithstanding all these sacrifices, thou at all turn from following me, I will do thus and thus. Many of us think when we have spent a whole day in fasting, and our hearts have been enlarged and have offered up a great sacrifice to God, that we may take the more liberty afterward: no, though you offer "twenty-two thousand oxen, and one hundred and twenty thousand sheep," yet, if after this thou shalt at all forsake me, all that thou hast done shall be rejected. Therefore those sacrifices that are not joined with offering up of ourselves, are such as God will make us ashamed of; but if together with our sacrifices we offer up ourselves, which is our reasonable service, we shall never be ashamed. Therefore, you that are poor and weak in parts, and have but little grace, yet, if that little be true, though your hearts are not so enlarged perhaps as others' in prayer, and you look upon your sacrifices as mean, and as unworthy to be tendered up unto the great God; but dost thou then offer up thyself to him as a sacrifice? It is true, my parts are weak, and my abilities are poor and mean, but, O Lord, what I am, and what I can, I tender unto thee; here, Lord, take soul, body, life, estate, liberty, and all I enjoy, I tender them all unto thee as a sacrifice: I say then, peace be unto thee, the sacrifices thou lightly esteemest God will not make thee ashamed of, but he accepts thy poor services when together with them thou offerest up thyself; whereas if thou didst not tender thyself as a sacrifice, though thy services were ten thousand times more glorious than they are, they would be all cast back as dung in thy face.

6. Be humbled after all your best services. Take no glory to yourselves, but be vile in your own eyes, when you perform any duty that seems to have any excellency in it, and which perhaps others regard as having much. If your hearts be elated with it, the glory of it is gone, and it is that which you must be ashamed of, though now you be honoured for it, and pride yourselves in it.

Lastly, Tender up all in Christ, in the worthiness of his infinite sacrifice. Christ is that sacrifice which is well-pleasing unto God, and all others are pleasing unto him only through the merit and worthiness of the Lord Jesus Christ, who has tendered up himself unto God the Father as a sacrifice to heal all our sacrifices, and to take away all their shame. 1 Pet. ii. 5, "Ye also, as lively stones, are built up a spiritual house, an holy priesthood, to offer up spiritual sacrifices, acceptable to God;" how? "by Jesus Christ." Mark, you are as "lively stones," and lively stones "built up," not merely stones lying here one and there another, but "lively stones built up" in a holy communion, that is the meaning, built up "to offer sacrifices," and that "spiritual sacrifices." But mark, though our sacrifices be never so spiritual, yet they cannot be acceptable to God but by Jesus Christ; that is the sacrifice the saints shall glory in and bless God for to all eternity, which shall take away the shame of their sacrifices, and by its all-sufficient merit render them acceptable unto God. Thus, through the good hand of the providence of God, we are come to the end of this fourth chapter.

CHAPTER V.

Ver. 1. *Hear ye this, O priests; and hearken, ye house of Israel; and give ye ear, O house of the king; for judgment is toward you, because ye have been a snare on Mizpah, and a net spread upon Tabor.*

THIS chapter is the beginning of another sermon of Hosea, preached, as some think, in the reign of Pekah, son of Remaliah, king of Israel, whom you read of 2 Kings xv., probably toward the end of his reign, which was about the same time that Ahaz reigned in Judah, when that horrible confusion was brought into religion, he having placed the altar that he brought the fashion of from Damascus in the house of God; therefore the Lord here inveighs by his prophet not only against Israel, but also against Judah. The sum of the chapter appears to be this:

I. A summons of all sorts to judgment, ver. 1.

II. Accusation and condemnation of Israel by themselves, ver. 2—5.

III. Judah brought in as guilty, and sentence passed upon her, ver. 5, 6.

IV. Israel and Judah conjointly arraigned and condemned, ver. 7—14.

V. The good effects resulting from the judgments of God, ver. 15.

I. In the summons remark these three several words.

"Hear ye. Hearken. Give ear."

"Hear ye, priests."

"Hearken, ye house of Israel."

"Give ear, O house of the king." Hence,

Obs. 1. When God comes in ways of judgment, he expects we should seriously incline our minds to what he is doing. We should not only "hear," but "hearken," and "give ear:" God then will force audience. We are bound to hearken and to give ear to God's commanding word; but if we refuse it, he will have us to hear and give ear to his threatening word; and if that be refused, he will force us to hear and give ear to his condemning word; for so it is here, "Hear ye, hearken, give ear," for judgment is against you all.

There are three classes named here, "priests, people, house of the king."

All sorts are cited to judgment, for corruption was gone over, and judgment comes against all. Hence,

Obs. 2. Generality in sins is no means to escape God's judgments.

With men this may be a means to escape punishment; One and all is a word of security. When soldiers combine in the same offence, and cry, One and all, they escape with impunity. But it is not so with God, he regards not the number of those involved in the offence. Men think, I do but as others do, and I shall escape as well as they. With men this is somewhat, but with God nothing; though all sorts offend, yet there is never a whit the more security thereby unto any. We have a notable scripture confirming that, Nah. i. 12, "Thus saith the Lord; Though they be quiet, and likewise many, yet thus shall they be cut down, when he shall pass through." Though they be many, yet thus shall they be cut down.

Obs. 3. The priests have usually been the causes of all the wickedness in, and judgments on, a nation. He begins with them, "Hear, O ye priests," as the principal cause of all the evil; first of the evil of sin, and then of the evil of punishment; calling them priests, not that they were true priests, for they were not of the tribe of Levi, but merely so reputed. So Jeremiah saith, chap. xxiii. 15, "From the prophets of Jerusalem is profaneness gone forth into all the land;" and there are many passages of Scripture which plainly attribute the evil of nations to priests. And has it not been so with us? and is it not so at this day? There was never a more filthy sink of scandalous, superstitious priests in a kingdom than of late amongst us, as has begun, and will yet further appear to you. There has been an accusation against our parliament, that orthodox, grave, godly divines have been ejected. I suppose you begin now to see what kind those grave, orthodox, godly divines were: evident and plain proofs exist, but it shall yet be made much more manifest in the eyes of all.

Obs. 4. The people will go the way the king and priests go. "And hearken, ye house of Israel." By the "house of Israel," is meant the common people. "Priests" first, the "house of Israel" next, and the "house of the king" last. And the house of Israel is set between the priests and the house of the king, because by these two, the corruption of the priests and of the house of the king, all were influenced: the evil of the people came from them both, partly from the priests, and partly from the house of the king, and between them both the people were undone. If but one of them be right there is great hope of much good; but woe to a people when both of them are corrupt, both priests and the house of the king! Though the house of the king should be corrupt, yet if the priests and ministers kept up the truth, and vigour, and life of religion, things would go reasonably well in a kingdom, and though religion might be persecuted, yet its life would not become extinct. Whatever laws magistrates may enact against the ways of God, except ministers yield compliance, those laws will not be brought to prevail with the consciences or practice of the people. Jeroboam and the other princes saw it was in vain for them to think to prevail with the people except they could gain the priests, therefore it was the great design of Jeroboam to get them over on his side, which he easily did, because all preferment came from him, he raised whom he would.

But mark, might not the people excuse themselves and say, What should we do? On the one side authority enjoins us, on the other side our ministers teach us to do thus and thus, what shall we do? might they not think to excuse themselves?

No, judgment is against you, O "house of Israel;" notwithstanding the example of the priests and the house of the king, yet you are not to be excused. A great many reasons may be given why sinful compliance in the people may not be excused. I remember Arias Montanus, on this scripture, lays down this for a rule, That no king can make any law but by the people; they cannot, saith he, make laws by themselves alone, the people must consent to them some way or other; therefore the people are involved in all the wicked laws in a kingdom. It is not enough therefore for you to say, Such and such laws are made, and we cannot help it; we are to know, it is not merely the will of a king that is a law to a kingdom, but laws enacted imply the sanction of the people. This answer he gives, and quotes a heathen in support; and although in Scripture and elsewhere, there are instances of absolute authority, yet many kings are limited in their power; and in these times especially the people are not to be excused in their evil.

Now this shows evidently that God would have every one examine what is taught and commanded him by his superiors. The people are here cited to judgment, and placed between the priests and the king's house; though the priests taught, and the king's house enjoined, the observance of superstitious rites, yet they must be judged. It is then, I say, clear, that God would have every one examine what is taught and commanded him by his superiors, and judge himself of the rule of his actions, for they must each give an account unto God.

But you may say, Shall it be left to every one to judge of the truth of what is taught, and of the lawfulness of what is commanded? If so, what order can there be?

To answer that, Whatever inconvenience may result, it appears evidently to be a truth, for we must answer unto God for our actions, therefore we must know the rule of our actions; therefore, first, let the inconvenience be what it will, the truth is good. But, secondly, I say this, that every one must judge so far as concerns his own act; he cannot judge as far as regards the magistrate's act, what is fit for him to command, nor with respect to the minister, what is fit for him to teach, but he may and ought to judge so far as his own act is concerned As I must answer before God for what I do, I must so judge it, but if I be taught and commanded by authority one thing, and I judge another, I go on mine own peril, that is, if I do not judge right, I sin against God, and incur punishment from him, and I must run the hazard; but to judge that which must be the rule of my act, is a certain right belonging to every man.

Obs. 5. Kings and princes must have sin charged upon them, and be made to know that they are under the threats of God, as well as others. "Give ye ear, O house of the king." There is here an "O" prefixed, "Give ye ear, O house of the king," for though it comes in last, yet it is the principal; for what harm can superstitious and idolatrous priests do, except they be countenanced by the "house of the king," that is, the king himself, and his courtiers; "Give ear," therefore, "O house of the king."

"For judgment is toward you." Mark, he does not attribute all this evil to wicked counsellors that got into the house of the king, but charges it directly upon the house of the king itself. Evil princes may be as great a cause why there are evil counsellors, as evil counsellors why there are evil princes. Evil counsellors usually see what the design of a prince is, and what is suitable to his disposition, and they cherish that with their wicked counsels. But were the designs and dispositions of princes right, they might have counsellors about them to further that which is right too. Certainly it is no excuse for princes to countenance the evil, and then to say they were advised to such and such courses; for if the teaching of the priests, and the commands of princes, do not excuse people, but they must judge as having to answer for themselves, then counsellors about princes cannot excuse them. It is the unhappiness of princes to have none about them to charge them personally with their guilt, I mean, to show them, in the name of God, the evil and the danger of their sins. It was wont to be said, (as I have before told you,) *Da Ambrosios et plures habebimus Theodosios*, Let us have Ambroses and we shall have Theodosiuses, because of his freedom of spirit with that emperor. And to another emperor, Valentinian, he said, *Noli te extollere imperator, si vis diutius imperare, esto Deo subditus*, Do not lift up thyself, O emperor, if you *will* be emperor longer, if you *will* reign longer, be willing to be subject unto God. And we know with what freedom of spirit the prophets in former times spoke even to kings' houses. As Samuel to Israel, 1 Sam. xii. 25, "If ye shall still do wickedly, ye shall be consumed, both ye and your king." So Elijah to Ahab, Thou art he that troublest Israel. So Elisha to Jehoram, 2 Kings iii. 13, 14, "What have I to do with thee?" (and yet Jehoram came to the prophet in a humble manner;) "What have I to do with thee? Get thee to the prophets of thy father and the prophets of thy mother." And, "Were it not that I regard the presence of Jehoshaphat the king of Judah,

I would not look toward thee nor see thee." This he said to a great king. Others, in the primitive times, have addressed princes with similar boldness; and a great cause of the evil of these latter days has been the flatteries of courtiers, therefore, saith the prophet here, "Hear ye, O house of the king." Kings are great indeed above other men, but what are they before the great God? "He shall cut off the spirit of princes; he is terrible to the kings of the earth," Psal. lxxvi. 12. "When they were but a few men in number; yea, very few, and strangers in the land. When they went from one nation to another, from one kingdom to another people; he suffered no man to do them wrong: yea, he reproved kings for their sakes," Psal. cv. 12. He reproved kings for the sake of his own people, when they were but few in number, and went wandering from one nation to another, and said, "Touch not mine anointed;" that is, touch not my saints. He gave kings warning that they should take heed how they did so much as touch his church, touch his own people; God's people are there called his anointed, and it is said unto kings, that they should not touch his anointed that were so few and wandered up and down from one nation to another. Say thus even to the house of the king. But observe further,

Obs. 6. Though kings are to be reproved for sin, some due respect ought to be shown to them. The house of the king is named last here, is named after the house of Israel. Why so? Not that the house of Israel were more guilty than the house of the king, but because the house of the king could least endure reproof, could hardly bear reprehension, therefore, in wisdom, so far the prophet would go; he would begin with the other, and in his censures of it introduce the house of the king.

"Judgment is toward you," saith the prophet. המשפט here is taken either actively or passively. Actively, *pro actu judicii*, so Junius, it was their part to judge out of the law; and he would read it thus, Judgment is yours, O house of the king; you ought to judge the people in righteousness. But I rather think that it is here to be taken passively; that is, that God calls you to judgment, to suffer judgment, judgment is toward you, or against you. And observe, I beseech you, the difference between the beginning of the 4th and 5th chapters. In the 4th, it was but a controversy, a strife that God had with them; "Hear the word of the Lord, ye children of Israel: for the Lord hath a controversy with the inhabitants of the land." But here it is come to judgment; that which before was but a contending with them, is now come to a judgment of them, to a passing of sentence upon them, judgment is against you, sentence is out upon you. The former was God's pleading against them, and this now is God's judging of them. Hence,

Obs. 7. When God pleads against us, let us not disregard. If we do so when he begins to plead his cause with us, if we neglect it because judgment is not upon us, it will proceed to a sentence. God has laid his plea against many a man in his word, and perhaps some of you see and know it; and God lays his plea against many a man in his conscience; but he neglecting this plea of God laid against him in his word and in his conscience, has afterward received the sentence of death in his soul, which has sunk his heart into despair. Many a man has had God speaking against him in his word and in his conscience, I say, and *there* has been God's controversy; he has been laying his plea there, and thou hast gone on in thy sin, and at length, it may be, there comes the sentence of death on thy soul, that thou dost as it were feel, as some have said they have felt, God passing a sentence of death upon them in this world which has sunk them into endless despair; it has been a day of special judgment to them, they have heard, as it were, God delivering from his throne this sentence against them, Thou art a dead man, a lost man. Oh take heed of neglecting God's pleas, lest they come to judgments.

"Judgment is against you." Why? what is the cause?

"Ye have been a snare on Mizpah, and a net spread upon Tabor."

Mark, God passes not judgment but he gives the cause for it. Men are rash, and will pass judgment on persons and things that they know not. Sometimes you hear men railing against some: ask them, Do you know them? No. What have they done? Neither do they know that, only it is generally reported that such men disturb the peace of the kingdom. But in this they deal not righteously. God passes not judgment without giving a full and sufficient cause why he does it; "Ye have been a snare on Mizpah, and a net spread upon Tabor."

There is much of the mind of God in these words. Some take "Mizpah" appellatively, *pro speculatione*, you have been a snare upon the watch, for so צפה *(speculor)* from whence the word cometh, signifies; and *speculatio* they take to be those over whom they should watch, as *congregatio pro congregatis, circumcisio pro circumcisis*, so *speculatio pro custoditis*. As if God should charge them thus, You should have been watchmen, you priests, and you of the king's house, but you have been a net to insnare them; you should have been *speculatore*, but you have been *venatores et aucupes*, you have been fowlers and hunters of my people. Theodoret reads it *pro speculatoribus*, that is, you spread a net for the watchmen, you superstitious priests, you house of the king, and you people generally, you spread a net for your faithful watchmen; if you have any watchmen that are more watchful than others, you seek, if possible, to insnare them. So they understand it, and though it does in some measure express the meaning of the words, yet I think it cannot be received here, for as the word Tabor is taken properly, not appellatively, so I think ought the word Mizpah. Mizpah and Tabor were the names of two mountains in the land of Israel, the first signifying a watch, and the other, Tabor, a high place, so called by way of eminency, because it was a famous and high mountain.

Now both these mountains were very eminent among the people of Israel. Mizpah some think to be the mountain where Laban and Jacob met, Gen. xxxi. 49, and that it was so called by Laban, "for he said, The Lord watch between me and thee, when we are absent one from another." And in Judg. xx. 1, we find, the children of Israel gathered together as one man, unto the Lord in Mizpah.

So of Tabor, Psal. lxxxix. 12, where it is joined with Hermon, which was famous also, as Cant. iv. 8, "Come with me from Lebanon, my spouse, with me from Lebanon: look from the top of Amana, from the top of Shenir and Hermon." Hermon is but badly designated in the versified translation of the Psalms (and a great many similar mistakes occur): "The little hill Hermon," Psal. xlii. 6; whereas the truth is, Hermon was a high and famous hill. In the Psalms it is, "I will remember thee from the land of Jordan, and of the Hermonites, from the hill Mizar;" Mizar, indeed, signifies small, but they make it as if it were an appellative to Hermon. But the Psalm is rather to be interpreted thus, I will remember thee, O Jerusalem, wherever I am, in all quarters of the world, from Jordan, which lay on the east of Jerusalem, from Hermon, a high mountain in the north, and Mizar, that is, the south, because the mountains of the south were small; as if he should say, Whether I be east, or north, or south, from the temple, I will remember Jerusalem.

So that the Psalm should not be rendered as if Mizar were a mere appellative to Hermon, "the little hill Hermon;" for Hermon was a high and eminent hill, and is joined with Tabor, Psal. lxxxix. 12, which was so famous, that it was a proverbial speech among them to say, As Tabor amongst the mountains. To the Christian too it is full of interest, as being the mount of transfiguration. Josephus, in l. iv. cap. 21, of the Wars of the Jews, saith it was 30 stadia high, and on the top, 20; now a stadium is 125 paces, or 625 feet; and the summit lay as equal as if it had been made by the art of man, and was very fertile and full of trees, and altogether a very pleasant and delightful place.

Plin. lib. 2. cap. 23.

Now God chargeth them, that they had "been a snare on Mizpah, and a net spread upon Tabor." According to some, these mountains are taken synecdochically, for all high places, and these metonymically, for all the superstition and idolatry committed upon them; and then the meaning is, Your idolatry upon these high places has been a net and a snare to the people.

But I rather think the sense to be metaphorical, thus, These mountains were places very delightful, which the gentry of the kingdom frequented much in hunting, and where they were wont to spread their nets and set their snares for fowls and beasts. Now saith God, You "have been a snare on Mizpah, and a net spread upon Tabor;" that is, You watchmen, and others that join with you, have been as huntsmen that have laid snares for the souls of my people, as they lay snares on Mizpah and Tabor; God thus charging them with laying snares for the souls of his people, and hunting them and catching them in their ways of superstition and idolatry. The gospel is called a net in the Scripture, and the ministers of the gospel are to spread it, but the cords and twists of that net are precious, they are the blessed truths, the holy mysteries, of the gospel; and happy are they that are caught in that net. Superstitious priests and governors have their nets too, that they spread and catch the souls of the people in, but their nets are made of other manner of stuff. So Jeroboam and the rest of the princes would not at first attempt to force the people by violence to adopt a false religion, but artfully sought to allure their hearts into a love of it, and would spread for the people unawares their nets, whose meshes were woven with the threads and lines of such cunning devices as,

1. The plea of authority. Does not authority command you to do thus and thus?

2. The sanction of the priestly office. Do not the priests, the holy fathers, do thus and thus? and have you more understanding than they; more wit than all the statesmen and the king's house, and more than all your teachers too?

3. We do not alter our religion, we hope we worship the same Jehovah that you worship.

4. The things required of you are not of much importance, mere circumstances of place: you worship at Jerusalem, it is but worshipping at Dan and Beth-el here before these two images; you shall not worship the images, but worship in this place.

5. All we aim at is your own good; for that was Jeroboam's pretence: It is too much for you to go up to Jerusalem, to go twice a year so long, and tedious, and dangerous a journey; no, saith he, I tender the good of my people more, therefore let them worship here.

6. The example of the majority. The ten tribes, the multitude, adopt these rites, Judah and Benjamin only differ from them, why should you desire to imitate their fastidious scrupulosity?

7. Their long-continuing prosperity. Has not Israel prospered as much as Judah? Has not God been with us as much as with them? Judah pretends he worships God aright, we are sure God is with us.

8. Reproaches cast on the true worshippers of God; as in the 7th chapter of this prophecy, ver. 3, "They make the king glad with their wickedness, and the princes with their lies." That is, this was their cunning device, to raise all the reproaches they possibly could against the true, forward, and zealous worshippers of God, especially against the prophets and ministers; and therefore in Amos, who prophesied at the same time, you find that Amaziah said, the land could not bear his words; they were even enough to excite sedition among the people, yea, what are these that oppose the king's laws but rebels? These were the snares which they set to catch the people, to make them out of love with the true worship of God. Thus they were "a snare on Mizpah, and a net spread upon Tabor."

Thus it has been with us; how cunningly have men laid their nets amongst us to catch souls! They say, it is but yielding a little to a thing enjoined by authority, besides, it is really unimportant, and is countenanced by the example of many learned and godly men; yea, and why should you hinder yourself of the good you may do? It is after all a mere matter of circumstance, connected with decency and order, and consistent with much devotion, and by yielding as far as we can, we may gain papists; none but a company of simple people oppose these ancient customs, which can plead the precedent of the fathers of the church, yea, of many martyrs who have shed their blood. Thus many souls have been caught as a bird in a snare, with these lines and twigs thus cunningly twisted together; and so caught that they could not tell how to get out, but being once involved in the meshes, were insnared more and more: as a bird once caught in the net, by its very flutterings is the more entangled; so men when they yielded a little, could not tell where to stop, but at last have gone so far, and been so completely insnared, as to be wholly unable to extricate themselves, but by their very efforts have become more deeply involved; and, the truth is, at length even their consciences have ceased to disquiet them: as a bird, that is perhaps at first alarmed when the net is but stirred, but after a little loses its fear; so many men of tender consciences have at first shrunk from superstitious vanities, but being caught by cunning arguments and devices, have, after a few faint efforts to disenthral themselves, succeeded in quieting their consciences, and calmly acquiesced in their captivity. Oh how many have been thus led captive! This was the design of the adversary amongst us, if possible to subdue the consciences of men; a design worthy of the father of lies, from whom it emanated. Even in their taverns and feasts, they were plotting and studying what it was that would best overcome the scruples of such and such men, and endeavoured to suit the temptation to the character and circumstances of each. It may be the old ceremonies would catch some; others perhaps would break through the old, therefore there must be new ones devised; these again might not suit others, but the book of Liberty on the Sabbath, that would be a proper bait; if it failed, then the oath of canonical obedience. Thus they laid nets for the consciences of men, knowing that if they could but once silence them, they might do with them what they would; certainly they saw that there was no way to make them their own, to make them *filii ecclesiæ*, sons of the church, as they called it, but by first giving a sop to their consciences. Many men have found this to be true by experience, and we have seen it: they have come with all the flatteries they could to some, that have stood out many years, and by whose ministry perhaps God has done good; and having but once induced them to yield a little, though with fear and trembling, yet have they presently concluded that certainly they were secured, and then heaped all their injunctions upon them in rapid succession, until their consciences were altogether subdued. And as it is with some birds and beasts, that when caught are presently fatted up; so it was with some ministers and others, when once insnared in their nets, they presently had livings and preferment, bishoprics, chaplaincies, and the like: and as some other birds when caught are forthwith nipped in the head, or have their limbs broken; so they dealt severely, maliciously with others, and ceased not until they entirely crushed them. Thus acted those amongst us that have been "a snare on our Mizpah and a net spread upon our Tabor;" but blessed be God that their snare is broken, and our souls are escaped as a bird out of the hands of the fowler, Psal. cxxiv. 7. My brethren, do not you think you would have been all involved one after another in these their superstitious ways, seeing how in a few years they have prevailed? But God looked from heaven and pitied the souls of his people, and heard their groans and sighs. Oh, many a poor minister has gone home to his wife, and having no other way of maintenance, has, out of fear of losing his living, yielded to their superstitious injunctions; but think you how he has wrung his hands, and could not sleep that night, but lay tossing on his bed with a dismal conscience. Well, the Lord has heard these cries and broken our snares, and our souls are delivered. God forbid such a judgment should ever befall us again, and that God should bring these fowlers amongst us to insnare our souls as they have done.

But there is another interpretation of this text which well consists with this, and I think is agreeable to the mind of the Spirit. Mizpah and Tabor I take in their own proper sense; "You have been a snare on Mizpah, and a net spread upon Tabor," that is, that they really did spread snares and nets on those very mountains, which stood between the two chief cities of Israel and Judah, Samaria that belonged to the ten tribes, and Jerusalem that appertained to Judah and Benjamin. Now Jeroboam and the other princes, his successors, placed watch-towers on these two mountains, and there set men to be as spies, to see who went from Israel to Judah. There were some conscientious persons that would not be contented with that worship which was set up by authority, but must now and then be stealing to Jerusalem at the times appointed: now the priests counselled those that were in authority, saying, We shall never have peace till we catch these men, who must be going to Jerusalem, therefore let there be some device to apprehend them: then others suggested, that as most of them, when going, passed by Mizpah and Tabor, those two places would serve to set towers on for watchers, who might surprise every one of them. Now this counsel pleased the princes very well, and thereupon, (as I find in Arias Montanus, who cites it out of the Jewish histories,) there were two towers set upon these mountains for this very purpose. This God charges them with, and for this, judgment is out against them. Oh, this is that which provokes God exceedingly, and will bring fearful judgment upon a people, when magistrates and ministers will seek to catch poor souls that would worship God in his own right way.

And has it not been so in our late High-commission court? when there was but a mere reader in a country town, that could do nothing else, if there were any eminent preacher near, and poor souls that were hungering after the bread of life would go to hear him, they would set men on purpose to note down the names of such, just as Jeroboam did here. The Lord has a special eye on poor souls thus oppressed and insnared, to relieve them in due time; and blessed be his name, he has done much for us, in relieving and delivering us from these men, against whom the judgment of God is this day gone forth. What is become of their proctors and summoners, and of all that rabble rout that were catchers and hunters of such poor souls as were desirous of worshipping God in his own way?

Ver. 2. *And the revolters are profound to make slaughter, though I have been a rebuker of them all.*

The Lord by his prophet proceeds in his charge against Israel for their idolatry.

"The revolters." The apostates, those who once rendered me the worship I required; but they are revolted. The brand of a revolter is an ignominious brand, especially when God himself charges this upon any; Once you were full of zeal in the ways of God, but you are revolted, you are apostates. There can be no blacker brand on a people or a man than this is, He is an apostate, a revolter. We must understand this their revolting especially in reference to their falling off from the true worship of God to their idolatry.

"Are profound;" העמיקו they are grown very deep in this their way of idolatry. At first they began but with a little, but by degrees they reached the very depths. When men enter on the ways of idolatry, they know not whither they shall go. They think perhaps, at first, to go but thus and thus far, but before they are aware they are sunk into the very depths.

Obs. 1. It is a dangerous thing to venture on the beginnings of false worship, especially when the tide is flowing in. If a man stand on the shore of the sea when the tide is coming in, and thinks, The water is but shallow now, I may venture to stand here; still it comes insensibly on, and he thinks it is not much deeper than before: but if he venture too long he may soon be swallowed up and sunk in the very depths of the sea. Thus it has been with many; they have been beguiled, have thought they might yield thus and thus far, but little thought of the tide that was coming in. It is true, if it had been going out there had not been so much danger. They truly are deceived in their opinion of the first Reformers, who say they were wont to yield somewhat for peace sake; but then the tide of superstition was on the ebb; and yet it was not without danger that they yielded so far as they did: but of late the tide has been coming in, and these gradual compliances have drawn many into the very depths of superstition, where they have been irrecoverably lost.

"Are profound," they are grown profound, that is, their hearts are got very deep in these ways; (so I find some interpret it, and not improbably;) they are grown deep; that is, they are deeply rooted in these ways, so that there is little hope of ever drawing off their hearts from them; they have continued in them a great while, and now they plead antiquity and custom.

Calvin in loc.

Obs. 2. It is a dangerous thing to be deeply rooted in superstitious ways. What a great deal of stir is there in dealing with them that are deeply rooted in false ways of worship! By custom they become deeply rooted.

"Are profound," they are grown "profound," that is, they have revolted from God exceeding much, deeply revolted. It denotes the greatness of their revolting. In Isa. xxxi. 6, there is such an expression, "They have deeply revolted;" they have not only forsaken somewhat of my worship, but they have deeply, exceedingly revolted from me. So in chap. ix. of this prophecy, ver. 9, "They have deeply corrupted themselves;" they have very much, exceedingly corrupted themselves.

"Are profound," they are grown deep, that is, (as

some would have it,) they grow deeper in their ways of idolatry than God does in the ways of his worship: as thus, They will punish more the breaking of any of their rules in their invented worship, than God punishes the breach of his commands. So I find Mercer, that learned interpreter, quoting Rabbi Jarchi as having this expression, *Qui non ascendit transgreditur; qui offendit occidetur:* He who ascends not (to the feast) transgresses; he that offendeth (so) shall be slain. God only accounts him a transgressor that comes not up to the feast at the appointed time; but they say, whosoever doth not come shall be put to death. They will go further in the punishment of the breach of their superstitious enactments, than God does in punishing of the breach of his holy law. So they are grown deep. Yea, they would seem to go further, to be more zealous and earnest for their ways of idolatry, than God himself is for his ways of holy worship.

And have we not found this, that revolters, superstitious idolaters, have grown deep thus? that is, they will punish the breach of their superstitious ways more deeply than God punishes the breach of his law; they will insist more on time, and will be more eager to have their laws fulfilled abundantly, than the true worshippers of God are eager to have the law of God fulfilled.

But though I think the Holy Ghost hath a reference to these things, the main and principal scope of the word I conceive to be this, according as you have it in your translations, They are grown "profound;" that is, They are very subtle in their ways of idolatry, they lay their snares deep.

We spake before of the snares of idolaters; now here the Holy Ghost charges them with being profound, that is, They are subtle, they lay their snares very deep: as fowlers and hunters (to follow the metaphor) will go into low places and ditches, that so the birds may not perceive them; so the Holy Ghost here saith, these are content to go deep, they are deep in their plots, they will deny themselves in any thing almost, and will be content to lie very low, so be it they may further their own ends. You find in many great promoters of superstition and idolatry, that they will crouch and seem to be very affable and courteous, and in many things even deny themselves, and all to further their own ends; thus they are profound in their subtilty: according to that expression we have in Psal. x. 9, 10, "He lieth in wait secretly as a lion in his den: he lieth in wait to catch the poor: he doth catch the poor, when he draweth him into his net. He croucheth, and humbleth himself, that the poor may fall by his strong ones."

This should teach us to be willing to deny ourselves in our own ends that we may promote the true worship of God; for idolaters will crouch, and bow, and deny themselves in many things, for the promotion of their idolatry. There are many depths, many subtleties in their ways; their powers are strained to the utmost to maintain their superstition; and men that have strong parts and good wits, what a gloss are they able to put upon the worst things in the world, especially when aided by the father of lies! The Scripture tells us of "the depths of Satan," Rev. ii. 24. Satan in his instruments has deep arts, and goes beyond many poor weak and simple people. And we have in Scripture the "devices" of Satan, 2 Cor. ii. 11, τὰ νοήματα, the reasonings of Satan. And then the methods of the devil, Eph. vi. 11, τὰς μεθοδείας, the deep policies of the devil; and in nothing more exercised than in the maintenance of false worship; gravity and seeming profound learning appear to countenance it. This was just the way of idolaters at these times, they were grown profound in this their way. Hence,

Obs. 3. The hearts of apostates are the most deeply rooted in wickedness.

No men are so deeply rooted in wickedness as apostates. The revolters are grown deep, that is, are deeply rooted in this their way of wickedness, and amongst other wickedness, above all in the ways of superstition and idolatry. Apostates, if they grow superstitious and idolatrous, are the most deeply rooted in those ways, yea, and the most profound and subtle in them. Hence you might observe in your own experiences the practices of our prelates, they would choose to themselves chaplains of such as had fallen off and apostatized from that strictness which they seemed as puritans to profess in former times; they thought their choicest and best men were such as arose out of the ashes of a puritan, as they themselves were wont to express it; knowing that those that were formerly seemingly strict in their practice, were best acquainted wherein the consciences of godly men were most tender, and most familiar with their habits and places of resort, and therefore the most likely to prove the fittest agents.

Obs. 4. Idolaters, especially apostates, are profound and deep.

We had need therefore to beware of those that are superstitious when they come with the greatest show of arguments: they are deeply rooted, and can hardly be got to abandon their superstitions; we had need likewise be deeply rooted in the truths of God, or they will certainly undermine us. The Scripture tells us, that "the Spirit of God searcheth the deep things of God," 1 Cor. ii. 10; revealeth the mysteries of Christ. Those that have that Spirit of God that searcheth those deep things of God, are the only persons that are likely to stand out against the deep policies of idolaters. And the truth is, every godly man and woman, though never so meanly gifted, yet are more profound than the greatest scholar in the world that is wicked and superstitious; for they have the Spirit of God, that searcheth the deep things of God; and this it is that keeps their hearts from being insnared by all the profoundness of false worship.

Obs. 5. Idolaters are deep in their policies.

It should teach us then to labour to be wise in the worship of God. When we would maintain God in his worship, it should teach us to learn to seek to outplot them: they are full of their plots; why should not the Spirit of God teach us wisdom as well as the spirit of Satan teaches them? Why should we not exercise our parts energetically in the true worship of God, as they theirs in the way of superstition and idolatry? But we see it ordinarily otherwise, "The men of the world are wiser in their generation than the children of light," they are deeper in ways of policy, and so deceive such as are simple. If you take them on the first show of things, they will seem to come with such colour of arguments as will certainly deceive you. Therefore you should beg wisdom of God, that you might not be deceived through the subtlety of Satan in these men.

I find divers of the ancients have other interpretations of these words; I will not, however, spend further time in discussing them, because I think we have already had the meaning of the Holy Ghost in these words; therefore we will pass on. They "are profound "To make slaughter." To make slaughter! what does God intend by these words? He means by their making "slaughter," their sacrifices to their idols; and so by the sacrifices, which was the principal part of their false worship, he includes all their false worship; they were deep in all their false worship, naming the chief for the rest.

But why does he call their sacrifices, making "slaughter?"

In way of reproach. God will not honour them by saying, They offered me sacrifice; no, but it is, "to make slaughter." As if God should say, I regard all your sacrifices as no better than slaughter, your temple no better than shambles, and your priests no other than butchers. Thus contemptibly doth God speak of the sacrifices of those that choose their own superstitious ways. Isa. lxvi. 3, "He that killeth an ox is as if he slew a man; he that sacrificeth a lamb, as if he cut off a dog's neck; he that offereth an oblation, as if he offered swine's blood:" and yet there God speaks of the sacrifices of Judah, not of Israel. Let the sacrifices be for the matter of them what God requires, and offered in the place which God has appointed; yet when men make their sacrifices their own righteousness, and think to put off God by them, I regard them no more, saith God, than the cutting off of a dog's neck. But these sacrifices of Israel had a twofold error in them: First, they were not offered in the place that God would have them. Secondly, they rested upon them likewise; therefore are they called no other than slaughter. Hence observe,

That whatsoever worship is tendered up to God, if it be not his own, or if in that worship (though it be his own) we choose our own ways, God accounts it an abominable thing, whatsoever show of devotion it may have.

The words "to make slaughter," God uses not merely to show the contempt he has of all their sacrifices, but by that he secretly insinuates the cruelty of the priests and of the princes to those that would not yield to their idolatries, their grievous persecution of them, even unto blood. They "are profound," saith God, they are grown deep in their idolatry, they are grown to the depth of malice, so that their hearts are enraged against those that will not conform, even unto blood: No matter what becomes of them, no matter if they were all hanged, a company of precise and scrupulous fools, that pretend conscience, and do nothing else but trouble the state. Do not Jeroboam and the council command these things? The kingdom can never be well till it be rid of them.

"Though I have been a rebuker." Though I have been an instructor, or corrector; so the word may be rendered, as well as a rebuker. And "have been," or am, or will be, you may put it which way you will, is not in the text, but simply, "though I a rebuker," eruditor, corrector of them all. As if God should say, They cannot plead ignorance; indeed, were it that they never had any means, then they might have some pretence for what they do, but I have been an instructor and rebuker of them all.

ואני

This particle, "I," hath reference either to the prophet, or to God himself.

1. The prophet: and then, either actively or passively.

מוסר

"I have been a rebuker," or I have been rebuked; so some render it.

1. "I," the prophet, "have been a rebuker." From thence the note is,

Obs. 6. The ministers of God must rebuke sin.

2 Tim. iv. 1, 2, "I charge thee before God, and the Lord Jesus Christ," saith Paul to Timothy. And among other charges, this was one, that he should rebuke the offenders. And Tit. i. 13, "Rebuke them sharply," ἀποτόμως, cuttingly, so the word signifies. Tit. ii. 15, "Rebuke with all authority."

This is the work of the ministers of God, to rebuke "with all authority," to rebuke "cuttingly," when there is cause for it.

And, indeed, the spirits of sinners are base and vile, and a minister of God, coming in his Master's name, is above the highest of them. And if the rebuke be administered in a gracious manner it will make the proudest sinner tremble. Let them seem never so scornful outwardly, yet, I say, let a minister of God come in God's name, and speak as the oracle of God, he may make the proudest and stoutest sinner to quail under his rebukes; for their spirits are vile. And though it seems grievous for the present to those that are rebuked, yet they will bless their reprovers afterward, if God bless the rebuke; and others will curse them that would not rebuke them in their evil ways.

2. If we refer this to God himself, "I have been a rebuker;" that is, not I the prophet only, but I the Lord have been a rebuker of them all; the observation is,

Obs. 7. When the ministers of God rebuke according to the oracles of God, God rebukes. And if there be any means in the world to humble the heart of a sinner, it is this, to see that God rebukes him in his word. You may put these two notes together: 1. God rebukes in his word; and, 2. This is a great means of humbling the heart of a sinner. Thou comest to the word, and findest thyself rebuked for such and such evils that thou art conscious to thyself of; know it was God rebuked thee that day, and he will call thee to account for those rebukes which he there gave thee. Thou camest, perhaps, to hear what the minister would say, but thou foundest before thou wentest that thou wert rebuked for such and such secret evils thou art conscious to thyself of; know, I say, God rebuked thee at that time, and look to it, God will call thee to an account for his rebukes.

But God rebukes not only by his word, but sometimes by his works too; when he manifests himself against sinners, suiting his works so as to show evidently that he sets himself against them, then, I say, God rebukes them for some special evils, although they will not see it. Isa. xxvi. 11, "Lord, when thy hand is lifted up, they will not see: but they shall see." God lifts up his hand to rebuke wicked and carnal men, and evidently sets himself against them, and they will not see: but they shall see. Hence,

Obs. 8. Idolaters' hearts are stubborn. They were profound to make slaughter in their ways of superstition, though I was a rebuker of them all; they cared not for my rebukes, they regarded not my words, their hearts were stubborn and stout against them. *Verbi contemptus, idolatriæ comes*, saith Mercer upon the place, The contempt of God's word is the companion of idolatry. Common experience tells us how your superstitious, false worshippers slight the word of God; they are above it, they speak jeeringly of the Scripture and of warrants from God's word; and extol the fathers and antiquity, and such and such writers, but the word of God they usually contemn and scorn.

Thus it was here, they regarded not what God said in his word. Idolaters are very stout against the word of God, and contemn it. None of its commands nor rebukes but they withstand. Poor vile worms that they are! who are they, that they should dare to resist the rebukes of the infinite holy God? Know, however thy spirit rises against his word, it will certainly cast thee. The psalmist, in Psal. lxxvi. 6, saith, "At thy rebuke, O God of Jacob, both the chariot and horse are cast into a dead sleep." And so Psal. lxxx. 16, "They perish at the rebuke of thy countenance." And Psal. civ. 7, "At thy rebuke they fled." And Psal. xviii. 15, "The foundations of the world were discovered at thy rebukes." The rebukes of God have a great deal of power in them, heaven and earth cannot stand before them; how then can that stubborn heart of thine succeed in its opposition?

Let us not be troubled, my brethren, nor discouraged, at the stoutness of idolaters. They have always resisted the rebukes of God in his word, and therefore let us not think it much though they now withstand the evident truth of God, and the works of God, that apparently make against them. They were tormented with the wrath of God, but "they repented not to give him glory," Rev. xvi. 9. Many men are ready to think their cause is good, because their spirits are so resolute to slight all that appears against them. Let not us have higher thoughts of them because of this, for it has always been the course of idolaters to stand out stoutly against all the rebukes of God in his word and works, because the Lord has an intent to destroy them. Hence,

Obs. 9. Sin after rebukes is exceeding sinful. It is too much to neglect God's commands, but to stand out against any intimation of his displeasure is a greater evil. God expects that the heart of sinners should in such a case melt before him; and it was the commendation of Josiah, that when the law was read, his heart melted; and indeed an ingenuous spirit is soon rebuked. But when the heart of a sinner is got above all rebukes, then it hardens exceedingly, and treasures up wrath against the day of wrath. We ourselves cannot bear others to be insensible to our rebukes, we cannot endure them to be disregarded by a child or a servant. How shall the infinite God bear our slighting of his rebukes?

O let us charge this sin upon our souls. How often has God rebuked me in his word and in his works, and yet, the Lord knows, this wretched and stubborn heart of mine has stood out against it all! Certainly this resisting of the Holy Ghost will lie one day heavy upon thy conscience. Nothing will increase the burden of sin more than this, that I have sinned, and that in my sin I have stood out against the rebukes of God. As in Prov. v. 12, 13, "And thou mourn at the last, when thy flesh and thy body are consumed, and say, How have I hated instruction, and my heart despised reproof!" The words are spoken of one gallant, a brave young gallant, that blustereth it out in the world, and carries all before him, and cares for nothing that is said; but when the hand of God is upon him, and his flesh and body are consumed, then he begins to lament his condition, Oh, how have I despised reproof, and have not inclined mine ear to them that instructed me! This is the aggravation of sin indeed.

And that we may humble our souls for our standing out against God's rebukes, add but this consideration, that God has such rebukes in reserve as will force us to yield. If we stand out against his rebukes in his word and lesser chastisements, against his loving rebukes, let us know that God has "furious rebukes;" so they are called in Ezek. v. 15; xxv. 17. When thou comest to the word, or when thy parents, or thy governors, or thy friend, rebuke thee for thy sins, God rebukes thee in them, and these are loving rebukes; but if thou rejectest these, know, God has "furious rebukes" for thee one day, yea, "rebukes with flames of fire," Isa. lxvi. 15.

"Of them all." This (if you apply it to the prophet) shows his impartiality. And thence,

Obs. 10. Prophets' rebukes must be impartial rebukes: not like cobwebs, to take small flies and to let the great ones go through; they must be impartial. Oh how many prophets have sharpened their rebukes against those that have been truly conscientious, and have saddened their hearts even out of their pulpits; but have let those that are loose go quiet away; nay, not only quiet, but rejoicing! When the hearts of the saints have been saddened, they have sharpened their rebukes against these; but the looser of the parish, or, many times, the great ones, have gone away rejoicing. Thus, if you take the words, "I have been a rebuker of them all," actively.

But if passively, as some do, They have rebuked the prophet; as if he should say, They have been profound in their idolatrous ways, and I have been faithful in preaching to them, and what has been my recompence? All of them have rebuked me. All of them; not only their priests, not only their chief and great men, have rebuked me, they indeed might with some show of reason bitterly inveigh against me; but all the people have done it too. I have been a rebuke to all the people, they have all been bitter against me, and sharpened their very tongues against me; Oh, say they, here is one that likes not our manner of worship, he must have another kind of religion, he tells us that we must all go up to Jerusalem and worship there, and nothing but that will be accepted. Thus they scorned and rebuked him, and even flew in his very face. Hence,

Obs. 11. It is a hard thing for a few men to stand out against a state in matters of religion.

If there be but some few unto whom God hath shown another way, and the generality differ from them, certainly those few are likely to meet with hard treatment, and to be a rebuke, not only to ministers, but generally to all the people; they must expect to be under the rebukes of all sorts. Thus it was with the prophet, and with all that went his way, he was a rebuke unto them all.

Ver. 3. *I know Ephraim, and Israel is not hid from me: for now, O Ephraim, thou committest whoredom, and Israel is defiled.*

"I know Ephraim." This is *Notitia judicialis, non approbationis*, A knowledge to judge, not a knowledge of approbation.

"I know Ephraim;" that is, I know all his shifts, all his evasions and his cunning devices, all his plots, pretences, and base ends. These may be hid from men, but I know them all, they are not hid from me. Mark, first, "I know Ephraim," and then, I know Israel.

First, "Ephraim." By "Ephraim," as you have heard before, we are to understand the princes, the great ones, amongst them, because Jeroboam was of the tribe of Ephraim. "I know Ephraim," that is, I know the politic ends of all the great ones amongst them: they profess to man that they desire to worship me, and say, God forbid that they should change religion; and they cry out against all that would excite such suspicions of them amongst their good people. But "I know Ephraim," saith he, I know what his aim is, I know what his thoughts are, and what was plotted at such a time, and what his chamber counsels with certain priests were; I know what correspondence he has with some that corrupt my worship, and all that follow him and favour him, I know them thoroughly, all their devices and depths. I know what has been working these many years; how he seems as if he would serve me, but I know that what he does is merely to serve his own ends. I know how the poor are deluded by his fair and solemn protestations, they think he means nothing but well, and that none but a company of precise people are jealous of him; but I know what they intend, and what their ways are, whatsoever colour they put upon them. "Ephraim," that is, the great ones, the princes, persuade the people that Jeroboam and his successors aim at nothing else but to reform things for the best, but I know that matters are far otherwise; "I know Ephraim."

"Israel is not hid from me." That is, the people; they pretend that they do but as they are taught, and that they merely submit to authority, and would rejoice indeed if things were otherwise, and matters reformed more in accordance with the word of God; yet some things must necessarily be yielded to for peace sake. True indeed, they say, these prophets of the Lord, and some others, are good and honest men, and would have us to do otherwise; but things are not yet clear, and the course they recommend, though in apparent conformity with the Scriptures, may bring us a great deal of trouble and inconvenience; for peace sake then we must be contented to yield to the judgment of such and such learned and wise men; and though we yield in these matters, yet our hearts are right for God. But saith God, "Israel is not hid from me.

"Israel." That is, the base, temporizing, revolting, superstitious spirits of the people, they are not hid from me; their unwillingness to yield themselves to my government, their love to their ease and estates, the reluctance of their carnal hearts to venture and suffer any thing for my truth and ordinances. Israel, in these his distempers of heart, is not hid from me; all these things are plain before me; he may blind men and deceive his own conscience, but he cannot hide it from me, saith God. From whence the observations are these:

Obs. 1. God's eye is upon the secrets of men's hearts. Certainly, therefore, hypocrites must needs be atheists; they that think to put off God with outward shows, must needs deny God, as if God did not see the secret turnings and windings, plottings, contrivances, and aims of their hearts.

And then, oh the patience of the infinite God! that notwithstanding he sees what villany there is in the world, coloured over with religious protestations and professions, yet he bears with it. I know, saith he, I know what all their ends and aims are, and what kind of success they desire; although they colour and cover them all over with such protestations of religion, and a professed for its establishment. Oh the infinite patience of God, that can bear with men who attempt to veil their iniquities under solemn protestations and professions of religion! At this exhibition of his patience we must needs wonder.

Again, God knows all the hearts and secret aims of men; let us then pray to him to make our own hearts known to ourselves. He knows them, and except we be upright in our wish to know, and unfeignedly desire of God that he would show us, our own hearts, we possibly may, after many duties performed, perish for some secret sin that we were ourselves unconscious of. I say, it is possible for persons to go on a long time in the profession of religion, and to make conscience of all known duties, yet to perish at last for some sin that they know not to exist in themselves.

You will say, This is a hard thing; what shall become of us then?

To mollify this therefore a little, take this along with it: Except thou hast a heart unfeignedly willing to know and search itself, and earnest with God that he who knows thy heart would make it known to thyself: if, indeed, thy heart be thus upright, that thou canst appeal to God and say, Lord, I know that I have a vile, false, and hypocritical heart, and much evil may lurk secretly in it, that I have not known all this while, an evil such as I may justly perish in; but, good Lord, make it known to me, let me know the worst of myself, let me know the evil that is in me, and my purpose is to resist it: if thou hast such a heart, thou hast no cause to think that thou shalt perish for any evil ways in thee. But if thou hast any secret evil in thyself, and dost not in the uprightness of thy heart unfeignedly desire to know it, that so thou mayst forsake it, and get thyself rid of it, and canst not appeal to God that thou art willing to have it made known unto thee, thy condition may be dangerous, notwithstanding all the duties thou performest.

Obs. 2. God's eye upon our hearts and ways, is a special means to humble us. "I know Ephraim," is brought in as a means to humble Ephraim, to humble Israel.

No more powerful means in the world to humble the heart, than to remember that God looks upon our hearts and ways. The discovery of our evil to others may be some means to humble us. Oh how it would abase men, if God should discover to their friends and acquaintance all that evil that is in their hearts! And hereafter, at the great day of judgment, when the secrets of all hearts shall be disclosed, how will the wicked and ungodly be abased before men and angels! We read of the adulterer in Job xxiv. 17, that the morning is to them even as the shadow of death; and if any recognise them, they are then as in the terrors of the shadow of death. Wicked men (especially adulterers, for it is spoken of them) hate the light, and the morning is unto them as the shadow of death. Now I argue, if the knowledge that men have of our secret wicked ways is so terrible to a guilty conscience, what is it then when this guilty conscience shall have real apprehensions of the infinite God! He has seen thee when thou hast been such a wretch in such an inn, in such a tavern, in such a secret place. He has seen what thou hast said and plotted; yea, what thou hast thought and plotted. Look upon God thus seeing thee, and try if it will not humble thy heart. O labour to humble thy heart by this, How unwilling was I to know such a truth! how glad when I got a thing out of my conscience, that would have forced me to measures I was reluctant to adopt! and whatever I pretended, love to myself, to my ease, to my estate, made me decline this truth of God; and God saw all this. When we feel such base workings within, such plottings and contrivings of our hearts for our own selves and for our carnal ends and aims, let us consider that the eye of God is upon us. Let us conceive we hear the voice of God from heaven saying to us, I know what you are plotting, I know what your aims are, I know the base workings of your spirits. Did we but apprehend God thus speaking from heaven to us, as here he speaks by the prophet, "I know Ephraim, and Israel is not hid from me," it would be a special means to humble our hearts for evil present, and to prevent evil for the future.

"Now." There is in this word a great emphasis: Even still Ephraim goes on in wickedness; he has gone on a great while, and even now when I am coming against him, he continues still in his wickedness. Hence,

Obs. 3. God will deal with men according to their present ways.

In what he finds them for the present, he will deal with them for that especially. Not but that when he finds them in evil for the present, he will call them to an account for all things that are past too; but he especially suits the punishment to their present iniquities.

I note this the rather, to show to sinners this useful lesson: Whatsoever thou wast before, though thou hast continued a long time in thy wickedness, yet if thou hast but now a repenting heart to return unto God, there might be hope and help for thee. O consider this, thou wretched sinner. As if God should say here, Ephraim has continued wicked a long time, but if he had now a heart to return to me, it should be well with him; but even now, to this very moment, "Ephraim committeth whoredom:" so say I to the vilest sinner in this place, whatsoever thou hast been, here is salvation, if now at this instant thou hast a heart to turn to God: thou canst not tell whether God will ever give thee another now: if thou return *now* unto him, and repent and believe, thou mayst be saved; but if God come upon thee after this exercise, and find thee continuing in thy sinful ways, and say, Even now, yet for all this, this sinner continueth in his sin, this will be a heavy thing indeed. So here he comes to Ephraim, "Now, O Ephraim!" He makes an exclamation against him; O Ephraim, after all the means that have been used to recall thee, yet still, O Ephraim, thou continuest in thy idolatry.

And, "Ephraim, thou committest whoredom," thou dost it; thy sin is greater in this, for thou carriest the people with thee, and there is little hope of reformation till the great ones reform; if Ephraim commit whoredom, Israel must needs be defiled; so it follows:

"Israel is defiled." There is a twofold defilement of the people of Israel.

1. Defiled morally; that is, by their wicked works: as here, by their murders, and thefts, and adulteries.

2. "Israel is defiled;" that is, they defile my worship, and that defiles them. They have defiled my worship, and consequently are defiled themselves. And that I take to be especially meant here. "Israel is defiled;" that is, among other ways of defilement, they mingle with heathens, and bring them in to defile my worship. In Isa. xlvii. 6, God threatens to defile his sanctuary, and to pollute his inheritance: that is, when he suffers, by his just judgment, idolaters and heathens to come into his sanctuary, to mingle with his inheritance.

And then, Israel is defiled another way; that is, Israel mingles his own inventions with my worship; and Israel brings in, or suffers the heathen to come in to my worship, and so my worship is defiled, and they are defiled in consequence. Whence,

Obs. 4. Defiled worship exceedingly defiles the souls of people.

Nothing defiles the souls of men more; and, among other defilements in worship, the mixing with wicked and ungodly men, with such as God would not have come into his sanctuary, is especially injurious.

But you will say, Does the mixture of the wicked and ungodly defile the worship of God, or defile others in it? Is the sacrament of the Lord's supper the worse if wicked men partake of and unite in that rite? Am I the worse for it, or is the sacrament the worse, is that worship defiled? How may we refer this defilement of Israel to our defilement at this time? Is there any church in the world but has wicked ones in it? And will you say that they are defiled, and that the worship is defiled, because there are wicked amongst them? Then we can go no where in the world but we must be defiled, and the worship must be defiled.

Many think they may from this argue fairly, that there being a mixture in the best churches, therefore if mixtures make the communion defiled, then all are defiled. It comes fully in my way to speak to this point, and I shall do it briefly.

First, I know none who hold any otherwise but that, the best church in the world may have wicked men creep in and continue amongst them. Who knows the hearts of men when they come in? and therefore the best churches may have wicked men amongst them. This, I say, all men grant; therefore this objection, Will not there be wicked men in the best church? can have no strength in it, for no one denies it; and therefore they that make it, fight with a shadow.

But, secondly, I lay this for another position, which I think all will grant also, That the sacrament is not defiled to the receivers merely by the presence of the wicked. I verily believe every one will grant this; for my part I know none who denies this to be a truth, namely, that the sacrament is not defiled to the right receivers of it, merely because of the presence of wicked men. No one affirms the contrary to this, but all that I know of, even those that are the strictest in church order and discipline, will grant this to be a truth.

But then you will say, How shall we distinguish mixture of communion, or mixture of worship?

Not merely because wicked men are there. But, first, a congregation is then defiled, if they do not use the power that Christ has given to every church, of casting out all the scandalous persons that are amongst them. Now if any church shall (under what pretence soever, as saying they have no power, or that the power is taken from them, or the like) neglect this duty, viz. to cast out those that are unworthy, then the church is defiled, and their communion is defiled. So that their communion is not defiled because the wicked are there, but because they neglect the duties of casting them out. For let a man be a hypocrite, it is not the duty of the church to cast him out till he discover himself; but if then the church perform not its duty as it ought in his expulsion, then it is defiled. And the example of the incestuous Corinthian, in 1 Cor. v., plainly proves this. "A little leaven" (saith the apostle) "leaveneth the whole lump." What is that lump there? The church communion; and the leaven is the incestuous person; and the apostle gives order to cast him out, lest the "whole lump," the whole communion, should come to be defiled. So churches come to be defiled.

Again further, Not only churches come to be defiled, but, secondly, particular persons and communicants come to be defiled, if they neglect the duty that belongs to them as Christians. That is, Christ requires this, If thy brother offend thee, go and tell him his fault between thee and him alone; but if he will not hear thee, then take with thee one or two more; and if he shall neglect to hear them, tell it to the church. Now if thou hast done this thy duty to all scandalous persons in the congregation, then the sin rests on the church, thou mayst receive the sacrament with comfort, though wicked men be admitted to it: so that though the communion be defiled, that is, defiled to those that are guilty, to those that have neglected their duty; yet, if you but do your duty, then, though wicked men may be there, you may receive the sacrament with comfort; for though the communion may be defiled in respect of others who have neglected their duty, yet to you it cannot be defiled. Now then, to conclude this with that place in Psal. cxix. 1, Blessed is the man that is "undefiled in the way." Blessed are those men that in their way, in the course of their lives, keep themselves from defilement, and especially keep themselves from defilement in the ways of God's worship. Blessed is he whose heart is cleansed from secret filth, that does not defile himself in the vain, carnal plots and cunning fetches of wicked men.

Obs. 5. A defiled nation is near to ruin.

"Israel is defiled." He speaks of Israel that is ready to fall, for so it follows, ver. 5, "Israel and Ephraim shall fall;" and here just before he tells us, that Israel is defiled. When clothes are so defiled that they cannot be purged, we usually cast them out; so when there is defilement and filth amongst a people and they will not be purged, the Lord utterly rejects them. While God is indeed purging a nation, there is hope. As for example, though a garment be much defiled, yet if you see care taken and cost bestowed to cleanse it, that proves that there is an intention to preserve it. So while the Lord is adopting means to purge a nation, there is much hope that the Lord intends to save that nation. And we may comfortably hope that this is God's intention toward us. God knows, we have been a defiled people, and have defiled ourselves; never a one of us but may lay his hand upon his heart, and say, I have been defiled, and so may deserve to be an outcast. But behold, the Lord is bestowing cost upon us, and he is cleansing and purging us, and therefore we may hope that the Lord will not utterly reject us.

But no marvel that the Lord lets us and our brethren lie abroad in frosty nights. Many complain of much hardship, many of our brethren are sent from their comfortable houses, and are now fain to lie in the fields in the cold. No marvel, I say; this nation has been defiled. When clothes are much defiled, it is not enough to wash them and rinse them, but you lay them abroad in frosty nights. Yea, there are some defilements that cannot be taken away but by fire; and if the Lord will not only wash us and rinse us and lay us abroad, but put us into the fire for to cleanse us at last, blessed be his name.

Ver. 4. *They will not frame their doings to turn unto their God: for the spirit of whoredoms is in the midst of them, and they have not known the Lord.*

Here lies the evil. Though we be defiled, if God be about to cleanse us, there is hope; but if the words that follow in this 4th verse be applied to us, then we are a lost people indeed. Israel is defiled indeed, but Israel may be brought back again to the true worship of God. No, saith God, Israel is not only defiled, but he will not frame his doings to turn unto his God.

"They will not frame their doings to turn unto their God." The words in the original are very elegant, לא יתנו מעלליהם לשוב אל-אלהיהם Jerome and Vulg. render them, *Non dabunt cogitationes*, They will not give themselves to think of such a thing as turning unto the Lord. Mercer and Castellius, *Non dabunt operam*, They will not do their endeavours to turn unto the Lord. Tremellius, *Non adhibent actiones*, They do not apply any action of theirs any way to turn to the Lord. Drusius and Pagninus, *Non permittunt opera, et factu sua*, Their custom in their ways of sin will not suffer them to turn to the Lord. And the Septuagint and Calvin, thus, Οὐκ ἔδωκαν τὰ διαβούλια αὐτων, They give not their counsels, their studies, to turn to the Lord. These several translations I find of the words. And by all these conjoined, we may arrive at the knowledge of the meaning of the Spirit of God here; for the words are somewhat strange, therefore we need all the light we can get to find out their sense.

"They will not frame their doings." They will not give their mind to turn to the Lord, they will not put forth themselves into any posture that way. It is true, we can do nothing without the Lord, but yet the sin lies in our wills rather than in our power, therefore the will is charged by God. They cannot turn unto God of themselves, but yet they may do somewhat, they may bend their thoughts upon it, they may think of it, they may attend upon the means. But, saith the Holy Ghost, they will do nothing tending that way, they will not so much as set themselves into any kind of posture of turning unto me. This is to show what little hope of good there was in them for time to come. They are far enough from turning unto me, saith God, there is no such inclination in them, they are fully bent another way; though they cannot do it of themselves, yet they will not so much as give their minds to think of the means. Israel will not frame his doings to turn unto his God.

1. He will not so much as set his heart to think of any thing that will bring him unto God. Not so much as to think, Are my ways right or not right? What if it should prove that my ways are not right, what shall become of me then? This were one step God-ward, if a man but thus framed his doings to turn unto God; if he had but such thoughts as these, Lord, what am I doing? What is my way? Am I right or no? What if it should prove that my ways are not right, what will become of me? This were somewhat. But, saith God, these are far from any such hesitating thoughts in their sinful course, they run on violently and heedlessly, and will not so much as frame their minds to turn unto me.

2. Though a man cannot turn to God, yet through the common work of God's Spirit he may do this, he may be willing to hear and consider what is said for the ways of God. But, saith he, they are carried on with prejudice against the ways of God; let what will be said, they will not frame themselves to consider.

3. They will not wait upon God in the use of means. It is true, we are poor, weak, and ignorant creatures; but if we would wait upon God to know his mind, if we would set our faces that way, it may be God will reveal himself more clearly unto us. In Jer. l. 5, when God intends good to a people, it is promised, that "They shall ask the way to Zion, with their faces thitherward." True penitents will be inquiring after the ways of God with their faces standing thitherward. But, saith God, they will not do this, they will not set themselves to inquire thus after the mind and ways of God.

4. They will not apply the rule of the word to their actions. Whatsoever they see will make for their own ends, that they will follow, but they will not frame their doings so far as to take the rule of the word and apply it to their actions.

5. The light and power they have they will not use. They will not break off even gross offences, things that they cannot possibly but see to be evil. Though they cannot fully and immediately turn to God, yet there are some things so gross that they cannot possibly but see they are evil: yet, saith God, they will not so much as discontinue them, they will not use their power to reform them; and if they thus will not use that light which they have, what should they have more?

6. They will not join in with the work of God. When he is in his way toward them, when he himself is about to frame them, when he has them in his hand, they will oppose his work, they will not join in with it to frame themselves to turn unto God. But, Rom. viii. 7, it is said, "The carnal mind is not subject to the law of God, neither indeed can be." Therefore, in 2 Chron. xxx. 8, Hezekiah exhorteth the priests and the people, that they should not be "stiffnecked," but "yield themselves unto the Lord;" mark, the yielding of themselves unto the Lord is contrary to stiffneckedness. But now this people are stiffnecked, they will not yield themselves unto the Lord; though by his gracious dealings with them he is framing them to turn them unto himself, they oppose and stand out against God's work. Just as when you have a child that you would fain frame to such a gesture, and you take him and put him into such a way; but now he is so far from doing of it, that he wriggles up and down and will not suffer you to frame him. Why, saith God, I have been framing them myself, I have not only shown them what they should do, but my works have been so toward them that I have been framing them, but they are stiffnecked, they will not be framed, they will not join with my work in framing of them, they will break out in their wicked ways even at the very time when I am framing of them to turn them unto myself; according unto that expression you have in Hos. vii. 1, "When I would have healed Israel, then the wickedness of Samaria was discovered;" that is, when I was about to turn them unto me, then, even at that time, they break out in their violence and wickedness.

7. They will adhere to their old customs, to their former ways, to what they have received from their forefathers, and been trained up in, these they will keep to; but to frame themselves to turn unto the Lord, that they will not.

8. They will take and improve to the uttermost every advantage they can have against the ways of God. Those that are against framing of themselves to turn unto the Lord when God is about to turn them, discover it in this, that if at the time there be any advantage that their corrupt hearts can possibly take of the ways of God, they will take that and improve it to the uttermost: just as a child, if untoward, will take any advantage of you; so it is with those people who have no heart to turn unto the Lord. There is no preparation of their hearts, what then shall I do with

them? saith God: if their hearts were in any preparation it were somewhat, but they are not. We read in 2 Chron. xx., that the high places were not taken away, because the people had not prepared their hearts to turn unto the Lord. It is similar to this expression in the text, the people were not in a teachable, in a convertible frame of mind. The Lord grant that this Scripture may not be true of us at this day; that the reason why there remains so much evil in God's worship is, because the people have not prepared their hearts, they do not frame their doings to turn unto the Lord. It was a charge upon Rehoboam, in 2 Chron. xii. 14, that "He did evil, because he prepared not his heart to seek the Lord." But you will say, What power had he to turn unto the Lord? he was a wicked man. Yea, but this wicked man, though he had no saving grace, yet is charged for doing evil in that he did not prepare his heart to seek the Lord. God therefore expects that a people, though not able to turn to him thoroughly, yet should have their faces Zion-ward; and as a people in general, so every soul in particular.

Some that are not yet turned to the Lord, yet are in a way of turning, in a readiness to receive what God shall reveal. This is a happy condition. If God shall see a nation, though it be not fully reformed, ready to receive what he shall reveal, oh, this is a happy thing. As the Scripture saith, John iv. 35, "the fields are white already to harvest," that is, there was a preparation in the hearts of people to receive the gospel; they are ready to embrace what the mind of God is, when it shall be revealed unto them. Oh that this might be said of this people, they are willing to hear, consider, and observe, what God shall speak.

God is about to bring us out of superstition, both his works and word are tending that way; but there are multitudes of people that will not frame their doings to turn unto the Lord, their spirits are perverse, they are full of prejudice, froward, and reluctant to be convinced. The apostle Peter bids the saints, in Acts ii. 40, save themselves from that untoward generation. O, let not this charge be upon us, that we are an untoward generation, that God is framing us for good, but we will not frame our doings to turn unto the Lord. As we see a workman, when he has a piece of timber that is knotty and will not work in his hand, he casts it into the fire; or as clay that is not well tempered, will not work in the hand of the workman, he many times casts it away in anger, It will not work in my hand, what shall I do with it? The Lord is hewing of us by his prophets, and seeking to frame this nation to his will; O, let us work in God's hand, let us join in his design, and yield ourselves to the work of God, that the Lord may not cast us into the fire.

If we will not frame our doings to turn unto the Lord, he may break us, break that frame that we raise in our own imaginations. Perhaps we are framing to ourselves a strange kind of commonwealth, to enjoy our ease, and honours, and prosperity, and so we build castles in the air. O, but let us rather frame our hearts to turn unto the Lord. If we will not, God may put us into the fire again. A workman, you know, puts the iron into the fire that it may be worked into the form he wishes; and still the iron is hard and it will not frame to his hand, then he subjects it to the fire and hammer again. So the Lord hath begun to put us into the fire that we may frame our doings to turn unto him; and if these we have been in will not bring our hearts to a framable disposition, the Lord may return us to the fire again and again. And let not us complain of the heat of God's fire, but rather let us complain of the waywardness of our own hearts, that we do not frame our doings so as to turn unto the Lord.

But yet, through God's mercy, we cannot say but that there are many of every rank, here and throughout the rest of England, that are framing themselves to turn unto the Lord. Let us take notice of God's goodness, therefore, and enlarge a little on the proofs of this.

1. They have abolished what is sinful. It was a great plea among us, First let us know what we shall have, and then we will cast out this that we have. This was a plea fomented by the antichristian party; but, certainly, it was the way of God; and we have cause to bless God for it, that it put into the heart of the parliament and of the kingdom, to be willing to put down, and to cast out, and that by a solemn oath, by lifting up hands unto the most high God, whatsoever was naught.

2. Their willingness to be directed aright. The parliament has called an assembly, such as I believe never yet was in this nation, nor scarce in any other, men of gravity, judgment, and holiness, such as they thought might best direct them in the ways of God; and they profess that whatsoever shall be revealed to be the right way, they will walk in it. This is a good frame of heart.

3. Their solemn day of humiliation. The assembly has begun with such a day to humble themselves before God, that the Lord may guide them to direct aright those that had them. There was never such a work in England before that was begun with such a day of humiliation. Did your convocation ever keep such a day unto God, to beg of him directions in the work?

Let not people be discontented, or cast any slanders or calumnies upon them, because of some particular failings: for you must know, when God looks upon kingdoms and states, he does not so much regard particular actions as the general tendency; now that there is so much done in a public way, that there is so much framableness, though there be much failing in particulars, yet we have cause to bless God. It is true, those that would fain have a perfect reformation, would have men thoroughly frame themselves presently, and set up all presently without any more ado, and banish all presently. I suppose this results from a good intention, from love to Christ and his ordinances: but we must know it is not so easy to reform a whole nation that has been so corrupted and defiled; therefore, though there be not so perfect a reformation at present, yet let us bless God for what is done, that there is so much framing of the doings of the nation to turn unto the Lord, and not murmur and repine because all is not done that we desire.

And though perhaps they may never bring the work thoroughly to the pitch we desire, yet I make no question but what the parliament and assembly have done, will be enough to lay a foundation for another generation, if they bring it not to perfection themselves. Oh that the Lord would yet further frame our hearts and doings to turn unto him!

Has God at any time put into your heart a framable disposition to turn unto the Lord? Has God begun to make you think of your ways? Has he begun to excite fear in your hearts concerning your eternal estate? Has he wrought in you some desires to know him, to attend upon him in the use of means? Make much of this framable disposition, for it is very pleasing unto God; God complains where it is not, therefore he likes it where it is; and improve it: oh happy had it been with many had they improved that framable disposition that God had wrought in them! Cannot you remember, when sometimes you came to the word, what a melting frame of spirit you had? and in such an affliction you were as iron put into the fire, fit to be moulded into any form? But what is become of this disposition? Is it not worse with you now than before? Have you not lost it? The time was when the word excited in you good desires and dispositions, and you have thought, Oh, now I hope God will turn me to himself; I hope I shall never be at such a pass again as I have been: and thou didst begin to abandon such and such a corruption. This was a good frame, and if you had gone alone and sought God, and prayed of him to advance and perfect this work, it had been well with you; but you have fallen upon other business, and gone into company, and, it may be, on the next temptation have been overcome, and your hearts have been hardened. Iron, you know, when it has been once in the fire, and is grown cold, is more unmalleable than before: so it is with many, after they have been in some measure wrought upon by the word, and broken down by affliction, they have been more unframable than they were before.

And let us make much of it likewise in others. Is there any friend, or child, or kinsman, or acquaintance of yours, brought into this framable disposition? does the Lord begin to melt and soften their hearts? Is the Lord, by such a sermon, or by such an affliction, beginning to work upon them? Oh let me advance it as much as I can. The devil does so, when he sees us in a framable disposition to sin, he sets tempters on work to improve it; and we know it was the way of idolaters, when they saw England in a framable disposition to idolatry, what abundance were sent amongst us to improve it! Oh the mercy of God toward England, that when we were framing our doings to return to idolatry, the Lord comes and puts the frame of England more from thence than before it was! O let not us lose this framableness; though it is not so much as we desire, yet let not us lose what it is. England would be in a lamentable condition if it should lose what it has got from God already. Yet further on this,

Obs. 1. Apostates seldom have any inclination to turn unto God.

No meltings of spirit, no yieldings, but their hearts are hardened, and they depart further and further from God; for so he speaks of Israel as an apostatizing people. I dare almost challenge you all, when did you ever know a notorious apostate turn unto God? Very rarely. I will not say it is impossible, but with respect to apostates that are men of parts, and have gone far from God, if they have but proceeded so far as to be persecutors or contemners of the truth, as these Israelites here were, when did you ever know any of them to turn unto God? "They will not frame their doings."

"Their God." Their God: 1. By profession. 2. Their God who has showed much mercy to them, and has done them much good. 3. The God who is yet willing to be their God. They will not return unto him.

This is the aggravation of their sin, that they will not turn to such a God. What! not turn to him whom they profess to be theirs, whom they flatter with their mouths, and say that all their good and happiness is in him? not to him who has so blessed them all their days? not to him who is yet willing to be reconciled to them? Oh this is a sore and bitter evil indeed, that they will not turn to this God.

But yet there is a further thing observable here.

Obs. 2. True repentance is not only to leave evil and to do good, but to turn unto God as our God: "*Their* God."

To turn to God as a God in covenant with us; as a God in whom is our portion and happiness; as a God willing to be reconciled. Here indeed is the very formality of repentance. A man may, by the terrors of the law, turn from the practice of a sin; he may, by the strength of natural conscience and self-interest, set upon good duties; but here is no true repentance. True repentance is this, when we look upon God as tendering himself to us as a covenant God in Christ, and so we turn unto him. In Jer. iii. 22, "Return, ye backsliding children," (saith the Lord,) "and I will heal your backslidings." Now mark the answer of true penitents; "Behold, we come unto thee; for thou art the Lord our God." So when God calls to a sinner, Return, O return unto the Lord, for he is willing to be your God in an everlasting covenant; he manifests his grace toward you in his Son, and offers you mercy there; yea, he is willing to heal all your backslidings and forgive all your sins: and a sinner answers, "Behold, we come unto thee; for thou art the Lord our God:" true, indeed, we have sought after vanity, but now our good, our happiness, is in thee; "we come unto thee, for thou art the Lord our God:" here is true repentance.

"For the spirit of whoredoms." Here is the reason why they turn not unto the Lord, "The spirit of whoredoms is in the midst of them."

1. Many understand by this, that evil unclean spirit that possessed them. And then the observation is,

Obs. 3. It is God's just judgment to give men over to the devil to be blinded and hardened, when they forsake him and his truth.

Do not excuse thy sin by saying it is the devil that tempts thee, for this may prove its aggravation, that by the just judgment of God thou art now given up to be under the power of the devil, and to be acted upon by him. As in Eph. ii. 2, the Scripture speaks of the miserable estate that men are in by nature, dead in sin, the children of wrath; and amongst other aggravations of their misery, this is not the least, they walk according to "the spirit that now worketh in the children of disobedience." The word translated "worketh," ἐνεργουντος, implies an effectual, internal activity; and this is an aggravation of their misery, and not any excuse to them for their sin. Thou hast rejected the good Spirit, the holy Spirit of God; and now the spirit of whoredom, an unclean, vile spirit, works in thee.

2. By "the spirit of whoredoms," others understand a violent inclination to uncleanness, both spiritual and bodily, confirmed by indulgence. We have had this phrase before, in chap. iv. 12. The spirit of fornication. So then, saith the prophet, they will not turn to the Lord, for there is a violent inclination of spirit, an impetus with which they are carried on in the ways of wickedness, that there is little hope of turning them to God. "The spirit of whoredoms," that is, the efficacy that there is in that wicked disposition of their hearts to carry them on so violently. In 2 Thess. ii. 11, the Scripture saith, that because men love not the truth, the Lord gives them up to the efficacy of error: "And for this cause God shall send them strong delusion, that they should believe a lie;" so it is in your translations, but the words, ἐνέργεια πλάνης, signify the efficacious inworking of error, to carry them on irresistibly from error to error. We find sometimes, in men carried on to erroneous opinions, such an impetus of spirit, such an efficacy of the error in them, which so hurries on their hearts, that they cannot calmly or quietly listen to any thing calculated to undeceive them. That is a spirit of error; God gives them up to the efficacy, the spirit, the activity, the power of error, to believe a lie.

"Is in the midst of them." That is, it is come into them, and sitteth as a king and ruleth in their hearts. An evil spirit may beset the godly, may compass them about, but it gets not into their midst, they keep it out from the throne, it does not reign over them. The coming into the midst of them, denotes the full possession that this unclean spirit, this impetus and strong inclination of mind, has over them. And therefore you find, in Prov. viii. 20, that it is said of wisdom, "I lead in the way of righteousness, in the midst of the paths of judgment." That is, wisdom not only brings men to the verge of God's ways, to be a little taken with their outside, but brings them into "the midst of the paths of judgment;" that is, they come wholly into them, so that they even take full possession of them. So in 1 Sam. iv. 3, "Let us fetch the ark of the covenant of the Lord out of Shiloh unto us, that, when it cometh among us, it may save us." The force of the Hebrew is, that it may come into the midst of us, and there have full power to do us good and save us. They depended much on the ark, and yet it failed them. By the way, we may depend too much on a good cause; the cause may be good, and yet, depending on it, and neglecting to reform our own lives, we may fail as they did here.

בקרבם

Many men receive an evil spirit quickly into their midst, when, God knows, the good Spirit of the Lord stands knocking at the door of their hearts, and cannot have entertainment even in the outer room.

"And they have not known the Lord." That is, they know not my greatness, my holiness, they know not what a jealous God I am. Idolaters have low and mean apprehensions of God. The right knowledge of God will lead the heart to seek after the worship acceptable to him; but when men know not God, and discern not his glory, greatness, and excellency, they think to put him off with their own devices and will worship, their own fancies and conceits. A soul that rightly apprehends what God is, dares not tender up to God any worship but his own.

Now from the connexion of these words, "The spirit of whoredoms is in the midst of them, and they have not known the Lord," a specially important observation flows.

Obs. 4. Impetuousness of spirit blinds the mind.

"The spirit of whoredoms is in them;" and then follows, "they have not known the Lord." Whatsoever is said then against their way cannot convince them. Men do not consider how they come to be blinded, although ordinary experience points out the manner: when the mind is possessed by passion, love, fear, sorrow, or any other strong affection, and carried out powerfully to the object which excites them, it will not listen to, will not understand, any thing urged against it; the voice of reason is unheeded, charming never so wisely. Some have a spirit of sluggishness, and they love their ease; a spirit of covetousness, and they must have their estates; a spirit of ambition, and they must have their honour and respect; a spirit of pride and self-love, and they must not on any account grant that they are ignorant and mistaken; therefore they cannot see the truths, the ways of God. But now let God humble such men, let the edge of their spirits be taken off, let him come and but mortify these their prevailing lusts, and then they with ease begin to see that which they could never see before; then a mere hint of any truth moves their hearts; whereas before, all the means of conviction were unavailing.

O my brethren, when we come to examine truths, let us look to our spirits. "Blessed is the man that feareth the Lord;" him will the Lord teach in his right way. When a man, humbling his soul before the Lord, and being jealous of his own spirit, examines a truth, and cries to God to subdue what is evil in him, and to give him a teachable heart to discover the truth; suppose that yet he cannot find it; let such a man walk according to the light whereunto he has attained, and he may rest in hope that God in due time will show him more. But that which is evil in God's eyes, and in the eyes of the saints, is, when men are hindered from seeing a truth by a spirit of opposition to it. No gracious heart can take it ill, if he see one that has a spirit subject to God, a spirit wherein the fear of God appears, in an unfeigned desire to know what the mind of God is: suppose that for the present I cannot make such a man understand what I would, yet so long as his spirit is thus submissive to God, I have no cause to be provoked against him, but to treat him with all love, meekness, and gentleness, and expect that God in due time will reveal himself unto him. But when one professes to desire to know the truths and mind of God; and yet there appears a spirit of opposition, pride, and vain-glory; oh, this it is which is grievous in the eyes of God, and wearisome to his saints.

Ver. 5. *And the pride of Israel doth testify to his face: therefore shall Israel and Ephraim fall in their iniquity; Judah also shall fall with them.*

Mark, as there is a connexion between a spirit of whoredom and not knowing God, so there is a connexion between not knowing God and the pride of Israel. They know not the Lord, and the pride of Israel doth testify to his face. From whence,

Obs. 1. Ignorance and pride usually go together.

There are no men so conceited of their knowledge as the ignorant. For where there is knowledge, there a man sees that he knows but little, and is able to discover his own deficiency; but an ignorant man is not able to discover his own ignorance, and therefore usually he is proud. You shall have many men, and women too, that will pretend such abundance of knowledge, and their hearts are puffed up, because they have got some expressions more than others have, as if they were somebody, and had some manifestations of things to them more than others have; yet come and examine things at the bottom, and the truth is, they are ignorant of the very principles of religion. 1 Tim. vi. 4, "He is proud, knowing nothing," saith the text; and yet he speaks of those that are full of vain questions and janglings about matters of religion, that will come with such objections and curiosities of questions, yet the Holy Ghost saith, he is proud and knows nothing. And certainly, the man that is there spoken of is a man as much conceited of his knowledge as you can conceive a man to be, as appears plainly in the text.

But now, wisdom and humility, they likewise go together too. "With the lowly is wisdom," Prov. xi. 2. If the heart be brought under God, put in a gracious, humble, lowly frame, with the lowly there is wisdom, the Lord delighteth to reveal himself to the humble.

"The pride of Israel." The Seventy read the words otherwise: The injury and the wrong that Israel has done unto God, shall be brought down, shall be humbled: for I suppose their meaning in that translation is, that whereas Israel by his wicked ways has wronged and been injurious to God, he shall be humbled for it, he shall be brought down and made to know what it is for him so to wrong God. And indeed, those that corrupt God's worship are the greatest wrongers of God in the world, they do the greatest injury unto God.

ταπεινωθήσεται ἡ ὕβρις τοῦ Ἰσραήλ.

But we may safely keep to the translation in your books, as more suitable to the original than that of the Seventy, and then the observation is,

Obs. 2. Idolaters are proud men, and idolatry is a proud sin.

The scope of the prophet here is chiefly to rebuke them for their false worship; though he speaks of other sins, yet that is the main. "The pride of Israel doth testify to his face;" Israel will have their own way of worship and forsake God, O proud hearts that they have! Idolatry is a proud sin. In all disobedience against God there is much pride: pride of the heart is manifested not only in clothes and in fine things, but in disobedience against God; and as in all sin there is pride, so in a more peculiar manner in the sin of idolatry. For,

1. Idolaters regard the true worship of God as a mean thing, as a thing beneath them. Their way of worship is pompous, fine, and splendid; but the true worship of God is poor, low, and mean. All your superstitious and idolatrous people look thus on the simplicity of the ways and worship of God.

2. They presume to put more dignity on a creature than God has, to put more honour on places than God and nature have imposed. God has made them thus and thus, but I will exalt them higher, and put an excellency, a spiritual, yea, a divine excellency upon them; for so idolaters take upon themselves to do, and this is horrible pride.

3. They prescribe the form of God's worship. The worship of God is the dearest thing he has in the world; and for any creature to take upon him to prescribe which way he shall be worshipped, is the most notorious pride in the world.

4. They honour what is a man's own because it is his own, rather than what is God's. Do not you see it plainly in all superstitious, idolatrous people? As in that one thing of days? God has set one day apart for the honouring of himself, and for the celebration of the birth, death, resurrection, and ascension of Jesus Christ, and of the whole work of our redemption: how is that day slighted and neglected! But what a horrible wickedness is it accounted not to keep that which man sets apart by himself, that day which is of man's appointment! Men will set apart a day for the honour of Christ, and insist that Christ is quite forgotten if that day be forgotten, and Christ is much dishonoured if that day be not regarded. I appeal to you, who sets it apart? whose is it? Is it God's, or is it yours? God's? Certainly, if such a thing were so acceptable to God as men conceive it to be, we should have some little hint, somewhat in the book of God regarding it. We have the story of all the acts of the apostles, what they did in several places, and there is not the least mention of any such thing of their honouring Christ, by setting a day apart for the celebration of his nativity: we have the epistles to several churches upon several occasions, and we find no notice taken of any such thing in any church they established. Surely therefore it is men's own, there is nothing in God's word for it, how highly soever it is honoured. But we have enough in Scripture for God's own day, the Lord's day; it is appointed by God himself to be a day of thanksgiving for the birth, resurrection, and ascension of Christ, and for the whole work of our redemption: but man, out of his pride, will have another day, and so set his post by God's post; he thinks it is not honour enough to Christ to put the celebration of his birth, death, resurrection, ascension, all together in one day; no, he thinks it conduces more to the honour of Christ to have several days, one for his birth, another for his resurrection, and another for his ascension; whereas God hath put all into one, and would have his Son honoured by the observation of that one day.

וענה בפניו "Doth testify to his face." In the original it is, answereth to his face. When any thing is returned suitable to the work expended, that is said to answer that work: as, when the ground brings forth corn for the husbandman, then it answers to the seed and labour of the husbandman; Gen. xxx. 33, "So shall my righteousness answer for me," saith Jacob to Laban, I shall have that which is suitable to my righteousness. So here, The pride of Israel answereth to his face, that is, the fruit of their pride shall be, in the punishment of it, fully answerable to its sinfulfulness: so I find many render it. Micah i. 2, "Let the Lord God be witness against you," testify against you, (it is the same in Hebrew,) or answer you according to your sins, in the way of punishment. When the Lord brings suitable judgments, full up to the measure of men's sins, those judgments do answer; yea, and witness against them, they witness to the faces of those men the guilt of those sins.

Well, but we will rather take it, and so it is to be understood I think, according to what you read in your books, "The pride of Israel doth testify to his face:" that is, the pride that appears in Israel doth fully testify the horrible wickedness and obstinacy that is in Israel, it testifies it to his face. It is true, you cannot see the heart; but pride in the heart seldom lies there long secret, for it is a sin that must be aboveboard; pride must vent itself, in that its glory consists. You could not see the vileness and wickedness that was in a sinner's heart before; but now this sin "pride" that is sent forth, is a loud witness against him of the evil that dwells within.

There is a secret pride, and a witnessing pride. Isa. iii. 9, "The show of their countenance doth witness against them; and they declare their sin as Sodom, they hide it not," but manifest it outwardly in their very countenance: it is taken from harlots; some that are at first departed from their husbands keep things very secretly, and you shall perceive them demure in their countenance; but at length they come to be bold and impudent in their filthiness, and you may perceive adultery in their very countenance, and they witness openly in their words and looks the wickedness of their hearts. As that sin of adultery, so almost all sins are witnessed where pride is discovered. No sin disgraces men more than pride, and that is the curse of God upon it. Pride seeks for the greatest honour to a man, and there is nothing that doth more dishonour him. Why? Because pride doth testify that there is a woeful deal of evil in that man's heart: as I will instance a little.

A man that differs in judgment from his brethren in divers things, pretends this, he cannot see the truth of God, which he would fain see; he cannot do as his brother, for his conscience bindeth him otherwise. But, you will say, every man pleads conscience; how shall we know whether it be the stoutness of his heart, or the tenderness of his conscience? Thus, if this man behaves himself humbly, and the rather humbly in all other things, because he cannot see as his brother in some particulars, and so is in danger to be an offence to his brother, and therefore his soul is humbled;* this is a good witness that it is conscience, and not mere obstinacy, that makes him differ. But now, if his behaviour be high and proud when he differeth from his brother, and he does not consider it as an affliction to him that he cannot see as his brother, but censures him, and thinks that it is either through his weakness or his wilfulness that he will not see, and so carries himself high and proudly before his brother, this witnesseth to his face that it is stubbornness and singularity. Thus his pride testifies to his face the inward wickedness of his heart.

And as in a church, this is a principle, that though a man be guilty of many and great sins, yet he is not to be cast out but for obstinacy. You will say, How shall we know that obstinacy is in a man's heart? I know many observe such and such rules for it, as, if you do not reform when certain learned men tell you what they would do, &c. But we say, if, after an offence and admonition, any one in a congregation conducts himself proudly, this, his proud behaviour, witnesseth to his face, that it is not out of tenderness or scruple of conscience that he yields not to what his

* Or, that his brother does not see what he does. This passage must be understood, 1. Of lesser differences. 2. Not absolutely nor always, but in things wherein one is not clear; for if he be, he cannot but think it is at least weakness in that particular, (though in others he may judge him stronger than himself,) that he does not see the same with him.

brethren would have him, but through the stoutness of his heart. His " pride testifieth to his face."

The pride of men's hearts witnesses much against them. I remember I have read in Bede, a story of a synod or assembly of divines, held in England in the time of Austin, then bishop of Canterbury. On convening together they went to a holy anchorite, to advise with him, whether they should yield to what Austin desired to impose on them? and he replied, If he be a man of God, yield to him; if not, stand out against him. They answer, A man of God! how shall we know that, whether he be a man of God or no? Whereupon he said, If he be humble; for Jesus Christ saith, " Learn of me, for I am meek and humble in heart:" if he be a humble man, he is a man of God, and then learn of him. But how shall we judge of his humility? say they: and he replied, You shall perceive it by his behaviour: let him arrive at the place of assembly before you, and if then you perceive him behave himself imperiously, proudly, not so much as to rise to show you any respect, then take it for granted that he is a proud man, and reject what he imposes; but if he be meek, humble, and lowly in his demeanour to you, then regard what he saith. So when they came to the assembly, Austin sat in his chair, in a proud, imperious manner, and would not stir to any of them: upon that they rejected whatsoever he said, for according to the counsel of the holy man, his pride did witness to his face that he had a vile and a wicked heart, and did not come to them in the name of Christ.

That which comes from the humble and lowly is much to be regarded. Humility does witness to the face of a man, that he knows much of the mind of Christ; and pride witnesses to the face of a man, that he is not acquainted with the mind of Christ.

The word גאוך here translated " pride," I find that a learned interpreter, Livelius, because in itself it signifies excellency, thinks it refers to God, who swears " by the excellency of Jacob," Amos viii. 7; and so interprets it thus, That God who is the excellency of Israel, in whom Israel should glory, is he that doth witness against them. And I find some incline to this; but the other I conceive rather to be the scope of the Holy Ghost, taking the word as it is translated for " pride," and the " testifying to his face" for an open, apparent witnessing, so as to render it manifest.

" Therefore shall Israel and Ephraim fall in their iniquity." Ephraim is the princes of Israel; they were proud because of the honour they had. And Israel, the people, they were proud because they had great men to bear them out, and they could plead authority for what they did. But they shall both fall, both Ephraim and Israel. Hence,

Obs. 3. The fruit of sin is a casting down.

It is here said, they shall fall, rather than that they shall be punished, in reference to what went before; for there he had spoken of the pride of Israel: and from thence further

Obs. 4. Pride goes before a fall. God will cast down the proud; and certainly, when those that are proud fall, they must needs fall very low, because a proud man lifts up himself on high, and you know, according to the height, so is the fall: now a proud man lifts up himself so high indeed, as even to exalt himself above God, therefore his fall must needs be very great. And upon this I remember Bernard remarks, Here is the reason why a proud man can have no grace from God. Why? God is the fountain of grace, and it is a rule in nature, that the stream that comes from a fountain ascends no higher than its source. Now God being the fountain of all grace, surely grace cannot rise higher than God himself; but a proud man lifts himself up above God, therefore he is above grace, grace cannot reach him.

1. A proud man goes from God, as if he could live without him; for that is the pride of men's hearts, when they have outward prosperity they go from God, as if they could live without him.

2. He goes against God, as if he were able to resist him.

3. He goes beyond God, as if he made himself the end of all his actions.

4. He lifts up himself above God, as if there were more excellency in him than in God. He lifts up his will above God, and that two ways:

(1.) He desires his will to be followed rather than God's.

(2.) Whereas God is contented to have his will only in just and good things; a proud man saith, I will have my will, whether it be just or not. Come and deal with a proud man and say, Do you well in this? is this fit? I will have my will, is the reply: this is more than God challenges to himself. God will have his will in nothing but what is good and just; thou wilt have thy will whether it be just or no: thus thou goest beyond God, and liftest up thyself above him, therefore surely thou shalt fall.

I need not show you any example of the fall of proud men; this our age manifests it clearly enough. How hath God cast a stain on proud, superstitious men! You know what a height they were grown to, two or three years since; and now two, if not three, kingdoms have lifted up their hands to the most high God to extirpate them. Their pride did testify to their faces, and no marvel that they are fallen; and the Lord cast them so far down, that they may never be able to rise up in their pride again.

" In their iniquity." The Hebrew ב בעונם signifies for, as well as "in;" fall for their iniquity, as well as in their iniquity. But to keep to the word, they shall " fall in their iniquity." Surely they fall hard who fall in their iniquity, they fall so as to break their bones, yea, ofttimes to their utter destruction.

My brethren, these are falling times, and if we fall in our iniquities, great and grievous shall be our fall; but if our iniquities be removed by faith and repentance, though we should fall, yet we shall fall into the bosom of our Father, and into the arms of Jesus Christ. How much better is it, seeing that men are like to fall, to labour then to remove our iniquities beforehand, and not to fall in them! And if we fall not in our iniquity, but in the cause of God, and on account of the grace given unto us, then we may be of more use in our fall than we were in our standing. As it is with corn, which falling into the ground fructifies, and is more profitable then than when it was in the granary; so many godly men, many young ones, that are fallen within these two or three years, not in or for their iniquity, but in the cause of God, and in the exercise of their graces. They are fallen indeed, but fallen into the arms of God, and into the bosom of Christ; and they are as fruitful in their fall as they were in their standing, for no question but God will cause much fruit and a plentiful harvest for England to arise in consequence.

"Judah also shall fall with them." Mark, first Ephraim shall fall, and then Judah, for indeed Ephraim was first in sin. The ten tribes first forsook the true worship of God, and they brought in Judah together with them, and the text saith, that " Judah shall fall with them." This is here mentioned to aggravate Ephraim's sin, and the judgment attendant, thus; This shall lie heavy on Ephraim one day, that not only he has ruined himself, but ruined Judah too; brought Judah into his sin, and involved him in his plagues. Hence,

Obs. 5. It is a great aggravation for any one to think what misery he brings others into, when God truly enlightens his conscience. It may be God's hand is upon thee for thy sin. This is grievous. Oh but, together with the sin, have not I by my counsel, by my example, by my countenance, brought others into sin? And I have brought them into misery as well as myself: it may be there are many in hell at this time whom I have holpen thither. It is true, God's hand is upon me: I am falling, and whither I shall fall I know not; I see hell open, and I may fall into it; however, I am afraid of this, that there are some fallen into hell already, of whose sin I was the cause; and is it possible that I should be preserved out of it? must I not follow them and fall thither too, when they are there already through my wickedness? You, therefore, that have associated with, and led others to wickedness, many of your companions may be dead and gone, without any manifestation of repentance; you had indeed need to be thoroughly humbled.

Obs. 6. It is no plea, you see, for any one to say, I will follow the example of others. If you will follow the example of others you must perish with others. Judah follows the example of Ephraim, and Judah must fall with Ephraim.

Obs. 7. If God's people comply with wicked men, they must expect to fall with them in outward judgments. Judah was the only people God had on the earth, and as Israel is a type of the apostate church so is Judah a type of the true church; yet it seems that Judah, though the true church and the only people of God, very much complied with Israel; and complying with Israel in false worship, they must fall with them. Come out from amongst them, my people, lest, being partakers of their sins, you be partakers of their plagues too. And this, I make no question, is the reason why so many of God's servants fall at this day, they have conformed to the times and defiled themselves; though we cannot say so of every one of them that fall in this cause, yet it is to be feared it has been the case with many. And it may be, though we dare not determine of God's ways, for the thoughts of God's ways in mercy are higher than our thoughts, higher than the heavens are above the earth, yet we have cause to fear that many, if not most of this generation, shall fall before God brings forth this glorious work of his in saving our Zion.

But here is a difficulty; in the first chapter you heard that God, though he threatened Israel, yet said, "I will have mercy upon Judah;" but here he saith, Ephraim shall fall, and Judah shall fall with him. Now for the reconciling of that, we are to know that though Judah fall with Israel, yet there shall be a great deal of difference in their fall. Israel, the ten tribes, shall be brought into captivity so as never to return again; I mean, never to return from their captivity as Judah did; Judah was to return again after seventy years: so Judah fell with them, but they fell not as they fell. Though the saints therefore may be scourged with rods, yea, with scorpions, as they are at this day, as well as wicked men, yet the Lord does not, will not, take his loving-kindness from them.

There is yet one particular more to be observed, and it is from the Hebrew particle גם, "Judah *also* shall fall with them;" and I question not but the Spirit of God holds forth this note from it.

Obs. 8. The falling of the saints with wicked men is of special consideration. There is much in it; some special matter to be considered of in the falling of God's people with the wicked. Indeed it is that which, in these days, puts us to a stand; we wonder at the ways of God, his judgments are past finding out: we must adore them in what we do not understand. That the hand of God should be stretched out against the wicked, against such as have corrupted his worship by their own superstitions, is no marvel; but that so many of his dear saints, so precious in his eyes, in all the surrounding countries, should suffer such hard things, and fall together with the wicked, we are at a stand, and know not what this means. What! Judah fall also with Israel, when God had no other people on the face of the earth? surely there is some great matter in it. It is, I say, of special consideration: and there are many things that God would have us seriously to observe in the fall of his people together with wicked men.

1. How holy a God he is. He spared not his own Son, and he spares not his dearest ones. He will give the dearly beloved of his soul into the hands of his enemies. God had but one Son that never sinned against him; but he has not one son that never was afflicted by him. And therefore we have no cause to wonder that the godly sometimes suffer, for his own Son did.

2. None must presume on former services. When Israel forsook God Judah did cleave to God's true worship, and in that God was much honoured. But Judah must not rely on that; Oh, I have done service for God, when others forsook him I cleaved to him; and so think to take more liberty afterward. No, saith God, though Judah has much honoured me, and adhered to my worship, when Israel, the ten tribes, forsook me, yet if Judah shall afterwards comply with Israel, Judah shall likewise fall. None must presume upon former services. It is customary with men, if they have been useful in some things, to begin to take liberty to themselves to do what is not convenient, thinking that because they have done some service they must not now be contradicted in any of their desires. Thus we find it often among men, and from this many amongst us have fallen. How many have there been, that in the beginning of this parliament, and at the commencement of these wars, have done good service for the commonwealth; and afterwards began to be high and proud, and they must have what they will, and none must contradict them, but every body must submit unto them! and so through their pride, though they have done good service, yet afterward they fall. Let every one take heed of this, both in regard of God, and also with respect to man. You that have been most forward in the public cause, never think to presume because of what you have done; but walk humbly now, and be serviceable still, for otherwise you may fall, notwithstanding your services, as Judah did.

3. God engages himself to no people if they transgress. "Judah also shall fall:" by that God declares that there are no men, though never so useful, but he can do without. Perhaps you may think, if you desert the cause, where will there be any to stand up in your room? Take heed, though you may think you are the most useful man, either in the ministry, or in the city, know that God can do without you, and you may fall as well as other men.

4. If his own people fall with the wicked, what then may wicked men expect? If such things be done to the green trees, what shall be done to the dry? If judgment begin at the house of God, where shall the wicked and ungodly appear?

Ver. 6. *They shall go with their flocks and with their herds to seek the Lord: but they shall not find him; he hath withdrawn himself from them.*

Shall they fall? No, they have a way to prevent it; they will pacify God with the multitude of their sacrifices, their flocks and their herds, they are content to spend those all in sacrifices unto God; and shall this people fall? There is much to be observed from every word here; the interpretation is not difficult, and the observations I shall pass briefly.

"They shall go." ילכו *Ibunt huc et illuc, modo ad*

hunc, modo ad illum montem, as interpreters render it; They shall run up and down, from one place to another, from one sacrifice to another, in a kind of hurry of spirit. And from that word there may be this observed:

Obs. 1. Those who depend on duties are in a distraction of spirit when their duties prevail not. They often change their duties, but they change not their hearts. Many think, Well, I have done thus; yea, but if I shall add this to what I have done, then I shall prevail: whereas those that do their duties in obedience to God, and go out of themselves and depend for their acceptance on a higher sacrifice, on Jesus Christ; these go on with much sweetness and quietness of spirit, though for the present they see not the thing performed which they aim at in their duties: their spirits are not in a hurry and in a distraction as the spirits of others that depend upon their duties.

Obs. 2. God contemns the services of hypocrites, of superstitious and idolatrous apostates. "With their flocks and herds." He means, with their sacrifices, but he gives them not the name of sacrifices, but only "their flocks and herds," for they are not worthy of that name.

Obs. 3. It is a sad thing when God will not own as his what we tender up to him. "Their flocks and their herds." Mark, they make use of their own, according to their own mind, in their own ways, to worship me as they list; and therefore God doth not call them his, doth not own them as his, but he terms them "*their* flocks and *their* herds;" What they do, saith God, what they offer, is their own, their flocks and their herds, I will not own them: so in our sacrifices of prayer and praise, typified by those legal sacrifices, in which we seem to tender up ourselves wholly unto God; for God to say, All that you have presented all this while in your prayers, I own not, these are none of mine, they are all your own; this were indeed a sad thing.

There is no such way to put an excellency upon any thing we have, upon our parts, abilities, or estates, as this, to tender them up first unto God; and if God shall please to own them, then to receive them again out of his hands; we shall then receive them with abundance of sweetness and excellency. But here he calls them, "*their* flocks and *their* herds;" though they were tendered unto God in sacrifice, yet he will not say they are his, but their own. Thus it is with all hypocrites, and formal and superstitious persons, in their services. Self is the principle of what you do, and therefore all your services remain your own, you serve yourself rather than God in them.

Herein lies the sweetness and true comfort of a man's estate, or of whatsoever he possesses, when he shall consecrate and devote them all to God so that they remain no longer his own. This is a sacrifice that God is well pleased with. These are my talents, saith God, this is my estate, here I return to you again: and when a man shall take what he has as having first consecrated and devoted it to God, and receiving it out of God's hand again, O, this adds a sweetness and a blessing to it. All we have is God's, as he is the first cause of all; but mark, God rejoices as much, if not more, in a second right that he has to our possessions, namely, by our tendering up all to him in a gracious manner, as he does in the first right of being the cause of all. I beseech you observe this, God has a twofold right to the estates, parts, and abilities of his people. First, he has a right to them as he is the cause of them; I gave them to you, therefore they are mine. But secondly, when his servants by an exercise of grace shall offer them up again to him, Now, saith God, they are mine by a second right; and this second right to them, they being tendered up to me in a holy manner, is the right that I rejoice in; and this will be most comfortable to you. O my brethren, let us not deprive God of this second right to all we have, or are, or can do, for this will not at all weaken our right, but strengthen, sweeten, and bless our possessions abundantly.

Obs. 4. Superstitious and idolatrous people are abundant in their services. "They shall go with their flocks and with their herds."

They are content to go with all their flocks and their herds to seek after God; thousands of rams and ten thousand rivers of oil, any thing to offer up unto God; but mark, it is in their own form, and on their own ordinances, men will expend in abundance; on God's, as little as possible, as might be again instanced in in regard of setting of days apart for God.

Natural conscience tells us, that when we have to do with God in our services, great things are suitable to a great God. Your papists, in times of straits, have a kind of praying which continues for forty hours together; but it is in their own way, they will be abundant enough in that. Many of you think much to spend a quarter of an hour in a morning or in an evening in seeking God in your families; when superstitious and idolatrous people are abundant in those services, in seeking God in their own way.

But observe, though superstitious and idolatrous people be abundant in their services to their idols, yet they are not infinite in them. But the saints of God, if their spirits be right, are enlarged to a kind of infiniteness in God's service. As thus, they would still know more of God's mind, do more, and are never satisfied with what they do. There is no idolatrous and superstitious person, but confines himself within some limits, and thinks that when that task is over, when the forty hours are elapsed, the work is done: but now here is the difference between a natural work and a spiritual; a natural work is always a limited work, but a spiritual work has always an infiniteness in it; thus, though I am not able to do what is actually infinite, yet my heart is infinite in this, that it is never satisfied, but it would fain have more, and if I were able to do ten thousand times more than I do, yet my heart would be as eager to do more as it was at first; I should not think I am any nearer to the end of my journey than I was at the first day; for I am to deal with an infinite God, therefore let my services be never so great and many, yet still my ardent desires are to rise higher and to do more. Here is the supernatural work of grace, which goes beyond all the idolatry in the world.

Obs. 5. Superstitious and idolatrous people will spare no cost in their worship.

They will go with their flocks and with their herds, bestow all their estates on the service of their idols. How shameful is it for us to be so niggardly in the true service of God! Never men had larger opportunities to honour God with their estates than at this present time. And certainly men should rather rejoice that they have an opportunity to serve God with their estates, than murmur that his service requires the sacrifice.

"They shall go with their flocks and with their herds, to seek the Lord."

Obs. 6. There is a time when vile and wicked men shall see a need of God. "They shall go with their flocks and with their herds to seek the Lord."

Though wicked men, when they have all about them suitable to their carnal desires, slight and neglect God, yet there is a time when they shall be brought into such a condition that they shall see their need of him. O, let us remember this in the midst of our prosperity! We find by experience that God does bring men to times wherein they see need of him; oh, therefore, now the love and mercy of God, the pardon of our sins, and peace with God, how precious should they be in our eyes!

It is good to make God our friend, whom we are sure we shall one day have need of. We all conclude that it is a point of wisdom to make such a man our friend, of whom we can certainly say, we shall one day have need of him. O, let us be sure to make God our friend, for certainly one day we shall have need of him. Blessed are those souls who have an interest in that God whose friendship all the world shall one day require.

Obs. 7. All pretend to seek God. "They shall go with their flocks and with their herds to seek the Lord."

Whatsoever they do, they do it for the honour of God, and for the service of God, and out of respect to him; and why should not we do this and this? we have good aims and good intentions, do we not seek to honour God in what we do? When those idolaters of Israel set up the calf, they proclaimed a day to Jehovah, a day for the honouring of God, and pretended that what they did was out of respect to God, and to honour him. The worst men and the most superstitious will yet profess to honour God. So it is again in regard of those days that men have set apart for God, and it is that which has settled men in the superstitious observation of them, that it is for the honour of Christ; What! (say they,) shall we not honour the birth of our blessed Saviour? what profaneness, what a disrespect is this to the Lord Christ! Well, let others do what they will, for our parts we will observe it, for hereby we shall do honour to our blessed Saviour. So the papists, for the adoration of images, say, What! not regard nor reverence the image, the picture of our blessed Saviour, and of the holy saints? And the truth is, if it be duly weighed, there is the same reason for images of Christ and his saints, as for days set apart to the honour of Christ by man's invention; and there is as fair a pretence for honouring Christ by setting up his image before me to remind me of him, as by keeping a day of mine own appointment for the same purpose. There is (I say) the same reason for both, and whatsoever argument any man shall bring me against the one, I dare undertake to prove it good against the other.

We are, my brethren, to take heed of men that pretend to honour God. These here will seek the Lord, though in a false and superstitious way. But those that pretend to honour God, prevail much with weak and scrupulous minds. As the greatest heretics that have ever been in the church have been great pretenders to godliness, many there are at this day that, out of pretence to honour Christ, have leavened the hearts of people with dangerous errors, and especially corrupted the young converts; for as soon as ever God is pleased to work upon any, to convert them unto himself, they love Christ, their hearts are taken with him, and they honour free grace that has pardoned the sins of their youth, of which they have such a fresh sense. Now, false teachers take advantage of this, and, therefore, if they bring any thing to them that hath the name of Christ, and the gospel, and free grace, they know they will greedily imbibe it; and many dangerous errors sweetened with such pretences are strongly maintained. By this means their leaders attain their own ends, and they see it not.

Obs. 8. Superstitious and idolatrous men are most abundant in their services in the time of affliction.

"They will go with their flocks and their herds:" when in extremity, then God shall have any thing from them. Self-love drives men far and enlarges them much. Men in a storm are content to cast out much of that which is precious to them; "They poured out a prayer when thy chastening was upon them," Isa. xxvi. 16. They are straitened in prayer, it comes out by drops, before, but when thy chastening is upon them, then they pour it out. And this is the baseness of our hearts, that we can find enlargement for God only when it is suitable to our own ends. Those whose hearts are more enlarged in adversity than in the enjoyment of mercies, had need of self-examination.

Obs. 9. Carnal professors think to make God amends for former and present evils of their hearts and lives by outward performances.

If they bring their flocks and their herds, much sacrifice, they think that will suffice. But let us learn to take heed of this vanity, of thinking to make God amends for former or present sins by any sacrifice we can perform to him thus. Some of you, perhaps, that are negligent in your relative duties; servants, children, stubborn and perverse against parents and governors; wives and husbands mutually neglecting their duties; and you think, though you indulge yourselves in those things, yet, if you pray much, and hear much, and speak of good things, and be forward in the profession of religion, that will make amends for the neglect of your duties. O take heed of this, you that are forward in your profession, and abundant in the performance of holy duties; take heed of this deceit of your hearts, to think to put off God with these things, and thereby to compensate for the neglect of your duties. Some are accused of injustice, uncleanness, and great wickedness, and yet they think to put off all this, by going with their flocks and their herds. Herein consists their sinfulness, they rest in the bare duties. But the saints have a further sacrifice to offer to God, to be a sweet savour before him. They have first the sacrifice of Jesus Christ, which these sacrifices typified; and then they have their souls and bodies, which they tender up to God as a reasonable sacrifice.

"But they shall not find him." From hence,

Obs. 10. If God be to be found any where, he is to be found in his ordinances. "They shall go with their flocks and with their herds, but they shall not find him."

These sacrifices were materially good, but yet they should not find God in them. When the Lord appointed the tabernacle to be erected, (a type of the ordinances we now enjoy,) he said, "Where I will meet you;" and again the second time, "There I will meet with thee," Exod. xxix. 42, 43. If God be to be found any where, it is in the performance of holy duties.

Obs. 11. To find God in them should be the end of all holy duties.

It should be so, and they pretended that end here. When either God is coming unto us in mercy, or when we are drawing near to God in duty, we must be restless till we find him, especially in the latter. Many, I beseech you observe this, many perform duties, but do not look at finding God in them. They do not examine after the duties are done, Have I met with God in this or that duty? Have I met with God this day in the word? I have been in my closet, and there I have prayed; have I found God in prayer? Found God! what is that? You should never be quiet in the performance of holy duties till you meet with God one of these two ways; 1. Either by finding God coming to you in the communication of himself, and the sweetness of his love and mercy; or, 2. Your own hearts drawing nearer unto him. And in either of these ways we find God.

Obs. 12. God will not be always found when sought.

"They shall go with their flocks and with their herds, but shall not find me." Thus men are never like to meet with God:

1. When they seek him in any superstitious way. These kind of formal, superstitious worshippers of God, did much, spent much time in God's worship; I appeal to their own consciences, and to all that knew their lives, did any thing of God appear in them? It might be manifested from their frothy, vain, and carnal conversations, that they never met with God in those ser-

vices. When God is sought, but not in his own way, he will not be found.

2. When we seek ourselves rather than God, then he will not be found.

3. When we do not seek God as a God; that is, when we tender him only external, and not soul services; when we seek him not with uprightness and in the integrity of our hearts; when we seek him not with those high and reverent apprehensions of him, with that fear of his name suitable to such an infinite God as the Lord is; then God will not be found.

4. When we seek him too late. There may be a seeking of God too late. Seek him while he may be found. Oh then, we had need lose no opportunity of seeking God, for he will not be always found. And this is just with God; for God often seeks us when we will not be found, and therefore it is just that he should not be found when we seek him.

"He hath withdrawn himself from them." When the saints of God seek him in a holy way, he is presently found. "Then shalt thou call, and the Lord shall answer; thou shalt cry, and he shall say, Here I am," Isa. lviii. 9. Perhaps they do not take notice of God; he is many times with us and stands by us, he is present, and we know not that he is there. But now, that we may know that he is there, he makes that promise, that when we seek him as we ought to seek him, he will say, "Here I am."

The word חלץ here translated "withdrawn himself," may be as well rendered, *divisit se*, or *eripuit se*; he has divided, yea, snatched himself from them; that is its force: they go to seek him, and cry after him; God snatches himself from them, as one that refuses their friendship. Hence,

Obs. 13. God delights not in the services of superstitious and formal professors; but with the humble and contrite heart is his delight. The flocks and the herds of the wicked are rejected, and God withdraws himself from them, but small things from the saints are accepted. As in 1 Sam. vii. 9, when holy Samuel there offered but a sucking lamb for a burnt-offering to the Lord, presently "the Lord thundered with a great thunder on that day upon the Philistines, and discomfited them; and they were smitten before Israel." Here are herds and flocks, and yet God withdraws himself; but Samuel there offers but a poor sucking lamb, and presently the Lord thunders with a great thunder upon their adversaries. So in Rev. viii. 4, 5, after the incense, with the prayers of the saints, were offered up, there followed "voices, and thunderings, and lightnings, and an earthquake." Great things are effected by small services of the saints when offered in uprightness, but the greatest services of hypocrites and formal professors God regards not, but withdraws himself from them.

Obs. 14. It is a sad thing when God withdraws from the creature, when he seeks him in distress. As in 1 Sam. xxviii. 15, when Saul was seeking God, and God was departed from him, mark what Saul saith, "I am sore distressed; for God is departed from me." And in chap. ix. 12, of this prophecy, "Yea, woe also to them when I depart from them!" saith God. Oh, that is a sad condition! It is a sign that,

1. God puts dishonour on a people, as I showed you more largely when I spake of the rejecting of their sacrifices. What greater dishonour can it be to a people, than for God to take more pleasure in their howlings under his wrath, than in their cryings to him for mercy? And yet to such a condition may a people, nay, your own soul, be brought. I say that God may take more pleasure in your howlings under his wrath, than in your cryings to him for mercy, and that in your temples, if you do not reform as well as cry to him; and this is confirmed by Amos viii. 3, "And the songs of the temple shall be howlings in that day, saith the Lord God." As if he should say, The songs of the temple were loud, but I will take more pleasure in their howlings than in their songs. And Isa. xxix. 1, "Woe to Ariel, to Ariel, the city where David dwelt!" &c.; and ver. 2, "Yet I will distress Ariel, and there shall be heaviness and sorrow: and it shall be unto me as Ariel." The text seems to be obscure at the first reading, but the meaning is this: By Ariel is meant Jerusalem, the city where David dwelt, the place where the sacrifices were offered unto God; Ariel signifying an altar of God, God's altar that did devour the sacrifices like a lion. Now, saith God, thou shalt be to me as Ariel; thou Jerusalem, where my famous altar was, where so many famous sacrifices were offered, thou shalt be to me as Ariel; that is, you indeed offer many sacrifices unto me, but yet continue in your hypocrisy, and in your wickedness; know, saith God, I will make that city as an altar on which your blood shall be offered, and I will take as much pleasure in the sacrifice of your blood offered on this altar, as in all the sacrifices that were offered on the altar from whence the city had its name; your name shall be Ariel, that is, your city shall be stained with your blood as the altar was with the blood of the sacrifices. God rejects and casts out the services of such as are superstitious and ungodly.

2. No creature can help us; they will say, How can we help when God will not? he has withdrawn himself.

3. Some great judgment must then be expected; as when a poor petitioner goes to the prince with a petition, and the prince turns his back upon him; Surely, thinks he, now some evil is nigh me.

4. No protection from any evil can then be expected; God has withdrawn himself.

5. Then conscience flies in one's face: Oh, the blessed God is gone, and mercy is gone, and Christ is gone, and that for those sins of mine, those lusts of mine, that lay so near my heart. Oh how terrible will it be to conscience, when God shall appear to withdraw himself!

6. It is a forerunner of God's eternal withdrawing himself from the soul, and from the body too.

The saints had rather have God's presence, though angry, than God withdrawing himself from them. When God withdraws himself but a little, they can never rest till he has returned again: "O cast me not from thy presence," saith David.

My brethren, when we perceive God withdrawing himself in any degree from us, let us stir up ourselves, and cry mightily, as the church, when apprehensive that God was leaving her, Jer. xiv. 9, "Leave us not." God goes by degrees from a people; first, it may be, to the threshold; and Jeremiah, a holy prophet, saw him withdrawing from them. Carnal hearts do not perceive how God withdraws himself from a people by degrees, but those that are acquainted with the mind of God, and search into the word, are able to discern this, and they cry, Lord, leave us not, if thou be gone, all is gone.

Yea, but does not God withdraw himself from his saints? how then is this a judgment peculiar to idolaters, and wicked, superstitious persons?

The answer is this, God indeed withdraws himself sometimes from his saints, but not in the same manner as from the wicked. For in his withdrawings from the saints,

1. They yet retain good thoughts of him in his absence, whereas the wicked pine, and vex, and fret against him. As, in the absence of her husband, a faithful wife still retains good thoughts of him as of her husband, and continues to love him, whereas with the adulteress it is far otherwise: so wicked men do, upon God's withdrawing of himself in judgments and afflictions, begin to have hard thoughts of God, and to say, If this is to serve God and to walk in his ways, what

good have we got by all that we have done? But now you shall observe in the Canticles, when Christ had withdrawn himself from the church, she still calls him her King, and her Beloved, still gives him honourable titles.

2. He draws their hearts to cry more earnestly after him. As a mother will playfully withdraw and hide herself from her child, loving to hear its cries after her, and to witness its anxiety to come into her arms; so the Lord loves to hear his children cry after him, to come to him. The Lord shall hear none of our cries in heaven, for there we shall always be with him; but here he sometimes withdraws from us, that he may hear us cry after him.

3. He leaves some light behind him, that they may see which way he is gone. As when a torch or candle is taken out of a room, yet you may see some glimmering light which way they went; so when God withdraws himself he is wont to leave some glimmering light, that his people may see which way to follow him.

4. His bowels yearn toward them. Jer. xxxi. 20, " Is Ephraim my dear son?" &c. I thought of him and my bowels yearned, saith God, or " my bowels were troubled." He has an eye towards them for much good in all his withdrawings.

5. Nothing then will satisfy them till God return. When God withdraws himself from others, they will seek after vanities to make up the want of his presence, as an adulteress in her husband's absence will seek other lovers. But the language of the saints is, If God be gone, I will enjoy nothing else, at least I will be satisfied in nothing else, till I have his presence again.

6. He yet does not utterly forsake them; as David prays, Psal. cxix. 8, " I will keep thy statutes: O forsake me not utterly." It seems that then God had somewhat withdrawn himself from David, yet mark, his heart was toward God, " I will keep thy statutes;" thou hast forsaken me in some degree, yet I will keep thy statutes still, " O forsake me not utterly." If thou canst say thus, Indeed God has withdrawn himself from my soul, yet, though I have not that comfort in him that my soul desires, I will keep his precepts as long as I live, I will do what I can to honour him; thou mayst pray with comfort, Lord, " O forsake me not utterly."

As those that are godly may depart from God, but yet, as in Psal. xviii. 21, " I have not wickedly departed from my God," they do not depart from God as other men do; so God may depart from the godly, but yet not so as he departs from the wicked.

Let us take heed of withdrawing from God, of withdrawing our souls from any way of truth. If in prosperity we withdraw from God, and think we can live without him, he will make us know in adversity that he too can be blessed without us. It is usual for men in prosperity to get on without God well enough; but when thou comest into adversity, the Lord will make thee know, though thou perishest as dross and dung from the earth, yet he will remain a blessed God without thee to all eternity. God has no need of us. If thou dost think thou canst do well enough without him, he will show that he can do well enough without thee.

Ver. 7. *They have dealt treacherously against the Lord: for they have begotten strange children: now shall a month devour them with their portions.*

In the words before, the Lord threatened to withdraw himself from Israel. When they shall seek him with their flocks and herds, they shall not find him. A dreadful sentence! but what is the cause? Why will God in a time of mercy withdraw himself from his creatures, though they seek him with their flocks and with their herds?

There is reason enough for it, and it is given here, " They have dealt treacherously against the Lord."

The word בגדו here translated, dealing treacherously, signifies *perfide agere*, to deal perfidiously, they have been perfidious; and likewise *decipere*, to deceive, they deal deceitfully; but it especially means that fraudulent dealing that takes place in breaking of covenants, and is often applied to men violating the marriage bond, as in Mal. ii. 14, 15.

I find Luther translates it, they have contemned the Lord; and so, according to some, it is often rendered; and thence takes occasion to ask, What! do they seek the Lord with their flocks and herds, and yet despise God? how can these consist? They seem as if they would greatly honour God, yet here they are charged with contemning and despising him. To this he answers, Whatsoever pretences men make of honouring God, yet, if they do not obey and keep to his word, and that especially with respect to his worship, they are guilty of contemning and despising God. We may abound in outward services, and yet, in the mean time, our hearts despise God, contemn his authority and majesty.

But the word ordinarily is used according to our translation of it here, " They have dealt treacherously," they have been false with me.

And mark the connexion: they come to seek me with their flocks and their herds, but I have withdrawn myself from them, for " they have dealt treacherously." Hence we would briefly

Obs. 1. When the ungodly come to seek God, God looks on the wickedness of their hearts.

" They have dealt treacherously." As if God should say, Here comes a company of base, false-hearted hypocrites, ungodly wretches, to seek me, with their flocks and herds. Are they like to be heard? are they like to be regarded in all their services? no, they are base and perfidious, they have vile, wicked, and cursed hearts.

O consider this, you that have not yet washed away your sins in the blood of Christ, and made your peace with God: the guilt of your sin is yet upon you, and its filthiness yet adheres to you: you come to God in prayer, and seek him, and cry unto him for mercy: know, that all the wickedness that ever you committed in the whole course of your lives, is fresh in the presence of God; God looks upon all as if it were now present. O, learn therefore to cleanse thy heart in the blood of Christ, by faith in him, and by repentance; and then, though thou hast been vile heretofore, when thou comest to seek the face of God, thy sins shall not be remembered before him. So much for the connexion.

But for the words themselves, and first, in their proper signification, "They have dealt treacherously;" the meaning is, they make a great show of religion, but it is only for their own ends, and under that show they do that which dishonoureth me, they betray my glory. Here is treacherous dealing indeed, treachery against the God of heaven; these are treacherous spirits, to make professions and protestations of religion, to make any use they can of religion, so far as it will suit their own turns, but when it proves unprofitable, to cast it off; yea, if it prove contrary to them, to persecute it. This is treachery against God in a high degree.

Again, " treacherously," in that they break their covenant with God; that is the special treachery here intended, they have broken that covenant in which they were engaged. They gave up themselves to be the Lord's, but they have basely forsaken and dealt treacherously with him. So that this treachery relates either to the oath of allegiance to God as our King, or to the covenant that we make with him as our Husband. And thence,

Obs. 2. The sins of such as are in covenant with God are sins of treachery. They are sins of a deeper dye than other men's sins. Other men's sins are transgressions against, and disobedience to, the will of God; but they are not so properly treachery: but the sins of those that are engaged to God in covenant have another impress upon them than the sins of other men, their sins are treachery against God. And we know there is nothing accounted more vile amongst men than treachery; it is the highest possible expression of our indignation against a man to say, Such a man take heed of, he is a treacherous man. Certainly the sins of those that have engaged themselves unto God, go nearer to the heart of God than other men's sins do; they are more dishonourable to him, they provoke the eyes of his glory more.

O let us then look back to what we have done ever since we first entered into covenant with God, ever since we first gave up our names to him; and let us charge our souls with this aggravation of our sins: O my soul, what hast thou done? Thou hast not only trespassed and disobeyed as others, but thou hast been treacherous against the Lord. Let us keep ourselves from sin, and awe our hearts and strike fear into our spirits with this meditation, What! shall I, that have so deeply engaged myself to God, now forsake and deal treacherously with him?

Let us take heed of this evil of dealing treacherously with God, not only in regard of the particular covenants between God and our own souls; but, in a more special manner, let us take heed of breaking our public covenants. England has been guilty of great sins against God, but England never entered into such solemn covenants with God as of late; therefore, if we keep not our covenants with God now, England's sins will prove to be greater than they were before, they will prove to be treacherous sins. Do not account your entering into covenant with God at any time to be a slight matter; do not trifle with him: when you come to the sacrament, there you renew your covenants; perhaps in your closets in the day of your affliction you renew your covenants; but especially when you come in a solemn way to join with the people of God, to bind yourselves in a covenant with God to amend your lives, and inquire after the true worship of God, and to conform yourselves according to his word; O now take heed what you do; to walk now as you formerly have done, this is a treachery against the God of heaven. Certainly God expects much from us after such a covenant as we have lately entered into, one of the most solemn covenants that ever was made; and a national covenant too, and therefore more to be regarded than a private; yea, a uniting covenant, that unites two nations, if not three, together; and a covenant that is more for the kingdom of Christ, and more directly against the kingdom of antichrist, and the antichristian party, than ever yet was made since the world began. Antichrist quickly arose, and made much opposition; but for two nations so solemnly to lift up their hands to the most high God to oppose all antichristian government, is that which, if it be kept as carefully as it is made solemnly, is the greatest honour that Christ ever yet had in regard of his government here upon earth. And we had need look to it, because it is such a mighty work that it should engage our hearts, and make us thankful that we ever lived to see God bring about such a strange thing in our generation. I appeal to you, was it possible four years ago for any man in the world, yea, for an angel, to conjecture such a thing as this, that two nations should join together, that the representative body of the kingdom, and the assembly of divines, in one day should be lifting up their hands to the most high God, to do their utmost to extirpate prelacy, that is, government by archbishops, bishops, archdeacons, deans, &c. Now the more miraculous the work of God is in bringing this strange thing about, the more bonds lie upon us to keep that covenant with God. O, therefore, let us not now add treachery to all our former apostacy, for our sins now will prove sins of treachery.

But if it be such an aggravation of our sins, to be covenanters with God, if we neglect our engagement, then it were better (perhaps some will say) never to enter into covenant; for it seems, if we had not taken the covenant there, our guilt would not have been so aggravated.

The answer to that is this, A carnal heart alone is sorry for its engagement to God, either because of afflictions that are in the ways of God, or because the obligations of obedience to God are stronger, or because the danger of breaking them is greater. Perhaps, when thou art engaged to God and his ways, thou meetest with many afflictions in those ways; take heed of repenting of thy engagement because of them. Perhaps thou seest thyself so strongly bound that thy conscience will now fly in thy face on the slightest transgression; O, take heed of receding from thy engagement notwithstanding. For one whose heart is gracious, certainly will never repent of his engagement, though there be more danger attendant on his sin now than before; why? because he hates his sin. Now let there be never so much danger to keep me from that which I hate, I will never be sorry for that: as for instance, suppose there be a deep gulf, that if I fall into will destroy me, I tremble to come near it; but there is a fence to keep me off full of sharp iron spikes, which, if I should but try to get over it, will gore and prick me; shall I be sorry that such a fence exists, when it is but set there to keep me from destroying myself? So a gracious heart will never be sorry that it is engaged in the ways of God, and that if it should break the engagement there would be an aggravation of its sin; for why? the very engagement is but as a strong fence to keep me from that which I would be loth to come to, which would destroy me. And those that begin to think their engagement to God and his ways to be a hard thing, and could wish for more liberty, will certainly deal treacherously with God, yea, their hearts are even already departing from God. Take heed of this, it is a step to apostacy, (remember it, my brethren, it is an important caution,) it is, I say, the first degree of apostacy, for any man to begin to be sorry that he is so deeply engaged to God and his ways. All the true saints of God, when they are engaged, bless God that ever they were engaged.

"Against the Lord." Against Jehovah. This is the vileness of man's heart. Though God be never so gracious, so merciful, so faithful; though he be never so blessed, so glorious in himself and worthy of all honour; yet so vile is man's heart that it will deal treacherously with even God himself. To deal treacherously with a friend, with a fellow creature, is an evil; but to deal treacherously with the infinite and blessed God is a far greater evil. When vexed yourselves with the treachery of others, O, consider how treacherously God is dealt with in the world. Thou dost think none was ever so dealt with, ever so wronged, as thou art; God is more wronged, more contradicted, more treacherously dealt withal, than any ever were. And how many are there that think it a dishonour to them even to be suspected of treacherous dealing, and will often say, What! deal treacherously with my friend? I were not worthy to live if I should! yet these men deal treacherously with God every day.

Thus much for this charge, For "they have dealt treacherously against the Lord. Next he shows wherein.

"For they have begotten strange children." That is

a further aggravation, that they have not only sinned themselves, but have sought to propagate their sin and their wickedness: for it might otherwise be said, True, Israel has sinned very grievously against the Lord, but may there not be hope of the generation succeeding? No, for they bring up their children in the same superstition, idolatry, and wickedness, that they themselves walk in. That is the meaning, "They have begotten strange children;" they should beget children to God, but they beget them to idols, and so this wickedness, this treachery against God, is propagated from one generation to another, there is a succession of it; as are the old, so are the young.

When any draw others to evil ways, they are said in Scripture to make them children of the devil, to beget them as children of the devil. Matt. xxiii. 15, "Ye compass sea and land to make one proselyte; and when he is made, ye make him twofold more the child of hell than yourselves;" you beget him to the devil. So parents, first, by way of natural generation, beget children to themselves, and then, by educating their children in ways of wickedness, beget them the second time to the devil. And they are called "strange children," because God will not own them: They are none of mine, saith God, they are strangers from me, I will have nothing to do with them. The words being thus opened, the observations are these:

Obs. 3. Parents have the charge of their children committed to them by God.

It is implied here, that it is their duty to look to beget their children to God, and to take heed that they be not begotten to the devil. For Ephraim, the ten tribes, are here charged, that whereas they should have brought forth their children for God, and so they should belong to God's inheritance, and God should have owned them; now they beget them to their idols, and they are strange children. God certainly does not give you children to beget them for the devil and for hell. It should be a sad thing to parents to think, Here is a child coming from my loins, conceived in my womb, an enemy unto God; what! shall such come forth out of my loins? shall a firebrand of hell be conceived in my womb? Certainly it should go to the heart of a parent to see his child estranged from God, though he were not the cause of it; but much more when a parent shall come to be convinced, this child is thus wicked and ungodly, and as he has received the seeds of his corruption from me at the first, so those seeds were nourished up by my example and encouragement, I have led him to such wickedness. Woe to such parents! and such children may even curse the time that they were born of such parents, and rather wish they had been of the generation of dragons and offspring of vipers. When God gives you children, he expects that you should labour that there may be a succession of godliness in the world, that not only you should be godly, but that you should bring up your children to be so too. "He established a testimony in Jacob, and appointed a law in Israel, which he commanded our fathers, that they should make them known to their children: that the generation to come might know them, even the children which should be born; who should arise and declare them to their children," Psal. lxxviii. 5, 6. This is the way of God, he commands you to make known his statutes and laws to your children, that the generation to come might know them, and not that you should bring them up in wickedness and superstition. I have read that the Romans were wont to sue such parents as were not careful of the education of their children. Therefore Cicero, inveighing against Verres, saith, *Quod filium tuum, &c.*, You have not only done thus and thus yourself, but you have educated your son among the intemperate, in riotousness, in feasting, in drinking, amongst wantons and unclean persons, and by this means you have not only wronged your child, but the commonwealth. Thus he laid his action against him. Now how might heathens shame us in this, who account those to deserve punishment not only from God, but from men, that are not careful of the education of their children! There is a great deal of reason for it, and it were very good now that there were a law of a similar nature enacted on this ground, because the commonwealth has a part in the children as well as the parent; and the parent not being careful to bring up the child in the fear of God, wrongs the commonwealth as well as the child, and therefore ought to be punished by the commonwealth.

Obs. 4. Children are usually as their parents and education are. The parents were idolaters, they were ungodly and strangers from God; their children are so too. In many families we see that the father is an enemy to God, and the son an enemy to God, and the grandson the same, and so there goes on a line and a succession of wickedness, profanity, and enmity against God. It is usually so.

Therefore let those children that are born of and brought up under godly parents, bless God for such a mercy. It may be, if thou hadst been born and brought up of papists, thou wouldst have been a papist thyself. If thou hadst been born of a malignant, of one that is a stranger to and a contemner of God, thou wouldst have been so too.

And seeing it is thus usual for children to be as their parents, oh, then, what a mercy is it for God to work by his grace in any child born of wicked parents! This is not an ordinary mercy. Some born of godly parents bless God that by that means they are kept from wickedness; but there are some born of and brought up by wicked parents, to whom God is so gracious, that, in a more than ordinary way, he goes further in mercy to them, and works grace in their hearts notwithstanding. This is his extraordinary mercy, a mercy that thou art to admire at throughout all eternity, that notwithstanding thy birth and education, yet God should reveal himself unto thee.

But how vile are they that, being born of good parents, are yet wicked! It is customary for such as are born of wicked parents and have wicked education, to be wicked, to be strange children; but for those that have godly parents and godly education, for them to be wicked and strange children, this denotes wickedness in the extreme.

Obs. 5. It is a dangerous thing for children to follow the example of their parents in wickedness. It is from hence that they are called "strange children," they are strangers to God. It is not enough for them to plead, I did as my father or as my mother taught me. No, if thy parents be wicked and superstitious, and they bring thee up accordingly, and so thou art wicked and superstitious thyself, know that, notwithstanding this excuse, God looks upon thee as a strange child, thou hast no part nor portion in him, thou art an alien, thou art estranged from God.

Children therefore had need to examine their parents' ways and actions; and above all, the children of superstitious people, for nothing is more naturally handed down in succession, than idolatry and superstition. Never plead then, We do but as our forefathers have done. That place in Peter one would think should for ever stop the mouth of that plea, 1 Pet. i. 18, 19, "Ye were not redeemed with corruptible things, as silver and gold, from your vain conversation received by tradition from your fathers; but with the precious blood of Christ, as of a lamb without blemish and without spot." Mark the text, that the being redeemed from our vain conversation, received by tradition from our fathers, is so great a mercy that it cost the blood of Jesus Christ. If God accounts it such a mercy, that he is willing to lay down the blood of his Son to purchase it for a poor creature, shall not this creature prize this mercy? And yet you think it rather to be a mercy to go on in the ways that you have received by tradition from your fathers, and you conceive their example a strong plea. Mark what you do; you do in effect say, We look on the blood of Jesus Christ as a common, as a worthless thing. He shed his blood to redeem thee from that which thou thinkest is worth nothing to be redeemed from. Thou thinkest it a good thing to go the way of the traditions of thy fathers; and Christ saith, I account it so great an evil, that rather than any that belong to me shall go on in that way, I will lay down my blood, my life, to deliver him from it.

Obs. 6. When succeeding generations are wicked, there is little hope of a people. I have withdrawn myself, saith God, I have done with them; and afterward he tells us, that they shall be desolate, "for they have begotten strange children:" the children, the generation that is rising up, are idolaters too, they go as their fathers did; and what hope is there of them? When in a vineyard, or orchard, not only the old trees are rotten, but the young are likewise corrupted and blasted, then there is little to justify the bestowing of any great cost on it.

Much care is to be had therefore of the succeeding generation. And there is no better criterion, whereby we may divine (as they say) what God intends to do with a nation, than this, the state of the children: look at the young that are rising up in that nation, and by that you may come to divine what God intends to do with the next generation. Here we have much cause to bless God for his mercy toward us, in that with regard to this particular, he has in a great measure (we hope) taken away the sign of his dreadful wrath. I say, in a great measure; for we still have a great many of the young generation prepared and ready to make riots and tumults to maintain their fathers' or their masters' old superstitions; and if ever there be any stirs in a kingdom about such things, (as superstition and idolatry can seldom be banished from a kingdom without them,) they are usually begun by the young; what, if you take away their holidays from them, you take away their lives. I make no question, but, so far as is fit, times of recreation will be allowed them; and there is good reason for it, though such superstitious days be taken from them. But because many of their masters and parents who adhere to the old superstition, still countenance their observance, and they obtain consequent liberty in them, therefore they had almost rather lose their lives than lose them, and being heady and naught, are easily induced to raise tumults and make seditions for them. But though there are many that are very vile in this respect, and, such as they are, are the saddest omen of God's displeasure against a nation; yet, on the contrary, we should wrong the grace of God, if we should not observe his goodness towards us in the workings of his Spirit on the young amongst us. Yea, many whose parents and masters have been superstitious, wicked, and ungodly, have, we find, been delivered by the Lord, and are now not willing to sully themselves with the "vain conversation received by tradition;" they begin to know the Lord, and to inquire after God. And blessed are you of the Lord; you are our hope, that God intends us good, and that he will not let out the wild beasts to devour us, but will rebuke them for your sakes. And although, perhaps, many of these gracious young ones may perish, yea, many have been slain already in this cause, yet let not others that remain behind be discouraged; for it is an argument that God intends for us some great and special mercy, in that he is willing to venture such precious ones for the procuring of it. We may well reason thus, that if so much precious young blood, that might have lived to serve God, be shed in this cause, when God comes to grant to England mercy, he will grant such mercy as will be worth all their blood; and that mercy must needs be great, that shall be worth all the blood of those that are so precious, who might have lived so many years to serve God in this world.

They who have defiled themselves with superstitious vanities, are not likely to share in this mercy, nor to be employed by God to prepare it for the succeeding generation. But because God has a love to the young generation that are godly, therefore he has reserved much mercy for many of them to see and enjoy; and others of them that are not likely to see it, yet he will be so gracious to them, that he will employ them in ushering in that mercy: and whether it is better to be made instrumental for the glory of God and the good of another generation, or to live to see the fruit of this, is hard to determine. Certainly, those that in one generation are made so instrumental, as to lay the groundwork of mercy for another generation, are as happy as that other generation that comes to reap the fruit of their labours and sufferings; and those that do come to reap the fruit of their labours shall bless God for them, and when they enjoy the good and liberty of the gospel, they will bless you to all generations. Therefore, let there be no discouragement to godly young ones, though it pleaseth God to cut off many by death in this cause, for God hath some excellent end in it beyond all our reaches.

Obs. 7. God takes it exceeding ill at men's hands, that they should corrupt the young. This note is as full in the words as any other. God takes it exceeding ill, it is a part of treachery against God, for any to be a means to corrupt the young. Take heed what you do in this matter; those young people that are rising up, and beginning to inquire after godliness, take heed that you hinder them not, especially parents and governors; O let your consciences fly in your faces, when you begin to curb them for their forwardness. Many times your minds cannot but misgive you, when you think, I have been wicked and evil most part of my days, I spent, God knows, many of my years in vanity and profaneness; here are young ones that begin betimes to inquire after God, and yet, wretch that I am, my heart rises against them.

And as those that hinder the young are to be rebuked, so such as seek to corrupt them by false opinions. Certainly it is that by which God is much provoked at this day; and, as, on the one side, there is hope of mercy because so many of the young begin to inquire after God, so I know no such dreadful proof of God's displeasure against this nation as this, that as soon as the young begin to know Jesus Christ, there are presently corrupt errors infused into them, and that under the notion of honouring Christ, and free grace, and the gospel, so much the more; whereas indeed they are none other than principles of libertinism and looseness, and such as will even eat out the heart of godliness. Certainly, the Lord has a quarrel against such as corrupt the young by their false principles: for there are none so ready to imbibe errors as they, especially young converts, who begin to inquire after the ways of God: and these their corrupters have this advantage, they come not to them to persuade them to profaneness, but they come with seeming pretences of giving honour to Christ, and of magnifying free grace, and in the mean time sow amongst them seeds destructive of the power of godliness. To corrupt the young, and, when they begin to inquire after and to know God, to do that which may estrange them from him, excites the wrath of God; and it is a greater proof than any other of God's displeasure against us, that it is so common and frequent at this day.

"Now shall a month devour them with their portions."

"A month." I find interpreters much perplexed about this expression. Many think that God aims at one special month, and they tell us, that in one month in the year, which answers to our July, there were many grievous things to befall the Jews, both in former and in latter times, as if that were a more ominous month than any other. I will not spend time to speak further of that.

But there is certainly somewhat else in this expression. I find a parallel passage to this in Zech. xi. 8, where the Holy Ghost speaks of three shepherds that God will cut off in one month; "Three shepherds also I cut off in one month; and my soul lothed them, and their soul also abhorred me." This is the most exact description of your superstitious idol shepherds, even such as we have at this day amongst us in many places. "My soul lothed them," saith God, "and their soul also abhorred me." Who more hate the power of godliness than such men? and whom does the soul of God more abhor? "I cut them off in one month," saith God. By "month" I conceive two things meant.

1. The Jews in those times were wont to have their days of reckoning with their workmen and with their debtors usually at the beginning or ending of every month, and this expression seems to allude to that custom of theirs; "now shall a month devour them," that is, the time of their month shall come when I will reckon with them, and when that fixed time shall come of my reckoning, they shall be undone, they shall be devoured and destroyed. Hence,

Obs. 8. God has set a time to reckon with sinners. Though he be patient for a long time, yet he has a month, a set time appointed, and he will not go beyond that time.

Obs. 9. The time of reckoning with sinners, is the time of their destruction. The time of their reckoning will be the time of their destruction.

2. Many interpret it thus, a little short time shall devour them; it shall not be long, it shall not be a hundred and twenty years, as it was when he threatened the old world, but it shall be very speedy; as if God should say, When once I begin with them, a month shall make an end of the work. And indeed what will a month do when God lets the sword (for that was the judgment here threatened) come upon a nation! What a great deal of havoc have the enemy made in a month, in many parts of England! Into what a miserable condition have many that were rich, and had great estates, been brought within that time! so that God seems to refer to the Assyrians that were let out upon them; Let them but once come, saith he, and they will not be long about the work, a month's time shall devour them.

Luther, and some agree with him, thinks that by the "month" is here meant their solemnities and new moons, and that so it has reference to their superstition and idolatry. But that I think to be too far from the meaning: I rather conceive that by "a month" is meant the short time of their destruction, when once the adversary comes in upon them.

"With their portions." I find the Seventy translate חלקיהם τοὺς κλήρους ἀυτων, their lots. And it may be so rendered, because in the division of the land of Canaan, that which they had for their estates was given to the ten tribes at first by lot. Well, saith God, I gave you your estates by such a special providence of mine, by lot; but though I did thus measure them out, otherwise than the estates of any men on the earth, yet a month shall devour your lot, all that you had in that appointment of my special providence shall now be devoured. From thence an observation arises of exceeding use to us:

Obs. 10. The more special the providence of God is toward us in mercy, the more grievous are his judgments if subsequently provoked.

That mercy I had by such a special hand of God's providence, that I can relate from point to point, how strangely the Lord wrought to bestow it upon me. Well, thou canst speak of God's providence and bless his name, and thou dost well in so doing; but then, take heed thou dost not abuse that mercy that thou enjoyest by the special hand of God's providence; take heed of provoking God to come and devour that mercy. So it is threatened here, "a month shall devour their portion," their estates that they had by special lot shall now be destroyed because of their sins.

But further, if we take it according to the translation in your books, which is likewise suitable to the original, "a month shall devour their portion," that is, all their outward estates, all their riches, all their outward comforts, all that they have, and account as their portion, a month, a little time, shall destroy. And from thence there are these two observations:

Obs. 11. A carnal heart has his portion in this world only. Here is his portion, he has his portion in this world.

Obs. 12. The poor condition of the greatest in the world; his portion is no other, but a month may devour it. If thou hadst the whole kingdom, and many kingdoms, for thy portion, and this were all, thou hadst a poor pittance for one who has an immortal soul, for one made for eternity, a month may devour it. That man is but a poor man who has no other portion but that which a month may devour. But now, the saints have God himself for their portion, a portion which neither month can devour nor time destroy, but which they shall enjoy fresh and green, lively and full, and that to all eternity; a portion which lives for ever, and secures their everlasting life too.

Ver. 8. *Blow ye the cornet in Gibeah, and the trumpet in Ramah: cry aloud at Beth-aven, after thee, O Benjamin.*

The prophet, seeing how little impression his denunciations made on the hearts of this people, therefore, in the name of the Lord, assumes another character, and speaks in this verse as a general commanding an immediate alarm, as if the enemy were already at the gates; "Blow ye the cornet in Gibeah, and the trumpet in Ramah." As if he should say, You have often heard that the Lord would bring the sword upon you, now it is come, it is come; the enemy is even ready to break into your cities, to rifle your houses, to ravish your wives, to murder your children: "Blow ye the cornet in Gibeah, and the trumpet in Ramah: cry aloud at Beth-aven, after thee, O Benjamin." It is a summoning of them, as if one should come to the city and cry, The enemy, the enemy is at the gates, arm, arm! so the prophet here, that he might rouse the hearts of those that are stupid and senseless, saith, I have often in the name of God threatened that he would bring the sword upon you, but you continued insensible; know, that the Lord is now upon you in wrath, the enemy is come, now is the time for your destruction; blow ye the trumpet, set yourselves in battle-array, make what resistance you can, for now wrath and misery are upon you. That generally is the scope of the words, but there are yet three things to be considered for their further explication.

I. Why Ramah and Gibeah are particularized.

II. Why "cry aloud at Beth-aven."

III. The meaning of the words, "after thee, O Benjamin."

I. Ramah and Gibeah. I find many take these words not as proper names for cities, but to signify the hills and high places of the country. And the Seventy indeed translate them, ἐπὶ τοὺς βουνοὺς, ἐπὶ τῶν ὑψηλῶν, upon the hills, and upon the high places; for Ramah signifies a high place, and Gibeah, by way of excellency, a hill. And they would interpret it as if the Lord should say to the prophet, Go to the highest places in the country, the highest hills, and there let the cornet and the trumpet be blown, as an alarm to awaken the whole land. And then the observation would be,

Obs. 1. When a people is in danger of God's wrath, it is high time for them to be awakened.

It is then fit that it should be made known to them. Not only that they should go to the governors, and those that are in high places of authority, but go where they may make known the danger to all the people of the land. It is true, it is fit the governors should be awakened in the first place, but if they be awakened and not the people, it will prove to little purpose. Many men of late of vile spirits could not endure that ministers should warn people of dangers, or tell them of the forerunners of God's displeasure against a nation; at such things being preached in public auditories, their spirits were mightily incensed: but it is the way of God, in times of public dangers, to have the people made acquainted.

But further, Ramah and Gibeah were two eminent cities, and belonged both to the kingdom of Judah. They were indeed in the tribe of Benjamin, but Benjamin and Judah were joined in one kingdom under the house of David, and the other ten tribes separated under Jeroboam. Now these two cities were of some eminence in the kingdom of Judah, and it is likely were strongly fortified. Now God is here threatening judgment against Judah, as he did before, when he said, "Judah also shall fall with them;" therefore saith he, "Blow ye the cornet in Gibeah, and the trumpet in Ramah," in the most eminent places of Judah, in the most fortified, and let us see how they are able to resist the misery that is coming upon them.

But further, I find the Chaldee paraphrast explains it as if the meaning were, because that Gibeah was the city of Saul, and Ramah the city of Samuel, therefore God threatened judgment for their making of a king against his will, and for their disobedience to the words of Samuel. But I think this is somewhat too far-fetched.

II. "Cry aloud at Beth-aven." Beth-aven I believe to be the same city as that Beth-el where was one of the calves, and which belonged to the ten tribes; and the majority of interpreters confirm this opinion.

Now this Beth-el, which signifies the house of God, is called here Beth-aven, the house of vanity, because of the idol that was set up there. Therefore mark the emphasis, when he speaks of Ramah and Gibeah, he saith, Blow the cornet and the trumpet: but when of Beth-aven, הריעו "Cry aloud," howl out, O Beth-aven, for that was the great place of superstition. He nameth this city rather than Dan, (where the other of the two calves was placed,) because it was so near to the kingdom of Judah.

III. "After thee, O Benjamin." That is, Benjamin was close to this Beth-aven, and adjoining the kingdom of Israel. Now, saith God by the prophet, the wrath of God shall come out against Israel, Ephraim shall be left desolate, and Beth-aven shall howl and cry out, and you, Benjamin, that are so near them, take you heed to yourselves, "after thee, O Benjamin," thy turn will be next. You have reason to look to yourselves when your neighbour's house is on fire; so saith God here, Howl, Beth-aven, "after thee, O Benjamin:" Benjamin lay near Beth-aven, and when Benjamin saw the wrath of God against the ten tribes, and in that city of Beth-aven, Benjamin should look to itself. That is the meaning of the Holy Ghost in these words. Now for the notes of observation.

Obs. 2. When danger is apprehended as present and real it affects the heart most.

The Lord had threatened the sword many times by the prophet, and their hearts were secure and insensible; but now he comes and presents it as present and real to them, "Blow ye the trumpet," the danger is now at hand, it is here, saith the prophet. There is a great deal of difference between men's hearing of wars and rumours of wars, and the very reality of the evil itself when it comes before their eyes. This judgment of war, of the sword, has been threatened against this nation long ago. I dare appeal to you, who for twenty years remember the common strain of almost all the godly ministers in the kingdom, was not their usual theme this, to show what were the forerunners of God's judgments against a nation? Ever since I was a youth, and took any notice of sermons, I know nothing that sounded in mine ears more frequently than that. In almost all places in the kingdom, it was the usual custom of all your eminent ministers to search into God's word to see what were the sins that brought public judgments upon a nation, and to apply them to England. But this was ordinarily slighted. Some indeed of our brethren that feared the Lord and his judgments, and thought that they foresaw a storm, withdrew themselves, and were scorned and contemned for their labours. But now we see the thing that was feared and threatened is come, it is upon many countries, and do we not now form far different conceptions of it than when we only heard of it? In those countries where the sword has been raging, do not they apprehend the evil of war in another manner than they ever did when they heard it merely threatened in sermons? Oh when it indeed comes in its real form, it affects men far otherwise than the rumour of it. Those men that continually have their ears filled with the noise of the drum and trumpet, with the neighing of horses, and roaring of the cannon, will tell you that war is a dreadful thing indeed. So it is in all other afflictions that are threatened; how little is the threat regarded! but when they come indeed, oh then how do the hearts of men sink within them! Now God is coming against me, now wrath is upon me, saith the guilty soul, how far it may go I know not; I heard often of such things, now it is come, it is come! Oh the dreadful apprehensions that are in men's hearts of the wrath of God when it is come! whereas before, when threatened, it is never feared.

And this is a rule, an everlasting rule, That the less a judgment is feared when threatened, the more dreadful apprehensions there are of it in the heart when once it cometh to be executed.

Obs. 3. Ministers of God must realize the things they preach to the people.

They should study all ways and means they can to make what they preach to the people appear real to them, and not mere notions. So the prophet here, he had preached often of the judgments of God, of the sword, but this would not do, therefore now he strives to make what he had delivered appear in the most vivid manner possible to the eyes and hearts of the people, as the only way to benefit them. It is not therefore enough for a minister barely to tell the people truths, to state to them what danger they are in, but by all conceivable means to make this stand out in bold relief before them. We know how Ezekiel acted when he threatened the captivity, he went and made before them a kind of siege to render it real to them. So Jeremiah and other prophets. Now though ministers cannot do as they did, yet they are to study all manner of expressions in their power to invest things with the greatest possible reality. And indeed this is a great part of the skill of a good minister. The art of preaching, I say, lies especially in this, to make things appear real to the souls of the hearers. As, when we come to tell you of the danger of sin and of the wrath of God due to it, we tell you this, and we quote Scripture for it, perhaps it stirs not the heart; but if we can so present God's wrath to you, hold it up so vivid and real before your eyes as to induce you to bethink yourselves in what a situation you would be if now all creatures were taking their leaves of you, if now you were standing before the great God to receive the sentence of condemnation, if God were now at this instant coming upon you; if, I say, we could so preach as that you should apprehend these things as real, more good might be so done in one quarter of an hour than perhaps in divers years before. The power of a ministry consists much in this. And I suppose some of you know by experience what it is that I mean by the ministers making things real to your hearts. Have not you sometimes found some truths made so real out of the word, brought so home to your consciences, that you have thought that you have even stood before the throne of God, and that God was even then pronouncing sentence against you? Some have expressed it thus, Such a time I went to hear the word, and methought that I were summoned before the great God to judgment, I saw the Lord God himself speaking to me, I had represented before mine eyes the wickedness of my life, my danger, the wrath of God, and I felt even the very flashes of hell-fire on my conscience. Now God was in the word indeed when the reality of things was thus presented to my soul. And certainly it is the aim and endeavour of godly ministers in their studies, not only to wear out an hour or two in speaking on a text, but, with the blessing of God, to present such and such truths in the greatest possible reality to the souls of their audience. Such was the prophet's method, who not only tells them of their danger, but speaks as if it were at hand, and makes it thus real before them.

Obs. 4. Ministers, if their embassy of peace be slighted, must denounce war.

For they know that God must have honour one way or other, either by people subjecting themselves to him, or by God's avenging himself upon them. Honour God must have; although you may think his word will pass unfulfilled, yet faithful ministers know God must have honour one way or other; either willingly you must come in and give it to him, or he will force it out from you. If the joyful sound of mercy be not received, the dreadful sound of war must fill your ears.

Obs. 5. God's displeasure against sin is the principal cause of war in a land.

So it is here, "They have dealt treacherously against the Lord: for they have begotten strange children: now shall a month devour them with their portions. Blow ye the cornet in Gibeah, and the trumpet in Ramah," &c.; upon this ground, because of their treacherous dealing with God, and bringing up of their children in idolatry. When indeed danger comes on a nation, the people of the land are ready to lay it upon those that are most free from it. To whom do men at this day attribute the troubles of this nation, but to those that have throughout stood in the gap to prevent danger, and that have with more prayers and tears besought God than those their ready accusers? But in all ages the saints have been made the troublers of a nation: But is it not thou and thy father's house? saith the prophet, speaking even to Ahab himself. The troublers of our Israel lie not in the prophets, lie not in the ministers, of whom men say, they preach sedition.

And indeed, in a singular manner, Luther, that great instrument of God, was called the trumpet of rebellion: no new thing therefore is it, for the ministers of God, that first preach the word of reconciliation, and then seek to show people their danger, to be accounted by them the causers of their troubles, because they will not let them go on quietly in their ways, but in the name of God oppose and reprove them. But we know where our trouble lies, it lies in those that are most superstitious and idolatrous, they bring the sword: attribute it not to any other cause, it is the provocation of the most high God that brought these wars upon us. If therefore we be weary of war, let us be weary of our sins. I remember Polanus on this text has this note, and indeed he hinted it to me; In Hungary, a place which is near the Turks, and infested by their frequent incursions, the Jesuits attribute all the evils to the gospel preached and received there. But the Lord knows where to lay the burden right.

Obs. 6. Superstitious places and persons are in the greatest distress in the time of God's judgments.

"Cry aloud at Beth-aven." According to the interpretation I gave you, it was, being the place where one of the idols was set, full of superstition and idolatry. Now mark the difference, it is only, Blow the cornet and trumpet in Ramah and in Gibeah; but, "Cry aloud," or shriek out, and howl, O Beth-aven.

When God's hand comes out against a nation, it will fall heaviest upon those that are idolatrous and superstitious. It is true, God's hand has hitherto fallen heavy, and very heavy, upon many of our brethren, his own dear saints; but has it not also fallen heavily on the idolatrous and superstitious? However, mark the end, stay till God has done, and you will find that the hand of God will be heaviest on them; Howl, O Beth-aven. Those places that have been the nests of superstition and idolatry, are the places that his wrath will be most against. And indeed they do begin to howl and cry out already: for though some of God's people have endured much, yet, have two nations lifted up their hands to the most high God to extirpate God's people? No! but they have lifted up their hands to endeavour to extirpate the superstitious amongst us; therefore God's hand is heaviest against Beth-aven.

Obs. 7. In times of trouble the ungodly and superstitious are in the greatest perplexity.

Instead of repairing to God by faith and repentance, all that they have to do is to cry out and to howl. Howl, O Beth-aven: they were far enough from coming to humble their souls before the Lord, and graciously to accept of the punishment of their iniquity, and to bear the affliction laid upon them; oh no, their spirits were vexed and enraged, they could howl and cry out, and that alone. Is not this the way of many, apparently most diligent in their prayers and services, when they come into affliction? what do they then but vex and rage, howl and cry out? but are far from giving glory to God as he requires: They howled upon their beds, saith God, but they did not seek unto me. And God threatens this in Amos viii. 3, (who was contemporary with Hosea,) "The songs of the temple shall be howlings in that day." They had their singing service before, saith God, I will turn these into howlings; for their cries under affliction and trouble are no other before God. The Lord regards otherwise the cries of his people under oppression; they cry to God and send up their prayers of faith, and the incense of a broken heart, and God accepts them, and returns them answers of peace. But for the crying out of wicked and ungodly men under his hand, God regards it no more than howling. Thus it is here, Howl, O Beth-aven; much like those in Isa. li. 20, that, in the time of distress, are described to lie in the head of all the streets, as a wild bull in a net, filled with the fury of the Lord.

Obs. 8. It is an ill thing to have ill neighbours. "After thee, O Benjamin." Benjamin was near Beth-aven, therefore he must fare the worse for Beth-aven.

To dwell amongst ill neighbours is a dangerous thing, and we should take heed of it. I remember a commentator on this place gravely exhorts men, when they hire houses and farms, to inquire what neighbours were to be near them, and to take heed of dwelling nigh wicked men, for, saith he, when God's judgments come out against them you may smart, you being so near them they may singe you at least. I have often read of Themistocles, a heathen, that, having a farm to let, he published it, according to custom, at the market-place, and added, and there are good neighbours; thinking it were more comfortable for men to live near the good than the wicked.

Obs. 9. When the wrath of God is out against our neighbours, we had need look to it.

Though we have been in security before, yet if God's wrath come near to us we had need to stir. It is high time to look to ourselves when our neighbour's house is on fire. The truth is, we in England have been a long time in deep security, though Germany, though France, though the Low Countries, the Palatinate, Italy, and almost all the countries about us have been on fire, and the sword has raged amongst them, and it was threatened that it was likely we would be the next; and we were told that the sword takes its circuit, and that the Lord, going about to judge the nations of the earth, had already judged the surrounding ones; yet, because we felt nothing, though it was near us, we had no hearts to prevent it; therefore God is now come amongst us, even into our very midst. The truth is, we in England lay a great while as it were like a faggot on the fire: you know, when many faggots are on the fire the under ones become inflamed, and the faggots a little above begin to catch the fire, and the next above these grow black; now, if so be you would not have the uppermost faggot burnt, will you let it lie there, and say, Though the faggots below be burnt, yet this is not touched? is not that faggot, think you, in danger? So I compare several nations to faggots in the fire: it is true Germany was the under faggot, and was in the flame, and other faggots have been burning, and we in England lay as it were on the top of all, and it was a good while ere the flame reached us; and though we were warned to pluck ourselves as a fire-brand out of the fire, yet we through security lay still, and now the flame has caught us: yea, though we be now burning in many places in the kingdom, yet, because we find that the actual seat of the war is, it may be, twenty, thirty, or forty miles from us, how secure are we, as if God did not intend us at all, as if we had nothing to do to take notice of his hand upon our brethren! Wrath is pursuing, but because it is not upon us, oh the security and desperate folly that is amongst us! Just so it was in Germany, as travellers observed, if the wars were but a few miles from them they went on in their trading as quietly and securely as ever, till at length it came upon them and devoured them. Has it not been so in many places in England? May it not be said of many places amongst us, as here in the text, Ramah, and Gibeah, and Beth-aven, after thee, O Benjamin? So may we not name several towns, Banbury and Worcester, after thee, O Exeter, O Bristol? It may be, when the wars were in Shropshire, and Coventry, and other parts, those in Bristol and in Exeter thought they were free, and safe enough. And truly, though God has delivered us all this while, yet, if we be secure, it may be as well said of us, Exeter and Bristol, and after thee, O London.

But you will say, What shall we do when the hand of God is stretched out thus near us?

1. Humble our souls before God, go forth to meet this mighty God with repentance, cry mightily to him, that, if it be possible, his wrath may be appeased before it fasten upon us. As in Luke xiv. 32, it is said of those that are wise, when a great king came out against them with twenty thousand, they sent ambassadors to desire conditions of peace, when he was yet a great way off. Mark, when he was a great way off. So, we must not stay till God is come to our gates, till he be just upon us; but while this great King, the Lord God, is a great way off, at a distance, we must send to him, and meet him by repentance, by humbling our souls, and making our peace with him. Let not us think, It is true, the hand of God was against our brethren of Scotland, but they were quickly delivered; but I may say, After thee, O England. We have not done what our brethren did; for it is observed, that though the generality of that people were notoriously vile, wicked, and rude before these times, yet, partly through the covenant they have entered into, and otherwise, there is no question that, though much evil still exists there, and perhaps not the power of godliness so thoroughly as in many of God's people here, yet certainly a more general reformation has taken place among the common people than amongst us; which speaks hard things against us. O let us go forth and meet our God by repentance.

2. We should rise as one man, and help our brethren. For this has been our evil, that we have suffered the kingdom to moulder away, our brethren to be destroyed: Oh, saith one place, why need we trouble ourselves? and so the land is destroyed piecemeal. Certainly, it is the duty of the kingdom, and of those that remain, when they see their brethren, though at a distance, suffer so much wrong, to rise all as one man, to venture themselves for the relief of their brethren, and not think themselves secure because evil has not yet reached them. We see our brethren of Scotland were willing to come in with their help, and though the sword is far from them, yet, doubtless, some of them think of this very text; Now the trumpet is blown in England, in the northern parts, after thee, O Scotland: they think, after our turn is over, theirs is next, therefore they are willing, to prevent it, though it be in such a hard season as this, to help their brethren.

3. We should meet our danger before it comes. It is easier to keep an adversary at a distance than to repel him when he is closed with us. This has ever been the policy of wise men, rather to go out to meet an adversary than to think to have strength enough to repel him when he comes. Thus in general.

4. As kingdoms, so particular persons, should lay to heart God's impending judgments; as thus, Dost thou see God's hand upon thy neighbour? after thee, O sinner, thy turn may be next: is God's hand stretched out on your fellow servant, on your brother, on your dear friend? after thee, O sinner, thou art guilty of the same sin, thy turn may be next: is God's hand out upon thy companion? after thee, O sinner. O lay this to heart, think with thyself, It may soon come to be my turn. The very thought of this, when God has struck some with sudden death in a fearful manner, God has sanctified to some; What (thought they) if God strike me next? such a one is sent down, for aught I know, to his place, I may be the next! the thought, I say, of this has been so settled upon the heart of some, that it has been a means of their conversion. The Lord make it so to every sinner that sees his fellow, his neighbour sinner, struck before him.

Ver. 9. *Ephraim shall be desolate in the day of rebuke: among the tribes of Israel have I made known that which shall surely be.*

In the words before, you heard that the Lord, by the prophet, did not only threaten war, but summon the cities of Israel, Judah, and Benjamin, as if war were at the gates. But what if troubles do come, said they, we shall do well enough, they will have an end, and blow over again, we shall wear them out; we have been delivered out of great troubles, and so we may be out of these. No, it is otherwise now, Ephraim shall now be desolate, Ephraim, that is, the ten tribes, shall be desolate לשמה This word signifies something stupendous, the hand of God shall be upon them even to amazement, they shall come into desolation, in the time of his rebuke, in the day of his trouble. The words are plain; the observations from them are these:

Obs. 1. That the day of the afflictions of God's people is the day of their rebuke. See this proved in Numb. xii. 14, where Moses saith, "If her father had but spit in her face, should she not be ashamed seven days." When God afflicts his people he, as it were, spits in their faces; and ought not they much more to be ashamed? Whatever that wanton generation think or say, that God never chastises his people for sin, there is no doctrine more evidently contained in Scripture. But they tell us it was in the Old Testament; and herein they show their weakness and disposition to cavil; but they add, which seems to have some show of strength,

That it derogates from the satisfaction of Christ.

But the force of this is nothing, for Christ satisfied for them under the law, as well as for us; they were saved by the same satisfaction that we are, therefore if it now derogates from Christ's satisfaction under the gospel, it did then also under the law.

Obs. 2. God hath his set times for rebuke. As they have their days of sinning, so God will have his days of correcting: you have your days of prosperity now, riches, honour, and plenty in abundance, but remember, it may be the day of rebuke is coming. It is good to put this very case to ourselves. I have mercy now both for soul and body, and oh how comfortable is it, and how happy is my condition! but is there not a day of rebuke coming, when all these mercies will be taken from thee, and then what wilt thou do, O my soul? "And what will ye do in the day of visitation?" Isa. x. 3.

Obs. 3. When wicked men stand out against lesser judgments, they have cause to fear greater. Ephraim had days of lesser chastisements, but slighting them, God would try him no more: there are times in which God will utterly pursue sinners to destroy them, not for instruction, but destruction. The Lord has his houses of instruction, correction, and execution; when the first cannot effect God's end, the third shall, and yet the Lord be just and righteous; for the Lord has no need of us; what is it to him if we should perish everlastingly? he can have his glory from us in our damnation.

Obs. 4. It is a dreadful time when God so rebukes a people that he destroys them. When the hand of God shall be so upon them that he is resolved never to take it off again, even as it was upon Ephraim at this time, I intend not to reform, but to ruin him; this now is a most dreadful time: for,

1. All that wrath which they have treasured up breaks in then upon them. As wicked men treasure up wrath, so doth God, Rom. ii. 5. Now God lets out the flood-gates of his wrath against such a people.

2. All their sins come together into God's remembrance. "In the day when I visit I will visit their sin upon them," Exod. xxxii. 34. It may be you are for the present spared, but the time is coming that God will visit, and then look to it.

3. The cries of justice then prevail against such men. I speak of wicked men mingled and intermixed with the godly. In this day God will not call back his anger. There are times in which God does not stir up all his wrath, as in Psal. lxxviii. 38. Many times God's anger is coming against a nation, family, or person, but he calls it back again; but in this day of rebuke, God will not restrain his wrath, but let it forth to the uttermost.

4. Mercy leaves such a people. "An evil, an only evil, behold, is come," Ezek. vii. 5. But the place most remarkable for this is Ezek. xxii. 20, I will bring you into the furnace, and there I will leave you. God brings his people into great trouble sometimes, but never leaves them there. But there are some whom mercy leaves and forsakes in their troubles; and this is a most sad condition, for by this God shows that he will no more honour himself by their services, but by their sufferings. God saith thus, Seeing they would not give me my glory in a way of duty, I will extract and force it from them in a way of suffering.

5. The Lord then intends hurt to such a people. The Lord perhaps brings you out of an affliction, but in that deliverance he intends your hurt and not your good, Jer. xxiv. 9. I intend nothing but hurt to such a people in all my dealings.

6. All creatures desert such and dare not own them. God being against thee, the creatures cannot help in the least.

7. All their services are rejected. God will be no more entreated for them; now conscience smites and torments the spirits, and all the miseries that come upon them are but the beginnings of eternal sorrows; and this is a most sad case: therefore let us pray with David, Psal. vi. 1, "Lord, rebuke me not in thine anger;" and as the prophet in Jer. xvii. 17, "Be not a terror unto me." But now, because tender consciences are ready to think when God rebukes them, or lays any affliction upon them, that it is to ruin and destroy them; as the Israelites said, in Deut. i. 27, "Because the Lord hated us, he hath brought us forth out of the land of Egypt." In every difficulty they encountered they conceited God hated them in it, though he had so many times done them good. And has not this been the reasonings of our unbelieving hearts, and the murmuring of our spirits in our afflictions? O take heed of such, they are very displeasing unto God. There is a great difference between the rebukes of God upon the godly and the wicked, though perhaps rebuked both in one and the same affliction. As the apothecary breaks Bezar stones to powder, but is very careful not to lose the least grain of them; so the Lord's people, even in the furnace, are dear to him, and have then the greatest experience of God's love. When Jacob lay upon the ground, and had the stone for his pillow, even then he had that heavenly vision from God.

But now the question is, How shall we know whether those rebukes that are upon us are intended for our good or our hurt, our desolation or our restoration?

It may be known thus: if God's displeasures be such, that we find him more set against our sins than our persons, it is an argument that he intends our good, not our hurt, in his rebukes.

But you will say, This is as difficult as the other; how shall we know God aims at our sins, and not our persons? Thus:

If his rebukes work us to a humiliation for our sins, to a resignation of ourselves up to God's disposal, and to an acquiescence in the punishment of our iniquities; this is an argument that God aims at our sins, and not at our persons, in his rebukes, and so in them intends our good and not our hurt. But you will say, It is usual for wicked men in their afflictions to cry out, it was their sins that brought this upon them. But hereby we may discern the difference.

1. They cry out of their sins but *per accidence*, but of the judgment *per se*, the judgment troubles them more than their sins, the cause of the judgment: but the godly cry out of their sins *per se*, and of the judgment *per accidence*, their sin troubles them.

2. A child of God more desires the sanctification of an affliction than its removal; but the wicked care not for removing the cause of judgment, even sin, so the rod of correction be taken off.

"Among the tribes of Israel have I made known that which shall surely be." Some conceive that these words are spoken as the aggravation of this people's misery; and if so, the observations from them are,

Obs. 5. God smites not a people with judgment before he warns them. "Among the tribes of Israel have I made known."

Obs. 6. When God threatens he is real in his threatenings. "That which shall surely be." Ephraim thinks that God intends not him. Sinners think that when God warns them he is not in earnest, it shall not be; but God saith, It shall be. God esteems his word more than heaven and earth; nay, heaven and earth shall pass away, before the least jot or tittle of it shall fail; and cursed be that peace that has no other ground or foundation than this hope, that those things are not true which the ministers of the word from the word threaten against sinners. And yet this is the condition of many people, and it mightily provokes God, as you may see in Deut. xxix. 19—21, If notwithstanding what is written in this book "he bless himself in his heart, saying, I shall have peace; the anger of the Lord shall smoke against such a man." Oh the bitter, aggravating circumstances recorded in this scripture against such a sinner! Now if God will be so punctual in fulfilling his threatening word, how much more his word of promise! for God has not done so much to realize to you his threatenings as his promises. For,

1. God has not called such witnesses to confirm them. Sometimes, in the general, he calls the heavens to witness; "Hear, O heavens, and hearken, O earth, I have nourished up a people and they rebel against me;" but there are Three in heaven and three on earth who are witnesses, but not to the threatening word, 1 John v. 7, 8.

2. To the verifying of a promise there is not only God's faithfulness, but his faithfulness in Christ, all the promises are in him, yea and Amen: there is in God's promising word, not only his faithfulness, but his faithfulness in Christ, all the promises are made in Christ; so are not the threatenings, judgments have not such immediate relation to Christ.

3. Promises are not only God's covenant with his people, but his testament, and so more sure than a covenant; for a covenant may be broken by the one party, but a testament cannot, it being confirmed by the death of the testator: the promise on our part may be broken, but when we look upon them as confirmed by the death of the great testator Jesus Christ, we have strong consolation: as it is a great evil not to believe the threats of God, so it is also a great evil not to credit the promises of God. Christians, you wonder when wicked men believe not God's threatenings and his judgments to tremble at them. Know, O Christian, that not only men, but angels stand and wonder when thou dost not believe the promises of God, when they are so confirmed that we might believe and walk in comfort.

Obs. 7. The revealing of sin before judgment aggravates both the sin and the judgment. If a father should desire his child not to do a certain thing, nay, not only desire but forbid him, yea, threaten him with punishment if he did it; if he shall after all this gainsay his father's will, he puts a greater contempt upon his father, for he breaks through hedges and fences which should have restrained him: so when God shall forbid, yea, threaten if we break out, it puts a great contempt upon God.

1. The goodness of God is not honoured by us: when the Lord for our good shall warn us of our sins, that so we may prevent judgment, the desert of our sins, and we, notwithstanding, sin, it dishonours God's goodness.

2. The truth of God is not honoured: when we disobey, we do no other than try whether the word be true or no, whether God's words are yea and nay. O sinner, dost thou know what thou dost? thou temptest God, saying, Lord, there are such and such threatenings against sin, but I do not believe them, Lord, I will venture it, I will put it to the trial whether it be so or no.

3. It aggravates the sin: the judgment cannot but be the greater, thou canst expect but little pity from the goodness of God which thou hast slighted, when it warned thee of those judgments which are now upon thee, his mercy to remove them cannot be expected. God, by his ministers, warned me in such a sermon, but I went on and would not reform, and now there is matter for the worm of conscience to gnaw upon; that thou mayst say as Job, "What I feared is now come upon me;" and this is that which aggravates our misery. Have not the ministers of God now for these twenty years, especially in these latter seven years, made this the subject of their preaching, to warn us of judgments? and now the judgments of God are come upon us, God has vindicated the word of his servants.

But these words, though they may be thus understood, yet I conceive they bear a further signification, which is this: I have declared among the tribes what shall be finally irrevocable, without any change or alteration; I have formerly repented, and have been entreated, but now I will repent no more. They seem to contain God's unchangeable purpose for the desolating of this people; and being thus understood, the observation from them will be this:

Obs. 8. There is a time when there shall be no help to deliver from judgment. Though they should call, cry, mourn, weep, fast, and entreat, yet the judgment shall not be removed. As is said of Esau, "he found no place of repentance," Heb. xii. 17. There is a great mistake in the interpretation of that place made by many, who gather from it that there may be many tears shed, much sorrow found, and yet no true repentance; but the meaning of the words is this, he found no place for his father Isaac's repentance, though he cried and shed tears for the blessing, yet his father repented not that he had bestowed it upon Jacob: so that people may cry and humble their souls before God, yet shall find in God no place of repentance; nay, if the saints of God should all join together and pray for such a people they would not prevail; Ezek. xiv. 20, "Though Noah, Daniel, and Job" should pray for them, they should not prevail. O sinner, take heed this be not thy condition; thou hast perhaps godly parents and kindred, and they set themselves to seek God for thee, but God will deny them, their prayers shall not prevail for thee. This may be the case with nations and kingdoms, there may be true repentance found and turning to God, and yet no deliverance from outward affliction. I deny not but that true repentance shall deliver a soul from eternal wrath, from perishing in hell; but this I affirm, that there may be true repentance found, and turning to God, and yet no deliverance from a temporal affliction. And this I shall make good by two remarkable texts of Scripture. The first is in Deut. iii. 26. Moses had sinned, and God saith he should not go into the land of Canaan, which was a sore affliction to him: upon this, Moses, who we may be certain had repented him of that sin, prayed; yet see what he saith, "The Lord was wrath with me for your sakes, and would not hear me: and the Lord said unto me, Let it suffice thee; speak no more unto me of this matter." All his prayers and repentance could not deliver him from that outward affliction, and bring him into Canaan. The second text is in 2 Kings xxiii. 25, 26. In chap. xxii. we find the heart of the king melting when he heard the law read, and perceived the anger of the Lord against his people was provoked; he humbled himself, and the Lord told him that he should die in peace. And in chap. xxiii. the king sets upon reforming the people, enters into a solemn covenant with God, causes the people to join with him, pulls down the groves, destroys idolatry; and although it be said in ver. 25, that "like unto him was there no king before him," yet, in ver. 26, there is added, "Notwithstanding the Lord turned not from the fierceness of his great wrath, wherewith his anger was kindled against Judah." So that sometimes God is so set upon his threats, that they shall come to pass; God will make them good whatever ensues: this I conceive to be the meaning of these words; and so Mr. Calvin reads them. God may be so resolved against a man's eternal estate, that he will never show such a man or such a people mercy more; as we may see in those which were bid to the gospel supper: therefore we had need to gather ourselves together "before the decree bring forth," Zeph. ii. 1, 2. O let us in this kingdom take heed; through God's grace we are not yet left desolate, but have much mercy, even in this day of our rebuke; but what God will do one cannot determine; therefore it concerns us to prepare to meet our God, lest the wrath of God meet us, overcome and destroy us, till there be no remedy: though, through present mercy, we may say there is remedy, let us the rather tremble and be awakened, because God sometimes comes against, and is more quick with, a people that are not so openly and notoriously vile as others are, than with the most profane.

Ver. 10. *The princes of Judah were like them that remove the bound: therefore I will pour out my wrath upon them like water.*

But why is God so wrath with Israel? Have not the princes of Judah provoked him also?

Yea, God here speaks to them principally. It seems the people were not so bad, so sinful, as they, for in the next words he saith, that "Ephraim is oppressed and broken in judgment, because he willingly walked after the commandment."

Obs. 1. Princes must answer to God for all their doings: "The princes of Judah." Though they are above all men in power, and so are not so liable to give an account to man as others are, yet to God they must: those actions which are least obnoxious to men, are much to God.

"Were like." That is, not so much figuratively as really; it is usual in Scripture to put the word "like," for the thing itself, as thus, "The glory as of the only begotten of the Father." The princes of Judah were those that removed the bound; by the light of nature, and the law of God, it was a wicked thing to do so; you may see it forbidden by the law of God, Deut. xxvii. 17.

It was a custom among the heathens and the Romans, if any man removed the bound, the ancient landmark, to adjudge them, if poor, to slavery, to dig in deep pits; if rich, to banishment, and a forfeiture of the third part of their estates.

The princes of Judah broke down the bounds in a fourfold manner.

1. They took away other men's estates. God appoints men their bounds and estates, therefore it is not in the power of princes to take them at their pleasure. It was not in the power of Ahab to seize Naboth's vineyard; nay, not to force him to sell it: though a king, he thought it too much to take it by violence; and Jezebel, though a cruel woman, yet would not advise him to possess himself of it without some colour of law. Therefore princes have no right to the subjects' estates, nor liberty to seize them at their pleasure; though such principles of late have been infused into them by some, for which we this day suffer so heavily. In Isa. i. 23, their princes are said to be "rebellious, and companions of thieves." Now if all were their own they could not be thus classed. We would think that they of all men should not break bounds, for what is it they may not have if they would? Plutarch records an excellent conversation between Cineas and Pyrrhus, who was mightily bent on war with Italy, much to the purpose. Cineas thus addressed him: What shall we get if we overcome the Romans? We shall subdue, saith Pyrrhus, our great enemy, and be made possessors of a brave country. Cineas asked what he would do then? Then we will subdue Africa, Carthage, and Sicily. And what then? Then, saith Pyrrhus, we will feast, drink, and be merry. Cineas replied, Why may you not do so now, without shedding so much blood, putting yourself to so much trouble, and endangering your person. If princes would keep within their bounds, what hinders but that they may enjoy themselves and their comforts in peace and quiet, without the shedding of blood?

2. They broke all bounds. That is, they break all laws and liberties; they will not be bound by laws, saying thus, Laws were made for subjects, not for princes. And thus these princes broke the bounds. Hence we may see what corruption there is naturally in the hearts of men; and this is furthered by evil counsellors. When Cambyses desired to marry his sister, but questioned whether he might do it or no, he called his judges together to give him their advice, and they told him, there was indeed a law against it; but, added they, ye princes of Persia may do what you will. They were so far from dissuading him from that wicked act, that they encouraged him in it. And has not our time afforded such counsellors to our princes?

3. They broke the bonds of religion. Therefore interpreters conceive that our prophet Hosea prophesied in Ahaz's time, when he provoked God so by idolatry, setting up the abomination of desolation. And this is the great breach of bonds, when people provoke God. God has set bounds to his word, for his worship and service. Now, take heed that you go not beyond those bounds, for any pretence of decency or comeliness, suitable to the state and circumstances in which you live. God has permitted men to use great liberty in civil things, but none in his worship and ways. Oh what evil have popish princes done in this respect, in removing these bounds! And this is the main reason which makes papists so labour for the upholding and setting up of an arbitrary government, having thereby full liberty to break all bounds in religion.

4. They broke the bonds of their own covenants, and regarded them not. Such were the corruptions of those princes, they broke all sorts of bonds, civil, spiritual, covenanting bonds; nothing restrained them.

But has God left no means to keep in bounds princes as well as subjects?

To this I answer, Yea, certainly. Those who at first gave power for families and persons to keep these, never sanctioned their being broken by the great. The law of nature never gives power to destroy itself, especially in a kingdom where there are resources defensive and offensive, against any means that the greatest in power may raise to infringe the laws and liberties of men; for no subject of a prince but is also a subject of the state, and the state may deal with the instruments that it employs either defensively or offensively. Trajan, after he was made emperor, put a sword into his officer's hand to defend him while he defended the laws; but if he failed in his duty, bade the officer deal with him as a delinquent. It will be worth our pains and cost if, after all our troubles, we can but get the kingdom settled in its true rights and liberties; though our workmen, who are making up our breaches, through some negligence or miscarriage, suffer the wild beasts to break in, yet let not us murmur and repine, but be content, and bless God that we have means to help ourselves. A few years ago we thought our breaches so wide, that none could help or deliver us; now, then, that God has raised up for us helpers contrary to our expectation, let us bless God for them, and be content, and stir up ourselves to aid them. If the sea should break in upon a country, would you sit still, or let any by you rest that would not stir to make up the breach? A farmer is contented to see cattle run up and down in his ground, while his workmen are making up his hedges and fences to keep them out: so our workmen are making up the hedges, let us be contented to suffer awhile patiently. The truth is, those most complain of confusions and disturbances who have been most instrumental to make our breaches and distractions.

Thus the princes of Judah were like them that break the bound, and for thus doing the Lord threatens, in the following words, to "pour out his wrath upon them like water." They have passed their bounds in sinning, and my wrath shall pass its bounds upon them; they kept no bounds in sinning, and my wrath shall keep no bounds in punishing. The Hebrews were wont to express anger by עבר a word which signifies, going beyond bounds; intimating, that ordinarily in our anger we are apt to go beyond bounds. The sense then is, "I will pour my wrath upon them" in great abundance, "like waters." The judgments of God in Scripture are often set forth to us by this similitude of water, as in Isa. xxviii. 17; Nah. i. 8. Look, as their anger ran like water, so my wrath shall run upon them until they are consumed.

God's wrath is very hot against wicked governors, such as break the bounds of religion, laws, and covenants: the Lord is much displeased against the great when wicked. Numb. xxv. 4, the people of Israel committed a great evil in provoking God by their idolatry, joining themselves to Baal-peor, and the Lord said, "Take the heads of the people." The people offended by the encouragement of the governors, therefore their heads must off; the people sin, and the governors must suffer because they reproved not nor restrained, but countenanced them. Hence we may

Obs. 1. We had need pray much for princes. Fearful are the examples which historians report concerning the judgments of God upon wicked princes.

Leander, in the description of Italy, tells of a cruel tyrant, who persuaded himself that he must give an account to no man for what he did; at last God gave him into the hands of the people, who stripped him naked, bound him upon a plank, and drew him through the streets in the sight of all the people; then made a great fire, in which they heated tongs red hot; and, when they had done thus, proclamation was made in the market-place, that seeing he had wronged so many that it was impossible he could atone for the injuries he had committed, therefore all that had suffered by him should come and lacerate his flesh with these implements of torture.

Another fearful example we have of later date, in the massacre in France. Charles the Ninth, pretending much love and kindness to the Protestant party, invited them to a great marriage-feast; and, at the same time, issued a commission, whereby he called in those bloody miscreants, who cruelly murdered them: there he broke bounds; but see how God met with him in a most grievous disease, through the violence of which there spurted out blood from several parts of his body, so that, before he died, he wallowed in his own gore. God poured out his wrath upon them in blood who in their lifetime thirsted after blood.

Obs. 2. The bounds of religion and laws, as they keep in obedience, so they keep out judgments. Pure religion and good laws, as they are bounds to keep us in duty, so they keep judgments and wrath from us. And we ought to look on laws in both these points of view, not only as means to keep us in order and duty, but also to keep out wrath: if we break our bounds, we must look that wrath should break in upon us; therefore we had need do as men that live near the sea, when the sea breaks in upon them, they presently leave all other businesses, to make up the breaches. Our bounds are broken, and who is the occasion of it the Lord knows, and wrath is broken in upon us at our breaches; therefore let us now, as one man, endeavour to stay "the overflowing scourge."

Obs. 3. God punishes according to men's sins. They break the bounds, God breaks in with wrath upon them. Are they resolute in sinning? God will be as resolute in his judgments upon them: see Jer. xliv. 25: You have sworn and vowed to your superstitions, and I have sworn to bring judgment upon you, and it shall come to pass. Therefore when judgments are upon us, if we would have them removed, we should diligently observe what sins we are guilty of correspondent to the judgment; for many times we may trace the cause of a judgment by the sin that we are guilty of; and if we ever expect to have troubles removed, we must first remove their cause, sin.

Ver. 11. *Ephraim is oppressed and broken in judgment, because he willingly walked after the commandment.*

Wrath, in the former verse, was threatened against the princes of Judah, who removed the bounds; and here the Lord returns again to Ephraim, in this 11th verse; and in the 12th verse, to Judah and Ephraim both together; they being both a provocation to God, are plagued both together.

The word "oppressed," in the original is עשוק translated by Jerome, "calumniate," and by the Seventy usually understood in a like sense. We may interpret the words thus, Ephraim, by sycophants, suffers a great deal of wrong. When there are false reports raised against men, they suffer wrong by it: false reports are as a false medium, which represent things otherwise than they are. As a staff put into the water seems crooked, although in reality not so; so the actions of men in the reports of others may seem crooked, when in themselves they are straight and good. And thus was Ephraim broken in judgment; though his cause was good, yet was it wrested in judgment, and that without redress. Good causes are many times perverted by bad men; but the saints may support themselves with Paul's comfort, who cared not for man's judgment. In this signification the Septuagint usually take the word; but here they express it actively, thus, Ephraim has overpowered his adversaries, and so has trodden down judgment. But the words are well rendered in your books in the passive sense, "Ephraim is broken in judgment." *Concussus judicio: concussio* is a law

Κατεδυναστευσεν Ἐφραϊμ τὸν ἀντίδικον αὐτοῦ, κατεπατησε το κρίμα.

term, signifying such a kind of breaking and oppression as threatens the utter ruin and undoing of a man by law; as many rich men threaten to ruin their poor neighbours when they do them any wrong. Or, as corrupt and wicked magistrates, when they cannot bring the poor to say or do what they desire, will threaten to recompense it on them, if ever it lie in their power: of this Samuel clears himself, 1 Sam. xii. 3, "Whom have I defrauded? or whom have I oppressed?" (the word is the same as here;) that is, Have I used my power to threaten men to yield up their liberties, their rights, their enjoyments? This was the sin charged here on the great princes of the ten tribes.

עשקתי

"Broken in judgment." That is, not in God's judgment upon them, but in the judgment of their own cause, they were crushed in their estates, liberties, and laws, and that not only by their own magistrates and governors, but also by the Assyrian: by their own magistrates they were broken and oppressed, good men were discountenanced, just causes betrayed, the whole court corrupted, and the laws of the land, which should have maintained the bounds, were broken; they were so broken as a thing which is broken but not quite spoiled with the fall, some shreds of it may be made use of; so the generality of them were so broken that there was little right to be had for any wrong committed. And as they were thus oppressed in the prophet Hosea's time, so also in the time of the prophet Amos, who prophesied about the same period: Amos ii. 7, "They pant after the dust of the earth on the head of the poor." They did not only seek to bring poor men under them, but even utterly to destroy them, they sought to ruin them, and that by perverting of judgment. So Amos v. 11, their oppression grew to such a height that they took the wheat of the poor from them; if the poor had but gleaned a little wheat in the fields, as they brought it home they robbed them of it: this was the oppression which at this time prevailed among the ten tribes, from their own governors. But they were also oppressed by the Assyrian, who calumniated and reproached them, saying, Where is now your God, in whom you so much trusted? Thus much for the explication of these words. The reason follows:

"Because he willingly followed after the commandment." But some here may say, Why this? is there so much in this to provoke God?

Yes, this was a great sin; for the opening whereof, take notice of these three things.

1. Whose commandment they followed. The commandment of Jeroboam and his princes, men that had authority and power in their hands, yet it provoked God thus highly against them, that they followed the commandments of men who had authority over them. It may seem strange that this charge should be against Ephraim for this, no question but they pleaded thus, What! am I wiser than my governors? must not I do as they bid me?

2. What commandment it was that they followed. It was to worship the calves at Dan and Beth-el. He worshipped God, but in a false manner, and this provoked God so against him.

3. "He *willingly* followed after the commandment;" as soon as ever he was commanded he yielded, without any deliberation, or consultation with himself; whereas he should have stood it out, and have rather endured the loss of all, than yield to their commands: as the three children, who rather suffered the fiery furnace, than they would fall down before the image. Though the generality of them followed after the commandment, yet there were some found among Ephraim who would go to Jerusalem to worship in the place of God's appointment: so 2 Chron. xi. 16, those which set their hearts to seek God would go up to Jerusalem, and not follow Jeroboam to Dan and Beth-el: some knew that God would be worshipped in his own way and in his own place, but the generality of the people liked the commandment, because it was will-worship, which pleases man's nature best; and then it was most for their ease; and this was Jeroboam's plea, I love my people's ease, I would not be so harsh to them, therefore come, we will worship the true God still, it is but the circumstance of place, and that is of little importance. They then willingly followed after the commandment, and thereby encouraged Jeroboam in his wicked design. The Vulgate expresses it thus, they willingly followed after dregs; and the Hebrew seems to confirm this, signifying filthy dregs; and is rendered vanities, or vain things, by the Septuagint. If this be the meaning two things may be remarked:

הָלַךְ אַחֲרֵי־צָו
τῶν ματαίων.

1. That Jeroboam was willing to have the people enjoy their lusts, so he might compass his ends; he was content to give the people the full indulgment of their lusts, and therefore the baser sort clave to him. Jeroboam reasoned thus: I must rend the kingdom from David, but how shall I accomplish it? I must have the people to assist me in it, but how shall I gain them? I will let them have their pleasures in sin, they shall have their lusts without contradiction, and then the most will follow me, I shall be sure of the rude multitude, the profane in the kingdom.

2. After their filthy vanities; that is, after their idols, the calves which he had set up; for the Scripture sets forth the filthiness of idolatry by the basest things in the world.

Thus much of the words in that sense: but they are more full as read in your books, and more agreeable to the original, and afford many observations.

Obs. 1. It is a great judgment for a people to be under oppression. It is a very sad affliction for a nation, family, or person to be under oppression, and broken in judgment, when good men and good causes are crushed and slighted, and wicked men and bad causes prevail and prosper, when a man's innocency avails him nothing. Solomon, in Eccles. iii. 16, saith it is a great evil, when wickedness is got into the place of judgment. God has promised to deliver his people from this, "In righteousness shalt thou be established; thou shalt be far from oppression," Isa. liv. 14; but these times are not yet come, the greater part of the world is at this day under oppression. It is sad to have our estates and our liberties broken for conscience; conscience-oppression is the worst oppression: and this was our condition not long since, nay, and is the condition of many of our dear brethren in many places of this kingdom; has it not come to such a pass that the meanest, yea, the basest, persons in a city or country have had power enough in their hands to undo the best ministers in the kingdom, and that he who departed from iniquity made himself a prey? Oh with what an iron rod has the kingdom been ruled, parliaments broken, the edge of the law turned against the godly party! witness the banishing of men, ministers oppressed in their estates, in their liberties, but especially in their consciences, if they would not, like the fiddler's boy, be ready to dance after every pipe; insomuch that when the Lord gave us a little reviving, we were even as men in a dream. When, under all this, we were ready to say, We shall never be delivered, how is it possible that we should be rescued from the oppressors? how was heaven filled with our cries and earth with our moans! Thus it has been; and worse now it is in many places of the kingdom with many of our brethren; but let them and us be comforted in this, it was thus with Israel, when God delivered them out of captivity. To our adversaries that text may be applied, Isa. xxx. 12; they "trust in oppression;" what is their language but this? We will raise a great army and muster together strong forces, and then we will be masters of the field, and reduce the rebels. They trust in oppression, and make cruelty their arm of power; take away that, and their cause falls to the ground: but God's people are commanded the contrary in Psal. lxii. 10, "Trust not in oppression;" and for those that do oppress, they shall be like those in Isa. xxx. 13, "whose breaking cometh suddenly in an instant;" and you that have friends in oppression, send them for their comfort such scriptures as Psal. xii. 5, "For the oppression of the poor, for the sighing of the needy, now will I arise, saith the Lord; I will set him in safety from him that puffeth at him."

But you will say, True, God will arise, but not yet: these are good words, but we may suffer extremely in the mean time.

But mark what the Lord saith in the 6th and 7th verses of the same Psalm: "The words of the Lord are pure words;" and this word among the rest, that God will arise, and set his people in safety, from this generation to the end. And if any of your friends be in danger, send them Isa. li. 12, 13, "Where is the fury of the oppressor?" God will assuredly so work out things in his own time, that we shall be able to say, Where is now the fury of the oppressor? Now, if God has made us to know the smart of this sore and heavy burden, he looks that we should have very tender carriages and loving dispositions towards our brethren, especially towards their consciences; mark his charge concerning this, Exod. xxiii. 9, "Thou shalt not oppress a stranger:" why so? Oh, saith God, "for ye know the heart of a stranger." Perhaps there are some that walk close with God, who have tender consciences, which cannot yield to what may be imposed upon them by authority, Oh take you heed of oppressing these, God expects that you should use them with all lovingkindness.

Obs. 2. Idolaters are great oppressors. When was it that Ephraim was oppressed? When he walked after the commandment of Jeroboam. Changes in religion bring people to oppression. Therefore the Scripture sets forth antichrist by Egypt, because the people of God were there most grievously oppressed, and the woman in the Revelation is said to sit upon the waters. That story of a bishop who would oppress the people, is well known, who, when one standing up told him he could not do it by law, answered, that if there were any law against him he would carry it in his sleeves. Likewise that oppression of the Waldenses was very great, who, desiring that they might but enjoy the liberty of worshipping God in woods and groves, were refused. And was not this our condition some few years since, when the saints durst not appear for God in public, but only in private rooms and chambers?

Obs. 3. God has a righteous hand in delivering of men into the hands of unrighteous oppressors. "He willingly walked after the commandment," saith God. It may be your enemies, into whose hands I have delivered you, may deal unjustly and oppress you out of measure; yet am I just.

We are oftentimes ready to complain of instruments which oppress us, and never look at the hand of God that smites us by them. We should look within ourselves, and find the cause there which provokes God, what sins we are guilty of, and make our peace with God: and so likewise in the kingdom, this is the way to be delivered from our oppressors. I remember a story in Cedrenus concerning Phocas, who, having murdered his master the emperor Mamicius with his wife and children, usurped the empire, and opened a floodgate to all impiety: an honest poor man at that time was wonderfully importunate at the throne of grace to know a reason why that wicked man so prospered in his design; and was thus answered by a voice, That a worse man could not be found, but that the sins of Christians, and the city of Constantinople, required it. Sins unrepented of give strength to an enemy's side.

Obs. 4. A special cause of oppression is, people's following of false worship. We never read of Israel's great oppressions, but when they "walked after the command;" and it is very observable, after they once began to follow the commands of Jeroboam, the ten tribes never had any good kings, whereas Judah indeed sometimes had, because they kept something of God amongst them, the temple and some of its services. If we submit to wicked men in our consciences, no wonder if they are quickly usurpers over our estates.

Obs. 5. Our giving too much to men, God often punishes by making them the greatest instruments of our misery. If you will make governors gods, it is just with God to make them devils to you; for men made idols become devils. We should labour truly to inform ourselves of that obedience which we owe to governors, and yield them that and no more. If people will give that to men which is God's due, it is just with God to make them the greatest plagues to us.

Obs. 6. We may see here the evil nature of wicked men. Jeroboam and his princes are very fair and specious, give good words to the people, and all to gain their own ends; and when they had attained them, then they broke them in judgment, and oppressed them exceedingly: the more they are yielded to, the more they oppress. It is a sign of a base spirit, for men thus to abuse poor people. "The wicked boasteth of his heart's desire, and blesseth the covetous, whom the Lord abhorreth," Psal. x. 3.

Obs. 7. It is Satan's course to get false worship backed by authority. Satan's chief design is to get his worship into the throne, and to effect this he labours to corrupt the pure worship of God, and presses his own upon the people, backed with the command of authority; the devil knows that there is no way so likely to prevail with the people as this, that if authority commands, that overpowers all reason brought to the contrary. And this is the aspersion cast upon the godly at this very day, that they rebel against authority; an old subterfuge, which in all ages the devil has used to get advantages against the saints. This was Haman's argument, that it was not for the king's honour to suffer the Jews to live in his provinces. Sanballat and Tobiah would not suffer the people of God to build the temple; why? because they were factious people, disobedient to authority. So Paul himself was accused of sedition: and the false prophets tell the king that Amos was such a turbulent fellow that the land could not bear the words which he uttered.

Obs. 8. Man's authority is not a sufficient warrant. No evil may be committed under pretence of the commands of authority. Therefore the papists' blind obedience is too great a burden and bondage for man as man to bear; then much more as Christians. If God command any thing we must look more at the *quis* than at the *quid;* but in the commands of men we must look at the *quid*, what it is that is commanded, more than the *quis*, who commands; the commands of men may be such that the best obedience is to disobey. The pope, writing to Bernard, required a thing of him which was unlawful. Bernard returned this answer, I as a child do not obey, and I obey in disobeying. God's authority is that which we must look at in all our actions. Authority at the first was set up for the good of commonwealths, and not for their hurt, therefore it was no wonder that so many in former times did deny obedience to the unlawful commands of magistrates, when the edge of justice was turned against them; but now, since authority is good, harmonizing with the will of God, punishing sin and wickedness, who obeys more than those who formerly were accounted disobedient? Therefore it is a false reproach which is cast upon the professors of the gospel, that they are disobedient to governors, and contemn authority. Who are they that, in their estates, liberties, and lives, venture most in this cause? is it not the people of God? Nay, is not this used as an argument to godly soldiers to be content with the want of pay, because they are owners of this war? It is for religion and liberty they stand, it is conscience incites them to show themselves active for God, and venture largely for his sake, though they verily believe they shall never see a return of their cost: let but law and authority go on God's side, and then they will obey willingly.

It is true, authority against God must not be obeyed; but suppose the command be in indifferent things?

I answer, that absolutely indifferent things are not within the reach of the magistrate, he is to command that which in his conscience, and according to law, he conceives to be for the good of the commonwealth.

But in this case who must be judge?

The magistrate is to judge whether the thing be indifferent or no, and accordingly we are to yield obedience, if the contrary do not appear to be manifest.

But may not a man judge of his own actions? True, he may; but with a twofold peril, that if the course be right and sincere, he must adopt it; and if it prove light and false, then submit it to the magistrate's censure. Now if the magistrate should command any thing which you in conscience think is not right, according to the rule, you must disobey them, observing however these cautions:

1. With much suspicion and self-jealousy, thinking that they may understand better than we.

2. Pray and beg earnestly of God, with much humility, that he would discover the truth to you; and disobey them not presently, but upon serious deliberation.

3. Account it your affliction and trouble that you cannot agree with them, and make it not a matter of joy.

4. If in some things you cannot obey them, do it as secretly as you can, make not a public business of it; to prevent scandal, boast not of that which should be thy trouble and affliction.

5. You must be very modest in your refusal to comply, not proud and self-conceited, thinking yourselves above them, or better than they.

6. You must have a high and reverent esteem and respect to them, for their place' sake, although they require that from you which you cannot yield.

7. You must be careful to be so much the more obedient in other things; if in some things you cannot yield to them, in other things that you can you should be the more obedient, that so your masters and governors may see that it arises not from obstinacy, but conscience; and this will mightily convince masters and governors.

8. You must be so much the more conscientious in your walking with God in all things; if in some things you plead conscience, and be remiss in other things, your governors may justly say, that it is from caprice and fancy, not for conscience' sake.

9. If, after all this, the magistrate shall in a legal way inflict punishment upon you, you are to submit to it, and patiently to bear it, or else avoid the place.

Thus, observing these cautions, you may disobey magistrates or governors, in things which your conscience tells you are not according to truth.

Obs. 9. The more willing men are to sin, the greater is the sin.

The more of the will there is in any thing, if it be evil, the worse it is; if it be good, the better. Many men make this for their excuse in their evil actions, it was against their wills; this does not excuse, but where the will goes along with any thing, if evil, it is very evil indeed.

1. Now the will may be said to be in sin, when a man does those things which produce sin, or on which sin follows, or omits that which would keep him from sin: a drunkard, perhaps, does not will to swear, strike, and abuse men, yet, doing such things, although unconsciously, his will may be said to be in those sins, because he did not shun the things which led to them.

2. The will may be said to be in a sin, when a man shall, in difficulties, in which he must either sin or suffer, choose rather to sin than to suffer. This people here were commanded by Jeroboam to worship at Dan and Beth-el: but God commanded them to worship at Jerusalem; now for them to disobey God's command, and choose rather to obey Jeroboam's command than suffer Jeroboam's punishment, was a sin of willingness in them. When a man omits a duty commanded, for some attendant hardships, he sins willingly in that his omission.

Obs. 10. Willing obedience in evil brings much guilt upon a people.

This people should not presently have complied with the king's command, but petitioned against, yea, suffered punishment rather yielded; had they done so, they had done something; but no sooner was the command issued, but they willingly obeyed. Governors, perhaps unconsciously, command that which is not good, but if they see their people stand out against it, then they will begin to bethink themselves. There is much evil in this obedience, for by this you mightily enrage them against those that, by reason of the tenderness of their consciences, cannot obey. It is recorded of Louis XI., that being about to confirm unlawful edicts, many of the nobility came to him in their scarlet gowns to petition him not to do it, and if he would proceed, that he would take their lives away; for they told him they would rather die than live to see the confirmation of such unlawful commands; whereupon the king, struck with their coming in such an unusual manner, stayed his hand, and refused to sign. Oh how happy are princes and people in such nobility! Had Ephraim done thus, they had done well in it, and might have had comfort from it.

Obs. 11. Commands for false worship easily prevail. Witness in this kingdom; when King Edward would have reformed the mass, what rebellion arose in Cornwall! but when Queen Mary set it up, how did people please themselves in such abominations! So in our days, what command issued by bishops met not with present obedience?

Obs. 12. It is the duty of Christians willingly to obey God. What a shame is it that we should not willingly obey the commands of God, when devils and wicked men have some that will obey them willingly! How do you think to follow after God, and put off all thoughts of him till you come to lie on your death-beds? Our hangings-off from God mightily hinder our comforts.

But you will say, Were we but assured that they were the commands of God, we would obey them.

But if we would examine, we should find that it is oftener our own unwillingness to obey, than any uncertainty about the commands of God, that hinder us. There are many things in which the Scriptures are dark, yet if things can be fairly inferred from Scripture, we are to obey; otherwise, how can we be said to obey with the obedience of faith, as we are commanded? Now, how can we be said to obey with the obedience of faith, if we must have reasons for every thing?

But how shall we know God's mind in matter of worship?

In this case we are to compare things together and

weigh them seriously, and so get out the result and mind of God, and follow that, although for the present there want demonstrative reason to make it out clear. And thus much for the words so understood.

Now from the other reading of the words, after the Vulgate latin, *post sordes*, we may

Obs. 13. It is the way of bad princes to give liberty to men's lusts.

Now surely that way which has so much of sin in it, cannot be the safe way for men to walk in.

Obs. 14. Idolatry is filthy stuff.

Therefore you that are so pleased with them, and take such delight in superstitious vanities, much good may you do with them; for our parts that truly fear God, we desire the pure ordinances of Jesus Christ.

Ver. 12. *Therefore will I be unto Ephraim as a moth; and to the house of Judah as rottenness.*

God made a great difference between Judah and Israel; but they joined in the same sins, and God couples them in the same wrath: "Therefore will I be unto Ephraim as a moth, and to the house of Judah as rottenness."

"Therefore." Why? wherefore? It has reference to the words we spake of the last day, they "willingly walked after the commandment." Because they followed the unlawful commands of Jeroboam and his princes, "therefore will I be unto Ephraim as a moth:" that for Ephraim.

And it is likely the same cause might exist for God being "to the house of Judah as rottenness." Had they resisted the unlawful commands of those in power all might have been well; but they thought that perhaps some disturbance would arise in the state, Oh, it is better for us to obey, that we may be at peace; but while they, to free themselves from apprehended disturbance and to enjoy their own quiet, would obey unlawful commands, the secret curse of God rested on their estates: "Therefore" (saith the Lord) "I will be unto Ephraim as a moth, and to the house of Judah as rottenness." A secret curse there was on peace so procured.

In the opening of these words, and presenting the mind of God to you in them, there are these five or six things to be considered.

1. The reading of the words.
2. Their scope, what it is that God intends by them.
3. The reason of the difference of the expression, A moth to Ephraim, and rottenness to Judah.
4. What time this refers to; when was God a moth to Israel and rottenness unto Judah?
5. How and in what respects God may be said to be a moth and rottenness to a people.
6. The several observations to be drawn from it.

All this is necessary for the opening of this twelfth verse.

כעש וכרקב

Καὶ ἐγὼ ὡς ταραχὴ τῷ Ἐφραΐμ, καὶ ὡς κέντρον τῷ οἴκῳ Ἰούδα.

I. The reading of the words. The Seventy read the words a little different from our English version, *ταραχὴ καὶ κέντρον, conturbatio ac stimulus*, I will be a trouble unto Ephraim and a prick unto Judah; I will trouble, prick, goad, and vex them. The blessed God, who is a rest to his people, is a trouble, a prick, and goad, to vex his enemies, the ungodly. The Vulgate and Jerome read it thus, *Ego tanquam tinea Ephraim*, I will be as a moth unto Ephraim; the first word as in our books; but the second, *quasi et putredo domui Judæ*. Others, as Munster, Leo, Juda, Drusius, render it *quasi et teredo*. Teredo is a worm that eats out the heart of the strongest wood. *Minutissimus vermiculus*, saith Luther on the place; and Pliny saith it is the worm that breeds in ships at sea, and eats out the heart of the strongest oak planks: but yet often translated rottenness, because the worm causes that wood to be rotten. Prov. xii. 4, "A virtuous woman is a crown to her husband; but she that maketh ashamed is as rottenness in his bones:" there the same word occurs; a woman whose behaviour is such in company as makes ashamed, is rottenness to a man's bones, be they never so strong. That for the reading.

II. The scope of these words, what it is that God intends by them; which is, that judgment should come, 1. Secretly, 2. Gradually, 3. Insensibly.

That wrath which I intend to let out upon Ephraim and Judah shall come,

1. Secretly; as the moth doth eat the garment secretly, so my wrath shall be, there shall be no noise of it for a while.

2. Gradually; I will go on by degrees: a moth and rottenness do not consume the garment or the wood all at once, but step by step.

3. Insensibly; they shall not so much as perceive it, they shall not see for a long time how my wrath is out against them, and yet it shall consume them. That is the scope.

III. The reason of the difference of the expression, A moth to Ephraim, and rottenness to Judah. If God intended only to show his secret, gradual, insensible judgment, then one expression might have sufficed. But the reason of the different terms used is, Israel was to be destroyed sooner than Judah: Judah should hold out longer than Israel, though both of them were to be destroyed at length. As strong wood holds out longer though there be a worm in it, than a garment attacked by moths; so Judah held out above a hundred years after this threat, after this rottenness began in them, longer than Israel did; for the time that this moth was in Israel (of which we shall speak presently) to Israel's captivity, was but two or three and forty years; but from the time of God's being a rottenness to Judah to his desolation, one hundred and threescore years elapsed.

IV. To what time doth this refer? when was God a moth unto Ephraim and rottenness to Judah? To show that fully would require some time; I will refer you to the scriptures which contain the account, both when the moth and when the rottenness began. From 1 Kings xv. 8, to the end of the 17th chapter of 2 Kings, you may find the time when God was a moth to Ephraim: and for Judah, in 2 Kings xvi., when God was rottenness unto Judah, even from Ahaz's time to the time of their being carried away captive into Babylon, which was about a hundred and sixty years. And besides the Scriptures, Josephus, in lib. ix. cap. 12, and lib. xv. towards the latter end, and lib. x. cap. 10, likewise sets forth the condition both of Ephraim and of Judah, when the Lord was a moth to the one and rottenness unto the other.

V. How and in what respects God may be said to be a moth and rottenness to a people. Indeed the same thing is signified in both these expressions, only (as I have told you) the first implies a quicker despatch of Israel, and the second a more slow judgment on Judah, but both issuing in the same results. Now God is a moth and rottenness to a people many ways.

1. In the very spirits of people. There is a secret way of God's wrath upon a people in their spirits, which is not perceived in the world. As, 1. When the spirits of men in a nation grow weak and cowardly; that shows a judgment of God upon them that is as a moth to them. And so it was in Israel, as you may find in 2 Kings xv., &c., where their governors did what they pleased, and the people laid down quietly and dared not to appear in the least to find fault with their actions. 2. When a base sloth of spirit seizes on the hearts of a people, a dull sordidness, a minding of low things, and

disregard of worthy and honourable achievements; when men are thus, then God is as a moth and rottenness to them. 3. When there are jealousies and divisions. As a moth in a garment, and rottenness in wood, secretly dissever and waste the threads and fibres, so secret jealousies and secret divisions in the minds of men, by the disunion they create, consume and destroy them. 4. Base compliance for their own ends. 5. Falseness of spirit in the trust committed to them. When you see this prevail, especially in those that are put in public trust, then is God a moth and rottenness to that people. And that is the first, A moth and rottenness in the spirits of men.

2. In men's counsels. As, 1. In blindness; that they shall not be able to see the plots of their enemies; they shall not know their own advantages, nor how to improve what they have; they shall not hit upon the right means to relieve themselves. There shall be a perplexity and contradiction in their counsels, and they shall be insnared in their own folly. 2. In blasting their projects: God may not appear outwardly in a hostile and terrible manner, but his secret curse rests upon their counsels, and so is a moth and rottenness to them.

3. In their tradings. Trade shall decay amongst them, and they shall grow poorer and poorer, no man knows how. There shall be a secret curse upon their tradings and estates, that no man can give a cause of.

4. In the chief instruments they make use of for their good; taking away their chief ones secretly, when nobody takes notice of them. As with rotten wood, one little piece drops down after another; so in a state and kingdom, chief instruments shall be taken away, and no one notice it; sometimes one, and then another, and then another after him; so they shall moulder away by degrees, and those that remain shall be blasted in their esteem among the people. Those that God gives ability to do them good, and might be very useful and serviceable unto them, yet, though they live amongst them, they shall be so blasted by reports one way or other, that they shall not be able to do them much good. And when you see this prevailing in a kingdom, then God is a moth and rottenness to them.

5. In their enterprises: when in their actions and enterprises there is division amongst them; not only division in their spirits, but in their actions, one goes one way and another another way, they scarce can agree in any thing, and so all their enterprises are brought unto nothing.

6. In their warlike power and strength. There shall be a great charge upon the people and much shall be gathered together, but no man shall know how it is spent; it shall moulder away, so that every one shall complain of the charge and of what goeth from him, but nobody almost can see what it comes to.

7. In their religion. A secret curse of God on them, that their religion should be corrupted, that their wine should be mixed with water, their silver with dross; that when they desire to purify their religion, there shall be such mixed and contradictory opinions, as to manifest that there a secret moth and rottenness, even a secret curse of God, rests. These seven ways God may be said to be a moth and rottenness to a people.

Now, from all these, arise these observations, which we should take special notice of as nearly concerning us.

Obs. 1. God may be in a way of wrath against a nation or individual, and yet meanwhile be very patient and long-suffering toward them.

Therefore no people must think themselves secure because that God appears not in the height of his displeasure. Neither let any think themselves safe because God is patient towards them. As in the greatest afflictions of the saints there are glimpses of God's goodness, so in the greatest prosperity of the wicked, when God is most patient towards them, there are some footsteps of his wrath. No child of God is ever in such a dark night, but he has some beams of God's goodness; and no wicked man is ever in such a height of prosperity, but he has some workings of God's wrath against him.

Obs. 2. God many times lets out his wrath against a people in little things.

"I will be a moth and rottenness." They are both little things. What is a moth? And that which is translated rottenness, is one of the least of worms, a worm that eats into the heart of the wood, and so produces rottenness. As there may be much poison in small drops, so there may be much wrath in little things. You know the wrath of God was shown much on the Egyptians in the plagues of lice and flies; and so it may be let out against thee in very small and contemptible things; things thou little thinkest of, and passest by unheeded, may be means of great wrath in the hands of God.

Obs. 3. When God lets out his wrath in small things, it is contemptible to carnal hearts.

The carnal in Israel and Judah little thought of the extent of the impending evil, but slighted and contemned all that the prophet could threaten, for it was but "a moth and rottenness." It has been so amongst us. With what contempt did many hear the threatenings of God's ministers against England! And why? Because some dreadful judgment did not rest visibly on the nation; though meanwhile the wrath of God and the fruits of his displeasure were amongst us. Men are seldom sensible of little things. As they little consider God's mercies in small things, so in the same they little regard God's wrath. As it is an argument of a gracious heart to bless God for his mercies in small things, so likewise it proves that the heart is right when in small things it is observant of God's displeasure. If God but hold up his finger, presently to take notice and to be sensible of it, is an argument of a gracious heart. As it is an argument that that flesh is full of life which is sensible of the least touch, so that heart is full of grace when it is impressed by the least token of God's displeasure. But when we are in such a frame of mind that, except God strikes us in some terrible manner, we are not sensible of his displeasure, this is a sign of the callosity and hardness of our hearts.

Obs. 4. Though carnal hearts slight and contemn God's wrath in small things, yet it will eat them out at last. It will bring them down, it will destroy them, if it be neglected. You know, in Exod. viii. 25, the plague of flies brought down the spirit of Pharaoh more than all the previous judgments; he said before that he would *let* the people go, but he never *bade* them go till then. God is able to bring down the stoutest and proudest spirit by little things. He can eat out the heart of the strongest wood by this little worm; and so by the least of his judgments can abase the stoutest and proudest.

Obs. 5. God is slow in punishing. He punishes by degrees at first: yea, his punishing is as a moth, and as a little worm in the wood, it is a long time before they do any hurt. This is to show that God's wrath is at first but slow. And by this we are taught to do even as God himself doth, to be "slow to wrath;" in our wrath and displeasure against our brethren, to be slow as God is slow; not presently to fly in the faces of our servants or of our children when they displease us. God deals not so with us, but is a long time before he bring on us any sensible evil. The Romans used to have the rod and the axe carried before their magistrates, to show that they began by lower punishments at first, and proceeded gradually to the infliction of the extreme penalty.

Obs. 6. God has secret judgments to bring upon a

people. In 2 Kings iii. 17, "Thus saith the Lord, Ye shall not see wind, neither shall ye see rain; yet that valley shall be filled with water." There shall be a filling with water though you see neither wind nor rain; you shall not know whence it comes, yet the valleys shall be filled with water. So, often the judgment of God is out against a people, against a family, or an individual, and no one can tell whence it comes. As God has many secret blessings for his people, so he has secret curses against the ungodly. Let us take heed of secret sins, for God has secret wrath in store to avenge secret sins. Many of you that find the hand of God out against you, and know not wherefore, examine your own hearts, whether there be not in you many secret sins against the Lord. It was so at this time when God came to be as a moth unto Ephraim, for in 2 Kings xvii. 9, speaking of the very period this prophecy relates to, the text saith, that the children of Israel did secretly that which was not right in the eyes of the Lord: therefore just was God in this, to be as a moth, to pour forth his displeasure secretly. Take you heed of secret sins, lest God consume you by secret judgments.

Obs. 7. Our corruptions within breed our trouble and our undoing. Whence comes the moth but from the very cloth itself that it corrodes? it is bred there: and this worm is bred in the wood that it consumes. "A moth shall eat them," seems to have been a proverbial speech amongst the Hebrews, when they would express the perishing of any by their own counsels and ways; as the Latins, *Fabrum constringi compedibus quas ipse cuderat,* The workman is fettered with those fetters he makes himself: and so that proverb of ours, To nourish a snake in a man's own bosom, is something of the same import; that is, the evil which befalls us is bred within us; the wrath which consumes us is engendered by our internal corruptions. As the bird furnishes out of its own plumage the feather to wing the shaft for its own destruction, so from our own sins results our own misery. From the uncleanness of a nation or a particular soul comes its evil; therefore if we should read the words according to the Vulgate, they followed *post sordes,* after the filth of Jeroboam, then the elegance of the expression would be increased; it was those filthy ways of Jeroboam that caused these moths to be bred. From our uncleanness comes our consumption: as from the impurity of the body many evils are bred, so from the want of purity in the spirit. Therefore we should be willing to take pains in the work of repentance, yea, though it be somewhat troublesome to the flesh, yet better wear out clothes a little by washing them than let them rot in their dirt. True, washing of clothes wears them a little, but filth soon engenders corruption and decay: so the work of repentance may put you to pain and wear out your bodies a little, but if you let your hearts alone in the filth of sin, misery must ensue. Take heed of suffering any sin to remain undisturbed in your hearts, it will breed a worm, (for so this word rottenness signifies,) it will breed a worm, the worm of conscience, that may prove the worm that never dieth.

Obs. 8. God's wrath, though secret, many times eats out men's spirits and makes them unuseful. Therefore it is compared to a moth, and to rottenness, to a worm in the wood: as the moth eats out the strength of the garment, and renders it unserviceable for any thing; and as the worm in like manner eats out the strength of the wood; so the secret wrath of God many times eats out men's spirits, and makes them very unuseful in the places where they are set. How many have had excellent parts when young, and have been very useful; yet the uncleanness of their spirits has bred a worm that has eaten out the excellency of those parts, and before they have died they have been as a moth-eaten garment and rotten wood! indeed there has been the same bulk and as goodly an appearance as before, yet, if you come to make use of them, they as much differ from their former selves as a moth-eaten garment from itself, or rotten wood from the same material unaffected by decay.

Obs. 9. Though others go before them, yet they shall follow not long after. This note is drawn from the diversity of the expression, a moth to Ephraim, and rottenness to Judah. God indeed will deal more quickly with Ephraim, and consume them sooner in his wrath, but Judah shall follow not long after. A matter of serious reflection for any people, that, though others are consumed before them, yet it will not be long before they shall follow. Germany and other countries have gone before us: we cannot prophesy as here the prophet did, but yet, except God prevent by an extraordinary hand, we may follow not many years after; and who knows how soon? And, to apply it individually, it may be such a friend of thine is gone, the hand of God has consumed him and eaten out his very heart, and he is perished as filth and dung from the face of the earth; and thou art yet alive: and is there not rottenness in thee? is not the secret wrath of God eating out thy heart? He is gone a little before, but thou art like to follow within a little while after. What great matter is it though thy companion be struck dead and gone to hell, and thou left alive, when thou shalt follow not long after? It is in this case as with persons who travel together; perhaps one outrides another, and so comes to his inn a little sooner than the rest of his company, but before he is lighted off his horse, or gone to his chamber, the others have arrived also: so perhaps God's hand strikes one dead and sends him to hell, yet within a while the rest will follow after. Therefore consider, when God's hand is upon any to strike them dead, I may follow not long after. A moth to Ephraim and rottenness to Judah.

Obs. 10. What a poor creature is man. God, in expressing himself thus to be a moth and rottenness, speaks with a kind of contempt against the pride of Ephraim and Judah: they were haughty and proud, but, saith God, a worm shall consume them. In Job iv. 19, it is said of men, that they "dwell in houses of clay, whose foundation is in the dust, which are crushed before the moth." It is a strange expression, I know not any such in Scripture to show the weakness and vanity of man. Indeed to be crushed before a lion is not so much; but that he should be crushed before a moth, that a moth should be able to crush a man, marks strongly the weakness that is in man. Wherein is he to be desired? he is but vain, yea, vanity itself, when he can be crushed before a moth. And so, what are the great kingdoms of the world? let them be never so proud and haughty, yet they are but as rottenness, and a worm may consume them.

Obs. 11. How low God condescends that he may express his meaning to men. It is a very strange expression, for the high and glorious and dreadful God, whom the angels themselves adore, to say of himself, that he will be as a moth, and for this infinite and blessed Deity to say of himself, that he will be as rottenness. Dare any creature have used such a low and mean comparison respecting God, if we had it not in his own word? Yet this high and glorious God condescends thus low only that he might the more easily reach, and the more surely affect, our understandings. Surely we should be willing to appear very low, to do any service for God, seeing God is pleased thus to humble himself to our apprehensions.

Obs. 12. It is a sad thing for divers neighbouring countries, professing the same religion, and living in the midst of a common enemy, to have God's hand against them at the same time. A moth to Ephraim, and rottenness to Judah. These ten tribes, and Judah together with Benjamin, were the only professing people that God had, and they lived in the midst of the heathen, their common enemy; now this is the dreadful threatening, that the hand of God should be out against them both together. And of this we have special occasion to take notice at this day. In many ways God's wrath has been out against us in England, not only as a moth and rottenness, but so long, and to such an extent, that the ruin and decay it has occasioned have become manifest. But, blessed be God, that he has been gracious to our brethren near us, (I mean our brethren of Scotland,) and that the same judgments that have been upon us, have not been upon them at the same time; that though God's hand be out against us, yet that the same hand was not stretched out at the same time against them. For so we may compare England and Scotland to Ephraim and Judah, brethren living near together, and living in the midst of common enemies. Had the Lord, at the same time, been moth and rottenness there, as he was here, what had become of us? That is, had there been the same divisions in Scotland that there were, that there are still, in England, what had become of us at this day? Oh! it is a mercy of God which we must notice and bless his name for, that though he were a moth to us, by exciting divisions, dissensions, jealousies amongst us, whereby we were weakened and unable to help ourselves, and became a prey to the common enemy; yet, though at the same time nothing was more aimed at than to create the like divisions in Scotland, that he has delivered them from that judgment, that he has not been in that respect a moth and rottenness unto them. How had the common enemy rejoiced and boasted had this object been attained! This was God's great mercy unto us, whereas it was threatened against Israel and Judah that his wrath should be against them both at the same time.

Ver. 13. *When Ephraim saw his sickness, and Judah saw his wound, then went Ephraim to the Assyrian, and sent to king Jareb: yet could he not heal you, nor cure you of your wound.*

"When Ephraim saw his sickness, and Judah saw his wound." The word translated "his sickness," is from one implying grief and sickness. And the word translated "wound," from a word that signifies *colligavit*, he hath bound up; either because of the corruption of the body that is gathered together, or because of the binding up of it with cloths.

הלין חלה Æger fuit.

מזרו זור comprimere atque colligare.

"When Ephraim saw his sickness, and Judah saw his wound:" that is, God at length made them to see what a crazy condition both their civil and church state were in, how wounded they were, how like to perish, and ready to die. In Isa. vii. 1, and succeeding passages, you may find the sickness of Judah, and how Judah saw it. When Rezin, king of Syria, and Pekah, son of Remaliah, came against Judah, the heart of the king and the heart of his people were moved, as the trees of the wood are moved with the wind; then Judah became sensible of his sickness and dangerous condition. How Ephraim saw his wound, we shall see further presently, when we examine what remedy for it they sought to obtain.

Wrath was out against Ephraim and Judah some time, and had almost consumed them before they would take notice of it. Hence,

Obs. 1. The pride of man's heart will not easily be brought to see and acknowledge the hand of God. "Lord, when thy hand is lifted up, they will not see," Isa. xxvi. 11. They will not acknowledge the hand of God against them, but would rather make it appear to the world that all is well with them. So it was for a long time with Ephraim and Judah, but at length they saw their sickness and their wound.

Obs. 2. God will force men to be sensible of his hand out against them; he will make them to see their sickness and their wound. Micah vi. 13, "Therefore also will I make thee sick in smiting thee," saith God; I will smite thee, and I will make thee sensible of my stroke: so in that forecited place of Isa. xxvi. 11, "Lord, when thy hand is lifted up, they will not see; but they shall see, and be ashamed," saith God: I will make them to know and to be sensible of my stroke; the sickness shall so grow upon them, the anguish of the wound shall be so great, that they shall be sensible.

Obs. 3. Men more readily see their wound than their sin. They see their sickness and their wound, but here is nothing of their sin. This is usual with carnal hearts in their afflictions, to look at nothing but their wound and their sickness; they regard nothing but to get that healed; seldom will you hear them cry out of their sin. Thus it was with Israel and Judah; and is the way of carnal hearts.

Obs. 4. Men will not seek for help till they be made sensible of their misery. "Then went Ephraim to the Assyrian, and sent to king Jareb." And this is true spiritually; till God wounds the soul, and it is made sensible of its sickness, it seldom, yea, never, sends out for help; but when he strikes, it cries for aid. And many times it is with soul-affliction as it is here with outward affliction, they seek for help, but seek it in a false way. They "went to the Assyrian, and sent to king Jareb."

You will say, When did they do so?

To explain this, we must refer to the Kings, for though you have this prophecy of Hosea placed in your Bibles at a great distance from the book of Kings, yet this prophet and others prophesied in the time of the kings, and therefore their history will much help to a right understanding of the predictions delivered. First, then, Ephraim begins to send to the Assyrian and to king Jareb. In 2 Kings xv. 19, there you read that Menahem, who was king of the ten tribes, gave Pul the king of Assyria a thousand talents of silver, that his hand might be with him to confirm unto him the kingdom. Mark, that his hand might be with him to confirm the kingdom. It seems, this king of Israel saw his kingdom to be in a crazy condition, saw his sickness and his wound; therefore he sends to the king of Assyria, and gave him a thousand talents of silver, that he might confirm the kingdom in his hand; and in the 20th verse, you shall find that his subjects were obliged to pay it, "Menahem exacted the money" (saith the text) "of all the mighty men of wealth" in Israel. Oh what do subjects often suffer to satisfy the humours of their rulers! And in 2 Kings xvii. 4, you find that Hoshea, another king of Israel, sent messengers, for help, to So, king of Egypt. And as to that Jareb, which is named here, some say that it was a principal city in Assyria; others, that it was a special name of the kings of Assyria; but others, and very likely with truth, do not make it the proper name of a man, but a word of appellation, according to its signification; for Jareb means *defensorem*, the defender, or avenger. Therefore, when Gideon's father spake to the people concerning his son's casting down the altar of Baal, and cutting down the grove that was by it, he saith, "Will ye plead for Baal? will ye save him? if he be a god, let him plead for himself:" thereupon they called Gideon's name Jerub-baal, he that defended them from, or took vengeance on, Baal. So here they sent to the king of Assyria, as to one that should be their defender or avenger: they do not seek to God, but they sent to king Jareb, the prophet saith, as their defender. As often in scorn we call men by the name of that which they undertake to be; so, because they trusted in the king of Assyria as their defender or avenger, therefore God, in contemptuous irony, calls him Jareb; They sent to their defender, but they little thought of me. So much with respect to Ephraim.

And then as to Judah, though he be not particularly named, because Ephraim was the most forward and the first that sent for help, yet doubtless the prophet here rebukes Judah as well as Ephraim; for in 2 Kings xvi. 7, Ahaz king of Judah sent to Tiglath-pileser king of Assyria to come up and save him out of the hand of Rezin and Pekah, kings of Syria and Israel, that did rise up against him: and in 2 Chron. xxviii. 16, you find Judah again sending for strange helps, unto the kings of Assyria. The words being thus opened, the observations are these:

Obs. 5. Carnal hearts seek to the creature for help in time of difficulty.

They saw their sickness, they saw their wound; what did they then? They "went to the Assyrian, and sent to king Jareb." They look to no higher causes of their trouble than second causes, therefore they seek to no higher means for their relief than second causes. They regard their troubles as such as befall other men as well as them, and so look not up unto God. They are led by sense, and the second causes are before them and near to them, but God is above them and beyond them, and his ways are often contrary to sense; they know little of God, and have less interest in him; therefore it is that they little mind God in their straits, but send for help unto the creature.

This is the way of carnal hearts at this very day. What helps do they send for but creature helps? Therefore, my brethren, let us not fear our adversaries much, for their strength is in the arm of flesh; and we know they take no other course but to strengthen themselves in the creature; they know no other help; they little regard God in all their ways; let them have what they will, yet pray they cannot, they have little heart to go unto God; they curse and swear, yea, and tell us that it was never worse with them than when they prayed most: all their help, then, is on this side heaven, and therefore not much to be feared; they have that carnality of heart in them which was here in Ephraim and Judah, when they were a people to be destroyed, and were given over by God to seek for help only in the creature, to go to the Assyrian and to send to king Jareb.

As it is in temporal, so it is sometimes in spiritual distress. When God strikes the soul of men with sicknesses, and wounds their consciences, what course do they take? they seek not to the Lord that smote them, but to the creature, for help; they go to their companions, to their trading, to their shops, to their pleasures, &c., and strive in them to find relief for their souls. This is the way of carnal hearts, to seek to the creature for help, both temporal and spiritual, when they are smitten.

Obs. 6. There is much guilt contracted by resting on creature helps. Thus it was with Israel and Judah; they contracted much guilt in that manner. And we find that God is greatly incensed with such as do so. In 2 Chron. xxv. 6—9, when Amaziah king of Judah, in a time of danger, hired a hundred thousand men out of Israel, which were idolaters, the Lord would not suffer him to make use of them, but bids him send them away; "Let not the army of Israel go with thee, for the Lord is not with Israel." Yea, "but what shall we do" (saith the king) "for the hundred talents which I have given to the army of Israel?" Be content, the prophet replied, rather to lose the hundred talents, than to make use of such wicked men as they that have forsaken the true worship of God.

It is a great question among many, whether it be lawful to make use of wicked men in any cases, especially in public affairs of kingdoms; to send for their help in time of public danger, to think to strengthen ourselves by the ungodly. Peter Martyr, in his Comment on Judges, chap. iv. 17, handles this question, How far leagues may be made with idolaters and wicked men? and gives two reasons why their aid should never be sought in any of our straits. First, then, there will be by this means danger of their infecting us with their idolatrous spirit and superstitious usages. But, secondly, and especially, if you send for their help, how can they unite with you in prayer to God to bless you? and when you have gotten the victory, how can you join together in praising God? And indeed this is as strong an argument as possible, not to make use of the help of wicked men in the public affairs of a kingdom. They truly are unfit to join together in fighting, that cannot join together in prayer and in praising of God. And yet this is very natural to most men, yea, good men are sometimes guilty of this, of seeking too much to the wicked for help in times of difficulty. Asa, though otherwise a godly king, in 1 Kings xv. 18, is blamed in that he sent to Benhadad the king of Syria to help him; and in 2 Chron. xvi. 9, Hanani the seer told him that he had done foolishly in so doing, for, saith he, you require not such aid; "For the eyes of the Lord run to and fro throughout the whole earth, to show himself strong in the behalf of those whose heart is perfect toward him." So that it proved that in this thing Asa's heart was not perfect with God, because he sought for help from the wicked, and relied not upon the Lord. And it is very observable of this king, that though a good man, and, it seems, a soldier, yet he was very angry with the seer: "Then Asa was wrath with the seer, and put him in a prison house:" what! shall a prophet contradict him in his warlike affairs? I must have soldiers, old soldiers, about me; talk as you will of good men, and that God will be with those that can pray, I must have those that can fight, those that are soldiers. I would it were not so at this day. Isa. xxx. 1, 2, "Woe to the rebellious children, saith the Lord, that take counsel, but not of me; and that cover with a covering, but not of my spirit!" wherefore do they this? "that they may add sin to sin." This is a strange charge, "Woe to the rebellious children," that go on in their own ways, and "take counsel, but not of me," and that cover things over with vain pretences, "but not by my spirit;" yea, and all is, "that they may add sin to sin!" And what is this sin? It follows presently, "That walk to go down into Egypt, and have not asked at my mouth; to strengthen themselves in the strength of Pharaoh, and to trust in the shadow of Egypt!" "And have not asked counsel at my mouth," saith God. They think to strengthen themselves by Pharaoh, and never ask counsel of me. It is rebellion, it is a following of their own counsels, a covering over things, but not by God's Spirit, an adding sin to sin, to seek for help from wicked and ungodly men.

Revetus on this text treats at large about this very question, of forming leagues with idolatrous and wicked men; and saith, That for whole kingdoms, on any pretext whatever, to call in the help of ungodly men against those that are of the same religion, is unlawful and sinful. Still he thinks it may possibly in some cases be allowed, but it would require a great deal of time to discuss fully every case, and to give all the requisite cautions. But certainly it would appear, that some amongst us, and their cause, have little to do with God when they seek for such helps as they do, and rely so much upon them; when they send for papists, for Irish rebels, for atheists, and care not who they have, so be it they may further their own designs, and deliver themselves from the hand of God that is out against them. They cannot but be sensible that his hand is out against them, yet they vainly look for creature help, and for aid from some arm of flesh. And on the contrary, this is an argument of the faithfulness of others, who though a party low and ready to be trodden down, yet have been so far from seeking help from, or protection of, wicked men, that though fair proffers have been made them, yet have they resolved to venture the loss of all in a good cause; let success attend it or no, whether they attain the liberty they desire or not, yet are they content to venture their estates, their lives, and all in that cause, and not to provide for themselves by the help of such as they see to be evil, and whose ways and designs they see are not conformable to the will of God.

And if to seek to wicked men for help and protection be so sinful, what is it then for men, in times of straits, to seek to the devil for help? Surely that must be much more sinful, to use those ways that are in themselves directly evil, as lying, swearing, cheating, cozening, and the like. For you to think to help yourself by those means in times of difficulty, is as if you should say, I see God does not help me, I will try what the devil will do. Certainly, by iniquity shall no man be established, Prov. xii. 3. Art thou in a strait under any affliction? never think of seeking to help thyself by unlawful means, for they cannot avail thee. And that will appear more evident from the words that follow.

"Yet could he not heal you, nor cure you of your wound." The Assyrian could not help, Jareb could do no good; yea, indeed they were so far from helping Israel and Judah, that they made the wound greater: for Israel was afterwards carried away captive by the Assyrian to whom he sent for help; and as to Judah, we read in 2 Chron. xxviii. 20, that when Ahaz sent for help to Tilgath-pilneser, king of Assyria, he came to him indeed, but he distressed him, and strengthened him not. Whence we may

Obs. 7. Creature comforts avail little in the day of God's wrath. God's wrath was out against Ephraim and Judah, and they would fain seek to the creature for help, but unavailingly. Creatures can afford little aid in the day of God's wrath, they are all as a broken reed, that rather pierces than supports a man's hand. So the Scripture saith of riches, that they also avail not in the day of wrath. All the creatures will say to you, If God help you not, how can we aid you? They are but as a tree in a storm; you may run under it, and perhaps for a time it may afford you some shelter, but if the storm rage on, what protection can the leaves yield? The creature may refresh you a little, but if God's wrath continue, what effectual benefit can you receive?

καὶ οὐ μὴ διαπαύσῃ ἐξ ὑμῶν ὀδύνη.

But the words, "yet could he not heal you," the Seventy translate, he shall not so much as ease, or even in a small degree mitigate, your grief. Sometimes by seeking to creature comforts a man may think he gets some relief, but the truth is, it ends in trouble and sorrow. A man that thus seeks for help to the creature when God has wounded him, is as a stricken deer; the deer runs up and down from one bush to another to seek for ease, but still the blood falls fast. What relief can bushes yield to a poor deer while the arrow remains fast in his body? God often strikes his arrows into the sides of people, and they run up and down to the creature, to this bush and to the other, for help, but little or none can they obtain. Some little, and of brief duration, I confess they may occasionally get, as in the case of Ahaz, when Rezin and Pekah came against him. Ahaz received some present aid from Tilgath-pilneser, king of Assyria; but afterwards (as we shall show you when we come to another point) it did him little good, for God's hand was out against Judah so much the more dreadfully.

Obs. 8. Of all things men rest on for help, wicked men are like to prove most helpless. They leave you in the hour of your need, as the scribes and Pharisees did Judas, when he was brought into straits by his sin, and in the anguish of his spirit came and said, "I have sinned, in that I have betrayed the innocent blood." "What is that to us?" say they, "see thou to that." There was all the comfort he could get from them. They were ready to draw him into the sin, but when he had committed it, then, "What is that to us? see thou to that." Such comfort you are like to have from your wicked companions in times of difficulty; they will draw you into that which is evil, but afterwards, when they come to visit you suffering under the rod of the Almighty for the very sins they have tempted you to commit, what miserable comforters will they prove! So true is it, you can obtain no help from the wicked in the hour of your need.

Obs. 9. The best men are not to be depended on in times of difficulty. God has given us experience at this day, that every man is vanity. So the Scripture saith, Verily every man is vanity. Cease from man, for wherein is he to be esteemed? Had we no other stay but man, what should become of us? Therefore, neither to the Assyrian, no, nor to any living, are we to send for help, otherwise than as instruments in the hand of God. He pronounces a curse upon him "that trusteth in man, and maketh flesh his arm, and whose heart departeth from the Lord;" and saith, "he shall be like the heath in the desert, and shall not see when good cometh; but shall inhabit the parched places in the wilderness, in a salt land and not inhabited," Jer. xvii. 5, 6.

Ver. 14. *For I will be unto Ephraim as a lion, and as a young lion to the house of Judah: I, even I, will tear and go away; I will take away, and none shall rescue him.*

That which is here translated in your books, "a lion," the Seventy render, a panther, which is one of the swiftest and fiercest creatures in the world. God's wrath for strength is compared to a lion, and for swiftness to a panther. To a lion, because though most strong and terrible, yet, as naturalists say, If you fall down and submit he will show mercy. Thus God is a lion, strong and fierce in his wrath, yet merciful to those that submit unto him.

The word שחל here translated "lion," differs from ארי the term generally employed, in that it signifies a fierce lion. And so you have it in Job iv. 10, "The roaring of the lion, and the voice of the fierce lion," שחל so that God threatens here to be a fierce lion. Of this creature, Gesner, in his History of Animals, saith, that nature has so ordered it, that because the lion is so fierce of himself, he has always a kind of a quartan fever, or ague, upon him, to mitigate or calm his fierceness. And it were well with many if it were so with them; many that are fierce and of lion-like spirits in the service of their lusts, and for the gratification of their passions, but sheepish enough in the cause of God.

But mark, God was before a moth and a worm, but now he is become a lion. I will be a moth unto Ephraim, and a worm unto Judah; for so you may translate it. And now, "I will be unto Ephraim as a lion, and as a young lion to the house of Judah." Why a lion? that is, he will appear in the fierceness of his wrath against Ephraim.

But what is the reason of the difference of the expressions here? As he said before, he would be a moth to Ephraim and rottenness to Judah; so here, he will be a lion to Ephraim, and a young lion unto Judah. The reason is the same as before. As there it was designed to show, that though God intended the destruction both of Ephraim and of Judah, yet Ephraim sooner, and Judah later; so here, though God would be terrible in his wrath to Judah, yet he would be more so to the ten tribes: and so we find, that though Judah was carried into captivity, yet that captivity lasted but for seventy years, and Judah returned again; but Israel was torn in pieces so that he never revived. They were both sinners, but Judah retained somewhat of God's true worship, therefore God would show them a little mercy. Though wicked men will the less spare the saints because of their godliness, and will take the more advantage of their frailties because they are professors, yet God will pity them. The observations from hence are these:

Obs. 1. When God's lesser afflictions work not, God will be most terrible. You heard of the moth and worm before; they are the lesser afflictions, and it seems they did not move their hearts to repentance, nor bring them unto God; therefore does God turn to be a fierce lion unto Ephraim, and a young lion unto Judah. God's wrath is as Elijah's cloud, that at first appeared but as a hand-breadth, but within a while overspread the whole heavens. It is as the thunder, which at a distance sounds low and indistinct, but stay a while, and the peals are loud and terrible. It is as the fire, at first struggling for life, but which, when fanned by the wind, bursts forth in irresistible fury. As in that known place, Lev. xxvi. 18, "And if ye will not yet for all this," saith the Lord, "hearken unto me, then I will punish you seven times more for your sins;" and again, ver. 21, "seven times more;" and ver. 24, "yet seven times." God will increase in his wrath, from being as a moth and as a little worm, to be like a lion. Such degrees there are in his anger. You had need look to it when the hand of God is stretched out even but a little against you; though it be but as a moth and as a worm, yet, if you disregard it, it may increase: for as great a difference as exists between a moth and a fierce lion, such a difference may there be between present wrath and that which awaits you. Thus the Lord often deals with men's spirits; causes secretly the worm of conscience to gnaw them, and some disquiet and trouble ensue; but, notwithstanding, they go on still in their sins, and at length God comes upon them as a lion, tearing their souls. Did you never see a sinner lying on his death-bed in anguish of mind, God's wrath, like the paws of a lion, preying on the very caul of his heart, whilst he lies roaring out he is damned, he is damned! and now he sees, yea feels, the heat of the wrath of God against him. Thus God comes as a lion to prey upon those that will not regard the gnawings of the worm: when the worm was but little and small, they slighted it, and that caused God to bring the greater judgment. So it is with families; God comes upon families sometimes in a little sickness, in a child or in a servant, and that is not regarded; afterwards God comes with plague of pestilence, or some other dreadful judgment.

So in kingdoms, the Lord comes first with light judgments, and then with heavier. As in Ireland, for many years together, the Lord was as a moth and rottenness; but of late how like a lion has he there appeared! how has he torn and rent that kingdom in a most dreadful manner!

Yea, the truth is, the Lord had been to England as a moth and rottenness; and this very text I question not but some of you have heard many years ago applied to it, when those that preached from it little thought that ever God's hand should be so stretched out against many parts of England as it is at this day. In many parts of this kingdom the Lord is now as a lion. "The lion hath roared, who will not fear?" Amos iii. 8. Oh it is time for us all to fall down to the ground before the Lord. It is true, God has not yet come to this city as a lion to tear and rend it as other places in the country; but yet we have heard the roaring of the lion abroad, and God calls us to fall down before him that he may not come and tear us likewise. Certainly, the Lord will have glory of his creature; God has sworn by himself, and the word has proceeded out of his mouth in righteousness, that every knee must bow to him, and every tongue confess his name: every creature must submit to him, and if lesser judgments will not do it, God will lay every sinner upon his back, he will come as a lion to tear him in pieces.

But further, mark what is between these two, being a moth and a lion; between these two it is said, "Ephraim saw his sickness, and Judah saw his wound; then went Ephraim to the Assyrian, and sent to king Jareb:" and now saith God, "I will be unto Ephraim as a lion." Hence,

Obs. 2. Our seeking out for ourselves in times of affliction refuges of lies provokes God. The Lord looks upon this with indignation: What! when I appear in my displeasure, do they seek to escape it by sending to the Assyrian and to king Jareb? upon this the indignation of God rises high, and he becomes a fierce lion to them. Josephus reports, that in the factions in Jerusalem, Antiochus being called in by one party proved the ruin of both. This is the honour God expects, that in our affliction we should not fly from, but humble ourselves before him; if we do not, his anger, his jealousy, arises to a fearful height, he will pursue in the fierceness of his wrath. The way is not to fly from God, but to fall down before him, to lie at his feet. No one can abide the slighting of his anger. If a parent or a master be slighted by the child or the servant, it incenses him more: so when men make light of the anger of God, and think that there is power enough in any creature to pacify him, this causes the wrath of God to burn more fiercely against them. You have as notable an example as any in the book of God, in Isa. vii., compared with 2 Kings xvii., where you find that Ahaz in the time of his distress sought to the king of Assyria, though God offered him a sign by the prophet that he himself would deliver him. But mark, on this the Lord threatens that he would bring upon him and upon his people days, the like whereof had not come since the day that Ephraim departed from Judah; such days God would bring upon them, more dreadful than ever yet came upon Judah, and that because when they were in straits they sought for help from the Assyrian. And as in outward dangers, so in spiritual, a man shall seek for help from God. Does God wound thy spirit, does he make it sick, and dost thou seek to unlawful means for help? dost thou go to thy company, to music, to good cheer, to relieve thee? Oh this provokes God against thee! This is just as if a man in a fever should take a draught of cold water: true, for a while he may have a little ease; but the disease returns with greater violence: so those that in trouble of conscience seek for carnal helps, by their vain tampering only render their condition worse.

Antiq. lib. 12. cap. 6, 7.

"I, even I, will tear." The main thing wherein God expresses the dreadfulness of his wrath here in this place, is the tearing of them as a lion. We may take in pieces that which we purpose to mend for future service, but when we tear a thing we intend to use it no more. This expression marks the greatness of God's wrath, as in Psal. l. 22, "Consider this, ye that forget God, lest I tear you in pieces." Now this tearing here refers to the letting in the Assyrian upon Israel, and the Babylonian upon Judah. And the main observation from it, and which is indeed seasonable for these times of ours, is,

Obs. 3. When God in wrath causes war in a kingdom, then God teareth.

I will send the sword amongst you, I will send the Assyrian against you, and then I will tear you. The judgment of war is a tearing judgment. God's wrath never appears more dreadful than in letting out the wrath and rage of provoked enemies upon a people. The teeth and claws of this lion are no other than spears, and swords, and poleaxes; the mouth of this lion is no other than the roaring cannon, from whose mouth proceed fire and smoke, and sudden death. Here you may see stout and strong ones struck down by thousands in a moment; here one man's arm is torn from his shoulders, there another man's leg is rent from his body; here one dying lies wallowing in his own blood, there another weltering in his gore, all mangled and wounded. "Every battle of the warrior is with confused noise, and with garments rolled in blood;" death reigns in the field, and triumphs, which side so ever falls. And as in 1 Sam. iv. 17, when there was a great slaughter among the people, and one told Phinehas's wife that her husband and her brother-in-law were dead, she bowed herself and travailed, for her pains came upon her:" so when news comes home to the poor fatherless children and widows, Your husband is dead, and your father is dead; oh what tearing of hair, wringing of hands, rending of clothes, lifting up the voice and crying, until the noise thereof reaches to heaven! My brethren, war is a tearing judgment, it is *malum complexum*, a compound sorrow. The cup that is now in the hand of the Lord "is full of mixture," Psal. lxxv. 8; full of bloody ingredients, of fire, famine, pestilences, murders, rapes, cruelties, and all miseries; the Lord tears now indeed. Oh how is the husband rent from his wife, and haled to prison by cruel and bloody soldiers! How are men's estates and possessions torn from them in tumultuous outrages! their pleadings and cries rejected with scorn and contempt, and the bodies of their wives and children, and their own too, abused in the rage and malice of the insulting adversary! And of all wars, civil wars are the most dreadful; there God tears indeed; there the brother contends with the brother, and the father bathes his hand in the blood of his own son. Thus the Lord has been a lion in many parts of this kingdom. Alas, our brethren abroad cannot say as they in Jer. iv. 5, "Assemble yourselves, and let us go into the defenced cities;" they stand afar off, and are afraid to come out of the land of their captivity, because of the oppressing sword. Yea, and in this heavy judgment that is upon us, never was God's name so torn as it is now by bloody oaths and hideous and unheard-of blasphemies. And what more do our adversaries desire, but to tear the saints and to trample them under their feet?

My brethren, time it is for us all to rend our hearts, even to tear and rend our very hearts within us, because the Lord is come out against us as a tearing lion, devouring on every side. The Jews were wont when they heard the name of God blasphemed to rend their garments. We hear of the dreadful blasphemies of our adversaries, their rending and tearing of the name of God; oh how should we rend our hearts rather than our garments, and mourn with more than ordinary sorrow at this desecration of the name of the Most High! And the rather because we have escaped for the present, and our estates and bodies are yet uninjured. Our sins have passed into the cups of our brethren, have increased their miseries, and have been those claws and teeth that have torn them. Thus the Lord is raised from a moth and worm even to a tearing lion.

Obs. 4. God has a righteous hand in the worst actions of men. Though the Assyrians and Babylonians did this, yet, saith God, I will be as a lion to tear them. We cry out that men are so vile and wicked, but you must look up to God who directs all. The most horrid wickedness ever committed, the betraying of Christ, and the crucifying of the Lord of life, the Scripture saith, was done by the fore-determined counsel of God, Acts ii. Therefore let those that have had their estates, their husbands, and their children torn from them by wicked men, let them know that the Lord has had a hand in it. Though men be wicked, yet the Lord is righteous; let them justify God in all. This is God's glory, that he can have a hand in the most hideous wickedness in the world, and yet remain righteous notwithstanding: therefore he saith here, "I, even I, will tear." He not only owns it, but would have people to take special notice that he directs all. Oh the use that we might make of this to ourselves, if in all those dreadful judgments that are upon us, and the yet heavier ones that have befallen some of our brethren, we could but believe that the hand of God has done it! I, even I, have done it: and in this one verse, I is repeated four times: let the thing be never so hideous to you, yet know that I am the great orderer and disposer of all, and I have some great thing to bring to pass by all this that is come upon you. And certainly, though the misery be great that some parts of the kingdom endure, yet because God's hand is so much in it, therefore we must know that he has some great thing to bring to pass by these his dispensations toward us.

Obs. 5. God has a righteous hand in the worst actions. What the wicked Assyrians and cursed Babylonians did, that God is said here to do; and in the sin of Judas, the most horrible that ever was, God not only permitted, but ordered all, Acts ii. 23. This is God's glory, and yet to be free from the evil of sin. Many knots there are about this, that men exercise their wits to untie; but *Cum veniet Elias*, (as the Hebrews use to say when gravelled, When Elias cometh we shall understand,) there is a time when all difficulties shall be easily reconciled. You whose estates have been torn from you, and it may be many of your dearest friends, consider that it is God that is the lion tearing.

Obs. 6. The hand of God is more immediate in some judgments than in others; "I, even I;" and the more immediate the more remarkable: There shall not only come judgments upon you, but I will bring them, they shall be such that you shall see that I am in them. In some judgments, God makes so much use of the creature, that sinners can see little of his hand in them; but in some others, they can easily discern it. Belshazzar trembled at the hand-writing, and his thoughts were troubled within him; why so? the hand struck him not at all, but he saw it to be the hand of God, the hand of the Deity was in it, Dan. v. 5, 6, and this made him to tremble. Gen. vi. 17, "Behold, I, even I, do bring a flood." And that wrath which is out against us at this time, is the hand of God in a special manner; God may well say to us, "I, even I, will tear" ye, O England. Oh how has God manifested himself to us in these latter years since the wars began! As we ought to take notice of God's judgments on kingdoms, so also on families and particular persons: as a godly heart is observant of God's hand in mercies, and as coming from him they are most sweet; so, on the contrary, he takes notice of God's hand in every judgment to be humbled under it: "I will establish my covenant with you," Gen. ix. 11; and Isa. xliii. 19, 25, "I, even I, am he which blotteth out thine iniquities." As mercies are then most sweet when we see them come from God's immediate hand in the way of special providence, so God's hand remarkable in judgments must be regarded. For,

1. Hereby the heart becomes humbled, when it considers that it is God which appears against him: Not devils, nor men, but God, that God in whom I live, and

from whom I receive every blessing that I enjoy. This it was that troubled Christ, more than all the wrong which the scribes and Pharisees did to him, when he considered that it was his God; "My God, my God, why hast thou forsaken me?" When the saints see God's hand against them in any thing, this troubles them and humbles them more than any thing else.

2. It is a special means to render the heart patient. Psal. xxxix. 9, "I was dumb, I opened not my mouth; because thou, Lord, didst it." See it in Eli, "It is the Lord, let him do what seemeth him good:" and in Christ himself, Shall not I drink of the cup which my Father shall give me? Is God my God, and doth this come from my Father? I will take it, I am sure it will do me no harm, but much good.

3. By this means the soul is put upon the inquiry, why this affliction has come, what may be the cause of this trouble. When we see nothing but man the instrument used in an affliction, we regard it not so much, it never leads us to soul-search and trial of ourselves; but when God is seen in a cross, the soul begins to consider, What have I done? what aileth thee, O my soul? Thus did the church, Micah vi. 9, "Hear ye the rod, and who hath appointed it." There are letters written upon God's rods, which the man of wisdom can read.

4. It causes the soul to receive content and satisfaction in nothing but God alone, and in peace with him. When we look upon judgments only in the second cause, we are apt to think that second means will make up the breach again, which sin has made; as they in Isa. ix. 10, 12, "The bricks are fallen down, but we will build with hewn stone:" "for all this his anger is not turned away:" why so? In the 13th verse we have the reason; "For the people turneth not unto him that smiteth them, neither do they seek the Lord of hosts:" they would not see the hand of God, nor give glory to him, for if they did, they would say as this people, in the next chapter, "Come, and let us return unto the Lord: for he hath torn, and he will heal us; he hath smitten, and he will bind us up." Thus much for the doubling the expression.

Obs. 7. When God intends ruin and desolation to a people, it is impossible for any to deliver them out of his hands. "I, even I, will tear and go away." When lions tear their prey, they are not afraid of what they have done, but walk majestically before the dead carcass, as it were bidding defiance to all other creatures; they run not away as the fox, but walk as it were in state, for so the words in the original imply: "I, even I will tear." As if God challenged all the creatures in heaven or earth to grapple with him, "I, even I, will tear." It implies how God will deal with Judah, he will not be afraid of them, he will not come against them in secret, but publicly.

אַף

The judgment at this time upon our enemies is not a secret, but an open one, the Lord deals not subtlely and by craft with them, as they do with his people; but though the Lord deal as a lion, tearing and rending them, yet they will not see him, neither are they able to resist him, nor can any rescue themselves out of his hands: let the means in God's hands be never so weak, yet when he is in a way of wrath there shall be no delivery from him. Isa. xxvi. 6, "The foot shall tread it down:" tread down what? "the lofty city:" what feet? "even the feet of the poor, and the steps of the needy." In Jer. xxxvii. 10, the Lord tells them, that though they "had smitten the whole army of the Chaldeans, and there remained but wounded men among them, yet should they rise up every man in his tent, and burn their city with fire."

Obs. 8. When God comes against a people, he defies the strongest, and greatest in power, and most confident in an arm of flesh, to deliver themselves out of his hands. Isa. xxiv. 21, "And it shall come to pass in that day, that the Lord shall punish the host of the high ones that are on high," in their greatest pride, in the midst of their greatest victories and conquests. And it is very observable, that since our enemies gained their greatest advantages they have lost the most; God then pulled them down when they were most proud, and God will go on in his work though men are never so proud and strong: therefore it is our wisdom to resign ourselves into his hands, yea, though they be hands of chastisement; for although no power can rescue out of his hand, yet by humbling ourselves, falling down before him, willingly submitting to him, we may change the operations of his will. God had rather that men voluntarily gave him his glory than compelled him to extort it from them.

Ver. 15. *I will go and return to my place, till they acknowledge their offence, and seek my face: in their affliction they will seek me early.*

"I will go." God repeats it again, which notes, 1. The glory of the work, that he is not ashamed of what he has done: and God's people ought to resemble God in this; let their actions be warrantable, such as they may with comfort own and stand to, yea, suffer for, if requisite. 2. The irresistibility of God's work, as if he should say, Let any try whether they can oppose me. 3. And chiefly it implies, I will bring them into captivity, and there I will leave them. Whence,

Obs. 1. It is a heavy judgment for God to tear and wound, and then to leave a people. God saith, If they return not, I will rend and tear them, make them very miserable, and in that condition will I leave them, I will be a stranger to them, and will not own them. Ezek. xxii. 20, "As they gather silver, and brass, and iron, and lead, and tin, into the midst of the furnace, to blow the fire upon it, to melt it; so will I gather you in mine anger and in my fury, and I will leave you there, and melt you." God in another place promises to be with his people in the fire and in the water; but there is a time that God's people may so provoke him, that he will bring them into the fire and there leave them. When the Philistines fell upon Saul, it was a sad time for him, because God had left him. Oh how terrible was it when God left Christ upon the cross but for a little while! This we all deserve, and this is the portion of the damned in hell. While the judge is present upon the bench the malefactor has hope, but when he departs, hope departs. Therefore the church prays, "Lord, leave us not:" "Thou art my hope in the day of evil," Jer. xiv. 9; xvii. 17. God is said to be the "strength" of his people, in Psal. xxxvii. 39. Now, if their strength be gone, they must needs be weak. Christ rebukes his disciples for fearing when he was in the ship with them: but when God leaves a people, oh what cause of fear is there then! The church implies as much, Jer. xiv. 9, "Thou art in the midst of us; leave us not;" we are in a sad condition already, yet, O Lord, do not thou leave us.

Now, if we would not have God leave us, let us take heed we do not leave God. Would you have God for you in adversity, then be you for God in prosperity, nor forsake him when he is afflicted, that is, when his people and cause suffer. Many will be for the saints and own the cause of God when all things go well, and their side prospers; but in trouble they forsake them, as if they knew them not. Know that in thus doing thou leavest God, and God may justly leave thee in thy affliction. But now, it is God's promise to his people, that he will not leave them, Psal. xxxi. 7, 8; xxxiv. 17, 18. God may bring thee into the power and jurisdiction of the evil, but wait thou on the Lord and he shall deliver thee. We are wont to say when we are in any trouble, to our dear friends, What! will you also leave me? will you not now own me, and stand by me? As Christ himself said to his disciples, "Will ye also go away?" God will never leave his people in this manner. The shepherd may allow his dog to hunt the sheep and to bark at them, in order to bring them together, but never suffers him to worry and kill them: so God may permit the wicked to hunt the saints, and perhaps sometimes to fasten upon them, but then God will call them off again, for his promise is, as in Heb. xiii. 5, "I will never leave thee nor forsake thee;" in which words we have in the Greek five negatives to affirm the truth of this conclusion, that God will never forsake his people. I will not, not leave you. Yea, but the people of God might say, But, Lord, we seem to the eye of the world to be forsaken. No, saith the Lord, I will not, not, not forsake you. There are two negatives to leaving, and three to forsaking; from whence we may see how strongly God has engaged himself for his people's security.

οὐ μή σε ἀνῶ, οὐδ᾽ οὐ μή σε ἐγκαταλίπω.

"And return to my place." These words are something difficult. What is God's place? Is God contained in any place? God is rather the place of the world, than the world his place. "I will return to my place;" that is, I will go to heaven again: not that God is there only contained, but that is the place from which he reveals himself most, there his holiness shines forth most gloriously. There is but little manifestation of God in this world, compared with what there is in heaven; the glory of all the world is but as a dungeon to that place of God's special presence; and we are like children born in a dungeon, who think there is no better place because they never saw better; but heaven is our Father's place, and Christ, who is our elder Brother, is gone thither before us, to provide mansions for us; let us therefore have conversations in heaven answerable to the holiness of that place. This world is like the out-housing, stables, or kennels, belonging to some palace or stately building; and even as these are very inferior to the rooms in the house, so is the pomp and state of this world to heaven. God has given the world to worldly men for their portion, but the saints have a better inheritance reserved for them, even in heaven.

Deus est habitaculum mundi, non mundus habitaculum ejus.

"And return to my place." When was God from his place? when did he come from thence? Thus: when he did rend and tear them, appearing against them as a lion, and as a young lion; then it was as if God should come down to rectify and set in order things which were amiss, as we may see in the case of Sodom, Gen. xviii. 21, "I will go down now, and see whether they have done altogether according to the cry of it which is come unto me:" the sin of Sodom brought God from his throne. So in Isa. xxvi. 21, "Behold, the Lord cometh out of his place to punish the inhabitants of the earth for their iniquity: the earth also shall disclose her blood, and shall no more cover her slain." God compares himself to a prince on his throne, who goes from his place of state into countries to quiet mutinies and rebellions among his people. Hence,

Obs. 2. Sin disturbs heaven and earth. God cannot be quiet in heaven for sinners; just then is it for God to trouble sinners on earth.

Obs. 3. In times of public judgment God leaves his majesty in heaven, to set things in order on earth. And surely it will be to their cost when God thus comes; do but view the terribleness of his approach, in Psal. xviii. 9, 12, "He bowed the heavens also, and came down: and darkness was under his feet. At the brightness that was before him his thick clouds passed, hail stones and coals of fire" were under his feet. God seems to speak as a father to his children; What! must I come to you, will you force me to come among you? if I do, it shall be to your cost.

Obs. 4. God's administrations to his people may sometimes be such as if he regarded them not. "I will return to my place." When I have afflicted them I will go to heaven, and there will I sit, and my administrations shall be such towards them as if I regarded them not; as a prince that goes from the tribunal to his seat of dignity, and regards not the poor prisoner. God's people may be so left in the hands of the wicked, that they may think God has forsaken them, and given them over into their power, and conclude that God is gone and has now hid himself for ever. As a poor child in misery in one country, and his father in another, thinks thus, I am in trouble and sorrow, and I have a father, but he is in another country, and I know not when he will return; so God may return to his place, and the soul may seek him, but he be gone. Yet the saints should be encouraged, notwithstanding, to look up to God, and know, though God be gone, yet there is a way to bring him down again. In Psal. xviii. 6, God was in his heavenly temple, and his people cried to him in their distress; then the Lord "bowed the heavens, and came down." Let me make haste, saith God, I must go to the help of my people; therefore, that I may make speed, let the heavens bow before me. So in Isa. lxiv. 1, 2, the church cries out, "Oh that thou wouldest rend the heavens, that thou wouldest come down!" True, Lord, thou art in heaven, and there dwell thy majesty and glory; but oh that thou wouldest come down and help us! Prayer, as it will rend the heavens to get up to God, so it will rend the heavens for God to come down to man. Lord, if thou wilt go to thy place, then what will become of thy glory? In the world thou hadst service and honour done to thee by the creature, thy saints offered sacrifice to thee; though sometimes thou, God, didst seem to answer, I care not for this, I can and will have honour to myself in some other way.

Revertar ad habitaculum sanctitatis meæ. Chald. Paraphrase.

Obs. 5. When the wicked are in perplexity, then God enjoys himself in his perfection, Ezek. x. 4. When they are in wrath and sorrow, and God receives not that external service from them which he has had, "I will return to my place," saith he, and enjoy myself in my glory. And this aggravates the misery of the damned in hell: We are here in eternal torments and horror, but what does God lose by this? he is reposing in blessed beatitude in the midst of his own perfections.

Obs. 6. God sometimes turns his back upon sinners, until they acknowledge their sin: "Till they acknowledge their offence." This is the best way for God to deal with some kind of men; let them but feel a little of the smart of trouble, and then they will consider. Many who are wilful will do so and so, their wills shall be their law; now the best way to tame such is to let them see and feel the evil of their ways. So saith God, My prophets and my messengers can do them no good, therefore let them alone: 1 Kings viii. 47, "If they shall bethink themselves and repent."

Obs. 7. God humbles himself to behold what is done upon earth. It is a kind of self-denial in God to regard man at all. As it is a mighty condescension in a prince to come from his throne to visit and comfort poor men in dungeons and prisons: surely such prisoners have occasion to honour such a prince, for he comes from his throne to visit them; how much more then have we need to honour God for his love towards us!

But to examine more closely the words in the original; they are, till they become guilty in their own hearts, and acknowledge themselves to be so. יאשמו signifies to offend, to be guilty, to be desolate, and to sacrifice for sin; all these significations the root אשם will bear.

Until they become guilty. Were they not guilty

before? Would God have them more guilty? No; but God would have them convinced of their sin, accuse themselves for it, justify him in all, and lastly, with sorrow and shame, acknowledge themselves to be sinners before God and men. It is true, as soon as ever the sin is committed, the sinning person incurs guilt; but then he is especially said to be guilty, when his own acknowledgment confirms the sentence of the law.

But when was this disposition wrought in them? has it ever yet been? or is it still to be fulfilled and accomplished?

I answer, that it was in part made good at their coming out of captivity: hence Daniel, chap. ix. 5, in the name of the whole church, speaks after this manner, "We have sinned, and done wickedly, and have rebelled, even by departing from thy precepts," &c. How many terms are used to express their departure from God! Also in Ezra ix. 13, 15, and in Neh. ix. 16: all these three lived after Hosea, though in our Bibles placed before him. This text is fulfilled again in Jer. xxxi. 18; Ephraim was then guilty when he was found bemoaning himself. Again, it was fulfilled when Christ was preached, Acts ii. 37, "When they heard this, they were pricked in their heart." And certain it is, this prophecy had reference to Christ. But this scripture shall principally be fulfilled at the calling of the Jews, then they shall become guilty: Zech. xii. 10, "They shall look upon me whom they have pierced, and they shall mourn for him."

Obs. 8. So long as men prosper in their sins, they will contest even with God himself. Mal. iii. 7, "But ye said, Wherein shall we return?" Is not this the speech of many proud spirits? being taxed about any crime, they presently answer, Wherein have we offended? This is remarkable in Saul, 1 Sam. xv. 13, when he told the prophet he had performed the commandment of the Lord. Samuel labours to convince him of his sin, saying, "What meaneth then the bleating of the sheep in mine ears, and the lowing of the oxen which I hear?" yet, after continued expostulations, in the 20th verse Saul replies, "Yea, I have obeyed the voice of the Lord." It was otherwise with David when the prophet came to him; "I have sinned against the Lord," was the ready answer, 2 Sam. xii. 13. It is a good sign of a soul truly humbled, when it joins issue at once with the word.

Obs. 9. Affliction sanctified brings men to see and acknowledge their sins. God in afflictions marks men out, and then conscience will prey upon them, as Simeon and Levi fell on the men of Shechem, for then they are sore and unable to resist. In time of affliction thou shalt find conscience hard enough for thee: what pangs have men in their sickness! saying, as he in Prov. v. 12, "How have I hated instruction, and my heart despised reproof!" Oh what a deal of guilt is opened and discovered in affliction! Afflictions are to the soul as earthquakes to the ground, which opens the graves and discovers abundance of filth.

Obs. 10. It is a sign of a hard heart not to confess when God's hand is upon us. Even Pharaoh did this: and it is that which God requires: Joshua bids Achan, "My son, give, I pray thee, glory to the Lord God of Israel, and make confession unto him." Confession gives glory to God, and when thou standest out in this thing, thou opposest God in his glory. Latimer reports of a man in his time, who was to be executed at Oxford for some villany, that many means were used to induce him to confess the act, but none could prevail: being cut down, after hanging the appointed time, they perceived he was not quite dead, and by the use of means brought him to himself, when he confessed all circumstances. This example may show us thus much, not always to conclude men are not guilty when they confess nothing; there is that stoutness in the hearts of men, that they will rather venture damnation than yield to men.

Obs. 11. God will have glory from us. If we do not acknowledge our guilt by lesser judgments, he will continue, yea, even increase them, till we confess and give glory to him. Our unwillingness to do this, is often the reason that we are so long under trouble: sin in the conscience lies as purulent matter in a sore, requiring to be let out before ease can be obtained. God calls for confession, and no true peace otherwise can be enjoyed; O therefore, sinner, confess and give glory to God. How many are there who have lain a long time under anguish of spirit, till they have freely and fully confessed the sins which lay heavy and burdensome on their conscience! Neglect not this duty when you are called to it, it is an ordinance appointed by God for the easing of troubled souls; and when you cannot get peace any other way, having used other means, and yet God withholds the light of his countenance, then are you called to confess to others. See what course David took, and how he sped, Psal. xxxix. 2—4, "I was dumb with silence, I held my peace, even from good;" I roared and was vexed, but I said, I would confess my sin, and shame myself for them, and then thou forgavest the sin of thy servant. Mark here, there was some sin which lay upon David's conscience, and he could not get peace in again; what course takes he? I (said he) did but say, I would confess; and then thou forgavest my sin, thou didst then seal a pardon to me. O take this course, and thou shalt have the like success. God comes to thee in a sickness, and saith, Sinner, guilty, or not guilty? give God then the glory of a humble confession. It is true, to confess offences against men to men, there may be danger in it, making us liable to trouble; but confession of offences against God never causes trouble.

"And seek my face;" that is, my favour, my Son, and my ordinances, for, in general, God's face is nothing else but God's manifestation of himself in his love, in his Son, or in his ordinances; and it is a most blessed thing thus to behold God's face, Rev. xxii. 4: this is what David so earnestly prayed for, "Lord, lift up the light of thy countenance upon me:" one sight of God is better than all the world. To see God any way is sweet, but to see him in Christ is surpassing excellent: in the world, we have nothing of God but his mere footsteps, but in Christ is the great manifestation of the wisdom, mercy, and love of God to poor, lost man. And in the ordinances, too, God communicates himself in an especial manner. In these three things are shown to us the meaning of those words, "and seek my face." The observations from them are these:

Obs. 12. It is not enough to acknowledge our sins, but we must seek God's face. The heart, in the work of humiliation, must be active: the soul which is truly humbled before God, must be lively and active after God, else our humiliation is worth nothing in his sight. When the heart is sullen and desponding in its humiliation, God looks not at it. Thus in Ezek. xxxiii. 10, we read of some who are said to "pine away" in their sin. Many, when God begins to afflict them with their sins, and to excite some trouble in their minds, pine away in their iniquity, are deterred from duty, and lie down under their trouble discontented and melancholy; and this is a very bad sign: therefore here is the test whether our trouble of conscience be genuine or not; if it arises from melancholy, it dulls the heart, banishes all spirit and activity, and renders it wholly unfit for service; but if true, it enlivens the soul, animates the mind, though naturally dull and inactive, and makes the whole man energetically zealous, it puts the soul in ways of activity for God, when in the service of God. The melting of lead consumes the lead, but the melting of silver refines and purifies it: so the trouble of a carnal heart melts and consumes it, but a gracious spirit will abide the fire, and come out purer and better; therefore repentance is expressed by a word implying activity, Isa. lv. 1, "Come ye, buy, and eat; yea, come, buy wine and milk." Matt. xi. 28, "Come unto me." A true penitent heart is in an active, coming posture, fitted for any service.

Obs. 13. When God leaves his people, he leaves something behind him, which causes the heart to seek after him; the soul has her eyes upon God, looking after him. Therefore, much are they to be reproved, who are so full of their sad conclusions and desperate forebodings, I am undone and lost for ever, there is no hope, to hell I must go: but a gracious heart, in the darkest night of sorrow and trouble can see some glimpses of light and comfort, saying as that good man, Ezra x. 2, "Yet there is hope in Israel concerning this thing;" and as the church in Isa. xlii. 24, "Who gave Jacob for a spoil, and Israel to the robbers? did not the Lord, he against whom we have sinned?" What follows? "Thus saith the Lord that created thee, O Jacob, and he that formed thee, O Israel, Fear not," Isa. xliii. 1.

Let us lay up this to support our spirits with in sad times; we know not what days await us, yet surely we cannot be in a sadder condition than Ephraim was in here, to have God to be to us as a moth and as a lion to tear and devour us. Many make their conditions worse by their desperate conclusions. Austin observes, that David prayed earnestly that he might not be cast out from that face which he had offended. Is God angry with us or the kingdom? let us not run away from him, but earnestly seek him.

Obs. 14. True repentance is not so much to seek our own ease, as God's face. The face of God is more in the heart and thoughts of a true penitent, than its own ease: 2 Chron. vii. 14, "If my people, which are called by my name, shall humble themselves, and pray, and seek my face, and turn from their wicked ways; then will I hear from heaven, and will forgive their sin, and will heal their land." We may seek our own good, but we must go beyond it; it is God, and not ourselves only, which we must seek after in our seekings after God. This has been the practice of the saints: Psal. lxiii. 1, "O God, thou art my God; early will I seek thee: my soul thirsteth for thee, my flesh longeth for thee in a dry and thirsty land, where no water is;" not for water "in a dry and thirsty land," but for thy face. So Isa. xxvi. 8, "Yea, in the way of thy judgments, O Lord, have we waited for thee; the desire of our soul is to thy name, and to the remembrance of thee." We seek God in our days of humiliation, and that earnestly; but what are our ends? Is it that we may have our peace, our ease, our estates, and our lives? We may indeed desire and seek for these, but do we seek the face of God more even than these? if so, we may hope that our requests will be granted.

But what is God's face? *Ut amplecterentur verbum et cultus in verbo propositos, hoc proprie est facies Dei, quo se revelat, et nobis conspiciendum offert:* It is the word, and God's worship propounded in the word, &c., saith Calvin, as upon this place, so on that, "Seek ye my face." Whence,

Obs. 15. God's ordinances and worship are his face. The soul never knows God or has close communion with him, as in these; in other things darkly, in these with open face. The creatures are but his footsteps; these his countenance, whereby we know him better than by the other.

Obs. 16. Repenting hearts are solicitous about God's ordinances. As soon as they begin to know God and themselves, they begin to disrelish those ways of worship which satisfied them before.

Obs. 17. The worship of God, his name, and his

ordinances, should be the objects of our great concern in times of public calamity. Though our sufferings are great, yet we should pray, Lord, take care of thy great name, ordinances, and worship, which are dearer to us than any thing in the world; therefore, O Lord, whether we have peace and liberty or not, our estates or not, take care of these and it suffices; let England enjoy but thy name, thine ordinances, and the government of thy Son, and we have enough. Lord, thou knowest our peace, our lives, and estates are dear to us, and we desire them all; but thy gospel, thy presence, and the manifestation of thy face are dearer than they all, and other things are sought by us in subservience to these. Oh that this frame of spirit were found in us! then how soon would the Lord return and heal all our breaches, and destroy our enemies, and settle us in a sure peace! 1 Kings viii. 44—53.

"In their affliction they will seek me early." Hezekiah sends to the prophet, Isa. xxxvii. 3, and tells him that it was "a day of trouble, and of rebuke, and of blasphemy," as it is with us at this day; "wherefore," saith he, "lift up thy prayer for the remnant that is left:" and saith my text, "In their afflictions they will seek me early." Now when men's minds are dejected and cast down with every rumour of fear, Providence seems to have presented them here a very seasonable subject of meditation, especially if you connect these words with the beginning of the following chapter, as is done by the Septuagint and Jerome, who read them thus: "In their affliction they will seek me early: come, and let us return unto the Lord: for he hath torn, and he will heal us; he hath smitten, and he will bind us up." The first words are a prophecy of what the Lord will work in his people Judah, "In their affliction they will seek me early," and then follows the ready response of the church, "Come, and let us return unto the Lord:" this was God's design in tearing them. And now from the connexion of these two, God's wounding, and their returning unto him again,

Obs. 18. That which God aims at in his administrations to his elect he will accomplish. In my tearing them I aim at their good, and I will effect it. God useth many means, his word, his works, and his encouragements, and all these are of very great force and power to accomplish his gracious purposes; and though in the ungodly they do not, yet in the elect they are efficacious; God leaves not them to the means, but he will see that the means effect that good which they require. When God sends the gospel to any place, it meets with two sorts of people, reprobates and elect; now God does to them all that is fit for him to do, and if they do not or will not receive it, he goes his way and leaves the reprobates to themselves, but the elect he follows after with the means, and accomplisheth the good he aims at. Some express it thus, A man has his servant and his child sick of the stone; he provides a remedy for both; brings the surgeon to his servant, tells him that he is willing to be at the cost, but the servant refuseth, choosing rather to suffer the misery and pain than undergo the operation: the master seeing this goes away, and comes to his child, who refuses likewise; but from him the father goes not away, but commands his child to be bound, and will see the surgeon perform his office. So God offers the means to all; the reprobates refuse it, God lets them alone; the saints refuse it also, but God will not permit this, but sets the means home upon them by his almighty power.

But touching the words themselves, "They will seek me early," the Hebrew has but one word ישחרנני to express all these by, as if he should say, They shall morning me, they shall come in the morning of their time and seek me. For the further opening these words,

שחר The morning before light, or the dawn. In Kal it is, denigrare, nigrum esse: in Pihel, mane quærere. Sept. ὀρθριοῦσι.

What time does this seeking of God refer to? when did the Jews thus seek God? It refers to these three periods:

1. When the seventy years were at an end. And this was fulfilled in Dan. ix., Ezra ix., and Neh. ix.; then they sought God early, when their sorrows and oppressions were greater than in Egypt, as Jeremiah in the Lamentations expresses it.

2. Under their captivity and oppression by the Romans. When Christ came into the world, three thousand were converted at one sermon which Peter preached to them, Acts ii., and multitudes came in daily, Acts xxi. 20.

3. At the calling of the Jews, who are now in a most sad and deplorable condition; then shall this be principally fulfilled.

How did they seek God in any of these times early? for in Daniel's time, he saith, "All this evil is come upon us; yet made we not our prayer before the Lord our God, that we might turn from our iniquities, and understand thy truth," chap. ix. 13: they never prayed to God in all the time of their captivity with any seriousness till the end of it came. Then for the second time, how did they seek God early at Christ's coming, when the Scripture tells us, John i. 11, that "He came unto his own, and his own received him not?" they crucified him, and were very bitter enemies to him, even to the death. And for the third time, the calling of the Jews, how did they seek him early? for it is two thousand three hundred years since this prophecy was spoken, and yet they have not sought God; how then is this fulfilled, that they sought God early? To this interpreters answer,

1. This is to be understood not in respect of the time, but as soon as they came to be illuminated, to have their eyes open, to see any thing of the truth, in the morning of their day of grace; as in Cyrus's time, and suddenly at Peter's sermon, and hereafter, when the coming of the Son of man shall be as the lightning: this time seems to be called the day-star arising in their hearts, 2 Pet. i. 19. The calling of the Jews shall be suddenly, therefore, in Rev. ii. 28, they are promised "the morning-star," that is, some beginnings of a day of grace; those which overcome shall partake of the good of that day, and then shall be the time in which the people shall seek God early.

2. "Seek me early," may mean, seek me diligently; as Prov. vii. 15, "Therefore came I forth to meet thee, diligently to seek thy face, and I have found thee." I came forth to seek thee early in the morning; the word is the same with this in the text. And thus this was fulfilled in the time of their captivity; Neh. iv. 17—20, they built the walls diligently, or earnestly, having their weapons in one hand, and their tools in the other. So the spouse sought Christ diligently; and in the apostles' time, Acts ii. 37, they cry out, "Men and brethren, what shall we do?" And when the Jews are called, it is prophesied of them, that they shall be as doves flying to the windows, Isa. lx. 8. Hence,

Obs. 19. In the sorest and greatest afflictions which befall the people of God, God intends their good. I will return unto my place, that they may seek me early: in all this that is come upon them, I intend them no hurt, but every way much good. Isa. xxvii. 9, "By this therefore shall the iniquity of Jacob be purged; and this is all the fruit to take away his sin." The 14th verse of Isa. xxvi., compared with the 19th verse of the same, shows God's different dealing in afflicting the wicked and the godly. In the 14th verse we have God's dealing with the wicked, "They are dead, they shall not live; they are deceased, they shall not rise;" the wicked are dead, and being dead, shall never rise: but in the 19th verse, when he speaks of the saints, he saith, "Thy dead men shall live, together with my dead body shall they arise." The Scriptures make a marked distinction between the anger of God and the anger of men: men in their anger seek the destruction sometimes of those against whom they are incensed; but God loves in his anger; the spring of his anger to his people is love. The outward administrations of God both to the wicked and the godly may be one and the same, yet the root from whence they come very different, they may be love and kindness to the one, but wrath and hatred to the other.

Obs. 20. God has little honour in this world. God here speaks of his own people, they seek him, but it is but seldom, except when in afflictions; and if the service they perform be small, what has he from other men? If men make use of you for their necessities and in their extremities only, you take it unkindly, and think they serve themselves more than respect you. Oh how ill may God take it then from us, when he seldom or never hears from us but in our extremities!

Obs. 21. Times of afflictions are times for seeking God. This is the apostle's advice, "Is any among you afflicted? let him pray," James v. 13. And Isa. xxvi. 16, "Lord, in trouble have they visited thee, they poured out a prayer when thy chastening was upon them:" "they poured out a prayer," to thee, not by drops now and then, but a strong, unbroken stream; "a prayer," in the singular number, denoting that they made their prayers but as one continued act: the word לחש rendered there "prayer" signifies incantation, as in words used for such a purpose there is supposed to be much efficacy; so here, their prayers were very powerful to prevail with God. The voice of prayer is well-pleasing to God when fervent.

In the time of affliction the soul sees that it has to deal with God; the false medium, the delusive glosses wherewith sin was wont to be disguised, are then removed, they see sin as sin. Luther saith, that many of Paul's Epistles could not be understood but by the cross. Men in prosperity can dispute against the truth, and grow wanton with it; but let God but lay his hand upon them, how easily will they yield! Afflictions awaken the conscience, so that the truths of God come with more power: "He openeth also their ear to discipline, and commandeth that they return from iniquity," Job xxxiii. 16; xxxvi. 10. Did not God command them before? Yes, but not with the same power and efficacy.

Obs. 22. When the Lord is pleased to work grace in the heart, that heart is taken off from all creature helps. They dare not go with Ephraim to king Jareb; they dare not go to councils or to armies for relief, but to God; how are they then to be blamed who seek to the devil for help in distress! To rest on men is evil, much more upon the devil. Do any of you go to enchanters or wizards to find God? you may seek him, but shall not find him.

Obs. 23. We are not to be discouraged in seeking God, though afflictions drive us to it. This people sought God, but their afflictions constrained them to do so, yet God accepted them.

Sit not down despairing in your afflictions, saying, God will never be gracious, our seeking him is to no purpose. It is true, as Jephthah said to the people, "Do you now come to me in your distress?" so God may justly say, Do you now come to me in your sorrows and miseries, when you cast me off in your prosperity? I confess it is very dangerous to put off seeking God till then, but if then God be pleased to work upon your hearts, be not discouraged, but seek him still. So Joel saith, that in his affliction he sought the Lord: but did the Lord answer him? Yea, his requests were granted.

Obs. 24. An acceptable seeking of God must be an early seeking. Now, men are said to seek God early,

1. In the morning of their years. When the young

make this text true in the letter of it, it is well-pleasing to God. It may be God laid his hand on thee in thy youth, and then revealed the knowledge of himself to thee, thy misery by sin, thy remedy in his Son, so that the church's prayer was thine, Psal. xc. 14, "O satisfy us early with thy mercy." How many sins are by this prevented! Your father or master, if godly, would give a world (if they had it) that they had begun sooner to serve the Lord, and to seek him early; therefore bless God who has put it into your hearts to seek him. John was the young disciple, and he in his youth began to know Christ; and of all the disciples none had such respect showed them as John, for it is said that he lay in Christ's bosom, and Christ loved him.

2. In the morning of God's revealing himself. As soon as ever God begins to discover himself, we should then seek him early; the soul should say, as Paul, "I was not disobedient unto the heavenly vision;" "neither conferred I with flesh and blood," Acts xxvi. 19; Gal. i. 16. Has God set up a light in your consciences? and has it discovered to you your misery? and have you hearkened to its voice? What have you done since? Is sin reformed? Are you changed in the inner man? Is Christ formed in you, and exalted upon his throne in your hearts? Is your will subjected to the will of God, and your whole man delivered up to the government of God? Blessed of the Lord art thou if it be so. But contrariwise, is sin let in, and liked as well as ever, after these stirrings and convictions of conscience? Then are you far from the number of those who are early seekers of God.

3. When we seek him with fervency and diligence. When God's hand is out against us, he then looks that we should seek him with intentiveness of spirit. See how the church seeks God, Isa. xxvi. 9, "With my soul have I desired thee in the night; yea, with my spirit within me will I seek thee early." When was this? In a grievous night of affliction, when they were in great troubles; then to seek God early, with their spirits within them, is most emphatical. So Acts xii. 5, prayer was made by the church for Peter "without ceasing;" it was continued prayer, prayer stretched out: even so ought our prayers to be lifted up with fervency. True prayer is active and working; the fervent prayer of the righteous prevails much with God, James v. 16. Lively, working prayers are prevailing prayers.

But what is it to seek God diligently? When we seek him,

1. With all other things under our feet, when all other things are contemned in comparison. When the soul is carried out after God with a panting, longing desire, as the hart after the water-brooks.

2. With our whole heart. The heart is not divided in the work, every part is employed; as Jehoshaphat, 2 Chron. xx. 3, "feared, and set himself to seek the Lord," gave himself wholly to the work.

3. When the soul bears down all difficulties in seeking God, when nothing shall keep him off his work; as Jacob wrestled with God, and would not let him go till he blessed him, Gen. xxxii. 24—26. So the woman of Canaan, how earnestly did she seek to Christ for her daughter, and would not be discouraged by difficulties! Matt. xv. 22—25.

4. When no means are neglected to be used whereby that which we seek may be obtained. The soul tries every means, and follows God in all his ways, that it may find him; as the poor woman who followed Christ from place to place to touch the hem of his garment; Christ could not be hid from her.

5. When we resolve even to die in the pursuit; when it is our constant practice living, and our resolutions dying; as Jacob, the nearer the dawning of the day approached, the more earnest was he. How contrary are the practices of too many, who at the first seek God early, and earnestly too, yet after a while leave off and grow cold! Oh that it were not thus with us at this day! The Lord has brought us low at this time, yea, our condition is sad. True, there is a spirit of seeking abroad in the land, but now God calls for a quickening of this. "Be fervent in spirit, serving the Lord;" in the original it is, ζέοντες, boiling in spirit; let us so seek him now, that hereafter we may praise him. "They shall praise the Lord that seek him: your heart shall live for ever," Psal. xxii. 26. How sweet are those mercies which are won by prayer, and worn with praises! Therefore now stir up the gift that is within you: you that never prayed before, pray now; and you that have prayed before, quicken your diligence and double your care. How much better is it to seek God than men! to cry to God for mercy than to cursed men! God might have made your condition as the condition of your brethren. How many are this day fleeing for their lives, and begging mercy at the hands of barbarous, bloodthirsty, merciless monsters! and you are yet in peace, seeking your God, for yourselves and them.

But it may be asked, Why should we seek God? Can we do any thing to move God? Will God be the sooner entreated by us?

I answer, No, the words mean not that we can alter or change God's mind; but such exhortations as these are to fit and prepare us for mercy, to raise our spirits to a suitable frame and disposition for mercies expected and desired. And thus we leave this rich mine of the fifth chapter, which has been so fruitful in affording many choice truths; and come to the sixth, a rich mine also of heavenly and most seasonable directions, no less useful than the former.

CHAPTER VI.

In this chapter we have,

I. Israel's true repentance, ver. 1—3.

II. A sad complaint of the feigned repentance of many in Israel, ver. 4.

III. A further upbraiding of Israel for its unkind dealing with God, ver. 5—11.

I. Israel's true repentance, manifested in their resolution to return to him who had smitten them, their confidence in his mercy, and their blessing themselves in their happy condition now they were returned.

Ver. 1. *Come, and let us return unto the Lord: for he hath torn, and he will heal us; he hath smitten, and he will bind us up.*

These words are an excitation of the mind, not the body, to return to God; they also show the mighty spirit which came on this people at this time, as if they had said, Well, our princes have deceived us, and our prophets have deluded us and led us aside; we have been false in our worship, wrong in our practices, and have incurred the displeasure of God: but now, "come, and let us return," we are resolved to fall down and humble ourselves before him: "he hath smitten us, and he will bind us up." The Septuagint, and also Jerome, understand these words to refer to the practice of surgeons, who are wont to put deep and long tents into sores which they desire not merely to skin, but thoroughly to heal. So that here are marked Israel's dangerous disease, and their great corruptions, and that in their afflictions; and God's design not to let them die of the disease, or perish under his hand in the curing, but to heal them, and that thoroughly. A woman whose breasts are sore must have them thoroughly tented before they be healed, and she bids the surgeon to make her cure complete, though it be long and painful. So saith God, This people are very sorely wounded, and their cure will be very long and tedious, sore and painful, yet I will heal them. And the people saith, seeing it is thus, "Come, and let us return;" it matters not, though our healing cost us dear and be painful, it is enough that God will heal us. Let our disease be never so grievous, "come, and let us return." A man that has a mortal wound about him, what pain would he not be willing to endure were he certain of being cured! This people conceived themselves so wounded, that if God had not undertaken to relieve them they must have perished; but in that God had undertaken the cure, they were confident they should be healed.

Obs. 1. When God's time of mercy is come, he puts a mighty spirit of seeking into men. God's time was come for Israel's deliverance, and now God puts an active, stirring spirit into them; therefore they say, "Come, let us return:" before, their spirits were heavy and dull, like men in a lethargy; but now, their minds are quickened for God, and they say, like those in Isa. ii. 3, "Come, and let us go up to the mountain of the Lord, to the house of the God of Jacob;" and, as in Isa. xliv. 5, they willingly and cheerfully call themselves by the name of Jacob, and subscribe with their hand unto the Lord, and surname themselves by the name of Israel. As a ship whose sails are filled with a full and strong wind, they go on gallantly against all opposition: there is a spirit infused into them, such as Epaphras desires with fervent prayers for the Colossians, chap. iv. 12, "that ye may stand perfect and complete in all the will of God." Now will effectual and thorough reformation take place. At the time of antichrist's destruction, God has promised to put such a spirit into the hearts of the people, that all his tyranny shall not be able to stand before them: God will breathe upon the spirits of men, and they shall rise up powerful in his might.

Now, considering God's power, let not us despair concerning the great works which are doing in our times. Let men be never so base and perfidious, when God's time is come he will speak the word for deliverance. What a miserable, senseless condition was the world in a little before Luther's time! But when he came, what a spirit was raised in the people! And what a spirit has there been excited amongst us, and that suddenly, when we were in such bondage, and, although born free, likely to be slaves and vassals subjected to the wills of some twenty or thirty men! And what a spirit did God raise in our brethren of Scotland, when he was about to do them good, and to break the neck of the yoke of their tyranny! Oh then what a cursed thing it is for any to quench, keep under, or resist such a spirit as this when it arises within them!

Obs. 2. A joint turning to God is very honourable to God. "Come, and let us return." It is much honour to God when but one soul is turned to him, but when many are converted there is much glory, a multitude of praises then offered up to God; as in Rev. v. 11, "And the number of them which stood round about the throne was ten thousand times ten thousand, and thousands of thousands." And so Rev. xix. 6, "The voice of a multitude, saying, Alleluia, for the Lord God omnipotent reigneth."

Obs. 3. Times of mercy are times of union. Oh it is very sad when men will go every one their own way; but when men join together, saying, Come, and let us set about the Lord's work, every one encouraging each other, then there is hope the times of mercy are nigh that people. But our misery is the divisions and the rendings asunder that are amongst us. God is much displeased at this, and it certainly is one great hinderance to the entrance of mercy, that, notwithstanding God has us in the fire and threatens even our consuming, yet we will not join and unite together.

Obs. 4. True penitent hearts seek to get others to join with them. Oh how glad are they to see any coming on with them to seek the Lord! and how careful are they to give encouraging examples, to persuade them with all gentleness, saying, Come, let us go up to the house of the Lord, we have found the Lord very gracious to us; O come, he is good still, yea, and good to you, if you will come to him! If the husband have found God good to him, he will persuade the wife, the child, the servant, to come to Christ. Thus much of their resolution to return: the reason follows:

"For he hath torn, and he will heal us." Hence,

Obs. 5. In times of the greatest sufferings a truly penitent heart retains good thoughts of God. God has torn, and wounded, and smitten us; what then? shall we run away from God, and think hardly of him? No, think well of him and bless his name, even when you receive the hardest measure from God. This the people of God in former times have done: in all their miseries how careful were Nehemiah, Ezra, and Daniel to acquit and justify God! yea, the church in the time of her desertion retains Christ as a King, and calls him so, Psal. xliv. And as they dare not entertain hard thoughts of God, so neither of his cause nor his people. Many are like bad servants, who while they have every thing fitting, can give their master's family a good report; but let them be crossed, and go away in discontent, how vilely do they speak of it! or as sturdy beggars, who whilst they find relief and succour, can give good words; but let them be sent away empty, and then what terms are sufficiently abusive? so when things go well with the cause of God and his people, they will be on God's side. Oh take heed of being sorry that you have been so far engaged in it; this is a base and vile spirit. See how low the church was in affliction, Psal. xliv. 12—16, "by reason of the enemy and avenger:" yet in ver. 17, although "All this is come upon us," what then? is not God good, and his cause good that we maintain? No, God forbid such a thought should enter into us: Although "all this" evil "be come upon us, yet," she saith, "have we not forgotten thee, neither have we dealt falsely in thy covenant." Oh let us lay up this truth as a mighty comfort and stay to us in these times, and a good incitement to prayer; for mark, in the 23rd verse, "Awake, why sleepest thou, O Lord? arise, cast us not off for ever." Those can pray to purpose, who in the sorest afflictions can manifest the most fear of God, and exercise notwithstanding the most love toward him and his ways.

Obs. 6. A penitent heart is not a discouraged heart. It is a heart that sinks not down in discouragements, saying, (as some do,) We are a lost people and undone, there is no hope, we had been better never have ventured as far as we have. It dares not draw conclusions from what has been, to what is, and what will be; this it regards as too presumptuous. David in the cave can trust in God, and hide himself under God's wing, Psal. lvii. 1. So long as there is a God in heaven, such a soul will expect help from him, will expect mercy notwithstanding his severity and justice; the severity of justice in God cannot keep him from waiting for and expecting what God has promised: if the soul can but get over this difficulty, the deep gulf of God's justice, it will easily surmount all the dreadfulness of man's displeasure. A repenting heart is a purified, and therefore not a discouraged, but a sustained heart; while men of unclean and unholy minds are always jealous of God, and of his dealings toward them: oh let it appear that we are not thus, by the cleanness of our lives and the purity of our conversations. Carnal hearts are not discouraged when they have carnal helps to underprop them, and shall we be afraid of any difficulty who have God for our help? Remarkable is 1 Sam. iv. 9, with regard to the speech made by the Philistines. On the coming of the ark into the camp of Israel, they were put into great fear; yet how do they encourage themselves! "Be strong, and quit yourselves like men, O ye Philistines, that ye be not servants to the Hebrews, as they have been to you: quit yourselves like men, and fight." So say I, Let us be courageous in these times, and fight for our liberties, our laws, and our religion: did we but spend that strength in returning to God which we do in discouraging thoughts, oh how soon would help come for us out of the sanctuary! Now though we must not be discouraged when helps and means fail, yet, like the prophet, our confidence must be mingled with deep humility for our sins which cause these breaches, Hab. iii. 15—18. We should improve our humiliation as they did, Judg. xx., who, though in a good cause, a cause which God approved of, yet lost forty thousand men in the prosecution of it. What did they then? leave it off, and run away? No, but summoned fresh courage and resolution, fasted and prayed, and humbled themselves before the God of their fathers, and then prospered. Oh let us be humbled, that we may not be discouraged!

And as we must not be discouraged, so must we not falsely encourage ourselves: as they said, "The bricks are fallen down, but we can build with hewn stone;" so say not, This army is lost, but we can raise another quickly. Let us only encourage ourselves in the Lord our God, but take heed of resting too much in the goodness of our cause. 1 Sam. iv. 3, the people said, "Let us fetch the ark of the covenant of the Lord out of Shiloh unto us, that, when it cometh among us, it may save us out of the hand of our enemies:" they thought the bare having of that among them would deliver them. Know that it is not the goodness of our cause that can bear us up, and carry us through difficulties, if we do not turn to the Lord.

Now, that your spirits may not sink under these troubles, let me give you a few props to lean upon.

1. If we have been faithful in our work, we may have this testimony, that what is our duty as creatures, is performed by us; and know, though there were many weaknesses in our performances, yet we have to deal with a God who loves sincerity in infirmities.

2. If we suffer, God suffers more. This should mightily encourage us in sufferings, when God is contented to be our partner.

3. God sees further than we, and knows what is best for us. When the wars first began we promised ourselves a present end of them, and we thought it would be best; but God saw otherwise; and now we are sensible that if we had obtained peace at the first we should not have known what to have done with it, it would even have undone us by this time.

4. Things are not more difficult now to God than they were at the first; God knows as well how to deliver in the greatest straits, as if none at all existed.

5. God usually works by contraries, bringing light out of darkness; saving Israel in the Red Sea, when in the greatest danger of drowning.

6. God will be seen in the mount. God has his time, his set time, to appear for his people, and before that time come he will not show himself. The soul is very prone in misery to run into a double extreme, either of presumption or despair; presumption, that puts the evil day far off; and unbelief, that puts the good day far off: therefore take heed of both these.

But could we have the encouragement of this people, could we say that we have returned, it were something.

Now for this, know, that if the consideration of God's healing mercy is more prevailing with us to turn than any misery whatsoever, if we are willing and desirous to turn, the other may be made good, that God is willing to heal and bind us up. Can we but make out the first part of our turning, I dare affirm the second, of God's healing; though the means employed may be very painful, the Lord may put a deep tent into us to eat out our putrified flesh, yet we ought more earnestly to desire a thorough and sound healing, than an easy and perhaps transient cure.

Obs. 7. When God intends good to a people, he gives them intimations of his love. How did this people know that God would heal them, and that he would bind them up? Thus they argued it, from God's goodness, from his name, and from his covenant. Oh would God but put into our thoughts to consider the mercy of God to us in the covenant.

But I fear this would be presumption in me, may some say.

I answer, No, if thy believing and resting upon the promise sanctifies the heart, and does not make it secure; if thy laying hold upon the promise more breaks the heart, renders it more humble and submissive, it is a right supporting the heart upon the promise, and not presumption.

Obs. 8. Apprehension of mercy causes the heart to turn. Many say, God will not be gracious, mercy is past, there is no hope, therefore we will give over waiting. No, but let us seek him still, and wait longer for mercy to come.

Obs. 9. The saints make their healings not a fruit of their returning, but of God's mercy. Many poor souls think that they must not believe till they are so far humbled, and so much broken. This is an error; we should exercise our faith more upon God's healing than our returning, and this will cause us to be humbled; humiliation will soon follow. Good works are a good nurse to faith; but if we make works the mother of faith, that faith is not right, it rests not on Scriptural grounds.

Ver. 2. *After two days will he revive us: in the third day he will raise us up, and we shall live in his sight.*

God's works are comments on his word; and I have often had occasion to notice this in explaining this prophecy: as Christ said of that scripture, Luke iv. 21, "This day is this scripture fulfilled in your ears;" so may I now say of this scripture, how literally has God fulfilled it in us! In the last discourse you heard of God's wounding and of his healing; how has he graciously healed us, and literally fulfilled these words towards us! "After two days he will revive us." But two days after our humiliation he revived us, and the third day we lived in his sight; and if we follow on to know the Lord we shall know more of his counsel, and though the darkness of the night be not yet over, yet the morning is prepared.

But may we conclude, as this people, that God will revive us, and that we shall live in his sight? If we can prove our turning unto God, and our returning from sin, the other may be made good, that he will revive us in our sorrows.

The scope of these two verses is to express a further confidence of repenting, believing Israel in God's goodness: before he smote them, and now he would revive them. But before this reviving comes perhaps we may be as dead men, yea, lie a day, that is, a certain time, as dead men, forsaken and forgotten of God; yea, we may lie the second day also, that is, a second time wherein we expected help the enemy may triumph over us; yet "we shall live in his sight," that is, all shall see, that the eye of God was on us for good: he will revive us, and God shall be in our sight as we shall be in his;

glorious things is he about to make known to us; though it be night now, yet know his mercy is coming, even as the morning follows the dark night. This is the sum of these words.

Yet, for the further opening of them, know that interpreters are greatly perplexed to discover what is meant by "two days;" some think it spoken of the Jewish captivity; others, of the second coming of Christ, the Messias.

The meaning of the words "after two days," appears to be, that although God do not come presently, yet, "after two days," he will come; mercy, though it stays long, yet will come. Two days in Scripture signifies a short time; as Numb. ix. 22, "Whether it were two days, or a month, or a year, that the cloud staid upon the tabernacle." Mercer quotes R. Abrah. Ezræ Fil. as saying, that wounds and gashes in a man's body pain and smart more at two days' end than at first; so God may let us lie in the smart of pain and sorrow two days, but in the third day mercy shall follow.

Interpreters generally conceive these words to have reference also to the two days that Christ lay in the grave; and Luther saith that this is the scripture which Paul refers to in 1 Cor. xv. 4, that Christ "rose again the third day according to the Scriptures:" what scripture? why this, "the third day he will raise us up, and we shall live in his sight;" and though the text notes the confidence which repenting Israel had in God's mercy towards them, yet it refers also to Christ, as if they should say, Our straits and miseries may be great, and we may lie in them a while, as did Christ, but he was raised the third day, and so shall we. Calvin saith, that God gave a famous and memorable example of Israel's mercy after their captivity by Christ's rising from the grave; and this may well be meant of Christ, as that scripture shows, Hos. xi. 1, "When Israel was a child, then I loved him, and called my son out of Egypt:" who would have thought that this had reference to Christ, had not the Scriptures applied it to him, in Matt. ii. 14, 15, "And departed into Egypt: and was there until the death of Herod: that it might be fulfilled which was spoken of the Lord by the prophet, saying, Out of Egypt have I called my son?" How darkly was Christ shadowed out in the Old Testament! as by Jonas in the whale's belly three days. Oh what cause have we who live in gospel-times, when Christ is manifested so clearly, to bless God! what dark and mystical intimations had they of Christ in those days, when this, and that of Jonas in the whale's belly, were some of the clearest!

When at any time God would comfort his people in distress, what does he do? he reveals a prophecy of the Messiah to come; as in Isa. vii. 14; ix. 6; and Zech. ix. 9: and so here, God having smitten, wounded, and torn them, comes and heals them, promising them that they shall revive and live in his sight.

But here now Luther makes an objection, If these words had reference to Christ they should run thus, *He* shall live in his sight, not *we;* and he answers it himself, that it denotes the efficacy of his resurrection, not only for himself, but for many others.

1. "We shall live in his sight;" לפניו before his face, that is, his favour shall be towards us for mercy. As the turning the face away shows anger, so the turning of God's face towards us signifies favour.

2. We shall see his face with comfort, and rejoice in the sight of it.

3. We shall eye his face in acts of obedience, and he will eye our duties with acceptance.

4. It implies security in his presence. As in the presence of a king his very presence is our security and safety; so, "we shall live in his sight," that is, we shall be safe in his presence. The observations from hence are,

Obs. 1. God's own people may not only be smitten and wounded by God, but may lie for dead in their own eyes, and in the eyes of all about them, for a time: see it in the case of Heman, Psal. lxxxviii. 10, 14, "Wilt thou show wonders to the dead? shall the dead arise and praise thee? Lord, why castest thou off my soul? why hidest thou thy face from me?" And in Ezek. xxxvii. 3, we read of dry bones which should be made to live; and Rev. xi., the witnesses shall be slain and lie dead in the streets, the beast shall overcome them; the generality of those that stand for Christ shall be slain by the beast, and overcome by his power.

The reason of this may be, because God can work about his glory by contrary means. When God fetches out his glory from the afflictions of his people, it costs him not so much nor so dear as when he brings it out of sin: now if God's glory be so dear to him, that he will suffer sin to be in the world, thereby to fetch his glory out of it, why should we be unwilling that God should suffer afflictions to be upon us, seeing by them he procures glory to himself? "In the greatness of thine excellency thou hast overthrown them that rose up against thee," Exod. xv. 7. How should God manifest his glorious power in raising them up, were they never brought low? In heaven God will so manifest his glory to us that we shall not need such dark shadows to give it prominence.

If this be so, take heed of drawing darker conclusions from God's dealings than they will bear, as to say, The Lord has forsaken us, and God will have mercy no more upon us; he has forgotten to be gracious, he has left his cause and turned his back upon his inheritance. We should labour to be well informed in the grounds upon which his cause stands and is maintained, and which may uphold us in the maintenance of it; for know that God may put thee to the trial, and if thou art not thoroughly grounded thou wilt apostatize.

Obs. 2. God leaves his people in that dead condition for a time; the first day they may look for help, and it may not come; and the second day he may let them lie, and that after their seeking of him. This people said, "Come, and let us return unto the Lord;" yet what do they add? "After two days he will revive us;" it must be some time first. God is a great God, and his creature must wait. There is much grace exercised in an afflicted condition, when the soul quietly submits to God, and patiently tarries the Lord's leisure, let his dealing be never so hard towards it. God sometimes answers his people's prayers presently when they seek him, so that it may not only be said, in the evening, but, in the morning hast thou heard me; not only this day, but the next also. See 1 Kings xviii. 38, 44, where Elijah prays, and the Lord heard him presently; but he prays again, and then the Lord defers: in ver. 38, he prays for fire to come down to consume the sacrifice, and it did so; but in ver. 44, of the same chapter, he prays again for rain, and see in what a posture he prays; yet he obtained his petition with much difficulty, he sent his servant seven times, and at the seventh it was but a little cloud; at first God heard him presently, but he prays again, and then mercy comes slowly and with difficulty; yet God was not angry with Elijah. So Daniel prays, and was heard presently; but the people pray, and pray earnestly, yet they were not answered.

Oh, therefore, let us take heed of an impatient and froward spirit in trouble, of being weary of well-doing, and of growing careless in holy services, because an immediate answer comes not; this as much as any thing shows the rottenness of our spirits, and is as evident a sign of a hypocrite as any we have in Scripture.

Obs. 3. The time of God's reviving his people is neither long in God's nor in the saints' account. It is but "two days;" "the third day he will raise us up, and we shall live." "As birds flying, so will the Lord of hosts defend Jerusalem," Isa. xxxi. 5. He has promised not to contend for ever: and in 1 Pet. i. 6, "Though now for a season, if need be, ye are in heaviness through manifold temptations;" in the original it is, If now, if need be; so that there is great need of afflictions before God sends them. So 2 Cor. iv. 17, afflictions are "for a moment," for a very little time. Faith lifts up the soul on Pisgah, and enabling it to realize the valley of Achor, the door of hope, as lying between it and mount Zion, creates patience in midst of the greatest sufferings. It is a sign of a distempered spirit to complain of the length of an affliction; a gracious heart desires more its sanctification than its removal; we might have been swallowed up in the gulf of eternal misery. "Yet once, it is a little while, and I will shake the heavens, and the earth, and the sea, and the dry land; and I will shake all nations, and the Desire of all nations shall come," Hag. ii. 6, 7; but Christ came not until five or six hundred years afterwards. Our impatience makes affliction seem long.

Obs. 4. Faith realizes God's reviving mercies in the saddest condition. When their help is gone, in the mount of man's extremity will God be seen. We should reason thus, Because God's people are in great extremity, it is a sign that God will arise and help them; and not despair. As before the morning light is the thickest darkness, so let us never be discouraged at the increase of afflictions, for they show the time then hastens on for deliverance. And this faith makes present and shows to the soul life in death, favour in frowns, love in strokes. Faith discerns a great difference between the strokes of God on the saints and upon the wicked; as Isa. xxvi. 14, compared with ver. 19, "They are dead, they shall not live; they are deceased, they shall not rise." When God strikes wicked men, their wounds forerun death here, and eternal death hereafter; when he smites them in their cause, in their names, or estates, it is to undo them. But now, mark the 19th verse, "Thy dead men shall live, together with my dead body shall they arise." Some think that these words denote the glorious security of the church, that though men and means fail, yet faith can see deliverance in the womb of an infinite wisdom, power, and faithfulness: faith revives other graces when seeming dead, and puts life into them, much more into our dead conditions. It is reported of the crystal, that it possesses such virtue, that its very touch quickens other stones, and imparts to them lustre and beauty. It is true of faith, that it removes present evils, and approximates distant good. Psal. xci. 7, "A thousand shall fall at thy side, and ten thousand at thy right hand; but it shall not come nigh thee:" this is a very strange speech, that a man may be in a place where a thousand shall fall by him, and ten thousand at his right hand, and yet he not be touched by the disease. By faith the soul enjoys this security. Psal. lx. 6, "God hath spoken in his holiness; I will rejoice, I will divide Shechem, and mete out the valley of Succoth:" the thing was not yet done, yet they rejoiced in it as present. Faith enables a dead and barren womb to conceive and bring forth, it raises up a dead son out of the ashes; Abraham bids his servants to stay at the bottom of the hill, and expect his coming; oh strong was his faith in this thing!

Ut vives aliis lapidibus pretiosis extinctis, solo attactu luscitaret. Guliel. Paris.

How unbeseeming are our spirits, and how is our faith manifested to be weak and poor, when a mercy promised is within sight, ready to be fulfilled, and yet we are impatient and froward if it come not just as we desire; when we are full of such despairing conclusions against ourselves or the cause of God, saying, Alas, all is now gone, we are left desperate, God has forsaken his cause! O let us take heed of pleasing ourselves with such carnal arguments and objections, for they mightily provoke and dishonour God, and hinder much good which else we might enjoy.

But were I worthy, I could think that then I might entertain some hopes.

In this case, exercise faith upon Christ even in thine unworthiness; and though thou mayst die and not see the harvest, nor reap the fruit of thy prayers, yet know, the generations to come shall, and this may comfort thee. So Jacob's speech when he lay a dying, "Behold, I die; but God shall do much more for you." The cause may be trodden down for a while, and God may hide himself, but know, that he will keep with thee his covenant which he never yet broke; so long as Christ is thine and thou art his, God's covenanted faithfulness is also thine. What if those that stand for Christ and his cause be sometimes beaten, must they therefore give over? No, but venture still: and, if our sins hinder not, though we may lie dead to-day, and to-morrow, yet the third day we may live in his sight.

Obs. 5. Mercies after two days' death, are reviving mercies. "After two days will he revive us." Promises in times of afflictions are sweet indeed; oh, then, how much more deliverance! Such mercies are resurrection mercies, which God sends after killing afflictions. And such mercies has the Lord given us at this very day; the Lord has revived us when almost dead, therefore would we give God the glory, and render to him due and seasonable praise for such seasonable mercies. Let us observe these rules.

1. Look back to the former base unbelief of your hearts, and chide them, upbraid them with this now, O vile heart of mine! did not I begin to say, Alas, I am undone, all is lost, my hopes are now abortive? was not I sorry that ever I was so engaged as I am, were it to do again I would be better advised? did not I think the neutrals, those who "came not to the help of the Lord against the mighty," far better off than I, and wish myself in their condition? How has the Lord been dishonoured by me! what secret repinings and grudging thoughts have I had even against God himself, because of the various dispensations of his providence! Say now, O base, vile, unbelieving heart, how has the Lord confuted thee, and made thee to see thy shame and ignorance, in believing sense rather than faith!

2. Has God bestowed reviving mercies on you? then be willing to give God the glory of them, and resign them up to him on this ground, because they have been forfeited by your unbelief. An unbelieving heart forfeits all mercies before it has them: true, God gives many precious ones to sad, froward, discontented spirits; but you cannot receive them with the same comfort as others, because they are forfeited, and though God through his bounty suffers you to enjoy them, yet you are in fear continually lest God should exact his forfeiture. O believe your mercies in the promise through all the difficulties.

3. Remember the covenants which you made to God in the times of your trouble, and keep them. It is a provoking sin to break covenant with God, God complains of it against Israel: "When he slew them, then they sought him: and they returned and inquired early after God. Nevertheless they did flatter him with their mouth, and they lied unto him with their tongues: for their heart was not right with him, neither were they stedfast in his covenant," Psal. lxxviii. 34, 36, 37. Oh how usual is it with men in any misery to covenant largely with God, and presently to forget what they have done! this is a sign of a false heart, therefore take heed of it. Lay more weight upon the covenants which you make, if ever you mean to give God real praise for any mercy.

4. Consider how much better it is to give God the

glory of a mercy willingly, than force him to extort it from you in wrath: God is better pleased with active praise, than passive, for his mercies. Consider, glory he *will* have. O oblige him not then to force what is so due to him from you. If you give not God the glory of the mercies you possess, he in wrath may take them from you: and had not God given us this reviving mercy, it might have been our case to have been forced to give God his glory in a passive manner.

5. Whatever God calls for now from you, be willing to give up to him freely. Whatsoever we would have gladly given for such a mercy in our misery, had God indented with us for it, let us be ready and willing to give him now the mercy is come; had we known our danger, and the miseries which would have flowed in upon us had not mercy prevented, and God said, What are you content to do, to suffer, to part with, that you may be delivered out of this danger, and possess the contrary mercy? Seeing then God has given us such a mercy without this indenting, make this an argument to give freely unto God that which he now requires. You have been, perhaps, in bodily fears, and danger of death by some sickness; now, if God had called for your estates, would you not have given them to him? Do that now which you would then have done.

6. Lay up against unbelief for time to come. Has God remembered us in our low estate? let us say with David, "We will trust in him so long as we live;" we will never determine, as formerly, either against ourselves or the cause of God; we will never more entertain hard thoughts of him, but are resolved to do what belongs to us as creatures, and leave the success of the business to God. Apply this any way, and it will be very useful. Has God helped thee in any soul-trouble? revived thee in the depths of sorrow, when he had hid himself from thee? lay up such passages of God toward thee against all the risings of unbelief; resolve upon this, that thy soul shall rely on him for help whatsoever becomes of thee: this is to give God the glory of reviving mercies. Thus, in Psal. xviii. 1, 2, David appropriates God to himself, and gathers from that strength and support. He was at this time in such great straits by reason of Saul's persecution, that he gave up all for lost; "I shall one day perish by the hands of Saul." "All men are liars," he exclaimed; the prophets of God, Gad and Nathan, are liars; they tell me that I shall be king, that I shall sway the sceptre in Israel, but I am more like to be killed and betrayed, surrounded as I am by deceitful and bloodthirsty men. Soon, however, he recalls his words, and confesses that he spake unadvisedly with his lips: "In my haste I said, All men are liars." And here in this 18th Psalm, where he praises God for that mercy which formerly he would not believe, he addresses him by eight titles, all of them calculated to strengthen his faith: "My rock, my fortress, my deliverer; my God, my strength in whom I will trust; my buckler, the horn of my salvation, my high tower:" from all these titles of God, as his God, he derives encouragement and support. In all the Scripture I know not so short a text so full of matter for the strengthening of faith as this is; and it is faith's special work to realize God as ours in all these relations. Oh how beautiful would our praises for reviving mercies show, could we but exercise our faith thus upon all these titles of God as our God!

Obs. 6. The real sight of deliverance strongly inclines the soul to turn to God. The people made this use of approaching mercy: What! will God after two days deliver and revive us? Come then, and let us return unto him; let us not any longer stand out, but come in, that he may revive us and raise us up. When the soul sees mercy coming, it beholds God outbidding all other temptations, and overpowering all difficulties; and happy are they who by faith can discern it afar off, and are thereby stirred up to turn to God. When God sends such thoughts as these into the soul and settles them on the mind, I am now in a very good condition, well, and in health for the present, but where may I be within two days? I enjoy peace, and have every thing that heart can desire, both for necessity and delight, but within a short time where may I and these be? these are thoughts calculated to strike awe into the soul of the sinner. But, on the contrary, to believers very comfortable and full of sweetness: I am in great and extreme misery, but after two days it will pass away, then, oh where shall I be? in heaven, in joy and blessedness, for evermore at rest with my Saviour! This made Paul overlook all his afflictions; 2 Cor. iv. 17, It is true I am under great afflictions, but they are but light, and but for a moment; and what shall I have then? An eternal weight of glory. Therefore Christians should not be always poring over their afflictions, but look up to mercy, and review their comforts as well as their discouragements; consider, that within two days God will raise us up again, and this will mightily raise our spirits and quell the tumults in our hearts. As we should be sensible of God's hand to be humbled for our sins which have caused him to afflict us, yet should we take care that we do not destroy ourselves by our fears.

Obs. 7. The apprehension of the death and resurrection of Christ is a special help to faith in affliction. Many things may aid, but the consideration of Christ's resurrection most of all: when the soul shall exercise faith thus; I am thus and thus afflicted and in misery, so was Christ, and much more: though he were the Son of God, the first begotten of the Father, and so blessed for ever; yet he was delivered up into his enemies' hands, scorned, persecuted, spat upon, nay, crucified, and put to a shameful death. My condition for the present is not so, but if it should be so it is no more than Christ's was; in this his great sorrow all his friends forsook him, a thing which much aggravates their misery who are in straits; and doubts and fears oppressed his followers, insomuch that the two disciples which went to Emmaus said, "But we trusted that it had been he which should have redeemed Israel." To what a low condition did God thus bring Christ! and yet this was the greatest work that ever was done, and the most glorious to God. Was the church ever in a lower condition than Christ himself was? yet Christ was raised and delivered out of all; yea, this was a special end of his deep abasement, to be a comfort and a pattern to his churches in like trials: and seeing this is held forth to us in a clearer way than it was to the Jews under the law, we should make more use of it than they did. Was Christ so low that the wrath of God was upon him for satisfaction even to death? this surely was a deep and horrible pit. And is there any hope that ever he should be raised from it? Yea, then was God's time to show his power, and to declare him to be his Son. And now God thus speaks to his people in all their straits: Did my power raise my Son in such a low estate? it is able also to raise you. As the apostle argues in 1 Cor. xv., If Christ be not risen, the dead are not raised, &c.; so from thence I also infer, that the church must rise because Christ is risen. If the church does not rise, Christ is not risen; and if so, "then is our preaching vain, and your faith is also vain:" therefore raise up your saddened spirits on this ground, Christ is risen, and I also shall rise with him. It was wont to be the salutation of the Christians in ancient times, *Christus resurrexit,* Christ is risen: so the saints, though brought very low, may conclude that yet that power which raised the Head, will, in his time, raise the body and make it glorious with himself.

"And we shall live in his sight." As Israel was repenting, so it was believing Israel also; and as their believing furthered their repentance, so their repentance furthered their faith; they were confident that they should live in his sight. Hence,

Obs. 8. When God grants mercies, he would have his people to be of lively spirits. The meaning of the Spirit in this text is, that however the saints may seem as dead when the wicked prevail over them, yet, when God gives rest and life, they shall be lively and full of spirit: God loves not to see his people sad and dejected, when, in reality, they have cause for the greatest joy.

Obs. 9. When God is reconciled to a people, his face is towards them. He looks then upon them and loves them: Rev. xxii. 4, "And they shall see his face." God deals not with us as David did with his son, 2 Sam. xiv. 24, "And the king said, Let him turn to his own house, and let him not see my face." But if God be once reconciled, all the frowns in his face are turned into smiles, he is all lovely towards his saints.

Now how incongruous a thing is it, that when God smiles we should lower! And as God smiles when we humble ourselves, so should we look cheerfully on our children and servants on their submission.

Obs. 10. God's people account their life to be in God's favour. Hypocrites desire only the enjoyment of mercies, and if they obtain that they are contented, though they enjoy not the presence of God at all in them: but with the saints it is otherwise; although they have precious mercies, and yet God not present in them, they content not them; if they have health and not God's presence in it, if they have peace and not their peace with God, it satisfies not them; this is their cry, Lord, "let me see thy countenance, let me hear thy voice; for sweet is thy voice, and thy countenance is comely," Cant. ii. 14.

Obs. 11. The Lord's mercies to his people are settled mercies. He not only gives them the prospect, but the real possession, of mercy. We are revived and raised. Yea, but we may die again. No, "we shall live in his sight," we shall live before him. Mercies to the saints are not the fruit of God's patience, for then they would not be settled mercies; but they come from the covenant of grace, and so are called, "the sure mercies of David," Isa. lv. 3.

Obs. 12. Faith raises the soul high. "He will revive us," and "he will raise us up." Is that all? No, but "we shall live in his sight." It is a proof of a very carnal heart, to be contented with low mercies, to be put off with any thing: it pleases God well, when his people will not be put off with small mercies. Though it is true, we must be thankful for the least mercy, and content with it in opposition to murmuring, yet we must not rest therewithal satisfied; but if thy faith be true, it will expect more; and if it hath got a promise from God, it will improve it to the utmost extent that the promise will bear; and when it hath one promise fulfilled, it will look out for the answering of another. We do not approve of such a craving disposition in a beggar, but God is much delighted with it in his people.

Obs. 13. The eye of God on his people is their comfort. The saints have much comfort from God's eye; whereas it is the greatest terror to the hypocrites, that God sees them, that they are continually in his sight; "If one know them, they are in the terrors of the shadow of death," Job xxiv. 17. It is no wonder that they would fain hide themselves from his presence, "for the eyes of the Lord are over the righteous, and his ears are open unto their prayers: but the face of the Lord is against them that do evil," 1 Pet. iii. 12. The saints account it their privilege that God sees them; and it is a very good sign of sincerity, when the soul can look up to the clear beams of the Sun of righteousness without fear or apprehension; as the eagle, when she would prove her young, holds them up in the sight of the sun, to try if they can endure with steady, undazzled gaze its effulgent brightness.

Obs. 14. It is the great care of the saints to walk as in God's sight. Psal. xvi. 8, 9, "I have set the Lord always before me: because he is at my right hand, I shall not be moved:" I will not fear, I have set him before me; "therefore my heart is glad, my glory rejoiceth: my flesh also shall rest in hope." This text is spoken chiefly of Christ; and if Christ must be kept from falling by setting the Lord always before him, much more must we. Not that he was in danger of falling as we are, but this is to be understood as Heb. v. 8, which speaks of obedience learned by sufferings; looking at God helped him to obey, and to stand in obeying; as the apostle saith, 2 Cor. ii. 17, What we speak, it is as in the sight of God in Christ; that is, What we say, it is in the power and efficacy of Christ. But how comes this to pass, that they thus preach? why as in the sight of God? We thus preach, his power enables.

Obs. 15. The eye of God upon his people is their safety and security. "The eyes of the Lord are over the righteous," 1 Pet. iii. 12. As a child thinks itself safe if it be in the parent's presence, so the saints should look upon themselves as very secure in the sight of God. A philosopher in danger of shipwreck in a starry night, could say, Surely I shall not perish, there are so many eyes of Providence over me. Could a philosopher speak thus, and may not a Christian say much more, that he shall not perish, seeing God's providential eye is over him?

Ver. 3. *Then shall we know, if we follow on to know the Lord: his going forth is prepared as the morning; and he shall come unto us as the rain, as the latter and former rain unto the earth.*

This scripture is very full, and pregnant with sweetness, and the interpretation unattended with difficulty.

"Then shall we know, if we follow on to know." "If" is not in the original, which runs thus, ונדעה נרדפה לדעת And we shall know, and we shall follow on to know. The word signifies to follow one as eagerly as a man which persecutes another, and persecutes him as Paul did the saints, with full purpose of mind: when men thus follow on to know, God will reveal himself more. Luther applies these words to Christ, and the gospel revelation of him, setting men's minds on fire by the truth so clearly discovered, and inflaming them with such love to it that they follow on to know it. But although these words have reference to Christ, yet, primarily, they are to be understood of God's delivering his people out of captivity. Then they shall know. What shall they know? That they shall live in his sight. When God delivers them, then they shall know,

1. God's faithfulness in his covenant made to our fathers: we know very little of it now, but the time is coming when we shall know it clearly.

2. The works of God's wisdom, all working for his people's good in their lustre and beauty.

3. The excellency of God's power, how it overrules all things, and how it is exerted for the saints' good.

4. The mercy of God acting every way for their best advantage: we are now in great misery, and our troubles increase, and we cannot see how mercy is working for good; but then we shall know.

5. The mind of God: we are now in much darkness, not only with respect to outward troubles, but to soul-trials; we know very little of God now at the best, but then we shall know him clearly.

6. The vanity of all worldly pomp and glory, and the folly of all carnal confidence: men are now ready to call the proud happy, and bless the workers of iniquity, and run to king Jareb; but then we shall

know that God is able to deliver his people out of all straits.

7. That it is not in vain for the people of God to seek him, even then, when all human helps and hopes fail; then they shall know that there is a power and efficacy in prayer, as God's ordinance, to help them in difficulties.

8. The meaning of many prophecies which are now very dark and obscure, and yet contain much sweetness for the churches of God: and whether this will be worth knowing, let discerning men judge.

9. The glorious purposes and decrees which God has had from all eternity for our good: God has glorious purposes, although we for the present know them not, but we shall know them; there is a time that all these things, and much more than these, shall be revealed.

"We shall know, if we follow on to know the Lord." "If" is not in the original, but put in to fill up the sense; but if we take the words literally, "we shall know, if we follow on," then the sense runs thus, Does God reveal himself to his people? and do his people lay hold of the opportunity? if so, they shall know more. But if you take the words without the "if," thus, You know, and follow on to know; the meaning is, That when God begins to show mercy he will go on to show mercy; so that these words are a motive to turn to God, or an expression of their confidence in God. God was now in the dark, his presence clouded towards them, and the enemies scoffed and mocked at them, saying, "Where is now your God?" The people answer, We shall know our God again, and he will discover himself to our comfort, but to your shame. The observations are,

Obs. 1. True penitents turn to God that they may know God. As there must be some knowledge before turning to God, so we turn to God that we may know him more; and the desire of knowing him should not be so much to deliver from hell, as to be fitted thereby to do him more and better service. If the hypocrite have but so much service and knowledge as to manage thereby to attain his own ends, he is satisfied; but a gracious heart dares not rest in such content.

Obs. 2. No man can turn to God, but as God's face is towards him. We cannot turn to God except God turn first to us: "When he giveth quietness, who then can make trouble?" Job xxxiv. 29.

Obs. 3. When God comes to his people in mercy, he reveals to them much of himself; and according to the degrees of his coming to them, are the manifestations of himself unto them, either more or less; he gives them something in this life, an earnest at the beginning, and at death the full payment, the perfect enjoyment of all promised good. Faith can see a glory in God, even in the darkest seasons; but in the times of light, then it can see abundance of mercy.

Therefore it is Christian wisdom to take notice of the mercies we enjoy, else we cannot glorify God's name. Oh how much of the faithfulness, power, wisdom, goodness, and mercy of God in turning the counsels, plots, and devices of the wicked to our good, we might have known, had we but been diligent observers of his providence! Those who see not the glory of God now shining brightly in the world, have very little light in themselves, but must needs be very dark, or strangely negligent in the observation of the good things they enjoy from God. Of John, who saw the future blessed estate of the church, the temple of God, the ark of the testament was kept in the holy of holies, Rev. xi. 19, when none of the people could see it, it is said that he should prophesy again, Rev. x. 11; not that he should arise again and prophesy, but the time is coming that the Revelation shall be as clearly understood as if John had written a new revelation. Just so in Isa. xxx. 26, a scripture parallel to the text, the Lord promises, when he binds the breach of the people, and heals the stroke of their wound, "the light of the moon shall be as the light of the sun;" knowledge shall wonderfully increase, there shall be very glorious manifestations of God to his people. And that passage in Isaiah shows plainly that our present text refers to that time in which God will exalt his church, and make it glorious in the eyes of all beholders.

Obs. 4. The knowledge of God is a very comfortable thing to the saints. They speak here triumphantly, "Then shall we know, if we follow on to know;" any thing of God makes gracious hearts to spring with joy and gladness. It is the happiness of the saints in heaven to know God, and to have the sight of God: and so it is here; "This is eternal life, to know thee, and Jesus Christ, whom thou hast sent;" not only to know him, but to know him as he appears for his church's deliverance. How many are now in heaven blessing God that ever their eyes beheld these days! Nay, certainly, should God but let our forefathers out of their graves to see what a turn things here have taken, and how their prayers have been answered, they would be as men astonished. If it be so comfortable to see and know God in this life, what will it be in heaven, where nothing shall intervene to darken this sight of God!

Obs. 5. The more men turn to God, the more they shall know of him; yea, this we may be sure of, whatever else we here enjoy. "All this evil is come upon us; yet made we not our prayer before the Lord our God, that we might turn from our iniquities, and understand thy truth," Dan. ix. 13: if we understand thy truth and turn from our iniquities, we shall know more of the truth. "The pure in heart shall see God," Matt. v. 8. Oh the sweet light which purified minds enjoy! to these God reveals his secrets, and acquaints them with the mystery of his covenant, Psal. xxv. 14. The great rabbies of the world are ignorant of these things, they are mysteries unto them; and this is the reason of it, because they turn not unto God, neither labour to know God.

Obs. 6. Those that know something of God desire to know more. He that is learned covets after more knowledge. None, truly, but the ignorant, are enemies to learning; those that never knew the worth of it, are they that cry it down; therefore those who are contented with little, nay, and think their little sometimes too much, are of poor, mean, and base spirits, far from following on to know the Lord.

Obs. 7. A gracious heart puts forth strong endeavours in the use of means to increase in the knowledge of God. He will let no time escape, neglect no opportunity, in which knowledge may be increased, Dan. ix. 13. This was Solomon's prayer, 1 Kings iii. 9, "Give, therefore, thy servant an understanding heart;" in the Hebrew it is, לב שמע Give thy servant a hearing heart. Though God had discovered himself wonderfully, yet he desires that God would further manifest himself to him. Therefore they are very foolish that think they know enough of God, and are contented with what they know; it is a great blessing of God to have a hearing ear and an understanding heart. Therefore what a fond opinion is it, and what a sluggish spirit does it manifest, to be satisfied with the knowledge of former times! What! say they, shall we be wiser than our forefathers? We are, indeed, to bless God for the knowledge of our forefathers, and say, as Master Greenham did, "I bless God for what our forefathers knew;" but also add with him, "I bless God also that he has kept back some of his counsels to communicate to this generation." It is an argument of a poor spirit to rest satisfied with small measures of knowledge; the light three or four hundred years ago was dim, and in these days our light is poor and weak to that which shall be revealed, especially with respect to the worship and order of God's house. Therefore had not we need to "follow on to know the Lord?" Therefore God forbid that any should scorn at the new lights which God discovers, but rather let us be humbled for our ignorance, and now begin to follow on earnestly and perseveringly to know the Lord. No new truth indeed in respect of the word is revealed, but with regard to the manifestation of them to us they may be said to be new.

Obs. 8. It is a blessed thing to take notice of God's revealing himself. Oh how happy a thing had it been for many of us, if, when God first began to stir our hearts, we had followed on to know the Lord! How sad it is for many to look back to former days! what glorious and sweet manifestations had they then of God's love! but, through worldly cares and sluggishness of spirit, all is lost: they are now in the dark, and cannot speak of God to edification: whereas many who are younger, and have kept their communion with God, know more of God, and are able to speak more sweetly of his goodness, than they. And you who thus know God in your youth, bless him that he has brought you to this light, and make much of it; for as Christ said to Nathanael, John i. 50, "Because I said unto thee, I saw thee under the fig tree, believest thou? thou shalt see greater things than these;" so do you bless God for what you do know, and God will reveal more.

Obs. 9. Those who "follow on to know the Lord," shall know more of him. "The diligent hand maketh rich." It matters not though thy parts be weak, thy abilities mean, thy failings many, if Christ be thy Teacher it matters not, thy weaknesses shall not hinder his instructions; Christ teaches the weak as well as the strong, nay, accounts it his glory to teach such; nay, the Father himself is not ashamed to instruct them. Christ gives thanks to his Father, that he has revealed these things to babes and sucklings. Christ is a meek, gentle, lowly Teacher, very mild and loving, he will neither upbraid his followers with their weakness, nor discourage them in their dulness. Christ speaks to poor, weak, burdened sinners; "Come unto me, all ye that are weary and heavy laden;" who then will be discouraged? No, to thy soul he will give wisdom liberally, and infuse into thee the principles of saving knowledge. Col. i. 10, "That ye might walk worthy of the Lord unto all pleasing, being fruitful in every good work, and increasing in the knowledge of God." Great are the treasures of knowledge which a diligent Christian may obtain. "Continue," or draw out, "thy lovingkindness unto them that know thee," Psal. xxxvi. 10. Thou hast some glimmering knowledge of God, some spark of Divine light; bless God for it, and follow on perseveringly to know the Lord, and then thou shalt know more. It is a heavy curse that is denounced on those women in Timothy, that are "ever learning, and never able to come to the knowledge of the truth," 2 Tim. iii. 7.

But many a poor soul may here object, If this be so, I fear it is my condition, that the means aggravate the sins that I commit, and leave me inexcusable.

To answer thee, If thou art not one who follows divers lusts, and make them thy practice, thou art not among those who are "ever learning, but never able to come to the knowledge of the truth." If thou followest on to know God, God will follow thee on with mercy.

Obs. 10. One mercy makes way for another; a less prepares for a greater. God beholds all things at once with one view of his providential eye, and it is his happiness so to do; but the saints cannot do this, they must know a little now, and more at another time. And do not our times make good this text? The Lord will grant one deliverance now, and another reviving the next day, and all to usher in a greater. The Lord first smote us, and within two days did he revive us, and the third day we lived in his sight; and since that deliverance we have followed on to know the Lord, and God has revealed himself more in his power, wisdom, and faithfulness; and, if it be not our fault, we may know more of his workings. Oh that we had hearts to follow on the Lord in repenting, believing, and turning to him! he would follow us with mercies, and all the good that we can wish for, one after another. God makes wicked men to know more wrath, and the drops of his anger here are but the beginning of the deluge of miseries which are their portion; they sink, and sink, and their sinking must be to all eternity. Oh the difference which there is between God's dealing with the saints and with the wicked! though the saints may be under a cloud for the present, yet they shall know the Lord, the sun will appear again; the Lord will follow on his work, though we neglect ours, and glorious shall be the issue. Were it not a glorious thing, if a man had lived from the beginning to this day, and might live to the end of the world, to see what God did in former times, what God doth now, and what he will do to the end of the world for his poor churches? The saints shall live to all eternity to see these glorious things. God did glorious things in the first six thousand years, and surely the next six thousand shall be still more glorious, but in eternity God will do most of all: then the saints of God, those which "follow on to know the Lord," shall be put into the real possession of all those glorious things which God has been doing from all eternity.

"His going forth is prepared as the morning." Jerome conceived these words to be meant of Christ; he shall come as the morning, being called the "Sun of righteousness," and "the Morning-star;" and he conceives that it may have reference to the title of the 22nd Psalm, "A Psalm of David, to the chief Musician upon Aijeleth Shahar;" that is, the morning hind; to wit, Christ, who was sent forth as the morning hind, and hunted in his infancy and in his life, as the hind is pursued by the hounds.

But if we take the words simply as they lie before us, they appear an expression of Israel's confidence in God after a night of trouble. The word נכון "prepared," signifies also decreed, it is decreed upon as the morning and the evening, as the day follows the night by a decree. Children, when they see the sun going down, will often cry, because they think he will never rise again; so the wicked in their straits cry out, We are undone, this darkness will never be over: yea, and such is the baseness of our unbelieving hearts, we think when the clouds of sorrow begin to arise, and blackness to cover the sun of our prosperity, mercy will never break through, light will no more appear. But more particularly,

Obs. 11. Times of afflictions are night times. This is implied here: we may have a long time of sorrow and misery, a dark tempest may overtake us, yet know, that a morning will come. They are called night times for three reasons.

1. Because of their uncomfortableness. Darkness is very terrible. Drexelius tells us of a young man, very fearful of darkness, who, on God striking him with a dangerous sickness, insomuch that he could not sleep, tumbling up and down in his bed, uttered these words, If this darkness be so terrible, what is eternal darkness! and this proved the means of his conversion. Well, therefore, may affliction times be called night times, times of darkness.

2. They are times that often put an end both to public and private service. The night is the time in which the brute creatures, which in the day time keep close, come forth for their prey. Therefore the apostle's exhortation is seasonable, Let us work while it is called to-day, before the night cometh, when no man can work.

3. Night times are times of danger. Many of our

brethren can testify to this in these times. When is the time that wicked men prey upon the saints, and the wild beasts go out to devour, but in the dark? so, when do men meditate upon terror and create fears to themselves, but in the night of their afflictions and sorrows?

Obs. 12. The time of deliverance is the morning, the morning after the sad and dark night. As light is comfortable in the morning after a sad, dark, and stormy night; so is deliverance after trouble. The morning is very desirable, as appears, Psal. cxxx. 6, "My soul waiteth for the Lord more than they that watch for the morning: I say, more than they that watch for the morning." God's mercies after afflictions are very sweet, as the light approaching in the morning is to the labouring man going forth to his work. When God has work for men to do, he expects that they should go forth to it, and show themselves in it. As the sun when it rises begins to show itself in its brightness and glory, so ought every Christian to shine in the work and service of God after deliverance. In a sickness, or when some strait is upon thee, thou art hindered in God's service, and in thy work; well, then, when God bestows on thee the morning of a deliverance, go forth and manifest thy zeal for him, be not ashamed of his cause in the bright noon-day of mercy.

Obs. 13. The church has no afflictions unfollowed by a morning. The morning will come, either to churches in special, or persons in particular; and we hope this time is coming to us; therefore let dominion be given to the Lord in the morning; yea, and let dominion be given to the righteous in the morning, and this seems to be the meaning of Rev. ii. 26, 28, "To him that overcometh, will I give the morning-star." There may be great contentions, grievous miseries, in this night of afflictions; but be encouraged, to him that overcometh will I give this morning-star of comfort and deliverance.

Obs. 14. It is God's presence which constitutes the saints' morning. As the stars may impart some light, and yet the brightness of all combined cannot form the light of day, but when the sun appears there is day forthwith; so God may make some comfort arise to a soul from secondary and inferior means, but it is he himself alone who, by the shining of his face, and the smiles of his countenance, causes morning.

Obs. 15. God's mercies to his people are prepared and decreed. They are set and determined, "Thy going forth is prepared as the morning:" the word I showed you in the original signifies decreed. Jer. xxxiii. 20, "Thus saith the Lord; If ye can break my covenant of the day, and my covenant of the night, and that there should not be day and night in their season; then may also my covenant be broken with David my servant." Here we have both the text and the note from it; as is the covenant of God's decree with day and night, morning and evening, called a covenant because it is sure and certain, so also is the covenant which God has made to Christ and to his church firm and sure; and it is a ground of strong consolation to the saints to consider, that mercies which they want are set and decreed mercies, and therefore they may wait for them with patience.

Obs. 16. The saints in the night of their affliction can comfort themselves in this, that the morning is coming. It is night yet, but the morning will come, it is approaching: the assurance that the morning is dawning upholds the saints' spirits in the night of their sorrows. The tempest-tossed mariner in the gloom of night, the weary traveller in his dark and lonesome journey, comfort themselves with this, that the morning light is coming. It is far better to be in darkness, and expect the dawn, than to be in the light, and to know or fear that darkness is coming, and light will never return more.

Obs. 17. The saints' night is darkest a little before their deliverance; as a little before the dawning of the day the darkness is most dense and terrible. So it was in Egypt a little before Israel's deliverance, and their return out of captivity. And this should mightily encourage us, in these times, not to be disheartened though our miseries should increase, for the darker and the bigger the cloud is, it will the sooner break; therefore wait with patience.

Obs. 18. God's mode of deliverance is gradual. As the day breaks by degrees, so the saints shine gradually in their lives, answerable to the light which God imparts. We would have instantaneous deliverance; light, and perfect noon-day forthwith; but this is not God's mode of dealing with his people. A child knows not that it is day till it be very light indeed; but the wise can discern the first streaks in the horizon. Oh that we were so wise to discern God's dealings in the workings of providence towards us!

"And he shall come unto us as the rain." God so glories in this part of his creation, that he wonders when men do not fear him who is the giver of rain: "Neither say they in their heart, Let us fear the Lord our God, that giveth rain," Jer. v. 24; there is so much of my glory in this very one creature, that men's hearts must be very hard that will not praise me for it. And God is elsewhere styled, "the Father of rain." The mention of it here refers to that country in which the prophet spake; to Canaan, where they had rain, not so frequently as we have, but twice a year especially, viz. at seed-time, to soften the ground, and a little before harvest, to fill up the corn in the ear. The apostle James seems to allude to this, chap. v. 7, "The husbandman waiteth for the precious fruit of the earth, and hath long patience for it, until he receive the early and latter rain:" so should we, for God's time of delivering his people, his interpositions shall be as seasonable as the former and latter rain. The observations from these words are,

Obs. 19. What the rain is to the corn, God's blessing is to his people. We depend as much upon God for blessing and mercy, as the seed upon the rain for growth and increase; without the rain the corn will be but as "the parched places in the wilderness," which is the curse branded upon the wicked, Jer. xvii. 5, 6. Hence we may see what poor creatures we are, depending upon such a thing as the rain is in itself, and learn from that to consider how entirely we depend on the infinite God for all the blessings we enjoy.

Obs. 20. The church should increase under the rain of God's blessing. As the earth is not unthankful for the rain, but sends forth corn, grass, and flowers; so should we always, after the receiving of mercies, return unto God in duties. We would think it strange if the earth, after all the cost man has bestowed upon it, and after the sweet and seasonable showers of rain, should be barren and fruitless. O man, condemn thyself: the word is compared to rain; and how many times have the sweet showers and droppings of the word lighted upon thee, and yet thou hast remained barren and unfruitful! Deut. xxxii. 2.

Obs. 21. God's mercies to his people are both seasonable and suitable: "as the latter and former rain unto the earth." The Lord comes to wicked men in a way of general providence; but to the saints as rain in seed-time and harvest, with much fulness. How should this teach us our duty to wait with patience upon God, as the husbandman for the appointed weeks of harvest! James v. 7. If mercies always came when we would have them, they would prove judgments to us; that which in itself is a mercy, coming untimely, proves an affliction; God sent his people Israel a king, but he proved a heavy judgment to them. It is God's mercy unto you to defer his gifts till the full time. We exclaim, Our troubles are great, and continue long; we had thought to have seen a period to these times, our wars at an end, and peace settled in our kingdom; and now we see, if they had indeed ended when we desired, what a misfortune it would have been to us. How many that observe God's dealings can say, that if such a mercy had come when they wished for it, it had ruined them! therefore God's time is the best time. Hence we find that the saints have often blessed God when he has crossed them in their desires, and has denied them the thing which they so importunately asked. The Lord has sent us the former rain seasonably, at the beginning of the summer, to prepare the earth for fruit; but now there are scorching heats in the kingdom, heats of displeasure in the country, in the city, nay, almost in every family. Let us then now with patience wait, and the latter rain in its season will assuredly come.

Is God so seasonable in his mercies towards us? Let us be seasonable and suitable in our duty; let us bring forth fruit unto God in due season, as the godly man in the 1st Psalm is said to do; for in this consists the excellency of service. Therefore it is no other but a temptation of Satan, that, when men are called to pursue their necessary avocations, then stirs them up to prayer or hearing: these are not the motions of the Spirit, for they are seasonable; for God never puts the soul upon extremes, the performing of two contrary duties at one and the same time. It is an excellent sign of a gracious heart, to account a season for service, a mercy; and the lack of opportunity, a misery. Certainly it is a great judgment of God upon a man, to be unserviceable in a season of service. Jude, ver. 12, describing the corruptions of the gospel by life and doctrine, in his time, saith, they were "trees whose fruit withereth, without fruit, twice dead, plucked up by the roots;" trees corrupt even in the time of autumn, when their fruit should come in abundantly. Thus it is with many men, when God expects the most fruit from them, they show themselves most corrupt and vile. These mightily provoke God. And how many such have we amongst us at this day, who, when God calls them to service, manifest the rottenness which is in their spirits! Many when they are in a poor condition think, Oh had I such a man's estate, what a deal of good would I do with it! had I such parts and abilities as some have, and as much time, and as many opportunities afforded me, how would I lay them out for God! O foolish hearts, who, when they can do nothing, would do most, and when they may do most, do nothing at all.

Obs. 22. God's mercies to his people are varied according to their necessities. "The latter and the former rain." Toward the seed-time they wanted rain, and God sends it them. Now, as God may call us to a variety of services, according to the variety of mercies, let not us content ourselves in that we have done something, employed our heads, or hands, or purses; but willingly devote every power and adopt every expedient to subserve his cause. God has employed thee this day in one service, he has another for thee to do the next; be willing and ready to be set on work, and bless God that he deigns to employ thee in his service.

Obs. 23. When God has begun in mercy with his people, he will go on. If God should give only the former rain, the seed would not fructify and increase without the latter rain: faith will believe that God will not lose the glory of former mercies, for want of succeeding ones: faith believes that God will never begin a work, and leave it incomplete. Let not us then begin to obey God, and then leave off and lose all that we have done; let us consider that the vows of God are upon us, the many prayers we have put up, and let us not now lose the return of them. How many in the days of their youth followed on to know God, and found the sweetness of the word to be as the former and the latter rain unto them! Do not now lose all which you got in your youth, by denying him service in your age.

Obs. 24. God's mercies to his people procure much good. They are not empty shells, there is in them all they profess to contain, all God promises to give.

Obs. 25. The deliverances of God's people come from heaven. They spring not out of the earth; if ever God's people are delivered, there must be a Divine, Almighty power put forth, else it will never be a deliverance in mercy.

Obs. 26. God's people's deliverances cannot be hindered. Why? Because they come from above. They are as the light of the sun, and as the rain that comes upon the earth: who can hinder the sun from shining, the rain from falling? who can interrupt night and day? so, who can hinder the rain of mercy from falling on a people prepared for it?

Obs. 27. We should make a spiritual use of God's works in his creatures. We see after the coldest winter there comes a summer, after a drought great rain: let not us, in the times of cold and dark afflictions sent by God, conclude that mercy is quite gone, that God has shut up his loving-kindness in forgetfulness; no, but let us rest assured that there will be a return of mercy which shall revive us.

Ver. 4. *O Ephraim, what shall I do unto thee? O Judah, what shall I do unto thee? for your goodness is as a morning cloud, and as the early dew it goeth away.*

Luther interprets these words as a further expression of mercy to this people Israel, and not in the light of a reproof; as if the Lord had said to them, O Israel, my people, I have been very good and gracious to you in the land of Egypt, delivered you from the tyranny and oppression you were under there, and I have been with you in the wilderness, and I have brought you into the land of Canaan; but what are these? all temporal mercies; I have greater than these to bestow upon you in gospel times. But to this interpretation this objection will arise:

What shall we understand by the next words, "your goodness is as a morning cloud?" how can this be said? Luther to this answers thus, "Your goodness;" that is, the goodness of God, which is yours by covenant, and by purchase procured for you; this mercy of God shall refresh your parched souls, as the morning cloud does the earth after a long drought.

But the words "goeth away," and their goodness being but "as a morning cloud," taken together, the sense leads us to interpret it as a breaking off from the discourse about the promise of mercy, to a convincing of Ephraim and Judah of formality in their attempts at reformation; they all passed off, as the morning cloud which vanishes away, and as the early dew that comes to nothing.

Jerome thinks that it is God's mercies towards them which thus pass away; he would not leave them quite without hope, they should have some mercy, but it should not abide nor stay with them. But the genuine sense of the words I conceive to be, an upbraiding of the formality that generally prevailed in their pursuit of reformation; therefore, "O Ephraim, what shall I do unto thee?" As if the Lord should say, You put me to a stand, you even nonplus me in this thing; what, therefore, shall I do unto thee?

Here in general we may observe the change of the prophet's voice: in the beginning of the chapter it is all mercy, and their repentance sweetly join in with the mercy promised them; but now he begins to upbraid them for their hypocrisy, incorrigibleness, and inconstancy in the ways of God: a very good pattern for ministers who have to deal with varieties of people.

" O Ephraim, what shall I do unto thee? O Judah, what shall I do unto thee?" To open these words more particularly: the expression "what shall I do unto thee?" implies either compassion or expostulation.

I. Compassion; as if he should say, O Ephraim, it is in my heart to do thee good, but nothing will work upon thee, therefore, "O Ephraim, what shall I do unto thee?" Like that expression in Isa. v. 4, "What could have been done more to my vineyard, that I have not done in it?" were there any other further course to be taken, any thing else to do, I would do it? Now from this sense of God's compassionating them, we may,

Obs. 1. That God grieves not willingly the children of men; he is even forced to it: at the very time they are grieved by afflictions, God is troubled for their miseries. Can any tell me, men or angels, nay, I appeal to yourselves, can you tell me what I should do more to you than I have done? If you can, I would do it. God expostulates with them; he comes not suddenly upon them, punishment is the last measure he adopts with his people.

And so it should be with us to those under us, as our children or servants; all means of prevailing must be tried before correction; exhort, advise, reprove, and pray for them: have you first taken this course? else you can have little comfort in correcting them. This is God's way, though you perhaps see it not. He here meets an objection which repining Israel might seem to make: We are believers, to us the promises belong; why might not the Lord bring mercy to us without using such means as smiting, wounding, killing, and parching? No, saith God, I could not otherwise bring about mine own ends. Oh, therefore, let us check such thoughts. God brings us low by afflictions; he could do it by mercies, but then the end which he aims at would not be so fully accomplished.

Obs. 2. We should not think much to lose our pains with others. God has taken pains and been at cost with this people, and he has lost all; and God seems here to mourn over it: I have used this admonition, and that counsel, yet still you continue hypocritical; "O what shall I do unto thee?" yet God does not leave them or grow weary of his pains, he persists still in the means likely to do them good. In this should the saints imitate God: if this course prevail not, try a second; if it succeed not, adopt a third, perhaps that may, and success will amply repay all the pains. And thus much for the words in the sense of compassion: but now,

II. Expostulation, to humble them, or to convince them of their sin. Hence,

Obs. 3. It is a special means to humble men, to lead them to consider what measures have been adopted for their good. Would we be seriously affected with sin, and humbled for sin? then let us go alone and call our souls to account, whether means have not been used sufficient to do us good: consider what means they have been, judgments, national, domestic, and personal; mercies, reproofs out of the word, admonitions from friends, terrors and checks of conscience: when they have thus passed in review before you, charge conscience to speak to thee the truth, and when it doth, give it leave to upbraid thee thus; What! so unprofitable, so stout and stubborn, so froward and impatient, so unthankful and so unbelieving, notwithstanding all this? This would be a means singularly calculated to show the soul its real condition. But, alas! most men put off and shun such a course as this; the devil knows its efficacy, and he strives mightily to lead the soul off from it to such excuses as these, Had I the means others have, I should be more fruitful: I was reproved, but it was done too openly; had it been in private and with more love, by such a one and in such a place, it would have done more good. Infinite are the false pretences of an ungodly heart, and the cunning devices of Satan's subtlety in the soul; but when the Lord comes truly to humble the soul, that soul will charge itself home throughly for its sins, in all their circumstances and all their aggravations.

Obs. 4. Such is the perverseness of men's hearts, that God many times seems to be in a strait what to do with them. "What shall I do unto thee?" God was here even at a stand, he was fain to consult with himself about them. See in other scriptures how God expresses this; Exod. xxxiii. 5, "Therefore now put off thy ornaments from thee, that I may know what to do unto thee:" and Deut. xxxii. 5, "They have corrupted themselves, their spot is not the spot of his children: they are a perverse and a crooked generation." The words in the original refer to the manner of דור עקש ופתלתל wrestlers, who wave up and down, that if the one thinks to have the other here, he is winded the other way: so this people eluded God's dealings. Therefore, Acts ii. 40, we are commanded to "save ourselves from this untoward generation," σκολιᾶς, crooked or perverse, so that none can do them good. God's ministers are often put to a stand with such, like those in Christ's time, whom neither John nor Christ himself could please; when John came, they exclaimed against his rigour and harshness; and when Christ came, mild and gentle, of him they said, he was "a wine-bibber, and a friend of publicans and sinners."

But it may be objected, God knew not what to do; how is this? could not God have put forth his almighty power and turned their hearts, and that immediately? how then is it said, God knew not what to do?

To this I answer, that God was not bound to do this, for God had used all means to prevail with Ephraim and Judah, which the most loving and compassionate friend could have employed. Suppose a man were in such a condition, that, for his cure, all the doctors of physic in the country where he lived were gathered together, and consulted, but their prescriptions availed nothing; would not this set forth in aggravated colours the danger of the disease, and the difficulty of the cure? All this is in God, and much more, and it is put forth for the good of souls; I have put forth more power, wisdom, love, and mercy than man can do. Now shall this be an aggravation in respect of the creature, and not of the Creator? All means to do you good have been put forth excepting my almighty power, and yet the work is not done.

Obs. 5. The condition of people is sad, when no means will do them good. Then that fearful judgment may be pronounced upon them, Jer. vi. 30, "Reprobate silver shall men call them, because the Lord hath rejected them." Ezek. xxiv. 13, "Because I have purged thee, and thou wast not purged, thou shalt not be purged from thy filthiness any more, till I have caused my fury to rest upon thee."

Obs. 6. It goes very near the heart of God, to see those that are nigh unto him perverse in their ways. What! for Judah to forsake me? It is sad to find crosses and untowardness in Ephraim; but to meet with them in Judah, where my ordinances are in a special manner, and they so near unto me, and I so tender of them! It is strange to behold of what knotty, crabbed spirits God's own people sometimes are! A piece of wood may be sound, yet full of knots and very tough. What goes nearer a man than to find crossness in his wife, his children, or friend? from a stranger it matters not so much. Even so God is more affected by the unkindness of his people than the wickednesses of the ungodly.

Obs. 7. It is not enough to worship God better than

others, if we be of perverse spirits. This was the sin of Judah, because they had the ordinances in a purer way, and worshipped God better than Ephraim, they thought they might continue in this their sin. Oh that this were not England's sin at this day! let us be humbled for it, that we may escape their judgment.

"Your goodness." The word חסדכם properly signifies piety and godliness, but in a more extended sense, kindness, mercy, and goodness. But why *your* goodness? Yours, because either of God's goodness toward them, or the goodness, the holiness, which was in them, 1. God's goodness towards them, which is sometimes by imputation called ours, as in Rom. xi. 31, "That through your mercy they also may obtain mercy;" by that mercy which God bestowed on you, you may encourage the Gentiles to come in. 2. Their goodness; either to their brethren, or their piety and holiness, both these were "as a morning cloud, and as the early dew that goeth away." If the first signification of them be taken, then the sense runs thus:

God's goodness to them was as the morning cloud; that is, they, by their sin, had driven away God's mercy and goodness from them, even as the wind carries the dust before it: God was apparently about to bestow mercies, and they, by their sins, put them all away from them. Bernard saith, that the wind of their unthankfulness drove away the floods, much more the dews, of mercy from them. Now God forbid that this should be our condition: the clouds of mercy are over us, and the dews of mercy are upon us; now should we, by our sins, drive these away from us, how woeful will be our case! Therefore let us not only pray to have the dews, but also the clouds to shower down rivers of mercy. Though I do not think this to be the principal scope of the words, yet it may afford us useful meditation; but the words seem properly to signify their own goodness, which may be taken for,

I. Mercy and compassion towards one another; because, in the 6th verse, God calls upon them so earnestly for mercy, notwithstanding all their shows and promises of reformation; these were all but hypocritical, like those in Jer. xxxiv. 15, 16, of whom God saith, "And ye were now turned, and had done right in my sight, in proclaiming liberty every man to his neighbour;" but they had polluted his name again, by causing those servants formerly set at liberty to return, and bringing them into subjection: so people who are for a time pitiful and very merciful, afterwards often grow cruel and hard-hearted.

Let us take heed of so evil a disposition. When together we sometimes can join in love and unity, pitying each other, and bearing with each other's infirmities, bearing Christian admonition patiently; but these good words and fair shows often vanish and come to nothing. Where are those refreshing showers of love and friendship which you were wont to water each other with in your Christian societies? In the room of these there now grow nothing amongst us but the lusts of pride, passions, and sad dissensions, which parch and dry up all those good seeds of love and gentleness.

I desire to press this the more, because the Scripture is pleased to make use of this expression of the dew to express the sweetness of a Christian spirit, Psal. cxxxiii. 1, 3, "Behold, how good and how pleasant it is for brethren to dwell together in unity!" How pleasant is it? It is "as the dew of Hermon, and as the dew that descended upon the mountain of Zion:" as that refreshed the grass, so this affection of mercy and love the saints. He compares it not to a dew that dried up presently, but to a dew which descended down; and "there the Lord commanded the blessing, even life for evermore." There. Where? Even in the communion of his saints. This is spoken particularly of church fellowship. Oh, then, take heed that your mercy and bounty in relieving your brethren and persecuted saints, be not as the dew "that goeth away." The Lord has not made his mercy, no, not his mercy in dewing the earth, "as a morning cloud" that vanishes away and comes to nothing. Oh let not our mercy and love be mere shows and proffers, devoid of truth and reality! they should truly come like showers upon those who have been parched with the burning rage and malice of the adversary. The Lord expects more from us now with regard to this duty than at other times; we must not only pity and give good words, saying, Alas, my brother; and alas, my sister, I would I could help you, the Lord pity and relieve you; you must not only do thus, but relieve them with your money and provisions. Is it not with too many of us as it was with those in James ii. 15, who say to a brother, "Depart in peace, be ye warmed and filled," but give them not wherewithal to do it? what good does this passing cloud do them? But perhaps you will say, that your sympathies have not been thus evanescent; you have bedewed the saints in their need, you have given something; but still it may have been but a poor pittance, and that out of your abundance: know, that this is not sufficient, your dew must be constant, and proceed on in degrees of mercy; yea, we should rejoice that God gives us an opportunity, and do what we do, not forcedly or repiningly, but with a willing mind. Thus much of the words in this signification of mercy.

II. General goodness and piety; and in this sense there is much of the mind of God in the words, they are as full of marrow and sweetness as can be desired. Now in that God should express godliness and piety by such a word as mercy,

Obs. 8. The necessity of this grace of love and brotherly kindness. Though by nature men are passionate and rugged, grace will mollify them; of covetous men it will make liberal and free-hearted, for grace is part of the Divine nature. Nothing is so communicative as God, the highest good; and according to the height of any creature is its communicativeness. As the sun, being sublime and excellent, is most communicative; so a gracious man: has he parts? they are not for himself, but for the church. Has he an estate? he distributes and communicates of it to the saints; and according as grace arises in the soul, will communicativeness arise. A true Christian is not close-handed.

Obs. 9. The excellency of this grace of mercy. When we wish to express the whole of any thing by a part, we do not select an inferior part, but some of its great characteristics; as by prayer many times is expressed the whole worship of God, "Whosoever shall call upon the name of the Lord shall be saved," Rom. x. 13.

"As a morning cloud, and as the early dew." In these words God charges this people with three things whereby their notorious hypocrisy was expressed.

1. Their vacuity and emptiness; their words were empty sounds, they were "clouds without water," as Jude expresses it, ver. 12. It is the high commendation of Christians to be full of God, of Christ, and full of grace and knowledge; of which Ephraim had a show, but it was but a show.

2. Their falseness and dissembling; they had a heart and a heart, that is, they were double-minded toward God, they dealt treacherously with him.

3. Their inconstancy and fickleness. As often the clouds, all black and lowering, portend rain, but in a short time are dispersed by the wind, and the sky becomes again perfectly clear; even thus it was in their goodness, though they made glorious shows in their reformation, yet were they all empty, false, and inconstant. Thus it was in the general in the reformation of the land, things were reformed but by halves, and in their particular turnings it was but as the morning

cloud; many times there were great appearances of reformation, but they were like the early dew which presently goeth away. The ten tribes and Judah made such beginnings in reformation, and setting up the worship of God, that if God were truly worshipped by any people in the world it would be by these; they would set God up high in their thoughts, high in their practices; and this was very burdensome to the Spirit of God; therefore he saith, "What shall I do unto thee, O Ephraim? What shall I do unto thee, O Judah?"

We find glorious shows of reformation come to nothing, as appears in many instances. 2 Kings ix., x., Jehu made great shows: when Joram asked him, "Is it peace, Jehu?" he answered, "What peace, so long as the whoredoms of thy mother Jezebel and her witchcrafts are so many?" And, in the 10th chapter, what a slaughter doth he make of the priests of Baal! Well, what was the result of all this? read but on in the chapter, ver. 29, 31, and it is said, "Howbeit from the sins of Jeroboam the son of Nebat, who made Israel to sin, Jehu departed not." What a cloud of hopes was there in Ahab's time! 1 Kings xviii. 39, all the people cried, "The Lord, he is the God; the Lord, he is the God;" upon the miracle which was wrought by Elijah's prayer, when the fire came down and consumed the sacrifice: but this all vanished in the people, and respecting Ahab himself the text saith, he "did sell himself to work wickedness in the sight of the Lord," and "did very abominably in following idols," so that "there was none like unto him," 1 Kings xxi. 25, 26. When the prophet comes to him after he had killed Nabal, and tells him of his sin, he falls down and humbles himself, insomuch that God himself takes notice of it, and, upon it, pronounces a transmission of his punishment, that he would not "bring the evil in his days, but in his son's days." God bids the prophet see how he humbled himself, and that not in a show, as if his heart were not touched and affected, but he did truly humble himself in his kind. But now, did no reformation follow upon this? No, none at all. It is very hard to bring great men to reform themselves; where have we such an example since Theodosius the emperor, who although guilty of rash effusion of blood, yet, coming on a sabbath to the place of public worship, would have received the sacrament: Ambrose, seeing him approaching, goes and meet him at the door, and thus addresses him, How dare those bloody hands of yours, which have shed so much innocent blood, lay hold of the body and blood of Christ? Which speech so startled him that he went away, and was humbled for his sin, and afterwards came and made his public confession, and then was admitted to communion. Whence we may see, that kings, yea, emperors, have been kept back from the sacrament. But did this humiliation of Ahab come to nothing? If we look but into the 22nd chapter, we shall find him of a proud, haughty spirit, resolved upon his own will, contrary to the will of God; he would go up to Ramoth-gilead, and when Jehoshaphat asked him, "Is there not here a prophet of the Lord besides, that we might inquire of him?" he said, "There is yet one man; but I hate him;" and this was after his humiliation. And is it not thus with us? Many times, when judgments are upon us, how penitent and humbled are we! but if the rod be removed we grow proud and stubborn forthwith. So in Judah, how did that young king Joash begin! 2 Chron. xxiv. 4, he "was minded to repair the house of the Lord," and gave commandment to the priests and the Levites to gather money for the purpose with haste, and, although a very young prince, was so zealous, that he blamed the high priest for his inactivity; and, ver. 10, it is said, "all the princes and all the people rejoiced, and brought in, and cast into the chest." What did this produce? surely some glorious effect. Mark now the 17th verse: "After the death of Jehoiada came the princes of Judah, and made obeisance to the king." And what then? "Then the king hearkened unto them;" they then began to get him on their side, very likely by sinful compliances and flattering speeches, for the text saith, that he "hearkened unto them. And they left the house of the Lord God of their fathers, and served groves and idols;" they forsook their religion, and then "wrath came upon them:" while they kept the truth, it preserved them; but turning from the rule, what outrages do they commit, and what did they suffer! Ver. 21, 22, they conspire against Zechariah and stone him; the blood of a prophet's son is now nothing to them, and the king forgets the faithful services of Jehoiada the father, and consents to his death: oh to what a height of sin is this young zealous prince come! How many sad examples have we in these our days like this of Joash! how many are there who in their youth promised well, but the fair hopes prove to be but "as a morning cloud," their timely beginnings end in apostacy! Another example we have in Amaziah, 2 Chron. xxv. 2. Amaziah, in the 6th verse, had hired a hundred thousand of Israel to go with him to the war, and for their hire had given them a hundred talents of silver. But there came a man of God to him, saying, that he must not use them. "And Amaziah said to the man of God, But what shall we do for the hundred talents which I have given to the army of Israel? And the man of God answered, The Lord is able to give thee much more than this." He had no security for it, but only God's word, and that from the mouth of a man; what then? Amaziah obeyed presently, and separated the allies out of Israel; but yet, ver. 14, "it came to pass, after that Amaziah was come from the slaughter of the Edomites, that he brought the gods of the children of Seir, and set them up to be his gods, and bowed down himself before them, and burnt incense unto them." Thereupon, ver. 15, God sends him another prophet; and now see how the spirit of the man is changed. In the former verses the man of God comes to him and crosses his design, and yet he hearkens unto him, and obeys the command of God in that which entailed present and certain loss; but here, when the prophet reasons with as much mildness and love as possible, "Why hast thou sought after the gods of the people, which could not deliver their own people out of thine hand?" they could not rescue or save their people from thee, and wilt thou serve them? yet in the 16th verse mark the answer: "The king said unto him, Art thou made of the king's counsel? forbear; why shouldest thou be smitten?" Dost thou know what is our design in this? The prophet forbears, but what follows? "I know that God hath determined to destroy thee, because thou hast done this, and hast not hearkened unto my counsel." The truth is, when we see men unruly, stubborn, and wilfully rejecting counsel, especially after some good workings and stirrings, it is a fearful sign that God purposes to destroy them. As that wicked king at one time could call the prophet his father, yet afterward be enraged against him; so some may be friends to the saints at one time, and at another their bitter enemies.

And as the Scripture is full of such examples, so also are ecclesiastical histories. When Domitian, a most cruel persecutor of the Christians, came to the crown, he could not endure blood to be shed, no, not even in sacrifices. Of Nero also it is reported, that for five years he was so pitiful and full of mercy, that when they came to him to sign the sentence for the execution of a malefactor, he exclaimed, Oh that I had never learned to write! And yet where had the commonwealth of Rome, or the church of God, a more desperate enemy or cruel persecutor? God grant this may never be our case. What had we at the first, in the beginning of the par-

Quam vellem literas non didicisse.

liament, how did they show themselves, and what great things did they perform! stood against arbitrary government, impeached great ones, executed justice on some peers! What a mighty spirit was raised in the countries to second and stand by the parliament! Now where is the man that ever thought such a party of lords and commons would be found to join with a company of papists, atheists, malignants, and Irish rebels, against the cause of God and the gospel, and every thing that is truly good? Oh most horrid apostacy, that this morning cloud, which in the beginning shone so gloriously, should thus vanish and come to nothing! And private men, though perhaps not so bad as some in public stations, yet how cold and flat-spirited are they! private interest and their own selfish ends ruling in them more than the prosperity of the public; nay, so we can gain our own ends, though with loss to the public, we care not. Oh what shall God do with us, who are such an untoward people? Change but the name, and this scripture is ours; O England, "what shall I do unto thee?"

Mutato nomine.

Your spirits for reformation are down, you care not for a deliverance, but are willing to crouch under your burdens; but let me tell you, should these beginnings of reformation prove to be as the "morning cloud and early dew," we will be the most miserable people in the world, and procure to ourselves and posterity the greatest curse that ever befell a nation; yea, the generations that are yet unborn may, if we neglect this great opportunity, curse our times. Therefore, be encouraged to venture in this work, and still own the cause, for God will own it; and never leave it, that so the work may be finished, and we may say with the saints, "Lo, this is our God; we have waited for him," and he hath heard us. We should consider that it is a mercy the Lord has made use of such false-spirited men to benefit his people; and seeing the Lord is gone so far in the work, let us entreat him that he would follow it on, and not only bedew us, but even wet us to the root. There is a very remarkable promise in chap. xiv. 5 of this prophecy, "I will be as the dew unto Israel: he shall grow as the lily:" they shall have the dew, and be like the lily: but the lily is a poor, weak, fading thing; but, saith God, he shall "cast forth his roots as Lebanon," my mercy shall be perfected towards them. The Lord grant this promise may be made good to us. And thus much of their reformation in the general, as it concerned the public state and church.

Now touching the particular reformation of themselves, and their hypocrisy in it: the observation from thence is,

Obs. 10. For any to make good beginnings, and let them fall again, is grievous to God, and dangerous to themselves. Psal. lxxviii. 36, 37, "Nevertheless they did flatter him with their mouth, and they lied unto him with their tongues. For their heart was not right with him, neither were they stedfast in his covenant." What then? Ver. 58, 59, "They provoked him to anger with their high places, and moved him to jealousy with their graven images." God then "greatly abhorred Israel;" they were as "a deceitful bow," hypocritical in all their ways, which the Spirit of God cannot endure, for these reasons:

1. The Spirit of God is a holy Spirit; but this is a slight, fickle, vain, and unsound spirit.

2. The Spirit of God is unchangeable, and constant in all its motions; but this spirit is altogether changeable. It is said of God, that there is no shadow of change in him; and in such a heart as this is there is no shadow of constancy.

3. Such men as these stifle the very conceptions of the Spirit of God in them. It is accounted murder in a woman to stifle the conception in her womb, or in any way to hinder it; now if this be such a vile thing, is it not much more to stifle the conception and first breathings of the Spirit in the soul? Oh take heed of this!

4. There can be no trust reposed in such men as these; they are fit for no employment, neither God nor man can confide in them, or use them for any service, yea, we ourselves cannot endure to have to deal with such, they are so fickle and wavering.

5. They manifest by this, that there is no fear of God before their eyes; for were the fear of the great God in them, it would overawe them so that they durst not act thus.

6. This is a great pollution of the name of God. Jer. xxxiv. 16, when they had professed to set their servants free, they called them to servitude again, and in this, God saith, they polluted his great name.

7. This is an argument that the things of God and matters of religion are looked upon by you as things indifferent; when thou hast a mind to them thou canst use them, or thou canst let them alone; and this greatly dishonours the Spirit of God.

8. This shows that such people never, even at the first, had any sound principles in them; far from the life of Christ, which is said to be a stedfast life, and the life of every saint should be like unto his, "their heart was not right with him, neither were they stedfast in his covenant."

Now, as it is grievous to God and to his Spirit, so it is very dangerous to ourselves. For,

1. We lose many an opportunity, many a soul-stirring, which at our first awaking we have had. When the soul is first convinced, oh the many stirrings and good motions which are in it! any thing would then take impression upon the heart; but when we go back, a callous insensibility begins to overspread the heart.

2. The inconstant can never grow to any eminency of grace and godliness, even though there be truth at the bottom. It is said of Reuben, Gen. xlix. 4, "Unstable as water, thou shalt not excel." Men that do but very little, yet that still progress in godliness, though their parts be weak, and their performances mean and imperfect, may attain to something; but those who at the first do a great deal, run very fast in their youth, and afterward grow cold again, are very bad: the cooling after heating is very dangerous, as to the body, so more to the soul.

3. This hardens the heart very much. When the spirit is cooled after a heating, it is like water which, being hot and cold again, is more cold than it was before; or like iron heated and quenched, is harder than before.

4. This aggravates all other sinning. What! wilt thou sin thus, after God has appeared thus?

5. This spoils the acceptableness of all our other services, be they never so specious. As a man that has a child lunatic, in his fits and moods he is very senseless and sottish, but in his *lucida intervalla* he comes to himself and speaks sensibly and well; now if a man should see him at this time he would think he ailed nothing: so there are many who seem to be eminent Christians for the present, but let a temptation present itself, or lust within stir, and they are overcome.

6. There is nothing will more damp the heart when it comes before God in duty. God may say to thee, O soul, how darest thou come before me in such a duty as this, when thou knowest thou art guilty of breach of promise, and falsifying covenant with me? This will be an eating corrosive on thy spirit. God may say to thee, How canst thou expect that I should be constant in my mercies toward thee, when thou art so inconstant in thy duty to me? This inconstancy toward God, brings wavering in faith, and unsettledness in our confidence God-ward; the one makes way for the other; inconstancy in duty, and wavering in believing.

How should this stir us up to look to our own hearts,

seeing they are so fickle and deceitful! Let us watch over and daily suspect them. John ii. 23, 24, it is said of the people, that many believed in Christ, because of the miracles which he wrought; yet Christ would not commit himself unto them. So Deut. v. 29, there is a people that made large promises to God, that they would walk in all the statutes and ordinances of their God. Now, saith God, this people say well, they are good words, but "Oh that there were such an heart in them!" God regards no work you do, except he find it rooted in you. "If ye continue in my word, then are ye my disciples indeed," John viii. 31: no true disciple of Christ without abiding in Christ. "All flesh is grass," Isa. xl. 6; that is, whatsoever is done by fleshly principles, every duty, though never so fair in outward appearance, if it come from a principle of flesh, is but as the grass; and as the grass withereth and its flower fadeth, so will these specious outside duties vanish away. Therefore look to your heart, and above all keepings, keep it very diligently; for if the root be sound, the branches will be so too, and the fruit thereof good and profitable.

Obs. 11. It is a very dangerous thing to let beginnings die. Therefore, would you be preserved from such an evil as this, of fickleness and inconstancy, take my counsel in these particulars.

1. Rest not in sudden flashes and stirrings of spirit. Perhaps at a sermon some truth or other that nearly concerns thee, is pressed home upon thy conscience, and it begins to stir the heart and warm the affections; now, do not think the work is now over, or that the hazard of miscarrying to all eternity is passed; no, thou must rise higher and go further than this, or else thou art undone for ever. This is that rock upon which many poor souls split to their everlasting destruction, therefore look to your hearts in time.

2. Labour to get your hearts off from all earthly engagements. That man can never stand constant toward God who is entangled with the snares and cares of this world. He whose heart is constantly fixed upon God, though he does but little in the way of duty, in comparison of many a mere professor, yet shall hold out, when the most glorious hypocrite in the world shall fall to the ground.

3. Take heed of secret sins. They will undo thee if loved and maintained: one moth may spoil the garment; one leak drown the ship; a penknife stab and kill a man as well as a sword; so one sin may damn the soul: nay, there is more danger of a secret sin causing the miscarrying of the soul, than open profaneness, because not so obvious to the reproofs of the word; therefore take heed that secret sinnings eat not out good beginnings.

4. Often examine how things stand with your hearts. Say, O my soul, how is it with thee? how stand matters between God and thee? Come, my soul, there was a time that there was such and such good motions in thee, what is now become of them? at the first thou wert very forward and active for God, such a chamber, such a closet, can witness the intercourse God and thou hadst; thou didst then walk close with God and his fear was in thee. This, if observed, would be a special help to keep the heart upright: but I fear many a minister may say of his people, as Paul did to the Galatians, Where is now the blessedness which you spake of? Gal. iv. 15.

5. Never trust your hearts after spiritual comforts and revivings. When in any ordinances thou hast met with God's presence, and he has shone upon thee in love, and thou hast got a smile from Jesus Christ, have a care of your hearts, and expect and prepare for temptations. Many, when they have within good desires and hopeful beginnings, think that the work is past and the danger is over; and then comes a temptation of Satan, and encounters with them, and they are basely foiled, and lose their peace. Great consolations usually precede great temptations. In Matt. iii. 17, God testifies that Jesus Christ is his beloved Son, "This is my beloved Son, in whom I am well pleased;" and in the very next chapter tells us how he was led "into the wilderness to be tempted of the devil." Often, too, after the greatest mercies follow the greatest miseries: see how well Christ knows this; John xii. 12, he comes riding in pomp to Jerusalem, and the people magnified him, crying out, "Hosanna to the Son of David;" yet, ver. 27, he cries out, "Father, save me from this hour."

6. After good desires and motions of the Spirit humble yourselves. Make yourselves base and vile in your own eyes, that so you may grow downward in the root: it is very dangerous when beginnings run upwards presently, but when they show us our sins and unworthiness then they work kindly. If there be no moisture at the root of the tree, though there be never so many blossoms, they will die, vanish, and come to nothing; so if your joys and secret raptures of soul are not moistened in the tears of sorrow and humiliation, they will blow off and be shaken down by the next temptation; but when the inward workings of joy in the heart operate as well to humiliation as consolation, when they work both ways, then will not your goodness be as the early dew that goeth away, and as the morning cloud which soon vanisheth. In Psal. cx. 3, it is prophesied that in the times of the gospel Christ's people shall be willing in the day of his power; Christ's power shall be put forth upon his people to subdue their wills to the will of God; so that if we find this effect of Christ's power in us, then may we be sure that our goodness shall not be evanescent.

7. Rest not in stirrings and beginnings, except you find that they tend to unite you to Christ. As soon as your hearts begin to work, you should stop a little and ask yourselves what of Jesus Christ is there in these motions; Have I more of his righteousness, wisdom, and love than I had before? Only such stirrings of heart as bring Christ into the soul will hold and stand fast. That is very observable which we read concerning the manna, Exod. xvi. 14, that the dew which was upon the ground passed away, but the manna abode still: so the good affections and desires which are in many are even like the dew, which, as soon as the sun is up, is gone presently: now if you would not have the efficacy of them gone, try what manna there is left behind, what of Christ is strengthened. Is your faith propped, your love inflamed, your humility increased? then it is something. The Israelites could not feed on the dew, but the manna was their nourishment. So, how is it with you when the fervour of your spirits has abated? can you then feed upon Christ, this spiritual manna? Look what word of promise then takes up its abode in your hearts, and how your hearts are affected with it: such as find the promise remaining when the dew is gone, and that these promises are as sweet now as they were when first the affections were excited, such a soul will hold out, and his righteousness shall not be as the morning cloud or early dew that passeth away.

Ver. 5. *Therefore have I hewed them by the prophets; I have slain them by the words of my mouth: and thy judgments are as the light that goeth forth.*

"Therefore have I hewed them by the prophets." We would think there were little connexion in these words, yet there is a very fit one. "Therefore," that is, because they are so fickle and inconstant, *therefore* have I caused my prophets to deal sharply with them to cut them to the heart. I would not have dealt thus with them, but that I have no other means left, seeing they are so vain, so slight in their spirits; and this resource I try, that, if possible, they might be brought to see with what a God they have to deal. The apostle, in Titus i. 13, gives command to "rebuke them sharply, that they may be sound in the faith;" sharply, that is, cuttingly, rebuke them cuttingly. My prophets have been as an axe, as an axe that cuts hard, knotty wood, or as the instruments of carvers in stone, which cut hard, rough things. "I have slain them by the words of my mouth." The Sept. refer these words to the prophets, and render them, *Διὰ τοῦτο ἀπεθέρισα τοὺς προφήτας ὑμῶν· ἀπέκτεινα αὐτοὺς ἐν ῥήματι στόματός μου·* Therefore have I hewed your prophets; I have slain them by the word of my mouth. And Jerome saith, they relate to the time of Elijah, 1 Kings xviii. 40, who slew many of Baal's prophets; and to Jehu's time, who did the same, 2 Kings x. 25. Thus they interpret it; and in this you have an objection of the people answered, who might plead thus: True, we have been led aside and have not worshipped God as we should do, but it is our priests and our prophets who have seduced us; we did but as we were taught, and if we have gone astray, our prophets and our priests have misled us. Nay, saith God, you cannot plead so, for you have seen my hand out against the prophets sufficiently, I have cut them off. Though I conceive not this to be the meaning of these words, yet from this sense this useful observation may be drawn:

Obs. 1. When God comes against false prophets, he looks especially that people should not do as they have been taught by them. In Ezek. xiii. 9, a woeful judgment is denounced against the false prophets, for prophesying peace when God's purposes were set against Jerusalem for destruction. Their judgment was, that they should not come into the assemblies of his people; and, my hand shall be against them; and mark, "ye shall know that I am the Lord." They shall then know more particularly that I am the Lord God, when my hand is thus out against them. It is a powerful means to convince a people, when they see the hand of God out against their false teachers; and if so, how should the people of England be convinced of the evil of that way they so admire and extol, when the hand of God is so heavy upon its superstitious time-servers and maintainers!

But there are some, as Pareus and others, who refer the word to the good prophets; and so in a twofold sense they are said to be slain.

1. In their charge. I have sent them, saith God, to deliver my message to this people, and they have flown in their faces and killed them, and I account it as if I had done it, because I set to the work: and this was spoken at the time when the prophets were grossly abused, when Zechariah the prophet delivered his message to king Joash, and was slain for it, 2 Chron. xxiv. 21; as saith Acts vii. 52, "Which of the prophets have not your fathers persecuted?" But now here is their encouragement against all the ill usage and the hardships which they meet with in their work; I look upon it, saith God, as if I did it myself: therefore certainly God will not let them go unrewarded. 1 Sam. xxii. 23, David saith to Abiathar, "Abide thou with me, fear not: for he that seeketh my life seeketh thy life: but with me thou shalt be in safeguard." David was the occasion of the death of Abiathar's father, and therefore especially cared for him; and shall not God much more? So that, have you a friend, a brother, or a father, slain for, or in, the cause of God, shall not God take his part? yea, he will. Ahimelech was slain accidentally for the cause of David, and yet would David deal well with Abiathar: but, saith God, thy friend was slain, standing for me, and owning my cause; he shall lose nothing by it, for I will deal well with thee, and preserve thee alive for his sake.

2. In their ministry. It has been so heavy that it has even killed them, I have so burdened them with work that I have even slain them; so that this people cannot say, they have not been warned, or that they have had no prophets among them, or that their prophets have been idle, that they have had no work to do: and certainly it is a good death for a minister to die preaching. Pareus makes much use of this, and saith, How much more honourable to die in doing God's work, than by committing sinful acts of intemperance, uncleanness, &c.! Men cannot spend their strength better than in God's service. Oh let that people who have such ministers look to it, that they bring forth fruit answerable in some proportion to the cost bestowed on them. And if you understand the passage thus, then God seems to speak grievingly, Oh what shall I do with this people? What means have been used, what losses have I sustained by them! I have spent many choice servants among them, the lives and strengths of such spirits have been spent upon them of whom the world was not worthy. Oh what shall I do unto such a people? Surely a people enjoying such a ministry had need look to their profession. May not this be said of many congregations in London? Has not God sent many choice spirits among you to do you good? and have they effected the end for which they were sent? If not, woe to you! When God spends the lives of his choicest and most precious servants, if he have not a considerable value and return in people's fruitfulness, it will mightily provoke and incense him against them: God highly esteems the lives and strengths of his ministers, they are valued more than to be spent and wasted upon unfruitful people, who neither care for them nor their ministry.

Oportet episcopum concionantem mori.

But to come more particularly, and according to the genuine sense of the words, this slaying refers itself to the people. Now the word slays in these two respects:

1. In its denouncing of judgment upon men; for what the word threatens it is said to do: Jer. xviii. 7, 9, "At what instant I shall speak concerning a nation, and concerning a kingdom, to pluck up, and to pull down, and to destroy it;" "And at what instant I shall speak concerning a nation, and concerning a kingdom, to build and to plant it;" we should look upon both as performed.

2. In its operation, it has a mighty efficacy to lead impenitent sinners to ruin; it is as a two-edged sword, which does execution every way: Isa. xi. 3, it makes men "of quick understanding in the fear of God:" and God is said to consume antichrist by the breath of his nostrils, and by the word of his mouth; yea, the word is of such a force, that sometimes it brings death in a literal sense to those who withstand and oppose it. Ezek. xi. 2, Pelatiah gives wicked counsel in the city, and the prophet is commanded to prophesy against him; and in the 13th verse we read, that when the prophet prophesied Pelatiah died: thus God often makes the word so powerful in the mouths of his servants that it presently strikes men dead. Gualter observes from hence, that the power of the word appears in this, that it awakens, convinces, and terrifies the consciences of men, so that they go home and become self-murderers; and the truth is, it is often nothing else but the word working powerfully to their ruin and destruction.

Or the words may be taken hyperbolically. As men that are oppressed and in misery exclaim, Ye kill me, I am not able to endure it, you will be the death of me! the prophets came so close to them, that they cried out, Oh they will kill us, we are not able to suffer them! Luther saith, that by these words, "I have slain them by the words of my mouth," is meant the law; by the law thou hast slain them; and by the word "prophets" he saith is meant, that part of doctrine which is necessary to be preached, to prevent the abuse of the doctrine of the gospel, which otherwise men would be ready to pervert: and he further adds, that those who deny the use of the law were not fit even to be suffered to exist. I mention this of Luther the rather, because those who deny the obligation of the law, urge so strongly his authority to countenance their error.

"Thy judgments are as the light." That is, passively: Thy threatenings upon them, or the execution of those threatenings upon them, shall break out as the light; though they have slain my prophets, and think thereby to free themselves from those judgments which they threatened against them. No, saith God, for all this I will make known my threatenings which they have denounced against them. When the prophet Jeremiah had delivered the message of God to the princes and the priests, they laid hold on him, and said, He should surely die, Jer. xxvi. 8. Now see what the prophet saith in the 14th and 15th verses, "As for me, behold, I am in your hand: do with me as seemeth good and meet unto you. But know ye for certain, that if ye put me to death, ye shall surely bring innocent blood upon yourselves, and upon this city, and upon the inhabitants thereof: for of a truth the Lord hath sent me unto you to speak all these words in your ears." You think, perhaps, that when the minister is gone his words are no more: no, they shall lie upon you, and shall break out so manifestly that they shall clearly convince you. Though formerly they pleaded for themselves, as they in Isa. lviii., yet let them entertain never so good a conceit of themselves, I will discover them to be but base hypocrites; I will show you such clear demonstrations of the ways of righteousness in which you should have walked, that all shall discern what you are, and it shall appear as clear as the light wherein you have strayed from the rule.

Again, the words may be taken actively; and then the sense is, My power shall so appear upon them, that their righteousness and holiness shall appear as the light. And then, though my judgments were smart and tedious at the first, yet you shall not repent it; you shall see so much good resulting, as will make you amends for all. Or thus, I have sent my prophets among this people for this very end and purpose, to make this people a righteous people, and that they may manifest this as clearly as the light. Thus you have the meaning of the words; the observations follow.

Obs. 2. Inconstancy in religion provokes God's anger. The waverers and unstable in religion require to have cutting truths preached to them; "Therefore have I hewed them," saith God, "by the prophets:" and as God's ministers must deal thus with their people, so must every man in particular who loves his own soul; and if so be thy soul be precious in thy eyes, thou wilt willingly deal sharply with thyself, and say, O wretched heart that I have, to let such stirrings die, such motions of the Spirit come to nothing! Dost thou know whom thou hast to deal withal, the great and infinite God? and for what thou hast to deal with him, for nothing less than eternity? and hast thou stirrings of heart about this? and dost thou let them die? this provokes God.

Obs. 3. Many men's hearts are like knotty timber and rough stones. "I have hewed them." The longer men continue in their sins, the knottier they are. As timber which has lain long soaking in the water is tough and hardened; so men's spirits that are soaked in their evil ways, oh how untoward are they, and how hard a thing is it to fasten any thing that is good upon them! So that when we see men's spirits tough, stubborn, and hard to be wrought upon, let us think of this text, "I have hewed them by the prophets."

That this is spoken of a people, whose goodness was as a morning cloud, and the early dew which passeth away:

Obs. 4. Although the goodness of many be but as the dew, yet is their evil hard and settled. The goodness of many is like the softness of a plum, soon crushed; but their wickedness is like the stone in the plum, hard and inflexible: so that you may here see, grace and truth consist not in good motions, stirrings, and desires, for these may be where the heart is not melting, soft, nor tender; the heart is not changed, for were the heart kindly wrought upon, it would kindly yield to the power of the word, and, when it comes against their sins, would take part with it.

Obs. 5. God's ministers are hewers. "I have hewed them by the prophets." Elsewhere they are called God's workmen, and here hewers, and that in these two respects; either to prepare them for God's building, or to cast them into the fire; these are God's ends in sending his ministers, his hewers: now they hew all, good and bad, to take them off from their own rootings, and make them as beams in God's building, or to be as an axe laid to the root of their souls. It is recorded of Solomon's temple, that, "when it was in building, there was neither hammer, nor axe, nor any tool of iron heard in the house;" the materials being prepared, fitted, and squared beforehand: so those which will be members of God's temple hereafter, must be hewed and fitted for it here; therefore John is said to be one sent to make rough things plain, to level great mountains, mountains of sins, crabbed and rugged spirits. By this you may see what a hard task the minister's labour is, and why Jeremiah resolved that he would speak no more in the name of the Lord to the people. The work of a minister is more laborious than the work of a carpenter, as Chrysostom expresses it; for, saith he, when the carpenter has wrought hard all day, he goes home, and on his return in the morning finds matters as he left them; but we hew and take pains, and leave our people, but on our return find them worse than before.

Obs. 6. When the ministers of the gospel meet with such rough, cross, and untoward spirits, they must deal with them accordingly.

"I have hewed them by the prophets;" my prophets have done their work upon them. God seems to speak to the prophets, to bid them sharpen their tools, make their instruments keen, preach suitably unto them, saving some with fear, as the apostle Jude speaks, ver. 23. I wonder what they can say to this scripture, who cry out against ministers for preaching the law, when the text saith plainly, "and others save with fear." Therefore let those that are the ministers of the word have a care that they sharpen their tools by the word, putting an edge upon them, that so they may encounter successfully the greatest oppositions.

Obs. 7. When the ministers hew, God hews. "I have hewed them," saith God, whereas it was the prophets that did it. Is the word sharp, and does it come close at any time? then look to God as the cause. Is the tool sharp, and does it cut? then look to the hand that directed the stroke, and know that if God hew thee, he will have his will upon thee, he will accomplish the end he aims at. When God hews thee, if thou dost not work under his hand to make something of for use, he will throw thee into the fire: as a workman in anger throws away the piece he is at work upon into the fire; so saith God, This man or this woman are good for nothing, I will throw them into the fire. Take heed, you who have stirrings and motions unto good, and yet have your secret lusts, beloved bosom corruptions, know that God may cut you down for the fire; and thou mayst already in his purpose be thus cut down, though thou livest under the ordinances in the bosom of the church. As the fig tree was cut down, yet had leaves for a while, green and flourishing; so know, it is possible for a man to make a glorious profession, and perform many duties, and yet to be but a vessel of wrath, one cut down in wrath by the stroke of the word. This cutting down is like to that which we find in Luke xiv. 24, "For I say unto you, That none of those men which were bidden shall taste of my supper;" and yet these men had their stirrings and motions. Oh! the consideration of this should make sinners to tremble, that it is possible for men, yea, for men professing godliness, to be cut down by the word of wrath, and that, while they are living and well. Now God may be said to cut a man down for vengeance, when he in judgment determines and secretly resolves against him, that no means nor mercies shall do him good; and now, woe indeed to that man against whom God is thus resolved and determined! But that none may be discouraged and disheartened by this, but the rather awakened, know, that so long as God still strives with thee, and is yet working upon thee by his word and Spirit, he has not yet determined against thee, thou art not past hope of cure; therefore improve the seasons, and do not abuse this that hath been said; let it support you against despair, but not encourage you to presume.

Obs. 8. God's ministers are God's tools; and as tools by working are worn out, so are God's ministers. But when the work goes on, the labourer thinks not much though the tools are worn: so God, when he sees people come in and accept of mercy, is content to bear the loss of the wearing of his tools. And as men reckon not only for the work done, but also for the wearing of the tools, and the more precious the tool is, the more account is made of it; so will God, also, not only reckon for the lives of his servants, but also for their strength, and the weakening of their bodies by their manifold labours. Therefore people had need to look to it, that their fruit correspond with what God expends on them; for know, that God sets a high price upon the lives of his choice servants, and he will have a valuable consideration for them, either in you or upon you; and woe be to you if God forces the price of such blood as theirs is in your ruin!

Obs. 9. God's ministers are God's mouth to his people. "I have slain them by the words of my mouth." "If thou take forth the precious from the vile, thou shalt be as my mouth," Jer. xv. 19. And look, what is threatened by them, is threatened by God; and the promises which they open and press upon a soul in distress, is done by God himself, and it is to be looked upon as God speaking to thee in particular.

Obs. 10. The word of God is of great power, and full of efficacy. "I have slain them by the words of my mouth." The word is like a two-edged sword, which smites every way and doth execution: every time men hear the word, it is for life or for death. Deut. xxxii. 46, 47, "Set your hearts unto all the words which I testify among you this day; for it is not a vain thing for you; because it is your life:" it is your life which lies upon it, therefore look ye to it. So in Rev. xi. 5, "And if any man will hurt them, fire proceedeth out of their mouth, and devoureth their enemies: though the witnesses be as olive branches, yet if any wrong them they must be killed by devouring fire.

But if the word be of such efficacy, of a slaying nature, why should we hear it?

We are bound to hear the word as our duty: and when we come, we should present our lusts before the edge of the word: were sin thus presented before it, it would only slay the sin, and not the person. When the word comes, it will slay the one, either your sins, or your souls; therefore, if you would have your souls saved, put your sins to death. The upright need not fear coming to the word; but such as are resolved to keep their sins, the word will slay both them and their sins.

Obs. 11. God's judgments lie concealed while men go on prosperously in sin. They see them not; they sin, and judgment appears not; and, therefore, they take liberty and imbolden themselves in their sins.

Obs. 12. When judgments do come, they break out. "Thy judgments shall break forth." Judgments were working their ruin before, they did not sleep: when judgments come, they break out upon sinners: as mighty waters, being stopped in their course, when they work over the interruption, run the faster.

Obs. 13. God has his time to punish sins openly; as they sin secretly in the dark, God will punish openly in the light, to make them ashamed.

Obs. 14. God will have his time to convince men by his judgments; then their filthiness shall be punished.

Now God's judgments may be said to break forth as the light, to convince men, in three ways:

1. When the thing threatened in the word comes to pass.

2. When the judgment inflicted is suitable to the sin committed.

3. When it is executed by a remarkable hand upon the sinner, then that judgment breaks forth upon a man as the light.

Obs. 15. God's judgments are gradual. They break forth as the light, not all at once, there is the morning light and the mid-day; as mercies to the saints are gradual, so are judgments upon the wicked. There is much to be learned by this breaking out of judgment as the light. Isa. xxvi. 9, "When thy judgments are in the earth, the inhabitants of the world will learn righteousness." Micah vi. 9, "The man of wisdom shall see thy name: hear ye the rod, and who hath appointed it." Prov. xxviii. 5, "Evil men understand not judgment: but they that seek the Lord understand all things;" they shall learn much. Examine your hearts by this, and see what you have learned by these judgments that are broken out upon us so manifestly, that the greatest atheist in the world may learn, that "the Lord, he is the God," as the people cried out in 1 Kings xviii. 39.

Obs. 16. When God sends a ministry to a people, it is to discover his way and worship. The Lord makes their righteousness to appear and break forth as the light; he will have his way and worship appear as clearly as the light, his way shall not be hidden from them.

Obs. 17. The more powerful the ministry is, the more terrible shall judgments be, if despised. Your consciences shall echo upon this ground in your ears, "The Lord is righteous in all his ways," justly am I punished. Oh the sad cries of many in their sicknesses and on their death-beds! How many times have I been warned by the word! but I slighted warnings, I regarded them not, warnings have been no warnings to me, therefore justly am I in misery.

Oh that the consideration of this might be more prevalent and work more upon us, than ever God's quickness in his judgments has wrought towards those that stand out against a quick, searching ministry.

Ver. 6. *For I desired mercy, and not sacrifice; and the knowledge of God more than burnt offerings.*

This scripture having much of the mind of God in it, and much difficulty in the understanding of it, I read no further at this time. Here we have a reason of God's severe expression in the former verse, where it was said that God had hewed them by the prophets, and slain them by the words of his mouth. Why was God so severe against them? Because he would not be put off with their sacrifices. They bolstered up themselves with these, objecting against the prophet when he pressed them to mercy and to the knowledge of God, Why, are not we abundant in serving of God? burnt-offerings are not neglected by us, and why should not we be accepted? No, saith God, "I desired mercy, and not sacrifice;" never tell me of your sacrifices and burnt-offerings, so long as there is no mercy among you. "Therefore have I hewed them by the prophets, and slain them by the words of my mouth;" you are so attached to these outward things, that I must hew you off from them. This sentence is quoted twice by Christ himself in the New Testament, Matt. ix. 13; xii. 7, which, as it does not occur in any other place, notes its great importance.

"For I desired mercy." חפצתי signifies to desire or to will a thing with great complacency or delight; as if God should say, Mercy is a thing so pleasing to me, that I desire it at my heart. God's great mercy in reconciling the world unto himself by Jesus Christ, is more worth than all the sacrifices in the world; but this is not the mercy meant in the text. Heb. x. 5, 6, "Sacrifice and offering thou wouldest not, but a body hast thou prepared me: in burnt-offerings and sacrifices for sin thou hast had no pleasure." There is no mercy like this, the mercy of God in his Son Jesus Christ. But the mercy here spoken of is the mercy of man, and the word for mercy here, is, in the original, the same as is used for goodness in the 4th verse. The meaning then is, I desire mercy; that is, not the mercy of God, but mercy to man, mercy to ourselves; and so Christ interprets it, Matt. xii. 7, "If ye had known what this meaneth, I will have mercy, and not sacrifice, ye would not have condemned the guiltless." As if Christ should say, God in some cases would have men provide for themselves, though they thereby neglect the strict observance of the sabbath: "I will have mercy," as to ourselves, so to others, mercy to men, either to their bodies, or to their souls; mercy to the body every one will grant, but it ought to be especially to the soul, as we may gather from Christ's other quotation of these words, Matt. ix. 13, "Go ye and learn what that meaneth, I will have mercy, and not sacrifice: for I am not come to call the righteous, but sinners to repentance." This word "mercy" is a synecdoche comprehending all the duties of the second table under one. "I will have mercy, and not sacrifice:" by "sacrifice" is meant, synecdochically, all instituted ordinances and worship, all the affirmative precepts of the second and fourth commandments, all ordinances then commanded them, or that ever should be enjoined; and this appears from Christ's applying the text, in Matt. xii. 7, to the sanctification of the sabbath: and in Matt. ix. 13, Christ quotes it in reference to an ordinance, (whether true or not, human or Divine, matters not,) the separation of the Jews from publicans and sinners; and tells them, that in a case of mercy they might eat with them, thereby gaining an opportunity to do good to their souls: so that from those two you see a clear warrant for the interpretation of this text.

חסד

Now, in the further clearing of it, I shall answer some questions, satisfy some objections, and raise certain observations.

I. I shall answer some questions. And,

1. What is an instituted ordinance? There are natural ordinances, and instituted duties. Now what is the difference between them?

For the unfolding of this, know, that by natural duties we understand such duties as we owe to God as God, to men as men, which, if there had been no law to bind us to the performance of, yet would they have been fulfilled by us, being engraven on the heart by the finger of God himself. Such duties, for instance, as the first commandment binds us to, to have no other gods but the Lord, to fear this God and him alone, to love him before all and above all, to trust in him for help at all times: these are duties to be done as unto a God; nature itself dictates the performance of them.

Then there are duties to be performed unto men, as honouring of parents, speaking the truth, not deceiving one another; these duties are radicated in the heart, that were there no law of God to bind men, yet it were in men's hearts to do them. Now these duties must not yield to mercy. But by instituted duties, I mean those which, if God had not revealed, had not been duties, neither would men have been bound to their performance: as, for instance, the sacrifices under the law, by bullocks and goats; sacrifices of such a kind, were they not revealed by some prophet to be in accordance with the mind of God, had not been obligatory. So our church ordinances of sacraments, Christian admonition, and the like, are such as flow from God's prerogative, and not necessarily from his nature. Natural duties, then, refer to attributes in God's nature and character; instituted, to the expression of his will.

2. But how did God say here, "Mercy, and not sacrifice?" Did not God require sacrifice as well as mercy?

Yea, God did require sacrifice as well as mercy; but we must understand this with these limitations:

1. I will have sacrifice, but not without the spirit. Sacrifices without the spirit joined with them are nothing worth. When spiritual worship is joined with their outward sacrifices, then they are accepted. Instituted worship separated from natural worship is not regarded.

2. Not sacrifices to make atonement for their sins. The people thought by their sacrifices to make atonement for their lives, though never so vile and base; but, saith God, I will not have it thus, I will have it only typical, in relation to Christ. But they left out Christ in them: therefore, saith God in this sense, "I will have mercy, and not sacrifice."

3. Not sacrifice; that is, of your own. They had many sacrifices of their own, which God neither required, nor would accept of from them. "I will have mercy, and not sacrifice."

4. Not sacrifices; that is, such as are injuriously gotten. The Jews were a very oppressing, grinding people; they would be much in sacrifices, but it was out of the rights of the poor; they would oppress and grind the poor, and then think to atone for all by their sacrifices: in this case, "I will have mercy, and not sacrifice."

5. Not sacrifices; that is, comparatively, mercy rather than sacrifice. This negative, in Scripture, is often used to mark inferiority, as in Prov. viii. 10, "Receive instruction, and not silver; and knowledge rather than fine gold." "Receive instruction, not silver;" that is, rather than silver. God's requiring of knowledge does not forbid men seeking estates, but it shows us rather, that knowledge is to be chosen in preference. So Paul is sent to preach the gospel, and not to baptize; that is, rather than to baptize, for Paul did baptize in some places. So saith God here, "I will have mercy, and not sacrifice;" that is, Let me have both; but if both cannot be had, let me have mercy of the two, I do so much delight in it, that if I cannot have mercy and sacrifice together, I prefer mercy.

3. Why should God require mercy rather than sacrifice?

Because mercy is good in itself, but sacrifice is good only in reference to something else; the good of sacrifices consists only in their reference to Jesus Christ.

Mercy is good in itself, but sacrifice is only good because commanded by God's prerogative, God's command constitutes its goodness.

Mercy is part of God's image in man, but sacrifice is not; and by how much God's image in man surpasses any other excellency, by so much does mercy excel sacrifice.

All instituted worship was made for man, not man for it; but for natural worship man was made, and not it for man, therefore must it needs be more excellent. Christ's reasoning warrants this, "The sabbath was made for man, not man for the sabbath." Now this cannot be said of natural worship, of the duties of fearing God, loving of God, trusting in God.

There is more self-denial in a duty of mercy than in any sacrifice. To do good to the poor, and that in obedience to God's command, argues more self-denial than the offering up to God of sacrifices.

Mercy is *æternæ veritatis*, an eternal, everlasting duty; it was always, and shall be so, and the habit of it shall continue to all eternity. Though in heaven there be no objects to be delivered out of misery, yet this disposition of mercy remains even there.

Sacrifice is a typical duty for the obtaining of the pardon of sin, but mercy is a moral duty. Now, that which is a moral duty, is better than that which is but to further us in the obtaining of pardon for a moral offence, committed against the great God.

Because sacrifices are but to further us in natural duties. To what end serve sacraments, and why do I partake of them, but to strengthen my faith, increase my love, and to further my appetite in hearing God's mind? Why do I hear the word of God, but that it may turn me unto God? Now the end is better than the means for the attaining of the end; therefore upon these grounds God may be said to desire mercy rather than sacrifice.

4. What are these cases in which God will have mercy, and not sacrifices?

The principal are these ten.

1. If a beast should be in danger of losing its life by any casualty upon the Lord's day, God allows us to forbear all church ordinances at that time, rather than let the beast perish; but because this liberty is allowed by God to men in this case, yet you must not think that a beast is better than all God's ordinances.

2. In the case of the poor; and that I conceive to be the principal scope of the words in the text. These people wronged, oppressed, and tyrannized over the poor, and then thought to make amends to God by their sacrifices and offerings. Men must not lay out so much of their estates either in superfluities, or for the maintenance of God's true worship, as to hinder them in their benevolence and charity to the poor; no ordinance of God should hinder us in showing mercy to the least member of Jesus Christ. Although those which are next us ought to be first relieved, yet know, it is a shame that others should be neglected and forgotten; yea, it is a reproach to the ways of God, that profane men should be more liberal to the poor, that more hungry bellies should be fed and naked backs clothed by them, than by those who profess religion, and would seem to honour God most. Do not think this will be sufficient to excuse you before God, when the cry of the poor shall come up before him, that you have been at such and such charges for the ordinances and worship of God: no, in this case God will have mercy.

3. Mercy to parents, to relieve parents in their necessity, is a case in which God will have mercy, and not sacrifice. If Providence so order that our parents should stand in need of our help, and we are able to aid them, it is our duty to do it, though by this means we are deprived of God's ordinances. You ought rather to regard the relief of parents than the observation of the sabbath, if the case require it. You may be ready to think thus, Had not I better let my parents alone? I must obey the command of Christ, who saith, Matt. x. 37, "He that loveth father or mother more than me is not worthy of me." But there is in this matter a mistake. "Is not worthy of me," only means, if your parents should counsel, advise, persuade, entice, or command you to the practice of evil, or to the omission of any good, or the breach of any command; and upon your refusal they should be angry with you, that you will not obey them, but follow the command of God, and not go out of God's way; in this case father and mother are to be forsaken for Christ and the gospel, but in no case if th[illegible] stand in need of your help; as is enjoined in Mark vii. 11, "But ye say, If a man shall say to his father or mother, It is Corban, that is to say, a gift, by whatsoever thou mightest be profited by me; he shall be free." Now *Corban* signifies a gift consecrated to God; and the Jews thought that if they could apply the word Corban of any thing, they were exempted from all duty to their parents in that respect: It is true, I had an estate, but I have consecrated it to God, and church services; and though I owe duty and respect to you, as my parents, yet more to God, as my Creator. This is most vile and abominable, and reproved by Christ himself. Possidonus, in the Life of Austin, reports, that he condemned parents who gave their estates away to monasteries, and pious uses, as they thought, and neglected their children: so for children to neglect and slight parents in the time of their necessity, and think to excuse it with the plea of having given it to the church, and being now unable to do any thing more, this will not suffice. This was the old way of papists, to get people to give to their mother the church. I find a tradition cited by some of the Jews, as used by them; when they fell out and were thoroughly angry one with another, they would tell him he should never have any benefit in any thing which they had, and this they called Corban. In Matt. xv. 5, it is called "a gift," the gift of the altar. Therefore some of the heathens forbade this oath Corban; and yet this was the oath that these did swear by. And by some it is used in a similar manner even at this day, as thus; when any that we are related to have thoroughly angered us, we are wont to say, Well, you shall never be a penny the better for me: this is no other than this oath Corban which they used to swear by in this place.

4. Where the good of souls is concerned. And this is Christ's case, Matt. ix. 13, "Go ye and learn what that meaneth, I will have mercy, and not sacrifice: for I am not come to call the righteous, but sinners to repentance." Though men ought to prize ordinances, and to highly esteem God's worship, yet if it should so happen that instituted worship and mercy to souls come together, and interfere with each other, and both cannot be done, the former may be reverently omitted, and the work of mercy to the soul attended to before it. We are ready to think that nothing must give way to instituted worship, but certainly immortal souls are of more worth than ordinances. Paul was of such a disposition, that he could wish himself out of heaven and become an anathema for his brethren, that souls might be saved.

5. In case of human societies, and for the quiet state of kingdoms, and yet this without prejudice to God's ordinances. God has allowed to men the art of navigation: we read, Solomon sent ships to Tarshish to fetch gold; and were it not for this text, I could not see any warrant for the estrangement from ordinances attendant on it; when men shall be three or four years out, perhaps, and never hear sermons nor receive sacraments: and yet it is lawful upon this ground, that God will have the peace of states and quiet of kingdoms preserved and maintained, he will rather dispense with men in the use of his own ordinances, for the prosperity of civil states: therefore Solomon is not reproved for sending ships to Ophir for gold.

6. In the case of church societies, when the people of God are scattered and cannot meet together, God is content in such cases his people should be without ordinances, and yet incur no sin: as is clear in the case of the children of Israel all the time the church was in the wilderness, even for forty years together they wanted circumcision; but when they came to the borders of Canaan, and were about to enjoy any settlement, then they were circumcised again, and had the passover,

which before they could not partake of. So that in some cases, and upon some grounds, the people of God may be without ordinances, and that for a long time, and yet incur no sin; and upon this ground in the text, "I will have mercy, and not sacrifice." Therefore this may be the reason of those words which Christ spake to his disciples, "I have yet many things to say unto you, but ye cannot bear them now:" so may we say, Christ has many truths to reveal which people are not yet able to bear, therefore he withholds the revelation of them at present.

7. In respect to our bodies: and this is Christ's case in Matt. xii. 7, "If ye had known what this meaneth, I will have mercy, and not sacrifice, ye would not have condemned the guiltless." God's care of the bodies of men is such, that he will rather have men do the one than the other, he will rather have mercy than the duty. Christ pleads not here for the disciples, that this was not a breach of the sabbath; but the case was such that their bodies required it, it was a case of mercy, and now God would rather have the mercy than the duty. A servant perhaps thinks much to stay at home, to tend a child or look to the house, upon the Lord's day; he objects, Why should I not go to the church? Is not my soul of greater worth and price than this child, or this house? Now these people go upon a good principle, yet err in their application of it: as, for instance, a father commands his child to do two services for him, the one to wait on him at table, the other to clean his shoes. To wait upon his father at table he is willing to do, because it is creditable; but the other he grumbles at, and is discontented. Now in which does he show most obedience? Surely in fulfilling the meanest command. So God requires of us two sorts of duties, one the more honourable, the other more mean, yet perhaps the meaner, a work of mercy. God is wonderfully careful of our bodies, and would have us also careful of the bodies of others. Men ought not to macerate their bodies. God does not require weak, sickly bodies to spend whole nights in fasting and prayer; God in this case will have mercy, and not sacrifice.

8. With regard to our own estates. But here some may say, What! may we regard our own particular estates before the service of God? Yea, in some cases we may, as thus: Suppose we were in the assembly at public ordinances, and there should be a fire in the town, or thieves breaking into a house, we might lawfully leave the ordinances to quench the fire, or to apprehend the thieves and save our goods. Numb. ix. 10, if a man were in a journey, and in the mean time the passover were to be delivered, he might go on in his journey, and do his business, and yet incur no sin. So may we, if in a journey or on special business, if not undertaken in slight or contempt of the ordinance, we may go on without sin; God will have mercy.

9. In the times of persecution, God allows his people to discontinue some ordinances; as is clear in Acts viii. 1. There was at that time a great persecution against the church which was at Jerusalem, so that the church was scattered and could not assemble to enjoy church-fellowship, and yet it was no sin to them: it had been an unjust charge if any had come and said, What! do you prize your lives so highly, and fear the loss of them more than the ordinances of God? Will you not unite in church-fellowship and constant assembling of yourselves together, because you think you shall suffer by it? No; in such a case, God will have mercy, and not sacrifice.

10. In the case of some eminent service for God. As in the case of Nehemiah; he being the king's cupbearer must attend to it; and when he was to go up to Jerusalem, asked the king's leave; and when he had finished his work he returns to the king again to serve in his place: though he wanted the ordinances in the king's court, which he might have enjoyed at Jerusalem, yet, that he might be more serviceable in the church's cause, he is contented to deny himself in his own comforts. These are the cases, with others of the like nature, in which God will have mercy, and not sacrifice.

II. I shall satisfy some objections that may be made against this.

1. But men's hearts are deceitful, and they may pretend cases of mercy when there is no such thing in hand.

Know, though in such a case thou couldst not do it, yet do not thou judge another man that may or can do it. The rule is difficult, it is true, yet do not thou envy another man's grace, to whom God has given power to manage his business with Christian wisdom. Thou thinkest that if thou wert in such places and hadst such temptations as others have, thou shouldst miscarry, and aim at self in them; yet do not thou judge another man that may do it in sincerity, do not thou judge another man's duty through thy weakness. God's servants in this world are as his stewards: now we know that a steward has not every particular enjoined him by his lord, but only general rules given to order particulars according to prudence, faithfulness, and zeal; for the exercise of these three graces are required in a steward, prudence and wisdom, faithfulness and trust, care and zeal. So does God give general rules for the ordering of a Christian life; and these general rules being observed, particular cases are to be ordered in prudence, faithfulness, and zeal; wisdom to judge, faithfulness in doing, zeal to keep up life and spirit in action; and where there is a miscarrying through frailty, God will have mercy.

2. But it may be asked, Can any duty of the second be more excellent than the duties of the first table; of the one, God being the object; of the other, man?

The duties of the first table are to be understood, either for the substantial and internal duties of the heart, or some superadded duties materially connected with them: then there are duties of the second table, some more substantial, some superadded: now if we compare the internal and substantial duties with the superadded duties, there the substantial are above them, and to be preferred before them, they having God for their immediate object; yet in some cases God is pleased to indulge with men so far, that he will let the duties of the second table, duties of mercy towards men, take precedence even of the more substantial duties of the first table; so in the duties of the second table to men, some, which are but circumstantial and not so necessary, God allows should be done, when others more fundamental shall lie still omitted, yet without sin.

3. But if God's ordinances are duties, can they be omitted at any time, and that without sin? Are they duties or not duties?

For answer, Take notice, there are two sorts of precepts, negative and affirmative; a negative binds *semper, et ad semper*, always and at all times; but an affirmative binds only *semper*, but not *ad semper*, always, but not at all seasons; at one time we may omit a thousand actions which are to be done, but we cannot do many actions at one and the same time: therefore, for affirmative duties, if they be done in their season, God accepts of them as done continually; as for that command, Pray continually, if it be done in its season, God looks upon it as done continually, and always done. If Providence should so order it, that another duty require to be done at this instant, the duty which I was going to perform ceases then to be a duty to me at this time. If two good things come together, but one can be done at a time, so that the other is not a duty at that time to you, which otherwise is a duty; else if this were not, man would be necessitated to sin, and all the grace, and mercy, and assistance of God could not help, if two affirmative precepts were thus obligatory at the same time; therefore this must be remembered for a truth, that when two affirmative precepts come together, the one is a duty to be performed, the other not.

But what say you to the case of Daniel? when he knew that the writing was signed, he went into his house and prayed more earnestly, Dan. vi. 10. Might not he have saved his life according to this rule, "I will have mercy, and not sacrifice?" yet his was a sacrifice that he tendered up to God, it was more than a prayer.

Daniel was then called to manifest Jehovah to be the true God, for he was forbid at the time, by a decree, to pray to any God, or ask a petition of any man save of the king, during thirty days. Now, had he done this, he had denied the true God, and acknowledged Darius to be God. The thing he had to profess was higher than the sacrifice, it was a duty of the first commandment, a manifestation of God to be the true God; and the case standing thus, who is the God that must be prayed unto? Daniel resolves it, saying, I will pray to no God but the true God. And surely, in such a case, profession is to be made whatever becomes of mercy; yea, in a lesser case of sacrifice than this, if profession of faith is involved, it is turned from a duty of the second table to a duty of the first, and must be done as a duty of the first: as thus, Suppose a man be forbid to do a duty which formerly he has constantly performed, and esteemed lawful, and his forbearing of it shall be to them a testimony of his denial of that truth which he formerly held; in such a case he is called to suffer the hardest things imaginable, yea, to sacrifice life itself, if necessary, rather than to omit that duty, or to do the least thing which, to the enemies of the truth, may interpretatively be a sign of denial. The doing of such a duty against such a command is a witnessing to the truth, and not offering up of sacrifice. It is not always that a man is called to this; but if it ever come to this case, interpretatively to deny a truth of God, then must we suffer rather than obey in such a thing, though never so small. And this was the case of the primitive times, they would rather suffer the loss of life, estates, and all, than do that which interpretatively should be a profession of the denial of any of the least truths of God. Tertullian reports of a soldier, who, when all the rest of his fellows carried bays on their hats, in testimony of their worship of a false god, carried a sprig in his hand, and on being asked the reason, answered, I am a Christian; this manifested him to be so, and he at the last suffered death rather than yield. How many among us would think this a small matter, and had it been their case would have done it! yet this man, regarding it as a note of distinction, chose rather to lose his life than comply; and this act of his was approved of, as lawful, by learned and godly men. If we lived in the times of our forefathers, when the question was, Who is a Christian, or who is not? and this by way of distinction, the case would then be different, changed from a sacrifice to a precept and duty of the first commandment. There was a time that the saints would not assemble together because of the persecution, Acts viii. 1; but at another time they would not forsake joining together, whatever became of them: when their assembling was made a note of distinction, who was a saint, who not; who held for such a truth, who would not; in this case, for them not to have assembled together had been a great sin in them, and interpretatively a denial of the truth.

4. But if God will have mercy in case of outward things, saving our estates and preservation of our persons rather than his own ordinances, is not this to prefer the body to the soul? &c.

The preservation of a man's outward estate and condition is to be considered in a threefold respect.

1. As it is in itself: and when a man shall love his estate only in reference to itself, certainly it is sin to regard it before sacrifice.

2. As it enables us to do service for God and our brethren: and this is in a higher respect than the other, of loving our estates for ourselves.

3. As a duty in such and such cases, that so I may be made more serviceable for God, and for his people. Now in this case it is an act of religion; the saving of our estates, as well as praying or hearing of a sermon, in this case is an act of sacrifice, for I do it in obedience to God, for religious ends; though the thing itself be an outward act, yet thus done it is an act of religion, for by this I manifest both my love to God and religion.

5. But is not a man bound to part with much of his estate, yea, and to suffer much, for the enjoyment of the ordinances?

Yea, certainly, very much: we ought both to give and to suffer much for the enjoyment of ordinances; yea, we should choose rather to live in a poor condition, so we may enjoy the ordinances in their purity, than to be in a rich condition and want the ordinances; we are to be liberal ourselves, and careful in exciting others to be so, even till it come to the case of unmercifulness, and then God will have mercy, and not sacrifice. But when may it be said to come to a case of unmercifulness, in which God will have mercy, and not sacrifice?

1. When a subsistence is so denied, that the subject would be destroyed; in this case God will rather have mercy than instituted worship performed to him.

2. When a greater opportunity is denied to do good to our own souls and brethren, than this is of enjoyment of the ordinances; then surely God will have mercy, and not sacrifice. It is impossible to give particular rules in every thing; this is left to the sanctified prudence of the saints.

6. But is not this the justifying of, and consenting with, those that took up innovations, and read the service book?

I answer, No; this Scripture gives no warrant for any such, for there is a great difference between the yielding to that which may pollute and defile the ordinances, and to forbear an ordinance: we must not do any thing to pollute an ordinance, though it were to save our lives; but the forbearing of an ordinance, and that for a long time, may be done, and yet without sin.

7. But is it not a greater mercy to enjoy ordinances than estates? we think it a great mercy, yea, and we have many mercies in the enjoyment of them, and though we suffer many hard things, meanwhile we enjoy communion with God and Jesus Christ in them.

Certainly the mercy is very great, and much communion is to be had with God in his own ordinances rightly administered, and happy are those souls which find this effect by the ordinances and communion with God:

But yet know, that the maintenance of the subject is to be more regarded than the comfort of it, though it be spiritual. But now have a care of turning what I have said into poison; do not ye say that you may now do any thing for the preservation of the subject; we must not do the least thing by which an ordinance may be polluted and defiled.

To be serviceable in public use is more than to enjoy ordinances; as for a minister to preach Jesus Christ to a people, is a greater mercy than his particular good can be; and this has been the judgment of all the churches, yea, it has been the practice of the churches to send forth men to preach the gospel, and to open the things of the kingdom to them, when they could not enjoy the ordinance of the sacrament: Paul would have been content to have been anathema for his brethren; the being of public use to the churches was a greater good to him, and more in his esteem, than his own private gain. Thus far of the objections; ten observations follow answerable to these.

Obs. 1. Carnal hearts which make little conscience of their duties, and are very cruel in their dealings towards men, yet may be contented to submit to instituted worship. This very scripture, "I will have mercy, and not sacrifice," is a secret rebuke to such people. Such were those in Jer. vii. 4, who cried, "The temple of the Lord, The temple of the Lord;" and yet were very wicked in their dealings. Those hypocrites in Isa. lviii. could be content to submit to instituted worship, frequent in solemn duties of fasting and prayer, yet were such as did smite with the fist, oppress, and grind the poor. In Ezek. xxiv. 21, the sanctuary was accounted their strength, the excellency of their strength, and that which their eyes did pity, and yet were they very wicked; and, in the 25th verse, their minds were on it, their hearts did love it, yet they themselves were carnal.

Because men may be exercised in instituted worship without any power of godliness, the outward act of performance is a very easy work to flesh and blood, there is little difficulty in it.

Because it has the most show of the power of godliness; they seem to be as sincere as any in their worship, there is a great show in the flesh, in the outward man; whereas God's worship is inward, soul worship, which carnal hearts cannot endure, nor do they desire it, it is outside worship which they prize. Now God forbid that any should have low conceits of ordinances, because wicked men join in them.

Obs. 2. Carnal men think to satisfy their consciences by joining in outward ordinances. Thus did they in this place think to put off God and their own consciences, by living in the external acts of worship, while they continued in the love of known sin. What a deal of stir had the prophet to convince these hypocrites of this their wickedness!

Obs. 3. God and men's consciences will not be put off. God will despise both it and them. The heathen gods would not be put off with such outsides, in the judgment even of the heathen themselves. Plato saith, What a vile thing is it to think, that the gods will be put off with gifts! No, these are despised by them, they look that the soul should be just. And Seneca, It is not fat sacrifices, but inward performances, that God regards.

Obs. 4. The Lord has a high esteem of mercy; and it appears in this, that he will have it preferred before sacrifice, and this is called, a "sacrifice acceptable," and a sweet savour in God's nostrils, Phil. iv. 18. Chrysostom saith, that he had rather work a work of mercy than a miracle: and surely that must needs be high in God's eyes and esteem, which he pays so dear for.

O Christians! imitate God in this, let your esteems of mercy be raised higher than ever before, from this that you have heard concerning its excellency. The works of mercy are glorious works, there is more in such than in those acts of religion which men think are more spiritual. I speak the more of this, because it is a scandal which is laid upon godly men by the men of the world, that they are miserable and close-handed; now in this we should labour to convince the world by the practice of mercy.

Obs. 5. It is the Christian's skill, when two duties come together, which to choose. This is a snare in which many Christians are caught and foiled; they think both must be done at the same time, whereas the one is the duty, the other not.

Obs. 6. Though the object of an action be spiritual, yet it is not a sufficient ground to prefer it before another action, whose object may be but natural. The ordinances of God have God for their object, and the enjoying of communion with him; yet in the performance of other actions which may be only natural, I may show more obedience to God than in offering up of sacrifice.

Obs. 7. If God's own worship may be forborne in case of mercy, how much more men's institutions and inventions! Oh what a vile spirit is there in those men who will not suffer their superstitious vanities to give place to mercy! men must be undone in their bodies and estates, rather than their wills be disobeyed! The prelatical faction have themselves confessed, that the cross, the surplice, and the rest of that trash, were their own institutions; yet ministers must be silenced, bodies imprisoned, families starved, and thousands of souls destroyed, rather than their wills should not be fulfilled. Oh the intolerable pride of these men! had they been God's institutions, yet might they have been forborne. What did these men's actions say but this, Let Christ never be revealed to thousands and millions of souls, rather than these ceremonies shall be omitted or neglected?

Obs. 8. God will have mercy rather than disputing about sacrifice. Suppose there be a truth in that which is disputed about, yet God in this case will have mercy rather than sacrifice, rather than mercy shall be neglected he will have sacrifice omitted. We have ordinances and plenty of preaching, but the Lord knows how soon we may be deprived of them; let us not then dispute and wrangle away our mercy.

But must we not inquire after truth, and at this time also?

God forbid we should deny or speak against any which shall search into, or inquire after, truth, yea, at this time, when a case of mercy requires it; but, when young converts are taken off from fundamental truths, and led into errors, and souls hindered from coming in to Christ, in this case we should abstain from contending.

But young converts must abstain from all appearance of evil, and labour to come to the knowledge of Christ's will in every point.

True, they must, but this must be done orderly, they must first be established and grounded in fundamentals, and then they have liberty to do this; that rule is perpetual and holds in this case, Rom. xiv. 1, "Him that is weak in the faith receive ye, but not to doubtful disputations." Now let no man say, the point was a case of indifferency: some would eat herbs out of conscience, others would forbear; now certainly it is a sin to do that out of conscience which God neither regards nor commands: the thing itself here was indifferent, yet in this case they must not receive them to doubtful disputations; now, if not to doubtful disputations, then surely not to disputation to hold up error, and to insnare and betray young beginners in godliness. In Acts xv. 24, "certain" are spoken of, "which went out" from the apostles, and "troubled" the disciples "with words subverting their souls." The words in the original signify, as if a man had been packing up wares to send beyond the seas, and one should come and scatter and undo all again which was packed up; or as soldiers, who having packed up their artillery, their bag and baggage, are forced to undo it all suddenly again: so did these false teachers unvessel, scatter, and bring them all into confusion, labouring to subvert them from the faith.

Ἀνασκευάζοντες τὰς ψυχὰς ὑμῶν.

Obs. 9. Mercy must be preferred before our own wills and lusts. God is contented, that we may perform our duties to our brethren, to forbear his own ordinances; and shall we stand upon our wills and humours? O proud spirit, that exalteth thyself against the Lord; we must be content to deny ourselves very far for the public good, and for our brethren's sake, since God is pleased to bear with men so far, as for a time to be without that honour, which he should have from men in their acknowledgment of him in public service.

Obs. 10. Men must be contented to forbear their institutions with those who cannot yield in their consciences to them. But let there be peace and quiet maintained by us; we should indulge and bear each with other in such cases, of mercy especially; there should not be the urging of lesser things upon tender consciences with such severity as to undo them, though they be God's ordinances.

But if this be so, then what hinders but men may do what they list?

No. What has been said has been limited only to instituted worship, and so, punish them they may, but not to their ruin; nay, in these controversies in which men are so divided, some thinking this course, others thinking another, to be agreeable to Christ's ordinance, things ought not so to be urged, as to undo the other party that opposes; certainly such a practice as this is contrary to the rule of mercy in this text. Is it not cruelty to insist, that men must unsatisfy themselves presently, and lay down their opinions upon such a day as shall be appointed them.

But you will say, It is sufficient that learned and godly men hold this opinion, they find sufficient to satisfy them, and we may mistake.

To this I answer, that those who are ignorant in any respect, must understand the grounds on which men hold their opinions. If their reasons satisfy you, then it is something; but to say, I must hold such and such things because others do, and I ignorant of their grounds, this is folly; for as we must not have an implicit faith, so we must not have an implicit judgment, to hold an opinion because others hold it. And thus I have given you the mind of God in this scripture, so far as God has revealed it to me for the present.

It follows,

"And the knowledge of God more than burnt-offerings." For the understanding of these words, I shall first answer some questions, and then give you the observations.

1. What knowledge of God is here meant?

Certainly not a knowledge barely notional. but such as is joined with faith and obedience, a practical knowledge, which brings the heart to love and embrace the truth: Isa. liii. 11, "By his knowledge shall my righteous servant justify many."

2. Why is the knowledge of God joined to mercy here? was it not full enough before, "mercy, and not sacrifice?"

Because as God accepts not mercy without sacrifice, neither does he regard knowledge without mercy. Men are here in the extremes on both sides: some are very merciful, as the papists, but withal very ignorant of the knowledge of God and his ways; that, as the apostle saith of love, If I should give all my goods to the poor, and my body to be burnt, it were nothing; so, if we be never so merciful, and ignorant, it availeth nothing. Others have much knowledge, yet are very rugged and hard-hearted. Now when mercy and knowledge are thus separated, God regards them not; but when they meet together, then are they well-pleasing in his sight.

3. Why is knowledge only named here, whereas there are many duties of the first table, as well as this?

Because both of the excellency and necessity of the knowledge of God; the knowledge of God has an influence on all the duties of God's worship.

Because many are very much exercised in instituted worship, yet very ignorant in the knowledge of God. It was so then, and is so now in our days; many who contend for ordinances and Christ's government in his church, are yet very ignorant of Christ's redeeming the world, the way of God in reconciling himself and sinners together; ignorant of the attributes of God, and their working for his people's good: therefore he requires the knowledge of himself to be in men principally.

4. Why is the knowledge of God put after mercy, it being better than mercy?

The knowledge of God is not set after mercy because mercy is to be preferred before knowledge, but because mercy is more apparent, most convincing to men: now when people are convinced of one duty, they are the sooner convinced of another; conscience will easily convince them of what is God's mind.

5. But why is it said burnt-offerings, rather than peace-offerings and sin-offerings, which we read of?

Because these have more respect unto God than other offerings, as has been shown to you at other times, with the differences between burnt-offerings and other offerings: as if the Holy Ghost should say, I require mercy and not sacrifice, and the inward worship of God, faith and knowledge, rather than any natural worship. The notes from hence are these:

Obs. 11. The duties of the first and second table are to be joined together. Mercy and sacrifice, knowledge of God and burnt-offerings, when in their place, are acceptable, therefore let us take heed of separating that which God has joined.

Obs. 12. The knowledge of God is a most excellent thing. This is that which sanctifies God's name, and manifests him to be very glorious in the world. Paul accounted all things but loss and dung in comparison of the excellency of this knowledge of Christ. Instruct then your children and servants in this knowledge, else how can God have his glory from them? How few are there which glorify God as God! and the reason is, because of the ignorance which is in their minds, Eph. iv. 18.

Obs. 13. Men may be very diligent in instituted worship, and yet very ignorant. None so acted in their instituted worship as these people, yet none so ignorant as they.

That you are forward in instituted worship is your commendation, but take heed this be not your sin, to be ignorant of fundamental things. It is the great design of the devil to set up the man of sin, to keep men in darkness and ignorance. Many who think themselves, and would be thought to be, opposers of antichrist, even by their very questioning of fundamentals of religion, and disputings about their new opinions, raise him up; the devil is wont to darken the truth of Christ and religion, by casting a veil over it: therefore, you that are guilty of this distemper, take heed, though you have light in some things, that a veil be not drawn over those things which do more nearly concern you, and are of greater consequence.

Obs. 14. Soul-worship must be preferred before all other worship. We must not give God a carrion service, a carcass without a soul. Strong are the expressions in Scripture which are used against such outside, formal worship. Isa. i. 11—13, God professes of them, that he regards them not, he is full of them, his soul loathes them, they are iniquity, and a trouble to him, they are looked upon as a burden to him, such as God will hide his eyes from, and when they make many prayers he will not hear them. In this one scripture we have fourteen expressions against outside, formal duties, beside the four which we find in Isa. lxvi. 3. Thus you have the mind of God in this short but full sentence.

Now God forbid that what hath been said out of this scripture should be sinfully abused to carnal indulgence.

Ver. 7. *But they like men have transgressed the covenant: there have they dealt treacherously against me.*

Here is an argument, that mercy in the former verse is to be understood in a large sense; why? because it is the very substance of the covenant; they have been hard-hearted, cruel, and unmerciful, and thereby have transgressed the covenant. I am merciful in the covenant, and my grace is free and full to sinners there; but they have transgressed the covenant by being cruel and unmerciful: "But they like men have transgressed the covenant."

"Like men;" that is, like Adam; these men have sinned after the similitude of Adam's transgression. Rom. v. 14, speaks of those who "had not sinned after the similitude of Adam's transgression:" but these, as they have old Adam in them, so they have dealt with me as he did; and as he for his sin was cast out of Paradise, so these men have deserved to be cast out of the good land. But Vatablus, and Tremelius, and others, read the words thus, They have broken my covenant as a man, they thought that I had been as their fellow creature; as they made it their practice to break covenants with men, so they thought to do with God: so they have transgressed my covenant. This sense may be admitted; and hence it would be seasonable to observe, that the cause of breach of covenant with God is, because we consider not that it is with God that we make our covenants.

But the words are more usually read, as in our books, "But they like men have transgressed the covenant;" that is, not as I, who, like a God, have kept covenant; but they, like such men as themselves, i. e. weak, inconstant, frail, unfaithful creatures, have transgressed, Job xxxi. 33.

But may not this seem to be an excusing or diminution of their sin to say, "They like men," implying the common frailty of human nature, "have transgressed?"

No; it is rather an aggravation of their sin. Therefore the word here translated "men," is אדם used for man in his corrupt estate, for weak, frail men; and so distinct from that which signifies generous and strenuous men: אישים and so the comparison is not only between God and man, but between the several degrees of men.

Or thus, They have transgressed my covenant like men; that is, not like my people. Saints that are of my church, they have not transgressed my covenant so. Their ways have been the ways of ordinary men, and as such they have transgressed my covenant. The two last senses are principally meant here.

"My covenant." The covenant of God we usually divide into two parts; but the Scripture, to me, seems to hold forth a threefold covenant: the one of works, that which was made with Adam in Paradise. The second, that which was made with Abraham, the covenant of grace; the tenor of which is this, I will be thy God, and the God of thy seed after thee. Then the covenant made with them on Mount Sinai. Now the covenant here cannot be meant immediately of the covenant of works, nor of the covenant of grace, for this covenant here referred to is one especially made with them, and therefore must be understood of that at Mount Sinai, made many hundred years after the others; yet mediately it has reference to that of works, and of grace.

And were this knot rightly understood and untied, the Antinomians and we might easily be reconciled; for we grant that believers are delivered from the law in respect of the power of it, as condemning; from its rigour, but not from its duties; for the things commanded in the law were duties before the law was given, the law was written in the hearts of the saints from the beginning. But the opening of this point would require a whole exercise, and I shall reserve it to some other time.

Now, then, the covenant which they transgressed was the covenant at large, but especially that covenant which God made with them when they came into the land of Canaan.

"They transgressed;" the word is עברו they went over; the covenant was betwixt them and their sins, and they went over it to their sins, the bank was not high enough to keep them and their sins asunder.

"There;" they transgressed the covenant שם *there*, in that good land of Canaan into which God had brought them, and given them possession: so the Chaldee.

Again, "There" they transgressed the covenant, there where God had hewed them by his prophets, and thought to work them to good.

Lastly, "There," that is, in the covenant itself, and that in those things wherein they thought they kept the covenant, and thought they honoured me most; in those things they broke the covenant.

"Have they dealt treacherously." The Sept. renders it κατεφρόνησε μοῦ, they have despised me; they have forsaken me, and chosen other lovers; even as a woman leaves her own husband to whom she was engaged, and goes to other men. It denotes the heart's joining to some other rather than God, so as to be willing to leave the Lord, and, either out of affection to some other, or for private advantage, to forsake God and his cause, nay, to promote and further that which is against God. The notes from the words are these:

Obs. 1. It is God's goodness that he enters into covenant with such poor creatures as we are. It is made an aggravation of their sin here, that they falsified the covenant. The love of God in entering into covenant with such mean, worthless creatures, should constrain duty from us in the most difficult precepts, and that with willingness.

Obs. 2. God is constant in his covenant with men. This is in opposition to their unfaithfulness; they deal falsely with God in the covenant, but God is constant in his covenant, he confirms it with the strength of a giant. Dan. ix. 27, "And he shall confirm the covenant with many for one week." The word there והגביר signifies, he confirms the covenant like a giant, or a mighty strong man: they, as weak men, break covenant with me, but I with strength confirm my covenant: therefore David saith, 2 Sam. xxiii. 5, "Yet he hath made with me an everlasting covenant, ordered in all things, and sure."

Obs. 3. Man's nature is very weak and unsettled. "They like men have transgressed the covenant." We must not lay too much upon men, for when most unfaithful they act but like men. Oh what folly is it in men to forsake the eternal God and run to the creature! We trust our servants in our businesses, and shall we not trust God much more? The word saith, "All men are liars;" nay, "every man at his best state is vanity." Psal. lxii. 9, "Surely men of low degree are vanity, and men of high degree are a lie: to be laid in the balance, they are altogether lighter than vanity."

Obs. 4. The apprehension of our obligations should keep us within covenant. Oh never let be said, that our sins are so strong that they break covenant to attain their desires. It is a sign of a most vile, wretched spirit, so to desire sin, as to break over this bond of the covenant. Think of this, all you that are so easily overtaken with sin; when a temptation to any sin comes, say thus, Such a sin I would have, and my desires are after it, but did I never covenant against it? and what! shall I be so wicked as to break my covenant for it?

Obs. 5. Breach of covenant is a most grievous aggravation of sin; it provokes God highly against that people or person. "There have they dealt treacherously against me." Deut. xxix. 24, 25, "Even all nations shall say, Wherefore hath the Lord done thus unto this land? what meaneth the heat of this great anger? Then men shall say, Because they have forsaken the covenant of the Lord God of their fathers, which he made with them when he brought them forth out of the land of Egypt." What cause have we to bless God that he hath not destroyed us for breach of covenant with him! Why should not our condition be the condition of this people here in Deuteronomy? Had God turned his hand and let our enemies prevail, this might have been our case.

Obs. 6. God expects that of his people which every one cannot do. They must not plead they are flesh and blood as other men, God would have you more than men; you must remember that you are saints and members of Christ, and therefore must live as the redeemed of the Lord. In 1 Cor. iii. 3, "Are ye not carnal, and walk as men?" the apostle rebukes the Corinthians for this; God looked that they should walk beyond other men, and that which the apostle makes the ground of his reproof, they make their excuse. Jesus Christ descended from on high, to this end, to purchase a peculiar people to himself, that might yield him honour in the world, beyond that which he has from other men. We should live as those which have the Divine nature in them; we should beware of passion and anger, even as God is slow to anger. How far are those from doing any eminent thing for God, who cannot deny themselves in their wills and passions, and have not even common humanity!

Obs. 7. Our keeping covenant with God is the effect of his grace; we have not that power of ourselves; therefore let us bless God for this mercy.

Obs. 8. Men may do many services and yet be covenant-breakers. It is possible for a man to have committed the sin against the Holy Ghost, and yet be a professor of Christ and the gospel; therefore we had need look to our hearts.

Obs. 9. We may be covenant-breakers even in those things in which we seem to be most religious. But may this be in the duties of God's worship? Yea, it may be, thus; when men shall think to cover any sin they live in, by their performing of duties, this is treacherous dealing, and playing false in the covenant.

Obs. 10. The sins of saints which break covenant are sins of a double dye; other men's sins are rebellions against God, but theirs are treacheries.

Obs. 11. The want of the right knowledge of God is the main cause of breach of covenant. Dan. xi. 32, "And such as do wickedly against the covenant shall he corrupt by flatteries: but the people that do know their God shall be strong, and do exploits." Who shall be corrupted by flatteries; those that know God? No, they shall be strong, and do great exploits; such shall be employed by him in his work.

Obs. 12. There can be no keeping covenant with God, where there is unmercifulness to men: let there be never such professions and expressions of religion in words, if there be cruelty and unmercifulness, there can be no keeping of covenant with God, Heb. iii. 10.

Obs. 13. The consideration that it is with God that we break covenant, is a humbling consideration. Against me who am their God, who have protected them from dangers, delivered them in straits, against me have they thus sinned. As, if a man should carefully bring up a poor child, and this child, when he came to years, should abuse and wrong him, would not this be ingratitude and unkindness indeed? so the consideration of what a God it is that we break covenant with, wonderfully aggravates our unkindness.

Ver. 8. *Gilead is a city of them that work iniquity, and is polluted with blood.*

We read in Numb. xxxii. 1, of the land of Gilead, which Reuben and the half tribe of Manasseh possessed, on the other side of the river; in it were divers cities of refuge, which were the cities of the Levites; one of them, the most famous, which gave name to the whole country, was Gilead: which thing is usual among us at this day; whole counties receiving their names from some eminent place in them, as Northampton, Northamptonshire; Leicester, Leicestershire. This city of Gilead, in which were the priests, should have been holier than the rest, but it was polluted, and from thence the rest of the places of the kingdom.

"That work iniquity." The words are פעלי און and signify, "that work iniquity," or vain things, with energy and effectually, as Pagnine saith פעל means, *agere cum energiâ et effectu.*

"And is polluted with blood," עקבה מדם supplanted or overturned with blood; the Levites who dwelt there have undone the city. How many cities are supplanted and overturned by the priests which live in them, by their cruelties, by their subterfuges, and subtle excuses for sin and wickedness! They supplanted these cities of refuge, which were for those who had shed blood at unawares, they flying to them being secure; and that they did in these four ways:

1. By taking those in which were wilful murderers, whereas the city was for the shelter of those who had killed any unawares; now these men would judge wilful murder to be but manslaughter, as we call it. And I wish our kingdom be not deeply guilty of this sin, even by this very distinction, when men in their passions shall make nothing of killing a man, and it is but accounted manslaughter; certainly God will never account it so, but even wilful murder.

2. By refusing to take in those whom of right they should, except they had good store of money to give them. When some that were poor applied for admittance, they would refuse or delay them, and by that means they were often taken by the pursuer of blood; for these priests were to judge of it.

3. By casting those out which were in, and could not be a source of gain to them: often they delivered such to the avenger of blood, when they should have protected them.

4. By their cruelty to those that would not join with them in their false worship. Perhaps they might some of them be men of tender consciences, and could not join with them in their superstitious worship; now these priests, perhaps, would complain of them to the magistrate, that they were troublesome persons and bred divisions, and by this means they got them out of the cities of refuge. And has not this been our case of late? Thus they supplanted these cities of refuge. The observations are,

Obs. 1. That through man's wickedness the best ordinances of God are corrupted. These cities of refuge were for special use, ordinances of God set apart for the saving, and they made them a means and instrument for the shedding, of blood. The sacrament is an ordinance set apart by God for union and communion; and what more prevents this than its abuse? men's coming unprepared separates tender consciences from joining with them. So likewise in civil ordinances for men's outward good, how have they been perverted! where have they tyrannized more, and used more cruelty and injustice, than in the very courts for the administration of justice? and such as should have seen equity performed, were the greatest instruments of oppression and mischief.

Obs. 2. We must not always judge of places from

former circumstances. Gilead was a city famous for God's worship, yet now how defiled with blood! So Rome, how famous was it for the worship of God! yet now it is become the very filth of abomination.

Obs. 3. Places set apart for God's worship, if corrupted, become the worst of all. Gilead a city of refuge, yet where was there ever such a defiled and corrupted place? So in our universities and colleges, what superstitions and vanities have abounded! even like Augeus' stable, a place of filthiness and vileness. And this is no new thing, for Gregory Nazianzen reports of Athens, that it was the most full of superstitions, and acknowledges it a great mercy that God preserved him and Basil from those infections.

Obs. 4. To be a worker of iniquity is most abominable. "Gilead is a city of them that work iniquity." God's people sometimes are overtaken by sin, but they are never workers of iniquity; for the Scripture tells us, that he which works iniquity is of the devil.

Obs. 5. The clergy, if wicked, are the worst of all. No men can work out or bring to pass their own ends as they can. The priests were in Gilead, and they were the men who wrought the mischief. And have not our times sealed to this truth? Who have been so vile and wicked as our corrupted clergy? but how has God broken the plots, and crossed the designs, of these vermin!

Obs. 6. A wicked clergy overwhelms whole nations. These were they which overturned this city of Gilead: and thus would they have done to us, had not God, in his infinite wisdom and mercy, prevented their hellish plots.

Obs. 7. False worship and tyranny are joined together. Wherever you see tyranny there conclude there is false worship: therefore we had need to pray hard for the ordinances in their purity, that we may not have false religion, and consequent tyranny. Luther tells us, that the devil is a liar and a murderer; so that where there is a lie in God's religion, there is murdering.

Obs. 8. There are none so cruel as wicked clergymen; so they may have their wills and lusts satisfied, though it cost the blood of thousands of souls, they care not.

Obs. 9. Cruelty in the clergy is the worst of all; for it is required of them to be men of peace: but who are the great incendiaries of our times, and fomenters of these wars, but the vile, wicked clergy?

Ver. 9. *And as troops of robbers wait for a man, so the company of priests murder in the way by consent: for they commit lewdness.*

This verse has much of the former in it.

"Troops of robbers." The kingdom of Israel had their troopers robbing and spoiling up and down; and who were these robbers, but their priests? their priests were turned robbing troopers. And have not we this text literally fulfilled at this day in our kingdom? The gown is cast off and the armour put on, and now they are turned troopers. They were before murderers of souls, and now they are turned murderers of men's souls and bodies both; so that we might send their gowns after them, and say, as Joseph's brethren said to their father Jacob, Do not you know this? is not this your son Joseph's coat?

"Murder in the way." They stood in the way to rob; how was this? in what way did they rob? Jerome putting this question to a Jew, his answer was, That at the time of the passover, and the pentecost, the people used to come to Jerusalem, and as they were going in their journey, these priests would stand in the way and slay them: they were the least suspected of any; Gilead was a city which should have defended them from robbers, and they were turned robbers themselves. The notes are these:

Obs. 1. Wicked ministers are most outrageous against those that leave them, and cannot join with them in their superstitious and false worship. The priests were so.

Obs. 2. Wicked men, especially wicked priests, wait to do mischief; how much more should God's people wait for opportunities to do service for God, and for his people!

Obs. 3. Many people are nearest undoing when they think themselves most secure. It was the case of these poor travellers here; they thought themselves most safe and secure, and then were they slain and murdered by these wicked, robbing priests.

Obs. 4. Wicked men abuse the esteem which others have of them. These priests were the least suspected, and reputed harmless, innocent men, as at this day; and in other things, as in theft, many servants who are trusted by their masters, abuse their masters' confidence, and so are the more false.

Obs. 5. Judges are least called to an account for their wrongs, and therefore are the more bold to sin. These priests were to judge of murder done by others; now instead of judging others' murders, they murdered themselves; now who should judge of their murders? There follows,

"By consent:" the word is שכמה taken by Luther and others for the city Shechem, which stood near Jericho; and he saith, that Christ, in the parable of the man which fell among thieves between Jericho and Jerusalem, had respect to this place of Hosea. But I shall interpret it as in our translation, because I find it in another scripture signifying "consent:" "Then will I turn to the people a pure language, that they may all call upon the name of the Lord, to serve him with one consent," Zeph. iii. 9. The word is שכמה with one shoulder, and is a metaphor taken from oxen yoked together.

When God's people join together in a work, it should be a shame for any to withdraw from them. Thus these priests murdered by consent, they set to their shoulder in this wicked work, the one was not ignorant of what the other did. The note hence is,

Obs. 6. Wicked men can join together in wickedness, how much more should the saints join together for God! What shall we say to those differences which are made amongst us? It is not long since we were under antichrist's yoke; and were we not galled and pinched? Then why will you not take Christ's yoke on you, which is easy and light?

"They commit lewdness." זמה עשו They studied wickedness, they plotted for it.

Obs. 7. None so plot wickedness as clergymen. Gilead is that wicked city of robbers; there the priests consulted together and plotted their wickednesses.

Obs. 8. Plotted wickedness is the most vile. Exod. xxviii. 6, the ephod was to be made of "cunning work," of a work which had much thought in it; so it is in the original. That work is very good which has much thought and consideration in it; and that sin is wicked, with an aggravation, which is thought of and meditated upon; then it is lewdness. Think of this, all you that do plot and think of your sins before you do commit them: in those sins there is lewdness.

מעשה חשב
Opere excogitato.

Luther renders the original here, "they do whatsoever they think," which may also be the force of the word "lewdness;" he saith that they had a proverb in Germany, that the monks were so wicked that there was nothing so bad which they could think of, but they would dare to do it. None so bold in sin, or dare to venture themselves so far, as wicked clergymen. Many men are vile and wicked enough, but they want capacity and confidence to vend and utter it; but these wicked priests could do it, calumniate and reproach without fear, these have impudent, bold faces; and concerning such I say no more but this, "The Lord rebuke them."

Ver. 10. *I have seen an horrible thing in the house of Israel: there is the whoredom of Ephraim, Israel is defiled.*

The Lord proceeds further in his complaint against Israel.

"I have seen an horrible thing." שעריריה a thing that may make the hairs of our head to stand on end; the Seventy translate it by φρικώδη, a word of something similar import, signifying, a storm in the sea. This word sometimes signifies the devil, as in Lev. xvii. 7, "They shall no more offer their sacrifices לשעירם unto devils, after whom they have gone a whoring."

Tremelius, in his comment, observes, that the letters are more than ordinary in this word here, to increase its signification; as if he had said, It is a horrible thing, a very horrible thing! What is this horrible thing? It was this, Ephraim had defiled himself. Whence,

Obs. 1. Idolatry is a very horrible sin. To worship a false god, and that for politic ends, as they did here, is a most horrible thing; to preserve their estates and their liberties, they fell from the true worship of God to worship at Dan and Beth-el. Jer. ii. 11, 12, "Hath a nation changed their gods, which are yet no gods? but my people have changed their glory for that which doth not profit. Be astonished, O ye heavens, at this, and be horribly afraid, be ye very desolate, saith the Lord:" and chap. xviii. 13, "The virgin of Israel hath done a very horrible thing:" and chap. xliv. 4, "Oh, do not this abominable thing that I hate." God does not put an aggravation upon this sin beyond what is in it. It is usual with men, if any thing be done against them, to make it very horrible with circumstances and aggravations; but God never does so. A notable example we have of man's aggravating an offence, Dan. iii. 14, "Nebuchadnezzar spake and said unto them, Is it true, O Shadrach, Meshach, and Abed-nego, do not ye serve my gods, nor worship the golden image which I have set up?" "Is it true?" the words in the original are, What desolations have these made, not to obey me! This is the manner of proud hearts, but not God's, he never speaks more against a sin, or punishes men more for sin, than it deserves. We can look upon God's judgments as horrible, but where is the man that looks upon sin as horrible? It may be you tremble at gross sins, but where is the man that trembles at false worship? The apparitions of the devil are very horrible to us; and sin is here expressed by the same words as the devil.

הצדה of Desolatio, Mont. צדיה in Niphal Desolari.

Obs. 2. Though we may seem to colour sin over, yet God sees it. "I have seen an horrible thing in the house of Israel."

Obs. 3. Idolatry is a provoking sin, but especially in the house of Israel. "I have seen an horrible thing in the house of Israel."

"There is the whoredom of Ephraim, Israel is defiled." Ephraim was the tribe of Jeroboam, and by Ephraim is to be understood the court and the nobles; there, saith God, did I see this abominable thing. Where the common people are generally wicked in a nation, it is a sign of much evil; if the gentry are profane, it is much worse; but if the nobility and those at the court are idolaters, it is night indeed. If Ephraim be vile, it is no marvel if Israel be defiled.

Ver. 11. *Also, O Judah, he hath set an harvest for thee, when I returned the captivity of my people.*

These words are something difficult; I shall show the meaning of them, thus: Judah has wrapped up herself in the same offence, in the same transgression received from Ephraim, the ten tribes, and it has grown up to a harvest of judgment, which has its set, appointed time. But when? "When I returned the captivity of my people." This refers to the time mentioned in 2 Chron. xxviii. 6, where you find these three things: 1. The harvest set for Judah. 2. The captivity of Judah. 3. The return of their captivity. The harvest was set when "Pekah, the son of Remaliah, slew in Judah an hundred and twenty thousand in one day; because they had forsaken the Lord God of their fathers." What a harvest was here set! and the text saith, they "were all valiant men."

But what was it that provoked the Lord thus against them? Because they had forsaken the Lord, the God of their fathers. God's judgments in Scripture, cutting down a people, are compared to a harvest; Joel iii. 13, "Put ye in the sickle, for the harvest is ripe." But where was this captivity? In 2 Chron. xxviii. 8, "And the children of Israel carried away captive of their brethren two hundred thousand, women, sons, and daughters." But when was their return? In the 9th verse, the prophet comes to them, and in the 11th tells them, they must deliver up their captives which they had taken from their brethren: these were brethren, as is clear, yet behold their rage! yet, in the 15th verse, see how this affected them; they clothed, fed, and restored all their captives again presently. See the mighty power of the word to still the rage of the stoutest spirits. Oh that it might do so with us at this time, as it did here with this people! this would be a kindly work indeed. So that by this you may see what the harvest in the text is.

The notes from hence are,

Obs. 1. The sins of a people are seeds for a harvest of judgment, as their good actions are for a harvest of mercy.

Obs. 2. God has a fixed time for judgment; and though you have a time, yet know it is fixed; therefore sow as fast as you can, there will come a harvest ere long.

Obs. 3. In the time of God's judgments, he remembers mercy for his people. He has set a time for the return of their captivity.

Thus you have, I conceive, the genuine sense of these words. There are some that read them thus: Judah, since you are guilty also, you shall not enjoy your peace nor your lands in quiet, till God return your captivity; Israel shall not enjoy their harvest, but Judah shall.

Now that which makes me think this is not the meaning, is this, because the Lord still goes on to threaten Judah; I have "set an harvest for thee."

Some others interpret it thus: When God was about to turn away their captivity, Judah did so harden Israel in their way, that it was the cause of my hardening my heart against them, and not returning their captivity. Israel might think thus, Though we are bad, and in many things amiss, yet Judah, who are a people nearer to God than we, is also defiled.

Obs. 4. Many are ripened for judgment by the example of others, especially of great professors, and chiefly of professing and reforming churches, that have the name of pure worship in them. Let such be very wary what they practise, especially in a time of reformation, lest they harden others in their corruption.

CHAPTER VII.

Ver. 1. *When I would have healed Israel, then the iniquity of Ephraim was discovered, and the wickedness of Samaria: for they commit falsehood; and the thief cometh in, and the troop of robbers spoileth without.*

THIS chapter is filled with complaints wholly against Israel. The two former chapters brought in Judah with them, but this chapter is spent wholly against Israel. Luther saith, that by the reading of this chapter, we may see that the church has always evils of one and the same kind, even at this day such as in those times. We have had a clear and lively pattern of this held forth to us in our times concerning our evils.

"When I would have healed Israel." Before, God took upon him the person of a husband, that would have recalled his adulterous wife: but in this chapter, he compares himself to a surgeon, who would have cured a wounded person; and his people he compares to such; but coming to cure them, he found their wound worse than he expected. As sometimes when a surgeon first comes to a wound, he thinks it not so bad and dangerous as indeed it is found on probing it, and all this while perhaps the patient remains very quiet and still; but when put to pain by searching of their wound, then they are froward, and struggle: So, saith God, many ways and means have I used to do them good, judgments, reproofs, and exhortations, but they grow worse and worse, the sins of Ephraim break forth, the sins of the court work out, and the sins of Samaria (which was the chief city) show themselves. In Isa. vii. 9, "The head of Ephraim is Samaria:" as if the wickedness of the court were complained of by some in the country.

"Then the iniquity of Ephraim was discovered, and the wickedness of Samaria" did appear. The prophet looks upon Ephraim, the wicked court, and Samaria, the profane city, and sees death in the face of both; the sin of Ephraim and Samaria is in the head, which speaks them in a dangerous condition, Lev. xiii. 44. They add iniquity to iniquity, which shows their perverseness; and "he that is of a perverse heart shall be despised," Prov. xii. 8.

"The wickedness," ורעות their wickednesses: "When I would have healed Israel, then the sin of Ephraim was discovered, and the wickednesses of Samaria."

Obs. 1. In great cities there is all manner of evils.

But now, when was God about to heal these ten tribes? to what period does this refer? Some interpret it to be, when God went about to cure the evils and the abominations that were in Rehoboam's reign, which was a very sad time: had he hearkened to the counsel of his wise, grave counsellors, it had been well for him and his people; but giving credit to the counsel of his young, inexperienced men, he endangered the very life of his kingdom by it; and when, through the pride of his heart, he would not hearken, God rent the greatest part of the kingdom from him, and gave it to Jeroboam; and now, when there were such hopes of delivering them from these their oppressions, then did the iniquity of Ephraim appear, then did they oppress and crush those which would not yield to their superstitious idols and false worship. But this cannot be the meaning of this passage, for at this time the ten tribes were not divided, nor broken off, neither was Samaria built, as we see in 2 Kings xvi. If this be not the time, then to what time does this refer? Surely to the period of Jehu's reign, who was made the surgeon of those times, who was anointed in Gilead, the city of surgeons: for God saith, "Is there no balm in Gilead, no physician there?" God used Jehu for the doing of a great deal of work for their cure, he destroyed and dissipated Jezebel and the priests of Baal; and when this was doing, the great courtiers of Ephraim and the citizens of Samaria came and gave him their counsel: Jehu, take heed what you do; be wise, consider what you do in such cases as these, take heed you do not overdo: you have done enough in destroying Baal's priests and putting down idolatry; but if, moreover, you pull down Dan and Beth-el, and suffer the people to go up to Jerusalem, you will lose all. Then farewell all obedience, your kingdom is lost. Then the citizens of Samaria come and tell him, that if he go on thus, they shall be undone and lose all their trading, and shall be separated: And why should this be, seeing there is no need of it? we may worship at Dan and Beth-el as well, and it will be more for our ease. This might be the language of the people; and in this the iniquity of Ephraim and the sin of Samaria appeared; and this was wickedness with a high hand. The observations are these:

Obs. 1. The sins of a kingdom are the sores of a kingdom. Isa. i. 6, "From the sole of the foot even unto the head there is no soundness in it; but wounds, and bruises, and putrifying sores." First in regard of their sins, then in regard of their miseries.

By this we may see that wicked men are the sores and wounds of a nation, parish, and family; therefore one having three wicked daughters calls them the imposthumes, or cankers, of his family; even so, wicked men defile wherever they come. Oh that people would think of this their condition! Thou that art a wicked man runnest up and down with filthy stuff, more odious in God's eyes than a lazar in our eyes.

As sin, so afflictions and miseries are the wounds of a kingdom, family, or person; and if we will not be sensible of the one wound made by sin, God will make us sensible of the other by suffering them. Our kingdom is like the man which fell among thieves as he went from Jericho to Jerusalem. Does not the nation lie now a bleeding? and where is the man that pities it? nay, are not men so far from pitying these wounds, that multitudes flock together to take advantage of our sores, even like the flies which suck out content and sweetness from the sores of poor creatures; I mean those who strive to suck out the blood of the kingdom in their offices and places, men that are altogether for themselves, and how they may make themselves and theirs great in the world, though the nation lie a bleeding. Aristotle tells us of a man, whose sores the flies using constantly to suck and lie upon, his friend coming by him, and seeing them upon him, beat them off; the man was discontented at it, saying, Alas! what have you done? I thought, replied his friend, I had done you a good turn. O no, for when these are off fresh ones will come, that will suck me worse than the others did before. Had we not those that did suck us before? have we forgotten those oppressions? shall we have worse now? It follows,

"When I would have healed Israel." Hence,

Obs. 2. The Lord is the healer of a people. It is he alone that can do it, and none but he; we may use many means to be healed, but all in vain, except the Lord heal us with pardoning and sanctifying mercies: Jer. xvii. 14, "Heal me, O Lord, and I shall be healed; save me, and I shall be saved: for thou art my praise." So Psal. lx. 2, "Heal the breaches thereof; for it shaketh." How many are there that would go about to heal our wounds slightly! Jer. viii. 11. We are like many silly persons, who, feeling a little pain of their wounds, will needs have them skinned up and healed presently, and then they putrify and are worse than ever. But the Lord is the healer of his people, and when he heals he does it effectually. Many encouragements we have in Scripture to seek to God for healing, as the promise of God, 2 Chron. vii. 14, "If my people, which are called by my name, shall humble themselves, and pray, and seek my face, and turn from their wicked ways; then will I hear from heaven, and forgive their sin, and will heal their land." Mark the connexion of these words; first seek to be forgiven, and then healed; if we should be healed before pardoned, woe be to us, we should then be undone! Isa. lvii. 16—18, "I will not contend for ever, neither will I be always wroth: for the spirit should fail before me, and the souls which I have made. For the iniquity of his covetousness was I wroth, and smote him: I hid me, and was wroth, and he went on frowardly in the way of his heart." Now what may we think will become of him? Surely, now, nothing but desolation and destruction. No, saith God, "I have seen his ways, and will heal him: I will lead him also, and restore comforts unto him and to his mourners." Jer. iii. 22, "Return, ye backsliding children, and I will heal your backslidings." Oh that the answer of this people might be ours: "Behold, we come unto thee, for thou art the Lord our God."

Now the Lord cures accurately: as surgeons cure by purgation and allaying the misery; so the Lord heals his people by taking away the cause and the malignancy of that trouble which is upon them. So, thou that art under any particular trouble or affliction, if God sanctify that trouble by removing its cause, God may be said to heal, though the affliction be not quite taken away.

Then God may be said to heal by fomentation, as surgeons use to do, when the part is able to resist and oppose that which would feed the humour: so when the Lord puts strength into the soul to oppose disquieting and vexing thoughts, that sinks into the soul from its afflictions: now, where this work is accomplished, the soul is healed.

Obs. 3. God does not always will things according to his omnipotent power. "I would have healed Israel;" that is, I would and I did use all the means calculated to heal them.

But it may be objected, If God see that we are unable of ourselves to be healed, how can we be healed, when we have not the power?

Now, for answer to this, we must know, that men are not healed proceeds not so much from the want of ability as want of will; men do not do what they can, therefore they do not *will* to be healed. God does not make men unwilling, but speaks to us after the manner of men; though there be also an inability, yet because men think not of that in not turning, or because the inability is chiefly in the perverseness of the will, it is not a metaphysical inability, as I may so speak, but a formal wilfulness; and though men think that God is altogether to blame that they are not healed, God will make this one of his works at the day of judgment, to clear himself from those aspersions. Now men are so proud, that they think themselves too good and too lofty for God; but God will clear up all, and show himself to be righteous in their destruction.

Obs. 4. Much wickedness often lies hid in a kingdom, or person, till the means of cure appear. It was thus with Paul, Rom. vii. 9, "I was alive without the law once; but when the commandment came sin revived, and I died;" yet, notwithstanding, God, by his almighty power, helped him over all difficulties. As, when a man begins to repair an old house which is rotten and decayed, he does not conceive the trouble of it, till he comes to remove the rubbish; who would imagine the wickedness that is in many men's hearts, which discovers itself when the means comes? Had not God set many servants in good families, the vileness and the vanity of their spirits had not discovered itself. Certainly this is our condition. Some few years since there appeared much wickedness in England, but how much more since God has sent the means to cure it! as appears,

1. By a bitter spirit of malignancy against the power of godliness. No people so wicked as we were before, but now our wickedness is grown to a spirit of malice and opposition against the word and the saints. At the first, men cried out for a reformation, and cried down bishops; but when God's people began to rejoice, of a sudden what a desperate spirit of pride and malignancy was there raised to oppose strenuously the reformation so much desired! and this aggravated by a malice which, 1. Blinds men's eyes, so that they cannot see their misery by reason of the falsities, and flatteries, and treacheries used against Scotland, Ireland, and England. And, 2. Makes them, rather than they will be subject to the yoke of Christ, willing to be slaves to the worst of men, yea, to their vilest lusts: and doth not this show a desperate spirit against God?

2. A base, sordid spirit, that will rather endure perpetual slavery by vile men, than incur any risk.

3. A treacherous spirit. When men betray kingdoms, overthrow states, and deceive the trust and confidence reposed in them, undermine and destroy parliaments, does not this manifest a most vile spirit in the people of this kingdom? Heretofore the commonalty could not be brought to fight against the Scots, yet now there can be found a gentry to fight against the parliament.

4. A blasphemous spirit. This sin abounded before, but how much is it now increased! nay, are there not now new oaths invented and pressed?

5. A cruel, bloody spirit. Some few years since who could have imagined the cruelties that have been used by Englishmen?

6. A spirit of division. We should have thought that in a time of public calamity we should have sodered together; when there was private persecution more love was expressed; and that which makes the rents now the more sad is, that they are between the best people.

7. An oppressing spirit. Men formerly oppressed are now turned oppressors themselves. What doth this but presage what these would have done had they had the power in their hands? This iniquity is now discovered.

8. A spirit of envy. How are active men in public places envied and spited! and how many now stand neutral, and upon this very ground, because they see others not so rich as they employed! therefore they sit still and fret themselves, and seek to hinder them that are active in public service, and so the work is hindered.

9. A spirit of superstition. Would ever any man have thought that the parliament should ever have had such a party to oppose them in their reformations? We might rather have thought that there would have been a general spirit rising against these superstitious vanities, to have banished them for ever. Oh what misery do these rotten teeth put this kingdom to at this very day! This iniquity is also discovered.

10. A wanton spirit. Such opinions as were never known before, doubting of the immortality of the soul, that there is no visible church upon the face of the earth; and all this under the name of Christ and free grace. Now what does all this but show, that when God would have healed us, then did our iniquities appear? What sad presages are these of approaching miseries!

11. An unmerciful spirit. Every one seeking his own, and how he may make him and his great in the world, and neglecting the poor and those that are in distress. We have cause to say, O Lord, what shall become of us? Know this, that I may not altogether discourage you; though our times are miserable, yet are they not altogether like unto Israel. It cannot be denied but that our court has imitated Ephraim, which was their court; yet though the city of Samaria did join with Ephraim, the city with us has not sided with the court, but the bulk of it has kept faithful with their God; for which mercy the children yet unborn will have cause to bless God.

Obs. 5. When a people grow worse upon the means of healing, it is a sign that their condition is desperate. Isa. i. 5, "Why should ye be stricken any more? ye will revolt more and more." Jer. li. 9, "We would have healed Babylon, but she is not healed." Ezek. xxiv. 13, "In thy filthiness is lewdness: because I have purged thee, and thou wast not purged, thou shalt not be purged from thy filthiness any more, till I have caused my fury to rest upon thee." Now, certainly, had not God found a party in this kingdom which closed with him when he would have healed us, we might have had occasion to make use of this scripture. How just were it with God to leave such a people as we are in our healing, because we are so impatient under the rod! Arias Montanus quotes out of Hippocrates, that the physicians in his time were bound by an oath to leave under their wounds to perish, such as were incorrigible, and would not endure the surgeons to cure them. When a man is engaged in a bad cause, and means are used to convince him, yet ofttimes he will become worse. Oh the vileness of men's spirits! We had need take heed that the cause we engage in be good, for how many men are there who defile their consciences, rather than yield to take shame to themselves for their sin! Oh what cause have we to fall down and be humbled for our iniquity, and to say as they in Jer. xiv. 18—20. So for particular towns and places where God sends the gospel, the means of grace, and that people is the worse for it, they have cause to tremble, and not to cry out against the preaching of the word as if that were the cause of it: this were most wicked and abominable. It was thus in Christ's time. We never read of any possessed with devils before Christ came; now shall we say it had been better that Christ had not come? O blame not the ministry, but your own hearts; and consider of this, you that God is working upon, the Lord comes close by the ministry of his word to heal you, and then you discover your wickedness and rotten hearts. The Lord stirs such a conscience, and begins to heal such a soul. Now it is the devil's policy to spoil such beginnings. Now, thinks the devil, if I can make such a soul commit a sin against conscience, or live in the omission of any known duty, the word then will never more work to benefit such a man. I have heard of one who, being troubled in conscience for committing that great sin of uncleanness, the devil tempting him to commit it again, told him if he would he should never be troubled more for it; the poor man yielding, and venturing upon it again, after he had done it was indeed never tempted again, nor troubled more, but lay afterward in a languishing, senseless condition, and so died. O take heed of this, you that are convinced in your consciences of the evil of such and such courses, for it is the great policy of the devil to make thee, who art convinced in conscience, to sin against conscience, and then he thinks the work is lost; the devil does not much fear the word's working upon him whom he has prevailed upon to live in secret known sins, and to venture upon the commission of sins against conscience. You who are under God's healing hand, be silent, and submit quietly: be not froward, you that are in troubles of conscience, hearken for a word from God; as the men of Ben-hadad did from that king, in 1 Kings xx. 33, they hearkened diligently whether any words of comfort fell from him, and caught at them hastily. Know that it were just with God to make you as the people spoken of in Isa. vi. 10. This concerns all, but especially those that are in trouble of conscience. Those that God begins to stir and work upon, take heed, I say; does Christ himself begin to work upon you? does he desire to heal you? is he willing to offer his blood to cure you by applying it to your wounded consciences? Let not the corruptions of your hearts now break forth, take heed now of sins against conscience, lest he let you perish in your lusts. Be willing to let God alone to do his work in you, lie quiet and still, take heed of murmuring and repining speeches, but follow on the work begun, and beseech him not to leave you till it be completed in you, and the great hazard of your miscarrying over. Little do you imagine those sins will weigh down and burden conscience which now you commit against its light. What a torment will it be to thy conscience to think, that at such a time I felt Jesus Christ coming to heal my soul in the ministry of his word; oh happy had it been for me, if I had lain under his hand, and kept his salve upon my sore! but because it was for the present troublesome, I cast it off, and went into such company, and listened to such temptations, and by this means have wounded my soul anew most desperately; and now what can I expect, but that the Lord should for ever forsake me, and leave me to die in my sins and wallow in my blood, and his eye not pity me, and make me to inherit the curse of that people, whose ears should be deaf that they should not hear, whose eyes should be blind that they should not see, and be converted, and I should heal them?

"They commit falsehood; and the thief cometh in, and the troop of robbers spoileth without." Furthermore, in these words the prophet shows in what particulars their iniquity did appear: they committed falsehood, they wrought a lie in regard of their falsehood, their false worship; and then in regard of their oppression, wronging one another, but especially in falsifying their trust one to another, and in their relations, not performing the duties which their relations called for, and bound them unto; so the word in the original שקר properly signifies. "They commit falsehood;" that is, they commit such a sin as the breaking of that duty which the law of their relation calls for from them. The notes hence are,

Obs. 6. It is the description of a wicked man, to commit falsehood. As the godly man is said to be for the truth, and to do the truth; so wicked men are against the truth, and go contrary to the truth: as the devil is said not to abide in the truth, even such are these who commit falsehood, and work a lie.

Obs. 7. It is a forerunner of great mischief, when people are false in their relations. In Micah vii. 5, 6, it was an ill time when all sorts of people were so unfaithful in their relations.

Obs. 8. There is much secret wickedness committed by men of false religions. "And the thief cometh in, and the troop of robbers spoileth without." Such as these are secret and cunning workers of mischief in church and state. Gal. ii. 4, "Because of false brethren unawares brought in, who came in privily to spy out our liberty which we have in Christ Jesus, that they might bring us into bondage." It is a great evil in a commonwealth to have secret oppressors, but far worse to have public spoiling. We have had much of the first formerly, and the Lord knows how much more of the second we may further taste of: I verily believe, there is none that ever thought the enemy would have spoiled in such a manner as he has done, and that ever Englishmen would have endured it; and we are the first people that ever endured such oppressions, that were not slaves before; and what the counsels and thoughts of God are in this thing concerning us we cannot tell. "Violence and spoil is heard in her; before me continually is grief and wounds." What then? "Be thou instructed, O Jerusalem, lest my soul depart from thee," Jer. vi. 7, 8. The first part of this scripture is ours at this day, grief and wounds are continually before us: but "be thou instructed," O England. In what? In this, that dreadful breach which sin has made between the king and parliament; be instructed in this. Jer. xv. 13, "Thy substance and thy treasures will I give to the spoil without price, and that for all thy sins, even in all thy borders." So Isa. xlii. 22, 24, "But this is a people robbed and spoiled; they are all of them snared in holes: they are for a prey, and none delivereth; for a spoil, and none saith, Restore. "Who gave Jacob for a spoil, and Israel to the robbers? did not the Lord, he against whom we have sinned?" Who among you will give ear and hearken to this? Men are wicked and tyrannical; but who is he that has given this our land to the plunderers? Is it not the Lord? Therefore we should look beyond the troubles, the hand that strikes, to God, who gave them their commission, and delivered us up into their hands. When God gives up a people to the robbers and spoilers in such a kind, his wrath is said to come upon them; as in the 25th verse, "Therefore he hath poured upon him the fury of his anger, and the strength of battle."

Ver. 2. *And they consider not in their hearts that I remember all their wickedness: now their own doings have beset them about; they are before my face.*

"They consider not in their hearts." ובל־יאמרו ללבבם They say not to their hearts. This phrase in other scriptures is used for saying in their hearts. Jer. v. 24, "Neither say they in their heart, Let us fear God, that giveth rain." And in Eccles. i. 16, considering, is communing with our own hearts; I spoke, or consulted, with my heart. From this phrase of speaking thus to our hearts, we may,

Obs. 1. It is a good thing to be often speaking with one's own heart, thus: O my soul, how is it with thee? how stand things between God and thee? what terms standest thou in for eternity? canst thou look upon God's face with comfort and not be afraid? what guilt is there in thy conscience? canst thou behold eternity and rejoice in the thoughts of it? Such meditations and questionings as these would be very profitable for the soul. Many people can talk abroad in company of these things, but where is the man that sets apart time to question with his soul about these? Psal. iv. 4, "Stand in awe, and sin not: commune with your own heart upon your bed, and be still." There are in the soul many times boisterous distempers, but then we should cause a silence and a calm in our hearts, bid them be still. There are great distempers in that family where the husband and the wife go two or three days together, and speak not one to another; so there is no less distemper in that soul, which can go two or three days without questioning itself, and examining its condition. But what is it they should speak? This,

"That I remember all their wickedness." The Vulgate renders it thus, Lest they should consider. Do not you think that God remembers the sins of your forefathers only, that they were vile and wicked; no, but I also remember the sins that are present before me. But the reading of the words in your books is most agreeable to the original; therefore Luther saith, that these words are a reproof of their security: the princes, they feel not the judgment, although the principal actors in the wickedness; and although the common people suffer much, yet they attribute their sufferings to any thing rather than to their sins. Hence,

Obs. 2. God remembers the wickedness of people, though long since committed. As we may see in the case of Amalek, God remembers this their wickedness many hundred years after; 1 Sam. xv. 2, "Thus saith the Lord of hosts, I remember that which Amalek did to Israel, how he laid wait for him in the way, when he came up from Egypt." Amos viii. 7, "The Lord hath sworn by the excellency of Jacob, Surely I will never forget any of their works." Nay, they are not only remembered, but recorded: "The sin of Judah is written with a pen of iron, and with the point of a diamond," Jer. xvii. 1. Every oath, every lie, yea, and every vain thought, which thou hast committed, and continuest in under an impenitent condition, know, that thy sins are remembered; and that thou mayst be sure of it, see what is said, Job xiv. 17, "My transgression is sealed up in a bag, and thou sewest up mine iniquity." They are sealed in a bag: as the clerk of assize seals up the indictments, and at the assizes brings his bag and takes them out; even so will God; as God has his time to seal up men's transgressions in his bag, so he will have his time to take them out, to reckon with sinners for them, and then woe to them! Deut. xxxii. 34, "Is not this laid up in store with me, and sealed up among my treasures?" It is sealed up to be remembered, though perhaps committed forty or fifty years ago; and it is thy sin if thou dost not remember them, when and where they were committed; and if thou wilt not, know, that God has his time to make thee know them.

Obs. 3. Wicked men consider not that God remembers their sins. In Psal. xciv. 5—7, they commit horrible wickednesses, daring sins, yet they force themselves not to believe that God takes notice of them and remembers them; "they say, The Lord shall not see, neither shall the God of Jacob regard it." The Jews tell us, that when Jeroboam's hand was dried up, the false prophets told him that this was but by chance, and so kept him from thinking of God that had smitten him. Did men consider that it is God that remembers them, it would work humiliation in them, and stop them in their sins. Were the danger that sin brings men into always in their eye, they would think it both a great madness and folly to sin against God. Joshua thought it so; Is the iniquity of Peor a small thing in your eyes, that you should add more to it? Didst thou know that God remembers the sins of thy youth and thy maturer age, thou wouldst fear that, on the next sin thou committest, God might bring upon thee all thy previous transgressions. As a man that has used his body to drink poison, for a time may do well, but at last he is overcome, and destroys himself; so the next sin which thou committest, though it be less than former transgressions, it may set all the rest on working: as, suppose there be many barrels of gunpowder in a room, and a few grains lie scattered about, and a spark falls into that, and so fires all the rest; so thy former sins are as the barrels of gunpowder, the next sin thou committest, especially if a sin against knowledge, may be the grains which set all the rest on work to pull down judgment upon thee. There is no argument so powerful to keep men from their sins, as the consideration that God sees and knows them all, and will remember them.

Obs. 4. When God punishes for sin, he manifests that he remembers sin. 1 Kings xvii. 18, the woman of Zarephath questions the prophet, saying, "What have I to do with thee, O thou man of God? art thou come unto me to call my sin to remembrance, and to slay my son?" God's hand being upon her, brought her sin to remembrance. How do the consciences of men dictate this to them in their afflictions, This cross is for such a sin, this misery for such a base lust that thou wouldst have fulfilled at such a time; God now puts thee in mind of such an act of uncleanness, such a time thou wert cruel and hard-hearted. This is clear in Joseph's brethren, whose sin was committed twenty-two years before trouble came upon them. You that have committed many sins a long time ago, and think they are forgotten, it is not so; even if the guilt of them be taken away by Christ, know that there will come a time in which thou shalt be put in mind of them: as a man that in his youth gets many a bruise and rub, which then he undergoes well enough, and never complains of; but when he grows old, or has an infirm body, then every rain and change of weather will remind him of the previous injuries: but this is the saints' privilege, that God never so remembers their sins, as to condemn them for their sins. It follows,

"All their wickedness: now their own doings have beset them about; they are before my face." Luther saith, their studied wickedness, their contrived iniquities, have beset them round about, or their doings have compassed them round. These words have reference to malefactors, who shift up and down, but at the last are beset and seized: just so their sins had beset them, that they could no way escape. Or, as soldiers beleaguer a town, and will not let any in or out; so men by their sins are besieged, and brought into such a condition that there is no way for comfort to come at them, or for them to avoid the judgments which are coming upon them: men's sins are like the six men in Ezek. ix. 2, "And, behold, six men came from the way of the higher gate," to beset the gates of the city. And know, O thou bold sinner, that God has his time to beset thee with thy sins and his judgments, to awaken thy conscience by setting thy sins in order before thee; and this is the great reason why men cry out in the horror of their consciences, because they are beset with their sins. What a sad condition were this city in, if beleaguered with a hundred thousand men! Every man's sins are worse, and endanger a man more, than millions of enemies can do; man shall need no other enemy than his own iniquity: thine own iniquity shall find thee out, it shall find thee as in a snare. Prov. v. 21, "For the ways of man are before the eyes of the Lord, and he pondereth all his goings:" that is, I so remember their sins, as if they were all present before me, committed at this very instant; so that thou art to consider that God does not only remember thy sins, but they are before God's face, so that God never can look about him, but they meet his view. Thou hast committed a sin, and perhaps art troubled for it, but after a while thou forgettest it, and the trouble is blown over; but God looks upon it as now presently committed: for as there is no beginning of eternity, so there is no succession. If thou wert to go to the Lord's table, thou wouldst not go in a drunken fit, or immediately after an act of uncleanness; but God at that very instant looks upon thee as drunken, unclean, and filthy, though the act may be past many years before.

Ver. 3. *They make the king glad with their wickedness, and the princes with their lies.*

"They make the king glad." First, By their ready compliance with his commands regarding false worship. The king and the princes were glad to see their edicts willingly yielded to and obeyed: at first, when the commands came from Jeroboam to change the way of God's worship, they had cause to fear that it might not take with the people, there would be some difficulty to make them change the way of God's worship; but when they saw it go on currently without contradiction, they rejoiced.

Secondly, By their flattering of him in his wicked ways. They not only yielded to his unlawful edicts, but commended them, and applauded him for his care and tender respect for them, in shortening their journey, that they should not go so far as Jerusalem to worship; and they flattered him in this extremely, telling him that this was the way to establish his kingdom.

Thirdly, By their own wickedness and profaneness. At this the king was glad; and why? because he then knew his design was accomplished; he had made them wicked in their lives, by letting them have their will in evil, and now he no longer feared their scrupling to worship the calves at Dan and Beth-el. Thus they made the king glad. Hence,

Obs. 1. Wicked people are easily led aside by the examples of their governors. Which way superiors go, the multitude will go: if they observe external decorum, they will do the same; if they do wickedly, they will do so likewise; though they do not love their prince, yet, that they may have their prince's favour, they will sin against God.

Obs. 2. It is wickedness for any people to obey the unlawful commands of their governors. This people might think this was no sin in them; What! must we not obey our governors, and be subject to authority? yet we see the Holy Ghost calls it wickedness. So how many are there, who for their worship have no other authority but their superiors, their governors! this will never pass current in God's account.

Obs. 3. It is a vile wickedness to flatter princes. Yet, how has this been the constant course of courts! It is reported of Dionysius, that when he spit, his flatterers would lick it up, and say, it was sweeter than honey. It is vile in the people to flatter, and more vile in princes to love to be flattered. Cyril on this text saith, Had the fear and love of God been in this people, it would have kept both them and their princes; it would have balanced their spirits, and enabled them to have withstood such wicked commands.

Obs. 4. It is a most vile thing to make any glad with, or to be made glad by, wickedness. Yet how many are guilty of this sin! Some are so hardened in their wickedness, that they will make others drunk, and then laugh at them when they have done so: how far are these from David's temper, whose eyes ran down with tears because men kept not the law; and horror took hold upon him! There is no greater sign of a desperate heart hardened in sin, than to laugh at sin in others, and make a sport of it in themselves; and the higher men are in place and dignity, the greater is the aggravation of their sins: for princes, who are set to be punishers of sin and a terror to evil-doers, to rejoice at iniquity is most horrible! Prov. xxix. 12, "If a ruler hearken to lies, all his servants are wicked."

"With their wickedness." Note,

Obs. 5. The king is in a sad condition, when his ends must be accomplished by the wickedness of the people. Such are the dispositions of these men, that they will do any thing rather than suffer the least punishment; as amongst us some men have no conscience left in them to check them; but these precise puritans, as they term them, will suffer and die rather than sin against God and wrong their consciences. Now these priests and their officers, whom the prophet here speaks of, they would reason thus: If I should cross the king's mind I would lose my place, be put out of my office, and suffer a great deal of trouble: and rather than they will run such risks, they will join any design to ruin that which crosses them, yea, though it be the worship of God. Œcolampadius saith, that bad princes are always enemies to the strict ways of religion; and such as are the strictest in those ways, and walk most agreeable to the word, and are tender in their conscience, fearful to sin against it, these are disregarded and discountenanced, but those that are most wicked are accounted the best subjects, and these they will trust; therefore, where there is no religion, slavery soon follows: that people may be brought to any thing, who have lost their religion; but where profession is maintained, it will teach men to stand for their liberties, and not to yield against the truth. But what! does religion teach men rebellion? does it deny obedience to governors? No, by no means; religion teaches obedience to governors, and the more religious any man is, the more obedient he will be to lawful authority: the gospel commands obedience to governors, but not to tyranny, not to the mere wills and humours of others, God never made such a difference between men; religion never teaches disobedience to lawful authority, to such as rule in the Lord.

"And the princes with their lies." Luther refers this to the lie of their false worship, their idolatry, which the Scripture calls a lie, Rom. i. 25, "Who changed the truth of God into a lie, and worshipped and served the creature more than the Creator." This is not, however, the full meaning and scope of the words; but thus:

They put their false glosses upon their false worship, to make it to take with the people and with the princes. The priests did not only submit and yield to them themselves, but encouraged the people, telling them it was decent and comely in the worship of God.

Or thus: By denying whatsoever may hinder them in their false worship. If the prince should by any means hear that his commands were not likely to take with the people, and so his ends be defeated, they would boldly come and affirm the contrary; or if they had an ill success, they would deny it, and say they had none, it was but a slander which was put upon them by these factious puritans; they would make the princes believe they had good success, when their designs were crossed and hindered.

But chiefly, they made "the princes glad with their lies," by raising slanders and evil reports upon the names and persons of those who might stand in the way to cross and hinder them, they blasted such men as were in credit in the eyes of the people; and those in authority loved this at the heart, this was mighty pleasing in the eyes of the princes: and this certainly was the plot of the priests who, at that time, were enemies to the true worship of God.

The notes are,

Obs. 6. All idolatry is but a lie in God's esteem, he looks upon it as a deceitful thing.

Obs. 7. Idolaters are wont to further their false worship by lies; to tell of their good success when they have none; and when matters turn out ill, to say their success is as good as heart could desire; but this in special was their trick, to slander and disgrace those that stood in their way. The text in Jer. xx. 10, saith that they waited for the prophet's halting, and said, "Report, and we will report;" do you say the thing, and we will affirm it, we will spread it abroad; report, and let us alone with it then, we will never stand examining the truth of it, we heard it reported, and that is sufficient. In later times, what calumnies and reproaches were by the papists raised against Luther! men set on work on purpose to do it. You may perceive my strait at this time, how loth I am to rake in these filthy puddles, and yet led by this scripture so fully to it, that I must either balk the mind of God, or else touch upon these jarring strings; but I shall, for peace' sake, for the present wave it, and reserve it to its more convenient place; howbeit, this will stick to some whose course it has been: but how vile and wicked is this course! for what recompence can such possibly make for the wrong done? The evils of slander are many.

First, It cannot be expected that an answer should suddenly come to clear away the reproaches. Secondly, When an answer is come, it will be but one's yea and another's nay. Thirdly, If it should be satisfactory, all the amends that can be made is a recantation, I am sorry, I was misinformed, I had letters of it; and this is a poor requital. Fourthly, It is a question whether ever the answer shall spread as generally as the calumny.

Obs. 8. It is an evil thing to make men glad with lies. This was their sin here, they had made the princes glad with their lies.

You had need look to yourselves when you hear reproaches and slanders against instruments of public good. Do you secretly love and cherish them? If you do, it is a sign there is rottenness in your hearts. It is evil to sow reports and slanders, but to harrow them in is worse: he that reports, is he that sows slanders; and he that carries the report and spreads it, is he that harrows it in.

Ver. 4. *They are all adulterers, as an oven heated by the baker, who ceaseth from raising after he hath kneaded the dough, until it be leavened.*

This verse needs but little opening, and the rather, because the 6th verse has much to the same effect.

"They are all adulterers, as an oven heated by the baker:" either spiritual or corporeal adulterers. Is the heat of either like to an oven? Therefore let every one take heed of that which may kindle this fire, either of corporeal or spiritual adultery: 1. An inward heat. 2. Violent, that turns every thing to its own increase. 3. A heat abiding, collected, and resting; not of a hearth, which scatters the heat, but as the heat in an oven.

Now if wicked, sinful heat be so kept in and compacted, how much more should our heat be kept in and compacted for God, in the duties of his worship! When we come to prayer, perhaps we have a little heat, but it is scattered and confused: if a man were to heat a pot upon the fire, he would take it ill if another should scatter the fire abroad. The devil comes and scatters our heat, and spoils us in our affections: now, we should oppose the devil in this. It follows,

"Who ceaseth from raising after he hath kneaded the dough, until it be leavened." Jerome and others greatly aid in understanding these words, by a tradition of the Jews, which was this: They say, the intent of Jeroboam for altering of religion was very hot, but not knowing how it would take, they sent abroad spies to see how the people stood affected, and gradually to leaven them; they thought if this their design were urged upon them of a sudden, it would not take, but if by degrees, it might gain upon men's minds. Thus Jerome and Cyril. As, when the baker ceases from kneading, he does not presently put it into the oven, but lets it lie, that the leaven may run through it; so Jeroboam and his princes were like this baker, they were set upon their design, and it they would have, but they would have the people first leavened previous to their putting it into execution: and Cyril adds, that those who went to persuade the people, artfully told them it would be for their ease and profit not to go up to Jerusalem, but to petition the king, that he, out of his princely love and wisdom, would permit them to worship at Dan and Beth-el. And here lay the top of the plot; the king's design, so much desired by him and his princes, must yet be brought about by the people, they must petition to the king that he would grant this liberty to them, to worship at Dan and Beth-el, and that they might not go up to Jerusalem. By this you may see, how wicked and wise idolaters are for the accomplishment of their purposes; by this means princes obtain their ends, and their plots remain undivulged.

Behold the cunning plots of the devil, to delude poor souls in matters of worship; therefore, we had need to look to our ways, we have to deal with cunning princes and subtle men.

This means was of late used among ourselves; our bakers have been kneading their dough, but they had heated their oven too hot, and so their cake proved over-baked, abortive, and came to nothing; and we have cause to bless God, who gave them up to this violence of rage. These in Jeroboam's time were wise enough to carry on their designs with moderation, policy, and secrecy, and so succeeded; our enemies were not.

And as wicked men do stay and are contented to wait, till the fittest time comes for the accomplishment of their wicked plots, so the devil is contented to wait; he first tempts the soul to sin, and when the temptation has prevailed, he stays and lets the sin work a while, therefore take heed of letting a temptation prevail; do not roll it up and down in your thoughts, saying, What if I should do such a thing? what if I should not? now know, that the devil is a leavening your hearts, and when your hearts are thus leavened, he will come in with such strength of temptation that you shall not be able to resist him; therefore, as Christ bade his disciples beware of the leaven of the scribes and Pharisees, so take heed of this leaven of Satan. In this the devil deals as God does with a sinner in the gospel. The gospel is compared to leaven in Matt. xiii. 33. God leavens the heart with some truth or other, and there lets it lie and soak a while in the soul; he casts into the soul some truth, and does not presently urge it on the soul with violence, putting it forthwith upon difficult duties, which it is not capable to perform at the first, but lets these truths lie, soak, and spread in the heart, till such time as the disposition and savour of the heart be moulded and changed into the truth; and then the Lord comes in with other truths, and works them upon the heart, which it was neither fit nor capable of before. And it were wisdom in the ministers of the gospel to take this course, not violently to urge strict and hard duties upon new converts; but press the gospel to them, and there let it lie and soak a while upon the spirit: and blessed is that soul which is thus leavened; the Lord will carry on this work to perfection; these beginnings, the Lord, in his time, will finish.

Ver. 5. *In the day of our king the princes have made him sick with bottles of wine; he stretched out his hand with scorners.*

There is no preposition "in" in the Hebrew, it is only, יום מלכנו The day of our king. The people being leavened with Jeroboam's idolatry, now make their acclamations in honour of their king, and rejoice in the forms of worship which he and his princes had set up, and would not regard the requests and petitions of some few who desired it might not be established; and though they were bound in conscience to go up to Jerusalem, yet, notwithstanding, the king would send forth his edicts, to tell the people there should be no more going up to Jerusalem, but to Dan and Beth-el; now at this they rejoice, and cry out, Oh the day of our good king, which has set his good people at liberty, and eased us of our great journey to Jerusalem, to the danger of the kingdom, and is an enemy to those precise people!

This day of their king, was either the day of his birth, or his coronation-day, or the day in which he set up the calves at Dan and Beth-el. Now it cannot be imagined but that there were some murmurings amongst some of the people, they were not all inclined to consent to the setting up of the calves; therefore they did it by a stratagem, taking advantage of the mirth and triumph in the day of their king. Or thus: If the people were not thoroughly leavened by this means, they would take this course; Come, we will go set up our king, and magnify our king, and this will prepare the people to receive any thing he enjoins. Let the citizens be in their gowns, and the gentry in their array, and let the king be amongst them, and show himself courteous and loving to the people, and now let us cry out, Oh our good king! This is the day of our king!

Those who refer this day to the day of his birth,

Obs. 1. That we never read in Scripture of any godly king that celebrated his birth-day, but of three wicked kings, Pharaoh, Gen. xl. 20; Jeroboam, in this text; and Herod, in Mark vi. 21: not that it is altogether unlawful to celebrate or observe a birth-day, or a coronation-day, if it be observed with two cautions:

1. That it be not made as a holy-day, a holiness put upon it; for God never gave that power to man, to set a day apart as holy for his use.

Obj. What! may not man set days apart for humiliation or thanksgiving? Yea, he may. Then what is the difference between God's setting of days apart for holy uses, and man's doing the same?

Answ. The difference lies in this: time and things set apart by God for holy employments and services, besides that they make the duties more holy, and the ordinances more solemn and spiritual, than they are upon a day which man appoints, (for man's appointment puts no holiness upon the duties which are done upon those days,) there is a continued holiness in them, as in ministers, &c.; but there is no more holiness in days and times set apart by man for God, than there is holiness put upon the paper on which the Bible is printed: the printer takes out so many reams of paper from his heap, and sets them apart to print the Bible; now will any man think this paper is more holy than the rest?

2. Provided that God do not at that time call for some other duty or service from us. Man must not so tie himself, by any institution of his own, as to cross God's providence: as suppose I have set a day apart for thanksgiving, providence may so order, that God that very day may call for a day of humiliation; now if I should keep a thanksgiving day, and so cross providence, being called to humiliation, I should sin. These two things being observed, I know nothing to the contrary but that it may be lawful to observe a day. A man may remember his birth-day with this view, to be humbled for not doing the work we are called unto; so men married may, at the revolution of the year, bless God for the mercies they have enjoyed in that ordinance entered into on that day: but how many are there who have little cause to remember either that, or their birth-day! nay, may they not rather, with Job, curse the day of their birth? Suppose you should hear a voice from heaven this day, that you must die and not live, that this must be the last day you should live, tell me then, could you bless God for the day of your birth? would the thoughts of it be delightful to you? Philip the Third, king of Spain, who lived so strictly that he never committed any gross crime, or known sin willingly; yet, when he came to die, is reported to have cried out, Oh that I had never reigned! that I had lived a private life in the wilderness, that I might not have to answer for not doing the good, or hindering the evil, which I might have done! It is a sad thing, when men come to die, not to be able to look back with comfort to their past lives, to a faithful discharge of their duties: had Jeroboam kept his birth-day in this manner, there had been no evil in it; but his keeping of it was only to satisfy the flesh, till he himself was sick with wine: in such days, Bacchus and Venus have the greatest portions.

Obs. 2. Festival days are usually made distempering days, days of provocation. "Made sick with bottles of wine." This wine is like that in Deut. xxxii. 33, "Their wine is the poison of dragons, and the cruel venom of asps:" this wine of asps makes the spirits warm, and the body sick. Job knew the danger of feasting; therefore, when his children were feasting, he was sacrificing. They made the king drunk with wine. This was the way which they took to gain the king. And is not this the course which is taken now in our days, to betray the young gentry into base filthiness? This was the plot of these priests, first to make the king drunk, and then they could do any thing with him, could get any edict from him to serve their own base ends, to suppress the precise and godly among them.

Obs. 3. Drunkenness is an old court sin. See how the prophet, Isa. xxviii. 1, fills his mouth with woes and threatenings against the drunkenness of Ephraim; "Woe to the crown of pride, to the drunkards of Ephraim!" The court, the crown of Ephraim, was at Samaria. A miserable thing it is, that those who have the most opportunity for God, should spend their time in such beastly vanities, and do to their bodies and souls as Richard the Third to his brother, drown them in a butt of sack.

Obs. 4. Drunkenness brings diseases. "Be not among wine-bibbers, among riotous eaters of flesh; for the drunkard and the glutton shall come to poverty." How many are there which carry about with them the marks of their lusts, as Paul carried about him the marks of the Lord Jesus! Men will venture much for their lusts, but if Christ call them to suffer any thing for him, then they are tender and sickly; but let their estates, healths, and credits stand in the way to hinder them in the pursuit of sinful desires, they will break through them all: now, a shame is it for a Christian not to do more for God, than these men will do for their lusts. Timothy is commanded to drink but a little wine, and that for his refreshment, to help nature; but when men drink and make sots of themselves by it, what diseases does this bring on them! The Scripture tells us, that the saints' bodies are the temples of the Holy Ghost; do you think that such a body as this is like to be a temple? no, but rather like matter for the very sink of hell, where all filth shall be fuel for everlasting burning. How canst thou answer the weakening of thy strength by this lust, when God demands all thine energies? It may be thou wilt say, thou wert never dead drunk; but wert thou never so distempered as to weaken thy powers, and make thee unfit for service? How sinful then is the practice of those that drink others' healths, till themselves are sick through excess!

Obs. 5. Drunkenness is most of all vile in governors, men of place and power. Prov. xxxi. 4, "It is not for kings, O Lemuel, it is not for kings to drink wine; nor for princes strong drink." It is not for them; and why? because they are above us, and how can any man endure to be under drunken beasts? they are gods, and how vile and abominable is it to have drunken gods! Therefore the Carthaginians made a law, that none of their magistrates in the time of their magistracy should drink any wine.

Obs. 6. It is much more vile to make others drunk, than to be drunk ourselves. Therefore in Esth. i. 8, "the drinking was according to the law; none did compel: for so the king had appointed to all the officers of the house, that they should do according to every man's pleasure:" none were compelled to drink more than they were willing. You may think they express a great deal of love to you, in drinking to you, and pressing you to drink; but when they have overcome you, then will they laugh at you, and make you a scorn; especially if they can get you who are professors of religion to be overtaken. Therefore you had need above all men to take heed of this sin, for if you fall, religion suffers, and the name of God is evil spoken of by your means; therefore Christ himself warns his disciples to take heed of surfeiting and drunkenness. Therefore you that are professors had the more need to take heed of this sin, and mind this exhortation of Christ.

Obs. 7. Drunkenness is especially vile when we pretend to praise God. When God shows thee mercy, and thou pretendest to praise him for it, then to take liberty to exceed in creature indulgence, this is most abominable. We have had many days of thanksgiving to praise God for his mercies; if we have been excessive in the use of the creatures, be humbled, it is an ill requital of God for his mercy.

"He stretched out his hand with scorners." לצצים here translated "scorners," is variously rendered by the Sept. by λοιμων, pestilent persons, Psal. i. 1, and Prov. xxii. 10; by ἀκολαστος, untamed, or wanton, Prov. xxi. 11; and elsewhere, by ὑπερηφανεις, proud, and ἀφρονες, without understanding.

κακοὺς. A word signifying evil men, because scorners are full of all kinds of evil.

Luther translates the word by κακοὺς, evil workers, and interprets it of false teachers, that delude the people and deprave the Scriptures; and this kind of scorning, by perverting the Scripture, is the worst of all others, it is most abominable. Job xx. 14, "His meat in his bowels is turned, it is the gall of asps within him;" the word in such men's spirits is turned into bitterness. These scorners, who were they? The nobles and the princes, the officers in the court, these were the men who scorned at the people for going up to Jerusalem to worship, and thereby forfeiting the king's favour, their places at court, their honours and preferments, and all for a mere circumstance, and a trifle, as they thought; and this was at the time of their feasts and jovialities, when they might both harden the hearts of the king and people. Now "he stretched out his hand" to them, that is, 1. He encouraged them, and gave them his hand to kiss. How unlike is this to God, of whom Job saith, that he will not give his hand to the wicked, to malignants! Job viii. 20. 2. To stretch forth his hand is to put forward any work, or further designs on foot; as Herod furthered the wicked designs of the high priests and scribes in persecuting Christ, he "stretched forth his hands," Acts xii. 1. "He stretched out his hand with scorners." Scorners are the basest of people, and, as if he were a common companion for them, this king put off all princely dignities, and made himself their associate, if they could but in any way further his designs. Hence,

Obs. 8. Sensual courtiers are for the most part great scorners. Experience proves this.

Obs. 9. Times of feasting are usually times of contemning all religion. Then they think none live such brave lives as they do; when they are thoroughly heated with wine, then they have a flout and a scorn for every one; then God himself is reproached by them, and his saints had in disgrace. Psal. xxxv. 16, "With hypocritical mockers in feasts, they gnashed upon me with their teeth." There are many who carry things very fair in the eyes of the world, who seem to be Christians, yet, when they come among scorners, have their scoff and private jeer; these are odious in God's sight. Where is there more scorning and scoffing, than in princes' courts, and great men's tables? If a court chaplain had but heard any thing of a puritan, or of a private meeting, was it not their music? Thus they informed the king, that they were none but a company of precise fools, giddy-headed people, and the king received this news with joy, it made him merry, and he gave them thanks for their pains. Oh how far is this below a true princely spirit!

Obs. 10. The right way of worship is by carnal hearts accounted a very slight thing; and God's people, who stand for God's ordinances in their purity, are regarded as foolishly precise.

Obs. 11. The devil has ever been wont to hinder reformation, by raising up men of pestilent wits to scorn at religion: and this way the devil prevails very much; when he cannot prevail by persecution, he gains much this way. Men that are of any spirit cannot endure scorning; therefore we read of mocking to be a cruel persecution in Heb. xi. 36, "And others had trial of cruel mockings." And Ishmael's mocking is said to be persecution. In the primitive times, they would set up an ass's head and a book by it, to show that they professed to learn, and yet were as simple as an ass. I have heard of a scholar in Queen's college, who professed he had rather suffer the torments of hell, than endure the contempt and scorn of the puritans. And this is the devil's old way: but men will not be jeered out of their inheritance, and God will scorn such scorners, Prov. iii. 34. That place is famous in Lam. iii. 62, 63, "The lips of those that rose up against me. Behold their sitting down, and their rising up; I am their music." What then? "Render them a recompence, O Lord, according to the work of their hands. Give them sorrow of heart, thy curse unto them."

Obs. 12. When kings' hearts are against religion, they shall never want wits to further their designs. History confirms this.

Obs. 13. Unhappy is that kingdom where princes give their hands to scorners, and deny it to the people of God. It was a happy and blessed time with that people in 2 Chron. xxxv. 1—3, when the prophets of God were encouraged by the king himself.

Ver. 6. *For they have made ready their heart like an oven, whiles they lie in wait: their baker sleepeth all the night; in the morning it burneth as a flaming fire.*

These words set forth the strength of Jeroboam's and his princes' desires to set up false worship, and their subtlety in taking opportunity and lying in wait to leaven the people. The notes are from the similitude.

Obs. 1. The heat of their hearts was so violent, that it did devour all that opposed it. As fire devours all combustible things, so they devoured all kinds of reason brought against them and their way; what was advanced in contradiction to their worship, was like straw or wood in an oven, they were so strongly set upon it, they devoured all presently. Therefore at any time, when we come to men, and see them wilfully bent upon their way, it is to no purpose to speak to them; but let them alone, and let God but humble them upon their sick-beds, and then they will hearken. No dealing with bees in a hot day, but at night there is.

Obs. 2. God will be hot in judgment as men are hot in sin. God will make as little of them as they do of God's people. "For, behold, the day cometh, that shall burn as an oven; and all the proud, yea, and all that do wickedly, shall be stubble: and the day that cometh shall burn them up, saith the Lord of hosts, that it shall leave them neither root nor branch," Mal. iv. 1.

"Whiles they lie in wait." Though they are as hot as an oven, yet they do not run headlong, imprudently, but wait their opportunity. And should not this be our wisdom in the ways of God, not to "make haste?" Isa. xxviii. 16. Let not our desires be so eagerly set after any thing, but that we can be willing to be without it, or patiently to wait God's time for it. They are as hot as an oven, and yet not cooled because they have not their desires presently fulfilled. So must we take heed of having our hearts cooled, when we have opportunities to further any design we have on foot for God and his cause. Though they had not opportunities to further their plots, yet they waited still, and were not discouraged. How many times do people, when God sends but a little famine of the word amongst them, grow cold, and lose all their heat!

"Their baker sleepeth all the night." It is as if men, who have a common oven, were to put fuel into it, and let it burn till they called their customers together, and when this was done, then slept. So the people were leavened. These people, by their bakers, were prepared; they had heated their oven, and now they thought they might go to sleep, they might be quiet. And did not our bakers do thus? they had heated their oven, but blessed be God, who disappointed them in their way. When these bakers slept, their oven heated notwithstanding, but ours grew cold.

Obs. When we think subtle adversaries to be most secure, they are still driving on their designs. Thus it was in Ireland, and here amongst us, even in their greatest shows of peace in their treaties. The truth is, if ever we will have the fire quenched, which now burns so violently, we must take away the incendiaries, and stirrers up of these unnatural wars. Though opportunities for work may cease, let not the fire of our good cause go out, let the oven be hot still. At the first their oven did but begin to heat, now it is all in a flame: at the first they would use fair means with the people, and persuade them with good words, and answer their arguments; but when their oven was hot, when they had brought their designs to maturity, and got power into their hands, then it is now no longer, Will ye worship at Dan and Beth-el? and, That is your best course; no more attempt to satisfy the consciences; but, To prison with them; such a prison for such, and the other strong hold for the rest. This has ever been the course of those who would set up any false worship.

Ver. 7. *They are all hot as an oven, and have devoured their judges; all their kings are fallen: there is none among them that calleth unto me.*

Not only Jeroboam and his successors, but also princes and people, at length grew hot in the pursuit of that great design of altering religion, insomuch that no man might dare to show himself against them. Many of the people, at first, scrupled to yield to their new way; but having overcome their consciences, now nothing troubles them; they not only yield themselves, but violently constrain the consciences of recusants. But this similitude we met with in the 4th verse of this chapter, and then opened it, and therefore pass it over here. It follows,

"And have devoured their judges." Jerome observes on this, that it is not probable but some of their judges had some light in them, to see that the altering of religion could not but be against their laws; yet, seeing both the princes and the people were set violently upon it, they also yielded.

Such are the vile, base, and low spirits of men in honour, and this honour depending upon the favour of kings, that, rather than hazard their places, and lose their gains, they will yield to any thing; and, to please the king, will tell him the law is for him, the bonds of the kingdom cannot control him. Micah iii. 10, 11, "They build up Zion with blood, and Jerusalem with iniquity. The heads thereof judge for reward, and the priests thereof teach for hire, and the prophets thereof divine for money." The princes and the prophets ask for a reward. The princes desire to infringe on some rights of their subjects, but to cover the vileness and injustice of the action, would ask the judges whether it were legal or no; now the judges, for their own profit, encouraged him, and told him it was lawful, he might do it. How have our judges imitated these! Though men had some integrity at the first, yet, the heat arising so high in the princes and nobles, yea, and in many of the high court of judicature, they could not endure it. Thus we see how one time answers to another in wickedness. The princes' designs increase in strength when they have got the judges to countenance and support them.

Others interpret it thus, They have mischieved and ruined their judges that did oppose them; and Mercer, that learned interpreter, in support of this sense quotes a tradition of the Jews, That the princes and rulers had so wrought upon the people, that they should come to the king with a humble petition, in which they should desire and entreat him to give them leave to set up an idol, which they did. When they came, the king put them off, telling them it was late in the evening now, and bade them return in the morning.

In the morning they came exclaiming, Arise, and set us up an idol. No, saith he, your sanhedrim will not give consent to nor suffer it. We have taken a course with them, replied they, we have killed them: which is the usual means persecutors adopt with those who seem likely to oppose them in their plots.

Or thus, They had devoured their judges and their princes by treachery. And this story refers to that in 2 Chron. xiii., a chapter of as much treachery as we read of. "All their kings are fallen;" that is, into that false worship into which Jeroboam was fallen. And it is very observable, that all the kings of the ten tribes were wicked. From Jeroboam the first, to the captivity, there were eighteen kings, and all of them wicked and naught; and the reason of this was, that the modes of false worship suited with their politic ends; so that the observation from it may be,

Obs. 1. It is a hard thing to take men off from their strong engagements. It was a work so difficult, that all the prophets could not do it. It is very hard, especially when their engagements are in matters of importance. They were wise, politic men, and therefore could not choose, in all probability, but see, how point blank their ways went against God's mind; even Jehu himself, who was raised up so high by God, on purpose to root out idolatry, and did root out idols and Baal's priests, yet followed the calves, as well as his predecessors.

Therefore never wonder to see men obstinate, and not be convinced of the evil of their ways; this text shows clearly that many are willing to deny themselves in small things, but when it comes to great things they flinch and hang off; therefore we see what snares places of honour are to most men. Many ministers see the evil of ceremonies, and are convinced that they sin if they yield to them, and rather than sin they will leave their livings; but when did you ever see a bishop deny himself? when was it ever known that a prelate so far submitted to lay down his great dignities and fat livings for his conscience? It follows,

"There is none among them that calleth unto me." 1. They were presumptuous and confident in their way, and none of them would ask counsel of me; notwithstanding their judges were devoured, they sought to other helps, or rested in their outward prosperity: or, 2. They are sottish and stupid, and call not unto me, though all be in a confusion in the state, their judges devoured, &c.

Obs. 2. When governors set up false worship, it should quicken our prayers. Micah vii. 7, "I will look unto the Lord; I will wait for the God of my salvation: my God will hear me." So in Acts iv. 29, "And now, Lord," hear us. The Christians there got into a corner, and made their complaints and moans to God of the evil of the times; and do but observe the rise and ground of their prayers, "And *now*, Lord," hear us. They do as men that would leap a great way, take their rise upon a hill to further them: so these people make the miseries of the times their encouragements, not their discouragements. It is a desperate sign to see men sink under their discouragements, and murmur against God. Oh let us go to God and make our moan to him, and let us die calling upon his name; let David's resolution be ours, Psal. cxvi. 2, "I will call on the Lord as long as I live." And this is a very good argument that the cause of God will stand: if our spirit of prayer hold, the cause of God will hold; but if that go down, fear the sinking of the cause.

Ver. 8. *Ephraim, he hath mixed himself among the people; Ephraim is a cake not turned.*

"Ephraim, he hath mixed himself." There is a great evil charged upon Ephraim, and that is observable, he hath mingled himself among the people; the people did not so much seek to him, as he to them. Some here understand by "Ephraim" the court, because Jeroboam was of the tribe of Ephraim; and Cyril hath this note from thence, that it is a great dishonour for them that are in place of honour, to suit themselves and their minds to those that are of base, low spirits among their people; men of place and power should be men of honour and worth. But we take "Ephraim" here for the people of the ten tribes, for so it is more often taken in Scripture. They were guilty of this sin, in mixing themselves with the people, that is, the Gentiles, in these five regards:

1. In their marriages. The seed of the Israelites was too precious to mingle with the Gentiles; this was forbidden in Deut. vii. 3; and the good man Ezra, chap. ix., in the day of humiliation, confessed this sin unto God against them: and it was typified of the Christians under the gospel, that they should not mix themselves with the wicked and ungodly of the world; they must marry in the Lord: it is a sad affliction to be unequally yoked. It is reported of Maxentius, a cruel tyrant, that it was his custom to judge some malefactors to death after this manner, viz. To have a dead man chained to the living man, till the living man was killed by the dead man. How many living men have dead wives, and living wives dead husbands! Oh how comely a thing it is to see the delight of our eyes the delight of God's eyes!

2. They mingled God's worship with their superstitions and idolatries. They had not wholly defiled the worship of God, yet they had mixed themselves. Jeroboam had been in Egypt, where he had seen their idolatrous heifer, and he was much taken with it, therefore he would imitate them in his calves. 2 Kings xvii. 33, 34, in one verse it is said they feared the Lord, and in the next verse it is said they did not; "They feared the Lord, and served their own gods.—Unto this day they do after the former manners; they fear not the Lord." Never let us satisfy ourselves in mixtures of worship: though we have never so much true worship among us, God will never be put off with such excuses.

3. They mixed themselves in their persons, and suffered others to join with them. Neither must Christians suffer the wicked to join with them in matters of worship; and surely if fornicators, adulterers, and profane men are crept in, they must (when discerned) be cast out speedily. Now if such as these must be cast out when crept in unawares, then surely such must not be received in when known beforehand. And certainly a bare confession of faith is not sufficient to admit a man to the ordinances, for those that are vile and wicked in their lives, may make a verbal and outward confession; men may confess with their mouths, and yet deny all in their lives; as if a man should confess his faith in English, and deny it again in Latin: yet if any should creep into a church in which thou art bodied, if thou dost thy duty in admonishing them, and if they will not be warned to profess against them, thou mayst certainly, yea, and with good conscience, partake of the ordinance notwithstanding.

4. In their leagues and covenants they mixed themselves. They made covenants and leagues with other people, which was forbidden them in Exod. xxxiv. 12, "Take heed to thyself, lest thou make a covenant with the inhabitants of the land whither thou goest, lest it be for a snare in the midst of thee." Deut. vii. 2, "And when the Lord thy God shall deliver them before thee; thou shalt smite them, and utterly destroy them; thou shalt make no covenant with them, nor show mercy unto them." Isa. xxx. 2, 3, "That walk to go down into Egypt, and have not asked at my mouth; to strengthen themselves in the strength of Pharaoh, and to trust in the shadow of Egypt! Therefore shall

the strength of Pharaoh be your shame, and the trust in the shadow of Egypt your confusion."

5. They were mixed in their societies with other people. Psal. cvi. 35, "They were mingled among the heathen, and learned their works;" they served their idols, which were a snare unto them. It is a very dangerous thing to be mixed with a wicked society. "And the mixt multitude that was among them" (people that came out of Egypt) "fell a lusting," Numb. xi. 4. The mixt multitude fell a murmuring; this is an affliction in any society, but especially in church societies. But suppose Providence cast me into a family where there are such as these? In such a family thou mayst be as oil in water unmixt; put never so much water amongst oil, the oil will be above it, swimming upon the top. Psal. xxvi. 9. "Gather not my soul with sinners, nor my life with bloody men:" if you would not be gathered with them in the day of judgment, do not you gather to them now in communion in ordinances, nor in intimate society. The Lacedemonians would not suffer a stranger to be with them above three days; and shall we associate ourselves with such as are strangers to God? God had made a great difference betwixt Israel and other people, they were a people separated from all the people of the earth, Exod. xxxiii. 16; in the original it is, marvellously separated, or set apart, for God; they were a people whom God did own in a more peculiar manner, and his eye was upon them for good, therefore it did not become them to mix with other people.

"Ephraim is a cake not turned." We read this expression and make little of it, but there is very much concerning us in it. Mark well the expression; the repetition of the word Ephraim, "Ephraim is a cake not turned." The prophet here speaks in a condoling manner, O Ephraim, what! my dear son, and do thus? Ephraim was a cake not turned in these four respects:

1. In their plots and counsels. They did not turn their designs and proceedings up and down; they thought of one way of false worship, but not of another; to wit, at the time which might have carried on their plots, they did not weigh circumstances.

2. In their indifference. You could not tell what to make of him; he was so indifferent that it mattered not much to him whether God were God or Baal, 1 Kings xviii. 21. How many men are of this garb among us, both in their opinions and practices!

3. Their perverseness. Although heavy afflictions were upon them, that they lay as it were burning upon the coals, and took no means for their help and cure, they cried out, and lay howling upon their beds, yet they turned not to the Lord; they could not devise a way to escape, they were good for nothing, as a cake not baked; like those in Jer. iii. 5, "Will he reserve his anger for ever? will he keep it to the end? Behold, thou hast spoken and done evil things as thou couldest." Just thus it is with souls in their spiritual estates; in terrors of conscience and sorrow for sin, they lie pining away in their iniquities, and take no course to deliver and help themselves. When thou art in this condition thou shouldst be acting upon God, and looking after him; thou shouldst not lie scorching and burning upon the coals of thy transgressions, but shouldst make out after the mercy of God in Jesus Christ.

4. Luther and Vatablus make the sense of the words to note the greediness of Ephraim's adversaries; they were like a man pinched with hunger, who, coming to food, falls upon it presently, and eats the cake forthwith, and will not stay till it be baked; thus Ephraim's adversaries fell upon him. But this I conceive not to be the meaning of the words, but the second and the third.

Ver. 9. *Strangers have devoured his strength, and he knoweth it not: yea, gray hairs are here and there upon him, yet he knoweth it not.*

"Strangers have devoured his strength." By "strength" we must understand Ephraim's rich and warlike power; and here we may see the poor shifts and strength of carnal hearts: the Almighty is the strength of the saints; such a strength is God, that all the devils in hell, nor men on earth, cannot take away from them. Strangers devoured the strength of Ephraim. Such as were not in covenant with God may rob the saints of their outward supports and comforts: a good cause may miscarry when the managers of it are rested upon, and too much confidence placed in them. We see how just it is with God to cross and turn the designs of men against themselves when they forsake him; and this is a great curse, when wicked men are suffered to take away what we have and do enjoy in our estates and liberties: and metaphorically this may be applied to our spiritual strength; we should take special care that strong lusts do not devour our strength for God: and this is the reason of our flatness in duties. You often complain of deadness in prayer; examine whether there be not some secret lust which takes away your strength. And is it a misery for strangers to devour the strength of our bodies and estates? much more of our spirits.

"And he knoweth it not." The note from hence is this,

The hearts of the wicked strongly work after their lusts. Although they meet with never so many difficulties in their way, yet they know them not. But in good they know every little difficulty they meet with, and have repenting thoughts in them that ever they were so engaged in a good cause; but their own ways, the ways of their lusts, trouble them not. It follows,

"Yea, gray hairs are here and there upon him." That is, such miseries as make them gray. There were at this time many troubles upon the ten tribes, often afflicted by the Assyrians plundering and spoiling of them. And it is no strange thing to see men gray with very grief and sorrow. Scaliger tells us of a young man, whose hair, through the extreme trouble of his spirit, was turned all gray in one night. How much more should our spirits be affected with the miseries of our times!

Or, their miseries were so long upon them, that they made them gray. They were lasting sorrows; they were old in sin, and God made them old in miseries and punishments for their sins. Thus Germany has been gray-headed for many years together, in respect of the length of their miseries.

Or, they have been a long time, and might have gained more knowledge of me, and got large experiences of the goodness of my ways, yet they know me not, nor my ways. The whiter men's heads are, the blacker often are their sins: it is a most dreadful sight to see a white head and an old sinner. I have read of one Eleazar, who would not do any thing which might seem to be evil, because he would not spot his white head. Gray hairs should be a strong argument to move men to walk blamelessly in their lives.

Or, they had many symptoms of their ruin and destruction upon them; as gray hairs show that men's ends are near. Men that are gray, and would not be thought to be old, will pluck out their white hairs; but if there be gray hairs upon us, let us know they are admonitions to us, and warnings of our ruin, Heb. viii. 13. There are many symptoms of a kingdom's gray hairs: I shall instance some of them; as,

1. Oppression in courts of justice.

2. Idolatry and superstition in God's worship and ordinances.

3. The secret curse of God upon men and their estates.

4. The taking away of the valiant and righteous men out of the kingdom, is a sad gray hair in that kingdom. A kingdom where these gray hairs are is in a dying condition; and happy were it for us if these gray hairs were not to be found amongst us: we have lain a long time at the grave's mouth, and yet many gray hairs continue still, and what God will do with us we know not. How covetous and self-seeking are men in these days, notwithstanding God's wrath burns so hot, threatening an utter desolation of all! We had need therefore to prepare for a dying kingdom.

"And he knoweth it not." Does not this speak our condition likewise? Gray hairs are here and there and we know it not. How have the ministers of God forewarned us long since of these times! but we would not regard them, both they and their message were slighted. This people was so stupified they knew not who it was that smote them, nor for what it was they were smitten.

Ver. 10. *And the pride of Israel testifieth to his face: and they do not return to the Lord their God, nor seek him for all this.*

In the fifth chapter we opened words similar to these, only the scope of the place is different. They would not take notice of God's hand, but proudly braved it out, and would not learn his meaning in the rod. Let us, on the contrary, learn humility, to accept of the punishment of our iniquities, submitting, and acknowledging that our Father hath smitten us and spit in our face. Whence,

Obs. 1. God expects we should turn upon afflictions. He "sealeth their instruction;" "he openeth also the ear to discipline, and commandeth men" thereby "that they return from iniquity," Job xxxvi. 10.

Obs. 2. Afflictions, if not sanctified, will never turn the heart.

Obs. 3. It is a great aggravation of men's sins not to turn under afflictions.

Obs. 4. Though afflictions may work repentance, yet such repentance is seldom true; it will not often sustain the trial; yet people should try and see what it will do. Repentance coming from afflictions has a promise: Lev. xxvi. 41, 42, "If then their uncircumcised hearts be humbled," if then, even when my hand is upon them, "they accept of the punishment of their iniquity:" "then will I remember my covenant with Jacob," "and I will remember the land."

Obs. 5. True repentance is rather a seeking of God's face, than our own ease from afflictions.

Ver. 11. *Ephraim also is like a silly dove without heart: they call to Egypt, they go to Assyria.*

The word פותה translated "silly," signifies easily seduced, persuaded to any thing. We are wont to say that children and fools are easily persuaded to any thing. Men that are hardly persuaded to believe in God, and what God saith, are yet often easily induced to believe errors. These thought themselves very wise in going to Egypt, but they did very foolishly, 2 Kings xvii. 4; the leaving of God's ways and following our own is very foolishness. How many, when it has been too late, have cried out of this their folly! From whence this may be observed:

Obs. 1. Though men may be misled by others, yet are they not excused. This will not excuse them before God at the great day, to say, Others did thus, and I followed them, thinking them to be in the right.

"Without heart;" that is, without understanding. Prov. vi. 32, "But whoso committeth adultery with a woman lacketh understanding." Chap. x. 21, "The lips of the righteous feed many: but fools die for want of wisdom," or for lack of wisdom. Now of all creatures the dove is the most silly: as appears,

1. The dove defends not her young ones as other creatures do; the hen and other flying creatures will preserve their young ones, but the silly dove lets them go quietly. So was Ephraim, in this respect, like unto the dove, they were destroyed and made a prey of by others, yet never laid it to heart. The Lord in mercy look upon us. Is not this our case? We suffer our brethren to be destroyed and made a prey of, and never lay it to heart, because we for the present are quiet.

2. The dove will keep by the place of her nest although you take it away. Yea, Pliny reports of some doves which will fly many miles to their nests. Even in this also is Ephraim like unto a silly dove; where he was many years ago there he is still. And so it is with many men; they know and are convinced that such company, which they have frequented, has done them mischief, and yet they cannot leave them: here is a silly dove without understanding indeed.

3. Doves, though swift in their flying, yet being dull in preventing of danger, are easily caught with the net. So was Ephraim easily insnared and preyed upon by his enemies.

4. The dove is delighted in the beauty of her feathers, and prides herself in the clapping of her wings, and cutting of the air, as it were. Ephraim was priding herself in her ornaments. We are very ready and prone to imitate the creatures in that which is evil, but not in that which is good. There are some good properties in doves which they would not follow, as their innocency and simplicity, their unity and chastity, meekness without gall, cleanliness, and purity. *Prudentia absque bonitate malitia est, et simplicitas absque ratione stultitia est.* From whence we may

Obs. 2. Godliness does not sanction men in their folly. When men will not go from the rule, but adhere to that as the guide in all cases of their lives, this is godly simplicity. It is matter of wonder to see how subtle men are to damn themselves. Those are only wise men who are truly godly; they then begin to be wise when they begin to be godly. Our simplicity may aggravate our misery, but it can never bear us out in it, nor excuse it. True godliness will undermine all sinful simplicity; therefore take heed of putting that upon the Spirit of God which is nothing but the simplicity of our own hearts. "Be ye therefore wise as serpents, and harmless as doves."

Ver. 12. *When they shall go, I will spread my net upon them; I will bring them down as the fowls of the heaven; I will chastise them, as their congregation hath heard.*

In the former verse the Lord, by the prophet, charges Israel for their silliness as the dove; but, as silly as they were, they thought to provide for themselves well enough by their going to Egypt; but, it being out of God's way, it proved but silliness, for God was resolved to meet with them. "When they shall go, I will spread my net upon them;" my providence shall so begirt and straiten them, that although they may seem to escape, yet they shall be insnared. This place has reference to 2 Kings xvii. 4, the Assyrian was God's net to take them in. The emphasis of the word lies here,

"My net," in the pronoun "my." Men by their cunning and policy may bring men into great trouble and straits; but when God sets himself, by his attributes of wisdom, power, and justice, to bring a people down to ruin, they shall be taken, they shall not escape. The notes are:

Obs. 1. It is just that those who go out of God's way should be insnared. Job xviii. 7, "The steps of his strength shall be straitened, and his own counsel shall cast him down." Chap. xxii. 10, "Therefore snares are round about thee, and sudden fear troubleth thee." How many can from experience testify to this, who, going out of God's ways, have met with snares! It is God's curse upon the wicked, that their table shall become a snare to them: and in Isa. viii. 14, he threatens that he would be "for a stone of stumbling and for a rock of offence to both the houses of Israel, for a gin and for a snare to the inhabitants of Jerusalem." And therefore in straits it is good to think thus, Where am I? what am I doing? am I in my way or no? have I not followed my own counsel and left God's? If we have, mark what God saith, "I will bring them down as the fowls of the heaven." You think to escape by flying, but when you imagine you are the most secure, then I will meet with you.

Obs. 2. God may for a time let wicked men prosper in their ways, insomuch that they may think all danger is past; but when they are high, then is God's time to pull them down; at the highest God can reach them; yea, even then it is God's delight to pull them down. A remarkable text we have to this purpose in 2 Sam. xxii. 28, "But thine eyes are upon the haughty, that thou mayest bring them down." Thine eyes are upon them; that is, as a fowler sets his eyes upon a bird that sits on high, which he would take in his snare or net. The proud and haughty spirits fly on high, and think themselves very secure, and bless themselves in their way; but God's eyes are upon them, waiting for a fit time to pull them down. A philosopher, on being asked what Jupiter did in the highest heaven, replied, He pulls down the haughty, and exalts the humble. Obad. 3, 4, "The pride of thine heart hath deceived thee, thou that dwellest in the clefts of the rock, whose habitation is high; that saith in his heart, Who shall bring me down to the ground? Though thou exalt thyself as the eagle, and though thou set thy nest among the stars, thence will I bring thee down, saith the Lord." Thus also of that proud king of Babylon in Isa. xxiv. 21, "And it shall come to pass in that day, that the Lord shall punish the host of the high ones that are on high, and the kings of the earth upon the earth." This cannot be understood of the devil, but of the king of Babylon, whom God threatens to pull down.

"I will chastise them." The word translated "I will chastise," signifies both to bind, and to chastise, or instruct.

First, I will bind them: sinners shall be bound with the cords of their lusts.

Secondly, I will chastise and instruct them; noting that chastisements should be with instructions. "I will chastise them."

"As their congregation hath heard." Moses and the prophets have instructed them, but they disregarded them; but I will make good what they said of them.

Obs. 3. Sinners had need to regard what they hear out of the word of God, for it will take hold on them some way or other. Zech. i. 6, "But my words and my statutes, which I commanded my servants the prophets, did they not take hold of your fathers?" O thou impenitent sinner! take heed how thou goest on in thy wicked ways, for know, that all the power in God is engaged to make good his word against thee. Therefore when Christ sends forth his disciples to preach the gospel, he engages all his power to make good what they, in his name and according to his mind, deliver. "And Jesus came and spake unto them, saying, All power is given unto me in heaven and in earth. Go ye therefore, and teach all nations. And, lo, I am with you alway, even unto the end of the world," Matt. xxviii. 18—20. Oh how should we, from this consideration, be stirred up to hear the word with trembling!

Obs. 4. When judgments come upon impenitent sinners, it is a humbling consideration for them to reflect, that that word which they heard in the congregation was true. How do multitudes on their sick beds prove this to be true! Now God makes them believe the truth of that word which before they had slighted. It is the office of the Spirit of God to bring the forgotten word into the minds of the saints: John xiv. 26, "But the Comforter, which is the Holy Ghost, whom the Father will send in my name, he shall teach you all things, and bring all things to your remembrance, whatsoever I have said unto you." But God is wont by another manner to bring the word into wicked men's minds, even by his strokes, and that not for their comfort, but for their horror and destruction.

Ver. 13. *Woe unto them! for they have fled from me: destruction unto them! because they have transgressed against me: though I have redeemed them, yet they have spoken lies against me.*

"Woe," in Scripture, sometimes signifies pity, sometimes misery; here it is be understood of misery.

"For they have fled from me." The word here interpreted "fled from," signifies to wander. It is a woeful thing to depart from God, much more to wander from God. Woe be to you, when I depart from you! but if you depart from me, what will you do? In wandering from God, thou wanderest from the only infinite good; and then, where wilt thou rest the sole of thy foot? what shall comfort thee in the time of thy distress? It is evil to wander from God, but much more to make haste from God. It is the devil's plot and custom, to hurry backsliding sinners from God, that they should not consider what they do, and whither they are going; he posteth them on in their evil ways, "as a bird hasteth to the snare, and knoweth not that it is for his life," Prov. vii. 23. Oh how earnest should the saints be after God! not to be kept off with impediments, but, with David, in Psal. lxiii. 8, follow hard after God; and Psal. cxix. 60, "I made haste, and delayed not to keep thy commandments." It follows,

"Destruction unto them!" This is always the end of such as depart from God: and happy were it if thou couldst see it beforehand. Oh how many, when they have come to see the end of their ways upon their death-beds, have given a most dreadful shriek, as seeing themselves past recovery!

"Because they have transgressed against me." They have not only sinned against me, but have broken covenant also; they have dealt perfidiously with the Lord. Before, God said he would chastise them; but now, he would destroy them, make an end of them. Utter ruin is the portion of those that break covenant with me.

"Though I have redeemed them." Some read it in the future: Though I would, and was ready to do it; yet, they say that the way of worship I prescribed is not so successful, and no such blessing follows it; they say my prophets threaten nothing but judgment and utter desolation: now, saith God, all these are lies, it is no such matter, I was ready to do them good. But the future is often used for the preter-tense in the Hebrew, and so here: the sense is, I have not only redeemed them out of Egypt, but very often since out of the hands of their enemies. And the story which this scripture refers unto, is in 2 Kings iv. 27. The Lord wonderfully prospered them in their wars; "And the Lord said not that he would blot out the name of Israel from under heaven: but he saved them by the hand of Jeroboam the son of Joash." It follows,

"Yet they have spoken lies." That is, they attributed their redemption to those helps which they had, or to their idols, saying in this manner: Other people that served not God were delivered as well as we; we see not so much of God's hand in our deliverance as you speak of. Or else, They fathered their errors upon me because I delivered. Now, saith God, in this you lie against me. They made false interpretations of God's mercies; as, that God was no such enemy to this way of worship, because he had redeemed them. The notes are:

Obs. 1. God's redeeming mercies, are great aggravations of our sin. When God delivers, and we attribute it to any thing in us, or that we have done, it is mighty provoking to God, because it takes away his glory in delivering.

Obs. 2. Such as take occasion to sin more freely against God after deliverance, give God the lie. As they in Jer. vii. 10, said, they were "delivered to do all these abominations." Or, as Philip, that wicked king of Spain, being delivered in a storm, said it was to this end, that he might root out all the Lutherans. So, are there not many so vile, who, being delivered in a sickness, or from any great danger, think it is that they might sin more freely? which is a most horrible wickedness, and lying against the Lord.

Obs. 3. For a man to urge any false doctrine upon another, is a lying against God. Therefore take heed how you bring scriptures to prove any error which you or others hold, for God will look upon it but as a lying against him. It is a dangerous thing to counterfeit the king's stamp; and is it not much more to counterfeit the truths of God, by errors seemingly maintained by Scripture?

But to apply this spiritually: many whom God has redeemed from sin, hell, and wrath to come, the hazard of their miscarrying being over, yet dare not, will not say, that God has showed mercy unto them; they are ever complaining, that they are still in their sins, that there is no work of God's Spirit upon them; or if they do grant there is some change, that God has done something for them, yet are they full of fears that it will pass away, that God will leave them at the last. Now take heed of this kind of speaking, beware what you say, lest you be found liars against the truth of God in your hearts.

"Against me." Luther, upon these words, takes much notice of God's speaking so in his own person: They have departed from me, they have transgressed against me, done wickedly against me, spoken lies against me, called not upon me, &c. Hence,

Obs. 4. The great evil of sin lies in this, that it is against God. This consideration laid David very low; "Against thee, thee only, have I sinned." And this it is which humbles a gracious heart, that it should sin so unkindly against God.

Obs. 5. The more directly a sin is against God, the greater is the sin. For now God suffers more immediately in his glory, and that aggravates the sin.

Ver. 14. *And they have not cried unto me with their heart, when they howled upon their beds: they assemble themselves for corn and wine, and they rebel against me.*

"And they have not cried unto me." The Seventy render it, Καὶ οὐκ ἐβοήσαν πρὸς μὲ αἲ καρδίαι αὐτῶν, Their hearts have not cried to me. Where we may see, that it is not enough to cry with the mouth, except the heart cry as well as the mouth. We read of Moses, that though he spake not a word that is expressed in the text, yet he prayed: it is the working of the heart that is the heart of prayer. Therefore, when Elijah prayed, it is said, he prayed in praying, James v. 17. And by this we see the great difference there is in praying. Heart-prayer pleases God. A workman who wants words to express himself, yet may be able to perform his business very well in God's account; so he that is able to express himself in fine language, eloquent sentences, and multitudes of words, may yet not pray at all: therefore, when you pray, look that your hearts go along with the duty, otherwise, your cries will be but as the prayers in the text, which are called howlings, and that in these four respects:

Oratio est res ardua, et magni laboris, est opus difficillimum ideo rarissimum. Luther.

1. The hideousness of their cry; crying unto God as the heathens used to their idols; and so the Hebrew seems to imply, intimating something remarkable, by setting a letter more than ordinary to this word, howling. Thus the heathen Indians at this day howl to their gods.

ייליל

2. Their distempered and unquiet spirits: they were in their spirits very turbulent, in their lives unquiet, and froward in their carriage in prayer. Even thus it is with many in trouble of conscience, they are very boisterous, make much noise. The shallowest waters make the greatest noise, but the deepest rivers run the stillest so those that have the deepest sense of sin, and are kindly troubled for it, are quiet, still, and submissive, under God's hand. And certainly such a boisterousness of spirit under the sense of sin, is not from the Spirit: although there may be some legal terrors when God has subdued the heart to himself, the heart will seek earnestly for mercy, and yet in a quiet, humble way.

3. Their pain. The brute beasts in their pain and trouble will cry out and roar: even thus did these men here, the extremity of the misery they were in forced howling from them. No men complain more of judgments when they are executed, than those that were least sensible of them when they were threatened. Carnal hearts cry out altogether of the misery of the times; the judgment it is that troubles them, more than its cause, sin. See this between Pharaoh and David, Saul and David. Saul cries, he cries to Samuel, saying, I have sinned, and done foolishly, yet honour me, I pray thee, before the people. David, he confesseth his sin, and accepts of the punishment of his iniquity; Lord, it is I that have sinned; as for these sheep, what have they done? Pharaoh, he cries to Moses, that he would pray to God to deliver him from the plagues that were upon him. David, he cries to God, "Lord, take away the iniquity of thy servant." If iniquity be done away, judgment will soon be removed, sin being the cause of all misery.

4. Because God regarded their cries no more than the howlings of beasts: Amos viii. 3, "The songs of the temple shall be howlings in that day." As the prayers, so the sacrifices: in Isa. lxvi. 3, they are but as the cutting off a dog's neck; and their cries were but as the cries of that dog whose neck was cut off. In their pride they were wont to speak contemptuously of God, his ways, and servants; and so God contemns and scorns them, their prayers, and their sacrifices: Prov. i. 26 is verified here; he will laugh at their destruction, and mock when their fear cometh. Oh how vile are wicked men in God's eyes when they are in trouble and misery! None so vile but we pity and relieve them; but for the infinite, merciful, pitiful God, who is full of goodness, and has bowels of tender love and compassion, for him to have in derision the cries of his creature, oh the consideration of this is most sad! oh vile is the sin which makes man thus odious!

And here we see what little use there is of wicked men's spirits; they are of no use, there is for them in the places where they live nothing that they can do. Thou canst easily sin, and bring down judgments by thy sins; but when they are come upon thee, what wilt thou do? Perhaps thou wilt pray and cry to God: God abhors thy prayers, thy cries are abomination unto him: it is the saints' prayers that are so acceptable unto him; "The prayer of the upright is his delight," Prov. xv. 8. The least sigh which comes from a godly heart, is such a strong cry that it fills heaven and earth, so that (as I may speak with reverence) God can hear nothing else but that, because he both prepares their hearts to pray, and prepares his ear to hear; therefore we find in Scripture such expressions as these, Psal. x. 17; and Neh. i. 6, the good man prays that God's ear would be attentive, and his eyes open, that he might hear the prayers of his servant. Psal. lxxxvi. 1, "Bow down thine ear, O Lord, hear me: for I am poor." 1 Pet. iii. 12, "His ears are open to their prayers." And Psal. lxxxvi. 6, God gives his ear to their prayers and attends to the voice of their supplication. What does all this hold forth to us but this, that the prayers of saints are very delightful to him, they are pleasant music in his ears? Were there no other difference between the godly and the wicked than their prayers, it were sufficient to make men out of love with the ways of sin, and join with the saints in the ways of holiness. The saints send up sweet breathings, and God takes pleasure in them: the wicked howl and cry out, and God rejects them.

"Upon their beds." Men in their prosperity go up and down uncontrolled in their wicked ways, but when God confines them to their chambers and their sick beds, then they howl.

"They assemble themselves for corn and wine." The Vulgate renders it *ruminabant*, not *comedebant*, like beasts they feed; the Seventy, *κατετέμνοντο*, they cut themselves, as Baal's priests; but it rather signifies to assemble. 1. They flock together that they might get corn and wine; so they had it, they did not care what became of God and his ordinances. 2. Assemble to feed themselves with the wheat; so they might be pampered, they looked at nothing else. 3. Or, more probably, were assembled at their temples to cry for wheat. The notes are these:

Obs. 1. The vilest men in times of common calamity will assemble themselves to pray to God. Now, certainly, if they will pray to have trouble taken away when upon them, it is our duty to pray to prevent danger ere it comes.

Obs. 2. When hypocrites assemble, it is for themselves, not for God; for corn and wine, and outward mercies. Were it not that they wanted some outward good, God would seldom or never hear from them.

Obs. 3. Hypocrites seek God more for sensual things than for others. We assemble together in our fasts to seek God, but what is it for? if only or principally for outward things, it is but carnal and not spiritual seeking.

"And they rebel against me." 1. *Præ frumento*, when they are fed like unto the ox when it is fed fat, they kick against their master. Or, 2. They rebel after they have assembled themselves; when once the duty is over, they go to their old courses again, and undo all their prayers: as Jer. v. 3, "Thou hast stricken them, but they have not grieved; thou hast consumed them, but they have refused to receive correction." We should from hence,

Obs. 4. Duties should mightily engage us against sin. Hast thou in prayer either confessed sin, or asked mercy of God to pardon thy sins? Know, there lies a great engagement upon our hearts now to be humbled for our sins, and to walk according to our prayers. Dost thou in prayer beg power against thy sins? and in thy life dost thou rebel against God? Are there not many who will be long and very earnest in prayer, and judge themselves for their sins, yea, and in words justify God, if he should for ever condemn them for their sins, and yet afterwards rebel anew against God? Oh, may it not be said, Is this the man that even now was in heaven in prayer, and is now, as it were, in hell in his conversation? methinks the very next time thou goest to pray to God, thy mouth should be stopped, and thou shouldst not be able to speak unto him: as we read Origen was, when he had apostatized; coming to preach again, and reading that text in Psal. l. 16, 17, "What hast thou to do to declare my statutes, or that thou shouldest take my covenant in thy mouth? seeing thou hatest instruction, and castest my words behind thee;" his mouth was presently stopped, and he was not able to speak a word more. So thou prayest to God, and after thou hast prayed, thou goest and sinnest freely again: O thou wretch, tremble at this; go and humble thy soul before God for thy sins, and tremble at coming thus into God's presence. I put this dilemma to you: either you pray against your sins, or you do not; if not, O consider how thou art departed from God; if thou dost pray against them, then how darest thou live in those sins which thou hast prayed against? Tertullian has an excellent observation to the purpose: Prayer must always be with remembrance of God's precepts, lest we are as far from God's ear as his precepts are from our hearts. But further,

"They rebel against me;" that is, when their own turns are served, and their own ends satisfied, then they rebel against me; as if now they had no more need of God, nor never should want help from him. Oh how many are there, who upon their sick beds cry out to God, that he would pardon their sins, and show them mercy, making large promises to God of future service that they would do! God has taken them at their words, and raised them up again and restored them to strength. And what have they done? Nothing, but rebelled against him more than formerly, and are like the wild ass that snuffeth up the wind.

Ver. 15. *Though I have bound and strengthened their arms, yet do they imagine mischief against me.*

God in this verse compares himself to a skilful surgeon, who binds up broken arms and wounds: so God had often bound up their arms when broken by the enemies. In 2 Kings xiv., there we find God bound up their broken arms.

Obs. 1. God alone can bind up broken arms.

Obs. 2. To be sinful after great mercies is a great aggravation of sin. God finds us, as surgeons do their patients, all out of joint, and crying out from pain, Oh that I had ease! I would give my estate that I might be cured! and when the surgeon has used his skill, and cured you of your pain, and given you some ease, if then you should stand disputing with him for a shilling matter, would it not be an unworthy act? and would not the man think his time and skill ill bestowed? Oh how many people are there who deal thus with God; haggle and shuffle it with God in their distress! Oh if God will deliver them, what promises do they make, but when they have peace and quiet forget again!

Obs. 3. It were an argument of an excellent spirit indeed, if, when after our strength is restored and any mercy anew given to us, we would study how we might glorify God with the same. Have our arms been broken, and has God bound them up for us? O let us now use them for God. But this people were far from such a disposition, they imagined evil against God. As if a patient, cured of some desperate wound or disease, should seek to stab his surgeon or physician.

"They imagine mischief." The word רע signifies all kinds of evil; and to imagine mischief is in some respects worse than to practise it; it was not a weakness or sin of infirmity in them, for it was an imagined mischief, it was a most vile, provoking sin, for it did aim at the dishonouring of God himself: they who live in sin, live as if they were born for nothing but to do mischief to God.

What was this mischief they imagined against God? Why thus, When the arm was broken, they were more remiss in urging and pressing their false worship: as if God should say, Now they are low and in trouble they want opportunities, and have not that power to set up and press forward their designs against my true worship and servants; but now that their arms are bound up, and they have a little more ease and liberty, now they set their wits to work to invent mischief against my people and worship. And it may be, this is the cause why the Lord keeps our arms still broken, that we might learn to submit; for when at any time God has begun to bind up our arms, how have many improved all opportunities to set up themselves and their ways!

Ver. 16. *They return, but not to the most High: they are like a deceitful bow: their princes shall fall by the sword for the rage of their tongue: this shall be their derision in the land of Egypt.*

"They return, but not to the most High." They make shows, yea, do something. This verse refers to the story of Jehu, who did very much; there were very great beginnings in his time to cast out idolatry, but neither did he nor the people come up to the full height that God required of them, but would have some mixtures of their own. And thus it is in many people's reformation, they are very hot in the beginning; and even among us, how high did the hearts of people rise! but what a damp is there since that time! though, blessed be God, great things are done amongst us. But, saith God, that is not yet done amongst them which I would have done; it is true, they honour me indeed, but it is as the nations round about them honour their gods, they do not honour me as the infinite, eternal, First Cause of all things. People should so labour to reform themselves, that they may hold forth the honour of God as he is infinite, glorious, eternal, and having all power in his hands. The observations from the words are these:

Obs. 1. God is the most high God, the Supreme Majesty of heaven and earth. He is so high, that he humbles himself to behold things done in heaven; it is a stooping in him that he takes notice of things in heaven, surely, then, much more for things done on the earth. Surely, then, he is a high God, and whenever we come before him in prayer, we should come before him as to a God who is so glorious, and high above all things, that betwixt him and us there is an infinite distance.

Obs. 2. A true penitent should have this high God always in his eye. And great would be the efficacy of such a sight as this upon the spirit, it would be very profitable for the soul. For,

1. It would make the soul to be very serious with God, not daring to dally with him who is infinitely above it.

2. It would make the soul abhor itself in dust and ashes, Job xlii. 6: there is nothing humbles the soul more than this sight of God's majesty.

3. It shows the soul the infinite evil which there is in sin.

4. That there is no standing out against this high God: I must crouch before him, for he will prevail against me.

5. That he is infinitely worthy of all that I am or have, and all that I can do: and this very thing would answer all temptations against God.

6. It would inform us that it is not every sorrow and slight mourning for sin that will serve, but it must be such a sorrow as is becoming such a God.

7. In this sight of God I behold that which has power in it to raise my soul above all things here below: self, the world, and all creature-comforts, all things must be looked upon as under our feet, else we cannot close with God.

8. I see, by this sight, enough in God to make me blessed, and that I may bless myself in him, in the loss of all the world; there is enough in him to make me amends for all the troubles I have met withal for him. These are the thoughts of a true penitent heart, concerning God. Now the soul can say, The Lord is God, and there is no such God as the Lord. And by this, your thoughts of God, you may put your repentance to the trial, whether it be of the right kind or no. Have you sorrowed for sin, as before such a glorious, high God as the Lord is, that those that see your humiliations, may see glory, and honour, and praise, written upon them to the Lord? The want of this these people here were charged with: and this has often been our case. The Lord help our reformers to carry on the work of reformation begun, as before the high God. If we lose this opportunity, we lose such an opportunity as yet was scarce ever granted to any nation upon the face of the earth. Now proud, wicked men may lift themselves high in the world, and be thought to be somebody for it; but it is the low, broken, penitent soul, which is the high man, because he returns to the high God.

They return, but it is not to the yoke, as some render the words, they will not come under obedience to God's commands; for there is no difference, but in the points, between עֹל *jugum* and עַל *altissimus:* and if we understand the word thus, then it notes, that they promised much, and made many fair shows of doing much, but would not come under the yoke; they will still be sons of Belial, without yoke. So many people, upon exhortation and entreaties, will promise fair, they will return, and they will do much; but when it comes to see the yoke, they flinch back and hold off, Oh, it is too hard for them.

"They are like a deceitful bow." Thus did their progenitors; they trod in the same steps: Psal. lxxviii. 57, they "kept not his testimonies; but turned back, and dealt unfaithfully like their fathers: they were turned aside like a deceitful bow." Now a bow is deceitful two ways.

1. When it causes the arrow to turn from them against whom it was levelled, and recoil upon him that shoots it. These people were God's bow; Zech. ix. 13, God saith, I have bent Israel as my bow to shoot at evil-doers. How vile and wicked is it for those, into whose hands God has committed power to execute justice and judgment against evil-doers, to turn all their power against the saints, and those who work righteousness.

2. When it carries away the arrow quite contrary to the aim of the archer. Many of these acted thus, they had good aims, and intentions, and purposes, but yet they carried the matter quite contrary; these words refer to Jehu's time, he was notoriously "a deceitful bow:" "Come, see my zeal for the Lord;" yet, a hypocrite. O let us look to our hearts, there may be secret warpings in them, which may cause us to miscarry for ever, if we take not heed; many who have good intentions, good purposes, aims, and desires, may yet, almost unconsciously, have some secret warpings which may make them miscarry to all eternity. A man may with a deceitful bow aim at a beast, and yet kill a man; so many may think they strike at sin, and yet, with that very goad, may at the same time wound the saints.

"Their princes shall fall by the sword." These were they who had the chief hand in the setting up of false worship, and in oppressing those that would not join with them: now God would reach these great ones. In times of battle, princes stand at a distance, secured by their life guards; they put on others and think to be safe themselves; they will bring others into straits and miseries, and care not though thousands be slain in a battle, they shall do well enough: but, saith God, They shall not so escape, "their princes shall fall by the sword," it shall not distinguish them from others.

"For the rage of their tongue." Δι' ἀπαιδευσιαν, so the Sept. render the words. They raged against God, his people, and ordinances, and thought themselves too big to be contradicted. We may note here,

Obs. 3. When men grow very wicked, they grow outrageous; like mad-men, there is no ruling of them, there is such a world of wickedness in them they take a liberty to say what they please. We find many strong expressions about the tongue in Scripture: as,

1. Job v. 21, it is called a "scourge;" therefore the saints are promised to be delivered from it.

2. Psal. lvii. 4, "a sharp sword." Prov. xii. 18, "the piercings of a sword;" and in chap. xxv. 18, "A man that beareth false witness against his neighbour is a maul, and a sword, and a sharp arrow."

3. It is compared to "fire;" yea, said to be "set on fire of hell," James iii. 6; to the "coals of juniper," Psal. cxx. 4, which are quickly kindled, but abide long. All these expressions, with others, we find about the tongue of the wicked. But now, see what is said of the tongues of the saints: Cant. iv. 11, "Thy lips, O my spouse, drop as the honeycomb: honey and milk are under thy tongue." And Prov. x. 20, "The tongue of the just is as choice silver."

4. An outrageous tongue is such a poison as poisons itself, which no other poison doth: other poisons hurt no further than they are applied, they cannot poison at a distance; but this is such a strange working thing that it will both hurt, and so destroy men, that they shall never recover themselves, and this it will do at a distance. These men have such dispositions, that they will let none pass without a lash of their tongue. Now, the Lord, he will not let such escape, he will scorn the scorners. When these men are in their rage, none are spared, no, not God himself; but Christ will convince them of their hard words. Consider, how, in your families, or in some companies, you have been guilty of the rage of the tongue in these respects. It follows in the last words,

"This shall be their derision in the land of Egypt." When they come to Egypt they think to find that they will help and befriend them; No, saith God, instead of helping, they shall scorn them. One part of the rage of their tongue, was in speaking basely of the worship of God and of his people; and now the Egyptians shall speak basely to them: Why do you come to us for help? Where is your God, that you so boasted of? Therefore just is it with God, that those who forsake him and his help, and go to men for succour, should by them be made a scorn. Oh it is a most grievous judgment for God's people to be made a scorn by such, the Egyptians! And it should be our care and duty, not to put our brethren into such straits, that the poor saints of God should be forced to go to the wicked for help, lest they should reproach them, saying, Why do you come to us? What! cannot your holy brethren relieve you? Do you expect help from us? But, in special, this is their derision in the land of Egypt, the rage of their tongue and mutual contentions. When the Egyptians shall see this, they shall deride them, and regard them as the greatest possible objects of scorn.

The Lord deliver us from this judgment! When were there such divisions amongst us as at this day? Oh the rage of the tongue, which abounds in every place! The devil himself has a chief stroke in this rage, and, as well as our adversaries, laughs to see it prosper and increase; and what should move us more to agree one with another than this, the consideration of the woeful scorn and derision we should be to them, if God should deliver us up into their hands? Now, as this, their rage, was a symptom to them of their ruin, so the Lord grant that we may betimes repent of it, lest it prove also unto us a sign of utter ruin and desolation. Thus, through the Lord's help and assistance, we have gone through this seventh chapter, and showed you the meaning of the Holy Ghost in it.

CHAPTER VIII.

Ver. 1. *Set the trumpet to thy mouth. He shall come as an eagle against the house of the Lord, because they have transgressed my covenant, and trespassed against my law.*

THE prophet still continues the denunciation of judgment against Israel, with the declaration and aggravation of their sins.

"Set the trumpet to thy mouth." Let there be a full, free, and open manifestation of the sin and the danger of Israel. The same commandment here given to the prophet, we have in Isa. lviii. 1, "Cry aloud, spare not, lift up thy voice like a trumpet, and show my people their transgression, and the house of Jacob their sins."

Obs. 1. Ministers must not only be trumpeters of the gospel, trumpeters of mercy and peace, but trumpeters of judgment and of war. They are set to warn people of danger, and woe to them if they do not! God will require their blood at their hands. However the spirits of people may be against the free and bold work of the ministry in denouncing judgments, yet the spirits of God's ministers must go on in their way. Luther, for the freedom and boldness of his spirit, in inveighing against the sins of the times, and threatening God's judgments, was called the trumpet of rebellion. If a town be besieged by the enemy, the crying of children or women must not hinder the beating up of the drums, nor the roaring of the cannon. God takes it exceeding ill at his ministers' hands, to be mealy-mouthed when his wrath is incensed; and therefore he calls the watchmen that did not give warning by an ignominious name, "dumb dogs, that cannot bark," Isa. lvi. 10. Pliny relates, that, when the Gauls scaled the capitol of Rome, the dogs which were set to keep it, being fed too full, lay sleeping, and did not give warning; they therefore not only hanged them up, but every year the Romans, in memorial, on that day hung certain dogs upon an elder tree in the city, crucifying them alive, by way of punishment, as it were; and upon this ground it is thought that the Romans so hated that kind of death. And therefore the death that Christ died was the more cursed. God is exceedingly provoked against his watchmen if they give not warning.

Book xxix. chap. 4.

Obs. 2. God's ministers must not be weary of their work, though they see little good result. Hosea had proclaimed war before this, in the name of the Lord, but he must do it again; so far from being weary, or discouraged, his spirits must rise in intenseness, strength, and fervency. Before, Hosea's voice was the voice of a man; but now, it is the sound of a trumpet. Let wickedness stop her mouth, but let the mouths of God's servants be opened; yea, let a trumpet be set against their mouths, in declaiming against the wickedness of the times in which they live.

Obs. 3. The denunciation of threatening in the name of God, is a terrible sound. If men be not afraid of this trumpet, and awakened by it, there is a time that shall awaken them, when the archangel shall blow his trumpet. Those who are most awakened, and fear the sound of this trumpet, shall have the most comfort when the trumpet of the archangel shall blow.

"He shall come as an eagle." Luther thinks this prophecy meant against Judah, because of the subsequent mention of "the house of the Lord." And then this eagle must be understood of Nebuchadnezzar, who is called an eagle, Ezek. xvii. 3; Jer. xlviii. 40. But rather I think it refers to the Assyrian, for the prophet here is prophesying against the ten tribes, and seems to take away the two great confidences on which they leaned, which were these:

First, That they had made a league with Egypt, which was nigh; as for the Assyrian, he was a great way off, and there was not so much danger to be apprehended from the Assyrians.

Secondly, They imagined they had "the house of the Lord" with them, and worshipped the true God. Now the prophet takes away these two. "He shall come as an eagle against the house of the Lord;" that is, the Assyrian; Shalmaneser is called an eagle, because he was to come with an army. It may be his ensign was an eagle, or, as some parts of armies are called wings, so here an army is compared to an eagle. To show to them that their danger is not so far off as they imagined, "He shall come as an eagle," that is, swiftly, with mighty force and vehemency. He shall have an eagle's spirit, an eagle's eye: the eagle is quick-sighted, and the spirit of an eagle is not easily daunted. Yet it is observable, that in the law the eagle was an unclean bird, though the king of fowls, and of a brave spirit; God would not have the eagle offered in sacrifice, but rather the dove. God often regards not eagles' spirits, those that soar aloft and fly on high, but receives dove-like spirits, such as are of a meek and quiet temper. But "he shall come as an eagle," swiftly, that is upon the prey before it is aware.

Obs. 4. Men flatter themselves when danger is at a distance from them. If it be not just upon them, they think themselves safe; but God can bring evil suddenly and irresistibly upon them. "He will lift up an ensign to the nations from far, and will hiss unto them from the end of the earth: and, behold, they shall come with speed swiftly," Isa. v. 26. Gaulter applies this place to the Turks coming suddenly from the uttermost part of Europe, yea, from Asia, into Germany, and so into Spain, Sicily, and Italy. God, to punish the contempt of the gospel, brought them suddenly upon them. However, the Lord has delivered us hitherto from foreign nations; we think ourselves secure because God has put work enough into their hands for the present, with the Danes, French, and Spaniards; but how easy is it for the Lord in an instant, even when there is no fear of them at all, to bring them swiftly!

Obs. 5. All the swiftness, fierceness, quick-sightedness, and spirit of an enemy is from the Lord. If an enemy be swift in his course, quick-sighted and fierce, and has a strong spirit, we are to attribute it to the Lord.

Obs. 6. Wicked men, in satisfying their rage and malice, are as eagles; much more should we be in our service for God. If they, to satisfy their rage, are as eagles, we should imitate them in this, and even be much more so, in the service of God.

"He shall come as an eagle against the house of the Lord." Interpreters differ much about this phrase, "against the house of the Lord." Because Hosea prophesied against the ten tribes, Luther and others think that this clause must be meant against Judah, as if God, threatening Israel, should say, Do not you think to escape, for the enemy shall come as an eagle, even "against the house of the Lord." But we need not strain it so, for it may be meant against the ten tribes notwithstanding this expression, and for this reason; because they called the eminent place, where one of their calves was set up, Beth-el, the house of God; and so ironically here the houses of their idols may be called "the house of the Lord," because they chose those houses and places instead of the house of the Lord. "He will come against the house of the Lord;" that is, against that which you account so: but I think that is not satisfactory, but rather this; the church of Israel, though very corrupt, yet, before their actual divorce, is called "the house of the Lord:" so that from thence the note is,

Obs. 7. God does not presently cast away a church so as to unchurch it, though it be guilty of many heinous sins. Great sins do not *ipso facto* unchurch a church, therefore there should be much patience before any decline from a church by way of renouncing it.

Obs. 8. It is a high expression of the privilege of a true church, yea, though it be very corrupt, that it is the house of the Lord. But you will say, What do you mean by a true church? I take it for the present nothing but this; Any united company of saints who set up what ordinances of God they know, is a church, wherever it is; and here God dwells, here God keeps house; and it is good keeping house with God. He is worse than an infidel that provides not for his own house; certainly God will provide for his own house. Moses was faithful in all the house of God, that is, in all the church of God. What, then, though thou dwellest in a poor cottage, if thou art a member of the church of God, if God give thee this blessing, to dwell in his own house, you are well enough. In Psal. xxvi. 8, "Lord, I have loved the habitation of thy house, and the place where thine honour dwelleth." The church is not only God's house, but the house wherein the honour of God dwells. Princes may have some houses where they retire for a time, but they have some principal houses to show their magnificence and glory; and such a house is the church of God to the Lord. All, then, who are in the church, especially officers, must behave themselves and be faithful in it as in the house of God: "He shall come against the house of the Lord."

Obs. 9. Though we are God's house, yet the enemies may be suffered to come upon us. It will not profit us, if we transgress the covenant. Joab was plucked from the horns of the altar; and so may we be plucked even out of the house of God. God's own house is no security to sin and wickedness.

"Because they have transgressed my covenant." God loves to clear his justice, and to show the cause of the evil that comes upon us; he would have it clearly charged upon ourselves, that they may not put it off to God's decree, that they were predestinated to such and such evils. The Lord has his time to charge all the evils that come upon sinners upon themselves; Thy destruction is of thyself. The bond between God and his church is his covenant, and all the good or evil of a church depends upon the covenant; and therefore it was the way always of the people of God, when they were far declined from God, to return to him by way of renewing covenant. "All the paths of the Lord are mercy and truth unto such as keep his covenant," Psal. xxv. 10; especially now all our good depends upon the covenant, more than formerly the good people of the Jews did, because the Lord has sealed the covenant with the blood of Jesus Christ actually, which was not so then. But we had this expression formerly, when we opened the covenant of the Jews, and showed what kind of covenant it was.

"And trespassed against my law." ועל־תורתי פשעו Calvin saith, that, further to convince them, and show that it was not through ignorance they transgressed, they could not say, Lord, what is thy covenant? For, saith God, I made it known clearly in my law, they had it plainly set out in my law. The heathen can know the mind of God only by looking into the book of the creature, where it is written but very darkly, and they can see but little of it there. Yes, saith God, but my people have my law, where my mind is written plainly; they may see it, and know what my covenant is with them, and therefore their sin is so much the greater, they have transgressed against my law. The Seventy translate these words, καὶ κατὰ τοῦ νόμου μου ἠσέβησαν, and against my law they have dealt ungodlily: the words seem especially to refer to the worship of God commanded in the law, they have not worshipped me according to my instituted worship; for though God looks at every part of his law, yet more especially at that which relates immediately to his worship. פשעו properly signifies, they have prevaricated against my law, they have made a show that they would do what my law requires, but they do quite contrary. What people is there in the world but will make some show that they would obey God's law? no people but say it is fit that they should be obedient to God's law; still what variety of opinions and practices are there among men, and yet all will father their opinions and practices upon God's law; and mark, but they prevaricate in this; they pretend one thing, but go quite the contrary way: and this is that which God charges upon his people, on account of which he would send his enemies, even an eagle, upon them.

Ver. 2. *Israel shall cry unto me, My God, we know thee.*

In the Hebrew the words somewhat differ from our translation, there Israel is placed first, but in the Hebrew last, לי יזעקו אלהי ידענוך ישראל To me they shall cry, My God, we know thee, Israel. The words thus read have more elegance in them, and hint some observations that would hardly arise from our version.

If you read it as it is in our Bible, then it is only a speech of God to them.

But if you read it according to the Hebrew, To me they shall cry, My God, we know thee, Israel, they seem to put God in mind who they were; as if they said, We are Israel, who know thee, remember we are not strangers to thee; They shall cry unto me, My God, we know thee, Israel. It is Israel that cries to thee, O my God!

Or, as if they put God in mind of their father Israel, in whom they placed confidence; They shall cry to me, My God, we know thee, Israel; O remember our father Israel, and deal graciously with us for his sake. Just like those who cried, "We have Abraham to our father;" so this people, in the time of their affliction, would cry to God that they had Israel to their father, who prevailed as a prince with God; and therefore they hope they shall fare the better for Israel.

Or thus, They shall cry to me, My God, we know thee, Israel; that is, we know thee to be the God of Israel, we have known thy ways in former times for the good of thine Israel. Remember, Lord, how thou hast wrought for them, and work now for us in the same manner. Thus there is more in this word, Israel, if you set it in the last place in the verse, than if you set it in the beginning.

Obs. 1. In affliction men see their need of God. So the Chaldee paraphrase upon this place, When I bring straits upon them, they always pray before me, and say, Now we see plainly that we have no other God besides thee; O, redeem us, because we are thy people Israel.

Obs. 2. Even hypocrites and the vilest wretches, in the time of their distress, will claim interest in God, and cry to him. Those who have departed most from him, will be ready to claim an interest in him in their distress. What impudence was it for this people, who had so grossly departed from God, and so contrary to their light, to come boldly and claim their interest in him in the time of their affliction! Truly, we see the same spirit in men at this very day, the most wicked and ungodly man or woman will be ready in afflictions to claim interest in God. I appeal to you, if one should take the circuit of the congregation, and speak particularly to every one, Do you hope that God is your God? every one would be ready to say, Yes, we hope he is. This is the impudence of men's hearts, who will take liberty to go on rebelling and fighting against God all their lives, and yet in the time of their distress claim an interest in him.

Obs. 3. Knowledge and acknowledgment of God in an outward and formal way hypocrites think will commend them much to God in time of affliction. They expect favour from him because they have made some profession of God. "We know thee;" as if they said, Lord, we were not as others who forsook thee; we continued Israel still; we did not turn to be heathens. It is very difficult to take away men's spirits from trusting in formality, in outward worship; We are all Christians, say they, we are not turned heathens. Oh how sweet and comfortable is it then to have a true interest in God! in the time of affliction, to be able to say, in truth, Lord, we know thee; and blessed be thy name, Lord, we have known thee; we have had experience of thy goodness, faithfulness, mercy, love, and tender compassion towards us; we have known thee an infinite, all-sufficient good; thou hast satisfied our souls with thy love; the light of thy countenance has been the joy of our hearts. O blessed be the time that ever the Lord made himself known to us; we can say, Lord, we have known thee, and, therefore, now, Lord, have mercy upon us. Let us all learn to make more of our interest in God, and to labour to know him more and more, that we may have this comfort in our afflictions, and be able to say in truth, O Lord, thou art our God, we have known thee. If hypocrites think it so great a comfort that they are Israel, what is it then to be a true Israelite, in whose heart is no guile!

Obs. 4. Degenerate children think to have favour for the sake of their godly parents. We have known thee, Israel. Children should imitate the virtues of their godly parents, and then they may draw comfort from the godliness of their parents.

Obs. 5. Hypocrites, though degenerate, will not only think to fare better for their godly parents, but to have the same mercy as their godly parents had. They little think of the difference there is between Israel heretofore, and that Israel now so basely degenerated.

Ver. 3. *Israel hath cast off the thing that is good: the enemy shall pursue him.*

They cry, We have known thee; but they "cast off the thing that is good;" they profess to know God in words, but in works they deny him. What is it to say, We know God, and yet to "cast off the thing that is good?"

זנח here translated "cast off," signifies, hath put off a great way, yea, hath abominated the thing that is good; not only forsaken the thing that is good, but cast it off with a kind of abomination.

"Israel hath cast off the thing that is good." That is, first, cast off God himself, who is, as Anselm speaks, that good in which there is all good: God, the highest and chief good, they have cast him off. Secondly, "the thing that is good," indefinitely; that is, they will not be ordered by any rule, they care not for the good of any one, but only to have their own lusts satisfied.

Bonum in quo omnia bona. Anselm.

But that which I think is most properly aimed at by this phrase, "the thing that is good," is, the worship of God, my worship: they say, We know thee, but in the mean time they cast off that good thing, that which I hold indeed to be the thing that is good. Hence,

Obs. 1. The true worship of God is the good thing, by way of excellence. We account our estates are goods, we speak of the goods of such a man. Are our estates such good things? Oh what then is the worship of God! The worship of God is good by way of excellence above all our goods, the good thing that a spiritual heart can prize, that which God delights in, and wherein his people enjoy so much communion with himself; the thing by which God lets out so much good to his people; it is the safety, protection, and blessing of a kingdom. Where the purity of God's worship is, all other good things will follow; that is the good thing; and it is a sign of a gracious heart, to prize the worship of God in its purity, above all good things that a kingdom can enjoy.

Obs. 2. God's own worship, though such a good, is repelled, and cast off as evil, if it suit not the carnal hearts of men. The spirits of men rise against it, they will not so much as examine things in a peaceable and quiet way, but by prejudice; because they see it not suitable to their own ways, their spirits rise, abominating that which God himself prizes.

Obs. 3. Though at first men only leave God, forsake the thing that is good, yet at length they grow to such ripeness in sin, that they cast it off with abomination. Merely to neglect that which is good is an evil; but to cast off that which is good as an abomination, shows the sin of a people is grown to a great height, that they are near to judgment indeed. Men who have been very forward in the profession of religion, and who seemed to love the thing that is good, by degrees have their hearts drawn from the ways of God; and now they cannot bear the sight or the hearing of those things in which they delighted. Their hearts rise against any who practise them; they shut their eyes, and stop their ears, and with violence repel the truth; as those in Jer. xliv. 16, As for the word of the Lord that thou hast spoken to us, we will not hear thee. Oh, are there not some present, who thought they had received much sweetness in the ways of God, and now have not only left them, but their hearts rise against them; and if any thing be spoken for them, cast it off, and even abominate it? Let such take heed that God cast not them off. "If thou seek him, he will be found of thee; but if thou forsake him, he will cast thee off for ever," 1 Chron. xxviii. 9. O my brethren, let us take heed of casting off the thing that is good; we may pass over many truths of which God has convinced us, but let us take heed of casting off any truth, for then we are ripe to judgment, then the Lord may justly cast us off for ever.

Obs. 4. If the hearts of wicked men be so vile as to cast off God and his worship, how much more should we cast off with abomination, that which is abomination itself! How much more should we cast off false worship with abomination, and say, Get thee hence! and, in the same manner, all kind of evil and sin that would stick so fast upon us! "Abhor that which is evil," Rom. xii. 9; abhor it as you would abhor hell itself; such is the force of the original, Ἀποστυγοῦντες τὸ πονηρὸν. Thus we should learn from wicked men casting off what is good, to cast off that which is evil and wicked.

Obs. 5. Whatever knowledge we have of God, or profession we make of worshipping him, yet if we cast off the thing that is good, it deprives us of any interest we have in God, and of any comfort in crying to God in our afflictions. I beseech you, take notice of this; They "cry to me, My God, we know thee;" but, saith God, they have "cast off the thing that is good." Though it be meant of the worship of God principally, yet it is spoken indefinitely; and to cast off violently, and that against light, any thing that is good, any truth of God, deprives the soul of comfort and interest in God, or crying to God in the time of distress. O sinner, how dearly dost thou pay for thy beloved sin! at what a costly rate dost thou buy every beloved lust of thine, when it deprives thee of all comfort and interest in God, that otherwise thou mightest have in crying to God in the day of distress!

Obs. 6. When the good of duty is cast off, evil of punishment will come in. "The enemy shall pursue him." By casting off that which is good, we cast off mercy and protection; we open a door to all kind of misery: if we retain that which is good, we retain God; but when that which is good is cast off, we lie exposed and naked to all kind of misery, for God owns us not.

Ver. 4. *They have set up kings, but not by me: they have made princes, and I knew it not: of their silver and their gold have they made them idols, that they may be cut off.*

Here we have their civil apostacy, the other was a moral apostacy. "They have set up kings, but not by me." Though all government is dependent on God, yet we are to know that God had an especial hand in the government of the people of the Jews. It was not merely civil, but a spiritual, and a kind of divine kingdom and typical government that God set over them, to typify the government of Christ. And hence we are to take this caution; we may easily be led into many errors, if we argue, That because the kings of Israel and Judah did so, therefore it is in the power of any king to do the same now; for certainly there was much difference between government in that state, and government now. State and church were mixed together, and the government was typical, to set forth the kingdom of Jesus Christ. Therefore, though God now leaves states at liberty to set up what government may best suit them, yet that was not permitted to the Jews; they were to have only that government which God revealed from heaven, for their civil state. When, therefore, they would change the form of their government from judges to kings, God said, they had rejected him in casting it off.

"They have set up kings, but not by me." Some think that this has reference to the choosing of a king at first, because they did it without God's warrant; and so they have set up kings, but not by me. But I rather think it refers to Jeroboam and his successors; they set up Jeroboam and his successors, but not by God. This, you will say, is a strange opinion, for Scripture clearly states that it was from God that Jeroboam should be king, and that the ten tribes should be rent from Solomon's posterity for the punishment of Solomon's sin. So 1 Kings xi. 29—31. The prophet Ahijah the Shilonite comes to Jeroboam, rends the garment of Jeroboam in twelve pieces, and saith to him, "Take thee ten pieces: for thus saith the Lord, the God of Israel, Behold, I will rend the kingdom out of the hand of Solomon, and will give ten tribes to thee." The Lord sent his prophet to tell him expressly, that he would rend ten tribes from the house of Solomon, to give them to him; and yet here it is said, "They have set up kings, but not by me." Again, in chap. xii. 15, Rehoboam "hearkened not unto the people; for the cause was from the Lord, that he might perform his saying, which the Lord spake by Ahijah the Shilonite unto Jeroboam the son of Nebat." It was from the Lord that Rehoboam gave such a churlish answer, it was from the Lord that he was left to such a tyrannical, cruel spirit, that the Lord might fulfil the word that he had spoken by Ahijah the Shilonite.

Abulensis thinks that the ten tribes for the matter of the thing did no more than was right, and he gives this reason,

Abulensis in 1 Reg. 12. Quæst. 8. T. 9.

These tribes were free tribes, but Rehoboam would bring them into slavery, and reign over them as a tyrant; therefore they might lawfully depart from him and make to themselves a new king. And then he puts the cause, viz. a people, or commonwealth, first gave the power to kings and princes, but upon certain conditions; therefore, as they first gave power to them, so they may diminish it if they abuse it, and tyrannize over them. When a people choose a chief governor, they do not give themselves to him as a man gives to his friend a piece of money, or a horse, that is, give all out of their own possession, and that he may do with them what he will, but upon certain conditions.

Now, though I do not altogether approve of what he has said, because at least the case between people and princes now is different from what it was; then God challenged a peculiar prerogative over them for ordering their government; yet thus far in divinity is true: There is more reason that people should now have more power to cast off tyranny than there was, because now none arrives at government over others, orderly and ordinarily, but by agreement; therefore if the agreement and law of the country be elective and not hereditary, or that males shall only inherit, or that they may deliver themselves from tyranny, so far certainly God allows in his word.

But now, to answer the case more clearly, "They have set up kings, but not by me;" though God had foretold that the ten tribes should be rent away from the house of David, and that Jeroboam should be set up, yet they did not this thing in a lawful manner, for they should have consulted with God about the manner of it, and when God would have it done. It was not enough that God foretold it should be done, but when they did it they ought to have consulted God, and have been directed by God. They did not aim at fulfilling the prophecy, for the people generally merely minded their own passions and lusts, and looked no further. Though God overruled it to fulfil his own counsels, yet they aimed at no such thing.

Obs. 1. We may do the thing which God would have done, and yet sin highly against God. God would have Jeroboam set up, but as they only looked at the matter, and did not observe God's way, God rejected them.

Obs. 2. In doing that which God would have done, yet if we do not know that it is God's mind, we sin against God. Though we do the thing that God would have done in his secret will, yet we sin against God if we know it not to be his revealed will. Now no action can be good, not only materially good, but formally also, but that is which is done in obedience to God; and that shows the dangerous condition of ignorant people, all their actions are sin, because they know not in them God's mind.

Obs. 3. To go about great businesses without consulting with God, is sin. Even the heathens were conscious of this, therefore Publius Scipio would never enter upon any great business without first going to the capitol to pray to the gods.

Obs. 4. Alteration in civil government is a great business. God had need be much consulted, especially if there be any church work mingled with it. Never was there a time when England required such consulting with God as this. Now England is about the greatest and weightiest business that ever it had since it was a nation. The very alteration but of an officer is a great matter, and requires much consulting with God, and especially if it be in the church. Our Saviour's conduct in sending out his twelve apostles as officers for the church is very observable: he was in prayer all night before, then in the morning he calls his disciples, and so sends forth twelve of them, and gives them his commission; but he makes preparation in praying to God all night long, Luke vi. 12, 13. Surely those that are about choosing church officers, ministers of God to be their pastors and teachers, had need spend days and nights in prayer. Here they did not consult God in setting Jeroboam over them, and therefore, saith God, they have made them kings, but not by me.

Obs. 5. When we are about great businesses, we must look at God's designs. We must take heed of our passionate wills, and our own self-ends, else we do it not by God. In civil affairs, a magistrate may do that which is just, but if he is urged by his passion, this is not by God: and so in church affairs, if the elders excommunicate, the party may deserve it, but if they be guided by passion and self-ends, this is not done by God. "They have set up kings, but not by me."

And then, further, as the people sinned, and God would not own that which they set up, so Jeroboam sinned too. Jeroboam might say, Lord, didst not thou send thy prophet to tell me that I should have the ten tribes, and yet wilt thou not own me? No, God would not own him; because,

1. Jeroboam did not seek God.
2. Jeroboam did not stay God's time. David was anointed by God, and though he had many opportunities to take away Saul's life, and to gain thereby the kingdom, yet he would not, but waited till he saw the time was come that he should be brought to the kingdom. But Jeroboam would not do so.
3. Jeroboam's ends in taking the kingdom were not right.
4. Jeroboam did not administer the kingdom for God, and therefore God would not own him. And so some read the words, They have not administered the kingdom by me; but administering the kingdom by their own lusts, therefore I will not own them.

Obs. 6. We can have no comfort of God's mercies if we stay not God's time.

Obs. 7. When we have a mercy promised, we must take it by lawful means. "He that believeth shall not make haste," saith the Scripture. Many there are so greedy of places, preferments, and other things they desire, that they make as much haste to obtain them as if they feared that if they stay for the orderly coming into the place they desire, they must go without it. What blessing, then, can there be in that which we would seek to get in our haste, without God?

Obs. 8. When we have a mercy, if we improve it not for God, we thereby deny that we are indebted to him for it. God has given thee an estate, or honours, or preferment. What doest thou? Dost thou now abuse this for thine own lusts? If so, thou hereby deniest that thou hast had it from God. "They have set up kings, but not by me." I will not own that. Why? Because in the form of their administration they have renounced any right I have to their government. And so the Seventy translate the words, 'Εαυτοῖς ἰβασίλευσαν, They have reigned to themselves.

Yea, but it may be said, How were the people that were living now guilty of this? It was long since the people did thus set up Jeroboam, and rend themselves from the house of David; how came these to be guilty of this?

The answer is, That they, continuing and retaining the government of Jeroboam upon the same ground their progenitors first raised it, are guilty of their sins. Children, imitating their parents' sins, contract their parents' guilt.

And Mercer, on this place, quotes a Hebrew, David Kimchi, as saying, that now, when the people saw what Jeroboam and his successors did, that they would keep them from going to Jerusalem before the Lord, and make them to serve idols, and forsake God's true worship, they should have driven him from the kingdom. Such was his opinion: but it is scarcely correct; we cannot do so merely for religion, except the law of the country will bear us out in it. War is not to be undertaken merely for maintaining religion immediately, but for maintaining those laws by which religion is established, and the civil right that men have to the practice of their religion confirmed. So wars may be undertaken; but in a place where the laws of the kingdom were utterly opposed to religion, to take up arms were unjustifiable, except those laws were previously annulled by competent authority.

But now our taking up arms is justified in this, because we do it to maintain the civil right that we have to the practice of our own religion: so that our case is not the case of the Christians among the heathen. There is a law of nature (I confess) beyond the right of any law, and the right in that cannot be given away by any predecessors. But because the mischief would be infinitely great, if it were left to every man to judge when by this law of nature he might resist; therefore there is a necessity that men should, for their particular, suffer, rather than so resist; it is necessary for us to stay till we be helped in some orderly, legal manner. I say, the God of order never leaves people to such miserable inconveniences and mischiefs; and therefore, in the case of individuals, they are rather to suffer, though they should be tyrannized over against the law of nature.

But certainly, a state, or country, may judge when the law of nature, and the right of a kingdom that the law of nature gives, besides that which is given by positive laws, are to be maintained. The right of the law of nature is never taken away by positive enactments.

"They have made princes, and I knew it not." They made some in a very sinful manner, and God might well say, I knew not them. But God speaks of them all, not only of those, but even of Jeroboam himself, and Jehu, who though in part set up by God, yet he saith of them, "I knew it not;" that is, I approve it not, I approved it not as they did it; I let them alone in their way, and let them go on: as if God should say, I neither did, nor will, take cognizance of what they do to bless them in it. When we seek not God for a mercy, when we enjoy it God will not even own it to be his.

The Seventy translate the words, *καὶ οὐκ ἐγνώρισάν μοί*, and they have not made it known to me. When we ask not God's mind, and seek not a mercy from God, we act as if we would get it without his knowledge. We must tell God what we would have, before we presume to take it; and by this means we may go to God with more comfort for help and direction, if we meet with straits. Whereas, otherwise, whatsoever difficulties occur, if we should seek to God to help us in them, God would say, I knew nothing of the matter, you undertook it without me, and you must shift for yourself in it; look to it now as you can, sink or swim, I will have nothing to do with it. We are wont to put off men in this manner, if they will go and undertake a business of their own heads, and then in their difficulties apply to us for aid; Nay, as you undertook it without me, so go on without me. However, I make no question but now many thousands of the servants of God in this great business of the state, where they meet with so many difficulties, can go to God and say, Lord, we did advise with thee, and we undertook this in obedience to thee, and now, Lord, help us in our straits. Oh! it is a comfortable thing to have previously advised with God, for then we can apply to him with confidence in all our difficulties.

Further, there are these two notes from this:

Obs. 9. God knows how to make use of men's sins. They sinned, and yet God brought about his own ends by it.

Obs. 10. God often suffers sinners to prosper for a long time. Even this kingdom of Israel, that was thus set up without God, did prosper outwardly for two hundred years together; therefore this is no argument to God's owning a business; it is but as a cipher; add a figure to it indeed, then it will make somewhat; if you can warrant it is God's work, then you may, when it prospers, have comfort.

"Of their silver and their gold have they made them idols." See the ill success of their actions, and all because God was not sought. Whatsoever we do to satisfy our passions and lusts for our own ends, without seeking God, must be attended with bad results. Though God suffered this kingdom to prosper outwardly, yet woeful, mischievous fruit ensued upon the alteration of their government without God; it fell into, and continued in, idolatry for two hundred years. We had need take heed to our hearts that we be upright, and seek God, in setting up any new form of government, lest, though it be so very specious to our eye, that we may think that we are delivered from many yokes and burdens, yet such effects may result that we may thereby be brought under a bondage still more grievous. They cast off the house of David because of the burdens that were upon them, but yet have they brought greater upon themselves; for now Jeroboam and his successors lay a very heavy yoke upon their very consciences, the yoke of idolatry: the burden before was upon their backs and shoulders, but now it comes to be a burden upon their consciences, and that is worse to bear.

"Of their silver and their gold have they made them idols." God here instances their zeal in their idolatries; they were content to contribute their silver and gold for their idols, they had rather be without them than without their idols. Covetous spirits had rather be without God, and Christ, and his ordinances, than without their silver and gold; let them have their silver and gold, and let God, and Christ, and his ordinances go. Yet these idolaters say, Let us have our idols, and let our silver and gold go. Yea, they parted with their gold and silver to make them gods; but many of you keep your gold and silver and make them gods too. The sun (saith Austin) is a more beautiful thing than thy money, but it is not thy God. That which brings in silver and gold, drossy, carnal minds love; but if it brings not this in, they care not for it whatsoever it be. Chrysostom has another expression: A covetous man is not delighted with the beauty of heaven, nor with the motion of the sun. Why? Because the sun does not send forth golden beams into his house.

Aug. de Disciplina Christ.

Chrysost. in Matt. xxviii. Hom. 84.

"That they may be cut off." The word עצבים translated "idols," signifies things that cause much labour; and then follows, "that they may be cut off;" as if he should say, They are at a great deal of charge to undo themselves. Many men make their own damnation chargeable to them. "Of their silver and their gold have they made them idols," saith God, "that they may be cut off." My end was that they might be cut off, whatsoever their end was. When we are busied in compassing our own ends, God may be working our ruin even by those very things we bless ourselves in, and from which we expect great advantage. O consider this, while I am plotting for myself, and blessing myself in hope of gain, God's thoughts, and counsels, and workings, and ends may be cross to mine, even intending my ruin, my eternal ruin!

Obs. 11. Whatsoever we do, from which evil necessarily follows, is accounted by God as if we brought the evil designedly on ourselves. Surely they set not up silver and gold with an intention to destroy themselves; but because destruction necessarily follows, therefore God accounts it done on purpose. Thus in Prov. viii. 36, "All they that hate me love death." Surely no man loves death; but when you do cast off the instruction of wisdom you, as it were, say you love death: as here, "that they may be cut off."

Ver. 5. *Thy calf, O Samaria, hath cast thee off; mine anger is kindled against them: how long will it be ere they attain to innocency?*

"Thy calf, O Samaria." He calls the idol a calf by way of contempt. But why is it called the calf of Samaria? We read only of two, and neither was set up in Samaria; yet here it is called, "Thy calf, O Samaria." The reason is this, that Samaria was the chief city; and because the calf was maintained by the power, and riches, and countenance of the chief city of the land, therefore it is called the calf of Samaria. Where the chief city is corrupted, the whole land will quickly become corrupt; and where that stands right, it goes well with the whole land. That is the reason why the adversaries seek to corrupt and overthrow our chief city. As all depended on what Samaria did, therefore the corruption of false worship is attributed to Samaria, it is "thy calf, O Samaria." So if God had not moved the hearts of the people of this city, but we had brought popery in, it might have been said, it was the popery of London. Whereas, on the other side, if God please to work their spirits to go on to the end aright, children yet unborn may have cause to bless this city, and say, This is the reformation for which we may bless London.

"Hath cast thee off." Hath cast thee off from me; so some have it. But rather as you have it in your books, "Thy calf hath cast thee off."

Obs. 1. Though idolaters promise themselves safety and protection by their idols, yet they will fail them at last. All you that go on in sin, know that its ways will fail you at last; as they say, the devil leaves the witches when imprisoned. When Judas went to the scribes and Pharisees in the anguish of his spirit, and cast down the money, and said, "I have sinned in that I have betrayed the innocent blood;" "What is that to us?" say they, "see thou to that." Therefore the best way is to cast off our sin and wickedness first. But God will not do thus, he will not cast off his people in the time of trouble; and when our unbelieving hearts fear that God will cast us off in the time of trouble, we make God an idol, as if God would do as the idols did. We may, in God's cause, be brought into straits, but God will never cast us off in them: when in difficulties we are ready to think ourselves utterly forsaken, but then God may be working the greatest good for us. We have a most notable scripture for that in Isa. xlix. 13, 14, "Sing, O heavens; and be joyful, O earth; and break forth into singing, O mountains: for the Lord hath comforted his people, and will have mercy upon his afflicted." But mark, "Zion said, The Lord hath forsaken me." All around were in a singing condition; and God calls the heavens to sing, and the earth to be joyful, and the mountains to break forth into singing, because of the great work that God was accomplishing for his people: "But Zion said, The Lord hath forsaken me, and my Lord hath forgotten me." And so it is with particular souls, they are ready to say, The Lord hath forsaken me; but God will not do so.

"Mine anger is kindled against them." When wicked men are brought into the greatest straits, then God's wrath is hottest, and then also conscience upbraids most. As men's countenances sometimes change red and pale with anger; so here, metaphorically, God's anger is said to be "*kindled* against them." Though the superstitious may think that outward, pompous worship pleases God most, yet we see here that it stirs up his anger and kindles his wrath.

"How long will it be?" Men's hearts are stubborn in their own ways, they will not be drawn off from them; wicked men will be true to their own principles.

Obs. 2. There is a stubborn constancy in evil, as well as a gracious constancy in good. "How long will it be?"

Obs. 3. God is very patient: "the riches of his goodness, and forbearance, and long-suffering."

Obs. 4. Continuance in sin is no excuse, but an aggravation of sin, it makes it grievous to God. When God chastises us, we are ready to cry, "How long, Lord?" "Will he retain his anger for ever?" Know, that our continuance in sin is as great a burden to God's Spirit; he cries out, When will they be made clean? when shall it once be? "O Jerusalem, wash thine heart from wickedness, that thou mayest be saved. How long shall thy vain thoughts lodge within thee?" Jer. iv. 14.

"Ere they attain to innocency." The words are לא יוכלו נקין they cannot innocency, that is, they are so deeply engaged that they cannot attain to innocency: when men are engaged in evil ways they cannot deliver themselves. The observations are,

Obs. 5. We should take heed of engagements in that which is evil.

Obs. 6. If, by custom in evil, we have no power to get out, this will not excuse us. In 2 Pet. ii. 14, "Having eyes full of adultery, and that cannot cease from sin;" this is the aggravation of sin, not its excuse. A learned man of late renders this, they cannot bear innocency: and indeed, according to the Hebrew, this may as well as any thing else be added for explication; for, as we have observed, the original is, they cannot innocency, the word attain not being in the Hebrew; and to this he gives the following interpretation, suiting very well with the time wherein Hosea prophesied; They cannot bear with those who will not join with them, but will go to Jerusalem to worship, and who seek to free themselves from defilements in the service of God. There is nothing in the world wherein men can less bear one with another, than in dissensions about the worship of God, and commonly the nocent party is the most bitter; as the Lutherans were worse in their ways than the Calvinists, especially in respect of superstition, but were a great deal more bitter against the Calvinists than the Calvinists against them; it was a saying of Calvin, Though Luther should call me devil, yet I would honour him as a servant of Jesus Christ.

Non poterunt ferre innocentiam.

The word נקין here translated "innocency," signifies purity, or cleanness: whatsoever holiness may seem to be in false worship, yet is it not clean; but God's worship is clean, "the fear of the Lord is clean:" such wickedness attends it, as if God should say, You are never like to wash off the guilt of it as long as you live. It is not so easy as men think, to get off the guilt of superstitious worship. We cannot but acknowledge, to our own shame, that we have formerly sullied ourselves with superstition: we had need wash and rinse our hearts again and again, and be willing to lay abroad a frosting whole nights, that we may be cleansed from the filth that we have contracted; yea, we should not think it much, nor marvel, though the fire of God's wrath come out against us and burn hot and long; if it be but to purge, and not to destroy us, it is well: for it is not easy to be cleansed from superstition; it is only the blood of the immaculate Lamb that is able to wash away its stains; its filth sticks very fast.

Ver. 6. *For from Israel was it also: the workman made it; therefore it is not God: but the calf of Samaria shall be broken in pieces.*

The prophet proceeds in his conviction of Israel's sin, with the threats of God against it.

"For from Israel was it." That is, their idolatry

was from themselves; it was hard to get them off from their idolatrous worship, for it was from themselves. Others worshipped idolatrous images, as being deceived, being made to believe that they came from their gods; as that wise town clerk of Ephesus, in his grave, sage speech, Acts xix. 35, said, their image "fell down from Jupiter;" or else they were such as were brought from the temples of other people, whose original they knew not. But, saith God, My people are more sottish than any, for from Israel themselves come these their images that they worship, they have set them up themselves; they know that the other day they were but pieces of wood, overlaid with gold and silver; for their calves were idols that Israel invented themselves, not the same (as some think) with the Egyptian Apis, for that idol was a live bullock with several spots and divers things wherein it differed from the calves that Israel worshipped, so that the calves of Israel's worship were their own invention. Hence there are these notes:

Obs. 1. None are so sottish in wickedness as apostates. Israel was more sottish than any people.

Obs. 2. To be devisers and inventors of evil, and especially of any thing false in the worship of God, is a great aggravation of sin. Those that are the first inventors and devisers of wickedness, and especially of any false worship, are most wicked and abominable before God. It was from themselves.

Obs. 3. Men hold fast by their own inventions in the worship of God. This is given as a reason why they could not be brought off from that false worship; it was from themselves. And hereby men show that they honour their own fancies and wills above the will and the mind of God: we will a great deal more easily part with the worship of God that comes from God, than with worship that comes from ourselves.

"Also." "For from Israel was it also." There is somewhat in that "also;" and it is this, As formerly in the wilderness they set up a calf, so here again, "from Israel was it also." Former examples of God's wrath against their progenitors will not deter them, they still follow the guise of their ancestors in false worship.

Obs. 4. No sin is more hereditary than idolatry. "From Israel also." Hence, the second commandment alone threatens to visit the sins of the fathers upon the children.

"The workman made it; therefore it is not God: but the calf of Samaria shall be broken in pieces." There are two arguments, why their calf was "not God."

I. "The workman made it."

II. It "shall be broken in pieces."

I. "The workman made it." It is the greatest folly to look upon that which derives its excellency from ourselves, as superior to us, and that in the highest degree; to forsake the God that made us, and to make that to be a god unto us which we have made ourselves. The father looks upon his child as inferior to him, because he was the instrument of his being, and so he well may; and if one be maintained or raised by another, he is expected to be serviceable to him. In both these relations we stand to God, but idolatry makes men go against the very principles of reason. They fashion the idol, and yet account it their god: they are made and sustained by God, and yet forget him. Hence, especially,

Obs. 5. Man cannot by any act of his own deify a creature. They "made it, therefore it is not God." Man cannot so much as impart holiness to a creature, much less divinity; all the workmanship of man, by his consecration, or any thing that he can do, cannot make stones and mortar holy, so that, in case of need, it should be a sin to put them to a common use. Man takes too much upon him to think to raise the creature so near to divinity; he cannot, by any work of his, so put religious respect on a place, or on any thing else, that God there shall be nearer to him, or he nearer to God. Whatsoever is of man's work, in God's worship, perishes in the using of it; surely then man's creation cannot be God. "The workman made it; therefore it is not God."

Indeed there is a creation of man which the Scripture speaks of, that is called god, not truly, not God really, but metaphorically; thus in 1 Pet. ii. 13, kings and governors are called man's creation, man made them; and you know the Scripture calls governors gods. "I have said, Ye are gods," Psal. lxxxii. 6; but it is added, "ye shall die like men:" this text shows, if man made them, they cannot be truly gods; and the former scripture tells us, that kings and governors are man's creation; in your books it is translated man's "ordinance," but it is in the original κτίσις ἀνθρωπινὴ, man's creation. Man made them, and *therefore* they are not gods; therefore we must not give them the honour of a God, to subject our consciences unto them; no, neither are we bound to subject our outward estates, and liberties, and lives to their humours and lusts, for to the mere will of God alone are we all subject.

If all the art and skill, power and riches, of all the men in the world were put together, and all the wisdom and power of angels, and all the created excellency in all things and in all creatures, joined to it, yet this surely could not be a God to us; I say, if we conceive all art, skill, power, and riches, of all the world, brought together into one man, yea, all the skill and power of angels put into him too, and if he were able to extract all the excellencies out of all creatures, and combine them in himself, yet could he not be a God unto us; because he was made. And shall we say further, God himself, by his infinite power, cannot make any thing to be a God to us; nay, if God himself were made, he could not be God: therefore, surely that which the workman hath made cannot be a God.

How vile then are our hearts, and how do we debase ourselves, to subject ourselves to every vanity, as if it were a God, whereas all the power in God himself cannot so exalt a created excellency, as to be a God to us! How vain is the heart of men that makes pleasure their god, as the voluptuous, his belly; that makes money their god, as the covetous; that makes honour and the applause of men their god, as the ambitious! Bernice and Agrippa came with great pomp, with much fantasy, μετὰ πολλῆς φαντασίας, Acts xxv. 23; all the excellency of their pomp was but a show, a mere fantasy.

In this God shows the excellency of an immortal soul, that it is such, that only an infinite, eternal being, like himself, can be a God to us.

But further, This is an argument against the idol of the mass: a common priest, vile perhaps in himself, makes it a god: what kind of a divinity must it be? Can there be a greater stumbling-block to Jews, Turks, or heathens, to keep them from embracing the Christian religion, than this, that Christians should make their god, and then eat him? That is the first argument: "The workman made it; therefore it is not God."

II. It "shall be broken in pieces." "But the calf of Samaria shall be broken in pieces," "therefore it is not God." No God, surely! He speaks here with indignation, It is not God, it is a calf; as doth the psalmist, Psal. cvi. 20, "They changed their glory into the similitude of an ox that eateth grass." It "shall be broken in pieces," it shall not be able to help itself, much less help them; it shall be as Dagon before the ark, broken all to pieces.

Jerome on the place saith, that he learned from a Hebrew, that this word (which is not a verb, but a noun, signifying, breaking in pieces) carries with it the idea of a web, such as you see at some times of the year in the fields, upon the grass, thin webs, like spiders' webs, that presently dissolve into atoms; so that their calf shall, like them, dissolve and come to nothing. All the confidence and hopes in any thing we set up in the place of God, are such to us. What difference is there between such a thing and "a strong rock," and "an high tower," such as God is to his people.

And again, The word signifies saw-dust, that comes from timber that is sawn, and so it "shall be broken in pieces:" look, as the calf in the wilderness was ground even to dust, to powder, and Moses made the people drink of it in water; so God will serve this calf. Hence,

Obs. 6. Idols are to be broken in pieces. So God commanded, Exod. xxxiv. 13; Deut. vii. 5; Ezek. xx. 7; with many other scriptures; and thus godly magistrates have ever done, broken idols in pieces. And blessed be God for what has been done of late among us, that so many idols, and especially that great idol which was in the most eminent place of the city, God put a spirit into those in authority to break in pieces. This must be done by the magistrate, as those in authority alone possess power over public places.

I remember Austin in his sixth discourse on Christ's sermon, speaking of Deut. xii. 1—3, saith, First you must possess the land, and then you shall overthrow their altars; and thence notes, That it is for those alone who have the possession of the land to break the idols in pieces. In the city of Basil, we read, that every Ash Wednesday (as they call it) is observed a festival, instead of the popish fast on that day, because of the burning of popish images. And though we have no warrant to observe such a day as a holy day, yet certainly as a day of outward, civil rejoicing, we have cause to observe those times wherein notorious and abominable idols have been broken in pieces.

Obs. 7. Whatsoever may be broken in pieces, we are not to make our god. Now, all creatures in the world are subject to breaking: your estates are in danger to be broken in pieces, therefore they are not gods; that is the argument of the Holy Ghost here: yea, it may be many of your estates are broken in pieces already; oh what poor gods were they then to you! and so with any other creature whatsoever: therefore let us "trust in the Lord for ever: for in the Lord Jehovah is everlasting strength," Isa. xxvi. 4.

Obs. 8. Deifying a creature makes way for the destruction of that creature. "The calf of Samaria shall be broken in pieces," because it was made an idol. If you would use your estates to fit you for God's service, you might keep them; but if you set them up in God's place, it is just with God that they should "be broken in pieces." Yea, if you set your husband, your wife, your child, your friend, in the place of God, they must be broken to pieces; broken to pieces, at least with respect to you. Many great instruments of God, God has been fain to break to pieces, because that men have set them up in the place of God, and made even gods of them.

Ver. 7. *For they have sown the wind, and they shall reap the whirlwind: it hath no stalk: the bud shall yield no meal; if so be it yield, the strangers shall swallow it up.*

"For they have sown." Sowing is a laborious work, and this idolatrous people were very laborious, took a great deal of pains, about their false worship. Hence,

Obs. 1. Idolaters are laborious; they are willing to take pains and go through many difficulties for the furtherance of their false worship. Those that sow must be abroad in the wind and the cold. Let not us be sluggish then in the true worship of our God, let us be willing to pass through many difficulties to promote his cause.

Obs. 2. Idolaters sow in hope. Sowing is a labour without any present profit coming in by it, the benefit of the labour lies in the future expectation. We are forthwith weary of a little labour, except we receive some present return; we cannot wait for the blessing of "the former and the latter rain" upon our endeavours; we must be always reaping, or else we are wearied and discouraged. Idolaters would work hard though they get nothing for the present; how much more should we labour for God in expectation of the harvest that God has provided!

Obs. 3. Idolaters labour to maintain their false worship for the sake of posterity. "For they have sown." Sowing is a work for the maintenance of the succession of provision from one generation to another: so idolaters are not content to enjoy their idolatries during their own times, but adopt means to continue the enjoyment to future generations. Thus we should do, and with great reason, in the true worship of God; not think it enough to enjoy it ourselves, but use all means in our power, that we may leave it to our posterity; that we may sow for posterity as well as ourselves, that we may leave a stock of provision for our children afterwards. Through God's mercy our forefathers did so, and we have reaped the harvest of their seed; and as through their endeavours we have enjoyed much of the worship and of the truths of God, let us likewise sow for those that will succeed us.

Obs. 4. Idolaters observe their seasons. "For they have sown." Sowing is a work that must be done in its season, or it is done in vain: so idolaters mark the times fit for the furtherance of their false worship; much more should we for the worship of God. We have had a fair season, and have seemed to be very busy; the Lord grant we do not sow the wind, as follows in the next words.

"The wind." "They have sown the wind." This is a proverbial speech, signifying the taking a great deal of pains to little purpose; as if a man should go abroad in the fields, and spread his hands about with effort, and yet grasp nothing but air. The wind is an empty creature in respect of things solid, therefore the Scripture often makes use of it to signify the vanity of the hopes and laborious endeavours of wicked men: you find several expressions in Scripture illustrative of this; as, "Labouring for the wind," Eccles. v. 16; "feeding upon the wind," Hos. xii. 1; "bringing forth the wind," Isa. xxvi. 18; "inheriting the wind," Prov. xi. 29; and here, in the text, "sowing to the wind."

Obs. 5. Many do nothing all their lifetime, but sow the wind; they labour and toil, but what comes of it? It is no good account to give to God of our time, to say that we have taken a great deal of pains; we may take pains, and yet "sow the wind."

Who are those that sow the wind?

1. Some students; men that spend their thoughts and strength about things no way profitable to themselves or others, such sow the wind; with a great deal of earnestness they do just nothing, for what they do is but a trifle. Many scholars study night and day, tire themselves with reading, and musing, and writing, and yet are no way useful; either their studies have been in useless things, raking among rubbish and lumber, or else they know not how to turn to advantage their reading and learning. And indeed it is a pitiful object to behold one who has been all his days a great student, has risen early and gone to bed late, grudged the very time of his meals, yet a useless man in the place where he is, and of no service, after all, to church or common-weal: such a man has all his days "sown the wind."

2. Idolaters; all those who take pains and are at great cost in superstitious worship, all their intentions that they have to honour God, come to nothing, it is

but a sowing the wind: and this is that which is here especially meant, they sow the wind. All idolatrous worshippers but sow the wind: how many papists are there, that dare not for their lives but rise at the hours that they have vowed, and spend them at their beads, wear out their bodies by their fastings and watchings, deny themselves the use of the creatures, wear sackcloth, lie very hard, tire their bodies by pilgrimage, forsake the revenues that their progenitors have left them, vow perpetual virginity, shut themselves up in cloisters! What a deal of labour and toil is all this to the flesh! and it is for conscience' sake, with a desire to honour God, and to afflict themselves for their sins. And yet this, not having warrant from God, being but "will-worship," is but sowing the wind; they lose all their labour, cost, and charge, all their thoughts, and devotions.

3. Formalists; such as content themselves in the outward part of God's worship, having no power nor life of godliness in the services they perform. You have many that do things out of custom, content themselves in the outward act, dare not for their lives neglect prayer, not one morning nor evening, nor at other times, and are often with God's people in fasting, or coming to hear the word; but yet all this while, not having the life and power of godliness in these their duties, they do but sow the wind, they lose all their labour; and when they come to die, and desire comfort from what they have done, they shall find nothing but the wind to feed upon, they will have no solid comfort to satisfy their souls in the day of their distress.

4. The vain-glorious; they who do all that they do out of vain-glory, who, to set up themselves among others, spend a long time in prayer, and an ostentatiously scrupulous observance of all rites and ceremonies, a principle of vain-glory actuating them throughout; these have been but sowing the wind. Men of public gifts, who do abundance of good in the church of God and in the commonwealth, but are moved thereto by a principle of self and vain-glory, lose all, they sow but the wind.

5. Carnal politicians; these leave the rule of the word, and carry on their actions altogether by the rules of carnal policy, thinking to effect great things by their devices. These, despising the word and worship of God as things beneath them, sow but the wind while they profess to be engaged in weighty matters. The people here were moved by carnal policy, and God calls it all but sowing the wind: they thought they had framed to themselves a notable piece of work, but, saith God, it is but sowing the wind.

6. Such as serve themselves of sin; such as seek to shift for themselves by sinful means when they are in any straits, and forsake lawful courses to help themselves out of trouble; these are they that sow the wind to themselves, nothing will come of all the labour they take. Now to apply this:

1. The church of God may have much comfort in this, that all their enemies, in all they do, but sow the wind; they can never prevail, be not afraid of them.

2. Life is the seed-time for eternity: it is an evil and dangerous thing therefore now to sow the wind, to lose this seed-time, and to have nothing for our souls to feed upon to all eternity. Oh! how sad will it be when we are entering on eternity, to see then that we have all our lifetime but "sown the wind!" Did men consider that their actions were seeds for eternity, certainly they would take more heed what they do. Men are very careful of their seed; what husbandman that is to sow his ground would go into a market to buy chaff, to buy blasted stuff to be his seed? no, he would buy the largest and plumpest corn he could get for seed. So should we be careful of all our actions, for they are such seed as must bring forth a harvest of eternal happiness, or else eternal sorrow; and especially we had need look to our seed when God gives us a fair opportunity of sowing. All hypocrites, formalists, and false worshippers, sow the wind, their actions are but as the wind; but the servants of God, whose works come from faith, and are indeed godly, they sow to immortality and glory, their seed will bring forth a glorious harvest. I remember that Luther, though a man that seemed to beat down works very much, yet has this passage concerning works: Take works out of the cause of justification, and no man can too magnificently commend good works that come from faith. And speaking of a good work that comes from faith, he saith, Any one good work is a more precious thing than heaven and earth. Yea, he himself, though no merit-monger, yet extols good works that come from faith, and saith, The whole world is not sufficient reward for one good work resulting from faith. Indeed the works of the saints have a great deal of excellency in them, one gracious work has more of the glory of God in it than all the creation of heaven and earth besides: I say, the whole frame of heaven and earth has not so much of the glory of God in it, as one good work that comes from the grace of God in the hearts of the saints; and my reason is this, because a good work that comes from the grace of God in the hearts of the saints, is a reflection of spiritual life, that is, of the very life of God, as the Scripture calls it, the life of God, and the Divine nature. Now an action of spiritual life more sets forth the glory of God than any glory that God has passively; the glory that he has in the frame of the heavens and earth is but a passive glory, but here the very glory of God is reflected upon his own face, it is a glory of spiritual life. A man does not account one so much honoured in an image that is drawn of him, as when he sees his child act as he himself acts, his own character impressed on the offspring. Now all the frame of heaven and earth is not so much as a picture, it is but as the footsteps of God, the skirts of his glory; but in one gracious action of the saints God sees his child act as he himself doth, he sees the workings of his own holiness and his own virtues; we show forth the virtues of him that "hath called us out of darkness into his marvellous light," 1 Pet. ii. 9.

3. Ministers must most of all men take heed that they sow not the wind. God has made them seeds-men of that eternal seed, his word, and they fail to sow it truly, when, 1. They are loth to take pains, or to be at the charge for good seed, they sow husks and chaff, and bring merely empty words to their people. 2. When they do take sufficient pains, but bring their own fancies and counsels instead of the precious immortal seed of the word: in both these cases they do but sow the wind. The Seventy translate the words which we render "for they have sown the wind," thus, for they have sown things corrupted by the wind. Those actions that pride corrupts, will never bring forth good fruit.

כי רוח יזרעו "Οτι ἀνεμόφθορα ἔσπειραν.

"And they shall reap the whirlwind." As we sow, so shall we reap. The word in the Hebrew (Tremelius upon this place observes) has a syllable more than usual added; and that, saith he, to increase its signification; to note, that this is not only a whirlwind, but a most terrible whirlwind. And mark, he does not say they sow the wind, and they shall reap the wind; no, there is more in the harvest than in the seed; if men will "sow the wind," they must expect to "reap the whirlwind." If thou hast but a little pleasure in thy sinful ways, thou must expect a great deal of misery as their fruit. Their labour shall not only be in vain, but much evil shall come, sudden and violent destruction. All sinful actions are like the sowing of the wind in the earth: now we know, if windy vapours get into the earth, they break forth into whirlwinds, they cause earthquakes;

סופה turbo, hic סופתה.

so wicked actions break forth into violence and irresistible evils, and will cause heart-quakes at last. Great is the power of the whirlwind, the Scripture describes it as very great; so, in 1 Kings xix. 11, it "rent the mountains, and brake in pieces the rocks." Sabelicos reports, that Cambyses' soldiers being at dinner in a sandy place, there arose a whirlwind and drove the sand upon them so that it covered them all. And yet, what is the wind, but many vapours conjoined? and yet what mighty strength is in them! By the way, this meditation may be raised here: What! shall the conjunction of many such weak things as vapours prevail so mightily? what then must be the strength of the infinite God, to which nothing can be added! Add many vapours together, and they form strong winds, which rend up the mountains by the roots. If many weak things put together (I say) prove thus powerful, what must be the strength of an infinite God, to which no strength can be added! But out of the words,

Obs. 6. It is just with God, that those who sow the wind should reap the whirlwind; should be brought into trouble and vexation, into miserable and irremediable distresses. You that spend your time about trifles, whereas God sets you in the world on work of great importance, it is just with God that you should have horror on your spirits hereafter, when he shall make you see how you have spent that time upon which eternity depended: and you that spend your time in false worship, and so think to put off God with your own inventions, it is just with God that you should reap the whirlwind. Ye formalists, who spend your strength and time in the observance of mere external rites, and never sanctify the name of God, it were just with God that horror, and distress, and trouble should fill your souls. And you, ye hypocrites, who aim at your own vain-glorious ends, whereas you should desire to bring glory to the name of God, it is just with God that fearfulness and trembling should possess you. How many have lain upon their death-beds, and cried out, Oh I have done all in hypocrisy! and so horror of conscience has been as a whirlwind to their souls. Carnal politicians, too, that have left God, and sought to provide deliverance for themselves and others out of difficulties by sinful courses, the Lord often brings into most dreadful straits, and, the worm of conscience gnawing upon them, they find by sad experience that they have reaped the whirlwind. And indeed we begun of late to corrupt the worship of God, and were carried on by carnal policy, and did sow the wind; and how has the Lord now made us in great measure to reap the whirlwind! Job saith the whirlwind comes from the south; but indeed the truth is, we have had whirlwinds coming from the north and west, and may yet have whirlwinds coming from all parts of the kingdom; for what has the land done of late, but "sown the wind?" Let us not wonder, though God at this day speak unto us out of the whirlwind, as once he did to Job.

Yea, but many may say, That which we have sown has some substance in it, it is not only the wind, for we see that it comes to a blade, it comes forth.

Yea, but, I beseech you, observe the words that follow,

"It hath no stalk: the bud shall yield no meal: if so be it yield, the strangers shall swallow it up." It may be a stalk may come forth; but, saith God, it shall be crushed before it comes to the bud. But what if it does bud? It shall be blasted, it shall "yield no meal." But what if so be it yield meal? Then "strangers shall swallow it up," saith God. This serves most elegantly to show God's watching over an apostatizing people for evil, and that howsoever they may seem to prosper for a while, yet at the last the curse of God will be their ruin.

Obs. 7. Sometimes wicked actions may seem to prosper, though God's curse is upon them. God may let them come to a stalk, or to the bud, or to the meal; this notes the possibility. It may come to the stalk, possibly to the bud, possibly to the meal, but then all shall come to nothing.

My brethren, we have found it so by experience; as it was here with this people, in their wicked idolatry and their carnal policy, has it not been so with our adversaries? some of their actions God has crushed presently; others have grown up to a blade, and have seemed to have meal in them, but then the curse of God has come upon them. Oh the uncertainty and the vanity of the comforts of ungodly men! When can they bless themselves in any one project? When it comes up to the blade? No, saith God, it shall not come to a stalk: God watches so that it seldom comes so far. Well, but then may they bless themselves if it has risen up to a stalk? No, not then either, God's curse is on them. But if it bud, may they not then bless themselves? Our projects, say they, begin to bud, and thrive bravely, may we not bless ourselves now? No, God still watches over you for evil. But what if it come to a full issue, "yield meal," and they be ready even to feed upon the fruit of their projects, may they not then think all is sure? No, the curse of God pursues them, "strangers shall swallow it up." Blessed be that God who has thus followed our adversaries: how often have they blessed themselves, and when some designs have succeeded according to their desires, thought all was well, and then God's curse came upon them! We are, my brethren, too unbelieving, too ready to fear if we hear of any thriving in any measure of our adversaries; if any stalk appear, and especially if they begin to bud, O, then we think they ripen; and we do not look up to the great God, who delights in blasting the projects of the adversaries. As the blessing of God is upon the good actions of his people, so the curse of God is upon the wicked projects of his enemies. God may seem often to leave many a good action, but he carries it through at length, though many things conspire to crush it in the very bud. God carries good projects through many difficulties, and crushes wicked projects through much prosperity.

Obs. 8. To have our desires satisfied for a while, and then destroyed, is a great judgment. But that it should be so is just in God; for ordinarily we are thus in our obedience, which usually withers before it comes to any ripeness; if it get up to the stalk, it may be, it comes not to a bud; if to meal, some strange lust or other comes in and devours it. Oh how often do our strange lusts devour our good actions, when ready to be performed! Of how many in their youth have we thought that very gracious seed began to sprout forth, and that the seed grew to a stalk, and when they came to act for themselves, that it budded in gracious actions; in their middle age we thought it yielded meal; but in their old age strange lusts came and devoured all. It is a great judgment for strangers to devour our estates which we have acquired by a great deal of labour; but truly, for strange lusts to come to devour thy hopeful beginnings, is a far greater judgment. Many have laboured diligently all their lives, and that which they have done has seemed to come to something; and the truth is, in the conclusion the devil has had the advantage of all.

And God seems to be out against us in some degree, even in the ways of his judgments, at this day. Thus as many of the adversaries' projects, so many of ours, the Lord has blasted before they come to a stalk; and when they have budded the Lord has blighted them, by the unfaithfulness of some or others; in the midst of our greatest expectations, the Lord has seemed to blast us, and what God will do with us we know not; only let us make sure that our seed be good, and though this does not prosper, or that does not succeed, yet at last God will bring the greater harvest upon us.

Ver. 8. *Israel is swallowed up: now shall they be among the Gentiles as a vessel wherein is no pleasure.*

"Israel is swallowed up." Israel had made leagues among other people, till they were even swallowed up by them. And truly, my brethren, if great care be not had, there is much danger in making leagues with other nations, lest in time of our need they should encroach upon us, and at length even impose upon us laws. It was so with Israel; by their league with other people they at length became subject to their laws, and were swallowed up by them. And thus many of the people of God, yea, of the churches of God, by mingling themselves with the world, are even swallowed up, so that they lose their beauty, and at length no difference appears between them and those who surround them. None certainly can expect that any church in the world can continue without a mixture of wicked men and hypocrites, but it is one thing when they creep in unawares, and another when the fence is broken down, so that it is very hard to discern the appearance of a church amongst them: thus it was with Israel.

"Now shall they be among the Gentiles as a vessel wherein is no pleasure." By these words, vessel of no pleasure, is meant, a vessel that is for the carrying up and down of excrements; only the Scripture, when it mentions such vile things, speaks euphemistically; but that is the force of the word: as if he should say, My people shall be in a vile, contemptible condition among the Gentiles, as a vessel that is fit for nothing but excrements. Thus Jehoiachin is threatened, Jer. xxii. 28, though a great man, to be as "a vessel wherein is no pleasure." They had wasted their substance in seeking help from the Egyptians and Assyrians, and these made a prey of them: so long as any thing of value remained, they made much of them, but their estates being once wasted by them, they regarded them as vile and contemptible. And this is the way of wicked men, while they are serving their own turns upon any, they will flatter and caress them, but when their end is gained, then they treat them with scorn and contempt. None, when their estates are consumed, are more scorned and contemned than professors of religion who have basely crouched to wicked men, and sought to shelter themselves under them: therefore let us learn wisdom, and venture with caution to make use of men, and not please ourselves in their commendations, if they have ends of their own to serve; when they have attained them, they will scorn you, and look upon you as base and contemptible.

Again, "A vessel wherein is no pleasure." The Seventy translate it, σκεῦος ἄχρηστον, an unprofitable vessel. But there is certainly more intended in this expression; a vessel employed in base and contemptible uses; Israel shall be so employed; and thereby they shall find a difference between my service, and the service of their enemies. Oh it is a sad expression, What! Israel a vessel employed and received to empty out excrements! Israel were a people "precious" and "honourable" in the eyes of God, Isa. xliii. 4. "An holy people unto the Lord," God's "peculiar people," "above all the nations that are upon the earth," Deut. xiv. 2. "The Lord's portion," Deut. xxxii. 9. God's "inheritance," Isa. xix. 25. God's "peculiar treasure," Exod. xix. 5. God's "glory," Isa. xlvi. 13. God's "delight," Isa. lxii. 4. Israel were "the dearly beloved of my" (God's) "soul," Jer. xii. 7; and yet now Israel is become a vessel fit only for excrements! Oh what a change does sin make! They were holy vessels, employed in holy services, in attending upon God and his worship, so as no people were; but now, see the ruin and degradation brought upon them by sin! How doth sin vilify men, employ them in base services, most degrading to an ingenuous mind! A young Spartan being taken by Antigonus, and sold for a slave, whilst employed by his master in any thing creditable, he did it; but when he bid him go and empty a vessel wherein is no pleasure, No, saith he, I will not serve you in such matters; and his master being angry with him, he went to the top of the house and cast himself off, rather than be forced to obey. And certainly there is nothing so beneath the excellency of an immortal soul as sin, for by means of it, though high in thine own thoughts, thou comest to be a vessel for the very devil to empty his excrements into: and that is lower than to be a scavenger employed in collecting the filth of the street; yea, as low as if thou wert condemned to go from morning to night, to carry away the filth in thy very hands and mouth. Some men are vessels of mercy, chosen vessels, vessels of honour fitted for the Master's use: and it is an infinite mercy of God to us, when we have deserved to be cast out as vessels wherein there is no pleasure, that God should take us out of the common lump, and should employ us to be vessels of his sanctuary; whereas others are vessels of wrath, used only in base services that are beneath the excellency of an immortal soul.

Yea, some there are who have been eminent in the church heretofore, who have been vessels filled with the gifts, I do not say graces, of the Holy Ghost, but now they are vessels in which there is no pleasure. Many of the saints, heretofore, have been refreshed by those gifts of the Holy Ghost that have been in them, but now their gifts are gone, they are fit for nothing but the meanest services; yea, some of them filled with poison, vessels wherein neither God nor man can take pleasure: yea, and some very forward professors of religion, that once were as the polished sapphires, are now turned apostates, are become more black than the coal; they were as golden vessels in the house of God, and are now become "vessels wherein is no pleasure." Demosthenes once desired the Athenians not to make a urinal of a wine pot; to employ men, that had been eminent, in base services. But now men whom God himself heretofore made use of for great services in church and state, the Lord has left to be "vessels of no pleasure." O remember, all you, from whence you are fallen! Thy heart is now exercised upon low things, thy work, it may be, now is only to further the wicked designs and desperate malice of other men; and dost thou think to be a vessel of glory, to stand before the presence of the holy God, and join with saints and angels in the eternal praises of his name? O remember from whence thou art fallen, and rest not till the Lord has been pleased to purge thee, and make thee fit for thy Master's use, and to become a vessel of honour in thy Master's house.

Ver. 9. *For they are gone up to Assyria, a wild ass alone by himself: Ephraim hath hired lovers.*

The Lord, by the prophet, proceeds on in his charge against the ten tribes.

"For they are gone up to Assyria." They look not up to the high God for help, but "are gone up to Assyria;" Assyria is higher in their eyes than the God of heaven. How vile a thing is it to forsake confidence in God out of suspicious thoughts of him! for so it was here, they retained suspicious thoughts of God, as if he would leave them in their extremity, and therefore forsook they him, and sought for help elsewhere; they expect more good, more faithfulness, more love, not only from the creature than from God, but from the very enemies of God than from God himself; yea, that people that professed interest in God, that would seem to bless themselves in this, that God was their God, even they looked to have more good and to find more faithfulness in the very enemies of God than in God himself. Let the heavens be astonished at this wickedness: and yet this evil abides deep-rooted in the hearts of the children of men.

"A wild ass." This the Scripture mentions in divers places, as one of the most unruly, untamable, and fierce of all creatures; such as cannot be brought to be serviceable, nor to live with, no, nor even to keep company with, their own kind, but they run up and down in the wilderness alone. In Job xi. 12, mention is made of this creature; "For vain man would be wise, though man be born like a wild ass's colt." And in Job xxxix. 5, "Who hath sent out the wild ass free? or who hath loosed the bands of the wild ass?" And, to name no more, in Jer. ii. 24, "A wild ass used to the wilderness, that snuffeth up the wind at her pleasure; in her occasion who can turn her away? all they that seek her will not weary themselves; in her month they shall find her." Those that desire to know more of the nature of this beast, may find divers things in Pliny and other naturalists. But now we are only to speak of it as the Scripture suggests.

Pliny, l. 8. cap. 40.

Why does God compare Ephraim and the ten tribes to the wild ass?

For two reasons. 1. To show the extreme stubbornness and fierceness of this people. Wicked men that have forsaken God and are left to themselves, not only become like to savage creatures, but to savage creatures of the worst kind, they run up and down satisfying the lusts of their own hearts irresistibly, and bear down all before them; they stamp, and rage, and are mad when at any time they are opposed in their wicked ways: this is the scope of the Holy Ghost here; thus Ephraim was when he was opposed. Do you not find many such, many that are so resolved on ungodliness and sin, that they will hear nothing, they snuff at the wind and all that is said against them, and madly pursue their own ruin? Jeremiah saith, "in their month you shall find them;" that refers to the very last month which the wild ass goes when with young, then, when great with young, and not till then, can it be dealt with. Some historians say that the wild asses are so fierce, that they will tear asunder armour of proof; but "in their month" they are so big that they cannot wield themselves, and then "you shall find them." So, though sinners be never so stubborn, yet God has his month, and perhaps then "you shall find them." When at any time you find your children, or servants, or others, stubborn and stout against whatsoever is said to them, and even raging in their madness, for the satisfying of their wicked wills, you may remember this text and creature; they are as wild asses that are alone by themselves. And of all wicked men, idolaters are the most stubborn and stout in their impieties; their hearts are set upon their idols; yea, as the phrase of Scripture is, in Jer. l. 38, "they are mad upon their idols." Nothing can be said to those whose hearts are taken with false worship; nothing will prevail with them without an exertion of the infinite power of God; no sinners are more bold, more untamable and fierce in their ways; and therefore is it, that if they be opposed in their superstitions such tumults arise, stones flung against windows where God is truly worshipped, any thing in the world, they care not what. Because they think themselves condemned in their sinful ways, therefore they run like wild beasts in a furious manner, even against those that worship God better than themselves.

2. By way of contempt. As in Job xi. 12, "Vain man would be wise, though man be born like a wild ass's colt:" he would fain think himself somebody, yet he is a most base and vile creature. And if any of you be not so fierce in your wicked ways as some others are, if God has tamed your spirits by his word and Spirit, bless him for it; for all men are "born like a wild ass's colt," they are mad upon their wickedness even to their own ruin. But because stoutness and stubbornness evermore proceed from pride, and none think it such a dishonour as the stubborn for their wills to be crossed in any thing, therefore the Scripture casts the more contempt upon them, and calls such "wild ass's colts;" and indeed there are none more contemptible in the eyes of God than stout sinners.

"Alone by himself." This expression tends to show that Ephraim and the ten tribes would have their own wills "alone." There are these two things implied in it:

1. That they would be under no government, but alone by themselves, and have liberty to do what they list, acknowledging no commander; and so the Chaldee paraphrase, Because that they would walk in the evil of their own lusts, and acknowledge no commander. And thus many at this day love to be alone, that is, to live at their own hand, to be from under government.

2. That they were unfit for society, they were so furious and fierce in their ways. "Alone by himself." Some are of such untoward and perverse dispositions, that they can agree with no one, so that they are only fit to live in solitude. I suppose you have met, in your families, with those that are so extremely perverse in their ways, and of such untoward and crooked dispositions, that they are fit to live in no society: to them this reproof of Ephraim is applicable.

"Ephraim hath hired lovers." אהבים loves. Before, they put their confidence in the Assyrians, Egyptians, and others, and now they make them their loves. Our observations are these:

Obs. 1. Where we place our confidence, there our love should be placed. If God be the confidence of our hearts, let our love be placed there; yea, let God be our loves, in the plural number, for so it is here, they "hired lovers." She would fain have the Assyrians to love her. When God is forsaken, and we have lost our interest in God's love, no marvel though there be such a seeking after the creature's love. Men that forsake God, seek to make up what they have not in God, in the creature; as a dog, when he has lost his master, is ready to follow every one he meets with.

Ob . 2. The unlovely will use unworthy means to purchase love. "Ephraim hath hired lovers." Because they had nothing lovely in themselves, therefore they seek even to hire love; though the truth is, love cannot be hired nor purchased: although men may fawn, and flatter, and crouch, that they may gain the love of others, yet if they be unlovely in themselves, although those whom they fawn on and flatter may use them for their own turn, yet the truth is, they will despise them in their hearts, and often discover to their intimate friends how they scorn and contemn them. Therefore, if others would secure love, they themselves must have some excellency and loveliness, for love cannot be hired.

Obs. 3. Idolaters will not stand upon terms if they may have their idols. "Ephraim hath hired lovers." This shows the shamelessness of the ten tribes in seeking after their false worship. Other harlots are hired to commit uncleanness, but Ephraim, in its spiritual whoredoms, will be at charge for their idols. So in Ezek. xvi. 33, 34, "They give gifts to all whores: but thou givest thy gifts to all thy lovers, and hirest them, that they may come unto thee on every side for thy whoredom. And the contrary is in thee from other women in thy whoredoms, whereas none followeth thee to commit whoredoms: and in that thou givest a reward, and no reward is given unto thee, therefore thou art contrary." As if God should say, You are more vile and base in your uncleannesses than any in the world besides; for others receive rewards, but you are so set upon your filthy lusts that you will give rewards that you may commit your abominations. They care not how they debase themselves, they will not stand upon honour and respect, but let them have their false worship, they will submit to any thing. Oh! why then should we stand hesitating thus in matters wherein the honour of our God and the public good lie at stake? Why should we not be willing to suffer shame and disgrace, any thing, rather than the public good should not go on, than the service of God should be hindered? If others will not seek to us, yet, if good may be done, if God may have glory, let us seek to them. Though others be never so vile in their carriage towards us, yet let us do what we can to win and convince them, let us be willing to lie under their feet that God may be glorified. If others will not join in a good work, except they may have the honour of it, let them have it, provided the work go on. Let the work go on, and if they will stand for the glory, let them have it; so God may be lifted up, let us be willing not to be seen. This is that which often hinders the success of God's cause. Men stand upon terms, and will not go on in a good cause, but break off if others be preferred before them. If two called to carry a long piece of timber through a narrow passage, should stand striving who should go foremost, one saying, I will go first, the other, Nay, but I will go first, they could never carry the timber; if one have one end, and the other the other end, and they cannot agree which should go first, and he that goes after thinks himself dishonoured because his fellow goes before him, they can never carry it through, but must lay it down. So it is many times with a good cause, it is like a piece of timber upon two men's shoulders, which must go through a narrow passage, and one saith, Why should not I have the glory of it? and the other saith, Why should not I have the glory of it? and whilst men stand wrangling who should have the greatest glory, in the mean time the public cause is exceedingly hindered. Let us be willing to submit, and debase ourselves any way, so be it the true worship of God prosper.

Obs. 4. It is an evil thing to be drawn to false worship, or bodily uncleanness, upon any terms. "Ephraim hath hired lovers." Hope of the greatest gain, or deliverance from the greatest affliction, should not prevail. But for a man or woman to seek after the ways of sin, to be at cost that they may have their lusts gratified, is more base and abominable. Certainly uncleanness should be cast off with indignation, though we be tempted to it with never so much gain; but for one to be set upon uncleanness, so as to seek after it, and to spend their husbands' estates that they may have free course for the indulgence of their lusts, is a most abominable thing indeed; and yet many are thus guilty, both in regard of bodily and spiritual adultery.

Josephus, lib. xviii. cap. 4.

Ver. 10. *Yea, though they have hired among the nations, now will I gather them, and they shall sorrow a little for the burden of the king of princes.*

These words at first seem to be dark, and yet we have much of the mind of God in them, and much concerning ourselves.

"Yea, though they have hired among the nations." This God still takes ill, that they should go to the nations for help when God had made their condition so much above the nations; for in their going to them they did, as it were, say, that all the love, and mercy, and protection from the great God toward them, was no more than the nations had; they did, as it were, hold forth to the world that the nations were rather in a better condition than themselves, in that they would go to them for their help: and this went very near to the heart of God; for God had expended the very strength of his love and the riches of his mercy upon this people, and after he had done so much for them, that they, under the pressure of some slight afflictions, should go to the nations that did, for the present, prosper somewhat outwardly better than themselves, oh, this was exceeding grievous to the heart of God! And thence the observations are,

Obs. 1. It is a very great evil for the people of God to conclude, when wicked men prosper a little more than they, that therefore they are in a better condition than themselves. This is an evil that affects very much the heart of God; and yet this ordinarily prevails, in some degree or other, among the people of God. I appeal to your consciences in this very thing; though sometimes your souls have had sweet refreshing from the Lord in the enjoyment of communion with him, yet, when God's hand has been out against you, when you have seen others prospering, though you knew them to be wicked and ungodly, their ships coming home safe and richly laden, and their trading in a flourishing condition, do you not then sometimes find such thoughts rising within you, as if these men were in a better condition than yourselves? Oh! know that the least thoughts of such a kind exceedingly grieve the Spirit of God by which you are sealed, that because they have a few loaves more than you, though you have all the riches of God and Christ, though you have the inheritance of saints, yet that you should think them in a better condition than yourselves. How ordinary is it, upon this ground, for those that have professed themselves to be godly, rather to withdraw from the afflicted saints, and seek correspondence with the wicked in their prosperity! God would have his people see such an all-sufficiency in himself in their saddest condition, that they need not go out from him for help, but still wait upon him and keep his way. The Lord, by his prophet, rebukes Jehoshaphat, in 2 Chron. xix. 2, for helping the ungodly, and loving them that hate the Lord. And is it not as great an evil to seek the love of the wicked and ungodly, and ask help from them that hate the Lord? Certainly the evil is very great, it argues the very little love that we have to God, it charges God with unfaithfulness, as if, though he has engaged himself to his people, he would leave them in their need; this encourages the wicked in their wickedness, and it charges God with that which is accounted one of the vilest things among men, the abandonment in the time of trouble of those employed in our work. We look upon such men as employ others in any service, and then leave them to shift for themselves in their straits, we look upon them as vile men, unworthy to be dealt withal. Now will we charge God with this which degrades even men? And besides, it is a most desperate folly so to do; for when thou art thinking to provide for thyself by correspondence with ungodly men, it may be thou wert at that time just at the very point of deliverance. It is God's usual way to come to help his people when they are in the greatest straits; and therefore it is the greatest folly when we are in straits to think of shifting courses, so that then we must forsake our own mercy in thinking of shifting courses. In straits, above all times, Christians should take heed of thinking of shifting courses, because then, above all times, those are the times for God to show his mercy, and just then. Wilt thou then be forsaking him? Oh! it is that which should lie near to your hearts. If any of you have been guilty of this, let but the word of God bring this upon your spirits this day; Oh! how do I know but at that very time when I took such a shifting course, that was the very time that God was about to do my soul good, and of doing good for my body? and yet then I deprived myself of good, that goodness and mercy of God! It follows yet,

"Now will I gather them." This gathering is referred by interpreters, either to the nations whom they sought unto, or to themselves. "I will gather them;" that is, that nation; or, I will gather you. If to the nation, then the meaning is,

Notwithstanding you hire the nations, yet I will gather them against you; they shall be strengthened against you with the same money that you hire them withal, I will turn it against you: and now you have provided fair for yourselves, have you not?

Obs. 2. Many times when we think to provide best for our peace, we make the greatest provision for our ruin. God often makes people work their own woe and ruin themselves, and nothing tends more fully and directly to undo them than what they do themselves; thus God overrules the counsels and thoughts of men.

What a vain thing is it to plot against God, when God can turn men's arrows against themselves! None often are greater instruments of God's wrath against us than we are ourselves; yea, and those with whom we seek most to correspond; and it is just with God it should be so, that if we will leave him, to seek correspondence with wicked men, it is just with God, that, of all men in the world, those should be the men that will be made the executioners of God's wrath upon us.

אקבצם a קבץ colligere.

But now, if to Israel; I will gather them among the nations. The word here for gathered, is sometimes used in an army for gathering dead bodies slain in battle. You think to have the nations to aid, but you shall be as a company of dead bodies in an army, and so lie in heaps. But I find that Calvin takes it as having reference to the former verse. This people are wild, and run up and down, this way and that way, to shift for themselves; but I will gather them, that is, I will keep them in: so the words likewise may signify, I will keep them in, I will gather in their spirits, there shall be some dispensation of providence to restrain them, I will keep them from those ways wherein they would presently have ruined themselves.

Colligam eos, retinebo eos. Calvin in loc.

Obs. 3. People many times run headily on in evil ways that will certainly ruin them; but when God's time for the execution of his wrath is not yet come, the Lord restrains them and keeps them in from such ways; though their hearts be set upon them to their own undoing, yet they shall not go on in them; I will pity them who cannot pity themselves. But then follows the greatest difficulty in this verse,

"And they shall sorrow a little for the burden of the king of princes." This has more darkness in it, and yet, upon the searching into it, we shall see it clear, and pregnant with many excellent truths. There are these five things to be inquired into for the opening of these words:

I. Who is here meant by "the king of princes."

II. What was this the burden of "the king of princes."

III. When was this fulfilled, that they should "sorrow for the burden of the king of princes."

IV. Why called, "the burden of the king of princes."

V. What is meant by sorrowing "a little."

These five considerations will clear the text. Indeed we cannot see the full meaning of the Holy Ghost, without in some measure understanding them.

I. Who is meant by "the king of princes?" We are here to understand the king of Assyria, because he was a great king, whose nobles were princes; and we find this both in sacred and profane history. 2 Kings xviii. 24, "How then wilt thou turn away the face of one captain of the least of my master's servants?" And in Isa. xxxvi. 13, "Hear ye the words of the great king, the king of Assyria." And so Josephus, Book I. chap. 10, saith, That before Sodom's destruction, the Assyrians were lords of all Asia: so that the Assyrian was a great king, and here called "the king of princes."

Thus God suffers his enemies to grow great in the world; an Assyrian, a dog, a wicked wretch, under the curse of God, and yet a great king, even "the king of princes." Luther has such an expression concerning the empire of Turkey; It is, saith he, but a crumb that the great Master of the family doth cast to dogs. What are your estates then? Certainly, though never so great in the world, what are any of your estates to the whole Turkish empire? And if that be but a crumb that the great Master of the family casts to a dog, you should never then bless yourselves in the enjoyment of a little of the world. But though the Assyrian may be called "the king of princes," in regard of his power over some great men, yet our Lord Jesus Christ is peculiarly the "King of kings, and Lord of Lords." In Rev. xix. 16, "He hath on his vesture and on his thigh a name written, King of kings, and Lord of lords."

Why was it written "upon his vesture," and why "upon his thigh?" "Upon his vesture;" that is, he will appear openly to be the King of kings: there was a time when Christ seemed to be, as it were, a servant under the dominion of antichrist, but now his name shall be "upon his vesture," openly. And then, "upon his thigh;" that is, upon his lower parts, his church militant, it shall have the kingly power among them for its good, so that they shall be above the nations, according to the prophecy in Isa. lx. 13, "I will make the place of my feet glorious;" that is, the church in their low condition. He saith not, he will have the name upon his crown, but "upon his thigh," that is, upon his lower parts, upon his people that were in a low condition; he will make the very place of his feet to be glorious, even there shall be written, "King of kings, and Lord of lords."

II. What was this his burden? "The burden of the king of princes." This burden was the taxes imposed upon the people, whereby they maintained their correspondence with this king of Assyria. Correspondence with wicked men is burdensome, for the more they are sought and yielded to, ordinarily, the more exacting, generally, they are; and whatsoever they for a while do for you, is indeed to serve their own ends: this Israel brought upon themselves; for they would go to Assyria, and they found the Assyrians burdensome to them.

When men will follow their own ways, and think to have more ease in them than in God's, it is just they should find those ways burdensome. I am persuaded there is not one in this congregation but has experienced this; when you think your ways will bring more ease to you than God's ways, have you not found your ways burdensome?

III. When was this fulfilled? "They shall sorrow a little for the burden of the king of princes." For the mourning of the prophet we must refer to the history of the kings, and in 2 Kings xv. 19, 20, you find the time when this prophecy was fulfilled. "Pul the king of Assyria came against the land: and Menahem gave Pul a thousand talents of silver, that his hand might be with him to confirm the kingdom in his hand. And Menahem exacted the money of Israel, even of all the mighty men of wealth, of each man fifty shekels of silver, to give to the king of Assyria." This was one burden. And then, in ver. 29, "In the days of Pekah king of Israel came Tiglath-pileser king of Assyria, and took Ijon, and Abel-beth-maachah, and Janoah, and Kedesh, and Hazor, and Gilead, and Galilee, all the land of Naphtali, and carried them captive to Assyria." This was a further burden. At these two times was this scripture fulfilled.

IV. Why called "the burden of the king of princes?" In speaking of the burden that was upon the people, why does he apply to the Assyrian such an epithet? It seems to be a diminution of their burden rather than any aggravation; for he speaks of sorrowing but a little, as if it should not be so great a burden as would afterwards be upon them; noting thus, that they were burdened awhile with taxations from a great king, but they should afterwards come under the power, and be subject to the wills and lusts, of all kind of base people, of the very dregs of the nations: and it is not so great an evil to be under the power of men of rank and quality, no, not under their oppression, as to be under the oppression of people that are of mean origin and condition, the very refuse of a nation; to come to be under their power is a great deal worse.

And by the way, this should teach those that are of mean breeding, and of mean condition, if they be put into any place of power and authority, to take heed how they behave themselves, for their oppression will be the most grievous to an ingenuous spirit. And there is a great deal of danger of their growing more oppressive than such as were born to greatness, and their oppression becoming so intolerable as to bring the greatest confusion, if not well looked to. Therefore, here, when he would lessen the burden, he saith, You " shall sorrow a little for the burden of the king of princes."

V. What is meant by sorrowing a little? " They shall sorrow a little." They complained; but, saith God, Why complain of this? this is but a small burden to that which you are like to have; there is a burden of another kind coming on you: and hence the notes are,

Obs. 4. When sinners have brought trouble upon themselves, they complain much; but when they complain, they are to consider, that what they feel is but little to what is coming after. There are burdens upon you, and you are complaining of them, as if they were the greatest that ever were upon people. O sinner! when you are complaining of your burdens, know, that these burdens that are upon you may prove to be but very trifles in comparison of what is likely to come upon you afterwards; for that is the scope of the Holy Ghost here, " They shall sorrow a little for the burden;" as if he should say, There is another manner of sorrow in store: and so it occurred, for afterwards the Assyrians carried them all away captives, and the basest of all the people came to set their feet upon them; therefore saith the Holy Ghost, " They shall sorrow a little for the burden." As the mercies of God to his saints, which now they have, are but a little, they may be said to rejoice but a little for present mercies; so the burdens upon the ungodly are but a little, but if they return not to God upon what they now feel, God has greater burdens than those under which they are so impatient.

Obs. 5. Taxes upon men's estates are but a little burden in comparison of being brought under the power of the enemy. Though there be sore taxes upon you, as here there were fifty shekels of silver laid upon every man that was able, yet those taxes are but small burdens in comparison of being given up to the power of the enemy; they would lay burdens indeed upon us, burdens upon our consciences, our estates, our lives, our liberties, whatsoever we are or have must be under their mercy: now we are troubled, but then their little finger will be more heavy than the loins that now are upon us; although we dare not say but some may find present burdens very burdensome.

Obs. 6. Taxes are but little burden in comparison to the carrying of our brethren into captivity. Though we enjoy our estates ourselves, yet if God lay his hand upon any of our brethren, though in remote parts of the kingdom, we should account this to be a burden. Not only their taxations were a burden, but the carrying away of their brethren that were beyond the river.

If there were no other sin among us, it were just with God to bring the enemy upon us, and then we should find that there were other manner of burdens.

But there is another burden that we are not sensible enough of, and that is, the captivity of our brethren in the remote parts of this land. Oh how little sensible are we of it, because we feel it not ourselves!

Obs. 7. It is God's mercy to bring lesser evils upon us, thereby to prevent greater. You shall sorrow a little, I will not undo you presently; but return to me, or else you are utterly undone. But this is my mercy, I will bring afflictions upon you by piecemeal, and if you do not return to me, then you shall be utterly lost: for so this people were, they were carried away captive, and have never returned, even to this day. O, does God come to you in your family, or person, or estate? O let us consider of this.

Obs. 8. The consideration of little burdens upon us, should move us to turn to God. It should break our hearts, and cause us to seek the face of God, that we may prevent greater evils, that otherwise will certainly come. The Lord, in his dealing towards us, seems as if he were loth to lose us, and that this nation should perish: oh that this might work kindly upon our hearts, to prevent greater evils, that we might not be made a spectacle of the wrath of God to all surrounding nations.

But further, the words translated, " they shall sorrow a little," are by some rendered, they have begun a little for the burden of the king of princes: and so, in Deut. ii. 25, a word that comes from the same root is translated. Then the sense would run thus: That which they have felt is but the beginning of what is like to come; my wrath is let out upon them in some degree already, and do you not see how it is begun to burn upon them? and by that which was lately before your eyes you may believe my threatenings. Hence,

Obs. 9. God's judgments against wicked men are the beginnings of further judgments. In Deut. xxxii. 42, " I will make mine arrows drunk with blood, and my sword shall devour flesh; and that with the blood of the slain and of the captives, from the beginning of revenges upon the enemy." All this is but " from the beginning of revenges;" when I come so terribly upon them it is but " the beginning of revenges." We are ready to think, if there be miserable slaughters, surely God has been revenged enough upon this people. No, all this may prove but " the beginning of revenges." I may say so concerning ourselves, though the Lord many times has made the sword drunk with blood, yet it may prove to be but " the beginning of revenges." Truly we cannot say that, from the time that these judgments have been upon us, we have begun to turn to God; yea, the estate of the kingdom is far worse than it was at the beginning of this present heavy stroke. In Matt. xxiv. 6—8, " Ye shall hear of wars and rumours of wars: see that ye be not troubled: for all these things must come to pass, but the end is not yet. For nation shall rise against nation, and kingdom against kingdom: and there shall be famines, and pestilences, and earthquakes in divers places. All these are the beginning of sorrows."

Obs. 10. God expects from men, that though they be not sensible of his threats, yet, when he begins to execute his wrath upon them, they should begin to turn a little to him. O, it were well with us if we did prevent God's heavy wrath by our repentance. Numb. xvi. 46, " Moses said unto Aaron, Take a censer, and put fire therein from off the altar, and put on incense, and go quickly unto the congregation, and make an atonement for them: for there is wrath gone out from the Lord; the plague is begun." Oh how should we all make haste! We cannot only say the plague is begun, the plague of civil war, which is the greatest of all plagues, but it has gone on to a great length.

Ver. 11. *Because Ephraim hath made many altars to sin, altars shall be unto him to sin.*

It was the charge of God in Scripture, that there should be but one altar for sacrifice; and there was another which was made afterwards for incense, and no more. In Deut. xii. 3, we have the charge of God that there should be none other made; "Ye shall overthrow their altars, and break their pillars, and burn their groves with fire; and ye shall hew down the graven images of their gods, and destroy the names of them out of that place." And then, ver. 13, 14, "Take heed to thyself that thou offer not thy burnt-offerings in every place that thou seest, but in the place which the Lord shall choose in one of thy tribes." And in chap. xxvii. 5, "Thou shalt build an altar unto the Lord thy God, an altar of stones: thou shalt not lift up any iron tool upon them." And according to this Joshua acted, Josh. viii. 30; and hence the circumstances narrated in chap. xxii. 11—34. Now, for the altar of God, I shall first show you a little the meaning of its form and structure, and then the reason why God would have but this one altar. In Exod. xx. 24, there is an injunction of God for the altar of sacrifice; "An altar of earth thou shalt make unto me, and shalt sacrifice thereon thy burnt-offerings," &c. Here observe that, That when God would have an altar made for sacrifice it must be but an altar of earth; but if it should be of stone, thou shalt not lift up any tool upon it. Why, one would think that to carve and paint the stones, and to do any thing to embellish them, would be better than to have the stones rough. No, saith God, whatsoever you may think of adorning my altar by carving and painting it, "if thou lift up thy tool upon it thou hast polluted it:" all man's devices in the worship of God, though never so pompous, do but pollute. And, quite contrary to our high altars, they must not go up upon steps, that their nakedness be not discovered thereon; noting, that when we come into the presence of God we should take heed of spiritual nakedness, and the pride and vanity of our spirits in prayer. God would have them make an altar so as not to go up upon steps, lest their nakedness should be discovered. But now, in Exod. xxvii. 1, 2, you find an altar of shittim wood overlaid with brass: you will say, Why was the first of earth, and the other overlaid with brass? The reason was, because that the one was to be made when they were in an unsettled condition, and the other afterwards when they were in a more stated condition than formerly, and that it might endure a long time. But mark, it must be according to God's direction, except God reveal that it should be of shittim wood and overlaid with brass, they were not so to make it.

And then, the second altar was the altar of burnt incense, and that you have in Exod. xxx. 1—3, and that was to be overlaid with pure gold. That of brass it was, because there were sin-offerings to be offered upon it; but now the altar of incense was the altar just before the veil against the mercy-seat, where there was only incense offered, which was to signify the intercession of Jesus Christ, presenting his merits, and the prayers of all his people, to the Father. The prayers of the saints are compared to incense; and there are many things observable about the altar; it is said that there should be four horns, and in Rev. ix. 13, "I heard a voice from the four horns of the golden altar which is before God." Now St. John speaks of times that should be; he heard a voice from the four horns of the altar; that is, from all the prayers of the saints in the four corners of the earth, a voice came forth and did great things in the world. Certainly, my brethren, the prayers of God's saints in all the corners of the world is that which makes the world ring. A learned man has said, If there be but one sigh from a gracious heart, it fills the ears of God so that he hears nothing else. Nay, what is in Rev. viii. 3, about this altar of incense, is observable: "And another angel came and stood at the altar, having a golden censer, and there was given unto him much incense, that he should offer it with the prayers of all saints upon the golden altar which was before the throne." Thus we see, that in our time we are to make use of this golden altar that is before the throne, all our prayers are to be offered up upon that, which was a type of Jesus Christ; and our prayers, except they be mingled with the incense which Christ offered himself upon the golden altar, cannot be accepted. And likewise what we read in Exod. xxx. 3, deserves to be noted, "and thou shalt make unto it a crown of gold round about;" to typify the intercession of Christ, and the prayers of the saints. You may see by this that Christ's intercession, and the prayers of the saints, coming from faithful hearts, are accounted the very glory of Jesus Christ; he regards it as his dignity and glory to make intercession for his people, and to take the poor prayers of his people and present them to his Father: he considers that his crown is set upon his head, when you exercise your faith on him, that he may present your prayers with his intercession to the Father; but when you think to be heard yourselves, and do not exercise your faith upon Christ, you do, as it were, take off the crown from off his head. The points of difference between the altar here enjoined to be made by Moses, and afterwards really so made, and the altar appointed in the times of the gospel, are very remarkable.

1. Christ is our altar in the gospel. So Heb. xiii. 10, "We have an altar, whereof they have no right to eat which serve the tabernacle;" that is, such as shall still pertinaciously adhere to the ceremonies of the law have no right to partake of Jesus Christ.

2. The gospel-altar was larger, more comprehensive. There is a prophecy of the altar that the church shall have, in Ezek. xli. 22: the altar under the law, the text saith, was to be a cubit long, and a cubit broad; but that which was to be in the time of the gospel, must be three cubits high, and two cubits long: and this imports, that there shall be a larger extent of the service of God under the gospel than under the law. Mal. i. 11 much confirms this: "For from the rising of the sun even unto the going down of the same my name shall be great among the Gentiles; and in every place incense shall be offered unto my name, and a pure offering: for my name shall be great among the heathen, saith the Lord of hosts."

3. It was set before the veil by the ark of the testimony, before the mercy-seat. It was to stand in the holy of holies, but just before the veil, right against the mercy-seat. And by this you are helped to understand Heb. ix. 4, which, as some take it, seems to differ from this. It is said there, that the holiest of all had the golden censer; by which they understand the golden altar, in which the censer was. But we shall find that the golden altar did not stand in the holy of holies, for we read, in Exod. xxx. 6, "And thou shalt put it before the veil that is by the ark of the testimony, before the mercy-seat that is over the testimony." Interpreters reconcile it thus: it is not said here that the golden censer, or altar, if we so take it, was *in* it, but it *had* it. That is, it was for the use of the holy of holies, and it stood just before it, and just against the mercy-seat; so that the high priest, when about to go into the holy of holies, was to take a censer and incense from this altar, and so enter the holiest of all.

Calvin.

But note, in that the altar of incense stands just against the mercy-seat, and yet there is a veil between the mercy-seat and it; so, when we offer up our incense upon the merits of Christ and his intercession, though we cannot, by the eye of our bodies, see the mercy-seat, yet we must act our faith upon it. And further, it is observable, that the incense must be burnt upon this altar at the very time when the lamps were to be trimmed and lighted; so Exod. xxx. 7: and that was to note this to us, that we are to join the word with our prayers, and not to come ignorantly to God, but labour to enlighten our souls with the lamp of his word, when we come to offer up to him our incense.

4. There is a command, that no strange incense shall be offered upon it. This is to teach us, that we must take heed of bringing any thing to God, to offer him in prayer, but what comes from the Spirit of God; only God's own incense. Take heed (I say) of bringing unsanctified parts, or any thing but that which is from the Spirit of God.

5. Once a year an atonement was made upon the horns of the altar with the blood of the sin-offering; though the sin-offering was not offered upon it, yet once a year an atonement was made upon it with its blood. This is to note, that even by our incense we, for our part, defile the altar. And thus I have a little digressed, yet still to open up Scripture to you, to show to you the meaning of God's altars.

But why did God account it so heinous a crime to make any other altars besides these?

The reasons are these:

First, Because these altars typified these two things:

1. The altar of burnt-offerings typified this, That Christ was to be the only sacrifice. There should be no other sacrifice to pacify God's wrath but only Jesus Christ, who was both the sacrifice and the altar also, for his human nature was offered to God upon the merits, as it were, upon the worthiness of his Divine nature: Heb. ix. 14, "How much more shall the blood of Christ, who through the eternal Spirit offered himself without spot to God, purge your conscience from dead works to serve the living God?" This altar did signify the offering of Jesus Christ. As if God should say, Know, that what endeavours you do or can use to satisfy my justice and my wrath, it is to no purpose, there is nothing but only my Son, and that offering, that shall satisfy my wrath. And now for them to make more altars, it was to deny that great point of religion, that there was only the sacrifice of Christ to satisfy God.

2. The incense altar typified this, That in Christ only all our services, which are our spiritual sacrifices, are accepted of God. There must be no altar but this for the sacrifice, and the other for incense; God would have this doctrine kept pure from that time and for ever, that none of our spiritual sacrifices can be accepted any other way but only as they have reference to Jesus Christ, that altar which the Lord has appointed.

Secondly, That they might be the bond of the church. Because the people of the Jews were a national church, therefore there was to be a national worship, all the nation was to join, not only apparently, but really, in the very same individual worship; and this was the bond of their national church. Now, for my part, I know none living that hold a national church in these days in this sense, that is, as of Divine institution, and joined in one, by God's commanding any common national worship. Where there are in nations a great many of the saints of God, that they may be called a national church we dispute not; but when people talk of a national church in the strict sense of the word, they understand not its meaning. It is not enough to have the same kind of worship, as now, we all pray and read the word in all congregations, we have all the same sacraments; but to constitute us a national church we must have a common altar, and unite together in a common worship. If the nation of the Jews had worshipped the same God, after the same manner, in divers temples and upon divers altars, this had not been a national bond to them; but by coming up to the same temple, and offering upon the same altars, and when the sacrifice and incense were offered they were offered for them all conjointly, this was the thing that united them into a church union, different from any possible church union amongst us, till we have similar institutions. Our worship implies nothing but a personal union, but for thousands of congregations to be bound by institution to join in the very same bond of worship, in the very same individual act, such a union we have not in these days. Unless we understand this aright, we understand not the reason why they had but one altar for burnt-offerings and one altar for incense.

But now it may be said, That it does not seem to be such a sin to erect altars, (for that is the sin charged here upon Ephraim, that they "made many altars,") for the Scripture speaks of many altars that were God's altars; thus Elijah complains, 1 Kings xix., that they had cast down God's altars, They "have thrown down thine altars;" now this was spoken after the time of the law, when there were but only two altars appointed by God, the altar for burnt-offerings and the incense altar, and the prophet did not mean them.

Divines answer this thus, That this is spoken of those altars that the patriarchs and others had built to sacrifice upon to God, before the time that the law was given by Moses for that one only altar of sacrifice. For it was lawful, before the command, to build divers altars, but afterwards it was not.

Yea, but still the objection will be, How could it be a sin to cast down those altars, when they were of no further religious use? for after the command of God for that one altar, then the others were to be demolished. Was it not commended in the godly kings, that they cast down high places, and cut down groves? though some of them formerly were for the true worship of God, yet, after God had appointed a peculiar place for his worship, and those other places were abused to superstition, then they were to be cast down: and so there is no question but all other altars built for religious uses were to be cast down, after God's own altars were made. To this I would answer thus,

That the evil that Elijah complains of, was the profaneness of the people, their casting off all fear and reverence of God; because they did not cast down those altars out of love to God and his worship, and through a holy determination that they would not suffer any thing that might lead to superstition, that was not the principle whereby they were actuated in casting them down, but they were led thereto by malice and rage against religion, and to satisfy their lusts. And thus, if men oppose that which is indeed superstitious, yet not out of a true love to God and his honour, nor a sincere desire to set up and to maintain his true worship, but in bitterness and rage, merely to gratify their own selfish purposes; though, I say, the thing be evil that these men oppose, yet God will not own their actions as any service to him, it is a sin in them to cast down that which should be cast down, if they do not cast it down out of a right and gracious principle: then what evil is it for men in bitterness of spirit to oppose that which is in itself good, if God account it a sin to oppose that which should be opposed, if it be through bitterness of spirit, and not through gracious principles!

Obs. 1. Man's inventions in God's worship are rejected of God. "Ephraim hath made many altars." Whatsoever is made by man in religious worship, is rejected of God; the very spirit and life of the second commandment consist in this. "Thou shalt not make unto thee any graven image;" that instances but one thing, but by that we are to understand every thing pertaining to Divine worship; the very life and the very spirit of the second commandment, I say, lies in this, the making to ourselves. If God will appoint ceremonies significant of heavenly things, to raise our hearts on high, we are to use them with reverence and respect; but we must not presume in this to imitate God: that is the ground of all superstitious ceremonies, because they find God makes some, they think that they may presume to make others; now it is a sin against the second commandment for us to presume to make any thing in matters of Divine worship.

Obs. 2. There is no stop in superstitious worship. "Ephraim hath made many." If men leave the rule they know not where to stay: hence the multiplying of things thus among the papists, five hundred altars in some one temple. And Austin, in his 19th Epistle, complains of the multitude of ceremonies that were in the church in his time. What complaints would he have now! All things in the church were full of presumptions, they did multiply one thing after another; and indeed, let the right way once be left, and there are no limits. O, let us take heed how we multiply in God's worship. There is much controversy between the papists and us about multiplying in the worship of God.

Omnia in ecclesia presumptionibus plena. Aug. Epist. 19.

We would have but one Mediator, they would have many; we would have but one rule of faith, but they will give power to pope and church to make articles of faith; we would have but one object of worship, they would have many; we would have but one sacrifice, they would have many oblations for the quick and dead; we would have but one satisfaction, they would have many; we would have but one merit, they would have many: and thus, by multiplying, the unity of the church is divided: but we must keep to the unity that we find in the Scripture.

Obs. 3. We are ready to imitate our forefathers in evil, but not in good. "Ephraim hath made many altars." Their forefathers were mightily incensed against the supposed addition of but one altar to God's altars, but they will not imitate their forefathers in this good thing, in standing up for that one true worship of God, Josh. xxii. 11. If you ask the reason why their progenitors were so zealous for God's own altar, and yet now their children after them make many altars, the reason may be this, which will afford a note of very great use to us; When their progenitors came first into the land of Canaan, and Joshua, according to the commandment of God by Moses, set up an altar, they, seeing the goodness of God towards them, were much affected with it; but after they had enjoyed the land a while, after they begun to be settled, to be warm in their nests, and to prosper in the land, then they ventured upon this way of corrupting of God's worship by multiplying altars; and when they had once ventured and escaped unpunished, then they thought they were sure, might go on with impunity: and so by degrees they come to this excess in superstitious worship. The note is,

Obs. 4. We must take heed lest any distance of time make us not to fear the threatening denounced on the breach of the commandment. They were afraid of the breach of the commandment soon after it was given; but when some time had elapsed, and they were settled in prosperity, then they ventured to transgress: hence I say, our note is, That we must take heed that the distance of time, or our settling in a prosperous condition, do not make us to fear the commandment less than we did at first. And for this you have a most excellent scripture in Deut. iv. 25, "When thou shalt beget children, and children's children, and ye shall have remained long in the land, and shall corrupt yourselves, and make a graven image, or the likeness of any thing, and shall do evil in the sight of the Lord thy God, to provoke him to anger." "When thou shalt beget children, and children's children, and ye shall have remained long in the land," then thou shalt make graven images. There was not so much fear that when they came *first* into the land they should make graven images; they were then but just delivered out of their bondage, God had made known his glorious word unto them, their hearts were warm with love and gratitude; but after they had lived long in the land, they began to forget God and make graven images. Just so it is with us; when we are newly come out of afflictions, then our hearts are a little warm, and we would serve God according to his own way; but after we have continued long in the land, and been a while in a prosperous condition, and find all things around us pretty well, oh! then we begin to be cool, and forget the Lord and his ways. It has been always so, and it is so now, not only in particular persons and nations, but churches too. Ordinarily when people are delivered from superstitious vanities, and come to worship God in his own way, at first they enjoy the ordinances of God in their purity, oh how glad are they! and they bless God, and their hearts are warmed and enlarged, and their hearts do close one with another, and there is a sweet union between them: but after they have lived a while in the land, after they have lived a while in the ways of God, and enjoyed him a little, they begin to grow more cool and dead, and fall to wrangling and contending, and so all that spirituality and heavenly ardour that they had before vanish and come to nothing. I beseech you remember Deut. iv. 25; take heed, after you have abode a while in such a condition, that you forget not God.

Obs. 5. Every age adds something to idolatry and false worship. "Ephraim hath made many altars:" hath multiplied altars, so Jerome; and the Seventy, hath gone on in way of multiplication. They had some altars at first, which their forefathers made, and they afterwards made more, and so every succeeding generation added to them. O my brethren, let the true worship of God, then, not only continue, but multiply. Idolaters will not argue thus, Why should we be wiser than our forefathers? no, they will go beyond their forefathers in false worship; and yet, how many among us will thus plead against reformation, Why should not we content ourselves with what our forefathers did? our forefathers knew not of such new ways of worship as you tell us of. But now, my brethren, if our forefathers reformed a little, let us bless God for what they did; but let us add more, to raise up the worship of God yet higher and higher, as in Psal. lxxi. 14, "But I will hope continually, and will yet praise thee more and more;" the words may be read thus, I will add unto thy praise, O Lord. Thou hast had praise, indeed formerly thou hadst praise from others; but I will do something to add to thy praise, I will praise thee more and more. So every generation should strive to praise God more and more, to add to God's praise, to find out more of God's truths, to add to the purity of God's worship, and to cast out superstition more than their forefathers have done: our forefathers are to be much commended for having done what they did, and (I say) we are to bless God for them, that the Lord put such a spirit into them; but know, that that which was accepted from our forefathers will not be accepted from us, God expects that we should add to his praises. Men desire to add more and more to the estates of their progenitors, and so your children will add a little to the estates that you leave them; and so men account it their ambition to raise their families. My brethren, we should have a

, Multiplicavit, Jerome. 'Επλήθυνεν, Sept.

holy ambition to exalt ourselves more and more in every age, by the practice of religion: as Jehu said in 2 Kings x. 18, "Ahab served Baal a little, but Jehu shall serve him much." As he said, though feignedly, of false worship, we should say, with sincerity, of the true worship of God, Our fathers have served the Lord a little, but we will serve him more; we have more mercies than they had, more light than they had; if they served God a little, we will serve him much.

Obs. 6. God still remembers the first and chief actors in sin. "Ephraim hath made many altars to sin." He speaks to the ten tribes, and yet only names Ephraim, because the governors were of that tribe. The chief in a family, by whom the whole family is corrupted, and the chief in a town or country, God has an eye upon, and though others escape they shall not. Ephraim hath multiplied altars to sin; they intended not to sin, it was not their intention when they made altars that they might sin, they thought they pleased God, but God accounts it sin, and a provocation to him. Hence observe further,

Obs. 7. Whatsoever names we give to things, it may be, God will give them other names and titles. We may say that it is devotion, God will say it is superstition; we may say it is good intention, but God may say it is presumption; we may say it is prudence and wisdom, but God may give it another name, and say it is temporizing, time-serving; God is wont to give other names to things than we do. In the Scripture they call their images their "delectable things," Isa. xliv. 9; God calls them "detestable things," Ezek. xxxvii. 23. No question, if you would ask them why they built altars, they would say, to the honour of God; but saith God, "Ephraim hath made many altars to sin."

Obs. 8. When men's hearts are set upon false ways of worship, it is just with God to let them have their desires to the full. "Altars shall be unto him to sin." That is, thus; seeing they *will* have them, they *shall* have them; they shall have enough of them, let them go on in their way, let them multiply their sin. They keep a great deal of stir for it, and have it they must, they refuse to see the light, they are prejudiced against the way of God's worship; let them have their desires, let them have, saith God, governors to establish by their authority, and teachers to defend by subtle arguments, what they wish for: they multiply altars to sin, and they shall be to sin, even to harden them; their hearts are set upon them, and they will have them, and love them, and they shall be hardened in them. This is the heavy judgment of God, to give men their hearts' desires in what is evil. And as it shall be to them for sin, so it shall be to them for misery, the fruit of sin; for so sin is taken very frequently in Scripture for the fruit of sin; they will have them to sin, and they shall find in them the fruit of sin, misery.

Ver. 12. *I have written to him the great things of my law, but they were counted as a strange thing.*

There appears a greatness in the very sound of this verse, and there is as much in it as the sound doth import; and therefore, though we pass over other things more briefly, yet because there is very much of God's mind in this, we should wrong the Scripture if we should pass over this too slightly.

"I have written to him the great things of my law." This is made an aggravation of their sin, They multiply altars to sin, and yet, saith God, "I have written to him the great things of my law;" they find no such things in my written law: and what that written word of God, against those many altars, was, you had the last day; but in that these are made sins because they were against the written word of God, thence,

Obs. 1. Whatsoever is urged or practised in matters of worship, must have warrant out of the written word of God. It was sin. Why? Because I have written to them (saith God) the great things of my law, and they counted it a strange thing; though that which they did had a great deal of seeming devotion in it, yet it was otherwise than they found written in my law.

This question should be put to any that tender to us any form of worship, or doctrine of religion, under any specious show whatsoever, Where is it written? "To the law and to the testimony," saith Isaiah, chap. viii. 20: "if they speak not according to this word, it is because there is no light in them:" they may seem very judicious and wise, but if they speak not according to this word, they have no light in them; not only to the law and testimonies, but to the written law and testimonies; this must be the standard at which all doctrines and modes of worship must be tried. Many may put fair colours on their proceedings, that they tend to the common peace, and a great deal of good may result from them, and the like; but is it written? Did I ever command it? saith God. Policy may say it is fit, reason may say it is comely, and experience may say it is useful, but doth the written law say it should be? Nay, it is not enough to say, that we cannot say it is forbidden, but where is it written? In matters of worship this is a certain rule. Tertullian, about the crowning of the soldier with bays, saith, If it be affirmed, It is lawful, because the Scriptures do not forbid it; it may equally be retorted, It is therefore not lawful, because the Scriptures do not command it. No matter what the thing be, saith Luther, in matters of religion, we must look who it is that bids it, who it is that commands it; never, I beseech you, in any point of religion argue thus, Why, what hurt is there in it, is it not very comely? I cannot think but it may do a great deal of good. These arguments are weak arguments in matters of worship; to them all we must answer, Is it written? As Christ replied to the devil and his temptations, "It is written;" so, if you can, bring a written word against what they would have you to do, or let them show where what they enjoin is written. In Exod. xxxix. we find it said, at least ten times, they did according to what the Lord had commanded Moses; and in the conclusion of the chapter, Moses blessed the people: the people are blessed when in the matters of worship they keep to what is commanded.

And again, As we must not make our own conceptions the rule for worship, so neither the opinions of learned men, nor custom, nor antiquity, must be the rule, but what is written: "I have written to them the great things of my law;" they must keep to that. Whatsoever use we may make now of the opinions of ancients and the like, yet, if the ancients themselves were alive, they would abhor the use that many make of their quotations. Cyprian, in one of his epistles, speaking of his predecessors, saith, We must not look what this man or that man before us did or taught, but what he that was before all, namely, Christ, who alone is "the way, the truth, and the life." And so Augustine has a passage to the same effect, in which, speaking of the ancients, he saith, Even granting them all due respect, yet for us to think that we may not reject from their writings some things, because they were learned men, is inadmissible: for such, he adds, I will be in respect of the writings of other men, and such would I have those that understand my writings be to me, I will not so esteem the writings of any before me as to think that nothing should be cast out nor mended, neither would I have any think so of my writings. And so Ambrose, Where the Scripture is silent we must not speak. Thus we see, that though men at present, for the maintaining of that which is evil, will make use of quotations and antiquities, yet that those very ancients whom they cite as authorities abhorred this; and Christ and his apostles quoted none of the learned men before them, but only Moses and the prophets.

But you will say, Though we must not take other men's writings as the rule, yet they may help us to understand the Scripture aright.

Luther, I remember, saith, that the Scriptures should rather help us to understand men's writings, than men's writings to understand the Scripture; that many will make men's writings a judge and rule for understanding the Scriptures, not the judge of truth, but the rule for understanding aright the Scriptures, whereas (saith he) the Scripture should rather be the rule for understanding them.

And so Hilary saith, He is the best interpreter of Scripture, that takes the sense rather out of the Scriptures themselves, by comparing one passage with another, than brings to it any new meaning: therefore the understanding of Scripture is more by Scripture than by the writings of any man living. And yet still we may, doubtless, make use of the gifts of God in others, but so as to keep us close to the written word for the rule; yea, and for the meaning of the rule, they may help us to see whether the Scripture will justify this truth, or this sense: for there lies the mistake; most people think, that whatsoever any man writes, if it be contrary to the word, we may not receive it, but we must understand the word in the sense in which they take it: now we must not go so far; for the Scripture is written, not only that we might know what the rule is, but that we might understand the meaning of the rule, by comparing Scripture with Scripture; now so far as the writings of men will help us to discover the meaning of Scripture by Scripture, so far we may make use of them; but we cannot say, this is the meaning, because it is the opinion of such and such learned men; they should compare one Scripture with another, show you the history of the time, and give you the reasons for their interpretation: and this is the use of writers for understanding the Scriptures. Then you will say, Why do we make use of writers so much? Why, because they show how one scripture has reference to another, and relate the history connected with the passage.

The sense of things is to be resolved in the Scripture itself, and therefore we must keep ourselves very close to what is written.

"Written." It was not so at first, but delivered from hand to hand; but afterwards, when the church began to multiply, then the word was written. And this is a mighty blessing of God, that we may have the mind of God written, so as to look into it, and search to know it, by reading it over and over again, and taking it into our hands. When we are lying upon our beds, if we light a candle in the night, we may be reading and looking into the mind of God. If we should only hear that there were such a book in the world, in China, in the uttermost parts of the habitable globe, a book that God had written, or that God had employed men to write by an inspiration of his own Spirit, and wherein he had revealed the great counsels of his will concerning man's eternal estate; if we should hear that such a book had come down even from heaven, and that in the uttermost parts of the earth, oh what a longing desire should we have to see it! Who but would give their whole estate to have a week's or a fortnight's time to see and read in such a book? if one could, he would be willing to travel to the end of the world to enjoy such a privilege. No man need say, Shall I go to the uttermost parts of the earth? for it is in your hands, it is in your houses; the book wherein the great God has written his mind, has written all things unto you which concerns your eternal salvation, is that same which you have in your hands. However we prize it now, heretofore it has been prized at a high rate; how many of the martyrs would venture their lives to keep but a few leaves of Scripture in their houses! And how vile is it then for us to neglect the reading of this written word! One Theodorus, a physician at Constantinople, sent to Gregory the Great a great sum of money for the redeeming of captives: in his reply Gregory much commends his liberality, yet takes occasion to blame him for not reading the Scriptures; and uses this expression, The Emperor of heaven, the Lord of the angels and men, has sent to you that which concerns your life, and will you neglect to read it with a fervent, with a zealous spirit? He would not but blame him even when he sent such gifts to him, it grieved him so to think that one so bountiful to the distressed should neglect the reading of the Scriptures. Many have excellent parts, and yet find but little relish for the Scriptures. No books that are written should take us off from this written word; although we have cause to bless God abundantly for what is written, for those excellent helps which we have, yet we must take heed that no written book in the world take us off from this written word of God. Luther therefore saith, I even hate mine own books, and I oftentimes even wish that they were burnt, that they might perish. Why? Mark his reason, Because I fear lest they should be any kind of hinderance to men, or withdraw them from reading the Scriptures: and he forthwith proceeds to commend the Scriptures: They are the only fountain of all wisdom; and further, I am even terrified, I tremble, at the example of the former age in this respect, because many divines spent so much time in reading Aristotle, and Averres, and other writers, and spent so little time in reading Scripture. And the truth is, it was that which brought so much ignorance into the world in the time of the school-men, which was a time of great learning, and yet the time of the greatest ignorance in the mysteries of godliness, because they minded Scripture very little, but only turned things into questions and disputes that tended not according to Scripture. Though we may make use of the labours and gifts of other men, yet look we especially to the written word, and let not other writings take us off from that. Hence we say, the Scripture, by way of excellency. We must keep ourselves to the written word, and take heed of being led aside by any traditions of men; that is a most detestable derogation from the written word. Yet we find the council of Trent, speaking of the Scriptures, saith in one of its canons, We do receive Scripture, and reverence Scripture; but moreover we receive and reverence traditions with the same affection of piety and reverence as we do the Scripture. These are the very words that all papists are born to hold, and for them to deny any council were death unto them. It argues men to be in the dark, so to regard written verities. The Jews are vain in their imaginations, and understand the Scripture so little, because they mind traditions as much as Scripture, and more; for they say, Divide a man's life into three parts, one part must be spent in reading Scripture, and two parts more in the two several parts of the Talmud, which is their traditions; and some of them say that this is one tradition among them, that Moses studied the Scripture in the day-time, and those Talmudical traditions during the night. It is indeed night work, and a sign that the world is so much in darkness, because they have so much respect to traditions, and neglect the written word of God, which we must regard more than if one came from the dead, or if an angel from heaven came and preached to us.

Concil. Trid. sess. 4. decret. prim.

But you will say, We must not look to it more than

if God should reveal any thing to us, suppose by a voice from heaven.

We have warrant to regard more the written word of God than the voice of God from heaven. In 2 Pet. i. 19, the voice that came down at the transfiguration in the mount is referred to, but saith the apostle, "We have also a more sure word of prophecy," more even than that was; that is, we are not so likely to be deceived by resting upon the written word, as if we look for revelations from God. "We have a more sure word of prophecy," therefore it is not so much after revelations that we are to look, (especially in such times as these,) but to the written word of God. There is a generation of men rising now, if not risen, that begin to have low thoughts of the Scriptures of God, and think to understand the mind of God otherwise; finding his written word keeps their hearts too close and lays too strong bonds upon them, because they would fain be loose, they would fain imagine to themselves other ways for the discovery of God's mind; but when they are dead, when their souls, it may be, are perished eternally in hell, the written word of God shall stand and be honourable in the eyes of his saints.

Βεβαιότερον λόγον.

"I have written." The prophet saith not *he* hath written; but he brings in God, saying, "I have written." And that for these two reasons:

1. To put the greater emphasis upon it, for it is more for God himself to come and say, "I have written;" as if a father or master say to his child or servant, I command you to do such a thing, it is more than if a brother or fellow servant should say, My father or my master has bidden you to do such a thing.

2. Whosoever were the penmen of the word, it is I that write it, I take it upon myself. The word is so much his, that God claims not only the truths that are in the word, but the very inditing; and in 2 Pet. i. 21, it is said of holy men, they "spake as they were moved by the Holy Ghost," ὑπὸ Πνεύματος ἁγίου φερόμενοι; they were not only moved, but carried on with a kind of violence, to write what they did. Both in their speaking and in their writing, "I have written."

"To him." From this form of expression,

Obs. 2. We should look upon the Scripture as concerning ourselves. Here is a letter written to every one of you individually, therefore it is in the singular, "I have written to him." Each must regard the Scripture as written to him or her particularly. God has written a letter to thee that thou shouldst not commit adultery, nor swear, nor steal, and that thou shouldst keep the sabbath, and that thou shouldst not lie, and that thou shouldst reverence him, and love him, and fear him; all such kind of rules has God from heaven written to thee, and it is a marvellous help to obedience, and to awaken men's consciences, when they apprehend them as written to them. Psal. cxix. 105, "Thy word is a lamp unto my feet, and a light unto my path." It is not a light that I see at a distance, a great way off; but as a light held to my feet, that I make use of for the ordering of mine own steps.

Many there are that seem to rejoice in the word of God, as a light to reveal truths unto them for matter of discourse, but they use it not as a lamp to their own feet, and a light to their own paths; and therefore follows, ver. 106, "I have sworn, and I will perform it, that I will keep thy righteous judgments:" I have looked upon thy word as a lamp to my own feet, as a thing nearly concerning myself, and then I have sworn and I will perform, I have sworn that I will keep thy righteous judgments. It is a mighty means to stir up a man's spirit, and quicken him to obedience, to look upon the word as written to himself: as thus, when you come to hear out of God's word, and God directs the minister so that you apprehend it as spoken to you, it will stir and awaken you; Oh, methought this day every word the minister spoke was directed to me! And so every word in the Scripture that concerns thee, God writes to thee; and conceive it so, and it will be a mighty means to stir thee up to obedience. As, if a man be asleep, a great noise will not awaken him so soon, as if you call him by his own name; so when the word of God comes as to ourselves in particular, it is a mighty means to stir the heart.

Obs. 3. Though the word concerns all men, yet it is written to the church in a more especial manner. "I have written to him." As you find in the Revelation all the epistles were written to the churches, and indeed all the word of God is in a more especial manner addressed to the church; there are some things concerning all mankind, but that which God aims at more especially, is the church. First, the church of the Jews; they had that great privilege, that the oracles of God were committed to them: therefore, in Rom. iii. 1, 2, when the apostle had taken them off from resting in many of their outward privileges, he brings an objection; But then may some say, "What advantage then hath the Jew?" he answers, "Much every way; chiefly, because that unto them were committed the oracles of God." In this thing they had much advantage over all the people in the world, that to them were committed the oracles of God: God gave Jacob his law, it was the inheritance of his people; it was written to them, and through them transmitted to his church. This is a great honour which God puts upon his saints; God makes his church to be the keeper of his records, the court of rolls, as it were; therefore they should look to it that they be kept faithfully, that they be not corrupted, for then they do falsify their trust. The church has the keeping of Scripture, but gives no authority to Scripture. In John v. 46, 47, Christ saith, "Had ye believed Moses, ye would have believed me: for he wrote of me. But if ye believe not his writings, how shall ye believe my words?" Mark, Christ would have the authority of his words to be much strengthened by the writings that were before in Scripture, "If ye believe not his writings, how shall ye believe my words?" But now, on the contrary, the papists will say, If ye believe not our words, how can ye believe their writings? they will take upon them more than Christ: Christ saith, "If ye believe not his writings, how shall ye believe my words?" they say, If ye believe not our words, how can ye believe their writings? for they take the authority of Scripture to depend upon their words. It is written to the church, and committed to the church, but the authority comes not from the church.

"The great things of my law." By "law" here we are to understand the whole word of God, and not the law as distinguished from the gospel; and so the word means, being derived from one signifying to teach, the law is a doctrine that is taught; and so, though sometimes it may be distinguished from some other parts of Scripture, yet now we are to understand the whole mind of God in his word; when you read in Psal. cxix., how David loved God's law, it is not the ten commandments, but the mind of God revealed in his word.

תּוֹרָה lex, a יָרָה docuit.

"The great things of my law." The Vulgate renders it, *multiplices leges*, the manifold laws, the multiplicity of my laws; and the words in the Hebrew seem a little to favour it. Thence these two things might be argued:

אכתוב־לו רבו תורתי

1. That the word is full and perfect; that in it we have rules for every thing that concerns the ordination of our lives God-ward: in his word there is a multiplicity of laws and rules for all our ways.

2. That there are manifold excellences in God's law; as the manifold wisdom of God is in Christ, so the manifold excellences of God are kept up together in the

word of God. The Seventy translate it by πλῆθος, the fulness, or multitude, and according to that, Tertullian has an expression, I adore the fulness of the Scripture. Oh the multitude of excellent things there are there! and the fulness that is in them! I find this word translated by many of excellent signification, and indeed the Hebrew will bear to be differently rendered. Some translate it, the precious thing, the magnificent thing, the excellent thing, the honourable things of my law; as in Acts ii. 11, they spake "the wonderful things of God;" τὰ μεγαλεῖα τοῦ Θεοῦ, it is more than the great things, the magnificent great things of God. Now the things of the word are glorious and honourable, and very great, they are to be looked upon as great things, the things of God's word: that is the first and most important.

Adoro plenitudinem Scripturarum. Tertul.

And then, The things that concern God's worship are to be looked upon as great things, for it has reference to them also; but the expression aims at that which is more general; "the great things of my law," the honourable, magnificent, and glorious things. Now the things of the law were great things, because,

1. They are from the great God, and they have on them the stamp of his authority. In every truth, in every thing that is written in God's law, there is the awful authority of the great God, that binds kings and princes in chains, that lays bonds upon the conscience, such as no created power can: when we come to hear the word, we come to it either as to a sovereign, to receive laws from it, or as to a judge, to receive from it the sentence of death; it has the dreadful authority of the great God in it, and therefore every thing that is in the word is to be looked upon as a great thing. A piece of parchment, and a little wax, and a few lines, what are they? but having the authority of the great seal of England, they are to be looked upon as important. The things of God's law are great things, for great authority attends them.

2. The lustre of the great God shines in them. Take all the creatures that ever God made in heaven and earth, and there is not so much glory of God in sun, moon, stars, sea, plants, and all things in the world, as there is in some few sentences of Holy Scripture, therefore they are great things. Psal. cxxxviii. 2, "Thou hast magnified thy word above all thy name." The name of God appears in his great work of creation and of providence; we are to look upon God's name as very great; yet "Thou hast magnified thy word above all thy name," it is more than all God's names besides. It may be, when there are some extraordinary works of God in the world, as thundering, lightning, and the like, we are ready to fear, and say, Oh how great God appears in these great works! Were our hearts as they ought to be when we read the word, we would tremble at that more than at any manifestation of God in all his works since the world began; and if so be, thou dost not see more glory of God in his word than in his works, it is because thou hast little light in thee; let the world think of the things of God's law that are written, as they will, yet they are the great things of his law.

3. They are the great mysteries of God's will. The great counsels of God about the souls of men, about his way to honour himself, to bring mankind to himself and to eternal life, are contained in the word; counsels and mysteries so great that the angels themselves desire to look into them. As in Prov. viii. 6, it is said of wisdom, "Hear, for I will speak of excellent things;" so the word of God speaks of excellent things, right excellent things, such great mysteries of God's wisdom as should engage our thoughts, yea, and do engage the thoughts of angels, and shall yield admiring employment to angels and saints to all eternity. Psal. cxix. 27, "Make me to understand the way of thy precepts: so shall I talk of thy wondrous works." Mark how these are joined together: "Make me to understand the way of thy precepts: *so* shall I talk of thy wondrous works." Why, David, couldst not thou see the wondrous works of God in the book of the creature, in heaven and earth? O no; "Make me to understand the way of thy precepts: so shall I talk of thy wondrous works." We often talk about vain and slight things, because we have nothing else to talk of; but did we understand the way of God's precepts, we should be furnished with discourse of the wondrous works of God.

4. They are of great concernment. The things of God's law are of great concernment, for all our present good or evil depends upon them. Prov. iii. 22, They are "life unto thy soul, and grace to thy neck." So saith Moses in Deut. xxxii. 46, "Set your hearts unto all the words which I testify among you this day, which ye shall command your children to observe to do, all the words of this law; for it is not a vain thing for you, because it is your life." There is, too, a curse annexed to the breach of every thing in God's law; "Cursed be every one that abideth not in every thing that is written in the book of the law." Is it not a great matter then? Certainly nothing in the law can be looked upon as unimportant, when the curse of God is annexed to the breach of every thing written in it. We have there the casting of our souls for eternity; and is not that a great matter? Did we come to hear the word, or did we read the word, as the word by which our eternal condition must be decided, we would look upon it as a great word.

5. They have great power and efficacy upon the hearts and consciences of men. When God sets home the things of his law, they will bring down the proudest and the stoutest, they will enlighten the blindest mind, and convert the hardest heart in the world; the law has a mighty power upon the soul, and therefore it is great.

6. They make all that receive them great: they make them great, even because they have but the keeping of them, much more then if they receive them. In Deut. iv. 8, "What nation is there so great, that hath statutes and judgments so righteous as all this law, which I set before you this day?" What nation so great as you are? Why, wherein are we greater than other people? Wherein? In this: "What nation is so great, that hath statutes and judgments so righteous as all this law, which I set before you this day?" This was that which made the people of Israel a great nation, beyond all the nations in the world; they were not great in multitude, but in that they had the law of God, and the great things of his law, revealed to them. The Lord honours a nation highly when he reveals the things of his law to them; how great then does a soul become that embraces those things, that has all those great and good things revealed in the law made over to it as its own! Surely that soul is in a high and honourable condition.

7. They are great in God's esteem; they are great, because the great God thinks them so. That is to be accounted great, which the most judicious and wise men in the world judge to be so. Indeed that which a child thinks great may not be so; a child may think a bauble a great thing: so we may think things great indeed; we think the things of the world are great, estates, riches, and honours, these we deem great things; but what are these in God's eyes? God despises all these things. But that which the great God will think to be a great thing, certainly that is indeed great. Now mark what a high esteem God has for his word in that place, where Christ saith, "Till heaven and earth pass, one jot or one tittle shall in no wise pass from the law, till all be fulfilled," Matt. v. 18. As if Christ should say, The Lord will rather withdraw his

power from upholding heaven and earth, than from making good any one jot or tittle of his law. You may think it a little matter to break God's law, but God thinks it a great matter, and God would have us to make a great matter of every thing that is written in God's law. I am the more willing to enlarge on this, because I know it is the ground of all the wickedness in men's hearts and lives, that they look upon the law as a little matter: well, though they dare sin against God's law for the attainment of very trifles, yet God saith, I will rather lose heaven and earth, than one jot or one tittle of my law shall fail; and he will make it appear one day, that the things of his law are great things. "He will magnify the law, and make it honourable," Isa. xlii. 21. Some amongst us, considering neither what they say nor what they do, running away with the very word law, think to vilify it, saying, What have we to do with the law? Let them do what they will, yet God "will magnify his law;" and as it is great in the thoughts of God, so it is, and shall be for ever, great in the thoughts of the saints. The Lord will have his people, to the end of the world, entertain high thoughts of his law. The saints look upon the law of God as so great, that they had rather suffer all devisable miseries and torments, than willingly break it in any one particular; surely he accounts it great, who is willing rather to lose estates, liberty, yea, and life itself, in the midst of tortures and torments, rather than offend the law of God in any one thing, though he might escape all if he would; Nay, saith a gracious heart, let all go rather than I will venture to break one jot or tittle of the law of God. Men of the world think such to be fools, Why, they say, will you be content to suffer so much, lose all your friends? what! venture your fair estates, run the risk of being immured in a prison, or even losing your life? The world lightly esteems God's commandments, and deems men who are observant of them more precise than wise; but if God would but show to you how great a thing his law is, and all the threatenings which are revealed therein, you would account your estates, and lives, and all your comforts, as little and poor in comparison. Hence, in Rev. vi. 9, "I saw under the altar the souls of them that were slain for the word of God, and for the testimony which they held." Wherefore were they slain? Surely it was for some great matter that they would venture their lives. It was for "the word of God, and for the testimony which they held." And thus the saints of God have ever accounted the law of God a great thing. "I have written to him the great things of my law."

From what has been advanced, we may further

Obs. 4. The word contains matter to exercise the greatest minds. Many men cannot endure to spend their thoughts and time about trivial matters; whereas others think it happiness enough, if they can, by the meanest employments, procure subsistence. Oh, let all those of high aspirations exercise themselves much in the law of God; here are objects fit for great minds, yea, objects that will elevate the greatest: and indeed none in the world are truly great but the saints, for they exercise themselves in the great counsels of God. We account those men the greatest that are employed in state affairs: now the saints are lifted up above all things in the world, and regard them all as little and mean, and are exercised in the great affairs of the kingdom of Jesus Christ. Hence the Lord would have the kings and the judges to have the book of the law written, Deut. xvii. 18, 19; and it is reported of Alphonsus, king of Arragon, that in the midst of all his great manifold occupations, he read over the Scriptures fourteen times with commentaries. How many have we, men of great estates, and claiming to be of great minds, that scarce regard the law of God! they look upon his law as beneath them. Books of history and war they will peruse with diligence, but for the Scripture, it is a thing that has little in it.

Obs. 5. It is a special means to obedience to have high thoughts of God's law. That is the reason why the prophet here speaks thus, "I have written to him the great things of my law, but they were counted as a strange thing." As if he should say, If they had had the things of my law in their thoughts, they would never so have acted. Psal. cxix. 129, "Thy testimonies are wonderful; therefore doth my soul keep them:" I have high thoughts of thy testimonies, I look upon them as glorious things, I see in them much of thyself, and "therefore doth my soul keep them." He saith not, therefore do I keep them; but, therefore doth *my soul* keep them; my very soul is in this, in keeping thy testimonies, for I look upon them as wonderful things. It is a good sign that the Spirit of the great God is in a man, when it raises him above other things, to look upon the things of his word as the only great things in the world. "All flesh is grass, and all the goodliness thereof as the flower of the field: the grass withereth, the flower fadeth, but the word of our God shall stand for ever," Isa. xl. 6, 8. There is a vanity in all things of the world, but in that which the word reveals, in that there is an eternity: we should therefore admire at nothing so as at the word, and we should greatly delight in God's commandments; an ordinary degree of admiration or delight is not sufficient, but great admiration and great delight there should be in the law of God. And all arguments drawn from God's law should powerfully prevail with you. Temptations to such and such evils may assail you, and you may say they are strong temptations, but that which is in God's law should be stronger than they all: there is more in God's law than there can be in any temptation whatsoever. Know, it is dangerous for us to regard any thing in God's law as inconsiderable, so as to think it no great matter, though in that particular we depart a little from the rule of the word: Prov. xiii. 13, "Whoso despiseth the word shall be destroyed;" that is, looks upon any thing in God's word as a light thing. One, when convinced that things undertaken were evil, was wont to say, that he must make bold with God Almighty sometimes. Do not you make bold with God's word, and secretly jeer at those who are so scrupulous that they cannot venture a little? Remember Prov. xiii. 13, "Whoso despiseth the word shall be destroyed:" take the least thing that you think so despicable in God's law, and venture on the breach of it, God will make it a great matter; for when you have broken the law in the least thing, all the angels in heaven, and men in the world, cannot satisfy God for that wrong. If they should come and say, Lord, here is a poor creature who has broken thy law but in this one thing, which he thought to be a little matter, we are content to be ten thousand years in torments to satisfy its requirements: Nay, saith God, that will not satisfy the broken law. Therefore take heed of despising God's law, or despising any thing that is revealed by him, for certainly it will prove a great matter; and when the law has been broken, let us not deem the transgression slight, and think it is to be atoned for at the last by a "Lord have mercy upon me."

Obs. 6. The worship of God is a great matter. Every thing in God's worship is to be looked at as a great matter: they may think it a matter of indifferency whether they do it or no, at least in some things; my brethren, let us learn to know that every thing in the worship of God is important; God regards it much; God saith not that he is jealous for any thing, but for his worship. Uzzah thought it a little matter to go and catch the ark, and especially with a good intention: True, the law of God is, that it should be carried upon men's shoulders, but may it not as well be carried in a cart? he thought it but a little matter, yet was it in its consequences great. So, that which we think little in God's worship, may prove of moment. So Uzziah, in 2 Chron. xxvi., doubtless, thought it no great matter to go into the temple and offer sacrifices, Is it not as fit for a king to offer it as a priest? It was in the temple, and agreeable to the true form, and Uzziah, because he was a great man, thought he might venture, (for there you find that he had an army of three hundred thousand and seven thousand and five hundred soldiers,) yet, notwithstanding, God smote him. And Nadab and Abihu, too, thought it no great matter to go and offer strange fire; It is not expressly forbidden in God's word, they said: but it was a great matter before God, for God came with fire from heaven to destroy them. Hence it is that God in his word would set out the glory of his worship, and make them to think every thing connected with it great, that so they might not have their hearts taken with any false worship. Ezek. vii. 20, "As for the beauty of his ornament, he set it in majesty;" (and hereby God aggravates their sin of idolatry, My worship and service, I made it as beautiful and glorious as possible;) "but they made the images of their abominations and of their detestable things therein." So in Jer. xvii. 12, "A glorious high throne from the beginning is the place of our sanctuary." Mark what follows, ver. 13, "O Lord, the hope of Israel, all that forsake thee shall be ashamed, and they that depart from me shall be written in the earth, because they have forsaken the Lord, the fountain of living waters." As if God should say, Oh the insensate hearts of men, when I present unto them such a glorious worship of mine, yet they turn to their own vile inventions, and regard it not! I beseech you, brethren, labour to look upon God's worship as a glorious thing. But now the reprehension follows:

"But they were counted as a strange thing." Herein consists the wickedness of people, that though God shows forth his glory in his word, yet they look upon it as "a strange thing," as a thing that they shall get little good by if they obey, or little hurt by if they disobey. We might now show wherein this people did account God's worship a strange thing, and what particulars of his law they accounted strange things; but this especially deserves to be noticed, they accounted it a strange thing, that God should so stand upon it, that he must needs be worshipped in Jerusalem, at the temple, and at no other altar, whatsoever came of it. Now, because they thought that if the people went to Jerusalem to worship, it would be very prejudicial to the state, this was "a strange thing," and that which they could see no reason for. So people are ready to think, if any thing be propounded for the worship of God out of the word, Yea, but is it consistent with peace? it may cause contention to insist now upon such things. First, men will frame troubles in their own thoughts, and put them upon God's worship; whereas indeed they do not bring such trouble, but if they be examined they may consist well enough with the peace of states. I make no question but this is one especial thing aimed at by the Holy Ghost here, that they accounted God's law, that very law of his which required them to worship at Jerusalem, "as a strange thing;" they could not see why they might not venture to worship him elsewhere, especially when in their eyes it seemed to favour the peace of the civil state.

Now they accounted this, and the other particulars of God's law, "as a strange thing" in four respects.

1. As a thing that did not much concern them. They took not to heart the breaches of God's law, neither did they much regard the keeping of it, it was no great matter to them; they made account that what they did in that respect was *ad libitum*, that much did not depend upon it, either good or evil: as a stranger accounts it not to concern him what the master commands; or as we account it no great matter what strangers do, what clothes they wear, or what course they take, we let them pass by without concern.

2. In their apprehensions; they could not discern their reason. As we term a thing strange that we do not understand, and for which we can see no reason; so they in the text, that God should say thus and thus, when we cannot see that any account can be given for it, they are "strange things:" strange things that they did not apprehend the reason of. And especially, among other things of God's law, (as was said before,) the form of God's worship was a very strange thing to them; that God should so insist that he must be worshipped no where in the way of public worship but at Jerusalem, at the temple, no sacrifices must be offered but there; yea, that though people dwelt a great way off, though, as they thought, it would bring a great deal of disturbance into the kingdom of Israel, yet that God should so insist upon it, and that the prophets should urge with such fervency, their going to Jerusalem at all risks, they accounted this a strange thing. And indeed it is very strange to people to think, that we must look to the exact way of God's worship, whatsoever trouble or disturbance results from it, we must not in the least go against the mode that he has established: this is a strange thing to carnal hearts. And Luther, on the place, seems to interpret it, as if this text had especial reference to this note that I am now speaking of: They did condemn, saith he, and contemn the prophet's sermons, as a doctrine dangerous to the commonwealth; especially the doctrine about going up to Jerusalem to worship, they thought it was hurtful to the commonwealth, and therefore condemned it. What strange thoughts have carnal hearts of many parts of God's law! they think them foolishness, even those very things wherein the wisdom of God is revealed to the children of men, those things wherein are the deep counsels of God concerning man's eternal estate.

3. There was no suitableness between their hearts and the doctrine; they did not make the law of God familiar to them as that which suited their minds. As a man turns almost instinctively from company altogether unsuitable to him in language, customs, and pursuits; so when the law of God suits not the dispositions of our hearts, our ends, our ways, our very hearts turn from it as from a strange thing: whereas indeed our hearts should be familiar with the word of God; his word and the things contained therein should not be as strange things to our souls, but, as the Holy Ghost saith, it should be as our kinswoman, and as our delight continually. Prov. vi. 21, 22, "Bind them continually upon thine heart, and tie them about thy neck. When thou goest, it shall lead thee; when thou sleepest, it shall keep thee; and when thou awakest, it shall talk with thee." There should be a familiarity between our hearts and the commandments of God; when going to bed, when we rise up, when we walk in the way, we should be conferring about the things of God's law, to make them familiar to us, that we may not be estranged from them. God sees that men's hearts would quickly be estranged from his law, therefore he commanded that by all such means and ways they should endeavour to make it familiar to them.

4. They used the word as a stranger; that is, for their own ends only. As usually when strangers come into a country, and all travellers know it, the natives either treat them slightly, or if they do seem to show any respect, it is merely for their own advantage: so they accounted the law a strange thing, that is, they made use of the law merely to serve their own ends; so far as obedience to the law suited them, so far they yielded to it, and no further. Now it is very observable,

that those who were so zealous in their false worship, that, as the text saith, they did multiply, and had special regard to, their altars; yet the law, they accounted that "as a strange thing."

Obs. 7. Superstitious people, although very zealous in their own observances, are yet very negligent in God's mode of worship; they little regard that. Indeed their own altars were accounted great things, on their own ordinances they did not care what they expended; but as for God's institutions, they are as "a strange thing" unto them. We have seen very evidently, and do see it in great part to this day, how those that are very zealous in their own superstitions are the most negligent in God's ordained worship: to instance; you know, in late times, what a deal of stir men made with the ceremonies and modes of worship which they themselves had appointed; how zealous and devout were they in them! when they came in public congregations to bow and cringe, and perform other ceremonies, which they said the decency of God's worship required, how resolute were they for them, even so that the mouths of the most godly ministers must be stopped if they refused to conform! Yet these very men would scorn and jeer at strictness in God's ways, and slight any man that would be conscientious in them, and accounted all rebels who would not, in obedience to authority, adopt their ceremonies. For men to be conscientious about little things (as they termed them) in God's law, seemed strange; whereas they would urge men to obey to the uttermost every particular of their own; and so, in another respect, they would persecute to the uttermost men that worked but to get bread for their families on their holy-days, and yet could publish Books of Sports for the profanation of the Lord's day. And thus the great things of God's law were "as strange things," but their own things were great matters. Surely, if it were such a great matter to observe, for instance, the festival of Christ's nativity, we would have some hint of it from the beginning of Matthew to the end of the Revelation, but God no where mentions it. And mark, those people that stand most upon such festivals, stand least upon God's sabbaths. Many think it a strange thing for men not to pay regard to such festivals; Why may not we keep the birth of our Saviour? Now, that you may not think it so, do but consider this, that when God has set apart any thing for a holy use, it is no strange thing; but it would be strange in man to venture to imitate God in the things of his worship, to do that in God's worship which God himself has done before. Thus God has set apart a holy time, viz. the sabbath; it is set apart to solemnize the whole work of redemption, the nativity of Christ, his life, death, resurrection, ascension, and the coming of the Holy Ghost; God, I say, has set the sabbath apart that we might have a holy-day to keep the remembrance of them all. Now, when God has appointed one day, for man to dare to venture to set another apart, this is presumption. So, because Christ has set outward elements and sacraments to be a remembrance for his body and blood, for man to say, Christ has named bread and wine, why may not I also appoint something? this you would all say were a great presumption. Certainly the presumption is the same in the former.

Obs. 8. It is a dangerous thing for men to have their hearts estranged from God's law, and from the other spiritual truths that are in God's word; from the knowledge of that law in which they have been educated, and of which heretofore they have made profession. Thus it was with this people, they had been educated in God's law, and professed that, whatsoever God should reveal, they would obey; but now, notwithstanding, their hearts were estranged. Oh! let men take heed of this for ever.

You that have had good education, have been brought up in the knowledge of God's law, and have had its gracious principles infused into you in your youth, take heed now of being estranged from those truths which heretofore have been familiar to you, and of which you have made profession; take heed, I beseech you, of the several degrees of the estrangement of the heart from the law of God. I will but name them, to show how the hearts of men do become estranged.

1. They are less frequent in intercourse with God. A man that has a familiar friend does not estrange himself suddenly, but by degrees; it may be they visit one another less than they were wont to do, and yet there is no contention between them, but by degrees they grow to be strange, and then at length become very enemies. And thus it is with men's hearts; when men grow strange from the word, that they were acquainted withal before, they begin to call things in question, whether they be so or no, and especially those things which most concern the mortifying of sin, and the strictness of holiness.

2. Their delight in the truths of God abates. They were wont to take abundance of delight in meditating on the word; oh how sweet was it in the night season! and to confer about God's word with others was their great joy; but now this is abated, and many things, of which before they were very confident, they now begin to doubt.

3. They begin to have some hard thoughts of God's word. So some that heretofore prized the word, and regarded its truths as the joy of their hearts, yet now begin to entertain hard thoughts of the word.

4. They begin to wish that many things in the word were otherwise than they are; they cannot see enough to persuade them of their falsity, but, growing estranged from the word, they wish they were not true.

5. They begin to listen to things which are against the word. There was a time when they never would regard any thing advanced against the strictest requirements of holiness, but now are they ready to listen to objections. As a man, when intimate with his friend, cannot endure to hear any thing said against him, but being estranged from him, he can drink in any scandal greedily.

6. They become reluctant to search throughly into truths; they put off serious thoughts, and will not examine candidly into things as they were wont to do, but will rather search into any thing that may make against the truth than that which will work for it. I beseech you, observe such workings of your hearts.

7. There will be an engagement in some practice not allowed by the word. Then a man grows further estranged from his friend, when he not only refrains from coming into his company, but will engage himself with others that are against him.

8. Former weighty arguments are now weak. There was a time when certain things were thought to have very great weight in them, but now they are nothing, they are "accounted as a strange thing." Just as when a man is estranged from his friend; he thought before he had a great deal of excellency in him, but now he esteems him not; this argues the estrangement of his heart from him.

9. They at length violently reject the truths of the word, they grow to be open enemies to the truth. Some that have been familiar with God's word and truth, and made profession of them, and seemed to love them, have by these several degrees grown to be strangers from them, and at length enemies to them. Apostates have ever proved to be the most desperate enemies to the truths of God. Take heed, therefore, of the estranging of your hearts from the truths of God, lest you afterwards prove enemies to God: it is an evil thing to account his law "a strange thing;" how much more to account it an enemy to us, and our hearts to be ene-

mies to it! Isa. v. 24, "Therefore as the fire devoureth the stubble, and the flame consumeth the chaff, so their root shall be as rottenness, and their blossom shall go up as dust." Why? "Because they have cast away the law of the Lord of hosts, and despised the word of the Holy One of Israel." O, let us ever take heed of this; and therefore let our prayer be that of the prophet David, in Psal. cxix. 18, 19, "Open thou mine eyes, that I may behold wondrous things out of thy law." And then follows, "I am a stranger in the earth; hide not thy commandments from me." Lord, I account myself a stranger here in the world; O, let not thy word be a stranger to me. I beseech you, observe this; those who account themselves "strangers in the earth," will never account the law of God "a strange thing" to them; but such as account themselves to be the inhabitants of the world, they will have God's law to be a stranger to them. Observe it, and you will find this to be true. When your hearts begin to close with the things of the world, you do not meditate in God's word so much as you did before, nor delight to read it; but if you can keep your heart from the things of the world, using them as if you used them not, then this will be your prayer, Lord, "hide not thy commandments from me." "Thy word is sweet unto me as honey and the honey-comb."

Obs. 9. That which men's corrupt hearts will not close with as a rule of holiness, they put upon Christ, as if Christ had delivered them from it. Many will estrange themselves from the law of God by too much familiarity with the world; but for people to conclude, because they now know more of Christ, that therefore they should be greater strangers to the law than they were before, this is indeed a strange way of estranging our hearts from God's law. The Holy Ghost, foreseeing such a generation would arise in the times of the gospel, who would boldly assert, that whatsoever the people of God were bound to under the Old Testament, yet under the New they had nothing to do with the law of Moses, very remarkably, at the very close of the Old Testament, annexes to a prophecy of Christ the words, "Remember ye the law of Moses my servant." "Unto you that fear my name shall the Sun of righteousness arise with healing in his wings," Mal. iv. 2. To you that fear my name shall Christ arise. What then does it add? then you shall have nothing to do with the law when Christ arises? No; mark the 4th verse, "Remember ye the law of Moses;" almost the last words thus carrying the requirements of the Old Testament into the New; as if the Holy Ghost should say, Now I have done revealing all my mind about the Old Testament, and you must never expect any more prophets, nor any further revelations, till the time of the New; when, instead of the prophets, you shall have the "Sun of righteousness arise." Well, then, we shall never have any thing to do with the law of Moses more? Nay, but, saith the Holy Ghost, then "Remember ye the law of Moses my servant."

Ver. 13. *They sacrifice flesh for the sacrifices of mine offerings, and eat it; but the Lord accepteth them not; now will he remember their iniquity, and visit their sins: they shall return to Egypt.*

"They sacrifice." The Jews might object, Why, how do we account the law of God "a strange thing?" do not we continue to offer our sacrifices to God? Why do you say we account the law a strange thing? From the connexion, therefore,

Obs. 1. Men may continue in the outward profession and performance of duties of religion, and yet the great things of God's law may be a strange thing to them. They do offer sacrifices still, and yet they accounted God's law "as a strange thing" to them. Do not think it sufficient that you continue in the outward profession of religion; nay, shall I say more? I question not, but a man may continue in outward duties and yet apostatize from God, so far as to commit the sin against the Holy Ghost; and that is evident from the example of the scribes and Pharisees, whom Christ charges with committing the sin against the Holy Ghost, although they continued to observe a great deal of outward strictness in religion: therefore you may apostatize far from God, though you do not forsake the public ordinances of God.

"Flesh." God calls all their sacrifices "flesh;" that is, in contempt; as if he should say, You sacrifice, indeed, I have a little flesh from you, but do you think that this is the thing which I look for in my offering? I expect faith and obedience, I expect the work of faith relying on him who is typified by all your sacrifices; but as you want that inward spiritual worship in your souls, I account your sacrifices but flesh.

Obs. 2. Most people offer nothing to God in all their sacrifices but "flesh." Their offerings are flesh; that is, even in your prayers, in your hearing, in your receiving, you offer sacrifice, but all is but "flesh;" God has the outward man, and it may be you have fleshly ends in what you do, and fleshly, carnal hearts. Many a man has excellent gifts in prayer, and seems to offer up an excellent sacrifice to God; but it is nothing but flesh, there is little of the Spirit of God, of the sanctifying Spirit, it may be, nothing. A man may preach excellently, yet in fleshly wisdom, nothing but fleshly excellency. O my brethren, what are our sacrifices if they be nothing but "flesh?" You know what the Scripture saith, "All flesh is grass, and all the goodliness thereof is as the flower of the field: the grass withereth, the flower fadeth: but the word of our God shall stand for ever," Isa. xl. 6, 8. All a man's parts, all things are but flesh that come not from the sanctifying work of the Spirit of God by the word, and will pass away; but the word of God, that is, the impression of the word of God upon the soul by the sanctifying work of God's Spirit, abides for ever. You may have got a great deal of fleshly excellency, so that others may admire your gifts and parts; but this flesh is as grass, it will come to nothing, and all your esteem will pass away "as the flower of the field." Let us take heed, my brethren, that our sacrifices be not flesh, for though they may glitter a while in the world, within a few years all will be as grass and will come to nothing.

"For the sacrifices of mine offerings." God commanded them to sacrifice flesh. Yet here seems to be an accusation; not, however, that they sacrificed, nor that they sacrificed nothing but the outward part, flesh, but rather thus: In the burnt-offering all the whole sacrifice was tendered up to God; but in the peace-offering some part of it belonged to the offerer, so that when they came to offer that, they came with their friends, because they were to partake of it. Now, saith God, "They sacrifice flesh for the sacrifices of mine offerings;" that is, they change mine ordinance; whereas I looked for burnt-offerings, the whole offerings, from them, they will rather offer peace-offerings, wherein they shall have part of the flesh for themselves, that they may take content therein. Thus I find interpreters carry it, and I verily think it to be the meaning of the Holy Ghost. So that from hence the note is,

Obs. 3. To aim at self in serving God eats out all true devotion. When there is a duty to be done, part of which God requires, and we show respect to God in it, and in the other part we enjoy ourselves, such duties men can be content well enough to perform; but the truth is, that part which concerns themselves generally eats out all the true devotion to God; although the worship be pretended, yet self-respects the heart is most upon: as for instance, the keeping of festivals they liked well enough, and we do not read so much about their non-observance, because in them there was something agreeable to the flesh: but now for the day of their fasts, God saith, "Whosoever afflicts not his soul, that soul shall be cut off." They had not so much mind to that in the tenth day of the seventh month, therefore God threatens, that whosoever did not afflict his soul that day, it should be cut off. And so you shall find it. That is the reason indeed why men are so much set upon their festivals; they pretend God's worship, and honour to their blessed Saviour, and the like; but the truth is, it is their appetite, their sports, and the licence to the flesh, that they aim at. I warrant you, let the time (as now it falls out) be the time of a fast, it will not be so much regarded; and for any man to keep a festival, when God by his providence calls to fast, certainly that man regards his own carnal lusts rather than God. And that by which all these festivals are upheld is, because that, together with a show of religion, the flesh gets so much gratification; but the performance of duties wherein God is served, and nature denied, is a great testimony that the Spirit of God is in our hearts: when we can offer up our burnt-offerings wholly to God, and ourselves denied, they are testimonies that the Spirit of God is in us. As in 1 Kings xiii., you read of the lion which slew the prophet that went contrary to God's commandment. Now the lion was specially sent by God to do this; and that there might be a testimony to that effect, therefore the text observes, that the lion stood by the carcass and did not meddle with it after it was once slain. It was the nature of the lion to have fed upon the carcass, but here was an argument, that what the lion did was from God. So, when any man shall perform a duty merely for God, and in that duty shall deny himself, shall be content to part with honours or preferment, that is a sign God is in it. And so in this public service: Oh, who would not venture himself for the public cause? But there is a public pay too as well as the public cause! But now, if a man, though he has not that which he expects, yet is content to venture himself as much as he did before, God is in this man, certainly, when he can thus do a work and deny himself in that work. And truly we should be willing so to do; why? because God requires not of us any self-denial that can do us any hurt. God would never have us deny ourselves in things that immediately concern our communion with himself and our eternal good. God expects self-denial, but it is only in those things that concern this present life. Now when God is so propitious to us that he will let us sometimes enjoy ourselves in the required duties, surely when he requires self-denial, and that in things of inferior moment, we should not hesitate to deny ourselves in them.

"But the Lord accepteth them not." As if he said, I would not have them, I was not pleased with them. Here,

Obs. 4. Whatsoever our services be, if self be regarded, all is rejected. Not only if sin be regarded, "If I regard iniquity in my heart, the Lord will not hear my prayer;" but if self be regarded, our services may please ourselves, but cannot please God. And for this you have a remarkable scripture in Amos v. 22, "Neither will I regard the peace-offerings of your fat beasts." Amos was contemporary with Hosea, and seems specially to refer to the very same thing as Hosea here, so that his words may help us to understand the passage before us. "Neither will I regard the peace-offerings of your fat beasts:" observe, they are their "peace-offerings;" he saith not, I will not accept the burnt-offerings of your fat beasts; but "the peace-offerings," because of their peace-offerings they ate part themselves; and saith God, Let your offerings be never such fat beasts, yet I will not accept them: so, let your duties be never so zealous and abundant, yet, if performed with a regard to self, God accepts them not.

"Now will he remember their iniquity." They offered their sacrifices that their sins might be done away, and had they exercised faith upon Christ the true sacrifice, their sins would have been blotted out; but they offering with a regard to themselves, it is said of them, "Now," for all this, "will he remember their iniquity."

Obs. 5. Men may perform great services, exercise themselves much in holy duties, and yet their sins remain unexpunged on God's file. It is indeed a sad thing for a man to kneel down and pray with woeful guiltiness upon his spirit, and rise up with the same sense of guilt that he knelt down with; and perhaps he has gone on and prayed and received the sacrament for these many years together, and every sin that was upon him when he first began is upon him now; whereas those that in holy duties exercise their faith upon Christ their Mediator, and with the act of faith tender up him to the Father, whatsoever sins were upon them before are now done away.

Obs. 6. However God may for a while forbear to come upon wicked men for their sins, yet he has his time to remember them all; to remember, that is, by his judgments to make it appear to them that he does remember them, when they think that he has forgotten them. 1 Sam. xv. 2, "Thus saith the Lord of hosts, I remember that which Amalek did to Israel, how he laid wait for him in the way, when he came up from Egypt." I remember what he did; why, this was four hundred years ago that he spoke of. We may commit a sin when in our youth, and feel nothing of it till we come to be old, and then God may remember it against us: as many when young, their bones full of marrow and their veins of blood, feel not their present excesses; but in old age, then it aches in their flesh and bones, and then they remember their licentiousness and carelessness in their youth. And so many young people commit sin, and conscience never troubles them for it, and they think all is forgotten; but many years after the sin is committed, God remembers it, and makes them remember it too. Joseph's brethren had committed that sin against their brother two and twenty years before they were compelled by God's dispensations to say, "We are verily guilty concerning our brother," Gen. xlii. 21. Many things might be said to this point which I cannot now insist upon, only this take with you; Let all you that are young, yea, and others too, take heed what you do in sinning against God, for that which you do now may be remembered against you many years after; perhaps twenty, thirty, forty years hence, God may come upon you for your present actions. Methinks this should be to young men a constraining motive to take heed of wicked lives, Youth's sins may prove to be age's terrors.

Oh! is it not a great deal better that God should remember "the kindness of thy youth" than the sins of thy youth? Jer. ii. 2. You that are young, begin, I beseech you, to be godly betimes, that God may remember "the kindness of your youth." How blessed is the condition of the saints in comparison of the wicked! "God will remember their sins no more;" he will "bury in the depths of the sea" the transgressions of his people. Numerous expressions of similar import occur in the word of God.

But further, "*Now* will he remember their iniquity;" that is, in the time of their holy duties. Now this is a sad thing, that God should not only remember a man's sin, but even then when he is about to offer sacrifices to God; as in Heb. x. 3, it is said, "In those sacrifices there is a remembrance made of sins every year;" that is, it was a note of their guiltiness every time they came to offer sacrifice, and their sacrifices did not do away their sins fully, now will he remember them. But when they offered in a careless and ungodly manner, surely such sacrifices would bring their sins into remembrance indeed.

Obs. 7. God remembers the sins of the wicked especially in the performance of holy duties; and that upon these two grounds:

1. Because then we come into God's presence. We then come before his eyes in a more especial manner. We are in God's eyes always, but holy duties the Scripture speaks of as a more especial drawing nigh to God. If a malefactor that has committed an offence a long time since, and thinking it forgotten, should presume to come into the presence of the king or judges, this presumption, were he discovered, would be deemed an aggravation of his guilt: so when the wicked are bold to draw nigh to God, although their consciences tell them that they have not sought to do away their sins by faith and repentance, this puts God into remembrance (to speak of God after the manner of men).

2. Their holy duties are aggravations of their sin, therefore God will remember them then rather than at any other time. As thus: the Jews in the text come to sacrifice for their sins, the language of which rite certainly was, Lord, I acknowledge I do deserve death myself for the sins which I have committed, and I can only have peace with thee through the sacrifice of thy Son that I believe is to come: now for them to come and virtually to say so, and yet continue still in their sin, this aggravated their guilt; it was a sin of infirmity before, it is a sin of presumption now. So, when men presume to come before God in prayer who have heretofore lived wickedly, and thus testify the respect which they profess they owe to him, while yet their consciences tell them that they do wickedly depart from God in their lives; when, I say, in prayer they confess and name their sins before God, and tell him what sinners they are, and yet still their hearts do close with these their sins, what an aggravation is this! yea, they come to judge themselves for their sins, and yet still to continue in them. O my brethren, if you did but think how such prayer aggravates our sins, it would make your hearts quake and tremble. But I speak only to those that, being hypocrites, live still in their sins; their holy duties being but aggravations, no marvel though God then remember their sins in a more special manner. We have cause to wonder that God does not come upon some of us in his wrath, while we are in the midst of our holy duties: as Pilate came upon the Galileans and mingled their blood with their sacrifices; so, while we compare the lives of men with their prayers, it is indeed a marvel that God does not mingle their blood with their sacrifice. O take heed, any of you that are conscious to yourselves of your hearts closing with any known sin, take heed the next time you go into God's presence in prayer, and confess your sins, and judge yourselves, that God does not then remember your sins. "Now will he remember their iniquity," even in the time of their holy duties: you think that is the time in which you most please God, but it may prove to be the time of God's remembering your iniquities against you.

"And visit their sins." God visits either in mercies or judgments; and in the godly visiting, it is to be understood concerning those things that seemed before to be neglected, as, in Gen. xxi., God visited Sarah after apparent neglect: and so, in Exod. iv., he visited the children of Israel; that is, when he seemed wholly to have neglected them: and so, I will "visit their sins;" though they may think I have neglected them, yet I will "visit their sins." Whence,

Obs. 8. God visits men's sins when they think he neglects them most. God has his time to make diligent inquiry for all their sins. In Exod. xxxii. 34, "In the day when I visit, I will visit their sin upon them;" then all their sins shall come up together. And that is the reason that God is content to bear with wicked men, and wink at their sins for the present; why? because God has a day to visit them: This sin which they commit now, they shall not hear of it till a great while hence, but I have a day to visit, and then this and the other sins shall appear. Days of visitation heretofore were wont to be called days of vexation, but the day of God's visitation will be a day of vexation indeed to ungodly men. Micah vii. 4, "The best of them is as a brier; the most upright is sharper than a thorn hedge: the day of thy watchmen and thy visitation cometh; now shall be their perplexity." In Isa. x. 3, "And what will ye do in the day of visitation, and in the desolation which shall come from far? to whom will ye flee for help? and where will you leave your glory?" So I may say to many guilty consciences, "What will ye do in the day of visitation?" Poor sinner! thou canst tell now, thou canst go home and be merry, and do what thou list; but what wilt thou do "in the day of visitation?"

They will return, or, as we translate it, "they shall return to Egypt." And so it denotes,

1. The course they would take when God was about to visit them. "They will return to Egypt." Whither will ye flee "in the day of visitation?" We will flee into Egypt, say they; if the Assyrian power grow too great, we will go into Egypt for help. And this may seem to refer to 2 Kings xvii. 4, where "the king of Assyria found conspiracy in Hoshea; for he had sent messengers to So king of Egypt."

Obs. 9. Carnal hearts, when God is visiting them for their sins, are plotting how to shift for themselves. Vain deluded soul! thy thoughts should be, How may I make my peace with God? how may I seek the face of God? thou art thinking of various shifts, whereas thou shouldst only be thinking of reconcilement with God. And thus it is with kingdoms; when God is visiting kingdoms, you find many that sit at the stern, exercise all their thoughts about carnal helps, whereas their great thoughts should be, how they might fall down before God, and make peace between God and the kingdom: thus it was here, I will visit them, and they think to return to Egypt.

2. Their judgment. "They *shall* return to Egypt." It is threatened that they should return to Egypt at the latter end of Deut. xxviii.; there it is as a close to all the former judgments, "And the Lord shall bring thee into Egypt again."

Obs. 10. It is one of the most dreadful judgments upon a nation, after God has delivered them from a bondage, to return them into the same again. And as it was grievous to bring them back into the bondage of Egypt, so more to return us into a spiritual Egypt. If we should again come fully under the power of those that have persecuted us and oppressed us, our bondage would indeed be seven-fold more than it is: and yet what cause have our hearts to tremble, when we think how we abused the beginning of the deliverance we have had! But of all judgments, let us pray to be delivered from that judgment, that we may never be returned again to our prisons.

Obs. 11. It is just with God, that those who inherit their progenitors' sins, should inherit their progenitors' judgments. You continue in their sins, you shall have their judgments also.

Quest. But were they ever carried into Egypt? was this threat ever fulfilled?

Ans. No, they were not carried captive into Egypt, but they fled into Egypt for refuge, and there lived and died miserably, Jer. xliv. Hence,

Obs. 12. All places are places of misery when God forsakes a people, as all places are comfortable when

God is with a people. Many seek to help themselves, and perhaps they in part obtain what they would have; but the very answering of their desires ofttimes proves to be the execution of the wrath of God upon them. You have a mind to go to Egypt, you "shall return to Egypt," saith God.

Ver. 14. *For Israel hath forgotten his Maker, and buildeth temples; and Judah hath multiplied fenced cities: but I will send a fire upon his cities, and it shall devour the palaces thereof.*

"For Israel hath forgotten his Maker." They have forgotten their Maker, but I will remember them, saith God.

Obs. 1. God punishes for sins when men are most secure: whereas if you would remember your sins, God might forget them; or if you would remember God, your sins should not be remembered. It is an abominable thing for us to forget God, from whom we received our memory, and by whom we are remembered; we should never have been thought of if God had not given us what we have, and therefore for us not to think of God is a vile sin. Now, God is forgotten when he is not honoured, when he is not regarded as our confidence, help, refuge, our only good, when he is not obeyed; if we do but remember sin, we cannot but honour him. How many forget what manifestations once they had of God! they are passed by from them, and other things occupy their thoughts. Oh what manifestations of God have many of your souls enjoyed, and what communion with your heavenly Father! how has God's Spirit shone upon you! and you thought you should never forget those things; but now other things are in your hearts: such have cause to fear that they are under much wrath, that they should so forget their Maker. God challenges remembrance under this title: "Remember now thy Creator in the days of thy youth," Eccl. xii. 1. There is no creature but the rational, that can reflect upon the cause of their being, the first cause, and therefore God would not lose the honour from this creature. "The ox indeed knoweth his owner, and the ass his master's crib;" the beasts can take notice of those that bring them good things; but to reflect upon the cause of their first being, I say, that is proper to the rational creature, and therefore it is an honour that God expects from you, and will not relinquish.

The words "his Maker," imply not here God's giving them their being, but God's advancing and blessing them, so as to bring them to that happy condition which now they were in: "Israel hath forgotten his Maker," they have forgotten the God who has thus advanced them. So I find the word rendered, 1 Sam. xii. 6, "The Lord that advanced Moses and Aaron;" in the original, יהוה אשר עשה את-משה ואת-אהרן the Lord that *made* Moses and Aaron; that is, when God called them to the public work, God, as it were, then made them. Indeed for a man to be called to public service is a great honour from God, God then makes a man: we often use that phrase ourselves, if a man be raised to any preferment, such a man is made for ever. He whom God casts his favour upon, and delights to use in public service, is indeed a made man.

Obs. 2. God's favour makes a man. You have an excellent scripture for this in Isa. xliii. 7, "I have created him for my glory, I have formed him; yea, I have made him." Here are these three words together. God doth not satisfy himself with saying, I have given him his being, or all that he has, but he makes use of these three different words to signify how all our good comes from himself: I do not know a similar expression in Scripture. I have brought him out of nothing; then, secondly, I have formed him, I have put beauty and glory upon him; yea, and thirdly, I have made him, I have raised him to the height of all. God has created us all; but has he formed us? We are to look at God's forming as well as at his creation, how God forms and fashions us unto his own will.

Obs. 3. The greater height of excellency God raises any man to, the more vile is his sin in forgetting God. Many men will remember God when they are low, but when God has advanced them, then they forget him, and that is worse. But there follows,

"And buildeth temples." How is God forgotten, and they building temples to the honour of God? You accuse us of forgetting God our Maker; what people in the world remember God as we do, when we are at such charges about his worship?

The word היכלות translated "temples," signifies also palaces. The church is indeed God's palace. But note from hence,

Obs. 4. When God is worshipped in any way but his own, then God is forgotten. Papists set up images, and say it is to remind them of God; but the truth is, they forget God in them.

Obs. 5. When men's hearts depart furthest from God, then are they many times most forward in superstitious worship. We know that in the primitive times the hearts of men did close most with the power of godliness, and were more sincere in their worship; but afterwards, when they came to have peace, and temples, in and after Constantine's time, then they forgot God most, and grew superstitious. When the Christians worshipped God in dens and caves of the earth, they remembered God more than when they had glorious temples built for them. Men that have departed from God must have something to satisfy their consciences. Of late, how desperately was our kingdom departing from God, and setting itself against all the power of godliness; yea, and for the building of temples too, that is, for a more pompous and glorious external worship! but they forsook the temples of God, and persecuted them; the saints of God, the true temples of the Holy Ghost, were neglected.

But you will say, Why is it a sin to build temples? I answer, It was in them,

I. A sin of hypocrisy.

II. A sin of superstition.

I. A sin of hypocrisy: they would persecute those that would go to worship at the true temple, and yet bestow so much cost in building temples of their own. And many of the ancients have many large invectives against all such as shall bestow a great deal on outward buildings, and yet let the poor saints want.

II. A sin of superstition: they would not go to Jerusalem, to the temple that God had appointed, yet they would set up temples of their own. There are many that hate the true temple, and the true church, that is, the communion of saints; yet magnify the outward buildings, as if they were the only church. So the Jews, when God would have them build his own temple, were slack enough: in Hag. ii. 2, 4, 9, what a deal of trouble had God by his prophet to get them to build his temple! but their own temples they would build.

But wherein was the superstition manifested in their building temples?

Thus: it is a sign of superstition for any men to put holiness on any buildings of their own. There were three things that made the temple at Jerusalem a holy temple; and none of them can be attributed to any other place in the world.

First, It was set apart by God, so that it was a sin to use it for any other than a holy purpose.

Secondly, It sanctified the very duties that were performed.

Thirdly, It was a type of Jesus Christ. There were

these three things peculiar to the temple at Jerusalem. And therefore you must learn for ever from hence, that no argument can be drawn from the temple at Jerusalem for the holiness of temples now. Hence mark,

1. It is a sign of superstition to set apart a place, so that it should be a sin to use it for any common purpose.

2. It is still worse to set apart a place so as to think that the very place should sanctify the duty, because the temple of Jerusalem did so. Now, for a man to think that his prayers are sanctified because they are within such a building, is superstitious: hence a company of poor ignorant people must go behind a pillar and pray, as if they were accepted the more because of the place. True, indeed, when we come and join with the church, our prayers are accepted, because it is in a way of ordinance. Chrysostom exclaims against this superstition, saying, Jeremiah when in the mud could pray, Job on the dunghill, and Jonah in the belly of the whale; and therefore, why should we confine God's hearing of prayer to such and such places? Besides dedication, the heathens had enchantments: *Ab auguribus inaugurabantur, suis auguriis sanctiora reddebantur; hoc nisi fieret, templa esse non poterant* (*teste* Varrone) *sed ædes sacræ dicebantur.* Men have been very profuse in this, both heathens and Christians, and yet I find that some of the heathens thought God too great to be worshipped within any building. Zeno, the philosopher, thought that temples must not be built; and the Persians, who worshipped the sun, thought that the whole world was its temple, and would have none other. The Magi, too, persuaded Xerxes to burn all the temples of Greece, because they shut up God within walls. Some of the heathens had such thoughts of God, though ordinarily they were very abundant in building of temples to their idols. Josephus recounts Herod's desire to seem to honour God by building a glorious temple, even that same temple which was standing in Christ's time. He would make it as large and glorious as Solomon's was, and so he laid out a great sum of money upon it, in building it with blocks of white marble, twenty-five cubits long, eight cubits high, and about some twelve cubits broad: thus superstitious he was, and yet he was ungodly. And so many, to gratify inclinations of their own, care not what they expend; but in those things which God requires they are slack enough.

Chrysost. Hom. 79. ad populum.

Josephus, l. 15. c. 14.

"And Judah hath multiplied fenced cities." Judah, seeing God's judgments upon Israel, does not use the judgments of God upon their brethren, so as to consider their own sins, and fall down before the Lord, and be humbled in his sight; but when they saw that God's hand was against the ten tribes, all their care was to fortify themselves; Let us build strong cities, that we may be delivered from the miseries that are come upon our brethren. This is the course carnal hearts pursue; when God expects that they will be put upon humiliation and repentance, and look to it and consider whether they have not the same sins among them that were among their brethren, they regard nothing but carnal means. It is lawful to build strong cities, to fence ourselves against enemies; yea, but we had need lay the foundation of them in humiliation and reformation; and when they are built, they may not be rested in, for, saith God, "I will send a fire upon his cities, and it shall devour the palaces thereof." We must not bless ourselves in any strong places as if they could deliver us from the wrath of God. I have read of a city, that, fearing their enemies, sent to a neighbouring prince to come and help them, and charged their ambassadors to tell him what strength they had. But, saith the prince, have you got a cover to defend you from heaven? if not, I will not meddle with you: you must have something to ward God's wrath from you, you are so wicked; and except you have something to deliver you from that, I will not assist you. So, though we have strong walls, yet we must look for a cover from heaven, which is our peace with God through Jesus Christ.

Obs. 6. Men are more desirous to secure themselves from outward calamities than from God's wrath. "Judah hath multiplied fenced cities." Of outward safety men think they have never enough, to secure themselves from poverty and from their enemies, but security from God's wrath they little regard. In spiritual things we are content with a little, but when it comes to temporal security, we think we can never be too safe; and indeed, this will show you what your hearts are most set upon, that which you endeavour to secure yourselves most in, that is your chiefest good. A gracious heart will never say, May I not go to heaven though I do no more? but, Can there any thing more be done? does God require any thing more of his creature? God that knows all things, knows my heart is ready to do all things that he has revealed to me; and if there were any thing more to do, oh that I knew it, that I might fulfil even all righteousness!

"But I will send a fire upon his cities." They "multiplied cities," saith the text, "but I will send a fire." Hence,

Obs. 7. When we bless ourselves most in our own thoughts we should consider, But what are God's thoughts? We think we will do thus and thus, and save ourselves by this or the other means. Poor wretch! thou sayest thou wilt do thus and thus; yea, but think, what if God's thoughts, at the same time, be otherwise? Thou art plotting to save thyself, but God is plotting to destroy thee: what if there prove to be a disjunction between God's thoughts and thy thoughts? Wicked men have plots and devices for themselves, but God comes with his disjunctions, I will do thus and thus. Our enemies have had their plots, but God has been pleased to come in with his disjunctions, his thoughts have not been as their thoughts, blessed be his name.

Some interpret these words, "But I will send a fire," It may be that they think their forts are so strong that they cannot be beaten down, "but I will send a fire" to burn them down.

But I rather think this fire is meant metaphorically, I will send their enemies, which shall be as a fire; and so enemies are often called "a fire" in Scripture.

Obs. 8. By whatsoever means fire comes, God's hand is to be looked to in it. "But I will send a fire." If there has been a fire in your streets or houses, you will inquire by what means it came: but look up to God; whatsoever the means were, it is God that sends the fire.

Obs. 9. Brave things are subject to God's devouring fire. "And it shall devour the palaces thereof." As when the disciples looked upon the fair buildings of the temple and wept, and Christ said, "There shall not be left here one stone upon another;" so when we look upon our brave palaces, let us consider how quickly the fire of God's wrath may come, and not leave a stone upon a stone. And let us strive continually to look up to that place where Christ is gone to prepare mansions for us, and to that building that is eternal in the heavens, made without hands.

CHAPTER IX.

Ver. 1. *Rejoice not, O Israel, for joy, as other people: for thou hast gone a whoring from thy God, thou hast loved a reward upon every cornfloor.*

HERE begins another of the prophet's sermons. Gualter thinks this the sixth that Hosea preached to these ten tribes, wherein he still pursues the course he had commenced, convincing of sin, and threatening of wrath against Israel. This sermon was preached in a time when Israel seemed most prosperous and joyous.

"Rejoice not, O Israel, for joy." These words, according to interpreters, refer to one of these two periods:

I. When Israel, the ten tribes, obtained some special victory over their enemies. Or,

II. When Menahem made a league with the Assyrians.

I. When Israel, the ten tribes, had obtained some special victory over their enemies. This may refer, either to the time mentioned, 2 Kings xiii. 25, when Jehoash beat Benhadad three times, and recovered the cities of Israel;

Or, the time spoken of in 2 Kings xiv. 13, 14, "And Jehoash king of Israel took Amaziah king of Judah, and came to Jerusalem, and brake down the wall of Jerusalem. And he took all the gold and silver, and all the vessels that were found in the house of the Lord, and in the treasures of the king's house, and hostages, and returned to Samaria." This certainly was a time of great jollity and mirth among the ten tribes, as was also in the time of Jeroboam, 2 Kings xiv. 28, and in the time of Pekah, 2 Chron. xxviii., where the text saith, ver. 6, 8, They "slew in Judah an hundred and twenty thousand in one day, which were all valiant men. And the children of Israel carried away captive of their brethren two hundred thousand, women, sons, and daughters, and took also away much spoil from them, and brought the spoil to Samaria." Now in this time their hearts were much elated, for, in ver. 9, 10, the prophet Oded came to them and said, "Behold, because the Lord God of your fathers was wroth with Judah, he hath delivered them into your hand, and ye have slain them in a rage that reacheth up unto heaven. And now ye purpose to keep under the children of Judah and Jerusalem for bondmen and bondwomen unto you: but are there not with you, even with you, sins against the Lord your God?" It seems almost the same expression as we have here in the text; as if he should say, Now you purpose to keep the children of Judah and Jerusalem for bondmen and bondwomen, and you insult and rejoice, and you think you have gotten the day and have prevailed; "but are there not with you, even with you, sins against the Lord your God?" just as here, "Rejoice not, O Israel, for joy, as other people; for thou hast gone a whoring from thy God:" as if he should have said, Though God has given you a victory, and you think you have matter for much joy, yet,

"Rejoice not, O Israel, for joy, as other people." Why? Because your conquest is over your brethren, therefore rejoice not as "other people," as the nations around you would rejoice in slaying them.

Obs. 1. That is a sad war in which the conqueror has cause to be sad at the very conquest. If other people had gotten the victory, they might triumph; why not? but though you have prevailed, yet these are wars in which you should not triumph in, for by this means the nation of the Jews is becoming weaker, and in more danger to be made a prey to the common enemies; do not, therefore, you rejoice as other people might rejoice in such a conquest. And indeed such are our wars and victories at this day; we must not rejoice in our conquests as other people, not so as the French or Spaniards would if they prevailed against us, or as we might over foreigners; for our conquests weaken our own nation, they involve the destruction of our brethren, and therefore we are not to rejoice for joy as other people.

II. When Menahem made a league with the Assyrians. We read, 2 Kings xv. 19, that Menahem, king of the ten tribes of Israel, made a league with the Assyrian, that great king, "that his hand might be with him to confirm the kingdom in his hand."

Now when leagues of pacification and association are confirmed, nations are wont to triumph and rejoice, and by outward expressions to manifest their great satisfaction at them: Oh! now there is a peace made, now we shall grow stronger than ever we were, and be delivered from many troubles that heretofore oppressed us. So Israel blessed themselves in the Assyrian, in that they had got such a rich and mighty prince on their side; now that they had made their peace with him, they thought themselves secure, and contemned all threats, and derided all that the prophets said against them; now did the malignants among them lift up their heads and insult over them that would say, God's judgments would follow them if they did not join with God's people in his true worship; they sung away care, and none thought of any danger on account of their sin; they could not endure to hear of any apprehensions that might disturb their jollity and conceited happiness, whereof they promised to themselves the continuance. But now saith the Lord, by the prophet, "Rejoice not, O Israel, for joy, as other people;" be not too confident with whom you have made such a sure league, for they may prove to be your undoing, may prove to be the instrument of greater wrath from God than you have ever yet experienced: and indeed so it was, the Assyrians with whom they made this peace, and in whom they rejoiced much, proved to be the greatest instrument of wrath to the ten tribes. You have made your peace with him, and now you rejoice; but you have not made your peace with God, saith the prophet; and what good can your pacifications, can peace struck with them, do, so long as still ye go a whoring from your God, and break your peace and covenant with him daily. "Rejoice not, O Israel."

Obs. 2. Leagues wherein we much rejoice, may prove occasions of sorrow. They are called peace and union, but suddenly they may change their names, and be called a massacre; they may bring ruin and destruction on a nation, especially if the foundation of the peace be not laid in reformation. As long as a nation is departing from God, they have no reason to rejoice in any peace.

When people have been worn out with wars, they are greedy of peace of any kind, they care not with whom they make it; Oh nothing but peace, let us have that! and if there be but a peace concluded once, upon never such unsafe terms, Oh, the bells must ring, and bonfires must be made. This seemed to be the condition of the people at this time, but saith God, You are deceived, this peace will prove your undoing: "Rejoice not, O Israel, for joy, as other people: for thou hast gone a whoring from thy God."

But the observations which we may draw from the two periods referred to, that in which they gained advantages over their enemies, and that in which they made their peace, viewed conjointly, are such as these:

Obs. 3. Carnal hearts bless themselves in outward prosperity, in health, strength, friends, as if all were well with them, although they be under much guiltiness, though there be fearful breaches between God and their souls. How things are between God and them they care not, so be it outward things prosper; if there be no punishment for sin upon them, the guilt and pollution

Seculi lætitia est impunita nequitia. Aug. in John, Tract. 12.

of sin never trouble them. Augustine in his Tract. upon John, saith, The joy of the world is nothing else but their wickedness unpunished; if God do not punish them presently, then they have a great deal of joy. And in Amos vi. 4—6, you have the description of the people of Israel more at large (for Amos prophesied in the same time that Hosea did): "That lie upon beds of ivory, and stretch themselves upon their couches, and eat the lambs out of the flock, and the calves out of the midst of the stall; that chant to the sound of the viol, and invent to themselves instruments of music, like David; that drink wine in bowls, and anoint themselves with the chief ointments: but they are not grieved for the affliction of Joseph." Well; have not you more reason, you afflicted and distressed saints, to rejoice in God without the world, than they have to rejoice in the world without God? Shall not all the wrath of God that hangs over the heads of wicked men, and all the guilt which is upon them, damp their joy when they have but meat, and drink, and clothes, and a little outward prosperity; and shall the loss of a few creature comforts, such as many reprobates have to the full, damp your joy, when you have an interest in all there is in God, in Christ, in the world, in heaven, in eternity? When in all this you may rejoice, how unreasonable is your dejection!

Obs. 4. When men rejoice, they should consider whether God approves of their joy. These rejoiced, but the prophet comes in the name of God and saith, "Rejoice not." When therefore we find ourselves inclined to rejoice, we should consider whether God approves of it. The rejoicing of many is so little in accordance with the mind of God, that they dare not so much as consult about the matter with God, or their own consciences: the more some can prevail with their own consciences to be silent, the more joy they have; yea, some there are that have so much guilt on their spirits, that they can have no joy, but when they can contrive, by some means or other, to lull their consciences to sleep; when their consciences are asleep they are fain to snatch a little joy: now, cursed be the joy that cannot stand with the free working of a true enlightened conscience.

Obs. 5. Men may prosper, and yet have little cause to rejoice. All outward prosperity may consist with the heavy wrath of God hanging over the sinner's head; he may be upon the very brink of destruction, and yet prosper outwardly. Outward prosperity may come in wrath; the poison of God's curse may be in the wine as well as in the water: the ungodly poor have their water poisoned, and wicked men, that are rich and prosperous, have their wine poisoned; and what difference is there between drinking poisoned water and poisoned wine? The swelling of carnal hearts in their prosperity, is a sign that it is poisoned to them. Outward prosperity, as it may come in wrath, and consist with wrath, so it may make way to wrath, by it the vessels of wrath may be fitted to destruction: God often has a further aim in suffering wicked men to prosper than they are aware of. As Haman, when invited by Esther to a banquet, inferred that he was honoured above all the nobles in the land, and went away rejoicing, and told his friends of the great honour that was put upon him; but Esther had a design in it far other than Haman thought of, she designed not to honour, but to destroy him: so many, whose estates God raises, draw inferences from his dealings with them far other than ever he intended; they think God has blessed them, whereas, in truth, God is working their ruin and destruction. As a painted face is no argument of a good complexion, so a prosperous estate is no argument of a good condition.

Obs. 6. Carnal hearts in their joy are immoderate, their spirits are elated, and they think not of setting bounds to their joy; so the words import, "Rejoice not for joy;" if you will rejoice, let there not be mere joy, but some kind of mixture in it. There should be a mixture of reverence and fear in our rejoicing; we should, in this world, "rejoice with trembling."

Whatsoever blessings we have from God, yet should we, in our present state, "rejoice with trembling," remembering,

1. Our unworthiness of any good we receive, a deep sense of which should mingle with our joy.

2. The afflictions of our brethren.

3. The uncertain and vanishing nature of all those things in which we rejoice.

Put these three things always into the cup of your joy; else it will be too sweet, and clog the stomach.

"Rejoice not, O Israel, for joy, as other people." That is,

1. Be not taken with the world's jollity. The apparent happiness of others that are in a different way from us, is many times a great temptation to draw the heart to them.

2. Imitate them not in their modes of rejoicing. Dancing, and many other ways of rejoicing, they had in their idolatrous feasts: we must not imitate idolaters in their triumphs. This was the sin of many in the primitive times; because they had newly come out of heathenism, they would turn the heathenish feasts into Christian feasts, and heathenish customs, whereby they were wont before to honour their idol gods, into Christian rites: and they thought this was very good, that whereas before they thus honoured idol gods, they now thought, if they did but turn these to honour Jesus Christ, they would be accepted. No, this was a great sin, and brought a great deal of evil into the Christian world, and we do to this day feel its effects: indeed, herein is the original of the observation of this time, both of your Christmas and New-year's day; they are but transferred from heathenish observances to the honour of Christ and of the saints. I remember this time * two years, through mere providence that Scripture came in our way, "I will take away their solemn feasts;" and there I showed how these came, instead of the heathenish rites. Now, saith the Holy Ghost here, "Rejoice not, O Israel, for joy, as other people," do not you imitate them; they have their idolatrous feasts, but do not you as they. We must not take liberty to imitate heathens and idolaters in their worship, though we think thereby to tender our respects to God.

3. "Rejoice not as *a* people," for the word *other* is not in the original. Do not you rejoice as if you were to continue a people still, for you are to be carried captive, and not to continue as a people; you have brought yourselves into such a condition that you are not to look upon yourselves as a people: do not rejoice, no, not as a people. It is a miserable spectacle to see those who are ready to be destroyed, jolly and merry, as if no such thing impended. It is said of the dolphin, that it sports most at the approach of a storm. So, when the storm of God's wrath is arising upon a people, then they are most jolly and merry.

4. Rejoice not profanely. Others rejoice, and scorn at the threats of God: so Ephraim had mixed himself amongst the nations, and treated with scorn what was said by the prophet. Do not rejoice profanely, do not rejoice presumptuously, promising to yourselves continuance in your prosperity.

5. You have not such cause to rejoice as others. "Rejoice not, O Israel, for joy, as other people." Why? Israel! though you be Israel, yet there is not so much cause for you to rejoice, as for other nations. Israel, the

* Preached in Christmas.

ten tribes, prided themselves in their privileges above other people, and despised all in comparison of themselves: but now God tells them, that their sins had brought them into a worse condition than other people were in, and they must not rejoice so much as they. From thence this profitable note may be raised:

Obs. 7. Many who look with scorn upon others as mean and low, may yet be in a worse state than they. For instance, you may be a man of parts and in esteem, and engaged in high employments for church and commonwealth; another is in a mean, low condition, of weak parts and of little use; and yet such guilt may rest upon you, that you may not have such cause to rejoice as this poor man has whom you so contemn. It may be you have excellent gifts in prayer, and are an eminent professor; others may be vile in your eyes, they are no professors at all: if all were known, you have not such cause to rejoice as they whom you contemn.

Obs. 8. Although we enjoy the same blessings that others do, yet we may not have always the same cause to rejoice. I say, it may be others have more cause to rejoice in a little than we in abundance. Do not say in your hearts, Others are merry and cheerful, why should not I be so too? I have as good an estate as such a one, and as fair a dwelling, and as comely children, and why should not I be merry? But it may be there is not such a breach between God and him as between God and thee, it may be there is not so much guilt upon his spirit as upon thine, therefore thou must not rejoice as he does; though thou hast the same outward blessings, yet it follows not that thy joy should be similar. You have cause rather to reflect, Such and such men are cheerful indeed, yea, they may, for they have not provoked God as I have done, I am conscious of sins which I believe they are free from. A man afflicted with a sore disease, when he sees others merry thinks with himself, Yea, indeed you may be merry, but if you felt what I do you would have little cause to rejoice.

Obs. 9. It is a great aggravation of men's misery, to see others rejoice when they cannot. It is not for them to rejoice as others do; that which is the cause of rejoicing to others you have had and abused, you have abused like mercies of God, and now you must not rejoice as other people. Luke xiii. 28, is very notable for this, "There shall be weeping and gnashing of teeth, when ye shall see Abraham, and Isaac, and Jacob, and all the prophets, in the kingdom of God, and you yourselves thrust out." This is the aggravation of your misery, to see others in a happy and rejoicing condition, and "you yourselves thrust out." As, if a man lay confined in a prison near the street, on a day of triumph and festivity, and should hear in his dark dungeon the mirthful voices of the rejoicing multitude as they pass to and fro, this would be a great aggravation of his misery; Yes, would he think, they who have their liberty may rejoice, but I must not rejoice as they do. And this will be the aggravation of the misery of the damned hereafter, when they shall see Abraham, Isaac, and Jacob, and all the prophets, in the kingdom of God, and themselves cast out: it may be the father shall see his child in the kingdom of God, and himself in hell, being cast out: they shall rejoice eternally when I must be in everlasting torments. The reason follows,

"For thou hast gone a whoring from thy God." The ground of joy or sorrow is, the terms that are between God and us. Sin has an evil in it to damp all our joy. If we would have joy in any thing, let us take heed of defiling it by sin. Of all sins, the sin of forsaking God, or corrupting his worship, is such an evil as is sufficient to take away all the joy of a nation. If we have forsaken the true worship of God, we have little cause for joy, though peace and outward prosperity may attend us; whereas a people retaining it, whatever be their condition, have indeed cause to rejoice. Yea, and as a whole nation, so individuals in it, if their consciences tell them that they have not complied with the times, and gone a whoring from God in ways of false worship as others have done, they have cause to rejoice, whatsoever befalls their nation; whereas the others, that have complied, though the nation should prosper never so much, yet have little cause to rejoice in that joy. Let us therefore be solicitous about nothing so much as about the true worship of God.

Yea, but this people might say, Suppose we have some corruptions in the worship of God, yet do we retain more than other nations. Nay, saith God, "thou hast gone a whoring," and so you are more guilty than other nations.

Obs. 10. That which we deem a trifling deviation in God's worship, God may call a gross corruption. True, might they say, we may fail in some circumstances, we go not up to Jerusalem to worship; but still we worship the true God, and we observe the law of Moses. No, saith the Lord, "thou hast gone a whoring from thy God."

But still, Why may not we rejoice as other people? surely we are not worse idolaters than they, therefore, though we may not rejoice *more* than others, yet why not *as* others? They make idols to be their gods; there is nothing so vile among us as among the surrounding nations. From God's charging them more than others,

Obs. 11. A nation may be free from the gross evils that there are in another nation, and even have many good things that the other has not, and yet be in a worse condition. You will say, How can this be?

Thus: some of their sins may have greater aggravations, which may make their condition (all things considered) worse. We, in this land, have heretofore much rejoiced in this, that we have had the doctrine of religion purer among us than almost any people; and certainly, except for some few that of late days have sought to corrupt it, it must be confessed that the doctrine hath been kept very pure in the main points; and in some things we have even gone far beyond other reformed churches, as in our observance of the sabbath, and worship paid to God in our families. Never had God more honour from any people in the world than he has had from us in these and many other respects; but yet, notwithstanding, it seems by God's present dealings with us, that he is more provoked with us than with other people: and the truth is, take these one or two things, the bitterness of our hatred against the power of godliness, and our persecution of it, and I think never was any people so guilty as we have been. In other reformed churches men may be as forward and zealous as they will, and yet meet not with persecution as here; others may have kept the sabbath more loosely, yet they never persecuted the strict observers of it, nor, as here generally, attempted to stop the mouth of the faithful ministry. So it may well be said to us at this day, "Rejoice not, for joy, as other people."

Yea, but still, If we be idolaters, (would the ten tribes say,) they are so too.

There was one particular aggravation in the case of Israel that was not among other people, and that was this, No other people would forsake their gods as Israel had forsaken theirs, Jer. ii. 10, 11; there was never such a thing as for a nation to change their gods; even Kedar, one of the basest of nations, would not do so: Go to Kedar, and see, and search diligently whether any nation hath ever forsaken their gods; but you have forsaken me. From thence we may

Obs. 12. To be constant to ill principles is not so great an evil as to be false in good principles. God, I say, accounts it not to be so great an evil for men to be constant to their principles, though they be evil, as to forsake the good. As now, if a man has been brought up all his days in superstition, and thinks verily that is the right, certainly this man is not so guilty before God as another who has been educated in the true worship of God, and has made profession of it, and yet afterward doth apostatize and backslide. God had rather that men should keep to their principles, though evil, than entertain good principles and forsake them. There are none so vile in God's eyes as apostates: there is not so much sordidness and baseness of spirit in those men that adhere constantly to their principles, though evil, as in those who betray their principles, although good.

Obs. 13. The sins of God's people are the greatest sins of all. The sins of the saints are the greatest sins of all, and they are to mourn more than any. In Amos iii. 2, "You only have I known of all the families of the earth; therefore I will punish you for all your iniquities;" your sins are greater. And that in Rom. ii. 9, "Tribulation and anguish, upon every soul of man that doeth evil, of the Jew first, and also of the Gentile." And we have these two excellent texts in Jeremiah; chap. xviii. 13, "Ask ye now among the heathen, who hath heard such things: the virgin of Israel hath done a very horrible thing;" that is the aggravation, that it is the virgin of Israel that has done such a horrible thing. But especially chap. xxxii. 30, "For the children of Israel and the children of Judah have only done evil before me from their youth." Now Jerome raises a question upon this: What! the children of Israel and Judah only done evil from their youth? Have none done evil but they? And to this he answers, He that has the knowledge of God and goes from it, he alone sins in the eyes of God: as for unbelievers, they sin too, but it is as if God saw it not, and as if God minded it not; as he saith in Acts xvii., He winks at the days of their ignorance. We read of the Philistines, that they ventured to carry the ark upon carts, 1 Sam. vi. 7. God did not show himself provoked against their doing so: but when the Levites presumed to carry it upon carts, 2 Sam. vi. 3, the Lord makes a breach upon them, and strikes Uzzah with death. He bore with it in the Philistines a little before, and it may be they presumed, and thought, The Philistines carried the ark upon a cart, why may not we? That which God will bear from others he will not bear from his own; their sins are against covenant, and that mightily aggravates the sins of God's people.

O remember this, you that do often covenant with God in prayer. How often do you renew your covenant with God! What promises do you then make, and yet afterwards prove false and vile! Such as you must not rejoice as other people. You view with disgust a drunkard reeling in the streets, and with abhorrence hear a swearer blaspheming the name of God; yea, but their sins may not be so great as the vanity of thy spirit, the looseness of thy heart, and those secret sins of which thou art guilty. And why? Because thou hast so covenanted and bound thyself to God. The drunkard was never made sensible of his sin, nor felt the wrath of God upon his conscience; but it has visited thy conscience, and thou hast engaged thyself to God, if he would show mercy, thou wouldst walk holily and strictly before him. Now, dost thou think that thy sins are as the sins of other people? They never had such soul-quickening ordinances, but go up and down to taverns and alehouses, and their hearts never know what a powerful sermon means: had they enjoyed such blessings as thou hast, then likely it would be with them far better than now. And the name of God is not so much polluted by them as by thee. Thou professor of religion, the eyes of all men are upon thee, and in thy sin thou dost not only disobey God, but thou dost pollute his holy name; thou art a stumbling-block unto others, and the cause of the hardening of many hundreds in their sins, and therefore thy sin certainly is worse than others'. It would be a great point to show how the sins of the professors of religion are worse than others. It is not enough for them to say, We are all sinners. No, we must not excuse ourselves thus, that others are guilty as well as we, when we consider what aggravations there are in our sins more than in the sins of others. It is a sign of a very carnal heart to think to excuse itself thus: True, I sin, but others sin as well as I do. Yea, but a true penitent heart will not only consider itself a sinner, but what aggravations are there upon his sin more than upon the sins of others; and so will charge itself: True, such and such sin, but had they experienced what I have, it would not be so with them; my sin, that has broken through so many terrors of conscience, and that God has sought by such means to keep me from, is a sign of the violence of my spirit indeed. It is, therefore, an abominable thing to make our profession in holy duties a medium to make our sins less. Dost thou think that this is a means to make thee escape that wrath? Certainly not, but a great aggravation of thy sins.

We have a generation of men among us, that, because they are believers, therefore say, they need no sorrow for their sin, they must have only joy. Now, certainly, thy being a believer may aggravate thy sin, may make it so much the more vile, and may pierce thy heart so much the more; for if thou art a believer thou knowest what the pardon of thy sins cost; therefore, certainly, God's mercies towards thee are the aggravations of thy sins. The truth is, suppose our sins were not so great as the sins of some other people are, yet it is not always an argument that we may rejoice as other people.

Why so? you will say.

Thus: suppose our sins be but equal, or less than the sins of other people, yet it is more than we know, whether God will pass by our sins as he does the sins of others. What if God, out of his prerogative, damn thee for a little sin, and save others who have committed great sins? We have such examples in Scripture; the thing that God cast away Saul for, in itself was not so much as that which David afterwards was guilty of; Saul might have said, This is an offence, but is this like murder and adultery? yet God pardons David, and casts away Saul. Do not you, then, think to rejoice as other people; why, may not God do with his mercy as he pleases, it is his own? God may pardon one, and damn thee eternally.

"Thou hast loved a reward upon every cornfloor." Israel saw the nations round about her have a great deal of plenty upon their cornfloors, which they attributed to the serving of their idol gods, therefore Israel thought to comply with them out of love to their abundance; and since then she prospered more, she thought; and this she loved, by this she was exceedingly hardened in her ways of idolatry, and blessed herself in them. This is the scope. God made many promises to provide for Israel in his service, but they thought to get more in following the ways of the Gentiles than in following God's ways: like some, who, though they have liberal provision from their husbands, yet, hoping to get more from others, to gratify their vanity and love of pleasure, leave their husbands, and "forget the covenant of their God," Prov. ii. 17. Just thus it was with Israel; though she might have God's care over her, and provision for her in the ways of his worship, yet, beholding the Gentiles living more bravely, she would follow after them. At first (as you heard) she hired lovers herself, but now she loves "a reward upon every cornfloor," now she expects greater advantage; this indeed was what urged her on. She might have many pretences, she might plead that she did not see why she might not do such and such things, they were not directly contrary to God's word; but whatsoever pretences she made in the altering of God's worship, yet the great matter that prevailed with her heart was this, she "loved a reward upon every cornfloor." And thus it is with very many that are superstitious; speak to them of their ways, they will have very many fair pretences, they think that they have this and that warrant out of the Scripture for it; but all the while they have a secret regard to their living, trading, estates, and friends, and this biases their hearts and minds. But divers things before to the same purport have been spoken of, and we shall here only

Obs. 14. Idolaters love outward prosperity, because it is a reward of their service to their idols. So the sweetness of our comforts should consist in this, that they come from God as a reward of our faithfulness. When idolaters look upon their plenty and attribute it to their idol gods, shall it be so much the sweeter to them? let all our comforts be so much the sweeter to us, when we look upon them as coming from God as a reward of our faithfulness. In Psal. cxix. 56, David saith, "This I had, because I kept thy precepts." You will say, Can we look upon any thing as a reward of our righteousness? Free grace and the gospel reward may stand together; God may reward according to our works, though not for our works, and God is pleased to call it so for the encouragement of his people. Outward prosperity, if it follow our keeping close with God, is very sweet, as the cipher when it follows the figure doth add to the number, though it be nothing in itself.

Ver. 2. *The floor and the winepress shall not feed them, and the new wine shall fail in her.*

As a father, when he sees his admonitions not regarded by a stubborn child, withdraws his allowance from him; so God deals here, You have had many admonitions, now I will withdraw your allowance.

"The floor and the winepress." He doth not say the field, but "the floor," I will let them bring their corn to the floor; and he does not say the vine, but "the winepress."

Obs. 1. God often lets wicked men come near the enjoyment of a mercy, and then cuts it off: as many times the saints come near afflictions, and when they are at the very brink, then deliverance arrives.

Obs. 2. God is wont to strike wicked men in those things on which their hearts are most set. They would have their floor and winepress to afford them plenty, in that thing God strikes them. Now observe whether, in God's ways that are against you, he does not strike you especially in that on which your hearts are most set; if he does, know there is the finger of God, and God would have you take special notice of it.

"And the new wine shall fail in her." ותירוש יכחש בה the new wine shall lie to them. So in Hab. iii. 17, "The labour of the olive shall fail," כחש shall lie; that is, it shall not perform what it seems to promise to you.

Obs. 3. All creature promises we shall find but a lie; but the promises of the word shall never fail. Whatsoever you promise to yourselves, I say, let it be grounded upon the word; but if you promise to yourselves great matters from any creature, you will find a lie in the conclusion. We often lie to God in not answering our good beginnings, and it is just with God that the creature should even lie to us, and not accomplish what they seem to promise to us.

Obs. 4. Men will be disappointed at last in that which they think to get in a way of sin. The way of the wicked shall deceive them, they shall not find what they expected therein. The saints shall find more than ever they expected from God, but the wicked shall find less than that which they expected from the creature. But there is not much difficulty in this verse, therefore we pass it over briefly.

Ver. 3. *They shall not dwell in the Lord's land; but Ephraim shall return to Egypt, and they shall eat unclean things in Assyria.*

"They shall not dwell in the Lord's land." Before, God was to them as a father taking maintenance away from them, leaving them to suffer want; but here his anger increases, and he puts them out of his house: as a father first withdraws allowance from his perverse son, and when that will not do, then he thrusts him out of his house; so doth God here: "The floor and the winepress shall not feed them;" and not only so, but, saith God, "They shall not dwell in the Lord's land." I will cast them out of my house, cast them out of my land; I will not suffer Ephraim to dwell any longer there.

God would make them to know that it was his land, that they were but tenants at will, and enjoyed the land upon conditions of obedience, as appears in Lev. xviii. 26; and in Lev. xxv. 23, we read of an ordinance of God, that no land in Canaan should be sold for ever, but only to the year of jubilee; the richest, that bought never so much land, could not buy it for ever, he could not have such a tenure as runs amongst us, "to have and to hold for ever." But you will ask why. The reason is given in the same verse: "The land shall not be sold for ever:" why? "for the land is mine; for ye are strangers and sojourners with me;" I have brought you to the land, and ye are but sojourners with me in my land. God may dispose of all as he pleases. It is a good meditation for us to dwell upon, that we are God's stewards; the Lord is the great landlord of all the world. When you go abroad into the fields, you that are godly may see more land than is your own, but you cannot see more than is your Father's.

"The Lord's land." This may be said of all the land in the world, he that is thy Father is the great landlord of the world. Men respect their landlords and are afraid to displease them, but how little respect is given to this great landlord! "The earth is the Lord's, and the fulness thereof;" but, though all the world be "the Lord's land," yet this land of Canaan was "the Lord's land" more peculiarly in many respects:

1. It was a land that God "had espied" as a special place for his people, Ezek. xx. 6. God was overlooking all the world; Where should I have a good land (or country) to set my people? and the text saith, God had espied this for them.

2. It was the land of promise. In Heb. xi. 9, "By faith he sojourned in the land of promise, as in a strange country." No land in Scripture is called the land of promise but only this.

3. It was a land given by oath, Gen. xxiv. 7.

4. It was a land which the Lord brought his people into, by "a mighty hand and with an outstretched arm."

5. It was a land divided by lot; not only all the land, but every piece in it, and the possession that any man had, was ordered by God himself, by lot.

6. It was a land wherein God dwelt himself, a land that God called his own rest; "This is my rest for ever," Psal. cxxxii. 14; and God sware unto them that hardened their hearts in the wilderness, that they should not enter into his rest; that is, that they should not enter into the land of Canaan. It was the land wherein were the ordinances and the worship of God, and his honour dwelt there, and so it had a peculiar blessing upon it above every land on the face of the whole earth.

7. It was a land over which God's eye was in a more special manner: there is a most excellent scripture for that in Deut. xi. 12, "A land which the Lord thy God careth for; the eyes of the Lord thy God are always

upon it, from the beginning of the year even to the end of the year."

8. This land was typical of the rest of the church in heaven, for so the apostle, in Heb. iii. 11, seems to apply Psal. xcv. 11, "Unto whom I sware in my wrath that they should not enter into my rest." And so in 1 Chron. xvi. 15—18, it is said, "Be ye mindful always of his covenant; the word which he commanded to a thousand generations; even of the covenant which he made with Abraham, and of his oath unto Isaac; and hath confirmed the same to Jacob for a law, and to Israel for an everlasting covenant, saying, Unto thee will I give the land of Canaan, the lot of your inheritance." Mark, that he would give unto them the land of Canaan; this must be remembered to a thousand generations, and it must be a law to Israel afterwards. Certainly this notes that God aimed at more by the land of Canaan than merely to possess them of so much ground.

9. Various titles are given to this land: a "holy land," Zech. ii. 12; "an exceeding good land," Numb. xiv. 7; "a pleasant land, a goodly heritage," Jer. iii. 19; "as the garden of Eden," Joel ii. 3; "the glorious land," Dan. xi. 16, 41; "the glory of all lands," Ezek. xx. 15; and here in my text, "the Lord's land." Now from all these titles we are not only to take notice of this, that it would be a great judgment of God to drive them out of such a good land; but,

Obs. 1. It is a great judgment of God to drive men out of a land for sin. Truly, sometimes, when you travel abroad where there are fair prospects, you cannot but meditate thus: Oh how vile would be our sins, if they should provoke God to cast us out of such a good land as this is! And most of the titles, though not all, given to the land of Canaan, may be applied to our land; and certainly, if God should proceed in his wrath to cast us out, it would be a heavy judgment to consider of, "They laid the pleasant land desolate." Howsoever wicked men may cry out of God's servants, that they are the cause of the trouble of the land, yet certainly it is the wicked and ungodly, they that are false in the worship of God, who lay "the pleasant land desolate." Also, we might here observe, that to be cast out of those mercies that God by an extraordinary providence has brought to us, is a sore and a grievous evil.

Obs. 2. The excellency of the state of the church of God. The rest of Canaan was a type of the rest that God has in his church, and all those that are members of the true church of God partake of it. To enjoy God in his ordinances, is to enjoy that which is typified by all this.

O believer, thou hast a good land, there is an abundance of excellent privileges belonging to the church of God; and as it is a judgment to be cast out of such a land as this was, so it implies what a great judgment it is to be cast out from the church of God, or for God to deny to give to us the blessing of his church. You know what a great affliction it was to Moses, to think that he should not come into that good land; and how earnestly did he pray to God to be admitted into Canaan! Certainly it is that which we should pray for, that we might live to come into that Canaan into which God is bringing his people: now let us not murmur as they did in the wilderness, "and were destroyed of the destroyer," 1 Cor. x. 10; but let us go on, and be as Caleb and Joshua, of another spirit, and not fear our adversaries, but go on in God's way, and the Lord will bring us into the good land. True, we have deserved to be cut off in the wilderness; but certainly God has a Canaan yet to come for his people, the Lord has great things to do for his church; and there are many expressions upon which some think that God even will make use of this Canaan yet, to be the place of the manifestation of his chief majesty and glory in this world: but, however that be, yet the Lord has a sure Canaan for his people.

"But Ephraim shall return to Egypt, and they shall eat unclean things in Assyria." The returning to Egypt we have had before. But besides that, they shall be brought to such poverty and misery as to eat unclean, polluted bread, whereas before they had abundance. Peter would eat nothing that was unclean till God warned him; but the Assyrians would bring them unclean meat and bid them eat. They would say, We cannot, this is against our religion, and against our consciences. Your consciences! what do we care for them? eat it or starve: so they were forced to eat.

Obs. 3. It is a great misery to be brought under those who have no regard to the consciences of men.

But that which is especially aimed at here is, God would take away all notes of distinction between them and the heathen. This prohibition of meats was a means to keep them from mixing with the heathen, but now saith God, All is gone, let them go and eat unclean things; as for the covenant with me, it is wholly abolished, I will own them no more than the very impure heathen: they would make leagues with the Assyrians; well, they shall partake with them, and be filthy and unclean as they. As they defiled God's worship by mixing heathenish pollutions with it, now God gives them up to all heathenish uncleanness; as they were like the heathens in inward impurity, so let them be, saith God, in outward abominations.

Obs. 4. It is just with God, that those who will make leagues with wicked men, should eventually be enthralled in their abominations. They were indeed at a distance from them before, but when once the peace is made, they come now to be all one with them.

Obs. 5. When men are inwardly unclean, God cares not for their outward cleanness. Thus many professors of religion defiling their consciences, and becoming like the wicked in inward sins, God at length gives them up to themselves, that there should be no difference between them and the wicked in their outward abominations. Have you not known some examples of this?

Obs. 6. It is a fearful sin for the saints to join with the ungodly in impure worship. There might be as much excuse for eating things unclean as one could imagine; Why, Lord, they might say, shall we starve? True, they might doubtless eat that which was unclean rather than starve, but yet their misery was great misery, that they could have nothing to eat but that which was unclean: but now this is not only an affliction, but sin, and indeed the moral of it is to show the great evil that there is in joining with any mode of false worship; to unite in false worship is a great evil, and an argument that God is about to disclaim us. Cyprian from this place dehorts Christians from communicating with wicked ministers, *Ne sibi plebs in hoc blandiatur*, &c. But I do not speak of not joining in worship if there be unclean ones there, ministers or people; and I am persuaded, if it be thoroughly weighed, no one will be found to be of that opinion; for it is impossible but in time some that are ungodly will creep unawares into every church: but this is not that which causes many to forbear communion, but some things being actually done that their consciences tell them to be sin. But if these matters of offence be removed, and the worship kept pure, and liberty given to every one to deliver their own souls by faithfully rebuking and admonishing, and a power exist in exercise in the church to cast out the unclean, no doubt, though some be admitted, men may communicate.

Ver. 4. *They shall not offer wine offerings to the Lord, neither shall they be pleasing unto him: their sacrifices shall be unto them as the bread of mourners;*

all that eat thereof shall be polluted: for their bread for their soul shall not come into the house of the Lord.

The prophet, in the name of God, proceeds to denounce further threatenings on Israel, and this in the 4th verse is a very dreadful one.

"They shall not offer wine-offerings to the Lord." In their offerings there was wont to be wine and oil, to note cheerfulness in God's service: thus in Numb. xv. 5, 6, "The fourth part of an hin of wine for a drink-offering shalt thou prepare," and "thou shalt prepare for a meat-offering two tenth deals of flour mingled with the third part of an hin of oil." But now all joy shall be taken away, there shall be nothing but sadness and sinking of spirit under their misery, no wine-offering. Hence,

Obs. 1. It is just with God to take joy from those who abuse it to their lusts.

Obs. 2. This makes an affliction grievous indeed, when the joy in God's service is gone. "They shall not offer wine-offerings;" all their joy and comfort in the service of God shall be gone; they shall not only have sorrow in their outward afflictions, but every time they engage in any service of God, their hearts shall be dejected. There was a time when some of you were wont to offer "wine-offerings to the Lord," that is, to have much joy and comfort in the service of God; but is it not all gone? where are your "wine-offerings to the Lord?" You can now go through duties, but your hearts are heavy and dull in the performance of them; there is no sweetness, no enlargement of spirit, all the worship of God is now a burden unto you. Surely, no affliction is so great as God's duties becoming burdensome. So long as the saints have a wine-offering for the Lord in holy duties, so long as their spirits in the discharge of them can be free and joyful, their afflictions are not very burdensome, they are well enough: this is more delightful to them than all the wine in the world, for as they can say of God's love, "Thy love is better than wine," so can they say of their love to God, Our love to him is more comfortable to us than any wine of earth. Now, though they be in afflictions, and their estates are gone, so that they have no wine to drink themselves, yet if they have their "wine-offerings" to offer to the Lord, this makes glad the hearts of the saints, more than the hearts of all the men in the world can be gladdened, when their corn, and their wine, and their oil increase.

"Neither shall they be pleasing unto him." Whatsoever their offerings be, they shall not be grateful unto him; God will take no delight in them, they will be but sour things to his palate; whereas the offerings of the saints in his own way, do cheer the very heart of God. "Neither shall they be pleasing unto him;" nothing that is tendered to God from them shall be pleasing to him: No, saith God, now I will have other ways than your offerings in which to glorify myself upon you, I will rather glorify myself by your miseries, they shall be sweet and delightful to me.

"Their sacrifices shall be unto them as the bread of mourners; all that eat thereof shall be polluted."

כלחם אונים The Hebrew may be taken substantively or adjectively, as thus, the bread of mourning, or the bread of mourners; now, by "the bread of mourners," is here meant unclean bread, for so it is interpreted afterwards, It shall be unclean.

But why is the bread of mourners unclean? This text has reference to Numb. xix. 11—14, where you read, that the dead body of a man defiled whatsoever touched it; yea, whatsoever came near it, even all those that came to the place where the dead body was, to mourn with the friends for the dead, became unclean. And it is observable, that the dead body of a beast did not make men so unclean (by legal uncleanness) as did the dead body of a man. The dead body of a beast made one unclean only till the evening, Lev. xi. 27, whereas the dead body of a man made one unclean seven days. And this was to note that there were more remarkable expressions of the anger of God on the sin of man in the dead body of a man, than in the dead body of a beast; one made unclean but "till evening," the other "seven days." But the reason why there was this uncleanness from the dead body, was to note,

1. The uncleanness that there is in sin, in dead works, that those that did meddle with them were polluted; yea, the uncleanness incurred in coming near to sinners, all that was in the tent was polluted.

2. How little pleasing to God funeral rites are, they were made unclean by them; for this "bread of mourners" is the bread that they eat at their funerals. The Gentiles mourned for their dead inordinately; and God would have a difference between his people's mourning for the dead and their mourning, because that he would sustain his people's faith, and the hope of resurrection from the dead; whereas had they had liberty to mourn so excessively as the heathens did, the very faith and hope of resurrection from the dead might in time have been almost extinguished; therefore God would have them take heed of that, and consequently ordained in the ceremonial law, that all the mourners for the dead should be unclean for a certain length of time. As for any that indulge their natural affections without restraint in their mourning for the dead, I would apply to them the words of Jer. xxxi. 15, 16, "Thus saith the Lord; A voice was heard in Ramah, lamentation, and bitter weeping; Rahel weeping for her children refused to be comforted for her children, because they were not." But now, "Thus saith the Lord; Refrain thy voice from weeping, and thine eyes from tears: for thy work shall be rewarded, saith the Lord; and they shall come again from the land of the enemy." Let us not then weep as others, let us not mourn as others that have no hope; remember that the mourners for the dead under the law were to be unclean for seven days.

3. That God would have cheerfulness in his service, and therefore "the bread of mourners" is accounted polluted. So in Lev. x. 19, when Aaron had an occasion for mourning as great almost as any man ever had, (his children, that were so eminent in office, having been destroyed by such a visible hand of God,) and Moses was angry that the priests had "not eaten the sin-offering," Aaron said to him, "If I had eaten the sin-offering to-day, should it have been accepted in the sight of the Lord?" It would have been but as "the bread of mourners." I that have been struck this day, and am in such a dreadful condition, would God have regarded the sin-offering? God required joy in his services, Deut. xii. 7, 18; and hence that profession in Deut. xxvi. 13 was required, "Then thou shalt say before the Lord thy God, I have brought away the hallowed things out of mine house, and also have given them unto the Levite, and unto the stranger, to the fatherless, and to the widow, according to all thy commandments which thou hast commanded me: I have not transgressed thy commandments, neither have I forgotten them." And then, ver. 14, there follows, "I have not eaten thereof in my mourning." They were to profess this to God, that they had not eaten thereof in their mourning; this was to show, that sacrifice offered with a sinking heart, in sorrow, is not pleasing to God; "God loveth a cheerful giver." We must not pine away in our iniquities, sullen dejection of mind, even in sorrow for sin, sours our spirits and services, and makes them unacceptable to God. There is a groaning and a sighing one to another, or rather, against one another, that is condemned in Scripture

in James v. 9: the words in your Bibles are, "Grudge not one against another," but in the original, Μὴ στενάζετε κατ' ἀλλήλων; Sigh not, or groan not, one against another. Many in company are of a dull, pensive spirit, sighing and groaning, and making their society burdensome: saith the Holy Ghost, Do not sigh and groan one to another. There is a sullen dejection of soul that is as unpleasing to God as it is to men, it pollutes the heart, and pollutes duty.

But (you will say) is all mourning forbidden, that here the Holy Ghost should say, "Their sacrifices shall be unto them as the bread of mourners?" Christ saith, "Blessed are they that mourn;" and the sacrifice of God is "a contrite heart."

True, an evangelical sorrow is accepted, but that has sweetness in it; it is not bitter, it is not a mourning that causes dejection or sullenness, or straitness of spirit, but it enlarges the heart and makes it active for God. Hence, in Ezra ix., although we read before that Ezra was astonished at the sin of the people, yet saith he, at ver. 5, "And at the evening sacrifice I arose up from my heaviness;" when the time came that I should sacrifice unto God, my heaviness did not hinder me in the performance of my holy duties. But how many are there that sink down in their heaviness, and when God calls upon them to any duty, they cannot arise, they are so dejected! Shall God accept such service as theirs? You may please yourselves in it, and think it is humiliation, but there may be much pride in dejection; there is no spirit so proud as the devil, and yet no spirit so dejected. Lead, we know, melts soonest, but it consumes in the melting; and many times the spirit may be ready to sorrow and melt upon every occasion, but the melting is such as consumes its strength and unfits it for the service that God calls for; now those services which you in such a mourning way tender up to God, are not accepted of him. Remember this text, "Their sacrifices shall be unto them as the bread of mourners."

Gualter observes on this, God would not accept of the offering of mourners, they were unclean, yet many seek to get their greatest gain from funeral mournings: and he proceeds to inveigh against such; the priests and officers that use to tend upon funerals for gain, he calls vultures and crows, as such flock to dead bodies; and those who support themselves by funerals, sepulchral dogs.

Theophylact also, on these words, "the bread of mourners," observes, That it means the things offered to God gotten by oppression, as thus; Suppose any get an estate by oppression, it may be they are at home and merry, while the poor children or widow is mourning for those morsels that thou art rejoicing in. But the first note most accords with the mind of the Holy Ghost, the mourning that has respect to the funerals, and so especially to the dejection of spirit in holy duties.

"For their bread for their soul shall not come into the house of the Lord." We may understand by the words "their bread for their soul," First, Their oblations generally, not only bread; but their oblations: as Mal. i. 7, "Ye offer polluted bread upon mine altar;" bread is there taken generally for all kinds of offerings upon God's altar. So, "their bread for their soul," that is, those offerings which they offered for the very life of their souls.

Obs. 3. It is a sad thing when God rejects a creature who would seek to him for his very life. These people had rejected the voice of the Lord at the temple, and kept others from going thither; they thought sacrifices elsewhere would serve the turn as well; but now they shall be unable to bring any acceptable sacrifices to the house of the Lord, though they should desire to do it for their very souls. Thus many, who in the time of their prosperity neglect and slight the worship of God, and think it of little moment, afterwards, when they see their very lives, their souls, lie at his mercy, then would they fain seek to God, they see they are undone if God be not merciful to them; yet then God rejects them, their offerings then, "their bread for their soul, shall not come into the house of the Lord," that is, will not be accepted of God. When a man is crying for an alms, to be rejected is something; but when a man is crying for his soul, then to be rejected, and by God himself, this is more grievous.

Secondly, The bread that they have to maintain their lives, for so we find the Scripture calls the soul, the life of a man, in Matt. vi. 25: "Is not the life more than meat?" Οὐχὶ ἡ ψυχὴ πλεῖόν ἐστι τῆς τροφῆς; "Is not the *soul* more than meat?" It is here the bread for the soul, that is, the very bread necessary to maintain their lives; although they should be willing to offer that to the Lord, it shall not come unto him. Now this is as if the prophet should say to them, You cannot now be brought to offer your superfluity to God, but your condition shall be such, that if you would offer the very bread you have to preserve your lives, God will not accept it. As if a man were so poor that he were ready to starve, and yet for all that would say, Well, though I starve, yet I will offer this I have to live on to God, rather than use it myself; now you would think this a proof of a great deal of devotion; but the case shall now be, that though you should seek God with such earnestness, yet the heart of God shall be so hardened against you that your offerings will not be accepted.

Obs. 4. Those who in time of prosperity are loth to deny their ease, or to lay out any thing of their superfluity for God, may yet be willing to pluck out their very eyes, and tear their very flesh, in indignation for their sin, and God not vouchsafe to regard them. Therefore, by this, learn to seek God while he may be found, and not to stand upon your own terms with God in the day of your prosperity, and to say, I cannot spare this and that for him. If we deny God now what is his due, though we would give to him hereafter that on which our lives depend, yet it shall not be accepted.

Thirdly, That they shall have no more bread than will serve for their present exigences. They shall have nothing to bring to the house of the Lord; they shall be so put to it when they are in captivity, and shall be kept so strictly, as to have nothing but bread and water, nothing but supplies for present need, they shall be far enough from having any thing to offer to the Lord, to be accepted of him; if they should think of bringing any thing to the house of the Lord, alas! what have they? nothing but a little bread to sustain life.

Obs. 5. To have no estate to offer to the service of God, in the ways of his public worship, is a great affliction.

Ver. 5. *What will ye do in the solemn day, and in the day of the feast of the Lord?*

There was a time, saith God by the prophet, that you would not suffer any to go up to the feasts; but now you shall be far enough from Jerusalem, or any other place of worship, and the very remembrance of those solemn days, which were days of rejoicing, Numb. x. 10, shall be grievous to you: "What will ye do in the solemn day, and in the day of the feast of the Lord?" Thus some interpret it, they make those feasts to be the feasts in which they should have gone up to Jerusalem; but I take not this to be scope of the Holy Ghost here, but rather thus: by "the solemn day, and feast of the Lord," is meant, the solemn day of God's wrath and vengeance upon them. Now, to confirm this, I shall show, that in Scripture the day of God's wrath is called, first, "The solemn day;" and, secondly, "The day of the feast of the Lord."

First, "The solemn day," is the day of God's wrath. "Thou hast called as in a solemn day my terrors round about, so that in the day of the Lord's anger none escaped nor remained," Lam. ii. 22. "The solemn day" is there "the day of the Lord's anger."

Secondly, The day of God's feast. That time when God doth execute his wrath upon wicked men is the day of a feast to God. Besides other texts, in Rev. xix. 17, 18, it is said, "And I saw an angel standing in the sun; and he cried with a loud voice, saying to all the fowls that fly in the midst of heaven, Come and gather yourselves together unto the supper of the great God; that ye may eat the flesh of kings, and the flesh of captains, and the flesh of mighty men, and the flesh of horses, and of them that sit on them, and the flesh of all men, both free and bond, both small and great." It is a solemn day, a day of the execution of God's wrath, wherein God executes wrath publicly, and brings much wrath together. And yet it is termed "the supper," the feast, "of the great God." "Thou hast called as in a solemn day my terrors round about." You know that in the day of a petty sessions there may be some justice administered, but more privately; but in a day of solemn assize, when there is a full gaol delivery, then judgment is done publicly. So God executes justice sometimes on particular men, but yet has he his solemn day to execute his judgments publicly before all, and then the Lord feasts.

The day of execution of God's wrath upon wicked men is a day of feast, for these reasons:

1. Because their feast days were days of slaying sacrifices; so they should now be slain, and God would account their bodies even as sacrifices slain for this great feast of his. In Isa. xxxiv. 6, "The Lord hath a sacrifice in Bozrah, and a great slaughter in the land of Idumea." And in Zeph. i. 7, 8, "Hold thy peace at the presence of the Lord God: for the day of the Lord is at hand: for the Lord hath prepared a sacrifice, he hath bid his guests. And it shall come to pass in the day of the Lord's sacrifice, that I will punish the princes, and the king's children, and all such as are clothed with strange apparel." "He hath bid his guests." Here is the feast of God, and the slaughter of great men, the dishes as it were of sacrifice that God would have at this his feast; the executioners of God's wrath are now his priests, to kill his sacrifices. Soldiers and executioners are turned the priests of God, to kill his sacrifices for this his feast. Hence, in Jer. vi. 4, "Prepare ye war against her," is in the original, קדשו עליה מלחמה *sanctify* the war against her; and in another scripture, the executioners of God's wrath are called God's "sanctified ones."

2. A day of feasting is a day of rejoicing; this day of the execution of God's wrath upon sinners, especially great sinners that escape men's hands, is a day of rejoicing to God, as in a day of feast. The word חג here translated "feast," signifies also dancing, it is a day wherein the Lord's heart doth, as it were, leap within him because of joy; God rejoices in the execution of his righteous judgments upon them: therefore God's wrath in Scripture is called "wine;" and the wicked are said to wring out and drink the dregs of his cup, Psal. lxxv. 8. When sinners continue impenitent, the Lord is as much delighted in the execution of his justice, as men can be in drinking of wine. So Deut. xxviii. 63, "And it shall come to pass, that as the Lord rejoiced over you to do you good, and to multiply you; so the Lord will rejoice over you to destroy you, and to bring you to nought." And Ezek. v. 13, "Thus shall mine anger be accomplished, and I will cause my fury to rest upon them, and I will be comforted." This is a strangely fearful expression. Let us, then, my brethren, take heed how we rejoice in sin; God may rejoice in the execution of his judgment upon us due to our sin. Men have their days of joy and mirth in sin; and God has his days of rejoicing in the execution of his wrath. Oh how sad is the condition of a creature when the infinitely merciful God shall rejoice in his ruin! Surely then, if God so rejoice in the execution of his wrath upon wicked men, the saints also may rejoice. "The righteous shall rejoice when he seeth the vengeance: he shall wash his feet in the blood of the wicked," Psal. lviii. 10: an allusion to the custom of those countries, where they were wont after their travels to wash their feet with cold water, to refresh them: so the blood of the wicked should be refreshment to the righteous. Now this is not an insulting joy over them, but a rejoicing in the honour that God has, and in the good that results to the church by the execution of his vengeance upon such men. So there follows in ver. 11 of the same Psalm, "So that a man shall say, Verily there is a reward for the righteous: verily he is a God that judgeth in the earth." The saints may look upon wicked men when they see them executed, and pity them as men; but still they may rejoice in this, that they see a spectacle before them verifying such scriptures, "Verily there is a reward for the righteous; verily he is a God that judgeth in the earth." And in Psal. lii. 6, "The righteous also shall see, and fear, and shall laugh at him." Mark, though he may rejoice, yet he must have fear mixed with it, "he shall see," and "fear," and "shall laugh." And note, that scripture is spoken of Doeg, a most desperate enemy to God's people, and one who watched every opportunity to do them mischief, and especially to do mischief to David. He it was who came and stirred up Saul against David, and this 52nd Psalm contains a prophecy of his destruction, yet, saith the Spirit of God, "The righteous also shall see, and fear, and laugh;" though they rejoice, yet must they have fear mixed with their joy. If a man can keep his heart spiritual, sanctifying God's name in the beholding of such an object, as that of men eminent in wickedness being brought to execution, he may lawfully, according to the mind of God, feast his eyes on the sight. Such a day is called "the feast of the Lord;" and the Lord is not wont to feast himself, but he calls his saints to feast with him. In Prov. xi. 10, "When it goeth well with the righteous, the city rejoiceth: and when the wicked perish, there is shouting." And that it should be so, accords with God's mind. And therefore, although Christians especially should be far from proudly insulting, even over such men, yet, when God lays an object before them wherein they see the answer of many prayers, and the fruit of the cries of many thousands that were oppressed, yea, of many thousand conscience-oppressed ones; if, I say, at the stroke of God, they, with hearts lifted up to him, give a shout that ascends to the heavens, this pleases God, and the holy angels; it is music fit for "the day of the feast of the Lord."

"Ye." Yea, but saith the Holy Ghost here by the prophet, "What will ye do?" When God makes this his feast in the execution of such as were eminently wicked, the saints may rejoice and bless his name; he bids them then, as it were, to look and see, Is it not good to wait upon me? The saints may do so and bless God; but, "What will *ye* do in the solemn day, and in the day of the feast of the Lord?" Ye wicked, "what will ye do" in that day? what will become of all your jollity? what will become of all your stoutness and wilfulness, of all your pride, of all your scorning, of all your vain hopes, when this "solemn day" draws nigh, when "the feast of the Lord" comes. In Isa. x. 3, we have a scripture parallel to this, "What will ye do in the day of visitation, and in the desolation which shall come from far? to whom will ye flee for help? and where will ye leave your glory?" You can tell what to do now, you have your lusts and pride to serve, and stand it out stoutly now; but what will you do in the day of visitation, when God's "solemn day," and "the day of the feast of the Lord," shall come. Oh! what can they do but, as the great and mighty men in Rev. vi. 16, 17, call "to the mountains and rocks, Fall on us, and hide us from the face of him that sitteth on the throne, and from the wrath of the Lamb: for the great day of his wrath is come; and who shall be able to stand?" Those who are now the most bold and presumptuous in their sins, when this "day of the Lord" comes, shall be in the most miserable perplexity, not knowing what to do; unwilling to bear that which is upon them, and unable to avoid it, they will not know what course to take. "What will ye do in the solemn day, and in the day of the feast of the Lord?" For then,

1. All your comforts will be gone, all those things with which your hearts closed, and made as gods.

2. Now God himself will fight against you: "Howl ye; for the day of the Lord is at hand; it shall come as a destruction from the Almighty," Isa. xiii. 6. It may be you look only upon the agents employed, and flatter yourselves with hopes of escape: your hopes are vain, it is "a destruction from the Almighty," and therefore what can you do?

3. Conscience in that day will terrify you.

4. You shall not know whither to go for help. To the creature? it cannot help you; your vain hopes in the creature have their very heartstrings broken; you thought that you might obtain aid there, but now you see they cannot help.

5. Then the very thoughts of God must needs be terrible to you; and then what will you do?

6. These miseries are but the beginning of sorrows, this "day of the Lord" is but a preparation for another still more solemn. Oh! what will ye do in the day of the Lord? My brethren, though you can discern no blenching in their countenances, yet did you but see the black bosom, and the woeful guilty spirit by sin within, you would know that the soul could not tell what in the world to do in the day of the Lord. It is strange what a man may do even before death, in the presence of men, although his own conscience testifies against him; and though men are ready to be taken with dying men's expressions, yet there is often much deceit in them.

But you will say, What a man professes when he is ready to die, certainly must needs be a truth.

Bishop Latimer has a remarkable story concerning this in one of his sermons. As he was riding he came where an execution was about to take place; when the people saw him they made way, and he went up to speak with the man; but neither he, nor any that were about him, could get him to give glory to God by confessing the crime for which he was to be executed: he persisted that he was not guilty. At length they turned the ladder, and when they thought life extinct, they cut the rope and took him down; but after a little, they saw some motion, and by rubbing and chafing him restored animation, so that he was able to speak, and then he confessed all; that he was guilty of those very things, which, when about to die, he had strenuously denied. Thus it is possible for men in the stoutness of their hearts, even at the last, rather to venture their souls than confess their guilt; and well may they who have ventured their souls so much before upon other things, think that they may make bold with God even at such a time.

But, however, in this "day of the Lord," this day of public calamity, there will be much dejection of spirit in the wicked, they will not know what to do; but the servants of God, who have walked conscientiously before him, will know what to do in such a day. For,

1. They can bless God that ever they knew him, that ever they knew his ways, that ever he put it into their hearts to fear his name.

2. They can exercise their faith upon that word in which the Lord has caused them to trust, they can make it to be the support of their souls and the joy of their hearts, even in such a day.

3. They can sanctify God's name in his righteous judgments, they can see mercy and the love of a Father in the sorest and heaviest afflictions that befall them.

4. They can ease their souls by pouring them forth into the bosom of a gracious and reconciled Father.

5. They can see beyond all these present evils immortality and glory; they can see on the other side, a little beyond these troubles and afflictions, an everlasting joy and day of peace in store for them. A Job can tell what to do, he can profess that though God slay him, yet will he trust in him, Job xiii. 15; xix. 25. A David can tell what to do; "I remembered thy judgments of old, O Lord; and have comforted myself," Psal. cxix. 52. An Habakkuk can tell what to do; "Although the fig tree shall not blossom, neither shall fruit be in the vines; the labour of the olive shall fail, and the fields shall yield no meat; the flock shall be cut off from the fold, and there shall be no herd in the stalls: yet I will rejoice in the Lord, I will joy in the God of my salvation," Hab. iii. 17, 18. Thus you see the saints know what to do in such a day; and this is the excellency of grace, that it can never be put so to it in any strait, but it can tell what to do: as David said to Achish, in 1 Sam. xxviii. 2, "Surely thou shalt know what thy servant can do;" so the saints, in times of public calamity, should set their graces so on work that all may see what their faith, and humility, and patience, can effect; their actions should say, Surely you shall see now what the servant of the Lord can do. If one should say to any who have made profession of godliness, You spake much of the excellency of grace, but what can you do with it? The answer that such a one may well give is this, When you are utterly at a loss what to do, or which way to turn yourselves, yet, through God's mercy, my way is clear. Grace is able to carry a man through fire and water; this faith of mine, and the grace that I have gotten by the word at which you can scorn, do, through God's mercy, enable my soul to rejoice, yea, to triumph, in tribulations. Can you do that? You can rejoice now when you are in a tavern; but in the day of tribulation, when a dismal day shall come to the world, what will you do? I thank God, I have that which can rejoice my heart even in such a day; and the inwrought operation of the word, and prayer, and the ordinances, can enable me to do that which you cannot do; and surely it is something when a man, in times of tribulation, can so carry himself above all, that men or devils are unable to confound him.

Ver. 6. *For, lo, they are gone because of destruction: Egypt shall gather them up, Memphis shall bury them: the pleasant places for their silver, nettles shall possess them: thorns shall be in their tabernacles.*

But do you say to us, What will we do in such a day? Why, we know well enough what to do, we have a way to help us; if all your threatenings should befall us, yet we can have help. It is not likely that all this misery and desolation which you prophesy of will come suddenly; then surely we know what to do, we will go to Egypt, which is not far off; and if we cannot live here in our own country, we will go to Memphis, which is a brave city, and there we may live well enough. Many of us are merchants, and Memphis is as great a place for merchandise as where we live, and we will go thither.

Obs. 1. Carnal hearts have always some devices to provide for themselves. Indeed it is this that takes off the hearts of men from humbling themselves before the Lord, and making their peace with him; they think they may in some manner escape God's strokes, therefore they do not fall down with trembling hearts before the Lord, and cry unto him, "Lord, what wilt thou have us to do?" Were it not for this vain conceit, what humiliation would there be before the Lord, what submission to him, what seeking of him! "Thou art wearied in the greatness of thy way; yet saidst thou not, There is no hope: thou hast found the life of thine hand; therefore thou wast not grieved," Isa. lvii. 10. Thou thoughtest thou couldst tell what to do, therefore thou wert not grieved. When God intends mercy to men, he takes them off from their vain hopes, and from all their carnal reasonings. When the hearts of men are brought to this, to cry, "Men and brethren, what shall we do?" and as Jehoshaphat, "We know not what to do; but our eyes are up unto thee;" I say, when men's hearts, taken off from all their shifts, come to this, As for any thing in ourselves, we know not what to do, but only our eyes are up unto thee; then is mercy at hand, and never till then. And therefore all the time that you are reasoning in your own imaginations, you are far from mercy.

"For, lo, they are gone because of destruction: Egypt shall gather them up, Memphis shall bury them." The prophet here speaks as if the thing were done already. Although they were in Samaria, and in the cities of Israel, yet, saith the prophet, "Lo, they are gone." The wrath of God was too hot for them in their own country, and away they are gone, and betaken themselves to Egypt for refuge. Hence,

Obs. 2. Carnal hearts will rather make any thing their refuge in difficulties, than God. My brethren, just these, for all the world, have been, I fear, and it may be yet are, the thoughts of many among us. Ministers of God, say they, denounce judgments, affirming that God has a controversy against us, and we already see some tokens of God's wrath upon us. Well, let the worst come that can, we hope to shift some way or other; we may escape to Holland, or Germany, or France, or New England, and there make shift to live. And these back doors that their eyes are upon, have made them less solicitous about, and less helpful in, the great things that God calls aloud on all to unite in with all their strength, that they may deliver their own land from the heavy wrath that hangs over it. Well, notwithstanding men's thoughts are bent on various expedients, all will prove vain. You think, saith God, to flee some where; you will be disappointed, for "Egypt shall gather you," and "Memphis shall bury you;" my wrath and sore displeasure shall so pursue you. It is a vain thing for men to seek to flee from the presence of God. But certainly, in some cases a man may flee from danger; as when they see that their work is done in one place, and God in his providence opens them a door to another: but if, out of distrust and slavish fear, when God calls for further work in a place, and there is no other door opened by providence, they attempt to break a way for themselves, to make provision for the flesh, they may expect wrath to pursue them wheresoever they go, their safest places may prove to be their graves; "Egypt shall gather them up," as they gather dead bodies; "Memphis shall bury them." Memphis was a principal city in Egypt, now well known to your merchants and mariners by the name of Grand Cairo. It was then called Memphis, as some think, from the name of one of the king of Egypt's daughters. It was very famous for the pyramids and sepulchres of the kings, and stood very commodious for traffic, being situated on the river Nile. It contained a multitude of streets; I am loth to name the number, for indeed it appears incredible; only this is remarkable, that generally all the streets had at each end of them two gates, so that they might be locked up as separate towers, and the inhabitants immured from all communication with the rest of the city. The Holy Ghost may allude to that in saying "Memphis shall bury you." Now, say they, We will go to Memphis, a brave place for traffic, and a very commodious city, a safe city, that has all the streets shut up like so many towers; we will go and find safety there. Yea, but "Memphis shall bury you," saith God.

Obs. 3. It is a great affliction to be forced to leave one's own country, and die in a strange land. The Lord has sent many of his servants into other countries to live among strangers; some there are that have gone of their own accord, yet, through God's mercy, they have not so gone but God has given them liberty to return again; and though their going has been (as you know) much aspersed of late, yet, when more weighty work permits, I make no question but you will be so fully satisfied as to acknowledge a special hand of God even in their going. But the Jews especially accounted it a great misery to die out of their own land. Buxtorf, in his book called The Jewish Synagogue, relates a tradition of the Jews to this effect: they believe that the resurrection of the Jews at the great day shall be at Jerusalem, that wheresoever any of the Jews have died, yet they shall arise at Jerusalem; therefore many of them who lived a great way off, when they began to grow old, would leave their stations, and go as near to Jerusalem as they could: for their tradition adds, that the bodies of those who are interred at a distance shall come through passages of the earth all along to Jerusalem, and that they may prevent the trouble of coming so far under the ground, therefore in old age they go to dwell near Jerusalem. This is the vanity of spirit to which they are left. But though that be a vanity, yet certainly it is an affliction to any to live and die out of their own country: but if it be a great evil to flee from one's own country for fear of destruction, and to have the place they flee to made as their grave, what a far greater evil is it for men, merely out of love of gain, to leave places where before they did, or might, enjoy communion with the saints; to leave the ordinances of God to go to dwell among papists, or heathens, where they cannot have the freedom of God's worship! Now it is just with God, that such as these are should find those places to be labyrinths of miserable perplexity to them, seeing they, out of love to gain, thus venture themselves. Therefore let men take heed how they go, for any private ends, from places where God's worship may be had, to places where they cannot enjoy it.

"The pleasant places for their silver, nettles shall possess them: thorns shall be in their tabernacles." The words מחמד לכספם translated "the pleasant places for their silver," mean also the desire of their silver. This may refer,

1. To their furniture of silver, that nettles shall grow where are now their "pleasant places for their silver" and household stuff, that they took so much delight in; as in Lam. i. 7, "Jerusalem remembered in the days of her affliction and of her miseries all her pleasant things that she had in the days of old." Mark but these two things from this text, "Jerusalem in the days of her affliction and of her miseries." My brethren, there may be days of affliction, and yet no days of misery; the saints may meet with days of affliction, but yet they may not be days of misery. But when the wicked meet with days of affliction, they meet likewise with days of misery. But the thing for which especially I quote this text is this, Jerusalem then, "in the days of her affliction and of her miseries, remem-

bered all her pleasant things that she had in the days of old." So here it is threatened that nettles shall grow in "the pleasant places for their silver;" then shall they too remember the delights they had there, when all shall be so utterly destroyed.

2. The places where they hid their silver. As you know in times of war men will hide their silver, hoping they may return for it again. But, saith God, you shall go far off from it. I make no question but another generation may find treasures of silver in those countries in the midst of "nettles" and "thorns."

3. To their delightful houses adorned with silver, that were so glorious in their eyes. All now is gone, saith God, and nettles and thorns shall grow up and shall *inherit* them; so the word יירשם translated "shall possess them" means. You hope to leave these brave houses to your children to inherit; but now, saith God, I have other heirs for your houses, thorns and nettles shall inherit them. It is a lamentable spectacle to see places, where fair buildings have been, overgrown with nettles and thorns; as probably will happen if these wars in divers places of this kingdom continue. Of Troy it has been said, Corn grows where Troy stood: it was made a ploughed field. But to have nettles grow is worse; for where the plough goes there are inhabitants, but nettles and thorns speak of desolation. Travellers tell us, that in many places of Germany there are nothing now but bushes and nettles where splendid buildings once stood. The Lord deliver us from such a heavy stroke! It is threatened also in Isa. xxxii. 13, "Upon the land of my people shall come up thorns and briers; yea, upon all the houses of joy in the joyous city." Would it not be a sad spectacle to see, in such a city as this, the buildings overthrown, and nettles and thorns growing rank in our fairest streets? Yet sin is thus ruinous. And then in Isa. xxxiv. 13, "Thorns shall come up in her palaces, nettles and brambles in the fortresses thereof: and it shall be an habitation of dragons, and a court for owls;" the owls shall keep court there. In our courts we know what abundance of sin there was; now the owls shall keep court there instead of those who lived so delicately in them. Sin, my brethren, is a leprosy that infects the very doors of our houses. There is a notable passage in 2 Kings xxv. 9, where it is said of Nebuchadnezzar, that "he burnt the house of the Lord, and the king's house, and all the houses of Jerusalem, and every great man's house burnt he with fire." There is a great deal of sin usually committed in great men's houses; and at this day how have the great men of the land, almost in all places, showed a spirit of malignity against the work of reformation! Oh how just with God is it that their houses should suffer! as is here threatened in my text. Many of them have been spoiled already, and if God give them not hearts speedily to see the evil of their ways, it is very probable that within a few years this text of mine shall be fulfilled upon them all.

Seges est, ubi Troja fuit.

It may be Israel thought, though the war did keep them from their houses for a while, nay, though they should be broken down, yet their lands would remain, they could not be alienated. Nay, saith God, flatter not yourselves with thinking to return again to them, for you never shall, for nettles and thorns shall possess them.

Ver. 7. *The days of visitation are come, the days of recompence are come; Israel shall know it: the prophet is a fool, the spiritual man is mad, for the multitude of thine iniquity, and the great hatred.*

"The days of visitation are come, the days of recompence."

Obs. 1. God has his set time for the execution of his judgments. "The days of visitation." What good is it to a malefactor that he is let alone a while in the prison, when he knows that such a day of the month must be the day of his execution?

Obs. 2. Our judgments are none other but recompences. "The days of recompence." You may have vain pleas and reasons to justify yourselves; but when God comes to visit you, he will deal with you in a way of recompence proportionable to your deeds. If you would fall down and acknowledge your sins and your need of mercy, then it may be you may find mercy; but if you will stand to justify yourselves, then expect that God, when he comes, will come in a way of recompence.

And now, my brethren, what a desperate venture is this, that men will venture to deal with God in a way of recompence, whereas you may be dealt with in a way of mercy!

You will say, Who are those whom God will deal with in a way of recompence?

Certainly those who will attempt to justify themselves, and say, God knows I do what I can, and this is not so much my fault as others'. Let them expect that God, when he comes to deal with you, will have your pleas fully examined; and if it prove that your pleas will hold, you shall have accordingly; and if your pleas shall be found false, then you shall be dealt withal in a way of justice. Will you venture? dare any of you venture to stand it out on your pleas? If you say you do what you can, you will be tried by it, and you shall be recompensed accordingly; and if it be found indeed that you do what you can, you shall be saved; but if it be found you have not done what you could, you shall perish eternally. Will you venture? Certainly, whatsoever you stand pleading to justify yourselves by, you may expect that God will deal with you accordingly.

"Are come." Twice "are come;" as it is said, "Babylon is fallen, is fallen." Israel was about to be recompensed for her transgressions, and would therefore hardly be moved with any apprehension of danger, accordingly you have the "come" twice repeated.

Obs. 3. The apprehension of present evil terrifies the soul. You have a remarkable text for this in Ezek. vii. 6, "An end is come, the end is come;" and then the next words, "it watcheth for thee; behold, it is come." In one little verse three times, "An end is come, the end is come; behold, it is come." And in the verse before, it "is come," and in the verse after, it "is come;" five times God tells them that it "is come." Then saith my text,

"Israel shall know it." Here our observations are,

Obs. 4. Wicked men will not know till they feel; when they are struck, then they will know. The best knowledge of God's displeasure comes from the causes, but if men will not know from thence, they shall know from the effects. In their prosperity they had many false prophets who soothed them with flatteries, so that they were kept from knowledge; but now when they had felt God's stroke, then they should know: but he does not tell you what they should know. They should know these things:

1. What a great God they had to deal with.
2. How vile a thing sin is.
3. The vanity of all their shiftings.
4. The dreadfulness of Divine wrath.
5. The faithfulness of God's prophets.
6. The wisdom of those who dared not do as they did.
7. The folly and vanity of all the false prophets that did before seduce them; they should know that "the prophet is a fool, the spiritual man is mad." The knowledge we gain of these things in the season of

affliction, is knowledge of a different kind to that which we have in the hour of our prosperity. A German divine in an affliction said, In this disease I know what sin is, and how great is God. And yet he was a divine, why did he not know before? No, truly, he never before so knew what sin and God were.

Obs. 5. The knowledge men gain of God in the time of affliction, is a working knowledge. "Israel shall know it." I appeal to yourselves; how many of you, in the time of your sickness and afflictions, have known things after another manner than ever you knew them before?

"The prophet is a fool, the spiritual man is mad."

Obs. 6. In the time of affliction men cry out, that those who seduced them are fools. One who died not long since, near the Exchange, lamented bitterly his having kept company with lewd ministers, who encouraged him in his ways, and hardened him against religion and the saints of God.

We know how men have closed with wicked ministers, and how they have hardened themselves in scorning at religion and puritans, and yet have had cause on their death-beds to cry out against those who deceived them, telling them that they need not be so strict and so pure: take heed now how you be deceived by accounted-spiritual men. In that text of Isaiah they found by experience, that the prophet was but "a fool," and that those who had such glorious spiritual titles were but "mad;" and if you take not heed, some of you hereafter may have abundant reason on your death-beds to cry out against certain ministers amongst us, who persuade you after the same example.

Obs. 7. It is no excuse for men to be led aside by their ministers. The reason that they were given up to such prophets follows:

"For the multitude of thine iniquity, and the great hatred." Thou hadst a wicked and vile heart, which hated God's people and the ways of godliness, and therefore it was just with God to give thee up to those whom now thou seest to be fools and mad. O, it is just with God, when men's spirits are against his true prophets, to leave them to ministers that undo their souls everlastingly! But if you understand this of the true prophets, the sense will run thus: You shall know in the time of your visitation, whether they were madmen and fools or no: it was from the multitude of your iniquities, and great hatred against the ways and people of God, that you accounted them so; you made many exceptions against them, but the truth is, you saw nothing; but the malignity of your hearts lay at the bottom, you accounted them fools and madmen because of the multitude of your iniquities. Men who are not so able to judge of matters sometimes controverted, yet may have this rule to help them to judge of ministers and their cause:

What is the side men incline most to, as they grow most in godliness? and what side do men incline most to, as they grow more loose and formal in their ways?

If there be parties, and you are not able to judge which is in the truth, some good men being on one side, and some on the other, take, I say, this rule as a help: What is the side men most incline to, as they grow in godliness? and what side is that which men most cleave to, as they grow most loose and most formal? When men whose multitude of iniquities increases, and according to their increase so they incline to a party, I cannot but suspect its goodness; more especially if, besides, I see that the more conscientious men are, and the more the fear of God prevails in them, and the more strict they grow in their ways, they do the more incline to the other side; I cannot but think that there may be much of God there. And yet it is true, it must be granted, that the greatest heretics that ever were have pretended great holiness. But still, if this opinion were not of God, those that did indeed grow up in true holiness, the more holy they were, the less would they savour that way, though it had never such a pretence of holiness. And if it be but a pretence of holiness, and not true, then certainly the more loose and formal professors grow, the more will they close with that way (if it be but a pretence). So it is here, their hearts were taken off from the true prophets of God, through the multitude of their iniquities; the more loose they became, the more were their hearts taken off from the true prophets of God.

Ver. 8. *The watchman of Ephraim was with my God: but the prophet is a snare of a fowler in all his ways, and hatred in the house of his God.*

In the former verse God charged, as the cause of much evil in Israel, the false prophets, but yet through the people's sin; for it was through the multitude of their wickedness that they were so guided by those false prophets, whom they followed in the time of their prosperity: but he would have a time wherein they should know their "prophets" were but "fools," and "the spiritual man" but "mad." In this 8th verse the same is continued, "The watchman of Ephraim was with my God: but the prophet is a snare of a fowler in all his ways, and hatred in the house of his God."

"The watchman." Those who profess themselves watchmen, take upon themselves glorious titles. Prophets and ministers of God are called "watchmen:" and these made great profession that they would be as careful to foresee, and labour as much to prevent, danger to the people as any others could; they professed to be very useful to the people, and to be full of zeal for God, but they were "a snare;" and this title of theirs, and this their profession, proved to be a snare to the people.

Obs. 1. Many vile things are hidden under fair and glorious titles, as many excellent things are disgraced by base and ignominious ones. You know what a deal of evil was lately covered over amongst us, by names and titles, as the clergy and the church; and likewise what abundance of good was defamed by epithets such as conventicles, puritans, and the like; and now the titles of things may be changed, but yet remain as dangerous as before. Let people ever take heed and examine what lies under them, and let them not be led away, one way or other, either by fair and specious, or by ignominious, titles; ordinarily, people that do not examine things thoroughly are taken with names and titles. But somewhat of these heretofore.

"Of Ephraim." The people of Israel, the ten tribes, had no mind to the true watchmen, because they threatened hard things against them; they were willing to close with those who preached things more pleasing, so that they might set one against another, and obtain quiet; although the truth was, that these watchmen of their choice were a most grievous snare to them.

Thus many who have carnal hearts, and are not able to bear the evincing and threatening power of the word in the mouths of true, faithful watchmen, seek to help themselves by the opinions and judgments of other ministers, concluding they are safe when they have the countenance of some that are learned, especially if also they have a repute for godliness, for so certainly the watchmen here spoken of had; and then they can set the opinions and judgments of one against those of the other; they think they are safe now and may be quiet; yet this proves a dangerous snare.

Obs. 2. When there is clear conviction of a truth, it is a dangerous thing, out of an unwillingness to yield to it, to seek the opinions of others. I confess, when a man out of love to the truth, that he may be confirmed therein, or that he might know fully what the truth is, for him to seek help from others is a good thing; but if out of distaste to a truth, if because the heart is weary of it, and would fain not have it to be true, because it may bring some trouble, if upon that ground he goes to seek the opinions of others, hoping to find them contrary, that so he may have something to quiet his mind; this is a great snare to the souls of those who have been guilty of it.

"Of Ephraim." Ephraim had watchmen as well as Judah. Hence,

Obs. 3. No cause so ill but will have some that have the repute of being wise, learned, and judicious men to maintain it.

"Was with my God." They professed more than ordinary judgment in the knowledge of God's mind, and acquaintance with his ways, and yet they were snares to the people. Whence,

Obs. 4. Every man in his erroneous opinion pretends to be with God, and for God; without this indeed he could never be a snare to those who profess themselves to be the people of God.

Obs. 5. It is a great grief to those who have the true knowledge of God, and interest in him, to see others who maintain that which is evil, yet pretend that they know God, and are zealous for his glory. "With my God." The prophet seems to speak in grief and trouble; These watchmen of Ephraim, those among the ten tribes, they will pretend to be for God, to be for "my God."

Vatablus further observes on this, Ephraim made to himself a watchman, and would hear him together with his God; like madmen, would attend to man as to God, and so would worship idols and God too, they would seem to respect the true as well as the false prophet, which is mere madness.

Obs. 6. They would not wholly depart from God, and yet they would maintain false worship, they would mingle both together. "The watchman of Ephraim was with my God."

"But the prophet is a snare of a fowler in all his ways." That is, he catches poor simple, deluded souls, as a fowler catches the bird, laying baits pleasing to it, and hiding the snare that presently comes upon it: so, saith he, the watchmen of Ephraim do. They come to the people with very fair and specious pretences, which they labour to instil into them, and do not discover what inferences they intend afterwards to make, or what their designs are; for the present they come to them, and desire them to yield to things that seem to be as fair as any thing in the world, and with much pretence that it is only for their own advantage, and that they intend them nothing but good: now, when they have brought them to yield to such things, they know that some inferences may be drawn from them, that will make them to yield to other things, which, had they been presented to them at first, they would never have agreed to; but the inferences lay hidden as the snare does, and they, not foreseeing the consequences, are brought to yield to such things, that afterward they cannot tell how in the world to avoid further compliance. Thus "the prophet is a snare of a fowler," who lays things which seem at first very plausible, intending however afterwards to bring the people to yield to other things, that would be abhorred if presented to them at the first.

My brethren, as long as you live take heed of such snares of watchmen. God would not have you submit to any thing, nor do any thing, but out of faith.

Obs. 7. You must have ground from Scripture, and especially in the matters of God's worship, before you yield or submit to any thing; for otherwise, though things may seem to be very fair at first, yet they may prove to be but snares before you are aware.

"And hatred in the house of his God." Some understand this of the false prophets, thus:

1. The watchman was an object of God's hatred, in God's house. Wicked officers in the church, bringing in their superstitions, and importuning and urging the delusions of their own hearts, seeking to comply with the times to preserve themselves in credit and esteem, and in the enjoyment of their livings, these are an object of God's hatred; there are none whom God hates more than such kind of watchmen in his house. And at this day we see how God has cast shame and rebuke into the faces of such. They are hatred by way of exclamation: *ô rem odiosam et abominandam domo Dei!* Oh hideous and abominable thing, that such watchmen should be pertaining to the sanctuary!

2. Watchmen are hatred, by way of efficiency; that is, they cause hatred, they cause my people to hate the true prophets, and the servants of God that would worship God in his own way. And, indeed, no men in the world are such causes of the hatred of the faithful ministers and saints of God, as wicked watchmen. Who were the men that stirred up hatred and persecution against the saints and people of God in former times, but evil and wicked ministers?

"And hatred in the house of his God."

I find some who understand this, and not without some probability, of the true prophets, and then the sense would be:

1. You accounted the prophets of the Lord, who declared the mind of the Lord faithfully to you, to be no other than fools and madmen; but you shall know that they were no fools, that they were no madmen. So I find in 2 Kings ix. 11, "Wherefore came this mad fellow to thee?" saith the captain of Jehu; and in 2 Chron. xxxvi. 16, "They mocked the messengers of God." So Ezekiel's friends and acquaintance are thought to have bound him, as thinking him mad, chap. iii. 25. And so we read in the Gospel of Christ's kinsfolk, that they laid hands upon him; and Paul, in 2 Cor. v. 13, saith, "Whether we be beside ourselves, it is to God." The true prophets were scorned and contemned as spiritual madmen; but, saith the Lord, They shall know in the time of their visitation whether they were so or no: you shall find by your woeful experience, that these were no such madmen as you thought them to be. In affliction men have more honourable esteem of the true prophets of God than at other times; those that were jeered at before, as so wise, so precise and holy, and of such tender consciences, are often, when the hand of God is upon men, sent for by their very mockers, in preference to any other men, to pray for them. So we read of the people of Antioch, though many of them voted for the banishment of Chrysostom, yet, being terrified by an earthquake, they immediately sent for him again.

Theodoret. lib. 5. cap. 34.

2. Still, take it as concerning the true prophets, and it means, even Ephraim wanted not watchmen to show them their danger in departing from God; though the ten tribes did decline from God, yet such was God's goodness to them, that they had watchmen that were faithful even among them.

"Was with my God." That is, they had watchmen who acted as having to deal with God and not with men, as sent from God, as pleading for God; and hence they could not be taken off from their object, either by threats or flattery: they might have had preferment as well as others, and needed not have been the butt of the hatred and malice of men no more than others, if they would have done as others did. No, but they were "with my God," the fear of the great God was upon their spirits, and they dared not do as others did; they resolved to approve themselves faithful to God; come of it what would, they went on in their way, they left their means and estates, their liberties, and their lives, all to God; it was for God to provide for them, it was for them to look to it, that they continued faithful to God. And thus the sense runs, If these were true prophets that were among the ten tribes, then it is as an aggravation of Ephraim's sins, that though they had many false prophets, yet they had watchmen who did continue faithful with God.

Obs. 8. The people of God rejoice when they see faithful ministers keep close to God. "Was with my God." When they see them, not set upon their own designs, not temporizing, but making it their bent and aim to magnify God, and to bring men to the knowledge of him, oh! they rejoice in this. So the prophet speaks with a joy, (if it be spoken of the true watchmen,) Oh! blessed be God that, notwithstanding all the defection of the times and consequent corruptions, yet there were watchmen among Ephraim that were faithful with God, men who had no other designs but to set up God, and were willing to deny themselves in any thing, so be it they might bring souls to their Master.

And certainly it greatly rejoices the saints to see ministers of God pure and upright in this respect, to have no designs of their own, but to set up the honour of God among the people. But even these prophets, faithful as they were, yet were accounted no other than "a snare of a fowler," and even "hatred in the house of their God;" they are accused of being politic, subtle men, who have cunning plots and devices to set up their own way, they are as bad as Jesuits: such aspersions as these the devil casts upon them, and gets many good people to drink in these calumnies, and those who otherwise were accounted godly, and of great use in the house of their God, are now become even "hatred in the house of their God;" the devil has so prevailed to bespatter and asperse them with stories and reports, that even though most faithful with their God, yet are they now looked upon as the troublers of the times, as snares to people; yea, as "hatred in the house of their God," and that even by many who otherwise have good affections: by no way does the devil drive on his own designs more efficaciously than by thus making the most painful, faithful, zealous ministers of God become even "hatred in the house of their God," even among good people that are professors of godliness. Thus Jer. xviii. 22, "They have digged a pit to take me, and hid snares for my feet." And Isa. xxix. 21, They "lay a snare for him that reproveth in the gate."

"Hatred in the house of his God."

Understanding this still of the true prophets, the sense proceeds thus: Yet he continues in the house of his God, he makes this his encouragement, that he is in the house of his God, in God's work, though he be hated for it. God's ministers should not be offended though they find the like dealings among the professors of religion now, but should still continue with all faithfulness in the work and employment which God sets them about, and then all aspersions will wipe off in time, they will vanish and come to nothing.

Calvin interprets this somewhat differently from what has been said, in a middle way between both, and if not according to the full scope, yet it comes very near; he takes the former part of the verse to relate to the true, the latter part to the false prophets, as if Hosea would speak thus: There was a time that Ephraim had watchmen with my God, and with his people, they had Elisha, and Elijah, but now the prophet is "a snare of a fowler," and "hatred," "in the house of" "my God." This is a woeful change in places where people have had watchmen that were godly, wise, zealous, faithful with God, but now these are gone, many of them banished, and many of them with God in heaven, and they have now others among them, as a just judgment of God, who are a snare to them, and hatred in the house of God; these who have succeeded those blessed servants of God, are like the storms and tempests, which often succeed fair and sunshiny weather. If we understand it thus, for the true prophets in the former part of the verse, and the false prophets in the latter, then there is a special emphasis in the change of the phrase "my God" and "his God," "the watchman with my God, "and "hatred in the house of his God;" the God of the true watchmen and the God of the false prophets are not the same; those who pretend to worship God, and yet worship him in a false way, worship in reality another, and not the same God: no marvel then though there is hatred between true and false prophets; they must needs have hatred one against another who have divers gods. "My God," and "his God," and yet both pretended to be for the same God.

Yea, but, saith the prophet here, whatsoever their pretences are, they teach not people the worship of God in a right way, God is not their God. Who they are that have most interest in God, let God himself judge; not by giving the one more of the favour of the times than the other, for the false prophets had more of this now; but, 1. By the clearer manifestation of the Spirit of God in men. 2. By the witness of men's consciences when they are going to appear before God. And, 3. By what Christ shall own at his appearing. Oh that I could tell how to sweeten these times! God, by providence, has cast me upon this scripture, and I know not how to give you the mind of God regarding it but by being thus plain.

I shall only add one observation made by Arias Montanus on the words, "hatred in the house of his God." He saith the phrase is taken from such men as live in great families, and who have a great deal of power with their lords, (being continually at their tables and bed-side,) and abuse it to cause hatred, and at length to undo others and themselves. So were these prophets in the house of God; they seemed to have much intimacy with God in his house; but the truth is, they abuse this their intimacy to the injury of others, and their own eventual ruin.

Ver. 9. *They have deeply corrupted themselves, as in the days of Gibeah: therefore he will remember their iniquity, he will visit their sins.*

"They have deeply corrupted themselves." העמיקו שחתו Their wickedness has deeply rooted itself, so the word signifies; there is little hope to prevail with them, labour as you may, their superstitious and idolatrous ways have gotten such deep root in their hearts. Sin, and especially that sin of superstition, so deeply roots itself in the hearts of men, if it be let alone but a little time, that there is no getting of it out.

And indeed there is little hope of our ever seeing the reformation now in hand attain its full beauty and perfection, until even God himself, either by some extraordinary manifestation overthrow the prevalent superstitions, or at least by his own hand remove those from amongst us that have such superstitious and idolatrous principles rooted in them. We wonder that men cannot be weaned from such ways. Oh, they are deeply rooted, and it is not an easy matter to eradicate them. It is a blessed thing to take sin betimes; and you that are young, who have not other wickedness, and especially superstition, rooted in you, it is likely God will make use of you to bring this reformation to perfection; it may be, when others are dead and gone, you shall see what God intended in all these stirs that have been among us. By experience we have found superstition is deep rooted indeed, and that the love of it still abides in the heart; that though men be content not to practise the superstitions they did before, because now the times do not favour them, yet they cannot be brought to leave them off as sinful, but as inconvenient.

You have but few men, I had almost said but few ministers, especially of those who were at all forward in superstitions, and did not before account them a burden, who, though they do leave them off at this time, can be brought to acknowledge them to be sinful, and so to charge themselves with sinning against God in them. They are content to relinquish them as things inconvenient, and perhaps burdensome to other men; but the leaving them off thus shows, if the times should favour them again, there is a principle retained in their hearts, so that they would be in readiness to submit to them again, and to practise them as formerly; this bitter root of superstition abides in their hearts: that is the meaning of this phrase, they are deeply rooted, that is, their superstition and false worship are deeply rooted in their hearts. Well, let their superstition be rooted as deep as it will, yet, as Christ saith in Matt. xv. 13, "Every plant which my heavenly Father hath not planted shall be rooted out," God will either root thee out, or the superstition of thy heart out of thee. And seeing the false worshippers have superstition so rooted in their hearts, oh how should the true worshippers of God have the truth rooted in their hearts, never to be eradicated! So St. Paul in Col. ii. 7, "Rooted and built up in him, and stablished in the faith, as ye have been taught, abounding therein with thanksgiving."

"As in the days of Gibeah."

This must cost us a little further time to open fully. Rooted in their evil ways, "as in the days of Gibeah." What has this reference to? The Scripture speaks of the city Gibeah as notable for two things: First, As being the city of Saul, and consequently some apply this thus: that as heretofore they cast off my government when they chose Saul to be king over them, so now they reject me again.

Secondly, As the scene of the circumstances narrated in the 19th and 20th chapters of Judges. You find there the story of a Levite, whose concubine went from him and played the harlot. He went to fetch her again, and as he was returning home would not be persuaded by his servant to go to Jebus, because its inhabitants were "not of the children of Israel," but he would "pass over to Gibeah" of Benjamin, there expecting certain protection; yet he found it quite otherwise, the people of that city were abominably wicked, and they came in the night, and "beset the house round about, and beat at the door," and desired the person who had received him into his house to bring him forth, that they might "know him;" but they obtaining him not, get his concubine, and "abuse her all the night until the morning," when she is found dead at the door of the house. Upon which horrid thing, being committed in a city belonging to the people of God, this Levite takes a knife and cuts his concubine (being dead) "into twelve pieces, and sent her into all the coast of Israel," and bade them think upon it, and consider what should be done. "And it was so, that all that saw it said, There was no such deed done, nor seen, from the day that the children of Israel came up out of the land of Egypt." Wherefore all the people, "from Dan even to Beersheba," assembled to consult what should be done, and they resolve to go against the city of Gibeah. In the 11th verse of the 20th chapter the text saith, "All the men of Israel were gathered against the city, knit together as one man;" and in the 13th verse they require the delinquents to be delivered up to them. "But the children of Benjamin would not hearken to the voice of their brethren the children of Israel;" but gathered themselves together, even "twenty and six thousand men that drew sword," to side with "the inhabitants of Gibeah, which were numbered seven hundred chosen men." Who would have thought that among the people of God there could have been raised an army to defend such "children of Belial?" But the people of Israel were resolved such notorious wickedness should not go unpunished; and they "arose, and asked counsel of God, and said, Which of us shall go up first to the battle against the children of Benjamin?" And the Lord directs Judah to go up first; but the Benjamites the first day got the victory, and slew two and twenty thousand men. Upon that the children of Israel went up to God again, and wept before the Lord, and God gave them leave to go again, and they went, and the Benjamites came out again and slew eighteen thousand more. These wicked malignants got the victory two days, and slew forty thousand of the children of Israel, that went not only by God's leave, but by his desire; for two days together they fell before those wicked and vile wretches, but they knew that their cause could not but be good, and they were resolved they would go to God again, and humble their souls before him, and fast, and pray; and then they overthrew those wicked Benjamites, and men of Gibeah. And whereas twenty-six thousand came out against Israel, twenty and five thousand and an hundred men were slain by the sword, and the city of Gibeah burnt with fire: so God executed wrath upon them at length. This is the story to which the prophet refers, and many things might be observed from it in reference to the purposes for which the prophet quotes it: in his time they stood out to defend wicked ones, as the children of Benjamin had done. And it concerns us fully now, our wars are undertaken on almost the very same grounds; for what is the main cause of them but to fetch delinquents to the execution of justice? And who would have thought that delinquents, under whose burdens we groaned in former times, and whom we accounted the great scourge of the nation, should find an army to defend them? Perhaps sometimes we may be overcome by them, and they may for a while prevail; but let us fast before God, and humble ourselves more thoroughly, and certainly God will also in our times own his own cause.

Obs. 1. When men to whom we seek for protection deal falsely with us, their wickedness is great in the eyes of God. This Levite passed over from Jebus to Gibeah, thinking to have had protection there, and yet these deal vilely towards him. Does any man put himself under any of you for protection, and do you abuse the confidence reposed in you? This surely is an abominable thing in the eyes of God.

Obs. 2. We may meet with worse usage from those who profess religion, than from those who profess it not. It may be, if they had gone to Jebus they would not have met with such ill usage as they did at Gibeah. Sometimes they who make profession of religion are guilty of more ill usage to the servants of God than others that are profane and ungodly, yea, or of another religion. Oh! let men take heed how they behave themselves toward their brethren, that they may not have cause to say, Lord, were we among the Indians, or among some moderate papists, or under some of the prelates again, we should not find such hard usage as we do from some of our brethren who profess thy name and seek reformation: it were, indeed, a sad thing (I say) if ever there should be cause for the servants of God to make such moans to Heaven, and send up such cries to God.

Obs. 3. God may regard those as unholy and unclean who make a fair show of religion. Whereas Israel thought themselves holy and devout for God in the multitude of the sacrifices and devout services which they performed, yet God looks upon them as filthy and wicked, even as the Sodomites of Gibeah. "They have deeply corrupted themselves," saith God, "as in the days of Gibeah:" notwithstanding your fair shows and your sacrifices, yet you are looked upon as thus vile and abominable before God. God will not be put off with words of reformation and outward service, for men may have such base ends in it, and may mix so much of themselves to corrupt the right way of God and to keep out his right service, under pretext of serving him more truly, that this may make them and their performances most odious to God. Such is the clear and plain note from thence. We do not read of such abominable filthiness of body as was in the days of Gibeah, but because of the corruptions of his worship, the Lord considered that they had deeply corrupted themselves, as "in the days of Gibeah."

Obs. 4. For men to stand up impudently and boldly in the defence of wickedness committed is abominable in the eyes of God. Thus they did "in the days of Gibeah." And thus you are ready to do; not only to commit horrible wickedness and sins, but to stand in its defence. There is this desperate stoutness of spirit and hardness of heart in many men, that when they are once entered into the ways of sin, rather than they would yield and submit, they will venture the undoing of themselves: the men of Gibeah did so, and they were undone accordingly.

Obs. 5. To join with others in defence of evil is worse than to stand out ourselves in evil. Yet how many have we of the gentry and nobility of the kingdom, that do not only seek to defend themselves, but join with the greatest malignants amongst us, with those that are the greatest causes of evil, and were like to have been the utter undoing of us all! To defend them from justice they will venture the ruin of their own families; whereas, had the malignants been given up, they might have saved their estates, families, and all. Oh that ever God should leave men in such horrible wickedness as this! This is just as it was "in the days of Gibeah."

Obs. 6. Those who defend wickedness may for a while prosper; even the men of Gibeah and the Benjamites prospered.

Obs. 7. The defenders of wickedness must at last perish. Twenty-five thousand and a hundred of these twenty-six thousand perished, with all the men of Gibeah, and the city was burnt. So, let men stand out as stubbornly and stoutly as they will, and say, What care we? we will lose our lives and estates rather than submit and yield: well, you may lose all at length: you may perhaps prevail for a time; but let not men's hearts be hardened by that, nor let any of the other side be discouraged, for certainly those that stand desperately out in defending wickedness shall perish at last: so did the Gibeonites.

Obs. 8. The sins of the forefathers are an aggravation of the children's sins. Yea, but what is this to us? might the prophet's auditors say. Certainly, it is much to you, for these sins of your forefathers "in the days of Gibeah" aggravate your present sins. And yet, such is the delusion of many poor people, that they excuse the present sins by the sins of former times. As thus; suppose ministers or others should complain of the sinfulness of the times, and declaim against it, you will hear some say, Why do they keep such a stir about the wickedness of the times? were they not as bad heretofore as they are now? Oh wretched delusion! The great aggravation of thy guilt is, that thou livest in the sins of thy forefathers: thou art, it seems, the child of wicked parents, and how just had it been with God to have cut thee off presently for their sins! and dost thou say, that thy wickedness is no other than the wickedness of thy forefathers? Certainly, if the times be as evil as they were heretofore, they are thereby worse, for the evil of our forefathers is an aggravation of our present evils, if we continue in them. As the treachery of a parent would be no excuse for the treachery of a child, no excuse for him to say, My father was a traitor: so for me to excuse the sins of the present times by the sins of former times, and say, they were as bad formerly as now, is reasoning of just a similar kind; but this is not the reasoning of the Spirit of God, he aggravates the sins of Israel in Hosea's time with the sins that were in the days of Gibeah. God may let men alone in their wickedness for a long time, until they grow to the full height of their iniquities, and then he visits them. When the sins of the Amorites were full, then he visited them.

"Therefore he will remember their iniquity, he will visit their sins." This phrase, of God's remembering iniquity and visiting sin, we had before, therefore we pass it over, and proceed to the 10th verse.

Ver. 10. *I found Israel like grapes in the wilderness; I saw your fathers as the firstripe in the fig tree at her first time: but they went to Baal-peor, and separated themselves unto that shame; and their abominations were according as they loved.*

The scope of the Holy Ghost in this, is to upbraid the ten tribes for their wretched, ungrateful dealing with God; their sin is aggravated by God's love towards them and their forefathers.

"I found Israel like grapes in the wilderness; I saw your fathers as the first-ripe in the fig tree at her first time." That is, as when a traveller in the parched wilderness, dry, weary, and faint, comes to a place in which unexpectedly he finds clusters of grapes, from whence he has abundance of cooling refreshment; oh how grateful must this be to such a man! Such delight, saith God, had I in your forefathers. He names grapes and figs here, because they are the most delightful of all kinds of fruit to weary travellers. Now if it be so, that God has such delight in his people in this their wilderness state, how should God be their delight when they are in the wilderness! Oh! let God in his ordinances be to us in our troubles and afflictions, as grapes to the weary traveller, and "as the first-ripe in the fig tree at her first time." Surely, if God will account us so delightful to himself, there is great reason that we should in return delight in him. Some of God's servants have been forced to flee into the wilderness, and though they have not had such outward refreshments as we have had who have sat here under our own vines and fig trees, yet God has made them to find grapes in the wilderness; they have sat under God's protection and ordinances, as a man in the wilderness would sit under a vine of grapes, and refresh himself with them.

Obs. 1. We should lay to heart God's love to our fathers, and seek to continue it to ourselves. "I saw your fathers as the first-ripe in the fig tree at her first time." It is a sad thing to look upon degenerate children, who have had fathers in whom God took delight. Your fathers were as clusters of grapes, that did refresh the very soul of God: as it is said of wine, that it doth cheer both God and man; so the grace and holiness of your forefathers, oh how refreshing were they to the heart of God! But what are you, what delight can God take in your sour and bitter fruits, in your corrupt and degenerate spirits? Oh! it is a comfortable thing when a child is able to say, as Exod. xv. 2, "My God," and "my father's God." God was my father's God, and delighted in my father, and, blessed be his name, he is my God, and I hope he has some delight in me. You who are the children of fathers in whom God delighted like as in "grapes in the wilderness," it is a mighty engagement for you to look to yourselves, that your hearts and lives be not corrupt, but that, following the steps of your fathers, God may delight likewise in you. But further,

"As the first-ripe in the fig tree at her first time."

There is a great deal of elegance in these expressions. The fig tree bears twice in the year, and here it is, " the first-ripe at the first time." Their fathers were as delightful as grapes in the wilderness, and as the figs, " the first-ripe in the fig tree at her first time."

Now we know that we prize the first-ripe fruits, many will give almost any price for them. We say, when they at first appear, that they are ladies' meat, or longing meat: now the Lord is pleased to condescend to express his love to his people, and to speak of it, as the love of a longing woman to fruits when they first come into season; as a woman has a longing desire after such things, so, saith God, my soul has longed after you to do you good, I have taken as much pleasure in you as ever woman could take when her longing desires were being most delicately gratified. This is the meaning of the Holy Ghost here, and many expressions of similar import occur in Scripture; as in Jer. xii. 7, God's saints are called " the dearly beloved of God's soul;" and in the 10th verse, " my pleasant portion ;" in Exod. xix. 5, the " peculiar treasure" of God; and here, " grapes in the wilderness," and " the first-ripe in the fig tree at her first time." This is God's exceeding goodness to us, though we be sapless in ourselves, and have nothing in us to afford delight, yet, out of his own free grace, God is willing to express himself thus to his people. Oh what delight should we have in God, who takes such delight in his servants! These expressions may well lead us to meditate also on the delight which God has in the young, who begin to give themselves up betimes to him; the Lord loves " the first-fruits," and " the first-ripe" of things: so Micah vii. 1, " Woe is me! for I am as when they have gathered the summer fruits, as the grape-gleanings of the vintage: there is no cluster to eat: my soul desired the first-ripe fruit." So, by way of allusion at least, we may apply it to God. God is a longer; for what? for the first-ripe fruits, the first of your years: graciousness, when it first buds out in youth, oh how pleasing is it to God! In Exod. xxiii. 19, God would have " the first of the first-fruits," he would not only have the first-fruits, but " the *first* of the first." God insists much on the first still. And in Lev. ii. 14, you read, that the Lord is so eager to have the first-fruits, that he will not stay till they be ripe, he will have the "green ears of corn dried by the fire." As many women will not stay until the thing be ripe in the course of nature, but if they can have it ripened by any art, they will have it so; so, saith God, my longing after the first of things is so, that I will not stay till they be fully ripe, but the corn, though it be green ears, if they may be dried by the fire, I will have them. So in Cant. ii. 12, 13, "The flowers appear on the earth; the time of the singing of birds is come, and the voice of the turtle is heard in our land; the fig tree putteth forth her green figs." And in chap. vi. 11, "I went down into the garden of nuts to see the fruits of the valley, and to see whether the vine flourished, and the pomegranates budded." Oh, the Lord looks up and down in congregations, that are as the gardens of God, to see such. And so in chap. vii. 12, "Let us get up early to the vineyards; let us see if the vine flourish, whether the tender grape appear, and the pomegranates bud forth: there will I give thee my loves." O let us go and see whether the tender grape appear, or the pomegranate bud. " There will I give thee my loves." Where God sees grace beginning and budding in young ones, there God manifests himself; " there will I give thee my loves." O, begin to be godly betimes; you satisfy the heart of your longing God, as the first-fruits satisfy the longing woman.

"But," saith God, "they went to Baal-peor, and separated themselves unto that shame." What! a *but* come after all this? God is manifesting his delight in them as in "grapes in the wilderness," and "the first-ripe in the fig tree at her first time;" and yet, behold, a *but* follows.

Obs. 2. The greatness of God's love is not enough to engage carnal hearts. This is an evil and a sore thing to see. There was a time that God accepted of this people and delighted much in them, but now they are departed. Oh how wont are people to degenerate! a few years since, how forward and zealous were many for God, and for reformation; but within a while they grew cold, and dead, and formal, and began to leave off all their good beginnings, and decline from God and from his truth.

"They went to Baal-peor, and separated themselves unto that shame." God complains of this people as a husband of an adulteress: Though I delighted in her and loved her, though she had all the content she could desire, yet she forsakes me, and gives up herself to impurity and uncleanness. I beseech you observe, nothing affects an ingenuous heart more than the waste of love; such had rather ill bestow money than love. So, certainly, it goes to the heart of God that his love should be ill bestowed upon people. Notwithstanding, saith God here, all my love to their forefathers, whereby they might have drawn an argument that they would have blessings on themselves, if they continued in the ways of their forefathers, yet they forsook me; " they went to Baal-peor, and separated themselves unto that shame."

Obs. 3. The more shameful any thing is, the more abominable is it to forsake God on its account. It were an abominable thing to forsake God for the gaining of heaven and earth, if they could so be gained; but to forsake God for a Baal-peor, God takes this ill indeed.

Obs. 4. There is no evil so base or shameful to which a carnal heart is not ready to cleave, to the forsaking of the blessed and glorious God. Many, indeed, are so set on base things, that they are content to part with all the good that there is in God and Jesus Christ, if they may but obtain them, yea, content for their sake to undo themselves to all eternity.

Obs. 5. So to leave God, as to give up ourselves to baseness and wickedness, is most abominable. To be overtaken with sin is vile, but to give up ourselves to wickedness is truly abominable: and yet of this many are guilty. At first, perhaps, sin is fair-mannered, and saith, Do but dally with me at first; but after a while the soul insensibly abandons itself to the most wretched sinful courses: this is the case of many an apostate, they had some comfort before in God and in Christ, but having tampered with sin until they have become habituated to it, they have lost all their spiritual comforts; and now saith this desperate soul, I cannot have comfort in God and Christ, and therefore I will have it in the satisfying of my lusts. O my brethren, what a shame is this, to be guilty, so far as thou art able, of shaming even God himself and Jesus Christ! So in Heb. vi. 6, apostates are said to put Jesus Christ "to an open shame:" an apostate, that leaves the ways of God and separates himself to his lusts, puts the Lord Jesus Christ to an open shame. Oh how should God's people separate themselves for the Lord, and be wholly his, seeing idolaters separate themselves to their idols! Let them look upon themselves as a people separated for the Lord.

"And their abominations were according as they loved." This may be understood,

1. As they loved, so they were guided; they were not guided by the word, nor by any Divine rule, nor by right reason, but "according as they loved," they followed what they had a mind to, never regarding what the mind of God was.

Obs. 6. The judgment is soon gone when the heart is taken. Ordinarily people love not that way to which the rule guides them, but that to which their affections tend. It is very sinful for men to be carried on merely by the violence of their affections, and especially this is evil in the matters of God's worship; in it we may not do things as we like, that is, because we think such things are very fair, and there appears to us no hurt in them. We must examine whether we have warrant out of the word for them; we must not follow our inclinations, but bend them to that rule.

2. They were abominable as they loved; they were turned into the very likeness of that which they loved. And indeed our affections render us in some measure like that on which they are fixed. The understanding turns the object into a likeness to it, but the heart is turned into the likeness of its object.

Austin, Ep. 52, ad Maced., expresses himself in a remarkable manner respecting this. Such is every man as his love is. Does a man love the earth? he is earth. Does a man love God? what shall I say, he shall be even God too. And indeed the Scripture saith we are partakers of the Divine nature. Oh what care then had we need exercise about the object on which we set our affections! Dost thou love a thing base and filthy? then thy soul is base and filthy too. Dost thou love the glorious and blessed God? then thy soul is made like to God. Choose, therefore, good objects for thy love; love the Lord, and love his holy ways; love things that are excellent and glorious, and by the loving of these thy heart will have an excellence and glory put upon it; but if thou lovest that which is drossy and filthy, thy heart will become degenerate and base likewise. Man's soul is like the chameleon, changed into the colour of the object it looks upon.

Plin. lib. 8. cap. 33.

3. That which is here translated in the concrete sense, I find may be as well rendered in the abstract, They were abominable as their love; and so it is understood by some: that is, they were abominable as the idols were which they loved, and their idols were called love, in the abstract; as a man calls his wife his love, so they called their idols their love; and they were abominable as their love, that is, as abominable as Baal-peor was, so abominable were they. So the psalmist, "They that make idols are like unto them."

4. I think the especial scope of the Holy Ghost in these words has reference to what you read in Numb. xxv. 1. You find there the people of Israel, by the wicked counsel of Balaam, were enticed to commit uncleanness with the daughters of Moab, and by them drawn to the worship of their idols. So their love to the daughters of Moab drew them to serve Moab's idols.

"Their abominations were according as they loved;" that is, setting their love upon these wicked women, they were enticed by them first to uncleanness, and then to idolatry. Solomon's wives also drew him to idolatry.

Obs. 8. It is usual for people to adopt the religion of those whom they love: if their hearts be taken with any, it is usual for them to adopt their religion; according to their kindred, according to their friends, according to the stock that they marry into, so is their religion. You will find many that have been forward in the cause of religion, grow cold because they have married into families without the savour of religion, and now they conform to their wives' dispositions; according to what they love, so their religion either burns hotter or grows cooler: it was thus usually said of Ahab for his wickedness, Such a one was his wife; and so of another king, The daughter of Ahab was his wife: their religion was according as they loved. And, my brethren, if those who are in a false way can draw whom they love to it, then certainly those in the truth should also labour to draw those whom they love to embrace the truth. Wicked wives will draw their husbands to that which they love, to idolatry, to false worship; popish wives have drawn more husbands to their popery, than godly wives (I fear) have drawn husbands to the truth: why should not gracious wives labour to win their husbands to good by love, as well as wicked wives to entice them to wickedness by their love? And, indeed, those who would gain others to good must first gain their love. The women of Moab gained the love of the people of Israel, and then prevailed on them to serve their gods. So, if you would benefit any, first labour to gain their love: let godly wives act so towards their ungodly husbands. How would you gain them? Not, surely, by reproachful speeches, but (though they be never so evil) walk lovingly towards them, that they may be convinced that your souls truly love them, and so by your loving carriage gain their love; that is the way to win them to your God. So we are told of many of the women in the primitive times that had heathenish husbands, that by their gracious, loving carriage they won them over to the truth. And so ministers, if they would win people to God, must walk before them in such a gracious, holy, loving manner, that they may gain their love, and then they will win their souls: if there be wrangling between minister and people, there is little hope of any good. And so with your neighbours and friends, if you would win them to God, gain first their love yourselves, for it is a mighty motive in matters of religion for people to do as they love.

Ver. 11. *As for Ephraim, their glory shall fly away like a bird, from the birth, and from the womb, and from the conception.*

"As for Ephraim." A pathetical expression; he makes a stop at Ephraim; O Ephraim! how sad, how much to be lamented, is thy condition!

"Their glory." By it is meant, all their pomp, riches, strength, prosperity, but especially their numerous progeny, in which they did so much glory. Ephraim, the ten tribes, prospered very much, and were far more numerous than Judah. This scripture refers to their state especially in the time of Jeroboam II., of which you read, 2 Kings xiv. Ephraim then prospered very much.

Obs. 1. A numerous progeny is accounted a glory. "Their glory." So in Prov. xvii. 6, "Children's children are the crown of old men;" the Seventy render it καύχημα, the glory of old men. Parents are wont to glory and pride themselves much in their children; for,

1. By their children they themselves are multiplied.

2. What excellency soever there is in the child, they look upon it as their own, and on themselves as the cause of it: men and women love themselves much, and because children are, as it were, portions of themselves, therefore they glory in them.

3. They have thereby hope of continuation from generation to generation; and in this hope they glory.

But let parents learn to give God the glory of their children, and to bring them up for him, and then they may rejoice in them indeed, as a great mercy of God. In Prov. x. 1, "A wise son maketh a glad father; but a foolish son is the heaviness of his mother." Why is a wise son said to be the gladness of the father? does not a mother rejoice in a wise son too? And why is a foolish son said to be the sorrow of the mother? does not the father sorrow and mourn for a foolish son? The Holy Ghost, not without reason, expresses himself thus, "A wise son maketh a glad father," and that for two reasons.

1. The father usually has a more strict hand over his son, to educate him to wisdom, than the mother. Mothers, too often, by weak indulgence, spoil their children; they cannot endure that they should suffer

any hardship, and hence their children prove foolish and fit for nothing, and great sorrows to them.

2. A wise son is fit for employment abroad in the world, and therefore rejoices the heart of his father; but a foolish son is fit for nothing but to remain at home with his mother, and as he grows up, to grow stout and stubborn against her. If, then, children be a glory to their parents, they should labour to be such, that they may indeed be a glory and not a shame to them. Many, instead of being a glory to their parents, are a great shame to them, as Augustus Cæsar, who had three daughters that were wicked, used to call them his three imposthumes, and his three cankers upon his body. And so children, that should be the glory of their parents, and the glory of a family, too often shame and disgrace both. And if you expect that your children should be a glory to you, you must not be a shame to them: sometimes children are a shame to their parents, and sometimes parents are a shame to their children.

Tres Vomicas, tria Carcinomata. Aug.

"Shall fly away like bird." This admits of two expositions.

I. Men glory in their outward pomp and prosperity, and their children, but all these "shall fly away like a bird." That is, 1. Suddenly. 2. Swiftly. 3. Irrecoverably.

A bird, encaged perhaps many months, on some opportunity gets out, and is gone in a moment, suddenly, so swiftly too that you cannot follow her, and irrecoverably, that you can never take her. All outward glory is uncertain: in Prov. xxiii. 5, it is asked, "Wilt thou set thine eyes upon that which is not? for riches certainly make themselves wings; they fly away as an eagle toward heaven;" fly away like a bird, and that bird the eagle, that flies so swiftly that there is no getting her again. How many lately in Ireland, and in our own land, have had estates in the evening, and all has been gone away swiftly like a bird before the morning! they have been rich in the morning, and have been even beggars in the evening. Let us take our hearts off from glorying in all outward excellencies, and seek that glory which is abiding, constant, and everlasting. We should look upon all outward comforts now as upon the wing; if ever we had cause to do so, at this day we have especial cause. We cannot now reason thus, We have enjoyed such prosperity thus long, and therefore we shall have a continuance of it. No, all outward comforts fly away like the bird: that comes in one moment which before came not in many years. In Jer. ix. 23, 24, "Thus saith the Lord, Let not the wise man glory in his wisdom, neither let the mighty man glory in his might, let not the rich man glory in his riches: but let him that glorieth glory in this, that he understandeth and knoweth me, that I am the Lord which exercise loving-kindness, judgment, and righteousness, in the earth: for in these things I delight, saith the Lord." Your delights are in other vain things, in estates, in bravery; but in these things I delight, saith the Lord God, and if you will glory, do you glory in those things in which I myself delight: your glory in the midst of your prosperity flies from you like a bird; but the Lord, the glory of his own people, in the midst of their adversities flies to them like a bird. I say, the glory of the wicked in the midst of their prosperity flies from them, but the Lord God, who is the glory of the saints, flies to them in their afflictions. Thus in Isa. xxxi. 5, "As birds flying, so will the Lord of hosts defend Jerusalem; defending also he will deliver it; and passing over he will preserve it." "As birds flying;" it is a metaphor taken from the bird when she sees the young ones in any danger of the kite, she flies with speed to save them: As birds flying, so will I defend Jerusalem. Your glory departs in the midst of your prosperity, but the glory of the saints flies to them in their adversity.

II. The glory of their posterity "shall fly away like a bird;" that is, the Lord will cut off their numerous posterity, their young men, in whose number they gloried, so that there shall be few left among them.

Obs. 2. Godliness brings blessings swiftly, and wickedness causes them to depart as swiftly. The blessing of God upon Abraham's seed came very swiftly after it began to come; and now God threatens it shall go away as swiftly. As you may find it if you observe the story of the increase of the seed of Abraham, from the time of their going into Egypt. But threescore and ten souls went down into Egypt; but when they came out of Egypt, but two hundred and fifteen years afterwards, (for the four hundred and thirty years are to be reckoned from the promise to Abraham until their coming out of Egypt, and it is clear that there were two hundred and fifteen years from the promise to their going down into Egypt,) there came up, from twenty years old and upwards, men of war, six hundred thousand, three thousand, five hundred and fifty; besides the Levites, who, with the males from a month old and upwards, were twenty and two thousand, besides the women and all the other children: and this was in the time of their bondage. Thus the glory of Abraham's seed came very swiftly. And now it shall fly away like a bird, they shall decrease more than they did increase.

"From the birth, and from the womb, and from the conception." God's curse follows the wicked close; sometimes in their birth; sometimes in the womb; sometimes hindering the conception. You see how God has us at advantage, how he has us in his hand at every turn; he might, if he had pleased, have smitten us in our conception; if he had spared us there, stifled us in the womb; if spared there, made us stick in the birth.

Wherefore learn we to acknowledge God's mercy in the general, that he is patient, and long-suffering, and gracious unto us: let us consider the several passages of his mercy, to bless God not only for our general preservation, but that he preserved us in the very conception, preserved us in our mother's womb, and then in the birth; and then in the cradle, in our childhood, in our youth, in our middle age, and in our old age; for we lie at his mercy at every point of time.

"Their glory shall fly away like a bird, from the birth, and from the womb, and from the conception:" of some I will hinder the conception, some others in the womb shall die, others shall perish in their birth, and so at every time my curse shall follow them; "from the birth, and from the womb, and from the conception."

Ver. 12. *Though they bring up their children, yet will I bereave them, that there shall not be a man left: yea, woe also to them when I depart from them!*

"Though they bring up their children, yet will I bereave them." It is here threatened that a fearful judgment from God will pursue and overtake them, though they escape that curse under which others suffer.

Obs. 1. Many think all is well when they have escaped judgments that have come on others; but know, thy preservation from such may be thy reservation to greater judgments that God intends for thee afterwards.

Obs. 2. The loss of children in hopeful maturity is a loss indeed. It is a judgment to be deprived of children in the womb, in the birth; but when you have endured much pain in bearing and bringing forth your children, much labour and trouble in bringing them up, when many a thoughtful care has been expended on their education, and they now begin hopefully to arrive almost at men's and women's estate, and you think to have comfort in them, for God then to take them away, is indeed very sad to parents, such a bereavement bows down their hearts exceedingly: yet such things as these have befallen many heretofore; and parents, though the condition must be acknowledged very sad, yet must they in such a case submit to God's hand. Perhaps some of you have in the breeding of your children endured much, and through many difficulties they have been brought till they have grown up almost to men's and women's estates; and perhaps they have been obedient and hopeful, and you trusted to have had them as the staff of your age; and yet God suddenly has made them fly away like a bird; perhaps by drowning, or some other untimely end, the Lord has suddenly torn them from you. You will say, My condition is more than ordinarily sad. Therefore God calls you to sanctify his name in a more than ordinary degree, to exercise grace more than ordinary; and the exercise of grace in such an extraordinary stroke of God upon you may be as great a comfort and blessing to you as the enjoyment of your child would have been. If a tender mother, after breeding and bringing up a child with care, and pain, and labour, should have him taken away by some untimely death, (as you call it,) she would think her condition the saddest of any living. Perhaps some such may be here, or know some of their friends who have had such a hand of God upon them; be but convinced of this one thing, which I know you cannot deny, that the exercise of grace suitable to this work of God that is now upon thee, or against thee, take it as thou wilt, I say, the exercise of thy grace suitable to this work of God, is a greater good to thee than the life of thy child could have been; it could never have done thee that good which the exercise of grace may do thee in this condition, when it is suitable to this stroke of God upon thee. And this indeed is the only way to make up any losses, be it a child, be it a husband, or the dearest friend, a wife, or thy estate, yet the exercise of thy grace is better than the enjoyment of them all.

"Yet will I bereave them, that there shall not be a man left." ושכלתים מאדם yet will I bereave them, that they be not men. Sometimes God lets children live, and yet they never come to be men; he strikes them in their understandings, that they are bereaved of them so far that they never attain the stature of men's minds. I remember it is reported of Sir Thomas More, that his wife was mightily desirous of a boy, (that was her word,) and she had one that proved a fool; whereupon her husband said to her, You were never quiet till you had a boy, and now you have one that will be all his life a boy.

"I will bereave them, that there shall not be a man left." I rather think the meaning of these words is, I will take them away, that they shall not live to be men, strong men of war. You boasted yourselves that you had so many of your children that were such valiant men of war before, but I will bereave you of them, saith the Lord.

"Yea, woe also to them when I depart from them!" "Yea, woe also to them!" there is added the "yea," or surely, "also," as if the Holy Ghost should say, Why do I threaten this or the other evil? the great evil of all, the rise of all evils, is God's forsaking them. "Yea, woe also to them when I depart from them!"

God departs from a people, or a particular soul, when he withdraws his goodness and mercy from them; and the reason why wicked men for a time enjoy good things is, because God's time is not yet come to depart from them; but when God's time is come to depart from them, then all vanishes suddenly: as the light continues so long as the sun is in the firmament, but as soon as ever it is gone, the darkness of the night begins to approach.

Obs. 3. It is God in the creature that upholds it. The general presence of God with his creature maintains its strength, and health, and comforts; and upon God's departing, all vanishes and comes to nothing. Thou hast thy prosperity now, and thou thinkest thou mayst enjoy it still; but how canst thou tell but God may suddenly depart? and then all is gone. The alteration of man's condition is not only from natural causes, but has reference to a higher source, God's departing. Carnal hearts think themselves safe if they do not see how natural causes shall work their ruin; yea, but know that thy prosperity, or thy adversity, depends not upon natural causes, but upon a higher cause; though thou hast the confluence of all natural causes working for thee, yet, if God pleases to withdraw himself, thou art a lost creature.

And so it is with a kingdom. When God is pleased to depart from a kingdom, he takes away wisdom from the wise, gives them up to their own perverse counsels, blinds them that they cannot foresee their danger nor discern means of help, so that they adopt measures as if they intended to destroy themselves. If God do but leave them, whatsoever their wisdom was before, all their endeavours shall be blasted and come to nothing. And in this especially we should sanctify and acknowledge God's name, acknowledge our immediate dependence upon him for all the outward good we enjoy, whatsoever second causes may concur to aid us.

Wicked men will not observe his hand in their discomforts; they cry out of this and the other as the cause of their evil, but it is God's departing from them that is the great thing they should lay to heart. Particular evils must not be compared with this of God's departing. Whatsoever our condition be, yet, if God be not departing, we are well enough; Though in the fire, though in the water, I will be with thee, saith the Lord. Mark the ground of the confidence of the saints in the time of affliction: in Psal. xlvi., (Luther's Psalm it is called, that is, a Psalm that Luther was wont to call to his friends to sing, when he heard of any danger, or of any sad occurrence,) "Therefore will not we fear, though the earth be removed, and though the mountains be carried into the midst of the sea; though the waters thereof roar and be troubled, though the mountains shake with the swelling thereof. The heathen may rage, and the kingdoms be removed:" yet all shall not trouble us. Why, what is the ground? "The Lord of hosts is with us; the God of Jacob is our refuge." These same words are repeated twice in the Psalm, "The Lord of hosts is with us." he is not departed; "the God of Jacob is our refuge:" *therefore* no great matter what men can do unto us. But if one be in misery and God departed, oh how dreadful is his condition! It was a dreadful speech of Saul, "I am sore distressed; for the Philistines make war against me, and God is departed from me," 1 Sam. xxviii. 15. Oh, when the Philistines make war upon a people, when there are enemies at our gates, and our consciences tell us that God is departed from us, this is a sad condition. It was a woeful speech of Saul, God is now departed when I have most need of him. Woe to men then! For,

1. The root of all our evils is very deep when God is departed. They lie not in this or that particular, we might make shift to get over them, the spirit of a man might sustain his infirmity; but the root of the evil lies in the departing of God; and what can the creature do when God is departed? As the king of Israel, when the woman said, "Help, my lord, O king," replied, "If the Lord do not help thee, whence shall I help thee?" And as all creatures say, If God be departed, we cannot help, nay, the very devil cannot help if God be gone: so in 1 Sam. xxviii. 16, when Saul was sore distressed and would raise up Samuel, the devil, who came in the likeness of the prophet, said, "Wherefore then dost thou ask of me, seeing the Lord

is departed from thee?" No creatures in the world, nor devils, can do good when God is departed; then evil is indeed altogether evil. An evil may have much good in it, and God may sanctify it for abundance of blessings to his people, so long as he continues with them; but if he be gone, then the evil is only evil: and if God be gone all protection is gone, and therefore thou art liable to evils of every kind. And however for the present the things that remain seem to be good, yet the blessing is gone if God be not with thee. And this evil that is upon thee is no other but the forerunner of eternal evil; and the creature certainly then must needs sink when God is thus departed. Oh! if it be so woeful a thing for God to depart from a people here in this world, in regard of the withdrawing of outward things and mercies from them, what is it then for the Lord to depart for ever from the soul! What an alteration does the departing of the sun make! Take a delightful sunshine summer's day, and how beautiful is it! Now compare that with a winter's dark, dismal night; what makes the difference between these two? The presence of the sun in the one, and its absence from the other. This is but the presence, or the departing, of one of God's creatures. Oh! if that makes such a difference in the world, what must the presence or the departing of the infinite God do to the soul! Let the saints who enjoy God's presence prize it, and pray as the prophet did, "Lord, leave us not."

How vain is the heart of man, that *will* depart from God! If thou depart from him, he departs from thee too; and woe to thee, whatsoever thou hast, when the Lord is departed from thee!

The Lord departs from individuals, as well as from kingdoms and nations, and woe to them also! When God departs from particular persons, he withdraws his common gifts and graces, and the comforts that they were wont to have; he curses all means for their good; and gives them up to temptations: those are the three special things that God does in departing from a soul. 1. He withdraws the common gifts and graces which it had, and the consequent comforts. 2. He curses the means that would do them good. And, 3. He gives them up to the strength and power of temptation.

You will perhaps say, Many a soul that desires further presence of God, may from these observations fear that God is departed.

Now though God may, doubtless, in some degree withdraw himself even from his saints, so that they may fear that he is departed from them; yet one evidence remains to thee, let thy condition be never so sad, if thou art a saint; God does not so depart from his saints, but he leaves behind some lustre, some little glimmering of himself, which serves to show the soul which way God is gone, and to draw the heart of a poor sinner after him, and make it restless and unquiet till it come into his presence again. When God departs from hypocrites, he departs so that he leaves nothing behind him, not so much as to make them follow on after him, and so they turn away and seek to make up the loss of God in something else; but a saint of God, that has God beginning to depart in any degree, will not turn aside to seek to make up the loss of God in any thing else, but he still has so much of God as strongly to carry out his heart after him, so that he looks, and sighs, and groans, and cries after the Lord. David, in Psal. cxix. 8, shows us that God was in some degree departed from him, in his own view at least; but mark this expression, "I will keep thy statutes: O forsake me not utterly." O Lord, methinks I feel that thou art going, I feel that I have not those comforts and those stirrings of thy Spirit which I was wont to have, but, O Lord, yet for all this, "I will keep thy statutes;" I am resolved, though I should never have further comforts from thee, yet, Lord, "I will keep thy statutes;" do with me what thou wilt, I will do what I can to honour thee; "O forsake me not utterly." So long as thy heart can close with this text, and say, as David, Lord, "I will keep thy statutes;" though I feel not thy presence with me as I was wont to do, yet, Lord, I will do what I can to honour thee; though I be in a sad condition, and thou seemest to leave me, yet, Lord, "I will keep thy statutes; O forsake me not utterly;" so long, I say, as thou canst adopt David's words as thine own, it is an evidence God is not so departed as he is wont to depart from hypocrites, and wicked and ungodly men. And if it be so woeful a thing when God departs, truly then when God is about departing we had need cry mightily to him, both for kingdoms and particular souls. When a malefactor stands before the judge, and is crying for mercy, if the judge prepare to leave the bench, he lifts up his voice, and shrieks out indeed, Good my lord, have mercy! for he sees, if the judge once quit the bench, he is a lost man: so when we see God going, we should indeed be earnest in our pleadings. Many footsteps of God's departing from us there have been, and are, and yet still God leaves a light behind; yea, blessed be God, he is not so departed, but that he has left so much of himself as that we may know where to find him.

Ver. 13. *Ephraim, as I saw Tyrus, is planted in a pleasant place: but Ephraim shall bring forth his children to the murderer.*

"Ephraim, as I saw Tyrus, is planted in a pleasant place." What! God departed? Woe to us when God departs from us! Why, but Ephraim might bless himself in his prosperous condition, Ephraim might say, Why do you speak of God's departing? We are in a good condition, it is but your melancholy fears that make you speak so; we were never stronger, never had better fortifications, were never more prosperous, than at present. This, as I have told you, has reference to the time of Jeroboam II., 2 Kings xiv. The prophet grants it, that they were in a prosperous estate; Ephraim was like Tyrus, "planted in a pleasant place." Tyrus was a rich city, and of exceeding strength, situated much like (as it is reported) to that famous city in Italy, Venice, on a rock in the sea, about seven hundred paces from the land. Tyre was a place of exceeding strength. Quintus Curtius, lib. 4. de Reb. gestis Alexandri., saith, that Alexander in his conquest had more to do to conquer Tyrus than all Asia besides, it was such a mighty and strong place. Pliny, lib. 5. cap. 19, saith, the compass of it was nineteen miles. It was the general mart of almost all the world, and was consequently very full of people: to this especially the prophet refers, when he saith, Ephraim was like Tyrus; because Ephraim did so glory in his numerous progeny, and Tyrus was a mighty populous place. Pliny saith, three other ancient cities came out of it, as Leptis Utica, and that great Carthage, which was but a spring out of this root; that Carthage, which was so famous a city, that it contended for a long time with Rome for the monarchy and dominion of the whole world. Yea, and Gades, divided, as it was, from the rest of the earth, was peopled by a Tyrian colony. But we need not so much recur to these authors, for in Ezek. xxvii. 3, 4, you have the city Tyrus described as a most brave, rich, and glorious city: "O thou that art situate at the entry of the sea, which art a merchant of the people for many isles, Thus saith the Lord God; O Tyrus, thou hast said, I am of perfect beauty. Thy borders are in the midst of the seas, thy builders have perfected thy beauty." And then, ver. 33, "When thy wares went forth out of the the seas, thou filledst many people; thou didst enrich the kings of the earth with the multitude of thy riches and of thy merchandise." Now saith the Lord here, Ephraim is thus; she said to herself, that she was so prosperous, and strong, and rich every way, she was like to Tyrus; I grant it, saith the prophet, and I have seen it so, Ephraim is thus, even when God is departing from her. Hence,

Obs. 1. God may depart from a kingdom, or an individual, in the time of their greatest prosperity. When thou art nearest eternal misery, thou mayst be at the very summit of outward prosperity. Physicians say that the uttermost degree of health in the body, is the next step to sickness: it is indeed true, that the highest degree of outward prosperity is often but the forerunner of ruin. Oh! let us learn never to trust in our prosperity, but always to walk with fear and trembling before the Lord: never let us think that we are safe and well because we have outward things as we desire; we may have them so, and yet that very night the word may come, "This night shall thy soul be required of thee," as you know was the case with the rich man in the Gospel; when he had his barns full, and was deliberating what to do, the Lord said, "Thou fool, this night shall thy soul be required of thee." And Nebuchadnezzar, at the very time when he was glorying in the magnificent palace he had made, the word came forth against him. But further, it should especially teach us that,

Obs. 2. As we should trust in no outward prosperity, so, not in any fortifications, however strong. Tyrus was an invincible place, as it seems, yet God could pull it down. Nor are we to trust in the multitude of soldiers. This example is as pointed as any to teach men to trust in no external advantages whatsoever.

Calvin renders this somewhat differently, and truly not without some probability: I saw Ephraim, that thou wert planted in a pleasant place, as in Tyrus; and interprets it thus, Thou art a plant like to the plants that were in Tyrus. Indeed the word בנוה translated "pleasant place," signifies also a building, because they are wont to build in the most delightful places; it likewise signifies a secure place of habitation. Now (saith he) Tyrus was upon a rock, and therefore they had little ground for orchards, or gardens, or plants, but only such as were made by art, and with a great deal of cost: and as men, when they are striving with nature, if they mean to do any thing at all, will do it to purpose, and fetch out the most curious plants, and bestow a great deal of cost to cover them from the coldness of the winter; so Ephraim was compared to such a plant, that is, God was at a great deal of charge for it, and very careful he was to preserve it. As before God compared his love to his people to a longing woman, that longed for the first-ripe fruits; so here God compares his respect to his people to the care expended on a tender plant in a garden made on unlikely ground, at abundant cost and charge; look, what care would be taken to preserve such plant in covering and keeping it from the frost, such was my care towards Ephraim, howsoever they have served me. Thus, saith Calvin, to aggravate their sins, God shows his care of them. But, adds the text, for all this, though my care hath been thus over them, yet they "shall bring forth their children to the murderer."

Obs. 3. God never shows so much respect to any, but that upon their forsaking him wrath follows. Yet, after all this, "Ephraim shall bring forth his children to the murderer;" as if their children had been born for no other end but to satisfy the mouth of the sword, to be objects of the fury of the murderer.

"But Ephraim shall bring forth his children to the murderer." Sometimes indeed in war men are led forth even by the treachery, or the spite at least, of their commanders, only that they might be a prey to the murderers. If any wicked officers in an army have a spite against a man, or any particular company of men, ordinarily this is most against the godly men in the army, they will set them upon the most desperate service on purpose that they might be cut off, or at least fall into the hand of the murderer. As David, for his own ends in another way, would set Uriah in the forefront, and would have others withdraw from him, on purpose that he might fall by the enemy. Many children have been brought forth to the murderers even in this way.

Obs. 4. The curse of God goes forward from the parents to the children. It is for the sin of the parents that the children are to be brought forth to the murderers. And especially the curse rests not upon idolaters, but goes on to their children. There are two branches in this observation:

1. The curse of God stays not upon the parents, but goes towards the children; Deut. xxviii. 18, "Cursed shall be the fruit of thy body;" and especially to the children of idolaters. So Psal. cxxxvii. 8, 9, "O daughter of Babylon, who art to be destroyed; happy shall he be, that rewardeth thee as thou hast served us. Happy shall he be, that taketh and dasheth thy little ones against the stones." And Isa. xiii. 18, "Their bows also shall dash the young men to pieces; and they shall have no pity on the fruit of the womb; their eye shall not spare children." So in the second commandment, the Lord there threatens to visit the sins of the fathers upon the children, of them that hate him, to the third and fourth generation.

You will say, Why should children suffer for their parents' sins?

You will kill young vipers and snakes though they never have stung; so, God sees guilt enough in the children of wicked men and of idolaters, so that in justice he may destroy them; but he the rather destroys them because they be the children of such. When a man commits treason he deserves death for his own crime, but if the king hear that his father and grandfather were traitors, he shall die the rather because of them. So it is true, the children of the godly have sin and guilt in them, as well as the children of wicked men; but the children of wicked men, having guilt of their own, and so liable to God's justice, God will take the advantage the rather to do justice on them because of their parents' wickedness and ungodliness; and this is righteous enough with God.

And the children of idolaters, above all, shall not be spared, especially those that live to many years, because no sin is so much strengthened by appealing to the example of forefathers as superstition and idolatry. Why should we be wiser than our forefathers? What is the argument for our superstitious vanities, but our forefathers did thus? And therefore is it observable, that in none of the commandments does God threaten judgments upon the children but in the second commandment, and that because no commandment is so broken from the example and plea of forefathers as the second; and therefore let the children of idolaters and false worshippers look to it that they repent from the sins of their forefathers. Instead of pleading for the sins of your forefathers, you should fall down and humble your souls on account of them; or otherwise that is the very reason that God will punish the sins of the forefathers upon the children, because their fathers did worship God in a false way, and they will do so too.

2. This is a special fruit of God's curse upon children, that they shall be brought forth to the murderer. In times of war, if you make not your peace with God, it is just with God that things should be ordered so that your children should be brought forth to the murderers. O you tender-hearted mothers, who are loth that the wind should blow upon your children,

look upon them and pity them; how can you endure to see their blood gush out? how can you endure to see your little ones dashed in the streets, or upon the pikes of the soldiers? If your hearts cannot endure this, seek to make your peace with God, to deliver yourselves and your children from a curse which has befallen many. We know not what these wars may bring forth: what they have done in Ireland we have heard much of, how the parents have seen their children brought forth to the murderers; and though it is true, in many cities and places where the enemy has come, they have not generally, at least, broken forth into such abominable cruelties as this; but who knows what a summer or two may bring forth? for, certainly, where war continues it drives on with more and more rage.

You will say then, Oh! let us make peace upon any terms.

No, let it rather be your care to make your peace with God; that is your way to deliver your children from being brought forth to the murderers; for if it be a false peace, it may but hasten the evils you apprehend. The curse of God is especially severe in this, when it shall come to pass before their very parents' eyes, for so the prophet speaks, as if they should be brought forth even before them. Many of the heathens have very pathetical expressions about the sad condition of parents, when their children are slain before their eyes: as that of Priam over his son Polites, slain by Pyrrhus, May the gods, if there be any divinity in heaven which regards such things, retribute you for this! Thou hast even sprinkled the blood of the child upon the father's face. He was not able to refrain, though he saw himself ready to die next, but cries to the very heavens to revenge it. And how sad is the story of the emperor Mauritius, whose sons, and wife, and daughters, were brought and slain before his very eyes! If your children did but understand this text that I am now opening, they would even look upon you and cry with tears in their eyes, O father! mother! repent, repent, and seek God for yourselves and for us; repent and make up your peace with God, that we may not be brought forth to the murderers.

Dii (si qua est in cœlo pietas, quæ talia curet) præmia reddant debita, patrios fœdasti funere vultus. Virg.

But if this be so great an evil, for parents to have their children to be brought forth to the murderers here, how great an evil then is it for parents to bring forth children to be fuel for God's wrath for all eternity, to be firebrands for the everlasting burnings. You then that are parents, look upon your children and soften your hearts by such thoughts as these: Oh! what a sad thing would it be that such a babe that came out of my womb should be a firebrand for God's wrath to burn upon to all eternity! Oh! how had I need pray, and bring up my children in the fear of God, lest I should be such an unhappy father, as out of my loins not only to bring forth a child to the murderers, but for the devils in hell! But let not this discourage you that are godly to venture your children in lawful wars; in such a cause if you be willing to sacrifice your children to God, and they be brought forth even to death, yet are they brought forth to martyrdom, rather than to the murderer. Thou shouldst rather rejoice that thou hast a child to bring forth in such a cause, than be overpressed with sorrow that the life of thy child has been taken away by the murderer; and some of your children, though with the loss of their own lives, have been a means to keep you and us all from the hand of the murderer, to keep the city and the kingdom from being overrun with tyranny, idolatry, and all kinds of profaneness; and the good which has been thus effected, may compensate the lives of your children. Rev. xii. 11, 12, "And they overcame him by the blood of the Lamb, and by the word of their testimony; and they loved not their lives unto the death. Therefore rejoice, ye heavens, and ye that dwell in them." When parents shall be willing to give up their children in the cause of God, even children, having made up their peace with God, shall be willing to sacrifice themselves in his cause; and then when they "love not their lives unto the death," there shall be joy in heaven, and they shall overcome in dying, even as Jesus Christ overcame in his death. I remember I have read of Xenophon, that when sacrificing to some idol god, he wore a crown upon his head, and there came news to him, that his child was dead, and he presently pulled his crown from off his head in token of sorrow; but then asking how he died, answer was made, that he died in the wars; whereupon he called for his crown again. So perhaps some of you have lost your children, nature cannot but work; yea, but then ask how they lost their lives; they lost them valiantly, in a work that did as much concern the glory of God as ever any war did, and seeing they died so, rather bless God than be so sorrowful that they fell into the hand of murderers.

Ver. 14. *Give them, O Lord: what wilt thou give? give them a miscarrying womb and dry breasts.*

Upon the declaration that they shall be brought forth to the murderer's hand, then follows, "Give them, O Lord: what wilt thou give? give them a miscarrying womb and dry breasts."

Some think this was an imprecation by a spirit of prophecy, as if the holy prophet had his heart filled with the wrath of God: "Give them, O Lord: what wilt thou give? give them a miscarrying womb and dry breasts."

But rather, according to most interpreters, I think this expression is one of commiseration; that is, foreseeing the lamentable condition that the ten tribes should be in ere long, the prophet pities their condition, and would fain come in and pray for them, and begins, "Give them, O Lord:" and then he stops, as if he should say, but, O Lord, what shall I say for them? "Give them;" but, Lord, I know not what to ask for them, I am at a stand when I consider what they are, and their many previous mercies, what warnings they have had, how hardened they are in their sin, and how thy word is gone forth; but yet, "Give them, O Lord:" shall I say, Lord, give them deliverance, give them peace, give them prosperity still? Lord, I dare not, that I cannot ask; all means have been used to bring them unto thee, and yet they stand out against thee: thou knowest they are dear to me, they are of my flesh, and I should be glad that they might be saved; but thy glory is dearer to me than they are, and therefore for that I cannot pray: but yet, "Give them, O Lord: what wilt thou give? give them a miscarrying womb and dry breasts." What! shall the enemies be let out upon them? shall they and their children be made a prey to the murderer? Lord, rather let no more be born of them, rather let those children that otherwise should have been born, and might have lived in their own land, Lord God, let them not be born rather than come to so great misery. So he doth not pray for "a miscarrying womb and dry breasts" absolutely, but comparatively.

Obs. 1. Men's sins often make God's ministers and saints at a loss what to say in prayer. Truly, though there has been a mighty spirit of prayer through God's mercy in the kingdom, yet, considering that since God has shown himself willing to deliver us, and Christ has been coming even upon his white horse, in peace, to take the kingdom to himself, as great a spirit of malignity has appeared against Christ and his saints as ever was in the kingdom, it puts many of the ministers and saints of God to a nonplus in their prayers, and straitens their very hearts in the day of their fasting; when they are to seek God, that the Lord would give forth mercy, they know not what to say. The Lord knows that our present condition is more unfit for mercy than at the very first day. Thus a nation, thus particular people, may put the servants of God to a stand in their prayers, and straiten their hearts. Oh! had people gone on in the embracing of reformation as they seemed to do at the first, how enlarged would the hearts of the saints have been in prayer! O Lord! give England mercy, give England deliverance!

Obs. 2. The fruitfulness and barrenness of the womb are from God. "Give them; give them a miscarrying womb and dry breasts." This is from God. In Gen. xxx. 1, 2, when Rachel cried for children, "Give me children, or else I die," the text saith, that "Jacob's anger was kindled against Rachel; and he said, Am I in God's stead?" The learned Paulus Phagius saith that the Hebrews have this tradition, that there are four keys in God's hand, which he gives not into the hand of any angel:

1. The key of the rain. "The Lord shall open unto thee his good treasure, the heaven to give the rain unto thy land in his season," Deut. xxviii. 12.

2. The key of food. "The eyes of all wait upon thee; and thou givest them their meat in due season. Thou openest thine hand, and satisfiest the desire of every living thing," Psal. cxlv. 15, 16.

3. The key of the grave. "Behold, O my people, I will open your graves, and cause you to come up out of your graves," Ezek. xxxvii. 12.

4. The key of the womb, Gen. xxx. 1, 2.

These four keys God keeps in his own hand, and therefore God's providence is to be observed in this, and there ought to be a submission to his hand in it.

Obs. 3. Sin may bring such evil times upon a people that those who live in them had better not been born, or died before such times arrived. "Give them a miscarrying womb and dry breasts." Children that should live to endure all the miseries of those times that are coming, had been better not have been born, or have died long before such times, saith the prophet. We must take heed of wishing this upon every little affliction that befalls us. Some, if their children do but anger them, wish they had never been born, or that they had died many years ago; but this is wicked frowardness against God himself; those that are so ready to wish their children had not been born, are the least sensible of the sin that causes the affliction upon which they wish such things.

"Give them a miscarrying womb and dry breasts." There may be many reasons for this prayer of the prophet; as,

1. Such miserable havoc might be made that parents might even wish that they never had any children.

2. Cruel tyranny might be exercised on their souls and bodies.

3. They might be drawn from God by false religion, and so be in a condition worse than if they had not been born.

Hence parents to whom God denies children, or from whom he takes them away, should quiet themselves in God's arrangement, especially in such times as these. It may be God has taken away your children to deliver them from greater evils; as in the house of Jeroboam there was but one child that had any good in it, and saith God, "That child shall die; because in him there is found some good thing toward the Lord God of Israel," 1 Kings xiv. 12, 13. So that God takes away many that he loves, and lets others live for whom he has not so much regard.

Yes, some may say, if I were sure that their souls were safe, I would be content, though God took them away.

That is true indeed; if your children were saved, what loss were it for them to be taken away and received to heaven, and there to live for ever with Christ, not to sin or sorrow more? But, however, you may satisfy yourselves by these reflections:

1. That they are under an indefinite promise, though not a universal.

2. Suppose they should not be saved, yet it were better they should be taken away than live to sin more against God. They might have lived to have done a great deal of mischief in the world, if they were such as God did not intend to save; therefore quiet thyself. God sees further than thou dost, when he either denies thee children, or takes them away, in such times as these.

3. Times when public evils are threatened are good times to die in. If it be better not to be born in evil times, then certainly it is no great evil to die in evil times. Good men are taken away from the evil to come. As, if a woman's breast were to be lanced, or cut off, would not the tender father take the children out of the room in the mean time? Who knows but God may have the breast of his church, our mother, to be even cut off for a time, and now oblige her to suffer heavier things than ever she has done. If God then take away his tender children, that will not be able to bear such a sight as that, what great evil is it? So we read, when God's glory was to pass by, he puts Moses into the hole of a rock; and truly the graves of the saints are but as the holes of the rock till the glory of God's justice passes by a people.

4. If the sins of parents may be the cause of such things to children, that they had better never been born, let parents take heed that they lay not up such wrath for an inheritance for their children; their children afterwards may even wish they never had been born of such parents. If parents be careless in the education of their children, and bring them not up in the fear of the Lord, hereafter their children may curse the time that ever they were born of them, and say, Oh that I rather had been of the offspring of vipers, or the generation of dragons, than that I had come of such parents! Oh that my mother had had a miscarrying womb, or that she never had had breasts to give me suck! Certainly, this will one day be the voice of many children against their parents. Look to it, that there be not a father nor mother in this place that may give cause to their children thus to wish they had never been born of such parents. And, certainly, if the enduring of sorrows and misery in this world may put them into such a condition, what then will sin, and being the authors of miseries to others, do? Those children that are abominable and wicked in their lives, and are causes of mischief to others, with how much cause may it be said, that it had been better their mother's womb had miscarried: as it was said of Judas, that it had been better that he had never been born. And so it may be said of many at this day. What abundance of evil are they the cause of to others! What woeful disturbances, distractions, and calamities do some men bring upon a nation! Had it not been better that their mothers' wombs had miscarried, and their breasts had not given them suck?

And again, What horrible wickedness are some guilty of! How many mothers this day have cause to say, Oh that my womb had miscarried of such a child! that my breasts had never given such a child suck! that ever one should have come out of my womb to do so much mischief, to take up arms to fight against his country, and against the saints, for the establishment of slavery and tyranny! Oh that these breasts of mine had never nourished such, for it may be they will prove very murderers! Certainly, if ever there were a time to wish their wombs had miscarried, and their breasts had never given suck, these are the times many may do so. Christ saith, in Luke xxiii. 29, "Blessed are the barren, and the wombs that never bare, and the paps which never gave suck." I say, concerning many in this kingdom at present might this be said. If any prophet could have foreseen that thou shouldst have been an actor in so much mischief as has been done in this kingdom of late, thou wouldst have said Amen to his prayer when he cried against thy mother, Lord, give this woman "a miscarrying womb and dry breasts."

Ver. 15. *All their wickedness is in Gilgal: for there I hated them: for the wickedness of their doings I will drive them out of mine house, I will love them no more: all their princes are revolters.*

"All their wickedness is in Gilgal: for there I hated them." What this Gilgal was, I opened in chap. iv. ver. 15. It was a place very famous for many remarkable things: stones were set up in remembrance of the great mercy in crossing the Jordan, there was the first passover after their deliverance, and there, too, they were circumcised: "And the Lord said unto Joshua, This day have I rolled away the reproach of Egypt from off you. Wherefore the name of the place is called Gilgal unto this day," Josh. v. 9. They were not circumcised during all that time in the wilderness, from whence it was called Gilgal, because the reproach was there rolled away. There, too, they first ate the fruit of the land. But now they have rendered this place of many mercies, the most abominable in the country; for because there were such great things done in Gilgal, they thought that it was a holy place, and therefore might justify their superstitious rites: God afterwards chose another place for his worship, yet they thought to sacrifice and worship in Gilgal; they thought it might be justified, because it was a place where such great things had been done. Now, saith God, I never intended that; "all their wickedness is in Gilgal."

Obs. 1. The superstitious are proud to put holiness upon places in which remarkable occurrences connected with religion have taken place. This we have had occasion to speak of before, and therefore I pass it.

"All their wickedness." That is, their chief wickedness; as if God should say, There is a great deal of wickedness among them, there are murders, and thefts, and abundance of other evils, breaches of the second table; but yet, above all, their wickedness is at Gilgal; they think to make use of that place where I showed so much mercy to them, they think to justify their superstitious worship by performing it there, but I will have them know that I hate this: "there I hated them," saith God, I abhor this whereby they think to justify themselves.

Obs. 2. Above all sins, the sin of idolatry makes a people hated of God. Because in that sin men think, by their own forms of worship, to atone to God for their wickedness; they present their own ways of worship, to justify themselves in all other kind of wickedness.

Obs. 3. To take occasion to sin from God's mercy, is that which God especially hates. They had met with much mercy at Gilgal, and they made it an occasion to their wickedness. To make that which should engage us to God to be an occasion of wickedness against God, is abominable in God's eyes. As you read in the law, you must not seethe a kid in its mother's milk, Exod. xxiii. 19; that which is the milk to preserve the kid, must not be a means for a second death; to seethe or boil it in its mother's milk, saith God, is unnatural cruelty: so for us to turn those things which should be a means to engage our hearts further to God into an occasion of further sinning against God, is abominable; "*there*," saith God, "I hated them."

But further concerning Gilgal. Their idolatrous priests told them, as is probable, that that place was a holy place, and that surely God, who had appeared so to them there, would accept of their services in that place rather than in any other; and so, though God afterwards chose another place, yet still they doted upon this Gilgal, and that which was so famous for God's worship, became as infamous for superstition and wickedness.

Polanus on the text compares Wittenberg in Germany to this Gilgal. Those places where the Lord has been peculiarly gracious to people, the devil seeks especially to corrupt. Wittenberg was the beginning of the Reformation by Luther; now, saith he, the devil has made it the theatre of divers heresies: so here, that place which had been the scene of the greatest mercy, is the place of the greatest wickedness; the devil envies it so much the more, and all their wickedness is here.

"All their wickedness." That is, their chief wickedness: their superstition and idolatry is the chief and the great wickedness that provokes God against a people; not only because of the presumption in it, but because it is an inlet to all other kind of wickedness.

Obs. 4. Where there is false worship in any place, all manner of wickedness follows. People stick to their superstitions more than to any thing, and therefore that is the chief wickedness; yea, and they think by them to satisfy God for their other sins; all their wickedness is there.

Obs. 5. To sin where there are the testimonies of God's abundant mercies, is very abominable. That is a great aggravation of sin, to sin in the face of the testimonies of the mercies of God. What! where so much mercy, yet there to be wicked and abominable? Does God fill thy family, thy chamber, thy closet, thy bed, thy shop, with the testimonies of his mercy? Take heed how thou sinnest *there* where there are abundant testimonies of God's mercy to witness against thee, to the aggravation of thy sin.

"All their wickedness is in Gilgal: for there I hated them." I find some interpreters, and that not one or two, but many, (and that makes me speak of this interpretation,) that refer this wickedness to the casting off the government that God had appointed, and introducing a new form: Gilgal was the place where they would have Saul to be their king, and cast off the government by judges that God had appointed among them; now this was the ground of all their other obstinate wickedness, and God remembers this a long time after, and saith, "All their wickedness is in Gilgal; for there I hated them."

Ar. Mon. and some Hebrew interpreters.

Obs. 6. It is hateful to God to cast off the government to which God would have us subject. The Jews had both their civil and ecclesiastical government by Divine institution, they were both mixed in one there. And though now we have not our civil government by Divine institution, but it is left to the creation of man, according as in prudence men in several countries shall think best; but ecclesiastical government certainly is as much by Divine institution now, as ever it was; and it must be so, because it is spiritual, and nothing can work in a spiritual way upon the inward man, but that which is by Divine institution: therefore whatever the government be, (I will not meddle with the particulars,) yet we must take heed how we cast off that which is appointed by God, for that is hateful in his sight: "there I hated them." We had need therefore search and examine to find what that is, and if we think it be not so clear as their government was to them, we must take so much the more pains to examine, and not think it long that there is so much time spent in seeking to find out what the government should be, for it is no light matter. Many think it but a circumstance, and that we need not trouble ourselves so much about it, nor spend so much time in searching it out. Learn henceforth to look upon it as a great matter, as a matter upon which the welfare or the evil of a kingdom much depends, for so it was here; Because they cast off, saith God, the government that I would have, "there I hated them."

Obs. 7. Some sins provoke God to anger, and some to grief, but some to hatred: "there I hated them." It is dreadful when our sins provoke hatred. This is the great difference between the sins of the saints and others; the sins of the saints may anger God, may grieve God, but the sins of others provoke God to hatred. "There I hated them."

Obs. 8. Sometimes God manifests his hatred in the very places where men sin against him: "*there* I hated them." As a man's spirit will rise if he come to a place where he has been wronged by any; so saith God, every time he looks upon Gilgal, Oh, there was this wickedness committed, "there I hated them."

"For the wickedness of their doings I will drive them out of mine house." They shall remain no longer in a church state, they shall remain no longer in my house.

Those who, under the colour of being under the church of God, yet live in the ways of wickedness, God will unchurch them even in regard of the outward appearance of a church estate; "I will drive them out of mine house." This is a dreadful expression: for a father to take his child or servant, and drive them out of his house, denotes great indignation: to be driven out of God's house is a sore evil, that makes all other evils indeed to be evil, as abiding in God's house is a great blessing, and recompenses the want of many outward blessings. If any of you that have been servants to great men, have been driven out of their houses for conscience' sake, yet if God take you into his house you are well enough; and for that you have a famous scripture in Psal. lii. 8, "But I am like a green olive tree in the house of God: I trust in the mercy of God for ever and ever." Upon what occasion was this Psalm penned? When David was driven out of the house of Saul by means of Doeg, who so exasperated Saul against him, that David was driven from his house, so that he dared not come into it. What comfort had David then? "But I am like a green olive tree in the house of God;" though I cannot be in Saul's house, and enjoy its privileges, yet, blessed be God, that I may be in his house, and there thrive and prosper as a green olive tree.

Obs. 9. God cannot endure wickedness in his house, "For the wickedness of their doings I will drive them out of my house," neither should we. As God accounts it his dishonour to have wickednesss and wicked men in his house, so should we in the church regard the ungodly. We must not make God's house an unclean place for all; the profane should be driven out, as Christ drove out the buyers and sellers out of the temple; yea, and so should all Christians drive out of their families wicked and ungodly servants: "He that worketh deceit shall not dwell within my house: he that telleth lies shall not tarry in my sight," saith David, Psal. ci. 7. It is a dishonour for any who make profession of religion, that though they be not themselves scandalous in their own lives, yet there are those in their house that live scandalously, their servants are as wicked as any; this is a dishonour to religion: God drives out wickedness out of his house, and do you expel it from yours.

"I will love them no more." By "love" here is meant, the communication of outward good things, for that carnal hearts account to be the only love of God: indeed, if they may have outward prosperity here in this world, they make that an argument of God's love to them. Well, saith God, though you have had many such fruits of my love, yet I will love you no more, I will take away all those privileges and good things which you have enjoyed. There are privileges and good things that come from no other love but that which may be taken away; oh, let not us be satisfied with such, let us be satisfied with nothing else but that which comes from everlasting love! You may have your outward estates, you may have comely bodies, health, strength, success in your labours, yea, you may have church privileges, and yet all this not come from the everlasting love of God, that can never be taken away: these fruits of God's love may be taken from you, and God may say as concerning all these, I will love you no more; but there are fruits of love, the sanctifying graces of God's Spirit, the fruits of electing love, and God can never say of these, I will love you no more.

"No more." After the many deliverances this people had in a way of love, God resolves with himself that he will have done with them, he "will love them no more," he will deliver them no more. God may withdraw the sense of his love from his people for a while, but yet manifest it again; the afflictions of the saints are but a little cloud that soon passes over, the sun soon breaks in again upon them, and love shines; but the sun of the wicked and ungodly sets, and never rises again. This is dreadful, when a man's ruin, or a people's ruin, is thus sealed by God; whatever mercies you have had heretofore, yet now there is an end of all; adieu, mercy, adieu, love; I had gracious manifestations of them once to my soul, but they are now gone; I must never enjoy them more, God has now changed his administration toward me, I must expect nothing but wrath, nothing but ruin, from the hand of his sore displeasure, and to be sunk everlastingly. Oh, let not thy provocations of God be continued, do not add to them. I have dealt falsely with God, dallied and trifled with the Lord, many times promising fair, but when I was delivered then have I dealt wickedly with thee, O Lord: but now, Lord, no more. Oh, take heed, if thou addest any more to thy wickedness, lest that this dreadful sentence be pronounced in heaven against thee, I will love thee no more. The words in the original are, לא אוסף אהבתם I will add no more love: I have done enough already, I will do good to this wretched creature no more; my goodness and mercy have had their turn; now, Spirit, strive with them no more; ordinances, no more do them any good; mercy, meddle no more with them: "I will love them no more."

"All their princes are revolters." This is a very strange expression. What "all?" Yes, even from Jeroboam to Hosea's time, all the princes of Israel were wicked men, for two hundred and fifty years, in all successions every one was naught, false, and ungodly, all were revolters. The paranomasia in the original is elegant, שריהם סוררים princes revolters, its force cannot well be expressed in our version. The Seventy render the latter word by ἀπειθοῦντες, men that could not be persuaded; all their princes were men that could not be persuaded; they were set upon their own way, their own ends, and would have their own politic fetches; and let prophets, let any of the godly, attempt to show them the mind of God, they were resolved on their own way, they would follow this course at all risks, for it they would venture even their lives, and the loss of their estates.

Obs. 10. Men great in power and authority think it a dishonour to alter their minds; such men will go on desperately, to the ruin of themselves and of their kingdoms, r‥her that hearken to counsel. Luther on the place has this expression; Being elated by their power, they would be above the word itself; they thought it much that their hearts should submit to the authority even of God's word. This is the wickedness of men's hearts, when they grow great they swell above the word of God.

Elati potentia volebant superiores esse verbo. Luther.

"All their princes are revolters." Some of them

made some kind of show when they came first to the crown, and raised great hopes that their times would be better than before, and that things that were evil in former princes' reigns would now be reformed, but within a while they went all the same way: thus Jehu, and so some others, promised fair at first, but they all turned to be revolters. From whence,

Obs. 11. The nature of creature engagements. See what they will work in the hearts of men when in the pursuit of their honours, their preferments, their great places of dignity, and power, and profit, and gain; see what they will do. Evil princes being engaged, and afraid of losing their power, if any should go to Jerusalem to worship, all went in one stream, not one of them was taken off from their great engagements; indeed many in smaller matters may be drawn off to God, but if it come to a great matter, then none. Thus it has happened with us. Perhaps some poor ministers, with small livings, would discern the truths of God, and the sinfulness of ceremonies; but where did your deans and bishops? where did any of the prelates that had great engagements? they would never see the truth that now almost every body sees, their great engagements hindered them. And so the great engagements of princes hindered them, though the truth was clear enough.

Obs. 12. According to people's interests so they are; as they see those above them go that have power over them, that way people will go. Ephraim is wicked, because "all their princes are revolters." Those that are in places of power drive the people along before them. God has little honour in the world but as it suits men's interests.

Obs. 13. Princes, though they should be used with reverence, yet must not be flattered; their sins must be showed plainly unto them, though they can hardly bear it. "All their princes are revolters." "Touch the mountains and they will smoke;" touch the great men, reprove but them, and presently the heat of their wrath rises, and they smoke even with indignation. But yet those that are faithful about them should trust God with their places, and estates, and with their lives. Oh had we but those about princes that would deal faithfully, and show them how far the guilt and the evil of blood may be upon them! certainly it would be otherwise with us than it is at this day, had we but Latimers and Deerings. Of Latimer it is said, that sending a book to King Henry the Eighth, he wrote in the first page of it, "Whoremongers and adulterers God will judge." And Deering, in his sermons even before the queen, speaking of disorders of the times, said, "These and these things are thus and thus, and you sit still and do nothing. May we not then well say with the prophet, It is the mercy of the Lord that we are not consumed, seeing there is so much disobedience both in subjects and in prince." Certainly much good might come had we now men of such spirits as heretofore lived.

Obs. 14. When princes successively are wicked, there is little hope of good to a people. The saints under the persecution of one groan and cry to God, but another comes and oppresses them more. We had need therefore pray for those in high places, for princes, for it concerns much the people, as we shall presently see more at large.

Ver. 16. *Ephraim is smitten, their root is dried up, they shall bear no fruit: yea, though they bring forth, yet will I slay even the beloved fruit of their womb.*

"Ephraim is smitten." הכה אפרים God had threatened Ephraim long before, but now "Ephraim is smitten;" not threatened only, but smitten. The phrase imports as if he were smitten from heaven by a thunderbolt, as if in a dreadful manner God himself smote him.

Obs. 1. God will not always forbear sinners. "Ephraim is smitten." He threatens a long time, but he smites at last. God may be a long time bending his bow, and making his arrows ready, and preparing the instruments of death, but at length he smites, and when he smites he smites terribly. How sad is the condition of a wicked man, who has had many warnings, and toward whom God has showed much patience, but of whom at length this is the news that one neighbour tells another, Oh, such a man is smitten of God, the wrath of God has pursued and has overtaken him, the fearful stroke of God is upon him! This certainly will be said of all wicked, impenitent, secure sinners. What sad reports are there at this day in all countries about us, even throughout the world! What is the news throughout the Christian world almost but this, England is smitten, the Lord has smitten her? The Lord has indeed smitten us with a dreadful stroke, and he still continues to smite us. Isa. v. 25 is made good upon us this day, "The anger of the Lord is kindled against his people, and he hath stretched forth his hand against them, and hath smitten them:" mark what follows, "the hills did tremble," (oh that our hearts did,) "and their carcasses were torn in the midst of the streets:" (and so it has been with us:) yet "for all this his anger is not turned away, but his hand is stretched out still." And thus it is with us. And the principal cause that is there given of such woeful smiting is, as you may observe in the 20th and 23rd verses, the perverseness of men's spirits in turning things quite contrary to the mind of God. As thus, "They call evil good, and good evil; they put darkness for light, and light for darkness; put bitter for sweet, and sweet for bitter: they justify the wicked for reward, and take away the righteousness of the righteous from him." This is the cause of this smiting; and never was there such perverseness in the hearts of men to turn things quite contrary, to cry truth for falsehood, the ways of sedition for the ways of Christ, to cry out against the saints that are for peace, as the great troublers of the kingdom, and in many places to "justify the wicked for reward." What favour have many malignants! and those that have most appeared in the cause of God, how are they discountenanced! This is the cause why God should smite us, and why our carcasses should be torn in the very streets. The Lord has smitten us this day, as he did the people in 1 Kings xiv. 15, "The Lord shall smite Israel, as a reed is shaken in the water," (and then there follows,) "he shall root up Israel out of this good land." So it is here, "Ephraim is smitten, their root is dried up." The Lord this day has smitten us "as a reed is shaken in the water." That which men cried up at first, they cry down again presently after; wavering and inconstant in all their ways, they know not indeed what they would have. The Lord has smitten us so that he has fetched blood, yea, the Lord has smitten us by those that should have protected us; and that is a sore smiting, to smite us by the hand of such as should protect us. Such a threatening is denounced in Zech. xi. 6; oh how is it made good upon us this day! the text there saith, "I will no more pity the inhabitants of the land, saith the Lord; but lo, I will deliver the men every one into his neighbour's hand, and into the hand of his king, and they shall smite the land; and out of their hand I will not deliver them." It is a very strange scripture, I know not the like in all the book of God. God threatens to smite this people, and how? "I will deliver the men every one into his neighbour's hand, and into the hand of his king, and they shall smite the land." Why is it so great an evil to be delivered into the hand of our neighbour, and into the hand of our king? Truly at this time it seems it was. The Lord thus smites us this day, he smites us sorely by giving us up to smite one another. We smite one another with the tongue. In Jer. xviii. 18, "Come, let us smite him with the tongue," say they. When was there ever such smiting with the tongue as there is now? yea, even good men smite one another. There was a time when the prophet desired to be smitten by the righteous; in Psal. cxli. 5, "Let the righteous smite me; it shall be a kindness: and let him reprove me; it shall be an excellent oil, which shall not break my head." But now we may justly cry out to God, Lord, let not the righteous smite me: the very smiting of the righteous is a sorer smiting this day than the smiting of enemies; yea, and worse too. In Isa. lviii. 4, they "fast to smite with the fist of wickedness;" that may imply too with the pen; and to smite with the pen is a sorer smiting sometimes than smiting with the sword. And they smite with the sword too, for brother is against brother, and father is against child, and child against father; and this is a forerunner of God's smiting the earth with a curse. In Mal. iv. 5, 6, the very close of the Old Testament, Elijah is prophesied to come, and to "turn the heart of the fathers to the children, and the heart of the children to their fathers, lest" (adds the text) the Lord "come and smite the earth with a curse." Oh that Elijah might come amongst us! otherwise, what can be expected but the Lord's smiting the land with a most dreadful curse? When were fathers against children, and children against fathers, as now, and that in matters of controversy? It was wont to be a proverbial speech among the Jews, when they had any knotty controversy that they could not untie, When Elias shall come, then we shall know the meaning of this. We may say at present, Well, because we see what controversies and what differences in judgment exist, the Lord Christ (whose forerunner Elias was to be) will come ere long, and open all things to us: the Messias will come again and tell us all, and satisfy us in all our difficulties, and put an end to all our disputes. But for the present the Lord smites us, not only by the sword, but he smites us as he smote the men of Sodom, "with blindness," Gen. xix. 11. The curse threatened in Deut. xxviii. 28, 29, is even now upon us, "The Lord shall smite thee with madness, and blindness, and astonishment of heart; and thou shalt grope at noonday, as the blind gropeth in darkness, and thou shalt not prosper in thy ways: and thou shalt be only oppressed and spoiled evermore, and no man shall save thee." O my brethren, how is this fulfilled at this day! with what blindness, and madness, and astonishment are the people of this land smitten! If God smote not men now with blindness, it is impossible but they should see what should be done in such a time as this. Indeed now almost every man in the kingdom cries of being oppressed and spoiled evermore.

We thought that when the spoilers and oppressors who were amongst us had passed away, that we were safe and well. Oh! but it is renewed again, and now come the spoilers the second time, and the third time, spoiling evermore; and this is the fruit of God's smiting men with blindness and madness. And yet who is it that returns to him that smites him? But, Lord, seeing thou art smiting, oh that thou wouldst smite once more, smite these rocky hearts of ours; if thou wilt but smite there, that might free us from other strokes; then might gush out tears of repentance, then might we smite every man upon his own heart, and turn unto thee.

From the connexion of this and the preceding verse,

Obs. 2. When God suffers rulers to revolt, the people are smitten. "All their princes are revolters;" and, "Ephraim is smitten." Pray then much for your rulers; and let not them that have the chief government in their hand think it strange that people inquire into their actions, and that they use all means in their power to keep them upright; for if they revolt they not only undo themselves, but undo us. It concerns us to inquire how it is with them, and to be solicitous about them; and they must not bid us that are beneath them to let them alone and meddle with our own business, and follow that which concerns us, as certainly what they do does indeed much concern us: were it indeed that if they miscarried they only should be smitten, then we had less to do to look after them; but if they revolt we are smitten. If a child should, in all humility and reverence, beseech his father to leave off certain sinful courses, or to take heed that he be not misled by certain counsels, and his father should say, Concern yourself about your own business; the child might well answer, O father, I hear in the word of God, that God doth visit the sins of the fathers upon the children, and I may suffer for these sins of yours when you are dead and gone, therefore I beseech you, consider what you do: so I say, if we should petition and labour with our governors in all humility to take heed of any evil counsel, and they should bid us look to our own concerns, we may well answer, We have heard in the word, that when the "princes are revolters," "Ephraim is smitten;" that if governors revolt from any former protestations, the people are likely to suffer. It is, we know, from the revolting of many of our lords and members of the high court that we have been smitten as we have been. How many of them have now revolted to the enemy! their revolting has been the cause of our being thus sorely smitten.

Obs. 3. The compulsion of authority does not excuse sin. It cannot free Ephraim from being smitten because their governors are evil; they cannot excuse their sin by that. Perhaps the people would plead thus; What could we do? we could not help it, those that were in power enjoined such things, and if we did not obey them they would undo us; we were not able to bear their smiting of us, therefore we were forced to yield. Oh! better endure the smiting of man than the smiting of God; "It is a fearful thing to fall into the hands of the living God."

Obs. 4. The apprehension of God's hand in smiting should humble the hearts of sinners. Thus in 2 Chron. xxvi. 20, it is told of Uzziah, that when he saw that he was smitten, though he were stout and proud before, yet then "he hasted to go out" of the temple. There is no longer standing out, for the Lord has smitten. So when we apprehend God smiting, there is no standing out against the great God, we had need make haste to reform.

"Their root is dried up." But though we be smitten we hope we may grow; we may lose our leaves and some of our boughs, but we hope that we shall spring again. Perhaps these are the vain apprehensions of some men, who never look to making their peace with God. No, saith God, I will not only smite to take off your leaves and branches, but I will smite the very root; "their root is dried up." There is difference between the pruning and lopping of a tree, and the drying up of its root; there may be help so long as the root remains alive. I will never trouble myself any further (saith God) with them; I have already smitten off their boughs, and that has done no good, I will dry up the very root now. It is a great aggravation of God's smiting when he smites at the root. Every smiting is not a drying up of the root. It is the base unbelief of our hearts, the discontentedness, frowardness, sullenness of our vile spirits, that makes us thus conclude almost upon every stroke of God, that he intends our undoing; if he but smite us so that a few leaves or branches are removed, we are presently ready to conclude that God intends to blast us, and to dry up the very root, and ruin us utterly. How often in our unbelief, when tried by temptations, and the leaves of our comforts, our enlargements, and the like, have been shaken off, how often do we conclude, Oh! the Lord is coming against me, and he will certainly blast all, all that I seem to have, the very root of all my hopes and comforts, will presently be blasted! This is the evil of our hearts, and springs from our sullen, froward unbelief. It may be God intends only to prune thee and to take away superfluities, that so the sap may go down more to the root, that thou mayst more exercise the root-graces, humility, patience, faith, self-denial; God perhaps smites only to make the sap go down more to nourish these root-graces, though thou concludest that he will dry up the root presently. In this smiting wherewithal the Lord has smitten us we hope that he intends not to dry up the root, but we may say of it as in Isa. xxvii. 7, "Hath he smitten him, as he smote those that smote him? or is he slain according to the slaughter of them that are slain by him?" The godly party may suffer much, but I make no question but the ungodly party has suffered as much; and "by this shall the iniquity of Jacob be purged; and this is all the fruit to take away his sin." And in the 4th verse God tells us, that "fury is not in him:" God is fain to make an apology to his people when he is smiting; Though I smite you, yet not so as I smote those that smote you, but "I stay my rough wind in the day of the east wind," and "fury is not in me:" "by this shall the iniquity of Jacob be purged," the end of all is "to take away his sin."

Obs. 5. God has his time to dry up the roots of sinners, and the roots of nations. 1. God dried up the roots of many that have made fair profession in former times; they had no other root but only parts, and common gifts, and morality, and this root God dried up. Many fair and glorious professors, how are they this day blasted! sapless, dry spirits, and useless in the world, even at this time when there is so much service required of them! And by being dried up, what are they but prepared for the fire? Old, withered, sapless professors, I say, whose "root is dried up," are fitted for nothing but the fire; they are like those spoken of Jude 12, corrupt trees, δένδρα φθινοπωρινά, trees that are corrupt in the autumn. Thus it is with many professors, at the time when God expects fruit, they are sapless, corrupt, dried up by the root; and what then are they fitted for but for the fire?

2. God has his time to dry up the root of nations, as in Isa. v. 24. Now we might seek to understand what the root of a nation is, but I think we need not in this place, because it is sufficient by way of metaphor, to show that God does not only afflict a nation, but designs its utter ruin and destruction.

Yet a word or two on this point.

What was the root of Ephraim?

1. The covenant that God made with them. And when God intends to break his covenant with them, because they broke theirs, then he dries up the root; and therefore in the next chapter you find that God charges them with dealing "falsely in making a covenant," Hos. x. 4.

2. The godly in Ephraim. So Isa. vi. 13, "But yet in it shall be a tenth, and it shall return, and shall be eaten: as a teil tree, and as an oak, whose substance is in them, when they cast their leaves: so the holy seed shall be the substance thereof." So here, "the holy seed shall be the substance thereof." The holy seed in a kingdom is as the root and substance of it; and yet such is the perverse wretchedness of men, that, in stirring against them, they would root out the very root of the nation.

3. The vigour and power of the fundamental laws in a kingdom are as the root of it, from whence springs all its outward peace and comfort.

4. The blessing of God upon the wisdom and faithfulness of those in place, that is as the root of the good of a nation; in these things especially consist the roots of a nation.

We hope that God will not wholly dry up our root, only let us take heed of this: though there be indeed a difference between the covenant of God with the nation of the Jews, and any covenant that God makes with any nation at this day, yet if we be false in the covenant that we make with God, this may root us out; let us look to it that the vigour and power of the fundamental laws of the kingdom be maintained, and that the godly be not discountenanced; let us not set ourselves to root out them, for in so doing we do but seek to root out ourselves; and let us pray that the blessing of God may abide upon those that are in place of power; and while these things continue we may hope that the Lord intends, though he may scatter and break us in pieces, yet to suffer a root to abide, and, notwithstanding all our misdeeds, to preserve it to his own glory. There will be a root of the saints that shall flourish till Jesus Christ comes again: "The root of the righteous shall not be moved," Prov. xii. 3; though the righteous may be lopped from all their outward comforts, yet their root must not be moved, that lies deeper than any creature power is able to reach. But there is a root, oh that God would dry it up! a root that the Scripture speaks of, Deut. xxix. 18, a root of bitterness, "that beareth gall and wormwood." Oh what bitter fruit does that root bear amongst us! Oh that God would indeed dry it up!

"They shall bear no fruit." They would bring forth fruit to themselves, and seeing they would bring forth no other fruit but to themselves, they shall bring forth no fruit, saith God. How happy were we if God would say to the root of bitterness that we speak of, as he said to the fig tree, "Let no fruit grow on thee henceforward for ever!" Matt. xxi. 19. Oh that such a curse from God would fall upon the root of bitterness which is in the hearts of so many, that we might never hear the evil language, the evil speeches of people, and the bitter expressions which we have heard heretofore!

"Yea, though they bring forth, yet will I slay even the beloved fruit of their womb." מחמדי translated here "beloved," signifies also desirable, the desires of their womb. Children are the desires of the womb, that is, women are very strong in their desires after them, "Give me children, or else I die," said Rachel. Indeed harlots care only for their lust, and would have no fruit of their womb; an excellent emblem are they of the vanity of many preachers, who, if they can satisfy their lusts, and show their wit and parts, care not for any fruit at all, care not for begetting any children to God. The same word here used for desires, and translated "beloved," is likewise in other scriptures similarly rendered: Dan. ix. 23, O man "greatly beloved:" O man of desires. So in Dan. x. 11, where Daniel is called, "a man greatly beloved," it is, a man of desires. And so in Prov. xxxi. 2, "What, my son? and what, the son of my womb? and what, the son of my vows?" You see with what a great deal of affection Solomon's mother speaks, "my son," "the son of my womb," and "the son of my vows," or desires. But indeed the word is there properly rendered, "the son of my *vows*." I made vows to God, if God would give thee me, I would given thee up to God, and by vows dedicated thee to his service: "what, the son of my vows!" Women therefore should look upon their children as the children of their vows, and show forth their love to them in the way that God would have them. We have a strange scripture in Tit. ii. 4; "the aged women" are there commanded to "teach the young women to love their husbands, to love their children:" it is a strange thing that a mother must be taught to love her children. Thy child is "the beloved fruit" of thy womb, but yet thou must be taught by God, taught by his people, and by his word, to love thy children in a right and holy way; take heed of loving them so as to provoke God to take them from you, take heed that they be not slain for your sakes. Many mothers have slain the fruit of their womb by loving them too much. Do not honour your children above God, as Eli did: when you look upon their natural comeliness, consider they have that in them, and that too by your means, which, except they have another birth, will make them objects of God's eternal hatred. They are the beloved fruit of your wombs, and you look upon them and see that they are sweet and comely babes; yea, but think withal that through you they are so conceived and brought forth, that if they have not another birth, though they be objects of your joy by being born to you, yet they will be objects of God's hatred by being born in sin by you, Psal. li. 5: you may look upon them as objects of your delight, but God may look upon them as those whom he has appointed to death. Alas, those poor, sweet babes, what hurt have they done? God sees enough in them that in his justice he may slay them. But in this that he saith, he will "slay even the beloved fruit of their womb," or the desirable fruit,

Obs. 6. If what is dear to God be not dear to you, even the very fruit of your womb shall not be regarded by him. That is the scope of the threatening. Here, saith God, is a people to whom my honour, my ordinances, my saints are not dear; therefore even the desirable things of their womb, the very "beloved fruit of their womb," that which goes more to their hearts than any thing in the world, that which is the dearest to them, I will slay in mine anger. If you would have what is dear to you dear unto God, let that which is dear to God be dear unto you.

Ver. 17. *My God will cast them away, because they did not hearken unto him: and they shall be wanderers among the nations.*

"My God will cast them away." Not their God, but *my* God. There is much to be observed from hence.

Obs. 1. Let all the world forsake God, a faithful soul will not. Hosea lived in wicked times, all the ten tribes generally had departed from God; but still "*my* God," my soul shall keep close to God; I have chosen the Lord to be mine, and I have found such soul-satisfying good in him, that he shall be mine for ever; here will I rest for ever; I have chosen the way of God's true worship, I will not conform myself to the common mode of worship where I live, but I will choose God to be "my God," whatsoever the world doth. Such was the prophet's constancy and such should be ours.

Obs. 2. In evil times, when others forsake God, yet a gracious soul can claim God as its God: yea, and especially when times of trouble come, when sore evils are ready to fall upon the people generally, yet here is the comfort of a gracious heart, "*my* God." Blessed be God for the interest which I have in him; they may take away my house, my estate, my means, but they cannot take away "my God;" in him I have interest still, which they cannot take from me. This was the comfort of Micah, in chap. vii.: he describes the evil of his times, "The good man is perished out of the earth: and there is none upright among men: they all lie in wait for blood; they hunt every man his brother with a net," ver. 2. "The best of them is a brier: the most upright is sharper than a thorn hedge," ver. 4. "Trust ye not in a friend, put ye not confidence in a guide: keep the doors of thy mouth from her that lieth in thy bosom," ver. 5. But after all, in the 7th verse, he exclaims, "Therefore I will look unto the Lord; I will wait for the God of my salvation: my God will hear me." O my brethren, there may come times ere long that the knowledge of God, and interest in him, may be worth to us ten thousand thousand worlds.

Obs. 3. It is no presumption for individuals to challenge a special interest in God, in way of distinction from the multitude. "My God." How singular was Hosea at this time! This people might think him very presumptuous: What, as if nobody had interest in God but he! Is not God our God as well as his? He is bold to speak this in way of distinction: You may forsake God and his worship, but I have cleaved to God, he is "*my* God." So in 1 John v. 19, you may see how singular John was: "We know that we are of God, and the whole world lieth in wickedness." How could the world take such an expression? What are you? A few poor people; and yet "we know," saith he, "that we are of God, and the whole world lieth in wickedness." What are you more than others? Yes, John knew, and would not be discouraged to affirm, that the world did lie in wickedness; and yet, "we know that we are of God."

Let not men then be offended at the fewness of those who keep the truth, and the multitude of those who forsake it. In the life of Phocion the Athenian, Plutarch relates, that there was once an oracle of Apollo Delphias read before the people, which said, That although all the people agreed, yet there was one man amongst them who dissented from them. Now the people were startled at this; but Phocion stepping forth before them all, bid them never seek further for the man, for it was he, who liked none of all their doings; and yet Phocion at length gained as much respect from them as ever any man did, and they chose him forty times to be their prætor. And so, let never so many go on in a way for which thou canst not see light in thy conscience, keep to thy principles, only examine them thoroughly. The respect we owe to ourselves and to others, calls us to make a narrow scrutiny. We should think we may possibly be rather in an error than they, and we ought to give all due reverence to the judgments of men more in number, more learned, perhaps, and more wise, than ourselves; praying to God above all to show us his mind, and searching our own hearts to see that there be nothing particular to bias or prejudice them. After all such endeavours to find out the truth, if God still persuade our consciences, we should not be discouraged because the greater part go the other way, but keep to that which our consciences tell us is the right. Thus it was with Hosea, though they went generally another way, yet he could exclaim in truth, "My God."

Obs. 4. It is a dreadful thing for wicked men to be declared against by the godly. "My God will cast them away." Those who have interest in God, who know God's mind, know that such a God as he is cannot have communion with such people. Thus Isaiah speaks at the latter end of the 57th chapter, "There is no peace, saith my God, to the wicked." He puts the emphasis there; he saith not, "There is no peace to the wicked," saith God, but "saith *my* God." Oh! when those that have an interest in God, and keep close communion with him, and thereby come to be much acquainted with his mind, when they shall declare concerning you, "There is no peace," do not slight it. If any of them should say, If I know any thing of the mind of God, if I have any interest in God, certainly there can be no peace to thee in such a way as thou art in; take heed of slighting such warnings from men that are godly and humble. True, many that make very great profession of religion, may be bold to suspect and to censure others, who, may be, are better than themselves; but if I see one that walks humbly, strict in his way, holy, and heavenly, and self-denying in other things, if such a man should but have any suspicion of my condition, I had need look to it, it should daunt my heart to have such a Christian look upon me but with a suspicious eye.

Obs. 5. When men are violent in wickedness God will be violent in his judgments. "My God will cast them away," with violence and with anger, as a man takes his stubborn child or servant, and thrusts them out of his house. So Lam. ii. 6, "He hath violently taken away his tabernacle." They abused that ordinance of God, abused his tabernacle, and he has taken it violently away. O unworthy, wretched people, that should enjoy mine ordinances so, and abuse them! "He hath violently taken away," as in anger and indignation against them.

Take heed of being violent in the ways of sin. You will cast the cords away, and cast away the truths, Psal. ii.; Isa. v.; take heed thou becomest not a castaway thyself: those that are so ready to cast away God's truths, it is just with God that he should cast them away, as a man casts away a loathsome thing. They cast away their idols "as a menstruous cloth, and say unto them, Get thee hence," Isa. xxx. 22. You perhaps cast away the truths of God as loathsome now, but the Lord will one day cast thee away as a filthy and loathsome thing.

"Because they did not hearken unto him." "My God will cast them away." But why? "Because they did not hearken unto him." This is a notable sentence, saith Luther, and worthy to be written upon all our walls. Indeed there is much in it; they would hearken to such and such, and to the rules of their policy, and to their own ends, but not to God. Hence the special point to be observed here is,

Hæc notabilis est sententia, et digna quæ in omnibus parietibus scribatur. Luther.

Obs. 6. In what concerns God's worship we must hearken to God. The not hearkening to God is that which provokes God to cast away a people with indignation. "My God will cast them away, because they did not hearken unto him!" Perhaps other duties we may know by the light of nature; but when we come to matters of worship, there God must be hearkened to, and none else. God expects that his creature should hearken to him in what he saith; we should be all as the servant was with his ear bored, Exod. xxi. 6. Christ himself had his ear bored, he would hearken to what his Father said; therefore Psal. xl. 6 saith, "Mine ears hast thou opened," or bored: Christ was as a servant with his ear bored, to note that he would have his ear at the command of his Father. And who or what are you, that you should have your ears free? In Isa. xxviii. 23, mark what several expressions we have about calling to hearken; "Give ye ear, and hear my voice; hearken, and hear my speech." In one little verse there are these four; "give ye ear," "hear," "hearken," "hear." Oh, God expects that we should have a hearing ear; and that is the way for wisdom. In 1 Kings iii. 9, Solomon prays, "Give therefore thy servant an understanding heart;" but in the Hebrew it is, a hearing heart; that I may have a hearing heart, so as to be able to judge thy people. They that have not a hearing heart, have not an understanding heart. The not hearkening to God comes from the pride of heart. In Jer. xiii. 15, "Hear ye, and give ear; be not proud: for the Lord hath spoken." There is no such pride as the turning away our ears from hearkening to God. And turning away our ear from the law of God is that which makes God turn away his ear from hearing our prayers; it is an evident sign of coming destruction. In 2 Chron. xxv. 16, mark what the prophet saith to Amaziah, "I know that God hath determined to destroy thee, because thou hast done this, and hast not hearkened unto my counsel." Dost thou come to the word, and not hearken to the counsel of God in his word? It is an evident sign that God intends to destroy thee. Oh hear! "hear, and your souls shall live," "your souls shall live." Indeed here lies the ground of almost all the evil in professors of religion, the not hearkening to the truth. I suppose those that make profession of religion, if they have enlightened consciences, dare not sin against a known truth; but now here is the evil of thy heart, and look well to it. Thou dost say, If I knew it were a truth I would not go against it. Yea, but the corruption of thy heart makes thee unwilling to hearken to it, you would fain have such a thing not to be a truth. I appeal to you, have you never felt some corruptions thus stirring within you, that when you see that if you should be taken off from the side you have espoused, a great deal of ease and liberty and outward comforts would be gone, your hearts are very loth that that should be true, and therefore you are not willing to hearken with a clear heart, so as to entertain the truth, when proved? It is the sign of a gracious heart, to be willing to retain every truth, to be willing to let the truth prevail, whatever it be; but the lusts of men's hearts hinder them from hearkening, and render them loth to receive those truths that most affect them. But when any shall be able, in the presence of God, upon an examination of their hearts, to say, O Lord, let thy truth prevail, thou knowest that I am willing to hearken to every truth of thine; though it should pluck away all my outward comforts, I would fain know thy truth, thy very strictest truths, those which most concern thy glory, and thy true worship. Whatever becomes of my credit or estate, Lord, let thy truth prevail in my heart. It is, I say, a gracious heart that will thus hearken to God and his truth. But, as Jeremiah saith, men have "uncircumcised ears, that cannot hear;" through the corruption that is in their spirits, they cannot hearken to those things which seem to make against them.

"They shall be wanderers among the nations." These last words contain the threatening.

Obs. 7. It is a judgment to have an unsettled spirit. A spirit wandering up and down, unable to settle to any thing, sometimes in this place, sometimes in that; sometimes in this way, and sometimes in another; this is a judgment of God. Solomon saith, "Better is the sight of the eyes than the wandering of the desire," Eccles. vi. 9. The wandering of men's appetites and desires work them a great deal of vexation.

Obs. 8. Those who are cast away out of God's house can have no rest; they go about like the unclean spirit, seeking rest, but can find none. The church of God and his ordinances are God's rest, "This is my rest for ever," Psal. cxxxii. 14, and should be the rest of the hearts of his people; and they are indeed the rest of the hearts of those that are gracious. But alas, poor soul! who art wandering from God, whither goest thou? where indeed will be thy rest? It was the curse of God upon Cain, to be a wanderer up and down upon the face of the earth.

But you will say, May not men be wanderers; that is, may not they be cast out of their habitations and countries, and wander up and down, and yet not be cast off from God?

True, we read in Heb. xi. 37, that the Christians "wandered about in sheepskins and goatskins; of whom the world was not worthy." But that was in a way of persecution for God, and for his truth: it was not because they would *not* hearken, but because they *would* hearken. And though thou shouldst be forced to to wander from thy brethren, and the sweet habitation that thou hadst, and thy friends, and art perhaps fain wander up and down even for thy life, yea, but canst thou say, Yet I hope I am not one of God's cast-aways? It is one of God's epithets in which he glories, that he "will gather the outcasts of Israel." Man has cast me out, yea, but I bless God, I carry a good conscience with me. Such need not be troubled at their wandering state, as can carry a good conscience with them. You are cast out from your friends; yea, but still thou hast the bird that sings in thy bosom. Canst thou say, I have not cast away thy commandments, Lord? Indeed, if a man's conscience tell him that he has cast away God's commandments, then, if he wanders, it is dreadful to him. What though thou art wandering from thy house, from thy outward comforts, yet not from God's commandments; "Cast me not away from thy presence," saith David; though thou art cast out from thy friends, yet not from God's presence. Here it is, "They shall be wanderers among the nations;" and Psal. xliv. 11, "Thou hast scattered us among the heathen." It was a great judgment of God to be scattered among the nations, for they were a people that were separated from the nations, and not to be reckoned among the nations, they were God's "peculiar treasure." This curse is upon the Jews to this very day; how are they wanderers among the nations!

Obs. 9. We should prize the communion of saints. Let us learn what a blessing it is to live among our own people, especially among the saints, in the enjoyment of God's ordinances; let us make use of it now, lest God teach us what it is by casting us away and making us to wander among the wicked and ungodly: then your consciences will fly in your faces, and tell you, Oh what blessed times, what sweet communion, we once had! but we began to neglect the prize that God put into our hand. Oh if we were where once we were, we would meet often, and pray, and confer, and would labour to edify one another in our most holy faith, and warm one another's spirits, not spending all our time in wrangling and jangling; but now those times are gone, and we are cast away, and are wandering up and down among wicked and ungodly people. Truly there has not been a time for many years when the communion of the saints has been so little improved as at this day; we now wander, as it were, among ourselves, and little converse one with another, what we should do living together. Just were it with God to bring this judgment upon us, that we should wander among wicked people here and there, and that we should not be privileged to see the face of saints, to have converse or communion with them.

CHAPTER X.

Ver. 1. *Israel is an empty vine, he bringeth forth fruit unto himself: according to the multitude of his fruit he hath increased the altars; according to the goodness of his land they have made goodly images.*

GUALTER makes this the beginning of Hosea's seventh sermon. The argument is like that of the former, upbraiding and threatening. Hosea had to deal with tough and stout spirits, and therefore he still strikes with sharp rebukes and severe threats.

"Israel is an empty vine." The church is often in Scripture compared to a vine, as in Psal. lxxx. 8, "Thou hast brought a vine out of Egypt: thou hast cast out the heathen, and planted it." And in that known place, Isa. v. 1, "Now will I sing to my well-beloved a song of my beloved, touching his vineyard."

The church is here compared to a vine, and that for many reasons:

1. No plant has a more unpromising outside than the vine; how mean is its appearance! it looks so weather-beaten, rugged, grizzled, and weak with its hollow stalk: and such is the church; the outside of it is very unpromising, little beauty and comeliness; as Christ himself had little beauty and excellency in his outward form.

2. The vine is the most fruitful plant that grows out of the earth. That great naturalist, Pliny, tells of very strange fruitfulness of some kind of vines; in lib. 14. c. 4, he tells of ten culei, about eighteen hundred gallons, that an acre of vines brought forth in a year; nay, in the first chapter of the same book, he tells of one stock, one single vine, planted by Livia the empress, which yielded a hundred and eight gallons of good wine yearly. The vine is a very fruitful thing, though unpromising in the outside. And what fruit indeed is there brought forth to God in the world but by his churches? and God expects much fruitfulness among his people; however, as you shall hear, they are charged with being empty.

3. No plant requires so great care as the vine; what a deal of pains are bestowed in dressing, underpropping, and pruning it, what constant looking to it requires! And the Lord has the greatest care of his people, of his church: he accounts it no dishonour to be the husbandman himself; as he is said to be in John xv.: and in Isa. xxvii. 3, you have a most admirable expression of God's taking care of his church, as his vine; "I the Lord do keep it; I will water it every moment: lest any hurt it, I will keep it night and day." I will keep it, and I will water it, and that "every moment;" and again, "lest any hurt it, I will keep it night and day." And this is the vineyard that he speaks of in the beginning of this chapter, and it was the vineyard that brought out red wine, the best sort of wine. Those that bring forth the best sort of wine, shall have the best of God's care, and charge, and protection over them.

4. The vine is the most depending plant in the world; unable to underprop itself, it must have props more than other plants, and therefore nature has given it tendrils by which it catches hold upon any thing near it. And so the church, weak in itself, the most depending thing in the world, depends upon the props that God affords it. You have an excellent place illustrative of this in Isa. xxvii. 2, 3, where the Holy Ghost, speaking of "a vineyard of red wine," saith in the 4th verse, "Fury is not in me;" which shows that there should come a kind of great storm and tempest, but he would not have his people to be discouraged. "Fury is not in me." And then in the 5th verse, "Let him take hold of my strength, that he may make peace with me, and he shall make peace with me." "Let him take hold of my strength;" that is, speaking to his church as a vine, In the time when my fury is abroad, yet do you, like the vine, which catches hold upon a pole, and there underprops itself, so take hold of my power, act but faith upon it in time of storms and tempests, and you shall have peace; thus, though never so much troubled abroad in the world with others, yet in me the church may, nay shall, have peace. It is the nature of the vine to catch hold upon that which is next it, especially in time of storms; and so when the strongest oaks are rent in pieces, yet the vine, clinging to its supports, abides unharmed.

5. If it be not fruitful, it is the most unprofitable thing in the world. I suppose you are familiar with Ezek. xv. 2—4, "What is the vine tree more than any tree, or than a branch which is among the trees of the forest? Shall wood be taken thereof to do any work? or will men take a pin of it to hang any vessel thereon? Behold, it is cast into the fire for fuel:" it is not meet for any work; the vine is meet for nothing, not to make a pin, if it be not fruitful. And no people in the world are so unprofitable as professors of religion, if they bring not forth the fruit of godliness. The world may be rid of such people better than of any else.

6. A vine is the most spreading of plants, it spreads larger than other plants, and fills a great deal of room with its branches; and so is intimated by the promise of the church in Isa. xxvii. 6, "Israel shall blossom and bud, and fill the face of the world with fruit."

7. The vine is the softest and most tender of plants, the emblem of peace; the sitting under our vines is used to set forth peace. And so the people of God should be of tender, soft spirits, not like the bramble, nor the thorn; if we sit under thorns and brambles we may be pricked with them, but sitting under the vine, there is nothing but sweetness and delight.

"Israel is a vine," yea, but he is an "empty vine." The word in the original is בוקק Israel is an emptying vine; the sense is much the same, an empty vine, or an emptying vine: that is, though there be much cost bestowed upon Ephraim, so that he might be fruitful, yet he makes himself empty. This shows how he comes to be an empty vine; not because God's mercy is scant to him, but he makes himself so by his sin; what sap and moisture he has, he pours it forth into other things, and so is empty himself.

Israel was a vine full of clusters, refreshing God himself; as you heard in chap. ix., he was to the Lord as grapes in the wilderness, as a vine that did bring forth grapes in the wilderness, sweet to a weary and thirsty traveller. Israel was once such; yea, but now he is come to be "an empty vine," though he grows in the vineyard of God, and not in the wilderness.

"An empty vine," and no marvel, for, as you have heard in the latter end of the former chapter, he would not hearken to the Lord, he would not hear the word of the Lord, and so the Lord threatened to cast him away. Whence Luther observes, The word is like a fruitful rain, there can no true fruit be without the word. Those that will not hearken to the word, no marvel though they be empty; it is the word that makes fruitful, it is that which is as the fruitful rain: those that leave and forsake the word, observe how fruitless they become, what empty spirits they have. When heretofore they were forward in hearing the word, and loved it, and delighted in it, then they were fruitful; but since they have been taken off from the word, you find their spirits empty, and their lives empty. No men in the world so empty as those who would worship God in another way than the word appoints; men that would think to worship God after their own fancies and ways, oh how empty are they in all the duties their will-worship dictates!

Verbum tanquam fœcunda pluvia, sine verbo nulli possunt veri fructus. Luther.

Obs. 1. Emptiness in those who profess themselves to be God's people, is a very great evil. Oh, it is a grievous charge to be brought against those who grow in God's vineyard, who profess themselves to be God's, that they are empty, "an empty vine." When we would speak of a man contemptuously, as having no natural or acquired excellency in him, we say such a one is an empty or light fellow; and that is the meaning of the word which you have in Matt. v. 22, "Whosoever shall say to his brother, Raca, shall be in danger of the council;" the word Raca signifies empty, and imports as much as if he should call his brother an empty, worthless fellow. So in James ii. 20, "But wilt thou know, O vain man, that faith without works is dead?" The words are, ὦ ἄνθρωπε κενὲ, O empty man; Knowest thou not, O empty man, "that faith without works is dead?" Many keep a great deal of noise about faith, and God's free grace, and yet are extremely empty men, and understand little of the true excellency of the covenant of grace: Knowest thou not, O empty man, "that faith without works is dead?" Speak as much as thou wilt of faith and God's grace, yet if there be no works thou art an empty man. Nature will not endure emptiness; some of the philosophers have said, that the world would rather be dissolved than that there should be any vacuity; creatures will move contrary to their nature rather than they will suffer a vacuity. Certainly a vacuum in the souls of God's people is the worst possible vacuum: for,

1. It is unnatural.

2. It is a dishonour to their Root. Christ has all the fulness of the Godhead in him, and of his fulness are we to receive grace for grace: to grow upon him, upon such a Root, and yet to be empty, oh what a dishonour is this to Jesus Christ!

3. It frustrates the Lord of all the care, and cost, and charge he expends. If thou wert another plant, that grew in the wilderness, it were not much; but a vine, and one in God's vineyard, and yet fruitless, oh this is a sore evil!

4. There is no blessing upon thy soul if thou art "an empty vine;" as in Isa. lxv. 8, "As the new wine is found in the cluster, and one saith, Destroy it not; for a blessing is in it." If there be wine in the cluster, then a blessing is found in it, but otherwise destroy it. No blessing is found in those that are of empty spirits.

5. If there be grace, it cannot but bear fruit. It is an evil in a vine to have but a little sap, to shoot forth in leaves and bear no fruit: yea, but what is that to grace, which is the Divine nature itself, the most glorious thing in the world? Therefore for Christians to be without fruit is an exceeding great evil. Dost thou know what fruit is? One gracious action that comes from the sap of the root that is in Christ, is more worth than heaven and earth; one single gracious act, I say, is more worth than heaven and earth. Oh, the fruit of the saints is fruit to eternity, and to be without this fruit must needs be a great evil. Those that are empty and without fruit are said, in John xv. 6, to be but ὡς κλῆμα, "*as* a branch," and then such a branch as must be cut off. God will cut off those branches; he will cut them off from their profession, and suffer them to fall so that they shall not continue to the end.

6. Common gifts shall be taken away. Oh, how many that heretofore seemed to flourish, yet, bearing no fruit, but leaves only, now their leaves are gone, their common gifts are taken away from them; they are not only withered, but cast away, cast away from God, and out of the hearts of the saints; and men shall gather them, the men of the world shall catch them, and shall make use of them, and they shall be cast into the fire and burned; cast into the fire, not for a fiery trial, but that they may be burned: these are the threatenings against those that bear no fruit. It is the glory of God's people, to be filled with "the fruits of righteousness," Phil. i. 11; to "be filled with the Spirit," Eph. v. 18; yea, to "be filled with all the fulness of God," Eph. iii. 19. Oh how contrary is this to emptying! And filled indeed the saints should be with fruit, because they are the very fulness of Christ, "the fulness of him that filleth all in all." In Eph. i. 23, the church is said to be the fulness of Jesus Christ himself; and shall the church be an empty vine, when it is the very "fulness of him that filleth all in all?"

7. An empty spirit is a fit dwelling-place for the devil. In Matt. xii. 44, he findeth the house empty, and then comes in: where the devil sees an empty spirit, there is a fit place for him to enter. It is an evil thing for you to grow upon God's ground and to cumber it, to cumber any part of God's ground; it may be, if thou wert gone, there might be another in thy family, or place, that might bring forth fruit to God; God might have more rent, but thou hinderest: for all his possessions in the world the great rent is, the fruit that the church brings forth. As in Cant. viii. 11, it is said, that Solomon let out his vineyard, and it brought him in a thousand pieces of silver for the fruit of it; so God, he lets out his vineyard, and his rent is, the fruit that the saints bring forth to him. What glory has God in the world, if those that profess themselves to be his people should be empty?

8. God does not let us sit under empty vines; our vines have been fruitful vines, shall we then be empty vines ourselves?.

9. The Lord has justly made this our vine bleed for its emptiness; it bleeds, and is in danger to bleed to death; it has brought forth little fruit, and therefore it is just with God that he should let this vine now bleed even to death.

10. The evil of emptiness is great according to the greatness of opportunities. To be empty when God puts great opportunities of great service into our hands, and expects an energetical fulfilment of them, is surely most vile. Oh, my brethren, that we were but sensible of this!

But if it be an evil thing to be empty, what then is it to bring forth "the grapes of Sodom," and "the clusters of Gomorrah?" to bring forth the wine of the gall of asps, wild grapes? And yet a great deal of such fruit has been brought forth; and truly the fruit that most men bear now, is wild grapes at the best. If men do any thing, yet they do so mingle the vanity of pride, the sourness of their own spirits, the rigidness of their own nature, with what they do, that all is but ungrateful to God.

Well, to conclude this, about the emptiness of the vine: O let us prize fruitfulness more, and say, as the vine that is brought in in Judg. ix., "Should I leave my wine, which cheereth God and man, and go to be promoted over the trees?" Oh! so, shall we leave our fruitfulness for any earthly advantage in the world? Let us account it a greater advantage to bring forth much fruit to the glory of God, than to glory in any earthly good. No matter what becomes of us, so we may be but fruitful: though God dung us, though he cast all the filth and reproaches in the world upon us, yet if God will make this but cause us to be fruitful, it is no great matter.

But further, from the manner of the phrase: Israel is a vine emptying itself.

That is an aggravation of emptiness, when we empty ourselves; when God is not wanting to us in means, but we are in their use. And what is the cause of emptiness, but the pouring out our strength and spirits on our lusts and the world? No marvel though we have no fruit for God, and strength in his service, when we let out all to other things.

The Vulgate renders it, *vitis frondosa*, a leafy vine. The Sept. εὐκληματοῦσα, a vine that brings forth goodly branches. And our version, "an empty vine." "Empty;" that is, all the strength and juice of it is let out in the goodliness of the branches and leaves. So, many professors in these days empty out all the strength that they have, and all their parts, merely into leaves; and have goodly branches, make goodly outward profession, and give goodly words, and will speak much of religion; but nothing but leaves, nothing but words, all this while.

Pliny, lib. 17. cap. 22, saith of vines, that it is fit (at least for two years together after their planting) to cut them down to the very ground, that they may not sprout out in leaves, and so lose their juice and strength at the root. And truly this is that which has marred the hopeful beginnings of many young people in these times, they have presently sprouted out into leaves; for never was there a more hopeful time of young people than at the beginning of this parliament, and no greater encouragement was there than from them at that time; I will not say it is wholly lost, but oh how many of them that began to understand the ways of God have let out all their strength in leaves, and contests, and disputes, and wranglings, and strange kind of opinions, and little fruit is come of any thing! nay, there is little savour at all in their spirits. Oh how happy had it been if God had kept them down in humiliation to the very ground for a year or two together! Now any work of humiliation is a thing that is altogether laid aside, all presently sprout out into leaves. My brethren, whatsoever may be said, or whatsoever heretofore has seemed to be preached, to the contrary, yet certainly, if rightly understood, they have been but doctrines that must of necessity be acknowledged. We do not press humiliation as the condition of the covenant of grace, we look not at it so, but humiliation keeps the spirits of men low, and empties them of themselves; keeps them down, (I say,) and renders them a great deal more fruitful, so that they cannot run up as mere leaves, and spend their strength in vain, outward show. How many of those amongst us are fallen off again, not only to be slight and vain, but even to be wicked and ungodly, because they were not kept down low for a while; but God ordering things so that they should live in times of liberty, oh how luxuriant have the leaves of their profession been! When God lets a people grow rank, and prunes them not, they quickly grow barren. We had never so many rank Christians growing out in luxurious branches as at present; they think they have overtopped all, because they can talk more than others do; whereas there are some poor Christians that grow low to the ground, and when they get a little comfort it is gone away from them presently, who yet walk humbly before God, and nobody takes notice of them, they are despised and contemned; but these will grow and be delightful to the palate of God, when such rank professors as those shall wither and be cast out. The pruned vines bring forth the best fruit: compare Isa. v., with chap. xxvii. In the 5th chapter God complains of his vineyard, that when he looked for grapes it brought forth wild grapes. There the prophet speaks of the time before the captivity; but in the 27th chapter there is a scripture that seems to refer to the times after the captivity, and there the vineyard of God is said to be "a vineyard of red wine;" and God speaks much unto it what it should be after the time of the captivity, it should bring forth the best kind of wine, for then God pruned it. They thought that God would come in a furious manner upon them; no, saith he, "Fury is not in me," my intent hereby is "to purge away the iniquity of Jacob." The vines that are pruned bring forth the best and the most fruit.

But I find other interpreters render this text thus, Israel is a spoiled vine. And Luther refers it to the emptying of the abundance of her riches and prosperity. Indeed these two go together, emptiness of fruit, and being emptied of our comforts and prosperity, being spoiled. Israel has spoiled herself, and I have for her sins let the spoilers come among her, and so have emptied her of all her good: even while she enjoyed her outward prosperity, she was emptied of the blessing of God upon her; but afterward the Lord emptied her of all her outward good also.

Obs. 2. Sin will empty a land of all the blessings God has bestowed. Sin is an emptying thing, sin empties lands, and families, and persons of all their outward comforts. In Isa. xxxiv. 11, God threatens "the line of confusion, and the stones of emptiness," for sin. And oh how has it emptied many parts of our land! how has sin emptied us! what empty houses are there in many places! Houses that were wont in every room of them to be filled with costly furniture, now the owners look upon the walls and see them bare and destitute: chests, too, that were filled with such brave clothes heretofore, now are broken to pieces: and those places which were filled with diet and plenty are now empty; barns empty, purses empty, and bellies empty; yea, the veins of men emptied even of their very blood. Oh how are we a spoiled vine now at this day! The vine that a while since was so delightful to God and man, and so glorious even in the esteem of all round about us, yet now, how has the Lord sent his emptiers to empty us! as in Nah. ii. 2, "The Lord hath turned away the excellency of Jacob, as the excellency of Israel: for the emptiers have emptied them out, and marred their vine branches." This text is fulfilled towards many parts of this kingdom at this day.

"He bringeth forth fruit unto himself." This is very strange, "empty," and yet bring forth fruit; if he brings forth fruit, how empty? Yes, it may very well consist: "he bringeth forth fruit *to himself;*" he is empty with respect to any fruit he brings forth to me, but yet has juice and sap enough to bring forth fruit to himself. Oh how many that are barren towards God, and have no abilities to do any thing for him, yet, when they come to do any thing for themselves, how active and stirring are they! when you put them upon any duty for God, then they are weak, and unable, and the like; but in a matter that concerns themselves, there they have spirit enough, and too much a great deal. If parents have children that sin against God, they scarcely notice it; but if they offend against themselves, oh how do their spirits rise, and what rage is there in the family! The truth is, were our hearts as they should be, if we have no strength for God we should have none for ourselves; and whereas we excuse ourselves, saying that we are weak in our memories, and unable to resist temptation, and can do nothing for God, we should take a holy revenge upon ourselves, and say, Certainly, if I can do nothing for God I will do nothing for myself; if I cannot rejoice in God I will not rejoice in myself; and if I cannot take care for God I will not take care for myself. To be barren to God and fruitful to ourselves, this is a great disproportion.

"Unto himself." The Vulgate renders it, *fructus adæquatus est ei*, his fruit is like to himself; he bringeth forth fruit like to himself.

Obs. 4. Men of base principles will do base things, corrupt hearts will have corrupt ways. An ingenuous spirit sometimes wonders to see the ways of many so base and vile as they are; men in public employment who have opportunity to do God a great deal of service, and when it comes to it, how sordidly and basely do they carry themselves, not caring what becomes of the public good, of God, and kingdoms, and churches, so be it they may scrape but a little to themselves! Yea, but do not wonder, it is fruit suitable to themselves; they are men of base spirits, of base, corrupt principles, and therefore they bring forth fruit like themselves, fruit like the stock. So many times children are like their parents; their parents are wicked, and they wicked accordingly. Like an imp or branch of such a stock, such are the fruits of many.

"He bringeth forth fruit unto himself." That is, in all that he does he aims at himself, he has regard to his own ends, to fetch about his own designs, to bring his own plots to an issue, and all must be subservient to them. Ephraim had many designs and plots to make themselves rich, and all their strength and ability were made to subserve their own designs. It was said of Judah in their captivity, in Zech. vii. 5, 6, They did fast, and eat, and drink to themselves; all that was done was with a view to themselves; whereas the fruit that they should have brought forth, should have been to God, and not to themselves. There is a very sweet place for that in Cant. vii. 13, "At our gates are all manner of pleasant fruits, new and old, which I have laid up for thee, O my beloved." Thus should every gracious heart say, and especially then when God makes your hearts most fruitful with pleasant fruit, new and old. Have ye at any time found your hearts enlarged and melt towards God, and felt full liberty in his service? Take heed now that this pleasant and sweet fruit new from God, and the old experiences which you have had heretofore of his goodness, be not but as fruit brought forth to yourseves; let not corruption reap that which God has sown. You know it is a curse that one should sow and another reap: it is God that sows, and shall the flesh reap now? and shall the devil reap? Oh! let not these sweet fruits, especially the fruit of enlargement in prayer, and the fruit of abilities to do God service in any public work, let them not be as fruit for yourselves, do not take the glory of them to yourselves, but let this fruit be for your Beloved. When at any time you find your hearts most fruitful, graces most fully exercised, O think thus, I will lay up this for my Beloved, I will lay the experiences of the goodness of God unto me, that may fit me to glorify God more than heretofore. Oh that is sweet indeed, when God comes in with fruit, and we lay it up for our Beloved! God is to have all our fruit. You observe in Cant. viii., that Solomon let out his vineyard; but mark, in letting it out he must have a thousand pieces of silver, and the husbandmen must have two hundred: if God afford us some wages for what we do, let not us attempt to take the greater part to ourselves; let Solomon have the thousand, and let us be contented if we may have two hundred; but ordinarily we take the greater sum, and return the less to God in any fruit. But observe further the 12th verse, the difference between Solomon's vineyard and Christ's vineyard; Solomon let out his vineyard, but Christ saith, "My vineyard, which is mine, is before me:" there is noted this difference, that Jesus Christ takes the care of his own vineyard, he does not let it out, "it is before him." And therefore if we have any thing, we must not have it so much for our wages as free gift; for Christ does not let out his vineyard as Solomon did, but he keeps it and dresses it himself, and therefore it is fit that he should have all the fruit. In Isa. lxi. 3, "That they might be called trees of righteousness, the planting of the Lord, that he might be glorified." Such should the saints be, they should bring forth fruits unto God. And in Phil. i. 11, "Being filled with the fruits of righteousness, which are by Jesus Christ, unto the glory and praise of God." So should the saints be, and all the fruits they bear.

But carnal hearts aim at themselves; all that they do, they act from a principle within themselves, and no further, and therefore they cannot go beyond themselves. It is an argument that all thou doest has a principle not higher than self, when thou actest for thyself; whereas the principle that the saints act by, is the principle of grace derived from heaven, and therefore carried to heaven, as the water is carried as high as the fountain from whence it comes, Eccles. i. 7. A selfish heart is a narrow heart; but a gracious heart is a heart enlarged, it enlarges itself to infiniteness; such is the property of grace, though it cannot be infinite, yet it is enlarged to infiniteness. Those that work for themselves, the truth is, lose themselves in their working, and lose all their fruit; it is thy worst self that thou aimest at. There is a kind of selfishness which we may aim at; that is, if we can make God to be our own end, our happiness, as the saints do. In such a case no men in the world may do more for themselves than the saints: yea, but how? because they make more of their own good to be in God than themselves, and they make themselves to be more in God than in themselves, and therefore they have themselves more than any, but they have themselves in God. And no men lose themselves more than those that seek themselves most. "He that will lose his life, shall save it." Those that will aim at themselves, what is that but a little money, and credit, and esteem of men? O poor, base, vile heart, hast thou nothing else but this? whereas all the glory that is in God himself may be thy portion, and thyself may be in it; so that if God himself be happy, thou mayst be happy, because God himself may come to be thy portion; and is not that a better self to be emptied into God? but therein thou darest not trust God, nor thyself to empty thyself into God, but certainly that is the way to enjoy thyself. "For all seek their own," (saith the apostle,) "not the things which are Jesus Christ's," Phil. ii. 21. Oh! this selfishness, it is vile at all times, but never so vile as at this time; for men now to look and aim at themselves, especially those in public places, is the most abominable and the most foolish thing in the world. Mariners in the time of a calm may look to their several cabins, but during a storm, then to be painting and making fine their cabins, were worse than foolish; how would they deserve to be pulled out by the ears, and to be cast into the sea, that should then be looking to their own interests! What is your joy more than the joy of others? and what are you that you must have ease and content more than others? If ever God calls us to be emptied of ourselves, certainly it is in such times as these are. But we should chiefly,

Obs. 5. It is all one to be an empty Christian, and to bring forth fruit to oneself. Men think that which they bring forth to themselves is clear gain; but this is an infinite mistake, for that which is for thyself is lost, and that which is for God is gained. Professors that are selfish are empty. Many of you complain of emptiness and unfruitfulness, here is the reason, You are so selfish. That prayer is an empty prayer, though never so full of words and excellent expressions, whose end is self: many of the saints, in joining with persons, find their prayers to be such, though there be excellent words, because they see selfishness. Men that aim at self, had need be cunning to keep it from being seen. Let self be seen in a duty, though it be never so glorious outwardly, yet it is loathsome in the eyes of the very saints. Let but a man appear to be affected with himself in what he does, with the tone of his voice, or carriage, or gesture, or any thing else, we know how abominable it is in the eyes of all. And so for sermons, where they are selfish, certainly they are empty things; and so I might instance in every other thing that men do. The fulness of the spirit in a prayer or sermon, or any other duty, is the seeking to lift up the name of the blessed God in the duty, in that consists its fulness. Many of weak parts and very poor abilities, yet having their hearts upon God in a duty, there is a fulness in their service; there is more in that weak expression, in those sighs and groans, than in all the eloquence of your empty hypocrites, they not being filled with all the will of God; so Col. iv. 12 should be rendered: it is in your Bibles, "That ye may stand complete in all the will of God;" but the original is πεπληρωμενοι ἐν παντὶ ϑελήματι τοῦ Θεοῦ, being filled with all the will of God. If thou wouldst have a fulness in what thou doest, a fulness in a prayer, a fulness in thy service, in any thing thou doest, be filled with the will of God, and not with thy self-ends. You know empty vessels will break when you set them at the fire, and so will selfish spirits; those that are selfish, quickly grow empty. You that are merchants know, that if your factors abroad trade for themselves, they seldom do any great matters for you. I have known merchants that have therefore been chary to permit their men to trade for themselves. And God loves not to see us trading for ourselves, but only as we trade for him, and so account that to be for ourselves. And here is an evident demonstration that your selfishness will make you empty for God. How many are there that complain of emptiness! Oh! they cannot do this, and they cannot do that! Why? because except they find comfort, and that coming in which they aim at, they have no mind to any duty. They go to prayer, and strive to pray, and they come away and say, Oh the empty prayers that we make! But what is the reason that you cannot pray as you would? You have no heart to pray. If you would have enlargement in prayer, and present answer of your prayer to get what you would have, O, then your hearts would be much let out in prayer, and then you would have a mind to pray; but now, though it be your duty to pray, because you thereby tender up the worship that a creature owes to God, that is no argument to put you upon prayer: so self appears in your very prayers. But now try this way, try this way but to get above yourselves once, and be emptied of yourselves; look with a more single eye to God when you go to prayer, let this be the great motive, O Lord, this is that worship which I as a creature owe to thee, the strength of my body and soul are due to thee; and though I have not enlargements and comforts, though I feel not that I get by duty to myself, yet, in obedience to thee, and that I might lift up thy name, and that I might worship thee, I am resolved to go on in such duties as thou requirest of me: try but this way, and see whether you will not grow more fruitful in prayer than you did before.

But to pass that, I find that Pareus and others render the words thus, An empty vine he is, although he treasure up fruit unto himself: and so we may understand emptiness by that word which I have opened to you, a spoiled vine; he is a spoiled vine, and he is emptied of all his prosperity, and riches, and glory that he had, although he seeks to treasure up unto himself. They seek to treasure and enrich themselves, to lay up and provide for themselves now, that they may have store by them come what will come; but this will not do, saith God, Israel must be a spoiled, empty vine for all this. And here we may profitably

Obs. 6. When God is spoiling a nation, it is vain for men to think to provide for themselves. Certainly it is not the time, when God is spoiling and emptying a nation, or other parts of the kingdom, for men to have their thoughts intent on scraping together an estate to themselves even out of the evils of the times, by places and by offices to enrich themselves; certainly there can be little honour or little comfort in such an estate. It surely is the very frame and guise of a vile spirit to think of enriching itself in such times as the present. What God may cast men into by extraordinary providence at any time, or on account of some eminent services, we speak not of; but certainly, if God in his mercy shall put an end to such times as these are, and men shall prove to be rich after this storm is over, who had not some eminent providence of God to cast it upon them, I say, whosoever shall so appear rich after these times, it will be little honour to him or his posterity, but rather be the most dishonourable riches ever gained in the world. In Jer. xlv. 4, 5, the Lord saith to Baruch, who was a good man and yet in this much misguided, "Behold, that which I have built will I break down, and that which I have planted I will pluck up, even this whole land. And seekest thou great things for thyself? seek them not." I am breaking down that which I have built, and plucking up what I have planted, and doest thou seek great things for thyself? seek them not. In Acts viii. 20, saith Peter to Simon Magus, "Thy money perish with thee." So may I say to many, Is this a time for men to treasure to themselves, for men to have their chief care now to gain riches? Oh! it is just with God to say to thee, Thy riches perish with thee. Whosoever now will make it his chief care, and think now it is a time of trouble, and now I may gain thus and thus, and it will not appear; I say, those that shall make this to be their care now, to take advantage of these times to treasure up to themselves, just were it with God to say of them and their riches, Thy money and thy riches perish with thee. There follows,

"According to the multitude of his fruit he hath increased the altars; according to the goodness of his land they have made goodly images." Here you have the unthankfulness of Ephraim; you have had his barrenness, and selfishness, in the two former expressions, and now here his unthankfulness. The devil loves superstitious and idolatrous people to have good lands and good possessions, that he may be served accordingly; idolaters serve their idols according to the lands and possessions that they have; "according to the multitude of his fruit" were the multitude of his altars. And certainly it is great reason why all the papists are so desirous to get England, and contribute so much that they might but get into England, and get possession here, for in no place could they have more goodly images, and more brave things, than here in England; the fruitfulness of this land is that which makes it such an object to the antichristian party, and to the devil; he thinks that, might the popish party get here, oh the brave things that I should have here! I begin to have fine altars, but if they had possession of all the riches in the land, then what golden monuments should I have! We began to have great charges laid out upon temples, (as they called them,) but certainly if they should prevail now, you should have them build them up to the very skies, such pinnacles and glorious things there would be; for the land is a great deal more fruitful and goodly than it was heretofore, it is improved mightily now. What brave buildings were there in our forefathers' time! witness these that we have near us, Westminster, and Paul's, and the like. I remember Latimer, in one of his sermons before the king, tells of his father, a man of good hospitality, and that kept a horse for the king, that the portion he gave with his daughter was some five pounds. So I say, if that men were so poor and mean in former times, and yet from superstition raised such edifices, certainly, if the superstitious party had the possession of the land now, there would be brave things done; and therefore the devil, seeing that, strives to bring it into their power.

Obs. 7. To make God's blessings the means to increase our wickedness, is an abominable thing; to increase our sins according to the increase of God's blessings. How many may be charged with this, That when they were of low and mean estates, then God had more service from them than he has now they are of higher estates! the higher they are raised in their estates, the lower they are in the work of God: as it is observed of men that grow very fat, they have so much the less blood. And so the fatter men are in their estates, many times the less blood and life, and less spirits, they have for God. There are many reasons against this.

1. Certainly this is against the ingenuity of a Christian, to be less for God when he has most from him; when his own turn is served, then to turn his back from the Author of all his good.

2. This is a main Christian principle, that the good of an estate consists in this, That it gives a proportionably large opportunity for the service of God. This is a great Christian principle about estates; an estate affords either a less or greater opportunity for God's service; upon this principle does a Christian go in the enjoyment of his estate. Now for a man to be less for God, or more for that which is evil, the better his estate is, he thereby goes against that great Christian maxim.

3. Yea, and it is against thy prayers for a sanctified use of thy estate. Does God give thee an estate? I hope thou dost seek that this may be sanctified. Now for thee to do less for God, and more for that which is evil, by the increase of thy estate, thou dost go against a sanctifying prayer.

But yet the chief point of all I take to be this: Mark here, They do "according" (for there lies the very strength of these words): "according to the multitude of his fruit," and "according to the goodness of his land they have made goodly images." There is a great deal of elegancy in the Hebrew, so that from these two expressions, "according," and "according," here is the note: That the love that idolaters bear to their idols, it is proportionable to what abilities they have to show their love; "according to the multitude of his fruit," and "according to the goodness of his land." When idolaters are low they will yet do what they can, and as they grow up they will do more.

לארצו הטיבו מצבות

Virgil has a very fine expression of the idolater toward his idol there: We now make thee but of marble, but if so be our flock does increase, and we have as many lambs as we have sheep, we will make thee of gold.

Nunc te marmoreum pro tempore fecimus: at tu, si fœtura gregem suppleverit, aureus esto. Ecl. 7.

And thus the true worshippers of God should do in their service to God that which is proportionable; if they be able to bestow but marble for the present, if God raises their estates their marble is to be turned into gold: and not only in regard of their estates, but of the gifts and means they have, their abilities; know that that which God will accept of when thou art low in thy gifts, and means, and parts, will not serve turn when God increases thee in them all. Have you more than others? Account it your shame that it should be said of any in the world, That there is such a one that has less mercies than I, and yet God has more service from him than he has from me. There is no proportion between many of your increases for God, and your increases from God. Now you must look to the proportion, to make it as exact as can be, my increase from God, and my increase for God. O, be often paralleling these two together, and see whether one do not by far exceed the other; and be not at rest, O Christian, except thou canst make a meet return: those who are rich, must be rich in good works. In 1 Tim. vi. 17, 18, God "giveth us richly;" therefore "be rich in good works." It is not enough for a rich man to give sixpence or twelvepence for some great service, but he is to be rich in good works, and for relieving distressed ones, and the maintenance of the gospel; he is to be rich in good works, and to account his riches to be as well in his good works as in his estates. Thou hast so much comings-in more than others, thou art rich in that; yea, but what works go from thee more than others? art thou rich in that? If we should judge the riches of men and women by their good works, how many rich men would there be accounted very poor! Every man must be serviceable as God has blessed them, 1 Cor. xvi. 2. O, this meditation would be of very great use to those whose estates are blessed by God: think thus, Is there such a distance between what service I do for God and the service others do, as there is between what I receive from God and what others receive from God? This meditation (I say) would be very useful. Cast up your accounts thus: Consider, what service do others for God, and what do I? I do as well as others. True, but is there as much distance between the service that I do and the service my poor neighbour renders, as between my estate and his estate? You perhaps can look upon poor people carrying tankards, earning dearly tenpence or twelvepence a day, and you have many hundreds a year coming in; now is there as much difference? You would be loth to be in such a condition as those are in; oh, but is there as much difference between the glory that God has from you, and the glory that God has from them? It may be, some of them, after having been hard at work all day, when they return home, and get alone with their wives and children, fall a praying, and with tears bless God for their bread and drink.

And perhaps you, in your many hundreds a year, and many dishes at your table, are but discontented and froward. O consider, that though God has raised you above others in estates, yet you are lower than many others in good works. If a man's estate has increased you shall quickly see it in his clothes; his house and his furniture shall be finer than before, the increase will manifest itself that way; but can you see it in his good works more than before? does such a man more for the service of God than before, more for the relieving of the woeful necessities of his poor brethren? If men come finer to the Exchange than their wont, persons are ready to think, What, is this man grown richer than he was before? You should (if God does raise your estates) make it appear in being forward with good works, in good works that are chargeable, so that men may take notice of your riches by your rich works, rather than your rich clothes. Except there be a proportion between our plenty and our prosperity, there is no evidence that our prosperity comes in mercy; but if a proportion, then not only an evidence that our prosperity comes in mercy, but a good addition to the good of our prosperity. If a merchant's ship come home, and he has gotten a thousand pounds by the voyage, now if God raises his heart proportionably to the furtherance of the gospel, that is more than ten thousand pounds: a man would account it well if he had gotten so much and he could employ it to get ten times as much more. Think but thus: By being proportionable in service for God, thou dost increase the blessing thou hast received in thine estate ten-fold. Thou often thinkest of the blessing of God in giving thee an estate more than before, and others think of it, Oh what a blessing such a man has! yea, but think of the blessing that should follow; has God given him or her a heart to do a great deal of service? The second blessing is the great blessing indeed. When David had rest, he presently thinks of building God a house, and that in a manner proportionable to what God had blessed him with. And that is very observable in the difference between Moses's altar and Solomon's altar: you know Moses was in times of affliction, and his altar was five cubits long and three cubits broad; and Solomon's was twenty cubits long and ten broad: Moses was low for outwards, Solomon was high; therefore Moses's was five cubits high and three broad, and Solomon's was twenty cubits long and ten broad. God does proportion his goodness to what we do for him; why should not we also proportion our service to what he does for us? Therefore when God blesses any of you in your outward estate, it is very good to do somewhat presently, as thus. A man perhaps heretofore had but a little stock, and lived in a parish where he had but poor and mean preaching; now God raises his estate, and his house is better, his clothes better, why then should not I have better preaching for my soul? And so, many other ways, if God has blessed you with good preaching, then help your poor neighbours some way or other, that the gospel may be furthered by God's blessing, and that as he has prospered you.

"They have made goodly images." כטוב לארצו הטיבו מצבות an elegant paranomasia, according to their good lands, so "goodly images." Now this word that is translated "goodly," signifies also beauty: they that were good benefactors to their images, made their images beautiful. The same word is used in the story of Jezebel, where she is said to tire her head, she made herself a "goodly" head. Oh how great a shame is it to do so much for images, dead images, and to do so little for the images of God! Shall idolaters not care what cost they bestow upon their dead images, and shalt thou see one bearing the lively impress of the image of God, naked, and hungry, and miserable, and wilt thou deny them? Every man has the image of God in some measure, even wicked men; but especially in those that are godly there is a renewed image, there the very life of God, the Divine nature, appears: and what a charge will this be, when God shall bring idolaters at the day of judgment against thee, that shall have bestowed so much upon their dead images, whilst thou hast let these images of God suffer want! Certainly, so long as there are any bearing God's image upon them that want, and want miserably too, for thee to think of increasing thy estate now, and to be richer than in former times, argues great and vile insensibility.

"Goodly images." Men are taken with outward shows, but to a spiritual heart the ordinances of God, though they be never so plain, are goodly things. A spiritual heart sees a goodliness in all God's ordinances; carnal hearts see goodliness only in their outward bravery, and outward pomp and glory. Pareus observes on this, Here we see the vain distinction that papists make between their images and idols; we see here they are charged for making goodly images.

Ver. 2. *Their heart is divided; now shall they be found faulty: he shall break down their altars, he shall spoil their images.*

"Their heart is divided; now shall they be found faulty." My brethren, I know that you would be willing enough that I should, in such a point as this is, go beyond an expository way, seeing God has cast me upon it; but as this point has been fully handled in a treatise of mine already printed,* (to which I shall refer you,) I shall pass it, and proceed to the following words.

"He shall break down their altars, he shall spoil their images." The divisions of this people were much about the rites of worship, most of them contending for false modes against the true: they would have their images and their altars honoured; but God saith he will break them down, and spoil them; Ye keep a stir for them, but you shall not have them. But he will "break down their altars;" *decollabit*, the word comes from a root that signifies a neck; and so that which you have in your books translated "break down," is, break their necks; he will break the necks of their altars. Ternovius, a learned interpreter, observes upon the place, that it has an allusion to that which they were wont to have upon their altars, *ornamenta quasi capitella*, ornaments which were as heads or crowns upon their altars; yea, but saith the Lord, I will break the necks of them all. "He shall break down their altars, he shall spoil their images." The notes from thence are briefly these:

Decollabit יערום a ערף cervix. Vatabl.

Obs. 1. Though men strive never so much to maintain that which is evil, God will break it; they may by their contending and seeking have it a while, but God will break the neck of it at last, it shall come to nothing.

Obs. 2. Though men be convinced of an evil, yet if the temptation abide they will recur to it again. "He shall break down their altars." Why? they were convinced before of the evil of them, for so in the former words, "now shall they be found faulty," they shall acknowledge themselves guilty in contending so much for them. Well, but, saith God, though you are convinced of your guiltiness, yet that is not enough, I will break them down; for otherwise, if they remain, they may be snares unto you: to prevent that evil, the evil temptations are to be taken away as far as possible. You acknowledge yourselves guilty when my hand is upon you, but you will turn to it again if the temptation be not removed, therefore will I break down your altars, and spoil your images.

* Irenicum: Heart-divisions opened, &c.

Obs. 3. Superstitious altars and images are to be taken away. It is the magistrate's work to take away those that are in public places; but I have spoken of that before, and shall not recur to it now; only if you meet with any superstitious pictures and images, you must not keep them, and say, What hurt will these do? though they do not hurt now, yet they may afterwards: you are not to sell and make gain of them, but do as God does, break them down and spoil them, that they may not hereafter be snares to others.

Obs. 4. Those things to which we give that respect which is God's due, are liable to the stroke of God. They gave to their altars and images the respect due to God; God's Spirit rises against that; "he shall break down their altars, he shall spoil their images," saith God. So, whatsoever it be to which you give that respect which God challenges to himself, you may expect that God will spoil it and break it down. If you give to your estates the respect due to God, you make an idol of them, and may expect that God will break them; yea, to your children, your names, your bodies, parts, whatsoever you have, if you rob God of that respect which is due to him, and give it unto them, expect that God will break such things.

Obs. 5. If it be God's will to break down that which is evil in his worship, let us take heed that we have no hand to set it up; that we do not endeavour to set up false worship, for it is in God's heart to break it down: let us not set up idols, either in our hearts, or elsewhere.

Obs. 6. We must not break down superstitious and idolatrous things to make up our own broken estates. We should labour to abolish those things, and not seek our own benefit by them; as certainly many do in breaking down things that are naught and superstitious, they endeavour to make up their broken estates, and that is all they truly aim at. But, saith God, I will break them down and utterly spoil them: so should we, and look not to our own advantage.

"He shall break down." I find some interpreters render the words thus, it shall break them down, and so apply it to their divided hearts. The pronoun translated "he" is relative, and the antecedent, according to the former exposition, is in that last verse of the former chapter where he had spoken of God; but according to this interpretation the antecedent is, "Their heart is divided;" their hearts, their very dissensions, their divisions, shall break down their altars, and spoil their images. From such an interpretation we might profitably

Obs. 7. Men's divisions and contentions break the neck of that which they contend for; especially when men in their contentions are violent, furious, outrageous, and heady, they do usually by their rage and passion break down and spoil the very thing that they would fain maintain; and their party is very little beholden to such as thus act in a spirit of contention. You know those furious, violent prelates, did not they break the neck of their prelacy merely by their fury and outrageousness? And in any party it always happens, that those who are the most furious and outrageous do the least service to their party, and many times are the very break-neck of their party, and of their cause: it shall break them down.

Ver. 3. *For now they shall say, We have no king, because we feared not the Lord; what then should a king do to us?*

What! break down our altars, and spoil our images? No, the king will maintain them against you all: let the prophets say what they can, and a company of precise fools oppose them as they will, we have the king on our side, he will rather lose his crown than he will lose these things, he will stand for them to his very life, and therefore we do not fear that they shall be broken down. No, that will not serve your turns, (saith the prophet,) your king shall not be able to help himself, much less to help you in those superstitious ways that you would have.

"For now they shall say, We have no king." They rejoiced and gloried much in their king, they relied altogether upon their king; no matter for the prophets, they have the king's commandment, for what they have done they can show the king's broad seal, and they were sure that they had the king's heart with them, their king would bear them out in all. They cared not therefore what they did, so be it they had the countenance of their king, that he would defend them; and not only defend, but, by being zealous and forward for his ways, they hoped to have promotion by him; they did not fear to be questioned for any thing, no matter whether they went against law or not, they could shelter themselves under the power and favour of the king: the pomp and glory of the court were a great thing in their eyes, and made them bold in their idolatry and oppression; because of the power and greatness of the king, who should control them in any thing that they did? But now, (saith the prophet,) you have had your day; you have had your time that you could thus shelter yourselves under the power of the king, and do what you list, and oppress, and rage, and nobody durst meddle with you because of the power of the king, but now the case is altered.

"For now they shall say, We have no king." Had they no king? Yes, Hoshea was their king; but the meaning is, it is all one as if we had no king, his power is so broken that, the truth is, he cannot help us. Drusius, upon the place, saith, He cannot protect us, which is the duty of the king, and therefore it is as if we had none. "Now they shall say, We have no king;" alas, he is not able to save himself, he can do nothing for us, his pomp, his power, and glory are in the dust; he is distressed himself, and we are miserably disappointed of our hopes, we are undone. Who can help us now? whither shall we go? what shall we do? Our consciences upbraid us now for our bold, presumptuous wickedness. Oh how far were our hearts from the fear of the Lord! we dared the God of heaven and all his prophets, we boldly ventured upon those ways which we were told, yea, which we knew in our very consciences, were a provocation to the Lord; we set up our own worship, we pleased ourselves, we made our wills to be the rules of all our actions, we took liberty to satisfy our lusts, we mingled our own ways with God's ordinances, we subjected religion to public ends, we were rigid and cruel towards those who differed from us, we upheld the authority of the king against God and his people; and now God has justly brought this distressed estate upon us, that the king's power, in which we so trusted, is broken, and in a manner gone. Oh, now we see we feared not the Lord; we have none now to help us, we now know what it is not to fear the great God; God is above us, and therefore now what can a king do to us? What could he do for us, suppose we had him again? alas, our misery is beyond his help; seeing God is provoked with us, and has forsaken us, what should a king do for us? And thus, in this short paraphrase, you have the scope of the words, as if the people should have spoken in this manner.

Ac si non esset, nam is quem habemus, non potest nos protegere, quod est officium regis. Drus.

But now the question is, what times does this refer to? "Now they shall say, We have no king," &c. When did they say so?

The times that this refers to seem to be those which we read of, 2 Kings xvii. In that chapter you find the times that this has reference to; then they might well say, "We have no king." The observations from it are,

Obs. 1. It is a great evil for a people not to have the protection and the blessing that might be enjoyed in the right government of a king over them. It is a great evil, and they complain of it as such, and so far their complaint is right, that they are now deprived of the protection and good that otherwise they might have had from the right government of a king over them.

And, my brethren, our condition is even such in regard of the personal presence and protection of a king; in those respects we may almost use the same words as here, and say, We have no king among us. And whether is it better for a people to have no king, or to have no protection from their king? But that which is contrary to protection is a question fitter to be discussed and determined in a parliament than in a pulpit; and to them I shall leave it.

But the church of God shall never have cause to make this complaint, that they have no king: in Psal. xxix. 10, 11, "The Lord sitteth King for ever. The Lord will give strength unto his people; the Lord will bless his people with peace." In Psal. xlv. 6, "Thy throne, O God, is for ever and ever: the sceptre of thy kingdom is a right sceptre." Psal. cxlv. 13, "Thy kingdom is an everlasting kingdom, and thy dominion endureth throughout all generations." Psal. cxlix. 2, "Let the children of Zion be joyful in their King."

"Because we feared not the Lord." Here

Obs. 2. It is a great evil not to fear the Lord. "Fear ye not me, saith the Lord, which have placed the sand for the bound of the sea?" It is an evil and a bitter thing, that the fear of the Lord is not in men. For God is a great God, infinitely above us, clothed with majesty and honour; trembling frames of heart become his presence. None like unto the Lord: great and marvellous are his works; oh! who would not fear him? God has infinite authority over us, to save, or to destroy; he has us all at an infinite advantage, by the least word of his mouth to undo us. His wrath is insupportable: "Who among us shall dwell with the devouring fire? who among us shall dwell with everlasting burnings?" Isa. xxxiii. 14. Darest thou, a vile wretch, presume to rebel against any word of the Lord, when the next word may sink soul and body into the bottomless gulf of eternal horror and despair? Who art thou that dost not fear the Lord? Dost thou not fear the commanding word of the Lord, when the next word that proceeds out of his mouth may be a destroying word, to undo body and soul for ever?

Obs. 3. In times of prosperity, when men have the favour and countenance of great ones, there is little fear of God among them. "We feared not the Lord." Oh! those times when we had the favour and countenance of great men, there was little fear of God among us. So long as men have any confidence in the creature, so long they see no need of God, their hearts are swollen with pride, God is not in all their thoughts; they say to God, Depart from us, we do not desire the knowledge of thy ways. They set their hearts and tongues against the God of heaven, they can venture upon any thing then; to tell them it is sin against God, nothing at all affects them. How vile and foolish are the hearts of wicked men, that the enjoyment of such poor things as they have in the creature, should imbolden their hearts against the great God of heaven and earth! Yet thus it is, men little consider that even those things which their hearts do so much rest upon, are absolutely at the disposal of this God whom their hearts do not fear.

But let the saints of God take this note with them, Shall creature confidence take men's hearts off from God's fear? then let God's fear take your hearts off from creature confidence. Certainly this is far more reasonable. Oh! it is infinitely irrational that creature confidence should take the heart from God's fear; but it is infinitely rational that God's fear should take our hearts off from creature confidence.

Obs. 4. The taking from a people the protection and benefit they might have by kingly power, is a punishment for their want of the fear of God. "We have no king," we are deprived of the benefit and the protection we might have by kingly power; it is "because we feared not the Lord." What evil we feel in this, let us attribute it to the want of the fear of God in ourselves, and in the people of the land. We complain of those that are about the king, and of her that lies in the bosom of the king, and of the evil of his own heart in part; but whence is it that God has left him, either to them, or to any evil in his own spirit? The Lord in this punishes the sins of the people. It is usual for God to punish the sins of the people by leaving governors to evil courses; in 2 Sam. xxiv. 1, you have a remarkable scripture for this, "And again the anger of the Lord was kindled against Israel." And what then? "And he moved David against them to say, Go, number Israel and Judah." "The anger of the Lord was kindled against Israel, and he moved David against them." To what? God lets temptations be before David, to lead him into a sin that might bring evil upon the people. It was because the anger of the Lord was kindled against Israel. It is because that a people fear not God, that the Lord leaves kings, leaves their governors, to those evil ways to which they are attached; and therefore learn we, when we hear of any evil done by the countenance of kings, or of any in power, learn we to lay our hands upon our own hearts, and say, Even this is because we feared not the Lord. How easy had it been with the Lord to have wrought upon his heart! oh what prayers have been sent up unto the Lord for the heart of one man! never since the world began have more prayers been proffered for the heart of one man. But the Lord has seemed even to shut his ears against the prayers of his people; now let us lay our hands upon our hearts, God has denied our prayers, it is because we have not feared him. Now certainly there has been but little fear of God amongst us, and little fear of the great God is still to this day amongst us.

Obs. 5. The times of God's wrath and judgments force acknowledgment from men that they did not fear God. When God comes against them in ways of wrath, now they can acknowledge that they feared not God. Had the prophet come to them before and told them, Oh! you are a wretched, vile people, there is no fear of God among you. Why, wherein do not we fear God? As in Mal. i., they would not be convinced; but now, when the wrath of God is upon men, now they shall say, We see now apparently we feared not the Lord. As Cardinal Wolsey, when in distress, is reported to have said, Had I but served God as well as I served the king, it would have been otherwise with me than it is; but I sought to please the king rather than God, and now I am left in this distressed estate. He would have scorned that any should have told him before that he pleased the king more than God; but afflictions will draw forth acknowledgment: for in afflictions God appears dreadful to the soul, it is no dallying, and trifling, and putting off then; we see we have to deal with an infinite, glorious, and dreadful God. And in times of affliction conscience will assert its rule over men, it will not be quieted and stilled as in the season of prosperity; but it will speak, as Zebul, in Judg. ix. 38, "Where is now thy mouth, wherewith thou saidst, Who is Abimelech?" So saith conscience in times of affliction to wretched creatures, Where now is that bold and presumptuous heart of thine? Thou didst scorn at fearing and trembling before God, and slightedst his word; but where now is that proud, wretched heart of thine? In times of affliction men's hearts are abased and humbled, and therefore are ready to say, It is because we feared not the Lord. Mark here,

They do not when in affliction and trouble say, There were a company of factious people who would not yield to any thing, and we may thank them for all this; you hear no such words, O no, but it is, "Because we feared not the Lord."

Obs. 6. When the heart is humbled, it will not put off the cause of evils to other men or other things, but will charge itself as the cause of the evils that are upon it. Oh how much better, my brethren, were it for us to see the want of the fear of God by his word to us, and his Spirit in us, than by his wrath against us, or his stroke upon us. Let us every day examine our hearts, How has the fear of God been in me this day? has the fear of God actuated and guided me in all my thoughts, counsels, and actions this day? How happy were it whenever we lie down to rest to have such a short meditation, Has the fear of God been the thing that has acted, and governed, and guided me in my course this day? But there follows.

"What then should a king do to us?" Suppose we had him; now he is gone, but if we had him, what good would he bring to us? As if they should say, We speak much concerning our king, but now we have not the king with us as he was; yet if he were with us again, what should he do for us? what would our condition be better than it is? And indeed, what good had their kings done for them? The people of Israel were very desirous of a king, they must needs have a king, God yielded to their desires in giving them Saul; then afterwards they must have a king again, so they had Jeroboam, and he must be the king of the ten tribes. Their first king was given in God's wrath, and almost every one of the kings of Israel was a plague to them; what had they done for them? All the time they had judges they were in a better case; Israel was in a far better case when they were ruled by the government of God. And Peter Martyr, in his preface to the Book of Judges, observes three things wherein Israel was better when they were under judges, than kings.

First, All the time they had judges, they were not led captive out of their own country as afterwards.

Secondly, Whenever they were oppressed, and God raised them up a judge, he did always prevail so as to deliver them from their oppression, before he had done he delivered them from their oppression; that is to be observed in the story of the judges, but their kings did not so.

Thirdly, We find not any one of their judges charged or condemned by God as evil, and executing unrighteous judgments among them, as the kings are; Such a one did evil in the sight of the Lord, and such a one did evil; almost every one of the kings of Israel did so. God does not charge the judges so; it was otherwise therefore with them after they had kings. And the truth is, that Christ has been but little beholden to, I may say, the most of our kings; yea, little beholden to most of the kings that have lived upon the earth; and he has taken as little care of the greater part of them: as they have taken little care of his honour, so he has taken little care of the greater part of them. Of all the sixty-three Roman emperors elected by the senate, historians agree that but six had such protection from God as to die a natural death, but six of threescore and three: there were twenty-nine of the emperors that did not reign above twenty-five years and some months; yea, there were twelve of them that reigned but three years and some months: see what havoc was made of them: they regarded not the honour of Jesus Christ, but were enemies unto him, and he regarded as little their safety. From hence the notes are these:

Obs. 7. When God forsakes a people, nothing can do them good. "Except the Lord build the house, they labour in vain that build it," Psal. cxxvii. 1. "What then should a king do to us?"

Obs. 8. It is just with God to make those things unuseful to men which they sinfully dote upon, and put their confidence in. They sinfully doted upon kings, and put their confidence in them, and God does now justly make the power of kings unuseful to them. "What then should a king do to us?" If we dote upon them, it is just with God to make them unuseful to us. Or if we dote upon our credit and names, and so upon kings and princes; if men expect preferment from them, it is just with God to blast all their hopes, that they should be forced to say, Now I see God fights against him, as well as against me. Thus the people spake in respect of their kings.

This scripture may well be a comment upon that text in Psal. cxlvi. 3, "Put not your trust in princes, nor in the son of man, in whom there is no help." Do not put your trust in princes, have no confidence in them; if you put your trust in them, they will be unuseful to you. And Chrysostom upon that very psalm has this note: Whereas they would say, Oh, he is a prince! Saith Chrysostom, Let me tell you that which you perhaps will wonder at; because he is a prince, therefore put not your trust in him. And he gives this reason, Because who is in a more unsafe condition than they? Are not they fain to have their guards go about them to protect them? In times of peace, even in a city that is ruled by good laws, yet are they fain to have the instruments of war round about them to protect them; and therefore put not your confidence in them, because they are princes. But then, in the Psalm, they are called to put their confidence "in the Lord, which made heaven and earth, the sea, and all that therein is; which keepeth truth for ever." Alas, you may put confidence in princes, but they will not keep truth; they will make fair promises to you, that you shall have some great matters by them, but they use you but to serve their own turns; but put your trust in the Lord. "The Lord shall reign for ever;" kings do not reign for ever, they are the children of men, the breath is in their nostrils; but "the Lord shall reign for ever, even thy God, O Zion, unto all generations."

Obs. 9. How great an evil is it to a people then, whose complaints are, What doth a king not do against us? Musculus, upon the forenamed Psalm, (those that read his comment shall find that note in it,) saith, You are not to put your trust in princes that are the children of men, they are but men; yea, but what shall we say to those that are cruel oppressors, that are rather like tigers and such kind of wild beasts among men, that seem not to be children of men, how shall we put our trust in them? Oh! it is a sad condition indeed that a people is in, when they have this cause to complain, when they shall have cause to cry out and complain, Oh how, how doth he run from place to place, plundering, spoiling, breaking, tearing, destroying wheresoever he comes! That people is in a sad condition. What shall he do for us? nay, what doth he not do against us continually? and all this, because we have not feared the Lord.

See here the alteration of the spirits of these men towards their king. King; not long ago they put their confidence in their king, and gloried in their king, and now, "What shall a king do to us?" Hence the note is,

Obs. 10. God can soon make a great change in the hearts of people in reference to their kings; that even those that did dote and admire him, and own no other God but their king, shall even turn their hearts and say, What can a king do for us? The least turn of God upon the hearts of people will make such a change as this is.

Obs. 11. The difference between the blessed estate of God's people, and the wretched estate of wicked men. Those who fear God can say, What shall a king, what shall men, what shall devils do against us? but other men in their straits, What shall they do for us? We are in a distressed condition, and what shall they do for us? But the people of God are never in such a distressed condition but they are able to say, What shall men or devils be able to do against us? for God is our protector.

Obs. 12. The more stoutness and sinful creature confidence there is in any, the more do their hearts sink in desperation when they come to be crossed in their hopes. They were very stout and full of creature confidence before they were brought into misery, and now what low, sordid spirits have they! now they sink in desperation. None have their hearts sink in desperation more than those who in the ruff of their pride are the most bold and presumptuous against God and his servants.

Obs. 13. A carnal heart is not led by experience of the vanity of creature confidence to seek after God. "What then should a king do to us?" Their hearts sink in regard of any hopes that they have from their king. But yet you read nothing of their hearts being set upon God, and mourning, and working towards God; when they are taken from the creature they say not thus, Now we see our vain confidence in our king, and what hopes we had of preferment in him God has crossed; well, we will go and seek to make the King of heaven our portion. No, no such thing comes from them as this. Their heart lies sullen and sinking, it has no interest in God, and cannot go to him to make up what it wants in the creature. But it is otherwise with a gracious heart; The hand of God has taken off my confidence in the creature, yea, but I hope it is in mercy to my soul, that I might have the more confidence in God, and that God might have the more glory from me; and therefore I hope that this taking off my heart from the creature, will for ever unite my heart more to the Lord than ever heretofore it has been. Yea, this is a gracious work indeed, when the heart is taken off from creature confidence and brought nearer unto the Lord.

Ver. 4. *They have spoken words, swearing falsely in making a covenant: thus judgment springeth up as hemlock in the furrows of the field.*

They are convinced of their sin, that they have not feared God, they cry out of their misery, "What then should a king do to us?" But mark what follows; they were not gained to God ever a whit the more, but when taken off from their hopes one way, see how they set upon another.

"They have spoken words." Luther here saith, this is a Hebraism, for, they have anxiously consulted; that the Hebrews are wont so to express an anxious consultation; and for that he quotes Isa. viii. 10, "Take counsel together, and it shall come to nought; speak the word, and it shall not stand." So then the words here would signify, they get together and contrive one with another what they shall do in such a case as this, how they may any way help themselves. As we read of the people of God in Mal. iii. 16, "They that feared the Lord" met one with another and spake together; so these wicked wretches, that were thus disappointed of their hopes, met together, and spake one to another, some such words as these:

Our case is very sad, oh! who should have thought such things should have befallen us? We are as much crossed of our hopes as ever any men were; we made account we should have overrun them, and they would have been but as bread unto us, we should have made a prey of them, and all their estates would have been ours long before this time. Those prophets who told us that God was against us, those ministers that encouraged people in the name of God, and those people that differed from us, now we see that their words are fulfilled, and what they thought would come, is now come upon us; now is come to pass what such precise ones among us, whose consciences would not submit to our ways and the way of our king, said. Surely they cannot but look upon us as a most wretched, miserable, forsaken people, now we are like to lose our houses, estates, honours, and all those delightful things which we hoped might have made our lives prosperous and jocund. Oh! what shall we do in such a distressed state as this? We had almost as good die as endure such a miserable life as we are like to live, at the mercy of men who we know scorn and hate us. Is there no way to help ourselves? cannot we get some to join with us? can we call in no help from any strangers? no matter what compliances in return they demand. Thus they toss up and down, not knowing what in the world to do in their conference.

Or thus; May we not yet possibly make up some peace though we be in this distressed condition? Whatsoever propositions they shall proffer to us, we will, rather than fail, yield to them all; we may perhaps get some advantage hereafter, or be in some means in a better case to revenge ourselves than now we are. If they will have us take the covenant, and nothing else will satisfy them, we will do it; and when we have taken it, perhaps they may put some of us in places of trust, and so we may privately work about our own ends, and drive on our own designs that way better than in any openly hostile manner. And if together with their covenant they will have oaths, we will take them too; and if we cannot agree to their oaths or covenant hereafter, we will say, We were forced to it, and therefore they do not bind us. Some such kind of communication it is like they had. And could you hear the communication of our adversaries when they get together in those straits that God has brought them into, you would likely hear some such kind of stuff as this is, they spake such words one to another.

"They have spoken words, swearing falsely in making a covenant." דברו דברים אלות שוא כרת ברית Others refer this to the times of the prophet's threatening, or when they saw their danger imminent. The Chaldee paraphrase has it thus, They spake violent words; that is, they rage and fret, they speak proud, swelling words, they swear and curse: What! shall our images be broken down, shall we be brought under and made to serve our enemies? We scorn it, we defy all that shall attempt it. We will do this and that, we will have our minds, we will die for it else; we will enter into leagues, we will get such and such to conjure together with us, and surely make our party good. Thus they speak of the great things that they will do: thus they speak words, in making a covenant with oaths of vanity, for so you may render the original. And indeed, if men could prevail with great words, and daring expressions, and bold resolutions, and desperate oaths, and wicked curses, then may some hope to prevail against the God of heaven and his saints; but saith he, These things shall do them no good. And indeed these things should never move us, though we hear our adversaries speak proud, swelling words, and say what they will do, threaten monstrous things, let us not be troubled at it, for they do but hasten the wrath of God against themselves. In the mean time, while they are swearing, and cursing, and making brags, and boast what they will do, the counsels of the Lord work their ruin, and bring about surely the good of his people. But further,

"They have spoken words, swearing falsely in making a covenant." What has this reference to? What covenant did they make? and wherein did they swear falsely? Some think it refers to the covenant which the people made with Jeroboam at the first, and so with his successors; that is thus, The people came to him and took their oaths, and entered into solemn league, that they would support him in the breach which he made from the house of David, and stand by him in opposing those who would not yield to him in the alteration of worship: for their princes would not probably have been so strongly set upon the alteration of the ways of worship, had not the people joined themselves freely to them by oaths and covenant: now when they saw that the people came in flocking and willing to yield to the oath which the king would give them, upon this they the rather confirmed Jeroboam in his purpose. I find that Arias Montanus and Vatablus thus interpret the words.

But now others, and that more probably, understand this covenant and swearing to be the covenant they made with the Assyrians and with the Egyptians, the story of which you have in 2 Kings xvii. Hoshea "sent messengers to So king of Egypt, and brought no present to the king of Assyria, as he had done year by year." First, he had covenanted with the king of Assyria, and that was broke; and then they would covenant with So king of Egypt; and so they sware falsely in making a covenant with the Assyrians and the Egyptians. Now the observations are,

Obs. 1. Carnal hearts, in their straits, take shifting courses. They have no God to go to, and so, as a dog that has lost his master, they will follow after any for relief.

Obs. 2. It is an evil thing for professors, in straits, to combine with wicked men. God professes he will not take the wicked by the hand, neither should we. It is a sign the cause is evil, when men can have no other help but by combining with the wicked and ungodly. Just thus it is at this day with the adversaries to the parliament; all men generally that make any profession of godliness, see they cannot have help from God, therefore they combine, and bring into covenant Irish rebels, papists, Turks, or Jews, any in the world, to help themselves withal: this is the wickedness of men's hearts.

Obs. 3. No trust is to be reposed in the oaths or covenants of the wicked. Let their protestations be never so solemn, their oaths, their covenants, it is but only to gain time to work about some advantage, that they cannot effect for the present, while they have any opposition. If they have not things under their power as they desire, they will promise you any thing in the world; but when once they come to get power in their hands, then who shall require the fulfilling of their promises, their oaths, their covenants? And therefore, certainly, when we have to deal with those whom we have experienced to be false, we must ever retain this conclusion, except we see an apparent change in their hearts; for it is not enough that they are willing to take covenants, that is no new thing; but till we see that God has wrought some mighty work upon their hearts we must carry this conclusion, Certainly, if they can, they will ruin us, therefore our condition cannot be safe till it is such that they can do us no hurt.

Obs. 4. Breaking covenant, though with wicked men, is a wickedness which God will punish. I have heretofore spoken of falseness, and falseness in covenant and promises, and shown you the example of Saul and Zedekiah, therefore I shall not look back to those things. God loves human societies, which cannot be preserved but by faithfulness; Faithfulness (it is the speech of a heathen) is the common safety of all men. I remember I have read of the Romans, that, by the light of nature, they did so esteem of faithfulness in covenants, that

Fides, commune hominis præsidium. Cicero.

they built and dedicated a temple to it, as to a goddess; and in that temple all their leagues, truces, covenants, and bargains were made, which were so religiously observed, that whosoever broke them was to be held as accursed, and unworthy to live in human society. The Egyptians too would punish perjury with death. Among the Indians the fingers and toes of perjured persons were cut off. And I have likewise read, when Tissaphernes the Persian warred against the Grecians, he broke covenant with the Grecians, and thereupon Agesilaus rejoiced greatly, saying, By this means he has made the gods his enemy and our friend; wherefore let us boldly give him battle. We know how our enemies have broken their covenants from time to time, and the very conditions which they have made themselves, yea, even lately in that town which we hear such good of now; in that we hope the Lord is even revenging himself upon them for breaking covenant in that very place. Now, my brethren, as even the very heathen are convinced that this is so great and dreadful an evil, what cause have we to lay our hands upon our hearts this day in respect of that part of our covenant which concerns one another, for certainly since the time of our solemn covenant there was never more treachery than there has been in England, and in Scotland too; there has been as much treachery since that time as ever yet was since either of them were a nation: we have been false one to another so far as relates to ourselves. But further,

"They have spoken words, swearing falsely in making a covenant." Calvin, in his notes on this scripture, understands this oath and covenant not to be a covenant to men, but their covenant with God, in promising repentance and new obedience; and so they spake only words, "swearing falsely," they did but deceive him in swearing and making a covenant. And this indeed is a sore and dreadful evil, to swear to the high God, and to covenant with him, to draw so nigh to him, and yet to be false. God threatens in Lev. xxvi. 25, that he will send a sword to avenge the quarrel of his covenant; and when we see the sword rage so as it doth, we may have cause to fear that the Lord has a quarrel against us, in avenging our falseness in the late covenant that has been made. And that we may see further our guiltiness and evil in swearing falsely in making a covenant, we must know that many ways our hearts may be false in our covenants with God. It is a dreadful evil to be false any way in covenant with God: any of you that upon your sick-beds have been solemnly promising to God reformation if God restored you, if you be false, O know, that the Lord has a quarrel against you, and he has a dreadful evil to charge upon your souls. How many of you have been false in your private covenants! But to be false in public covenants, that is most dreadful. But our hearts may be false divers ways: as,

1. If we make our covenant merely upon politic grounds. If we make the solemn worship of God, wherein we express our fidelity for reformation of religion, to be merely subservient to politic grounds, here is a falseness of heart, we are false in swearing thus, and making a covenant; we do not sanctify the name of God as we ought.

2. If we put on it false interpretations we are false; when we shall make our covenant a mere snare to our brethren. Let us consider how far any of us are guilty of this, and let the Lord judge between us. I say, when we seek to make it a snare even to our brethren. How have those been accused for the breach of this oath, in things which have not accorded with the points that are in controversy with our brethren! as if this oath were put upon all men to determine most abstruse and difficult points of controversy, to bring men to submit to such things as are very abstruse and difficult

to understand: this were to make an oath a snare, and to take the name of God in vain in a fearful manner. Certainly the Lord never would have oaths put to men to this end, that men that are of different ways and opinions in controversial things, should be forced by means of an oath to be of the same judgment, and to do the same things: this is a great abuse of this oath, wheresoever it is urged so far. Certainly no man is guilty of the breach of this oath and covenant, that shall but endeavour as far as he can to understand what the mind of God is, and then to practise according as he understands, though he should mistake; as in that part of the covenant regarding the point of schism, the thing itself being a sin, we may as well swear against it, as David did to keep God's commandments, Psal. cxix. 106; but now, if David did labour to understand God's commandments, and practised as far as he did understand, suppose he did not understand all things aright, it might be his weakness, but not his perjury. So let us be in point of schism, or any other point of the covenant; if men do endeavour to understand what is schism by the Scripture, and accordingly do, in their several places, by what means their consciences tell them is lawful, endeavour to oppose it, though they should not think that to be schism which their brethren account schism, or perhaps is so, yet they are not forsworn. This is evil, to make a covenant to be a snare unto us, and our hearts so far are false in it.

3. Then is the heart false in making a covenant, when it does not fulfil it according to the nature of it, when it goes quite opposite to its tenor. As, since our covenant has been made, when were there ever greater divisions? our covenant is for unity. When more profane ungodliness? our covenant is against it. When more injustice? our covenant is against all such things; and yet, since England was a nation, never did stronger cries ascend to heaven for these sins, than since our covenant. Therefore certainly there is a great breach between God and us in this respect.

4. When men make their covenant to be a cloak for malignity; that is, though they have malignant and vile, wicked spirits, yet they can but take the covenant, and then all is well. Here they swear falsely in making a covenant. After this their covenant there is a great deal of injustice among them.

"Thus judgment springeth up as hemlock." By "judgment" some understand the judgments of God, and then the sense is, Those wicked ways of yours are the seeds that bring up God's judgments, as hemlock, bitter and deadly. There is a truth in this interpretation, though I think it is not the full scope of the words here; but it may be, the Holy Ghost would hint some such thing unto us in it, that our actions are as seeds, and sown here, they will bring forth according to their nature. Wicked actions, when sown, will bring forth bitter fruit, will bring forth hemlock. It may be, saith he, you look for peace and prosperity; but, contrary to your expectation, behold hemlock and bitterness. I beseech you, take heed of preparing to yourselves a potion of hemlock against you lie sick and are cast upon your death-bed: a man has sown his field, he thinks to have a good crop of corn, but judgment, the judgment of God, comes up, and there is hemlock instead of it.

But because I think this not to be the scope of the place, therefore I pass it by, and rather think that by "judgment" is here meant, righteousness, equity, and justice.

That whereas there should be righteousness, equity, and justice; behold, instead, there springs up a crop of oppression, unrighteousness, and injustice, that is bitter as hemlock. I rather think that this must be the meaning, because I find that in divers scriptures injustice is compared to bitter things, yea, to hemlock itself: in Amos v. 7, "Ye who turn judgment to wormwood, and leave off righteousness in the earth." And in Amos vi. 12, "Ye have turned judgment into gall, and the fruit of righteousness into hemlock." I will not stand to open the former text, but you see the Scripture charges the people, by this expression, of sinning against judgment and righteousness, that they turned it to hemlock.

Now I find three things especially recorded of this herb.

First, It is a very venomous herb; therefore I find Pliny records of it, in the 25th Book, 13th chapter of his Natural History, that the Athenians were wont to give it to malefactors that were condemned to die. And Socrates, that was so wise a man among them, because he did not yield to their gods, but spake against them, maintaining there was but one God, therefore they adjudged him to die by drinking hemlock.

Secondly, I find the same author saith of it, that the leaves are somewhat like to coriander, but more tender, and with a strong, stinking smell, and the seeds like to aniseed. So justice seems to have a very fair pretence sometimes, and to do things that are very good; under very fair pretences men are very unjust: the leaves when they come up one would think there should be such a fine fruit, one would think to have coriander or anise, but the truth is, it comes to hemlock at last.

Thirdly, That which Jerome reports of it in his comment on my text, where he saith, that hemlock grows up very stiff and full of joints, and that at the joints it puts forth stalks, which not only sprout upwards and bear fruit, but downwards to form roots; and he saith that every branch, if it has but a joint in it, will serve instead of a seed; yea, he saith, if any pieces fall on the ground, they will grow up so as that it will be very hard to extirpate them. And truly thus it resembles injustice, which, if let alone but a little, oh how quickly it multiplies and spreads itself through the whole land!

Pliny too observes, That the root of it is hollow, and so unfit for any use at all. And so are the hearts of the unjust, hollow hearts and unfit for any thing.

That the leaves are beneficial for swellings, and sore eyes. And God turns even the injustice that is many times among a people to be medicines to his people against their swellings, and to open their sore eyes.

That if hemlock be drank in wine, it will certainly kill a man, and that without remedy. So if men be unjust, and take delight in their injustice, and scorn and contemn those that they can oppress, such men are in a desperate condition indeed.

And lastly, That this herb kills by cold; that if the leaves or seeds get the mastery of any, they feel themselves begin to wax cold in their inward parts, and so die inwardly. Oh! how many who have been very hot and zealous, yet, having gotten power into their hands and unrighteously used it, have grown cold in that in which they were formerly zealous, and still grow colder and colder; and thus their unrighteousness is like to prove their death!

"In the furrows of the field." Calvin puts this question, Why doth he not say, It springs up in the field, but "in the furrows of the field?" And he gives this answer to it, Where there are furrows in the field, there has the plough come that has broken up the field; and it is to prepare for good seed when the field is laid in furrows, and therefore less tolerable for hemlock to spring up there than in the field that is not ploughed, or in other unprepared ground. When a field is ploughed and prepared for seed, and one would hope to have much advantage by his field, to have much justice and righteousness in a country; where we see there have been great works of God to cast out those that were

Calvin. Expos. Cur potius supra sulcos agri, quam in agro?

unjust before, and the expectation of all the people is, that certainly now there will be nothing but righteousness and judgment; when, instead of that, comes up injustice and oppression; as hemlock, when it springeth up in such a field that is so prepared for justice; this is a sore evil; the Lord is much provoked against, and so complains of it, "that judgment springeth up as hemlock in the furrows of the field."

Obs. 1. That people is in a sad condition, and it is a sign the Lord has forsaken them, that they are near ruin, when in those places where there is most likelihood of justice and equity, there exist injustice and oppression. Oppression and injustice in places where God expects righteousness and equity, is a sad omen, a forerunner of great evil to places. It is God's complaint, in Isa. v.; just before he threatened the utter spoiling of his vineyard, he gives this reason, "I looked that it should bring forth grapes, and behold, it brought forth wild grapes." And he mentions, among the wild grapes, injustice: there it is called "wild grapes," as "hemlock" here, for both are very sour, and bitter before the Lord. Injustice in places from whence justice may be expected, is by the Lord accounted a most fearful, a ruining, sin. In Amos v. 12, "I know" (saith the Lord) "your manifold transgressions and your mighty sins." Now the word translated "mighty sins," in the Hebrew signifies your bony sins, because the strength of a man is in his bones; and therefore he calls the strength of that sin bony; it is a very strong sin, it cannot easily be resisted. Your sins have great bones in them, saith he; and what are they? You afflict the just, you take a bribe, that you may turn away the poor in the gate from their right: those are their great and their mighty sins. In Jer. xxii. 15—17, "Did not thy father eat and drink, and do judgment and justice? and then it was well with him?" Again, "He judged the cause of the poor and needy; then it was well with him:" and, "Was not this to know me? saith the Lord." Let men talk never so much of reformation, and of setting up the worship of God, and of casting out false worship, yet if they rejoice in injustice and oppression instead of that, God will not take himself as known. "But," saith he, "thine eyes and thine heart are not but for thy covetousness, and for to shed innocent blood, and for oppression, and for violence, to do it." And in Amos v. 21, is a remarkable place for this, "I hate," saith he, "I despise your feast days, and I will not smell in your solemn assemblies." You have many feast days, and days of thanksgiving; you bless me for what I do for you, but I will not care for your days of thanksgiving. Why? In the 24th verse, "But let judgment run down as waters, and righteousness as a mighty stream." As if he should say, Keep as many days of thanksgiving as you will, I care for none of them, except "judgment run down as waters, and righteousness as a mighty stream." Mark here the expression of the Holy Ghost; judgment and righteousness is compared to a river; that is, it should be common for all, that the poorest might come and take of it as well as the richest: it must not be like a pond, or well, enclosed for a man's private use, "But," saith he, "let judgment run down as waters, and righteousness as a mighty stream," as a river; it must be as a river. Now, you know, from the Thames every poor person may come and fetch water for their relief. So justice should be like the water in the Thames, that the poorest of all may have it for the very fetching of it. But till then, saith he, I regard none of your days of thanksgiving. And so in Isa. lviii., there is one special reason why the days of fasting were not regarded, it was because of their oppression of the poor, and their uncharitableness, and their injuriousness in the courts of justice. We have now many days of fasting and thanksgiving, more than ever yet England knew, and we may think that God will smell a sweet savour; but oh! this hemlock coming up "in the furrows of the field" will imbitter all, for if ever God did look for righteousness and judgment from a people, then certainly he looks for righteousness and judgment from us at this day. Oh! for us now, that stand in need of so much mercy, that cry for mercy, that we should be oppressing at such a time as this, it is a most dreadful thing. What! is all the cost that God has bestowed upon us come to this, that there should be no other fruit but hemlock come up in the furrows of the field? all the cost of God and man, all the works of God towards us, do they come but to this issue, only to bring forth hemlock? Were there ever more cries, were there ever more bitter moans and complaints, because of injustice, than of late have been in this land? Never were people so frustrated in their expectations. When indeed such as were notoriously wicked were in place, then we expected nothing but hemlock; but now they are cast out, and others come in, we hoped that there had been such a preparation that nothing but fruits of righteousness would have come up. But now, to be oppressed by them that are in the places of former oppressors, this is grievous. Lord, what is man? In Isa. lix. 9, it is said, "Therefore is judgment far from us, neither doth justice overtake us: we wait for light, but behold obscurity; for brightness, but we walk in darkness." This light is especially spoken of the light of justice; as if they should say, The land once indeed was dark, all the courts of judicature, and all the men that had places to judge in, were darkness, we had nothing but darkness; yea, but now we waited for light, we hoped now there would be reformation; it is spoken after their many days of fasting and prayer; but yet, behold darkness, behold oppression still. Oh! many who are come empty into places of power suck harder than some former oppressors did. And what will be the end of these things? How many poor men travel many times far, expecting fruits of justice, but they meet with hemlock! they sigh and lift up their eyes and hearts to heaven, sending up their moans to God, Lord, is this the fruit of our labour? do our hopes come to this? what! must we go home with sad hearts, and be made a scorn and prey to those that are wicked round about us? Oh! these are sad moans at such times as the present.

My brethren, it were easy to name many stalks of hemlock that there are come up amongst us instead of righteousness and judgment. I will name one or two.

First, That such as have been notoriously malignant, yea, such as have been upon actual war, should yet, upon any slight acknowledgment, or from having for their own ends taken covenant, get into committees, and have power there over the well-affected party who have been most forward from the first; that now those who hate them, and have spirits full of bitterness against them, should have power over them to tax them as they please; power over their estates, their liberty; power to order the affairs of the country round about them, and to revenge themselves upon them because they were so forward in the beginning; what grows in the furrows here but bitter and venomous hemlock? Where the fault lies, that we cannot determine; but such men, doing such things, in such places, it is nothing but "hemlock in the furrows of the field."

Secondly, Here is another stalk of hemlock, That poor men, taken from their families, who were the only means of support to their wives and children, yet should be so left without pay themselves, that their wives and children are destitute of bread and clothing; and officers in an army, who were but mean men heretofore, and knew scarce how to live, should now live bravely, glister in their gold and silver lace; what is this but hemlock? Is not here injustice and oppression? that thousands should want food, that widows and children should cry out for bread, who lived pretty well heretofore; and others who before knew not how to live, yet now shall be brave in a far higher way than ever formerly; is not here hemlock that grows up "in the furrows of the field?" I know not neither where to charge this, but yet we see hemlock doth come up.

But now, though we might name many other stalks of hemlock, yet certainly take this caution along with you.

Every man in times of distraction, such as those wherein we live, must account to suffer something, things cannot be carried on with that equity as if all things were settled among us; therefore, though we may in a humble and peaceable way make our moans one to another, and seek to inform those that are in power, and petition, yet it ought to be our care, whatever we suffer in our particular, to preserve as far as we can the honour of our supreme court; better many suffer individually hard things, than the honour of that should not be kept up, for by not maintaining that we make way to suffer worse things than ever yet we have done. For how would we have help when we meet with wrong and injustice? Under God there are but three ways, two extremes, and one middle, for men to have right in case of injustice.

1. The king's arbitrary power, acted by those that are about him. We have tasted enough of this hemlock heretofore; would we think to have our help that way? We know what that hemlock means.

2. The appeal to the people. That were a remedy worse than the disease, for then all would seem to come to be in a confusion that way; if the people, the generality of the people, should take up the matter, we should then have nothing but murders and robberies. Then the meanest man in the kingdom, if he has but as strong arms and legs as the richest of all, he is presently equal with them, when things come to be redressed by the tumultuous people.

3. Therefore the third means of help in case of injustice is, the mean, that is, our parliament, which, as things are now, is the only regular help that we can have. If therefore we see or feel some things amiss, we may be sensible and seek help too, but in a peaceable and humble way of petitioning, being more tender of their honour than of our own private right. And an appeal to Heaven there may be likewise; but by an appeal to either of the two extremes, certainly in that we make our remedy worse than the disease. Pray much for them therefore, that there may not one stalk of hemlock rise up among them, or any seed fall down from them, but that they may be as the field which the Lord has blessed, full of the fruits of justice and righteousness; that themselves, and this city, and the kingdom, may be the habitation of justice; that mercy and truth may meet together, that righteousness and peace may kiss each other; that truth may spring out of the earth, and righteousness look down from heaven, Psal. lxxxv. 10, 11.

Now there is one note more, that I find in Tremelius, Pareus, and many others, on the words, "the furrows of the field." In the latter end of the word translated "field," there is, say they, a *jod*, which by some is considered paragogical, or a formal addition only, but by others as an affix for the plural number; and so they translate it thus, hemlock in the furrows of my field. And that is a great aggravation. Hemlock in the furrows of any field is an evil: but what! my people, men that profess godliness? what! those that profess to set up reformation, yet hemlock there in the furrows of my field? Oh this is sad and evil indeed! In Jer. xxxi. 23, "Thus saith the Lord of hosts, the God of Israel; As yet they shall use this speech in the land of Judah and in the cities thereof, when I shall bring again their captivity; The Lord bless thee, O habitation of justice, and mountain of holiness." When I bring their captivity again, and own them to be mine, then there shall be such eminent justice and holiness that this speech shall be used, "The Lord bless thee, O habitation of justice, and mountain of holiness." So if we would have any evidence to our souls that God does own us, and that we are his, and God indeed has delivered us from our captivity, we should labour that justice and holiness may be so eminent that all the people about us may say, The Lord bless this land, the "habitation of justice, and mountain of holiness." Both must go together; we must not think to raise up the ordinances of God, and cast out superstition, but we must be "the habitation of justice," as well as "the mountain of holiness," if we be the land that the Lord has blessed.

Ver. 5. *The inhabitants of Samaria shall fear because of the calves of Beth-aven: for the people thereof shall mourn over it, and the priests thereof that rejoiced on it, for the glory thereof, because it is departed from it.*

"The inhabitants of Samaria shall fear." You heard before that they were convinced in their consciences that they did not fear God: "For now they shall say, We have no king, because we feared not the Lord." They feared not God, but now they shall fear: "The inhabitants of Samaria shall fear."

Obs. 1. That those that fear God least, are most afraid of every thing else. Where the fear of God is not, other base fears will be; and so much the more, the less we fear God. Oh how much better were it that our fear were set upon God, than upon other things! You must love something; were it not better that your love were placed upon God than on any thing else? And you must fear something; were it not better that your fear were upon God, than any thing else? And you must rejoice in something, and sorrow, and the like. Fear is a very troublesome affection if misplaced. O, learn to place your affections right, place them upon God. By the fear of God you shall come to fear nothing else; oh how excellent is God's fear! This one thing sets out the excellency of the fear of God; that where the fear of God is settled in the heart, all other base fears are rooted out. Would not you be glad to be delivered from creature fears, especially you that have lived in many dangers a few months since? Oh, if you might be delivered from the fears of the creature, how glad would you be! Here is the only way; let the fear of God be strong in your hearts, and the fear of the creature will not prevail with you. You see it clearly in the example of Habakkuk, Hab. iii. 16, "When I heard, my belly trembled; my lips quivered at the voice: rottenness entered into my bones, and I trembled in myself." But now, Habakkuk, why trouble yourself with so much fear? Mark, a great good came to him by it; "that I might rest in the day of trouble, when he cometh up unto the people." When there shall be a coming up unto the people, and the enemy shall prevail, and when "the fig tree shall not blossom, neither shall fruit be in the vines; the labour of the olive shall fail, and the fields shall yield no meat; the flock shall be cut off from the fold, and there shall be no herd in the stalls;" when things shall be brought into the very saddest condition, so that men shall be at their wit's end, and know not what in the world to do; then, saith he, "I will rejoice in the Lord, I will joy in the God of my salvation." When God spake, then "my belly trembled, and my lips quivered at the voice." Yea, but when men came in the greatest rage, and when all things were dark, and dismal, and black abroad, yet then did I "rejoice in the Lord, and joy in the God of my salvation;" all fear was gone. Men can rejoice in the time of their prosperity, but in times of affliction then they fear; whereas those that fear the Lord in their prosperity, in the season of their affliction may most rejoice. Nazianzen, in his 12th Oration, saith well, This is our care, that we are afraid of nothing more than that we should fear any thing more than God. That is his expression. Here is an excellent fear, a fear rightly set. Would you fear? fear to fear any thing more than God, and then your fear is set right: but if you do not, &c. Though men that have no fear of God may seem to have bold spirits, and it seems to result from the greatness of their spirits that they will not fear God, yet these men in the time of danger are the most base, cowardly men in the world. I will give you a notable instance for this: Manasses was a proud and insolent man, that seemed to be fearless of any threatening of God, and scorned his prophets; but mark, when he came into danger, 2 Chron. xxxiii. 11, where did they find Manasses? He was run into the bushes; this brave, bold-spirited man, that dared God and his prophets, and cared not for what was said, yet in danger what a base, low spirit had he! he runs and hides himself in the midst of bushes and briers.

This is the temper and guise of the spirits of men that will not fear God.

"Because of the calves of Beth-aven." You know what they were, those that Jeroboam set up in Dan and Beth-el, the golden calves.

Luther, upon the place, moves a question; What a wonderful thing is it (saith he) that Jeroboam should be so bold as to set up calves to worship, when there is that eminent story of God's revenging himself for the people's worshipping a calf that Aaron set up, that at one time cost the lives of twenty-three thousand men, and yet that Jeroboam should presume to set up calves again to worship! It was a strange, bold attempt, saith Luther, it was a wonderful thing that he should be so bold, and that he should prevail with the people. Luther thus answers this question: The truth is, there is nothing so horrible and vile but people in a little time will be brought to yield to; if great ones, by their example and by their endeavours, labour to set it up, it will be set up; and, be it never so vile, never so abominable, the people will be brought to receive it. That is his answer.

And truly we find it so, that let people seem to abhor things never so much, yet if they find it be the wish of great ones, and if it be once set up in a way of power, they yield to it. One would think it an impossible thing, God having now cast so much odium upon our prelates, for the people of England ever to be brought to yield to them, and I make no question but many of you say so when you meet together; but do not deceive yourselves, if so be that those had prevailed that sought to prevail against us, we should quickly have the spirits of people turned, and as much for prelates, and ceremonies, and altars, (the generality of the people I mean,) as here they were for these calves again, though they had that sad story in their ears continually, of so many thousands that were slain for calves before.

"Because of the calves of Beth-aven." Why, were there many calves at Beth-aven? Indeed there were calves at Dan and Beth-el, but there was but one at each of them. This Beth-aven and Beth-el were the same. Jeroboam was so subtle to set up the calf at Beth-el, because the place took its name from God; but here the Holy Ghost calls it Beth-aven, a house of vanity, or iniquity. We may call things by names that may hold up some honour and respect, but God will give another name to these things on which we would fain put honour.

He calls it "Beth-aven," and "the calves of Beth-aven." Why, were there many calves at Beth-aven?

Now the answer that some give is this: There was but one at Beth-el indeed; but both Beth-el and Dan may have the name Beth-aven, (for they are both houses of vanity,) and so "calves" mentioned here in respect of them both.

Others thus: "The calves of Beth-aven." As if the prophet should say, Set up as many calves as you will, they shall not help you if you had a thousand of them.

But rather, as I find Arias Montanus, with others, say, they are called the calves of Beth-aven, because, according to the example of the calf that was set up at Beth-aven, their workmen made other little ones for their houses. Like as Demetrius the silversmith made shrines for Diana's temple, and it was his trade also to make little temples in silver, either to hang about their necks, or to be set up in their houses as ornaments; so probably the calf set up at Beth-aven had so much honour put upon it, that they had little things like to it made of wood, or silver, or gold, according to their estates; and so had them in their families; and therefore they are called "calves," in the plural number. And if this were so we might have a good note:

Obs. 1. That the true worshippers of God should labour to bring his true worship into their families. They would bring the calf into their families, or houses; so should we bring the ordinances and worship of God into our families, and not content ourselves with public worship, but have private worship too: they did not content themselves with a calf abroad, but had them at home in their houses or families.

But further, some remark, They are called the calves in the feminine gender, the she-calves, by way of contempt.

"The inhabitants of Samaria shall fear, because of the calves of Beth-aven." Why "the inhabitants of Samaria?" The calves were not there. Samaria was their chief city; as London is to England, so Samaria was the chief city to the ten tribes. "The inhabitants of Samaria shall fear." Samaria was a very strong city; and when the Assyrians came and carried away the ten tribes captive, they took all the country round about before they took Samaria. It was with Samaria as with London in these sad times; when there have been wars round about in England, London has been safe for these three years together. And so when there were wars in all Israel, yet Samaria continued safe; yea, not only when some towns, but when every town was taken, Samaria was so strong as to be able to endure a siege for three years together: thus you find in 2 Kings xvii. 5, that the king of Assyria came and besieged Samaria three years: yet, this being so, the text saith, "The inhabitants of Samaria shall fear, because of the calves of Beth-aven." That is, though they were a strong city, yet when they heard that their gods were taken away, yea, when they did but hear that Beth-el and Dan were in danger of having their gods taken away, they felt this; and though they themselves were safe in their outward condition for the present, and had strength enough to resist the enemies, yet they were afraid; that is, there was a solicitous fear in them about the calves of Beth-aven before they were taken, and when they were taken their hearts were daunted, and they knew not what in the world to do. Thus you see the meaning of the words. Whence,

Obs. 2. In times of danger our hearts should be most solicitous about the worship of God. It was so in the season of their danger, their hearts were especially solicitous about Beth-el, where they had the worship of their gods. So are idolaters solicitous in time of danger, not so much because of their outward peace, (it is not said that they were afraid because the enemies would come and take their corn, or their estates,) but for Beth-aven, where the calves were, they feared. When there is any danger, the honour of God, his church, his ordinances, should lie nearest to our hearts: thus it was with old Eli; "Eli sat upon a seat by the wayside watching: for his heart trembled for the ark of God," 1 Sam. iv. 13. He had his sons in the army, yet his heart did not tremble for them, nor that if the enemies should prevail he was likely to lose his estate, and there would come woeful misery upon the land; no, his heart trembled not for these, but for "the ark of God." I appeal to you, what was that which your hearts trembled most for in the time of our greatest danger? Was it for "the ark of God?" was it because of his ordinances? Oh! if they prevail they will trample the ordinances of the Lord and the saints of God under feet. The true worship of God, and the power of godliness, did your hearts tremble because of this? Certainly if your hearts were right they would do so. What! shall idolaters tremble because of their calves, and shall not our hearts tremble because of our God? 1 Kings viii. 44, 45, "If thy people go out to battle against their enemy, whithersoever thou shalt send them," what should they do? "and shall pray unto the Lord toward the city which thou hast chosen, and toward the house that I have built for thy name: then hear thou in heaven." In prayer they must look towards the city and the temple; for the temple was a type of Christ, so the city was a type of God's ordinances, where the people went up to worship. Oh! that should be in our eyes. The city where the ordinances of God are, when we go to war let that be in our eyes, and let that make us fight valiantly; and when we are praying to God, let us not pray so much that we may be delivered from our adversaries, as that the temple and the city of our God may be preserved.

Obs. 3. Cities that are strong and safe themselves, should be sensible of the miseries of others. "The inhabitants of Samaria shall fear." God knows how far we have been wanting in this very thing; if a stranger had come out of another country into London, and walked about the streets, could he have imagined that there were such civil wars in this land as there are, such wonderful desolations as have been made in other parts? Oh how little did we lay the afflictions of others to heart, because they were at some distance from us! Oh the mercy of our God, that has not brought us into the same evils and miseries! this one sin had been enough to have provoked God against us, because we were so little sensible of the miseries of the surrounding countries and cities. This Samaria was full of wickedness, yet when they heard what dangers Beth-el and Dan, and their other cities, were in, oh, they were mightily affected with it. Learn we from hence to be humbled for our shortcomings in this respect, and if ever the Lord should yet try us further, let us learn to be sensible of the miseries of others that are about us.

Obs. 3. There is no staidness of heart in resting upon any thing but the living God. They that stay themselves upon any thing else, if any afflictions or dangers happen, their hearts are filled with fear presently. They are afraid "because of the calves." When their calves are gone, all their confidence is gone, and then their hearts are overwhelmed with fear. When men have nothing to rest upon but their own inventions, their own ways, no marvel though they fear in times of danger; they begin to bethink now that all that they rested upon is vanity: yea, the service of God, that men in times of prosperity can rest upon and can satisfy their consciences withal, yet in time of danger it will not do; no inventions of men, no external duties of religion, especially such as are mixed with superstition, will then uphold the heart from being overwhelmed; it is only the confidence in the living God, the union of our souls with Jesus Christ, and enjoyment of communion with him in his own ordinances, that can comfort our souls in time of danger. So it is said of the godly in Psal. cxii. 7, 8, "He shall not be afraid of evil tidings: his heart is fixed, trusting in the Lord. His heart is established, he shall not be afraid." It is again repeated; let evil tidings, come what will, his heart is fixed, because he trusts in the Lord.

"For the people thereof." Here he speaks of the calf of Beth-aven in the singular number, for the people *of it*, that is, of the calf; for so I find the word "thereof" referred by most interpreters, to the calf, not to Samaria. From thence the note would be,

Obs. 4. Idolaters dedicated themselves to their idols, they were the people of the idol. Those that were the very peculiar treasure of God and his own people, now are called the people of the calf, for they have none to go to for help, but only to that idol of theirs; they had forsaken God.

"Shall mourn over it." Though certainly at first the setting up of the calf could not but be a very strange thing to the people of Israel, yet after a little they were used to it, and paid it worship; and it took their very consciences, so that they loved it, and when it was taken away they mourned, and were in extreme distress and trouble.

Obs. 5. Idolaters do mourn when their false worship is taken from them. At this day, my brethren, how do many mourn after the superstitious vanities and customs that they were wont to have! Now prelates, and service-book, and altars, and such kind of things are taken away, and when they meet together they exclaim, Oh! now all religion is gone! So they persuade poor people in remote parts, that the parliament has taken away all religion; and there is a great mourning in their spirits, they think they know not how in the world to serve God if their book be taken away from them: and I make no question it has been a cause that many have taken up arms, merely to defend such their superstitious vanities and customs. They mourn for their wonted burials for the dead, and would almost as lieve lose their lives as such kind of things. I remember I have read of some Indians that were wont to worship an ape's tooth, a religious relic among them; and that when it was taken from them, they so mourned its loss that they came and offered a very great price, even many thousands, to redeem this their ape's tooth, because it was a religious relic. And so we have men this day who, though their superstitious vanities and customs be no better than a very ape's tooth, yet mourn over them, and would be willing to part with a great proportion of their estate to redeem them again, they mourn after their calves.

Oh! how then should we mourn after the true worship of God, how dear should that be to our souls! For if calves, superstitious relics and customs, apes' teeth, and such things be so dear to idolaters; oh! those ordinances of God in which our souls have met with so much soul-refreshings and communion with God, in which so much of the Spirit of God and such enlightenings have been imparted to our souls, oh! how should we mourn after them! You that have gotten any thing by the word or by his ordinances, that have ever known what it has been to have communion with God in them, you should think with yourselves, If these should be taken from me, then I should have cause to mourn indeed. I have lost much of my estate, and my friends, many of them are gone, and these are a cause of mourning; oh! but if I should lose the ordinances and worship of God, what cause would there be then of mourning!

"And the priests thereof that rejoiced on it." The priests especially mourn. The word here translated "priests," is in the Hebrew כמרים and I find the word from whence it comes signifies three things.

1. To sound aloud: and so some think that therefore they are called Chemarims, because of the clamorous sounds they were wont to make in their superstitious worship: just as we were wont to have bellowing in the cathedrals, so they were wont to have, and therefore were called Chemarims, because of their mighty noises and sounds that they were wont to have.

2. To burn, or to be hot: and so Luther understands the word, and saith, that they were called Chemarims from their burning desires after their ways of false worship.

3. To be black from burning; because those things that are burnt are made black. When the flame first takes hold upon a thing it makes it black: and so Chemarims are as much as black ones, or indeed black coats,* in allusion to the black garments that they were wont to use. And I find in 2 Kings xxiii. 5, that this word here rendered "priests," is there used for "idolatrous priests." Those black coats that were then, accounted it a kind of religion to go in black, and from thence they derived the name. And though certainly it is fit for the ministers of the gospel to go gravely and decently, and not to express lightness and vanity in their garments, yet so to regard black, as if necessarily they must wear black coats, and no other garments will serve the turn, savours of superstitious vanity. Though gravity be required in their very garments, yet to stand so much upon the very colour may be dangerous; and for those that are looked upon as religious men, that they should be tied and bound to it, is, I say, evil. They were wont to do so here: and so almost all your heathens and superstitious people have had always a special colour for the garments of their priests; so the Turks have green, others different colours. Thus much for the name Chemarims.

"The priests that rejoiced on it;" that is, they that did exalt over the calves. The priests got the king on their side, and made the calves brave, and had a splendid kind of worship, and many pompous ceremonies; the priests gloried in this, for they had a special hand in all, and because they had the countenance of authority for their calves, they were able to crush any that spake against them, they "rejoiced on it," saith the text.

But now it is threatened, that they shall mourn; those priests that did so glory in their calves, (as who were they that did glory so much in pompous altars and other outward adornings, as your priests?) they exulted and had all under them, and would quickly crush a man reluctant to yield to them; they did even brave it over all, and call themselves sometimes the triumphant clergy, just like your Chemarims; but now here they were like to lose all, and they mourned.

Polanus, on this very place, refers it to the fat livings, parsonages, prebendaries, deaneries, and bishoprics, and such kind of preferments. Oh how do our prelates and their satellites mourn this day for the loss of these things! Thus they that did so rejoice to expect preferment, are gone now, the world is at an end with them, and they mourn one to another because of the loss of such things as these are: and long may they mourn upon this ground. In Rev. xviii. such people are well set forth: upon the fall of Babylon, the text saith, that "the merchants of the earth shall weep and mourn over her; for no man buyeth their merchandise any more:" then in ver. 14, "The fruits that thy soul lusted after are departed from thee:" and in ver. 15, "The merchants of these things, which were made rich by her, stood afar off, weeping and wailing." Those that were made rich by the whore of Babylon stand afar off, weeping and wailing. And so weep and wail those made rich by the prelates, and by superstitious vanities; and blessed be God that we see them mourn that did so triumph and rejoice over the people of God; blessed be God that he has so changed things, that now they hang down their heads and mourn, even because of their calves that are taken from them.

"For the glory thereof." They sought to make them as glorious as they could, and they accounted them very glorious. Now shall wicked men, idolaters, account their idol worship glorious? Oh how glorious should the worship of God be in our eyes, the true spiritual worship of God! Let the true ministers of God learn not to glory in the flesh, but desire to "know nothing but Jesus Christ, and him crucified."

"Is departed." For divers years together the worship of the calves had a great deal of glory put upon it, but it went away. And so you know what glory was upon our prelates, and such kind of worship as they of late set up, but "the glory thereof is departed." And look to it, whatever the inventions of men are, if unsanctioned by God, the glory will depart from them.

Ver. 6. *It shall be also carried unto Assyria for a present to king Jareb: Ephraim shall receive shame, and Israel shall be ashamed of his own counsel.*

"It shall be carried unto Assyria for a present to king Jareb." What king Jareb was you heard in the fifth chapter: his name signifies a helper: as now the king of France is designated The most Christian king; our king, The defender of the faith; so king Jareb was called The helper. Now the calves are to be sent to king Jareb, that was their help. Some think that they sent it for a present, but the text will not bear that; but his soldiers, taking Dan and Beth-el, send the calves to king Jareb as a trophy, as that which they knew he would much rejoice in: they rested much upon king Jareb as a help to them, and now their form of worship, their very religion, is at Jareb's disposal, for he has now the calves in his hand, to do with them what he will.

Obs. 1. Our dependence on men for help is dearly bought, if it comes to that, that they shall have the disposal of our religion. Jareb was their helper, and they would have him to help them; but now their calves are sent to him for a present, and Jareb has the disposal of them for their religion.

Obs. 2. Idolaters are wont to rejoice much when they get one another's gods. As when the Philistines got the ark, they rejoiced much, they carried it to Dagon's temple. Also the enemies of the church will rejoice much if they can get the power to trample upon our religion; they will rejoice much if they can get your estates, but they will rejoice more if they can do what they will with you in regard to your religion. Oh! this would be that which would make them glad at the very heart, if they could control us in our worship. Oh! let us know this beforehand, that we may cry to God the more earnestly, that whatever the Lord gives them power over, he would not give them power over our religion; for at that they most aim.

"Ephraim shall receive shame, and Israel shall be ashamed of his own counsel." Jerome upon the place refers to this tradition of the Jews: That the priests of the calves had taken away the golden ones and set up calves of brass instead, only gilt over with gold; and now the king of Israel, when he was in straits, sent these calves to king Jareb for a present to pacify his anger, and the

See Schickard's Prodromus, or his Bechinath Haperuchim.

* This is the rabbins' interpretation of the word, (and they apply it to the popish monks and nuns,) which Calvin rejects, and expounds it to signify, either their clamorous noise in worshipping, as 1 Kings xviii. 27, or to be a common name whereby those idolatrous priests were known, as 2 Kings xxiii. on which place see Munster's Annotations.

king of Assyria, supposing that the calves were of gold, rejoiced, but afterwards, when he found that they were of brass, he sent messengers to the king of Israel to tell him how he had cozened him, and thereupon the king and all the people were ashamed. But this is but a tradition of theirs, and not very probable. But I rather take the following to be the true interpretation:

"Ephraim shall receive shame, and Israel shall be ashamed;" that is, their hopes shall fail them, and they shall see their counsels come to nothing, and this shall cause them shame and confusion of face. The ten tribes "shall receive shame." Failing in our hopes makes us to be ashamed. They had good hopes they should prevail because of their calves, but now their calves are taken from them, and now they are ashamed. So Job vi. 20, "They were confounded because they had hoped; they came thither, and were ashamed:" they hoped to have relief, but had not, and therefore they were ashamed; the disappointment of hopes causes great shame. Oh, then, what shame and confusion will there be at the great day, when we shall be disappointed of our last hopes! If we had been disappointed of our hopes now in respect of our adversaries, oh what shame would have been upon the people of God! our adversaries would have cast shame upon us, and said, What is become of your fastings and prayers? As it is likely the Assyrians did when they took the calves; Oh, now we have gotten your gods, said they; and upon this the people were ashamed: and so if our adversaries had prevailed they would have reviled us in like manner. My brethren, we have cause to bless the Lord from our souls that he has delivered us from such a temptation, as to be ashamed of our hopes; though the truth is, if we considered aright we should not have been ashamed, for our hopes were not so much in the saving of our estates, as in this, that God would acknowledge his own cause in the end; and so our hopes would not have failed: yea, but if they had but apparently failed, if the enemy had but seemed to have prevailed, I say, it would have been a mighty temptation for us to have been ashamed of our hopes. Oh! blessed be God for preventing this, that the Lord has not even for a season made his people ashamed of their hopes and prayers! The ministers of God can stand up and look comfortably on their congregations, because they incited people, and encouraged their hearts in this cause; and they have comfort to their souls in this, that when things were at the lowest, yet still they could place their hopes on God, and believe yet in God that he would go on in such a cause as this is; and the Lord has not caused the expectation of his poor people to fail. But if it be shame (I say) now to be disappointed in some present hopes, O remember, in the midst of earthly disappointments, what shame would it be before men and angels if it should prove that any soul in this place should be disappointed of their last hopes! Thou hast hopes of salvation, and of eternal life, and if it should prove, when all secrets are to be made public before the Lord Jesus and his angels, that all thy hopes are but delusions, what would become of thee? David prays, "O Lord, let me not be disappointed of my hope." Let that be thy prayer, especially in regard of thy last hopes. In 1 John ii. 28, we are counselled to "abide in him; that, when he shall appear, we may have confidence, and not be ashamed before him at his coming." Oh, that is the comfort of the saints, that they shall not be ashamed at the coming of Jesus Christ; and many that are not ashamed now, yet at the coming of Jesus Christ, oh the shame that shall be cast upon them! But the main emphasis lies in the words that follow.

"Of his own counsel." Now what was that counsel? What? why it was this. The counsel that was between Jeroboam and his princes and the priests, together with some eminent men of the people, first, for the setting up of false worship; secondly, for the forcing of all men that belonged to the ten tribes to forbear going to Jerusalem. This was thought a notable plot, a notable counsel, they considered it to be the only means to keep things in peace among them. Why, (say they,) if we shall suffer every one that has a fancy in his head, to go to Jerusalem to worship, we shall have nothing but confusion; and therefore let us take such a course that people shall have a place to worship in, and a form to worship by: it is but only a few that are so strict that they must needs worship in Jerusalem, and therefore let us determine this, that we will have a constant form obligatory on every one, and we will have no more going to this Jerusalem to worship, but they shall be content to worship at Dan and Beth-el, and this will keep things in peace. Now this counsel seemed to be a fine plot to keep things in order. But, saith the Lord, "Israel shall be ashamed of his own counsel;" though they think those men who advise thus sage and wise, yea, even good men, and earnest for peace, and so cry up mightily the counsel, yet the Lord "sitteth in the heavens," and "laughs," and saith, "Israel shall be ashamed of his own counsel." Perhaps now, whilst they are permitted to carry all before them, they bless themselves in their counsel, and think it very excellent, and approved of by God; but when my time shall come, when they shall see what evil it brings upon them, then they shall be ashamed of their counsel.

Obs. 3. Men's own counsels bring shame to them, especially in religion. Men naturally are very blind in the things of God, they do not see far in them; their hearts are full of corruptions, which strongly bias them: we may instance some.

1. There is much self-love in men: any thing that is men's own is much regarded, a great deal more than truth that is another man's; if it be their own they mind that, but let another man speak that which has truth, it is little regarded. There is in men's hearts much violence to maintain their own counsels, and therefore it is very like that their counsels will bring them to shame. There is nothing that men can bear to be contradicted in, less than in their counsels. And the more men are set upon their own counsels, the more likely are they to bring them shame in the conclusion.

2. A judgment from God comes upon men's spirits, if they *will* follow out their own counsels; I say, there is ordinarily a judgment of God upon them to leave them to folly when they rest upon their own counsels. So it is threatened in Psal. lxxxi. 11, 12, as a great judgment of God upon men, to give them up to their counsels: "My people would not hearken to my voice; and Israel would none of me. So I gave them up unto their own hearts' lust: and they walked in their own counsels." Oh! it is a terrible place; I beseech you consider it well: these are times wherein every one is plotting; oh! tremble at these words, "I gave them up unto their own hearts' lust; and they walked in their own counsels." Men's own counsels bring them to shame; ofttimes they come to nothing after they have made a great deal of stir, so that they are fain to sit down, and there is an end of all their labour; perhaps they have laboured to advance their counsels by much evil, much sin, much heart-burning, and when it comes to all, there it lies, there is an end of it; thus they are ashamed of their counsels. Yea, many times the counsels of men work quite contrary; God much glories in this, in making use of men's own counsels to bring them into snares. What has brought our adversaries into snares but their own counsels? What brought the prelates down but their own counsels? so that they would bite their very fingers for what they did in their protestation. God has been pleased to deal thus graciously

for us, to bring our enemies into snares by their own counsels. So in Job xviii. 7, it is said of the wicked, "his own counsel shall cast him down." And Psal. ix. 16, "The wicked is snared in the work of his own hands. Higgaion. Selah." You have not those two words conjoined elsewhere in the whole book of God. It seems to imply that it is a thing to be meditated on very much, that "the wicked is snared in the work of his own hands." O consider this work of God, in bringing men down by their own counsels!

It is just that it should be so; for men provoke God by their counsels, Psal. cvi. 43. Oh! the Lord looks upon the counsels of men, and is much provoked by them, and therefore just it is with him to make their counsels so to be a snare to them, that they should be ashamed of them at the last. It concerns us therefore, my brethren, to look to our counsels, what they are. I will give you a few rules about them, that they may not bring you shame.

First, Keep out from your counsels those things that would hinder you. As,

1. False principles; be not actuated in your counsels by false principles.

2. Wicked men; take heed that they do not join with you in your counsels; as in Job xxi. 16, "Lo, their good is not in their hand: the counsel of the wicked is far from me:" and so in Job xxii. 18. O keep out wicked men from your counsels.

3. Your own ends; take heed how they come in: if any of a man's own ends come into his counsels, they will warp them.

4. Conceitedness, and pride; when you come to counsel, O take heed of a conceited spirit, in leaning to your own understanding; God is wont to blast such.

5. Flesh and blood. "I conferred not with flesh and blood," saith Paul, Gal. i. 16: I did not look to carnal excellency, but laid all such aside; they would have advised me to this and that, and I should never have done as I did if I had consulted with flesh and blood.

6. Passion and frowardness. "He taketh the wise in their own craftiness: and the counsel of the froward is carried headlong," Job v. 13. If once you find in your counsels your hearts begin to be hot, rather break off; take heed of resolutions formed at such a time. It is a safe way for you, if you would consult about business of moment, as soon as heat appears to fall to prayer; we had need of cool and quiet spirits when we are consulting: as, if you would weigh a thing exactly with gold scales, (as in counsels we should weigh things very exactly,) you would not weigh in the midst of a wind: when men's passions begin to be up they weigh things as a man would weigh gold abroad in the wind; they cannot weigh exactly. Take heed then of passion in your counsels.

Divers other things there are that spoil our counsels, that we should be aware of. And if we would have our counsels right, then observe these further rules.

1. Look up first to Jesus Christ, that great Counsellor. He is called in Isa. ix. 6, the "Counsellor;" it is he that is "wonderful in counsel." God has entitled his Son the "Counsellor;" he is to be the counsellor of thy soul for thine eternal estate, yea, and to be thy counsellor for all matters of religion, and the worship of God: look up then to him.

2. Pray much. If you would not have your counsels miscarry, pray much. In Prov. viii. 14, "Counsel is mine," saith wisdom, representing Christ. That which some note respecting the counsel of Ahithophel and the counsel of Hushai, is very remarkable. The counsel of Ahithophel, the truth is, if we examine it, was the wiser counsel of the two; and Absalom loved Ahithophel exceedingly, and his counsel was ordinarily accounted as the oracle of God; yet then, because God had an intent to bring down his counsel, it was rejected, and the counsel of Hushai embraced; God thus heard the prayer of David when he prayed, "Lord, turn the counsel of Ahithophel into folly." And let us pray much that God would be with our counsellors, that there may be none among them like those spoken of in Ezek. xi. 2, "These are the men that devise mischief, and give wicked counsel in this city;" and that likewise the Lord would sway counsels, and that men would yield to that which is the safest and the best counsel, to that which is the best in the eyes of God. Many times, when a company meet together, there are some things cursorily mentioned that are neglected by the company, whereas if God were with them to guide them, that very thing perhaps would sway all their counsels: let us then pray much. "Guide me with thy counsel, and afterward receive me to glory," Psal. lxxiii. 24. Oh, especially in matters that concern our souls and religion, we should pray much that God would guide us by his counsel, and so bring us to glory.

3. Let the fear of God be strong in your hearts when you come to ask counsel. Oh, it is a good thing when any are going to counsel about matters of consequence, for them to possess their hearts beforehand with the fear of the great God, and then they will counsel well: you have a notable scripture for this in Ezra x. 3, Come, let us go to do "according to the counsel of my lord, and of those that tremble at the commandment of our God." It may be there are some with greater depth of understanding; yea, but have they the fear of God in them? is there hope that they are guided by the Lord? let us take heed to do "according to the counsel of those that tremble at the commandment of our God." Do you see a man whose heart is possessed with the fear of God and his word? if his parts be but ordinary, you may expect that God will be with him rather than with those that are bold and presumptuous, and slight the word of God.

4. Be sure to look at the word, especially in matters of religion; and think not thus, I nreason and prudence such a way were better, and would more conduce to peace. Luther saith, Reason is a most deadly enemy even to faith, it is dangerous to reason in matters of faith; and so in matters that regard the worship of God. Keep to the word therefore in all your counsels, and in them all labour for sincerity of heart: what makes men miscarry in their counsels is this, that their hearts are biased with some lust or other, and therefore when any thing is spoken to them suitable to their inclinations, that they embrace; and if any thing be spoken to them that is otherwise, they reject it. Oh, it is just with God to answer thee according to the idol that is set up in thine own heart.

5. Take heed of being put off with any fair shows. When the Lord is leaving any, yet he will suffer those that give evil counsel to mix a great many good things with that which is evil. As some that will put a few brass shillings into a great bag of money; the rest is all good current money, yea, but here are some brass shillings amongst it. So sometimes in the midst of a great deal of good counsel, there is a little mixture that may turn all: therefore those that would counsel, especially in public affairs, had need have their eyes about them, and poise every word and line, and examine every particular, or otherwise they may quickly come to be ashamed of their own counsel.

6. God has promised to direct the humble, therefore come with humility in your counsels, and be sure in what is evidently right to follow; and then you may with the more confidence expect God to help you in other things.

7. Consult with indifferent judgment.

8. If the thing affect others, think what we would desire if we were in their case.

9. Consider whether the attaining of your object, though good, may not occasion more evil than the thing is worth: if it be not of present necessity, *(non deliberandum de necessariis,)* the rubs attending it may show it is not good at this time, or not thus, or not for me.

Obs. 4. Times of affliction make men ashamed of that which they would not be ashamed of before. "Ephraim shall receive shame, and Israel shall be ashamed of his own counsel:" and so also Jer. ii. 26; Zeph. iii. 11. Sir Walter Raleigh well saith, "When death comes, which hates men and destroys men, it is believed; but God, that makes and loves men, is not regarded. O eloquent, O mighty death! whom none could advise, thou art able to persuade." That is, men that would never be persuaded by any thing else to believe that they were not right, yet when death appears it can persuade them. Now afflictions are an evil; but how eloquent are afflictions! what power have they to persuade men that they were wrong, who would not be persuaded by all the arguments in the world before! In afflictions "Israel shall be ashamed of his own counsel." O, I beseech you, let us take heed of this, let us not go on headily in our own counsels till God bring us into misery, and we be forced to cry out of our own counsels, and be ashamed of them.

Ver. 7. *As for Samaria, her king is cut off as the foam upon the water.*

"As for Samaria, her king is cut off." Before, God threatened that they should be ashamed of their counsels, and what that counsel was I told you. Ashamed of our counsel! we hope not, we shall maintain it; our king is for us, he will venture his life, his kingdom, that he may maintain us in our way.

Your king, saith the prophet, he shall be "as the foam upon the water," even the king of Samaria.

Yea, but our king is in a strong town, in Samaria, a great city, and so strong as to be able to sustain a siege for three years together. And yet the king of Samaria, though he had gotten the chief city in the kingdom to be fully for him, and so much victuals and strength as he could hold out for three years, yet (saith the Lord) he shall be "as the foam upon the water."

"As the foam upon the water." The word קצף translated "foam," sometimes signifies the foam that is in a man who is extremely angry, as in Zech. i. 2. Your king that doth foam in anger when he is crossed "shall be as the foam upon the water," saith God. Now hence,

Obs. 1. Ungodly men in their greatest power and rage, are, if God comes upon them, nothing but "foam," poor weak creatures that vanish and come to nothing. The foam when the waters rage makes a great show above them, but stay a while, and it vanishes and comes to nothing. Your king that rages and is above others, and thinks he has a great deal of power, in a while comes to nothing. The Scripture compares men in their greatest power to things of the greatest vanity; there are, in scriptures that I will mention to you, nineteen or twenty different particulars, wherein men in their greatest power are compared to that which has nothing but vanity; yea, there are such expressions in Scripture, to set out the meanness, vileness, and baseness of men in the greatest power, that it would make Christians that understand Scripture, and that are of the same judgment with their Father, with God, as he has revealed himself in his word, never to be afraid of the power of men. I will name them distinctly to you thus:

The Scripture sometimes calls even kings and great ones a mere noise, nothing more; so in Jer. xlvi. 17, "Pharaoh king of Egypt is but a noise."

They are but as small dust: "The multitude of thy strangers shall be like small dust," Isa. xxix. 5.

They are but as chaff: "The terrible ones shall be as chaff that passeth away," Isa. xxix. 5. Who would be afraid of a noise, small dust, and chaff?

They are as nothing: "Behold, all they that were incensed against thee shall be as nothing," Isa. xli. 11.

They are "as tow," Isa. i. 31; put a little fire to tow, and it quickly comes to nothing.

They are as dung: "As dung for the earth," Psal. lxxxiii. 10.

They are as straw that is trodden for dung: "As straw is trodden down for the dunghill," Isa. xxv. 10.

They are compared sometimes to a beast that has a hook in his nostrils; so Isa. xxxvii. 29, God will put a hook in his nose: now who would be afraid of a beast that has a hook put into his nostrils?

They are as stubble, and as "stubble fully dry," ready for the fire, Nah. i. 10.

They are as rottenness, and "their root shall be as rottenness," Isa. v. 24.

They are as scum: "Her scum shall be in the fire," Ezek. xxiv. 12.

They are as smoke: "As smoke is driven away, so drive them away," Psal. lxviii. 2.

They are as grass: "As the grass on the housetops, and as corn blasted before it be grown up:" all these you have together in Isa. xxxvii. 27.

They are "as wax that melteth before the fire," Psal. lxviii. 2.

They are "as the fat of lambs," Psal. xxxvii. 20.

They are as "a worm," Job xxv. 6.

They are vanity, lighter than vanity, their "best state is altogether vanity," Psal. xxxix. 5.

They are as snow melting before the sun, Job xxiv. 19.

They are as the light of a candle: "The candle of the wicked shall be put out," Prov. xxiv. 20.

And lastly, They are a lie; even great men and princes; for so saith Psal. lxii. 9, "Men of high degree are a lie."

Thus, my brethren, we see how the Scripture heaps up expression upon expression. It might have been very profitable to have insisted upon all these particulars, and to have opened them, to show you how contemptibly the Holy Ghost speaks of men in their great power.

Now if we could gather these scriptures together, and put them all into one, and so present the power of great men to us, and by these things have the same judgment of them that God has, it would tend mightily to deliver us from the fear of man. "As for Samaria, her king is cut off as the foam upon the water."

Ver. 8. *The high places also of Aven, the sin of Israel, shall be destroyed: the thorn and the thistle shall come up on their altars; and they shall say to the mountains, Cover us; and to the hills, Fall on us.*

I confess, from these words to the end of the 11th verse there appears, at the first reading, much obscurity; yet they are like to a mine, the outside barren, but within much and precious treasure.

Israel, the ten tribes, confided in two things, and so strengthened themselves against all that the prophet could say against them.

First, In the power of their king. Now that is gone. That is as foam, saith God: confide not in the power of the king, think not that will bear you out, for he shall be "as the foam upon the water."

Secondly, In their sacrifices. They were a religious people, and very costly in their devotions, and they confided much in that. Well, for this second confidence, thus saith the Lord; "The high places also of

Aven, the sin of Israel, shall be destroyed: the thorn and the thistle shall come up on their altars." Though never so pompous in their eyes, yet they are "the high places of Aven:" they were called before Beth-aven, the house of vanity; now Aven, vanity itself. That place was no other than Beth-el, whose name signified the house of God, where one of the calves was set up. Now the name of this place did a great deal of hurt among the people; Oh! to go up to Beth-el, the house of God! therefore God would take away that name, and calls it Beth-aven first, and then Aven, that is, instead of calling it the house of God, I will have it called the house of vanity. און signifies vanity, yea, iniquity itself.

Obs. 1. God stands much upon taking people off from specious names put upon any things made use of in false worship; he stands much upon it, for whereas before he had changed it from Beth-el to Beth-aven, he changes it now from Beth-aven to Aven: God would obliterate the name of Beth-el, and make it to be accounted by the people to be nothing but iniquity and vanity.

Obs. 2. The more of the nature of sin any thing has, the more vile and abominable it is. Therefore God speaks of it by an expression that conveys somewhat of its aggravated nature—"the sin of Israel," sin in the abstract; more than if he had said, the sinful things of Israel. "The sin of Israel," that is, their idolatrous worship.

Obs. 3. Their false worship is the great sin; and it was the greater sin in Israel, because that their holiness was typical, and did especially consist in instituted worship. It is true, God would have true holiness if ever they came to heaven, but that holiness upon which they were called a holy people, was in their instituted worship; and it was typical, to set forth the true holiness that should be in all the members of the church now; therefore God was much provoked with their pollutions in instituted worship, their holiness consisting so much in it.

Obs. 4. We may so abuse the creatures of God, as not only to make them sinful to us, but even to turn them into sin, as it were. Thus their idols, and the creatures that they abused to sin, are here called their sin, "the sin of Israel;" and many men abuse their bodies so that they may be called sin itself.

Well, that which they accounted holy, you see God accounts not only sinful, but "sin," and saith, it "shall be destroyed."

Obs. 5. When any ordinances of God's appointment are abused, they are but to be purged; but if they be inventions of men, they are to be destroyed. "The high places also of Aven, the sin of Israel, shall be destroyed." We must learn for ever to take heed of meddling with, or putting any thing of our own in the place of, God's worship. We may think in reason this may be good as well as that, we see no evil in it; why may not this form then be as good as that? Yea, but God looks upon things according as he himself requires them: and therefore Calvin, I remember, on this place saith, God often pronounces those things that may please us, sin and sacrilege, and would have them destroyed. Let us therefore rest in his judgment; it is not our part to dispute about matters of worship: we must not dispute and say, Why may not this be? this may be for a good use, and a great deal of good may be the result; we must not stand disputing with God, and debating the matter with him; for though it may be very specious in our eyes, yet it may be very odious and abominable to the eyes of God.

Obs. 6. Even all those things that evil men make use of for sin shall one day be taken from them. "The high places also of Aven, the sin of Israel, shall be destroyed." You shall not always have the creatures of God to abuse to sin; there will be a time when God will deliver his creatures from this vanity to which they are now subject.

Obs. 7. Man's sin brings destruction upon the creatures. "The high places also of Aven, the sin of Israel, shall be destroyed." Sin is as poison in a glass, that causes the glass to be broken and cast upon the dunghill.

"The thorn and the thistle shall come up on their altars." This expression denotes,

First, The great devastation that shall be made in those places where they had altars, which took place especially in Samaria, which was besieged for three years together. The enemies had Beth-el in their own hands, and they manifested their rage forthwith upon their altars, and upon all their religious things; they pulled them down and made them lie in heaps of rubbish, so that in the space of three years the very thistles and thorns grew up in their place. It is usual to express the devastation of a place by saying, that the grass shall grow where the houses were, where the city was there shall corn grow: so here, "the thorn and the thistle shall come up on their altars."

Secondly, It is an expression of indignation, as if God should have said, I will take more delight to see the thorns and thistles grow out of the very rubbish of the altars, than in all their images and brave pictures and gildings. Just as if it had been said about seven or eight years ago of the Service-book, Oh, now you honour it much, and it must be bound and gilt bravely, and strung curiously; but this that you so idolize now, within a while shall be but waste paper, it shall be thrown to the mice and rats to eat! this would have been an expression of like indignation against it, as is here uttered against the altars.

Obs. 8. If it be sad that places of false worship should not be frequented as formerly they were wont to be, how much more sad is it that places of true worship should be neglected! As thus, They were wont to go to Beth-el to worship at their altars: yea, but, saith God, they shall go no more thither, but those places shall be filled with nettles, thorns, and thistles: they accounted that sad. Yea, but we should account it sad that the paths to the true worship of God should not be beaten as in former times: where there was an altar, as it were, for the worship of God, those places then were frequented much; but had our adversaries had their wills, we should have had "the thorn and the thistle" grown up in them.

Obs. 9. If it be so sad to have such an ill succession here in false worship, sad to false worshippers, what sadness is there for the true worshippers of God to have an ill succession in the church! Truly much like, methinks, it is, when there has been in a place a godly and a powerful ministry, and afterwards, for the sins of the people, God takes it away, and instead thereof comes up a pricking thorn, a brier, a thistle, a nettle, an unworthy man, of no gifts or graces, who can only gall and prick, and do hurt and mischief; this is a succession like to that which God here threatened, that thistles and thorns should succeed their altars. Jerome on the place seems to hint some such kind of meditation, when he saith, Instead of true doctrine, there shall be a wilderness of very corrupt doctrine; where there was true doctrine taught, now it shall lie waste as a wilderness.

Solitudo pessimæ doctrinæ. Jer. in loc.

Obs. 10. God accounts the ruin of the most glorious things abused to sin, a more pleasing object than when those things were in the greatest pomp and glory. The buildings and the altars were splendid, but God looked upon them as more glorious when pulled down and grown over with thorns and briers. And so if a man have a very beautiful, comely body, and abuse it to sin, when God shall strike him, and he shall be covered with worms as a filthy carcass, God will look upon that as a more lovely sight than his body decked with all kind of ornaments. Better that the creature perish, though it be the most glorious creature in the world, than that it be abused to sin.

Obs. 11. Those things which men account highly of in the matters of worship, when God lets in their enemies they contemn. They accounted highly of their calves, but when the Assyrians came they contemned them, and pulled them down. It is not only so in respect of false worship, but of true; those things that we highly esteem and bless God for, and think what infinite pity it is that they should not be continued, yet if God should let our adversaries in they would scorn them. As now, such liberties as these are, what infinite pity were it that people should be deprived of them; but if God should let our adversaries in upon us they would scorn and contemn these things, as the Assyrians did those which the Israelites accounted to be as God.

"And they shall say to the mountains, Cover us; and to the hills, Fall on us." This is an expression to show,

First, The dreadfulness of their misery. It should be a misery so great as to make them weary of their lives, should make them rather desire death than life.

Secondly, Their wonderful desperation. In the apprehension and sense of this their misery they would have no whither to go for help, but their hearts should despair, and all the relief that they should expect was, to have the mountains fall upon them, and the hills to cover them. Now this expression I find Christ afterwards makes use of in setting forth the misery of the destruction of the Jews by the Romans, Luke xxiii. 30; and the Holy Ghost, in speaking of the misery of the antichristian party, when the wrath of God should come out upon them, saith, their misery shall be so great, that their princes, and great men, and mighty men, and chief captains, shall call upon the mountains to fall upon them, and the hills to cover them, Rev. vi. 15, 16. The reverend Mr. Brightman, on that very scripture, saith, that it was fulfilled in the time of Constantine, when the heathen emperors were vanquished: and he applied it to Dioclesian, who was so terrified in apprehension of the wrath of the Lamb, that he drank poison and so killed himself; to Maximian, who hanged himself; and to Galerius, who died of a most noisome and filthy disease. Maximinus, too, that he might prevent his death, likewise murdered himself; and Maxentius ran into the Tiber to hide himself in its waters. And thus they sought by different violent deaths to hide themselves from the sight of the Lamb.

I suppose all of you understand clearly that it is meant as an expression of great anguish and desperation; but yet, that we may see why the Holy Ghost makes use of this expression rather than others, and discern clearly its appropriateness, you must know that the land of Canaan (the scene of the prophet's present predictions) was a land full of mountains and hills, and these mountains were, many of them, stony and rocky; and the Jews were wont therefore to dig places in them for safety in the time of great danger, constructing them so, that by the narrowness of the ingress they might be able easily to keep out an enemy. Josephus saith, that thieves and robbers too were wont to make use of such caves and dens in the mountains and hills. To such places this scripture alludes, and by this you may be helped to understand divers other passages; as Isa. ii. 19, "And they shall go into the holes of the rocks, and into the caves of the earth, for fear of the Lord, and for the glory of his majesty, when he ariseth to shake terribly the earth." They should go then into the holes of the rocks and caves of the earth, for they were wont to use such things there much. And so Psal. xi. 1, "In the Lord put I my trust: how say ye to my soul, Flee as a bird to your mountain?" In times of danger they were wont to flee to those mountains. And Psal. cxxi. 1, "I will lift up mine eyes unto the hills, from whence cometh my help:" not only to the temple, but to the hills, because in time of danger they were wont to think of the hills. But, saith David, I lift up my heart to God, and that shall be to me instead of a hundred refuges in hills. And Psal. xxxvi. 6, "Thy righteousness is like the great mountains." This is said not only because the mountains stand steadily and strongly, but because they were places of refuge and shelter. The saints have refuge in the faithfulness of God; and as they used to run to the holes in the mountains, so God is called a strong rock for the righteous to run to. God is as a rock, not only because the faithfulness of God is steady as a rock, but because, as they had caves and holes in the rocks that they were wont to run to in time of danger, so his faithfulness affords a refuge to his people in every time of need: therefore is God called "a Rock." And it is said, "The strength of the hills is his also," Psal. xcv. 4. And Psal. xciv. 22, "The Lord is my defence; and my God is the rock of my refuge."

Josephus, Antiq. lib. 14. cap. 27. De Bello Judaic. lib. 1. cap. 12.

But yet further, that we may more fully understand the meaning of this expression; When in times of danger they ran to the caves in the mountains, and to the rocks, they considered when there, Oh, if the enemy should come upon us, how sad would our condition be! Oh that rather this mountain that is now over us would sink down and fall upon us, rather than that the enemy should take us! This I regard as the meaning and origin of this phrase; they despised the mountain of God, the going up to his mountain, but now they would be glad to have these mountains crush them in pieces.

Obs. 12. The alteration which God can make in cities and kingdoms. They who were proud and scornful erewhile, are now so distressed that they would think themselves happy to be crushed by mountains and hills.

Obs. 13. How great is the misery of falling into the hands of our enemies. Israel knew how cruelly the Assyrians had treated others, therefore, when they came against them, and besieged them for three years together, they desired to die under the mountains rather than to fall into their hands. Josephus, in one of the forenamed places, gives us a notable story of this, telling us of some that fled into the mountains and holes for safety, and Herod pursued them; among others there was an old man, who had seven children and his wife with him, and who, rather than fall into Herod's hands, called his children one by one to the mouth of the cave that he had made in the mountain, and with his own hands killed them in succession before the enemy, afterwards he put to death his wife, and when he had cast their dead bodies down the rock, he threw himself down headlong after them; so he slew himself, and all he had, rather than he would fall into the hands of his enemies. Certainly this is a wonderful exhibition of misery. Some of you perhaps have seen or felt somewhat, but all that has been nothing to what was like to happen, had the enemies gotten full power. Let us bless God then that we are delivered from that, that we have no such cause to cry out to the mountains to cover us, and to the hills to fall upon us.

Obs. 14. There is nothing so fearful as the wrath of God. One would think that which these poor people desired here dreadful enough, to have the mountains fall upon them, and the hills to cover them; but it is not so dreadful as God's wrath: take all the terrors in the world, they are nothing to the wrath of the Almighty when fully apprehended: sometimes the wrath of God lies more heavy on a man's conscience than a thousand mountains. And, my brethren, if it be so dreadful in outward judgments, how dreadful is it like to be when it shall come to be fully poured out upon the wicked and ungodly! "In those days shall men seek death, and shall not find it; and shall desire to die, and death shall flee from them," saith Rev. ix. 6. Oh! when God's wrath appears against the ungodly, it will be dreadful, especially when the full vials of it come to be poured out.

Obs. 4. To live in lingering misery, is worse than present dreadful death even in this world. I remember Suetonius tells of Tiberius Cæsar, that one whom he had condemned to death petitioned him that he might have his despatch; whereupon Tiberius replied, Sir, you and I are not friends yet, you must not die, you must be kept in misery. It is often worse than death to be kept in lingering misery; it is so, even in regard of the miseries of this world; oh how much worse than death is it then to be kept under the wrath of God to all eternity! How fearful is it to live in misery for ever, then, and never to die! Why it is better, certainly sense would apprehend it better, for a man to be despatched presently, than to live in lingering misery: yet, if we knew all, it were better for the wicked to live in the greatest misery in this world, than to die the fairest death; thou wert better to live as a dog, a toad, yea, as a stock-log at the back of the fire, (if it were possible,) than to die, if thou knewest all that hereafter in hell awaits thee, being wicked: *then* thou shalt not die, though it would be the greatest happiness to thee. If thou shouldst after a thousand years cry to God, O Lord, that mountains might fall upon me! the Lord would answer, You and I are not friends yet: and if after a thousand years more thou shouldst cry, O Lord, that I might be crushed to pieces! the Lord would answer you still, You and I are not yet friends. I tremble, saith Bernard, to think of that, that I should fall into the hands of living death, and of dying life, where men do not die that they might for ever cease to exist, but die that they may for ever die; they are always dying, but never die, but are kept by the almighty power of God on purpose that they might be fuel for his wrath, and subjects for his revenging justice. O consider this, you that are so ready to desire death, because you are at any time in a lingering misery. Is a lingering misery so evil? Then what will be the lingering evil of eternity!

Nondum tecum in gratiam redii. Sueton. l. 3. c. 6.

Bernard, lib. 5. de Confid.

Obs. 15. The wonderful misery of wicked men in their affliction. They have no whither to go for help; they have not God, they have no refuge but the mountains and hills; and what is their refuge there, but that they may fall upon them? Oh the difference between a saint of God and a wicked man in times of affliction! When in times of affliction, thou (if thou art wicked) shalt rage and be mad, and know not whither to go, and the uttermost help that thou canst think to have is from the hills and mountains to fall upon thee; then the saints of God shall be able to look up to heaven, and cry, Heaven is open for us, open to receive my soul. Angels, come and guide it, and bear it in. O arms of mercy, bowels of mercy, spread open yourselves to embrace me! Here is a difference. And is not this better than to cry to mountains to fall upon thee, and hills to cover thee? And yet such a difference in men's estates do sin and godliness make.

Obs. 16. The wonderful evil of despair, what a dreadful thing is desperation. The greatest benefit it suggests is to be crushed in pieces: so the help that many have, is but a halter to strangle them, a knife to murder them, or the water to drown them. Desperation is truly a dreadful thing. Francis Spira, surrounded by its horrors, cried out, Verily, desperation is hell itself. Upon all this, Luther concludes with this exhortation: Let us stir up ourselves to the fear of God, let us flee idolatry, let us beautify the word by our holy lives, and pray to Christ that we may escape such things as these, which God inflicts upon the contemners of his word. If you would not come into this wonderful despairing condition, O learn to fall down before the word; fear God *now*, that you may not despair *then*. You that contemn, and slight, and scorn the word now, this may prove to be your portion ere long, this desperate cry may be the greatest ease that your forsaken souls can have.

Ver. 9. *O Israel, thou hast sinned from the days of Gibeah: there they stood: the battle in Gibeah against the children of iniquity did not overtake them.*

"O Israel, thou hast sinned from the days of Gibeah." "O Israel," I am speaking this to you, it merely concerns you, you have sinned from the days of Gibeah. You think your sin is not so heinous as to merit these dreadful threatenings, that you should come to this desperate condition; Why, say the men of Israel, what means the prophet in being so terrible in his threatenings? pray what is our sin? Yes, you have sinned as in "the days of Gibeah," or "from the days of Gibeah," as in your books; or it may be read, beyond, or more than in "the days of Gibeah." "From the days of Gibeah;" from what time was that? You may read the story of Gibeah in Judg. xix., xx., and their sin. I shall not need to spend much time now in opening what Gibeah was, or the nature of its sin, because that in chap. ix. 9, of this prophecy, I met with those words, "They have deeply corrupted themselves, as in the days of Gibeah." But not only the 19th and 20th chapters, where we have the story of their horrible wickedness in abusing the Levite's concubine, but likewise the 18th, which speaks of Micah's idol, and the idolatry that was prevalent among the people, is here referred to.

Now, you have sinned, as "from the days of Gibeah;" that is, your forefathers of old have committed idolatry and sin against me, and you are grown rooted in your sin, and have taken it from your forefathers. For that sin of the Levite's concubine was very ancient. It seems to have been committed between the time of Joshua and the time of the Judges. For though events be set in Scripture so that one seems to follow another, yet they do not so always in point of time. But my reason why that sin of the Levite's concubine seems to have been then, is this: because you find in that story of the 19th of Judges, when the Levite was passing on, his servant would have had him go into Jebus, but "his master said unto him, We will not turn aside hither into the city of a stranger, that is not of the children of Israel; we will pass over to Gibeah," Judg. xix. 12. So that it seems Jerusalem was not then taken in by the children of Israel; but if you read the 1st chapter of Judges, you shall find that Jerusalem was taken, it was taken before you read of any particular judge; therefore this sin that was in the days of Gibeah was very ancient. You have sinned of old, saith he, and you have continued in the succession of sin of old. If you take it "*from* the days of Gibeah," we might thus interpret it.

But it is rather, I think, to be taken comparatively, Your sin is more than the days of Gibeah, it is greater, whatever you think of it. You think you worship and serve God, yet the truth is, was that sin horrible, that a whole city should come together to force a Levite's concubine till she was dead at the door? was that a horrible sin? yea, and was it horrible for them to stand to defend it? Your sin is greater. Why?

1. That was but one particular act, it was all done in one night; but you go on in a constant, settled way.

2. That was a sin but of some few of the people; your sin is more general.

3. That sin they had not so much means to resist, nor so much experience of the ways of God as you, and therefore your sin is greater than the sins that were in "the days of Gibeah."

4. Because that, continuing in the commission of sins which God made use of your forefathers to revenge, you greatly provoke God. That is the meaning: and for further opening of that sin I shall refer you to that which I delivered on chap. ix.

But understanding their sin as either "*from* the days of Gibeah," or "*more* than the days of Gibeah," the observations are,

Obs. 1. The sins of ancestors continued in are attended with aggravations. We are ready to excuse our sin, and say, Why, we do nothing but that which our forefathers did. Yea, but it may be that your sins are greater than the sins of your forefathers, because they had not such means. This would answer those that plead for old superstitious vanities, Why should we be wiser than our forefathers? But know, that if you continue in their sins, it is worse in you than in them.

Obs. 2. God takes it very ill that those men, or the posterity of those, whom he uses as instruments to punish sin in others, and to reform others, yet should be guilty themselves of the same, or greater, sins. Oh! (saith the prophet,) you may justly expect to have the mountains to fall upon you, and the hills to cover you, for you are more wicked than "in the days of Gibeah;" though I used your forefathers to punish that great sin, yet you continue to be more vile than they were that were punished by your forefathers. O my brethren, God cannot endure to see that wickedness continued in men, which they have been employed to punish in others. What! shall we, or any in this generation, be used to execute the anger of God on superstitious people; and shall we continue in the sin of superstition? shall we be used to cast out men's inventions, and shall we bring in men's inventions? Yea, shall we be used to punish oppression, and tyranny, and injustice; and shall we continue in oppression, tyranny, and injustice? Oh! this will cry to heaven, when it shall be said, God stirred you up to make you an instrument to cast out such oppressing courts, and tyranny, and certain men that were so cruel to godly people; you were employed to cast them out, and you now succeed them in like oppressions, and tyranny, and injustice, and you make my saints cry to heaven for the burdens that you lay upon them. Oh! this would be very heavy. Take we heed, that when God uses us, or our forefathers, to reform any evil, take heed that it be never said, that those evils continue in their children after them.

Our Reformation, as the punishment of the sin of Gibeah, cost much blood; much has been shed to punish oppressors, to bring in delinquents, to cast out those that have been burdens to the people of God. Therefore, as it was an aggravation of guilt in their posterity to continue in that sin, whose punishment had cost so much blood; so, the more it costs to cast out our oppressing courts, &c., the more fearful will our sin be if we continue in oppression ourselves. You complain sometimes of ministers, if they reprove sins, and be guilty of the same sins they reprove you of; you account that very evil, and so indeed it is. So it may be as well said of magistrates, for them to punish sins, and yet continue in them themselves, is very evil.

"There they stood." Either this must be meant,

I. Of the men of Gibeah, that they stood, and the battle did not overtake the children of iniquity. Or,

II. Of the men of Israel. There the men of Israel stood, and their battle did not overtake the children of iniquity.

I. If it be meant of the men of Gibeah, then the expression marks their stoutness, they would stand it out, "there they stood." Though they had committed such a horrible wickedness, and there was a desire only to have the real delinquents punished, yet they combine together, and would stand it out; they stood stoutly to maintain the wickedness that was committed, especially after their first success: they fought, and in both days they slew forty thousand; now, having conquered in the first battle, this did hearten them; yea, they had the day the second time, and that made them stout in their way. Success will imbolden men in their wickedness. God many times gives success designedly to harden the hearts of men, that they may stand it out to their ruin, for so it proved to the Benjamites. Be not troubled then at the success of adversaries, God gives them success but to lead them to ruin.

II. If you take these words, "there they stood," to refer to the men of Israel, it would cost one a great deal of time to lay before you the variety of interpretations given to them. I will, therefore, only give you what I think may be the scope of the Holy Ghost, or at least what may be fairly derived from the words.

"There they stood." That is, when the men of Israel saw, in their battle at Gibeah, that they did not prevail at first, and that their brethren stood out stoutly, and that they themselves had lost so many thousand men, upon this they were at a stand. "There they stood," they knew not what in the world to do, to think that in so good a cause, in a work in which they had warrant from God to engage, yet that they should have such ill success: "there they stood."

Obs. 3. Men had need be very well grounded in a good cause when they meet with much difficulty. I believe since this cause that we have been about in England has been begun, many, through unbelief and cowardice, have been at a stand; they stood, and knew not which way to go: Lord, is this the cause of God? is this the truth of God? What! can his cause have such ill success? Many men's spirits fluctuate with the success.

"There they stood;" that is, though they were at a stand, and somewhat troubled, yet they persisted in their work; notwithstanding the difficulties they met with, they would not fly off, but "there they stood" to it; they were resolved, whatever ill success they had, to go on in the work to which God had called them.

"The battle in Gibeah against the children of iniquity did not overtake them." When they did fight against the children of iniquity, yet the battle did not overtake them, to wit, the Benjamites, not the first day, but they were foiled twice: though I know some interpret this otherwise, yet this seems to me the most genuine explication.

But why does the prophet introduce it here? The men of Israel, to whom Hosea prophesied, might say, You tell us, that our sin is as in "the days of Gibeah," yea, let us but have success the first day, and the second day, we hope we shall do well enough. Nay, saith the prophet, your sin is worse; you may not think that your case is so good as the Benjamites, the battle did not overtake them, but it shall overtake you: and upon this ground the prophet brings in this, that the battle did not overtake them, granting that which they would object, yet so as not to suffer it to make for them, but to take away their hopes of escape.

Obs. 4. The children of iniquity may escape once, and again: though men be children of iniquity, yet the battle may not overtake them. The account in Judges is a story as well calculated to take away the seeming success in an ill cause, and disappointment in a good cause, as any I know in all the book of God. It did not overtake them at first. God's wrath follows many men in this world, and yet for a long time overtakes them not, he oft calls it back: Psal. lxxviii. 38, "But he, being full of compassion, forgave their iniquity, and destroyed them not: yea, many a time turned he his anger away, and did not stir up all his wrath." But at length God's wrath overtakes men. "My words and my statutes, which I commanded my servants the prophets, did they not take hold of your fathers?" Zech. i. 6. I sent out my threatening words, and they escaped a long time, but at length my words took hold of them. As the dog may follow the hare barking a great while, but at length overtaking, he springs upon it, and tears it; so, did not my words take hold upon your forefathers?

Calvin gives another interpretation of these words, and some other notes upon them, but I think that the foregoing is their main and genuine scope.

Ver. 10. *It is in my desire that I should chastise them; and the people shall be gathered against them, when they shall bind themselves in their two furrows.*

"It is in my desire." God speaks here as one that has forborne a length of time, and now longs to satisfy himself.

Tremelius upon the place notes, that the form of the word for chastising here is unusual, and adds, that perhaps God would express some more than ordinary punishment. Luther renders באותי ואסרם *Valde cupide eos castigabo*, Exceeding desirously will I chastise them. It is in my will to chastise them. O blessed God, do not we find in thy word, that the works of thy justice are said to be thy "strange works," and that thou art not willing to grieve the children of men, that mercy pleases thee? but where do we ever find that justice was so pleasing to thee?

It is true, though at first God seems to forbear the execution of justice as a thing he has no mind to, yet if sin be stubbornly continued in, now God desires it as a thing than which there is nothing more pleasing to him. He is burdened with men's sins, and desires to bring punishments upon them, as a man under a great burden desires to be eased; "Ah, I will ease me of mine adversaries, and avenge me of mine enemies," saith the Lord, Isa. i. 24: and in Ezek. v. 13, you find that God in threatening of wrath saith, that he would do thus and thus, and he would be comforted; and in Prov. i. 26, it is said that he "will laugh at the calamity of the wicked, and mock when their fear cometh;" and in Rev. xiv. 10, the wrath of God is called "the wine of his wrath," because he takes so much pleasure in the execution of it. The reasons for this are,

1. God's justice is God himself, as well as any other attribute.

2. God delights to vindicate his honour, therefore the word for chastisement signifies sometimes the vindication of a man's honour. The honour of God is dear to him. Your peace and comforts may be dear to you; yea, but my honour is more dear to me.

3. In chastisements God fulfils his word; the word of God would be slighted and contemned else. Now this pleases me therefore, to chastise them, to fulfil my word upon them.

Oh the fearful evil of sin, that brings the creature into such a condition, that God's heart is delighted in every evil that sinful creatures suffer! This must needs be a sad condition indeed, for the merciful God, that delights so much in doing mercy, yet now to look upon a sinner under his wrath, and to delight in it, and love it, and be well pleased to see the creature, even the work of his own hands, in such sufferings. Hereafter there will be pure justice, God will delight in the destruction of sinners in hell, in the execution of his justice upon them; he will there do nothing else but rejoice in it, there shall be nothing but joy in God's heart to see the execution of his justice upon sinners to all eternity; yea, and God will call all the angels and saints to come to rejoice with him: Come, ye angels and saints, and rejoice with me; here is a wretched sinner that was stubborn and rebellious against me in the time of his life, and see how my power has overtaken him, see the dreadfulness of my wrath, come and rejoice with me for ever in this my wrath. This will be the condition of sinners eternally in hell.

Consider this, you that have a desire to sin, a mind to sin, you that derive delight and comfort from sin. Is it in your will to sin? It is God's will to punish. Can you rejoice in sin? God can rejoice in the execution of his wrath. Are you resolute upon your sin? God can be resolute in the ways of his wrath. When God chastises his servants for their infirmities, he does it as a thing to which he has no mind at all, and therefore saith the apostle, "*If need be*," we fall into many temptations, 1 Pet. i. 6; and they are but *seeming* grievous; even he himself is afflicted in all their afflictions, Isa. lxiii. 9. David would have Joab go against Absalom, but saith he, "Deal gently for my sake with the young man, even with Absalom," 2 Sam. xviii. 5; so, when God chastises his servants, he sends an affliction; Go, saith he, and scourge such a one; yea, but deal gently with him for my sake. The bowels of David did yearn towards Absalom, even when he sent Joab to fight against him; so the bowels of God do yearn towards his people, even when he sends afflictions upon them. But when he comes to deal with the wicked and ungodly, I will do it to purpose, saith God, I will delight in it, yea, I will be comforted in it.

"And the people shall be gathered against them." That is, I will chastise them thus, by gathering people against them. The Assyrians, when they gathered against them, did it merely to serve their own ends; yea, but saith God, I have a hand in it, I will gather them against them. And certainly God had a mind to chastise them, when he would gather enemies against them. The Assyrians, perhaps, would never have dared to presume to come against Israel, if God had not had a hand in it: and certainly we could never have imagined it possible, that so many should be gathered together thus publicly, in this land, to maintain wickedness, and to fight to make themselves slaves, except that God had a mind to chastise England.

But I find that others read it thus:

I will chastise them according to my mind: and so the word will bear.

The Septuagint read it, κατὰ τὴν ἐπίθυμίαν μοῦ. *Juxta desiderium meum.* Vulg. According to my desire.

Œcolampadius on the place saith, God prescribed a certain time to this people to come in and repent, but saith God, You shall not prescribe me how long I shall stay, but I will do it when I please, both as regards the time and the degree of the chastisement.

Obs. 1. When God has a mind to bring about a thing, he will in his own time gather the people. I remember, in the life of Pompey, when some asked him, what they should do when the enemies came against them? that he replied, Let me but stamp upon the ground of Italy, and I shall have men enough. That, in him, was an idle vaunt, but it is a true one in God; let him but stamp with his feet, and he can gather people enough together.

Obs. 2. God will choose with what rod he will scourge us, according to his own mind, both as regards the degree and the kind. Under many afflictions we mourn and repine, and these discontented expressions come from us, Oh, I could bear any thing but that! But is it fit for thee to choose thine own rod? God might have said also, I had rather you had committed some other sin. It may be, because that is the affliction most cross to thy spirit, that therefore God will have it; God sees that that is more for his honour, and perhaps for thy good. Therefore let us learn to submit to the will of God. Is it fit that thou shouldst choose thy sin and thy rod too? No, stay there; if thou wilt choose thy sin, God will have liberty to choose thy rod.

"When they shall bind themselves in their two furrows." באסרם לשתי עינתם These words appear very obscure at first, and I find a mighty deal of puzzling among interpreters about them. The difficulty is in the word עינתם here translated "furrows;" the same letters, omitting the points, may be rendered, their two sins; or, by substituting for one of the letters another much like it in form, their two eyes: in all these three acceptations the sense may go reasonably well. As thus:

First, And they shall bind themselves in their two sins. Or you may take it of God's threatening what he would do; I will bind them for their two sins; so I find Arias Montanus and others translate it.

The Septuagint render it *ἐν τῷ παιδεύεσθαι αὐτοὺς ἐν ταῖς δυσὶν ἀδικίας αὐτῶν*, I will chastise them for their two sins; and so it may be, chastise as well as bind, for the words that signify binding and chastising are very cognate. I will chastise them for their two sins. When he binds them he will chastise them. And so I find Luther understands it.

Vincere אסר
Castigare יסר
Propter geminum peccatum ipsorum. Luther.

And then they think it refers to the two calves of Dan and Beth-el; or the two sins of bodily and spiritual adultery: or otherwise it has the same sense with that in Jer. ii. 13, "My people have committed two evils; they have forsaken me the fountain of living waters, and hewed them out cisterns, broken cisterns, that can hold no water."

Secondly, As it is in your books, "they shall bind themselves in their two furrows;" that is, I will bring their enemies upon them, and they shall yoke them like oxen that are yoked to plough, they shall bring them into servitude, and into bondage, they shall make them plough in their two furrows, that is, do double work. So Polanus, who saith, they shall put double tasks upon them, and make them work in a servile way. And I the rather think this is the meaning of it, because the Holy Ghost pursues this metaphor in the following verse, thus, "And Ephraim is as an heifer that is taught, and loveth to tread out the corn."

Polanus in loc.

Thirdly, Adopting the alteration in letters proposed, the sense would be, they shall yoke them as oxen are yoked, eye to eye. They yoke the oxen even, and set eye to eye; so the enemies shall come and yoke them, so that they shall be like beasts to do their work; and this shall be the condition of Ephraim that has this fair neck.

"They shall bind themselves in their two furrows." Some others, among whom is Calvin, understand by this, they shall covenant together. When the enemy comes upon them, then they shall join together in covenant, as oxen that are yoked together; Judah and Israel shall join together, and they shall be in their furrows, in their trenches, as England and Scotland in the late war. So when the people are gathered together, they shall bind themselves together, and lie together in their several trenches. So I find some interpret it, but this appears foreign to the chief and genuine scope of the passage.

I understand it thus; they shall be brought into miserable bondage, they shall be like oxen: and so saith one interpreter upon the place, When you see oxen yoked together, then be reminded of the yoke of the enemy; you live daintily and bravely now, but when God shall let out the enemy upon you, you shall serve as slaves, yea, as beasts.

Ver. 11. *And Ephraim is an heifer that is taught, and loveth to tread out the corn; but I passed over upon her fair neck: I will make Ephraim to ride; Judah shall plough, and Jacob shall break his clods.*

In the 2nd verse you heard much of the divisions of Ephraim, and of the ten tribes; but in the latter end of the 10th verse you heard how God would join them together. But how should they be joined? It should be in their bondage, they should be bound together in their furrows. Now, though it be in your books, "they shall bind themselves," which has likewise a sense which we spake to then; yet you may as well read the words, they shall bind them together, and so carry the sense, that they should be bound in their furrows, like oxen yoked in the plough; they would not come in together under God's yoke, but they shall come in together under the yoke of the adversaries: and that I think is the principal scope of the words, "they shall bind them in their two furrows." They that were so divided in their prosperity, when they come into bondage, shall, by their enemies, be bound together. It was said of Ridley and Hooper, they could not agree together till they were in prison, but then they harmonized well. And so when we were heretofore in our bondage we could agree better together than now. Oh it were just with God to bring us again under the bondage of our enemies, and bind us in our furrows together!

But Ephraim thought herself far from this. No, Ephraim is not for ploughing work, Ephraim loves to tread out the corn, but not to plough. They were wont in those times, instead of thrashing out the seed from the chaff, to have beasts to tread it out, or to draw instruments whereby the seed was separated from the husk. Now there are some things to be remembered here.

First, There was no yoke upon them while they were treading out the corn.

Secondly, They were then not to be muzzled, but to feed as they pleased, and this by the command of God, Deut. xxv. 4.

Now this was a very easy work for them, to be without yoke, to run up and down in the corn, and so fatten themselves; they had enough to feed on, certain food, and present food; whereas those heifers that went to plough were fain to be abroad in the storms, and cold, and wind, and work all day long, and perhaps had no food till night; this was a hard work, and Ephraim did not love such. This seems to have reference to some of the ten tribes, who would stay in their country, and worship at Dan and Beth-el, and would not go up to Jerusalem. Oh, that was hard; and it was better for them to stay in the land, where they might enjoy their possessions, their shops, their tradings, their friends; that was easy, but to go to Jerusalem might cost them their estates, it would excite opposition against them, and they must leave all and go for the worship of God, to worship God according to his own way, they must for a time leave all: this was a ploughing work in respect of the other. Now Ephraim, those that live among the ten tribes, loved no such hard work. From whence there are many excellent points to be observed.

Obs. 1. It is a sign of a carnal heart, to be set upon easy, to the avoidance of difficult, work in God's service. "Ephraim loveth to tread out the corn." It is a dangerous thing to desire more ease in God's work than God would allow.

Obs. 2. The carnal and hypocrites can be well content with those services which bring with them present comfort and encouragement. When they did tread out the corn, there was present supply. So it is with men, when they can have present maintenance. Ternovius, a learned man, upon this very scripture observes, Where men see not present gain coming in, they despise Christ; but where they may have to eat for the present, there they may be easily brought to believe any service or worship that is, for the present, countenanced by the state. From Numb. vii. 9, we see that God allowed no cart to the children of Kohath to carry the ark, and they sinned in putting it upon one, 2 Sam. vi. So, where men may enjoy certain revenues, whether they work or not, or whether they work negligently or not, it is a great temptation; much greater than in a man's enjoying encouragement on uncertainties, and on the assurance that he shall have it no longer than he labours, and labours to purpose; but when men have certain revenues coming in, though they labour by themselves or by others, though negligently or industriously, it is a great temptation.

Ubi non vident quæstum rident Christum, ubi datur ut edant, adduci possunt ut credant. Ternov. in loc.

Obs. 3. To labour for present accommodation only to themselves, is a sign of carnal hearts. A generous spirit will labour for posterity. If none should plough, how would there be corn to tread out? We must be willing to plough though we have not present food, though we should have nothing till night, yea, though we should have nothing till the night of death; yea, throughout all our lives we should be willing to plough in hope. Ephraim loved not that work. That is a generous spirit, that is willing to endure difficulty here, though he finds no present returns, yea, though none reap the benefit but posterity.

This may be also applied to soul work, in our seeking to God. Many are content to pray, and follow God and his ordinances, so long as they may have present comfort, but if that fails they have no heart to the duty. Now we should be willing to plough, that is, to endure difficulty, though we have no present returns.

This is that which causes so many to perish in the world, they must have present content; whereas the saints of God are willing to trust God though they have nothing in this world, to trust him to have their wages in the world to come.

"But I passed over upon her fair neck." By her easy work in treading out the corn, and not having the yoke upon her neck to plough, she became very delicate, her skin was white and tender. "Her fair neck," or, the goodness of her neck, טוב צוארה Her neck, through her prosperity, had become delicate, nothing must trouble her; let others, if they will, engage in works attended with trouble and difficulty, for her part, she was tender and delicate, and must endure no burdens, no difficulty at all.

Obs. 4. The evil of outward adornings. "Her fair neck."

Many are proud of their fair necks and skins, so proud that they grow in consequence extremely wanton; they must lay open their fair necks, that others may see them, see how white they are, what fair skins they have; and put black patches likewise, to set off their beauty and the whiteness of their skins; and if that suffice not, they will even lay over them a paint, to make them fair if they be not otherwise so: nothing but ease, and delicacy, and pleasure is for them, as if they came into the world for no other end but to live bravely and be looked upon; as if mankind and all creatures must work and suffer to provide for these nice and delicate wantons, who yet are of no use at all in the world. Certainly God never gave any great estates for no other use, but only to be brave withal, and to keep their skin white. Whatsoever estates we have, yet except we endeavour to be useful in the world in proportion to those estates, we can have little true comfort in what we enjoy: the comfort of the lives of rational creatures certainly lies not in a fair white skin; their comfort is in being useful in the places where God has set them, their good consists in that. Man is born to labour, and there must be labour one way or other, every one is bound to labour. These fair white skins, and fair necks, oh what foul souls many of them have! their beauty is but skin deep. Filthy and abominable are many of them in the eyes of God, and in the eyes of those who know the corruptions of their hearts. How would these fair necks be able to bear iron chains for Christ? to be nailed to the stake, to have such a neckerchief put upon them as Alice Driver had? The story is in the Book of Martyrs. When they put the chain about her neck to nail her to the stake, she gloried in it, and blessed God for it. Yes, but this Alice Driver was wont to plough, (for so it is said a little before,) her father brought her up to plough, and not so delicately; she could endure then an iron chain upon her neck for Christ. Hard breeding is fittest for Christian suffering.

"But I passed over upon her fair neck." Some interpret the words as expressing God's indulgence, as if he was content to let Ephraim prosper and thrive in their way, and not to bring any hard bondage upon them; but the interpretation which I find others give is more probable: I came upon her fair neck, and made the yoke to pass over. So Jerome upon the place saith, When this phrase, "I passed over," is applied to God, not only here, but always in Scripture, it is in a way of threatening; and it may very well be here a threatening expression following the similitude taken from husbandry.

In the same allegorical manner Ephraim is compared to "an heifer that is taught," as if he should say, he would not willingly work. Whence,

Obs. 5. God looks upon dainty, tender, delicate people, who mind nothing but their own ease and convenience, with indignation. What! Ephraim must be so tender and delicate, that nothing must come upon "her fair neck?" I will make the yoke to come upon it, saith God. When people through their delicacy must be altogether tended, and have all things serviceable to them, and they of no use at all, God cannot bear it. And as for the eminency of any of you, either in estates or honours in the world, above others, it ought not to be the cause of envy, for it is God that puts the difference between one and the other. We do not envy that some should go finer than others; but this neither God nor man can endure, that any should have so much *in* the world, and yet be of so little use *to* the world, should be through their delicacy as if they were born for nothing else but, like babies, to play withal. I will make the yoke to pass over them, saith God. Though you do not put your hands to servile labour, there are other manner of works; but then, through your delicacy, if you meet with any difficulty, you will do nothing for God: the Lord looks upon such dispositions with indignation, as sinful, and has his time to bring them to hardness. How many delicate and fair necks, that could not endure any difficulty, has God brought the yoke upon in these days! persons that were so nice and tender, and complaining of every little difficulty in any work that God would have them to do. God has made the yoke to pass over their heads, and to lie heavy upon their necks. God threatens this to the daughters of Babylon, to the antichristian party especially, in Isa. xlvii. 1, 2, "Come down, and sit in the dust, O virgin daughter of Babylon, sit on the ground: there is no throne, O daughter of the Chaldeans: for thou shalt no more be called tender and delicate. Take the millstones, and grind meal: uncover thy locks, make bare the leg, uncover the thigh, pass over the rivers." And then in the 3rd verse, "Thy nakedness shall be uncovered, yea, thy shame shall be seen: I will take vengeance, and I will not meet thee as a man." That which you cannot endure so much as to hear of now, (your very ears are so delicate, as well as your necks,) *that* I will bring upon you. O my brethren, how much better is it to be willing to endure hardships for God, than to be brought to hardships by our adversaries; and rather to put our necks under the yoke of Jesus Christ, than to have God put our necks under the yoke of his wrath and displeasure! But God has his time to bring upon them hard things; and therefore, though God spares your bodies, that you need not put them to the servile tasks that others do, yet be so much the more willing to do service for God otherwise. Venture yourselves among your kindred; that is the work to which God calls ladies. You meet with carnal friends that are honourable and of great rank in the world, now, to espouse in the midst of them the cause of God, is as hard a work as to labour with one's hands, and may do a great deal more service. When you come into carnal company, be willing to put forth yourselves to endure hardships in that way which God calls thee to, and God will accept of it; but if, through thy delicacy and niceness of mind, thy spirit comes to be as delicate as thy skin is, and thou must not displease any, nor suffer any thing for God, it is just with God to bring thee to suffer in spite of thy heart.

"I will make Ephraim to ride." We regard this as a further threatening; in Scripture it is applied both to mercy and judgment: thus to mercy, in Isa. lviii. 14, "Then shalt thou delight thyself in the Lord; and I will cause thee to ride upon the high places of the earth." And to judgment, in Job xxx. 21, 22, "With thy strong hand thou opposest thyself against me. Thou liftest me up to the wind; thou causest me to ride upon it, and dissolvest my substance." Other scriptures might be shown where this expression is in a way of judgment. And so it is thought by interpreters here to refer to the speedy captivity of the ten tribes. As if God should say, By his ease, and by his much feeding in treading out the corn, he is grown so fat and lusty that there is no ruling of him; yea, but, saith God, I will ride him; though he kicks and spurns and is so unruly with his fat feeding, yet I will put such a curb into his mouth, that I will order him and rule him as I please. Ephraim was like a pampered horse that is kept at full feeding, none could ride him; yea, but, "I will make Ephraim to ride," saith God.

Obs. 6. God has ways to curb those who through their prosperity are delicate and unruly; though they may champ upon the bit, and foam at the mouth, and stamp again, yet God will rule them: "I will make Ephraim to ride."

"Judah shall plough;" that is, Judah shall for a long time take pains and go through many difficulties in the ways of my worship, and shall suffer much while Ephraim lives delicately. Judah did indeed suffer much more difficulty and hardship than the ten tribes. But I think this scripture refers especially to those two passages that we find, the first in 2 Kings xviii. 4—8, and the other in 2 Chron. xxviii. 6. 2 Kings xviii. records the great reformation that Hezekiah made in the worship of God in Judah and Jerusalem. And then Judah's suffering you have in 2 Chron. xxviii. 6, where it is said, that "Pekah the son of Remaliah slew in Judah an hundred and twenty thousand in one day, which were all valiant men." It is a very strange scripture. Israel, the ten tribes, were worse than Judah: Israel forsook the true worship of God; Judah kept themselves to the true worship; and yet God let Israel so prosper that they so prevailed against Judah and the tribe of Benjamin, as to slay in one day a hundred and twenty thousand valiant men. Oh what lamentation and wailing must have been in the country then, that of two tribes a hundred and twenty thousand valiant men should be slain in one day! We think it is a dreadful battle when three thousand are slain in the field, but here is a battle in which a hundred and twenty thousand are slain in one day, and that out of two tribes. And in 2 Kings xiv. 13, "And Jehoash king of Israel took Amaziah king of Judah, the son of Jehoash the son of Ahaziah, at Beth-shemesh, and came to Jerusalem, and brake down the wall of Jerusalem," &c. Thus Judah and Benjamin, those two tribes that kept to the worship of God, were sorely afflicted by Ephraim, the ten tribes which had forsaken the worship of God. Strange are the counsels of God concerning men.

"Judah shall plough;" that is, they shall endure a great deal of trouble in the reforming what is amiss among them. Whence,

Obs. 7. It is an honour for men to labour and go through difficulties for God while others are labouring for their ease. Be not troubled that you see other people can take liberty to themselves to provide incomes to live bravely. Does God give you a heart in the mean time to be willing to go through hard work for him? Envy them not, thou art in the better condition, thou art ploughing for God; while they are providing for their own ease, thou art doing God service; oh! thou art far the happier.

"Judah shall plough." Take the ploughing for the hard things they *suffered*, as well as the hard things they *did* for God, and thence,

Obs. 8. Let none boast that they live more at ease than others. Others suffer more hardship than thou; do not think that God loves thee more than others. God loved Judah at this time more than Ephraim, and yet Ephraim lived bravely, and prevailed over Judah. Judah was God's true church, and Israel had apostatized from God, and yet one had more outward prosperity than the other. Thus many times those upon whom God's heart is more set, suffer hard afflictions; and those on whom God's heart is not so much fixed, enjoy their prosperity.

O, I beseech you, consider this well; for at this day, how many of our brethren are there in the western parts, on whose backs the ploughers have ploughed deep furrows, while we have been here as it were treading out the corn! Let not us think that God loves us more than them; they may be more dear to God than we: Judah was far more dear to God than Israel, and yet Israel must live jocundly and bravely.

O consider this, you that are of greater rank. All your life is treading out the corn: you see your poor neighbours endure much hardship, O think not that you are higher in God's thoughts than they; they may be more dear to God than you, and yet they may be put to difficulties, and you may live bravely all your lives.

But it may seem to weaken the foregoing observation, that the ploughing is spoken of as future, "Judah shall plough." The Hebrews, however, ordinarily make use of the future and preter tense promiscuously. But if you take it in the future sense, that they shall plough hereafter, it may signify the captivity of Judah, that they shall be carried into captivity, and so be brought under by the Babylonians.

"And Jacob shall break his clods." By "Jacob" we must understand the ten tribes. As if God should say here, that Judah shall be put to some difficulties, yet Jacob, the ten tribes, must be put to more. Judah shall be carried into captivity; yea, but Jacob shall break the clods. Though Judah shall plough, yet the breaking of the clods is worse than the ploughing, for it is more servile; for the ploughman is the chief, he goes on in ploughing, but it is his servant or boy whom he sets to break the clods after him. So, though Judah shall be brought to difficulties, yet Jacob shall be put to more difficulties; for the captivity of Judah was great, yet it was not so great as Jacob's.

"Judah shall plough, and Jacob shall break his clods;" that is, Judah's clods. The expression we have here, with the reference it has to Judah, intimates, according to some, That there shall be a time, though now you that are the ten tribes are so delicate and proud above Judah, and Judah so much lower than you, that you despise him; yet the time shall come that you shall be glad to join with Judah, and be as a servant to Judah, to break his clods, when God shall restore his people again: Judah shall return from his captivity, and shall be taking pains in the service of God; and it shall be well for you if you can but come and be as his servant.

Obs. 9. Though God may have mercy upon those afterwards who forsake his true worship, and join them with his people, yet, if this mercy place them in the meanest condition among God's people, they should be willing to submit to it. Those that have dishonoured God and shamed themselves in times of trial, by forsaking his truths, it is a mercy if ever God unite them to his church again; but if he does bring them to join it, they should think it a great mercy, and be willing to be in the meanest condition. What! must those think to be masters and lords, who have forsaken God and his truth, and have been very false for their own ends in times of trial, shall they think in times of reformation to bear all before them? Oh! it is a mercy if they be but admitted to break the clods, to join with those servants of God that have been faithful, and willing to serve him through difficulties.

Ver. 12. *Sow to yourselves in righteousness, reap in mercy; break up your fallow ground: for it is time to seek the Lord, till he come and rain righteousness upon you.*

The Holy Ghost still goes on in this allegory of husbandry, continuing in the exhortation the metaphor that he had used in the threatening. In the midst of his threats he falls to exhorting.

Obs. 1. Though the sins of a people be great, and judgments near, yet exhortations are to be used. Who knows what an exhortation may effect, even with the worst people in the world? There were many things spoken concerning Israel, which one would have thought should have discouraged the prophet to meddle with exhortation; but God would have him yet exhort. One cannot tell what an exhortation may do, in the most desperate hardness of men's hearts, and pride and stoutness of men's spirits; therefore the prophet exhorts them, as if he should say, Well, if you would not plough, if you would not come under the yoke and be put into the furrows, as you were threatened before, why then, sow to yourselves. O, be willing to break up the fallow ground of your hearts, and sow to yourselves in righteousness, and so you shall reap in mercy.

"Sow to yourselves in righteousness, reap in mercy." I find some of the ancients interpret this somewhat wildly.

"Sow in righteousness;" that is, (saith Jerome upon the place,) Sow in the law, in obedience to the law, and reap in the grace of the gospel; that is, you shall sow in the works of the law, and reap in the gospel: but this seems far-fetched.

As Jerome is somewhat too legal, so Luther (because his heart was much in the gospel, and he was wont to view all scriptures, as far as possible, as expressing the grace of the gospel) inclines somewhat too much to the other extreme.

"Sow in righteousness." What are the seeds of righteousness? That is, saith Luther, the doctrine of the gospel tendering the righteousness of Jesus Christ: the attending to, and embracing, this doctrine of the gospel, that there is righteousness in Jesus Christ alone, this is sowing in righteousness; for what other righteousness is there but this? When reason would ascend to the highest degree of righteousness, what does it? Only this, to conclude righteousness to be, to depart from evil and do things that are good. But what righteousness is this? But the Scripture righteousness teaches a man to know that he has no good at all in himself, that all his evil is pardoned in Jesus Christ; this is the righteousness of the gospel, and this is the seed of all good works. I name this, though I can hardly conceive it to be the scope of the prophet here; yet a very good meditation arises from it, which I see noticed by that useful man in the church of God, Luther, who goes on to say, What madness and blindness in the adversary is there, that will urge people to sow, and yet reject and cast off this seed that they should sow, that is, the doctrine of the imputation of the righteousness of Christ by faith! Why, saith he, in all pulpits they cry out to men for good works, that they should sow in righteousness; but where have they their seed? Certainly the truth which he inculcates here is excellent. How vain is it for men to be taught to sow good works till they have got the seed! and the seed of all good works is, the righteousness that we have by Jesus Christ: and thereupon he rebukes those who blame the doctrine of the gospel as the means of licentiousness. A great many, when we preach, saith he, of the righteousness of Jesus Christ, think that we preach licentiousness, and that men may live as they list, but it is quite the contrary; when we preach the righteousness of Jesus Christ, we preach the seed of all good works; and from those who have this seed, good works will issue. But, saith he, further, they would have righteousness; but what righteousness? They slight the righteousness of God's making, the righteousness of his Son, but they must have righteousness of their own to tender up to God; and then, when they come to good works, they will slight God's good works, and they will be giving to God of their good works. The world doth neglect those works enjoined by him as light things, that is, the works of mercy, kindness to the saints, &c. No, they will have none of these, they will have other brave works, to build churches, and temples, and monasteries, and to lavish out gold about them, they are their chiefest good works: they will not deign to do the work as it were of a servant, but aim rather to be a benefactor to God; for, in relieving thy poor brother when none but thyself and God know it, thou dost the work of a servant, but to build brave temples and monasteries, and lavish out gold upon them, this is for you to be a benefactor to God. Thus much for Luther's speech.

"Sow to yourselves in righteousness." We know of the prophet, though he would lead the people to Christ, yet his preaching was chiefly legal. "Sow righteousness;" that is, Go on in the works of righteousness, those works that are right, and just, and equal, such as you may give a good account of before God and man: as if he should say, Do not you think to put me off merely with outward services, with offering sacrifices, and the pomp of ceremonial, perhaps, superstitious, worship, I will never accept of these things; but let me have righteousness, let there be the works of righteousness; according to the rules of righteousness, so work. And the Jews, if they did but perform generally the external works of righteousness, might have external mercies. If indeed they did some works of righteousness, and not others, then they could not expect mercy from God; but though there were no saving grace in them, yet if they did but perform the external works of righteousness, and there was a proportion between one and another, there seems to have been an external covenant that they were under for outward mercies for their outward righteousness: not but that I think for heaven they must have had true grace and godliness, as the saints must have now; but external mercies were more annexed to external duties than now amongst us.

You will say, We have external promises too.

Yea, but they are attached to godliness *in* Christ Jesus.

Now from the words we may

Obs. 2. The actions of men are seeds, such seeds as will certainly come up. Other seeds may die in the ground, and rot, and never come up; but there is never an action which thou performest, but will come up one way or other, it will come up to something.

Obs. 3. The seed sown will come up after its kind. The seeds of tares will not come up to wheat, but will continue tares, and so the wheat, wheat: all our actions will come up after their kind. Men neglect their actions, and think that when they have done, it is over, they forget what they did yesterday or the day before; but though you may forget it, yet it will come up in the same kind, though you think not of it. I remember Pliny reports of some parts in Africa, that when they sow their seed, they go away, and never look after it for many months together: so it is with many men, they sow, but they never mind what they have done, and quite forget what their seed has been, till they must come to reap. But certainly thine actions lie there, and will grow up to something.

Obs. 4. As the seed lies in the ground rotting awhile, but afterwards comes up, so it is with our actions; they seem as if they were quite forgotten, but they will come up; yea, and good actions seem as if they were wholly lost many times: well, though the seed doth rot, rot in the ground for a time, yet it will come up afterwards.

Obs. 5. The seed, when sown, comes up through the blessing of God upon it. No endeavour of the husbandman can make the seed come up, but he must leave it to the blessing of God; so the seeds of our actions must be left to God. God's justice will make the seeds of the wicked come up, and his goodness and mercy will make the seeds of the saints come up; leave thine actions to the blessing of God.

Obs. 6. The better the seed is, for the most part the longer it lies under ground. When you sow wheat and rye, you sow them in the autumn of the year; but when you sow barley and oats, you sow them in the spring, and they do not, as the wheat, endure frost and snow. Even so the best of our actions lie longest under ground.

Obs. 7. The ministers of God are sowers of the seed of the word; and the hearers should be sowers too. The minister sows the word in thine ears, and then thou shouldst take it from thence and sow it in thy heart, thy life and conversation.

Obs. 8. If our actions be seeds that we sow, then large opportunities of doing much service for God should be our riches; like a large field, that is sown with good grain; if thou hast a heart to improve those opportunities.

Oh that we would but consider of this, that when the Lord gives any a large opportunity for service, God lets them out so much land; Go, (saith God,) you must husband so much land, and sow it for mine advantage. Many of you that are poor, have not a foot of land in the world, and you think that landed men are happy men: does God give you opportunity of service to honour him? Oh! thou hast got a great deal of land, the meanest of you that have opportunities of service; God lets you out his land, you have abundance of land and ground given to you by God: and a man should account himself rich according to the opportunity of his service; as men in the country account themselves rich according to the land that they have to plough and sow. In Lev. xxvii. 16, it is said, "If a man shall sanctify unto the Lord some part of a field of his possession, then thy estimation shall be according to the seed thereof." The meaning is, that if a man will sanctify a piece of land to God, you shall prize it not according to its extent, but according to the seed it is fit to receive. So the opportunities that are fit to receive much seed, should be accounted rich opportunities. And we should esteem the price of our lives to be according to the seed thereof: Thou livest such a year, what is thy life worth? It is according to the seed thereof. And so for these four or five last years, oh what opportunities have we had for service for God! now they are to be prized according to the seed thereof, that is, as our service and work were in those years. Then certainly, if we must estimate our lives according to the opportunity of service for God, then these last five years we may reckon as fifty. It is a great blessing to have a good seed time; the Lord has blest us with this good seed time. Oh now, what a folly were it for a man out of base penuriousness to refrain from sowing his ground, because he is loth to venture his seed! or through love of his ease loth to go abroad; it is somewhat cold, and he will keep by the fire-side, and will not go abroad to sow his seed. Oh! thus it is with us, through our base unbelief we will venture nothing for God, we are loth to put ourselves upon any difficulty; this is our folly.

Obs. 9. It is not every seed that will serve. Be sowers, but sow "in righteousness;" let it be righteousness, let it be precious seed. Thus, in Psal. cxxvi. 6, they are spoken of as "bearing precious seed" with them. Oh! there are many who sow venomous seed, that will bring forth poisonous fruit; all their days they have been sowing nothing but seed of unrighteousness. Yea, in this field that God has given to us, of opportunity of service for him, what have many done? what have they sown? They have sown salt in it; that is, they have sown their passions, they have sown contention and the seeds of discord, and that has been the cause why that our field, those opportunities which we have enjoyed for God, has been so unproductive: there has been so much salt, the salt spirits of men and women have been so manifested in their passions and frowardness, and their contentions one against another, that it has made us barren. Thus, Prov. vi. 14, "Frowardness is in his heart; he deviseth mischief continually, he soweth discord." And ver. 19, it is made one of the things which the soul of God abhors, that a man should "sow discord." And so in Prov. xvi. 28, "A froward man soweth strife." Oh! how many are there amongst us that go from one place to another, and tell you such a tale, and such a report, and sow nothing but strife and discord! such the Lord hates. What! in such a time as this is to sow discord! there could never have been a time more unfit to sow the tares thereof. Oh! let men take heed of sowing discord now; God calls for the seed of righteousness.

"And reap in mercy." I find many interpret this, mercy to men: that is, sow the seeds of righteousness, and let the fruits of mercy be abundant amongst you. But to carry it according to that which is more like to be the scope of the Holy Ghost, we are to understand by "mercy," the mercy of God. Now two things are to be observed in this phrase:

First, That it is in the imperative mood, "reap in mercy," not, ye shall reap in mercy.

Secondly, In the original it is, לפי־חסד *ad os misericordiæ*, in the mouth of mercy.

Now to explain these words accordingly.

First, That it is in the imperative mood, "reap in mercy;" not, ye shall reap in mercy. This signifies these two things:

1. The certainty of the mercy they shall have.
2. The readiness of the mercy, that it is ready at hand for them to possess; just as if one should say to you in your shops, Let me have this commodity, and

here take your money, that is, here is your money ready and certain.

Secondly, In the mouth of mercy. Now if the translators had rendered it thus, Sow in righteousness, and reap in the mouth of mercy, it would have been obscure; but those who understand the original, know that the mouth of a thing is often used for the proportion and measure of a thing. As thus in Lev. xxvii. 16, "Thy estimation shall be according to the seed thereof." Now the Hebrew is, Thy estimation shall be to the mouth of the seed, that is, according to the proportion of the seed so shall the estimation be. And so you have it in Exod. xvi. 16, "Gather of it every man according to his eating;" that is, to the mouth of every man, in a proportion according to what is fit for every man.

"Sow to yourselves in righteousness, reap in mercy." Thus, "Sow in righteousness;" it is a poor seed that we shall sow: now God saith not, you shall reap "in righteousness," but "in mercy," from the mouth of mercy. You take out of the mouth of the sack, and sow your poor proportion, but when you come to reap, you shall reap, if you be faithful, according to the proportion of mercy; what is fit for a merciful God to do, what is suitable to the infiniteness of my mercy, that shall you reap. It was so with the Jews, if their obedience was but external, yet they should have mercy beyond that outward obedience: but if it be applied to those who live in the times of the gospel, indeed that which comes from you, being so mixed as it is, is but poor, yet you may expect to reap, not according to what you do, but according to what may manifest the infinite mercy of an infinite God. Every one, let them be never so weak, and employed in never such poor and mean services, yet, if their hearts be upright, they shall not reap according to the meanness of the work, nor the poverty of the service, but look, what glory and happiness is suitable for an infinite God in way of infinite mercy to bestow, that they shall have in the mouth of mercy, suitable to mercy. Thus you have the meaning of the word.

Obs. 10. As a man sows, so shall he reap. Though he shall reap more than he sows, yet he shall reap in the same kind. If he sow wickedness he shall not reap mercy; but he that sows righteousness shall reap mercy. It is a mocking of God, for men to think that though they sow wickedness yet they shall reap mercy; therefore saith the apostle, in Gal. vi. 7, "Whatsoever a man soweth, that shall he also reap. God is not mocked." If thou thinkest to reap mercy when thou sowest wickedness, thou mockest God to his very face. If a man should sow tares and say, I shall have a good crop of wheat, would you not think that man mad? or he should think you a fool to believe him, were he to tell you so. So for you to think that either God or man should believe that you should have mercy when you sow not righteousness, it is, I say, to mock God; and know, "God is not mocked; for what a man soweth, that shall he also reap;" and thy fruit shall be another manner of fruit, thou shalt rent that which shall be bound in bundles, and thou bound together with it, and cast into unquenchable fire. But of those that sow righteousness, not a seed shall be lost, they shall be recompensed for all their pains, and labour, and sufferings. For so saith the Lord, Psal. cxxvi. 5, "They that sow in tears shall reap in joy." There shall be an assuring fruit to those that sow in righteousness, for true gospel-righteousness is the most precious thing in the world, more worth in one of its righteous acts than heaven and earth. God will not lose that seed, it is precious seed; there is more of God in one righteous act of a godly man, than there is in all the works of creation and providence, (angels and saints excepted,) yea, than in all the whole frame of creation.

The reason is this, Because in all the creation God's glory is manifested but passively, God works there and holds forth his glory passively; but in the righteous acts of the saints, there is an active glorifying of God; there is an act of the very image of God, and the life of God: the Divine nature is there, and therefore there is more of God in the working of righteousness than in any thing else besides.

Oh, let the saints rightly estimate the actions of righteousness; though there be much evil mingled, yet there is a great deal of the glory of God in every action. If we were but grounded in this principle it would make us abound in the work of the Lord. So in the morning and in the evening let not thy hand rest, trust God with thy seed, do not be deterred with this difficulty and the other: "He that observeth the wind shall not sow; and he that regardeth the clouds shall not reap," Eccl. xi. 4. Is it a duty that God requires of thee; do not think, Oh, but it is windy, and ill weather: no, but sow thy seed, "sow it in righteousness," and commit it to God, and thou shalt reap. Blessed are those who have sown much for God in their life-time! Oh the glorious harvest that these shall have! the very angels shall help them to take in their harvest at the great day; and they need not take thought for barns, the very heavens shall be their barns. And oh the joy that there shall be in that harvest! the angels will help to sing the harvest song that they shall sing who have been sowers in righteousness: but oh the confusion of face which will be upon those who were not willing to endure difficulty in ploughing and sowing! "The sluggard will not plough by reason of the cold; therefore shall he beg in harvest, and have nothing," Prov. xx. 4. In harvest he will be crying for mercy, Lord, mercy now. But what fruits of righteousness? No fruits of righteousness, no mercy. "Reap in mercy!" an expression as remarkable as we have in the whole book of God; not reap in righteousness, but "reap in mercy."

Obs. 11. After all we do, yet we have need of mercy. Let us be the most plentiful in sowing the seeds of righteousness, yet we are unprofitable servants after we have done all, and must "reap in mercy."

But surely an act of righteousness has much in it.

Yea, but all the good of it is God's, so much as there is in it of evil is ours; and after we have done all, we had need come to God as beggars to cry for mercy. Those who have lived the most holy lives, yet woe to them if they have not mercy, if they have not righteousness beyond their own, if mercy come not in to plead for them! Woe to Abraham, Isaac, and Jacob, if mercy plead not for them! if at the great day they have nothing to tender up to God but their own righteousness, they are certainly lost and undone for ever. All that we can do is infinitely unworthy of the majesty of God. In 1 Chron. xxix. 14, when the people offered so much to God for the building of his tabernacle, mark how David was affected with it; "Who am I, and what is my people, that we should be able to offer so willingly after this sort? for all things come of thee, and of thine own have we given thee." And in 1 Chron. xxii. 14, when David had provided "an hundred thousand talents of gold, and a thousand thousand talents of silver," for the building of the temple of God, besides "brass and iron without weight," yet after all he exclaims, Out of my poverty have I offered this. So Arias Montanus renders בעניי In your books it is, "in my trouble I have prepared" this, but the word signifies poverty as well as trouble and affliction. And so saith David, after all this, Yet in my poverty have I done this; whereas this was a mighty thing that was offered. I remember Sir Walter Raleigh, in his History of the World, part 2. chap. 17. sect. 9, reckons up the sum of what David there prepared for the temple of the Lord, and makes it more than any king in the world is worth; he makes it to come to three thousand three hundred and thirty-three cart loads of silver, allowing two thousand weight of silver, or six thousand pounds sterling, to every cart load, besides threescore and seventeen millions of French crowns: and yet when he had done all, Out of my poverty have I done this. As if he should say, Lord, what is this in respect of thee who art the great God? If thou wilt but accept of this, I shall be infinitely bound to thee.

O my brethren, let us ever learn after all our duties not to be proud, but keep your hearts low and humble before God. Has God enabled us to sow in righteousness? our hearts are puffed up presently: oh no, thou must keep thy heart still under. Alas! such is the pride of our spirits, if we be but enlarged a little in prayer we are ready to be puffed up presently. Oh! what is this to the service which a creature owes to the blessed and eternal God! Hadst thou spent all thy time since thou hadst any understanding, night and day, in the work and service of God, hadst thou been the greatest instrument of God's service that ever was in the world, yet thou hast cause to lie down at God's mercy-seat and cry, Mercy, Lord, mercy for a poor wretched, vile creature, after thou hast done all; we are so unable to do any thing ourselves. Luther saith, The very act of thanksgiving is from God. And therefore be humbled, and cry, Grace, grace to all that has been: and let all public instruments not take too much upon them, but lie low before the Lord. Oh! did we but know God we would indeed be low after our duties.

Ipsa gratiarum actio. Luth.

To lay down one's life for God you will say was a great service. Cyprian's prayer at his martyrdom contained these two remarkable expressions; Lord, I am prepared to pour forth the very sacrifice of my blood for thy name's sake; yea, Lord, I am prepared here to suffer any torment whatsoever. These two expressions he used. You will say, Now surely this man might stand upon his terms with God. But he goes on: But when thou dost lift up thyself to shake the earth, Lord, under what cleft of the rock shall I hide myself, to what mountain or hill shall I call to fall upon me and cover me? As if he should say, Lord, though I be here ready to give up my body to be massacred for thee, to give up my blood to be an offering, and to suffer any torment, yet when I consider what a God I have to do withal, if thou shouldst deal with me as I am in myself, oh I must cry to the rocks to cover me, and the hills to fall upon me. This should teach us to keep our hearts low and humble after we have done the greatest work whatsoever. One of the German divines when at the point of death was full of fears and doubts, and some said to him, You have been so employed, and have been so faithful, why should you fear? He replied, The judgments of man and the judgments of God are different; I am to go before the great and all-seeing God. Though it is true, God would not have us daunted with any terrible apprehensions of him, yet he would have us be possessed with reverence, so as to be humbled when we think what a God it is we have to do withal: you must "reap in mercy." Oh! this shall be the song of the saints to all eternity, Mercy, mercy: "Not unto us, Lord, not unto us, but unto thy name give glory," Psal. cxv. 1.

Obs. 12. God will give abundantly above our works. Oh, it is a point that has very much encouragement to poor troubled sinners that are low. Raise up thy faith: it is not what thy work is; though it be low and mean, and though there be many failings in thy work, yet is there uprightness in it; and if thou hast sown the seeds of righteousness, thou shalt reap according to what shall honour the mercy of an infinite God at last. When Alexander was giving a gift to a poor man, he dared not receive it, it was too great. Yea, but, said Alexander, though that be too great for thee to receive, yet it is not too great for me to give. So I may say to poor souls, when they hear of these glorious promises. Their hearts are ready to think, This is too good news to be true, too great a mercy for me to receive. So it is as thou art in thyself, but if God will give according to the proportion of his mercy, it is not too great for him to give.

Now thus it is that God will deal with those that are in covenant with him, that have all their fruit from the seed of righteousness, Christ in the heart. I say, the Lord will deal with them according to the proportion of infinite grace.

Take this one meditation, That where there is any uprightness, when thou shalt come to reap from God, thou shalt reap so much as must manifest to all angels and saints to all eternity, what the infinite mercy of an infinite God can do; and that is enough, one would think: the poorest Christian, who does but the least for God, when he comes to reap shall have a harvest that must manifest the infinite riches of the infinite mercy of God, and what he is able to do for the exaltation of a creature to glory. Comfort thyself in this, in thy poor, low condition, and in the performing of thy poor services.

"Break up your fallow ground: for it is time to seek the Lord, till he come and rain righteousness upon you."

"Break up your fallow ground," &c.: the prophet exhorted them in the words before, to sow in righteousness, that they might reap mercy.

But you must not sow without ploughing, that were a preposterous way; therefore, though the words come after, yet the thing is to be done before. Look that you plough up the fallow ground: you have been sinful and ungodly in your way, it will not be enough for you now to set upon some good actions, We will do better, we will do such and such good things that God requires of us: no, that is not the first work you must fall upon, but it must be to plough, to "break up your fallow ground."

Obs. 13. The hearts of men naturally are as fallow grounds, nothing but thorns and briers grow upon them, they are unfit for the seed of the word.

When he bids them plough up their fallow grounds, these three things are implied:

First, The work of humiliation. The truths of God, both of the law and of the gospel, must get into their hearts, and rend them up, even as the plough rends up the ground.

Secondly, That weeds, thorns, and briers must be turned up by the roots, the heart must be cleared of them. It is not enough to pluck out a weed or a thorn here and there, but we must plough up the ground, turn all upside down, and get rid of all the beggarly stuff and thorns that were in our hearts heretofore.

Thirdly, Get a softness in your hearts: as when the ground is ploughed, that which was before hard on the outside, and baked by the heat of the sun, being now turned up presents a soft mould, prepared to receive seed.

There are many evils in us that we would reform, but we have not been humbled for them, for our ceremonies, and subjection to false government of the church. Who has been humbled for these things, as sin? We reform them as things inconvenient, but not being humbled for them as sin, the very roots of these things are in the hearts of many, so as, if times should change, a distinction would serve their turn to come and submit to them again; so that we sow before we plough. In Jer. iv. 3, you have this exhortation carried a little further; "Break up your fallow ground, and sow not among thorns." They must not think to mingle that which is good with that which is evil: it may be a few good seeds are brought into a business; yea, but there is a great deal of evil. My brethren, take heed of being so deceived; many, though they do not intend to deceive you, yet they may deceive you by mixing some good things with a great many evil; and therefore examine things. But I note this place in Jeremiah the rather from the consideration of the time of its delivery, which was about the time of Josiah. Now that was a time of great reformation; but saith Jeremiah, What though you do many things? you sow among thorns, you do not plough up the ground, you are not humbled, your sins are not taken up by the roots; and therefore, though a great deal of ill stuff seems to be cast out, and many good things are set up in the worship of God, which were not formerly, yet you must plough, plough up your fallow grounds. The Holy Ghost joining them together, "Sow in righteousness," and "break up your fallow ground," I would have you observe, That there are some that do sow and not plough, and there are others that do plough and not sow, but we must join both together.

There are that do plough and not sow; that is, they (it may be) are troubled for their sins, much humbled perhaps on account of them, but they do not reform, after their humiliation there does not follow reformation. Now as reformation, where humiliation has not gone before, usually comes to little purpose, so humiliation, where reformation follows not after, comes likewise to little purpose.

In Isa. xxviii. 24, a similar image is applied to God; "Doth the ploughman plough all day to sow?" to note that God observes his times, and that we must not be offended because that he does not things as we would have him always, that is, he lets wicked men prosper sometimes, and the godly suffer afflictions: as if the Holy Ghost should say here, Let God alone with his work, God observes his times and seasons: as the ploughman does, he does not always plough; so God has his times and seasons, and knows when to relieve, and when to afflict, his church, and when the wicked shall prosper, and when they shall be brought into adversity: God instructs the ploughman to know his season, and he knows his own, therefore be not offended. And so should we know our seasons, and observe our times for humiliation and reformation. But this for the reformation of a state.

But the ploughing of the heart is the thing that is here especially intended, and I desire to apply it particularly to every individual. Those who have such sore necks that they cannot bear the yoke, yet must all hold the plough here spoken of. Now for this ploughing of your hearts, it is to get in truths into your spirits, that may rend up your hearts. I will name some few truths that are as it were the ploughshare; you should not only know them, but labour to get them into your hearts.

1. Such is the vileness of every sin, that it separates the soul from God, and puts it under an eternal curse. This one truth you must get deep into your hearts, it will help to unloosen the roots of the thorns and briers that are there, the settled apprehension of this truth.

2. There is such a breach between God and the soul by sin, that all the power in all the creatures in heaven and earth is not able to make up this breach: here is a sharp ploughshare to get into the heart.

3. By nature I am fully engaged in this controversy with God, my heart is full of it, all the faculties of my soul are filled with that heinous sin.

4. Every action throughout my whole life, in my unregenerate estate, was nothing else but sin, nothing else but sin, and that too of a vile nature.

5. If any sin be pardoned to me it is by virtue of a price paid that is more worth than ten thousand worlds. Now here is the gospel as well as the law, for the ploughing is but the spiritual using of the law; for you must take notice that the law, as law, accepts of no humiliation for sin, but viewed in the light of the gospel it does tend to humiliation: the law in the gospel humbles the soul so as to do it good. Now therefore get the truths that the law, having reference to the gospel, requires, and see what they will do in thy soul: you must work them in. And let conscience be put on to draw this plough: these are as the ploughshare, and the working of conscience is the drawing of this plough; when the plough stops, (as when it meets with a thorn and brier,) a strong conscience will draw it on, and will rend up by the roots the thorns and briers. Though these truths put you to pain, yet you must be content to draw them on in the soul; and if these and the like truths be got into thy soul, and thou be at plough, and thy conscience be drawing, I shall say unto thee, God speed the plough; yea, God speed these truths which conscience is drawing on in the soul, for they may tend to a great deal of good, to prepare thee for the seed that may bring forth righteousness and mercy to thy soul for ever. I confess it is a hard work to plough thus; indeed only to hear sermons, and talk and confer of good things, these things are pretty easy; but to go to plough, to plough with such truths as these are, to get up the thorns and briers by the roots, this is a very hard task: but we must be willing to do it, and to continue ploughing; as the fallow ground must not only be ploughed once, but it may stand in need of ploughing the second and third time before it be fit for the seed to be cast in; and so with our hearts. It may be some of you have been ploughing, and have got in some truths; yea, but many weeds and thorns have grown up since, and you must to ploughing again: it may be many years ago since you have been thus ploughing, and your hearts have lain fallow ever since; do not think it enough that once you have been humbled, but be often ploughing up this fallow ground; it is far better to have the plough get into your hearts, though it be sharp, than to have the sword of God's justice upon you. We have in these times a wanton generation, that cannot endure to go to plough, they would be doing nothing but taking in the sweet, treading out the corn. But this ploughing they cry out of merely through wantonness, and sinful self-indulgence; they would have nothing but jollity and licentiousness in their hearts and ways; yet the Scripture, in Luke ix. 62, compares the ministers of the gospel to ploughmen; "No man, having put his hand to the plough, and looking back, is fit for the kingdom of God," not fit to be employed in the administration of the gospel. These men talk of humiliation for sin, but they reject that, than which nothing more humbles for sin, the price that was paid for sin in the blood of Jesus Christ: there is no such sharp ploughshare as that. If I were to preach one sermon in all my life for the humbling of men for sin, I would take a text that might show the great price that was paid for it, and therein open the breach which sin has made between God and man's soul; but they will not make use even of the gospel as a plough to plough the heart for the work of humiliation.

Well, God has prospered this work heretofore, and notwithstanding all the wantonness of men's spirits this way, yet, I say still, God speed the plough; God speed this way of ploughing the hearts of men, and getting in those truths calculated to humble the hearts of men for their sins. These were the truths which God blessed in former times, and none ever lived so much to the honour of the gospel. For this generation that is come up, they talk of the gospel, but they live not to the honour of it, the gospel has not honour by them, nor has Jesus Christ. But the former generation of men, though in some things they might fail, yet certainly God blessed them in their way, so far as it was according to truth.

No marvel though these men bring forth such little fruit of righteousness, it is because they sow among thorns; presently they are blown at the top, and full of confidence, but their seed is among thorns, and therefore it doth not prosper. And thus much for this expression about the ploughing up of fallow grounds, both in reference to general reformation and humiliation, and concerning men's souls in particular.

"For it is time to seek the Lord." Here we may

Obs. 14. It is a mercy that there is yet time for you to seek the Lord. It might have been past time with you for seeking the Lord, God might have forced his honour from you in another way, have fetched out his glory from you in your eternal ruin. Oh! it is a mercy that God will be sought of you; and therefore "break up your fallow ground," and "sow in righteousness;" "for it is time to seek the Lord." Oh! you that yet live loaded with years and guilt, remember this scripture; yet you have "time to seek the Lord," and it is a wondrous mercy; if you but understood the extent of it, you would fall down with your faces upon the ground, and bless the Lord that you have yet time to seek him. What do you think those damned creatures in hell would now give, if it might be said of them, that they have time to seek the Lord? if they might have but one hour more to seek the Lord with any hope of obtaining mercy from him? What you are now, they were not long since. Oh! do you fear and tremble, lest, if not seeking the Lord, you ere long be as now they are; so that it shall be said of you, Time is gone, time to seek the Lord is past; God will not now be sought of us. Oh "seek the Lord while he may be found, and call upon him while he is near." When divers ministers and others were attempting once to comfort a woman of Cambridge under great terror of conscience, she regarded them with a ghastly look, and gave them only this answer, Call time back again. If you can call time back again, then there may be hope for me: but time is gone.

Oh that we had hearts to prize our time, to seek the Lord therefore "while he may be found." When thou goest home, fall down upon thy face before the Lord, and bless him that yet "it is time to seek the Lord." It is time for the public, through God's mercy, yet to seek the Lord. It might have been past time; and who almost that desired to know any thing of God's mind for these last seven or eight years or more, but did think that England's time of seeking God was even "clean gone for ever?" But the Lord has been pleased to lengthen out our time to seek him; and this we should prize and make use of.

Obs. 15. It is high time now to seek the Lord. For,

First, God has shown much patience and long-suffering toward you, and there is a time in the which the Lord saith he will be weary with forbearing; therefore the Lord having suffered thus long with you, it is high time for you to seek him, lest he should say, that he was weary in forbearing, and would forbear no more. It is fit you should seek the Lord at all times, but now it is high time, when God hath been so long-suffering towards you; how do you know but that the time for the end of patience is at an end?

2. Mercy is even going, and judgments are threatened: as if the prophet should say, If ever you will seek him, seek him now; God is going, and judgments are at hand, and therefore it is high time for you to seek the Lord. As a prisoner pleads whilst the judge is on the bench, but if he sees the judge ready to rise, then, knowing that if he depart he is undone for ever, he lifts up his voice, and cries out, Mercy, mercy. So it is now high time for you to seek the Lord; high time, mercy is going, judgment is at hand; God, as the Judge, is going off the bench; now cry, cry out for your lives, or you are undone for ever.

This may well be applied to us, both in general, and in the particular. It is high time for us; God has shown himself about to depart from us, yet still he lingers; a company of his saints have been crying, and as the Lord has been going from us, they have lifted up their voice, and so he yet grants us time.

Obs. 16. This time is an acceptable time. God now calls upon you, and holds forth the sceptre of his grace towards you, therefore it is now an acceptable time to seek God; seek him now, and he will be found. 2 Cor. vi. 2, "Behold, now is the accepted time; behold, now is the day of salvation:" while you enjoy the means of grace, while God is offering mercy in the gospel, it is the accepted time, it is the time to seek the Lord. The misery of man is therefore great, because he knows not his time. In Eccl. viii. 6, 7, the wise man saith, "Because to every purpose there is time and judgment, therefore the misery of man is great upon him; for he knoweth not that which shall be." Oh! this is true of us, we know not our time, and therefore is our misery great upon us. "And when he was come near, he beheld the city, and wept over it, saying, If thou hadst known, even thou, at least in this thy day, the things that belong unto thy peace! but now they are hid from thine eyes," Luke xix. 41, 42. Missing of time is a dangerous thing; that may at one time be done with ease, which cannot with all possible labour be effected at another. Thou canst not tell what may depend on one day, on one minute; perhaps even eternity may depend upon this moment, upon this day. A man goes abroad from his family and gets into company, perhaps into an alehouse or tavern to drink, and there spends the day in wickedness; thou dost not know but on that time the day of thy eternity may depend, it may be cast upon that day: as Saul was cast upon that sacrificial act of his; "For now" (saith Samuel) "would the Lord have established thy kingdom upon Israel for ever. But now thy kingdom shall not continue," 1 Sam. xiii. 13, 14; so God may say to thee, Well, notwithstanding all thy former sins, I would have been content to have passed by them, if thou hadst sought me this day. The consideration of this would make us take heed how we spend even a single day. A mariner may do that at one time which he cannot possibly do at another. He has now a gale of wind, and may quickly get over sea; but if he stay till another time, though he would give his heart's blood to get on, he cannot. And so sometimes thou hast such gales of the Spirit of God, as may do good to thy soul for ever; take heed thou lose them not, if thou losest them thou mayst be undone for ever. Oh! it is fit to wait upon God for our time; and if God give us time, let us take heed we do not trifle and say, We shall have time hereafter. Therefore in Phil. ii. 12, the apostle saith, "Work out your own salvation with fear and trembling:" and there follows, ver. 13, "For it is God which worketh in you both to will and to do of his good pleasure." What connexion is there? If God work the will and the deed, why need I work at all? Nay, the connexion is thus, Do you work out your salvation with fear and trembling, take all opportunities you can, let the fear of God be upon you so as to omit no opportunity; for you do absolutely depend upon God, so that if he withdraw himself from you, you are undone for ever, for you can do nothing of yourselves, it is God that worketh the will and the deed. As if we should say to a mariner, Be careful, take advantage of your wind and sail, for all your voyage depends upon God; if you neglect your opportunity, you are gone. It is time for the youngest of all to seek the Lord; as soon as ever you begin to have the dawning of reason, it is time for you to seek the Lord; oh that you did but know your time! But what time is it for the old, for those who have neglected seeking the Lord the most part of their lives? is it not high time for you to seek the Lord, who have spent so much of your lives in vanity and folly? The time you have is uncertain; and yet suppose you should live so long a period as in the course of nature you might, yet many of you cannot have as much time to seek the Lord as you have had in departing from God, you cannot have so much time to honour God as you have had to dishonour him: and therefore is it not time for you to seek the Lord? I remember it is said of Themistocles, that when about to die, at the age of a hundred and seven, he was grieved on this account, Now I am to die, when I begin to be wise. And certainly it cannot but be a grief to any to think, Through God's mercy, the Lord has begun to work grace (I hope) in my heart, yea, but as soon as I begin to know God, and have any heart to serve him in this world, I must be taken out of it. It was a proverbial speech once, (you find it in Plutarch's Lives,) Weighty things to-morrow. Oh! take heed this proverb be not fulfilled concerning you, Weighty things to-morrow. Take weighty things, things of infinite consequence, while you have time. Let weighty things be regarded now.

But further, certainly it is time now for England to seek the Lord, for many reasons.

1. Never any nation in the world had a greater opportunity for seeking and honouring God than we have had. We were like to have been befooled of our opportunity of getting mercy from God; but the Lord has betrusted us with it again after it was got even out of our hands; oh! let us then catch hold of it now, and bless God that we have it even restored to us again, and let it be a strong argument upon us now to seek the Lord.

2. Certainly it is time in a more special manner now for us, because that things are in so great a confusion, that all are at their wits' end almost. Alas! our wise counsellors at the stern, are fain to depend upon mere providences and casualties, and the truth is, there is such a confusion of things, that if God should say to the wisest man in the land, Well, do you contrive which way you think things should be best, and I will carry out your suggestions, they could scarce tell what to say, or on what to determine, such confusion prevails.

3. We thought it was time to seek the Lord, when we were in great danger from the adversaries, when we apprehended that they would come to our very gates: surely it is as great time to seek the Lord now, when he has delivered us from our enemies, that we may not devour one another. And when God has given us some rest from them, and said, Well, all that before you were afraid of was, that the enemies would prevail, and then you could do nothing, but I have quelled their power in a great measure, and commenced the work of reformation, oh! we are now at a stand, and know not what to do, and we go on in such crafty ways one against another, that every one is at a stand. Oh then, it is time for us to fall down upon our faces, to seek God to direct us, to regard the great opportunity that God has put into our hands.

4. We now want only light to know what to do; and therefore whereas heretofore we have sought to God for power that we might be able, now we are to seek to him for light, that we may know how to improve our ability. There are these two things in seeking God; praying to him, and labouring to put ourselves into that way and disposition wherein God is wont to meet with his people, and communicate himself to his people.

"Till he come and rain righteousness upon you."

The word יורה here translated "rain" sometimes signifies to teach; and the Scripture makes use of that similitude of rain, for doctrine, because of the likeness of doctrines distilling as the rain. Accordingly some interpret it, Ply the work until he teaches righteousness; and so regard it as a prophecy of the Messias: "Sow righteousness," and "break up your fallow ground, for it is time to seek the Lord," till the Messias come and teach you the righteousness of God. So they paraphrase it. But take it as it is here,

"And rain righteousness." And then there are these things in it:

I. The signification of the word "righteousness."

II. What is meant by "raining righteousness."

I. By "righteousness" is meant,

1. That God will deliver them from oppression; that though they have unrighteous dealing with men, yet they shall have righteous dealing with him. And this is a great mercy to a people, for God to undertake that there shall be nothing but righteous dealings betwixt them and himself.

2. The fruit of God's faithfulness in the fulfilling of all those promises of his for good unto them, wherein the Lord does style himself righteous. If you will now break up, saith he, your fallow ground, and seek the Lord, the Lord will deliver you from oppression; and the Lord will make good all his faithfulness to you, according to all that good word that he has promised.

II. By "raining righteousness" is meant,

1. That all their good and help must come from heaven as the rain doth; as if the prophet should say, If you look to men, yea, to men in public place, you have little hopes that there should be such righteous dealings, or to expect that the good word of God in all his promises to his people should be fulfilled; yea, but look to heaven, saith God, "I will rain," it shall come down from heaven by ways that are above nature, and beyond the power of man, "I will rain righteousness." Seek him therefore till he rain righteousness; be not discouraged though you should see public men carry things never so unrighteously, yet seek the Lord till he rain righteousness.

2. The plenty of righteousness, that righteousness shall come in abundance. It may be now, some men may meet with some righteous dealings, and be encouraged when things are at the best among men, but this righteousness comes but by drops; yea, but seek the Lord till he "*rain* righteousness." What is it to have a few drops of water? You may go into your garden, and with a little pot of water water the herbs; yea, but when it rains down water, then the earth is refreshed. And so saith the Lord here, Seek me till I come with a shower of righteousness, and rain it down upon you.

3. The working so graciously in the works of my righteousness to you, as shall make the seeds that you have sown to be fruitful, to grow up to the honour of my name, and to your good. Now there are many godly amongst you, and they sow righteousness, they do many good actions; but, alas! kept down still by the scorching heat of the oppressors. In places where oppression prevails, many godly, truly godly, persons sow much seed of righteousness, but little good comes of it, all is kept down: yea, but saith the Lord, Seek me till I rain righteousness; I will rain from heaven such showers that shall be the fulfilling of my promises to you, that shall make all your righteous actions grow up to the praise of my name, and the good of your brethren. Oh what a blessed time, when there shall be nothing but righteous dealings, and all the faithfulness of God shall be fulfilled, and there shall be plenty!

Obs. 17. God will come to sow righteousness in time. Those that plough and sow in righteousness, God will come in his grace and goodness to them: "To him that soweth righteousness shall be a sure reward,"

Prov. xi. 18. Be not discouraged, you that sow righteous seed; for it is not with the seed of righteousness as with the seed that is sown in the earth, for if that do not come up within a certain time, it will never come up; but you cannot say so of the seed of righteousness, it will come up.

Obs. 18. God sometimes comes not presently in raining righteousness upon his people that do sow righteousness. "Seek the Lord, *till* he come and rain righteousness:" as if the prophet should say, You have hearts to seek the Lord, to be humbled, and reform, to sow in righteousness; well, be not discouraged, continue seeking, stay till he doth rain righteousness. After the seed is sown, you would fain have a shower the next morning, but, may be, it will not fall so soon, stay till God's time: God does not always hear the prayers of his people so as to answer them when they would. It is very observable concerning Elijah, at one time when he cried for fire to come down upon the sacrifice, it came down presently; but when he cried for rain, he was fain to send his servant seven times: Elijah did not get rain from heaven so soon as fire from heaven.

Obs. 19. Those that seek aright will continue seeking God "till he come and rain righteousness." There is an excellent scripture in Psal. ci. 2; saith David, "I will behave myself wisely in a perfect way. O when wilt thou come unto me? I will walk within my house with a perfect heart." As if he should say, Why, Lord, it is thy presence I desire more than a thousand worlds, and I will endeavour to behave myself "within my house," in my family, not only in the presence of others, but in my family, in the most "perfect way;" Lord, "when wilt thou come unto me?" It seems God did not come and manifest himself presently: though David did behave himself in a perfect way in his house, yet David professes he would wait still. Many scriptures may be given for this, and many arguments why a gracious heart will not leave over seeking till the Lord comes.

It is the Lord I seek, and he is a great God, and fit to be waited on, though he come not presently. We think it is a matter of state, because of the distance that there is between one and another, to make them stay; why should we think much that we should wait upon the great and infinite God? And, perhaps, you pray and find no benefit; it is fit for you to wait upon God. There is an infinite distance between God and you; seek and wait till he comes.

There are many motives to continue seeking God.

1. That in so continuing to seek, we are doing our duty. This is a very great evil among many; they are praying and seeking God, but they only have their eyes upon what they shall get by seeking God, and if nothing comes of it, then they are discontented; whereas the mere consideration that in patient seeking thou art doing thy duty, should be enough to quiet thy heart.

2. Thou certainly canst not be better engaged than in seeking God. Whither wilt thou go? If thou leavest seeking God thou turnest from thine own mercy to vanity. And hast thou a temptation to leave off seeking God? shalt thou get any thing by it? Certainly thou canst not do better, and therefore seek the Lord, "seek the Lord till he come." Isa. xxx. 18, is a most excellent scripture to uphold the heart in seeking God, though God do not seem to come: "The Lord is a God of judgment; blessed are they that wait for him." You have not judgment, you know not when it is a fit time that things should be done; but "the Lord is a God of judgment," he knows how to do things in judgment, and therefore "blessed are they that wait for him." Think of this, and deny your own judgments and your own thoughts, and know that you are waiting upon the Lord, who is "a God of judgment," infinitely wise, to come to his people in a fit season, and to come so that at last you would not wish that he had come sooner.

3. All the while you are waiting, God is working good. We are waiting at men's doors, and they take no notice of it; but if we knew, all the time we are waiting, that our petition were reading and they in consultation about it, and we were only detained for the issue of the consultation, it would satisfy us. And so a gracious heart may be assured of this. Hast thou sought the Lord in the truth of thy heart? The thing is not come yet, but ever since thou hast sought the Lord, the heart of God has been thinking of that thing which thou soughtest him for, and wilt not thou go on to seek God still, till he doth come?

4. While thou art seeking God, thou art not altogether without some dews. Indeed God does not come and rain in showers that righteousness which he will hereafter, but surely thou hast dews, thou hast some encouragements; do not slight those dews of God's grace which thou art receiving, for then thou mayst stay the longer before the showers of righteousness come; rather prize the dews, and the showers of righteousness will come the sooner. Many Christians, though they have many dews of God's grace upon their hearts to refresh them, yet, because they have not showers, think they have nothing. What! hast thou no dews of grace? what is it that keeps thy heart so tender as it is? thou wouldst not for a thousand worlds wilfully sin against God: certainly, if thy heart were hardened the truths of God would not so affect it. Indeed the ra n comes in a visible manner; yea, but there are dews of grace that come in a secret way: thou dost not, indeed, see the comings in of those dews of grace upon thy heart, yea, but others may see their effect.

5. When the Lord does come, he will come more fully a great deal. It is recorded of Glover, the martyr, that when he had been seeking God for the raining of righteousness, and become willing to give his life for God, and yet God had absented himself from him, he complained to his fellow, Austin, that God was not come. Well, but, saith his friend, he will come; and give me a sign before you die, if you feel the Spirit of God come to your heart. The poor man was to be burnt the next day, and continued all night in seeking God, and yet he came not; yea, the sheriff came to carry him to the stake, and his heart still remained dead. But he went on till he came within view of the stake, and then the Holy Ghost came into his heart, and filled him with joy, so that he lifted up his hands and voice, and cried, He is come, he is come. Now there came a shower of righteousness upon his heart; he was content to seek the Lord till he came.

Obs. 20. Those who are content to seek God till he come, his coming will be to them with plentiful showers in raining righteousness. Oh how many cursed apostates are there that will curse themselves one day for not continuing to seek God till he came! Perhaps some here have had some convictions of conscience, and because they have not had encouragement, presently they have become discouraged; and so thou hast basely gone back, and now God has left thee, and thou art become a base, useless hypocrite, a dishonour and a disgrace to religion, and all because thou wouldst not stay till God came. Oh! but others have staid God's time, and God came at length so fully that now they bless his name that they did stay. I remember I have read of Columbus, who first discovered the West Indies, that his men were even weary, he was so long in sailing, and so they resolved they would return back again; so all their labour had been lost. But Columbus came to them with all entreaties to go on a little time, and at length prevailed with them to continue the voyage but three days longer. So they were content to venture three days, and within those three days they began to see land, and so discovered those parts of the world of which before we knew nothing. Now, what a miserable thing had it been if they had come back and lost all their voyage! Thus it is with many a soul sailing towards heaven and eternal life. Thou hast been a long time tossed up and down in the waves of the sea, the waves of temptation and of trouble, and thou thinkest it is best to return: oh! stay a while, do not limit thy pursuit to three days, but go on; it might haply be said of some, that had they proceeded in their voyage but three days more, they might have come and seen, whereas now they have lost all. Oh, "seek the Lord" then, "till he come and rain righteousness upon you."

Obs. 21. The help of those who seek God is from heaven. "Till he come and rain." They do not so much expect help from the creature as from heaven, to it they look up for their help. When all comforts in creatures fail, they look upwards and there see their help.

Obs. 22. The effect of God's coming to his people after seeking, is to make them fruitful; "till he come and rain righteousness;" that is the end of the mercy of God in coming to people. It may be you would have God come; but wherefore? to bring comfort unto you? No, the end of God's coming to his saints is to make them fruitful. And this would be an argument of the sincerity of your hearts in seeking God: when you are seeking him, what do you seek him for? only for comfort, and peace, and to ease you from troubles? Yea, but do you seek God that you may be fruitful? The hypocrites seek to have grace that they may have comfort, but the godly seek comfort that they may have grace; so it is, that God may "rain righteousness." I am as a dry ground, oh that God would come with the influence of his grace to make me fruitful in the works of holiness! Many of you would have comfort, (as now in these days men's ears are altogether set upon comfort,) but is your comfort the showers of God? does it make the seeds of righteousness fructify in your hearts? Certainly you can have little comfort in that which is not, as rain from heaven, to bring up the fruits of righteousness in your hearts and in your lives.

Obs. 23. God's coming with blessings upon those who seek him, is righteousness; that is, the good that they have as a fruit of seeking of him, is the fulfilling of God's word, for which God's faithfulness was engaged. Jesus Christ had purchased it by his blood, and they had before a bond for whatever good they received from God.

This consideration should much help us, both in our seeking God, and in the enjoyment of our comforts. When we are seeking God we are not seeking him merely as for a gratuity. Though in reference to us it is only free grace, but to Christ it is righteousness, it is that which Christ has purchased. Therefore saith St. John, "If we confess our sins," he does not say, God is merciful to forgive them, but "God is faithful and just to forgive our sins," 1 John i. 9. And so, when you receive a mercy from God, you are not to look upon it as a mere alms, though in reference to yourselves indeed it is so; but in reference to Christ, your Head, it is righteousness, it is that which Christ has purchased, that which God gives you as a fruit of his faithfulness, as well as of his own free grace: when thou art seeking of God let not the eye of thy faith be only upon the grace and mercy, but upon the very righteousness, of God.

Obs. 24. Though the good we do results in our own benefit, yet God rewards it as if he gained by it. God makes promises to us, that if we do thus and thus we shall enjoy such and such mercies. "Sow to yourselves in righteousness, reap in mercy." When we sow, God gives us leave to aim at ourselves; but yet when God comes to reward us, he rewards us as if it were only for him and not for ourselves, he rewards us in ways of righteousness.

And thus much for these words, raining righteousness. God has rain of another kind for the wicked and ungodly: "Upon the wicked he shall rain snares, fire and brimstone, and an horrible tempest," Psal. xi. 6.

Ver. 13. *Ye have ploughed wickedness, ye have reaped iniquity; ye have eaten the fruit of lies: because thou didst trust in thy way, in the multitude of thy mighty men.*

Notwithstanding all exhortations, and all offers of mercy, yet you have gone quite contrary, saith the prophet. Instead of breaking from your iniquities, you have ploughed them.

"Ye have ploughed wickedness;" that is, you have taken pains to propagate that which is evil, both in yourselves and others. That is the ploughing of wickedness. "The ploughing of the wicked is sin," Prov. xxi. 4; that is, their endeavours, their labour is especially for the furtherance of sin, the very strength of their spirits is let out for the promotion of their wickedness. So Job iv. 8, "Even as I have seen, they that plough iniquity, and sow wickedness, reap the same:" to plough means to endeavour and labour for iniquity, for so the word חרש here translated "to plough," signifies, to frame, work, or endeavour any thing with all our might. You have set your hearts altogether upon this work of furthering wickedness, in thinking of it, in plotting about it, in stirring up of one another, and doing all you can in your endeavours for the furtherance of wickedness.

Yea, you have been willing to go through all difficulties to accomplish your wicked intentions; as we read in Micah vii. 3, a scripture which shows remarkably the strong endeavours of wicked men after their sin, they "do evil with both hands earnestly." It is a very strange text; they are willing to take pains and to put forth all their energies in their sins.

Oh how many are there who take more pains to go to hell, than others do that go to heaven! they will so struggle and suffer for their sins, be willing to break with their friends, to venture their estates, to hazard their healths, to accomplish their sinful lusts; yea, to do any thing in the world, to compass their wickedness. Yet will they not plough for God, but complain of any little difficulty in his ways; whilst no difficulty in the ways of sin can deter them. Oh what a wicked and wretched heart is this, to be offended with every difficulty in God's ways, and yet be content to endure all bitterness in the ways of sin! Oh that we were but as instrumental for God, and willing to plough as hard for him, as others do for sin! When you shall come to die, and to reap the fruit of your labour, what terror do you think will this be, when your consciences tell you that you have taken more pains in the ways of wickedness than ever you did in the ways of God! As Cardinal Wolsey exclaimed when he was about to die, Oh! had I but served God as diligently as I have served the king, he would not have deserted me in my grey hairs. So when you come to die, and your consciences say, Oh that I had but broken as much sleep for prayer and seeking of God; oh that I had but ventured my estate, and name, as much in the ways of God as in the ways of sin! it had been happy for me; is it possible that any of you can die in peace, when your consciences shall tell you that you never took those pains for God which you have done for sin? In a good motion for God, if others engage you will join, but you will not plough hard for it; but in things that are suitable to your own lusts, you will not only join with others, but move it yourself, and plough hard for it. Oh what a pity is it, that men's parts and strength should be so expended on that which is evil! How instrumental might men of active spirits be for God if their necks were but in God's yoke! but they, all the days of their lives, have their necks in the devil's yoke, and are ploughing continually for him, and they will reap accordingly.

Now this ploughing wickedness referred especially to their false worship; there they endeavoured strenuously, they ploughed hard to get up their false worship, their worship at Dan and Beth-el, and not to go to Jerusalem to worship.

"Ye have ploughed wickedness." You do not hear of any sowing; for the truth is, there needs no sowing for wickedness, there needs but the preparation; do but plough, that is, do but prepare the ground, and wickedness will come up of itself. When you plough righteousness you must sow the seeds of righteousness.

"Ye have reaped iniquity." That is, you have your heart's desire, you have brought about your own ends, you have what you ploughed for. Sometimes men plough and take a great deal of pains in that which is evil, and God crosses them; but at other times God lets them reap: that is, You labour to promote such a thing, though it be not according to God's mind, and it may be God will let you have it; well, you plough for it, and you shall have it: and dost thou bless thyself in that? Oh, woe to thee! it is a woeful harvest that thou hast. It is a fearful curse for any to have their heart's desires in their sin satisfied. It were a thousand times better that thy ploughing were to no purpose at all, that all thy labours and endeavours were quite lost: thou art loth to lose thy endeavours in the ways of sin, but it were a thousand times better that thy endeavours were all lost than that thou shouldst attain that which thou ploughest for.

But I find the word עולתה here rendered "iniquity," is used also in Scripture to signify, the punishment of iniquity; the Hebrews having the same word to signify sin, and the punishment of sin.

Or thus, which I think the Holy Ghost somewhat aims at, You plough wickedness, and reap iniquity. The ploughing was for their false worship, and their reaping was iniquity. I beseech you here

Obs. 1. The fruit of false worship is the increase of sin in a nation. "Ye have ploughed wickedness," for so afterwards it is called, the "great wickedness;" and the fruit of that is the increase of much sin, it brings forth a harvest for sin. When men have striven to set up any false worship, and succeeded, what is the fruit? There grows presently a formality in religion, men have a religion, and yet they enjoy their lusts; for the true worship of God alone will not stand with men's lusts, therefore when men set up any kind of false worship, this will be the fruit, there will be a formality in religion, and this will please men exceeding well, for they can live in worldliness and licentiousness. And verily, my brethren, one main thing that makes carnal, loose hearts contend so much for a loose kind of worship, is that they may have so much the more liberty to sin. Endeavouring for this kind of evil will result in the reaping of iniquity.

"Ye have eaten the fruit of lies." What are those lies of the which they eat the fruit?

1. Those arguments by which they justified themselves in their iniquity. Yea, but they are but the fruit of lies. They would set up a way of false worship, but they would have some reasons for it, they would have some arguments to defend it, and those, oh, how they hugged and closed with them; and let any one bring and show them that such a thing may be proved thus and thus by such an argument, now, because they had a mind to the thing, their hearts closed upon those arguments; and they fed upon it, it did them good at their hearts.

2. The comforts which they had from their false worship. In the way that you set up you have a great deal of comfort, and you are very glad that it thrives. It is but a lie, saith God.

3. The hopes they entertained when their false worship was established. They had such hopes that all should be so well, and that there should be no more trouble between them and Jerusalem. But you feed upon lies, saith God.

4. The interpretation of God's dealings, in blessing them in their false worship. All kind of outward blessings which they had they interpreted as the goodness of God to them for that which they had done: as that is usual in places where there is any thing in matters of religion altered, though it be not right, yet you shall have men that are for that way, whatever blessing comes upon a nation, they will interpret it as the fruit of that. Yea, but this will come to nothing.

5. The false reports that they raised against those who opposed their false worship. There were many that would not yield to their modes of false worship, and upon that reports were raised concerning them, what kind of men they were, and what they had done; and when these reports were brought to them of the other way, they did them good at their hearts. Yea, but "ye have eaten the fruit of lies:" many men's breakfasts, and dinners, and suppers, are nothing else but "lies." Surely, now, this will breed no good nourishment. And why is it that we have such a deal of ill blood amongst us? Simply because that men have such coarse food.

"Because thou didst trust in thy way, in the multitude of thy mighty men." Israel, the ten tribes, had two great confidences, that are expressed in this latter part of the verse.

I. In their way; that is, in the way of religion that they had chosen for themselves, and which was distinct from the way of Judah, from the true worship of God.

II. In their mighty men; that is, the power they had in their state.

These are two great confidences of people.

I. Confidence in their way. "Thou didst trust in thy way." They were confident that was right, and were not willing to hear any thing to the contrary: and if they did, yet their hearts were so biased by their false worship, that any thing that was said to the contrary was nothing to them; they were very confident that no one could say any thing to purpose against them; No, we have so many understanding, learned men for this way, no question it is right, none but a company of silly, weak men, follow any other course.

Thus they trusted and pleased themselves in their way, and sought to harden themselves and one another in it. They have got the day, they have, doubtless, laid all upon their backs who have opposed them; there is a great deal more reason for this than for any other procedure; there is no way of peace to the state, to the kingdom, but this; that which others would have, namely, to go to Jerusalem to worship, is most unreasonable. Yea, they think that God is well pleased with their devices, and that they do good service in opposing and persecuting those who are not of their way. Thus they trust in their way.

Obs. 2. That which is a man's own way he is very ready to trust in, and to esteem highly. We have for this a notable scripture in the book of Judges, chap. ii. 19, expressing well the strength of spirit that is in men when their way is of their own devising; "They ceased not from their own doings, nor from their stubborn way." I beseech you observe this, it is but a different expression, *own doings*, and *own way;* the doings were their own, such things as they had contrived to themselves, their *own* way; and then they ceased not from them, they were stubborn in them because they were their own. "The way of a fool is right in his own eyes; but he that hearkeneth unto counsel is wise," Prov. xii. 15. "A fool," one that understands a little, yet if the way be his own, he will not hearken to counsel, he thinks he needs not counsel with any; he is so strong in it because it is his own way. It is a hard thing to get men out of their own contrivances in matters of religion: and therefore what God saith of all the heathen, in Jer. ii. 10, 11, is observable; "Pass over the isles of Chittim, and see; and send unto Kedar, and consider diligently, and see if there be such a thing. Hath a nation changed their gods, which are yet no gods? but my people have changed their glory for that which doth not profit." No nation but God's own people would change their gods; why? because the gods of the nations were of their own making. Men adhere strongly to their own inventions. "Thou didst trust in thy way." As when an object is too near the eye, the eye is not able to see it, so as to discern the evil that may be in it; so the evil that is near oneself, very near, that is one's own, it is very hard to see. If a man's heart be engaged in a way of his own, he will be ready to father it upon God himself, and say, It is God's way; and he will be ready to think that all other ways, different from his, are men's own.

None are more ready to charge others with pride than the proud; and none more ready to charge others of adhering to their own way, than those who most stick to their own conceits: it is one mark of such a man's heart, to think that whosoever differs from him, is perversely stubborn in his own conceits and his own ways.

It is difficult to make such will-worshippers acknowledge that their ways are of their own devising; but however men may attempt to deceive themselves or others, and even ascribe to God their own inventions, yet the Lord will one day discover all their ways, and show how much of their own is in them. We have a notable text for that in Prov. xxi. 2, "Every way of a man is right in his own eyes: but the Lord pondereth" or weigheth "the hearts." Mark, "Every way of a man is right in his own eyes: but the Lord pondereth the hearts:" that is, Though we choose ways to ourselves, and think they are right, and are ready to declare that our ways are God's ways, that we may justify ourselves so much the more; but saith the text, "the Lord pondereth the hearts;" that is, God weighs exactly how much there is of his own, and how much there is of our own in it. Oh! it were a happy thing if we were able to do so; it is a great part of the skill of a Christian to be able so to ponder his own ways, as to know how much of God and how much of himself is in a thing. Very few in the world know this; there is scarce any action that the best of us do, but there is somewhat of self in it, somewhat of God it may be, and somewhat of self; but now here is the skill, to be able to weigh how much of God and how much of ourselves is in an action. Your goldsmiths can presently tell you how much gold and silver is in a vessel, but an unskilful man looks upon it and thinks it all gold. Oh! it were an excellent skill to be able in all our actions thus to ponder all our ways, to know how much of God and how much of ourselves is in them; it is for want of this spiritual discernment that we miscarry so often. "Every way of a man is right in his own eyes: but the Lord pondereth," God weighs men's actions, to see how much of himself and how much of us there is in them.

But now, then, is it so, that it is in the hearts of men to trust so much in their own way, because it is their own? Oh what a shame is it, then, that we should not have our hearts close with, and trust in, God's way! Let a way be never so base and vile, yet if it be a man's own, his heart closes with it, and trusts, and is strong in it: oh, then, when the way is apparently God's, why should we be so fickle and unsteady as we are almost always in it? Make but the way of religion to be thine own, and then thou wilt be strong enough in it; but till that time comes, till we have given up our wills to the will of God, and we have made God's will to be our own will, we are never likely to be strong in the ways of God. When there is but one will between God and us, when God's interest is our interest, when God's glory is our glory, then shall we become strong. Oh! happy are they who have so given up themselves to God, that they look upon their own good to be more in God than in themselves: to look upon one's own good, and will, and the comforts of our hearts, and the happiness of our lives, to be more in God than in ourselves, is the work of grace that leads to perseverance in godliness. Thus it is between man and wife; when the wife comes to make the will of her husband her own, then she loves him strongly, and constantly: so when God's will is made to be our own, then we will follow God's will strongly, and shall persevere in it.

II. Confidence in their mighty men; "in the multitude of thy mighty men." This made them very confident in their way: why, they had an army to back them, they had an army to fight for them, to maintain that way of theirs, they had countenance from men of power, they had strength enough to crush any that should oppose them.

Obs. 3. When the outward strength of a kingdom goes along with a way of religion, men think it must needs be right, and that all its opponents are but weak men. Mark the connexion: "Thou didst trust in thy way;" that is, (as I find it generally interpreted,) their way of religion; and then "in the multitude of thy mighty men;" these two are put together: and generally men will trust in, and incline thus to, the strongest side, and the scale would turn were the strength of the mighty men to go another way; as now, suppose that the strength of the kingdom of the ten tribes had resolved to go up to Jerusalem to worship, and not to worship at Dan and Beth-el, do you think there would have been almost any considerable party that would not have gone up to Jerusalem, but worshipped at Dan and Beth-el? but when the strength of the kingdom held the other way, when the mighty men and the way of religion countenanced each other, the generality of the people went that way that the mighty men went. This is the vanity and the exceeding evil of men's hearts, that which way soever the mighty men go, that way they will trust in. There are very few who will deliberately say, I will go that way in which I see the mighty men; but there is a secret bias which inclines the minds of men to hearken to what may be said for that way, and not willingly to listen to what may be said for another. It is such a bias as makes them willing and ready to let in any probability; if there be but the least probability for the way in which the mighty men go, they take in that, and that makes way for another and another likelihood; and so, imbibing more and more, they become so confirmed for that way, as to put off the strength of any thing that can be said against it, except it be so apparent, as that they must be forced to sin against their consciences directly if they listen not to it. I say, when the spirits of men are biased by seeing the strength of the kingdom go in a way, though (perhaps) they may lay some good at their hearts, yet there is that corruption in man's heart, that except we can make the other way so clear, that, notwithstanding all possible shifts and every kind of reasoning, they shall be so self-condemned, that their own consciences shall tell them they go directly against their light, I say, except we can come thus, we cannot prevail with men's hearts, when the sway of a kingdom goes another way. And there are many truths of God that concern his worship, which cannot be made so clear but that a man may have such a diversion to satisfy his conscience in this, That I in going another way do not go against my conscience: God would have us adopt that which is most likely to be his mind, without any consideration of any outward respects. Oh how will outward respects turn the balance! In Rev. xiii. 3, when power and authority were given to antichrist, " all the world wondered after the beast." So it is ordinarily, that way which the mighty men go men's hearts will generally follow. Oh the little honour that Jesus Christ has by us! Our hearts are swayed for the most part by carnal arguments and carnal motives.

Obs. 4. Great armies are the confidence of carnal hearts. " In the multitude of thy mighty men." When they can get together a great army of a multitude of mighty men, let there be never such threats in the word, yet if they think they have strength enough to bear them out, they bless themselves therein. Oh! let us take heed of this carnal confidence. Through God's mercy the Lord has given us now, that we have the multitude of mighty men on our side; let us take heed that our faith do not ebb and flow with our armies. I will give you one scripture that shows how far a gracious heart should be from making flesh his arm; " Cursed be the man," saith Jer. xvii. 5, " that maketh flesh his arm." And how far a godly man was from trusting in an army of mighty men, we have in 2 Chron. xiv. 11; " It is nothing" (saith Asa) " with thee to help, whether with many, or with them that have no power." Why, Lord, though we have no power, yet thou canst help us. Why did Asa speak thus? Had he no power? You shall find in the chapter a little before, that Asa had five hundred and fourscore thousand valiant fighting men, almost six hundred thousand, at the very time when he is pleading with God, " Lord, it is nothing with thee to help, whether with many, or with them that have no power." We account it a great army if we have twenty, or thirty, or forty thousand men; he has almost six hundred thousand men, and yet goes to God and prays, Lord, thou canst help where there is no power.

But yet further, from the connexion of these two, their trust in their way, and in the multitude of their mighty men: from thence,

Obs. 5. Those who trust to any way of their own, had need of creature strengths to uphold them. They had indeed need of bladders under their arm-holes, if they trust in a way of their own. But now, if the way in which a man confides be the way of God, why then, though all outward helps and all worldly encouragements should fail him, though we should see the creatures at never so great a distance, yet the heart that puts its trust in God has enough to uphold it; here is the difference between men trusting in their own way, and in God's. Indeed when men trust in their own way, so long as the sun shines upon their path, and they have external helps, they can go on confidently; but let outward helps fail, and their hearts sink within them.

But now, when the heart is upright with God, and trusts in the word and promises, then it is able to say with Habakkuk, chap. iii. 17, " Although the fig tree shall not blossom, neither shall fruit be in the vines; the labour of the olive shall fail, and the fields shall yield no meat; the flock shall be cut off from the fold, and there shall be no herd in the stalls; yet I will rejoice in the Lord, I will joy in the God of my salvation." Whatsoever becomes of armies, and of the policy of men, of friends, and all outward things, yet I will bless myself in the Lord, and bless the time that ever I knew God and his ways; my heart yet is confident it is the way of God, and upon this his way I can venture my state, my liberty, my life, yea, and my soul; let all things seem to be under a cloud, and never so dismal, yet my heart is steady, and is fixed in this way of God into which the Lord God graciously has drawn my heart.

Oh, this is an excellent thing. Examine your hearts in this respect, whether, when at any time you have seen things go very cross, your hearts have not shaken.

I remember an observation which some make about John the Baptist. After he was cast into prison, he sends two of his disciples to know whether Christ were the Messias, or no: they think that though before he was cast into prison he did know that he was so; " Behold the Lamb of God!" but when once he came to sufferings, there was some shaking of his spirit. So it is ofttimes with men, when things do somewhat shine upon them, and they have some outward encouragements, they go on, and are persuaded that their way is right; but when things fall cross, and the hearts of men are opposed, and they are like to meet with more evils than ever they made account of, then they begin to call things into question, and ask, Is this the right way? Oh! it is a sign that there was much failing in thy heart at first, when in the time of outward afflictions thou comest to call in question whether it be the way of God or not.

Ver. 14. *Therefore shall a tumult arise among thy people, and all thy fortresses shall be spoiled, as Shalman spoiled Beth-arbel in the day of battle: the mother was dashed in pieces upon her children.*

As if the prophet should say, You have the militia on your side, and you think you shall be able to drive on your design, as having all the strength with you: but what if there should be seditious tumults within you? what though the power of the enemy without come not upon you, cannot God work your ruin in a way that you think not of? Oh how suddenly may God suffer the discontentments of people to break forth into rage and fury, so that intestine tumults shall arise, and bring all into the most miserable confusion!

Obs. 1. Tumults are a token of the great wrath of God on a city or country. " Therefore shall a tumult arise among thy people;" a threatening of God's severe wrath against these people, who were so confident in their way. A man may avoid external dangers to his body, but a distemper within may be his death. Fearful miseries come upon cities and countries when tumults arise: these two things have been their main cause:

1. Great oppressions.
2. Engaging numerous parties in matters controversial.

These conjoined are very dangerous, for men will carry on what they have begun, if once they be engaged in it. To engage a rude multitude in a business, especially if it be controversial, is a very dangerous thing; for we know not what they may do to pursue and follow their engagements. When the multitude is in a rage, they are like a tiled house on fire, which you cannot approach when once the flames have reached the tiles, as they fly so about your face: so in tumults, there is no coming near to talk to them, to convince them, but they are ready to fly presently upon you. And none are so cruel as the vilest of people when they are got together in a head: men of no blood care not what blood they shed. " A poor man that oppresseth the poor is like a sweeping rain which leaveth no food," Prov. xxviii. 3. Oppressions are great, the evil of tyranny is very great; but the evil of tumults is still greater. We see it many times in men of mean rank, sometimes in those committees which some of you complain of. Now men could bear oppression a great deal more easily from those who are much above them, but the oppression of our equals, or of abjects, is intolerable; if they come to get power any way, they are likely to be more oppressive than others. We have cause to bless God for delivering of us from tumults in this respect.

I might show you most dreadful examples of tumults in history. Josephus speaks of many, for when God was at last about to destroy the Jews by the Romans, their utter ruin was prepared by tumults and seditions among themselves. In his second Book of the Jewish Wars, chap. 11, he speaks of one Eleazar and Alexander that raised a tumult, and murdered as they went men, women, and children, and so made havoc of the country, that the nobles of Jerusalem were fain to come out clothed with sackcloth and ashes upon their heads, to beseech them that they would have pity upon their country, and upon their wives and children, and upon the temple; the nobles, with sackcloth and ashes upon their heads, came to assuage the rage of this tumult, so grievous was it. And in his sixth Book, chap. 11, he saith, that being in some straits for food, if any places in the city had their doors shut up, they suspected that there was meat in them, and would presently break in, and seize whosoever they found by the throat, so as to force the meat half chewed out of their very mouths; and if any of them should let it go down before they could lay hold on their throats, they would use them most cruelly for doing so. And in another place he saith, that the citizens suffered so much by them, that when the enemies took the city they thought it rather a relief than an increase to their misery. My brethren, we should rather bear much than foment tumults; take heed of that, you know not what the end of such things will be. In Amos ii. 2, it is said, "Moab shall die with tumult;" and here, "A tumult shall arise among thy people."

"Therefore shall a tumult arise among thy people." When God intends utterly to destroy a people, he suffers tumults to arise among them, as one of his sorest scourges. I find some take the word "tumult" to refer primarily, if not altogether, to the confusion of the hearts of people, when the enemies should come upon them, that they should be all in a confusion, not knowing what to do through fear and terror. As suppose on a sudden an army should come against a city, people would be wringing their hands, and running up and down from place to place, pale and terror-stricken, and confounded in their minds. Thus God threatens it should be with them. As if he should say, You are jolly and brave now, but when the Assyrians come upon you, then shall your hearts fail, and terror and perplexity shall possess you, your women and your children shall cry out for fear, and you shall be unable to aid them. This is the sense which some give it, but the former is not to be rejected.

It is a mercy that God has not tried us thus: we live in our houses, and follow our tradings, and lie down and sleep in quietness, and rise again; but we cannot imagine what woeful distractions there would be in the spirits of people in the city, if there were a considerable army encamped round about it. Perhaps some of you here have been in places where the enemies have come suddenly, so that you know what this tumult in the spirits of men and women means. Bless God (I say) that the Lord has delivered us from such tumults as these. The power and providence of God in the government of the world by a few, so keeping the people from tumults, and from bringing all to confusion, are to be acknowledged, and his name to be sanctified.

The word שאון translated "tumult," seems indeed to import this, signifying, the crying of fearful creatures, of those that are terrified and scared. Oh! it is a great mercy for men to be so stablished that, in the apprehension of dangers, they can find their hearts unperplexed, being stayed upon God. Of a righteous man it is said in Psal. cxii. 7, "He shall not be afraid of evil tidings: his heart is fixed, trusting in the Lord:" but it is a still greater blessing, when we see the armies before us, and hear the neighings of horses and clattering of the spears, *then* to be fixed. Oh! we should labour in the time of peace to make our calling and election sure. In Psal. lvii. 7—9, "My heart is fixed, O God, my heart is fixed: I will sing and give praise. Awake up, my glory; awake, psaltery and harp: I myself will awake early. I will praise thee, O Lord," &c. When does David thus cry to awake, and to give glory to God, and sing praise, and declare that his heart was fixed? When Saul persecuted him, and he was in danger of his life: Saul pursued him to take away his life, yet, even then, saith David, "My heart is fixed, O God, my heart is fixed: I will sing and give praise." So in Psal. xlvi. 2, 3, "We will not fear, though the earth be removed, and though the mountains be carried into the midst of the sea; though the waters thereof roar and be troubled, though the mountains shake with the swelling thereof. Selah." This Psalm was wont to be called Luther's Psalm, for in times of trouble he would say, Come and let us sing the 46th Psalm. Many scriptures we might cite to this purpose. Of Archimedes the mathematician it is recorded, that when the city of Syracuse was taken, he continued, in the midst of the sack and carnage, intent upon the drawing of his lines, so that when the soldiers burst in on him with their naked swords he was drawing his mathematical figures. Which of you, if at prayer, or any serious duty, you should hear of the breaking in of adversaries, could have your hearts at such a time fixed in a settled, constant way upon God.

As outward tumults in cities and countries are very great evils, so are likewise spiritual tumults in the heart, when God seems to come against the soul as an enemy, or the apprehension of his absence causes trouble and distraction of the heart. Thus in Psal. xl. 2, "He brought me up also" (saith the psalmist) "out of an horrible pit." Now the word is in the original the very same that we have here, from the pit of tumultuousness. It is as if he should say, My heart was sometimes fixed indeed, but at other times it was in a tumultuous condition, when I apprehended God not coming in according as I expected; yea, but the Lord did bring me up out of the pit of tumultuousness. Oh! has not this been the condition of some of you in time of trouble of your spirit, when you have apprehended the absence of God from you? Your hearts have been all in a tumult; has the Lord delivered you? Remember the Psalm, "The Lord has brought me up also out of the pit of tumultuousness;" I was in a tumultuous condition, my heart was even overwhelmed, but the Lord has delivered me out of the pit of tumultuousness. And then in Psal. lxi. 2, "From the end of the earth will I cry unto thee, when my heart is overwhelmed: lead me to the rock that is higher than I." Remember that scripture likewise.

מבור שאון Foveâ tumultûs.

"And all thy fortresses shall be spoiled." What are strong holds for the safeguard of a people, when the strong God is against them? You have made lines and fortifications, yea, but the strong God is against you. "All thy strong holds shall be like fig trees with the first-ripe figs: if they be shaken, they shall even fall into the mouth of the eater," Nah. iii. 12.

And now, my brethren, blessed be God we know this scripture to be true in a way of mercy, God has made our enemies so to us; and not in a way of judgment: God might have made our strong holds so to them, this scripture might have been fulfilled thus, "All thy fortresses shall be spoiled," that is, though we have made fortresses, we might have heard, first of this and then of the other strong hold in such a place having been spoiled, this castle and the other castle taken, and we might have even been amazed with the news, and have said, How does God fight against us, that though we had such strong holds, and men enough to man them, yet for all that they have been but as "the first-ripe figs," which, "if they be shaken, even fall into the mouth of the eater!" How were our hearts dejected when we heard but of one strong hold (Bristol) being taken from us. But I say, through God's mercy, this summer the Lord has made this text good unto us; all thy strong holds, not all ours, but all the enemies', how have they been spoiled generally! Oh! the Lord has appeared glorious this way, and has made this last summer to be a continual miracle of mercy to us in this very respect. "All thy fortresses shall be spoiled."

"As Shalman spoiled Beth-arbel."

Jerome reads it, As Salmana was destroyed by the house of him that vindicated Baal in the day of battle. And so all that follow the Vulgate refer this to the story that we have in Judg. viii., where Gideon slew Zalmunna the prince of Midian; and so they take Arbel as an abbreviation for Jerubbaal. The Holy Ghost seems to make that great judgment of God upon Zalmunna to be exemplary, as in Psal. lxxxiii. 11, "Make all their princes as Zebah, and as Zalmunna;" but the letters in the Hebrew here are different, and we do not read of Gideon, though he did use very much severity upon Zebah and Zalmunna, that he dashed the mother upon the children.

ארבאל ירבעל

Luther thinks it is meant of some notable act of cruelty upon some place very near to them, the particulars whereof we have not recorded in Scripture. Indeed the name Beth-arbel we find not in the canonical Scripture; but in 1 Macc. ix.2, such a place is mentioned, which afterwards became very famous for the great overthrow which Alexander the Great gave to Darius: so that it is as if the Holy Ghost should say, Did you not hear of that horrid, savage slaughter, which Shalman caused in Beth-arbel, when the mother was dashed in pieces upon her children? they regarded not sex nor condition, the tender-hearted mother, embracing her children, was dashed in pieces upon them: such dreadful wrath of God your Beth-el may expect.

בית ארבאל domus dei insidiatoris.

Beth-arbel signifies the house of the insnaring god, the god of policy and subtlety. It seems the people that called this city by this name, had a god which they honoured as the god of subtlety; and they trusted in it, expecting that thereby all their enemies would be insnared. Therefore called they their city Beth-arbel, the house of the insnaring god. But now this would not do, the more they sought by subtlety to undermine their enemies, the more were their enemies enraged; and therefore when they came upon them they spoiled them, and dashed the mother upon her own children. We might from this very word,

Obs. 2. We should not think by our plots and policies to prevail, if God be against us. Do not think to put off God by plots and policies, and to avoid dangers that way; this people did so, because they had a Beth-arbel, a god of policy, they thought to prevail, but their misery was so much the greater. Mothers and children were dashed in pieces one against another. If you make Arbel, policy, to be your god, you may expect so much the more the rage of God, and of the instruments of his wrath against you.

And let men take heed how they seek to deceive and cozen other men, for there is no such way to encourage one man against another, as to attempt to undermine him by policy: deal not so with your friends, acquaintance, and neighbours, you will encourage them so much the more.

Obs. 3. When God lets out the fury and rage of war, the cruelty is great. "The mother was dashed in pieces upon her children." We read in Psal. cxxxvii., concerning idolaters, that when the Lord lets out his wrath upon the parents, he will let it out upon the children too; "Happy shall he be, that taketh and dasheth thy little ones against the stones." It is a very strange phrase. And in Isa. xiii. 16, "Their children also shall be dashed to pieces before their eyes." I remember, Ursine, in his comment on that place of Isaiah, quotes this 137th Psalm; and he has first this note, That though God does thus execute his wrath, yet usually, because it is so dreadful, and there is so much savageness in the thing in man's eye, therefore God is wont to do it by wicked men, and we never read that he made use of his own saints to execute that wrath. And then to that doubt, Is it not said in the Psalm, "Happy shall he be, that taketh and dasheth thy little ones against the stones?" which words seem to approve of the deed; he, and Calvin, and others, answer thus, That it means not that they are blessed in their persons, or heirs of eternal blessings of mercy; but it is a prophetical wish that they might have the blessing of success in the work, as an execution of God's wrath and God's justice: though the instruments did it to execute their savage cruelty, and so sinned in it; yet the prophet looks upon the justice of God in it, and, speaking in the spirit of prophecy, wishes success to them in such a work, that the justice of God may go on and have its course.

Obs. 4. The sins of parents ofttimes come upon their children. What has the poor infant done? Oh! you tender-hearted mothers, consider of this, how far your sin may reflect upon your children. If ever you should see bloody soldiers to come in in a terrible way, (as sometimes you have apprehended,) and they should dash you upon your children, consider it is your sin that has done it.

But you will say, Shall the children suffer for the fathers' sin?

Do not we read that God will visit the sins of idolaters unto the third and fourth generation? Indeed were your children innocent, had they no original sin, then it were another matter; but now, considering they have enough in them to make them subjects of God's wrath, God may take advantage the rather because of thy sin; and therefore take heed, and especially take heed to God's worship, for we do not find in Scripture where any children are so threatened as the children of idolaters are.

Obs. 5. The judgments of God near to us should awaken us; we should think, Why may it not be upon ourselves? This was a heavy judgment of God upon some city near, and God would awaken them. Oh, what we have heard has been upon our brethren in other parts, and we have been sottish, and not sensible of it, because it has not just come upon our gates: the Lord expects when we hear of any dreadful evil upon others, that we should tremble and fear before him. And then one thing further note from hence:

"The mother was dashed in pieces upon her children."

Shalman שלמן signifies, one that is peaceable; one that is peaceable, and yet he shall exercise his cruelty so as to dash the mother upon her children: this is not one that bears cruelty in his name, not a tiger, but a Shalman, a peaceable man, as his name signifies, and yet thus cruel when he comes to have power!

Obs. 6. Men who have peace in their names, and peace in their mouths, and peace in show, yet when they come to have power oftentimes are very cruel. We were like to have found it so; if our adversaries had prevailed, this city especially might have been made a

Beth-arbel, and mothers dashed upon their children. It is true, when the adversaries did prevail in any place they did not do so, but it was not through any pity, but out of fear; but had they gotten the day, then we might have expected even dashing of the mother against the children.

Ver. 15. *So shall Beth-el do unto you because of your great wickedness: in a morning shall the king of Israel utterly be cut off.*

"So shall Beth-el do unto you." What! shall Beth-el rise up against the rest of the ten tribes, and come and destroy mother and children together? That is not the meaning.

But Beth-el shall do it; that is, Beth-el is the cause of this, that dreadful slaughter that is like to be among you, it shall come from Beth-el. Who would ever have thought that?

Obs. 1. Miserable judgments ofttimes arise from causes we little think of. From Beth-el should come this slaughter and dreadful bloodshed. And as that more generally, so more particularly this:

Obs. 2. From places of idolatry come the greatest evils to kingdoms. As it is very observable, on the contrary, from the places of God's worship comes the greatest good. So Psal. lxxvi. 2, 3, "In Salem also is his tabernacle, and his dwelling-place in Zion. There brake he the arrows of the bow, the shield, and the sword, and the battle." Did God break them there? Was there a fight in Zion, and in Salem? No, that is not the meaning, but in Zion and Salem, where God's tabernacle was, those servants of God who were there worshipping and praying to God, got the victory. So we may say, that in such a place, that was fasting and praying in the time of our battles, there God brake the arrow and the bow. Where the true worship of God is, from thence comes the good of a kingdom. And so in Isa. xxxi. 9, "Whose fire is in Zion, and his furnace in Jerusalem." The Lord is there threatening the enemies of his people, and he saith, that "his fire is in Zion, and his furnace is in Jerusalem;" there God has his furnace, and from thence it shall go to destroy the adversaries. And so, on the contrary, where idolatry is set up, and false worship maintained, from thence come evils and miseries upon us.

"Because of your great wickedness."

The words are, מפני רעת רעתכם because of the wickedness of your wickedness; so the Hebrews express the superlative degree, by a genitive case, the evil of the evil, the wickedness of the wickedness.

Obs. 3. False worship is the great sin by which especially God is provoked against a people. Whence, let us not make light account of the worship of God, for how little soever God's worship is in our eyes, yet in his sight it is a great matter; and though you think that the sins against God in the matter of his worship be but small, yet God saith, it is the "great wickedness," it is the wickedness of wickedness. And great wickedness it may be called, not only in respect of its nature, but from its many attendant aggravations.

Obs. 4. God takes notice not only of men's sins, but of the aggravation of their sins. Oh! let us do thus; not only look upon your sins and acknowledge yourselves to be sinners, but look upon the aggravations of your sins; This sin committed against so many mercies, so many prayers, and resolutions, and vows, and covenants, and so many deliverances that I have had: labour to lay the aggravations of your sins upon your hearts; this is the way to humble them before the Lord. Indeed the saints of God need not seek to excuse their sins, they need not be afraid to lay them in all their aggravations on their hearts, in all their aggravations. Greaten your wickedness before the Lord; do not, as ordinarily people do, extenuate your sins, for if there be any possible extenuation, Jesus Christ will find out that in his pleading. Christ is your advocate who sits at the right hand of the Father, and it is his work to plead your cause, and therefore if there can be any thing to extenuate a sin he will do it. You know that, in his sojourn in this world, when his disciples did offend very much in that sleepiness of theirs, so that when their Master was to suffer they could not watch with him one hour, that sin might have been aggravated with abundance of circumstances, but saith Christ, "The spirit indeed is willing, but the flesh is weak," Matt. xxvi. 41; he extenuates and excuses. Now that which Christ did there, he will be ready to do in heaven, for thou that art a saint.

Obs. 5. Wrath is proportioned to the greatness of the sin. Great wickedness and great wrath go together, and therefore according to the greatness of our sins should be the greatness of our humiliation. For so it is said of Manasses, that he humbled himself "greatly:" and in Lam. i. 20, where the church is humbling itself before God for the great wickedness and the great wrath that was upon them; "Behold, O Lord; for I am in distress: my bowels are troubled; mine heart is turned within me; for I have grievously rebelled." Mark, here you have these two points together; the church aggravates her sin, "I have grievously rebelled;" and what then? "O Lord; I am in distress: my bowels are troubled; mine heart is turned within me." Oh! remember this text, you whose consciences tell you of grievous rebellions.

"In a morning shall the king of Israel utterly be cut off."

Now, to understand this, we must consider to what it refers, what king of Israel this was, and when this was fulfilled. It refers to the account in 2 Kings xvii., and the king of Israel here spoken of is Hoshea, Israel's last king, therefore it is said that he shall "utterly be cut off;" for he and all his family were utterly cut off, there was an end of the kingdom of Israel, that had continued so long provoking God. I have forborne, saith God, the kings of Israel a long time, but now they shall "utterly be cut off" in Hoshea.

This king of Israel's spirit was stout enough against God and his prophets. My brethren, it is not the stoutness of the greatest men upon earth to say, they will, and they will; yea, they will venture their lives and kingdoms. Why, if they will, God will too, he has a will as well as they; at length God's will grows as strong as theirs, and proceeds against them, and against their very families: "the king of Israel shall be utterly cut off."

Kings of the earth suffer little from men. What a brave thing is it for a man to be able to go up and down in countries, and rend, and tear, and oppress, and bring thousands into woeful miseries and extremities, and yet be afraid to suffer nothing at all himself! Therefore it is fit for God to take in hand those men that are above the power of their fellow men; when men cannot deal with them, the Lord himself takes them in hand, and they are so much the more under the immediate justice of the infinite God.

"Shall the king of Israel utterly be cut off."

But when shall this be? "In a morning." There is a sad morning coming.

Cyril interprets it thus: God in his patience is compared to a man asleep, and in the execution of judgment he is said to awake; God brings his righteous judgments to light every morning. But that is a little too forced.

Secondly, "In a morning;" that is, early, betimes. So in Jer. xxi. 12, "O house of David, thus saith the Lord; Execute judgment in the morning." So the king of Israel shall be early cut off; and indeed this king of Israel was early cut off, he did not reign above eight or nine years at most. God takes some in the morning of their time, in their youth, when their day is but as it were dawning; some sinners he apprehends sooner than others. "In a morning shall the king of Israel utterly be cut off."

Thirdly, "In a morning;" that is, even when the light comes, when they have hopes of further good, then he shall "utterly be cut off;" which comes yet nearer and more full to the sense and scope of the Spirit of God here. And so if you read the story in the book of Kings, you find, when Hoshea was about to be cut off, he had entered into a league with the king of Egypt, and thought that now "a morning" would arise, and he should have a brave day, and live many merry days now; and when he thought the light of this morning was beginning to dawn, God came to cut him off.

Obs. 6. When people think that now light is breaking out, after a long night of darkness, then God's displeasure breaks forth upon them. We cannot but acknowledge that the Lord has granted us a morning light, but let us fear and tremble, for the time of God's displeasure is sometimes in the morning. When we think we have light breaking forth, God may have other ways to bring darkness upon us than we are aware of; we know how dreadful a day it was with Sodom after a sunshine morning. It is very observable, the difference of God's dealing with his own people, and with those that are carnal and of the world. Compare this scripture with Zech. xiv. 7. Here, "In a morning shall he be utterly cut off." But in Zech. xiv. 7, where God is speaking of mercy to his people, he speaks of a day that should be known to God, and saith, "At evening time it shall be light:" he comforts his people thus; but when he threatens the wicked he saith, When the morning comes it shall be darkness. The Lord is wont to turn the darkness of the saints into light, and to turn the light of the wicked and ungodly into darkness. Oh, let us learn to fear that God then who is able to turn light into darkness, and darkness into light. "Seek him," saith Amos v. 8, "that turneth the shadow of death into the morning, and maketh the day dark with night." He can "turn the shadow of death into morning." Suppose there be the greatest darkness upon you, God can make that a morning of light; and suppose there be a morning of light, God can turn that into darkness. Many, because they have a morning, bless themselves, and think all must needs go on according to their desires; it is very customary for men, especially when compassing some notable design of their own, if it prosper in the beginning, they think all will go on. Oh, thou mayst be utterly deceived; thy designs may have a morning, and then God may cut off thee and thy designs, and all thy thoughts may even then perish. We read that Saul had many victories after that God had pronounced that he should be rejected. And therefore we had need fear *that* God, who can turn the morning into darkness, and darkness into light.

Obs. 7. God loves to draw forth great sinners to the light; not to come upon them in the dark, but to bring forth his judgments in the morning, openly and clearly. God discomfited the host of Egypt "when the morning appeared," Exod. xiv. 27.

Obs. 8. God will be quick in his work. "In a morning he shall be cut off;" that is, suddenly. They thought by their power to hold it out; No, saith God, I will not make a day's work of it, it shall be in the morning; so the Vulgate turns it, It shall pass as the morning, as the light of the morning quickly passes over. As the king of Israel is compared to the "foam," so he is here compared to the "morning." Now, my brethren, to close this chapter, Oh what alteration of things God is able to make in a morning! They (it may be) the day before, and over-night, were jolly and merry, and blessed themselves in their way; they had confidence in their "way, and in the multitude of their mighty men;" but "in a morning" all is spoiled. God can "in a morning" make mighty alterations in a kingdom, and in cities, and families, and individuals. My brethren, who knows what a day may bring forth? who knows what a morning may bring forth? "Thus saith the Lord God; n evil, Aan only evil, behold, is come. An end is come, the end is come: it watcheth for thee; behold, it is come. The morning is come unto thee, O thou that dwellest in the land: the time is come, the day of trouble is near," Ezek. vii. 5—7. As if God should say, All this while that thou hast been in the act of the pride of thy heart and vanity of thy spirit, I did determine, that such a morning such an evil should come; and it is come, it is come, saith God; the morning is come. O think, when you lie down at night, what thou hast done this day; do not dare to lie down, but first make thy peace with God; thou knowest not what may be in the morning: and when thou risest up in the morning, look up to God, and seek blessing and mercy from the Lord, for though thine eyes be opened, and thou come to see the morning light, yet, before it be quite gone, thou knowest not what may befall thee. Seek, therefore, to make thy peace with God, both in the night and in the morning, for great changes may come to thee both in the night and in the morning, that thou never thoughtest of in all thy life.

CHAPTER XI.

Ver. 1. *When Israel was a child, then I loved him, and called my son out of Egypt.*

THIS chapter is made by some the sixth sermon of Hosea's prophecy. The scope of it is this: To clear God from severity, and to upbraid Israel for ungrateful and stubborn carriage, against mercies and means; and yet to promise mercy to the remnant, to his elect ones. This extends to the end of the 11th verse. As for the 12th verse, though made a part of this chapter, yet it were more aptly a great deal joined to chap. xii.; and so it is by some.

At the close of the preceding chapter there were dreadful threatenings against Israel, that the mothers should be dashed in pieces upon their children, and the king utterly cut off. But now, does not this argue God to be a God of rigid severity? Where is the mercy, goodness, and clemency of God towards his people? What! to have the mother dashed in pieces against her children; to cut off the king of Israel utterly? Yes, saith God, for all this I am a God of mercy and goodness, for I have manifested abundance of mercy already, and am ready still to manifest more; but you have been a stubborn and a stout-hearted people against me. And from this general scope,

Obs. 1. God stands much upon the clearing of himself to be a God of love and mercy. Whatsoever becomes of the wicked, yet God will make it clear before all the world, that he is a God of much mercy. God takes it very ill that we should have any hard thoughts of him; let us not be ready to entertain such thoughts of God, as if he were a hard master. I remember Luther saith, That the general scope of the Scripture is, to declare the Lord to be a God of mercy and goodness; the whole Scriptures, saith he, aim especially at this, that we should believe and be confident that God is a gracious and

Tota Scriptura hoc præcipue agit, ne dubitemus, sed certo speremus, confidamus, et credamus Deum esse misericordem, benignum, patientem. Luth.

merciful God. And this is the scope of this chapter. Let us rather charge ourselves of wickedness, and ungrateful dealings with God, and let us for ever justify God, and acknowledge him to be not only a righteous, but a gracious God: though thou and thousands such as thou art shall perish to all eternity, yet the Lord shall be acknowledged a God of mercy before his angels and saints for evermore. But thus much for the scope.

"When Israel was a child."

That is, at his first beginning to be a people, in his young time my heart was towards him. Indeed, the heart of God was to Israel, that is, Jacob, the father of the tribes, before he was born, before he had "done any good or evil," Rom. ix. 11, 12. But here it is spoken not of the father, but of the tribes.

"When Israel was a child." That is,

I. When he knew little of me.

II. When he could do little for me.

III. When there was much vanity and folly in him, as there are generally in children.

IV. When he was helpless and succourless, and knew not how to provide for himself.

Excussit כּעַר significat eum, qui crebro jugum parentis vel heri excutit et quamvis כִּי Ternov. in loc.

But further, Ternovius, a learned commentator on this prophecy, thinks that נער here translated "a child," intimates the stubbornness of Israel against God, one that has often shaken off the yoke of parents, or of a master; and so כי here translated "when," sometimes signifies although; Although Israel was a child, a froward and perverse child, that shook off the yoke, yet then I loved him. And what a child Israel was when God loved him, you may find in Ezek. xvi. 4, 5, "And as for thy nativity, in the day thou wast born thy navel was not cut, neither wast thou washed in water to supple thee; thou wast not salted at all, nor swaddled at all. None eye pitied thee, to do any of these unto thee, to have compassion upon thee; but thou wast cast out in the open field, to the lothing of thy person, in the day that thou wast born." Then in the 6th verse, "And when I passed by thee, and saw thee polluted in thine own blood, I said unto thee when thou wast in thy blood, Live; yea, I said unto thee when thou wast in thy blood, Live." Again and again is the command of mercy given. And then in the 8th verse, "Now when I passed by thee, and looked upon thee, behold, thy time was the time of love; and I spread my skirt over thee, and covered thy nakedness: yea, I sware unto thee, and entered into a covenant with thee, saith the Lord God, and thou becamest mine."

Well, but wherein did God manifest that he did love Israel when he was a child?

Mark that 8th verse, "Now when I passed by thee, and looked upon thee, behold, thy time was the time of love; and I spread my skirt over thee, and covered thy nakedness: yea, I sware unto thee, and entered into a covenant with thee, saith the Lord God, and thou becamest mine."

The love of God to Israel is expressed in these three particulars.

First, God "entered into a covenant" with him. Oh, it is a great mercy of God, and a fruit of great love, that such an infinite God would be pleased to make a covenant with his people, to bring them into covenant relation with him: all mankind was in covenant with God at first, but falling from that first covenant, God took into covenant with himself only a peculiar people, and made this distinguishing grace a fruit of his great love.

Secondly, "Thou becamest mine:" that is, I had separated thee for myself, and took thee for a peculiar one to me, and intended special mercy and goodness to thee; "thou becamest mine," so as that I should have a special propriety in thee, and thou shouldst have a special propriety in me.

Thirdly, I confirmed all this by an oath, "I sware unto thee." Was not here love, for God to covenant, to take in to such propriety, and to swear that we should be his? Thus "when Israel was a child, then I loved him."

Now the observations are these:

Obs. 2. It is the privilege of the church and of the saints, to be beloved of God. God loves his people, this is their privilege, he loves them with a special love. In Jer. xii. 7, they are called, the "dearly beloved of my" (God's) "soul;" see how God loves his people. God delights in his saints, and there is nothing in the world that should sanctify a gracious heart more than this, that God loves him; and as God's love is extraordinary to them, more than to other people, so their love again should be reflected upon God in a more than ordinary way. Nothing can be a recompence to love, but love: that is certain, love is never satisfied but with love; and therefore, seeing God professes love to his people, he expects love from them; therefore he will not be satisfied with any duties you perform, unless they flow from love. Love must have love; and know, that you cannot prize God's love more than God prizes yours; there is nothing in heaven and earth that God prizes more than the love of his saints, and therefore, if ever God's love, or God's prizing of your love, may gain love, O you saints, love the Lord.

Obs. 3. It is a great aggravation to sin, to sin against love. For to that end God here shows that he loved them, that he might aggravate their sin so much the more, and clear himself. Often in the days of your humiliation, and at other times, you regard your sin as aggravated, as it is against knowledge, and does a great deal of hurt, and brings you under dreadful threatenings, provoking the wrath of an infinite God against you; these are things calculated to humble your hearts for sin; but this still more, that your sin is against love, that though God has shown much love to you, yet you sin against a loving and a gracious God. God begins with this aggravation, it being his scope here to clear himself, and to convict his people of ungratefulness: "When Israel was a child, then I loved him." Sins against love are great sins indeed.

Obs. 4. It is very useful to call to mind God's old love. "When Israel was a child, then I loved him." His love to us when we were children; yea, his love to our forefathers. For a nation, too, to consider the ancient love of God to it at its first beginning, is of very great use; nay, brethren, it would be of very great use to us to consider God's ancient love to England. And I will give you one remarkable proof of it, that it was the first nation which ever God set his heart upon to bring into the fold of the gospel, the first nation in the world that by public authority submitted to the gospel; and certainly God remembers that love of England. So we find it recorded. True, indeed, we cannot give Scripture proof for this, because it was since the time of any Scripture; but so far as we may credit early records, we find it, of all nations upon the face of the earth, the first that received the gospel with the countenance of public authority. And this is not a little matter; certainly the Lord remembers "the kindness of" our "youth," and the old love of England, its "first love," in receiving the gospel. Indeed God caused the gospel to be preached to other places before it was to England; but no place by the countenance of public authority received it so soon as England did, and therefore, in that respect, England may be said to have been the very first-fruits of the gospel. Oh, it is good for us to consider of that, and many good uses we may make of God's ancient love; when we see any further expressions of it, the thoughts of his former love may encourage us to believe that surely God intends its continuance.

Centur. Cent. 2. Cap 2. Tit. de Propagation. Ecclesiæ ex J. Balæi Catal. Rossæi Brittania.

And then for ourselves individually, it is very good for us to look back to his ancient love. Some of you (I suppose) in this place may say, that God loved you when you were children: When I was a child, I had such and such expressions of God's love toward me; it was love that I was born of Christian parents, and educated in Christian doctrine, that I was delivered from such and such dangers, yea, (it may be,) God began to reveal himself to me betimes. And if you would call to mind all the loving passages of God's providence since you were children, you might have matter of meditation sufficient. Many of you complain that you cannot find matter for meditation: I will give you a rule to help you in meditation at any time, it is this: when you cannot meditate of other things, but you are presently bewildered and know not whither to go, then turn yourselves to this; to think of all the gracious passages of God's providence towards you ever since you were children; and this theme the weakest may be able to pursue with profit.

Obs. 5. All God's old mercies remain engagements to duty, and aggravations to sin. "When Israel was a child, then I loved him." It is spoken of to aggravate their sin, and further to engage them to duty. Remember that the love and mercies of God to you when you were children, are engagements to duty when you are old, and aggravations of your sin: sins against old mercies are the greatest sins. Oh that you should sin against that love of God to you when you were children! God began with you then, and has continued his love and mercy to you ever since; oh then make this an aggravation of your sin in the day of your humiliation, charge it upon your own souls, These and these sins have I committed; though God loved me, though his mercy and goodness were toward me when I was a child, and have followed me ever since, yet I have walked unworthy of all that love and mercy. Know, that though you may forget the old love of God, yet the Lord remembers it; he remembers his old mercies, and he remembers your old sins.

Obs. 6. Let not our hearts sink in despairing thoughts, though we see that we are able to do but little for God, and though we are unworthy of his love. Though there be much vanity and folly in our hearts and in our lives, yea, though there has been much stubbornness, yet still let not our hearts sink in despairing thoughts. "When Israel was a child, then I loved him." They could do little for me, and they knew little of me, and they were vain, and foolish, and stubborn, and yet "I loved them." Certainly, the dealings of God toward Israel are as a type of his dealings toward his saints, as the afflictions of Israel are typical with respect to the church: and as we gather an argument for patience in afflictions, when we read how God dealt with the people of Israel in the wilderness; so also should our faith be strengthened by the long-suffering and tender mercy shown them: though they were unworthy, and poor, and weak, yet God loved them. Therefore you, poor people, that find yourselves weak in understanding, alas! you know little, and can remember little, of that which is good, and you can do little for God; Yea, I find (perhaps saith one) much frowardness and stubbornness in my heart against God; but do you bewail it? if so, let not your hearts be discouraged, do not think that these are things that will hinder the love of God; God's heart may be towards you notwithstanding all this; God's love does not find, but makes the object lovely; therefore God can love though thou knowest little, and canst do but little.

But you will say, He *can* love, but *will* he love? If I did but know that, my heart would find peace.

To that I answer,

First, When you hear that God loved Israel when he was such a child that "none eye pitied him," this is enough to help you against any concluding thoughts against God's love, for God loved his people Israel when they were as unworthy as you are.

Secondly, The readiest way for you to know with certainty whether God will love you or not, is, 1. To raise up your faith, if you are able, upon such grounds as this, The consideration of his love to his people when they were unworthy.

2. In quietness and meekness of spirit to lay thyself before the Lord as an object of his pity. Thou dost not think thyself worthy to be an object of love, yet lay thy heart before God as an object of pity, and there resolve to wait till the time of love shall come, till God shall make known that his heart is toward thee for good. It is not the way for thee to be froward and vexing, because of thy unworthiness, meanness, poverty, and baseness, and so to determine that on account of these he will not love thee; no, I say, the way for thee to have the sense of God's love, is this, when thou seest there is no worthiness in thee why he should love thee, yet to remember that there is enough in thee to make thyself an object of his pity.

Obs. 7. God's love begins betimes to his people, let not his people's love be deferred too long. God is beforehand with you in love, and whenever we begin to love him it is upon this ground, "because he first loved us." You who are young, love God betimes, for if you be such as ever shall be saved, God did not only love you when a child, but he loved you before you were born, before the foundations of the world were laid. Oh! it is a pity that the first springing of your love should not be bestowed upon God. Certainly old love is the best love; as old love in God is sweet, so old love in the saints: it is a sweet thing to think that God loved me from a child; but then, if I can say this too, I loved God from a child, this will make it sweeter: put but these two together, and what is wanting to the comfort of one's life? God loves that love which is from a child; "I remember thee, the kindness of thy youth," Jer. ii. 2: God loves the love of young ones, the love of children. How sweet will old age be to thee if thou canst say, Lord, through thy mercy I have loved thee from a child, and that is an evidence that thou didst love me when I was a child! How many are there now old, whom God loved when they were young, that would give ten thousand worlds, if they had them, that they had known and loved God sooner than they did! I say, those whose eyes God enlightens, and hearts God converts to himself, would give ten thousand thousand worlds that they could but say this, Oh that I had but loved God from a child! You who are children and young ones, do you begin betimes to love God, that, if you live to be old, you may say, that God loved you from a child. It was an excellent speech of Austin, when it pleased God to work upon his heart, Lord, I loved thee too late. And so it will be with any that begin to love God, they will say that they loved God too late; this tardy affection will be the great burden to their souls.

Nimis sero te amavi. Aug.

"And called my son out of Egypt."

"And called;" that is, by Moses and Aaron, I sent them to call them out of Egypt and to bring them from thence. This seems to refer to Exod. iv. 22, where the Lord directs Moses to go to Pharaoh, and to speak on this wise, "Thus saith the Lord, Israel is my son, even my first-born." So in Jer. xxxi. 9, "I am a father to Israel, and Ephraim is my first-born."

"My son:" the Seventy render it in the plural, *τὰ τέκνα αὐτοῦ*, his sons; but in the original it is לבני *my son;* thus, although the Holy Ghost speaks of all the people in general, yet he puts them in the singular number, and in their very community calls them the son of God.

Obs. 8. The church is related to God as a son to the father, yea, the very first-born. What God speaks of the people of Israel is especially intended towards his saints, which are the true Israel of God; they have the privilege to be sons unto God, to be children. "Seemeth it to you," saith David, "a light thing to be a king's son-in-law?" What then do you think it is to be son to the King of heaven and earth, and heir of heaven and earth? "Is Ephraim my dear son?" Jer. xxxi. 20. This is the privilege therefore of the saints, that God deals with them as sons; "I will spare them," saith the Lord in the prophet Malachi, chap. iii. 17, "as a man spareth his own son that serveth him." And the special privilege that they have from this is, that they are not under the law as slaves, in reference to God; those that are in the state of slavery are under this law, Do, or die; if thou dost offend but in the least thou shalt perish for ever, the curse of the law is upon thee. But the sons of God are brought into another condition, not to be under that law; they indeed, if they do offend, may be corrected and chastised, Psal. lxxxix. 30—32; but they are never under the law of the sentence of eternal death for their offences. There is a great deal of difference between the administration of God towards slaves, and towards sons: this is the great privilege of sonship, that thou art not under the law, but art brought under another law, even the law of Jesus Christ; that though thy sin indeed, of its own nature, if God should deal with thee in justice, would be enough to put thee under an eternal curse, yet being a son, God puts thee under another law, and deals not with thee by that which pronounces a curse against every sin.

Obs. 9. Let wicked men take heed how they use the saints, for they are God's sons; they are not slaves, they are the sons of the eternal God. "Is Israel a servant? is he a home-born slave? why is he spoiled?" Jer. ii. 14. How comes it to pass that Israel is so dealt with? What! is not Israel a son, and "Ephraim my dear son?" Jer. xxxi. 20.

When any of the people of God are under the power of any men, God looks upon them as sons; and if they deal hardly with them, God will inquire and say thus, Is such a one a slave? had he been a slave I would not so much have cared for your dealing thus with him, but he is a son. You find in the Acts that they were afraid when they heard that Paul was a Roman. When thou knowest thou hast to deal with a son of God, know that though thou hast not liberty to misuse any, yet when thou misusest him, thou dost it at thy special peril.

Obs. 10. The saints are not only sons in their particular relation, but in their community. The whole community of the church, as members, are but as one son: "I called my son out of Egypt;" he speaks of the whole body of Israel. Now the Lord looks upon the community of his church as one son, in the singular number; one, not in outward incorporation and visible government, but in spiritual union and communion with their common Head. Many privileges belong to the church of God in their community, as well as in their particular relation. And they should labour to unite themselves much together, seeing God joins them together in the singular number. Oh! the Lord loves unity in his church.

Obs. 11. God's sons are not exempt from sore and grievous evils in this world; though they be sons, yet they may be in Egypt: "And called my son out of Egypt." So in Jer. xii. 7, "I have forsaken mine house, I have left mine heritage; I have given the dearly beloved of my soul into the hand of her enemies." Though "the dearly beloved of God's soul," yet "given into the hand of her enemies." Though God's son, yet in Egypt. So with the church under antichrist; for above twelve hundred years God gave up his sons into that spiritual Egypt.

We must not think therefore, as soon as we come under grievous afflictions, that God has cast us off from being sons; though they were in Egypt, yet still they were "my son." Now we are ready to think, that if God bring us into sore afflictions then we are no more sons; no, thou mayst be delivered up to the power of the enemy, and yet no slave, no enemy, but a son of God still. Deut. xxxii. 10, is much to be observed, where it is said of the people of Israel, that they were "in the waste howling wilderness," and yet they were "as the apple of God's eye." So thou mayst be delivered up to suffer sore things, to be banished from thy house and home, and to wander up and down "in the waste howling wilderness," and yet remain "as the apple of God's eye." It is a strange sight indeed to see a child of God, an heir of heaven, a co-heir with Jesus Christ, one dearer to God than heaven and earth, subject to the power, the caprice, and lusts of wicked, base, ungodly men; yea, it may be, for a time slaves to Satan; I say, even those whom God has an eternal love to are ofttimes for a season slaves to Satan; but then they have not the comfort of this sonship, nor do they know it: but now they may know themselves to be sons, and yet slaves to the humours of wicked and ungodly men, and than this there is not a stranger sight in the world; I believe the angels in heaven do not see a stranger sight, nor one at which they more admire, than a godly man under the lusts of wicked men. This is God's permissive work for the present, but he intends to manifest himself in another way hereafter: for the present he fetches about the glory of his own ends this way, he lets even his own dear sons be in Egypt; but God has his time to deliver his people and call them out of Egypt: it is but a call, and it is done; it is as easily done as a man that gives a call for such a one out of such a place. Let our bondage be never so great, it requires but a word from God to deliver us.

Obs. 12. It is a great mercy to be called out of Egypt. This the Lord here brings as a great testimony of his love to them, that he called them out of Egypt. In Exod. xii. 42, "It is a night to be much observed unto the Lord for bringing them out from the land of Egypt:" to be called from that Egypt was a fruit of love; and so to be called from spiritual Egypt, (for man's natural estate is a spiritual Egypt,) to be called from antichristian Egypt, is a great fruit of love: and as it is a fruit of love, so it is an aggravation of sin, for so it is brought, "I called my son out of Egypt," and yet they did thus and thus.

If God remembered this mercy, of calling them out of Egypt so many years before, as an aggravation of their sin, how much more may the Lord make that an aggravation of our sin, that he called us so lately out of our Egypt! In many ways I might show you that we were under as great, if not a greater bondage than the Israelites were under in Egypt. And there has been as outstretched an arm (though not so obvious to sense) in calling us, as in calling them out of Egypt. Now let not this be an aggravation of our sin, that the sound of our cries under the yoke of our bondage is not yet out of our ears, and the very sores of our shoulders through their yokes not yet thoroughly healed, and yet we grow to be wanton, foolish, vain, proud, cruel, oppressing one another, and abusing our liberty. Oh! our sin must needs be accounted exceeding great before God.

Well, but yet we see not all, nor even the chief part, of the mind of God in this expression, for we find that, in Matt. ii. 15, the Holy Ghost cites this scripture which now I am opening to you, and interprets it of Jesus Christ. When Jesus Christ was fain to fly into Egypt to save his life, the Holy Ghost saith, that it was to fulfil that "which was spoken of the Lord by the prophet, saying, Out of Egypt have I called my son."

It is a very strange interpretation, of which, however, we have other similar in the New Testament; and Jerome on the place saith, that Julian and some of the Jews, with others who hated the Christian religion, took much advantage of this quotation of Matthew in their arguments against the authority of the gospel, saying, Surely it proves Matthew very unskilful in Scripture, that he should make such a quotation as this, when it is apparent that it is spoken of the calling of the people of Israel out of Egypt. And truly we should never have thought that there had been such a meaning in this place of Hosea, had we not found it so interpreted by the Holy Ghost. But before we open this, and show how this scripture is rightly quoted by the evangelist, I would observe, that we may see by this interpretation, both of Matthew, and divers other places in the New Testament, that there is much more of the mind of God in the Old Testament than was generally known to them who lived in those times. Which of the Jews could have so interpreted "I have called my son out of Egypt?" that is, Jesus Christ, after his birth, shall be persecuted and forced to fly for his life, and that into Egypt, and he shall come again out of Egypt; who could have thought this to be the intention of the Holy Ghost? Things were not understood till they came to be fulfilled, and then their accomplishment interpreted the prediction. And the truth is, as in the Old Testament so in the New, there are a great many scriptures of which we understand yet but little; the time of our ascertaining their full meaning, is reserved to the period of their fulfilment. Many such prophecies we have in the Revelation and other places, that are (I am confident) as dark to us as this place of Hosea was to the Jews; and there is as excellent a spiritual meaning in many places of the New Testament hidden from us, that will hereafter be revealed clearly to the church of God, as there were in the Old Testament; I know not whether I may say as many as those, but certainly as much hidden from us. Jesus Christ, the Lamb slain from the beginning of the world, is he who shall open the book that is sealed, Rev. v., as a fruit of his death; it is the Lamb, as he is a Lamb slain from the beginning of the world, that shall open the book that is sealed. There are many things in the book of God that are sealed to us this day, and it is the purchase of the blood of Jesus Christ to open it; and when his time comes, it shall be opened to us.

See Bucer on Matt. xxviii., p. 197.

"And have called my son out of Egypt."

Interpreters, I find, do much weary and tire themselves and their readers about the aptness of this as quoted in Matthew: their manifold opinions may, perhaps, be reduced to these three heads:

First, Some think that Matthew quotes this but only by way of allusion or similitude; that there is a similitude between Christ's going to Egypt and returning, and the people of Israel's going to Egypt and returning; but that is a frigid and a poor interpretation, and against what is said in Matthew, that Christ was taken down into Egypt, that the Scripture "might be fulfilled."

Secondly, Junius, that learned man, thinks that the very literal sense of the place, is rather a prophecy of Christ's going into Egypt and returning again, than of the people of Israel doing the same: and so, in his sixth parallel, (Paral. lib. i.,) he saith, It is as if God should say, I have threatened that I will utterly destroy the king of Israel, but shall I therefore wholly destroy Israel? No, no, I will not do that for my Son's sake; for though Israel is unworthy and receive not my Son, and by my Son's going into Egypt it is declared that they are so unworthy of him that they should never have my Son come among them again, yet he shall come among them again, and that shall be an evidence to them, that I will not cast off my people Israel. This is a very spiritual and good interpretation; and we find often that, when the Lord did promise mercy to his people, and would give an evidence that he would not destroy them, he was wont to give a promise of Jesus Christ; as in Isa. ix. 6, "Unto us a child is born, unto us a son is given;" he seals the promise that he will not cast off his people by promising the Messias. So Junius thinks that the Lord here seals this promise of mercy to the people of Israel, that he will not utterly cut off his own people; why? because he will call his Son out of Egypt. But yet I cannot think this altogether satisfactory, and will give you that which may more clearly appear to be the mind of God.

Thirdly, This scripture in Hosea was intended not only to show what was past, that God did indeed call his people out of Egypt, but to typify God's future intentions. Other instances occur in which many things spoken in the Old Testament literally of other matters, yet, apparently, are meant typically of Jesus Christ; as Exod. xii. 46, compared with John xix. 36: in Exodus, in the institution of the passover, God saith, "Not a bone of it shall be broken;" now in John xix. 36, it is said, when the soldiers came to break the bones of the two thieves that were upon the cross, through the ordering of Providence they found that Christ was dead, and so they brake not his bones. One would think now that this were a mere accidental thing; but yet the Holy Ghost saith, "These things were done that the Scripture should be fulfilled, A bone of him shall not be broken." Thus you see in things apparently very accidental, God has a special work, and often intends great things by what seem in our eyes to be of little moment. What more light thing than that, that they should not break the bones of Christ? though clearly meant at first literally concerning the paschal lamb, yet it had an ultimate typical reference to Jesus Christ. Compare two other scriptures together, 2 Sam. vii. 14, with Heb. i. 5: the words in Samuel apparently concern Solomon, "I will be to him a father, and he shall be to me a son;" but now the apostle, in Heb. i. 5, applies them to Christ, and saith, "To which of the angels said he at any time, Thou art my son, this day have I begotten thee? And again," saith he, "I will be to him a Father, and he shall be to me a Son?" These refer primarily to Solomon, and typically to Jesus Christ. So the words of the prophet here refer literally to Israel going into Egypt and returning back again, but yet have a further typical bearing on what would be done with Christ, that he should go to Egypt and return back again.

Obs. 13. God has an eye to Christ in all he does, all his works some way or other have reference to Jesus Christ: indeed God's carrying his people to Egypt and bringing them back again, was one of his greatest works, but still in that he had an eye to Jesus Christ.

Obs. 14. It will be one great part of the glory of the saints hereafter, to see how God had reference to Jesus Christ in all his great works in the world. Now we look upon things and witness their influence, but we do not discern their reference to Jesus Christ; hereafter it will be a special part of the glory of the saints, that they shall see how in all the works of God he had regard to Jesus Christ. In the work of creation; God would not have created the world but for his Son: in the fall, and in every thing, he purposed the magnifying of the great work of his Son; and those who had a special work of the Spirit of God in those times did understand God's meaning, though ordinarily they did not. I remember one learned interpreter, to show how they might understand God's mind by his types, thus expresses himself: As it was with Jonathan, when he carried his bow and arrows into the field to notify to David whether he should fly away for fear of Saul, or return back again. Now when Jonathan shot his arrows, he said to his lad, "Behold, the arrows are on this side of thee, take them;" or, "Behold, the arrows are beyond thee." Now the youth knew no more but that he was to look for the arrow, but David knew more, that when he said it was beyond him, then he should do thus, and when it was on this side, then he should do thus. It expresses very well the difference of the types and the letter of things: those who knew but merely the letter, were like Jonathan's lad, that did but only according to what Jonathan said; but David knew the intention of the mind of Jonathan, and so was able to make use of it. Oh! it is an excellent thing to be able to understand the mind of God in his word; it is a fruit of the love of Jesus Christ to his saints. And certainly if the people of Israel had but known this, when they first went into Egypt, and returned back again, that the Lord aimed at Jesus Christ in it, would it not have been a comfort to them? If they had known that God intended to make them conformable to his Son, would not this knowledge have supported them? Then certainly it must needs be a comfort to the saints to know now, that in all their sufferings they have a conformity to Jesus Christ; we know it now, and that the reason why we suffer is to make us conformable to Jesus Christ: the Jews did not know that this was the reason why God would have them suffer, but we know it, and therefore in all our sufferings we should exercise our faith in the sufferings of Jesus Christ. Do we suffer thus and thus? he did so, to take away the sting of our sufferings. And in a special manner, you that have been driven from house and home, and compelled, perhaps, to fly for your lives, and to go among strangers; still your suffering is not so great as was the suffering of Jesus Christ; he fled for his life when he was but an infant, and did not only fly to strangers, but to his enemies, to the Egyptians: you are driven but from one part of England to another. O, exercise your faith in this. It was a very strange work of God's providence, that presently after he was born he must fly for his life. You that are obliged to carry your children with you, O remember how Joseph and Mary were obliged to do it; and their flight was a great deal worse than yours, for they had no resource but to fly to Egypt. Now supposing it was by land, for which many reasons may be given, they were compelled to fly almost a hundred miles through the desert wilderness where there were no habitations: you fly from one town to another, and find relief; they were fain to fly above a hundred miles through the very desert between the land of Canaan and Egypt. Now, though it is true the people of Israel were forty years in the wilderness; but not through the length of the place, as three days' journey might have carried them into the land of Canaan, had not God delayed them, and suffered them to entangle themselves on account of their stubbornness and rebellions; yet, although we have no reason to conclude that Joseph's flight into Egypt was as tedious, certainly it must needs have been sad and miserable: it cannot be conceived that any of your flights should be so sad and miserable as that was, for they could not carry any provision with them, but were fain to fly in a private way to save the life of Jesus Christ. Oh, how often do you think did Joseph and Mary look upon this babe when they were flying through the desert wilderness, and think, What! is this the Son of God; is this the Saviour of the world; is this he that should be the Redeemer of Israel; is this he that is God and man; is this he that is the Second Person in Trinity, that presently after he is born we must fly for his life through a desert wilderness? Oh the strange work of God in the very work of man's redemption! Things were so low and poor, and seemed to go on in such a contrary way, as would have staggered any one's faith, that Jesus Christ should do such great things as he afterwards did. O my brethren, this is the way of God, to task the faith of men, especially at first. So it was with Christ's flight into Egypt.

Ver. 2. *As they called them, so they went from them: they sacrificed unto Baalim, and burned incense to graven images.*

"As they called them." That is, Moses and Aaron, and other prophets and ministers of God sent unto them, called them to serve the Lord, and to worship him according to his own way. And especially they called them from idolaters and false worship.

As I called them, καθὼς μετεκάλεσα αὐτοὺς, Sept. That is, though they were so called, I called them, yet they went from them. When the means of God are so powerful, to resist then is a very great evil. "If our gospel," that is, our gospel preached with so much plainness and power, "be hid, it is hid to them that are lost," 2 Cor. iv. 3. But take it here,

"As they called them." That is, look what earnestness there was in Moses and Aaron, and other ministers of God, to call them from their evil ways, so much stubbornness and stoutness was it for them to resist. Calvin thinks it is, Because they called them, therefore they went from them. That is, they went from them for the very nonce, as we are wont to say. Because Moses would have us do thus and thus, we will for that very reason do just the contrary.

"So they went from them." That is, turned their backs upon them: like stubborn children and servants, when they are called they will not hear, but turn their backs upon you; so did they to Moses. From whence,

Obs. 1. It is a mercy of God to have God's ministers calling us to obedience. Who are we that God should send his messengers after us? What need has God of us? Suppose we go on in the ways of death, and perish, what shall God lose by it? But this is God's mercy, that he will call after us. God might say, If you *will* go, go on and perish everlastingly. Oh, but he doth not so.

Obs. 2. It is as great a mercy of God to call us out of sin to duty, as to bring us out of affliction, and we should account one as great as another. We think it a great mercy if the Lord will call us out of an affliction; but when God calls us out of sin to duty, do you think that that is as great a mercy? If you do, it is a sign of a sanctified heart indeed. You are in sickness and under great extremity; if God should say, I will give out my word to deliver you, that would be a sweet word, you would say; yes, but when God gives forth his word to call thee out of thy sin to a duty, thou shouldst as joyfully take a hint of that word of God too. O, prize God's call to you from sin to duty, as much as from misery to prosperity.

Obs. 3. It is a great aggravation of men's sins, if they be called to duty after God has called them out of misery, and they obey not. After thou comest out of an affliction, whether bodily or spiritual, God expects thou shouldst as diligently hearken to his call that calls thee to duty, as thou didst take hold of his mercy when he held it to thee to deliver thee out of thine affliction. Charge thy soul thus, Oh wretched heart that I have! I called to God, and he has heard my call, and delivered me; and now he calls me to duty, and shall I stop mine ears against God's call? Oh how just were it for God to leave me in misery, when I turn my back to him when he calls me to duty!

Obs. 4. For men not only to disobey God's call, but to turn away themselves from it, and from those who speak to them in his name, betokens a high degree of sinfulness. In Jer. ii. 27, "They have turned their back unto me, and not their face;" and so Jer. xxxii. 33, "They have turned unto me the back, and not the face:" that is more than not to obey, it signifies to refuse to obey, to resolve not to obey. In Jer. xviii. 17, God threatens them that, "in the day of their calamity," he would show them his back too. As, when a traitor is petitioning his prince, so long as the prince is but willing to parley with him, and to read his petition, there is hope; but if the prince turn his back and will not look upon his petition, then hope is gone: so there is hope that we may bring persons to obedience so long as they will hearken to the word, but if once they turn their backs, then there is little hope: and when God turns his back upon sinners, woe unto them! Remember, you that turn your back upon calls to obedience, O remember that scripture in Jer. xviii. 17, that God threatens in the day of your calamity he will turn his back on you. Men do not attain to this wickedness at once; at first they are loth to be convinced that such a thing is a truth, but at length, when the evidence of truth comes clear, they in a desperate way turn their backs upon it, and resolve not to hearken to it. A striking instance you have of this in Jeremiah. At first they said that Jeremiah did not speak the word of the Lord, but afterward, "As for the word that thou hast spoken unto us in the name of the Lord, we will not hearken unto thee," Jer. xliii. 2; xliv. 16.

Obs. 5. It is yet a higher wickedness to have our corruptions irritated and provoked by the word. "As they called them, so they went from them." When men's hearts are as lime, that the showers of the word serve only to inflame them, their condition is sad indeed; when the clearer evidence they have of the word, and the more power with which it is preached, the more desperately wicked they become. We find it so in some places, and you wonder at it; but wonder not, for where the word does not convert, it hardens.

Obs. 6. God's free grace is very great and very strong. The Lord was merciful to his people that were thus stubborn and stout, but the more they were called to obedience the more wicked they grew, and yet God's mercy continued towards them for a long time together; and indeed, in that God should set his heart and love upon such a people as this, is almost one of the greatest helps against despair that we know of. Do but look into the book of God, and read of the people of the Jews, what a wretched, froward, perverse, stubborn, stout-hearted nation they were, and yet that the God of all the people of the earth should choose them to be his peculiar people; oh the free grace of God! nothing God has more at heart than to honour free grace. I confess I had thought to have spent some time in showing you the extreme stubbornness of the Jews, with the special view of magnifying the free grace of God towards such an unworthy people: you find that God does so himself; when he speaks of his mercy to that people, he gives them this notice, that he would have them to know, that what he did for them was not for their own righteousness: thus Deut. ix. 6, "Understand therefore, that the Lord thy God giveth thee not this good land to possess it for thy righteousness; for thou art a stiffnecked people:" as if God should say, I magnify free grace: whereas I might have chosen some other people that might have been more yieldable to my hand, I chose you, that it might appear that all that I did was out of free grace. In Psal. lxxviii. 8, "their fathers" are called "a stubborn and rebellious generation;" they seemed to be of strong spirits, but their strength was against the truth; and though stubbornness has a seeming glory in it, yet the truth is, its strength is but very weakness. Thus Ezek. xvi. 30, "How weak is thine heart, saith the Lord God, seeing thou doest all these things, the work of an imperious whorish woman!" They are said to be strong-hearted, "imperious," but saith the Holy Ghost, "How weak is thine heart!" And you shall find in Scripture that they are called stiffnecked, and iron-sinewed, impudent and rebellious children, that walked contrary to God, and had hardened their hearts and made them like an adamant; so Stephen saith, Acts vii. 51, "Ye do always resist the Holy Ghost:" moreover it is very observable, if you examine the Scriptures, that presently after they came out of the land of Egypt, within three days after God had shown them such a miraculous work they fell to murmuring; nay, they did not stay so long, for it is said in Psal. cvi. 7, "They provoked the Lord at the sea, even at the Red sea." In Exod. xvi. 2; xvii. 2, the people chide with Moses. So throughout Exodus, Numbers, Deuteronomy, Judges, and the Kings, you find them continually rebelling, a people with an iron sinew against God; and yet for all that the Lord makes choice of this people, and loves them: oh! free grace, the free grace of God! When your children are stubborn and stout against you, and you think it a grievous affliction to you, reflect, none in the world are so crossed with stubborn children as God himself.

And though any of you should find your hearts very stubborn, yet for all that do not allow them to sink into despair, for God's grace is free to overcome even stubbornness of heart, as it did here. You have a most remarkable confirmation of this in Exod. xxxiv. 8, 9, "And Moses made haste, and bowed his head toward the earth, and worshipped. And he said, If now I have found grace in thy sight, O Lord, let my Lord, I pray thee, go among us; for it is a stiffnecked people." Their being "a stiffnecked people" was no argument of despair, that God should not go among them; but Moses uses it as an argument with God, Lord, they are "a stiffnecked people," yet "let my Lord, I pray thee, go among us;" "and pardon our iniquity and our sin, and take us for thine inheritance." We may by the way here note how the Chaldee paraphrase renders this, Let the majesty of the Lord go among us; the majesty or divine presence: the Hebrews call it Shechinah, שכינה which they usually distinguish from God the Father, and say there is no coming before the blessed high King without the Shechinah. So our Saviour more plainly, John xiv. 16. But to return:

Obs. 7. None should despair. God holds forth by this example that he would have none sink with despair, but be brought in by his free grace, notwithstanding the stubbornness of their hearts against him.

Now as for the latter part of this 2nd verse, respecting their sacrificing to Baalim, and burning incense to graven images, I shall not enter upon it, as I have spoken of it fully before.

Ver. 3. *I taught Ephraim also to go, taking them by their arms; but they knew not that I healed them.*

Here we have the third degree of God's goodness towards Ephraim, the fruit of his love; he called them out of Egypt, and he called upon them by his prophets, and he taught them to go.

"I taught Ephraim also to go, taking them by their arms." God here compares himself to a nurse, or to a tender parent, that carries along the child, guiding it by the hand and feet, and in rugged, foul places, taking it up in the arms; such were my dealings towards Ephraim, saith God. In Psal. lxxvii. 20, God is said to lead them by the hand of Moses and Aaron, like a flock of sheep. But here he is said to lead them like a nurse or a parent; and this expression seems to have reference to Deut. i. 31, "In the wilderness, where thou hast seen how that the Lord thy God bare thee, as a man doth bear his son, in all the way that ye went:" look, as a man leads his son by his hand, and when he comes to difficulties, bears him up and takes him in his arms, so did the Lord thy God deal towards thee "his son;" and, as a loving parent, taught thee how to go in thy way out of Egypt, and led thee all through the wilderness until he brought thee into Canaan.

When they came first out of Egypt they knew not which way to go no more than a child, and if God had then left them, certainly they had perished; their way was very full of difficulty, and God did seem to lead them about, but the Scripture saith, "he led them forth by the right way," Psal. cvii. 7. Though they were forty years in the wilderness, whereas they might have gone through within a few days, yet still they were led in "the right way," God "taught them to go."

Obs. 1. When God calls his people out of afflictions, they know no more than a little child how to guide themselves in their way. We think if we be delivered from such and such an evil we are well; but when God does grant deliverance, if he should leave us there, we would quickly spoil ourselves, and turn our mercies into miseries. The pride of men's hearts inclines them to self-confidence, hence they get many a knock and bruise. Oh how many stumble and perish because they will be going themselves, and not depend upon God's hand!

We find this by experience: God has in a great measure called us out of Egypt, and we hope that he intends a Canaan to us, yet, what children are we! we do not know how to take a step in our way; oh how often since have we been at a stand, in a maze, not knowing which way to take, this or that! and how often, alas, have we fallen and gone astray! If ever people required God to teach them how to go, we do so at this day; our path is an untrodden path, and there are many stumbling-blocks in our way, and we often stumble and fall in them. Poor children do not more require the hand of the parent or nurse, when they go upon the ice or in slippery ways, than we need the hand of God upon us to lead and guide us in these our ways.

Obs. 2. The way in which God often leads people, may be a way of much difficulty. He "taught Ephraim also to go," and "led him forth by the right way." If we inquire what that way was; it was the way through the wilderness, yea, the way before they came into the wilderness, before they came to the sea: thus, Exod. xiv. 9, "The Egyptians pursued after them, all the horses and chariots of Pharaoh, and his horsemen, and his army, and overtook them encamping by the sea, beside Pi-hahiroth, before Baal-zephon." They were in a very strait way, the sea before them, Pharaoh and all his army behind them, and they were "encamping by the sea, beside Pi-hahiroth," at the mouth of those mountains which compassed them round about; and they were "before Baal-zephon," that is, The god of watching, the god which the Egyptians believed did watch those that went out of their country without permission. Yet, under the eye of this their watching-god, hemmed in between mountains, the sea before them and a great army behind them, God "taught them to go." In what way does God teach them to go? God "taught them to go" even through the sea. And when they have gone through the sea, is all the evil over? No, they must go into the waste howling wilderness, and there be led about for forty years together; and yet God here reckons up such guidance of them as a fruit of his love.

So long as we are in God's way, though it be difficult, yet have we cause to bless him that we are in it; and let not us be troubled at the difficulties we meet with, when we see God before us, leading us in our way.

Obs. 3. The more difficult their way is, the more care God has of his people. We do not find such an expression of God's care to teach them in any other way but when they went first out of Egypt; because then their way was the most difficult, therefore God took upon him in a special manner their guidance.

Be not discouraged at your difficulties, but when you are in your way, and your conscience tells you that it is not a way that you have chosen to yourselves, look up to God for guidance, cry to him; as you find in Psal. cvii. 6, "They cried unto the Lord in their trouble;" and then, ver. 7, "he led them forth by the right way." Mark how these two are joined together; "They cried unto the Lord in their trouble," and "he led them forth by the right way." When you are in straits, cry to God in your trouble, and the Lord will lead you forth "by the right way." When we have been in the greatest straits, and have had the hardest way to go, how has God taken us up in his arms! Through God's mercy, though we be very weak, yet we are gone on a great way from Egypt, even bondage in our spiritual Egypt. It is unthankfulness in people to say, We are in as bad a condition as ever we were. What God may bring us to through the unthankfulness of men we know not; but certainly, through God's mercy, we have been led along a great way on our journey. God has taught us to go; it has not been the wisdom nor foresight of men that has carried us so far on in our way, no, we have found, apparently, we are not much beholden to the wisdom of men for that way in which we have been carried, but it is God that has come in in our straits. We see by what has fallen out, how otherwise we should have perished in our way, or even returned back again into Egypt: how often have we been ready to think, Would things were with us as heretofore! oh! such has been the peevish discontent of our spirits, that we have been thinking of turning back into our Egypt: as it was with Israel of old, though God was with them in their way, yet often they thought of returning back again. We have been ready to think of by-ways for ourselves, and every one to trust to his own devices; and what cross paths have we walked in, first one way, and then another, undoing what we have done! first engaging men, and then discouraging the same men that we have encouraged; though they have continued the same, yet our spirits toward them have not remained unchanged. We may apply to ourselves Jer. xxxi. 22, which is spoken in reference to their way, coming out of their captivity; "How long wilt thou go about, O thou backsliding daughter?" We may well say to England at this day, Oh, how long wilt thou go about? that is, shifting this way and that, and not daring to trust God in his way. We are afraid, that if we should go on in the right path in which God guides us, that we should miscarry, and therefore we go about, and that is the reason it is so long before we have our deliverance; we follow our own way, and do not submit ourselves to the guidance of God. God makes to his people an excellent promise in Jer. xxxi. 9, in reference to the guiding of them in their way from their captivity: "They shall come with weeping, and with supplications will I lead them: I will cause them to walk by the rivers of waters in a straight way, wherein they shall not stumble: for I am a father to Israel, and Ephraim is my first-born." This is a passage very suitable to the scripture we are now opening. It is a fruit of fatherly love to guide us in a straight way, and keep us from stumbling. But mark how this shall be done; "They shall come with weeping, and with supplications will I lead them;" there must we weeping and supplication, to cry to God for guidance in our way: as a poor child, if it be left a little by the mother or nurse, stands crying for support and guidance; so it should be our care, in all our straits, not to fly upon this or that instrument, but to cry to God to lead us forth by the right way. We may apply this to God's guidance of the soul from spiritual Egypt; when God brings the soul out of spiritual bondage he guides it in the way to the heavenly Canaan. You whom the Lord is bringing out of your spiritual bondage, look up to God to teach you how to go. Why? For the way on which you have entered is a hard way, a straight way, and narrow way; it has many stumbling-blocks in it, and many by-paths near it, that are very like to it: your way is a very slippery way, and you had need be taught how to go; else you may slip and fall, and grievously wound yourselves. You that are young beginners in the way of religion, be not too confident in your own understanding and your own strength. Many poor children, for want of the care of their nurses, have gotten such falls when they were children that have lamed them and made them go crooked all their days: and so it has been with many young professors of religion; because they have been too bold and confident in their own understanding, the Lord has left them to such falls that they prove but crooked all the days of their profession; and though they do go on in the ways of religion, they are but maimed and crooked professors. And truly we have very great cause to fear, that they who survive but a few years, to see the present young professors of religion live to be something old, I say, we have cause to fear that those that live to see it, will see a great many maimed and crooked professors among them; for many young ones in these slippery times, that venture so much upon the ice, upon doubtful things that they understand not, get such falls and bruises as are like to stick to them as long as they live. Oh, let young ones take heed of venturing upon doubtful things, let them look up to God to make their way plain before them, and not lean to their own understandings, lest (I say) they meet with falls attended by bruises that they may feel another day.

Obs. 4. Seeing God makes it a fruit of his love to teach his people how to go, when you see others slip and stumble in their profession of religion, bless God for his mercy towards you, that he teaches and upholds you in your way. As when a man is riding upon the road in winter time, it may be he sees some before him whose horses get into holes and stumble, to the great danger or even serious injury of their riders; now, if you should see a man thus falling and breaking his leg or arm, would you not have cause to bless God that delivered you from such a mishap: so, when you see professors of religion falling in the ways of their profession, O bless God that he teaches you in your way, upholds and guides you. In slippery ways you will take hold of the hands of tender women to guide them; and so God does with you: know, the whole course of your way from spiritual Egypt to spiritual Canaan, is so covered with ice and so rugged, that God is fain throughout it all to take you by the hand. Oh the goodness of God, to condescend thus to his poor creatures, to compare himself to a nurse! Oh how often would we run into harm's way (as we are wont to say) if God did not lead us!

Obs. 5. Take heed, you who are weak, and have need of teaching, that you be not wayward and wanton, that you be not foolish and unruly, and that you do not wilfully run into rugged and slippery ways. God indeed is as a nurse to teach you how to go; yea, but be not you as wayward and froward children, that sometimes tire their nurses. It is more difficult to teach some children than others how to go, they are so froward and wilful that, if the eye of their nurse be from them but never so little, they will go their own way. O take heed you be not among those froward, wilful children, that will still be going their own way.

Obs. 6. God's ministers and all of us should labour to follow God in this his tender care of others. We should be like our Father. God takes a delight in teaching weak ones how to go, and in guiding them in their way. Truly, we that profess ourselves to be God's children, should imitate our Father: and especially God's ministers should take a delight to help weak ones on in their way; yea, to carry them in their very arms. That which God is said here to do, is elsewhere ascribed to Moses, as in Numb. xi. 12, "Have I conceived all this people? have I begotten them, that thou shouldest say unto me, Carry them in thy bosom, as a nursing father beareth the sucking child, unto the land which thou swarest unto their fathers?" It seems Moses, though he thought it to be very hard to bear so many people in his arms, (as it were,) yet God gave that commission to him, and he did it according as he was able, carrying the people as a nurse or a parent carries the sucking child in their bosom.

Obs. 7. God's ministers must not be discouraged though they meet with those that are very froward. We are as froward in reference to God, as any can be in reference to us; and therefore ministers, when they meet with young professors, and other beginners in the ways of godliness, and find them often untoward and peevish, should not because of that cast them off; but consider, if God had cast off you because of that, what would have become of you? No, instruct with meekness even them that oppose themselves; though they kick and spurn, yet instruct them with meekness. In 1 Thess. ii. 7, we have a notable pattern how a minister should carry himself in this respect; "But we were gentle among you, even as a nurse cherisheth her children." Thus ministers should be of gentle spirits, and know that God places them to teach children how to go in their way. So we find in Tit. i. 7, that they must not be "soon angry;" ministers must not be of angry dispositions. You would be loth to put your children to froward nurses, their very milk would some way savour of them, and injure your children; it is a special qualification, and necessarily required in a nurse, that she be of a gentle and patient disposition. Now God's ministers are compared to nurses; and do not think the comparison too mean, for God himself is compared to a nurse, when he saith, "I taught Ephraim also to go, taking them by their arms."

Obs. 8. That the love and tender care of parents and nurses in bringing up children, and enduring much trouble with them, imposes a great obligation on children when grown up to requite with duty and due respect their parents and nurses; and if they do not, it greatly aggravates their guilt. You that are grown up from children, remember the care, the sorrow, and the trouble of your bringing up, and be ashamed of your undutifulness. How is it that you have all your limbs, but from the care of your parents and nurses? You are to bless God for the care of those to whom you were committed when children, and know that you owe due respect unto them for it. He is an apostate to the great law of nature, who violates charities due to parents and nurses. I remember I have read of the Pisidians, a certain heathen people, that when they were feasting at any time, the first-fruit of all their feast they would offer to their parents, as thinking it unseemly for them to rejoice in the use of the creature, without showing due honour to their parents, from whom they had their being and education. Heathens have ever condemned and punished undutifulness in children; and the law of God (we know) does punish a stubborn child with death.

"But they knew not that I healed them." Many times children, though there be a great care to teach them how to go, yet will by their very venturesome wantonness get many a knock and bruise. So it was with this people; Indeed my care was towards them, but they would go their own way, and often to their own hurt. Well, did God therefore reject them, and say, It is through your own fault that you have gotten these bruises and maims? No, "I healed them," saith God. Though they were never so froward, and got thereby many bruises, yet my pity was so great, that I healed those very wounds and bruises occasioned by their own wilfulness.

Though in the reading of this we may pass it easily by, yet it is as remarkable a scripture as most we have in the book of God. What is the reason our consciences do so misgive us, and that we are so afraid that the Lord will leave us to ourselves? Our accusing consciences tell us this, that we may thank ourselves for our state; the Lord showed us another way, but we, through our sinful frowardness, would take our own. Can we then think that the Lord will have care of us in our sores that we got ourselves by our wilfulness? Yes, (saith God,) such was my compassion towards Ephraim, that I taught them how to go; and yet they got bruises; but still "I healed them."

Obs. 9. God will not cast off his children though they get hurt; yea, though they get hurt by their own sin, yet the Lord is so gracious as to heal them. There are remarkable words respecting this in Isa. lvii. 17, 18, "For the iniquity of his covetousness was I wroth, and smote him: I hid me, and was wroth, and he went on frowardly in the way of his heart." "He went on frowardly" when "I smote him." What then? In the 18th verse, "I have seen his ways." One would have thought there should have followed, I will therefore smite him, and plague him, and make him to know what it is to deal so frowardly and perversely with me; but behold the goodness of the Lord! God's "ways are not our ways, neither are his thoughts our thoughts," for he saith, "I have seen his ways, and will heal him: I will lead him also, and restore comforts unto him and to his mourners." I will not say, I will never lead him more, because he would not regard my teaching, but go his own ways and get many bruises; no, I have seen his ways, and will heal him, and lead him, notwithstanding.

O be not discouraged when you have gone out of God's way, but be troubled and ashamed; make use of this promise; the Lord sees the frowardness of his people, and yet will heal them, and lead them, and restore comfort to them.

And, my brethren, thus has the Lord dealt graciously with us in our inconsiderate, foolish, sinful courses. How often have we in this land been brought low by them! we have been sore wounded, yea, in danger of bleeding to death, by the falls that we have got; we have often given up all for lost, as it were; men's ways have been so perverse and cross, and there has been so little hope of any good, that sometimes, when we have met together, we have even said, All is gone, we are but betrayed, and therefore there is little hope of any good. Have not we oftentimes said thus? but the Lord has come in and healed us, and that scripture in Isa. lvii. has been made good to us; the Lord has beheld the frowardness of our ways, and yet has healed us, and has led us. You have gone on in such and such ways, saith God, and you have even undone yourselves in them, and you were despised, and others squandered away your estates, and nothing came of it; well, you knew not what to do, I will lead you in ways that you do not think of, in such ways as you have the least hopes of good by, I will lead you on in those ways, and restore comfort to you. My brethren, the ways by which the Lord has this last summer restored comfort to England, were they ways that any of you thought of this time twelvemonths? Certainly, it was never in the imaginations and thoughts of men to be brought by such ways as the Lord has led us in, and by which he has restored to us comfort; the Lord saw that the old army was not the way to restore comforts to England, and he has devised other means, new-modelled our army: well, let God's healing of the bruises that we got in walking in our own ways make us thankful, and careful that we run not wilfully into any such ways any more, that we be not still more venturous and more careless; if we be, God may suffer us to break our bones; for though God be patient, and loving, and merciful, yet he has time to leave men to the perverseness of their own ways. It may cost us dear before we are healed, if God leave us; though God may not take away his love to cast us wholly off, yet we may be forced to cry again and again with David, "Restore unto me the joy of thy salvation;" "make me to hear joy and gladness; that the bones which thou hast broken may rejoice," Psal. li. David would go out of his way, and he fell so as to break his bones; Oh "that the bones which thou hast broken may rejoice." When God heals us, he expects that we should take notice of his work, and acknowledge in it his hand.

"But they knew not that I healed them." I healed them, saith God, but they knew not that I healed them.

Obs. 10. God does us much good that we know not of: "but they knew not that I healed them." I say, God does us much good that we know not of, not only in preventing mercies, but in healing mercies; we attribute our healing to this and the other cause, but it is God in the use of means, sometimes even beyond means, though means oftentimes have been used without any good result, till at last God by a secret and invisible blessing comes and heals us. We must not envy at the honour due to instruments; but certainly, by the healing that we have had this last summer, we have cause to look beyond all men and means; and though God has used means, yet we should attribute all the glory immediately to God. Oh! let not us by our pride and stoutness, our oppression, our foolishness, make it appear that we do not acknowledge that God has healed us: God stands much upon being acknowledged to be the healer of his people, because it is his glory. In bodily healings we are ready to acknowledge those that heal us; what thankfulness is given to physicians when they have been instruments of good to us! Before the cure, what would men give! all their estates, that they might be healed of such a disease; but when healed, it may be, some will neglect the physician; but only those of base spirits, for men generally are very ready to show gratitude in such a case: how gainful therefore is the practice of physicians that God makes use of to heal men's bodies! Louis XI. of France allowed his chaplains twenty shillings a month, but his physician, one John Cottière, ten thousand crowns; four crowns must serve his chaplain, while ten thousand are barely sufficient for his physician; so gainful is the practice of the latter, because men are more sensible of the healing of their bodies than the healing of their souls.

Well, any of you who have been in great sickness and distress of body, yea, and in distress of soul too, and are healed, do not now, by the inconsiderateness of your minds, and the abuse of your strength in the ways of sin, manifest that you do not know that God has healed you; both in respect of national healing, and in respect of personal healing, let every one make use of those words of David, Psal. ciii. 1—3, "Bless the Lord, O my soul: and all that is within me, bless his holy name:" and again, "Bless the Lord, O my soul, and forget not all his benefits: who forgiveth all thine iniquities; who healeth all thy diseases." Oh that we were able to join these two together now, "Who forgiveth all thine iniquities," and "healeth all thy diseases!" Healing is a mercy indeed, but how much more sweet a mercy when it is a fruit of forgiveness! God has in great measure healed the land and nation, oh that we could say that he had forgiven us! Our healing without our forgiveness will be to little purpose; and therefore, in the times of our greatest wounds, we should cry for forgiveness in the first place, and not be satisfied with any healing without forgiveness of our sins. And so particularly, God, it may be, has healed some of you, or some in your families, of bodily diseases, and has been pleased to relieve you in your sad condition; yea, but can you put both together, bless the Lord who has forgiven all the iniquities of my family, and healed all their diseases? Do not satisfy yourselves with any thing short of this; when thou findest the *one*, "all thy diseases" healed, be not satisfied except by faith thou canst see the *other*, "all thine iniquities" forgiven.

Ver. 4. *I drew them with cords of a man, with bands of love: and I was to them as they that take off the yoke on their jaws, and I laid meat unto them.*

This is a great verse, and it will be very hard to pass over it in an expository way only.

"I drew them with cords of a man, with bands of love."

Here is a fifth expression of God's love. Two occurred in the former verse, "I taught them to go," and "I healed them," and others preceded them; now here is the fifth, "I drew them with cords of a man, with bands of love." God still aggravates his mercy that they may see the aggravations of their sin. There is no such way to be kindly humbled for sin, as to see it has been committed against much mercy.

"I drew them with cords of a man."

Some understand this as if it were a proper name, with the cords of Adam, for the word is אדם a man of red earth.

But it is rather to be taken appellatively; "with the cords of a man," that is, I did not deal with them like beasts, which must be drawn or forced on with violence; my way was not thus with them, to draw them and force them on with iron chains or strong cords about them; no, saith he, I dealt with them like men, "I drew them with cords of a man." Which denotes these three things:

I. I dealt with them rationally, as men, not as beasts, and so sought to draw them.

II. I dealt with them gently, not with rigour and violence, but as a man, for they were human; so my ways were ways suitable to their humanity: as the Scripture sometimes speaks of the rods of men, I will chastise them with the rods of men, by which some think is meant, I will deal with them gently.

III. I dealt with them honourably, in a manner suitable to that respect which is due to man. I considered that they were men, made at first according to my image, that they were the most excellent creatures that I had upon the earth, and therefore I dealt with them in a way suitable to preserve the honour of their human nature, rationally, gently, honourably.

I. Consider how God dealt rationally with this people.

1. The statutes which I gave them were according to the very principles of right reason, therefore, in Deut. iv. 6, he saith, "Keep therefore and do them; for this is your wisdom and your understanding in the sight of the nations, which shall hear all these statutes, and say, Surely this great nation is a wise and understanding people. Why? Mark the 8th verse; "What nation is there so great, that hath statutes and judgments so righteous as all this law, which I set before you this day?" Mark, all the nations that are about you shall say, What nation is there so wise, that has statutes and judgments like this nation? surely then my law had abundance of reason in it, reason sufficient to convince, not only you, but all the nations round about you. "I drew them with cords of a man," that is, rationally.

2. God strengthened it with many arguments, which is some way beyond the manner of men. If the Lord had but only given forth his law, and left men to discover its meaning, it had been enough; yea, but the Lord "drew them with cords of a man," that is, added to his law many arguments and reasons to show its equity. Now men think it enough if they give out a law, you are not used to have the proof and the reason of it; yea, but saith God, "I drew them with cords of a man;" I gave them a law that had reason in it, and explained that reason: as, if we should go no further than the very moral law, see how God begins, "I am Jehovah thy God, which have brought thee out of the land of Egypt;" every word containing a reason to back the law. "I am Jehovah;" therefore obey. I am "thy God;" therefore obey. I am thy God "which have brought thee out of the land of Egypt;" therefore obey. You thus see how the Lord argues his law by the strength of reason.

3. Yea, he not only employs reason, but many persuasions, and motives, and exhortations, as man deals with man: if you read the 4th, 5th, and 6th chapters of Deuteronomy, you shall find all these, calculated to allure to obedience as well as to convince; motives and persuasions being as the "cords of a man," to draw man as a rational creature.

4. If they had any objections, I answered them all. Do you not find when you come to hear the word, that it meets with every secret objection? you can have no secret objection against any thing that God requires, but at some time or other the word meets with it.

5. Yea, I called them to reason with me, therefore I dealt with them like rational creatures; as in Isa. i. 18, "Come now, and let us reason together, saith the Lord;" see how God deals with people after the manner of men: as now, if you should fall out with a neighbour, who, it may be, is froward and humorous, when you are able to overcome your own passion, you go to him and say, I pray thee let us reason the case together, and if it be yours, take it; so God saith, Let us reason the case together, be not carried on with humour and passion, but let us come and fairly reason the case one with another.

6. God earnestly desires that they would but consider of things. In Deut. xxxii. 29, "O that they were wise, that they understood this, that they would consider their latter end!" Now when you have to deal with the froward and passionate, if by the strength of reason you could control your own passion, you would be ready to express yourselves thus, Oh that I could but find such a man exercising his reason, that he were but wise, that he would but weigh things! Thus God saith concerning his people, Oh that they were wise, and considered, and understood!

7. God pleads with them after the manner of men. In Jer. ii. 35, "Behold, I will plead with thee, because thou sayest, I have not sinned." Thou art righteous in thine own thoughts; come then, I will plead with thee, and convince thee, saith God. As now, if any wrong you, and yet will not acknowledge their fault, perhaps some of turbulent spirits will make them know that they have wronged them by casting them into prison; but God does not do so, he pleads the case with them.

8. The Lord will appeal to their own consciences whether they have dealt well with him, yea or no; he will make them to be the judges. In Isa. xlvi. 8, "Remember this, and show yourselves men: bring it again to mind, O ye transgressors:" do not be led on like beasts in your passion and humour, show yourselves but men, and do but remember, and think of it. I will leave it to you to judge: "Judge, I pray you, betwixt me and my vineyard," Isa. v. 3. And then again, "Are not my ways equal? are not your ways

unequal?" Ezek. xviii. 29. Now all these expressions are to show how God drew them with the "cords of a man," rationally.

II. He drew them gently. As if God should say, I have not driven them on with rigour, but I have dealt gently with them, like men. Indeed as to one who was always striking a youth, or servant, or man, you would be ready to say, You have not to do with a beast, or a dog, but with a man: saith God, I remembered I had to deal with a man, and therefore I dealt gently. There are these six or seven particulars, in which God expresses his dealing *gently* with them.

1. I suited myself to their very dispositions. This now is to deal in a gentle way. As a schoolmaster looks upon his scholars not as a company of beasts, but as the children of men, and therefore considers their dispositions and tempers, and, if he be a wise schoolmaster, suits himself thereto, and draws them on with such ways and cords as are suitable to human nature: so I do, saith God, I lead them gently, drawing them as "with cords of a man."

2. I observed when they were in the best temper, and have sought to work upon them then. If you that are wives will deal with your husbands like men, observe when they are in a good temper, and then seek to draw them. God does so: I observed when they were in the best possible temper, and then I came upon them to draw them with the most strength.

3. I gave them time to consider. Though they were never so untoward, yet I did not instantly chasten them, but gave them time to bethink themselves: many scriptures we might adduce on this point. Now when we fly upon others presently, without thus giving them time to consider, we deal not with them like men, but beasts; but "I drew them," saith God, "with cords of a man."

4. I hired them to obedience by my gifts. I do not only in an imperious way command them to obey at their peril, but I have come and hired them to the ways of obedience, and gave them gifts to draw them, and so I dealt with them like men.

5. When they did not obey, I considered whether it were through weakness or wilfulness, and, putting a difference between them, dealt with them accordingly.

6. In all afflictions that were brought upon them, I considered that they were but men of weak natures, and could not bear much; I did not lay on as if I were laying upon an ox, or some such creature that had much strength to bear, but I considered that they were men, and their natures tender, and I laid on my strokes gently: as you know the prophet speaks in Isa. lvii. 16, "I will not contend for ever, neither will I be always wroth: for the spirit should fail before me, and the souls which I have made." The Lord looks upon the weaknesses of his people, and therefore will not contend, lest their spirits should fail before him.

7. In their afflictions I sympathized. So you know what the Lord saith, "In all their afflictions I was afflicted," Isa. lxiii. 9. As a tender father, or wise master, if he strike the child or servant, the very blows, in a manner, will be felt by himself; but it is not so with you when you strike a beast. So saith God, when I afflicted them, it went to my very heart, and I was afflicted as well as they.

III. He drew them honourably. That is, so that the honour and respect which were any way due or suitable to such a creature were preserved.

1. My instructions ever exceeded my corrections. I never inflicted more stripes than I gave instructions. It is a dishonour to mankind for any superior to give more blows than instructions; but I dealt with them like men, suitable to the respect which is, in a manner, due to human nature.

2. Whatsoever spark of ingenuousness remained in them, I took care to preserve it. If there were but a spark of this virtue in any of them, I not only did not quench it, but took great care to preserve it in all my dealings towards them.

3. I aimed at their good as well as mine own glory in all things. Many scriptures confirm this. When you strike beasts, you do not consider of the good of the beast, but of the benefit you may derive by the furtherance of your work; but when you strike men, you should regard their good as well as your own advantage. No parent should strike a child, but with reference rather to the benefit of the child than to the gratification of their own humour: when you strike merely for your own advantage, without aiming at the good of those you punish, you deal not with them like men, but like beasts.

4. In all my dealings I still held forth hope of reconciliation upon their returning unto me. Though they deserved never so much, and I seemed to come against them in the harshest manner, yet I never so dealt against them but there was hope preserved that, on their repentance, I would be reconciled to them: this is to deal with them like men. When you, parents or governors, deal with any that offend you, never be so harsh as not to leave, though they be very evil, some hope that upon their coming in they may be reconciled to you.

5. In all my dealings with them, though they were hard sometimes to flesh and blood, yet I put a difference between them and other people. Other people were to me in comparison but as dogs, but these as men, yea, as free-men. So in Jer. ii. 14, "Is Israel a servant? is he a homeborn slave? why is he spoiled?" What! Israel a servant, a home-born slave? No, he must be looked upon as a free-man. So in Isa. xxvii. 7, "Hath he smitten him, as he smote those that smote him?" No, I look on them in a different respect, and as men, yea, as free-men, and deal with them accordingly.

6. Whensoever they began to return, I met them half way. I did not stand it out to the uttermost, to discourage their hearts, but I met them half way in all their returnings. And did not God deal honourably with them? Indeed, if you desire to treat contemptuously those who have offended you, you say, Let them wait; but if to honour others, if we see them but coming afar off, we go forth with haste to meet them, as the father of the prodigal did: so saith God, I did not deal with them in a contemptuous manner, but "I drew them with cords of a man," and honourably entreated them.

Thus you have this expression opened, "I drew them with cords of a man."

Now there are divers things to be observed on these three points.

Obs. 1. The ways of God are very rational, so that they may draw any man of understanding to love them. If man's nature were not degenerated, if we did but stand right in regard of our principle of reason, it were impossible but the ways of God should draw us, at least to an outward obedience to them: there is no reason in your ways, but there is reason in God's ways; and therefore, if you had but the hearts of men, though you had not the hearts of saints, you would be constrained to approve at least of God's ways, and drawn to an outward conformity with them. If men were not besotted with their lusts, and did but bethink themselves of the ways of God, they certainly never would be so confident in their wickedness. "If thy people," saith Solomon, 1 Kings viii. 47, "shall bethink themselves in the land whither they were carried captives:" there is so much reason in God's ways, that if one did but bethink himself. "I considered," saith David, Psal. cxix. 59, "my ways, and turned my feet unto thy testimonies." Oh, it is a great mercy to have a considering heart; and it is a great judgment of God to leave any to a slight and vain spirit, not to weigh and ponder things. Most people are led on in a continued hurry of passion, like to the horse in the battle, and no man saith, What have I done? O, couldst thou but attain so much power over thy passion and the violence of thy lusts, as to get alone and weigh God's ways, surely thou couldst not but be convinced that the ways of God are better than thy ways, they are so rational.

Obs. 2. The way to prevail with men, is to deal with them in a rational way. The way that I took to prevail with this people, was to draw them with the cords of men. Certainly the means God adopts to prevail with people are the best.

Therefore those who would prevail to bring any to adopt their views, should deal with them in a rational way: so the Spirit of God, in John xvi. 8, "And when he is come, he will reprove the world of sin;" that is, he shall come with demonstration, for so ἐλέγξει literally signifies; to convince by way of demonstration so clearly, that one cannot possibly deny. And so the apostle saith, Our preaching was ἐν ἀποδείξεί πνεύματος καὶ δυνάμεως, in the "demonstration of the Spirit and of power," 1 Cor. ii. 4: mark, "in the demonstration of the Spirit," and so in "power." This concerns ministers more especially: if ministers would speak powerfully to people, let them speak in demonstration, the demonstration of the Spirit indeed it must be, there is a spiritual reason in the Scripture. Ministers must not think to scare men into the ways of godliness, though I know sometimes God makes use of the bare terrors of the law; but the main thing whereby ministers must have hope to do good to their people, must be by preaching convincingly, to overcome their very reason as far as possible, and to set the law of God so before them, that if they will but judge between God and their own souls, they shall condemn themselves, and approve of God. That ministry is likely to be the best soul-saving ministry, which meets with every objection of their hearts, and at every turn reveals their secrets. O remember you preach to men, and therefore make use of that reason which you find in Scripture. I know reason alone will never do it; but yet when God works to the salvation of souls, he works upon them after the manner of men, and therefore the ministers of God, that are co-workers with God, should work in a manner correspondent.

And not only ministers, but magistrates too, must labour to draw them with the cords of men, that is, by reason rather than violence, in difficult cases of conscience. In such things as men cannot be convinced, and yet are not wilfully ignorant, they must not make prisons and fines their arguments, these are not the cords of men: indeed in civil matters, that carry in their very face the light of common equity and justice, magistrates need not stay to persuade or convince, but may enforce obedience by punishments; but in all things of a more dubious nature, and that, from their connexions and consequences, are difficult to be understood, and are controverted even among godly and wise men, there they must proceed with tenderness and caution: people must first be instructed and informed, and then, if they do not oppose wilfully, but seem to desire to understand, and yet cannot, they must not be dealt with in a way of violence. That is not to deal with men like men, to force them to things for which they discern no reason, and with all their labour are unable to understand; certainly in such cases forbearance must be shown; and especially the rather, because that Christ, by an apostle, has charged us not to yield to any thing in matters of religion, till we understand the reason of it; "Whatsoever is not of faith, is sin." When Christ saith thus, that we must not receive a thing because such and such men enjoin it, till we examine and understand it for ourselves; surely, then, the uttermost that the power of violence and force may do is this, to make men examine things; but it should proceed no further. And so parents and masters should use conviction rather than correction.

Obs. 3. It is a great aggravation of men's sin, to stand out against reason, not to be drawn by these "cords of men." Many stand out against the ways of God, while yet their consciences fly in their faces and condemn them. Oh what a wretch thou art, that though the Lord has sought to draw thee with the "cords of a man," with reason, and has convinced thee, yea, has gotten the cords into thy conscience, and would pull thee to himself, thou wilt not be drawn by them! this is indeed an aggravation of your guilt. Some vain reasonings can draw man to sin as a cart-rope: They "draw iniquity with cords of vanity, and sin as it were with a cart-rope;" that is, their vain reasonings that they have for their sin, twisted together, make a strong cart-rope to draw iniquity. Oh! shall not God's cords be as strong as the devil's cords or man's cords? Many there are, though God seems to draw them with these "cords of a man," yet whose lusts are so strong, that, like pampered horses in a team, they will break the cart-ropes, break all their harness to pieces; their unruly spirits even say like those in Psal. ii., "Let us break their bands asunder, and cast away their cords from us." Well, thou shalt one day be held by the cords of thine own sin, (as the Scripture speaks,) and thy conscience shall lash thee with those cords of conviction that failed to draw thee. Shall not the cords of conviction draw thee from thy sin? they shall serve to be as whips to lash thy soul even to all eternity. Know that the rules of right reason and Scripture reason shall stand, when thou, and thousands of such wilful fools as thou art, shall perish eternally. And these are the notes for God's dealing in a rational way.

Obs. 4. Man's nature, if not degenerated, is loving and gentle. So saith God, "I drew them with cords of a man;" that is, gently, in accordance with man's nature, as fair means will work upon it rather than rigid severity: hence, in ordinary speech, kindness is called humanity, Let men have some humanity in them, that is, let them be courteous; to be courteous and to show humanity we use as synonymous. So that the nature of men, though fallen, yet if not twice dead, and overcome by its corruptions exceedingly, is naturally kind and gentle.

O, you that profess religion, labour to be eminent in courteousness, in gentleness, in humanity; know that grace, though it does elevate above humanity to Christianity, yet it does not take away humanity. No, it raises it higher; and therefore, seeing there is something left in man's nature of gentleness and fairness, surely those that have grace and a principle within to curb corruption, should covet earnestly these most excellent gifts.

Obs. 5. We should draw our relations with gentleness. Seeing that gentleness is the cords of men, we should use it to draw on to goodness those whom we desire. Ministers, parents, governors, neighbours, observe the dispositions of those you have to deal with, suit yourselves to them, labour so to gain their hearts if possibly you can; and that they may have good thoughts of the ways of godliness, manifest no bitterness, nor sourness. Did not God gain upon your hearts by gentleness? But if God did come in a harsh way to your apprehensions at first, yet know, there is no such distance between you and your neighbours, your children, or servants, as there is between God and you; therefore it is for you to deal with your fellow creatures in a gentle, kind manner. If a hunter would get his game, he does not make a hooting and noise, but steals on them gently and quietly; and so, if you would win souls, you must attract and allure them by "the beauties of holiness." Learn this, you that are of harsh tempers, who do nothing but attempt to terrify to good, saying, If you will not do thus and thus, I will deal with you thus and thus: O, try what gentleness will do; do not so domineer over others as to think that it is for you to satisfy your wills upon them, but labour to be all things to all men.

And never chastise children nor servants but with grief; and put a difference between weakness and wilfulness; and let your hand be heavy on them only upon mere necessity, when all other means have been tried unavailingly: God deals thus with his people.

Obs. 6. Gentle means rejected, aggravate sin. As now, if you can bring gifts to a man, you can quickly blind his eyes: we have found that man's nature, even in the place of justice, loves gifts; they are the cords of men, suitable to their natures indeed. Now God does thus (as I may so speak) bring gifts; but if God shall not prevail with his gifts, this will be a great aggravation of your sin.

Obs. 7. Always preserve the honour of inferiors. It is a rule that will be very helpful to those that have young ones to bring up; though the fault be great, yet put them not to so much shame before others, as they shall have no esteem or honour to lose, they will grow desperate then; and so long as the bridle of shame is on them, you may keep them from much evil. And this is the reason that your gaol-birds never almost come to any good; why? because they have no honour to lose, all is gone already, and therefore they grow desperate. Nothing is more suitable to a man's nature to deter from evil, than the fear of the loss of respect and of honour; and therefore the very doom of the damned at the day of judgment is thus expressed, they shall rise "to shame and everlasting contempt," Dan. xii. 2. "To shame," that is as much against human nature as any thing: and therefore you that have to deal with men, take heed how you deal; always keep such a hand over them, as those that are under you may see that they have yet some honour to lose; do not deprive yourselves of such a means to bridle your children or servants. Some of you have for your servants persons of good birth in this city, divers have children well born and well educated; use them accordingly, draw them with correspondent cords: if you be of meaner birth and education, and had hard breeding, and were drawn by iron cords, do not think to deal thus with others who have had better breeding than yourselves, but deal with them fairly, with due consideration of what suits their quality and condition.

Obs. 8. How will the shame and confusion of men be aggravated hereafter, who disregarded God's using them in an honourable manner! This is the way to bring shame and confusion upon you for ever, as hereafter men and angels, and your own consciences, shall say: Just it is with God to punish me with eternal shame and confusion; why? for God had respect to me when I lived, and dealt with me honourably, seeking to draw me with the cords of a man; and it is just that now he should give me my portion among devils and reprobates, and that he should no more regard me as a creature, but rather hate and abhor me as a devil, for I would not regard his dealing with me as a man. This will justify God in that wrath which will one day fall on you.

Obs. 9. Not to be drawn to our duty but by violence and strength, is bestial. Brute beasts can roar and cry out when the pain is upon them; and so it is with many men, they never cry out of their sins, never fear God, never yield to his hand, but only when his strokes are upon them, then they cry out and bellow like beasts. Well, God delivers them; but they turn to their lusts as formerly, and as soon as they are delivered forget their vows and covenants with God; they sin again, and God comes upon them again, and again they bewail their sins: Oh that we had spent, say they, our time in praying, and in lamenting our sins, which we spent in such and such company! This is when God's hand is upon you, and the effect of the hearing of his word: to be drawn by the word is to be like a man; not to be moved but by blows evidences a bestial and brutish heart. Charge yourselves with this brutishness of spirit; I fear some of you have cause to say, In all the course of my life my heart has never yielded to God, but just when his strokes have been upon me. I beseech you, brethren, deal with God like men; God deals with you like men.

Obs. 10. The Lord deals with us suitably to our nature. "I drew them with cords of a man." O let us then deal with God, as far as we are able, suitably to his nature. What! does God regard us as men? let us then regard him as God, let us glorify God as God. When the Lord has to deal with us he considers we are men; when we have to deal with God, let us consider he is God; and as the Lord is pleased to condescend to us as men, O let us labour to ascend to him as God.

"With bands of love."

"Bands," that is, thick cords; not only with "cords," as before, but thick cords, so בעבתות here translated "bands" signifies; for its primitive עבת means to wreath, and to thicken with wreathing; as you see those that make cords and lines, take their hemp and form one wreath, and then another, twisting many of them together, so as to make a strong cord.

"With bands of love;" that is, with such bands as have many wreaths in them, many plies joined together to make them a strong cord, a cord as strong as a cart-rope: so I find the same word used in Isa. v. 18, where it is said, "Woe unto them that draw iniquity with cords of vanity, and sin as it were with a cart rope!" The word וכעבות there translated "cords," is the same that occurs in the former part of our verse, the "cords of a man;" but now the other, "and sin as it were with a cart rope," is the same word here rendered, the "bands of love;" that is, a thick rope, as of a cart, with many wreaths in it: so that though the former word, "cords," in your English, seems to imply as much as the latter, "bands," yet, according to the Hebrew, this is especially emphatical. As indeed when we come now to open the "bands of love" with which God did draw this people, we shall find many cords wreathed and twisted together to bind them fast to God. An expression somewhat parallel to this occurs in Jer. xxxi. 3, "With loving-kindness have I drawn thee."

I drew them "with bands of love;" that is, I used them in a loving way; if love could have gained them, could have overcome their enmity, and bound them to me, they have wanted no love, saith God: whereas their sins deserved the bands of iron, instead, they have had "bands of love."

If you ask me what were those "bands of love," by which God drew this people of Israel unto himself, I answer,

1. Separation from all other people. God did wonderfully separate this people from all the nations in the world, to be a people unto himself, and that out of love; and this was a great fruit of love, and a strong wreath to bind them, that God should set his heart upon this to be his own people above all other people in the earth. In Exod. xxxiii. 16, "Wherein shall it be known that I and thy people have found grace in thy sight? is it not in that thou goest with us? so" (saith he) "shall we be separated, I and thy people, from all the people that are upon the face of the earth." It is in your books, only, shall be separated, but ונפלינו signifies wonderfully separated, we shall be wonderfully separ-

Mirificemur præ omnibus pop. Munster.

ated from all the nations of the earth. Indeed the Lord did wonderfully separate this people from all the nations of the earth, and this only out of love, and not from any excellency he saw in them. "The Lord did not set his love upon you, nor choose you, because ye were more in number than any people; for ye were the fewest of all people," Deut. vii. 7.

Obs. 11. The Lord does not always stand upon the greatest number. Indeed our argument is, that so many go in such a way, and so few in another, and so surely God is most like to approve of that which the majority adopt. No, God does not always stand upon number: "I did," saith he, "not choose you because you were more in number than any people, for you were the fewest of all people;" therefore it was only love that made the Lord choose this people at first, and separate them from other nations.

2. Election of the parents and their seed. "I chose you, and your seed also." And this was a great mercy: If I had but only set my heart upon yourselves, it had been somewhat, but it was upon you and your seed, so as to bring you and your seed into covenant with me. There are two twists (as I may so say) in this band of love, that he should choose them and their seed, and bring them both into covenant, for thus you have it in Deut. iv. 37, "Because he loved thy fathers, therefore he chose their seed after them;" and in Ezek. xvi. 8, the text saith, "Thy time was the time of love; and I sware unto thee, and entered into a covenant with thee, saith the Lord God, and thou becamest mine." The time was a time of love; and that made the Lord to enter into covenant with this people. God showed it was a time of love indeed, that he would take such a people as this was, and enter into covenant with them.

3. God's setting his heart upon them to delight in them. I made them my portion, my inheritance, my treasure, the dearly beloved of my soul, my glory, a royal diadem to myself; I could show you Scripture for every one of these expressions: Deut. vii. 6, "The Lord thy God hath chosen thee to be a special people unto himself;" a "special people," and he gives them all those epithets. Surely these are "bands of love."

4. Pitying them in their afflictions. If so be at any time they were in any afflictions, I pitied them, and looked upon them with the eye of mercy, and relieved them, and redeemed them out of their afflictions: "In his love and in his pity he redeemed them," Isa. lxiii. 9.

5. God engaged all his attributes for their good. I set on work all my wisdom, and my power, and my mercy, to do them good above all nations, working great wonders for them. Now for this we shall not need to cite any particular passage, the whole story of God's carrying them from Egypt through the wilderness to Canaan, and there providing for them, is a sufficient testimony. So, in Isa. lxiii. 9, we named before God's redeeming of them, he adds this too, "and carried them all the days of old." The Lord never was so glorious in his power towards any people as towards them, the right hand of his power and excellence was stretched out for them, Exod. xv.

6. A continued watchful eye over them. "With bands of love." I had a continual watchful eye over them and their land, mine eye was upon their land where they dwelt for good, above all other lands that were upon the earth: "A land which the Lord thy God careth for: the eyes of the Lord thy God are always upon it, from the beginning of the year even unto the end of the year," Deut. xi. 12. Canaan was a land that God cared as little for as any place of the earth before his people came into it, a land wherein God was as much dishonoured as in any other place; but now when his people came into it, it is a land that his eye is upon, that the Lord takes care of, from the beginning of the year to the end of the year: such respect did God show to his people.

7. He gave them his oracles, the revelation of his will. This was another notable fruit of the love of God to this people. "In Judah was God known: his name was great in Israel." "He showeth his word unto Jacob, his statutes and his judgments unto Israel. He hath not dealt so with any nation: and as for his judgments, they have not known them," Psal. cxlvii. 19, 20. This was a notable privilege that Israel had above all other people. In Rom. iii. 1, it is asked, "What advantage then hath the Jew? or what profit is there of circumcision?" In ver. 2, the apostle replies, "Much every way:" the Jew has much advantage every way above all other people of the earth. Why, wherein? "Chiefly, because that unto them were committed the oracles of God." Other men had the book of nature, they could see God's name, as it were, written in the characters of that book; yea, but the special things of God, the counsels of God concerning the eternal state of the children of men, were not then revealed: but saith he, I gave to this people my oracles, I revealed to them those counsels of mine concerning man's eternal state, I opened to them my whole heart and soul, all that I would have known to the children of men for that time I opened to them. Oh this is a band of love indeed, to have the oracles of God committed to a people.

8. The Messiah was to come of them. This was the eighth twist (as it were) in these "bands of love," to make them a great cable to bind them unto God. I set my heart so upon, as to have the Messias to come from them, in whom all the nations of the earth should be blessed. I rather chose this people than another to have my Son to be born of them, to be of their stock.

9. A law, the sum of which was nothing but love. I showed before, that the law of God had strength of reason in it, and so God "drew them with the cords of a man," that is, his law was rational. So here he draws them "with bands of love," gives them a law, the sum of which was nothing but love, as thus: What is the sum of the first and second table of the law? The sum of the first table is, "Thou shalt love the Lord thy God with all thy heart, and with all thy soul;" and the sum of the second table is, "Thou shalt love thy neighbour as thyself:" so that love is the sum of the whole law.

10. God gave them more than any else could offer. He outbid all temptations. Whatsoever good, pleasure, delights, honour they could expect in following any thing else, I showed them that they might have all these and much more in myself; there was nothing they could have in following after any of their false worship, but I made it appear that they might have as much in myself, I outbid all temptations in order to encourage them in my ways. Accordingly, throughout the whole Scripture, we find the Lord propounding himself to his people as a lovely object, on purpose to draw their hearts away from all other things which might seem to be lovely, that he might have the whole soul to himself.

11. He heard all their prayers. Whensoever they were in any want, if they did but cry to me, I heard them. "What nation is there so great, who hath God so nigh unto them, as the Lord our God is in all things that we call upon him for?" saith Moses, Deut. iv. 7.

12. And lastly, I have done so much for them, that it cannot be conceived that I should have done more. "What could have been done more to my vineyard, that I have not done in it?" Isa. v. 4. Let any one speak what more love they could conceive posssible from a God to his people than I have shown. So that put all these together, and you see how God drew this people "with bands of love." Now this for the explication: our observations from hence are,

Obs. 12. Love has strong bands; yea, "strong as death," Cant. viii. 6. None are so strongly bound together as friends that are bound in love. The bands of nature are not so strong as the bands of love. "A friend is nearer than a brother," saith the Scripture. The bands of love are the strongest bands, they are a twisted band. For,

1. Love is in itself a lovely thing to behold, there is an amiableness in love to attract the eye and the heart. So Cant. vii. 6, "How fair and how pleasant art thou, O love, for delights!" How fair and how pleasant is love! Take "love" for the affection of love, it is fair and pleasant for delights; and when the beloved is called by the name "love," it shows that love is very amiable and very beautiful.

2. Love has in it much sweetness, much power to insinuate itself into the heart. Base, adulterous love we know has a great deal of power to insinuate itself into the heart; so in Eccl. vii. 26, the hands of the whorish woman are called "bands;" how much more attractive power must dwell in true, gracious love!

3. Love is generative, love has a great generative power to beget love. Augustine saith, There is no greater provocation to love, than to begin to love. Love can draw iron hearts. *Magnes amoris amor*, love is the loadstone of love, it will draw love, and, wherever it is, beget love.

Nulla est major ad amorem provocatio, quam prævenire amando. Aug.

4. Where love is got into the soul it commands all the faculties and understanding. Look, what a man loves his powers are exercised about: if a man love his sin, his understanding will work for it; oh what subtle arguments will men have for the sin they love! a man's heart will be very subtle to argue for the object of its regard. So, on the contrary, when once the Lord has taken the heart with love, this love commands the understanding, and then all reasonings are for God, and the soul hearkens to none that are against him, or against his ways. If a man's heart be taken with love to a woman, he will hear nothing against her; but if his mind be alienated from her, then every report against her he will readily receive, and even aggravate to the uttermost. So when a man's heart is taken with the things of God and of religion, it will hear nothing against them; but if the ways of God cease to please, then they are glad if they can hear any thing that makes against them. Love commands all the faculties of the soul, the understanding and the thoughts; it commands the will and affections; it commands the body, and estate, and liberty; it commands all that a man has, or is, or can do. Love has the absolute commanding power of all; oh! love has strong bands.

5. Love makes all services for the beloved delightful; it not only commands, but renders the obedience easy: "I will rest in my love, and rejoice over them with singing," saith God. When the heart is once taken with love, I say, it not only does that which is good for the object of its regard, but does it with delight.

6. Love knows not any bounds, it never sets itself any limits, but would even infinitely prevail.

7. In its service love knows no weariness. The soul is never weary in the actings of love. Men that love their pastime will sit up all night and never be tired; so with those who love the ways of God, though the flesh may be weak, yet the spirit flags not.

8. Love is strong, so that it stands out against all oppositions, nothing can prevail against it. "Love is strong as death." "Many waters cannot quench love, neither can the floods drown it," Cant. viii. 6, 7.

9. Love rejoices in suffering; not only delights in doing, but delights in suffering. If one that loves another shall suffer for him whom he loves, he will rejoice in those sufferings.

10. And lastly, Love seeks not its own, suffers not itself to be itself, (as it were,) to be at its own disposal. The heart once taken with love is no longer its own, but gives itself into the possession of that which it loves. Join all these together, and you may see that love has strong bands.

Obs. 13. Let us do as God does; that is, labour to cast the bands of love upon those with whom we have to deal. It is God's way to bind his people to himself, "I drew them with bands of love." Then, saith God, I have enough, I have them secure enough, if I get them within the bands of love. Oh, if you would draw any to you, let it be by love. You that are ministers, and especially appointed to the work of drawing others to God, what should you do? Open the love of God to them, present the grace of the gospel to souls, labour to work upon their hearts by all the mercies of God; by the mercy of God tendered to them, received by them, and bestowed upon them: there is no such way to draw souls to God as this. "Repent, for the kingdom of heaven is at hand," Mark i. 15, that is, the preaching of the gospel. The first of all Christ's sermons, and of his disciples', was, "Repent, for the kingdom of heaven is at hand." As if he should say, O sirs, look about you, consider your ways; there is a glorious kingdom now at hand, a kingdom of righteousness and mercy, wherein the glory of the grace of God is revealed to the children of men in another way than ever formerly. This is the way to bring men to repentance. True, it is good to use all means, to show the greatness, and the justness, and the holiness of God, and the like; but the prevailing argument above all to bring men to repentance is, that "the kingdom of heaven is at hand:" and indeed we would do so if we considered that repentance is a gospel grace; it comes not by the law, the law recognises it not, but the gospel, and therefore to present the love of God to the children of men as manifested in the gospel, is the way to draw to repentance. We have a notable story in the Book of Martyrs, as also in Eusebius's Ecclesiastical History: John the apostle having committed a young man who was very hopeful to the care of a bishop, the youth afterwards proved to be very wicked, associated himself with thieves, and so became in time the captain of a company of thieves and robbers; with them he lived in the mountains, wholly bent on slaughter, murder, and extreme cruelty. After this, John comes to this bishop, and bids him restore to him the charge which he and Christ had committed to his custody; whereupon the elder, looking down with a heavy countenance, sobbing and sighing, said, He is dead. John inquiring when, and by what kind of death, he answered, He is dead to God, for he is become the captain of a company of thieves in such a place. The apostle then, rending his garments in great sorrow, said, Prepare me a horse, and let me have a guide. And so he rode in haste, and, being come to the place, is stopped by the thieves' watch. The apostle neither flies nor resists, but saith, For this purpose came I hither, bring me to your captain. He, in arms, stood awaiting his approach; but when he perceived that it was John, he was struck with shame, and fled away. The old man, forgetful of his years, pursues him flying, and cries, My son, why fliest thou from me thy father, unarmed and old? O son! tender my case; be not afraid, as yet there remains hope of salvation, I will undertake for thee with Christ. And thus he runs after him, crying, that yet there was hope of mercy and pardon, and that he would die for him. He, hearing this, first stood still, turning his countenance to the ground, next shook off his armour, then trembled for fear, and wept bitterly; so that this "band of love," this affectionate concern of the apostle, broke his heart, and he returns back and

Book of Martyrs, lib. 1. Euseb. lib. 3. cap. 20.

falls weeping upon the neck of John, and became afterwards an eminent Christian.

Whatever may be thought of this story, yet certainly there are no such bands as these of love to draw the hearts of people to God. Have you to deal with stony hearts? the way is to lay them upon the soft pillow of the gospel, and so you may break them. Lay a stone upon a stone, and it starts from you and does not break; but if you lay it upon a pillow, you may presently break it with a hammer. The word is compared to a hammer; yea, but we must labour to lay the hearts of people upon the pillow (as it were) of love, upon the grace of God in the gospel, that is the way to subdue them. None are so bound to God as those who are bound to him by love: those that are bound to God by fear, unmixed with love, their bands will not hold, they will seek quickly to break through their restraints; none (I say) that are held to God by the bands of fear alone, but will seek after any occasions to break those bands, and if they can but get any opportunity, they will, and commonly at last do, break through them: but now, those who are held by bands of love, are bound for ever unto God.

Obs. 14. When men cast off the sweet of their sin by the sweet of the love of God, then they will never return to their sin again. If it be only the bitterness of the law, and its punishment, that makes them cast off sin, they will be ready to turn to their sin again; but when it is cast out by the sweet of love, when one sweet enters for another, such hold on their way. Austin, speaking of a sweet of sin, saith, Thou, Lord, didst cast out those sweetnesses, and thou didst enter in thyself instead of them, who art more sweet than any pleasure whatsoever. And it was from hence that he held on so in his way, because God, casting out the sweet of sin, instead thereof did himself enter into his soul. Oh, said he then, how sweet it is to want those sweetnesses! No marvel though grace be so persevering, and we read so much of perseverance, especially in the times of the gospel, because that there are none truly converted to God, but have that sweet come into their souls through love, which is more delightful to them than all the sweet they had by sin before.

Aust. Confess. lib. 9. cap. 1.

Never be afraid, you whom God is beginning to turn to himself, never be loth to part with any sweetness you had in the ways of sin, for by turning to God you shall find a thousand times more in God and his ways. Oh, they are things that you love, and you are loth to part with them; yea, but when you are turned to God, God will be as lovely to you as ever any thing in the world was. If the ice be but broken over-night by the husbandman, when he comes the next day he finds it frozen up again; but let the sun dart on it his warm beams, and then it runs down in streams: so the breaking of the heart by the terrors of the law, is but like the breaking of the ice with a pole by the husbandman to give the cattle drink; but when the love of God comes to the heart, then the corruptions of the heart dissolve, even as the ice dissolves when the warm beams of the sun rest upon it.

The way, therefore, to gain the hearts of men is by love. And we should the rather do it, because it is the great design of God in the gospel, to manifest his love to the children of men; he has in it opened his heart, and the treasures of his love. What is the gospel, but the manifestation of the treasures of the love of God? those eternal loving-kindnesses of God towards mankind are all displayed in the gospel; and no minister can be a faithful minister of the gospel, who does not endeavour to open this heart-love of God to the children of men in Jesus Christ. Oh! it is a pleasant work to be a minister of the gospel in this respect, to be always searching into the treasures of love, and to array them before souls to win them unto God.

And then, likewise, if you have to deal with men, you must labour to draw them with the bands of love. In Phil. ii. 1, 2, " If there be therefore any consolation in Christ, if any comfort of love, if any fellowship of the Spirit, if any bowels and mercies, fulfil ye my joy, that ye be like-minded, having the same love," saith the apostle. Oh! let it be through love that you come to be " like-minded;" and do not think to force men into the same mind, by using bitter language and expressions to them if they differ in judgment from yourselves. But if there be any love, be of the same mind; labour to get into one another's hearts, if you would do good one to another. A minister, if he would do good to his people, must labour to get into their hearts, that the people may love him: therefore it has been observed, that your wrangling ministers and bitter men, who, if they be but crossed in any thing, presently vent their own bitterness, never do any good at all; but those that are willing to deny themselves, and to suffer for the cause of the gospel, prevail most. So, if you would do good to any of your kindred, do what you can to get into their hearts; labour to win their love, and so you may be a means to draw them to the ways of God: if once they be persuaded that you love them, you may then reprove any thing that is evil in them, and persuade them to any thing that is good, they take nothing ill from you. Therefore men of sour and bitter spirits labour under a great disadvantage in compassing their designs; if they speak any thing, though never so good, yet is it rejected, because that people think it proceeds not from love. But on the other side, let one of a sweet and loving disposition speak never so harshly, yet the party will take it well, because he knows he loves him. Oh! these "bands of love," my brethren, they are mighty strong. When you meet together in any society, if you would effect your object, do not seek to get your will by wrangling and frowardness, but by "bands of love." I confess there are some of such perverse spirits, that the more advances are made, the further they recede, they have even lost all ingenuousness; but if you have to deal with men whom you believe to be gracious and upright, then do not think to gain any thing from them but by love.

These " bands of love," in the text, the devil seeks to break; his great design is, to make men have hard thoughts of God and his ways, to make them believe that God hates them, and that though they have some good things from him for the present, yet that the heart of God is not towards them; and so he labours to make a separation between the soul and God. In like manner he strives to break the "bands of love" between Christian and Christian. That was a fearful judgment which we read of in Zech. xi. 14, when the staff that was called " Bands" was broken, intimating, as a judgment, the disruption of the brotherhood between Judah and Israel, and the ruin attendant on their rejection of Christ. When the staff of " Beauty," "the covenant which God had made with all the people," was broken, the "other staff, even Bands," "the brotherhood between Judah and Israel," was " cut asunder."

My brethren, never were the "bands of love" more broken among Christians than they are now. We read of " bands of love," but what is become of them? They are broken. They were in former times twisted in so many wreaths, (as I told you the original signifies,) that one would have thought they could never have been broken; but now, on every occasion, we find they snap asunder. Oh how justly might God bind us with iron bands, seeing that the "bands of love" will not bind us! God has cut the cords of divers of our yokes asunder, and has broken the bands of the oppressor, and now, behold, we break the "bands of love."

Oh! unworthy wretches that we are, we look with a jealous eye one upon another, every one shifting for himself, there are no "bands of love" in our hearts. Of the wicked it is said in Scripture, "there are no bands in their death," that is God's patience; but woe to us, we live without bands! and that results from our sin, and the wrath of God upon us. In Eccl. iii. 8, it is said, there is "a time to love." When is the time? Certainly, if ever there were a time to love, this surely is it.

O Divine love! whither art thou gone? hast thou left the earth as unworthy of thy beauty and glory? Oh that thou wouldst come again into the hearts of the saints, and bind them together! The want of the "bands of love" every one complains of; Oh those soul-refreshing and soul-ravishing meetings that we were wont to have! But, especially, we find the bands of public love quite gone, and quite broken: read but over 1 Cor. xiii., and see the effects of love there, and by that you will find the "bands of love" quite gone. Love, the scripture tells us, "thinketh no evil," it puts the best interpretation possible on all things. Now surely there is great want of love amongst us, that when men, in the uprightness and sincerity of their hearts, desire to find out the mind and will of God, and that merely out of conscience, because they dare not go any further than they see the mind of God go before them, therefore they shall be judged to be a stiff-necked people, and to be the great hinderers of reformation. Is this the best interpretation that possibly can be made of things? Can there be no other grounds why they differ from their brethren, but merely stiff-neckedness? how if it shall be owned by Jesus Christ at the great day, that it was out of sincerity, because they desired to know the mind of Jesus Christ fully, and yet they could not see what their brethren say they did? We should put on every thing the best possible interpretation. Love "hopeth all things," and "beareth all things;" now for such public striking against any such forbearance, and crying out that we would have a toleration of all things in religion; for this is their great argument, whereas they know in their consciences that their brethren do join with them in the doctrinal part and in the main points of religion, and the things wherein they differ are matters of no such great moment, but may be forborne with peace enough if men's hearts were peaceable and still; now to infuse that into the people's heads, that if forbearance be shown in any thing, there must be a toleration of all things, surely this is not a fruit of love, this is not that which the Holy Ghost saith, that love bears all things. I am loth to proceed, lest it should serve as an occasion of stirring up any spirits, and so hindering the fruit of love: let me say, on the contrary, there may be too eager censure the other way, that is, we may too readily accuse such as are of a different way and judgment, that they do it altogether out of their self-ends and self-aims. I verily believe, that those brethren on the other side who do differ, may be conscientious in their way, and do it out of zeal to God, and to what they apprehend to be truth; we should apprehend one another so, if we see corruption of heart manifested in nothing else but merely in the judgments and opinions. Now if both could but thus judge each of other, that they both are upright in what they pursue; one side imagines that their party follows God's mind, and the other that the side which they espouse is the Lord's side: let us judge now that they do it in uprightness, except it appears some other way, then we should quickly close and join hearts together, if we had such upright opinions one of another: the more it is the design of the devil to break those bands of brotherhood and of love, the more should we labour to unite together; we should countermine Satan.

And you who are superiors, labour you to gain your inferiors by love. Do not say of them, They are of untoward dispositions, and how can my heart be towards them to love them? Oh! none of your inferiors are more untoward to you than you are to Christ; and Christ, if he should not love you because of your untowardness, what would become of you? Now consider this, when your servants and children are untoward, Why should that hinder love, whereas my untowardness does not hinder the love of Christ to me? I remember to have read of Monica, Austin's mother, that some of her neighbours who had Christian husbands wondered how she and her husband, who was a heathen, managed to live so lovingly together. Our husbands, said they, are Christians, and yours a heathen, and yet you live more lovingly with him than we do with our husbands. She answered them, It may be, when your husbands do any thing that provokes you, you are presently froward with them; but I labour to overcome my husband by love, and so to gain his heart to me, and thereby we live so lovingly together; Christianity teaches me to perform the duties of a wife to my husband, though he be a heathen. I verily believe there are many godly couples, who for want of love live worse than when one yoke-fellow is carnal. You will say, How can that be? Yes, though there be godliness, yet there may be such frowardness and passion as may cause wonderful disturbance: but on the other side, where there is godliness and love, there is such an overcoming with love, that though the man be wicked and never so harsh, yet, having the nature of a man in him, he will be overcome by love. Would you then be united more than you have ever yet been? Labour to cast the bands of love one upon another; let the husband study how to overcome his wife with love, and so the wife the husband, and then there will be a sweet union indeed. And so for masters and servants, there should be love there to unite one to another: though the master be above the servant, yet the master should account his servant's regard a happiness: there is not such a distance between you and your servants, as between God and you. Oh! it is a sweet thing when a man can say in his family, I bless God, all my family love me; and whatsoever they do, they do it out of love to me. It may be you are harsh towards your servants, and you will make them do what you command them to do, and they dare not do otherwise: yea, but what is that? do your servants love you? do they do all for you out of love? you might have as much and a great deal better obedience from your servants than you have, if it sprang from love. And so likewise in a family, when one servant loves another: as it was said of David in 1 Sam. xviii. 22, "all his servants love thee," all Saul's servants did love David; so servants should labour to live so in families that all the other servants should love them.

But you will say, They are so wicked, how can I hope to have love from them?

Yes, though they cannot love thee because thou art godly, yet godliness has something in it common to the excellency of man's nature.

Yea, and magistrates should labour to gain those subject to them by love. As the greatest in a family, if he be a lord, or an earl, should not think it too much to gain a servant by love; so those intrusted with the greatest power in government, should not think it too much to gain the affections of their meanest subjects. We see it was thus with David, 1 Chron. xxviii. 2, "Then David the king stood up upon his feet, and said, Hear me, my brethren, and my people." What a sweet expression respecting a great prince! "Then David the king stood up upon his feet, and said, Hear me, my brethren, and my people;" he did not sit down magisterially, and say, My people, and you that are my subjects and servants, I command you to do thus and thus; but he stands up to them, and saith, "Hear me, my brethren, and my people." This was a way to gain the hearts of people to him. You know Absalom sought in a false way to steal away the hearts of people by a gentle carriage. I have read of John the Second, of Portugal, that he chose for his emblem a pelican, because when her young have been bitten with serpents, she feeds them with her own blood, and thereby cures them: thereby he would testify his readiness to let out his blood for the good of his subjects, for the healing of his subjects; he would not feed upon his subjects' blood, but he would rather let out his own blood for their good. This is the commendation of a prince, not to seek to feed upon his subjects' blood, and to raise up his honour and prerogative by shedding it; but to love them so as to be willing to let out his own blood for their good, if required. The maxim that some have laboured to infuse into princes, I had rather be feared than be loved, is a maxim beseeming only tyranny, and no way suitable to an ingenuous mind. Certainly that man, be he what he will, who is actuated by such a principle, is a man of a sordid and base spirit; a man of a generous, ingenuous mind would rather be beloved than feared. Let every man seek to gain another by love. If you strive to gain any but by love,

Timeri quam diligi malo.

1. You are not likely to prevail.
2. If you do prevail, there will be more previous trouble than fruition will repay.
3. When you do prevail, and men do as you would have them, they dare not do otherwise; yes, but they hate you: what good is it for a man to have his will upon another, if in the mean time he hate him?
4. If you do not prevail by love, they will do no more than just needs must. And this is the reason, indeed, why hypocrites are hide-bound toward God, why they do so little for him; God has never gained their hearts by love, but only by fear, and therefore they will do no more for God than of necessity they must; whereas (as I said before) love never propounds bounds.
5. If you do not get them by love, they watch for all opportunities to fling off. Now what a poor gain is this, to gain one with a deal of trouble, and for him to do what I would have him, and yet to hate me, and to do no more than needs must, and then to watch for all opportunities to appear against me! Wherefore, my brethren, to close this, let us follow after and provoke one another to love; you will find sweetness in your own love, sweetness in the very exercise of it, and sweetness in the fruits of others' love.

Obs. 15. As love has such bands in it, let us make use of the love of God to bind our hearts to him. You have heard that love has bands; you have heard too that we should do as God does. Is this then God's way? Oh! let us make use of all the love that ever God has shown to us to gain our hearts to him.

This would be a large theme to speak of, if we should attempt to open to you what the love of God has been to you, how much love God has shown to the nation, and to ourselves, to gain our hearts. Oh the many twists of this cord! it is a strong cord indeed to bind us to God. This is that which God seeks by all his love, to work our hearts to love.

Not to speak now of the love of God to you as to creatures, nor as to men; but to speak a little of his love to you as you are saints. I shall show you very briefly what strong cords of love God has cast upon you, to gain your hearts to love him. God's love, then, to you is,

1. Eternal. Before ever you were born the bowels of God yearned towards you (as I may so speak with holy reverence). God was twisting these bands of love from all eternity that he might gain your hearts; and thinking that at such a time such and such persons shall live upon the earth, I will make preparation by such bands of love now as, when revealed to them, shall unite and fasten them close to myself. It was love from eternity. Oh the transactions that were between the Father and the Son from all eternity to manifest love to your souls! the great counsels (I say) that were transacted between the Father and the Son before the world was, were about these your bands of love.

2. Elective and separating. When he left many thousands, he set his heart upon you. Mal. i. 2, "Was not Esau Jacob's brother? saith the Lord: yet I loved Jacob." So, wert not thou of such a family? and yet thou seest how God has cast off a great part of that family, and yet has he loved thee! Wert not thou such a one's brother, such a one's sister, that remained wicked and ungodly, and, it may be, died so? and yet God has loved thee; he has passed by so many great ones in the world, and so many of thy kindred, and rather pitched his love upon thee. It is a love of choice, and therefore might the rather gain thee to thy God.

3. Free. "I will love them freely," Hos. xiv. 4. "The Lord did not set his love upon you, nor choose you, because ye were more in number than any people; for ye were the fewest of all people," Deut. vii. 7. God there would manifest his love to his people to gain their hearts to him: "The Lord did not set his love upon you," saith he, "because you were more in number; but," as in ver. 8, "because the Lord loved you." It is a strange mode of arguing, "The Lord did not set his love upon you because you were more in number," but the Lord did set his love upon you "because he loved you." He could go no higher; there can be no other reason why the Lord should love you, but because he did love you. We are wont to say, It is a woman's reason to say, I will do such a thing because I *will* do it. Now if any of you would have a reason why God loved you, why thus, He loved me because he loved me. The Lord did not set his love upon you for this reason; but he did set his love upon you because he loved you; so it is a free love. Oh let the freeness of it be another ingredient, so as to bind your hearts unto him.

4. God so loved you that he gave his Son for you. "God so loved the world, that he gave his only begotten Son," John iii. 16. Sometimes it has been in the thoughts of men, whether there might not be more worlds than this our world. Certainly God in his infinite power might make a thousand worlds more glorious than this, such worlds that the meanest creature in them might be as high in excellency above the sun, as the sun is above a piece of earth. But now this we may know, let there be never such excellent creatures made, they cannot have a greater fruit of love than mankind has from God. Oh! this is the love of God to mankind, and calls aloud to the children of men to love God; here is a fruit of love beyond that shown to angels, for the Lord took not upon him the nature of angels, but the nature of man.

5. He has given himself too, as well as his Son. Not only given the Second Person in the Trinity, but himself. He does not think it enough to give heaven and earth to thee to be thy portion, but he will make himself thy portion, he will be thy God. You would think it a great matter if God should say, Well, all this world I will give for thy portion; yea, that I may give thee a testimony that I love thee, I will make another world for thy sake, and make thee the lord of it all: but in that God has given thee his Son, and given thee himself, this is a greater degree of love; and the soul of man, were it so enlarged as it might be, yea, so as grace does enlarge the hearts of the saints, such a soul would

say, Lord, what wilt thou give me, if thou givest me not thy Son, if thou givest me not thyself? though I be less than the least of thy mercies, yet, except I have thyself as my portion, all else is not sufficient for me. Well, saith God, that thou mayst know that my heart is set upon thee for good, I will give thee my Son, I will give thee myself and my Spirit. Oh, what love is this to the children of men, that ever we should live to have our ears filled with such a sound from heaven!

6. God so loves his people, that, in comparison of his saints, he cares not what becomes of all the world. Thus, Isa. xliii. 4, "I have loved thee; therefore will I give men for thee, and people for thy life." If thy case be so that it shall not be well with thee without great evils that shall come upon the generality of the children of men, and people, and nations; I do not so much care for them, (saith God,) my heart is upon you, so much so, that, in comparison of you, I care not what becomes of all the world. Oh the love of God to his saints!

7. A pardoning love. "Unto him that loved us, and washed us from our sins in his own blood," Rev. i. 5. You do not hear it said, that Christ has loved us and purchased great kingdoms for us, has made us lords, and earls, and countesses, and so loved us; no, but "unto him that loved us, and washed us from our sins in his own blood." Now it is a good argument that the love of God is upon you, if you account this to be a great fruit of love, to wash you from your sins by the blood of Jesus Christ. Surely if he will do so much for you, as shall cost him so dear as his own blood, he loves you; the love of Jesus Christ broke through the difficulties, for when there were such transactions between the Father and Son about redeeming the soul, God said, If thou wilt take upon thee to deliver them from their sin, thou must come thyself and be made a curse for their sins. And Jesus Christ replied, Lord, thy will be done in it, yet let me deliver them from their sin; though I lose my life, though it cost me my blood, though I be made a curse, whatsoever it cost me, yet let their sins be washed from them. He has washed us from our sins at the price of his own blood. Oh the love of Christ to his saints! what bands of love have we here! I have seen some who, that they may twist and bind their cords the more fast, will wet them: the cords of the love of Jesus Christ are wet with his own blood.

8. A conforming love puts loveliness on the creature, even God's own nature. If one could say any thing greater than has been said, this, one would think, should be very high and great: for God so to love us, as to make us partakers of the Divine nature; so to love us, as to put his own life into us, to enable us to live the very same life as himself does; so to love us, as to put his own image upon us; oh, this is the love of God to his saints!

9. He loves thee with the very same love wherewith he loves Jesus Christ himself. Thus John xvii. 26, "That the love wherewith thou hast loved me may be in them," saith Christ to the Father. Oh to have the same love as that with which the Father loves Christ! Is not this a strong band to bind thy heart to God? If God had loved thee only so as to give thee an estate and honours here in this world, this were no other than the love which the reprobate may have; and will this love satisfy thee? Oh the difference between the love of God to his saints and the love of God to other men! he loves the great ones of the world, that are wicked, with no other than the love wherewith he loves a reprobate; but he loves the saints with the same love wherewith he loves his Son; and this love will bring thee one day to be one with the Father and with the Son: is it not then a strong band of love to gain thy heart to himself?

10. A love of communion. God delights in communion with his saints: God indeed does all this for his saints, puts the Divine nature and the life of God into them, and sets so much love upon them; why? that he might have a people to enjoy everlasting communion with him. I would fain, saith God, have some creatures that might live with me, to enjoy communion with me; that might live to see my face, and to behold all the glory that I intend to manifest to all eternity. O blessed God! hast not thou the angels that are with thee to enjoy thy glory, to have communion with thee? No, saith God, but I would have these poor creatures that are so low and mean in the world, I would have them raised up to enjoy communion with myself. This is the end of God's bestowing any grace upon his saints, it is that he might raise them to enjoy communion with him, and to delight in him, and he to delight in them; that he might have creatures to communicate the treasures of his goodness to, and that thou mightest communicate what thou art able to him. Surely Christ does not account himself full without his saints; and therefore you find in Eph. i. 23, that the church is called "the fulness" of Jesus Christ; and therefore he prays, "Father, I will that they also, whom thou hast given me, be with me where I am," John xvii. 24: I shall not account myself full except they be with me, and see my glory. Oh the love of Jesus Christ to his saints!

11. A sweetening and sanctifying love. Thou mayst see love in every thing; though thou hast now less of the creature than others have, yet thou hast it out of love; on all thy mercies thou mayst see the eternal love of God to thee. The Lord from all eternity saw that such a kind of life was the best calculated to further the eternal good he intended for me, and therefore he has chosen to place me in this condition. Oh how sweet may the life of any be when they can reason after this manner, Well, this condition in which now I am in, the Lord from eternity saw the fittest condition to work my heart to himself, and therefore it is that I am in this estate rather than another. And then thou findest daily by experience how the Lord has helped thee in thy straits, and heard thee in thy prayers, and answered thy desires. This I told you, in the opening of the text, was a fruit of love to the people of Israel, and so it has been with thee.

12. An overcoming love. God's love overcomes all our unworthiness, both before and after conversion. He foresaw all, yet still his love was not quenched toward thee, but saith the Lord, My love shall break through all. Many times you set your love upon some who prove untoward and unworthy, and you think with yourselves, Could I have but foreseen this untowardness they should never have had my love: but now the Lord foresaw all thy ill requitals, and yet it did not hinder the love of God towards thee.

13. In the love of God there is the love of all relations. As now, the love of a father towards a child; the Lord takes upon him the relation of a father: the love of a husband; the Lord takes upon him the relation of a husband: and the love of a friend too, a friend "that sticketh closer than any brother."

14. God's love is an everlasting and unchangeable love. This crowns all, his is a love that shall never be quenched. He that the Lord loves, he loves unto the end; "he will rest in his love," Zeph. iii. 17; Jer. xxxi. 3. If thou knowest that he has loved thee in his Son, thou hast hereby an "everlasting consolation;" let heaven and earth meet together, let there be what changes and alterations there will, yet there is "everlasting consolation" for thee, if thou knowest but this love of God, 2 Thess. ii. 16.

Now, my brethren, all this I have done that your hearts may be gained unto God. And what wilt thou do now? Wilt not thou now love the Lord thy God? shall not all this love of God to thee in Christ constrain thee? "The love of Christ constraineth us," saith the apostle, 2 Cor. v. 14. "O love the Lord, all ye saints;" if the Lord has thus loved you, love ye the Lord, all ye his saints. Then God is love himself, he is the element of love; and whither should love go but up to its kindred element? Air desires to be in its proper place; and earth will descend to its proper place: the proper place of love is God, God is (as it were) the element of love, for so the Scripture saith, "God is love; and he that dwelleth in love, dwelleth in God," 1 John iv. 16. O labour to be rooted and stablished in love: "That ye, being rooted and grounded in love, may be able to comprehend with all saints what is the breadth, and length, and depth, and height; and to know the love of Christ, which passeth knowledge," Eph. iii. 17—19. Being rooted in love, thereby ye come to comprehend with all saints the breadth, and length, and depth, and height, and to know the love of Christ, which passeth knowledge. Neither the strength of natural parts nor learning so teach us the love of Christ as love; get but your hearts "rooted and grounded in love," and you will come to understand the glorious things of the gospel in another manner than ever you did. And mark what follows, "that ye might be filled with all the fulness of God." Had we not such an expression in Scripture, we should not dare to make use of it. What! for a poor creature to be filled with "God," to be filled with "the fulness of God," to be filled with "all the fulness of God?" This is the reason why Christians are so scant in their obedience, and empty in their spirits, because they are not acquainted with this "breadth, and length, and depth, and height" of "the love of Christ." O know that God prizes thy love, and is satisfied with nothing but thy love. In Cant. vii. 12, "There will I give thee my loves," saith the spouse. When thou comest to the ordinances to hear the word, to receive sacraments, or to prayer, yet if thou comest not to give the Lord Christ thy "loves," it is nothing; "There will I give thee my loves." Christ prizes love at a high rate; and that love which will serve for other things, certainly will not serve Christ. He loves thee too little (saith Augustine) who loves any thing besides thee, or will not love that thing for thee. You may love wife, and children, and friends, yea, but you must love them all for God; when you see any thing lovely in them, think it is but a beam of the loveliness of God. And thus I have endeavoured now to raise your hearts to God by love: the Lord has cast bands of love upon your souls; oh that, by the ministry of his word this day, these bands may be somewhat strengthened, that you may go away with your hearts more strongly than ever united to the love of God!

But there is one point more observable in these "bands of love" by which God draws people to himself.

The scope of the prophet here in mentioning these "bands of love," is to aggravate their sin; from whence,

Obs. 16. Nothing more aggravates sin than that it is committed against love. God has three bands to bind us to obedience.

1. The band of his law.
2. The bands of afflictions.
3. The bands of love.

But now to break the bands of the commandments, and the bands of afflictions, and the bands of love too, this aggravates sin very much.

O thou sinner! charge thy sin with this aggravation. What! sin against such a God, such love? Oh what a vile heart have I! Augustine saith, The spirit is too hard, which, though it will not bestow, yet will not requite love. O let not there be such a hardness in the spirits of the saints. Thou didst not begin with God to love, thou didst not begin to bestow love; be not so hard towards God as not to requite love. Do not we see how base, adulterous love can gain upon men's hearts? what strong bands that love has! The giving of gifts and bribes, what bands they are to tie men's hearts, and hands, and tongues! And shall not the love of God, and the fruits of that love, be a stronger band to tie thy heart unto him? Nothing goes more to the heart of man or God than the abuse of love; a man can better bear the abuse of his money, the abuse of any thing, than of his love. God's Spirit is grieved with his saints: we do not read that the Spirit of God is grieved with the wicked; God may be "angry with the wicked every day," but not grieved; but when the saints sin against him the Spirit of God is grieved, because their sins are against love. When thou sinnest against God, the Lord looks upon thee, as Cæsar once upon Brutus: What! thou too, my son? What! thou whom I have so loved? What! break all those bands? When we read in the 2nd Psalm of the kings and princes of the earth, who said, "Let us break their bands asunder, and cast away their cords from us," we think that is great rebellion; but for thou that professest thyself to be God's, it is a greater evil to break these "bands of love." O thou, my son, my child, thou on whom I have bestowed so much love, yet thou to sin against me! When thou art committing any evil, conceive with thyself as if God were looking upon thee, and pleading with thee, by all those fruits of his love that ever thou hast received from him; and wilt thou yet sin against him for all this? We read in Luke xxii. 61, 62, when Peter had sinned, Christ did but look upon him, and he "wept bitterly:" oh! Peter saw love in the looks of Jesus Christ; and therefore we know, when Christ afterwards came to him, he pleaded with him with this argument of love, "Lovest thou me?" and "lovest thou me?" Oh! when he saw the eyes of Christ so sparkling with love, and then considered that he had sinned against that Christ who had so loved him, had broken all those "bands of love," then "he went out, and wept bitterly." The word in Mark xiv. 72, is ἐπιβαλὼν, breaking out in weeping; so it may imply the force employed in doing any thing; he did break out, break out in weeping, he was not able to bear it, his heart burst even in sunder, when he considered how he had burst asunder the "bands of love." What! after such manifestations of mercy and goodness, such warmings of heart in communion with Jesus Christ? O my soul! what canst thou find in any ways like God's ways? canst thou find the like love and the like sweetness in any as thou hast done in God? yet for all these unkind, unloving dealings, God follows thee with love, his heart is yet open unto thee. As a man may go from the sun, and yet still the beams of the sun follow and warm him; so the hearts of the saints do many times decline from God, yet they have the warm beams of love following after them to draw their hearts again to him. Oh! return, return into this bosom of infinite love, here thy soul may have everlasting embracings.

"And I was to them as they that take off the yoke on their jaws, and I laid meat unto them."

Here is a fruit of love in delivering them from their bondage. As a husbandman who is merciful to his beast will not tire it too much with hard labour, but takes off the yoke, lifting it up with his hands, and gives it food; so did I, saith God, I did not tire Ephraim with labour and servitude. When you were in Egypt, and often afterwards when under your enemies' yokes, I freed you from your bondage; as the husbandman, when the beast has been ploughing and begins to be hot, lifts the yoke up to cool the neck that the beast may refresh itself.

"As they that take off the yoke on their jaws."

Because of some instruments, some bridle that was fastened to the yoke that was on their neck and put into their jaws. Therefore this phrase, "As they that take off the yoke on their jaws."

Luther on the place understands this of that spiritual ease which there is in the yoke of Jesus Christ; and so saith, The Lord by his Spirit helps us to obey; he does not only command, and tell us what to do, but assists us with his Spirit, and gives us power, and lifts up the yoke, and bears it together himself with us; and hence saith Christ, "My yoke is easy, and my burden is light." Indeed it is an easy yoke in comparison of the law: the law saith, Do this, and live; do not, and die: the law takes advantage upon every infirmity, it admits not of endeavours without performances, it gives no strength to what it commands: but the yoke of Christ is easy; Christ "continues strength;" there is never a command without an appropriate promise of strength, as an artery that runs together with the veins. And Christ accepts of endeavours; his yoke is far easier than the yoke of the law.

We must not think this too far-fetched, because we find that the Holy Ghost in the New Testament interprets the beginning of this chapter concerning Christ, which we would never have thought to have been meant of Christ, "I called my son out of Egypt." Now if so be that God had an eye to Christ in the words, "I called my son out of Egypt," why should we not think that Christ might be also referred to, when he saith, "I was to them as they that take off the yoke on their jaws;" I delivered them from the yoke which neither they nor their fathers could bear, and I brought on them the more easy yoke of the gospel?

But though the Holy Ghost may have had an eye to this, yet that which is primarily and literally meant is, the deliverance from oppression, I delivered them from the oppressions that were upon them. Whence then the observations are,

Obs. 17. Deliverance from oppression is a great mercy. Oh what ease is there in it! how does it cool our necks! "I have broken the bands of your yoke, and made you go upright," Lev. xxvi. 13. We had once heavy yokes upon us, that made us stoop, we stooped under them; but through God's mercy these bands of our yokes are in a good measure broken, so that we may go upright; and woe to us if we go not upright now! In Ezek. xxxiv. 27, "They shall know that I am the Lord, when I have broken the bands of their yoke, and delivered them out of the hand of those that served themselves of them." My brethren, if ever God manifested himself to be the Lord towards us, it has been in breaking the bands of the yokes that were upon us, and in delivering us from those who served themselves of us. We were under a proud and cruel generation of men, that minded themselves, and cared not what became of the consciences, estates, liberties, or lives of men, if only they could have their humours and their lusts gratified; and what means could we see for the deliverance of ourselves from their yoke? But the Lord has appeared; and then, saith the text, "They shall know that I am the Lord;" if we did not know that God was the Lord before, yet now we may know him. And the truth is, such have been the wonderful works of God towards us in the breaking of our yokes, that methinks it were enough to convince an atheist; those of you who have been heretofore troubled with temptations of atheism, the strange ways of God towards this nation in freeing of us from the yokes which have been upon us, may convince you of a God, may make you say, Surely there is a God in heaven that beholds the ways of the children of men; "the Lord, he is God." Then "they shall know that I am the Lord."

Oh that upon the manifestation of God in this way of mercy we may come to know that God is the Lord! The Lord might have forced us to have known that he was the Lord by laying more grievous yokes upon us, by bringing us under more dreadful evils than we have ever yet experienced; but the Lord has rather been pleased to choose another way, to make us to know that he is the Lord by taking our yokes off from us. This God has done.

Obs. 18. To grow wanton after deliverance from yokes is very sinful. This arises naturally from the scope of the context here, which is, to aggravate their sin so much the more; as if he should say, I have taken off the yoke from your jaws, and yet now you are wanton, and kick and spurn with the heel against me. What! now when we come to have a little more liberty, and begin to feel our necks freed of those yokes that were upon them, shall we begin to frisk, and spurn, and kick, and that against God himself, who has taken the yoke from off us? Oh, this is very dreadful. What! to abuse our liberty from bondage to all manner of licentiousness in horrid and wanton opinions, in wicked and abominable practices? certainly this is an ill requital of this fruit of love, in lifting up the yoke from off our jaws. This is a very great evil which we are this day guilty of; if ever there were a people guilty of this evil, of kicking and spurning against God so soon as he has taken off the yoke from their jaws, then we are at this day. Could any have believed, if it had been revealed from heaven but six years since, that within six years this people of England should be delivered from those sore yokes under the burden of which they cried to heaven, yea, that the Lord would work in a miraculous way to deliver them; and yet, upon their deliverance, there should be such wantonness, such horrid, blasphemous opinions, and wicked, licentious ways, even among the very professors of religion; could it have been believed? Certainly if our godly forefathers that were under the yoke, and that cried to God for deliverance, were to rise out of their graves now, and hear a full narration of all that liberty which God has granted to his people in England, in the breaking of all those yokes of tyranny, both in the civil and in the ecclesiastical state, they would presently think that they should see wonderful, glorious results from all this in England; but if, after conversing for a little time with men, they were to hear such monstrous opinions, and to see the extreme licentiousness and wantonness in the hearts of men, as expressed in their actions, they would be ready to spit in the very faces of their children, to disown with contempt those that now live in such times as the present. The wantonness of our hearts in abusing our deliverance is very evil in these respects:

1. It hardens our adversaries. Our former oppressors, the prelates and others, will not they say, (or do not you give them occasion to say,) Now you see what is the fruit of casting us out; was there such wantonness before? were there such horrid opinions when we had power? We kept down all such things, in our time of authority we could easily curb them; but you see what extravagancies there are, how men run wild, as soon as our power is taken from us. By this means they are hardened: and others that are of a prelatical spirit are hardened, and begin to think, Surely the other is the better way. And indeed if this be a good argument, if the keeping men in union, and suppression of errors by violence, prove the truth of any way, or of any government, it may as well prove prelatical as any other, for we know that they kept men by violence from venting such notorious errors; but shall we, because there is not this tyranny upon us, be more erroneous, and more wanton in our spirits?

Omnes licentia deteriores sumus.

2. It darkens the glory of this great work of God.

The Lord has been pleased to magnify his name in the deliverance of these kingdoms from the yoke; now what should be the care of all the people of God, but to seek to magnify the great work of God, to make it beautiful and glorious before the eyes of all? But now, by this wantonness and licentiousness, men do darken the glory of God, and obscure its lustre and beauty. In Psal. cxlix. 4, the Lord promises to beautify the meek with salvation; "He will beautify the meek with salvation:" now the Lord has wrought so towards us as to beautify us with salvation, and indeed there is a great beauty in the salvation which he has wrought; but this does (I say) darken the glory of God, and takes away the beauty of the work of God in our salvation. What! has God done all this for us, that men might turn wanton, and run wild into monstrous opinions and blasphemies? Oh, woe to thee! how unfit art thou to live in such a time as this is, to darken the glory of such a glorious work as God has wrought for us here in England!

3. It deprives others of just liberty. It is on your account who are so wanton, and run so wild in your opinions and in the looseness of your lives, that the discreet, and wise, and holy, and peaceable, who desire to make use of their liberty in Christ, must be denied it for your sakes. Whatever denial they have of that liberty which they would use in a gracious and peaceable way for the honour of God, will one day be laid to your account, for by your wantonness it is occasioned.

4. It may bring the yoke on us again, or be the means of bringing others under heavier bondage.

5. It justly prejudices rational men against liberty, and inclines them to think that they shall do God good service by laying heavy yokes upon men who thus dishonour his name. If ever, instead of the great strings that have tied yokes upon you, you should have lesser strings, and these meaner instruments of oppression should be multiplied to tie still heavier yokes upon you, thank yourselves, you are the cause of it. "The yoke of my transgressions is bound by his hand," Lam. i. 14. The Lord may justly bind the yoke of your transgressions upon you. Oh that God would humble us for the abuse of our freedom from our yokes! Oh let us take heed of this, and say with ourselves, Surely this is not the use that we should make of our deliverance; no, but rather this use, we will rather so much the more willingly take the yoke of Jesus Christ upon us. In Exod. xii. 25, after the people of Israel were delivered from the yoke of Egyptian bondage, presently it is said, "ye shall keep this service;" speaking of the passover, that was to be kept upon their deliverance from Egypt, "ye shall keep this service." The word there for "service" is עבדה the same that is used sometimes for their service and bondage under the Egyptians; as if the Lord should say, You were once in service indeed, there was a service that the Egyptians required of you, a servile service it was, and your necks were under it; now I will work thus miraculously to deliver you from that servility, and you shall keep this my service, which is a great deal better than the service under your enemies. And indeed this should be the use; we were slaves to our adversaries, let us be willing now, seeing we are free-men, to be servants of Jesus Christ, and to take his yoke; but the growing wanton upon the removal of our yoke is a great aggravation of sin. "Because thou servedst not the Lord thy God with joyfulness, and with gladness of heart, for the abundance of all things; therefore shalt thou serve thine enemies which the Lord shall send against thee, in hunger, and in thirst, and in nakedness, and in want of all things: and he shall put a yoke of iron upon thy neck, until he have destroyed thee," Deut. xxviii. 47, 48.

Obs. 19. Oppression of others after deliverance from oppression is a crying sin. If this be a mercy that we should bless God for, that we are delivered from the yokes of men, and the abuse of it in our wantonness be a great sin, then it must needs be an aggravation of our guilt, to begin to lay yokes one upon another. If it be the mercy of God to take off your yokes, we should seek to take the yokes off from our brethren, to make their ways as easy to them as we possibly can, and not devise means to pinch their consciences; conscience oppression of all oppressions is the most grievous. There was heretofore a generation of men, who studied what would pinch conscience most, and that which they found most likely to do so, they would urge to the uttermost upon men; this was devilish; I hope we have not many so vile as these were. Though such and such opinions and ways may serve our turn, we should consider whether they may not be burdensome to others.

Well, but though they be burdens, if they be truths, why should they not be urged?

Nay, suppose they be truths, yet, except they be necessary, let not men be instrumental in imposing them upon others: if a necessity exists, then no plea can be admitted. Some men, however, are so happy (if I may so call it) that they have a latitude in their judgments, that which way soever the times turn they can find out a distinction to help themselves, that so their fair necks should never come under a yoke: it is their singular good fortune that their judgments always suit with the times.

I will not condemn such men, for possibly it may be God gives them to see further than others do; but yet, by this they have ease: but now, were these men ingenuous, they should consider their brethren thus: I have a latitude, and I could conform myself to the complexion of the former times, as, now times are changed, I can to the present; but some others, whom I have reason to judge as faithful and as gracious as myself, have no such latitude; it falls out unhappily for them, for in former times their judgments could not suffer them to do what was enjoined them, they were fain to suffer, and to be deprived of estates, and livings, and whatsoever they had; well, now the times are changed, it happens that their judgments cannot conform to the alterations the changed times bring along with them; and yet surely this arises not from frowardness, nor perverseness, for take *these* men in all things else, I find them as conscientious, as spiritual, as myself. Alas! must they now suffer, and shall I add to their afflictions? shall my hand be used to lay the yoke on them and to press it hard? God forbid; I will rather study, though I will not yield any truth, but stand to defend whatever I am persuaded in my conscience is a truth, yet I will rather study as far as I possibly can to ease them, and to make their lives comfortable. I know God has given them ability and hearts to do him service, and it may be as much as I; oh why should they be hindered and discouraged in their work? I will study what latitude there may be for them. This were somewhat like, this were ingenuousness indeed, this would truly savour of a good spirit, and be a gracious testimony of your thankfulness to God for breaking off the yokes that were upon you. My brethren, when our yokes are taken away or lifted up, we must have regard to others as well as ourselves, and not think or say, Let them bear, let their necks bear; oh no, what are our necks more than theirs? If God pities his people and will lift up the yoke, let us do what we can to put under our hand to relieve others, although we bear somewhat ourselves. Some men glory in imposing burdens; but it is not such a glorious thing to lay yokes upon others, the glory is in lifting up the yoke from off them. This is the glory of God, to take off the yoke from the jaw and from the neck. Christ professes his "yoke is easy," his "burden is light;" oh! let not ours then be hard and heavy, if Christ's be easy. And especially in these days of our fasting and prayer, oh! let us be very careful to lift up the yoke from off our brethren as far as possibly we can without sin. "Is not this the fast" (saith God) "that I have chosen? to loose the bands of wickedness, to undo the heavy burdens, and to let the oppressed go free, and that ye break every yoke?" Isa. lviii. 6. "Is not this the fast that I have chosen,—that ye break every yoke." And in the 9th verse, "Then shalt thou call, and the Lord shall answer; thou shalt cry, and he shall say, Here I am. If thou take away from the midst of thee the yoke." Still mark how God urges this removal of the yoke, when you come to fast: Is this the fast that I require, to do thus and thus? no, saith he, but "to undo the heavy burdens, and to let the oppressed go free, and that ye break every yoke:" and again, if you shall do so, "Then shalt thou call, and the Lord shall answer; thou shalt cry, and he shall say, Here I am." God stands much upon this in the days of our fasting, that we lay no burdens and yokes upon our brethren, but that we do what we possibly can to take off yokes, that we may be able to appeal to God, Lord, thou knowest that I do as much as I can, and I pray that thou wouldst direct me in mine endeavours to render comfortable the lives of those whom I believe to be faithful and conscientious.

This is not to give liberty to every kind of licentiousness and blasphemy, but when I see that certain things may consist with godliness, and godly and peaceable men have many doubts among them, and especially seeing I hold these my present views but a short time, and did not see heretofore as now I do, I will do what I possibly can with a good conscience, that my brethren may enjoy thy ordinances in what liberty thou wilt afford unto them. This savours like the spirit of a Christian indeed.

And, likewise, you that are in any authority, seeing God accounts it his glory to take off the yoke from his people, O, be you tender towards them that are under you; as magistrates, as governors, as parents, as masters, lay not, my brethren, too heavy yokes on your children and servants: fathers should "not provoke their children to wrath," and masters should be gentle towards them that are under them, knowing they have also a Master in heaven. Give them therefore whatever liberty may consist without sin, even outward liberty; keep them not continually at work, but afford them some times of recreation and refreshment. True, your holy-days are taken away, but surely there is no such likely way to bury them in oblivion, that they should never be thought of again, as to have some set times for servants and children to recreate themselves. It is, too, the only way to keep the sabbath pure; for if they have no recreation during the week, they will have it on the sabbath, or return once more to their former superstitious holy-days. The beast must not always be ploughing, sometimes the yoke on his jaws must be taken off.

"And I laid meat unto them."

Faciam eos edere quietè. Luth.

Luther saith, I so wrought for them, that they should eat their meat quietly: as if the prophet should say, You did not provide for yourselves your meat, God prepared it for you, and came and laid it before you. Thus God laid meat before them when he rained manna from heaven; when the quails were he provided them. Whence,

Obs. 20. Mercies prepared, provided, and laid before us, are to be prized. When we receive a mercy, I say, that did not cost us much, but is prepared and set before us, it is to be prized.

How many of you have all your mercies prepared for you! when you go abroad on business, you take no care for provision at home in your families, you do but rise and dress, and go abroad, it may be to a sermon, or other company, and return home again; you have your tables spread, and find full dishes upon them, without any care of yours, all is prepared for you. O, consider the mercies of God towards you in this thing. Whereas many poor people are fain, before they can get bread for their families, their wives and children, to work hard; but the Lord lays meat before you. God is to be acknowledged in this.

אט a נטה descendere fecit.

The propriety of the word is, I made it to descend; it came down from heaven, it was neither too high nor too low, but it came just to you, fitted for you: which teaches us further,

Obs. 21. In receiving our food, we must look up to heaven. We are more beholden to the heavens than to the earth for our bread. God is to be acknowledged in that "he satisfieth the poor with bread," yea, and that he satisfies the rich with bread; the richest of you all are to see how it comes from heaven: I made it to descend. I say we should look from whence our very food descends, it descends from heaven. Lift up thine eyes to heaven when thou art eating meat; be not as the swine under the tree, that looks downward to the acorns, but never upward towards the branches of the tree from whence the acorns fall; but look up to heaven from whence thy meat and thy provision did descend.

Obs. 22. The service of God's people is easy, and their provision bountiful. "I was to them as they that take off the yoke on their jaws, and I laid meat unto them." Now the service of many of your servants is hard, and their provision very penurious, you would have them do your hard labour, and yet provide little food for them; oh, this is the basest of all cruelties, to put servants to hard labour, and yet not to provide comfortably for them for their food.

But, my brethren, the main thing that I would note from hence is, How great are the mercies of God to us, who has eased our yoke this day, and laid meat too before us! My brethren, who would have thought four years since, that there would be civil wars for almost four years together in our land; and such cruel, bloody wars, and so general throughout the whole kingdom; and that yet we should at this day have provision so plentiful as we have? Did not all say, even at the first year when the wars began, Surely things will be very scarce? many began to lay in corn and other provision, and we had cause enough to fear; but behold the bountifulness of the love of God, that has eased our yokes, and has laid meat before us, that "the poor is satisfied with bread," and there are "no complainings in our streets;" we have not only our bread, but our tables filled. What difference do you see in the tables of men now from former times! If a stranger should come into this kingdom, hearing what miserable wars there have been, (as bloody and cruel as ever were in any kingdom,) and yet see every man's table so filled, he could not but stand and wonder: certainly strangers think our condition to be far more sad in respect of provision than it is. Let us not then be wanton with our plenty. We were wont to say, If we might have but bread and cheese and the gospel, it were good cheer; now, my brethren, we have food of earth, and the bread of life too. What! is it sweet to be freed from outward bondage, and to have meat laid before us? how sweet is it then to be freed from spiritual bondage, and to have the food of life laid before us! yet this is our condition. Our blessing specially consists in this, in having our spiritual yokes taken off from us, and having the bread of life laid before us in a more plentiful measure than ever we had: was there ever a time that this city had so much meat laid before it for the soul, as at this day? The misery of other parts of the kingdom is your mercy; the Lord grant that you do not loathe and despise your manna: God has ways enough to cut you short.

Ver. 5. *He shall not return into the land of Egypt, but the Assyrian shall be his king, because they refused to return.*

To give you first a short paraphrase of the words, (for there is no difficulty in them,) and then the notes of observation: it is as if the prophet should say,

Howsoever he thinks to help himself with ease, to shelter himself in Egypt, yet he shall not, but he shall go into captivity into Assyria; for all the means which have been used would not bring him to return.

The observations then are,

Obs. 1. That which hardens men's hearts against threats in their sin, is some expedient that they have in their thoughts; Let the worst come that can be, yet I have such and such a relief.

My brethren, it is a great mercy of God to be so wholly taken from all carnal props, from all vain shifts and hopes, as to be thoroughly convinced that there is no help in any thing, or in any creature, in heaven and earth, but only in turning to God, and casting the soul down before mercy; If that saves me not, I am undone for ever. When the heart comes to this, God is working in a gracious and merciful way: I see my sin, my affliction that is upon me, and feel it; though my heart would be shifting this way and that way, yet God has convinced me nothing can do me good, I am lost and undone whatever course I take, except I return to God, and humble my soul before him, and seek his face, and obtain his mercy.

Obs. 2. A stout heart cares not whither it goes, rather than it will return to God. "He shall not return into the land of Egypt." It was a very strange perverseness to think of this shift, to go back to Egypt. Why, was not Egypt the place of their bondage, and the Egyptians still retained their cruelty? and yet they thought of this help, that they would turn to Egypt rather than to God. So the prodigal will rather go to the swine to feed upon husks, than to his father. And some stubborn children care not what miseries they suffer, rather than they will come and humble themselves to their parents; they will hang themselves, and drown themselves, and seek their fortune, as they are wont to say, rather than be persuaded to come in and submit themselves; no, never as long as they live, though they die, yet will they not: and thus their hearts are stout. But while they think they are stout against their parents, they are stout against God too, and God has ways to bring men's stout hearts to yield.

Obs. 3. Stubborn hearts, though God be dealing with them in mercy, will, foolishly and desperately, if any thing cross them, wish to return to their former condition of misery. If you make any thing that God does an argument to a stubborn heart for duty, if it pleases him not, he will reject all that is done for him, and say he had rather be as he was before, Let me go into Egypt again. This is their unthankfulness, that because they are vexed and crossed in some one thing, they will foolishly and desperately wish that they were returned to their former condition.

Oh, thus it is with many of us; how foolishly, how wickedly, have we thought and said it was better with us before than now, let us return to our former condition! this is thy folly and thy desperate wickedness. But saith the text, "He shall not return," though he thinks of returning: as if the Holy Ghost should say, Do not please yourselves to think it is but to return to Egypt, that you can no where be worse off than you are now; God has worse things in store for them who harden their necks.

And, my brethren, this is our case this day; let not us think of returning to our former condition; certainly, were we to attempt to return, our condition would be far worse than before, our danger far greater. This is certain, to the view of any men that have their eyes open, that our condition in England must, if we return, be far worse than before. Many say, Oh, we were thus and thus in former times, and if we were now but as then we should do well enough! O, let us not think so; we must certainly be far worse off than we were, for if we think of returning it will not be to Egypt, but to Assyria.

Obs. 4. God knows how to cross the wills and mar the plots of wicked men. They please themselves with their devices, they will do thus and thus; if they be put to this shift, then they have a second, and a third. Yea, but there is a God in heaven who has determined otherwise.

Never were wicked men more crossed in their plots than they are at this day; they have said that they would do thus and thus, but God has said they should not, and they have not.

Now God in his mercy defeats the sinful projects of his people; but when the wicked are crossed in their sin, it is because God has other ways to bring about greater evils on them: "the Assyrian shall be his king." Well then, whatsoever any man's thoughts and desires are, the Lord deliver us from turning into Egypt again. And likewise the Lord grant the Assyrian may not be our king.

"But the Assyrian shall be his king." The Lord deliver us from both Egypt and Assyria. Why an Assyrian? why was he threatened to be their king? You shall find that he was one of a cruel and proud heart; the Assyrians were generally so, a generation of men cruel, proud, stout, and hard-hearted. "O Assyrian, the rod of mine anger," saith God, Isa. x. 5; and in ver. 7, "It is in his heart," in the heart of the king of Assyria, "to destroy and cut off nations not a few." And in the 12th verse, "Wherefore it shall come to pass, that when the Lord hath performed his whole work upon mount Zion and on Jerusalem, I will punish the fruit of the stout heart of the king of Assyria, and the glory of his high looks." Oh! it it is a sore evil to be subject to the rage of a proud and stout-hearted man, who *will* set his heart against God himself; who, though God fights against him, yet will stand it out; and though his design is crossed, yet will not come in; who will not give glory to God though his will cost him the blood of many thousands, but will go desperately on, regarding more his own will and lusts than the blood or lives of millions. How sad and dreadful is the condition of those who have such a stout heart to reign over them, armed with power, inflated with pride, enraged with cruelty! This is that which the Lord threatens here; and why? "because they refused to return." I beseech you observe this; "He shall not return into the land of Egypt," saith God, "but the Assyrian shall be his king, because they refused to return." From whence further,

Obs. 5. If we will not do God's will, God will cross us in our own. They would have their will, they *would* return, but they shall not, saith God; they will not return to me, therefore they shall not return whither they will themselves. God can cross us in our own wills at every turn. Foolish men! who will presume to cross God in his will, when God has them at such infinite advantages to cross them every way in every thing! If you cross God in that in which he delights, you may expect God will cross you in that in which you most delight.

O, when you are crossed in any thing that you have set your thoughts and heart most upon, commune with yourselves thus; Have not I crossed the mind of God, in that upon which God most set his heart? It is a good way, my brethren, to take a holy revenge upon ourselves, and if we cannot get our hearts to work for God as they *ought*, not to suffer them to work for ourselves as they *would*.

Obs. 6. God is not so much displeased at our sins, as at our not returning. He saith not, that the Assyrian should rule over them because they have sinned, but because they refused to return. "Because they would not return." It is too much that thou hast sinned, but as soon as ever thou hast sinned it concerns thee to think of returning; God expects as soon as ever the sin is noticed, that thou shouldst presently begin to return. It is dangerous to continue in the least sin; this aggravates thy sin dreadfully, and endangers thy sealing up to wrath everlasting.

Obs. 7. To refuse to return, notwithstanding means used, and mercies tendered, is a fearful aggravation. *Not* to return is evil, but to *refuse* to return, notwithstanding means used and mercies tendered, oh this is fearful indeed.

O lay this to heart, thou convicted sinner; what offers of mercy has God made to thee! what callings to mercy hast thou heard, outward calls in providence, and inward calls by the Spirit of God! Oh how has God called after thee, "Return, return, thou Shulamite;" return, return, return, thou wretched, wilful sinner; O, come in and return! What means of all sorts hast thou had to cause thy heart to return to God! and yet standest thou out? Think of what the Spirit saith in Job ix. 4, "Who hath hardened himself against him, and hath prospered?" What! dost thou think to harden thyself against God, and yet to prosper? "Who hath hardened himself against him, and hath prospered?" And mark what follows; "Which removeth the mountains, and they know not: which overturneth them in his anger. Which shaketh the earth out of her place, and the pillars thereof tremble." And yet cannot thy heart be overturned, can it not tremble? In this, that thou refusest to return, thy sin is aggravated above the sin of the devils themselves, for we do not know that ever the devils *refused* to return, for they were never offered mercy; God did never offer the devils mercy, God never sent to preach to them, either by his ministers, or word. Return, and ye shall have mercy; here is a price paid, here is a salvation for you, your sins may be pardoned: the devil had never such an offer. Who knows what the devil might do if such an offer were made to him? But now these offers are made to thee, and thou refusest to return. O return, therefore, thou sinful soul that art wandering from God in the ways of death and destruction, this day give in thine answer: as we read in Jer. iii. 22, where the Lord calls his backsliding children, "Return, ye backsliding children, and I will heal your backslidings." Mark the answer they give to God, "Behold, we come unto thee; for thou art the Lord our God." Oh that there might be such an answer given this day from some backsliding soul that is turned from God! O poor soul! whither art thou gone? God calls this day to thy soul, Return, return; and professes that he is willing to heal thy backslidings. O give in this answer, "Behold, we come unto thee; for thou art the Lord our God." Oh that some soul might this hour refuse no longer to return. Why wilt not thou return? God is content to return to thee: thou art turned from God, and God in the ways of his administrations is turned away from thee; but mark the promise in Jer. viii. 4, 5, "Thus saith the Lord; Shall they fall, and not arise? shall he turn away, and not return? Why then is this people of Jerusalem slidden back by a perpetual backsliding? they hold fast deceit, they refuse to return."

Some interpret the words here, "Shall he turn away and not return," of God. The Lord is not so turned back, but he is ready to return; oh! why shouldst thou backslide with "a perpetual backsliding?"

"Because they refused to return." The word מאנו translated "they refused," may signify they scorned. What! talk to him of returning, tell him of his sin against God, and its greatness, and the greatness of the danger, and the threatenings of God against his sin? he despises all these things, these are poor things to scare children withal; tell him of the mercies of God in pardoning his sin, he slights all. This humiliation now for sin, this breaking off of sinful courses, they deride the motions of them, they scorn to return. Hence, further,

Obs. 8. Scornful spirits, when called upon in the bowels of mercy to return from their evil ways, do not only refuse to return, but also scorn and slight what is said to them. Well, howsoever thou dost scorn and contemn it, know there are some who admire at God's mercies in calling thee to return, who admire at mercy tendered to themselves, and prize it more than all things in the world; they turn to the Lord with all their souls, nothing in all the world can stop them; they bless God that ever their ears heard the call of God, wooing them to return, and they would not for ten thousand thousand worlds but they had heard it, and felt the Spirit of God working their hearts to return to him.

Ver. 6. *And the sword shall abide on his cities, and shall consume his branches, and devour them, because of their own counsels.*

"And the sword shall abide on his cities." They relied on their cities and therefore refused to return; but saith the Lord here, וחלה חרב בעריו "The sword shall abide on his cities." The Vulgate and Jerome translate it, The sword has begun on their cities.

If we understood it thus we might derive a very profitable meditation.

Obs. 1. It is time for a people to return, when God doth but whet, or draw out, his sword. "At what instant I shall speak concerning a nation, and concerning a kingdom, to pluck up, and to pull down, and to destroy it; if that nation, against whom I have pronounced, turn from their evil, I will repent of the evil that I thought to do unto them," Jer. xviii. 7, 8. Oh! happy had it been for us, if, when the sword begun with us, we had turned from our evil.

But we must rather take it as in our version, and so the words are more proper, "The sword shall abide on his cities."

The evil of the sword I have already opened in the latter end of the former chapter, but that which I here would note is, The abiding of the sword upon their cities. From whence,

Obs. 2. The abiding of the sword is a sore judgment. So it was here, for afterwards, in the reign of Hoshea, was this prophecy fulfilled, when Samaria was besieged for three years together. When God threatens fearfully, he threatens the abiding of the sword; "the bathing it in heaven," its being "filled with blood," "made fat with fatness," and that it "shall devour," and "shall be satiate," and "made drunk with blood." All these six expressions you have in two scriptures, Isa. xxxiv. 5, 6, and Jer. xlvi. 10. Oh! this a dreadful thing, for the sword to abide. It has abode long on Germany, the Lord has been angry with them for almost these thirty years: we think three or four years long for the abiding of the sword amongst us.

But if it be such a fearful judgment for the sword to abide, how vile are they that seek to prolong its abiding on a people, and that for their own advantage! Oh! that is a cursed thing; such men live upon blood, every draught they drink they drink blood, who have endeavoured the prolonging of the sword upon this kingdom for their private advantages.

My brethren, we have cause to bless God, that he

has raised up instruments* for us, who have hazarded the shortening of their own lives to shorten the war, who have done their work of late as if they took it by the great. There is a froward and envious generation of men, who will say of some, because in certain things they differ from them, that they would be glad that these troubles might continue, because then they might have the more liberty. But we see these men, though of different judgments, do not contrive measures to continue the trouble, but hazard themselves to conclude it as soon as possibly they can, and that to admiration, doing things in the winter season, that is not ordinarily heard of among other nations; and all this, that the sword may not abide upon their country, but that peace may be hastened: on such surely the blessing of God must rest.

Obs. 3. The sword has its commission from God, and will abide as long as God will have it. He that is the Lord of hosts, gives the commission to the sword, and till he recalls his commission the sword shall go on. We may think the wars at an end; oh! let us look to it that we may make up our peace with God, and then we may hope it; but otherwise the Lord may cause "a serpent to come out of the cockatrice's egg," the Lord may kindle fires otherwise than we can imagine; therefore saith God, "The sword shall abide." It may be they thought, that indeed if the enemy come he will not stay long; but, saith God, he "shall abide."

I verily persuade myself, that there were many, yea, and some of the wisest in this kingdom, who persuaded themselves at the beginning of the taking up of the sword, that it would scarce have held twelve months together, it was so impossible to have foreseen the abiding of the sword so long upon us as it has. Yea, but if God gives commission it must abide: there is a notable text for that, in Jer. xlvii. 6, 7, "O thou sword of the Lord, how long will it be ere thou be quiet? put up thyself into thy scabbard, rest, and be still." Mark the answer there: "How can it be quiet, seeing the Lord hath given it a charge?" It must go on, it must abide, seeing the Lord hath given it a charge.

Obs. 4. It is a sad thing for the sword to be in the field, but still worse for the sword to be in the cities, for in the cities is the strength of the kingdom. "And the sword shall abide on his cities." When the sword comes into the cities, oh the fearful sights of houses fired, of streets running with blood, the hideous noise of shrieking women and children! Josephus, in his account of the Jewish Wars, reports of Jerusalem, that when the Romans came against it and took it, the narrow streets were so filled with dead bodies that there was no passage; and he adds, that the streets ran with the blood of the inhabitants, and many things set on fire, were quenched with the blood of men and women which deluged the streets, so dreadful was the sword there. The number of those that were slain and died during the time that the sword was stretched out against that one city, he saith, was eleven hundred thousand, it having been surrounded when crowded with strangers at the time of the celebration of the passover. Oh! for the sword to come to populous cities is very dreadful.

Joseph. de. Bello Judaic. lib. 7. cap. 7.

And the more dreadful it is, the greater is the mercy of God to our city; the Lord has so wholly delivered it from the sword that it has not come upon it at all. If the sword had come to this city, oh! it would have raged indeed; for this was the butt of the malice of the adversaries, their fury was reserved for this city: but the Lord has protected it, it has been the city of the Lord of hosts, the Lord has commanded that no army should meddle with it for hurt: Isa. xxxvii. 35, "I will defend this city," saith God, "to save it for mine own sake." Yea, it is for God's own sake indeed that he has said to the sword, "Go through the land;" and indeed quite through the land, except this city, and a few surrounding counties about it: as in Ezek. xiv. 17, "Or if I bring a sword upon that land, and say, Sword, go through the land," &c. The sword has even devoured from one end of the land to another, and yet this city is preserved, and not only preserved, but made a refuge and a succour for all the godly party flying from the rage of the sword. "Great is the Lord, and greatly to be praised" in this city, preserved by the Lord; except it had been preserved by the Lord, the watchmen certainly had waked "but in vain," Psal. cxxvii. 1.

"And shall consume his branches, and devour them."

The "branches," that is, the towns and villages about the city; for the cities in a kingdom are like the root or the body of a tree, while the villages or towns are as the branches; and here are threatened both city and branches.

And this city has been as a great body of a tree, that has sent out juice, and sap, and succour to all the towns and villages in the kingdom. When the sword is upon the city, there is little hope that the villages shall escape. Isa. xiv. 31, "Howl, O gate; cry, O city, thou, whole Palestina, art dissolved." When the city cries, then whole Palestina is dissolved. No marvel then, though there has been such plotting in this city, by making divisions, besides other treacherous and villanous ways, to bring the sword upon it to spoil it. What efforts have there been to betray us, one plot upon another! as soon as one is broken up, presently another is formed, and all against this city. Oh what a pleasant sight would it have been to our adversaries, to have seen it in confusion, and wallowing in its own blood! But the more there is depending upon it, the more carefully should all that love peace, and the welfare of the kingdom, labour for its good; every one should labour for the peace of it, that it may be a city compacted with unity within itself, that all that are godly and faithful therein may unite together, and every one bear the infirmities of his brother; that there may be no grating upon one another's spirits, no exasperation, no stirrings-up of violence one against another, especially against those that are gracious and peaceable. The more plotting, and falseness, and treachery there is against this city, the more faithfully should we labour for its good, yea, and the more should we increase our prayers for it. So Psal. lv. 9—11, "I have seen violence and strife in the city. Day and night they go about it upon the walls thereof: mischief also and sorrow are in the midst of it. Wickedness is in the midst thereof: deceit and guile depart not from her streets." What then? In the 17th verse, "Evening, and morning, and at noon, will I pray, and cry aloud: and he shall hear my voice." What saith the psalmist? "I have seen violence and strife in the city," yea, and "deceit and guile depart not from her streets." What shall I do then? "Evening, and morning, and at noon, will I pray." We complain of contentions, and divisions, and strifes in the city, and that there are so many plots and treacheries against the city; O let not us only talk of these things, but increase our prayers in frequency and fervency. Let there be no family without prayer to God in it, evening and morning at least; and if you prayed twice a day before, then pray thrice a day now, because of the strife, and treachery, and deceit in the city; and the Lord will hear our voice. And he concludes the Psalm thus, "Bloody and deceitful men shall not live out half their days; but I will trust in thee." Let them be never so bloody-minded, and desire never so much to imbrue the city in blood, yet saith the text, "Bloody

* The new-modelled army. Ann. 1645, 1646.

and deceitful men shall not live out half their days; but I will trust in thee."

"Because of their own counsels."

The evil, folly, and danger of men's own counsels, we we have spoken to, in the 10th chapter, 6th verse, "Ephraim shall receive shame, and Israel shall be ashamed of his own counsel." Now only a word here in reference to the abiding of the sword upon them.

The sword has abode upon us divers years: the wisest amongst us did not think the sword would have continued so long as it has done; and yet who can tell when there will be an end of these things?

Among other evils, certainly this evil of our own counsels is a great evil, that has made the sword to abide upon us: every man follows his own counsel, one man for his friend, and another for his friend. Men's own counsels, both in parliament, in city, in the army, in the country, throughout the kingdom, have been a great cause of the abiding of the sword so long a time upon us.

"Their own counsels." The Vulgate renders it, connecting it with the foregoing words, *Sua consilia comedent capita eorum,* shall eat up, or destroy, their heads. Those men that seemed to be the wisest and most full of counsel among them, even they were the cause of the continuance of this evil upon them. Montanus and Vatablus render it, their counsellors; because those that put them upon such counsels were the cause of the abiding of the sword. So in Ezek. xi. 2, of Jaazaniah and Pelatiah, princes of the people, it is said, "these are the men that devise mischief, and give wicked counsel in this city." God has an eye upon such as "give wicked counsel in this city," as the men that are the causes of the evil that is upon it. There is nothing more useful in troublesome times than counsel, if set aright; and nothing more dangerous in troublesome times than counsel, if it be wrong. The Lord deliver us, both parliament, army, city, and kingdom, from our own counsels. This will ever be; men will ever follow their own counsels, till they be taken off from their own designs and their own ends, till they can trust God with his work, and be willing to have their own private advantage swallowed up in the public good. Squint-eyed and selfish counsel will destroy us, if God be not infinitely merciful to us; yea, and it may be there are some well-intentioned for God, who yet in their counsels may be led aside by carnal principles: as for instance, many of good intentions, many who desire the furtherance of the kingdom of Christ, and can appeal to God that their hearts are sincere in their desire, think that there is no such way for the furtherance of the kingdom of Christ, as by the correspondency of it with the kingdoms of the world. This they regard as a sound fundamental principle; but certainly they are mistaken, for as the kingdom of Christ is not of this world, so the way to promote it is not by endeavouring the correspondency of it with the kingdoms of this world. God has laid the great work of man's salvation, the greatest work that concerns the glory of his name, in that which is foolishness to men; and almost all the great works of God, especially those that have a more immediate subserviency to the kingdom of his Son, he brings about, not by man's counsel, but by ways and means which seem folly to the counsels of men carnally wise. "For it is written, I will destroy the wisdom of the wise, and will bring to nothing the understanding of the prudent," 1 Cor. i. 19.

Ver. 7. *And my people are bent to backsliding from me: though they called them to the most High, none at all would exalt him.*

"And my people are bent to backsliding." Sometimes they may begin to reform, but they are quickly off again, for there is a principle of apostacy in them. "My people are bent to backsliding." If they do any thing in the way of reformation it is upon some external motive; their hearts are inclined another way: they are like a bough of a tree bent contrary to its nature by an external force; it may be for the present it yields, but there is in it an inclination, a propension, to return whither its own nature carries it. Thus it was often with Israel, upon some extraordinary work of God they would do such and such things, but they were as a deceitful bow that soon starts back.

My brethren, let us search our hearts. There was a great forwardness of reformation in the beginning of the parliament; how did men stir then! their spirits seemed to be then otherwise disposed than now: but it appears that in many of them it was only a spirit against those that had oppressed them, and a triumphing and rejoicing in having their wills upon them, and in the novelty of the change of things, but their hearts remained as carnal, drossy, and vain as ever. Therefore when men's wills were a little satisfied, and they saw that the godly people of the land began to rejoice, hoping for greater freedom than ever for, and countenance of, the religious party, and they found that there were some difficulties in the work of reformation, and that thereby their lusts should be curbed, that they should not, as before, have a licence to sin, upon this their hearts "are bent to backsliding;" that is, they fall off from the godly people of the land, with whom they formerly closed, and seemed much to rejoice in, their hearts are now against them as much as ever they seemed with them; yea, their hearts do vex and fret at any liberties they may possibly enjoy, or at any work of reformation that is begun. Thus it is with the nation at large, men's hearts "are bent to backsliding."

And if we look at men individually, their hearts "are bent to backsliding" from the ways of godliness which they began to profess, as thus: many young ones, and others, who have had workings on their hearts, and have made great profession of religion, yet, never having had their hearts changed, start back now; and that for many reasons.

1. God's ways have been unsuitable to them, and therefore they have found them hard and tedious.

2. To other things they have had a greater inclination, only they have been kept from them by the strength of conviction and external motives.

3. They have grown weary of the ways of God: that is a third degree, weariness of the ways of God.

4. They have watched all advantages how they might get off from their profession.

5. They have been sorry that they have engaged themselves so much as they did.

6. Any objections against such ways they greedily embrace, and diligently improve.

7. They are very ready to take any offence.

8. They watch for offences.

9. Any opinion that will give them a liberty from that straitness which they made profession of before, they are willing to embrace and entertain; if there be any practice that may give them any more liberty, they fall presently to it, and so they come to backslide. Now their actual backslidings are but a fruit of the bent of their spirits; their spirits were bent to backsliding before, and what they do now is but a fruit of the inward inclination. Let such know, that if they have no need of the ways of godliness, the ways of godliness have no need of them; the ways of godliness shall be justified and honoured, when they shall perish and be swept off as filth and dung from the face of the earth. I will leave only that scripture with them, "If any man draw back, my soul shall have no pleasure in him," Heb. x. 38.

But I find תלואים למשובתי which we translate "bent to backsliding," rendered variously; and indeed the Hebrew does seem to countenance divers readings. Calvin, Pareus, and others of our later writers, render the words *suspensi sunt*, they are as men hanging in suspense; for תלואים they say, translated by us "bent," signifies a propension to a thing; and is accordingly rendered by them, in suspense; the Septuagint favours this, translating it by ἐπικρεμάμενος. Now then, if the translation of the word be thus, which is for aught I know as suitable, or rather more so, than our version, why then there are these two things mainly in it.

First, They are in suspense; that is, they being in straits know not what to do. I find in Deut. xxviii. 66, the same word that here is translated "bent," is there rendered "shall hang in doubt;" "thy life shall hang in doubt before thee;" and that makes me the rather think that this interpretation may set out the mind of the Holy Ghost in this scripture. So then the meaning would be this:

They see themselves in such a sad condition that they know not which way to turn; they see their plots take not, their designs prosper not, they see God is out against them; and they would fain devise new plots, but they see as great an unlikelihood to prosper in their new, as in their former plots; what the issue of them may be they know not: thus are they in suspense and in doubt, not knowing which way to turn themselves.

And blessed be God who has put our adversaries in suspense and doubt: this is a judgment of God upon men who cannot trust God in his right and holy ways; they must have ways of their own, they must follow their own counsels, and these their own counsels insnare them, and bring them into most miserable straits, from whence they know not how to extricate themselves. God makes the ways of the righteous plain to them; but the counsels of men's hearts bring them into straits. They thought to deal wisely for themselves, but the truth is, their counsels, in which their wisdom was much applauded, bring them into such miserable straits and extremities, that they know not what to do.

Populus meus dubitat an velit redire ad me. Luth.

Secondly, Luther has a very good interpretation of this, reading the words thus: My people doubt whether they will turn to me or not; they see they profit not in their way, their consciences misgive them, they have some thoughts of returning to me, sometimes they are persuaded it is best for them to return; but the corruption of their own hearts stirs up temptations, and when they are presented to them, they know not what to do; they give many onsets, but they come not off freely; my people do hang in doubt and suspense, and do not come off freely to my way.

Populus meus hæsitat se convertere ad legem meam. Chald. Paraphrase.

And this is according to the Chaldee paraphrase, My people hesitate to convert themselves to my law: there are tossings to and fro in their minds, they are in doubt, and come not to a full resolution.

Obs. 1. It is a great evil for men to strive with their consciences. When their consciences put them upon the ways of God, they think there is good in God's ways, and that God is not well pleased with their present courses, and that it might be well for them if they reformed; yea, but then, on the other side, there come in temptations, and there are such difficulties in the way, I shall discountenance such and such great ones, I shall have opposition from some whom my measures will displease, I shall hazard myself, and the like; I must deny myself and go against the hair in many things, I must cross my heart in certain things on which it is strongly bent; why may I not do well enough in some other way, without so much trouble to myself? Thus their hearts reason within them: and yet again at other times serious thoughts begin to work, and their consciences thus to stir, Have not I to deal with a holy and glorious God? how if things shall prove otherwise than they are apprehended by me? what good will it do to me to cozen my own soul? were it not better for me to return? Oh that I could but tell how to speak this day to such as are perhaps yet in suspense! It may be there are some such here this day; they cannot be quiet in their present state, when they awake in the night season their consciences trouble them, and yet when they come abroad among company then that carries them away again; and thus their lives do as it were hang in suspense, and they are vexed and troubled in their own thoughts, not knowing what to do. Oh that I could (I say) speak to such hearts this day, that I could but tell how to present to them some determining thoughts! I will but in a few words suggest four or five meditations to such, that may help them to come to a determination; for the truth is, this is the cause almost of all the wickedness of such as have enlightened consciences under the means of grace, they do not come to a full determination. If thou art in suspense, let me cast into the scale these thoughts:

1. These stirrings now upon thee, which put thee thus to oppose the ways of sin, and bring thee so far as to be in suspense, know, they are the work of the Holy Ghost in thee; I do not say, that all going against such stirrings and workings is *the* sin, that *unpardonable* sin; but this I say, the sinning against those stirrings and workings of thy conscience is *a* sin against the Holy Ghost: take heed then of sinning against the good Spirit of God; the Holy Ghost has begun to conceive in thee, take heed thou dost not destroy the child in the womb. We know it is murder to destroy a child in the womb, when it is but beginning to be conceived; and thou that art in this suspense, thou hast a conception of the Holy Ghost in thee; take heed of murdering it.

2. If the Spirit of God leaves thee after this, thou wilt be more hardened than ever: let this be in thy thoughts. Thou hast stirrings of conscience, and some propension to the ways of God, but yet thy corruptions hang off; look to thyself while these workings of God are upon thee, if they leave thee they will leave thy heart harder than before.

3. In matters of such infinite consequence, certainly the safest way is the best way. It is not enough for thee to say, Is it necessary? and why must I do thus and thus? and what need it? and may not I do well enough without it? But when thou art reasoning about matters that concern eternity, though thou canst not fully satisfy thy mind, yet to take the safest way is the best way; and that thou art upon the safest way, is enough to countervail whatever trouble thou mayst meet with; though it should not be absolutely necessary that thou shouldst take such a course in such a particular, yet if thy conscience but suggests to thee, that this way is safer than the other, to go the safest way is best.

4. There is more evil in the least sin, than there can be good in whatsoever all the creatures in the world can tender to thee. Resolve upon this; this is a certain, undeniable principle: There is more evil in the least sin, than there can be good in all that all the creatures in the world can tender to thee.

5. It is best for me to do that now, which I would wish I had done if I were now to die. Put that meditation into the scale. Art thou in suspense, inclining now this way, now that, whether fully to come off from those ways of sin that thou art upon, or no? put this fifth thought into the scale, It is best for me now to do that which I would wish I had done if I were now to die. This will tend mightily to weigh down abundance of temptations that may be put into the other scale; and so thou mayst come to a determination, and deliver thy soul.

"Bent to backsliding," rendered by Calvin and others, they are in suspense, the Vulgate translates, My people hang in a kind of hope that I will return, and that all may be well with them at last; that though they do thus and thus, yet all may be well with them at last; God has often delivered them out of great afflictions, and why may not he deliver them still? And so they hang in expectation of God's coming to them. So they make למשובתי here translated "backsliding," to be a returning, a returning of God. I confess the word has something in it that signifies returning; but those who are skilful in Hebrew say, it is not used in a good sense, but in an evil; it is rather a going from, than a returning. Still, as the Vulgate has it, the hope of God's returning, and that things may be well, is the cause of the hardening of many hearts in sin; they hang as it were in the air, thinking that it may be well with them, and that things may not prove so bad as they hear. But cursed is that hope of comfort which has nothing else to ground upon, but only, It may be things are not so bad as we hear out of the word.

"Though they called them to the most High." That is, the prophets and messengers of God "called them to the most High," they wanted not means in the ministry of the word, they were called to "the most High," that is, to God. Now that God is "the most High," we have shown, chap. vii. 16, where he has also the title of "the most High." You who are highest, look upon God as above you; know that God looks upon you, and all men that are lifted up in the pride of their own hearts, as infinitely below him.

"They called them to the most High;" that is, they called them in the ministry of the word, that they might,

1. Know him; that is, that they might know him, "the most High," to be the infinite, supreme, glorious Majesty; that they might know the infinite distance which there is between God and the creature, and that they might know him to be the highest end of all things, so as to work after him submissively.

2. Acknowledge him; that they might thus fear him, that they might worship him, and love him, and trust in him, as the most high God.

3. Submit their wills to him whose will is supreme above all, and especially in matters of worship.

4. Come to have this high God as their God, and enjoy him as their portion. Thus the prophets "called them to the most High." Whereas their hearts were drossy, and low, and base, they minded only the satisfying of their flesh, and having their wills one upon another; their hearts hung down to their devised worship, which, though suitable to their public ends, and carrying great wisdom in their adoption of it, yet God would not own; God despised that worship of theirs with which they thought to honour him: the prophets therefore called them from these base, drossy things, to the most high God. Hence,

Obs. 2. Men's hearts naturally sink down to low and mean things; things unworthy of their souls, unworthy of that excellent nature with which they are endued. Men indeed have swelling hearts in their base, sinful way, but this very pride is their disease. The heart of man wants a true elevating principle, and the knowledge of "the most High" would more dignify and exalt it than pride can ever do: sin, wheresoever it is, debases man's nature.

Obs. 3. It is the end of the ministry of the word, to call to the most high God those who have their hearts grovelling after low and base things. Have not you found this fruit of the ministry of the word in your hearts, calling you many a time to the most high God from the vanities on which your hearts were fixed, telling you of the great and glorious Being with whom you have to deal in all your ways, who will have to deal with you to all eternity? I question not but many of your consciences have found this, even a word darted into your hearts that has called you from low, base things to the high and blessed God.

Obs. 4. It is a great and sore evil to stop our ears against the calls of the word. What! not answer to God's call? Does God call you, and you not answer to him? We say to a child, Your father calls you, or to a servant, Your master calls you, will you not answer? Oh! to shut our ears against the call to the most high God is a dreadful thing, it will lie heavy upon thee one day; those calls which thou hast had in thine ears will prove to be terrors in thy heart. Certainly, though thou lettest go the invitations of the word calling thee to the most high God, remember this, the calls which thou hast to the high God, being neglected by thee, will prove terrors in thy heart. Poor creature, to what dost thou listen? what invitations engage thy heart, that the calling to "the most High" cannot overcome thee?

Obs. 5. The calling "to the most High," is a special means to cause those that are in suspense to come to a full resolution. In Psal. xcvii. 9, "Thou, Lord, art high above all the earth: thou art exalted far above all gods." What follows in the 10th verse? "Ye that love the Lord, hate evil." God is a high God above all gods; hate evil then; set yourselves against evil, be resolved in the ways of God. When you are called to "the most High," you may see how infinitely worthy God is of all glory from you, what infinite good there is in him, and what infinite power he has to avenge himself of you, if you neglect his call; therefore there is a mighty deal of force to cause resolution. In Acts vii. we have a notable speech of Stephen concerning Abraham. Abraham was called from his father's house, and it cannot be imagined but that he had many thoughts to keep his heart in suspense; when called from his kindred, and all the contentment and comfort he had there, it is impossible but flesh and blood would suggest many thoughts to Abraham to keep his heart in suspense. But what led Abraham's heart to resolve fully what to do in such a case? The text saith, "The God of glory appeared to him," Acts vii. 2; it was not only God, but "the God of glory." My brethren, when God is calling you off from all creature comforts, from all things that may quiet your hearts in the world, and you have strong temptations to keep you in the ways of sin, let but the God of glory appear to you, and this will engage your hearts, this will bring them to a full resolution. Oh! blessed, blessed are those souls to whom, though they have continued long in suspense, yet at length the God of glory has appeared in the midst of their doubts and temptations.

And if there be such a force in this, then learn to present before thy soul that is in such a suspense, the glory of the great God; look up to this great God; It is the infinite high God to whom I am called. O thou hesitating, wavering soul, look up, and answer this call of God unto himself, answer it thus:

O Lord, thou art an infinite, blessed, glorious Being, the Supreme Being of all. I am a poor, vile worm, that lies under thy feet, and it is of thy mercy that thou wilt vouchsafe to look towards me; thou mightest have let me gone on in my baseness, and have suffered me to perish to all eternity, without giving me any call to thyself; but now that thou shouldst give me a call to thyself, thou, the high, and glorious, and blessed Lord, this is mercy: Lord, I come, and with fear and trembling fall down before thee, saying, "Lord, what wilt thou have me to do?" Those who have been wavering and afterwards settled, have found that this has been the thing which has settled them, some dreadful authority of the high God that has come to their hearts in some truth beyond their former experience.

Obs. 6. The true worship of God is an elevating thing. Then are they called to "the most High," when they are called to the true worship of God, for it raises the soul to "the most High." Men's inventions are low, base, and unworthy things. O consider whether thou findest this in the worship of God? Dost thou find thy soul raised up to "the most High" in his worship? if not, thou dost not worship God aright. Let no man look upon the worship of God as a low, mean thing; know, when thou art worshipping God, thou hast to deal with "the most High," whom angels worship and adore, with that God who is far above all creatures in heaven and earth: thus thou art to regard the worship of God. Oh how far are most men from this in their worship of God! very few there are that lift up their hearts to "the most High," even in the duties of worship. And so it follows in the words,

"None at all would exalt him." Why, If God be the most high God, how can he be exalted?

I answer, he is so high, that he cannot be more high than himself, God cannot be more excellent than he is in himself. God cannot make himself better than he is, nor more glorious in himself than he is; therefore no creature can make him more than he is: all that all the creatures in heaven and earth can do for God, can add nothing to him. "Blessed be thy glorious name, which is exalted above all blessing and praise," Neh. ix. 5.

Yet then God accounts himself to be exalted, when he is known and acknowledged as the high, supreme, first Being; when we fear him as a God; when we humble ourselves before him as before a God; when we are sensible of the infinite distance there is between him and us; when we are willing to lay down what we are, or have, or can do for the furtherance of his praise; when his will is made the rule of all our ways, and especially of his worship; when we make him the last end of all; when it is the great care of our souls and work of our lives to do what possibly we can, that he might be magnified and lifted up in the world; and when we account the least sin a greater evil than can be recompensed by all the good which heaven and earth can afford us: when we do thus, God accounts himself exalted by us. And this is the work that we all have to do, to give up ourselves to the exalting of the name of this blessed God. He is worthy, so worthy of honour from us creatures, that though ten thousand millions of men and angels should perish eternally for the furtherance of the least degree of his honour, he is worthy of it all; and therefore let us know it to be our work to endeavour in our places to exalt him: and blessed is that man or woman, who when about to die is able to say, O Lord, thou hast been high in my heart; thy wisdom I have adored, and submitted mine unto it; thy will I have honoured, and yielded mine likewise to it; and it has been the great care of my soul that I might, according to the ability given unto me, do something in my place to lift up thy name: such may go out of the world in peace, as having in some measure fulfilled their mission into it.

O you whom God has exalted, let it be your care to exalt God; and especially ye saints of the Lord, know God has exalted you on high, and expects that you should lift up his name: he has lifted you up out of the depth of misery, from the nethermost hell, he has joined you to, and made you one with, his Son, he has loved you with the same love wherewith he loved his Son, with him he has made you heirs, even "joint-heirs," he has given his angels to be ministering spirits to you, he has made it his great design to honour himself in your eternal good, he has prepared a crown of glory for you; O then, do you join together to exalt the name of this God who has lifted up you who were such poor vile worms, let the high praises of this God be in your hearts and mouths for ever. Thus Psal. cviii. 4, "Thy mercy is great above the heavens, and thy truth reacheth unto the clouds:" mark what follows in the 5th verse, "Be thou exalted, O God, above the heavens; and thy glory above all the earth." O Lord, we see thy mercy is exalted above the heavens, and thy truth to the clouds; then, Lord, be thou exalted above the heavens, that is, in our hearts and in our lives. Oh that God may be exalted in an answerable way above the heavens in what we do for him, as he has been exalted above the heavens in what he has done for us. Let us all exalt God's name: in either our everlasting destruction or salvation he will be glorified; let us pray that our safety may be identified with his glory.

My brethren, God has exalted himself of late in our eyes, in a glorious manner. "Be thou exalted, Lord, in thine own strength," Psal. xxi. 13. The Lord has exalted himself in his own strength: but mark what follows, "so will we sing and praise thy power." O let us sing and praise the power of God, who has of late so exalted himself in his own strength, and for the good of his own people.

Obs. 7. God has little honour in the world. "None at all would exalt him." Men seek to exalt themselves, but none to exalt God; every man follows his own ways and his own lusts, but the blessed and glorious God is exalted by few, or none. Men will arise to lift up antichrist, the kings of the earth will give their power to the beast, but none will exalt the Lord. Oh let this grieve the hearts of the saints, to see that the blessed God, so blessed in their eyes, should be exalted by so few.

And consider, every one of you, how little he has been exalted by you in all your ways. And why should you vex and fret that you have not honour and respect, when the blessed God, so infinitely worthy of honour and glory, is yet respected by almost none. Well, let this be our resolve from it; the less glory I see God have from the children of men, the more let me labour to honour him.

"None at all would exalt him;" so your version reads it: Luther and others, however, offer another interpretation, which, although not so good, may consist with the original, לא ירומם for if you observe the words, "him" is not there: they accordingly render it, there is none that lifts up himself; and explain it thus, Men are in a sleepy, sullen mood, that when God calls them, they will not stir up themselves to listen. And Luther makes use of this similitude, As a stubborn servant, or child, when the master calls him, will not stir and lift up himself to his call, there are none will lift up themselves; drossy, base, drowsy spirits, that are sleepy, and sink down to base, low things, they will not lift up themselves when they are called to the most high God. "They called them to the most High, there is none that lifts up himself."

It is a great evil to give way to a dead, dull sullenness of heart. When you come to the ministry of the word, you come with hearts dead and sinking down with discouragements. Now, when God calls, you should stir and lift up your hearts to close with those truths of God which do concern you; and it is a great evil in many, when they hear excellent truths which might do them good, that yet they do not lift up their hearts to close with those truths.

Ver. 8. *How shall I give thee up, Ephraim? how shall I deliver thee, Israel? how shall I make thee as Admah? how shall I set thee as Zeboim? mine heart is turned within me, my repentings are kindled together.*

Here, according to Luther, ends the 11th chapter, and the 12th begins at the next verse.

For the words themselves, we have not in all the

book of God a more full expression of the pathetical affections of mercy and compassion in God.

"How shall I give thee up, Ephraim?"

I beseech you observe, God was in the midst of his threatenings of judgment, and of charging them with their sin: "The sword shall abide on his cities, and shall consume his branches, and devour them, because of their own counsels. And my people are bent to backsliding from me: though they called them to the most High, none at all would exalt him." How! not one would come in? what should follow? One would think, Now let wrath pursue them, let the curse of the Almighty overtake them; one would wonder that it did not: but mark a greater wonder; after charging them with this wickedness, and in the midst of threatenings of the most dreadful judgments, God exclaims, "How shall I give thee up, Ephraim?" &c.

The Lord here takes upon him (as it were) the person of a loving father towards a stubborn and rebellious child. The child has gone away from the father, and has continued in its stubbornness; it may be the father sends after it; it will not come, it will not return, but goes on perversely. The father has many workings in his heart to cast it off; He shall never be the better for me, let him beg his bread from door to door, he is unnatural. Yea, but in the midst of these resolutions, and these sad thoughts towards the child, there comes a turning of his heart on a sudden: How shall I give it up? how shall I disinherit it? how shall I do it? It is my child, though stubborn; why may it not return? why may not yet God work good upon it? It is very evil, but how shall I give it up? I know not how in the world to bring my heart to it. Thus the Lord breaks out here. Here we have in your books four *hows:* "How shall I give thee up, Ephraim? how shall I deliver thee, Israel? how shall I make thee as Admah? how shall I set thee as Zeboim?" I confess in the Hebrew there are but two, yet they have the sense of four, and accordingly the interpreters insert them; How? how? how? how shall I do it? There are four interrogations here, and four answers. Four pathetical interrogations that God asks as it were himself:

First, "How shall I give thee up, Ephraim?"
Secondly, "How shall I deliver thee, Israel?"
Thirdly, "How shall I make thee as Admah?"
Fourthly, "How shall I set thee as Zeboim?"

And to these there are four answers, as thus:
First, "Mine heart is turned within me."
Secondly, "My repentings are kindled together."
Thirdly, "I will not execute the fierceness of mine anger."
Fourthly, "I will not return to destroy Ephraim."

These are the four answers; and for the last of them two reasons are given:
First, "I am God, and not man."
Secondly, "The Holy One in the midst of thee."

Now what the force of these reasons is we shall see when we come to them. But now to open to you briefly the words in a way of paraphrase, and then the several doctrinal notes from them.

"How shall I give thee up, Ephraim?" or, as some read it, What shall I do to thee, Ephraim?

I am as it were at a stand what to do; as the father, that with the rod in his hand comes to correct, and lets the rod fall out of his hand, his affections work so strongly.

What shall I do? As if God should say, Oh, were there but any repentings, I would rejoice; yea, I would accept them were they but ever so little. Could I but tell how to vindicate mine honour in any other way than by your destruction, I would do it; oh, what shall I do? It is your foolish, wilful stubbornness, going on in such a vile, sinful way, that puts God to such a stand. What shall I do? God seems here to have his heart troubled within him, much like that in Exod. xxxiii. 5, when God was offended with the people, "Put off thy ornaments from thee," saith he, "that I may know what to do unto thee." It is a strange expression; as if he should say, Come and fast and pray, "put off thine ornaments," and humble yourselves before me, that I may know what to do to you: oh! why may there not be some hopes? "Put off thine ornaments," if there be but any repentings.

Or if you take it as it is in your books, "How shall I give thee up, Ephraim?" then the scope is, Thou art upon the very brink of destruction, in the very mouth of ruin; wrath and misery stand waiting only for my giving thee up; oh! but how shall I do it? but I cannot tell how to find in my heart; how shall I do it? "How shall I give thee up, Ephraim?"

"Ephraim." This word contained a strong argument to move the compassion of God. If thou wert indeed the refuse of the world, I would not so much care for many thousands of them; but thou art "Ephraim," "my pleasant child," "my dear son," Jer. xxxi. 20. "How shall I give *thee* up, Ephraim?"

"How shall I deliver thee?" As if he should say, Justice calls for thee, that I would deliver thee up to her; justice pleads that thou art her due; but how shall I do it? how shall I do it? how shall I deliver thee? "Mine heart is turned within me."

The Septuagint and Vulgate render the words, How shall I protect thee?

The mistake arises from this: the same radical letters in the Hebrew that stand for delivering, signify likewise a shield, and therefore they translate it, How shall I protect thee as with a shield? but the sense is much the same, thus, How shall I protect such a one as thou art? how shall it be for mine honour that thou shouldst be under my protection? Men, indeed, do abuse their power to give protection to others, (and you know there has been a great abuse of this kind since the parliament began,) but saith God, How shall I do it? that is, I who am a holy and infinite God, how shall I protect such a one as thou art?

[a] אמגנך tradidit
clypeus מגן protexit
גנן a.

"How shall I deliver thee, Israel?" "Israel;" here is another argument: Israel, I remember thy father, I remember that mighty prince who wrestled with me and prevailed, and I account it my glory to be the glory of Israel and his seed. What! art thou the posterity of Israel, of one so dear to me, of a prince that heretofore so prevailed with me in prayer? what! art thou his posterity? "How shall I deliver thee, Israel?" When God looks upon them he sees them sinful and wretched, but when he looks upon what they were in reference to their forefathers, "How shall I give thee up, Israel?"

"How shall I make thee as Admah? how shall I set thee as Zeboim?"

Admah and Zeboim were the names of two of the five cities of the plain; now four of these five cities were destroyed by fire from heaven for their wickedness, and one only spared for Lot's sake. But this Admah and Zeboim were two of the cities on which the judgments of God were most terrible. The apostle Jude in his Epistle, ver. 7, saith, they, with "Sodom and Gomorrha," "are set forth for an example, suffering the vengeance of eternal fire." Now, saith God here, the truth is, you have provoked me as much as Admah and Zeboim have done, their sins were not greater than yours, and as great wrath belongs to you as to them; but oh! how shall I do it? "How shall I make thee as Admah? how shall I set thee as Zeboim?" how shall I constrain my heart to such a measure?

Jerome on the place moves this question, Why does he mention Admah and Zeboim, and not Sodom and Gomorrah?

The answer which he gives is this: Judah is compared in their sin to Sodom and Gomorrah, Isa. i.; Ezek. xvi.; for Judah had more means than Israel had, Judah had the temple amongst them, and therefore their sin was more aggravated. So Sodom and Gomorrah were the chief sinners; Admah and Zeboim did but as it were follow their example, and, by so doing, inwrapped themselves in the same judgments; but yet their sin was not altogether like Sodom's and Gomorrah's; therefore Judah, that had more means, is compared to Sodom and Gomorrah, and the ten tribes to Admah and Zeboim.

"Mine heart is turned within me."

Luther, according to his usual way in magnifying the grace of God, saith here, It is as if the heart that is stirred with anger for the sins of men, were not the true heart of God; and therefore saith he, "Mine heart is turned to me," mine own heart: now I have mine own heart indeed, when I have thoughts of peace; when I had thoughts of wrath it was not as it were mine own heart. So in Isa. xxviii. 21, God calls his execution of judgment, "his *strange* work." God's *own* heart is affected with our evil, and even turns with mercy towards us. So, Mine heart is come to me, saith God, as if it were gone before.

Cor inversum, cor concitatum ira propter peccata hominum, non sit verum Dei cor, verum Dei cor quod afficitur malis nostris, quod ardet commiseratione. Luth. Expos.

But otherwise, "Mine heart is turned within me;" that is,

As when a man's heart is much affected with love and compassion, there is the working of the spirits and blood round about it, and within it mighty motions and stirrings; so, saith God, methinks I find all my blood, as it were, and spirits, so working and stirred, that I find my heart even turning up and down within me, when I come to the execution of wrath. And then,

"My repentings." That is, those thoughts of God by which he came to do such things as men do in their repentings.

"Are kindled together." That is, all the thoughts that could possibly be mustered together to turn my heart from the dictates of justice to the ways of mercy, conjointly conspire (saith God) to kindle a flame within me. As a number of brands being laid together make a great flame; so all those thoughts, presented together, mightily stir and burn within me.

Oh, this is the goodness of God to his people, to have all things that in any way may be a motive to do them good, to come together before him, and make a fire in the very bosom of God. All the reasonings, as it were, of my heart being joined together for them, have kindled a fire, so that I cannot hold, but I must needs vent myself thus, "How shall I give thee up, Ephraim?"

But you will say, Why does God express himself thus? God might, without any more ado, pardon, and help, or deliver; why then should he express himself thus? To this Calvin answers, He accommodates himself to our weakness. God, who disdained not to take man's nature upon him, disdained not to personate a man who, being much wronged, is reasoning in himself what to do; his heart is full of pity, his bowels yearn, and he would fain find a way for mercy; and when provocation of execution comes into his mind, it is as a dagger to his heart: Oh, how shall I do this?

Accommodat se ruditati nostræ. Calv.

God personates such a man, and saith, How shall I do it? and mercy and justice are introduced to plead the case, both against and for Ephraim.

Justice comes in and pleads, Lord, their sins are great and many; their mercies have been great, the means which they have had have been exceeding many, thou hast been patient a long time towards them, and this thy long-suffering has been abused, their hearts are still hardened, thy name is blasphemed because of them. These arguments are advanced against them. But then mercy steps up and pleads, But, Lord, art not thou a God? Thou art a God: these actions indeed may overcome men, but shall they overcome thee? Is not this Ephraim? are not they thy people? are they not in covenant relation with thee? Spare them, Lord, for their forefathers' sake, for Abraham's sake, for Israel's sake, who was so mighty with thee. Remember, Lord, "the kindness of their youth," the wonders that thou hast done heretofore for them, when they were stubborn and rebellious. Lord, thou hast many of thine elect among them, and wilt thou then utterly consume them? When the Lord hears mercy thus pleading against justice, he exclaims, How shall I do it? I cannot do it. Thus you have seen the opening of the words, with the paraphrase.

Thus you have the words explained and paraphrased, and if any one of you should think that I do not confine myself to a mere brief exposition of this scripture, I may even answer you, How shall I do it? it were a very great burden upon one, to open such scriptures as these in an auditory that desire to have something spoken to their hearts, and to pass them over with a mere brief exposition. But for the notes, the first observation is,

Obs. 1. The greatness of men's sin hinders not the working of the bowels of God's mercies towards them. "None at all would exalt him:" they followed their own counsels, and did what they list, yet, "How shall I give thee up?" I will give you a like instance, and that is as remarkable a one as we have in all the book of God. What sins were greater than the sins of Jerusalem against Christ when he lived? yet Christ looks on Jerusalem, and weeps over it; weeps over it, when he considered of its destruction. Yea, and mark, though Jerusalem was guilty of the blood, yea, took away the very life, of Christ; yet when Christ was risen again, one of the first things recorded of him, is his saying to the disciples going to Emmaus, "That repentance and remission of sins should be preached in his name among all nations, beginning at Jerusalem," Luke xxiv. 47. Repentance and remission of sins preached to all nations: oh, but surely Jerusalem must be left, Jerusalem that did slay the prophets, and was so injurious, yea, Jerusalem which put Jesus Christ to death; though all nations should have repentance and remission of sins preached to them, yet one would think Jerusalem now should be excepted. No, saith Christ, "*beginning at Jerusalem;*" Jerusalem shall be the first place where I will have repentance and remission of sins preached, even that Jerusalem which took away my life; I will have repentance and remission of sins preached there first of all. Truly God's mercies are beyond man's iniquities.

My brethren, consider on this, first, If the bowels of God's mercies work towards us, notwithstanding our great sins, why should not the bowels of our compassions work towards our brethren, notwithstanding their infirmities? why should we, upon every little discontent, cast off all pity and love to our brethren? What! such great unworthiness in us, and yet it move not God to cast us off, but still, "How shall I give thee up?" O, when you look upon your brethren with whom your hearts did once close, and who were to you as your own souls, in the contemplation of being any instruments of evil to them you should have such reasonings as this, How shall I do it? I see infirmities in them, yea, but notwithstanding my great sins, God saith of me, "How shall I give thee up?"

Secondly, Why should great afflictions for God hinder our hearts working to him, when our great sins against God hinder not God's heart from working towards us? Why should any great afflictions for God hinder our hearts working towards him? Surely if

God will be merciful to us notwithstanding our sins, we should go on in the ways of obedience to him notwithstanding any consequent afflictions.

Obs. 2. Sinners are at the very mouth of misery, the brink of destruction, when they think not of it; nothing is required but for God to give them up.

Obs. 3. Nothing but God's free mercy keeps us from being destroyed; "It is of the Lord's mercies that we are not consumed."

Obs. 4. Sin puts God to a stand. How shall I do it? It brings disorder into the world; God must set his infinite wisdom on work to bring things about to his own glory. Sin has brought disorder and confusion; Now, saith God, I must set mine infinite wisdom on work to bring glory out of this confusion. If God has any good intentions to thee, know, thy sin lays such difficulties in God's way to find out a channel for his mercy toward thee, as puts him to a kind of stand; as thus, for God to find out a way that all the wrong which sin has done to him should be atoned for, and yet thy soul saved, is the hardest thing in the world. Thou canst commit sin easily, but (I say) when the sin is committed, for God then to discover a way whereby all that dishonour which is done to him may be made up, (as it must be, for otherwise all the disorder will not be brought into order,) and yet thy soul saved, is the hardest thing in the world; and were not God a God infinite in wisdom, he would never be able to devise the means of reconciliation. God does seem, as it were, to be at a stand; How shall I act so as to save these sinners, and yet not wrong myself? Oh this should humble us for our sins! As if a child should do so much evil as to bring himself into such briers and troubles, that if his tender father, being affected with his sad condition, would help him, he is put to abundance of difficulties, and is fain to beat his brains, and study ways and means how he shall contrive to save this his child from utter undoing: now if the child has any ingenuousness in him, he will not think, It is no great matter, so be it I be delivered; oh! but this will break his heart, Oh what troubles have I brought my father into! It is thus with us in reference to God, if we look upon God thus as personating a man.

Obs. 5. The salvation of a sinner breaks through a great many reasonings and workings of God's heart. How shall I do it? saith God. We little think what reasonings there are many times between mercy and justice about our lives, about our souls; could we but hear them as they debate in heaven regarding us, it would go to our hearts. The great salvation that comes by Christ was not determined without many reasonings between mercy and justice; there was presented to God whatsoever justice could say, and whatever mercy could say: What! (saith God,) must my son be under my wrath, and be made a curse, for the satisfying of justice? yet this must be; justice requires satisfaction; how can it be done without the Son of God being made a curse for man's sin? Such reasonings there are in the heart of God about man's salvation. In 1 Sam. xxvi., we read of Abishai and David's debating about Saul's life: "God," saith Abishai to David, "hath delivered thine enemy into thine hand this day: now therefore let me smite him," &c. No, saith David, "destroy him not." And thus they reasoned one with another. Saul was in a very dangerous situation when there was that reasoning about his life: in a like state are we many times; the justice and mercy of God reason about our lives and souls. Oh, how do we depend upon God for our lives and souls! and if we be saved, we are saved through many reasonings.

Obs. 6. According to the relation a sinful people have to God, so God finds it a difficult thing to execute wrath upon them. How shall I do it? The wrath of God is many times brought to the birth, and God cannot, as it were, (to speak after the manner of men,) know how to put strength to it to bring it forth. This is the reason that in Scripture we have such sending after sinners, and crying to them to return, such earnest wishes, Oh that they would return! and such pleadings with them, They will not come in, and return: this is the reason why we read of the Lord whetting his sword, and bending his bow, and preparing his arrows.

Why, is not God ready at any time to execute judgment upon a sinner?

No, he will be whetting, and bending, and preparing, and all because it is a work that he is loth to go through with (as it were): and this is the reason why God will not stir up his wrath, or if it be stirred up, he will call it back again. Lam. iii. 33, "The Lord doth not afflict willingly nor grieve the children of men;" and all this is, because it is God's nature to be merciful; mercy pleases him, and the Lord perfectly foresees, and has perfectly in his view, all the reasons that might move him to mercy, and stand in the way of his justice: as now thus:

1. The many prayers of the saints. Justice must break through all the prayers of all the saints of God that are in such places; and this is not an easy matter. We account it not an easy matter to break through a mighty army. God cannot come to a people that he is related to, and is worshipped by, but he must break through an army, the army of the prayers of his people: now saith God, How shall I do it? a mighty array of the prayers of my people stands between me and them.

2. The little ones, yea, the children of his own people, in a place. You know when God was about to destroy Nineveh, he looked upon the many thousands that could "not discern between their right hand and their left hand," Jon. iv. 11. But when God comes to destroy a kingdom that worships him, he looks upon those many infants, and sees in many of them the posterity of his servants. As they are but little ones, that moves his bowels; they have not been guilty of those sins wherewith their parents have sinned: And as they are, many of them, the little ones of mine own precious servants, how shall I destroy this place, even for their sakes?

3. God considers that he has but little worship in the world. There are but few in the world who worship him at all; And though it is true there are such mixtures in worship here, that in respect of that I cannot accept of what they have done, yet it is somewhat that I am worshipped; there are very few in the world that own me to worship me at all.

4. Services formerly rendered to him in that place. True, thinks God, but few there honour me now, but there are many of my servants that have done much, and suffered much; how many have I that have stood out to witness for me, and my truth! Certainly, my brethren, the Lord, in saving any kingdom when in danger, if it be a place that he has been honoured in, and where his people have suffered much for his name's sake, then he remembers it: and there is not a louder argument, next to the blood of Jesus Christ, in the ears of God, to save a place from ruin, than the blood of his people that has been shed for him; and therefore such a place is beholden to all that have suffered there for God.

5. The remnant of his saints. Some are yet left. And would I have saved Sodom if there were but ten righteous persons? now I will reckon how many I have here; not ten, or a hundred, but (it may be) God shall find thousands of righteous persons. Now the blood of my Son pleads for them, and how then shall I give them up?

6. A foresight of the miseries of the afflicted. Oh! their very cries are in mine ears already. If I should deliver them up into the hand of their enemies, oh the

extremity they would endure! how would they be plundered of all they have, put into prison, and miserably tormented! what shriekings and cries would there be, even from my people that serve me! Methinks mine ears are filled already with their cries beforehand. Often when we speak of the sorrows and miseries of people, before they come we are a little affected with them, but when we are eye-witnesses of them we are much more moved; as if any of you have seen the woeful miseries of those that have been under the power of their adversaries here, your hearts must have been affected indeed: but now all these miseries are present before God, as if they were now in real being, and therefore, "How shall I give thee up?"

7. The insulting triumph of the adversary. If I should deliver them, they will not honour me, they will blaspheme, they will scorn at their prayers and fastings, and at all their trusting in God, and at their good cause; What is become of your good cause, they will say, and of your so laying claim to God as you have done? Now the Lord foresees these blasphemies and insultings of the proud adversaries, how they will triumph, and tread upon his saints as dirt under their feet.

8. Many of mine elect are to come out of their loins, and therefore though I do not preserve the kingdom for their own sakes, yet for those elect ones that come out of their loins. If I should deliver them up to the rage of the enemy, then the line of my election would even be cut asunder, and therefore, "how can I give thee up?" I shall wrong myself in this thing, in giving them up I shall cut asunder even the very thread of election.

9. Other objects of wrath. If my wrath must be satisfied, let it run out upon others, "who will set the briers and thorns before me, that I may go through them and burn them up together."

10. The affliction of the saints is God's own affliction. True, they will suffer very much, but in all their afflictions I must be afflicted too; I foresee how their afflictions will affect mine own soul.

11. I am bound to fetch good out of all their evils. Suppose I should give them up; yea, but then I must work for mine own glory, and fetch out good from all their sufferings; and will it not be as easy for me to be patient towards them, as to work good from their sufferings when they are given up? God reasons in this manner.

12. If I destroy them, what glory shall I have? I shall have the glory of my justice; yea, but it will be but passively: and will that be much, to have justice so glorified? I have enough in hell to glorify my justice in a passive way.

13. Lastly, Mercy may yet work upon their hearts. Who knows but if yet I continue the gospel amongst them, and deliver them from their present great straits, who knows but their hearts may be turned to me?

O my brethren, I question not but at this day all these reasonings have been in the heart of God concerning England. When we have been at the very pit's brink, the Lord has been often saying even concerning England, "How shall I give thee up," England? "how shall I make thee as Admah? how shall I set thee as Zeboim? mine heart is turned within me, my repentings are kindled together." Before the parliament, when forces were raised against our brethren of Scotland, then said the Lord, "How shall I give thee up?" And then at Edge Hill, and at Brainford, and at Newbury, and Marston Moor, and Nazeby fight, we were at every one of them even at the point of being delivered up to the rage of the enemy; and then came in these reasonings of the heart of God, Oh! how shall I make them as other people, as Germany, or other nations? besides other mercies in former times, as in 1588, and the powder treason, these have been the workings of the bowels of God towards us, a poor, wretched, and sinful people. And let us now learn to acknowledge whence our preservation is. It is not from this man, and the other man, so much as from the reasonings of the heart of God thus for good to us-ward.

Hence let us learn what to do when temptation to any sin comes. What! is it thus with God? does God say when we are in danger of being destroyed, How shall I do this? Then when tempted to sin against God, let us say, How shall I do this, and sin against God? Joseph reasoned thus: when he had as fit an opportunity to sin as almost a man could have had, yet presently there came this reasoning into his heart, How shall "I do this great wickedness, and sin against God?" Reason itself dictates this. When God has fit opportunities to destroy us, God's mercy reasons within him; so when we have our temptations to sin, our hearts should consider, Oh! how shall I do this, and sin against the Lord my God? Let us present to our souls every argument against sin. Men will gather pleas for their sins; and so we should gather all we possibly can against them. It were *well*, my brethren, if men after they have sinned would say, Oh! what have I done? But it is *better* if men before they have sinned would say, How shall I do it? Oh! certainly our minds are very barren, that we have not, upon every occasion when a temptation comes, pleadings within to move us against it. Indeed after a sin is committed, men then can think of this and the other reason. Oh! it would be ill for us if God should thus deal with us, first deliver us up and destroy us, and then think of this and that which might have been done to have preserved us: therefore God, just when the danger comes, thinks of every thing calculated to avert ruin from us; so, when the temptation to a sin comes, then should we think of every motive that might deter us from its commission.

Obs. 7. A choleric disposition is none of God's image. When God comes to execute anger he cannot do it, but he must have a How shall I do it? before he does it, he must make a stop. Proneness to anger, suddenness to let out wrath, is not the image of God in any, man or woman.

When any of you are about to do any thing, especially against your brethren, against those to whom you are related, be not over-passionate, reason the case first in thine own heart: How shall I do this? True, I think they are in the wrong, but what good will result if I do thus and thus? Are they not those with whom I have had sweet converse, and whose godliness I have witnessed? Would it not be more for the honour of God if I forbore? Will any good come to the public? Shall not I rather serve the designs of the enemies with such sharpness and bitterness? will they not laugh and scorn at religion? Oh, how shall I do this? Oh, when we have workings in our own thoughts as bitter as gall, if, before we vent them, we would but put this question to ourselves, How shall I do this? by presenting all the arguments we possibly can to stop our anger, much good would result.

Yea, when ministers have prepared something to deliver, yet if there be any tartness in it, they should think, How shall I do this? what may come of it? I may vent myself, but what good will result? what glory to God? what advantage to the church? We should make many pauses, and many stops to our anger. As sometimes, when travelling in the country, you come upon some steep hill, you find that the countrymen lay here and there in several places something to turn the current of the water, for otherwise it would gore too much if it should run down swiftly, but when it has some stop it does not do so much hurt. Oh how does the anger of men gore deep! Why? Because it runs down headily, and violently, having nothing to stop it. Men in anger are very full of thoughts and resolutions, and all the reasonings of their hearts in their anger tend to nothing else but to heat their hearts more; all their thoughts work that way, till their hearts are made fiery hot, and so they burst out and cannot stay; they muse upon nothing else but that which may further their anger and displeasure: and those that are barren enough in their thoughts otherwise, yet are very quick in invention, and witty in the letting out of anger and wrath. But this would be your wisdom, had you the image of God prevailing in you, when you find anger stirring in your bosom, to rather muster up reasons that may qualify and allay it, and to muse upon those things which may serve to be a stop to it for the present, as God doth here. Oh! did men but pause, and say, How shall I do this? what peace and quiet might we have among us!

Obs. 8. Saints may be bold in seeking God in prayer. What! does God find it hard to him to execute wrath, does he muster up all possible arguments to stop his anger, and consider continually how he may manifest goodness and mercy? Why, then, if thou hast any arguments to plead with God for mercy, thou mayst come up with boldness and freedom to him; he is ready to receive thee, for thou bringest unto him that which is exceedingly suitable to him, suitable to his very heart. What! dost thou apprehend that the displeasure of God is out against thee, or against a land to which God is in any wise related? hast thou any arguments at all to plead with God in prayer? God gives his creature leave to plead with him, as if he were a man: come, then, with a free spirit, come cheerfully, and full of hope, for thou comest now to do that which God's heart is full of. Could a man know the thoughts of other men, and what most occupied their minds, and could he suggest thoughts to them suitable to what was passing within, what entertainment would he have! When a poor sinner, then, (if a penitent sinner,) comes to God, and suggests any arguments for mercy, I say thou dost suggest that of which the heart of God was full, and which is exceedingly suitable to it: thy pleadings mercy has been pleading already; and mercy carries on those arguments with a great deal more strength than thou art able to do, but it takes it well at thy hand to present any arguments to it. Thou art loth to perish, and God is as loth thou shouldst perish. If God give thee a heart to come to him to stop wrath, thou comest to him to do a work as acceptable to God as it can possibly be unto thee. When thou apprehendest judgment ready to be executed, look up to mercy; it may be the Holy Ghost may raise an act of faith, which will set on work the bowels of God's mercy. That which is very ready to work, a little thing will set on work; the least act of faith then would certainly constrain God to show mercy. Mercy has been pleading a great while, and justice pleading: mercy calls thee in to help, and to assist her to plead for thee, and who knows but the casting voice stays for thy coming in? though there have been pleadings in God's heart, yet the dispensations of God may be such that the casting voice shall not be given till thy pleadings are heard; by them the matter may be determined.

Obs. 9. How different were the dealings of the Father with his own Son. Do the bowels of God thus work towards poor sinners, pleading for them when wrath is ready to be executed; then we may here see the great difference between God's dealings with his saints and with his Son. When God comes to deliver up his people to punishment, for their sakes he saith, "How shall I deliver thee?" We do not find that God said so concerning his Son. God did deliver up his Son to wrath without a How shall I do it? yea, the heart of God was in it; there is no such expression of reluctancy about this work, but the Scripture saith that "it pleased the Lord to bruise him." Indeed it was for glorious ends which God had in view. Why so? God might have ends enough to bring forth his glory in our bruising; but yet, notwithstanding any thing that he might effect, he saith, How shall I do it? God doth not delight to grieve the children of men, but God did grieve his Son, he bruised him, and it pleased him to bruise him. You find such an expression in Isa. liii. 10; and in Psal. xl., "In the volume of the book it is written of me, I delight to do thy will." It was the will of God that Christ should come and suffer what he did. When Ephraim was bemoaning himself, God's bowels were troubled within him, he lets the rod fall out of his hand; thus, in Jer. xxxi. 18—20, when Ephraim was bemoaning himself, mark how God's bowels of mercy work, but the Scripture saith, that "God spared not his own Son;" God would spare Ephraim. Jesus Christ did bemoan himself when he cried out, "If it be possible, let this cup pass from me;" and, "O God, my God, why hast thou forsaken me?" Oh what a bemoaning of himself was this! and yet in Rom. viii. 32, it is said, "He that spared not his own Son;" he did not spare him, notwithstanding all the moans that he made to him, but he delivered him up. We read here, and divers times in Scripture, of God's repenting of the execution of justice upon sinners; but when he speaks of Christ, "I have made him a Priest for ever;" that is, so as he should be a sacrifice, both the Priest to offer, and the sacrifice itself: in Heb. vii. 21, "The Lord sware, and will not repent." Oh, certainly it was from this work of God, the delivering up of his Son, that the Lord has such working of bowels towards sinners when wrath comes to be executed: "How shall I give thee up?"

Obs. 10. The saints that walk close with God must needs be very secure. If the Lord deal thus with rebellious sons, what will he do with a son that serves him, that walks close with him? Though a son be very vile, very sinful, yet there is a "How shall I give thee up?" O, then, thou whose conscience witnesses of thy sincere endeavour to walk close with God continually, know that thy estate must needs be secure.

Obs. 11. When God delivers up his own people to any judgments, it is for some weighty cause. Never does any affliction come to them, but it breaks through many reasonings of God's heart; God intends by it something great. Does judgment begin at the house of God? It is because the Lord has some great intents to bring forth, and not because the Lord takes pleasure in the moans of his people, in the sorrows and sufferings of his servants; for certainly these bowels of compassion would not let such sore and grievous evils pass, if there were not some great ends and purposes of God to bring about.

Obs. 12. There is a difference between the day of patience and the times of wrath. For the sake of the godly there God's patience speaks thus towards the body of the people, "How shall I give thee up?" But there is a time that God will laugh at the destruction of sinners, and "will mock when their fear cometh," when he will execute his wrath, and be comforted, as the Scripture speaks. There is a time indeed when God saith, "How shall I give them up?" but there is another time wherein God gives forth "the wine of his wrath," Rev. xiv. 10. "The wine;" it delights the Lord as wine does a man. When indignation shall be as wine to God, then mercy and patience shall hold their peace, for they have had then their glory already, they will never speak more; but turn over the sinner to justice, yea, plead to justice against the sinner.

Obs. 13. If God thus hastens not judgment against us, we should not hasten it against ourselves. But let us make use of these dealings of God for the breaking of our hearts, and causing them to return unto him; let not us assist justice to our own destruction; seeing mercy pleads against the execution of wrath, let us take heed of new provocations: when God ponders the letting out of his wrath, let not us pull it upon our own heads; seeing God keeps off, and forbears, let not us hasten it. If Sodom had but known God's reasonings with Abraham in its behalf, one would have thought it would have broken the very hearts of Sodom. And let us consider the reasonings of God in this, and lay them to our hearts to break them, and think thus with ourselves, Lord, why should it be so hard with thee to deliver me up, when it is so easy with me to sin against thee? No pleadings have stopped me in the course of my sin, the word has pleaded, conscience has often pleaded, but I have not been stopped; oh, why should any pleadings stop thee in the course of thy wrath? The Lord cause such workings to be in our hearts to break them, considering, that indeed it is through the pleadings of mercy that any of us are alive, that we are out of the nethermost hell. And thus much for those words, "How shall I give thee up, Ephraim? how shall I deliver thee, Israel?" There follows.

Obs. 14. God's people are subject to as sore evils as the worst of men. "How shall I make thee as Admah? how shall I set thee as Zeboim?" Indeed, the sins of the saints have such great aggravations, that if God should deal with them according to a covenant of works, and not in a covenant of grace, their condition would be sadder than the vilest and most wicked. In Amos ix. 7, God saith, "Are ye not as the children of the Ethiopians unto me, O children of Israel?" You have had, indeed, deliverances, and so have they; and what are you better than the children of the Ethiopians unto me, if I should look upon you as in yourselves? Therefore in Isa. i. 10, the princes of Judah are called the "rulers of Sodom," and the people, the "people of Gomorrah." And in Lam. iv. 6, "The punishment of the iniquity of the daughter of my people is greater than the punishment of the sin of Sodom." Ezek. xvi. 48, "As I live, saith the Lord God, Sodom thy sister hath not done, she nor her daughters, as thou hast done, thou and thy daughters." "As I live;" God swears to it, that Sodom was not guilty of such great sins.

You will say, Yea, but we are delivered from such evils, by being under another covenant.

Yea, but that should not at all hinder the work of your humiliation, but rather further it, considering what you are in yourselves.

Obs. 15. When sinners are nearest to judgment, yet bowels of mercy are working towards them. When they deserve to be as Admah and Zeboim, even then, saith God, "How shall I give thee up? how shall I make thee as Admah? how shall I set thee as Zeboim?"

Obs. 16. Those that are in relation to God have a great privilege, which others have not. Thus, as if God should say, Let Admah and Zeboim perish if they will, let fire and brimstone come from heaven and eternal fire pursue them, what care I for Admah and Zeboim? but "how shall I make thee as Admah? and set thee as Zeboim?" I know not how to find in my heart to make *thee* so. Those in relation to God have a great privilege, which others have not; God disposes his mercies as he pleases.

It may be, some of you think that your sins are not so great, or not greater than the sins of others, and therefore you may escape as well as they. No, you may mistake in that; God may save some that are guilty of greater sins than you, and yet damn you, damn you for sins less than theirs. God's mercy is his own; if God will destroy Admah and Zeboim eternally, who can speak against God's dealings with them? But "how shall I make *thee* as Admah? how shall I set *thee* as Zeboim?" God knows how to make a difference between man and man. Let none presume, and say, Because others commit as great sins as I, I may escape as well as they; no, thou reckonest in this without thine host; God may make a great difference between his dealings with them and with thee, and still do thee no wrong, for the mercies of God are his own.

Obs. 17. If God be unwilling to make his people like the wicked in punishment, let not them make themselves like to them in sin. Does God put a difference between reprobates and his people in punishment? Oh, let the saints then labour to put a difference between themselves and such as are of the world in respect of sin; let that be no argument to them, Such and such do thus, and why may not I do so too? that is no argument with God. I have destroyed such and such, and why may not I destroy thee? that argument will not prevail with God. Thou committest such a sin, and I have some in hell whom I sent thither for the same sin: this argument prevails not with God. O, let not such an argument prevail with thee, that because such and such sin, therefore thou too wilt venture.

Obs. 18. Though God be never so much inclined to mercy, yet this doth not hide from his eyes the sins of his own people. He still sees them, he sees what they are in themselves, and he sees what would become of them if they were left to themselves. Now I am in a way of mercy towards you, yet I look upon you now as such as have deserved to be as Admah and Zeboim: do not think that because my mercies work towards you, that therefore your sins are not before mine eyes; I know your iniquities, and yet am gracious and merciful.

And is it so? Neither then should the hope, or encouragement, of mercy from God, hide our sins from us. As the thoughts of God's mercies to us do not hide our sins from him, so our hope of mercy from God should not hide our sins from our own eyes; but at the very time we think of the greatest mercy, we should look upon ourselves as, in ourselves, the most wretched, miserable, forlorn creatures.

"Mine heart is turned within me."

The word נהפך here translated "is turned" signifies some great stirring, some change into another condition, and not only denotes (as I see several interpreters observe) that God changes the sentence of his wrath, yet without any change in God's nature.

But I think the words besides have another special meaning, and that is, they denote the strong affections in God: in all this we must speak of him after the manner of men; as now, we know that strong affections in us, whether they be affections of love, or of joy, or of anger, carry the heart along with them, and cause in it very strong motions. I will give you one scripture that has this very phrase, which will show you the meaning is not "turned within me," that is, in a way of change, so much, as that it denotes the strong motions that are in the heart of God toward sinners: in Lam. i. 20, the church is lamenting her sin, and expressing the mighty workings of heart which she felt in herself by reason of her sin, and of her affliction, and there the same expression occurs that you have here: "I am in distress: my bowels are troubled; mine heart is turned within me." The meaning there is not that I am changed in my heart, so as to be turned from my sin; but that I find a mighty moving in my heart, through the mighty workings of it, and the strong affections of my heart. You may make my heart to leap within me, (as we say sometimes,) or pant, or ache within me. Any kind of strong affections makes strong stirrings in the heart. So here, "my heart is turned within me," I find strong motions and mighty stirrings in my heart.

Obs. 19. Strong movings of the heart of a penitent after God, give strong encouragement to come to God, for there are strong motions in God's heart after him. "My heart is turned," there are mighty strong movings in my heart for mercy to you. Do you find such movings in your hearts as you never before were acquainted with? before your hearts lay dead, and dull, and nothing would stir them, and now you find them mightily moved; do your hearts work strongly towards God? be encouraged in those stirrings; there are as strong stirrings in God's heart towards sinners.

Obs. 20. Let arguments of obedience to God cause stirrings in our hearts; let them not lie dead and dull within us. As arguments for mercy, oh how stirring are they in God's heart! If any argument for mercy toward sinners be propounded, the heart of God mightily stirs. Oh what arguments do you often meet with coming from the word, which one would think might work upon the heart of a devil to draw to obedience, and yet your hearts lie dead and dull under all those powerful arguments! Oh how unsuitable are your hearts to God! Do you expect that God's heart should work strongly towards you to do you good, and yet nothing stir in you?

Obs. 21. Let us not think it too much to have our hearts turned from strong resolutions to do evil. "Mine heart is turned within me," turned in respect of the revoking of the sentence. Men often have strong resolutions to a thing, and they see arguments that might turn them, but yet, they have resolved, and they are loth to change their thoughts and resolutions: oh! take heed of this, for God expresses himself after the manner of men. There have been many times strong resolutions found to destroy thee eternally, but the Lord does that which man would do when he changes his resolutions, though there be no change in God's nature; and he would, by expressing himself after this manner to us, inculcate this, that we should take heed we stand not upon our resolutions when there are arguments to the contrary, but be willing to have it known that now we are otherwise minded than before.

"My repentings are kindled together."

Surely God repents not as man does. You know the answer of divines, viz. that his administrations are such as if he did repent: but the word נחומי here translated "repentings," comes from נחם which signifies as well to comfort as to repent, noting that repentance and comfort are very near akin one to another: as the Hebrews express sin and punishment by the same word חטא so they do repentance and comfort.

"Are kindled." My bowels yearn within me; which expression you have in Gen. xliii. 30, Joseph's "bowels did yearn upon his brother;" and 1 Kings iii. 26, when the mother of the child saw it would be cut to pieces, "her bowels yearned upon her son:" the word "yearned" there is the same here with "kindled," her bowels kindled within her.

"Are kindled together."

Whatsoever might cause any repentings, they all come together, they lie glowing at the heart. The notes are these:

Obs. 22. God's repentings are mighty encouragements to prayer. When we present arguments to God for mercy, to think, that those arguments which we present, and all other that possibly may be presented, lie glowing at God's heart, yea, they lie glowing warm at the heart of God; they are not only before God, but there they lie as a number of sticks collected together and glowing, and ready to flame out; so all considerations that any way may serve to benefit the saints, do lie glowing together at the heart of God. It may be sometimes, when we come in prayer, alas! we are straitened in our own bowels, perhaps we cannot express ourselves, it may be but in one or two particulars we are able to give vent to our feelings, and that which comes out of our hearts comes very cold; but when we are straitened in our own bowels, and can express but little for ourselves, if we be such as belong to God's covenant, we must know that all considerations for our good that possibly men and angels can express, are all with God, all of them lay in a heat at God's heart. I do not know such a full expression as this is of repentings kindled: "kindled together."

Obs. 23. We must gather together as many arguments as we can to kindle repentance within us. Surely there is all the reason for it in the world. Does the Lord gather all together that may be for our good, and lay them upon his heart, and there keep them till they kindle and work powerfully upon his heart for our good? then, when we would repent, (for there is reason that we should repent as well as expect that God should for us,) we should be gathering all arguments we possibly can, and never leave till we find them kindled and warm at our hearts.

Oh! many of you have sometimes one argument that sticks at your hearts, and at another time another; at such a time some one truth darted in, and took possession of your hearts, and you would say as those that went to Emmaus, Did not we find our hearts burn within us? So you found truths coming in successively at such sermons. Yea, but now could you get but all the arguments for repentance that ever God darted into you together, and work them upon your hearts, and never leave till they be kindled, and continue crying to God, as Elisha did, till he got fire to come from heaven to consume the sacrifice; O Lord, my heart has a deal of watery stuff in it, that will not kindle, till the fire of the Holy Ghost descends; oh that it were with us, as David in Psal. xxxix. 3, "My heart was hot within me, while I was musing the fire burned:" so we should go into our closets, and gathering all things together that we can, to work upon our hearts, continue musing till we find the fire burning within us; nay, our hearts so inflamed, as to break forth with our tongues, to say, The Lord, he is God, he is worthy for ever to be feared, and honoured, and served; I have lived like a base and sinful, wretched creature, without a God in the world, but the Lord is God, and worthy to be honoured with my body, and soul, and estate, with my name, and liberty, and life, and whatsoever I am, or can do: now if it would break forth in such a resolution, how excellent would it be! Oh! let us be humbled, I beseech you, for the coldness of our hearts, that nothing can kindle there. What a damp is there upon our spirits, that when any argument is laid it goes out presently! We have truths laid upon us when we come to the word, but our damp hearts quench them all, they do not kindle. Many are witty enough to gather arguments for sin, and lay them upon their hearts, and so to kindle wickedness within; as in Psal. xli. 6, where you have a notable scripture of wicked men that came to David; "If he come to see me, he speaketh vanity: his heart gathereth iniquity to itself; when he goeth abroad he telleth it." All things that might suit with their wicked hearts, and for the furtherance of their ungodly ways, they gathered together for the encouraging and strengthening of themselves in their wickedness: so it should be the care of the saints to gather all things that might further repentance in them. That is the reason why wicked men are so hot in that which is evil, they gather arguments together; and hence it is that wicked men, when they have been in wicked company, come from it so hot in their resolutions to sin; why? because they have gathered a great deal together to inflame their hearts: and so should the saints, when together in holy communion and fellowship, be gathering one from another, every one should afford something to lay (as it were) to kindle the fire. But how? Laying their light ends together, and not their dead ends.

Obs. 24. Our mercies to others should not be cold, but burning. Let us be merciful, as our heavenly Father is merciful; that is, not only wishing good to others, but let there be kindled mercies within us so ardent that we may not be able to confine them. I suppose many of you, especially of estates, have had many thoughts that you would do this and this for such good uses, and you see some reason why it should be so; yea, but now, have these arguments burnt in your hearts, so as to cause you to break forth into resolutions? Well, though I have had thoughts and inclinations to make use of my estate thus and thus, yet I have been kept off; but now they are kindled in my heart, and I am resolved upon it. Thus it was with God, and let it be so with you.

Ver. 9. *I will not execute the fierceness of mine anger, I will not return to destroy Ephraim: for I am God, and not man; the Holy One in the midst of thee: and I will not enter into the city.*

"I will not execute the fierceness," the burning, "of mine anger," חרון אפי

True, your sins, and arguments against you, did lie at my heart, and did even burn it; but I will not execute that; I will execute the kindling of my mercy, but not the kindling of mine anger. Mark the several phrases, "repentings are kindled" in the way of mercy, and wrath is kindled; there was burning wrath, and burning mercy, but that which prevails is, the burning mercy. I will not execute the burning of mine anger. Why? For "my repentings are kindled together."

But how was this true? Was not Israel carried into captivity, and continued there many years, and never yet returned again (as some think); and when they were carried into captivity, for three years together there was a siege at the city? and yet God saith here, "I will not execute the fierceness of mine anger."

That which before was said, will sufficiently answer this: "How shall I make thee as Admah? how shall I set thee as Zeboim?" that is, though God did suffer them to be carried away captive, and their enemies prevailed against them, yet he did not make them as Admah, nor set them as Zeboim; the fierceness of God's anger, the burning of the anger of God, was not out against them. And, even in their carrying into captivity, the Lord had respect to his elect ones, and to this very day he purposes to do them good: and so we shall find in the next verse, that there is a promise of their returning from their captivity; and, therefore, though they were for a long time to continue there, yet still God did "not execute the fierceness of his anger."

Sin indeed stirs up anger, and fierce anger, in God. The Septuagint translate the words thus, *Οὐ μὴ ποιήσω κατὰ τὴν ὀργὴν τοῦ θυμοῦ μοῦ*, I will not do according to the anger of my wrath; that is, in extremity, I will not do thus with you. There were mighty stirrings in God's heart, pleadings of justice and pleadings of mercy, but God's mercy overcomes, gets the day, as it were; mercy triumphs over justice.

Obs. 1. The stirrings of mercy in our hearts should rather prevail with us than the stirrings of wrath. When we have workings this way and that way, we should consider which is the most benign side. The arguments had need be very much stronger for wrath than for mercy: if the arguments have any equality, or nearly any equality, in them, certainly the arguments for mercy should prevail: they do so with God's heart; O, be you like God in this.

Obs. 2. Stirrings for God should rather prevail with us than temptations to sin. Have not you found it thus many times in yourselves? You have had stirrings in your hearts to certain duties, and at the same time temptations to certain sins; now I put it to your consciences, as in the name of God, cannot you tell how the temptations to sin have often got the day? You have been rather carried from God to your base, sinful lusts, and your conscience has been overcome; conscience has pulled, and the drawings of the Spirit have been very powerful, but yet temptations have been more powerful, and you have yielded: oh, be ashamed of this, that it should ever be said, that, at such a time, conscience and temptations strove together within you, and temptations overcame conscience.

Obs. 3. God's mercies do not free his people from all fruits of displeasure. "I will not execute the fierceness of mine anger." My brethren, this is not meant merely of the times of the law; for this anger of God upon them is to this very day. But yet it is not "fierceness of anger," like that of Admah and Zeboim: there are, doubtless, among them the elect ones of God at this day. God will not have this called "the fierceness of anger:" it is displeasure, it is captivity, long captivity; they are a reproach and a by-word to the world; and yet there has not fallen on them "fierceness of anger." Our discontented hearts are ready to call every little affliction "fierceness of anger:" Oh how fierce is God! if we suffer ever so little. Yet did we indeed but know what anger our sins deserve, we would learn not to call every affliction that is upon us, no, nor our greatest afflictions, "fierceness of anger."

Obs. 4. We should acknowledge mercy, though we suffer hard things. If yet we be not utterly, nor everlastingly, cast off, let us acknowledge mercy. It is a mercy that "my repentings are kindled." "I will not execute the fierceness of mine anger." Why? Because they were not as Admah and Zeboim.

Let us then all learn this, Whatsoever afflictions are this day upon us, though it may be we are ready each of us to think our own afflictions to be the greatest of all, yet learn thou, I say, to bless God that fire has not been rained from heaven to consume thee and thy family; for this might have been thy portion, this "fierceness of anger."

"I will not return to destroy Ephraim."

God here compares himself to a captain that comes with his soldiers to a town. I suppose many in this place may easily understand the meaning of this word, by what they have seen and felt themselves. Soldiers come to a town, pillage, and leave it; and so the poor people think, Soldiers have been here, and we hope we shall do well enough now, as the worst is over: but it may be, within a month or two after the same soldiers come again, and utterly ruin the place and strip them of all. But now saith God, "I will not return to destroy Ephraim;" that is, Though I lay my hand upon them, and afflict them, and take away many comforts from them, yet when I have done that, there I will leave them, I will not come back again with a purpose utterly to ruin them; this I might do, I might return upon them with one evil upon another, but I will not do so.

Obs. 5. Sinners should not be secure when some evil is upon them, and think now they know the worst. No, God may justly return upon them again and again. If thou turnest not to God under thy affliction, God may justly return upon thee to ruin thee. Indeed, if thy afflictions have been such as have caused thy heart to return to God, thou mayst then hope that God will not return upon thee; but if so be thou behavest thyself frowardly under thy afflictions, thou mayst justly expect the return of God.

Obs. 6. God is very gracious to his people when evil is upon them. He will not add and add sorrow till he utterly destroy them, but he will forbear that he may have some subject for his mercy, he "will not contend for ever."

"For I am God, and not man."

Here is an argument that is very full; "I will not execute the fierceness of mine anger, I will not return to destroy Ephraim: for I am God, and not man."

God before personated a man in those yearnings of his bowels, that is, when God would express his mercy, he came in the most familiar way to reveal it; but when he comes to speak of anger, there he would have us know that he is not like to a man in the way of anger. With respect to mercy, saith he, if there be any man on earth specially remarkable for mercy, know that I am like him; but with regard to anger, I am not like man. God is very desirous that we understand fully his heart in the ways of his mercy, but when he speaks of the execution of his wrath, I will not do that; why? "for I am God, and not man." Mark the strength of this expression, "for I am God, and not man." The difference between God and man in the execution of wrath, you will find it very useful to consider: we shall proceed therefore to discuss it, and then draw from it several observations.

1. Man is of a weak spirit, not able to rule his anger. If men be but a little excited with anger, it is turned into rage, and there is no rule at all; but I am not man, saith God; I am God, I am no man, it is not with me thus, I am not of a weak spirit, I am able to rule my anger; and can repress it in the midst of the expression of my greatest wrath. "I am God, and not man;" the word is not אדם but איש a strong man, or a noble man; I am אל God, a strong God, and able to rule anger so as man cannot.

כי אל אנכי ולא־איש

2. Man is of a revengeful and cruel disposition, and cares not what he does so that he may have his lusts; but I am of a loving, sweet, and tender disposition; "I am God, and not man."

3. Man, many times, because he has not satisfaction within his own heart, therefore is in a rage with every body; he flies upon others, not so much for any thing that they do, but because of the disquiet of his own heart: but "I am God, and not man," I am infinitely all-sufficient of myself, and there is no disquiet in me; all is at rest and quiet within me, and this makes me to be of such a quiet disposition toward my creatures.

4. If there be any mercy in a man, it is but very little, a little matter will stop the current of man's mercy; but "I am God, and not man," there are infinite mercies in me, an infinite current, and the current of the mercy that is in me cannot easily be stopped, for "I am God."

5. Man is of a fickle and inconstant disposition, but "I am Jehovah, I change not, therefore ye sons of Jacob are not consumed."

6. If man passes by an offence, it is from some motives or some persuasions from without; if there be none of these, he is severe and rigid: but "I am God, and not man;" I have enough in mine own heart to persuade me; though there be no arguments from without, there is enough within me, in my own bowels, to persuade me, for "I am God."

7. Man thinks it a dishonour to him to begin reconciliation with those that have offended him; What! shall I go and disgrace myself to begin with my inferior? let him begin with me if he will: this is man's disposition; but "I am God, and not man," I account it my glory to begin the work of reconciliation, there is not such a disposition in me as in man.

8. Man cannot foresee the consequences that may follow upon his forbearing or pardoning of offences, and therefore he is loth to do either; but "I am God, and not man," I have infinite wisdom, and can foresee all the results.

9. Man cannot work good out of evil shown toward him, and that makes him not forbear; but "I am God, and not man;" I know how to work mine own ends, and the glory of my name, out of all the sins of my people.

10. Man, though he promises much mercy, yet ofttimes, if those to whom he promises mercy offend him, he will recall his promise again; and he thinks he may do so justly; all man's promises are but conditional: yea, but "I am God, and not man," I do not so; though I know beforehand there will be many weaknesses and infirmities in my creature, yet I have some promises that are absolute promises to my elect ones, and I will not recall them, though they be unfaithful and sinful. Man not only recalls promises when there is occasion given, but many times through unfaithfulness. Therefore Brentius, an approved divine, remarks on this place, The word is *Ish*, not *Adam;* and so he translates it, I am God, and not a noble man; you shall not have such dealings with me as from your great men, many of whom make great and fair promises, and you depend upon them, but they will deceive you, as is said in Psal. lxii. 9, "Surely men of low degree are vanity, and men of high degree are a lie:" your courtiers and great men, how do they deceive the expectation of those that are with them, especially in their need! they leave them in the lurch many times; but "I am God, and not man;" you shall not have such unfaithful dealings from me.

11. If man forbears and passes by offences now, he cannot have the offenders again at advantage when he pleases, and therefore he thinks he had best avail himself of the present opportunity; but "I am God, and not man," my creatures I have always at advantage; I can spare them now, for I can have them under my feet again, and again, and again, and therefore I have no such reason to take advantage of my poor creatures as one man has of another.

12. Man is bound to positive rules of justice that are set to him; but "I am God, and not man;" I will have mercy on whom I *will* have mercy, and whom I *will* I harden, Rom. ix. 18.

Obs. 5. Goodness and mercy is that wherein God glories. It is true, the Lord is high above man in all excellencies; but mark here, how he glories that he is "God, and not man," in the execution of wrath. Many glory in their anger, and make that to be their excellency; oh they are brave men, and of brave spirits; when they can vent their wrath, when they can rail and speak evil, and make others submit to them, and strike or punish them, why now they are brave men; I will make you do thus and thus: as in a family, you shall have sometimes a poor man or woman manifest abundance of pride of spirit, as if they were princes and monarchs, they will do thus and thus, and they think themselves of brave spirits; but mark, God glories in this, that he does not execute the fierceness of his anger.

I am infinitely above man. Wherein, O Lord, art thou above them? I am above them in this, that I can rule mine anger, and am merciful to those beneath me. Herein lies God's glory.

My brethren, this scripture (were there no other) shows that passion and anger debase man. God glories in his long-suffering and patience towards his creature. Thus in Numb. xiv. 17, "And now, I beseech thee, let the power of my Lord be great, according as thou hast spoken." What had God spoken, or where had he spoken any thing? Mark, this scripture refers to the latter end of Exod. xxxiii., where God promised that Moses should see his glory, and in chap. xxxiv. God made his glory pass by him; and what was it? "The

Lord, the Lord God, merciful and gracious, long-suffering, and abundant in goodness and truth," &c. Now here Moses refers to this, and lays hold upon it, as if he should say, O Lord, was not there a time that I was pleading with thee? and didst not thou promise to show me thy glory? and was it not "the Lord, the Lord God, merciful and gracious, long-suffering, and abundant in goodness and truth, keeping mercy for thousands, forgiving iniquity and transgression and sin." Why now, Lord, manifest thy glory; now, Lord, show thyself to be a glorious God. In doing what? Mark the 19th verse of that chapter of Numbers, "Pardon, I beseech thee, the iniquity of this people:" such is God's glory, and such the manifestation of his power. One would think that the power of God should rather be manifested in the destruction of sinners; no, the power of God is manifested in mercy rather than in misery and destruction: and we find, that those who come nearest to God are the most loving, and gracious, and merciful; yea, if they do but come near to God as far as possibly natural men may, their conformity appears in their love, forbearance, meekness, and gentleness. Even the heathens could say, The greater any one is, the more placable is his anger; a generous mind is not easily moved. And so they compare the lion, and bears, and wolves together: The lion, said they, is a magnanimous creature, therefore it is enough to fall down before it; but for wolves and bears, they insult over the prostrate; so those who have the most magnanimous spirits have likewise patient, and forgiving, and pardoning spirits. This note is as cross to a carnal heart as it almost possibly can be, I mean, to one who gives way to the lusts of his passion, for he thinks himself only magnanimous when he can vent his anger; often, were it not for the dread of being accounted a fool, he would forbear his anger. Yet know this, anger is not thy honour; it makes thee base in the eyes of thy servants, and children, and wife; it makes them look upon thee and despise thee, when they see thee coming into thy house like a mad fool, and drunken, as it were, with thy passion.

6. If God were like man, sinners could not be forborne. As if God should say, The truth is, your sins were such as, were not I God, it were impossible that I could bear: for so it is, though we think not of it; the evil of sin is so great, that if all the patience, in all the men that ever existed since the world began, were combined in one man, if he knew the great evil that there is in sin, he would destroy the world, he would not forbear, if his heart were but holy, as God is holy: "The Holy One of Israel in the midst of thee."

Obs. 7. It is a good way to exercise faith in God's mercy, to look upon God as God, as a Being beyond us, beyond any creature; for so this is therefore expressed, to the end that the people of God might exercise faith in beholding God as God. That is the way to help thee in thy faith: wouldst thou exercise faith upon God? look upon him as God, and do not conceive him to be as a man. It is true, to look upon him sometimes as a compassionate man is a little help, but that will not alway suffice. Perhaps it would help a little some that are here to reflect thus: If thou hadst to deal with the most merciful man that ever lived upon the face of the earth, wouldst not thou hope then that thou mightest be saved if he had the disposal of thy eternal state? Suppose there were a judge of the most tender spirit in the world, and all the relentings that ever were in all men's hearts met in him; if this judge had the disposal of thy eternal state, thou wouldst hope for mercy: but would it not help thee to know thou hadst to deal with one infinitely above that judge? That judge were a cruel tyrant, a savage tiger, in comparison of this God. God is "God, and not man," he is infinitely above man in the ways of his mercy. Many times by looking on God as ourselves we are first bold in sin, and afterwards sink down in despair in our sin. So in Psal. l. 21, "Thou thoughtest I was altogether such an one as thyself," saith God; that is, because I was patient and long-suffering towards thee, thou thoughtest I was like a man. A man, though he be a little offended, you think you may please him again; and so you thought I was like to yourselves, therefore you went on in your sins. This is one of the devil's stratagems: he first makes us look upon God like ourselves, and so we think that God has no greater hatred to sin than we have; but then, when we have once committed the sin, and the devil would tempt to despair, he makes us look to God as like to ourselves; that is thus, I find that I could not forgive such a one if he had so wronged me; and therefore from God they expect no mercy, regarding God as like to man, nay, like a corrupt man. Oh what a dishonour is this to God, that because thou thyself hast such a froward, perverse, cruel heart, that thou canst not forgive, thou therefore lookest upon God as if it were as hard for him to forgive as for thee! My brethren, the looking upon God as God, would help against many discouraging thoughts in poor sinners: as thus,

1. My sins are very great; men will forgive little offences, but God is "God, and not man," and therefore great mercies are little in comparison to him.

2. I have sinned against many offers of mercy; but God is "God, and not man," and God's mercy is such as brings in men that have refused the offers of mercy.

3. None is so sinful as I; but God is "God, and not man," and therefore he is above thee in the ways of his mercy: God has more mercy yet than ever he did manifest to any one creature in the world, and though I be the vilest of all sinners, yet let me look upon God as "God, and not man."

4. I am unworthy of any mercy from God. Indeed, if you had to deal with a man it might hinder; but God is "God, and not man," therefore it is not unworthiness that hinders mercy in God, mercy pleases God.

5. I am like to be of no use to God. True, if you were to deal with a man, he might not be pleased; but God stands in no need of you, or of any of his creatures, for he is, "God, and not man;" thou dost not honour God, as God, if thou dost not cast thy soul upon his mercy, as the mercy of God.

If I put this to thee, I hope the glory of it will be so great as will keep it from being abused. What! dost thou think thy condition is grievous? but dost thou think that such mercy as this which now I am naming would not serve the turn, that thou shouldst have such mercy as an infinite God should therefore manifest, to that end that he might show to men and angels to all eternity, what the power of his infinite mercy can do? Would not this mercy serve thy turn, such a mercy as is spoken of, Eph. ii. 4—7? I will name it again, abuse it at your peril: suppose thy condition so low, yet would not this serve thy turn, such mercy as an infinite God would show, to that end that he might make appear to men and angels to all eternity, what he is able to do in the infiniteness of his mercy? would not this serve thee, and help thee, and heal thee? Now this is tendered to thee in the gospel, even in Christ as an object of thy faith; and the very presenting of this is a work of the ministry of the gospel, that it might draw acts of faith, for it has a power to draw forth faith, yea, to beget faith; the very presenting such a thing as this is, has a quickening power in it. True, if you look upon God only as a merciful man, the glory is not such as that the shining of it upon the soul will add life: as now, the shining of the moon, or a hundred torches, will never beget life in a garden, but the shining of the sun will do it; so the apprehending of the mercy of God any other way but as God, as God in Christ, will never beget life in the soul. Look then on him in the infiniteness of his mercy, whose thoughts of mercy are beyond ours, as high as the heavens are above the earth; this is the way to beget faith. Therefore those who cannot believe take very ill courses for themselves, whilst they dwell only on such things as may discourage them, and think that this is pleasing to God: certainly the way to beget or raise faith in thy heart is, to look upon God as God in Christ.

Yea, but you will say, The truth is, this that you speak of, that God is "God, and not man," is rather a discouragement to my heart; it is God that I have sinned against, and not man: as in one sense it may encourage, so in another it discourages me: "Against thee, thee only have I sinned," saith David, Psal. li. And, indeed, this is the most piercing thought in a truly penitent heart, My sin is against God; I have lived so long without God, and in my sins have struck at God himself. Oh, wretch that I have been! I have been guilty of darkening the glory of the great God in the world. Now I will answer thee this in a word.

And is this that which aggravates thy sin in thy heart? Does this work upon thy heart most? Canst thou appeal to God, that of all the considerations of sin that ever thou hadst in thy life, nothing grieves thee so much, as that it is committed against God, because God is so glorious, so infinitely worthy of honour from all his creatures? Be of good comfort, and take encouragement from this point, and mark what I am saying; and with that I shall close all:

If the consideration of the glory of God above man thus aggravates thy sin to thy humiliation, then it will aggravate the mercy of God to thy consolation as well. If thou workest this thought upon thy heart, My sin is against "God, and not man," and therefore my heart is humbled; then the Lord would have thee to make use of the consideration of his glory as a God for thy comfort: God is "God, and not man," in the dispensations of his mercy.

"The Holy One in the midst of thee." God glories much in his holiness, and that in the midst of his people.

God is here said to be "the Holy One,"

To show that the anger he would let out should be unmixed with evil; that what considerations might be required to order and guide it should not be wanting. Men's angers are very unclean, there is much smoke and filthy stuff in the fire of their wrath. But in Exod. xv. 11, God is said to be "glorious in holiness;" and in Rev. xv. 7, God's vials of wrath are "golden vials."

Let us labour to be holy in our anger. This is a rare thing: if there be any corruption in man's heart it usually appears in his anger.

Obs. 8. God delights to show the glory of his holiness in mercy, and in pardoning rather than in avenging sin.

Obs. 9. God's faithfulness is a special part of the glory of his holiness.

Hence see how holiness will help our faith. And we should learn to manifest our holiness in our faithfulness. I am holy to make them holy, to sanctify them to myself.

"In the midst of thee." Casting the beams of his glory on every side of him.

But how "in the midst," when they were so vile, and cast off from being his people, a sink of idolatry and wickedness? "In the midst," in respect of some of his elect saints.

Obs. 10. God continues among a people for his elect's sake. The saints should consider of God, a holy God in the midst of them, and accordingly behave themselves. Lev. xxvi. 12, "I will walk among you, and will be your God, and ye shall be my people." And 2 Cor. vi. 16, speaks of a union still closer, "I will dwell in them, and walk in them."

Obs. 11. Men of place and government should be in the midst of those that are under them, carrying themselves holily; yea, though those subject to them should be froward, pettish, and sinful, yet they should carry themselves according to rule in all holiness, gravity, wisdom, and moderation.

Rivet, Ternovius, and some others, think that here is *enallage numeri*, a change of the number, holy, for holy ones, or saints: rendered so it would refer to the destruction of Sodom; *there* were no righteous, *here* are "the holy ones in the midst of thee."

Obs. 12. The saints are of great use where they live. They are the cause of mitigation of judgments.

"And I will not enter into the city."

Luther thus, God would signify himself to be merciful to scattered Israel among the Gentiles, *ut tamen non redeant ad politiam Mosaicam*, but so that they should not return to the Mosaical law.

Cultum meum non ponam in unâ tantum civitate, sed per totum mundum. Luth.

But it is rather to be taken in reference to the manner of God's proceedings in the destruction of Sodom; after he had done conferring with Abraham, he entered into the city, and destroyed it by fire and brimstone.

Obs. 13. God many times stands at the gates of a city, ready to enter in and destroy it, but humiliation in prayer, and reformation, keep him out.

God has not yet entered thus in here. Oh! let not our sins cause a merciful God to go out, and a provoked God to enter in.

Ver. 10. *They shall walk after the Lord: he shall roar like a lion: when he shall roar, then the children shall tremble from the west.*

"They shall walk after the Lord."

They shall not walk after their own inventions any more, nor after the lusts of their own hearts, nor after the examples or counsels of men, but after the Lord; they shall see God before them, their hearts shall be drawn after him; as they shall see God in his various administrations, so they shall turn. Which way soever God leads them, though in paths they have not known before, and in which few others walk, yet "they shall walk after the Lord."

In difficult paths, though never so dangerous to outward appearance; yea, though God should lead them from their dearest comforts, their sweetest contents, and though it do not appear to them whither the way tends, what God means to do with them; yet, seeing God before them, they shall be willing to walk after him. They shall account the way in which God is, the best, the safest, and the most comfortable. "These are they which follow the Lamb whithersoever he goeth. These were redeemed from among men, being the first-fruits unto God and to the Lamb," Rev. xiv. 4. "They shall walk" in a constant, steady course of obedience, "after the Lord."

It is the Lord, the blessed, glorious God, whom their souls love; whom they desire to honour; to whom they have given up souls, bodies, lives, liberties, names, estates, whatsoever they are, have, or are able to do. When Peter heard it was the Lord, he threw himself into the sea, that he might walk after him there. Thus the soul converted to God loves to walk after God.

"They shall walk after the Lord." This may be spoken of the church, as walking after the Lord in times of reformation, especially that famous "time of the restitution of all things," when God shall call home his people, the ten tribes, who yet are scattered up and down, wandering and groping in darkness. "They shall walk after the Lord;" the Lord shall be a Captain to them, leading them along as his redeemed ones, working by them glorious things in the earth, and bringing them through all opposition to places of rest, and fulness of all good. God shall appear in such visible administrations of his mighty power, that they shall say, Lo, this is our God, this is the Captain of the host of the Lord, yea, it is even the Lord himself; we will join together and follow him, whose wisdom, faithfulness, and courage is infinite; we will follow no other but him, and be in subordination to none else. The sight of such a Captain going before them shall put life, courage, and magnanimity into them, whatsoever they were before. Hence,

Obs. 1. It is the infinite goodness of the Lord, to be the Captain of his people.

Obs. 2. It is the honour, safety, happiness of the saints, to have God before them, to be walking after him.

"He shall roar like a lion."

If God appear thus it will make them fly from him. No, they shall, notwithstanding this, walk after him.

Obs. 3. The awful majesty of God, in his wonderful and dreadful works, causes the wicked, guilty conscience to fly from him; but the saints shall follow after, and cling to him. Isa. xxxiii. 14, 15, "The sinners in Zion are afraid; fearfulness hath surprised the hypocrites. Who among us shall dwell with the devouring fire? who among us shall dwell with everlasting burnings? He that walketh righteously, and speaketh uprightly." Acts v. 13, 14, "And of the rest durst no man join himself to them: but the people magnified them. And believers were the more added to the Lord, multitudes both of men and women." Psal. xlvi. (Luther's Psalm) ver. 2, 3, "Therefore will not we fear, though the earth be removed, and though the mountains be carried into the midst of the sea; though the waters thereof roar and be troubled, though the mountains shake with the swelling thereof." Ver. 6. "The heathen raged, the kingdoms were moved: he uttered his voice, the earth melted." But, ver. 7, "The Lord of hosts is with us; the God of Jacob is our refuge." Nahum i. 2, "God is jealous, and the Lord revengeth; the Lord revengeth, and is furious; the Lord will take vengeance on his adversaries." Ver. 3, "The Lord hath his way in the whirlwind and in the storm." Ver. 5, 6, "The mountains quake at him, and the hills melt, and the earth is burned at his presence, yea, the world, and all that dwell therein. Who can stand before his indignation? and who can abide in the fierceness of his anger? his fury is poured out like fire, and the rocks are thrown down by him." Now mark ver. 7, "The Lord is good, a strong hold in the day of trouble; and he knoweth them that trust in him." Joel iii. 15, 16, "The sun and the moon shall be darkened, and the stars shall withdraw their shining. The Lord also shall roar out of Zion, and utter his voice from Jerusalem; and the heavens and the earth shall shake: *but* the Lord will be the hope of his people, and the strength of the children of Israel." Hab. iii. 17, 18, "Although the fig tree shall not blossom," &c., "yet I will rejoice in the Lord, I will joy in the God of my salvation."

Oh the blessing of a clean conscience! it looks on the terror of the law, and of God, with comfort. Where there is neighing of horses, beating of drums, rattling of pikes, roaring of cannons, yet if a friend be the general, we fear not. All the terror there is in God, is comfort to the saints; the wicked have the dark side of the cloud, the saints the bright. Deut. xxxiii. 2, "He came with ten thousands of saints: from his right hand went a fiery law for them." Ver. 4, "Moses commanded us a law, even the inheritance of the congregation of Jacob." Neh. ix. 32, "Now therefore, our God, the great, the mighty, and the terrible God, who keepest covenant and mercy." Psal. xlvii. 1, 2, "O clap your hands, all ye people; shout unto God with the voice of triumph. For the Lord most high is terrible."

Be godly, and keep conscience clean, in these latter times; train up your children in ways of godliness.

"He shall roar like a lion." The roaring of the lion, Plutarch saith, invites the rest of the beasts, there is something for them.

But when was this? Many think, when the Babylonian monarchy was broken by Cyrus; then Belshazzar's knees beat together, and then the captivity returned, and divers of the ten tribes joined in the return. But this is spoken of the body of them; and if any such remarkable return had taken place, Ezra would not have left out their genealogies.

Others refer it to the times of the gospel, Heb. xii. 26, "Yet once more I shake not the earth only, but also heaven." The voice of the gospel, "Repent," and, "He that believeth shall be saved; but he that believeth not shall be damned," was a terrible voice. When secure minds (saith Luther) hear that salvation belongs to none but those that are baptized, and that believe in the name of Christ, they indeed tremble, and are solicitous concerning their future state. When Junius read the first chapter of the Gospel of John he was terrified.

But I take this to be meant rather of some notable work of reformation and calling in of these ten tribes to join with the church. The Lord will roar to terrify the hearts of their adversaries, that they shall not be able to hinder their return. Hence,

Obs. 4. When God's time is come for a thorough reformation in the world, he will make the earth tremble. Psal. cii. 16, "When the Lord shall build up Zion, he shall appear in his glory." It has been his way in his appearing for his church: Psal. lxxvi. 7—9, "Thou, even thou, art to be feared: and who may stand in thy sight when once thou art angry? Thou didst cause judgment to be heard from heaven; the earth feared, and was still, when God arose to judgment, to save all the meek of the earth." Ver. 12, "He shall cut off the spirit of princes: he is terrible to the kings of the earth." Isa. xxxiv. 4, "All the host of heaven shall be dissolved, and the heavens shall be rolled together as a scroll: and all their host shall fall down, as the leaf falleth off from the vine, and as a falling fig from the fig tree." Ver. 5, "For my sword shall be bathed in heaven." Ver. 6, "The sword of the Lord is filled with blood, it is made fat with fatness." Ver. 7, "Their land shall be soaked with blood." Ver. 8, "For it is the day of the Lord's vengeance, and the year of recompences for the controversy of Zion." Ezek. xvii. 10, "Shall it not utterly wither, when the east wind toucheth it?"

At the raising of Christ's kingdom, "Thy right hand shall teach thee terrible things," Psal. xlv. 4. "The kings of the earth, and the great men, and the rich men, and the chief captains, and the mighty men, and every bondman, and every free man, hid themselves in the dens, and in the rocks of the mountains; and said to the mountains and rocks, Fall on us, and hide us from the face of him that sitteth on the throne, and from the wrath of the Lamb," Rev. vi. 15, 16. "There shall be a time of trouble, such as never was since there was a nation: and at that time thy people shall be delivered," Dan. xii. 1. As when Egypt was smitten there were signs and prodigies, so now, in all places, admirable wonders in all the elements of the world; because,

Prodigia miranda per omnia elementa mundi. Lactan. lib. 7. cap. 15.

1. The ungodly have been cruel against the saints: Psal. lxxiv. 4, "Thine enemies roar in the midst of thy congregations."

2. The wicked will be secure, yea, his own people and will stand in need of roaring to awaken them.

3. The adversary will be stout and proud: *Confundetur omne jus, et leges peribunt,* All right will be overturned, and laws perish.

4. The difficulties will be great, so that Christ asks if he "shall find faith on the earth" at his coming, faith that ever his work shall be brought about, Luke xviii. 8. There will be mighty changes of things. Hence,

Obs. 5. God can soon make mighty alterations. Despair not then, though wicked men strengthen themselves never no much. "Be not ye afraid of them: remember the Lord, which is great and terrible," Neh. iv. 14. "Thou shalt not be affrighted at them: for the Lord thy God is among you, a mighty God and terrible," Deut. vii. 21.

Obs. 6. We should learn to prepare for those times.

"When he shall roar, then the children shall tremble from the west."

"The lion hath roared, who will not fear?" Amos iii. 8. There shall be mighty stirrings of heart; men's hearts shall shake within them, so that there shall be way made for people whose hearts are awakened to come into the church. The enemies shall be struck with such astonishment, that they shall not hinder; their violence and rage shall be abated. They shall say, as did once the Egyptians, Let us take heed what we do, the Lord fights for them.

And the hearts of those whom God intends to call shall be awakened, the slightness and vanity of their spirits shall be taken away. The awe on their hearts shall make them fear; they shall be roused from their sluggishness; they shall make haste to come in to join with the people of God. Fear causes haste, so the word used here signifies, and it is so rendered by some. Men delay and trifle, till God strikes their hearts with fear. *Spiritus Sanctus nescit tarda molimina,* The Holy Ghost likes not lazy labouring. "Thy children shall make haste," Isa. xlix. 17.

יחרדו Turpide accurrent, Tremel. Properabunt, Vatablus in notis.

"Then the children shall tremble from the west."

Those afar off, which were most unlikely. "The isles shall wait for his law," Isa. xlii. 4. The Mediterranean, the mid-land sea, is in the west. See Isa. xlix. 1, 12. Hence,

בנים מים Filii maris.

Obs. 7. There are like to be great stirrings in the western parts in the times referred to here by the prophet.

Ver. 11. *They shall tremble as a bird out of Egypt, and as a dove out of the land of Assyria: and I will place them in their houses, saith the Lord.*

"They shall tremble as a bird out of Egypt;" being struck with fear they shall hasten, so the original may signify.

יחרדו Advolabunt, Vulgat.

This some think was fulfilled when divers of the ten tribes joined with Judah in their return from captivity, for the monarchy of the Assyrians was subdued by the Persians, whose king was Cyrus. Therefore it is thought that the same liberty was given in Assyria for the ten tribes, as in Babylon for Judah. And not long after, Cambyses, the son of Cyrus, overcame the Egyptians, Herodotus, lib. 8, and Justin, lib. 10. And it is likely that he would be favourable to the ten tribes, as his father had been to Judah.

But Ezra, as was noted above, in likelihood would not then have omitted their genealogies. However, in the great restoration of things, this will be fulfilled. The Jews were strongly set to go to Egypt; now they shall as strongly desire to get out, to join with the churches: fly as a bird, not come as a snail; get over all difficulties; their elevated spirits raising them, they consider not earthly, drossy things. Now all their desire is to join with the saints, that they together with them may "walk after the Lord."

"And as a dove out of the land of Assyria."

1. Doves are sacred there, Euseb. Preparat. Evang. lib. 8. 5.

2. They are terrified with the least noise. *Terretur minimo pene stridore columba.*

3. Doves fly swiftly. "Oh that I had wings like a dove!" saith the psalmist, Psal. lv. 6.

4. They fly by flocks. "Who are these that fly as a cloud, and as the doves to their windows?" Isa. lx. 8.

5. It may be doves migrate from Assyria at certain times of the year, as several sorts of fowls do with us in their seasons.

"And I will place them in their houses, saith the Lord;" that is, I will provide lockers for them: he follows the former metaphor of doves.

God's people have been tossed up and down, they have had no abiding in their houses. But "I will place them in their houses, saith the Lord." Hence,

Obs. 1. God has his time to place his people in their own houses in rest, quietness, and safety; to deliver them from violence and wrong. "Moreover I will appoint a place for my people Israel, and will plant them, that they may dwell in a place of their own, and move no more," 2 Sam. vii. 10.

Obs. 2. It is a good work to be instrumental in providing, that those who live godly and are peaceable may abide quietly in their houses, and not be tossed up and down, because they cannot conform their belief or practice to others' standard. The tossing such up and down, though it may be from a zeal for Christ, yet Christ will never own.

Obs. 3. They that "walk after the Lord," shall be placed in their houses. They were willing to leave their houses that they might follow him, and now God places them in them.

Learn, then, to trust God with your houses, resolve to follow the Lord whithersoever he goes; he has a time to place his people in their houses, when others, who dared not trust God, shall wander in darkness.

Obs. 4. This must be the work of the Lord, it is only he can do it. "Saith the Lord." That mercy that comes beyond all means, it is the sweetest mercy. No matter what the means be, whether any or no, so that you have a word of God for the thing.

Ver. 12. *Ephraim compasseth me about with lies, and the house of Israel with deceit: but Judah yet ruleth with God, and is faithful with the saints.*

The Lord having manifested the bowels of his tender compassion towards Ephraim, the ten tribes, proceeds further to show what was that which stopped the way and course of his grace, of the grace that otherwise might have been let out unto them.

"Ephraim compasseth me about with lies, and the house of Israel with deceit." סבבני besets me round with lies; I am, in respect of the sin of Ephraim, (that is, of the governors,) and of the house of Israel, (that is, the people,) I am, in respect of their sins, as a man beset round, who would have egress, but when he goes one way, there he is stopped, and another way, he is stopped there too. God compares himself to such a man, as if, in going on in the ways of mercy, he is there stopped by some course of sin, and entering on another path, he is there stopped again.

"Ephraim compasseth me about with lies;" that is, with false worship, for that is a lie with false pretences; they put fair glosses upon things, but all are but lies; they have beset me with politic shifts of their own devising.

These did beset God, yea, and beset the prophet too, for so I find some turn it; they think it is spoken as in the person of the prophet, the prophet complaining that he was beset with lies; that they might, as far as they could, prejudice his ministry, and take off its power in their hearts, they beset him with lies, with false reports of this and the other thing. Upon which one has that note: A faithful divine, a preacher, is nothing else but, as it were, a centre to which all the lines of falsehood tend; it is a great plot of the devil to draw his lines, and to let them make the ministers of God (whom God uses as any instruments of good unto his people) to be as the centre of them all.

Theologus fidelis nihil aliud est, quam centrum, ad quod omnes lineæ dolorum tendunt. Meisner in loc.

But I rather take it as spoken in the name and person of God. "Ephraim compasseth me about with lies;" that is, they not only seek to blind men, but they would (if it were possible) deceive me, saith God. And indeed, when men seek to blind their own consciences, what do they but seek to deceive God? In the very act of worship (saith God) they are false; they profess honour and service to God, but they lie unto him, even when they are worshipping him.

Obs. 1. Many in their prayers, in the solemn act of worship, beset God with lies. Oh how many come into the presence of God, and there profess to God to acknowledge his greatness, his glory, his majesty, his power, his sovereignty, his dominion over them, and profess a great deal of fear of the name of God! and yet God knows it is not in their hearts, it is but as a lie to God. When they are worshipping God, they acknowledge their sin, and judge themselves for their sin, as if they were very much humbled and troubled on account of it; but God knows that all this is but a lie, there is no such humiliation of their hearts before God as their expressions would seem to convey: especially when they are the mouth-pieces of others, they cry to God for grace, and would fain above all things in the world have his grace; but God knows it is but a lie, all their prayers are even a besetting God with lies.

O, consider how far any of you, especially in praying with others, have been guilty of this, which is so marked with condemnation. Psal. lxxviii. 36, "They did flatter him with their mouth, and they lied unto him with their tongues." The word יפתוהו translated "flattered," signifies deceived, They deceived him with their mouth.

Why, can God be deceived?

No; but they did what lay in them to deceive him; if it were possible for God to have been deceived they would have deceived him. No marvel though men deceive men as they do: many that are of upright hearts, wonder when they hear that men's spirits can be so false; no marvel, I say, when God himself complains of being deceived by them; that is, they are so false, and do so beset God with lies, that, if it were possible, he himself should be deceived.

Obs. 2. Many also beset the business and affairs that they manage with lies. That is, thus, they plot with themselves how they may handsomely contrive to put together a goodly number of lies, that so they may beset men's understandings. There are such cunning attempts in the world to beset the understandings of men, that men shall not know what to say to things; and yet, whilst they cannot tell how to believe them, neither do they know what to say, things are so contrived. Deceitful men think with themselves, If such a thing shall be questioned, then I have such a shift to put it off; and if another thing shall be doubted of, then I have such a report, and such a fair pretence, to make it good. And thus they beset businesses with lies, and beset men's understandings.

"But Judah yet ruleth with God, and is faithful with the saints."

This of Judah's ruling with God, Luther, Meisner, and others think has reference to the story which you find in 2 Kings xviii., of Hezekiah's great reformation. Truly, if it be so, then it appears that this people had continued very long in besetting God and his prophet with lies, for then the prophet had been threescore years and ten a prophet to this people, and had been for that period showing to them their sin; for from the time of Hosea's prophecy to the beginning of Hezekiah's reign, it will appear to be above threescore and ten years, and still the prophet is complaining of this people, at that time when Judah did thus rule with God, that they still continued besetting God with lies. I would from this,

Obs. 3. When men are once engaged in shifts and lies, they grow pertinacious in them, there is little hope of their recovery. Then, let what will be said against them, let God's hand never so much appear, let the truths be never so clear before them, they go on pertinaciously when once they are engaged in such a course.

"Judah yet ruleth with God, and is faithful with the saints."

That is, Israel, the ten tribes, was not encouraged by her sister Judah's example, for Judah did otherwise; though the ten tribes did beset God with lies thus, their worship was all false, and nothing but a lie, yet Judah continued still in the true worship of God.

Obs. 4. Though examples of evil in others are no excuses, yet where there is no such temptation the sin is so much the greater. If indeed Israel could have said thus, You indeed complain of our false worship; who do otherwise? Does not Judah do so as well as we? do not they follow the same course? we took our example from them. No, Israel could not say so. This would not have wholly excused, but it might somewhat have extenuated, their guilt; evil examples do somewhat lessen, but not wholly excuse. Yet when there is no examples at all, but men take up evil of themselves, and are rather examples to others, this is a great aggravation of their sin. Again note, that,

Obs. 5. To continue in false worship when there is a right way held forth by others, aggravates the sin. If indeed we could say, We have been all our days brought up in this way, we knew no better, we saw none that held forth to us any other way; this might be some palliation. But they could not say so, for "Judah yet ruled with God;" Judah held forth the right way of worship according to the mind of God, and therefore the sin of Israel is here aggravated.

Obs. 6. It is a great commendation to continue in the true worship, when others fall off. "Judah yet ruleth with God." It was more to the commendations of Judah to continue in the true worship, after Israel had broken off; for in Israel were the ten tribes, more in number, and more flourishing as a kingdom a great deal than Judah; yet for Judah to hold on in the right worship of God, when so many fell off from it, and when a more flourishing kingdom than itself had continued so many years in false worship, this was a great commendation. Indeed there is a great temptation in this, when we see a multitude go another way; the devil prevails thereby much to draw men's hearts to that way; but the stronger the temptation is, the greater is the commendation of those who shall stand out. What though there be but a few, and you see others who walk contrary in seeming present prosperity, yet if thou canst hold on in the way of truth, in the way of God's worship according to his word, God looks upon this as a thing very pleasing to him; it is a very great commendation to those who do thus, and God takes it kindly from them: Judah does thus, whatsoever Israel does.

There were many evils, and those very gross, in Judah, but yet saith the prophet Hosea here, "Judah yet ruleth with God." Why? For the prophet Hosea was a prophet to Israel, he was not sent to Judah to inveigh against Judah, but to the ten tribes; and therefore, though there were many evils in Judah, he takes not so much notice of their evils, as of the evils of the ten tribes. Whence we may further

Obs. 7. We should be more severe with those that are nearest to us, when they dishonour God, than with others. As now, a minister is not so much to inveigh against those over whom God has not set him, but if there be any evil in those that belong to his charge, there he should deal more plainly; and so for others, you are not so much to meddle with others who do not concern you, as with your own family, those that are under your immediate charge. True, we should not see God dishonoured, but we should some way or other (as God calls us to it) testify for him; but the main thing that we should look to is, those that are under our charge: many are very indulgent towards those that are under their charge, and very busy and bitter against others.

"Judah yet ruleth with God." Jerome upon this place tells of a tradition that the Jews have here about Judah's rule, and it is this: When the people came out of Egypt, and Pharaoh pursued them, and the Red Sea was before them, and the mountains on either side, they were mightily terrified; yet God bade Moses to command them to go on. The people thought with themselves, Whither shall we go? and so were afraid. Now Judah had a spirit (say they) beyond the rest, and was the first tribe that ventured to go into the sea, and from thence obtained the principal place among the tribes. This is but their tradition.

But the meaning here is, that the kingdom of Judah yet continued according to God's mind in the house of David, and maintained the true worship, and so ruled with God. There are divers excellent notes further from hence:

Obs. 8. To enjoy but little with God, is better than much without God. As thus, The kingdom of Judah was but small in respect of the kingdom of Israel; yea, but "Judah ruleth with God." As here in a kingdom, so in an estate: hast thou a small estate? yea, but hast thou it with God? oh! it is a great deal better than to have a great estate and have much guiltiness with it, to have it without God. Israel maintained their rule by shifts; and that is a great evil. Though thou hast thy desires, yet if thou dost compass them, and still maintain them, by shifting courses, it is a sore and great evil, thou canst have little comfort in their enjoyment; for this is the meaning of the prophet, as if he should say, Israel ruleth, but how did they get and maintain their rule? It was in false, sinful ways. It may be thou hast thy will over thy brother; yea, but thou hast it in a sinful way: thou blessest thyself in that thou hast thy will, but thou hast little cause, if thou knewest all. Israel did not rule "with God."

Luther in loc.

Luther, on the place, saith, Papists dare not venture to embrace the true doctrine, for fear their rule should be lost. So it is with many people, they are afraid of the loss of their rule, if they should entertain the true ways of God's worship; they think that the true ways of God's worship cannot consist with their rule and power, and therefore they had rather retain them, and let the true worship of God go. Thus it was with Israel.

Or thus: "Judah yet ruleth with God;" that is, Judah, continuing in a right way of worship, does so reform as he rules in an honourable condition; Judah rules with God. Judah, reforming as he does, "ruleth with God," is in an honourable condition. Here, further,

Obs. 9. To serve God is to reign. The kingdom that serves God reigns indeed; yea, that individual who serves God reigns. It is an honourable thing to serve God; the Lord Christ "has made us kings" unto his Father, so honourable is the service of God.

"Judah yet ruleth with God." The Vulgate understands ruling with God thus, Judah descends, or comes down, as a witness with God. And indeed the difference, though it may seem to be very great in English, yet in the Hebrew it consists in the points, not in the letters. Ribera maintains this reading, and suggests these two remarks on it:

Testis descendit cum Deo. Vulg.

adhuc עַד testis עֵד
à רד damnatus est
רוד descendit ירד

First, When others leave the true worship of God, Judah continues, and so witnesses for God. Whence,

Obs. 10. God has never been without some witnesses to his truth. And in evil times, when others do forsake God and his worship, then for people to be willing to venture, and appear any way to witness for God, is a very honourable thing. Oh! it is a blessed thing to be a witness to the truth; Therefore was I born, saith Christ, that "I might bear witness to the truth." Those that are faithful and upright in evil times are God's witnesses.

Secondly, He descends, that is, he is content to be in a lower condition, so that he may witness for God; though Israel be in a more flourishing condition, and we be kept low, it is no great matter so that we may be God's witnesses. Hence,

Obs. 11. A gracious heart shrinks not from humiliation which affords the opportunity of witnessing for God. I see, indeed, others in the world, they are brave, and have the countenance of the times, and have all things according to the desires of the flesh; but we are kept low. It is no matter, so that we may but witness for God: let others take the outward glory and bravery of the world, let us be witnesses *with* and *for* our God.

"And is faithful with the saints." He is faithful, that is, he continues in the right government God would have him, and in his true worship.

Obs. 12. To forsake the true worship and government God has appointed, is unfaithfulness; and cleaving to it, especially through much difficulty and suffering, is a special part of faithfulness. It is an evil not to be faithful with the state in civil affairs, but not to be faithful with God in matters of religion is a greater evil.

Obs. 13. God has a special eye to a state's faithfulness with him in point of worship. Though there may be otherwise many evils, yet if they be faithful to him in point of worship, God has a special regard to that.

Obs. 14. Faithfulness consists in a constant persisting in good. It is not faithfulness only to profess good, but to continue in our profession. Judah "is faithful with the saints." I find divers learned men take this to be an enallage of the number, and instead of "with the saints," read, with the Holy One; for we may find instances in Scripture where the plural number is used for the singular, as in Josh. xxiv. 19, כי־אלהים קדשים "for he is an holy God." The word translated "holy" there is in the plural number, as here, and yet it must be understood and read in the singular, "he is an holy God;" and so some read here, faithful with the holy God.

But to take it as you find it in your Bibles, "faithful with the saints;" that is, with Abraham, Isaac, and Jacob, with Moses, with the prophets, with the forefathers; with them he continues faithful.

Or, faithful with such as are sanctified, the true priests of God, that God had sanctified to himself; faithful with the sanctified ones. Whereas Jeroboam took "of the lowest of the people," and made them priests to God, Judah would have no other priests but the sanctified ones of God.

Or, lastly, faithful with the people of God. For all of Israel that were holy, that were godly, that were the saints, and were not detained by some special hand of God, went up from the ten tribes to Judah, to the true worship of God; now Judah entertained them, and used them well, and was faithful to them. But, on the contrary, Israel, the ten tribes, were unfaithful, by using the saints of God evilly that would worship God according to God's own way; they were cruel and oppressing, and unfaithful to them, but Judah was faithful towards such, embracing and encouraging them. For us to go on in faithfulness, though we have none to join with, is a commendation; and the ways of God are excellent, whether any or no do join with us in them. But it is a great encouragement to be faithful with the saints; that is, to go on in those ways in which we see the saints walk: and to join with the saints, with such as are the choice saints of God, greatly encourages and strengthens the people of God in their way. "Faithful with the saints." Oh! it is good to be with the saints, even with the scattered remnant; a great deal better is it than to be with abundance of the men of the world.

Obs. 15. We should look more at the example of a few saints, than at the examples of thousands of loose and carnal professors. Judah "is faithful with the saints." It is true, the example of no man is to be a rule; but when the most gracious and holy saints adopt certain ways, it gives them a sanction, and mightily encourages and confirms others in them.

CHAPTER XII.

Ver. 1. *Ephraim feedeth on wind, and followeth after the east wind: he daily increaseth lies and desolation; and they do make a covenant with the Assyrians, and oil is carried into Egypt.*

"EPHRAIM feedeth on wind." We read, in chap. viii. 7 of this prophecy, that they had "sown the wind," and should "reap the whirlwind;" and now they feed according to what they sowed, and of what they reaped. They did sow the wind, and here they feed on wind.

Feeding on wind, is a proverbial speech, to note,

1. The following after vain, unprofitable things. When men please themselves in their own conceits and in their own counsels, and walk in ways that are, and will certainly be, unprofitable to them, they are said to feed on wind. When men think to please God with their own inventions, to escape danger by their own shifts, to prevail against the saints by their deep counsels and fetches, they feed upon wind; when men promise to themselves great matters by ways of their own, that are not God's, they feed upon wind: and for all this the prophet rebukes the ten tribes.

2. The swelling pride and elation of heart. You know, according to the food so will the body be; those that feed on wind must needs have hearts puffed up with conceitedness of themselves, and contempt of others that are not in the same way as themselves: they lie sucking imaginary content and sweetness in their own ways; they are full of themselves; wheresoever they come they must needs vent themselves, they are so full of their wind; they feed on wind, yet one prick of disappointment will quickly let out all the wind from such bladders, they are quickly amort and dead in the nest if they be disappointed.

3. Dependence on carnal, creature comfort. Evil men that live upon carnal, creature comforts, upon the applause of men, upon honours, they likewise feed on wind, and are puffed up for a while; but any prick of God's appearing against them lets out the windy stuff, and quickly they are dead. Any member of the body that is puffed up with wind seems to be greater than any other part, but it is not stronger; no, it is consequently the weaker: and so it is with the hearts of men, that are puffed up with windy conceits and with creature contentments, they have no strength by this inflation; though they seem stronger, yet when they are called either to do or to suffer for God, they then appear to be very weak, and therefore will change as the wind changes. Pliny, citing as his authority Democrates, who has written a whole book on the chameleon, observes of that animal, which is said to feed upon wind, That there is no creature in the world more fearful than the chameleon, and the reason that it is so changeable (for it will change into every kind of colour, according to that to which it is joined) is this very timidity of its nature engendered by its food. And truly, it is a very good description of men that feed upon wind; they seem big when they have no opposition, what will they not then do; they will do such and such great matters: but the truth is, none are of more fearful hearts than those who are puffed up with the wind of their own conceits; when God comes to cross them, or they are called to suffer in their ways, they will quickly turn to any colour, this or that; because they do but feed on wind, therefore is their might weakness, and they have no strength at all in them.

4. The turbulent, unquiet disposition of such. We know that the wind raises tempests and storms; and so men that are puffed up with the wind of their own conceits, are the men that raise such tempests and storms in the places where they live. My brethren, the saints have better food to feed upon, food that makes them more solid and more staid. While the men of the world feed on the wind of applause, on their own conceits, on their own vain counsels and plots, and upon the creature, and think to satisfy their cravings thereby; the saints feed on the mercy and all-sufficiency of God; they feed upon his word and promises, and upon the covenant of grace; they feed upon Jesus Christ, whose "flesh is meat indeed," and whose "blood is drink indeed," and so they come to have strength in them, for their food is food indeed. Others, feeding on the wind, are filled with their own devices, and hence it is that they cannot savour nor relish heavenly things; the breathings of the Spirit of God are not entertained by them, because they are filled with their own wind: but the saints are willing to empty themselves, and to receive into their souls the Holy Ghost, and the blessed things which the Holy Ghost brings; Christ comes in to sup with them, and they to sup with him, Rev. iii. 20; and thus are they nourished to eternal life, and fitted for any service or any suffering to which the Lord is pleased to call them: their food is different from the food of other men.

"And followeth after the east wind." This east wind, especially in those countries, is noted as a wind exceedingly hurtful to man and beast. We also have a proverb of the east wind; The east wind blows good neither to man nor beast; but more especially in that country. So we find in Gen. xli. 6, "And, behold, seven thin ears and blasted with the east wind sprung up after them." And in Ezek. xvii. 10, "Shall it not utterly wither, when the east wind toucheth it?" And in Job xv. 2, "Should a wise man utter vain knowledge, and fill his belly with the east wind?" When you see men talk and utter vain things, they do but seek to fill their bellies with the east wind. The east wind was so hurtful because attended with a heat of the sun that made it dry and scorching in those countries; therefore the Septuagint translates this *καύσωνα*, the scorching wind; and the Vulgate renders it, *æstus*, heat.

Now you will say, What does the Holy Ghost mean here? It is to hold out a very excellent truth to us:

Obs. 1. Creature comforts will prove but wind. Those who seek to satisfy themselves with such, and to stay themselves on their own counsels and their own inventions, not only deceive themselves, and will be disappointed at last in their expectations, but they will find these their ways to be very pestilential, hurtful, and dangerous, they will find that they will undo them, and bring them to utter misery. Oh how many have undone themselves with their own counsels! Were men but merely disappointed of their vain hopes, there were a great evil in that; but if disappointment were the only consequent evil, it were not so much. But you must not escape so; you that *will* feed upon the wind, and bless yourselves in your own ways, you must expect to meet with wrath and misery; these ways whereby you may think to shift from danger will bring you into danger. Oh! how many on their sick-beds, and death-beds, have cried out in the bitterness and trouble of their souls, for following of their own conceits and counsels, and the ways of other men! they see now that they are undone, undone by those ways: Oh! we have fed upon the wind, and we find evil ways that pleased us then torment us now, we find them to bring anguish, sorrow, and trouble upon us.

Obs. 2. It is a grievous thing, when troubles come, to have nothing within us to bear us out but the wind. Suppose men meet with the rough east wind, or storms and tempests befall them, yet if they have had solid food, whereby they come to get good blood, and marrow, and spirits, they may be able to bear it; but when the body is empty and meets with tempests, oh, this is very grievous to the poor frame. So it is with many when they meet with afflictions; but the saints have such solidity within them as bears them out; but other men that are empty, that have fed upon the wind all their days, have nothing to bear them out in great afflictions, but their hearts sink down in horror and despair.

"He daily increaseth lies." Ephraim, the ten tribes, all the day long increaseth lies, that is, he has new plots, and new devices, and new shifts for himself; he increaseth lies, new opinions and new reports; so we are to understand the word in its latitude. "He daily increaseth lies," and that,

First, In matters of doctrine; there "he daily increaseth lies," having once forsaken the truth. If the truth be once forsaken, men know not whither they shall go: Grant but one error, we are wont to say, and a thousand will follow, and they will multiply abundantly, especially some errors; there are some such breeding lies, that, if they be granted, there must be a great many others to maintain them. Never was there such an increase of false doctrine, of lies in that sense, as at this day. In Rev. xii. 15, when the dragon could not prevail against the woman, that is, the church, by bloody persecutions, then, saith the text, the dragon "cast out of his mouth water as a flood after the woman, that he might cause her to be carried away of the flood;" this was the policy of the devil, first labouring by violence to prevail against the church, but when he could not do that, then he "cast water out of his mouth like a flood;" that is, as interpreters observe, he laboured to undo the church by a deluge of error and heresies, when he could not ruin it by open violence. Truly this scripture is even fulfilled concerning us this very day: the Lord has been pleased to curb the dragon, and those that were his instruments in open and violent persecution, so that they cannot persecute the truths as they were wont to do; and now then this is the way of the devil, this dragon sends out of his mouth a flood of errors and heresies after the truth, after the church, labouring to swallow up all by this flood. And certainly we are in a great deal of danger at this day in this respect; there is a flood and deluge of all sorts almost of old errors, and many of them extremely dangerous, and men are serviceable to the dragon in this thing more than they are aware of. Oh that we could but see the subtlety of Satan in this continual increasing of lies! for these four or five years there has been an increase such as could never have been thought of; certainly if some of our forefathers that were holy and gracious should rise out of their graves, and see and hear such things as may be seen and heard in our days, they would stand amazed, and wonder how it were possible that ever England should be filled with such horrible opinions and customs as have prevailed in these latter times: so that now there lies the hope of the devil, by increase of such lies to eat out godliness and religion. This indeed seems to be the most hopeful design conceived by the devil in these latter times: men's hearts are carnal, loose, and sensual, and therefore they are prepared to receive these lies; and hence they multiply apace. But yet let none multiply them more than they are, by putting among them some truths, by shutting in truths in the midst of them, to make *them* appear likewise to be lies, and to be taken as honest men are when by any accident they are gotten in the company of lewd people, they are apprehended upon suspicion, merely because they are in their company. This is one of the devil's choicest devices, to shuffle in some truths among them, and because he could not have them suspected otherwise, they must be taken upon suspicion because they are there among them. Let not men gather these lies together to the end that they may oppose some truths thereby, but, as the prophet speaks, "What is the chaff to the wheat?" if men will speak of lies let them inveigh against them, and only against them, and make it appear that that is the work of their spirits, merely to oppose them, and not under such a pretence to make other things, which yet they cannot prove to be false, appear to be odious and monstrous, merely by shuffling them together among such horrible and damnable lies.

Secondly, Lies against the prophets, against the saints, and against the ways of God. And certainly there was never the like multiplying as there is at this day in this sense too; men carry their multiplying glasses along with them up and down. A lie at first is like a stone cast into the water: you know a stone when cast in makes a little circle, and then that another, and that another, every succeeding circle greater than the former; and so it is with many lies, at first they appear not so great, but they gain strength as they go, *acquirunt vires eundo*. There are many ways of multiplying and increasing lies.

1. By carrying about reports, and so making one lie generate many.

2. By misreporting of reports; that is, by putting reports into another dress, according to what men themselves apprehend; and that which is a truth when it comes to be examined nakedly, yet will, being put into another dress or arrangement, seem to be very false.

3. By adding to reports. Every man, according to his spirit, draws consequences, and when he has drawn them, he connects them with the report, as if they were part of the original, whereas they are but the comment.

4. By inventing new ones they come to increase and multiply; because such and such falsehoods will not do the feat, more shall then be added to them.

5. By maintaining lies by lies, as if men, being once engaged in a business, must defend themselves. If once they have misreported a thing, there is no help for it, but now it must be defended one way or other, somewhat must be done to establish it: as many times is the case with your servants; a servant has done a thing amiss; well, this servant seeks to cover it by a lie, and when once he has told one, he must tell a great many more to defend that one: and thus it is with men.

And truly, my brethren, seeing that this scripture does so by providence come in our way, let me speak thus much to you from it. It is one of the strangest things that ever occurred in the world, that there should be such strange reports of things that are matters of fact, yea, that one godly man, or company of men, should say one thing, and others, whom we think godly, should say quite contrary, and both in matters of fact: * I say, the consideration of this might indeed well make men stand amazed; for there is no sin that is more against the ingenuousness of a gracious heart, than a deliberate lie; to speak against a man's knowledge, and against a man's conscience, is one of the greatest sins against the ingenuousness of a gracious heart; and yet, even such as we think to be godly and gracious, issuing reports so contradictory to each other, and that about matters of fact, what shall we say to this?

To a friend who wrote to Austin about the allowability of telling an official lie, he answered, He must not tell a lie, no, not to save the whole world. Now what a difference is there in the hearts of men in these days! Truly, I do not know a greater temptation to atheism at this day than this is; for what will men think? There certain religious men speak thus, and others whom we account as religious speak quite contrary. Is there any religion in the world? We see so much contradicting one against another, surely one side much be false. It is this, I am verily persuaded, that is the cause of much atheism amongst us, and if God be not pleased to prevent one way or other, it will open a wide door to atheism in the nation. Some rejoice at these things, and nothing is more pleasing to them when they meet together; whereas they should be matter for our humiliation, we should mourn for them, to see how God is thus dishonoured, and what abundance of hurt is thereby like to come to souls. But now therefore, a little to quiet our hearts, that we may not be in danger of turning atheists by it, let us consider from whence comes it, that so many lies should be increased and multiplied.

1. Both sides may be right. They report according to their own apprehensions of things; and apprehending them in a different way, and on different principles, both of them may think they are in the truth, and yet one may contradict the other. For it is very much according to the principles of men's spirits in any thing, especially if a business has many things depending on it, and there are many circumstances to be laid together, to connect them as best suit their own apprehensions and principles. In such cases both parties may think they are in the truth, and contradict one another, and yet neither of them speak against their consciences: this (I say) may possibly occur even among good men.

2. Men do not always speak from their own knowledge, but are ready to take up the reports of those in whom they place confidence. When men see those whom they love of their side and way, they are very confident in their reports, and speak, not from being eye-witnesses themselves; and so they may come to contradict one another, and yet not do violence to their consciences: this is indeed the evil of giving too easy credit to reports. But though it be an evil, yet it comes not from a wilful violation of their consciences.

3. Sometimes when men report, they do not report all. Reports are cross one to another; yea, but did you hear all, or do you report all? It is a bad thing when a man will take one part of a thing and report it; another man may come and report the quite contrary; whereas if all were brought together and the whole series of things laid before them, there might appear such agreement in essentials as would unite both parties. Bring things to the original, and then you see how they agree: as now, sometimes in Scripture there are divers renderings; yea, but by bringing them all to the original, we come to see wherein their differences harmonize. And so with reports, bring them to the original, and you may help yourselves and others to see, when partial statements are rejected, a foundation for entire agreement.

4. Reports are contradictory, but that may arise rather from men's memories, than from any thing in the things themselves; I say, the contradiction may exist merely in the memory.

Let us learn then, my brethren,

First, To take heed of spreading reports to the dishonour of religion.

Secondly, To search into rather than report a matter; if you hear any thing which you think must surely be a lie, to go to the party, or get some that are acquainted with them to go to them, to see whether they can satisfy you in the thing. Many men stand and wonder at a report, whereas if they, or any friend for them, would but inquire into the matter, they might have such a plain history of the things related to them as would fully satisfy them.

Thirdly, To take heed of being inventive. Men still follow after new vanities; if they find not satisfaction in one, they are not moved thereby to seek the true God that they may have satisfaction, but seek for it in other things. Oh let us consider thus; I find no satisfaction in this; yea, but is it not because I forsake the Lord God, in whom there is all satisfaction? let me repair to God, and in him I shall find all fulness. No, but they take another course; I have not satisfaction in this thing, then I will seek for it in something else: and so they go from one false way to another, and in this sense increase lies. I will have new devices to shift off truth. The consciences of men will not be put off with old shifts; they have satisfied their conscience a while with one device; yea, but it will be put off no longer with that, they must have another; and when conscience comes to apprehend the weakness of that, then another. Oh, take heed of being inventive for the satisfying of conscience. Thine inventions may prove judgments in the hand of God.

"And desolation."

When men embrace their own vain conceits, and hopes, and false ways, they think they have gotten a great catch; but the truth is, they embrace their own ruin; mark how they are joined together, "He daily increaseth lies and desolation," "desolation" is the fruit of "lies;" and moreover, desolation is increased by lies; the more sin the more desolation, you will perish the more dreadfully. "A false witness" (saith Prov. xix. 9,) "shall not be unpunished, and he that speaketh lies shall perish." But he that walks uprightly walks surely. Prov. xii. 12, "The lip of truth shall be established for ever; but a lying tongue is but for a moment:" it may bluster a while and deceive many; yea, but it is "but for a moment."

"And they do make a covenant with the Assyrians."

That is, that they might have power to crush their brethren of Judah, they seek to make a covenant with the Assyrians, thinking to strengthen themselves thereby. You have found this charged upon them many times in this prophecy, in chap. x. particularly; their making a covenant with wicked men is repeated again and again, to show the heinousness of their sin, in forsaking God to join with the ungodly, and to teach us this lesson:

Obs. 3. When people are guilty of a sin, the prophets of God should beat upon it again and again. I shall not need to speak any further of this.

"And oil is carried into Egypt;" that is, they carry oil for gifts, and merchandise. The land of Canaan abounded much in oil, while there was little or none

* See the Apology of the Dissenting Brethren; and the Assembly's Answer to it.

in the land of Egypt, and therefore it was a great merchandise to carry oil from the land of Canaan into Egypt. So in Ezek. xxvii. 17, "Judah, and the land of Israel, they were thy merchants: they traded in thy market wheat of Minnith, and Pannag, and honey, and oil, and balm." But oil was (as it were) the staple commodity.

Now, my brethren, Egypt you know is a type of antichrist, and Canaan a type of the church. Egypt has no oil, no oil grows there; no, there are gall and wormwood, but there is no oil; but oil is in the land of Canaan. My brethren, what are we but almost like Egypt this day? We would be loth to return into Egypt to our former bondage, but we even turn ourselves to be as Egypt, we have little oil among us. What! is God bringing us to Canaan? how comes it to pass there is no more oil then? Oh! the oil that is among us (if there be any) is rather the oil of scorpions than any thing else; men's spirits, and men's pens and tongues, are even full of this oil, as if the ink made in these days was made of the oil of scorpions. Israel (the ten tribes) would send oil to Egypt, to gain the favour of Egypt; that they might have their wills over their brethren, they would be at a great deal of cost, and part with their oil. O my brethren, shall it be so with us in a spiritual sense; that we may have our wills over our brethren, shall we part with our oil? Why do not we say as the fig tree, "Shall we leave our sweetness to come and reign over you?" So, shall we leave our oil, that is, the suppleness, the gentleness, the tenderness of our spirits, shall we yield these, that we may prevail over our brethren? Oh how many were of supple, tender spirits, and loving one towards another! yet, out of a desire to prevail against their brethren, have parted with their oil, even with the tenderness and suppleness of their spirits. Remember, Egypt has no oil, oil is the produce of Canaan.

Ver. 2. *The Lord hath also a controversy with Judah, and will punish Jacob according to his ways; according to his doings will he recompense him.*

This verse I shall presently pass over. But the first part is very observable.

"The Lord hath also a controversy with Judah." Calvin saith of this, It is a wonderful thing. Did not God say, that "Judah yet ruleth with God, and is faithful with the saints;" and now saith, "The Lord hath also a controversy with Judah?"

Mirum est, &c. Calv. in loc.

I find some therefore would reconcile it by rendering it thus, "The Lord hath also a controversy *for* Judah;" but this seems a little strained: but if we read it as rendered in our version, "The Lord hath also a controversy *with* Judah," four reasons may be given why, after God had said that "Judah yet ruleth with God, and is faithful with the saints," he adds, He "hath also a controversy with Judah."

1. To show that God does not so look at the good of his people, but that he sees their evil too. You know those passages in Rev. ii., where, when God commends certain churches for doing thus and thus, he adds, "Nevertheless I have somewhat against thee," I do not so observe your good, as that your evil should escape me. My brethren, some there are, that if there be any evil in men, can see no good in them; this is wicked. But there are others, that if there be any good in them, can see no evil; this is too much indulgence, they err in both extremes.

2. Men are very apt to excuse their evil by their good. I mean thus, that such as embrace the true worship of God, are right there, they *will* have pure ordinances, and the worship of God conformable to the word; but because of that, though there be some looseness and negligence in their ways otherwise, they attempt to silence conscience; and think they are the true worshippers of God, and have the ordinances of God in their purity and power, and so think to swallow down all, much looseness, much carnality, much pride, much sensuality, much hypocrisy: because they retain the true worship of God, they seek to satisfy conscience. Oh! take heed of this; Judah retained the true worship of God, yet "the Lord hath also a controversy with Judah," and the Lord Jehovah may have a controversy against you also.

3. That Israel might neither think God or the prophet partial. The ten tribes might say, Does God threaten us? Is not Judah as bad as we? are there not evils among Judah as well as amongst us? are we only the sinful people? No, (saith the prophet,) I acknowledge there is much evil in Judah, and therefore "the Lord hath also a controversy with Judah," and Judah is not like to escape: delude not yourselves with the vain hope, that because others are bad, therefore you may escape; no, they are bad, and therefore God has a controversy against them. This may be a useful note to us; men are very ready to put off the evils which they are guilty of with this, I am not worse than others, I do such a thing amiss, and others do the same as well as I; and so they think to escape that way. O thou weak, vain man, why wilt thou deceive thy soul with this? Dost thou think that another man's evil will excuse thy sin? Thou art a vain man, and knowest not the way of God.

4. To show the ten tribes how much more must they expect the displeasure of God. If with Judah, who retains the true worship of God, yet, for some other evils, God has a controversy, then what will become of Israel, who has those same evils, and rejects the true worship of God too? As if the prophet should say, Your condition is far worse, therefore doth the Lord say, "The Lord hath also a controversy with Judah," that he might aggravate the evils of Israel: like that of Peter, "If the righteous scarcely be saved, where shall the ungodly and the sinner appear?" If so be that with the church which has the pure ordinances God is yet displeased for their sin, how much more will he be displeased with them who are corrupt in his worship! Therefore men should not bless themselves with such discourse as this, Why, others have evils as well as we. Yea, but if God will punish them for their evils who have fewer, and a great deal more good, than thou, how much more will he punish thee! Oh! if those that are the dear saints of God, that worship him in truth and sincerity, shall not escape scot-free for the evils among them; O, then, what will become of thee who art a wicked and vile wretch, and hast no good at all? If a Moses, that had done God so much service, yet for one sin of passion, in that he once spake unadvisedly with his lips, was shut out of the land of Canaan by the Lord, and commanded to speak no more to him of that matter; what will become of thee, who hast a passionate, froward spirit, of thee, who never hast nor wilt do God such service, what will become of thee? Oh, how mayst thou look to be shut out! This use you must make of the sins of others, and God's dealings with them. And saith he,

"And will punish Jacob according to his ways."

There are two questions necessary for the opening of this.

First, Why the ten tribes are called by the name of Jacob? we never read that they are called by the name of Isaac, and of Abraham.

Now the answer to this is very satisfactory, thus: The people of God are called in Scripture by the name of Jacob, and of Israel, Jacob's other name, rather than by the name of Abraham and Isaac, because they, though they were godly, and were the father and grandfather, yet in Abraham's family there was a wicked son as well as a good one; likewise from Isaac's loins there came Esau as well as Jacob; but from Jacob's loins there came none but were of God's church. Jacob's sons were the twelve patriarchs, and therefore the posterity is called by the name of Jacob, rather than that of Abraham or Isaac: "I said not to the seed of Jacob, Seek ye me in vain."

Secondly, Why is Jacob mentioned in this place?

Because the prophet intends presently, in the words that follow, to bring the example of Jacob to them before he was Israel, to aggravate their sin in order to their humiliation; and therefore here he names Jacob, to take away that vain plea of their hearts. Whereas they would say, Are not we the posterity of Jacob, have not we Jacob for our father? Well, (saith he,) I will punish Jacob; and I will show you presently, that you have no such cause to boast yourselves that you have Jacob to be your father. So, with most interpreters, I understand this.

"According to his doings will he recompense him." Of this part of the text I shall speak nothing, because in chap. iv. ver. 9, we had the very same words.

Ver. 3, 4. *He took his brother by the heel in the womb, and by his strength he had power with God: yea, he had power over the angel, and prevailed: he wept, and made supplication unto him: he found him in Beth-el, and there he spake with us.*

This prophet inveighing against the sins of these ten tribes, and threatening judgments, in these words takes away the plea which he saw was in their hearts against what he had said; We are the children of Jacob, and why do you thus charge us, and threaten us in the name of God? was not Jacob our father? as in Christ's time they pleaded that Abraham was their father.

Now in these words the prophet takes away this plea: You may bless yourselves in that Jacob was your father, but it will do you little good, for you are a degenerate offspring. True, God was very gracious to Jacob, and Jacob was very dear to God; it is otherwise with you, Jacob worshipped God after another manner than you do. The prophet therefore sets before this people here, in the words read, God's mercy to Jacob, and Jacob's graciousness in his behaviour toward God, that he might upbraid those children of Jacob who walked so unworthy of such a gracious father as Jacob was.

Now how this is set forth we shall speak to presently, only from the general scope of the passage we notice this one instruction:

Obs. It is a great reproach to wicked children, to hear of the graciousness of their parents. It should be a matter of much humiliation to them to hear of the relation that their parents had to God, and how zealously they worshipped him; children that have had gracious parents, should look upon it as a shame to them when at any time the graciousness of their parents is but mentioned before them. A king of Poland was wont to carry the picture of his father, of whom he had honourable esteem, in a plate of gold about his neck; and when he was about to do any matter of great importance, he would take this picture and kiss it, and use these words, God grant that I may now do nothing remissly, nothing unworthy of my father. O, you that have had gracious ancestors, think often of them, and when you are tempted to sin, reflect, Is not this unworthy of my ancestors? would they have done thus? Children should so walk as the virtues of their fathers should not die in them, but they should hold them forth. As Ambrose, in an oration on the commendations of Theodosius, saith, Though Theodosius be gone, yet surely, so long as his son lives, Theodosius will live among us. He meant thus, that the virtues of that excellent emperor would certainly live in his son, who was so hopeful. Oh! it is an excellent thing when the virtues of gracious parents live in their children; and it is a very evil thing when the parents are dead, yea, and their virtues are dead in respect of their children, nothing of them appears in them: they love to inherit their lands and estates, but it were far better to inherit their virtues and their godliness. But the people of Israel did not inherit the godliness of Jacob, and did not lay to heart the goodness of God towards their father Jacob, so that the prophet here now lays it all open before them, and to that end makes use, in the two verses which I have read to you, of three remarkable circumstances narrated of Jacob. They are recorded in Genesis, and there is in them much of the mind of God.

I. His taking his brother by the heel in the womb, Gen. xxv. 26.

II. His wrestling with the angel, Gen. xxxii. 24—32.

III. His interviews with God at Beth-el, Gen. xxviii. 10—22; xxxv. 9—15.

I. His taking his brother in the womb. "He took his brother by the heel in the womb." You must refer to Gen. xxv. 26, to know the mind of God in this; there you find that in the womb of Rebekah there was a striving between Jacob and Esau before they were born, and at their birth Jacob puts his hand out and takes his brother by the heel, from whence he had his name Jacob, which signifies a heel, and from thence a supplanter. And Esau obtained his name because he was hairy when born, because he was as it were a man already, a man made in the womb. Saith Luther, When Esau was born, and they saw him so hairy, they thought he was the man that would do very great and famous things in the world, and from thence he had his name Esau: now Jacob in his birth takes by the heel this very Esau, of whom such high expectations were entertained. A most wonderful history, saith Luther on the place, this of Jacob's thus taking his brother by the heel.

יַעֲקֹב à עָקַב supplantavit.
עֵשָׂו à עָשָׂה operatus est.

Habet nomen à faciendo; hic ille vir qui præclare omnia faciet. Luth.

But what is the meaning of this? (you will say;) why does the prophet instance this? What is this to the ten tribes, that Jacob took his brother by the heel? what good would this do the people to whom Hosea was prophesying? and what did he aim at? Was this story to be a means to humble the people for their sins? how could it do it? Therefore we must know that the scope and meaning of this great work of God, in Jacob's taking "his brother by the heel in the womb," was to show,

1. The free election of God. Esau was the first-born, and so in an orderly course the birthright should have descended on him and on his posterity, for such was the custom, the blessing was wont to go along with the first-born, and with their posterity; (in which the first-born was a type of Christ, who is called, "The first-begotten of all creatures;" and the blessing upon the first-born was a type of the blessing that we have by Christ;) now, though this in an orderly way belonged to Esau, as being the first-born, yet Jacob's taking of him by the heel was a certain token from God that Jacob should supplant him, and that he should get from him the birthright, and so the blessing; and in that Jacob should thus get the blessing, though he were the younger, and this sign was given of it when he was in the womb, this showed the free election of God, that it was through God's mere free grace that Jacob had the blessing rather than Esau, and that consequently the posterity of Jacob were in a better condition than the posterity of Esau. It was only the free grace of God, not from any excellency in Jacob, any worthiness in him more than in Esau, for God thus presignified the good which he intended to Jacob, "the

children being not yet born, neither having done any good or evil," Rom. ix. 11.

Though Esau was the elder and stronger, a hairy, active, stout man, and Jacob a plain man, yet Jacob is chosen, Esau is rejected; and God pre-signifies this by his taking his brother by the heel. Now in this sense it concerneth the people very much.

As if he should say, What! you are the posterity of Jacob, and not of Esau, and you glory in this; well, how comes it to pass so great privileges are attached to the posterity of Jacob rather than to the posterity of Esau; how comes this? Is it not from the free grace of God in choosing one rather than the other, and that in the very womb? As in Mal. i. 2, 3, "I have loved you, saith the Lord. Yet ye say, Wherein hast thou loved us? Was not Esau Jacob's brother? saith the Lord: yet I loved Jacob, and I hated Esau." In this I manifested my free love, even unto this people, that though Esau was Jacob's brother, and eldest brother, yet I loved Jacob and hated Esau. So in Rom. ix. 11—13, "For the children being not yet born, neither having done any good or evil, that the purpose of God according to election might stand, not of works, but of him that calleth; it was said unto her, The elder shall serve the younger. As it is written, Jacob have I loved, but Esau have I hated." Now that this took place in the womb was to show God's free grace.

If any should say, But God foresaw that Jacob would be a better man than Esau;

I answer, If it were of foreseen works, there were no argument in this to prove God's free election; but the apostle makes it to be an argument to prove God's free election of Jacob rather than Esau, because he chose them in the womb.

Luther, on Gen. xxv., has an excellent discourse on this subject, concerning God's rejecting the pride, pomp, and vanity of the world, and choosing the things that are mean and contemptible in the eyes of the world; and it was an emblem of it, in that God would rather choose Jacob the "plain man," than Esau the hunter, and the hairy man; I say, this shadowed forth that the Lord intends to reject the brave things of the world, its gallantry, glory, and pomp, and will rather choose the mean and contemptible things of the world. Who can persuade (saith Luther on the place) the pope, and Charles the Fifth, the French king, and the like, that they, being great in the world, yet are contemptible in the eyes of God, and God has rather chosen despised and contemptible things than them? And that was the scope of the prophet, that they should consider of the free grace of God towards Jacob, and so be humbled. And we should hence,

Obs. 1. We are to acknowledge God's election of our forefathers, and all the good we enjoy by such a choice, to be a fruit of free grace. Others were before God as well as our forefathers; as now, when God brought the gospel first to England, other nations were before God as well as it, it was mere free grace that pitched upon them rather than others, and we enjoy the blessing of it to this day; let us not sin against this free grace of God showed to our ancestors.

O s. 2. Those who enjoy great blessings, either temporal or spiritual, from God's mercy to their ancestors, are to consider and devoutly acknowledge the free grace of God. As now, such of you as are rich and great in the world, whence is it that your ancestors were more rich than others, and were not beggars as well as others? was it not free grace, the free, undeserved goodness of God? The ancestors of others were before God in "the same lump," Rom. ix. 21, and that God should pitch upon your ancestors to be honourable in the earth and rich, and you enjoy the benefit of it in this world, ascribe to his discriminating mercy. It may be, too, some elder brother, though honourable and rich, is rejected, and families rise from the younger brother rather than the elder; it was so here, Jacob that was the younger afterwards came to have the blessing, and Esau was rejected. Sometimes the posterity of the elder brother proves wicked; it was so here, religion flourished in the family of Jacob, and not in the family of Esau.

Look back to this, and see what cause you have to bless God, and how you are engaged to his free grace towards you in regard of your ancestors; as here, the prophet would have this people look back to the free grace of God to their father Jacob.

2. How eagerly Jacob desired the blessing. "He took his brother by the heel in the womb." That is, as if he should say, Your father Jacob was greedy of the blessing, greedy of the birthright; there was a secret instinct of God on the spirit of Jacob when he was in the very womb, which rendered him so desirous of the blessing of the birthright, that he would do what he could to get it from his brother. As if the prophet should say, Oh, but you that are his posterity are carnal, you do not regard the privilege of the birthright, nor the attendant blessing; being carnal, you care not which way the blessing goes, so that you may but live and have your ease and contentment to the flesh; oh, you are not like your father Jacob, who eagerly desired this blessing.

We are to make use of this for the humbling of our souls, thus: Some of you that have had your parents in your youth gracious and godly, and greedy after the things of God, how negligent have you been! Oh how negligent have I been! how careless is my spirit, and slight and vain! yea, though come to years, yet do I little regard that which my parents were eagerly desirous of when very young.

3. The prevailing of the people of God against the wicked at last. "He took his brother by the heel in the womb." God made Jacob a famous and notable type in this work, that certainly the saints, though they may seem to be low and mean for the present, yet shall they get advantage, ultimately, over the men of the world. The men of the world are set out by Esau; they ruffle abroad in the world, and are of fiery hot spirits, as Esau was, and they have great things in the world for a time, and the saints are under them, as Jacob was under Esau; but certainly the saints shall prevail against all the Edomites, all the Esaus, if I may so speak; there is a time coming in which they shall supplant them, and get the power over them, in which the godly shall prevail at length against all the wicked and ungodly in the world. You should consider it as if the prophet said to them, You are seeking to provide for yourselves in your sinful ways. Oh! if you did but consider, that the faithful, though they be persecuted for a time, and in a low condition, yet they shall get the power over all the great ones in the world, it would be otherwise with you than it is now. So the Scriptures tell us, that at length they shall have the dominion: Dan. vii. 18, "The saints of the most High shall take the kingdom;" and in ver. 21, "I beheld, and the same horn made war with the saints, and prevailed against them." But how long? Ver. 22, "Until the Ancient of days came, and judgment was given to the saints of the most High; and the time came that the saints possessed the kingdom." And ver. 27, "The kingdom and dominion, and the greatness of the kingdom under the whole heaven, shall be given to the people of the saints of the most High;" there is a time that it shall be given to them. And Psal. xlix. 14, "The upright shall have dominion over them in the morning." This was typified in this notable work of God in Jacob's taking Esau by the heel to supplant him.

4. The providence of God, how it extends towards infants, even in the very womb. The very striving of children in the womb is not without providence; there

was a mighty providence of God in this, to pre-signify the greatest things of God that are revealed in the Scripture. Now, though there be no such extraordinary and great things set forth by the ordinary stirrings of infants in the womb, yet certainly there is no stirring of the child in the womb, but it is with some providence of God, and God has his eye upon, and his hand in, the working even of the very child in the womb.

5. The secret ways of God in working upon infants. Though they have not the use of reason, yet, saith Luther here, there may be mighty workings of God even upon their spirits, in a secret way that we are not able to understand. And thereupon he exclaims against such as deny baptism to them, because they deem them not capable of any work of God upon them. The denying of baptism upon that ground, he calls a very odious and impious opinion; for, saith he, as it is with children, they have their nourishment in the womb in another manner than when they are born; so the work of God upon their spirits may be such as when they are in the womb, and when they are little ones, before they come to the use of reason, that may be far different to what the work of God is upon them when they come afterwards to have the use of reason.

Odiosum et impium dogma Anabaptistarum, qui ideo pueris baptismum negant, quia sensu ac menta careant, nec intelligant quæ cum eis aguntur. Luth. in loc.

6. That men who prove remarkable in their lives, have many times, in their very birth, notable presages of their future exploits. So Jacob here; "He took his brother by the heel in the womb." So Moses, by what occurred at his birth, by his strange and wonderful deliverance afterwards, and by his being brought into Pharaoh's court, gave a presage of what he would be; and so John Baptist gave early intimations of his important mission; and so other accounts tell us, that of men who have been famous for good or evil, there have been presages at their birth. Of Nero, who did such monstrous things, it is said that he was born with his heels forward. And of Dominicus, that great persecutor of the saints, that when his mother was with child, she dreamed that she had in her womb a wolf, with a firebrand in his mouth; and he even proved to be so, for he was one of the first that stirred up persecution against the saints by fire. Your papists turn it quite otherwise; I remember one of them interpreting this providence of God, in sending the mother of Dominicus (who was the father of the Dominicans) such a dream, saith it was to signify, that by the splendour of his holiness and doctrine he should inflame the whole world: experience, however, taught far otherwise. Now I note this only to show the vanity of men's spirits in interpreting ways of providence merely according to their own humours. And thus much for that remarkable circumstance recorded of Jacob, that "he took his brother by the heel in the womb." Now follows the next, and that is,

II. His wrestling with the angel. "And by his strength he had power with God."

This story refers to Gen. xxxii. In the preceding chapter you find that God, having bid Jacob return into the land of his fathers, and to his kindred, promised him that he would be with him in his journey; yet mark, though God had made him go this journey, and had promised that he would be with him in it, yet Jacob, for all that, meets with as hard things in the way as almost we can read, or hear, that any one ever experienced. He had an express command of God to go, and a promise that he would be with him in the journey; yet it would ask some time to show the many hard things which Jacob met withal in it; but, amongst others, this was a very sad one, that being to go by the land of Seir, the country of Edom, where his brother Esau lived, he sent messengers before him, not being altogether without some fear that the old grudge still remained in the heart of his brother, and that now, having an opportunity to satisfy his desire upon him, he might take advantage of it. As he feared, so he found it, for having sent messengers to his brother, they return again to him, and bring him word that his brother was coming against him with four hundred men; so manifesting, by the manner of his coming, that he did intend mischief against Jacob. And now, upon this, the heart of Jacob was much distressed; so the text saith, Gen. xxxii. 7, "Then Jacob was greatly afraid and distressed;" vehemently afraid, and great straits were upon his spirit. Now, being in such great straits, Jacob seeks to provide for himself; he did not presently conclude and say, We are utterly undone, but he would see what could be done; so, though he knew the fury of his brother, yet, if it were possible but to save some part of his company, he would do it, and so he prudently divides them in the way that he conceived best for their safety. But though he dealt thus prudently, yet, *that* he trusted not to, but seeks unto the Lord; he would go to prayer in the great strait and extremity he was in. So in ver. 24, "And Jacob was left alone; and there wrestled a man with him until the breaking of the day;" which cannot be interpreted otherwise than that he was waiting upon God to know his mind, and to seek God. And when he was alone, there comes out one in the form of a man, wrestling against him as though he likewise intended to destroy him; and this was no other than God himself, the Lord Jesus Christ. That it was Christ appearing in human shape, and not an angel, is clear from ver. 5, where he is called Jehovah, God of hosts; and you find, in Gen. xxxii. 30, that "Jacob called the name of the place Peniel; for," saith he, "I have seen God face to face, and my life is preserved." God comes and appears against him as an enemy, even at that time in which this holy man Jacob was in such great straits; and yet Jacob, though God did thus appear against him, did not sink in his heart, but stirred up all the strength that he had, and wrestles even with God himself, thus appearing like an enemy, and "had power" at length, "and prevailed." One would have thought that there had been enough to have sunk Jacob's spirit, the distress that he was in at that time, his brother coming with four hundred men ready to destroy him, he left alone, one coming out and wrestling with him; yet, "by his strength he had power with God, and prevailed." This is as remarkable a relation as any we have in the Old Testament.

"He had power with the angel," that is, with God, when he came and wrestled with him in a time of so great extremity. I beseech you here to

Obs. 3. It is God's way sometimes with his best and dearest saints, in their greatest dangers, and in their greatest afflictions and troubles, to seem to come forth as their enemy. When God came and wrestled with Jacob, and seemed to be as an enemy to him, was the time of the greatest extremity that one would think it possible for a man to be in, you cannot apprehend greater distresses, or greater cause for distress, than Jacob had at this time; a poor man with a few women and children and cattle, and his brother who owed him a grudge, and had sought his death, coming with four hundred men in an hostile manner, and he "left alone," yet at this time God appears like an enemy to him; this was sad, a very heavy condition indeed. As God did with Jacob, so with Christ himself; God never so appeared outwardly against Christ, as when his disciples left him, just in the night when he was to be betrayed, then he was in an agony, and sweat drops of water and blood; yea, and when he was in the hands of his enemies, and lift up to the cross, and made a derision of to all the world, yet then he cries, "My God, my God, why hast thou forsaken me?" Forsaken at that time in so great distress! Jacob in this was even a type of God's forsaking Christ in times of such great distress. And so we find in Job, when he was in his great distresses, yet "the terrors of the Almighty" were upon him: and Heman, with divers others whom we might name. This is a point of very great concernment to us. O, be not discouraged, ye people of God, if at any time ye be brought into a condition like Jacob's. His story is of very great concernment to you; God's ways towards him shadowing forth what they are like to be to other saints afterwards, even to the end of the world, namely this; That the most eminent and most precious saints of God must not think to be excused even from this condition, that when they are brought into the greatest outward afflictions that possibly can be imagined, God may not even at that time appear against them like an enemy. Oh! this is the saddest condition conceivable, to one who has any acquaintance with God. Many poor servants of God in affliction will say, As for these afflictions, they are heavy indeed upon me, my estate gone, or husband gone, or wife gone, and my friends leave me in this condition; yea, and it may be the hand of God is upon me in sickness, and so one trouble after another: but though these things are heavy, had I but the light of the face of God upon me it would be nothing to me; had I but those comforts which once I enjoyed in the assurance of God's love, all would not be much to me; but now, when all these outward comforts are gone, I see God appearing like an enemy to me so as he never did before. Does God deal thus with any of his people? am I not a reprobate? For God is wont, when his people are in affliction, to appear with the light of his face to comfort and encourage them; but he has not done so to me: even at this time I find God more terrible to my soul than I have ever yet found him, and therefore surely I am but a cast-away. I make no question but some of you may know the meaning of such temptations as these in the time of your afflictions, or if you have not known the meaning of them hitherto, you may hereafter; and you that have known, or hereafter shall be brought to know, what these things mean, O, treasure up this scripture, it will be worth a world to you; for the devil will mightily strengthen himself with this, What, are not you a cast-away? Surely God has rejected you, else he would never appear against you in your afflictions if he had any love to you.

Answer, I say, the temptation thus:

I have read in the book of God, and heard that even thus God dealt with my father Jacob, who was so precious to him.

Yea, but was not he in some way of sin?

No, he was in the way in which God bade him go, and yet even then, in his so great distress, God wrestled with him, never wrestled more with him than then, and seemed even then, at such a time as that was, to come against him like an enemy. Oh! treasure up this, that your hearts may not sink in despair, when the greatest afflictions and spiritual desertions meet together.

"By his strength he had power with God."

It appears that when God came thus against him to wrestle with him, God intended no hurt to him, it was but to stir up his strength, and to prepare him for great deliverance, and for choice mercies; God at this very time did intend to Jacob as great a mercy as ever he gave to any of the children of men in this world, and that was this, That he should have strength to prevail with God, that he should have his name changed and be called Israel, a prince prevailing with God, and so be honourable to the end of the world, and be set up as a type to strengthen the faith and to comfort the desponding hearts of all future saints; I say, it was as great a mercy as ever any mere child of man had in this world, and that at the very time when Jacob was in almost the greatest conceivable depth of affliction. Therefore here,

Obs. 4. God sometimes brings the deepest affliction when he intends the greatest mercy. Do not therefore conclude, Never any was so afflicted as I have been: why, Jacob might have said so, and yet God had never greater thoughts of mercy towards him than he had then. Therefore remember this again, when tempted to think, Never any was so afflicted as I have been: grant it, yet it may be there is mercy intended for you at this time, such as never yet was granted to any of the children of men before; it is possible it may be so, it was so with Jacob, and therefore let not your faith flag.

"By his strength he had power with God." In this his great distress he does not lie down as a man discouraged, but he stirs up what strength he had, and falls a wrestling with this man, even with God, thus appearing against him as an enemy. Oh! thus should the seed of Jacob do, you that are the seed of Jacob, for so specially praying Christians in time of distress are called. "I said not to the seed of Jacob, Seek ye me in vain," Isa. xlv. 19. They are not called the seed of Abraham, but of Jacob; because Jacob was so eminent in praying in such great extremity, you that are the seed of Jacob should do so. Every little opposition that comes upon a sluggish heart, upon one of low and mean principles, presently damps his spirit, makes him yield and bows him down, and he is ready to say, All is gone. Oh! art thou of the seed of Jacob? The seed of Jacob should never think their condition to be so sad, but there may be recovery. Is it a great affliction that is upon me? am I in great distress? let me so much the more stir up my strength. When Alexander was in a great danger he exclaimed, Now there is a danger fit for the mind of Alexander. So, does God bring into great straits? now there is a strait fit for a gracious heart, for one that is partaker of the Divine nature to encounter: stir up therefore what strength thou hast; do not say, I shall never be able to overcome this difficulty; do not say so, for you are not in greater straits than Jacob was at this time, and yet mark, Jacob had power, and stirs up his power. It may be you have such strength as will do more than you are aware of; the grace of God is mighty in the hearts of his saints. Have you never been enabled to do more than ever you thought you should have been? Jacob stirs up his strength, he does not lie down sullen and discouraged, as is usual for Christians to do; if God does but afflict them, and especially if he draws but the light of his face a little from them, presently they lie down discouraged, and will not be comforted. Oh! thou dost not show thyself to be of "the seed of Jacob," thou hast not the spirit of thy father Jacob in thee.

"By his strength he had power with God." "Strength:" what strength? you will say.

He had very great bodily strength, he wrestled partly with bodily strength; as in Gen. xxix. 8, 10, you find that Jacob was a very strong man of his body, for the stone of the well which the shepherds were fain to meet together to roll away, Jacob took and rolled away presently: but certainly he had strength beyond his ordinary bodily strength at this time; God raised a bodily strength beyond whatever he had, and likely beyond whatever man had before. God increased Samson's bodily strength to a great pitch; and the power of God was seen in that, and may be seen much in the elevating of nature in a creature; as the Scripture saith, the body that "is sown in weakness, is raised in power," 1 Cor. xv. 43. Luther saith, That men's bodies shall be raised to such strength, that they shall be able to toss mountains as a man tosses a ball. And Anselm has an expression of like import, That the saints shall be so strong in the world to come, that if they will they can shake the earth at their pleasure. Surely much bodily strength was here to wrestle with an angel. You know the power of an angel; one in one night could slay above fourscore thousand men; and yet here Jacob himself wrestles with an angel; that is, with the Messenger, the Angel of the new covenant, the Son of God, the Second Person in the Trinity. But especially Jacob's spiritual strength, his soul-wrestling, was great; the wrestling of faith within him was at that time very great, it was the irresistible might of man's weakness, when made strong τῇ ἐνέργειᾳ τοῦ Θεοῦ, by the in-working of God.

Obs. 1. When God strives against his servants, he gives them correspondent strength. Here Jacob was in great extremity, and God comes and wrestles against him, but God gives him strength proportionable to his wrestling. O, take this for thy comfort and encouragement. Many times thou art ready to reason thus, Alas, I am not able to endure a little affliction, what shall I do if I meet with a greater affliction? certainly then I should sink. O, be not discouraged with such unbelieving thoughts, for though thou art weak, and it is as much as ever thou canst do to stand under thy present burden; know assuredly, if greater burdens come, there will come greater strength too: there was answerable strength put into Jacob to wrestle with those difficulties to which he was called. God will not suffer us to be tempted beyond our strength.

"By *his* strength." What! Jacob's strength? Mark, the strength that God puts into us, though it be God's own, yet when we have it, and work by it, God accounts it as ours; it is called Jacob's strength, though the truth is it was God's strength; God himself wrestling with him gives him strength, and yet he will account it Jacob's own strength. Hence, further,

Obs. 5. It is a great honour to manifest much strength in wrestling with God in prayer. In this was the honour of Jacob, with his strength he prevailed with God. We should not come with weak and empty prayers, but we should put forth strength; if a Christian has any strength in the world for any thing, he should have it in prayer. According to the strength of the fire, the bullet ascends; so according to what strength we put forth in prayer, so is our prevalence. This strength of Jacob was a type of the spiritual strength which God gives his saints when they have to deal with him: and we find in the New Testament mention of very great strength that the saints have by the grace of God. In Eph. iii. 16, "That he would grant you, according to the riches of his glory, to be strengthened with might by his Spirit in the inner man." Mark what expressions are here, That they might "be strengthened," be strengthened "with might," and "with might by his Spirit," the Spirit of God, and "in the inner man;" and all this "according to the riches of his glory." Such strength a Christian may attain to; I say, a Christian may here in this world attain to such strength; there is might added to strength, and the Spirit of God to enable him to that might, and that in the inner man, and that according to the riches of God's glory. Surely the strength is great that is by the Spirit of God, but such strength as shall manifest the glory of the Spirit of God, yea, such strength as shall manifest the riches of the glory of the Spirit of God, this is the strength attainable for Christians, even here in this world: this is the strength which the apostle prays for the Ephesians. O, let us be ashamed of our weaknesses, seeing such strength is to be had. Jesus Christ is the Lion of the tribe of Judah, he has strength, and of his fulness we may come to receive grace for grace. O, let us not be satisfied with faint desires and wishes, when Jesus Christ is tendered to us as the fountain of strength.

Now I appeal to you Christians, Do you walk so that your strength manifests that such riches of the glory of God dwell in you? There is another scripture, "Strengthened," saith Col. i. 11, "with all might, according to his glorious power." Mark, "with *all might*, according to his glorious power." Thus Christians should seek to be strengthened with all might, according to the glorious power of God. To what? "Unto all patience and long-suffering with joyfulness." "Unto all patience." It may be, you have strength to bear some afflictions, and have some patience; but are you strengthened with "all might?" and are you strengthened according to the glorious power of God, unto "all patience?" And it may be, for a time you seem to have some patience; but hath patience had her perfect work in you? and is it to all "long-suffering?" Though the affliction continue a great while, will you patiently hold out to "long-suffering," and that "with joyfulness?" This is the glory of Christians, to have strength with God, the glorious power of God strengthening them "with all might," "unto all patience and long-suffering," and that "with joyfulness." "By his strength he had power with God, and prevailed;" he was as a prince with God: as in Gen. xxxii. 28, "For as a prince hast thou power with God;" so here, whereas it is said in your books, "he had power with God," the words שרה את-אלהים may be as well translated, he was a prince with God; and then it is repeated, "yea, he had power over the angel," וישר אל-מלאך ויכל he was a prince against the angel, and so prevailed.

Obs. 6. The way to prevail with men is, to prevail with God. Esau came against Jacob to destroy him, and he was afraid, but God gave him a certain evidence that he should prevail; Thou hast prevailed with me, saith he, and there is no fear of prevailing with all the men of the world, now thou hast prevailed with God. This indeed, and especially in these times, were a very useful topic to enlarge upon; that the way to prevail with men is, to prevail with God. What are all the powers of men? they are all at the disposal of God; the work is done when thou hast but prevailed with God. Thou hearest of great dangers that there are abroad in the world, but do thou get alone in thy closet, and fall a wrestling with God, and continue wrestling till thou dost feel thy faith wrestling with God, then thou mayst come down and conclude the work is done: none shall ever prevail against those who have so much interest with God; these may live joyfully in the world, never need fear the power and the rage of wicked men, they have that within them that helps them to prevail with God, and certainly man cannot prevail against them. Our rough brethren have come out against us, as here Esau, this rough brother of Jacob, came out against him, and yet Jacob, prevailing with God, prevailed against Esau. And blessed be God, that when our rough brethren have come enraged against us, there have been some amongst us who have prevailed with God, and by prevailing with God have prevailed over them, and against them. But though we are delivered from these rough brethren, yet we have rough ones of another kind still, that are against us. Oh, but let us carry ourselves blamelessly and inoffensively towards them, who yet behave themselves roughly and furiously against us, and so seek to prevail with them by a constant carriage of innocence and blamelessness of life before them, and thereby convince them, if it be possible, of all their mistakes. But above all, let us seek to prevail with God, and then God may turn their hearts, yea, the hearts of our roughest and most furious brethren, whose mouths are so opened, and whose pens are so plied against us; let us, I say, prevail with God, that so at length they may come and fall upon our necks as Esau did, and give us the right hand of fellowship: such things are not impossible. Let us not be troubled more than God would have us, but seek God, and wrestle with him: it is in vain to stand wrestling with them, giving ill word for ill word, and pen for pen, that is not the way; but wrestle with God, and walk convincingly before them, and so you may turn the hearts of your rough brethren, and that in a little time. Surely it is not more impossible to soder the spirits of brethren that seem not to be at so great a distance and so imbittered one against another as were Esau and Jacob, it is not more impossible for God now to soder them, than it was for God to soder the spirits of those brethren, that their meeting should be one of peace.

In this prevailing of Jacob against Esau we have a type of the church's prevailing against all the ungodly: though the enemies may be strong and furious, certainly the people of God shall prevail. As before in Jacob's taking Esau by the heel, there was a type that the people of God shall supplant all the wicked; so Jacob's prevailing at this time, presignifies that certainly the churches shall prevail; let men do what they will, and be as bitter as they will, the Jacobs shall prevail at length.

"Yea, he had power over the angel, and prevailed." If you look into the story you shall find that he did prevail, but it was after he had wrestled a great while. Constancy in wrestling with God will overcome at length, though we do not prevail at first, as Jacob did not, but was wrestling all night, and day broke, and then he prevailed. O, be not discouraged though you prevail not at first. Oh! I have been seeking God thus long, and have not prevailed. But go on still, you know not but that may be done in one hour that has not been done a long time before.

Mark further, Jacob after he was lame prevailed. Jacob had been wrestling all night, and got nothing; then the hollow of his thigh was touched and he became lame: now surely he will be overcome. Shall he prevail now? he that could not prevail in the midst of vigour and strength is not like to prevail now. But *then* Jacob "had power over the angel, and prevailed." Oh, this is very useful and seasonable for us.

Obs. 7. The time for the church to prevail is when she is most weak: when most unlikely to prevail, when she is lame, then is the time for her to prevail. We are ready to think, Oh, if we could not effect it when we had so much strength, is it like to be done now when our strength is so impaired? Now by this Jacob came to be more humbled when his thigh was touched, so that he was lame. God uses to damp means, and to bring even the sentence of death as an introduction to the greatest mercies.

Further, Though Jacob had a strong adversary against him, and he wrestled long with him, and he had become lame, yet, continuing wrestling, he grew more resolute towards the latter end; for you never read of Jacob being so peremptory before, "I will not let thee go, except thou bless me." The hollow of Jacob's thigh having been touched is one thing very demonstrative of the sad condition he was in; but this likewise should have been noticed, that the angel would have been gone, God would have been gone and have left him in that affliction, but then Jacob's spirit grew up more with a greater resolution than he had before, "I will not let thee go, except thou bless me." It seems that Jacob now more clearly than before discerned that he was God. This should be our way in our dealings with God, that when God brings us into the lowest condition, and seems as if he would leave us, we should stir up our spirits then, and be more resolute and strong than before. Oh! it is time now for the heart to bestir itself, when God is ready to go away. Do not say, God *will* be gone, and therefore sink down sullenly; it is time for thee then to stir up all that thou hast, and to act faith more then: as if Jacob should say, I will try yet one fall more, I will not yield the cause yet, certainly I must not perish: true, all things seem against me, as if I should be destroyed, but it must not be; faith begins to stir; has not God bid me come here? have I not his word? did not God say, he would do me good in this journey? and though it is true, the providence of God seems to work against me, yet the word of God works for me, and I will try whether shall prevail, God's word, or God's providence. Thus Jacob wrestles: "I will not let thee go;" as if he should say, I have the word for what I do, and God has bound himself by covenant, and so, though heaven and earth meet together, although I see my brother coming against me, and God departing from me, and all threatening ruin, yet I will believe still that there is mercy for me. This was Jacob's last turn, (as I may so say,) the trying as it were the last fall in this his wrestling, in opposing the word that he had with the work of God towards him. And here we would especially,

Obs. 8. It is our duty in every situation not to lay so much weight upon any work of God as upon the word of God. Let us build upon the word rather than fear the works, for it has been the usual way of God when he has given out a word, that his works have seemed to go quite cross, as not only in our father Jacob, but even in our father Abraham. What was the word of God to Abraham? There were two promises made by God to Abraham: 1. That he would bring him into a land that flowed with milk and honey. And, 2. That he would make his seed as the stars in the firmament. Well, here was God's word, but how was God's work? The very next thing that you hear of Abraham was, that after he had left all his friends, and had come into Canaan, he was ready to starve presently: now the word is, Thou shalt be brought into a land flowing with milk and honey; and as soon as ever he comes into that land he was ready to starve. Here is a land indeed!

2. That his seed should be as the stars of heaven. Abraham was twenty-five years after this before he had a child. He grew old, and also his wife. Well, at length he had one, and God commands him to sacrifice that one. What a work is here! how quite contrary to the word! Well, Isaac was saved; forty years elapse before he married; here are sixty-five years gone from the promise, and there is but one of his seed that must be as the stars of heaven. At length Isaac married, and he was twenty years without a child; here are eighty-five years and but only one birth from him; yea, and after that it appears that Jacob was above fourscore years before he married and had any children; thus there are between eight and nine score years gone, and but only Isaac and Jacob. How does the work of God here seem to contradict his word! It is the way of God, and therefore let us never trouble ourselves about God's works; he came indeed afterwards with his works and fulfilled his word to the uttermost, but for the present they seemed to be against it. O, lay up this as a lesson, you will have use for it many and many a time. It follows,

Obs. 9. Prevailing at last will recompense all our strivings. "And prevailed." Jacob was fully recompensed; he speaks of it as a recompence of Jacob after his striving; it was a hard wrestling, but he prevailed at length. And so it will be with all the people of God; let them go on and wrestle, and though things be hard for the present, when mercy comes it will pay for all. Thou wilt hereafter see no cause of repenting that thou continuedst wrestling with God; O, thou wilt see cause to bless God. Blessed be God that kept up my heart all this while: God knows that many times it was ready to sink, but if I had left off, what had become of me? I had lost the mercy that I now find; but I continued through God's mercy, and now he is come at length. Prevailing recompenses all our labour and trouble in seeking.

Well, he prevailed; but what is this to this people of Israel? Thus; this was to show their base degeneracy, as if he should say, Oh, of what a brave spirit was your father Jacob! but you are a base people, you subject yourselves to heathens, to idols: your father would not have subjected himself to any creature in the world, yea, he would wrestle with God himself when he had his word for it; but Jacob's posterity can crouch to the humours of men in the worship of God, and do any thing to save their skin: you are unworthy to be counted his posterity. Jacob's posterity indeed should be prevailers above the world's temptations. What! shall we yield to a base lust, when Jacob would not yield to the Almighty, but prevailed with him? are we of the seed of Jacob now? Oh, we are of low, mean spirits, led aside of every vanity, and overcome with every difficulty. But how did he prevail? in what way did he put forth this his strength? It follows;

"He wept, and made supplication unto him."

This weeping of Jacob is not recorded in the history of Genesis, nor, except here, in all the book of God. His supplication is recorded, but not his weeping; therefore his weeping was conveyed by tradition, or otherwise by revelation. There are many ridiculous conceits of the Jews and some old writers about this; they say it was the angel that wept, and prayed Jacob to let him alone. But to take it generally, as our divines do, that Jacob wept, and made supplication, and so prevailed with God; Jacob's heart was so pressed with his condition, that it caused tears to gush forth from him; and no marvel though tears came from him, for his heart could not but be full, when he came to think thus with himself: What! after I have served such a hard service under Laban my uncle, and God bade me come away from him, which I took to be such a great and merciful deliverance from God, yet how soon was I in danger of my life, even my uncle Laban pursuing me, but God delivered me there; and must I now fall into the hand of my brother? is the day come for him now to have his rage upon me? I see little other likelihood; his strength is great, and God himself appears against me, and I have been wrestling a great while, and I can get nothing from God, but that it is likely here I must die and perish; yea, and that God should leave me thus as he does, that God should appear a greater enemy to me than my brother Esau, and lame me! oh, now, is not this a sign that God intends to destroy me? yea, God would be gone too when I am in such a strait. All this makes him weep. As when a poor child is in straits and is crying to the mother, she beats it, and leaves it in its difficulties; can you then blame the child though it cry? So it was here; Jacob was in straits, and was seeking God, and God beats and afflicts him, and would be gone; oh, this does press tears out of the eyes of Jacob; What will become of me now? As if Jacob should have said, Were I to perish alone it were not so much, but my wives perish, and how can mine eyes endure to see their destruction? yea, it may be they will be ravished before mine eyes by these rude soldiers. These kind of workings in Jacob spirit you cannot but conceive must draw tears; he wept before the angel, considering this his sore distressed condition.

And on the other side, the reasonings of his faith would make him weep too, when he considered, Yea, but surely I am in the way of God, though I be in a great deal of danger; I have the promise and covenant of God with me; I have to deal with the holy, blessed and gracious God in all my ways; who knows but that my extremity may be God's opportunity? The heart of my brother is certainly in the hand of God, and all creatures are in God's hands too. Now the actings of faith, as well as those of fear and trouble, would make one weep; and it were well if we could weep on both sides. Sometimes you roll in your thoughts all the aggravations of your afflictions, and they make you weep: now, can you roll in your thoughts the aggravations of God's goodness and mercy, and can they make you weep? The end why God brought Jacob into this condition, to fall a weeping before the angel, was, that he might humble him, and break his heart, before he gave him deliverance; for it was one of the greatest honours (as we intimated before) that God conferred on Jacob, or ever on any man; therefore God would bring him very low before he would raise him so high, and make him fall a weeping, as well as praying, before he should have the mercy. Oh, this is God's way; he will bring men very low, to humble them before they shall have mercy; therefore when men's hearts are high and lofty, stout and hard, they are not in a way of mercy from God; but when men's hearts begin to break, thaw, and melt, and are tender, then they are on the threshold of mercy, as here. So we find it often in Scripture, that God, intending mercy, first breaks the heart and melts it by mourning and sorrowing: as Josiah, you know that was his condition, his heart melted when he heard the law, and God sends presently a promise of mercy to him. And in Jeremiah, the Lord promises his people, that he will bring them with weeping, and with supplications; that shall be their way to Zion.

Obs. 10. Heart-breaking, with tears before God, becomes the most generous and magnanimous spirit. It is an excellent thing to see a man of a brave spirit, strong and full of courage in service *for* God, yet melting, tender, and soft in his dealings *with* God. If you should see now a great captain or general, brave and magnanimous when abroad in the field about any difficult work, but when before God in prayer, weeping like a child, mourning and lamenting, and his heart breaking as soon as a child's; the manly, undaunted courage, and the broken-hearted, child-like simplicity, would extort respect. Spirits of such a mould are excellent, spirits that can turn according to what God calls them to, this way or that, can be stout and hardy in a work that demands stoutness, and can be soft, tender, and yielding where such qualities are required. Thus was our father Jacob. Oh, to have tender-hearted captains and generals, to have courageous, yet broken-hearted, spirits, to mix the work of grace thus, is most excellent, and it becomes the most brave and prudent spirit in the world, not only to fall down to prayer, but to weep before the Lord. Some men think it too low a thing to fall a weeping in prayer, as if it were womanish and childish; oh, it is an argument that thy heart is carnal and base, to think that it arises from want of understanding; I say, the thought is evil, and originates in the much corruption of thy heart. No man ever shed more tears in the presence of God than David, that brave and prudent captain. But to go far higher, I will set before you the example of Jesus Christ; Heb. v. 7, saith, "Who in the days of his flesh, when he had offered up prayers and supplications," how? "with strong crying and tears." Even Jesus Christ, the Son of God, God blessed for ever, he that was equal with the Father, the Lion of the tribe of Judah, he that had all strength and power, and had all the treasures of wisdom hid in him, and in whom the fulness of the Godhead dwelt bodily, yet when he had to deal with the Father, he offers up "prayers and supplications, with strong crying and tears." Does it become the Captain of our salvation in his seeking of God to weep? know then, it is not unbecoming any man or woman. Are you of the seed of Jacob? then, when you would prevail with God, labour to work your hearts even so as to express your affections, outwardly labour to do it in prayer, it will help to break thy heart. As a broken heart will cause outward expressions, so outward expressions will be a further cause to break the heart. And work thy heart by all arguments thou canst to come to that tenderness and softness, that thou mayst be like the Captain of thy salvation. When thou art crying to God, cry even with tears before him; and when thy heart is so broken with tears, then exercise thy faith upon the prayer of Jesus Christ. Now it is through the Spirit of Jesus Christ that my heart thus breaks, but I do not rest upon these; God forbid that I should rest upon my enlargements, upon my breakings of heart; no, but I will rest upon the breakings of Jesus Christ, who in the days of his flesh did send up mighty cries with tears unto God, and prevailed.

Obs. 11. Prayer is the great prevailing ordinance with God. "He made supplication." It has been the great engine that has carried things on in the world. When, in Rev. viii. 4, 5, "the prayers of the saints" were offered up, "there were voices, and thunderings, and lightnings, and an earthquake." Prayers of the saints can move heaven and earth; they can prevail with the God of heaven and earth. The praying legion was called the thundering legion. And Luther saith of prayers, They are our guns, our cannons; our prayers can prevail more that cannons. The saints have always put their great strength in prayer. Psal. cix. 4, is a very observable Scripture, "For my love they are my adversaries." But what then? But I pray. In your books it is, "but I give myself unto prayer." The words "give myself" you may observe printed in another distinct character, (which is to note that they are not in the original, but added by the translators, and in that they dealt faithfully,) but if you read it as in the Hebrew, "For my love they are my adversaries:" but I pray: as if he should say, That is my refuge, I account prayer my great help; they are my adversaries, and rail upon me, but I will not rail upon them again; when they oppose me I will not oppose them again. But I pray; I will pray to my God, and I believe that I have help enough there to resist all mine enemies. Jacob prevailed over the angel by supplication. It is a good sign of a gracious heart to lay the weight of business upon prayer. But I will not enter into this commonplace of the excellency, or power, of prayer and supplication, but only this, It is not every prayer that will prevail so with God.

Bombardo nostræ.

What prayer will then?

Such a prayer as Jacob's was, in Gen. xxxii. 9—12. In it there are many excellent ingredients.

1. Faith in the covenant of God. "And Jacob said, O God of my father Abraham, and God of my father Isaac." Upon this faith in the covenant the strength of any prayer most depends. Indeed to have strong expressions and affections in prayer is good; but strength of faith in the covenant of God is the greatest strength of prayer, and it was with this strength that Jacob prevailed. "O God of my father Abraham, and God of my father Isaac;" as if he should say, O thou God, that hast entered into covenant with my father Abraham and Isaac, remember thy covenant, O God, I rest upon it, upon the covenant of grace which thou hast made with them; for so certainly that with Abraham and Isaac was the same, for it is said, that "the sign of circumcision was a seal of the righteousness of faith," Rom. iv. 11. "And in thy seed shall all the nations of the earth be blessed," Gen. xxii. 18. There was the covenant of grace. Now, O Lord God, it is the covenant of grace that I rest upon in these my straits. When you are in any strait, and go to God in prayer, if you can have recourse to the covenant of grace, and act your faith upon God's covenant with you, oh! that will be a strong prayer. When there are but words in prayer, they vanish as the wind, but when there is much faith in prayer, that makes it to prevail; "the prayer of faith," that is prevalent, saith the apostle James, chap. v. 15.

2. His appeal to God, that he was in the way in which he had set him. He could appeal thus to God; "Thou which saidst unto me, Return unto thy country, and to thy kindred." Why, Lord, am I out of my way? Am I not in the way which thou hast set me? I met with difficulties in my way, but, Lord, thou saidst to me, "Return unto thy country;" thou biddest me return. That is an excellent ingredient in prayer, and adds much strength, when the soul in prayer can come to God and say, O Lord, this and that difficulty has befallen me, but, Lord, I am in the way thou hast set me, I am doing thy work, I am not out of my way. For any to be out of the way which God has set them in will mightily damp their hearts in prayer. And it is a mighty encouragement to prayer, and carries it on with mighty strength, when the soul can appeal to God, Lord, whatsoever straits I meet withal, yet I am in thy way.

3. The pleading of a particular promise: "And I will deal well with thee." God made a promise to Jacob in particular, that he would deal well with him in his journey that he went. And though it is true, the great strength is in the great promise, the covenant of grace; yet it adds much strength likewise to use particular promises that concern the very business we are about; and it is a very good thing, when we go about a business that has difficulty in it, to search the word, and to see what promises there are that more particularly concern the business we go about.

4. A deep sense of his own unworthiness. Ver. 10, "I am not worthy of the least of all the mercies, and of all the truth, which thou hast showed unto thy servant." The soul prevails when it comes with humility before God in prayer, and is truly sensible of its unworthiness of any mercy. Lord, I am not worthy of the least crumb of bread, but rather worthy to be cast out from thy presence for ever: it is an easy matter for persons to have such words in their mouths, but to have this indeed in their hearts in prayer, adds very much strength to prayer.

5. The acknowledgment of the mercy that he had received, and of the truth of God in fulfilling promises. Both add much strength to prayer, to take notice of what God has done for us, to observe how he has, in great measure, fulfilled his word for us. When we are praying, we many times are sensible only of what we would have, but not of what we receive; and the vehemency of our desires after what we would have, takes away our apprehensions, and hinders our acknowledgment of the mercies we have had already. But when thou comest to prayer, whatsoever thy state be, though in never such great straits, yet acknowledge what thou hast already, be willing to praise God in thy lowest condition.

6. Remembrance of former meanness. "For with my staff I passed over this Jordan; and now I am become two bands:" that is a further expression of his humility, and God's further mercy.

7. A thorough conviction of the importance of what he prays for. "Deliver me, I pray thee, from the hand of my brother, from the hand of Esau: for I fear him, lest he will come and smite me, and the mother with the children." Lord, I do not utter words without feeling, for, Lord, as I am crying to thee for help against my brother, I do apprehend my great extremity; Lord, I fear him, lest he come and smite me, with the mother and the children.

When we come to prayer, we must not have words,

fine and puffed up, but with little in them, but there must be as much sense of the thing that we pray for, as the words that we speak do seem to import and carry with them: many times we have great words and little sense, and that makes our prayers so empty.

8. Strong arguments. Though it is true, that what we can say to God cannot move God, yet it may move our own hearts; and God would have us to use strong arguments in prayer. "And thou saidst, I will surely do thee good, and make thy seed as the sand of the sea, which cannot be numbered for multitude," ver. 12. As if he should say, Lord, how will thy promise be fulfilled? Didst thou not say that my seed should be as the sand of the sea? Now if the mother and children be cut off, what will become of thy promise?

God is so indulgent as to suffer us to plead our cause with him. And these pleading prayers are strong prayers; he wept, and made supplication, so he prevailed with God. Now, labour you (if you be of the seed of Jacob) to pray as your father Jacob did. But so much shall suffice for that second history, about Jacob's prevailing with the angel.

III. His interviews with God at Bethel. "He found him in Beth-el, and there he spake with us."

The words in the original are, בית-אל ימצאנו ושם ידבר עמנו He *will* find us in Beth-el, and there he spake with us. As if it were an encouraging word of the angel to Jacob, that God would find him in Beth-el; and indeed the words would bear such an interpretation, but, as the learned know, the future is often used for the preter tense in the Hebrew, and it is more agreeable to the context to read them as you have them in your Bibles, "He found him in Beth-el, and there he spake with us;" that is, he found Jacob in Beth-el, and spake to Jacob, and in speaking to Jacob he spake to us all.

Now for the opening of this history, and showing how it suits with the scope of the prophet in this place. We read in Scripture of two meetings which God and Jacob had at Beth-el, and this text in Hosea seems to refer to them both.

1. When for fear of danger he fled from his brother, when his brother had mischievous thoughts against him, after he got the blessing from him, Gen. xxviii. 10.

2. When God appeared to him after he came out of Padan-aram, Gen. xxxv. 9—15.

1. He finds him in Beth-el, Gen. xxviii. 10; yea, indeed, for as Jacob lay asleep with a stone under his head, he saw a vision of angels ascending and descending from heaven, and God speaking excellent things unto him. Hence,

Obs. 12. God finds his people many times when they little think of him. He comes to his people in ways of mercy when they scarce dream of it: Jacob was but in a dream at this time, and yet God came in very wonderful ways of mercy towards him.

Oh how often has God found us in this way! how often may many of you say, that the Lord has come unexpectedly to you in ways of mercy, which you could never have expected. Oh, when unexpected mercies come, we should consider that God has found us; our sins might have found us, whereas the mercies of God have found us out.

2. The other time that God found Jacob was, Gen. xxxv. 9—15, when he was in great distress, after his daughter Dinah had been defiled, and his sons Simeon and Levi had committed that great outrage against the Shechemites, so great as to fall on the city, and slay all the males. Upon that Jacob and all his family were in great danger of being destroyed, for the act was so foul, that it could not but make all the people (as Jacob thought) to abhor him, and "to gather themselves together against him, and to slay him," Gen. xxxiv. 30. The distress of Jacob was doubtless very great; his daughter defiled by one uncircumcised, his two sons committing such an outrage, and himself and his house in danger of being destroyed utterly by them; for who would have thought but that all the inhabitants of the land should have risen against him, and have cut him off? Now the next thing that we hear of, God meets with him at Beth-el, and speaks very gracious things to him there; and he did not only speak to *him*, but there "he spake with *us*."

That is, God meeting with Jacob in Beth-el, that which he spake to him there concerned us as well as it concerned Jacob. An expression to the same purpose we have in Psal. lxvi. 6, "He turned the sea into dry land: they went through the flood on foot: there did we rejoice in him:" for indeed the mercy of God towards the Israelites, which at that time did rejoice them, was a matter of rejoicing for us. Whatsoever is written, is written for our learning, it is as if God spake to us. That which God spake to Abraham, I am God all-sufficient; walk before me, and be upright; he spake that to us, he spake that to thee and me. That which God spake to Joshua, "I will never leave thee, nor forsake thee," Josh. i. 5, that the apostle, to the Hebrews, applies to the Christians at that time, Heb. xiii. 5; that he spake to us, he spake it to thee and me, if we be believers. That which God spake to the distressed and afflicted ones in Psal. cii. 17, "He will regard the prayer of the destitute, and not despise their prayer;" that he spake to us, for in ver. 18 it is said, "This shall be written for the generation to come." And that which God spake to Jacob at these two several times in Beth-el, is written for the generations to come, is written for us. Well then, what was it? what was the special thing which God spake to Jacob when he found him at Beth-el? and what was that to us? I will show you many things; there are nine or ten notable things to be observed by us, which God spake to us at Beth-el.

Obs. 13. The foundation of the comfort of the saints is in the covenant of God. "There he spake with us." When he appeared to Jacob, what said he to him? "I am the Lord God of Abraham thy father, and the God of Isaac," Gen. xxviii. 13. Jacob was flying for his life then, and this was to comfort him in his danger, "I am the Lord God of Abraham thy father, and the God of Isaac;" then he spake this to us, that the foundation of the saints' comforts in the times of their distresses, is the covenant of grace which God has made with them, and their fathers before them.

Obs. 14. The seed of Jacob are the inheritors of the land of Canaan; for so he told him, "The land whereon thou liest, to thee will I give it, and to thy seed." Now this concerns us, that the seed of Jacob shall inherit the land of Canaan, that was typified by it. There are some who think that yet there shall be an inheritance of the land of Canaan by the faithful seed of Jacob, but, however, this certainly "he spake to us," that all the seed of Jacob are the inheritors of the land of Canaan one way or other in the literal, or in the typical sense.

Obs. 15. Mercies promised should be believed, even when there is great unlikelihood of their fulfilment. So he spake to us there. He tells Jacob there, when poor and solitary with his staff, and no provision but a stone for his pillow, he tells him then that his promise shall be made good, and his seed become so great as to inherit the land of Canaan. How unlikely was all this at such a time! but God would have him to exercise his faith upon the promise even then, when there was such a great unlikelihood of its accomplishment.

Obs. 16. The multiplying of the church is a great blessing; for, saith he, thy seed shall be thus and thus, as the sand of the sea shore; I will increase my church abundantly from thy loins.

Obs. 17. Saints, even the strongest, have need of renewing of promises. God renews the same promise to him that was made before to Abraham, that his seed should be great; but the truth is, that the promise, though as certain as before, yet had been a long time.

Obs. 18. The blessing which comes to the world, comes by the promised Seed. He tells him, that in his Seed all the nations of the earth should be blessed: the great blessing of the world is by the promised Seed, by Jesus Christ.

Obs. 19. It was in God's heart, thousands of years ago, to do good to us Gentiles; though at that time we were as dogs, yet it was in God's heart to bless us. Oh, this is a comfortable speech to us, it concerns us Gentiles in a more special manner than it did them to whom Hosea at this time prophesied.

The presence and protection of God are the only encouragement of the saints in their ways. So in ver. 15, saith God, "Behold, I am with thee, and will keep thee in all places whither thou goest;" this he spake to us, this the saints should make high account of.

Obs. 20. God is still working towards the fulfilling of promises; for so he tells him, "I will not leave thee until I have done all that which I have spoken to thee of;" though you cannot see how my administrations towards you do any way work for the fulfilling of my promise, yet know I will not leave you till I have fulfilled all my promises.

Obs. 21. The mercy and faithfulness of God are constant. However things may go with us here for a while, yet the mercy of God continues, the line of God's mercy is not cut asunder, but his faithfulness carries it on till all the good that he has promised, or that faith can believe, is granted to us; for so he tells Jacob there, "I will not leave thee, until I have done all that which I have spoken to thee of." All this God "spake with us," the first time of his meeting with Jacob in Beth-el.

Now the second time that he met with Jacob in Beth-el, is spoken of, Gen. xxxv. 10, and there see what God "spake with us." God changes Jacob's name to Israel, confirms his promise and covenant to him again as before, remembers his wrestling, and his prevailing with him: and in that God tells us he remembers our fervent prayers; after they are gone, his heart is yet upon them. A general view of all he spoke to us there, would lead us to observe,

Obs. 22. The saints have need of the confirmation of mercies, especially of the covenant.

Obs. 23. God's presenting himself to the soul as God Almighty, is a great help to faith. We find in Scripture that God very seldom, when he speaks of his almighty power, speaks of his willingness to do good; for that God would have his people take for granted, it is implied in the covenant which he made with them at first. "I am God Almighty," saith he here; thou hast had experience of my almighty power in turning the heart of thy brother: and now thou art in a great danger; because thou art few in number, thou art afraid of the people of the land; but "I am God Almighty;" there is little power in thee, but in me power dwells. The consideration of God's almighty power, is that which should help the saints in the midst of all their straits and afflictions.

When Jacob was afraid of being cut off because he was few in number, now God presents himself as God Almighty, and blesses him now with fruitfulness, and tells him he will multiply him to "a nation and a company of nations," "and kings shall come out of thy loins." In all this we have an excellent lesson that God speaks to us.

Obs. 24. God delights to revive his people in their fears with suitable mercies. Jacob was never in greater fears than on those two occasions; yet now the Lord comes at this time of his great straits, and tells him of multiplying him to many nations, and that kings should come out of his loins; at that time when he was afraid that the nations should come and destroy all that belonged to him, God tells him that kings should come out of his loins. Oh, the Lord delights to revive his people in their fears, and that with suitable mercies!

Oh, it should teach us to be tender-hearted towards the saints that are in fears and troubles, and to labour to comfort our brethren with seasonable and suitable mercies! And especially after great conflicts that is observable; for Jacob had been wrestling with God not long before, and after these great conflicts God comes with the manifestation of great mercies. This God spake to us there, that we should not be discouraged, though God bring us into great conflicts; because after those times are the seasons for God to speak to us things the most comfortable, and the most encouraging. There God "spake with us." Thus you see the third story opened to you, and its useful import, I know scarce a scripture fuller than these two verses.

And the reason why the prophet brings this third story to upbraid this people is, as if he should say thus:

First, Your father Jacob worshipped the true God in Beth-el; you worship the calf in Beth-el (for you know that in Dan and Beth-el the calves were set up). Are you the children of Jacob? did Jacob worship an idol in Beth-el? No, God found him in Beth-el, and God spake with him there; but you worship a calf in Beth-el.

Secondly, God made gracious promises to your father Jacob in Beth-el; you slight them, you regard them not, you go to shifting courses for yourselves, and dare not rely upon promises as your father Jacob did.

Thirdly, You pollute the place which God had made his house, that place where there were such gracious manifestations of God you pollute. It is an aggravation of sin, to sin in those places where God has showed much mercy.

And then, lastly, You are gone from the covenant which your father Jacob made with God at Beth-el. Your father Jacob (as God renewed his covenant) entered into covenant himself with God at Beth-el, and saith, that the Lord should be his God; but have not you forsaken that covenant? You do not stand to the covenant which your father Jacob made at Beth-el.

Ver. 5. *Even the Lord God of hosts; the Lord is his memorial.*

He that appeared to your father Jacob was no other than the Lord of hosts, Jehovah, and Jehovah is his memorial.

Your father Jacob conversed with God, he had great power with the great God, the Lord of hosts, Jehovah. You forsake this God, you see no such excellency in him, you rather turn to idols.

"The Lord God of hosts." But how does the prophet make use of this title of God, "The Lord God of hosts?"

It is in reference to those hosts of God that appeared to Jacob a little before he met with his brother Esau, when, after having wrestled with God, and having his name changed, the text saith, "The angels of God met him. And when Jacob saw them, he said, This is God's host," Gen. xxxii. 1, 2. This refers to that place. The hosts of God appeared to Jacob just upon this time of his wrestling, and the text saith there, "he called the name of that place Mahanaim," that is, two hosts, or two camps. Saith Hosea, The Lord of hosts is his name; as if he should say, It is the same Lord that was the Lord of hosts that appeared to Jacob your father a little before his wrestling; it is the same God, he remains the same God still, and your sin is against that God, even against the Lord God of hosts.

Now for this title, "The Lord God of hosts." That which you see this morning, may remind you a little of it, yet I shall not speak much of it now, because you that have been auditors here, and others too, may know, that even in this place I have preached on that glorious name of God, the Lord of hosts, and likewise some years since published my exposition on it,* because God did then appear to England in that title, the Lord of hosts, more fully than in former times. Therefore I endeavoured to open it as I was able unto you, to show what glory of God was in that name, that we in this land might especially learn to sanctify it; and since that time the Lord has given us more occasion to sanctify that name of his than formerly; indeed this title, Lord of hosts, as well as Jehovah, is the memorial of God, and should be to the posterity that remains; we should tell the posterity after how the Lord has manifested himself as the Lord of hosts amongst us. If ever God appeared in the glory of this title in any country or nation, he has done it here: it is from the Lord of hosts that our armies have so prevailed; one that has but half an eye (as we are wont to say) can see it. Had God wrought our victory by a company of old, brave, gallant soldiers, and by mighty armies, then the glory of God as the Lord of hosts had been eclipsed in some measure; but whereas such great things have been done, as scarce any history can tell us of, since Joshua's time, here, in this very kingdom, within these twelve months, and that by the weakest, the feeblest instruments, how will the Lord of hosts be in "his memorial," if these transactions be set out to the life, lustre, and verity of them! children yet unborn will learn to magnify God by this name of his. That such things should be done by an army so contemptible in the eye of flesh and blood as this our army was, none other surely than the Lord of hosts appeared for us.

And in that God has manifested himself for his own people so much, I will give you one scripture which I do not remember I made use of then, to show you what the hosts of God are besides the sun, moon, and stars, and the works of creation in general. Besides all these, God has two special armies, the saints and the angels; these I may call Mahanaim, the two hosts of God. Respecting the angels, I shall not need to give you Scripture: but with regard to the people of God, that they are called "the hosts of the Lord" in way of distinction from all other of the hosts of God, is manifest from Exod. xii. 41, where the people of Israel going forth from Egypt, the text saith, "And it came to pass at the end of the four hundred and thirty years, even the selfsame day it came to pass, that all the hosts of the Lord went out from the land of Egypt." What were they but God's people? the church is called there "the hosts of the Lord." God's own people God glories in as his hosts in way of distinction from all other people. And so in Cant. vi. 4, the church of God is said to be "terrible as an army with banners." And through God's mercy the Lord has manifested what great things he can do by such an host, by an army that has had so many of his chosen ones among them; they have been the hosts that God, the Lord of hosts, has taken so much delight to be the Captain of, and to go forth withal. But thus much for that name, "the Lord of hosts;" what use the prophet makes of that name we shall speak to presently, how it is a doctrinal point that he builds his exhortation upon, "Therefore return unto the Lord."

"The Lord is his memorial:" Jehovah is his memorial.

This name Jehovah is a name in which God glories much, for indeed it is the name of God's being, which expresses that more fully than any other name of God; this, and that name of God, "I am that I am," which comes from the same root, and is in effect the same with this name Jehovah; I say, God glories in this above all his names: and therefore in Deut. xxviii. 58, "That thou mayest fear this glorious and fearful name," Jehovah, thy God; in your books it is, "The Lord thy God," but in the original, Jehovah, thy God. God looks upon this name as his glorious and his fearful name, and would have people to take heed that they look to this, that they "fear this glorious and fearful name, Jehovah thy God." This name the Jews keep a mighty stir about, and think they find great mysteries in it; they have such superstitious reverence for it, that they will not so much as pronounce it; they call it the ineffable name; and if it be written, they think it is a very wicked thing to tread upon the paper which contains it. But it is very observable here how cross the superstition of men is to God; they in reverence to God will not so much as mention this name, because, they say, it is a name in which God so much glories: and yet mark here, my text saith, this name is God's "memorial," God would have this name mentioned above any of his names, it is the name by which he would be remembered to all generations. So in Exod. iii. 15, you find, that God speaking of this his name, Jehovah, Jehovah Elohim, Jehovah in covenant, saith, that he would be known by it to all generations: "This is my name for ever, and this is my memorial unto all generations." It might indeed well be wished that the very word Jehovah had been retained in your English version (Lord printed in capitals always indicates its presence in the original). There is much then in this name:

First, It sets forth the glory of God more than any name, because above all names it shows that God has a being from himself, in which much of the glory of God consists; this is proper to God: and indeed from this one principle, that God is from himself, we come to understand almost all things that can be known of God by any light of nature, by any natural understanding, unaided by Divine revelation. The knowledge of God in Christ is above both, being matter of pure revelation; but the knowledge of God as Adam at first knew him, and as the creature can know him by any natural light, derives its greatest strength from this principle, That God has his being from himself: and from this follows,

1. That he is the First Being of all things.
2. That he is the Supreme Being, he is above all.
3. That he is an Eternal Being, he can have no beginning, because it is from himself.
4. That he is an Infinite Being, that there are no bounds at all to his being; for whatever is bounded, is bounded by something without it; but God being from himself, and having no cause, can have nothing to limit and bound his being.
5. That there is all being in God; whatever has any being, it must be either that that is the first, or from the first: he is an Absolute Being of himself, having it from himself, and therefore all being is eminently contained in God himself.
6. That whatsoever is in God, is God himself; from this name Jehovah, he is an Absolute Being, nothing but himself: this is the difference between God and any creature. Whatsoever is in the creature, is not the being of the creature. A man has wisdom; now the wisdom of a man is one, and the essence of the man is another, thing; but it is not so with God, whatsoever you can say of God, is God; the wisdom of God, is God; the mercy of God, is God; the justice of God, is God himself; and so all the attributes. We often conceive of the attributes as if they were distinct from the being; when we say, God is wise, as if God were one

* The glorious Name of the Lord of Hosts: the title of a book of the author's, being one of the first in defence of the wars on the parliament's side.

thing, and wisdom were another; but certainly if we would apprehend God as in himself, we cannot apprehend him so; as if his wisdom were one thing, and God another; or his mercy one thing, and God another: so that the truth is, nothing can properly be predicated of God, because when a thing is predicated there is a difference between the subject and the predicate, but there is no such distinction with respect to God; but whatsoever can be said of God, is God himself; and much of the glory of God appears in this one thing, in this, I say, that all that is in God is God himself. The understanding God thus, helps us to see God in his glory as much as any way whatsoever; few people however apprehend this, but look upon God as a creature, and so think God is some excellent thing that has so many excellencies in him: but to understand it aright, we should know that all that is said of God is God himself, and therefore all but one being in God; wisdom, mercy, justice, power, life, holiness, and faithfulness appear many diverse things to us, but in God all are but one excellency. As now, the beams of the sun appear diverse to us, they shine through a blue glass, and there is a blue reflection, and a green glass, and then it is green, and a red glass, and then it is red, but yet all constitute but one beam. So the infinite, first, absolute Being of all, appearing in his several workings and in his several administrations, seems to be several; but they all form but one being that is in himself: such is the signification of the name Jehovah.

7. All the being of the creature depends upon God, is from God originally, and so depends upon God every moment. Every time you hear the name Jehovah you should be put in mind of this, that as all creatures had what they had from God at first, so they do absolutely depend upon God every moment for their being, and for their every good.

8. God being thus Jehovah, will give a being to all his promises, and to all his threatenings. And therefore when he appeared to Moses, to tell him that he would fulfil the promise made to his people, to bring them out of Egypt, he tells him that though he had appeared to Abraham by the name El-shaddai, God-all-sufficient, yet he had not appeared to him by the name Jehovah; which is as much as if he should say, Yea, indeed, when I spake to Abraham, I made a promise to him, that I would give him such a land, and thus and thus, but I did not give a being to the promises; but now I come to make way for the fulfilling of this promise, now I appear to be Jehovah: thus Jehovah is God's "memorial," that is, every time you read the name Jehovah, or hear that name Jehovah, then you should meditate on these things, and contemplate God as Jehovah in all these different aspects. And thus for the opening of these two names. The observations from them are,

Obs. 1. Though God be never so strong and terrible in himself, never so great and glorious, yet faith has strength to wrestle with him. Jacob had power with God. God! what God? The Lord of hosts, Jehovah, the great and glorious God. And yet Jacob wrestles with this Lord of hosts, God-Jehovah, and prevails with him.

So that hence Christians should learn to raise up their spirits when they have to deal with God. If God has given them faith, they should be daunted neither by God's terror nor his greatness. Thou dost sometimes look upon God as the great Creator of heaven and earth, the great Lord of hosts, the infinite Jehovah, and the lustre of his glory seems to amaze thee; be not afraid. O thou believing soul, if thou art a seed of Jacob, notwithstanding all the terribleness, and all the glory, that there is in God, and the infinite distance that there is between him and us, which his name Jehovah sets out unto us, yet thou mayst wrestle with this God, even with this God, and prevail. Many poor Christians are much daunted and discouraged with the sight of the greatness of God; but this text is a very great help to silence the apprehension of such. Indeed it is for ungodly men, to whom God is an enemy, to be daunted with the apprehension of the greatness of God; but to the seed of Jacob, even when Jacob prevailed it was with this God, that is, the Lord of hosts, whose memorial is Jehovah.

Obs. 2. The greatness and glory of God in these his names is a great aggravation of sin. Oh, the Lord is infinitely terrible, he is the Lord of hosts, Jehovah, and yet you wretched creatures have departed from, and sinned against, this God. Oh, it is a fearful aggravation of men's sin, that their sin is against such a God, the Lord of hosts, whose name is Jehovah; nothing can humble the soul of a sinner more effectually than the sight of the Lord in his glorious attributes. When thou comest to know with what a God thou hast to deal, this will make thee see the greatness of thy sin. Therefore the prophet sets God in his glory before this people, that they should come to see their great sin, and that there should be a stop given to the course of their hearts, which were running on in the ways of unrighteousness.

Obs. 3. God is the same to us as he was to our forefathers, if we forsake him not. He was thus to your father Jacob, the Lord of hosts, Jehovah; and his memorial is still the Lord of hosts, and Jehovah, and therefore you might have this God to appear the Lord of hosts for your good as well as he did to your forefathers, and you might have God appear to be Jehovah for you as well as he did to Jacob, if you forsake him not. O wretches! that you should forsake this God, whom you might have to be the Lord of hosts and Jehovah to you.

O, let us learn this, when we read in Scripture, or hear from our forefathers, how God has appeared heretofore for his saints, for our forefathers, to reflect, God is the same God still, and we may come to have as much good from this God as ever any had since the world began; there is no shortening of his power, and no darkening of his glory, but with whatsoever power God has wrought, in whatsoever glory he has appeared, in former times, he may manifest the same for us now. It is a mighty argument for people to keep close to God and be faithful with him even because of this.

Obs. 4. There is no need of images to keep God's remembrance. The glorious titles of God and his attributes, and the manifestation of himself in his works, is the best memorial of God; that is our way, the way of man to make to himself memorials. God has made himself "a memorial." When you read in the word this glorious title of God, Jehovah, it is a better memorial of God than all the images in the world are, and we may better sanctify God's name, and have our hearts better wrought upon, by such titles of God, than by all kind of images whatsoever.

Obs. 5. God manifests his glory, that he may be remembered from generation to generation. "The Lord God of hosts; Jehovah is his memorial;" as if he should say, God then manifested himself as Jehovah, and he would be remembered in other ages to be so; what God does to his people in one age, he not only expects to have his name sanctified for that present, but he would have it laid up from age to age, and would be honoured in all generations from those great manifestations of himself in some one age.

My brethren, oh that we had hearts to do this! Oh that we could make this God his memorial! that we could lay up what God has manifested of himself in this age, for the benefit of another age! I hope God will one way or other provide means for the recording of the famous things that God has done in this age, that it may be a memorial to the posterity afterwards; for certainly our age cannot give God the glory that is due unto his name for what he has done; we had need labour to continue it to posterity, that the ages to come may remember what God has done to give glory to him; it is his memorial.

Obs. 6. This name of Jehovah, the memorial of God, affords matter for a very useful meditation. You that say you cannot meditate, your meditations are barren; would you help yourselves in meditation to have a holy memorial of God, think much of the name Jehovah, remember what has been hinted to you from that name, and what is contained in it.

Ver. 6. *Therefore turn thou to thy God: keep mercy and judgment, and wait on thy God continually.*

"Therefore." Here comes the application now; the two preceding verses contain the doctrine, this is the use, "Therefore turn thou to thy God;" so that this "therefore" has reference to all that the prophet had said concerning Jacob, and to these titles of God; as if he should say thus:

I. You had such a gracious father that did thus prevail with God, to whom God did so appear, "therefore turn thou to thy God."

II. God is "the Lord of hosts," therefore turn to him.

III. "Jehovah is his memorial," therefore turn to him.

I. The reference it has to their father Jacob affords us this note:

Obs. 1. The consideration of our godly forefathers is a great argument to turn us to God. O you children who have had parents that were wrestlers with God, are you wicked now? Consider what parents you had, and turn you therefore to God. In 2 Tim. i. 3, "I thank God," saith St. Paul, "whom I serve from my forefathers with pure conscience." Oh! it is a great comfort to a man or woman if they can say thus, "I thank God, whom I serve from my forefathers with pure conscience:" my forefathers served God, my grandfather, or grandmother, or father, or mother, was godly; and I thank God even from them that I serve God: God is "my God," and "my father's God," Exod. xv. 2.

II. The consideration of God as "the Lord of hosts," is a mighty motive to cause us to turn to God. Wilt thou go on in ways of enmity against the Lord of hosts, the Lord of hosts, who has angels and all creatures to fight for him? Wilt thou, a poor worm, stand out against this God? Thou that goest on in a way of wickedness, know thou fightest against the great Lord of hosts. What were it for a drunken fellow to come and think to oppose but such an army as goes out of the city at this time? but for a poor wretched worm to think to stand against the infinite God, the Lord of hosts! oh! it were infinite boldness and presumption, and desperate madness; therefore turn to the Lord. All the while thou art going on in ways of wickedness, thou art fighting against the Lord of hosts.

And, on the other side, if thou hadst but a heart to turn to the Lord, oh how joyful would this title be to thee, that that God which is thy God, is the Lord of hosts, is the Lord of all the hosts in the world! We are not afraid now to see soldiers, and to hear the beating of drums, and shooting of guns, when we know that all are our friends; but if we should have heard the beating of drums, and neighing of horses, and the guns of our enemies, that would have struck fear. So one that hath turned to God, need not fear any army, any creatures; why? all is commanded by God their Father. Oh the joy, peace, and security that a heart may have which is turned to God! In Acts xxvii. 23, 24, Paul saith, "There stood by me this night the angel of God, whose I am, and whom I serve, saying, Fear not, Paul." Mark, There stood before me the angel of God. Did not that terrify him? "The angel," that is but one of the members of the hosts of God; any one angel has a great deal of terror in him sometimes, for there is much of the glory of God in angels, and we know that their appearing has struck terror into many men. But now, saith Paul, the angel said, "Fear not;" if it be the angel of God, "whose I am, and whom I serve," then I need not fear; yea, let God muster up all his hosts, and appear to one that has turned to him, if he can say thus, "Whose I am, and whom I serve," these hosts will say, "Fear not." Therefore turn to the Lord, because he is the Lord of hosts.

III. God is Jehovah, therefore should we turn to him. There is a great deal of force in this name to cause sinners to turn to him, for this name Jehovah has as much terror in it to a guilty, ungodly soul, as any thing we read of in all the book of God. I say, put all together that we read in the book of God, yet if we did but thoroughly understand the name Jehovah, we should see as much terror in it to a guilty conscience, and a sinful soul that goes on in the ways of wickedness, as almost all that is mentioned of God that might be terrible. As thus,

Jehovah. If he be Jehovah, he has power over every thing that has a being to torment thee with it, for he has all being in himself, all being is from him, and he disposes of all; therefore whatsoever thing has any being in it, this God has the power over it, to make use of it to torment thee withal. Do but consider what power some little creature, if it be in some part of a man's body, has to produce torment; a little gravel in the kidneys, or stone in the bladder, poor and weak in itself, but being in that place, what torture does it bring! Now if they have such power to torment thee, then what power have all things in the earth, and the infinite God that has all essence, and all being, and can dispose of all things as he pleases, to bring pain, misery, and torment to a sinner! It is a very humbling consideration to a sinner.

And, on the other side, if there be any power in any thing that has a being to bring any comfort, it is all in God, for God has all in him eminently. As now, one creature has power to torment in one way, another in another way; and so one creature has power to comfort us one way, another another; but all this is eminently in God. The gravel torments one way, the gouty humour in the veins torments another way, and fire and the sword torment after another manner, and burning fever, fire without and fire within, and the stinging of serpents, all torment after different manners; now all power of all things is in God eminently, in him is the quintessence of all things, and therefore the power of God is able to bring all sorts of torments at one time in one thing. As now, suppose several herbs of several virtues, if these herbs were all distilled into one water, then a drop of that has the virtue and efficacy, it may be, of forty several herbs; so now, (if I may so compare,) God has all kind of power in himself, and is able to put forth in one instant all the power and efficacy that there is in all creatures in heaven and earth, either to torment or to comfort us. If one herb has one sweetness, and a second another, and the third another, how sweet will be the distillation of them all together. Now all sweetnesses being in God eminently, oh what comfort is there in God to the soul! Thus, either way, the name Jehovah affords full matter for meditation, either to humble us for sin by the dreadfulness of his wrath, or to comfort and encourage us by the reflection that there is all being in God eminently, and that all depend absolutely upon him; therefore turn to God, because he is Jehovah.

Obs. 1. The excellency of the saints is an argument to turn us to God. When both together, the excellency of Jacob and the excellency of God, this is set as an argument to turn to the Lord. Turn to me.

But they might say, Do not we turn to God? we do serve God. Thence further,

Obs. 2. We depart from God in the midst of our services when we perform them not in God's way. They did worship God after a fashion, but God did not account that worshipping of him, but departing from him; therefore turn to God.

"Turn thou."

That is, every one of you; do not stand objecting and cavilling against what I say, but turn to God every one of you. "Turn thou to thy God." Thou art Israel, thou art the posterity of that great prevailer with God, therefore turn *thou* to God. The note of observation from hence, which, if you lay it to heart, you will find it of very great use, is this:

Obs. 3. Every one should consider what peculiar arguments there are that concern him in particular to turn to God. "Therefore turn thou to thy God." There is a great deal more reason why *thou* shouldst turn to God than others.

Oh that every one of us here in this place would but in our meditations labour to recall all those particular arguments that concern ourselves, that might turn us to God! Do not take it in the general, Turn to God because he is your Creator, turn to God that you may be saved: this concerns all. But consider what special reasons thou hast, as thus: Consider what special manifestations of God have been vouchsafed to thee; what special offers of grace have been made to thee; what special workings of the Holy Ghost there have been upon thy heart; what special illuminations of God's Spirit there have been within thee; consider what special dangers thou hast been in; what special vows and covenants thou hast made to God, and yet hast departed from him afterwards; consider what special engagements thou hast had: these are but hints to lead you to lay to heart all the arguments that may concern you especially to turn to thy God. "Therefore turn thou to thy God." Do not thou look upon others, and think thus, I do as others do: yea, but thou hast more reason to turn to God than others, there are more arguments to persuade thy heart than others, "Therefore turn thou to thy God." And this is a great mercy of God towards any, when he darts powerfully those special considerations and arguments that concern their souls to turn to God: we come to hear the word, and to hear the nature of repentance, and the motives to repentance, but that generally concerns all, and does not much move our heart; but at another time it pleases God to suggest something out of the word that concerns us in particular, and this affects our hearts more powerfully than all the rest. As if a man be asleep, though there be a great noise, perhaps it does not awaken him, but let one call him by his name, and speak particularly to him, and that will awaken him when a greater noise will not do it: so, though there be general reasons for turning to God, they do not so much prevail with people, as when God speaks to us by name, and saith, Turn *thou* to God. There are these special arguments why *thou* shouldst turn to God rather than others. Many times you will say, If ever any were bound to God, then I am: then turn thou to God because thou art more engaged than others.

"To thy God."

That is, though you have departed from him, yet he has not so wholly cast you off, but he may yet be *thy* God. From whence,

Obs. 4. The sight of any relation to God, or hope of mercy from him, is a special means to draw the heart to turn to him. He may yet be *thy* God, God has not left thee; O thou wretched, sinful soul, who knows but that he may be thy God, and thy God to all eternity? Thou mightest have been past hearing of any possibility of God's being thy God, and therefore turn to God, turn to *thy* God.

"Keep mercy and judgment."

Want of mercy, in the 4th chapter of this prophecy, was charged upon this people, that there was no mercy in the land. And so in divers other places, want of justice. Now, "turn thou to thy God; keep mercy and judgment." From the context,

Obs. 5. In our turnings to God, we must reform our special sins. It is not enough for any to turn to God, and leave some gross sins; but is there any sin more special than another, that you have lived in before your turning to God? reform in that sin above all. None can ever have any sure argument that their repentance is true, though they have left many sins, if they have not left their special sins. There is some special sin that thou hast lived in, what sayest thou to that?

Obs. 6. It is nothing for people to reform in God's worship, except they reform also in the duties of the second table. The duties of the second table, mercy and judgment; "Turn thou to thy God; keep mercy and judgment." Many seem to be forward in duties of instituted worship, which is very good; we are to honour God, God is jealous in that business: but now, together with that, if we be not conscientious in the duties of the second table, of mercy and judgment too, it is nothing; all will vanish and come to nothing except thou livest righteously and mercifully with men also, as well as worship God aright; do not think to put off thy conscience with the duties of worship, except thou dost "keep mercy and judgment." This we would observe generally; but more particularly,

Obs. 7. A heart truly turning to God, must needs be very merciful to men. God expects that from all who turn to him, that upon thy turning to God, thy bowels should yearn towards thy brethren, and turn to them in love, and in mercy, and meekness, and gentleness, and forgiveness. For when thou turnest to God, is it not the mercy of God that draws thy heart? If it be not that, thy turning is not right; never any turned to God rightly but their hearts were taken with God's mercy; and can thy heart be taken with God's mercy, and thou not merciful to thy brethren? Many professors of religion think little of this, but I find the Scripture makes as much of this as of any thing but faith itself, faith in the covenant of grace. These three things the Scripture holds forth, and urges very much upon men, faith, mercy, and unity. The two latter are thought to be of little or no moment with men, but certainly the Lord Christ lays much upon mercy towards men, that all that are his members should be of merciful and of uniting dispositions one towards another. Oh, it is mercy in which the Scripture makes religion to consist: James i. 27, "Pure religion and undefiled before God and the Father is this, To visit the fatherless and widows in their affliction." And in James ii. 13, "Mercy rejoiceth against judgment." This will help us in the time of straits, and in the season of danger, that we have been merciful towards our brethren, for so I understand the words, "Mercy rejoiceth against," or over, "judgment:" not that God's mercy is *more* than his judgment, and that, though a sinner has deserved judgment, yet God's mercy will prevail, and triumph over it; but I take the text to refer to mercy in man, and not mercy in God, that is, thus; When man has had a merciful heart towards others, towards his brethren, that then if he should live to meet with affliction, live to a time of judgment, times of common calamity, common dangers, that mercy which he has exercised towards his brethren in the time of his prosperity will cause his soul to triumph in the midst of all dangers. In the time of affliction mercy rejoices over judgment: Let judgment come, let afflictions come in the world, let there be never such hard times among the nations, yet I have a testimony to my conscience, the Lord has given me a merciful heart towards my brethren that are in misery, and I that am but a poor creature, who have but a drop of mercy to that God whose mercy is infinite as the ocean of mercy, will not that God be merciful to me much more? Keep mercy therefore, you that turn to God, be of merciful dispositions towards your brethren. Oh! this is wanting among many professors of religion, they are of cruel and harsh dispositions, rigid, sour, and severe towards others, they care not what becomes of them. O, be merciful to your brethren; you that are turned to God, show it in this, that you keep mercy.

"And judgment."

That is, righteous judgment among men. Thou canst not turn to God from thy unrighteousness, and to a righteous God, and yet still not be righteous towards men. Many texts of Scripture I might have shown you, that commend this grace of righteousness; and it is made the great promise to the church in its glorious state, that righteousness shall prevail there, that her people shall be a righteous people.

But further, "and judgment." Not only judgment in doing no man any wrong, and righteousness in dealing; but a manifestation of thy hatred against sin, by the execution of judgment.

Obs. 8. Where there is a true turning to God, there must be righteousness among men. Certainly, if turned from thy unrighteousness towards a righteous God, then thou wilt be turned likewise from thy unrighteousness towards thy fellow men.

Obs. 9. Those who are in authority must manifest their hatred against sin, by the execution of judgment. Though in thine own cause thou mayst forbear, yea, thou shouldst be merciful; but when public manifestation of hatred against sin requires justice, then there is no place for sparing; when God calls thee, in any public place, to manifest hatred against sin, then (I say) thou mayst not think of sparing.

But you will say, Oh, I must pity, and show mercy.

Well, if you would be merciful, be merciful in your own cause. Many will plead for indulgence to malefactors, yet in their own business they have no indulgence to those who offend them. It beseems a judge to be very pitiful when he is wronged himself, but it beseems him to be very righteous and just when the public calls him.

Obs. 10. Mercy is first, and judgment afterwards. "Keep mercy and judgment." The Scripture makes a difference between our respect to mercy and judgment: thus, Micah vi. 8, "What doth the Lord require of thee, but to do justly, and to love mercy, and to walk humbly with thy God?" A pre-eminence must be given to mercy, mercy must not only be shown, but loved; justice must be done.

Obs. 11. The mixture of mercy and judgment is very comely. "Keep mercy and judgment." The Scripture joins them very often: "I will sing of mercy and judgment," Psal. ci. 1. "He that followeth after righteousness and mercy findeth life, righteousness, and honour," Prov. xxi. 21. "Unto the upright there ariseth light in the darkness: he is gracious, and full of compassion, and righteous," Psal. cxii. 4. And in Jer. ix. 24, the Lord seems to glory in this his righteousness as well as in his mercy: saith the Lord, Let no man glory in the flesh; "but let him that glorieth glory in this, that he understandeth and knoweth me, that I am the Lord which exercise loving-kindness, judgment, and righteousness, in the earth:" let him glory in this, that he knows that I am such a God; this is my glory, that I am both righteous and merciful.

Now for the several rules: First, When mercy should be shown. Secondly, When judgment should be executed. How men should be directed to mix both these together.

First, Mercy should be shown,

1. When men offend by infirmity, through weakness, and not through wilfulness.

Oh that we would consider of this! Our brethren that sometimes differ from us in judgment and in practice, consider, Do they appear, in any of their ways, to be wilful in their way? can you take it upon your consciences, that it is through obstinacy or any wicked principles that they walk otherwise than you? does it not appear in all their other ways that they walk humbly and conscionably, that if they be in the wrong, yet it is through mere weakness that they cannot discern the truth, which thou thinkest thou dost see? Now thou shouldst be merciful towards them, and carry not thyself in a rigid, severe, bitter, and harsh way towards them, but in a merciful way; mercy when the offence arises from infirmity.

2. When the offender is already sensible of his offence.

3. When there may be as much good done by a fair, gentle, and merciful carriage, as by a harsh and rigid demeanour.

4. Especially when any begin to feel passion arise in their hearts, and a spirit of revenge to stir in them, above all times, then is the time for mercy. Examine thy heart, thou hast to deal with thy brother; now see whether there do not begin to arise passion and revenge in thy spirit towards him, now is the time for mercy; it is not the fit time for judgment, it is not a fit time to give judgment, nor for thee to execute judgment, but now is the time for mercy.

Secondly, Judgment should be "kept," especially,

1. When called to manifest hatred against sin.

2. When the public good requires it; when you cannot be merciful to one, but you must be cruel to another. As in many things wherein men would be merciful, the truth is, the mercy they show to some is cruelty to others; and when thou hast the least interest in a business, then there is the most like to be the time for judgment.

"Keep mercy."

"Keep;" not only do some acts of mercy, but "keep mercy."

Many men, in some good moods, oh how pitiful are they! how merciful! but come to them at another time, and how rigid, how sour are they then! how bitter, how cruel, how harsh are they! We have found it so by experience. You can say of such a man, Oh! what sweet converse had we together, and what a sweet-tempered man he was! how loving, how meek, how gentle, how pitiful! But come to him now, how harsh and rugged! yea, extremely bitter in his expressions, mightily turned, as if he were not the same man. "Keep mercy," *keep* it. Does God at any time melt thy heart, and make thee apprehensive of thy need of mercy? does thy heart begin to bleed towards thy brethren? O, keep it, keep this temper; the Lord keep this in the thoughts and purposes of thy heart for ever. It should be the care of Christians, not only to do that which is good, but to keep their hearts in such a constant frame. Oh that some of you would but call to mind the days of old! Was there not a time in which your hearts did melt towards your brethren, and you had sweet converse and communion with them; what is become of those spirits now? O, turn to that gracious, sweet temper again; and if ever God reduce you to that temper, keep it. Consider what is it that has changed my heart, what has brought me to it. Now if God does discover how thou hast lost that sweetness of thy heart, oh! labour to repent and turn to God, and resolve, If ever God bring me to that temper again, (as sometimes, through his mercy, I have felt,) I hope, through his grace, that I shall keep myself in that temper. Oh! how happy were it with us, if, when God brings our hearts into a good temper, we had but hearts to keep them in the same! "Keep mercy."

"And judgment." "Keep judgment" too. In some acts you find men very just, while in others they will be false enough. But now it should be our care to be as is said of God in Jer. l. 7, "the habitation of justice:" so also it should be in the courts of justice, they should be indeed "the habitation of justice." Perhaps sometimes, in some one cause, a man may have justice in a court; yea, but if it be not so in all causes, and at all times, justice is not "kept." Justice should be always at home; a court should be always the habitation of judgment. And so it should be in families, and in individuals. It may be thou wert some time just in thy ways; yea, but then thou hadst not a temptation to unjust dealing. Some men, by a temptation, are brought to such unjust dealing, that if a man had said some years ago that thou wouldst have done such things, you would have been ready to exclaim, "What, is thy servant a dog, that he should do this great thing?" 2 Kings viii. 13. When a man is once engaged in any unjust way, he will go on; therefore *keep judgment*.

"And wait on thy God continually." That is, do not satisfy yourselves in duties of mercy and judgment only, but worship God; for by waiting on God is meant the exercise of spiritual graces, wherein the worship of God consists, wherein we come to make God to be our God. As it is not enough for men to think they worship God, and yet make no conscience of the second table; so neither is it enough for men to make conscience of the second table, and not to worship God. It may be some of you are very just; yea, but what worship of God is there in your families, and in your own hearts? Do your souls worship God, and sanctify the name of God in all your ways? Therefore to the words, "Turn thou to thy God, keep mercy and judgment," is added, "and wait on thy God continually."

"Wait on thy God." Let us consider how we are to wait on God.

1. In faith. The basis or foundation of waiting, is faith; to believe there is good in God, help, supply in him, and in him alone, however contrary things seem to be. I believe there is help in God alone, and not in those base ways into which my corrupt heart before led me.

2. In the use of the means which God has appointed for the attaining of my desires.

3. In an earnest looking out for mercy. I believe here is mercy, and no where else; I attend on God for it in the use of these means, and I look out for mercy.

4. In quiet submission in the mean time, though God stays long. That is true waiting, not to be discontented, not to have my heart sink, though God stays long.

5. In seeking God all the while. That soul that does this, may be said to wait on God.

Obs. 12. A turning heart is a waiting heart. The heart that turns truly to God is taken off from all creature contentments, so as to rest in them, and looks up to God for all help, and for all supply. And this waiting is of very great use to those that are turning to God. Consider of it; is any of you about the work of turning to God? has God begun to make a turn in any of your hearts? Know, that when you are turning to God, you are very like to meet with a great many things that may discourage you, many suggestions of the devil and your own hearts: Why should not I go back again? What good have I gotten by reading and praying? I get nothing by it, all will come to nothing at last. Temptations are like to come thick and threefold upon the heart of a sinner turning to God. I am confident I am speaking in this to the hearts of all that know what it is to turn to God; there was a time that thou wert departing from God, and then thou wentest on quietly, but ever since God has begun to turn thy heart, oh the thick and threefold temptations of the devil that have come to thee! Now this is a very seasonable exhortation; Turn to God and wait upon him, be not discouraged; notwithstanding all difficulties, fears, temptations, and discouragements, from men, and devils, and thine own heart, yet wait upon God and keep in his way.

Oh! it had been happy had this exhortation been set home upon the spirits of many to whose hearts the Lord was beginning to give a turn. Not long since the Lord was beginning to turn thy heart to himself, and thou didst meet with some things that discouraged thee, which has turned thee quite off again. Oh! had but this exhortation come seasonably then, "Turn thou to thy God, and wait upon him;" oh! it had been happy for thee. The Lord make it seasonable now to thee! Oh! remember this text, "Turn thou to thy God," and "wait upon him continually."

"Wait." Oh! there is reason that thou shouldst wait upon God. Thou sayest, If I had comfort, and if I were sure I should be saved at last, though I have discouragements from men, yet, if I had but comfort from God, then I could be content: yea, but wait, wait for comfort, wait for peace, wait for assurance; God is a great God, and is worthy to be waited on. There are some reasons why we should wait upon God.

1. Men that are above others will take state upon them, and they will be waited on. God is great, and therefore wait upon him.

2. We are vile creatures and unworthy, and therefore let us wait. If a beggar should rap and rap, and you come and see it to be a beggar, your heart rises upon him; if he beg, he must wait if you be busy. We are beggars, and therefore it is fit we should wait.

3. God has waited on us a long time. How long did God wait upon thee? It may be thou wert twenty years old before thou didst begin to turn to God, perhaps thou wert thirty or forty years old, and God was waiting upon thee to be gracious all that time; God was waiting for opportunity to do thee good, therefore wait thou now upon God.

4. What we wait for is worth our waiting. If a man believed there were nothing but scraps to be had at last, then he would not wait so long; but if he hoped some great thing was to be gotten, then he would wait. When beggars come to a mean house, they knock at the door and stay a little, and if they give them nothing, away they will go; but if they come to great houses, or coaches, they will wait, though it be long, and run a great way after them. That which we wait for is worth thousands of worlds; we wait for the pardon of sin, we wait for the assurance of God's love, we wait for the shedding abroad of the Holy Ghost in our hearts; we wait for rich treasure, and know that there is enough to be had in God: your waiting will pay for all.

5. It is a great part of God's worship to wait upon him. It is not the worship of God, only to pray, and hear the word, and receive sacraments; but when you are waiting you are worshipping of God.

6. God is all this while preparing mercy for you. Suppose a scrivener write something for you; well, the thing is not yet done; yea, but he is writing as fast as he can. Know, O thou soul who art turning to God, all the while thou art waiting God is working; God is setting all his attributes on work for thy good while thou art waiting, and therefore wait on thy God.

7. God is infinitely wise, and he knows when it is best for us to have the mercy, he knows the times and seasons; wait then still upon God, for "the Lord is a God of judgment." Alas! we are hasty, we cannot judge when the time is fittest, but God is "a God of judgment," and therefore wait upon him: should we have a mercy just when we would, our mercy would undo us, and therefore let us wait.

O my brethren, we have as much encouragement here in this land to wait upon God as ever any people had. We would fain have had the wars ended, and we began to murmur and repine because it was not done, Oh, but we will not wait; therefore we will not turn; and those that turn to God least will wait least upon him, and those that turn to God most will wait most upon him. Do not you see that God has wrought abundance of good for us by deferring what we would have? Suppose we had had no opposition at the beginning of the parliament, but that the king had agreed, and said, You shall have your desires. Our desires then were limited to some few things, as the abolition of ship money, tonnage and poundage of monopolies, &c., and the granting of triennial parliaments, and the like. Now what abundance has God wrought by deferring what we would have had! Oh, it is good for people to wait upon God. Let us look back to our murmurings and repinings all this while; true, we have suffered something; yea, but has not God wrought good out of our sufferings? And suppose there should be fears of new storms arising, oh, let us not say we will wait no longer. Take heed of foolish resolutions of your own. God is wisest, leave God to do his own work; keep the way of God and go on in your duty, and then let God work his own ends, either by war or peace, as he pleases, only "wait thou upon thy God."

"Continually." It is fit for us to wait. Yea, but we have waited a long time. Well, but yet know that you are at the right door. Suppose a man be knocking at a door, and he has knocked a great while and nobody comes, he begins to think it is not the right door, but somebody tells him that it is, and thereon he stays: so we may assure our hearts thus much, we are at the right door certainly, and let us not think to go away, we shall find somebody within, God will appear at length. What! shall we lose all for want of waiting a little while longer? Thus it is with many wretched apostates, that have taken a great deal of pains in seeking after God a great while, and for want of waiting a little longer they have lost all. Oh, let there be this resolution in your hearts, If I die and perish, yet I will die and perish waiting upon God. Certainly the soul which has this resolution will never come to despair; yea, there is no such way for the hastening of mercy, as for a soul to lie flat at the feet of God: Let God do what he will with me; if I perish, I will perish waiting upon him; though he kills me, I will trust in him, and stay upon him. You have waited; how long, I pray? Oh, you have been waiting and seeking God it may be this half year, or twelve months. What is that, I pray? O thou wretched soul! thou hast deserved eternal flames, and wilt thou grudge waiting on God a few years? If God would keep thee waiting all thy days, (as he has done many,) and at the last manifest himself unto thee, thou hast cause to bless God for ever; and therefore do not grudge though thou hast been waiting a while, and it may be, though thy time is come, yet God's time is not come. The time which you call long, God calls not so; one day with God is as a thousand years; it is no time with God, and therefore do not complain of the length of thy time. But for waiting, and that "continually," there are further reasons.

1. Your betters have waited longer. Read but Psal. lxxxviii., and there you will find one better than you who waited all his time. The Lord was pleased to work grace upon him when he was young, his heart was turned to God then; and you may find in the text, that from his youth up, the terrors of God were upon him. "Wait thou upon thy God continually."

2. You cannot better yourself. Whither wilt thou go, poor soul? now you are seeking God, you have not what you would have, whither will you go? Can you mend yourself any way? if you cannot, then wait upon God "continually."

3. It may be before God began to turn thy heart, thou didst think mercy was easy to be obtained, that it was nothing to believe; thou didst wonder that people spake so much of the hardness of believing, in thine eyes it was easy. Well, the Lord is now working upon thy heart, and would humble thee for those slight thoughts which thou hadst of faith; the Lord will have thee to know, that believing in his grace requires a mighty work of God, even the same power which raised Jesus Christ from the dead. Be humbled for thy slight thoughts about the work of faith, and know, that this (it may be) is the thing which God intends in so long keeping thee so low, that thou mayst come to see that faith requires the mighty power of God to work it; that so thou mayst give glory to God whenever thy heart shall be raised by the work of faith to believe in him, and to be enabled to triumph in him, and say, "Lo, this is our God, we have waited on him," and this is the God of my salvation. And therefore, you that are turning to God, wait upon your God continually.

Ver. 7. *He is a merchant, the balances of deceit are in his hand: he loveth to oppress.*

This scripture, though it seem somewhat harsh, and hard to read, yet it may be a good providence of God that has brought it before us at this time.

The scope of the prophet and connexion here is, We may exhort, but so long as their hearts are covetous, and set upon their way of getting gain, they will never regard what we say; they will not turn to God, they will not hear of it, but will rather turn a deaf ear to all entreaties. This indeed is the guise of men who have great dealings in the world, and whose hearts are set upon their riches, let the most glorious truths possible be set before them, yet they are as nothing to them. We read in Luke xvi. of Christ himself preaching before a company of men, and some of them being very covetous; mark what the text saith, ver. 14, "And the Pharisees also, who were covetous, heard all these things: and they derided him," they blew their noses at him, so the word signifies, they scorned him. Christ spake of excellent and divine mysteries, some of his auditors had dealings in the world, and great estates, and they scoffed at his words: Tell us of such things as these! tell us of ways of gain, how we may come to enrich ourselves. Similar seems to have been the disposition of some of the auditors of Hosea at this time, therefore saith he,

ἐξεμυκτήριζον.

"He is a merchant." The word כנען here translated "a merchant," signifies a Canaanite, and may be rendered according to the very letter, He is a Canaanite, for in Hebrew the word for Canaanite and merchant is the same. Thus Job xli. 6, "Shall they part him among the merchants?" among the Canaanites: and Prov. xxxi. 24, She "delivereth girdles unto the merchants;" the Hebrew is, to the Canaanites. Now the reason why a merchant and a Canaanite are synonymous in Scripture is, because the country of Canaan was much given to merchandise, and indeed much to deceit. As astrologers were called Chaldeans, because Chaldea was famous for mathematicians; and robbers and thieves were called Arabians, because the inhabitants of Arabia were addicted to theft; so because Canaan had so many merchants, therefore a Canaanite and a merchant were designated by the same term.

But here the Holy Ghost calls them not Israelites, mark, he saith not, You are an Israelite, but a Canaanite; and that by way of upbraiding them, as if because they had degenerated so much from Israel, spoken of before, he would not call them Israelites, but Canaanites.

Obs. 1. Men by their sin may lose the honour of their progenitors.

Obs. 2. Though the calling of a merchant is not only a lawful, but a very honourable employment, yet the abuse of it may make it very contemptible. If it be abused and corrupted it may become very contemptible; for so here the Holy Ghost does cast such a word upon them, to show how, through their corruption, they had rendered contemptible a calling that was honourable, and brought ignominy upon themselves; for though merchants that are subtle may, in the pride of their hearts, rejoice in their craft and cunning, and think that they can circumvent others by their deceit, and get money by over-reaching them, they may glory in this, as if it were a great excellency in them, but the Holy Ghost casts contempt upon those; "He is a merchant," a Canaanite, and "the balances of deceit are in his hand."

"The balances of deceit are in his hand." The Lord abhorred their "balances of deceit," yea, and professed that they are an abomination to him, if you read Lev. xix. 35, 36, "Ye shall do no unrighteousness in judgment, in meteyard, in weight, or in measure. Just balances, just weights, a just ephah, and a just hin, shall ye have: I am the Lord," I am Jehovah. If you will acknowledge me to be the Lord, to be Jehovah, be just in your dealing, have no unjust balances, let there be no injustice in your trading. And in Deut. xxv. 13—16, "Thou shalt not have in thy bag divers weights, a great and a small. Thou shalt not have in thine house divers measures, a great and a small. But thou shalt have a perfect and just weight, a perfect and just measure shalt thou have: that thy days may be lengthened in the land which the Lord thy God giveth thee. For all that do such things, and all that do unrighteously," (mark,) "are an abomination to the Lord thy God." Much stress is laid upon it. You think you may take liberty in such things. No, saith the text, all that do such things are "an abomination to the Lord thy God;" deceit in trading is not only a thing that God forbids, but a thing that God abominates. Dost thou profess any interest in God? hast thou any hope that God should be merciful to thy soul, to do thee any good? dost thou think that God is thy God? know, this is an abomination then to thy God, to that God in whom thou professest to have some interest. Prov. xi. 1 confirms this, "A false balance is abomination to the Lord; but a just weight is his delight," God takes pleasure in that.

"The balances of deceit." We are to regard this as a synecdoche for all kinds of deceit in trading, though only balances are here mentioned; not only deceitful balances, but measures, and tale, and lights, and mixtures, when they shall mix water and other things with any commodity to make it heavier, or mix bad with good ware, or, by some of their many arts, put a deceitful gloss and appearance on things; or use deceitful words, and make many protestations, yea, even swear deceitful oaths, with regard to the original cost and quality; and deceitful books, and deceitful reckonings; all such things are here condemned, and he who practises them is termed "a Canaanite." Yet those have their due honour that are righteous in their dealing; but such as make profession of merchandise, and are not righteous in their dealings, cannot think much that the Scripture should call them, by way of upbraiding, "a Canaanite."

Even a joining with others in deceit is included in this: as if a man, who knows the way they take is to cozen others, yet to get gain he will be content to join with them to partake a part of their gain: these things, and perhaps your own consciences would tell you of abundant more that you know of, of the mysteries of iniquity that there are in trading. As we read of those in the Revelation, that were under the power of antichrist, they might not buy nor sell, except they had the mark of the beast upon them. And the truth is, among a great part, if not most, of our buyers and sellers, there is the mark of the beast upon them, deceitfulness and falseness among them; and because this is thought to be so light a matter, therefore the Scripture lays the more weight upon it. And so much as the time will give me leave, I shall labour to lay some weight upon this, of deceitfulness in ways of trading.

"The balances of deceit are in his hand." Hereby (saith a learned interpreter on the place) is intimated a continual and perpetual study and endeavour to deceive, he has it at hand, it is in his hand continually.

Innuitur continuum ac perpetuum studium. Meisn. in loc.

In the forecited place, Deut. xxv., men are forbidden to have a false weight in their bag; you must not keep a false weight in your house, much less in your hand.

Or, it may be, he alludes to those that have a sleight of hand to make the balances turn one way or the other, so that their customers shall not perceive it.

"He loveth to oppress." What oppression is there in trading? If I buy a commodity and sell it again, what oppression can there be? There may be oppression in trading, as thus:

1. In monopolizing commodities. When a few men get a trade into their own hand, and make such use of it for themselves that poor men who have been brought up to it, and have no other means of livelihood, are not able to live by it, this is oppression. Certainly this monopolizing in trading is a great oppression: the Lord has in great measure delivered us from it, but yet not wholly, there is a great cry against it in many parts of the land still.

2. When men take the advantages of the weaknesses of those with whom they deal in their trading; but especially when they take advantage of men's necessities, that is, if such a man must sell his commodity, now for men to take advantage of his necessity, and therefore beat it down, so as even almost to undo a man in the very things he is necessitated to sell. I verily believe you know the meaning of such things as these are.

Or now, those who work upon the like necessity in buying, as sometimes when men must at a certain season bring over certain commodities, you will let them lie to the last, that so you may have them at any rate; and so when you come to know that men must needs have a commodity of you, then to raise the price so as they cannot live upon it, this is even to drink their very blood, this is oppression.

3. In wronging the poor of their rightful wages. There are many poor men, that are servants to you who are merchants and tradesmen, they live upon their labour, and they must come and fetch commodities of you, that they may live; now you, knowing their necessity, that they must have your work, therefore beat down their wages, and give not unto them so that they may maintain their families. You will say, I do not wrong them, if they do not, others will. It may be, but it does not excuse you.

4. In the oppression of debtors. When tradesmen have gotten poor men into their debts, then they will make them that they shall buy of them, and of none other, and so will put off on them their braided ware, and that at a dear rate. You will say, We sell it them. Yea, but you force them to buy of you; for if they

should go from you, then you fall upon them, and put them into prison, or evil entreat them some other way. This is to love to oppress, to take the advantage of men's necessities when they are grown poor. Certainly these things are grievous to the Spirit, and abominable in the eyes of God. These are rebuked here; and that you may see that there is a great deal of evil in these "balances of deceit," and oppression in trading, do but consider these particulars:

1. Observe how this is introduced in my text, as opposite to turning to God. "Turn thou to thy God;" then presently, "He is a merchant, the balances of deceit are in his hand; he loveth to oppress." Those who endeavour to get gain to themselves by any deceit or oppression, these are men that yet have not turned to God. Thou hast not turned to Jehovah, thy heart is not turned to him, thy heart is turned to the earth, the earth is thy portion, and the things of the earth thine inheritance; it is not God that thou hast chosen, thou hast not turned unto him.

2. Thou dost certainly not know the nature of sin, who darest venture the least sin for the greatest gain; had God ever enlightened and awakened thy conscience to see the true nature of sin, thou wouldst rather lose all thy estate, and be clothed with rags all thy days, than willingly commit the least sin to get the greatest estate. It was a saying of Austin, That there must not be so much as an officious lie; that is, a lie when a man intends no hurt, but good; yet this must not be told, saith he, no, not to save the souls of all the world. Surely then a lie must not be told to get twelve pence in a bargain, or five shillings, or fifty shillings, or five pounds; it must not be told to save the souls of all in the world. Now to tell a lie to deceive others as well as thyself, surely God has not yet laid the weight of sin upon your souls; the day is yet to come, that you shall know (perhaps to all eternity) what the weight and burden of sin mean.

3. Certainly you do not trust in God; you may speak of trusting in God, but it is apparent by this, that you have jealous thoughts of God, that you do not believe that God takes care of you. And here is not only sin, but an evidence of your misery; you are in such a condition, that your own consciences condemn you, and tell you that God takes no care of you, for did you believe that God cared for you, had a care over your body, estate, and soul, then wouldst thou leave all to God; I will cast my care upon God, I will go on in God's way, and leave all other things to him. But now, when a man is low in the world, and would fain rise higher, or would provide a certain portion for his children, and he falls to deceiving, and thinks to obtain it that way, the plain explicit English of it is, For my part, I dare not trust God to take care for me, and that which I think God does for me is not enough; if I trust to God's blessing, I may be a poor man, my children may be poor: I dare not then trust to promises, nor protections, nor providences, but I must take my own way. The truth is, the language practically amounts to this, I cannot get an estate by God, and therefore I will see what I can do by the devil.

4. All duties of religion that thou performest are rejected by God. You who are conscious to yourselves of falseness in your trading, and, it may be, have gone on many days and years in your ways, I say, all the duties of religion that you perform are rejected by God; you *will* deceive, and yet come to hear, and deceive again, and yet hear, and so make the duties of religion subserve as a colour to your deceit. Who would suspect that a man so forward in matters of religion should be so deceitful? Oh! cursed is that wickedness above all wickedness; it is aggravated by this, when thou makest religion to be a colour of deceit, know that God casts all thy profession and duties as filth and dung back again in your face. "Thou hast," saith Ezek. xxviii. 18, "defiled thy sanctuaries;" how? "by the multitude of thine iniquities, by the iniquity of thy traffic." By the iniquity of thy *traffic* thou hast defiled thy sanctuaries. You go abroad, and there you traffic, and deceive, and put off false commodities, and have false reckonings, and the like: now you come into the sanctuary; oh, but you defile the sanctuary by the multitude of your iniquity; and among other iniquities, the iniquity of your traffic is that which especially defiles the ordinances of God to you. In Micah vi. 8, when those hypocrites had said, What shall we do? shall we come with "thousands of rams, or with ten thousands of rivers of oil?" saith the prophet, "He hath showed thee, O man, what is good; and what doth the Lord require of thee, but to do justly," &c.? As if he should say, Though you come with all these things, it is all to no purpose, whatsoever offerings you offer to God, it is all nothing, except you "do justly."

5. There is a curse mingled with every thing which thou dost enjoy. Though, it may be, some things are gotten honestly, yet (I say) there is a curse mingled in all things thou doest, it venoms and poisons every thing thou doest. In Zech. v. 2, 3, there was a flying roll of twenty cubits, and the breadth of it ten cubits: "then said he unto me, This is the curse that goeth forth over the face of the whole earth;" for whom? "for every one that stealeth shall be cut off," &c. Every bit of meat which thou dost eat at thy table, thou mayst look upon as dipped in the curse of God: I have gotten this by deceit. Thou wouldst be loth to have every bit of meat rolled up in dirt and so put into thy mouth; but know, O fraudulent man! thine every bit of meat is rolled up in the curse of God.

6. Surely thou, who art guilty of this deceit in the way of trading, canst not pray if thou comest to prayer; surely thy conscience is very blind, for when thou art conscious to thyself of deceit, how canst thou come into the presence of a righteous God? Canst thou say, O righteous Father? darest thou come into the presence of such a holy and righteous God, who professes to abominate thy ways? Surely thy conscience must be very blind, if thou dost not understand the evil of thy sin. It may be, at first, in thy trading, thy conscience did trouble thee for a little time, thou hadst misgiving thoughts; but thou hast worn them out, and so art ready to bless thyself that thou hast gotten over such a difficulty as that is: thy condition is far worse. Or if not, if thy conscience be not seared with a hot iron, then thou wilt be terrified. I verily think that those who have any light left in them dare not go to prayers. Oh! dost thou so prize a little gain, as to take away the freedom of thy spirit, and the holy boldness of thy heart in prayer? Oh how shouldst thou say to gain, Get thee hence as a menstruous cloth!

7. Know, that if thou shouldst come to make use of thy estate in any good work, God rejects it. Isa. lxi. 8, "For I the Lord love judgment, I hate robbery for burnt-offering." What! will you get by deceit an estate, and come and offer it to me? I abhor it, saith God. Chrysostom saith, Why dost thou despise and dishonour God thus, in bringing unclean things to him? it is a reproach to God: a man who has gotten an estate by deceit, if he brings his estate to any service of God, he thereby reproaches God.

8. Know that God will avenge such things. It may be the poor man whom thou oppressest in thy trading cannot right himself upon thee, because a bargain is a bargain, you will say. Yea, but God will come over with the bargain again; it may be you have done with him in your bargain, but God has not done with you.

You will say to him, You saw what it was, and you bought the thing of me as it was, and I have nothing to say to you; but God has much to say to you on this point. Mark those two scriptures: first, in Micah vi., the Lord having shown what he did require, that men should be just in their ways, adds, in ver. 11—13, "Shall I count them pure with the wicked balances, and with the bag of deceitful weights? for the rich men thereof are full of violence, and the inhabitants thereof have spoken lies, and their tongue is deceitful in their mouth. Therefore also will I make thee sick in smiting thee." O, when God comes to smite thee, he will make thee sick to purpose; sickness to such men as have defiled consciences in their trading is dreadful sickness indeed: as if God should say, You shall have no great content in what you have; I will be avenged on you for what you do; either you or your heirs shall not enjoy it. But the second text is one which concerns Christians very much, a place that cannot possibly have escaped the notice of those of you that are exercised in Scripture, 1 Thess. iv. 6, "That no man go beyond and defraud his brother in any matter." You must not go beyond your brother. Your brother is weak; you will say, Let the weaker look to it as well as he can. No, you must not take advantage of his weakness, he is your brother; you must not defraud him, no, not "in any matter:" why? "because that the Lord is the avenger of all such, as we also have forewarned you and testified."

And know, this day the Lord forewarns you once more, and by the ministry of his word does testify against you in this respect; and if you *will* go on in any way of deceit, you go on against the very strength of the word and strength of conscience this day, and this word preached this day to you shall certainly testify against you another day.

9. How terrible will death be to such men, when they shall leave the sweet of all their estates, and carry nothing but the guilt of all with them! In Job xxvii. 8, "What is the hope of the hypocrite, though he hath gained, when God taketh away his soul?" Sometimes men seek to deceive, and they are discovered, and so rendered base and contemptible to all the world; yea, but sometimes they may carry it so cunningly, that they shall never be discovered perhaps in this world, but they shall gain, and say with Ephraim here, "I am become rich, I have found me out substance;" but "what is the hope of the hypocrite, though he hath gained?" what profit shall it be, though thou hast gained the whole world and thou shalt lose thy own soul?

10. Thou must restore, if thou hast any estate now, or if thou dost ever get one; restoration must be made, or thou canst not expect to find mercy from God, all thy sorrow, cries, and prayers are vain; without restitution, there cannot be expectation of pardon and forgiveness. The ancient speech that all divines in all ages of the church have closed withal was, There must be restitution of that which is falsely gotten; if it be in thy power to do it, thou must restore it, or else thou canst not have any hope of mercy; those sweet morsels which you have swallowed must be vomited up again. And therefore, you that are apprentices, take heed of being deceitful to please your masters, for if you have a hand in it you must restore. I will give you Scripture and reason, why it is impossible that any kind of repentance can be accepted of God without restitution.

1. Because, if I have power to restore, all the while I do not restore I continue in the sin; I do not only wrong the man just the very hour I have deceived him, but all the while I keep that which is his in my hand: this is the reason why that repentance can never be accepted of God, which consists with a wilful continuance in the sin that a man seems to repent of. Do I repent of my sin, and yet wilfully continue in the sin? I say, *wilful*, for I have it in my hand to restore. Oh, but I shall undo myself. Yea, but that is wilful still; is it better for thee to keep an estate or to keep a sin? Now, certainly any man that has any light must needs acknowledge thus much, That if I truly repent me of my sin, I must, as far as I possibly can, undo my sin; can I say, I am heartily sorry for a sin, when I do not what I can to undo that sin?

2. There are divers scriptures commanding restitution; I will give you two or three. Ezek. xxxiii. 14, 15, "Again, when I say unto the wicked, Thou shalt surely die; if he turn from his sin, and do that which is lawful and right; if the wicked restore the pledge, give again that he had robbed, walk in the statutes of life, without committing iniquity; he shall surely live, he shall not die." He does not "walk in the statutes of life," except he "give again that he had robbed." So in Numb. v. 6, 7, you have the law about restitution: "When a man or woman shall commit any sin that men commit, to do a trespass against the Lord, and that person be guilty; then they shall confess their sin which they have done." Is this all? No; mark: "and he shall recompense his trespass with the principal thereof, and add unto it the fifth part thereof, and give it unto him against whom he hath trespassed." He must confess his sin; yea, but that is not enough, he must recompense the party. This is a most excellent scripture. Mark, it is said here, "If a man shall commit any sin that men commit, to do a trespass against the Lord;" it is not only against man, but "against the Lord," against the rule of justice which the Lord has set for the maintaining of order and human society in the world. And then observe further: "If a man or woman shall commit any sin that men commit, to do a trespass." You will say, I do no other than all tradesmen do. Mark the text, "If a man or woman shall commit any sin that men commit;" as if the Holy Ghost should say, I confess it is a common sin, but though it be ordinarily committed by men, though there should be confession of that sin, yet if there be not restitution, it will do you little good. I remember Latimer, in one of the sermons that he preached before King Edward, speaking of this very point of restitution, saith, that the first day that he preached about it there came one and gave him twenty pounds to restore; the next time he preached another brought him thirty pounds; and on another occasion there came another and gave him two hundred pounds ten shillings. He uses this homely expression, "Restore what you have gotten, else you will cough in hell, and the devils will laugh at you." Certainly it is that which will lie heavy upon conscience; gravel in the kidneys will not grate so upon you as a little guilt on your consciences. I myself knew one man who had wronged another but of five shillings, and it seems he did not much regard it, the sum being so small; yet God awakening his conscience fifty years after, he could not rest till he had restored that five shillings. And therefore know, that though it be many years since you have gotten any thing by deceit and wrong, yet God will (if he has a love to you) constrain you to restore it. Oh what foolish lusts are the lusts of covetousness! As the apostle saith, Those that will be rich fall into many foolish lusts: this sin of covetousness and deceitfulness brings men into foolish lusts, and makes men pierce themselves through with many sorrows. And oh that God would pierce them with some sorrow this day, that they might never have one night's quiet rest, till they at least resolve in their hearts that they will commence the work of restitution.

And even those of you that have made false agreements with your creditors, if God awakens your consciences, I see not how you can quiet them till you satisfy your creditors: these things will not be peace another day.

Now the Lord convince those that, hearing the word of God, are guilty, and know that God will call for an account of this thing, and of this text that through providence has been preached to them this day.

Ver. 8. *And Ephraim said, Yet I am become rich, I have found me out substance: in all my labours they shall find none iniquity in me that were sin.*

In the verse before Ephraim is charged for being a "merchant," for having "the balances of deceit in his hand," and loving to oppress. But "Ephraim said, Yet I am become rich."

"Yet." The particle אך signifies, here, nevertheless; as if they should say, Let the prophet say what he will, let him inveigh against me as he pleases, I know not what he means by his deceit and oppression, I am sure I gain well by it. "Yet I am become rich;" I am sure I prosper in this way, and that is enough for me.

"I have found me out substance." The word און here translated "substance," signifies sometimes iniquity, labour, violence, rapine, affliction, riches, an idol; all these things this word signifies: indeed most of them, if not all, are usually accompaniments of riches in the hands of the wicked.

The Greeks call riches ἀναψυχὴν, rest, refreshing to the soul. They account the great refreshing and rest to their souls to be in their riches, however acquired.

"Substance." Those things which the prophet tells us of are but notions, imaginations; but in what I have found there is "substance;" to have an estate, and riches, and incomings, in them is substance. "I have found me out substance." Hence,

Obs. 1. Wicked men will have something to say for themselves, though their ways be never so foul. The prophet brings heavy charges against them, "the balances of deceit," and loving to oppress, and other sins before named; yet Ephraim saith; he hath somewhat to say. It is a very hard thing to stop the mouths of wicked men, and especially of the rich wicked; wicked men that prosper in their wickedness, say what you will, you cannot stop their mouths. The work of conversion is not so much as begun till the mouths of sinners be stopped, till they be so convinced of their evil ways that they have nothing to say for themselves.

Obs. 2. Wicked men may prosper for a while in their evil courses. "Ephraim said, Yet I am become rich." It is true, sometimes God meets with wicked men, and curses them in their way, so that they have not their desire satisfied; but often they have, they do become rich, they get their hearts' desires: Job xxi.; Psal. lxxiii., and many other places.

Obs. 3. Wicked men attribute to themselves their prosperity and riches. "I am become rich, I have found substance." They do not look up to God, indeed they dare not; those whose gains are sinful, dare not acknowledge God in them. This is the evil of getting any thing in a way of sin, that a man cannot come to God and say, Lord, I bless thee that thou hast given me this. No, his conscience would fly in his face. Wicked men attribute all to themselves: this is a very wicked and vile thing. Deut. vi. 12, "Then" (speaking of their having houses and lands in Canaan) "beware lest thou forget the Lord," and only look at thyself, and attribute all to thyself. The "great and goodly cities," "and houses full of all good things," are given to thee by the Lord thy God, "which sware unto thy fathers."

Obs. 4. Carnal hearts account riches the only substantial things. "I have found me out substance." They think there is no substance in other things. You speak of spiritual things, of communion with God, of faith in Jesus Christ, and of the promises, they are but poor dry things, that have no substance in them; but tell me of gain, and incomings, there is some savour there, in them there is substance. Indeed nothing gives substance to spiritual things but faith: in Heb. xi. 1, "Faith is the substance of things hoped for, the evidence of things not seen." Faith gives a substance to things spiritual, a believer looks upon them as substantial, and regards these outward things as imaginary. Carnal hearts think spiritual things imaginary, and an outward estate substantial: the word of God is quite contrary to these. Thus in Prov. viii. 21, wisdom saith, "That I may cause those that love me to inherit substance;" that is, as if nothing had a substance but only that which comes in by wisdom, by grace. We call rich men substantial men; Such a man, we say, is a substantial man; for indeed all the substance that the world looks after is riches, they account them substance.

Obs. 5. Carnal hearts much glory in their possessions. "I am become rich, I have found me out substance." They make their boast in what they have got, they bless themselves in their way. In Zeph. i. 9, it is spoken of the very servants of rich, covetous men, who seek to get an estate but to their masters, in a way either of violence or of deceit, they "leap on the threshold." They triumph, and leap in their rejoicings, that they have circumvented others, that they have got such and such things to their masters; much more then will the masters themselves leap and rejoice in the having their hearts' desires filled: they glory in it.

Obs. 6. Carnal hearts, that have gotten estates by sinful means, seek to relieve their guilty consciences with the consideration of the outward comforts they enjoy. The prophet charges them with their sin, charges the guilt of their sin upon them. But we are rich, say they, and we inherit substance. Wicked men will seek to relieve their consciences, their guilty consciences, by rejoicing in their riches, and in their estates, and in what they have got. In Isa. lvii. 10, you have a scripture somewhat suitable to this; "Thou hast found the life of thine hand; therefore thou wast not grieved." It may be, if a man goes on in an evil way, and does not prosper in it, God crossing him, then he begins to bethink himself, Is not this a sinful way? does not God oppose me in it? and then he begins to be grieved. But if he can find the life of his hand go on, and he prosper and have what he desires, then he will not be grieved, then his heart is hardened. Wicked men will set their riches and estates against all their guiltiness, and think they will countervail it. I beseech you, weigh this matter well, consider that there is no more full and sure sign of a worldly man than this, that he can think to relieve his conscience in the guilt of the least sin, by the enjoyment of the things of the world; that he can set the good things of the world against the guilt of sin, that he can put any thing in the world in the balance to down-weigh the least guilt of any sin. Herein is evidenced a worldly, wretched heart: thou dost bless thyself in thy great estate, but hast thou contracted no guilt at all in its acquisition? Thou canst not say but some guiltiness has been contracted; yea, but this contents thee, so much gain has been the result. Oh! thou art a wretched man, that canst set the gain in the world against the least guilt that thou hast contracted. Oh! it has been an ill bargain, riches got by guilt; thou hast made (I say) an ill bargain for thyself. Thou knowest not God, knowest not with whom thou hast to deal, that canst set any gain by sin for to countervail the evil of that guilt that thou hast committed for the getting of that gain of thine.

Obs. 7. Wicked men labour to persuade themselves that God is not altogether so displeased with them as many would persuade them. Surely, if my condition were so dangerous as you would persuade me to, I should not prosper so much in my way as I do, I should not get riches so as I do. Upon this they begin to think that God is of their mind, as in Psal. l. 21, "Thou thoughtest that I was altogether such an one as thyself." We find by experience that when men are under affliction, when God's hand is upon them, they begin to think that he does not like their ways; but when they go on and prosper they are ready to think that God approves. There is a notable story concerning the mother of Lombard, Gratian, and Comestor, (the first, the Master of the Sentences; the second, the compiler of a great part of the pope's law, the Decretal Epistles; the third, the author of the Scholastical History, the best man and book of the three,) all famous men, and all three bastards; now when their mother came to make her confession to the priest, she could not acknowledge much evil in her whoredoms, nor find her heart much grieved or troubled on account of them; and when the priest urged her to repent and do penance, she replied that the thing might be evil which she did, yet that the prosperity and eminent usefulness of three such sons might well cover her transgressions. Thus it is ordinarily; men think the magnitude of the sin lessened by the greatness of the success. The people they may laugh at me, (saith a covetous man,) but I applaud myself at home, as I contemplate the money in the chest; so long as I see comings-in, let men talk what they will, I cannot believe that things are so bad as they report, that God is so much against me, my prosperity surely is an indication of his favour. These are the reasonings of a carnal heart. Of Dionysius it is related, that when he had committed sacrilege, and had a good voyage after it, he said, You tell me of sacrilege, but see what a good voyage the gods themselves have granted me. Oh, these are heathenish reasonings, and yet I fear they are not altogether rooted out of such as profess themselves Christians. "Ye who go down to the sea in ships, who do business in great waters," it may be if you meet with an ill voyage, then you begin to recollect yourself, What sin have I been guilty of? but now, if your voyage be prosperous, though you have contracted much guilt upon your spirits while you were at land, yet prospering in your voyage, you never think but all is well. Oh no, a good voyage is no sign of the absence of guilt; as sometimes I have told you, that a painted face is no sign of a good complexion: it may be it is the curse of God upon thee that does let thee so to prosper; and if God had any love to thee, he would not let thee to prosper so, he would cross thee in thy ways, that so thou mightest bethink thyself. Another, perhaps, has been as wicked as thou, and yet the Lord had a love to him, and he crossed him in his ways, so that he has begun to bethink himself, and cannot rest till he gets the guilt of his sin done away; but for thee, God's heart it seems is not yet towards thee, he has no love to thee; and if he lets thee go on and still prosper in a course of sin, this is the fruit of reprobation: and certainly there can scarcely be a greater note of reprobation than prosperity in sin. This is what we should all pray to God to deliver us from; Lord, let us never prosper in sin; if thou seest our way to be naught, that we thereby contract guilt upon our spirits, Lord, let us not thrive and prosper; if we do, a thousand to one but we are undone for ever.

Populus me sibilat, at mihi plaudo ipse domi simul ac nummos contemplor in arcâ. Hor.

Videtis quam bona navigatio, ab ipsis diis, sacrilegis tribuatur. Val. Maximus, lib. 1. cap. 2.

"And Ephraim said, Yet I am become rich, I have found me out substance."

Ephraim thus put off all that the prophet spake. So when Christ was preaching to the Pharisees, the text saith, Those that were rich derided him. Rich, covetous men slight any thing that is said against them, for they have wherewithal, they think, to relieve their consciences against all their guilt. Well, though thou mayst think to relieve thy conscience for the present, it will not always be so; there is a time that conscience *will* speak, and will not be put off with those idle conceits.

Obs. 8. The saints believe the word against sense, and carnal hearts believe sense against the word. Herein lies the difference between a godly man and a wicked; I say, one that is godly and has faith, believes the word against sense; Let me go on in a way which I know is God's way, though I do not prosper, yet I have peace in it, I do not repent me of it: but a wicked man will believe sense against the word; Let the word say my way is never so dangerous, yet if by sense I find that I prosper in it, that shall suffice me. "Yet I am become rich, I have found me out substance."

"In all my labours." That is, in all that I get by my labours.

"They shall find none iniquity in me that were sin." That is, let them search, they shall not find in me that which is sin. As if they should say, No, I abhor what you say; to oppress, cheat, and cozen, who can prove it? let any prove if they can that I cheat, or get any thing in a false way; I dare any to come and say it; is there any law that can take hold of me? "They shall find no iniquity in me;" though there be some little matter, yet there is nothing for which the law of the land can take hold of me; and if my way be such as no man can take advantage against me by the law, why should I be thus condemned? That is the meaning of these words. Hence,

Obs. 9. Evil things often have good names. "In all my labours." The truth is, that which is meant here, is that which they had got by oppression and deceit, and they call it by the name of their labours. So covetousness is called by the name of good husbandry, and following their callings, and the art and mystery of their callings. Many think to silence their consciences by such shuffling of names.

Obs. 10. It is very hard to convince covetous men of their iniquity. Rich, covetous men are much conceited in themselves. "The rich man is wise in his own conceit," Prov. xxviii. 11. You shall sometimes see a man that gets riches; and as we say of some when we look upon their wit, we wonder at their wealth; and others when we look upon their wealth, we wonder at their wit to get an estate: they have wit only to get money, but for any thing else they are ignorant, poor, weak men, especially in matters of religion; as weak as children are they, and yet wise in their own conceits, for they have got that which they see all the world runs after. It is very hard to convince covetous men of their falseness, that they get any thing in a sinful way.

Again, There is no sin more hard to convince a man of than covetousness; and yet the apostle saith, 1 Cor. v. 11, that it is a sin for which a man is to be cast out of the church. When almost did you ever hear of a covetous man convinced? what example can you almost ever bring of one that has been covetous and rich, and got his estate in a false way, that shall come and give glory to God, and acknowledge his sin, and cast up his sweet morsels again? Covetousness is a besotting, a blinding sin: Who shall find any iniquity in me? what do I but that which I may do?

Obs. 11. As it is hard to convince, so it is difficult to charge, covetous men with their sin. For so according to some it is, Who dares charge me? It is a very dangerous thing to charge a rich man of any evil, for he has his purse by his side, and can tell how to revenge himself on you.

Obs. 12. Men may in words profess what they themselves are guilty of to be an abominable thing. "They shall find none iniquity in me that were sin." If I should be false, that were a very horrible and vile thing. Go to all tradesmen one after another, and tell them of cheating, and cozening, and deceiving; they will scorn your words, It were a wicked thing, one were unworthy to live. How often, when tradesmen have a mind to cheat, will they profess, that if they should cozen and cheat, they were unworthy to trade any more! Oh what cauterized consciences have many men, that give up themselves to gain, and make Mammon their god! Luther renders it, God forbid that I should be found wicked in my actions. Many deep in guilt will clap their hands on their breasts, and when you charge them with having cheated and cozened you, Oh, God forbid that I should do so! they exclaim; and although their consciences will tell them that they have done so, they will be ready to take their oaths, and swear, and use such curses that they never did such a thing, or never had such a thing; and when their books are false, they will swear that they are true.

Absit ut deprehendar sceleratus in meis factis. Luth. in loc.

Obs. 13. Wicked men care not, so others cannot accuse them. If they can carry it so closely that men shall not see it, then they bless themselves; all is well and fair, if they have cunningly contrived their wickedness, that men cannot charge them with it. Who shall find iniquity in me that were sin? Well, though you think yourselves well enough because men cannot find out your sin, yet God can find it out, "be sure your sin will find you out;" God has his time to find out iniquity that will be sin to you, and there is much between God and your consciences, though men cannot charge you. Oh, but if so be that God would but discover to the world what he is able to charge you with, how loathsome would many of you appear to your neighbours! how unfit would you be to trade with men! or who would meddle with you? Now certainly your condition is not the better because it is kept so secretly that men cannot charge you; perhaps it would be better if they could, for it might bring you sooner to be humbled for it. You think now, because you have only to deal with God, you can do well enough with him. Do you think it such a matter to deal with the infinite, holy, and glorious God? Servants would be troubled if their masters knew their deceit and cozening; but if a little child knew it they care not for that; so men think it is no matter if God know it, but they are loth that men should know it, that will bring shame and disgrace to them. O carnal, wicked, atheistical heart, that cannot be satisfied if men know the evil, but can rest content though God is conscious to it!

Obs. 14. A carnal heart extenuates its guilt. Indeed the words may be interpreted, Who shall find iniquity in me? if they could find it, I would acknowledge it to be a great sin. But I rather take it thus, Who shall find any great iniquity in me? It is but a little overreaching, a little craft and cunning, the matter is not great. Well, that which thou dost account little, the Lord will one day account great; the overreaching and defrauding thy brother, though it be but a sleight of hand, God will find one day to be a great matter.

Obs. 15. A soul which God is humbling for good, rather aggravates his sin. That is the way of a true convert, he labours rather to aggravate his sin, to bring all the circumstances he can to make his sin heavy upon his soul. Oh! I find I cannot get my heart to break for my sin, I cannot apprehend the evil of my sin as I would in the greatness of it, and therefore, oh that God would help me to see its magnitude! He studies all the attendant circumstances to make his sin great in his own eyes. But now, a heart that is not wrought upon to a work of repentance, all that he labours for is to lessen his sin, and to have all the reasonings that he can in a way of diminution of his sin. Oh, this is an ill sign!

It is a very ill sign, first, when a man resists conviction as long as he can. Secondly, when, after he can stand out no longer, then he begins to extenuate his guilt: It is no more than others do; and how should I maintain my family? and I hope men may make the best of what they have. Oh! if the Lord once show thee the evil of sin, all these reasonings will vanish before thee, and thou wilt fall down and humble thyself before God, as one worthy for ever to be cast out from the presence of the Lord; for in this, that thou darest not trust in him, thou seekest to hell to provide for thyself and family, rather than thou wilt depend upon God.

Obs. 16. If wicked men can but escape the danger of law, that is all they care for. "They shall find none iniquity in me that were sin;" that is, by the law. Oh how many are there whom you may easily convince of having been very false! You speak to their consciences. Yea, but what is that? can you take your advantage? Take your advantage if you can, say they. Now if it were not for atheism in men's hearts, it would be the greatest advantage of all, that a man is able to charge his conscience. What witness have you for such a thing? I have your conscience. Oh, they are glad of that: if they hear that you have no other witness, they think they can do well enough. Now that is an argument of atheism in men's hearts, that they think they are well enough, whatsoever they do, when law cannot take hold on them. Well, there is a court of conscience to sue thee in, and justice will sue thee in that court, and cast thee one day, though man's law cannot.

Ver. 9. *And I that am the Lord thy God from the land of Egypt will yet make thee to dwell in tabernacles, as in the days of the solemn feasts.*

The connexion is this: You say you are grown rich by those sinful ways of yours; "I am become rich, I have found me out substance." You think now you have no need of me, you have found substance other ways, and I am forgotten by you; but you should remember that "I am the Lord thy God, which brought thee out of the land of Egypt:" there was a time when you had need of me, a time when you knew not what to do without my help, and were in great affliction; then I delivered you with a mighty hand; you should remember those old mercies of mine. Oh, but you are ungrateful, you do not think what I have done for you in bringing you out of the land of Egypt. If I be the same God still, why might not you live upon me, and receive as much good from me, as others? You will go and seek to shift for yourselves by false ways, and forsake me. Am not I the Lord? that "God which brought you out of the land of Egypt?" have not I, by what I have done for you, shown plainly to you that you might as well provide for yourselves by me as by any other god, by my ways as well as by any other ways that you take? Can any god work for you so as I have done? Is there that good to be got in those ways of sin which there is in mine? "I that am the Lord thy God from the land of Egypt;" not only at that time delivering you, but ever since providing for you, and graciously preserving you, and doing you good many ways, from the time that I have been a God to you; and yet you do thus wretchedly forsake me. In all your straits I have helped you, in all your necessities I have supplied you, in all your difficulties I have relieved you, in all your distresses I have delivered you, in all your burdens I have eased you; the whole course of my providence has been gracious to you; from the very time of your coming out of the land of Egypt, how did I provide for you in the wilderness, afterwards by judges, and then I raised you up kings! "I that am the Lord thy God from the land of Egypt."

Obs. 1. When men prosper in sin, they forget what God has done for them in former times. As if he should say, You do not remember that I am "the

Lord thy God from the land of Egypt." Now you are "waxen fat" and have your hearts' desires; but remember there was a time when you were low enough, and cried and made your moan to me in your affliction; remember those days. Oh how ordinary is it for us in our prosperity to forget God's mercies in delivering us from affliction! Not long since we were low enough, but the Lord has in great measure delivered us from our Egypt, and presently, as soon as God has delivered us, every man begins to think of enriching himself and to intrigue for estates; presently (I say) we have forgotten our sad condition, the time of our mourning, of our praying. Oh how contrary is the disposition of our hearts now to what it seemed to be a little while ago, when under sore and sad afflictions!

Obs. 2. God takes notice of men's unthankfulness. God looks upon a people that walk so vilely: What! are these the people that I have done such things for? What God has done for us is (to speak after the manner of men) fresh in his memory.

And if we could have what God has done for us afresh in our minds upon the commission of new sins, it would be a mighty means to humble us.

Obs. 3. Old mercies are great engagements to duty, and great aggravations of our neglect of it. But we have had occasion to speak of these things before.

"Will yet make thee to dwell in tabernacles, as in the days of the solemn feasts."

Some read it by way of interrogation, thus, What! shall I, the Lord that brought thee out of the land of Egypt, yet make thee to dwell in tabernacles? Shall I yet continue my wonted love to you as to make you to keep your feast of tabernacles still with joy, as you were wont to do yearly? shall I do thus? saith God.

Calvin gives a peculiar interpretation, different from all; as if God should say thus, It is a wonderful thing that you should be so forgetful of my great mercy in bringing of you out of Egypt, it is so out of your minds that I had need work over that deliverance again: what! shall I cast you out of your houses, and bring you into captivity again, and then deliver you, and bring you into the wilderness to dwell in tabernacles again? shall I again go over my work? It is so much gone out of your minds and hearts, that such a repetition seems needful to quicken your spirits. Thus Calvin interprets this passage, and he is generally as just as any. This interpretation may be well applied to us, thus:

Let us consider ourselves, that if all God's merciful dealings towards us were to begin again, if we were to go through all those straits, and fears, and sorrows that we have passed through, our hearts would shake within us: as a mariner that has passed through dangerous seas, thinks, If I were to pass over these again, it would be hard and grievous. Now let us consider, if God should but reduce us to the same condition that we were in seven years ago, and say, You shall pass through all those straits, and return into the condition you have been in; it would be very sad to us to think of, the bare apprehension would make our hearts quake. I verily believe scarce any of you who have been at all observant of the providence of God towards you, but would be very loth to venture all again, would be loth that God should go over with you in all those providences. And yet God is the same God still, and may do it; yea, but flesh and blood would shake at it. Now do not show yourselves so unworthy of God's gracious dealings with you, as to put him to it to bring you into straits again, to renew what he has done unto you. Thus we apply Calvin's interpretation.

Many regard the words as a mere threat, and no otherwise: I did indeed bring you from the land of Egypt, but I will bring you into tabernacles again. As if God should say, I will cast you out of your brave, stately palaces, your city and country houses, and you shall come into the wilderness again, and dwell in tents and tabernacles. Thus the many interpret it.

But I rather think the words contain a consolatory promise, whereby the Holy Ghost invites them to repentance; as if God should say thus, Though you have indeed deserved to be cast out of your dwellings, and to be brought into tents and tabernacles in the wilderness again, yet I remember my ancient goodness towards you, and my covenant with your father Abraham; I am the same God that brought you out of the land of Egypt, therefore return and repent, and I will be with you in as much mercy as ever I was; whatever the breaches have been for time past, I will now be as gracious to you as I have ever been; as you have celebrated the feast of tabernacles with abundance of rejoicing, so I will continue this your prosperous estate, you shall from year to year have cause to rejoice in this your solemn feast. All their feasts were feasts of rejoicing; "They have made a noise in the house of the Lord, as in the day of a solemn feast," Lam. ii. 7; but now this feast of tabernacles was especially a feast of rejoicing, and that you have in Lev. xxiii. 40, where they are commanded to rejoice in this feast, for it was after the ingathering of their corn and wine. In Deut. xvi., where this feast is further spoken of, it is said at the end of ver. 15, "Thou shalt surely rejoice;" it is not only you may, but a command, look to it that you do rejoice in this feast of tabernacles; so that the feast of tabernacles was a very joyful feast. Now saith God, "I that am the Lord thy God from the land of Egypt," I will yet make thee rejoice, as in the feast of tabernacles. From hence we have these notes:

Obs. 4. God loves to give hopes of mercy to sinners upon their repentance. God loves to draw the hearts of wretched, vile sinners, by giving them hopes of mercy upon their repentance. So in 1 Sam. xii. 19, 20, they confessed their sin, their special sin, in asking a king, above all; but saith Samuel, Though "ye have done all this wickedness, yet turn not aside from following the Lord." So Ezra x. 2, "Yet now there is hope in Israel concerning this thing." God sees that if there be not hope, men will grow desperate in their wickedness. "There is no hope: no, for I have loved strangers, and after them will I go," Jer. ii. 25. Oh! it is good for sinners to see there may be still hope.

And God's ministers, when they have to deal with sinners, though very wicked, yet should give them some line of hope to catch at; though they be even drowned in their covetousness in the world, and in their guiltiness, yet should we cast to them a line of hope; there is nothing revealed to exclude the possibility of thy soul yet at length being saved. Oh let men take heed of despairing, determining conclusions against themselves.

Obs. 5. It is not the greatness of any sin that can be ground enough for a desperate determining conclusion. To any who say, God will never show mercy; I reply, No magnitude of sin, no accumulation of aggravated circumstances, can be ground enough for thee to say, God will never show mercy; it is a proud, sullen, desperate spirit of thine to make such conclusions: thou mayst indeed, and thou oughtest to say, It were just with God not to show mercy, the Lord might justly cast me out of his sight; but to say that he *will not* show mercy, is more than thou, or any angel in heaven, can say; and therefore, O wretched, sinful, guilty consciences, and especially you that have been apostates, that have forsaken God and his truths, yet return, return. O return, thou Shulamite, thou mayst possibly find God as merciful to thee as ever he was; there is hope of mercy for thee still, and if thou dost perish eternally, it will rather be for some future, than for any past, transgression; if God let thee live, if he let thee live to-night, I say, thou wilt rather perish for the sins committed this moment, than for all the sins committed in all thy life-time before.

But now thy continuance in impenitency is a new sin; thy continuing to reject the grace of God, and abiding still in thy unbelief, this indeed may cause God to bring over again all thy former sins, and reckon for them. Oh! this consideration might draw the heart of the most wretchedly wicked sinner to God.

Is it so, that it is not for any of my past sins that I am like to perish, but if I perish I shall perish rather for continuing in evil, than for what evil I have committed? Oh! the Lord forbid then that I should continue, let me this day stop. The Lord would have hopes of mercy cast to the vilest and most wicked.

And let us be merciful, as our heavenly Father is merciful; that is, let servants and children, that have offended you, see that upon their returning they shall find as much favour from you as ever they did. Sometimes governors, when provoked, behave themselves so rigidly towards their inferiors, that it makes them even desperate: God deals not so with you; be ye then merciful, for God is merciful.

And as God shows himself unchangeable towards his people in goodness, so it beseems us to be. If we have shown respect any way to other, either in speeches or otherwise, if they appear to be what they were, it beseems us to be towards them as then; let them but appear to be what they were when such respect were shown to them, and, according to the example of God, it beseems us to show ourselves to them again and again, to what we then did. " I that am the Lord thy God from the land of Egypt, will yet make thee to dwell in tabernacles."

Obs. 6. The consideration of what God has done, should help our faith in believing what he will do. May not he who has delivered us thus far, deliver us yet further? I am the Lord that has delivered you from Egypt. O, let us make use of what God has done for us, to help our faith to confide in him for further grace. The truth is, God has done so much for England, that not more remains to be done than has been done; and if there be but as much of the power, goodness, and mercy of God manifested towards us for the next five or six years, as for these last six, certainly it will be as glorious a nation as ever was upon the face of the earth: it will be the beginning of the new Jerusalem, if God should continue so as he has done. And why may not the Lord, that has brought us out of Egypt, bring us to rejoice as in the feast of tabernacles?

And so spiritually; God, who at first did enlighten thy mind, and brought thee from Egyptian darkness, is certainly able to do as great things for thee still, and to finish the work he has begun for thee. How many are there who, though they have found God's mighty hand upon them in giving a turn to their hearts, and bringing them out of "the gall of bitterness" and "the bond of iniquity," yet, when they feel but their corruptions a little stirring, are ready to think that they shall perish one day by the hand of those same corruptions? When we were enemies, were we not reconciled to him? God has given the deadly wound to thy sin, he has *mortified* thee, and the truth is, there is not more to be done to bring thee to heaven who hast the least degree of grace than God has already done; by giving thee the least measure of grace, he has made a greater alteration in thy estate from one that is in an estate of nature, than the alteration will be from thy conversion to the height of glory; that alteration will not be so much, neither will it require such a great power of God to make thee a glorious saint in heaven, as it required to make thee of a child of wrath, a child of God: thou hast the better half, the most eminent power of God is put forth already; for our change from grace to glory will be but gradual, but our change from nature to grace is total; and therefore, let thy faith be helped from what God has done, to believe what he will do.

"I will yet make thee to dwell in tabernacles."

Albertus and others regard this, "I will yet make thee to dwell in tabernacles," as a promise of their return from captivity, that they must again, in the land of Jewry, keep the feast of tabernacles.

I confess, were this a promise to Judah, I should think this to be the meaning of it; but because it is to Israel, who never returned, I shall follow those who think it refers to the times of the gospel, and to all the true Israel of God that should be converted to the faith; and I think it has reference to that, because we find so often, in this prophecy of Hosea, things apparently far off applied to the times of the gospel.

"I will yet make thee to dwell in tabernacles." In the spiritual sense thus, The Lord has his time, though he seemed to cast off these ten tribes, yet to bring the Jews, and all the Israel of God, into his church, and to build for them in it several tabernacles. And there in several churches, as in so many several tabernacles, they shall have the feast of sweet things, of "fat things," of "wine on the lees well refined," Isa. xxv. There shall they keep a feast, and there shall their hearts rejoice, and be "satisfied as with marrow and fatness."

My brethren, the Lord has delivered us in great measure from Egypt: all the difficulty now is about the building of tabernacles; for the present there is very little matter to make tabernacles of amongst us. I remember Mr. Ainsworth, on Exod. xxv. 2, citing R. Menahen, tells of a tradition of the Jews, which observed there was no iron stuff for the building of the tabernacle. (Truly our hearts are mostly iron, and hard one towards another, and therefore not fit matter for tabernacles.) In 1 Kings vi. 7, there was no iron tool, either, heard in the building of the temple. O my brethren, iron tools will not do the work for the building of God's tabernacle, we must have tools of another kind. There are no tabernacles almost yet, wherein the saints, either of one judgment or of another, have much rejoicing; the glory of God has not yet filled the tabernacles which we have built. What God intends towards this generation, whether ever to bring them into those tabernacles that he here promises, I know not; but surely that God which has brought us out of Egypt, will bring either us, or the posterity after us, a generation of his own people, to keep the feast of tabernacles with rejoicing.

Ver. 10. *I have also spoken by the prophets, and I have multiplied visions, and used similitudes, by the ministry of the prophets.*

This is a further declaration of God's goodness to this people, and an upbraiding of them for their wickedness, when they have had so many means; as if God should say, They have not wanted the revelation of my will, I have spoken by my prophets, and multiplied visions. Heb. i. 1, seems to have reference to this, "God, who at sundry times and in divers manners spake in time past unto the fathers by the prophets;" πολυμερῶς καὶ πολυτρόπως, in several sorts of ways God revealed himself in former times.

"I have also spoken by the prophets, and I have multiplied visions."

There is not much difficulty in the words. The notes briefly are these:

Obs. 1. It is God that speaks by his prophets. Though the prophets and the messengers of God are mean, yet so long as they speak to you in his name, the authority of what they say is above any. They may be under their auditors many ways, but the message they bring is above them; though they are weak, yet the power of God goes along with what they speak, to make it good; and therefore you shall find when Christ sent his disciples to preach, saying, "Go and teach all nations," he first said, "All power is given to me in heaven and in earth," and then followed, "Go ye *therefore* and teach all nations;" as if he should say, All the power that is given to me shall go along with your teaching. It is the Lord that speaks, the Lord Christ that speaks in his word by his messengers; "He that heareth you, heareth me; and he that despiseth you, despiseth me."

The word does little good till men come to apprehend this, that it is God that speaks by his messengers. 1 Thess. ii. 13, the apostle saith, that they received the word, "not as the word of men, but as it is in truth, the word of God." That is observable of Samuel; God called to Samuel, and Samuel thought it had been Eli that spake, and all that time God would not reveal his mind to him, till at length Samuel returned this answer, "Speak, Lord; for thy servant heareth," 1 Sam. iii. 9. Mark, God would reveal his mind to Samuel then, and not before. So it is here; you come to the word, and you come to hear the gifts of such men, such a man has excellent gifts, and abilities, and delivery, and such kind of things; God reveals nothing to you, you have heard a sound, and that is all, and no more is revealed to you than if you heard an oration in a school: but when God shall be pleased to dart this thought into your minds, I am now going to hear that which is the word of God himself, the word of that God that is my judge, and that must be my judge at the great day; now see whether God will not make himself known to you, that so you shall say, Methinks I never heard sermon before in all my life; I have come and heard a man preach, but I never heard God preach before; it was not as the word of God, but as the word of such a man. God expects that men should "tremble at his word," and therefore look upon it as *his* word.

Obs. 2. It is a great mercy to a people for God to reveal his mind to them by his prophets. What would all the world be but as a dungeon of darkness, were it not for the prophets and ministers of God? they are as "the light of the world," and "the salt of the earth," Matt. v. 13, 14, the world would rot and be unsavoury were it not for the ministry of the word in the world. And so we find, that when God would make a special promise to his people, he promises them, that they shall have their teachers; "And though the Lord give you the bread of adversity, and the water of affliction, yet shall not thy teachers be removed into a corner any more, but thine eyes shall see thy teachers," Isa. xxx. 20. Oh! here is a promise to a gracious heart. But to another it is nothing. What! shall the ministry of the word countervail the loss of my estate? God does not say, I will take away from you your afflictions; oh no, but "thine eyes shall see thy teachers;" perhaps your eyes shall never see your money and estates again, but your eyes shall see your teachers. Kings on their coronation days are wont to give great gifts to show their magnificence; then the conduits will sometimes run wine: now, when Christ ascended up to be crowned on high, what were the great gifts that he gave to the world? "He gave some, apostles; and some, prophets; and some, evangelists; and some, pastors and teachers," Eph. iv. 8, 10. These are the great gifts of Jesus Christ upon his ascension into heaven and taking the crown of glory; as if Christ should say, Shall I give a magnificent gift to the world like a prince, like the King of heaven? I will give gifts unto men, I will give them apostles, prophets, pastors, teachers: that is the great, magnificent gift that Jesus Christ has given to the world, oh that we could learn to prize it! I remember I have read, in Chrysostom's time, that the godly men, when he was silenced, were so affected with it, that they had rather the sun did withdraw his beams and not shine in the world, than that the mouth of Chrysostom should be stopped; they so prized the word of God by his mouth. Oh that men could learn to prize it more, at a higher rate! And you that are citizens, show you esteem it highly in this one thing: many of you here have your city and your country houses, but what little care have we to seat ourselves in places where we shall have faithful ministers of God to reveal the mind of God to us! If you come to seat yourselves any where, you scarce take it into consideration to give a penny the more because of a faithful minister, or a penny the less if it has none; oh! this shows the extreme neglect of God, and of his ordinances. How few country villages about the city are supplied with faithful preachers! Faithful prophets are a great blessing of God.

Obs. 3. God will take account of what becomes of the word, labour, and pains of his prophets. So he here upbraids Ephraim with them. God will take account of all the spirits that his ministers spend, of every drop of their sweat, and of all their watchings in the night; I sent my prophets, rising early, and going to bed late; God will take account of all, and you shall know that there has been a prophet among you; the ministers shall be brought out to say and testify, Lord, I was in such a place, and I revealed thy mind thus unto them; they could not but be convinced, and yet still they continued in their wickedness.

Obs. 4. It is a great mercy for God to declare his mind again and again. "I have multiplied visions," saith God. It were a mercy for God but once to tell us of his mind, and if we will not come in at first, for ever to cast us off; but "I have multiplied visions." In Jer. xviii. 7, God saith, "At what instant I shall speak," &c.; and God may justly expect, that "at what instant" Christ is preached, that people should come in, for indeed their commission seems to run very quick; "Go ye into all the world, and preach the gospel to every creature. He that believeth and is baptized shall be saved; but he that believeth not shall be damned," Mark xvi. 15, 16; as if Christ should say, There shall be quick work made with men. But yet the Lord is gracious to men, to multiply visions one after another, to reveal his mind at sundry times and in divers manners: the Lord is long-suffering; though our hearts be not moved at one time, yet still he would try, and he would have his ministers do so too. "In meekness instructing those that oppose themselves; if God peradventure will give them repentance to the acknowledging of the truth," 2 Tim. ii. 25. It was a great aggravation of Solomon's sin, that he departed from God after the Lord had appeared to him twice: "And the Lord was angry with Solomon, because his heart was turned from the Lord God of Israel, which had appeared unto him twice," 1 Kings xi. 9.

Oh how may God upbraid us with this, that not twice, but twenty, yea, a hundred times he has appeared to us! May not your consciences tell you, that at such and such a time you have had the visions of the Almighty, and yet you have stood out against them, yea, against them again and again? O my brethren, the multiplying of visions greatly aggravates the sin of our resistance. It was the comfort of Paul at his conversion, that he "was not disobedient unto the heavenly vision," Acts xxvi. 19. Oh how happy were it for you if upon the first vision your hearts would come in! Oh that you could but say, Though it is true, I lived at such a time and place in ignorance and darkness, I knew little of God, yet the first time I came to hear the word, wherein the mysteries of the gospel were revealed, I bless God my heart yielded: so the apostle blesses God for the effect that the word had upon the Thessalonians from the first day, even until that time.

"And used similitudes, by the ministry of the prophets."

This is a very strange expression, occurring no where else that I know of in the book of God. I will not trouble you with divers readings or interpretations, to me it seems to show the aggravations of men's sins, that they hearkened not to the word, though it was brought down to the level of their understandings by similitudes.

Exponit Deus in verbo similitudinem sui, hoc est, pingit voluntatem suam. Luth. in loc.

Obs. 5. The Lord takes account of the manner of men's preaching, as well as the things they preach. Men may have their sins aggravated, not only for standing out against the word, but against the word so and so delivered. The main necessary truths of God are made known to you all; yea, but some of you have them made known to you in a more sweet and winning way, in a more convincing manner, than others have, and God takes account, not only of the message you hear, but of the manner of its delivery.

Obs. 6. The revealing the word by similitudes is very useful and profitable; for it conduces much to make truth go to a man's heart before he is aware, and to impress it upon the memory; many remember the simile, and so the truth which it conveyed. It is reported of the Marquis Galeacias, a nobleman of great estates, and near of kin to the pope, that once coming but to hear Peter Martyr preach, by a mere simile that he used, God smote his heart, and made it the means of his conversion. The simile was thus: Peter Martyr in his discourse had occasion to say, Men may think very hardly of God and his people, but this is because they do not know him; as suppose a man a great way off sees a company of excellent dancers, the musicians are playing, and there is exact art in all that they do; at the distance he regards them as a company of mad-men, but (added he) as he draws nearer and nearer to them, and hears the melodious sound, and observes the art that they use, then he is much taken and affected: and so it is with you; you are a great way off, and look from a great distance upon the ways of God, and so you think his people mad; but could you but come to observe what excellency is in them, it would take captive your hearts. God blessed such a similitude as this to that great man's heart, so that though his wife and children lay imploring at his feet, yet he came to Geneva, and there continued a godly man all his days. But we should take some heed here.

Peter Martyr on John xx. See the Life of Galeacim.

1. Similes should be brought from things known.

2. We must not urge similes too far, we must take heed of a luxuriant, wanton wit.

3. And they must be very natural, plain, and proper, or else man will appear in them rather than God.

Obs. 3. Slight not the word when it comes by a simile. "And used similitudes." You will say, This is but a simile. But though it be, yet God is speaking to thy heart in it.

Obs. 4. Take heed that you do not rest in the pleasantness of the simile. Many come to the word to have their fancies touched and pleased, more than any thing else: do not play with similes; look rather at what you can see of God in them, than how far they savour of the wit of man.

Ver. 11. *Is there iniquity in Gilead? surely they are vanity: they sacrifice bullocks in Gilgal; yea, their altars are as heaps in the furrows of the fields.*

What Gilead was you have heard before in chap. vi. ver. 8, "Gilead is a city of them that work iniquity." It was a city of the priests beyond Jordan, where the priests that were beyond the river lived. Sometimes it is taken for the Mount Gilead, where Jacob and Laban met and made a covenant one with another. Here neither is excluded; but most, I find, refer it to the city of the priests. And what Gilgal was you had opened to you in chap. ix. ver. 15, "All their wickedness is in Gilgal." Now Gilgal was the place where they were circumcised on this side Jordan, and belonged to Judah. Gilead belonged to Israel, Gilgal to Judah.

"Is there iniquity in Gilead? surely they are vanity: they sacrifice bullocks in Gilgal."

The latter part of this passage the Septuagint render, *ἄρα ψευδεῖς ἦσαν εν Γαλαὰδ ἄρχοντες θυσιάζοντες*, surely the princes sacrificing in Gilead are vanity. And indeed the word שורים translated "bullocks" is much akin to שורים which signifies princes, the difference mainly consisting in a tittle on the right hand or on the left, and so there might easily be a mistake. But to read it as it is here, "They sacrifice bullocks in Gilgal," great sacrifices; and they think to put off God with their great sacrifices, sacrificing bullocks, but all in vain.

The places having been spoken of before, we may proceed at once to see what the scope of the Holy Ghost is here. "Is there iniquity in Gilead?"

"Is there?" an interrogation; it is as if he should say, Who dare say there is iniquity in Gilead? Gilead! what! the city of the priests, iniquity there! who will charge Gilead, where the priests are, with iniquity? What! are you wiser than all our priests? Just like to the plea which some heretofore have had, What! do not our ministers do thus? Is not this their opinion? shall we not regard what our ministers do? "Is there iniquity in Gilead?" is there iniquity among them? do they not join in this way? This seems plainly to be the scope of this charge, "Is there iniquity in Gilead?" It is the city of the priests! is there iniquity there? what! in a place where they use to meet, where they dwell?

"Surely they are vanity," saith the prophet. Even these priests of Gilead, on whom you rest so much, are but vanity; you may give up your consciences and your ways to them, because they come and persuade you that such a thing is to be done, and you must do it, and so by giving up your consciences and ways to them you may be led into much evil.

"Surely they are vanity." Though they be your priests, though they be learned men, and should understand the way of God, yet they have their own interests too, they drive their own designs; they keep not the truth of God, but they follow their own minds. "Surely they are vanity." Those ways to which they persuade you, God allows not of, they will prove vanity. Let the learned note, even wise, learned, understanding men, priests who seemed to be much for God, may yet be vanity.

Obs. 1. Whatsoever is presented in the worship of God, if not by God's appointment, is mere vanity. "Surely they are vanity," even Gilead.

Again, This Gilead being on the other side of Jordan, was taken by the Assyrians, and its inhabitants were first carried away captive, as appears, if you read 2 Kings xv. 29. Those that were on the other side Jordan were carried captive first, and Gilead among the rest; so that it is probable that this prophecy was delivered after the capture of Gilead by the enemy, before the rest of the tribes were taken: and then the force of his argument is this:

There is iniquity in Gilead; yea, and Gilead has smarted for her iniquity; though they promised themselves peace, yet all proved but vanity: yea, they smarted very dreadfully, for in Amos i. 3 it is said, that Gilead was "threshed with threshing instruments of iron." Now Amos was contemporary with Hosea, and speaks of the wonderful miseries that had befallen the city of Gilead. As if the prophet should say, Do not you know there is iniquity in Gilead? has not God declared it by his severe wrath upon Gilead? have not they proved vanity? What then can Gilgal expect? They yet sacrifice bullocks, they are guilty of the same sin of false worship as Gilead was. God had appointed but one place to worship in, but they had abundance of sacrifices, and had their altars as common as the very heaps of stones in the fields.

Obs. 3. When God's judgments have been against any for sin, all guilty of the same sins have cause to fear, and not promise safety to themselves though they be spared a while.

But further, and chiefly, Gilead had smarted thus and thus, and the prophet now speaks to Gilgal, which belonged to Judah: Look to yourselves; if Gilead has smarted thus, you are like to suffer as much or even more; for Gilead did not own the temple; the ten tribes (you know) had forsaken the temple, and were further removed from God in their very profession; but Gilgal belonged to Judah, and so nearer to God in outward relation, they professed a greater care of his worship: now, saith he, What! shall God be thus avenged of Gilead for false worship? how then shall Gilgal escape, that profess a greater nearness to God in his worship, and yet for all that corrupt God's worship, and "sacrifice bullocks;" "yea, their altars are as heaps in the furrows of the fields?" Hence,

Obs. 4. Those whose principles and professions are nearer to God than others, if they be superstitious, God will be sorely avenged upon them: those (I say) whose principles and profession come most near in the matters of worship.

We may look at this point as nearly concerning ourselves; thus, if a superstitious, prelatical ministry and people had the wrath of God pursuing them, as it has been heavy upon them, then those who shall profess to come near in the point of reformation, whosoever they be, this side or the other, who profess to come nearest, if they mingle their own inventions in worship, God will be more sorely displeased with them: the more piety and holiness, the more we profess to come close to the word of God, and yet withal mingle our own inventions, the more is God displeased; Gilgal offends more than Gilead.

"Their altars are as heaps in the furrows of the fields." As husbandmen use to gather their stones that kept the corn from growing, and every furrow almost some of them were laid in a heap; so, saith he, their altars were as common as those heaps of stones.

Or it may have reference to some of their superstitious or idolatrous customs. In the furrows of the fields they had many altars built to sacrifice, that they might seek God for the fructifying of their land; such a kind of worship of God as afterwards the heathens rendered to their *dii terminales*, for a blessing on their lands; and, following their example, the papists. And heretofore in England you know it was customary in procession-weeks for the men, when they went up and down their perambulation, in the bounds of their fields to set up crosses and crucifixes, and to have prayers read, and psalms sung, which were intended not merely to show the bounds of their parish, but to invocate God for his blessing upon their fruits. By making and setting up crosses in the bounds of their fields, they thought there so came a blessing upon their corn, and therefore, at certain times of the year especially, they would go to their crosses, and offer their prayers there, that they might have their corn and pastures more blessed. Thus we see superstition and idolatry are ever the same, among the Gentiles, among the papists, and lately among ourselves; they all had their altars "as heaps in the furrows of the fields."

Or in a way of threat, as some interpret it, Their altars shall be broken down, and they shall be "as heaps" of stones "in the furrows of the fields:" so in Jer. xxvi. 18, "Zion shall be ploughed like a field, and Jerusalem shall become heaps;" as God threatened them, so their altars are here threatened to be broken down, and to be as heaps in the field; God will regard their fine and costly altars no more than rubbish and heaps of stones in the fields.

Ver. 12. *And Jacob fled into the country of Syria, and Israel served for a wife, and for a wife he kept sheep.*

God by the prophet here again introduces Jacob. He had spoken before of his wrestling with God and prevailing, and yet again the prophet recurs to his history, because he saw that the people of Israel, when charged with their sins, and threatened with the anger of God, still had recourse to Jacob their father, and thought because they were the seed of Jacob, therefore God would not deal so severely with them; therefore still the prophet seeks to lead them off from such a mode of reasoning.

"And Jacob fled into the country of Syria." As if he should say thus, You pride yourselves in your father Jacob; yea, but consider in what a mean condition Jacob was, and if any privilege comes to you as being his seed, it results from the mere free grace of God, and not from any excellency there was in your father Jacob. He would take off the conceit of excellency in their father Jacob, for whose worthiness they thought that God surely would not forsake his posterity, though very wicked: as if he should say, Consider what a poor condition your father Jacob was in:

First, He was a poor exile, fain to flee for his life, even from his father's house. And then when he did flee, he fled to his uncle; and what was he there? a poor servant; he lived in two hard apprenticeships (as it were) with his uncle Laban; he found him to be a very hard master to him for seven years, and for seven years after that he behaved himself roughly and rigidly towards him, ofttimes changing his wages. Saith he, Do not forget the meanness of Jacob: he fled thus; and when in Syria he would marry, he had no dowry, but was fain to serve for a wife, his condition was so low and mean. That is the first reason why the prophet brings in Jacob here again, to take them off from too high a conceit of Jacob their father, that they should not rest themselves in him, nor pride themselves in his excellency.

Secondly, That he might show what their father Jacob was, how unlike to him were his posterity, for he was patient and humble under long and hard afflictions: as if he should say, He was content to serve, and to be in a low and mean condition; but you are proud and haughty, you can bear nothing, you must be high and brave, and must conform yourselves to other nations. Your father Jacob was content to serve a long time for a wife, seven years, and seven years again, and went on in a humble and patient way, and kept close to God all that while: it is not so with you who are his posterity.

Thirdly, He brings in the example of Jacob, to show how wonderful the providence of God was towards him, in carrying him to his uncle's house, and providing there for him; in protecting him against his uncle Laban; in raising his estate, for he went over with his staff in his hand, but the Lord raised him to be two bands: the providence of God was such towards your father Jacob. As if the prophet should say, You speak of your father Jacob, oh that you would but so consider him as to be what he was, to be patient and humble under God's hand, and to wait upon God's providence to work good for you: no, but you will be providing and shifting for yourselves, and you dare not trust to God as your father Jacob did. Thus, in these three respects, you see something of the intention of the prophet in introducing again Jacob.

But this will not suffice for the exposition of this notable scripture; we must refer to the story of Jacob, as narrated Gen. xxviii. and xxix.

This verse refers to both,

I. His flight from the house of his father Isaac to Syria, to Laban, Gen. xxviii.

II. His serving Laban for his wives those twice seven years, Gen. xxix.

I. Jacob's flight into Syria. From this you may derive much instruction. It was ordered for two ends:

1. To save his life. Esau threatened the life of Jacob, and by the counsel of his mother he fled to his uncle Laban's, until the wrath of Esau should be appeased.

2. God purposed good out of his evil; he designed him advantages from his flight. Many times God is pleased to turn the flights of his people to their abundant good: they may flee because of their enemies, and think that if they can but have their lives for a prey they will do well; yea, but God may have a further end, and intend abundance of good to them, even that they shall find more mercy in that place where they flee but to get a shelter for their lives, than ever they had in all their lives before. Many that have fled from persecution of ungodly men, though they have fled from their father's house, and from their own country, yet in their flight have found greater mercies there than ever they did in all their lives before; they can tell great stories of the mercies of God to them in the places of their exile. So it was here with Jacob: one purpose of God in his flight was, that he might provide a wife for himself out of his mother's kindred, for so he was charged by his father, to get a wife of the daughters of Laban, Gen. xxviii. And further observe, as Isaac foresaw that Jacob was like to endure a great deal of trouble and affliction in this his flight, he renews the blessing upon him. And thus God is wont to do when he sees his people in a way wherein they are like to suffer sore and hard afflictions; he prepares them by renewing his blessing upon them, by a fresh manifestation of himself to them. His father's blessing did help much to carry Jacob through all his afflictions, and the renewing of God's blessing suffices to carry the believing soul through many and deep waters.

II. Jacob's serving for his wives those two seven years. When Isaac sent Jacob away, he sent him in a very mean condition, without any such provision as Abraham's servant had when he went to seek a wife for Isaac; in Gen. xxiv. 10, we read Abraham sent with his servant a great deal of provision, and ten camels, and earrings, and bracelets, and the like; but Jacob is sent away to seek for a wife with only a staff in his hand.

If it be said, that the reason why he was sent so meanly was, that he might not be discovered on account of the rage of Esau.

Though that might be a reason of his first going away in so mean a condition, yet that could not be the reason why Isaac should not afterwards send after him; but we never read that Isaac sent any servant after him, but sent him away with his staff in his hand, having only the blessing of God upon him. Therefore it is more probable, that God thereby did mean to train up Jacob in a low condition, in an estate of affliction, to patience, and humility, and dependence upon God.

Well then, he flees to Syria to his uncle Laban; when he comes there he serves him, yea, he was a servant to him for even twenty years together in a low condition, Gen. xxxi. 38; and during all this time he found Laban, though his kinsman, very rough to him; as many times young people, coming to their kindred, find them at first very rough and harsh towards them. Laban was very churlish, yea, even very false, to him, yet Jacob goes on, and endures "in the day the drought," and "the frost by night." Isaac his father was alive at this time, and yet we never read that during it he sent to him, a thing much to be wondered at; we read of no intercourse between them all this while, but Jacob lives apart from his father, though a rich man and a great man, and goes on in a humble, patient, and quiet way, depending upon God to make an issue out of all his sufferings; and God did at length make a very glorious issue out of all, though Laban used him hardly. Now, being Isaac's son and having the blessing, one would have thought that Laban should have been willing to have bestowed a daughter upon him; nay, but he is obliged to serve for a wife, and when he has served, is deceived with a Leah, which was a very great injury to Jacob, but Laban urged her upon him. It is very great cruelty in guardians, or parents, or any that have the government of others, to force wives upon them for their own private advantage; those matches seldom come to good; though God turned this to good, yet I say these forced matches seldom come to good, they are the undoing of many. Jacob desired to have the wife that he had served for. Nay, saith Laban, Gen. xxix. 27, "Fulfil her week," the week of the festivity of her marriage, that is, confirm the marriage with Leah first; for Laban knew that except he had willingly afterwards gone in to her, he had not been bound to her as a husband: Laban would have him own her for his wife, and then, said he, we will agree together, you shall serve seven years more for Rachel, and you shall have her also. But now we must not understand this as if Laban kept Rachel from Jacob till he had served "yet seven other years," that is, completed fourteen years; no, he did but fulfil the week of Leah, and then Laban gave Rachel to him, yet upon condition that he should afterwards serve seven years for her also: this is plainly what was required of him. And as an evident demonstration that Rachel was given to Jacob before her seven years were completed, it appears from the story that Leah had no children until Rachel was married to Jacob, and yet all the twelve patriarchs were born to him within the compass of the twenty years that he was with Laban. Now if the first had not been born till after the fourteen years' service, it could not possibly be, that all of the rest should be born within the six remaining years; for we find in the story that Leah had four children one after another, and then left off bearing, and then she gave Zilpah to Jacob, who bare two sons, and after that Leah had another son and a daughter, and all this before Rachel had any children: so that it must needs be understood that Rachel was given to Jacob at the end of the first seven years, yet that he served two seven years for these two wives.

Now the Lord was pleased to turn this to a great deal of good, though it was hard service and bondage; these two wives that Jacob served so long for, were made the two greatest instruments of good that ever have been in the church before or since, excepting only the virgin that brought forth Christ; for by these two was the house of Israel built up, twelve tribes came of them and of those that they gave to Jacob, but the Holy Ghost reckons the building up by these two; and from them the blessing that was wont to be upon a married condition was proverbially taken; in Ruth iv. 11, the elders said to Boaz, "The Lord make the woman that is come into thine house like Rachel and like Leah, which two did build the house of Israel:" this was the common blessing on a married condition,

The Lord make this woman like Rachel and like Leah, that built the house of Israel.

Why like these two, rather than Sarah?

Because they built up the house of Israel, and all that came from them were of the church. Oh it is a great blessing in a married condition to build up the house of God. Though thou shouldst serve hardly for a wife, yet if God makes thy marriage so blessed to thee, as to enable thee thereby to build up the church of God, that is a blessed marriage: those that are married, and their friends, in their prayers, should pray to God for such a blessing; Oh that the Lord would make this woman to be a builder up of the house of Israel!

But from the prophet's introducing here the flight and servitude of Jacob, we may

Obs. 1. Such as pride themselves in their ancestors, should look back to their mean condition. Some are very high in their conceits because they have such and such ancestors; it may be two or three degrees off they were great, but look but a little further, and they were but mean tradesmen, or yeomen in the country: here the prophet would take these off from priding in their ancestors. It is a great vanity for any to pride themselves in their ancestors. Plato said, all kings came from ploughmen, and all ploughmen from kings. Because some are great and rich by some providence or other, they think themselves above the common sort of mankind, they look upon others with contempt: "Look unto the rock whence ye are hewn," saith the prophet, Isa. li. 1, "and to the hole of the pit whence ye are digged."

Obs. 2. Patience, and humility, and dependence upon God in times of long-continued afflictions, much commend the grace of God in any. I say, when any shall be patient, and humble, and depend upon God in times of long affliction, this much commends the grace of God in them.

O let me urge this, 1. Upon any of you that are in hard services. If I were to speak to a congregation of apprentices, that had hard services, and rough masters, and cruel mistresses, I would charge them not to fret and vex, not desperately to fling off and say, Why should I bear such services? Do not in a desperate mood determine to go and seek your fortunes, as they are wont to say. Many young men have undone themselves through the roughness of their masters and mistresses to them in their apprenticeships, and though the evil will be upon themselves, yet God will require this at their masters' and mistresses' hand. This is a sign that there is no fear of God, that because they are in hard services, therefore they should resort to desperate courses. It may be your brother or sister has an excellent service, more liberty, better wages, and better provision, than you have; yet, seeing God in his providence has disposed of you to such a hard service, look up to God, and wait upon him continually to work good through it; God may intend good to you in such a service more than you are aware of.

2. As for any of you that are come out of hard services, look back to them, and consider how you behaved yourselves in them. Are you the seed of Jacob? If you be, though your service has been hard, yet have you gone on patiently, and humbly, and in dependence upon God, as Jacob did; and God will remember this for good to you afterwards. Yea, but now, did not you behave yourselves proudly and stubbornly, and so make your service so much the more hard, by provoking your governors? O, look back to these things, and consider how far you are from being of the disposition of Jacob, that you profess to be your father. Many apprentices in their hard services have done that which they have cause to repent of afterwards.

Obs. 3. Love will carry through long service. "Israel served for a wife." Love is ashamed to complain of difficulties. Oh, so it would be if we loved God; we would not then complain of his service as difficult.

Obs. 4. A good wife is a great blessing of God, though she has no portion. Though a man serve for her, yet is she a great blessing from God; there is a more special mercy of God there, than there is in giving men an estate. He served long, and long, even for a wife.

Luther, on the place, speaks much about the blessing in marriage of a good wife. Certainly, saith he, Jacob did not serve so long that he might have a companion of his life with whom there should be nothing but railing, scolding, and wrangling; no, but he looked upon marriage as the school of all virtue, for so should a married estate indeed be.

Non tam longo tempore servivit Jacob ut haberet sociam vitæ, cum quâ perpetuo rixaretur, tanquam scholam omnium virtutum matrimonium cupide ingressus est. Luth. in loc.

Obs. 5. Children should not marry without or against their parents' consent. If you profess yourselves to be of the seed of Jacob, (for so the godly are called in Scripture,) be like to your father Jacob in this, in being obedient to your parents in your matches. Jacob had a charge from his father to take a wife in Laban's family, and therefore he would rather serve seven years, and seven years afterwards, than seek a wife any where else. There is no greater disobedience in the world, than that of children, in the case of marriage, flinging off the yoke of subjection to their parents. Luther urges this point exceeding much. Civil laws require the consent of parents in all lawful marriages; and so the authority of sacred Scripture declares to us, that those marriages have been ever happy that have been with the consent of their parents. And again, (saith he,) experience testifies that those marriages have been for the most part unhappy, that have been without the consent of parents; certainly the blessing of God is not upon them; you may think to please yourselves in the gratification of your lusts for a week or two, but it is just with God that you should live miserably all your days who make no more conscience of disobedience to your parents in your matches. And if any of you here present be guilty in this respect, know that the Lord rebukes you this day, commands you to go alone and humble yourselves, and to bewail that sin of yours, which is certainly very great: you had need, both husband and wife together, to fast and pray to God to remove the guilt of that sin, that so you may have a blessing upon your married estate, and upon your posterity.

Ver. 13. *And by a prophet the Lord brought Israel out of Egypt, and by a prophet was he preserved.*

Still the prophet goes on to show their meanness in their ancestors. Your father Jacob was thus a poor exile, and fain to serve for his wife. It is true, Joseph was a while in prosperity; but when Joseph was dead, all your ancestors then were in Egypt as miserable bond-slaves; they were there as bond-slaves, and how should they get out? there was no apparent way, Pharaoh, a mighty king, opposed to them, they without friends or armies to help them. God indeed sent them a prophet, Moses; and what was he? one that had been a poor shepherd for forty years together in the wilderness: and when this prophet was to go into Egypt to deliver them, was it likely that he should ever succeed? He went into Egypt in a mean and low condition; "He took his wife and his sons, and set them upon an ass, and he returned to the land of Egypt," Exod. iv. 20; and when he came there the children of Israel would not own him, and Pharaoh would not let Israel go: how should this one Moses deliver them? nay, their bondage increased when Moses came to them. Yet "by a prophet" (the text saith) "the Lord brought Israel out of Egypt, and by a prophet was he preserved." This was a mighty work of God, to bring Israel out of Egypt by a prophet, and to preserve them in the wilderness. And by the way, you read in Exod. xxxviii. 26, there were numbered of males "from twenty years old and upward, six hundred thousand and three thousand and five hundred and fifty;" and in Numb. i. 46, in the second year after they went out from Egypt, you find that there was just the same number, besides Levi, whom God had taken for himself to be his portion: thereby God would show that none should lose any thing that they did for him. How often, when men have been willing to give any thing to God, has God made it up in one year!

But to return, I introduce this to show the great work of God, that by a prophet he brings such a number out of Egypt, and preserves them in the wilderness, using no means for their preservation or guidance but a mean prophet: by him he provides water, and meat, and clothes for them; defends them against their enemies, that they should not come and destroy them; when they were in any danger, helps them; when stung by the serpents, shows them what they should do to be healed; and by him, a mean prophet, composes all their differences. Such was the mighty work of God towards them.

He does not say, "the Lord brought Israel out of Egypt," but "by a prophet the Lord brought Israel out of Egypt, and by a prophet was he preserved." This was to show,

First, Their very low and mean condition, that they had no succour nor help in the sight of human reason; human reason could no way help them, they had none but a poor prophet.

Secondly, That God in their deliverance would appear himself, and would work such a glorious work by his own hand.

Thirdly, To upbraid this people to whom Hosea then preached, for the abuse of his prophets. There was a time (saith he) a prophet stood you in stead: now you care not for the prophets, they may speak what they will, but you care not for them; but there was a time that a prophet stood you in stead, however stout and proud you are now. I find divers interpreters observe this, and among the ancients Cyril of Alexandria especially, showing how instrumental a prophet had been for good to them. Had not God blessed the endeavours of a prophet for good to your forefathers, where had you been at this day?

Obs. 1. The consideration of the shiftless estate of our ancestors should humble us much. And if the consideration of our ancestors' estate should humble us thus, how much more when we consider our own! Oh, lately, how shiftless were we! And the truth is, though there were armies raised, yet God would not so much as look at them, but rather looked at his prophets, and his servants; the praying people were the main and principal means that helped us in that condition: and this should humble us; we should take heed of growing haughty and proud when we are delivered, considering how shiftless we were but a little while ago; and therefore, if now we have gotten peace, and prosperity seems to be following in, let us guard against pride; look back to that shiftless, poor condition that you were in a little while ago.

Obs. 2. When God works great things for his church, his way is to work it by very small means. Little means God uses when he intends the greatest mercies to his church. God's deliverance of his people from Egypt, was a type of the deliverance of his churches to the end of the world from their bondage and afflictions. And God sends them a prophet, and he must deliver them: "By a prophet the Lord brought Israel out of Egypt, and by a prophet was he preserved." Though God did it, yet God speaks of the prophet as the great instrumental means for their help. God takes delight in this, when he does good to his people, not to make use of such great means, as when he works his own ends towards other people: when God intends good towards other people, he will do it in a more natural way, by natural means; but when he comes to work good for his own, he will do it in a more supernatural way; for mercies are so much the sweeter by how much the more God is in them; the more we see the finger of God in a mercy, the sweeter it is. And above all things, the Lord accounts himself glorified in his people's depending upon him in the want of all means; the Lord accounts this his glory, that he may be an object of the rest of the souls of his people, that when they are in any straits, in any afflictions, yet they can look upon God as an object for their rest, and can say, "Return unto thy rest, O my soul."

O consider this, ye servants of God, when in straits and difficulties; remember, that God accounts it to be that in which he rejoices, as the special glory of his name, that his servants shall make him in their straits the rest of their souls: and this is the reason why he is wont to work so much good for his people by such poor and weak means.

Obs. 3. It is a great aggravation of men's sins, if they grow naught and wicked after God has in a more than ordinary manner appeared for their good. If then they grow naught and wicked, when God has appeared from heaven for their good, and wrought beyond all natural means, and set them upon their legs again, and delivered them, it much aggravates their sins.

Obs. 4. Unkindness to, and abuse of, such as are related, though but by succession, to those whom God has used to be instruments of our deliverance, is a very great evil. This I think the Holy Ghost especially intends here. By a prophet the Lord brought them out of Egypt, and by a prophet he preserved them; and what! do you now treat unkindly and abuse prophets? Divers good things God had done for his people by prophets, as by Moses here, so afterwards by Samuel, and Elijah, and Elisha; great things in the matters of state God had done for this people by prophets, and therefore he takes it very ill that they should so abuse and slight the prophets.

This shows, 1. A base levity of spirit. 2. An abominable ingratitude of spirit and vile injustice: and God will avenge these things. We have a remarkable illustration in Judg. viii., ix. In the former, ver. 33—35, it is said, "And it came to pass, as soon as Gideon was dead, that the children of Israel turned again, and went a whoring after Baalim, and made Baal-berith their god. And the children of Israel remembered not the Lord their God, who had delivered them out of the hands of all their enemies on every side: neither showed they kindness to the house of Jerubbaal, namely, Gideon, according to all the goodness which he had showed unto Israel." Gideon had been such a famous instrument of good to Israel, that they received forty years' prosperity by him; but as soon as he was gone, the people went a whoring from God, and then they were unkind towards his posterity. So in chap. ix. 6, "And all the men of Shechem gathered together, and all the house of Millo, and went, and made Abimelech king." And Jotham one of Gideon's sons, expostulates with them, and tells them the parable of the trees that desired a king; and, in ver. 19, 20, saith, "If ye then have dealt truly and sincerely with Jerubbaal and with his house this day, then rejoice ye in Abimelech, and let him also rejoice in you: but if not, let fire come out from Abimelech, and devour the men of Shechem, and the house of Millo; and let fire come out from the men of Shechem, and from the house of Millo, and de-your Abimelech." As if he should have said, God will avenge this. What! did God make my father an instrument of so great good to you, and do you so ill requite all his kindness and service? The Lord judge, and if it be so indeed, as now I charge you, let this be a manifestation of God's displeasure, that "fire come out from Abimelech," &c. As if he should say, Do not think that you can have peace and quiet in your present courses; you think you have provided well for yourselves in setting up Abimelech, and you now bless yourselves therein; We shall have peace, say you: oh no, the displeasure of God will go on and pursue you, and there will be a fire among yourselves; and it is just with God that it should be so, for this ingratitude of yours towards those who have been so instrumental for your good. The Scripture holds out this, that this is one way for God to avenge himself upon a people that shall be ungrateful to such as have been instrumental for good to them, that they shall have a perverse spirit mingled among themselves, that when they think to provide for their own ease and peace, they shall have a fire kindled among them, so as in the conclusion to devour each other. These people, in Judg. viii. 22, were very zealous for Gideon, when God had delivered them by his means; "Then the men of Israel said unto Gideon, Rule thou over us, both thou, and thy son, and thy son's son also:" they made great promises then, they were then mightily affected. We were in a dangerous condition, say they, and were like to have been in perpetual bondage under our enemies, but God has stirred up thee, and blessed thee, and therefore thou, and thy son, and thy son's son shall rule over us. They were mightily affected with this mercy of God when it was fresh, but presently after you shall find they "remembered not the Lord their God, who had delivered them," nor Gideon, the instrument of God's mercy to them; but requited the posterity of Gideon as ill as if he had been one of their greatest enemies.

O my brethren, this is a sore and grievous evil, the Lord cannot endure ingratitude.

Ver. 14. *Ephraim provoked him to anger most bitterly: therefore shall he leave his blood upon him, and his reproach shall his Lord return unto him.*

"Ephraim provoked him to anger most bitterly." It is true, (saith God by the prophet,) that I loved your father Jacob, and I have magnified myself towards his posterity, in the great and wonderful things which I have done for them; but you have been a wretched people, and provoked me most bitterly: as if he should say, Gentleness, sweetness, and love, dwell in God, if he be not provoked; if there be any anger, it is from men's provoking him.

You have provoked me bitterly, in bitterness: you have provoked, you have imbittered my Spirit against you, by your bitter sins; you make my Spirit, that is so sweet of itself, to be bitter against you.

The word תמרורים signifies sometimes to exalt and make high; and accordingly Tremelius, Vatablus, Calvin, and others, translate it, high places, You have provoked me with the high places. Indeed that was a special sin, the sin of idolatry, which provoked God most bitterly against them.

But it is more full to translate it according to the more strict signification of the word, You have provoked me in bitternesses, you have been very bitter against my saints that would go from Samaria to worship at Jerusalem. I have shown in this prophet how bitter the ten tribes were against any that would separate from them and go to worship at the temple. You have provoked me in that bitter sin of abusing my prophets, in that ingratitude of yours towards those whom I have made instrumental for your good; you have provoked me in sinning against such great mercies; you have forsaken the living God, the fountain of all good, and have turned yourselves to vanity; you have provoked me to anger most bitterly. From whence,

Obs. 1. God is not angry but when he is provoked. Neither should we be; let us be as our heavenly Father is: saith God, "Ephraim provoked him to anger."

Obs. 2. Sin provokes God, puts God to stir up his anger, puts it to the trial whether there be any anger in God or no. So Heb. iii. 9, "Your fathers proved me," ἐδοκίμασαν, they tested me, they would put it to trial whether there was such anger in me. Wicked men indeed do so; they hear much of the anger of God against sin, and they put it to trial, they will see whether it be so or no; they dare not say so in words, but their actions do so. Oh, it is a dreadful evil to provoke God. 1 Cor. x. 22, "Do we provoke the Lord to jealousy? are we stronger than he?" Can you stand it out with God? Is it not folly to provoke a man that is a superior, that has power over you, and can crush you? O wretched, bold heart, that darest stand it out to provoke the eyes of his glory, to provoke the Holy One of Israel! What, to provoke him that can stamp you into hell presently! to provoke him that has the point of the sword of justice at your hearts! but yet this is the boldness of ungodly men; a man that dares not provoke his landlord, yet will dare to provoke God.

Obs. 3. It is a great evil to provoke one another to wrath, but a greater evil to provoke to wrath God. In Eph. vi. 4, parents are charged not so much as to provoke their children to wrath; and wilt thou then provoke God? If we will provoke one another, let us "provoke unto love and to good works;" to a kind of acrimony of love, Heb. x. 24. So in Gal. v. 26, it is said, "Let us not be desirous of vain-glory, provoking one another;" προκαλούμενοι, calling forth one another's corruptions, that is the meaning of it; Let there not be a desire of vain-glory, provoking one another, calling forth one another's corruptions. Oh! it is an evil thing that we do call forth the corruptions of one another so. Was there ever times like the present? men provoking one another, and stirring up one another to envy, wrath, and malice; O, take heed of this, wonderful mischiefs have resulted from it. What mischief do you think will come then of provoking God to anger? Consider this, especially you that are of passionate spirits; if a wife, a servant, or a child, do any thing amiss, you are presently all on fire; oh that you would reflect, What! shall I, a poor worm, be so soon provoked with a fellow creature if he displease me? O Lord, what a wretch am I then, that dare provoke the infinite God! What, can I think my anger to be so terrible to a child, a neighbour, a servant? oh, how terrible is the anger and wrath of an infinite God against a creature when he is provoked! I cannot bear it, whoever provokes me; why should I think that the infinite God should bear with me when I provoke him? Oh that the passionate would consider! But further:

"Bitterly."

"Most bitterly." Gualter has a very good expression about this; and especially in speaking of idolatry as provoking God: Just as if a wife that had broken her covenant, and used many unlawful dalliances, should attempt in like manner to manifest regard to her own husband, and he aware of her falseness. Oh what a bitter provocation would this be! a husband would not bear it. Just so did this people do in their idolatries; in idolatry they go a whoring to idols, and will tender up to God himself that kind of worship which they give to their idols: oh this is a bitter provocation.

Obs. 4. Though sin of its own nature does provoke God, yet there are some sins which provoke him more than others. "Ephraim provoked him to anger most bitterly." So Heb. iii. 8, "Harden not your hearts, as in the provocation," ἐν τῷ παραπικρασμῷ, in the time of bitterness. Oh, some things, as hardness of heart and false worship, imbitter God's Spirit; yea, many times even those things wherein we think we do God a great deal of service imbitter his Holy Spirit. Oh, there are many men who think they serve God in doing that which provokes him bitterly. We know what the Scripture saith, that when they shall deal thus and thus with the saints they shall think that they do God good service: they may have a good intention in what they do, and yet provoke God bitterly. Oh let us not rest in good intentions; I question not but this people pleaded their intentions to the prophet. Well, whatsoever their intentions were, yet by their actions they bitterly provoked God.

And as there are some sins that are as bitter clusters, "their grapes are grapes of gall, their clusters are bitter," as the Holy Ghost saith, Deut. xxxii. 32; so God will be as bitter against those that provoke him bitterly, "They shall be devoured with bitter destruction," Deut. xxxii. 24. Oh, for the creature to forsake God is "an evil thing and bitter," Jer. ii. 19; and it will be bitterness in the end, as Abner said to Joab, 2 Sam. ii. 26, "Knowest thou not that it will be bitterness in the latter end?" Oh, those dalliances of thine will be bitterness in the end; those sins of thine that are the most pleasing to thee, as they are bitter to God, so God will make them bitter to thee one day. "Her end is bitter as wormwood," Prov. v. 4; though the beginning is sweet as "an honeycomb" to you, yet the Holy Ghost saith, that "her end is bitter as wormwood." So Jer. iv. 18, "Thy way and thy doings have procured these things unto thee; this is thy wickedness, because it is bitter." My brethren, we are charged in Scripture to take heed of being bitter one against another; the husband is charged not to be bitter against his wife, Col. iii. 19. It is an evil thing when in a family there is bitterness. Oh, but when the Spirit of the eternal God is bitter against a people! You wives who have such a bondage upon you, who find it evil to have such bitterness from your husbands, oh but then look up to God, is God's Spirit sweet to you? it is a blessing to have the Spirit of God sweet. There is a generation of men that have God's Spirit bitter towards them, by their being bitter one against another. In Eph. iv. 31, it is said, "Let all bitterness, and wrath, and anger, and clamour, and evil speaking, be put away from you, with all malice:" this is the charge of God; as we would obey him in any thing, we are charged to put away "all bitterness, and wrath, and anger, and clamour, and evil speaking." Oh what a spirit of bitterness prevails among us! how bitter are our words and speeches! In Psal. lxiv. 3, wicked men are said to "whet their tongue like a sword, and bend their bows to shoot their arrows, even bitter words." If ever bitter words did fly like arrows about our ears, they do at this day; I verily believe that England never understood, as lately, what bitter words meant. In Rev. viii. 11, it is said, "the third part of the waters became wormwood; and many men died of the waters, because they were made bitter." My brethren, sometimes the third part of sermons are wormwood, are bitter: oh, I would to God that we could not sometimes say the same of prayer; bitterness in prayer, in writing, in speaking, in conferring one with another, do not you think that this much provokes God? Yea, even those men that were wont to draw down sweetness on one another's spirits in prayer, what do they now? they cannot meet together but with bitter spirits, one imbittering the other, as if there were nothing but gall and wormwood among us. Let me apply that scripture in James iii. 11, "Doth a fountain send forth at the same place sweet water and bitter?" What! those that were of such sweet natures and dispositions, and by grace much more sweet, does there now nothing but bitterness come out of such fountains? one would wonder to see men's natures so changed besides the work of grace. Oh, shall out of the same fountain come forth "sweet water and bitter?"

"Therefore shall he leave his blood upon him." That is, he shall bring his sin upon his own head: Those that will be wilful in sin, their blood be upon their own heads; that is the meaning. Never stand excusing any more; you have warning enough; if you will go on in your way, the blood be upon your own head, you will undo yourselves and there is no help. Mark the phrase, "Therefore shall he leave his blood upon him."

Obs. 5. When God brings the guilt and the punishment of sin on a man's own head, and there leaves it, that is sad indeed. In 2 Sam. xii. 13, it is said, that when Nathan came and rebuked David for his sin, on David's confessing his sin Nathan said to him, "The Lord also hath put away thy sin;" גם־יהוה העביר חטאתך which is translated by some thus, The Lord hath made thy sin to pass away: oh, that is a happiness indeed, when it may be said of God, he has made the sin and the guilt to pass away from the sinner. But on the other side, when God leaves the sin, with its attendant guilt, upon the sinner, as if God should say, Here is the guilt of sin upon the head of such a man, and let it abide and lie, I shall leave his blood upon him; as in Ezek. xxii. 20, the Lord saith, "So will I gather you in mine anger and in my fury, and I will leave you there." The Lord many times brings his saints into the fire of afflictions, but he will not leave them there; but when he brings the wicked into the fire, there he leaves them.

"And his reproach shall his Lord return unto him." That is, they do what lies in them to bring a reproach upon me the living God, as if there were not an all-sufficiency in me, but I will make the reproach to turn upon their own heads; yea, they reproach my saints too, but I will make this to return upon their own heads. O take heed of doing any thing to bring a reproach upon God.

You will say, Can the creature bring a reproach upon God?

I might show you divers ways: I will instance but one,

Apostatizing from God. When professors of religion, that have been very forward and seemed to rejoice in the ways of God and to rely upon him, forsake God to follow after their vain lusts, I say, these do bring a reproach upon God himself. In Heb. x. 29, they are said to do "despite to the Spirit of grace," they wrong and bring a reproach upon the Spirit of grace. And Heb. vi. 6, it is written, they put the Son of God "to an open shame;" they make him a reproach before all. As when you cart people up and down the city you hold them out as a scorn; so they put the Son of God to open shame; they do (as it were) hold forth the Son of God to open shame. There is more good to be had in a whore than in Jesus Christ, and God, and the blessed Spirit; that is the language of a whoremonger, and all apostates, however diversified, their sins are like-minded.

ἐνυβρίσας.

παραδειγματίζοντας.

Well, ye apostates, from whence is it that the people of God are reproached, but because of you? Do you then bring a reproach upon God, upon his name, upon profession, upon his saints? the Lord has ways to turn the reproach upon yourselves; and usually such men as these, before they die, God puts to open shame, he leaves them to such vile courses as they come to be a shame, a by-word, a scorn, and cast out as dung and filth, not only to the churches, but from such as have any kind of civility or morality at all. O, take heed of bringing a reproach upon God, and so upon his saints. O, let the saints go on in a constant way of holiness and faithfulness; God will wipe away their reproach, the Lord will return the reproach upon the heads of such as seek to reproach them. But when there comes a reproach upon the wicked, it shall be another manner of reproach than upon the saints, it is called "a perpetual reproach;" the reproach of the saints is not a perpetual reproach, but when it is upon the ungodly it shall be a *perpetual* reproach; and in Jer. xlii. 18, those two things are joined together, "a curse, and a reproach." So Neh. iv. 4, "Hear, O God, for we are despised; and turn their reproach upon their own heads." Sanballat and Tobiah did reproach the servants of God, who sought in the uprightness of their hearts to honour God; but, Lord, "turn their reproach upon their own heads," saith Nehemiah.

And truly this is the best way, when the servants of God are reproached; though they may by lawful means seek to vindicate their names, yet their chief resource is to pray, Lord, turn the reproach upon the heads, or into the bosoms, of our adversaries.

Obs. 6. God will be Lord, let the wicked do what they can. "And his reproach shall his Lord return unto him." "His Lord;" what! is God the Lord of this people? "His Lord;" as if the prophet should say, You reject God and will not be in subjection to him, you will not own him to be your Lord; but he will be your Lord in spite of your hearts. Christ has purchased to be Lord over the world, and he will be Lord over all, over all apostates, hypocrites, wicked men; let them do what they can, Jesus Christ will be Lord over them in spite of their hearts.

Oh it is a blessed thing to give up ourselves willingly to the subjection of Jesus Christ. If we say, "We will not have this man to rule over us," Christ will say, But I will rule over you; "I have sworn by myself, the word is gone out of my mouth in righteousness, and shall not return, That unto me every knee shall bow, every tongue shall swear," Isa. xlv. 23. "Be still, and know that I am God," Psal. xlvi. 10. So I say to the most troublesome and tumultuous spirit, that would cast off the yoke of God; Be still, thou wretched, thou proud spirit, and know that God is the Lord, he will prevail against you. God made Julian to know this, when struck by a dart he cast his heart blood into the air, with an O thou Galilean, thou hast overcome me! And so all wicked men shall be forced to say one day, Well, though I would cast off the commands of God behind my back, and break his cords, yet the Lord has overcome me; and though I perish to all eternity, yet God will be God blessed for ever, and Lord of the whole earth.

Julian the apostate.

CHAPTER XIII.

Ver. 1. *When Ephraim spake trembling, he exalted himself in Israel; but when he offended in Baal, he died.*

THIS chapter is partly legal and partly evangelical. Legal; charging this people with their sin of idolatry and of ingratitude, showing them God's wrath, partly already inflicted, and further threatened them, to the 14th verse, and again in the 15th and 16th verses, there returning to further threats; but in the 14th verse there is something mixed of the gospel in the midst of these charges and threats. Ephraim would have put off all the evil that came on him upon God; but God charges Ephraim himself with it: all the change of Ephraim's condition from what it had been, comes from his own sin; and the evil that is like further to come upon him will be for his own sin.

"When Ephraim spake, trembling;" not, when Ephraim spake tremblingly; but, when Ephraim spake, (there should be a stop,) trembling; as much as if it were said, there was trembling when Ephraim spake, those that heard him did tremble. When Ephraim spoke, there was trembling. There was a time when Ephraim was very honourable among the tribes, when the very speaking of Ephraim had great power, and took great impression upon whomsoever he spake to. Yea, though Ephraim was the younger brother, that came of Joseph, yet, by the guidance of the hand of God upon Jacob's hand, the blessing came upon him more especially; and so from time to time God put much honour upon this tribe of Ephraim, according to the blessing he had from Jacob, when his right hand did lay hold upon the head of Ephraim. Joshua was of the tribe of Ephraim, and when Joshua spake what trembling was there among all the people! what mighty power and authority had he! And you read in Judg. viii. 1, 2, in their speaking to Gideon, what trembling they caused, and what yielding presently ensued: "And the men of Ephraim said unto him, Why hast thou served us thus, that thou calledst us not, when thou wentest to fight with the Midianites? And they did chide with him sharply. And he said unto them, What have I done now in comparison of you? Is not the gleaning of the grapes of Ephraim better than the vintage of Abi-ezer?" And so in Judg. xii., when Ephraim came to fight with Jephthah they had thought to have done the same, they spake great and swelling words; Ephraim took much upon him, and made account that all should tremble and shake when he spake.

"He exalted himself in Israel." Jeroboam was of the tribe of Ephraim, and so it refers in a more especial manner to him, and his house, the princely power being put upon that tribe of Ephraim in Jeroboam, and they having power in their hands prevailed very much at the first, and caused trembling in all those to whom they spake. As if the Holy Ghost should say, There is a great change now in Ephraim, he is not now as he was, nor likely to continue so. Ephraim presuming upon his excellency, and upon his strength and worth, ventured to sin, "he offended in Baal," that is, in a way of idolatry, for so Baal sometimes is a general word for an idol: Jer. ix. 14, "But have walked after the imagination of their own heart, and after Baalim," after their idols. And the Chaldee paraphrase seems to allow of this; They did sin, in that they did worship idols.

"When he offended in Baal." But though this is meant immediately of Jeroboam, including his calf, yet it has special reference to the idolatry that was afterwards in this princely tribe, in the successors of Jeroboam, and in a more special manner in Ahab; 1 Kings xvi. 31, he did not satisfy himself in worshipping of the calves, but added this, to worship Baal, the god of the Sidonians.

"He died."

"He died." His spirit even died; he was of a stout, but afterwards came to be of a low, base, and sordid spirit, and so "died." They were under the sentence of death; Jeroboam's house was cut off, and Ahab's house cut off; and the people died at last; they became vile and contemptible, so that every body could insult them. When a lion is alive and roars, he is terrible to all the beasts; but the most timorous thing will run over, or trample upon, a dead lion. So Ephraim was terrible to all about him, but when he had "offended in Baal" his honour was taken from him, and he was fain to crouch to every one; and the wrath of

God pursued and never left him, nor his family, nor the people, but they died and came to nothing. Oh the poor spirit that there was in this tribe after they "offended in Baal!" In 1 Kings xx., you shall see what a low and mean spirit they had: whereas before, when they spake men trembled, none could make them tremble; but there, ver. 1—4, it is said of Ben-hadad, the king of Syria, that he "gathered all his host together;" "and he sent messengers to Ahab king of Israel into the city, and said unto him, Thus saith Ben-hadad, Thy silver and thy gold is mine; thy wives also and thy children, even the goodliest, are mine. And the king of Israel answered and said, My lord, O king, according to thy saying, I am thine, and all that I have." They had a low and mean spirit, yielding to any thing; and yet of a perverse, froward spirit, to be cruel over those that were under them: the Lord was departed from them, and so their spirits were gone, and they were as a dead carcass, which every one could insult with impunity. Thus you have the general meaning of this scripture; yet we shall consider it more particularly when we examine it in reference to Jeroboam. But from what has been said, there are these observations:

Obs. 1. It is an honour to have respect from others when we speak, to have what we say received with reverence and respect, showing that it impresses the hearts of others, and is not cast out as a vain and worthless thing. Thus Job describes his honour, chap. xxix. 9, 10, "The princes refrained talking, and laid their hand on their mouth. The nobles held their peace, and their tongue cleaved to the roof of their mouth." And in the 21st verse, "Unto me men gave ear, and waited, and kept silence at my counsel." A great honour it was to Job, that when he spake his speech was so regarded.

Let children, and servants, and all inferiors, learn to give due honour to those whom God has set above them; not to scorn at nor slight their words, nor when they speak to them to go away and smile and jeer; but it is fit when a father speaks to his child, that the child show reverence and respect in its very countenance and carriage; and so when masters speak to their servants, and superiors to their inferiors. But especially let us give God such honour when he speaks, oh let there then be trembling! Should inferiors honour their superiors by showing reverence when they speak? O let us give this to God. "Bless the Lord, ye his angels, that excel in strength, that do his commandments, hearkening unto the voice of his word," Psal. ciii. 20. The angels excel in strength; and what! do they slight and disregard the word of God? Oh no, they hearken unto the voice of his word, showing for it a reverent respect; and it infinitely beseems us, when God speaks, to "stand in awe," and "do his commandments."

Obs. 2. Those who are in place of power over others account it their honour, not only that those under them should regard, but that they should tremble at what they say. Man greatly delights to lift up himself above others, and to lord it imperiously over them: we might give divers examples of men who have had great power in their hands, who, when any thing has displeased them, would speak so as to make others to shake and tremble: nay, not only men in great place will do this, but you will find the same disposition in men that are very mean and of a very low rank. And in families too, how many when they do but speak to their wives, though they be collateral, and not directly under them, yet how imperiously will they speak, yea, so as even to make the house shake almost! and so with their servants and children; and this they account their glory. My brethren, though this be often through much distemper, and pride, and vanity in men, to delight to make all that are under them to tremble when they speak, yet this is an honour due to God, and God expects it from us; for the Lord is infinitely above us, we are all under the feet of God, and at his disposal, both for our present and eternal state.

And it is fit for us therefore to show reverence to God when he speaks, to have a heart to tremble at his word, that is what God looks for. So Isa. lxvi. 2, "To this man will I look," saith the Lord, "even to him that is poor and of a contrite spirit, and trembleth at my word:" the word that God speaks is that which has the dreadful authority of God in it; it is that which binds conscience, that word which, if thou obeyest not, will bind thee over to eternal death. It becomes the greatest monarchs in the world to tremble when God speaks: oh! who art thou that canst stand against the voice of God? Oh, bold and hard of heart art thou, that canst stand out against God's voice. "The voice of the Lord is powerful; the voice of the Lord is full of majesty," Psal. xxix. 4. And Hab. iii. 16, "When I heard, my belly trembled; my lips quivered at the voice: rottenness entered into my bones, and I trembled in myself." This is the honour that is due to God. Oh, it is a comely thing to see a congregation sit even trembling under the word of God, manifesting their hearts to be affected with the authority and majesty of that which God speaks; for "the voice of God is full of majesty."

"When Ephraim spake, there was trembling."

This the prophet mentions as an aggravation of his sin and misery afterwards. As if the prophet should say, There was a time that God did subdue the hearts of people, so that Ephraim had a great deal of authority over those that were under him; "when Ephraim spake, there was trembling." Whence, with Pareus,

Obs. 3. The subjection of the hearts of men to those in authority, is a work of God, God is to have the glory of it. It is from God that the hearts of multitudes are brought under some few, so as to fear them, and to receive what they speak with trembling. Thus we read in Josh. iv. 14, "On that day the Lord magnified Joshua in the sight of all Israel; and they feared him, as they feared Moses, all the days of his life." Before Moses's death Joshua was but his servant, and we do not read that he was so magnified among the people that they feared him. No, the fear was then upon Moses, because Moses was in place of authority; but when Moses was taken away, and Joshua was to succeed him, then the Lord magnified him, the Lord put a lustre upon him, and the Lord caused the people to fear him, as they had feared Moses. It is a work of God to cause people to fear magistrates. So in Dan. v. 19, "For the majesty that he gave him," that is, that God gave the king, "all people, nations, and languages, trembled and feared before him." It is God that puts majesty upon governors, to make those that are under to fear. Psal. lxxvii. 14 deserves to be noted; it is there said of God, "Thou art the God that doest wonders." What are those wonders and marvellous things? If you read, you shall find among others, "Thou leddest thy people like a flock by the hand of Moses and Aaron;" that is reckoned among the wonders and marvellous things that God did, that he did lead his people "like a flock by the hand of Moses and Aaron." That so great a multitude should be so led by the hands of two, is a wonderful work of God, God is to have the glory of it: it is for the maintaining of government and order in the world, that God so subdues the hearts of many under few.

Obs. 4. The meaner the beginnings of men are, the more imperious oftentimes they prove in power. "When Ephraim spake, there was trembling." This was the younger brother, and had power, not according to the ordinary common course, but by a special providence of God; and so we very often find that men of mean quality and inferior rank, if any providence raises them above others, they prove the most imperious.

Obs. 5. Sin will bring men's honour down. "But when he offended in Baal, he died." Though there was a time that every one reverenced Ephraim, and did much regard what they spake, yet, they falling to sin and wickedness, it is just with God to bring their honour and esteem down, to bring them into the dust, and to make them vile and contemptible in the eyes of those that ere while did reverence them. We find this threatened both to magistrates and ministry. With respect to magistrates, in Job xii. 21, "He poureth contempt upon princes:" God pours contempt; though they had very great honour and esteem, yet through their sin contempt is thrown upon them. And then for those in the ministry, in Mal. ii. 9, "Therefore have I also made you contemptible and base before all the people." "The priest's lips should keep knowledge," and those that were faithful were very honourable; but when they became "partial in the law," that is, when they began to turn the word of God to their own ends, the Lord made them vile in the eyes of the people. The main charge against them was, that they were "partial in the law;" they would handle the word of God partially, what they could get to drive on their own ways by, they would improve that to the uttermost, and turn the word which way they pleased; they thought by this means to prevail, and to get esteem of the people, yet this was the thing that God threatens, to make them thereby to be vile and contemptible in the eyes of the people. When people come to discover that men do indeed drive on their own designs and their own ends in the ways of God, nothing will take away their repute and their honour more. Oh the great change that there is in the honours and esteem of men! God for their sin casts them out, and there pours contempt on their names, as those who have outlived their honours, even in the very hearts of the saints. Indeed when there is a change in the outward condition from prosperity to afflictions, then wicked and carnal men will not regard those whom they before honoured. As in Job's case, in chap. xxix. he tells us how he was honoured, and regarded, and reverenced where he lived in prosperity; but when he was in affliction, chap. xxx. 1, he saith, "But now they that are younger than I have me in derision, whose fathers I would have disdained to have set with the dogs of my flock." This is our wickedness, to change our minds of the esteem of men because of their prosperity or adversity; it evidences great vanity of spirit: surely, if now God by his providence has brought down, in regard of his outward estate, one who has been high in place and godly in the exercise of his functions, he is yet to be honoured still, continuing in his integrity and holiness. But now I speak of this as a judgment of God upon men, when God casts out their names from the very hearts of the saints, and that worthily too, when they deserve to be looked upon as dead carcasses, though heretofore in much honour and esteem. Heretofore they were as gardens that had many sweet flowers, excellent common gifts, for which they were respected; but now like gardens overgrown with weeds, which no man regards. As houses that were hung with costly hangings, but afterwards pulled down and nothing left but the bare walls; so their gifts were very precious. As houses once opulent, which their owners have deserted, leaving nothing but bare walls, it may be mice and vermin run up and down in rooms that were once hung bravely; so it is with many who had excellent gifts, which were highly honoured and esteemed by people that knew them, but now the hangings are gone, there is nothing but vermin running up and down in their spirits. Oh what a mighty havoc sin will make! how it will bring men's honours down!

Let men therefore take heed of trusting in their former repute, for let them have done what they will heretofore, yet if they depart from God their honour will depart too. Men that are in place of authority, or in the ministry, had need consider this point well; for it is a matter of great moment for them to keep up their repute and esteem, that they may be the more useful, and do service, not only for themselves, but for God. And it is one of the great designs of the devil, to seek to cast dirt upon those whom God is wont to use as instruments for good: oh, it concerns them to look to it that they be chargeable with nothing justly.

It is very observable how God remembers Ephraim for dishonour a long time after. In Revelation, chap. vii., where the tribes are reckoned up, only two tribes are left out, Dan and Ephraim; Ephraim is not mentioned there by his own name, but by the name of Joseph; and the reason that is given is, because those two tribes were ringleaders in idolatry. If you read Judg. xviii., you find the children of Dan there setting up "the graven image;" and you know the great changes that Ephraim made in the worship of God, by Jeroboam's setting up of calves, and so afterwards sinning in Baal: hence the great dishonour by omission that God put on them afterwards.

"When Ephraim spake."

"Spake" what? What did Ephraim speak when he caused trembling? Our observations hitherto have been general, but referring it to Jeroboam, that was of Ephraim, and so to his courtiers, what did they speak? They spake these two things, and so caused trembling in the hearts of the people.

I. About the alteration in the government, about the taking off the ten tribes from the house of David; "What portion have we in David? neither have we inheritance in the son of Jesse," 1 Kings xii. 16. When this was mentioned, there was trembling; it did certainly at first cause the people's hearts to shake, they thought it was a very great matter, they knew not what would come of it; what! to forsake the house of David, and to have a change of government? this caused many thoughts of heart, and much trembling, lest evil might result. "When he spake, there was trembling," but, "he exalted himself." Notwithstanding such concussions of spirit, yet Jeroboam went on in his way, and would venture the worst; let come of it what would, he would on, "he exalted himself." But then afterwards he sins in his idolatry, as his successors sin in their Baal, and then "he died;" God struck him, and his family, and so the ten tribes. From whence our notes of observation are,

Obs. 6. Alteration in government is a matter of very great hazard and difficulty. Men that have to deal in any kind of alteration in matter of government, had need be very wise in their carriage in it in respect of the people, for much depends upon them. When there was any alteration in government there was trembling, mighty fears and troubles in the hearts of the people.

Obs. 7. Resolved spirits will break through difficulties.

Obs. 8. When God intends to have a work accomplished, he will raise up men to go through with it, notwithstanding any difficulties there are in it. "He exalted himself." Though the people's minds were very much troubled, and there was a great deal of shaking throughout the land, yet he lifts up himself; he had some encouragement from the prophet, and otherwise, so that he *would* go through with the matter. It was a purpose which God had purposed, that he might fulfil what was threatened to Solomon for his former sin.

Obs. 9. If the workers together with God, after duties are accomplished, rest in their own parts or strength, so as to forsake and sin against God, it is just with him to leave them, that they shall vanish and come to nothing. "He exalted himself," and prevailed in what he spake, notwithstanding the trembling of the people; and now, having got himself warm in the nest, and strong in his kingdom, he lifts up himself in another manner, and forsakes God, and trusts in his own strength, and then he dies; God casts him off.

Men had need take heed, though they be carried through many and great difficulties by a spirit more than ordinary, they had need take heed (I say) that afterwards they do not walk in their own strength, but walk humbly before God; if they forsake God, they will die and perish.

II. About the alteration in religion: this likely caused more trembling than the other. What did Jeroboam speak? That now they were not to go up to worship at Jerusalem, God did not stand upon such things; no, they might save themselves that long journey: and so there was a calf set up at Dan and Beth-el, and they must go and worship there: this was a mighty alteration in their worship. And surely when this was mentioned first to the people, there could not but have been great trembling; the spirits of the godly surely would tremble at such a motion, they would look upon it as a most dreadful curse of God upon the kingdom, that there should be such a change in the matters of religion, from truth to falsehood; and even among others, too, there was a general trembling, for men have some kind of conscience with regard to religion and the worship of God, and this was so flat against the word, that where there was but any conscience of God they could not but have had some fear, they could not tell what might come of it, and therefore there could not but be a very great concussion of spirit in the people of the land. At first this was so; but yet afterwards their spirits became dead spirits, that he might do with them what he would; and so they joined with Jeroboam, and even with Ahab, and sinned more and more.

Obs. 10. Alteration in religion is a very difficult business. It cannot be expected but the hearts of people will stir much upon the alteration of religion; though it be from worse to better, yet the hearts of people will stir very much at first. When the Reformation from popery took place here, what a stir was there! they were presently ready to take up arms in Cornwall. What ado was there for the book of Common Prayer! so that the king was fain to write to them, that it was no other than the sum of what they had before, only translated into English, with some amendments. And certainly the casting out of prelacy has caused a great deal of trembling; a great ado there is. How hard it is to get but a single rotten tooth out of a man's head! it costs a great deal of pain and trouble. Though the wars were undertaken for the maintenance of our liberties, as subjects and men, and for the civil right we have to our religion also; yet we see that the very thoughts of any kind of change whatever in matters of religion, causes the hearts of men to shake and to be unsettled. A change in matters of religion, even though from the worse to the better, is an affair of great moment, and therefore requires much prayer. If it cause trembling when the change is from the better to the worse, it will likewise cause trembling where it is changed from the worse to the better; and therefore it requires that all the godly should join all their strength together, against those that would oppose their strength against it.

Obs. 11. Men of resolute spirits will go on, even in matters of religion, though it be from the better to the worse. You may say, The people will not bear nor endure it. Yea, but they will venture to go on with their way and design, though it be from the better to the worse; but now, if the change be from the worse to the better, then it is a special gift of God to give men hearts to persevere, notwithstanding difficulties.

Obs. 12. Gradual encroachments under fair shows further designs. "He exalted himself," though there were "trembling:" that is, he succeeded in this his change of religion, not by open violence presently, but he carried things on by fair shows, one thing after another, and so prevailed with the people. This is the way to compass an object.

Obs. 13. God's long-suffering must not be abused. "but when he offended in Baal, he died." Though God may suffer men to make some alterations in religion, though they be for the worse, and let them prosper, yet if they will grow from one degree to another in forsaking God, then God comes upon them with his wrath, and they die; if they know not where to hold, God will not continue patient towards them any longer.

Obs. 14. A family or people from which God has withdrawn his protection and blessing, is as a dead carcass. "He died." I understand similarly Matt. xxiv. 28, "For wheresoever the carcass is, there will the eagles be gathered together." Though it is true that this is spoken about the coming of Christ, yet I do not think that the carcass is Christ, and the saints the eagles, although it has been interpreted so by several; but Christ's coming, here meant, is his coming against Jerusalem, his coming in his judgments against the people of the Jews: they were now as a dead carcass, God having forsaken them; and the eagles, birds of prey, would come upon them: this might refer particularly to the Romans, whose ensign is the spread eagle. The body of the Jews that had forsaken God and his truth, and so were but as a dead carcass, would become the prey of those eagles. A people or family that forsakes God and his worship is as a dead carcass, the prey of the spoiler.

Obs. 15. Corruption of worship causes God thus to withdraw from a people, and make them to be as a dead carcass. "But when he offended in Baal, he died." As it was said of Troy, so long as they kept the Palladium, the image of Minerva, Troy was impregnable, but when that was gone, then was it overcome and spoiled; so when God's worship, which is the life and safety of a place, is corrupted and gone, then cometh death. Though I do not think that God always observes the same strictness in matters of worship as with the Jews; for the Jews certainly, though they had a covenant of grace in which God dealt with them, yet they had too a special covenant which God made with them, respecting their being in the land of Canaan. Now indeed God goes by general rules, that is, to punish the disobedient and to reward those that are godly, his ways now towards nations and people, with regard to outward punishments and mercies, are but according to general rules; but his administration towards the Jews, besides general rules, were according to a special covenant made with them about their living in the land of Canaan, either prosperously, or in adversity.

Obs. 16. When wicked men are most active in evil, yet then may they be under the sentence of death. When they seem to have the greatest power to do what they list, yet then they may be as a dead people. "When he offended in Baal, he died." If you will but observe the story, for these prophets cannot possibly be understood without reference to the history in Kings and Chronicles: observe but the account in the Kings: when was it that Ephraim "offended in Baal?" It was in Ahab's time; they were never more active for their idolatrous ways than then, nor was there ever more violence or cruelty exercised on the prophets of the Lord; for then Jezebel had her hundred prophets set at her table, but the prophets of God were fain to be hid in a cave, and Elijah to shift for his life: and yet "when he offended in Baal, he died." Died! why he seemed to be full of life, and activity, and vigour, and thought to do what he list, and to trample all under feet that would stand against that way of worship. But for all this their bravery and pride they were dead, saith the Holy Ghost, they were a base people, and under the sentence of death; God was gone from them, and they were decaying, and so they should deny him more and more till they utterly perished. "When he offended in Baal, he died."

Ver. 2. *And now they sin more and more, and have made them molten images of their silver, and idols according to their own understanding, all of it the work of the craftsmen: they say of them, Let the men that sacrifice kiss the calves.*

"And now they sin."

The family of Ephraim and the ten tribes, for so Ephraim is taken for Jeroboam sometimes, and sometimes for the whole tribe, and sometimes for the governors, and sometimes for all the ten tribes as distinct from Judah.

"Now they sin more and more."

From whence I beseech you observe the taking in the people now together with Ephraim: at first it was, "when *he* offended in Baal, he died;" but now it is said, "*they* sin more and more:" all the people join with him in sin.

At first, when he began to speak about the alteration of religion, the people trembled to think of it; but it seems afterwards they could swallow it down well enough, they could join with Jeroboam, yea, and Ahab too, "more and more;" let them impose what they would upon them, they could yield to it.

Obs. 1. Use makes a mighty alteration in men's spirits. How many men's hearts and ways are different from what they seemed to be! If one had mentioned formerly such things as they do now, they would have trembled. If about six years since one could but have presented in a map all our speeches and actions one against another, and told us how things should be, our hearts would have shaken, and we would have trembled at the very thoughts of it; but now "more and more" we go on, and God knows whither we shall go: oh the alteration that a little time makes in men's spirits! Now (saith he) they are a dead, heartless people; you may do what you will with them; they will now do things altogether opposed to their former principles. A man would wonder that this people, who were so astonished at the bare thoughts of the change in religion, should now be swallowed up in idolatry.

Obs. 2. The sudden affections and sudden expressions of people are never to be regarded. Though people may seem to be up and very forward in their affections and expressions, yet, I say, never rest too much upon them. Nothing is more uncertain than the spirits of the multitude, and therefore it is the most irrational thing for any of wisdom to think to carry things that way for a constancy; you may find them forward in one way at one time, but they will be quickly off again, and that which one time they will extol, at another time they will cry down; and such alteration of spirits these times will be a witness to, I believe, as great as ever occurred from the beginning of the world. "Now they sin more and more."

Mobile vulgus.

"And now."

There is a great emphasis in this particle, "now." "They sin more and more;" that is, even "now," when the very sentence of death was out against them, even "now" they do it. Thus did Ahab in 1 Kings xvi. 30, "And Ahab the son of Omri did evil in the sight of the Lord above all that were before him;" he added evil to evil. From whence,

Obs. 3. When destruction is nearest evil men are most wicked. Now their sin ripens apace: when the scum grows highest, then it is nearest the fire; and so the nearer it is to the fire the higher it will grow. It is a great sign that the times of men are not long, when they grow notoriously wicked. See a man that hitherto has been forward in that which is good, he may have failings, and yet the Lord may pity him; but now let this man grow to be very wicked, not only to abate of his profession, but to become openly sinful, expect the ruin of that man suddenly, it will not tarry long.

Obs. 4. It is a great aggravation of men's wickedness to sin after God threats, and in the times of judgment, when they are under God's hand. Oh, when God appears against us we should presently submit, at the least holding up of his finger: but this is the pride of men, not to stoop even when the hand of God is against them, and the rather because they would justify their sin; if they should stoop and yield on the hand of God coming out against them, this would debase them, but they rather will stand out the more that they might justify their sin, that they are not as men would take them to be.

Obs. 5. When men have lost their credits, honour, and esteem through the just judgment of God, they grow more base and vile in their sinful ways than ever. Ephraim had a great deal of esteem and honour, but he lost it through God's just judgment, and now he, and the people together, "sin more and more." We find this usual, that men's esteem and credit, though they have very base hearts within all the while, yet will keep them in a very fair way; and, on the contrary, many who have lived very fair so long as they had esteem and credit, yet if their credit be but cracked, and their esteem gone, will prove very base and sordid. As in a garden, if a man have but a few weeds in it, he will have them pulled up; but if it be overgrown with weeds, then he cares not much for it, but lets it run more and more: so in men's hearts, though there be something amiss in them, and yet their names kept up, they will reform; but if once they have fallen, so that their honour, credit, and esteem are gone, they go on further and further in wickedness. Or as it is with a man when he has a new garment, he is afraid at first of every little spot, and much more of a rent; but when afterwards the garment becomes much sullied, he becomes careless of it, he never stands brushing of it as before: it is thus for all the world with men in respect of their hearts and of their lives, and therefore it is good for them to look to it betimes, when their names begin but a little to be lost, when they may see the just hand of God beginning to come, then to reform; for if they let themselves go upon liberty, they will grow vile and abominable. "They sin more and more."

Obs. 6. There is no stop in apostacy. Let men once apostatize from God, and there is no stop then; they cannot tell whither they may go, if once they begin to roll down. A man may think thus, I will but roll thus far, and there I will stop. No, if once you begin to roll, you will roll and roll down to the bottom; you know not whither you may roll, or where you may fall. If a man should leap into the water, and say, I will sink but thus far, to the middle and no farther, this were but folly; you will sink more and more: so it is with apostates; I verily believe those that did make slight at first, did not think that they should go so far, Oh, God forbid that they should do things so vile and so abominable! yea, but when once they are rolling, when once they are sinking, they roll and sink more and more, till they roll into the bottomless pit of hell; they sink more and more, till they sink into the very bottomless gulf, into such things as they would before have shrunk from with abhorrence. There is a curse upon the wicked in Psal. xxxv. 6, "Let their way be dark and slippery; and let the angel of the Lord persecute them." When men *will* go out of the ways of God into slippery paths of their own, it is just with God that an evil spirit should drive them on in those ways. As in your travelling in champaign countries, a highway goes to such a town, and another lies close by it, and you, it may be, choose the wrong one, and so go on and think it will bring you to the place where you are travelling; but it winds so that you go further and further from the right road, perhaps many miles before you are aware of it: so it is in apostacy; it may be, at first, when men depart from the ways of God they think it not of much moment, but then these evil ways wind gradually, and, it may be, almost imperceptibly, widening the distance between them and God. "They sin more and more."

I will give you the steps of an apostate's departure from God.

1. Some slight sin against knowledge, though never so little, for sin of mere infirmity I cannot call apostacy; but if it be ever so little a sin *against knowledge*, it breaks the bond of obedience: when you will venture to do that which you know is against God, this bond of obedience being broken, no marvel though you fall and "sin more and more."

2. Every act of sin tends to increase the habit. Corruption grows by acting; as with grace, every act of grace extends grace in the heart of a man; and the way to grow in grace is, to act grace much; so that when you are acting your grace, you do not only that which is your duty, but you are growing in grace: so when you are acting of corruption, you are not only doing that which is evil, but you are increasing the tendency to it; and therefore every sin that causes us to decline from God, makes us to go more and more from God.

3. Every sin against conscience weakens the work of conscience. The authority of conscience will quickly be weakened when it is once broken; break but off the yoke of conscience, and conscience will be weaker than it was before. The first time a man sins against conscience, his conscience, having a great deal of strength in it, mightily troubles him; but having had a flaw, (as it were,) it grows weaker. I remember a notable story which that reverend and famous divine, Dr. Preston, relates of one in Cambridge, who, after having committed a great sin, had this temptation, Do the act again, and your conscience will trouble you no more: this temptation prevailed with him, he did it again, and then he grew a very sot indeed, and went on in his wickedness. Every sin does somewhat to weaken conscience, and therefore one that falls off from God will "sin more and more."

4. A man loses his comfort in God according to the degree of his departure from him. For some kind of comforts hypocrites may have; as there may be common gifts of the Spirit to enable them to do service, so there may be common gifts of the Spirit to comfort them, they may taste of the powers of the world to come. Many have some flashes of joy; but when they are departed from God they cannot have so much comfort as they were wont to have, and when they have not that comfort they must have it some way, and are fain to go sharking up and down to get it some where else: I cannot have that comfort in God which I was wont to have; I was wont, when I was troubled, to go and read the word, I could find comfort there; let me go into good company, I could find comfort there; but in the presence of God I could find comfort; but now I cannot: and so the heart must have comfort some way or other, and therefore goes more and more from God.

5. When one has sinned against God, holy duties become very unsuitable to his soul. It is a more difficult thing to engage his heart in them than before, and so he comes to neglect duties, and by neglecting them his corruption grows. They were a powerful means to restrain corruption; for when a man is abroad and inclined to licence, yet when he thinks thus, Yea, but before I go to bed I must pray, and how shall I then beg grace from God, when now I wilfully sin against him? this curbs a man: so long as he can keep any kind of suitableness between his heart and holy duties, though he should fail in some things, he would quickly recover; but when he begins to have holy duties so veiled as to leave them off, then he will "sin more and more," for the curb is removed.

6. The presence of God is terrible to an apostate. He cannot think of God without some terror; before he would often think and speak of God, but now he puts off the thoughts of God, the thoughts of him and his presence being terrible; it must needs be that he must wander up and down even more and more, be as a Cain wandering away from the presence of God.

7. The thoughts of whatsoever might turn an apostate's heart to God, are grievous to him. If he thinks of turning to God, presently will be presented to him some difficulty that will make him even put off all those thoughts, and rather give himself liberty to his own ways.

8. One sin cannot be maintained without another. As now, you find when one man has done wrong to another, he knows not how to carry it out but by doing him more wrong, to crush him if he can. And so there are divers sins that have many sins depending upon them; if a man be engaged in a business that is sinful, that he may carry it on successfully he must commit a great many other sins, and so fall off more and more.

9. The pride of men's hearts is such, that they will attempt to justify transgression. Men love to justify what they have done; when they have sinned, they will grow more resolute and violent, that all people might think that their hearts recoil not in the least. You think many times when you see men very strong and violent in an evil way, that surely they are fully satisfied in it; oh! you are mightily mistaken in that, they may be very violent and very strong in their way, only that they may persuade other folk, though their own consciences tell them that they are not satisfied. Thus the pride of men's hearts makes them "sin more and more."

10. When men have gone far in sin, they grow desperate. They little hope ever to recover themselves, and therefore "sin more and more."

11. God in his just judgment withdraws himself from apostates. God withdraws those gifts and common graces that they had, and saith, Let them go on; "he that is filthy, let him be filthy still."

12. God gives up apostates to their corruptions, and to the power of the devil. It is a dreadful thing when the church does it, although it be for the salvation of the soul, and for the destruction of the flesh, 1 Cor. v. 5; but when God delivers up one to his corruptions, it is for the soul's destruction: Do you rule him, saith God, because he would not be ruled. No marvel then though an apostate "sin more and more."

O, stand with all your might against the beginning of sin; tremble, and stop on the threshold. Had this people done so, at the first they trembled, oh, had they but kept that trembling heart continually, it would have preserved them from abundance of evil: and so, do not some of you remember that there has been a heart-trembling and hesitancy at the very thought of those things which, it may be, some of you now practise? oh, happy had it been for you had you kept such a frame! You young beginners, you tremble at temptations, you tremble at the thoughts of sin, at the first rising of corruption in your hearts; oh keep this frame, and regard not that boldness of spirit which there is in some. Some venture to the edge of the precipice, but it is a dangerous situation; rather keep a trembling, sin-fearing heart, for if you lose that, and begin but to tamper with some sin, if the devil thus beguile you, it is most likely that after the first offence you will sin more and more, and never pause till you are wholly involved in the snares of the devil.

And let us learn, my brethren, to be more and more in the ways of God, as apostates are more and more in the ways of sin. Oh that it were so with us! Let us not content ourselves to do a little for God, but still more and more, as David, in Psal. lxxi. 14, " I will yet praise thee more and more," I will add to thy praise, so the original signifies: Lord, some praise thou hast had in the world, oh that I could live to add any thing to it! " I will yet praise thee more and more."

Obs. 7. Idolatry is a very growing sin. " When he offended in Baal, he died," and now " they sin more and more." Gross idolatry has grown upon men under fair pretexts and upon plausible principles.

My brethren, do but break this one bond in the matters of worship, that all worship must be by institution, I say, all the worship of God must be either that which is written in man's heart, or that which is in the word by institution: if so be that men will break this, and venture to exalt any creature beyond what God, either in a work of nature or by an institution, has raised it, then begins superstition; this, I say, is the fruitful source of all false worship, to raise any creature higher than God, either in nature or by institution, has raised it; do but venture to put upon any one ceremony more than nature or Divine institution has put upon it, and you know not where you shall stop. You know to what a height of idolatry popery is grown, but it began fair at first. And so we were going to most vile and abominable idolatry; but by what steps? We had broken the bond of regulating the worship of God by the word, and were bringing in men's own reason and inventions, and were beginning to put a religious respect upon that which God had never done: now do but grant such a licence in the least matters, and then you know not whither you will run in the way of idolatry, you will " sin more and more."

Oh let reformation be to us as idolatry is to wicked men, let us not rest in any degrees, but still reform more and more: idolaters will not stand still, oh why should they then who seek to reform stay their hands?

" And have made them molten images of their silver."

They were at great charge in making them, and so went on strongly in their way; though it cost them much, yet still they would go on.

" They have made them molten images."

Tertullian inveighs much against the maker of any images for religious services, and saith, It is not enough for you to say, We will not worship them, but you must not make them.

" Of their silver."

" Their silver" is put for their money; silver is used in divers languages for money in general. The calves were of gold, but it is said they were of silver, because the people contributed their money; and other images they added to them that they made by their money: their idolatry was chargeable to them. To avoid trouble in going to Jerusalem, and expenses in their sojourn there, they would not go to Jerusalem to worship; but they were willing to part with their silver for their idolatrous worship. Though men will not have God's service to be chargeable to them, yet their own ways are often so.

" And have made them molten images of silver, and idols according to their own understanding." The word עצבים translated " idols" signifies griefs, or things that do terrify or cause grief: and indeed idolatry will bring grief, and men of superstitious, idolatrous spirits are often filled with fears. But this is all " according to their own understanding," that is, as they thought fit themselves, such as should be suitable to their own ends, they took the liberty to tender up their respects to God according to their own inventions; and hence indeed comes superstition. Hence come the great corruptions in the worship of God; when men *will* interpose their own understandings, will leave the simplicity of the rule, and go their own way; when they think that the worship of God is not pompous enough of itself. They who do not worship God in a spiritual way, will labour to make up the want of the spiritual part by the addition of many externals, invented by " their own understanding;" and because such things in the service of God are rational to them, they think they must be acceptable to God, and therefore wonder that any should oppose them.

Calvin on this very text has most memorable expressions against men bringing their own understandings into the worship of God; saith he, * Here the worship of God is spoken of, in which whatsoever is of man's prudence, whatsoever is the dictate of mere reason, must yield, prudence and reason must give way; yea, whatsoever are the counsels of men, they must not judge by sense, by reason, or by prudence, in the matters of God's instituted worship; if they do permit themselves in the least degree, they do nothing but defile the worship of God. And again, he saith, This is the very principle whereby men must be taught to worship God aright, that they must be made fools first themselves. If men will come to worship God, they must deny and lay down their understandings, they must not so much as allow themselves to be wise. And thus he heaps these expressions one upon another, adding, Let them listen to the word of God alone, for this condemns whatsoever is pleasing to the judgment and reason of men.

God is indeed little beholden to men's understandings in those two things, matters of worship, and of faith. Respect, it may be, for the man, may somewhat the more make such an expression pass current, that it is the very principle of right worshipping of God for men to be fools. Hence many of the learned men of the world have accounted them fools and simple men; as heretofore the Nonconformists, were not they so accounted because they would not yield to those things which were imposed upon them? yea, we must be fools. It is true, when once we have an institution men's prudence and reason are required to guide us in the right management of it; but to raise up any thing in the worship of God beyond what I have warrant for in the word is no where allowed. In such a case it is not enough for men to say; This is good, and what hurt is there in it? and without this there will come a great deal of stir; and can any reasonable man deny its excellence? I say, when we come to matters of worship, wherein we expect a presence of God for a spiritual work on the soul of man, all these arguments we must lay aside, they are inadmissible. I cannot here argue for a thing, that it is good, and that I have need of it, and therefore must have it; but I may argue, that it is good, and that I have need of it, because instituted. Luther, likewise, saith, In matters of worship we must not regard so much *what the thing is*, but *who it is that commands it;* do not let us lean to our own understandings. Thus much for their sin of idolatry.

* Hoc agitur de cultu Dei, in quo cessare debet quicquid est prudentiæ, quicquid est rationis in hominibus, quicquid consilii et omnis eorum sensûs; nam si hic tantillum sibi permittunt, nihil aliud quàm Dei cultum vitiant. Hoc principium est rite colendi Dei, ut homines stulti fiant neque permittant sibi sapere, sed tantum prebeant aurem Deo; Hic damnat quicquid arridet judicio hominum vel rationi. Calv. in loc.

But further, they thought to carry themselves in a prudential way, but the Lord condemns it as sottish; they thought they were very wise in it, yea, but their wisdom was very foolishness. For there follows,

"All of it the work of the craftsmen: they say of them, Let the men that sacrifice kiss the calves."

As if he should say, What a sottish thing is this, that when they themselves put all its excellency on the creature, they will yet worship it, and say to the men that sacrifice, "Kiss the calves!" Whereas God challenges worship on this ground, because he is himself the supreme, the only source of all excellency.

Obs. 8. Those who trust most to their own understandings in matters of worship, God gives most up to sottishness. I say, if men will venture to go according to their own understandings in worship, God may justly give them up to sottishness, and none are given up more than those who think to be most prudential and wise. In Isa. xxix. 13, God saith, "Their fear toward me is taught by the precept of men." What then? "Therefore, behold, I will proceed to do a marvellous work among this people, even a marvellous work and a wonder." What is the marvellous work, what is the wonder? "The wisdom of their wise men shall perish, and the understanding of their prudent men shall be hid." What! they will lean on their own understandings in my worship, and they will prescribe what I should have, and they think they are very wise in what they do; I will do "a marvellous work and a wonder." What is this? I will cause "the wisdom of their wise men to perish, and the understanding of their prudent men shall be hid;" they shall be left to sottish and absurd ways, that all that are about them shall see that they are judicially blinded.

O my brethren, we see this fulfilled at this day; those that will venture upon their own understandings in worship, how hath the Lord left them to blindness! though men of excellent parts in former times, yet their parts begin to be blasted.

And observe it, you will find this to be the case more and more: such men as bring their own understandings into God's worship, I say, the Lord will blast at one time or other, so that others shall see, and take notice, and stand and wonder at it.

"All of it."

"All of it." As if he should say, If there were any thing of God in it, possibly it might be accepted, but when it is all of man——.

This may be said of many of our services; they are all of man, there is nothing of God, nothing of the spirit of Christ in them; no marvel though they vanish, and we vanish in them.

"They say of them, Let the men that sacrifice kiss the calves." זבחי אדם עגלים ישקון The Seventy render these words thus, *Θύσατε ἀνθρώπους, μόσχοι γὰρ ἐκλελοιπασι·* which interpretation the Vulgate likewise adopts. In zeal to their idols they sacrificed men. According to which reading the sense would be, Those are worthy to kiss the calves that sacrifice men. This was forbidden, Lev. xviii. 21, and xx. 2. But it was done in a perverse imitation of Abraham, who would have offered up Isaac. It prevailed much among the heathen; the king of Moab sacrificed his eldest son, who should have reigned in his stead, 2 Kings iii. 27; and Tertullian saith, Apolog. cap. 9, that it continued till the time of Tiberius. Lactantius, Just. lib. i. cap. 21, records of the Carthaginians, that being vanquished by Agathocles, king of Sicily, they thought the gods were displeased with them, and that they might appease them, they sacrificed two hundred of the noblemen's sons.

The place where the Jews sacrificed men, was in Tophet, in the valley of the son of Hinnom. Hinnom is derived from a word signifying to lament, and roar, because of the noise of those that were sacrificed; whence Gehenna.

Tophet, of a word signifying to beat on a drum; which they used, not only to drown the noise, but all the kindred of the sacrificed person did rejoice with timbrels and dances in great mirth, till the sacrifice was fully consumed. The Hebrews are quoted by Selden De Diis Spris., *Cognati omnes tympanis et chordis summa cum lætitia exultant quoad omnino combustus fuerit.*

But to pass by that interpretation, and to take it as it is read in our books: by these words they call upon the sacrificers, and encourage them in their idolatrous ways.

"Kiss." The kiss is a ceremony of worship; Psal. ii. 12, "Kiss the Son;" but also it expressed their love and delight, as well as their homage. Hercules' chin, in Sicily, was worn bare with kissing, saith Cicero. And if they could not reach the chin, then they kissed the hand. Hence Job xxxi. 27, "If my mouth hath kissed my hand." How foolish were they, to forsake the blessed God to worship calves! How should we be forward and cheerful in the worship of the blessed God, in coming to kiss the Son!

Pliny, lib. 28. cap. 2.

Obs. 9. It is false worship, to give religious respect to any creature, by kissing, as well as by bowing to it. I know no reason why a book may not be set up to be bowed to, as well as to be kissed, in taking an oath. The lifting up of the hand to the high God, in an oath, we find in Scripture, therefore that is safe.

Ver. 3. *Therefore they shall be as the morning cloud, and as the early dew that passeth away, as the chaff that is driven with the whirlwind out of the floor, and as the smoke out of the chimney.*

Here are four elegant similitudes to set forth Ephraim's weak, vanishing condition; God's power over them, the swiftness of the punishment, its violence, and his utter desolation, so that his place shall not be found.

1. "A morning cloud." Ephraim was risen, seemed to threaten great things, overcast the leaves like a cloud; but on the brightness of God's justice appearing, all was dispelled. Their "goodness" (chap. vi. 4) was "as a morning cloud, and as the early dew;" now they shall be so themselves.

2. "Early dew." The dew seems to bespangle the grass; but the sun rising, it is soon dried up. Ephraim's estate was beautiful, but the heat of God's wrath consumes all presently.

3. "Chaff." כמץ signifies the smallest of the chaff, the dust of the chaff-heap, and that abroad, where their floors were, and a whirlwind coming upon it. Psal. xxxv. 5, "Let them be as chaff before the wind: and let the angel of the Lord chase them."

Obs. 1. Many, when they begin to be unsettled, the angel of God, as a messenger of wrath, drives on apace to misery.

4. "Smoke." "The smoke out of the chimney," it seems to darken the heavens, but presently it is scattered. The original signifies a chink or hole; because in Judea there were not such chimneys as we now use, but as it were windows, or open places in the upper part of the house, or in the wall, as at present in Norway and Sweden, saith a learned interpreter upon the place. We may hence,

מארבה significat foramen, in Judæâ non fuerunt tales camini, qualibus nos hodie utimur, sed fenestræ superiore parte domûs, vel in paviete, quemadmodum hodie in Norwegiâ, et Sueciâ. Ternov. in loc.

Obs. 2. The vanity of proud men. Here God compares to such mean, vile things, persons that heretofore were so lofty. So 1 Kings xiv. 10, Jeroboam's house is threatened to be destroyed, "as a man taketh away dung, till it be all gone."

Why then should wicked men be feared who are

thus before the Lord? Do not bless yourselves in any prosperity, never think yourselves settled; for when you are most prosperous, and likely to continue so, yet are ye but "as the morning cloud;" yea, as "the early dew," "the chaff," "the smoke."

Ver. 4. *Yet I am the Lord thy God from the land of Egypt, and thou shalt know no god but me: for there is no saviour beside me.*

"Yet I am the Lord thy God." This is spoken,

I. As an aggravation of their sin. "Yet I am the Lord thy God;" as if he should say, You have thus provoked me, notwithstanding I am the Lord thy God. I have done very great things for you and for your forefathers.

Obs. 1. It is very evil to sin against great works of mercy. When we do any thing for another wherein we think we might gain him to ourselves for ever, and he yet—this is very grievous.

II. By way of encouragement. "Yet I *am* the Lord thy God;" I am ready to show thee the like mercy still. This is to break their hearts, and to provoke them to come in to the Lord. He speaks to an apostate people; as if he should say, Were you yet what you sometimes seemed to be, oh how gracious should I be to you! I am yet whatever I seemed to be to you; why are you so perverse towards me? Jer. ii. 2, "I remember thee, the kindness of thy youth, the love of thine espousals, when thou wentest after me in the wilderness, in a land that was not sown."

III. As a strong argument to obedience. "Yet I am the Lord thy God." When the will of God is once known, saith Luther, on Gen. xxvii., we are no further to dispose of rights, because neither parents, lords, nor masters have this title, "I am the Lord thy God."

"From the land of Egypt." As if he should have said, What a state had you been in, if I had not delivered you out of Egypt, from the iron furnace, a low, base employment! ye had been bond-slaves, and might have spent your days there in sorrow and trouble. Consider then, 1. Your low estate. 2. How your strength might have been spent. 3. When this anguish was upon you, what crying to me, and my delivering of you! Hence note, that,

Obs. 2. Deliverance from Egypt is a proof of God's being our God.

But does this concern us?

Much. There is a spiritual Egypt from which we have been delivered, as the apostle makes use of the paschal lamb in a spiritual sense, 1 Cor. v. 7. The power, severity, and holiness of God, appear in the delivery of his people from Egypt; so also in our deliverance from antichrist, as Rev. xv. 2, 3, the church is brought in singing the song of Moses (which the children of Israel sung for their deliverance from Pharaoh) for its deliverance from antichrist. Pharaoh was the dragon in the waters, Psal. lxxiv. 13, 14, so is antichrist, Rev. xii. The city of Zurich engraved the year of their deliverance from antichrist upon pillars in letters of gold.

"And thou shalt know no god but me."

That is, Thou shalt effectually acknowledge, worship, serve, love God as a God; no other.

Obs. 3. The end of God's great work is, that he may be known to be a God, a sincere, gracious, and holy One. The knowing God to be a God, is a special part of that worship which is due to God.

To acknowledge God to be God, is to know him in his excellency, majesty, and glory, above what is known of him by the light of nature.

This cannot but have a mighty operation on the heart. For,

To know God to be a God, is, 1. To know him to be the first Being of all. 2. The infinite, all-sufficient God. 3. The fountain of all good to his saints.

1. This must needs gain the heart to him. 2. There is no worship of God where this is not. 3. Where this is all follows. 4. The right knowledge of God keeps from false worship. "But now, after that ye have known God, or rather are known of God, how turn ye again to the weak and beggarly elements," the Jewish ceremonial worship? Gal. iv. 9.

"Thou shalt know no god but me." This is the first commandment, of which Luther saith, All duties flow from that great ocean of the first commandment, and again return thither. We see the prophets to be most exercised in the use of the first commandment.

Obs. 4. It is not good to know idolaters' worship at all. For this is spoken in the text by way of opposition: "Thou shalt know no god but me;" that is, thou shalt be acquainted with no other worship. As in Deut. xii. 30, "Take heed to thyself, that thou inquire not, saying, How did these nations serve their gods?"

Therefore those that are not grounded, (and who is so grounded if it be against the precept of God?) should not even inquire after, much less go to see, the worship of idolaters.

Obs. 5. Nothing should be known or acknowledged to have any good in it, but with an infinite distance between it and God. "Thou shalt know no god but me;" that is, nothing but with a difference from me, as much as between God and the creature; "For who in the heaven can be compared unto the Lord? who among the sons of the mighty can be likened unto the Lord?" as saith the psalmist, Psal. lxxxix. 6, and elsewhere. There is an infinite distance between God and every creature: we may know creatures as creatures, but nothing as God, but God.

Obs. 6. We should know and acknowledge God when we are in misery and straits. So the church, "Verily thou art a God that hidest thyself, O God of Israel, the Saviour," Isa. xlv. 15. Many in time of prosperity will know God and acknowledge him; but when troubles come, they change their thoughts.

"For there is no saviour beside me." Hence the observations are:

Obs. 7. God delights to manifest himself a Saviour God. Thus Jer. xiv. 8, "O the hope of Israel, the Saviour thereof in time of trouble." Isa. lx. 16, "Thou shalt also suck the milk of the Gentiles, and shalt suck the breast of kings: and thou shalt know that I the Lord am thy Saviour and thy Redeemer, the mighty One of Jacob;" and lxiii. 1, "Who is this that cometh from Edom?—I that speak in righteousness, mighty to save." And Acts v. 31, speaking of Christ, "Him hath God exalted with his right hand to be a Prince and a Saviour, for to give repentance to Israel, and forgiveness of sins." There is his glory, and there should ours be also. He might manifest himself a God in our ruin.

Obs. 8. Saving mercies are great mercies.

Obs. 9. Though God does more for us than any, yet he receives not so much from us.

Obs. 10. No creature can do us any good further than God enables it.

Obs. 11. Our faith should be exercised on God as a Saviour, to whom there is none like. "Be strong in the Lord," (saith the apostle,) "and in the power of his might," Eph. vi. 10: if our dangers are more than any, yet our Saviour is more than any also. "I will call on the Lord, who is worthy to be praised: so shall I be saved from mine enemies," 2 Sam. xxii. 4.

Obs. 12. God must be acknowledged in all salvation. "They forgat God their Saviour, which had done great things in Egypt," Psal. cvi. 21.

Obs. 13. We should make use of all God's saving mercies, to engage our hearts to him. For, 1. God saves from such evils as none else can. 2. He saves some from as great or greater than ever he has. 3. God saves from all evil. 4. Without means. 5. Above means. 6. Contrary to means. 7. None saves but by him. "There is no God else beside me; a just God and a Saviour; there is none beside me," Isa. xlv. 21. 8. God saves in all modes of saving, 2 Sam. xxii.; Psal. xviii.

But will he be such a Saviour to me in my condition?

Yes; he expresses himself thus in the midst of threats; in that chapter of Isaiah just cited, ver. 22, he saith, "Look unto me, and be ye saved, all the ends of the earth:" even then when he threatens, look up to him as a Saviour above all. God magnifies this his title every day, to some in one manner, to some in another: time is coming when he will magnify this in saving them wholly from all evil.

Obs. 14. Though God does us more good than any, yet for our hearts not to be with him as with other things, is vile.

Obs. 15. Happy are they who have an interest in this God. If we have interest but in one man that is able to do us good, we bless ourselves in it.

Obs. 16. We are never safe but when our peace is made with God.

Obs. 17. Unless you pray to God as a God, having all power to save, you pray to an idol. Isa. xlv. 20, "They have no knowledge that set up the wood of their graven image, and pray unto a god that cannot save."

Obs. 18. God is not worshipped as God, but when he is worshipped as a Saviour. It is not to say God is our God, but to rely on him as a Saviour.

Ver. 5. *I did know thee in the wilderness, in the land of great drought.*

"The wilderness," where there grew not one grain of corn. You who were so poor in the wilderness, depending on me for every morsel of bread; yet after, when you were fed, how proud and wanton grew you! "But Jeshurun waxed fat, and kicked——then he forsook God which made him, and lightly esteemed the Rock of his salvation," Deut. xxxii. 15. In Ezek. xvi. 49, the Sodomites are condemned for behaving themselves contemptuously against the poor; but these do it against God.

God evidences this his knowledge and acknowledgment of them as his people, in leading them through the wilderness, by several instances and expressions: he takes notice of this wilderness, Deut. viii. 15, "Who led thee through that great and terrible wilderness;" *Luctus ubique pavor, et plurima mortis imago.* He knew them as "a peculiar treasure above all people; a kingdom of priests, an holy nation," Exod. xix. 5, 6. "He kept him as the apple of his eye;" as an eagle beareth her young ones on her wings, "so the Lord alone did lead him," Deut. xxxii. 10—12. They "lacked nothing," chap. ii. 7. He led them "with his glorious arm," Isa. lxiii. 12.

Now God knew them in the wilderness, 1. In respect of their sin, which he visited. 2. In regard of their wants, which he provided for. We may connect both thus:

They went three days and found no water; and when they found it, it was so bitter they could not drink of it. Then he sweetened it by a miracle, Exod. xv. 22, 23, 25. Then in the wilderness of Sin they complained that the whole assembly would be slain with hunger; then came manna, a rain of manna, Exod. xvi. They loathed manna, and then quails were sent, Numb. xi. They "pitched in Rephidim, and there was no water," so that they were "almost ready to stone" Moses; then water out of the rock is given them, Exod. xvii. 1—6. But, ver. 8, "Then came Amalek and fought with Israel:" when Moses held up his hand Israel prevailed; and when Moses's hands hung down Amalek prevailed; at last Joshua discomfited them, ver. 9—13. Exod. xviii., Jethro is sent to refresh them, with Moses' wife, and his two sons; and chap. xix., xx., God gives them his law. Numb. xii., Miriam and Aaron contend with Moses: that sedition God rebukes. Numb. xiii., spies being sent, they discourage the people, yet God leads them on. Numb. xvi., Korah, Dathan, and Abiram conspire, upon which the earth opens and swallows up the rebels. "But," ver. 41, "on the morrow all the congregation," a hundred forty and seven thousand, murmur against Moses and Aaron for it; upon which the plague comes. They had other idols besides the calf, Amos v. 25, 26; Acts vii. 42, 43. Numb. xxi., "King Arad the Canaanite fought against Israel, and took some of them prisoners." Ver. 5, Their souls loathe manna, fiery serpents are sent. Ver. 23, Sihon, king of the Amorites, comes out against them and fights. Ver. 33, Og, the king of Bashan, goes out against them. Chap. xxii., Balak sends Balaam to curse them. Chap. xxv., The people "commit whoredom with the daughters of Moab," and go "unto the sacrifices of their gods" at Baal-peor, upon which a plague ensues. Chap. xxxi., They war with Midian, slay their five kings, destroy their cities, women, children, flocks, thirty-two thousand women that had not known man they take captive. And in this war they lost not one man, ver. 49. Now our observations are:

Obs. 1. Man's wickedness strangely contrasts with God's goodness: God knew their sin and yet destroyed them not; they receive mercies and yet sin.

Obs. 2. It is a great mercy for God to know a man in time of distress. This is God's way. Men know in prosperity; but let us make God our friend, he will be a friend otherwise than men will be.

Obs. 3. We should not be dejected in times of trouble; that is the time for God to know thee: be willing to follow God in any estate.

Obs. 4. God's knowing us in distress is a mighty engagement. Let us look back to the times when we were in trouble.

Obs. 5. Let us know God's cause when it suffers, and know our brethren in their sufferings.

Obs. 6. God's knowledge is operative and working; it does us good. Our knowledge of God should be so too. To sin against our knowledge of God is evil, but to sin against God's knowledge of us is worse.

Ver. 6. *According to their pasture, so were they filled; they were filled, and their heart was exalted; therefore have they forgotten me.*

You heard in the preceding verse of the gracious providence of God towards his people while they were in the wilderness: "I did know thee in the wilderness, in the land of great drought." God glories much, and mentions often, his care over, and goodness to, his people in the wilderness. When they had got out of the wilderness into the land of Canaan, where there was much pasture, they thought themselves to be well, that now they could live of themselves; and so they lived to themselves, and in a little time destroyed themselves: the truth is, they were in a worse condition then than when they were in the wilderness, for, saith he, "According to their pasture, so were they filled; they were filled, and their heart was exalted; therefore have they forgotten me. Therefore I will be unto them as a lion: as a leopard by the way will I observe them: I will meet them as a bear that is bereaved of her whelps."

We do not hear such terrible things against them when they were in the wilderness.

"I did know thee in the wilderness," but now it is otherwise.

From the connexion note first,

Obs. 1. It is better to want the comforts of the creature, and to have God's protection, than to have abundance of the creature, and depend on ourselves. We do not love a dependent life, but it is safest; many have more of God's presence with them, and protection over them, when they are in the wilderness, when they are in adversity, than they have when they come into prosperity, when they come to enjoy abundance of the creature: God knows them when they are in afflictions, and they know God; but when they become prosperous, God neither knows them so much, nor they know God so much.

Examine, I beseech you, when you were low; say, had you not more of God's presence with you then than you have now? Did not God know you more then? did not you know God more then? had you not more sweet communion in those times than you have now? Oh, God made you know him by gracious visitations of his Spirit, and there were gracious workings of your spirit towards him. Are not you grown flat, dead, drossy, and carnal now more than before? do not you seek greedily after the world to fill yourselves therewith? and do not you begin to be exalted in your own hearts? do not you begin to be puffed up? have you no friends that are so? If you know but any of your friends that, when they were lower than they now are, knew God better than now they do, and God knew them, and there was more sweet converse between God and them, put them in mind of this text: "I did know thee in the wilderness, in the land of great drought. According to their pasture, so were they filled; they were filled, and their heart was exalted; therefore have they forgotten me." God deliver them from the remaining part of the text, "I will be unto them as a lion; as a leopard by the way;—as a bear that is bereaved of her whelps." You seldom find in Scripture any of God's saints worse for afflictions; give me any one example: for my part, I know not one in all the book of God that came worse out of an affliction than when they went in; but I can tell you of many, even of God's dear people, that came worse out of prosperity than when they came in. Therefore it is observable in 2 Chron. xvii. 3, it is said in commendation of Jehoshaphat, that he walked in "the first ways" of David his father. David his father at first was in an afflicted estate, afterwards in a more prosperous condition; he was hunted like a partridge at first, but when he came to prosperity his ways were not so good, therefore the Holy Ghost puts a commendation on his "first ways" rather than upon his after ways. I fear it may be said so of some, that their first ways, when they were low, were a great deal better than their after ways. This for the connexion.

"According to their pasture, so were they filled." According to the fatness and riches of the land when they came into it they were filled; they fell upon whatever sensual pleasure they could enjoy to the uttermost of their means. They would improve all the means and opportunities they had to give contentment to the flesh; "so were they filled." Thus you see men that love to live in the gratification of the flesh up to the height of their means, will be sure to have satisfaction if possible; if they go abroad and see any thing that may give content to the flesh, they resolve to have it if they can when they come home. According to all the means that they have, so they will have the flesh satisfied. How happy were men if they were so wise for their souls, if according to the means of grace we sought to fill our souls! Oh, how does the Lord lead us in green pastures, and yet what empty souls have we!

"According to their pasture, so were they filled." But can we say, that according to the green pastures in which God leads us, so are we filled? We live in green pastures, and yet are we empty. Here we see that men regard their bodies, regard the sensual pleasures of the flesh abundantly more than spiritual, as if there were a greater good in sensual delights than there is in all spiritual comforts.

"According to their pasture, so were they filled; they were filled." Twice we have "filled."

A little will serve man's desires in spiritual things, but they will fill, and fill themselves again, in things sensual.

It notes the greediness of their spirits in falling upon those contentments which they had for the flesh. When they came into a fertile land "they were filled; they were filled:" such is the nature of carnal men, to fall with greediness on creature-comforts, and to think on nothing but filling themselves, filling, filling. In Psal. lxxviii. 29, you may see what their disposition was; even before they came into their fat pastures, when God but in the wilderness granted them flesh, "they did eat," saith the text, "and were well filled." So it is in your books, but the force of the Hebrew is, they were filled very much, they were filled exceedingly, they filled themselves to the uttermost. Prov. xxiii. 5, well describes the greediness of men's hearts after carnal contentments; "Wilt thou set thine eyes upon that which is not?" speaking of riches: thus it is in your books, "Wilt thou set thine eyes upon that which is not?" but the more correct translation is, Wilt thou make thine eyes to fly upon that which is not? When a carnal heart sees any opportunity of enjoying carnal contentments, he makes his eyes to fly upon them, to fly upon them with eagerness: great is the greediness of a carnal heart!

"According to their pasture, so were they filled."

They thought of nothing but filling themselves, whereas other thoughts should have mingled with their self-gratification, when God brought them into their fat pastures. True, we may enjoy what God gives us; yea, but we must not only seek to fill ourselves, but we are to labour to mix such thoughts as these with the good things which we enjoy. As thus, now:

1. Here I enjoy abundance of good in the creature; whence have I all this? is it not from God? They did not think of this, so be it they might fill themselves. As the swine under the acorn tree seeks to fill the belly, but never looks from whence the acorns come; so carnal hearts fill themselves, but never look whence the blessings come; whereas a gracious heart takes the comforts of the creature that God affords, but, while it is receiving them, it looks up to God the principal of all.

2. What do I think God aims at? God gives me abundance of the creature, but what is God's end? is it only to satisfy my flesh? has God no further end than this?

3. I now possess these contentments, but what opportunities have I by these to do good more than before? Surely these are not given me merely to pamper the flesh, but are given me as large opportunities of service for God.

4. Now I enjoy abundance. What is the rule that God has set in the word for the ordering of my heart in the time of plenty?

5. I have much now in the world more than before; but oh my unworthiness! how unworthy am I of these comforts! unworthy of the least morsel of bread, and yet my table is furnished, and I am filled. Carnal hearts fall upon their dishes, and pour down their full cups, and never think of their unworthiness, how unworthy *they* are of the least drop of water.

6. God gives me abundance of the creature; but what is it that makes the difference between me and others? Some others are empty enough, their bellies are empty, their houses empty, their cupboards empty; but I am filled: why should God deal thus with me rather than with others?

7. I enjoy abundance here in the creature; but is there not danger, is there not a snare in the possession? Have not I a naughty, vile heart? How if these should prove to be temptations to me to draw my heart from God? were I not better without them? In the Epistle of Jude, ver. 12, it is spoken of as an evidence of carnality, that they feast, "feeding themselves without fear;" they fall upon what is before them and fill themselves, but "without fear:" whereas we should never enjoy fulness in the world, but with fear; fear of the snare that there may be in the abundance.

8. I have abundance; but what uncertainty is there in all these things! I have it now, but how quickly may it be gone; these things taken from me, or I from them!

9. I have much, and therefore I have a great account to give to God of these my pastures; this my fulness will make my account so much the greater.

10. I have much: oh, but, considering how little service I do for God, may not I fear that this which I have is to be my portion?

11. Do not many obligations attend on my possession? That fulness which I have, does it not more fully engage me unto God than others? Carnal hearts are void of these thoughts in the enjoyment of their fulness, they care not, so be it they can but fill themselves, how they get, or how they use their abundance.

O my brethren, our hearts should be filled with these thoughts in our fulness; but it is with most as in Isa. lvi. 12, "Come ye, say they, I will fetch wine, and we will fill ourselves with strong drink; and to-morrow shall be as this day, and much more abundant:" there is all that they care for.

Those especially fall most greedily upon carnal contentments that have been kept short a long time. So it was here.

"I did know thee in the wilderness, in the land of great drought. According to their pasture, so were they filled." "They were filled," they minded nothing but filling themselves, they gormandized; as it is usual with them that have lived very sparingly and meanly before, if they come to a full diet they fill themselves so greedily, as even sometimes to distemper themselves, and occasion plagues and grievous diseases: when a man has fasted to starving almost, he had need be very careful what he does when he comes to a full table. Physicians will not suffer men that have fasted long to eat much: it brings many diseases on soldiers and others, because sometimes they want much, and sometimes they have abundance, and so they spoil themselves; as we read of Saul's men, that they fell upon the cattle so that they did eat the blood. Oh let us take heed of this; it should be a seasonable lesson to those who have known what emptiness has meant in these times, and are now going into their countries again, and to enjoy their possessions: oh let them take heed how they fall upon the comforts of the creature greedily; they should rather prepare themselves beforehand, and season their hearts with those thoughts, that may keep them from the danger of fulness. And when they come to their houses and lands, and begin to stock them again, they should think, Oh, what were those sins of mine when I was here before in my house, and enjoyed fulness! how little honour had God by my abundance before! Let me now remember all my murmurings and repinings when God took away my estate, and let me seek to make peace with God even for them. In the time of my distress, I cried to God, and I was afraid that I should never enjoy my estate again; and has God given it to me? oh let me improve it better for his service than ever I have done. Such thoughts men should have when they come to their estates again, and not fall upon them as if they only sought to make up for interrupted pleasures, and thought of nothing else. There is a great deal of danger here, God has ways to make men cast out their sweet morsels when they regard nothing but the filling of themselves.

"And their heart was exalted."

This their fulness puffed them up: pride is a disease that ordinarily follows fulness. It is hard, saith Bernard, to be in honour without swelling. Pride is the disease of prosperity; so, Psal. lxxiii., David describes the prosperity of the wicked, and in ver. 6 adds, "Therefore pride compasseth them about as a chain; violence covereth them as a garment:" and hence that caveat of the apostle, 1 Tim. vi. 17, "Charge them that are rich in this world, that they be not high-minded." "Charge them," saith the apostle, for it is usual for men that are rich, that are full, to be high-minded. "Charge them, that they be not high-minded." Because,

Difficile est esse in honore sine tumore. Bern.

1. That these things in the world are great things in their eyes, yea, they are the only good things to a carnal heart; they are his happiness, and therefore he blesses himself in them, and is puffed up on account of them.

2. When they enjoy fulness in the world, then their lusts are satisfied, then they have fuel for their lusts, which makes them grow mighty high.

3. They can live of themselves and depend upon none, and this essentially puffs them up. In Psal. x. 5, speaking of proud men in prosperity, the psalmist saith, "As for all his enemies, he puffeth at them." They care for nobody in the world, they can live of themselves; others depend upon them, and they depend upon none, and this elates them.

4. They conceive some excellency in themselves. Why, they have more than others; as if it were because they had more excellency in themselves, and were more worthy than others; they are not common people, but are called out from among others as the prime and chief, as if there were more worth in them: this puffs them up.

5. They see all desire what they have; they see a great distance between them and others, and those that are under them do highly esteem them. "They call the proud happy;" the rich have many flatterers. "They were filled, and their heart was exalted," not only above men, but above God. Psal. lxxiii. 9, "They set their mouth against the heavens, and their tongue walketh through the earth." They will speak against every one when they are high themselves, scorning at the ways of God, and at his saints. When do wicked men that are of scornful spirits, scorn and speak most roughly against the people of God and his ways, but when they are filled? when at taverns they have filled themselves with wine and good cheer, then they scorn, and blaspheme, and "set their mouths against the heavens, and their tongues walk" throughout the city and country, against parliament, and all indiscriminately; their tongues are free when they are filled. Hence Psal. xxxv. 16, "With hypocritical mockers in feasts, they gnashed upon me with their teeth." In the time of their feasts, when they were filled, then they were "mockers," and "they gnashed upon me with their teeth." Abundance of evil is done by scorning and contemning at feasts; and in that respect their wine, with which they then fill themselves, may be called, as in Deut. xxxii. 33, "the poison of dragons, and the cruel venom of asps;" for as it fills their bodies with heat, so their spirits with rage and malice. And especially those who were heretofore

low, if they come to be filled, their hearts are most exalted. Oh the sad examples we have of this at this day! many not long since in a low and mean condition, having gotten places, they have got estates and power in their hands, oh how are their hearts exalted! Would you ever have thought to have lived to have seen such a change in their spirits as at this day? In how many ways do they discover their pride now they are promoted!

1. In their estrangement towards those that they were familiar with heretofore. They keep aloof from you; they are filled, and now their hearts are exalted.

2. Their carriage is very high and lofty; you must wait now if you would but speak to them.

3. Now they need no advice or counsel. They were wont to communicate themselves to you, and to be willing to hearken to advice and counsel; yea, but they are filled now, and their hearts are exalted, as if the exaltation of their estates put more wit into their heads.

4. Now they are harsh; to those that are under them they speak harshly and ruggedly, and care not for any under them. When they lived formerly among their neighbours, then they would complain of the harshness and rigidness of others, but since they are filled they are as harsh as any; and so before, when they were low, they cried out of oppression, but when they come once to be in place themselves, and to be filled, then they act as others: hence that in Psal. lxxiii. 8, "They speak wickedly concerning oppression: they speak loftily:" if you complain of oppression, they speak thus. It is spoken of wicked men in prosperity.

5. They show their pride. When they are filled they cannot bear contradiction now as they were wont, they cannot now endure reprehension.

6. Those mercies which not long since they would have highly prized, they now slight, they are now in their eyes as mean things.

7. All the use they make of what they enjoy now more than before, is to get higher and higher, for that alone they use it all. Those who have been low and mean in their estates, now they begin to be filled their hearts are exalted; and thus do they discover the exaltation of their hearts. Oh! but this is a great and a sore evil, for so it is rebuked by the prophet. O thou that hast thy heart exalted on being filled, it is a sign that thou hast a poor, low spirit of thine own, to be so lifted up with those things which thou dost enjoy.

For, 1. What low and mean things are they! What are they but crumbs that the Master of the family casts to dogs?

2. They are such things as make thee never a whit the better, nor the more excellent. Indeed it is said, that knowledge puffs up the heart, for it puts an excellency upon the man; but the heart of the wicked is little worth, let him have never so much prosperity.

3. Those things in which thou pridest thyself, are no other than may be, and have been, the portion of a reprobate. They are no other than may consist with God's eternal hatred of thee, and his eternal wrath against thee.

4. They are such things as may come from God's wrath, and like enough they do; and when thou art filled with, and thereby puffed up by them, it is a sign that there is a curse mixed with them. If a man comes to a table and eats, and then swells presently, God be merciful to me, am I poisoned? saith he. If thou fillest thyself, and art puffed up, it is an argument thy prosperity is poisoned, the curse of God is on it. Had not you rather have the coarsest diet, were it only wholesome, than the daintiest dish with poison in it? Is it not better to have the russet coat that is not dangerous, than a velvet coat that has the plague in it? Thy condition, if thou knewest it, may be was a great deal better before. Oh that any considerations might abate the elation of men's spirits, that are so puffed up with outward prosperity!

5. Thou art less filled with spiritual good than before; that which is substance thou hast lost, and thou art filled with wind.

6. Ere long what thou hast must be taken away.

7. Perhaps the right to what thou dost enjoy, is but the right that a malefactor has to his supper before the day of his execution.

8. The evil of any one sin is a greater evil than all thy prosperity is a good; if it but occasion any one sin to thee, it brings more evil upon thee than all the filling thou hast is good unto thee.

9. Thou art filled; but oftentimes it falls out so, that the very time for God to let out his wrath upon wicked men is when they are most filled. Job xx. 22 remarkably confirms this: "In the fulness of his sufficiency he shall be in straits:" it is an expression to be noted; they think they have sufficient now to live of themselves, but "in the fulness of their sufficiency they shall be in straits." And in ver. 23, "When he is about to fill his belly, God shall cast the fury of his wrath upon him." And in Psal. lxxviii. 29—31, "So they did eat, and were well filled: for he gave them their own desire; they were not estranged from their lust. But while their meat was yet in their mouths, the wrath of God came upon them, and slew the fattest of them." Oh, thy fulness is no cause for thee to lift up thy heart, for when thou art fullest, then is the time for God's hottest wrath to be let out upon thee, thine abundance but prepares thee for slaughter. How much better is it for the beast to feed on the common and live, than to be brought into fat pasture and prepared for the butcher! When thou wert feeding on the common, thou wert in a way of preservation; but now thou art come into the fat pasture, it is to prepare thee for slaughter: be not exalted then in thine own heart because of thy fulness.

10. It may be God has respect to others in thy fulness, it is not in regard to thee.

11. Hereafter thou mayst perhaps curse the time that ever such an estate befell thee, curse the time of thy fulness. Perhaps upon thy sick bed thou mayst lie and wish, Oh that I had kept my shop still, and been continued in my low condition! I had gone out of the world with a great deal less guiltiness than now I am like to appear before God with. Oh, be not exalted because thou art full.

"Therefore have they forgotten me." Proud men forget God; "The wicked, through the pride of his countenance, will not seek after God," Psal. x. 4. They have forgotten what need they had once of me, what cries they sent up to me, what moans they made before me; they have forgotten how gloriously I wrought for their deliverance, and all their consequent engagements to me; they have forgotten to acknowledge me, or sanctify my name, in all the good they enjoy. Oh, this is a sore and great, and yet an ordinary, evil; as soon as we have our turns served, God is minded no more. "They remembered not his hand, nor the day when he delivered them from the enemy," Psal. lxxviii. 42. Oh, it should have been in their memory, to have sanctified the name of God in their great deliverance; but when they were delivered they rememembered it not. "Call upon me in the time of trouble, and I will deliver thee, and thou shalt glorify me," saith God. We call upon God in the time of trouble, and God hears us, and delivers us, but the latter part is forgotten; and that soon too; "They soon forgat his works," saith Psal. cvi. 13: sometimes we forget before the work is quite accomplished. Oh! the Lord deliver us from this great evil. Shall I say, Deliver us? I may say, not deliver us *from* this evil only, but *out* of it, for it is upon us already. Oh the great things that God has done for this land within these six years! Never, since Joshua's or Moses's time, was there a story of God's working for a people so wonderful as the story of this last six years would be if faithfully recorded; and yet, though the Lord be going on in his ways of mercy towards us, we have forgotten. Oh, does it not appear so? What do men look after? Every man his own advantage and ends, seeking to fill themselves, minding nothing else. And what mighty haughtiness of spirit is there in many men within this six years! Oh how have we forgotten the Lord, forgotten those instruments that God has made use of for good to us! God had more honour from us when there was not the hundredth part done for us; now we (as it were) shake our ears, and, let God do as he will, we hope we can contrive to shift pretty well for ourselves. Oh! the Lord deliver this city out of, and from, this evil of forgetting the Lord when we are filled. Your trading is becoming more abundant now than formerly; now the country begins to be open, and they repair to the city for all. Oh, the Lord deliver this city from surfeiting by their fulness, and from this sin of forgetting the Lord. Oh that we could but say, That the Lord having restored the trading to the city, and that in a measure exceeding former experience, that we are resolved to sanctify the name of God more than ever we did. Oh! do you remember God every time you see customers come into your shops, every time you see the waggons come out of the country into your streets, do you bless God? and how is he therefore honoured among you? Oh that it were so! It is a sore and grievous evil to forget the Lord, after he has granted us fulness; it is a horrible ingratitude, as if there were nothing to be regarded but ourselves. And especially dangerous, because,

1. It is against many previous warnings of God. If you read Deut. vi. 10—12, and viii. 10—20, you shall find there how the Lord charges his people: "When the Lord thy God shall have brought thee into the land, when thou shalt have eaten and be full, then beware lest thou forget the Lord." "Then beware lest thou forget:" again and again this is inculcated, showing how prone we are to forget the Lord in our fulness. Oh that you, whom Providence has brought here this morning, would consider these scriptures! Now God is beginning to come in with more fulness than before; O, beware that you forget not the Lord God in the midst of your fulness; let there be as much or more prayer in your family than there was in former times, that you may have a sanctified use of the fulness which you now enjoy. Yea, to forget is worse than beastly. "The ox knoweth his owner, and the ass his master's crib; but Israel doth not know, my people doth not consider." If the ox be but fed, he knows his owner. Who is it that feeds you? Is it not the Lord? and will you forget him? Oh! this will lose the blessing of all you enjoy, and your hearts will grow wicked beyond what you can imagine; you cannot imagine the evil that your hearts will grow to, if you forget God in the enjoyment of that estate in which God sets you.

2. It is a sin that God knows not how to pardon. For so he expresses himself, Jer. v. 7, "How shall I pardon thee for this!" As if he should say, Though I be a God of infinite mercy, yet here is a sin I know not how to pardon. Why, saith he, when I had fed them to the full, they committed adultery, and they abused that fulness. Oh! "how shall I pardon thee for this?"

3. If ever you have need of God again, how will conscience be stopped? With what face could you go to God again for help, if brought low? conscience will presently say, You were once empty and God filled you, and what honour had God from you? No, your hearts were exalted, and you forgot God.

4. To forget the Giver in the enjoyment of his gifts, is most foolish. We depend upon God in the midst of all our fulness as much as before, every moment we lie at God's mercy; though perhaps you are not sensible of it, yet certainly it is so.

5. Your forgetting God will make you forget yourselves; and just it may be with God to forget you, and to change the course of his administration towards you. Oh! take heed then of being exalted, and of forgetting the Lord, in your fulness.

Truly, brethren, God had rather have his people fall into almost any sin than pride, and consequent forgetfulness of him. Therefore you find in Scripture, that God will rather set the devil upon his people, than have their hearts exalted. As Paul, lest he should be lifted up above measure, he had a thorn in the flesh, the buffeting of Satan. God had rather see the devil buffet his people than see their hearts exalted.

Yea, he had rather suffer them to fall into any other sin. Charge your souls, then, against this, as David; "Bless the Lord, O my soul, and all that is within me, bless his holy name; bless the Lord, O my soul, and forget not all his benefits," Psal. ciii. 1, 2. See what a charge he puts upon his soul; "O my soul," thou hast received many benefits from the Lord, and there is this deadness in thee; if but left to thyself, thou wilt forget the Lord, and this will be a sore evil in thee; "bless, then, the Lord, O my soul, and forget not all his benefits." Oh that you would go home and charge your souls not to forget the Lord and all his benefits! let husband put wife in mind with this charge, and wife the husband, but especially yourselves in secret, between God and yourselves, to charge your souls not to forget his benefits. On the contrary, the more we remember God in our blessings they will be,

1. The more sweet to us. You have a great many mercies, but when you forget God you lose the very sweetness of all your mercies. Oh! when you can see a mercy, and see the God of that mercy, then it is sweet: when I can see a mercy, and the fountain from whence it comes, and whither it tends, then the mercy is sweet: oh! therefore you deal foolishly in forgetting the Lord.

2. The more safe.

3. The more eminent will we be in grace. Oh what a lovely object is it to behold a man or woman heavenly and spiritual in the midst of all outward enjoyments! I say, the graces of such do indeed glister like diamonds, like most precious pearls; and therefore, remember the Lord in all the good things that you enjoy.

Ver. 7. *Therefore I will be unto them as a lion: as a leopard by the way will I observe them.*

Most dreadful expressions follow here. God is exceedingly provoked with the exaltation of men's hearts, and their forgetfulness of him in prosperity.

Is this the same God that spake so of Ephraim heretofore? "Is Ephraim my dear son?" Ephraim "my pleasant child." "How shall I give thee up, Ephraim?" "mine heart is turned within me;" "ever since I spake against him, I do earnestly remember him still," and "my repentings are kindled together." Is this the Lord that now will be "as a lion," "a leopard," "a bear bereaved of her whelps," "a wild beast," unto Ephraim? What! is this the God that heretofore carried them as eagles do their young upon their wings, and nourished them as the eagle nourisheth her young ones? Is this the God that was as a gracious father unto them, to whom this people were as "the dearly beloved of God's soul;" and now God "a lion," "a leopard," "a bear bereaved of her whelps," "a wild beast to tear them?" Is this the merciful God? Is it thus *that* God appears who is love and mercy itself? O my brethren, how dreadful does sin render God to his creature! But all this while there is no change in God's heart; God is the same in himself as before; the change is in the creature. The sun that softens the wax, the same sun hardens the clay. The same blessed, infinite, glorious Being, that does good to his creature in one condition, is in another aspect dreadful to the creature. "With an upright man thou wilt show thyself upright, and with the froward thou wilt show thyself froward," Psal. xviii. 25, 26. Above all, God sets himself out in a most terrible manner against those whose hearts in prosperity were exalted and forgot him.

Obs. 1. The Lord pities men, yea, sinful men, in the time of their adversity; but when they are at the height, and forget him, his anger is especially hot against them. I will cite one passage to show how God has regard to men in low conditions; but against those that are fatted up in prosperity, his anger burns most fiercely. Ezek. xxxiv. 16, "I will seek that which was lost, and bring again that which was driven away, and will bind up that which was broken, and will strengthen that which was sick: but I will destroy the fat and the strong; I will feed them with judgment." "That which was lost," "I will seek;" "that which was broken," "I will bind up;" "that which was sick," "I will heal;" but "I will destroy the fat and the strong; I will feed them with judgment." Here surely is a scripture full of comfort for the hearts of those that are in an afflicted condition. See how God regards such; but God has not such regard to "the fat and the strong," he "will feed them with judgment," and destroy them. The care and protection of God is more over the lost ones, and the broken ones, and the sick ones, than the fat ones and the strong ones; they are to be fed with judgment. "I will be to them as a lion;" and the reasons of this are,

1. Their hearts are very much hardened in their sin, their sin is grown to a height.

2. There are so many creatures that they have use of more than others, that do cry against them. Poor people have not so many creatures to cry against them as the rich have.

3. They can make friends to avoid the stroke of justice from men, but the poor fall under it unpitied; therefore God takes them into his hands and deals with them more severely.

4. When judgment comes upon them it is more observed, and therefore God to them will be "as a lion."

"As a lion." You have a parallel passage in Psal. l. 22, "Consider this, ye that forget God, lest I tear you in pieces, and there be none to deliver." Their hearts were exalted, they forgot God, "therefore I will be unto them as a lion."

1. A lion is the most terrible creature. "The lion hath roared, who will not fear?" Amos iii. 8. O my brethren, the threats of God should be to us as the roaring of a lion, and our hearts should tremble at them.

2. None can take away the prey from a lion. "As a young lion among the flocks of sheep; who, if he go through, both treadeth down, and teareth in pieces, and none can deliver," Micah v. 8. None can deliver out of God's hand.

3. A lion is strong, and crushes at once the whole compages of a man's bones. Alas! man, what is he? In Job iv. 19, he is said to be "crushed before the moth;" much more then before a lion: oh, then, much more before the Lord God when he comes as a lion!

4. The lion will narrowly mark any one that wounds her. If there were hundreds of men together, and one did but shoot at or wound her, she will be sure to mark that man. The Lord marks out those that sin against him, and that wound his name; they must not think to escape among others. The Lord's eye is upon them particularly.

5. The lion sleeps but little, and with her eyes open. So the Lord. As "he that keepeth Israel neither slumbereth nor sleepeth," Psal. cxxi. 4; so he that destroys his enemies does not slumber nor sleep.

6. The lion will fall upon no creature except from hunger or provocation. The Lord, though his wrath be terrible as a lion, yet is not so ready to fall upon his creature; it must be for some special end, or from some provocation, but then he falls terribly indeed.

7. It is observed of the lion, that if you do but fall down on the ground, and submit and yield, it will pass by, and will not tear and rend where there is a humble submission, whereas other creatures will. Oh! thus God is a lion, terrible, but yet only to those that stand out against him.

8. The naturalists observe of the lion, that it cannot endure to be looked asquint upon by any. Thus it is with the Lord; the Lord loves no squint-eyed Christians, I mean, none that have by-ends of their own: the Lord loves uprightness in our ways and dealings.

9. They say of the lion, that it is a great enemy to apes and wolves. So is God to flatterers and tyrants. Thus God is compared to a lion.

"As a leopard by the way will I observe them." כנמר על־דרך אשור The Seventy render this *κατά την ὁδὸν 'Ασσυρίων*, by the way of the Assyrian: so the Vulgate and Jerome.

The she-leopard is the same as that which they call a panther; and the Lord compares himself to it, because,

1. It is so fierce, that it presently flies in the face of a man. "As a leopard," I will fly in the very faces of such; such manifest much pride in their faces, and I will fly in their very faces, saith God.

Plin. lib. 10. cap. 37. Ælian. lib. 2. cap. 23. Scalig. Exerc. 208.

2. It is a very swift creature, Hab. i. 8. So the Lord will swiftly come against wicked and ungodly men, "as a leopard," swiftly, and overtake them.

3. A leopard watches its prey, being very subtle, to observe the fit times and opportunities to fall upon the prey. So the text, "As a leopard by the way will I observe them:" this strongly intimates the fearful wrath of God against wicked men. As in Jer. v. 6, "A leopard shall watch over their cities." I say there is much of God's wrath in this, it is very terrible; the Lord sets his infinite wisdom on work to watch fit times and opportunities to let out his wrath upon ungodly men. "I will watch over them for evil," as in another scripture is threatened. Those are truly in a sad condition whom the Lord watches over for evil: God watches over his people for good; but such as, when they are full, exalt themselves and forget the Lord, God watches over them for evil: they should be destroyed soon; But, saith God, I have a fitter time than now, wherein I will both get myself a greater name, and it shall be worse for them; in due time shall their feet slide. This is the reason why men live so long in their prosperity, and go on and satisfy their wills, because God is watching over them, and his time is not yet come.

4. When the leopard comes upon its prey, it leaps upon it suddenly. And so does the Lord to ungodly men; he comes in an hour that they expect not, and leaps upon them. And therefore you must not think that you are as well, because you are in as safe a condition, as you were a year or seven years since. It is as well with me, saith one, as it has been with me in all my life-time. What then? you may be never a whit the further off from dangers, for the way of God in bringing his wrath is many times sudden.

5. The leopard sometimes will sleep a very long time, even three days together, but after it awakes it is more fierce than before. And so the Lord, though sometimes he may be patient towards sinners, yet, when he comes to awake out of his sleep, he is more terrible:

"Then the Lord awaked as one out of sleep. And he smote his enemies in the hinder part: he put them to a perpetual reproach," Psal. lxxviii. 65, 66.

Ver. 8. *I will meet them as a bear that is bereaved of her whelps, and will rend the caul of their heart, and there will I devour them like a lion: the wild beast shall tear them.*

The third creature is the bear: "I will meet them as a bear that is bereaved of her whelps."

Ælian. lib. 5. cap. 14. Plin. lib. 8. cap. 36.

This creature is very fierce and terrible; accordingly we read in 2 Kings ii. 24, "There came forth two she-bears out of the wood, and tare forty and two children of of them." "Let a bear robbed of her whelps meet a man, rather than a fool in his folly," Prov. xvii. 12. She is fierce at all times, but above all, if she be "robbed of her whelps." It is observed that no creature loves her young ones more than the bear, and yet they are the most deformed of any; an emblem, it may be, of a man that loves his own deformed fancies. One interpreter remarks upon it: Oh, how will the Lord be in a holy rage, if his children be wronged, his own children, who bear his image; when the instinct of nature in this creature, the bear, incites it to such rage when she is robbed of such ugly things as her whelps are! 2 Sam. xvii. 8, saith Hushai to Absalom, "Thou knowest thy thy father and his men, that they be mighty men, and they be chafed in their minds, as a bear robbed of her whelps in the field." Thus the Scripture often compares exceeding fierceness and rage, to the fierceness of "a bear that is bereaved of her whelps;" therefore it is added here,

"And will rend the caul of their heart, and there will I devour them like a lion." Here he mentions the lion the second time. The word in your books is the same, but in the original it is somewhat different.

As the lion is named here the second time, we may observe, that when it comes on its prey it rends the body asunder, and loves to suck the blood and the fat that is about the heart; and as for the other parts, except in extreme hunger, it leaves them for other beasts to prey upon; but the heart, and the blood, and the fat about the heart, the lion loves to suck. And therefore saith God here, "I will rend the caul of their heart, and there will I devour them like a lion."

Luther well observes on this, The Lord here will do as a lion does, he more immediately will strike out their hearts, and punish them with spiritual plagues and judgments; and as for their estates and bodies, he will leave them to other beasts, and they shall plague them and punish them that way: they had a film upon their hearts, and instructions could not reach them; but God will tear that caul, will tear that film from off their hearts that kept off instructions. Oh! let us take heed of this that keeps out of our hearts the word of God, take heed of that for ever, for God has ways to tear this film from off thy heart.

As Bernard, putting his finger on his brother's side, who was a soldier, and disregarded his good instructions and admonitions, said, One day a spear shall make way to this heart for instructions and admonitions to enter: so I may say to such whose hearts have a film upon them, that what the preacher saith cannot find entrance, God may justly come and rend this caul from off thy heart that keeps out the admonitions of his word. Arias Montanus notes, that it may refer to the sending the plague upon their hearts, and leaving their estates and comforts to the Assyrians.

"The wild beast shall tear them." Why, did he not name wild beasts enough before? There was "the lion," and "the leopard," and "the bear," and "the lion" again, and yet he adds, "the wild beast;" as if he should say, If there be any terror, any dreadfulness, in any wild beasts whatsoever, there is that in my wrath, if you escape one wild beast another shall tear you; and now he comes to all wild beasts; put them all together, and such is the fierceness of my wrath. There arises from hence one excellent observation:

Obs. All the dreadfulness of all creatures in the world combined meets in the wrath of God. As all the good that is in all creatures together is in the love and mercy of God; so all things that can in any way bring any torment on, or torture to us, and the quintessence of all this is in God's wrath: "The wild beast shall tear them."

Lyra thinks that this prophecy was fulfilled when they were carried captive, and in their journey many died, and so they were cast into fields and devoured by wild beasts: and it is likely it may be fulfilled in part so; as usually, when soldiers carry an enemy captive, they throw them, if they be sick unto death, with little concern into a ditch, that is all they care for them. And so it was with this people; the Lord, though he knew them in the wilderness, and his protection was over them, yet now forgets them, and lets them be carried into captivity, and cast to wild beasts to tear and devour.

Some think that the expression of God's wrath by these beasts, has reference to the four monarchies, which God would make use of to be very terrible to his saints. In Dan. vii. you find the four monarchies of the world, the Babylonian, the Persian, the Grecian, and Roman monarchies, set forth in the same manner, as here the Holy Ghost sets out the wrath of God against Israel; for the truth is, those things that we have here in Hosea were to set forth God's ways to his people in after-times, and not merely when they were to be carried captive. In Dan. vii. 3, there appeared four great beasts; the first like a lion, by which was signified the Babylonish empire; the second like a bear, the Persian; the third like a leopard, the Grecian; for Alexander was as a leopard, exceeding swift, all his exploits he performed in twelve years, and was but thirty-three years old when he died. Moreover, they observe of the leopard, (which is named from a panther,) that its body smells exceeding sweet above all beasts; of Alexander's body, too, it was said, that it had a peculiarly sweet smell. Then the fourth being the Roman empire, mark how it is imaged, just as God here sets out his wrath; he names not any particular beast, but describes it as "dreadful and terrible, and strong exceedingly; and it had great iron teeth: it devoured and brake in pieces, and stamped the residue with the feet of it: and it was diverse from all the beasts that were before it; and it had ten horns." You know now that that was divided into ten kingdoms, or ten sorts of civil governments at several times.

Panthera, hinc leopardus. Arist. Histor. Animal. lib. 9. cap. 6.

Sleid. de quat. Imperiis. lib. 3.

This is the Roman empire, the power of which antichrist was to have; by both which the Lord would exercise his people, and be very terrible to his people, especially those people of his that were apostatizing people, that would worship him according to their own ways: God would be thus terrible to them wherever they lived; under any of the former empires, they should have God either as a lion, a leopard, a bear, or like this last-mentioned dreadful creature.

But you will say, Why do you speak thus? Or it may be people would speak thus to the prophet, O, why do you speak of God in this terrible manner? Is not our God a gracious and a merciful God? why then will you render God thus terrible? In answer the prophet saith:

Ver. 9. *O Israel, thou hast destroyed thyself; but in me is thine help.*

O, do not find fault with the dreadfulness of God, that God appears thus clothed in terrors to you; and do not blame the ministers of God, that they represent God in this dreadful manner before you. Though it is true, that God appears ready to destroy you, yet still the Lord is infinite, holy, and blessed, and a God of mercy and goodness in himself: "O Israel, thou hast destroyed thyself," thou mayst thank thyself for all this. Many of you, when you hear the terrors of God set before you, perhaps your hearts rise against them, and your spirits exceedingly loathe such manifestations. Why then do ministers make God appear so terrible, when he is such a merciful and gracious God? O, rather lay thy hand upon thine own heart and say, God indeed is thus gracious and merciful, but it is my wickedness arrays God in terrors. The judgments of God are called "strange things," because God delights not in the execution of wrath, in appearing like "a lion," "a leopard," and "a bear." That which pleases the heart of God, is to appear as a Father to do good to his people; but, "O Israel, thou hast destroyed thyself."

Obs. 1. This will one day aggravate men's judgments, that they are themselves the cause of all the evils which they suffer. You may think to put it over on God, and say, Oh how dreadful is God's justice! but God knows how to put it all upon yourselves. The destruction of sinners will appear to be from themselves; God will clear it up to all the world, before men and angels, and will clear it up to men's own consciences: the damned in hell shall not be able to speak against God's justice at all, but shall be forced to charge themselves with all the evil that is upon them: Oh! it was through this wretched, vile, and wicked heart of mine; God was not wanting to me in any means of good, but I had a rebellious heart, and I have brought all this evil upon myself; I have destroyed myself.

"O Israel, thou hast destroyed thyself." Destroyed himself! did not God, in the words immediately before, say, that he would "meet them as a bear that is bereaved of her whelps," and "rend the caul of their heart," that he would be as "a lion" to them, and as "a leopard?" and yet here he saith, "O Israel, thou hast destroyed thyself!"

Obs. 2. Though God makes use of instruments to execute severe wrath on a people, yet their destruction is to be attributed to themselves. "O Israel, thou hast destroyed thyself," thou mayst thank thyself for all this.

Perdidit te, Israel. Calv.

The original שחתך ישראל is by some rendered differently; by Calvin and many others, It has destroyed thee, Israel.

The old English translation, wherein Beza's (the Geneva) notes are, renders it, one has destroyed them: the word may be so translated; one has destroyed them, or, it has destroyed them, or, somewhat has destroyed them; as if God should say, Not I, but somewhat else has destroyed them.

Perdidit te rex tuus. Trem.

Tremelius translates it, thy king has destroyed thee; for so the context will bear. "Has destroyed us" (so are the words.) Has? what has? Why your king has destroyed you, saith Tremelius. Most of the Hebrews complete it thus, your calf has destroyed you, your idols have destroyed you. Aben Ezra, your feigned comforts have destroyed you. Drusius reads it interrogatively, Who has destroyed thee? Your fulness, of which ver. 6, or your own heart and wickedness, have destroyed you. The Greek thus, Τῇ διαφθορᾶ τοῦ Ισραὴλ τὶς βοηθήσει, Who shall give help to the corruption of Israel? Though the words be read so diversely, yet most agree in giving them the same meaning as your books; your own wickedness has destroyed you; your sinful, ungodly, idolatrous living, forsaking God and his ways, and putting confidence in an arm of flesh, that has destroyed thee.

Vitulus tuus. Rabb.

Consolatio fictitia Ab. Ezr.

Corrupit te. Drus.

"But in me is thine help." Those words are somewhat different in the original, for there are two ins, כי־בי בעזרך in me, in thy help. And so you may observe, that in your Bibles *is* is printed in a different character, which notes that it is not directly according to the original. In me, in thy help.

Drusius on the text saith, In me, in thy help; that is, I am in thy help, and thy help is in me. This seems to be according to the intention of the Holy Ghost, Whatsoever help thou hast, I am in it, and thy help it is in me. "In me is thine help."

Ego in auxilio tuo, et auxilium tuum est in me. Drus.

Pareus reads it, against thy help, and so supplies the word, thou hast rebelled against thy help. Thou hast destroyed thy help; why? because thou hast rebelled against thy help. The original will bear this, against thy help.

Quod in me in auxiliatorem rebellasti. Pareus.

But the other more full and general interpretation, and more in accordance with the original, is, thy help is wholly in me, and I am wholly in thy help; thou hast destroyed thyself, but thy help is wholly in me. This shall suffice for the reading of the words. Now for the several truths that are to be here held forth to us out of them.

Obs. 2. Men would fain put off their evils from themselves to God. Men are naturally loth to charge themselves with the evil that comes upon them, it is their ill hap, their ill fortune, their ill luck; or they could not help it, they did what they could; and so think to attribute it all to God; it is for want of means, for want of this or that thing which God denied to them, it is because God put them into such and such a condition; but never come to charge themselves. But the prophet speaks here in a compassionate way; O Israel, (saith he,) never stand charging it upon God, "thou hast destroyed thyself."

Obs. 3. God knows how to turn all the evil upon ourselves. Though we may think to lessen our evil by putting it upon God, God will turn it all upon our own heads, and make it clear to all the world that we were the cause of all the evils that were upon us, both temporal evils, and those evils that shall come upon such as shall perish eternally. It will be one of the great works at the day of judgment, to make it manifest to men and angels, that all the misery that comes upon the damned is from themselves; their own consciences will acknowledge it, and God will be justified before all: it will be found that the cause of man's perdition is not in the decree of God; God's decree damns none; their sin damns them, not the decree. For,

1. The decree of reprobation is but the leaving men to be dealt with in a way of justice. Whereas saith God, Here are some upon whom I am resolved to magnify my grace to all eternity, whatsoever comes between to hinder it, I am resolved that these shall be subjects for me to exercise my grace on to all eternity; that is election: but there are others whom I will leave to a way and course of justice, they shall have what they earn, and no otherwise. So that the decree is not the cause of men's damnation; their sin comes in between that and their damnation, so that they destroy themselves.

2. It infuses not any evil into them. You will say, Sin comes in between decree and damnation; but how comes sin in? Certainly not by any infusion from God, but by man himself, man himself is its author.

3. It is not by any coaction. You will say, Though sin in men is the cause of it, yet men cannot help it, men cannot but sin. Now to reply: 1. Man sins as freely as if he could do otherwise. God made man in

such a condition that he might not have sinned; and though it is now true that, through their fall, men cannot do that which is good, they cannot but sin, "having eyes full of adultery and that cannot cease from sin," as the apostle saith of some, yet they sin as freely as if they had power to keep from sin; sin pleases their wills, it is suitable to them: so it is true that the saints in heaven cannot but glorify God, but yet they glorify God with freedom too; they are so set in an estate of glory, that they cannot sin, but yet they honour God freely, that is, in honouring God they do that which is suitable to their own spirits. 2. Every sinner that perishes, murders himself. All that are damned eternally, all of them are self-murderers: this is a grievous thing: "O Israel, thou hast destroyed thyself." The more there is of self in men's destruction, the more grievous is their condition. It would make our hearts bleed to see a bird shot with an arrow feathered from its own body: all the judgments of God, all the arrows of the Almighty, that come against sinners, are as it were feathered by that which comes from sinners themselves, they are the cause of their own evils. The more self in sinners' destruction, the more hard is their condition. Self appears in sin,

1. When men bring misery upon themselves without any temptation. The less temptation, the more self: and some destroy themselves so, that it comes merely from themselves without any temptation.

2. When men's sins are plotted, contrived sins. The more plotting and contriving about sin, the more art thou the author of thine own evil or destruction.

3. When men sin, although warned beforehand of their sin. They are told beforehand of the evil, yet still are wilful in it, and will go on in it: such may thank themselves for their destruction.

4. When men, notwithstanding they are often stopped in their sin, and though God many times in the dispensations of his providence, and by his word, stays them in their course of sin, and yet still they *will* go on. Thank thyself if thou be undone.

5. The more means to the contrary they enjoy, the more enlightenings, the more drawings of the Holy Ghost to win them from their sin, and yet unavailingly.

6. When men's sins are of that nature, that they do not only deserve, but they actually work, their destruction. All sins deserve it, but some sins work it; as drunkenness, and some others which might be named; the very sin there destroys the sinner.

7. When men shall presume to venture further in any danger than they can help themselves out of. They think they will go but thus far, and no farther, and so they venture on beyond their power to help themselves; they destroy themselves.

Now this evil of self-destruction is so much the more grievous, when men destroy themselves in things in which they most bless themselves, in which they do most glory, and in which they promise to themselves the greatest good; if this proves to be their destruction, it is so much the more grievous. Oh, it is a sad thing to be a self-destroyer; for,

1. What pity can there be for such? Who will pity any who are the cause of all their own evil, who wilfully bring it upon themselves? You will say, Thank yourselves; who will pity you? Oh, this will be the condition of all that perish; neither God, nor angels, nor saints shall pity them; neither the father out of whose loins they came, nor the mother who bare them; they shall see that they have undone themselves.

2. The extreme vexation that there will be in men's spirits when they shall be convinced of this, when the Lord shall present to them all the means they have had, and all the mercies they have enjoyed, so that their consciences shall fly in their faces and tell them, You may thank yourselves for this, it was that wretched heart of thine that thou hast so talked of; I told you of this before; that pride, that hypocrisy, that *self-seeking*, and that falseness of thine, have brought thee to all this. Oh this will be an eternal vexation, it will be the matter for the worm to gnaw upon in hell hereafter, Oh, we have destroyed ourselves!

3. God will revenge this upon men; for no man has the power over himself; thou destroyest one of God's creatures in being a self-murderer, thou shalt be punished for destroying thyself. Because they have not the disposal of themselves, they are God's creatures. It is a greater sin for a man to murder himself, than his father or mother. Austin was wont to say, It is a greater sin than parricide, to be a self-murderer; and the reason he gives is, For the nearer the relation, the greater is the sin of the murder: as it is a greater sin for me to murder a kinsman than a stranger, a greater sin to murder a brother than a kinsman more remote, a greater sin to murder a father than a brother, so it is a greater sin for me to murder myself than my father; why? for I am nearer myself than my father: and so the sin is greater for any to lay violent hands upon themselves than upon another. You would think it a horrid thing if the devil were to come with a temptation, Go, take a halter and hang up your mother that bore you, or take a knife and cut your father's throat; but when you are tempted to murder yourselves the sin is still greater. Self-murder is a great evil, and yet all people in the world that perish are self-murderers. When we do but hear of a man that hangs or drowns himself, we think it is a very sad thing: now when you look upon wicked men going on in the ways of sin and destruction, look upon them as so many men running to drown themselves, and plunge themselves into the bottomless gulf; as so many men cutting their own throats, and hanging themselves, for so they assuredly do. Hence let us learn,

1. To charge ourselves with all the evil that is upon us. Do not so put it off, neither on God nor the devil, but charge ourselves still, for certainly we cause more evil to ourselves than all the devils in hell. *All the devils in hell could not undo us, if we did not undo ourselves.* We are ready to charge it upon wicked men, or temptations of the devil; and if not so, then upon God; for so you do, when any thinks to excuse his sin thus, God knows I do what I can: that is as much as if you should say, For my part, I am free of any evil that comes upon me, if I perish I am guiltless; I do what I can, and it is because God does not give me grace: thus you put it from yourselves on God. No, let us learn to charge ourselves with evil: a tender heart will take even that which is the devil's to himself, and a carnal heart will put over that which is from himself on the devil. Observe the difference between one that has a tender spirit, and another; when any temptation originating really with the devil comes, he presently charges his own heart, Oh what a wretched, vile heart have I! whereas it may be but mere suggestions and temptations of the devil, and not the steam and filth of his heart; but he judges his heart from those temptations, and thinks it is nothing but its uncleanness and filthiness. But you shall have another man that has a most filthy, wicked heart, and there come most abominable steams which break forth into foul diseases, and though it comes altogether from himself, yet saith he, The temptations of the devil lead me aside, and I cannot tell how to resist him. It is not from temptations, it is from thyself, from that wicked, unclean heart of thine; and were there no devils in hell at all, thou hast the seeds of all sin in thy heart, thine own uncleanness is their fruitful source.

2. To be afraid of ourselves, and to pray to God to be delivered from ourselves. *Better to be given up to the devil than to one's self.* You know the incestuous

person was delivered up to Satan, but it was for the destruction of the flesh, and the saving of his soul, 1 Cor. v.; but when one is given up to himself, it is for the damning of his soul: then we may well say by anticipation of the lost, "Thou hast destroyed thyself."

And, my brethren, we have cause to think of this very seriously likewise in respect of the kingdom and nation. Certainly, if ever this kingdom be destroyed, it must needs be written for the generations to come, Here is a kingdom that has destroyed itself. Certainly we cannot say it is from God, if we perish: what God will do with us we know not, but truly, this we may plainly see, that if God leaves us but a little more to ourselves, we are in a very fair way to destroy ourselves; and that after all that God has wrought for us. God has wrought like a God for us; but we, how do we deal for ourselves? Like men, shall we say? Oh no, like brute beasts: if men, mad-men, men that are appointed to destruction. It will be the saddest story that ever was in the world against a people, if so be that at length we perish, after God has done so much for us. Truly, now God has wrought like a God to deliver us from our common enemies, God has need to work as much for us like a God to deliver us from ourselves. Great have the works of God been in delivering us from the rage of those of whom we thought, and that justly, that they intended our destruction. If God should now say, Well, I have done my work, I have delivered you from those you were afraid of, and now I will leave you to yourselves, oh! we had cause to fall upon our faces, and say, O Lord, do not so, for it had been better that they had destroyed us; for if thou shouldst leave us to ourselves, our destruction would be a more bitter destruction. Do not we see how fast we run towards destruction? being but a little left to ourselves, what a perverse spirit is there now amongst us! We say sometimes of the prelates, The hand of God is against them; how have they brought themselves into a snare! Now they may stand and look upon us, and even laugh almost at us, and say, Well, let them alone; as we speak of some, Give them line enough and they will quickly hang themselves; Let them alone, and they will fall out one with another, and destroy one another, they will quickly ruin themselves if they be let alone. Oh, we have as much experience as any of the vanity of men's hearts, of their folly, pride, hypocrisy, and frowardness. Who could ever have thought this five or six years ago? If this had been presented as it were in a map to us, You shall be in great dangers, you shall have mighty enemies rise ready to swallow you up; but I will appear and work for you, I will put forth my glory, the right hand of my power and excellency shall appear for you; and when all this is done, you shall undo yourselves, and out of your own selves shall be your ruin, even from those in whom you much trusted, and much applauded, even they shall be cause of the evil; yea, and you who now think your hearts are so right, and have said, Oh, if God would but deliver us, how we would magnify his name! you yourselves shall be the cause of the evil of the kingdom. Had any said so of some of whom now our hearts have cause to shake within us, when we think, (as the prophet did of Hazael,) You shall do thus and thus, they would have been ready to answer, What! are we dogs? are we dead dogs, that we should do such things? Well, the Lord deliver us from ourselves.

"But in me is thine help."

We can easily destroy ourselves, but can we save ourselves? A child can break a glass that all the men in the country cannot mend. Every fool may do mischief to himself, yea, and to others, but can he help? It is God only that is the help of his people; it is not means that help, but God; yea, God much glories in that very thing, to be accounted the cause of all good; he would have all evil cast upon men, but all good from himself, even present good, and eternal good, he would have attributed to himself.

One, though a Jesuit, comments thus on these words, "In me is thine help." Hence it follows, (saith he,) that predestination, vocation, and grace, do not come from the foresight of the merits of those that are predestinated, but from God's predestinating, calling, preventing with his grace: these things are the help of God. Even from the mouth of a Jesuit we have this, thus acknowledging sometimes in their writings, and when they are serious, that neither predestination, nor vocation, nor grace, comes from any foresight of what man would do, but only from God's predestinating, calling, preventing the predestinated by his grace; and this is the help of God. God is the centre of all good, both present and eternal.

Inde sequitur, prædestinationem, vocationem, et gratiam non esse ex præviis prædestinatorum meritis; sed ex Deo prædestinantur, vocantur, gratiâ suâ prædestinatos præveniente: hæc enim sunt auxilium Dei. Cornel. a Lapide in loc.

Austin was wont to say, God does many good things in a man that a man does not himself; man does nothing which God does not that man may do. This point we must not speak at large to, but pass by presently, for we met with it before in the prophecy, where it was said, "There is no saviour beside me," chap. xiii. 4.

Multa bona facit Deus in homine, quæ non facit homo; nulla facit homo, quæ Deus non facit ut faciat homo. August.

"In me is thine help." That is, thy continued help; not only help for the present, but whatsoever help thou hast continued to thee, it is all in God. "Be thou their arm every morning, our salvation also in the time of trouble," Isa. xxxiii. 2; not only their help for the present, but they need still a continued supply and help every morning. We may here, further,

Obs. 4. There is no misery that man can bring himself to in this world, but there is help for it in God. Though thou hast destroyed thyself, yet in me is thy help; there may yet be help in God. As if God should say, I do glory in being a helper. It is God's glory to help men in misery; let it be ours.

It is the glory of many men to destroy, to do mischief; but it is the glory of God to be a helper.

Luther, on the place, saith, I desire to defend thee, to preserve thee, this indeed is to be a God. To be a helper, God glories in this. Oh that we could account it our glory to be helpful to one another!

Cupio te defendere, te servare, hoc vere esse, Deum esse. Luth. in loc.

Let us also look upon God in this his glory, and make him the object of our faith in times of distress. Let us not lie vexing and fretting under our misery, but lift up our eyes to God the Helper. Let no want of means, no unworthiness in us, cause our hearts to sink: those despairing temptations that say to us, There is no help in God, they are very sinful at any time, let the condition be never so bad.

You will say, I am a wretched creature, I have undone myself.

Well, though thou hast, yet desponding, despairing thoughts, which lead us to say, There is no help in God, are wicked and sinful. God accounts it his glory to help men even when they have destroyed themselves. There is a time indeed when there will be no help for sinners; but whilst in this world, we may say as Shechaniah, in Ezra x. 2, "Yet now there is hope in Israel concerning this thing." Oh make use of that scripture when thou seest thyself sink down even to the very gulf, oh, yet there is hope in the God of Israel for this very thing. Suppose thy condition be worse than any in the world, yet you know, it has not been known what God has laid up for them that love him; there is still help in God.

Yea, but will he help? O doubting soul, reason thus:

1. There is help in God, and he accounts it his glory

to be a helper. He accounts it not so much his glory to be a destroyer, no, that is his "strange work," but to be a helper, that is his great glory.

2. When men are most undone, even then is the time for God to help. "Thou hast destroyed thyself; but in me is thine help." Oh, come and return, there may yet be help for thee, though thou hast destroyed thyself.

"Thou hast destroyed thyself; but in me is thine help." This may be said in aggravation of their sin and stubbornness: Why dost thou not come in to me? have not I always been a help to thee in all times of straits and distresses? You are in great misery; now I am the same that I ever was, there is yet help enough in me: from whence,

Obs. 5. If the misery of those who have heretofore seen help in God increases, and they sink yet lower and lower, they had need examine themselves thoroughly. Surely they have shut the door against themselves for help, for God is never weary of doing good; "The Lord's hand is not shortened, that it cannot save; neither his ear heavy, that it cannot hear: but your iniquities have separated between you and your God," Isa. lix. 1, 2. I beseech you mark but this, there is a great difference between God and man in this helping. Men that are very kind and helpful sometimes, yet at other times will be very surly and harsh towards the same whom formerly they much befriended, and that not from any cause without, but merely from the temper of their own hearts, and the change that has taken place in their own spirits; not because those that they have been kind to are worse now than before, no, but because of a froward, surly, harsh humour that is risen up in themselves: you shall see such a difference in men who have been very sweet, loving, and helpful to you at some times; but come to them at other times, and you shall find them dogged, and surly, and harsh, and you cannot tell what has provoked them; it arises from nothing but a distemper within. Thus it is with men, but it is not so with God. "Thou hast destroyed thyself, but in me is thine help;" it is still; I have been thy helper all thy days, and still am the same God, ready to do thee good, and to help thee.

Obs. 6. The more God has helped any, the greater will be their destruction, if they be destroyed at last. "Thou hast destroyed thyself; but in me is thine help." I have been a help always, I was ever ready to help and to do good, and yet thou art undone. Oh, to be destroyed when God is at hand to help, to perish when there is a fountain just before us, as Hagar, this will be sad indeed! To perish in the midst of means, and in the midst of mercies, what an aggravation will this be to men's sins another day, when they are past the time of mercy to help, then to think, Oh how gracious was God to me while I lived!

And as a nation, too, we should apply this to ourselves. "Thou hast destroyed thyself; but in me is thine help." It will be the aggravation of our misery if we should yet perish. O my brethren, consider, shall all the great stories and remarkable accounts that we have given of God's mighty working in helping us, shall they be of no other use but to aggravate our miseries at last? It would be a sad termination.

Ver. 10. *I will be thy king: where is any other that may save thee in all thy cities? and thy judges of whom thou saidst, Give me a king and princes?*

First, to speak a little to the words as you have them in your books, for the Hebrew will admit of such an interpretation; and then I shall show you another reading, in my judgment, as suitable to the original.

"I will be thy king."

Notwithstanding all your plots, all your rage, I will govern you. "I will be thy king," and will do that which beseems me as the great King of heaven and earth; I will not be borne down by you with all your tumult, I will govern you, I will have mine own ends, do what you can; things shall not go as you will, but they shall go as I will have them; you would cast off my authority, but I will maintain it; "I will be thy king."

Obs. 1. It is a sad condition when God rules over a people in spite of their hearts. And yet God many times rules over people in spite of their hearts, whether they will or no; while they are plotting and striving for themselves this way and that, God is bringing about his own ends in their ruin. "The Lord reigneth; let the people tremble," Psal. xcix. 1. It is not thy fretting and wilfulness that will hinder the course of God's ordering things in the world, he will be King at last do what thou canst; while thou and thousand thousands such as thou art shall perish eternally, God will be King. Oh, it is infinitely better for thee to fall down before the Lord and say, Lord, thou art above us, thou hast power over us, thou shalt be our King for ever. It is always just with God to say, "I will be thy king;" but certainly God has not made such a distance between man and man that any should say, Notwithstanding my injustice, and the misery it entails on the people, yet "I will be thy king," I will have mine own ends, mine own will. The bond between kings and states certainly is mutual.*

"I will be thy king."

I will not cast off all care of them, I will not leave them to the mercy, or rather to the cruelty, of others; but let them come and return to me, and I will deal with them as a king to defend, to govern them, and to do them good.

That God should be King over a people is his mercy, and man's felicity. This should be our prayer, Lord, give us not up to be ruled by our lusts, but do thou rule over us; and, Lord, give us not up to be ruled by the lusts of wicked men, suffer not unjust and cruel men to rule over us, but do thou reign over us. Let us say, "The kingdoms of this world are become the kingdoms of our Lord and of his Christ; and he shall reign for ever and ever."

But the words are read otherwise, thus, in the old translation, where Beza's (the Geneva) notes are; I am, where is your king that may save thee in all thy cities? And I find most interpreters adopt this.

So the Septuagint, ποῦ ὁ βασιλεὺς σοῦ οὗτος, where is that your king. And the Chaldee paraphrase, where is your king that should save you in all your cities? The sense is much the same.

As if he should say, I am the same God that ever I was, but where is your king that should save you in your cities? Oh may the words read so pierce the hearts of some, if ever they have had any acquaintance with God, and known what communion with God has meant, to hear but God say these words, "I am," I am the same God that ever you knew me to be; but where is your king that should save you? And if, with Pareus, you read it as here, I will be, and there make the stop; I will be, what he had said before, as a lion, a leopard, and as a bear bereaved of her whelps; and then, where is your king that should save you?

Pareus in loc.

This is God's name, in Exod. iii. 14, "I am that I

* Vid. Bucer in Matt. xvii. 27. *Cuncta supremo magistratus concedenda propter conscientiam;* i. e. The supreme magistrate is to be submitted to in all things, but matters of conscience. He speaks of private men, not of those who by laws are appointed to be a screen between the prince and people, such as Calvin's Instit. lib. iv. cap. 20. sect. 31, saith the three estates in parliament are.

am," or, "I will be what I will be." So saith God here, I am, I will be; but then where is "thy king? where is any other that may save thee in all thy cities? and thy judges of whom thou saidst, Give me a king and princes?" My brethren, I am no prophet, and have not the spirit of one to prophesy of things before, or order scripture when it should be preached on and when not; I am, you see, pursuing my ordinary course, and meeting with this scripture, am bound (according to my ability) to demonstrate to you wherein its force lies. I hope your consciences will witness that there shall not be the least straining of it, but that I endeavour to give you the story, and the temper of the people at this time. It appears plainly that there were three things that they much rested upon: 1. The king. 2. The city. 3. The nobles. Put king, and city, and nobles together, and who can prevail against us? Saith God, "Where is thy king? where is any other that may save thee in all thy cities? and thy judges of whom thou saidst, Give me a king and princes?" These three they put together. If our king come to the cities he will have a party and strength there, and we know the cities are able to command all the country and kingdom. The militia, and a numerous company of men and riches, are congregated in the cities, and therefore the king, together with them, and the princes, the nobles of the land who favour him, these all surely render our condition safe; and yet in the midst of all these God asks them, by way of derision and insultation, "Where is thy king? where is any other that may save thee in all thy cities?" The notes from the words are,

Obs. 2. The things that carnal hearts rest upon will vanish. Where are they? saith God; what is become of them? You would encourage one another, and say, Come, we shall have a day yet, for we have this strength, and the king and nobles for us. Where are they? Those things on which carnal hearts rest will vanish and come to nothing.

Obs. 3. God loves to insult over men in their carnal confidences. For so, he doth not say here, Your king shall not save you, nor your cities shall not save you, nor your princes and nobles shall not save you; but, Where are they? in a kind of irony: God loves to insult over the carnal confidences of men. And we find in Scripture many such passages, as in Deut. xxxii. 37, "And he shall say, Where are their gods, their rock in whom they trusted?" And in Isa. xix. 12, "Where are they? where are thy wise men?" What! we have got statesmen, men versed in state affairs, we have them with us. But "where are they?" saith God. Thus the Lord insults over men that put their confidence in the flesh, and especially when they have been confident in their own ways, forsaking God, and so bringing themselves to misery; when they have brought themselves to misery by forsaking the ways of God, then God insults, Now where are these things in which you so confided?

And truly, even the saints, so be it they do it in a holy, humble way, may have some kind of triumph over ungodly men; only as so much carnality still adheres to them, there is danger, they had need keep their hearts very low: but if they do it in the strength of God, we have it in Scripture, "The virgin, the daughter of Zion, hath despised thee, and laughed thee to scorn." Only keep your hearts (I say) low, and you may come to see the glory of God, and then triumph in this, that God has heard your prayer, and has been with his people; and that though the enemy has had so much power and strength in the flesh, yet the Lord has disappointed them.

Obs. 4. It will greatly confound carnal hearts, when they shall be asked, Where is their confidence? They shall be found speechless. When they shall be asked, Where is your bravery, and pride, and the stoutness of your hearts? they shall be able to say nothing. Oh! this will pour confusion and shame upon them. Certainly, ere long, all carnal hearts that make their boast in the pomp and glory of the world shall be greatly confounded.

"Where?" I say, this confounding "where" will be asked of every wicked and ungodly man: what will they be able to say then? In Judg. ix. 28, we read of one "Gaal the son of Ebed," who said, "*Who* is Abimelech?" but in ver. 38, when Abimelech came with strength against him, Zebul said to him, "Where is now thy mouth, wherewith thou saidst, Who is Abimelech, that we should serve him?" When men are in their pride and bravery, then they scorn at God and men, they little regard any thing that is said to them; but when God brings them down low, then where is that mouth of thine that did so boast, and speak so proudly?

My brethren, let us learn from hence, therefore, to seek after, and rest upon, those things of which we may be able always to give an account where they are, if it should be asked us. The saints, if it should be asked them, Where is their God? can answer, It is the God of heaven that we have trusted in, the God that is in the highest heavens, and in the hearts of the saints; we can tell where our God is. It is just with God that wicked men should be insulted over, because they insult over the saints: if God do but seem to absent himself from his people, they will presently triumph over them, saying, Yea, where is your God? where are your prayers and fastings? Have not some of you heard such language many times in this kingdom? The saints of God can always give an answer to this "Where?" they can tell where their fastings and prayers are: but the wicked are not able to tell what is become of their confidences and boastings.

Therefore, O you saints of God, never be afraid of evil men, for ere long it will be demanded of them, where their pomp, and glory, and pride are, and they will not be able to answer.

"And thy judges of whom thou saidst, Give me a king and princes."

By judges, sometimes kings are meant, as Amos ii. 3, "I will cut off the judge from the midst thereof;" (he speaks, saith Drusius, of the king of Moab;) but we are to understand here their nobles and great men, upon whom they relied, for so they are called in Scripture. They had indeed judges before that time, when they said, "Give me a king and princes;" they had judges, but they were of meaner rank in comparison of those they had after: they had judges that by God's appointment governed them, but they were too mean for them; no, they must have a king, they must have princes, they must have judges that are kings and princes, great men, for these that they had to rule over them were but of their own rank, and this would not satisfy them, they must have such as were great ones, high above them: those were but ordinary men; what were they but the commons, of the same rank with other men, raised up but a little while ago from the grade of ordinary men? and why should we be ruled and governed by them? No, we must have a king, and nobles, and they must govern us: "Give me a king and princes." Read but the story of the judges, and you shall find that God had evermore appeared with them, I do not remember any one of them who prevailed not when God raised him up: but now this people regard them not; why? because they were but mean men of their own rank, though God did assist and prosper them so exceedingly.

Judices aliquando reges designant, ut Amos ii. 3, Exscindam judicem de medio tui. De rege Moab loquitur.

Obs. 5. Though God be much with men, yet if they be of a low rank, carnal hearts regard them not. Let them do never so great services, and be never so instrumental for the kingdom, even those that have had their estates, their liberties, and all preserved by them, and by the mighty spirit that God has put into them, yet, when the work is over, they look upon them but as mean, ordinary men, men of a common rank, and so let them go: after all the great things that God has done by them, still their thoughts and minds are upon others that are above them, upon princes, and nobles, and such men; they regard and rely more upon men in whom they see outward pomp and glory, than upon those who have evidently the presence of God with them. Oh, we see that that which has been is still to this very day.

"Of whom thou saidst, Give me a king and princes."

Where did they say so? They said so in 1 Sam. viii. 5, "Make us a king to judge us like all the nations." Indeed the word "princes" we do not find there, but here the Holy Ghost adds, "and princes;" but that must of necessity be supposed, for if there be a king, a king must have his court and nobles about him, and, as a fountain of honour, confer honour on the great men about him; so that though princes be not named there, yet the Holy Ghost supplies them as a thing that must of necessity be understood; Come, let us be governed by a king and the great ones attendant on him. But you will ask me,

What is the reason that nothing would satisfy them but a king and nobles?

If you read 1 Sam. viii., you will find that they were almost mad upon it, a king they must have, and would have. Oh! it was very grievous to Samuel's spirit: he told them their great sin, and the Lord said, "They have not rejected thee, but they have rejected me." Samuel told them what God said, and God bade Samuel tell them what a king they should have, that he would oppress them extremely, exercise arbitrary government to the full, take away their servants and children, and do with them what he pleases; You will be brought to be his slaves, any parasite at court may easily get your estates; you shall be accounted an offender for a word, and fined at pleasure; you shall be in most miserable bondage, if you have a king. But now after Samuel had told them all this, "Nay," say they, "but we will have a king." If any one should come and reason, Why do you desire a king so much? what will you get by it? do not you think that he will have your estates, your liberties, and all you possess, at his disposal? no one could deny this, they did not deny the least word that Samuel said, but they held their conclusion, "Nay, but we *will* have a king." What should make them thus? These seven reasons may be given for it.

1. For novelty's sake. They had tried other kinds of government before, but now they would have somewhat more. Men's spirits are very much given to change, though they can give no rational account why they desire it.

2. They might entertain some distrust of their former judges; because they were men of meaner rank, they might think that they should not be able to help them; Let us, say they, have a king that shall go before us in our wars. Though they had never so much experience of the judges, yet they thought there would be more good if they had great ones, and they were afraid that these men of a lower, meaner rank would fail them at last.

3. They might desire to be like other nations, because they loved pomp. What! say they, shall we see our neighbouring nations governed by those who have great pomp and glory, and shall we be governed by men that were but tradesmen a while ago? No, they would be like other nations.

4. Perhaps they had experienced some oppressions from the former judges. Though most of them were good, yet certainly there can be no human government but will afford some cause at one time or other for some to complain. Take the best government that can be in the world, yet, seeing it is a government of men and administered by men, there will be some cause or other at some period for complaint. Now this is the peevishness of men's hearts, that if there be but any condition wherein they suffer, they do nothing but complain of their suffering, and desire a change; and they never think of the inconveniences and sufferings that may result. They would be rid of these to whom they were now subject, and would have a king. These men angered them, laid on them some odious taxes; now, so be it they might get rid of them, they care not what they bring upon themselves; and therefore, "Nay, but we will have a king."

5. Out of a spirit of opposition against the way of God's appointment. God was their Governor, and their hearts rose against his rule, through a mere spirit of opposition, though they could give no reason why they might not be as well under it as any other: but it was God's way, and there is an opposition in the heart of man to any thing that has God in it.

6. They had some hopes that they should have more liberty for their lusts. Now, in their present form of government, there was more inspection over them, and they could not so easily corrupt their rulers; but in a merely human government, if they could but make a friend of their ruler, they might do what they list; if they would but consent to be a slave to him, they might make all their neighbours slaves to them: they had probably a great deal more hopes of licence for their lusts in this than their present government.

7. Many of them had hopes to get preferment this way. Let us have a king and princes, and we shall so get preferments and places in the court, therefore we will not be satisfied with any other way but this; we live in a mean, low condition without this, but we shall get preferments by the change, therefore give us a king.

But now this is observable, Though they thought they had a great deal of reason for themselves, yet after they had once smarted, and found indeed that there was upon them, after they had these kings and princes, more oppression than ever they were under in their lives; now was a time that Hosea could speak freely to them, and say in the name of God, Where is your king, and those men for whom you were so earnest? what good have you got? For it is observable, though they were never so eager upon having a king, yet, if you read the story in Samuel, when God did but thunder from heaven, then they exclaimed, "We have sinned." When they were under oppression, then Hosea could speak freely and plainly to them, Where is your king? and where are these men?

Obs. 6. Men will not hear so long as they do not suffer. If men be once bent upon a certain course, and have their estates about them, and countenance from great ones, speak what you will against their way, they will not hear you; but let these men smart, and find by experience the evil of their course, then you may speak to them and say, Do you think now that was wisely done, for which you were so eager? do you think you dealt well for yourselves? Oh then they will be ready to say, I confess I did not think so seriously of those things before, I looked only upon that which appeared good for the present, and now after-wit is bought, although it be dear, I see cause to repent.

My brethren, surely kings and nobles are great blessings of God when they are good. You see I have not in the least strained the place, but held forth to you its true scope. Let none go away and say, that I inveighed against kings, or nobles; certainly in themselves they are great blessings of God, and we must acknowledge it fitting to have a difference between man and man.

It is a slander that is upon a sort of people, as if they would have all things to lie level, and one to have as much honour as the other. God forbid we should have such a thought: let us give honour to those whom God would have honoured, and never envy nor grudge at their honour: if God pleases to send those that are good, I say, they may be great instruments of great blessings of God to us. But now mark the very next words that follow in the 11th verse. They would have a king.

Ver. 11. *I gave thee a king in mine anger, and took him away in my wrath.*

They were ready to say, Why do you thus blame us for our eager desire? did not God approve of it? God himself was content we should have one; God himself chose our first king, Saul, and appointed Samuel to anoint him. And if you understand it of the other king, Jeroboam, for so interpreters go, they might say, And Jeroboam also; did not God foretell by the prophet, that Jeroboam should have ten tribes? and did not the man of God tell us that this was from the Lord? And therefore why should you so much upbraid us about our kings? it is the mind and will of God that we should have them.

The answer of the prophet is: True, God did give you a king, and appointed Samuel to anoint him, and foretold that Jeroboam should be king over the ten tribes: yea, but it was in his anger; he gave you one indeed, but it was in his anger. You were so set upon it, that you would have one; If you will, take him, saith God, and take him with all that shall follow after: so that it was (as one speaks) rather from an angry God, than from an entreated God.

Ab irato, potius quam ab exorato Deo.

"I gave thee a king in mine anger." Saul and Jeroboam were given in anger, those primarily, as a punishment of their sin: Saul as a punishment of their sin in rejecting Samuel, and in their disobedience to Samuel, and the way of government that they had then. And Jeroboam was given as a punishment of their sin of idolatry, that was committed in Solomon's time (as also of their rebellion and apostacy): and yet it is said that God did it.

Obs. 1. God may have a hand in things wherein men sin exceedingly. They sinned in getting a king, they sinned exceedingly in setting up Jeroboam, and yet God has such a hand in it, that he saith, I gave them these things. Calvin, (and I the rather cite his words here, because the adversaries would cast that aspersion on him, that he held that God was the author of sin,) on this very place, saith,* From this place we learn, that God does so exercise his judgments, that whatsoever evil there is, it is to be ascribed to men; whatsoever good, to himself: God seems to direct this work wholly to his own providence. From hence let us learn soberly to admire the secret judgments of God; neither let us imitate those impure dogs: impure dogs! what are they that do therefore grin and bark at God, because they cannot understand how God doth use wicked men? because they understand not this, they conclude that God is the cause of sin. He calls them the impure dogs, because they understand not how God doth work in making use of wicked men, that God is the author and cause of sin. His spirit was much against this, and therefore it was an extreme slander upon him, as if he should hold such an opinion. That is the first. God may have a hand in things wherein men sin extremely, and yet he remain holy.

Obs. 2. Things that are very evil, may yet have present success. It was a very evil thing for them to desire a king at this time, and likewise for the people to rend from the house of David, yet both of them succeeded according to their desire. Let us then learn never to judge of the goodness of a thing by its success. Say some, I warrant you we will have this; and if they get what they desire, they think God approves of it: they may desire a thing, and be set upon it, and though much be said to the contrary, yet they may drive on their designs, and prosper in it; but this is no argument that God owns it as good: never judge of things by success.

Obs. 3. God's gifts are not always in love. "I gave thee a king," saith he, but "in mine anger." God's gifts are not always in love; no, they are in anger many times. Read but Numb. xi. 18—20, you shall find there God giving people their desires. He lets them have them, but how? "Say thou unto the people, Sanctify yourselves against to-morrow, and ye shall eat flesh: for ye have wept in the ears of the Lord, saying, Who shall give us flesh to eat? for it was well with us in Egypt: therefore the Lord will give you flesh." You have wept and cried, saying, "Who shall give us flesh?" "The Lord will give you flesh;" and "ye shall not eat one day, nor two days, nor five days, neither ten days, nor twenty days; but even a whole month, until it come out at your nostrils;" you shall have enough of it, even till "it be loathsome unto you:" why? "because that ye have despised the Lord which is among you." The Lord gave them their desires, because they had despised him. So you are ready to bless yourselves that you have what you would have, and think that therefore God regards you, whereas God gives you what you desire because you have sinned against him; if he were not angry with you, he would not give it. Saith Augustine, God many times in giving is angry, in denying is merciful. It is because he is angry that he gives you such things as you would have. So in Psal. lxxviii. 29—31, God gives them flesh according to their desires, but "while their meat was yet in their mouths, the wrath of God came upon them." If we had time a little to open this most excellent point, it might quiet our desires; for we might endeavour to speak of the several ways of God's giving, that, by comparing one thing with another, we might learn to distinguish whether a thing be given in love or in anger, come to know how much is in it of God's loving-kindness.

Dando irascitur, non dando miseretur. August.

But only now let me leave this with you about it, Take heed of immoderate desires for any worldly thing: take heed of saying, I must, and I will, and I will have it; whenever you find your hearts strongly rising to a thing, then be afraid, be afraid of having it, as much as you were of having any thing in your lives. No one can have any comfort in any thing as coming from God's love, until they can first quiet their hearts, and be willing to be at God's disposal, be willing to be without it; that is one main sign of God's giving in anger, or in love. When any find an eager desire after a thing, Oh it is very suitable to such and such a purpose; yea, but now if I can go alone and consider that God is wiser than I, and knows what is best for me; if I can labour to work my heart to this, Lord, if it be good for me, then I desire it; but if thou seest it would not be good, then Lord, here I am, do with me what seems good in thine eyes; as David did: surely nature could not but work strongly in his case, when leaving the holy city, yet he said, "If I shall find

* Ex hoc loco discimus, Deum sic exercere sua judicia, ut quicquid mali est, debeat hominibus ascribi: Deus videtur hoc totum dirigere sua providentia, discamus admirari sobrie arcana Dei judicia, neque imitemur impuros istos canes qui obganiunt, quia non possunt agnoscere quomodo Deus utatur etiam improbis hominibus, quia hoc non percipiunt, concludant Dominum esse causa peccati. Calv. in loc.

favour in the eyes of the Lord, he will bring me again, and show me both it, and his habitation: but if he thus say, I have no delight in thee; behold, here am I, let him do to me as seemeth good unto him," 2 Sam. xv. 25, 26. Yea, this was a trial indeed, and doubtless this temper of David's heart in his affliction was the thing that gave him so much enlargement to praise God, when he returned to the ark and city again. Had David vented himself in impatient complainings; What! must I go from the city of Jerusalem? how doth God deal with me! I am resolved I will return to Jerusalem and take possession of the city, whatsoever comes of it, though it even cost me my life; perhaps David might have gotten thither, but there would not have been so much love of God in it, as when he could give up himself to God's disposal. And so, if this people could have said thus, True, Lord, thou art our King, but we are despised because we are governed by men of such mean quality: and the truth is, God had promised them a king also, and therefore it was not such an evil thing to desire a king, the evil lay in the eagerness of their desire, they would have him now: if they had been but quiet, and said, Lord, thou dost tell us in thy word of a king that we shall have, Lord, fulfil this thy word, and for the present we are content to submit to thee, as long as thou thinkest fit; now, it may be, God would have given them a king then, or presently after, and so they might have had a holy and gracious king; but they *must* have him now, and so they had him with the anger of God. You remember the words of Rachel to Jacob, "Give me children, or else I die." She had a child and died; though it was not in God's anger as an enemy, yet it was a fatherly anger. O think but of this, you women that are so desirous of children, or any outward blessing. You, too, who are desirous of altering your condition, as in marriage, and must needs have such a one, although you beg your bread all your days, and although parents are against it, and you cannot, even yourselves, discern evidences of grace. Now, saith God, you shall have it, you shall join together, and you shall work your own misery by this eagerness of your spirit. O brethren, let us learn to be moderate in our desires, and commit them with our hearts to God.

"I gave thee a king in mine anger, and took him away in my wrath."

I have observed before that God's gifts are not always in love, and now, because it is an important point, there are two things which I desire to do very briefly.

I. To show you, how a man may know that what God gives him is given in anger, and not in love.

II. To draw some corollaries from the foregoing.

I. How we may know that what God gives is in anger, and not in love. It is a very hard thing to convince men, if they have their desires satisfied, that it is rather from anger than love. Men are so well pleased with the satisfying of their desires, that they can very hardly be convinced but that God intends good to them in it; and therefore you shall find, in 1 Sam. xii. 17, that God was fain to do one of his great and wonderful works to convince this people that the king whom he gave them there was given in anger rather than in love: "Is it not wheat harvest to-day? I will call unto the Lord, and he shall send thunder and rain; that ye may perceive and see that your wickedness is great, which ye have done in the sight of the Lord, in asking you a king." Samuel had before, in chap. viii., told them of their sin in asking a king, but they would not be convinced; "Nay," say they, "but we will have a king over us." Now saith Samuel, It is wheat harvest; and whereas it was a strange and wonderful thing for the Jews to have rain then, but though it be harvest time, yet it shall rain and thunder; and all to the end that you may be convinced of your great wickedness in asking you a king. They had not only had their desires granted before this time, but, as they thought, had them, in some wise, confirmed; for Saul had prospered after he had been a king: but yet for all that, (saith he,) I will give you an evident demonstration, that it is not in love that you have him, but it was your great wickedness in seeking you a king. "So Samuel called unto the Lord; and the Lord sent thunder and rain that day." And then, in ver. 19, "All the people said unto Samuel, Pray for thy servants unto the Lord thy God, that we die not: for we have added unto all our sins this evil, to ask us a king:" now we do acknowledge it to be a very great and sore evil indeed, though our king has prospered a while, yet God shows us now that it is an evil. And by this you may see that it is hard for men to be convinced, when they have according to their hearts' desires, that it is in anger rather than in love.

But to give you some notes, whereby you may be helped to see, whether what you have granted by God according to your desires be in anger or love:

1. When you desire a gift, rather than God in it. When your desires are for the gift rather than the Giver, you can have no comfort that there is love in it. There is no man that has to deal with another, if he knows that what he does desire from him, it is not out of love to him, but merely from the love of the gift, certainly, though he may give him for some other ends, yet he does not give it out of love. Those desires that are not out of love, are not satisfied from love. Love satisfies no desires that are not raised by love; love acts always upon love. Now God knows what the ground of our desires is; if we desire the gift rather than the Giver, rather than God in it, we can have no comfort that our enjoyments proceed from love. Whatsoever a gracious heart would have from God, yet this is the main thing in its desires, Oh, let me have God in them! such is my condition in this world, that God appoints that I shall not enjoy him immediately altogether, but I shall enjoy him through such and such mercies, oh then that I might have these mercies, that I might enjoy him in them! Certainly any thing that thou hast in satisfaction of such desires is out of love; but when thou lookest no further than the creature, wouldst have the thing, but lookest not at God in it, thou canst not expect the love of God to be conveyed by it.

2. When our desires are immoderate and violent. This was just the case of this people here: "Nay, but we will have a king over us," we must needs have him; whatsoever comes of it, we *will* have him. When God satisfies the desires of his people in his love, he first quiets their hearts, bringing them into a sweet and blessed moderation; but when men's hearts are so violent, that the thing they desire they must have, God many times saith, You shall have it then, take it: but then he speaks not in love, that is very remarkable: Numb. xi. and Psal. lxxviii. 29—31, and other passages, confirm this point. But I would further remark of that Psalm, that the Lord, after he had showed that he did not answer their desires in love, but in wrath, then, in ver. 31, saith, after the judgments of God had come upon them in the satisfying of their desires, that many of them were slain by God; and the parallel passage referred to in Numbers saith, "He called the name of that place Kibroth-hattaavah, because there they buried the people that lusted;" that is, The sepulchres of the lusts of their desires: God sets a brand upon that place, Here, saith he, are the graves of the desirers; they must needs have flesh, and they stood upon their desires, their desires must be satisfied; and here are the graves of the desirers, saith God. O remember, you that lust after evil things, remember when your desires are immoderate and violent, it is just with God to set a brand by some remarkable hand of his against you, and

say, Here is the mark of these desires that were so immoderate and so violent.

3. When God grants men their desires before the due time. They have what they would have, but they have it not in God's time. Children long with desire after green fruit, but if they could stay but a few weeks or months, one apple then would be worth a hundred when they are green; but they cannot stay, they must have the fruit when it is green; they have it, but it does them no good. So when we have our desires satisfied before the due time, it proceeds not from love. God had promised that Israel should have a king in due time, that there should come kings from the loins of Abraham; and in Deut. xvii. 14, there is a prophecy of the king they should have: yea, but they would not stay God's time, and therefore he was given not out of love. Psal. cvi. 13, it is said of those that did so lust that God gave them their lusts in his wrath, "they waited not for his counsel." That is noted there. Oh, we should be willing to wait for God's counsel. We would have the thing presently done; yea, but God's counsel works one thing after another, in mutual dependence, and we should be willing to wait for his counsel: if we will not mind God's counsel, but must have our desires satisfied, and that now, we cannot expect love in them, but rather wrath: he gives unto them in his anger.

4. When God grants us what we would have, but without the blessing. He grants the thing, but takes away the blessing of the thing, he takes away the comfort and satisfaction of it; "They shall eat, but they shall not be satisfied." So in Psal. cvi. 15, "He gave them their request, but sent leanness into their soul:" this is a similitude transferred from the body to the soul. Men may often have a dog's appetite, (as the physicians call it,) that is, a mighty greedy stomach, but they cannot digest what they eat, and so the body is lean; so here, they had a mighty desire, but as in the body many times there is such a disease that the meat turns not to nourishment, so in their souls, they had even that which their souls desired, yea, but their souls could not be satisfied. The body thrives not with what it eats when it has such a disease upon it; so, though the soul virtually has what it desired, yet it had a distemper with it; thus it could not be satisfied, nor thrive, nor prosper with what it had: "He sent leanness into their soul." How often are we greedily desirous of certain things, and think, Oh how happy should I be if I had them! It may be God lets you have your desires, but when he has he snatches away the comfort of it; you shall have a well, but it shall have no bottom, you shall not be able to get out the good and comfort in what you have. Surely God is not in it, for the blessing of God maketh rich, and addeth no sorrow with it; no, it brings comfort.

5. When that which we desire is merely to satisfy our lusts; merely that we might have our humours and lusts satisfied, that is all. We do not desire such and such things that by them we may be fitted for the service of God, we cannot give an account why these and these things should help us in the work of the Lord, but that we may go on as well without them; but they are suitable to our lusts. Oh! if God does give thee any thing to satisfy thy lusts, certainly he gives it in his wrath: as now, if a man have a disease in his body, and his enemy know what will feed his disease, he will gladly give it him that he may be the sooner despatched; no faithful physician, no loving friend, will give to any that which will feed their disease, but will rather take it from them in love. Oh! the Lord sees men's hearts set upon such and such lusts, and if certain things which they desire are granted them, their lusts will be fed by them; They shall have them, saith God. It is as dangerous a sign of reprobation as any thing, to give them that which shall be most suitable to their lusts, that shall most harden them; and on the other side, a token of the greatest love, when God shall take that from his children which he knows will but feed their lusts. Many diseases are such, that the only way to cure them is to keep the patient on a short diet; though they cry for food, and be very hungry, yet they must be kept very low; why? because the nature of the disease is such as will draw all nourishment to its own increase: and so God is fain to do with his own people, when he sees them sick of a disease which will naturally draw to its centre all the nourishment afforded.

6. When men are so eager that they care not whether the gift comes from a reconciled or a provoked God; it is all one to them: Let me have it; but whether it comes from God reconciled, or God provoked, they little care. In Numb. xi. is the notable story before referred to, of God's satisfying desires in his wrath. In the beginning of the chapter God is very much provoked with the people: "When the people complained, it displeased the Lord: and the Lord heard it; and his anger was kindled; and the fire of the Lord burnt among them, and consumed them that were in the uttermost parts of the camp. And the people cried unto Moses," and so the judgment was removed from them. But then, presently after, they fell to murmuring before ever any thing was done to reconcile God and their souls together. You do not read of any work of humiliation to seek reconciliation with God, between the time in which God manifested his sore displeasure against them, and that in which he satisfied their desires; no, they looked not at that, let them only have their desires; hence it came to be that their desires were satisfied in wrath.

Does thy conscience tell thee that there has been a time wherein God has been displeased with thee, and his anger has burst out against thee? Perhaps thou art in a better condition now than thou wast before; O, but tell me, hast thou humbled thy soul before God to make up thy peace with him? Has there been a day of atonement between God and thy soul? Has God's displeasure been out against thee, and now does he come and satisfy thee in what thou dost desire, before any thing has been done in falling down before him and seeking his face, and making peace? Thou canst not have comfort in this. Thy desires are satisfied rather in wrath than in mercy.

7. When God regards not our preparation for a mercy. Carnal hearts take no great care themselves of it, Let me have it, say they, our fitness matters not. It is your sin and wickedness not to regard the preparation of your hearts for what you have; and it is God's judgment to give it to you before you be prepared. A gracious heart, when it would have a mercy, is as careful to get the heart prepared for the mercy, as to obtain it. Those things would indeed suit me, but is my heart fit for such a deliverance? is my heart fit for such mercies? If it be thy care to prepare thy heart when thou art labouring for the mercy, surely, when it comes, it must be sweet indeed; but when there is no preparation before, thou canst not know that it is in love. We little think that we have need of preparation for mercies. If indeed God should threaten some judgment, we would think that we had need be prepared; but certainly there is as great need for preparation for mercies, to be able to make good use of them, as for afflictions, to be able to bear them. This I have likewise from Numb. xi. 18; it is said, "And say thou unto the people, Sanctify yourselves against to-morrow." There is a charge that they should sanctify themselves against to-morrow, for God would give them flesh. I do not find that they did do it, but when God promised to give them flesh, he bid them sanctify themselves; as if he should say, If that your desires

come before you have sanctified yourselves, it will be in wrath, not in mercy. O, therefore, when earnest to have your desires satisfied think thus, The Lord charges thee to sanctify thyself; do I take care of this? do I make it my endeavour to sanctify myself before the mercy comes? Then thou mayst have comfort in it, and not otherwise.

8. When we rest on the means we use, and seek not God by prayer. Whatever we enjoy that we get not by prayer before, or sanctified by prayer after, we cannot know that it proceeds from love. "Thou preventest him," saith David, Psal. xxi. 3, "with the blessings of goodness." God sometimes acts so towards his saints, but generally, when he intends a mercy from love, he first fills the heart with the spirit of prayer; when a mercy comes after much prayer, then it is surely a mercy from love. When the saints have been praying, and then God has come in with mercy, oh then they have gathered arguments of God's love to them; This I had because I sought thee: as Hannah did concerning Samuel: how did she rejoice in Samuel! "For this child I prayed," saith Hannah unto Eli; oh this is the mercy that I prayed for; therefore she called her child's name Samuel, one "asked of the Lord." And so when we can call every gift we have, Samuel, that is, a gift asked of God, a gift gotten by prayer, this is an argument of love. But otherwise we can have no assurance that it is from love. True, a king was not unlawful for them to desire, because they had such intimations in Scripture; but they acted not so much out of regard to them; no, they come to Samuel, and say, "Give us a king;" we do not read that they go to God for it. Such a great change of their state as that was, one would think, should have required divers days in seeking of God. It was a mighty change, to a new kind of government, from one that was of God's own appointment, to a form of government similar to that of the surrounding nations. Yet we find no days of prayer for this great change, and therefore it was in wrath that they had it. Therefore when you would have any thing, look not so much to come by it according to second causes, but be much in prayer, according to the excellency of the thing for which you seek.

9. When God gives our desires, but not a sanctified use of them. When God gives you the shell, but not the kernel, surely it is not in love. If your children should ask a nut of you, and you give them a nut that has no kernel, they will not think (if so be that you knew it) that it is in any great love. Truly, all the good things that wicked men have, they are but shells without kernels, they are not in love. The kernel of every blessing is a proportionable measure of grace to use it for God. You have a great desire that God should change your condition; if he should, and not give you a heart fit for that, you had better be without the change. You have a desire that God should prosper you in such a business; yea, but if he does not teach you how to abound, you had been better never to have abounded. Now it is not in love for God to give any success, except he gives a measure of grace proportioned to the success; therefore this you should all examine; The Lord has altered my condition, and many good things I have more than before; but what graces have I more than before? what exercise of grace, what work of grace, more than before? Certainly if it be in love it will be so.

10. When a secret curse attends what we have. If so be that a man should be very hungry, and have a mighty desire to satisfy himself, and he falls greedily upon his meat and eats it, but as soon as he has eaten it his body swells to an enormous size, surely he begins to think then that all is not well. Lord have mercy upon me, saith he, afraid that he is poisoned. So God gives you your desire, and as soon as you have it you begin to swell, you are bigger than you were before, your hearts are proud, and you can look scornfully upon others; oh, you are poisoned; this is an ill satisfying of your hunger, you are poisoned surely in this. In Isa. x. 16, you have a notable expression to this purpose; "Therefore shall the Lord, the Lord of hosts, send among his fat ones leanness; and under his glory he shall kindle a burning like the burning of a fire." Even such things wherein there appears to be a great deal of glory, such things perhaps as when your desires are satisfied you can glory in; oh you glory in such and such a mercy, such a good thing you have above others; but under this glory there is a burning kindled, there is a great deal of the wrath of God in it, a secret curse attends it.

11. When we regard not what becomes of others, so we have our desires satisfied. And this is from their example here. Let us have a king. A king! what shall become of Samuel then? has not he judged you, and been faithful with you? What! will you show yourselves so ungrateful to him for all the good he has done to you, as to reject him, and his house, and family? Oh, they cared not for that; Let us have a king; let what will become of Samuel and his house, what care they? And so when men are greedy in their desires, Let us have such and such a thing, but care not what becomes of others, it is another note of desires not granted in love.

12. When God, in satisfying of our desires, makes way for some judgment. Now indeed the thing that we have is comfortable, but stay awhile, and you shall see there is some judgment approaching by that very thing which you receive; and when the judgment is come, afterwards you will see how the mercy made way for it: very great judgments many times befall men, that are made way for by the satisfying of their own desires. God has many ways to prepare a path for his anger, often by giving you your desires; there is nothing more ordinary in experience than this, and therefore we need not stand upon it. If you will but examine the course of your lives, sometimes you may see, that if God had satisfied your desires in such and such things, it would have made way for the greatest misery that ever you had in all your lives; and when God denies sometimes to his people, they can confess, O Lord, I see that had I had my desires gratified, I had been undone. And on the other side, you will find that those things which you account the greatest mercies to you, do make way for the greatest evils; surely, then, they were not given in love.

13. When men are greedy of things to the disregard of the results; when they would have their desires satisfied in a foolish way, never minding what inconveniences may follow, but merely looking to their present comfort. Thus it was here; they would have a king; Samuel came and told them all the inconveniences that would follow upon it, how that they should have this affliction and the other; You that are so desirous of him, if he comes among you, he will bring you into slavery, your estates and your children shall be under his power, you will be in slavery to every courtier. Nay, but we will have a king for all this: they would needs change the way of government; Oh that we might have a king! and they would be brought more under law than before; for indeed in the time of the judges, you find that the people of Israel enjoyed a great deal of liberty, and obeyed the judges in a great measure voluntarily; you thus find but two tribes that followed Barak and Deborah, and so of Jephthah, and Samson, those that "offered themselves willingly among the people" followed them, Judg. v. 9; and with Gideon those of Ephraim "did chide sharply," Judg. viii. 1; so much freedom there was in the time of the judges. Yea, but we will have a king,

and we will all then be tied to the same thing, and be under the same power, and so there will ensue firm union: we shall no longer act each according to his own will, but all shall come in and join under the same law, and so we shall go on unitedly. Certainly this was their reasoning in their desire of having a king. Now this kind of union among the people, doubtless, was very good, but they considered not what inconveniences might result from their being thus chained together. Prisoners that are chained at a post are together all the day long; but would you have such a kind of union, would you be united with such chains? Consider, that with the union slavery may come upon you. But they did not consider any such things; No matter, say they, come, let us all be joined in one, and let the same law be upon every one. But now, how this would bring them under bondage and slavery in those things they would be loth to be brought under in, they considered not at all.

14. When men seek to have their desires satisfied merely because they love change. We cannot have any comfort that God's gifts proceed from love, when they are sought for out of a foolish, inconstant spirit. They thought they had been long enough under judges, and in a mere desire of novelty, not knowing what might come of such a change, demanded a king. And so people, though there be never so much good in a way, yet out of a novelty they would fain have a change; and if God grant them a change when they have no other ground but that for it, it is a sign that there is wrath in it, and not love.

15. When it is through impatience to submit to God in a former condition. It is ill when granted to gratify the appetite for novelty, but when given to impatience, then it is sure to be in wrath, and not in mercy. If your condition be changed, God has put you in a lower and meaner condition, it is true, it is lawful for you to desire a change; yea, but if you desire it because you cannot submit to God's hand, and it is given to you, then it is a sign that it is given in wrath: but when you have brought your hearts to this, Lord, here I am, dispose of me as thou pleasest, I am content to lie under thy hand, but, Lord, I look up to thee for mercy; consider I am a poor weak creature, and it is fit that thou shouldst have thy will, and not I mine; then if God make a change, you may have comfort that it is in mercy; but if you have it through impatience, you can have no comfort at all in it. It was just so here; they could not bear the hand of God in any present trouble that they had upon them, and so thought to help themselves by having a king, and God gave them one, but it was in his anger.

16. When our desires of further mercies make us forget former mercies. They would have a king that might go before them, and fight for them. Fight for them! did not God fight for them before? Oh, wonderful and glorious battles they had when they were under their judges, when they had Samuel to direct them, they never afterwards had more glorious victories than then: nay, you shall find in the whole story of the judges, that they did always prevail; and their judges generally were good, and guided them in God's ways; but the kings did not so, for the kings of Israel were none of them good, from the first to the last. O unthankful wretches that they are, so eager to have another condition, never minding nor blessing God for what they had, forgetful of all the good they had received. Samuel could appeal to them, "Whose ox have I taken? or whose ass have I taken? or whom have I defrauded?" 1 Sam. xii. 3. He had judged them righteously. But they forget all God's goodness and mercy towards them, and must change their condition. O, consider this, you that desire a change; be not unthankful for what you have had; if you be so eager to have more as to forget what you have had, if God should send you more your case is like to be worse than it is now. If one should take meat to eat before he has digested his previous food, because the new dishes brought to the table please his palate, this does not nourish him, but turns to evil humours, and so does him hurt; but if he would stay till he has digested what he has eaten before, then he might eat and be thereby nourished. You that would fain have more and more, have you digested what you have had? are you thankful for former mercies? has God had the glory of what you have had before? then, if God gives you any thing, you may have comfort to your souls that it comes out of love.

17. When men desire new things out of distrust of God, and make such conclusions of unbelief; Surely if God should not grant such and such things unto them, then they are lost and undone, and there is no way in the world to help them. Their desires are excited by distrust; whereas, (my brethren,) gracious desires are the fruit of faith, it is the prayer of faith that does good; it is faith that inflames the gracious desires which are sent up to God, they are sent up by the strength of faith, and not the strength of unbelief. It is the strength of unbelief that makes the desires of people so strong as they are, as thus: These people desired a king; why? because they could not trust God to have but only judges as they had before. Samuel was an old man, and his sons were naught, and they see themselves in a hard condition; yea, but now seeing God had not spoken to them about a new government, they should have had it from God, if at all, God should have chosen them one; but they thought that they must have one to go before them in their battles, or else they would miscarry, and they saw the princes of the earth that they went before their subjects in their battles, and therefore they would be like unto them, and durst not trust God in that way in which they were before. And therefore it was in wrath that God gave them their desires.

18. If, when God changes our condition, we bring the sins of our old condition into our new, we can have no assurance that the change proceeds from love. Our care should be, when our condition is changed, to ask, What were the sins of my former condition? what were the sins of my afflicted, my low condition? Let me take heed that I do not bring into my new state my former corruptions.

19. If we seek to attain our desires by unlawful means, certainly that is cursed. If God does let us prosper in ways that are unlawful in themselves, we cannot believe that what we enjoy proceeds from love, but from wrath.

I have the more willingly enlarged on this point because of its great usefulness.

II. Now then, by way of corollary, from all that has been said, let us learn,

1. To take heed that we quiet ourselves in our desires. Be not too earnest in your desires. Remember that scripture, 1 Cor. x. 6, "Now these things were our examples, to the intent we should not lust after evil things, as they also lusted." It refers to their lusting for their quails, here called "lusting after evil things;" though the things themselves were good, yet the manner of their lusting made them evil to them. These are for our example, that we should not lust so as they lusted. When you read Numb. xi. and Psal. lxxviii., and there find how they lusted after evil things, and how the wrath of God came upon them when they had their desires satisfied, remember that these things "are written for our admonition," 1 Cor. x. 11. And so when we read of their eager desires after a king, and what they met withal when they had him, it should teach us so far to moderate our desires, as to labour to regu-

late them by the word, and to subject them to the mind of the blessed God.

2. To prepare our hearts for what we have, and to seek proportionable grace for any thing that we do desire. Treasure up this lesson. When thou wouldst have a mercy from God, O seek proportionable grace, and prepare thyself for the mercy.

3. Not to be too much exalted when thou hast thy desires satisfied. Methinks this point might be as a prick, to prick the bladders of the pride of men's hearts. O, take heed, though you have prospered according to your desires. Saul prospered a great while, and yet it was in wrath. Certainly there is no great matter to be expected from such things as we may have in God's wrath, and therefore no cause to be exalted.

4. Never to draw any arguments of God's love, by our desires in outward things being satisfied. It is a vain conceit of people to think thus, God loves me; why? because I have desired such and such things, and God has given them to me. If a man were to go and choose a wife, and knew her face were painted, would he conclude, Surely here is one of an excellent complexion? No, he would rather suspect it. Truly it would be as just to infer that this woman's complexion, and the constitution of her body, are sound and good, as to conclude that my condition is good because God satisfies my desires.

5. Never to envy any men who have their lusts satisfied. There is little cause that you should envy them. Were you to see a man that loves wine drink some which you knew to be poisoned, or a man with a satin suit which you knew had the plague in it, there were no cause of envying either; water, or a leather suit, were a great deal better. God satisfies men many times, but it is in wrath, and to prepare them for slaughter.

6. To be content to wait patiently, and when our desires are denied. Oh, this is a point of very great use, to teach us patience when God denies us. Be patient and content when God denies you your desires, for you do not know what God may aim at in it.

7. Not to rest in what you enjoy, but to seek to know the source from whence it comes. And this I take to be as special a difference as any I know between a carnal and a gracious heart. A carnal heart thinks thus, If I have the thing, I care not for any more; but a gracious heart looks at the principle from whence it comes, he loves to look at the root and source. A gardener that owes the flowers, regards the root more than the flower a great deal; but a stranger is more pleased with the flower than with the root. So carnal hearts look only at flowers, but gracious hearts look at the root. I have such and such a thing, but have I an evidence of God's love? Look how high the head of the fountain is, so high the water will go, and no higher. Water will ascend as high as the place was from whence it descended. And so every mercy we have will carry us as high as from whence it came. If from common, general bounty, it carries us to God but in a common, general way; but if it comes in special love through Christ, it carries us to God in Christ.

8. To seek those gifts which God never grants to any but in love. There are some things of such a noble and excellent nature, that God never grants them to any but in love, they are precious things indeed. And this one consideration shows the difference, as much as any thing I know, between spiritual and temporal blessings. Temporal blessings, though they are in themselves good, and attended with many sweet accommodations, yet they are of such a low nature, that many times they come to men out of God's wrath; they may consist with wrath, yea, they may flow from wrath. But spiritual blessings, the graces of God's Spirit, those spiritual blessings wherewith we are blessed in Christ Jesus, are of such a nature that they can never come but from love, and out of love. From this you see, that a little grace is more worth than the enjoyment of all the world. God may give a man the empire of all the world, and he may do it in wrath, and the gift tend to the furtherance of wrath; but if you have but the least dram of grace, if you have but any spiritual knowledge of God in Christ, "this is life eternal:" "This is life eternal, that they might know thee the only true God, and Jesus Christ, whom thou hast sent," John xvii. 3. Faith; this is a precious gift. If thou hast any knowledge of the Divine nature, it comes from the infinite ocean of eternal love, and will carry thee to the infinite ocean of love. O, then, prize grace, seek after grace.

You whose hearts have been so eager and desirous after outward things, turn now the stream of your desires. I have been eager after such and such things; if I have them, yet I may have the wrath of God with them, and what good will they do me then? Oh, but I hear of things that are to be had, which I can never receive but in love, they are the privileges that come to the saints in Jesus Christ.

9. To bless God, if we know and find that what we have proceeds from love. You are to bless God for what you have; but in that he has given you your desires, and given them out of love too, here God blesses his blessings, and your blessings should be double, treble, seven, a hundredfold. The Lord has delivered me from such an affliction, and I find it is in love. As Hezekiah could say, when he "was recovered of his sickness," "Thou hast in love to my soul delivered it from the pit of corruption," Isa. xxxviii. 17; so I make no question but many of the people of God, even many of you that are before him this day, are able to say, Well, from the observations which I have heard this day upon this point, thus opened, I can say, to the glory of God, Out of love to my soul has he delivered me out of such an affliction, from such a sickness; out of love to my soul has he granted me such a mercy: I had been praying and crying to him for certain mercies, and out of love to my soul has he granted them to me. O, you may go away with comfort in what you have, be it never so little that God has given you. O, the Lord has given you a good portion, your lot is fallen into a good ground, you have a goodly inheritance, certainly you have a child's portion, go away and be satisfied in it.

And now, my brethren, though this, in a practical point of view, is the chief, I confess I have not yet come to that which is held forth in the very words, and that is about the giving of governors in God's wrath; I only have spoken concerning the giving of our desires generally: but now, for the particular, specific object of their desires, that God had given them a king in his wrath; that I confess is a point in which there may be much of the mind of God known, and which would require some time in fully opening. It would be hard to speak of such a point as this is without very great deliberation, and to have full scope when at any time I speak of it; and therefore I do not intend at this time to meddle with this point of God's giving kings in wrath, I shall rather defer it to the next day. Only one note further, and that is this:

Many get from their consciences the gratification of their lusts, as they strive to obtain from God the objects of their desires. They are very violent in their desires, and would fain have God grant them such and such things; at length, though it be a thing very displeasing to God, he saith, Let them have it. Just so it is in regard of conscience, for conscience is God's vicegerent in the soul of man. Now many men are very desirous of things which their consciences at first strongly oppose. Oh, they would fain have such and such things: saith conscience, You may not, you will sin against God, you will wound me, and bring sorrow and affliction on yourselves. This makes them pause; they are very much grieved that their consciences will not sanction their desires, and it may be they are so far enlightened that they dare not act without their approbation: now, although they may restrain themselves for a while, yet still their lusts are very violent, and they would fain have their consciences to yield to them; they labour therefore and struggle with them, and seek to find out some evasions and distinctions whereby they may either lay them asleep, so that they may not trouble them, or at length to satisfy their consciences so far as to extort from them permission to gratify their desires. Now their lusts, when they are grown hot, send up such steams into their understandings as hinder the work of conscience, conscience begins to be more dull in its work, not so quick in the apprehensions of its duty, nor in the exercise of it, as before; and at length, after much ado, when they have tired and wearied themselves, and tired conscience too, they at length do obtain even of their very consciences such things as they have a mind to; so that now their consciences begin to say to them, Seeing you have such a strong and earnest desire, do it: they do it with all eagerness, blessing themselves, and thinking they have gotten a great victory in that they have prevailed on their consciences to sanction their pursuits. It may be these men will say, If I thought it were against conscience, if conscience did tell me that it ought not to be done, I would not do it for a world. Yea, but, friend, how do you obtain leave of your conscience? There was a time that conscience was opposed; how comes it now to sanction? is it not through the violence of your spirits? You would needs have it, you were set upon it that you must have your liberty and preferment, your ease and content, and you must not suffer such and such things, and by this violence of your spirits you succeeded in prevailing over your consciences: now conscience lets you go on; but remember, conscience will tear you for it another day: you have prevailed over it so that it does not accuse you of your evil ways, but lets you go on; do you think you will not hear of it another day? O yes, certainly conscience, being God's vicegerent, will do as God will do in this case: when men importune for their desires of God, Why, saith God, let them have them; but do not you think that God will call them to an account for it? so it is here. As men shall hereafter pay full dearly for those things which God suffers them to have here; so many will pay full dearly for those things which conscience now gives them liberty to enjoy: though you have liberty, yet it is a liberty forced from conscience, and conscience will have another reckoning with you hereafter. You know how it was with Balaam, he desired, because of his preferment, to go to curse Israel, and though God did deny him once, yet he would ask again, and would not be satisfied till God said, at length, Go; yea, but for all that God met him in the way, and had like to have destroyed him. Just so do many with their consciences; it may be they see some preferment that they may get in such a way, and their consciences for the present have some tenderness, but they will ask their consciences, and if their consciences say No, they will ask again and again; and as, I say, God said at length to Balaam, Go, but said it to him in anger, and met him in the way, and had like to have destroyed him; so, though conscience may suffer thee to serve thy desires, yet will it one day come out with a drawn sword against thee, and be perhaps thy destruction.

Notes prepared by the author for another sermon on ver. 11, which (being prevented by the Lord's taking him to himself) he preached not.

Ver. 11. *I gave thee a king in mine anger, and took him away in my wrath.*

Obs. 1. Kings and princes sometimes are given to a people in anger. Job xxxiv. 30, "That the hypocrite reign not, lest the people be insnared." It is in anger if a hypocrite reign. Psal. cix. 6, "Set thou a wicked man over him: and let Satan stand at his right hand." Dan. viii. 23, 24, "In the latter time of their kingdom, when the transgressors are come to the full, a king of fierce countenance, and understanding dark sentences, shall stand up. And his power shall be mighty, but not by his own power: and he shall destroy wonderfully, and shall prosper." So it was said of the Agrigentines, that Phalaris was given to them as a plague, and Marius to the Romans. Anastasius Nicenus, Quest. 15, in Script., speaks of one in the time of Phocas, pleading with God, and saying, Wherefore, Lord, hast thou made Phocas emperor? The answer from heaven was, Because I could not find a worse. He tells also of the bishop of Thebais, who, being proud because advanced, had these words spoken to him: Wherefore, miserable man, art thou proud? Thou wert not made bishop because thou wast worthy, but because the city deserved such a bishop.

But it may be demanded, When are kings and princes given in anger? I answer,

1. When men are eager upon them. The men of Shechem were eager upon Abimelech, Judg. ix. 6; they had him, but in wrath; for, ver. 23, it is said, "Then God sent an evil spirit between Abimelech and the men of Shechem." And what the issue was we know.

2. When kings and princes are desired out of an opposition to what God would have them to be under, as here in the text: so 1 Sam. viii. 10, 19.

3. When such are given as were Saul and Jeroboam. For explication of this, observe,

I. What Saul was.

1. Tyrannical. 1 Sam. viii. 11, compared with the title of Psal. xviii.

2. Bold and venturous, to do things of his own head in God's worship. He sacrificed before Samuel came, 1 Sam. xiii. 9.

3. Hypocritical. He blessed Samuel, and pretended he had "performed the commandment of the Lord," 1 Sam. xv. 13; whereas he had rebelled against it, ver. 22, 23.

4. Rash. "Cursed," saith he, "be the man that eateth any food until evening," 1 Sam. xiv. 24; which was, first, a hinderance to the execution of vengeance, ver. 29, 30; and again, all the people heard not, and he had like to have executed the curse on his son Jonathan, if the people had not rescued him.

5. Hardly convinced. He stands in the defence of himself against Samuel the prophet, 1 Sam. xv. 20.

6. Greedy of gain. Samuel charges him with flying upon the spoil, 1 Sam. xv. 19.

7. A respecter of the people more than of the commandment of God. "I feared the people," saith he, "and obeyed their voice," 1 Sam. xv. 24.

8. A seeker of his own vain honour. "I have sinned: yet honour me now, I pray thee, before the elders of my people, and before Israel," 1 Sam. xv. 30.

9. Abandoned by God's Spirit. "But the Spirit of the Lord departed from Saul, and an evil spirit from the Lord troubled him," 1 Sam. xvi. 14.

10. Of a poor low spirit to help himself when God was departed. When he was troubled with the evil

spirit, he was fain to accept the poor help that music could afford him, 1 Sam. xvi. 17.

11. Subtle and crafty. David, speaking of Saul, saith, "They have prepared a net for my steps," "they have digged a pit before me," Psal. lvii. 6; cxlii. 3.

12. Proud and haughty. "For the sin of their mouth and the words of their lips let them even be taken in their pride," Psal. lix. 12. "Will the son of Jesse give every one of you fields and vineyards," &c., 1 Sam. xxii. 7.

13. Given to cursing. "And for cursing and lying which they speak," Psal. lix. 12.

14. Envious. When they had sung in the dance, "Saul hath slain his thousands, and David his ten thousands;" the text adds, "Saul was very wroth, and the saying displeased him;" "and Saul eyed David from that day and forward," 1 Sam. xviii. 6—9.

15. A hater of the saints. 1 Sam. xviii. 11, Saul cast his javelin at David, and said, "I will smite David even to the wall with it." And ver. 12, 13, "Saul was afraid of David, because the Lord was with him, and was departed from Saul. Therefore Saul removed him from him." And 1 Sam. xix. 1, "Saul spake to Jonathan his son, and to all his servants, that they should kill David." And ver. 17, he calls him his enemy, saying to Michal, "Why hast thou deceived me so, and sent away mine enemy, that he is escaped?"

16. Cruel. 1 Sam. xxii. 18, 19, he caused to be slain eighty-five priests; and smote the city of Nob, (the city of the priests,) "men and women, children and sucklings, and oxen, and asses, and sheep, with the edge of the sword." Psal. vii. 2, David prays for help, "lest he" (Saul) "tear my soul" (saith he) "like a lion, rending it in pieces." And Psal. lvii. 4, "My soul is among lions: and I lie even among them that are set on fire, even the sons of men, whose teeth are spears and arrows, and their tongue a sharp sword."

17. Treacherous: he pretends a benefit, intends a mischief. "And Saul said to David, Behold my elder daughter Merab, her will I give thee to wife: only be thou valiant for me, and fight the Lord's battles. For Saul said, Let not mine hand be upon him, but let the hand of the Philistines be upon him," 1 Sam. xviii. 17.

18. False of his word. "But it came to pass at the time when Merab Saul's daughter should have been given to David, that she was given unto Adriel the Meholathite to wife," 1 Sam. xviii. 19. And 1 Sam. xxvi. 21, Saul saith, "I have sinned: return, my son David: for I will no more do thee harm:" yet, chap. xxvii. 1, David was so pursued by him, that he fled to Achish king of Gath.

19. A disregarder of oaths. 1 Sam. xix. 6, "Saul sware, As the Lord liveth, he shall not be slain;" yet, ver. 10, 11, he would have smitten him to the wall with his javelin, and missing that, he sent messengers to murder him in his house.

20. Stout against his conscience, and all the means which God used to reclaim him. 1 Sam. xxiv. 17—20, "Thou art more righteous than I," &c. "I know well that thou shalt surely be king, and that the kingdom of Israel shall be established in thy hand," &c. Hence David, Psal. lix., praying against Saul, as appears in the title of the Psalm, saith, ver. 5, "Be not merciful to any wicked transgressors."

21. A preferrer of base men, and rejecter of good. David was his enemy, but Doeg a mighty man with him, 1 Sam. xxii. 18, 22.

22. He cares not for his own laws to satisfy his humours. Having suppressed wizards and witches, yet he seeks to them and promises them immunity, 1 Sam. xxviii. 9, 10.

23. Unwearied in his malice. He never rests, but follows David, as one hunts a partridge, from place to place; if disappointed one way, he tries another; sends to David's house, then to Naioth, then to Keilah, then to Ziph, then to Engedi, to Hachilah: "Saul sought him every day," 1 Sam. xxiii. 14. "Behold, he travaileth with iniquity," Psal. vii. 14.

24. One that could not be overcome by kindness, love, faithfulness, &c., 1 Sam. xxiv. 4; xxvi. 8, 9.

25. Vexed because he could not have his mind. They "return, and make a noise like a dog," vexed to lose his morsel, Psal. lix. 14, 15.

26. Desperate in forsaking God, and going to the devil for counsel, 1 Sam. xxviii. 7, and afterward wilfully kills himself, 1 Sam. xxxi.

II. What Jeroboam was.

1. One that seemed to be much for the good of the people, but when he had power in his own hands, then none more fierce, 1 Kings xi. 27. He cared not for the people, Hos. xiii. 1.

2. One whose carriage was very taking, diligent, industrious, and valiant, a man fit for rule, 1 Kings xi. 28. But when he had got power into his own hands, there was nothing but imperious domineering; as Tacitus saith of Galba, All men judged him fit for rule, till he ruled.

Omnium consensu capax imperii, nisi imperasses.

3. One who subjected religion to policy. "And Jeroboam said in his heart, Now shall the kingdom return to the house of David, if this people go up to do sacrifice in the house of the Lord at Jerusalem. Whereupon the king took counsel, and made two calves of gold," &c., 1 Kings xii. 26—28.

4. False, pretending one thing, and meaning another. He said unto the people, "It is too much for you to go up to Jerusalem: behold thy gods, O Israel, which brought thee up out of the land of Egypt," 1 Kings xii. 28.

5. Idolatrous. "But hast done evil above all that were before thee: for thou hast gone and made thee other gods, and molten images," 1 Kings xiv. 9.

6. A conscience oppressor. He laid snares for those that went up to Jerusalem to worship, as was noted, Hos. ix. 8.

7. A scorner. "He stretched out his hand with scorners," Hos. vii. 5.

8. Subtle. He ordained such a feast as was at Jerusalem, made a house of high places, and priests, that all might be furnished like the worship at Jerusalem, 1 Kings xii. 31.

9. Intemperate. "In the day of our king the princes have made him sick with bottles of wine," Hos. vii. 5.

10. One who despised the true ministers of God and loved a base clergy. "Made priests of the lowest of the people," 1 Kings xii. 31.

11. Enraged against the servants of God, and God himself, when opposed. "And it came to pass, when king Jeroboam heard the saying of the man of God, which had cried against the altar in Beth-el, that he put forth his hand from the altar, saying, Lay hold on him," 1 Kings xiii. 4.

12. Extremely stout, notwithstanding such a hand of God upon him. "After this Jeroboam returned not from his evil way, but made again of the lowest of the people priests of the high places," 1 Kings xiii. 33.

13. A slighter of God and his worship. "And hast cast me behind thy back," 1 Kings xiv. 9.

14. One who "did evil above all that were before him," 1 Kings xiv. 9.

15. One who trusted to his many men and policy, not regarding what is said to him about fighting against God, 2 Chron. xiii. 8, 12, 13.

16. One who, though conquered before God's servants, who relied on the Lord, so that he lost "five hundred thousand chosen men" at one time, yet continued in his evil, 2 Chron. xiii. 17.

17. One who for his own ends would make use of God's prophets, 1 Kings xiv.

18. A man of a base spirit. God threatens he will take his house away, "as a man taketh away dung," 1 Kings xiv. 10.

19. One whose family was such, that, except in one little child, there was found in it no "good thing toward the Lord God of Israel," 1 Kings xiv. 13.

20. One "who made Israel to sin." The common epithet the Scripture gives him.

21. One who ruined the kingdom by his sin. "He shall give Israel up because of the sins of Jeroboam," 1 Kings xiv. 16.

Yet for all this, "the days which Jeroboam reigned were two and twenty years," 1 Kings xiv. 20.

Seeing governors are sometimes given in wrath, let us pray that they be given to us in love. But there follows,

"And took him away in my wrath." As if he should say, Though they were evil, yet I took them away, to make way for worse.

Obs. 2. Oppressors are taken away, and greater oppressors come in their room.

Calvin, thus, I will take away this kingdom from you, which I see to be an occasion of blindness to you; for if it remain, I shall be nobody with you, nor will my word be of any authority.

Obs. 3. What God gives in anger never prospers.

Expect not therefore help from those men or things that God gives in wrath.

Sometimes God accepts of repentance when it is unfeigned, as in David's taking Bathsheba to wife, of whom he had Solomon, &c.; viz. if the thing itself be good.

Obs. 4. What God gives in anger cannot hold long with us. Caution, yet this kingdom of Israel continued twenty years.

Obs. 5. Those things that begin ill, prosper not usually. *Initium maledictum, finis maledictus*, Calvin in loc. The beginning is accursed, and so is the end. Thus many things begun in anger, end in wrath: this kingdom of Israel is an example of this from the beginning to the end. [But yet here also that holds, which the author noted above, ver. 9, that no condition is so bad, but there is help in God for it, and if so be that the continuance in it be not with sin, or the thing a sin in itself.]

Obs. 6. When men have enjoyed their desires in wrath a while, God rends them in fury from them. This is terrible indeed, for as it was given in indignation, all the while it was enjoyed it was abused. "While the meat was yet in their mouths, the wrath of God came upon them," Psal. lxxviii. 30, 31.

Pœnæ piorum ira, impiorum furor. Pareus.

But yet we must here note the difference which Pareus observes, That the calamities attendant on what God gives in displeasure, are indeed wrath to his own people, but to his enemies fury.

Obs. 7. God's removal of a wrathful gift, is often but an instance of more wrath.

But here are two questions: 1. How may we know when God takes away, and not in wrath?

1. When the comfort or creature which he takes from us, began to draw our heart from him, and it is seasonably removed to our sanctification. 2. When we can bless God and be thankful. 3. When God makes it up in himself, and in the comforts of his Spirit.

2. When does God take away a thing in wrath?

1. When it is given in anger.

2. When he takes it away by violence in some terrible manner. Psal. lviii. 9, "Before your pots can feel the thorns, he shall take them away as with a whirlwind, both living, and in his wrath." Psal. lii. 5, "God shall likewise destroy thee for ever, he shall take thee away, and pluck thee out of thy dwelling place, and root thee out of the land of the living." Lam. ii. 6, "He hath violently taken away his tabernacle;" as a man that is angry snatches away what he had given.

3. When he takes it in the hour of our need. Zeph. ii. 4, "They shall drive out Ashdod at noon day;" when they should have taken the benefit of their houses for shelter, and their meat for refreshment.

Tempus sane incommodissimum, iter gravissimum facientibus in æstate et in locis calidioribus. Drus. in loc.

4. When we murmur and complain inordinately of our affliction.

5. When we shift and shirk out for succour.

6. When there is nothing but bitterness, and only evil in the removal.

7. When one evil makes way to another evil, and none are sanctified. "He made a way to his anger," Psal. lxxviii. 50.

8. When the deprivation carries with it the marks of special sins; yea, when the sin itself is allowed to deprive us of a mercy: as when intemperance takes away health; ambition brings into disgrace; covetousness takes away riches. "This is my covenant unto them, when I shall take away their sins," Rom. xi. 27.

9. When it happens according to those misgiving thoughts which we have had, and to which yet we would not give heed.

10. When it brings sin into remembrance. "Thou makest me to possess the iniquities of my youth," Job xiii. 26. "Art thou come unto me to call my sin to remembrance, and to slay my son?" 1 Kings xvii. 18.

Wherefore seeing this is so fearful, let us pray, with David, "O Lord, rebuke me not in thine anger, neither chasten me in thy hot displeasure," Psal. vi. 1.

Obs. 8. Whether we have our desires, or whether they be taken away, yet still all may be in wrath. To this state our sins may bring us.

Obs. 9. Change of oppressing government by foreign power, is a sign of wrath.

Obs. 10. God's hand in a business excuses not man's sin; he can make use of man's sin to the furtherance of his ends, and yet be innocent.

Obs. 11. We must judge of nothing by success.

Samaria's Downfal;

OR

A COMMENTARY,

BY WAY OF SUPPLEMENT,

ON THE FIVE LAST VERSES OF THE

THIRTEENTH CHAPTER OF HOSEA;

WHEREIN IS SET FORTH,

EPHRAIM'S DIGNITY, DUTY, IMPENITENCY, AND DOWNFAL.

VERY SUITABLE TO, AND SEASONABLE FOR, THESE PRESENT TIMES.

WHERE YOU HAVE THE TEXT EXPLAINED, SUNDRY CASES OF CONSCIENCE CLEARED, MANY PRACTICAL OBSERVATIONS RAISED, WITH REFERENCES TO SUCH AUTHORS AS CLEAR ANY POINT MORE FULLY.

BY THOMAS HALL, B. D.

PASTOR OF KING'S NORTON.

Thus will I do unto thee, O Israel: and because I will do this unto thee, prepare to meet thy God, O Israel.—AMOS iv. 12.
A prudent man foreseeth the evil, and hideth himself.—PROV. xxii. 3.

Etsi Christus et apostoli minantur facinorosis, et graviter reprehendunt vitia; tamen prophetarum conciones ideo ad deterrendos malos aptiores, et ad timorem Dei inculcandum efficaciores sunt, quia semper certas pœnas flagitiosorum addunt, quas eventus postea ostendit non fuisse vanas.—LUTHER. in Præfat. ad Hoseam.

TO THE

RENOWNED CITY OF LONDON,

GRACE, MERCY, AND PEACE, BE MULTIPLIED.

A WORD spoken in season is much commended by the wisest of men, Prov. xv. 23, and xxv. 11. Yea, it is made one of Christ's excellencies, that he had "the tongue of the learned," that he should "know how to speak a word in season," Isa. l. 4. Such words are not only profitable, but also powerful, and carry abundance of convincing strength and force with them, Job vi. 25. This, principally, has imboldened me to dedicate this treatise to you. Had I searched for five verses throughout the whole Bible, I could hardly have found five together (all things considered) more suitable and seasonable for the present times.

In them we have an alarm for the drowsy, a corrosive for the impenitent, a cordial for the penitent, and many quickening considerations to move us all to a speedy preparing to meet our God in a way of unfeigned humiliation, before the decree bring forth, and the fierce anger of the Lord seize upon us.

Here we may see Ephraim's dignity, and Ephraim's downfal, and those sins which helped to bring him down; and in him we may read England's condition. The Lord has made us his Ephraim, he has laid his right hand upon us, he has made us the head of the tribes, he has set us above, when for our sins he might long since have laid us in the dust. Ephraim's sins were Ephraim's ruin; and if those sins be found in England which were found in him, what can we expect but the like judgments? for God is the same to the same sinners. If Samaria's sins be found in London, London must look for Samaria's judgments. God will not spare sin, wherever he finds it, be it in city or country. Sin has brought down greater cities than yours; as they had their times of rising, so of ruining; as of building, so of burning: witness Nineveh, No, Tyre, Babylon, and Jerusalem, sin has made them all a desolation. For my own part, I shall never expect that city or state should prosper, till God's church prosper; or that our houses should continue, when God's house lies waste; all our buildings will be but Nods and Babels, that is, unsettlement and confusion, till God's house be settled and exalted amongst us, Hag. i. 4—11. The sins of England I fear more than all the enemies in the world. It is not Spain or Italy, it is not France or Turkey, that I fear; though all nations should compass us about, yet, were we but an obedient people, I should not doubt but that in the name of the Lord we should destroy them. But it is the atheism, heresy, blasphemy, security, impenitency, apostacy, profanation of holy things, formality, hypocrisy, unrighteousness, division, and contempt of the gospel; these, even these, are the enemies that I fear; and if any thing destroy us, it is these abominations that reign amongst us. "Be thou instructed," therefore, O England, and thou, O London, the chief city thereof, lest the Lord's "soul depart from thee," and thou be made "desolate, a land not inhabited," Jer. vi. 8. God has borne long with our provocations, but he will not always bear, but will at last reconcile his patience with the fierceness of his fury. Let not therefore Satan delude any, as if these were but some melancholy conceits, some fearful fancies, or vain prognostications of some lying astrologers; but know, that these are certain assertions, grounded upon the infallible word of God, whose threatenings, as well as promises, are like to silver, that has been seven times purified, and thoroughly tried, Psal. xii. 6.

True, we have many privileges that others want, but no privileges can preserve an impenitent people from ruin: Jerusalem was highly privileged, and had the choicest preaching, a little before its downfal. The sins of a city and nation may be so great, that though Noah, Job, and Daniel (three men that could do very much with God, Ezek. xiv. 14) should stand before the Lord for them, yet they shall not prevail for a hardened, apostatizing people. Where such spiritual judgments go before, temporal judgments always follow, Isa. vi. 9—12. Sinning is worse than suffering; better see a people bleeding, than blaspheming; for by our sufferings God is glorified, but by our sins he is dishonoured.

We are a people that are much for liberty, we cannot endure a yoke; no, though it be Christ's easy yoke, yet we will not have him to reign over us; we will not serve him with gladness and singleness of heart in the abundance of all things, and therefore he may justly make us serve our enemies in the want of all things, Deut. xxviii. 47, 48. And as we are all for liberty, so he may justly proclaim a liberty for us to the sword, pestilence, and famine, Jer. xxxiv. 17.

God has humbled many in your great city, by sickness, poverty, and decay of trading, &c.; but have you been made humble thereby? He has sent the choicest of his ministers amongst you, and fed you (in a spiritual sense) with the finest of the wheat; but have you answered God's cost and care? and are you bettered by all his dispensations to you? Have you heard the voice of the rod, and who hath appointed it? or have you not rather fallen away more and more, and grown worse and worse? if so, how can you expect peace, when your apostacies and spiritual fornications are so many? 2 Kings ix. 17, 18.

But it is not for me to counsel you, who have so many living and dead counsellors at hand; I shall therefore betake myself to prayer, desiring that the good-will of Him that dwelt in the bush may dwell amongst you, that he would be for walls and bulwarks to you, and your glory in the midst of you; that he, by the Spirit of fire and of burning, would purge out of you every thing that offends, that your scum of blasphemy, heresy, hypocrisy, unrighteousness, &c., may no longer abide in you, but that the name of your great and famous city may for ever be Jehovah Shammah, The Lord is there. This is and shall be the prayer of

Your servant in the Lord,

THOMAS HALL.

King's Norton, Nov. 17, 1659.

TO THE READER.

HAVING occasion lately to peruse Mr. Burroughs on Hosea xiii. 13, I found that his commentary was defective, and that Mr. Burroughs (that prince of preachers) died before he had finished the chapter; whereupon I perused the remainder of the chapter, and finding it to be very pertinent to these present drowsy, dangerous times, and that no man had set upon it these twelve years, (for so long has Mr. Burroughs been dead,) having a little respite, in the strength of my God I undertook it, and by his assistance have at last completed it. True, it has cost me some pains, the most of these five verses being so turned and tortured, so intricate and perplex, admitting of so many various lections and senses, and interpreters so divided amongst themselves, that he had need of a great deal of prayer and patience that undertakes them. I think there are not many harder verses in the Bible than some of these, yet by a good hand of Providence I have gone through them, and have not balked any known difficulty, but have made all as plain and intelligible as possibly I could.

Many posthumous works have had supplements excelling their predecessors; this cannot be expected here. All that I can promise thee is this, that I have as fully and faithfully explained the text as I could. I have raised thence many useful observations, and given references (because I understand they are very acceptable to many) to such as enlarge upon any point more fully. Some common places are succinctly handled, and if any controversy occur, (according to my custom and calling,) they have a lash and a pass.

As for the fourteenth chapter, it is piously and pithily opened by two very grave, judicious men; so that now you have the whole prophecy completed. If thou reap any benefit, give God the praise, who is pleased to show light in the darkness, and strength in the weakness, of

Dr. Sibbs. Dr. Reynolds.

Thine in the Lord,

THOMAS HALL.

CHAPTER XIII.

VERSE 12.

The iniquity of Ephraim is bound up; his sin is hid.

THIS chapter contains the sum of the eleventh sermon of Hosea, wherein the prophet (like the sweet singer of Israel) treats both of judgment and mercy, and uses both drawing and driving motives (one or both of which usually work upon all ingenuous dispositions) to bring them to repentance. And since God has ordained the law to make way for the gospel, and humiliation to go before consolation, therefore the prophet denounces,

1. Judgments against Israel, and specially that of the sword, which should cut off his kings, destroy his kingdom, take away all their pleasant things, and make them a desolation: neither was God to be blamed for all this, for it was their own sins that had brought those evils upon them, viz. their idolatry, pride, carnal confidence, impenitence, stupidity, ingratitude, and forgetfulness of that God, who had raised them to great glory and dignity.

2. He sets forth the fierceness of God's wrath against them, ver. 7, 8. Great blessings when abused bring great judgments. Their sins had turned God, their great Benefactor, into a "lion," "a leopard," "a bear bereaved of her whelps," "a wild beast;"* and imbittered his soul against them. They dreamt they should find him a God all mercy; he tells them they are mistaken, for now they should find him a God full of fury.

3. Whereas they might think to escape because God had so long forborne them, the prophet, by a prolepsis, prevents this conceit: "The iniquity of Ephraim is bound up, his sin is hid;" that is, Ephraim thinks now he may take his pleasure, since his iniquity lies hid, and he has so long escaped; but mark what follows, ver. 13, "The sorrows of a travailing woman shall come upon him." As the pleasure of conception has the pangs of child-birth attending it, so this secure and pleasant people shall certainly meet with sorrow in the end; and therefore Ephraim is but "an unwise son," and guilty of great folly, in that he does not speedily make his peace with God.

4. Lest they should despair, he intermixes comfort with his threatenings, and allays the terrors of the law with the promises of the gospel, ver. 14.

5. Yet, lest they should grow secure, after a little interruption in the order of the words, he returns to denounce judgments, and tells them, that notwithstanding the promise of deliverance, yet first they must expect a desolation of the chief city and the kingdom, ver. 15, 16.

In this 12th verse we have briefly set forth the desperate and deplorable condition of God's people; they were come to that height of wickedness, and grown so stupid under God's strokes, that now they must expect no more pardon, nor look that God should bear any longer with them. So that in these words the Lord meets with the vain conceits of the loose persons of those times, who soothed themselves in their evil ways, and because the Lord suspended his judgments for a time, therefore they never apprehended them, but thought that the Lord was such a one as themselves, that is, no way displeased with their sins; but since he connived at them, they concluded he slept, and took no notice of them, but had utterly forgotten them. But they are much deceived, saith the Lord, for I have seen all their wickedness, and have sealed up all their sins till the due time of revealing them (which is now at hand) be come. It is true, I have borne long with them; let that offend none, for I have not forgotten their provocations, they are all bound up so that not one of them shall be lost, but they shall dearly reckon for them all together. As God has "a book of remembrance" wherein he records the good deeds of his people, which shall one day be published to their everlasting praise, Mal. iii. 16; so he has a book of remembrance wherein he records the wickedness of the wicked, which shall ere long be published to their everlasting shame. As the sin of Judah was "written with a pen of iron, and with the point of a diamond," so that it should not easily be blotted out, Jer. xvii. 1; so all the sins of Ephraim, from the time of Jeroboam's reign to their going into captivity, were bound up and sealed, that they might not be lost. Papers that lie loose and unbound are scattered with every wind, but when they are fast bound up and sealed, then they are safe and sure. Money that lies at random is lost, but that which is locked up in coffers is safe, and will be brought forth when need requires. So God had not forgotten Ephraim's sin, but had hid and sealed it up till the determined time to punish him was come; he had locked it up in his memory for a day of reckoning.

Yet, to leave no clod unbroken that we may find out the golden ore, I shall give you the grammatical reading of the words; for a good foundation is the strength of the building.

"The iniquity." עון the pravity and perverseness, the prevarication and crookedness, of Ephraim's ways is laid up.

"Of Ephraim." Ephraim was Joseph's second son, but it is here put for the ten tribes of Israel, of which Ephraim was one of the chiefest; so Hos. iv. 17; v. 3; vi. 4; vii. 8, 11; and their first king after the division was an Ephraimite.

"Is bound up." צרור The metaphor here implies special care and custody, and is borrowed from the men of the world, who are careful to lock up their money that it be not lost. The like expressions you may read, Deut. xxxii. 34; Job xiv. 17; xxi. 19; Lam. i. 14. So the iniquity of Ephraim was sealed and kept safe, to be brought forth in due time as a charge against him. Though men scatter their sins abroad and forget them, yet God bundles them up and remembers them; and as pardoning grace does loose the sinner, so sin unpardoned is said to be bound up and reserved for punishment, Matt. xvi. 19.

צרר gavit, custodivit, constrinxit quasi in fasciculum; ita Gen. xlii. 35; 1 Sam. xxv. 29; Prov. xiii. 22; xxx. 4.

"His sin." חטאתו The punishment of his sin. It is a frequent metonymy to put sin for the punishment of sin. So Lev. xx. 20; Numb. xii. 11; Ezek. iv. 4—6. *Peccatum ejus*, from *Chata*, to err, or wander from the mark: such is sin; it is a wandering and going astray from the law of God, it is an erring from the mark which we should always aim at, viz. the glory of God and our own salvation.

* Deus comparatur leoni sævo, quo nulla bestia truculentior. 2. Pardo in via observanti, quo nulla subtilior. 3. Urso catulis orbato, quo nulla sævior. 4. Cuivis immani bestiæ, siqua alia, prioribus immanior, sub genere continetur. Ternovius in loc.

צפינה abscondita est, a צפן recondidit, custodivit. Sic Job x. 13; Psal. xvii. 14; Prov. xxvii. 16; Jer. xvi. 17.

"Is hid." Not from God, but with God; it is laid up by him for a day of reckoning, when the Lord shall pour out the fierceness of his wrath on Israel. So that their sin is hid, not in mercy, but in judgment; not for protection, but for desolation. "Samaria shall become desolate." God lays up the sins of the wicked in store against a day of wrath, when he intends to punish them for all together, Rom. ii. 5.

Obs. 1. God is wondrous patient, and bears long with sinners. He is many years in laying men's sins up in his treasury. He does not immediately cut off sinners, nor always destroy wicked men in the act of sin, as he might do, (for so many sins as men commit, so many damnations they deserve,) but with much patience, and great long-suffering, he bears with "the vessels of wrath," Rom. ix. 22. He bore with the old world many hundred years, even till the whole earth was corrupt before him, and his Spirit tired out, as it were, with striving with them, Gen. vi. 3; 1 Pet. iii. 20. He spared Sodom so long that their sins cried to heaven for vengeance against them, Gen. xviii. 20, 21. He spared Amalek, too, four hundred years, 1 Sam. xv. 2, 3. He spared Israel here three hundred and sixty years ere he sent them into captivity, Ezek. iv. 4—6. He spared the Gentiles four thousand years, Acts xiv. 16, and bore with Jerusalem till they stoned his prophets, and would not be reclaimed, Matt. xxiii. 37. His vials of wrath are vessels of large extent, but narrow mouths; they pour out slowly, but drench deeply, and distil effectually God's wrath on the heads of his enemies, Rev. xvi. 1, 18, 19. Though we provoke him daily, yet he is patient towards us, "not willing that any should perish, but that all should come to repentance," 2 Pet. iii. 9; Rev. ii. 21. He sends his messengers in great compassion to us, "rising early" to stop us in our sinful courses, and so prevent our destruction, 2 Chron. xxxvi. 15; Jer. xxv. 4. Yea, he is not only patient, but "long-suffering," which is a further degree of patience, it is patience lengthened out, Exod. xxxiv. 6; Psal. ciii. 8; Jonah iv. 2. He waits, and waits long for our returning, crying, "Wilt thou not be made clean? when shall it once be?" Jer. xiii. 27. Were some good man to sit but one hour in the throne of God, and look down upon the earth, as God does continually, and see what abominable idolatries, blasphemies, heresies, homicides, perjuries, adulteries, persecutions, oppressions, were committed in that hour, he would undoubtedly in the next set all the world on fire. It is well, in this respect, that we have to do with God, and not with man. "I will not execute the fierceness of mine anger, I will not return to destroy Ephraim." Why so? "For I am God," most true in my promises, and of infinite patience, "and not man," who is mutable and passionate, and could not bear the daily indignities and provocations which are committed against me, Hos. xi. 9. Great then is the sin of those who abuse the patience and long-suffering of the Lord, adding sin to sin, and drunkenness to thirst; that draw on iniquity with the cords of vanity, and so treasure up wrath against the day of wrath. Impunity breeds in them impenitency; "Because sentence against an evil work is not executed speedily, therefore the heart of the sons of men is fully set in them to do evil," Eccl. viii. 11. Every word has its weight; these indulged sinners do not barely practise sin, but their heart is set on it; the very bent of their spirit is to evil indefinitely, that is, to all manner of evil, and that with resolution and purpose of heart, they follow it fully. As good men cleave to God and his ways with "purpose of heart," Acts xi. 23, and are married to him, Cant. ii. 16, so do these to sin and Satan, they are married to them, Hos. iv. 17. Impunity and prosperous wickedness make men insolent, Psal. lxxiii. 8, 9, impudent, Isa. iii. 9. And resolute in sin, Jer. xliv. 16, 17. Such are apt to think there is no God, or at least that he regards not things below; or that he is like themselves, approving of their ways, and that which they do is no sin, Psal. l. 16—22. Those gross hypocrites, that talked so much of God's word, but denied him in their works, being slanderers, adulterers, thieves, thought that because God was silent, and did not presently punish them, that therefore he approved of their wickedness. But mark what follows, there is a stinging *but*, "but I will reprove thee, and set them in order before thine eyes." Thou shalt know one day how I hated thy sins, by the punishments which I will inflict upon thee for them; and though now thou hidest them, yet then I will marshal them and set them in rank and order before thy face. Consider this, therefore, you that cast God's counsels behind your backs, and hate to be reformed, before he awaken your drowsy consciences, and rouse up that mastiff which lies sleeping in your bosoms, before you come to answer for all in the midst of flames. It is a sad and sore delusion wherewith Satan deceives millions of men, that because they are not presently punished, therefore they shall never be punished; and since God has forborne so long, therefore he will always bear, and they shall never hear more of their sins; hence it is that the wicked flatter themselves in their sins, Deut. xxix. 19; Psal. xxxvi. 1, 2; Isa. xlvii. 7.

Obs. 2. God's forbearance is no acquittance; though he bear long, yet he will not always bear. We see he bore long with the old world, Sodom, Jerusalem, &c., but at last they paid for all. Mercy abused turns into fury, and the preservations of wicked men are but reservations to greater wrath. God has leaden heels, but iron hands; the further he fetches his arm, the heavier will the blow come; the further he draws his arrow, the deeper will it wound. God's mill may grind soft and slow, but it grinds sure and small, and he will recompense his patience with the fierceness of his fury, Nah. i. 3, 6. Ever after the sweetmeats of sin, look for a sad and sour reckoning. There was never any that sinned against the Lord, be it never so secretly or subtlely contrived, but first or last the punishment of their sin found them out, Gen. iv. 7; Numb. xxxii. 23. As parents let their children alone till, after multiplied faults, they have committed some signal one, and then reckon with them for all together; so the Lord lets the wicked alone till they be ripe for ruin, Gen. xv. 16, and have filled up the measure of their sin, that wrath may come upon them to the uttermost, Amos i. 3, 6, 9, 11, 13. The whore of Babylon, that has so long made herself drunk with the blood of the saints, shall at last be burnt with fire; yea, it is said she is fallen already, to show the certainty of it, Rev. xiv. 8. God will avenge the injuries done to his church, though it be long first, Luke xviii. 6. When God has long held his peace, and been still, then he will cry suddenly, "like a travailing woman," and "will destroy and devour at once," Isa. xlii. 14.

Now, the Lord show mercy to England, and awaken us out of our deep security, for we have been a people that have exceedingly abused the patience and long-suffering of our God; as he has loaded us with mercies, so we have loaded him with our iniquities; we have made him to wait with our sins, and broken his heart with our abominations, Ezek. vi. 9. As we have been increased, so have we sinned against him; the more victories and success we have had, the more blasphemous and licentious we have been. Do we thus requite the Lord, O foolish and unwise? Is this the thanks we render to God for above a hundred years' preaching? Shall not the Lord visit for such sins as these, and will not his soul be avenged on such a nation as this? True, the Lord has borne long with us, but he will not always bear; but as he said to Ephraim here, so may I say to England, The iniquity of England is bound up, and her sin is hid till a meet time of punishment is come, which we have cause to fear is now at hand; and then God will reckon with us for all together, as we do with rebellious children. Remember your covenant-breaking, saith God. Item, Take this for your blasphemies, and that for your adulteries; take this for your heresies, and that for your atheism and apostacy; take this for your intolerable tolerations, and that for your reviling my messengers.

Obs. 3. This is a special device of Satan, first to tempt men to sin, and then to security in sin. To this end he persuades them they may do well enough; though they have done thus and thus, yet they shall hear no more of it. Thus he deluded our first parents; first he tempts them to sin, and then goes about to persuade them that they shall not die, nor be punished for their sin, Gen. iii. 4. He labours to free men from fear, that so they may be free to sin. In good things he separates the means from the end, and in evil he separates the end from the means. Thus this great deceiver of the whole world blinds men and deludes them, persuading them that what they have done, either is no sin, or if it be a sin, yet it is but a small one; or if it be a great one, yet it is not known; or if it be known, yet it shall never be punished. Thus seducers and false prophets, those devils incarnate, devils clothed with flesh and blood, like their father the devil, curse where God blesses, and bless where God curses. They daub over men's sins, and sew pillows under men's elbows, persuading men that the evils threatened shall never come, but they shall have peace, though God has said there is no peace to the wicked, 2 Kings ix. 18; Jer. viii. 11. Hence the apostle warns us thrice to take heed that no man deceive us with vain words, making us believe that we may be idolaters, covetous, fornicators, &c., and never be punished for it, 1 Cor. vi. 9; Gal. vi. 7; Eph. v. 6. "Be not deceived; God is not mocked:" you may, by your shifts, distinctions, and evasions, delude yourselves, and delude others; but there is no deluding God, who knows us better than we know ourselves. Carnal hiding of sin hinders the prosperity of the sinner, Prov. xxviii. 13; the more men hide them in this kind, the more God will reveal them; as we see in Saul, Achan, and David; what means did each of them use to cover his iniquity, but all in vain, for God brought it to the public view of all, 2 Sam. xii. 12. The only way to have our sins hid indeed, is plainly and sincerely to confess them, Psal. xxxii. 5.

Facit securos quos cupit esse captivos. Aug.

Obs. 4. It is a sore punishment to go unpunished for sin. When the Lord was angry with Ephraim, he bids "let him alone," and tells him that he will not punish him for his sin, Hos. iv. 14, 17; that is, Since Ephraim *will* go after idols, after idols he *shall* go, I will not by any punishment restrain him, but I will let him go on and prosper in his abominations to his utter confusion: and thus to be given up to one's own heart's lust, is a sign of God's highest displeasure. In this sense not to be stricken is the sorest stroke, Isa. i. 5, and for God not to be angry is the greatest anger; as to be stopped and corrected for sin is the greatest mercy, Psal. lxxxix. 32—34; xciv. 12, 13.

Obs. 5. Punishment is never nearer than when it is least feared. A great calm many times is the forerunner of a storm. When men cry, "Peace and safety, then sudden destruction cometh upon them," 1 Thess. v. 3. When the old world was eating, drinking, buying, building, marrying, and sleeping in security, then comes the flood. When Agag thought "Surely the bitterness of death is past," saith Samuel, Hew him in pieces, 1 Sam. xv. 32, 33. When men are at ease in Zion, a woe hangs over their heads, Amos vi. 1—8. When men look upon judgments as afar off, then God will defer no longer, Ezek. xii. 27, 28. Secure Laish becomes a booty to its enemies, Judg. xviii. 7, 27. The Amalekites, when they had taken Ziklag and were drunken, fearing no danger, were suddenly surprised and slain, 1 Sam. xxx. 16, 17. When the Philistines met to be merry and sport themselves with Samson, he brings the house upon their heads, Judg. xvi. 25, 29. Darius, in the midst of his cups was slain by the Persians, Dan. v. 30. And Babylon, that boasted she sat as a queen and should see no sorrow, had sudden plagues come on her, Rev. xviii. 7, 8.

Let no man then delude himself with the thoughts of impunity; for though conscience may sleep for a time, yet at last it will be awakened, and then the longer thy sins have been hid, the more will they rage against thee, especially at the day of judgment, that day of revealing the hidden work of darkness. God will then "bring every work to judgment, with every secret thing, whether it be good or evil," Eccl. xii. 14. God will then unlock his treasury, and those sins which are now sealed up shall be brought to open light; and those secret villanies which men would not have exposed for all the world, shall be written as with a beam of the sun upon their foreheads to their everlasting shame. Sinners shall then have no cause to say, "Where is the God of judgment?" Mal. ii. 17.

Let us therefore make a right use and improvement of the patience of God,* let it melt and humble us, and lead us to repentance. Let us, in this our day, know the things that belong to our everlasting peace, whilst the patience of God yet waits upon us, and he stands knocking at the door of our hearts, Rev. iii. 20, before the door of grace be shut against us, for then it will be too late. To quicken you, know that God in the end will reckon with you for all his patience and forbearance; the longer he has borne with you, the greater will your sin be. He takes an exact account of every day and year that he has borne with us; "Forty years long was I grieved with this generation," Psal. xcv. 10. He takes notice of every provocation; "They have tempted me now these ten times," Numb. xiv. 22: though you forget your provocations, yet God does not. Yea, he records every sermon that we hear, and the day and year that it was preached to us, Hag. i. 1.

Lastly, let us imitate God, and be followers of him as dear children, be patient as he is patient. Though we cannot be so by way of equality, yet by way of analogy and resemblance, in our degree and measure, we may and must: if he bear with us, we may well bear with our brethren; if he has forgiven us pounds, we may well forgive them pence. We should be "kind one to another, tender-hearted, forgiving one another, even as God for Christ's sake hath forgiven us," Eph. iv. 32; Col. iii. 13. Let our moderation and quietness of mind be made known to all, Phil. iv. 5; and if any man wrong us, let us melt them with our kindnesses, Rom. xii. 20, as David melted Saul, and made him weep, and confess that he was more righteous than himself. Even nature could say, It becomes a noble spirit to pass by injuries. When one told King John that his deadly enemy was buried there, and advised him to deface his monument; No, said the king, but I wish all the rest of mine enemies were as honourably buried. It was an excellent answer of Chrysostom to the Empress Eudoxa, and savoured of a sweet, mortified frame of spirit. If the queen (said he) will banish me, let her banish me; "The earth is the Lord's, and the fulness thereof." If she will saw me asunder, let her do it, the prophet

Aristot. Rhetor. l. 1. c. 14.

* Nemo sit deterior quia Deus est melior, toties delinquendo, quoties ignoscitur; quid enim indignius quam ex divina misericordia desumere argumentum ad divinam justitiam provocandam, et quia Deus libenter excipit pœnitentes, data opera velle fieri peccatores? Tertul. de Pœnit. c. 7.

Isaiah suffered as much. If she will, let her cast me into the sea, and there will I remember Jonah.

Ver. 13. *The sorrows of a travailing woman shall come upon him: he is an unwise son; for he should not stay long in the place of the breaking forth of children.*

In this verse the prophet goes on to denounce judgments against an obstinate and rebellious people, if by any means he might awaken them out of their security. By the sorrows of a woman in travail, he sets forth the sudden, sure, and sore destruction, which was even now coming upon the heads of those carnally-confident sinners. They promised themselves peace and prosperity, they had made a league with death, and had put the evil day far from their souls, and therefore drew near to iniquity, Amos vi. 3; no words nor warnings, no mercies nor judgments, could work upon them; therefore the Lord resolves to bear no longer with them, but speedily to surprise them with his judgments. "The sorrows of a travailing woman shall come upon him."

In this verse we have, I. A commination, or a judgment threatened, set forth by the similitude of the sorrows of a travailing woman; a metaphor very frequent in Scripture, wherein are set forth sudden, sharp, inevitable sorrows.

1. Pangs upon a woman in travail come suddenly and unexpectedly; sometimes whilst they are eating, drinking, sleeping, playing, and think not of the pains of travail: so the Lord threatens to bring upon this stupid people calamities which should be like the sorrows of a travailing woman, sudden and unexpected.

2. The pains of a woman in travail are sharp, exquisite, and extreme sorrows, the bitterness whereof that sex can witness.

Such pangs the Scripture often makes the emblems of extreme anguish and distress, Psal. xlviii. 6; Isa. xxvi. 17, 18; xxxvii. 3; Jer. vi. 24; xxii. 23; xlix. 24; Micah iv. 9, 10; Gal. iv. 19. So the calamities which were coming upon this people were not slight sorrows, but such as brought desolation with them. 2. The longer a dead birth is concealed and carried in the womb, the more dangerous and difficult is the travail. Ephraim had for a long time concealed his sin, and therefore now his pangs are like to be so much the more grievous. 3. If the birth be living, the greater the birth, and the longer they go with it, the sharper are the pangs. So the longer God bears with a people, and the more his patience is abused, the more terrible will his wrath be.

3. Inevitable and irresistible. There is no escaping when once the time of travail is come. *Cum adest hora, non datur mora.* So the set time of Ephraim's calamities was now at hand, which they should in no wise be able to avert or avoid.

II. A reason for this commination, taken from the folly of Ephraim; he is, and, for aught I see, for ever will be, "an unwise son," which appears in his stupidity and obstinate persisting in his sins, without any striving to get out of them by repentance. Ephraim is "an unwise son," for had he been wise he had not staid so long in the birth.

Lest Ephraim should reply, that a travailing woman is soon delivered, her pain may be sharp, but it is but short, she has hope not only of an end, but also of a birth, the joy whereof maketh her remember her anguish no more, John xvi. 21; the prophet proceeds, Ephraim "is an unwise son; for he should not stay long in the place of the breaking forth of children." Ephraim "is an unwise son," that sticks long in the birth, and so will be the death both of himself and his mother. He uses no means to facilitate the birth, or to help himself by passing through the strait gate of repentance. God stands over him, stretching forth his hands all the day long to wash off his filth, but he had no mind to come out of his filth, or to be washed from his wickedness, Ezek. xvi. 4, 9; rather than endure the pangs of regeneration, he will venture to stay a while though he be stifled for his pains. As if the prophet should say, Were Ephraim wise he would humble himself, and make his peace with God, that he might, by his mercy, be delivered fully from his miserable straits. If he were not utterly stupified, or rather mad, he would take notice of God's judgments impendent over him, and would imitate little infants, who strive to free themselves out of the straits and dangers of the birth. So would Ephraim have endeavoured to free himself by true repentance. But alas! so besotted and hardened is he in his sins, that he rests content with his carnal condition, never once striving or desiring to come out of this darkness into light, or to be brought from under the power of Satan unto God.

So that in these words the prophet notably inveighs against the stupidity and folly of God's people, in that they had rather be stifled in the filth of their sins, lie in the mouth of death, and under the pressures of God's wrath, to the destruction both of themselves and the church, (which he had before compared to a mother, Hos. ii. 2,) than extricate themselves out of this sin and misery by true repentance.

Obs. 1. Where sin precedes, sudden, certain, sharp, inevitable sorrows always follow. In the former part of the chapter we read of Ephraim's idolatry, pride, impenitency, &c.; now follows, "The sorrows of a travailing woman shall come upon him." Sin and punishment are inseparable companions, Gen. iv. 7, 14; xix. 15; Numb. xxxii. 23; Deut. xxviii. 15—68; hence the word which we render iniquity, signifies also pain and sorrow, because the workers of iniquity bring pain and sorrow upon their own heads, Job xxi. 19; Psal. xxxii. 10.

How then should we hate sin with a pure and perfect hatred! not only *odio inimicitiæ*, but also *odio aversationis;* hate it so as to turn from it. This is the cause of all our sorrows; we may thank our sins for all our sickness, pains, and plagues, Lam. iii. 39. We should therefore do by our sins, as the Jews did by Paul (whom they looked upon as their enemy); "when they saw him in the temple, they stirred up all the people, and laid hands on him, crying out, Men of Israel, help: This is the man, that teacheth all men every where against the people, and the law, and this place," Acts xxi. 27, 28. So should we encourage each other against sin, and lay violent hands upon it, saying, Men and brethren, help: this is it that destroys our people, lays waste our cities, opposes the law, defiles our duties, and incenses the Most High against us.

Let us therefore purge it out of our understandings, and mortify it in our affections. Considering,

(1.) What sin is in its own nature. It is poison, dung, vomit, filth, folly, madness, darkness, sickness, destruction, death. It turned angels into devils, men into beasts, light into darkness, life into death, and order into confusion.

(2.) What sin is in respect of God. It is a reproach and a contempt of him, 2 Sam. xii. 9; it is blasphemy, rebellion, enmity, Rom. viii. 7.

Obs. 2. Scripture language is modest. The mouth of the matrix is called "the place of the breaking forth of children." Thus Adam is said to know Eve; and David to go in to Bathsheba: and so adultery is called "stolen waters," Prov. ix. 17. The Holy Ghost knowing the power of our corruption, and how apt we are to be fired with filthy speeches, therefore, by euphemisms, puts seemly titles on unseemly things. The Scriptures not only command chaste and modest things, but they also speak chastely and modestly of those things.

Abominable then is the sin of the popish casuists, who speak so grossly of the secrets of women in their cases on the seventh commandment. By their obscene words they corrupt good manners, and rather incite than suppress sin. If men must answer for "every idle word," much more for sinful and immodest ones.

Obs. 3. It is a point of great folly to lie long under convictions, and yet never proceed to thorough conversion. The world is full of such unwise Ephraims, that are of a Laodicean temper, neither hot nor cold, that halt between two, or rather twenty, opinions. Their hearts are divided between God and the world, God and their idols, Hos. x. 2. They have their understandings enlightened, their affections stirred, and they are strongly convinced of the truth and comfort that are in God's ways, and yet there they "stay," they never proceed to a thorough conversion. They are almost, but not altogether, persuaded to be Christians; and so shall be almost, but not altogether, saved, Acts xxvi. 28. God has brought them to the birth, and there they stay, refusing to come forth. He would cure them, but they will not be cured; he would convert them, but they will not be converted, Jer. li. 9. Many have a name to live, and are not far from the kingdom of heaven, they come even to "the place of the breaking forth of children," but there they "stay long," too long. They were never fully brought off from their vain principles and practices, and therefore when a temptation comes, they return to them again, as the dog to his vomit.

Many go far, very far, so that they hear the word with some kind of faith and affection, with sorrow and joy, reforming many things, performing many good duties, both publicly and privately; being endowed with excellent gifts of knowledge, utterance, praying, and preaching, and shows of many graces, to the deceiving of themselves and many others; as Balaam, Saul, Ahab, Jehu, Herod, Judas, Demas, Ananias and Sapphira, and those apostates mentioned Heb. vi. 4—6; and yet for want of sincerity they lose all. It is said of king Joash, that he smote the ground twice or thrice and then stayed; whereupon the prophet was angry with him, saying, "Thou shouldest have smitten five or six times; then hadst thou smitten Syria till thou hadst consumed it," 2 Kings xiii. 18, 19. So many a man begins well, and subdues two or three lusts, it may be, but for want of thorough work in subduing them all, loses all. A man may go within a mile of some famous city, and yet for want of going that mile never come there. A man may bid within a shilling of some good bargain, and yet for want of that shilling lose it. The people of Israel went as far as Kadesh-barnea, and were within eleven day's journey of Canaan; and yet by reason of their sins many of them perished in the wilderness and never came there, save only Caleb and Joshua, who followed the Lord fully and sincerely, Numb. xiv. 34, xxxii. 8—13. It is sad when a man shall come near the kingdom of heaven, and yet never come there, Mark xii. 34: to sink within sight of the harbour; like Rachel, to die within a mile of Ephrath, Gen. xxxv. 16; to come within one stride of the mark, and yet miss it, that torments the soul. Many purpose well, and promise well, they begin to repent, and begin to reform, but they are ever beginning, and never bring any thing to perfection: like those "silly women" who were "ever learning, and never able to come to the knowledge of the truth," 2 Tim. iii. 7; like that hypocritical son, who said he would go, but "went not," Matt. xxi. 30, their cold and heartless essays come to nothing. These lose heaven many times for some one lust, as Judas for his covetousness, Esau for a mess of pottage, and the young man who had done much, yet in whom one thing was lacking, which marred all, Mark x. 21; if he could but have parted with that, he might have had Christ and happiness.

Inter cætera mala hoc habet stultitia, semper incipit vivere. Seneca.

O then deny yourselves universally, sell all for the pearl of price; you may buy gold too dear, but you can never buy Christ too dear. What if thou part with riches, pleasures, friends? thou shalt have better riches, pleasures, and friends, all shall be made up in a better kind; yea, thy friends and riches (if God see it good for thee) shall be given thee into the bargain, Matt. vi. 33.

It is true, conviction is very necessary, and an excellent preparative to conversion; as ploughing fits the ground for sowing, so does this fit the heart for grace: and therefore the first work of the Spirit is, to "reprove the world of sin," John xvi. 8. A man must by the law be convinced of his misery, before ever he will beg for mercy; and though all are not converted who are convinced, yet all are convinced who are converted. Men will not come to Christ till they see no other remedy. The malefactor cries not for a psalm of mercy, till he be cast. The prodigal never cares for coming to his father, till he comes to see and say, Here "I perish with hunger," Luke xv. 17. Men must be beaten out of their strong holds, like fish out of their holes, or else they will not come in; we may break hook and line too, to get out a great fish, but cannot, till he be half choked. First convince a man that his disease is desperate, and then persuade him to cut off a leg or an arm. First disarm men of all shifts and flattering dreams, and then you will bring them to their knees. Saul had many shifts, but Samuel refels them all, and at last brings him to, "I have sinned," 1 Sam. xv. 30. If you belong to God, he will effectually convince you in his due time; he that has begun a good work in you, will finish it; he that has brought to the birth, will give strength to bring forth; he that has brought you out of Sodom, will not rest till he has set you safe in Zoar; he perfects all his works in his people, Psal. lvii. 2.

This then is the first and great work of the Spirit, to convince men thoroughly of their lost and undone condition. This is virtually and fundamentally all; till this be done, no good can be done; we shall never be truly humbled, nor prize a Saviour, nor be fit for his service, nor be intrusted by him. Men must be convinced in themselves what they are in themselves, before Christ will reveal himself unto them. Christ will not pour the oil of mercy, but into broken hearts; nor be a physician to any, till they be sick of sin. Such will be ductible and tractable to his will. Paul, when unhorsed and humbled to the ground, is ready to do whatever Christ commands him, Acts ix. 6.

Naturally men have covers, false colours, cavils and excuses for sin; but when the Spirit comes with convincing power, it stops their mouths, and puts them to silence, so that they have nothing to say for themselves, Rom. iii. 19; they see themselves to be guilty, and such as cannot plead their own cause without an advocate. Whilst men are in their natural condition, they are full of self-righteousness, and filled with false notions. Like spiders, we are full of poison, and yet not sick of it, because it is our nature; but when the Spirit comes, it undeceives men, it rectifies their judgments, and confutes those vain conceits which before possessed them. It now clearly convinces them of the vanity of the creature, of the hatefulness of sin, and the necessity of a Saviour. Conviction is a clear and infallible demonstration, which takes away all a man's shifts, and does so nonplus him, that he has nothing to say for himself. When Christ had confuted the Pharisees, he took their cloaks from them: Now I have spoken to them, "they have no cloak for their sin," John xv. 22. Every natural man has some cloak and cover for his sin; but when the Spirit comes, carnal arguments are confuted, and the devil's strong holds are battered, 2 Cor. x. 4, 5; now he confesses he is poor and naked, lost and undone, without a Saviour; now he has no plea, nothing to pretend by way of excuse for himself. And this is the first form in Christ's school; he will never prove a good proficient in the higher form of the gospel, that has not first been convinced and abased by the terrors of the law. God will have men know what he has done for them, and his grace prized at a due rate, and respected by them. Christ is not Christ to any till sin be seen; neither can we bring you to any thing in Christ, till we have brought you to nothing in yourselves. When men are first broken up with the sight and sense of sin, then they may expect to be sown in righteousness, Hos. x. 12. Take heed then,

[1.] Of resisting the Spirit's convictions: do not drive, drink, or game them away; it is a sin against the Holy Ghost so to do, though not *the* sin against the Holy Ghost, Acts vii. 51. Many stifle the Spirit's convictions, like harlots, who destroy their conceptions that they may avoid the pangs of child-birth. Put not out God's light in thy soul, lest his Spirit strive no more with you in this kind, Gen. vi. 3. When God sends his ministers to preach, print, dispute, and convince you, yet if you will not be convinced, take heed lest he say, you shall not be convinced; and in his wrath he say, Means of grace never better this people, sacraments never comfort them, sermons never stir them; since they will be filthy, let them be for ever filthy, and since they will not be purged, they shall not be purged till they die. Thus for God not to strive is the sorest judgment, and a forerunner of some dreadful judgment upon a person or nation.

Many love to hear of privileges, but not of duties; of salvation, but not of sanctification; of heaven, but not of conviction and conversion, which is the way thither. Like the Israelites, that liked Canaan, but would not go through a wilderness to it. But a gracious soul is thankful for humiliation, as well as for consolation; and blesses God, when by his word and Spirit he convinces him of his misery, that so he may be fit for mercy. The sinner convinced of sin, is nearer heaven than the best natural man in the world. Publicans and harlots, that have no excuse nor apology for their gross sins, are in a more hopeful way of cure, than Pharisees, who think themselves righteous enough. Better (saith Austin) be a humble sinner than a proud innocent.

[2.] Of ignorance and unbelief, which are two great hinderances of conviction. When men know not their misery, nor believe the curses which yet are due to them, no wonder if such be unwrought upon.

[3.] Of quenching the motions of the Spirit in you, for if ever you be convinced, the Spirit must do it, John xvi. 8; all the men and ministers in the world cannot do it without the Spirit. We may tell you long enough of this and that sin which you have done, and all to no purpose, till the Spirit sets in with the work, and makes you sensible of sin; then, and never till then, it becomes effectual. Mark, therefore, when the Spirit moves in thee, and improve those opportunities for thy soul's advantage. For as, when children are come to the natural birth, it is God that must and can give strength to bring forth; so, much more in this supernatural birth, is his almighty assistance requisite.

O, then, follow on convictions till they come to conversion, be no longer unwise children, that "stay long" in the place of bringing forth. Be not almost, but altogether, Christians. Rest not content with a name of living, but live indeed. Beseech the Lord to bring thy soul out of this prison, tell him that Christ has proclaimed liberty to captives, and thou art one; thou hast been long in captivity to sin and Satan, beseech him now at last to free thee, and thy soul shall praise him. Be earnest, let God see that thy desires are real, and then he that has brought to the birth will give strength to bring forth.

[4.] Consider, if a man may attain conviction, and yet miss of conversion and salvation, what will become of those that were never yet convinced of their sin, nor had so much as the faith of devils, to believe and tremble. If Jehu that was zealous for God, and Ahab that humbled himself, and Judas that lived unblamably, and the Pharisees that prayed and fasted, and Herod that reformed many things, and Ananias and Sapphira that gave their goods to pious uses; if all these came short of heaven, where, oh where, will thousands amongst us appear, that come short of those who came short of heaven? Rest not then in thy dead and formal condition, but get a sound and thorough conversion. To quicken you, consider,

(1.) In so doing you will be wise children. Naturally we all desire to be accounted wise, the title of fool is odious to us; but we are never wise indeed, till convictions go on to thorough conversion. When the prodigal was enabled to determine to return, then, and not till then, did he come to himself, Luke xv. 17.

(2.) You shall have God's Spirit to assist you. The work indeed is hard, but such assistance will make it easy. The Spirit of God loves to be employed in such noble work as the destruction of sin, and the exalting of Christ in the soul. He is the Spirit of comfort and peace, but he lays the foundation of it in convincing us of our sin and misery.

(3.) It will make you profit more by sermons, sacraments, prayer, &c. When the soul is thus ploughed up with a sense of sin, then it is a fit soil to sow the seed of God's word in.

(4.) It will prevent abundance of sorrow. If Ephraim had not stayed so long in the place of bringing forth, it had been better with him, and he had prevented those desolations that after seized upon him.

(5.) By coming off fully to Christ, you will enjoy abundance of peace and comfort, which otherwise you will miss of. A thorough conversion brings joy, as a woman that is once delivered of her birth, forgets her sorrow for joy that a child is born into the world. The wise merchant, who sold all, and parted with every lust, for Christ, went away rejoicing, as having made a wise bargain. The Spirit lays the foundation of comfort, first in convincing men of their sin and misery, and then of an all-sufficient righteousness to free them from that misery, John xvi. 9, 10.

Obs. 4. Impenitent sinners are unwise men. Impenitent Ephraim is called "an unwise son;" though for number, power, and riches, he was the chief of the tribes. Hence impenitent sinners, and fools, are synonymous in Scripture, Prov. i. 7, 32; Psal. xiv. 1; Rom. i. 22; Tit. iii. 3. Though the blind world may admire, yet, in God's esteem, for all their parts and power, they are but fools and mad-men, 1 Sam. xxv. 25; Luke xii. 20; xv. 17; 1 Cor. ii. 14. It is a grief to parents when their children are fools, Prov. x. 1; xix. 13; and it is a trouble to God when his children are stubborn fools, that may, but will not, know the things that concern their peace. When men are wise to do evil, but averse to do good, when men forget the God of their mercies, and suffer seducers to mislead them, this speaks men fools, Deut. xxxii. 6; Gal. iii. 1. When men fear sufferings more than sin, and resist assistance when it is tendered them, and had rather be strangled in the birth than have strength to bring forth, all this proclaims men's folly.

Obs. 5. To be stupid under judgments is a sore judgment. To be sick, and yet to be insensible of sickness, is a deadly sign: yet so was Ephraim here; the pangs of a travailing woman were upon him, yet he "stays long" in the place of bringing forth, like a child that does not struggle or move for its own relief, which is mortal both to the mother and the child. It is made a note of a wicked man, that he cries not to God for help and deliverance, when he binds him with the cords of correction, Job xxxvi. 13. Men are stupid indeed, when they are wasted, and yet will not be warned; plagued, and yet not instructed, Isa. i. 5; ix. 13; Jer. v. 3; Amos iv. 6, 11. Yet such there have been, and are still, that are no whit affected with God's judgments upon them, nor repent they of their sins, though scorched with plagues, Isa. xlii. 25; Rev. ix. 20; xvi. 9, 11. And is not this England's sin? The pangs of a travailing woman are come upon us, and we are encompassed with dangers on every side; grey hairs, which are a sign of weakness, old age, and death approaching, are here and there upon us; yet we know it not, so as to make a right use of it, and to repent, Hos. vii. 9. The more pains God takes to cure us, the more we revolt both in doctrine and manners; and, therefore, since in our filthiness there is lewdness, and we will not be purged, we may justly fear that we shall not be purged, but as we have had our will, so God will have his will too: I will cause my fury to rest upon you, Ezek. xxiv. 13.

It will be our wisdom to foresee the plague, and hide ourselves; to mourn for the things we cannot mend; to keep ourselves free from the sins of the time, that so we may be kept free from those plagues which are certainly coming upon this sinful land: if any thing set us free from the sense of evil, it is the fear of evil, Prov. xxviii. 14; Hab. iii. 16.

Obs. 6. God owns his people even when they are guilty of great folly and stupidity. Ephraim is a son, though "an unwise son." The ten tribes under Jeroboam, Ahab, and the rest of those wicked kings of Israel, were sadly overgrown with idolatry, security, impenitency, &c.; and yet God owns them for his people to the last, and their circumcision as valid still. Jerusalem that killed the prophets, yet was owned by Christ for the church of God; and he preached unto them, even when he wept over them for their sins, and for the foreseen calamities which were coming on them. The church of Corinth, what carnality, divisions, and profanation of holy things were amongst them, and yet still styled "the church of God," 1 Cor. i. 2. Great, then, is the uncharitableness of those people, that cast off churches and people whom God has not cast off, and unchurch those whom God has not unchurched. The brother of the prodigal was angry at his father's kind reception of him, and calls him "this thy son," by way of proud disdain, and not this my brother, Luke xv. 28—30.

How many are angry at us for owning the Church of England for a national church, and her parochial assemblies for true assemblies, though the word and sacraments be rightly dispensed there! This savours strongly of Pharisaical pride, and too high conceits that some have of themselves and of their church way, in whose assemblies there may be found worse things than in many of those churches which yet they reject.

Ver. 14. *I will ransom them from the power of the grave; I will redeem them from death: O death, I will be thy plagues; O grave, I will be thy destruction: repentance shall be hid from mine eyes.*

This verse is a kind of parenthesis, and being taken entirely in itself, the context will run more smoothly. It is full of knots and difficulties, having almost as many interpretations as interpreters, and as many various lections as words.

"I will ransom them from the power of the grave; I will redeem them from death." Some read these words conditionally, and put in the word if, taking the verb in a different mood and tense, thus, If Ephraim were wise and would but repent, I would have ransomed him from death, I would have redeemed him from the power of the grave; that is, I would either have preserved him from captivity, or else I would have delivered him thence. This is true, but not from the text, for the word is אפדם I will ransom, I will redeem; and we may not change mood and tense to make a sense of our own, though never so good. The words therefore are to be taken simply in themselves, for a singular support to God's people in their deepest distresses; as containing in them a precious cordial, and a most comfortable evangelical promise, of a mighty redemption and glorious resurrection to the remnant according to the election of grace, whom God would have comforted in times of distress. It is usual with the prophets to intermingle comforts with their threatenings, to keep God's people from despair. So Hos. i., ii., xi.; Amos ix. 8—15. Before he had threatened destruction to the wicked, now he comforts the penitent. In the words we have,

1. The deep distress that God's people were in, they were in the hand of the grave, and in the jaws of death, i. e. they were as it were dead and buried in captivity. The word שאול signifies both the grave and hell.

מיד שאול e manu sepulchri, i. e. e summo periculo. Job v. 20; Psal. xlix. 16.

(1.) It is for the grave, Gen. xxxvii. 35; Prov. xxx. 16. (2.) For hell metaphorical, i. e. some deep distress, Psal. lxxxvi. 13. (3.) For the local hell, Prov. xv. 11. We may take in all these significations, for Christ has redeemed us from them all, and triumphed over them on the cross, Col. ii. 14.

2. A promise of their redemption from this their misery. "I will ransom them from the power of the grave." What is that? Why exegetically it is added, "I will redeem them from death;" that is, I will bring my elect out of their captivity, where they lay for dead, and this deliverance shall be to them a pledge of their resurrection to eternal life.

3. The manner how this shall be done, set forth by a prosopopœiacal apostrophe to death and the grave, whom he brings in as some living enemy, and therefore calls to him, saying, "O death, I will be thy plagues; O grave, I will be thy destruction." O death, thou seemest to be mighty and powerful, but I will wholly disarm thee; I will not only bite thee, but utterly destroy thee.

4. The certainty of this deliverance, drawn from the constancy of God in keeping his promise, and from the immutability of his decree. "Repentance shall be hid from mine eyes;" נחם יסתר מעיני I will never repent of the mercy which I have promised them, but my goodness to them shall be firm and unalterable. This sense suits best with the original and with the context, wherein God promises a choice mercy to his people. The Vulgate and Seventy render it, consolation is hid from mine eyes: true, נחם signifies consolation as well as repentance; but to render it as a threatening here, as if God should say, I am fully determined to destroy my people, for consolation is hid from mine eyes, is very improper, for it confounds the context, and the scope of the verse, which is to comfort, and not to disquiet God's people. In it the prophet, the better to strengthen their faith, highly extols God's almighty power; for in straits we are very apt to question that, Numb. xi. 13—23; Psal. lxxviii. 19. To an eye of sense, God's people, lying in captivity, were as dead men, and past all hope of recovery: Yes, saith the prophet, though ye were dead, yet God can raise you again, for he is Lord of death and hell, and has a sovereign power over them all; though death conquers all, yet he conquers death; though it be mighty, yet God is almighty, and there is nothing too hard for him; he will be the death of death, and if none will redeem you thence, he will.

The question is, of what redemption and deliverance does the prophet here speak, whether of a temporal or spiritual redemption? I answer, of both.

1. Literally the Lord promises to free his elect and penitent people from the grave of their captivity. Banished men are counted as dead men, especially in a civil sense, and the place of their banishment is as the grave. Now many of the remnant of Israel, after the destruction of their kingdom, joined themselves to the Jews, and with them came out of Babylon. Though, for their idolatry and ingratitude, he threatened perpetual banishment to them, yet, for the comfort of his people then, and of their progeny, he promises a redemption for them, Hos. i. 10; which was fulfilled about two hundred years after that Samaria was taken, when Cyrus proclaimed liberty to the Jews to go build the temple, Ezra i.

2. Typically it alludes to our spiritual and eternal redemption by Christ, and our conquest over death and hell by him. By Adam's sin, death came upon all men, Rom. v. 15; but Christ, by his resurrection, has freed us from the power of death, and has led it captive, which formerly led us captive, Psal. lxviii. 18; Eph. iv. 8. This is the redemption (saith Zanchy) which is principally and properly here meant: for though the people of Judah, after seventy years' captivity in Babylon, did return again out of it; yet the people of Israel, after that Samaria was taken, never returned again to their own land, for it was laid waste, and inhabited by strangers. It is usual with the prophets, suddenly to digress from their history to Christ, who was their scope, delight, and love; so that every hint and shadow in the Old Testament brought him to their remembrance: and then from Christ to recur to their history again. Thus it is here; and so Isaiah, prophesying of Cyrus, who should deliver Israel out of Babylon, in the same chapter prophesies of Christ the redeemer of his church, Isa. xlv.; and Ezekiel, having inveighed against idle and idol shepherds, presently turns his speech to Christ, who is the true Shepherd of his people, Ezek. xxxiv. 2—16: so Zech. ix. 9; xiii. 6, 7.

In this verse the prophet introduces death and the grave, as two tyrannical enemies, to whom he speaks in the name of the Lord Christ (as the apostle expounds it, 1 Cor. xv. 55) as a conqueror, saying, "O death, I will be thy plagues; O grave, I will be thy destruction." Or as the apostle from the Septuagint, (though in this text the apostle in some things varies from the present Septuagint, and so do other citations in the New Testament; which shows the folly of those, who equalize it with the original Hebrew,) "O death, where is thy sting? O grave, where is thy victory?" 1 Cor. xv. 55. The first Adam brought death into the world, but the Second Adam has abolished it.

Septuaginta a verbis et intellectu Scripturæ sæpe alienissimi sunt, et vel volentes vel ignorantes transtulerunt quæ defendi non possunt. Jerom.

Erotemata hæc insultoria sunt, et sarcasmi speciem habent. Estius.

There is some difficulty in the words, and therefore I shall open them particularly, and break every clod, that I may find out the golden ore in this glorious triumph over death, and notable encomium on the resurrection of the dead.

Piscator and others read the words interrogatively, as an insulting and triumphing interrogation, thus, O death, where are thy plagues? O grave, where is thy destruction? They are no where to be found, for Christ has removed them, and taken them out of the way of his people, so that now there is no hurt in death. This various reading comes from the ambiguous signification of the word אהי which is rendered by some, I will be; by the Septuagint, που, where; and the apostle, following the Septuagint, speaking to Greeks, and that in Greece, alleges a Greek text, as being most familiar and best known to them. The apostle gives the sense and meaning, but not the words, which is frequent in Scripture; the penmen being intent on the matter, were not curious in the words, but did add and alter what might explain and clear them: yet the prophet and the apostle are easily reconciled, thus, "O death, I will be thy plagues," i. e. I will pull out thy pestilent sting; "O grave, I will be thy destruction," i. e. I will get the victory over thee. I, the Lord Christ, will redeem them from death by paying a valuable price for their redemption; this none could do but I: yea, I will be the death of death, I will be its plagues and destruction; it shall never prevail against my people, for I will restore them to life again, 1 Cor. xv. 26, 54, 55. It is not I am, or I have been, but, I will be, thy destruction. Now, in Hebrew, the future tense oft expresses both the present and preterperfect tenses; it implies not only the time to come, but also the time present, and the time past; I am, I have been, and shall be for ever, death's destroyer. Christ was virtually the Lamb slain from the beginning of the world, and so was death's destroyer; but actually he conquered death and the grave, by lying dead in the grave, and by his almighty power raising himself thence again, so that death hath now no more dominion over him and his, Acts ii. 24.

Paulus versionem Septuagint. imitari videtur, quia ea versio potissimum nota erat Corinthiis. Sed interim non discedit ab Hebraicâ Veritate. Pet. Martyr.

אפדם significat non simpliciter liberare, sed pretio redemptionis redimere. Ita גאל significat jure affinitatis redimere, unde גאל affinis, ad quem pertinebat redemptio possessionum. Zanchy.

"O death, I will be thy plagues;" אהי דבריך מות not one or two, but many plagues, even so many as shall destroy thee. Thou didst destroy my people, but now I will destroy thee; thou didst triumph over them, but now I will triumph over thee, and lead thee, and all the enemies of my people, in triumph at my chariot wheels, Psal. lxviii. 18; Eph. iv. 8; for under death and the grave is synecdochically comprehended the conquest of all the enemies of our salvation; as sin, death, hell, Satan, banishment, imprisonment, poverty, sickness, tribulation, persecution, famine, sword, &c., over all these we are more than conquerors, even triumphers, through Christ that loved us, Rom. viii. 35, 37. He names only death, because death is "the last enemy that shall be destroyed," 1 Cor. xv. 26; yet, by an argument from the greater to the less, he comforts his people thus, If I can deliver you from death and the grave, then much more from banishment and captivity.

"O grave, I will be thy destruction," אהי קטבך שאול I will be thy rooting out and cutting off. The same word is used, Deut. xxxii. 24; Psal. xci. 6; Isa. xxviii. 2; and here implies, Thou didst destroy my people, but now I will destroy thee, so that they may now sing triumphantly, O death, where is thy pestilent sting, wherewith thou wast wont to torture and torment us? it is gone, it is destroyed by Christ, who is thy death, O death, and thy utter destruction. As a man that drinks a cup of poison, drinks that which will be his ruin; so the grave, by swallowing and devouring Christ, was conquered and killed by him. Of old they did celebrate the victories and triumphs of Achilles, Hercules, Alexander, Julius Cæsar, and the rest of the great conquerors of the world; but, alas, all those died and were conquered by death. Only Christ, the King and Saviour of his church and people, by his death has conquered sin, Satan, and death; and has made full satisfaction for us to the law and justice of God.

So that which the prophet speaks here of the restoration of the Jews in particular, the apostle applies to the general resurrection of the dead: "When this corruptible shall have put on incorruption, and this mortal shall have put on immortality, then shall be brought to pass the saying that is written, Death is swallowed up in victory. O death, where is thy sting? O grave, where is thy victory?" 1 Cor. xv. 54, 55; where the apostle quotes two texts, and it is usual with the penmen of the New Testament to refer to divers texts out of the Old Testament, and to unite them into one in the New. So Peter, speaking against Judas,

Acts i. 20, saith, "It is written in the book of Psalms, Let his habitation be desolate, and let no man dwell therein: and his bishoprick let another take:" the former part is taken out of Psal. lxix. 25, and the latter part out of Psal. cix. 8. So of Mark i. 2, 3, the former part is taken out of Mal. iii. 1, the latter from Isa. xl. 3. So Christ himself, Matt. xxi. 13, alludes to Isa. lvi. 7, and Jer. vii. 11. So here the apostle cites one text out of Isa. xxv. 8, "He will swallow up death in victory," בלע המות לנצח which the Seventy render, *κατέπιεν ὁ θάνατος ἰσχύσας*, death devours all; but this is contrary both to the sense of the prophet and the apostle, who speak not of the prevailing power of death, but of the power of Christ over death. Death is swallowed up in victory, and that great devourer of all is by Christ devoured. This promise is now fulfilled in the death of Christ, who has already destroyed the power of death for his people; and shall be completely fulfilled at the resurrection of the dead, when all corruption and mortality shall be totally taken away, and death shall be swallowed up in victory for ever. In the sense of this mercy, the apostle breaks forth, ravished as it were with the contemplation of this conquest over death, into a triumphant song, which all the saints shall sing at the last day: when they shall be totally freed from the captivity of death and the grave, then shall they insult over subdued death, and say, "O death, where is thy sting," wherewith thou wast wont to wound all creatures? "O grave, where is thy victory," by which thou hast hitherto kept the dead under by force, which now thou must render again, as not being able any longer to hold them under thy power? Rev. xx. 13, 14. It is only sin by which death has power over us; and it is the just rigour of the law which inflicts death upon us for sin. But thanks be to God who has given us the victory over sin, which is the cause of death, and over death, which is inflicted for sin, through Jesus Christ our Lord, by whom we obtain an immortal and incorruptible life. Thus the apostle has faithfully given us the sense of the prophet, though not his very words.

The sum and substance of all is this, Though Ephraim has been an unwise son, and has delayed his returning unto me, yet his impenitency and security shall not retard or disannul my faithfulness and truth to my people, I will never repent of those gracious promises which I have made to them, but will certainly fulfil them. Let not therefore my chosen, penitent ones despair as if there were no hope, no help for them; for I, their Saviour, will redeem them from the power of all their enemies, and cause them to rise from death (which had power over them through sin) to the glory of eternal life. So that now they may begin their triumphant song, "O death, where is thy sting? O grave, where is thy victory?"

Obs. 1. Though the Lord be terrible to the wicked, yet he is a tower to the righteous. Though plagues come suddenly and inevitably upon the wicked, like pangs upon a woman in travail, yet even then has the Lord a tender respect to his people, and will ransom them from the power of the grave. Isa. i. 24—27; iii. 10, 11. And though they should go into captivity with the wicked, yet God will set a distinguishing mark of mercy upon them, Ezek. ix. 4; Rev. vii. 3. In the midst of his judgments he remembers mercy, and has a tender care over his people, making them to be pitied of all that lead them captive, Psal. cvi. 46; wherever they go, they have his more especial presence with them to uphold and comfort them, Isa. xliii. 2, 3; Jer. xvi. 13—15; Micah iv. 10; Dan. iii.; vi. 22. When all forsake them, yet I will not forsake them, but will be "a little sanctuary" to them in their captivity, Ezek. xi. 16, 17. God is ever mindful of his covenant to his people, and in the midst of all confusions, he has an ark for Noah, a Zoar for Lot, a Midian for Moses, a Haran for Jacob, a cave for David, a grave for Methuselah, and Josiah, and a Pella for Christians. Elijah, that was zealous, and a man of fire for God in wicked times, was carried in a fiery chariot to heaven. Jeremiah, that witnessed against the corruptions of the times, how tenderly does the king of Babylon deal with him, when the king and his nobles lay in misery! Jer. xxxix. 11—14.

Obs. 2. The Scripture of the Old Testament is the word of God. The apostle shows us the divine authority of it, even in gospel times, by referring to this text, and another in Isa. xxv. 8, to prove the Divine mystery of the resurrection. About four hundred places are cited out of the Old Testament in the New. Both Testaments are the sacred word of the great God, and serve for mutual illustration and explanation.

Obs. 3. The Scripture lies not in the bare words and syllables, but in the sense and meaning. Hence it is that Christ and his apostles, citing texts out of the Old Testament, give us the sense and meaning of the place, but not the very words; so in a text sometimes they omit a word, and sometimes they add something for explanation' sake, as Matt. ii. 15, 23; xxvi. 31; Rom. x. 15—21. So Gen. ii. 24, compared with Matt. xix. 5, where *οἱ δύω*, they two, is added emphatically, not they twenty, shall be one flesh. So Deut. vi. 13, compared with Matt. iv. 10, where the exclusive particle, *μόνῳ*, only, which was not expressed in Deuteronomy, but tacitly and interpretatively understood, is added by our Saviour very significantly. So Isa. lxiv. 4, collated with 1 Cor. ii. 9, "Neither have entered into the heart of man:" these words are added by way of illustration by the apostle. So Isa. xxii. 13, "Let us eat and drink, for to-morrow we shall die." But the apostle puts it in the present tense, 1 Cor. xv. 32, "to-morrow we die;" and this he does for explication' sake, to express the desperate madness of those epicures, who would eat and drink securely, although they were to die presently. This shows the folly of the quaking Scripturists, (such there are in our days as well as anti-scripturists,) who take the bare words and syllables, and will not suffer any meaning or exposition to be given of them. Thus when they call for a proof of infant baptism, you must show them in so many words, Thou shalt baptize infants, else they will not believe you. Tell them, that generals include particulars, and that children are confederates, and in covenant with their parents, and therefore have right to the seal of the covenant; and that infant baptism now is as lawful as infant circumcision of old; yet this doth not satisfy, because they cannot read in so many letters, Thou shalt baptize infants. So the papists stick to the bare letter, "This is my body." Whereas that bread could not be his natural body, for Christ was then alive when he said, "This is my body;" and the apostle calls it bread four or five times after consecration, 1 Cor. xi. 23—28.

Perspicuum est apostolos et evangelistas in Veterum Scripturarum interpretatione, sensum quæsisse non verba, nec magnopere de ordine sermonibusque curâsse, dum intellectui res pateret. Jerom. ad Pammach.

The Scripture lies not in the bare and naked words, but in the scope and true interpretation of the words, which is, as it were, the soul and life of the Scripture. Hence Christ bids us not barely read, but search for the sense and meaning of the Scriptures, John v. 39. The lawyers have a saying, *mens legis est lex*, not the bare words, but the meaning of the law is the law.

Ne putemus in verbis Scripturarum esse evangelium, sed in sensu, non in superficie, sed in medulla, non in sermonum foliis, sed in radice rationis. Jerom. Com. ad Gal. i.

Obs. 3. Christ is the Lord. He who has power over death and hell is the Lord; but Christ has this power, Rev. i. 18; xx. 13, death and hell gave up their dead to Christ their Judge. It is he that by the price of his own blood has redeemed us from the hand of sin and Satan, from death and hell; what the prophet spake of Jehovah, the apostle applies to Christ, 1 Cor. xv. 54, 55.

Obs. 4. There is a holy harmony and sweet consent in the Scripture. There is no repugnancy, no real contradiction there; like stones in an arch, they mutually uphold and strengthen each other. The doctrine of the prophets gives light to the apostles, and the apostles again illustrate and explain the prophets. In both there is one and the same Spirit of truth, who "at sundry times, and in divers manners," has published one and the same truth to his people, Heb. i. 1, 2. They must not therefore be opposed, but composed; not made to contradict, but to confirm each other, Luke xxiv. 44.

Obs. 5. God's people, whilst in this world, may fall into deep distress and misery. They may be brought so low, that to a carnal eye they may seem dead and buried, past hope and help, not only in their own eyes, but also in the eyes of others. We have a notable instance for this, in Ezek. xxxvii. 1—15; the desperate condition of God's people in their Babylonish captivity, is there set forth by dead, dried bones, to an eye of sense past all hope or possibility of recovery; insomuch that God's own people, whose faith should not fail, cry out, ver. 11, "Our bones are dried, and our hope is lost: we are cut off for our parts." Yea, the prophet himself was staggered: the Lord asked him, ver. 3, "Son of man, can these bones live?" is it possible that ever such dry bones should live again? The prophet answers, "O Lord God, thou knowest:" it passes my apprehension to conceive how this should be, I know not how it should be effected; but, Lord, thou knowest what thou hast to do, and to thee nothing is impossible. This the Lord does in his wisdom, to draw us out of ourselves and all creature confidences, that in a holy desperation we may say with repenting Israel, "Asshur shall not save us; we will not ride upon horses: neither will we say any more to the work of our hands, Ye are our gods: for in thee the fatherless findeth mercy," Hos. xiv. 3.

Obs. 6. God in his due time will deliver his people out of the deepest distress. He is omnipotent, he can and will redeem Israel, not out of one or two, but "out of all his troubles," Psal. xxv. 22. Art thou weak? He can strengthen thee. Art thou sick? He can heal thee. Art thou dark? He can enlighten thee. Art thou dead? He can enliven thee. Hast thou lain in thy grave till thou stinkest again? So did Lazarus. Hast thou lain till thou art rotten? So did Israel in their Babylonish captivity, and yet were restored, Ezek. xxxvii. 11, 12. So in desertions we are apt to despond; when we walk in darkness, and can see no light, neither sun-light nor moon-light, neither star-light nor candle-light, but are like unto dry bones in a sepulchre, without life, without spirit, without strength, without comfort, and see no way of deliverance. Aye, but now is a time to live by faith, and not by sense, Isa. xl. 27—31; l. 10. Such is our weakness, that we art apt to "limit the Holy One of Israel," and to think that he can help us in lesser trials, and bring us out of petty crosses; but when some great waves of temptation come, then we are apt to question God's power and promises, and to say with David, "I shall now perish one day by the hand of Saul," 1 Sam. xxvii. 1. We are apt to say with Martha, If Christ had come a little sooner, he might have raised Lazarus, but "by this time he stinketh," and is past help, John xi. 39. Aye, but it is the better for that, for now Christ's power will be the more manifested, and his Father the more glorified. The more grievous thy disease, the greater will the praise of thy Physician be in thy cure; and we shall love much, when we see how much is forgiven; and therefore David makes it an argument to move the Lord to pity him, because his sins were great, Psal. xxv. 11. Remember, it is God's usual course to let men be dead and buried (as it were) in misery, and to bring things to extremity, and then appear, Gen. xxii. 14; Psal. xlvi. 1; when trouble comes, then he comes too. We read of three persons that Christ raised from the dead: one was dead, but not carried out, Mark v. 41. A second was dead, and carried out, Luke vii. 14. A third was dead, carried out, buried, and lay till he stunk in his grave, and that was Lazarus; Christ speaks but the word, "Lazarus, come forth," and he lives. God is never nearer to his people than when to a carnal eye he seems farthest off; as we see in the three young men that were cast into a fiery furnace, and Daniel into the lions' den. Sense and carnal reason would have said, God had now forsaken them, and there was no help, yet even then did they find the greatest help; so good it is to trust in God.

Obs. 7. Death in itself is a formidable enemy, and, considered as a curse due to impenitent sinners, is very terrible; even the most terrible of all terribles, as Aristotle calls it. It is armed with stings and plagues, and is therefore called an "enemy," 1 Cor. xv. 26; and "the king of terrors," even such a terror as is the chiefest and greatest of terrors, Job xviii. 14. Hence dreadful calamities are set forth by "the shadow of death," Job x. 21, 22; xvi. 16; xxiv. 17; Psal. xxiii. 4; Jer. xiii. 16; the "messengers of death," Prov. xvi. 14; and the "snares, sorrows, and terrors of death," Psal. xviii. 4, 5; lv. 4. It is this that snatches men, when they least think of it, from their dear relations, pleasures, riches, recreations, mansions, honours, which they love as their lives; and this must needs be terrible to a natural man, who has no assurance of better things when he dies. Hence such are said to be in bondage, and a slavish fear of death, all their life long, Heb. ii. 15. Whilst wicked men look upon death at a distance, and think it far off, they fear it not; but when God shall open their eyes by sickness, and summon them to appear before him, then, like Pashur, they are Magor-missabib, a terror to themselves, and all that are round about them, Jer. xx. 3, 4. Saul, though a king, and a valiant man, yet, when he heard that death was at the door, and he must die to-morrow, was so dispirited with this dismal news, that he fell into a deadly trance, and was not able to bear it; the fear of death had well nigh ended him before his death came, 1 Sam. xxviii. 19, 20. So Belshazzar, a mighty monarch, in the height of his mirth, is "greatly troubled," his countenance is changed, his thoughts trouble him, and his joints are loosed; but whence came all this terror and amazement? from fear of this king of fears, death, which suddenly after surprised him, Dan. v. This puts an end to all a wicked man's comforts and hopes; conscience shall now be awakened, and he must give an account of his stewardship. This made Louis XI., king of France, to command his servants, in his sickness, that they should not once mention that bitter word death in his hearing. Yea, even the godly, in a temptation, for fear of death, have not acted like themselves at other times; as we see in three of the greatest worthies that we read of in the Scriptures: first, Abraham, famous for faith, Gen. xii. 12, 13; xx. 2, 11; and David, famous for valour, 1 Sam. xxi. 12, 13; and Peter, for courage, yet to save his life Peter denied his Lord.

῞Ο θάνατος πάντων τῶν φοβερῶν φοβερότατον. Arist. Ethic. l. 3. c. 6.

See Caryl on Job xviii. 14.

Obs. 8. Death is a conquered enemy. Christ has disarmed him, and taken away his sting. He has redeemed his from the power of the grave, and swallowed up death in victory. Christ, by his death, has destroyed death, and "him that had the power of death, the devil," Heb. ii. 14. By suffering of that death which was due to us for our sins, he has destroyed the power of

Diabolus dicitur habere mortis imperium, non qua rex, sed qua tyrannus, vel qua carnifex qui habet imperium in eos qui morti propter facinora sua adjudicati et ipsius protestati traditi sunt. Gerhard.

O beatam illorum mortem qui participes facti sunt mortis Christi! Knox.

Satan, and taken away that advantage which he had against us by reason of sin, whose wages is death. Satan thought by death to destroy Christ, but Christ, by his death, destroyed his kingdom, and became more glorious by dying; like another Samson, he slew more at his death than in his life. So that now we are more than conquerors, ὑπερνικῶμεν, we are even triumphers through "him that loved us." He has triumphed over death, and all the enemies of our salvation, and we in him, our Head, triumph, 2 Cor. ii. 14; Col. ii. 14, 15. By lying in the grave he has sweetened our grave for us, so that now we may sleep in it as in a bed of down, Isa. lvii. 2; and our flesh may "rest in hope" of a glorious resurrection, Psal. xvi. 9. Now, if ever, we may sing that triumphant song, "O death, where is thy sting?" It is destroyed, abolished, gone. This strong man armed is overcome by a stronger than he. Neither the pleasures of life, nor the pains of death; neither the height of prosperity, nor the depth of adversity, nothing now can separate us from Christ, Job v. 20—22; Rom. viii. 35—39. Death may dissolve our corporal marriage, but it is so far from abolishing, that it perfects, our spiritual marriage; killed we may be, but conquered we can never be. Christ's victory is our victory, and all his conquests ours.

See Dr. Goodwin on Christ's Death and Resurrection, sect. 2, 3. p. 22. quart.

Tollitur mors non ne sit, sed ne obsit. Aug.

But if Christ, by his death, has destroyed death, why then do the godly die? To this I answer, Christ did not die to deliver us from sickness and death, but to free us from the curse that is in these. By his death he has pulled out the sting of death. The death of the body still remains, but the sting, and that which is penal, is taken away, so that it cannot hurt us; and therefore the text saith not, I will free you from death, but *è manu mortis*, from the destructive power of death; so as it shall have no dominion over you to hurt you, nor be able to separate you from Christ. As the apostle saith of sin, it is in us, but it does not reign in us. So die we must, but death has no dominion over believers, as it has over wicked men; it gets the victory over them, they die, and die eternally; but a believer's death is neither total, penal, nor perpetual.

1. It is not total. It seizes only on the body, the carcass, the outside; it goes to its dust, but the spirit returns to God that gave it, Eccl. xii. 7.

2. It is not penal, but profitable. In the grave we put off our filth, deformities, defects, infirmities, and mortality itself. It is our attiring house, to fit us for immortality and glory.

3. It is not perpetual, it is but a sleeping till the general resurrection, Rom. viii. 10, 11. Our conquest over death is partly fulfilled in this life, but it shall be consummate *in facto*, and fully completed at the resurrection. Then shall they "awake and sing, that dwell in dust," Isa. xxvi. 19. This upheld Job in the midst of all his sorrows, "I know that my redeemer liveth;" my comfort is, though I die, yet I have one to right me that lives for ever, Job xix. 25. David comforts himself with this, that God would redeem him from the power of the grave, and from the hand of hell; though riches cannot redeem the rich, yet God would redeem him, Psal. xlix. 15.

But I must part with wife, children, friends, pleasures. But know, all these losses will be made up in a better kind; as you may see at large in Mr. Byfield's Cure of the Fear of Death, at the end of his Marrow, p. 745; and Bp. Hall's Balm of Gilead, p. 141.

Let us then not fear death with a slavish fear. Christ died to free us from such a fear of death, Heb. ii. 15. A religious, prudential fear does well; fear it so as to arm yourselves and prepare for it, but not so as to be dejected under it. No wise man will fear a conquered enemy; if you truly believe in Christ, the conqueror of death, you need not fear death. Think on Christ when you think on death, and then you may in a holy sarcasm and contempt say, "O death, where is thy sting?" Christ has unstinged it, and, as it were, disarmed it; so that now we may safely put it in our bosoms: buzz it may about our ears as a drone bee, but sting it cannot, for Christ has taken away the guilt of sin, and has made that which was sometimes a curse to become a blessing, of a foe he has made it a friend, of a poison a medicine, of a punishment an advantage, Phil. i. 21, of the gate of hell a passage to heaven. It is now like the valley of Achor, "a door of hope;" that which was sometimes the king of terrors is now become the king of comforts, as making way for the enjoyment of the highest comforts. We part with a life of misery to enjoy a life of glory. We are wont to say, A fair exchange is no robbery; but such a change is our great advantage. Hence it is that the apostle, summing up a Christian's privileges and riches, sets down death as part of it, 1 Cor. iii. 22, not only life, but death is yours. He that can truly say, I am Christ's subject and servant, may as truly say, Death will be my preferment and high advancement. So true is that of Solomon, Eccl. vii. 1, the day of a man's death is better than the day of his birth. Then, and never till then, shall we rest from our labours, Job iii. 17; Rev. xiv. 13, and be perfectly freed from sin and all its attendant evils.

Look not therefore on death with philosophical eyes, as if it were the end of all our comforts, but look on it with Christian eyes, as the year of jubilee, the day of our coronation, and consummation of the marriage between Christ and our souls.

Non potest male mori qui bene vixerit. Aug.

A natural man, that looks upon death with an eye of sense, sees nothing but horror and terror in it; but a gracious soul, that looks on it with an eye of faith, sees life in death, light in darkness, and comfort in discomfort: though for a time he must lie in the grave, and death seems to have dominion over him, yet he as certainly sees a resurrection as if he were already in possession of it, and therefore he triumphs already in assurance of a total conquest through Christ; death is already swallowed up by him in victory, Isa. xxv. 8. Christ was his life, and therefore now death is his gain. He lived holily, and now he dies happily; he lived unto the Lord, and therefore he now dies unto him, Rom. xiv. 7, 8; 2 Cor. v. 15. His care was to keep a good conscience, and now he has the comfort of it, 2 Cor. i. 12.

Mr. Trapp.

Let atheists, then, and worldlings, and wicked men, fear death, who know no better life; but let the righteous, who has hope in his death, Prov. xiv. 32, embrace it, and bid it welcome, as the martyrs did, who went as joyfully to their stakes as others do to marriages. Witness all those living speeches of dying saints which shall shortly be published by an able and industrious hand to the world. Cyprian, hearing the sentence of death pronounced against him, said, Lord, I thank thee that now thou wilt free me from the bonds of the body. I shall not now lose my life, but change it for a better. Pomponius Algerius, in an epistle which he wrote to his friends from the delectable Hortyard of the Leonine prison, July 12, 1555, excellently saith, I shall tell you strange things, I have found a honeycomb in a lion's belly; in a deep dungeon I have found pleasantness; in a place of bitterness and the shadow of death I have found peace and hope of life. In the belly of hell I have found comfort. Where others weep, there do I sing for joy; and where others fear, there have I support. The good hand of my God has done all this for me. He that seemed sometime to be far from me, is now most present with me. He that I had but some glimpses of before, I now see face to face. He has turned my winter into a glorious spring; why should I fear any freezing cold, who am thus inflamed with the love of God? Let malefactors fear this prison, to me it flows with honey.

Obs. 9. God's decrees are infallible and unchangeable. Repentance is hid from his eyes, he knows not what it means. "God is not a man, that he should lie; neither the son of man, that he should repent," Numb. xxiii. 19; 1 Sam. xv. 29. He is Jehovah, he changeth not, Mal. iii. 6. His covenant he will not break, nor alter the thing that is gone out of his lips, Psal. lxxxix. 34, 35; cx. 4; Isa. liv. 9, 10; if he has decreed to show mercy to his people and to redeem them from the power of hell, all the devils in hell shall not be able to hinder it. It is not the counsel of men or devils, but the counsel of the Lord, that shall stand, Psal. xxxiii. 10, 11. If he has spoken it he will do it, yea, and the contrary plots of wicked men shall help to effect it, Acts ii. 23; Rom. ix. 11.

But is not God said to repent? Gen. vi. 6; Jer. xviii. 8; Amos vii. 3, 6. That is spoken, not properly, but after the manner of men, and according to our capacity, because his work is changed, though himself continueth unchangeable, for with him "is no variableness, neither shadow of turning." He is constant and faithful in performing all his promises to his people, 1 Thess. v. 24. "All the paths of the Lord are mercy and truth unto such as keep his covenant and his testimonies." They are mercy in promising, and truth in performing; not one thing shall fail of all the good things which God has promised to his people, Josh. xxiii. 14; though they be not presently fulfilled, yet in God's due time they shall be accomplished, for though God come not at our time, yet he never fails his own, Deut. xxxii. 35; Hab. ii. 3.

Obs. 10. Believers in this life may be assured of their salvation. Repentance is hid from God's eyes; whom he loves once he loves for ever. Not one of those that the Father has given to Christ shall perish, Matt. xviii. 14; John vi. 39. "The foundation of God standeth sure," more sure than the pillars of the earth or the poles of heaven, 2 Tim. ii. 19. The decree of election is there called, 1. A foundation. 2. A firm and sure foundation. 3. It is not a foundation of man's laying, but it is the foundation of God. 4. It is not a tottering, but a standing foundation, built on a rock, sealed and confirmed by the Spirit, counsel, and special knowledge of God; he "knoweth them that are his." Hence the covenant of the Lord made with his people is called "an everlasting covenant," 2 Sam. xxiii. 5; Hos. ii. 19, 20; and he has promised to plant his fear in their hearts, that they shall never depart from him, Jer. xxxii. 40. If they fall, yet they shall not be utterly cast down, for the Lord upholds them with his hand, Deut. xxxiii. 3; Psal. xxxvii. 24; Prov. ii. 7, 8; John x. 28. They stand not by their own strength, but are kept and guarded by his almighty power "through faith unto salvation," 1 Pet. i. 5. Common gifts and graces may fade and fail, but his gifts, that is, his peculiar, essential gifts, which appertain to salvation, are "without repentance," Rom. xi. 29.

Ver. 15. *Though he be fruitful among his brethren, an east wind shall come, the wind of the Lord shall come up from the wilderness, and his spring shall become dry, and his fountain shall be dried up: he shall spoil the treasure of all pleasant vessels.*

The prophet having comforted God's people, returns again to the denouncing of judgments against the wicked; and because similitudes make a deep impression, therefore he uses them. He sets forth, ver. 13, their distress by the pains of a woman in travail; and in this 15th verse, the spoil and havoc that should be made amongst them by Shalmaneser, king of Assyria, which he illustrates by a double similitude.

But, first, he prevents an objection which Ephraim might make; I am fruitful, and abound with riches, honours, strength, and therefore I fear no fall. Admit it be so, though Ephraim be "fruitful among his brethren," yet "an east wind shall come, the wind of the Lord shall come up from the wilderness, and his spring shall become dry, and his fountain shall be dried up: he shall spoil the treasure of all pleasant vessels."

On this verse there are almost as various interpretations as there be interpreters, so that I may say of it as Maldonate said of another text, *Nescio an hic locus facilior fuisset si nemo eum exposuisset*, This text had been plainer unexplained.

1. Some make the words a promise of great blessings to Ephraim after all his sorrows; Yet he shall be fruitful amongst his brethren. After the Assyrian had spoiled him of all his treasure, yet by the might of him that ransometh men from the grave, they shall be raised up. But this is a forcing of the words contrary to their genuine sense and meaning.

2. Others apply it to Christ, and say, He shall increase and multiply his elect both in number and glory at the last day. The very rehearsal of this is confutation sufficient.

Qui ad Christum refert, filum orationis non advertit. Mercer.

3. The Vulgate, leaving the Hebrew to follow the Septuagint, read it, *Ephraim dividet*, Ephraim shall divide amongst his brethren, and make a schism amongst them, therefore God will send the Assyrian against him. But the word is יפריא *crescet*, not *dividet*.

4. Lyra *hic delirat*, when he takes, or rather mistakes, the word for a division and separation at the end of the world, when the evil shall be separated from the good, and the goats from the sheep. Quite contrary to the scope of the text, which speaks of increasing, not of dividing; and of brethren, which sheep and goats were never yet accounted.

In the words then we have,

I. Ephraim's dignity from God's mercy to him.

II. Ephraim's downfal and consequent misery.

I. Ephraim's dignity flowing from God's mercy towards him. "Though he be fruitful among his brethren." He was the head of the tribes, Judah alone excepted, and that only in respect of dignity; for in number of men, and in power and riches, Ephraim excelled them all. The prophet alludes, 1. To Ephraim's name, which signified fruitful and flourishing; such as his name was, such was he; Ephraim was his name, and fruitfulness was with him; both the fruitfulness of the earth, and the fruitfulness of the womb; he was like a bough by a well-side, fruitful, and flourishing, whose branches run over the wall. He had the upper and the nether springs, the blessings of heaven above, and of the earth beneath, Gen. xlix. 22, 25. 2. He alludes to the blessing which Jacob his grandfather gave him on his death-bed; Ephraim "shall be greater than" Manasseh, "and his seed shall become a multitude of nations," Gen. xlviii. 19.

אפרים a פרה fructificavit, crevit, auctus fuit. Gen. xlix. 22.

II. Ephraim's downfal and consequent misery. God's mercies should have made him more fruitful and obedient, but he, like an unwise son, became more insolent, idolatrous, and disobedient, Hos. xiii. 5, 6. Therefore God will now sweep all away, and make him know the value of his mercies by the want of them.

"An east wind shall come, the wind of the Lord shall come up from the wilderness, and his spring shall become dry, and his fountain shall be dried up: he shall spoil the treasure of all pleasant vessels."

In which are contained,

1. The judgment threatened. "An east wind shall come." קדים רוח "an east wind." This wind usually is most violent and boisterous; when God is said to break ships, it is with "an east wind," Psal. xlviii. 7; when he divided the sea, it was with "a strong east wind," Exod. xiv. 21. It is a dry, sharp, searching, hurtful wind, destructive to the herbs and fruits of the earth, especially in those countries, Gen. xli. 6; Job xv. 2; Ezek. xvii. 10; xix. 12; Isa. xxvii. 8; Jonah iv. 8. Hence, great afflictions are compared to east winds, Job xxvii. 21; Jer. xviii. 17. This east wind is not to be taken properly, but metaphorically; by it is meant the king of Assyria with his forces, who should come from the east, and, like an east wind, should dry up and destroy all before him. In this sense, the violent Chaldeans are compared to an east wind, Hab. i. 9. And the Assyrian is also compared to an eagle, which comes swiftly, with great force and violence.

2. From whom this wind shall come. It comes not by chance or fortune, but it comes from God, and therefore it is called "the wind of the Lord;" that is, a mighty, strong, irresistible wind, carrying down all before it; such a one as God himself shall raise for the punishment of Ephraim, viz. that most cruel and most merciless Assyrian, sent by the Lord to avenge the quarrel of his covenant.

3. From whence it shall come. It "shall come up from the wilderness," where the winds blow most fiercely and vehemently, because they meet with no resistance. It was "a great wind from the wilderness" that brought the house upon Job's children, Job i. 19. This denotes the fierceness of the Assyrian against Israel, he shall rage unmercifully against him.

4. The hurt which this violent wind shall do. "His spring shall become dry, and his fountain shall be dried up." What is that? why exegetically there is added, ישסה אוצר כל־כלי חמדה "he shall spoil the treasure of all pleasant vessels." When the fountain is dried, the streams must needs fail. Allusion in this is made to the land of Ephraim, which abounded with fruits and springs, and it withal sets forth the great abundance of all things that Israel enjoyed; they had not drops, or ponds, or torrents, but constant springs of mercy, whilst others had only some streams thereof; they sat at the fountain head, they had the root, when others had but branches, Hos. ix. 16. We might paraphrase the whole thus: Since Ephraim and the rest of the tribes have rebelled against me, they shall be brought to utter desolation; all the springs of my blessings shall be taken from them, and all manner of happiness shall fail them; I will send the Assyrian amongst them, and he shall spoil all their treasures, and carry away all their ornaments; even their most precious and desirable things, though never so closely hid, this searching wind will find them out, be it gold, silver, jewels, costly ointments, perfumes, apparel, or any of the precious fruits of the earth: whatever desirable thing is hid and highly esteemed, either by the covetous, the voluptuous, or the lascivious, shall all become a prey to the merciless Assyrian.

אוצר Thesaurus proprié dicitur pecunia in terra abscondita, et latiori forma dicitur quicquid pretiosum est, sive illud in pecuniis, sive in bonis quocunque modo numeretur. Ezek. xxxviii. 13; Nahum ii. 9. Sanctius in loco.

כלי חמדה which we translate "pleasant vessels," signifies properly a vessel of desire, a Hebraism for very precious things. Hence Daniel is called איש־חמדות a man of desires; that is, a precious man, and greatly beloved, Dan. x. 11; a good land, ארץ חמדה a land of desire, that is, a most desirable land, Jer. iii. 19. So all pleasant things, whether gold, jewels, garments, are called things of desires, that is, precious things, 2 Chron. xx. 25; Dan. xi. 8, 38, 43. It is usual with the Hebrews thus to express the superlative degree by putting the substantive in the genitive case.

The sum of all is, Though Ephraim be high, and mightily exalted above his brethren, yet since he has not exalted my name who have exalted him, nor made my benefits and my mercies motives to duty and obedience, but has fought against me with my own favours, and abused my blessings to my dishonour, therefore I will bring the Assyrian upon him, who, like an east wind, shall blast him, utterly dash all his hopes, spoil his treasures, and carry him into captivity: so that he who was some time the head of the nations, shall now become the tail; he that was above, and was the terror of the nations, making them tremble when he spake, shall now become the scorn of the nations, and the contempt of the people.

Obs. 1. God's goodness is wholly free. He chooses not for seniority of birth, or excellency of parts, or worthiness of the person, but he loves whom he loves, and shows mercy to whom he will show mercy, Rom. ix. 15. Ephraim here, the younger brother, is preferred before Manasseh, the elder, and is advanced in number and dignity above him. This displeased Joseph, and oft displeases us; but what pleases God should please us, we should quiet ourselves in such dispensations as our Saviour did, Matt. xi. 26, "Even so, Father: for so it seemed good in thy sight:" that is, since it is thy good pleasure to hide the mysteries of salvation from the wise men of the world, and to reveal them to simple men and women, it contents me well, because it is thy good pleasure so to have it. We are apt to confine God's grace to the order of nature, and external accomplishments. Amongst all the sons of Jesse, even Samuel the seer would not have chosen David, the youngest and the least regarded, and therefore set to keep sheep, to be king of Israel; yet God makes choice of him, and passes over his brothers Eliab, Shammah, and Abinadab, goodly persons, great soldiers, and prime courtiers. God's blessing goes not by carnal seniority, but by spiritual grace and choice. He is wiser than the wisest, and often chooses where man leaves, and leaves where man chooses, as we see in Abel, Shem, Abraham, Isaac, Jacob, Judah, Joseph, who, although younger brethren, yet were preferred in favour before Cain, Japheth, Haran, Ishmael, Esau, Reuben, Simeon, Levi. This God does not only to magnify his sovereignty and free grace, but also to check our vain thoughts, who are apt to limit the Holy One of Israel to our ways and inventions.

See Jenkyn on Jude.

Obs. 2. God's ministers must use plain and familiar expressions for the better convincing of their people, both of their sin and misery. The prophet here uses similitudes from a travailing woman, from the east wind; and the Lord, by way of aggravation of their sins, tells them that he had spoken to them by his prophets, and had "multiplied visions," and given them much preaching, yea, and the better to convince them, he had "used similitudes by the ministry of his prophets," Hos. xii. 10. This is an excellent way of preaching, and prevailing, it both notably illustrates the truth, and insinuates itself into men's affections. Galeacius Caracciolus, an Italian marquis, and nephew to a pope, was converted by an apt similitude which he heard from Peter Martyr. Similitudes are more memorable, and suit best with the capacities of all; for thereby things are brought, 1. To our sense. 2. To our understanding. 3. To our memory. 4. To affection and practice. This made the prophets so frequently use them, Isa. v. 1, 2; Ezek. xvi. 3; Hos. xiv. 5—9. Nathan caught David with a parable, 2 Sam. xii. 1, 2, &c., and out of his own mouth condemned him. Christ, who spake as never man spake, whose words were full of power and authority, yet, the better to work upon his hearers, frequently used parables, from the sower, from leaven, from mustard-seed, flowers, feasts, from a treasure, &c., Matt. xiii.; xxiv. 32; Mark iv. 33; Luke xiii. 6; John xx. 6, 7, &c.

And the apostle Paul fetches similitudes from runners and wrestlers, &c., 1 Cor. ix. 24; 2 Tim. iv. 7.

We are naturally very incapable of the best things, 1 Cor. ii. 14, like a dull ass colt, untractable, Job xi. 12. We are slow to believe, and hard to perceive, the truths of God; Christ blamed his own disciples for it, Luke xxiv. 25. Plain preaching is the best teaching, it is the best way to convince and convert men; and if plain, familiar preaching will not work, certainly by dark, mysterious preaching it will never be effected. Hence Christ tells Nicodemus, that if when he had spoken of earthly things they believed not, how will they believe when he shall speak to them of heavenly things? John iii. 12. This made Paul, that he had rather speak five words in a known tongue to edify others, than ten thousand in an unknown tongue, 1 Cor. xiv. 19. That is the best preaching which sets forth things to the life, and makes them as plain as if they were written with a sun-beam.

We should therefore admire the riches of God's mercy to us in condescending to teach us so plainly and familiarly, using all means to convert us, and bring us home to himself; so that if any perish for want of knowledge, they may thank themselves, for God has left no means unessayed to do us good. He has used comparisons from things: 1. Natural. 2. Artificial. 3. Ceremonial. 4. Moral.

1. Natural. Thus, to show his tender love and care over his people, he alludes to a mother's love to her child, and to a hen, that with much tenderness gathers her chickens under her wings; and compares his people to "the apple of the eye," Psal. xvii. 8; Zech. ii. 8, which is guarded with many tunics, the better to preserve it from danger.

2. Artificial; from ploughing, sowing, silversmiths trying their metals in the fire, Psal. xii.; 1 Thess. v. 21.

3. Ceremonial. Psal. li. 7, "Purge me with hyssop," alluding to the cleansing of the lepers under the law.

4. Moral, Isa. lxvi. 12.

Many complain they are not book-learned. 1. Whose fault is that? thou canst not plead ignorance for want of means. 2. If thou couldst read never a letter, yet the book of the creature is written in such large characters, that he who runs may read them; had we but spiritual hearts, we might learn many spiritual lessons from them.

Obs. 3. The higher the mercy, the deeper the judgment if abused. "Though he be fruitful among his brethren, an east wind shall come." Fruitful Ephraim, that was the head of the tribes, and advanced above his brethren, is now for his sins made the most contemptible amongst them. Zanchy renders כִּי *licet* by *quoniam*, and understands the verse thus, *Quoniam Ephraim fructificavit*, &c. Seeing Ephraim is fruitful amongst his brethren, i. e. since he abounds in riches, power, and many privileges above the rest of the tribes, these shall be so far from saving him, that God will be more fierce against him for their abuse. Capernaum, that was exalted to heaven in the abundance of the means of grace, (for it was the city of Christ's residence, where he frequently cured the sick, preached, and wrought many miracles,) yet for ingratitude, unfruitfulness, and abuse of those means, was thrust down to hell; that is, it lost its privileges, and was brought to a very low and miserable condition; so that at this day the land is a desolation, not three houses standing where those three famous cities, Chorazin, Bethsaida, and Capernaum stood; and at last they shall be damned in hell too, for contemning so great salvation, when offered to them, Matt. xi. 23. As Ahasuerus said of Haman, who had abused his favour, Hang him on a gallows fifty cubits high, Esth. vii. 9; so will Christ say of such, Plunge them into hell so much deeper than others, because they rejected Christ when he was tendered to them. None sink so deep into hell as the lewd, licentious Christian. Favour abused increases sin, and men's offences are aggravated by their obligations. If Turks and Tartars shall be damned, debauched Christians shall be double damned, because they bring a reproach upon Christ and his ways, and open the mouths of the wicked to cry, Behold, these are the people of the Lord, see how loosely and unrighteously they live, Ezek. xxxvi. 20. Where the Lord has been a "valley of vision," and bestowed much preaching, if people answer not the Lord's cost, they must expect a burden of judgment to light upon them, Isa. xxii. 1. No place was punished like Jerusalem, because no place had better preaching and more privileges, Lam. iv. 6; Dan. ix. 12. They that have preaching, shall one day know what it is to have had prophets amongst them, Ezek. ii. 5, and shall pay full dearly for their contempt of them, 2 Chron. xxxvi. 15, 16; Prov. i. 24—27; xxviii. 9; Isa. v. 24, 25; xxx. 9, 12, 13; Jer. vi. 19; ix. 12, 13; Zech. vii. 11, 12; Matt. x. 14, 15. This is the reason why judgments usually begin at "the sanctuary," Ezek. ix. 6, and at "the house of God," 1 Pet. iv. 17; Rom. ii. 9; though it end not there, but go on to the wicked. The cup begins at Jerusalem, and then goes round to Egypt, Uz, Ashkelon, Ekron, Edom, Moab, and to "all the kingdoms of the world, which are upon the face of the earth," Jer. xxv. 15—33. The highest in preferment are first in punishment; and if this be done to Zion, woe to Babylon, Jer. xlix. 12. The sins of God's people are committed against greater light and love, and bring more dishonour to God, and disgrace to his truth, than the sins of others; and therefore of all men he will not spare them for their iniquities, as we see in Moses, Eli, David, Hezekiah, Zacharias, 1 Sam. ii. 27—30; 2 Sam. xii. 14; Luke i. 20. They are a people nearer to him than others, and therefore he will not bear with them as he does with those that know him not, Lev. x. 2, 3; Numb. xvi. 9; Amos iii. 2. A father will sooner correct his children if they offend, than strangers whom he does not know, Heb. xii. 5, 6. We can endure dung in our fields, which we cannot abide in our parlours. We suffer those briers to grow in the wilderness, which we cannot away with in our gardens. If they be open enemies, God can better bear it; but it highly provokes him to be wounded in the house of his friends; when he shall nourish and bring up children, and they shall rebel against him, he cannot, he will not, brook it, Isa. i. 2, 7. 1. To show his impartial justice to the world; 2. For the terror of others; 3. To take off the scandal that comes hereby to religion; he will punish sin wherever he finds it, Numb. xx. 12. He has his fire in Zion, and his furnace in Jerusalem, and is terrible in the assembly of his saints, Psal. lxviii. 35.

Professio religionis non aufert debitum, sed auget. Salvian.

Obs. 4. No privileges nor prerogatives can preserve a disobedient people from ruin. Ephraim here had many privileges, as you may see, Gen. xlviii. 16, 19, 20; Deut. xxxiii. 13—17, where, under the name of Joseph, Moses blesses Ephraim with the precious things of the heavens above, and the precious things of the earth beneath, as corn, wine, gold, silver, &c., and prophecies that the good will of him that dwelt in the bush should dwell amongst them; that is, God would show his special love to them as his peculiar people, and not only give them outward, but inward blessings also, and would so strengthen them, that no enemy should be able to stand before them; yet Ephraim, sinning against the God of those mercies, lost all. No privileges can shelter us if God be against us. He that raised us, can as easily ruin us; he that exalted us, can as easily abase us; he that made us famous for mercies, can quickly make us infamous for judgments, and consume us after he has done us good,

Josh. xxiv. 20. It is not silver, nor gold, Prov. xi. 4; Ezek. vii. 19; Zeph. i. 18, not men, nor might, that can save us, if God be against us, Psal. xx. 7, 8; Isa. xxii. 6—14; Nah. iii. 12. Many trust in their swords, and think by their valour and skill in war to defend themselves, and possess the land as their inheritance for ever; but God tells them, since they trust in the sword, that they shall fall by the sword, and be cast out of all, Ezek. xxxiii. 26—28. If he be against us, all is against us; and if he but stamp or hiss for an enemy, they presently come against us, Isa. v. 26. Jerusalem was strongly fortified, and no man thought that ever the enemy could have entered it, Lam. iv. 12; and if privileges could ever have preserved a sinful people from ruin, Jerusalem had never been destroyed, for they had more privileges than all the people in the world besides. It was called "the perfection of beauty," and "the joy of the whole earth;" "the city of God," Psal. xlvi. 4; "the city of the great King," Matt. v. 35. So famous was it for preaching, that it is called "the valley of vision," Isa. xxii. 1; and they were called, a peculiar people, a holy people, a people near to God, that knew his name, and were blessed by him above all people. They had godly magistrates, as David, Hezekiah, Josiah, &c., and zealous prophets, as Isaiah, Jeremiah, Ezekiel, &c., and afterwards, Christ and his apostles. To them pertained "the adoption, and the glory, and the covenants, and the giving of the law, and the service of God, and the promises; whose are the fathers, and of whom as concerning the flesh Christ came:" these eight privileges the apostle sets down together, Rom. ix. 4, 5. None better seated, none more strangely delivered, none had such signal providences, and glorious ordinances; all the world besides lay in darkness, they only were a Goshen, a land of light, God's glory, his pleasant portion, and delight, &c. So that if any people under heaven might have been secure in respect of privileges, it was Jerusalem; yet they, falling to atheism, idolatry, persecution of God's messengers, &c., are become a desolation. Sodom was a beautiful place, like the paradise of God, Gen. xiii. 10; Babylon was "the glory of kingdoms," Isa. xiii. 19; yet both the one and the other were destroyed for their lewdness and pride.

England is apt to boast of its privileges, and to tell what great things God has done for us. With thankfulness it must be acknowledged that God has done great things for us indeed: he has made us, as he did Ephraim here, the head of the nations, when for our sins we might have been the tail; he has set us above, when for our horrid apostacies, and hideous blasphemies, he might justly have laid us beneath; he has made us the terror of the nations, and given us victory upon victory, success upon success, and has prospered us by sea and land, blessed us with the best laws, and the best land (all things considered) in the world; and, as if all this had not been sufficient for us, he has given us the word and the sword, Moses and Aaron, magistracy and ministry, the best (I think) in the world. Besides the singular helps in print, those excellent tracts, both polemical and practical; compare but our large Annotations with the Dutch Annotations, and you will see what cause we have to be thankful in that respect.

All these things make us deeply indebted to our God; but had we ten thousand times more privileges than we have, yet if we walk not up to them, and answer them with obedience, we are an undone people. The greater our privileges, the nearer to judgment, if we abuse them. Shiloh was for a time privileged with the tabernacle and the ark, those visible pledges of God's special presence and residence amongst them; but they, abusing these mercies, were given up to judgments, Jer. vii. 12; and if England go on in sinning, as it has done of late, and proceed in its hypocrisy, blasphemy, apostacy, heresy, formality, profaneness, and abuse of God's favours, we must certainly expect some sweeping judgment. It is not privileges, it is not circumcision, nor uncircumcision, it is not those outward prerogatives, that make us acceptable to God, but a new creature, Gal. vi. 15; either new men, or no men in God's esteem. Let us then become a holy people, and we shall be a happy people. Let us answer our privileges with self-denying hearts and lives, that as God has done more for us than for others, so we may do more for him than others; that as he has given us distinguishing mercies, so we may answer them with distinguishing manners, not living like the men of the world, that the Lord may rejoice over us to do us good, and may show us yet greater things than these, Exod. xix. 4, 5.

Obs. 5. Abuse of mercies forfeits mercies. God had done much for Ephraim; he had not been to him a barren wilderness, or a land that was not sown, but he brought him out of the wilderness, miraculously delivered him out of Egypt, freely adopted him for his own, planted him in a fat pasture, even a land flowing with milk and honey, gave him his law, and sent to them many extraordinary prophets; but they, instead of exalting God, who had exalted them, grew proud and insolent, forgetting the God of all their mercies, and confiding in kings and princes, kissing the calves, and sacrificing to Baal, who could not save them, and then they died, Hos. xiii. 1—12. When they began to fight against God with his own mercies, and to abuse the health, wealth, and blessings which God had given them, to the dishonour of the Donor, then they lost their riches, strength, glory, kingdom, and all; then comes the Assyrian, like an east wind, and sweeps away all. Before his name was Ephraim, fruitfulness, but now God threatens them with emptiness, barrenness, dryness of roots, fruits, branches, springs, even the loss of all. As all the world had been witnesses of God's special favour to them, so now they should be witnesses of their just confusion. When men honour not the Lord with their riches, but kiss their own hands, and sacrifice to their own nets; when, like beasts, they bite the hand that feeds them, and crop the tree that shelters them, it is just with God to take all from them, Hos. ii. 8, 9. In Neh. ix. 7—25, we have a large catalogue of God's singular mercies. Ver. 26, we read how they abused those mercies; and then, ver. 27, 28, we read of God's judgments on them for abusing those blessings. So Psal. cvi. 9—11, we see God's mercies; ver. 13—39, we have the abuse of them; and ver. 40—42, the consequent judgments. It is usually seen, that where the Lord bestows the greatest mercies, there he oft receives the greatest indignities; where he gives most honour, there he receives most dishonour. When Jeshurun is fat and full, then he kicks, Deut. xxxii. 15. Ephraim here was a son, and had all the privileges of a son; the greater then was his sin to rebel against that God who had been so tender to him. He had,

1. Dilection. "When Israel was a child, then I loved him," Hos. xi. 1, 4.

2. Direction. "I taught Ephraim also to go," and sent Jonah, Amos, Hosea, and other prophets to instruct him, Hos. xi. 3.

3. Correction. As a father corrects his children for their good, so did God by Ephraim, Hos. v. 15; vi. 1, 2.

4. Provision. Fathers provide for their children; so did God for Ephraim: "I did know thee in the wilderness, in the land of great drought. According to their pasture, so were they filled; they were filled," Hos. xiii. 5, 6.

5. Protection. He was their King, who saved them from their enemies: "I will be thy king: where is any other that may save thee in all thy cities?" Hos. xiii. 10.

God has done as great things for England (all things considered) as ever he did for Ephraim; he has been a tender Father to us, he has blessed us abundantly both in church and state; he has broken the power and policy of many subtle Ahithophels and great Zanzummims, giants, and sons of Anak. He has made mountains a plain before us; and though fierce men have ridden over our heads, yet has he brought us through fire and water into a wealthy place. For England's sake he has sent to Babylon, and brought down all their nobles: he has bound even kings and princes in chains, and their followers in links of iron. He has made the wicked to bow before the good, and the evil at the gates of the righteous. No nation so blessed of our God as we, and no nation that has worse requited the Lord's blessings than we have done. As he has loaded us with mercies, so we have loaded him with blasphemies, heresies, apostacies; no favours can win us, no benefits bind us; if God had been our deadly enemy, we could not have acted more ignobly and disingenuously against him than we have done. It is a miracle of mercy that he yet continues his mercies to us, and that he has not long ago stripped us naked, as in the day when we were born, Hos. ii. 3. We have rendered evil to the Lord for all his goodness to us, and therefore we may justly fear that evil should pursue us, Prov. xvii. 13. If he shall be punished that renders evil for evil to man, what shall be done to him that renders evil for good, and that to his God who never did him hurt? The good Lord humble us for all our ungrateful and disingenuous walking before him, who has been so good and gracious to us; and grant, that at last we may know and acknowledge the God of our mercies, lest an east wind come and bereave us of all; for though at present we have peace and plenty, and fresh springs of mercy round about us, yet God can suddenly dry up all our springs, and bring a plundering Assyrian from the east or west upon us, (for those metaphorical winds, as well as the natural, are all his servants,) that shall quickly rob us of all our pleasant things. Let us not therefore flatter ourselves, and think that because at present we have peace, therefore no evil shall come upon us; for if England go on to sin after the rate as it has done of late years, adding drunkenness to thirst, sin to sin, and heresy to heresy, &c., the wrath of the Lord will certainly break forth against us; and then we that would not serve him gladly and sincerely in the abundance of all things, shall be made to serve in want and misery, that we may know the difference between his service, and the service of men, Deut. xxviii. 47, 48.

See Caryl on Job, Jenkyn on Jude, Manton on Jude.

Obs. 6. The judgments of God are irresistible. Let Ephraim be deeply rooted like a tree, or well founded like a tower, yet, if ever this east wind of God's displeasure do arise, it will pull him up by the roots, blow him down, and carry him into captivity, carry him into scarcity, carry him into infamy, yea, carry him to death, and then to hell. If the Lord gives but the word of command, he has winds in store to carry us into any of those sad coasts. Though great men are rooted in the earth like great mountains, (in their own conceit, and in the opinion of others,) yet they are but like tennis-balls in the hands of God, which he hurls at pleasure which way he pleases, as is excellently set forth, Isa. xxii. 18. With a word of his mouth he can speak his enemies into confusion; he can with more ease destroy them, than we can crush a moth in our windows, or tread a worm to death under our feet. How easily and irresistibly does a bar of iron break an earthen pot to pieces! Psal. ii. 9. There is not the least creature but is too strong for us, if God set it on. He did not vex Egypt with lions and leopards, but with grasshoppers, frogs, flies, and lice, to show his almighty, irresistible power, who can punish us by the most contemptible creatures. Thus he slew Popeleius and Hatto by rats and mice, Hermonactes was stung to death with bees, Pope Adrian was choked with a fly, Cassander was eaten with lice, Antiochus and Herod with worms. Thus we see God's omnipotency, and man's impotency, and must learn to fear him who is able to arm the least and weakest of his creatures, and make it strong enough to encounter and conquer sinful man.

Obs. 7. Cruel enemies are God's rod. They come not by chance, or of their own accord, but the Assyrian here is sent by God as the rod of his indignation against rebellious Ephraim; hence he is called "the wind of the Lord," as being more immediately sent by him. So Isa. x. 5—7, 15, the Assyrian is called God's "rod," "staff," "axe," "saw," with which God chastises "an hypocritical nation;" they can do nothing without a hand to move them. There is no evil in this kind, but it comes from God, Isa. xlii. 24, 25; xlv. 7; liv. 16; Jer. li. 20; Lam. iii. 1, 37; Amos iii. 6; Hab. i. 6. Hence Nebuchadnezzar, the king of Babylon, is called God's "servant," Jer. xxv. 9, whom he employed in his service for the correction of his people; and the wicked are called his "sword," Psal. xvii. 13. As the winds natural, so the winds metaphorical, are all at God's command, sent by him as executioners of his wrath upon a sinful people, Lev. xxvi. 25; Ezek. xiv. 17, 22.

But how can it stand with the justice of God to use such wicked, blasphemous instruments?

He that brings light out of darkness, and good out of evil, can make good use even of the sins of men. As a wise physician can so order poison, that it shall become a medicine, and can expel poison by poison; so the most wise God can extract good out of the actings of those evil ones, and what they intend for evil, he by his over-ruling providence disposes unto good.

For the clearing of this, we must take notice of a fourfold act of God in the actions of wicked men. There is an act, then,

1. Of inspection, whereby he sees all that is done, Job xxxiv. 21, 22; Psal. xciv. 7, 9.

2. Of permission, whereby he does actively suffer that to be done, which he has power to hinder, Psal. lxxxix. 40—42.

3. Of limitation or restraint, whereby he keeps in the wicked so that they cannot do any thing more or less than he will have done, Gen. xx. 6; Job i. 12.

4. Of direction and order, whereby the evil actions of wicked men (which are in themselves evil) are, by his most wise disposing and overruling providence, turned to good, Gen. xlv. 5, 7, 8; l. 20; Acts ii. 23, 24. The devil, Judas, Pilate, and the Jews, had ends of their own in crucifying Christ, but God had an end above their ends, and a plot above their plots, to which all their plots (though against their intents) were subservient. They did fulfil God's decrees against their wills.

But if they do only that which God foresees, permits, limits, and disposes, how can they be said to sin, and why does God punish them since they fulfil his will?

Because they do it not in obedience to God, but out of malice, covetousness, and self-ends, &c. Whatever they pretend, yet they intend nothing less than the doing of God's work, and the fulfilling of his will. Their end is to satisfy their lusts, to enlarge their borders by the conquest of countries and the spoils of the people, Isa. x. 7. This may,

1. Awe us; since in war we have not to do with men only, but it is God who is mighty in power, and terrible in judgment, that comes against us. If we had only to do with potsherds of the earth we might make some resistance, but when the Creator shall come against the creature, Omnipotency against impotency, who can stand? Isa. xlv. 9. He is the Lord of hosts,

and if he be against us, the hosts of heaven and the hosts of earth are against us also.

2. Comfort us in the midst of all our sufferings by the hands of cruel men, that yet they are but God's rods to chastise us for our good. Even they are his servants, and can do nothing without a commission from our Father, John xix. 11. They cannot curse where God does not curse, Numb. xxiii. 8. The very devil their master is chained and limited, and cannot devour whom he will, but only whom he may, that is, whom God permits him to devour. We are apt, like curs, to bite the stone, and not look at the hand that threw it, whereas we should always look at the hand of God in all our distresses (whatever the instruments be); then we shall be dumb and silent, when we see that it is God that has done it, Gen. l. 20; Job i. 21; Psal. xxxix. 9; 1 Cor. x. 13. The wicked are but God's scullions to cleanse us, his files to furbish us and scour off our rust, his millers to grind us, and make us fit manchet for our Lord's use. The Chaldeans were cruel persecutors, yet the Lord sends his people into the land of Chaldea for their good; he makes them to learn that many times in Babylon, which they would never have done in Zion, Jer. xxiv. 5. God can make a medicine of these vipers, and can dispose the worst things to his people's good, Rom. viii. 28. Their very persecutions shall spread the gospel, Acts viii. 1; Phil. i. 12, 19. So that in some sense we are beholden to our enemies, for they make us better.

3. Comfort us also, inasmuch as when those rods have done their work, themselves shall be burnt, Isa. x. 24—2. After Pharaoh had done God's work on Israel, God drowns him. After the Assyrian had done God's work upon his people, the Babylonians come and destroy him, and his flourishing empire, Nah. i. 2, 3. God suffers them for a time to vent their sin and malice, that his justice may be the more apparent in their downfal.

Obs. 8. Sin bereaves us of our most pleasant, precious, and desirable things. So, Jer. xv. 13; xx. 5; and Isa. lxiv. 11, where the church complains, that "all our pleasant things are laid waste." In which words, mark, 1. The generality of their loss; not some, but "all;" all their treasures, all their princes, all their palaces, all their riches, all their cities, sin had ruined all. 2. Their propriety in them; "our" pleasant things. To see another suffer, it may affect us, but not so deeply as when we ourselves suffer. 3. The excellency of the things which they lost; they were "pleasant" and desirable things. To lose base, contemptible things does not so much trouble us, but to lose our choicest things goes near us. 4. Which aggravates all, here is, 1. Conflagration, "Our holy and our beautiful house is burnt with fire." 2. A devastation and desolation, all is "laid waste."

So long as Ephraim was Ephraim, that is, faithful and fruitful, he flourished; but now that he had forsaken God, God forsook him, and lets in an east wind that destroys all. He that before was famous, and the head of the tribes, is now, since he has found out falsehood, and new lights, and new gods, become infamous, and the footstool of the tribes. So Hos. xiii. 1, "When Ephraim spake trembling, he exalted himself in Israel; but when he offended in Baal, he died:" that is, 1. When Ephraim spake trembling, or with trembling, (as it is in the original,) he was afraid of sin. Or, 2. When Ephraim spake, there was trembling; that is, he was once very awful to the rest of the tribes, so that when he spake, the rest of the tribes were ready to tremble. But when once he fell to idolatry, and worshipped Baal, he lost his reputation, and no reckoning was made of him. He that before was formidable, is now become contemptible both with God and man, at home and abroad. Now every paltry adversary tramples upon him without control, as the fearful hare on a dead lion. See thus how Ben-hadad, the king of Syria, insults over Ahab, who had "sold himself to work wickedness:" 1 Kings xx. 3, 4, "Thy silver and thy gold is mine; thy wives also and thy children, even the goodliest, are mine. And the king of Israel answered and said, My lord, O king, according to thy saying, I am thine, and all that I have." Look, as the worried cur falls upon his back, and turns up all fours, as craving quarter, so did this sordid idolater crouch to his enemy; when God was departed from him, he was even as a dead carcass. Whilst Israel kept close to God, and walked in his way, neither Balak nor Balaam, neither the devil nor his agents, could by their enchantments hurt them; but when by the wicked counsel of Balaam they were enticed to sin against God by committing whoredom with the daughters of Moab, then God's wrath breaks forth against them, and they die for it, Numb. xxv. 1; xxxi. 16. Hence a heathen could say, It is our sins that weaken our armies, and make them fly before their enemies. As all good is in God, the chiefest good, who is therefore called a sun for consolation, and a shield for protection, and the God of all comfort both inclusively and exclusively, Psal. lxxxiv. 11; 2 Cor. i. 3; so all the evil in the world may be seen in sin, which is the chiefest evil, as poverty, sickness, war, death, hell. Sin dries up all our springs, stops our fountains, spoils our treasures, and robs us of all our pleasant things; our pleasant land, our pleasant food, our pleasant raiment, our pleasant houses, pleasant children, sin, sin, sin bereaves us of them all. God turns "a fruitful land into barrenness, for the wickedness of them that dwell therein," Psal. cvii. 34; and therefore when any thing goes amiss with us, we should search for the sin that has done us the mischief; find out the Achan that has caused the trouble; find out the Jonah that has raised the storm; do justice on the one, and drown the other, and we shall have peace. We should slay that which otherwise will slay us, and ruin iniquity, which ruins our houses, lands, wives, children, "all our pleasant things." It is this enemy that robs us of our health, wealth, peace, plenty, ordinances, magistrates, ministers, and all our comforts.

Nostris peccatis barbari fortes sunt, nostris peccatis Romanus superatur exercitus.

You may say, We will hide our treasures that none shall find them. But mark, there is no hiding of yourselves, or substance, when God pursues, Jer. xi. 11. The wind of the Lord will pierce into the most secret places, and find out you, and all your hid treasures, Psal. xxi. 8; cxxxix. 7, 8; Isa. xiii. 16, 17; Amos ix. 2—4. God has those that watch for your riches, Jer. iv. 16, 17; and greedy soldiers that shall search for your hid treasures, Isa. x. 13, 14; xlv. 3; Obad. 6.

Let us then wean our hearts from those flying, fading, transitory things. What the prophet said of riches, "If they increase, set not your hearts upon them," may be fitly applied to all creature comforts; if friends increase, set not your hearts upon them; if children increase, or honours, or armies, or pleasant habitations, &c., yet set not your hearts upon them, but look upon them as things that have wings to fly from us in our greatest need. Lie loose, therefore, in your affections to all earthly enjoyments, that so whenever the Lord shall call for them by fire, sword, or any other way, it may not trouble you to part with them; make not idols of them in over-loving them, lest you lose them. It is great folly greedily to lay up treasures for we know not whom, Psal. xxxix. 6; Jer. xvii. 11; it may be for an enemy, as Ephraim here: little did he think that the merciless Assyrian should be enriched with his labours, and that the men whom their souls hated should be masters of all their desirable and pleasant things.

Since earthly things are so uncertain and fading,

"Lay not up for yourselves treasures on earth, where moth and rust doth corrupt, and where thieves break through and steal; but lay up for yourselves treasures in heaven," Matt. vi. 19, 20. Lay out your estates for God, his truth, his cause, his people, and the spiritual good of you and yours. This is to lay up treasures in heaven. Get grace, that is durable riches which will never leave you, and that better part which shall never be taken from you.

Ver. 16. *Samaria shall become desolate; for she hath rebelled against her God: they shall fall by the sword: their infants shall be dashed in pieces, and their women with child shall be ripped up.*

This verse contains the end of the sermon, and of the chapter, and therefore those interpreters do ill who make it to begin the next chapter, when this verse fitly coheres with the precedent verse: there the prophet showed how they should be plundered and lose their goods, here he tells them how they should be butchered and lose their lives. So that the prophet does not here begin a new sermon, but only confirms what he had spoken before of the destruction of Samaria, and the overthrow of the whole kingdom. So that the words are a clear and concluding exposition of the former similes; wherein we have,

תאשם desolabitur a אשם desolari, devastare, perire, quia peccatum est desolationis causa. A Lap. Leigh's Crit. S.

1. The dismal downfal of Samaria, "Samaria shall become desolate," תאשם שמרון The prophet labours to awaken them by foretelling the greatness of their punishment.

2. The meritorious cause of this sad destruction, viz. her rebellion, "for she hath rebelled." So that she has no cause to complain of God, as if he dealt hardly with her, for her own rebellion is the true cause of her destruction, and her great provocation has brought this upon her; as the church in the like case complains, "The Lord is righteous" in sending sword, plague, and famine upon us, "for I have rebelled against his commandment," Lam. i. 18.

באלהיה in Deum suum, emphaticé additur hoc pronomen; quia obliteraverant sua ingratitudine adoptionis divinæ beneficium. Rivet.

3. The aggravation of this their rebellion; it was not against man, but against God, yea, against "her God" in covenant, who had been so good and gracious to her both in temporals and spirituals, yet she most ignominiously casts off him, and prefers the calves, Hos. xiii. 2.

4. The manner of their destruction, or what kind of death they shall die, and that is by the sword, "they shall fall by the sword." They shall not only lose their treasure, and their land, but their lives also. He says not, all shall fall, but indefinitely יפלו "they shall fall;" that is, many of the inhabitants of Samaria, and of the kingdom of Israel, shall be slain by the Assyrian.

5. The better yet to awaken them out of their security, he sets forth the rage of the Assyrian, with its aggravations, telling them, "their infants shall be dashed in pieces, and their women with child shall be ripped up." They should not only die themselves, but their little ones also should perish with them.

"Samaria shall become desolate." Samaria was built by Omri, king of Israel, who "bought the hill Samaria of Shemer for two talents of silver, and built on the hill, and called the name of the city which he built, after the name of Shemer, owner of the hill, Samaria," 1 Kings xvi. 24. It was the royal city, even the chief city of the kings of Israel, where they kept their court, and had their special residence; there they reigned, and there they were buried. This was the metropolis, or mother city; all the other cities of the kingdom of Israel were called the daughters of Samaria, Ezek. xvi. 46, 55. In Augustus Cæsar's time, it was called Sebaste, and not long after was totally ruined. And here let it be noted once for all, that when the prophets speak of the ten tribes only, sometimes they call them Samaria, sometimes Ephraim, and sometimes Israel, Joseph, Jezreel, Beth-el, Beth-aven; but when they speak of the two tribes, they usually do it under the name of Judah, Jerusalem, Benjamin, and the house of David.

Samaria was a populous, strong, well-fortified city, there were in it horses, and chariots, and armour, 2 Kings x. 1, 2. It was every way well prepared to hold out against an enemy, as appears by the three years' siege of that potent enemy which lay against it; yet, notwithstanding all the fortifications, Samaria shall be made desolate, because of her sin. Samaria is here put for the inhabitants of Samaria, viz. the Israelites, and synecdochically for the whole kingdom of Israel, as distinct from the kingdom of Judah. The prophet names only Samaria, because it was the prime city, and all the rest were taken before; there was none left but Samaria, and sin brings down that also. This city was twice besieged, first by the Syrians in Ahab's time, 1 Kings xx. 1; 2 Kings vi. 24; and now by the Assyrians. Pul and Tiglath-pileser had before molested Israel, 2 Kings xv. 19, 29, and now comes Shalmaneser, a third king of Assyria. He besieges Samaria in the days of Hoshea, the last king of Israel; he takes it, and carries the inhabitants into captivity, from which they never returned, but were totally rooted up, having continued, from Jeroboam their first king, about two hundred and sixty years.

"For she hath rebelled against her God." The Lord had used all means to reclaim them, his Spirit had long striven with them in the ministry of those prophets which he had in compassion sent amongst them, as Jehu, Semaiah, Azariah, with Elijah, Elisha, Joel, Jonah, Amos, Micah, and specially this our prophet Hosea. How plainly does he tell them throughout his prophecy, of their idolatry, apostacy, ingratitude, and of the judgments which were coming on them for those sins! yet nothing will work upon them, but they persist obstinately in their sins, and therefore the Lord resolves to pour out his fury on them. Since they had imbittered his soul with their sins, and given him gall who had given them honey, and given him wormwood for his milk, therefore he now resolves to send on them bitter punishments, Hos. xii. 14.

מרה significat rebellare, apostatare, exacerbare, et ad amaritudinem concitare. Ruth i. 20; Lam. i. 18.

"They shall fall by the sword;" that is, they shall die by the sword; so the phrase is frequently taken in Scripture, as Lev. xxvi. 7, 8; Numb. xiv. 3, 43; 2 Sam. i. 12; Psal. lxxviii. 64; Ezek. v. 12; Hos. vii. 16.

Cadit et Ripheus justissimus unus qui fuit in Teucris. Virg.

"Their infants shall be dashed in pieces, and their women with child shall be ripped up." This sets forth the great rage and fury of the barbarous Assyrians, and withal implies the greatness of Samaria's sin, which provoked God to so great wrath. They should spare neither old nor young, no mercy should be showed to women or children, no sex, no age should escape unpunished; their little infants and sucklings, which usually are spared, yet now shall be dashed in pieces. Soldiers are wont to show mercy to women and children, unless sorely provoked; the Assyrians had besieged Samaria three years, and therefore they dealt the more severely with them. Fenced cities sometimes hold out long, but when taken they generally suffer much. Of such brutish inhumanity we read, 2 Kings xv. 16, where the tyrant Menahem ripped the infants of Tiphsah out of their mothers' wombs, because their fathers "opened not to him." These examples in no wise justify, much less excuse, the malicious cruelty of wicked men who despitefully slay the godly with their seed; such cursed Edomites shall surely and suitably pay for it, Psal. cxxxvii. 7; Amos i. 13. The Assyrians, who here dash in pieces Ephraim's children, had at last, by way of retaliation, their own so served, Nah. iii. 10.

The sum of all is this: O people of Israel, I have often told you what you will not believe, that your destruction is near; therefore now know, that whether you believe it or not, yet God will certainly and suddenly execute what he has decreed, and fulfil what he has spoken by me; neither have you any cause to complain of cruelty in God, since it is your own rebellion which has brought this judgment on your own heads. There have been no means wanting on God's part to do you good, he has sent his prophets rising early and coming late unto you. He would have cured you, but ye would not be cured, and therefore now ye shall never be purged; but your chief city, with the regions round about it, shall be made a desolation, your men shall fall by the sword, yea, your women and little children shall die without mercy.

Obs. 1. God usually warns before he smites. He sends Hosea to tell them before, "Samaria shall become desolate." He speaks before he strikes, and denounces judgments before he executes them. Seldom does he send any great judgment against his own people, but he tells them of it first. He lightens before he thunders, shoots off his warning pieces before his murdering pieces, and hangs out the white flag of mercy before the black flag of destruction. He deals not with us, as one did with Diogenes, who first brake his head, and then bid him take heed. But he first admonishes us to repent; thus he did to the seven churches of Asia before their destruction, Rev. ii. 5. He first cuts men down with the sword of his mouth, before he cuts them down with the sword of his hand, Hos. vi. 5. He first blows the trumpet, (and commands men so to do, Deut. xx. 10—12,) before he sends the sword, Hos. v. 8, 9; 2 Chron. xxxvi. 15, 16; Jer. vii. 25; xxvi. 18; Joel ii. 1; Amos iv. 12; Zeph. ii. 1—3.

Sometimes God warns,

1. By extraordinary and immediate revelation. Thus he warned the wise men that came to Christ not to go to Herod, but to return to their own country another way, Matt. ii. 12.

2. By prodigious signs and comets. These are the usual forerunners of some judgment approaching. They have a voice as well as the word; if they will not hearken to the voice of the first sign, yet they will believe the voice of the second, Exod. iv. 8. Christ tells us, that before the destruction of Jerusalem, there should be many fearful sights and signs, Luke xxi. 11, 25. And Josephus affirms, that before its destruction, for a whole year's space there appeared a comet like a sword. Before our German wars, there appeared a blazing comet in 1618.

3. By his ministers, Ezek. xxxiii. 2, 7, 8. Thus he warned the old world, a hundred and twenty years, by the preaching of Noah, before he drowned it, Gen. vi. 13. Before the destruction of Jerusalem, he sent Christ himself and his apostles to call them to repentance.

4. By his lesser judgments. 1. He comes as a moth, which eats one thread now, and another anon, and without any noise devours all. 2. As a worm, or rottenness, which eats out the heart of the strongest oak. 3. If that will not do, there lies a lion that tears all in pieces without resistance, Hos. v. 12, 14.

5. By his rods on others, as on the Palatinate and Savoy, &c.; so he sent the Jews to Shiloh, Jer. vii. 12: also by taking away eminent magistrates and zealous ministers, Isa. iii. 1—6.

6. By the motions of his Spirit; he knocks at the door of our hearts, and warns us to return, Rev. iii. 20.

And this he does, 1. In mercy to his people, that they might prepare to meet him, and so prevent his judgments; as those that believed the threatening of the hail, housed themselves and their cattle, and so were saved, Exod. ix. 18—21. He deals not with us like an enemy, who surprises his adversary unawares; but, like a faithful friend, he tells us of the storm approaching, that we might hide ourselves from it, 2 Chron. xii. 5—7; Job xxii. 29; Hab. iii. 16.

Calamitas dicitur ventura ut agente populo pœnitentiam non veniat. Jerome.

2. For the manifestation of his justice upon the wicked, who shall be made inexcusable, in that they had such fair warning given them, but they would not take it. Nineveh, at the preaching of one Jonah, repented and escaped; the Lord be merciful to England! how many hundreds of Jonahs have we had to call us to repentance, and yet we turn not, but fall away more and more! It is a sad aggravation of men's sins, and puts a sore sting into men's troubles, when conscience shall fly in their faces and say, Thou wast foretold of such judgments, and forewarned of such and such miseries, but thou contemnedst the voice of thy teachers, and didst set at nought all their counsels; and therefore now thou must expect no more pity or patience from God, but mayst justly expect that he should fulfil the word which he spake by his servants against thee.

Let then his warnings win thee, and his patience and long-suffering lead thee to repentance. Let not his admonitions be always lost upon thee. Be not still secure and senseless, like Lot's sons-in-law, who, when he warned them of danger approaching, "seemed as one that mocked," Gen. xix. 14; but how soon did they find that he was in earnest! So Isa. v. 19, they mocked at the prophet that told them of captivity and judgment, and bid him let them see the things he spake of; and they did so to their sorrow. And is it not so in our days? when we tell people of judgment approaching, and ready to seize upon them, they look upon it as some vain dream or melancholy fancy, till they are made to feel the contrary. See how dreadfully God threatens such secure, unbelieving sinners, Deut. xxix. 19—21.

Believe his timely warnings. Without faith all warnings are ineffectual; it is only Noah, that by faith feared and built an ark, that was saved, both he and his household, Heb. xi. 7.

Obs. 2. The ministers of God must apply the word to their people. The prophet preaches at Samaria against the sins of Samaria, and tells them to their faces, that for their rebellion they shall be made a desolation. Thus did all the prophets; they made Jerusalem to know her abominations, Isa. lviii. 1; Ezek. xvi. 2. So did Christ himself apply the word particularly to his hearers, Matt. xi. 21, 23; xxiii. 37, 38; John iv. 17, 18; so did the apostles, Acts ii. 36, 37. This is the only way to convince and convert men; what is spoken generally to all, few will apply to themselves, *Quod dicitur omni, dicitur nulli.*

Be not then offended at the plain and powerful preaching of the word. A plaister that is not applied, will never heal. A minister shall never profit his people, till he apply the word to their particular cases. Those whom the Lord intends for conversion, by his Spirit he sets the word so home upon their hearts, that they think the minister knows even all their secret thoughts.

Obs. 3. Judgments seldom go alone. Ephraim was plundered before, but now he must be butchered; before he lost his goods, now his life must go, which is more precious than all pleasant things, Job ii. 4. How oft do we read of sword, plague, famine, those three arrows of God, shot together against a rebellious people, Ezek. xiv. 21. As sins seldom go alone, so neither do judgments: see what a concatenation and chain of judgments is set down together, Deut. xxviii. 15—68

God wants not variety of judgments to inflict upon a sinful people, that they may know what a sad and bitter thing it is that they have provoked him. Pharaoh had ten plagues one after another. The trumpets and the vials in the Revelation came not single, but by sevens, bringing in mischief upon mischief, and plague upon plague, till he had consumed them, Deut. xxxi. 17; Jer. li. 31, 32.

Obs. 4. When lesser judgments do not mend a people, God usually comes with greater. If plundering will not mend Ephraim, desolation shall end him, Hos. v. 12, 14. When Chedorlaomer had plundered Sodom, and that did not better them, Gen. xiv. 11, at last comes fire from heaven and consumes them, Gen. xix. When gentle physic will not work out the peccant humour, the physician applies stronger. If gentle correction will not mend our children, we double our strokes. If one beating will not mend a people, God will plague them yet seven times more according to their sins, Lev. xxvi. 21, 24; Isa. i. 5; Jer. v. 3, 6. When no judgments will work upon Pharaoh, then he is drowned. When temporal judgments do not mend a people, he sends them to eternal. It is an ill sign when men are incorrigible under judgments, and become the worse for beating, Isa. ix. 13. Ahaz had a brand set upon him, to warn all others to take heed of this sinning sin: "In the time of his distress did he trespass yet more against the Lord: this is that king Ahaz." *That* king, that wicked, infamous, irreligious king, who "sacrificed to the gods of Damascus, which smote him." What madness is this, to serve such as beat their servants for their pains, and ruin them! for so it follows, "They were the ruin of him, and of all Israel," 2 Chron. xxviii. 22, 23.

Desperate sores must have desperate cures. Hard knots must have hard wedges. "Fitches are beaten out with a staff," but the cummin must have a rod, Isa. xxviii. 27. When the Lord had used all means to bring Israel to repentance, when he had sent blasting, plague, famine, and sword upon them, and yet they were impenitent, Amos iv. 6—11, he proceeds there in ver. 12, to tell them that now he would deal more sharply and severely with them. "Therefore thus will I do unto thee," i. e. thus terribly, thus dreadfully, in a more fierce and furious manner than ever: "Therefore thus will I do unto thee, O Israel: and because I will do this unto thee, prepare to meet thy God, O Israel." There is no meeting him in a way of opposition, or rising up against him; (for who ever hardened himself against God and prospered?) but meet him in a way of humiliation and repentance with prayers and tears, despatch those messengers to meet him on the way whilst he is afar off, that you may prevent the execution of God's wrath. A lion will not seize on a yielding prey; the bending reed is preserved, when the stubborn oak is pulled up by the roots, Isa. ii. 11, 12, &c. By this means we shall either remove the judgment, or get it sanctified, so that all shall be for good unto us, or else God will take us away, as he did Josiah, before the evil comes. We shall escape those trials we cannot bear, and be enabled to undergo those trials which we cannot escape.

Quid sit facturus tacet, ut dum ad singula pœnarum genera pendent incerti, pœnitentiam agant, ne inferat quæ minatur. Jerome.

Mittamus preces et lachrymas cordis legatos. Cyprian.

Obs. 5. Eminent places ofttimes are eminent in sin. In great cities there usually are great sinners. Jerusalem was a great city, and what great abominations were in it! murder, oppression, bribery, profanation of sabbaths and holy things, her princes were roaring lions, her judges ravening wolves, and the priests did violence to the law, Ezek. xxii. Babylon was a famous, wealthy, populous city, yet full of cruelty and pride, full of witchcraft and fornication, both corporal and spiritual, Jer. l. 31—38. The cities of Sodom and Gomorrah were full of crying sins, as pride, idleness, gluttony, inhumanity, and notorious uncleanness. And here in the text Samaria was full of idolatry and rebellion against God, 1 Kings xiii. 32; Isa. x. 10, 11; Hos. viii. 5: the lesser cities were called the daughters of Samaria, Ezek. xvi. 46, and those were like their mother. Great cities have great influence upon their neighbour towns; if they be idolatrous, superstitious, riotous, proud, profane, so will the places round about them be; if great Babylon be a harlot, she will quickly become "the mother of harlots and abominations," Rev. xvii. 5. We should not therefore desire to live in such populous places, (unless we be called by God to them, for then he will keep us, as he did Lot in Sodom,) but to go and live in them without a call, only for pleasure, or to see fashions, &c., is a sore temptation. We see travellers that go thus to such great places, return ofttimes infected both in body and soul. So true is that of one, *Nunquam inter homines fui, quin minor homo redii.*

Obs. 6. Such places as have been eminent for sin, usually are eminent for punishment. As we see in the old world, Sodom, Jerusalem, and Samaria here, for her sin, is made a desolation, Micah i. 6. When sin grows general and national, it brings national judgments, Isa. viii. 18; Jer. xi. 9, 11; Hos. iv. 1—3. When all Israel transgressed the law, no wonder if the curse come upon them, Dan. ix. 11. Many think to escape the better because they have so many companions, when the more general the sin, the nearer to judgment. If all nations sin, all nations must have the cup of God's wrath given them, Jer. xxv. 15; Mal. iii. 8, 9. It is as easy with God to destroy a world of men as one man, they are all but as a drop and a little dust to him, Isa. xl. 15—17. Multitudes of sinners increase wrath. When the Jews "assembled themselves by troops in the harlots' houses," then God would pardon them no longer, Jer. v. 7, 8. The more wicked the times and places are that we live in, the greater our praise will be if we be godly. To be good in good times and places, a hypocrite and formalist may be; but with Lot to be good in Sodom, and Job in the land of Uz, and with Noah in the midst of an ungodly world, and with Elijah to be righteous and zealous in the midst of an unrighteous and perverse generation, that is praiseworthy indeed, and argues much sincerity. It was the commendation of the church of Pergamos, that she professed Christ's name where Satan had his throne, and did not deny him in the days when Antipas, his faithful martyr, was slain, Rev. ii. 12, 13. Fly sin then, which brings destruction, not only on the sinner, but also on the very towns, cities, castles, and places where they dwell. As God has promised that peace and prosperity shall be in the dwellings of the righteous, Job v. 24; viii. 6; Prov. iii. 33, and that he will make a hedge about them, and all that they have, to preserve them from robbery, fire, molestation by evil spirits, and other calamities, Job i. 10; so, on the contrary, sin makes a man naked, and exposes him, and all that he has, to the curse of God. He will destroy the very dwellings of idolaters, swearers, cursers, bribers, &c., Job xii. 6; xv. 34; Zech. v. 4. The wickedness that has been practised in the great houses and castles of this land, has laid many of them in the dust, and we may look to be brought yet lower: we have brought God low in our judgments, low in our affections, low in our actions, low in his ordinances, low in his vicegerents and ambassadors; and therefore it is just with God to lay us low, and to debase us, who have so many ways debased him.

Obs. 7. No fortifications can preserve a sinful people from ruin. Let them make walls as high as heaven, and ditches as deep as hell, yet if sin reign within, it will bring all down. It is not a fleet by sea, nor forces by land, it is not a magazine of treasures, nor an arsenal of armour, that can preserve a wicked kingdom from ruin. As Samaria was a well-fortified, so it was a rebellious, idolatrous, sinful place, and this brought it down, Ezek. xvi. 46; xxiii. 4, 5; Hos. vii. 1; Amos iii. 9, 10; Micah i 5, 7. Though it were strongly fortified both by art and nature, and very large, about three miles in compass, yet Samaria's sin was Samaria's ruin. Nineveh was a populous, ancient, great, strong, wealthy city, yet her great sins laid her in the dust, and made all her strong holds drop like ripe figs, with little ado, into the mouth of the Chaldeans. Babylon a most ancient, ample, wealthy, well-fortified, potent, populous city, yet, abounding with sin, all her power and policy could not keep her from ruin. Jerusalem, that strong city, encompassed with mountains, towers, and bulwarks, fortified both by art and nature, and so powerfully protected by the Lord himself for many years together, to the admiration of all the world, that it was judged invincible; Lam. iv. 12, "The kings of the earth, and all the inhabitants of the world, would not have believed that the adversary and the enemy should have entered into the gates of Jerusalem;" yet Jerusalem's sin was Jerusalem's ruin; and, therefore, let none confide in cities, or any privileges whatsoever. We are apt in our distresses to run to well-fortified places, but in vain is salvation looked for from those creature confidences; if the Lord help not, how should these help? This is to forsake God, "the fountain of living waters," the Almighty, and all-sufficient, "a very present help in trouble," and to go to cisterns, "broken cisterns" of creature comforts, that will fail and forsake them in a time of trouble, Jer. ii. 13.

Obs. 8. Sin is a bitter thing. Samaria has rebelled, or imbittered (as the word is in the original) God, and "provoked him to anger most bitterly" by her sin, Hos. xii. 14. Ephraim's sins were bitter to God, yea, they were bitternesses, in the abstract, and in the plural number also. This may discover to us the cursed nature of sin, and the iniquity of our iniquities, which turns God's sweetness into bitterness, his patience into wrath, and his bowels into wormwood. If any thing can sadden God, and imbitter his soul, it is sin. To see every base lust preferred before him, to see Satan in the throne, the heart, and the Spirit of God kept out, must needs imbitter his Spirit against us. The Lord that made heaven and earth, and sustains the pillars of it, yet never complains of that burden; but sin is such a burden, that he oft complains of that, as tiring him out, Isa. i. 14, 24; xliii. 24; Amos ii. 13; and the bitterness thereof is as gall, which he cannot endure, Deut. xxxii. 32. God is all love and sweetness, and would not deal thus bitterly with us, did not our bitter sins provoke him to it.

Sin is bitter, 1. To God. 2. To Christ. 3. To the Holy Spirit. 4. To angels: 1. To good angels. 2. To the evil angels. 5. To men: 1. To good men. 2. To wicked men. 6. To states and kingdoms. 7. To the creatures. 8. In its effects: 1. Private. 2. Positive.

Sin is bitter,

1. To God, as we have seen before.

2. To Christ; it made him cry in the bitterness of his soul, "My God, my God, why hast thou forsaken me?" and made his soul heavy unto death. So bitter were our sins to him that they made him "a man of sorrows," Isa. liii. 3, and made him sweat, *non guttas sed grumos*, clots of blood, Luke xxii. 44. When Christ hung upon the cross, they gave him gall and vinegar to drink: every sin is as gall to him. "The Lord is righteous; for I have rebelled against his commandment," or, as it is in the original, because I have imbittered him; he is righteous in all his judgments on me, for I have imbittered him against me by my bitter sins, Lam. i. 18.

3. To the Holy Spirit of God. Nothing grieves it, and drives it out of the soul, but sin, Gen. vi. 3; Eph. iv. 30.

4. To the angels. 1. To the good angels: it is bitter and displeasing to them to see their Lord and Master daily provoked by a company of sinful, rebellious creatures; and should the Lord give them but a word of command, they would suddenly smite all the wicked dead, and revenge the dishonours done to him, as we see in Sennacherib's blasphemous camp, where one angel in one night killed a hundred fourscore and five thousand men.

2. To the evil angels: it has thrown them from heaven to hell, and of angels it has turned them into devils, and keeps them in chains of darkness to the judgment of the great day, Jude 6.

5. To man. 1. To good men: there is nothing so bitter to them as sin, nothing grieves them like this, that they have grieved the good Spirit of God. All losses, crosses, reproaches, are light with them in comparison of sin. The church of Ephesus could bear any affliction, but not sin, Rev. ii. 2. Good David oft complains of the burden of his sins, seldom of his sufferings, Psal. xxxviii. 4. So bitter a thing is sin to them, that it ofttimes makes them weary of their lives, and long to be dissolved that they may sin no more, Rom. vii. 24; 2 Cor. v. 4; it makes them a burden to themselves, Job vii. 20, and causes them to weep bitterly, Matt. xxvi. 75. Hence Job, chap. xiii. 26, calls sins bitter things, "Thou writest bitter things against me," what is that? "thou makest me to possess the iniquities of my youth."

2. To wicked men. Though whilst conscience sleeps they may think it a light matter, yet to an enlightened and an awakened conscience nothing is more bitter. This made Adam to hide himself, and Cain to complain that his sin was a burden too heavy for him to bear. Judas could not endure the bitterness of it, but went forth and hanged himself. Nothing so bitter as sin when it is once charged by God upon the conscience; of all heavy things this is the most heavy: "A wounded spirit who can bear?" Those that will not now believe it, yet shall one day find it, that it is an evil and bitter thing that they have sinned against God, Jer. ii. 19; iv. 18; Lam. iii. 15; Amos viii. 10; Prov. ix. 17, 18; xiv. 13; xxiii. 32; Gal. v. 19—21; Acts viii. 23. Solomon, who had found sweetness in the ways of the flesh, yet at last felt and acknowledged the bitterness of such courses, Prov. v. 3, 4; Eccl. vii. 26. Though sin may for a time seem sweet to the sinner, and it be a pastime to them to do wickedly, yet it will be bitterness in the end, the poison of asps is in it, Job xx. 12—14.

If sin then be so bitter, how comes it to pass that wicked men are no more sensible of it? To this I answer,

1. Their consciences are seared with the custom of sinning, which has taken away the sense of sin, so that now it is become connatural and pleasant to them, and so is not grievous. Poison in a toad is not troublesome, he is never sick of it, nor sensible of it, because it is natural to him; but poison in a man, a sheep, a dove, is deadly, because it is not in its proper place.

Elementum in suo loco non est ponderosum. Arist.

2. It is a spiritual bitterness; now wicked men have no spiritual life in them, they are dead in sin, and so are insensible of it.

3. The devil, that prince of darkness, keeps wicked men in darkness and ignorance, so that they know not the terrors of the Lord, nor what "a fearful thing" it is to fall into the hands of an angry God; and this makes men so fearless of sin. As we cannot desire what we know not, so we cannot fear it. A child that knows not what a terrible thing a lion or a bear is, will venture to provoke them; but a man of understanding will run

from them. It is fools who make a mock of sin, who never knew the danger of it; but the godly, who know its bitterness, will rather choose any misery than the least iniquity, any affliction rather than sin.

6. To states and kingdoms, and provokes the Lord to send bitter enemies against them, Hab. i. 6. The very land where wicked men dwell is sick of them, and cannot have ease till it has spewed them out. As a man that has poison in his stomach is not well till he be rid of it, and as the sea would not be quiet till Jonah was thrown overboard; so nations can have no rest till they have vomited up such wicked men, which, like corrupt humours, oppress and burden them, Lev. xviii. 25, 28; xx. 22. This is that bitter water which causes the curse to seize on persons and nations, Numb. v. 18, and brings upon them bitter destruction, Deut. xxxii. 24. Thus the ten tribes here were spewed out for their idolatry, when they were carried captive by Shalmaneser into the land of the Medes, from whence they never returned, 2 Kings xvii. 18. And the Jews were vomited up when they were carried captive into Babylon for the space of seventy years, 2 Chron. xxxvi. 21.

7. To the creatures. They all groan under the burden, and as a woman in travail longs to be disburdened and eased of her birth, so the whole creation travails in pain, and longs to be delivered from that bondage, vanity, and corruption, to which it is subject by reason of the sin of man, Rom. viii. 20—22.

8. In its effects, which are twofold: 1. Privative. 2. Positive.

1. The privative effects of sin are sevenfold: it deprives us of,

1. The favour of God, which is the very life of souls: "In his favour is life," Psal. xxx. 5.

2. God's fatherly care and protection over us, Gen. iv. 14; Exod. xxxii. 25.

3. The guard of the angels. Every godly man has not one angel, but a guard of angels about him, to keep him, whilst he keeps God's ways, Psal. xxxiv. 7; xci. 11, 12; Heb. i. 14.

4. Peace of conscience; a jewel of more worth than all the world. Adam, when he had sinned, was afraid, and hid himself. David, after his sin, complained of broken bones, his sight and sense of sin was as bitter to him as if he had broken all his bones, Psal. li. 8.

5. Our excellency. Purity is our excellency; it is sin, and only sin, that robs us of our glory, and makes us like other men. As Jacob said of Reuben when he had defiled his father's bed, "Thou shalt not excel," Gen. xlix. 4.

6. All true right to the creature. A wicked man is a usurper, though he may have a civil right, in *foro soli*, yet, in *foro poli*, he has a sanctified right to nothing. When men are in Christ, then, and not till then, all is theirs, 1 Cor. iii. 22.

7. Heaven and eternal happiness, Rev. xxi. 27.

2. The positive effects of sin are more especially three. It exposes us to all miseries, external, internal, and eternal.

Sin exposes us to miseries,

1. External, in body, goods, good name; we may thank sin for all our sicknesses, sorrows, sores, losses, plagues, poverty, &c., Deut. xxviii. 15—68; Lam. iii. 39.

2. Internal. It brings hardness of heart, the sorest of plagues; all the plagues of Pharaoh, all the sores of Job, and all the sorrows of Joseph, are nothing compared with it. This brings spiritual blindness, a reprobate sense, a spirit of slumber, and strong delusions, Isa. vi. 9, 10; Rom. xi. 8.

3. Eternal miseries both in soul and body; it brings sorrows endless, easeless, and remediless. So that there is no evil like the evil of sin, no plague like this plague. As piety has the promise, and carries its reward with it, and though no man should recompense it, yet the good we do is recompence itself; not only for, but in, the very keeping of God's commandments there is great reward, Psal. xix. 11; the act of keeping them is a reward as well as the issue. As every good work brings its reward with it, so every evil work brings its sorrow with it; and though no man punish it, yet it is a punishment to itself, it is *finis operis*, though not *finis operantis;* Jer. iv. 18, "Thy way and thy doings have procured these things unto thee." Sin is that which procures us all our sorrow, we should therefore hate it with a pure and perfect hatred, and get this cause of all our sorrows removed, and then the effect will cease.

Now is sin so bitter? 1. Then take heed of pleading for sin, or extenuating it. Put not sweet names upon so bitter a thing. There is a woe denounced against such as do so, Isa. v. 20, "Woe unto them that call evil good, and good evil; that put darkness for light, and light for darkness; that put bitter for sweet, and sweet for bitter!" Such look upon sin through the devil's spectacles, and then no wonder if they call drunkenness good fellowship, covetousness frugality, pride decency, &c. Such put a fair glove upon a foul hand, and false glosses upon filthy vices, the better to deceive. "But let no man deceive you with vain words, for even for these things cometh the wrath of God upon the children of disobedience." Call not therefore sin so as the corrupt world calls it, but esteem and call it as the word of God calls it. How is that? Why, it calls it an abomination, poison, sorrow, sickness, bitterness, filth, vomit, folly, madness, darkness, dung, death, &c.

When the judgment is thus truly convinced of the vileness of sin, it is an excellent preservation against sin.

2. If sin be so bitter, then sad is the condition of such as are insensible of its bitterness, who make that their recreation here which will be their damnation hereafter, who plead not only for infirmities (which yet no good man dares do) but also for enormities. They declare their sin like Sodom, impudently and impenitently; they thank God they never knew what the burden or bitterness of sin meant; but know, if sin be not bitter here, it will in another world be more than bitter.

And therefore this may comfort those that groan and grieve under the burden and bitterness of sin; such as make their sin their greatest sorrow, Christ will be unto them their greatest joy. Christ calls such, as it were by name, to come to him, Isa. lv. 1, 2; Matt. xi. 28. This qualifies a man, and fits him for Christ; when Christ sees of the travail of his soul in our souls, it delights him, Isa. liii. 10, 11. This sense of sin argues some spiritual life in the soul. Nature will not complain of nature, nor will corruption complain of corruption; it is only grace that makes us truly sensible of the bitterness of sin.

3. Pity those that groan under the burden and bitterness of sin. No sorrow like their sorrow, no burden like the burden of a wounded conscience. Add not affliction to the afflictions of those whom God has wounded, but pour the oil of mercy into their sin-sick souls. Be not like Job's friends, miserable comforters, and physicians of no value; if we must ease our enemy's ox or ass when he lies under his burden, shall we not much more ease our brother's soul? Exod. xxiii. 5. Be not harsh or hasty, be not sour and censorious, to such, but be meek and merciful, and so bear each other's burdens, Gal. vi. 1, 2.

Obs. 9. It is a sad aggravation of people's sins when they sin against *their* God. The God of all their mercies, the fountain of all their enjoyments; their God in covenant, whom they have avouched for their God, and vowed openly that he shall be their God, and they

Deus illorum esse dicitur, ut qui fœderis nexu conjunctus sit illis, quem jure societatis colere debebant, a quo non poterant citra perfidiæ crimen deficere. Wolf. in 2 Reg. xvii.

would be his people, to love, serve, fear, and obey him; yet, contrary to all vows, baptistical, eucharistical, personal, national, to fly from God, and to rebel against him, this is the height of sin, and makes it exceeding sinful, and provokes the Lord to say, "Lo-ammi, Ye are not my people," as he said to Ephraim, Hos. i. 9.

And is not this England's sin? God has taken us into covenant with himself, he has owned us above all the people in the world, he has made us the head and terror of the nations, he has done wonders for us at home and abroad, and made us his darling nation; whilst others swim in blood, we swim in blessings of peace; whilst others are weeping and wailing by the waters of Babylon, we dwell in an Eden, joy and gladness are found in us, thanksgiving and the voice of melody. He has made us his Ephraim, he has laid his right hand upon us, he has planted us in a fruitful soil, hedged us about with his gracious protection and good laws; he has removed from amongst us all the apparent impediments to our growth and fruitfulness; he has furnished us with choice persons, and those persons with excellent gifts and graces: he has a special care over us for good; and now he looks (as well he may) for the pleasant grapes of obedience, but behold the sour and wild grapes of confusion, disorder, error, and disobedience abound amongst us. We have broken all our covenants, we are not only sermon-proof, but we are also covenant-proof; no bonds so sacred, so strong, but we can as easily break them as Samson did the cords of the Philistines. So that what can we expect but that the Lord should take away his hedge of government both temporal and spiritual, breaking down the wall which defended us from our enemies, and letting in all the wild beasts that might destroy us? Justly might he withdraw his good hand of providence and protection from us, and expose us to all manner of rapine and ruin, for our apostacies and rebellions.

Hall on 2 Tim. iii. 3.

Obs. 10. Sin, especially the sin of rebellion, brings the sword upon a people. "They shall fall by the sword." This is God's last and great rod, and he never brings it forth till he be greatly provoked by his people's sins, Job xxxvi. 12; Isa. i. 20. When no other means will better a people, then comes the sword and cuts them off. God has three evil arrows, which he shoots at a rebellious people, viz. the sword, famine, and pestilence, Ezek. v. 16, 17; these are called "arrows," because they are sharp and deadly; and "evil," because of the misery and mischief which they bring: of all the three, the sword is the sorest, as appears by David's choice, 2 Sam. xxiv. 14; besides, the plague and famine are the usual attendants of war; where the sword goes before, there famine and pestilence usually attend.

Obs. 11. Little infants are great sinners. "Their infants shall be dashed in pieces."

1. That great sin and rebellion of Adam is imputed to them for sin; what he did, they did, we were all in the loins of that one man, Rom. v. 12.

2. They have not only original sin imputed, but imparted also; they have inherent original sin, which is radically, seminally, fundamentally all sin. The youngest child carries an old man of sin within him. We are no sooner born into the world, but we have a world of sin about us.

3. The sad diseases, pangs, and dismal deaths which seize on infants, are strong proofs of this point, their very dying speaks them sinners. "The wages of sin," be it original or actual, "is death," Rom. vi. 23. Original sin, which is the greatest sin in the world, cleaves to their natures, and makes them odious and abominable in God's sight, so that they are by nature children of wrath, and obnoxious to all his judgments. We are all *damnati antequam nati*, and so might justly have been sent from the womb to the tomb.

Obs. 12. Wicked parents bring judgments on their posterity. Their poor little ones fare the worse for them; Hos. ix. 12, 13, "Though they bring up their children, yet will I bereave them," and "Ephraim shall bring forth children to the murderer," who is God's executioner; so become parricides, rather than parents. Thus the old world was drowned, and their children with them; and the Sodomites were burnt, and their children with them. Achan was not only stoned himself, but his sons and daughters, yea, and his cattle, perished with him. The accusers of Daniel were slain by the lions, both they and their children, Dan. vi. 24. The Jews that rejected and crucified Christ, brought a curse not only upon themselves, but also upon their children, Matt. xxvii. 25, "His blood be on us, and on our children," which has now lain on them above sixteen hundred years.

It is just with God to cut off the wicked and their seed, as we kill the wolf with her whelps, and the fox with her cubs: though the young toad has not actually poisoned any, yet, because it has a poisonous nature in it, we destroy it. So does God by the children of the wicked, Gen. xix. 25; Numb. xvi. 32, 33; 1 Sam. xv. 3; Isa. xiii. 16; Jer. xliv. 7; Hos. x. 14. When men rebel against God and reject his ways, he will send against them a barbarous and cruel nation, that shall not regard the persons of the old, nor have compassion on the young, Deut. xxviii. 50; xxxii. 25; Ezek. ix. 6.

But are not infants called "innocents," Psal. cvi. 38; Jer. xix. 4? how then can it consist with the justice of God thus severely to punish them?

True, they are so called, but not because they have no sin; but, 1. In respect of those cruel men, who without any cause shed the blood of those little ones who had deserved no such thing at their hands. So the Assyrians here were guilty of great inhumanity, in killing those infants, and God in his due time retaliated it on them, Nah. iii. 10.

2. Though they may be called innocent in respect of any actual sin, yet they are not so in respect of original sin, which seminally and radically is every sin. The guilt of that sin cleaves to their natures, and makes them obnoxious to all tortures here, and eternal torments hereafter.

3. The sins of the parents may be also a moving cause, and may provoke the Lord to smite the parents with their children. Exod. xx. 5, the Lord threatens to visit the sins of idolatrous parents upon their children, because either they already walk in their fathers' sins, or else in time they would do so, or, it may be, worse, which God only knows.

3. God has a sovereign right and power over all his creatures; he is the potter, and we are his clay, he may do with his own what he pleases, he may make us or mar us, raise us or ruin us; and none may say unto him, What doest thou? He that gives life may take it away, how and when he pleases; his will is the rule of justice, yea, justice itself; we must therefore adore God's judgments when we cannot comprehend them, and know that, though they may be secret, yet they are always just.

4. Children are parts of their parents, part of their family and part of their substance, and God may justly punish the sinful parent in his child, as well as in his cattle and estate, because they do not only belong to him, but also are a part of him.

5. Sin committed by a particular member of a politic body is by a synecdoche, frequent in Scripture, attributed to the whole body, and does, in a measure, really belong to it. Thus Achan's sin, though not known to the people, yet made them all guilty, till he was put to death, Josh. vii. 11.

Vid. Lavater in Josh.

6. Yet these temporal judgments may be mingled with spiritual mercies; as we see in Jeroboam's child, who was taken away in mercy, because there was some goodness found in him, 1 Kings xiv. 12, 13. Especially the infants of God's people, that are in covenant with their parents, there is great grounds of hope that they have changed their temporal life for an eternal; and are freed from many sins, sorrows, and temptations, to which men that live to riper years are exposed; yea, if they should be cast away for their original sin, yet their damnation will be lighter than if they had lived longer. It had been good for reprobates if they had not been born, or that they had died as soon as they had been born, for then they would not have had so many sins to answer for.

Infantes sunt pars ecclesiæ; oportet eos cum ecclesia affligi, ut reddantur conformes filio Dei. Luther.

But has not God said, "The son shall not bear the iniquity of the father?" Deut. xxiv. 16; 2 Kings xiv. 6; Ezek. xviii. 20. It seems then to be cruelty to kill the children for the parents' sins, especially such as are unborn, and have not deserved such evils. To which I would answer,

1. It is true in respect of the Assyrians, it was cruelty and horrid barbarousness in them to kill poor harmless little ones, and God threatens to visit such sins upon the heads of such sinners.

2. It is not cruelty in God, for children are children of wrath as well as their parents; as all have sinned, so he may punish all without injustice. Besides, he permits and orders the cruelty of wicked adversaries to his own glory and his people's good. As for Deut. xxiv. 16, it speaks of God's restraining of magistrates, who may not punish the children for the fathers' offences. True it is, God finds cause enough in children themselves to punish them, but when they imitate their wicked parents, this hastens and heightens wrath, by adding sin to sin.

3. The son shall not bear the iniquity of the father, if he depart from the father's iniquity and do not walk in his steps. Ezek. xviii. 14, 17, "If he beget a son, that seeth all his father's sins which he hath done, and considereth, and doeth not such like," "he shall not die for the iniquity of his father." But if the son tread in his father's steps, he shall bear his own iniquity, and becomes accessory to his father's sin, by imitation, and approbation of it, Matt. xxiii. 32; Luke xi. 48, 50; the blood of former generations had not been required of that generation if they had not been as bloody as the former. But where old sins are continued and approved of by new acting of them, there the old sins, as well as the new, are justly punished. So that the threatening is not to be understood absolutely, but conditionally, viz. if the children do persist in their fathers' sins and walk in their wicked ways.

4. The son shall not bear the personal iniquities of the father in reference to eternal punishment; God will not damn a son simply for the sin of his father, it is a man's own sin which is his everlasting ruin, yet he may lay many temporal chastisements upon a good son for the sin of his father. The Lord, in Ezek. xviii. 20, 23, 32, seems to speak of eternal, and not of temporal punishment.

1. This should make parents fearful of displeasing God, lest they bring miseries, not only on themselves, but also on their children; their idolatry may bring a curse upon their children's children to many generations. No children in Scripture are threatened like the children of idolaters. In none of the commandments does God threaten to visit the sin of the fathers upon the children but only in the second, Exod. xx. 5. It is well observed by a pious and precious divine, that there are eight sins which do more especially bring judgments on a man's posterity; whereof the first is idolatry.

2. Adultery, 2 Sam. xii. 14.

3. Covenant-breaking, 2 Sam. xxi. 13.

4. Persecution of the godly, Matt. xxiii. 31—36; Psal. cxxxvii. 7.

5. Murder, 1 Kings xxi. 21; Jer. xv. 4.

6. Oppression, Job xx. 19—26; Hab. ii. 9.

7. Contempt of magistracy and ministry, Numb. xvi. 32, 41, 49; 1 Kings xiii. 33, 34.

8. When men pretend reformation, and intend themselves, as Jehu did, Hos. i. 4.

God is very pitiful and tender over infants, as appears in that he would not destroy Nineveh for the infants' sakes that were in it, Jonah iv. 11; and in the sacking of cities he commands them to spare infants, Deut. xx. 14; but it is the sin of parents which many times hardens God's heart against them, and makes him to delight in the destruction both of them and theirs; yea, and it hardens men's hearts against them so that they cannot but act such cruelty against them, as they never intended, as we see of Hazael, 2 Kings viii. 11—13. When the prophet Elisha wept, and told him what mischief he should do to Israel; "Their strong holds wilt thou set on fire, and their young men wilt thou slay with the sword, and wilt dash their children, and rip up their women with child;" "Hazael said, But what, is thy servant a dog, that he should do this great thing?" He then thought it a base and barbarous thing, when he was king Ben-hadad's servant, to act such inhuman cruelty upon the mothers with their infants. The prophet only tells him that he shall be a king, ver. 13, and then when he had changed his condition he would also change his manners, and commit all the abominations which he mentioned. Let parents then labour for grace, that they may leave a blessing, and not a curse, to their posterity, Gen. xvii. 7; Exod. xx. 6; Psal. cxii. 2. If you will not pity yourselves, yet pity your little ones, let not them fare the worse for you. It is ill being a wicked man's child, yea, their very beasts fare the worse for them; Achan was stoned, and his cattle with him, Josh. vii. 24, 25. The wicked Egyptians bring a murrain upon their cattle, Exod. ix. 3. As a good man is a public good, the family, city, kingdom, fare the better for him, yea, his cattle are spared for his sake; "The Lord shall sever between the cattle of Israel and the cattle of Egypt: and there shall nothing die of all that is the children's of Israel," Exod. ix. 4. God blesses the very cattle of his people, and if the creature could speak it would desire to serve those that serve God. Most parents provide inheritances for their children, but ofttimes they leave their sins with them too. It was a sad legacy that Joab left to his children, that one should be a leper, another a weakling, a third beg his bread, 2 Sam. iii. 29. So many a man, to one child he leaves his murder, to another his adultery, to a third his usury, to a fourth his swearing. Gehazi left a talent of silver behind him to his posterity, but he left the leprosy with it. Better want such men's lands and inheritances, than thus to inherit their sins too.

2. Let children be humbled then for their forefathers' sins, that they be not imputed to them, Lev. xxvi. 41. So did Nehemiah, chap. i. 6; and David, Psal. lxxix. 8, "O remember not against us former iniquities;" עונת ראשנים the iniquities of our forefathers. He that sees the sins of his predecessors, and is not humbled for them, approves of them, and so becomes accessory to them. Hence the Lord blames Belshazzar for not humbling himself for his father's sin and punishment which he knew of, Dan. v. 22. Let us therefore acknowledge ourselves to be the children of sinful parents, and say before God, "A Syrian ready to perish was my father," Deut. xxvi. 5; and, with David, "We have sinned with our fathers," Psal. cvi. 6; and,

with Daniel, chap. ix. 8, deprecate the punishment which is due to us for their sins. So Jer. xiv. 20.

3. Admire the patience of the Lord, that has borne so long with us who have been sinners from the womb. If little ones, who never sinned against the patience of God as we have done, endure such pangs, sorrows, sickness, and death, what may men of years look for, who have added to original corruption a numberless number of actual transgressions? If this be done to the green tree, what shall be done to the dry? If infants (who are innocents, and righteous comparatively) shall scarcely be saved, where shall the ungodly and rebellious sinner appear? If he spare not little ones that lie in their mothers' bowels, but suffer wicked men to drag them thence; where, oh where shall those wicked parents appear, who have been the primary cause of all this mischief and sorrow to them, and have been the authors and actors of that wickedness which has brought this misery on them? It should therefore be matter of great humiliation to us all, when we see the sharp and sore judgments that oft light upon little ones for their original sin.

As God's people were wont in extraordinary cases to bring their infants and sucklings with them to keep fasts, Joel ii. 16, the better to affect their hearts, and break them with sorrow for sin, which threatened destruction to them and their little ones; even this use should we make of the miseries of infants; when we see God's hand upon them, we should humble ourselves to think what judgments are due to us who have so many actual sins to answer for, which these little ones are free from. We should therefore mourn over them as David did for the people, As for these sheep, what have they done? it is I that have sinned. So let us say, As for these little ones, what have they done? it is we, even we that have sinned, and provoked the Lord to anger with our transgressions.

Me, me: adsum qui feci: in me convertite ferrum. Virg.

Obs. 12. Rebellion brings destruction. Samaria shall be made desolate, for she has rebelled. When God's heritage is as a lion that roars and rages against him, then he gives it into the hands of its enemies, Jer. xii. 7—11; iv. 17; xliv. 16, 17, 22; Lam. i. 18, 20; Micah vi. 13; Matt. xxiii. 38. Israel had sinned, and now the Assyrian destroys their cities, eats up their fruits, passes through their land, carries the people into captivity, and makes slaves and exiles of them in a strange country.

1. Rebellion is a capital sin; it is not every sin, (though every sin, more or less, has something of rebellion in it, being committed against that allegiance which we owe to God by the law of creation,) but it is an habitual obstinacy and stubbornness in sin; hence such are said to have necks of iron, and brows of brass, hard and uncircumcised hearts; they are called a froward generation, "lying children, children that will not hear the law of the Lord," Isa. xxx. 9; rebelling against the light, Job xxiv. 13.

It is reckoned amongst the greatest sins, and is compared to witchcraft, 1 Sam. xv. 23, which is the highest and most hideous idolatry in the world; it is a renouncing of God to follow the counsel of the devil. It is a sin that God will certainly visit, for his justice will not suffer it to go unpunished, Exod. xxxiv. 7; Isa. i. 2, 7.

For sins of mere infirmity there is a pardon in course; but sins of presumption, committed with a high hand against light and warning, are very dangerous, and therefore David prays of all sins to be kept from such, Psal. xix. 13. Those great sins call for great humiliation, before there can be any pardon expected, Exod. xxxiv. 7; 2 Chron. xxxiii. 12; Psal. lxviii. 18.

2. Do not envy the prosperous condition of rebellious sinners; though they may flourish for a time, and waters of a full cup be wrung out unto them, yet their feet shall slide in due time, and every threatening shall light upon them. They are rather to be pitied than envied.

3. As ever we desire to be free from desolation, let us fly those sins which cause it. Look what sins brought desolation upon Ephraim, those sins will bring desolation on England, if they reign amongst us; for God is the same to the same sinners.

Quorum exitus perhorrescis, eorum opera pertimescas.

Quest. But what were Ephraim's sins which brought desolation upon him?

Answ. Upon search I find them to be many, but about twenty signal ones there are which brought destruction on him. Whether they be not England's sins, as well as Ephraim's, the application will show.

Ephraim's sins then were, 1. Idolatry. 2. A ready complying with men's inventions. 3. Contempt of the true prophets. 4. Delight in false prophets. 5. Pride. 6. Hypocrisy. 7. Self-seeking. 8. Witchcraft. 9. Barrenness under the means of grace. 10. Ingratitude. 11. Covenant-breaking. 12. Security. 13. Anarchy. 14. Lukewarmness and neutrality. 15. Division. 16. Carnal confidence. 17. Incorrigibleness. 18. Oppression. 19. Atheism. 20. A fulness of sin. Lastly, Corrupt rulers.

1. Their first grand, bosom, beloved sin was idolatry. They forsook the Lord, and set up calves; when they should have cried, Kiss ye the Son and worship him, they cry, Kiss ye the calves, which Jeroboam has set up, and worship them, Hos. xiii. 1, 2; and this idolatry was universal, it was not in one, but in all their cities, 2 Kings xvii. 9—11; Ezek. xxiii. 4, 5.

This is a God-provoking and a land-destroying sin, it is the choosing (as it were) another husband, it breaks the covenant and the marriage knot between God and a people. It is a preferring of the devil before Christ, and dirty dunghill gods גללים before the living God, 2 Kings xvii. 12; Ezek. iv. 12; xiv. 10.

Whatever sinners may escape, yet idolaters are sure to pay for it. When men begin to choose new gods, the next news is, War is in the gates, Judg. v. 8; Psal. lxxviii. 58; Jer. xxii. 7—9; Micah i. 5—7. Many sorrows attend this sin, Psal. xvi. 4. This, even this, was that fatal sin which laid Samaria in the dust, Amos viii. 14; and therefore Hosea more inveighs against their idolatry, than against any other sin.

And is not this England's sin? Have not we chosen of late many new gods, and with Ephraim set up "idols according to our own understanding?" Hos. xiii. 2; and have made a light within us, and not God's word, the rule of our actions? We have forsaken his faithful ministers to follow calves, Socinian, Arian, Arminian, Anabaptist, Quaking calves. Moses bare with many provocations from the people of Israel, but when, in his absence, they set up a calf, he could bear no longer. Where can we go, but we meet with Jeroboam's calves? what town, city, county, is not pestered with them? These prophesy falsely, and too many love to have it so; but what will they do in the end thereof, when God shall call them to account for all their heresies and blasphemies? Jer. v. 31.

Besides the gross idolatry that still abounds in the land, many are falling openly to popery, and many, in their affections, hankering after the bewitching allurements of that Babylonish harlot. A sad omen of an approaching judgment, as France and Germany can testify.

And add to this the great worldly-mindedness and inordinate love of the world that abounds amongst us, which is idolatry in God's esteem, Col. iii. 5.

2. A second sin of Ephraim was a ready compliance with the inventions of men, Hos. v. 11; xi. 6; "Ephraim

is oppressed and broken in judgment, because he willingly walked after the commandment" and traditions of men, preferring them before God's commandments. Jeroboam no sooner commanded idolatry, than the people obeyed, 1 Kings xii. 32, 33. Omri, another of their kings, makes statutes for grosser idolatry, and even in those statutes did they walk, Micah vi. 16. And for this the Lord threatens to destroy them, Hos. v. 12, 14.

And is not this England's sin? Are not many, too many amongst us, more ready to hearken to a seducer than to a faithful teacher, and more ready to follow vanity than verity, preferring the chaff of men's inventions before the wheat of God's word? Let the ablest minister in the land preach in some towns, yet how many are there that prefer a railing, seducing sectary, who preaches the fancies and dotages of his own brain, before the faithful servants of God, that dispense his word sincerely!

This also is a sad presage of some approaching judgment.

3. Contempt of the true prophets. It was a rare age of prophets, they had the best preaching a little before their ruin. So great was the Lord's care over them, and so loth was he that they should perish, that he sent extraordinary prophets to them, more in number than he did to the kingdom of Judah, and by them he supplied the defect of the ordinary ministry of priests and Levites. They had Elijah, Elisha, Jonah, Amos, Micah, Joel, and Hosea, who prophesied to them about seven and forty years, besides Ahijah, Jehu, Iddo, Azariah, &c.; yet such was their obstinacy and perverseness, that no wooings nor warnings could work upon them; instead of hearkening to those messengers which the Lord in great compassion sent to them to reclaim them from their idols, they mocked, jeered, misused, and persecuted them, and looked upon them as a pack of cheats and deceivers that frighted people without a cause, till the wrath of the Lord broke forth against them, and there was no remedy; his anger was so fierce it could not be extinguished. When David sent messengers to comfort Hanun, and he abused them, David's anger was kindled against him, and it cost him dear, 2 Sam. x. 4. Contempt of the word is an infallible forerunner of judgment. When Eli's sons hearkened not to the counsel of their father, God cut them off. When Amaziah contemned the counsel of the prophet, it was a sign that the Lord purposed to destroy him, 2 Chron. xxv. 16.

Verbi divini contemptus tanquam via ad extremam impietatem cavendus est. Wolf.

And if this be an infallible sign of a nation's ruin, the Lord be merciful to England! never was the land so full of pious, painful, learned ministers, and never were any so coarsely and ungratefully dealt withal by many, as these are. What loads of reproaches and floods of bitter railings are cast out against us, not for any evil that we have done, but solely for discharging our duty, and stopping men in their sinful, heretical, destructive ways! we are their enemies only because we tell them the truth. Those that formerly were ready to pull out their own eyes to do us good, now are ready to pull out our eyes. Thus have we been wounded in the house of our friends. To be derided by Egyptians is threatened as a misery, Hos. vii. 16; but to be reproached by friends and professors is very grievous. The good Lord lay not this ingratitude and contempt to their charge. Though we bear, yet God will not always bear. When Moses is silent, then God arises; when he is dumb, then God speaks; when he is deaf, then God hears and stirs, Numb. xii. 1, 4. God will smite through the loins of those that rise against his messengers, and of those that hate them, that they rise not up again, Deut. xxxiii. 11.

It is not so much the minister as the ministry that is cried down; that which they should principally love us for, viz. for our work's sake, that is the ground of these men's hatred. As it was not the baron, but the barony, that was the traitor in tyrants' days; so, for the most part, it is not so much the man that they smite at, as the maintenance, the tithes, the glebe, and the ordinances of God wherewith they are intrusted.

4. Delight in false prophets. Elijah is persecuted, when eight hundred and fifty false prophets are entertained and fed, 1 Kings xviii. 4, 19; though they were fools and mad-men: Hos. ix. 7, "The days of visitation are come;" how doth that appear? why, "the prophet," the false prophet, "is a fool," and flatters the people with vain hopes; yea, "the spiritual man is mad;" that is, he who brags so much of the Spirit, and falsely boasts that he is inspired by the Holy Spirit, and that he speaks all as moved by it, this man is mad, he is smitten with a spiritual frenzy, doting upon his own dreams, and lunatic illuminations, and venting his brainsick notions instead of God's word. These priests Jeroboam (in his carnal policy) chose out of "the lowest of the people," (fit servants for such gods, calves suit well with calves,) which were not of the sons of Levi, who were set apart by God's special command for the service of his house, but "whosoever would" might thrust himself into the office, how unworthy soever, 1 Kings xiii. 33; but see what follows immediately, ver. 34, "This thing became sin unto the house of Jeroboam, even to cut it off, and to destroy it from off the face of the earth." This, even this, was that indelible sin which ruined both him and his family.

And is not this the sin of England? are not false prophets by many thousands preferred before the true? will not many go ten miles to hear a deceiver, that will not go two to hear a faithful minister of Christ? When men go by troops to such harlotry meetings, the Lord will visit for this, as well as for corporal harlotry, Jer. v. 7, 9.

The Quaking seducers are certainly led by this spirit of the devil, as will easily appear, if we consider the men, the matter, or the manner of their speaking.

1. The men, both speakers and hearers, are generally a profane generation, they are *mordaces et mendaces*, notorious railers and liars, like their father the devil.

2. The matter of their speaking. What is it? why, it is against ministers and their maintenance, against the coercive power of the magistrate, against Scripture, ordinances, &c.

3. The manner of their meeting. It is profane and tumultuous. A rout meet together, on a mountain, a common, or under some hedge, and there, without any praying before, some speak, others jeer, some dispute, some quarrel and fight, others take tobacco, (amidst such an unsavoury company they had need of some better antidote,) so that one would think they were at some bear-baiting, and not at the service of God. That men should be tolerated, yea and encouraged, to serve God, is commendable; but that men should be tolerated to blaspheme and worship the devil, is abominable.

2. What folly and madness have seized on the false prophets of our times, the swarms of blasphemous pamphlets do sufficiently testify to the world; the thousands and ten thousands infected by them plainly foretell that some judgment is at hand.

3. How many of Jeroboam's priests have thrust themselves into the work of the ministry, who vent heresies and blasphemies instead of truth! What toleration and countenance have been given to such, is known now to all the world. Foreign churches complain against us for it; and what cause we have to fear that wrath is coming upon us for this sin, let the wise reader judge. If ever that caution of our Saviour were in season, it is now, Matt. x. 17, "Beware of men."

Christ does not say, Beware of serpents, or devils, (he promised them power over these, Mark xvi. 17, 18,) but, "Beware of men."

1. Beware of wicked men, wolfish persecutors and bloodsuckers, who hate us "without a cause," Psal. lxix. 4: how much more, when by our unwise walking we shall expose ourselves to their fury and malice!

2. Beware of hypocrites, and seeming good men. The devil can transform himself into an angel of light, and oft appears in Samuel's mantle, the better to deceive; he is never more to be feared. It is this *sanctus Satanas*, this white devil, that does us most hurt: the swearing, cursing, black devil, every one cries shame of; but it is the preaching, praying, professing devil, who pretends to extraordinary sanctity and mortification, that deceives even many a good soul in its overmuch credulity. These are more dangerous (in some sense) to us, than the very devil himself; for if the devil should appear to us in his own native deformity, we should run from him for fear, no man would hearken to him: if the devil should come in person, and call men to the alehouse, or from their callings, who would obey? but when he comes to us in a friend, a wife, a bosom companion, he is not so easily perceived, and so we are sooner insnared; and therefore our Saviour saith not, Beware of Satan, but, Beware of those men who are the instruments of Satan: if they should come like angels, we should suspect them, if like beasts, we should shun them, if like fiends, we should fear them; but coming to us like men of the same profession with us, and professing great kindness to us, how soon are poor plain souls deceived! and therefore "beware of men," for as God loves to work upon men by the ministry of man, and sends them to such; so the devil, who is God's ape, loves to draw men from God, by men, viz. by seducers and deceivers, who are inspired, fitted, and filled by him for that purpose. If Ahab will not hear Micaiah, the true prophet of the Lord, the devil has four hundred false prophets at hand to deceive him. When he would seduce Adam from his obedience, he does not appear himself, but he sets Eve his wife upon him, and so prevails. When he would have innocent Abel slain, he does not do it himself, but he has a malicious Cain that will do it. When the devil would have Christ crucified, he has a Judas, a devil incarnate, ready at hand to betray him, John xiii. 2.

3. Beware even of good men. The devil can shroud himself under a Peter, and tempt our Saviour by him, Matt. xvi. 23; by his example he can compel the Gentiles to live after the Jewish manner, in observing the ceremonial law, Gal. ii. 14. The best of men are but men at best; they know but in part, they have their infirmities, and must have their grains of allowance; we may not therefore glory in men, nor pin our faith on their sleeves, because we know not whither they may carry it. The great sin of this age is, building on man; Such a holy man is for a toleration, and such a one holds such opinions. What tell you me of men? we must live by rule, not by example, neither may we follow any good man further than he follows Christ in his word, 1 Cor. xi. 1. Be it Paul, you must try his doctrine by the touch-stone of the word, before you trust it, Acts xvii. 11. Remember "every man" is "a liar," Rom. iii. 4, either actively, or passively; either by imposture, and of purpose, or else by impotency, and in event.

4. Beware of great men. We are apt to be led by their examples; if Prince such a one, or Sir Thomas such a one, rise, how apt are people to follow, without any consideration! Great men oft are great sinners, they have their native corruptions heightened by their pomp and prosperity, Job xxi. 7—15; Jer. v. 5. When great men are wicked men, and have great parts and great wits, they do great mischief, as Ahithophel, Catiline, &c. Beware then of following such great ones.

5. Beware of subtle seducers, pretenders to new light, Gen. iii. 5, to revelations, glorious mysteries, &c., Rom. xvi. 17; "inwardly they are ravening wolves," Matt. vii. 15. Poison in itself is dangerous, but never more dangerous than when mixed with honey. These have "men's persons in admiration," but it is for their own ends and advantage, Jude 16. And if ever this caution were seasonable, it is now, when there are so many jugglers and cheaters gone forth into the world. Their number is greater than formerly, and they act more subtlely and mystically; they act against Christ under the name of Christ, Matt. xxiv. 5, and that so cunningly and craftily, that, if it were possible, they would deceive the very elect, Matt. xxiv. 24; they have Jacob's voice, but Esau's hands; they talk divinely, as if they had no bodies, and live lewdly, as if they had no souls; hence it is that we are so oft admonished to take heed of them, Rom. xvi. 17; 2 Tim. iii. 5; 2 John 10.

But such cite Scripture. So did the devil, Matt. iv. 6.

But there is some truth in what they say. So there is in the mass, and in stage plays. It is the devil's usual practice, to mix some sugar with his poison to make it go down the better, and to mingle some truths with his errors; as the fowler mingles corn with his chaff, that he may catch the sooner. You will shun those that poison your bodies, O take heed of those that would poison your souls. No murder like soul-murder. Shun a seducer, as you would shun the devil himself, whose factor he is; and when he speaks fairest, and pretends most love, then fear him most. When Herod intended Christ's destruction, he then pretended devotion, Matt. ii. 8. When Absalom sought his father's kingdom, he pretends a vow at Hebron. When Saul would ruin David, he makes him his son-in-law, 1 Sam. xviii. 17. Beware then of men, who put fair gloves upon foul hands; who pretend pity, but act cruelty; who promise liberty when they intend thraldom.

But they are great professors. So were those that followed Christ, yet he would not trust them, for he knew the deceit that was in them, John ii. 24, 25. All is not gold that glitters, nor are all Israel that are of Israel; and therefore take heed whom you trust.

6. Beware of thy foes. We are beset round with them, and that both corporal and spiritual; we had need therefore to be sober, and watch, and to pray with David, Help me, O Lord, and that "because of mine enemies," Psal. xxvii. 11. Many there be that watch for our halting, we also should watch and countermine them. There is a cursed enmity in the wicked against the righteous, Gen. iii. 15; Psal. xxxvii. 14; so that they could even slay them all, as Cain did Abel, 1 John iii. 12, because by their light and life they reprove them. And this enmity is,

1. Natural, and so constant and delightful.

2. Intensive. As a good man loves good men, *appreciative et intensive, affectu et effectu*, with a high degree of affection, and shows it in his actions; so the wicked hate the godly with an inveterate, intensive hatred, they could even wish that they had more lives than one, that they might exercise their malice on them; antipathy is against the whole kind, they desire that even the name of Israel might be no more in remembrance.

3. Irreconcilable. Enemies may be reconciled, but enmities never, till nature be changed: when Saul is converted, and become a Paul, then, and not till then, he prizes whom before he persecuted.

4. Beware of thy friends and relations. By these the devil ofttimes does us more hurt than by our open enemies; and therefore when one was praying, Lord, deliver me from my foes; Nay, said one that heard

him, rather pray, Lord, deliver me from my friends. We usually shun our foes, and take heed of their counsel; but it is the devil in a friend that undoes us. The Italian proverb is, God keep me from the hurt of my friends, and I will see to my foes.

But it is my wife that persuades me, and shall I not hearken to her? If thy wife give thee good counsel according to the word, then, in all that Sarah shall say unto thee, hearken to her voice; else you must stop your ears against those sirens. How many wives have deluded their husbands, and drawn their hearts from God! Adam, by hearkening to Eve, undid himself and all his posterity. Solomon was besotted by his idolatrous wives, Samson betrayed by Delilah, and Job had undone himself had he hearkened to his wife's wicked counsel, Job ii. 9.

But it is my son, my brother, my kinsman, that counsels me. Even these may deceive you, if you take not heed; "A man's foes shall be they of his own household." What the Scripture speaks in case of persecution, is most true in case of temptation; brother shall betray brother, the father the child, and children shall rise against the father, Matt. x. 21, 36. Even Christ's brethren rose against him, John vii. 5; and the Jews, that were his kinsmen according to the flesh, were so fiercely set against him, that they preferred Barabbas, a robber, before him, and sought to stone him, Matt. xxvii. 20; John xi. 8. Thus Cain slays his brother, Ishmael persecutes Isaac, Esau Jacob, and Joseph's brethren sell him. So that if ever that counsel also were in season, it is now, Micah vii. 5, 6, "Trust ye not in a friend, put ye not confidence in a guide: keep the doors of thy mouth from her that lieth in thy bosom." Why so? "For the son dishonoureth the father, the daughter riseth up against her mother;" we may add, the servant against his master, the subject against his superior.

8. Beware of strangers. Try men before you trust them. Time discovers men's tempers; the heart of man is so deeply deceitful, that it requires some time to know it; and if it be not safe to trust relations, much less strangers. Hypocrisy is spun with a fine thread, and none are so soon deceived as the over-credulous; and therefore Solomon so oft blames men for trusting strangers, Prov. v. 20; vi. 1, 2. Christ's sheep will not follow strangers, John x. 5.

9. Above all, beware of that evil man thyself. It is a secret, subtle, daily, deadly, bosom enemy, which does us most mischief; we ourselves are the sorest enemies to ourselves, *Inimicorum pessimus, quia proximus*. All the devils in hell, and all the men in the world, could not hurt us, if we were but true to ourselves. It was a good prayer of St. Austin, Lord, deliver me from that evil man myself. The way to conquer Satan, is first to conquer ourselves. This is the highest and hardest martyrdom, to deny ourselves universally. Let us then walk wisely in this day of England's trial, remembering that the Scripture calls wicked men wolves for ravening, dogs for greediness, lions for cruelty, and foxes for subtlety. Any of these creatures, when enraged, are terrible, and we will take heed of them; but when the cruelty and subtlety of all these creatures shall concentre and meet in man, how great is the danger, and how had we need to "beware of men," especially when they come with fair pretences, and with "feigned words," veiling over foul matters, 2 Pet. ii. 3; calling pride, decency; error, new lights; hypocrisy, extraordinary sanctity; heretics, the servants of God! The devil knows that if sin should appear in its own proper colours, men would hate it, so ugly and loathsome is it. If Jeroboam had told Israel plainly, they must worship devils, when they worshipped the calves, who would have followed him?

5. They were full of pride. Hos. v. 5; vii. 10, "The pride of Israel testifieth to his face." They were proud of their riches, and proud of their buildings, and therefore the Lord threatens to "smite the winter-house with the summer-house," which they had built for pride and pleasure, Amos iii. 15.

And is not this England's sin? Was there ever more pride in heart, in habit, in hair, in vestures, gestures, words, and works? And does not pride ever go before destruction, and a high mind before a fall? But of this elsewhere at large.

6. Hypocrisy abounded amongst them; they were like a deceitful bow, that breaks and deceives the archer; they compassed the Lord about with their lies, crying, My Father, my Father, howling before him in their misery, when, alas, their righteousness was but as the morning dew which suddenly vanisheth away, Hos. v. 6; vi. 4; vii. 14, 16; viii. 2; xi. 12; 2 Kings xvii. 9. This made the Lord to reject and abhor both them and their services, Amos v. 21, 22.

And how does this sin reign in England from Dan to Beersheba, from east to west, from one corner of the land to another! Never was the land so full of praying and preaching, lectures, repetitions, private meetings, &c., and never such unmortified, unholy, unrighteous walking, unanswerable to those duties. This abuse and profanation of holy things makes the land to tremble under us, Ezek. xxii. 8. The land is full of science, but where, oh where, is the conscience? The voice is Jacob's voice, but the hands are the hands of Esau. Many talk like angels, but live like devils; they talk as if they had cloven tongues, but walk as if they had cloven feet. Most amongst us live directly contrary to their prayers. They pray against pride, and yet their pride is visible; they pray against worldly-mindedness, and yet they are notoriously worldly; they pray for self-denial, and yet are great self-seekers, &c. Oh this cursed hypocrisy, hypocrisy, hypocrisy, ruins all; it is that leaven that sours all our services, that coloquintida that makes our duties deadly. If any sin destroy England, it is this. God may bear with other sins, but this provokes him to his face, and is such a horrid mocking of him, that his soul abhors.

Odi improbum qui proba loquitur verba. Menander.

In oculis Dei nullum majus scelus est hypocrisi. Sultet.

7. The Israelites were great self-seekers. They brought forth fruit, but it was to themselves, Hos. x. 1; they were all for present profit and present pay, like the heifer that loves to "tread out the corn," (where she may eat as she goes,) but loves not ploughing, that is hard and hungry work, Hos. x. 11; they were all for liberty and ease, they could not abide God's yoke, and therefore the Lord tells them, that since they loved liberty so well, they should have enough of it, but to their ruin. Israel was a wanton heifer, the whole pasture could not contain nor content her, and therefore the Lord threatens to give her the liberty of the lamb in the wilderness, where it should be exposed to a thousand dangers and miseries, Hos. iv. 16.

And is not this the great sin of England? Was there ever less self-denial, and more self-seeking in the land? Where shall we find a plain, simple, single-hearted Jacob, that prefers God's glory before his own interest, and can be content to perish, so that God's name may flourish? Show me, O show me that man, that I may give thanks unto God for him.

Most men in our days are squint-eyed; they pray, hear, repent, fast, give alms, but still they have an eye to themselves in all their actions, Zech. vii. 5; Matt. vi. 2.

And as Ephraim, so England is all for liberty; liberty in church, and liberty in state; liberty in spirituals, and liberty in temporals. We have those that, like sons of Belial, can bear no yoke, none must reign over them. They must have liberty, liberty, liberty; and I will "proclaim a liberty for you, saith the Lord, to the sword, to the pestilence, and to the famine." This is the portion of such libertines, Jer. xxxiv. 17.

8. Witchcraft and enchantments. This also was a sin which helped to ruin Ephraim. They had familiarity with the devil, and by his aid they could divine and enchant, 2 Kings xvii. 17.

And was there ever more witchcraft in England than at this day? Oh this sinning sin grows rife amongst us. Those seducing, deluding, quaking sots and sectaries, that go up and down the land with their enchanting ribbons, and other diabolical practices, plainly show that too many of them are in league with the devil. They talk much of the Spirit moving and the Spirit leading them; their bastards, their railing, and their blasphemy, show that it is an evil spirit that leads them.

This sin helped to ruin the Jews: "Therefore thou hast forsaken thy people the house of Jacob, because they are soothsayers like the Philistines," Isa. ii. 6. If England be guilty of the like sin, it must also look for the like punishment.

9. Barrenness under the means of grace. God was not wanting in any means of grace to Ephraim, but Ephraim was an empty vine, and wanting to himself, Hos. x. 1.

This also is the great sin of England, we are dead under lively oracles, and fruitless under fruitful ordinances, and lean under soul-enriching means; like Pharaoh's lean kine, that devoured the fat ones, yet themselves were still lean, Gen. xli. 20, 21. We dishonour the Lord's pastures and discredit his ordinances by our unfruitfulness, and open the mouths of the wicked to cry, *Ecce quales sunt qui Christum colunt!* Behold how dead and dull, how base and barren, how unholy and unrighteous, these Christians are! Such barren ground is "nigh unto cursing," Heb. vi. 8. Which of us will plough the rocks, or sow the sands, or bestow cost upon ground which will bring forth nothing but briers and thorns? The barren fig tree was cut down, because it cumbered the earth, and made the ground about it the worse, Luke xiii. 6—9. The fig tree that had nothing but bare leaves of profession, was cursed for want of fruit, Mark xi. 13, 14. God will lay his axe to the root of those trees that bring not forth good fruit, Matt. iii. 10; and lay waste his vineyard, and command the clouds to rain no more rain upon it, when after all his cost and care it brings forth nothing but "wild grapes," Isa. v. 2—7. When the Lord comes to walk in the beautiful vineyard of his church, and finds a tree that flourishes not in so fruitful a soil, he will cut it down, it shall no longer cumber the ground.

Our great unfruitfulness under the rich means that we enjoy should deeply affect us. If Hannah wept for the barrenness of her body, how should we lament the barrenness of our souls, and cry, as Rachel, "Give me children, or else I die!" so, Give me grace, or I am undone; make me fruitful, or I perish for ever. Complain to God against it; the best and most fruitful Christians have made the saddest complaints against themselves. Holy Bradford, how oft did he lament over that deadness, unfruitfulness, unthankfulness, which cleaved to his nature! David, how oft does he beg for quickening grace! Do by your barren hearts, as men do by their barren grounds; they will dig, dung, drain them, and use all means to make them fruitful: so do you; pray, read, meditate, hear, confer, and use all means to get your dead hearts bettered, and your graces quickened.

Yet, lest any should deceive themselves, thinking that they grow in grace, when they do but deceive themselves, you must know that, 1. There may be a growing in gifts, when there is no growing in grace. Many a man knows more, and can pray longer, than formerly, and yet no growth in grace. True growth is principally internal in the root, in humiliation, sanctification, faith, obedience; it is a growing up. not only in some things, but in all things, Eph. iv. 15. True growth is universal, it is not only a growing in the head, (as some that have the rickets do,) but in heart, head, and every part. True growth, saith Aristotle, is a diffusing of nourishment to all the parts, the understanding, will, memory, affections, body, soul, all are bettered.

2. It may be you do grow, but do you grow answerably to all the means and mercies which God has bestowed upon you? They that have much, of them shall be much required. Where the husbandman bestows extraordinary cost, there he expects an extraordinary crop; and herein the best of us all have great cause to be humbled in the dust. Who can say he has answered the Lord's cost and care, and grown answerably to all those sermons, sabbaths, sacraments, good books, corrections, and all the other rich means which God has afforded us in these latter days? Oh what giants might we have been in the ways of grace and goodness, if every ordinance had been effectual upon our hearts! he that is weak amongst us might have been as strong as David, and he that is strong as David might have been as an angel of the Lord, for wisdom and purity, Zech. xii. 8. Like Saul, we might have been taller by the head and shoulders (in the ways of grace) than other men. Our leanness, and our lewdness, our barrenness, and unfruitfulness, our walking so unanswerably to the rich means of grace that we enjoy, certainly foretell a storm approaching.

10. Ingratitude, and abuse of God's mercies to the promoting of idolatry. The more God did for them, the less they did for him; their fulness bred forgetfulness, and the more they were increased, the more they sinned. Hence the Lord so oft complains of this sin, as provoking him more than all the rest, Hos. ii. 8; iv. 7; x. 1; xi. 3, 4; xiii. 5, 6. It was this sin especially that brought the sword upon them, Hos. ii. 9; xiii. 7. The prophet Amos also, who was contemporary with Hosea, notably sets forth the great ingratitude of this people in abusing God's mercies, Amos ii. 9—11.

And is not this that crying sin of England? Do we not fight against God with his own blessings, abusing our health, wealth, wit, peace, plenty, corn, wine, gold, silver, Scriptures, ordinances, yea, all our comforts and creatures, to the dishonour of the Giver of them? His mercies make us proud, his riches covetous, his peace secure, his food intemperate, and all his benefits serve us but as weapons to rebel against him.

And do we thus requite the Lord, O foolish and unwise? is this the thanks we give him for all his patience, preservations, success, and deliverances? Will not the Lord visit for these things? and shall not his soul be avenged on such a nation as this? Had England no more sins to answer for but this, even this were sufficient to make it a desolation, as it did Samaria.

11. Covenant-breaking. God had betrothed them to himself, and chosen them from the rest of the world, to become his people; "But they like men have transgressed the covenant; there have they dealt treacherously against me," Hos. vi. 7; x. 4. Like sons of Adam, they walked in his steps; though they were abundantly blessed by God, yet they revolted from him, and transgressed the covenant; *there*, even *there*, where they should have been most faithful, viz. in the covenant, there they dealt most falsely and perfidiously with him.

And is not this one of the crying sins of England? Never was there a wiser and better composed covenant in the nation, and never any worse performed; we have lifted up our hands to the most High, that we will (in our places and callings) extirpate heresies, and yet many walk as if they had taken a covenant to propagate them; many amongst us make no more of their covenants, than an ape does of his collar, which he can put off or on at his own pleasure.

Let any man but read all the branches of the covenant, and then compare with them our contrary walking; and he cannot but admire the infinite patience of the Lord, that he has not long since sent a sword to avenge the quarrel of his covenant upon us, Lev. xxvi. 25. We must not think to do such things, and escape, or to break our covenants with God, and then be delivered, Ezek. xvii. 15—20. If the Lord so sadly avenged the breach of covenant with a man, yea, with a heathen, and idolater, what shall be done to him who breaks his covenant made with the great God of heaven and earth? and if a good man will perform the covenant which he has made, though it be to his disadvantage, how great is their sin then, who perform not the conditions of such covenants as tend to their everlasting welfare! Psal. xv. 4. The Jews have a saying, that there is no punishment that befalls them, but there is in it a dram of the golden calf: so there is no misery that befalls England, but there is in it a dram of covenant-breaking.

12. Security. Though "strangers had devoured his strength," yet he knew it not; the Syrian and Assyrian had consumed him, and made a prey of him, yet such was his stupidity, that he knew it not, viz. with a practical, saving knowledge, so as to repent, and make a right use of it: "yea, grey hairs are here and there upon him," which were a sign of weakness, and old age, and approaching death; yet they laid it not to heart, Hos. vii. 9; but they were at ease in Zion, and trusted in the mountain of Samaria, putting the evil day far from them, and therefore a woe is denounced against them, Amos vi. 1, 3; ix. 10.

And was there ever more security and senseless stupidity in England than at this day? Do not the ministers of Christ generally complain that they see not that life, zeal, activity, tenderness, compunction, in their people, which formerly existed? Many applaud and flatter themselves with their gifts and external profession of sanctity, but the power of it is very much wanting amongst us. A great calm ofttimes is a forerunner of a storm; and great security is a great forerunner of some great judgment. When the old world was eating, drinking, buying, building, marrying, and thought not of a flood, then it came and swept them all away; when men cry Peace and safety, then comes sudden and swift destruction, 1 Thess. v. 3.

13. Anarchy. They "have devoured their judges, all their kings are fallen," Hos. vii. 7. They discovered their rage in their seditious and frequent conspiracies, to the devouring and destroying of their judges and magistrates, as appears in the frequent murders of their kings.

What anarchy and confusion is amongst us, he is a great stranger in our English Israel that knows not.

14. Lukewarmness. This is another sin that helped to ruin Ephraim. Hos. vii. 8, "Ephraim is a cake not turned," and so but half-baked, or dough-baked; *neque crudus, neque coctus*, neither hot nor cold, neither fish nor flesh, but of a middle, mongrel religion, halting between two, partly for God and partly for the devil, partly for Christ and partly for Baal: but God hates such halting, half-hearted doings; and therefore spews them out of his mouth, and sends them packing into captivity.

And is not this the sin of England? are we not a lukewarm generation, neither hot nor cold, that halt not between two, but two hundred opinions? We have a knee for God, and a knee for Baal; a tongue for Christ, and a tongue for antichrist; a tongue for truth, and a tongue for falsehood; like the harlot, we are all for dividing: but God will be served truly and totally, without halting or halving; he has made our whole hearts, and he will have all, or none at all. Oh, this sin of formality and lukewarmness cries for some judgment against us. Where is our zeal for God's glory? our mourning for the great dishonours that are done to his name? our crying out and witnessing against the blasphemies, heresies, juggling, and Satanical delusions that abound amongst us? Nay, do not many plead for a general toleration of all sorts and sects? and if under a colour they make a law against such, yet it is either made so wide that offenders creep through, or the rulers are so overawed that they dare only admonish when they should punish, and barely shave the head which of right should be cut off.

Now, will not the Lord visit for these things? and shall not his soul be avenged on such a cold and careless nation as this is?

15. Divisions. Ephraim was against Manasses, and Manasses against Ephraim; there was division upon division amongst them; their sins had divided them from their God, and now God in his just judgment sets a spirit of division amongst themselves to their destruction. Hos. x. 2, "Their heart is divided; now shall they be found faulty;" or, as some render the word, they shall be ruined. For desolations in a state oft follow divisions in the church, as we see in Poland, Germany, and elsewhere.

And was England ever more sadly divided and subdivided than at this day? What separations and subseparations are found amongst us? One is of Paul, another of Apollos; divisions in principles, divisions in practice, divisions in judgment, and divisions in affection; divisions in church, and divisions in state: for the divisions of England there be sad thoughts of heart. Jerusalem's divisions were Jerusalem's ruin; the Lord grant that England's divisions prove not England's ruin. These give the enemy great advantage against us, and encourage them to set upon us. When Israel and Judah were at variance, then comes Shishak the Egyptian and troubles Jerusalem, 2 Chron. xii. 2.

It is observed, that England was never conquered but when it was divided within itself.

Dum pugnant singuli, vincuntur universi. Tacitus.

Oh that God who has made our hearts would mend them, and unite them, that we may never lose our religion, laws, estates, persons, posterity, and all that is dear to us, and lay ourselves open to the malice of a bloody enemy, who has no way to overthrow us sooner than by our sinful dissensions.

16. Carnal-confidence. For this sin they are frequently reproved; one while they trusted in their kings; anon they go down to Egypt for help, and then seek to the Assyrian: they forsook the Lord, and trusted in an arm of flesh, which yet could not help them in their troubles, Hos. v. 13; vii. 11; xii. 1; xiii. 10.

And does not this sin abound in England? Have not we trusted in kings, princes, protectors, parliaments, armies, navies, &c.? We have leaned upon our staves, till we have broken them all, and ruined our carnal-confidences by idolizing them.

17. Incorrigibleness under lesser judgments. God had been as "a moth" to Ephraim, which consumed him by little and little; but since that did not better him, the Lord came as "a lion" against him, and tore him all to pieces, Hos. v. 12, 14. Like a good physician, he used all means to heal them, Hos. vii. 1, by his word, by his mercies, by his judgments; but since nothing would mend them, the Lord swears by himself, to root up them, and their posterity, for their stubbornness, Amos iv.

And is not this our sin? Has not the Lord used all gentle means, and spent all his lesser rods, in vain upon us? Who can say he has been the better for all the agues, fevers, taxes, poverty, sickness, or any of those lesser rods which God has laid upon us? May not the Lord complain of England as he did sometime of Israel for their incorrigibleness? Amos iv. 6—12. Thus and thus have I done to you, "yet have ye not returned to me, saith the Lord;" and therefore now will I bring some greater judgment on you, unless by repentance you "prepare to meet thy God," and so prevent his wrath.

Plectimur sed non flectimur, corripimur sed non corrigimur. Salvian.

18. Oppression and cruelty. They acted their oppressions on the poor in a violent, virulent manner, which brought destruction upon them, Amos iii. 9—12; iv. 2. They used false weights, and loved to oppress; they were all for getting, though it were by force and forgery, Hos. xii. 7.

And does not this sin reign amongst us? Was there ever more racking of tenants, and grinding of the faces of the poor? Was there ever more cozening, cheating, overreaching, and unrighteous dealing in the land, and that by some who pretend to an extraordinary measure of religion. I believe the like has not been known in the memory of man. Our forefathers had less light and knowledge, but there was far more plainness and single-heartedness in those days than characterizes ours.

I have but little dealing in the world, (had I less I should be well contented,) yet I must profess, that I can scarce tell where to find a plain, simple, single-hearted Nathanael. Let such know that God abominates them, Deut. xxv. 13—16, and will be avenged on them, 1 Thess. iv. 6. The whole land fares the worse for such. This was one of those sins, amongst the rest, that brought judgments on Jerusalem, and will certainly bring judgments on London, and the rest of our cities where such enormities abound, Ezek. xxii. 12, 29, 31.

19. Atheism. They forgot God days without number, he was not in all their thoughts. Hence the Lord so oft complains, that they knew him not, nor considered that he remembered all their doings, Hos. ii. 5, 8, 13; v. 4; vii. 2.

Atheism at this day is the crying sin of England; we are not in so much danger of papism now as of atheism. How has this God-provoking, land-ruining sin overspread the whole island! We have all sorts of atheism amongst us, mental, vocal, vital.

1. We have close atheists, and gross atheists; we have atheists contemplative, and atheists practical. Some are closer atheists, they do not directly and plainly cast God out of the world; yet these fools (who are the world's wise men) say in their hearts, "There is no God," Psal. xiv. 1. This kind of atheism is not so easily discovered, nor reproved, and so it wants that help which gross atheism meets withal.

2. Many that confess God in their words, yet deny him in their works, and by consequence deny his all-seeing eye and being, as if God took no notice of things below; these are practical atheists, Tit. i. 16. Eliphaz sets the brand of wickedness upon the forehead of this sin, Job xxii. 5, 13, 14; and God threatens to search, as "with candles," for such atheistical ones, that is, he will search narrowly, and sift them thoroughly, as the woman that lighted a candle to search for her lost groat, Zeph. i. 12. Yet atheism is frequently acted in the world in one degree or other: Psal. x. 4, "The wicked, through the pride of his countenance, will not seek after God;" that is, he thinks he has no need of him, but has enough in himself, and therefore he will not go to God: "God is not in all his thoughts;" a Hebraism, signifying he is in none of his thoughts, no, not in one of his thoughts or ways. The devil would fain make men not believe that which he himself cannot but believe, viz. that there is a God. This is one of the highest degrees of wickedness in the world. To deny God is so high a sin that it takes away all at once, the devil needs not come a second time. This is to sin against the greatest light; it is not only a sin against the light of Christianity, but against the light of nature, against the witness of the creature, and the whole creation. Such sin against the providence of God, and against the common consent of all nations. Tully could say, There was never any nation so barbarous as to deny that there was a God. I have seen a city without walls, but never any city but acknowledged a God. I have heard of some that have denied that there was a God; yet never knew the man, but, when he was sick, would seek unto God for help. Therefore, saith Seneca, they do but lie that say there is no God; they sin against the light of their own consciences; they who most studiously go about to deny God, yet cannot do it, but some check of conscience will fly in their faces: hence heathens have condemned some to death that denied there was a God. This is a mother-sin, and the root of all abominations, yea, in every sin there is a virtual, tacit, interpretative atheism; they say, as it were, in their hearts, that God does not see, Psal. xiv. 1—3; lxxiii. 11, 12; xciv. 5—9. This sin ruined Jerusalem, Ezek. ix. 9, and if it spread in England as it has done of late years, it will certainly ruin us also.

We all carry the root of this prolific sin about us, and in every sin there is a grain, at least, of atheism. When we are charged with it we are apt to say, as Hazael, "But what, is thy servant a dog, that he should do this great thing?" he would not believe that there was so much wickedness in him. "The Lord hath showed me that thou shalt be king over Syria," answered the prophet, and then thy corruptions will soon appear, when thou hast power and opportunity to act them. So say I, thou art a son of Adam, lapsed and fallen in him, thou hast the seed of this sin within thee, and when a temptation comes it will quickly discover itself to the world.

Take heed of polytheism, which is the ready way to atheism; the having of many gods is the ready way to have no God. An *omni* religion is the ready way to no religion. The world abounds with false gods. Our gods are,

1. Whatsoever we love more than God, that is our god: *Amor tuus, Deus tuus.*

2. Whatsoever we confide in more than God, is our god, Job xxxi. 24.

3. Whatever we glory and rejoice in more than God, Jer. ix. 23; Phil. iii. 19.

4. Whatever we ascribe efficiency to, Hab. i. 16. God will have all power ascribed to himself, Deut. viii. 12, 13, 17, 18.

5. Whatever we obey against the mind of God, be it friend or foe, men or devils, that we make our god.

20. Their sin was full, and they ripe for ruin. God had borne with their provocations about two hundred and sixty years, even till they had filled up the measure of their sins, and then he brought destruction on them.

Now Ephraim's sin was full in respect of, 1. Multitude. 2. Magnitude. 3. Strength. 4. Growth. 5. Impudency. 6. Obstinacy.

There was a fulness in respect of,

1. Multitude. 1. All sorts of sin abounded, both in doctrine and manners; there was idolatry, adultery, murder, witchcraft, lying, stealing, oppression, 2 Kings xvii. 9—11; Hos. iv. 1, 2; vii. 7; Amos ii. 6. 2. All sorts of sinners abounded, high and low, princes, priests, and people, all were idolaters, and delighted in false worship, Hos. v. 1; Micah vii. 3—6.

This universality of sinning is ever a forerunner of judgment: when all the old world had corrupted themselves, then came the flood; when all Sodom was wicked, and all Jerusalem rebelled, when "the mean man boweth down" to idols, "and the great man humbleth himself," then God will not forgive, Isa. i. 5, 6; ii. 9; Jer. v. 1—7; vii. 18, 19.

2. Magnitude; which is a forerunner of destruction. When the sins in themselves are great, as idolatry, witchcraft, hypocrisy, apostacy, and these sins are heightened by circumstances, being committed against great light, love, patience, &c. This was Ephraim's, I wish it were not also England's, case.

3. Strength. When men do wickedly "with both hands," that is, earnestly and actively, Micah vii. 3. When men "draw iniquity with cords of vanity," and study how they may do mischief with all their might, Isa. v. 18; Ezek. xxii. 6.

4. Growth. When men "sin more and more," as Ephraim did, Hos. xiii. 2, and grow "worse and worse," 2 Tim. iii. 13, persevering in their sin without end or measure, this also prognosticates ruin to a nation. The Lord did not presently destroy the Amorites, but suffered their sin to come to its fulness, that he might pour upon them the fulness of his fury; Gen. xv. 16, "The iniquity of the Amorites is not yet full." Though they were notoriously wicked, yet he bears with them till their sins were ripe for ruin. A woman must go her forty weeks till the child be come to perfection, and then comes her travail suddenly and surely. So sin has its conception, rise, reign, and ruin, Psal. vii. 14; James i. 15.

5. Impudency. When men declare their sins like Sodom, and openly profess their wickedness with "a whore's forehead" that refuses to be ashamed, Isa. iii. 9; Jer. iii. 3; vi. 15; Zeph. iii. 5.

6. Obstinacy. When nothing can reclaim a people, but they are resolvedly wicked, as Ephraim here, who was married to idols, and would not return, being deeply rooted in iniquity, Hos. iv. 17; v. 4; ix. 9. They sold themselves to do wickedly, 2 Kings xvii. 17; they would not be warned by the falls of others, whom God had punished before them for the same sins, 2 Kings xvii. 8—15, but rejected the counsel of his prophets, till the wrath of the Lord broke forth, and there was no remedy, as you may see, 2 Kings xvii. 7—24, where you have Ephraim's sins, and Ephraim's punishment, fully set forth.

Now what could the Lord do less than root up such a people, so obstinate under reproofs, so unthankful for mercies, so incorrigible under judgments, so incapable of repentance, so impatient of remedies, so impenitent under all the means of grace which God had afforded them?

Let us now reflect upon ourselves, and see whether Ephraim's sins be not England's sins: if so, parity of sins will bring parity of judgments; if our sins run parallel with those of Ephraim, we may justly expect Ephraim's downfal.

It is said of Lot, that his righteous soul was vexed with the sins of Sodom, 2 Pet. ii. 7, 8; the original signifies, his soul was racked and tormented when he saw the abominations of the Sodomites. These twenty sins which abound in England, and forebode some approaching judgment, should even rack and torment our souls with grief, that so we may be marked for mercy when judgment comes, Ezek. ix. 4; Hab. iii. 16.

ἐβασάνιζεν a βασανίζω, torques, a βασανος, lapis Lydius, cruciatus quivis.

Lastly, their rulers were corrupt, their kings, princes, judges, were idolaters, revolters, violaters of the law, bribers, &c., Hos. iv. 18, 19; v. 13; ix. 15; and the people were corrupted by them, for where the head is rotten, the members cannot be sound. Of all the twenty kings of Israel (after the division of the state) there was not one good from first to last, they were all idolaters; which serves to clear and vindicate the justice of God in the utter overthrow of those kings, and their kingdom, who had for the space of two hundred and thirty-seven, or two hundred and sixty years, abused the goodness and patience of the Lord.

On the whole matter, the counsel which the Lord gave to Ephraim, shall I give to England, Hos. xiv. 1—3. Return, O backsliding England, from thy atheism, apostacy, heresy, blasphemy, hypocrisy, formality, ingratitude, witchcraft, security, anarchy, and take with you words of sincere confession, and turn unfeignedly to the Lord; so will he receive you graciously, and accept both of your persons and performances.

Israel's Prayer in Time of Trouble,

WITH

GOD'S GRACIOUS ANSWER THEREUNTO.

AN EXPLICATION

OF THE

FOURTEENTH CHAPTER OF HOSEA;

IN SEVEN SERMONS,

PREACHED IN MARGARET'S CHURCH, AT WESTMINSTER, BEFORE THE HONOURABLE HOUSE OF COMMONS, NOW ASSEMBLED IN PARLIAMENT.

BY EDWARD REYNOLDS,

MINISTER OF THE WORD OF GOD AT BRAUNSTON IN NORTHAMPTONSHIRE, AND A MEMBER OF THE ASSEMBLY OF DIVINES.

PUBLISHED BY ORDER OF THE SAID HOUSE.

TO THE

HONOURABLE HOUSE OF COMMONS,

ASSEMBLED IN PARLIAMENT.

In obedience to your commands, I here humbly present to your view, what you were pleased with patience and readiness of affection lately to attend unto. I considered, that though the choiceness of the auditory might require the exactest preparation, yet, both the condition of the times, and the nature of the duty, called upon us to lay aside our ornaments. And therefore I spake with such plainness, as might commend the matter delivered rather to the conscience of a penitent, than to the fancy of a delicate hearer. The king of Nineveh was a king as well in his sackcloth as in his robes: and the truth of God is indeed fuller of majesty when it is naked, than when adorned with the dress of any human contribution, which many times takes from it, but never adds to it any value.

I looked upon you in your double relation, both common, as Christians, and special, as men intrusted with the managing of those arduous and most pressing difficulties under which this distempered kingdom is now groaning.

And for the quickening of those endeavours which belong to you in both these relations, I presented you both with the bottom of a nation's unhappiness, which is sin; and with the top of their felicity, which is God's free grace and favour: that by your serious cares to purge out the one and to procure the other, you might, by God's blessing on your consultations, dispel that black tempest which hangs over this kingdom, and reduce the face of things to calmness and serenity again.

When the children struggled together in the womb of Rebekah, she was thereupon inquisitive, "If it be so, why am I thus?" Gen. xxv. 22; and she addressed herself to God for a resolution. Surely this nation is become like the womb of Rebekah, the children thereof struggling together in their common mother; and when God has mercifully freed us from foreign enemies, brethren are become enemies to brethren, and by their enmities likely to tear and torment the bowels of their mother, and to ruin themselves.

And what have we now to do, but to inquire the cause of these sad commotions, Why are we thus? And surely the cause is chiefly where the disease is, within ourselves. We have been like the womb of Rebekah, a barren nation, not bringing forth fruits for the so many mercies with which God has filled us. So that now it is no wonder if God cause us to be in pain within our own bowels, and to feel the throes and "sorrows of a travailing woman," Hos. xiii. 13, ready to bring forth her own confusion, a Benoni or an Ichabod, a son of sorrow or a son of shame, to this hitherto so peaceable and flourishing kingdom.

All that we can comfort ourselves with in these pangs and qualms of distemper is, that there are some Jacobs amongst us, who, instead of supplanting their brethren, will wrestle and have power with God, Gen. xxxii. 24; Hos. xii. 3, 4. The people have often petitioned, sometimes his sacred Majesty, sometimes this Honourable House, which are his great council, many overtures and endeavours of accommodation have been tendered, and yet we cry out in our pangs, and have, as it were, brought forth wind, neither have we wrought any deliverance in the earth, Isa. xxvi. 17, 18.

I have here, therefore, presented a new petition, dictated and drawn up to our hands by God's own Spirit, to which both king and parliament, peers, and prophets, and people, must all subscribe, and offer it with prostrate and penitent hearts to Him who "standeth in the congregation of the mighty," and "judgeth among the gods," that he would "take away all" our "iniquity," and "receive us" into favour again, and accept of a covenant of new obedience, Psal. lxxxii. 1; Hos. xiv. 2.

And this petition God is pleased to anticipate with an answer of grace in the consequent parts of the chapter whence the text is taken, and that particularly to every branch of the petition. He will take away iniquity. His anger shall not punish, his love shall heal our backslidings, the greatness of our sins shall not hinder the freeness of his grace. He will do us good, and give us life, by the dew of his grace reviving us; and glory, clothing us, like the lily of the field, with the beauty of holiness; and stability, fixing us by his grace, as the cedars of Lebanon are fastened upon their roots; and growth, or enlargement, as the branches spread forth themselves; and continual vigour and plenty, as the olive tree, which is always green and fruitful; and glorious comforts by the sweet savour of the knowledge of God, which, like the spice trees of Lebanon, shall diffuse a spiritual perfume upon the names, and into the consciences, of penitent converts.

He will prevent us with the blessings of safety, as well as of sanctity and comfort; we shall, under his shadow, find shelter and protection from all our fears. Though, like corn, we be harrowed under the clods; though, like a lopped vine, we seem naked and reduced to lowness; though, like crushed grapes, we lie under heavy pressures; yet he will receive, and enlarge, and comfort us again; and when we are in our own eyes as fatherless children, he will set his eyes upon us as a tutor and guardian; he will hear, and observe, and answer, and pity us, enabling us to make good our covenant by his grace, and causing the fruit of his loving-kindness to be found upon us. Thus God is pleased to borrow the various perfection of other things to adumbrate the united and accumulated mercies which he promises to a turning and petitioning people.

You have the petition sent you from God, and his answer preventing you in all the members of it with the blessings of goodness. I have nothing else to do, but to beg of you, and of all this great people whom you represent, the subscription of your hearts and lives to this petition; and to beg of God, that he would graciously incline the hearts of this whole kingdom, rather to wrestle with him for a blessing, than to struggle and conflict amongst themselves for a curse. With which prayer I humbly conclude, commending your persons and your weighty affairs to his grace; and rest,

Your most humble servant in Christ,

EDWARD REYNOLDS.

From my study in Braunston, August the 8th, 1642.

CHAPTER XIV.

VERSE 1—3.

O Israel, return unto the Lord thy God; for thou hast fallen by thine iniquity. Take with you words, and turn to the Lord: say unto him, Take away all iniquity, and receive us graciously: so will we render the calves of our lips. Asshur shall not save us; we will not ride upon horses: neither will we say any more to the work of our hands, Ye are our gods: for in thee the fatherless findeth mercy.

THE blessing of Ephraim was, according to the signification of his name, fruitfulness, Gen. xli. 52; the fruitfulness of the earth, a bough by a well, and the fruitfulness of the womb, and of the breasts, Gen. xlix. 22, 25; Deut. xxxiii. 13—17. Contrary to which two blessings, we find in our prophet two judgments threatened against him for his sins; chap. xiii. 15, 16, "Though he be fruitful among his brethren, an east wind shall come, the wind of the Lord shall come up from the wilderness, and his spring shall become dry, and his fountain shall be dried up: he shall spoil the treasure of all pleasant vessels. Samaria shall become desolate; for she hath rebelled against her God: they shall fall by the sword: their infants shall be dashed in pieces, and their women with child shall be ripped up." And throughout the whole prophecy, (if you read and observe it,) you will find the judgments of God against Ephraim to be expressed by weeds, emptiness, barrenness, dryness of roots, of fruits, of branches, of springs, and by a curse upon their children; as, on the other side, the blessings here in this chapter renewed to Ephraim repenting, are all expressed by metaphors of fruitfulness, ver. 5—7.

From these two woeful judgments, against the fruitfulness of their springs, and the fruitfulness of their wombs, by the desolations of a bloody sword, our prophet takes occasion once more to awaken and drive them to a timely repentance, that so they may recover the blessing of their name; Ephraim may be Ephraim again, a plentiful, a fruitful, a flourishing people. That "when God's judgments are in the earth," they would then, at least, set themselves to "learn righteousness," that they may wash their feet in the blood of the wicked.

Παράδειγματί τοῖς ἄλλοις γίνεσθαι ἵνα ἄλλοι ὁρῶντες πάσχοντα ἃ ἂν πασχοι φοβούμενοι βελτίους γίνωνται. Plato apud A. Gel. l. 6. c. 14.

Of all nations under heaven this land of ours has had the blessing of Ephraim upon it, fruitfulness of the earth, abundance of plenty; fruitfulness of the womb, abundance of people. But our misery is, that the abundance of our sins has mightily outvied the abundance both of our plenty and of our people; sins, also, too parallel to those of Ephraim. And this parity of sins has no doubt called upon God for a parity of judgments. It is but a very little while since the Lord seemed to call for a north wind, as he does here for an east wind; two armies there met, ready to look one another in the face; but his heart turned, his repentings were kindled, he would not give up Ephraim then. He seems now once more to be drawing a sword, and having in vain "hewed" us by his "prophets," as he complains, Hos. vi. 5, to try whether hewing us by his judgments will work upon us. So that now, though I must read my text, "O Israel," yet I must apply it, O England, "return unto the Lord thy God; for thou hast fallen by thine iniquity. Take with you words, and turn to the Lord: say unto him, Take away all iniquity, and receive us graciously: so will we render the calves of our lips."

The whole context contains two general parts:

I. An invitation to repentance, ver. 1.

II. An institution how to perform it, ver. 2, 3.

Before we come to the particulars of the invitation, let us first briefly observe, That in the midst of judgments proposed against obstinate sinners, God reserves and proclaims mercy to sinners that are penitent. When a consumption is decreed, yet a remnant is reserved to return, Isa. x. 22, 23. The Lord will keep his "vineyard," when he will burn up "the briers and thorns" together, Isa. xxvii. 2—4. When a day of "fierce anger" is determined, the "meek of the earth" are called upon to seek the Lord, Zeph. ii. 3. When the Lord is coming "out of his place to punish the inhabitants of the earth for their iniquity," he calls upon his people to "hide" themselves in their "chambers," "until the indignation be overpast," Isa. xxvi. 20, 21. The angel which was sent to destroy Sodom, had withal a commission to deliver Lot, Gen. xix. 15. God made full provision for those who mourned for public abominations, before he gave order to destroy the rest, Ezek. ix. 4, 6. Men in their wrath will many times rather strike a friend than spare a foe; but God's proceedings are without disorder, he will rather spare his foes than strike his servants, as he showed himself willing to have done in the case of Sodom, Gen. xviii. 26. "Moses stood before him in the breach," and diverted judgments from Israel," Psal. cvi. 23. Yea, God seeks for such, Ezek. xxii. 30, and complains when they cannot be found, Ezek. xiii. 5; and if he deliver others for them, certainly he will not destroy them for others. However it go with the world and with wicked men, it shall go well with the righteous; there shall be a sanctuary for them when others stumble, and they shall pass through the fire when others are consumed by it, Isa. iii. 10, 11; viii. 14—16; Zech. xiii. 8, 9. The reasons of this tender care are,

1. God's justice. He will not punish the righteous with the wicked; he will have it appear that there is a difference "between him that serveth God and him that serveth him not," Gen. xviii. 23; Mal. iii. 18.

2. God's love to his people. He has "a book of remembrance" written before him, for them that fear him, and think upon his name. "And they shall be mine, saith the Lord of hosts, in that day when I make up my jewels; and I will spare them, as a man spareth his own son that serveth him," Mal. iii. 16, 17. Here is a climax and gradation of arguments drawn from love. In a great fire, and devouring trouble, (such as is threatened, Mal. iv. 1,) property alone is a ground of care; a man would willingly save and secure that which is his own, and of any use to him; but if you add to this preciousness, that increases the care. A man will make hard shift to deliver a rich cabinet of jewels, though all his ordinary goods and utensils should perish. But of all jewels, those which come out of the body are much more precious than those which only adorn it. Who would not snatch rather his child than his casket or purse out of a flame? Relation works not only upon the affection, but upon the bowels, Jer. xxxi. 20. And lastly, the same excellency that the word "jewel" adds to the word "mine;" the same excellency does "service" add to the word

"son." A man has much conflict in himself to take off his heart from an undutiful son. Never a worse son than Absalom, and yet how does David give a charge to the commanders to have him spared! How inquisitive after his safety! how passionately and unseasonably mournful upon the news of his death! But if any child be more a jewel than another, certainly it is a dutiful child, who has not only an interest in our love by nature, but by obedience. All these grounds of care and protection for God's people in trouble are here expressed; property, they are "mine;" preciousness, they are "jewels," treasures, ornaments unto me; relation, they are "sons;" usefulness, they are sons that "serve:" none could look on a thing so many ways lovely with the same eye as upon a professed and provoking enemy.

3. God's name and glory. He has spared his people even in the midst of their provocations for his name's sake, Deut. xxxiii. 26, 27; Josh. vii. 9. How much more when they repent and seek his face! He will never let it be said, that any seek the Lord in vain, Isa. xlv. 19.

But it may be objected, Does not Solomon say, that "all things come alike to all?" and that "no man knoweth either love or hatred by all that is before him?" Eccl. ix. 1, 2. And is it not certain and common, that in public desolations good as well as bad do perish? Does not the sword devour as well one as another?

True, God does not always difference his servants from wicked men by temporal deliverances; troubles commonly and promiscuously involve all sorts. But there are these two things in it to be considered:

1. Many times the good suffer with the bad, because they are together corrupted with them; and when they join in the common provocations, no wonder if they suffer in the common judgments, Rev. xviii. 4. Nay, the sins of God's people do (especially in this case) more provoke him to outward judgments than the sins of his professed enemies; because they expose his name to the more contempt, 2 Sam. xii. 14; and are committed against the greater love, Amos iii. 2; and he has future judgment for the wicked, and therefore usually begins here at his own sanctuary, Ezek. ix. 6; 1 Pet. iv. 17.

2. When good men, who have preserved themselves from public sins, do yet fall by public judgments, still there is a great difference in this seeming equality, the same affliction having, like the pillar that went before Israel, a light side towards God's people, and a dark side towards the Egyptians, God usually recompensing the outward evils of his people with more plentiful evidences of inward and spiritual joy. A good man may be in great darkness as well as a wicked man, but in that case he has the name of God to stay himself upon, which no wicked man in the world has, Isa. l. 10. The metal and the dross go both into the fire together, but the dross is consumed, the metal refined. So is it with godly and wicked in their sufferings, Zech. xiii. 9; Eccl. viii. 12, 13.

This reproves the folly of those who in time of trouble rely upon vain things which cannot help them, and continue their sins still. For judgments make no difference of any but penitent and impenitent. Sickness stands not on ceremony with an honourable person, but uses him as coarsely as the base. Death knocks as well at a prince's palace as a poor man's cottage; wise men die as well as fools. Yea, poison usually works more violently when tempered with wine, than with some duller and baser material. In times of trouble usually the greater the persons the closer the judgments. When Jerusalem was taken the nobles were slain, but the poor of the land had vineyards and fields given them, Jer. xxxix. 6—10.

Therefore in troubles we should be more humbled for our sins than our sufferings, because sin is the sting of suffering. That mercies should not win us; that judgment should not awaken us; that the rod should speak, and we not hear, Micah vi. 9; that the fire should burn, and we not feel, Isa. xlii. 25; that desolation should be threatened, and we not instructed, Jer. vi. 8; that the hand of God should be lifted up, and we not see it, Isa. xxvi. 11; that darkness should be upon us, and we not give glory to God, Jer. xiii. 16: this is that which should most deject us, in mercies to have been wanton, and in judgments senseless. Get repentance by an affliction, and then you may look on it as a traffic, and not as a trouble, like a merchant's voyage, which has pain in the way, but treasure in the end. No afflictions can hurt him that is penitent. If thou escape, they will make thee the more thankful; if not, they will bring thee the nearer and the sooner to God.

The way to be safe in times of trouble, is to get the blood of the Lamb upon our doors. All troubles have their commission and instructions from God, what to do, whither to go, whom to touch, whom to pass over. Be gold, and though the fire come upon you, you shall keep your nature and purity still. "Godliness," saith the apostle, "hath the promise of this life," and in that general promise one special clause, that we shall not "be tempted above that we are able," 1 Cor. x. 13; neither are there indeed any distresses against which there is not a refuge and escape for penitent sinners to some promise or other. Against captivity. "When they be in the land of their enemies, I will not cast them away, neither will I abhor them, to destroy them utterly," Lev. xxvi. 44. Against famine and pestilence. "If I shut up heaven that there be no rain, or if I command the locusts to devour the land, or if I send pestilence among my people; if my people, which are called by my name, shall humble themselves, and pray, and seek my face, and turn from their wicked ways; then will I hear from heaven, and will forgive their sin, and will heal their land," 2 Chron. vii. 13, 14. Against sickness. "The Lord will strengthen him upon the bed of languishing: thou wilt make all his bed in his sickness," Psal. xli. 3. Against poverty. "When the poor and needy seek water, and there is none, and their tongue faileth for thirst, I the Lord will hear them, I the God of Israel will not forsake them," Isa. xli. 17; Psal. lxviii. 10. Against want of friends. "When my father and mother forsake me, then the Lord will take me up," Psal. xxvii. 10; lxxii. 12. Against oppression and imprisonment. "Which executeth judgment for the oppressed: the Lord looseth the prisoners," Psal. cxlvi. 7. Against "whatsoever plague, whatsoever sickness there be," 1 Kings viii. 37, 38. He is the God of "all consolation:" how disconsolate soever a man's condition is in any kind, there cannot but within the compass of "all consolation" be some one or other remedy at hand to comfort and relieve him. And so much by the way of general preface from the words of the context, which leads us to consider,

I. The invitation to repentance: in which we have, 1. The matter of the invitation. 2. The motives contained in the invitation.

1. The matter of the invitation is conversion: without that, the hand which is lifted up in threatening will fall down in punishing; and where that is, God has "a book of remembrance" for his jewels, when his wrath burneth as an oven against the stubble, Isa. xxvi. 11; Mal. iii. 16.

But this conversion has two conditions in it. 1. It must be to the Lord. "O Israel, return unto the Lord." Not merely philosophical, to some low and general dictates of reason, such as Aristotle, or Plato, or Epictetus, or Plutarch, or the like heathen moralists could furnish us with, without self-denial, lowliness of spirit, or * faith in Christ.

Not merely political, to credit, or profit, or secular ends, † *propter famam, non propter conscientiam*, as the orator speaks, or as our prophet saith, "for corn and wine," Hos. vii. 14. As good be an empty vine, as bring forth fruit only to ourselves, Hos. x. 1.

But it must be spiritual, to the Lord. "If thou wilt return, O Israel, saith the Lord, return unto me," Jer. iv. 1. And not only "unto the Lord," for that may be done falsely and flatteringly, with a halting and divided heart, Jer. iii. 10. By the force of semi-persuasions, like that of Agrippa, Acts xxvi. 28, and Orpah, Ruth i. 14, complimenting with God, and then forsaking him. By the force of compulsory impressions, like that of Pharaoh and Israel in the wilderness, Exod. viii. 8; ix. 27—34; Psal. lxxviii. 34—37. ‡ Promises on the rack, and pride when there was respite again; thawing in the sun, and freezing in the shade; melting in the furnace, and out of it returning again to hardness; like the prophet's cake, burnt on the one side, and dough on the other. But it must be,

2. Even unto the Lord; so much the original word עד imports, a full, thorough, constant, continued conversion, with a fixed, rooted, united, established heart, yielding up the whole conscience and conversation to be ruled by God's will in all things, Joel ii. 12; Acts xi. 23; Psal. lvii. 7; Eph. iii. 17; Psal. lxxxvi. 11; Heb. xiii. 9.

2. The motives to this duty are two. 1. His mercy: "Return unto the Lord thy God;" he is yet "thy God:" no such argument for our turning to God as his turning to us. Adam looks on him as a judge, and hides; the prodigal looks on him as a father, and returns. As the beams of the sun shining on fire deadens its flame, so the shining of God's mercies on us should dishearten and extinguish our lusts. This is the use we should make of mercy. Say not, He is my God, therefore I may presume upon him; but, He is mine, therefore I must return to him. Because he is God, I will be afraid to provoke him; and because he is mine, I will be afraid to forfeit him. He is so great, I must not dare to offend him; so precious, I must not venture to lose him. His mercy is a holy mercy, which knows to pardon sin, but not to protect it. It is a sanctuary for the penitent, not for the presumptuous, Joel ii. 12, 13; Isa. lv. 6, 7; Jer. xxxi. 18; Hos. iii. 5; Psal. cxxx. 4; Acts ii. 38; Matt. iii. 2; Isa. lxiv. 9.

'Αγαθὴ ἡ τοῦ Θεοῦ δικαιοσύνη, καὶ δικαία ἔστιν ἡ ἀγαθότης αὐτοῦ. Clem. Alex. Stro. lib. 6.

2. His judgment, and that expressed rather as our act than his: "Thou hast fallen by thine iniquity." If mercies do not work upon love, let judgments work upon fear. Extremities are a warrant to importunities. Even heathen mariners in a storm will cry mightily upon God. When there is a deluge coming, is it not time for Noah to fear, and to prepare an ark? Heb. xi. 7. "What meanest thou, O thou sleeper," to lose the season and benefit of God's visitations? when there is a tempest over the ship, heavy distresses, and distractions both at home and abroad, to be so secure in thy wonted impenitency, as if thou hadst had no sins to procure these judgments, or no sense to feel them, Jonah i. 6; as if there were agreements and sealed covenants between thee and the sword, that it should not touch thee? If thou be falling, is it not high time to consider thy ways; to search and to judge thyself; to have thine eyes like the windows of Solomon's temple, broad inwards; to find out thine own provocations, and, as David speaks, to keep thyself from thine iniquity? Psal. xviii. 23.

Dant animum ad loquendum libere ultimæ miseriæ. Liv. lib. 29. Inops senatus auxilii humani ad Deos populum et vota vertit, &c. Liv. l. 3. Alex. Stro. l. 6. 6. p. 45 3. Edit. Heins. Sozom. l. 9. c. 6. Brisso. de Formul. l. 1. Aug. de Civ. Dei, l. 1. c. 33.

Εκαστος κακούργων ἐκφέρει τὸν αὐτοῦ σταυρόν. Plut. de Sera. Vindict.

Thus when in one and the same time mercies and judgments are intermixed, then is the most solemn season to call upon men for repentance. If we felt nothing but fears, they might make us despair; if nothing but mercies, they would make us secure. If the whole year were summer, the sap of the earth would be exhausted; if the whole were winter, it would be quite buried. The hammer breaks metal, and the fire melts it, and then you may cast it into any shape. Judgments break, mercies melt, and then, if ever, the soul is fit to be cast into God's mould. There is no figure in all the prophets more usual than this, to interweave mercies and judgments, like those elegancies which rhetoricians call ὀξύμωρα, to allure, and to bring into a wilderness, Hos. ii. 14. And this of all other is the ἡμέρα κρισιμος, as physicians call it, the critical time of diseased people, wherein the chief conjecture lies, whether they be mending or ending, according to the use which they make of such interwoven mercies.

Vossius Rhetor. l. 5. c. 12. sect. 7.

Vide Gorræi Definit. Medic. et Laurent.

I have cursorily run over the first part of the context, the invitation to repentance, as intending to make my abode on the second.

II. The institution how to perform it. Therein we have, 1. A general instruction, "Take with you words." 2. A particular form, what words they should take, or a petition drawn to their hands, "Take away all iniquity, and receive us graciously: so will we render the calves of our lips. Asshur shall not save us; we will not ride upon horses: neither will we say any more to the work of our hands, Ye are our gods: for in thee the fatherless findeth mercy."

1. A general instruction, "Take with you words." Of this I shall speak but briefly. It imports the serious pondering and choosing of requests to put up to God. The mother of Artaxerxes in Plutarch was wont to say, that they who would address themselves to princes, must use ῥήμασι βυσσίνοις, silken words. Surely he that would approach to God, must consider, and look as well to his words as to his feet. He is so holy and jealous of his worship, that he expects there should be preparation in our accesses unto him, Josh. xxiv. 19; John iv. 23; Eccl. v. 1, 2; Gen. xxxv. 2, 3; 1 Sam. xvi. 5; Isa. i. 15, 16; preparation of our persons by purity of life, Job xi. 13; preparation of our services by choice of matter, Job ix. 14; Luke xv. 17, 18; preparation of our hearts by finding them out, stirring them up, fixing them, fetching them in, and calling together all that is within us to prevail with God, 2 Sam. vii. 27; Isa. lxiv. 7; Psal. lvii. 7, 8; ciii. 1; 2 Chron. xxx. 19.

Quantum a præceptis tantum ab auribus Dei longe sumus. Tertul. de Orat. cap. 7.

The services which we thus prepare must be taken from him; they must not be the issues of our own private and fleshly hearts; for nothing can go to God, but that which comes from him. And this phrase seems to import these three things: 1. We must at-

* Non sunt bona quæ non de radice bona procedunt. Ea ipsa opera quæ dicuntur ante fidem quamvis videantur hominibus laudabilia, inania sunt, ut magnæ vires et cursus celerrimus præter viam. Aug. Enarr. in Phal. 31. Vide de Spirit. et Lite, c. 20, 21, 26. Contra Duas Epist. Pelag. l. 3. c. 7. ep. 106. De Fide et Operibus, c. 14. Contra Julian. lib. 4. cap. 3.

† Nihil ad ostentationem, omnia ad conscientiam refert. Pl. l. 1. epist. 22. Nihil opinionis causâ, omnia conscientiæ, faciam. Senec. de Vita Beata, c. 20.

‡ Semisauciam hac atque hac versare voluntatem. Aug. Confess. l. 8. c. 8. Plerique ipsius pœnitentiæ, &c. Ambro. de Pœnit. l. 2. c. 9. 'Επαλληλοι ἐπι τοῖς ἁμαρτήμασι μετὰνοιαι. Clem. Alex. l. 2. Strom. Irrisor est non pœnitens qui adhuc agit quod pœnitet, &c. Isidor. de Summo Bono. Senec. Ep. 120. Ambros. Offic. lib. 2. c. 22.

tend to his will, as the rule of our prayers, 1 John v. 14. 2. We must attend to his precepts and promises, as the matter of our prayers, 2 Sam. vii. 25. 3. We must attend to the guidance of his Holy Spirit, as the life and principle of our prayers, without which we know not what to ask, Rom. viii. 26; Zech. ii. 10; Job xxxvii. 19.

Vid. Aug. Epist. 105. Et Epist. 121. c. 65.

And prayers thus regulated are most seasonable and sovereign duties in times of trouble; the key which opens a door of mercy, the sluice which keeps out an inundation of judgments. Jacob wrestled and obtained a blessing, Hos. xii. 4. Amos prayed, and removed a curse, Amos vii. 1—6. The woman of Canaan will not be denied with a denial, Matt. xv. 24, 27. The people of Israel will beg for deliverance even when God had positively told them that he would deliver them no more, Judg. x. 13, 15. Jonah will venture a prayer from the bottom of the sea, when a double death had seized upon him, the belly of the deep, and the belly of the whale; and that prayer of his opened the doors of the leviathan, as the expression is, Job xli. 14, and made one of those deaths a deliverance from the other, Jonah ii.

Oh let the Lord's remembrancers give him no rest. There is a kind of omnipotency in prayer, as having an interest and prevalence with God's omnipotency; it has loosed iron chains, Acts xvi. 25, 26; it has opened iron gates, Acts xii. 5, 10; it has unlocked the windows of heaven, 1 Kings xviii. 41; it has broken the bars of death, John xi. 41—44. Satan has three titles given him in the Scripture, setting forth his malignity against the church of God. A dragon, to denote his malice, Rev. xii. 3; a serpent, to denote his subtlety, Gen. iii. 1; and a lion, to denote his strength, 1 Pet. v. 8. But none of all these can stand before prayer. The greatest malice, the malice of Haman, sinks under the prayer of Esther; the deepest policy, the counsel of Ahithophel, withers before the prayer of David; the hugest army, an host of a thousand thousand Ethiopians, run away like cowards before the prayer of Asa, Esth. iv. 16; 2 Sam. xv. 31; 2 Chron. xiv. 9—12.

Vid. Justin Martyr, Apol. 2. Tertul. Apolog. c. 5. 39, 40. Et ad Scapulam. c. 4.

How should this encourage us to treasure up our prayers! to besiege the throne of grace with armies of supplications! to deny a denial! to break through a repulse! He has blessed those whom he had crippled, Gen. xxxii. 25—28; he has answered those whom he did reproach, Matt. xv. 26, 28; he has delivered those whom he did deny, Judg. x. 13—16. He is "the same yesterday, to-day, and for ever," Heb. xiii. 8. If he save in six and in seven troubles, should not we pray in six and seven extremities? Job v. 19. Certainly, in all the afflictions of the church, when prayers are strongest mercies are nearest.

And therefore, let me humbly recommend to the cares of this honourable assembly, amongst all your other pressing affairs, the providing that those solemn days, wherein the united prayers of this whole kingdom should with strongest importunities stop the breaches and stand in the gaps at which judgments are ready to rush in upon us, may with more obedience and solemnity be observed, than indeed they have been of late. It is true, that here, and in other cities and populous places, there is haply less cause to complain. But who can without sorrow and shame behold in our country towns, men so inapprehensive either of their brethren's sufferings, or of their own sins and dangers, as to give God quite over, to let him rest, that they themselves may work; to come in truth to Jehoram's resolution, Why should we wait upon God any longer? to grudge their brethren's and their own souls and safeties one day in thirty, and to tell all the world that indeed their day's work is of more value with them than their day's worship? multitudes drudging and moiling in the earth, while their brethren are mourning and besieging heaven. I do but name it, and proceed to,

2. The particular form suggested to them, according to which their addresses unto God are to be regulated; which consists of two parts; 1. A prayer; 2. A promise. The prayer is for two benefits; 1. The removal of sin; 2. The conferring of good. In the promise or restipulation, we have, 1. Their covenant, wherein they promise two things; 1. Thanksgiving for the hearing and answering of their prayers; 2. A special care for the amendment of their lives. 2. The ground of their confidence so to pray, and of their resolutions so to promise; "For in thee the fatherless findeth mercy." We shall now meditate on the first of these, The prayer of the church in their fears and sufferings; wherein I shall begin, in the prophet's order, with their prayer against sin, "Take away all iniquity."

The word נשׂא rendered "take away," signifies, 1. To expiate, or make atonement by a sacrifice. So the scape goat (which was a sign of Christ our sacrifice as risen and living again) is said to carry the sins of the people into the wilderness, Lev. xvi. 22, thereby signifying Christ's taking our sins from us, John i. 29; Heb. ix. 28. 2. To forgive, which in the court of mercy is the taking away of sin, Psal. xxxii. 1, 5. 3. To remove or take away by destroying, Hos. i. 6; Job xxxii. 22; and sometimes by burning, 2 Sam. v. 21; Nah. i. 5: so sin is said to be destroyed, Rom. vi. 6, to be subdued, Micah vii. 19, to be purged away with the spirit of judgment and burning, Isa. iv. 4. The meaning then is, Take away all our sins from us, lay them upon Christ our sacrifice; for his merit pardon them, by his grace destroy and subdue them, that so, the root of judgments being removed, they likewise may therewithal be removed too. From hence the observation which I shall insist upon is this:

Obs. 1. When God threatens judgments, we in our conversion to him should pray against sins. Our eye of sorrow should be more upon that which dishonours him, than upon that which afflicts ourselves; more upon that which is contrary to his image, than upon that which is contrary to our own nature; more upon that which defiles, than upon that which pains us. Pharaoh cares for nothing but the removal of death, Exod. x. 17; Simon Magus for nothing but to have perdition and the gall of bitterness kept from him, Acts viii. 24; but good men, like wise physicians, cure the disease at the root, as Elisha did the waters by putting salt into the spring-head, 2 Kings ii. 21. The angel was smiting the people with a plague; David betakes himself to the right remedy, "Lo, I have sinned, and have done wickedly;" he goes not to the physicians, but to the altar to make atonement for sin, and so the plague was stayed, 2 Sam. xxiv. 17, 25. Destruction was threatened against Israel, for their calf, their murmurings, their rebellions; Moses stands in the breach to divert it, Psal. cvi. 23; but how does he do it? surely by praying against their sins, Exod. xxxii. 31, 32; xxxiv. 9; Numb. xiv. 19. A sick man was brought to Christ to be healed, Matt. ix. 2; Christ overlooks the disease, and begins at the sin, "Son, be of good cheer, thy sins be forgiven thee;" and this being forgiven, the malignity of the disease was removed, though the matter should have remained. This was the usual method of David in his troubles, to throw over those Shebas that had wrought his woe. "Blot out," "wash thoroughly," "cleanse," "create," "renew:" he is far more importunate for pardon and purging, than for ease and comfort, Psal. xxv. 18; xxxii. 4, 5; xxxviii. 3, 4; li. Complaining in trouble is the work of a man, but repenting is the work of a Christian, Lam. iii. 39, 40.

The reasons of this point are these three. 1. If a judgment should be removed while sin remains, it is not removed in mercy, but in anger; for many times God gives over punishing in displeasure, as a man throws away the rod when his scholar is incorrigible. "Why should ye be stricken any more? ye will revolt more and more," Isa. i. 5. If men be settled on their lees, and will not be reclaimed, there cannot a heavier punishment light upon them, than to be without punishment, to be left to themselves, and the fury of their own wills, speedily to work out their own perdition; that their own pleasures may become their plagues, and the liberty of their own lusts their sorest bondage, Hos. iv. 14; Psal. lxxxi. 11, 12; Ezek. xxiv. 13; Rom. i. 24, 28; Rev. xxii. 11.* God may take away in wrath that which he sent in anger, Hos. xiii. 11; as on the other side he may punish sin then when he forgives it, and may visit iniquity with rods then when he will not utterly take away his loving-kindness from a people, Psal. lxxxix. 32, 33; xcix. 8.

2. If a judgment be removed, so long as sin remains it is gone *cum animo revertendi*, either the same or a worse is likely to succeed, for God will overcome when he is judged, Rom. iii. 4. Pharaoh's stubbornness did not but increase his plagues. God will not endure that the pride of man should outvie his justice, Exod. ix. 17. If we do not take Christ's warning to go and "sin no more," we have great cause to fear his inference, that "a worse thing" will come unto us, John v. 14. If we do yet exalt ourselves, God will yet plead with us, Jer. ii. 9. If we will walk contrary to him, he threatens to do the like unto us, and to punish us seven times more for our sins, Lev. xxvi. 18—28. If we do not turn to him that smites us, then "his anger" in smiting shall not be "turned away, but his hand is stretched out still," Isa. ix. 12. God can bring clouds after rain, distresses in Ireland after distractions in Scotland, and distractions in England after distresses in Ireland, mischief upon mischief, and counsel against counsel, Manasseh against Ephraim, and Ephraim against Manasseh, to vex and weary out a sinful people, till they pine away in their calamities.

3. Sin being removed, though the affliction should not be removed, yet it is sanctified and turned into good. Repentance, like the philosopher's stone, can turn iron into gold, can make afflictions golden. So "the trial of your faith," that is, your affliction, is said to be "much more precious than of gold that perisheth," 1 Pet. i. 7. Whereas sin remaining is like copperas, which will turn wine or milk into ink. It converts the blessings of God into the provisions of lusts; cankers learning with pride, wit with profaneness, and wealth with luxury; like leaven, which turns a very passover into pollutions. As the pearl, which is an ornament to the woman who wears it, is a disease to the fish which breeds it; as the same perfume which refreshes a dove, is mortal to a vulture; as the same pillar and cloud was light to Israel, but dark to Egypt; the same deep a path to Israel, but a grave to Egypt; so the same blessings which by grace are converted into comforts, by sin are abused into dishonourable services, Hag. ii. 13. Sweet powders can make leather an ornament, when the sanies of a plague-sore will render a robe infectious. As it was said of Naaman, he was "a great man," an "honourable" man, "a mighty man in valour, *but* he was a leper," 2 Kings v. 1; so whatever other ornaments a man has, sin stains them with the foulest *but* that can be brought to deprave the fairest endowments. A learned man, a wealthy man, a wise man, an honourable man, but a wicked man. This makes all those other good things tributary to Satan.

Athe. l. 3. c. 13.

And therefore as the gold and silver of the Canaanites was to pass through the fire before it could be used by Israel, Numb. xxxi. 22, 23; so all other blessings bestowed on men must be "purged by the spirit of judgment and by the spirit of burning," through the purifying waters of repentance, before they can bring honour to their author, or comfort to their enjoyer. When Christ overcomes Satan, "he taketh from him all his armour wherein he trusted, and divideth his spoils," Luke xi. 22. How does he divide the spoils? Surely he makes use of that wit, wealth, power, learning, wisdom, influence, which Satan used against Christ's kingdom, as instruments and ornaments to the gospel: as when a magazine in war is taken, the general makes use of those arms which were provided against him, for his own service.

Τεύχεα συλήσας φερέτω κοίλας επι νῆας. Hom. Il. 11.

Qui se dedebant arma tradebant. Cæsar. de Bello Gallico, lib. 3.

And as sin thus corrupts blessings, so on the other side repentance sweetens judgments, and can turn afflictions into matter of comfort. As scarlet pulls out the teeth of a serpent, so this takes away the sting of a judgment. As wine draws a nourishing virtue from the flesh of vipers; as hot birds can feed upon iron, and purge their bodies by swallowing stones; so repentance, though it should not remove a judgment, yet it can feed upon it, and fetch meat out of the eater, and out of the strong sweetness, Judg. xiv. 14.

Plut. de Audiend. Poetis.

There are two evils in afflictions. They are a thorn in the flesh, as they are matter of pain, and a snare to the conscience, as they are matter of temptation; as there are two things in a chain or fetter, the heaviness whereby it loads, and the hardness whereby it galls, Isa. viii. 21; 2 Chron. xxviii. 22; Rev. xvi. 10, 11. Now as a prisoner, though he cannot make his chain lighter, yet, by lining it with wool or other soft things, he can prevent the galling; so repentance, though it take not away the pain of affliction from the flesh, yet by humbling the soul to bear meekly, with silence and quietness, the indignation of the Lord, and accept of the punishment of sin, Micah vii. 9; Lev. xxvi. 41; Jer. x. 19, it removes the temptation and malignity of it from the conscience. And thus as Protagoras by his natural dexterity ordered the burden which he was to bear with more ease and advantage; so piety makes judgments, by spiritual prudence, more easy to be borne, and the light yoke of Christ, as bladders in a deep water, bears up the spirit of men from sinking, and lightens every other burden. And therefore as he in Plutarch said of the Scythians, that though they had no music nor vines amongst them, yet they had gods; so whatever other things may be wanting to a people, yet if God be their God, they are not destitute of any happiness. Yea, as those roses are usually sweetest which grow nearest to ungrateful weeds; so the comforts of God's Spirit are strongest when a man is otherwise perplexed. It was promised to Josiah, that he should die in peace, and yet we find that he was slain in war, 2 Chron. xxxiv. 28; xxxv. 24. His weeping and humiliation altered the very nature of trouble, and made war to be peace to him.

A. Gel. l. 5. c. 3.

Plut. de Sanitate tuend.

Now for the use and application of this point: this serves,

1. To instruct us how to deprecate calamities when God shakes his rod over us. There is nothing in all the world that God is

Usque ad delictum hominis Deus tantum bonus, exinde

* Exaudit propitius, non exaudit iratus: et rursus non exaudit propitius, exaudit iratus. ——non parcit propitius, parcit iratus. Aug. contra Julian, lib. 5. cap. 4. Ad utilitatem quosdam non exaudis, ad damnationem quosdam exaudis. Id. in Psal. xxi. Magna ira est quando peccantibus non irascitur Deus. Hieron. Ep. 33. O servum illum beatum cujus emendationi Deus instat, cui dignatur irasci, &c. Tertul. de Patient. cap. 11.

judex et severus, &c. Tertul. contra Marcion. l. 2. c. 11, 14.

angry with but sin; for all other things are his own works, in the goodness of which he rested with singular complacency and delight. Sin is that against which God's arrows are directed; and as the arrow sticks in the butt to which the mark is fastened, so the judgments which are shot at sin must needs light upon us to whom sin cleaves. The way then to divert the arrow is to remove the mark. God does indeed sometimes bring afflictions, without respect to the provocations of sin, upon his best servants: as if a man should shape out of a mass of gold some excellent vessel, though the gold be never so pure, yet it must pass through the fire and the hammer again. But it is certain too, that no affliction comes in anger but with respect to sin. And the anger of God is the bitterest thing in any calamity.

Now to divert this, there is no way but to get sin removed. Take the bark from a tree, and the sap can never find its way to the boughs. Sin is the vehiculum which carries shame and sorrow to the soul. Take away that, and a judgment has no commission. You may find an error in it, if you be not the same men that you were when it issued forth, for God shoots no arrows to hurt the body of his Son. Job indeed complains that God's arrows were within him, Job vi. 4, but these were not for destruction, but for trial; as men shoot bullets against armour of proof, not to injure, but to test it. Job in this case was brought forth, not as a malefactor to suffer, but as a champion to triumph. Let a man take what course he can to keep off God's judgments, and hide himself in the closest protection that human power or policy can contrive; so long as he keeps his sin with him, God's arrows will get through at one joint or other, 1 Kings xxii. 34. A naked man with innocency, is better armed than Goliath in brass or iron.

Verberat et lacerat, non est sævitia, certamen est. Senec. de Prov. c. 4. Tentationibus non vincitur fides, sed probatur. Cypr. de Mort. Aug. de Civ. Dei, lib. 1. cap. 29, 30. lib. 4. cap. 3.

We are apt in our distress to howl and repine, to gnaw our tongues and tear our flesh in the anguish of our sufferings; like the silly hart, which runs mourning and bleeding, but never thinks of getting out the fatal dart that sticks in its side. We look upward, to see whether help will drop into our mouths; and we look downward, to see whether human succours will avail us, Isa. viii. 21, 22; but we look not each inward, to find out "every man the plague of his own heart," that we may be rid of that, 1 Kings viii. 38: and till this be done, sin as naturally draws and sucks judgments to it, as the loadstone does iron, or turpentine fire. Indefatigable have been the pains of this high court, to make up the breaches that threaten us, and to heal the land. Whence comes it that our distractions remain unremoved? Certainly our leaks are not stopped, our sins are not thrown away; we labour at the pump to get the water out, but we do not take care to cure the passage at which it enters in: we are old bottles still, and God will not "put new wine into old bottles," Matt. ix. 17. If men would spend their murmurings and reproaches rather upon their sin than upon their physicians, the work would be sooner done. When the temple of God was to be new built, and a public restitution of the face of things to glory and splendour was in agitation, the prophets call upon God's people then especially to repent, Hag. i. 7; Zech. i. 3. Impenitency puts obstructions to God's mercy, and to all noble enterprises. So long as our lives are as bad as before, how can we expect that our condition should be better? in that case mercies themselves become no mercies; as, in the case of repentance, judgments would be no judgments. If we turn from our evil ways, God has engaged himself by a solemn promise, that he will do us "no hurt," Jer. xxv. 6. Otherwise to busy ourselves in outward ceremonies of repentance, bodily fasting, and verbal praying, is indeed but to flatter God, and, if we could, to deceive him. And God will answer such men not according to the prayer of their lips, but according to the idol of their hearts, Ezek. xiv. 4, 5.

2. This teaches us how to pray against sin. It must be against all, and in all respects. In the Hebrew text there is a kind of unusual transposition of the words, כל־תשא עון the word for "all" is first. Methinks it intimates an intentness of the church upon that point, to have, if it were possible, all sin taken away at the very first. If there be one leak in a ship, one gap in a wall, one gate in a city unprovided for; it is enough to sink a ship, to drown a country, to betray a city. One little boy thrust in at a window, can unlock the door for all the rest of the thieves. It was but one Jonah that raised a tempest, but one Achan that troubled a camp, and one sin generally unrepented of were enough to undo a kingdom. Do not say it is a little one, and my soul shall live. Even the philosopher tells us, that sometimes ἀδικήματα ἐλάχιστα are μεγιστα, the smallest errors prove most dangerous. How little soever it be in its own nature, it becomes heinous by thy allowance. It is as much treason to coin pence as twenty-shilling pieces, because the royal authority is as much violated by the one as the other.

Arist. Rhet. I. 1. Et Polit. lib. 5. cap. 8.

This then we must first and principally remember, to set ourselves against all sin. In confession none to be dissembled, in supplication none to be excepted, in conversion none to be reserved; never give it over so long as any is left. O Lord, yet it works, yet it lives, yet it tempts, yet it pains me. Sin has not done accusing me, let not thy mercy have done forgiving my sin. Sin has not done rebelling in me, let not thy grace have done subduing my sin. When men kill snakes or vipers, so long as they see them pant, or attempt to thrust out a sting, they strike them. Sin, like the thief on the cross, when it is first nailed and kept from its old tyranny, yet will, as much as it can, revile, and spit out venom upon Christ. O, therefore, give it not over, break its legs, crucify it clean through, till it be quite dead. None can pray or turn to God in truth, or hope to be delivered from judgments in mercy so long as he holds fast any known sin. Can any man look to receive benefit by the blood of Christ, who hugs the monster that shed it? Is it not treason knowingly to harbour and entertain a traitor? Whosoever loves and holds fast sin, lies to God in every prayer that he makes.

This serves to reprove and humble us for our hypocrisy and halvings with God in our conversions from sin, and confessions of it: we are willing to pray for the pardon of them all, we would have none hurt us; but when it comes to parting, and taking all away, this we cannot away with. Some are fat, delicate, golden sins; we would fain spare these, as Saul did Agag, and hide them, as Achan did his wedge, 1 Sam. xv. 9; Josh. vii. 21. Herod hears John gladly in many things, but if he restrain him from his Herodias, he must expect to be himself restrained, Mark vi. 20. Agrippa will be almost a Christian, but altogether may chance to bring a chain with it, Acts xxvi. 28. Jehu will down with Baal and his priests, but he knows not how to part with his calves, lest he venture his kingdom, 2 Kings x. 30, 31. Policy is ever entering caveats against piety. Thus men stand bartering with Christ in the bargain of salvation, not considering that the purchase of heaven is like the buying of the sibyl's prophecy, the longer we stand off, the dearer every day it will cost us; the more tears, the harder repentance, the deeper sorrow, the stronger cries. These men know not the price of a soul, nor the worth of a Saviour.

Oh, if Christ should have served us so in dying for sin, as many of us serve him in turning from sin, what a condition had our souls been in! If he had died for some sins, and not for others; if he had been as unwilling to "save" us "to the uttermost," as we are to serve him to the uttermost; if he had stopped before he came to "It is finished," and left any one drop of that bitter cup for us to drink after him, would it not have caused our belly to swell, and our thigh to rot, and made us for ever incapable of any other mercy than only a less damnation? Numb. v. 21.

Well, beloved, Christ expects, that as he died for all sin, so we should die to all. He will be counted "worthy of all acceptation," before he will bestow himself, 1 Tim. i. 15. He will not suffer his blood and his mercy to mingle with sin, or to be a protection to it: he cannot endure mingling of the holy seed with the profane; swearing by the Lord, and swearing by Malcham, Zeph. i. 5; Samaritan services, to be for the Lord in one thing, and for the world and flesh in another, one step straight, and another crooked, 2 Kings xvii. 33; one speech Ashdod, and another Canaan, Neh. xiii. 24; to let our conversation be yea and nay, a mongrel service, In this I will do as you bid me, but in that I will not; like the Jews that would buy Christ's blood with money, but not take the money into the treasury; they were fearful to defile their chests, but not to defile their consciences: this Christ cannot away with. It is dangerous to say with the Pharisee, This I am not, and that I am not, Luke xviii. 11; or with the young man, This and that I have done, and in the mean time to have one thing lacking, to have one door locked up still to keep Christ and salvation from us, Mark x. 20. Whosoever keeps a covetous heart for the world, or a sensual heart for the flesh, or a proud heart for the devil, is unworthy of heaven by his own election, and would not go in thither if the door were wide open: he would not find there any fuel for these lusts, any Nabal, or Cosbi, or Diotrephes, with whom to converse. And surely he that allows himself in any one wickedness is, in God's construction, habitually guilty of all, James ii. 10; Luke xvi. 10; Ezek. xviii. 10—13.

Alternæ inter cupiditatem nostram et pœnitentiam vices sunt. Se[illegible] de Otio Sap. cap. 27. Maximum judicium malæ mentis fluctuatio. Ep. 120. Vir bonus ἀμεταμέλητος. Arist. Ethic. l. 9. cap. 46. τετράγωνος. Id. l. 1. c. 10. μοχθηροὶ τὸ βέβαιον οὐκ ἔχουσιν. Id. l. 8. c. 8.

Qui uno peccavit omnium reus est, peccans contra charitatem in qua pendent omnia. Aug. Epist. 29. Vid. Sen. de Benefic. l. 4. c. 26, 27. l. 5. c. 15.

Therefore in this case, as Samuel said to Jesse, "Are here all thy children?" if any be left "we will not sit down till he come hither," 1 Sam. xvi. 11; so we must conceive in our confessions and renunciations of sin, that Christ asks us, "Are here all?" if any be reserved, I will not take possession till that be cast out: there must not "an hoof" be left in Egypt, if God be to be served, Exod. x. 26. God's law, as well as man's, disallows inmates in the same house: he will not endure "a double heart;" he is "heir of all things," there lies no writ of partition in his inheritance; his title is so good that he will never yield to a composition; he will have all the heart or none, Psal. xii. 2; James i. 8; Psal. cxix. 104, 128.

4. We should therefore be exhorted (in time of trouble especially) to set about this great work, to fall foul of our sins; to complain against them to God, as the Achans that trouble Israel, as the corrupters and betrayers of our peace; to set ourselves in God's eye, and not to dare to lie to his Holy Spirit, by falseness or hypocrisy, as if we could reserve any one sin unmortified which he should not know of; but being in his sight to whom "all things are naked and opened," to deal in all sincerity, and to hate sin even as he hates it, Heb. iv. 13; Gen. xvii. 1; 2 Cor. ii. 17.

"Take away all iniquity." There are five notable duties to which these words lead us.

1. Sense of sin, as "an heavy burden," as the prophet David calls it, Psal. xxxviii. 4. Such sense our Saviour requires in true penitents, "Come unto me, all ye that labour and are heavy leaden," Matt. xi. 28. To conceive them heavier than "a millstone," Luke xvii. 2; than the weight of "mountains," Luke xxiii. 30. What apprehension had Peter's converts of sin, when they felt the nails wherewith they had crucified Christ sticking fast in their own hearts, and piercing their spirits with torment and horror! Acts ii. 37. What apprehensions had the poor jailer of his sins, when he came as a prisoner before his own prisoners, springing in with monstrous amazement and consternation of spirit, beseeching them, "Sirs, what must I do to be saved?" Acts xvi. 29, 30.

Consider it in its nature: a universal bruise and sickness, like those diseases which physicians say are *corruptio totius substantiæ*, unsoundness from head to foot, when "the whole head is sick, and the whole heart faint," Isa. i. 5, 6. And who does not feel such a universal languor to be a heavy burden? For a man that must needs labour, to have weights hung at his hands; that must needs walk, to have clogs fastened to his feet; how can he choose but cry out with the apostle, "O wretched man that I am! who shall deliver me from the body of this death?" Rom. vii. 24.

Consider it in the curse that belongs to it: "A roll" "written within and without" with "lamentations and mourning, and woe," Ezek. ii. 10.

Look outward, and behold a curse in the creature, vanity, emptiness, vexation, disappointment; every creature armed with a sting to revenge its Maker's quarrel.

Look inward, and behold a curse in the conscience, accusing, witnessing, condemning, haling to the tribunal of vengeance; first defiling with the allowance, and after terrifying with the remembrance, of sin.

Look upward, and behold a curse in the heavens, "the wrath of God" "revealed" from thence "against all ungodliness and unrighteousness of men," Rom. i. 18.

Look downward, and behold a curse in the earth; death ready to put a period to all the pleasures of sin, and like a trap-door to let down into hell, where nothing of sin will remain but the worm and the fire.

Look into the Scripture, and see the curse there described; an everlasting banishment from the glory of God's presence; an "everlasting destruction" by "the glory of his power," 2 Thess. i. 9; the Lord showing the jealousy of his justice, the unsearchableness of his severity, the inconceivableness of his strength, the bottomless guilt and malignity of sin, in the "everlasting destruction" of ungodly men, and in their everlasting preservation to feel that destruction. "Who knoweth the power of thine anger?" saith Moses; "even according to thy fear, so is thy wrath," Psal. xc. 11. It is impossible for the most trembling consciences, or the most jealous fears of a guilty heart, to look beyond the wrath of God, or to conceive too highly of it. As in peace of conscience, the mercy of God is revealed to believers "from faith to faith;" so in anguish of conscience, "the wrath of God is revealed" from fear to fear.

Anima in corpore erit non vivendi causâ sed dolendi. Aug. de Civ. Dei, l. 13. c. 2. Prima mors animam nolentem pellit a corpore, secunda nolentem retinet in corpore. Ibid. l. 21. c. 3.

A timorous man can fancy vast and terrible fears, fire, sword, tempests, racks, furnaces, scalding lead, boiling pitch, running bell-metal, and being kept alive in all these to feel their torment. But these come far short of the wrath of God, for, 1. There are bounds set to the hurting power of a creature; the fire can burn, but it cannot drown; the serpent can sting, but he cannot tear in pieces. 2. The fears of the heart are bounded within those narrow apprehensions which itself can frame of the evil which may be done. But the wrath of God proceeds from an infinite justice, and is executed by an omnipotent and unbounded power, comprising all the terror of all other creatures (as the sun doth all other light) eminently and excessively in it. It burns, and drowns, and tears, and stings, and bruises, and consumes, and can make nature feel much more than reason is able to comprehend.

Oh, if we could lay these things seriously to heart, (and yet these are but low expressions of that which cannot be expressed, and come as short of the truth itself as the picture of the sun in a table does of the greatness and brightness of it in its own orb,) should we not find it necessary to cry out, "Take away all iniquity?" this sickness out of my soul; this sword, this nail, this poisoned arrow, out of my heart; this dagger of Ehud out of my belly; this millstone, this mountain, from off my back; these stings and terrors, these flames and furies, out of my conscience? Lord, my wounds stink, my lips quiver, my knees tremble, my belly rots, I am feeble, and broken, and roar, and languish; thy wrath lies hard upon me, and thy waves go over my head.

Oh, if we had but a view of sin as it is in its native foulness, and did feel but a touch of that fury which God is ready to pour out upon it, this would stain all the pride of man, and sour all the pleasures of sin, and make a man as fearful to meddle with it, as a guilty woman with the bitter water which caused the curse, Numb. v. 21. Most true was that which Luther spake in this point; If a man could perfectly see his own evils, the sight thereof would be a perfect hell to him: and to this God will bring wicked men. "I will reprove thee, and set" thy doings "in order before thine eyes," Psal. l. 21. Make them take a view of their own hearts and lives, fuller of sins than the firmament of stars, or a furnace of sparks. "Now consider this, ye that forget God, lest I tear you in pieces, and there be none to deliver."

2. Confession; for he that cries to have sin taken away, acknowledges that it lies upon him. A full confession, not of many, but of all sins, either actually committed, or habitually comprised in our body of sin. As he in the Comœdian said, that he had invited two guests to dinner, Philocrates and Philocrates, a single man, but a double eater; so, in examination of ourselves, we shall every one find sins enough in himself to denominate him a double and a treble sinner. A free confession; not as Pharaoh's, extorted upon the rack, nor as that of Judas, squeezed out with anguish and horror; but ingenuous and penitent, arising from the purpose of a pious heart, that comes like water out of a spring, with a voluntary freeness, not like water out of a still, which is forced with fire.

Athenæus. lib. 1.

3. Weariness and detestation of all sin; for we call not to have a thing removed till we be weary of it. Thus we are taught in the Scripture to be ashamed and confounded, to loathe and abhor, to judge and condemn ourselves, to throw sin away as a detestable thing, though it be a golden or silver sin. A spiritual judgment looks on all sin as filthy and stinking, showeth a man to himself as a vessel full of dung, scum, excrements, and gives him no rest till he be thoroughly purged. For hatred is πρὸς τὰ γένη, against the whole kind of that which we hate, Psal. xiv. 3; xxxviii. 3; Ezek. vi. 9; xvi. 63; Isa. xxx. 22; 1 Cor. xi. 31.

Arist. Rhet.

4. An acknowledgment of our own impotency to remove sin from ourselves. We have no more power than a slave in chains has to get out of his bondage till another ransom him; than a dead body in a grave, till Christ raise it. Our iniquities take hold upon us and keep us down, that we cannot hearken or be subject to the will of God. If sin were not removed by a greater strength than our own, it would most certainly sink us into hell, Psal. xl. 12; Jer. vi. 10; Rom. v. 6, 8; vi. 23; viii. 7; Eph. ii. 1—5; 2 Cor. iii. 5.

5. An imploring of God's mercy and grace, that what we cannot do ourselves, he would be pleased to do for us. In works of art it is hard to build, but easy to destroy. But in works of sin, though our weakness is able to commit them, yet none but God's power is able to demolish them. None but Christ is strong enough to overcome "the strong man," Luke xi. 21. His person only has strength enough to bear the curse of sin; his sacrifice only merit enough to make expiation for sin; his grace only virtue enough to remove its pollution. Though we should take "nitre," and "much soap," our sin would remain "marked," Jer. ii. 22; but he comes "like a refiner's fire, and like fullers' soap," and can wash out all, Mal. iii. 2. His only business in coming into the world was, "that he might destroy the works of the devil," 1 John iii. 8.

Facile est momento, quo quis volet, cedere possessione magnæ fortunæ: facere et parare eam difficile atque arduum. Liv. 2. 24. Corpora lente augescunt, cito extinguuntur. Tacit. Vit. Agric.

Now the things for which we pray in this petition are these three. 1. Remission; that God would take away the condemnation of sin from us, by not imputing the guilt thereof to us, but would cause it to pass over on Christ, on whom he has laid the iniquities of his people, Isa. liii. 6; Rom. iv. 8. Such an expression the Holy Ghost uses, העביר The Lord has caused thy sin to pass over from thee to Christ, 2 Sam. xii. 13; which being obtained, all other judgments are *ipso facto* removed too, so far as they import proper and vindictive punishment.

2. Sanctification; that the virtue of Christ's death, and the grace of his Spirit, may subdue the power of sin, and cleanse and strengthen our consciences against the commands of it, and temptations unto it, Heb. ix. 14; Micah vii. 19.

3. Continued renovation; that as in sanctification begun we have power against all kinds of sin, so by the continual supplies of the Holy Spirit we may have further power against all degrees and remainders of sin. That Christ would purify our sin unto death, as our sin did him, and not give over mortifying it, till his blood be revenged of it to the uttermost, and our souls delivered from it to the uttermost.

I shall conclude the first part of the petition with a short word of exhortation to this honourable assembly. Those things which God works in us and bestows upon us by his grace, he also requires of us by his command: sometimes he promises to turn us, sometimes he commands us to turn to him; sometimes he bids us put away sin, and sometimes he promises to take it away from us, Isa. i. 16; Ezek. xviii. 31; xxxvi. 26; Heb. viii. 10—12; in the one showing us what is our duty, and in the other where is our help. And as this latter consideration calls upon our faith to pray, so the former upon our obedience to work. I shall therefore (right honourables) humbly offer a double exhortation to all of you.

Lex jubet, gratia juvat. Aug. Epist. 95.

First, That every one of you would seriously endeavour to "take away all iniquity" from his own person. And to this there lies upon you a double obligation: one with relation to the safety of your own souls; for whatever other honour, wealth, wisdom, learning, interest a man has besides, if sin have the predominancy, they are but Satan's magazine, and that man his servant, to employ them against God that gave them; and the more mercies wherewith any man has been trusted, the heavier judgment will be poured out upon the breach of that trust. Better be a wooden vessel to hold wine, than a silver vessel to hold excrements; better be a beggar with the treasure of God's grace, than a prince with the load of a man's own sins.

But there is a further tie upon you, with relation to the success of that honourable employment whereunto you are called. *Ita nati estis, ut bona malaque, vestra ad rempublicam pertineant.* God will be sanctified in all those that draw near to him, as well in civil as in sacred administrations. It is very hard for a person in whom sin rules, to be constantly faithful to any public and honourable service; for grace only establishes the heart, Heb. xiii. 9. Ahithophel, a man of great wisdom, falls from David; Joab, a man of great valour, falls from Solomon. And admit he be faithful, yet the sin of his heart sends out a prohibition to the wisdom of his head and the labour of his hand: he that will be a fit vessel for his Master's uses, must first of all "purge himself," 2 Tim. ii. 21; as we first cleanse a vessel before we use it. When Joshua was to negociate a public reformation, and to administer a public service, his "filthy garments" must be taken from him, and he must be clothed with "change of raiment," Zech. iii. 4. Let every one of you make his public service one argument more than he had before for his necessary reformation, and let the piety of your lives bear witness to the integrity of your honourable undertakings.

Tacit. Annal. lib. 4.

Secondly, As you must take away sin from yourselves, so make it your principal work to "take away all iniquity" out of the land. Liberty, property, privileges are sacred and precious things, not to be in the least manner betrayed; yea, in some sense we may look upon them, as the Jews upon their *Massora, tanquam legis et pietatis sepem*, as a fence and mound to religion itself. Arbitrary government would quickly be tampering in sacred things, because corruption in the church is marvellously subservient and advantageous to corruption in the state. But the most orient pearl of this kingdom is our religion, and the bitterest enemies to that are our sins. These are the snuffs that dim our candlestick, and threaten its removal; these the leaven that defile our passovers, and urge God to pass away and depart from us; these the obstructions between his sacred Majesty and you, and between both and the happiness of the kingdom. Think seriously what ways may be most effectual to purge this leaven out of the land. The principal sacrificial knife which kills and mortifies sin, is the knowledge of the word of God. It would have been a great unhappiness to the commonwealth of learning, if Caligula had (as he endeavoured) deprived the world of the writings of Homer, Virgil, and Livy. But oh, what an Egyptian calamity is it to have, in this sunshine of the gospel, thousands of persons and families (as I doubt not but upon inquiry it would appear) without the writings of the prophets and apostles! a Christian soldier without his sword, a Christian builder without his rule and square, a Christian calling without the instruments and balances of the sanctuary belonging to it. Oh that every parish, therefore, had an endowment fit for a learned, laborious, and worthy pastor, and pastors worthy of such endowments, that provision were made that every family might have a Bible in it, and (if by law it might possibly be procured) the exercises of religion therewithal! this would be the surest magazine to secure the happiness of a kingdom: that all reproachful titles, which the devil uses as scarecrows to keep back numbers from pressing in upon Christ's kingdom, were by law proscribed; that scandalous sins were by the awfulness and severity of discipline more blasted and brought to shame; that the Lord's house were more frequented, and his day more sanctified, and his ordinances more reverenced, and his ministers, which "teach the good knowledge of the Lord," more encouraged; in one word, that all the several fountains of the commonwealth were settled in a sound and flourishing constitution: that in every place we might see piety the elm to every other vine, the supporter to every other profession; learning adorned with piety, and law administered with piety, and counsels managed with piety, and trade regulated with piety, and the plough followed with piety: that when ministers fight against sin, with the sword of God's word, you who are the nobles and gentry of the land would second them, and frown upon it too; a frown of yours may sometimes do as much service to Christ, as a sermon of ours; and he cannot but take it very unkindly from you, if you will not bestow your countenance on him who bestowed his blood on you: that you would let the strictness of your lives, and the piety of your examples, put wickedness out of countenance, and make it appear (as indeed it is) a base and a sordid thing.

Sueton. in Calig. cap. 34.

If we would thus, in serious earnest, set ourselves against the sins of the land, no power, no malice, no policies, should stand between us and God's mercies; religion would flourish, and peace would settle, and trade would revive, and the hearts of men would be reunited, and the church be as a city compacted, and this nation would continue to be, as it has been, like the garden of Eden, a mirror of prosperity and happiness to other people; and God would prevent us, in the second part of our petition, with the blessing of goodness; as soon as ever iniquity were removed, he would do us good, which is the second thing here directed to be prayed for.

"And receive us graciously." וקח־טוב And take good, to wit, to bestow upon us; so taking is sometimes used for giving, thus: לקחת מתנות באדם "thou hast *received* gifts for men," Psal. lxviii. 18, is by the apostle rendered καὶ ἔδωκε δόματα τοῖς ἀνθρώποις, "and *gave* gifts unto men," Eph. iv. 8: and it is not improbable that the prophet here secretly leads us to Christ the Mediator, who first receives gifts from his Father, and then pours them forth upon his church, Acts ii. 33.

The meaning then is, Lord, when thou hast pardoned, weakened, mortified sin, go on with thy mercy, and being in Christ graciously reconciled to us, give further evidence of thy fatherly affection, by bestowing portions upon us. They shall not be cast away upon unthankful persons, we will "render the calves of our lips;" they shall not be bestowed upon those that need them not, or that know where else to provide themselves. It is true we have gone to the Assyrian, we have taken our horses instead of our prayers, and gone about to find out good; we have been so foolish as to think that the idols which have been beholden to our hands for any shape that is in them, could be instead of hands and of God unto us, to help us in our need: but now we know that "men of high degree are but a lie," that horses are but "a vain thing for safety," that "an idol is nothing," and therefore can give nothing, Psal. lxii. 9; xxxiii. 17; 1 Cor. viii. 4: that power belongeth unto thee, none else can do it; that mercy belongeth unto thee, none else will do it; therefore since in thee only "the fatherless findeth mercy," be thou pleased to do us good.

We will consider the words, 1. Absolutely, as a single prayer by themselves. 2. Relatively, in their connexion, and with respect to the scope of the place.

1. Absolutely: and from such a consideration of the words we

Obs. 2. All the good we have is from God; he only must be sought unto for it; we have none in ourselves; "I know that in me, that is, in my flesh, dwelleth no good thing," Rom. vii. 18; we can neither think, nor speak, nor do it, Gen. vi. 5; 2 Cor. iii. 5; Matt. xii. 34; Psal. xiv. 3.

And missing it in ourselves, it is in vain to seek for it in things below ourselves.

They can provide for our back and belly, and yet not

even that without God: the root out of which the fruits of the earth grow is above in heaven, the genealogy of corn and wine is resolved into God, Hos. ii. 21, 22. But if you go to your lands, or houses, or treasuries for physic for a sick soul or a guilty conscience, they will all return an ignoramus to that inquiry; salvation does not grow in the furrows of the field, neither are there in the earth to be found any mines or harvests of grace or comfort.

In God alone is "the fountain of life," Psal. xxxvi. 9; he that only "is good," he only "doeth good," Matt. xix. 17; Psal. cxix. 68: when we have wearied ourselves with having recourse to second causes, here at last, like the wandering dove, we must arrive for rest: "There be many that say, Who will show us any good? Lord, lift thou up the light of thy countenance upon us," Psal. iv. 6. From him alone comes "every good and every perfect gift," Jam. i. 17: whether temporal; it is his blessing that makes the creature able to comfort us, Prov. x. 2; Matt. iv. 4; 1 Tim. iv. 4, 5. The woman touched the hem of Christ's garment, but the virtue went not out of the garment, but out of Christ, Luke viii. 44. Or whether spiritual; sanctified faculties, 1 John v. 20; sanctified habits, Eph. ii. 8—10; Col. ii. 11, 12; sanctified motions, Phil. ii. 13; 2 Tim. ii. 25; glorious relations, in predestination, adoption, and Christian liberty, Eph. i. 5, 6; John i. 12; excellent gifts, heavenly comforts, all and only from him, 1 Cor. xii. 6; 2 Cor. i. 3; Rom. xv. 13: and that without change and alteration; he does not do good one while, and evil another, but goodness is his proper and native operation; he is not the author of sin, that entered by the devil; he is not the author of death, that entered by sin; but our destruction is of ourselves, Hos. xiii. 9. And therefore, though the prophet saith, "Shall there be evil in a city, and the Lord hath not done it?" yet he does it not but only as it is *bonum justitiæ*, good in order to his own glory; for it is just with God, that they who run from the order of his commands, should fall under the order of his providence, and doing willingly what he forbids, should unwillingly suffer what he threatens.

Concil. Milevit. can. 3, 4, 5. Concil. Arausic. secund. Aug. de Grat. et lib. Arb. cap. 21.

Vid. Tertul. cont. Marcion, l. 2. c. 14.

In one word, God is the author of all good, by his grace working it; the permitter of all evil, by his patience enduring it; the orderer and disposer of both, by his mercy rewarding the one, by his justice revenging the other, and by his wisdom directing both to the ends of his eternal glory. This serves,

1. To discover the free and sole working of grace in our first conversion, and the continued working of grace in our further sanctification. Whatsoever is good in us habitually, as grace inhering, or actually, as grace working, is from him alone as its author. For though it be certain, that when we will and do ourselves are agents, yet it is still under and from him; *Certum est nos facere cum faciamus, sed ille facit ut faciamus*, as the great champion of grace speaks; by grace we are that we are, we do what we do in God's service. Vessels have no wine, bags have no money in them, but what the merchant puts in: the bowls of the candlesticks had no oil but that which dropped from the olive branches. Things which seek no higher perfection than is to be found within the compass of their own nature, may by the guidance and activity of the same nature attain thereunto; but man, aspiring to a divine happiness, can never attain to it but by a divine strength: impossible it is for any man to enjoy God without God.

Aug. de Grat. Christi, c. 25. cont. 2. Ep. Pelag. l. 4. c. 6. De Perfect. Justitiæ, c. 19.

Aug. de Civ. Dei, l. 12. c. 9.

Aug. lib de Patientia, c. 18.

The truth of this point shows itself in five gradations:

1. By grace our minds are enlightened to know and believe him; for spiritual things "are spiritually discerned," Jer. xxxi. 33; Matt. xi. 27; 1 Cor. ii. 12—14.

Vid. Aug. de Grat. Christ. l. 1. c. 13, 14. et ep. 143.

2. By grace our hearts are inclined to love and obey him; for spiritual things are spiritually approved: he only, by his almighty and ineffable operation, worketh in us, *et veras revelationes, et bonas voluntates*, both right perceptions and good desires, Jer. xxxii. 39; John vi. 44.

Aug. de Grat. Christi, c. 24.

3. By grace our lives are enabled to work what our hearts love; without which, though we should will, yet we cannot perform, no more than the knife which has a good edge is able actually to cut, till moved by the hand, Rom. vii. 18; Phil. ii. 13; Heb. xiii. 20, 21.

4. By grace our good works are carried on to perfection. Adam, wanting the grace of perseverance, fell from innocency itself. It is not sufficient for us that he prevent and excite us to will, that he co-operate and assist us to work, except he continually follow and supply us with a residue of spirit to perfect and finish what we set about. All our works are begun, continued, and ended in him, 1 Thess. v. 23; 1 Pet. v. 10; Jude 24; John xvii. 15.

Vid. Aug. Enchirid. c. 32. De Grat. et lib. Arb. c. 6, et 17. Peto ut accipiam, et cum accepero rursus peto. Hieron. ad Ctesiphont.

Lastly, by grace our perseverance is crowned; for our best works could not endure the trial of justice, if God should enter into judgment with us, Psal. cxliii. 2; Isa. lxiv. 6. Grace enables us to work, and grace rewards us for working; grace begins and grace finishes both our faith and salvation, Phil. i. 6; Heb. xii. 2. The work of holiness is nothing but grace, and the reward of holiness is nothing but grace for grace.

2. To teach us how to know good from evil in ourselves. What we look on as good, we must see how we have derived it from God; the more recourse we have had to God by prayer, and faith, and study of his will, in the procurement of it, the more goodness we shall find in it. A thing done may be good in the substance of the work, and yet evil in the manner of doing it; as the substance of a vessel may be silver, but the use sordid. Jehu's zeal was rewarded as an act of justice, *quoad substantiam operis*, and it was punished too as an act of policy, *quoad modum*, for the perverse end, 2 Kings x. 30; Hos. i. 4. A thing which I see in the night may shine, and that shining proceed from nothing but rottenness. We must not measure ourselves by the matter of things done; for there may be *malum opus in bonâ materiâ*. Doeg prays, 1 Sam. xxi. 7, and Herod hears, Mark vi. 20, and hypocrites fast, Isa. lviii. 3; Matt. vi. 16, and Pharisees preach, Matt. xxiii. 2, 3; but when we would know the goodness of our works, look to the fountain, whether they proceed from the Father of lights, by the Spirit of love, and the grace of Christ, from humble, penitent, filial, heavenly dispositions: nothing will carry the soul unto God, but that which comes from him. Our communion with the Father and the Son, is the trial and foundation of all our goodness.

Rebus ad ima tendentibus in imo ponitur fundamentum; ecclesia vero in imo posita tendit in cœlum, fundamentum ergo nostrum ibi positum est. Aug. Enarrat. 1. in Psal. xxix.

3. To abase us in our own eyes, and stain all the pride and cast down all the plumes of flesh and blood, when we seriously consider that in us, as now degenerated from our original, there is no good to be found. Our "silver is become dross," our "wine mixed with water," Isa. i. 22. As our Saviour saith of the devil, "When he speaketh a lie, he speaketh" ἐκ τῶν ἰδίων, "of his own," John viii. 44; so when we do evil we work of our own, and κατὰ ἄνθρωπον, "as men," as the apostle speaks, 1 Cor. iii. 3. Our lusts are our own, James i. 14; our very members are of that body of sin which the apostle calls the "old man," with which it is as impossible to do any good, as for a toad to spit cordials, Rom. vii. 23; Col. iii. 5; Eph. iv. 22.

Men are apt to glory in their good hearts and intentions, only because they cannot search them, Jer. xvii. 9; and being carnal themselves, to entertain none but carnal notions of God's service. But if they knew the purity and jealousy of God, and their own impotency to answer so holy a will, they would lay their hands upon their mouths, and with Job "abhor themselves," Job xlii. 5, 6; and with Isaiah, bewail the uncleanness of their lips, Isa. vi. 5; and with Moses, fear and quake, as not being able "to endure that which was commanded," Heb. xii. 20; and with Joshua, acknowledge that they "cannot serve the Lord, for he is an holy God," Josh. xxiv. 19: they would then remember that the law of God is "a fiery law," Deut. xxxiii. 2, and the tribunal of God, a tribunal of fire, Ezek. i. 26—28; that the pleadings of God with sinners are "by fire and by his sword," and "his rebuke with flames of fire," Isa. lxvi. 15, 16; that the trial of all our works shall be "by fire," 1 Cor. iii. 13; that the God before whom we must appear is "a consuming fire," Heb. xii. 29. Go now and bring thy straw and stubble, thy drowsy and sluggish devotion, thy fickle and flattering repentance, thy formal and demure services, into the fire, to the law to measure them, to the Judge to censure them; nay, now carry them to thine own conscience, and tell me whether that will not pass the Father's verdict upon them. That which is fair in thine eye is filthy in God's.

Sordet in conspectu judicis, quod fulget in conspectu operantis. Greg.

4. For exhortation to these particular duties. 1. To patience and meekness under any evil that God may bring upon us; and that not barely because he does us good in other things, which was Job's argument, "What? shall we receive good at the hand of God, and shall we not receive evil?" Job ii. 10; but further, because the very evils that come upon us are oftentimes by him intended for good, as Joseph told his brethren, Gen. l. 20. We are not angry with the physician when he lances, diets, and restrains us of our will: he denies us our will, that we may have our will; a sick man is many times most faithfully served when he is crossed. I lop my trees, bruise my grapes, grind my corn, to fit it to the ends whereunto it tends. God's end is merciful when his hand is heavy. As John's roll was sweet in the mouth, but bitter in the belly, Rev. x. 10; so troubles may be bitter to the palate, but profitable to the conscience; like hot spices, that bite the tongue, but comfort the stomach, Isa. xxvii. 9; xlviii. 10; Heb. xii. 11.

Medicina etiam invitis prodest. Sen. ep. 98.
Quæ per insuavitatem medentur, emolumento curationis offensam sui excusant, et presentem injuriam superventuræ utilitatis gratia commendant. Tertul. de Pœnit. cap. 10.

And as it dictates patience in suffering evil, so in doing our duties, though we suffer contempt and reproaches for it. If we were to receive our rewards from men, their frowns might discourage us; but when we have done God's will, God himself will be our reward, and make his promises our comfort. Moses and Aaron, though their whole employments were for the good of Israel, were yet repaid with murmuring and discontent, and the people, like children, *qui cibum sumunt, sed flentes*, (to use the similitude of the orator in Aristotle,) repined at the food which their prayers obtained for them; yet nothing dismayed them from their duty. *Etiam post naufragium tentantur maria.* The woman of Canaan prays on when she is denied, and Jacob holds with his hands when his thigh is lamed. Our first care must be to be in our way, to be doing our duties, and then, though (as Solomon speaks) we should meet a lion in our way, we must not be dismayed; for angels are stronger than lions, and he has given "his angels charge over" us, "to keep" us "in all" our "ways," Psal. xci. 11. Yea, whilst we are with him, he is with us, 2 Chron. xv. 1.

Quisquis volens detrahit famæ meæ, nolens addit mercedi meæ. August. cont. literas Petiliani, lib. 3. cap. 7.

Rhetor. l. 3. c. 4.

Sen. ep. 81.

2 S

So that the way of the Lord is the surest and safest way for any man to walk in: "The way of the Lord is strength to the upright," Prov. x. 29.

2. To humility. If thou be a vessel of gold, and thy brother but of wood, be not high-minded, it is God that makes thee to differ; the more bounty God shows, the more humility he requires, 1 Cor. iv. 7; Rom. xi. 20. Those mines that are richest are deepest; those stars that are highest seem smallest; the goodliest buildings have the lowest foundations: the more God honours men, the more they should humble themselves; the more the fruit, the lower the branch on which it grows: pride is ever the companion of emptiness. Oh how full was the apostle, yet how low was his language of himself! "less than the least of all saints," "last" of apostles, "chief of sinners," no sufficiency to think, no abilities to do; all that he is, he is by grace: thus humility teaches us in our operations to draw strength from God, not from ourselves; in our graces to ascribe their goodness to God, and their weakness to ourselves, Eph. iii. 8; 1 Cor. xv. 8; 2 Cor. iii. 5; 1 Tim. i. 15; Rom. vii. 18.

Opulentissima metalla quorum in alto latent venæ. Sen. ep. 23.
Altissima flumina minimo sono labuntur. Q. Curt. l. 7.

3. To dependence and continual recourse to God, as the fountain of all good; to keep an open and an unobstructed passage between him and our soul. Say not, I have light enough in my house, I may now shut up my windows, for light within has dependence on immediate supplies from the sun without, and so has grace upon continual supplies from "the Sun of righteousness." God teaches even the husbandman to plough and thresh, Isa. xxviii. 26; in these things his direction is to be implored: meddle not then with great and high affairs without recourse to him; his name is Counsellor, and his testimonies are counsellors, let them be the rule and square of all your debates, Isa. ix. 6; Psal. cxix. 24. It is recorded for the honour of Scipio, that he went first to the Capitol, and then to the senate. But you have more noble examples. David is put to flight, he flees and prays, 2 Sam. xv. 26, 31; Hezekiah is at a stand in all his counsels, he sends to the prophet and prays, Isa. xlvii. 3, 4, 15; Jehoshaphat is in great distress, and knows not what in the world to do, but he prays, 2 Chron. xx. 6; Nehemiah is sore afraid, and hath a petition to make to the king, but first he makes one to God, and prays, Neh. ii. 3, 4. Whenever the children are come to the birth, and there is no strength to bring forth, all the world cannot furnish you with such another midwife as prayer, and recourse to God; it has delivered even graves of their dead. Therefore let me beseech you, whenever you meet with such difficulties as put you to a stand, that you know not what to advise or resolve upon, go to your closets, prostrate yourselves at His throne, whose honour it is to be seen in the mount; beg counsel of him "in whom are hid all the treasures of wisdom and knowledge." Let it appear that you seek his face to direct you, and his glory as the supreme end and design of all your consultations; and then try whether he be not a present help in trouble, and whether he will not magnify the wisdom of his counsel in the perplexity of yours.

Vid. Aug. de Grat. et lib. Arb. cap. 8.

Liv. lib. 26. A. Gel. l. 7. l. Valer. Max. l. 1. c. 2.

4. To fidelity, in the use of any good which God bestows upon us; for God gives not talents to men barely to enrich men, but to employ them: therefore as the vessel has one passage to let the wine into itself, and another to pour it out into the flagon; so we should not only fill ourselves by dependence upon God, but should supply ouselves by love and service to our brethren.

Right Honourables, this nation has put into your hands all that is outwardly dear to them, their persons, posterities, liberties, estates. In these sad and woeful distractions they look upon you as binders, and healers, and standers in the gap, and repairers of the waste places. God has called you to a high and a great trust; and the sad distempers of the church and state, the distresses and desolations of Ireland, the doubts, and fears, and convulsions of England, and in these two kingdoms the interest of all the protestant churches, call to you, like the man of Macedonia, in St. Paul's vision, "Come—and help us," Acts xvi. 9. Now in this great strait, when the children are come to the birth and there is no strength to bring forth, stir up the graces of God in you, call together all that is within you to call upon his name, improve the uttermost of your interests in him for the state of his church, manage every one of his gifts to the closing of those miserable breaches which threaten an inundation of calamity upon us all; wisdom, and learning, and piety, and prudence, are healing things. Remember (and oh that God would put into the hearts of this whole kingdom, from the throne to the plough, to remember) the fate of a divided kingdom from the mouth of truth itself. Oh that we would all remember, that misunderstandings, and jealousies, and divisions of heart, are a high evidence of God's displeasure, and that "through the wrath of the Lord of hosts is" a "land darkened," and, as it were, infatuated, when Manasseh is against Ephraim, and Ephraim against Manasseh, and every man eateth "the flesh of his own arm," Isa. ix. 19—21. Oh let us all remember what it cost Shechem and Abimelech, Judg. ix.; what it cost Benjamin, and the other tribes, even the loss of threescore and five thousand men, Judg. xx.: remember Priam and his children will laugh, Babylon will clap their hands, and wag their head; no such time for Shishak, the Egyptian, to trouble Jerusalem, as when Israel is divided, 2 Chron. xii. 2. Let it never be said of God's own people, that they are fallen into the curse of Midianites, and Ammonites, and Edomites, and Philistines, to help forward the destruction of one another. Oh that God would give this whole nation hearts to consider these things, that he would put a spirit of peace and resolved unity into their minds, to be true to their own happiness, and by how much the greater are the subtleties of men to divide them, to be so much the more firmly united in prayers to God, and in concord between themselves; that they may not expose their persons, estates, posterity, and (which is dearest of all) their religion, to the crafty and bloody advantages of the enemies of the protestant churches, who in human view could have no way to overthrow them, but by their own dissensions!

Ἦ κεν γηθήσαι Πρίαμος, Πριάμοιό τε παῖδες, Ἄλλοι τε Τρῶες μέγα κεν κεχαροίατο θυμῷ. Hom. Il. 1. 255.

Having thus spoken at large of the words of the prayer considered absolutely, we shall proceed to view them,

2. Relatively, in the scope and connexion of the prayer suggested to the judgment threatened. And here we would

Obs. 3. When temporal judgments are felt or feared, God's people should pray for spiritual mercies; human sorrows cannot overcome where the joy of the Lord is our strength. Thus the Lord seems to have taught his apostle; he was under some pressing discomfort, the messenger of Satan sent to buffet him, he prays for particular deliverance, and God answers him *non ad voluntatem sed ad utilitatem*, implying a direction to all such prayers, "My grace is sufficient for thee," 2 Cor. xii. 9. When thou feelest a thorn in thy flesh, pray for grace in thy heart; the buffets of Satan cannot hurt where the grace of God does suffice. So he directs us in time of plague and famine, to pray, and to seek his face, 2 Chron. vii. 14; to look more after his favour than our own ease; to be more solicitous for the recovery of his love than for the removal of his rod. This is a true character of a filial disposition. "In the way of thy judgments," even in that way wherein wicked men fling thee off, and give thee over, and quarrel with thee, and repine against thee, even "in the way of thy judgments have we waited for thee, and the desire of our soul is" more "to thy name" than to our own deliverance, Isa. xxvi. 8. True disciples follow Christ more for his doctrine than his loaves, and are willing to choose rather affliction than iniquity, John vi. 26.

Bonus qui non tribuit quod volumus, ut tribuat quod malimus. Aug. ep. 34.

The grace and favour of God is "life," Psal. xxx. 5, "better than life," Psal. lxiii. 3, and therefore must needs be the most sovereign antidote to preserve and to bear up the soul above all other discomforts; whereas if he be angry, no other helps are able to relieve us. Brass and iron can fence me against a bullet or a sword, but if I were to be cast into a furnace of fire, it would help to torment me, if into a pit of water, it would help to sink me. Now our God is "a consuming fire," Heb. xii. 29, and his "breath like a stream of brimstone," Isa. xxx. 33. Human plasters can never cure the wounds which God makes; where he is the smiter, he must be the healer too, Hos. vi. 1. All the candles in a country are not able to make day there, till the sun come; and all the contents of the world are not able to make comfort to the soul, till "the Sun of righteousness arise with healing in his wings." In a mine, if a damp come, it is in vain to trust to your lights, they will burn blue and dim, and at last vanish; you must make haste to be drawn upward if you will be safe. When God sharpens an affliction with his displeasure, it is vain to trust to worldly succours; your desires and affections must be on "things above," if you will be relieved. There is no remedy, no refuge from God's anger, but to God's grace. Blood-letting is a cure for bleeding, and a burn a cure for a burn; and running in to God is the way to escape him, as to close and get in with him that would strike you is the way to avoid the blow. In a tempest at sea, it is very dangerous to strike to the shore, the safest way is to have sea room, and to keep in the main still: there is no landing against any tempest of God's judgments at any shore of worldly or carnal policies, but the way is to keep with him still; if he be with us in the ship, the winds and the sea will at last be rebuked.

Calores caloribus onerando deprimimus et sanguinis fluxum defusa insuper venula revocamus. Tertul.

This then should serve to humble us for our carnal prayers in times of judgment, such as the hungry raven, or the dry and gaping earth, makes; when we "assemble" ourselves "for corn and wine," for peace and safety, and be in the mean time careless whether or no God receive us graciously. God much complains of it when he slew Israel; the rack made him roar, the rod made him flatter, but all was to be rid of affliction; it was the prayer of nature for ease, not of the spirit for grace, for "their heart was not right," Psal. lxxviii. 34—37. The like he complains of after the captivity: they fasted and prayed in the fifth month, (wherein the city and temple had been burned,) and in the seventh month, (wherein Gedeliah had been slain, and the remnant carried captive,) but they did it not out of sincerity toward God, but out of policy for themselves; and this he proves by their behaviour after their return. If you had indeed sought me, you would have remembered the words of the prophets when Jerusalem was inhabited before, and being returned, would now have put them to practice; but Jerusalem inhabited after the captivity is just like Jerusalem inhabited before the captivity: so that from hence it appears, that all their weeping and separating was not for pious, but politic reasons, Zech. vii. 4—7. And there is nothing under heaven more hateful, or more reproachful to God, than to make religion serve turns, to have piety lackey and dance attendance, and be a drudge and groom to private ends, to make it a cloak to policy, a varnish to rotten wood.

O then, when we weep and separate ourselves, let us not think to mock God with empty ceremonies of repentance, let us not assemble ourselves only to flatter away the rod from our back, and to get peace and security to our own persons, and then let the favour of God, the power of his grace, the comforts of his Spirit, be as unregarded as before; (as if we fasted and prayed only for our backs and bellies, not for our consciences or conversations;) for be we well assured, he who does not ask the things which he ought, shall not obtain the things which he asks: such a prayer begs nothing but a denial.

We have now many fasts together, we have prayed for making up our breaches, for repairing our ruins, for composing our distractions, for reducing this kingdom to a happy constitution, for a right understanding between the king and his great council. These prayers we have not found yet return, like Noah's dove, with an olive branch, a gracious answer to us again. What is the reason? Where is the obstruction? Is not he a God that heareth prayers? Is it not his title? Does he not glory in it? Certainly mercies stop not at God, but at us. We are not straitened in him, but straitened in our own bowels. If there come but a little light into a room, the defect is not in the sun, but in the narrowness of the window. If a vessel fill but slowly, the fault is not any emptiness in the fountain, but the smallness of the pipe. If mercies ripen slowly, or stop at any time in the way, it is not because they are unwilling to come to us, but because we are unfit to enjoy them. Our prayers, doubtless, in many cases, have not been words taken from the revealed mind of God, but from our carnal dictates.

We would fain have things well in our country, but have we hitherto looked after our consciences? The distractions without us, have they driven us to consider the distempers within, or to desire the things above? The unsettledness of peace in the kingdom, has it awakened us to secure our peace with God? We would fain have better times, but have we yet laboured for better hearts? we would fain have a right understanding between the king and his great council, but have we yet seriously set about having a more clear and sweet communion between us and our God? we long to see more good laws, but are we yet come to care for good lives? Every one cries out, "Who will show us any good?" but how few think on "the light of God's countenance!"

Hence, beloved, is the miscarriage of all our prayers. If we would "seek first the kingdom of God," we are promised other things by way of overplus and accession, as he that buys a treasury of jewels has the cabinet into the bargain. But when we place our kingdom in outward comforts, and let our "daily bread" shut all the other five petitions out of our prayers, no wonder if "the promise of this life," which is annexed to godliness, answers not those prayers wherein godliness is neglected. It were preposterous to begin the building of a house at the roof and not at the foundation. *Piety is the foundation of prosperity.* If you would have your sons as plants, and your daughters as polished corner-stones, your garners full, your cattle plenteous, no complaining in your streets, Psal. cxliv. 12—14; if you would have the king happy, and the church and the state happy, and peace and prosperity flourish again; let our chief prayer be, Lord, make us a happy people by being our God. Give us thyself, thy grace, thy favour, give us renewed hearts and reformed lives; let not our sins confute, and outcry, and belie our prayers, and pray them back again without an answer. And when we seek thee and thy Christ above all, we know that thou wilt "with him also freely give us all things." The spiritual good things which we beg, will either remove, or shelter and defend us from, the outward evil things which we suffer.

Quicquid mihi præter illum est, dulce non est: quicquid mihi vult dare Dominus meus, auferat totum, et se mihi det. Aug. Enarrat. 2. in Psal. xxvi.

Further, this serves for an instruction to us touching a sanctified use of God's judgments, or threatenings. When we learn obedience (as Christ did) by the things which we suffer, Heb. v. 8; when παθηματα are μαθηματα, that we are chastened and taught together, Psal. xciv. 12; when sufferings quicken spiritual desires, and the more troubles we find in our way, the more love we have to our country; when we can say, "All this is come upon us, and yet have we not forgotten thee," Psal. xliv. 17, 18; when we can serve God as well in ploughing and breaking the clods, as in treading out the corn, Hos. x. 11; when with Jonah we can delight in him even in the whale's belly, and suffer not our love of him to be quenched with all the waters of the sea; when we can truly say to him, Lord, love me, and then do what thou wilt unto me, let me feel thy rod rather than forfeit thine affection; when we can look through the anger of his chastisements to the beauty of his commands and to the sweetness of his loving countenance, as by a rainbow we see the beautiful image of the sun's light in the midst of a dark and waterish cloud; when by how much the flesh is the fuller of pain, by so much prayers are fuller of spirit; by how much the heavier are our earthly sufferings, by so much the stronger are our heavenly desires: when God threatens punishments, and we pray for grace, this is a sanctified use of God's judgments. And this we should all be exhorted to in the times of distraction, to make it the principal argument of our prayers and study of our lives, to obtain spiritual good things; and the less comfort we find in the world to be the more importunate for the comforts of God, that by them we may encourage ourselves, as David did in his calamity at Ziklag, 1 Sam. xxx. 6. When the city Shechem was beaten down to the ground, then the men and women fled to the strong tower and shut that upon them, Judg. ix. 51. "The name of the Lord is a strong tower: the righteous runneth into it, and is safe," Prov. xviii. 10. By thus striving for a sanctified use of God's judgments we shall,

1. More honour God, when we set him up in our hearts as our fear and treasure, and mourn more towards him than for the miseries we feel, and suspire more after him than all the outward contentment which we want.

2. More exercise repentance; for it is "the sorrow of the world" which droops under the pain of the flesh, but "godly sorrow" is most of all affected with the anger of God.

3. More prevail with God. The more heavenly the subjects of our prayer are, the more prevalent they must needs be with a heavenly Father; we have five spiritual petitions to the one for bread. The more suitable our prayers are to God's will, the more easy access they will have to his ear. The covenant of grace turns precepts into promises, and the spirit of grace turns precepts and promises into prayers. It is not God's will that we should live without afflictions, but our sanctification is God's will, 1 Thess. iv. 3. The more prayers proceed from love, the more acceptable to the God of love: now prayer against judgments proceeds from fear, but prayer for grace and favour proceeds from love.

4. Hereby we shall more benefit ourselves. God's grace is much better than our own ease; it gives us meekness to submit, it gives us strength to bear, it gives us wisdom to benefit by our afflictions.

God's favour is much better than our own ease, and is a recompence for sufferings beyond all their evils. A man would be contented to be loaded with gold, so he might have it for the bearing, though it be heavy, yet it is precious; and God's favour turns affliction into gold. If he give quietness, nothing can give trouble, Job xxxiv. 29; and if he keep back his grace and favour, nothing can give peace; neither wealth, nor honours, nor pleasures, nor crowns, nor all the world, with the fulness, or rather the emptiness, thereof, none of them can do us any good. Any thing which will consist with the reign of lust, with the guilt of sin, with the curse of the law, with the wrath of God, with horrors of conscience, and with the damnation of hell, is too base to be called the good of man. "To do justly, and to love mercy, and to walk humbly with thy God," this is *bonum hominis*, the good of man, Micah iv. 8; to "fear God, and keep his commandments," this is *totum hominis*, the whole end and happiness of man, Eccl. xii. 13.

O then get remission and removal of sin, get this *bonum hominis*, the oil of grace in your lamps, the peace of God in your hearts, the streams of the river of God in your consciences; and then, though the earth be moved, and the mountains shake, and the waters roar, whatever distractions, whatever desolations happen, *impavidum ferient ruinæ;* thou shalt find a chamber in God's providence, a refuge in his promises, a pavilion in the secret of his presence, to protect and to comfort thee above them all.

Ver. 2, 3. —*So will we render the calves of our lips. Asshur shall not save us; we will not ride upon horses: neither will we say any more to the work of our hands, Ye are our gods: for in thee the fatherless findeth mercy.*

In the whole context we have before observed two general parts, Israel's prayer, and Israel's promise. The prayer we have handled, and now proceed to,

II. The promise, wherein are two things to be considered: 1. The covenant itself. 2. The ground upon which they make it, God's mercy to the fatherless. First, then, of the covenant, wherein they promise two things: 1. Thanksgiving for God's hearing and answering of their prayers. 2. A speeial care for amendment of their lives.

"So will we render the calves of our lips." פרים שפתינו The apostle out of the Septuagint reads this, *καρπὸν χειλέων*, "the fruit of our lips," Heb. xiii. 15. It is the use of the Scripture to describe spiritual duties by expressions drawn from ceremonies and usages under the law; as repentance is called washing, Isa. i. 16; and prayer, "incense," Psal. cxli. 2; Rev. v. 8; and the righteousness of saints, "fine linen," in allusion to the garments of the priests, Rev. xix. 8; and Christ, "an altar," whereby both our persons and services are sanctified and accepted, Heb. xiii. 10; Rom. xii. 1; 1 Pet. ii. 5; Isa. lvi. 7. Thus here, the spiritual sacrifices of praise are called "calves," to show the end of all sacrifices, which were ordained for the stirring up of spiritual affections and praises to God, and also to intimate the vanity of ceremonial without real services. The beast on the altar was but a carnal, but the faith of the heart and the confession of the mouth was a reasonable, sacrifice. No point more insisted on in the prophets than this, Isa. i. 15; Micah vi. 6—8; Amos iv. 4, 5; v. 21; Psal. l. 13—15; lxix. 30—36. They had idolatrously dishonoured God with their calves of Dan and Beth-el, and they had carnally and superstitiously placed all worship and holiness in the calves of the altar; but now they resolve to worship God neither politicly, after human inventions, nor perfunctorily, with mere outward ceremonies, but spiritually, and from inward affections; for the lips are moved by the heart.

Habemus altare, viz. corpus Christi. Hesych. in Levit. lib. 8. cap. 4.

Vid. Tertul. contr. Judæos. cap. 5, 6. et de Oratione, cap. 1. Aug. de Civ. Dei, lib. 10. cap. 5. et Epist. 49.

Now, thanksgiving is further called "the calves" or sacrifices "of our lips," to intimate, that after all God's rich mercies to us, in pardoning our sins, and in multiplying to us his grace and spiritual comforts, we, like beggars, have nothing to return but the bare acknowledgments and praises of our lips, words for wonders: and those words, too, his own gifts; we cannot render them to him before we have received them from him. Psal. cxvi. 12, 13; Matt. xii. 34; 1 Chron. xxix. 16.

"Asshur shall not save us." To the general confession of sin intimated in those words, "Take away all iniquity," there is added here a particular detestation of their special sins, with a covenant to forsake them, lest waxing wanton with pardon and grace, they should relapse into them again. The sum is to confess the vanity of carnal confidence, betaking itself to the aid of men, to the strength of horses, to the superstition of idols for safety and deliverance. All which they are now at last, by their experience and by their repentance, taught to abandon, as things which indeed cannot, and therefore they are resolved shall not, save them.

By the Assyrian is here intimated all human succour procured by sinful correspondence, by a synecdoche of the part for the whole. But he is particularly mentioned, 1. Because he was the chief monarch of the world, to show that the greatest worldly succours are vain, when they are relied upon without, or against, God. 2. Because the Scripture takes notice often of it as their particular sin, the sending unto, relying upon, and paying him tribute for aid and assistance, Hos. v. 13; vii. 11, 12; 2 Kings xv. 19, 20. 3. Because instead of helping, he did greatly afflict them. Their flying to him was like a bird's flying into a snare, or a fish's avoiding the pole wherewith the water is troubled, by swimming into the net, 2 Kings xv. 29; Hos. xiii. 4.

"We will not ride upon horses." By "horses" we are to understand the military preparations and provisions which they made for themselves, both at home and from Egypt, 2 Chron. i. 16; Isa. xxxi. 1.

"Neither will we say any more to the work of our hands, Ye are our gods." By "the work of" their "hands" are meant their idols, which were indebted to their hands for any shape or beauty that was in them. The same hands which formed them were afterwards lifted up in worship to them, Isa. xliv. 10, 17; xlvi. 6—8; Jer. x. 3, 15; Acts xix. 26. Time was when we said, "These be thy gods, O Israel, which brought thee up out of the land of Egypt," Exod. xxxii. 4; 1 Kings xii. 28; but now we will not say so any more, for how can a man be the maker of his Maker?

"For in thee the fatherless findeth mercy." This is the ground of their petition for pardon and grace, and of their promise of praises and amendment, God's mercy in hearing the prayers, and in enabling the performances, of his people. It is a metaphor drawn from orphans in their minority, who are, 1. Destitute of wisdom and abilities to help themselves. 2. Exposed to violence and injuries. 3. Committed for that reason to the care of tutors and guardians to govern and protect them. The church here acknowledges herself an outcast, destitute of all wisdom and strength within, of all succour and support from without, and therefore betakes herself solely to God's tuition, whose mercy can and is wont to help when all other help fails.

This is the last link of that golden chain of repentance, made up of these gradations: 1. A humble address unto God. 2. A penitent confession of sin. 3. An earnest petition against it. 4. An imploring of grace and favour. 5. Thanksgiving for so great benefits. 6. A covenant of new obedience. And, lastly, A confidence and quiet repose in God.

Let us now consider what useful observations the words thus opened will afford. As we see that after they have petitioned for pardon and grace, they then restipulate and undertake to perform duties of thankfulness and obedience, we would, in general,

Obs. 4. True penitents, in their conversion from sin, and humiliation for it, not only pray to God for mercy, but moreover covenant to express the fruits of those mercies in a thankful and obedient conversation. When first we are admitted into the family and household of God, we enter into a covenant. Therefore circumcision, whereby the children of the Jews were first sealed and separated for God, is called "my" God's "covenant," Gen. xvii. 4, because therein God did covenant to own them, and they did in the figure covenant to mortify lust, and to serve him, without which they were in his sight but uncircumcised still. "Behold, the days come, saith the Lord, that I will punish all them which are circumcised with the uncircumcised," על-כל-מול בערלה upon all that are circumcised in uncircumcision, Jer. ix. 25. The nations joined in the following verse with Judah, who are said to be uncircumcised, did yet use circumcision, as the learned have observed; but being out of covenant with God, it is accounted to them as uncircumcision, and so was that of the Jews too when they broke covenant with God, Rom. ii. 28, 29; Acts vii. 51. And as the Gentiles being converted are called Jews, and said to be born in Zion, Psal. lxxxvii. 4, 5; Gal. vi. 16; 1 Cor. xii. 13; so the Jews living impenitently are called Gentiles, Canaanites, Amorites, Hittites, Ethiopians, Sodomites, Ezek. xvi. 3; Hos. xii. 7; Amos ix. 7; Isa. i. 10. In like manner baptism among Christians is called by the apostle συνειδήσεως ἀγαθῆς ἐπερώτημα εἰς Θεὸν, which the learned interpret the answer, or covenant, of keeping a good conscience towards God, 1 Pet. iii. 21. Ἐπερώτημα, a question or interrogation, which some would have to be the conscience making interpellation for itself to God; others, to be as much as δοκιμασία, the examining of a man's self, like that before the Lord's supper, 1 Cor. xi. 28. I rather take it as an allusion to the manner of John's baptism, wherein the people first confessed, and consequently renounced, sin; and being taken into Christ's service, or into that kingdom of God which was at hand, inquired what work they were to do. And we find the same word in Luke iii. 10, "And the people" ἐπηρώτων αὐτὸν, "asked him, saying, What shall we do then?" whereby is intimated, an engaging of themselves by a solemn promise and undertaking to the practice of that repentance unto which John baptized them. * Whence arose that grave form of the ancient churches, wherein questions were proposed to the person baptized touching his faith and repentance, renouncing the world, the flesh, and the devil, with a solemn answer and stipulation obliging thereunto. Which custom seems to have been derived from the practice used in the apostles' time, wherein profession of faith unfeigned, and sincere repentance, was made before baptism, Acts ii. 38; viii. 37; xvi. 33; xix. 4. This is the first dedicating of ourselves, and entering into a covenant with God, which we may call, in the prophet's expression, the subscribing, or giving a man's name to God, Isa. xliv. 5.

Visitabo super omnes populos incircumcisos. Versio Chald. Ἐπισκέψομαι ἐπὶ πάντας περιτετμημένους ἀκροβυστίας αὐτῶν. Septuag.

Herodot. l. 2. Artabanus apud Euseb. de Præparat. Evang. l. 9. c. 27. Orig. in Rom. l. 2. cap. 2.

Cameron. de Eccles. p. 34. Nec hoc novum Scripturis figrate uti translatione nominum, ex comparatione criminum, &c. Tertul. contr. Judæos, c. 8. et cont. Marcion, l. 3. c. 8.

Now the covenant between us and God being perpetual, "a covenant of salt," Jer. xxxii. 40; 2 Chron. xiii. 5. As we are to begin it in our baptism, so we are to continue it to our lives' end, and upon all fit occasions to repeat and renew it for our further quickening and remembrancing unto duties. So did David, Psal. cxix. 106; so Jacob, Gen. xxviii. 20—22; so Asa and the people in his time, 2 Chron. xv. 12, 13; so Hezekiah, 2 Chron. xxix. 10; xxx. 5, 23; so Josiah, 2 Chron. xxxiv. 31, 32; so Ezra and Nehemiah, Ezra x. 3; Neh. ix. 38.

De pacto salis, vid. Paul. Fagi. in Levit. ii. et Pererium in Gen. xix. 16, 17, 26. Stuck. Antiquit. Con. xiv. l. 1. c. 30. Sal duraturæ amicitiæ symbolum, Pier. lib. 31.

The reasons enforcing this duty may be drawn from several considerations.

1. From God in Christ, where two strong obligations occur; 1. His dealing with us. 2. Our relation to him.

1. His dealing with us. He is pleased not only to enter into covenant with us, but to bind himself to the performance of what he promises. Though whatever he bestow upon us is all matter of mere and most free grace, wherein he is no debtor to us at all, yet he is pleased to bind himself to acts of grace. Men love to have all their works of favour free, and to reserve to themselves a power of alteration or revocation. But God is pleased that his gifts should take upon them in some sense the † condition of debts; and although he can owe nothing to the creature, yet he is content to be a debtor to his own promise; and having at first in mercy made it, his truth is often engaged to the performance of it, Rom. xi. 35; Job xxii. 3; xxxv. 7, 8; Micah vii. 20.

Further, his word is established in heaven; with him there is no variableness, nor shadow of change; his promises are not yea and nay, but in Christ Amen, 2 Cor. i. 20; if he speak a thing it shall not fail, Josh. xxi. 45. He spake and the world was made; his word alone is a foundation and bottom to the being of all his creatures: and yet, notwithstanding the immutable certainty of his promises, when they are first uttered, for our sakes he is pleased to bind himself by further ties; free mercy secured by a covenant, and a firm covenant secured by an oath, Deut. vii. 12; Luke i. 72, 73; Heb. vi. 17, 18; that we, who, like Gideon, are apt to call for sign upon sign, and to stagger and be disheartened if we have not double security from God, we, whose doubting calls for promise upon promise, as our ignorance does for "precept upon precept," may, by "two immutable things, in which it was impossible for God to lie—have a strong consolation." Now if God, whose gifts are free, bind himself to bestow them by his promise; if God, whose promises are sure, bind himself to perform them by his oath; how much more are we bound to tie ourselves by covenant to God, to do those things which are our duty to do, unto the doing whereof we have such infirm principles as a mutable will and an unstedfast heart.

Quid est Dei veri veracisque juratio nisi promissi confirmatio, et infidelium quædam increpatio? Aug. de Civ. Dei, lib. 16. cap. 32.

2. Our relation to him. We are his, not only by a property founded in his sovereign power and dominion over us, as our Maker, Lord, and Saviour, Psal. c. 3; 1 Cor. vi. 19, 20; but by a property growing out of our own

* Aug. lib. de Fide et Operibus c. 9. Tertul. ad Mart. c. 2, et 3. et de Coron. Milit. c. 3, et 13. de Habitu. Mulieb. c. 2. de Spectacul. c. 24. et lib. de Idolatria. Apol. c. 38. Interrogatio legitima et Ecclesiastica. Firmilian. apud Cyprian. ep. 75. et ib. ep. 70, et 76.

† Dignaris eis, quibus omnia debita dimittis, etiam promissionibus tuis debitor fieri. Aug. Conf. l. 5. c. 9. Non ei aliquid dedimus, et tenemus debitorem. Unde debitorem? quia promissor est. Non dicimus Deo, Domine redde quod accepisti, sed redde quod promisisti. Aug. in Psal. xxxii. Cum promissum Dei redditur justitia Dei dicitur. Justitia enim Dei est quia redditum est quod promissum est. Ambros. in Rom. iii. Justum est ut reddat quod debet. Debet autem quod pollicitus est. Et hæc est justitia de qua præsumit apostolus promissio Dei. Bern. de Grat. et lib. Arbit. Licet Deus debitum alicui det, non tamen est ipse debitor, quia ipse ad alia non ordinatur, sed potius alia ad ipsum, et ideo justitia quandoque dicitur in Deo condecentia suæ bonitatis. Aquin. part 1. qu. 21. art. 1. Nulla alia in Deo justitia nisi ad se quasi ad alterum, ut sibi ipsi debitum reddat secundum condecentiam bonitatis, et rectitudinem voluntatis suæ. Scotus 4. dist. 46. qu. 1.

voluntary consent, whereby we surrender, and yield, and give up ourselves unto God, Rom. vi. 19; 2 Cor. viii. 4. We are not only his people, but his willing people, by the intervention of our own consent, Psal. cx. 3. We give him our hand; תנו־יד ליהוה give your hand unto the Lord, "yield yourselves unto the Lord," 2 Chron. xxx. 8, an allusion to the manner of covenants or engagements, Prov. vi. 1; xvii. 18; Ezek. xvii. 18. We offer up ourselves as a free oblation, Rom. xv. 16, and are thereupon called "a kind of first-fruits," James i. 18. We are his, as the wife is her husband's, Hos. ii. 19; Ezek. xvi. 8. Now such an interest as this ever presupposes a contract. As in ancient forms of stipulation there was asking and answering: *Spondes? Spondeo. Promittis? Promitto. Dabis? Dabo.* As in contract of marriage, the mutual consent is asked and given, Gen. xxiv. 58; so it is here between God and the soul, the covenant is mutual, Gen. xvii. 2. He promises mercy, to be our "exceeding great reward," and we promise obedience, to be his "willing people;" and usually according as is the proportion of strength in our faith to believe God's promises of mercy to us, such is also the proportion of care in our obedience to perform our promises of duty to him.

Junge ergo manus, et concipe fœdus. Statius.
Heus! ubi pacta fides, commissaque dextera dextræ? Ovid.

2. From ourselves. And here covenants are needful in two respects. 1. In regard of the falseness and deceitfulness of our corrupt hearts in all spiritual duties. The more cunning a sophister is to evade an argument, the more close and pressing we frame it; the more vigilant a prisoner to make an escape, the stronger guard we keep upon him. Our hearts are exceeding apt to be false with God. One while they melt into promises and resolutions of obedience, as Pharaoh and Israel did, Psal. lxxviii. 34—37, and presently forget and harden again. Lot's wife goes out of Sodom for fear of the judgments, but quickly looks back again out of love to the place, or some other curiosity and distemper of mind. Saul relents towards David, and quickly after persecutes him again, 1 Sam. xxiv. 16—20; xxvi. 1, 2. This is the true picture of man's heart, under a strong conviction, or in a pang of devotion, or in time either of sickness, or some pressing affliction, on the rack, in the furnace, under the rod, nothing then but vows of better obedience; all which do oftentimes suddenly vanish as "the early dew," and wither away like Jonah's gourd. Therefore, both to acknowledge and prevent this miserable perfidiousness of such revolting hearts, it is very needful to bind them to God with renewed covenants; and since they are so apt with Jonah to run away and start aside, to neglect Nineveh and to flee to Tarshish, necessary it is to find them out and to bring them home, and, as David did, to fix and fasten them to their business, Psal. lvii. 7.

Inversâ occasione ebullire saniem quæ latebat in ulcere, et excisam non extirpatam arborem in sylvam pullulare videas densiorem. Bern. Serm. 2. in Assum. Mar.

2. In regard of the sluggishness to duty natural to us. We are apt to faint and be weary when we meet with any unexpected difficulties in God's service, to esteem the wilderness as bad as Egypt; to sit down as Hagar did, and cry, to think that half way to heaven is far enough, and almost a Christian progress enough; that baking on one side will make the cake good enough; that God will accept of bankrupt payment, a noble in the pound, part of our hearts and duties for all. Now, to correct this torpor, this ὀλιγοψυχία, as the apostle calls it, 1 Thess. v. 14, this pusillanimity, and faint-heartedness in God's service, we must bind it on ourselves with renewed covenants, and put to the more strength because of the bluntness of the iron, Eccl. x. 10. A covenant does as it were twist the cords of the law, and double the precept upon the soul; when it is only a precept, then God alone commands it, but when I have made it a promise, then I command it and bind it upon myself. The more feeble our hands and knees are, the more care we should have to bind and strengthen them, that we may lift them up speedily, and keep them straight, Heb. xii. 12, 13; and the way to effect it is to come to David's resolution, "I am purposed that my mouth shall not transgress," Psal. xvii. 3. Mere empty desires will not keep weak faculties together; broken bones must have strong bands to close them fast again; a crazy piece of building must be cramped with iron bars to keep it from tottering: so if we would indeed "cleave unto the Lord," we must bring "purpose of heart," even strong resolutions, Acts xi. 23. Cleaving will call for swearing, Deut. x. 20. As it should be our prayer, so also our purpose, to have hearts united to fear God's name, Psal. lxxxvi. 11; whence the phrases of preparing, fixing, confirming, establishing, rooting, grounding, and other like, so frequently occurring in the Scripture, 2 Chron. xxx. 19; 1 Chron. xxix. 18; Eph. iii. 17; Heb. xiii. 9; James v. 8.

3. From regard to our brethren, that by a holy association and spiritual confederacy in heavenly resolutions, every man's example may quicken his brother, and so duties be performed with more vigour and fervency, and return with the greater blessings. If fire be in a whole pile of wood, every stick will burn the brighter, even the greenest wood will take fire in so general a flame. Men usually have more courage in the body of an army, where concurrent shoutings and encouragements do, as it were, infuse mutual spirits into one another, than when they are alone by themselves. David rejoiced in but recounting the companies and armies of God's people when they went up to Jerusalem in their solemn feasts, Psal. lxxxiv. 7. And therefore most covenants in Scripture were general and public, solemnly entered into by a great body of people, as that of Asa, Josiah, and Nehemiah, the forwardness of every man whetting the zeal of his neighbour, Prov. xxvii. 17.

4. From the multitudes, strength, vigilance, malice, assiduous attempts of all our spiritual enemies, which call upon us for the stronger and more united resolutions. For common adversaries usually gain more by our faintness, and divisions, than by their own strength.* Therefore soldiers use to take an oath of fidelity towards their country and service. And † Hannibal's father made him take a solemn oath to maintain perpetual hostility with Rome. Such an ‡ oath have all Christ's soldiers taken; and at the Lord's supper, and in solemn humiliations, they virtually renew the same, never to hold intelligence or correspondence with any of his enemies.

The first thing in a Christian man's armour mentioned by the apostle, Eph. vi. 14, is the § girdle, that which binds on all the other armour, (for so we read of girding on armour, Judg. xviii. 11; 1 Kings xx. 11,) and that girdle is truth. Which we may understand either doctrinally, for stedfastness and stability of judgment in the doctrine of Christ which we profess, not being "carried about with every wind of doctrine," but "holding fast the form of sound words," "knowing

* Μήτε ἀπολειψειν τὰ σημεία, μητε ἀλλο πραξειν μηδεν ἐναντίον τῷ δημῳ. Dionys. Halicarn. l. 10. Ποιήσειν τὸ προσταττόμενον ὑπερ των ἀρχόντων κατὰ δυναμιν. Polyb. l. 6. Præmia nunc alia atque alia emolumenta notemus sacramentorum. Juv. Sat. 16. Lips. de Milit. Rom. l. 1. Dial. 6.

† Liv. lib. 35. Appian. in Iberico et Lybico. Polyb. l. 3.

‡ Vid. Tertul. de Coron. Milit. c. 11.

§ Cingere est militare, apud Plaut. Et stare distinctum, erat pœnæ militatis genus. Sueton. Suidæ ζώννυσθαι est καθοπλιζεσθαι, et Ζώνη, δυναμις, unde dicitur Deus balteum regum dissolvere. Job xii. 18.

whom we believe," and the certainty of those things wherein we have been instructed, Eph. iv. 14; 2 Tim. i. 12, 13; Luke i. 4; or else morally and practically, for stedfastness of heart in the faithful discharge of those promises which we have made unto God, (for so faithfulness is compared to a girdle, Isa. xi. 5,) whereby we are preserved from shrinking and tergiversation, in times of trial and in our spiritual warfare. And this faithfulness, the more it is in solemn covenants renewed, the stronger it must needs be, and the better able to bind all our other arms upon us. Christ's enemies will enter into covenants and combinations against him and his church, Psal. ii. 1, 2; lxiv. 5, 6; lxxxiii. 5—8; Acts xxiii. 12; Jer. xi. 9; and our* own lusts within us will many times draw from us oaths and obligations to fulfil them, and make them *vincula iniquitatis*, contrary to the nature of an oath, 1 Kings xix. 2; Mark vi. 23: how much more careful should we be to bind ourselves to God, that our resolutions may be the stronger and more united against so many and confederate enemies!

This point serves, I. For a just reproof of those who are so far from entering into covenant with God, that indeed they make covenants with Satan his greatest enemy, and do in their conversations as it were abuse those promises, and blot out that subscription, and tear off that seal of solemn profession which they had so often set unto the covenant of obedience; such as those in the prophet's time, who had "made a covenant with death, and with hell" were "at agreement," Isa. xxviii. 15. Men are apt to think that none but witches are in covenant with the devil, because such are in the Scripture said to be "consulters with familiar spirits," Deut. xviii. 11; but, as Samuel said to Saul, "Rebellion is as the sin of witchcraft," 1 Sam. xv. 23, every stubborn and presumptuous sinner has so much of witchcraft in him, as to hold a kind of spiritual compact with the devil. We read of the serpent and his seed, Gen. iii. 15; of the dragon and his soldiers, Rev. xii. 7; of some sinners being of the devil, animated by his principles, and actuated by his will and commands, 1 John iii. 8; 2 Tim. ii. 26. Satan tempting, and sinners embracing and admitting the temptation upon the inducements suggested, has in it the resemblance of a covenant or compact. There are mutual agreements and promises, as between master and servant, one requiring work to be done, and the other expecting wages to be paid for the doing of it; as in buying and selling, one bargains to have a commodity, and the other to have a price proportionate. Thus we read in some places of the service of sin, John viii. 34; Rom. vi. 16; 2 Pet. ii. 19; and in others, of the wages belonging to that service, Heb. xi. 25; 2 Pet. ii. 15; Jude 11; and elsewhere of the covenant bargain and sale for the mutual securing of the service and of the wages, 1 Kings xxi. 25. Wicked men sell themselves, bargain and grant away their time, and strength, and wit, and abilities, to be at the will and disposal of Satan, for such profits, pleasures, honours, advantages, as are laid in their way to allure them; and thus do they as it were with cords bind themselves to sin, Prov. v. 22. Ahab bought Naboth's vineyard of the devil, and sold himself for the price in that purchase. Balaam, against the light of his own conscience, and the many discoveries of God's dislike, never gives over his endeavours to curse God's people till he had drawn them into a snare by the Midianitish woman, and all to this end, that he might at last overtake the wages of iniquity which he ran so greedily after, Numb. xxii. 21; xxiii. 1, 14, 29; xxxi. 16; Jude 11; Micah vi. 5; Rev. ii. 14; 2 Pet. ii. 15. Jezebel binds herself by an oath to murder, 1 Kings xix. 2. Judas makes a bargain for his Master's blood, and at once sells a soul and a Saviour, for so base a price as thirty pieces of silver, Matt. xxvi. 15. Profane Esau makes merchandise of his birthright, whereunto belonged the inheritance, or double portion, the princely power, and the office of priesthood, the blessing, the excellency, and the government, Gen. xlix. 3; 2 Chron. xxi. 3; all which he parts with for one morsel of meat, Heb. xii. 16; being therein a type of all those profane wretches, who deride the ways of godliness and promises of salvation, drowning themselves in sensual delights, and esteeming heaven and hell, salvation and perdition, but as the vain notions of melancholy men, having no other God but their belly, or their gain, Phil. iii. 19; 1 Tim. vi. 5.

Alterius esse non possunt nisi diaboli, quæ Dei non sunt. Tert. de Idolol. cap. 18. et de Habit. Mulieb. c. 8. de Cultu Fœmin. cap. 5.

Mane piger stertis, surge, inquit avaritia, eja surge, negas, instat, surge, inquit; non queo, surge. Pers. Satyr. 5.

So much monstrous wickedness is there in the hearts of men, that they add spurs and whips to a horse which of himself rusheth into the battle. When the tide of their own lusts, the stream and current of their own headstrong and impetuous affections, do carry them too swiftly before, they yet hoist up sail, and, as it were, spread open their hearts to the winds of temptation, precipitating and urging on their natural lusts by voluntary engagements; tying themselves yet faster to misery than Adam by his fall had tied them, and making themselves, not by nature only, but by compact, "the children of wrath." One makes beforehand a bargain for drunkenness, another contrives a meeting for uncleanness, a third enters into a combination for robbery and cozenage, a fourth makes an oath of revenge and malice; like Ananias and Sapphira, they agree together to tempt the Spirit of the Lord, Acts v. 9. Like Samson's foxes, they join together with firebrands to set the souls of one another on fire, as if they had not title enough to hell except they bargained for it anew, and bound themselves, as it were, by solemn obligations, not to part with it again.

Oh that every presumptuous sinner, who thus sells himself to do wickedly, would seriously consider those sad encumbrances which go along with this his purchase. Those who would have estates to continue in such or such a succession, as they themselves had pre-intended, have sometimes charged curses and execrations upon those who should alienate, or go about to alter the property and condition of them. These many times are causeless curses, and do not come. But if any man *will* make bargains with Satan, and *will* buy the pleasures of sin, he must know that there goes a curse from heaven along with such a purchase, which will make it at the last but a γλυκύπικρον, a sweet bitter, like John's roll, which was sweet in the mouth, but bitter in the belly, Rev. x. 10; like Claudius's mushroom, pleasant, but poisonous; that will blast all the pleasures of sin, and turn all the wages of iniquity in *aurum tholosanum*, into such gold as ever brought destruction to its owners. It is said of Cn. Seius, that he had a goodly horse, which had all the required perfections of stature, feature, colour, strength, proportion, comeliness, but withal this misery ever attended it, that whosoever became its owner was sure to die an unhappy death. This is the misery that always accompanies the bargain of sin; how pleasant, how profitable, how advantageous soever it may seem to be to flesh and blood, it has always calamity in the end, it ever expires in a miserable death. Honey is very sweet, but it turns into the bitterest choler. The valley of Sodom was one of the

Infusum delectabili cibo boletorum venenum. Tacit. Annal. lib. 12.

Vid. A. Gell. lib. 3. cap. 9.

Omnia illic seu fortia, seu honesta, seu sonora, seu canora, seu subtilia proinde habe ac si stillicidia mellis de libacunculo venenato, nec tanti gulam facias voluptatis quanti periculum. Tertul. ibid.

* Καὶ τους γε πρώτους αὐτῶν καὶ δυνατωτάτους ἐς ἀθέμιτων ὁρκωμοσιῶν ἀνάγκην προσηγαγε, παῖδα γαρ τινα καταθύσας, καὶ ἐπὶ τῶν σπλάγχνων αὐτου τὰ ὅρκια ποιήσας, ἔπειτα ἐσπλαγχνευσεν αὐτὰ μετὰ τῶν ἄλλων. Dion. de Catilina, l. 37. Inter cætera vid. Euseb. Hist. Eccles. l. 6. c. 8.

most delightful places in the world, but is now become a dead and a standing lake. Let the life of a wicked man run on never so fluently, it has a *mare mortuum*, a dead sea, as its termination. O, then, when thou art making a covenant with sin, say to thy soul as Boaz said to his kinsman, Ruth iv. 5, 6, At what time thou buyest it, thou must have Ruth the Moabitess with it; if thou wilt have the pleasures, the rewards, the wages of iniquity, thou must also have the curse and damnation that is entailed upon it; and let thy soul answer, as did the kinsman, No, I may not do it, I shall mar and spoil a better inheritance.

II. This may serve for an instruction to us touching the duties of solemn humiliation and repentance. We must not think we have done enough when we have made general acknowledgments and confessions of sin, and begged pardon and grace from God; but we must withal further bind ourselves fast to God by engagements of new obedience, as holy men in the Scripture have done in their more solemn addresses to God, Neh. ix. 38; Psal. li. 12—15; for without amendment of life prayers are but howlings and abominations, Hos. vii. 14; Prov. xxviii. 9. *Quantum a præceptis, tantum ab auribus Dei longe sumus.* No obedience, no audience. A beast will roar when he is beaten; but men, when God punishes, should not only cry, but covenant.

Tertul. de Orat. cap. 10.

To the performance whereof, that we may the better apply ourselves, let us a little consider the nature of a religious covenant. A covenant is a mutual stipulation, or a giving and receiving of faith between two parties, whereby they do unanimously agree in one inviolable sentence, or resolution. Such a covenant there is between God and true believers, he giving himself as a reward to them, and they giving themselves as servants to him. He willing and requiring the service, and they willing and consenting to the reward; he promising to be their God, and they to be his people, Heb. viii. 10. A remarkable form of joint and mutual stipulation we have, Deut. xxvi. 17—19, "Thou hast avouched the Lord this day to be thy God, and to walk in his ways, and to keep his statutes, and his commandments, and his judgments, and to hearken unto his voice: and the Lord hath avouched thee this day to be his peculiar people, as he hath promised thee, and that thou shouldest keep all his commandments; and to make thee high above all nations which he hath made, in praise, and in name, and in honour; and that thou mayest be an holy people unto the Lord thy God, as he hath spoken." Where we have both the mutual expressions of intimate relation one to another, and the mutual engagements to universal obedience on the one side, and to high and precious benefits on the other, growing out of that relation. For, because God is mine, I am bound to serve him; and, because I am his, he has bound himself to provide for me. There are two parts of the covenant: 1. That which consists in God's promise to be our God, which, in general, imports thus much, God's giving himself in Christ to us, and, together with Christ, all other good things. Benefits relative, in justification from sin, and adoption to sons. Benefits habitual, a new nature by regeneration, a new heart and life by sanctification, a quiet conscience by peace and comfort. Benefits temporal, in the promises of this life. Benefits eternal, in the glory of the next. Thus is Christ made of God to us wisdom, in our vocation, converting us to faith in him; righteousness, in our justification, reconciling us to his Father; sanctification, in our conformity to him in grace; and redemption, from all evils or enemies which might hate us here, and unto all glory which may fill and everlastingly satisfy us hereafter, 1 Cor. i. 30. This part of the covenant we are not now to consider, but, 2. That part of the covenant which concerns our engagement to God, wherein we promise both ourselves and our abilities to him, to be his people and to do him service.

Duorum pluriumve in idem placitum consensus. Ulpian. L. 1. ff. de pactis unde mutua ex fide data et accepta oritur obligatio.

The material cause of this covenant is whatsoever may be promised to God; and that is, 1. Our persons. 2. Our service.

1. Our persons. "We are thine," Isa. lxiii. 19. Giving our own selves to the Lord, 2 Cor. viii. 5; not esteeming ourselves our own, but his that bought us, 1 Cor. vi. 19, 20; and being willing that he who bought us should have the property in us, and the possession of us, and the dominion over us, and the liberty to do what he pleases with us;* being contented to be lost to ourselves, that we may be found in him, Phil. iii. 9. If sin or Satan call for our tongue, or heart, or hand, or eye, to answer, These are not mine own, Christ has bought them, the Lord has set them apart for himself, Psal. iv. 3; they are vessels "meet for the master's use," 2 Tim. ii. 21; I am but the steward of myself, and may not dispose of my Master's goods without, much less against, his will and commands.

2. Our services; which are, 1. Matters of necessity; 2. Matters of expediency; and, 3. Matters of praise. All which may be made the materials of a covenant.†

1. Matter of duty and necessity. As David by an oath binds himself to keep God's righteous judgments, Psal. cxix. 106. And the people in Nehemiah's time enter into a curse and an oath to walk in God's law, and to observe and do all his commandments, Neh. x. 29.

2. Matter of circumstantial expediency, which, in Christian wisdom, may be conducive to the main end of a man's life, or may fit him for any special condition to which God calls him. So the Rechabites promised their father Jonadab, and held that promise obligatory in the sight of God, not to drink wine, nor to build houses, &c., Jer. xxxv. 6, 7; because by that voluntary hardship of life they should be the better fitted to bear that captivity which was to come upon them; or because thereby they should the better express the condition of strangers amongst God's people, upon whose outward comforts they would not seem too much to encroach, that it might appear that they did not incorporate with them for mere secular, but for spiritual, benefits. It was lawful for Paul to have received wages and rewards for his work in the gospel as well of the churches of Achaia, as of Macedonia and others, as he proves, 1 Cor. ix. 4, 14; yet he seems upon the case of expediency, that he might "cut off occasion from them, which" desired "occasion," and might the better promote the gospel, to bind himself by an oath, (for so much these words, "As the truth of Christ is in me," do import, as the learned have observed,) never to be burdensome in that kind to those churches, 2 Cor. xi. 7—12. Lawful things, when inexpedient and gravaminous, may be forborne by the bond of a covenant.

3. Matter of thanksgiving and praise to God; in which case it was usual to make, and to pay, vows. "What shall I render unto the Lord for all his benefits toward me?" saith David; "I will take the cup of salvation," (as the use of the Jews was in their feasts and sacrifices of thanksgiving, Luke xxii. 17,) "I will pay

* Socrati cum multa multi pro suis facultatibus offerrent, Æschines, pauper auditor, nihil, inquit, dignum te quod dare tibi possim invenio, et hoc uno modo pauperem me esse sentio, itaque dono tibi quod unum habeo, meipsum. Seneca de Benef. lib. i. cap. 8.

† Sunt quædam quæ etiam non volentes debemus: quædam etiam quæ nisi voverimus non debemus, sed postquam ea Deo promittimus necessario ea reddere constringimur. Aug.

my vows unto the Lord." Whereby it appears that godly men, when they prayed for mercies, did, likewise, by vows and covenants bind themselves to return tribute of praise in some particular kind or other, upon their prayers being heard, Psal. cxvi. 12—14; cxxiii. 2, 3: so Jacob did, Gen. xxviii. 22; so Jephthah, Judg. xi. 30, 31; so Hannah, 1 Sam. i. 11, 27, 28; so Hezekiah, Isa. xxxviii. 20; so Jonah, chap. ii. 9; and so Zaccheus, to testify his thankfulness to Christ for his conversion, and to testify his thorough mortification of covetousness, which had been his master-sin, did not only out of duty make restitution where he had done wrong, but out of bounty engaged himself to give the half of his goods to the poor, Luke xix. 8.

The formal cause of a covenant is the plighting of our fidelity and engaging of our truth to God in that particular which is the matter of our covenant. Which is done two ways; either by a simple promise and stipulation, as that of Zaccheus; or in a more solemn way, by the intervention of an oath, or curse, or subscription, as in the case of Nehemiah and the people, Neh. ix.

The efficient cause is the person entering into the covenant; in whom these things are to concur:

1. A clear knowledge, and deliberate weighing of the matter promised, because error, deception, or ignorance, are contrary to the formal notion of that consent, which in every covenant is intrinsical and necessary thereunto. *Non videtur consentire qui errat.*

2. A free and willing concurrence. *In omni pacto intercedit actio spontanea*, and so in every promise. Not but that authority may impose oaths, and those as well promissory as assertory, Gen. xxiv. 3; 1 Kings ii. 42; Ezra x. 3, 5; as Josiah made a covenant and caused the people to stand to it, 2 Chron. xxxiv. 31, 32. But that the matter of it, though imposed, should be such in the nature of the thing as that it may be taken in judgment and righteousness, that so the person may not be hampered in any such hesitancy of conscience as will not consist with a pious, spontaneous, and voluntary concurrence.

3. A power to make the promise, and bind oneself by it. For a man may have power to make a promise which is not finally obligatory, but upon supposition; as a woman might for her own part vow, and by that vow was bound up as to herself, but this bond was but conditional, as to efficacy and influence upon the effect, to wit, if her husband heard it and held his peace, Numb. xxx. 3, 4, 14.

4. A power, having made the promise, to perform it. And this depends on the nature of the thing; which must be, first, possible, for *impossibilium nulla est obligatio.* No man can bind himself to things impossible. And next, lawful, in regard either of the necessity, or expediency, or some other allowableness in the thing. For *turpe est jure impossibile*, we can do nothing but that which we can do rightfully. Sinful things are in construction of law impossible, and so can induce no obligation. A servant can make no promise to the dishonour or disservice of his master; nor a child or pupil, contrary to the will of his parent or guardian; nor a Christian, to the dishonour or against the will of Christ whom he serves. In every such sinful engagement there is intrinsically *dolus, error, deceptio*, the heart is blinded by the deceitfulness of lust, Eph. iv. 18, 22; Heb. iii. 13; 2 Pet. i. 9; 2 Cor. xi. 3. And these things are destructive to the nature of such an action as must be deliberate and spontaneous. Promises of this kind bind to nothing but repentance.

Impia promissio est quæ scelere adimpletur. Juramentum non est vinculum iniquitatis. Vid. Caus. 22. qu. 4. Præstare fateor posse me fidem si scelere careat, interdum scelus est fides. Senec.

From these considerations we may learn what to judge of the promises which many men make of doing service to God.

1. Some join in covenants as the greatest part of that tumultuous concourse of people, who made an uproar against the apostle, were gathered together, they "knew not wherefore," Acts xix. 32. Such do not understand the things which they promise; as if a man should set his hand and seal to an obligation, and not know its contents or conditions. Such are all ignorant Christians, who have often renewed their covenant of new obedience and faith in Christ, and yet know not what the faith of Christ is, or what is the purity, spirituality, and comprehensiveness of that law to which they have sworn. As the apostle saith of the Jews, If they had known they would not have crucified the Lord of glory; we may say of many of these, If they knew the purity and holiness of those things which they have vowed to keep, they either would not have entered into covenant with God at all, or would be more conscientious and vigilant in their observation of it. It is a sign of a man desperately careless, to run daily into debt, and never so much as remember or consider what he owes. If there were no other obligation to tie men to the knowledge of God's will, this alone were sufficient, that they have undertaken to serve him, and therefore by their own covenants are bound to know him. For surely many men who have promised repentance from dead works, if they did indeed consider what that repentance is, and to what a strict and narrow way of walking it confines them, would go nigh, if they durst, to plead an error in the contract, and to profess that they had not thought their obligation had had engaged them to so severe and rigid a service, and so repent of their repentance. But in this case, ignorance of what a man ought to know, cannot void the covenant which he is bound to make, and, having made, to keep; but his covenant exceedingly aggravates his ignorance.

Qui per delictorum pœnitentiam instituerat Domino satisfacere, diabolo per aliam pœnitentiæ pœnitentiam satisfaciet, eritque tanto magis perosus Deo quanto æmulo ejus acceptus. Tertul. de Pœnitent. c. 5.

2. Some make many fair promises of obedience, but it is on the rack, and in the furnace, or as scholars under the rod. Oh if I might but recover this sickness, or be eased of this affliction, I would then be a new man, and redeem my mispent time. And yet many of these, like Pharaoh, when they have any respite, find out ways to shift and elude their own promises, and, like melted metal taken out of the furnace, return again to their former hardness. So a good divine observes of the people of this land in the time of the great sweat in king Edward's days, (I wish we could find even so much in these days of calamity on which we are fallen,) as long as the heat of the plague lasted, there was crying out of, We have sinned; mercy, good Lord, mercy, mercy. Then people of the highest rank cried out to the ministers, For God's sake tell us what shall we do to avoid the wrath of God. Take these bags, pay so much to such a one whom I deceived, so much restore to another whom in bargaining I overreached, give so much to the poor, so much to pious uses. But after the sickness was over, they were just the same as they were before. Thus in times of trouble men are apt to make many prayers and covenants, to cry to God, "Arise, and save us," Jer. ii. 27. "Deliver us only, we pray thee, this day," Judg. x. 15. They inquire early after God, and flatter him with their lips, and own him as their God, and Rock of salvation, and presently start aside like a deceitful bow. As Austin notes, that in times of calamity the very heathen would flock to the Christian churches to be safe amongst them. And when the Lord sent lions amongst the Samaritans, then they sent to inquire after "the manner of the God of the land," 2 Kings xvii. 25, 26. Thus many men's covenants are founded only in terrors of conscience. They throw out their sins as a merchant at

Quos vides petulanter et procaciter insultare servis Christi sunt in iis plurimi qui illum interitum clademque non evasissent, nisi servos Christi se esse finxissent. De Civ. Dei, l. 1. c. 1.

sea his rich commodities in a tempest, but in a calm wish for them again. Neither do they throw away the property over them, but only the dangerous possession of them. This is not a full, cheerful, and voluntary action, but only a languid and inconstant velleity; contrary to that largeness of heart and fixed disposition which Christ's own people bring to his service, as David and the nobles of Israel offered willingly and with joy unto the Lord, 1 Chron. xxix. 17.

3. Since a covenant presupposes a power in him that makes it, both over his own will, and over the matter, thing, or action which he promises, so far as to be enabled to make the promise; and since we of ourselves have neither will, nor deed, nor sufficiency, either to think or to perform, Rom. vii. 18; 2 Cor. iii. 5; Phil. ii. 13. We hence learn, in all the covenants which we make, not to do it in any confidence in our own strength, or in any self-dependence on our own hearts, which are false and deceitful, and may, after a confident undertaking, use us as Peter's used him; but still to have our eyes on the aid and help of God's grace, to use our covenants as means the better to stir up God's graces in us, and our prayers to him for further supplies of it. As David, "I will keep thy statutes;" but then, "O forsake me not utterly," Psal. cxix. 8. Our promises of duty must ever be supported by God's promises of grace; when we have undertaken to serve him, we must remember to pray as Hezekiah did, "O Lord, I am oppressed; undertake for me," Isa. xxxviii. 14. Our good works cannot come forth from us, till God first of all work them in us, Isa. xxvi. 12. He must perform his promises of grace to us, before we can ours of service unto him. Nothing of ours can go to heaven except we first receive it from heaven. We are able to do nothing but in and by "Christ which strengtheneth" us, John xv. 5; Phil. iv. 13. So that every religious covenant which we make has indeed a double obligation in it; an obligation to the duty promised, that we may stir up ourselves to perform it; and an obligation to prayer, and recourse to God, that he would furnish us with grace to perform it: as he that has bound himself to pay a debt, and has no money of his own to do it, is constrained to betake himself to supplications that he may procure the money of some other friend.

4. The final cause of a covenant is to induce an obligation where was none before, or else to double and strengthen it where one was before, to be *vinculum conservandæ fidei*, a bond to preserve truth and fidelity. Being subject to many temptations, and having backsliding and revolting hearts, apt, if they be not kept up to service, to draw back from it, therefore we use ourselves as men do cowardly soldiers, set them there where they must fight, and shall not be able to run away, or fall off from service.

Obligatio est juris vinculum quo necessitate astringimur alicujus solvendæ rei. Instit. lib. 3. T. 14. Vid. Gregorium. Tholos. de Repub. lib. 8. cap. 8.

III. This should serve to humble us on a twofold consideration:

1. Of the falseness and unstedfastness of our hearts, which want such covenants to bind them, and, as it were, fasten them to the altar with cords: as men put locks and fetters upon wild horses, whom otherwise no enclosure would shut in. Our hearts, as Jacob said of Reuben, Gen. xlix. 4, are "unstable as water;" "weak," as the prophet calls them. * Moist bodies (as water is) *non continentur suis terminis*, do not set bounds to themselves, as solid and compacted bodies do, but shed all abroad, if left to themselves; the way to keep them united together is to put them into a close vessel: so the heart of man can set itself no bounds, but falls all asunder, and out of frame, εἰς ἀνάχυσιν, as the apostle's expression is, 1 Pet. iv. 4, if it be not fastened and bound together by such strong resolutions. Sometimes men, either by the power of the word, or by the sharpness of some affliction, are quickened and inflamed to pious purposes, like green wood which blazes while the bellows are blowing; and now they think they have their hearts sure, and shall continue them in a good frame, to-morrow shall be as this day. But presently, like an instrument in change of weather, they are out of tune again, and, like the chameleon, presently change colour; and, as Chrysostom saith, the preacher, of all workmen, seldom finds his work as he left it. Nothing but the grace of God balances and establishes the heart, and holy covenants are an ordinance or means which he has been pleased to sanctify to this purpose, that by them, as instruments, grace, as the principal cause, might keep the heart stedfast in duty. If, then, Isaiah bewail the uncleanness of his lips, and Job suspect the uncleanness and wandering of his eyes, what reason have we to be humbled for this unstedfastness of our hearts, from whence the diffluence and looseness of every other faculty proceed!

Homil. 13. ad Popul. Antioch.

2. If we must bewail the falseness of our hearts that stand in need of covenants, how much more should we bewail their perfidiousness in the violation of covenants! that they take occasion even by restraint, like a river that is stopped in its course, to grow more unruly; or, as a man after an ague, which took away his stomach, to return with stronger appetite to sin again. To crucify our sins, and in repentance to put them, as it were, to shame, and then to take them down from the cross again, and fetch them to life, and repent of repentance; to vow, and "after vows to make inquiry," Prov. xx. 25; this is a very ill requital to Christ. He came from glory to suffer for us, and here met with many discouragements, not only from enemies, but from friends and disciples; Judas betrays him, Peter denies him, his disciples sleep, his kinsfolks stand afar off; yet he does not look back from a cross to a crown, and though he be tempted to come down from the cross, yet he stays it out, that he might love and save us to the uttermost: but no sooner are we out of Egypt and Sodom, than we have hankering affections to return, at the least to look backwards again. We engage ourselves to be ruled by the word of the Lord, as the Jews did, Jer. xlii. 5, 6; and with them, Jer. xliii. 2, when we know his word cavil against it, and shrink away from our own resolutions. Oh how should this humble us, and make us vile in our own eyes! God is exceeding angry with the breach of but human covenants, Jer. xxxiv. 18; Ezek. xvii. 18; how much more with the breach of holy covenants between himself and us! He threatens to revenge severely the quarrel of his covenant, Lev. xxvi. 25; and so doubtless he now does, and will do still, except we take a penitent revenge upon ourselves for it. And therefore,

Spumeus, et fervens et ab obice sævior ibit. Ovid. Senec. Nat. Quæst. l. 6. c. 17.

IV. Having entered into covenant, we should use double diligence in our performance of it, quickening and stirring up ourselves thereto by the consideration,

1. Of the stability of his covenant with us, even "the sure mercies of David," Isa. liv. 8, 9; lv. 3. To break faith with a false person were a fault, but to deceive him that never fails nor forsakes us, increases both the guilt and the unkindness.

2. Of his continued and renewed mercies. If he were a wilderness unto us, there might be some colour to repent us

Vid. Chrysost. in Psal. cxiii.

* Ὑγρον τὸ ἀόριστον οἰκειω ὅρω. Aristot. de Gener. et Corrupt. lib. 2. cap. 2. Hinc qui vitam agunt mollem, remissam, voluptuariam, in hanc et illam partem flexilem dicuntur. Βίον ζῆν τὸν ὑγρὸν καὶ διαῤῥέοντα. Chrys. Rom. xiii. xiv. et Suidæ, ὑγρὸς dicitur ὁ εὐκατάφορος εἰς τὰς ἡδονάς. Ejus animum qui nunc luxuriâ et lasciviâ diffluit. Terent. Heauton. Messallina facilitate adulterorum in fastidium versa ad incognitas libidines profluebat. Tacit. Annal. l. 11.

of our bargain, and to look out for a better service. But it is not only unthankfulness, but folly, to make a forfeiture of mercies, and to put God, by our breach of covenant with him, to break his with us too, Jer. ii. 5—8; xxxi. 31—34; Numb. xiv. 34; Jonah ii. 8.

3. Of our baptism and the tenor thereof, wherein we solemnly promise to keep "a good conscience," and "to observe all things whatsoever" Christ commands us, 1 Pet. iii. 21; Matt. xxviii. 19, 20. From which engagement we cannot recede without the note and infamy of greater perfidiousness. To take Christ's pay and do sin service, to be a subject to Michael and a pensioner to the dragon, to wear the livery of one master and do the work of another, to be an Israelite in title and a Samaritan in truth, this is either to forget or to deride our baptism, 2 Pet. i. 9, for therein we did as it were subscribe our names, and list ourselves in the register of Zion; and as it is a high honour to be enrolled in the genealogies of the church, so is a great dishonour to be expunged from thence, and to be "written in the earth," and have our names with our bodies putrify into perpetual oblivion, Jer. xvii. 13; Neh. vii. 64, 65.

Quis miles ab infœderatis, ne dicam ab hostibus regibus, donativum et stipendum captat nisi plane desertor et transfuga? Tertul. de Præscript. cap. 12.

4. Of the seal and witnesses whereby this covenant has been confirmed. Sealed in our own consciences by the seal of faith, believing the holiness of God's ways, and the excellency of his rewards, for "he that hath received his testimony hath set to his seal that God is true," John iii. 33; mutually attested by our spirits, feeling the sweetness of duty, and by God's Spirit, revealing the certainty of reward, Rom. viii. 16; and this in the presence of angels and saints, into whose communion we are admitted, 1 Cor. xi. 10; Heb. xii. 22; so that we cannot depart from this covenant without shaming ourselves to God, to angels, to men, and to our own consciences. Yea, the font where we were baptized, and the table where we have sacramentally eaten and drank the body and blood of Christ, and the very seats where we have sat attending to his voice, like Joshua's stone, Josh. xxiv. 22, 27, will be witnesses against us if we deny our covenant, though there be no need of witnesses against those who have to do with the Searcher of hearts and the Judge of consciences, that consuming fire whom no lead, no dross, no reprobate silver, no false metal, can endure or deceive, no Ananias or Sapphira lie unto without their own undoing.

5. Of the estate which these covenants refer to, and the tenor whereunto these services are annexed, which is "eternal life." After we have had patience to keep our short promises of doing God's will, he will perform his eternal promises of giving himself unto us. And who would forfeit an inheritance for not payment of a small homage or quit-rent reserved upon it? If we expect eternal life from him, there is great reason we should dedicate a mortal life to him. Let us not pay our service in dross, when we expect our wages in gold.

Having handled the general doctrine of our entering into covenant with God, I shall now proceed to the particulars to which they here engage themselves, whereof the first is a solemn thanksgiving, "so will we render the calves of our lips." All the sacrifices of the Jews were of two sorts: some were ilastical, propitiatory, or expiatory, for pardon of sin, or impetration of favour; others were eucharistical, "sacrifices of thanksgiving," (as the peace-offerings, Lev. vii. 12,) for mercies obtained, Psal. cvii. 22. With relation to these, the church here, having prayed for forgiveness of sin, and for the obtaining of blessings, doth hereupon, for the further enforcement of those petitions, promise to offer the peace-offerings of praise, not in the naked and empty ceremony, but with the spiritual life and substance, namely, the calves of their lips, which are moved by the inward principles of hearty sincerity and thanksgiving.

From hence we learn, that sound conversion and repentance enlarges the heart in thankfulness towards God, and disposes it to offer up the sacrifice of praise. And this duty here promised we may consider,

I. *Ut materiam pacti*, as the matter of a covenant or compact, which we promise to render to God in acknowledgment of his great mercy in answering the prayers which we put up to him for pardon and grace. It is observable, that most of those psalms wherein David implores help from God, are closed with thanksgivings to him, as Psal. vii. 17; xiii. 5, 6; lvi. 12, 13; lvii. 7—11; David thus by a holy craft insinuating himself into God's favour, and driving a trade between earth and heaven, receiving and returning, importing one commodity and transporting another, letting God know that his mercies shall not be lost, that as he bestows the comforts of them upon him, so he would return the praises of them unto heaven again. Those countries that have rich and staple commodities to exchange and return to others, have usually the freest and fullest traffic and resort of trade made to them. Now there is no such rich return from earth to heaven as praises; indeed to celebrate appreciatingly his goodness towards us is the only tribute we can pay to God. As in the flux and reflux of the sea, the water that in the one comes from the sea to the shore, does in the other but run back into itself again: so praises are as it were the return of mercies into themselves, or into that bosom and fountain of God's love from whence they flowed; and therefore the richer any heart is in praises, the more speedy and copious are the returns of mercy to it. God has so ordered the creatures amongst themselves, that there is a kind of natural confederacy and mutual negociation amongst them, each one receiving and returning, deriving to others, and drawing from others what serves most for the conservation of them all, and every thing by various interchanges and vicissitudes flowing back into the original from whence it came; thereby teaching the souls of men to maintain the like spiritual commerce and confederacy with heaven, to have all the passages between them and it open and unobstructed, that the mercies which they receive from thence may not be kept under and imprisoned in unthankfulness, but may have free course in daily praises to return to their fountain again. Thus Noah, after his deliverance from the flood, built an altar, on which to sacrifice "the sacrifices of thanksgiving," that as his family by the ark was preserved from perishing, so the memory of so great a mercy might in like manner by the altar be preserved too, Gen. viii. 20. So Abraham, after a weary journey, being comforted with God's gracious manifestation of himself unto him, built an altar, and "called on the name of the Lord," Gen. xii. 7, 8; and after another journey out of Egypt, was not forgetful to return to that place again, Gen. xiii. 4; God's presence drawing forth his praises, as the return of the sun in spring and summer causes the earth to thrust forth her fruits and flowers, that they may as it were meet and do homage to the fountain of their beauty. If Hezekiah may be delivered from death, Isa. xxxviii. 20; if David from guilt, Psal. li. 14; they promise to sing aloud of so great mercy, and to associate others with them in their praises: "Then will I teach transgressors thy ways," and "will sing to the stringed instruments." Guilt stops the mouth, and makes it "speechless," Matt. xxii. 12, that it cannot answer for one of a thousand sins, nor acknowledge one of a thousand mercies. When Jacob begged God's blessing on him in his journey, he vowed a vow of obedience and thankfulness to the Lord, seconding God's promises of

David omnes fere Psalmos in quibus Dei auxilium implorat, gratiarum actione claudit. Muis in Psal. x. 6.

mercy with his promises of praise, and answering all the parts thereof: "If God will be with me, and will keep me in this way that I go, and will give me bread to eat, and raiment to put on, so that I come again to my father's house in peace; then shall the Lord be my God." If he single out me and my seed, to set us up as marks for his angels to descend to, with protection and mercy, and will indeed give this land to us, and return me "to my father's house in peace;" then "this stone, which I have set up for a pillar" and monument, "shall be God's house," for me and my seed to praise him in: and accordingly we find he built an altar there, and changed the name of that place, calling it Beth-el, the house of God; and God, El-beth-el, the God of Beth-el. And lastly, if God indeed will not leave nor forsake me, but will give so rich a land as this unto me, I will surely return a homage back, "of all that thou shalt give me I will surely give the tenth unto thee." So punctual is this holy man to restipulate for each distinct promise a distinct praise, and to take the quality of his vows from the quality of God's mercies, Gen. xxviii. 13—22; xxxv. 6—15. Lastly, Jonah out of the belly of hell cries to God, and vows unto him a vow, that he would "sacrifice with the voice of thanksgiving," and tell all ages that "salvation is of the Lord," Jonah ii. 9. Thus we may consider praises as the matter of the church's covenant.

II. *Ut fructum pœnitentiæ*, as a fruit of true repentance, and deliverance from sin. When sin is taken away, when grace is obtained, then indeed is a man in a right disposition to give praises to God. When we are brought out of a wilderness into Canaan, Deut. viii. 10, out of Babylon to Zion, Jer. xxx. 18, 19, then saith the prophet, "Out of them shall proceed thanksgiving and the voice of them that make merry." When Israel had passed through the Red Sea, and saw the Egyptians dead on the shore, the great type of our deliverance from sin, death, and Satan, then they sing that triumphant song, Moses and the men singing the song, and Miriam and the women answering them, and repeating over again the burden of the song; "I will sing unto the Lord, for he hath triumphed gloriously; the horse and his rider hath he thrown into the sea," Exod. xv. 1, 20, 21. When a poor soul has been with Jonah in the midst of the seas, compassed with the floods, closed in with the depths, brought down to the bottom of the mountains, wrapt about head and heart and all over with the weeds, and locked up with the bars of sin and death; when it has felt the weight of a guilty conscience, and been terrified with the fearful expectation of an approaching curse, lying as it were at the pit's brink, within the smoke of hell, within the smell of that brimstone and scorchings of that unquenchable fire which is kindled for the devil and his angels; and is then, by a more bottomless and unsearchable mercy, brought to dry land, snatched as a brand out of the fire, translated into a glorious condition, from a law to a gospel, from a curse to a crown, from damnation to an inheritance, from a slave to a son; then, then only, never till then, is that soul in a fit disposition to sing praises unto God. When God has forgiven all a man's "iniquities," and healed all the "diseases" of his soul, and redeemed his "life from destruction," or from hell, (as the Chaldee renders it,) and crowned him "with loving-kindness and tender mercies," turning away his anger, and revealing those mercies which are "from everlasting" in election "to everlasting" in salvation, removing his sins from him "as far as the east is from the west;" then a man will call upon his soul over and over again, and summon every faculty within him, and invite every creature without him, to "bless the Lord," and to ingeminate praises to his holy name, Psal. ciii. 1—22. As David begins that Psalm with "Bless the Lord, O my soul," and ends it with "Bless the Lord, O my soul;" so the apostle, making mention of the like mercy of God to him, and of the exceeding abundant grace of Christ, in setting forth him who was "a blasphemer, and a persecutor, and injurious," "for a pattern to them which should hereafter believe on him to life everlasting," begins this meditation with praises, "I thank Christ Jesus our Lord;" and ends it with praises, "Now unto the King eternal, immortal, invisible, the only wise God, be honour and glory for ever and ever. Amen," 1 Tim. i. 12—17. It is impossible that soul should be truly thankful to God, which has no apprehensions of him, but as an enemy, ready to call in, or at the least to curse, all those outward benefits which, in that little interim and respite of time between the curse pronounced in the law and executed in death, he vouchsafes to bestow. And impenitent sinners can have no true notion of God but such. And therefore all the verbal thanks which such men seem to render to God for blessings, are but like the music at a funeral, or the trumpet before a judge, which gives no comfortable sound to the mourning wife, or to the guilty prisoner.

Ab æterno per prædestinationem in æternum per glorificationem. Bernard. serm. 2. in Ascens. Dom.

III. *Ut medium impetrandi*, as an argument and motive to prevail with God in prayer. For the church here prays for pardon, for grace, for healing, not only with an eye to its own benefit, but to God's honour. Lord, when thou hast heard and answered us, then we shall glorify thee, Psal. l. 15. "I will praise thee," saith David; "for thou hast heard me, and art become my salvation," Psal. cxviii. 21. It is true, if God condemn us, he will therein show forth his own glory, 2 Thess. i. 9, as he did upon Pharaoh, Rom. ix. 17; in which sense the "strong" and "terrible" ones are said to "glorify" him, Isa. xxv. 3, 5, because his power in their destruction is made the more conspicuous. But we should not therein concur to the glorifying of him. "What profit is there in my blood, when I go down to the pit? Shall the dust praise thee? Shall it declare thy truth?" Psal. xxx. 9; lxxxviii. 10, 11. "The living, the living, he shall praise thee," Isa. xxxviii. 19. This is a frequent argument with David whereby to prevail for mercy, because else God would lose the praise which by this means he should render to his name, Psal. vi. 4, 5; cxviii. 17. God indeed is all-sufficient to himself, and no goodness of ours can extend unto him, Job xxii. 2; xxxv. 7; yet as parents delight to use the labour of their children in things which are no way beneficial to themselves, so God is pleased to use us as instruments for setting forth his glory, though his glory stands in no need of us, though we cannot add thereto one cubit. He has made all men *in usus profundarum cogitationum suarum*, for the uses of his unsearchable counsels. "The Lord hath made all things for himself: yea, even the wicked for the day of evil," Prov. xvi. 4. Yet he is pleased to esteem some men "meet" for uses for which others are not, 2 Tim. ii. 21, and to "set apart" some for himself, and for those uses, Psal. iv. 3; Isa. xliii. 21. * God by his wisdom ordereth and draweth the blind and brute motions of the worst creatures to his own honour, as the huntsman does the rage of the dog to his pleasure, or the mariner the blowing of the wind to his voyage, or the artist the heat of the fire to his work, or the physician the bloodthirstiness of the leech to a cure. But godly men are fitted to bring

Deus suam gloriam quærit non propter se sed propter nos. Aquin. 22. qu. 32. art. 1. ad 1. m.

August. de Nuptiis et Concupis. lib. 2. cap. 16. Omnia propter se ipsum fecit Deus, omnia propter suos. Bern. ser. 3. in Die Pentecost.

* Est in malorum potestate peccare; ut autem peccando hoc vel hoc illa mala faciant, non est in illorum potestate, sed Dei dividentis tenebras, et ordinantis eas, ut hinc etiam quod faciunt contra voluntatem Dei, non impleatur nisi voluntas Dei. Aug. de præ. Sanct. c. 16.

actually glory to him, to glorify him operatively, 1 Cor. x. 30, 31; Eph. i. 11, 12. And this is that in which God chiefly delights.

Our Saviour bids his disciples cast their net into the sea, and when they had drawn their net, he bids them bring of the fish which they had then caught, and yet we find that there was on the land before a fire of coals, and fish laid thereon, and bread, John xxi. 6—10; thereby teaching us that he did not use their industry for any need that he had of it, but because he would honour them so far as to let them honour him with their obedience. And therefore even then when God tells his people that he needed not their services, he calls yet upon them for thanksgiving, Psal. l. 9, 14.

This then is a strong argument to be used in prayer for pardon, for grace, for any spiritual mercy, Lord, if I perish, I shall not praise thee, I shall not be meet for my Master's uses. Thy glory will only be forced out of me with blows, like fire out of a flint, or water out of a rock. But thou delightest to see thy poor servants operate towards thy glory, to see them not forced by power but by love to show forth thy praises. And this we shall never do till sin be pardoned. God can bring light out of light, as the light of the stars out of the light of the sun, and he can bring light out of darkness, as he did at first; but in the one case there is a meetness for such a use, in the other not. Now we are not meet subjects for God to reap honour from, till sin be pardoned, till grace be conferred. Then we shall give him the praise of his mercy, in pitying such grievous sinners; and the praise of his power and wisdom, in healing such mortal diseases; and the praise of his glorious and free grace, in sending salvation to those that did not inquire after it; and the praise of his patience, in forbearing us so long, and waiting that he might be gracious; and the praise of his wonderful providence, in causing all things to work together for our good; and the praise of his justice, by taking part with him against our own sins, and joining with his grace to revenge the blood of Christ upon them. A potsherd is good enough to hold fire, but nothing but a sound and pure vessel is meet to contain wine or any rich depositum.

IV. *Ut principium operandi*, as a principle of emendation of life, and of new obedience. Lord, "take away all iniquity," and receive us into favour, then will we be thankful unto thee, and that shall produce amendment of life: "Asshur shall not save us, we will not ride upon horses, neither will we say any more to the work of our hands, Ye are our gods; for in thee the fatherless findeth mercy." A thankful apprehension of the goodness of God in forgiving, giving, saving, honouring us, is one of the principal foundations of sincere obedience. Then the soul will think nothing too good for God, who has showed himself so good to it. "What shall I render unto the Lord for all his benefits toward me?" saith the prophet David, Psal. cxvi. 12: and a little after, "O Lord, truly I am thy servant; I am thy servant, and the son of thine handmaid;" that is, a home-born servant, thine from my mother's womb. It is an allusion to those who were born of servants in the house of their masters, and so were in a condition of servants. *Partus sequitur ventrem.* If the mother be a handmaid, the child is a servant too; and so the Scripture calls them *filios domûs*, children of the house, Gen. xiv. 14; xv. 3; xvii. 12; Lev. xxii. 11. His heart being enlarged in thankfulness, presently reminded him of the deep engagements which bound him to service even from the womb. True filial and evangelical obedience arises from faith and love. Faith shows us God's love to us, and thereby works in us a reciprocal love to him; "We love him, because he first loved us," 1 John iv. 19. This is the only thing wherein a servant of God may answer him, and may *de simili mutuam rependere vicem*, as Bernard speaks, return back to God what is his own gift. * If he be angry with me, I must not be angry again with him, but fear and tremble, and beg for pardon; if he reprove me, I must not reprove, but justify him; if he judge me, I must not judge, but adore him: but if he love me, I must take the boldness to love him again, for therefore he loves, that he may be loved. And this love of ours to Christ makes us ready to do every thing which he requires of us, because we know that he has done much more for us than he requires of us. "The love of Christ," saith the apostle, "constraineth us; because we thus judge, that if one died for all, then were all dead;" that is, either dead in and with him, in regard of the guilt and punishment of sin, so as to be freed from the damnation of it; or dead by way of conformity to his death, in dying unto sin, and crucifying the old man, so as to shake off its power and strength. And the fruit of all, both his dying and our loving, is this, "that we should not live unto ourselves, but unto him which died for us, and rose again," 2 Cor. v. 14, 15. Thus love argues from the greater to the lesser, from the greatness of his work for us to the smallness of ours unto him; if he died to give us life, then we must live to do him service.

† Fear produces only servile and unwilling performances. As those fruits which grow in winter, or in cold countries, are sour, unsavoury, and unconcocted, but those which grow in summer, or in hotter countries, by the warmth and influence of the sun are sweet and wholesome; such is the difference between those fruits of obedience which fear and which love produces. The most formal principle of obedience is love, and the first beginnings of love in us to God arise from his mercies to us being thankfully remembered; and this teaches the soul thus to argue, God has given deliverances to me, and should I break his commandments? Christ gave himself to redeem me from all iniquity, and to make me in a special manner his own, therefore I must be "zealous of good works," Tit. ii. 14; therefore I must "show forth the praises of him who hath called me out of darkness into his marvellous light," 1 Pet. ii. 9. No more frequent, more copious common-place in all the Scriptures than this, to call for obedience, and to aggravate disobedience, by the consideration of the great things that God has done for us, Deut. x. 20, 21; xi. 7—9; xxxii. 6, 7; Josh. xxiv. 2—14; 1 Sam. xii. 24; Isa. i. 2; Jer. ii. 5, 6; Hos. ii. 8; Micah vi. 3—5. In the law a ransomed man became the servant of him who bought and delivered him; and upon this argument the apostle calls for obedience: "Ye are not your own; for ye are bought with a price: therefore glorify God in your body, and in your spirit, which are God's," 1 Cor. vi. 19, 20. We have but the use of ourselves, the property is his, and we may do nothing to violate that.

V. *Ut instrumentum Divinæ gloriæ*, as a means and instrument of publishing God's praises. There is

* Si mihi irascatur Deus, num illi ego similiter redirascar? non utique sed pavebo, sed contremiscam, sed veniam deprecabor. Ita si me arguat, non redarguetur a me, sed ex me potius justificabitur; nec si me judicabit, judicabo ego eum, sed adorabo; si dominatur, me oportet servire; si imperat, me oportet parere; nunc jam videas de amore quam aliter sit. Nam cum amat Deus non aliud vult quam amari. Bern. serm. 83. in Cantic.

† Vere Christianus est qui plus amat Dominum quam timet gehennam, ut etiam si dicat illi Deus, utere deliciis carnalibus sempiternis, et quantum potes pecca, nec morieris nec in gehennam mitteris, sed mecum tantummodo non eris; exhorrescat et omnino non peccet; non jam ut in illud quod timebat non incidat, sed ne illum quem sic amat offendat. Bern. de Catechizand. Rudibus, c. 17.

an emphasis in the word "lips." Sometimes it is a diminutive word, taking away from the duty performed, as Matt. xv. 8, "This people honoureth me with their lips, but their heart is far from me;" but here it is an augmentative word, which enlarges the duty, rendering it more comprehensive. "I will sacrifice unto thee," saith Jonah, "with the voice of thanksgiving," Jonah ii. 9. God regards not the sacrifice if this be not the use that is made of it, to publish and celebrate the glory of his name. The outward ceremony is nothing without the thankfulness of the heart, and the thankfulness of the heart is too little except it have a voice to proclaim it abroad, that others also may learn to glorify and admire the works of the Lord. It is not enough to "sacrifice," not enough to sacrifice "the sacrifices of thanksgiving," except withal we "declare his works with rejoicing," Psal. cvii. 22. There is a private thankfulness of the soul within itself, when, meditating on the goodness of God, it does in secret return the tribute of a humble and obedient heart back again unto him, which is to praise God on the bed: and there is public thanksgiving, when men "tell of all the wondrous works" of God "in the congregation of his saints," Psal. xxvi. 7, 12; cxlix. 1, 5. Now here the church promises this public thanksgiving, it shall not be the thankfulness of the heart only, but of the lips too; as it is noted of the thankful leper, that he "with a loud voice glorified God," Luke xvii. 15. "The living, the living, he shall praise thee," saith Hezekiah. But how should they do it? "The fathers to the children shall make known thy truth," Isa. xxxviii. 19. There are some affections and motions of the heart which stop the mouth, being of a cold, stupefactive, constringent nature, as the sap stays and hides itself in the root while it is winter; such is fear and extremity of grief. "Assemble yourselves," saith the prophet, "and let us enter into the defenced cities, and let us be silent there; for the Lord our God hath put us to silence," Jer. viii. 14; Isa. x. 14. Other affections open the mouth, are of an expansive and dilating nature, know not how to be straitened or suppressed; and of all these, joy, and sense of God's mercy, can least contain itself in the compass of our narrow breast, but will spread and communicate itself to others. A godly heart is in this like to those flowers which shut when the sun sets and the night comes, and open again when the sun returns and shines upon them. If God withdraw his favour, and send a night of affliction, they shut up themselves and their thoughts in silence; but if he shine again, and shed abroad the light and sense of his love upon them, then their heart and mouth are wide open towards heaven in lifting up praises unto him. Hannah prayed silently so long as she was in bitterness of soul, and of a sorrowful spirit, but as soon as God answered her prayers, and filled her heart with joy in him, presently her mouth was enlarged into a song of thanksgiving, 1 Sam. i. 13—15; ii. 1—10.

Plutarch. de Capiend. ex Hostibus Utilitate. Arist. Problem. sect. 27.

There is no phrase more usual in the Psalms, than to sing forth praises unto God; and it is not used without a special emphasis. For it is one thing to "praise," and another to "sing praises," Psal. cxlvi. 1, 2. This is, to publish, to declare, to speak of abundantly, to "abundantly utter the memory of" God's "great goodness," that "one generation may praise thy works to another, and declare thy mighty acts," Psal. cxlv. 4, 7. And therefore we find, in the most solemn thanksgivings, that the people of God were wont in great companies and with musical instruments to sound forth the praises of God, and to cause their joy to be heard afar off, Neh. xii. 27, 43; Isa. xii. 4—6; Jer. xxxi. 7. This then is the force of the expression: Lord, when thou hast taken away iniquity, and extended thy grace and favour to us, we will not only have thankful hearts, every man to praise thee by himself; but we will have thankful lips to show forth thy praise, we will stir up and encourage one another, we will tell our children, that the generations to come may know the mercy of our God.

Apud poetas clarissimos laudes Deorum inter regalia convivia canebantur. Quintil. lib. 1. cap. 10. Nec aliter veri Dei laudes in conviviis Christianorum. Tertul. Apolog. cap. 39. Cyprian. lib. 2. epist. 2.

This is a great part of the communion of saints, to join together in God's praises. There is a communion of sinners, wherein they combine together to dishonour God, and encourage one another in evil, Psal. lxiv. 5; lxxxiii. 5—8; Prov. i. 10, 11. Eve was no sooner caught herself, but she became a kind of serpent, to deceive and to catch her husband. A tempter has no sooner made a sinner, but that sinner will become a tempter. As, therefore, God's enemies hold communion to dishonour him; so great reason there is that his servants should hold communion to praise him, and to animate and excite one another to duty, as men that draw at an anchor, and soldiers that set upon a service, are wont to do so with mutual encouragements, Isa. ii. 3; Zech. viii. 21; Mal. iii. 16. The holy oil for the sanctuary was made of many spices compounded by the art of the perfumer, Exod. xxx. 23—25, to note unto us that those duties are sweetest which are made up in a communion of saints, each one contributing to them his influence: as in winds and rivers, where many meet in one they are strongest; and in chains and jewels, where many links and stones are joined in one they are richest. All good is diffusive, like leaven in a lump, like sap in a root; it will find the way from the heart to every faculty of soul and body, and from thence to the ears and hearts of others. Every living creature was made with the seed of life in it, to preserve itself by multiplying, Gen. i. 11, 12. And of all seeds, that of the Spirit is most vigorous; and in nothing so much as in glorifying God, when the joy of the Lord, which is our strength, puts itself forth to derive the praises of his name, and to call in others to their celebration, 1 John iii. 9; 1 Pet. i. 23.

From all which we learn some means, amongst many others, whereby to try the truth of our conversion. 1. By the life and workings of true thankfulness to God for pardon of sin, and acceptance into favour. Certainly, when a man is converted himself, his heart will be enlarged, and his mouth will be filled with the praises of the Lord; he will acquaint others to what a good God he is turned. If he have found Christ himself, as Andrew and Philip, and the woman of Samaria did, he will presently report it to others, and invite them to come and see, John i. 41, 46; iv. 29. If Zaccheus be converted, he receives Christ joyfully, Luke xix. 6. If Matthew be converted, he entertains him with a feast, Luke v. 29. If Cornelius be instructed in the knowledge of him, he will call "his kinsmen and near friends" to partake of such a banquet, Acts x. 24. If David be converted himself, he will endeavour that other sinners may be converted too, and will show them what the Lord has done for his soul, Psal. li. 13. The turning of a sinner from evil to good, is like the turning of a bell from one side to another; you cannot turn it but it will make a sound, and report its own motion. He that has not a mouth open to report the glory of God's mercy to his soul, and to strengthen and edify his brethren, may justly question the truth of his own conversion. In Aaron's garments (which were types of holiness) there were to be golden bells and pomegranates, which (if we may make any allegorical application of it) intimates to us, that as a holy life is fruitful and active in the duties of spiritual obedience, so it is loud and vocal in sounding forth the praises of God, and thereby endeavouring to edify the church. Gideon's lamps and pitchers were accompanied with trumpets: when God is pleased to put any light of grace into these earthen vessels of ours, we should have mouths full of thankfulness to return to him the glory of his goodness.

And as that repentance is unsound which is not accompanied with thankfulness, so that thankfulness is but empty and hypocritical which does not spring out of sound repentance. We are wont to say that the words of fools are *in labris nata*, born in their lips; but the words of wise men are *e sulco pectoris*, drawn up out of an inward judgment. "The calves of the lips" are no better than the "calves of the stall" in God's account, if they have not a heart in them. Without this the promise here made to God would be no other than that with which nurses deceive their little children, when they promise them a gay golden new-nothing. Praise in the mouth without repentance in the heart, is like a sea-weed that grows without a root; like the pouring of balm and spices upon a dead body, which can never thoroughly secure it from putrefaction; like a perfume about one sick of the plague, whose sweet smell carries infection along with it.

Dicta factis deficientibus erubescunt. Tertul. de Patria, cap. 1.

It is not the mentioning of mercies, but the improving of them to piety, which expresses our thankfulness to God. God sets every blessing upon our score, and expects an answer and return suitable. He compares Chorazin and Bethsaida with Tyre and Sidon; and if their lives be as bad as these, their punishment shall be much heavier, because the mercies they enjoyed were much greater. The not rightly using mercies is being unthankful for them. And it is a heavy account which men must give for abused mercies, Deut. xxxii. 6; Amos ii. 9—16; Luke xiii. 7; Heb. vi. 7, 8. Sins against mercy, and under mercy, are "the first-ripe fruit;" when the sun shines hottest, the fruits ripen fastest, Amos viii. 1, 2; Jer. i. 11, 12. God does not bear so long with the provocations of a church, as of those that are not a people; the sins of the Amorites were longer in ripening than the sins of Israel. When judgment is abroad, it will begin at the house of God.

Μία ἀμοιβὴ κυριωτάτη, ταῦτα δρᾶν ἅ περ ἀρεστα τῷ Θεῷ. Clem. Alex. Strom. l. 7. Deum colit, quisquis imitatus est. Senec. Epist. 65.

2. But further, we should be so much the more earnestly pressed to this, by how much it is the greater evidence of our conversion unto God, and by how much more apt we are to call for mercies when we want them, than with the leper to return praises when we enjoy them. Ten cried to be healed, but there was but one that returned glory to God, Luke xvii. 11—19. Vessels will sound when they are empty; fill them, and they are presently dumb. When we want mercies, then with Pharaoh we cry out for pardon, for peace, for supplies, for deliverances; but when prayers are answered, and our turn served, how few remember the method which God prescribes, "Call on me in the day of trouble; I will deliver thee, and thou shalt glorify me," Psal. l. 15; yea, how many, like swine, trample on the meat that feeds them, and tread under foot the mercies that preserve them! How many are so greedily intent upon the things they desire, that they can neither see nor value the things they enjoy! *Omnis festinatio cæca est.* It is noted even of good king Hezekiah, that he "rendered not again according to the benefit done unto him," 2 Chron. xxxii. 25. Therefore we should be exhorted in our prayers for pardon and grace, to do as the church here does, to promise the sacrifices of thankfulness and obedience, not as a price to purchase mercy, (for our good extends not to God, Psal. xvi. 2,) but as a tie and obligation upon ourselves, to acknowledge and return the praise of mercy to him that gives it. And to this the apostle exhorts us, "Let your requests be made known unto God," not only "by prayer and supplication," but "with thanksgiving," Phil. iv. 6; 1 Thess. v. 17, 18; 1 Tim. ii. 1; which we find to have been his own practice, Eph. iii. 14—21. We should keep a catalogue of God's mercies to quicken us to duty, as well as a catalogue of our own sins to make us cry for mercy. And to this duty of thanksgiving we may be excited by the consideration of,

Seneca de Benefic. l. 3. c. 3. Liv. lib. 22.

I. God's greatness. "Great is the Lord, and" therefore "greatly to be praised," Psal. cxlv. 3. The praises of God should be according to his name, Psal. xlviii. 10; xcvi. 8. All things were made for no other end, but to return glory to him who made them. Because all things are "of him," therefore all must be "to him," Rom. xi. 36. And this the very figure of the world teaches us. For a circular line ends where it began, and returns back into its original point, by that means strengthening and preserving itself. For things are usually strongest when nearest their original, and the more remote from that, the weaker they grow; as a tree is strongest at the root, and a branch or bough next the trunk or stock, and the further out from thence, the smaller and weaker it grows; and the further it is from the original of its being, the nearer it is to not being. So all creatures are hereby taught, both for the preservation of that being which they have, and for the supply of those perfections which they want, as well as for the setting forth of the greatness of their Maker, (out of whose infinite being all finite beings are sustained and perfected,) to run back to God, for whose sake they are, and have been created. Rivers come from the sea, and therefore run back into the sea again; the trees receive sap from the earth, and within a while pay it back in those leaves that fall down to the earth again. Now as God has made all creatures thus to show forth the glory of his greatness, so he will have them do it by those principles, and in that manner of working, which he has planted in them. Inanimate and mere natural creatures are bid to praise the Lord, Psal. cxlviii. 8, 9; but this they do blindly and ignorantly, like the arrow which flies toward the mark, but understands not its own destination, being directed thither by an understanding without and above itself. And thus when any thing by the natural weight and inclination of its own form moves to the place where it may be preserved, or draws to it those further degrees of perfection whereby it may be improved, and have more of being communicated to it, it may truly be said to praise the Lord, in that it obeys the law which he planted in it, and is by his wise providence carried back towards him, to derive its conservation and perfection from the same fountain from whence proceeded its being. But now, reasonable creatures being by God enriched with internal knowledge, and that knowledge in his church exceedingly raised by his manifestation of himself in the word as their uttermost blessedness, he therefore requires that we should work actively, and with intention of the end for which he made us, guiding all our aims and inclinations towards his glory by that internal knowledge of his excellency which he has implanted in us, and revealed to us. And indeed all other creatures are in this sense said to glorify God, because the infinite power, wisdom, goodness, and perfection of God which are in their beings and workings so notably relucent, do become the object of reasonable creatures, to contemplate upon, and by that means draw forth admiration and adoration of him.

II. God's goodness. He deserves it at our hands. He gives more to us than we are able to render unto him. The sun shines on the moon with its own glorious light; the moon returns but a faint and spotted light upon the world. We can return nothing to God but that which is his own, 1 Chron. xxix. 16, and it is returned from us not with that purity with which it came to us. We cannot send forth a thought round about us, but it will return with a report of mercy, and that mercy calls for a return of praise. But above all, the goodness of God mentioned in the text, "Take away all iniquity, and receive us graciously," this calls for "the calves of the lips" to be offered, as in the new moons, with trumpets and solemnity, Numb. x. 10. The beams of the sun, the more directly they fall on the body of the moon, fill it with the more abundant light; so the more copious and remarkable God's mercies are to us, the more enlarged unto him should be our praises. Therefore true penitents that have more tasted of mercy, are more obliged to thanksgiving, Psal. cxlvii. 20. "Excellent speech becometh not a fool," Prov. xvii. 7; but "praise is comely for the upright," Psal. xxxiii. 1. For as God is most dishonoured by the sins of holy men when they are committed against light, and break forth into scandal, 2 Sam. xii. 14, so is he most honoured by the confession and praises of holy men, because they know more of his glory and goodness than others, and can report greater things of him. Wicked men speak of God by hear-say, and by notion only, but holy men by intimate experience; as the queen of Sheba knew more of Solomon's wisdom from his mouth than from his fame. He that sees but the outward court and buildings of a palace, can say it is a glorious place; but he that, like the ambassadors of the king of Babylon in Hezekiah's time, shall be admitted to see "the house of his precious things," and all the treasures of the palace, can speak much more honourably of it, 2 Kings xx. 12, 13. Every one might see and admire the stones of the temple without, who were not admitted to view the gold and curious workmanship within. The more intimate communion a man has with God as a Redeemer, the more glorious and abundant praises can he render unto him. Besides, praise is the language of heaven; the whole happiness of the saints there is to enjoy God, and their whole business is to praise him. And they who are to live in another country, will be more solicitous to learn the language, and fore-acquaint themselves with the manners and usages of that country, than they who have no hopes nor assurance of coming thither. As they who have hope to be like Christ in glory, will purify themselves, that they may in the mean time be like him in grace, 1 John iii. 2, 3; so they that have hope to praise him for ever in heaven, will "study the song of Moses the servant of God, and the song of the Lamb," before they come thither. And indeed none can praise God but they that can abase and deny themselves. Wicked men in all duties serve and seek themselves; but the very formality of praise is to seek God, and to make him the end of our so doing. The apostle exhorts us to offer ourselves "a living sacrifice," Rom. xii. 1; that is to say, to separate ourselves for God and for his uses. The sacrifice we know was God's, for his sake it was burnt, and broken, and destroyed. We must be such sacrifices; deny ourselves, be lost to ourselves, not serve, nor seek, nor aim at ourselves; but resolve to esteem nothing dear in comparison of God's honour, and to be willing any way, whether by life or by death, that he may be magnified in us, Acts xxi. 13; Phil. i. 20. Love of communion in natural creatures is stronger than self-love; stones will move upward, fire downward, to preserve the universe from a vacuity, and to keep the compages of nature together. How much more is, and ought to be, the love of God himself in the new creature stronger than self-love, whereby it seeks and serves itself! And without this all other services are but as Ananias's lie, lies to the Holy Ghost, keeping to ourselves what we would seem to bestow upon him. Lifting up the eyes, beating the breast, spreading the hands, bending the knee, hanging down the head, levelling the countenance, sighing, sobbing, fasting, howling, all nothing else but mocking of God. And we may say of such men, as the emperor of him that sold the glasses for pearl, (though in a sadder sense,) *Imposturam faciunt et patientur.* They deceive God, and fail in his precepts, and they shall be themselves deceived, and fail in their own expectations; for "the expectation of the wicked shall perish," Prov. x. 28.

Pretiosam vestem exigua quævis macula turpius decolorat. Nobis ad immunditiam minima quævis inobedientia sufficit, &c. Bernard. ser. de Triplici Custodia.

Est locus ubi vere quiescens et quietus cernitur Deus, locus omnino non judicis, non magistri, sed sponsi: sed heu rara hora, et parva mora. Id. ser. 23. in Cant.

Illa domus lætitiæ est, ista militiæ. Illa domus laudis, ista orationis. Bern. serm. 2. in Dedicat. Eccles.

III. By a consideration of ourselves, and that in a two-fold point of view. 1. Of our natural torpor and sluggishness to this duty. As the Dead Sea drinks in the river Jordan and is never the sweeter, and the ocean all other rivers and is never the fresher; so we are apt to receive daily mercies from God, and still remain insensible of them, and unthankful for them. God's mercies to us are like the dew on all the ground, our thanks to him like the dew on the fleece. We are like fishermen's wheels, wide at that end which lets in the fish, but narrow at the other end, so that they cannot get out again; greedy to get mercy, tenacious to hold it, but unthankful in acknowledging or right using it. The rain comes down from heaven in showers, it goes up but in mists. We sow in our land one measure, and receive ten; yea, Isaac received a hundred-fold, Gen. xxvi. 12; but God sows ten, it may be a hundred, mercies amongst us, when we scarce return the praise and the fruit of one. Our hearts in this case are like the windows of the temple, 1 Kings vi. 4, wide inward to let in mercies, but narrow outward to let forth praises. Now as husbandmen use, where the nature of land is more defective, to expend on it the more importunate labour; so, having hearts so earthly for the performance of so heavenly a duty, we should use the more holy violence upon them. And as the widow extorted justice from an unjust judge by her continual coming, Luke xviii. 5, we should press, and urge, and with ingeminated importunity charge this duty upon ourselves, as does the psalmist, "Oh that men would praise the Lord for his goodness, and for his wonderful works to the children of men!" Psal. cvii. 8, 15, 21, 31. 2. Of our own benefit. For indeed all the benefit which arises out of this duty redounds to us, and none to God. His glory is infinite, and eternally the same, there neither is, nor can be, accession to that by all our praises. When a glass reflects the brightness of the sun, there is but an acknowledgment of what was, not any addition of what was not. When an excellent orator makes a panegyrical oration in praise of some honourable person, he does not infuse any dram of worth into the person, but only sets forth and declares that which is to others. A curious picture praises a beautiful face, not by adding beauty to it, but by representing that which was in it before. The window which lets light into a house, does not benefit the light, but the house into which the light shines. So our praising of God serves to quicken, comfort, and refresh ourselves, who have interest in so good a God; or to edify and encourage our brethren, that they may be ambitious to serve so honourable a Master; but our praises add no lustre or glory whatever to God.

Ipse sibi omnia. Tertull. contra Praxeam, cap. 5.

But further, the right performance of this duty is founded on the due apprehensions of God's being good, and of his doing good, Psal. cxix. 68; or on his excellency in himself, and his goodness towards us. In the former respect it consists in adoring and extolling the great name of God, ascribing in our hearts and mouths all blessedness unto him, acknowledging his infinite majesty in himself, and his sovereignty over us his poor creatures, Exod. xv. 11; Micah vii. 18; and so covering our faces, and abhorring ourselves in his sight, Isa. vi.; Job xlii. 5, 6; not daring to question any of his deep, absolute, and most unsearchable counsels; but because all things are of him, to acknowledge that all things ought to be for and to him, and are to be reduced to the ends of his glory, by the counsel of his own will, Rom. ix. 20, 21; xi. 33, 36; Matt. xi. 25, 26; Psal. cxxxv. 5, 6; Job ix. 12; Eph. i. 11. In the latter respect, as he is the God in whom we "live, and move, and have our being," and hope for our blessedness; so it imports, first, a glorying and rejoicing in him as our alone felicity, Psal. xxxiii. 1; Hab. iii. 18; Phil. iv. 4. Secondly, a choosing and preferring him above all other good things, making him our end and aim, in life, in death, in doing, in suffering, Rom. iv. 7, 8. Thirdly, a thankful acknowledgment of all his mercies, as most beneficial unto us, and most gratuitous and free in regard of him, 2 Sam. vii. 18; Lam. iii. 22, 23. Lastly, a constant endeavour of a holy life, so to bring forth fruit, to do the will of God, and to finish his work which he has set us, so to order our conversation aright before him, as that he may have ascribed to him the glory of his authority over the consciences of men, and of the power of his love shed abroad in their hearts; and that all that see our conversation may say, Doubtless, the God whom these men serve after so holy a manner, for whom they despise all outward and sinful pleasures, is a holy and blessed God, infinitely able to comfort, satisfy, and reward all those that so conscientiously and constantly give up themselves to him, John xv. 8; xvii. 4; Psal. l. 23; Deut. iv. 6, 7; Matt. v. 16; 2 Cor. ix. 13; 1 Pet. ii. 12.

The second particular in their covenant is, amendment of life, and a more special care against those sins of carnal confidence, and spiritual adultery, whereby they had formerly dishonoured and provoked God. From whence there are two observations which offer themselves.

Obs. 4. True repentance and sound conversion, as it makes a man thankful for the pardon of sin past, so it makes him careful against the practice of sin for the time to come, especially those particular sins whereby he had formerly most dishonoured God, and defiled his own conscience. This doctrine consists of two parts, which we will consider asunder.

And first, of this care and purpose of amendment in general. When the poor converts who had been guilty of the most precious and innocent blood that ever was shed, began to be convinced of that horrible sin, and found those nails wherewith they had fastened the Lord of glory to a cross, pricking and piercing their own hearts, with what bleeding and relenting affections did they mourn over him! with what earnest importunities did they inquire after the way of salvation wherein they might serve and enjoy him! never were their hands more cruel in shedding that blood, than their hearts were now solicitous to be bathed in it, to be cleansed by it, Acts ii. 37. The poor prodigal, who is the emblem of a penitent sinner, when he came to himself again, or bethought himself, as the phrase is, 1 Kings viii. 47, (for we do never depart from God, but we do withal forsake and lose ourselves, and are transported with a spiritual madness from our right minds,) immediately grew to a resolution of arising out of that base and brutish condition, and of going home to his father, and by that means to his wit and senses again. So when, by John's preaching of repentance, men were turned to the wisdom of the just, (for all unrighteousness is folly and madness,) and were prepared for the Lord, we immediately find what a special care they had to be informed in the ways of duty, earnestly inquiring after that new course of obedience in which they were now to walk, Luke iii. 10, 12, 14. All true penitents are of the same mind with these in the text, "Neither will we say any more," and, "What have I to do any more with idols?" ver. 8; as Ezra in his penitent prayer, "Should we again break thy commandments?" chap. ix. 13, 14. "Christ being raised from the dead, dieth no more;" and when we repent of sin, it must be with a repentance "not to be repented of," Rom. vi. 9, 12; 2 Cor. vii. 10. "The time past of our life must suffice us to have wrought the will of the Gentiles," 1 Pet. iv. 3.

This care arises from the nature of true repentance, which has two names usually given it. 1. Μετάνοια, a change of the mind; the heart is framed to have other and truer notions of sin, of grace, of heaven, of hell, of conscience, of salvation, than it had before; for the mind of wicked men being defiled, they can frame to themselves none but impure apprehensions of spiritual things, as a yellow eye sees every thing yellow, and a bitter palate imparts to every thing its bitterness. 2. Μεταμέλεια, a change of the cares and endeavours of life; that whereas before a man made provision for the flesh, and his study and care was how to satisfy the lusts of his own heart, Rom. xiii. 14, what he should eat, what he should drink, wherewith he should be clothed; now his care is how he may be saved, how he may honour and enjoy God, Acts ii. 37; xvi. 30. The first question in repentance is, "What have I done?" Jer. viii. 6; and the next question is, "Lord, what wilt thou have me to do?" Acts ix. 6. And this care repentance works,

1. By a godly sorrow for sin past. It brings into a man's remembrance the history of his former life; makes him with heaviness of spirit recount the guilt of so many innumerable sins, wherewith he had bound himself as with chains of darkness; the loss of so much precious time mispent in the service of such a master as had no other wages to give but shame and death; the horrible indignities thereby offered to the majesty and justice of God; the odious contempt of his holy will and sovereign authority; the daring neglect of his threatenings, and undervaluing of his rewards; the high provocation of his jealousy and displeasure; the base corrivalry and contesting of sinful lusts with the grace of the gospel, and the precious blood of the Son of God; the gainsaying, and wrestling, and stubborn antipathy of a carnal heart to the pure motions of the Spirit, and word of Christ; the presumptuous repulses of him that stands at the door and knocks, waiting that he may be gracious; the long turning of his back, and thrusting away from him the word of reconciliation, wherein Christ by his ambassadors had so often besought him to be reconciled unto God: the remembrance of these things makes a man look with self-abhorrence on himself, and full detestation on his former courses. And he now no longer considers the silver or the gold, the profit or the pleasure of his wonted lusts, though they be never so delectable or desirable in the eye of flesh; he looks upon them as accursed things to be thrown away, as the converts did upon their costly and curious books, Acts xix. 19; Isa. xxx. 22; xxxi. 7. Sin is like a plaited picture: on the one side of it, to the impenitent, appears nothing but the beauty of pleasure, whereby it bewitches and allures them; on the other side, to the penitent, appears nothing but the horrid and ugly face of guilt and shame, whereby it amazes and confounds them. Thus the remembrance of sin past, (which they are very careful to keep always in their sight, Psal. li. 3,) does, by godly sorrow, work special care of amendment of life for the time to come, 2 Chron. vi. 37, 38; Psal. cxix. 59; Ezek. xvi. 61—63; xx. 43.

Πεινῶντι γὰρ ἀνδρὶ μάζα τιμιωτέρα χρυσοῦ τε κἀλεφαντος. Achæus Eretriens. apud Athen. lib. 6. cap. 20.

2. By a present sense of the weight and burden of remaining corruptions, which work, and move, and put forth what strength they can to resist the grace of God in us. As the time past wherein sin reigned, so the

present burden of sin besetting us is esteemed sufficient, and makes a man careful not to load himself wilfully with more, being ready to sink, and forced to cry out under the pain of those which he unwillingly lies under already. * A very glutton, when he is in a fit of the gout, or stone, will forbear those meats which feed such painful diseases. A penitent sinner is continually in pain under the body of sin, and therefore dares not feed so dangerous and tormenting a disease. † The more spiritual any man is, the more painful and burdensome is corruption to him, Rom. vii. 24; for sin to the new man is as sickness to the natural man. The more exquisite and delicate the natural senses are, the more are they sensible and affected with that which offends nature. Contraries cannot co-exist without strife. The Spirit will lust against the flesh, and not suffer a man to fulfil the lusts of it, Gal. v. 16, 17; the seed of God will keep down the strength of sin, 1 John iii. 9.

Φόβος βουλευτικοὺς ποιεῖ. Arist. Rhet. l. 2. c. 5.

3. By a holy jealousy, and godly fear of the falseness and backsliding of our corrupt heart, lest, like Lot's wife, it should look back towards Sodom, and, like Israel, have a mind hankering after the flesh-pots of Egypt, the wonted profits and pleasures of forsaken lusts. A godly heart prizes the love of God, and the feelings of spiritual comfort from thence arising, above all other things, and is afraid to lose them. It has felt the burnings of sin, the stingings of those fiery serpents, and has often been forced to befool itself, and to beshrew its own ignorance; and, with Ephraim, to smite upon the thigh. Like the burnt child, it dreads the fire, and dares not meddle any more with it; it considers the heaviness of God's frown, the rigour of his law, the weakness and fickleness of the heart of man, the difficulty of finding Christ out when he has withdrawn himself, and of recovering light and peace again, when the soul has wilfully brought itself under a cloud; therefore it will not venture to harden itself against God. Thus godly fear keeps men from sin, Job xxxi. 23; Psal. iv. 4; cxix. 120; Prov. xxviii. 14; Eccl. ix. 2; Jer. xxxii. 40; Phil. ii. 12.

4. By a love to Christ, and a sweet recounting of the mercies of God in him. The less a man loves sin the more will he love Christ. Now repentance works a hatred of sin, and thereupon a love of Christ; which love is ever operative, and putting forth itself towards holiness of life. As the love of God in Christ towards us works forgiveness of sin, so our reciprocal love, wrought by the feeling and comfort of that forgiveness, works in us a hatred of sin. A *direct* love begets a *reflex* love, as the heat wrought in the earth strikes back again a heat up into the air. The woman in the gospel having much forgiven her, "loved much," Luke vii. 47. "We love him because he first loved us;" and love will not suffer a man to wrong the thing which he loves. What man ever threw away jewels or money when he might have kept them? except when the predominant love of something better made these things comparatively hateful, Luke xiv. 26. What woman could be persuaded to throw away her sucking child from her breast to swine or dogs to devour it? Our love to Christ will not suffer us to cast him off, or to throw his law behind our backs. New obedience is ever joined to pardon of sin and repentance for it, by the method of God's decrees, by the order and chain of salvation, and arises out of the internal character and disposition of a child of God. We are not sons only by adoption, appointed to a new inheritance; but we are sons by regeneration also, partakers of a new nature, designed to a new life, joined to a new Head, descended from a new Adam, to whom therefore we are, in "the power of his resurrection, and the fellowship of his sufferings," to be "made conformable," Phil. iii. 10. The apostle uses many excellent and weighty arguments to enforce this upon us, Col. iii. 1—4: "If ye then be risen with Christ, seek those things which are above, where Christ sitteth on the right hand of God. Set your affection on things above, not on things on the earth. For ye are dead, and your life is hid with Christ in God. When Christ, who is our life, shall appear, then shall ye also appear with him in glory." 1. Our fellowship with Christ: we are "risen with" him; what he did corporally for us, he does the same spiritually in us. As a Saviour and Mediator, he died and rose alone; but as a Head and Second Adam, he never did any thing but his mystical body and seed were so taken into the fellowship of it, as to be made conformable to it. Therefore if he rose as a Saviour to justify us, we must, as members, be therein fashioned unto him, and rise spiritually, by heavenly-mindedness and a new life, to glorify him. 2. We must have our affections in heaven, because Christ is there. The heart ever turns towards its treasure; where the body is, thither will the eagles resort. 3. He is there in glory at God's right hand; and grace should move attracted to glory, as the smaller particles of matter to the larger mass. And he is there on our business, making intercession in our behalf, providing a place for us, sending down gifts to us. And the client cannot but have his heart on his own business, when the advocate is actually stirring about it. 4. We are "dead" with Christ, as to the life of sin; and a dead man takes no thought or care for the things of that life from whence he is departed. A man naturally dead looks not after food, or raiment, or land, or money, or labour; and a man dead to sin takes no more care how to provide for it. 5. In Christ we have a new life, therefore we should have new inclinations suitable to it, and new provisions laid in for it. A natural man feeds on worldly things by sense, a spiritual man on heavenly things by faith and conscience. We can have nothing from the first Adam which is not mortal and mortiferous; nothing from the Second which is not eternal and life-giving. Whatever the one gives us shrinks and withers into death; whatever the other, springs and flourishes into immortal life. Our life, therefore, being new, the affections which serve it, and wait upon it, must be new likewise. 6. This life is our own; not so any thing in the world besides. I can purchase in the world only to me and mine heirs for ever, but spiritual purchases are to myself for ever. And every man's affections are naturally most fixed upon that which is most his own. 7. It is a hidden life, the best of it is yet unseen, 1 John iii. 2; and though the cabinet which is seen be rich, yet the jewel which is hidden in it is much richer. And as there is a sinful curiosity in lust to look after the hidden things of iniquity, and to hanker after forbidden pleasures, so there is a spiritual curiosity or ambition in grace, to aspire towards hidden treasures, to press forward towards things that are before us, "to be clothed upon with our house which is from heaven." As Absalom, being brought from banishment, longed to see the face of his father, 2 Sam. xiv. 32; so the soul, delivered out of the land of darkness, never thinks it sees enough of light. When God did most intimately reveal himself to Moses, Moses did most earnestly beseech him to show him his glory, Exod. xxxiii. 11, 18. The more sweetness we find in the first-fruits, in so much of Christ as is revealed to us, the more strong are our affections to the whole harvest, to that abundance of him which is hidden from us. A few clusters of grapes

* Εἰ τοῖς μεθυσκομένοις ἑκάστης ἡμέρας ἀλγεῖν συνέβαινε τὴν κεφαλὴν πρὸ τοῦ πιεῖν τὸν ἄκρατον, ἡμῶν οὐδὲ εἷς ἔπινεν ἄν. Clearch. apud Athen. l. 14. c. 1.

† Conflictus miserabilis. Aug. de Nupt. et Concupis. l. 2. c. 1. Quo quis pejus se habet, minus sentit. Senec. Epist. 52.

and bunches of figs will inflame the desire of enjoying that Canaan which abounds with them. 8. It is "hid with Christ," so hid as that we know where it is. "Hid," so that the enemy cannot reach it, but not hid from the faith of the child. 9. It is hid "in God." It is life in the fountain, Psal. xxxvi. 9. Every thing is most perfect in its original source, and this is such a fountain of life as has in it fulness without satiety, purity without defilement, perpetuity without decay, and all-sufficiency without defect. Lastly, it is but hid, it is not lost; hid like seed in the ground; "when Christ," "the Sun of righteousness," "shall appear," this life of ours in him will spring up and appear glorious.

Now, next let us consider this care of repentance against a man's own more particular and special sins. "Asshur shall not save us; we will not ride upon horses: neither will we say any more to the work of our hands, Ye are our gods." Israel had been guilty of very many provocations, but when they come to covenant with God, and to renew their repentance, their thoughts and cares are most set against their carnal confidence and spiritual adultery; their most unfeigned detestations, their most serious resolutions, were against these their most proper sins. True repentance works indeed a general hatred of "every false way," Psal. cxix. 128, and suffers not a man to allow himself in the smallest sin. Yet, as the dog in hunting the deer, though he drive the whole herd before him, yet fixes his eye and scent on some one in particular, which is singled out by the dart of the huntsman; so, though sound conversion do work a universal hatred of all sin, because it is sin, (for hatred is ever against the whole kind of a thing,) though every member of the old man be mortified, and every grace of the new man shaped and fashioned in us, yet the severest exercise of that hatred is against the sins to which the conscience has been more enslaved, and by which the name of God has been more dishonoured. A man that has many wounds, if there be any of them more deep, dangerous, or nearer any vital part, than another, though he will tend the cure of them all, yet his chiefest care shall be towards that. As the king of Syria gave command to his army to single out the king of Israel in the battle, 1 Kings xxii. 31, so does repentance lay its batteries most against the highest, and strongest, and most reigning sin of the heart; and by how much the more a man prized it before, by so much the more does he detest it now. Before they counted no silver nor gold too good to frame their idols of, their ear-rings shall go to make them a calf, Exod. xxxii. 3; but when they repent, nothing can be too base to compare them, or to cast them unto, Isa. ii. 20; xxx. 22.

'Ὀργὴ περὶ τὰ καθ' ἕκαστα, τὸ δὲ μίσος πρὸς τὰ γένη. Arist. Rhet. l. 2.

Human nature is the same in all men, yet some faculties are more vigorous in some, and others in others; some witty, others strong; some beautiful, others proper; some have a quick eye, others a ready tongue; some for learned, others for mechanical professions; as some grounds take better to some kind of grain than to others: so in the new man, though all the graces of Christ are in some degree and proportion shaped in every regenerate person, yet one excels in one grace, another in another; Abraham in faith, Job in patience, Moses in meekness, David in meditation, Solomon in wisdom, Phinehas in zeal, Mary Magdalene in love, Paul in labour. And so is it in the old man too: though by nature we have all the members of original corruption, yet these put themselves forth in actual vigour differently. One man is more possessed by a proud devil, another by an unclean one; Ahaz superstitious, Balaam ambitious, Cain envious, Korah stubborn, Esau profane, Ishmael a mocker, the young man a worldling, Mark x. 22. According to different complexions and tempers of body, (by which habitual lust is excited and called forth into act,) or according to differences of education, countries, callings, converse, and interests in the world, so men are differently assaulted with distinct kinds of sin; and most men have their *peccatum in deliciis*, which they may more properly call their own, Psal. xviii. 23. And as this sin is usually the special bar and obstacle that keeps men from Christ, as we see in the example of the young man, Mark x. 22, and of the Jews, John v. 44; xii. 42, 43; so when Christ has broken this obstacle, and gotten the throne in a man's heart, then the chief work of repentance is to keep this sin from gathering strength again: for as they say of some kind of serpents, that, being cut in pieces, the parts will wriggle towards one another, and close and get life again; so, of all sins, a man is in most danger of the reviving of his own proper corruption, as being like the nettle, whose roots are so crooked, are so catching to the ground, that it is a work of much care to keep the ground clean of them after they are weeded out.

In eodem prato bos herbam quærit, canis leporem, ciconia lacertum. Senec. Ep. 108.

And therefore repentance sets itself particularly against that sin, as a special argument of sincerity. "I was also upright" (saith David) "before him, and I kept myself from mine iniquity," Psal. xviii. 23. And "he that is begotten of God" (saith the apostle) "keepeth himself," 1 John v. 18; which he does certainly with most vigilance there, where he is in most danger of being assaulted. Thus David had, in that great and scandalous fall of his, stained his conscience with impure lust, with the guilt of blood; and that not out of ignorance, or common infirmity, or sudden passion and surprisal of some hasty temptation, (which might haply have consisted with uprightness,) but seriously, and deliberately, using many cunning arts and carnal shifts of sinful wisdom to colour and daub it over; and further, by this means had given a great blow to the holy name of God, and caused his enemies to blaspheme, as Nathan tells him, 2 Sam. xii. 14: therefore, in his penitential psalm, these four things he principally insists upon, "a clean heart," deliverance from "blood-guiltiness," "truth in the inward parts," and opportunity to "teach transgressors" the way of God, that they may be converted, Psal. li. 6, 10, 13, 14. Thus Zaccheus; worldliness and defrauding had been his sin, restitution and liberality are the evidences of his repentance in special for that sin, Luke xix. 8. So Mary Magdalene; her sin had been uncleanness, her eyes vessels and factors for adultery, her hair a net platted and spread to catch sinners; she remembered her wanton kisses, her provoking perfumes: and now in her conversion, where her sin had been most prevalent, there her sorrow was most penitent, and her repentance most vigilant; her eyes vessels of tears, her kisses humbled, or rather advanced to the feet of Christ; her hair a towel to wipe off those tears which she judged too unclean to wash such holy feet; her ointment poured out upon a new Lover, who had anointed her with his grace, Luke vii. 37, 38. The sin of the jailer against Paul and Silas was cruelty, and the first-fruit of his repentance was courtesy; he "brought them out" of a dungeon into his own house, from the stocks to his table, became an host instead of a jailer, a surgeon instead of a tormentor, and "washed their stripes," Acts xvi. 19—34. This was Daniel's method of working repentance in Nebuchadnezzar, persuading a proud, oppressing tyrant to justice and mercy, Dan. iv. 27; and Paul's with Felix, preaching before a corrupt and lascivious judge of "righteousness, temperance, and judgment to come," Acts xxiv. 25; and with the learned and superstitious philosophers, in a learned discovery, making known to them their "unknown God," Acts xvii. 23. So John, the preacher of repentance, laid his axe to the root of every tree, to the radical and prevailing lust in every order of men; to extortion in the publican, and to covetousness in the people, to violence in the soldiers, to carnal confidence in the Pharisees, Matt. iii. 7; Luke iii. 9—14. And so Christ with the young man, "One thing thou lackest," Mark x. 21; and to the woman of Samaria, "Go, call thy husband," John iv. 16, when indeed he was an adulterer, and not a husband.

The reason of this care of repentance is, 1. Because in godly sorrow this sin has lain most heavy upon the conscience. Hereby God has been most of all despised and dishonoured, our consciences most wasted and defiled, our hearts most hardened, our affections most bewitched and entangled. It has been a master-sin, that has been able to command and to draw in many other servile lusts to wait upon it. Many wounds, even after they have been healed, will on change of weather affect the part wherein they were with acute pains; and therefore men usually are more tender of that part, and keep it warmer: as the apostle saith, that on our dishonourable parts we bestow the more abundant honour; so, on such an infirm and tender part, we bestow the more abundant care; and the like do we in those wounds of the soul which are most apt to bleed afresh.

2. Hereby (as was said before) we testify our uprightness. When we will not spare our beloved sin, nor roll it under our tongue, nor hide it in our tent; when we will not muffle nor disguise ourselves like Tamar, nor hide amongst the bushes and trees like Adam, or in the belly of the ship with Jonah, nor spare any wedge of gold with Achan, or any delicate Agag, any fatling sins, with Saul; but with David will show that we "hate every false way," by throwing the first stone at our first sin, that which lay nearest and closest to our bosoms, which the Scripture calls cutting off the right hand, and plucking out the right eye, Matt. v. 29, 30; as Cranmer put that hand first into the fire, with which he had before subscribed to save his life. The story of the Turkish emperor is commonly known, who being reported so to dote on one of his concubines, as for love of her to neglect the affairs of his kingdom, caused her to be brought forth in great pomp, and cut off her head before his bashaws, to assure them that nothing was so dear to him but that he could willingly part from it to attend the public welfare. This was an act of cruelty in him, but the like is an act of penitence in us, when we can sacrifice the dearest affections wherewith we served sin. Let Christ kill our Agag, though delicately appareled, and divide the richest of all our spoils. If we be learned, we shall direct all our studies to the fear of God, Eccl. xii. 12, 13. If rich, we shall lay up a foundation of good works against the time to come, and consecrate our merchandise as holy to the Lord, 1 Tim. vi. 18, 19; Isa. xxiii. 18. If wise, if honourable, if powerful, if adorned with any endowment, our business will be, with Bezaleel and Aholiab, to adorn the gospel with them all; from our gold to our goats' hair, to lay all out upon the sanctuary, Exod. xxxi.; to make those members and abilities which had been Satan's armour, and weapons of unrighteousness, to be now weapons of holiness, and dedicated unto Christ, Rom. vi. 19. This is the holy revenge which "godly sorrow" takes upon sin, 2 Cor. vii. 10, 11.

If many men who profess repentance, and think they are already long ago converted unto God, would examine the truth of their conversion by this touchstone, it would minister matter of much humiliation and fear to them, when their own heart would reply against them as Samuel against Saul; Hast thou indeed, as thou professest, done the work of the Lord in destroying Amalek, "what meaneth then this bleating of the sheep in mine ears, and the lowing of the oxen which I hear?" what mean these worldly and covetous practices, these lascivious or revengeful speeches, these earthly, sensual, or ambitious lusts? are these Agags spared and kept delicately, and canst thou please thyself in the thoughts of a sound repentance? Did Paul fear that his God would "humble" him for those that had not repented amongst the Corinthians, because there were envyings, strifes, and debates amongst them? 2 Cor. xii. 20, 21; and wilt thou presume on thy repentance, and not be humbled when thou findest the same things in thyself? Hast thou never yet proclaimed defiance to thy beloved sin? made it the mark of thy greatest sorrows, of thy strongest prayers and complaints unto God? Hast thou never stirred up a holy indignation and revenge against it? and above all things, taken off thy thoughts from the meditation and love of it? and found pleasure in the holy severity of God's book and the ministry thereof against it? made no covenant with thine eye, put no knife to thy throat, set no door before thy lips, made no friends of unrighteous mammon? Dost thou still retain hankering affections after thy wonted delights, as Lot's wife after Sodom? and are the flesh-pots of Egypt desirable in thy thoughts still? "Be not high-minded, but fear." There is no greater argument of an unsound repentance than indulgent thoughts, and reserved delight and complacency in a master-sin. The devil will diligently observe and hastily catch one kind glance of this nature, (as Ben-hadad's servants did, 1 Kings xx. 33,) and make use of it to do us mischief. David had been free from some of his greatest troubles, if he had not relented towards Absalom, and called him home from banishment; he no sooner kissed Absalom, than Absalom courted and kissed the people to steal their hearts away from him. As there are in points of faith fundamental articles, so there are in points of practice fundamental duties. And amongst them none more primary, and essential to true Christians, than self-denial, Matt. xvi. 24; and this is one special part and branch of self-denial, to keep ourselves from our own iniquity, and to say to our most costly and darling lusts, Get ye hence. Asshur away, idols away, I will rather be fatherless than rely upon such helpers.

Obs. 5. True repentance and conversion take off the heart from all carnal confidence, either in domestic preparations of our own, "we will not ride upon horses;" or in foreign aid from any confederates, especially enemies of God and his church, though otherwise never so potent, "Asshur shall not save us;" or, lastly, in any superstitious and corrupt worship, which sends us to God the wrong way, "neither will we say any more to the work of our hands, Ye are our gods;" and causes the soul in all conditions, be they never so desperate, so desolate, so incurable, to rely only upon God. It is very much in the nature of man fallen, to affect an absoluteness and a self-sufficiency, to seek the good that he desires within himself, and to derive from himself the strength whereby he would repel any evil which he fears. This staying within itself, reflecting upon its own power and wisdom, and by consequence affecting an independence of any superior virtue in being and working, making itself the first cause and the last end of its own motions; is by divines conceived to have been the first sin by which the creature fell from God, and it was the first temptation by which Satan prevailed to draw man from God too. For since next to God every reasonable created being is nearest to itself, we cannot conceive how it should turn from God, and not in the next step turn to itself; and by consequence, whatsoever it was in a regular dependence to have derived from God, being fallen from him, it does by an irregular dependence seek for from itself. Hence it is that men of power are apt to

Vid. Aug. de Civit. Dei, lib. 2. c. 1. Aquin. part. 1. Q. 63. Art. 3. Hooker, B. 1. sect. 4.

deify their own strength, and to frame opinions of absoluteness to themselves, and to deride the thoughts of any power above them, as Pharaoh, Exod. v. 2, and Goliath, 1 Sam. xvii. 8, 10, 44, and Nebuchadnezzar, Dan. iii. 15, and Sennacherib, 2 Kings xviii. 33—35; Isa. x. 8—14: men of wisdom, to deify their own reason, and to deride any thing that is above or against their own conceptions, as Tyrus, Ezek. xxviii. 2, 6, and the Pharisees, Luke xvi. 14; John vii. 48—52; Acts iv. 11; Isa. xlix. 7; liii. 3, and the philosophers, Acts xvii. 18, 32; 1 Cor. i. 22, 23: and men of morality and virtue, to deify their own righteousness, to rely on their own merits and performances, and to deride righteousness imputed and precarious, as the Jews, Rom. x. 3, and Paul before his conversion, Rom. vii. 9; Phil. iii. 6, 9. Thus natural is it for a sinful creature, who seeks only himself, and makes himself the last end, to seek only to himself, and to make himself the first cause and mover towards that end.

But because God will not give his glory to another, nor suffer any creature to encroach on his prerogative, or to sit down in his throne, he has therefore always blasted the policies and attempts of those who have aspired to such absoluteness and independency, making them know in the end that they are "but men," Psal. ix. 19, 20, and that the Most High ruleth over all; and that it is an enterprise more full of folly than it is of pride, for any creature to attempt to work its own safety and felicity out of itself. And as men usually are most vigilant upon their immediate interests, and most jealous and active against all encroachments thereupon; so we shall ever find that God singles out no men to be such notable monuments of his justice and their own ruin and folly, as those who have vied with him in the points of power, wisdom, and other Divine prerogatives, aspiring unto that absoluteness, self-sufficiency, self-interest, and independency which belong unto him only. And as he has by the destruction of Pharaoh, Sennacherib, Herod, and divers others, taught us the madness of this ambition; so does he by our own daily preservation teach us the same. For if God has appointed that we should go out of ourselves to things below us for a vital subsistence, to bread for food, to house for harbour, to clothes for warmth, much more has he appointed that we should go out of ourselves for a blessed and happy subsistence, by how much the more is required for blessedness than for life, and by how much the greater is our impotency to the greatest and highest end.

Yet so desperate is the aversion of sinful man from God, that when he is convinced of his impotency, and driven off from self-dependence, and reduced to such extremities as should in reason lead him back unto God, yet when he has no horses of his own to ride upon, no means of his own whereby to escape evil, he will still betake himself unto creatures like himself, though they be enemies to God, and enemies to him too for God's sake (for so was the Assyrian to Israel): "When Ephraim saw his sickness, and Judah saw his wound, then went Ephraim to the Assyrian, and sent to king Jareb," Hos. v. 13. If he must beg, he will do it rather of an enemy than of God, yea, though he dissuade him from it, and threaten him for it. Ahaz would not believe though a sign were offered him, nor be persuaded to trust in God to deliver him from Rezin and Pekah though he promised him to do it; but under pretence of not tempting God in the use of means, will weary God with his provocation, and rob God to pay the Assyrian, who was not a help but a distress to him, 2 Kings xvi. 5, 8, 17, 18; 2 Chron. xxviii. 20, 21; Isa. vii. 8, 13; xxx. 5.

Well, God is ofttimes pleased to waylay human counsels, even in this case too, and so to strip them, not only of their own provisions, but of their foreign succours and supplies, so that they have no refuge left but unto him. Their horses fail them, their Assyrian fails them, Hos. vii. 11, 12; viii. 9, 10. Their hope has nothing either *sub ratione boni*, as really good to comfort them at home; or *sub ratione auxilii*, as matter of help and aid to support them from abroad. They are brought as Israel into a wilderness, where they are constrained to go to God, because they have no second causes to help them. And yet even here, wicked men will make a shift to keep off from God, when they have nothing in the world to turn to. This is the formal and intimate malignity of sin, to decline God, and to be impatient of him, in his own way. If wicked men be necessitated to implore help from God, they will invent ways of their own to do it. If horses fail, and Asshur fail, and Israel must go to God whether he will or no, it shall not be to the God that made him, but to a god of his own making; and when they have most need of their glory, they will change it into that which cannot profit, Jer. ii. 11. Thus foolish was Jeroboam, as to think his kingdom should be established by two calves at Dan and Beth-el, and by that means rooted out his own family, and at last ruined the kingdom, 1 Kings xii. 28, 29; xiv. 10, 15; 2 Kings xvii. 21—23; Hos. viii. 4, 5; x. 5, 8, 15. Thus foolish was Ahaz, to seek help of those gods which were the ruin of him and of all Israel, 2 Chron. xxviii. 23. Such a strong antipathy and averseness there is in the soul of natural men to God, as that when they are in distress they go to him last of all; they never think of him so long as their own strength and their foreign confederacies hold out, and when at last they are driven to him, they know not how to hold communion with him in his own way, but frame carnal and superstitious modes of worship to themselves, and so in their very seeking him provoke him to forsake them; and the very things whereon they lean, go up into their hand to pierce it, Isa. xv. 2; xvi. 12.

Ex arbitrio, non ex imperio. Tertul. cont. Psychic. cap. 13.

Now then the proper work of true repentance being to turn a man the right way to God, it takes a man off from all this carnal and superstitious confidence, and directs the soul in the greatest difficulties to cast itself with comfort and confidence upon God alone. So it is prophesied of the remnant of God's people, that is, the penitent part of them, (for the remnant are those that came up "with weeping and supplications," seeking "the Lord their God," and asking "the way to Zion with their faces thitherward," Jer. xxxi. 9; l. 4, 5,) that they should "no more again stay" themselves "upon him that smote them," but should "stay upon the Lord, the Holy One of Israel, in truth," and should "return unto the mighty God," Isa. x. 20, 21. They resolve the Lord shall save them, and not the Assyrian. So say the godly in the psalmist, "An horse is a vain thing for safety; neither shall he deliver any by his great strength." "Our soul waiteth for the Lord: he is our help and shield," Psal. xxxiii. 17, 20. They will not say any more, "We will flee upon horses, we will ride upon the swift," Isa. xxx. 16. "At that day," saith the prophet, speaking of the penitent remnant, the gleanings of Jacob, "shall a man look to his Maker, and his eyes shall have respect to the Holy One of Israel. And he shall not look to the altars, the work of his hands, neither shall respect that which his fingers have made, either the groves, or the images," Isa. xvii. 7, 8. And again, "Truly in vain is salvation hoped for from the hills, and from the multitude of mountains," that is, from the idols (which they had set up and worshipped in high places): "truly in the Lord our God is the salvation of Israel," Jer. iii. 23. "Neither will we say any more to the work of our hands, Ye are our gods."

So then, the plain duties enjoined in the latter part of these verses are these:

1. To trust in God, who is all-sufficient to help; who is Jehovah, the Fountain of being, and can give being to any promise, to any mercy which he intends for his people; can not only work, but command; not only command, but create deliverance, and fetch it out of darkness and desolation: he has "everlasting strength;" there is no time, no case, no condition, wherein his help is not at hand, whenever he shall command it, Isa. xxvi. 4.

2. Not to trust in any creature. 1. Not in Asshur, in any confederacy or combination with God's enemies, be they otherwise never so potent. Jehoshaphat did so, and his "ships were broken," 2 Chron. xx. 35—37. Ahaz did so, and his people were distressed, 2 Chron. xxviii. 19—21. It is impossible for God's enemies to be cordial to God's people, so long as they continue cordial to their God. There is such an irreconcilable enmity between the seed of the woman and the seed of the serpent, that it is incredible to suppose that the enemies of the church will do any thing which may, *per se*, tend to the good of it, or that any end and design by them pursued can be severed from their own malignant interest. Let white be mingled with any other colour, and it loses its own beauty. It is not possible for God's people to join with any that are his enemies, and not lose thereby their own purity. He must be as wise and as potent as God, that can use the rage of God's enemies, and convert it, when he has done, to the good of God's church, and the glory of God's name, and be able at pleasure to restrain and call it in again. We must ever take heed of this dangerous competition between our own interests and God's; to be so tender and intent upon that, as to hazard and shake this. Jeroboam did so, but it was fatal to him, and to all Israel. The end of Judah's combining with the Assyrian was, that they might rejoice against Rezin and Remaliah's son; but the consequence of it, which they never intended, was, that the Assyrian came up over all the channels, and over all the banks, and overflowed, and went over, and reached "even to the neck," and if it had not been Immanuel's land, would have endangered its destruction. If Israel for his own ends join with Asshur, it will hardly be possible for him in so doing, though against his own will, not to promote the ends of Asshur against God's church, and against God himself. And yet the prophet would not have, in that case, God's people to be dismayed, or to say, "A confederacy," "A confederacy;" but to "sanctify the Lord of hosts himself," and make him their "fear," and their "dread," who will certainly be "a sanctuary" unto them, and will "bind up" his "testimony," and "seal the law among" his "disciples," when others shall "stumble, and fall, and be broken, and be snared, and be taken," Isa. viii. 6—18. If we preserve Emmanuel's right in us, and ours in him, all confederacies against us shall be broken, all counsels shall come to nought.

2. Not in horses, or in any other human preparations and provisions of our own. "Some trust in chariots, and some in horses: but we" (saith David) "will remember the name of the Lord our God," Psal. xx. 7. That name can do more with a sling and a stone, than Goliath with all his armour, 1 Sam. xvii. 45. It is "a strong tower" for protection and safety to all that flee into it, Prov. xviii. 10. Whereas horses, though they be "prepared against the day of battle," yet "safety is of the Lord," Prov. xxi. 31. Horses are "flesh, and not spirit," and their riders are "men, and not God;" and cursed are they that make "flesh" their "arm," and depart from the Lord, Isa. xxxi. 1—3; Jer. xvii. 5. No, not in a variety of means and ways of help, which seems to be intimated in the word riding, from one confederate to another; If Asshur fail, I will post to Egypt; if one friend or counsel fail, I will make haste to another; a sin very frequently charged upon Israel, Isa. xx. 5; lvii. 9; Jer. ii. 36, 37; Hos. vii. 11. These are not to be trusted in, 1. Because of the intrinsical weakness and defect of ability in the creature to help. Every man is a liar, either by imposture, and so in purpose; or by impotency, and so in the event, deceiving those that rely upon him, Psal. lxii. 9.

2. Because of the ignorance and defect of wisdom in us to apply that strength which is in the creature to the best advantage. None but an artificer can turn and govern the natural efficacy of fire, wind, water, to the works of art. The wisdom whereby we should direct created virtues to human ends is not in or of ourselves, but comes from God, Exod. xxxvi. 1, 2; Eccl. vii. 24; ix. 11; Isa. xxviii. 26—29; James i. 5.

3. Not in idols, not in corrupting the worship of God. Idols are lies, and teachers of lies, and promisers of lies to all that trust in them, Jer. x. 1—16; Hab. ii. 18; Rev. xxii. 15. An idol is just "nothing in the world," 1 Cor. viii. 4; and that which is nothing, can do nothing for those that rely upon it. Whatever a man trusts in, in time of trouble, must needs have these things in it to ground that confidence upon:

In idololatriâ mendacium, cum tota substantia ejus mendax sit. Tert. de Idololat. cap. 1. unde idolatræ dicuntur συκοφαντεῖν τὴν ἀλήθειαν. Clem. Alex. in Protrept.

'Εχθρῶν ἄδωρα δῶρα καὶ οὐκ ὀνήσιμα. Sophoc. in Aj.

Τὸ εὐπαθεῖν ὑπὸ τυράννου φοβερόν ἔστι. Plut. Apop.

1. A knowledge of him and his wants. Therefore we are bid to trust in God's providence over us for all outward good things, because he "knoweth" that we have "need" of them, Matt. vi. 32.

2. A loving and merciful disposition to help. A man may sometimes receive help from such as love him not, out of policy and in pursuance of other ends and designs; but he cannot confidently rely upon any aid which is not first founded in love. I ever suspect and fear the gifts and succours which proceed from an enemy; they will have their own ends only, even then when they seem to tender and serve me; therefore David singles out God's mercy as the object of his trust, Psal. lii. 8.

3. A manifestation of that love in some promise or other, engaging to assist. For how can I with assurance, and without hesitancy, expect help there where I never received any promise of it? Here was the ground of David's, Jehoshaphat's, Daniel's trust in God, the word and promise which he had passed to them, 1 Chron. xvii. 25—27; Psal. cxix. 42; 2 Chron. xx. 7; Dan. ix. 2.

4. Truth and fidelity in the care to make these promises good. This is that which makes us so confidently trust in God's promises, because we know they are all "yea and amen," that it is "impossible for God to lie," or deceive, or for any to "seek" his face "in vain," 2 Cor. i. 20; Josh. xxi. 45; Heb. vi. 18; Isa. xlv. 19.

5. Power to give being and effect to whatsoever is thus promised. That which a man leans upon, must have strength to bear the weight which is laid upon it. This is the great ground of our trusting in God at all times, even then when all other helps fail, because he is "I am," that can create and give a being to every thing which he has promised; because "power belongeth unto" him, and "in the Lord Jehovah is everlasting strength," and nothing is "too hard," no help too great, for him who "made heaven and earth," and can command all the creatures which he made to serve those whom he is pleased to help, Psal. lxii. 8, 11; Exod. iii. 14; Isa. xxvi. 4; Gen. xviii. 14; Jer. xxxii. 17; Psal. cxxi. 2; Matt. viii. 2. Now whosoever seeks for any of these grounds of trust in idols, shall be sure to be disappointed. Knowledge they have none, Isa. xliv. 9, and therefore love they have none, for how

can that love any thing which knows nothing? Truth they have none, neither of being in themselves, nor of promise to those that trust in them; the very essence of an idol is to be a lie, to stand for that which it is not, and to present that to which it is most unlike, Isa. xl. 18; xliv. 20; Jer. x. 14—16. And power they have none, either to hear or save, Isa. xli. 23, 24, 28, 29; xlv. 20; xlvi. 7. And therefore that repentance which shakes off confidence in idols, not only converts a man to God, but to himself: it is not only an impious, but a sottish thing, and below the reason of a man, first to make a thing, and then to worship it, to expect safety from that which received being from himself, Isa. xlvi. 6, 7. These are the three great props of carnal confidence, foreign interests, domestic treasures, superstitious devotions: when men "please themselves in the children of strangers," and have their land "full of silver and gold," and "treasures," full of "horses" and "chariots," and "full of idols;" when they hoard up provisions and preparations of their own, comply with the enemies of God abroad, and corrupt the worship of God at home; these are the things for which God threatens terribly to shake the earth, and to bring down and to make low the loftiness of man, if he do not (as Ephraim here by long and sad experience) penitently renounce and abjure them all, Isa. ii. 6—9.

And now, this is matter for which we all may be humbled. There is no sin more usual among men than carnal confidence, to lean on our own wisdom, or wealth, or power, or supplies from others, to deify counsels and armies, or horses and treasures, and to let our hearts rise or fall, sink or bear up within us, according as the creature is helpful or useless, nearer or farther from us; as if God were not a God afar off, as well as near at hand. This we may justly fear, God has, and still will visit us, because we do not "sanctify the Lord of hosts himself" in our hearts, to make him our "fear" and our defence, and that he will blow upon all such counsels and preparations as carnal confidence deifies.

Therefore we must be exhorted to take off our hopes and fears from second causes, not to glory in an arm of flesh, or to droop when that fails us; not to say in our prosperity, our mountain is so strong that we shall not be shaken; nor in our sufferings, that our wound is incurable, or our grave so deep that we shall never be raised again. But to make "the name of the Lord" our "strong tower;" for "they who know thy name will trust in thee." And for direction herein we must learn to trust in God,

1. Absolutely and for himself, because he only is absolute and of himself. Other things, as they have their being, so have they their working and power of doing good or evil only from him, Matt. iv. 4; John xix. 11. And therefore, till he take himself away, though he take all other things away from us, we have matter of encouragement and rejoicing in the Lord still, as David and Habakkuk resolve, 1 Sam. xxx. 6; Hab. iii. 17, 18. All the world cannot take away any promise from any servant of God; and there is more of reality in the least promise of God, than in the greatest performance of the creature.

Nihil rex majus minari male parentibus potest, quam ut abeat e regno. Senec. Epist. [illegible]0. Tua me non satiant nisi tecum. Bern. Soliloq. Ubi bene erit sine illo? aut ubi male esse poterit cum illo? Bern. ser. 1. de Adven. Dei.

2. To trust him in the way of his commandments, not in any precipices or presumptions of our own. "Trust in the Lord, and do good," Psal. xxxvii. 3. First fear him, and then trust in him; he is a "help" and "shield" only unto such, Psal. cxv. 11. It is high insolence for any man to lean upon God without his leave, and he allows none to do it but such as fear him, and obey the voice of his servants, Isa. l. 10.

Nolite sperare in iniquitate, nolite peccare in spe. Bern. ser. 2. de Advent. In viis custodiet, nunquid in præcipitiis? Bern. ser. 14. in Psa. Qui habit.

3. To trust him in the way of his providence, and the use of such means as he has sanctified and appointed. Though man lives not by bread alone, but by the word of blessing which proceeds out of the mouth of God; yet that word is by God annexed to bread, and not to stones; and that man would not trust God, but mock and tempt him, who would expect to have stones turned into bread. If God has provided stairs, it is not faith, but fury, not confidence, but madness, to go down by a precipice: where God prescribes means and affords secondary helps, we must obey his order, and implore his blessing in their use. This was Nehemiah's way; he prayed to God, and he petitioned the king, Neh. ii. 4. This was Esther's way; a fast to call upon God, and a feast to obtain favour with the king, Esth. iv. 16; v. 4. This was Jacob's way; a supplication to God, and a present to his brother, Gen. xxxii. 9, 13. This was David's way against Goliath; the name of the Lord his trust, and yet a sling and a stone his weapon, 1 Sam. xvii. 45, 49. This was Gideon's way against the Midianites; his sword must go along with the sword of the Lord, not as an addition of strength, but as a testimony of obedience, Judg. vii. 18. Prayer is called sometimes a lifting up of the voice, sometimes a lifting up of the hands, to teach us, that when we pray to God, we must as well have a hand to work, as a tongue to beg. In a word, we must use second causes in obedience to God's order, not in confidence of their help. The creature must be the object of our diligence, but God only the object of our trust.

Dii prohibebunt hæc, sed non propter me de cœlo descendent. Vobis dent mentem ut prohibeatis. Liv. l. 9. Κυβερνήτης εὐχόμενος τὸν οἴακα προσάγει, &c. Plut. de Superst.

Now, lastly, from the ground of the church's prayer and promise, we learn, that the way to mercy is to be in ourselves fatherless. "The poor" (saith David) "committeth himself unto thee; thou art the helper of the fatherless," Psal. x. 14; cxlvi. 9. When Jehoshaphat knew not what to do, then was a fit time to direct his eye unto God, 2 Chron. xx. 12. When the stones of Sion are in the dust, "the time to favour her, yea, the set time, is come," Psal. cii. 13. When Israel was under heavy bondage, and had not Joseph as a tender father to provide for them, then God remembered that he was their Father, and Israel his firstborn, Exod. iv. 22. Nothing will make us seek for help above ourselves, but the apprehension of weakness within ourselves. In those creatures that are weakest, nature has put an aptitude and inclination to depend on those that are stronger. The vine, the ivy, the hop, are taught by nature to clasp and cling and wind about stronger trees. The greater sense we have of our own vileness, the fitter disposition are we in to rely on God. "I will also leave in the midst of thee an afflicted and poor people, and they shall trust in the name of the Lord," Zeph. iii. 12; Isa. xiv. 32. When a man is proud within, and has any thing of his own to lean upon, he will hardly trust in God, Prov. iii. 5; xxviii. 25. Israel never thought of returning to her first husband, till her way was hedged up with thorns, and no means left to enjoy her former lovers, Hos. ii. 6, 7. When the enemy has shut up and intercepted all her passages to Dan and Beth-el, to Egypt and Assyria, that she has neither friends nor idols to flee to, then she thinks of returning to her first husband, even to God.

Now from hence we learn, 1. The condition of the church in this world, which is to be as an orphan, destitute of all succour and favour, as an outcast, whom "no man seeketh after," Jer. xxx. 17. Paul entertained low thoughts of the world, and the world thought as basely of him. "The world" (saith he) "is crucified unto me, and I unto the world," Gal. vi. 14. Before conversion, the world is an Egypt to us, a place of bondage; after conversion, it is a wilderness to us, a place of emptiness and temptations.

2. The backwardness of man towards grace; we go not to God till we are brought to extremities, and all other helps fail us. The poor prodigal never thought of looking after a father, till he found himself in a fatherless condition, and utterly destitute of all relief, Luke xv. 17, 18.

3. The right disposition and preparation for mercy, which is to be an orphan, destitute of all self-confidence, and broken off from all other comforts. "When the poor and needy seek water, and there is none, and their tongue faileth for thirst, I the Lord will hear them, I the God of Israel will not forsake them," Isa. xli. 17. God will "repent himself for his servants, when he seeth that their power is gone," Deut. xxxii. 36, when there is *dignus vindice nodus*, an extremity fit for Divine power to interpose. Christ is set forth as a physician, which supposeth sickness; as a fountain, which supposeth uncleanness; as meat, which supposeth emptiness; as clothing, which supposeth nakedness. He never finds us till we are lost sheep; when we have lost all, then we are fit to follow him, and not before.

4. The roots of true repentance. *Nos pupilli, tu misericors.* The sense of want and emptiness in ourselves, the apprehension of favour and mercy in God. Conviction of sin in us, and of righteousness in him, John xvi. 9, 10; of crookedness in us, and of glory in him, Isa. xl. 4, 5.

Hereby room is made for the entertainment of mercy; where sin abounds, grace will more abound, and the more the soul finds itself exceeding miserable, the more will the mercy of God appear exceeding merciful, Rom. v. 20: and hereby God shows his wisdom in the seasonable dispensing of mercy then when we are in greatest extremity; as fire is hottest in the coldest weather. God delights to be seen in the mount, at the grave, to have his way in the sea, and his paths in the deep waters. Mercies are never so sweet as when they are seasonable, and never so seasonable as in the very turning and critical point, when misery weighs down, and nothing but mercy turns the scale.

5. How to fit ourselves for the mercy of God, namely, to find ourselves destitute of all inward or outward comfort, and to seek for it only in him. Beggars do not put on scarlet, but rags, to prevail with men for relief:* as Ben-hadad's servants put on ropes when they would beg mercy of the king of Israel. In a shipwreck a man will not load him with money, chains, treasure, rich apparel; but commit himself to the sea naked, and esteem it mercy enough to have *tabulam post naufragium*, one poor plank to carry him to the shore. It is not exaltation enough to Joseph except he be taken out of a prison to honour.

6. That we should not be broken with diffidence or distrust in times of trouble, but remember it is the condition of the church to be an orphan. It is the way whereby Moses came to be the son of Pharaoh's daughter; when his own parents durst not own him, the mercy of a prince found him out to advance him; and when he was nearest to perishing, he was nearest unto honour.

Leg. 19. Cod. de Sacros. Ecclesiis. et Leg. 46. Cod. de Episcopis et Cler. sect. 1. 3. Vide Tholos Syntag Juris. l. 15. cap. 28.

In the civil law we find provision made for such as were cast out, and exposed to the wide world, some hospitals to entertain them, some liberties to comfort and relieve their misery. And a like care we find in Christ; the Jews had no sooner cast out the man that was born blind, whose parents durst not be seen in his cause for fear of the like usage, but the mercy of Christ presently found him, and bestowed comfort upon him, John ix. 35. This is the true David,† to whom all helpless persons, that are in distress, in debt, in bitterness of soul, may resort and find entertainment, 1 Sam. xxii. 2.

7. To behave ourselves as pupils under such a Guardian; to be sensible of our infancy, minority, disability to order or direct our own ways, and so deny ourselves, and not lean on our own wisdom; to be sensible how this condition exposes us to the injuries of strangers, for because we are "chosen out of the world, therefore the world hateth" us; and so to be vigilant over our ways, and not trust ourselves alone in the hands of temptation, nor wander from our Guardian, but always to yield to his wisdom and guidance. Lastly, to comfort ourselves in this, that while we are in our minority, we are under the mercy of a Father; a mercy of conservation by his providence, giving us all good things richly to enjoy, even all things necessary unto life and godliness; a mercy of protection, defending us by his power from all evil; a mercy of education and instruction, teaching us by his word and Spirit; a mercy of communion, many ways familiarly conversing with us, and manifesting himself unto us; a mercy of guidance and government, by the laws of his family; a mercy of discipline, fitting us by fatherly chastisements for those further honours and employments to which he will advance us; and when our minority is over, and we once are come to a perfect man, we shall then be actually admitted into that inheritance immortal, invisible, and that fadeth not away, which the same mercy which at first purchased, now prepares and reserves for us.

Ver. 4. *I will heal their backsliding, I will love them freely: for mine anger is turned away from him.*

In the former words we have considered both Israel's petition in time of trouble, and the promise and covenant in which thereupon they bind themselves. In these and the consequent words to the end of the 8th verse, we have the gracious answer of God to both, promising both in his free love to grant their petition, and by his free grace to enable them to perform the covenant which they had made.

The petition consisted of two parts: 1. That God would "take away all iniquity." 2. That he would do them good, or "receive" them "graciously." To both these God gives them a full and gracious answer: 1. That he will "take away all iniquity," "I will heal their backsliding." 2. That he would receive them graciously, do them good, and heap all manner of blessings upon them, which are expressed by the various metaphors of fruitfulness; opposite to the contrary expressions of judgment in former parts of the prophecy.

"I will heal their backsliding." This is one of the names by which God is pleased to make himself known to his people, "I am the Lord that healeth thee," Exod. xv. 26; and, "Return, ye backsliding children, and I will heal your backslidings," Jer. iii. 22.

Now God heals sin in a fourfold manner.

1. By a gracious pardon, burying, covering, not imputing them to us. So it seems to be expounded, Psal. ciii. 3; and that which is called healing in one place, is called forgiveness in another, Matt. xiii. 15; Mark iv. 12.

2. By a spiritual and effectual reformation, purging the conscience from dead works, making it strong and able to serve God in new obedience; for that which health is to the body, holiness is to the soul. Therefore "the Sun of righteousness" is said to "arise with healing in his wings," Mal. iv. 2; whereby we are to understand the gracious influence of the Holy Spirit conveying the virtue of the blood of Christ to the con-

* Mendici cum eleemosynam petunt, non pretiosas vestes ostendunt, sed seminuda membra, aut ulcera si habuerint, ut citius ad misericordiam videntis animus inclinetur. Bern. ser. 4. de Advent.

† David homines in angustiis constitutos et oppressos ære alieno in suam tutelam suscipiens, typus Christi est publicanos et peccatores recipientis. Gloss. Philolog. Sacr. lib. 2. p. 424.

science, even as the beams of the sun do the heat and influence thereof to the earth, thereby calling out the herbs and flowers, and healing those deformities which winter had brought upon it.

3. By removing and withdrawing judgments, which the sins of a people had brought, like wounds or sicknesses, upon them. So healing is opposed to smiting and wounding, Deut. xxxii. 39; Job v. 18; Hos. vi. 1, 2; Jer. xxxiii. 5, 6.

4. By comforting against the anguish and distress which sin is apt to bring upon the conscience. For as in physic there are purgatives to cleanse away corrupt humours, so there are cordials likewise to strengthen and refresh weak and dejected patients. And this is one of Christ's principal works, to bind and heal the broken in heart, to restore comforts to mourners, to set at liberty them that are bruised, and to have mercy upon those whose bones are vexed, Psal. cxlvii. 3; Isa. lvii. 18, 19; Luke iv. 18; Psal. vi. 2, 3. I am not willing to shut any of these out of the meaning of the text, and that for a twofold reason:

1. Because it is an answer to that prayer, "Take away all iniquity." The "all" that is in it, the guilt, the stain, the power, the punishment, the anguish, whatever evil it is apt to bring upon the conscience, remove it *all*, let it not do us any hurt.

2. Because God's works are perfect; where he forgives sin, he removes it; where he convinces of righteousness, to the pardon of sin, he convinces also of judgment, to the casting out of the prince of this world, and brings forth that judgment to victory, Matt. xii. 20.

"Their backsliding." Their prayer was against "all iniquity," and God in his answer thereunto singles out one kind of iniquity, but one of the greatest, by name. And that, 1. To teach them and us, when we pray against sin, not to content ourselves with generalities, but to bewail our great and special sins by name, those especially which have been most comprehensive, and proved the seminaries of many others.

2. To comfort them; for if God pardon by name the greatest sin, then surely none of the rest will stand in the way of his mercy; if he pardon the talents, we need not doubt but he will pardon the pence too. Paul was guilty of many other sins, but when he will magnify the grace of Christ, he makes mention of his great sins, a blasphemer, a persecutor, injurious; and comforts himself in the mercy which he had obtained against them, 1 Tim. i. 13.

3. To intimate the great guilt of apostacy and rebellion against God. After we have known him, and tasted of his mercy, and given up ourselves to his service, and come out of Egypt and Sodom, then to look back again, and to be false in his covenant, this God looks on, not as a single sin, but as a compound of all sins. When a man turns from God, he does as it were resume and take home again upon his conscience all the sins of his life.

4. To proportion his answer to their repentance. They confess their apostacy: they had been in covenant with God, they confess he was their "first husband," Hos. ii. 7; and they forsook him, and sought to horses, to men, to idols, to vanity and lies: this is the sin they chiefly bewail; and therefore this is the sin which God chiefly singles out to pardon and to heal them of. This is the great goodness of God toward those that pray in sincerity, that he fits his mercy *ad cardinem desiderii*, answers them in the main of their desires, "Be it unto thee even as thou wilt."

Aug. Confess. lib. 5. cap. 8.

"I will love them freely." This is set down as the fountain of that remission, sanctification, and comfort, which are here promised. It comes not from our conversion to God, but from God's free love and grace to us. And this is added,

1. To humble them, that they should not ascribe any thing to themselves, their repentance, their prayers, their covenants and promises, as if these had been the means to procure mercy for them, or as if there were any objective grounds of loveliness in them, to stir up the love of God towards them.* It is not for their sake that he does it, but for his own: The Lord sets his love upon them because he loved them, Deut. vii. 7, 8. "Not for your sakes do I this, saith the Lord God, be it known unto you," Ezek. xxxvi. 32. He "will have mercy on whom" he "will have mercy," Rom. ix. 15.

2. To support them, above the guilt of their greatest sins. Men think nothing more easy while they live in sin, and are not affected with its weight and heinousness, than to believe in mercy and pardon. But when the soul, in conversion to God, feels the heavy burden of some great sins, when it considers its rebellion, and apostacy, and backsliding from God, it will then be very apt to think God will not forgive nor heal such great wickedness; there is a natural Novatianism in the timorous conscience of convinced sinners, to doubt and question pardon for sins of apostacy, and falling after repentance. Therefore in this case God takes a penitent off from the consideration of himself by his own thoughts, to the height and excellency of His thoughts who knows how to pardon abundantly, Isa. lv. 7—9; Jer. xxix. 11; Ezek. xxxvii. 3. Nothing is too hard for love, especially free love, that has no foundation or inducement from without itself.

And because we read before, Hos. viii. 5, that God's "anger" was "kindled against them," therefore he here adds that this also should be "turned away" from them. Anger will consist with love; we find God angry with Moses, and Aaron, and Miriam, and Asa; and he does sometimes "visit with the rod" and "with stripes," where he yet does "not utterly take" away his "loving-kindness" from a people, Psal. lxxxix. 32, 33. A man may be angry with his wife, or child, or friend, whom he yet dearly loves. And God is said to be thus angry with his people, when the effects of displeasure are discovered towards them. Now, on their repentance and conversion, God promises not only to "love them freely," but to clear up his countenance toward them, to make them by the removal of judgments to see and know the fruits of his free love and bounty toward them. When David called Absalom home from banishment, this was an effect of love; but when he said, "Let him not see my face," this was the continuation of anger; but at last, when he admitted him into his presence and kissed him, then that anger too was turned away from him, 2 Sam. xiv. 21, 24, 33.

Aristot. Rhet. lib. 2. cap. 2.

These words then contain God's merciful answer to the first part of Israel's prayer, for the taking away of all iniquity, which had been the fountain of those sad judgments under which they languished and pined away. Wherein there are two parts: I. The ground of God's answer, his free love. II. A double fruit of that love: 1. In healing their backsliding. 2. In removing his anger and heavy judgments from them. We will briefly handle them in the order of the text.

"I will heal their backsliding." When God's people return to him and pray against sin, God, out of his free love, heals them of it. He first teaches them what to ask, and then tells them what he will give. Thus we find conversion and healing joined together, Isa. vi.

* Si vera sit gratia, id est, gratuita, nihil invenit in homine cui merito debeatur, &c. Aug. lib. de Patient. c. 20. et alibi passim. Ex se sumit materiam et velut quoddam seminarium miserendi.—Miserendi causam et originem sumit ex proprio: judicandi vel ulciscendi magis ex nostro. Bern. serm. 5. in Natali Dom.

10. "And they shall return even to the Lord, and he shall be entreated of them, and shall heal them," Isa. xix. 22. "Return, ye backsliding children, and I will heal your backslidings," Jer. iii. 22. Men, if they be injured and provoked by those whom they have it in their power to ruin, though they return, and cry *peccavi*, and are ready to ask forgiveness, yet many times, out of pride and revenge, will take their time and opportunity to repay the wrong.* But God does not so; his pardons, as all his other gifts, are without exprobration; as soon as ever his servants come back to him with tears and confession, he looks not on them with scorn, but with joy; his mercy makes more haste to embrace them, than their repentance to return unto him, Luke xv. 20; then out comes the wine, the oil, the balm, the cordials; then the wounds of a Saviour do, as it were, bleed afresh to drop mercy into the sores of such a penitent. Oh, though he be not a dutiful, not "a pleasant child," yet he is a child; though "I spake against him, I do earnestly remember him still: therefore my bowels are troubled for him; I will surely have mercy upon him," Jer. xxxi. 20. The Lord greatly complains of the inclination of his people to backsliding, and yet he cannot find in his heart to destroy them, but expresses a kind of conflict between justice and mercy, and at last resolves, "I am God, and not man;" I can as well heal their backsliding by my love, as revenge it by my justice; therefore "I will not execute the fierceness of mine anger," but I will cause them to "walk after the Lord," Hos. xi. 7, 9, 10. Yea, so merciful he is, that even on a hypocritical conversion, when his people did but flatter and lie unto him, and "their heart was not right with him, neither were they stedfast in his covenant;" yet the text saith, "he, being full of compassion, forgave their iniquity," (not as to the justification of their persons, for that is never without faith unfeigned, but as to the mitigation of their punishment,) "and destroyed them not: yea, many a time turned he his anger away, and did not stir up all his wrath" against them, Psal. lxxviii. 34—38. So Ezek. xx. 17, "Nevertheless mine eye spared them from destroying them, neither did I make an end of them in the wilderness."

Gravis quædam inter virtutes videtur orta contentio siquidem veritas et justitia miserum affligebant: pax et misericordia judicabant magis esse parcendum, &c. Vid. Bern. serm. 1. in Annunci.

Now the metaphorical word both here and so often elsewhere used in this argument, leads us to look on sinners as patients, and on God as a Physician. By which two considerations we shall find set forth fully to us the exceeding mercy of God in the pardon and purging away of sin.

Healing, then, is a relative word, and leads us, first, to the consideration of a patient who is to be healed, and that is here a grievous sinner fallen into a relapse. Healing is of two sorts; the healing of a sickness by a physician; the healing of a wound by a surgeon. And sin is both a sickness and a wound. "The whole head is sick, and the whole heart faint. From the sole of the foot even unto the head there is no soundness in it; but wounds, and bruises, and putrifying sores," Isa. i. 5, 6. A sickness that wants healing, a wound that wants binding, Ezek. xxxiv. 4. A sick sinner, that wants a physician to call to repentance, Matt. ix. 12, 13; a wounded sinner, that wants a Samaritan (so the Jews called Christ, John viii. 48) to bind up and pour in wine and oil, Luke x. 34.

Diseases are of several sorts, but those are, of all other, most dangerous that are in the vital parts; as all the diseases of sin are, and from thence spread themselves over the whole man. Ignorance, pride, carnal principles, corrupt judgment, diseases of the head; hardness, stubbornness, atheism, rebellion, diseases of the heart; lust, a dart in the liver; corrupt communication, the effect of putrid lungs; gluttony and drunkenness, the swellings and dropsies of the belly; despair and horror, the grief of the bowels; apostacy, a recidivation or relapse into all; an ear that cannot hear God speak, Jer. vi. 10; an eye quite closed up, that cannot see him strike, Isa. xxvi. 11; Jer. xliv. 18; a palate out of taste, that can neither savour nor relish heavenly things, Rom. viii. 5; lips poisoned, Rom. iii. 13; a tongue set on fire, James iii. 6; flesh consumed; bones sticking out, sore vexed and broken to pieces, Job xxxiii. 21; Psal. vi. 2; li. 8. Some diseases are dull, others acute; some stupifying, others tormenting. Sin is all; a stupifying palsy, that takes away feeling, Eph. iv. 19; a plague in the heart, which sets all on fire, 1 Kings viii. 38; Hos. vii. 4.

Let us consider a little the proper passions and effects of most diseases, and see how they meet in sin.

1. Pain and distemper. This, first or last, is, in all, sin, for it begets in wicked and impenitent men the pain of guilt, horror, trembling of heart, anguish of conscience, fear of wrath, expectation of judgment and fiery indignation, as in Cain, Pharaoh, Ahab, Felix, and divers others, Gen. iv. 13, 14; Exod. ix. 27, 28; 1 Kings xxi. 27; Acts xxiv. 25; Isa. xxxiii. 14; Heb. ii. 15; Rom. viii. 15; Heb. x. 27. And in penitent men it begets the pain of shame, and sorrow, and inquietude of spirit, a wound in the spirit, a prick in the very heart, Rom. vi. 21; Ezek. xvi. 61; 2 Cor. vii. 10; Prov. xviii. 14; Acts ii. 37. Penitency and pain are words of one derivation, and are very near of kin to one another. Never was any wound cured without pain, never any sin healed without sorrow.

2. Weakness and indisposedness to the actions of life. Sin is like an unruly spleen, or a greedy wen in the body, that sucks all nourishment, and converts all supplies to its own growth, and so exhausts the strength and vigour of the soul, making it unfit and unable to do any good. Whenever it sets about any duty, till sin be cured, it goes about it like an arm out of joint, which, when you would move it one way, falls back another. It faints, and flags, and is not able to put forth any skill, or any delight, to the performance of any good duty. Naturally men are "reprobate," or void of judgment, "unto every good work," Tit. i. 16. Godliness is a mystery, a spiritual skill and trade; learning, and use, and experience, and much exercise are required in its practice, 1 Tim. iii. 16; Phil. iv. 11; Heb. v. 13, 14. To be "sinners," and to be "without strength," in the apostle's phrase, is all one, Rom. v. 6, 8. And look how much flesh there is in any man, so much disability is there to perform any thing that is good, Rom. vii. 18. Therefore the hands of sinners are said to "hang down," and their "knees" to be "feeble," and their "feet" to be "lame," that cannot make "straight paths" till they "be healed," Heb. xii. 12, 13. If they at any time on natural dictates, or some sudden strong conviction, or pang of fear, or stirrings of conscience, attempt any good work, to pray, to repent, to believe, to obey, they are quite out of their element; they are wise to do evil, but to do good they have no knowledge; they presently grow weary of any attempts at well-doing, and cannot hold out or persevere in them.

Καθάπερ τὰ παραλελυμένα τοῦ σώματος, &c. Arist. Eth. l. 1. c. ult.

3. Decay and consumption. Sin wastes and wears

* Εἴπερ γάρ τε χόλον γε καὶ αὐτῆμαρ καταπέψη,
Ἀλλά γε καὶ μετόπισθεν ἔχει κότον, ὄφρα τελέσσῃ
Ἐν στήθεσσιν ἑοῖσι·—— Hom. Iliad. I.

Quæ in præsens Tiberius civiliter habuit, sed in animo revolvente iras, etiamsi impetus offensionis languerat, memoria valebat. Tacit. Annal. l. 4. Non enim Tiberium quamvis triennio post cædem Sejani, quæ cæteros mollire solent, tempus, preces, satias mitigabant, quin incerta et abolita pro gravissimis et recentibus puniret. Id. Annal. lib. 6. Vid. et. Aristot. Ethic. lib. 4. cap. 11.

Tabificæ mentis perturbationes. Cic. Tuscul. Quæst.

out the vigour of soul and body, feeds on all our time and strength, and exhausts it in the services of lust. Sickness is a chargeable thing, a consumption at once to the person and to the estate. The poor woman in the gospel, who had an issue of blood, "spent all her living upon physicians, neither could be healed of any," Luke viii. 43. So poor sinners empty all the powers of soul, of body, of time, of estate, every thing within their reach, on their lusts, and are as unsatisfied at last as at the first, Eccl. i. 8. Like a silkworm, which works out its bowels into a mass wherein itself is buried, so sin wearies men out, and sucks away their radical strength in its service, and yet never gives them over; but as Pharaoh's taskmasters exacted the brick when they had taken away the straw, so lust consumes and weakens natural strength, in the obedience of it; and yet when nature is exhausted, the strength of lust is as great, and the commands as tyrannous, as before, Isa. lvii. 10; Jer. ii. 25. We are to distinguish between the vital force of the faculties, and the activity of lust which sets them on work; that decays and hastens to death, but sin retains its strength and vigour still, nothing kills that but the blood of Christ: and the decay of nature arises out of the strength of sin; * the more any man, in any lust whatsoever, makes himself a servant of sin, and the more busy and active he is in that service, the more will it eat into and consume him, as the hotter the fever is, the sooner is the body wasted and dried up by it.

4. Deformity. Sickness withers the beauty of the body, makes it of a glorious a ghastly and loathsome spectacle. Go to the comeliest person living after a long and pining sickness, and you will not find them the same; a wan countenance, a shrivelled flesh, a lean visage, a hollow and standing eye, a trembling hand, a stammering tongue, a bowed back, a feeble knee, a swollen belly; nothing left but the stakes of the hedge, and a few sinews to hold them together. Behold here the picture of a sinner, swelled with pride, pined with envy, bowed with earthliness, wasted and eaten up with lust, "filthy" and loathsome as a dead carcass, Psal. xiv. 3; Ezek. xvi. 4, 5. When thou seest an unmerciful man, that has no compassion left in him, think thou beholdest Judas or king Jehoram, whose "bowels fell out by reason of his sore diseases," 2 Chron. xxi. 19. When thou seest a worldly man, whose heart is glued to earthly things, think on the poor woman who was "bowed together, and could in no wise lift up herself," Luke xiii. 11. When thou seest a hypocrite, walking crooked and unevenly in the ways of God, think upon Mephibosheth or Asa, lame, halting, diseased in their feet. When thou seest a proud, ambitious man, think upon Herod eaten up with vermin. O, if the diseases of the soul could come forth and show themselves in the body, and work such deformity there, (where it would not do the thousandth part so much hurt,) as they do within; if a man could in the glass of the word see the ugliness of the one, as plainly as in a material glass the foulness of the other; how would this make him cry out, "My head, my head;" "my bowels, my bowels;" "my leanness, my leanness;" "unclean, unclean!" No man thinks any shape ugly enough to represent a devil by; yet regard his original, and he was a most glorious creature; sin turns him into a serpent or dragon. There is something of the monster in every sin, the belly or the feet set in the place of the head or heart; sensual and worldly lusts set up above reason, and corrupt reason above grace.

Inflatus et tumens animus in vitio est. Sapientis animus nunquam turgescit, nunquam tumet. Cic. Tuscul. Quæst. l. 3. O curvæ in terras animæ et cœlestium inanes. Pers. Ut corpora verberibus, ita sævitia, libidine, malis consulis animus dilaceratur. Tacit. Annal. l. 6.

Now because the sickness here spoken of is a falling sickness, and that the worst kind of fall, not forward in our way or race, as every good man sometimes falls, where a man has the help of his knees and hands to break the blow, to prevent or lessen the hurt, and to make him to rise again; but as old Eli's fall, a falling backward, 1 Sam. iv. 18; where a man can put forth no part to save the whole, and so breaks and bruises himself thereby more dangerously. Therefore as it is a sickness which requires curing, so it is a wound which requires healing and binding. The ancients compare it to falling into a pit full of dirt and stones, where a man not only defiles, but miserably breaks and bruises himself. There is *contritio, solutio continui, suppuratio, sanies*, &c.; all the evils of a dangerous and mortal wound.

Add to all this, that in this diseased and wounded condition a man has, 1. No power to heal or to help himself, but in that respect he must cry out with them in the prophet, "Why is my pain perpetual, and my wound incurable, which refuseth to be healed?" Jer. xv. 18.

2. No desire, no will, no thought to inquire or send after a physician who may heal him; but is well contented rather to continue as he is, than to be put to the pain and trouble of a cure; yea, he pleases himself in the goodness of his own condition, Rev. iii. 17; Matt. ix. 12.

Libens ægrotat qui medico non credit nec morbum declinat. Arist. Ethic. lib. 3.

3. He is in the hands of his cruel enemy, who takes no pity on him, but by flattery and tyranny, and new temptations, continually cherishes the disease, 2 Tim. ii. 26.

4. When the true Physician comes he shuts the door against him, refuses his counsel, rejects his receipts, quarrels with his medicines; they are too bitter, or too strong and purging, or too sharp and searching; he will not be healed at all except it may be in his own way, Prov. i. 24, 25; 2 Chron. xxxvi. 16; Ezek. xxiv. 13; Matt. xxiii. 37; Jer. xiii. 11. Thus we have taken a view of the patient, sick, weak, pained, consumed, deformed, wounded, and sore bruised; without power or help at home, without friends abroad; no sense of danger, no desire of change; patient of his disease, impatient of his cure; but one means in the world to help him, and he unable to procure it, and, being offered to him, unwilling to entertain it: who can expect after all this, but to hear the knell ring for such, and to see the grave open to receive them?

Now let us take a view of the Physician. Surely an ordinary one would be so far from visiting such a patient, that in so desperate a condition as this he would quite forsake him; as their use is to leave their patients when they lie a dying. Here then observe the singular goodness of this Physician.

1. Though other physicians judge of the disease when it is brought to them, yet the patient first feels it and complains of it himself; but this Physician gives the patient the very feeling of his disease, and is fain to take notice of that as well as to minister the cure. "He went on frowardly in the way of his heart," saith the Lord, and pleased himself in his own ill condition; "I have seen his ways, and will heal him," Isa. lvii. 17, 18.

2. Other patients send for the physician, and use many entreaties to be visited and their case undertaken by him. Here the Physician comes unsent for, and entreats the sick person to be healed. The world is undone by falling off from God, and yet God is the first that begins the reconciliation; that which hinders it is in the world, and not in him: therefore there is a great emphasis in the apostle's expression, "God was in

* Ἄπληστος ἡ τοῦ ἡδέος ὄρεξις. Arist. Eth. l. 3. c. ult. Πονηρία τῶν ἀνθρώπων ἄπληστον τι.—Ἀπειρὸς ἡ τῆς ἐπιθυμίας φύσις. Id. Polit. l. 2. Naturalia desideria finita sunt; ex falsa opinione nascentia, ubi desinant non habent, &c. Sen. Ep. 16.

Christ, reconciling the world unto himself," not himself unto the world; he entreats us to be reconciled, 2 Cor. v. 19, 20. He is found of them that sought him not, Isa. lxv. 1; and his office is not only to "save," but to "seek that which was lost," Luke xix. 10.

3. Other physicians are well used, and entertained with respect and honour; but our patient here neglects and misuses his Physician, falls from him, betakes himself to mountebanks and physicians of no value; yet continues he his mercy, comes when he is forsaken, nay, repelled. "I have spread out my hands all the day unto a rebellious people," Isa. lxv. 2.

Medicos civitate donavit Julius Cæsar. Sueton. in Julio. cap. 42. Vis morborum pretia medentibus; fori tabes pecuniam advocatis fert. Tacit. Annal. lib. 11.

4. Other physicians have usually ample and honourable rewards for the attendance they give; but this Physician comes only out of love, heals freely; nay, is bountiful to his patient, not only heals him, but bestows gifts upon him, gives the visit, gives the physic, sends the ministers and servants who watch and tend the patient.

5. Other physicians prescribe a bitter potion for the sick person to take; this Physician drinks of the bitterest himself. Others prescribe the sore to be lanced; this Physician is wounded and smitten himself. Others order the patient to bleed; here the Physician bleeds himself. Yea, he is not only the Physician, but the physic, and gives himself, his own flesh, his own blood, to heal the soul of his patient; dies himself, that his patient may live. "With his stripes we are healed," Isa. liii. 5.

We should from all this learn, 1. To admire the unsearchable riches of the mercy of our God, who is pleased in our misery to prevent us with goodness, and when we neither feel our disease, nor desire a remedy, is pleased to convince us of our sins; "Thou hast fallen by thine iniquity:" to invite us to repentance; "Take with you words, and turn to the Lord:" to put words into our mouth, and to draw our petition for us; "Say unto him, Take away all iniquity," &c.: to furnish us with arguments; We are "fatherless," "in thee" such find "mercy:" to encourage us with promises; "I will heal," "I will love:" to give us his ministers to proclaim these mercies to us, and his Spirit to apply them. If he did not convince us that "iniquity" would be our "ruin," Ezek. xviii. 30, we should hold it fast, and be pleased with our disease, like a mad-man, that quarrels with his cure, and had rather continue mad than be healed, John iii. 19—21.

Molestus est somnium jucundum videnti, qui excitat. Sen. Ep. 102.

If, being convinced, he did not invite us to repentance, we should run away from him, as Adam did. No man loves to be in the company of an enemy, much less when that enemy is a judge. "They have turned their back unto me, and not their face," Jer. ii. 27. Adam will hide himself "from the presence of the Lord," Gen. iii. 8; and Cain will go "out from the presence of the Lord," chap. iv. 16. Guilt cannot look upon majesty; stubble dares not come near the fire; if we be in our sins "we cannot stand before" God, Ezra ix. 15.

If, being invited, he did not put words into our mouths, we should not know what to say to him. We know not wherewith to "come before the Lord," or to "bow" ourselves "before the high God," if he do not show us "what is good," Micah vi. 6, 8. Where God is the judge, who cannot be mocked or deceived, who knows all things, and, if our heart condemn us, is greater than our heart, and wherever we hide can find us out, and make our sin find us too, Gal. vi. 7; 1 John iii. 20; Numb. xxxii. 23; where, I say, this God is the judge, there guilt stops the mouth, and makes the sinner speechless, Matt. xxii. 12; Rom. iii. 19. Nay, the best of us "know not what we should pray for as we ought," except the Spirit be pleased to help "our infirmities," Rom. viii. 26. When we are taught what to say, if God do "not withdraw his anger," we shall never be able to reason with him, Job ix. 13, 14. "Withdraw thine hand far from me: and let not thy dread make me afraid. Then call thou, and I will answer: or let me speak, and answer thou me," Job xiii. 21, 22. If he do not reveal mercy, if he do not promise love or healing, if he do not make it appear that he is a God that heareth prayers, flesh will not dare to come near unto him, 2 Sam. vii. 27. We can never pray till we can cry, "Abba, Father;" we can never call unto him but in "the multitude of his mercies." As the earth is shut and bound up by frost and cold, and puts not forth her precious fruits till the warmth and heat of the summer call them out: so the heart, under the cold affections of fear and guilt, under the dark apprehensions of wrath and judgment, is so contracted that it knows not to draw near to God; but when mercy shines, when the love of God is shed abroad in it, then also is the heart itself shed abroad and enlarged to pour out itself unto God. Even when distressed sinners pray, their prayer proceeds from apprehensions of mercy; for prayer is the child of faith, and the object of faith is mercy, Rom. x. 14; James v. 15.

2. The way to prize this mercy is to grow acquainted with our own sickness, to see our face in the glass of the law; to consider how odious it renders us to God, how desperately miserable in ourselves. The deeper the sense of misery, the higher the estimation of mercy. When the apostle looked on himself as "chief" of sinners, then he accounted it "a faithful saying, and worthy of all acceptation, that Christ Jesus came into the world to save sinners," 1 Tim. i. 15. Till we be sick and weary we shall not look after a physician to heal and ease us, Matt. ix. 12; xi. 28; till we be pricked in our hearts we shall not be hasty to inquire after the means of salvation, Acts ii. 37. Though the proclamation of pardon be made to "whosoever will," Rev. xxii. 17, yet none are willing till they be brought to extremities: as men cast not their goods into the sea, till they see they must perish themselves if they do not. Some men must be bound before they can be cured. All that God does to us in conversion, he does most freely; but a gift is not a gift till it be received, Rom. v. 17; John i. 12; and we naturally refuse and reject Christ when he is offered, Isa. liii. 3; John i. 11, because he is not offered but upon these terms, that we deny ourselves, and take up a cross, and follow him. Therefore we must be wrought upon by some terror or other, 2 Cor. v. 11. When we find the wrath of God abiding on us, and our souls shut under it as in a prison, John iii. 36; Gal. iii. 22, and the fire of it working and boiling like poison in our consciences, then we shall value mercy, and cry for it, as the prophet does, "Heal me, O Lord, and I shall be healed; save me, and I shall be saved: for thou art my praise," Jer. xvii. 14. Things necessary are never valued to their uttermost but in extremities. When there is a great famine in Samaria, an ass's head (which at another time is thrown out for carrion) will be more worth, than, in a plentiful season, the whole body of an ox. Nay, hunger shall in such a case prevail over nature, and devour even the tender love of a mother, 2 Kings vi. 25, 28. As soon as a man finds a shipwreck, a famine, a hell in his soul, till Christ save, feed, deliver it, immediately Christ will be the desire of that soul, and nothing in heaven or earth valued in comparison of him. Then that which was esteemed "the foolishness of preaching" before, shall be counted "the power of God," and "the wisdom of God;" then every one of Christ's ordinances (which are "the waters" of the temple, for the healing of the sea, that is, of many people, Ezek. xlvii. 8; and "the leaves of the tree of life," which are for "the healing of the nations," Rev. xxii. 2; and the streams of that "fountain opened" in

Israel "for sin and for uncleanness," Zech. xiii. 1; and the wings of the Sun of righteousness, whereby he conveys healing to his church, Mal. iv. 2) shall be esteemed, as indeed they are, the riches, the glory, the treasure, the feast, the physic, the salvation of such a soul, Rom. xi. 12; Eph. iii. 8; 2 Cor. iii. 8, 11; iv. 6, 7; Isa. xxv. 6; Rev. xix. 9; Luke iv. 18; Heb. ii. 3; James i. 21; John xii. 50; Acts xxviii. 28. And a man will wait on them with as much diligence and attention as ever did "the impotent folk" at the pool of Bethesda, when the angel stirred the water; and endure the healing severity of them not only with patience, but with love and thankfulness; suffer reason to be captivated, will to be crossed, high imaginations to be cast down, every thought to be subdued, conscience to be searched, heart to be purged, lust to be cut off and mortified; in all things will such a sick soul be contented to be dieted, restrained, and ordered by the counsel of this heavenly Physician.

"Their backsliding." משובתם This word imports a departing, or a turning away again, from God. It is quite contrary, in the formal nature of it, to faith and repentance, and implies that which the apostle calls a repenting of repentance, 2 Cor. vii. 10. By faith we come to Christ, John vi. 37, and cleave to him, and lay hold upon him, Heb. vi. 18; Isa. lvi. 2, 6; but by this we depart, and draw back from him, and let him go, Heb. x. 38, 39. By the one we prize Christ as infinitely precious, and his ways as holy and good, Phil. iii. 8; 2 Pet. i. 4; by the other we vilify and set them at nought, stumble at them, as ways that do not profit, Matt. xxi. 42; Acts iv. 11; 1 Pet. ii. 7, 8; Job xxi. 14, 15. For a man, having approved of God's ways, and entered into covenant with him, after this to go from his word, and fling up his bargain, and start aside like a deceitful bow; of all other dispositions of the soul, this is one of the worst; to deal with our sins as Israel did with their servants, dismiss them and then take them again, Jer. xxxiv. 10, 11. It is the sad fruit of an evil and unbelieving heart, Heb. iii. 12. And God threatens such persons to "lead them forth with the workers of iniquity," Psal. cxxv. 5, as cattle are led to slaughter, or malefactors to execution. And yet we here see God promises healing to such sinners: "I will heal their backsliding."

Venire ad Christum, quid est aliud quam credendo converti? Aug. de Grat. et l. Arbit. cap. 5.

Transfugas arboribus suspendunt. Tacit. de Morib. Germ. Transfugas ubicunque inventi fuerint quasi hostes interficere licet, l. 3. S. 6. ad leg. Cornel. de Sicariis. D.

To understand this aright we are to know that there is a twofold apostacy. 1. An apostacy arising out of impotency of affection, and prevalency of lust, drawing the heart to look toward the old pleasures thereof again: it is a recidivation or relapse into a former sinful condition out of forgetfulness and falseness of heart, for want of the fear of God to balance the conscience, and to fix and unite the heart to him. This was the frequent sin of Israel, to make many promises and covenants to God, and to break them as fast, Judg. ii. 18, 19; Psal. cvi. 7—13. And this falling from our first love,* growing cold and slack in duty, breaking our engagements to God, and returning again to folly, though it be like a relapse after a disease, exceedingly dangerous, yet God is sometimes pleased to forgive and to heal it.

2. An apostacy which is proud and malicious, when, after they "have tasted the good word of God, and the powers of the world to come," men set themselves to hate, oppose, and persecute godliness, to do "despite unto the Spirit of grace," to fling off the holy strictness of Christ's yoke, to swell against the searching power of his word, to tread "under foot the Son of God," and to count "the blood of the covenant" "an unholy thing," Heb. vi. 5; x. 29. When they know the spirituality and holiness of God's ways, the innocence and piety of his servants, yet notwithstanding set themselves against them for that reason, though under other pretences, this is not a weak, but a wilful, and (if I may so speak) a strong, and a stubborn apostacy; a sin which wholly hardens the heart against repentance, and consequently is incurable. To speak against the Son of man, that is, against the doctrine, disciples, ways, servants of Christ, looking on him only as a man, the leader of a sect, as master of a new way, (which was Paul's notion of Christ and the Christian religion when he persecuted it, and for which cause he found mercy, for had he done that knowingly which he did ignorantly, it had been a sin not to be pardoned, Acts xxvi. 9; 1 Tim. i. 13,) thus to sin, is a blasphemy that may be pardoned: but to speak against the Holy Ghost, that is, to oppose and persecute the doctrine, worship, ways, servants of Christ, knowing them, and acknowledging in them a spiritual holiness, and *eo nomine*, on that very account, to do it, so that the formal motive of malice against them is the power and lustre of that Spirit which appears in them; and its formal principle, neither ignorance, nor self-ends, but very wilfulness, and immediate malignity; woe be to that man whose natural enmity and antipathy against godliness ever swells to so great and daring a height! "It shall not be forgiven him, neither in this world, neither in the world to come," Matt. xii. 32. That is, say some, neither in the time of life, nor in the point or moment of death, which translates them into the world to come. Others, not in this life by justification, nor in the world to come by consummate redemption, and public judiciary absolution in the last day, which is therefore called "the day of redemption," in which men are said to "find mercy of the Lord," Eph. iv. 30; 2 Tim. i. 18. For that which is here done in the conscience by the ministry of the word and efficacy of the Spirit, shall be then publicly and judicially pronounced by Christ's own mouth before angels and men, 2 Cor. v. 10. Others, shall not be forgiven, that is, shall be plagued and punished both in this life and in that which is to come. Give me leave to add what I have conceived to be the meaning of this place, though no way condemning the expositions of so great and learned men: I take it thus, by "this world" we may understand the church which then was of the Jews, or the present age in which our Saviour Christ then lived. It is not, I think, unusual in the Scripture, for the words age, or world, to be sometimes restrained to the church. Now, as Israel was God's "first-born," and "the first-fruits of his increase," Exod. iv. 22; Jer. xxxi. 9; ii. 3; so the church of Israel is called the "church of the first-born," Heb. xii. 23, and "the first tabernacle," and "a worldly sanctuary," Heb. ix. 1, 8, and "Jerusalem that now is," Gal. iv. 25. And then by "the world to come," we are to understand the Christian church afterwards to be planted; for so frequently in Scripture is the evangelical church called "the world to come," and "the last days," and "the ends of the world;" and the things thereunto belonging, "things to come," which

Vid. Bezæ Annotat. in 1 Joan. v. 16.

Vid. Isidor. Pelut. lib. 1. ep. 59.

Beza, Calvin, Cartwright against the Rhemists, Chemnit., Deodati.

Chrysost. et Theophylact. Broughton Explicat. Revel. cap. 21. p. 301, 302.

* Eorum qui peccant antequam Deum noverint, antequam miserationes ejus experti sunt, antequam portaverint jugum suave, et onus leve, priusquam devotionis gratiam et consolationes acceperint Spiritus Sancti; eorum inquam copiosa redemptio est: at eorum qui post conversionem suam peccatis implicantur ingrati acceptæ gratiæ, et post missam manum ad aratrum retro respiciunt tepidi et carnales facti—Eorum utique perpaucos invenias, qui post hæc redeant in gradum pristinum, nec tamen si quis hujusmodi est, desperamus de eo, tantum ut resurgere velit cito. Quanto diutius permanebit, tanto evadet difficilius. Bernard. serm. 3. in Vigil. Vid. ser. 35. in Cant. Aug. de Civ. Dei, lib. 16. cap. 30. Isid. Pelut. l. 1. ep. 13.

had been hidden from "the beginning of the world," "from ages and from generations," and were by the ministry of the apostles made known unto the church in their time, which the "prophets and righteous men" of the former ages did not "see" nor attain unto. Thus it is said, "in these last days" God "hath spoken unto us by his Son," Heb. i. 2; and, "unto angels hath he not put in subjection the world to come," Heb. ii. 5; and, Christ was made "an High Priest of good things to come," Heb. ix. 11; and, "the law having a shadow of good things to come," Heb. x. 1: and the times of the gospel are called "the ages to come," Eph. ii. 7, and "the ends of the world," 1 Cor. x. 11. Thus legal and evangelical dispensations are usually distinguished, the former as "time past," the latter as "last days" or "ages to come," Heb. i. 1, 2; Eph. ii. 7; Col. i. 25, 26; the one an earthly and temporary, the other a heavenly and abiding administration: and so the Septuagint render the original word אבי־עד Isa. ix. 6, "everlasting Father," which is one of the names of Christ, by Πατὴρ τοῦ μέλλοντος αἰῶνος, the Father of the world to come.

The meaning then of the place seems to be this: that sins of high and desperate presumption, committed maliciously against known light, and against the evidence of God's Spirit, as they had no sacrifice or expiation allowed for them in the former world, or state of the Jewish church, but they who in that manner despised Moses and his law, though delivered but by angels, died without mercy, Numb. xv. 27, 30, 31; Heb. ii. 2; so in the world to come, or in the evangelical church, though grace should therein be more abundantly discovered and administered unto men, yet the same law should continue still, as we find it did, Heb. ii. 2—5; vi. 4—6; x. 26—28; neither the open enemies of Christ in the one, nor the false professors of Christ in the other, committing this sin, should be capable of pardon.

This doctrine of apostacy, or backsliding, is worthy of a more large explication; but having handled it formerly on Heb. iii. 12, I shall but briefly

Obs. 1. We should beware of backsliding above all other sins, of falling in soul, as old Eli did in body, backward, and so hazarding our salvation. If once we have shaken hands with sin, never take acquaintance with it any more, but say as Israel here, "What have I to do any more with idols?" The church should be like "Mount Zion, that cannot be moved." It is a sad and sick temper of a church to toss from one side to another, and then especially when she should be healed, to be carried about with every wind.

Obs. 2. We should not be so terrified by any sin, which our soul mourns and labours under, and our heart turns from, as thereby to be withheld from going to the Physician for pardon and healing. Had he not great power and mercy, did he not "love freely," without respect of persons, and pardon freely, without respect of sins, we might then be afraid of going to him: but when he extendeth forgiveness to all kinds, "iniquity," "transgression," "sin," Exod. xxxiv. 6, 7, and has actually pardoned the greatest sinners, Manasses, Mary Magdalene, Paul, publicans, harlots, backsliders, though we should not presume hereupon to turn God's mercy into poison, and his grace into wantonness, (for mercy itself will not save those sinners that hold fast and will not forsake sin,) yet should we take heed of despairing, or entertaining low thoughts of the love and mercy of God; for such examples as these are set forth for the encouragement of all that shall "hereafter believe on" Christ "to life everlasting," 1 Tim. i. 16. And the thoughts and ways which God has to pardon sin are above our thoughts and ways, whereby we look on them in their guilt and greatness, many times, as unpardonable; and therefore are fit matter for our faith to believe and rely on, even against sense, Isa. lv. 6—9.

Now follows the fountain of this mercy.

"I will love them freely." God's love is a most free and bountiful love, having no motive or foundation but within itself, and his free love and grace is the ground of all his other mercies to his people; he shows mercy on whom and because he will. From the beginning to the end of our salvation, nothing is primarily active but free grace. Freely loved, Deut. vii. 7, 8. Freely chosen, Eph. i. 4—8. Christ the gift of free love, John iii. 16. His obedience freely accepted for us, and bestowed upon us, Rom. v. 15, 18. Justification free, Rom. iii. 24. Adoption free, Eph. i. 5. Faith and repentance free, Phil. i. 29; 2 Tim. ii. 25. Good works free, Eph. ii. 10. Salvation free, Tit. iii. 5; Acts xv. 11. Thus the foundation of all mercies is free love. We do not first give to God, that he may render to us again. We turn, we pray, we covenant, we repent, we are holy, we are healed, only because he loves us: and he loves us, not because he sees any thing lovely or amiable in us, but because he will show the absoluteness of his own will, and the unsearchableness of his own counsel towards us. We are not originally denominated good by any thing which flows from us, or is done by us; but by that which is bestowed on us. Our goodness is not the motive of his love, but his love the fountain of our goodness. None indeed are healed and saved, but those that repent and return; but repentance is only a condition, and that freely given by God, disposing the subject for salvation; not a cause, moving or procuring God to save us. It is necessary as the means to the end, not as the cause to the effect. That which looks least free of any other act of God, his rewarding of obedience, is all, and only, mercy. When we "sow in righteousness," we must "reap in mercy," Hos. x. 12. When he renders "to every man according to his work," it is because unto him "belongeth mercy," Psal. lxii. 12.

Cum quis propter nullam aliam causam donat, quam ut libertatem et munificentiam exerceat, hæc proprie donatio appellatur. Julian. D. de Donationib. lib. 1.

This is the solid foundation of all Christian comforts, that God loves freely. Were his love to us to be measured by our fruitfulness or conduct towards him, each hour and moment might stagger our hope; but he is therefore pleased to have it all of grace, "to the end the promise might be sure to all the seed," Rom. iv. 16. This comforts us against the guilt of the greatest sins, for love and free grace can pardon what it will. This comforts us against the accusations of Satan drawn from our own unworthiness. True, I am unworthy, and Satan cannot show me to myself more vile than, without his accusations, I will acknowledge myself to be; but that love which gave Christ freely, gives in him more worthiness than there is or can be unworthiness in me. This comforts us in the assured hope of glory, because when he loves he loves to the end, and nothing can separate from his love. This comforts us in all afflictions, that the free love of God, who has predestinated us thereto, will wisely order all things for the good of his servants, Rom. viii. 29—39; Heb. xii. 6.

Our duty therefore is, 1. To labour for the assurance of this free love. It will assist us in all duties; it will arm us against all temptations; it will answer all objections that can be made against the soul's peace; it will sustain us in all conditions, into which the saddest of times may bring us. "If God be for us, who can be against us?" Though thousands be against us to hate us, yet none shall be against us to hurt us.

2. If God love us freely, we should love him thankfully, 1 John iv. 19, and let love be the salt to season all our sacrifices. For as no benefit is saving to us which does not proceed from love in him, so no duty is

pleasing to him which does not proceed from love in us, 1 John v. 3.

3. Plead this free love and grace in prayer. When we beg pardon, nothing is too great for love to forgive: when we beg grace and holiness, nothing is too good for love to grant. There is not any one thing which faith can manage to more spiritual advantages, than the free grace and love of God in Christ.

4. We must yet so magnify the love of God, as that we turn not free grace into wantonness. There is a corrupt generation of men, who, under pretence of exalting grace, do put disgrace upon the law of God, by taking away the mandatory power thereof from those that are under grace, a doctrine most extremely contrary to the nature of this love. For God's love to us works love in us to him; and our love to him is this, that we keep his commandments; and to keep a commandment is to confirm and to subject my conscience with willingness and delight to the rule and preceptive power of that commandment. Take away the obligation of the law upon conscience as a rule of life, and you take away from our love to God the very matter about which the obedience thereof should be conversant. It is no diminution to love that a man is bound to obedience, (nay, it cannot be called obedience if I be not bound to it,) but herein the excellency of our love to God is commended, that whereas other men are so bound by the law that they fret at it, and swell against it, and would be glad to be exempted from it, they * who love God, and know his love to them, delight to be thus bound, and find infinitely more sweetness in the strict rule of God's holy law, than any wicked man can do in that presumptuous liberty wherein he allows himself to shake off and break its cords.

"For mine anger is turned away from him." When we return with sound repentance to God, then God is pleased to give more than ordinary tastes of the sweetness of his love, by removing judgments, which are the fruits of his anger, from us. This point falls in with what was handled before, on ver. 2. Therefore I shall briefly conclude with these two notes:

Obs. 3. God will have us look on all judgments as fruits of his anger, and take more notice in them of his displeasure than of our own sufferings. When wrath is gone out, the sword drawn, thousands and ten thousands slain in our coasts; Israel given to the spoil, and Jacob unto robbers; a land set on fire with civil flames, and none able to quench them; a kingdom divided within itself; a church which sometime was the asylum for other exiled and afflicted Christians to flee for shelter to, miserably torn by the foolish and unnatural divisions of brethren, and dangerously threatened by the policy and power of the common enemy, who studies how to improve these divisions to the ruin of those that foment them; our work is to make this conclusion: Our God is angry; a God that loves freely, that is infinite in mercy and pity, who does not afflict willingly, nor grieve the children of men: this should be our greatest affliction, and the removal of this anger, by a universal reformation and conversion to him, our greatest business. And I do verily believe that England must never think of outliving or breaking through this anger of God, this critical judgment that is upon it, so as to return to that cold and formal complexion, that Laodicean temper, that she was in before, till she have so publicly and generally repented of all those civil disorders which removed the bounds, and brought dissipation upon public justice; and of all those ecclesiastical disorders which let in corruptions in doctrine, superstitions in worship, abuses in government, discountenancing of the power of godliness in the most zealous professors of it; so that our reformation may be as conspicuous as our disorders have been, and it may appear to all the world that God has washed away the filth and purged the blood of England from the midst thereof, by the spirit of judgment, and by the spirit of burning.

Obs. 4. God's love is the true ground for the removal of judgments in mercy from a people. Let all human counsels be never so deep, and armies never so active, and cares never so vigilant, and instruments never so unanimous, if God's love come not in, nothing of all these can in any wise benefit a nation. Those that are most interested in God's love, shall certainly be most secured against his judgments. Hither our eyes, our prayers, our thoughts must be directed. Lord, love us, delight in us, choose us for thyself; and then, though counsels, and treasures, and armies, and men, and horses, and all second causes fail us; though Satan rage, and hell threaten, and the foundations of the earth be shaken; though neither "the vines," nor "the olive," nor "the fig-tree," nor "the fields," nor "the herd in the stalls" yield any supplies; yet we "will rejoice in the Lord," we "will glory in the God of" our "salvation," Hab. iii. 17—19; sin shall be healed, anger shall be removed, nothing "shall be able to separate us from the love of God, which is in Christ Jesus our Lord," Rom. viii. 39.

Ver. 5—7. *I will be as the dew unto Israel: he shall grow as the lily, and cast forth his roots as Lebanon. His branches shall spread, and his beauty shall be as the olive tree, and his smell as Lebanon. They that dwell under his shadow shall return; they shall revive as the corn, and grow as the vine: the scent thereof shall be as the wine of Lebanon.*

In these verses is contained God's answer to the second part of Israel's petition, wherein they desired him to do them good, or to "receive" them "graciously:" and here God promises them several singular blessings, set forth by various metaphors and similitudes, all answering to the name of Ephraim, and the ancient promises made to him, Deut. xxxiii. 13—17. These blessings are opposed to many visitations threatened in the former parts of the prophecy, under metaphors of contrary import. The dew of grace, is opposed to "the morning cloud, and the early dew that passeth away," chap. xiii. 3; lilies, olives, vines, spices, to the judgments of nettles, thorns, thistles, chap. x. 8; spreading roots, to dry roots, chap. ix. 16; a fruitful vine, bringing forth excellent wine, is here opposed to an empty vine, bringing fruit only to itself, that is, so sour and unsavoury, as is not worth the gathering, chap. x. 1; corn growing, instead of corn taken quite away, chap. ii. 9, instead of no stalk, and the bud yielding no meal, chap. viii. 7; fruit promised, instead of no fruit threatened, chap. ix. 16; wine promised, in opposition to the failing of wine, chap. ix. 2; sweet wine, opposed to sour drink, chap. iv. 18; safe dwelling, instead of no dwelling, chap. ix. 3; branches growing and spreading, instead of branches consumed, chap. xi. 6; green trees, instead of dry springs, chap. xiii. 15: and all these fruits the fruits as of Lebanon, which was the most fertile part of that country, a mountain full of various kinds of the most excellent trees, cedars,

* Sub lege est qui timore supplicii quod lex minatur, non amore justitiæ se sentit abstinere ab opere peccati; nendum liber nec alienus a voluntate peccandi. In ipsa enim voluntate reus est, qua mallet si fieri posset non esse quod timeat, ut libere faciat quod occulte desiderat. August. de Nat. et Grat. cap. 57. Et infra, Omnia fiunt facilia charitati, cap. 69. et, Non est terribile sed suave mandatum. De Grat. Christi, lib. 1. cap. 13. Suave fit quod non delectabat. De Peccat Merit. et Remis. lib. 2. cap. 17. Contr. 2. epist. Pelag. lib. 1. cap. 9. lib. 3. cap. 4. de Doctr. Christi, lib. 1. cap. 15. de Spiritu et Lit. cap. 3.

cypresses, olives, and divers others, affording rich gums and balsams; abounding also in the most medicinal and aromatic herbs, sending forth a most fragrant odour, whereby all harmful and venomous creatures were driven from harbouring there; and in the valleys of that mountain were rich grounds for pasture, corn, and vineyards, as the learned in their descriptions of the Holy Land have observed.

The source of all these blessings is the heavenly dew of God's grace and favour, (alluding to the abundance of dew which fell on that mountain,) descending on the church, as on a garden, bringing forth lilies; as on a forest, strengthening the cedars; as on a vineyard, spreading abroad the branches; as on an oliveyard, making the trees thereof green and fruitful; and as on a rich field, reviving the corn. Here is spiritual beauty, the beauty of the lily, exceeding that of Solomon in all his glory; spiritual stability, the roots of the cedars, and other goodly trees in that mountain; spiritual odours, and spices of Lebanon; spiritual fruitfulness, and that of all sorts and kinds for the comfort of life: the fruit of the field, "bread which strengtheneth;" the fruit of the olive trees, "oil to make his face to shine;" the fruit of the vineyard, "wine that maketh glad the heart of man," Psal. civ. 15.

We esteem him a very rich man, and most excellently accommodated, who has gardens for pleasure, and fields for corn and pasture, and woods for fuel, for structure, for defence, for beauty, and delight; and vineyards for wine and oil; and all other conveniences both for the necessities and delights of a plentiful life. Thus is the church here set forth to us as such a wealthy man, furnished with the unsearchable riches of Christ, with every kind of blessing both for sanctity and safety; as the apostle praises "the God and Father of our Lord Jesus Christ, who hath blessed us with all spiritual blessings in heavenly places in Christ;" namely, election to eternal life, adoption to the condition of sons, and to a glorious inheritance, redemption from misery to blessedness, remission of sins, knowledge of his will, holiness and unblamableness of life, and the seal of the Holy Spirit of promise, Eph. i. 3—13.

Θεμιστοκλῆς ὑπὸ βασιλέως ἔλαβεν δωρεὰν, τὴν Λάμψακον εἰς οἶνον, Μαγνήσιαν δ' εἰς ἄρτον, &c. Athenæus, lib. 1. cap. 23. Vid. l. 4. ff. de Censibus.

The scope of the words, thus showing that God singles out so many excellent good things by name in answer to that general petition, "receive us graciously," or do us good, suggests the following general observation.

Obs. 1. God often answers prayer abundantly beyond the petitions of his people. They prayed only for good in general, leaving it (as it becomes us, who know not always what is good for us) to his holy will and wisdom in what manner and measure to do them that good; and he answers them in particular with all kinds of good things. So in the former petition they prayed in general for the forgiveness of sin, and God in particular promises the healing of their rebellions, which was the greatest of their sins. God often answers the prayers of his people, as he did the seed of Isaac, with a hundredfold increase, Gen. xxvi. 12. As God's word never returns empty unto him, so the prayers of his servants never return empty to them; and usually the crop of prayer is greater than the seed out of which it grew, as the putting in of a little water into a pump makes way to the drawing out of a great deal more. Isaac and Rebekah had lived twenty years together without any children, and he grew now in years, for he was forty years old before he married; hereupon he solemnly prays to God in behalf of his wife, because she was barren, and God gave him more than it is probable he expected, for he gave him two sons at a birth, Gen. xxv. 21, 22. As the cloud, which rises out of the earth often in thin and insensible vapours, falls down in great and abundant showers; so our prayers, which ascend weak and narrow, return with a full and enlarged answer. God deals in this point with his children, as Joseph did with his brethren in Egypt; he not only put corn into their sacks, but returned the money which they brought to purchase it, Gen. xlii. 25. So he dealt with Solomon, he not only gave him wisdom and gifts of government, which he asked, but further gave him "both riches and honour," which he asked not, 1 Kings iii. 13. The people of Israel, when they were distressed by the Ammonites, besought the Lord for help; he turns back their prayers, and sends them to their idols to help them: they humble themselves, and put away their idols, and pray again, and the highest pitch to which their petitions mounted was, "We have sinned: do thou unto us whatsoever seemeth good unto thee; deliver us only, we pray thee, this day," Judg. x. 15; and God answered this prayer beyond its contents; he not only delivered them from the enemy, and so saved them, but subdued the enemy under them, and delivered him into their hands; he not only gave them the relief they desired, but a glorious victory beyond their desires, Judg. xi. 22. God deals with his servants as the prophet did with the woman of Shunem; when he bid her ask what she needed, and tell him what she would have him do for the kindness she had done to him, and she found not any thing to request at his hands, he sends for her again, and makes her a free promise of that which she most wanted and desired, telling her that God would give her a son, 2 Kings iv. 16. So many times God is pleased to give his servants such things as they forget to ask, or gives them the things which they ask in a fuller measure than their own desires durst propose them. David, in his troubles, asked "life" of God, and would have esteemed it a great mercy to have been merely delivered from the fear of his enemies; and God not only answers him according to the desire of his heart in that particular, and above it too, for he gave him "length of days for ever and ever;" but, further, settled the crown upon his head, and added "honour and majesty" to his life, Psal. xxi. 2—5.

And the reasons hereof are principally two.

1. We beg of God according to the sense and knowledge which we have of our own wants, and according to the measure of that love which we bear to ourselves. The greater our love is to ourselves, the more active and importunate will our petitions be for such good things as we need. But God answers prayers according to his knowledge of us, and according to the love which he bears to us. Now God knows what things we want much better than we do ourselves, and he loves our souls much better than we love them ourselves, and therefore he gives us more and better things than our own prayers know how to ask of him. A little child will beg none but trifles and mean things of his father, because he has not understanding to look higher, or to value things that are more excellent; but his father, knowing better what is good for him, bestows on him education, trains him to learning and virtue, that he may be fit to manage and enjoy that inheritance which he provides for him: so "we know not what we should pray for as we ought," Rom. viii. 26; and when we do know our spirits are much straitened, we have but a finite and narrow love to ourselves; but God's knowledge is infinite, and his love is infinite, and according to these are the distributions of his mercy. Even the apostle himself, when he was in affliction, and buffeted by the messenger of Satan, and vexed with a thorn in his flesh, besought the Lord for nothing but "that it might depart;" but God had a far better answer in store to the apostle's prayer, and purposed to do more for him than he desired, namely,

to give him a sufficiency of grace to support him, and to magnify his strength in the infirmity of his servant, 2 Cor. xii. 9. When the prophet had encouraged men to "seek" the Lord, and to "return" unto him, and that upon this assurance, that he will not only hear petitions for mercy and forgiveness, but "will abundantly pardon," or will multiply to pardon, that is, will pardon more sins than we can confess, (for with him there is not only "mercy," but "plenteous redemption," Psal. cxxx. 7,) he further strengthens our faith, and encourages our obedience to this duty, by the consideration of the "thoughts" of God, to wit, his thoughts of love, mercy, and peace towards us: "My thoughts are not your thoughts, neither are your ways my ways, saith the Lord. For as the heavens are higher than the earth, so are my ways higher than your ways, and my thoughts than your thoughts," Isa. lv. 6—9. He can pardon beyond our petitions, because his thoughts of mercy towards us are beyond our apprehensions, Jer. xxix. 10—14.

2. God answers prayers not always with respect to the narrow compass of our weak desires, but with respect to his own honour, and to the declaration of his own greatness; for he promises to hear us that we may "glorify" him, Psal. l. 15. Therefore he is pleased to exceed our petitions, and to do for us abundantly above what we ask or think, that our hearts may be more abundantly enlarged, and our mouths wide opened in rendering honour unto him. When Perillus, a favourite of Alexander, begged of him a portion for his daughters, the king appointed that fifty talents should be given to him, and he answered that ten would be sufficient; the king replied that ten were enough for Perillus to ask, but not enough for Alexander to grant.* So God is pleased many times to give more than we ask, that we may look upon it not only as an act of mercy, but as an act of honour; and to teach us in all our prayers to move God as well by his glory as by his mercy. So Moses, when he prays for pardon to Israel, lest God's name should be blasphemed, Numb. xiv. 15—19. So Joshua, when Israel turned their backs before their enemies: "What wilt thou do unto thy great name?" Josh. vii. 9. So Solomon, in his prayer at the dedication of the temple: "Hear thou in heaven thy dwelling-place, and do according to all that the stranger calleth to thee for; that all people of the earth may know thy name," 1 Kings viii. 43. So David, in his petitions for Israel, and for the performance of God's promise to the seed of David: "Do" all "as thou hast said. Let it even be established, that thy name may be magnified for ever," 1 Chron. xvii. 23, 24. So Asa: "O Lord, thou art our God; let not man prevail against thee," 2 Chron. xiv. 11. So Jehoshaphat: "O Lord God of our fathers, art not thou God in heaven? and rulest not thou over all the kingdoms of the heathen? and in thine hand is there not power and might, so that none is able to withstand thee?" 2 Chron. xx. 6. So Hezekiah, when he spread the blasphemies of Sennacherib before the Lord: "Now therefore, O Lord our God, save us from his hand, that all the kingdoms of the earth may know that thou art the Lord, even thou only," Isa. xxxvii. 20. So the church of God in the time of distress: "Help us, O God of our salvation, for the glory of thy name: and deliver us, and purge away our sins, for thy name's sake. Wherefore should the heathen say, Where is their God?" Psal. lxxix. 9, 10. As every creature of God was made for his glory, Prov. xvi. 4; Rom. xi. 36; so every attribute of God works and puts forth itself for his glory. If he show mercy, it is to show "the riches of his glory," Rom. ix. 23; Eph. i. 11, 12. If he execute justice, it is to "make "his power known," Rom. ix. 17, 22; 2 Thess. i. 9. When he puts forth his power, and does terrible things, it is to make his "name known," Isa. lxiv. 1—3. If he engage his truth, and make his promises yea and amen, it is for his own glory, and that his name may be magnified in doing what he has said, 2 Cor. i. 20; 2 Sam. vii. 25, 26. Whenever therefore we pray to God, and therein implore his mercy on us, his justice on his enemies, his truth to be fulfilled, his power, wisdom, or any other attribute to be manifested toward his people, the highest and most prevailing medium we can use, is the glory of his own name. God's ultimate end in working must needs be our strongest argument in praying, because therein it appears that we seek his interest in our petitions as well as and above our own.

This serves, 1. To encourage us unto prayer, because God not only hears and answers prayers, which is a sufficient motive to his servants to call upon him, "O thou that hearest prayer, unto thee shall all flesh come," Psal. lxv. 2; lxvi. 20; lxxxvi. 5—7; cii. 17; but because he oftentimes exceeds the modesty, the ignorance, the fearfulness of our requests, by giving to us more than we ask. When poor men make requests to us, we usually answer them as the echo does the voice, the answer cuts off half the petition. Like the hypocrite noticed by the apostle, James ii. 15, 16, when he saw a brother or sister naked, or destitute of daily food, would bid him "Depart in peace, be ye warmed and filled," but in the mean time would give him nothing that was needful; and so rather mocked than answered their requests. We shall seldom find among men Jael's courtesy, Judg. v. 25, giving milk to those that ask water, except it be as hers was, *δῶρον ἄδωρον*, *munus cum hamo*, an entangling benefit, the better to introduce a mischief: there are not many Naamans among us, that, when you beg of them one talent, will force you to take two, 2 Kings v. 23; but God's answer to our prayers is like a multiplying glass, which renders the request much greater in the answer than it was in the prayer. As when we cast a stone into the water, though but small in itself, yet the circles which it causes spread wider and wider till they fill the whole pond: so our petitions, though very weak as they come from us, and craving but some one or other good thing, yet gaining access to the fountain of life, and unsearchable treasure of mercy which is in Christ, are usually answered with many and more spreading benefits. The trumpet exceedingly strengthens the voice which passes through it; it is but as a silent breath as it comes from the mouth entering in at a narrow passage, but it issues forth with spreading and multiplied vigour: so our prayers usually go up confined to God, but they come down again with enlarged answers from him; as the root is but of one colour, when the flower which grows out of it is beautified with variety.

Seneca.

Spiritus noster clariorem sonum reddit, cum illum tuba, per longi canalis angustias tractum, patentiore novissime exitu effundit. Seneca Epist. 108.

Now this should be a great encouragement to us to call upon God with sincerity of heart, because he multiplies to pardon, because we "know not the numbers" of his salvation, Psal. lxxi. 15, we cannot count the sum of his thoughts towards us, Psal. cxxxix. 17, 18. If any man were so wealthy, that it were all one with him to give pounds or pence, and who usually, when asked for silver, would give gold, every indigent and necessitous person would wait on this man's mercy. Now, it is as easy with God to give talents as farthings, as easy to over-answer prayers as to answer them at all. It is as easy to the sun to fill a vast palace as a little closet with light; as easy to the sea to fill a channel as a bucket with water. He can satisfy with

* Περίλλου τίνος τῶν φίλων αἰτήσαντος προῖκα τοῖς θυγατοίοις, ἐκέλευσε πεντέκοντα τάλαντα λαβεῖν, αὐτοῦ δὲ φήσαντος ἱκανὰ εἶναί δὲκα· Σοὶ γέ ἔφη λαβεῖν, ἐμοὶ δ' οὐχ ἱκανὰ δοῦναι. Plutarch. Apophtheg.

goodness, and answer with wonderful and terrible things, Psal. lxv. 4, 5. Oh who would not make requests to such a God, whose usual answer to prayer is, " Be it unto thee even as thou wilt," Matt. xv. 28; nay, who answers us beyond our own wills and thoughts, Eph. iii. 20, and measures forth mercy by the greatness of his own grace, and not by the narrowness of our desires? The shekel belonging to the sanctuary was, as many learned men think, in weight double to the common shekel which was used in civil matters; to note to us, that as God expects from us double the care in things belonging to him above what we use in the things of the world, so he usually measures back double to us again; " good measure, pressed down, and shaken together, and running over," " into " our " bosoms," Luke vi. 38. When the man sick of the palsy was carried to Christ to be healed, Christ did beyond the expectation of those that brought him, for he not only cured him of his disease, but of his sin, gave him not only health of body, but peace of conscience; first, "Son, be of good cheer, thy sins be forgiven thee;" and then, " Arise, take up thy bed, and go unto thine house," Matt. ix. 2, 6. The thief on the cross besought Christ to remember him when he came into his kingdom, but Christ answers him far beyond his petition, assuring him that the very same day he should be with him in paradise, Luke xxiii. 42, 43. The poor man at the gate of the temple begged for nothing of Peter and John but a small alms, but they gave him an answer to his request far more worth than any other alms could be, namely, such an alms as caused him to stand in need of alms no longer, restoring him in the name of Christ to sound strength, that he walked, and leaped, and praised God, Acts iii. 6—8. In like manner God answers the prayers of his people, not always it may be in the kind, and to the express will of him that asks, but for the better, and consequently more to his real will than he himself expressed.

Si non secundum voluntatem, tamen ad utilitatem. Πράξω ἁ θέλετε, ἁ δὲ λέγετε παραιτήσομαι. Acrotatus apud Plutarch Laconic. Apophtheg.

2. To encourage us in prayer to beg for an answer, not according to the defect and narrowness of our own low conceptions, but according to the fulness of God's own abundant mercies. It would not please one of us if a beggar should ask of us gold or jewels, silk or dainties; we would esteem such a petitioner more full of pride and impudence than of want. But God delights to have his people beg great things of him, to implore the performance of " exceeding great and precious promises," 2 Pet. i. 4; to pray for a share in "the unsearchable riches of Christ," to know things which pass knowledge, and to " be filled with all the fulness of God," Eph. iii. 8, 18, 19; to ask things which " eye hath not seen, nor ear heard, neither have entered into the heart of man," 1 Cor. ii. 9; to ask not as beggars only for an alms, but as children for an inheritance, Rom. viii. 15, 17, 23; Gal. iv. 6, 7; not to ask some thing, or a few things, but " in every thing " to let our " requests be made known unto God," Phil. iv. 6, because with Christ he doth " freely give us all things," Rom. viii. 32, even " richly all things to enjoy," 1 Tim. vi. 17. As Alexander the Great was well pleased with Anaxarchus the philosopher when he desired a hundred talents of his treasurer: He does well, saith he, in asking it, and understands his friend aright, who has one both able and willing to give him so great a gift. God allows his children a spiritual and heavenly ambition, to covet earnestly the best gifts, 1 Cor. xii. 31; to aspire to a kingdom, and accordingly to put up to him great and honourable requests; to think what great things Christ has purchased, what great things God has promised and proposed to us, and to regulate our prayers more by the merits and riches of Christ, and by the greatness of God's mercies, than by those apprehensions which we cannot but have of our own unworthiness.

Plutarch.

Thus far from the general scope of the text, and though many particular observations might be raised from the special blessings enumerated, yet I shall briefly comprehend them all in the following:

Obs. 2. On those whom God loves and pardons, he pours forth the benediction of his grace and Spirit, as the dew of heaven, to quicken them to a holy and fruitful conversation. The promises set down in general terms before, " I will heal," " I will love," are here further amplified by many excellent metaphors, and elegant figures, nine in number, multiplied into so many particulars, partly because of the difficulty attendant on the belief of the promise; partly because of the dejected state of the people under the variety of their former sufferings, who are therefore by variety of mercies to be raised up and revived; and partly to represent the perfection and completeness of the blessings intended, which should be of all sorts, and suited to all purposes. The foundation of all the rest is this, that God promises to " be as the dew unto Israel:" for Ephraim having been cursed with much drought and barrenness, when God blesses him again, he promises to be to him as dew is to the weary and thirsty ground, which so refreshes it that the fruits thereof grow and flourish again. Lilies, flowers, trees, vines, corn, are very apt (especially in such hot countries as Judea) without much refreshing dew and showers from heaven, to dry up and wither away: so would Ephraim have been quite consumed by the heavy wrath of God, unless revived by the heavenly refreshments of his grace and Holy Spirit.

But we shall proceed now to consider the words themselves.

" I will be as the dew unto Israel." אהיה כטל לישראל Dew, in its natural signification, imports a comforting, refreshing, and encouraging, a calling forth the fruits of the earth, by gently and insensibly insinuating itself into the ground; and in that sense is mentioned as a blessing, Gen. xxvii. 39: in its mystical and spiritual sense, it signifies Christ, Psal. lxxii. 6; who by his holy word and heavenly grace, dropping down and distilling on the souls of men, Deut. xxxii. 2; Job xxix. 22, 23; by his princely favour and loving countenance, which " is as a cloud of the latter rain," Prov. xvi. 15; xix. 12; by his heavenly righteousness, and most spiritual efficacy, Isa. xxvi. 19; xlv. 8; so quickens, vegetates, and revives the hearts of men, that they, like dew " from the womb of the morning," are born in great abundance to him, as multitudes of men and believers are wont to be expressed in the Scripture by drops of dew, Psal. cx. 3; Micah v. 7. In one word, all that which dew is, to the fields, gardens, vineyards, flowers, fruits of the earth, after a hot and scorching day, the favour, word, grace, loving countenance, and Holy Spirit of Christ, will be to the drooping and afflicted consciences of his people.

Chrysost. in Psal. li. 7.

From this metaphor then we learn,

1. That we are naturally dry, barren, fruitless, and utterly unable to do any good, to bring forth any fruit unto God; like a heathy and parched land, subject to the scorching terrors of the wrath of God, and to his burning indignation. So Christ compares Jerusalem to a dry, withered tree, fitted for judgment, Luke xxiii. 31; and he assures us that out of him we can do nothing, John xv. 4, 5. In us of ourselves there dwelleth " no good thing," Rom. vii. 18; we are not of ourselves, as of ourselves, sufficient to any thing, 2 Cor. iii. 5: he is the sun that heals us, Mal. iv. 2; the rain that fertilizes us, Psal. lxxii. 6; the root from which we derive life and nourishment, Rev. xxii. 16. As natural, so much more spiritual, fruitfulness, has its ultimate reso-

lution into him, who alone is the father of the rain, and begetteth the drops of dew, Hos. ii. 21, 22; Job xxxviii. 28.

2. That the grace of God is like dew to the barren and parched hearts of men, to make them fruitful. There are many things wherein the resemblance stands.

1. None can give it but God; it comes from above, it is of celestial origin, the nativity thereof is from "the womb of the morning," Psal. cx. 3. "Are there any among the vanities of the Gentiles that can cause rain, or can the heavens give showers? art not thou he, O Lord our God? therefore we will wait upon thee: for thou hast made all these things," Jer. xiv. 22. And the like we may say in a more strict and peculiar sense of regeneration, that it is a spiritual and heavenly birth; it is "not of blood, nor of the will of the flesh, nor of the will of man, but of God;" there is no concurrence or active assistance of the flesh, or of any natural abilities, to a birth which is merely spiritual, John i. 13; iii. 5, 6; James i. 17, 18. Therefore Christ was pleased to go up into heaven, before he shed forth his Holy Spirit in abundance on the church, John vii. 39; xvi. 7; Acts i. 4, 5; to teach us that our conversion and sanctification come from above,* by a Divine teaching, by a spiritual conviction, by a supernatural and omnipotent traction, by a heavenly calling, by the will of him who alone can give a will to us: no voice can be heard by those that are dead, but "the voice of the Son of God," John v. 25; vi. 44, 45; xvi. 8—11; James i. 18; Phil. ii. 13; Heb. iii. 1; xii. 25: and withal to acquaint us whither the affections and conversations of men thus sanctified should tend, namely, to heaven, as every thing works towards its original, and every part inclines to the whole, Col. iii. 1, 2; Phil. iii. 20. In allusion to this metaphor of dew or rain, the Holy Spirit is said to be poured out upon the churches, Acts ii. 17; Tit. iii. 6. And the word of grace is frequently compared to rain. As it is the seed by which we are enabled to be fruitful, Matt. xiii. 19, so it is the rain which softens the heart, that it may be the better wrought on by that seminal virtue, Isa. lv. 10, 11; Heb. vi. 7; whereas false teachers are called "clouds without water," Jude 12, they have no fructifying virtue in them. None can give grace but God; it is heavenly in its nature, therefore it is so in its original; it "tarrieth not for man, nor waiteth for the sons of men," Micah v. 7: it depends not on the wills, concurrences, preparations, or dispositions which arise out of us, but it wholly prevents us; we are made active by it, but we are not at all antecedently active in fitting or disposing ourselves for it.

2. It is the fruit of a serene, clear, and quiet heaven; for dew never falls either in scorching or in tempestuous weather, as philosophers have observed. In like manner, the grace, favour, and blessings of God, are the fruits of his reconciled affection towards us: upon the wicked he rains storm and tempest, he showers down on them the fury of his wrath, and shows himself dark, cloudy, gloomy, terrible unto them, Psal. xi. 6; lxxxiii. 15; Job xx. 23; Nah. i. 3, 8; but unto those that fear his name he opens a clear and a gracious countenance, and, being reconciled to them, sheds abroad his love into their hearts, and his peace into their consciences, like Gideon's dew on the fleece and on the ground, as a special evidence of his grace: and therefore the psalmist compares the love and peace that is amongst brethren unto dew, which ever falleth from a calm, serene, and quiet sky, Psal. cxxxiii. 3.

Aristot. Meteorolog. lib. 1. cap. 10. Plin. lib. 2. cap. 60. l. 18. cap. 29.

3. It is abundant and innumerable. Who can number the drops of dew on the ground, or the hairs of little rain? (for so they are called in the original, כשעירם because of their smallness and number, Deut. xxxii. 2.) So Hushai expresses the multitudes of all Israel, 2 Sam. xvii. 12, "We will light upon him as the dew falleth on the ground." And the multitudes of believers are said to be born unto Christ by his sending forth the rod of his strength, as dew "from the womb of the morning," Psal. cx. 3, which we find verified, Acts ii. 41; v. 14, 16; vi. 7; ix. 31, 42; xix. 20. Such is the grace and favour of God to his people after their conversion; unsearchable, it cannot be comprehended or measured, nor brought under any number or account, Psal. lxxi. 15; cxxxix. 17, 18. Christ is compared to manna: he was the bread that came down from heaven, John vi. 50, 51; and manna came in mighty abundance, so that there was enough for every one to gather, Exod. xvi. 16. It had dew under it, and dew over it, as we may conjecture by comparing Exod. xvi. 14, with Numb. xi. 9; whereunto the Holy Ghost seems to allude when he speaks of "the hidden manna," Rev. ii. 17; though that may likewise refer to the pot of manna which was kept in the tabernacle, Exod. xvi. 32, 33; Heb. ix. 4; as our life is said to be hid with Christ, now he is in heaven, Col. iii. 3. By this dew coming along with manna, is intimated, that the mercies of God in Christ, his daily mercies, (which are said, with allusion, I suppose, to this manna, to be "new every morning," Lam. iii. 23,) and his hidden mercies, to wit, the inward comforts of his grace and Spirit, are all innumerable and past finding out. We may say of his mercies, as the psalmist of his commandments, "I have seen an end of all perfection," but these thy mercies are "exceeding broad;" more than eye hath seen, or ear heard, or the heart itself is able to comprehend, Psal. cxix. 96; 1 Cor. ii. 9.

Lud. Capel. Spicileg. page 132, 133.

4. It is silent, slow, insensible; while it is falling you cannot say, Here it is: it deceives the eye, it is too subtle to be discerned by it: it deceives the ear, it is too silent for that to hear it: it eludes the touch, and is too thin and spiritual to be apprehended. You see it when it is come, but you cannot observe how it comes. In this manner was God pleased to fill the world with the knowledge of his gospel, and with the grace of his Spirit; by quiet, small, contemptible, and, as it were, insensible means. "The kingdom of God cometh not with observation," that is, with any visible, notable splendour, or external pomp, (as the Jews expected the Messiah to come,) but it came with spiritual efficacy, and with internal power on the consciences of men, and spread itself over the world by the ministry of a very few despised instruments, Luke xvii. 20, 21; with respect to which manner of working the Spirit is compared to wind, which we hear and feel, but cannot tell "whence it cometh, and whither it goeth," John iii. 8. The operations of grace on the conscience are secret, and silent; you shall find mighty changes wrought, and shall not tell how they were wrought; the same man coming into the church one hour a swine, a dog, a lion, and going out the next in all visible respects the same, but invisibly changed into a lamb.

5. It is of a soft and benign nature, which gently insinuates and works itself into the ground, and by degrees moistens and mollifies it, that it may be fitted to the seed which is cast into it. In like manner the Spirit, the grace, the word of God, is of a searching, insinuating, softening quality; it sinks into the heart, and works itself into the conscience, and from thence makes way for itself into the whole man, mind, thoughts, affections, words, actions, fitting them all unto the holy seed that is put into them: as the earth, being softened

* Ita docet ut quod quisque didicerit, non tantum cognoscendo videat sed etiam volendo appetat, agendoque perficiat. Aug. de Grat. Christ. cap. 14. 24. et cont. 2. Epist. Pelag. lib. 1. cap. 19, 20. Vocatio alta et secreta. Epist. 107. Bernard. Sermon. Parv. serm. 66.

and mingled with the dew, is the more easily drawn up into those varieties of herbs and fruits which it maintains.

6. It is of a vegetating and quickening nature, it causes things to grow and revive again; therefore the prophet calls it "the dew of herbs," Isa. xxvi. 19, which are thereby refreshed, and recover life and beauty: even so the word and Spirit of grace, distilling upon the soul, as small rain upon tender herbs, and as showers on the grass, cause it to live the life of God, and to bring forth the fruits of holiness and obedience, Isa. lv. 10, 11. Those parts of the world which are under either perpetual frosts, or perpetual scorchings, are barren and fruitless, the earth being closed up, and the sap thereof dried away by such distempers. Such is the condition of a soul under wrath, that has no apprehensions of God but in frost or fire; for "who can stand before his cold?" Psal. cxlvii. 17; who can "dwell with everlasting burnings?" Isa. xxxiii. 14. Fear contracts and binds up the powers of the soul; more than any other affection it indisposes to regular action. But when the soul can apprehend God as love, find healing in his wings, and reviving in his ordinances, this love is of an opening and expansive quality, calling forth the heart to duty; love within, as it were, hastening to meet and close with love without, the love of obedience in us, with the love of favour and grace in God. I shut and bar my door against an enemy whom I fear, and look upon as armed to hurt me; but I open wide my door, my bosom, to a friend whom I love, and look upon as furnished with counsel, and comfort, and benefits to revive me. There is a kind of mutual love between dew and the earth; dew loves the earth with a love of beneficence, doing it good, and earth loves dew with a love of concupiscence, earnestly desiring and opening unto it. Such is the love between Christ and the soul, when he appears as dew to it; he visits the soul with a love of mercy, reviving it, and the soul puts forth itself towards him in a love of duty, earnestly coveting as well to serve as to enjoy him.

7. It is of a refreshing and comforting nature, tempering the heat of those hotter countries, and so causing the face of things to flourish with beauty and delight. So God promises to be to his people in their troubles "like a cloud of dew in the heat of harvest," Isa. xviii. 4. The spiritual joy and heavenly comfort which the peace and grace of God ministers to the consciences of believers, Rom. xv. 13; v. 1; Phil. iv. 4; 1 Pet. i. 8, is said to make the "bones flourish like an herb," Isa. lxvi. 14. (As, on the other side, of "a broken spirit" it is said, that it "drieth the bones," Prov. xvii. 22.) "Their soul" (saith the prophet) "shall be as a watered garden; and they shall not sorrow any more. I will turn their mourning into joy, and will comfort them, and make them rejoice from their sorrow," Jer. xxxi. 12, 13.

From all which we should learn, 1. To be sensible of our own personal and spiritual dryness, barrenness, emptiness of fruit and peace, hard hearts, withered consciences, guilty spirits, under our own particular sins; so in regard of the whole land, to take notice of that tempest of wrath, which, like an east wind out of the wilderness, drieth up our springs, and spoileth our treasures, as the prophet complains, Hos. xiii. 15, 16; and to be humbled into penitent resolutions, as the church here is. If God, who was wont to be as dew to our nation, who made it heretofore like a paradise and a watered garden, be now to it as a tempest, as a consuming fire, turning things upside down, burning up the inhabitants of the earth, causing our land to mourn, and our joy to wither, Joel i. 12, this is an evident sign, that "the earth also is defiled under the inhabitants thereof," Isa. xxiv. 4, 5. Therefore as our sins have turned our dew into blood, so our repentance must turn our blood into dew again. If ever we look to have a happy peace, we must make it with God: men can give peace only to our bodies, our fields, our houses, our purses, (nor that neither without his overruling power and providence, who alone manages all the counsels and resolutions of men,) but he alone can give peace to our consciences by the assurance of his love, which is "better than life." And if there should be peace in a nation, made up only by human prudence and correspondences, without public repentance, and thorough reformation in church, in state, in families, in persons, in judgment, in manners, it would be but like those short interims between the Egyptian plagues, Exod. viii. 15; ix. 34; a respiting only, not a removing of our affliction; like the shining of the sun on Sodom, before the fire and brimstone fell upon it, Gen. xix. 23, 24. We all cry and call for peace, and, while any thing is left, would gladly pay dear, very dear, to recover it. But there is no sure and lasting purchase of it, but by unfeigned repentance and turning to God; this is able to give peace in the midst of war. In the midst of storm and tempest, Christ is sufficient security to the tossed ship, Matt. viii. 24, 27. "This man" is "the peace" even "when the Assyrian" is in the "land," Micah v. 5. Whereas impenitence, even when we have recovered an outward peace, leaves us still in the midst of most potent enemies; God, Christ, angels, Scripture, creatures, conscience, sins, curses, all these are arrayed against us. The apostle tells us, that lusts "war against the soul," 1 Pet. ii. 11. There is a strong emphasis in the word "soul," the soul is more worth than all the world, nothing to be taken in exchange for it, Matt. xvi. 26. So long as we have our lusts unconquered, we are under a war the most woeful, which spoils us not of our blood, our money, our corn, our cattle, our houses, our children, but of the salvation of our immortal souls. Time will repair the ruins of other wars, but eternity itself will not deliver that poor soul which has fallen in the wars of lust.

Therefore, if you would have peace as a mercy, get it from God, let it be a dew from heaven on your conversion to him. A "king's favour" is said to be as "dew upon the grass," Prov. xix. 12, and as "a cloud of the latter rain," Prov. xvi. 15; and it would with all joyfulness be so apprehended, if by that means the blessing of peace were bestowed on these distressed kingdoms. How much more comfortable would it be to have it as a gift from God to a repenting nation! For God can give peace in anger, as well as war. A ship at sea may be distressed by a calm, as well as broken by a tempest. The cattle which we mean to kill, we first prefer to some fat pasture: and sometimes God gives over punishing, not in mercy, but in fury; leaving men to go on quietly in their own hearts' lusts, that they who are filthy may be filthy still, Psal. lxxxi. 12; Hos. iv. 14, 17; Isa. i. 5; Ezek. xxiv. 13. God was exceedingly angry with Israel when he gave them their hearts' desire, in sending them quails, Numb. xi. 32, 33. Many men get their desires from God's anger by murmuring, as others do theirs from his mercy by prayer; but then a curse attends them. Now therefore, when our own sword devours us, when our land is, "through the wrath of the Lord of hosts," so darkened, that "the people" thereof are "as fuel of the fire," "no man" sparing "his brother," "every man" eating "the flesh of his own arm," (the sad character which the prophet gives of a civil war, Isa. ix. 19, 20,) let us take heed of God's complaint, "In vain have I smitten your children, they received no correction," Jer. ii. 30. Let us make it our business to recover God. It is he that "maketh wars to cease unto the end of the earth," Psal. xlvi. 9. And it is he who poureth out upon men "the strength of battle," and giveth them "for a spoil" "to the robbers," Isa. xlii.

24, 25. A sinful nation gains nothing by any human treaties, policies, counsels, contributions, till by repentance they secure their interest in God, and get him on their side. God being prevailed with by Moses in behalf of Israel, after the horrible provocation of the golden calf, sends a message to them: "I will send an angel before thee; and I will drive out the Canaanite—unto a land flowing with milk and honey: for I will not go up in the midst of thee." And presently there follows in the next verse, "When the people heard these evil tidings they mourned," Exod. xxxiii. 2—4. What were "these evil tidings?" to have an angel to protect and lead them? to have their enemies vanquished? to have possession of a land flowing with milk and honey? was there any thing lamentable in all this? Yes; to have all this and much more, and not to have God and his presence, was heavy tidings to God's people. And therefore Moses ceased not to plead with God till he promised them his own presence again, with which Moses chose rather to stay in a wilderness, than without it to go into the land of Canaan: "If thy presence go not with me, carry us not up hence," Exod. xxxiii. 13—15.

2. Whatever our spiritual wants are, to look up to heaven for a supply of them. Neither gardens, nor woods, nor vineyards, nor fields, nor flowers, nor trees, nor corn, nor spices, will flourish or revive without the dew and concurrence of heavenly grace. Christ alone is "all and in all" to his church: though the instruments be earthly, yet the virtue which gives success to them comes from heaven. We shall thus consider the succeeding metaphors, as connected with and dependent on him who is emphatically "the dew" unto his spiritual "Israel."

"He shall grow as the lily." יפרח כשושנה The beauty of the lily, or, as the prophet David calls it, "the beauties of holiness," arise from "the dew of the morning," Psal. cx. 3. He is the ornament, the attire, the comeliness of his spouse. For his people to forget him, is for "a maid" to "forget her ornaments, or a bride her attire," Jer. ii. 32. The perfect beauty of the church, is that comeliness of his which he communicates to her, Ezek. xvi. 14. Of ourselves we are "wretched, and miserable, and poor, and blind, and naked;" our "gold," our riches, our "white raiment," we must buy of him, Rev. iii. 17, 18. He is the Lord our righteousness, whom therefore we are said to put on, Rom. xiii. 14. He has "made us unto our God kings and priests," Rev. v. 10; and being such, he has provided beautiful robes for us, as once he appointed for the priests, Exod. xxviii. 2; Rev. iv. 4; vi. 11; vii. 9. This spiritual beauty of holiness in Christ's church, is sometimes compared to the marriage ornaments of a queen, Psal. xlv. 14; Rev. xix. 7, 8; xxi. 2; sometimes to the choice flowers of a garden, roses and lilies, Cant. ii. 1, 2; sometimes to a most glorious and goodly structure, Rev. xxi. 10—27; sometimes to the shining forth of the moon, and the brightness of the sun, Cant. vi. 10; Rev. xii. 1. All the united excellencies of the creatures are too low to adumbrate and figure the glories of the church.

Et quæ divisa beatos efficiunt, collecta tenet. Claud.

"And cast forth his roots as Lebanon." ויך שרשיו כלבנון The root and stability of the church is in and from him; he is "the Root of David," Rev. v. 5. Except he dwell in us, we can neither be rooted nor grounded, Eph. iii. 17. All our strength and sufficiency is from him, Phil. iv. 13; Eph. vi. 10; 1 Pet. v. 10. The graft is supported by another root, and not by its own. This is the reason of the stability of the church, because it is founded on a rock, Matt. xvi. 18; not on Peter,* but on him whom Peter confessed; on the apostles only doctrinally, but on Christ personally, as "the chief corner-stone, elect, precious," in whom whosoever "believeth" "shall not be confounded," Eph. ii. 20, 21; 1 Pet. ii. 6. This is the difference between the righteousness of creation and the righteousness of redemption; the state of the world in Adam, and the state of the church in Christ. Adam had his righteousness in his own keeping, and therefore when the power of hell set upon him he fell from his stedfastness; there was no promise given to him that "the gates of hell" should "not prevail against" him; being of an earthly constitution he had corruptibility, mutability, infirmity belonging to him from the very principles of his being. But Christ, the Second Adam, is "the Lord from heaven," over whom death has neither claim nor power; and the righteousness and stability of the church are founded on, and have their original in, him. The powers of darkness must be able to evacuate the virtue of his sacrifice, to stop God's ears to his intercession, to repel and keep back the supplies and influences of his Spirit, to keep or recover possession against his ejectment, in one word, to thrust him away from the right hand of the Majesty on high, and to kill him again, before ever they can overthrow his church. As Plato compared a man, so may we the church, to a tree inverted, with the root above and the branches below. And the root of this tree not only serves to give life to the branches while they abide in it, but to hold them fast that none can prevail to cut them off, John x. 28, 29.

"His branches shall spread." ילכו יונקותיו The growth and spreading abroad of the branches of the church, is from him whose name is "the Branch," Isa. xi. 1; Zech. iii. 8. To him "the uttermost parts of the earth" are given for a "possession," and all "the kingdoms of this world are" to "become the kingdoms of our Lord, and of his Christ," Psal. ii. 8; Rev. xi. 15. In regard of his first dispensation towards Israel, God's first-born, the land of Canaan is peculiarly called Immanuel's land, Isa. viii. 8. But in regard of his latter dispensation, when he sent "the rod of his strength out of Zion," and went forth conquering and to conquer, and gave commission to preach the gospel to every creature, the whole world is now, under the gospel, become Immanuel's land, and he is "the King of all the earth," Psal. xlvii. 7; "King of kings, and Lord of lords," Rev. xix. 16. "The Gentiles" "come" in to the "light" of his church, and "kings to the brightness of" her "rising;" and "the nation and kingdom that will not serve" her "shall perish; yea, those nations shall be utterly wasted," Isa. lx. 3, 12. Now every country is Canaan, and every Christian church the Israel of God, and every regenerate person born in Zion, and every spiritual worshipper the circumcision; now Christ is crucified in Galatia, and a passover eaten in Corinth, and manna fed on in Pergamos, and an altar set up in Egypt, and Gentiles sacrificed, and stones made children unto Abraham and temples unto God: see John iv. 21; Mal. i. 11; Zeph. ii. 11; Gal. vi. 16; Isa. xiv. 1; xliv. 5; Zech. viii. 23; Rom. ii. 29; Psal. lxxxvii. 4, 5; Phil. iii. 3; Col. ii. 11; Gal. iii. 1; 1 Cor. v. 7, 8; Rev. ii. 17; Isa. xix. 19, 21, 23; Rom. xv. 16; Luke iii. 8; Eph. ii. 21. In Christ's former dispensation the church was only

* Paulum audi dicentem, Petra autem erat Christus. Aug. in Psal. lx. Super hanc Petram quam confessus es, super hanc Petram quam cognovisti dicens, Tu es Christus Filius Dei vivi, ædificabo ecclesiam meam. De Verbis Dom. serm. 13. Quid est super hanc Petram? Super hanc fidem: super id quod dictum est, Tu es Christus Filius Dei. Tract. 10 in Epist. 1. Joann. Felix fidei petra, Petri ore confesso, Tu es Christus Filius Dei. Hilar. de Trin. lib. 2. Super hanc confessionis Petram, Ecclesiæ ædificatio est. lib. 6. Ἐπὶ ταύτῃ τῇ πέτρᾳ, τουτέστι τῇ πίστει τῆς ὁμολογίας. Chrysost. in loc. Vid. Isid. Pel. lib. 1. Ep. 235. Casaub. Exercitat. ad Annal. Eccles. 15. c. 12 et 13. Sixt. Senen. l. 6. Annot. 68, 69

national, amongst the Jews; but in his latter dispensation it is œcumenical and universal, over all the world; a spreading tree, under the shadow of the branches whereof "shall dwell all fowl of every wing," Ezek. xvii. 23.

"And his beauty shall be as the olive tree." ויהי כזית הודו The graces of the Holy Spirit wherewith the church is anointed are from him. He is the olive tree which empties the golden oil out of himself, Zech. iv. 12. Of his fulness we all receive grace for grace, John i. 16. With the same Spirit are we anointed, animated by the same life, regenerated to the same nature, renewed into the same image, reserved unto the same inheritance, dignified in some respect with the same offices, made priests to offer spiritual sacrifices, and kings to subdue spiritual enemies, and prophets to receive teaching from God, and to have a duplicate of his law written in our hearts, 2 Cor. i. 21; John xiv. 19; 1 Cor. xv. 48, 49; Rom. viii. 17; 1 Pet. ii. 5; Rev. i. 6; John vi. 45; Jer. xxxi. 33.

Origo fontium et fluminum mare, virtutum et scientiarum Christus. Si quis callet ingenio, si quis nitet eloquio, si quis moribus placet, inde est. Bernard. in Cant. serm. 13.

"And his smell as Lebanon." וריח לו כלבנון The sweet perfume and scent or smell of Lebanon, which arises out of holy duties, the grace which drops from the lips of his people, the spiritual incense which arises out of their prayers, the sweet savour of the gospel which spreads itself abroad in the ministry of his word and in the lives of his servants, they have all their origin in him, and from his heavenly dew. Of ourselves, without him, as we are altogether unclean, Psal. xiv. 3; Prov. xiii. 5, so we defile every holy thing with which we meddle, Hag. ii. 13, 14; Prov. xxviii. 9; Isa. i. 11—15; insomuch that God saith, "I hate, I despise your feast days, and I will not smell in your solemn assemblies," Amos v. 21; they are all of them, as they come from us, "gall and wormwood," "their clusters are bitter," Deut. xxix. 18; xxxii. 32. But when the Spirit of Christ blows upon us, and his grace is poured into our hearts and lips, then the spices flow out, Cant. iv. 16; then prayer goes up like incense and sweet odours, Rev. v. 8; then, instead of corrupt, rotten, contagious communication, our discourses tend to edifying, and "minister grace to the hearers," Eph. iv. 29; then the savour of the knowledge of Christ manifests itself in the mouths and lives of his servants in every place where they come, 2 Cor. ii. 14.

"They that dwell under his shadow shall return." ישבו ישבי בצלו The shadow and refreshment, the refuge and shelter, of the church against storm and tempest, against rain and heat, against all trouble and persecution, is from him alone. He is the only defence and covering that is over the assemblies and glory of Zion, Isa. iv. 5. "The name of the Lord is a strong tower," into which "the righteous" run and are "safe," Prov. xviii. 10. So the Lord promises, when his people should be exiles from his temple and scattered out of their own land, that he would himself be "a little sanctuary" to them in the countries where they should come, Ezek. xi. 16. He is a "dwelling place" to his church in all conditions, Psal. xc. 1; xci. 1, 2; "a strength to the needy," "a refuge from the storm, a shadow from the heat," "an hiding-place from the wind," "a covert from the tempest," "a chamber" wherein to retire when indignation is kindled, Isa. xxv. 4; xxvi. 20; xxxii. 2. Every history of God's power, every promise of his love, every observation and experience of his providence, every comfort in his word, the knowledge which we have of his name by faith, and the knowledge which we have of it by experience, are so many arguments to trust in him, and so many hiding-places in which to flee unto him against any trouble. "What time I am afraid, I will trust in thee," Psal. lvi. 3. "Why art thou cast down, O my soul? and why art thou disquieted in me? hope thou in God," Psal. xlii. 5, 11. He "delivered," he "doth deliver," he "will deliver," 2 Cor. i. 10. Many times the children of God are reduced to such extremities, that they have nothing wherewith to encourage themselves but their interest in him; nothing to flee to for hope but his great name, made known to them by faith in his promises, and by experience of his goodness, power, and providence. This was David's case at Ziklag, 1 Sam. xxx. 6; Israel's at the Red Sea, Exod. xiv. 10, 13; Jonah's in the belly of the fish, Jonah ii. 4, 7; and Paul's in the shipwreck, Acts xxvii. 20, 25. God is never so much glorified by the faith of his servants, as when they can maintain their trust in him against sight and sense; and when reason saith, Thou art undone, for all help fails thee, can answer in faith, I am not undone, "for he hath said, I will never leave thee nor forsake thee," Heb. xiii. 5.

"They shall revive as the corn, and grow as the vine." יחיו דגן ויפרחו כגפן The power which the church has to rise up above her pressures, to outgrow her troubles, to revive after lopping and harrowing, to make use of * affliction as a means to flourish again, all this is from him. That in trouble we are not overwhelmed, but can say with the apostle, "As † dying, and, behold, we live; as chastened, and not killed; as sorrowful, yet alway rejoicing; as poor, yet making many rich; as having nothing, and yet possessing all things;" like the corn which dies and is quickened again; like the vine that is lopped and spreads again; all this is from him who is "the resurrection, and the life," John xi. 25; who was that grain of wheat, which dying, and being cast into the ground, brought forth much fruit, John xii. 24; the Branch which grew out of the roots of Jesse, when that goodly family was sunk so low as from David the king to Joseph the carpenter, Isa. xi. 1.

"The scent thereof shall be as the wine of Lebanon." כיין לבנון As God is the author of all these blessings to his people, so when he bestows them he does it in perfection; the fruits which this dew produces are as the fruits of Lebanon, most choice and excellent. If he plant a vineyard, it shall be in "a very fruitful hill," and with "the choicest vine," Isa. v. 1, 2; "a noble vine, wholly a right seed," Jer. ii. 21. When in any kind of straits we have recourse to the creature for supply, either we find it like our Saviour's fig tree, without fruit, or like our prophet's vine, as good as empty, the fruits thereof not worth the gathering, Hos. x. 1. "Their grapes are grapes of gall, their clusters are bitter," Deut. xxxii. 32; full of vanity, vexation, disappointment. Friends fail either in their love, or in their power; people cry Hosanna to-day, and Crucify to-morrow. "Men of low degree are vanity, and men of high degree a lie." Counsels clash, or are puzzled with intricacies and unhappy obstacles, like the wheels in Ezekiel's vision, that seem hampered in one another. Armies, like Reuben, "unstable as water," now rise, presently ebb and sink away. Treasures, like the mountains out of which they were first digged, barren and fruitless, fuel rather to feed our sins than water to

* Medicamenta quædam prius affligunt ut sanent, et ipsa collyria nisi sensum videndi prius claudant, prodesse non possunt. Aug. Qu. in Matth. qu. 14. Quo terreri deberet, illo ipso recreatur——contumeliam tenet curationis pignus, &c. Scult. cap. 42. Observat. in Matth. de Muliere Syrophænissa. Plures efficimur quoties metimur. Tertul. Apol. cap. ult.

† Ὀλίγοι καὶ πολλῶν δυνατώτεροι, αἰχμάλωτοι καὶ τοῦ βασιλέως ἰσχυρότεροι, ἀπολέσαντες πάτριδα καὶ πίστιν μὴ ἀπολέσαντες· γυμνοὶ καὶ ἐνδεδυμένοι, πτωχοὶ καὶ εὔποροι, καὶ ἐλευθέρων ἀμείνους, &c. Chrys. de Trib. Pueris, Ser. 2. in Psal. l.

quench our flames; matter of prey to the wicked, more than of help to the miserable. In one word, take any creature-helps in the world, and there will be something, nay, very much, of defect in them. All existence but God's is mixed with non-existence; and as every man, so every creature besides, is a liar, like Job's brook, (or friends which he compares thereto,) that vanishes into nothing when there is most need of it, Job vi. 15—18: a liar, either by way of perfidiousness, which promises and then deceives; or by way of impotence, which undertakes and then miscarries. But whenever God promises and undertakes to bless any man or any people, he carries on his work to perfection; his blessings are all milk and honey, dew and fatness, wine and oil, the fruits of Lebanon, full of sweetness and maturity. He perfects that which he begins concerning his servants, Psal. cxxxviii. 8; Phil. i. 6. There doth "not one thing" fail "of all the good things" he speaks concerning his people; they all come to pass, and not one faileth, Josh. xxiii. 14. The riches which are gotten by human lusts and sinful resolutions are attended with many and piercing sorrows, 1 Tim. vi. 10; but when God blesses a man with riches, he takes away all the sorrow from it, Prov. x. 22. The gifts of God are all of them like his works, "very good," Gen. i. 31; and bring after them into the soul a sabbath, a rest, and peace.

3. We should from hence further learn, to show forth the fruits of this heavenly dew, agreeably to the scope of the several metaphors which the prophet here uses, drawn from the consideration of a garden, forest, fruitful field; similitudes frequently used by the Holy Spirit, to denote the beauty, sweetness, fruit, comfort, shelter, protection, which the church of Christ affords to its members, Isa. xxxv. 1, 2; lviii. 11; Cant. iv. 12, 16; vi. 2; (as, on the other side, the wicked are compared to a dry desert, and barren wilderness, Isa. xxxv. 6, 7; xli. 18; Jer. xvii. 6;) and as these are promises in regard of God, and so matter of comfort, they are duties with respect to us, and so matter of obedience. He promises,

Tanta est floris lilii dignitas ut Homerus omnes flores vocaverit λείρια. Jul. Pollux. vid. Plin. lib. 21. cap. 1.

1. That his people shall "grow as the lily," which is the most beautiful of all flowers, Matt. vi. 28, 29; that they shall be gloriously clothed, like a king's daughter, with the garments of praise, and the spirit of holiness, Isa. lxi. 3; set forth by various metaphors of broidered work, and fine linen, and silk, and ornaments, and bracelets, and chains, and jewels, and crowns, Ezek. xvi. 8—13.

And as it is his promise, so it ought to be our duty and endeavour to adorn the gospel of Christ, to be in his garden as a lily, and not as a nettle or bramble; to walk as becometh godliness; to let our light shine before men, that they may be won to admire the amiableness of the Lord's tabernacle, and glorify God in the hour of their visitation; to be as lights in the midst of a crooked generation, Phil. ii. 15, or as "the lily among thorns," Cant. ii. 2; to make it appear that spiritual wisdom causes the "face to shine," Eccl. viii. 1; that holiness is indeed a most beautiful thing, which commends us to the eyes of God and angels; a robe worn by Christ the King of saints, and by which we are made like to him who is "the chiefest among ten thousand," and "altogether lovely," Cant. v. 10, 16. We should take heed of any thing whereby our holy profession may be blemished, and the name of God through us defiled: of such levity as is inconsistent with the majesty of holiness; such morosity as is inconsistent with the meekness of holiness; such drooping as is inconsistent with the joy of holiness; such stiffness and sourness as are inconsistent with the lenity of holiness. In one word, we should labour by the innocence, purity, elegance, fragrance, fruitfulness; by the winning ingenuity, the mild and humble condescension, the prudent insinuation, the meek, quiet, and graceful demeanour of a holy life; to "show forth the praises of him that hath called" us, and to "put to silence the ignorance of foolish men," who, like the foul, pretend to despise beauty, like dogs, bay at the shining of the moon, and "speak evil of those things which they know not," Jude 10.

2. That his church should "cast forth" her "roots as Lebanon." Though she should have the beauty of the lily, yet she should be freed from its frailness, its aptness to fade and wither, beautiful to-day, to-morrow drooping to death. But she should have stability like the cedar, which is one of the strongest of trees, and least subject to decay; therefore is the church compared to it, Ezek. xvii. 22, 23, and the temple said to be built of it, 1 Kings vi. 15, 16, to signify the strength and duration of the church, against which the gates of hell should not prevail. And we may by the way observe, that most of the things here mentioned by our prophet, are also noted to have been in the temple, or in its services: lilies, 1 Kings vii. 19, 22, 26; olive trees, 1 Kings vi. 23, 32, 33; spices for incense, wheat and oil for meat-offerings, wine for drink-offerings. God thus furnishes his people with those blessings which may be most properly dedicated to him,* teaching us, as often as we receive any gifts from him, presently to inquire what relation they have to his temple, how his name may be honoured, how his church may be served, how his gospel may be furthered, how his people may be edified and comforted by them, how all our enjoyments may be divided as spoils to Christ: the power of great men, Isa. lx. 3; the swords of mighty men, 1 Sam. xviii. 17, 25, 27; Judg. vii. 18; the wisdom of learned men, 1 Kings iii. 9, 28; the cunning of craftsmen, Exod. xxviii. 3; xxxi. 6; the wealth of rich men, Isa. xxiii. 18; Prov. iii. 9; Psal. xlv. 12; Isa. lx. 6, 9; 1 Tim. vi. 17—19. Abraham gave of the spoils to Melchizedek, Heb. vii. 4; and Israel of all their wealth to the tabernacle, Exod. xxxv. 21; and David and his people of their treasure to the temple, 1 Chron. xxix. 2.

Plin. lib. 16. cap. 40. Theophrast. Hist. Plant. l. 3.

And as it is his promise, that the church should thus take root, 2 Kings xix. 30; Jer. xvii. 8; so we should account it our duty to be firm, stable, constant, "unmovable" in the truth, and "in the work of the Lord," as "a house" "founded upon a rock;" to stand "rooted and built up" in the truth, that we may "hold fast the profession" thereof "without wavering," not being "carried about with every wind of doctrine," but knowing whom and what we have believed, 1 Cor. xvi. 13; Eph. iv. 14; Col. ii. 7; Heb. x. 23; to "stand fast," "being rooted and grounded in" the "love" of God, that we may be "strengthened with might" in his service, and may with "purpose of heart" cleave unto him, being established by his grace, Eph. iii. 17; Col. i. 11; Heb. xii. 28; xiii. 9. In the civil law, till a tree has taken root, it does not belong to the soil on which it is planted. So it is not enough to be in the church, except, like "a cedar in Lebanon," we "cast forth" our "roots," and are so "planted" that we "flourish in the courts of our God," and "bring forth fruit in old age," Psal. xcii. 12—14.

P. De acquirendo rerum dominio. l. 7. § 13. et Arborum furtim cæsarum, l. 3. § 3. Cod. de Rei vindicatione, l. 11.

3. That the church should spread forth her branches, and fill the earth, and grow to a great compass and extent, that she should send out "her boughs unto the sea, and her branches unto the river," Psal. lxxx. 8—11; Dan. ii. 35; that his church should be a universal

* Τεύχεα συλήσας, οἴσω ποτὶ Ιλιον ἱρὴν
Και κρεμόω ποτὶ νηὸν 'Απολλωνος ἑκάτοιο. Hom. Il. η.

Spolia in templis suspendere antiqui moris erat. Cic. de Nat. Deor. lib. 2. Liv lib. 10. Virgil. Æn. 7.

church over the whole world; that as, in regard of sin, the whole world lieth in the wicked one, 1 John v. 19, so it should have Christ for its propitiation, through faith, 1 John ii. 2. *Totus in maligno propter zizania, Christus propitiatio propter triticum.* "By one Spirit are we all baptized into one body," 1 Cor. xii. 13; and that one body made up of "all churches of the saints," 1 Cor. xiv. 33, even of "all nations, and kindred, and people, and tongues," Rev. vii. 9: no difference of persons, "neither Greek nor Jew, circumcision nor uncircumcision, Barbarian, Scythian, bond nor free: but Christ all, and in all," Col. iii. 11; no difference of places, "all that in every place call upon the name of Jesus Christ our Lord, both theirs and ours," 1 Cor. i. 2; no difference of times, "Jesus Christ the same yesterday, to-day, and for ever," Heb. xiii. 8.

Aug. Epist. 48.

And as this is his promise, so we should endeavour,

1. To grow ourselves in knowledge and grace; to let our profiting appear unto all men; to abound in the work of the Lord; to let our graces from the heart, like leaven from the middle of the lump, spread abroad, and find their way to all the parts and powers of soul and body, that the whole man may be "filled with all the fulness of God," and grow up "unto the measure of the stature of the fulness of Christ," Eph. iv. 13—16; Phil. iii. 12—14; 2 Pet. iii. 18; Heb. vi. 1.

2. To promote zealously the growth and progress of the gospel in others. This is the nature of grace, to manifest itself, and by that means to allure and gather others to its own quality. It is set forth in Scripture by the names of light, which shines abroad, of ointment and perfume, which cannot be hid, of leaven, and salt, which impart to other things their own nature and relish. Therefore the Holy Ghost was given in "tongues," "tongues like as of fire," with "a sound from heaven as of a rushing mighty wind;" all which have a quality of self-manifestation, and are calculated to attract attention. There is an excellent place to this purpose in Eph. iv. 15, 16, "But speaking the truth in love, may grow up into him in all things, which is the head, even Christ: from whom the whole body fitly joined together and compacted by that which every joint supplieth, according to the effectual working in the measure of every part, maketh increase of the body unto the edifying of itself in love." The apostle thus illustrates the manner of spiritual increase in the mystical body of Christ by the proportion of the growth of members in the natural body, and thereby teaches us, that,

1. There must be a fellowship between the head and members, which, in the mystical body, is here spoken of as twofold, εἰς αὐτὸν, and ἐξ οὗ; growing "into him," and receiving "from" him; looking in this work of growth on Christ, first, as the end to which all that growth aspires; secondly, as the fountain from whence it proceeds; that by growing we may have a more intimate and strong communion with him, by that virtue which we receive from him. So here are two necessary requisites to this duty of endeavouring the "increase of the body," to have Christ for our end to which we work, and for our fountain out of which we derive our ability of working. Every true member of Christ is intent and vigilant on the interest and honour of Christ; and it belongs to the honour of Christ to have a perfect body. The church is his "fulness," he esteems himself maimed and incomplete if that should be finally deficient in any thing requisite to its integral perfection; and hence it is that every true Christian puts forth the uttermost of his endeavours in his place to carry on the "increase" of his Master's body; as every true-hearted soldier is exceedingly desirous, and, according to his power, endeavours, that every company and regiment under his general's command may be in all its offices and members complete. Again, every member of Christ being to him united, from him receives of his fulness "grace for grace," and so works to the same ends as the Head. And as the water which first rises out of the fountain, stands not still where it began, but goes forward till it grows into a great river; so those who are joined to Christ as a fountain, do, by reason of that vital communion which they have with the fountain, carry on the growth of the whole body; and the more vigorous the life of Christ is in any part, the more actively does that part work towards the edification of the whole.

Vid. Cameron. de Eccles. p. 84—86.

2. A mutual communion of the members of the body within and amongst themselves: to which is first presupposed, the organical and harmonious constitution and compacture of the body into one, out of which arise the form and beauty, the strength and firmness, the order and fitness, that are in it to those works which are proper to it, intimated in those two words συναρμολογούμενον, and συμβιβαζόμενον, "fitly joined together and compacted." It is a metaphor drawn from carpenters and other artificers, who, by several joints, so coaptate and fit the parts of their work to one another, that being put together and fastened, there may one whole structure or body grow out of them; and in that body this accurate fitness and intimate connexion of the parts one with another, produce an excellent strength, a beautiful order, and a ready serviceableness of each part to the other, and of all to the whole. So Jerusalem is said to be as "a city that is compact together," Psal. cxxii. 3; as the ark (a type of the church) had the ribs, and planks, and parts thereof so closely fastened into one another, that no water could get in; and as in the tabernacle, all the curtains thereof were to be coupled together, Exod. xxvi. 3. So Christ is all for unity, and joining things into one; two natures united in one person, two parties reconciled by one Mediator, two people concorporated into one church; one family, one Father, one seed, one Head, one faith, one hope, one love, one worship, one body, one Spirit, one end, and one common salvation. Christ is not, loves not to be, divided, 1 Cor. i. 13. This is a fundamental requisite to the growth of the body, to the preservation of its unity. The building must be "fitly framed together," if you would have it grow "unto an holy temple in the Lord," Eph. ii. 21; Col. ii. 19. When there was most unity, there was the greatest increase in the church; when they were all of "one accord," of one heart, and one soul, then "the Lord added to the church daily such as should be saved," Acts ii. 46, 47. They that cause divisions and dissensions, do not serve the Lord Jesus, and therefore they cannot but hinder the progress of his gospel, Rom. xvi. 17, 18. As in the natural, so in the mystical body, *solutio continuitatis* tends to the paining and grieving of that Spirit by which the body lives, and by consequence hinders its growth, Eph. iv. 30, 31. Our growth is by the apostle distributed into growth "in knowledge," and growth "in grace," 2 Pet. iii. 18; and divisions in the church are of themselves great hinderances to both these: to knowledge, because the most usual breaches in the church arise out of diversities of opinion publicly asserted and insisted on by their authors and followers. And though accidentally, where truth is embraced, it is held with more care, and searched into with more accurateness, because of the errors that oppose it (as the fire is hottest in the coldest weather); yet corrupt doctrine, being of the nature of a weed or canker, in spreading and corroding further and further, it must needs consequently hinder the diffusion, and so the growth, of true knowledge. Nor does it less hinder the growth of grace; for while the people of God are all of one heart and of one way, then all their communion

Nulla multitudinis potentia nisi consentientis, id est, unum sentientis. Aug. de vera Relig. cap. 25.

runs into this one design of mutually edifying, comforting, supporting, encouraging one another in their "most holy faith;" but when they are divided and broken into factions by different judgments, if there be not a great abundance of humility and spiritual wisdom, the spirits of men run out into heats and passions, into perverse disputes, and mere notional contentions, which have ever been diminutions to the power of godliness, 1 Cor. iii. 3, 4. When there are schisms in the body, the members will not have care one of another, 1 Cor. xii. 25. Greatly therefore, even for this one cause, are the sad and dangerous divisions of these times to be lamented, when men make use of civil troubles to disturb, yea, to tear asunder, the unity of the church; when they set up, as in the times of the Donatists, altar against altar, and church against church, and make secessions from the common body, and then one from another, to the infinite content and advantage of the common enemies of our religion, and to the injury of religion itself. It were a blessed thing if we were in a condition conformable to the apostle's exhortation, to "speak all the same thing," to "be perfectly joined in the same mind and in the same judgment," to "be of one mind," and to "live in peace," 1 Cor. i. 10; 2 Cor. xiii. 11. But if that cannot be attained to, let us yet all learn the apostle's other lesson, wherein we are "otherwise minded," to depend upon God for revealing his will unto us; and whereto we have already attained, "to walk by the same rule," to "mind the same thing," to remember that every difference in opinion does not, ought not to dissipate or dissolve the unity of God's church. Even in Corinth, where the people were divided into several parties, yet they continued "one church," 1 Cor. xi. 18.

Non tulit Cælius assentientem sed exclamavit, Dic aliquid contra ut duo simus. Senec. de Ira, 3. lib. c. 8.

The body thus constituted, and compacted for the increase thereof, presents these requisite characteristics.

1. Members severally distinct from one another, some principal, others ministerial, all concurring differently to the service of the whole. If the heart should be in the head, or the liver in the shoulder, if there should be any unnatural dislocation of the vital or nutritive parts, the body could not grow, but must perish. The way for the church to prosper and flourish, is for every member to keep in his own rank and order, to remember his own measure, to act in his own sphere, to manage his particular condition and relations with spiritual wisdom and humility; the eye to do the work of an eye, the hand of a hand. Say not as Absalom, If I were a judge, I would do justice, 2 Sam. xv. 4; but consider what state God has set thee in, and in that walk with God, and adorn the profession of the gospel, Rom. xii. 3; 1 Cor. xii. 8; xi. 28, 29; 2 Cor. x. 13, 14; Eph. iv. 7. Remember Uzzah; it was a good work which he did, but because he did it out of order, having no call, God smote him for his error, 2 Sam. vi. 6, 7. There are excellent works, which, being done without the call of God, do not edify, but disturb the body, Rom. x. 15; Heb. v. 4. Every man must walk in the church "as God hath distributed" and "hath called," and "every man" must, "in the same calling wherein he was called," "therein abide with God," 1 Cor. vii. 17, 20, 24.

2. Joints and ligaments so fastening these members together, that each one may be serviceable to the increase of the whole, Col. ii. 19. There are bands which join the body to the Head, without which it can neither grow nor live, namely, the Spirit of Christ, and faith in him, 1 Cor. vi. 17; Rom. viii. 9; Eph. iii. 17: and there are bands which join the parts of the body to one another; as namely, the same Holy Spirit, 1 Cor. xii. 13; which Spirit of grace stirs up every member to seek the growth and benefit of the whole, 1 Cor. xii. 25, 26. The sincere love and truth which each member bears to all the rest, is called "the bond of perfectness," Col. iii. 14, and "the bond of peace," Eph. iv. 3. Now love is a most communicative grace, it will plant, and water, and feed, and spend itself for the good of the whole, it will deny itself to serve the body, (as Christ did,) Gal. v. 13.

3. A measure belonging to every part. Some are in one office, others in another, some have one gift, others another, and all this "for the perfecting of the saints," Eph. iv. 11, 12; 1 Cor. xii. 4, 11: one is able to teach, another to comfort, a third to convince, a fourth to exhort, a fifth to counsel, and every one of these are to be directed to the edification and growth of the whole, Rom. xii. 3—8; Eph. iv. 7. The apostle saith, that we are "fellow citizens with the saints," Eph. ii. 19. Now as amongst fellow citizens there is wont to be an intercourse of mutual negociation, one man has one commodity, and another another, and with these they usually carry on mutual barter; so amongst the saints, one man is eminent in one grace, another in another, and according to their mutual requirements, or abilities, they interchangeably minister to one another towards the growth of the whole.

Vid. Aristot. Ethic. l. 5. c. 8.

4. Ἐπιχωρηγία, the supply of service and the supply of nourishment which one part affords to another, and so to the whole. This is principally from the Head to the members, called by the apostle, "the supply of the Spirit of Jesus Christ," Phil. i. 19; of whose fulness we receive "grace for grace," John i. 16; into whose image we are transformed "from glory to glory," 2 Cor. iii. 18: but it is proportionably between the members amongst themselves; for as several particular ingredients make up one cordial, and several instruments concur to the perfecting of one ἀποτελέσμα, or consummate work, and the beauty of every thing arises out of the variety, order, and mutual serviceableness which the parts thereof have one to another; so in the church, Christ has so tempered it together, that they might all stand mutually in need one of another. Therefore we find the saints in Scripture communicating to one another their experiences, temptations, deliverances, comforts, for their mutual edification, Psal. xxxiv. 2, 6; John i. 41, 45; iv. 29; 2 Cor. i. 4, 6; Phil. i. 12—14; Col. ii. 1, 2. And God's dealings with saints in particular are therefore registered in the Scripture, both that we might learn thereby to build up one another, and that by their examples we might support our faith, and through patience and experience of the Scripture have hope, because what has been done to one is in the like condition applicable to every other, James v. 10, 11, 17; Rom. xv. 4; 1 Cor. x. 6; Heb. xiii. 5.

5. Ἐνέργεια, an effectual working, a δύναμις πλαστικὴ or πεπτικη, a faculty to form and to concoct the matter, which has been subministered, to life and nourishment: which is the work of faith, and of the Spirit of Christ; whereby the soul of a believer, being sensible of want, desirous of supply, and pressing forward to perfection, sweetly closes with whatsoever the measure of any other part has communicated to it, converting it to its own growth and nourishment, which the apostle calls the mixing of the word with faith, Heb. iv. 2. Thus far in respect of the growth of the church; but he further promises,

4. That the beauty of his church shall be as "the olive tree;" that as she should have the glory of the lily, the strength and extension of the cedar, so this spreading should not be a vain ostentation, but should have joined with it the flourishing and fruitfulness of the olive. Now the honour of the olive tree consists in two things, perpetual greenness, and most profitable fruit, which serves both for light, to cause the lamp to burn, Exod. xxvii. 20, and for nourishment, to be eaten,

Lev. vi. 15, 16: in the one respect it is an emblem of peace, it makes the face shine, Psal. civ. 15; and in the other it is an emblem of grace, and spiritual gifts, 1 John ii. 20. These are the two most excellent benefits which God promises to his people; "He will speak peace unto" them, Psal. lxxxv. 8; Isa. xxxii. 17; and he "will give" them "grace and glory," Psal. lxxxiv. 11.

And as he promises, so should we practise these things, and learn to beautify the gospel of Christ, first, with our good works, as the fruits of his grace, John xv. 8; secondly, with our spiritual joy and comfort, as the fruits of his peace; that others, seeing the light and shining forth of a serene, calm, and peaceable conscience in our conversation, may thereby be brought in love with the ways of God. These two mutually cherish and increase one another. The more conscience we make of fruitfulness, the more way do we make for peace; when the waters of lust are sunk, the dove will quickly bring in an olive branch: and the more the peace of God rules in the heart, the more will it strengthen the conscience and care of obedience, from these considerations: first, thankfulness for so great a blessing: secondly, fear to forfeit it: thirdly, wisdom to improve and increase it.

5. That his church shall be in "smell as Lebanon," and that "the scent thereof shall be as the wine of Lebanon," as elsewhere we find her compared to a garden of "all the chief spices," Cant. iv. 12, 14; she shall be filled with the sweet savour of the gospel of Christ. "Thanks be unto God," saith the apostle, "which always causeth us to triumph in Christ, and maketh manifest the savour of his knowledge by us in every place; for we are unto God a sweet savour of Christ," 2 Cor. ii. 14, 15: where there are two metaphors, one of a sweet ointment, the other of a triumph. The name of Christ is compared to an "ointment," Cant. i. 3; and the preaching of the gospel, which is making manifest the savour of this ointment, is called the bearing of Christ's name, Acts ix. 15. Now, this sweet savour is annexed to a triumphal solemnity, because in all times of public joy they were wont to anoint themselves with sweet oil, which is therefore called *oleum lætitiæ*, "the oil of gladness," Psal. xlv. 7; Isa. lxi. 3. (For in times of mourning they abstained from sweet ointments, 2 Sam. xiv. 2; Dan. x. 2, 3.) The gospel therefore being a message of "great joy," Luke ii. 10; a leading of "captivity captive," and the means whereby Christ goes forth gloriously, "conquering, and to conquer," Psal. xlv. 3, 4; cx. 2; Rev. vi. 2; therefore they who brought these good tidings are said to be as a "sweet savour," whose lips drop "sweet smelling myrrh," Cant. v. 13, and whose doctrine is compared to the "powders of the merchant," Cant. iii. 6; and the time of the gospel is called an "accepted time," "the day of salvation," 2 Cor. vi. 2; that is, a time of singular joy and solemnity, a continual Easter, or festival, 1 Cor. v. 7, 8: and herewithal he promises likewise, that his people should offer up spiritual incense and services to him in prayers, thanksgivings, alms, and good works, Ezek. xx. 40.

Convivia, ludi—pocula crebra, unguenta, coronæ, serta parentur. Lucret. lib. 4. Aderant unguenta, coronæ, incendebantur odores. Cic. Tusc. qu. l. 5. Vid. Athenæum, lib. 15. c. 11, 12.

And as he promises, so we should practise these things. Our care should be to let our lips and lives breathe forth nothing but grace and edification, Col. iv. 6; to be frequent in the spiritual sacrifices of prayer, thanksgiving, and good works, which may be as "an odour of a sweet smell" before God, Phil. iv. 18; Rev. viii. 4; to labour to leave behind us "a good name," not out of vain-glory, or an empty, ambitious affectation of honour, but out of the conscience of a holy life, which makes the name smell "better than precious ointment," Eccl. vii. 1.

6. That "they that dwell under his shadow shall return." Which words admit of a double sense, and so infer a double promise and a double duty. 1. We may by an hysteron-proteron understand the words thus, When Israel have repented and are brought home to God again, they shall have security, defence, protection, refreshment under the comforts of his grace, against all the violence of temptation, as a spreading tree affords a sweet shade to the weary traveller, and shelters him from the oppression of the heat; whereby is signified the secure, quiet, and comfortable condition of God's people under the protection of his providence and promises, Job vii. 2; Isa. iv. 6; Micah iv. 4; Zech. iii. 10.

And as he promises such a condition, so should we in all troubles not trust in an "arm of flesh," or betake ourselves to mere human wisdom and carnal counsels, which are too thin shelters against God's displeasure, or the enemies of the church; but we must fly to him to hide us, we must find spiritual refreshment in his ordinances, promises, and providence, get his wing to cover us, and his presence to be a "little sanctuary" unto us, and "the joy of the Lord" to be our "strength," Psal. lvii. 2; xci. 1; Isa. xxvi. 20; Neh. viii. 10. When the Lord comes out of his place to punish the inhabitants of the land for their iniquity; when flood and fire, storm and tempest, the fury of anger, the strength of battle, are poured out upon a people; when a destroying angel is sent abroad with a commission to kill and slay, Ezek. ix. 5, 6; when Death, the king of terrors, rides up and down in triumph, stripping men of treasures, lands, friends, honours, pleasures, making them a house in darkness, where master and servant, princes and prisoners, are all alike: to have then an ark with Noah, a Zoar with Lot, a Goshen in Egypt; to have one arm of this olive tree spread over us; to have one promise out of God's word, one sentence from the mouth of Christ promising paradise to us, is infinitely of more value to a languishing spirit than all the diadems of the earth, or the peculiar treasure of princes.

2. If we take the words in the order in which they lie, then the mercy here promised is, that when God shall restore and repair his church, they who dwell under its comforts shall return and be converted to the knowledge and obedience which shall be there taught them. When "the branch of the Lord" is "beautiful and glorious, and the fruit of the earth excellent and comely," then "he that remaineth in Jerusalem shall be called holy," Isa. iv. 2, 3; then every vessel in Judah and Jerusalem shall be inscribed, "Holiness unto the Lord," Zech. xiv. 20, 21; then "the heart also of the rash shall understand knowledge, and the tongue of the stammerers shall be ready to speak plainly," Isa. xxxii. 4.

And this should be the endeavour of every one who lives under the shade of this tree, under the purity of God's ordinances, under the pious government and constitution of such a church or family as is here described, especially in these times, when, on the one side, the world is so much loosened and estranged from us, and, on the other side, reformation in the church is so much to be desired, to convert and turn men unto the Lord. All endeavours after reformation in a church are miserably defective, when they come short of this, which should be the ultimate reason of them all, namely, the repentance and conversion to God of those that dwell under its shadow. When God promises to give to his church "the glory of Lebanon," and "the excellency of Carmel and Sharon," the consequence of this beauty and reformation in the church is, "the eyes of the blind shall be opened, and the ears of the deaf shall be unstopped. Then shall the lame man leap as an hart, and the tongue of the dumb sing: for in the wilderness shall waters break out, and streams in the desert. And the parched ground shall become a pool, and the thirsty land springs of water," Isa. xxxv. 2, 5—7. "The wolf," "the leopard," "the lion," "the bear," "the asp," "the cockatrice," shall be so turned from the fierceness and malignity of their natures, that "they shall not hurt nor destroy in all" the "holy mountain," but "a little child shall lead them," Isa. xi. 6—9. It is a great happiness and advantage to live under the shade of a godly government; many have reason to bless God all their days that they were in their childhood trained up in such a school where piety was taught them as well as learning, where they had means as well of conversion as of institution; that they lived in such a family where the master of it was of Joshua's mind, "As for me and my house, we will serve the Lord," Josh. xxiv. 15. Salvation comes to a whole house when the governor thereof is converted, Luke xix. 9; Acts xvi. 33, 34. I shall never look on a church as effectually reformed, till I find reformation work conversion; till piety and charity, justice and mercy, truth, humility, gentleness, goodness, kindness, meekness, singleness of heart, zeal for godliness and mutual edification, and the life and power of religion, shine forth more conspicuously than before. When the very "headstone" is brought forth, and the last work in the building of the temple finished, yet then must the people cry, "Grace, grace unto it," Zech. iv. 7; intimating that reformation is never indeed consummate till the blessing of God make it effectual to those uses for which it was by him appointed. Church reformation should be like Paul's Epistles, which always close with duties of obedience.

7. That "they shall revive as the corn, and grow as the vine." In which two expressions are set forth two excellent and wholesome consequences of affliction. 1. "The corn," though it die first, and suffer much from frost, hail, snow, tempest, yet, when the spring comes, revives and breaks through all. So God promises to his church, in the saddest condition, a reviving again, and that it shall be brought "forth to the light," Ezek. xxxvii. 12; Micah vii. 9. 2. "The vine," when pruned and lopped, will not only revive and spring again, but will bring forth the more fruit, and cast forth the more fragrant smell. So God promises to his people, not only a reviving out of their afflictions, (hence haply Christ was buried in a garden, to note, that death itself does not destroy our bodies, but only sow them; "the dew of herbs" will revive them again, 1 Cor. xv. 42—44,) but further, a profiting by afflictions, that we may say with David, "it was good for" us, when we find it yield "the peaceable fruit of righteousness" after we have been "exercised thereby," Psal. cxix. 71; Heb. xii. 11.

Semina non nisi corrupta et dissoluta fæcundius surgunt. Omnia pereundo servantur; omnia de interitu reformantur. Tertul. Apol. cap. 48.

And as he promises these things, so we should learn to turn these promises into prayer and into practice. When we seem, in our own eyes, cast out of God's sight, yet we must not cast him out of our sight, but, as Jonah in the whale's belly, and as Daniel in Babylon, pray towards his holy temple still, Jonah ii. 4, 7; Dan. vi. 10. The woman of Canaan would not be thrust off with a seeming rejection, nor utterly despond under a grievous trial of faith, but, by a singular acumen and spiritual sagacity, discerned matter of argument in that which looked like a denial, Matt. xv. 27. Soap and fuller's earth, when first put on, seem to stain and soil the clothes, yet their use and end is to purify them. And God's frowns and delays may seem to be the denials of prayer, when haply his end is to make the granting of them more full of profit and comfort. Therefore in all troubles we must not give over looking towards God, but say with Job, "Though he slay me, yet will I trust in him," Job xiii. 15.

And after all afflictions we must learn to evidence their fruit, to come out of them refined, as silver out of the fire; to have thereby our faith strengthened, our hope confirmed, our love inflamed, our fruit and obedience increased, our sins taken away, and our iniquities purged; to be chastened and taught, to be chastened and converted, Isa. xxvii. 9. If we have run away from our duties, and been cast into a whale's belly for it, when we are delivered let us be sure to look better to our resolutions afterwards: "After all that is come upon us for our evil deeds, and for our great trespass, should we again break" his "commandments?" Ezra ix. 13, 14. As Job's riches after his afflictions, so we should endeavour that our graces after our afflictions may be doubled upon us, and that the scent of our holy example may, like spices bruised, or the grapes of Lebanon crushed in the winepress, spread abroad a more fragrant smell before God and man, as "the smell of a field which the Lord hath blessed," Gen. xxvii. 27.

Lastly, He promises that all these should be fruits of Lebanon, of the best and most perfect kind: "The scent thereof shall be as the wine of Lebanon." There are many evidences of the goodness of God even in the lives of pagan men; we read of Abimelech's unwillingness to sin against God, Gen. xx. 4, 6, and of his and Ephron's singular kindness to Abraham, Gen. xx. 14, 15; xxiii. 10, 11, 15. No argument more common than this of the virtues, the temperance, prudence, justice, mercy, patience, fidelity, friendships, affability, magnanimity, of many heathen men; insomuch that some have presumed so far as to make them *ex congruo* meritorious, or dispositive to salvation. But all these are but "wild grapes," bitter clusters, the fruits of an empty vine, not worth the gathering in order to salvation. But the graces which God bestows upon his church are of a more spiritual and perfect nature, proceeding from faith in Christ, from love of God, from a conscience cleansed from dead works, from an intention to glorify God and adorn the gospel, from a new nature, and from the Spirit of Christ, conforming his servants to himself. They are not grapes of Sodom, but grapes of Lebanon.

Vid. Vegam. de Justif. lib. 6. cap. 18, 19, 20. Andrad. Orthodox. Explicat. l. 3. Maldonat. in Johan. 5. 6. Greg. Valent. To. 3. disput. 1. Qu. 2. punct. 1, et 4. Erasm. Præfat. in Qu. Tusc. Cic. Aug. contra Julian. Pelag. l. 4. c. 3.

And as he thus blesses us, in the like manner should we serve him; not offer to him the refuse, the halt, and blind, and maimed, for sacrifice; not give unto him of that which cost us nothing; but go to Lebanon for all our sacrifices, "covet earnestly the best gifts," press forward and labour to perfect holiness in the fear of God. Give to him our lilies, the beauties of our minority; and our cedars, the strength of our youth; and our olives, and grapes, and corn, and wine: whatever gifts he has bestowed on us, use them to his service and honour again; nor content ourselves with "the form of godliness," with the morality of virtues, with the outside of duties, with the seeds and beginnings of holiness, (he has none who thinks he has enough,) but strive how we shall outrun one another to Christ, as Peter and John did towards his sepulchre. It was a high pitch which Moses aimed at, when he said, "I beseech thee, show me thy glory," Exod. xxxiii. 18. Nothing would satisfy him but fulness and satiety itself. Be sure that all your graces come from Zion, and from Lebanon, that they grow in Immanuel's land: till Christ own them, God will not accept them. Moral virtues and outward duties, grapes of Sodom, may commend us to men; nothing but inward, spiritual, and rooted graces, the grapes of Lebanon, will commend us to God. To do only the outward works of duty, without the inward principle, is at best but to make ourselves like those mixed beasts, elephants and camels, in the civil law, *operam præstant, natura fera est,*

Leg. 2. P. ad Leg. Aquil. Senec. de Benefic. lib. 7. cap. 19.

Vid. Aug. de Civit. Dei, lib. 5. cap. 19, et passim. Greg. Arimin. 1. dist. 1. q. 3. art. 2.

which, though they do the work of tame beasts, yet have the nature of wild ones. Moral virtue, without spiritual piety, commends not any man to God; for we are not accepted of him but in Christ, and we are not in Christ but by the Holy Spirit.

Ver. 8. *Ephraim shall say, What have I to do any more with idols? I have heard him, and observed him: I am like a green fir tree. From me is thy fruit found.*

The conversion of Israel to God in their trouble was accompanied with a petition and a covenant; a petition imploring mercy and grace from God, and a covenant promising to him thanksgivings and obedience. And God is pleased in his answer to have a distinct respect to both these: for whereas they petition first for pardon, that God would "take away all iniquity," he promises to "heal their backsliding" and to "love them freely;" and whereas they pray for blessings, "receive us graciously," God likewise makes promises of that in great variety, expressed by the several metaphors of fertility, answering to the name and blessings promised formerly to Ephraim. All this we have spoken of under the four preceding verses.

Now, in this 8th verse, God is pleased not only graciously to accept, but further to put to his seal, and to confirm the covenant which they make, promising that by the assistance of his Spirit they should be enabled to do what they had undertaken. This is the greatest ground of confidence that we can have to bind ourselves in holy covenants to God, even the promise of his strength and assistance enabling us to keep covenant with him. Therefore when David had said, "I have sworn, and I will perform it, that I will keep thy righteous judgments," there follows a little after, "Accept, I beseech thee, the freewill offerings of my mouth, O Lord, and teach me thy judgments," Psal. cxix. 106, 108. David was confident that God would not only accept his covenant, but teach him how to keep it, and that made him the more confidently bind himself by it.

In the original the words are אפרים מה-לי עוד לעצבים Ephraim, what have I to do any more with idols? which therefore some would have to be the words addressed by God to Ephraim. But there is nothing more usual in Scripture than an ellipsis of the verb; and we find this very verb omitted, and yet necessary to be supplied, Isa. v. 9; and in this place the Chaldee paraphrast, and from him the best interpreters, with our translators, have supplied it thus, "Ephraim shall say:" and so we understand it to be God's confirmation of the promise which penitent Ephraim had made, and his undertaking for him that he should indeed be enabled to perform his covenant.

Solom. Glassius Grammat. Sacr. pag. 380, 654.

"What have I to do any more with idols?" It is *interrogatio cum indignatione*, an interrogation not only importing a negative, I will not any more have to do with them, but also a vehement detestation of them and indignation against them; as that of David to Abishai, 2 Sam. xvi. 10; and that of Elisha to Jehoram, 2 Kings iii. 13; and that of the devil to Christ, Matt. viii. 29.

Gloss. Rhetor. Sacra. Tract. 2. cap. 5.

"With idols." לעצבים signifies likewise sorrows and grief of mind, a fit word to express Israel's sin and repentance. What have we to do with these idols and sorrows any more? They can produce no good, they they can hear no prayers, they can work no deliverance, they can bring nothing but evil and anguish to us, and therefore we will not follow them or seek to them any more. Here, then, is a solemn detestation, as of all their other sins, so of that especially which had most dishonoured God, most wounded their own consciences, and procured most sorrow to themselves, with God's confirmation of it.

Next follow several promises of special mercies. 1. Of hearing and answering their prayers: "I have heard," or answered, "him," or, as others render it, I will hear him. 2. Of fatherly care and providence over them: "and observed him," or fixed mine eyes upon him. I have strictly considered his condition, that I might proportion thereunto my mercies. This is a significant expression, intimating, first, vigilant care, and most intent and solicitous inspection and providence: "Behold, the eye of the Lord is upon them that fear him, upon them that hope in his mercy; to deliver their soul from death, and to keep them alive in famine," Psal. xxxiii. 18, 19. Secondly, direction and counsel: "I will instruct thee and teach thee in the way which thou shalt go: I will guide," or counsel, "thee with mine eye," Psal. xxxii. 8. Thirdly, honour and exaltation: "He withdraweth not his eyes from the righteous: but with kings are they on the throne; yea, he doth establish them for ever, and they are exalted," Job xxxvi. 7. Lastly, it is an expression for hearing prayers: God is said to have his "eyes open unto the supplications of" his servants, to hearken unto them in all that they call upon him for, 1 Kings viii. 52; and "the eyes of the Lord are upon the righteous, and his ears open unto their cry," Psal. xxxiv. 15. The church had before professed herself to be an orphan, that stood in need of tuition and protection; and here God promises to cast his eye and to place his affection upon her, to look to her, to be her tutor and guardian, to govern her with his special providence and wisdom, to take notice of her wants and supply them, to take notice of her desires and fulfil them, to take notice of her condition, and accordingly in all respects to provide for her. 3. Of refreshment, from the heat and violence of temptations or any kind of afflictions: "I am like a green fir tree," which, being ever green, and casting forth a large shade, affords much comfort and refreshment to the weary traveller. 4. Because the fir tree, though refreshing in respect of its shade, is yet unfruitful, therefore he further promises to be a root of blessings, and all kind of spiritual graces, to them: "From me is thy fruit found;" that is, From me is, or shall be, thy fruit, as Mal. ii. 6, 7; 1 Pet. ii. 22; Zeph. iii. 13. The word נמצא "found" may here seem to imply and direct us to an inquiry after the foundation and original of the fruit here mentioned: Though all thy fruit of good works and new obedience may seem to proceed from thyself, and to be thine own, yet if thou be careful to inquire after their root, thou wilt find that they come "from me," though they grow upon thee, and that thou bringest them forth only by the help, supply, and vigour of my grace bestowed on thee; thou doest them, but the power and strength whereby thou doest them proceeds from me.

Certum est nos velle cum volumus; sed ille facit ut velimus. Certum est nos facere cum facimus, sed ille facit ut faciamus. Aug.

These words then are the sum of God's answer to the covenant of his people. They "render the calves of" their "lips;" God hears and accepts them: they renounce carnal confidence in men, in horses, in idols; and when they look off and turn away from these, then God looks on them with a fatherly eye of care, providence, counsel, and protection: "I have observed him." They will not "say any more to the work of" their "hands, Ye are our gods," nor any longer make lies their refuge; and God enables them to do as they have said, and affords comfort and refreshment to them, as the shade of a fir tree to a weary traveller. Lastly, they believe and acknowledge that when they are "fatherless," and destitute of all help, there is mercy in God to comfort and provide for

Ipse facit ut illi faciant quæ præcepit: illi non faciunt ut ipse faciat quod promisit. Aug. de Prædestin. Sanct. cap. 10.

them; and this God makes good too. Mercy of protection, "I am like a green fir tree;" and mercy of bounty and benediction, "From me is thy fruit found;" by the one defending them against their fears, by the other enabling them to their duties. Thus does God enlarge and proportion his mercy to the uttermost extent of Israel's prayer or promise, and when they have no help or comfort out of him, he himself becomes "all and in all" to them; making a thorough compensation for every thing which they part with for his sake, and causing them to find in him alone all that comfort and satisfaction to their desires, which in vain they sought for in other things.

The words contain these two general points: First, God's promise, enabling Israel to perform theirs: "Ephraim shall say, What have I to do any more with idols?" Secondly, God's special regard to their prayers, "I have heard him;" to their persons, "and observed him:" illustrated by two metaphors; the one importing protection and defence, "I am like a green fir tree;" the other, grace and benediction, "From me is thy fruit found."

"Ephraim shall say." This is God's speech and promise, setting to his seal and gracious ratification to the covenant which Israel made, ver. 2, 3, without which it would have been null and void: for as man, by believing, sets to his seal to the truth of God, John iii. 33; so God, by assisting, sets to his seal to the purpose of man: but with this great difference; man's seal is but a subscription and confession of that which was firm before; for all God's promises are "yea and Amen," and faith does not put certainty into the promise of God, Rom. iii. 3, 4; 2 Tim. ii. 13, but into the heart of man concerning the promises, Rom. iv. 16; 2 Tim. i. 12. But God's seal is a confirmation of the promise of man, and a rendering stable that which otherwise would vanish away; all our sufficiency is from him, we can neither will nor do any thing further than we receive from him both "to will and to do," Phil. ii. 13. Pharaoh made promise after promise, and broke them as fast, Exod. viii. 8, 28; ix. 28. Israel one while makes promises, and quickly starts aside like a deceitful bow, as ice which melts in the day and hardens again in the night, Psal. lxxviii. 34—38; Jer. xxxiv. 15, 16; to-day they will, and to-morrow they will not; they repent to-day, and to-morrow they repent of their repenting; like the sluggard in his bed, who puts out his arm to rise, and then pulls it in again; "Yet a little sleep, a little slumber, a little folding of the hands to sleep," Prov. vi. 10. So unstable and impotent is man in all his resolutions, till God say Amen to what he purposes, and establishes the heart by his own grace, Heb. xiii. 9. When the waters stood as a wall on the right hand and on the left of Israel as they passed through the Red Sea, this was a work of God's own power; for water is unstable, and cannot keep together, nor be contained within any bounds, by its own consistency. So difficult a work is it for the mutable wills and resolutions of men to be kept close to any pious and holy purposes. Hence,

Obs. 1. A penitent's conversion and covenant of new obedience derive their stability from the promise and free grace of God. They are not sufficiently provided for by any band, obligation, or covenant of our own, whereby we solemnly engage ourselves, except God be pleased by his free grace to establish and enable the heart to their performance. Israel here, in the confidence of God's mercy, prays for pardon and blessings; and in the confidence of his grace, promises reformation and amendment of life; but all this is but like a written instrument or indenture, which is invalid and of no effect till the parties concerned have mutually set to their hands and seals. Till God be pleased to promise us that we shall do that which we have promised to him, and does as it were make our own covenants for us, all will prove too weak and unstable to continue. The grace of God to the purposes of men is like oil to colours in a table or picture, which imparts to them an unfading freshness.

There is a necessary and indissoluble dependence of all second causes upon the first, without whose influence and concurrence they neither live, nor move, nor have, or continue in, their being, Acts xvii. 28; Heb. i. 3. He who is the first of causes and last of ends, employs and directs the necessary, voluntary, contingent motions and activities of all second causes, to whatsoever ends he himself is pleased to preordain. And this the natural and necessary concatenation of things requires, that that which is the absolutest, supremest, first, and most independent will, wisdom, and power of all others, should govern, order, and direct all other wills, powers, and wisdoms, inferior and subordinate to it, to whatsoever uses and purposes he who has the absolute dominion and sovereignty over all is pleased to appoint. It cannot be other than a marvellous diminution to the greatness of God, and a too low esteem of the absoluteness of that majesty which belongs to him, to make any counsels, decrees, purposes of his to receive their ultimate form and stamp from the previous and intercurrent causalities or conditions of the creature. This I have always looked on as the principal cause of those dangerous errors, concerning grace, free-will, and the decrees of God, wherewith the churches of Christ have been so miserably in the former ages, and in this of ours, exercised by the subtlety of Satan, and by the pride of corrupt-minded men; namely, the too low and narrow thoughts and conceptions which men have framed to themselves of God, the not acquiescing in his sovereign dominion and absolute power of disposing all things which he made according to the pleasure of his own will; into which I am sure the Holy Scriptures resolve all, Matt. xi. 25, 26; Rom. ix. 18, 21; xi. 33, 36; Eph. i. 5, 9, 11; Psal. cxxxv. 6.

Vid. Aug. Enchirid. ad Laurent. c. 95—98.

Even in the sinful actions of men, God's influence and providence have a particular hand: as actions, his influence; as sinful, his providence. 1. His influence, to the natural motion and substance of the action, though not to its wickedness; for this stands not in being or perfection, (else the Fountain of being and perfection must needs be the first cause of it,) but in defect and privation of perfection. As when a hand draws a line by a crooked rule, the line is from the hand, but its crookedness from the rule: or, as when a man goes lamely, the motion as motion is from the natural faculty, but the lameness of the motion is from the defect and viciousness of the faculty. A swearer could not utter an oath, nor a murderer reach out his hand to strike a blow, but by the force of those natural faculties which have all their being and working in and from God; but that these natural motions are by profaneness or malice directed to ends morally wicked, proceeds from the vitiosity and defect which are in the second cause, making use of God's gifts to his own dishonour. 2. The providence of God has a notable hand in the guiding, ordering, and disposing of those actions, as sinful, to the ends of his own glory, in the declaration of his power, wisdom, and justice, to which the sins of wicked men are perforce carried on, contrary to those ends which they themselves in sinning proposed. As an artificer uses the force of natural causes to artificial effects: as a huntsman uses the natural enmity of the dog against the fox or wolf, to the preservation of the lambs, which otherwise would be destroyed; though the dog itself by nature is as great an enemy to the lamb as the fox: as the Pharisees were as great enemies to religion as the Sadducees, yet

Vid. Aug. de Civ. Dei, lib. 11. cap. 17, et passim. Quintil. lib. 2. Instit. cap. 13. Plutarch. Sympos. lib. 5. c. 1.

Paul wisely made use of their enmity amongst themselves, for his own preservation and deliverance from them both: so nothing is more usual than for God to manage and direct the sins of men to the bringing about of his own purposes and counsels, Gen. l. 20; 1 Sam. ii. 25; 1 Kings ii. 26, 27; 2 Sam. xii. 11, compared with 2 Sam. xvi. 22; Isa. x. 5—7; Acts iv. 28; Psal. lxxvi. 10. But now to gracious actions, which belong not at all to nature *as nature*, but only as inspired and actuated with spiritual and heavenly principles, a more singular and notable influence of God is required, not only to the substance of the action, but more especially to its rectitude and goodness; for we have no sufficiency of ourselves, not so much as to the first offers and beginnings of good in our thoughts, 2 Cor. iii. 5: when we are bid to "work out" our "own salvation with fear and trembling," it must be in dependence on the power and in confidence of the aid of God; "for it is" he "which worketh in" us "both to will and to do," Phil. ii. 12, 13: when we covenant to turn unto God, we must withal pray to him to turn us, Lam. v. 21; Jer. xxxi. 18. God commands us to turn ourselves, and to make us a new heart and a new spirit, that we may live, Ezek. xviii. 30—32; but withal, he tells us that it is he who gives us one heart, and one way, and a new spirit, that we may walk in his statutes, Ezek. xi. 19, 20; Jer. xxxii. 39. He gives us *posse, velle, agere, proficere;* the power, to make us able; the heart, to make us willing; the act, to walk; the proficiency, to improve; the perseverance, to finish and perfect holiness. David cannot run in the way of God's commandments till he enlarge his heart, Psal. cxix. 32. Nothing can find its way to heaven, but that which comes first from heaven, John iii. 13; we cannot give to God any thing but of his own. "Who am I," saith David, "and what is my people, that we should be able to offer so willingly after this sort? for all things come of thee, and of thine own have we given thee," 1 Chron. xxix. 14.

Aug. de Civ. Dei, l. 12. cap. 9.

For the further understanding of this point, and of the sweet concord and concurrence between the will of man converted, and the effectual grace of God converting, we shall set down these few propositions:

1. That there is in man by nature a power or faculty which we call free-will, whereunto belongs such an indifferency and indeterminacy in the manner of working, that whether a man will a thing or not, choose it or turn from it, he in neither moves contrary to his own natural principles of working. A stone moving downward, moves naturally; upward, contrary to its nature, and so violently. But which way soever the will moves, it moves according to the condition of its creation; when thus it chooses one part of a contradiction, it retains an inward and fundamental habitude to the other, like those gates which are so made that they open both ways. So that as the tongue which was wont to swear or blaspheme, does, when it is converted, by means of the same faculty of speaking, newly sanctified, utter holy and gracious speeches; so the will, which, being corrupted, did choose "evil and only evil," being sanctified, does use the same manner of operation in choosing that which is good: the nature imparted to it at first remaining still one and the same, but being now guided and sanctified by different principles. This we speak only with respect to the natural manner of its working; for if we speak of liberty in a moral or theological sense, it is certain, that the more the will of man observes the right order of its proper objects and last end, the more free and noble it is, the very highest perfection of free-will consisting in an immutable adherence to God as the ultimate end of the creature, and all ability of receding or falling from him being the deficiency, and not the perfection, of free-will. And therefore the more the will of man casts off and rejects God, the more base, servile, and enslaved. In which sense we affirm against the papists, that by nature man, since the fall of Adam, has no free-will or natural power to believe and turn to God, or to prepare himself for faith and conversion.

Vid. Calvin. in Ezek. xi. 19, 20. et Aug. contr. 2. Epist. Pelag. lib. 1. cap. 2. et lib. 2. cap. 5.

Gibeuf. de Libert. Creat. l. 1. Melior est cum totus hæret atque constringitur incommutabili bono, quam cum inde vel ad seipsum relaxatur. Aug. de Doct. Christ. l. 1. c. 22.

2. In man fallen, and thereby universally in all his faculties leavened with vicious and malignant principles, there is a native corrupt force, which puts forth itself in resisting all those powerful workings of the word and Spirit of grace, which oppose themselves against the body of sin, and move the will to holy resolutions: for the wisdom of the flesh cannot be subject to the law of God, Rom. viii. 7. The flesh will lust against the Spirit, as being contrary thereunto, Gal. v. 17. An uncircumcised heart will always resist the Holy Spirit, Acts vii. 51. There is such a natural antipathy between the purity of the word and the impurity of the will of man, that he naturally refuses to hear, and snuffs at it, and pulls away the shoulder, and hardens the heart, and stops the ear, and shuts the eyes, and sets up strong holds and high reasonings against the ways of God, and is never so well as when he can get off all sight and thoughts of God, and be as it were without God in the world, Jer. v. 3; vi. 10; xvii. 23; xix. 15; Mal. i. 13; 2 Chron. xxxvi. 16.

3. According to the degrees and remainders of this natural corruption, so far as it is unmortified and unsubdued by the power of grace, it does proportionably put forth itself in withstanding and warring against the Spirit of God even in the regenerate themselves.* A notable example whereof we have in Asa, of whom it is said, that he "was wroth with" Hanani "the seer, and put him in a prison house," being "in a rage with him because" he reproved him for his carnal confidence, 2 Chron. xvi. 10. And the apostle in many words both states and bewails the warring of this "law of sin" in his "members" against "the law" of his "mind," so that when he did with the one serve the law of God, with the other he served the law of sin, and was unable to do "the good which" he "would," and "the evil which" he "would not" he did by the strength of sin that dwelt in him, Rom. vii. 14—25.

4. The will of God is set forth in Scripture in a twofold point of view: 1. There is *voluntas signi*, or that will of God whereby he requires us to work, and which he has appointed to be observed by us; his will signified in precepts and prohibitions. "This is the will of God," saith the apostle, "even your sanctification," 1 Thess. iv. 3. So we are said to prove, to try, to do, God's will, or that which is pleasing in his sight, Matt. vii. 21; Rom. xii. 2; John viii. 29. And, 2. There is *voluntas beneplaciti*, the will of his purpose and counsel, according to which he himself in his own secret and unsearchable good pleasure is pleased to work; for he "worketh all things after the counsel of his own will," Eph. i. 11. "Whatsoever the Lord pleased, that did he in heaven, and in earth, in the seas, and all deep places," Psal. cxxxv. 6. And no second causes can do any thing else, though they never so proudly break the order of God's revealed will, but what his "hand and counsel determined before to be done," Acts iv. 28. The will of God's precept and command is every day violated, resisted, and broken through by wicked

Aquin. Part. 1. qu. 19. art. 1.

* Habitat in eis, et mentem resistentem repugnantemque sollicitat ut ipse conflictus, etiamsi non sit damnabilis quia non perficit iniquitatem, sit miserabilis tamen quia non habet pacem. Aug. de Nupt. et Concupisc. lib. 2. cap. 2. contra Julian. Pelag. lib. 5. cap. 7.

men to their own destruction: "How often would I," "and ye would not!" Matt. xxiii. 37; Jer. xiii. 27. But the will of God's counsel and purpose cannot be resisted or withstood by all the powers of the world; the counsel of the Lord must stand; and those very agents that work purposely to disappoint and subvert it, by those very workings of theirs bring it to pass;* and when, by their own intentions, they are enemies to it, by God's wonderful ordering and directing they are executioners of it, Rom. ix. 19; Psal. xxxiii. 11; cxv. 3; Prov. xix. 21; Isa. xlvi. 10; Josh. xxiv. 9, 10.

5. According to this distinction of God's will, we are to distinguish his call. Some are called *voluntate signi*, by the will of his precept, when they have the will of God made known to them, and are thereby persuaded to the obedience of it in the ministry of the gospel: in which sense our Saviour saith, "Many are called, but few chosen," Matt. xx. 16; and to those who refused to come to him that they might have life, he yet saith, "These things I say, that ye might be saved," John v. 34, 40. Others are called *voluntate beneplaciti*, ordained first to eternal life by the free love and grace of God, and then thereunto brought by the execution of that his decree and purpose in the powerful calling and translating of them from darkness into light. And this is to be called *κατὰ πρόθεσιν*,† according to purpose, Rom. viii. 28, namely, the purpose and counsel of showing mercy to whom he will show mercy, Rom. ix. 18.

6. They who are called by the mere outward call or voice of Christ in the evangelical ministry, may, and do, resist this call, and so perish. Chorazin, and Bethsaida, and Capernaum, were outwardly called by the most powerful ministerial means that ever the world enjoyed, both in doctrine and miracles; and yet our Saviour tells them that they shall be in a worse condition in the day of judgment than Tyre, Sidon, or Sodom, Matt. xi. 21, 24. So the prophet complains, "Who hath believed our report? and to whom is the arm of the Lord revealed?" Isa. liii. 1; which the evangelist applies to the argument of conversion, John xii. 37—41; for so the hand or arm of the Lord is said to be with his ministers, when, by their ministry, men turn to the Lord, Acts xi. 21. And the same prophet again, or Christ in him, complains, "All day long I have stretched forth my hands unto a disobedient and gainsaying people," Isa. lxv. 2; Rom. x. 21: so disobedient and gainsaying, that we find them resolve sometimes directly contrary to the call of God, Jer. ii. 25; xviii. 11, 12; xliv. 15—28; Matt. xxiii. 37.

7. They who are called inwardly and spiritually, with a heavenly call, *vocatione altâ et secundum propositum*, with such a call as flows from the counsel and purpose of God for their salvation, though they do resist *quoad pugnam*, though corruption in them strive to bear up against the grace of Christ, yet they do not resist finally and *quoad eventum*, to the repelling or defeating of the operation of God's effectual grace;‡ but they are thereby framed to embrace, approve, and submit to that call, God himself working a good will in them, captivating their thoughts to the obedience of Christ, and disposing them to that which is pleasing in his own sight, Phil. ii. 13; 2 Cor. x. 5; Heb. xiii. 21.

And this is done by a double act.

1. An act of spiritual teaching, and irradiating the mind and judgment with heavenly light, called by the prophet the putting the law into the inward parts, and writing it in the heart, Jer. xxxi. 33; 2 Cor. iii. 3; and by our Saviour, the Father's teaching, John vi. 45, and the Holy Spirit's convincing of sin, righteousness, and judgment, John xvi. 8—11; and by the apostle, a "demonstration of the Spirit and of power," 1 Cor. ii. 4, a spiritual revelation of wisdom out of the word to the conscience, Eph. i. 17. For though we are to condemn fanatic revelations beside the word, and without it; yet we must acknowledge spiritual revelation, or manifestation of the Divine light and power of the word by the Holy Spirit in the minds of men converted: for the word of God being a spiritual object, does, to the saving knowledge of it, require such a spiritual quality in the faculty which must know it, that it may be able to pass a right judgment upon it; for spiritual things "are spiritually discerned," 1 Cor. ii. 14. It is true that hypocrites, and other wicked men, may have very much notional and intellectual knowledge of the Scriptures, and those holy things therein revealed, Heb. vi. 4; 2 Pet. ii. 21; but none of that knowledge amounts to that which is called the teaching of God, and a spiritual demonstration:§ for the mysteries of the gospel were to this end revealed, that by them we might be brought to the obedience of Christ; and therefore the knowledge of them is never proportionate or commensurate to the object, till the mind be thereby conformed to Christ, till the conceptions which are framed in us touching God, and sin, and grace, and heaven, and eternal things, be suitable to those which were in the mind of Christ, 1 Cor. ii. 16. Evangelical truths are not fitted to mere intellectual, but to practical, judgment. It is such a knowledge of Christ as may fill us with "all the fulness of God," Eph. iii. 18, 19; a knowledge that must work communion with Christ, and conformity unto him, Phil. iii. 10; a knowledge that must produce "a good conversation,"‖ James iii. 13. "He that saith, I know him, and keepeth not his commandments, is a liar, and the truth is not in him," 1 John ii. 4. We know not Christ till we know him as our chiefest good, as our choicest "treasure," as our "unsearchable riches," as "elect" and "precious," as "altogether lovely," "the chiefest among ten thousand," and "worthy of all acceptation," in comparison of whom all the world besides is as "dung." The knowledge of Christ is not seeing only, but seeing and tasting, Psal. xxxiv. 8; cxix. 103. And therefore they who, in one sense, are said to have known God, Rom. i. 21, are yet a little after, ver. 28, said not to have God in their knowledge. The philosopher well observes, That such as every man is in himself, such is the end to which he works, and such notions he has of that good which is his end. It is

Ὁποῖος ποθ' ἕκαστος ἐστι, τοιοῦτο καὶ τὸ τέλος φαίνεται αὐτῷ. Aristot. l. 3. c. 7.

* Multa fiunt a malis contra voluntatem Dei, sed tantæ est ille sapientiæ tantæ quo virtutis, ut in eos exitus sive fines quos bonos et justos ipse prescivit tendant omnia quæ voluntati ejus videntur adversa. Aug. de Civ. Dei, lib. 22. c. 1. Alii obediunt, alii ligantur; nemo leges omnipotentis evadit. Id. de Agone Christiano, c. 7. Vid. Bradwardin. de Causa Dei, lib. 1. cap. 32. et Hug. de Sanct. Victor. Sum. Sentent. Tract. 1. cap. 13. et de Sacrament. lib. 1. part. 2. cap. 19, 20. et part. 3. cap. 5, 6, 13, 14, 15. Anselm. lib. 1. cur Deus Homo, c. 15. Lombard. lib. 1. dist. 17.

† Vocatio alta et secreta quâ fit ut legi atque doctrinæ accommodemus assensum. Aug. Ep. 107. et de Prædestinat. Sanct. c. 16, 17.

‡ Illud nescio quomodo dicitur, frustra Deum misereri nisi nos velimus. Si enim Deus miseretur, etiam volumus; ad eandem quippe misericordiam pertinet ut velimus. Aug. ad Simplician. lib. 1. qu. 2. Hæc gratia quæ occulte humanis cordibus divina largitate tribuitur, a nullo duro corde respuitur. Ideo quippe tribuitur, ut cordis duritia primitus auferatur. De Prædestinat. Sanct. cap. 8. et contr. 2. Epist. Pelag. lib. 1. cap. 20.

§ Cibus in somnis simillimus est cibis vigilantium, quo tamen dormientes non aluntur. Aug. Confess. lib. 3. cap. 6. Sol non omnes quibus lucet etiam calefacit: sic sapientia multos quos docet non continuo etiam accendit. Aliud est multas divitias scire, aliud possidere: nec notitia divitem facit, sed possessio. Bernard. in Cant. serm. 23.

‖ Τήρησις ἐντολῶν γνῶσις τοῦ Θεοῦ. Basil. de Martyr. manante. Hominis sapientia pietas est. Aug. Enchirid. cap. 2. de Doctr. Christiana, lib. 2. cap. 6, 7. et lib. 1. cap. 35.

impossible therefore that a wicked, debased heart can ever look on any spiritual object as its last end, or as principally desirable. If I should see a man choose a small trifle before a rich jewel, however he should profess to know the excellency and to value the richness of that jewel, yet I should conclude that he did not indeed understand its worth aright. And, therefore, to the perfect and proper knowledge of supernatural, spiritual things, there is required a special work of the grace and Spirit of Christ opening the heart, and working it to a spiritual constitution proportionable to those truths about which it is conversant. The Scripture every where attributes this work to God, and his Spirit. It is he that giveth "an heart to perceive, and eyes to see, and ears to hear," Deut. xxix. 4. It is he that giveth "an heart to know" him, Jer. xxiv. 7. It is he that manifests himself to those who love him, John xiv. 21. It is he that reveals to us by his Spirit the things of God, 1 Cor. ii. 10. It is he that gives "us an understanding," 1 John v. 20, and that opens the understanding to "understand the Scriptures," Luke xxiv. 45; Acts xvi. 14. It is he that teaches us to call Christ our Lord, Matt. xvi. 17; 1 Cor. xii. 3; for the voice of carnal and corrupt reason is, "We will not have this man to reign over us," Luke xix. 14. Every man naturally frames and shapes his notions of doctrinal matters to the manner of his conscience and conversation, embracing that which is consonant, and rejecting that which is dissonant, Micah ii. 11; Isa. xxx. 10, 11. To the unclean every thing is unclean, because the very "mind and conscience" of such men "is defiled," Tit. i. 15. This, then, is the first work in effectual calling, the opening of the eye of the mind rightly to conceive of the things of God, of the guilt of sin, of the heaviness of wrath, of the peril of perishing, of the momentous import of damnation and salvation, of the things that concern its everlasting peace, of the righteousness of Christ, of the beauties of holiness, of the exceeding abundant weight of glory, of the comforts of the Holy Spirit, and the unspeakable and glorious joy shed abroad in the heart by believing. These truths the heart is so convinced of, as seriously to ponder them; they form the subject of its deepest and most solemn meditations.

Deum scire nemo potest nisi Deo docente: sine Deo non cognoscitur Deus. Iren. l. 4. c. 14. A Deo discendum est quid de Deo intelligendum sit, quia non, nisi se authore, cognoscitur. Hil. de Trin. l. 5.

2. An act spiritually inclining and effectually determining the will of man to embrace the ultimate dictate of a mind thus enlightened, and to make a most free, spontaneous, and joyful choice of spiritual good things thus rightly apprehended, on a clear and deliberate consideration of their excellency above all other things, Phil. iii. 8. This act of choosing the Lord for our portion and chiefest good, and of cleaving to him, we find often mentioned in the Scripture, Deut. xxx. 19; Josh. xxiv. 22; Psal. lxxxiv. 10; cxix. 30, 31, 173; Acts xi. 23; Heb. xi. 25: for when the soul of a man is so thoroughly, by God's teaching, convinced of the danger and misery of sin, wherein so long as a man continues, he lives only to dishonour God, and to undo himself; of the benefit of righteousness in Christ, whereby he is reconciled to God, and adopted into a glorious inheritance; and of the beauty of holiness, whereby he is conformed to Christ his Head, and fitted for the inheritance; these previous acts of heavenly teaching are always seconded with effectual operations on the will, suitable to themselves: for the liberty of the will does not consist in a peremptory indifference to any object whatsoever, (else there should be no liberty in heaven,) but in this, that being a reasonable appetite, it is apt to be led one way or another, to choose one thing or another, according to the dictates of reason, and *servato ordine finis*, with subjection to that which is made to appear to be the supreme end and happiness of the soul; for every faculty is naturally subservient to the ultimate good of that nature whereof it is a faculty, and should monstrously exorbitate from its use and end, if it should put forth itself to the destruction, or refuse to close with, that which is the happiness of the soul to which it pertains. As soon as ever, therefore, the Spirit of grace does, by such a spiritual and practical demonstration as has been described, set forth God in Christ as the supreme and most unquestionable end and happiness of the soul, there are, consequently, suitable impressions on the will, determining it to operations conformable to such a beautiful and glorious object, and enlarging it to run to this centre, to renounce all other things, and to cleave to this alone.

Operatur Deus in cordibus quid aliud quam voluntatem? Aug. Ep. 107. Certum est nos velle cum volumus, sed ipse facit ut velimus præbendo vires efficacissimas voluntati. Id. de Grat. et Lib. Arbit. cap. 16.

And these acts upon the will are effected:

1. By preventing grace, it is bended and excited to heavenly appetitions, and to the choice of such spiritual good things, the sovereign excellencies whereof have been so sweetly represented. Good is the object of the will; we cannot will evil under the notion of evil; and among good things, that which is by the practical judgment resolved to be best, and that by the teaching of God himself, (who neither is deceived, nor can deceive,) becomes the object of the will's election. And thus God, by his exciting grace, works in us *ipsum velle*, that very act whereby we choose Christ, and subscribe our name in the roll of his soldiers and servants, answering the call of God with a most cheerful consent.

2. By assisting and co-operating grace,* it is further enabled to put forth this good will into deed, and so to work towards its own salvation, Isa. xxvi. 12; 1 Cor. xv. 10.

3. By subsequent grace, it is carried on towards perfection, to finish what was begun, and so to proceed from the beginning of faith in vocation, to the end of faith in salvation, the Spirit of Christ working in us, as he himself did work for us to a *consummatum est*, "It is finished;" saving "them to the uttermost that come unto God by him," Phil. i. 6; Eph. iv. 13; Heb. vii. 25; xiii. 21.

And by this means the native obstinacy of the will, both in and after conversion, is subdued, so that it neither does nor can overcome the grace of God working effectually with his word. First, because of the purpose of God to show mercy where he will show mercy, which can in no wise be resisted. Secondly, because of the power of God in the effectual applying of that mercy to the souls of men, with admirable sweetness, with undeniable evidence, with ineffable persuasion, with omnipotent and invincible energy, which no hardness of heart is able to refuse, because the proper operation of it is to take away that hardness which would refuse it, and that by an act of power equal to that whereby Christ was raised from the dead, which all the world was neither able to hinder nor prevent, Eph. i. 19; Col. ii. 12; 1 Pet. i. 5. Thus we see, though we desire, and endeavour, and purpose, and covenant conversion and amendment of life; yet the whole progress of conversion, our promises, our covenants, our abilities, our sufficiencies to make good any thing, do all receive their stability from the grace of God.

From whence we learn, First, Not to put confidence in our own studies, vows, purposes, promises of new obedience. "All men are liars," no sooner left to

* Cooperando perficit quod operando incipit; ut velimus sine nobis operatur, cum volumus nobiscum cooperatur. Aug. de Grat. et Lib. Arbitr. c. 17. Enchirid. cap. 32 de Nat. et Grat. cap. 31. contr. 2. Epist. Pelag. lib. 2. cap. ult. Non mihi sufficit quod semel donavit nisi semper donaverit. Peto ut accipiam, et cum accepero, rursus peto, &c. Hier. Epist.

Vide Aug. de Corrup. et Grat. cap. 11.

themselves, but they become miserable spectacles of weakness and mutability. Even Adam in innocency, when he was to be supported and persevere by his own strength, though he had no sin or inward corruption to betray him, how suddenly was he thrown down from his excellency by Satan with a poor and slender temptation! how strangely did a creature of so high and noble a constitution exchange God himself for the fruit of a tree, believe a serpent before a Maker, and was so miserably cheated, as to suppose that by casting away God's image he should become the more like him! Who could have thought that David, a man after God's own heart, with one miscarrying glance of his eye should have been plunged into such a gulf of sin and misery? that so spiritual and heavenly a soul should be so suddenly overcome with so sensual a temptation? that so merciful and righteous a man should so greatly wrong a faithful servant as he did Uriah, and then make the innocent blood of him whom he wronged a mantle to palliate and to cover the wrong, and use his fidelity to convey the letters and instructions for his own ruin? Who could have thought that Lot, so soon after he had been delivered from fire and brimstone, and vexed with the filthy conversation of the Sodomites, should be himself inflamed with unnatural, incestuous lust? Who could have suspected that Peter, who had his name from a rock, should be so soon shaken like a reed? and after so solemn a protestation not to forsake Christ, though all else should, that he should so soon be driven with the voice of a maid from his stedfastness, and be the first to deny him, and that with oaths and curses? Surely "every man in his best estate is altogether vanity."

Ut Bellerophon literas in seipsum scriptas ferebat. Hom. Ili. 2. et Plut. de Curiositate.

Therefore it behoves us to be always humbled in our own sight, and to be jealous, 1. Of our original impotency to the doing of any good, to the forbearing of any evil, to the repelling of any temptation by our own power. "By strength shall no man prevail," 1 Sam. ii. 9. To be "sinners," and to be "without strength," are terms equivalent in the apostle, Rom. v. 6, 8. Nay, even where there is a will to do good, there is a defect of power to perform it, Rom. vii. 18; our strength is not in ourselves, but "in the Lord, and in the power of his might," and in the working of his Spirit in our inner man, Eph. vi. 10; iii. 16; Phil. iv. 13. If but a good thought arise in our mind, or a good desire and motion stir in our heart, or a good word drop from our lips, we have great cause to take notice of the grace of God that offered it to us, and wrought it in us, and to admire how any of the fruit of paradise could grow in so heathy a wilderness.

2. Of our natural antipathy and reluctance to holy duties; our aptness to "draw back unto perdition," to refuse and thrust away the offers and motions of grace; our rebellion which arises from the "law in" the "members" "against the law of" the "mind," Rom. vii. 23; the continual droppings of a corrupt heart upon any of the tender buds and sproutings of piety that are wrought within us: our aptness to be "weary" of the yoke, and to shake off the burden of Christ from our shoulders, Isa. xliii. 22; our natural levity and inconstancy of spirit in any holy resolutions, continuing but as "the early dew," which presently is dried up; beginning in the Spirit and ending in the flesh, having interchangeable fits of the one and the other; like the chameleon, now of one colour, again of another; now hot with zeal, now cold with security; now following Moses with songs of thanksgiving for deliverance out of Egypt, and quickly after thrusting Moses away, and in heart returning to Egypt again.* Such a discomposedness and natural instability there is in the spirit of man, that, like strings in an instrument, it is apt to be altered with every change of weather, nay, while you are playing on it, you must ever and anon new screw it; like water heated, which is always tending to reduce itself to its own coldness. No longer sun, no longer light; no longer Christ, no longer grace: if his back be at any time on us, our back will immediately be turned on him; like those forgetful creatures in Seneca, who, even while they are eating, if they happen to look aside from their meat, immediately lose the remembrance of it, and go about seeking for more.

3. Of the manifold decays and abatements of the grace of God in us; our aptness to leave our "first love," Rev. ii. 4. How did Hezekiah fall into an impolitic vain-glory,† as soon as God left him to himself, in showing all his treasures to the ambassadors of a foreign prince, thereby kindling a desire in him to be master of so rich a land! 2 Kings xx. 12, 13. How quickly, without continual husbandry, will a garden or vineyard be wasted and overgrown with weeds! How easily is a ship, even at the very shore, carried with a storm back again into the sea! How quickly will a curious watch, if it lie open, gather dust on the wheels and become out of order! Though, therefore, thou have found sweetness in religion, joy in the Holy Spirit, comfort, yea, heaven, in good duties, power against corruptions, strength against temptations, triumph over afflictions, assurance of God's favour, vigour, life, and great enlargement of heart in the ways of godliness; yet for all this "be not high-minded, but fear." Remember, the flower that is wide open in the morning when the sun shines upon it, may be shut up in the evening before night come. If the sun had not stood still, Joshua had not taken vengeance on the enemy, Josh. x. 13; and if the Sun of righteousness do not constantly shine on us and supply us, we shall not be able to pursue and carry on any victorious affections. While God openeth his "hand" thou art "filled," but if he hide his "face" thou wilt be "troubled" again, Psal. civ. 28, 29. Therefore take heed of resting on thine own wisdom or strength. Thou mayst after all this grieve the Spirit of God, and cause him to depart and hide himself from thee; thou mayst fall from thy stedfastness, and lose thy wonted comforts; thou mayst have a dead winter on the face of thy conscience, and be brought to such a sad and disconsolate condition, as to conclude that God hath "cast" thee "out of" his "sight," that he hath "forgotten to be gracious," and hath "in anger shut up his tender mercies;" to roar out for anguish of spirit as one whose "bones" are "broken;" thy soul may draw "nigh unto the grave," and thy life to the destroyers, and thou mayst find it a woeful and almost insuperable difficulty to recover thy life and thy strength again. It was so with Job, chap. x. 16, 17; xiii. 26, 27; xvi. 9, 13; xxx. 15, 31; xxxiii. 19—22: it was so with David, Psal. li. 8; lxxvii. 2—4: it was so with Heman, Psal. lxxxviii., and divers others; see Psal. cii. 3, 11; Isa. liv. 6, 11; Jonah ii. 3, 4. Therefore we should still remember in a calm to provide for a storm; to stir up the graces of God continually in ourselves, that they be not

* Μοχθηροὶ ἓν βέβαιον οὐκ ἔχουσιν οὐ δε γαρ αὐτοὶς διαμένουσιν οἵμοιοί ὀντες. Aristot. Eth. l. 8. Στασιάζει αὐτῶν ἡ ψυχὴ. Id. l. 9. c. 4. Hoc habent inter cætera boni mores, placent sibi et permanent. Levis est malitia, sæpe mutatur. Senec. Epist. 47. Maximum indicium est malæ mentis, fluctuatio. Epist. 120. Vid. Athenæum, l. 7. c. 19. Tertul. de Pall. c. 3.

† Lege imperiali interdicta vini, olei, liquaminis exportatio, ne barbari gustu illecti promptius invaderent fines Romanorum, Leg. 1. Cod. quæ res exportari non debeant. Et apud Chinenses, exteri in loca regni interiora non admittuntur, tantum in oris maritimis conceditur commercium. Boterus in catalog. Imperiorum.

quenched, 2 Tim. i. 6; so to rejoice in the Lord, as withal to "work out" our "salvation with fear and trembling," Psal. ii. 11; Phil. ii. 12, 13: never to let the grace of God puff us up, or make us forgetful of our own weakness; but, as the apostle saith of himself in regard of God's grace, "when I am weak, then am I strong," 2 Cor. xii. 10, so to say of ourselves in regard of our own natural corruption, when I am strong, then am I weak.

Secondly, This must not so humble us as to deject and dismay us, or make us give over the hope of holding out to the end, although our nature is so weak, our enemies so strong, our temptations so many: but we must withal be quickened by these considerations, with prayer to implore, and with faith to rely on and draw, strength from the word and grace of God; to have always the window of the soul open toward the Sun of righteousness, whereby the supplies of his grace to prevent, excite, assist, follow, establish us, and carry on every good thing which he has begun for us, may be continually admitted. This is one of the most necessary duties for a Christian, to hold constant and fixed purposes in godliness: the Scripture frequently calls upon us for them; that "with purpose of heart" we "would cleave unto the Lord," Acts xi. 23; that we would "continue in the grace of God," Acts xiii. 43; that we would be "rooted and grounded in love," Eph. iii. 17; that we would "hold fast the profession of our faith without wavering," Heb. x. 23; that we would be "stedfast, unmovable, always abounding in the work of the Lord," 1 Cor. xv. 58; that we would look to ourselves, that we "lose not those things which we have wrought," 2 John 8; that we would "hold fast" and "keep" the "works" of Christ "unto the end," Rev. ii. 25, 26. And it is that which godly men are most earnestly solicitous about, and do strive after with the greatest importunity: "I am purposed that my mouth shall not transgress," Psal. xvii. 3. "Unite my heart to fear thy name," Psal. lxxxvi. 11. "My heart is fixed, O God, my heart is fixed: I will sing and give praise," Psal. lvii. 7. Therefore in this case it is necessary for us to draw nigh to God, who only can ratify all our pious resolutions; who "giveth power to the faint, and to them that have no might" "increaseth strength," Isa. xl. 29; who only can settle and establish the hearts of men, 1 Pet. v. 10. The conscience of our duty, the sense of our frailty, the power, malice, and cunning of our enemies, the obligation of our covenant, should direct the soul perpetually to God for the supply of his grace, that that may in all our weaknesses be sufficient for us, and "hold" us "up" that we may be "safe," and may never through infirmity or instability of spirit violate our own resolutions, Psal. cxix. 117.

Thirdly, This is matter of great comfort to the godly, that in the midst of so many temptations, snares, impediments, amongst which we walk, not only the safety of our souls and security of our eternal salvation, but even our present condition in this life, our conversion, our obedience, all our pious purposes of heart, all the progress which we make in a holy conversation, do not depend on the weakness and uncertainty of a human will; but upon the infallible truth, the constant promise, the immutable purpose, the invincible power, the free love, the absolute grace, the omnipotent wisdom and working of God, who doth according to his own pleasure both in heaven and earth, and worketh all things after the counsel of his own will: "I am the Lord, I change not; therefore ye sons of Jacob are not consumed," Mal. iii. 6. We poor and weak men change with every wind, strong to-day, and weak to-morrow; fixed and resolute to-day, shaken and staggering to-morrow; running forward to-day, and revolting as fast to-morrow; no hold to be taken of our promises, no trust to be reposed in our covenants. Like Peter on the water, we tread securely one step, and, our faith failing, sink the next. All our comfort is this, our strength and standing rest not on ourselves, but on the rock whereon we are built, and in the power of God, by which we are "kept through faith unto salvation," "out of" whose "hand" none are able to "pluck" us; our very actions are wrought in us, and carried on to their end by the power of Christ, who has mercy, wisdom, and strength enough to rescue us, as from the power of hell and death, so from the danger of our own fickle and froward hearts. To see a man when he is half a mile from his enemy draw a sword to encounter him, or take up a stone to hit him, would be but a ridiculous spectacle; for what could he do with such weapons by his own strength at such a distance? But if he mount a cannon, and point that level against the enemy, this we do not wonder at, though the distance be so great; because though the action be originally his, yet the effect of it proceeds from the force of the materials and instruments employed, to wit, the powder, the bullet, the fire, and the cannon. It seemed absurd in the eye of the enemy, for little David, with a shepherd's bag and a sling, to go against Goliath, an armed giant; and it produced in his proud heart much disdain. But when we hear David mention the name of God, in the strength and confidence whereof he came against so proud an enemy, this makes us conclude weak David strong enough to encounter great Goliath, 1 Sam. xvii. 40—47. It is not our own strength, but the love of God, which is the foundation of our triumph over all our enemies, Rom. viii. 35—39.

But here some will say, Then we may be secure; if God's grace and power be our alone strength, then let us commit ourselves and our salvation to him, and in the mean time give over all thoughts and care of it ourselves, and live as we list; no act of ours can frustrate the counsel or the love of God. To this we answer with the apostle, "God forbid." Though the enemies of free grace do thus argue, yet they who have indeed the grace of God in their hearts have "not so learned Christ." For it is against the essential nature of the grace and Spirit of Christ, to suffer those in whom it dwells to give themselves over to security and neglect of God; for grace is a vital and active principle, and does so work in us as withal to dispose and direct us to working also. The property of grace is to fight against and to kill sin, as being most extremely contrary to it; and therefore it is a most irrational mode of arguing, to argue from the being of grace to the life of sin. "How shall we, that are dead to sin, live any longer therein?" Rom. vi. 2. If we be dead to sin, this is argument enough, in the apostle's judgment, why we should set our affections on things above, Col. iii. 2, 3. The grace of God not only serves to bring salvation, but to teach us to deny "ungodliness and worldly lusts," and to "live soberly, righteously, and godly, in this present world," Tit. ii. 11, 12. He who has decreed salvation as the end, has decreed also all the antecedent means to that end, to be used in a manner suitable to the condition of reasonable and voluntary agents; to whom it belongs, having their minds by grace enlightened, and their wills by grace prevented, to co-operate with the same grace in the further pursuance of their salvation. And if at any time corruption should in God's children abuse his grace and efficacy to such presumptuous resolutions, they would quickly rue so unreasonable and carnal a way of arguing, by the woeful sense of God's displeasure in withdrawing the comforts of his grace from them, which would make them ever after take heed how they again turned the grace of God into licentiousness. Certainly, the more the servants of God are assured of his assistance, the more careful they are in using it to his own service. Who more sure of the grace of God than the apostle Paul, who gloried of it as of that which made him what he was, "By the grace of God I am what I am;" who knew that God's "grace" was "sufficient" for him, and that nothing could "separate" him "from the love of Christ;" who knew whom he had believed, and that "the grace of our Lord was exceeding abundant" towards him? and yet who more tender and fearful of sin than he? who more set against corruption, more abundant in duty, more pressing to perfection? This is the nature of grace, to animate and actuate the faculties of the soul in God's service, to ratify our covenants, and to enable us to perform them.

Fourthly, As it is singular comfort to the servants of God, that their own wills and purposes are in God's keeping, and so they cannot ruin themselves; so is it also, that all other men's wills and resolutions are in God's keeping too, so that they shall not be able to purpose or resolve on any evil against the church, without leave from him. So then, 1. When the rage and passions of men break out, tribe divided against tribe, brother against brother, father against child, head against body; when the band of unity which was wont to knit together this flourishing kingdom, is broken like the prophet's staff, and therewithal the beauty of the nation miserably withered and decayed, (for these two go still together, Beauty and Bands, Zech. xi. 10—14,) we must look on all this as God's own work. It was he that "sent an evil spirit between Abimelech and the men of Shechem," for the mutual punishment of their sins, Judg. ix. 23. It was he who "turned" the "hearts" of the Egyptians "to hate his people, and to deal subtilly with his servants," Psal. cv. 25. He sent the Assyrian against his people, giving them "a charge to take the spoil, and to take the prey, and to tread them down like the mire of the streets," Isa. x. 6. He appointed the sword of the king of Babylon, by his overruling direction, to go against Judah, and not against the Ammonites, Ezek. xxi. 19, 22. He, by the secret command of his providence, marked some for safety, and gave commission to kill and slay others, Ezek. ix. 4, 5. It is he who giveth "Jacob for a spoil, and Israel to the robbers," and poureth out "upon him the strength of battle," Isa. xlii. 24, 25. If there be "evil in a city," in a kingdom, "the Lord hath done it," Amos iii. 6; Isa. xlv. 7. This consideration is very useful both to humble us, when we consider that God has a controversy against the land, and that it is he with whom we have to do in these sad commotions that are in the kingdoms; and to quiet and silence us, that we may not dare to murmur at the course of his wise and righteous proceedings with us; and to direct us, with prayer, faith, and patience, to implore, and in his good time to expect, such an issue and close, as we are sure shall be for his own glory, and for the manifestation of his mercy towards his people, and his justice towards all that are implacable enemies to Zion.

2. In the troubles of the church this is matter of singular comfort, that however enemies may say, This and that we will do, hither and thither we will go; though they may combine together, and be mutually confederate, and gird themselves, and take counsel, and speak the word, yet in all this God has the casting voice, Psal. lxxxiii. 2—5. There is little heed to be given to what Ephraim saith, except God say the same: without him, whatsoever is counselled, "shall come to nought;" whatsoever is decreed or spoken, "shall not stand," Isa. viii. 9, 10. We have a lively hypotyposis or description of the swift, confident, and furious march of the great host of Sennacherib towards Jerusalem, with the terror and consternation of the people in every place where they came, weeping, flying, removing their habitations; and when he is advanced to Nob, from which place "the hill of Jerusalem" might be seen, he there shook his hand against "the mount of the daughter of Zion," threatening what he would do unto it. And then when the waters were come to the very neck, and the Assyrian was in the height of his pride and fury, God sent forth a prohibition against all their resolutions, and that huge army, which was for pride and number like the thick trees of Lebanon, were suddenly cut down by "a mighty one," to wit, by the angel of the Lord, Isa. x. 28—34, compared with Ezek. xxxi. 3, 10; Isa. xvii. 12—14; xxxvii. 36. Therefore,

3. Our greatest business is to apply ourselves to God, who alone is "the Lord that healeth" us, who alone can join the two sticks of Ephraim and Judah, and make them one, Exod. xv. 26; Ezek. xxxvii. 19; that he would still the raging of the sea, and command a calm again. He can say, "Ephraim shall say" thus and thus: he has the hearts of kings, and consequently of all other men, in his hands, Prov. xxi. 1; and he can turn them, "as the rivers of water," "whithersoever he will:" as men by art can derive waters, and divert them from one course to another, (as they did in the siege of Babylon, as historians tell us, and the Scriptures seem to confirm it, Isa. xliii. 15, 16; xliv. 27, 28; Jer. l. 23; li. 36,) so he can sway, alter, divert, overrule the purposes of men as it pleases him; reconciling lambs and lions to one another, Isa. xi. 6; making Israel, Egypt, and Assyria agree together, Isa. xix. 24, 25. He can say to Balaam, Bless, when his mind was to curse, Josh. xxiv. 9, 10; he can turn the wrath of Laban into a covenant of kindness with Jacob, Gen. xxxi. 24, 44; and when Esau had the desired opportunity to execute his threats against his brother, he can then turn resolutions of cruelty into kisses, Gen. xxxiii. 4; and when Saul has compassed David and his men round about, and is most likely to take them, he can even then draw him off by a necessary diversion, 1 Sam. xxiii. 26—28. This is the comfort of God's people, that whatever men say, except God say it too, it shall all come to nothing. He can "restrain the wrath of man" whensoever it pleases him; and he will do it, when it has proceeded so far as to glorify his power, and to make way for the more notable manifestation of his goodness to his people, Psal. lxxvi. 10. And thus far of God's answer to the covenant of Ephraim. They promised to renounce idols, and here God promises that they should renounce them. But we shall here further, from the words themselves, more particularly,

Herodot. lib. 1. Xenophon, Cyropæd. lib. 7. Salianus. Anno mundi 3515. § 5. et 3516. § 22. Sir W. Raleigh, lib. 3. cap. 3. § 5.

Obs. 2. In true conversion God makes our special sin to be the object of our greatest detestation: "What have I to do any more with idols?" This point has been fully opened before.

Obs. 3. It is the nature of true repentance, to break sin off, Dan. iv. 27, and not to suffer a man to continue any longer in it, Rom. vi. 1, 2: "What have I to do *any more* with idols?" It makes men esteem "the time past of" their "life may suffice" them "to have wrought the will of the Gentiles," 1 Pet. iv. 2, 3; and is exceeding thrifty of the time to come, so to redeem it as that God may have all: it does not linger, nor delay, nor make objections, nor raise doubts whether it be seasonable to go out of Egypt and Sodom, or no: it uses not the sluggard's language *modo et modo,* "Yet a little sleep, a little slumber, a little folding of the hands to sleep;" nor Agrippa's language, "Almost thou persuadest me;" nor Felix's language, "When I have a convenient season I will call for thee:" but "immediately" resolves, with Paul, not to confer "with flesh and blood," Gal. i. 16; makes haste to flee from the wrath to come," while it is yet to come, Luke iii.

7. It makes no anxious nor cavilling questions, What shall I do for the hundred talents? how shall I maintain my life, my credit, my family? how shall I keep my friends? how shall I preserve mine interests, or support mine estate? but ventures the loss of all for "the excellency of the knowledge of Christ," Matt. xiii. 46; Phil. iii. 7, 8; it is contented to part with a sky full of stars for one Sun of righteousness. The converts that return to Christ, come like "dromedaries," like "doves," like "ships;" no wings, no sails, can carry them fast enough from their former courses unto him, Isa. lx. 6—9. Abraham "rose up early in the morning," though his duty involved the sacrificing of his only son, Gen. xxii. 3. David "made haste, and delayed not to keep" God's "commandments," Psal. cxix. 60. When Christ called his disciples, "they straightway left their nets," their "ship, and their father, and followed him," Matt. iv. 20, 22. Such is the mighty power of repentance; it does not give dilatory answers; it does not say to Christ, Go away now, and come to-morrow, then I will hear thee; I am not yet old enough, or rich enough, I have not gotten yet pleasure, or honour, or profit, or preferment enough by my sins; but presently it hears and entertains him. I have sinned enough already to condemn, to shame, to slay me; I have spent time and strength enough already upon it, for such miserable wages as shame and death come to; therefore I will never "any more" have to do with it. This is the sweet and most ingenuous voice of repentance; "That which I see not teach thou me: if I have done iniquity, I will do no more," Job xxxiv. 32. There is no sin more contrary to repentance than apostacy; for "godly sorrow worketh repentance to salvation," which the soul never finds reason to repent of, 2 Cor. vii. 10, 11. Let us, therefore, "take heed" of "an evil heart of unbelief, in departing from the living God," Heb. iii. 12; and of drawing "back unto perdition," Heb. x. 39; of dismissing our sins, as the Jews did their servants, Jer. xxxiv. 16, and calling them back again; for Satan usually returns with seven more wicked spirits, and maketh "the last state" of such a man "worse than the first," Luke xi. 26. Ground which has been a long time laid down from tillage to pasture, if afterwards it be new broken, will yield a much greater crop of corn than it did formerly when it was a common field; and so the heart which has been taken off from sin, if it return to it again, will be much more fruitful than before. As lean bodies have many times the strongest appetite, so lust, when it has been kept lean, returns with greater hunger to those objects which feed it. A stream which has been stopped, will run more violently being once opened again. Therefore in repentance we must shake hands with sin for ever, and resolve never more to tamper with it. But further,

Obs. 4. God hears and answers the prayers of penitents only: "I have heard him, and observed him." When a man resolves, I will have no more to do with sin, then, not till then, does his prayer find way to God. Impenitence clogs the wing of devotion, and stops its passage to heaven. The person must be accepted before the petition: Christ Jesus is the priest that offers, and the altar which sanctifies, all our services, 1 Pet. ii. 5; Isa. lvi. 7; and Christ will not be their advocate in heaven, who refuse to have him as their king on earth. The Scripture is on no point more express than on this. "If I regard iniquity in my heart, the Lord will not hear me," Psal. lxvi. 18: prayer is a pouring out of the heart; if iniquity be harboured there, prayer is obstructed, and if it do break out, it will have the scent and savour of that iniquity upon it. "The sacrifice of the wicked is an abomination to the Lord," Prov. xv. 8, both because it is impure in itself, and because it has no altar to sanctify it. "He that turneth away his ear from hearing the law, even his prayer shall be abomination," Prov. xxviii. 9. Great reason that God should refuse to hear him who refuses to hear God; that he who will not let God beseech him (as he does in his word, 2 Cor. v. 20) should not be allowed to beseech God, Prov. i. 24, 28; Isa. i. 15. His ear is not heavy that "it cannot hear," but iniquity separates between us and him, and hides his face that "he will not hear," Isa. lix. 1, 2; Ezek. viii. 18. "God heareth not sinners," John ix. 31; the prevalence of prayer is this, that it is the prayer of "a righteous man," James v. 16. And indeed no wicked man can pray in the true and proper notion of prayer. It is true, there is a kind of prayer of nature, when men cry in their distresses to the God and author of nature, for such good things as nature feels the want of, which God, in the way of his general providence and common mercies, is sometimes pleased to answer suitably to the natural desires of those that ask them. But "the prayer of faith" (which is the true notion of prayer, Rom. x. 14; James v. 15) goes not to God as the author of nature, but as the God of grace, and the Father of Christ; and puts not up mere natural, but spiritual requests to him, as to a heavenly Father, which requests proceed from the Spirit of grace and supplication, teaching us to pray as we ought, Zech. xii. 10; Rom. viii. 26, 27; Gal. iv. 6; so that they who have not the Spirit of Christ, enabling them to cry, "Abba, Father," are not able to pray a prayer of faith. Prayer, when right, has two wills concurring in it, our will put forth in desires, and God's will respected as the rule of those desires; for we are not allowed to desire what we will ourselves of God, but we must ask "according to his will," 1 John v. 14. Now, whensoever impenitent sinners pray for spiritual things, they ever pray contrary to one of these two wills: when they pray for mercy and pardon, they pray against God's will, for that which God will not give; for mercy is proposed to and provided for those that forsake sin, Prov. xxviii. 13; he who chooses to hold fast sin, does by his own election forsake mercy; for "the goodness of God leadeth to repentance," Rom. ii. 4: God's mercy is a holy mercy, it will pardon sin forsaken, but it will not protect sin retained. Again, when they pray for grace, they pray against their own will, for that which they themselves would not have: it is impossible that a man should formally will the holding fast and continuing in sin, (as every impenitent man does,) and with the same will should truly desire the receiving of grace, which is destructive to the continuance of sin. If a wicked man do truly will the grace of God when he prays for it, why does he refuse the same grace when he hears it in the ministry of the word offered to him? If God offer it, and he desire it, how comes it not to be received? Certainly, there is not any thing in the corrupt heart of man by nature, which can willingly close with any sanctifying grace of the Spirit of Christ. Self-denial is a concomitant in all acts of grace, and self-seeking in all acts of lust; and therefore, where there is nothing but lust, there can be no real volition of grace, which is so contrary to it.

This teaches us to have penitent resolutions, and spiritual aims, in all our prayers, if we would have them prevail at the throne of grace. We are now under the heavy calamity of a civil war, and very desirous we are that it should be removed. We suffer, and languish, and fret, and pine away, and we complain every where of want and violence; but who set themselves to cry mightily to God, and call on their souls, as the mariners on Jonah, "What meanest thou, O sleeper? arise, call

Solenne erat eos quibus puræ manus non erant sacris arceri. Brislon. de Formul. lib. 1. Etiam impiæ initiationes arcent profanos. Tertul. Apol. Quantum a præceptis tantum ab auribus Dei longe sumus. Id.

Interdum obnixe petimus, quod recusaremus si quis offerret—multa videri volumus velle, sed nolumus—Sæpe aliud volumus, aliud optamus, et verum ne Diis quidem dicimus. Sen. Epist. 95.

on thy God?" Haply we go so far, we pray, and yet receive no answer, because we "ask amiss," James iv. 1—3. We are troubled that our lusts are abridged of their fuel, or that our nature is deprived of her necessaries, and for these things we pray; but till our troubles bring us to seek God more than ourselves, make us more sensible of his wrath than of our own wants, more displeased at what offends him than at what pinches and oppresses ourselves, we cannot promise ourselves an answer of peace. The mariners cried, and the tempest continued still; Jonah was to be cast over; so long as there was a fugitive from God in the ship, the storm would not cease. Never can we promise ourselves any comfortable fruit from our prayers till the aim of them is spiritual, that God may be honoured, that his church may be cleansed and reformed, that our lives may be amended, that whatsoever forsakes God in us may be cast away. Till God's "whole work" be "performed upon Mount Zion and on Jerusalem," we cannot promise ourselves that he will call in his commission and charge to take the spoil and the prey, Isa. x. 12. And therefore our greatest wisdom is to consider what God calls for, to make it our prayer and endeavour that his will and counsel may be fulfilled. The more we make God our end, the sooner we shall recover our peace.

Obs. 5. Our performance of duty depends much on God's hearing and answering our prayers. Ephraim will have no more to do with idols, because God has heard him. Prayer is the key of obedience, and the introduction to duty. The principles of duty are, Wisdom to know and order; will to desire and intend; strength to perform and persevere: and all these are the product of prayer. "If any lack wisdom, let him ask of God," James i. 5. So Solomon, 1 Kings iii. 9. And, "Who am I, and what is my people," saith David, "that we should be able to offer so willingly after this sort? for all things come of thee," 1 Chron. xxix. 14. And the apostle prays for the Ephesians, that God would "grant" them, "according to the riches of his glory, to be strengthened with might by his Spirit in the inner man," Eph. iii. 16. The principles of duty are the fruits of prayer, and therefore the performance of duty much depends on the hearing and answering of prayer.

Obs. 6. When we renounce all carnal and sinful confidences, and cast ourselves wholly upon God, engaging his eye of favour and providence to us, this will be a most sufficient protection against all the cruelties of men: "I have observed him." One would think, when we hear a sword threatened, dashing of infants, ripping of women, the prophet should have called on them to take to them weapons to make resistance; (and certainly the use of means in such cases is necessary; the sword of the Lord does not exclude the sword of Gideon;) one would think, I say, "Take with you words," were but a poor preparation against a destroying enemy: yet this is all that the prophet insists on; When the Assyrian comes against you, do you "take with you words;" your lips shall be able to defend more than his armies can annoy. Words uttered from a penitent heart in times of trouble to God, are stronger than all the preparations of flesh and blood, because that way which prayer and repentance go, that way goes God too. Amalek fights, and Moses speaks to God in the behalf of Israel, and the lifting up of his hands prevails more than all the strength of Israel besides, Exod. xvii. 11, 12. One man of God that knows how to manage the cause of Israel with him, is "the chariot of Israel, and the horsemen thereof," 2 Kings ii. 12. What huge armies did Asa and Jehoshaphat vanquish by the power of prayer! 2 Chron. xiv. 9—15; xx. 1—30. Till God forbid prayer, as he did to Jeremiah, chap. vii. 16; xi. 14, and take off the hearts of his servants from crying to him in behalf of a people, we have reason to hope that he will at last entertain thoughts of mercy towards them, Exod. xxxii. 10, 14; and in the mean time, when they are reduced to the condition of fatherless children, he will be their guardian, his eye of providence and tuition will observe them and take care of them. "A father of the fatherless, and a judge of the widows, is God in his holy habitation," Psal. lxviii. 5.

Obs. 7. Whatsoever human wisdom, wealth, power, or other outward means men have wherewith to defend themselves, yet they shall never find any true and solid protection or shelter but in and from God, after sound conversion to him. "I am like a green fir tree." The fir tree, Pliny saith, casts not its leaves, and so yields a perpetual shade both in winter and in summer: thus sound conversion yields comfort in all conditions of life. "God is our refuge and strength, a very present help in trouble. Therefore will not we fear, though the earth be removed, and though the mountains be carried into the midst of the sea," Psal. xlvi. 1, 2; Hab. iii. 16—18. However it be, God is good to Israel, and it shall go well with the righteous; he will be for a sanctuary to his people, that they need not be afraid, Isa. viii. 12—14. If you would have your hearts raised above all the troubles of the world, get under this fir tree, cast yourselves under this protection, get into the chamber of God's providence and promises, and then, though the troubles of the world may strip you of all outward comforts, yet God will be all to you.

Obs. 8. Though good works be ours when they are done by us, yet they come from God, who enables us to do them; we bear them, but God works and produces them in us; the duty is ours, but the efficacy and blessing is his: "From me is thy fruit found." This falls in with what has been treated of before, and therefore I shall not now enlarge upon it.

Ver. 9. *Who is wise, and he shall understand these things? prudent, and he shall know them? for the ways of the Lord are right, and the just shall walk in them: but the transgressors shall fall therein.*

These words are a most pathetical close, and, as it were, a seal which the prophet sets to all the doctrine of his whole book, and the entire course of his ministry; implying, in their general sense, first, A strong asseveration of the truth of all those things which he had in the name of God delivered to them. Secondly, An elegant and forcible excitation of the people to a sad and serious pondering of them, laying to heart the sins therein charged, the duties therein required, the judgments therein threatened, the blessings therein promised. And thirdly, A tacit complaint of the paucity of those who were "wise unto salvation," and of the desperate use which wicked men make of the word of God, and the ministry of his grace; namely, to stumble at it, and to turn it into an occasion of ruin to themselves.

"Who is wise, and he shall understand these things? prudent, and he shall know them?" The interrogation here implies, 1. A secret exprobration of folly to his hearers, or the greater part of them; for so this kind of interrogation frequently in Scripture intimates either a negation, or at least the rareness and difficulty of the thing spoken of: as, "Who hath known the mind of the Lord, that he may instruct him?" 1 Cor. ii. 16. "Who shall lay any thing to the charge of God's elect?" Rom. viii. 33: these are negatives. "Who knoweth the power of thine anger?" Psal. xc. 11. "Who among you will give ear to this?" Isa. xlii. 23. "Who hath believed our report? and to whom is the arm of the Lord revealed?" Isa. liii. 1: these are restrictives.

Vid. Glassii Rhetor. Sacr. Tract. 2. cap. 5.

Who? that is, few or none are such. 2. An earnest wish and desire of the prophet. Oh that men were wise to understand these things, and lay them to heart! as, "Who shall deliver me from the body of this death?" that is, Oh that I were delivered, Rom. vii. 24. "Who will show us any good?" that is, Oh that any could do it, Psal. iv. 6. 3. A strong affirmation or demonstration wherein true wisdom does indeed consist; and what men that are truly wise will do, when the ways of God are by the ministry of his servants set forth before them; namely, ponder and consider their great and weighty import: as Jer. ix. 12, 13, "Who is the wise man, that may understand this?" namely, as it follows, "for what the land perisheth, and is burned up like a wilderness, that none passeth through? And the Lord saith, Because they have forsaken my law which I set before them." This is the character of a wise man, to trace to their proper origin the judgments that are upon a people, and not to allege *non causam pro causa*, a false cause. 4. A vehement awakening and quickening of the people to this duty of sad attendance on the words which he had spoken to them: as Exod. xxxii. 26, "Who is on the Lord's side? let him come unto me." And 2 Kings ix. 32, "Who is on my side? who?" So it is as if the prophet should have said, There are none of you who have been my hearers, but would willingly retain the reputation of men of wisdom and understanding, and would esteem it a high indignity to be handed down to all ages as fools and mad-men. Well, I have preached amongst you many years together, (sixty are the fewest that we can well compute, some say seventy, others, above eighty,) but, alas, what entertainment has mine embassage received? what operation or success has it had amongst you? are not the calves still standing at Dan and Beth-el? do not carnal policies prevail still against the express will of God? O, if there be any wise, any prudent men amongst you, (and oh that all God's people were such!) let them, now at length in the close of my ministry, show their wisdom, by giving heed to what I have declared from the Lord, that they may learn to walk in God's righteous ways, and may not stumble and perish, and "fall therein."

"Who is wise, and he shall understand these things? prudent, and he shall know them?" Two words are here used to express the wisdom which God requires in those who would fruitfully hear his word; * the one importing a mental knowledge of the things, and the other a practical and prudential judgment in pondering them, and in discerning their great and momentous importance to our eternal weal or woe. So the apostle prays for the Colossians, that they might be filled with the knowledge of God's will "in all wisdom and spiritual understanding," Col. i. 9. In mere notional things, which are only to be known for themselves, and are not further reducible to use and practice, the bare knowledge of them is sufficient. But in things the knowledge whereof is ever in order to a further end, there is required, besides the knowledge itself,† a faculty of wisdom and judgment to apply and manage that knowledge to, and for the advancement of, that end. Now, we know that theological learning is all of it practical, and has an intrinsical respect and a direct tendency to enforce worship and obedience: ‡ therefore it is called "the acknowledging of the truth which is after godliness," Tit. i. 1. "The fear of the Lord is the beginning of wisdom: a good understanding have all they that do his commandments," Psal. cxi. 10. "Keep therefore" his judgments "and do them; for this is your wisdom and your understanding," Deut. iv. 6. Therefore, besides the bare knowledge of truth, there is required wisdom and spiritual understanding, to direct that knowledge to those holy uses and saving ends for which it was intended.

"Who is wise, and he shall understand these things? prudent, and he shall know them?" The doubling of the interrogation thus, augments the force of the words, and denotes that it is the supreme and most excellent act of wisdom and prudence, so to know the word and ways of God, as with a practical judgment to ponder them in order to salvation.

"For the ways of the Lord are right." We are to understand hereby, 1. The ways of his judgments, and of his wonderful providence toward men; which, however, to the proud and contentious spirit of the wicked, they may seem perverse and inordinate, and to the eye of all men "unsearchable;" § are yet by spiritual wisdom acknowledged to be most righteous and holy, to have no crookedness or disorder in them, but to be carried on in an even and straight course to the ends whereunto his holy counsel directs them. "His work is perfect: for all his ways are judgment," Deut. xxxii. 4. When Jeremiah desired to plead with the Lord concerning his judgments, he yet premises this as a matter unquestionable, that God was righteous in them all, Jer. xii. 1.

2. The ways of his will, word, and worship. So the word is often taken in Scripture, to signify the doctrine which men teach, as Matt. xxii. 16; Acts xiii. 10; xviii. 25; xxii. 4; and damnable heresies are called "pernicious ways," in opposition to "the way of truth," 2 Pet. ii. 2; and the rites or rules of corrupt worship are called by the prophet "The manner of Beersheba," Amos viii. 14. These ways of God are likewise very straight, carrying men on in a "right" line to a happy end, Psal. xix. 8; whereas wicked ways have crookedness and perverseness in them, Psal. cxxv. 5: and this seems here chiefly to be meant, because there follows, "the just shall walk in them;" that is, they shall so ponder and judge of the righteous ways of God in his word, as to make choice of them for the way wherein they intend to walk, as the psalmist speaks, "I have chosen the way of truth," Psal. cxix. 30: whereas wicked men being offended at the purity of Divine truth, stumble and fall into perdition. Chald. Paraph.

The words thus opened, lead us to dwell especially on the powerful and pathetic call contained in them to the people of Israel, to consider maturely and obey implicitly the doctrines taught by the prophet throughout his whole ministration amongst them. The arguments which he uses are drawn from,

I. The character of the persons: "Who is wise, and he shall understand these things? prudent, and he shall know them?"

II. The nature of the doctrines taught: "For the ways of the Lord are right."

III. The twofold use made thereof by different kinds of men. 1. To the just, the Lord's ways are a way of happiness; "The just shall walk in them." 2. To the wicked, an occasion of stumbling; "The transgressors shall fall therein."

I. The character of the persons. And here two things present themselves: 1. The one intimated, their paucity. 2. The other expressed, their prudence.

* Duæ sunt partes rationis secundum philosophum, una ἐπιστημονικὴ, altera λογιστικὴ, quæ ratiocinamur et deliberamus in ordine ad mores. Vide Arist. Ethic. lib. 6. cap. 2. et cap. 8.

† Οὐ τῷ εἰδέναι μόνον φρόνιμος ἀλλα καὶ τῷ πράκτικος. Arist. Ethic. l. 7. cap. 11.

‡ 'Οἱ δ' ἂν μὴ εὑρίσκονται βιοῦντες ὡς ἐδίδαξε, γνωριζέσθωσαν μὴ ὄντες Χριστιανοὶ, κἂν λέγωσι διὰ γλώττης τὰ τοῦ Χριστοῦ διδάγματα. Justin Martyr. Apol. 2. Qui Christiani nominis opus non agit, Christianus non esse videtur. Salvian. de Gubern. Dei, lib. 4.

§ Judicia Dei plerunque occulta, nunquam injusta. Aug. Serm. 88. de Tempore. 'Αγαθὴ ἡ τοῦ Θεοῦ δικαιοσύνη. Clem. Alex. Vid. Tertul. contra Marcion. lib. 2. cap. 11—16.

1. The paucity of the persons. This is intimated, as we have seen, by the interrogative form of the words, and leads us to

Obs. 1. There are few who are "wise unto salvation," few who seriously attend to and manage the ministry of the word to that end. If there be any accidental lenocinium to allure the fancies, or excite the curiosity or customary attendance of men on the ordinances, elegance in the speaker, novelty and quaintness in the matter, credit or advantage in the duty, on such inducements many will wait on the word; some to hear "a very lovely song," Ezek. xxxiii. 32, others to hear some "new doctrine," Acts xvii. 19; some for the loaves, to promote their secular advantages, John vi. 26, having one and the selfsame reason for following Christ which the Gadarenes had when they entreated him to depart from their coasts. But very few there are who do it *propter se*, and with respect to the primary use and intention of it. Our prophet seems to do as the philosopher, who lighted a candle at noon to find out a man wise indeed; he seems to "run to and fro through the streets," and to "seek in the broad places thereof, if" he "can find a man, if there be any that executeth judgment, that seeketh the truth," as the Lord commanded the prophet Jeremiah, Jer. v. 1. How does the most elegant of all the prophets complain, "Who hath believed our report?" Isa. liii. 1; xlix. 4. How does the most learned of the apostles complain, that the preaching of the gospel was esteemed "foolishness!" 1 Cor. i. 23. Noah was a preacher of righteousness to a whole world of men, and yet but "eight" persons were saved from the flood, and some of them rather for their family's sake than their own, 1 Pet. iii. 20. Paul preached to a whole academy at Athens, and yet but very few were converted, Acts xvii. 34; some disputed, and others mocked, but few believed the things which they were not able to gainsay. Hezekiah sent messengers into all Israel to invite them to the true worship of God at Jerusalem, but they were "laughed" "to scorn, and mocked," and a remnant only "humbled themselves, and came to Jerusalem," 2 Chron. xxx. 10, 11; Isa. xvii. 6; xxiv. 13. Though a gun be discharged at a whole flight of birds, but few are killed. Though the net be spread over the whole pond, but a few fishes are taken; many thrust their heads into the mud and the net passes over them: and so most hearers busy their heads with their own sensual or worldly thoughts, and so escape the power of the word. Out of the richest mine there is much more earth and dross dug than pure metal. Christ's flock in every place is but "a little flock," Luke xii. 32; "few chosen," Matt. xx. 16; "few saved," Luke xiii. 23; "few there be that find" the "narrow way which leadeth unto life," Matt. vii. 13, 14. The basest creatures are usually the most numerous, as flies and vermin; those that are more noble are likewise more rare. "The people of the God of Abraham" are, in the Scripture style, "princes" and "noble," Psal. xlvii. 9; Acts xvii. 11; 1 Pet. ii. 9; and how few are there of such in comparison of the vulgar sort! They are indeed many in themselves, Heb. ii. 10; Rev. vii. 9, but very few, and widely scattered, when compared with the rest of the world.

Rari sunt qui philosophantur. Ulpian. P. de Excus. Leg. 5. Rari quippe boni, numero vix sunt totidem quot Thebarum portæ vel divitis ostia Nili. Juvenal. Sat. 13.

Τὰ μέγιστα μονοτόκα τῶν ζώων ἐστι. Arist. de Generat. Anima, lib. 4. cap. 4.

We must therefore learn not to be offended or discouraged by the paucity of sincere professors, no more than we are in a civil state by the comparative paucity of wise counsellors and politicians. It is no strange thing at all in any community to see the weaker part more numerous than the wiser. If but few attend the "right ways of the Lord," and "walk in them," remember it is a work of wisdom, and such wisdom as cometh from above, and has no seeds or principles in corrupt nature out of which it might be drawn; nay, against which all the vigour of carnal reason exalts itself; so that the more natural wisdom men have, the more in danger they are to despise and undervalue the ways of God, as being better able to reason and to cavil against them,* Matt. xi. 25; Acts iv. 11; John vii. 48; 1 Cor. i. 20, 28; ii. 8; 2 Cor. x. 5, 6. Therefore, 1. In the ministry of the word we must continue our labour, "though Israel be not gathered," Isa. xlix. 4, 5. We must stretch out our hands, though it be to "a disobedient and gainsaying people," Rom. x. 21; Isa. lxv. 2. "Whether they will hear, or whether they will forbear," we must speak to them, be they never so rebellious, Ezek. ii. 7. And the reason is, because the word is never in vain, but it doth ever "prosper in the thing whereto" God sends "it," Isa. lv. 11. If men be righteous, they "walk;" if wicked, they "stumble;"† and in both there is "unto God a sweet savour," 2 Cor. ii. 15. God's work is accomplished, his glory promoted, the power of his gospel commended, in the one and in the other; as the virtue of a sweet savour is seen as well by the antipathy which one creature has to it, as by the refreshment which another receives from it;‡ the strength of a rock, as by yielding firm support to the house that is built upon it, so by breaking in pieces the ship which dashes against it; the force of the fire, as well by consuming the dross as by refining the gold; the power of the water, as well in sinking the leaky as in supporting the sound ship. The pillar of the cloud was as wonderful in the darkness which it cast on the Egyptians, as in the light which it gave to the Israelites, Exod. xiv. 20; the power of the angel as great in striking terror into the soldiers, as in speaking comfort to the women, Matt. xxviii. 4, 5. 2. In attendance on the word, we must resolve rather to walk with the wise, though few, than to follow a multitude to do evil, and to stumble with the wicked, though they be many; rather enter the ark with a few, than venture the flood with a world of sinners; rather go three or four out of Sodom, than be burnt for company. We must not affect a capricious or fastidious singularity in differing unnecessarily from good men, being one for Paul against Apollos, another for Apollos against Cephas; but we must ever affect a holy and pious singularity in walking contrary to evil men, in shining "as lights" "in the midst of a crooked and perverse nation," Phil. ii. 15; for "the righteous is more excellent than his neighbour," Prov. xii. 26. Though there be but few in the way, there will be many in the end of the journey. As the tribes and families went up divided toward Jerusalem, but when come thither, "every one of them in Zion appeareth before God," Psal. lxxxiv. 7.

2. The prudence of the persons: and in that the prophet calls upon his hearers to attend to his doctrine by this argument, that it will be an evidence of their prudence and wisdom, we are led to

Obs. 2. True wisdom draws the heart to know aright, that is, to consider and ponder the judgments, blessings, ways, and word of God in order to the chief ends, and according thereto to direct all the conversation:

* Pudet doctos homines ex discipulis Platonis fieri discipulos Christi, &c. Vid. Aug. de Civit. Dei, l. 10. c. 29. et l. 13. c. 16. et Ep. 102.

† Ὑπακούουσιν εὐαγγέλιον παρακούσασι κριτήριον. Clem. Alex. in Protreph.

‡ Vultures unguento fugantur et scarabei rosa. Plin. et Ælian. Κανθάρους ῥοδίνῳ χρισθέντας μύρῳ τελευτᾶν λέγουσι. Clem. Pædag. l. 2. c. 8. Ὁ γὰρ Στωϊκὸς ἔρως, ὥσπερ οἱ κάνθαροι λέγονται τὸ μὲν μύρον ἀπολείπειν, τὰ δὲ δυσώδη διώκειν. Plutarch. Nissen. Hom. 3. in Cantic. Τὸν αἴλουρον ὀδμῃ μύρων ἐκταρατεσθαι καὶ μαίνεσθαι λέγουσι. Plutarch. in Conjugalib. Præcept.

"Who is wise, and he shall understand these things? prudent, and he shall know them?" In God's account, that knowledge which edifies not, is no knowledge at all, 1 Cor. viii. 2. None are his wise men who are not "wise unto salvation," 2 Tim. iii. 15; who do not draw their wisdom from his word, and from his commandments, Psal. xix. 7; cxix. 98, 99; Jer. viii. 9.

Ethic. lib. 6. cap. 7.

There is a twofold wisdom, according to the distinction of the philosopher, *σοφία κατὰ μερος* and *σοφία ὅλως*. The former signifies wisdom in some particulars:* thus we esteem every man who is excellent in his profession, a wise man, so far as concerns the managing of that profession; we account him such when he knows all the necessary principles and maxims of his business, the right ends thereof, and the proper conclusions deducible from those principles, and derigible to those ends. As to the latter, *σοφία ὅλως*, wisdom in general, and in perfection, it regards those principles, ends, and conclusions, which are universally and most transcendently necessary to a man's chiefest and most general good: and this the philosopher calls the knowledge of the most excellent and honourable things, or of the last end and chief good of man. Now the end, by how much the more supreme, perpetual, and ultimate it is, so much the more it has of excellency and goodness in it, as bearing thereby most exact proportion and adaptation to the soul of man; for the soul being immortal itself, can have no final satisfaction from any good which is mortal and perishable: and being withal so large and unlimited, as that its reasonings and desires extend to the whole latitude of goodness, being not restrained to this or that kind, but capable of desiring and judging of all the different degrees of goodness which are in all the whole variety of things, it can therefore never finally acquiesce in any but the most universal and comprehensive goodness, in the nearer or more remote participation whereof consists the different goodness of all other things.

'Επιστήμη τῶν τιμιωτάτων. Arist. Eth. l. 6. c. 7. Πολλῶν καὶ θαυμαστῶν ἐπιστήμη. Id. Rhet. lib. 1. cap. 37. et Metaphys. l. 2. c. 2.

This supreme and absolute goodness can indeed be but one, all other things being good by participation with that. "There is none good but one, that is, God," Matt. xix. 17. But because there are two sorts of men in the world, righteous and wicked, the seed of the woman and the seed of the serpent; therefore, consequently, there are two sorts of ends which these men do differently pursue. The end of wicked men is a happiness which they, out of their own corrupt judgments, shape to themselves, and to which they finally carry all the motions of their souls, called in Scripture "the pleasures of sin," and "the wages of unrighteousness," Heb. xi. 25; 2 Pet. ii. 15; that thing, whatsoever it is, to obtain which men direct all their other endeavours, as profit, pleasure, honour, or power. And there are mediums exactly proportionable to these ends; namely, "the lust of the flesh, the lust of the eyes, and the pride of life," 1 John ii. 16. And there is a wisdom consonant to these means, and fit to direct and manage these lusts to the attaining of those ends; which therefore the apostle calls *τὸ φρόνημα τῆς σαρκὸς*, the wisdom of the flesh or corrupt nature, Rom. viii. 7; and St. James, a wisdom "earthly, sensual, devilish," James iii. 15: "earthly," managing "the lust of the eyes" to the ends of gain; "sensual," managing "the lust of the flesh" to the ends of pleasure; and "devilish," managing "the pride of life" to the ends of power. But such wisdom as this God esteems very foolishness: "My people is foolish;" "they are sottish children, and they have none understanding." Why? "They are wise to do evil, but to do good they have no knowledge," Jer. iv. 22. Wisdom is only to that which is good; he is the wisest man who is simple and ignorant in the trade of evil, Rom. xvi. 19. "If any man among you seemeth to be wise in this world, let him become a fool, that he may be wise," 1 Cor. iii. 18.

On the other side, the true and ultimate end of righteous men, is Almighty God, as most glorious in himself, and most good to us; or the seeking of his glory, that he may be honoured by us; and of our own salvation, that we may be glorified by him. The fruition of him as the highest and first *in genere veri*, and the greatest and last *in genere boni*, the chiefest object for the mind to rest in by knowledge, and the heart by love; this must needs be the best of all ends, both in regard of its excellency, as being infinitely and most absolutely good; and in regard of its eternity, so that the soul having once possession of it, can never want that happiness which flows from it, John vi. 27. The proper means for the obtaining of this end, is the knowledge of God in Christ, as in his word he has revealed himself, to be known, worshipped, and obeyed; for there only does he teach us the way to himself: and true wisdom is the pursuing of this means in order to that end. For though many approaches may be made toward God by the search and contemplation of the creature, yet in his word he has shown us "a more" full and "excellent way," which only can make us "wise unto salvation through faith which is in Christ Jesus," 2 Tim. iii. 15; Prov. ix. 10; Eccl. xii. 12, 13; Jer. ix. 23, 24.

Fecisti nos ad te, et inquietum est cor nostrum donec requiescat in te. Aug. Confess. l. 1. c. 1. Omnis mihi copia, quæ Deus meus non est, egestas est. Lib. 13. cap. 8. Vid. de Trinit. lib. 8. c. 3. de Civit. Dei, l. 12. c. 1.

Beatitudo hæc duo requirit, fruitionem incommunicabilis boni, et certitudinem æternæ fruitionis. Vid. Aug. de Civ. Dei, lib. 11. cap. 13.

All the thoughts and wisdom of men are spent on one of these two heads, either the obtaining of the good which we want, or the avoiding and declining the evil which we fear. And by how much the more excellent and difficult the good is which we want, and by how much the more pernicious and imminent the evil which we fear, by so much greater is the wisdom which in both these procures the end at which we aim. Now, then, what are the most excellent good things which we want? Food is common to us with other creatures; raiment, houses, lands, possessions, common to us with the worst of men: take the most admired perfections which are not heavenly, and we may find very wicked men excel in them. All men will confess the soul to be more excellent than the body; and therefore the good of the former to be more excellent than that of the latter; and its chief good to be that which most advances it toward the Fountain of goodness, where is fulness of perfection, and perpetuity of fruition. The excellency of every thing consists in two things; the perfection of beauty wherein it was made, and the perfection of use for which it was made. The beauty of man, especially in his soul, consists in this, that he was made like to God, after his image, Gen. i. 26, 27; and his end and use in this, that he was made for God, first to serve him, and after to enjoy him: for "the Lord hath set apart him that is godly for himself," Psal. iv. 3. "This people have I formed for myself; they shall show forth my praise," Isa. xliii. 21. Therefore to recover the image of God, which is in "knowledge," "righteousness, and true holiness," Col. iii. 10; Eph. iv. 24; to work to the service and glory of God, John xv. 8; to aspire to and enjoy the possession and fruition of God, Exod. xxxiii. 18; Phil. i. 23; must needs be man's greatest good; and, consequently, to attend on the means thereof must needs be his greatest wisdom.

Vid. Aristot. de iis quæ bona sunt, et quæ meliora et majora. Rhetor. lib. 1. cap. 6. 7.

What is the most pernicious and destructive evil which a man is in danger of? Not the loss of any out-

* Μάγειρος ἐστιν οὐκ ἐὰν ζωμήρυσιν ἐχων τὶς ἔλθη καὶ μάχαιραν πρὸς τινὰ· οὐδ' ἄν τὶς εἰς τὰς λοπάδας ἰχθῦς ἐμβάλῃ. 'Αλλ' ἔστι τὶς φρόνησις ἐν τῷ πράγματι. Philemon apud Athenæum, lib. 7. cap. 11. et Liv. lib. 39.

ward good things whatsoever, for they are all in their nature perishable; we enjoy them on the very condition of parting with them again; no wisdom can keep them: "Meats for the belly, and the belly for meats; but God shall destroy both it and them," 1 Cor. vi. 13. Not the suffering of any outward troubles, which the best of men have suffered and triumphed over. But the greatest loss is the loss of a precious soul, which is more worth than all the world, Matt. xvi. 26; and the greatest suffering is the wrath of God on the conscience, Psal. xc. 11; Isa. xxxiii. 14; Heb. x. 31; Matt. x. 28. Therefore, to avoid this danger, and to snatch this "darling from the paw of the lion," is of all other the greatest wisdom. It is wisdom to deliver a "city," Eccl. ix. 15; much more to deliver "souls," Prov. xi. 30. Angelical, seraphical knowledge, without this, is all worth "nothing," 1 Cor. xiii. 1, 2.

Therefore we should learn to show ourselves wise indeed, by attendance on God's word. If the most glorious creatures for wisdom and knowledge that ever God made, the blessed angels, were employed in publishing the law of God, Acts vii. 53; Gal. iii. 19, and did with great admiration "look into" the mysteries of the gospel, and stoop down with their faces towards the mercy-seat, 1 Pet. i. 12; Eph. iii. 10; Exod. xxxvii. 9; it cannot but be also our chiefest wisdom to hide the word in our hearts, and to make it our companion and "counsellor," Psal. cxix. 24. We esteem him the wisest man who follows the best and safest counsel, and that which will most preserve and promote his interest, his honour, and his conscience. Herein was Rehoboam's weakness, that by rash and passionate counsels he suffered his honour to be stained, his interest to be weakened, and his conscience to be defiled with resolutions of violence and injustice. Now there is no counsel to be compared with that of God's word. It enlightens the eyes, it "maketh wise the simple," Psal. xix. 7, 8. It is able to make a man "wise" for himself, and "unto salvation," which no other counsel can do, 2 Tim. iii. 15, 16. No case can be put, though of never so great intricacy and perplexity, no doubt so difficult, no temptation so knotty and involved, no condition whereinto a man can be brought so desperate, no employment so dark and uncouth, no service so arduous or full of discouragements, in all which, so far as respects conscience and salvation, there are not most clear and satisfactory expedients to be drawn out of God's word, if a man have his judgment and senses after a spiritual manner exercised therein. That we are so often at a stand how to state such a question, how to satisfy such a scruple, how to clear and expedite such a difficulty, how to repel such a temptation, how to manage such an action, how to order our ways with an even and composed spirit in the various conditions whereinto we are cast in this world, arises not from any defect in the word of God, which is "perfect," and able to furnish us "unto every good work," but only from our own ignorance and imperfect acquaintance with it, who know not how to draw the general rule, and to apply it to our own particular cases. And this cannot but be matter of great humiliation to us in these sad and distracted times, when, besides our civil breaches, which threaten desolation to the state, there are so many and such wide divisions in the church; that, after so long enjoyment of the word of God, the Scripture should be to so many men as a sealed book, and they, like the Egyptians, have the dark side of this glorious pillar towards them still; that men should be "tossed to and fro" like children, "and carried about with every wind of doctrine," and suffer themselves to be bewitched, devoured, brought into bondage, spoiled, led away captive, unskilful in the word of righteousness, unable to discern good and evil, to prove and "try the spirits whether they are of God," always learning, and never able to come to the knowledge of the truth; and this not only in matters problematical, or circumstantial, wherein learned and godly men may differ from one another, and yet still the peace and unity of the church be preserved, (for things of this nature ought not to be occasions of schism, or secessions from one another,) but in matters which concern life and godliness, touching the power of God's law, the nature of free grace, the subjection of the conscience to moral precepts, confession and deprecation of sin in prayer to God; the distinguishing true Christian liberty from loose, profane, and wanton licentiousness, and a liberty to vent and publish what perverse things soever men please; the very being of churches, of ministers, of ordinances, in the world; the necessity of humiliation and solemn repentance in times of public judgments; the toleration of all kinds of religions in Christian commonwealths; the mortality of the reasonable soul, and other the like pernicious and perverse doctrines of men of corrupt minds, (the devil's emissaries,) purposely by him stirred up to hinder and puzzle the reformation of the church. These things, I say, cannot but be matter of humiliation to all that fear God, and love the prosperity of Zion; and occasions the more earnestly to excite them to this wisdom in the text, to hear what God the Lord says, and to lay his righteous ways so to heart, as to walk stedfastly in them, and never to stumble at them, or fall from them.

Videntur ipsi angeli ex scriptis evangelicis, et ministerio apostolico plurima didicisse. Vid. Chrysost. Hom. 1. in Johan. Gregor. Nyssen. Hom. 8. in Cantic. Theophylact. et Œcumen. in Eph. 3.

Μισῶ σοφιστὴν ὅστις οὐχ αὑτῷ σοφος. Plutar. de occulte vivendo.

Sunt quædam falsæ opiniones quæ ulcus non gignunt: sunt etiam errores venenati, qui animam depascuntur. Vid. Plutarch. de Superstit.

Now there are two things which the prophet, in this close of his prophecy, seems to intimate should chiefly engage the attention and animate the obedience of the wise and prudent in times of trouble; namely, 1. The judgments, and, 2. The blessings, of God; his righteous ways in his threatenings against impenitent, and in his promises made to penitent, sinners. These are the things which wise and prudent men will consider in times of trouble.

1. The judgments of God. There is a twofold knowledge of them; the one natural, by sense; the other spiritual, by faith. In the former way wicked men do abundantly know the afflictions which they suffer, even to vexation and anguish of spirit. They "fret themselves," Isa. viii. 21; "gray hairs are here and there upon" them from very trouble and sorrow, Hos. vii. 9; they gnaw "their tongues for pain," Rev. xvi. 10; "they pine away in their iniquities," Lev. xxvi. 39; they are "mad" in their calamities, have "a trembling heart, and failing of eyes, and sorrow of mind," Deut. xxviii. 34, 65. In the latter, or spiritual sense, wicked men discern not, so they are said in the Scripture, when they burn, when they consume, when they are devoured, not to know any of this, neither to lay it to heart, Isa. xlii. 25; Hos. vii. 9; Jer. xii. 11; and the reason is, because they know it not by faith, nor in a spiritual manner, leading them to God. They see not his name, nor bear his rod, nor consider his hand and counsel, in it; nor measure his judgments by his word, nor look on them as the fruits of sin, leading to repentance and teaching righteousness; nor as the arguments of God's displeasure, humbling us under his holy hand, and guiding us to seek his face, and to recover our peace with him. This is the spiritual and prudent way of knowing judgments, Micah vi. 9; Isa. xxvi. 8, 9; xxvii. 9; Lev. xxvi. 40—42. *Scire est per causam scire.* True wisdom looks on things in their causes; resolves judgments into their causes; our sins to be bewailed, God's wrath to be averted; it makes this observation upon them: Now I find by experience, that God is a God of truth; often have I heard judgments threatened against sin, and now I see that God's

threatenings are not empty wind, but that all his words have truth and substance in them. The first part of wisdom is, to see judgments in the word before they come, and to hide from them; for as faith, in regard of promises, is "the substance of things hoped for," and can discern a being in them while they are yet but to come; so, in respect of threatenings, it is the substance of things feared, and can see a being in judgments before they are felt. The next part of wisdom is, to see God in judgments, in the rods when they are actually come, and to know them as leading to him. And that knowledge consists in two things: first, to resolve them into him as their author; for nothing can hurt us without a commission from God, Job xix. 11. Satan spoils Job of his children, the Sabeans and Chaldeans strip him of his goods; but he looks above all these to God, acknowledging his goodness in giving, his power in taking away, and blesses his name, Job i. 21. Joseph looks from the malice of his brethren to the providence of God; "God did send me before you to preserve life," Gen. xlv. 5. If the whale swallow Jonah, God prepares him, Jonah i. 17; and if he vomit him up again, God speaks unto him, chap. ii. 10. Secondly, to direct them to him as the end; to be taught by them to seek the Lord, and to wait on him in the way of his judgments; to be more penitent for sin, more fearful and watchful against it; to study and practise the skill of suffering as Christians, according to the will of God, that he may be glorified, Psal. xciv. 12; cxix. 67, 71; Deut. viii. 16; Zech. xiii. 9; Isa. xxvi. 9; Heb. xii. 11; 1 Pet. iv. 16, 19.

Perdidistis utilitatem calamitatis et miserrimi facti estis, et pessimi permansistis. Aug. de Civ. Dei, l. 1. c. 13.

2. The blessings of God. There is a double knowledge of them; one sensual by the flesh, the other spiritual in the conscience. The former is but a brutish and epicurean feeding on them without fear, as Israel on the quails in the wilderness; as swine, which feed on the fruit that falls down, but never look up to the tree whereon it grew; to use blessings as Adam did the forbidden fruit, being drawn by the beauty of them to forget God, Hos. xiii. 6. But spiritual knowledge of blessings, is to taste and see the goodness of the Lord in them: to look up to him as their author, acknowledging that it is he who "giveth" us "power to get wealth," and every other good thing, Deut. viii. 17, 18; Psal. cxxvii. 1; Prov. x. 22; and to be drawn by them unto him as their end, to the adoration of his bounty, to the admiration of his goodness, to more cheerfulness and stronger engagements to his service; to say with Jacob, He gives me bread to eat, and raiment to put on, therefore he shall be my God, Gen. xxviii. 20, 21. He "giveth" me "richly all things to enjoy," therefore I will "trust in" him, 1 Tim. vi. 17. Catalogues of mercy should beget resolutions of obedience, Josh. xxiv. 2—14.

II. The nature of the doctrines taught. "For the ways of the Lord are right." This integrity the prophet urges as a motive to induce us to consider them the more maturely, and obey them the more implicitly. Now the doctrine of God's judgments, precepts, and promises, is said to be right divers ways.

1. In regard of their equity and reasonableness. There is nothing more profoundly and exactly rational than true religion; and therefore conversion is called by our Saviour conviction.* "And when he," the Spirit of truth, "is come," ἐλέγξει, "he will convince the world of sin, and of righteousness, and of judgment," John xvi. 8. There is a power in the word of God to stop the mouths and dispel the cavils of all contradicters; so that they shall "not" be "able to resist," or speak against, the truth that is taught, John xvi. 8; Tit. i. 9, 10; Acts vi. 10; Matt. xxii. 34. And the apostle calls his ministry, a declaration and a manifestation of the truth of God to the consciences of men, 1 Cor. ii. 4; 2 Cor. iv. 2. And Apollos is said mightily to have "convinced the Jews," "showing" or demonstrating "by the Scriptures that Jesus was Christ," Acts xviii. 28. Therefore the apostle calls the devoting of ourselves to God, our "reasonable service," Rom. xii. 1; and those that obey not the word, are called "unreasonable" or absurd men, that have not wisdom to discern the truth and equity of the ways of God, 2 Thess. iii. 2. What can be more reasonable than that he who made all things for himself should be served by the creatures which he made? that we should live to him who gave us our being? that the supreme will should be obeyed, the infallible truth believed? that he who can destroy should be feared? that he who rewards should be loved and trusted in? that absolute justice should vindicate itself against presumptuous disobedience, and absolute goodness extend mercy to whom it pleases? It is no marvel that the Holy Spirit brands wicked men throughout the Scripture with the disgraceful title of fools, because they reject that which is the supreme rule of wisdom, and has in it the greatest perfection and exactness of reason, Jer. viii. 9.

Demonstratio est syllogismus scientificus. Arist. poster. Analyt. lib. 1. c. 2.

Nullum scelus rationem habet. Liv. lib. 28.

2. In regard of their mutual agreement and harmony.† As that which is right and straight has all its parts equal and agreeing one to another, so all the parts of Divine doctrine are exactly suitable and conformed to each other. The promises of God are not yea and nay, but yea and Amen, 2 Cor. i. 19, 20. However there may be seeming repugnances to a carnal and captious eye, (which may seem designedly allowed for the exercise of our diligence in searching, and humility in adoring, the profoundness and perfection of the word,) yet the Scriptures have no obliquity in them at all, but all the parts thereof do most intimately agree one with another, as being written by the Spirit of truth who cannot lie nor deceive, who is "the same yesterday, and to-day, and for ever."

3. In regard of their directness to that end for which they were revealed to men, being the strait road to eternal life, "able to build" us "up, and to give" us "an inheritance," Acts xx. 32. In which respect the word is called "the word of this life," Acts v. 20, and "the gospel of" "salvation," Eph. i. 13; yea, salvation itself, John iv. 22; xii. 50; Acts xxviii. 28, as being the way to it, and the instrument of it, 2 Tim. iii. 15—17; James i. 21.

4. In regard of their conformity to the holy nature and will of God, which is the original rule ‡ of all rectitude and perfection. Law is nothing but the will of the lawgiver, revealed with an intention to bind those that are under it, and for the ordering of whom it was revealed. That will being in God most holy and perfect, the law or word, which is but the discovery of it, must needs be holy and perfect too; therefore it is called the "acceptable and perfect will of God," Rom. xii. 2; Col. i. 9. It is also called a "word of truth," importing a conformity between the mind and will of the speaker and the word which is spoken by him; in which respect it is said to be "holy, and just, and good," Rom. vii. 12.

* Elenchus est syllogismus cum contradictione conclusionis. Arist. Elench. l. 8. c. 1. Et ἐλέγχειν est certa argumentatione disputantem vincere. Steph. ex Platone.

† Οὐδεμία γραφὴ τῇ ἑτέρᾳ ἐναντία ἐστιν, αὐτος μὴ νοεῖν μᾶλλον ὁμολογήσω τὰ εἰρημενα, &c. Just. Mart. Dialog. cum Tryphon. Quod de suo codice Justinianus, verius de sacro codice affirmatur, contrarium aliquid in hoc codice positum, nullum sibi locum vindicabit, &c. Cod. de vetere Jure enucleando, l. 2. sect. 15. et l. 3. sect. 15.

‡ Non idcirco juste voluit quia futurum justum fuit quod voluit: sed quod voluit, idcirco justum fuit quia ipse voluit, &c. Hug. de Sacrament. lib. 1. part. 4. cap. 1.

5. In regard of their plainness and perspicuity. They are doctrines in which men may walk surely, easily, without danger of wandering, stumbling, or miscarriage; as a man is out of danger of missing a way, if it be straight and direct, without any turnings, and in no great danger of falling in it, if it be plain and smooth, and no stumbling-block left in it. Now such is the word of God to those who make it their way: a "straight" way, which looks directly forward, Psal. v. 8; Heb. xii. 13. An "even" and smooth way, which has no offence or stumbling-block in it, Psal. xxvi. 12; cxix. 165. True, there are *δυσνόητα*, hard things, to exercise the study and diligence, the faith and prayers, of the profoundest scholars; water wherein an elephant may swim. But yet, as nature has made things of greatest necessity to be most obvious and common, as air, water, bread, and the like; whereas things of greater rarity, as gems and jewels, are matters of honour and ornament, not of daily use: so the wisdom of God has so tempered the Scriptures, that from thence the wisest Solomon may fetch jewels for ornament, and the poorest Lazarus bread for life; but those things which are of common necessity, as matters of faith, love, worship, obedience, which are universally requisite to "the common salvation," (as the apostle expresses it, Jude 3; Tit. i. 4,) are so perspicuously set down in the Holy Scriptures, that every one who has the Spirit of Christ, has therewithal a judgment to discern so much of God's will as shall suffice to make him believe in Christ for righteousness, and by worship and obedience serve him unto salvation.* The way of holiness is so plain that simple men are made wise enough to find it out, and "the wayfaring men, though fools, shall not err therein," Psal. xix. 7; Isa. xxxii. 4; xxxv. 8; Matt. xi. 25. From all which

Obs. 3. We should take heed of quarrelling with any word of God, or presuming to pass any bold and carnal censure of ours on his righteous ways. When God sets his word energetically in its power on the spirit of any wicked man, making his conscience to hear it as the voice of God, it usually works one of these two effects: either it subdues the soul to obedience by convincing, judging, and manifesting the secrets of his heart, so that he falleth down on his face and worshippeth God, 1 Cor. xiv. 25; or else it does by accident excite and enrage the natural love which is in every man to his lusts, stirring up all the proud arts and reasonings which the forge of a corrupt heart can shape in defence of those lusts against the sword of the Spirit which would cut them off, as that which hinders the course of a river, accidentally enrages its force, and causes it to swell and overrun the banks. And from hence arise gainsaying and contradiction against the word of grace, and the ways of God, as unequal and unreasonable, too strict, too severe, too hard to be observed, Ezek. xviii. 25; snuffing at it, Mal. i. 13, gathering odious consequences from it, Rom. iii. 8, replying against it, Rom. ix. 19, 20, casting reproaches on it, Jer. xx. 8, 9, enviously swelling at it, Acts xiii. 45. There are few sins more dangerous than this of picking quarrels at God's word, and taking up weapons against it. It will prove "a burdensome stone for" "all that burden themselves with it," Zech. xii. 3; Matt. xxi. 44. Therefore whenever our crooked and corrupt reason offers to except against the ways of God as unequal, we must presently conclude as God does, Ezek. xviii. 25, that the inequality is in us, and not in them.† When a lame man stumbles in a plain path, the fault is not in the way, but in the foot. Nor is the potion, but the palate, to blame, when a feverish distemper makes that seem bitter which is indeed sweet. He that removes in a boat from the shore, in the judgment of sense sees the houses or trees on the shore totter and move, whereas the motion is in the boat, and not in them. Unclean and corrupt hearts have unclean notions of the purest things, and conceive of God as if he were altogether such a one as themselves, Psal. l. 21.

Obs. 4. We should come to God's word always as to a rule by which we are to measure ourselves, and take heed of wresting it to the corrupt fancies of our own evil hearts, as the apostle saith some men do "unto their own destruction," 2 Pet. iii. 16; Acts xiii. 10. Every wicked man, though not formally and explicitly, yet really and in truth, sets up his own will against God's, resolving to do what pleases himself, and not that which may please God, and consequently follows that reason and counsel which wait upon his own will, and not that word which reveals God's. Yet because he that will serve himself would fain deceive himself too, (that so he may do it with less regret of conscience,) and would fain seem God's servant, but be his own, therefore corrupt reason sets itself on work to excogitate such distinctions and evasions as may serve to reconcile God's word and a man's own lust together.‡ Lust saith, Steal. God saith, No, thou shalt not steal. Carnal reason, the advocate of lust, comes in and makes some evasive distinctions; I may not steal from a neighbour, but I may weaken an enemy, or pay myself the stipend that belongs to my service, if others do not: thus most innocent men may be made a prey to violent soldiers, who use the name of public interest to palliate their own rapacity. Certainly it is a high presumption to tamper with the word of truth, and make it bear false witness in favour of our own sins; and God will bring it to a trial at last whose will shall stand, his or ours.

Cesset voluntas propria et non erit infernus, &c. Vid. Bernard. serm. 3. de Resurrect.

Obs. 5. "The ways of the Lord" should be the boundary, both to the ministration of the preacher, and to the faith of the hearer. 1. To us in our ministry, that we deliver nothing to the people but the "right" "ways of the Lord,"§ without any commixtures or contemperations of our own. Mixtures are useful only for either of these two purposes, either to abate something that is excessive, or to supply something that is deficient, and to collect a virtue and efficacy out of many things, each one of which alone

* In iis quæ aperte in Scripturis posita sunt inveniuntur illa omnia quæ continent fidem, moresque vivendi. Aug. de Doct. Christian. lib. 2. c. 9. et Ep. 3. ad Volusian. et contr. Ep. Petilian. cap. 5. Vid. Theodoret. serm. 8. de Martyrib. s. 12.

† Ut vernula illa apud Senecam quæ cum cæca esset, cubiculum esse tenebrosum querebatur. Ἐν τῷ πυρέτειν πικρὰ πάντα καὶ ἀηδῆ φαίνεται γενομένοις——ἀλλ' οὐκέτι τὸ πότον ἀλλὰ τὴν νόσον αἰτιώμεθα. Plutarch. de Animi Tranquillitate.

‡ Βιάζονται πρὸς τὰς ἐπιθυμίας τὴν γράφην. Clem. Alex. Strom. lib. 7. Εἰς τὰς ἰδίας μετάγουσι δόξας. Ibid. Κλέπτουσι τὸν κάνονα τῆς ἔκκλησίας, ταῖς ἰδίαις ἐπιθυμίαις καὶ φιλοδοξίαις χαριζόμενοι. Ibid. Ἕλκοντες πρὸς τὴν ἕαυτῶν ὀργην τὸ εὐαγγέλιον, &c. Justin. Martyr. Ep. ad Zenam. Simplicitatem sermonis ecclesiastici id volunt significare quod ipsi sentiunt. Hieron. Ep. Vid. Aug. de Doct. Christian. lib. 3. cap. 10. Scripturas tenent ad speciem, non ad salutem. De Baptism. contr. Donat. lib. 3. cap. ult. Eas secundum suum sensum legunt. De Grat. Christ. lib. 1. c. 41. Sequitur voluptatem non quam audit, sed quam attulit, et vitia sua cum cœpit putare similia præceptis, indulget illis non timide nec obscure; luxuriatur etiam inoperto capite. Sen. de Vita Beata, cap. 13. Nondum hæc negligentia Deum venerat, nec interpretando sibi quisque jusjurandum et leges aptas faciebat, sed suos potius mores ad ea accommodabat. Liv. lib. 3.

§ Aurum accepisti, aurum redde; nolo mihi pro aliis alia subjicias; nolo pro auro aut impudenter plumbum, aut fraudulenter æramenta supponas; nolo auri speciem sed naturam plane. Vincent. Lirin. Lege Corneliâ cavetur ut qui in aurum vitii quid addiderit, qui argenteos nummos adulterinos flaverit, falsi crimine teneatur. L. 9. P. Leg. Cornel. de Falsis. Qui tabulam legis refixerit vel quid inde immutaverit, Lege Julia peculatus tenetur. L. 8. P. ad Leg. Jul. Peculat.

would have been ineffectual. And so all heterogeneous mixtures do plainly intimate either a viciousness to be corrected, or a weakness to be supplied, in every one of the simples which are by human wisdom tempered together in order to some effect. Now it were great wickedness to charge either of these on the pure and perfect word of God, and, consequently, to use deceit and insincerity by adulterating it, either by such glosses as diminish and take away from its force, as the Pharisees did in their carnal interpretations, (confuted by our Saviour, Matt. v. 21, 27, 38, 43,) or by such superinducements of human traditions as argue any defect, which they also used, Matt. xv. 2, 9. Human arts and learning are of excellent use, as instruments in the managing and searching, and as means and witnesses in the explication, of holy writ, when piously and prudently directed to such uses. But to stamp any thing of a mere human original with a Divine character, and obtrude it on the consciences of men, (as the papists do their unwritten traditions,) to bind to obedience; to take any dead child of ours (as the harlot did, 1 Kings iii. 20) and lay it in the bosom of the Scripture, and father it on God; to build any structure of ours in the road to heaven, and stop up the way; is one of the highest and most daring presumptions to which the pride of man can aspire: to erect a throne in the consciences of his fellow creatures, and to counterfeit the great seal of heaven for the countenancing of one's own forgeries, is a sin most severely provided against by God, with special prohibitions and threatenings, Deut. xii. 32; xviii. 20; Prov. xxx. 6; Jer. xxvi. 2. This therefore must be the great care of the ministers of the gospel, to show their fidelity in delivering only the "counsel of God" to his people, Acts xx. 27; to be as the two golden pipes which received oil from the olive branches, and then emptied it into the gold, Zech. iv. 12; first to receive from the Lord, and then to deliver to the people, Isa. xxi. 10; Ezek. ii. 7; iii. 4; 1 Cor. xi. 23; 1 Pet. iv. 11. 2. The people are hereby taught, first, to examine the doctrines of men by the rule and standard of the word, and to measure them there, that so they may not be seduced by the craftiness of deceivers, and may be the more confirmed and comforted by the doctrine of sincere teachers; for though the judgment of interpretation belong principally to the ministers of the word, yet God has given to all believers a judgment of discretion, to "try the spirits," and to search "the Scriptures," "whether those things" which they hear be so, 1 John iv. 1; Acts xvii. 11; 1 Thess. v. 21; for no man is to pin his own soul and salvation, by a blind obedience, on the words of a man who may mislead him; nay, not on the words of an angel, if it were possible for an angel to deceive, Gal. i. 8; 1 Kings xiii. 18, 21; but only and immediately on the Scripture: otherwise, when the "blind lead the blind," the leader only should "fall into the ditch," and the other go to heaven for his blind obedience in following his guides toward hell; whereas our Saviour tells us "both shall fall into the ditch," though but one be the leader, Matt. xv. 14; xxiii. 15. Secondly, having proved all things, to "hold fast that which is good;" with all readiness to receive the righteous ways of God, and submit to them, how mean soever the instrument be in our eyes, how contrary soever his message be to our wills and lusts. When God manifests his Spirit and word in the mouths of his ministers, we are not to consider the vessel, but the treasure, and to receive it as from Christ, who, "unto the end of the world," in the dispensation of his ordinances, "speaketh from heaven" unto the church, Matt. xxviii. 20; 2 Cor. v. 20; 1 Thess. ii. 13; Heb. xii. 25.

Vid. Davenant. de indice et norma fidei. Chap. 25. 31.

Isid. Pelut. lib. 3. Ep. 165.

III. The twofold use made thereof by different kinds of men.

1. To the just, the Lord's ways are a way of happiness: "The just shall walk in them." And this leads us to

Obs. 6. Obedience, and walking in the right ways of the Lord, is the end of the ministry; that the saints may be perfected, that the body of Christ may be edified, that men may "grow up into" Christ "in all things," Eph. iv. 11—15; that their eyes may be opened, and they turned from "darkness to light, and from the power of Satan unto God," Acts xxvi. 16—18. The prophet concludes that he has "laboured in vain" if "Israel be not gathered," Isa. xlix. 4, 5; without this "the law of the Lord" is "in vain made," "the pen of the scribes is in vain," Jer. viii. 8; better not know "the way of righteousness," than, having known it, "to turn from the holy commandment delivered unto" us, 2 Pet. ii. 21. We should esteem it a great misery to be without preaching, without ordinances, and so indeed it is; of all famine, that of the word of the Lord is the most dreadful; better be with God's presence in a wilderness, than in Canaan without him, Exod. xxxiii. 15; better "the bread of adversity, and water of affliction," than "a famine" "of hearing the words of the Lord," Isa. xxx. 20; Amos viii. 11: this is "mischief" "upon mischief," when "the law" doth "perish from the priest," and "a vision of the prophet" is sought in vain, Ezek. vii. 26; and yet it is much better to be in this case, without a teaching priest, and without the law, than to enjoy them, and not to walk answerably to them. Where the word is not a savour of life, it is a "savour of death unto death," exceedingly multiplying the damnation of those that despise it, 2 Cor. ii. 16; Matt. xi. 22, 24. 1. Those sins which it finds, it ripens; making them much more sinful than in other men, because committed against greater light and more mercy.* One and the same sin in a heathen, is not so heinous and hateful as in a Christian. Those trees on which the sun constantly shines, have their fruit become riper and larger than those which grow in a shady and cold place. The rain will hasten the growth as well of weeds as of corn, and make them ranker than in a dry and barren ground. 2. It superadds many more and greater; for the greatest sins of all, are those which are committed against light and grace, John ix. 41; xv. 22—24; sins against the law and prophets, greater than those which are committed against the glimmerings of nature, Ezek. ii. 5; iii. 6, 7; and sins against Christ and the gospel, greater than those against the law, Heb. ii. 2, 3; x. 28, 29: such are, unbelief, impenitency, apostacy, despising of salvation, preferring death and sin before Christ and mercy; judging ourselves unworthy of eternal life. 3. By these means it both hastens and multiplies judgments. The sins of the church are much sooner ripe for the sickle than the sins of Amorites; they are "nigh unto cursing," Heb. vi. 8; "summer fruit," sooner shaken off than others, Amos viii. 1; Jer. i. 11, 12. Christ comes "quickly" to remove his candlestick from the abusers of it, Rev. ii. 5. The word is a rich

Nihil est aliud scientia nostra quam culpa, qui ad hoc tantummodo legem novimus ut majore offensione peccemus. Salvian. lib. 4.

* Criminosior culpa, ubi status honestior.—Qui Christiani dicimur, si simile aliquid barbarorum impuritatibus facimus, gravius erramus; atrocius enim sub sancti nominis professione peccamus: ubi sublimior est prærogativa, major est culpa. Salvian. lib. 4. Possunt nostra et barbarorum vitia esse paria, sed in his tamen vitiis necesse est peccata nostra esse graviora—Nunquid dici de Hunnis potest, ecce quales sunt qui Christiani esse dicuntur? nunquid de Saxonibus et Francis, ecce quid faciunt, qui se asserunt Christi esse cultores? Nunquid propter Maurorum efferos mores lex sacro-sancta culpatur?—Evangelia legunt, et impudici sunt; apostolos audiunt, et inebriantur; Christum sequuntur, et rapiunt, &c. Ibid.

mercy in itself, but nothing makes it effectually and in the event a mercy to us but our walking in it.

Obs. 7. We never make the Scriptures the rule of our life and conversation, till we be first justified. Our obedience to the rule of the law written in the Scriptures, proceeds from those suitable impressions of holiness wrought in the soul by the Spirit of regeneration, which is called the writing of the law in our hearts, Jer. xxxi. 33; 2 Cor. iii. 3; or the casting of the soul into the *mould* of the word, *ὑπηκούσατε δὲ ἐκ καρδίας εἰς ὃν παρεδόθητε τύπον διδαχῆς*, Rom. vi. 17. We are never fit to receive God's truth in the love and obedience of it, till we repent and be renewed. "If God," saith the apostle, "will give repentance to the acknowledging of the truth," 2 Tim. ii. 25. "The wise in heart," that is, those that are truly godly, (for none but such are in the Scriptures accounted wise men,) these "will receive commandments: but a prating fool shall fall," Prov. x. 8; where by "prating" I understand cavilling, contradicting, taking exceptions at, and making objections against, the commandment, and so falling and stumbling. To such the apostle James saith, chap. i. 19, "Let every man be swift to hear," that is, ready to learn the will and to receive the commandment of God; but "slow to speak, slow to wrath," that is, careful that he suffer no pride and passion to rise up and speak against the things which are taught: as Job saith, "Teach me, and I will hold my tongue," Job vi. 24. For the only reason why men fret and swell, and speak against the truth of God, is because they will not work righteousness. "The wrath of man worketh not the righteousness of God," James i. 20. Therefore men are "contentious," because they love not to "obey the truth," Rom. ii. 8. Disobedience is the mother of gainsaying, Rom. x. 21. When we once resolve to "lay apart all filthiness," then we will "receive with meekness the engrafted word," James i. 21, and not before. None hear God's words but they who are of God, John viii. 47; none hear the voice of Christ but the sheep of Christ, John x. 4, 5. Christ preached is "the power of God, and the wisdom of God," but it is only "unto them which are called;" to others a stumbling-block, and foolishness, 1 Cor. i. 23, 24. "We speak wisdom," saith the apostle, but it is "among them that are perfect," 1 Cor. ii. 6. He that is subject to one prince, cares not greatly to study the laws of another; or if he do, it is in order to curiosity, and not to duty. So long as men resolve of Christ, "We will not have this man to reign over us," Luke xix. 14, so long either they study not his word at all, or it is in order to some carnal and corrupt ends, and not to obedience or salvation.

Hereby we may try our spiritual estate, whether we be just men or no; if we make God's word our way, our rule, our delight, laying it up in our hearts, and labouring to be rich in it, that we may walk with more exactness. It was an ill sign of love to Christ, the Master of the feast, when men chose rather to tend their cattle and grounds than to wait on him, Luke xiv. 18; an ill sign of valuing his doctrine, when the loss of their swine made the Gadarenes weary of his company, Luke viii. 37. There was much work to do in the house, when Mary neglected it all, and sat at her Lord's feet to hear his doctrine, and yet was commended by him for it. He was better pleased to see her hunger after the feast which he brought, than solicitous to provide a feast for him; more delighted in her love to his doctrine, than her sister's care for his entertainment, Luke x. 41, 42. This is one of the surest characters of a godly man, that he makes the word in all things his rule and counsellor, labouring continually to get thereby more acquaintance with God and his holy will, Prov. x. 14; John xv. 7; Col. iii. 16. It is his way; and every man endeavours to be skilful in the way which he is to travel. It is his tool and instrument; every workman must have that in readiness, to measure and carry on all the parts of his work. It is his wisdom; every one would be esteemed a wise man in that which is his proper function and profession. It is the mystery and trade to which he is bound; and every man would have the reputation of skill in his own trade. It is his charter, which secures all the privileges and immunities which belong to him; and every citizen would willingly know the privileges to which he has a right. It is the testament and will of Christ, wherein are given unto us "exceeding great and precious promises;" and what heir or child would be ignorant of the last will of his father? Lastly, it is the law of Christ's kingdom; and it concerns every subject to know the duties, the rewards, the punishments, which belong to him in that relation.

2. To the wicked the holy and right ways of the Lord, in the ministry of his word, become an occasion of stumbling: "The transgressors shall fall therein." And that in two manner of ways: 1. Of scandal, they are offended at them. 2. Of ruin; they are destroyed by them.

1. By way of scandal, they are offended at them. So it is prophesied of Christ, that as he should be for "a sanctuary" to his people, so to others, who would not trust in him, but betake themselves to their own counsels, he should be for "a stone of stumbling and for a rock of offence; for a gin and for a snare," Isa. viii. 14; "for the fall and rising again of many in Israel; and for a sign" to be "spoken against," Luke ii. 34. So he saith of himself, "For judgment I am come into this world, that they which see not might see; and that they which see might be made blind," John ix. 39. And this offence which wicked men take at Christ, is from the purity and holiness of his word, which they cannot submit to: "a stone of stumbling" he is, "and a rock of offence, even to them which stumble at the word, being disobedient," 1 Pet. ii. 8; 2 Cor. ii. 14, 15. Thus Christ preached was "a sanctuary" to Sergius Paulus the deputy, and "a stumbling-block" to Elymas the sorcerer; "a sanctuary" to Dionysius and Damaris, and "a stumbling-block" to the wits and philosophers of Athens; "a sanctuary" to the Gentiles that begged the preaching of the gospel, and "a stumbling-block" to the Jews that contradicted and blasphemed, Acts xiii. 42, 45: the former primarily and *per se;* for salvation was the purpose of his coming, there was sin enough to condemn the world before; "I came not," saith he, "to judge the world, but to save the world," John xii. 47. The other occasionally, not by any intrinsic evil quality in the word, which is "holy, and just, and good," and deals with all meekness and beseechings, even towards obstinate sinners;* but by reason of the pride and stubbornness of those men who dash against it; as that wholesome meat which ministers strength to a sound man, but feeds the disease of another that sits at the same table with him; the same light which is a pleasure to a strong eye, is a pain to a weak one; the same sweet smells which delight the brain, afflict the matrix when it is distempered; and none of this by the infusion of malignant qualities, but only by an occasional working upon and exciting of those which were before present.

Bonæ res neminem scandalizant nisi malam mentem. Tertul. de Veland. Virg. cap. 3.

Vid. Irenæum, lib. 5. cap. 27.

And there are many things in the word of God at which the corrupt hearts of wicked men are apt to stumble and be offended. As, 1. Its profundity and depth,† as containing great mysteries above the dis-

* Οὐχ αἱ γραφαὶ γεγόνασιν αὐτοῖς αἰτίαι ἀλλ' ἡ σφῶν αὐτῶν κακοφροσύνη. Athanas. de Synod. Arim. et Seleuc.

† Δεῖ μὴ λογισμοῖς ἀνθρωπίνοις διευθύνειν τὰ θεῖα, ἀλλὰ πρὸς τὸ βούλημα τῆς διδασκαλίας τοῦ πνεύματος τῶν λόγων ποιεῖσθαι τὴν ἔκθεσιν. Justin. Exposit. Fidei.

covery or search of created reason. Such is the pride and wantonness of sinful wit, that it knows not how to believe what it cannot comprehend, and must have all doctrines tried at its own bar, and measured by its own balance; as if a man should attempt to weigh out the earth in a pair of scales, or to empty the waters of the sea with a bucket. As soon as Paul mentioned the resurrection, presently the Athenian wits mocked his doctrine, Acts xvii. 32; and it was a great stumbling-block to Nicodemus, to hear that a man "must be born again," John iii. 4. Sarah has much ado to believe beyond reason, Gen. xviii. 12; and Moses himself was a little staggered by this temptation, Numb. xi. 21, 22. A very hard thing it is for busy and inquisitive reason to rest in an ὢ βάθος, "Oh the depth of the riches, both of the wisdom and knowledge of God!" and to adore the unsearchableness of his judgments, though even human laws tell us that the reason of law is not always to be inquired into.* The great heresies against the highest mysteries of Christian religion, the Trinity, the two natures of Christ, the hypostatical union, the Divinity of the Holy Ghost, had their first rise among the Grecians, who were then the masters of wit and learning, and esteemed the rest of the world barbarous; † and the old exception which they were wont to take at the doctrine of Christianity, was its "foolishness," 1 Cor. i. 23.

2. Its sanctity and strictness, as contrary to the carnal wills and affections of men: for as corruption deifies reason in the way of wisdom, not willingly allowing any mysteries above its own scrutiny and comprehension; so does it deify will with respect to liberty and power, and loves not to have any authority set over that which may confine or restrain it. As Joshua said to Israel, "Ye cannot serve the Lord, for he is a holy God," Josh. xxiv. 19, we may say of the law, We cannot submit to the law, because it is a holy law. "The carnal mind" "is not," cannot be, "subject to the law of God," Rom. viii. 7. Heat and cold will ever be offensive to one another; and such are flesh and Spirit, Gal. v. 17. Therefore, ordinarily, the arguments against the ways of God have been drawn from politic or carnal interests. Jeroboam will not worship at Jerusalem, lest Israel revolt to the house of David, 1 Kings xii. 27. Amos must not prophesy against the idolatry of Israel, for "the land is not able to bear all his words," Amos vii. 10. The Jews conclude Christ must not be let alone, lest "the Romans" "come and take away both" their "place and nation," John xi. 48. Demetrius and the craftsmen will by no means have Diana spoken against, because by making shrines for her they got their wealth, Acts xix. 24, 25. Corruption will close with religion a great way, and "hear gladly," and do "many things" willingly, and part with much to escape damnation; but there is a particular point of rigour and strictness in every unregenerate man's case, which, when pressed close upon, causes him to stumble, and to be offended, and to break the treaty. The hypocrites in the prophet will give "rams," and "rivers of oil," and their "first-born," "the fruit of" their "body for the sin of" their "soul:" "but to do justly, and to love mercy, and to walk humbly with" their "God;" to do away "the treasures of wickedness," "the scant measure," "the bag of deceitful weights," "violence," "lies," the "deceitful" "tongue," "the statutes of Omri," or "the works of the house of Ahab;" *durus sermo*, this is intolerable: they will rather venture "smiting" and "desolation," than be held to terms so severe, Micah vi. 6—16. The young man will come to Christ, yea, run to him, and kneel, and desire instruction touching the way to eternal life, and walk with much care in observation of the commandments; but if he must part with all, and instead of great possessions, take up a cross and follow Christ, and fare as he fared, this is indeed a hard saying; he that came "running," went away "grieved" and "sad," and on this one point do he and Christ part, Mark x. 17, 22. Herod will hear John gladly, and do many things, and observe and reverence him as a just and holy man; but in the case of Herodias he must be excused, on this issue he and salvation shake hands, Mark vi. 20, 27. This is the difference between hypocritical and sincere conversion: that goes far, and parts with much, and proceeds to almost; but when it comes to the very turning point, and ultimate act of regeneration, it then plays the part of "an unwise son," and stays "long in the place of the breaking forth of children," Hos. xiii. 13; as a foolish merchant, who, in a rich bargain of a thousand pounds, breaks upon a difference of twenty shillings. But the other is contented to part with all, to suffer the loss of all, to carry on the treaty to a full and final conclusion, to have all the armour of the strong man taken from him, that Christ may divide the spoils, Luke xi. 22; Psal. cxix. 128; to do the hardest duties if they be commanded, Gen. xxii. 3.

3. The searching, convincing, and penetrating quality which is in the word, is a great matter of offence to wicked men, when it cuts them to the heart, as Stephen's sermon did his hearers, Acts vii. 54. Light is of a discovering and manifesting property, Eph. v. 13, and for that reason is hated by "every one that doeth evil," John iii. 20; for though the pleasure of sin to a wicked man be sweet, yet there is bitterness in its root and issue; he who loves to enjoy the pleasure cannot endure to hear of the guilt. Now the work of the word is to "take" men "in their own heart," Ezek. xiv. 5; to make "manifest" to a man "the secrets of his heart," 1 Cor. xiv. 25; to pierce like arrows "the heart of the king's enemies," Psal. xlv. 5; to divide asunder the "soul and spirit," "the joints and marrow," and to be "a discerner of the thoughts and intents of the heart," Heb. iv. 12; Isa. xlix. 2. This act of discovery cannot but exceedingly gall the spirits of wicked men; it is like the voice of God unto Adam in Paradise, Adam, "where art thou?" Gen. iii. 9; or like the voice of Ahijah to the wife of Jeroboam, "I am sent to thee with heavy tidings," 1 Kings xiv. 6.

4. The plainness and simplicity of the gospel is likewise matter of offence to the wicked, 2 Cor. x. 10; and that partly for the preceding reason; for the more plain the word is, the more immediate access has it to the conscience, and the more effect upon it. Mere human elegance, fineness of wit, and delicacy of expression, oftentimes stop at fancy, and take possession of that, as the body of Asahel caused the passers-by to stand still and gaze, 2 Sam. ii. 23. And wicked men can be contented to admit the word any whither, so they can keep it out of their conscience, which is its only proper subject, 2 Cor. iv. 2. When I hear men magnify quaint and polite discourses in the ministry of the word, and speak against sermons that are plain and wholesome, I look upon it not so much as an act of pride, (though the wisdom of the flesh is very apt to scorn the simplicity of the gospel,) but indeed as an act of fear and cowardice; because, where all other external trimmings and dresses are wanting to tickle the fancy, there the word has the more weighty and downright operation on the conscience, and must consequently the more startle and terrify.

5. The great difficulty, and indeed impossibility, of

* Οὐδε γὰρ οὓς ἀνθρωποι νόμους τίθενται τὸ εὔλογον ἁπλῶς ἔχουσι καὶ παντοτε φαίνομενον. Plutarch de sera numinis vindicti. Non omnium quæ a majoribus constituta sunt ratio reddi potest, et ideo rationes eorumque constituuntur, inquiri non oportet. P. lib. 1. T. 4. Leg. 20, 21.

† Vid. Hooker. lib. 5. 3. Mater omnium hæreticorum superbia. Aug. de Gen. contr. Manichæos, lib. 2. cap. 8.

obeying the word in its strictness and rigour, is another ground of scandal; that God in his word should command men to do that which indeed cannot be done. This was matter of astonishment to the disciples themselves, when our Saviour told them that it was "easier for a camel to go through the eye of a needle, than for a rich man to enter into the kingdom of God," Mark x. 25. This was the cavil of the disputant in the apostle against the counsels of God, "Why doth he yet find fault?" if he harden whom he will, why does he complain of our hardness, which it is impossible for us to prevent, because none can resist his will? Rom. ix. 19. Now to this scandal we answer, first, that the law of God was not originally,* nor is it intrinsically or in the nature of the thing, impossible; but accidentally, and by reason of natural corruption, which is enmity against it. A burden may be very portable in itself, which he who is a cripple may not be able to bear. The defect is not in the law, but in us, Rom. viii. 3. Secondly, that of this impossibility there may be made a most excellent use,† that being convinced of impotency in ourselves, we may have recourse to the perfect obedience and righteousness of Christ, to pardon all our violations of it, Gal. iii. 21, 24. Thirdly, being regenerated and endued with the Spirit of Christ, the law becomes evangelically possible to us again;‡ yea, not only possible, but sweet and easy, Rom. vii. 22; 1 John v. 3; Matt. xi. 30: though impossible to the purpose of justification and legal covenant, which require perfection of obedience under pain of the curse, Gal. iii. 10; in which sense it is a yoke which cannot be borne, Acts xv. 10, a commandment which cannot be endured, Heb. xii. 20; yet possible to the purpose of the acceptation of our services done in obedience to it, the spiritual part of them being presented by the intercession, and the carnal defects covered by the righteousness, of Christ, in whom the Father is always well pleased. Fourthly, if any wicked man presume to harden himself in the practice of sin under this pretence, that it is impossible for him to avoid it, because God hardeneth "whom he will," though the apostolical increpation be answer sufficient, "Nay but, O man, who art thou that repliest against God?" Rom. ix. 20; yet he must further know, that he is not only hardened judicially by the sentence of God, but most willingly also by his own stubborn love of sin, and giving himself over to sinning with all greediness, and thereby actively brings on himself those indispositions to duty, so that the law being impossible to be performed by him is indeed no other than he would himself have it to be, as bearing an active enmity and antipathy unto it.

Cor lapideum non significat nisi durissimam voluntatem et adversus Deum inflexibilem. Aug. de Grat. et Lib. Arb. c. 14.

6. The mercy and free grace of God in the promises are to wicked men an occasion of stumbling, while they turn it into "lasciviousness," and "continue in sin that grace may abound," Rom. vi. 1; Jude 4; and venture to make work for the blood of Christ, not being led by "the goodness of God" "to repentance," but hardening themselves in impenitency because God is good, Rom. ii. 4. There is not any thing at which wicked men more ordinarily stumble than at mercy, as gluttons surfeit most on the greatest dainties; venturing upon this ground to go on in sin, because they cannot out-sin mercy; and to put off repentance from day to day, because they are still under the offers of mercy; making mercy not a sanctuary to which to fly from sin, but a sanctuary to protect and countenance sin; and so by profane and desperate presumption turning the very mercy of God into a judgment, and savour of death unto themselves, pretending liberty from sin that they may continue in it, and abuse God by his own gifts, Deut. xxix. 19, 20; Numb. xv. 30.

7. The threatenings of God set forth in his word, and executed in his judgments on wicked men, are great occasions of stumbling to them, when they are not thereby, with Manasses, humbled under God's mighty hand, but, with Pharaoh, hardened the more in their stubbornness against him. There is such desperate wickedness in the hearts of some men, that they can even sit down and rest in the resolutions of perishing, resolving to enjoy the pleasures of sin while they may: "To-morrow we die," therefore in the mean time "let us eat and drink," 1 Cor. xv. 32. "Behold, this evil is of the Lord; what should I wait for the Lord any longer?" 2 Kings vi. 33. There are three men in the Scripture that have a special brand or mark of ignominy set upon them, Cain, Dathan, and Ahaz. "The Lord set a mark upon Cain," Gen. iv. 15. "This is that Dathan," and, "This is that king Ahaz," Numb. xxvi. 9; 2 Chron. xxviii. 22. And if we examine the reasons, we shall find that the sin of stubbornness had a special hand in it. Cain's offering was not accepted, on this he grew wroth and sullen, and stubborn against God's gentle warning, and slew his brother. Dathan and his companions, sent for by Moses, return a proud and stubborn answer, "We will not come up," "we will not come up," Numb. xvi. 12, 14. Ahaz, greatly distressed by the king of Syria, by the Edomites, by the Philistines, by the Assyrian, and in the midst of all this distress stubborn still, and trespassing "yet more against the Lord," 2 Chron. xxviii. 22. It is one of the saddest symptoms in the world for a man, or a nation, not to be humbled under the correcting hand of God, but, like an anvil, to grow harder under blows; and a most sure argument that God will not give over, but go on to multiply his judgments still, for he will overcome when he judgeth, and therefore will judge till he overcome. In musical notes there are but eight degrees, and then the same are repeated again; and philosophers, when they distinguish degrees in qualities, usually make the eighth degree the highest: but in the wrath of God against those who impenitently and stubbornly stand out against his judgments, we shall find no fewer than eight and twenty degrees threatened by God himself; "I will punish you seven times more," and yet "seven times more," and again, "yet seven times," and once more, "seven times for your sins," Lev. xxvi. 18, 21, 24, 28. Thus wicked men do not only stumble at the word by way of scandal, but also,

Vide quæ de Sardanapalo, Nino, Bacchide, Xanthia, aliis, congessit Athenæus. Lib. 8. cap. 3. et lib. 12. c. 7.

2. By way of ruin, because they are sure in the end to be destroyed thereby; for the rock stands still, the ship that dashes against it only is broken. God's word is and will be too hard for the pride of men; the more they resist it, the mightier will it appear in their condemnation. The weak corn which yields to the wind is not harmed by it; but the proud oak which resists it is many times broken in pieces. The soul which submits to the word is saved by it; the soul which rebels against it is sure to perish. Therefore since the

* Non fuit impossibile quando præceptum est, sed stultitia peccantis impossibile sibi fecit. Gul. Paris. de Vitiis et Peccat. cap. 10. Neque enim suo vitio non implebatur lex, sed vitio prudentiæ carnis. Aug. de Spir. et Lit. cap. 19.

† Nec latuit præceptorem præcepti pondus hominum excedere vires: sed judicavit utile ex hoc ipso suæ illos insufficientiæ admoneri—Ergo mandando impossibilia non prævaricatores homines fecit sed humiles, ut omne os obstruatur, et subditus fiat omnis mundus Deo, quia ex operibus legis non justificabitur omnis caro coram illo: accipientes quippe mandatum, et sentientes defectum, clamabimus in cœlum et miserebitur nostri Deus. Bernard. Ser. 50. in Cantic.

‡ Lex data, ut gratia quæreretur, gratia data ut lex impleretur. Aug. de Sp. et Lit. c. 19. Omnia fiant charitati facilia. De Nat. et Grat. cap. 69. De Grat. Christ. cap. 9. De Grat. et Lib. Arb. cap. 15.

word comes not to any man in vain, but returns glory to God either in his conversion or in his hardening, it greatly concerns every man to come to it with meek, penitent, docile, tractable, believing, obedient resolutions; and to consider how vain and desperate a thing it is for a potsherd to strive with a rod of iron; for the pride and wrath of man to give a challenge to the justice and power of God; for briers and thorns to set themselves in battle against fire. As "our God is a consuming fire" himself, so his law is "a fiery law," Heb. xii. 29; Deut. xxxiii. 2; and his word in the mouths of his ministers "a fire," Jer. v. 14; xxiii. 29. If we be "gold" it will "purify" us; if "thorns," it will "devour" and feed upon us. "This is the condemnation," saith our Saviour, "that light is come into the world, and men loved darkness rather than light, because their deeds were evil," John iii. 19. There was condemnation in the world before, while it lay in darkness and in mischief, and knew not whither it went; but not so heavy condemnation as that which grows out of light. When physic, which should remove the disease, co-operates with it, then death comes with the more pain and the more speed. The stronger the conviction of sin is, the deeper will be the wrath against it, if it be not by repentance avoided. No surfeit more dangerous than that of bread, no judgment more terrible than that which grows out of mercy known and despised: "The word that I have spoken," saith Christ, "the same shall judge" you "in the last day," John xii. 48. Every principle of truth which is by the word begotten in the hearts of disobedient sinners, and is held down and suppressed by unrighteousness, lies there like fire raked up under ashes, which at that great day will kindle into an unquenchable flame. The word can bring much of hell upon the spirit of impenitent sinners here; it can hew, and cut, and pierce, and burn, and torment, and root out, and pull down, and destroy, and strike with trembling and amazement, sinners the proudest and most secure, Hos. vi. 5; Acts vii. 54; Heb. iv. 12; Isa. xlix. 2; Psal. xlv. 5; Rev. xi. 5, 10; Jer. i. 10; 2 Cor. x. 4; Acts xxiv. 25. We need no messenger from the dead to tell us of the torments there. All the rhetoric in hell cannot set forth hell more to the life than Moses and the prophets have done already, Luke xvi. 31. But oh what a hell will it be at last, when the word which warned us of it shall throw us into it! when every offer of mercy which we have refused, and every threatening of wrath which we have despised, shall accompany us to the tribunal of Christ to testify against us, and into the fire of hell to upbraid us with our own perdition! Oh the doleful condition of impenitent sinners! if they have not the word they perish for the want, and if they have it they perish doubly for the contempt of it. Oh that men would consider the terror of the Lord and be persuaded; and that they would learn so much wisdom as not to arm the very mercy of God against themselves! A bridge is made to give us a safe passage over a dangerous river, but he who stumbles on the bridge is in danger to fall into the river. The word is given as a means to carry us over hell into heaven, but he who stumbles and quarrels at this means shall fall in thither, from whence otherwise he had been delivered by it.

GENERAL INDEX.

A

B

D

E

F

L

M

T

U

Printed in the United States
135733LV00001B/20/A

9 781892 777942